January 23-25, 2013
Rome, Italy

Association for Computing Machinery

Advancing Computing as a Science & Profession

POPL '13

Proceedings of 40th Annual ACM SIGPLAN-SIGACT Symposium on Principles of Programming Languages

Sponsored by:

ACM SIGPLAN and ACM SIGACT

Supported by:

École Normale Superieure, Inria, Microsoft Research, Università di Verona, Facebook, CEA LIST, EADS, Google, IBM Research, Intel, Mozilla, Oracle, SELEX Sistemi Integrati, CINI, DAPA, JULIA Software, Monoidics, & NEC

Association for
Computing Machinery

Advancing Computing as a Science & Profession

The Association for Computing Machinery
2 Penn Plaza, Suite 701
New York, New York 10121-0701

ISBN: 978-1-4503-1832-7

Additional copies may be ordered prepaid from:

ACM Order Department
PO Box 30777
New York, NY 10087-0777, USA

Phone: 1-800-342-6626 (USA and Canada)
+1-212-626-0500 (Global)
Fax: +1-212-944-1318
E-mail: acmhelp@acm.org
Hours of Operation: 8:30 am – 4:30 pm ET

ACM Order Number: 549131

Printed in the USA

Chairs' Welcome

Welcome to Rome and to POPL 2013, the fortieth edition of the *ACM SIGPLAN-SIGACT Symposium on Principles of Programming Languages*. Rome is a beautiful town, with an incredible millennial history in culture, art, and science, and fantastic opportunities for enjoying the Italian lifestyle, historic sites and museums.

POPL 2013 is co-located with new and well-established conferences and workshops in programming languages and systems: 14th Verification, Model Checking, and Abstract Interpretation conference; Workshop on Synthesis, Verification, and Analysis of Rich Models; 15th International Symposium on Practical Aspects of Declarative Languages; Workshop on Partial Evaluation and Program Manipulation; 1st Interference and Dependence workshop; 1st Workshop on Behaviours and Types; Workshop on Data Driven Functional Programming; 7th Programming Languages meets Program Verification workshop; 2nd Program Protection and Reverse Engineering Workshop; and Off The Beaten Track: Underrepresented Problems for Programming Language Researchers. Confirming the long standing tradition and attention of POPL to students and young researchers, the Programming Language Mentoring Workshop and the TutorialFest will provide the necessary warm-up for a full immersion in POPL!

POPL 2013 had an absolute record of submissions: 238 papers have been submitted and reviewed, in single-blind process, by the Program Committee (PC) and the External Review Committee (ERC). Each paper has been reviewed by 4 reviewers: 3 from PC and 1 from ERC, except for PC-authored papers reviewed by ERC members only, with a load of up to 28 papers for some PC members and 6 for some ERC members. 12 further external reviewers helped in providing expert evaluations in specific situations. Ultimately 947 reviews have been produced and 85% of the papers submitted had at least one expert reviewer, as a proof of the great attention and effort spent in making the selection as rigorous as possible. The PC met in person in Paris over two days at *École Normale Supérieure*. All PC members were present at the meeting and, out of 238 submissions, 43 papers were accepted (18%). Our gratitude goes to the PC, ERC, and all outside reviewers and sub-reviewers for their attention, dedication and patience. We are firmly convinced that the POPL standard is the highest possible in Computer Science, and that the reviews produced are the best around. We thank the HotCRP software development team for providing a great tool in managing submissions, reviews and the final conference program set-up. The POPL 2013 program covers most topics in nowadays research in programming languages, including 4 outstanding invited talks by Georges Gonthier (Microsoft Research, UK), Andrew Myers (Cornell University), Shriram Krishnamurthi (Brown University and ACM Robin Milner Award), and Noah Goodman (Stanford University). Due to time constraints over 3 full days, POPL 2013 is structured in two parallel tracks. We did our best in order to reduce the possible overlap of topics among parallel sessions. Of course this can only be a partial solution and we apologize if you cannot attend all presentations you would like because of this.

A great support has been obtained this year from leading companies and institutions, enabling us to keep the access to the conference, in particular for students, relatively low-cost if considered the location. The contribution of start-up companies having their roots into our community and in particular into scientific achievements appeared in POPL is particularly welcome and deserves attention and gratitude.

Organizing POPL is an extremely complex job. This could not be possible without the help of a terrific group of volunteers, making the whole POPL 2013 Organizing Committee a super team! Our community is lucky in having the chance of benefit of their talent and dedication. Our gratitude goes also to the POPL Steering Committee, who gave us the privilege of serving the POPL community; former POPL 2012 General Chair John Field and Program Chair Michael Hicks for their invaluable advice; to the ACM team led by Debra Venedam; to Lisa Tolles of Sheridan Printing; to John Lateulere of Integrated Management Solutions; to Michael Moshell, Carole and Mandy Mann of Registration Systems Labs; to Liù Catena and the Parco dei Principi staff, in particular Fabrizio Barbieri, for their professional help in managing all details of the on-site organization. We also thank Andrea Masini (Università di Verona) for the fantastic POPL 2013 logo design! They all made this event possible.

We really hope that you enjoy POPL 2013 in Rome, Italy!

Roberto Giacobazzi
POPL 2013 General Chair
Università di Verona, Italy

Radhia Cousot
POPL 2013 Program Chair
École Normale Supérieure, CNRS & INRIA, France

Author Index

Session 3.A: Semantics

Session 3.B: Proofs & Verification

Keynote Address

Session 4.A: Concurrency & Design

Session 4.B: Separation Logic

Keynote Address

Session 5.A: Concurrency

Session 5.B: Security

Keynote Address

Session 6.A: Models & Semantics

Session 6.B: Synthesis & Verification

Session 7.A: Compilation

POPL 2013: 40th ACM SIGPLAN-SIGACT Symposium on Principles of Programming Languages

General Chair: Roberto Giacobazzi *(Università di Verona, Italy)*

Program Chair: Radhia Cousot *(École normale supérieure CNRS & INRIA, France)*

Local Arrangements: Liù Catena *(Università di Roma Tor Vergata, Italy)*

Publicity Chair: Viktor Vafeiadis *(Max Planck Institute – SWS, Germany)*

Treasurer: Bor-Yuh Evan Chang *(University of Colorado, USA)*

Workshop Co-Chairs: Matthew Might *(University of Utah, USA)*
David Van Horn *(Northeastern University, USA)*

Student Activities Chair: Tobias Wrigstad *(Uppsala University, Sweden)*

Steering Committee Chair: John Field *(Google, USA)*

Steering Committee: Thomas Ball *(Microsoft Research, USA – 2011 General Chair)*
Radhia Cousot *(École normale supérieure CNRS & INRIA, France)*
John Field *(Google, USA – 2012 General Chair)*
Roberto Giacobazzi *(University di Verona, Italy)*
Jeremy Gibbons *(University of Oxford, UK – SIGPLAN Vice Chair)*
Michael Hicks *(University of Maryland, USA – 2012 Program Chair)*
Graham Hutton *(University of Nottingham, UK – past SIGPLAN Vice Chair)*
Mooly Sagiv *(Tel Aviv University Israel – 2011 Program Chair)*
Jan Vitek *(Purdue University, USA – SIGPLAN Chair)*
Philip Wadler *(University of Edinburgh, UK – Past SIGPLAN Chair)*

Program Committee: Josh Berdine *(Microsoft Research, UK)*
Sebastian Burckhardt *(Microsoft Research, USA)*
William R. Cook *(University of Texas, Austin, USA)*
Nils Anders Danielsson *(Chalmers & Gothenburg U., Sweden)*
Işıl Dillig *(College of William & Mary, USA)*
Manuel Fähndrich *(Microsoft Research, USA)*
Xinyu Feng *(University of Sci. and Tech. of China, China)*
Andrew D. Gordon *(MSR & University of Edinburgh, UK)*
Manuel Hermenegildo *(IMDEA Software, Spain)*
Eric Koskinen *(New York University, USA)*
Xavier Leroy *(INRIA, France)*
Francesco Logozzo *(Microsoft Research, USA)*
Laurent Mauborgne *(IMDEA Software, Spain)*
Andrzej Murawski *(University of Leicester, UK)*

Program Committee (continued):

Peter O'Hearn *(University College London, UK)*
Benjamin C. Pierce *(University of Pennsylvania, USA)*
Sriram Rajamani *(Microsoft Research, India)*
Francesco Ranzato *(Università di Padova, Italy)*
Andreas Rossberg *(Google, Germany)*
Andrei Sabelfeld *(Chalmers & Gothenburg University, Sweden)*
Peter Sewell *(University of Cambridge, UK)*
Yannis Smaragdakis *(University of Athens, Greece & University of Massachusetts, USA)*
Martin Vechev *(ETH Zurich, Switzerland)*
David Walker *(Princeton University, USA)*
Tobias Wrigstad *(Uppsala University, Sweden)*
Kwangkeun Yi *(Seoul National University, Korea)*

External Review Committee:

Alex Aiken *(Stanford University, USA)*
Matthias Blume *(Google, USA)*
Gilles Barthe *(IMDEA Software, Spain)*
Lars Birkedal *(IT University of Copenhagen, Denmark)*
Hans-J. Boehm *(HP Labs, USA)*
Avik Chaudhuri *(Adobe Systems, USA)*
Swarat Chaudhuri *(Rice University, USA)*
Derek Dreyer *(MPI-SWS, Germany)*
Michael Emmi *(University Paris Diderot, France)*
Jérôme Feret *(INRIA, France)*
Cédric Fournet *(Microsoft Research, UK)*
Daniel Frampton *(Australian National U., Australia)*
Simon Gay *(University of Glasgow, UK)*
Giorgio Ghelli *(Università di Pisa, Italy)*
Benjamin Goldberg *(New York University, USA)*
Robert Grimm *(New York University, USA)*
Vineet Gupta *(Google, USA)*
Chris Hawblitzel *(Microsoft Research, USA)*
Jonathan Hayman *(INRIA, France)*
Michael Hicks *(University of Maryland, USA)*
Martin Hofmann *(Ludwig-Maximilians U., Germany)*
Ranjit Jhala *(University of California, San Diego, USA)*
K. Rustan M. Leino *(Microsoft Research, USA)*
Sorin Lerner *(University of California, San Diego, USA)*
Francesca Levi *(Università di Pisa, Italy)*
Yitzhak Mandelbaum *(SEI-CMU)*
Damien Massé *(University de Bretagne Occidentale, France)*
Isabella Mastroeni *(Università di Verona, Italy)*
Maged M. Michael *(IBM Research, USA)*

External Review Committee (continued):

Jan Midtgaard *(Aarhus University, Denmark)*
Todd Millstein *(University of California, Los Angeles, USA)*
Greg Morrisett *(Harvard University, USA)*
Leonardo de Moura *(Microsoft Research, USA)*
Andrew C. Myers *(Cornell University, USA)*
George Necula *(University of California, Berkeley, USA)*
Tamiya Onodera *(IBM Research, Japan)*
Jens Palsberg *(University of California, Los Angeles, USA)*
Prakash Panangaden *(McGill University, Canada)*
Erez Petrank *(Technion, Israel)*
Andreas Podelski *(University of Freiburg, Germany)*
François Pottier *(INRIA, France)*
Maurizio Proietti *(CNR, Italy)*
German Puebla *(University Politecnica de Madrid, Spain)*
Martin C. Rinard *(MIT, USA)*
Xavier Rival *(INRIA, France)*
Sukyoung Ryu *(KAIST, Korea)*
Francesca Scozzari *(University di Chieti-Pescara, Italy)*
Jeremy G. Siek *(University of Colorado, Boulder, USA)*
Armando Solar-Lezama *(MIT, USA)*
James Stichnoth *(Intel, USA)*
Eijiro Sumii *(Tohoku University, Japan)*
Tachio Terauchi *(Nagoya University, Japan)*
Ashish Tiwari *(SRI International, USA)*
Viktor Vafeiadis *(MPI-SWS, Germany)*
David Van Horn *(Northeastern University, USA)*
Arnaud Venet *(NASA Ames Research Center, USA)*
Janis Voigtländer *(University of Bonn, Germany)*
Mitchell Wand *(Northeastern University, USA)*
Eran Yahav *(Technion, Israel)*
Francesco Zappa Nardelli *(INRIA, France)*

Additional Reviewers:

Niklas Broberg
Michael Clarkson
Agostino Cortesi
Mike Dodds
Rupak Majumdar
Antoine Miné
Carroll Morgan
Frank Pfenning
James Riely
Noam Rinetzky
Andrey Rybalchenko
Minlan Yu

POPL 2013 Sponsors

acm SIGPLAN

SIGACT

Supporters

ECOLE NORMALE SUPERIEURE

Inria — INVENTORS FOR THE DIGITAL WORLD

Microsoft Research

UNIVERSITA DEGLI STUDI DI VERONA

facebook

cea list

EADS

Google

IBM Research

intel

mozilla

ORACLE

SELEX Sistemi Integrati — A Finmeccanica Company

cini — Consorzio Interuniversitario Nazionale per l'Informatica

DAPA — Digital Asset Protection Assn.

JULiA — software verification made easy

MONOIDICS

NEC

Engineering Mathematics: The Odd Order Theorem Proof

Georges Gonthier

Microsoft Research Cambridge
7 JJ Thomson avenue
Camdridge, UK CB3 0FB
gonthier@microsoft.com

Abstract

Even with the assistance of computer tools, the formalized description and verification of research-level mathematics remains a daunting task, not least because of the talent with which mathematicians combine diverse theories to achieve their ends. By combining tools and techniques from type theory, language design, and software engineering we have managed to capture enough of these practices to formalize the proof of the Odd Order theorem, a landmark result in Group Theory.

Categories and Subject Descriptors F.4.1 [MATHEMATICAL LOGIC AND FORMAL LANGUAGES]: Mathematical Logic – Mechanical theorem proving. J.2 [PHYSICAL SCIENCES AND ENGINEERING] – Mathematics and statistics.

Keywords theorem proving; proof engineering; group theory; mathematical components; Coq; ssreflect.

1. The Challenge of Computer Mathematics

This past year we were reminded that the "killer app" that led Alan Turing to the invention of Computer Science was the completely formal verification of mathematical theories and proofs. Yet while computation with mechanical contraptions has found useful applications in nearly every human activity, this original goal has remained elusive. Even with the latest computer proof systems, which have become very good at the verification of code and POPL papers, dealing with the proofs produced by working mathematicians can be most painful.

My experience with the formalization of the four-color theorem in 2001-5 indicated that the problem might not be a lack of automation, as is often believed, but a lack of expressiveness of the tools and methods used to describe mathematics. Even though the four-color proof uses only the most elementary combinatorics, its formalization had required new ways of organizing and writing theories and proofs – but hardly any general-purpose proof-finding automation.

This suggested that language and software engineering techniques could perhaps be applied successfully to mainstream mathematics. In 2006 I founded the Mathematical Components project at the Microsoft Research – Inria Joint Center to test this thesis, by developing a comprehensive formal algebra using the Coq system. The aim was to cover most of a math undergrad syllabus, and the work was to be driven and validated by the formalization of a famously difficult and important result in Group Theory, Feit and Thompson's Odd Order theorem. In September 2012, we finally prevailed.

POPL'13, January 23–25, 2013, Rome, Italy.
ACM 978-1-4503-1832-7/13/01.

2. The Odd Order Theorem

Feit and Thompson's seminal 1963 paper began with the deceptively short statement

THEOREM. All finite groups of odd order are solvable.

The 255 pages that followed exposed the most difficult and complex group theory proof of its time, drawing on most of elementary results in algebra (including matrices, polynomials, normed vector spaces, modules, algebraic number theory, and Galois theory), and advanced results in group theory (such as the Schur-Zassenhaus and Hall-Higman theorem, or the theory of exceptional characters). The ground-breaking paper introduced several novel techniques that would later play a key role in the full classification of finite simple groups (e.g., Thompson transitivity, tamely imbedded subsets, and signalizer functors). Its result has applications throughout group theory, and can be seen as the starting point of the classification itself. Yet it was considered a very difficult paper to read, before a revision in 1994 and 2000 simplified and filled several gaps in the exposition. All of this made the Odd Order proof the perfect test for a mathematical formalization project.

Even the expanded statement of the theorem is short, because it only involves two definitions:

DEFINITION. H is a *normal subgroup* of a group G iff H is the kernel of a homomorphism from G to a *factor group* G / H: one can compute "mod H" in G. This is written $H \lhd G$.

DEFINITION. A group G is *solvable* if there is a *normal series* $1 = H_0 \lhd H_1 \lhd \cdots \lhd H_n = G$.such that each factor H_{i+1} / H_i is abelian.

Indeed, a full formalization of the statement from basic logic (including the necessary arithmetic and combinatorics) takes only two pages. Note that any finite group has a maximal normal series whose factors are all simple groups (this is why the classification is so important); for solvable groups these factors will all be prime cyclic groups. Also, solvable groups are tied to the resolution of polynomial equations, the motivating application of group theory.

The Feit-Thompson proof is just as complex as the Odd Order statement is simple; it proceeds by studying a minimal counter-example G, gradually refining its structure until a contradiction is reached. This study consists of three unequal parts:

Local Analysis One studies the proper subgroups of G, which are all solvable by assumption. Using finite representation theory (matrices with coefficients in a finite field) one shows that their intersection has rank at most 2; in turn this implies that most of these groups closely resemble Frobenius groups, with two possible exceptions, similar to a finite field with its Galois group.

Character Theory One uses character theory (traces of matrices with complex coefficients) to extract information about G from the description of its subgroups. This is possible because characters have a Euclidean geometry, and there are isometries mapping certain subgroup characters to characters of G. The global norm inequalities imply that subgroups are exactly Frobenius, and that the two Galois exceptions occur exactly as well.

Generators and relations Using fiendish explicit calculations exploiting the relations between the finite fields embedded in G, one constructs a polynomial of degree q with $p > q$ roots in a field of order p^q; at last, contradiction!

The revised proof of the first part, by Bender and Glauberman, spans the 140 pages of volume 188 of the LMS series; the second part, by Peterflavi, spans 100 pages of volume 272, while the last is a mere 8-page appendix in volume 188. The prerequisites represent about twice that amount, from a variety of sources. The Coq formalization of the 1300 lemmas of the proof spans 47,000 LOC (out of 170,000 for the full archive).

3. Mathematical Components

The basic premise of project was that formalized theories would be more useful if they could be composed more freely, and that this could be achieved by replacing the rigid 19th century first order logic with CiC, the more modern dynamic higher-order logic supported by the Coq system. First order logic imposes an exact fit, at the symbol level, between the statement of the assumptions of a proof step and the facts that fulfil them. In CiC, parts of a statement can be executable, and matching is performed up to (functional) evaluation. Thus in principle it is possible to formulate theories so that they behave more like software components that automatically generate "glue code" to facilitate interoperability, rather than simple procedures that only work for a fixed data representation. Our challenge was to understand how this could be made useful in practice.

We realized early on that this flexibility was even more crucial for stating theorems than for proving them. Mathematical notation is cleverly honed to provide exactly the information needed to determine a mathematical object in a given context. Much of it makes little sense in the rigid, context-independent setting of first-order logic. For instance the factor group G / H we saw earlier depends on the multiplication operator used in G and H. This must be determined by the context, if we are to support the common practice of computing and equating G and H as sets, as in the statement of the isomorphism theorem $GH / H \simeq G / (G \cap H)$; the other isomorphism theorem $(G / K) / (H / K) \simeq G / H$, where the '/'s refer to three different multiplications, shows that "context" must be understood locally.

The solution to this overloading problem is the familiar "object" paradigm, specifically its functional programming equivalent, type classes. In fact in Coq type classes are significantly more powerful than in traditional functional programming, because they have an internal representation in the CiC logic as type-containing records. Instance inference is an integral part of type inference; it amounts to inverting projections of class records during higher-order unification, using a set of canonical instances declared by the user. It can supply both operations an properties, and be based both on types and data values. A single expression can exploit several type classes; for example in G / H a "finite group type" class is used to determine which multiplication is involved and to ensure that the definition is constructive, and a "group" class is used to ascertain that resulting set is actually a group (as long as G is).

In addition to supporting the traditional algebraic hierarchy of rings, vector spaces, fields, algebras, etc. our type classes can also recognize groups, sesquilinear functions, AC operators, subfields and even direct sums of subspaces. The extended type inference substantially helps the formalization process: it is not uncommon that a single line of LaTeX-like notation hides two pages of inferred annotations, and when we introduced the group class nearly half of our proof scripts vanished into type inference.

4. Big Theories, Big Theorems, Big Proofs

Software engineering techniques, albeit more mundane ones, are also instrumental in coping with the sheer size of the prerequisite theories. Ensuring that the 4200 definitions and 15,000 lemmas and theorems remain accessible requires a triple combination of namespace management (across modules), rational naming conventions (within modules), and effective search tools (in the IDE).

The distribution of formal proof lines is a close fit to a power (Pareto) law. This is a heavy-tailed distribution, which means that while most lemmas will have a very short proof (two lines or less), most proof lines will occur in the proof of large theorems, and that such proofs will get very large indeed. Thus the formalization of the Odd Order theorem accounts for 10% of the theorems, but 30% of the script lines, and includes a 1,200 line proof (for Theorem (9.11) in the character theory revised proof).

We also observed the need for large theorem statements: it is preferable to have one large theorem that collects all the facts about a given situation (e.g., the structure of an extremal p-group), rather than a plethora of factoids whose applicability must be justified separately. Our proof scripting language, implemented by the ssreflect Coq plugin, efficiently supports extracting a relevant fact subset from such a theorem.

In order to handle the big proofs, our scripting language helps enforcing explicit control and data flow. The latter also turned out to be an invaluable tool for mining the logical structure of a proof, uncovering in several cases major simplifications.

Finally, we identified several formal proof structures that cannot be expressed easily with the traditional assertion, case analysis and induction constructs. A general "without loss of generality" construct, was invaluable in capturing intricate symmetry arguments. A small library for three-way inequalities proved indispensable for formulating concisely circular inequalities.

Acknowledgments

The work described here was done in collaboration with the members and visitors of the Mathematical Components project: A. Asperti, J. Avigad, Y. Bertot, C. Cohen, F. Garillot, S. Le Roux, S. McLaughlin, A. Mahboubi, S. Ould Biha, R. O'Connor, L .Rideau, A. Solovyev, E. Tassi, and L. Théry.

Full Abstraction for Nominal Scott Domains

Steffen Lösch Andrew M. Pitts
University of Cambridge
{steffen.loesch,andrew.pitts}@cl.cam.ac.uk

Abstract

We develop a domain theory within nominal sets and present programming language constructs and results that can be gained from this approach. The development is based on the concept of *orbit-finite* subset, that is, a subset of a nominal sets that is both finitely supported and contained in finitely many orbits. This concept appears prominently in the recent research programme of Bojańczyk *et al.* on automata over infinite languages, and our results establish a connection between their work and a characterisation of topological compactness discovered, in a quite different setting, by Winskel and Turner as part of a nominal domain theory for concurrency. We use this connection to derive a notion of Scott domain within nominal sets. The functionals for existential quantification over names and 'definite description' over names turn out to be compact in the sense appropriate for nominal Scott domains. Adding them, together with parallel-or, to a programming language for recursively defined higher-order functions with name abstraction and locally scoped names, we prove a full abstraction result for nominal Scott domains analogous to Plotkin's classic result about PCF and conventional Scott domains: two program phrases have the same observable operational behaviour in all contexts if and only if they denote equal elements of the nominal Scott domain model. This is the first full abstraction result we know of for higher-order functions with local names that uses a domain theory based on ordinary extensional functions, rather than using the more intensional approach of game semantics.

Categories and Subject Descriptors F.4.1 [*Mathematical Logic and Formal Languages*]: Mathematical Logic—Lambda calculus and related systems; F.3.2 [*Logics and Meanings of Programs*]: Semantics of Programming Languages—Denotational semantics

General Terms Languages, Theory

Keywords Denotational Semantics, Domain Theory, Full Abstraction, Nominal Sets, Symmetry

1. Introduction

Various forms of symmetry are used in many branches of mathematics and computer science. The results in this paper have to do with using symmetry to extend the reach of computation theory from finite data structures and algorithms to ones that, although they are infinite, *become finite when quotiented by a suitable notion of symmetry*. We focus on higher-order functional computation with data that may involve unboundedly many different names and symmetries given by permutations of those names. A simple example of such data is the abstract syntax trees for a language involving binding constructs, such as the λ-calculus with named bound variables: infinitely many abstract syntax trees represent a particular λ-term, modulo permuting their bound names. This way of viewing α-equivalence via symmetry was the initial stimulus for the development of *nominal sets* [14]—a theory for mathematical structures involving atomic names (that is, names whose only attribute is their identity) based on name permutations and the notion of *finite support*; we review this concept in Section 2.

Nominal sets have been used to develop the semantic properties of binders and locally scoped names, with applications to functional and logic programming, to equational logic and rewriting, to type theory and to interactive theorem proving; see the bibliography [1]. The work by Montanari *et al.* [22] on the π-calculus and HD-automata provides a somewhat different application of nominal sets (an independent one, since it uses a notion of 'named set' that only subsequently was shown to be equivalent to nominal sets [15, 37]). The use of symmetries of names (of fresh communication channels in this case) to get finite representations of infinitely many states is at the forefront in their work. It has recently been subsumed and generalised in a programme of what one might call 'orbit-finite' automata theory [7, 8, 13, 23, 42].

In this paper we bring together the 'names and binders' and the 'orbit-finite state space' aspects of nominal sets. We observe that a key concept underlying the automata-theoretic research programme of Bojańczyk *et al.* [6], that of being an *orbit-finite subset*, turns out to subsume a notion of topological compactness introduced, for quite different purposes, by Winskel and Turner in their work on nominal domain theory for concurrency [40]. We explain the connection and use it to develop a version of the classic notion of *Scott domain* within nominal sets. (Previous work on denotational semantics with nominal sets [34, 39] has focussed on simpler notions of domain, analogous either to ω-chain complete posets, or to algebraic lattices.) A domain element is compact if it stands for a finite approximation of a computation. We define this notion for our setting (in Definition 5) and show that the functionals for 'there exists a name such that...' and 'the unique name such that...' are compact. Plotkin [30] famously proves that PCF with parallel-or is *fully abstract* with respect to conventional Scott domains, in the sense that two expressions have equal denotations if and only if they the have the same observable operational behaviour in all contexts. We obtain an analogous result for nominal Scott domains, through adding the above functionals, together with parallel-or, to a programming language for recursively defined higher-order functions with name-abstractions and locally scoped names. Thus this paper makes the following contributions.

- We show (Theorem 8) that a finitely supported subset of a nominal set is compact with respect to unions that are uniform-

POPL'13, January 23–25, 2013, Rome, Italy.

directed in the sense of Winskel and Turner if and only if it is orbit-finite.

- We use orbit-finite subsets to generalise the notion of Scott domain from ordinary sets to nominal sets; we prove that the category of nominal Scott domains is cartesian closed, has least fixed points and is closed under forming domains of name abstractions (Sections 5 and 6). Although there are infinitely many names, the nominal Scott domain of names has some strong finiteness properties. In particular, we show that the functionals for existential quantification over names and definite description of names are uniform-compact elements of their function domains (Examples 14 and 15).
- We define a language PNA (Programming with Name Abstractions) that extends Plotkin's PCF language with names that can be locally scoped, swapped, abstracted and concreted. In order to illustrate these facilities for programming with name abstractions, PNA has a nominal algebraic datatype for representing λ-terms. PNA's operational semantics is inspired by [19, 27]; in particular, its method for deconstructing name abstractions makes use of Odersky-style, 'scope-intrusive' local names. We give a simple denotational semantics for PNA using nominal Scott domains and prove that it is computationally adequate (Theorem 27).
- We extend PNA to a language PNA$^+$ with syntax, operational semantics and denotational semantics for parallel-or, for existentially quantifying over names and for definite descriptions of names. We prove that the nominal Scott domain model of PNA$^+$ is fully abstract: any two expressions are contextually equivalent if and only if they have equal denotations in the model (Theorem 30).

There are full abstraction results for higher-order functions with local names using the intensional approach of game semantics [3, 18, 41], but our Theorem 30 is the first such result we know of that is based on ordinary extensional functions. There is no similar result known for FreshML [35], which uses generative rather than Odersky-style local names to implement the features that PNA provides for programming with name abstractions; and yet PNA (extended with recursive types) is in principle as expressive as FreshML, in view of Lösch and Pitts [19]. Our proof of Theorem 30 seems novel compared with other proofs of full abstraction results in the literature. We only sketch it here—the details will be published elsewhere. On the other hand it gives rise to some open problems that we discuss in Section 10, together with a number of possibilities for future work exploiting the use of orbit-finite subsets within nominal domain theory.

2. Finite support

We are interested in the denotational semantics of programs written in languages featuring binding constructs involving names that can be tested for equality. To take symmetry into account, we fix some countably infinite set $\mathbb{A}$ (of 'atomic names') and consider finite permutations of $\mathbb{A}$, that is, bijections $\pi : \mathbb{A} \cong \mathbb{A}$ with the property that $\pi\, a = a$ holds for all but finitely many $a \in \mathbb{A}$. Recall that an *action* of such permutations on a set X is a binary operation $\_ \cdot \_$ satisfying $\mathrm{id} \cdot x = x$ (where id is the identity permutation) and $\pi' \cdot (\pi \cdot x) = (\pi' \circ \pi) \cdot x$ (where $\_ \circ \_$ is composition).

Actions of finite permutations of $\mathbb{A}$ on sets X and Y can be extended to their cartesian product $X \times Y$ by defining for each $x \in X$ and $y \in Y$

$$\pi \cdot (x, y) \triangleq (\pi \cdot x, \pi \cdot y). \tag{1}$$

More interestingly, given actions on X and Y, we get an action on the set of functions Y^X by defining for each $f \in Y^X$

$$\pi \cdot f \triangleq \lambda x \in X \to \pi \cdot (f(\pi^{-1} \cdot x)) \tag{2}$$

where π^{-1} is the inverse of the permutation π. In particular, taking $Y = 2 = \{\mathrm{true}, \mathrm{false}\}$, a two-element set with trivial action ($\pi \cdot \mathrm{true} = \mathrm{true}$, $\pi \cdot \mathrm{false} = \mathrm{false}$), we get an action on 2^X and hence on subsets of X: for each $S \subseteq X$

$$\pi \cdot S \triangleq \{\pi \cdot x \mid x \in S\}. \tag{3}$$

Programs, being finite syntactic objects, only involve finitely many atomic names in their construction; whereas the elements of a set X used to denote program behaviours may well be infinite mathematical objects. We wish to limit our attention to infinite behaviours that depend only upon finitely many atomic names, as doing so yields a richer and better behaved theory. We can make precise what it means to 'only depend upon finitely many atomic names' entirely in terms of symmetry, that is, in terms of the permutation action. An element $x \in X$ is *supported* by a set $A \subseteq \mathbb{A}$ of atomic names if every permutation π satisfying $(\forall a \in A)\ \pi\, a = a$ also satisfies $\pi \cdot x = x$. That is, permutations that preserve A also preserve x. We say that a set X equipped with an action of finite permutations of $\mathbb{A}$ is a *nominal set* if each of its elements is supported by some finite set of atomic names. In this case one can show that for each $x \in X$ there is a smallest finite subset of $\mathbb{A}$ supporting x, which we write as $\mathrm{supp}\, x$ [14]. We also write $a \# x$ to mean $a \notin \mathrm{supp}\, x$. Note that since $\mathrm{supp}\, x$ is a finite set and $\mathbb{A}$ is not, given x we can always find some $a \in \mathbb{A}$ satisfying $a \# x$.

Given a nominal set X, the subsets that possess a finite support with respect to the action in (3) are called *finitely supported subsets* of X. Not every subset is finitely supported. For example, when $X = \mathbb{A}$ (with action $\pi \cdot a = \pi\, a$), the only finitely supported subsets are those $S \subseteq \mathbb{A}$ for which either S, or $\mathbb{A} - S$ is finite. We write $\mathrm{P}_{\mathrm{fs}} X$ for the collection of all finitely supported subsets of X, and with the action in (3) this is a nominal set. Indeed it is the power object (in the sense of topos theory [17]) for a model of higher-order logic based on nominal sets. The main difference between this model and the classical one is that it fails to satisfy choice principles.[1] As we discuss next, this difference causes nominal domain theory to be something more than just 'classical domain theory carried out in the nominal model of higher-order logic'.

3. Uniform-directed joins

A key idea behind domain theory [5] is to give denotations to programs with potentially infinite behaviour as a limit of approximations. For domain theory based on approximation via a partial order (rather than a metric), limits are joins of chains (linearly ordered subsets), or more generally, joins of directed subsets (where every finite set of elements has an upper bound in the subset). So long as one considers chains of arbitrary (ordinal) length, classically there is no difference between using joins of chains and using directed joins [20]. However, the equivalence of the two approaches relies on the Axiom of Choice and, as we noted above, that fails to hold for nominal sets. Therefore, in the nominal version of domain theory, formulating limits in terms of joins of chains is more restrictive than using joins of arbitrary directed subsets. (Of course, both the chains and the directed subsets should be finitely supported, to make sense nominally.) Winskel and Turner [40] provide a compelling reason for restricting attention to joins of chains. They show that a key notion provided by the nominal approach, the operation

[1] The associated model of set theory goes back to work in the 1930s by Fraenkel and Mostowski, who devised it specifically to negate the Axiom of Choice [see 12, Remark 2.22].

of name abstraction, preserves joins of chains, but does not necessarily preserve joins of directed subsets in general. We give below a simplified version of the Winskel-Turner example of the failure of name abstraction to preserve joins of all finitely supported, directed subsets.

Definition 1 (name abstraction). A *nominal poset* is simply a nominal set D equipped with a partial order $\sqsubseteq$ that is respected by the action of permutations: $d \sqsubseteq d' \Rightarrow \pi \cdot d \sqsubseteq \pi \cdot d'$. Given such a D, we get a pre-order on $\mathbb{A} \times D$ by defining $(a, d) \sqsubseteq (a', d')$ to hold whenever we have $(a\ a'') \cdot d \sqsubseteq (a'\ a'') \cdot d'$ in D for some (or indeed, for any) $a'' \mathrel{\#} a, a', d, d'$. (As usual, $(a\ a')$ denotes the permutation that swaps a and a', leaving all other atomic names fixed.) We write $[\mathbb{A}]D$ for the poset obtained by quotienting $\mathbb{A} \times D$ by the equivalence relation associated with this pre-order, and $\langle a \rangle d$ for the equivalence class of (a, d). Defining a permutation action by $\pi \cdot \langle a \rangle d = \langle \pi\, a \rangle (\pi \cdot d)$, one can show that $[\mathbb{A}]D$ is also a nominal poset, with $\operatorname{supp}\langle a \rangle d = (\operatorname{supp} d) - \{a\}$. An element of $[\mathbb{A}]D$ is an abstract form of α-equivalence class for elements of D. It is abstract, because D itself may not consist of syntactic data—we just need to know how name permutations act on its elements.

Example 2. For any nominal set X, partially ordering the elements of the nominal set $\mathrm{P_{fs}}X$ of finitely supported subsets of X by inclusion, we get a nominal poset. Consider the case when $X = \mathbb{A}$. Given $a \in \mathbb{A}$, the name abstraction function $\mathrm{P_{fs}}\mathbb{A} \to [\mathbb{A}](\mathrm{P_{fs}}\mathbb{A})$ mapping each $S \in \mathrm{P_{fs}}\mathbb{A}$ to $\langle a \rangle S$ does not preserve all joins of finitely supported, directed subsets. For example, consider the directed subset $\mathcal{F} \in \mathrm{P_{fs}}(\mathrm{P_{fs}}\mathbb{A})$ consisting of all finite sets of atomic names. $\mathcal{F}$ has empty support and its join $\bigsqcup \mathcal{F}$ is equal to $\mathbb{A}$. However, fixing upon $a \neq a'$ in $\mathbb{A}$, one has $\langle a \rangle \mathbb{A} = \langle a' \rangle \mathbb{A} \neq \langle a' \rangle (\mathbb{A} - \{a\})$ and one can check that $\bigsqcup\{\langle a \rangle F \mid F \in \mathcal{F}\} \sqsubseteq \langle a' \rangle (\mathbb{A} - \{a\})$. So $\langle a \rangle (\bigsqcup \mathcal{F}) \neq \bigsqcup\{\langle a \rangle F \mid F \in \mathcal{F}\}$.

A motivation for using nominal rather than ordinary domains to do denotational semantics is precisely to gain access to this operation of name abstraction, which can be used to model language features involving binders. So finding a setting in which name abstraction preserves limits of approximations is crucial. It turns out that the problem with the directed subset $\mathcal{F}$ in the above example is its lack of what Winskel and Turner call *uniformity*: each $F \in \mathcal{F}$ is a finite set of atomic names and hence is supported by F itself. Thus, there is no single finite support for all the elements of $\mathcal{F}$.

Definition 3 (udcpos). Given a nominal set X, call a subset $S \subseteq X$ *uniformly supported* if there is a finite set $A \subseteq_{\mathrm{f}} \mathbb{A}$ that supports each $x \in S$. A *uniform-directed* subset of a nominal poset is a subset S that is both uniformly supported and directed. A *uniform-directed complete partial order* (*udcpo*) is a nominal poset that has joins $\bigsqcup S$ for all uniform-directed subsets S.

Lemma 4. *In a nominal poset D, every finitely supported chain C is necessarily uniformly supported. In particular, each $d \in C$ is supported by* $\operatorname{supp} C$. □

For a proof, see Turner [39, Lemma 3.4.2.1]. As Turner points out, using this lemma, the classic result of Markowsky [20] can be extended to show that *a nominal poset is a udcpo if and only if it has joins for all finitely supported chains.* So in effect udcpos give us a domain theory within the higher-order logic of nominal sets based on chain-completeness. As we will see in Section 6, they also give us access to the name-abstraction construct.

We model potentially infinite program behaviours in languages with names using denotations that are uniform-directed joins of approximations to the behaviour. Each approximation should be finite in a suitable sense. For classical domain theory this amounts to being compact (also known as 'isolated') with respect to directed joins. By analogy, we make the following definition.

Definition 5 (algebraic udcpo). An element $u \in D$ of a udcpo D is *uniform-compact* if for all uniform-directed subsets $S \subseteq D$, $u \sqsubseteq \bigsqcup S \Rightarrow (\exists d \in S)\ u \sqsubseteq d$. We write $\mathrm{K}D$ for the set of uniform-compact elements of D. We say that D is an *algebraic* udcpo if each of its elements is the join of a uniform-directed subset of $\mathrm{K}D$. D is ω*-algebraic* if in addition the underlying set of $\mathrm{K}D$ is countable.

Recall that a subset of a set is compact with respect to directed joins (unions) of subsets if and only if it is a finite set. Here we are restricting attention to a smaller class of joins, the uniform-directed ones. Therefore, we expect uniform-compactness to be a more liberal notion of finiteness. We show in the next section that it corresponds precisely to the notion of orbit-finite subset introduced by Bojańczyk *et al.*[2]

4. Orbit-finite subsets

The action of finite permutations of $\mathbb{A}$ on the elements of a nominal set X partitions it into *orbits*: two elements x and x' are in the same orbit if $x' = \pi \cdot x$ for some finite permutation π. For example $\mathbb{A}$ itself has just one orbit. $\mathbb{A} \times \mathbb{A}$ has two, namely $\{(a, a) \mid a \in \mathbb{A}\}$ and $\{(a, a') \in \mathbb{A}^2 \mid a \neq a'\}$, and in general $\mathbb{A}^n$ has always finitely many orbits. In contrast, the nominal set $\mathbb{A}^*$ of finite lists of atomic names has infinitely many orbits (since lists of different length cannot be in the same orbit).

Definition 6 (orbit-finite subsets). A finitely supported subset $S \in \mathrm{P_{fs}}X$ of a nominal set X is said to be *orbit-finite* if it is contained in the union of finitely many orbits of X.

Bojańczyk *et al.* investigate orbit-finite data structures and algorithms (for a generalised version of nominal sets over any 'Fraïssé symmetry'). Note that an orbit-finite subset may well have infinitely many different elements. For example, $\mathbb{A}$ is an orbit-finite subset of itself. In order to compute with orbit-finite subsets one needs an effective presentation of them and their operations. The following notion turns out to give an alternative characterisation of orbit-finite subsets that is suitable for calculation. It was introduced independently by Turner [39, Definition 3.4.3.2], Gabbay [11, Section 3.3; 12, Definition 3.1; 13, Definition 3.1] and Bojańczyk *et al.* [6, Section 8], whose 'hull' terminology we adopt here. (See also Ciancia and Montanari [9, Definition 6.10], whose 'closures' are hulls of the form $\mathrm{hull}_{\operatorname{supp} x - \{a\}}\{x\}$.)

Definition 7 (orbit-finite hulls). Let X be a nominal set. Given finite subsets $A \subseteq_{\mathrm{f}} \mathbb{A}$ and $F \subseteq_{\mathrm{f}} X$, define $\mathrm{hull}_A F \triangleq \{\pi \cdot x \mid \pi \mathrel{\#} A \wedge x \in F\}$, where $\pi \mathrel{\#} A$ means that π is a finite permutation of $\mathbb{A}$ that fixes each $a \in A$.

It is not hard to see that $\mathrm{hull}_A F$ is supported by A and contained in a finite union of orbits of X (namely the orbits of each $x \in F$). What is less obvious is that every orbit-finite subset is of this form. This follows from a key technical property of hulls, proved independently by Turner [39, Lemma 3.4.3.5] and Bojańczyk *et al.* [6, Lemma 3]:

$$(\forall A, A' \subseteq_{\mathrm{f}} \mathbb{A}, F \subseteq_{\mathrm{f}} X)\ A \subseteq A' \Rightarrow (\exists F' \subseteq_{\mathrm{f}} X)\ \mathrm{hull}_A F = \mathrm{hull}_{A'} F'. \quad (4)$$

This property can be used to prove the following theorem that makes the connection between orbit-finite subsets and the notion of uniform-compactness from the previous section. Consider the nominal poset $\mathrm{P_{fs}}X$ of finitely supported subsets of a nominal set X, the partial order being subset inclusion. It possesses joins for all

[2] Bojańczyk et al. [6, Section 3] use the term 'finitary subset' for what we call an orbit-finite subset.

finitely supported subsets, given by union, and hence in particular it is a udcpo.

Theorem 8. *An element of the udcpo* $\mathrm{P_{fs}}X$ *is uniform-compact if and only if it is an orbit-finite subset of* X*; and it is an orbit-finite subset of* X *if and only if it is equal to* $\mathrm{hull}_A F$ *for some* $A \subseteq_f \mathbb{A}$ *and* $F \subseteq_f X$*. Every* $S \in \mathrm{P_{fs}}X$ *is the uniform-directed join of the orbit-finite subsets contained in and with the same support as* S*. Thus* $\mathrm{P_{fs}}X$ *is an algebraic udcpo in the sense of Definition 5.* □

So there is the following analogy

$$\frac{\text{finite}}{\text{directed}}\text{sets} \sim \frac{\text{orbit-finite}}{\text{uniform-directed}}\text{nominal sets}$$

which we apply next to the classical notion of Scott domain that arose in the denotational semantics of higher-order functional programming languages [30, Lemma 4.4].

5. Nominal Scott domains

A *nominal Scott domain* D is by definition an ω-algebraic udcpo with a least element and joins for all finitely supported subsets that have upper bounds (or equivalently, by Theorem 8, joins for all orbit-finite subsets that have upper bounds).

Remark 9 (flat domains). If X is a nominal set, the *flat* nominal poset $X_\perp$ is given by $X \uplus \{\perp\}$, with partial order $d \sqsubseteq d' \Leftrightarrow d = \perp \vee d = d'$ and permutation action extending that on X by $\pi \cdot \perp = \perp$. It is easily seen to be a nominal Scott domain, with $\mathrm{K}(X_\perp) = X_\perp$.

Definition 10. The category $\mathbf{Nsd}$ has nominal Scott domains for its objects and for its morphisms the functions $f : D \to D'$ that are both *equivariant*, that is, $f(\pi \cdot d) = \pi \cdot (f\, d)$ holds for all finite permutations π and all $d \in D$, and *uniform-continuous*, that is, monotone and preserving uniform-directed joins.

Remark 11 (Winskel-Turner domain theory). The 'nominal domain theory for concurrency' of Winskel and Turner [40] introduces the notion of uniform-directed join and contains a characterisation of compact elements in terms of the hull construct from Definition 7. However, their domains are more specific than ours as they are based on path sets (downwards-closed subsets of preorders), which form prime-algebraic complete lattices. Modulo countability, their category $\mathbf{FMCts}_\emptyset$ is a full subcategory of $\mathbf{Nsd}$.

Theorem 12. $\mathbf{Nsd}$ *is cartesian closed.*

Proof. The terminal object is given by the trivial flat domain $\emptyset_\perp$. The product of D_1 and D_2 is given by their cartesian product, with permutation action as in (1) and partial order $(d_1, d_2) \sqsubseteq (d_1', d_2') \triangleq d_1 \sqsubseteq d_1' \wedge d_2 \sqsubseteq d_2'$. Exponentials $D_1 \to D_2$ have an underlying set consisting of all uniform-continuous functions $f : D_1 \to D_2$ that are finitely supported with respect to the usual permutation action for functions given in (2). The partial order on such functions is also given as usual, argument-wise: $f \sqsubseteq f' \triangleq (\forall d \in D_1)\ f\,d \sqsubseteq f'd$. For ordinary Scott domains, compact elements of the exponential are given by joins of finite, bounded sets of step-functions. Here, given uniform-compact elements $u_i \in \mathrm{K}D_i$ $(i = 1, 2)$, one can show that the *step-function*

$$[u_1\,,\, u_2] \triangleq \lambda d \in D_1 \to \text{if } u_1 \sqsubseteq d \text{ then } u_2 \text{ else } \perp \tag{5}$$

is in $\mathrm{K}(D_1 \to D_2)$; that a typical element of $\mathrm{K}(D_1 \to D_2)$ is the join of an orbit-finite, bounded set of such step functions (so in view of Theorem 8, $\mathrm{K}(D_1 \to D_2)$ is countable, because $\mathrm{K}D_1$ and $\mathrm{K}D_2$ are); and that every element of $D_1 \to D_2$ is a uniform-directed join of elements in $\mathrm{K}(D_1 \to D_2)$. □

We give some examples of uniform-compact elements of exponentials in $\mathbf{Nsd}$ associated with the flat domain of atomic names, $\mathbb{A}_\perp$. The examples show that although $\mathbb{A}_\perp$ has a countably infinite underlying set, it has very different uniform-compactness properties from the flat domain of natural numbers, $\mathbb{N}_\perp$ (e.g. the permutation action on $\mathbb{N}$ is *discrete*: $\pi \cdot n \triangleq n$). These examples will be important for the development in Section 7.

Example 13 (name equality test). Let $2 = \{\text{true}, \text{false}\}$ be a two-element, discrete nominal set. For each atomic name $a \in \mathbb{A}$, consider the function $eq_a : \mathbb{A}_\perp \to 2_\perp$ given by

$$eq_a\, d \triangleq \begin{cases} \text{true} & \text{if } d = a \\ \text{false} & \text{if } d \in \mathbb{A} - \{a\} \\ \perp & \text{if } d = \perp \end{cases} \tag{6}$$

for each $d \in \mathbb{A}_\perp$. Then using the notation from Definition 7 and (5), one finds that $eq_a = \bigsqcup \mathrm{hull}_{\{a\}}\{[a\,,\,\text{true}], [a'\,,\,\text{false}]\}$, where a' is any atomic name not equal to a. Thus from the proof of Theorem 12 we have $eq_a \in \mathrm{K}(\mathbb{A}_\perp \to 2_\perp)$.

Example 14 (exists name). For each $f \in \mathbb{A}_\perp \to 2_\perp$ define

$$exists_{\mathbb{A}} f \;\triangleq\; \begin{cases} \text{true} & \text{if } (\exists a \in \mathbb{A})\ f\,a = \text{true} \\ \text{false} & \text{if } (\forall a \in \mathbb{A})\ f\,a = \text{false} \\ \perp & \text{otherwise.} \end{cases} \tag{7}$$

Picking any $a \in \mathbb{A}$, one can show that $exists_{\mathbb{A}}$ is equal to

$$\bigsqcup \mathrm{hull}_\emptyset\{[[a\,,\,\text{true}]\,,\,\text{true}], [\bigsqcup \mathrm{hull}_\emptyset\{[a\,,\,\text{false}]\}\,,\,\text{false}]\}$$

and hence that $exists_{\mathbb{A}} \in \mathrm{K}((\mathbb{A}_\perp \to 2_\perp) \to 2_\perp)$.

Example 15 (definite name description). Note that the functions in Example 13 satisfy $eq_a = eq_{a'} \Rightarrow a = a'$. Hence for each $f \in (\mathbb{A}_\perp \to 2_\perp)$ we can define

$$the_{\mathbb{A}}\, f \triangleq \begin{cases} a & \text{if } f = eq_a \text{ for some } a \in \mathbb{A} \\ \perp & \text{otherwise.} \end{cases} \tag{8}$$

Then picking any $a \in \mathbb{A}$, one has $the_{\mathbb{A}} = \bigsqcup \mathrm{hull}_\emptyset\{[eq_a\,,\,a]\}$ and hence $the_{\mathbb{A}} \in \mathrm{K}((\mathbb{A}_\perp \to 2_\perp) \to \mathbb{A}_\perp)$.

Remark 16 (least fixed points). As for any cartesian closed category, Theorem 12 allows us to model typed λ-calculus using nominal Scott domains and equivariant, uniform-continuous functions. $\mathbf{Nsd}$ also supports the usual interpretation of recursively defined terms via least fixed points: for if $D \in \mathbf{Nsd}$ and $f \in (D \to D)$, then $\{\perp, f\perp, f^2\perp, \ldots\}$ is a uniform-directed subset of D (each element is supported by $\mathrm{supp}\, f$) whose join is $\mathrm{fix}\, f$, the least fixed point of f, by the usual Tarskian argument. Indeed for each nominal Scott domain D, the function assigning least fixed points gives us a morphism in $\mathbf{Nsd}$

$$\mathrm{fix} : (D \to D) \to D. \tag{9}$$

It is probably the case that $\mathbf{Nsd}$ has the 'algebraic compactness' properties (enriched over the category of nominal sets) needed to model recursive definitions at the level of types; *cf.* [5, Section 5] and [34, Section 3]. However, we have yet to check the details of this.

6. Abstraction, concretion and restriction

The following result is the basis for giving denotational semantics using nominal Scott domains to languages with name binding operations, such as the one considered in Section 7.

Theorem 17. *If* D *is a nominal Scott domain, then so is the nominal poset* $[\mathbb{A}]D$ *from Definition 1. The operation of name abstraction* $(a, d) \mapsto \langle a \rangle d$ *extends to a morphism* $\mathbb{A}_\perp \times D \to [\mathbb{A}]D$ *in* $\mathbf{Nsd}$ *once we define* $\langle \perp \rangle d \triangleq \perp$.

Proof. If $S \in \mathrm{P}_{\mathrm{fs}}([\mathbb{A}]D)$ is uniform-directed, then so is $\{d \in D \mid \langle a \rangle d \in S\} \in \mathrm{P}_{\mathrm{fs}} D$, for any $a \in \mathbb{A}$. The same holds if S is finitely supported and bounded from above. In both cases, picking $a \# S$, one finds that the join of S in $[\mathbb{A}]D$ is $\langle a \rangle (\bigsqcup \{d \in D \mid \langle a \rangle d \in S\})$. Thus, $[\mathbb{A}]D$ has uniform-directed joins and joins of bounded finitely supported subsets, and its least element is $\langle a \rangle \bot$ (for any $a \in \mathbb{A}$). The above description of uniform-directed joins in $[\mathbb{A}]D$ implies that $\langle a \rangle u \in \mathrm{K}(\langle \mathbb{A} \rangle D)$ if and only if $u \in \mathrm{K}D$ and (hence) that $[\mathbb{A}]D$ is ω-algebraic. It also implies that each $\lambda d \in D \to \langle a \rangle d$ is uniform-continuous. □

Algorithms that manipulate binders not only construct name abstractions, they also pull them apart. For example, FreshML [35] supports computation with name abstractions via a convenient form of pattern matching that allows bound entities to be named while guaranteeing invariance under α-equivalence. The mechanism underlying this form of deconstruction of name abstractions is most easily understood in terms of name 'concretion', to which FreshML's pattern matching can be translated. Given $D \in \mathbf{Nsd}$ and $e \in [\mathbb{A}]D$, for each $a \in \mathbb{A}$ with $a \# e$ there is a unique element $e \mathbin{@} a \in D$ satisfying $e = \langle a \rangle (e \mathbin{@} a)$, called the *concretion* of the name abstraction e at the atomic name a [14, Section 5]. Note that this operation is partially defined: to form $e \mathbin{@} a$ we require $a \# e$, meaning that a not in the support of e. For flat domains we will make concretion a total, uniform-continuous function simply by mapping the pairs where concretion is undefined to $\bot \in D$. However, for non-flat domains this is not possible, because in general it does not give a monotone function. For example in $[\mathbb{A}](\mathrm{P}_{\mathrm{fs}}\mathbb{A})$, $a' \in \mathrm{supp}\langle a \rangle \{a, a'\}$ (assuming $a \neq a'$), but we cannot define the concretion of $\langle a \rangle \{a, a'\}$ at a' to be the least element $\emptyset$ of $\mathrm{P}_{\mathrm{fs}}\mathbb{A}$ since $\langle a \rangle \{a\} \sqsubseteq \langle a \rangle \{a, a'\}$ and $(\langle a \rangle \{a\}) \mathbin{@} a' = \{a'\} \neq \emptyset$.

One way to deal with this partiality of concretion in a programming language is to enhance its type system with 'freshness assumptions' to ensure statically that name abstractions are only concreted at fresh names. This is the solution adopted by the original version of FreshML [28] and is the one chosen by Winskel and Turner in their language Nominal HOPLA [39, 40]. Later versions of FreshML use a conventional type system and enforce freshness conditions dynamically via the use of local names in expressions [35]—at the expense of purity [31]. We do the same with the language introduced in the next section, but achieve purity via the use of Odersky-style [24] local names rather than generative ones. These will be modelled by some extra structure on nominal Scott domains in the form of name restriction operations [27, Section 2.3] that enable us to give morphisms $[\mathbb{A}]D \times \mathbb{A}_\bot \to D$ in $\mathbf{Nsd}$ for the operation of name concretion.

Definition 18 (uniform-continuous name restriction). A *uniform-continuous name restriction operation* on a nominal Scott domain D is a morphism $r : [\mathbb{A}]D \to D$ in $\mathbf{Nsd}$ satisfying the structural properties: $a \# d \Rightarrow r\langle a \rangle d = d$ and $r\langle a \rangle (r\langle a' \rangle d) = r\langle a' \rangle (r\langle a \rangle d)$ for all $a, a' \in \mathbb{A}$ and $d \in D$.

We usually write $r\langle a \rangle d$ as $a \backslash d$ with the particular morphism r understood from context. Using this morphism, as in Pitts [27, Corollary 2.14] we can extend the partial operation of concretion to a total equivariant function $\_ \mathbin{@} \_ : [\mathbb{A}]D \times \mathbb{A}_\bot \to D$ satisfying

$$\left.\begin{array}{lcl} (\langle a \rangle d) \mathbin{@} a & = & d \\ (\langle a \rangle d) \mathbin{@} a' & = & a \backslash (a\, a') \cdot d \quad \text{if } a \neq a' \\ (\langle a \rangle d) \mathbin{@} \bot & = & \bot. \end{array}\right\} \tag{10}$$

The fact that this is uniform-continuous and hence determines a morphism in $\mathbf{Nsd}$ follows from the description of uniform-directed joins in $[\mathbb{A}]D$ in the proof of Theorem 17.

The following result shows that domains arising in the denotational semantics of higher-order functional programming with name abstractions (Section 7) all carry a uniform-continuous name restriction operation. The theorem can be proved by extending the results in Pitts [27, Section 2.3] from nominal sets to nominal Scott domains.

Theorem 19. *Every flat nominal Scott domain $X_\bot$ has a uniform-continuous name restriction operation satisfying*

$$a \backslash d = \begin{cases} d & \text{if } a \# d \\ \bot & \text{if } a \in \mathrm{supp}\, d \end{cases} \tag{11}$$

for all $a \in \mathbb{A}$ and $d \in X_\bot$. If $D_1, D_2 \in \mathbf{Nsd}$ have uniform-continuous name restriction operations, their product $D_1 \times D_2$ has one satisfying

$$a \backslash (d_1, d_2) = (a \backslash d_1, a \backslash d_2) \tag{12}$$

for all $a \in \mathbb{A}$, $d_1 \in D_1$ and $d_2 \in D_2$. If $D_1, D_2 \in \mathbf{Nsd}$ and D_2 has a uniform-continuous name restriction operation, then whether or not D_1 has one as well, the exponential $D_1 \to D_2$ has such an operation, satisfying

$$(a \backslash f)\, d = a \backslash (f\, d) \quad \text{if } a \# d \tag{13}$$

for all $d \in D_1$ and $f \in D_1 \to D_2$. Finally, if $D \in \mathbf{Nsd}$ has a uniform-continuous name restriction operation, then the name abstraction domain $[\mathbb{A}]D$ has one satisfying

$$a \backslash (\langle a' \rangle d) = \langle a' \rangle (a \backslash d) \quad \text{if } a \neq a' \tag{14}$$

for all $a, a' \in \mathbb{A}$ and $d \in D$. □

Remark 20. In the above theorem, the name restriction operation for exponentials is rather subtle. Property (13) at first seems like only a partial specification for the function $a \backslash f$, but in fact determines it uniquely, since it implies that for all $d \in D$

$$(a \backslash f)\, d = a' \backslash ((a\, a') \cdot f)\, d \quad \text{for any } a' \# (f, d) \tag{15}$$

[see 27, Theorem 2.10]. It is easier to see that (14) uniquely defines name restriction for name abstraction domains because given $a \in \mathbb{A}$, we can always choose a representative for the equivalence class $\langle a' \rangle d$ with $a \neq a'$.

Theorem 19 gives operations that adequately model locally scoped names in programming languages. For example, in retrospect one can see that Shinwell and Pitts [34] use the name restriction operation constructed as above for continuation domains of the form $(D \to 1_\bot) \to 1_\bot$ to adequately model the operational semantics of FreshML, which evaluates a local scope by generating a name that is fresh for the current state. In this paper we use Odersky's functional theory of local names [24], which is modelled in $\mathbf{Nsd}$ rather easily in view of the above theorem. The next section introduces a language corresponding to a simply typed fragment of FreshML [35], but with this kind of locally scoped name.

7. PNA: programming with name abstractions

The programming language PNA (Programming with Name Abstractions) is basically Plotkin's PCF [30] with names added. Like PCF, PNA has arithmetic constructs, call-by-name higher-order functions and fixed-point recursion. What distinguishes the two languages is that PNA treats names as first-class citizens and has constructs for locally scoping them, swapping them, testing them for equality, and for name abstraction and concretion. To exercise the use of name abstraction it also features a representative 'nominal algebraic datatype', namely a type for α-equivalence classes of λ-terms. For example, when *subst* is the PNA expression defined below, $\mathit{subst}\, e_1\, a\, e_2$ computes the λ-term obtained by capture-avoiding substitution of the λ-term represented by e_1 for all free occurrences of the variable named a in the λ-term represented by e_2.

$\tau \in \mathrm{Typ} ::=$	*types*
$\texttt{bool} \mid \texttt{nat} \mid \tau \times \tau \mid \tau \to \tau \mid \texttt{name} \mid \texttt{term} \mid \delta\,\tau$	
$e \in \mathrm{Exp} ::=$	*expressions*
x	variable ($x \in \mathbb{V}$)
$\texttt{T}$	truth
$\texttt{F}$	falsity
$\texttt{if}\,e\,\texttt{then}\,e\,\texttt{else}\,e$	conditional
$\texttt{0}$	number zero
$\texttt{S}\,e$	successor
$\texttt{pred}\,e$	predecessor
$\texttt{zero}\,e$	zero test
$(e\,,e)$	pair
$\texttt{fst}\,e$	first projection
$\texttt{snd}\,e$	second projection
$\lambda x : \tau \to e$	function abstraction
$e\,e$	function application
$\texttt{fix}\,e$	fixed-point recursion
a	atomic name ($a \in \mathbb{A}$)
$\nu a.\,e$	local name
$(e \rightleftharpoons e)\,e$	name swapping
$e = e$	name equality test
$\texttt{V}\,e$	variable term
$\texttt{A}\,e\,e$	application term
$\texttt{L}\,e$	lambda term
$\texttt{case}\,e\,\texttt{of}\,(\texttt{V}\,x \to e \mid \texttt{A}\,x\,x \to e \mid \texttt{L}\,x \to e)$	term case
$\alpha a.\,e$	name abstraction
$e\,\texttt{@}\,e$	name concretion
$c \in \mathrm{Can} ::=$	*canonical forms*
$\texttt{T} \mid \texttt{F} \mid \texttt{0} \mid \texttt{S}\,c \mid (e\,,e) \mid \lambda x : \tau \to e \mid a \mid \texttt{V}\,c \mid \texttt{A}\,c\,c \mid \texttt{L}\,c \mid \alpha a.\,c$	

Figure 1. Syntax of PNA

$$
\begin{aligned}
subst \triangleq\ & \lambda y : \texttt{term} \to \lambda x : \texttt{name} \to \\
& \texttt{fix}\,(\lambda(f : \texttt{term} \to \texttt{term}) \to \lambda y' : \texttt{term} \to \\
& \quad \texttt{case}\,y'\,\texttt{of} \\
& \quad\quad \texttt{V}\,x_1 \to \texttt{if}\,x_1 = x\,\texttt{then}\,y\,\texttt{else}\,y' \\
& \quad\quad \mid \texttt{A}\,y_2\,y_2' \to \texttt{A}\,(f\,y_2)\,(f\,y_2') \\
& \quad\quad \mid \texttt{L}\,z \to \texttt{L}\,(\alpha a.\,f(z\,\texttt{@}\,a))).
\end{aligned}
$$

Figure 1 gives the syntax of PNA. In the grammar for expressions, the part below the dotted line is what is added to PCF. There are two kinds of identifier in the language: *variables* $x, y, z, f, \ldots \in \mathbb{V}$ and *atomic names* $a, b, c, \ldots \in \mathbb{A}$. The sets $\mathbb{V}$ of variables and $\mathbb{A}$ of atomic names are disjoint and countably infinite. Both kinds of identifier may be bound and the language's binding forms are $\lambda x : \tau \to \_$, $\nu a.\_$, $\texttt{case}\,e\,\texttt{of}\,(\texttt{V}\,x \to \_ \mid \texttt{A}\,x\,x \to \_ \mid \texttt{L}\,x \to \_)$ and $\alpha a.\_$. We identify expressions up to α-equivalence of bound identifiers. For any expression e, we write $\mathrm{fn}(e)$ for its finite set of free atomic names and $\mathrm{fv}(e)$ for its finite set of free variables.

The reason for making a syntactic distinction between variables and atomic names is that they behave differently. Various properties of PNA, such as its typing judgement, are preserved by the operation of substitution of expressions for variables but are only preserved by permutations of atomic names rather than more general forms of substitution for names. The operation of simultaneous substitution of expressions $e_1, .., e_n$ for distinct variables $x_1, .., x_n$ in an expression e is written as $e[e_1/x_1, .., e_n/x_n]$, where the substitution avoids capture of both free variables and free atomic names by the language's binding forms. The operation of applying a finite permutation $\pi : \mathbb{A} \cong \mathbb{A}$ to an expression e is written $\pi \cdot e$. It

$$\frac{(x : \tau) \in \Gamma}{\Gamma \vdash x : \tau} \qquad \frac{c = \texttt{T} \mid \texttt{F}}{\Gamma \vdash c : \texttt{bool}}$$

$$\frac{\Gamma \vdash e_1 : \texttt{bool} \quad \Gamma \vdash e_2 : \tau \quad \Gamma \vdash e_3 : \tau}{\Gamma \vdash \texttt{if}\,e_1\,\texttt{then}\,e_2\,\texttt{else}\,e_3 : \tau} \qquad \frac{}{\Gamma \vdash \texttt{0} : \texttt{nat}}$$

$$\frac{\Gamma \vdash e : \texttt{nat}}{\Gamma \vdash \texttt{S}\,e : \texttt{nat}} \qquad \frac{\Gamma \vdash e : \texttt{nat}}{\Gamma \vdash \texttt{pred}\,e : \texttt{nat}} \qquad \frac{\Gamma \vdash e : \texttt{nat}}{\Gamma \vdash \texttt{zero}\,e : \texttt{bool}}$$

$$\frac{\Gamma \vdash e_1 : \tau_1 \quad \Gamma \vdash e_2 : \tau_2}{\Gamma \vdash (e_1\,, e_2) : \tau_1 \times \tau_2} \qquad \frac{\Gamma \vdash e : \tau_1 \times \tau_2}{\Gamma \vdash \texttt{fst}\,e : \tau_1}$$

$$\frac{\Gamma \vdash e : \tau_1 \times \tau_2}{\Gamma \vdash \texttt{snd}\,e : \tau_2} \qquad \frac{\Gamma, x : \tau \vdash e : \tau'}{\Gamma \vdash \lambda x : \tau \to e : \tau \to \tau'}$$

$$\frac{\Gamma \vdash e_1 : \tau \to \tau' \quad \Gamma \vdash e_2 : \tau}{\Gamma \vdash e_1\,e_2 : \tau'} \qquad \frac{\Gamma \vdash e : \tau \to \tau}{\Gamma \vdash \texttt{fix}\,e : \tau}$$

$$\frac{a \in \mathbb{A}}{\Gamma \vdash a : \texttt{name}} \qquad \frac{a \in \mathbb{A} \quad \Gamma \vdash e : \tau}{\Gamma \vdash \nu a.\,e : \tau}$$

$$\frac{\Gamma \vdash e_1 : \texttt{name} \quad \Gamma \vdash e_2 : \texttt{name} \quad \Gamma \vdash e_3 : \tau}{\Gamma \vdash (e_1 \rightleftharpoons e_2)\,e_3 : \tau} \qquad \frac{\Gamma \vdash e_1 : \texttt{name} \quad \Gamma \vdash e_2 : \texttt{name}}{\Gamma \vdash e_1 = e_2 : \texttt{bool}}$$

$$\frac{\Gamma \vdash e : \texttt{name}}{\Gamma \vdash \texttt{V}\,e : \texttt{term}} \qquad \frac{\Gamma \vdash e_1 : \texttt{term} \quad \Gamma \vdash e_2 : \texttt{term}}{\Gamma \vdash \texttt{A}\,e_1\,e_2 : \texttt{term}} \qquad \frac{\Gamma \vdash e : \delta\,\texttt{term}}{\Gamma \vdash \texttt{L}\,e : \texttt{term}}$$

$$\frac{\Gamma \vdash e : \texttt{term} \quad \Gamma, x_1 : \texttt{name} \vdash e_1 : \tau \quad \Gamma, x_2 : \texttt{term}, x_2' : \texttt{term} \vdash e_2 : \tau \quad \Gamma, x_3 : \delta\,\texttt{term} \vdash e_3 : \tau}{\Gamma \vdash \texttt{case}\,e\,\texttt{of}\,(\texttt{V}\,x_1 \to e_1 \mid \texttt{A}\,x_2\,x_2' \to e_2 \mid \texttt{L}\,x_3 \to e_3) : \tau}$$

$$\frac{a \in \mathbb{A} \quad \Gamma \vdash e : \tau}{\Gamma \vdash \alpha a.\,e : \delta\,\tau} \qquad \frac{\Gamma \vdash e_1 : \delta\,\tau \quad \Gamma \vdash e_2 : \texttt{name}}{\Gamma \vdash e_1\,\texttt{@}\,e_2 : \tau}$$

Figure 2. PNA typing rules

is defined by recursing into all sub-expressions and applying π to occurrences of atomic names. This is an action in the sense of Section 2 and makes the set Exp of PNA expressions into a nominal set. Since the elements of Exp are expressions up to α-equivalence, support in this nominal set is given by the finite set of free names of each expression.

PNA is a simply typed language. The grammar for types (Figure 1) extends that for PCF (in a version with products $\tau_1 \times \tau_2$) with a type $\texttt{name}$ of names, a type $\texttt{term}$ of λ-terms modulo α-equivalence, and name abstraction types $\delta\,\tau$. The inductively defined typing judgement $\Gamma \vdash e : \tau$ (read as 'in the environment Γ the expression e has type τ') is defined in Figure 2 by the usual rules for PCF and, below the dotted line, rules concerning names. The typing environments $\Gamma = \{x_1 : \tau_1, \ldots, x_n : \tau_n\}$ are finite functions from variables to types that track occurrences of free variables in e. Note that because there is only one sort of name, we do not bother to add a component to Γ tracking occurrences of free atomic names in e.

In Figure 3 we extend PCF's usual rules for an inductively defined big-step evaluation relation with the rules below the dotted

$$\frac{c = \mathtt{T} \mid \mathtt{F} \mid \mathtt{0} \mid (e_1\,,e_2) \mid \lambda x:\tau \to e}{c \Downarrow c} \qquad \frac{e \Downarrow c}{\mathtt{S}\,e \Downarrow \mathtt{S}\,c}$$

$$\frac{e_1 \Downarrow \mathtt{T} \qquad e_2 \Downarrow c}{\mathtt{if}\;e_1\;\mathtt{then}\;e_2\;\mathtt{else}\;e_3 \Downarrow c} \qquad \frac{e_1 \Downarrow \mathtt{F} \qquad e_3 \Downarrow c}{\mathtt{if}\;e_1\;\mathtt{then}\;e_2\;\mathtt{else}\;e_3 \Downarrow c}$$

$$\frac{e \Downarrow \mathtt{S}\,c}{\mathtt{pred}\,e \Downarrow c} \qquad \frac{e \Downarrow \mathtt{0}}{\mathtt{zero}\,e \Downarrow \mathtt{T}} \qquad \frac{e \Downarrow \mathtt{S}\,c}{\mathtt{zero}\,e \Downarrow \mathtt{F}}$$

$$\frac{e \Downarrow (e_1\,,e_2) \qquad e_1 \Downarrow c}{\mathtt{fst}\,e \Downarrow c} \qquad \frac{e \Downarrow (e_1\,,e_2) \qquad e_2 \Downarrow c}{\mathtt{snd}\,e \Downarrow c}$$

$$\frac{e_1 \Downarrow \lambda x:\tau \to e \qquad e[e_2/x] \Downarrow c}{e_1\,e_2 \Downarrow c} \qquad \frac{e(\mathtt{fix}\,e) \Downarrow c}{\mathtt{fix}\,e \Downarrow c}$$

. . . .

$$\frac{a \in \mathbb{A}}{a \Downarrow a} \qquad \frac{e \Downarrow c \qquad a \backslash c := c'}{\nu a.\,e \Downarrow c'} \qquad \frac{e_1 \Downarrow a_1 \qquad e_2 \Downarrow a_2 \qquad e_3 \Downarrow c}{(e_1 \rightleftharpoons e_2)\,e_3 \Downarrow (a_1\;a_2)\cdot c}$$

$$\frac{e_1 \Downarrow a \qquad e_2 \Downarrow a}{e_1 = e_2 \Downarrow \mathtt{T}} \qquad \frac{e_1 \Downarrow a \qquad e_2 \Downarrow a' \qquad a \neq a'}{e_1 = e_2 \Downarrow \mathtt{F}}$$

$$\frac{e \Downarrow c}{\mathtt{V}\,e \Downarrow \mathtt{V}\,c} \qquad \frac{e_1 \Downarrow c_1 \qquad e_2 \Downarrow c_2}{\mathtt{A}\,e_1\,e_2 \Downarrow \mathtt{A}\,c_1\,c_2} \qquad \frac{e \Downarrow c}{\mathtt{L}\,e \Downarrow \mathtt{L}\,c}$$

$$\frac{e \Downarrow \mathtt{V}\,c \qquad e_1[c/x_1] \Downarrow c'}{\mathtt{case}\;e\;\mathtt{of}\;(\mathtt{V}\,x_1 \to e_1 \mid \cdots) \Downarrow c'}$$

$$\frac{e \Downarrow \mathtt{A}\,c\,c' \qquad e_2[c/x_2, c'/x_2'] \Downarrow c''}{\mathtt{case}\;e\;\mathtt{of}\;(\cdots \mid \mathtt{A}\,x_2\,x_2' \to e_2 \mid \cdots) \Downarrow c''}$$

$$\frac{e \Downarrow \mathtt{L}\,c \qquad e_3[c/x_3] \Downarrow c'}{\mathtt{case}\;e\;\mathtt{of}\;(\cdots \mid \mathtt{L}\,x_3 \to e_3) \Downarrow c'} \qquad \frac{e \Downarrow c}{\alpha a.\,e \Downarrow \alpha a.\,c}$$

$$\frac{e_1 \Downarrow \alpha a.\,c \qquad e_2 \Downarrow a' \qquad a \neq a' \qquad \nu a.\,(a\;a')\cdot c \Downarrow c'}{e_1 \mathbin{@} e_2 \Downarrow c'}$$

Figure 3. PNA evaluation rules

line that concern names. The evaluation rule for local names makes use of the auxiliary definition in Figure 4. Thus the relation $e \Downarrow c$ defines when a PNA expression e evaluates to *canonical form* c. See Figure 1 for the grammar of canonical forms. As for PCF, we only evaluate expressions that are *variable-closed* in the sense that $\mathrm{fv}(e) = \emptyset$, though they may contain free atomic names for evaluation. This is because, unlike variables, atomic names are canonical forms. We also choose to evaluate under name abstractions, so that $\alpha a.\,e$ is in canonical form if and only if e is. This permits a representation of α-equivalence classes of λ-terms in PNA that is as simple as PCF's representation of numbers: they are in bijection with variable-closed canonical forms of type `term`. (It is certainly possible to give a different operational semantics in which one does not evaluate under name abstractions. The corresponding denotational semantics would make more use of lifting than does the one in Section 8.) To deconstruct name abstractions, PNA features an operational version of the total concretion operation discussed in Section 6. Its behaviour is given by the last rule in Figure 3 and corresponds to property (10).

$$\frac{c = \mathtt{T} \mid \mathtt{F} \mid \mathtt{0} \mid \mathtt{S}\,c'}{a \backslash c := c} \qquad \frac{}{a \backslash (e_1\,,e_2) := (\nu a.\,e_1\,,\nu a.\,e_2)}$$

$$\frac{}{a \backslash \lambda x:\tau \to e := \lambda x:\tau \to \nu a.\,e} \qquad \frac{a \neq a'}{a \backslash a' := a'}$$

$$\frac{a \backslash c := c'}{a \backslash \mathtt{V}\,c := \mathtt{V}\,c'} \qquad \frac{a \backslash c_1 := c_1' \qquad a \backslash c_2 := c_2'}{a \backslash \mathtt{A}\,c_1\,c_2 := \mathtt{A}\,c_1'\,c_2'}$$

$$\frac{a \backslash c := c'}{a \backslash \mathtt{L}\,c := \mathtt{L}\,c'} \qquad \frac{a \backslash c := c' \qquad a \neq a'}{a \backslash \alpha a'.\,c := \alpha a'.\,c'}$$

Figure 4. Partial operation of name restriction, $a \backslash c := c'$

As for PCF, the PNA evaluation relation is easily seen to be deterministic ($e \Downarrow c \wedge e \Downarrow c' \Rightarrow c = c'$) and type-sound ($\emptyset \vdash e : \tau \wedge e \Downarrow c \Rightarrow \emptyset \vdash c : \tau$). It is also equivariant:

$$e \Downarrow c \Rightarrow \pi \cdot e \Downarrow \pi \cdot c. \tag{16}$$

Remark 21 (Odersky-style local names). Evaluation of locally scoped names $\nu a.\,e$ makes use of Odersky's functional theory of local names [24], because that way of evaluating them fits the intended model of PNA using nominal Scott domains. Scopes intrude in a type-directed fashion, as can be seen in the partial operation of name restriction on canonical forms $a \backslash c := c'$ defined in Figure 4. This operation is partial because $a \backslash a := c$ holds for no c. Thus, unlike in Pitts [27], we choose to follow Odersky [24] and make $\nu a.\,a$ a stuck expression that does not evaluate to any canonical form and whose denotation is $\perp$. This has the advantage that there are no exotic values (value-closed canonical forms) of type `term`—the only values of that type correspond to α-equivalence classes of λ-terms. The use of Odersky-style local names means that the operational semantics of PNA is stateless, unlike the operational semantics of the more usual generative version of $\nu a.\,\_$ used in the ν-calculus [29]. At the same time, it is known to be as expressive as that version in as much as there is an adequate translation from generative into Odersky-style local names [19].

Definition 22 (contextual equivalence). As usual, a PNA *context* $C[\_]$ is an expression with a single sub-expression replaced by the place-holder '$\_$', and $C[e]$ is the expression that results from replacing $\_$ by an expression e (possibly capturing free variables and atomic names in e). Given well-typed expressions $\Gamma \vdash e : \tau$ and $\Gamma \vdash e' : \tau$, we write $\Gamma \vdash e \cong_{\mathsf{PNA}} e' : \tau$ and say that e and e' are *contextually equivalent* if for all contexts $C[\_]$ for which $\emptyset \vdash C[e] : \mathtt{bool}$ and $\emptyset \vdash C[e'] : \mathtt{bool}$ hold, it is the case that $C[e] \Downarrow \mathtt{T}$ if and only if $C[e'] \Downarrow \mathtt{T}$.

Example 23. Although PNA contains the expressions of the ν-calculus [29] as a subset, the two languages have different semantics for local names—Odersky-style for PNA versus generative for the ν-calculus. This affects properties of contextual equivalence in the two languages. For example, if $\Gamma, x:\tau \vdash e : \tau'$, then

$$\Gamma \vdash \nu a.\,\lambda x:\tau \to e \cong_{\mathsf{PNA}} \lambda x:\tau \to \nu a.\,e : \tau \to \tau' \tag{17}$$

is valid. However, this is not always the case in the ν-calculus [29, Example 2]. One can prove (17) by checking that this identity holds in the denotational model developed in the next section and then appealing to the computational adequacy result proved there (Theorem 27). On the other hand, analogues of some ν-calculus equivalences are also true for PNA, once one takes into account the fact that, like PCF, PNA is call-by-name but the ν-calculus is call-by-value. For example, here are call-by-name analogues of equivalences in Pitts and Stark [29, Example 4]

$$\begin{array}{l}\emptyset \vdash \nu a.\, \lambda x : \texttt{name} \to (x = a) \cong_{\mathsf{PNA}} \\ \lambda x : \texttt{name} \to \texttt{if}\ x = x\ \texttt{then F else F} : \texttt{name} \to \texttt{bool}\end{array} \tag{18}$$

$$\begin{array}{l}\emptyset \vdash \nu a.\, \nu a'.\, \lambda(f : \texttt{name} \to \texttt{bool}) \to eq\,(f\,a)\,(f\,a') \cong_{\mathsf{PNA}} \\ \lambda(f : \texttt{name} \to \texttt{bool}) \to \nu a.\ \texttt{if}\ f\,a\ \texttt{then T else T} \\ : (\texttt{name} \to \texttt{bool}) \to \texttt{bool}.\end{array} \tag{19}$$

Here eq : bool $\to$ bool $\to$ bool is an abbreviation for a boolean-equality test defined using conditionals. In contrast to the ν-calculus, where it takes some effort to prove equivalences like (18) and (19), for PNA these properties are easily seen to hold in the straightforward and computationally adequate denotational semantics that we describe next.

8. Denotational semantics of PNA

For each PNA type τ, we define a nominal Scott domain $[\![\tau]\!]$ by recursion on the structure of τ as follows.

- $[\![\texttt{bool}]\!] = 2_\perp$, the flat domain (*cf.* Remark 9) on a discrete nominal set with two elements, $2 = \{\text{true}, \text{false}\}$.
- $[\![\texttt{nat}]\!] = \mathbb{N}_\perp$, the flat domain on the discrete nominal set of natural numbers, $\mathbb{N} = \{0, 1, 2, \ldots\}$.
- $[\![\tau \times \tau']\!] = [\![\tau]\!] \times [\![\tau']\!]$, the product of nominal Scott domains.
- $[\![\tau \to \tau']\!] = [\![\tau]\!] \to [\![\tau']\!]$, the nominal Scott domain of finitely supported, uniform-continuous functions (Theorem 12).
- $[\![\texttt{name}]\!] = \mathbb{A}_\perp$, the flat domain on the nominal set of atomic names, $\mathbb{A} = \{a, b, c, \ldots\}$.
- $[\![\texttt{term}]\!] = (\Lambda_\alpha)_\perp$, the flat domain on the nominal set of α-equivalence classes of λ-terms [14, Theorem 6.2],

$$\Lambda_\alpha \triangleq \{t ::= a \mid \lambda a.t \mid t\,t\}/{=_\alpha} \quad (\text{where } a \in \mathbb{A}). \tag{20}$$

- $[\![\delta\,\tau]\!] = [\mathbb{A}][\![\tau]\!]$, the domain of name abstractions of the nominal Scott domain $[\![\tau]\!]$ (Theorem 17).

Typing environments are interpreted as finite cartesian products: $[\![\{x_1 : \tau_1, \ldots, x_n : \tau_n\}]\!] = [\![\tau_1]\!] \times \cdots \times [\![\tau_n]\!]$. Finite tuples $\rho \in [\![\Gamma]\!]$ can be interpreted as partial functions from variables to domains such that $\mathrm{dom}(\rho) = \mathrm{dom}(\Gamma)$ and $\rho(x) \in [\![\Gamma(x)]\!]$ for all $x \in \mathrm{dom}(\Gamma)$. We call such partial functions Γ-*environments*. If $\rho \in [\![\Gamma]\!]$, $x \notin \mathrm{dom}(\Gamma)$ and $d \in [\![\tau]\!]$, then we write $\rho[x \mapsto d]$ for the $(\Gamma, x : \tau)$-environment that maps x to d and otherwise acts like ρ.

For each well-typed expression $\Gamma \vdash e : \tau$ and Γ-environment $\rho \in [\![\Gamma]\!]$ we define an element $[\![e]\!]\rho \in [\![\tau]\!]$ satisfying the clauses in Figure 5, by recursion over the structure of e.[3] The clauses for syntax constructs from PCF are analogous to the standard denotational semantics of PCF in Scott domains. The functions π_1 and π_2 in the clauses for $\texttt{fst}\,e$ and $\texttt{snd}\,e$ are the first and second projection functions for pairs. fix in the clause for $\texttt{fix}\,e$ is the least fixed point function (9). The clauses below the dotted line in Figure 5 are for the new syntactic constructs of PNA. In the clauses involving expressions of type term, we use $[t]_\alpha$ to denote the α-equivalence class of the syntax tree t of a λ-term. We use the concretion function from (10) in the clause for concretion expressions $e_1 \,\texttt{@}\, e_2$. The clause for $\nu a.\,e$ makes use of the uniform-continuous name restriction operation that each $[\![\tau]\!]$ has by virtue of Theorem 19. Note that the side conditions in the clauses for $\nu a.\,e$ and $\alpha a.\,e$ are always satisfiable as we identify expression up to α-equivalence. One can reformulate these clauses without side

[3] Strictly speaking, it is by α-structural recursion [26] since we identify expressions up to α-equivalence of bound identifiers.

$$[\![x]\!]\rho = \rho\,x$$

$$[\![\texttt{T}]\!]\rho = \text{true} \qquad [\![\texttt{F}]\!]\rho = \text{false}$$

$$[\![\texttt{if}\ e_1\ \texttt{then}\ e_2\ \texttt{else}\ e_3]\!]\rho = \begin{cases} [\![e_2]\!]\rho & \text{if } [\![e_1]\!]\rho = \text{true} \\ [\![e_3]\!]\rho & \text{if } [\![e_1]\!]\rho = \text{false} \\ \perp & \text{otherwise}\end{cases}$$

$$[\![\texttt{0}]\!]\rho = 0$$

$$[\![\texttt{S}\ e]\!]\rho = \begin{cases} n+1 & \text{if } [\![e]\!]\rho = n \in \mathbb{N} \\ \perp & \text{otherwise}\end{cases}$$

$$[\![\texttt{pred}\ e]\!]\rho = \begin{cases} n & \text{if } [\![e]\!]\rho = n+1 \in \mathbb{N} \\ \perp & \text{otherwise}\end{cases}$$

$$[\![\texttt{zero}\ e]\!]\rho = \begin{cases} \text{true} & \text{if } [\![e]\!]\rho = 0 \in \mathbb{N} \\ \text{false} & \text{if } [\![e]\!]\rho = n+1 \in \mathbb{N} \\ \perp & \text{otherwise}\end{cases}$$

$$[\![(e_1\,,\,e_2)]\!]\rho = ([\![e_1]\!]\rho, [\![e_2]\!]\rho)$$

$$[\![\texttt{fst}\ e]\!]\rho = \pi_1([\![e]\!]\rho) \qquad [\![\texttt{snd}\ e]\!]\rho = \pi_2([\![e]\!]\rho)$$

$$[\![\lambda x : \tau \to e]\!]\rho = \lambda d \in [\![\tau]\!].\ [\![e]\!]\rho[x \mapsto d]$$

$$[\![e_1\,e_2]\!]\rho = [\![e_1]\!]\rho\,([\![e_2]\!]\rho)$$

$$[\![\texttt{fix}\ e]\!]\rho = \text{fix}([\![e]\!]\rho)$$

. . . .

$$[\![a]\!]\rho = a$$

$$[\![\nu a.\,e]\!]\rho = a\backslash([\![e]\!]\rho) \quad \text{if } a \mathrel{\#} \rho$$

$$[\![(e_1 \rightleftharpoons e_2)\,e_3]\!]\rho = \begin{cases} (a_1\ a_2)\cdot([\![e_3]\!]\rho) & \text{if } [\![e_i]\!]\rho = a_i \in \mathbb{A}\ (i = 1,2) \\ \perp & \text{otherwise}\end{cases}$$

$$[\![e_1 = e_2]\!]\rho = \begin{cases} eq_a([\![e_2]\!]\rho) & \text{if } [\![e_1]\!]\rho = a \in \mathbb{A} \\ \perp & \text{otherwise}\end{cases}$$

$$[\![\texttt{V}\ e]\!]\rho = \begin{cases} [a]_\alpha & \text{if } [\![e]\!]\rho = a \in \mathbb{A} \\ \perp & \text{otherwise}\end{cases}$$

$$[\![\texttt{A}\ e_1\,e_2]\!]\rho = \begin{cases} [t_1\,t_2]_\alpha & \text{if } [\![e_i]\!]\rho = [t_i]_\alpha \in \Lambda_\alpha\ (i = 1,2) \\ \perp & \text{otherwise}\end{cases}$$

$$[\![\texttt{L}\ e]\!]\rho = \begin{cases} [\lambda a.t]_\alpha & \text{if } [\![e]\!]\rho = \langle a\rangle[t]_\alpha \in [\mathbb{A}]\Lambda_\alpha \\ \perp & \text{otherwise}\end{cases}$$

$$[\![\texttt{case}\ e\ \texttt{of}\ (\texttt{V}\,x_1 \to e_1 \mid \texttt{A}\,x_2\,x_2' \to e_2 \mid \texttt{L}\,x_3 \to e_3)]\!]\rho =$$
$$\begin{cases} [\![e_1]\!]\rho[x_1 \mapsto a] & \text{if } [\![e]\!]\rho = [a]_\alpha \\ [\![e_2]\!]\rho[x_2 \mapsto [t]_\alpha, x_2' \mapsto [t']_\alpha] & \text{if } [\![e]\!]\rho = [t\,t']_\alpha \\ [\![e_3]\!]\rho[x_3 \mapsto \langle a\rangle[t]_\alpha] & \text{if } [\![e]\!]\rho = [\lambda a.t]_\alpha \\ \perp & \text{otherwise}\end{cases}$$

$$[\![\alpha a.\,e]\!]\rho = \langle a\rangle([\![e]\!]\rho) \quad \text{if } a \mathrel{\#} \rho$$

$$[\![e_1 \,\texttt{@}\, e_2]\!]\rho = ([\![e_1]\!]\rho) \mathbin{@} ([\![e_2]\!]\rho)$$

Figure 5. PNA denotational semantics

conditions [cf. 27, Figure 4]

$$[\![\nu a.\, e]\!] = a \backslash (\lambda \rho \in [\![\Gamma]\!].\, [\![e]\!]\rho) \tag{21}$$

$$[\![\alpha a.\, e]\!] = a \backslash (\lambda \rho \in [\![\Gamma]\!].\, \langle a \rangle ([\![e]\!]\rho)) \tag{22}$$

by appealing to the slightly subtle properties of the name restriction operation for exponential domains (Remark 20).

Notation 24. For the empty typing environment $\emptyset$, there is a unique $\emptyset$-environment, ρ_0. Given a variable-closed expression $\emptyset \vdash e : \tau$, we simply write $[\![e]\!]$ for $[\![e]\!]\rho_0$.

Using the developments from Sections 5 and 6 one can prove the following results.

Lemma 25. *The denotation of any well-typed* PNA *expression* $\Gamma \vdash e : \tau$ *is a well-defined, finitely supported and uniform-continuous function* $[\![e]\!] : [\![\Gamma]\!] \to [\![\tau]\!]$. □

Lemma 26 (PNA **soundness**). *If* $e \Downarrow c$, *then* $[\![e]\!] = [\![c]\!]$.

Proof. The proof is by rule induction for $\Downarrow$, using the following properties of the denotational semantics whose proofs we omit.

- **Substitution lemma** If $\Gamma \vdash e : \tau$ and $\Gamma, x : \tau \vdash e' : \tau'$, then $\Gamma \vdash e'[e/x] : \tau'$ holds and for all $\rho \in [\![\Gamma]\!]$ we have $[\![e'[e/x]]\!]\rho = [\![e']\!]\rho[x \mapsto [\![e]\!]\rho]$.
- **Equivariance lemma** $\pi \cdot [\![e]\!] = [\![\pi \cdot e]\!]$.
- **Restriction lemma** If $a \backslash c := c'$ with c and c' variable-closed canonical forms of type τ, then the uniform-continuous name restriction operation defined on $[\![\tau]\!]$ as in Theorem 19 satisfies $a \backslash [\![c]\!] = [\![c']\!]$. □

The following result allows one to establish PNA contextual equivalences by proving equality of denotations.

Theorem 27 (PNA **computational adequacy**). *Given* $\Gamma \vdash e : \tau$ *and* $\Gamma \vdash e' : \tau$, *if* $[\![e]\!] = [\![e']\!] \in [\![\Gamma]\!] \to [\![\tau]\!]$, *then* $\Gamma \vdash e \cong_{\mathsf{PNA}} e' : \tau$.

Proof. It is not hard to see that the denotational semantic is compositional, in the sense that $[\![e]\!] = [\![e']\!] \Rightarrow [\![C[e]]\!] = [\![C[e']]\!]$. So in view of Lemma 26 it suffices to show that if e is a variable-closed expression of type bool, then

$$[\![e]\!] = \text{true} \Rightarrow e \Downarrow \texttt{T}. \tag{23}$$

We prove this by devising a suitable logical relation

$$d \lhd_\tau e \quad (d \in [\![\tau]\!],\ \emptyset \vdash e : \tau) \tag{24}$$

between the semantics and the syntax of PNA. (See Streicher [38, Chapter 4] for a good exposition of this method of proving computational adequacy for the Scott domain model of PCF.) The definition of $\lhd_\tau$ is by recursion on the structure of the type τ:

$$d \lhd_\gamma e \triangleq d = \bot \vee (\exists c)\, e \Downarrow c \wedge [\![c]\!] = d$$
$$\text{for } \gamma = \texttt{bool}, \texttt{nat}, \texttt{name}, \texttt{term}$$
$$(d_1, d_2) \lhd_{\tau_1 \times \tau_2} e \triangleq d_1 \lhd_{\tau_1} \texttt{fst}\, e \wedge d_2 \lhd_{\tau_2} \texttt{snd}\, e$$
$$d \lhd_{\tau_1 \to \tau_2} e \triangleq (\forall d_1, e_1)\, d_1 \lhd_{\tau_1} e_1 \Rightarrow d\, d_1 \lhd_{\tau_2} e\, e_1$$
$$d \lhd_{\delta\, \tau} e \triangleq (\text{И} a)\, d \mathbin{@} a \lhd_\tau e \mathbin{@} a.$$

The definition is standard except for the last clause, which is for name abstraction types. There we use the *freshness quantifier* (Иa) of nominal logic [25]. Thus $d \lhd_{\delta\,\tau} e$ holds if and only if $d \mathbin{@} a \lhd_\tau e \mathbin{@} a$ holds for some $a \mathbin{\#} (d, e)$, or equivalently, for any $a \mathbin{\#} (d, e)$.

The proof that this logical relation is closed under restriction, abstraction and concretion

$$d \lhd_\tau e \Rightarrow (\forall a)\ a \backslash d \lhd_\tau \nu a.\, e \tag{25}$$

$$d \lhd_\tau e \Rightarrow (\forall a)\ \langle a \rangle d \lhd_{\delta\,\tau} \alpha a.\, e \tag{26}$$

$$d \lhd_{\delta\,\tau} e \Rightarrow (\forall a)\ d \mathbin{@} a \lhd_\tau e \mathbin{@} a \tag{27}$$

is not straightforward, and we omit the details here. Armed with those properties, the fundamental property of the logical relation follows by induction on the structure of expressions; in particular we get $\emptyset \vdash e : \tau \Rightarrow [\![e]\!] \lhd_\tau e$. This, combined with the definition of $\lhd_{\texttt{bool}}$ yields (23). □

Using Theorem 27 we can prove many contextual equivalences in PNA, such as those in Example 23, in a straightforward manner via the denotational semantics. For example (18) is proved by the following argument. Since we identify expressions up to α-equivalence, for any given $a' \in \mathbb{A}$ we can pick a representative expression $\nu a.\, \lambda x : \texttt{name} \to (x = a)$ such that $a \neq a'$, then

$[\![\nu a.\, \lambda x : \texttt{name} \to (x = a)]\!]\, a'$	
$= (a \backslash [\![\lambda x : \texttt{name} \to (x = a)]\!])\, a'$	by definition in Figure 5
$= a \backslash ([\![\lambda x : \texttt{name} \to (x = a)]\!]\, a')$	by (13), since $a \neq a'$
$= a \backslash \text{false}$	as $a \neq a'$
$= \text{false}$	
$= [\![\lambda x : \texttt{name} \to \texttt{if}\ x = x\ \texttt{then F else F}]\!]\, a'.$	

Similarly $[\![\nu a.\, \lambda x : \texttt{name} \to (x = a)]\!] \bot = \bot = [\![\lambda x : \texttt{name} \to \texttt{if}\ x = x\ \texttt{then F else F}]\!] \bot$. Hence $[\![\nu a.\, \lambda x : \texttt{name} \to (x = a)]\!] = [\![\lambda x : \texttt{name} \to \texttt{if}\ x = x\ \texttt{then F else F}]\!]$ and so (18) holds by Theorem 27. To prove example (19) one can combine the definition in Figure 5 with the fact that if $a, a' \mathbin{\#} f \in (\mathbb{A}_\bot \to 2_\bot) \to 2_\bot$, then $f\, a = f((a\ a') \cdot a') = (a\ a') \cdot (f\, a') = f\, a'$ (since $f\, a' \in 2_\bot$). In contrast to the situation here, properties like (18) and (19) for the ν-calculus, which uses generative rather than Odersky-style local names, can be hard to establish whether one uses operational or denotational techniques. See Tzevelekos [43], which focusses on an equivalence like (19).

9. Full abstraction for PNA$^+$

Plotkin [30] famously proves that the Scott domain model of PCF is computationally adequate, but not fully abstract: equality of denotations implies, but is not implied by, PCF contextual equivalence. Furthermore, he shows that the Scott model becomes fully abstract once one extends PCF with a parallel-or construct.

Moving to nominal Scott domains and PNA, Plotkin's negative result can certainly be extended to show that the converse of Theorem 27 fails to hold. We do not yet know what happens if one adds just parallel-or to PNA (see Section 10). However, adding not only parallel-or, but also operational versions of the uniform-compact functionals in Examples 14 and 15, we will show that the nominal Scott domain model is fully abstract for contextual equivalence in the extended language.

Note that this section does *not* give a full abstraction result for the more common generative local names used for example in FreshML or the ν-calculus. Generative names can be modelled adequately in **Nsd** through a continuation monad as described at the end of Section 6, but full abstraction fails in this model, because of the results of Stark [36, Page 66].

Definition 28. The language PNA$^+$ is obtained by extending PNA with expressions for parallel-or, for existentially quantifying over name ('there exists some x : name such that…') and for forming definite descriptions over name ('the unique x : name such that…'). The syntax, typing and evaluation rules for this extension are given in Figure 6. Contextual equivalence for the extended language $\Gamma \vdash e \cong_{\mathsf{PNA}^+} e' : \tau$ is defined in the same way as it is for PNA in Definition 22.

Remark 29. The addition of existential quantification and definite description is mainly motivated by the need for them in our proof of

$e ::=$ *expressions*
$\ldots$ (as for PNA)
e `por` e parallel-or
`ex` $x.\, e$ existential name quantification
`the` $x.\, e$ definite name description

$$\frac{\Gamma \vdash e_1 : \texttt{bool} \qquad \Gamma \vdash e_2 : \texttt{bool}}{\Gamma \vdash e_1 \,\texttt{por}\, e_2 : \texttt{bool}}$$

$$\frac{\Gamma, x : \texttt{name} \vdash e : \texttt{bool}}{\Gamma \vdash \texttt{ex}\, x.\, e : \texttt{bool}} \qquad \frac{\Gamma, x : \texttt{name} \vdash e : \texttt{bool}}{\Gamma \vdash \texttt{the}\, x.\, e : \texttt{name}}$$

$$\frac{e_1 \Downarrow \texttt{T}}{\texttt{por}\, e_1\, e_2 \Downarrow \texttt{T}} \qquad \frac{e_2 \Downarrow \texttt{T}}{e_1 \,\texttt{por}\, e_2 \Downarrow \texttt{T}} \qquad \frac{e_1 \Downarrow \texttt{F} \qquad e_2 \Downarrow \texttt{F}}{e_1 \,\texttt{por}\, e_2 \Downarrow \texttt{F}}$$

$$\frac{e[a/x] \Downarrow \texttt{T}}{\texttt{ex}\, x.\, e \Downarrow \texttt{T}} \qquad \frac{a' \# e \qquad (\forall b \in \mathrm{fn}(e) \cup \{a'\})\; e[b/x] \Downarrow \texttt{F}}{\texttt{ex}\, x.\, e \Downarrow \texttt{F}}$$

$$\frac{e[a/x] \Downarrow \texttt{T} \qquad a' \# (e, a) \qquad (\forall b \in (\mathrm{fn}(e) - \{a\}) \cup \{a'\})\; e[b/x] \Downarrow \texttt{F}}{\texttt{the}\, x.\, e \Downarrow a}$$

$$[\![e_1 \,\texttt{por}\, e_2]\!]\rho = por\,([\![e_1]\!]\rho)\,([\![e_2]\!]\rho)$$
$$[\![\texttt{ex}\, x.\, e]\!]\rho = exists_{\mathbb{A}}([\![\lambda x : \texttt{name} \to e]\!]\rho)$$
$$[\![\texttt{the}\, x.\, e]\!]\rho = the_{\mathbb{A}}([\![\lambda x : \texttt{name} \to e]\!]\rho)$$

Figure 6. PNA$^+$

full abstraction (Theorem 30). Existential quantification for numbers (rather than, as here, for names) occurs in Plotkin's original PCF paper [30], and definite description has a long history in logic, but it is harder to motivate from a programming language perspective. In fact, a definite description functional for numbers rather than for names is not computable. The computability of `ex` $x.\, e$ and `the` $x.\, e$ provide an example of the phenomenon of 'finite modulo symmetry' mentioned in the Introduction. For example, to prove `ex` $x.\, e \Downarrow \texttt{F}$, we just have to pick one of the infinitely many atomic names a' that do not occur free in e and then show $e[a'/x] \Downarrow \texttt{F}$ and $e[b/x] \Downarrow \texttt{F}$ for each of the finitely many atomic names b that do occur free in e. This works because the equivariance property (16) of evaluation implies that if $e[a'/x] \Downarrow \texttt{F}$, then $e[a''/x] \Downarrow \texttt{F}$ holds for any a'' not occurring free in e.

The denotational semantics of PNA$^+$ expressions is given by extending the definition in Figure 5 with the clauses at the bottom of Figure 6. Here $por \in \mathrm{K}(2_\perp \to 2_\perp \to 2_\perp)$ is the usual parallel-or function satisfying

$$por\, d\, d' = \begin{cases} \text{true} & \text{if } d = \text{true or } d' = \text{true} \\ \text{false} & \text{if } d = \text{false and } d' = \text{false} \\ \perp & \text{otherwise;} \end{cases}$$

$exists_{\mathbb{A}} \in \mathrm{K}((\mathbb{A}_\perp \to 2_\perp) \to 2_\perp)$ is as in Example 14, and $the_{\mathbb{A}} \in \mathrm{K}((\mathbb{A}_\perp \to 2_\perp) \to \mathbb{A}_\perp)$ is as in Example 15.

Theorem 30 (full abstraction for PNA$^+$**).** *For all well-typed expressions* $\Gamma \vdash e : \tau$ *and* $\Gamma \vdash e' : \tau$ *in* PNA$^+$, *we have*

$$[\![e]\!] = [\![e']\!] \in [\![\Gamma]\!] \to [\![\tau]\!] \Leftrightarrow \Gamma \vdash e \cong_{\mathsf{PNA}^+} e' : \tau. \qquad (\mathrm{FA}_\tau)$$

The sketch of the proof of this result occupies the rest of this section.

The extension of Theorem 27 to PNA$^+$ is straightforward and gives us the left-to-right implication in (FA_τ). Establishing the reverse implication inevitably leads to an investigation of the definability of elements of the nominal Scott domain model by PNA$^+$ expressions. However, our proof of the right-to-left implication in (FA_τ) does not exactly follow any of the proof patterns linking definability with full abstraction surveyed by Curien [10]. In particular, we only know that the uniform-compact elements of the nominal Scott domain $[\![\tau]\!]$ are definable in PNA$^+$ for certain types that avoid the use of function types $\tau_1 \to \tau_2$ in which the nominal Scott domain $[\![\tau_2]\!]$ might contain elements with non-empty support. So $\tau_2 = \texttt{nat}$ is OK, but $\tau_2 = \texttt{name}$ is not, for example. This leads us to make the following definition.

Definition 31 (simple types). Let Styp $\subseteq$ Typ be the subset of the collection of types (Figure 1) given by the following grammar:

$$\sigma ::= \texttt{nat} \mid \texttt{name} \mid \sigma \times \sigma \mid \sigma \to \texttt{nat}.$$

The following lemma is the key to the usefulness of simple types. It is where the presence of '`the` $x.\, e$' expressions in PNA$^+$ gets used.

Lemma 32. *Any type* τ *is a* PNA$^+$*-definable retract of a simple type* $\sigma \in$ Styp, *meaning that there are closed* PNA$^+$ *expressions* $\emptyset \vdash i : \tau \to \sigma$ *and* $\emptyset \vdash r : \sigma \to \tau$ *with* $[\![\lambda x : \tau \to r\,(i\,x)]\!] = id_{[\![\tau]\!]}$.

Proof. First note that because name abstraction satisfies a form of η-expansion ($[\![\alpha a.\,(e \mathbin{@} a)]\!] = [\![e]\!]$, if $a \notin \mathrm{fn}(e)$), each $\delta\,\tau$ is a PNA$^+$-definable retract of $\texttt{name} \to \tau$ (PNA-definable, in fact), via

$$i \triangleq \lambda x : \delta\,\tau \to \lambda y : \texttt{name} \to x \mathbin{@} y \qquad (28)$$
$$r \triangleq \lambda(f : \texttt{name} \to \tau) \to \alpha a.\, f\, a \qquad (29)$$

(*cf.* [27, Theorem 2.13]). Secondly, using '`the` $x.\, e$' expressions, we also have that `name` itself is a PNA$^+$-definable retract of $\texttt{name} \to \texttt{nat}$, via

$$i \triangleq \lambda x : \texttt{name} \to \lambda y : \texttt{name} \to \texttt{if}\; x = y \;\texttt{then 0 else S 0}$$
$$r \triangleq \lambda(f : \texttt{name} \to \texttt{nat}) \to \texttt{the}\, x.\, \texttt{zero}\,(f\, x).$$

Thirdly, again using '`the` $x.\, e$' expressions, one can also show that `term` is a PNA$^+$-definable retract of $\texttt{nat} \times (\texttt{name} \to \texttt{nat})$ (proof omitted). Finally, it is not hard to see that `bool` is a PNA$^+$-definable (actually PCF-definable) retract of `nat`.

Using these four facts, one can proceed by induction on the structure of types to show that each τ is a PNA$^+$-definable retract of some simple type. □

Lemma 33. *If* τ *is a* PNA$^+$*-definable retract of* σ, *then full abstraction at* σ *implies full abstraction at* τ, *i.e.* $(\mathrm{FA}_\sigma) \Rightarrow (\mathrm{FA}_\tau)$.

Proof. Given i and r as in Lemma 32, suppose (FA_σ) holds and that $\Gamma \vdash e \cong_{\mathsf{PNA}^+} e' : \tau$, then we have $\Gamma \vdash i\, e \cong_{\mathsf{PNA}^+} i\, e' : \sigma$ by compositionality of $\cong_{\mathsf{PNA}^+}$. Thus by (FA_σ), for any $\rho \in [\![\Gamma]\!]$ we have $[\![i]\!]([\![e]\!]\rho) = [\![i\, e]\!]\rho = [\![i\, e']\!]\rho = [\![i]\!]([\![e']\!]\rho)$. We know that $[\![i]\!]$ is injective since it has a left inverse $[\![r]\!]$, and hence $(\forall \rho \in [\![\Gamma]\!])\; [\![e]\!]\rho = [\![e']\!]\rho$. Thus $[\![e]\!] = [\![e']\!] \in [\![\Gamma]\!] \to [\![\tau]\!]$. □

Combining these two lemmas, to prove Theorem 30 it suffices to show that (FA_σ) holds for all simple types $\sigma \in$ Styp. As surveyed in Curien [10], this follows from definability of all uniform-compact elements of the nominal Scott domains $[\![\sigma]\!]$. That is, for all $u \in \mathrm{K}[\![\sigma]\!]$ we wish to prove that $u = [\![e]\!]$ for some variable-closed PNA$^+$ expression $\emptyset \vdash e : \sigma$.

Remark 34 (definability of uniform-compact elements). Are all the uniform-compact elements of the nominal Scott domain $[\![\tau]\!]$ definable in PNA$^+$, for *any* type τ? We introduced simple types because we did not find a way to prove such a definability result at all types. We succeed in showing uniform-compact definability at simple types essentially because the codomains of simple functions are restricted to `nat`, which makes life much easier in this setting. If all the definable retracts used in our proof of Theorem 30 were actually definable *embedding-projection pairs* (in the sense that $[\![\lambda x : \sigma \to i\,(r\,x)]\!] \sqsubseteq id_{[\![\sigma]\!]}$ holds), then uniform-compact definability at simple types would immediately imply uniform-compact definability at any type.[4] Unfortunately for name abstraction types, (28) and (29) do *not* form an embedding-projection pair. There remains the possibility that embedding-projection pairs as above can be used to show uniform-compact definability at all types for a simpler language without name abstraction, such as the $\lambda\nu$-calculus of Odersky [24] extended with fixed points.

The proof of uniform-compact definability at simple types in principle follows the structure of the traditional proof by Plotkin [30]. A modern account of this proof can be found in Streicher's book [38]. However, in our nominal setting many uses of finite subsets in the traditional proof are replaced by uses of orbit-finite subsets and their presentation as orbit-finite hulls (Theorem 8). The definition of $\mathrm{hull}_A F$ involves existential quantification over finite permutations of $\mathbb{A}$, and for the definability proof we need to reduce this to existential quantification over elements of $\mathbb{A}$. This is where the presence of $\mathtt{ex}\,x.\,e$ expressions in PNA$^+$ gets used (along with a traditional use of `por`) to prove the following two crucial lemmas. Neither is trivial to prove. In particular Lemma 36 works by a subtle case distinction over all the different ways the atomic names in the supports of u and u' can overlap.

Lemma 35. $\bigsqcup \mathrm{hull}_A\{[u\,,\mathrm{true}]\}$ *is* PNA$^+$*-definable for every* $\sigma \in \mathrm{Styp}$, $u \in \mathrm{K}[\![\sigma]\!]$ *and* $A \subseteq_{\mathrm{f}} \mathbb{A}$.

Lemma 36. *Suppose that* $\sigma \in \mathrm{Styp}$ *satisfies*

- *for all* $v, v' \in \mathrm{K}[\![\sigma]\!]$ *that do not have an upper bound in* $[\![\sigma]\!]$, $[v\,,\mathrm{true}] \sqcup [v'\,,\mathrm{false}]$ *is* PNA$^+$*-definable.*

Then $\bigsqcup \mathrm{hull}_A\{[u\,,\mathrm{true}], [u'\,,\mathrm{false}]\}$ *is* PNA$^+$*-definable for any* $u, u' \in \mathrm{K}[\![\sigma]\!]$ *and* $A \subseteq_{\mathrm{f}} \mathbb{A}$ *satisfying:*

- *for all finite permutations* $\pi : \mathbb{A} \cong \mathbb{A}$ *satisfying* $\pi \# A$ *(see Definition 7), it holds that* u *and* $\pi \cdot u'$ *do not have an upper bound in* $[\![\sigma]\!]$.

Using these two lemmas one can show by simultaneous induction on the structure of $\sigma \in \mathrm{Styp}$ that

- u and $[u\,,\mathrm{true}]$ are definable for all uniform-compact elements $u \in \mathrm{K}[\![\sigma]\!]$, and
- $[u\,,\mathrm{true}] \sqcup [u'\,,\mathrm{false}]$ is definable whenever $u, u' \in \mathrm{K}[\![\sigma]\!]$ are uniform-compact elements that do not have an upper bound in $[\![\sigma]\!]$.

Most of the work lies in the case for functions types, which for simple types are of the form, $\sigma \to \mathtt{nat}$. By Theorem 8 and 12 each uniform-compact element u of $[\![\sigma \to \mathtt{nat}]\!]$ can be represented by $u = \bigsqcup \mathrm{hull}_A F$ for some $A \subseteq_{\mathrm{f}} \mathbb{A}$, $F = \{[u_1\,, n_1], .., [u_k\,, n_k]\}$, $u_1, .., u_k \in \mathrm{K}[\![\sigma]\!]$ and $n_1, .., n_k \in \mathbb{N}$. One has to perform another induction on the size of F and make a case distinction based on the existence of $[u'\,, n'], [u''\,, n''] \in F$ such that for all $\pi \# A$ the compact elements u' and $\pi \cdot u''$ have no upper bound in $[\![\sigma]\!]$. Using Lemmas 35 and 36 the proof goes through following the structure of Streicher [38, Theorem 13.9], thereby showing full abstraction for PNA$^+$.

10. Open problems

1. *Failure of full abstraction in the nominal Scott domain model. Is* **Nsd** *fully abstract for just* PNA+`por`*? Is it necessary to add both* $\mathtt{ex}\,x.\,e$ *and* $\mathtt{the}\,x.\,e$ *to* PNA+`por` *in order to obtain full abstraction?*

   We do not yet have examples of contextually equivalent expressions in PNA+`por`, PNA+`por`+ex, or PNA+`por`+the that have different denotations in **Nsd**. Probably the method of logical relations can be adapted to establish such contextual equivalences, but we have yet to pursue this.

2. *Is there a fully abstract model of* PNA *based on games in nominal sets?*

   Just as PCF is of more interest from a programming point of view than PCF+`por`, we regard PNA (suitably extended with recursive types) as a 'pure' version of FreshML that is potentially useful for functional programming with syntactical data involving binders. Game semantics provided an interesting solution for the original full abstraction problem for PCF [4, 16], and its nominal version has provided computationally useful, fully abstract models of generative local state [3, 18, 23, 41]. Can nominal game semantics provide a similar thing for PNA?

3. *Is there a nominal Scott domain semantics for the form of nominal computation embodied by the* Nλ *language* [6]*?*

   With Nλ, Bojańczyk *et al.* extend the simply-typed λ-calculus with a collection type—representing orbit-finite subsets (Section 2) via a syntax for orbit-finite hulls (Definition 7).[5] It is natural to consider adding fixed point recursion to this language, with a denotational semantics using nominal domains rather than nominal sets. The denotational semantics of such an extension of Nλ will require the development of *orbit-finite* power domains $\mathsf{F}_{\mathrm{n}} D$ in **Nsd**, whose uniform-compact elements are orbit-finite subsets of the uniform-compact elements of D.

4. *What recursive domain equations can be solved in* **Nsd***?*

   In his thesis, Shinwell [33, Section 4.5] shows that the traditional method for constructing minimally invariant solutions for locally continuous functors of mixed variance can be applied to the simple notion of nominal domain given by nominal posets with joins of finitely supported ω-chains. This can be extended to udcpos and we expect it can also be used for nominal Scott domains, but we have yet to check the details. An interesting alternative approach is to develop a nominal version of Scott's information systems [32] and construct solutions for recursive domain equations via inductively defined nominal sets of information tokens. We have begun to develop such a theory of *nominal Scott information systems* in which the role of finite sets is replaced by orbit-finite nominal sets [unpublished]. From a logical point of view [2], nominal information systems are presentations of non-trivial nominal posets *with all orbit-finite meets*, rather than just finite meets. We expect this machinery can be used to good effect for the orbit-finite power domain construct mentioned above, as well as for a version for nominal Scott domains of Moggi's monad for dynamic allocation [21, Section 4.14] featuring a *freely generated* uniform-continuous name restriction operation [27, Remark 2.8].

11. Conclusion

The results in this paper provide further evidence for how a semantic theory (domain theory in this case) is enhanced by using nominal sets: we gain the ability to model constructs involving names and their symmetries while preserving many aspects of the classical theory. The complications arising from the use of nominal sets

[4] Thanks to a referee for pointing this out.

[5] Their paper [6] is concerned with general 'Fraïssé nominal sets'. Here we restrict our attention to the 'equality symmetry' and nominal sets in the original sense.

are feasible and somehow orthogonal to the other developments. At the same time, their use gives access to new constructs that are far from trivial. This is the case for the notion of *orbit-finite subset*, which formalizes the important idea of finiteness modulo symmetry within nominal sets. We agree with Bojańczyk *et al.* [6] that this is an important notion with many potential applications. Here we have used it to develop a nominal domain theory that, via our full abstraction result, has a good fit with higher-type computation involving local names and name abstractions.

Acknowledgments

Lösch gratefully acknowledges the support of a Gates Cambridge Scholarship. This research was also supported by ERC Advanced Grant *Events, Causality and Symmetry* (ECSYM). We thank Michael D. Adams and the anonymous referees for their helpful comments.

References

[1] URL `http://www.citeulike.org/group/11951/`.

[2] S. Abramsky. Domain theory in logical form. *Annals of Pure and Applied Logic*, 51:1–77, 1991.

[3] S. Abramsky, D. R. Ghica, A. S. Murawski, C.-H. L. Ong, and I. D. B. Stark. Nominal games and full abstraction for the nu-calculus. In *Proc. LICS 2004*, pages 150–159. IEEE Computer Society Press, 2004.

[4] S. Abramsky, R. Jagadeesan, and P. Malacaria. Full abstraction for PCF. *Information and Computation*, 163(2):409–470, 2000.

[5] S. Abramsky and A. Jung. Domain theory. In *Handbook of Logic in Computer Science, Volume 3. Semantic Structures*, chapter 1. Oxford University Press, 1994.

[6] M. Bojańczyk, L. Braud, B. Klin, and S. Lasota. Towards nominal computation. In *Proc. POPL 2012*, pages 401–412. ACM Press, 2012.

[7] M. Bojańczyk, B. Klin, and S. Lasota. Automata with group actions. In *Proc. LICS 2011*, pages 355–364. IEEE Computer Society Press, 2011.

[8] M. Bojańczyk and S. Lasota. A machine-independent characterization of timed languages. In *Proc. ICALP 2012, Part II*, volume 7392 of *LNCS*, pages 92–103. Springer-Verlag, 2012.

[9] V. Ciancia and U. Montanari. Symmetries, local names and dynamic (de)-allocation of names. *Information and Computation*, 208(12): 1349–1367, 2010.

[10] P.-L. Curien. Definability and full abstraction. In *Computation, Meaning and Logic, Articles dedicated to Gordon Plotkin*, volume 172 of *ENTCS*, pages 301–310. Elsevier, 2007.

[11] M. J. Gabbay. A study of substitution, using nominal techniques and Fraenkel-Mostowski sets. *Theoretical Computer Science*, 410(12–13): 1159–1189, 2009.

[12] M. J. Gabbay. Foundations of nominal techniques: Logic and semantics of variables in abstract syntax. *Bulletin of Symbolic Logic*, 17(2): 161–229, 2011.

[13] M. J. Gabbay and V. Ciancia. Freshness and name-restriction in sets of traces with names. In *Proc. FOSSACS 2011*, volume 6604 of *LNCS*, pages 365–380. Springer-Verlag, 2011.

[14] M. J. Gabbay and A. M. Pitts. A new approach to abstract syntax with variable binding. *Formal Aspects of Computing*, 13:341–363, 2002.

[15] F. Gadducci, M. Miculan, and U. Montanari. About permutation algebras, (pre)sheaves and named sets. *Higher-Order Symb. Computation*, 19:283–304, 2006.

[16] J. M. E. Hyland and C.-H. L. Ong. On full abstraction for PCF: I, II and III. *Information and Computation*, 163(2):285–408, 2000.

[17] P. T. Johnstone. *Sketches of an Elephant, A Topos Theory Compendium, Volumes 1 and 2*. Number 43–44 in Oxford Logic Guides. Oxford University Press, 2002.

[18] J. Laird. A game semantics of names and pointers. *Annals of Pure and Applied Logic*, 151(2):151–169, 2008.

[19] S. Lösch and A. M. Pitts. Relating Two Semantics of Locally Scoped Names. In *Proc. CSL 2011*, volume 12 of *Leibniz International Proceedings in Informatics (LIPIcs)*, pages 396–411, 2011.

[20] G. Markowsky. Chain-complete p.o. sets and directed sets with applications. *Algebra Universalis*, 6:53–68, 1976.

[21] E. Moggi. An abstract view of programming languages. Technical Report ECS-LFCS-90-113, Department of Computer Science, University of Edinburgh, 1989.

[22] U. Montanari and M. Pistore. π-Calculus, structured coalgebras and minimal HD-automata. In *Proc. MFCS 2000*, volume 1893 of *LNCS*, pages 569–578. Springer-Verlag, 2000.

[23] A. S. Murawski and N. Tzevelekos. Algorithmic games for full ground references. In *Proc. ICALP 2012, Part II*, volume 7392 of *LNCS*, pages 312–324. Springer-Verlag, 2012.

[24] M. Odersky. A functional theory of local names. In *Proc. POPL 1994*, pages 48–59. ACM Press, 1994.

[25] A. M. Pitts. Nominal logic, a first order theory of names and binding. *Information and Computation*, 186:165–193, 2003.

[26] A. M. Pitts. Alpha-structural recursion and induction. *Journal of the ACM*, 53:459–506, 2006.

[27] A. M. Pitts. Structural recursion with locally scoped names. *Journal of Functional Programming*, 21(3):235–286, 2011.

[28] A. M. Pitts and M. J. Gabbay. A metalanguage for programming with bound names modulo renaming. In *Proc. MPC 2000*, volume 1837 of *LNCS*, pages 230–255. Springer-Verlag, 2000.

[29] A. M. Pitts and I. D. B. Stark. Observable properties of higher order functions that dynamically create local names, or: What's new? In *Proc. MFCS 1993*, volume 711 of *LNCS*, pages 122–141. Springer-Verlag, 1993.

[30] G. D. Plotkin. LCF considered as a programming language. *Theoretical Computer Science*, 5:223–255, 1977.

[31] F. Pottier. Static name control for FreshML. In *Proc. LICS 2007*, pages 356–365. IEEE Computer Society Press, 2007.

[32] D. S. Scott. Domains for denotational semantics. In *Proc. ICALP 1982*, volume 140 of *LNCS*, pages 577–613. Springer-Verlag, 1982.

[33] M. R. Shinwell. *The Fresh Approach: Functional Programming with Names and Binders*. PhD thesis, University of Cambridge, 2005.

[34] M. R. Shinwell and A. M. Pitts. On a monadic semantics for freshness. *Theoretical Computer Science*, 342:28–55, 2005.

[35] M. R. Shinwell, A. M. Pitts, and M. J. Gabbay. FreshML: Programming with binders made simple. In *Proc. ICFP 2003*, pages 263–274. ACM Press, 2003.

[36] I. D. B. Stark. *Names and Higher-Order Functions*. PhD thesis, University of Cambridge, Dec. 1994.

[37] S. Staton. *Name-Passing Process Calculi: Operational Models and Structural Operational Semantics*. PhD thesis, University of Cambridge, 2007.

[38] T. Streicher. *Domain-Theoretic Foundations of Functional Programming*. World Scientific, Singapore, 2006.

[39] D. C. Turner. *Nominal Domain Theory for Concurrency*. PhD thesis, University of Cambridge, 2009.

[40] D. C. Turner and G. Winskel. Nominal domain theory for concurrency. In *Proc. CSL 2009*, volume 5771 of *LNCS*, pages 546–560. Springer-Verlag, 2009.

[41] N. Tzevelekos. *Nominal Game Semantics*. PhD thesis, University of Oxford, 2008.

[42] N. Tzevelekos. Fresh-register automata. In *Proc. POPL 2011*, pages 295–306. ACM Press, 2011.

[43] N. Tzevelekos. Program equivalence in a simple language with state. *Computer Languages, Systems and Structures*, 38(2):181–198, 2012.

The Sequential Semantics of Producer Effect Systems

Ross Tate
Cornell University
ross@cs.cornell.edu

Abstract

Effects are fundamental to programming languages. Even the lambda calculus has effects, and consequently the two famous evaluation strategies produce different semantics. As such, much research has been done to improve our understanding of effects. Since Moggi introduced monads for his computational lambda calculus, further generalizations have been designed to formalize increasingly complex computational effects, such as indexed monads followed by layered monads followed by parameterized monads. This succession prompted us to determine the most general formalization possible. In searching for this formalization we came across many surprises, such as the insufficiencies of arrows, as well as many unexpected insights, such as the importance of considering an effect as a small component of a whole system rather than just an isolated feature. In this paper we present our semantic formalization for producer effect systems, which we call a *productor*, and prove its maximal generality by focusing on only sequential composition of effectful computations, consequently guaranteeing that the existing monadic techniques are specializations of productors.

Categories and Subject Descriptors D.3.1 [*Programming Languages*]: Formal Definitions and Theory—Semantics

General Terms Languages, Theory

Keywords Effects, Monads, Effectors, Productors, Thunks

1. Introduction

Effects have been around since the beginning of programming languages. After all, even programs written in the lambda calculus have effects: some programs diverge and some programs disregard their inputs. How these effects interact determines the semantics of a program, leading to strict or lazy evaluation depending on what choices are made. Yet, despite their prevalence, effects and their behavior remain fairly mysterious, especially when one considers how thoroughly data and types have been formalized. We view effects and types as complementary systems, so by improving our understanding of effects to match that of types we hope to broaden the perspective of programming languages as a whole.

Before we go any further, we should define what we mean by an effect, since this term has come to have different meanings in different communities. For some an effect is a classification of a computation determined by some analysis [17, 19, 22, 23, 30–32, 34]. For others an effect is synonymous with a monad [3, 9, 12, 13, 38]. Indeed, Wadler and Thiemann illustrated the intimate connection between the former type-and-effect perspective and the latter computational-effect perspective [38], which we will refine within this paper. What we mean by an effect is a classification of a computation independent of the values of its inputs and outputs. For example, "writes to the heap" is an effect but "writes to the heap only if the input integer is non-zero" is not. Thus, whereas types classify the inputs and outputs of computations, effects classify the internals of computations, forming complementary classification systems. More specifically, we are avoiding imposing the complexity of dependent classification systems in addition to the complexity of reasoning about effects in a language-independent manner.

This informal definition is much broader than what many might consider an effect. For example, "disregards its input" satisfies our definition: though it mentions the input to the computation, the meaning of this classification does not depend on the actual value of that input. Similarly, "uses variable `x`" satisfies our definition. These effects correspond to the use of context. They are often disregarded since many consider freely accessible persistent contexts to be a basic part of programming languages, even though such contexts are not necessarily present in resource-constrained or stack-based languages. When we realized this assumption, we had to reconsider our own notion of effect. What we found is that effects like "uses its input multiple times" can be formalized as *consumer* effects because they reason about how a computation consumes its inputs. In fact, many fundamental of behaviors of programming languages reflect these consumer effects. Unfortunately, in order to keep this paper focused, we must consider consumer effects to be outside of the scope at hand. Instead, we will focus on the much more familiar dual notion that we call *producer* effects.

A producer effect reasons about how a computation produces its outputs. For example, "may throw an exception instead of producing its output" or "may examine and alter the heap before producing its output" are familiar producer effects. Here is where most existing work on effects lies, and so likewise here is where we focus our attention. The reason that producer effects are so common is that they are intimately tied to the notion of thunked computations, meaning computations which have been delayed so that they can be treated as values. Indeed, we will define an effect as a producer effect if all computations with that effect can be thunked as "pure" computations for a domain-specific notion of purity. From this basic property, we will prove that the sequential semantics of all producer effects can be formalized by our framework. As a result, Moggi's monads for his computational lambda calculus [20], Wadler's indexed monads [38], Filinski's layered monads [5], and Atkey's parameterized monads [2] are subsumed by our framework, and we will illustrate how these various formalizations arise from simple assumptions on the producer effects at hand, as well as how those assumptions restrict the kind of information that the effect system can track. As an example, we present an effect system for ensuring shared memory is accessed only in critical regions, the

POPL'13, January 23–25, 2013, Rome, Italy.

semantics of which is guaranteed to be inexpressible by these existing systems because it violates their assumptions. However, we show how the semantics can easily be formalized with our framework to prove that the effect system prevents race conditions.

Just as we restrict our scope to producer effects, we also restrict it to sequential composition of computations. There are many other forms of composition, such as multiplicative composition (for parallelism and for adjacent subexpressions), additive composition (for branching), and coinductive composition (for recursion and for loops). We choose sequential composition because that is where existing research has focused its efforts. We focus on just the one form of composition so that we may address its challenges in full. We believe many of the insights and techniques in this paper can be adapted to other forms of composition, though there is still plenty of interesting work to be done there.

With our semantic framework, which we call *productors*, we provide a powerful solution to the problem of formalizing the sequential semantics of producer effects. This solution is not tied to common assumptions such as freely accessible persistent contexts or higher-order functions, enabling us to delve into more interesting semantic domains as well as narrow down the fundamental aspects of programming languages. Because it is so general, not only does our framework provide a means for specifying the semantics of programming languages or first steps towards improving the extensibility of programming languages, it also provides a meta-language for discussing effects and their properties. We will demonstrate how such a meta-language illuminates the constructs in existing languages, particularly in prior formalizations of effects.

This paper begins by first providing an example of an effect system greatly simplified for sake of exposition (Section 2). Then we present monads and how they formalize the semantics of an effect, albeit in a slightly different light than prior such explanations (Section 3). Afterwards, we adapt this approach to our example effect system, showing where and why monads need to be generalized (Section 4). That concludes our example-driven portion of the paper. We then move on to formalizing effect systems as effectors and effectoids (Section 5). We follow that by formalizing their semantics as productors and productoids (Section 6). With these formalisms established, we illustrate how a variety of existing semantic frameworks are special cases of productors arising from extra assumptions on the structure of the effect system at hand (Section 7). We then show what basic properties of a language with effects guarantee all its effects are producer effects and so formalizable using productors (Section 8). Finally, we remark on higher-level insights, opportunities to expand existing semantic techniques, and further directions to take our research in order to meet our goal of providing an abstract language for discussing and formalizing programming languages (Section 9).

2. Effects for Locking

Effects are a classification of computations independent of the explicit inputs and outputs of those computations. Sometimes effects are superimposed on top of an existing language in order to identify optimization opportunities or potential bugs [19, 31, 32, 34]. Other times effects are integrated into the type system [1]. For example, Java has checked exceptions, and Haskell uses monads in order to combine laziness and side effects. In this paper we will demonstrate how patterns in applications of effects lead to patterns in the semantics of effects. To demonstrate that these are just patterns and not necessarily inherent to effects, we present a toy language that breaks from all of these patterns.

Our toy language Crit, shown in Figure 1, has explicit synchronization and shared memory, limited for simplicity in that there is only one lock and one shared integer. Clearly this is just a subset of a more realistic language with branches, functions, and actual parallelism, as well as a much richer type system. However, our intent is just to address sequential composition, so we strip down the language to sequential composition. Nonetheless, even the semantics of this very simple language cannot be formalized using existing frameworks, at least not in a way that allows the semantics to prove the desired properties of the effect system. In particular, the effect system for this language is intended to prove that whenever a lock is acquired it is subsequently released (without being acquired again beforehand) and every use of shared memory occurs within such a critical region.

$$\frac{}{x:\mathbb{Z}, y:\mathbb{Z} \vdash z := x + y \dashv z:\mathbb{Z} \mid \mathfrak{E}}$$

$$\frac{}{\varnothing \vdash \mathbf{acquire} \dashv \varnothing \mid \textsf{locking}} \qquad \frac{}{\varnothing \vdash \mathbf{release} \dashv \varnothing \mid \textsf{unlocking}}$$

$$\frac{}{\varnothing \vdash x := \mathbf{get}() \dashv x:\mathbb{Z} \mid \textsf{critical}} \qquad \frac{}{x:\mathbb{Z} \vdash \mathbf{set}(x) \dashv \varnothing \mid \textsf{critical}}$$

$$\textit{Prop}\,\frac{\Gamma \vdash p \dashv \Gamma' \mid \varepsilon}{\bar{\Gamma}, \Gamma \vdash p \dashv \bar{\Gamma}, \Gamma' \mid \varepsilon} \qquad \textit{Sub}\,\frac{\Gamma \vdash p \dashv \Gamma' \mid \varepsilon \quad \varepsilon \leq \varepsilon'}{\Gamma \vdash p \dashv \Gamma' \mid \varepsilon'}$$

$$\textit{Seq}^2_{\fatsemi}\,\frac{\Gamma \vdash p \dashv \Gamma' \mid \varepsilon \quad \Gamma' \vdash p' \dashv \Gamma'' \mid \varepsilon' \quad \varepsilon \fatsemi \varepsilon' \mapsto \varepsilon''}{\Gamma \vdash p; p' \dashv \Gamma'' \mid \varepsilon''}$$

Figure 1. A toy language Crit with critical-region effects

$$\textsc{Eff} = \{\mathfrak{E}, \textsf{locking}, \textsf{unlocking}, \textsf{critical}, \textsf{entrant}\}$$

$$\mathfrak{E} \leq \textsf{critical}, \textsf{entrant}$$

$\downarrow \fatsemi \rightarrow$	$\mathfrak{E}$	locking	unlocking	critical	entrant
$\mathfrak{E}$	$\mathfrak{E}$	locking	unlocking	critical	entrant
locking	locking	—	entrant	locking	—
unlocking	unlocking	critical	—	—	unlocking
critical	critical	—	unlocking	critical	—
entrant	entrant	locking	—	—	entrant

Figure 2. The effect system for Crit

Before we get into the effect system, let us explain Crit at a high level. The judgement $\Gamma \vdash p \dashv \Gamma' \mid \varepsilon$ indicates that the program p consumes context Γ as its input, produces context Γ' as its output, and has overall effect ε. Note that Crit is linear: every value created is used exactly once. There is one exception: an integer stored to the shared state via **set** can be read multiple times via multiple **get**s. We can do this because it is possible to implement a duplicating function $\mathbb{Z} \multimap !\mathbb{Z}$ in linear type theory. One could make Crit non-linear by restricting its types to ones which have such a duplicating function. We chose not to because it is orthogonal to the concerns of sequential composition and would make the denotational semantics of Crit unnecessarily complex.

Next, consider the five primitive statements of Crit and their effect. We give addition the effect $\mathfrak{E}$, which we call the basic effect, and which more generally can be used for all effects not related to locking (such as non-determinism or memory allocation). The statement **acquire** has the effect locking because overall it changes the state of the lock from free to occupied. Dually, **release** has the effect unlocking because overall it changes the state of the lock from occupied to free. Lastly, **get** and **set** have the effect critical because they must occur inside a critical region.

Finally, consider the three general-purpose rules. *Prop* allows unused context to propagate through a program *without altering the effect*. While this is not necessary, and indeed is not possible for all effect systems (e.g. low-level stack-based effect systems), we will show how this relates to the notion of strength used in existing semantic frameworks. *Sub* conveys the notion of subeffects analogous to subtyping. $Seq^2_{\circ}$ specifies how effects sequence statically. These rules can easily be used for other languages, so we give their specifics separately in Figure 2. Note that Figure 2 has an additional effect entrant used to indicate code that enters and leaves a critical section (possibly multiple times), so though the code restores the state of the lock it first needs the lock to be free in order to execute.

This effect system has a number of unusual attributes. First, the effects do not form a lattice. In particular, ε is not a subeffect of every effect. Second, not all effects can be sequenced, not even necessarily with themselves. This means that effects can influence the typability of a program. Third, the order of the effects matters. locking before unlocking is considered entrant but the reverse is not allowed at all. All these attributes have important consequences on the denotational semantics of Crit and on the insufficiency of existing frameworks. But before we discuss those we should present the basics of denotational techniques for effects.

3. Monads

In 1958, Godement invented standard constructions [7], which became known as (Kleisli) triples, which became known as monads. In 1988, Moggi migrated the concept of monads from the category-theory community to the programming-languages semantics community [20]. In 1990, Wadler carried this concept over to the functional-languages community [35, 36], and in 1993 these concepts were realized as monadic programming and added to Haskell to make I/O more convenient and to embrace imperative functional programming [12], blurring the line between imperative programming and pure programming. This progression has made monads the most well known technique for formalizing the semantics of effects. Here we show how a monad formalizes an effect, but in a way that highlights opportunities for generalization.

Propagating an Effect Consider the expression $(64 \div x) + 1$ (using integer division). Focus on the problem that $+$ expects its first argument to be an integer but the $\div$ in the first argument may fail to produce one because $\div$ is a partial operation. In other words, $\div$ has the partial effect. We might represent this by saying that $\div$ has type $\mathbb{Z} \times \mathbb{Z} \xrightarrow{\text{partial}} \mathbb{Z}$. We want to formalize what it means to have the partial effect. Moggi observed that we can do so by modifying the return type of $\div$ [20]. In particular, we can view $\div$ as a function that returns an integer *or* a failure code. We can define an algebraic data type P_{partial} to represent these two cases:

$$P_{\text{partial}}(\tau) = \text{success}(\tau) \mid \text{failure}$$

Then we can formalize $\div$ as a *pure* operation $\mathbb{Z} \times \mathbb{Z} \to P_{\text{partial}}(\mathbb{Z})$.

When a failure occurs, any subsequent computations need to propagate this failure. In particular, if $64 \div x$ fails, then $(64 \div x)+1$ should fail as well. Thus, $(64 \div x) + 1$ also has the partial effect. We can do this by making the pure computation $\lambda v.v + 1$ from $\mathbb{Z}$ to $\mathbb{Z}$ instead take a $P_{\text{partial}}(\mathbb{Z})$ and return a $P_{\text{partial}}(\mathbb{Z})$. This is achieved with a *map* operation:

$$\begin{aligned} map_{\text{partial}} &: \forall \alpha, \beta.\ (\alpha \to \beta) \to (P_{\text{partial}}(\alpha) \to P_{\text{partial}}(\beta)) \\ map_{\text{partial}}(f) &= \lambda px.\ \textbf{case}\ px \begin{cases} \text{success}(x) \mapsto \text{success}(f(x)) \\ \text{failure} \quad\ \ \mapsto \text{failure} \end{cases} \end{aligned}$$

Thus *map* turns a pure computation into one which takes an effectful argument and propagates the effect. In this case, map_{partial} indicates that if a failure code is present then all computation should be bypassed and the failure propagated. Using *map* we can formalize the semantics of $(64 \div x)+1$ as $map_{\text{partial}}(\lambda v.v + 1)(64 \div x)$. We *map* the computation after the effectful operation so that it can take an effectful argument, then pass the effectful result to this mapped computation which propagates the effect. Thus if $64 \div x$ fails so does the entire expression.

This pair of a type constructor $P : \text{TYPE} \to \text{TYPE}$ and a function on computations $map : (\tau \to \tau') \to (P(\tau) \to P(\tau'))$ is called an *(endo)functor* (on the category of types) provided it satisfies a few additional equalities which we do not repeat here, and this is just one part of a monad. In the setting of effects, the type constructor P indicates how a production of the effect can be described as data so that effectful computations can be represented as pure computations with a modified return value, and the function *map* defines how to propagate the effect through pure computations.

Sequencing Effectful Computations Now consider a slightly more complex example: $(64 \div x) \div y$. Here we are sequencing two effectful computations. We can use the functor representation of the partial effect in order to formalize this expression:

$$map_{\text{partial}}(\lambda v.v \div y)(64 \div x)$$

The type of this formalization, though, is $P_{\text{partial}}(P_{\text{partial}}(\mathbb{Z}))$, since the computation we mapped, namely $\lambda v.v \div y$, also has the partial effect. Although having a doubly partial value allows us to determine which $\div$ failed, in this case we are only concerned with whether *any* $\div$ failed. That is, we want the effect of $(64 \div x) \div y$ to be partial rather than (conceptually) partial^2. We can accomplish this by using a monadic *join* operation to turn doubly partial values into (singly) partial values:

$$\begin{aligned} join_{\text{partial}} &: \forall \alpha. P_{\text{partial}}(P_{\text{partial}}(\alpha)) \to P_{\text{partial}}(\alpha) \\ join_{\text{partial}}(ppx) &= \textbf{case}\ ppx \begin{cases} \text{success}(\text{success}(x)) \mapsto \text{success}(x) \\ \text{success}(\text{failure}) \qquad \mapsto \text{failure} \\ \text{failure} \qquad\qquad\qquad\ \ \mapsto \text{failure} \end{cases} \end{aligned}$$

Note that in this example there is only one effect in the whole system, and this is why we can use a single monad. Some semantic frameworks generalize from one effect to multiple effects by using multiple monads, but our semantic framework provides a more general system in which these approaches are special cases.

Making Pure Computations Effectful With the above structures we can sequence a non-empty list of effectful computations interspersed with pure computations together into a single effectful computation. Monads have one more component that enables an *empty* list of effectful computations (from a type to itself) to be turned into a single effectful computation. This structure also enables pure computations to be turned into effectful computations. It is known as the unit of the monad, in this case turning pure values into partial values:

$$\begin{aligned} unit_{\text{partial}} &: \forall \alpha.\ \alpha \to P_{\text{partial}}(\alpha) \\ unit_{\text{partial}}(x) &= \text{success}(x) \end{aligned}$$

While it is important to be able to treat pure computations as effectful computations in order to handle computations uniformly, a system with many effects need only have one effect with a unit in order to accomplish this. Recognizing this is important since it allows effects to express significantly more concepts, as we will demonstrate later.

Coherency The operations for monads have a variety of equalities which must hold, known as the identity and associativity laws. We do not repeat those laws here, rather we convey their significance. Consider the expression $(((64 \div x) \div y) \div z) + 5$. This is essentially five computations sequenced together: 64, $\lambda v.v \div x$, $\lambda v.v \div y$, $\lambda v.v \div z$, and $\lambda v.v + 5$. Using the structures above we can sequence these computations (maintaining order) in a variety of ways depending on how we combine consecutive pairs and whether we turn pure computations into effectful computations or simply use functorial structure to propagate effects through them, but the result should be the same no matter which way is used. We call this concept semantic coherency, and the monad laws are necessary and sufficient to ensure this for sequential composition.

4. Semantics for Locking

With monadic techniques in mind, let us consider how we might define a denotational semantics for Crit. First, we need to choose a semantic domain on which to define all of our operations. Choosing a good semantic domain can enable the semantics to automatically ensure useful properties. In this case, we want to ensure that **acquire**s match up with **release**s one-to-one, and **get**s and **set**s happen only inside critical regions.

Selecting a Semantic Domain To this end, we opt for linear type theory as our semantic domain, since linear type theory already has a notion of counting built into it. We use an abstract type L to denote a free lock and an abstract type C to denote the capability to access shared memory. An abstract operation *acquire* converts a free lock L to a capability C, and an abstract operation *release* does the reverse. An abstract operation *get* fetches the value of the shared state provided a capability C is present, and an abstract operation *set* replaces the value of the shared state provided a capability C is present. Of course, L and C actually stand for $\mathbb{Z}$, but by hiding that information and ensuring every primitive operation consumes and produces one L or C we are guaranteed that every *acquire* matches up with a *release* and all *get*s and *set*s occur in between. These abstract constants and their types are summarized below.

$$\begin{array}{rr} L : \text{TYPE} & C : \text{TYPE} \\ acquire : L \multimap C & release : C \multimap L \\ get : C \multimap C \otimes \mathbb{Z} & set : C \otimes \mathbb{Z} \multimap C \end{array}$$

Representing Effectful Values Next, we must specify how to represent productions of each effect as data. While we could define $P_{\varepsilon}(\tau)$ as simply τ, we want to emphasize that ε represents all effects not related to locking. For example, ε could be non-determinism, in which case $P_{\varepsilon}(\tau)$ would be $\mu t.\ \tau \oplus (\tau \,\&\, t)$. As such, we simply assume $P_{\varepsilon}(\tau)$ is some monad with operations map_{ε}, $join_{\varepsilon}$, and $unit_{\varepsilon}$, along with an operation $strength_{\varepsilon}$ of type $\forall\alpha,\beta.\ \alpha \otimes P_{\varepsilon}(\beta) \multimap P_{\varepsilon}(\alpha \otimes \beta)$ which we will explain later.

As for the impure effects, their semantics all have the form:

$$T_{S,S'}(\tau) = S \multimap P_{\varepsilon}(S' \otimes \tau)$$

$T_{S,S'}$ transforms the state from S to S'. In particular, the impure effects transform between L and C:

$$\begin{array}{rr} P_{\mathsf{locking}} = T_{L,C} & P_{\mathsf{unlocking}} = T_{C,L} \\ P_{\mathsf{critical}} = T_{C,C} & P_{\mathsf{entrant}} = T_{L,L} \end{array}$$

Thus a computation with the locking effect must have access to a (necessarily unique) free lock L, do some computation with effect ε, and complete with a (necessarily unique) capability to access shared memory C still available.

Formalizing Primitive Operations Once we have determined how to represent an effect, we can give semantics to the primitive effectful computations. The strategy formalizes the semantics of a judgement $\Gamma \vdash s \dashv \Gamma' \mid \varepsilon$ as a term in linear type theory with the type $(\bigotimes\Gamma) \multimap P_{\varepsilon}(\bigotimes\Gamma')$. With this in mind, we define the semantics of the primitive effectful computations in Figure 3.

Note that the semantic domain guarantees that only one portion of code can hold the lock at a time. Thus, just the fact that these primitives can be expressed in that semantic domain ensures that they preserve that property. This helps a language designer determine how they can safely extend the language, since now they need only check that any potential new constructs are expressible in this domain.

Propagating Effects Next, we have to define how effects propagate through pure computations. Since the impure effects have the same shape, they also use approximately the same map operation:

$$map_{T_{S,S'}} = \lambda f.\lambda g.\lambda s.map_{\varepsilon}(\lambda\langle s', x\rangle.\langle s', f(x)\rangle)(g(s))$$

$$\begin{aligned} [\![x:\mathbb{Z}, y:\mathbb{Z} \vdash z := x+y \dashv z:\mathbb{Z} \mid \varepsilon]\!] &= \lambda\langle m,n\rangle.unit_{\varepsilon}(m+n) \\ [\![\varnothing \vdash \textbf{acquire} \dashv \varnothing \mid \mathsf{locking}]\!] &= \lambda\langle\rangle.\lambda l.unit_{\varepsilon}(\langle acquire(l), \langle\rangle\rangle) \\ [\![\varnothing \vdash \textbf{release} \dashv \varnothing \mid \mathsf{unlocking}]\!] &= \lambda\langle\rangle.\lambda c.unit_{\varepsilon}(\langle release(c), \langle\rangle\rangle) \\ [\![\varnothing \vdash x := \textbf{get}() \dashv x:\mathbb{Z} \mid \mathsf{critical}]\!] &= \lambda\langle\rangle.\lambda c.unit_{\varepsilon}(get(c)) \\ [\![x:\mathbb{Z} \vdash \textbf{set}(x) \dashv \varnothing \mid \mathsf{critical}]\!] &= \lambda n.\lambda c.unit_{\varepsilon}(\langle set(c,n), \langle\rangle\rangle) \end{aligned}$$

Figure 3. Semantics of the primitive effectful computations of Crit

Sequencing Effectful Computations The most challenging semantic component is sequencing effectful components. Here is where we have to stray from monads. After all, not all of these effects are monads. For example, there is no *join* operation for locking. To see why, recall that a locking computation needs a free lock to be available and then removes that free lock, turning it into a capability. Thus, immediately after a locking computation there is no free lock available, so there cannot be another locking computation that needs a free lock.

Fortunately, our effect system is designed to address precisely this problem. In Figure 2, locking ⨟ locking is intentionally undefined so that such programs are disallowed and we do not have to worry about sequencing two locking computations. This suggests how we might generalize monads for sequencing computation. Suppose we had functions $p : A \multimap P_{\varepsilon}(B)$ and $p' : B \multimap P_{\varepsilon'}(C)$ representing effectful computions with *different* effects. Furthermore, suppose $\varepsilon \fatsemi \varepsilon'$ were defined as ε''. Then we should be able to combine p and p' into a function of type $A \multimap P_{\varepsilon''}(C)$ representing a computation from A to C with effect ε''. So far, we can use map to get the following function:

$$\lambda a.map_{\varepsilon}(p')(p(a)) : A \multimap P_{\varepsilon}(P_{\varepsilon'}(C))$$

This function essentially produces a doubly effectful value like with monads, but this time with two *different* effects. So, like with monads, we need some way to turn this doubly effectful value into a (singly) effectful value with just effect ε''. Thus, whenever $\varepsilon \fatsemi \varepsilon'$ is defined as ε'' we need the following operation to sequence the two effectful computations:

$$join_{\varepsilon,\varepsilon'} : \forall\alpha.\ P_{\varepsilon}(P_{\varepsilon'}(\alpha)) \multimap P_{\varepsilon''}(\alpha)$$

For Crit there are four major categories of such sequencings: (1) basic followed by basic, (2) impure followed by basic, (3) basic followed by impure, and (4) impure followed by impure.

The first is simply assumed to be defined as discussed before:

$$join_{\varepsilon,\varepsilon} = join_{\varepsilon}$$

The second is fairly simple to define:

$$join_{T_{S,S'},\varepsilon} = \lambda f.\lambda s.join_{\varepsilon}(map_{\varepsilon}(strength_{\varepsilon})(f(s)))$$

Note that this is simply the result of sequencing the linear function $f : S \multimap P_{\varepsilon}(S' \otimes P_{\varepsilon}(\alpha))$, viewed as a computation with effect ε, with $strength_{\varepsilon} : S' \otimes P_{\varepsilon}(\alpha) \multimap P_{\varepsilon}(S' \otimes \alpha)$, also viewed as a computation with effect ε. What $strength_{\varepsilon}$ is doing is pulling the context of the state S' produced by f *into* the effectful value $P_{\varepsilon}(\alpha)$ so that it can be accessed by subsequent computations. Unlike in Haskell, $strength_{\varepsilon}$ does not exist for all monads in linear type theory. One notable exception is the error monad: $1 \oplus \tau$. This is why languages with both errors and locks have to have special constructs for handling the case when an error is thrown by a thread holding a lock. Similarly, this is why many languages have constructs for resource-sensitive data in the face of errors, such as C#'s `using` construct for `IDisposable` objects. Also, we were careful to define non-determinism using & rather than ⊗ (which corresponds to the (non-empty) list monad used by parsers) since the former has linear strength whereas the latter does not.

Moving on, the third is only slightly more complex to define:

$$join_{\mathfrak{E},T_{S,S'}} = \lambda\hat{f}.\lambda s.join_{\mathfrak{E}}(map_{\mathfrak{E}}(\lambda\langle s,f\rangle.f(s)))(strength_{\mathfrak{E}}(s,\hat{f})))$$

Here we have an S-state s and $\hat{f}$ is an $\mathfrak{E}$-effectful value containing a function expecting an S, so once again we have to use $strength_{\mathfrak{E}}$ and $map_{\mathfrak{E}}$ to give the contained function f access to the state s. This results in a doubly $\mathfrak{E}$-effectful value, so we use $join_{\mathfrak{E}}$.

The fourth case is the most interesting regarding this paper:

$$join_{T_{S,S'},T_{S',S''}} = \lambda f.\lambda s.join_{\mathfrak{E}}(map_{\mathfrak{E}}(\lambda\langle s',g\rangle.g(s'))(f(s)))$$

Note that it is only defined when the intermediate state S' agrees for both effectful computations, in which case it results in a $T_{S,S''}$-effectful computation. In fact, when we consider just the impure effects we get an instance of Atkey's parameterized monads [2], a connection we will discuss in Section 7.

With these components we can define the semantics of $Seq^2_{⨾}$:

$$\frac{[\![\Gamma \vdash p \dashv \Gamma' \mid \varepsilon]\!] = f \qquad [\![\Gamma' \vdash p' \dashv \Gamma'' \mid \varepsilon']\!] = f' \qquad [\![\varepsilon ⨾ \varepsilon' \mapsto \varepsilon'']\!] = join_{\varepsilon,\varepsilon'}}{[\![\Gamma \vdash p; p' \dashv \Gamma'' \mid \varepsilon'']\!] = \lambda g.join_{\varepsilon,\varepsilon'}(map_{\varepsilon}(f')(f(g)))}$$

Coercing Effectful Computations Crit has another feature, namely subeffects, that we could not encounter with monads since there was only one effect. Like subtypes, the intuition for subeffects is that there is a way to coerce computations pertaining to the subeffect into ones pertaining to the supereffect. As such, whenever $\varepsilon \leq \varepsilon'$ holds, we need an operation with the following form:

$$coerce_{\varepsilon,\varepsilon'} : \forall\alpha.\ P_{\varepsilon}(\alpha) \multimap P_{\varepsilon'}(\alpha)$$

With Crit, we can define such coercions from the basic effect to an impure effect whenever the input and output states match up, namely for critical and entrant:

$$coerce_{\mathfrak{E},T_{S,S}} = \lambda\hat{x}.\lambda s.strength_{\mathfrak{E}}(s,\hat{x})$$

Using these coercions we can define the semantics of *Sub*:

$$\frac{[\![\Gamma \vdash p \dashv \Gamma' \mid \varepsilon]\!] = f \qquad [\![\varepsilon \leq \varepsilon']\!] = coerce_{\varepsilon,\varepsilon'}}{[\![\Gamma \vdash p \dashv \Gamma' \mid \varepsilon']\!] = \lambda g.coerce_{\varepsilon,\varepsilon'}(f(g))}$$

Propagating Context There is only one rule left to handle for Crit. *Prop* is in a sense orthogonal to the concerns of sequential composition, yet it is so common in languages that we include it for sake of discussion. Suppose we have some function $f : \bigotimes\Gamma \multimap P_{\varepsilon}(\bigotimes\Gamma')$ denoting the semantics of $\Gamma \dashv p \vdash \Gamma' \mid \varepsilon$. We want to extend f so that it propagates the values of an additional context $\bar{\Gamma}$ through the computation. It is easy to define the following function that does at least part of the job:

$$(\bigotimes\bar{\Gamma}) \otimes f : (\bigotimes\bar{\Gamma}) \otimes (\bigotimes\Gamma) \multimap (\bigotimes\bar{\Gamma}) \otimes P_{\varepsilon}(\bigotimes\Gamma)$$

So the issue is that we need to somehow pull the $\bigotimes\bar{\Gamma}$ inside the P_{ε} so that we have the necessary $P_{\varepsilon}((\bigotimes\bar{\Gamma}) \otimes (\bigotimes\Gamma))$.

This issue should look familiar, since when sequencing the impure effects we needed some way to pull state inside of $P_{\mathfrak{E}}$, and so we use the same technique we used there. In particular, we need every effect to have a *strength* operation:

$$strength_{\varepsilon} : \forall\alpha,\beta.\ \alpha \otimes P_{\varepsilon}(\beta) \multimap P_{\varepsilon}(\alpha \otimes \beta)$$

We already assumed such an operation has been defined for $\mathfrak{E}$, so we need only define it for the impure effects. Again, the *strength* operations for the impure effects all have the same form:

$$strength_{T_{S,S'}} = \lambda\langle x,f\rangle.\lambda s.map_{\mathfrak{E}}(swap)(strength_{\mathfrak{E}}(x,f(s)))$$
$$swap = \lambda\langle x,\langle s',y\rangle\rangle.\langle s',\langle x,y\rangle\rangle$$

Note that this *strength* need only be defined for types α that can occur in a context Γ. So, if one were to extend Crit to be non-linear and ensure all Crit types τ had an operation $\tau \multimap\ !\tau$, then the effects could use a non-linear strength. This way Crit's effect system could be extended with exceptions, so long as one were to carefully track and define the interaction of exceptions with locking. However, since we already need the basic effect to have linear strength, we make no such restriction on the types occurring in Γ here.

We mentioned that *Prop* is not necessary for sequential composition; it comes from the notion that the context is freely accessible. In low-level stack-based languages, effectful operations may be required for even just accessing the context. Sometimes the context can be extended, but only if the effect is altered as well. For example, in a low-level stack-based language, it is occasionally the responsibility/privilege of the exception handler to clean-up/work-with the stack that existed at the point the exception was thrown. Such a language might have an effect of the form $\mathsf{exc}(\hat{\Gamma})$ where $\hat{\Gamma}$ is the state of the stack at the point the exception was thrown. Denotationally, the effect may be represented as $P_{\mathsf{exc}(\hat{\Gamma})}(\tau) = \tau \oplus \bigotimes\hat{\Gamma}$. Should the stack be extended prior to throwing the exception, then this must be encoded in the effect. As such, this language might have a rule like the following:

$$\frac{\Gamma \vdash p \dashv \Gamma' \mid \mathsf{exc}(\hat{\Gamma})}{\bar{\Gamma},\Gamma \vdash p \dashv \bar{\Gamma},\Gamma' \mid \mathsf{exc}(\bar{\Gamma},\hat{\Gamma})}$$

Thus this effect has no need for strength. We emphasize this example both to illustrate the origin of strength present in many existing formalizations and to illustrate the wide variety of languages our framework is capable of handling.

$$Seq_{⨾}\ \frac{\Gamma_0 \vdash p_1 \dashv \Gamma_1 \mid \varepsilon_1 \quad \ldots \quad \Gamma_{n-1} \vdash p_n \dashv \Gamma_n \mid \varepsilon_n \qquad [\varepsilon_1,\ldots,\varepsilon_n] \overset{⨾}{\mapsto} \varepsilon}{\Gamma_0 \vdash p_1;\ldots;p_n \dashv \Gamma_n \mid \varepsilon}$$

Figure 4. Assumed typing rule for effect systems

5. Effectors

While so far we have been focusing on our example language Crit, the intent of this work is to apply to nearly all effect systems. In this section, we introduce *effectors* to formalize effect systems as they pertain to typing sequential composition of programs. In the next section, we then present our semantic framework for effectors. Following that, we show how existing semantic frameworks fit within our own. Finally, we show what common properties of a language and its effect system guarantee that the semantics can be formalized with our framework.

For the sake of formalizing effect systems, we assume the unknown language at hand admits the rule $Seq_{⨾}$ in Figure 4. The language may (and should) admit many other rules as well; we simply need to know that it admits at least $Seq_{⨾}$. The symbol $\overset{⨾}{\mapsto}$ is a relationship from lists of effects to effects, so that $[\varepsilon_1,\ldots,\varepsilon_n] \overset{⨾}{\mapsto} \varepsilon$ indicates that ε is the overall effect of sequencing computations with effects ε_1 through ε_n in that order. $Seq_{⨾}$ informs us that the effects of computations are independent of their specific inputs and outputs, granting the modularity one would expect from an effect system. Thus we do not concern ourselves with some form of dependent effects. Note that we intend $Seq_{⨾}$ to include when n is 0, corresponding to typing the empty program. The following shorthands may further elucidate the meaning of $\overset{\fatsemi}{\mapsto}$:

$$\begin{array}{ccc} \not\varepsilon \mapsto \varepsilon & \text{means} & [] \overset{\fatsemi}{\mapsto} \varepsilon \\ \varepsilon \le \varepsilon' & \text{means} & [\varepsilon] \overset{\fatsemi}{\mapsto} \varepsilon' \\ \varepsilon \fatsemi \varepsilon' \mapsto \varepsilon'' & \text{means} & [\varepsilon, \varepsilon'] \overset{\fatsemi}{\mapsto} \varepsilon'' \end{array}$$

$Seq_{\fatsemi}$ may not seem like much to work with, but it actually provides some very useful structure. In particular, it is important to realize that given a sequence of computations, say $[p_1, p_2, p_3]$, the syntax $p_1; p_2; p_3$ could be parsed as a whole or as $(p_1; p_2); p_3$ or as $p_1; (p_2; p_3)$ or even as $(); p_1; (); p_2; (); p_3; ()$ with the empty program interspersed. As such, one can show that, should $[\varepsilon_1, \varepsilon_2] \overset{\fatsemi}{\mapsto} \varepsilon'$ and $[\varepsilon', \varepsilon_3] \overset{\fatsemi}{\mapsto} \varepsilon$ hold, then we can assert that $[\varepsilon_1, \varepsilon_2, \varepsilon_3] \overset{\fatsemi}{\mapsto} \varepsilon$ also holds *without changing the effects of programs*. In light of this, we formalize effect systems as follows:

Definition (Effector). A set EFF along with a relation $\overset{\fatsemi}{\mapsto}$ between List(EFF) and EFF satisfying the following two properties:

$$\begin{array}{cc} \textbf{Identity} & \textbf{Associativity} \\ \forall \varepsilon, \varepsilon'.\ \begin{array}{c} \varepsilon = \varepsilon' \\ \Downarrow \\ [\varepsilon] \overset{\fatsemi}{\mapsto} \varepsilon' \end{array} & \forall \vec{\varepsilon}_1 \ldots \vec{\varepsilon}_n, \varepsilon.\ \begin{array}{c} \exists \varepsilon_1 \ldots \varepsilon_n. (\forall i. \vec{\varepsilon}_i \overset{\fatsemi}{\mapsto} \varepsilon_i) \wedge [\varepsilon_1 \ldots \varepsilon_n] \overset{\fatsemi}{\mapsto} \varepsilon \\ \Downarrow \\ \vec{\varepsilon}_1 +\!\!+ \ldots +\!\!+ \vec{\varepsilon}_n \overset{\fatsemi}{\mapsto} \varepsilon \end{array} \end{array}$$

The identity rule says that sequencing an effectful computation with no other computations should have (at least) the same effect. The associativity rule says that, should one partition a list of effectful computations and sequence each partition together and then sequence each of those results together, sequencing the original list all together should have (at least) the same overall effect. This formalization may seem rather foreign with respect to existing work on effects. However, when an effector is *semi-strict*, meaning the associativity implication is actually an if-and-only-if, there is an equivalent monoid-like definition more akin to prior work:

Theorem 1. A semi-strict effector can equivalently be defined as an *effectoid*: a set EFF along with a unary relation $\not\varepsilon \mapsto -$, a binary relation $- \le -$, and a ternary relation $- \fatsemi - \mapsto -$ satisfying:

$$\begin{array}{lrc} \textbf{Identity} & \forall \varepsilon, \varepsilon'. & \begin{array}{c} \exists \varepsilon_\ell.\ \not\varepsilon \mapsto \varepsilon_\ell \wedge \varepsilon_\ell \fatsemi \varepsilon \mapsto \varepsilon' \\ \Updownarrow \\ \varepsilon \le \varepsilon' \\ \Updownarrow \\ \exists \varepsilon_r.\ \not\varepsilon \mapsto \varepsilon_r \wedge \varepsilon \fatsemi \varepsilon_r \mapsto \varepsilon' \end{array} \\ \textbf{Associativity} & \forall \varepsilon_1, \varepsilon_2, \varepsilon_3, \varepsilon. & \begin{array}{c} \exists \bar{\varepsilon}.\ \varepsilon_1 \fatsemi \varepsilon_2 \mapsto \bar{\varepsilon} \wedge \bar{\varepsilon} \fatsemi \varepsilon_3 \mapsto \varepsilon \\ \Updownarrow \\ \exists \hat{\varepsilon}.\ \varepsilon_2 \fatsemi \varepsilon_3 \mapsto \hat{\varepsilon} \wedge \varepsilon_1 \fatsemi \hat{\varepsilon} \mapsto \varepsilon \end{array} \\ \textbf{Reflexive} & \forall \varepsilon. & \varepsilon \le \varepsilon \\ \textbf{Congruence} & \forall \varepsilon, \varepsilon'. & \not\varepsilon \mapsto \varepsilon \wedge \varepsilon \le \varepsilon' \implies \not\varepsilon \mapsto \varepsilon' \\ & \forall \varepsilon_1, \varepsilon_2, \varepsilon, \varepsilon'. & \varepsilon_1 \fatsemi \varepsilon_2 \mapsto \varepsilon \wedge \varepsilon \le \varepsilon' \implies \varepsilon_1 \fatsemi \varepsilon_2 \mapsto \varepsilon' \end{array}$$

Proof. The proof can be found in the technical report [33]. □

Semi-strict effectors are common because compositional type systems are common. Conceptually, if $Seq_{\fatsemi}$ is actually an if-and-only-if, then the effector for the language is semi-strict. Note that $\not\varepsilon \mapsto \varepsilon$ does not necessarily imply ε is an identity in the usual sense for monoids. It simply means that pure computations (particularly the empty program) can be given the ε effect. We call such effects *centric* effects.

The effect system for Crit is defined as a congruently preordered partial monoid. This works because congruently preordered partial monoids are equivalent to *principalled* effectoids. A principalled effector is one where for every list of effects $\vec{\varepsilon}$ such that $\vec{\varepsilon} \overset{\fatsemi}{\mapsto} \varepsilon$ holds for some effect ε there exists a minimal such ε with respect to $\le$. Principalled effectors are common for the same reasons principalled type systems are common, such as simplifying type checking and type inference.

Note that not all effectors are semi-strict, especially ones used in analyses. For example, an analysis may say that `x := *p` has the read effect and that `*p := x` has the write effect but then give `x := *p; *p := x` the $\not\varepsilon$ effect even though generally those effects would combine into the read-write effect. The analysis is using information not contained in the descriptions read and write, namely that the same value and pointer is used in both heap uses, to reason that the program's semantics factor through the operation coercing pure computions into read-write computations and so can be treated as pure. In general, such effectors typically arise when an analysis uses more detailed reasoning intraprocedurally but coarser reasoning interprocedurally. Thus, while effectoids are extremely common, the generality of effectors is necessary to capture existing effect systems.

6. Productors

At last, we present our semantic framework for sequential composition of effectful computations, which we call a productor. Our goal is to give a denotational semantics to $Seq_{\fatsemi}$ in such a way that all the many possible parsings of $p_1; \ldots; p_n$ are guaranteed to produce the same semantics. Our fundamental assumption is that the semantics of the judgement $\Gamma \vdash p \dashv \Gamma' \mid \varepsilon$ can be represented as a morphism $[\![\Gamma]\!] \to P_\varepsilon([\![\Gamma']\!])$ for some function-on-objects P_ε.

Definition (Productor for an effector $\langle \text{EFF}, \overset{\fatsemi}{\mapsto} \rangle$). A category **Sem** with endofunctors $\{\langle P_\varepsilon, map_\varepsilon \rangle\}_{\varepsilon \in \text{EFF}}$ and natural transformations $\{join_{[\varepsilon_1,\ldots,\varepsilon_n],\varepsilon} : P_{\varepsilon_1} \circ \cdots \circ P_{\varepsilon_n} \to P_\varepsilon\}_{[\varepsilon_1,\ldots,\varepsilon_n] \overset{\fatsemi}{\mapsto} \varepsilon}$ such that $join_{[\varepsilon],\varepsilon}$ is always the identity transformation and the following diagram commutes whenever all terms are defined:

$$\begin{array}{ccccc} & & P_{\varepsilon_1} \circ \cdots \circ P_{\varepsilon_n} & & \\ & \overset{join_{\vec{\varepsilon}_1,\varepsilon_1} * \ldots * join_{\vec{\varepsilon}_n,\varepsilon_n}}{\nearrow} & & \overset{join_{[\varepsilon_1,\ldots,\varepsilon_n],\varepsilon}}{\searrow} & \\ P_{\vec{\varepsilon}_1} \circ \cdots \circ P_{\vec{\varepsilon}_n} & & \xrightarrow[join_{\vec{\varepsilon}_1 +\!\!+ \ldots +\!\!+ \vec{\varepsilon}_n,\varepsilon}]{} & & P_\varepsilon \end{array}$$

Notice the similarity between the commutativity requirements for productors and the implicational requirements for effectors. The idea is to ensure that the many ways that a sequence of programs may be typed all correspond to the same semantics. In other words, the specific proof used to type check a program should be irrelevant to its semantics. In the technical report [33], we ensure precisely that for the following denotational semantics of $Seq_{\fatsemi}$:

$$\frac{[\![\Gamma_0 \vdash p_1 \dashv \Gamma_1 \mid \varepsilon_1]\!] = f_1 \quad \ldots \quad [\![\Gamma_{n-1} \vdash p_n \dashv \Gamma_n \mid \varepsilon_n]\!] = f_n \qquad \left[\!\!\left[[\varepsilon_1, \ldots, \varepsilon_n] \overset{\fatsemi}{\mapsto} \varepsilon\right]\!\!\right] = join_{[\varepsilon_1,\ldots,\varepsilon_n],\varepsilon}}{[\![\Gamma_0 \vdash p_1; \ldots; p_n \dashv \Gamma_n \mid \varepsilon]\!] = f_1; map_{\varepsilon_1}(\ldots(f_n)); join_{[\varepsilon_1,\ldots,\varepsilon_n],\varepsilon}}$$

One might wonder why we worry about parsing ambiguity. After all, a language could always parse sequential composition left-associatively, like Haskell does. The reason is that by addressing ambiguity concerns we also address the kind of program transformations one would intuitively expect from sequential composition. For example, should $f()$ be defined as $p_1; p_2; p_3$, $g()$ as the empty program, and $h()$ as p_4, then one would expect $f(); g(); h()$ to have the same semantics as $p_1; p_2; p_3; p_4$. This is precisely what our commutative diagrams ensure.

We have proven that when the effector is semi-strict there is an equivalent definition of productors that may appear more familiar for those acquainted with existing semantic frameworks:

Theorem 2. A productor for an effectoid $\langle \text{EFF}, \not\varepsilon, \le, \fatsemi \rangle$ can equivalently be defined as a *productoid*: a category **Sem** with endofunctors $\{\langle P_\varepsilon, map_\varepsilon\rangle\}_{\varepsilon\in\text{EFF}}$ along with natural transformations $\{unit_\varepsilon : \mathbf{Sem} \to P_\varepsilon\}_{\vec{\varepsilon}\mapsto\varepsilon}$ and $\{coerce_{\varepsilon,\varepsilon'} : P_\varepsilon \to P_{\varepsilon'}\}_{\varepsilon\leq\varepsilon'}$ and $\{join_{\varepsilon,\varepsilon',\varepsilon''} : P_\varepsilon \circ P_{\varepsilon'} \to P_{\varepsilon''}\}_{\varepsilon\,⨾\,\varepsilon'\mapsto\varepsilon''}$ such that $coerce_{\varepsilon,\varepsilon}$ is always the identity morphism and the following diagrams commute whenever all terms are defined:

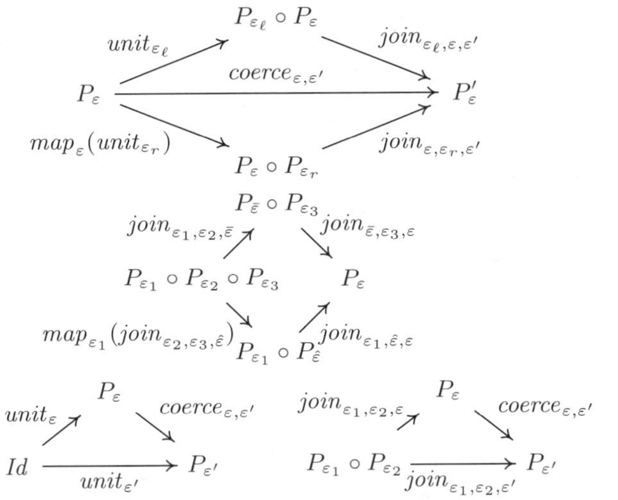

Proof. The proof can be found in the technical report [33]. □

The implicational requirements of an effectoid is essential to the above theorem. Using a productoid for a *pre*-effectoid, meaning an effectoid not necessarily satisfying the relevant implications, can indeed result in ambiguous semantics. Figure 5 provides a toy example of such.

The intuition behind this example is that pure represents no effect, err represents a possible error, and hndl indicates an error handler has been specified (more precisely the $\forall\alpha.\alpha$ must be a natural transformation – note that sometimes there can be many inhabitants of $\forall\alpha.\alpha$, such as differing error messages or even `null` in object-oriented domains). A primitive err-effectful operation **error**() throws an error, and a primitive hndl-effectful operation **handle**(h) sets the handler. The definition of $join_{\text{hndl},\text{hndl},\text{hndl}}$ indicates that, if the handler is set twice in a row, the second handler should be used in place of the first one.

The interaction of handlers and exceptions is defined solely by the $join_{\text{hndl},\text{err},\text{pure}}$ operation. In particular, this definition indicates that, should an exception be thrown, then the previously set handler should be used to handle the exception and proceed with normal execution. The result is that a computation has effect pure only if a handler has been set every place an exception might be thrown.

One can check that these operations do indeed satisfy the requirements of our definition in Theorem 2. However, supposing h_1 and h_2 are handlers, the following pure-effectful program still has two possible semantics:

$$\textbf{handle}(h_1); \textbf{handle}(h_2); \textbf{error}(); \textbf{error}()$$

In particular, the program can result in h_1 *or* h_2. The program results in h_1 if **handle**(h_2) gets matched up with the first **error**() (via $join_{\text{hndl},\text{err},\text{pure}}$), sequencing into a pure-effectful computation so that then **handle**(h_1) can be matched up with the second **error**() (via $join_{\text{hndl},\text{err},\text{pure}}$), sequencing into a pure-effectful computation resulting in h_1. The program results in h_2 if **handle**(h_2) overrides **handle**(h_1) (via $join_{\text{hndl},\text{hndl},\text{hndl}}$) and the two **error**()s are combined (via $join_{\text{err},\text{err},\text{err}}$), so that then **handle**(h_1); **handle**(h_2) can be matched up with **error**(); **error**(), sequencing into a pure-effectful computation resulting in h_2. Thus, the specific proof used to show the program has effect pure actually influences the program's semantics, violating semantic coherency.

$$\text{EFF} = \{\text{pure}, \text{err}, \text{hndl}\}$$
$$\forall\varepsilon.\quad \text{pure}\,⨾\,\varepsilon \mapsto \varepsilon \quad \varepsilon\,⨾\,\text{pure} \mapsto \varepsilon$$
$$\text{err}\,⨾\,\text{err} \mapsto \text{err} \quad \text{hndl}\,⨾\,\text{hndl} \mapsto \text{hndl} \quad \text{hndl}\,⨾\,\text{err} \mapsto \text{pure}$$

$$P_{\text{pure}}(\tau) = \tau \quad P_{\text{err}}(\tau) = P_{\text{partial}}(\tau) \quad P_{\text{hndl}}(\tau) = \tau \times \forall\alpha.\alpha$$

$$\begin{aligned}\forall\varepsilon.\quad & join_{\text{pure},\varepsilon,\varepsilon} &&= join_{\varepsilon,\text{pure},\varepsilon} = identity\\ & join_{\text{err},\text{err},\text{err}} &&= join_{\text{partial}}\\ & join_{\text{hndl},\text{hndl},\text{hndl}} &&= \lambda\langle\langle x, h'\rangle, h\rangle.\langle x, h'\rangle\\ & join_{\text{hndl},\text{err},\text{pure}} &&= \lambda\langle px, h\rangle.\textbf{case}\ px \begin{cases}\text{success}(x) \mapsto x\\ \text{failure} \mapsto h\end{cases}\end{aligned}$$

Figure 5. A semantically incoherent pre-effectoid and productoid

This productoid was designed by intentionally devising a pre-effectoid that violates our associativity requirement for effectoids. For example, hndl ⨾ hndl $\mapsto$ hndl and hndl ⨾ err $\mapsto$ pure hold, but there is no $\hat\varepsilon$ such that hndl ⨾ err $\mapsto \hat\varepsilon$ and hndl ⨾ $\hat\varepsilon \mapsto$ pure hold. As such, one cannot progressively transform either proof into the other using the required equivalences on the productoid, so they can produce different semantics.

This illustrates the subtleties of semantic coherency for effect systems addressed by our framework. Because the pre-effectoid does not satisfy the appropriate requirements, the productoid does not extend to a productor. Although not immediately apparent, in general a productor actually has more equational requirements than a productoid in order to maintain semantic coherency; it just happens to be that the implicational requirements of an effectoid imposes enough structure on its productoids to ensure they satisfy those additional equational requirements. In general, additional structure on the effector at hand imposes structure on its productors. This interplay will be a common theme during our discussion of existing semantic frameworks for effects.

7. Existing Frameworks

While the components and requirements of a productor can be described concisely, the high-level nature of this description can be daunting. As such, it is helpful to see how existing semantic frameworks for effects can be seen as special classes of productors. We start with the simplest such framework: monads.

Monads A monad $\langle M, map, unit, join\rangle$ is a productor for the effector with one effect ε and with $\vec{\varepsilon} \overset{⨾}{\mapsto} \varepsilon$ always holding. M is simply P_ε; map is map_ε; $unit$ is $join_{[],\varepsilon}$; and $join$ is $join_{[\varepsilon,\varepsilon],\varepsilon}$. The equational requirements for a monad are precisely those required by our definition of productor.

More generally, for any effector with an effect ε such that $\vec{\varepsilon} \mapsto \varepsilon$ and $\varepsilon\,⨾\,\varepsilon \mapsto \varepsilon$ hold (called a centric *idempotent* effect), any productor's representation of ε is necessarily a monad.

Monad Morphisms A monad morphism $coerce$ from a monad $\langle M, map, unit, join\rangle$ to another monad $\langle M', map', unit', join'\rangle$ is a natural transformation from M to M' such that the following diagrams commute:

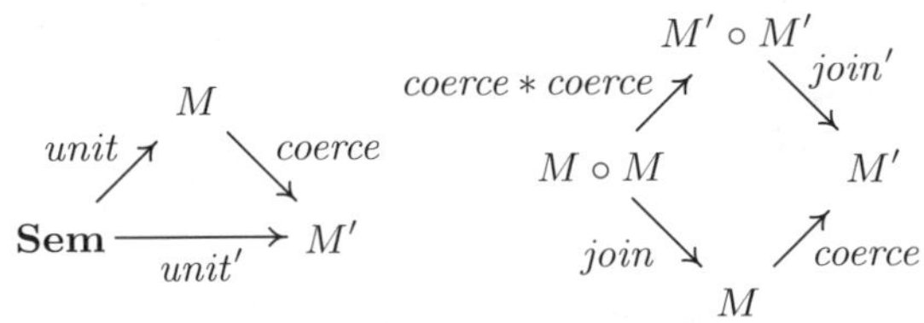

These equational requirements ensure that implicit coercions for effectful computations do not affect the semantics of the program, in the same spirit as Reynolds' requirements for implicit coercions for data types [28].

As we mentioned, monads correspond to centric idempotent effects. Furthermore, given two such effects ε and ε' with the additional property that ε is a subeffect of ε', then the equational requirements for productors guarantee precisely that the corresponding natural transformation $coerce_{\varepsilon,\varepsilon'} = join_{[\varepsilon],\varepsilon'}$ from P_ε to $P_{\varepsilon'}$ is a monad morphism. Thus both the concepts of monads and monad morphisms are special cases of productors.

Indexed Monads Program analysis is one of the most common applications of effect systems. Such analyses typically use what is known as a type-and-effect system [19, 22, 32], which taints code with a collection of atomic effects. For example, Talpin and Jouvelot taint code with how it accesses various heap regions [31], and Abadi showed that the dependency core calculus essentially takes this approach as well [1]. Abstractly, these effect systems form a join semi-lattice, and the combined effect of a sequence of computations is the join ($\sqcup$) of the effects of the individual computations, with pure and empty computations being given the $\perp$ effect [3, 13].

Wadler and Thiemann famously showed that one of Talpin and Jouvelot's effect systems can be formalized by what has become known as an indexed monad [38]. An indexed monad is a join semi-lattice of monads connected by monad morphisms. The semantics of sequencing effectful computations was defined by coercing both computations to the least common supermonad and then using the $join$ of that monad. They did this for a single effect system, but with our framework it is easy to determine that join semi-lattice effectors are intimately connected to indexed monads, and in these cases the semantics of sequential composition are guaranteed to be defined with this $coerce$-then-$join$ strategy.

To see why, consider the following properties of an effector where sequential composition of effects coincides with a lattice-join operation. They are guaranteed to be *centric* effectors, meaning all their effects are centric effects. They are guaranteed to be *idempotent*, meaning all their effects are idempotent. Lastly, they are guaranteed to be *increasing*, meaning whenever $\vec{\varepsilon} \overset{\fatsemi}{\mapsto} \varepsilon$ holds then all elements of $\vec{\varepsilon}$ are subeffects of ε.

The first two properties already guarantee that a productor represents all effects as monads and furthermore all coercions between such effects must be monad morphisms. Thus a productor for any centric idempotent effector must be a network of monads and monad morphisms, like an indexed monad. All we have left to do is show why sequential composition must take the $coerce$-then-$join$ strategy:

Theorem 3. Any increasing centric idempotent effector is semi-strict. For any productor of an increasing idempotent effector, $join_{\varepsilon_1,\varepsilon_2,\varepsilon}$ is determined by $coerce_{\varepsilon_1,\varepsilon}$, $coerce_{\varepsilon_2,\varepsilon}$, and $join_{\varepsilon,\varepsilon,\varepsilon}$.

Proof. First, suppose $\vec{\varepsilon}_1 +\!\!+ \ldots +\!\!+ \vec{\varepsilon}_n \mapsto \varepsilon$ holds. Since the effector is increasing, all effects in each $\vec{\varepsilon}_i$ must be subeffects of ε. Since the effector is centric and idempotent, $[\varepsilon, \ldots, \varepsilon] \mapsto \varepsilon$ holds for all arities. These and the definition of effector imply that $\vec{\varepsilon}_i \mapsto \varepsilon$ holds. Thus, since $[\varepsilon, \ldots, \varepsilon] \mapsto \varepsilon$ also holds, the effector is semi-strict.

Second, suppose $\varepsilon_1 \fatsemi \varepsilon_2 \mapsto \varepsilon$ holds. Since the effector is increasing, $\varepsilon_i \leq \varepsilon$ holds so $join_{[\varepsilon_i],\varepsilon}$ must exist. Since the effector is idempotent, $[\varepsilon, \varepsilon] \mapsto \varepsilon$ holds so $join_{[\varepsilon,\varepsilon],\varepsilon}$ must exist. Then by definition of productor since $[\varepsilon_1] +\!\!+ [\varepsilon_2]$ equals $[\varepsilon_1, \varepsilon_2]$, $join_{[\varepsilon_1,\varepsilon_2],\varepsilon}$ must equal $(join_{[\varepsilon_1],\varepsilon} * join_{[\varepsilon_2],\varepsilon})\,;join_{[\varepsilon,\varepsilon],\varepsilon}$, which is the longhand form of $(coerce_{\varepsilon_1,\varepsilon} * coerce_{\varepsilon_2,\varepsilon})\,;join_{\varepsilon,\varepsilon,\varepsilon}$. □

In the other direction, let us consider what kind of effectors indexed monads can handle. Suppose an effector is represented by an indexed monad. Then that effector can be faithfully extended so that it is a principalled, idempotent, increasing, centric, and furthermore *commutative*, meaning if $\vec{\varepsilon} \overset{\fatsemi}{\mapsto} \varepsilon$ holds then $\vec{\epsilon} \overset{\fatsemi}{\mapsto} \varepsilon$ holds for all permutations $\vec{\epsilon}$ of $\vec{\varepsilon}$. This tells us three things: the effector cannot guarantee properties that depend on an effectful computation occurring; the effector cannot guarantee properties that depend on the order of effectful computations; and the effector cannot guarantee properties that depend on the frequency of effectful computations.

First, we know that an effector represented by an indexed monad cannot have effects that guarantee an effectful computation occurs, since all effects are centric. In Crit it is important to distinguish computations that *must* lock from those that *might* lock in order to ensure shared-memory accesses occur in critical regions. In particular, the effector must not confuse a pure or empty computation for one that definitely locks, so that whatever effect ε used to identify definite locking cannot satisfy $\epsilon \mapsto \varepsilon$ and so cannot be centric. As such, indexed monads cannot be used for effectors that guarantee locking or guarantee responsiveness (e.g. a server always producing a response for each request).

Second, we know that an effector represented by an indexed monad cannot guarantee properties dependent on the order of operations, since the effector is commutative. In Crit it is important to distinguish accessing shared memory *after* acquiring a lock from accessing shared memory *before* acquiring a lock. Yet, if the effector were commutative, then $\mathsf{locking} \fatsemi \mathsf{critical}$ would necessarily equal $\mathsf{critical} \fatsemi \mathsf{locking}$ so such computations would be indistinguishable in the effector. As such, indexed monads cannot be used for effectors that need order sensitivity.

Third, we know that an effector represented by an indexed monad cannot guarantee properties dependent on the frequency of operations, since each effect is idempotent. In Crit it is important to distinguish acquiring a lock once from acquiring a lock multiple times since Crit prevents reentrant code. However, if $\mathsf{locking}$ were idempotent, then $\mathsf{locking} \fatsemi \mathsf{locking}$ would have to equal $\mathsf{locking}$ so that multiple acquisitions would appear the same as a single acquisition. As such, indexed monads cannot be used for effectors that want to track the quantity of effectful operations.

These limitations of indexed monads were part of why we endeavored to find a more general framework. The discussion here illustrates that, not only are there advantages to having a more general semantic framework, but our formalizations provide a useful language for discussing effectors, another reason why we began our investigations. It also bears some importance for effect analyses, since our findings indicate that lattice-based effectors have some severe limitations in what they can determine about a program. We hope these insights will encourage investigations into new analytical techniques and new semantic techniques.

Layered Monads Filinski introduced the semantic technique of *layered* monads [5]. A layering of a monad $\langle M', map', unit', join'\rangle$ over another monad $\langle M, map, unit, join\rangle$ is a natural transformation $layer : M \circ M' \to M'$ satisfying certain equational properties. $layer$ looks very much like our $join$ operation for effects $\top$ and $\perp$ should $\perp \fatsemi \top \mapsto \top$ hold. Indeed, Filinski's equational requirements for layerings are simply our equivalent requirements for productoids of an increasing centric idempotent effectoid, and Filinski uses the $layer$ operation to sequence a $\perp$ computation followed by a $\top$ computation, as our framework would do with the corresponding $join$ operation.

In more recent work [6], Filinski allows users to build a tree of monadic subeffects, with non-termination at the root of the tree, so that programmers could build their own effect system. Any effect system designed in such a way is guaranteed to be an increasing centric idempotent effector and so has many of the key limitations that we discussed for indexed monads. However, there is one significant difference: indexed monads necessarily correspond to *total* effectors whereas Filinski's tree of subeffects may not be total. An effector is total if for every list of effects $\vec{\varepsilon}$ there is some effect ε such that $\vec{\varepsilon} \overset{\fatsemi}{\mapsto} \varepsilon$ holds. This is not necessarily a limitation of Filinski's approach, though. It has the advantage that it can express user effects that are incompatible with each other. This is an important property for a modular language where users should be able to design their effects without worrying about what other effects may be present elsewhere in the system should they never meet each other.

Parameterized Monads Atkey made the observation that many effect systems have to do with transitioning from one state to another [2]. Indeed, most of the effects in Crit are used to indicate the required incoming state of the lock and the guaranteed outgoing state of the lock. As such, Atkey designed a *parameterized* monad to address this common case, and showed how parameterized monads can formalize a variety of concepts such as composable continuations [4, 37]. A parameterized monad is (equivalently)

- a category $\mathbf{S}$ of states and primitive transitioning operations
- a functor $\langle T, map\rangle : \mathbf{S}^{op} \times \mathbf{S} \to (\mathbf{Sem} \to \mathbf{Sem})$
- an extranatural transformation $unit : \forall s.\ Id \to T(s, s)$
- an extranatural transformation

$$join : \forall s, s', s''.\ T(s, s') \circ T(s', s'') \to T(s, s'')$$

satisfying equational requirements we do not repeat here.

This should look slightly familiar. In fact, the productor corresponding to just the impure effects of Crit is a parameterized monad. The category $\mathbf{S}$ is just the discrete category with objects *free* and *occupied*. The extranaturality conditions hold automatically since the category is discrete.

Now, it is important to note that a parameterized monad does two things simultaneously: it specifies how to sequence computations *and* it specifies the semantics of primitive operations. For example, our semantics for **acquire** and **release** could be adapted into a parameterized monad for the free category generated by the graph with two objects and a morphism between them in each direction. However, the intent of our framework is only to formalize sequential composition of computations, so we focus on a restricted subset of parameterizations. In particular, we focus on parameterized monads where $\mathbf{S}$ is thin, meaning there is at most one morphism between any two states. Such an $\mathbf{S}$ is actually a preorder, and so represents states with a substate relation.

Given such a set of states S and a substate preorder $\le$, define an effectoid $\mathcal{E}_{\langle S,\le\rangle}$ as follows:

- EFF is $S \times S$, so that the effect $\langle s, s'\rangle$ represents computations that transition from state s to state s'.
- $\mathfrak{E} \mapsto \langle s, s'\rangle$ holds iff $s \le s'$ holds.
- $\langle s'_1, s_2\rangle \le \langle s_1, s'_2\rangle$ holds iff $s_1 \le s'_1$ and $s_2 \le s'_2$ hold.
- $\langle s'_1, s_2\rangle \fatsemi \langle s'_2, s_3\rangle \mapsto \langle s_1, s'_3\rangle$ holds iff $s_1 \le s'_1$, $s_2 \le s'_2$, and $s_3 \le s'_3$ hold.

Due to their definition, all effectors formalizable by parameterized monads are of this form.

Theorem 4. Given a set of states S and a substate preorder $\le$, there is a one-to-one correspondence between parameterized monads for the category $\langle S, \le\rangle$ and productoids for the effectoid $\mathcal{E}_{\langle S,\le\rangle}$.

Proof. Given a parameterized monad $\langle T, map, unit, join\rangle$ for $\langle S, \le\rangle$, define the productoid for $\mathcal{E}_{\langle S,\le\rangle}$ as follows:

- $\langle P_{\langle s,s'\rangle}, map_{\langle s,s'\rangle}\rangle = T(s, s')$
- $unit_{\langle s,s'\rangle} = Id \xrightarrow{unit_s} T(s, s) \xrightarrow{map(s \ge s, s \le s')} T(s, s')$
- $coerce_{\langle s'_1,s_2\rangle,\langle s_1,s'_2\rangle} = map(s'_1 \ge s_1, s_2 \le s'_2)$
- $join_{\langle s'_1,s_2\rangle,\langle s'_2,s_3\rangle,\langle s_1,s'_3\rangle} =$

$$\begin{array}{r} T(s'_1, s_2) \circ T(s'_2, s_3) \\ map(s'_1 \ge s_1, s_2 \le s_2) * map(s'_2 \ge s_2, s_3 \le s'_3)\downarrow \\ T(s_1, s_2) \circ T(s_2, s'_3) \\ join_{s_1,s_2,s'_3}\downarrow \\ T(s_1, s'_3) \end{array}$$

The necessary equivalences hold due to the equational requirements of parameterized monads.

Given a productoid $\langle P, map, unit, coerce, join\rangle$ for $\mathcal{E}_{\langle S,\le\rangle}$, define the parameterized monad for $\langle S, \le\rangle$ as follows:

- $T(s, s') = \langle P_{\langle s,s'\rangle}, map_{\langle s,s'\rangle}\rangle$
- $map(s'_1 \ge s_1, s_2 \le s'_2) = coerce_{\langle s'_1,s_2\rangle,\langle s_1,s'_2\rangle}$
- $unit_s = unit_{\langle s,s\rangle}$
- $join_{s,s',s''} = join_{\langle s,s'\rangle,\langle s',s''\rangle,\langle s,s''\rangle}$

The necessary equivalences hold to due to the equational requirements of productoids.

These two processes are clearly inverses of each other. □

Now that we have seen how parameterized monads fit within our framework, let us consider the expressiveness of parameterized monads. First, a parameterized monad is *not* a family of monads. While $T(s, s)$ forms a monad since the input and output are the same, this is not the case for $T(s, s')$ whenever s and s' are not equivalent to each other. This is because $\mathfrak{E} \mapsto \langle s, s'\rangle$ holds only when s is a substate of s' and $\langle s, s'\rangle \fatsemi \langle s, s'\rangle \mapsto \langle s, s'\rangle$ holds only when s' is a substate of s. So, the effectoid $\mathcal{E}_{\langle S,\le\rangle}$ is *neither* centric, idempotent, nor increasing in general. Thus the very notion of distinct states is inexpressible by indexed monads and layered monads, indicating how powerful parameterized monads are.

Parameterized monads have their limitations, though. For example, information-flow effect systems [29] and contextual effects [21] do not meet the requirements of Theorem 4 and so cannot be formalized using parameterized monads. Interestingly, though, should we allow EFF for $\mathcal{E}_{\langle S,\le\rangle}$ to be just a subset of $S \times S$ rather than all pairs of states, then we can represent information-flow effect systems and contextual effects. For example, in [29] the states are levels of secrecy, so EFF contains only those pairs $\langle s, s'\rangle$ where s is a lower level of secrecy than s', since inputs can be propagated to outputs. Thus, Theorem 4 suggests such effect systems must be formalizable by something very similar to a parameterized monad.

Even such generalizations are still too restrictive for some effectoids. For example, the full effectoid for Crit *including* the basic effect $\mathfrak{E}$ cannot be formalized by a parameterized monad. The issue is that, ignoring substates since they are orthogonal to the following concerns, a parameterized monad can only have one effect between any two states. However, both $\mathfrak{E}$ and critical computations are permitted when the lock is acquired and finish with the lock acquired. If we wanted to prevent race conditions, then we would want to distinguish $\mathfrak{E}$ and critical computations since we should allow critical computations be ran in parallel with $\mathfrak{E}$ computations but not with other critical computations. Furthermore, if we wanted to track other effectful attributes that are state agnostic, such as non-determinism, then we would need multiple effects between any two states. Even just an indexed monad can be viewed as having many effects between a single state, showing why non-trivially indexed monads cannot be formalized by parameterized monads. Thus, while parameterized monads are expressive, there are still useful effectoids inexpressible even by generalized parameterized monads but still expressible by our framework.

Arrows and Freyd Categories Arrows [8], another generalization of monads, are a little difficult to discuss because they are simultaneously too general and too restrictive. First, they have three components, which we describe informally:

- a way to sequentially compose arrows
- a way to turn a pure computation into an arrow
- a way to propagate additional context through an arrow

These three components must satisfy equalities which essentially indicate that the arrows form a category, the pure computations form a pure subcategory, and a pure computation can be executed alongside an arrow without altering the overall effect of the arrow.

In fact, the above intuition behind the equational properties has been formalized. Heunan and Jacobs proved that arrows are equivalent to Freyd categories [10], an attempt to formalize arbitrary effectful computations. Informally, a Freyd category [26] is a premonoidal category [25] (a category with a notion of extending morphisms to propagate context) with a wide cartesian monoidal subcategory of pure morphisms that can be executed alongside other morphisms without altering their overall effect.

Note that an important aspect of the above descriptions is the notion of extending and propagating context. Herein lies our primary criticism of arrows and Freyd categories. What we determined is that nearly all of their structure has to do with extending and propagating context. If one removes the components that are present to serve those roles (i.e. anything using $\otimes$), what remains is just a category of effectful computations with a wide subcategory of pure computations. That is, arrows and Freyd categories say nothing about sequencing effectful computations besides the fact that sequencing pure computations results in a pure computation (not to mention they only handle one effect). So, while arrows generalize strong monads, they do so at the cost of discarding most of the useful structure to work with. It is for this reason that we focused on producer effects; our investigations suggest that being as general as possible means not providing any structure beyond a category with a distinguished subcategory.

8. Generality

The intent of this work is not to generalize prior semantic frameworks for effects, but to design the most general such framework possible. However, as we just mentioned while discussing arrows, the most general framework possible is not very useful. As such, we focused on producer effects and defined productors for formalizing producer effect systems. Here we show how a few language properties guarantee that the semantics of sequential composition forms a productor.

Figure 6 extends the language assumptions made in Figure 4. Again, while we assume these rules can be imposed upon the language at hand, we expect the language will have a different syntax and more rules in addition to those we assume.

Figure 6 introduces two new judgements. The judgement $\Gamma \vdash p \dashv \Gamma'$ indicates that p is a pure program with input Γ and output Γ' for some notion of purity. In prior work, this separation usually is termed as values versus computations. For example, OCaml restricts type generalization to values rather than arbitrary computations [39]. However, not all notions of purity may be restricted to values. For example, Haskell's notion of purity includes exceptions and non-termination. Here we let the designer determine their own notion of purity. Then we will show how effectful computations can be expressed by a productor on pure computations for whatever notion of purity the designer decided upon.

The other new judgement $\vdash p \overset{\varepsilon}{\underset{\Gamma\ \Gamma'}{=\!=}} p'$ indicates that p and p', viewed as ε-effectful computations from Γ to Γ', are semantically equivalent. When ε is absent, then they are semantically equivalent

$$\textit{Seq}\ \frac{\Gamma_0 \vdash p_1 \dashv \Gamma_1 \quad \ldots \quad \Gamma_{n-1} \vdash p_n \dashv \Gamma_n}{\Gamma_0 \vdash p_1; \ldots; p_n \dashv \Gamma_n} \qquad \textit{Seq}_{\varepsilon}\ \frac{\Gamma \vdash p \dashv \Gamma' \quad \Gamma' \vdash p' \dashv \Gamma'' \mid \varepsilon \quad \Gamma'' \vdash p'' \dashv \Gamma'''}{\Gamma \vdash p; p'; p'' \dashv \Gamma''' \mid \varepsilon}$$

$$\textit{Thunk}\ \frac{\Gamma \vdash p \dashv \Gamma' \mid \varepsilon}{\Gamma \vdash \lfloor p \rfloor_{\varepsilon} \dashv (\!|\Gamma'|\!)_{\varepsilon}} \qquad \textit{Exec}\ \frac{}{(\!|\Gamma|\!)_{\varepsilon} \vdash \mathbf{exec}_{\varepsilon} \dashv \Gamma \mid \varepsilon}$$

$$\textit{Eq}_{\beta}\ \frac{\Gamma \vdash p \dashv \Gamma' \mid \varepsilon}{\vdash \lfloor p \rfloor_{\varepsilon}; \mathbf{exec}_{\varepsilon} \overset{\varepsilon}{\underset{\Gamma\ \Gamma'}{=\!=}} p} \qquad \textit{Eq}_{\eta}\ \frac{\Gamma \vdash p \dashv (\!|\Gamma'|\!)_{\varepsilon}}{\vdash \lfloor p; \mathbf{exec}_{\varepsilon} \rfloor_{\varepsilon} \underset{\Gamma\ (\!|\Gamma'|\!)_{\varepsilon}}{=\!=} p}$$

Figure 6. Typing and semantic rules that guarantee productors

when viewed as pure computations. While not explicitly stated in Figure 6, we assume semantic equivalence is congruent with respect to sequential composition, implicit coercion of pure computation into effectful computation, and thunking.

Figure 6 also introduces three new meta-operations. The operation $\lfloor - \rfloor_{\varepsilon}$ maps an ε-effectful program to a pure thunked version of that program, delaying its execution and treating it as a value. In OCaml, given an (ε-effectful) expression e, $\lfloor e \rfloor_{\varepsilon}$ would be `fun () ->` e, effectively delaying the evaluation of e by turning it into a function waiting for an input, namely `()`. The operation $(\!|-|\!)_{\varepsilon}$ maps a context Γ to the context representing a thunked ε-effectful computation that would produce Γ whenever it is executed, i.e. the output of a thunked computation $\lfloor p \rfloor_{\varepsilon}$. In OCaml, $(\!|\tau|\!)_{\varepsilon}$ would be `unit ->` τ. Lastly, the operation $\mathbf{exec}_{\varepsilon}$ is the program that finally executes a thunked ε-effectful computation. In OCaml, $\mathbf{exec}_{\varepsilon}$ would be $-$ `()`, i.e. the program finally passing `()` to the thunked computation of the form `fun () ->` e. Note that, while our OCaml example defines the operations by wrapping the relevant program or context, other examples may be done by a more in-depth translation. For example, if a language has sum types, then thunking an exception-throwing program can be done by recursively translating the entire program to inject left or right instead of throwing an exception and to use pattern matching to explicitly propagate the exception. Thus a language does not have to be higher order in order to satisfy the requirements of Figure 6.

The rules in Figure 6 formalize a number of language properties, some of which are obvious, and some of which are fundamental to the notion of producer effects. *Seq* indicates that pure computations are closed under sequential composition. Note in particular that the empty computation is pure. $\textit{Seq}_{\varepsilon}$ indicates that sequential composition of effectful computations with pure computation preserves the effect of a computation. This formalizes the idea that the effect of a computation is not dependent on the values of its inputs or outputs. Note that these rules combined with using the empty computation for $\textit{Seq}_{\varepsilon}$ admit the following:

$$\frac{\Gamma \vdash p \dashv \Gamma' \qquad \varepsilon \mapsto \varepsilon}{\Gamma \vdash p \dashv \Gamma' \mid \varepsilon}$$

Thunk and *Exec* formally evidence the notion of producer effects. First, any effectful computation can be thunked into a pure computation by modifying only the output in a uniform manner. Second, there is a similarly effectful computation that executes a thunked computation. $\textit{Eq}_{\beta}$ and $\textit{Eq}_{\eta}$ essentially correspond to β- and η-equivalence for these constructs.

Note that these are not the only rules of the language; they are simply properties that may be superimposed upon a language. In particular, there can be (and typically are) many rules that operate on contexts of form $(\!|\Gamma|\!)_{\varepsilon}$ so that $\mathbf{exec}_{\varepsilon}$ is not necesarilly the only operation that can be performed on a thunked computation. Nonetheless, regardless of what additional rules the language at hand may have, so long as it admits at least the rules in Figures 4 and 6 then it is guaranteed to be an instance of our framework.

With these we can finally present our fundamental theorem:

Theorem 5. If a language with an effector $\langle \text{EFF}, \overset{\circ}{\mapsto} \rangle$ admits at least the rules in Figures 4 and 6, then there is a productor $\langle (\!|-|\!), \mathit{map}, \mathit{join} \rangle$ using pure computations modulo semantic equivalence as **Sem**, such that the language admits the following:

$$\frac{\Gamma_0 \vdash p_1 \dashv \Gamma_1 \mid \varepsilon_1 \quad \ldots \quad \Gamma_{n-1} \vdash p_n \dashv \Gamma_n \mid \varepsilon_n \quad [\varepsilon_1, \ldots, \varepsilon_n] \overset{\circ}{\mapsto} \varepsilon}{\lfloor p_1; \ldots; p_n \rfloor_\varepsilon \overline{\overline{\Gamma_0\, (\!|\Gamma_n|\!)_\varepsilon}} \lfloor p_1 \rfloor_{\varepsilon_1}; \mathit{map}_{\varepsilon_1}(\ldots(\lfloor p_n \rfloor_{\varepsilon_n}))\,; \mathit{join}_{[\varepsilon_1,\ldots,\varepsilon_n],\varepsilon}}$$

Proof. Define the productor as follows:

- $P_\varepsilon(\Gamma)$ is already defined as $(\!|\Gamma|\!)_\varepsilon$
- $\mathit{map}_\varepsilon(p) = \lfloor \mathbf{exec}_\varepsilon; p \rfloor_\varepsilon$
- $\mathit{join}_{[\varepsilon_1,\ldots,\varepsilon_n],\varepsilon} = \lfloor \mathbf{exec}_{\varepsilon_1}; \ldots; \mathbf{exec}_{\varepsilon_n} \rfloor_\varepsilon$

In the technical report [33], using Eq_β, Eq_η, and congruence. Here we prove only the desired semantic property of sequential composition, using approximately the same proof strategy.

First, there is an important lemma: given pure programs p and p' from Γ to Γ', if $p; \mathbf{exec}_\varepsilon$ is semantically equivalent to $p'; \mathbf{exec}_\varepsilon$, then p and p' are semantically equivalent. The lemma assumptions and congruence imply that $\lfloor p; \mathbf{exec}_\varepsilon \rfloor_\varepsilon$ is semantically equivalent to $\lfloor p'; \mathbf{exec}_\varepsilon \rfloor_\varepsilon$. Eq_η then tells us that the former is semantically equivalent to p and the latter to p'. Thus, by transitivity, p and p' are semantically equivalent.

Now, to prove that $\lfloor p_1; \ldots; p_n \rfloor_\varepsilon$ is semantically equivalent to $\lfloor p_1 \rfloor_{\varepsilon_1}; \mathit{map}_{\varepsilon_1}(\ldots(\lfloor p_n \rfloor_{\varepsilon_n})); \mathit{join}_{[\varepsilon_1,\ldots,\varepsilon_n],\varepsilon}$, due to our lemma we can instead prove $\lfloor p_1; \ldots; p_n \rfloor_\varepsilon; \mathbf{exec}_\varepsilon$ is semantically equivalent to $\lfloor p_1 \rfloor_{\varepsilon_1}; \mathit{map}_{\varepsilon_1}(\ldots(\lfloor p_n \rfloor_{\varepsilon_n})); \mathit{join}_{[\varepsilon_1,\ldots,\varepsilon_n],\varepsilon}; \mathbf{exec}_\varepsilon$. So, $\lfloor p_1; \ldots; p_n \rfloor_\varepsilon; \mathbf{exec}_\varepsilon$ is semantically equivalent to $p_1; \ldots; p_n$ by Eq_β. From Eq_β and the definition of *join*, $\mathit{join}_{[\varepsilon_1,\ldots,\varepsilon_n],\varepsilon}; \mathbf{exec}_\varepsilon$ is semantically equivalent to $\mathbf{exec}_{\varepsilon_1}; \ldots; \mathbf{exec}_{\varepsilon_n}$. From Eq_β and the definition of *map*, $\mathit{map}_{\varepsilon_i}(p); \mathbf{exec}_{\varepsilon_i}$ is semantically equivalent to $\mathbf{exec}_{\varepsilon_i}; p$. Using that fact and Eq_β, we know that $\lfloor p_i \rfloor_{\varepsilon_i}; \mathit{map}_{\varepsilon_i}(\ldots(\lfloor p_n \rfloor_{\varepsilon_n})); \mathbf{exec}_{\varepsilon_i}; \ldots; \mathbf{exec}_{\varepsilon_n}$ is equivalent to $p_i; \lfloor p_{i+1} \rfloor_{\varepsilon_{i+1}}; \mathit{map}_{\varepsilon_{i+1}}(\ldots(\lfloor p_n \rfloor_{\varepsilon_n})); \mathbf{exec}_{\varepsilon_{i+1}}; \ldots; \mathbf{exec}_{\varepsilon_n}$. Via induction, $\lfloor p_1 \rfloor_{\varepsilon_1}; \mathit{map}_{\varepsilon_1}(\ldots(\lfloor p_n \rfloor_{\varepsilon_n})); \mathbf{exec}_{\varepsilon_1}; \ldots; \mathbf{exec}_{\varepsilon_n}$ is equivalent to $p_1; \ldots; p_n$. Taking advantage of congruence, then $\lfloor p_1 \rfloor_{\varepsilon_1}; \mathit{map}_{\varepsilon_1}(\ldots(\lfloor p_n \rfloor_{\varepsilon_n})); \mathit{join}_{[\varepsilon_1,\ldots,\varepsilon_n],\varepsilon}$ is also equivalent to $p_1; \ldots; p_n$. Therefore the desired semantic property holds. □

Example Our toy language Crit does not actually satisfy the requirements of Figure 6. This illustrates that Figure 6 is sufficient but not necessary for our framework, demonstrating that our framework is useful even for formalizing languages without a notion of thunks. Nonetheless, for sake of illustration, we show how we might extend Crit so that it models Figure 6.

A sufficient extension of Crit is shown in Figure 7. Semantically we assume the usual β- and η-equivalences. The first extension is a singleton type Unit. The second and more important extension is effectful function types. In particular, $\tau \xrightarrow{\varepsilon} \Gamma$ represents an ε-effectful function accepting a τ as input and during execution assigning values of the appropriate types to the variables in Γ. Thus this extension is like the computational lambda calculus with multiple effects mixed with a register-based language.

With this language we can define the required judgements and operations in Figure 6 as follows:

$$\Gamma \vdash p \dashv \Gamma' \equiv \Gamma \vdash p \dashv \Gamma' \mid \mathfrak{E} \qquad (\!|\Gamma|\!)_\varepsilon \equiv t : \mathsf{Unit} \xrightarrow{\varepsilon} \Gamma$$
$$\lfloor p \rfloor_\varepsilon \equiv t := (\lambda u.\langle\rangle := u; p) \qquad \mathbf{exec}_\varepsilon \equiv u := \langle\rangle; t\ u$$

That is, a pure computation is one with the basic effect $\mathfrak{E}$. Thunking works by turning the computation into a function waiting for a

$$\frac{}{\varnothing \vdash u := \langle\rangle \dashv u : \mathsf{Unit} \mid \mathfrak{E}} \qquad \frac{\Gamma, x : \tau \vdash p \dashv \Gamma' \mid \varepsilon}{\Gamma \vdash f := \lambda x.p \dashv f : (\tau \xrightarrow{\varepsilon} \Gamma') \mid \mathfrak{E}}$$

$$\frac{}{u : \mathsf{Unit} \vdash \langle\rangle := u \dashv \varnothing \mid \mathfrak{E}} \qquad \frac{}{f : (\tau \xrightarrow{\varepsilon} \Gamma), x : \tau \dashv f\ x \vdash \Gamma \mid \varepsilon}$$

Figure 7. Crit extended with effectful functions

Unit value, eliminating that unit value, and then finally running the computation. That function is stored into variable t so that thunking results in an output context of the form $t : \mathsf{Unit} \xrightarrow{\varepsilon} \Gamma$. Executing a thunked computation, then, simply involves storing the unique value of Unit into a variable and then calling the thunk with that variable as the argument, thus causing the body of the function to finally execute.

These definitions clearly satisfy the requirements of Figure 6. Thus, our fundamental theorem implies that the semantics of extended Crit can be formalized with a productor defined on just the extended Crit computations with the basic effect $\mathfrak{E}$. Furthermore, the theorem shows how to construct this productor.

Closed Freyd Categories Now we would like to revisit existing frameworks to see what insights the assumptions in Figure 6 can offer. As we discussed, while Freyd categories offer a lot of useful structure for working with contexts, they provide little structure regarding sequential composition. However, Power and Thielecke recognized that strong monads arise for *closed* Freyd categories [27]. This is no surprise given our theorem, since the structures that makes a Freyd category closed are essentially the assumptions in Figure 6. Similarly, Atkey defined a notion of *parameterized* Freyd categories [2], and observed that closed parameterized Freyd categories gave rise to parameterized monads. Again, the additional structure for a closed parameterized Freyd category corresponds to the assumptions in Figure 6, so this result is no surprise given our theorem.

9. Conclusion

We have presented productors, a semantic framework for sequential composition of computations with producer effects, a concept we were able to formalize abstractly. In particular, we showed why the widespread notion of thunking makes producer effects so common. In our discussions of existing frameworks, we argued why it is important to restrict our attention to producer effects. We illustrated how monadic frameworks fit within productors, and used our framework to illustrate how properties of the effect system at hand give rise to various semantic structures.

In all this discussion, we have elided the higher categorical connections. For example, productors can be viewed as functors from the effector to the 2-category of categories. This higher perspective suggests some ways to adapt the framework to more specialized forms of computation. For example, by changing the target 2-category to that of premonoidal categories (i.e. categories with a notion of propagating context), one arrives at productors that can propagate context, such as a strong monad. Or, by using the 2-category of categories and *partial* functors, one can drop the implicit assumption of Theorem 5 that $(\!|\Gamma|\!)_\varepsilon$ is defined for all contexts Γ even if there is no ε-effectful computation with Γ as its output. In another direction, while we chose to present effectors along the line of lax List-monad algebras in **Rel**, they can equivalently be described as thin multicategories [15]. It would be interesting to investigate how the concepts for multicategories translate to effectors and productors. For example, a representable thin multicategory is equivalently a total principalled effectoid (equivalent to a congruently preordered monoid).

Our preliminary investigations into the dual concept of consumer effects and consumptors have been very intriguing. The traditional notion of context seems to be well described as a consumptor. Strength appears to be formalizable as an interplay of this consumer effect with the producer effects. Similarly, non-linear uses of inputs also seem best described as a consumptor. After all, an intuitionistic implication $P \Rightarrow Q$ translates to linear implication $!P \multimap Q$ with a modification on the *input* rather than the output. The ! modality is a comonad, which is a special class of consumptors just like monads are a special class of productor. Furthermore, it seems that strictness and laziness arise as two dual ways to make such a consumptor interact with producer effects.

Finally, while we have discussed what the semantic framework for producer effects should look like, we have not investigated how to actually build productors. With monads, there have been a variety of techniques for composing monads [11] (though interestingly many of these, such as distributive laws [14], arise as special cases of our framework), building monads from monad transformers [16], or combining algebraic monads [24] with tensors and sums [9]. We would like to see how these concepts extend to productors. For example, the coproduct of two monads is relatively simple to define [18], but at first thought it is not clear whether the coproduct of two effectors and respective productors would be simpler or more complex. Also, transformers such as for exceptions rely heavily on the presence of a $unit$ operation, so one wonders if they are restricted to just centric effectors. By reexamining these techniques in this new light, we expect to acquire a better understanding of their fundamental structure.

With this framework we aim to lay new grounds for the foundations of programming languages. Of course, there are still many more forms of composition to formalize the semantics of, but we have already begun transferring the strategy taken here to those settings and found some fruitful results. In the end we expect to have composable frameworks for formalizing the many roles effects have in programming languages. We hope this work will provide a new means to abstractly formalize, expand, and communicate programming languages.

Acknowledgements In addition to our anonymous reviewers, we thank John C. Baez, Thomas Ball, Daniel Brown, Jeffrey S. Foster, Michael Hicks, Ohad Kammar, Daan Leijen, Sorin Lerner, Daniel Marino, Andrew Myers, Patrick Rondon, Michael Shulman, and Zachary Tatlock for their valuable feedback on the research, its context, and our writing.

References

[1] Martín Abadi. Access control in a core calculus of dependency. In *ICFP*, 2006.

[2] Robert Atkey. Parameterised notions of computation. *JFP*, 19:335–376, July 2009.

[3] Nick Benton, John Hughes, and Eugenio Moggi. Monads and effects. In *International Summer School on Applied Semantics*, 2000.

[4] Olivier Danvy and Andrzej Filinski. A functional abstraction of typed contexts. Technical report, University of Copenhagen, 1989.

[5] Andrzej Filinski. Representing layered monads. In *POPL*, 1999.

[6] Andrzej Filinski. Monads in action. In *POPL*, 2010.

[7] Roger Godement. *Topologie Algébrique et Théorie des Faisceaux*. Hermann, 1958.

[8] John Hughes. Generalising monads to arrows. *Science of Computer Programming*, 37(1-3):67–111, May 2000.

[9] Martin Hyland, Gordon Plotkin, and John Power. Combining effects: Sum and tensor. *Theoretical Computer Science*, 357(1):70–99, 2006.

[10] Bart Jacobs, Chris Heunen, and Ichiro Hasuo. Categorical semantics for arrows. *JFP*, 19:403–438, 2009.

[11] Mark P. Jones and Luc Duponcheel. Composing monads. Technical report, Yale University, New Haven, CT, USA, December 1993.

[12] Simon Peyton Jones and Philip Wadler. Imperative functional programming. In *POPL*, 1993.

[13] Richard B. Kieburtz. Taming effects with monadic typing. In *ICFP*, 1998.

[14] David J. King and Philip Wadler. Combining monads. In *ETAPS*, 1992.

[15] Tom Leinster. *Higher Operads, Higher Categories*. Cambridge University Press, 2004.

[16] Sheng Liang, Paul Hudak, and Mark Jones. Monad transformers and modular interpreters. In *POPL*, 1995.

[17] John M. Lucassen and David K. Gifford. Polymorphic effect systems. In *POPL*, 1988.

[18] Christoph Lüth and Neil Ghani. Composing monads using coproducts. *ACM SIGPLAN Notices*, 37(9):133–144, 2002.

[19] Daniel Marino and Todd Millstein. A generic type-and-effect system. In *TLDI*, 2009.

[20] Eugenio Moggi. Computational lambda-calculus and monads. In *LICS*, 1989.

[21] Iulian Neamtiu, Michael Hicks, Jeffrey S. Foster, and Polyvios Pratikakis. Contextual effects for version-consistent dynamic software updating and safe concurrent programming. In *POPL*, 2008.

[22] Flemming Nielson and Hanne Riis Nielson. Type and effect systems. In *ACM Computing Surveys*, 1999.

[23] Hanne Riis Nielson, Flemming Nielson, and Torben Amtoft. Polymorphic subtyping for effect analysis: The static semantics. In *LOMAPS*, 1997.

[24] Gordon Plotkin and John Power. Notions of computation determine monads. In *FoSSaCS*, 2002.

[25] John Power and Edmund Robinson. Premonoidal categories and notions of computation. *Mathematical Structures in Computer Science*, 7:453–468, October 1997.

[26] John Power and Hayo Thielecke. Environments, continuation semantics and indexed categories. In *TACS*, 1997.

[27] John Power and Hayo Thielecke. Closed Freyd- and κ-categories. In *ICAL*, 1999.

[28] John C. Reynolds. Using category theory to design implicit conversions and generic operators. *LNCS*, 94:211–258, 1980.

[29] Nikhil Swamy, Nataliya Guts, Daan Leijen, and Michael Hicks. Lightweight monadic programming in ML. Technical report, Microsoft Research, 2011.

[30] Jean-Pierre Talpin. *Theoretical and Practical Aspects of Type and Effect Inference*. PhD thesis, École des Mines de Paris and University Paris VI, Paris, France, 1993.

[31] Jean-Pierre Talpin and Pierre Jouvelot. Polymorphic type, region and effect inference. *JFP*, 2:245–271, 1992.

[32] Jean-Pierre Talpin and Pierre Jouvelot. The type and effect discipline. *Information and Computation*, 111(2):245–296, 1994.

[33] Ross Tate. The sequential semantics of producer effect systems. Technical report, Cornell University, 2012.

[34] Andrew P. Tolmach. Optimizing ML using a hierarchy of monadic types. In *Types in Compilation*, 1998.

[35] Philip Wadler. Comprehending monads. In *LISP and Functional Programming*, 1990.

[36] Philip Wadler. The essence of functional programming. In *POPL*, 1992.

[37] Philip Wadler. Monads and composable continuations. *LISP and Symbolic Computation*, 7:39–56, January 1994.

[38] Philip Wadler and Peter Thiemann. The marriage of effects and monads. *Transactions on Computational Logic*, 4(1):1–32, 2003.

[39] Andrew K. Wright. Simple imperative polymorphism. *LISP and Symbolic Computation*, 8(4):343–355, 1995.

Copatterns

Programming Infinite Structures by Observations

Andreas Abel

Department of Computer Science,
Ludwig-Maximilians-University Munich,
Germany
andreas.abel@ifi.lmu.de

Brigitte Pientka
David Thibodeau *

School of Computer Science,
McGill University, Montreal, Canada
bpientka@cs.mcgill.ca

Anton Setzer †

Computer Science,
Swansea University, Wales, UK
a.g.setzer@swan.ac.uk

Abstract

Inductive datatypes provide mechanisms to define finite data such as finite lists and trees via constructors and allow programmers to analyze and manipulate finite data via pattern matching. In this paper, we develop a dual approach for working with infinite data structures such as streams. Infinite data inhabits coinductive datatypes which denote greatest fixpoints. Unlike finite data which is defined by constructors we define infinite data by observations. Dual to pattern matching, a tool for analyzing finite data, we develop the concept of copattern matching, which allows us to synthesize infinite data. This leads to a symmetric language design where pattern matching on finite and infinite data can be mixed.

We present a core language for programming with infinite structures by observations together with its operational semantics based on (co)pattern matching and describe coverage of copatterns. Our language naturally supports both call-by-name and call-by-value interpretations and can be seamlessly integrated into existing languages like Haskell and ML. We prove type soundness for our language and sketch how copatterns open new directions for solving problems in the interaction of coinductive and dependent types.

Categories and Subject Descriptors D.3.3 [*Programming Languages*]: Language Constructs and Features—Data types and structures, Patterns, Recursion; F.3.3 [*Logics and Meanings of Programs*]: Studies of Program Constructs—Program and recursion schemes, Type structure

General Terms Languages, Theory

Keywords Coinduction, Functional programming, Introduction vs. elimination, Message passing, Pattern matching

* David Thibodeau acknowledges financial support by the Graduiertenkolleg *Programm und Modellanalyse* (PUMA, 2008–) of the *Deutsche Forschungsgemeinschaft* (DFG) and by the *Undergraduate Student Research Award* (USRA) of the *Natural Sciences and Engineering Research Council of Canada* (NSERC).

† Anton Setzer has been supported by EPSRC grant EP/G033374/1, Theory and applications of induction-recursion. Part of the work was done while the author was a visiting fellow of the Newton Institute, Cambridge.

POPL'13, January 23–25, 2013, Rome, Italy.

1. Introduction

Representing and reasoning about infinite computation plays a crucial role in our quest for designing and implementing safe software systems, since we often want to establish behavioral properties about our programs, reason about I/O interaction and processes, and establish liveness properties that eventually something good will happen. While finite structures such as natural numbers or finite lists are modelled by inductive types, infinite structures such as streams or processes are elegantly characterized by coinductive types. Inductive types are now very well understood and supported by functional languages and proof assistants, whereas the theoretical foundations and practical tools for coinductive types lag behind.

For example, in the Calculus of (Co)Inductive Constructions, the core theory underlying Coq [INRIA 2010], coinduction is broken, since computation does not preserve types [Giménez 1996; Oury 2008]. In Agda [2012], a dependently typed proof and programming environment based on Martin Löf type theory, inductive and coinductive types cannot be mixed in a compositional way. For instance, one can encode the property "infinitely often" from temporal logic, but not its dual "eventually forever" [Altenkirch and Danielsson 2010].

Over the past decade there has been growing consensus [Setzer 2012; McBride 2009; Granström 2009] that one should distinguish between finite, inductive data defined by constructors and infinite, coinductive data which is better described by *observations*. This view was pioneered by Hagino [1987] who modeled finite objects via initial algebras and infinite objects via final coalgebras in category theory. His development culminated in the design of symML, a version of ML where one can declare *codatatypes* via a list of their destructors [Hagino 1989]. For example, the codatatype of streams is defined via the destructors `head` and `tail` which describe the observations we can make about streams. Cockett and Fukushima [1992] took up his work and designed a language *Charity* where one programs directly with the morphisms of category theory. But while Charity was later extended with pattern matching on (initial) data types [Tuckey 1997], no corresponding dual concept was developed for codatatypes (called final data types in Charity).

In this paper, we take a first step towards building a type-theoretic foundation for programming with infinite structures via observations. Dual to pattern matching for analyzing finite data, we introduce *copattern* matching for manipulating infinite data and describe coverage for copatterns. In order to focus on the main concepts and avoid the additional complexities that come with dependent types, for instance, the need to guarantee termination or productivity, we confine ourselves to simple types in this article.

Our theoretical treatment of patterns and copatterns takes inspiration from the growing body of work which relates classical and linear logic to programming language theory via the Curry-Howard-Isomorphism; more precisely, we build on the duality between (finite) values as right-hand side proof terms and continuations or evaluation contexts as left-hand side terms of sequent calculus [Curien and Herbelin 2000; Wadler 2005; Kimura and Tatsuta 2009]. Following Zeilberger's [2008b] deep analysis of focused proofs in linear sequent calculus [Andreoli 1992] and its relationship to pattern matching and evaluation order in programming languages, we distinguish between positive types which characterize finite data and negative types which describe infinite data. While values are matched against patterns, evaluation contexts are matched against copatterns. Our notion of copatterns extends previous work by Licata, Zeilberger, and Harper [2008] to treat least fixed-points as positive types and greatest fixed-point as negative types, and we recognize copatterns as a *definition scheme* for infinite objects.

More precisely, we regard copatterns as *experiments* on black-box infinite objects such as functions, streams and processes. Infinite objects can be defined by a finite, covering set of observations, which are pairs of experiment (copattern) together with its outcome (defining term). We take the distinction between the finite / initial / positive and the infinite / final / negative serious and give introduction rules and patterns for the former and elimination rules and copatterns for the latter. This leads to a core functional language based on natural deduction instead of the sequent calculus formulation explored in by Zeilberger [2008b] et al. [Licata et al. 2008].

Our contributions are the following:

1. We show how copatterns complement the syntax of existing functional languages and enable a style of programming with infinite objects by observations (Section 2.2). There is no need to move to a different programming paradigm such as classical logic [Curien and Herbelin 2000; Wadler 2003] or the morphisms of category theory (Charity).
2. We describe a non-deterministic algorithm for checking copattern coverage and prove that *well-typed* and complete *programs do not go wrong* (Section 5). The construction of a covering set of copatterns corresponds to the interactive construction of a program as in Agda and Epigram (Section 2.1).
3. We explain how copatterns can be a fruitful paradigm in rewriting and dependent type theory. In *rewriting*, definition by observations lead naturally to *strongly* normalizing rewrite rules and a semantics without infinitary rewriting [Kennaway and de Vries 2003] (Section 2.3). In dependent type theory, they overcome the subject reduction problem of the Calculus of (Co)inductive Constructions [Giménez 1996] (Section 2.4).

The remainder of this article is structured as follows: We informally describe copatterns in Section 2 and explain in detail their benefits in programming, rewriting and type theory. In Section 3, we define formally our core language with copatterns and its static semantics. We then describe its operational semantics together with copattern matching in Section 4. Coverage of copatterns together with the type safety proof is presented in Section 5. We briefly describe a prototype implementation of copatterns for Agda in Section 6, before we conclude with a discussion of related work (Section 7) and an outlook to further work (Section 8).

2. Copatterns and Their Applications

In this section we explain copatterns (Section 2.1) and flesh out the arguments started in the introduction. We illustrate how copatterns impact functional programming (Section 2.2), rewriting (Section 2.3), and dependent type theory (Section 2.4).

2.1 From function definition to copatterns

We introduce copatterns in the scenario of interactive program construction by refining the left hand side of a function definition step by step. As we will see, copatterns arise naturally as the generalization of definition by pattern matching.

As an example, we construct the infinite stream $N, N-1, \ldots, 1, 0, N, N-1, \ldots, 1, 0, \ldots$ of natural numbers via an auxiliary function $\mathsf{cycleNats} : \mathsf{Nat} \to \mathsf{Stream\ Nat}$ such that $\mathsf{cycleNats}\ n = n, n-1, \ldots, 1, 0, N, N-1, \ldots, 1, 0, \ldots$.

Before we begin, let us define Stream Nat as a recursive record type containing the possible observations we can make about streams. These observations are also referred to as destructors, since they allow us to take apart streams.

$$\begin{array}{l}\mathsf{record\ Stream}\ A = \{\ \mathsf{head} : A, \\ \qquad\qquad\qquad\qquad\ \ \mathsf{tail}\ \ : \mathsf{Stream}\ A\ \}\end{array}$$

Now we will construct cycleNats step-by-step, similar to the interactive editing in Agda [Norell 2007] and Epigram [McBride and McKinna 2004]. The starting point is the template:

$$\begin{array}{lcl}\mathsf{cycleNats} & : & \mathsf{Nat} \to \mathsf{Stream\ Nat} \\ \mathsf{cycleNats} & = & ?\end{array}$$

Since a function is an infinite object, we define it by *observation* rather than giving its value (a λ-abstraction) directly. However, we cannot give a value of $\mathsf{cycleNats}\ n$ for every natural number n, instead, we apply cycleNats to a *generic* natural number, the pattern variable x.

$$\mathsf{cycleNats}\ x \quad = \quad ?$$

Application to x, which we write as $\cdot\ x$, is our first instance of a copattern, an *applicative copattern*. It is, in this case, a generic *experiment* on cycleNats. The observation of its outcome determines cycleNats.

We are left with the task of constructing a Stream of natural numbers. We can make two principal experiments on a stream: we can observe its head and its tail, and the outcome of these two experiments determines the stream. These experiments give us two new copatterns: $\mathsf{head}\ \cdot$ and $\mathsf{tail}\ \cdot$, called *destructor copatterns*, and lead to the next refinement of our definition of cycleNats:

$$\begin{array}{lcl}\mathsf{head}\ (\mathsf{cycleNats}\ x) & = & ? \\ \mathsf{tail}\ \ (\mathsf{cycleNats}\ x) & = & ?\end{array}$$

The observed head of $\mathsf{cycleNats}\ x$ is just x. To determine the tail, we need to split on the pattern variable x:

$$\begin{array}{lcl}\mathsf{head}\ (\mathsf{cycleNats}\ x) & = & x \\ \mathsf{tail}\ \ (\mathsf{cycleNats}\ 0) & = & ? \\ \mathsf{tail}\ \ (\mathsf{cycleNats}\ (1+x')) & = & ?\end{array}$$

This generalizes the applicative copattern form $\cdot\ x$ to $\cdot\ p$ where p is a *pattern*, as usual, a term built from constructors, literals, and uniquely occurring variables only. We finally can fill the remaining two holes and complete our definition of cycleNats:

$$\begin{array}{lcl}\mathsf{head}\ (\mathsf{cycleNats}\ x) & = & x \\ \mathsf{tail}\ \ (\mathsf{cycleNats}\ 0) & = & \mathsf{cycleNats}\ N \\ \mathsf{tail}\ \ (\mathsf{cycleNats}\ (1+x')) & = & \mathsf{cycleNats}\ x'\end{array}$$

The infinite object cycleNats, a function yielding streams, is defined via the complete set of copatterns $\{\mathsf{head}\ (\cdot\ x), \mathsf{tail}\ (\cdot\ 0), \mathsf{tail}\ (\cdot\ (1+x'))\}$ where $\cdot$, the hole, is a placeholder for the function cycleNats. It is determined by the following set of observations, i. e., experiments mapped to their results:

$$\begin{array}{ll}\mathsf{head}\ (\cdot\ x) & \mapsto x \\ \mathsf{tail}\ \ (\cdot\ 0) & \mapsto \mathsf{cycleNats}\ N \\ \mathsf{tail}\ \ (\cdot\ (1+x')) & \mapsto \mathsf{cycleNats}\ x'\end{array}$$

2.2 Copatterns in functional programming: Restoring a missing symmetry

Destructor copatterns are a useful addition to functional languages even if no coinduction is involved. In the following we evolve an implementation of the state monad typical for Haskell to demonstrate why the absence of general copatterns breaks symmetry, and how copatterns restore it.

A first implementation defines the type State $S\ A$ of a stateful computation with result A just as a synonym for $S \to (A \times S)$. The monadic operations return and $\gg=$ ("bind") are given in an applicative style.

$$\begin{array}{lcl} \mathsf{State}\ S\ A & = & S \to A \times S \\ \mathsf{return} & : & A \to \mathsf{State}\ S\ A \\ \mathsf{return}\ a\ s & = & (a,\ s) \\ \_\gg=\_ & : & \mathsf{State}\ S\ A \to (A \to \mathsf{State}\ S\ B) \to \mathsf{State}\ S\ B \\ (m \gg= k)\ s & = & \mathsf{let}\ (a,\ s') = m\ s\ \mathsf{in}\ k\ a\ s' \end{array}$$

Returning a in state s yields the pair (a, s) of result and unchanged state, and executing the sequence $m \gg= k$ in state s first executes m : State $S\ A$ in state s, resulting in a value $a : A$ and a new state s', in which we run the continuation k applied to a. The code explains itself nicely if the application to s is read as *in state s*.

There are reasons to move away from type synonym State $S\ A$ to a bijection between the monadic type State $S\ A$ and its implementation as $S \to A \times S$. For instance, in Haskell, type synonyms interact badly with type-class based overloading, and instead, State $S\ A$ is implemented as a single-field record type with projection runState and constructor state.

$$\begin{array}{lcl} \mathsf{record\ State}\ S\ A & = & \mathsf{state}\{\mathsf{runState} : S \to A \times S\} \\ \mathsf{runState} & : & \mathsf{State}\ S\ A \to S \to A \times S \\ \mathsf{state} & : & (S \to A \times S) \to \mathsf{State}\ S\ A \end{array}$$

As we update our implementation of the monad operations, we are in for an unpleasant surprise: We can only partially keep up the applicative style, more precisely, only on the right hand side of =, the expression side. Here, we only have to prefix the monadic values m and $k\ a$ with the projection runState. But on the left hand side, the pattern side, we cannot do the same change, since projections are not allowed there. Instead we have to turn the l.h.s. application to s to a r.h.s. λ-abstraction over s, and prefix it with constructor state.

$$\begin{array}{lcl} \mathsf{return} & : & A \to \mathsf{State}\ S\ A \\ \mathsf{return}\ a & = & \mathsf{state}\ (\lambda s.\ (a,\ s)) \\ \_\gg=\_ & : & \mathsf{State}\ S\ A \to (A \to \mathsf{State}\ S\ B) \to \mathsf{State}\ S\ B \\ m \gg= k & = & \mathsf{state}\ (\lambda s.\ \mathsf{let}\ (a,\ s') = \mathsf{runState}\ m\ s \\ & & \qquad \mathsf{in\ runState}\ (k\ a)\ s') \end{array}$$

The projection bits are still nice to read, e. g., runState $m\ s$ reads as *run m in state s*, however, the definition of $m \gg= k$ as *the stateful computation, that if you pass it state s, ...* is a bit bumpy. The symmetry is broken.

Copatterns, which allow projections also on the l.h.s., restore the symmetry and allow a smooth definition of the monad operations again.

$$\begin{array}{lcl} \mathsf{return} & : & A \to \mathsf{State}\ S\ A \\ \mathsf{runState}\ (\mathsf{return}\ a)\ s & = & (a,\ s) \\ \_\gg=\_ & : & \mathsf{State}\ S\ A \\ & \to & (A \to \mathsf{State}\ S\ B) \\ & \to & \mathsf{State}\ S\ B \\ \mathsf{runState}\ (m \gg= k)\ s & = & \mathsf{let}\ (a,\ s') = \mathsf{runState}\ m\ s \\ & & \mathsf{in\ runState}\ (k\ a)\ s') \end{array}$$

It reads *if you run* return a *in state s, you get* (a, s); and *to run* $m \gg= k$ *in state s, run m in s, obtaining a value a and a new state s' in which you run k a.*

2.3 Deep copatterns in rewriting: Strong normalization for corecursive definitions

In the following we argue that copatterns help to integrate infinite objects into term rewriting, without having to change the standard reduction semantics.

A popular example of programming with infinite objects is the creation of the stream of Fibonacci numbers. It is concisely defined as

$$\mathsf{fib} = \mathsf{cons}\ 0\ (\mathsf{cons}\ 1\ (\mathsf{zipWith}\ \_+\_\ \mathsf{fib}\ (\mathsf{tail\ fib})))$$

Herein, cons is the stream constructor, head and tail the projection, and zipWith _+_ yields a stream by applying addition pointwise to a pair of streams (here: fib and tail fib).

Clearly, reading this equation as a rewrite rule, the computation of fib does not terminate under the standard semantics, which is *rewrite when the left hand side matches*. Using infinitary rewriting [Kennaway and de Vries 2003], fib converges to the Fibonacci stream

$$\mathsf{cons}\ 0\ (\mathsf{cons}\ 1\ (\mathsf{cons}\ 1\ (\mathsf{cons}\ 2\ (\mathsf{cons}\ 3\ (\mathsf{cons}\ 5\ \ldots$$

However, we are interested in the *strong normalization* of a term rewriting system since this yields a decision procedure for equality (which then implies decidability for checking dependent types).

We can revert to a non-standard rewriting semantics: label the definition of fib as *corecursive* and only unfold it when its value is demanded, e. g., by a projection. This solution, for instance taken in Coq [Giménez 1996], does not help with our particular definition of fib either, since tail fib appears in its own unfolding, leading to infinite reduction. A workaround exists: we could introduce a mutually defined auxiliary stream fib′ which denotes the tail of fib.

But copatterns provide a principled and scalable solution. Mechanically, transforming the definition of fib into copatterns yields

$$\begin{array}{rcl} \mathsf{head\ fib} & = & 0 \\ \mathsf{head\ (tail\ fib)} & = & 1 \\ \mathsf{tail\ (tail\ fib)} & = & \mathsf{zipWith}\ \_+\_\ \mathsf{fib\ (tail\ fib)}. \end{array}$$

These equations are actually fulfilled by our first equation for fib, but now we take them as *definition* of fib. The rewrite system is terminating; neither fib nor tail fib can be reduced by itself because none of the three defining copatterns matches.

Our syntax allows us to delay unfolding of corecursion until the *whole copattern* is matched. Copatterns, in particular, deep copatterns such as nested projections tail (tail ·) give us greater flexibility for corecursive definitions than non-standard semantics.

2.4 Copatterns in dependent type theory: Reclaiming subject reduction

Following the lead of the functional programming language Haskell, the dependently typed language Coq introduces both finite and infinite trees via constructors. However, this leads to fundamental problems. For example, the Calculus of (Co)Inductive Constructions, the core theory underlying Coq [INRIA 2010], lacks subject reduction. This issue is already described in Section 3.4 of Giménez' thesis [1996]. Oury [2008] brought it back to the attention of the community. A detailed analysis has been given by McBride [2009].

Let us recapitulate Oury's counterexample to subject reduction, as reproduced in Fig. 1: Given a coinductive type U with constructor in that takes just an argument of type U, the (extensionally) sole inhabitant u of U can be constructed as the fixed point of in. The definitions force and eq seem "pointless" [Chlipala 2012, p. 91]

U		a codata type
in	$: \mathsf{U} \to \mathsf{U}$	its only (co)constructor
u	$: \mathsf{U}$	an inhabitant of U
u	$= \mathsf{cofix\ in}$	infinite succession of ins
force	$: \mathsf{U} \to \mathsf{U}$	extensionally, an identity
force	$= \lambda x.\,\mathsf{case}\, x\, \mathsf{of}$ $\mathsf{in}\ y \Rightarrow \mathsf{in}\ y$	
eq	$: (x : \mathsf{U}) \to x \equiv \mathsf{force}\ x$	
eq	$= \lambda x.\,\mathsf{case}\, x\, \mathsf{of}$ $\mathsf{in}\ y \Rightarrow \mathsf{refl}$	
$\mathsf{eq_u}$	$: \mathsf{u} \equiv \mathsf{in\ u}$	
$\mathsf{eq_u}$	$= \mathsf{eq\ u}$	

Figure 1. Oury's counterexample.

but are in fact a major tool in Coq proofs about corecursive definitions such as u since they wrap a case-distinction around a cofix that triggers reduction: While unrestricted reduction of cofix f to f (cofix f) would diverge immediately, the following two rewrite equations for matching coinductive data maintain strong normalization:

$$\begin{array}{lll} \mathsf{case}\,(\mathsf{in}\ s) \quad \mathsf{of\ in}\ y \Rightarrow t & = & t[s/y] \\ \mathsf{case}\,(\mathsf{cofix}\ f)\ \mathsf{of\ in}\ y \Rightarrow t & = & \mathsf{case}\,(f\ (\mathsf{cofix}\ f))\ \mathsf{of\ in}\ y \Rightarrow t \end{array}$$

Now, the closed term eq u simplifies via

$$\begin{array}{lll} \mathsf{eq\ u} & = & \mathsf{case\ u\ of\ in}\ y \Rightarrow \mathsf{refl} \\ & = & \mathsf{case\,(cofix\ in)\ of\ in}\ y \Rightarrow \mathsf{refl} \\ & = & \mathsf{case\,(in\ (cofix\ in))\ of\ in}\ y \Rightarrow \mathsf{refl} \\ & = & \mathsf{refl} \end{array}$$

to the single constructor refl of propositional equality _≡_, which means that u and in u must be definitionally equal. Yet they are not, since u does not reduce to in u unless under a case distinction. Subject reduction is lost! As Giménez notes, subject reduction holds only modulo an undecidable equality on types that allows unrestricted fixed-point unfolding, but this is not what can be implemented in proof assistants for Intensional Type Theory with decidable type checking.

The culprit is that the rule for dependent matching is also available for coinductive data, i. e., in case of U we have the rule

$$\frac{\Gamma \vdash u : \mathsf{U} \qquad \Gamma,\, y : \mathsf{U} \vdash t : C(\mathsf{in}\ y)}{\Gamma \vdash \mathsf{case}\ u\ \mathsf{of\ in}\ y \Rightarrow t : C(u)}$$

The rule substitutes a constructed term in y for term u in type C, which may trigger reduction of case expressions in C that are not possible without the substitution. For instance, force (in y) reduces to in y, while force x does not reduce to x. This is exploited in the typing[1] of eq, which leads to the loss of subject reduction in the end.

The deeper reason for this dilemma is that coinduction is just understood as constructing infinite trees; coinductive structures are just non-well-founded data structures in Coq. However, even in dependent type theory, infinite objects are better understood through their elimination rules [Granström 2009; Setzer 2012], i. e., observations. Looking at Oury's example, it seems wrong to regard in as a *constructor*. Rather, it should be *defined* in terms of the only observation out : U → U (same for the infinite structure u : U):

$$\begin{array}{lllcllll} \mathsf{in} & : & \mathsf{U} \to \mathsf{U} & \qquad & \mathsf{u} & : & \mathsf{U} \\ \mathsf{out\ (in}\ y) & = & y & & \mathsf{out\ u} & = & \mathsf{u} \end{array}$$

The equations we have written are now exactly the reduction rules, no restricted unfolding of cofix has to be taken into consideration. This makes definitional equality and, thus, type checking more perspicuous, for the user it is a what-you-see-is-what-you-get equational theory. Dependent pattern matching on coinductive types U is no longer available and subject reduction is restored. The "pointless" tricks like force and eq, necessary to deal with edges of dependent pattern matching, are also obsolete.

While we do not develop a dependently typed language with copatterns in this article, we have illustrated the shortcomings of uniformly modeling finite and infinite data via constructors and highlighted the potential of copatterns in the dependently typed setting.

3. A Core Functional Language with Copatterns

In this section, we introduce a core language with recursive data types for modeling finite data and recursive record types[2] for modeling infinite data. The term language is redex-free, which allows for a *complete* bidirectional type checking algorithm.

We then proceed to define patterns and copatterns which allow us to define functions, records and programs—which can be type-checked by an extension of the algorithm. Function definitions will be modeled as sets of rewrite rules.

3.1 Types

We distinguish between *positive* types, 1, $A \times B$, and $\mu X D$, and *negative* types, $A \to B$ and $\nu X R$. This polarity assignment is inspired by focusing proofs in intuitionistic linear logic [Andreoli 1992; Benton et al. 1993]. Our types 1, ×, and μ correspond to the positive connectives 1, ⊗, and a combination of ⊕ and least fixed point, resp., and they classify finite data. The types → and ν correspond to the negative ⊸ and a combination of & and greatest fixed point, resp., and classify infinite data. Linearity will show up in the typing rules for patterns and copatterns, even though ordinary terms need not be linear.

In terms of categorical languages [Hagino 1987; Cockett and Fukushima 1992], positive types are *left objects* or *initial datatypes*, and negative types are *right objects* or *final datatypes*.

A, B, C	$::= X$	Type variable
	$\mid P$	Positive type
	$\mid N$	Negative type
P	$::= 1$	Unit type
	$\mid A \times B$	Cartesian product
	$\mid \mu X D$	Data type
N	$::= A \to B$	Function type
	$\mid \nu X R$	Record type
D	$::= \langle c_1\ A_1 \mid \cdots \mid c_n\ A_n \rangle$	Variant (labeled sum)
R	$::= \{d_1 : A_1, \ldots, d_n : A_n\}$	Record (labeled product)

Figure 2. Types.

Figure 2 introduces positive types P, negative types N, and types A which can be either positive or negative. Variants D serve

[1] Since refl : in y ≡ force (in y), by dependent pattern matching case x of in $y \Rightarrow$ refl : $x \equiv$ force x, thus, eq x : $x \equiv$ force x.

[2] Our terminology should not be confused with recursive records in object-oriented language foundations, e. g., by Abadi and Cardelli [1994].

to construct possibly recursive data types $\mu X D$, and records R list the fields d_i of a possibly recursive record type $\nu X R$.

In our non-polymorphic calculus, type variables X only serve to construct recursive data types and recursive record types. As usual, $\mu X D$ ($\nu X R$, resp.) binds type variable X in D (R, resp.). Capture-avoiding substitution of type C for variable X in type A is denoted by $A[C/X]$. The set $\mathsf{FTV}(A)$ of free type variables of a type expression A is defined in the standard way. A type is *well-formed* if it has no free type variables; in the following, we assume that all types are well-formed.

Datatypes Datatypes $C = \mu X D$ for $D = \langle c_1\, A_1 \mid \cdots \mid c_n\, A_n \rangle$ are recursive variant types. They could be called *algebraic* types. We write D_{c_i} for A_i. The constructor c_i of C takes an arguments of type $A_i[C/X]$, i. e., $D_{c_i}[C/X]$. Non-recursive data types can be represented by a void μ-abstraction μ_D. Like in SML, a constructor that requires no argument formally takes an argument of the unit type 1. Examples:

$$\begin{array}{lcll} \mathsf{List}\, A & = & \mu X \langle \mathsf{nil}\, 1 \mid \mathsf{cons}\, (A \times X)\rangle & \\ \mathsf{Nat} & = & \mu X \langle \mathsf{zero}\, 1 \mid \mathsf{suc}\, X\rangle & \\ \mathsf{Maybe}\, A & = & \mu\_ \langle \mathsf{nothing}\, 1 \mid \mathsf{just}\, A\rangle & \\ 0 & = & \mu\_ \langle\rangle & \text{(positive empty type)} \end{array}$$

Record types Record types $C = \nu X R$ with $R = \{d_1 : A_1, \ldots, d_n : A_n\}$ are recursive labeled products. They could be called *coalgebraic* types. The destructor d_i, if applied to a record of type C, returns the ith field which has type $A_i[C/X]$, or, with a "R_d" notation, $R_{d_i}[C/X]$. The destructors are applied in postfix notation to a term t as $t.d_i$. As for data, non-recursive record types are encoded by a void ν-abstraction ν_R. Examples:

$$\begin{array}{lcll} \mathsf{Stream}\, A & = & \nu X \{\mathsf{head} : A, \mathsf{tail} : X\} & \\ \mathsf{Colist}\, A & = & \nu X \{\mathsf{out} : \mu\_ \langle \mathsf{nil}\, 1 \mid \mathsf{cons}\, (A \times X)\rangle\} & \\ \mathsf{Vector}\, A & = & \nu\_ \{\mathsf{length} : \mathsf{Nat},\ \mathsf{elems} : \mathsf{List}\, A\} & \\ \top & = & \nu\_ \{\} & \text{(negative unit type)} \end{array}$$

Both D and R can be seen as finite maps from a set of labels (constructors and destructors, resp.) to types, with application written D_c and R_d. We write $c \in D$ and $d \in R$ to express that a label is in the domain of the corresponding finite map.

In this article, both $\mu X D$ and $\nu X R$ are just *recursive types* rather than inductive and coinductive types resp. Since D and R are not checked for functoriality and programs are not checked for termination or productivity, resp., there are no conditions that ensure $\mu X D$ to be a least fixed-point inhabited only by finite data, and $\nu X R$ to be a greatest fixed-point that hosts infinite objects which are productive. However, we keep the notational distinction to allude to the intended interpretation as least and greatest fixed-points in a total setting.

3.2 Terms and typing

Next we describe terms which constitute the targets of our rewrite rules. Terms are given by the following grammar:

$$\begin{array}{rcll} e, t, u & ::= & f & \text{Defined symbol (e.g. function)} \\ & \mid & x & \text{Variable} \\ & \mid & () & \text{Unit (empty tuple)} \\ & \mid & (t_1, t_2) & \text{Pair} \\ & \mid & c\, t & \text{Constructor application} \\ & \mid & t_1\, t_2 & \text{Application} \\ & \mid & t.d & \text{Destructor application} \end{array}$$

Terms can be identifiers (variable x, defined symbol f), *introductions* (tuple $()$, (t_1, t_2), constructed term $c\ t$) of *positive* types (1, $A \times B$, $\mu X D$), or *eliminations* (application $t_1\, t_2$, projection $t.d$) of *negative* types ($A \to B$, $\nu X R$). Constructor applications choose a variant and fold the recursive type; destructor applications unfold the recursive type and select a component of the record. Missing, by intention, are eliminations for positive types like tuple projections and *case*; these are replaced by *pattern matching*. Dually, we omit introductions for negative types, such as λ-abstractions and record values; instead we have *definitions by copattern matching* (see 3.4).

$\boxed{\Delta \vdash t : A}$ In context Δ, term t can be assigned type A.

$$\frac{\Delta(x) = A}{\Delta \vdash x : A}\,\mathrm{T_{Var}} \qquad \frac{}{\Delta \vdash f : \Sigma(f)}\,\mathrm{T_{Fun}} \qquad \frac{}{\Delta \vdash () : 1}\,\mathrm{T_{Unit}}$$

$$\frac{\Delta \vdash t : D_c[\mu X D/X]}{\Delta \vdash c\, t : \mu X D}\,\mathrm{T_{Const}} \qquad \frac{\Delta \vdash t : \nu X R}{\Delta \vdash t.d : R_d[\nu X R/X]}\,\mathrm{T_{Dest}}$$

$$\frac{\Delta \vdash t_1 : A_1 \to A_2 \quad \Delta \vdash t_2 : A_1}{\Delta \vdash t_1\, t_2 : A_2}\,\mathrm{T_{App}}$$

$$\frac{\Delta \vdash t_1 : A_1 \quad \Delta \vdash t_2 : A_2}{\Delta \vdash (t_1, t_2) : A_1 \times A_2}\,\mathrm{T_{Pair}}$$

Figure 3. Typing rules for terms.

Typing *Contexts* Γ and Δ denote finite maps from term variables to well-formed types. To ensure linearity in pattern typing, we write Δ, Δ' for the *disjoint union* of finite maps Δ and Δ', i. e., $\mathsf{dom}(\Delta) \cap \mathsf{dom}(\Delta') = \emptyset$. We write $\cdot$ or simply nothing for a finite map with empty domain, and we usually drop the braces when giving a context explicitly as set of pairs $\{x_1 : A_1, \ldots, x_n : A_n\}$. We assume a global *signature* Σ which maps defined symbols f to their type.

The rules for the typing judgement $\Delta \vdash t : A$ are given in Figure 3. Note that, since we have no binder on the term level —no λ, in particular—, Δ remains fixed in all the rules. Assumptions in Δ describe the type of pattern variables occurring on the left hand side of a rule and are synthesized when analyzing copatterns. For each term constructor there is exactly one typing rule, so we trivially obtain the usual inversion lemmata.

In the following, whenever we have a judgement J (e.g. a typing judgement), we write $\boxed{\mathcal{D} :: J}$ to indicate that $\mathcal{D}$ is a derivation of J using the rules for J. Usually our proof proceeds by induction on a derivation of our judgement and we write in this case "by induction on $\mathcal{D}$". Some of our judgements are algorithmic, i. e., partial functional relations. Unless stated otherwise, all arguments to these relations are inputs.

Bidirectional Type Checking Our language naturally supports overloading of constructors and destructors, when employing a bidirectional type checking algorithm [Pierce and Turner 1998]. Supporting overloading is convenient in practice and leads to elegant, compact and readable code. With bidirectional checking, overloading comes for free since a constructor c gets its meaning in the context of a data type—to type check a constructed term $c\ t$ we push its type $\mu X D$ in. Dually, a destructor d only has a meaning in the context of a record type $\nu X R$, which is inferred from head t in the projection term $t.d$. Overloading projections is standard in object-oriented programming (here, projections correspond to method calls), and has contributed to the success of the OO paradigm. Constructor overloading is also emerging, e. g., in the dependently typed languages Agda [Norell 2007] and Epigram [McBride and McKinna 2004].

Given a typing context Δ, we infer the type A of identifiers and eliminations (judgement $\Delta \vdash t \Rightarrow A$), while we check introductions against a given type A (judgement $\Delta \vdash t \Leftarrow A$). The

$\boxed{\Delta \vdash t \Rightarrow A}$ In context Δ, the type of term t is inferred as A.

$$\frac{}{\Delta \vdash f \Rightarrow \Sigma(f)}\ \mathrm{TC_{Fun}} \qquad \frac{\Delta(x) = A}{\Delta \vdash x \Rightarrow A}\ \mathrm{TC_{Var}}$$

$$\frac{\Delta \vdash t_1 \Rightarrow A_1 \to A_2 \quad \Delta \vdash t_2 \Leftarrow A_1}{\Delta \vdash t_1\ t_2 \Rightarrow A_2}\ \mathrm{TC_{App}}$$

$$\frac{\Delta \vdash t \Rightarrow \nu X R}{\Delta \vdash t.d \Rightarrow R_d[\nu X R/X]}\ \mathrm{TC_{Dest}}$$

$\boxed{\Delta \vdash t \Leftarrow A}$ In context Δ, term t checks against type A.

$$\frac{\Delta \vdash t \Rightarrow A \quad A = C}{\Delta \vdash t \Leftarrow C}\ \mathrm{TC_{Switch}} \qquad \frac{\Delta \vdash t \Leftarrow D_c[\mu X D/X]}{\Delta \vdash c\, t \Leftarrow \mu X D}\ \mathrm{TC_{Constr}}$$

$$\frac{}{\Delta \vdash () \Leftarrow 1}\ \mathrm{TC_{Unit}} \qquad \frac{\Delta \vdash t_1 \Leftarrow A_1 \quad \Delta \vdash t_2 \Leftarrow A_2}{\Delta \vdash (t_1, t_2) \Leftarrow A_1 \times A_2}\ \mathrm{TC_{Pair}}$$

Figure 4. Type-checking rules for terms.

rules are given in Figure 4. Type checking is trivially sound, but it is also complete without the need for any additional type annotations.

THEOREM 1 (Soundness of type checking).

1. If $\mathcal{D} :: \Delta \vdash t \Rightarrow A$ then $\Delta \vdash t : A$.
2. If $\mathcal{D} :: \Delta \vdash t \Leftarrow A$ then $\Delta \vdash t : A$.

Proof. Simultaneously by induction on the derivation $\mathcal{D}$. □

For simply-typed lambda-calculus, bidirectional type checking is not complete and typically requires type annotations. It fails for redexes $(\lambda x t)\ u$, since the type of a λ is not inferred. In our case, since for a type we have either introduction or elimination, we lack the usual redexes, thus, bidirectional type checking is actually complete.

THEOREM 2 (Completeness of type checking). *If $\mathcal{D} :: \Delta \vdash t : A$ then $\Delta \vdash t \Leftarrow A$, and if A is a negative type, then $\Delta \vdash t \Rightarrow A$.*

Proof. By induction on $\mathcal{D}$. Note that a proof of $\Delta \vdash t \Rightarrow A$ is sufficient, since this trivially implies $\Delta \vdash t \Leftarrow A$ by $\mathrm{TC_{Switch}}$. □

3.3 Patterns and copatterns

The driving force behind computation in our language is pattern and copattern matching. Pattern matching allows us to compensate for the missing eliminations for positive types, while copattern matching compensates for the missing introductions for negative types. In the following, we present (co)patterns and their typing.

Patterns

p	::=	x	Variable pattern
	|	$()$	Unit pattern
	|	(p_1, p_2)	Pair pattern
	|	$c\, p$	Constructor pattern

Copatterns

q	::=	$\cdot$	Hole
	|	$q\, p$	Application copattern
	|	$q.d$	Destructor copattern

The postfix application of a projection d in $q.d$ corresponds to the prefix application $d\ q$ we used in the introduction, to conform with Haskell and Agda syntax. Note that, in contrast to convention in the ML dialects, projection does *not* bind stronger than application, i. e., $f\ x\ .d$ is to be read $(f\ x).d$. Our style saves parentheses when writing nested copatterns.

Pattern typing is defined in Figure 5. It computes a context Δ containing all the variables in the pattern. A (co)pattern p (or q) must be linear, that is, each variable in Δ appears exactly once in p (or q, resp.). Again, there are two modes for pattern typing. The checking mode, denoted by $\Delta \vdash p \Leftarrow A$, works on patterns p and follows the checking mode for regular typing. The inference mode, denoted by $\Delta \mid A \vdash q \Rightarrow C$ works on copatterns q and additionally computes its type C from the given type A of the hole.

$\boxed{\Delta \vdash p \Leftarrow A}$ Pattern p checks against type A, yielding Δ.

$$\frac{}{x : A \vdash x \Leftarrow A}\ \mathrm{PC_{Var}} \qquad \frac{\Delta \vdash p \Leftarrow D_c[\mu X D/X]}{\Delta \vdash c\, p \Leftarrow \mu X D}\ \mathrm{PC_{Const}}$$

$$\frac{}{\vdash () \Leftarrow 1}\ \mathrm{PC_{Unit}} \qquad \frac{\Delta_1 \vdash p_1 \Leftarrow A_1 \quad \Delta_2 \vdash p_2 \Leftarrow A_2}{\Delta_1, \Delta_2 \vdash (p_1, p_2) \Leftarrow A_1 \times A_2}\ \mathrm{PC_{Pair}}$$

$\boxed{\Delta \mid A \vdash q \Rightarrow C}$ Copattern q eliminates given type A into inferred type C, yielding context Δ.

$$\frac{}{\cdot \mid A \vdash \cdot \Rightarrow A}\ \mathrm{PC_{Head}} \qquad \frac{\Delta \mid A \vdash q \Rightarrow \nu X R}{\Delta \mid A \vdash q.d \Rightarrow R_d[\nu X R/X]}\ \mathrm{PC_{Dest}}$$

$$\frac{\Delta_1 \mid A \vdash q \Rightarrow B \to C \quad \Delta_2 \vdash p \Leftarrow B}{\Delta_1, \Delta_2 \mid A \vdash q\, p \Rightarrow C}\ \mathrm{PC_{App}}$$

Figure 5. Type checking for patterns and rewrite rules.

Again, there is a one-to-one connection between pattern constructors and pattern typing rules. A standard inversion lemma holds for all rules in Figure 5.

3.4 Programs

A program $\mathcal{P} ::= (\Sigma, \mathsf{Rules})$ consists of a signature Σ mapping defined symbols f to their types and a collection Rules of rewrite rules. For each symbol f defined in the signature, $\mathsf{Rules}(f)$ gives the rewrite rules for f as a set of pairs $(q \mapsto e)$, called *observations*, which define the behavior of f. We require a dedicated symbol $\mathsf{main} \in \Sigma$, called the *entry point*, that determines the value of a program. Execution of a program means rewriting main with the Rules until no more rewriting is possible.

The informal syntax used in the introduction can be mechanically transformed into programs of form $\mathcal{P}$. For instance, the definition fib of the stream of Fibonacci numbers corresponds to the following entries in Σ and Rules.

$$\Sigma(\mathsf{fib}) \quad = \nu X\{\mathsf{head} : \mu Y \langle \mathsf{zero}\ 1 \mid \mathsf{suc}\ Y\rangle\ ,\ \mathsf{tail} : X\}$$

$$\mathsf{Rules}(\mathsf{fib}) = \left\{ \begin{array}{ll} \cdot\ .\mathsf{head} & \mapsto \mathsf{zero}\ () \\ \cdot\ .\mathsf{tail}\ .\mathsf{head} & \mapsto \mathsf{suc}\ (\mathsf{zero}\ ()) \\ \cdot\ .\mathsf{tail}\ .\mathsf{tail} & \mapsto \mathsf{zipWith}\ \_+\_\ \ \mathsf{fib}\ (\mathsf{fib}\ .\mathsf{tail}) \end{array} \right\}$$

A complete program needs also entries for zipWith and _+_, and a symbol main. The type of main should be positive, otherwise the result of the program is an unprintable infinite object. Here, main could be a function listing the first 42 elements of the Fibonacci stream—we leave the details to the imagination of the reader.

A program $\mathcal{P}$ is well-typed if $\vdash \mathcal{P}$ as given in Figure 6, which in essence says that any rule $(q \mapsto u)$ for any defined symbol f must be well-typed. A first result, proven in the next section, is that during the execution of a well-typed program we never encounter a term which is ill-typed.

4. Evaluation and Type Preservation

In this section, we define program evaluation in terms of a small-step reduction relation. To decide whether a rewrite rule can fire,

$\boxed{\vdash q[f] \mapsto u}$ Check rewrite rule.

$$\frac{\Delta \mid \Sigma(f) \vdash q \Rightarrow C \quad \Delta \vdash u \Leftarrow C}{\vdash q[f] \mapsto u}\ \mathrm{TC}_{\mathrm{Rule}}$$

$\boxed{\vdash \mathcal{P}}$ Check program.

$$\frac{\mathsf{main} \in \Sigma \quad \forall f \in \Sigma,\ (q \mapsto u) \in \mathsf{Rules}(f).\ \vdash q[f] \mapsto u}{\vdash (\Sigma, \mathsf{Rules})}\ \mathrm{TC}_{\mathrm{Prg}}$$

Figure 6. Well-typed rules and programs.

we match evaluation contexts against copatterns. We prove that reduction preserves types.

4.1 Evaluation contexts

Evaluation contexts E are elimination terms with a hole in head position. They generalize copatterns q in that they allow arbitrary terms e instead of just patterns p in argument positions.

E	$::=$	$\cdot$	Hole
	$\mid$	$E\,e$	Application
	$\mid$	$E.d$	Projection

The hole $\cdot$ can be considered as a special variable. We write $E[t]$ as shorthand for $E[t/\cdot]$. Typing $\Delta \mid A \vdash E : C$ for evaluation context E is defined in Figure 7. This judgement holds iff $\Delta, x : A \vdash E[x] : C$ for a fresh variable $x \notin \Delta$. Well-typed evaluation contexts compose.

LEMMA 3 (Composition of contexts). *If $\mathcal{D} :: \Gamma \mid A \vdash E_1 : B$ and $\mathcal{E} :: \Gamma \mid B \vdash E_2 : C$, then $\Gamma \mid A \vdash E_2[E_1[\cdot]] : C$.*

$\boxed{\Delta \mid A \vdash E : C}$ In context Δ, evaluation context E eliminates type A into type C.

$$\frac{}{\Gamma \mid A \vdash \cdot : A}\ \mathrm{ET}_{\mathrm{Head}} \qquad \frac{\Gamma \mid A \vdash E : \nu X R}{\Gamma \mid A \vdash E.d : R_d[\nu X R/X]}\ \mathrm{ET}_{\mathrm{Dest}}$$

$$\frac{\Gamma \mid A \vdash E : B \to C \quad \Gamma \vdash e : B}{\Gamma \mid A \vdash E\,e : C}\ \mathrm{ET}_{\mathrm{App}}$$

Figure 7. Typing rules for evaluation context.

4.2 Pattern matching

Matching a term t against a pattern p, if successful, yields a substitution σ such that $p[\sigma] = t$. Pattern matching is defined in terms of a judgement $t =^? p \searrow \sigma$ whose rules appear in Figure 8. Herein, a substitution σ is a finite map from variables to terms; we write $\cdot$ for the empty map, t/x for the singleton mapping x to t and σ, σ' for the disjoint union of two maps σ and σ'. Substitution typing $\boxed{\Gamma \vdash \sigma : \Delta}$ simply means that for all $x \in \Delta$, we have $\Gamma \vdash \sigma(x) : \Delta(x)$.

While matching patterns p is standard, matching copatterns q is straightforward as well. The hole $\cdot$ serves as "anchor" and in an implementation it seems wise to match "inside-out", i. e., start at the hole and proceed outwards.

4.3 Reduction and type preservation

The only source of computation in our language is a defined function symbol f in an evaluation context E that matches the copattern q of one of the rules $(q \mapsto u) \in \mathsf{Rules}(f)$. Such an $e = E[f]$ is a redex which can be *contracted* to another expression e', written $\boxed{e \mapsto e'}$. The precise rule for contraction is:

$$\frac{E =^? q \searrow \sigma}{E[f] \mapsto u[\sigma]}\ (q \mapsto u) \in \mathsf{Rules}(f)$$

One step reduction $\boxed{e \longrightarrow e'}$ is defined as the compatible closure of contraction, i. e., e *reduces* to e' if e' results from contraction of one redex in e. We omit the standard inductive definition of $e \longrightarrow e'$.

Our first major result is that reduction preserves types. We assume a well-typed program, i. e. all rewrite rules are well-typed.

THEOREM 4 (Subject reduction). *If $\Gamma \vdash e : A$ and $e \longrightarrow e'$ then $\Gamma \vdash e' : A$*

Subject reduction is a consequence of the following statements: Substitution preserves types, (co)pattern matching yields a well-typed substitution, and contraction preserves types.

LEMMA 5 (Substitution). *If $\mathcal{D} :: \Delta \vdash u : C$ and $\mathcal{E} :: \Gamma \vdash \sigma : \Delta$ then $\mathcal{F} :: \Gamma \vdash u[\sigma] : C$ for some $\mathcal{F}$.*

Proof. By induction on $\mathcal{D}$. □

LEMMA 6 (Adequacy of pattern matching). *If $\mathcal{D} :: \Delta \vdash p \Leftarrow A$ and $\mathcal{E} :: \Gamma \vdash e : A$ and $\mathcal{F} :: e =^? p \searrow \sigma$ then $\Gamma \vdash \sigma : \Delta$.*

Proof. By induction on $\mathcal{F}$. □

LEMMA 7 (Adequacy of copattern matching). *If $\mathcal{D} :: \Delta \mid A \vdash q \Rightarrow C$ and $\mathcal{E} :: \Gamma \mid A \vdash E : B$ and $\mathcal{F} :: E =^? q \searrow \sigma$ then $C = B$ and $\Gamma \vdash \sigma : \Delta$.*

Proof. By induction on $\mathcal{F}$. □

LEMMA 8 (Correctness of contraction). *If $\Gamma \mid \Sigma(f) \vdash E : C$ and $\vdash q[f] \mapsto u$ and $E =^? q \searrow \sigma$ then $\Gamma \vdash u[\sigma] : C$.*

Proof. By assumption, we have

$$\mathcal{D} :: \frac{\overset{\mathcal{D}_1}{\Delta \mid \Sigma(f) \vdash q \Rightarrow B} \quad \overset{\mathcal{D}_2}{\Delta \vdash u \Leftarrow B}}{\vdash q[f] \mapsto u}$$

since it is the only rule that could have been used.

$\boxed{t =^? p \searrow \sigma}$ Term t matches with pattern p under substitution σ.

$$\frac{}{t =^? x \searrow t/x}\ \mathrm{PM}_{\mathrm{Var}} \qquad \frac{t =^? p \searrow \sigma}{c\,t =^? c\,p \searrow \sigma}\ \mathrm{PM}_{\mathrm{Constr}}$$

$$\frac{}{() =^? () \searrow \cdot}\ \mathrm{PM}_{\mathrm{Unit}} \qquad \frac{t_1 =^? p_1 \searrow \sigma_1 \quad t_2 =^? p_2 \searrow \sigma_2}{(t_1, t_2) =^? (p_1, p_2) \searrow \sigma_1, \sigma_2}\ \mathrm{PM}_{\mathrm{Pair}}$$

$\boxed{E =^? q \searrow \sigma}$ Evaluation context E matches copattern q returning substitution σ.

$$\frac{}{\cdot =^? \cdot \searrow \cdot}\ \mathrm{PM}_{\mathrm{Head}} \qquad \frac{E =^? q \searrow \sigma}{E.d =^? q.d \searrow \sigma}\ \mathrm{PM}_{\mathrm{Dest}}$$

$$\frac{E =^? q \searrow \sigma \quad t =^? p \searrow \sigma'}{E\,t =^? q\,p \searrow \sigma, \sigma'}\ \mathrm{PM}_{\mathrm{App}}$$

Figure 8. Rules for pattern matching.

By Lemma 7, using $\mathcal{D}_1$ and both assumptions we have that $C = B$ and $\Gamma \vdash \sigma : \Delta$. Then, by Substitution (Lemma 5) and $\mathcal{D}_2$, we conclude that $\Gamma \vdash u[\sigma] : C$. □

Finally, the subject reduction theorem follows:

Proof of Theorem 4. By induction on the reduction relation, with contraction being the only interesting case:

$$\Gamma \vdash E[f] : B \quad \text{and} \quad \frac{E =^? q \searrow \sigma}{E[f] \mapsto u[\sigma]} \ (q \mapsto u) \in \mathsf{Rules}(f)$$

By well-typedness $\vdash q[f] \mapsto u$, we obtain from Lemma 8 that $\Gamma \vdash u[\sigma] : B$. □

5. Copattern Coverage and Progress

A fundamental property of strongly typed languages is *type soundness*; in the words of Milner [1978] "well-typed programs do not go wrong". This means that well-typed programs either produce a value or run forever, but never get *stuck* by encountering an invalid operation, like adding a function to a string or calling a number as one would call a function. For our language, there are three reasons why a program is stuck, i. e., no reduction step is possible yet we have not reached a printable value:

1. Missing rule. We might have defined a function $f : \mathsf{Nat} \to A$ but only given a rewrite rule $f\ \mathsf{zero} \mapsto \ldots$. In this case, $f\ (\mathsf{suc}\ n)$ is stuck. In this section, we give rules for *copattern coverage* that ensure no rewrite rules are forgotten.
2. Ill-typed term. The term $f\ \mathsf{nil}$ is stuck even if we have given a complete implementation of $f : \mathsf{Nat} \to A$. However, ill-typed terms like $f\ \mathsf{nil}$ are already excluded by type checking and the type preservation theorem.
3. Infinite object. The term f does not evaluate by itself; it is an underapplied function. However, just as the typical interpreter, we consider terms of negative types as values. As a consequence, our notion of value is not syntactic, but type-dependent.

As main technical result of this section and the article, we prove type soundness, syntactically [Wright and Felleisen 1994], by showing the progress theorem for a call-by-value strategy.

5.1 Values and evaluation contexts

Values are defined using a new judgment $\Delta \vdash_v e : A$ to mean that the expression e is a value of type A under the context Δ. We also use v to denote an expression which acts as a value. Whether an expression is considered a value or not depends also on its type, in particular, each expression of negative type N is considered a value—the rules are given in Figure 9.

$\boxed{\Delta \vdash_v e : A}$ In context Δ, e is a value of type A.

$$\frac{\Gamma \vdash x : A}{\Gamma \vdash_v x : A}\,\mathrm{V_{Var}} \qquad \frac{\Gamma \vdash_v v : D_c[\mu X D/X]}{\Gamma \vdash_v c\ v : \mu X D}\,\mathrm{V_{Const}}$$

$$\frac{}{\Gamma \vdash_v () : 1}\,\mathrm{V_{Unit}} \qquad \frac{\Gamma \vdash_v v_1 : A_1 \quad \Gamma \vdash_v v_2 : A_2}{\Gamma \vdash_v (v_1, v_2) : A_1 \times A_2}\,\mathrm{V_{Pair}}$$

$$\frac{\Gamma \vdash e : N}{\Gamma \vdash_v e : N}\,\mathrm{V_{Neg}}$$

Figure 9. Rules for values.

LEMMA 9 (Inversion for values). *The following hold for $v \neq x$.*

1. If $\Gamma \vdash_v v : 1$ then $v = ()$.

2. If $\Gamma \vdash_v v : A_1 \times A_2$ then $v = (v_1, v_2)$, $\Gamma \vdash_v v_1 : A_1$ and $\Gamma \vdash_v v_2 : A_2$.

3. If $\Gamma \vdash_v v : \mu X D$ then $v = c\ v'$ for some $c \in D$ and $\Gamma \vdash v' : D_c[\mu X D/X]$.

We dualize the notion of value for terms to evaluation contexts, introducing a judgement $\Delta \mid A \vdash_v E : C$ (see Figure 10). It accepts those well-typed evaluation contexts E that have values in all argument positions. The idea is that if E is "long enough", i. e., if C is a positive type, then $E[f]$ is a redex because one of the defining copatterns for f has to match E. This would not necessary be the case if the arguments in E were not values.

$\boxed{\Delta \mid A \vdash_v E : C}$ E is an evaluation context with only values in application arguments.

$$\frac{}{\Gamma \mid A \vdash_v \cdot : A}\,\mathrm{EV_{Head}} \qquad \frac{\Gamma \mid A \vdash_v E : \nu X R}{\Gamma \mid A \vdash_v E.d : R_d[\nu X R/X]}\,\mathrm{EV_{Dest}}$$

$$\frac{\Gamma \mid A \vdash_v E : B \to C \quad \Gamma \vdash_v v : B}{\Gamma \mid A \vdash_v E\ v : C}\,\mathrm{EV_{App}}$$

Figure 10. Rules for value evaluation contexts.

The following two propositions enable us to analyze non-empty value evaluation contexts from the inside out; they will be used in Theorem 12.

LEMMA 10 (Splitting a function evaluation context). *If $\mathcal{D} :: \Gamma \mid B \to C \vdash_v E : A$ and $E \neq \cdot$ then $E = E'[\cdot\ v]$ with $\Gamma \vdash_v v : B$ and $\Gamma \mid C \vdash_v E' : A$.*

Proof. By induction on $\mathcal{D}$. □

LEMMA 11 (Splitting a record evaluation context). *If $\mathcal{D} :: \Gamma \mid \nu X R \vdash_v E : A$ and $E \neq \cdot$ then $E = E'[\cdot.d]$ with $\Gamma \mid R_d[\nu X R/X] \vdash_v E' : A$.*

Proof. By induction on $\mathcal{D}$. □

5.2 Coverage

Figure 11 defines a judgment to indicate that a list of copatterns covers all eliminations of a given type A. The judgment is $A \lhd \mid (\Delta \vdash q \Rightarrow C)$ or, more generally, $A \lhd \mid \vec{Q}$ where $\vec{Q} = (\Delta_i \vdash q_i \Rightarrow C_i)_{i=1,\ldots,n}$ is a set of non-overlapping copatterns q_i with their type C_i and context Δ_i, each satisfying $\Delta_i \mid A \vdash q_i \Rightarrow C_i$.

The rules to construct a covering set of copatterns are not syntax-directed. To check whether a given set of copatterns $\vec{Q}$ for a type A is complete, we non-deterministically guess the derivation of $A \lhd \mid \vec{Q}$, if it exists. Although this NP-algorithm is not the best we can do, we are confident that we can adopt existing efficient coverage algorithms [Norell 2007] for our language.

The initial covering is given by the axiom $\mathrm{C_{Hole}}$. We can refine a covering $\vec{Q}$ by focusing on one copattern Q and either *split the result* of negative type or split one of its variables of positive type. Result splitting at function type $B \to C$ applies the copattern q to a fresh variable $x : B$, at record type $\nu X R$ we take all projections $(q.d)_{d \in R}$. Splitting a variable x replaces it by unit $()$, a pair (x_1, x_2) or all possible constructors $(c\ x')_{c \in D}$, in accordance with the type 1, $A_1 \times A_2$, or $\mu X D$ of the variable.

Let us revisit the example of the function cycleNats from the introduction and walk through the rules for coverage. With the following shorthands for types

$$\begin{array}{lcl} \mathsf{Nat} & = & \mu X \langle \mathsf{zero}\ 1 \mid \mathsf{suc}\ X \rangle \\ \mathsf{StreamNat} & = & \nu X \{ \mathsf{head} : \mathsf{Nat}, \mathsf{tail} : X \}, \end{array}$$

$\boxed{A \lhd | \vec{Q}}$ Typed copatterns $\vec{Q}$ cover elimination of type A.

Result splitting:

$$\frac{}{A \lhd | (\cdot \vdash \cdot \Rightarrow A)}\,\mathrm{C_{Hole}} \qquad \frac{A \lhd | \vec{Q}\,(\Delta \vdash q \Rightarrow B \to C)}{A \lhd | \vec{Q}\,(\Delta, x : B \vdash q\,x \Rightarrow C)}\,\mathrm{C_{App}}$$

$$\frac{A \lhd | \vec{Q}\,(\Delta \vdash q \Rightarrow \nu X R)}{A \lhd | \vec{Q}\,(\Delta \vdash q.d \Rightarrow R_d[\nu X R/X])_{d \in R}}\,\mathrm{C_{Dest}}$$

Variable splitting:

$$\frac{A \lhd | \vec{Q}\,(\Delta, x : 1 \vdash q \Rightarrow C)}{A \lhd | \vec{Q}\,(\Delta \vdash q[()/x] \Rightarrow C)}\,\mathrm{C_{Unit}}$$

$$\frac{A \lhd | \vec{Q}\,(\Delta, x : A_1 \times A_2 \vdash q \Rightarrow C)}{A \lhd | \vec{Q}\,(\Delta, x_1 : A_1, x_2 : A_2 \vdash q[(x_1, x_2)/x] \Rightarrow C)}\,\mathrm{C_{Pair}}$$

$$\frac{A \lhd | \vec{Q}\,(\Delta, x : \mu X D \vdash q \Rightarrow C)}{A \lhd | \vec{Q}\,(\Delta, x' : D_c[\mu X D/X] \vdash q[c\,x'/x] \Rightarrow C)_{c \in D}}\,\mathrm{C_{Const}}$$

Figure 11. Rules for copattern coverage.

the signature entries for cycleNats are the following:

$$\begin{array}{lcl} \Sigma(\mathsf{cycleNats}) & = & \mathsf{Nat} \to \mathsf{StreamNat} \\ \mathsf{Rules}(\mathsf{cycleNats}) & = & \left\{ \begin{array}{lll} \cdot\, x & .\mathsf{head} & \mapsto x \\ \cdot\, (\mathsf{zero}\,()) & .\mathsf{tail} & \mapsto \mathsf{cycleNats}\ N \\ \cdot\, (\mathsf{suc}\ x) & .\mathsf{tail} & \mapsto \mathsf{cycleNats}\ x \end{array} \right\} \end{array}$$

To check coverage, we start with the trivial covering and successively apply the rules until we obtain the copatterns of cycleNats. Since $A = \mathsf{Nat} \to \mathsf{StreamNat}$ stays fixed throughout the derivation, we omit it and just write the copattern list $\vec{Q}$. We start with $\mathrm{C_{Hole}}$.

$$(\cdot \vdash \cdot \Rightarrow \mathsf{Nat} \to \mathsf{StreamNat})$$

We apply x to the hole by $\mathrm{C_{App}}$.

$$(x : \mathsf{Nat} \vdash \cdot\, x \Rightarrow \mathsf{StreamNat}).$$

Then we split the result by $\mathrm{C_{Dest}}$.

$$\begin{array}{l} (x : \mathsf{Nat} \vdash \cdot\, x\ .\mathsf{head} \Rightarrow \mathsf{Nat}) \\ (x : \mathsf{Nat} \vdash \cdot\, x\ .\mathsf{tail} \ \Rightarrow \mathsf{StreamNat}) \end{array}$$

In the second copattern we split x via $\mathrm{C_{Const}}$, reusing the variable name x.

$$\begin{array}{llll} (x : \mathsf{Nat} & \vdash \cdot\, x & .\mathsf{head} & \Rightarrow \mathsf{Nat}) \\ (x : 1 & \vdash \cdot\, (\mathsf{zero}\ x) & .\mathsf{tail} & \Rightarrow \mathsf{StreamNat}) \\ (x : \mathsf{Nat} & \vdash \cdot\, (\mathsf{suc}\ x) & .\mathsf{tail} & \Rightarrow \mathsf{StreamNat}). \end{array}$$

Finally, we apply $\mathrm{C_{Unit}}$, replacing x by $()$.

$$\begin{array}{llll} (x : \mathsf{Nat} & \vdash \cdot\, x & .\mathsf{head} & \Rightarrow \mathsf{Nat}) \\ (\cdot & \vdash \cdot\, (\mathsf{zero}\ ()) & .\mathsf{tail} & \Rightarrow \mathsf{StreamNat}) \\ (x : \mathsf{Nat} & \vdash \cdot\, (\mathsf{suc}\ x) & .\mathsf{tail} & \Rightarrow \mathsf{StreamNat}) \end{array}$$

The lists of copatterns $\vec{q}$ for type A generated by the splitting rules is complete in the sense that every closed value context E eliminating A into a positive type P actually matches one of the copatterns q_i.

THEOREM 12 (Matching with a covering copattern). *If $\mathcal{D} :: \cdot \mid A \vdash_v E : P$ and $\mathcal{E} :: A \lhd | (\Delta_i \vdash q_i \Rightarrow C_i)_{i=1..n}$, then there are E_1, E_2 such that $E = E_1[E_2[\cdot]]$, $E_2 =^? q_i \searrow \sigma$ for some i, $\cdot \mid A \vdash_v E_2 : C_i$ and $\cdot \mid C_i \vdash_v E_1 : P$.*

To prove this theorem, we use the following statements.

LEMMA 13 (Splitting a pattern variable). *Let $\mathcal{D} :: \Delta, x : A \mid B \vdash q \Rightarrow C$ and $\mathcal{E} :: \mid B \vdash_v E : C$ and $\mathcal{F} :: E =^? q \searrow \sigma$.*

1. *Assume $A = A_1 \times A_2$ and let $q' = q[(x_1, x_2)/x]$. Then $\Delta, x_1 : A_1, x_2 : A_2 \mid B \vdash q' \Rightarrow C$ and $E =^? q' \searrow \sigma'$ with $\sigma = \sigma'[x \mapsto (\sigma'(x_1), \sigma'(x_2))]$.*
2. *Assume $A = \mu X D$ and let $q' = q[c\,x'/x]$ for some $c \in D$. Then $\Delta, x' : D_c[\mu X D/X] \vdash q' \Rightarrow C$ and $E =^? q' \searrow \sigma'$ with $\sigma = \sigma'[x \mapsto c\,\sigma'(x')]$.*
3. *Assume $A = 1$ and let $q' = q[()/x]$. Then $\Delta \vdash q' \Leftarrow C$ and $E =^? q' \searrow \sigma'$ with $\sigma = \sigma'[x \mapsto ()]$.*

Proof. First, prove an adaptation of these statements for patterns p and values v instead of copatterns q and evaluation contexts E. Then, prove this lemma by induction on $\mathcal{F}$. □

Proof of Theorem 12. The theorem is proved by induction on the coverage derivation $\mathcal{E}$. The variable splitting cases $\mathrm{C_{Pair}}$, $\mathrm{C_{Const}}$, and $\mathrm{C_{Unit}}$ follow from Lemma 13. We consider the rules for result splitting.

$$\text{Case } \mathcal{E} :: \frac{A \lhd | \vec{Q}\,(\Delta \vdash q \Rightarrow B \to C)}{A \lhd | \vec{Q}\,(\Delta, x : B \vdash q\,x \Rightarrow C)_{i=1,\ldots,n}}$$

By induction hypothesis, the statement holds for one of the patterns in $\vec{Q}\,(\Delta \vdash q \Rightarrow B \to C)$. If the pattern has been chosen from $\vec{Q}$, we are done. Thus, without loss of generality, $E = E_1[E_2[\cdot]]$ and $\cdot \mid A \vdash_v E_2 : B \to C$ and $\cdot \mid B \to C \vdash_v E_1 : P$ and $E_2 =^? q \searrow \sigma$.

If $E_1 = \cdot$ then $P = B \to C$, which is a contradiction since P is a positive type. If $E_1 \neq \cdot$, then $E_1 = E_1'[\cdot\ v]$ with $\cdot \vdash_v v : B$ and $\cdot \mid C \vdash_v E_1' : P$ by Lemma 10.

Thus, let $E_2' = E_2\ v$ and $\cdot \mid A \vdash_v E_2' : C$ by $\mathrm{EV_{App}}$, and $E_2' =^? q\,x \searrow \sigma, v/x$ by $\mathrm{PM_{App}}$.

$$\text{Case } \mathcal{E} :: \frac{A \lhd | \vec{Q}\,(\Delta \vdash q \Rightarrow \nu X R)}{A \lhd | \vec{Q}\,(\Delta \vdash q.d \Rightarrow R_d[\nu X R/X])_{d \in R}}$$

Analogously, using Lemma 11. □

5.3 Progress

We are ready to show that evaluation of a well-typed program does not get stuck, provided that all definitions come with a complete set of observations. First we note that closed terms are either values or eliminations of a defined symbols. Such an elimination is either a value evaluation context or contains a closed non-value.

LEMMA 14 (Decomposition). *If $\cdot \vdash e : A$ then either*

1. *$e = (), A = 1$,*
2. *$e = (e_1, e_2), A = A_1 \times A_2$,*
3. *$e = c\,e', A = \mu X D$,*
4. *$e = E_2[E_1[f]\ e']$ where $\cdot \mid \Sigma(f) \vdash_v E_1 : B \to C$ and $\cdot \mid C \vdash E_2 : A$ and $\not\vdash_v e' : B$ for some f, some evaluation contexts E_1, E_2, some term e' and some types B, C.*
5. *$e = E[f]$ for some f, E with $\cdot \mid \Sigma(f) \vdash_v E : A$.*

Proof. By induction on e. We only show the cases $e = e_1\ e_2$ and $e = e'.d$. The other cases are trivial.

Case $\vdash e_1\ e_2 : A$. Then by inversion $\vdash e_1 : B \to A$ and $\vdash e_2 : B$. By induction hypothesis $e_1 = E[f]$ with $\cdot \mid \Sigma(f) \vdash_v E : B \to A$ for some f, E or $e_1 = E_2[E_1[f]\ e']$ for some f, E_1, E_2, and e' where $\cdot \mid \Sigma(f) \vdash_v E_1 : B' \to C', \cdot \mid C' \vdash E_2 : B \to A$ and $\not\vdash_v e' : B'$, as the 3 other cases are impossible. In the former case, if $\not\vdash_v e_2 : B$, we can obtain case 4 by letting $E_2 = \cdot, E = E_1$ and $e_2 = e'$. This gives us $e_1\ e_2 = \cdot[E[f]\ e_2]$. If $\vdash_v e_2 : B$, then, by $\mathsf{EV}_{\mathsf{App}}$, $\cdot \mid \Sigma(f) \vdash_v E[f]\ e_2 : A$ and $E' = E\ e_2$. In the latter case, we have $E_2[E_1[f]\ e']\ e_2 = E_2'[E_1[f]\ e']$ by setting $E_2' = E_2\ e_2$.

Case $\vdash e.d : A$. Then by inversion, $\vdash e : \nu XR$ for some R. By induction hypothesis, $e = E[f]$ and $\cdot \mid \Sigma(f) \vdash_v E : \nu XR$, or $e = E_2[E_1[f]\ e']$ where e' is not a value. In the former case, $e.d = E[f].d = E'[f]$ and $\cdot \mid \Sigma(f) \vdash_v E.d : R_d[\nu XR/X]$ by $\mathsf{EV}_{\mathsf{Dest}}$. Otherwise, $e.d = E_2[E_1[f]\ e'].d = E_2'[E_1[f]\ e']$. □

Finally we prove progress under the assumption that every definition f is complete, written $\Sigma(f) \lhd\!\mid \mathsf{Rules}(f)$.

THEOREM 15 (Progress). *If $\mathcal{D} :: \vdash e : A$ then either $\vdash_v e : A$ or $e \longrightarrow e'$ for some e'.*

Proof. The proof is done by induction on e. By Lemma 14, we have five possible cases. Since the four first cases follow by a simple induction argument, we only present the last case.

Here $e = E[f]$ and $\cdot \mid \Sigma(f) \vdash_v E : A$. If A is negative, then e is already considered a value and we are done. Otherwise, since by assumption $\Sigma(f) \lhd\!\mid \mathsf{Rules}(f)$, we can apply Theorem 12 and obtain E_1, E_2 such that $E = E_1[E_2[\cdot]]$, $E_2 =^? q_i \searrow \sigma$ for some $q_i \in \mathsf{Rules}(f)$, plus $\cdot \mid \Sigma(f) \vdash E_2 : C_i$ and $\cdot \mid C_i \vdash_v E_1 : A$. Thus, by our reduction rules $E_2[f] \mapsto u_i[\sigma]$ where $(q_i, u_i) \in \mathsf{Rules}(f)$ and so $E_2[f] \to u_i[\sigma]$. We conclude that $E_1[E_2[f]] \to E_1[u_i[\sigma]]$. □

6. Extensions and Implementations

Our core language misses introduction rules for functions and objects, thus, we do not have lambda abstractions or record expressions. However, we can embed sets of behaviors $\{\vec{q} \mapsto \vec{u}\}$ into the expression syntax and obtain *anonymous objects* that subsume λ abstractions, SML's anonymous functions defined by pattern matching, and record expressions:

$$\begin{array}{lcl}
\lambda x t & = & \{\cdot\ x \mapsto t\} \\
\begin{array}{l}\mathsf{fn\ nil} \quad\quad\ \Rightarrow \mathsf{false} \\ \mid \mathsf{cons}\ x\ xs \Rightarrow \mathsf{true}\end{array} & = & \left\{\begin{array}{ll}\cdot\ \mathsf{nil} & \mapsto \mathsf{false} \\ \cdot\ (\mathsf{cons}\ x\ xs) & \mapsto \mathsf{true}\end{array}\right\} \\
\mathsf{record}\{\mathsf{fst} = t_1; \mathsf{snd} = t_2\} & = & \left\{\begin{array}{ll}\cdot.\mathsf{fst} & \mapsto t_1 \\ \cdot.\mathsf{snd} & \mapsto t_2\end{array}\right\}
\end{array}$$

Of course, bidirectional type checking is no longer complete since anonymous objects can only be checked against a given type, but can appear in elimination position.

Copatterns have been added to the development version[3] of Agda [Agda team 2012]. Currently, projection copatterns are not part of the core of Agda, they are parsed but then translated into record expressions. This does not give the full flexibility of copatterns, but allows us to experiment with them. Full copatterns in the core would allow us to exploit the benefits of deep projection copatterns and mixed projection/application copatterns, but for that, Agda's coverage checker has to be extended to copatterns. To accomplish this, further research is required, because dependent pattern matching is a far from trivial enterprise [Coquand 1992; Schürmann and Pfenning 2003; Goguen et al. 2006; Norell 2007; Dunfield and Pientka 2009].

Another prototypical implementation of copatterns exists in MiniAgda [Abel 2012]. In MiniAgda, one can certify termination and productivity using sized types [Hughes et al. 1996; Barthe et al. 2004; Abel 2007]. Copatterns provide the right syntax to decorate corecursive definitions with size variables that witness productivity.

[3] Available from the darcs repository `http://code.haskell.org/Agda`.

7. Related Work

Our work builds on the insight that finite datatypes correspond to initial algebras and infinite datatypes correspond to final co-algebras. This was first observed by Hagino [1989] and was the basis of categorical programming languages such as symML [Hagino 1987] and Charity [Cockett and Fukushima 1992]. Categorical programming languages typically support programming with the morphisms of category theory; while they do provide iteration, they do not support general recursion and pattern matching. In Charity, support for pattern matching on data types was added [Tuckey 1997], but it lacks support for copattern matching.

Our type theoretic development of copatterns exploits the duality of positive and negative types which is well known in focused proofs [Andreoli 1992]. Previously, focusing has been applied to pattern matching [Zeilberger 2008a; Krishnaswami 2009] and evaluation order [Zeilberger 2009; Curien and Herbelin 2000]. Closest to our work from a theoretical point of view is the work by Licata, Zeilberger and Harper [2008] where a language based on the sequent calculus is described which supports mixing LF types with computation-level types. The weak representational function space of LF is classified as a positive connective and admits pattern matching using constructor patterns; the strong computation level function space is classified as negative connective which is defined by destructor patterns. The accompanying technical report also describes briefly how to add ν-formulas to the proposed system. However, in their work, (co)pattern matching happens at the *meta level*; this is like replacing induction by an ω-rule. Our work provides an *object-level* syntax for copatterns and an *algorithm* for copattern coverage.

Kimura and Tatsuta [2009] extend Wadler's [2003] Dual Calculus to inductive and coinductive types, treating the constructor for inductive data as value constructor and the destructor for coinductive data as continuation constructor. However, they do not introduce recursive values or recursive continuations nor pattern and copattern matching, but allow only iteration over finite data and coiteration into infinite data.

Agda, in its currently released version 2.3.0, already avoids Coq's subject reduction problem. Infinite objects are created via *delay* ♯ and analyzed via *force* ♭, the corresponding operation on types is *lifting* ∞. In spirit, this approach mimics the standard trick in call-by-value languages such as ML and Scheme to encode lazy values by *suspensions*, i. e., functions over the unit type. The two-edged dependent pattern matching on infinite objects is ruled out, since one cannot match on functions.

Agda's coinduction is informally described by Danielsson and Altenkirch [2010], but it lacks solid theoretical backing. Indeed, compositionality is lost, because any data type that uses lifting is coinductive [Altenkirch and Danielsson 2010]. For instance, a data type of trees with infinite branching realized via streams host automatically infinitely *deep* trees, even if that is not expressed by the data type definition. Our work reinterpretes lifting as the generation of a mutual recursive record type that contributes the coinductive part to the data type. Forcing is interpreted as destructor and delaying as a mutual definition by destructor pattern. This way, we provide a standard semantics for coinduction in Agda and recover compositional construction of data types.

8. Conclusion

In this paper, we have presented a type-safe foundation for programming with infinite structures via observations. We model finite data using variant types and infinite data via record types. Pattern matching of finite data is extended with its dual notion of copattern matching on infinite data. While we do not consider termination and productivity in this paper, we guarantee that the functions are covering, i.e., they are defined on all possible inputs.

Copatterns lay a foundation for finitary rewriting with infinite objects. They are also an excellent candidate for representing corecursive definitions in type-theoretic proof assistants such as Coq and dependently typed languages like Agda.

In the future, we plan to extend the presented work to full dependent types. There are two main theoretical issues we need to tackle: first, extension of copattern coverage to dependent types, and secondly, checking termination and productivity of functions to guarantee strong normalization. A candidate for the latter task are sized types [Hughes et al. 1996; Barthe et al. 2004; Abel 2007] as already implemented in MiniAgda [Abel 2012]. Further, we aim at developing a denotational model for languages with copatterns. It seems that semantics based on orthogonality [Parigot 1997; Vouillon and Melliès 2004] provides a good starting point for this investigation.

From a practical point of view, we plan to fully integrate copatterns into Agda for a perspicuous and robust foundation of coinduction.

Acknowledgments

The first author thanks Thierry Coquand and Nils Anders Danielsson for email exchange about copatterns and the regular participants of the Agda Implementor's Meetings from 2008 on for lively discussions on copatterns and the best way to integrate coinduction into Agda. During an invitation to McGill University by the second author, much of the theory of copatterns was already worked out. He is also grateful towards Tarmo Uustalu and James Chapman for an invitation to the Institute for Cybernetics in Tallinn in November 2011. During that visit, the implementation of copatterns for Agda began. We also thank Jacques Carette and the anonymous referees for suggestions to improve this paper.

References

M. Abadi and L. Cardelli. A theory of primitive objects. Untyped and first-order systems. In M. Hagiya and J. Mitchell, editors, *Theoretical Aspects of Computer Software*, volume 789 of *Lect. Notes in Comput. Sci.*, pages 296–320. Springer, 1994.

A. Abel. Mixed inductive/coinductive types and strong normalization. In Z. Shao, editor, *Proc. of the 5th Asian Symp. on Programming Languages and Systems, APLAS 2007*, volume 4807 of *Lect. Notes in Comput. Sci.*, pages 286–301. Springer, 2007. ISBN 978-3-540-76636-0.

A. Abel. Type-based termination, inflationary fixed-points, and mixed inductive-coinductive types. *Electr. Proc. in Theor. Comp. Sci.*, 77:1–11, 2012. Proceedings of FICS 2012.

Agda team. The Agda Wiki, 2012.

T. Altenkirch and N. A. Danielsson. Termination checking in the presence of nested inductive and coinductive types. Short note supporting a talk given at PAR 2010, Workshop on Partiality and Recursion in Interactive Theorem Provers, FLoC 2010, 2010.

J.-M. Andreoli. Logic programming with focusing proofs in linear logic. *Journal of Logic and Computation*, 2(3):297–347, 1992.

G. Barthe, M. J. Frade, E. Giménez, L. Pinto, and T. Uustalu. Type-based termination of recursive definitions. *Math. Struct. in Comput. Sci.*, 14 (1):97–141, 2004.

N. Benton, G. M. Bierman, V. de Paiva, and M. Hyland. A term calculus for intuitionistic linear logic. In M. Bezem and J. F. Groote, editors, *Proc. of the 1st Int. Conf. on Typed Lambda Calculi and Applications, TLCA '93*, volume 664 of *Lect. Notes in Comput. Sci.*, pages 75–90. Springer, 1993. ISBN 3-540-56517-5.

A. Chlipala. *Certified Programming with Dependent Types*. MIT Press, June 2012. Unpublished draft.

R. Cockett and T. Fukushima. About charity. Technical report, Department of Computer Science, The University of Calgary, June 1992. Yellow Series Report No. 92/480/18.

T. Coquand. Pattern matching with dependent types. In B. Nordström, K. Pettersson, and G. Plotkin, editors, *Types for Proofs and Programs (TYPES'92), Båstad, Sweden*, pages 71–83, 1992.

T. Coquand. Infinite objects in type theory. In H. Barendregt and T. Nipkow, editors, *Types for Proofs and Programs (TYPES '93)*, volume 806 of *Lect. Notes in Comput. Sci.*, pages 62–78. Springer, 1993.

P.-L. Curien and H. Herbelin. The duality of computation. In *Proc. of the 5th ACM SIGPLAN Int. Conf. on Functional Programming (ICFP 2000)*, SIGPLAN Notices 35(9), pages 233–243. ACM Press, 2000. ISBN 1-58113-202-6.

N. A. Danielsson and T. Altenkirch. Subtyping, declaratively. In C. Bolduc, J. Desharnais, and B. Ktari, editors, *Proc. of the 10th Int. Conf. on Mathematics of Program Construction, MPC 2010*, volume 6120 of *Lect. Notes in Comput. Sci.*, pages 100–118. Springer, 2010. ISBN 978-3-642-13320-6.

J. Dunfield and B. Pientka. Case analysis of higher-order data. *Electr. Notes in Theor. Comp. Sci.*, 228:69–84, 2009.

E. Giménez. *Un Calcul de Constructions Infinies et son application a la vérification de systèmes communicants*. PhD thesis, Ecole Normale Supérieure de Lyon, Dec. 1996. Thèse d'université.

H. Goguen, C. McBride, and J. McKinna. Eliminating dependent pattern matching. In K. Futatsugi, J.-P. Jouannaud, and J. Meseguer, editors, *Algebra, Meaning, and Computation, Essays Dedicated to Joseph A. Goguen on the Occasion of His 65th Birthday*, volume 4060 of *Lect. Notes in Comput. Sci.*, pages 521–540. Springer, 2006. ISBN 3-540-35462-X.

J. Granström. *Reference and Computation in Intuitionistic Type Theory*. PhD thesis, Mathematical Logic, Uppsala University, 2009.

T. Hagino. A typed lambda calculus with categorical type constructors. In D. H. Pitt, A. Poigné, and D. E. Rydeheard, editors, *Category Theory and Computer Science*, volume 283 of *Lect. Notes in Comput. Sci.*, pages 140–157. Springer, 1987.

T. Hagino. Codatatypes in ML. *J. Symb. Logic*, 8(6):629–650, 1989.

J. Hughes, L. Pareto, and A. Sabry. Proving the correctness of reactive systems using sized types. In *Proc. of the 23rd ACM Symp. on Principles of Programming Languages, POPL'96*, pages 410–423, 1996.

INRIA. *The Coq Proof Assistant Reference Manual*. INRIA, version 8.3 edition, 2010.

J. Kennaway and F. de Vries. *Infinitary Rewriting*, volume 55 of *Cambridge Tracts in Theoretical Computer Science*, chapter Chapter 12 in Term Rewriting Systems, pages 668–711. Cambridge University Press, 2003.

D. Kimura and M. Tatsuta. Dual calculus with inductive and coinductive types. In R. Treinen, editor, *Rewriting Techniques and Applications (RTA 2009), Brasília, Brazil*, volume 5595 of *Lect. Notes in Comput. Sci.*, pages 224–238. Springer, 2009. ISBN 978-3-642-02347-7.

N. R. Krishnaswami. Focusing on pattern matching. In Z. Shao and B. C. Pierce, editors, *Proc. of the 36th ACM Symp. on Principles of Programming Languages, POPL 2009*, pages 366–378. ACM Press, 2009. ISBN 978-1-60558-379-2.

D. R. Licata, N. Zeilberger, and R. Harper. Focusing on binding and computation. In F. Pfenning, editor, *Proc. of the 23nd IEEE Symp. on Logic in Computer Science (LICS 2008)*, pages 241–252. IEEE Computer Soc. Press, 2008. ISBN 978-0-7695-3183-0. Long version available as Technical Report CMU-CS-08-101.

C. McBride. Let's see how things unfold: Reconciling the infinite with the intensional. In A. Kurz, M. Lenisa, and A. Tarlecki, editors, *3rd Int. Conf. on Algebra and Coalgebra in Computer Science, CALCO 2009*, volume 5728 of *Lect. Notes in Comput.,Sci.*, pages 113–126. Springer, 2009. ISBN 978-3-642-03740-5.

C. McBride and J. McKinna. The view from the left. *J. Func. Program.*, 14 (1):69–111, 2004.

R. Milner. A theory of type polymorphism in programming. *J. Comput. Syst. Sci.*, 17:348–375, Aug. 1978.

U. Norell. *Towards a Practical Programming Language Based on Dependent Type Theory*. PhD thesis, Dept of Comput. Sci. and Engrg., Chalmers, Göteborg, Sweden, Sept. 2007.

N. Oury. Coinductive types and type preservation. Message on the coq-club mailing list, June 2008.

M. Parigot. Proofs of strong normalization for second order classical natural deduction. *J. Symb. Logic*, 62(4):1461–1479, 1997.

B. C. Pierce and D. N. Turner. Local type inference. In *Proc. of the 25th ACM Symp. on Principles of Programming Languages, POPL'98*, San Diego, California, 1998.

C. Schürmann and F. Pfenning. A coverage checking algorithm for LF. In D. Basin and B. Wolff, editors, *Proceedings of the 16th International Conference on Theorem Proving in Higher Order Logics (TPHOLs 2003)*, volume 2758 of *Lect. Notes in Comput. Sci.*, pages 120–135, Rome, Italy, September 2003. Springer.

A. Setzer. Coalgebras as types determined by their elimination rules. In P. Dybjer, S. Lindström, E. Palmgren, and G. Sundholm, editors, *Epistemology versus ontology: Essays on the foundations of mathematics in honour of Per Martin-Löf.* Springer, 2012. To appear.

C. Tuckey. Pattern matching in Charity. Master's thesis, The University of Calgary, July 1997.

J. Vouillon and P.-A. Melliès. Semantic types: A fresh look at the ideal model for types. In N. D. Jones and X. Leroy, editors, *Proc. of the 31st ACM Symp. on Principles of Programming Languages, POPL 2004*, pages 52–63. ACM Press, 2004. ISBN 1-58113-729-X.

P. Wadler. Call-by-value is dual to call-by-name. In C. Runciman and O. Shivers, editors, *Proc. of the 8th ACM SIGPLAN Int. Conf. on Functional Programming (ICFP 2003)*, pages 189–201. ACM Press, 2003. ISBN 1-58113-756-7.

P. Wadler. Call-by-value is dual to call-by-name - reloaded. In J. Giesl, editor, *Rewriting Techniques and Applications (RTA 2005), Nara, Japan*, volume 3467 of *Lect. Notes in Comput. Sci.*, pages 185–203. Springer, 2005. ISBN 3-540-25596-6.

A. K. Wright and M. Felleisen. A syntactic approach to type soundness. *Information and Computation*, 115(1):38–94, 1994.

N. Zeilberger. Focusing and higher-order abstract syntax. In G. C. Necula and P. Wadler, editors, *Proc. of the 35th ACM Symp. on Principles of Programming Languages, POPL 2008*, pages 359–369. ACM Press, 2008a. ISBN 978-1-59593-689-9.

N. Zeilberger. On the unity of duality. *Ann. Pure Appl. Logic*, 153(1-3): 66–96, 2008b.

N. Zeilberger. *The Logical Basis of Evaluation Order and Pattern-Matching*. PhD thesis, Carnegie Mellon University, 2009.

A. Agda Examples

The development version of Agda has experimental support for copatterns which can be turned on by option `--copatterns`. In the following we present a few examples for copatterns in Agda syntax.

Colists Colists have a coinductive type with an embedded variant type. In Agda this is represented as mutual recursion between a coinductive record type and a data type.

```
mutual
  data μColist (A : Set) : Set where
    []   : μColist A
    _::_ : (x : A) (xs : νColist A) → μColist A
  record νColist (A : Set) : Set where
    coinductive
    field out : μColist A
open νColist
```

Our first function lets us append a νColist to a List. It is defined by recursion on the list.

```
open import Data.List using (List; []; _::_; map; concatMap)
append : {A : Set} → List A → νColist A → νColist A
out (append []        ys) = out ys
out (append (x :: xs) ys) = x :: append xs ys
```

Note the overloading of constructor _::_ for lists and colists.

We can also define a zipWith function for colists defined as a pair of mutually recursive functions. One is acting on νColist, the other acting on μColist.

```
mutual
  zipWith : {A B C : Set} → (A → B → C) →
            νColist A → νColist B → νColist C
  out (zipWith f xs ys) = zipWithμ f (out xs) (out ys)
  zipWithμ : {A B C : Set} → (A → B → C) →
             μColist A → μColist B → μColist C
  zipWithμ f []        ys        = []
  zipWithμ f (x :: xs) []        = []
  zipWithμ f (x :: xs) (y :: ys) = (f x y) :: (zipWith f xs ys)
```

Another example is an unfold function. Suppose we have a set of states S and a set of values A corresponding to the observation we do at some particular state. Then, given a function taking a current state and outputting a new state and its value, or no state at all if it is a terminal state, and given an initial state, we can build a colist of values of all states visited.

```
open import Data.Maybe using (Maybe; nothing; just)
open import Data.Product using (_×_; _,_)
mutual
  unfold : {A S : Set} → (S → Maybe (A × S)) → S →
           νColist A
  out (unfold f s) = unfoldμ f (f s)
  unfoldμ : {A S : Set} → (S → Maybe (A × S)) →
            Maybe (A × S) → μColist A
  unfoldμ f (just (a, s)) = a :: unfold f s
  unfoldμ f nothing       = []
```

Breadth-first traversal of non-wellfounded tree Finitely branching but potentially infinite deep trees can be represented by a coinductive record with two fields, a label and a list subs of subtrees.

```
record νTree (A : Set) : Set where
  coinductive
  field label : A
        subs  : List (νTree A)
open νTree
```

If we have a forest List (νTree A), we can extract the labels in a breadth-first manner by first taking all the roots, then concatenating all the subtrees and recurse. To ensure productivity, we distinguish the empty forest from the non-empty forest.

```
bf : {A : Set} → List (νTree A) → νColist A
out (bf [])        = []
out (bf (t :: ts)) = label t ::
                       append (map label ts)
                              (bf (concatMap subs (t :: ts)))
```

bf is productive since it is guarded-by-constructors [Coquand 1993]: it directly outputs either the empty colist or the non-empty colist, and since append xs ys only adds elements in front of ys. The latter is not yet tracked by Agda's termination and productivity checker, thus, the termination checker rejects this code. Productivity checking using sized types, as realized in MiniAgda, does work for bf, and it is our goal to bring coinduction in Agda to the same level of expressiveness as in MiniAgda.

Cache and I/O Efficient Functional Algorithms

Guy E. Blelloch Robert Harper

Carnegie Mellon University

guyb@cs.cmu.edu rwh@cs.cmu.edu

Abstract

The widely studied I/O and ideal-cache models were developed to account for the large difference in costs to access memory at different levels of the memory hierarchy. Both models are based on a two level memory hierarchy with a fixed size primary memory (cache) of size M, an unbounded secondary memory organized in blocks of size B. The cost measure is based purely on the number of block transfers between the primary and secondary memory. All other operations are free. Many algorithms have been analyzed in these models and indeed these models predict the relative performance of algorithms much more accurately than the standard RAM model. The models, however, require specifying algorithms at a very low level requiring the user to carefully lay out their data in arrays in memory and manage their own memory allocation.

In this paper we present a cost model for analyzing the memory efficiency of algorithms expressed in a simple functional language. We show how some algorithms written in standard forms using just lists and trees (no arrays) and requiring no explicit memory layout or memory management are efficient in the model. We then describe an implementation of the language and show provable bounds for mapping the cost in our model to the cost in the ideal-cache model. These bound imply that purely functional programs based on lists and trees with no special attention to any details of memory layout can be as asymptotically as efficient as the carefully designed imperative I/O efficient algorithms. For example we describe an $O(\frac{n}{B}\log_{M/B}\frac{n}{B})$ cost sorting algorithm, which is optimal in the ideal cache and I/O models.

Categories and Subject Descriptors D.3.1 [*Programming Languages*]: Formal Definitions and Theory; F.2.2 [*Analysis of Algorithms and Problem Complexity*]: Tradeoffs and Complexity Measures; F.3.2 [*Logics and Meanings of Programs*]: Semantics of Programming Languages

General Terms Algorithms, Design, Languages, Performance, Theory.

Keywords cost semantics, I/O algorithms

1. Introduction

On today's computers there is a vast difference in cost for accessing different levels of the memory hierarchy, whether it be registers, one of many levels of cache, the main memory, or a disk. On current processors, for example, there is over a factor of a hundred between the time to access a register and main memory, and another factor of a hundred or so between main memory and disk, even a solid state disk (SSD). This variance in costs is contrary to the standard Random Access Machine (RAM) model, which assumes that the cost of accessing memory is uniform. To account for non uniformity several cost models have been developed that assign difference costs to different levels of the memory hierarchy. The widely used I/O [2] and ideal-cache [9] models both assume a two level memory hierarchy with a fixed size primary memory (cache) of size M, an unbounded secondary memory partitioned into blocks of size B. Cost is measured in terms of the number of block transfers between primary and secondary memory—all other operations are considered free. The parameters M and B are considered variables for the sake of analysis and therefore show up in asymptotic bounds.

Algorithms that do well in these models are often referred to as I/O efficient or cache efficient—in this paper we will generically use the term cache efficient. The theory of cache efficient algorithms is now well developed (see e.g. the surveys [4, 6, 10, 15, 17, 22]) and the models indeed much more accurately capture the relative cost of algorithms on real machines than the RAM model does. This is true both in the context of algorithms that must run off disk when there is not enough main memory, and also in the context of algorithms that can fit in main memory, but not in various levels of the cache. For example, the models properly indicate that a blocked or hierarchical matrix-matrix multiply is much more efficient than the naïve triply nested loop ($\Theta\left(\frac{n^3}{B\sqrt{M}}\right)$ vs. $\Theta(n^3)$). In the RAM they have equal costs. The models also indicate that properly implemented versions of mergesort and quicksort are reasonably cache efficient but that samplesort and multiway mergesort are more efficient, and in fact optimal. Correspondingly all the fastest disk sorts indeed use some variant of samplesort or multiway mergesort, as the theory predicts [19].

Although the study of cache efficient algorithms has been very successful in identifying algorithms that are fast in practice, not surprisingly designing and programming algorithms for these models requires a careful layout of memory and careful management of space. Both temporal and spatial locality is critical in achieving good bounds. Spatial locality is important since memory is moved in blocks of size B, corresponding to either cache lines or memory pages. For example although merging two arrays of integers is reasonably efficient, the cost of merging two linked lists will depend on how the links are laid out in memory and needs to be considered with care. Care is also needed when allocating and freeing memory since touching unused memory incurs a cache miss. It is therefore important to reuse freed space immediately rather than returning it to a pool which might be evicted by the time it is reused—a generic memory allocator or garbage collection scheme will likely not do the right thing. To properly manage this problem, memory

POPL'13, January 23–25, 2013, Rome, Italy.

is typically preallocated and fully managed by the user/algorithm designer.

Needless to say, this form of programming is inconsistent with functional programming, especially when using recursive data types such as lists or trees. However, it is known experimentally that by using certain standard memory allocation schemes purely functional programs (no side effects) can be reasonably cache efficient with regards to both spatial and temporal locality [7, 8, 12, 23]. We give two examples.

Firstly, consider applying `map` with some simple function (e.g. increment) over a list of integers, and then applying the same `map` to the output. If the allocator keeps a pointer that gets incremented on each allocation, then after the first `map` all the cells of the list will be allocated adjacently. On the second `map` since the allocations are adjacent, reading the whole list will only incur $O(n/B)$ cache misses, where B is the block size, and evicting the newly generated blocks will also incur only $O(n/B)$ misses. This gives $O(n/B)$ cost, which asymptotically matches the cost of an optimal array version in an imperative setting. If the list were in an arbitrary order, the cost would be $O(n)$. All we have done is noted that the temporal locality of the allocations will lead to spatial locality of how they are laid out in memory.

Secondly, consider a block recursive matrix multiply on two $n \times n$ matrices. Such an algorithm will never require more than $O(n^2)$ live space but if recursion stops at problems of a constant size it will allocate a total of $O(n^3)$ space. Assuming that the maximum live space fits within the cache we should be able to run our matrix multiply with only $O(n^2/B)$ cache misses, needed for loading the two matrices and storing the result, but this would require being careful about reusing freed space that is already in cache. Fortunately generational garbage collectors have approximately this effect [8]. In particular if we make the first generation smaller than the size of the cache (M) then we will reclaim the memory whenever the allocation area fills, and reuse memory that is already in cache. This does not quite work in general since what is live at the time of the minor collection might get bumped from cache, but it gives some indication that it is not hopeless to make the natural recursive matrix multiply algorithm, as well as similar recursive algorithms, cache efficient.

We show that one can indeed implement cache-efficient algorithms in a call-by-value functional setting using recursive data types, and get provably efficient bounds on cache complexity. In particular we show that one can express algorithms at a high level using standard techniques and achieve optimal asymptotic performance when implemented on the ideal cache. Of course we do not expect the algorithm designer to understand the intricacies the garbage collector works in order to analyze their algorithm. Instead our approach consist of providing a reasonably high-level cost semantics that abstracts away from implementation details such as the garbage collection method, but still admits precise analysis of the cost of an algorithm on a two-level memory architecture. We then describe a provably-efficient implementation of the language on the ideal-cache model. We show that by using this implementation the costs analyzed in the high-level cost model asymptotically match the number of cache misses in the underlying ideal-cache model. The general idea of using high-level cost models based on a cost semantics along with a provable efficient implementation that maps the cost onto a lower level machine model has previously been used in the context of parallel cost models [5, 11, 13, 21].

Our high-level cost model consists of an operational semantics for a call-by-value variant of PCF in which we make explicit the allocation of and access to data objects. The store consists of three parts: a main memory, an allocation cache and a read cache. Both caches have size M and the memory is organized in blocks of size B (both measured in terms of abstract data objects). Data can migrate from the allocation cache to memory and from memory to the read cache, always in blocks of size B. Allocations are made in the allocation cache, and if the number of live objects in the cache exceeds M, then the B oldest locations are evicted to memory as a block, having unit cost. The read cache contains a subset of the memory blocks. A read has no cost if its location is in the read or allocation cache, otherwise it requires loading a block from memory into the read cache, having unit cost, and possibly ejecting an existing block. Hence the only costs are for evicting a block from the allocation cache or loading a block into the read cache. Since we are only concerned with measuring the traffic between main memory and cache memory, garbage collection for main memory is not modeled, but we do account for the detection of live objects, and their migration to main memory, when the cache limit is exceeded.

The provable implementation uses a generational collector to maintain the allocation cache. It uses a nursery of size $2M$ and allocates until the space runs out. It then traces the nursery for the live data. If there is $L > M$ live data, then $L - M$ locations are written to memory in blocks of B, leaving the nursery with at most M locations. The implementation allocates the stack in the heap and must amortize the cost of loading old stack frames against other operations since they are not modeled in the high-level cost semantics. We emphasize that the algorithm designer need not know anything about the garbage collector or how the stack is managed to analyze their algorithm; these concepts are only part of the provable implementation. The cost model is described in Section 3 and the provable implementation is described in Sections 4 and 5.

To demonstrate the utility of our approach, in Section 6 we describe some general techniques for analyzing the cost of algorithms in our model and show three examples of how to analyze the cost of algorithms in the model: mergeSort, k-way mergeSort and matrix multiply. Importantly our results on sorting and matrix multiply match the bounds for algorithms implemented directly in the ideal-cache model ($O\left(\frac{n}{B}\log_{M/B}\frac{n}{B}\right)$ and $O\left(\frac{n^3}{B\sqrt{N}}\right)$ respectively). The bounds for sorting are optimal. Because of our provable implementation bounds these results imply that on the ideal-cache model our algorithms written in a functional style using lists and trees are asymptotically as efficient as the low-level imperative programs. To analyze the algorithms we introduce the notion of a data structure being compact with respect to a traversal order. This is the way we capture the spatial locality of data structures in a language that has no explicit way to express memory layout.

Related Work

Although there has been a large amount of experimental work on showing how good garbage collection can lead to efficient use of caches and disks ([7, 8, 12, 23] and many references in [14]), we know of none that try to prove bounds for algorithms for functional programs when manipulating recursive data types such as lists or trees. Abello et. al. [1] show how a functional style can be used to design cache efficient graph algorithms. They however assume that data structures are in arrays (called lists), and that primitives for operations such as sorting, map, filter and reductions are supplied and implemented with optimal asymptotic cost (presumably at a lower level using imperative code). Their goal is therefore to design graph algorithms by composing these high-level operations on collections. They do not explain how to deal with garbage collection or memory management.

2. Background

I/O and Caching Models

The two-level I/O model of Aggarwal and Vitter [2] assumes a memory hierarchy consisting of main memory of size M and an unbounded secondary memory.[1] Both memories are partitioned into blocks of size B of consecutive memory locations. All computation must be performed from main memory, which is treated like a standard RAM, but there is an additional instruction for moving a block of memory from secondary memory to main memory and one for moving the other way. The cost of an algorithm is analyzed in terms of the number of block transfers—the cost of operations within the main memory is ignored. Many algorithms can be analyzed in this model and it is perhaps surprising how accurately it is able to capture the relative performance of algorithms. In their original work, for example, Aggarwal and Vitter showed tight upper and lower bounds for sorting n keys, with I/O cost $\Theta\left(\frac{n}{B}\log_{M/B}\frac{n}{B}\right)$. The two algorithm that match this bound are a multiway mergesort and a distribution sort, which are the standard algorithms used for disk based sorting, and they both perform significantly better than quicksort or standard mergesort. These algorithms are more efficient since they do not need to pass over the data as many times.

The I/O model can capture either the distinction between cache and main memory or between main memory and disk. In the first case the memory size corresponds to the cache size and the block size to the cache-line size, and in the second case the memory size corresponds to the main memory size and the block size to the page size (or whatever the transfer size between the disk and main memory is). One might note, however, that while the I/O model assumes two address spaces and the user explicitly moves data between them, a machine with caches assumes a single address space and makes its own decisions about what gets evicted from cache, e.g., using a least recently used (LRU) policy.

The ideal-cache model [9] can be used to better model a cache. It is similar to the I/O model but assumes the primary memory is treated as a cache with an ideal eviction policy. In particular the programmer only accesses one address space and a block is brought into the cache when a memory location is accessed whose block is not already in cache. Bringing in a block might require evicting another block from the cache. The model assumes that the best decision is always made, which is to evict the line used furthest in the future (the optimal off-line replacement policy). Since in practice we don't know the future, this is not possible on-line, but it is proved by Sleator and Tarjan's seminal work on competitive paging [20] that an LRU policy is always competitive with the optimal strategy (within constant factors in time and cache size). Therefore from a theoretical point of view the models are asymptotically the same. In this paper we will be using the ideal-cache model for simplicity although the results are also apply to the I/O model.

The ideal-cache model is often used in the context of cache-oblivious algorithms. These are simply algorithms for which the algorithm does not make any decisions based on the cache parameters M and B, although of course the analysis of cache complexity will depend on M and B. The advantage of cache-oblivious algorithms is that since they are oblivious to the cache parameters they work across multiple levels of a cache hierarchy simultaneously. Most of the algorithms in this paper are cache oblivious, but our k-way mergesort is not. We leave it as an open question whether it is possible to develop an I/O-efficient cache-oblivious sorting algorithm in our model.

Cache Efficient Algorithms

We now review some basic well known results on cache efficient algorithms in the imperative setting. The functional algorithms we present in Section 6 are based on the algorithms described here, but do not require arrays or explicitly memory management. We first consider mergesort. Throughout our discussion we assume that the elements being sorted each fit in a single machine word. All cache efficient algorithms we know of for sorting store the input and output elements directly in arrays.

First consider merging two arrays of keys A and B into an output array C of length n (as usual we assume the inputs are sorted in A and B in increasing order). The standard sequential algorithm for merging starts at the beginning of each array keeping a finger on each, finding the the lesser of the two keys at the fingers, copying this key to C, and incrementing the appropriate finger. This algorithm has a cache complexity $O(n/B)$ as long as $M \geq 3B$. This can be seen by noting that at any given time we only need one block from each of A, B and C resident in cache, and that we fully process the block before needing the next block. Therefore every block is only needed once.

For mergesort we assume the standard divide-and-conquer version, which recursively sorts each half of the array and then merges the result. Since merging as described cannot be done in place we have to be specific on how to manage memory. In particular allocating a new array for the result and then freeing the two old arrays using a general purpose memory allocator will likely not lead to the desired bounds (unless one can ensure special properties of the memory allocator). Instead the algorithm needs to pre-allocate a temporary array of length n and pass parts of this array to all subcalls. In particular mergesort could take as arguments both the input array and an equal length temporary array. The result is returned in the input array and the temporary array is used to merge into. Although these optimizations are relatively obvious and standard to programmers of imperative code, we bring them up to emphasize the care that needs to be taken to ensure the cache bounds—it is not simply an issue of reducing the number of calls to the memory allocator, it can actually asymptotically affect the cache bounds.

The cache complexity of this mergesort can be analyzed by considering two cases. The first is when the full computation fits in cache. In this case the two arrays need only be loaded into cache once and all the work can be done in cache. The problem fits in cache as long as $2n + \log n \leq M$, where the $\log n$ accounts for the stack size. The second case is when the problem does not fit in cache. In this case we have to pay for the cache misses on the two recursive calls plus the cache misses of the merge. This gives the following recurrence for the cache complexity $Q(n)$:

$$Q(n) \quad = \quad \begin{cases} 2Q(\frac{n}{2}) + O(\frac{n}{B}) & 2n + \log n > M \\ O(\frac{n}{B}) & \text{otherwise} \end{cases} \qquad (1)$$

The solution to this recurrence can be derived by noting that the top $\log_2(2n/M)$ levels of the recursion do not fit in memory while the lower levels do. The total cache complexity across each of the upper levels is $O(n/B)$ so the total overall cache complexity is $O(n/B \log_2(n/M))$. We note that this does not match the optimal cache complexity for sorting but is significantly better than simply assuming every access is a cache miss—specifically, a factor of $B \log n/(\log n - \log M)$ better. For sorting 10^{12} words in a memory with 10^9 words and a block size of 10^3 words, it is about a factor of about 4000 better. Quicksort has basically the same complexity as mergesort, although in the expected case. This is because scanning the input array to split it into the lesser and larger elements can be done using two fingers like in merging so again each block only needs to be loaded once.

We now describe a sort that is optimal for the I/O model. The idea is instead of partitioning the input array into two and recursively calling sort on each, to partition the input array into k parts, sort each part, and then merge all the parts. Since instead of having just two arrays to merge we have k arrays, we require a k-way merge. Without going into too much detail, such a merge

[1] Aggarwal and Vitter also considered a version of the model with "parallel" disk access, but most interesting results are explained with the single disk version.

can be implemented using one block of memory for each of the inputs needing to be merged as well as one block for the output. We keep a finger on each input and on each step select the minimum key at the fingers, move it to the output buffer and increment that finger. As long as all input blocks, the output block and any data for maintaining the fingers fit in cache, then the k-way merge will run with cache complexity $O(n/B)$, which is the same as the binary merge. Since there will be k input blocks and 1 output blocks, the space needed for the blocks is $(k+1)B$. Therefore accounting for overheads everything will fit in cache as long as $ckB \leq M$, or equivalently $k \leq M/(cB)$ for some constant c. We therefore pick k to be as large as possible, giving $k = M/(cB)$ As in the two way merge we need to be careful about allocation and preallocate temporary arrays to copy the output. We again can analyze the algorithm by considering the case when the problem fits in memory and when it does not. This gives the recurrence:

$$Q(n) \quad = \quad \begin{cases} \frac{M}{B}Q(\frac{n}{M/cB}) + O(\frac{n}{B}) & nc' > M \\ O(\frac{n}{B}) & \text{otherwise} \end{cases} \qquad (2)$$

where c and c' are constants, but n, B and M are variables. This solves to $O(n/B \log_{M/B}(n/B))$. This bound matches the lower bound for sorting in the I/O model [2] and hence also the ideal-cache model. The k-way mergesort is therefore asymptotically optimal.

3. Cost Semantics

In this section we define an *evaluation dynamics* that assigns a cost to a complete execution of a program. Following the I/O model, the cost measures the *cache complexity*, which is defined to be the traffic caused by the transfer of objects between the main memory and the memory cache. Accesses to objects in cache are considered to be cost-free, whereas migration of objects from cache into memory and from memory into the cache are charged unit cost. The dynamics is based on a two-level model of storage that includes a fixed-size allocation cache and a fixed-size read cache together with a main memory of unbounded size.

The evaluation dynamics provides the basis for assessing both the correctness and the cache complexity of programs. It is formulated at a sufficiently abstract level to free the programmer from having to reason directly about the compiler and run-time system, but is sufficiently concrete as to admit an implementation with a provable bound on its cache complexity. Thus, we may achieve the same overall results as are obtained using only low-level machine models in previous work on I/O algorithms, while working at the much more practical level of abstraction offered by functional programming languages.

We give the dynamics of a call-by-value variant of Plotkin's PCF language [18]. The syntax of expressions is summarized by the following grammar:

$$\begin{array}{rcl} e & ::= & x \mid \mathtt{z} \mid \mathtt{s}(e) \mid \mathtt{ifz}(e; e_0; x.e_1) \mid \\ & & \mathtt{fun}(x, y.e) \mid \mathtt{app}(e_1; e_2) \end{array}$$

The conditional tests whether a number is zero or not, and passes the predecessor to the non-zero case. Functions are equipped with a name for themselves to allow for recursion. The typing rules are standard, and are omitted here for the sake of concision. (See, for example, Chapter 10 of [13].)

For illustrative purposes natural numbers are treated as heap-allocated data structures of unbounded size (as will become evident shortly). It is straightforward to extend the language to account for a richer variety of data structures, including sum, product, finite sequence, and recursive types, and to account for typical hardware-oriented concepts such as machine words and floating point numbers.

Storage Model

Following Morrisett, *et al.* [16], the dynamics distinguishes *large* from *small* values, with large values being allocated in memory and represented by a location, and small values being those that are manipulated directly. In the present case the only small values are locations, but it is also possible to consider, for example, fixed-sized numbers as forms of small value. Correspondingly, all other forms of value (numbers and functions) are large. We also allocate *stack frames*, which reify the control state of evaluation, in memory. A *memory object* is either a large value of a stack frame.

The two-level memory model is parameterized by two constants, the *block size* B, and the *cache size* $M = c \times B$ determined by some constant c representing the number of blocks in the cache.

A *memory* μ is a finite mapping assigning a memory object to each of a finite set dom(μ) of abstract locations. The memory may grow without bound. (We do not consider here the separate problem of garbage collection for main memory, for which see Morrisett, *et al.* [16].) As a technical convenience, we assume that locations are divided into two classes, *value locations*, l, and *stack locations*, s, and require that a memory map value locations to large values and stack locations to stack frames. When the distinction is immaterial, we speak simply of locations and objects in memory.

A memory μ comes equipped with an equivalence relation $l \equiv_\mu l'$ over dom(μ) specifying that l and l' are *neighbors* in μ. Additionally, we require that each equivalence class in the domain of a memory is of size B. A memory whose domain consists of a single equivalence class of size B is called a *block*. The *neighborhood* nbhd(μ, l) of a location $l \in \text{dom}(\mu)$ is the restriction of μ to the neighbors of l in μ, a single block. The *expansion* $\mu \oplus \beta$ of a memory μ by a block β such that $\text{dom}(\beta) \cap \text{dom}(\mu) = \emptyset$ is the memory μ' that agrees with μ and β on their respective domains and for which $l \equiv_{\mu'} l'$ iff $l \equiv_\mu l'$ or $l \equiv_\beta l'$.

There are two forms of cache mediating access to memory. A *read cache* ρ for a memory μ is the restriction of μ to a finite set of locations of size at most M. The *contraction* $\rho \ominus \beta$ of a read cache ρ by a block $\beta \subseteq \rho$ is the read cache ρ' such that $\rho = \rho' \oplus \beta$. A *nursery* ν is a finite mapping that associates an object to each a finite set dom(ν) of locations. A nursery comes equipped with a linear ordering $l \prec_\nu l'$ of dom(ν), called the *allocation ordering*. If $l \prec_\nu l'$ we say that l is older than l' and that l' is newer than l in ν. The *extension* $\nu[l \mapsto o]$ of a nursery ν binding a location $l \notin \text{dom}(\mu)$ to an object o is the nursery ν' such that (1) $\nu'(l) = o$ and $\nu'(l') = \nu(l')$ for each $l' \in \text{dom}(\nu)$, and (2) $l' \prec_{\nu'} l$ for every $l' \in \text{dom}(\nu)$. The *contraction* $\nu \ominus \beta$ of a nursery ν by a block $\beta \subseteq \nu$ is the restriction of ν to $\text{dom}(\nu) \setminus \text{dom}(\beta)$.

The *live* locations live(R, ν) in a nursery ν relative to a subset $R \subseteq \text{dom}(\nu)$ consists of those locations in dom(ν) that are (transitively) reachable from locations in R. The *scan* scan(R, ν) of a nursery ν with respect to a subset $R \subseteq \text{dom}(\nu)$ is the block β of consisting of the oldest B live locations in live(R, ν). (See Morrisett, *et al.* [16] for formal definitions of these standard concepts.) It will be an invariant of the dynamics that the nursery contains at most M live objects relative to the roots of the computation.

A *store* σ is a triple (μ, ρ, ν) consisting of a memory μ, a read cache ρ for μ, and a nursery ν such that $\text{dom}(\nu) \cap \text{dom}(\mu) = \emptyset$. The *domain* of a store σ is defined by $\text{dom}(\sigma) = \text{dom}(\mu) \cup \text{dom}(\nu)$. An *initial store* is a store in which the main memory contains only large values and in which the read cache and allocation area are empty.

Evaluation Dynamics

The overall goal of the evaluation dynamics is to define the evaluation of a closed expression by an inductive definition of a relation between an expression and its value, which is always small, and its cost, a non-negative integer. The cost is computed by tracking the

$$\frac{\sigma \,@\, \mathtt{z} \uparrow^n_R \sigma' \,@\, l'}{\sigma \,@\, \mathtt{z} \Downarrow^n_R \sigma' \,@\, l'} \tag{3a}$$

$$\frac{\left\{\begin{array}{c} \sigma \,@\, \mathtt{s}(-) \uparrow^n_{R \cup \mathrm{locs}(e')} \sigma' \,@\, s' \quad \sigma' \,@\, e' \Downarrow^{n'}_{R \cup \{s'\}} \sigma'' \,@\, l'' \\ \sigma'' \,@\, \mathtt{s}(l'') \uparrow^{n''}_R \sigma''' \,@\, l''' \end{array}\right\}}{\sigma \,@\, \mathtt{s}(e') \Downarrow^{n+n'+n''}_R \sigma''' \,@\, l'''} \tag{3b}$$

$$\frac{\left\{\begin{array}{c} \sigma \,@\, \mathtt{ifz}(-; e_2; x.e_3) \uparrow^{n_1}_{R \cup \mathrm{locs}(e_1)} \sigma_1 \,@\, s_1 \\ \sigma_1 \,@\, e_1 \Downarrow^{n_1'}_{R \cup \{s_1\}} \sigma_1' \,@\, l_1' \\ \sigma_1' \,@\, l_1' \downarrow^{n_1''} \sigma_2 \,@\, \mathtt{z} \quad \sigma_2 \,@\, e_2 \Downarrow^{n_2}_R \sigma' \,@\, l' \end{array}\right\}}{\sigma \,@\, \mathtt{ifz}(e_1; e_2; x.e_3) \Downarrow^{n_1+n_1'+n_1''+n_2}_R \sigma' \,@\, l'} \tag{3c}$$

$$\frac{\left\{\begin{array}{c} \sigma \,@\, \mathtt{ifz}(-; e_2; x.e_3) \uparrow^{n_1}_{R \cup \mathrm{locs}(e_1)} \sigma_1 \,@\, s_1 \\ \sigma_1 \,@\, e_1 \Downarrow^{n_1'}_{R \cup \{s_1\}} \sigma_1' \,@\, l_1' \\ \sigma_1' \,@\, l_1' \downarrow^{n_1''} \sigma_3 \,@\, \mathtt{s}(l_1'') \quad \sigma_3 \,@\, [l_1''/x]e_3 \Downarrow^{n_3}_R \sigma' \,@\, l' \end{array}\right\}}{\sigma \,@\, \mathtt{ifz}(e_1; e_2; x.e_3) \Downarrow^{n_1+n_1'+n_1''+n_3}_R \sigma' \,@\, l'} \tag{3d}$$

$$\frac{\sigma \,@\, \mathtt{fun}(x, y.e) \uparrow^n_R \sigma' \,@\, l}{\sigma \,@\, \mathtt{fun}(x, y.e) \Downarrow^n_R \sigma' \,@\, l} \tag{3e}$$

$$\frac{\left\{\begin{array}{c} \sigma \,@\, \mathtt{app}(-; e_2) \uparrow^{n_1}_{R \cup \mathrm{locs}(e_1)} \sigma_1 \,@\, s_1 \quad \sigma_1 \,@\, e_1 \Downarrow^{n_1'}_{R \cup \{s_1\}} \sigma_1' \,@\, l_1' \\ \sigma_1' \,@\, l_1' \downarrow^{n_1''} \sigma_1'' \,@\, \mathtt{fun}(x, y.e) \quad \sigma_1'' \,@\, \mathtt{app}(l_1'; -) \uparrow^{n_1'''}_R \sigma_2 \,@\, s_2 \\ \sigma_2 \,@\, e_2 \Downarrow^{n_2}_{R \cup \{s_2\}} \sigma_2' \,@\, l_2' \quad \sigma_2' \,@\, [l_1', l_2'/x, y]e \Downarrow^{n_2}_R \sigma' \,@\, l' \end{array}\right\}}{\sigma \,@\, \mathtt{app}(e_1; e_2) \Downarrow^{n_1+n_1'+n_1''+n_1'''+n_2+n_2'}_R \sigma' \,@\, l'} \tag{3f}$$

Figure 1. Cost Dynamics

$$\frac{l \in \mathrm{dom}(\rho)}{(\mu, \rho, \nu) \,@\, l \downarrow^0 (\mu, \rho, \nu) \,@\, \rho(l)} \tag{4a}$$

$$\frac{l \in \mathrm{dom}(\nu)}{(\mu, \rho, \nu) \,@\, l \downarrow^0 (\mu, \rho, \nu) \,@\, \nu(l)} \tag{4b}$$

$$\frac{l \notin \mathrm{dom}(\rho) \cup \mathrm{dom}(\nu) \quad |\mathrm{dom}(\rho)| \leq M - B}{(\mu, \rho, \nu) \,@\, l \downarrow^1 (\mu, \rho \oplus \mathrm{nbhd}(\mu, l), \nu) \,@\, \mu(l)} \tag{4c}$$

$$\frac{l \notin \mathrm{dom}(\rho) \cup \mathrm{dom}(\nu) \quad |\mathrm{dom}(\rho)| = M \quad \beta \subseteq \rho}{(\mu, \rho, \nu) \,@\, l \downarrow^1 (\mu, \rho \ominus \beta \oplus \mathrm{nbhd}(\mu, l), \nu) \,@\, \mu(l)} \tag{4d}$$

$$\frac{|\,\mathrm{live}(R \cup \mathrm{locs}(o), \nu)| < M \quad l \notin \mathrm{dom}(\nu)}{(\mu, \rho, \nu) \,@\, o \uparrow^0_R (\mu, \rho, \nu[l \mapsto o]) \,@\, l} \tag{5a}$$

$$\frac{|\,\mathrm{live}(R \cup \mathrm{locs}(o), \nu)| = M \quad \beta = \mathrm{scan}(R \cup \mathrm{locs}(o), \nu) \quad l \notin \mathrm{dom}(\nu)}{(\mu, \rho, \nu) \,@\, o \uparrow^1_R (\mu \oplus \beta, \rho, (\nu \ominus \beta)[l \mapsto o]) \,@\, l} \tag{5b}$$

Figure 2. Reading and Allocation

movement of objects among the components of the store, charging one unit of cost whenever a block of objects must be moved to or copied from main memory, and charging zero cost otherwise. (So, for example, a computation that runs entirely in cache will be assigned zero cost, consistently with the I/O model.) To account for the memory traffic involving values, the dynamics makes explicit the allocation of objects in the nursery, their eviction to main memory when the capacity of the nursery is exceeded, and their movement into the read cache as they are required by the computation. To account for the memory traffic attributable to the implicit control stack, the dynamics also allocates (but does not otherwise use) stack frames, and ensures that any data that would appear in the stack is kept live by the dynamics.

These considerations lead to the evaluation judgment

$$\sigma \,@\, e \Downarrow^n_R \sigma' \,@\, l$$

stating that the expression e, when evaluated with respect to a store σ such that $\mathrm{dom}(\sigma) \supseteq \mathrm{locs}(e)$ and to roots $R \subseteq \mathrm{dom}(\sigma)$, results in a modified store σ', a location l representing the (large) value of the expression, and a cost n representing the cache complexity of the execution. The modifications to the store consist of allocations in the nursery, migrations of objects from the nursery to the main memory, and copying of objects from the main memory to the read cache. All memory traffic occurs in blocks of B objects, corresponding to loading a cache line or reading a block from disk. The roots R represent locations that are to be kept live by virtue of their being present in the implicit control stack or expression under evaluation.

The evaluation judgment is defined by the rules in Figure 1, making use of two auxiliary judgments for reading and allocating objects defined in Figure 2. It may be helpful to read through the rules once while ignoring all but the evaluation judgments to see that the rules define a conventional eager dynamics for a functional language. On such a reading the root set plays no role, and can be ignored. Moreover, the cost assignment has no significance under such a simplification.

Next, let us consider the roles of the *read* judgments $\sigma \,@\, l \downarrow^n o \,@\, \sigma'$ and the *allocate* judgments $\sigma \,@\, v \uparrow^n_R \sigma' \,@\, l$, where v is a value, in the dynamics. The quoted read judgment states that the result of reading location l in store σ results in the object o and the modified store σ', and has cost $n = 0$ or $n = 1$. The cost is non-zero only if the read causes a block to be loaded into the read cache. The modified store represents the possible effect of loading a block into the read cache. The quoted write judgment states that allocating the large value v in store σ results in a modified store σ' and location $l \in \mathrm{dom}(\sigma')$, and has cost $n = 0$ or $n = 1$. The cost is non-zero only if the allocation causes the eviction of a block from the nursery in order to maintain the live-size invariant. The read and allocate operations in the dynamics record the memory traffic engendered by the creation and examination of values during computation.

It remains to consider the role of the allocation judgments of the form $\sigma \,@\, s \uparrow^n_R \sigma' \,@\, f$, which represent the allocation of a stack frame in the store at stack location s. The purpose of allocating these frames is purely to ensure that the cost assigned to a computation is accurate with respect to the underlying implementation. Although an evaluation semantics has no explicit control stack, it is nevertheless the case that an implementation must allocate space for the representation of the control state, and this space allocation does influence the cache behavior of the computation. It may not, therefore, be ignored. Our method for accounting for the memory effects of the control stack is to allocate explicitly frames that would appear in the control stack to ensure that space usage is properly accounted for, and that required liveness information (to be detailed shortly) is properly maintained. The frames are denoted as $\mathtt{app}(-; e_2)$ and $\mathtt{app}(l'_1; -)$ in the cost dynamics.

With this in mind, let us examine in detail Rule 3f in Figure 1. We are to evaluate and determine the cost of $\mathtt{app}(e_1; e_2)$ in store σ with given roots R. First, we allocate a stack frame s_1 representing the pending evaluation of e_2 during the evaluation of e_1. This frame is now considered live, even though it does not appear in any expression under consideration. Accordingly, we evaluate e_1 relative to the store containing this frame, treating the just-allocated stack pointer to be live (as indicated by $\Downarrow_{R\cup\{s_1\}}$). This results in a location l'_1, which we then read from the store to obtain a function abstraction (as would be guaranteed by the static type discipline omitted here). We then create another frame s_2 corresponding to the suspended application of the function at location l'_1, and evaluate e_2 with this stack pointer considered live (as indicated by $\Downarrow_{R\cup\{s_2\}}$) to obtain location l'_2. Finally, we evaluate the function body, replacing the "self" variable by l'_1 and the argument by l'_2. The overall cost of the computation is the sum of the costs of each of these steps, which are given either inductively or by the uses of the read and allocate judgments. Observe that this rule properly accounts for tail recursion in that no extra space is held during tail recursive calls (as indicated by $\Downarrow_R$).

It remains to explain the read and allocate judgments defined in Figure 2. The read judgment assigns cost zero to any read from a location in either the nursery or the read cache (Rules 4b and 4a). Such reads have no effects, and hence induce no cache traffic. A read of a location that is only in main memory induces a load of the neighborhood of that location (a block of memory) into the read cache. If there is sufficient room for it in the read cache, the block is added to the cache and the contents is returned, at a cost of one unit (Rule 4c). If there is insufficient room in the read cache, a block is selected non-deterministically to be replaced by the required block, and once again a unit cost is charged to the read (Rule 4d). At the end of the section we discuss the use of non-deterministic eviction.

The allocate judgement defines the procedure for creating new objects in the store. Of course, new objects are considered newer in the allocation ordering than the objects already present in the nursery. If the new object fits within the nursery, it is allocated there at zero cost (Rule 5a). If the new object will not fit within the nursery, then the block consisting of the oldest B live objects in the nursery is evicted to main memory, making room for the newly allocated object; such an allocation is charged unit cost (Rule 5b). It is important to our method that the oldest objects be evicted from the cache as a block forming the neighborhood of each of its locations. Whether an object fits within the nursery is determined as follows. The nursery is *full* if the number of *live* objects in it is exactly M. (It is for the sake of assessing liveness that the allocation judgment is parameterized by a root set.) Eviction of a block reduces this to at most $M - B$ objects, so that the next $B - 1$ allocations will not cause an eviction. Thus we are, in effect, charging at most $1/B$ units of cost to each allocation (less if objects die before needing to be evicted).

It is essential to our results that the liveness of objects in the nursery may be assessed *without accessing main memory*. Given roots R we need only trace objects in the nursery itself, and need never consider locations lying outside of it. This is ensured by two properties of the dynamics. First, since the model is purely functional, the dependency graph of objects in the nursery is acyclic; an object may only refer to objects allocated earlier in the computation as defined by the allocation ordering. Second, implicit stack frames are explicitly allocated in the nursery to ensure that liveness may be assessed solely by examining the nursery itself, starting from the root set. Put another way, an object in the nursery cannot be live solely because of a pointer from main memory back to the nursery. This property is a consequence of immutability and the explicit allocation of stack frames in the semantics.

In Section 6 we will make use of a *deep copy* operation on values of certain types. In the illustrative language considered here this operation is definable on natural numbers as follows:

$$\mathtt{fun}(copy, x.\mathtt{ifz}(x; \mathtt{z}; x'.\mathtt{s}(\mathtt{app}(copy; x')))).$$

Calling this function on a number n has the effect of creating a "fresh copy" of n in the heap. No such operation is definable, or required, for function types. Deep copying is easily extended to product, sum, and inductive types, but would need to be provided as a primitive for base types such as fixed precision integers or floating point numbers.

Discussion

We briefly discuss some of the motivation for the decisions we made in formulating the dynamic semantics. The overall goal is to allow a simple analysis for the algorithm developer while capturing all the costs needed to prove asymptotic implementation bounds.

The separate allocation cache is important both for convenience of analysis and properly accounting for costs. It ensures that all short lived allocations never need to be allocated to memory. For a subcomputation in which the maximum footprint of live data allocated fits in the allocation cache, the user need not worry about any costs for any temporary memory. In a block matrix multiply on $n \times n$ matrices, for example, once $kn^2 \leq M$ for some small constant k, the only cost that needs be considered is the cost of reading the input and evicting the output. This is the case even though the multiply will allocate a total of $\Theta(n^3)$ space. It is also important that the partitioning of locations into blocks is not decided until locations are evicted from the allocation cache, which ensures that only live data is ever migrated to memory. If blocking were to be decided on allocation, for example, then by the time the objects are evicted most of the objects in a block may no longer be live. This would break the bounds we give in Section 6.

The cost semantics accounts for the allocation of stack frames in order to account for the space required to manage the control state of evaluation. This is particularly important in the case that no allocation is associated with the creation of a frame, for then there is no possibility to amortize the space required for the frame against the allocated object. Note that the semantics only models the space taken by the frames in the allocation cache and the cost of evicting them. It does not model any costs associated with reloading them into the read cache. As described in the next section, in a lower level model this can be amortized against the cost of evicting the frames in the first place.

It is important that the stack frames be heap allocated. A crucial invariant we require is that all live data in the allocation cache can be determined solely through the caches. If we had a separate stack cache it could allow for the eviction of a stack frame that references data in the allocation cache, breaking the required invariant. There are other techniques to handle this problem but we found that allocating the stack frames in the heap is the easiest.

Our model is non-deterministic in the choice of what block is evicted from the read cache in the case of a read miss. In our provable implementation bounds we show that if there is a (non-deterministic) execution that gives certain cache complexity then we can guarantee those bounds on the ideal cache model (within constant factors). When analyzing an algorithm this allows one to consider any policy for eviction. This is possible because the ideal cache makes the optimal decisions and will therefore be at least as good as the policy the user assumes. The justification for the ideal cache model is given in Section 2.

4. Abstract Machine

The abstract cost of a computation assigned by the evaluation dynamics given in the preceding section is validated in two stages. First, in this section we define an abstract machine with an explicit control stack, and show that the evaluation dynamics accurately predicts the behavior of the abstract machine with respect to both the outcome and the cost of the computation. Second, in Section 5 we show how to implement the basic operations of the abstract machine with only a small overhead. Taken together these two arguments demonstrate that the evaluation semantics provides an accurate model of the cache complexity of a program when implemented as described in these two steps.

The abstract machine takes the form of a labeled transition system between states of two different forms:

1. Evaluation state: $\sigma @ k \rhd e$, where $k \in \mathrm{dom}(\sigma)$ is a stack pointer, and $\mathrm{locs}(e) \subseteq \mathrm{dom}(\sigma)$, stating that e is to be evaluated on stack k relative to store σ.
2. Return state: $\sigma @ k \lhd l$, where $k, l \in \mathrm{dom}(\sigma)$, stating that small value l is to be returned to stack k relative to store σ.

The control stack is represented by a stack location, k, that refers to a linked list of frames, either the empty stack, written $\bullet$, or a frame together with another stack location, written $f;k$. The label on a transition is either 0, 1, or 2, and specifies the amount of work to be charged for that transition.

The rules given in Figure 3 define the abstract machine. Their overall form is standard (see, for example, Chapter 27 of [13]), with the main differences being that allocation and reading of values is made explicit, just as in the evaluation dynamics, and that the stack is explicitly represented as a linked data structure in the store. The multistep transition judgment $s \overset{n}{\mapsto}{}^{*} s'$ means that there is a finite, possibly empty, sequence of transitions from s to s' whose labels sum to n.

THEOREM 4.1 (Correctness of Evaluation Dynamics). *Let σ_0 be an initial store, let e_0 be a closed expression such that $locs(e_0) \subseteq dom(\sigma_0)$. Let the abstract machine be equipped with one additional block in the read cache, and let k_0 be a reserved stack location not used in the evaluation dynamics. If*

$$\sigma_0 @ e_0 \Downarrow^n_{\emptyset} \sigma @ l,$$

then there is an evaluation

$$\sigma_0[k_0 \mapsto \bullet] @ k_0 \rhd e_0 \overset{m}{\mapsto}{}^{*} \sigma'[k_0 \mapsto \bullet] @ k_0 \lhd l'$$

such that

1. *the results are isomorphic, $\sigma @ l \cong \sigma' @ l'$, and*
2. *the cost m is at most $3n$.*

The relation $\sigma @ l \cong \sigma' @ l'$ states that the reachable graph from l in σ is isomorphic to the reachable graph from l' in σ'.

Theorem 4.1 states that the outcome of a computation on the abstract machine is the same, up to choice of locations, as the outcome of the same computation according to the evaluation dynamics. Moreover, the total cost of the machine execution (measured in accordance with the I/O model described earlier) is at most a small constant factor larger than the cost assigned by the evaluation dynamics. The content of the theorem amounts to a proof that the space required by the control stack in a computation may be managed so as not to interfere with space usage of the computation itself.

The correctness proof may be decomposed into three major components. The first obligation is to relate the outcome of the evaluation dynamics to that of the abstract machine, disregarding, for the moment, the cost. The required correspondence is proved

$$\frac{}{\sigma @ k \rhd l \overset{0}{\mapsto} \sigma @ k \lhd l} \quad (6a)$$

$$\frac{\sigma @ \mathtt{z} \uparrow^n_{\{k\}} \sigma' @ l}{\sigma @ k \rhd \mathtt{z} \overset{n}{\mapsto} \sigma' @ k \lhd l} \quad (6b)$$

$$\frac{\sigma @ \mathtt{s}(-);k \uparrow^n_{\mathrm{locs}(e')} \sigma' @ k'}{\sigma @ k \rhd \mathtt{s}(e') \overset{n}{\mapsto} \sigma' @ k' \rhd e'} \quad (6c)$$

$$\frac{\sigma @ k \downarrow^n \sigma' @ \mathtt{s}(-);k' \quad \sigma' @ \mathtt{s}(l) \uparrow^{n'}_{\{k'\}} \sigma'' @ l'}{\sigma @ k \lhd l \xmapsto{n+n'} \sigma'' @ k' \lhd l'} \quad (6d)$$

$$\frac{\sigma @ \mathtt{ifz}(-; e_2; x.e_3);k \uparrow^n_{\mathrm{locs}(e_1)} \sigma' @ k'}{\sigma @ k \rhd \mathtt{ifz}(e_1; e_2; x.e_3) \overset{n}{\mapsto} \sigma' @ k' \rhd e_1} \quad (6e)$$

$$\frac{\sigma @ k \downarrow^{n_1} \sigma' @ \mathtt{ifz}(-; e_2; x.e_3);k' \quad \sigma' @ l \downarrow^{n_2} \sigma'' @ \mathtt{z}}{\sigma @ k \lhd l \xmapsto{n_1+n_2} \sigma'' @ k' \rhd e_2} \quad (6f)$$

$$\frac{\sigma @ k \downarrow^{n_1} \sigma' @ \mathtt{ifz}(-; e_2; x.e_3);k' \quad \sigma' @ l \downarrow^{n_2} \sigma'' @ \mathtt{s}(l')}{\sigma @ k \lhd l \xmapsto{n_1+n_2} \sigma'' @ k' \rhd [l'/x]e_3} \quad (6g)$$

$$\frac{\sigma @ \mathtt{fun}(x, y.e) \uparrow^n_{\{k\}} \sigma' @ l'}{\sigma @ k \rhd \mathtt{fun}(x, y.e) \overset{n}{\mapsto} \sigma' @ k \lhd l'} \quad (6h)$$

$$\frac{\sigma @ \mathtt{app}(-; e_2);k \uparrow^n_{\mathrm{locs}(e_1)} \sigma_1 @ k_1}{\sigma @ k \rhd \mathtt{app}(e_1; e_2) \overset{n}{\mapsto} \sigma_1 @ k_1 \rhd e_1} \quad (6i)$$

$$\frac{\left\{\begin{matrix} \sigma @ k \downarrow^{n_1} \sigma_1 @ \mathtt{app}(-; e_2);k_1 \\ \sigma_1 @ \mathtt{app}(l_1; -);k_1 \uparrow^{n_2}_{\mathrm{locs}(e_2)} \sigma_2 @ k_2 \end{matrix}\right\}}{\sigma @ k \lhd l_1 \xmapsto{n_1+n_2} \sigma_2 @ k_2 \rhd e_2} \quad (6j)$$

$$\frac{\sigma @ k \downarrow^{n_1} \sigma_1 @ \mathtt{app}(l_1; -);k_2 \quad \sigma_1 @ l_1 \downarrow^{n_2} \sigma_2 @ \mathtt{fun}(x, y.e)}{\sigma @ k \lhd l_2 \xmapsto{n_1+n_2} \sigma_2 @ k_2 \rhd [l_1, l_2/x, y]e} \quad (6k)$$

Figure 3. Abstract Machine

by induction on the derivation of evaluation judgment. Specifically, we prove that if $\sigma @ e \Downarrow^n_R \sigma' @ l$, then for any stack pointer k,

$$\sigma @ k \rhd e \mapsto^{*} \sigma @ k \lhd l.$$

The proof proceeds along standard lines, as described, for example, in Chapter 27 of the second author's textbook [13]. The same choice of locations may be made in the machine derivation as were made in the evaluation derivation, because the sequence of value allocations is precisely the same in both forms of dynamics.

The next step of the proof is to show that the abstract machine performs the same sequence of value reads in the same order as specified by the evaluation dynamics. This may be proved along with the correspondence described in the preceding paragraph. The argument relies on two important properties of the evaluation dynamics:

1. Any read of a value location is either a read of a location in the initial store, or a location that was allocated earlier in the evaluation.
2. Stack frames are allocated, but never read, in order to ensure that eviction of blocks from the nursery occurs in exactly the order imposed by the stack-based abstract machine.

A deterministic nursery eviction policy is required to ensure that the memory reads correspond exactly between the evaluation dynamics and the abstract machine. We can assume whatever policy is used the the dynamic semantics is also used by the abstract machine.

It remains to show that the stack reads employed by the abstract machine do not impose an asymptotically significant cost beyond what is predicted by the evaluation dynamics. Without special provision, access to the control stack would interfere with the allocation of data in the read cache, invalidating the cost given to the computation by the evaluation dynamics. To avoid this we make use of a dedicated read cache block in the abstract machine, which we will call the *stack cache block*, and explicitly manage this cache block as follows. Whenever a stack location is read from main memory, its neighborhood is loaded into the stack cache block, evicting the block that currently occupies it. We will argue that the cost of loading the stack cache can be amortized across the execution sequence, even if the same block is loaded into the stack cache more than once, a possibility that will be detailed shortly. The validity of the argument depends on two special properties of the run-time stack, namely that each allocated frame is read exactly once in a complete computation, and that the preceding stack frame is always older than the current one. Given such an amortization, it is then clear that the overall cost of execution on the abstract machine is bounded by a small constant factor of the cost ascribed to it by the evaluation dynamics, establishing the theorem.

To complete the proof, we describe the amortization of the cost of stack management in more detail. As an invariant we put a "dollar" on every memory block that contains a stack frame, except if it is the youngest such block and resides in the stack cache block, in which case it has no "money" associated with it. When the abstract machine evicts a block containing a stack frame from the allocation cache we spend three dollars—one for the eviction itself, one to put a dollar on the evicted block, and one to put a dollar on the block that is in the cache stack block. This third dollar might be needed to maintain our invariant since that block, if there is one, will no longer be the youngest memory block containing a stack frame. Now when the abstract machine loads a block into the stack cache block from memory we spend its dollar for the load. All blocks with older frames have a dollar on them already by the invariant, so the invariant is maintained. In summary we spend 3 block transfers (worst case) per block that is evicted from the allocation cache.

We finally note that there is no need to explicitly maintain the stack cache block in the abstract machine semantics since we are assuming an "ideal cache". Therefore as long as the cache has an extra block available, then the cache policy will do at least as well as the one we described.

5. Provable Implementation

In this section we describe an implementation of the abstract machine given in Section 4 in the ideal cache model with the same asymptotic cost. The efficiency proof for the implementation takes account of two issues that are treated abstractly in the evaluation semantics and in the abstract machine. The main issue is how to implement the allocation judgment defined in Figure 2. Rules 5a and 5b make reference to liveness of the data, and evict a block consisting of the oldest B live objects in the nursery. To ensure that the predicted costs are realized in practice we must argue that these conditions can be met by an implementation. The second issue is that we must account for the size of the stored objects (values and frames) that may appear in a computation, and account for the cost of handling these objects in an implementation.

Define the *size* of a machine state $\sigma_0 @ k_0 \triangleright e_0$ be the sum of the size of e_0 and the size of any function in σ_0. This may be thought of as the size of the program, including any λ-abstractions that may be present in the initial store.

THEOREM 5.1. *Fix an initial state $\sigma_0 @ k_0 \triangleright e_0$ of size s_0, and consider a complete computation*

$$\sigma_0 @ k_0 \triangleright e_0 \overset{m}{\longmapsto} \sigma @ k_0 \triangleleft l$$

with s_1 objects in the final store, σ. This computation be simulated in the ideal cache model with cache complexity $c \times m$ for some constant c, provided that words are of size at least $d \log(\max(s_0, s_1))$ for some $d > 0$ and that the cache has at least $(4M + B) \times s_0$ words. (The constants c and d are independent of σ_0, k_0 and e_0.)

Theorem 5.1 states that the implementation asymptotically realizes the work attributed to the computation by the evaluation semantics, and hence validates the algorithm analysis performed using that semantics.

The requirement on the word size in Theorem 5.1 ensures that all objects are addressable by a word-sized pointer, and accounts for the sizes of the objects themselves in storage. (A closure can be as large as the initial program.) The requirement on the cache size in Theorem 5.1 ensures that we may implement the abstract memory hierarchy with no more than a small constant factor of overhead in a manner that we now describe. (The $B \times s_0$ additional words account for the stack cache described in Section 4; it remains to discuss the implementation of allocation.)

The allocation judgment defined in Figure 2 relies on an assessment of the live size of the nursery, and on the eviction of blocks from the nursery to ensure that the nursery contains no more than M live objects. As we note earlier, the liveness of data in the nursery may be assessed without reference to the main memory; the liveness computation takes place entirely within the cache. Rather than assess liveness, possibly evicting a block, on each allocation, we instead amortize these costs across multiple allocations according to the following strategy. We reserve $2M \times s_0$ words of cache memory for the allocation area to accommodate at least $2M$ objects. Objects are allocated by maintaining a pointer into the nursery area, incrementing it on each allocation until $2M$ objects have been allocated, at which point the nursery space is exhausted. When this occurs, we perform a compacting garbage collection that preserves the allocation order of objects, simultaneously evicting as many blocks as necessary to obtain a live size of M objects in the nursery. After compaction, allocation continues as before until the nursery is again exhausted.

As long as there is sufficient space, allocation takes constant time. When a garbage collection is required, the cost may be attributed to the allocations of the live data in the nursery, so that in an amortized sense garbage collection is cost-free [3]. It is easy to see that no object is evicted to main memory using this implementation that would not have been evicted in the abstract sense. However, the evictions will, in general, happen later than predicted by the semantics. As a result, fewer objects may be live at the time of eviction, and so fewer blocks overall may be moved to main memory. As a result of this compression effect, two locations that were neighbors in the evaluation semantics may be in two different blocks in the implementation. To account for this, two blocks must be loaded to ensure that neighboring objects in the semantics are loaded into the read cache together. Thus we require $2M \times s_0$ words of cache in the ideal cache model to account for the M objects in the read cache.

With regards to the eviction policy from the read cache we note that an ideal cache will always choose an optimal policy (furtherst in the future). It will therefore do at least as well as any policy assumed by the abstract machine.

This completes the proof of the implementation bound stated in Theorem 5.1.

6. I/O Efficient Algorithms

We now describe algorithms analyzed in the model and prove bounds on their cache complexity. In particular we will consider mergeSort, k-way mergeSort and a recursive block matrix-matrix multiply. We will show that the k-way mergeSort and the matrix-matrix multiply analyzed in our model match the best bounds for the ideal-cache. Furthermore the implementations are completely natural functional programs using lists and trees instead of arrays.

Preliminaries

Before describing these algorithms we discuss some general issues and techniques that will be important in the analysis. For simplicity the semantics described in Section 3 only defines natural numbers. In the discussion in this section we assume the semantics have been augmented with some basic types including base types that fit in a machine word (machine integers, floats, and Boolean), sum types, product types, and recursive types made from products and sums. As with the RAM and I/O models, we assume that for an input of size n that machine words can store $O(\log n)$ bits. Hence a machine integer will be bounded by n^k for some constant k.

Since sorting (and matrix multiply) can be defined as higher order polymorphic functions we need to be careful about the size of the element type and cache complexity of the element function when analyzing overall cache complexity. For this purpose we define the notion of a *hereditarily finite* (HF) values. At the base any value of basic types that fit in words are HF. Inductively any sums or products of HF values are HF. A value of function type is HF iff for every HF argument of the domain type the function yields a HF argument of the range type, using only constant space in the process. In sorting we assume the elements themselves and the comparison function are hereditarily finite. In matrix multiply we assume the elements, addition, and multiplication functions are hereditarily finite.

It is important that the data structures that are traversed by our algorithms are laid out in an order that makes accessing them efficient. In our model the only way to control the layout of data structures is to allocate them in the desired order. We could try to define the notion of a list being in a good order in terms of how the list is represented in memory. This is cumbersome and low level. We could also try to define it with respect to the specific code that allocated the data. Again this is cumbersome. Instead we define it directly in terms of the cache complexity of traversing the structure. By traversing we mean going through the structure in a specific order and touching (reading) all data in the structure. Since types such as trees might have many traversal orders, the definition is with respect to a particular order (e.g. pre-order). For this purpose we define the notion of "compact".

DEFINITION 6.1. *A data structure of size n is* compact *with respect to a given traversal order if traversing it in that order has cache complexity $O(n/B)$ in our cost semantics with $M \geq kB$ for some constant k.*

We can now argue that certain code will generate data structures that are compact with respect to a particular order.

To keep data structures compact not only do the top level links need to be accessed in approximately the order they were allocated, but anything that is touched by the algorithm during traversal also needs to be accessed in a similar order. For example, if we are sorting a list it is important that in addition to the "cons cells", the keys are allocated in the list order (or, as we will argue shortly, reverse order is fine). To ensure that the keys are allocated in the appropriate order they need to be copied whenever placing them in a new list. This copy needs to be a deep copy that copies all components. If the keys are machine words then in practice these might be inlined into the cons cells anyway by a compiler—in fact

```
fun traverseL [] = []
  | traverseL h::R  = let val _ = touch h
                      in traverseL R end

fun traverseR [] = []
  | traverseR h::R  = let val R' = traverseR R
                          val _ = touch h
                      in R' end

fun map f [] = []
  | map f h::R   = f(h)::map R

fun map f [] = []
  | map f h::R   = let val R' = map R
                   in f(h)::R' end
```

Figure 4. Traversing a list in two orders, and examples of `map` that use each of the orders.

```
fun mergeSort less [] = []
  | mergeSort less [a] = [a]
  | mergeSort less A =
let
  fun merge(A,B) =
    case (A,B) of
       ([],B) => B
     | (A,[]) => A
     | (Ah::At, Bh::Bt) =>
          if (less(Ah,Bh))
          then !Ah::merge(At,B)
          else !Bh::merge(A,Bt)
  val (L,H) = split A
in
  merge(mergeSort(L),mergeSort(H))
end
```

Figure 5. Code for `mergeSort`.

optimizing compilers such as MLton can even inline product and sum types. However, to ensure that objects are copied we will use the copy operation described in Section 3, writing `!a` to indicate copying of a.

Although it might seem that there is only one "canonical" way to traverse a list, there are actually two. In the first all the elements of the list are visited on the way down the recursion, and in the second the elements are visited on the way back up. The order in which the elements are visited is reversed. The two versions are illustrated by the code in Figure 4. Fortunately if an algorithm is compact for one traversal it is compact for the other. This is because to be compact under either traversal requires that adjacent elements are allocated in the same block (neighborhoods in memory), and hence will be efficient in both directions. The fact that the orders are effectively equivalent is important since it means the model is quite robust relative to programming styles. For example the two implementations of the `map` function shown in Figure 4 will both be efficient if the list is compact with respect to either traversal. Furthermore the output is compact with respect to either traversal. This is true even though in the first case all elements are allocated first and then all cons cells, while in the second case they are interleaved.

Sorting

We now consider analyzing sorting in our cost model. We first consider mergeSort. We assume a vanilla purely functional version of mergeSort on lists as shown in Figure 5. We will not cover the definition of `split` since it is similar to merge. Note the only difference from a standard mergeSort is the use of the copy (`!`)

before the Ah and Bh. As discussed earlier this is important to ensure the result of the merge is compact. We note that for a list to be compact all its elements must be constant size. The interesting aspect of the code is that the cache complexity of this code in our model and hence when mapped onto the ideal cache using the implementation in section 5 matches the bounds for the array version discussed in Section 2.

To analyze the mergeSort we first analyze the merge.

THEOREM 6.2. *For a HF function* `less`, *and compact lists A and B, the evaluation of* (`merge less A B`) *starting with any cache state will have cache complexity* $O\left(\frac{n}{B}\right)$ *(*$n = |A| + |B|$*) and will return a compact list as a result.*

Proof. We consider the cache complexity of going down the recursion and then coming back up. Since A and B are both compact we need only put aside a constant number of cache blocks to traverse each one (by definition). Recall that in the cost model we have a nursery ν that maintains both live allocated values and place holders for stack frames in the order they are created. In `merge` nothing is allocated from one recursive call to the next (the cons cells are created on the way back up the recursion) so only the stack frames are placed in the nursery. After M recursive calls the nursery will fill and blocks will have to be flushed to the memory μ (rule 5b in Figure 2). The merge will invoke at most $O(n/B)$ such flushes since only n frames are created. On the way back up the recursion we will generate the cons cells for the list and copy each of the keys (using the !). Note that copying the keys is important so that the result remains compact. The cons cells and copies of the keys will be interleaved in the allocation order in the nursery and flushed to memory once the nursery fills. Once again these will be flushed in blocks of size B and hence there will be at most $O(n/B)$ such flushes. Furthermore the resulting list will be compact since adjacent elements of the list will be in the same block (neighborhood). □

We now consider mergeSort as a whole.

THEOREM 6.3. *For a HF function* `less`, *and compact list A, the evaluation of* (`mergeSort less A`) *starting with any cache state will have cache complexity* $O\left(\frac{n}{B}\log\frac{n}{M}\right)$ *(*$n = |A|$*) and will return a compact list as a result.*

Proof. As with the array version, we consider the two cases when the input fits in cache and when it does not. The mergeSort routine never requires more than $O(n)$ live allocated data. Therefore when $kn \leq M$ for some (small) constant k all allocated data fits in the nursery. Furthermore since the input list is compact, for $k'n \leq M$ the input fits in the read cache (for some constant k'). Therefore the cache complexity for mergeSort is at most the time to flush $O(n)$ items out of the allocation cache that it might have contained at the start, and to load the read cache with the input. This cache complexity is bounded by $O(n/B)$. When the input does not fit in cache we have to pay for the merge as analyzed above plus the recursive calls. This gives the same recurrence as for the array version (Section 2, equation 1) and hence solves to the claimed result. □

We now consider a k-way mergeSort using lists and a tree based heap for the k-way merging. The code is shown in Figure 6. The sort partitions the list into k parts, sorts each part recursively, builds a priority queue (PQ) out of the resulting parts, and pulls keys one by one out of the PQ adding them to the output list. The only slightly tricky part is maintaining the priority queue. The idea is each of the sorted lists is placed at a leaf. When pulling elements from the root of the PQ, the value is removed from the root and the

```
datatype 'a pq = Leaf of 'a list
               | Node of 'a * 'a pq * 'a pq

fun kWayMergeSort _ _ [] = []
  | kWayMergeSort _ _ [a] = [a]
  | kWayMergeSort less k L =
let
  fun getMin Leaf [] = NONE
    | getMin Leaf (a::_) = SOME(a)
    | getMin Node (a,_,_) = SOME(a)

  fun join(L,R) =
    case (getMin(L),getMin(R)) of
        (NONE,_) => R
      | (_,NONE) => L
      | (la,ra) =>
          if less(la,ra)
          then Node(la,delMin(L),R)
          else Node(lb,L,delMin(R))

  and delMin (Leaf (_::R)) = Leaf(R)
    | delMin (Node (_,L,R)) = join(L,R)

  fun merge H =
    case getMin(H) of
       NONE => []
     | SOME(a) => let val r = merge(delMin(H))
                  in !a::r
                  end

  fun buildPQ [a] = Leaf(a)
      buildPQ A =
        let val (L,H) = partition 2 A
        in  join(buildPQ(L),buildPQ(R))
        end

  val LL = partition k L
  val SL = map (kWayMergeSort less k) LL
  val HL = buildPQ SL
in
  merge HL
end
```

Figure 6. K-way Merge Sort.

two children are joined, which recursively pulls the value from the child with the smaller root. We don't show the code for `partition`, which simply partitions a list into k equal length parts (within 1). Although the code is somewhat involved the analysis of the cache complexity is relatively simple since most of the data allocated for the tree-based priority queue becomes unreachable before it needs to be flushed to memory.

THEOREM 6.4. *For a HF function* `less`, *and compact list A, the evaluation of* (`kWayMergeSort less k A`) *starting with any cache state and with an appropriate* k *(*$\approx M/B$*) will have cache complexity* $O\left(\frac{n}{B}\log_{M/B}\frac{n}{B}\right)$ *(*$n = |A|$*) and will return a compact list as a result.*

Proof. As usual once the input size is less than n/c for some constant, the whole problem fits in cache and we just pay to load the input and write the output, which will have $O(n/B)$ cache complexity if the input and output are compact. When the problem size does not fit in cache we note that with $k = \frac{1}{c}M/B$ for some constant c we can fit the head of each recursively solved list in the read cache, assuming each is compact. Therefore traversing all lists will use $O(n/B)$ cache complexity. Furthermore the size of the priority queue is proportional to k so the live part easily fits within the allocation cache. We have to be careful, however, since the

```
datatype 'a M = Leaf of 'a
              | Node of 'a M * 'a M * 'a M * 'a M

fun mmult + * (Leaf a) (Leaf b) = Leaf(*(a,b))
  | mmult + * (Node(a1,a2,a3,a4)) (Node(b1,b2,b3,b4)) =
let
  fun madd (Leaf a) (Leaf b) = Leaf(+(a,b))
    | madd (Node(a1,a2,a3,a4)) (Node(b1,b2,b3,b4))
      Node(madd(a1,b1),madd(a2,b2),
           madd(a3,b3),madd(a4,b4))

  val mm = mmult + *
in
  Node(madd(mm(a1,b1),mm(a2,b3)),
       madd(mm(a1,b2),mm(a2,b4)),
       madd(mm(a3,b1),mm(a4,b3)),
       madd(mm(a3,b2),mm(a4,b4)))
end
```

Figure 7. Matrix Multiply.

allocation cache is shared with the stack frames, which could eject some of the data allocated by the PQ. But since at any given time much less than half of the allocation cache (only $k = O(M/B)$ of it) is used by the PQ, we can charge all such ejections against the ejected cache frames (we charge for every cache frame). We can also charge reading them back into read cache against the cache frames.

Going down the recursion of the merge therefore requires $O(n/B)$ cache complexity to account for loading the k recursively solved lists, and ejecting the n cache frames. Coming back up the recursion again requires $O(n/B)$ cache complexity for ejecting the list and the copied keys. The resulting list is compact for list traversal since it is allocated in list traversal order (tail of the list first). This gives us the recurrence in equation 2 from Section 2 which solves to the desired result. □

Matrix Multiply

Our final example is matrix multiply. The code is shown in figure 7 (we have left out checks for matching sizes). This is a block recursive matrix multiply with the matrix laid out in a tree. It is therefore an interesting example of a tree data structure. We define compactness with respect to a preorder traversal of this tree. We therefore say the matrix is compact if traversing in this order can be done with cache complexity $O(n^2/B)$ for an $n \times n$ matrix (n^2 leaves). We note that if we generate a matrix in a preorder traversal allocating the leaves along the way, the resulting array will be compact.

THEOREM 6.5. *For HF functions* $*$ *and* $+$, *and compact* $n \times n$ *matrices A and B, the evaluation of* (mmult + * A B) *starting with any cache state will have cache complexity* $O\left(\frac{n^3}{B\sqrt{M}}\right)$ *and will return a compact matrix as a result.*

Proof. Matrix addition has cache complexity $O(n^2/B)$ and generates a compact result since we traverse the two input matrices in preorder traversal and we generate the output in the same order. Since the live data is never larger than $O(n^2)$ the problem will fit in cache for $n^2 \leq M/c$ for some constant c. Once it fits in cache the cost is $O(n^2/B)$ needed to the load the input matrices and write out the result. When it does not fit in cache we have to do 8 recursive calls and four calls to matrix addition. This gives the recurrence.

$$Q(n) = \begin{cases} 8Q(\frac{n}{2}) + O(\frac{n^2}{B}) & n^2 > M/c \\ O(\frac{n^2}{B}) & \text{otherwise} \end{cases}$$

This solves to $O\left(\frac{n^3}{B\sqrt{M}}\right)$. The output is compact since each of the four calls to madd in mmult allocate new results in preorder with respect to the submatrices they generate, and the four calls are made in preorder. Therefore the overall matrix returned is allocated in preorder. □

7. Conclusion

The idea of distinguishing the abstract cost semantics of language from its concrete implementation originates with Blelloch and Greiner's work on parallel programming [5, 11]. The chief benefit of their approach is that it provides a useful abstraction to the programmer that accounts for the complexity of a program, while simultaneously providing a guide to the implementor for how to achieve the complexity bound (with stated overhead). This work extends that methodology to account for the I/O complexity of a program in terms of two parameters, the cache block size (measured in objects) and the number of cache blocks. The programmer reasons at the level of the evaluation semantics, the implementor makes use of the provable implementation strategy to realize the predicted complexity. In the present case the essence of the proof is to argue that conventional implementation techniques, which rely on a run-time control stack and copying garbage collection, can be deployed to meet the abstract bounds given by the semantics of a functional language. The separation between the semantics and its implementations allows the programmer to work at the level of the code itself, and avoids having to reason in terms of the details of the compiler and run-time system (or, even worse, to be forced to drop down to a C-like level in which the programmer explicit manages storage allocation for each application).

Using the approach we are able to express algorithms in a standard high-level functional style using recursive data types (lists and trees), analyze them using a model that captures the idea of a fixed size read and allocation stack, but no details of the run time system, and yet match the asymptotic bounds for the ideal cache achieved by designing them using arrays and explicit and careful memory management in the imperative setting. For sorting the bounds are optimal.

One direction for further research is to integrate (deterministic) parallelism with the present work. Based on previous work we expect that the evaluation semantics given here will provide a good foundation for specifying parallel as well as sequential complexity. One complication is that the explicit consideration of storage considerations in the cost model given here would have to take account of the interaction among parallel threads. The amortization arguments would also have to be reconsidered to account for parallelism.

Another direction is suggested by the special treatment of the run-time stack described in Section 4. The stack is, after all, a particular data structure that is used implicitly by each program. This use could be made explicit, in which case it would be useful to understand more generally what properties of it allow for its efficient (in terms of cache complexity) implementation. These might well generalize to other data structures, and we it may be useful to develop a type system to capture these special properties.

Finally, although we are able to generate an optimal cache-aware sorting algorithm it is unclear whether it is possible to generate an optimal cache-oblivious sorting algorithm in our model.

Acknowledgments. This work is partially supported by the National Science Foundation under grant number CCF-1018188, and by Intel Labs Academic Research Office for the Parallel Algorithms for Non-Numeric Computing Program.

References

[1] J. Abello, A. L. Buchsbaum, and J. Westbrook. A functional approach to external graph algorithms. *Algorithmica*, 32(3):437–458, 2002.

[2] A. Aggarwal and J. S. Vitter. The input/output complexity of sorting and related problems. *Commun. ACM*, 31(9):1116–1127, 1988.

[3] A. W. Appel. Garbage collection can be faster than stack allocation. *Inf. Process. Lett.*, 25(4):275–279, 1987.

[4] L. Arge, M. A. Bender, E. D. Demaine, C. E. Leiserson, and K. Mehlhorn, editors. *Cache-Oblivious and Cache-Aware Algorithms, 18.07. - 23.07.2004*, volume 04301 of *Dagstuhl Seminar Proceedings*, 2005. IBFI, Schloss Dagstuhl, Germany.

[5] G. E. Blelloch and J. Greiner. Parallelism in sequential functional languages. In *FPCA*, pages 226–237, 1995.

[6] Y.-J. Chiang, M. T. Goodrich, E. F. Grove, R. Tamassia, D. E. Vengroff, and J. S. Vitter. External-memory graph algorithms. In K. L. Clarkson, editor, *SODA*, pages 139–149. ACM/SIAM, 1995. ISBN 0-89871-349-8.

[7] T. M. Chilimbi and J. R. Larus. Using generational garbage collection to implement cache-conscious data placement. In S. L. P. Jones and R. E. Jones, editors, *ISMM*, pages 37–48. ACM, 1998. ISBN 1-58113-114-3.

[8] R. Courts. Improving locality of reference in a garbage-collecting memory management system. *Commun. ACM*, 31(9):1128–1138, 1988.

[9] M. Frigo, C. E. Leiserson, H. Prokop, and S. Ramachandran. Cache-oblivious algorithms. In *FOCS*, pages 285–298. IEEE Computer Society, 1999.

[10] M. T. Goodrich, J.-J. Tsay, D. E. Vengroff, and J. S. Vitter. External-memory computational geometry (preliminary version). In *FOCS*, pages 714–723. IEEE Computer Society, 1993.

[11] J. Greiner and G. E. Blelloch. A provably time-efficient parallel implementation of full speculation. *ACM Trans. Program. Lang. Syst.*, 21(2):240–285, 1999.

[12] D. Grunwald, B. G. Zorn, and R. Henderson. Improving the cache locality of memory allocation. In R. Cartwright, editor, *PLDI*, pages 177–186. ACM, 1993. ISBN 0-89791-598-4.

[13] R. Harper. *Practical Foundations for Programming Languages*. Cambridge University Press, 2013. (Draft available at `http://www.cs.cmu.edu/~rwh/plbook/book.pdf`.).

[14] R. Jones and R. Lins. *Garbage Collection: Algorithms for Automatic Dynamic Memory Management*. Wiley, 1996.

[15] U. Meyer, P. Sanders, and J. F. Sibeyn, editors. *Algorithms for Memory Hierarchies, Advanced Lectures [Dagstuhl Research Seminar, March 10-14, 2002]*, volume 2625 of *Lecture Notes in Computer Science*, 2003. Springer. ISBN 3-540-00883-7.

[16] J. G. Morrisett, M. Felleisen, and R. Harper. Abstract models of memory management. In *FPCA*, pages 66–77, 1995.

[17] K. Munagala and A. G. Ranade. I/o-complexity of graph algorithms. In R. E. Tarjan and T. Warnow, editors, *SODA*, pages 687–694. ACM/SIAM, 1999. ISBN 0-89871-434-6.

[18] G. D. Plotkin. LCF considered as a programming language. *Theor. Comput. Sci.*, 5(3):223–255, 1977.

[19] M. Rahn, P. Sanders, and J. Singler. Scalable distributed-memory external sorting. In F. Li, M. M. Moro, S. Ghandeharizadeh, J. R. Haritsa, G. Weikum, M. J. Carey, F. Casati, E. Y. Chang, I. Manolescu, S. Mehrotra, U. Dayal, and V. J. Tsotras, editors, *ICDE*, pages 685–688. IEEE, 2010. ISBN 978-1-4244-5444-0.

[20] D. D. Sleator and R. E. Tarjan. Amortized efficiency of list update and paging rules. *Commun. ACM*, 28(2):202–208, 1985.

[21] D. Spoonhower, G. E. Blelloch, R. Harper, and P. B. Gibbons. Space profiling for parallel functional programs. In J. Hook and P. Thiemann, editors, *ICFP*, pages 253–264. ACM, 2008. ISBN 978-1-59593-919-7.

[22] J. S. Vitter. Algorithms and data structures for external memory. *Foundations and Trends in Theoretical Computer Science*, 2(4):305–474, 2006.

[23] P. R. Wilson, M. S. Lam, and T. G. Moher. Caching considerations for generational garbage collection. In *LISP and Functional Programming*, pages 32–42, 1992.

On the Linear Ranking Problem for Integer Linear-Constraint Loops

Amir M. Ben-Amram
The Tel-Aviv Academic College
amirben@mta.ac.il

Samir Genaim
Complutense University of Madrid
samir.genaim@fdi.ucm.es

Abstract

In this paper we study the complexity of the Linear Ranking problem: given a loop, described by linear constraints over a finite set of *integer variables*, is there a linear ranking function for this loop? While existence of such a function implies termination, this problem is not equivalent to termination. When the variables range over the rationals or reals, the Linear Ranking problem is known to be PTIME decidable. However, when they range over the integers, whether for single-path or multipath loops, the complexity of the Linear Ranking problem has not yet been determined. We show that it is coNP-complete. However, we point out some special cases of importance of PTIME complexity. We also present complete algorithms for synthesizing linear ranking functions, both for the general case and the special PTIME cases.

Categories and Subject Descriptors F.2.0 [*Analysis of Algorithms and Problem Complexity*]: General; F.3.1 [*Logics and Meanings of Programs*]: Specifying and Verifying and Reasoning about Programs

General Terms Verification, Theory.

Keywords Ranking Functions, Termination, Linear Constraints.

1. Introduction

Termination analysis has received a considerable attention and nowadays several powerful tools for the automatic termination analysis of different programming languages and computational models exist [1, 21, 27, 43]. Much of the recent development in termination analysis has benefited from techniques that deal with one loop at a time, where a loop is specified by a loop guard and a (non-iterative) loop body.

Very often, these loops are abstracted so that the state of the program during the loop is represented by a finite set of integer variables, the loop guard is a conjunction of linear inequalities, and the body modifies the variables in an affine linear way, as in the following example:

$$\begin{array}{l} \textit{while } (x_2 - x_1 \leq 0, x_1 + x_2 \geq 1) \textit{ do} \\ \qquad x_2' = x_2 - 2x_1 + 1, x_1' = x_1 \end{array} \tag{1}$$

where tagged variables represent the values at the completion of an iteration. When the variables are modified so that they are not affine linear functions of the old ones, the effect is sometimes captured (or approximated) by means of *linear constraints*. E.g., the C language loop "`while (4*x>=y && y>=1) do x=(2*x+1)/5;`", which involves integer division, can be represented by linear constraints as follows (since `2*x+1` is always positive)

$$\begin{array}{l} \textit{while } (4x_1 \geq x_2, x_2 \geq 1) \textit{ do} \\ \quad -2x_1 + 5x_1' \leq 1, 2x_1 - 5x_1' \leq 3, x_2' = x_2 \end{array} \tag{2}$$

Linear constraints might also be used to model changes to data structures, the variables representing a size abstraction such as length of lists, depth of trees, etc. [17, 34, 35, 43]. For a precise definition of the loop representations we consider, see Sec. 2; they also include *multipath loops* where alternative paths in the loop body are represented.

A standard technique to prove the termination of a loop is to find a ranking function. Such a function maps a program state (a valuation of the variables) into an element of some well-founded ordered set, such that the value descends (in the appropriate order) whenever the loop completes an iteration. Since descent in a well-founded set cannot be infinite, this proves that the loop must terminate. This definition of "ranking function" is very general; in practice, researchers have often limited themselves to a convenient and tractable form of ranking function, so that an algorithm to find the function—if there is one—might be found.

A frequently used class of ranking functions is based on *affine linear functions*. In this case, we seek a function $\rho(x_1, \ldots, x_n) = a_1x_1 + \cdots + a_nx_n + a_0$, with the rationals as a co-domain, such that (i) $\rho(\bar{x}) \geq 0$ for any valuation $\bar{x}$ that satisfies the loop guard; and (ii) $\rho(\bar{x}) - \rho(\bar{x}') \geq 1$ for any transition that starts in $\bar{x}$ and continues in $\bar{x}'$. This automatically induces the piecewise-linear ranking function: $f(\bar{x}) = \rho(\bar{x}) + 1$ if $\bar{x}$ satisfies the loop guard and 0 otherwise, with the non-negative rationals as a co-domain but ordered w.r.t. $a \preceq b$ iff $a + 1 \leq b$ (which is well-founded). For simplicity, we call ρ itself a *linear ranking function* instead of referring to f.

An algorithm to find a linear ranking function using linear programming (LP) was found by multiple researchers in different places and times and in some alternative versions [3, 20, 25, 36, 38, 42]. Since LP has a polynomial time complexity, most of these methods yield polynomial-time algorithms. Generally speaking, they are based on the fact that LP can precisely decide whether a given inequality is implied by a set of other inequalities, and can even be used to generate any implied inequality. After all, conditions (i) and (ii) above are inequalities that should be implied by the constraints that define the loop guard and body. This approach can, in a certain sense, be *sound and complete*

Soundness means that it produces a correct linear ranking function, if it succeeds; completeness means that if a linear ranking function exists, it will succeed. In other words, there are no *false negatives*. A completeness claim appears in some of the references,

POPL'13, January 23–25, 2012, Rome, Italy.

and we found it cited several times. In our opinion, it has created a false impression that the Linear Ranking problem for linear-constraint loops with *integer variables* was completely solved (and happily classified as polynomial time).

The fly in the ointment is the fact that these solutions are only complete when the variables range *over the rationals*, which means that the linear ranking function has to fulfill its requirements for any rational valuation of the variables that satisfies the loop guard. But this may lead to a false negative if the variables are, in fact, integers. The reader may turn to the two loops above and note that both of them do not terminate over the rationals at all (for the first, consider $x_1 = x_2 = \frac{1}{2}$; for the second, $x_1 = \frac{1}{4}$ and $x_2 = 1$). But they have linear ranking functions valid for all integer valuations, which we derive in Sec. 3.4.

This observation has led us to investigate the Linear Ranking problem for single-path and multipath linear constraint loops. We present several fundamental new results on this problem. We have confirmed that this problem is indeed harder in the integer setting, proving it to be coNP-complete (as a decision problem), even for loops that only manipulate integers in a finite range. On a positive note, this shows that there *is* a complete solution, even if exponential-time. We give such a solution both to the decision problem and to the synthesis problem. The crux of the coNP-completeness proof, and the corresponding synthesis algorithm, is that we rely on the *generator representation* of the transition polyhedron defined by the loop constraints. We provide sufficient and necessary conditions for the existence of a linear ranking function that use the vertices and rays of this representation.

Another positive news for the practically-minded reader is that some special cases of importance do have a PTIME solution, because they reduce (with no effort, or with a polynomial-time computation) to the rational case. We present several such cases, which include, among others, loops in which the body is a sequence of linear affine updates with integer coefficients, as in loop (1) above; and the condition is defined by either an extended form of *difference constraints*, a restricted form of *Two Variables Per Inequality* constraints, or a cone (constraints where the free constant is zero). Some cases in which the body involves linear constraints are also presented. All the algorithms presented in this paper have been implemented, and can be tried out online (see Sec. 5).

Our results should be of interest to all users of linear ranking functions, and in fact their uses go beyond termination proofs. For example, they have been used to provide an upper bound on the number of iterations of a loop in *program complexity analysis* [2, 3] and to automatically parallelize computations [24, 25]. We remark that in termination analysis, the distinction between integers and rationals has already been considered, both regarding ranking-function generation [13, 22] and the very decidability of the termination problem [9, 16, 45]. All these works left the integer case open. Interestingly, our results provide an insight on how to make the solution proposed by Bradley et al. [13] complete (see Sec. 6).

This paper is organized as follows. Sec. 2 gives definitions and background information regarding linear constraint loops, linear ranking functions and the mathematical notions involved. Sec. 3 proves that the decision problem, denoted LinRF($\mathbb{Z}$), is coNP-complete, and also presents an exponential-time ranking-function synthesis algorithm. Sec. 4 discusses PTIME-solvable cases. Sec. 5 describes a prototype implementation. Sec. 6 surveys related previous work. Sec. 7 concludes.

2. Preliminaries

In this section we recall some results on (integer) polyhedra on which we will rely, define the kind of loops we are interested in, and formally define the *linear ranking function* problem.

2.1 Integer polyhedra

We recall some useful definitions and properties which can all be found in [41]. A *rational convex polyhedron* $\mathcal{P} \subseteq \mathbb{Q}^n$ (*polyhedron* for short) is the set of solutions of a set of inequalities $A\mathbf{x} \leq \mathbf{b}$, namely $\mathcal{P} = \{\mathbf{x} \in \mathbb{Q}^n \mid A\mathbf{x} \leq \mathbf{b}\}$, where $A \in \mathbb{Q}^{m\times n}$ is a rational matrix of n columns and m rows, $\mathbf{x} \in \mathbb{Q}^n$ and $\mathbf{b} \in \mathbb{Q}^m$ are column vectors of n and m rational values respectively. We say that $\mathcal{P}$ is specified by $A\mathbf{x} \leq \mathbf{b}$.

The set of *recession directions* of a polyhedron $\mathcal{P}$ specified by $A\mathbf{x} \leq \mathbf{b}$ is the set $\mathcal{R}_\mathcal{P} = \{\mathbf{y} \in \mathbb{Q}^n \mid A\mathbf{y} \leq \mathbf{0}\}$. For a given polyhedron $\mathcal{P} \subseteq \mathbb{Q}^n$ we let $I(\mathcal{P})$ be $\mathcal{P} \cap \mathbb{Z}^n$, i.e., the set of integer points of $\mathcal{P}$. The *integer hull* of $\mathcal{P}$, commonly denoted by $\mathcal{P}_I$, is defined as the convex hull of $I(\mathcal{P})$, i.e., every rational point of $\mathcal{P}_I$ is a convex combination of integer points. It is known that $\mathcal{P}_I$ is also a polyhedron. An *integer polyhedron* is a polyhedron $\mathcal{P}$ such that $\mathcal{P} = \mathcal{P}_I$. We also say that $\mathcal{P}$ is *integral*.

Polyhedra also have a *generator representation* in terms of vertices and rays, written as

$$\mathcal{P} = \text{convhull}\{\mathbf{x}_1, \dots, \mathbf{x}_m\} + \text{cone}\{\mathbf{y}_1, \dots, \mathbf{y}_t\}\,.$$

This means that $\mathbf{x} \in \mathcal{P}$ iff $\mathbf{x} = \sum_{i=1}^m a_i \cdot \mathbf{x}_i + \sum_{j=1}^t b_j \cdot \mathbf{y}_j$ for some rationals $a_i, b_j \geq 0$, where $\sum_{i=1}^m a_i = 1$. Note that $\mathbf{y}_1, \dots, \mathbf{y}_t$ are the recession directions of $\mathcal{P}$, i.e., $\mathbf{y} \in \mathcal{R}_\mathcal{P}$ iff $\mathbf{y} = \sum_{j=1}^t b_j \cdot \mathbf{y}_j$ for some rational $b_j \geq 0$. When $\mathcal{P}$ is integral, there is a generator representation in which all $\mathbf{x}_i$ and $\mathbf{y}_j$ are integer.

Complexity of algorithms on polyhedra is measured in this paper by running time, on a conventional computational model (polynomially equivalent to a Turing machine), as a function of the *bit-size* of the input. Following [41, Sec. 2.1], we define the bit-size of an integer x as $\|x\| = 1 + \lceil \log(|x| + 1) \rceil$; the bit-size of an n-dimensional vector $\mathbf{a}$ as $\|\mathbf{a}\| = n + \sum_{i=1}^n \|a_i\|$; and the bit-size of an inequality $\mathbf{a} \cdot \mathbf{x} \leq c$ as $1 + \|c\| + \|\mathbf{a}\|$.

For a polyhedron $\mathcal{P} \subseteq \mathbb{Q}^n$ defined by $A\mathbf{x} \leq \mathbf{b}$, we let $\|\mathcal{P}\|_b$ be the bit-size of $A\mathbf{x} \leq \mathbf{b}$, which we can take as the sum of the sizes of the inequalities. The *facet size*, denoted by $\|\mathcal{P}\|_f$, is the smallest number $\phi \geq n$ such that $\mathcal{P}$ may be described by *some* $A\mathbf{x} \leq \mathbf{b}$ where each inequality in $A\mathbf{x} \leq \mathbf{b}$ fits in ϕ bits. Clearly, $\|\mathcal{P}\|_f \leq \|\mathcal{P}\|_b$. The *vertex size*, denoted by $\|\mathcal{P}\|_v$, is the smallest number $\psi \geq n$ such that $\mathcal{P}$ has a generator representation in which each of $\mathbf{x}_i$ and $\mathbf{y}_j$ fits in ψ bits (the size of a vector is as above). For integer polyhedra, we restrict the generators to be integer. The following theorems may be found in [41, Th. 10.2, p. 121] and [41, Cor. 17.1a,17.1b, p. 238] (citing [32]) respectively.

THEOREM 2.1. *Let $\mathcal{P}$ be a rational polyhedron in $\mathbb{Q}^n$; then $\|\mathcal{P}\|_v \leq 4n^2\|\mathcal{P}\|_f$ and $\|\mathcal{P}\|_f \leq 4n^2\|\mathcal{P}\|_v$.*

THEOREM 2.2. *Let $\mathcal{P}$ be a rational polyhedron in $\mathbb{Q}^n$; then $\|\mathcal{P}_I\|_v \leq 6n^3\|\mathcal{P}\|_f$ and $\|\mathcal{P}_I\|_f \leq 24n^5\|\mathcal{P}\|_f$.*

2.2 Multipath linear-constraint loops

A *single-path* linear-constraint loop (*SLC* for short) over n variables $x_1, \dots, x_n$ has the form

$$\textit{while } (B\mathbf{x} \leq \mathbf{b}) \textit{ do } A\begin{pmatrix}\mathbf{x}\\ \mathbf{x}'\end{pmatrix} \leq \mathbf{c} \qquad (3)$$

where $\mathbf{x} = (x_1, \dots, x_n)^\mathrm{T}$ and $\mathbf{x}' = (x_1', \dots, x_n')^\mathrm{T}$ are column vectors, and for some $p, q > 0$, $B \in \mathbb{Q}^{p\times n}$, $A \in \mathbb{Q}^{q\times 2n}$, $\mathbf{b} \in \mathbb{Q}^p$, $\mathbf{c} \in \mathbb{Q}^q$. The constraint $B\mathbf{x} \leq \mathbf{b}$ is called *the loop condition* (a.k.a. the loop guard) and the other constraint is called *the update*. The update is called *deterministic* if, for a given $\mathbf{x}$ (satisfying the loop condition) there is at most one $\mathbf{x}'$ satisfying the update constraint. The update is called *linear* if it can be rewritten as $\mathbf{x}' = A'\mathbf{x} + \mathbf{c}'$ for a matrix A' and vector $\mathbf{c}'$ of appropriate dimensions. We say that the loop is a *rational loop* if $\mathbf{x}$ and $\mathbf{x}'$ range over $\mathbb{Q}^n$, and that it is an *integer loop* if they range over $\mathbb{Z}^n$.

We say that there is a transition from a state $\mathbf{x} \in \mathbb{Q}^n$ to a state $\mathbf{x}' \in \mathbb{Q}^n$, if $\mathbf{x}$ satisfies the condition and $\mathbf{x}$ and $\mathbf{x}'$ satisfy the update. A transition can be seen as a point $\binom{\mathbf{x}}{\mathbf{x}'} \in \mathbb{Q}^{2n}$, where its first n components correspond to $\mathbf{x}$ and its last n components to $\mathbf{x}'$. For ease of notation, we denote such points by $\mathbf{x}'' = \binom{\mathbf{x}}{\mathbf{x}'}$. The set of all transitions $\mathbf{x}'' \in \mathbb{Q}^{2n}$ will be denoted, as a rule, by $\mathcal{Q}$. The transition polyhedron $\mathcal{Q}$ is specified by $A''\mathbf{x}'' \leq \mathbf{c}''$ where

$$A'' = \begin{pmatrix} B & 0 \\ & A \end{pmatrix} \qquad\qquad \mathbf{c}'' = \begin{pmatrix} \mathbf{b} \\ \mathbf{c} \end{pmatrix}$$

Note that we may assume that $\mathcal{Q}$ does not include the origin, for if it includes it, the loop is clearly non-terminating (this condition is easy to check). Hence, $\mathcal{Q}$ is not a cone (i.e., $m \geq 1$ in the generator representation). The polyhedron defined by the loop condition $B\mathbf{x} \leq \mathbf{b}$ will be denoted by $\mathcal{C}$ (the condition polyhedron).

A *multipath* linear-constraint loop (MLC for short) differs by having alternative loop conditions and updates, which are, in principle, chosen non-deterministically (though the constraints may enforce a deterministic choice):

$$loop: \ \bigvee_{i=1}^{k} B_i\mathbf{x} \leq \mathbf{b}_i \Rightarrow A_i \begin{pmatrix} \mathbf{x} \\ \mathbf{x}' \end{pmatrix} \leq \mathbf{c}_i$$

This means that the i-th update can be applied if the i-th condition is satisfied. Following the notation of SLC loops, the transitions of an MLC loop are specified by the transition polyhedra $\mathcal{Q}_1, \ldots, \mathcal{Q}_k$, where each $\mathcal{Q}_i$ is specified by $A_i''\mathbf{x}'' \leq \mathbf{c}_i''$. The polyhedron defined by the condition $B_i\mathbf{x} \leq \mathbf{b}_i$ is denoted by $\mathcal{C}_i$.

For simplifying the presentation, often we write loops with explicit equalities and inequalities instead of the matrix representation. We also might refer to loops by their corresponding transition polyhedra, or the sets of inequalities that define these polyhedra.

2.3 Linear ranking functions

A linear function $\rho : \mathbb{Q}^n \to \mathbb{Q}$ is of the form $\rho(\mathbf{x}) = \vec{\lambda} \cdot \mathbf{x} + \lambda_0$ where $\vec{\lambda} \in \mathbb{Q}^n$ is a row vector and $\lambda_0 \in \mathbb{Q}$. For ease of notation we sometimes refer to a linear function using the row vector $(\lambda_0,\vec{\lambda}) \in \mathbb{Q}^{n+1}$. Next we define when a linear function is a *linear ranking function* (LRF for short) for a given rational or integer MLC loop.

DEFINITION 2.3. Given an MLC loop with $\mathcal{Q}_1, \ldots, \mathcal{Q}_k$ as transition polyhedra, and a linear function $\rho(\mathbf{x}) = \vec{\lambda} \cdot \mathbf{x} + \lambda_0$. We say that ρ is a LRF for $\mathcal{Q}_1, \ldots, \mathcal{Q}_k$ iff the following hold for any rational point $\binom{\mathbf{x}}{\mathbf{x}'} \in \mathcal{Q}_i$

$$\vec{\lambda} \cdot \mathbf{x} + \lambda_0 \geq 0 \qquad (4)$$

$$\vec{\lambda} \cdot (\mathbf{x} - \mathbf{x}') \geq 1 \qquad (5)$$

and we say that it is a LRF for $I(\mathcal{Q}_1), \ldots, I(\mathcal{Q}_k)$ iff (4,5) hold for any integer point $\binom{\mathbf{x}}{\mathbf{x}'} \in I(\mathcal{Q}_i)$.

Intuitively, (4) and (5) requires that $\rho(\mathbf{x}) \geq 0$ and $\rho(\mathbf{x}) - \rho(\mathbf{x}') \geq 1$ respectively. For *rational* loops this must hold for all rational transitions, and for *integer* loops it must hold for all integer transitions. Clearly, the existence of a LRF implies termination of the loop.

Note that in Def. 2.3 we require ρ to decrease at least by 1, where in the literature [38] this 1 is sometimes replaced by $\delta > 0$. It is easy to verify that these definitions are equivalent.

DEFINITION 2.4. The decision problem *Existence of a LRF* is defined by

Instance: an MLC loop.
Question: does there exist a LRF for this loop?

The decision problem is denoted by LINRF($\mathbb{Q}$) and LINRF($\mathbb{Z}$) for rational and integer loops respectively.

It is known that LINRF($\mathbb{Q}$) is PTIME-decidable [36, 38]. In this paper, we focus on LINRF($\mathbb{Z}$).

3. The general case is coNP-complete

In this section we show that the LINRF($\mathbb{Z}$) problem is coNP-complete; it is coNP-hard already for SLC loops. We also show that $LRFs$ can be synthesized in deterministic exponential time.

This section is organized as follows: in Sec. 3.1 we show that LINRF($\mathbb{Z}$) is coNP-hard; in Sec. 3.2 we show that it is in coNP for SLC loops, and in Sec. 3.3 for MLC loops; finally, in Sec. 3.4, we describe an algorithm for synthesizing $LRFs$.

3.1 coNP-hardness

We prove coNP-hardness in a strong form. A number problem (a problem whose instance is a matrix of integers) **Prob** is strongly hard for a complexity class, if there are polynomial reductions from all problems in that class to **Prob** such that the values of all numbers created by the reduction are polynomially bounded by the input bit-size. Assuming NP≠P, strongly NP-hard (or coNP-hard) problems cannot even have pseudo-polynomial algorithms [26].

THEOREM 3.1. *The* LINRF($\mathbb{Z}$) *problem is strongly coNP-hard, even for deterministic SLC loops.*

Proof. The problem of deciding whether a polyhedron given by $B\mathbf{x} \leq \mathbf{b}$ contains no integer point is a well-known coNP-hard problem (an easy reduction from SAT may be found in [31]). We reduce this problem to LINRF($\mathbb{Z}$). Given $B \in \mathbb{Z}^{m \times n}$ and $\mathbf{b} \in \mathbb{Z}^m$, we construct the following integer SLC loop

$$while \begin{pmatrix} B & -I \\ 0 & -I \end{pmatrix} \begin{pmatrix} \mathbf{x} \\ \mathbf{z} \end{pmatrix} \leq \begin{pmatrix} \mathbf{b} \\ \mathbf{0} \end{pmatrix} \ do \ \begin{pmatrix} \mathbf{x}' \\ \mathbf{z}' \end{pmatrix} = \begin{pmatrix} \mathbf{x} \\ \mathbf{0} \end{pmatrix}$$

where $\mathbf{x} = (x_1, \ldots, x_n)^{\mathrm{T}}$, $\mathbf{z} = (z_1, \ldots, z_m)^{\mathrm{T}}$ are integer variables, and I is an identity matrix of size $m \times m$.

Suppose $B\mathbf{x} \leq \mathbf{b}$ has an integer solution $\mathbf{x}$. Then, the loop does not terminate when starting from this $\mathbf{x}$ and $\mathbf{z}$ set to $\mathbf{0}$, since the guard is satisfied and the update does not change the values. Thus, it does not have any ranking function, let along a LRF.

Next, suppose $B\mathbf{x} \leq \mathbf{b}$ does not have an integer solution. Then, for any initial state for which the loop guard is enabled it must hold that $z_1 + \cdots + z_m > 0$, for otherwise $z_1, \ldots, z_m$ must be 0 in which case the constraint $B\mathbf{x} - I\mathbf{z} \leq \mathbf{b}$ has no integer solution. Since the updated vector $\mathbf{z}'$ is deterministically set to $\mathbf{0}$, the guard will not be enabled in the next state, hence the loop terminates after one iteration. Clearly $z_1 + \cdots + z_m > z_1' + \cdots + z_m' = 0$, so we conclude that $z_1 + \cdots + z_m$ is a LRF. □

Note that in the above reduction we rely on the hardness of whether a given polyhedron is empty. This problem is coNP-hard even for bounded polyhedra (due to the reduction from SAT in which variables are bounded by 0 and 1). This means that even for loops that only manipulate integers in a rather small range, the problem is coNP-hard. The parameter "responsible" for the exponential behavior in this case is the number of variables.

3.2 Inclusion in coNP for SLC loops

To prove that LINRF($\mathbb{Z}$) is in coNP, we show that the complement of LINRF($\mathbb{Z}$), the problem of *nonexistence* of a LRF, is in NP, that is, has a polynomially-checkable witness. In what follows we assume as input an SLC loop with a transition polyhedron $\mathcal{Q} \subseteq \mathbb{Q}^{2n}$. The input is given as the set of linear inequalities $A''\mathbf{x}'' \leq \mathbf{c}''$ that define $\mathcal{Q}$. The proof follows the following lines:

1. We show that there is no LRF for $I(\mathcal{Q})$ iff there is a *witness* that consists of two sets of integer points $X \subseteq I(\mathcal{Q})$ and $Y \subseteq I(\mathcal{R}_{\mathcal{Q}})$, such that a certain set of inequalities $\Psi_{WS}(X,Y)$ has no solution over the rationals; and
2. We show that if there is a witness then there is one with bit-size polynomial in the input bit-size.

To make sense of the following definitions, think of a vector $(\lambda_0,\vec{\lambda}) \in \mathbb{Q}^{n+1}$ as a "candidate LRF" that we may want to verify (or, in our case, to eliminate).

DEFINITION 3.2. We say that $\mathbf{x}'' = \left(\begin{smallmatrix}\mathbf{x}\\ \mathbf{x}'\end{smallmatrix}\right) \in I(\mathcal{Q})$ is a witness *against* $(\lambda_0,\vec{\lambda}) \in \mathbb{Q}^{n+1}$ if it fails to satisfy at least one of conditions (4) and (5). The set of $(\lambda_0,\vec{\lambda})$ witnessed against by $\mathbf{x}''$ is denoted by $W(\mathbf{x}'')$.

DEFINITION 3.3. We say that $\mathbf{y}'' = \left(\begin{smallmatrix}\mathbf{y}\\ \mathbf{y}'\end{smallmatrix}\right) \in I(\mathcal{R_Q})$ is a *homogeneous component of a witness* (h-witness) against $(\lambda_0,\vec{\lambda}) \in \mathbb{Q}^{n+1}$ if it fails to satisfy at least one of

$$\vec{\lambda}\cdot\mathbf{y} \geq 0 \tag{6}$$

$$\vec{\lambda}\cdot(\mathbf{y}-\mathbf{y}') \geq 0 \tag{7}$$

The set of $(\lambda_0,\vec{\lambda})$ h-witnessed against by $\mathbf{y}''$ is denoted by $W_H(\mathbf{y}'')$.

The meaning of the witness of Def. 3.2 is quite straightforward. Let us intuitively explain the meaning of an h-witness. Suppose that $\mathbf{x}''$ is a point in $\mathcal{Q}_I$, and $\mathbf{y}''$ is a ray of $\mathcal{Q}_I$. Then a LRF ρ has to satisfy (4) for any integer point of the form $\mathbf{x}''+a\cdot\mathbf{y}''$ with $a>0$; letting a grow to infinity, we see that (4) implies the homogeneous inequality (6). Similarly, (5) implies (7).

DEFINITION 3.4. The set of $(\lambda_0,\vec{\lambda}) \in \mathbb{Q}^{n+1}$ witnessed and h-witnessed against respectively by $X \subseteq I(\mathcal{Q})$ and $Y \subseteq I(\mathcal{R_Q})$ is defined as

$$WS(X,Y) = \bigcup_{\mathbf{x}''\in X} W(\mathbf{x}'') \cup \bigcup_{\mathbf{y}''\in Y} W_H(\mathbf{y}''). \tag{8}$$

LEMMA 3.5. *Let $X \subseteq I(\mathcal{Q})$ and $Y \subseteq I(\mathcal{R_Q})$. If $WS(X,Y) = \mathbb{Q}^{n+1}$, then there is no LRF for $I(\mathcal{Q})$.*

Proof. Let $WS(X,Y) = \mathbb{Q}^{n+1}$. For any $(\lambda_0,\vec{\lambda}) \in \mathbb{Q}^{n+1}$, we prove that $\rho(\mathbf{x}) = \vec{\lambda}\cdot\mathbf{x}+\lambda_0$ is not a LRF. If $(\lambda_0,\vec{\lambda}) \in W(\mathbf{x}'')$ for some $\mathbf{x}'' \in X$, then the conclusion is clear since conditions (4,5) do not hold. Otherwise, suppose that $(\lambda_0,\vec{\lambda}) \in W_H(\mathbf{y}'')$ for $\mathbf{y}'' \in Y$. Thus, $\mathbf{y}''$ fails to satisfy one of conditions (6,7). Next we show that, in such case, there must exists $\mathbf{z}'' \in I(\mathcal{Q})$ that fails either (4) or (5).

Case 1: Suppose (6) is not satisfied. That is, $\vec{\lambda}\cdot\mathbf{y} < 0$.

Choose an arbitrary $\mathbf{x}'' = \left(\begin{smallmatrix}\mathbf{x}\\ \mathbf{x}'\end{smallmatrix}\right) \in I(\mathcal{Q})$, and assume that $\rho(\mathbf{x}) \geq 0$, since otherwise ρ fails (4) and is not a LRF. Note that for any integer $a \geq 0$, the integer point $\mathbf{z}'' = \mathbf{x}'' + a\cdot\mathbf{y}''$ is a transition in $I(\mathcal{Q})$, and $\mathbf{z}'' = \left(\begin{smallmatrix}\mathbf{z}\\ \mathbf{z}'\end{smallmatrix}\right) = \left(\begin{smallmatrix}\mathbf{x}+a\cdot\mathbf{y}\\ \mathbf{x}'+a\cdot\mathbf{y}'\end{smallmatrix}\right)$. We choose a as an integer sufficiently large so that $a\cdot(\vec{\lambda}\cdot\mathbf{y}) \leq -(1+\rho(\mathbf{x}))$. Now,

$$\begin{aligned}\rho(\mathbf{z}) &= \vec{\lambda}\cdot(\mathbf{x}+a\cdot\mathbf{y})+\lambda_0\\ &= \rho(\mathbf{x}) + a\cdot(\vec{\lambda}\cdot\mathbf{y}) \leq \rho(\mathbf{x}) - (1+\rho(\mathbf{x})) = -1\end{aligned}$$

So ρ fails (4) on $\mathbf{z}'' \in I(\mathcal{Q})$, and thus cannot be a LRF.

Case 2: Suppose (7) is not satisfied. That is, $\vec{\lambda}\cdot(\mathbf{y}-\mathbf{y}') < 0$.

Choose an arbitrary $\mathbf{x}'' = \left(\begin{smallmatrix}\mathbf{x}\\ \mathbf{x}'\end{smallmatrix}\right) \in I(\mathcal{Q})$, and assume that $\rho(\mathbf{x}) - \rho(\mathbf{x}') \geq 1$, since otherwise ρ fails (5) and is not a LRF. Define $\mathbf{z}''$ as above, but now choosing a sufficiently large to make $a\cdot(\vec{\lambda}\cdot(\mathbf{y}-\mathbf{y}')) \leq -(1+\rho(\mathbf{x})-\rho(\mathbf{x}'))$. Now,

$$\begin{aligned}\rho(\mathbf{z}) - \rho(\mathbf{z}') &= \vec{\lambda}\cdot((\mathbf{x}+a\cdot\mathbf{y})-(\mathbf{x}'+a\cdot\mathbf{y}'))\\ &= \rho(\mathbf{x}) - \rho(\mathbf{x}') + a\cdot(\vec{\lambda}\cdot(\mathbf{y}-\mathbf{y}'))\\ &\leq \rho(\mathbf{x}) - \rho(\mathbf{x}') - (1+\rho(\mathbf{x})-\rho(\mathbf{x}')) = -1\end{aligned}$$

So ρ fails (5) on $\mathbf{z}'' \in I(\mathcal{Q})$, and thus cannot be a LRF. □

Note that the condition $WS(X,Y) = \mathbb{Q}^{n+1}$ is equivalent to saying that the conjunction of inequalities (4,5), for all $\mathbf{x}'' \in X$, and inequalities (6,7), for all $\mathbf{y}'' \in Y$, has no (rational) solution. We denote this set of inequalities by $\Psi_{WS}(X,Y)$. Note that the variables in $\Psi_{WS}(X,Y)$ are $\lambda_0,\ldots,\lambda_n$, which range over $\mathbb{Q}$, and thus, the test that it has no solution can be done in polynomial time since it is an LP problem over the rationals.

EXAMPLE 3.6. Consider the following integer SLC loop:

$$while\ (x_1 \geq 0)\ do\ x_1' = x_1 + x_2, x_2' = x_2 - 1$$

Let $\mathbf{x}_1''=(0,2,2,1)^{\mathsf{T}} \in I(\mathcal{Q})$ and $\mathbf{y}_1''=(1,-2,-1,-2)^{\mathsf{T}} \in I(\mathcal{R_Q})$. Then, $\Psi_{WS}(\{\mathbf{x}_1''\},\{\mathbf{y}_1''\})$ is a conjunction of the inequalities

$$\{2\lambda_2+\lambda_0 \geq 0,\ -2\lambda_1+\lambda_2 \geq 1,\ \lambda_1-2\lambda_2 \geq 0,\ 2\lambda_1 \geq 0\} \tag{9}$$

The first two inequalities correspond to applying (4,5) to $\mathbf{x}_1''$, and the other ones to applying (6,7) to $\mathbf{y}_1''$. It is easy to verify that (9) is not satisfiable, thus, $WS(\{\mathbf{x}_1''\},\{\mathbf{y}_1''\}) = \mathbb{Q}^3$ and the loop does not have a LRF. This is a classical loop for which there is no LRF.

Lemma 3.5 provides a sufficient condition for the nonexistence of LRF, the next lemma shows that this condition is necessary. In particular, it shows that if there is no LRF for $I(\mathcal{Q})$, then the vertices and rays of $\mathcal{Q}_I$ serve as X and Y of Lemma 3.5.

LEMMA 3.7. *Let the integer hull of the transition polyhedron $\mathcal{Q}$ be $\mathcal{Q}_I$=convhull$\{\mathbf{x}_1'',\ldots,\mathbf{x}_m''\}$+cone$\{\mathbf{y}_1'',\ldots,\mathbf{y}_t''\}$. If there is no LRF for $I(\mathcal{Q})$, then $WS(\{\mathbf{x}_1'',\ldots,\mathbf{x}_m''\},\{\mathbf{y}_1'',\ldots,\mathbf{y}_t''\})=\mathbb{Q}^{n+1}$.*

Proof. We prove the contra-positive. Suppose that

$$WS(\{\mathbf{x}_1'',\ldots,\mathbf{x}_m''\},\{\mathbf{y}_1'',\ldots,\mathbf{y}_t''\}) \neq \mathbb{Q}^{n+1}.$$

Then, there is $(\lambda_0,\vec{\lambda}) \in \mathbb{Q}^{n+1}$ that fulfills (4,5) for all $\mathbf{x}_i''$ and (6,7) for all $\mathbf{y}_j''$. We claim that $\rho(\mathbf{x}) = \vec{\lambda}\cdot\mathbf{x}+\lambda_0$ is a LRF for $I(\mathcal{Q})$.

To see this, let $\mathbf{x}'' = \left(\begin{smallmatrix}\mathbf{x}\\ \mathbf{x}'\end{smallmatrix}\right)$ be an arbitrary point of $I(\mathcal{Q})$. Then $\mathbf{x}'' = \sum_{i=1}^m a_i\cdot\mathbf{x}_i'' + \sum_{j=1}^t b_j\cdot\mathbf{y}_j''$ for some $a_i, b_j \geq 0$ where $\sum_{i=1}^m a_i = 1$. Now, we show that $\mathbf{x}''$ and ρ satisfy (4,5) which means that ρ is a LRF for $I(\mathcal{Q})$:

$$\begin{aligned}\vec{\lambda}\cdot\mathbf{x}+\lambda_0 &= \lambda_0 + \sum_{i=1}^m a_i\cdot(\vec{\lambda}\cdot\mathbf{x}_i) + \sum_{j=1}^t b_j\cdot(\vec{\lambda}\cdot\mathbf{y}_j)\\ &= \sum_{i=1}^m a_i\cdot(\vec{\lambda}\cdot\mathbf{x}_i+\lambda_0) + \sum_{j=1}^t b_j\cdot(\vec{\lambda}\cdot\mathbf{y}_j)\\ &\geq 0+0=0\\ \vec{\lambda}\cdot(\mathbf{x}-\mathbf{x}') &= \sum_{i=1}^m a_i\cdot(\vec{\lambda}\cdot(\mathbf{x}_i-\mathbf{x}_i')) + \sum_{j=1}^t b_j\cdot(\vec{\lambda}\cdot(\mathbf{y}_j-\mathbf{y}_j'))\\ &\geq 1+0=1\end{aligned}$$

□

Note that the solutions of $\Psi_{WS}(\{\mathbf{x}_1'',\ldots,\mathbf{x}_m''\},\{\mathbf{y}_1'',\ldots,\mathbf{y}_t''\})$ in Lemma 3.7 define the set of all $LRFs$ for $I(\mathcal{Q})$ (see Sec. 3.4).

EXAMPLE 3.8. Consider again the loop of Ex. 3.6, and recall that it does not have a LRF. The generator representation of $\mathcal{Q}_I$ is

$$\mathcal{Q}_I = \text{convhull}\{\mathbf{x}_1''\} + \text{cone}\{\mathbf{y}_1'',\mathbf{y}_2'',\mathbf{y}_3''\}$$

where $\mathbf{x}_1''=(0,1,1,0)^{\mathsf{T}}$, $\mathbf{y}_1''=(0,-1,-1,-1)^{\mathsf{T}}$, $\mathbf{y}_2''=(0,1,1,1)^{\mathsf{T}}$ and $\mathbf{y}_3''=(1,-1,0,-1)^{\mathsf{T}}$. Then, $\Psi_{WS}(\{\mathbf{x}_1''\},\{\mathbf{y}_1'',\mathbf{y}_2'',\mathbf{y}_3''\})$ is a conjunction of the following inequalities

$$\begin{array}{llll}\lambda_2+\lambda_0 \geq 0 & -\lambda_2 \geq 0 & \lambda_2 \geq 0 & \lambda_1-\lambda_2 \geq 0\\ -\lambda_1+\lambda_2 \geq 1 & \lambda_1 \geq 0 & -\lambda_1 \geq 0 & \lambda_1 \geq 0\end{array} \tag{10}$$

The inequalities in the leftmost column correspond to applying (4,5) to $\mathbf{x}_1''$, and those in the other columns to applying (6,7) to $\mathbf{y}_1''$, $\mathbf{y}_2''$, and $\mathbf{y}_3''$ respectively. It is easy to verify that (10) is not satisfiable. Thus, $WS(\{\mathbf{x}_1''\},\{\mathbf{y}_1'',\mathbf{y}_2'',\mathbf{y}_3''\}) = \mathbb{Q}^3$.

COROLLARY 3.9. *There is no LRF for $I(\mathcal{Q})$, iff there are two sets $X \subseteq I(\mathcal{Q})$ and $Y \subseteq I(\mathcal{R_P})$ such that $WS(X,Y) = \mathbb{Q}^{n+1}$.*

The next lemma concerns the bit-size of the witness.

LEMMA 3.10. *If there exists a witness for the nonexistence of LRF for $I(\mathcal{Q})$, there exists one with $X \subseteq I(\mathcal{Q})$ and $Y \subseteq I(\mathcal{R_Q})$ such that $|X \cup Y| \leq n+1$; and the bit-size of $X \cup Y$ is polynomial in the bit-size of the input.*

Proof. Recall that by Lemma 3.7, if $I(\mathcal{Q})$ has no LRF, then

$$WS(\{\mathbf{x}''_1,\ldots,\mathbf{x}''_m\},\{\mathbf{y}''_1,\ldots,\mathbf{y}''_t\}) = \mathbb{Q}^{n+1}$$

or, equivalently, $\Psi_{WS}(\{\mathbf{x}''_1,\ldots,\mathbf{x}''_m\},\{\mathbf{y}''_1,\ldots,\mathbf{y}''_t\})$ has no solution. A corollary of Farkas' Lemma [41, p. 94] states that: if a set of inequalities over $\mathbb{Q}^n$ has no solution, there is a subset of at most n inequalities that has no solution. Since the set of inequalities $\Psi_{WS}(\{\mathbf{x}''_1,\ldots,\mathbf{x}''_m\},\{\mathbf{y}''_1,\ldots,\mathbf{y}''_t\})$ is over $\mathbb{Q}^{n+1}$, there is a subset of at most $n+1$ inequalities that has no solution. This subset involves at most $n+1$ integer points out of $\{\mathbf{x}''_1,\ldots,\mathbf{x}''_m\}$ and $\{\mathbf{y}''_1,\ldots,\mathbf{y}''_t\}$, because every inequality in $\Psi_{WS}(\{\mathbf{x}''_1,\ldots,\mathbf{x}''_m\},\{\mathbf{y}''_1,\ldots,\mathbf{y}''_t\})$ is defined by either one $\mathbf{x}''_i$ or $\mathbf{y}''_i$ (see eqs. (4–7)). Let these points be $X \cup Y$, then $|X \cup Y| \leq n+1$ and $\Psi_{WS}(X,Y)$ has no solution, i.e., $WS(X,Y) = \mathbb{Q}^{n+1}$.

Now we show that $X \cup Y$ may be chosen to have bit-size polynomial in the size of the input. Recall that the input is the set of inequalities $A''\mathbf{x}'' \leq \mathbf{b}$ that define $\mathcal{Q}$, and its bit-size is $\|\mathcal{Q}\|_b$. Recall that the points of $X \cup Y$ in Lemma 3.7 come from the generator representation, and that there is a generator representation in which each vertex/ray can fit in $\|\mathcal{Q}_I\|_v$ bits. Thus, the bit-size of $X \cup Y$ may be bounded by $(n+1) \cdot \|\mathcal{Q}_I\|_v$. By Th. 2.2, since the dimension of $\mathcal{Q}$ is $2n$,

$$(n+1) \cdot \|\mathcal{Q}_I\|_v \leq (n+1) \cdot (6 \cdot (2n)^3 \cdot \|\mathcal{Q}\|_f) \leq 96n^4 \cdot \|\mathcal{Q}\|_b$$

which is polynomial in the bit-size of the input. □

EXAMPLE 3.11. Consider $\Psi_{WS}(\{\mathbf{x}''_1\},\{\mathbf{y}''_1,\mathbf{y}''_2,\mathbf{y}''_3\})$ of Ex. 3.8. It is easy to see that the inequalities $-\lambda_2 \geq 0$, $\lambda_1 \geq 0$ and $-\lambda_1 + \lambda_2 \geq 1$ are enough for unsatisfiability ($n+1$ inequalities, since $n = 2$). These inequalities correspond to $\mathbf{x}''_1$ and $\mathbf{y}''_1$, and thus, they form a witness for the nonexistence of LRF.

THEOREM 3.12. LINRF($\mathbb{Z}$) $\in$ coNP *for SLC loops.*

Proof. We show that the complement of LINRF($\mathbb{Z}$) has a polynomially checkable witness. The witness is a listing of sets X and Y of at most $n+1$ elements and has a polynomial bit-size (specifically, a bit-size bounded as in Lemma 3.10). Verifying a witness consists of the following steps:

Step 1: Verify that each $\mathbf{x}'' \in X$ is in $I(\mathcal{Q})$, which can be done by verifying $A''\mathbf{x}'' \leq \mathbf{c}''$; and that each $\mathbf{y}'' \in Y$ is in $I(\mathcal{R_Q})$, which can be done by verifying $A''\mathbf{y}'' \leq 0$. This is done in polynomial-time. Note that according to Lemma 3.5 it is not necessary to check that X and Y come from a particular generator representation.

Step 2: Verify that $WS(X,Y) = \mathbb{Q}^{n+1}$. This can be done by checking that $\Psi_{WS}(X,Y)$ has no solutions, which can be done in polynomial-time since it is an LP problem over $\mathbb{Q}^{n+1}$. □

3.3 Inclusion in coNP for MLC loops

In this section we consider the inclusion in coNP for MLC loops. For this, we assume an input MLC loop with transition polyhedra $\mathcal{Q}_1,\ldots,\mathcal{Q}_k$ where each $\mathcal{Q}_i$ is specified by $A''_i\mathbf{x}'' \leq \mathbf{c}''_i$.

The proof follows the structure of the SLC case. The main difference is that points of the witness $X \cup Y$ may come from different transition polyhedra. Namely, $X = X_1 \cup \cdots \cup X_k$ and $Y = Y_1 \cup \cdots \cup Y_k$ where each $X_i \subseteq I(\mathcal{Q}_i)$ and $Y_i \subseteq I(\mathcal{R}_{\mathcal{Q}_i})$. We rewrite Lemmas 3.5, 3.7, and 3.10, Cor. 3.9, and Th. 3.12 in terms of such witnesses (the proofs are the same unless stated otherwise).

LEMMA 3.13. *Let $X = X_1 \cup \cdots \cup X_k$ and $Y = Y_1 \cup \cdots \cup Y_k$, where $X_i \subseteq I(\mathcal{Q}_i)$ and $Y_i \subseteq I(\mathcal{R}_{\mathcal{Q}_i})$. If $WS(X,Y) = \mathbb{Q}^{n+1}$, then there is no LRF for $I(\mathcal{Q}_1),\ldots,I(\mathcal{Q}_k)$.*

LEMMA 3.14. *For $1 \leq i \leq k$, let $\mathcal{Q}_{iI} = \text{convhull}\{X_i\} + \text{cone}\{Y_i\}$ be the integer hull of $\mathcal{Q}_i$, and define $X = X_1 \cup \cdots \cup X_k$ and $Y = Y_1 \cup \cdots \cup Y_k$. If there is no LRF for $I(\mathcal{Q}_1),\ldots,I(\mathcal{Q}_k)$, then $WS(X,Y) = \mathbb{Q}^{n+1}$.*

Proof. The proof follows that of Lemma 3.7. We pick $(\lambda_0,\vec{\lambda}) \in \mathbb{Q}^{n+1} \setminus WS(X,Y)$ and show that $\rho(\mathbf{x}) = \vec{\lambda} \cdot \mathbf{x} + \lambda_0$ is a LRF for each $I(\mathcal{Q}_i)$. This is accomplished by performing the same calculation, however referring to X_i and Y_i when proving that ρ is a LRF for $I(\mathcal{Q}_i)$. □

COROLLARY 3.15. *There is no LRF for $I(\mathcal{Q}_1),\ldots,I(\mathcal{Q}_k)$, iff there are two sets $X = X_1 \cup \cdots \cup X_k$ and $Y = Y_1 \cup \cdots \cup Y_k$, where $X_i \subseteq I(\mathcal{Q}_i)$ and $Y_i \subseteq I(\mathcal{R}_{\mathcal{Q}_i})$, such that $WS(X,Y) = \mathbb{Q}^{n+1}$.*

LEMMA 3.16. *If there exists a witness for the nonexistence of LRF for $I(\mathcal{Q}_1),\ldots,I(\mathcal{Q}_k)$, then there exists one, with $X = X_1 \cup \cdots \cup X_k$ and $Y = Y_1 \cup \cdots \cup Y_k$, where $X_i \subseteq I(\mathcal{Q}_i)$ and $Y_i \subseteq I(\mathcal{R}_{\mathcal{Q}_i})$, such that $|X \cup Y| \leq n+1$; and the bit-size of $X \cup Y$ is polynomial in the bit-size of the input.*

THEOREM 3.17. LINRF($\mathbb{Z}$) $\in$ coNP.

Proof. The difference from that of Th. 3.12 is that the witness is given as $X{=}X_1 \cup \cdots \cup X_k$ and $Y{=}Y_1 \cup \cdots \cup Y_k$. Thus, the verifier should use the appropriate set of inequalities to check that each $\mathbf{x}'' \in X_i$ is in $I(\mathcal{Q}_i)$, and that each $\mathbf{y}'' \in Y_i$ is in $I(\mathcal{R}_{\mathcal{Q}_i})$. □

EXAMPLE 3.18. Consider the following integer MLC loop

$$\begin{array}{lrcl} \textit{loop}: & x_1 \geq 0, x_2 \geq 0 & \Rightarrow & x'_1 = x_1 - 1 \\ & \vee\, x_1 \geq 0, x_2 \geq 0 & \Rightarrow & x'_2 = x_2 - 1, x'_1 = x_1 \end{array}$$

It is a classical MLC loop for which there is no LRF. The integer hull of the corresponding transition polyhedra are

$$\begin{array}{rl} \mathcal{Q}_{1I} = & \text{convhull}\{\mathbf{x}''_1\} + \text{cone}\{\mathbf{y}''_1,\mathbf{y}''_2,\mathbf{y}''_3,\mathbf{y}''_4\} \\ \mathcal{Q}_{2I} = & \text{convhull}\{\mathbf{x}''_2\} + \text{cone}\{\mathbf{y}''_5,\mathbf{y}''_6\} \end{array}$$

where $\mathbf{x}''_1{=}(0,0,-1,0)^{\mathrm{T}}$, $\mathbf{x}''_2{=}(0,0,0,-1)^{\mathrm{T}}$, $\mathbf{y}''_1{=}(0,0,0,-1)^{\mathrm{T}}$, $\mathbf{y}''_2 = (0,0,0,1)^{\mathrm{T}}$, $\mathbf{y}''_3 = (0,1,0,0)^{\mathrm{T}}$, $\mathbf{y}''_4 = (1,0,1,0)^{\mathrm{T}}$, $\mathbf{y}''_5 = (0,1,0,1)^{\mathrm{T}}$ and $\mathbf{y}''_6 = (1,0,1,0)^{\mathrm{T}}$. Let us first consider each path separately. We get

$$\Psi_{WS}(\{\mathbf{x}''_1\},\{\mathbf{y}''_1,\mathbf{y}''_2,\mathbf{y}''_3\}) = \left\{ \begin{array}{l} \lambda_0 \geq 0, \lambda_1 \geq 1, \\ \lambda_2 \geq 0, -\lambda_2 \geq 0 \end{array} \right\} \quad (11)$$

$$\Psi_{WS}(\{\mathbf{x}''_2\},\{\mathbf{y}''_4,\mathbf{y}''_5,\mathbf{y}''_6\}) = \{\lambda_0 \geq 0, \lambda_2 \geq 1\} \quad (12)$$

Both (11) and (12) are satisfiable. In fact, their solutions define the corresponding $LRFs$ for each path when considered separately. For the MLC loop, we have that $\Psi_{WS}(\{\mathbf{x}''_1,\mathbf{x}''_2\},\{\mathbf{y}''_1,\ldots,\mathbf{y}''_6\})$ is the conjunction of the inequalities in (11) and (12), which is not satisfiable. Thus, while each path has a LRF, the MLC loop does not. Note that the inequalities $\lambda_2 \geq 1$ and $-\lambda_2 \geq 0$ are enough to get unsatisfiability of (11,12), thus, $X{=}\{\mathbf{x}''_2\}$ and $Y{=}\{\mathbf{y}''_2\}$ is a witness, and consists of less than $n+1$ points ($n = 2$ in this case).

3.4 Synthesizing a linear ranking function

Although the existence of a LRF suffices for proving termination, generating a complete representation of the LRF is important in some contexts, for instance complexity analysis where a LRF provides an upper bound on the number of iterations that a loop can perform. In this section we give a complete algorithm that generates $LRFs$ for MLC loops given by transition polyhedra $\mathcal{Q}_1,\ldots,\mathcal{Q}_k$. The following lemma is directly implied by lemmas 3.13 and 3.14.

LEMMA 3.19. *For* $1 \leq i \leq k$, *let the integer hull of* $\mathcal{Q}_i$ *be* $\mathcal{Q}_{iI} = \text{convhull}\{X_i\} + \text{cone}\{Y_i\}$, *and define* $X = X_1 \cup \cdots \cup X_k$ *and* $Y = Y_1 \cup \cdots \cup Y_k$. *Then,* $\rho(\mathbf{x}) = \vec{\lambda} \cdot \mathbf{x} + \lambda_0$ *is a LRF for* $I(\mathcal{Q}_1), \ldots, I(\mathcal{Q}_k)$, *iff* $(\lambda_0, \vec{\lambda})$ *is a solution for* $\Psi_{WS}(X,Y)$.

The following algorithm is clearly implied: (1) Compute the generator representation for each $\mathcal{Q}_{iI}$; (2) Construct $\Psi_{WS}(X,Y)$; and (3) Use LP to find a solution $(\lambda_0, \vec{\lambda})$ for $\Psi_{WS}(X,Y)$.

EXAMPLE 3.20. Consider again Loop (1) from Sec. 1. The integer hull of the transition polyhedron is

$$\mathcal{Q}_I = \text{convhull}\{\mathbf{x}''_1, \mathbf{x}''_2\} + \text{cone}\{\mathbf{y}''_1, \mathbf{y}''_2\}$$

where $\mathbf{x}''_1 = (1,1,1,0)^{\mathrm{T}}$, $\mathbf{x}''_2 = (1,0,1,-1)^{\mathrm{T}}$, $\mathbf{y}''_1 = (1,1,1,-1)^{\mathrm{T}}$, and $\mathbf{y}''_2 = (1,-1,1,-3)^{\mathrm{T}}$. Then, $\Psi_{WS}(\{\mathbf{x}''_1, \mathbf{x}''_2\},\{\mathbf{y}''_1, \mathbf{y}''_2\})$ is the conjunction of the following inequalities (we eliminated clearly redundant inequalities)

$$\left\{\begin{array}{lll} \lambda_1 + \lambda_2 + \lambda_0 \geq 0, & \lambda_1 + \lambda_0 \geq 0, & \\ \lambda_1 + \lambda_2 \geq 0, & \lambda_1 - \lambda_2 \geq 0, & \lambda_2 \geq 1 \end{array}\right\} \tag{13}$$

which is satisfiable for $\lambda_1 = \lambda_2 = 1$ and $\lambda_0 = -1$, and therefore, $f(x_1, x_2) = x_1 + x_2 - 1$ is a LRF. Recall that this loop does not terminate when the variables range over $\mathbb{Q}$, e.g., for $x_1 = \frac{1}{2}$ and $x_2 = \frac{1}{2}$ (see Fig. 1(A)).

Let us consider now Loop (2) from Sec. 1. The integer hull of the transition polyhedron is

$$\mathcal{Q}_I = \text{convhull}\{\mathbf{x}''_1, \mathbf{x}''_2, \mathbf{x}''_3, \mathbf{x}''_4, \mathbf{x}''_5, \mathbf{x}''_6\} + \text{cone}\{\mathbf{y}''_1, \mathbf{y}''_2\}$$

where $\mathbf{x}''_1 = (4,16,1,16)^{\mathrm{T}}$, $\mathbf{x}''_2 = (1,4,0,4)^{\mathrm{T}}$, $\mathbf{x}''_3 = (2,8,1,8)^{\mathrm{T}}$, $\mathbf{x}''_4 = (1,1,0,1)^{\mathrm{T}}$, $\mathbf{x}''_5 = (4,1,1,1)^{\mathrm{T}}$, $\mathbf{x}''_6 = (2,1,1,1)^{\mathrm{T}}$, $\mathbf{y}''_1 = (5,0,2,0)^{\mathrm{T}}$ and $\mathbf{y}_2 = (5,20,2,20)^{\mathrm{T}}$. Then, the set of inequalities $\Psi_{WS}(\{\mathbf{x}''_1, \ldots, \mathbf{x}''_6\},\{\mathbf{y}''_1, \mathbf{y}''_2\})$ is the conjunction of the following inequalities (we eliminated clearly redundant inequalities)

$$\left\{\begin{array}{l} \lambda_1 \geq 1,\ 4\lambda_1+\lambda_2+\lambda_0 \geq 0,\ 4\lambda_1+16\lambda_2+\lambda_0 \geq 0, \\ 2\lambda_1+\lambda_2+\lambda_0 \geq 0,\ \lambda_1+4\lambda_2+\lambda_0 \geq 0, \\ 2\lambda_1+8\lambda_2+\lambda_0 \geq 0,\ 5\lambda_1+20\lambda_2 \geq 0,\ \lambda_1+\lambda_2+\lambda_0 \geq 0 \end{array}\right\} \tag{14}$$

which is satisfiable for $\lambda_1 = 1$, $\lambda_2 = 0$ and $\lambda_0 = -1$, and therefore, $f(x_1, x_2) = x_1 - 1$ is a LRF. Recall that this loop, too, does not terminate when the variables range over $\mathbb{Q}$, e.g., for $x_1 = \frac{1}{4}$ and $x_2 = 1$ (see Fig. 1(C)).

If we consider both loops (1) and (2) as two paths in an MLC loop, then to synthesize $LRFs$ we use the conjunction of the inequalities in (13) and (14). In this case, $\lambda_1 = \lambda_2 = 1$ and $\lambda_0 = -1$, is a solution, but $\lambda_1 = 1$, $\lambda_2 = 0$ and $\lambda_0 = -1$ is not. Therefore, $f(x_1, x_2) = x_1 + x_2 - 1$ is a LRF for both paths, and thus for the MLC loop, but not $f(x_1, x_2) = x_1 - 1$.

Given our hardness results, one cannot expect a polynomial-time algorithm. Indeed, constructing the generator representation of the integer hull of a polyhedron from the corresponding set of inequalities $A''_i\mathbf{x} \leq \mathbf{c}''_i$ may require exponential time—the number of generators itself may be exponential. Their bit-size, on the other hand, is polynomial by Th. 2.2. This is interesting, since it yields:

COROLLARY 3.21. *Given an MLC loop with transition polyhedra* $\mathcal{Q}_1, \ldots, \mathcal{Q}_k$, *where each* $\mathcal{Q}_i$ *is specified by* $A''_i\mathbf{x} \leq \mathbf{c}''_i$. *If there is a LRF for* $I(\mathcal{Q}_1), \ldots, I(\mathcal{Q}_k)$, *there is one whose bit-size is polynomial in the bit-size of* $A''_i\mathbf{x} \leq \mathbf{c}''_i$, *namely in* $\max_i \|\mathcal{Q}_i\|_b$.

Proof. As in the last section, we bound the bit-size of each of the generators of $\mathcal{Q}_{iI}$ by $\|\mathcal{Q}_{iI}\|_v \leq 6(2n)^3 \cdot \|\mathcal{Q}_i\|_f \leq 48n^3 \cdot \|\mathcal{Q}_i\|_b$ for an appropriate i. This means that the bit-size of each equation in $\Psi_{WS}(X,Y)$, having one of the forms (4), (5), (6), or (7) is at most $5 + 48n^3 \cdot (\max_i \|\mathcal{Q}_i\|_b)$. Let $\mathcal{P}$ be the polyhedron defined by $\Psi_{WS}(X,Y)$, then $\|\mathcal{P}\|_f \leq 5 + 48n^3 \cdot (\max_i \|\mathcal{Q}_i\|_b)$. If $\Psi_{WS}(X,Y)$ has a solution, then any vertex of $\mathcal{P}$ is such a solution, and yields a LRF. Using Th. 2.1, together with the above bound for $\|\mathcal{P}\|_f$ and the fact that the dimension of $\mathcal{P}$ is $n+1$, we conclude that there is a generator representation for $\mathcal{P}$ in which the bit-size $\|\mathcal{P}\|_v$ of the vertices is bounded as follows:

$$\|\mathcal{P}\|_v \leq 4 \cdot (n+1)^2 \cdot \|\mathcal{P}\|_f \leq 4 \cdot (n+1)^2 \cdot (5 + 48n^3 \cdot (\max_i \|\mathcal{Q}_i\|_b))$$

This also bounds the bit-size of the corresponding LRF. □

We conclude this section by noting that the algorithm induced by Lemma 3.19 works also for LINRF($\mathbb{Q}$), if we consider $\mathcal{Q}_i$ instead of $\mathcal{Q}_{iI}$. This can be easily proven by reworking the proofs of Lemmas 3.13 and 3.14 for the case of $\mathcal{Q}_i$ instead of $\mathcal{Q}_{iI}$. We did not develop this line since the main use of these lemmas is proving the coNP-completeness for LINRF($\mathbb{Z}$). This, however, has an interesting consequence: LINRF($\mathbb{Q}$) is still PTIME even if the input loop is given in the generator representations form instead of the constraints form. Practically, implementations of polyhedra that use of the *double description method*, such as the Parma Polyhedra Library [5], in which both the generators and constraint representations are kept at the same time, can use the algorithm of Lemma 3.19 judiciously when it seems better than algorithms that use the constraints representation [36, 38].

4. Special cases in PTIME

In this section we discuss cases in which the LINRF($\mathbb{Z}$) problem is PTIME-decidable. We start by a basic observation: when the transition polyhedron of an SLC loop is *integral*, the LINRF($\mathbb{Z}$) and LINRF($\mathbb{Q}$) problems are equivalent (a very similar statement appears in [22, Lemma 3]).

LEMMA 4.1. *Let* $\mathcal{Q}$ *be a transition polyhedron of a given SLC loop, and let* ρ *be a linear function. If* $\mathcal{Q}$ *is integral, then* ρ *is a LRF for* $\mathcal{Q}$ *iff* ρ *is a LRF for* $I(\mathcal{Q})$.

Proof. Let $\mathcal{Q}$ be integral. ($\Rightarrow$) Suppose that ρ is a LRF for $\mathcal{Q}$, then it is also a LRF for $I(\mathcal{Q})$ since $I(\mathcal{Q}) \subseteq \mathcal{Q}$. ($\Leftarrow$) Suppose that ρ is a LRF for $I(\mathcal{Q})$, it thus satisfies (4,5) of Def. 2.3 for any integer point in $\mathcal{Q}$. However, by definition of an integer polyhedron, every rational point in $\mathcal{Q}$ is a convex combination of integer points from $I(\mathcal{Q})$, this proves that ρ satisfies conditions (4,5) for any rational point as well. To see this, choose an arbitrary rational point $\mathbf{x}'' = \binom{\mathbf{x}}{\mathbf{x}'} \in \mathcal{Q}$. It can be written as $\mathbf{x}'' = \sum a_i \cdot \mathbf{x}''_i$ where $a_i \geq 0$, $\sum a_i = 1$ and $\mathbf{x}''_i \in I(\mathcal{Q})$. Thus, $\mathbf{x}'' = \binom{\mathbf{x}}{\mathbf{x}'} = \binom{\sum a_i \cdot \mathbf{x}_i}{\sum a_i \cdot \mathbf{x}'_i}$, and

$$\begin{aligned} \rho(\mathbf{x}) &= (\vec{\lambda} \cdot \sum a_i \cdot \mathbf{x}_i) + \lambda_0 \\ &= \sum a_i \cdot (\vec{\lambda} \cdot \mathbf{x}_i + \lambda_0) \geq 0 \end{aligned}$$

$$\begin{aligned} \rho(\mathbf{x}) - \rho(\mathbf{x}') &= (\vec{\lambda} \cdot \sum a_i \cdot \mathbf{x}_i) - (\vec{\lambda} \cdot \sum a_i \cdot \mathbf{x}'_i) \\ &= \sum a_i \cdot \vec{\lambda} \cdot (\mathbf{x}_i - \mathbf{x}'_i) \geq 1 \end{aligned}$$

□

The above lemma provides an alternative *complete* procedure for LINRF($\mathbb{Z}$), namely, compute a constraint representation of its integer hull Q_I and solve LINRF($\mathbb{Q}$). Note that computing the integer hull might require exponential time, and might also result in a polyhedron with an exponentially big description. This means that the above procedure is exponential in general; but this concern is circumvented if the transition polyhedron is integral to begin with; and in special cases where it is known that computing the integer hull is easy. Formally, we call a class of polyhedra *easy* if computing its integer hull can be done in polynomial time.

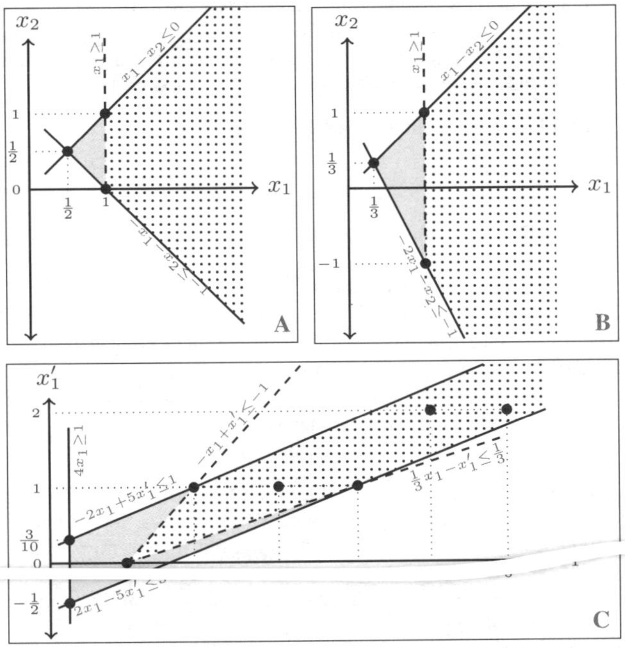

Figure 1. The polyhedra associated with three of our examples, projected to two dimensions. Dashed lines are added when computing the integer hull; dotted areas represent the integer hull; gray areas are rational points eliminated when computing the integer hull.

EXAMPLE 4.2. Consider again Loop (2) of Sec. 1. The transition polyhedron is not integral, computing its integer hull adds the inequalities $-x_1 + x_1' \leq -1$ and $\frac{1}{3}x_1 - x_1' \leq \frac{1}{3}$ (see Fig. 1(C)). Applying LINRF($\mathbb{Q}$) on this loop does not find a LRF since it does not terminate when the variables range over $\mathbb{Q}$, however, applying it on the integer hull finds the LRF $f(x_1, x_2) = x_1 - 1$.

COROLLARY 4.3. *The* LINRF($\mathbb{Z}$) *problem is PTIME-decidable for SLC loops in which the transition polyhedron $\mathcal{Q}$ is guaranteed to be integral. This also applies to any easy class of polyhedra, namely a class where the integer hull is PTIME-computable.*

Proof. Immediate from Lemma 4.1 and the fact that LINRF($\mathbb{Q}$) is PTIME-decidable. □

COROLLARY 4.4. *The* LINRF($\mathbb{Z}$) *problem is PTIME-decidable for SLC loops in which the condition polyhedron $\mathcal{C}$ is guaranteed to be integral, or belongs to an easy class, and the update is linear with integer coefficients.*

Proof. We show that in such case the transition polyhedron $\mathcal{Q}$ is, in fact, integral, and thus Cor. 4.3 applies. Let $\mathcal{C}$ be integral, and the update be $\mathbf{x}' = A'\mathbf{x} + \mathbf{c}'$ where the entries of A' and $\mathbf{c}'$ are integer. Let $\mathbf{x}'' = \binom{\mathbf{x}}{\mathbf{x}'} \in \mathcal{Q}$, that is, $\mathbf{x} \in \mathcal{C}$ and $\mathbf{x}' = A'\mathbf{x} + \mathbf{c}'$. Since $\mathcal{C}$ is integral, $\mathbf{x}$ is a convex combination of some integer points. I.e, $\mathbf{x} = \sum a_i \cdot \mathbf{x}_i$ where $a_i \geq 0$, $\sum a_i = 1$ and $\mathbf{x}_i \in I(\mathcal{C})$. Hence, $\mathbf{x}' = A'(\sum a_i \cdot \mathbf{x}_i) + \mathbf{c}' = \sum a_i \cdot (A'\mathbf{x}_i + \mathbf{c}')$ and

$$\mathbf{x}'' = \begin{pmatrix}\mathbf{x}\\ \mathbf{x}'\end{pmatrix} = \begin{pmatrix}\sum a_i \cdot \mathbf{x}_i\\ \sum a_i \cdot (A'\mathbf{x}_i + \mathbf{c}')\end{pmatrix} = \sum a_i \cdot \begin{pmatrix}\mathbf{x}_i\\ A'\mathbf{x}_i + \mathbf{c}'\end{pmatrix}$$

Now note that $\binom{\mathbf{x}_i}{A'\mathbf{x}_i + \mathbf{c}'}$ are integer points from $I(\mathcal{Q})$, which implies that $\mathbf{x}''$ is a convex combination of integer points in $\mathcal{Q}$. Hence, $\mathcal{Q}$ is integral. □

Corollaries 4.3 and 4.4 suggest looking for classes of SLC loops where we can easily ascertain that $\mathcal{Q}$ is integral, or that its integer hull can be computed in polynomial time. In what follows we address such cases: Sec. 4.1 discusses special cases in which the transition or condition polyhedron is integral by construction; Sec. 4.2 shows that for certain cases of *two-variables per inequality* constraints the integer hull can be computed in a polynomial time; Sec. 4.3 discusses the case of octagonal relations; Sec. 4.4 shows that for some cases LINRF($\mathbb{Z}$) is even strongly polynomial; and Sec. 4.5 extends the results to MLC loops.

4.1 Loops specified by integer polyhedra

There are some well-known examples of polyhedra that are known to be integral due to some structural property. This gives us classes of SLC loops where LINRF($\mathbb{Z}$) is in PTIME. The examples below are all from [41], where the proofs of the lemmas can be found.

LEMMA 4.5. *For any rational matrix B, the* cone $\{\mathbf{x} \mid B\mathbf{x} \leq \mathbf{0}\}$ *is an integer polyhedron.*

COROLLARY 4.6. *The* LINRF($\mathbb{Z}$) *problem is PTIME-decidable for SLC loops of the form*

$$\textit{while } (B\mathbf{x} \leq \mathbf{0}) \textit{ do } \mathbf{x}' = A'\mathbf{x} + \mathbf{c}'$$

where the entries in A' and $\mathbf{c}'$ are integer.

Recall that a matrix A is totally unimodular if each subdeterminant of A is in $\{0, \pm 1\}$. In particular, the entries of such matrix are from $\{0, \pm 1\}$.

LEMMA 4.7. *For any totally unimodular matrix A and integer vector* $\mathbf{b}$, *the polyhedron $\mathcal{P} = \{\mathbf{x} \mid A\mathbf{x} \leq \mathbf{b}\}$ is integral.*

For brevity, if a polyhedron $\mathcal{P}$ is specified by $A\mathbf{x} \leq \mathbf{b}$ in which A is a totally unimodular matrix and $\mathbf{b}$ an integer vector, we say that $\mathcal{P}$ is totally unimodular.

COROLLARY 4.8. *The* LINRF($\mathbb{Z}$) *problem is PTIME-decidable for SLC loops in which (1) the transition polyhedron $\mathcal{Q}$ is totally unimodular; or (2) the condition polyhedron $\mathcal{C}$ is totally unimodular and the update is linear with integer coefficients.*

As a notable example, difference bound constraints [7, 10, 11] are defined by totally unimodular matrices. Such constraints have the form $x - y \leq d$ with $d \in \mathbb{Q}$; constraints of the form $\pm x \leq d$ can also be admitted. In the integer case we can always tighten d to $\lfloor d \rfloor$ and thus get an integer polyhedron.

It might be worth mentioning that checking if a matrix is totally unimodular can be done in polynomial time [41, Th. 20.3, p. 290].

4.2 Two-variable per inequality constraints

In this section we consider cases in which the input loop involves *two-variable per inequality* constraints ($TVPI$ for brevity), i.e., inequalities of the form $ax + by \leq d$ with $a, b, d \in \mathbb{Q}$. Clearly, polyhedra defined by such inequalities are not guaranteed to be integral. See, for example, Fig. 1(B).

Harvey [29] showed that for *two-dimensional* polyhedra, which are specified by $TVPI$ constraints by definition, the integer hull can be computed in $O(m \log A_{max})$ where m is the number of inequalities and A_{max} is the magnitude of the largest coefficient.

DEFINITION 4.9. Let T be a set of $TVPI$ constraints. We say that T is a *product of independent two-dimensional $TVPI$ constraints* ($PTVPI$ for brevity), if it can be partitioned into $T_1, \ldots, T_n$ such that (1) each T_i is two-dimensional, i.e., involves at most two variables; and (2) each distinct T_i and T_j do not share variables.

LEMMA 4.10. *The integer hull of $PTVPI$ constraints can be computed in polynomial time.*

Proof. According to [41, Sec. 16.3, p. 231], a polyhedron $\mathcal{P}$ is integral iff each of its *faces* has an integer point. A face of $\mathcal{P}$ is obtained by turning some inequalities to equalities such that the resulting polyhedron in not empty (over the rationals). Clearly, if T_1 and T_2 are two sets of inequalities that do not share variables, and their faces have integer points, then all faces of $T_1 \cup T_2$ have integer points. Thus, $T_1 \cup T_2$ is integral. Partitioning T into independent $T_1, \ldots, T_n$ and checking that each is two-dimensional can done in polynomial time. Computing the integer hull of each T_i can be done in polynomial time using Harvey's method. □

The above approach can easily be generalized. Given any polyhedron, we first decompose it into independent sets of inequalities, in polynomial time (these are the connected components of an obvious graph), and then check if each set is covered by one of the special cases for which the integer hull can be efficiently computed.

COROLLARY 4.11. *The* LINRF($\mathbb{Z}$) *problem is PTIME-decidable for SLC loops in which: (1) the transition polyhedron $\mathcal{Q}$ is PTVPI; or (2) the condition polyhedron $\mathcal{C}$ is PTVPI, and the update is linear with integer coefficients.*

EXAMPLE 4.12. Consider the following SLC loop, as an example for case (1) of Cor. 4.11

$$\begin{array}{l} \mathit{while}\ (4x_1 \geq 1, x_2 \geq 1)\ \mathit{do} \\ \quad 2x_1 - 5x_1' \leq 3,\ -2x_1 + 5x_1' \leq 1,\ x_2' = x_2 + 1 \end{array} \tag{15}$$

Applying LINRF($\mathbb{Q}$) does not find a LRF since the loop does not terminate when the variables range over $\mathbb{Q}$, e.g., for $x_1 = \frac{1}{4}$ and $x_2 = 1$. The transition polyhedron is not integral, however, it is $PTVPI$ since it can be divided into $T_1 = \{4x_1 \geq 1, 2x_1 - 5x_1' \leq 3, -2x_1 + 5x_1' \leq 1\}$ and $T_2 = \{x_2 \geq 1, x_2' = x_2 + 1\}$. It is easy to check that T_2 is already integral. Computing the integer hull of T_1 adds the inequalities $-x_1 + x_1' \leq -1$ and $\frac{1}{3}x_1 - x_1' \leq \frac{1}{3}$. See Fig. 1(C). Now LINRF($\mathbb{Q}$) finds the LRF $f(x_1, x_2) = x_1 - 1$.

EXAMPLE 4.13. Consider the following loop, as an example for case (2) of Cor. 4.11

$$\begin{array}{l} \mathit{while}\ (-x_1 + x_2 \leq 0, -2x_1 - x_2 \leq -1, x_3 \leq 1)\ \mathit{do} \\ \quad x_1' = x_1,\ x_2' = x_2 - 2x_1 + x_3,\ x_3' = x_3 \end{array} \tag{16}$$

Applying LINRF($\mathbb{Q}$) does not find a LRF since it does not terminate over $\mathbb{Q}$, e.g., for $x_1 = x_2 = \frac{1}{2}$ and $x_3 = 1$. The condition polyhedron is not integral, but it is $PTVPI$ since the constraints can be divided into $T_1 = \{-x_1 + x_2 \leq 0, -2x_1 - x_2 \leq -1\}$ and $T_2 = \{x_3 \leq 1\}$. It is easily seen that T_2 is already integral; computing the integer hull of T_1 adds $x_1 \geq 1$. See Fig. 1(B). Now LINRF($\mathbb{Q}$) finds the LRF $f(x_1, x_2, x_3) = 2x_1 + x_2 - 1$. Note that the update in this loop involves constraints which are not $TVPI$.

4.3 Octagonal relations

$TVPI$ constraints in which the coefficients are from $\{0, \pm 1\}$ have received considerable attention in the area of program analysis. Such constraints are called *octagonal relations* [37]. A particular interest was in developing efficient algorithms for checking satisfiability of such relations, as well as inferring all implied *octagonal* inequalities, for variables ranging either over $\mathbb{Q}$ or over $\mathbb{Z}$.

Over $\mathbb{Q}$, this is done by computing the *transitive closure* of the relation, which basically adds inequalities that result from the addition of two existing inequalities, and possibly scaling to obtain coefficients of ± 1. E.g., starting from the set of inequalities $\{-x_1 + x_2 \leq 0, -x_1 - x_2 \leq -1\}$, we add $-2x_1 \leq -1$, or, after scaling, $-x_1 \leq -\frac{1}{2}$. Over $\mathbb{Z}$, this is done by computing the *tight closure*, which in addition to transitivity, is closed also under tightening. This operation replaces $ax + by \leq d$ by $ax + by \leq \lfloor d \rfloor$. For example, tightening $-x_1 \leq -\frac{1}{2}$ yields $-x_1 \leq -1$. The *tight closure* can be computed in polynomial time [4, 30, 39]. Since the tightening eliminates some non-integer points, it is tempting to expect that it actually computes the integer hull. It is easy to show that this is true for two-dimensional relations, but it is false already in three dimensions, as we show in the following example.

EXAMPLE 4.14. Consider the following loop

$$\begin{array}{l} \mathit{while}\ (x_1 + x_2 \leq 2, x_1 + x_3 \leq 3, x_2 + x_3 \leq 4)\ \mathit{do} \\ \quad x_1' = 1 - x_1, x_2' = 1 + x_1, x_3' = 1 + x_2 \end{array} \tag{17}$$

Note that the transition polyhedron is octagonal, but not integral. Applying LINRF($\mathbb{Q}$) does not find a LRF, since the loop does not terminate over $\mathbb{Q}$, e.g., for $x_1 = \frac{1}{2}$, $x_2 = \frac{3}{2}$, and $x_3 = \frac{5}{2}$. Computing the tight closure does not change the transition (or condition) polyhedron, and thus, it is of no help in finding the LRF. In order to obtain the integer hull of the transition (or condition) polyhedron we should add $x_1 + x_2 + x_3 \leq 4$, which is not an octagonal inequality. Having done so, LINRF($\mathbb{Q}$) finds the LRF $f(x_1, x_2, x_3) = -3x_1 - 4x_2 - 2x_3 + 12$.

Although it is not guaranteed that the tight closure of an octagonal relation corresponds to its integer hull, in practice, it does in many cases. Thus, since it can be computed in polynomial time, we suggest computing it before applying LINRF($\mathbb{Q}$) on loops that involve such relations. The above example shows that this does not give us a complete polynomial-time algorithm for LINRF($\mathbb{Z}$) over octagonal relations.

EXAMPLE 4.15. Consider the following SLC loop

$$\mathit{while} \left(\begin{array}{ll} -x_1 + x_2 \leq 0, & -x_1 - x_2 \leq -1, \\ x_2 - x_3 \leq 0, & -x_2 - x_3 \leq -1 \end{array} \right) \mathit{do}$$
$$x_1' = x_1,\ x_2' = x_2 - x_1 - x_3 + 1,\ x_3' = x_3$$

The condition polyhedron is octagonal, but not integral; moreover, it is not $PTVPI$. LINRF($\mathbb{Q}$) does not find a LRF (indeed the loop fails to terminate for $x_1 = x_2 = x_3 = \frac{1}{2}$). Computing the tight closure of the condition adds $-x_1 \leq -1$ and $-x_3 \leq 0$, which results in the integer hull. Now LINRF($\mathbb{Q}$) finds the LRF $f(x_1, x_2, x_3) = x_1 + x_2 - 1$.

A polynomial-time algorithm for computing the integer hull of octagonal relations is, unfortunately, ruled out by examples of such relations whose integer hulls have exponentially many facets.

THEOREM 4.16. *There is no polynomial-time algorithm for computing the integer hull of general octagonal relations.*

Proof. We build an octagonal relation $\mathcal{O}$, such that the minimum number of inequalities required to describe its integer hull $\mathcal{O}_I$ is not polynomial in the number of inequalities in $\mathcal{O}$.

For a complete graph $K_n = \langle V, E \rangle$, we let $\mathcal{P}$ be defined by the set of inequalities $\{x_e \geq 0 \mid e \in E\} \cup \{\sum_{v \in e} x_e \leq 1 \mid v \in V\}$. Here every edge $e \in E$ has a corresponding variable x_e, and the notation $v \in e$ means that v is a vertex of edge e. Note that $\mathcal{P}$ is not octagonal. It is well-known that $\mathcal{P}_I$, the matching polytope of K_n, has at least $\binom{n}{2} + 2^{n-1}$ facets [41, Sec. 18.2, p. 251], and thus any set of inequalities that defines $\mathcal{P}_I$ must have at least the same number of inequalities. Now let $\mathcal{O}$ be defined by $\{x_e \geq 0 \mid e \in E\} \cup \{x_{e_1} + x_{e_2} \leq 1 \mid v \in e_1, v \in e_2\}$, which includes $n + n \cdot \binom{n-1}{2}$ *octagonal inequalities*. It is easy to see that the integer solutions of $\mathcal{P}$ and $\mathcal{O}$ are the same, and thus $\mathcal{P}_I = \mathcal{O}_I$. This means that any set of inequalities that define $\mathcal{O}_I$ must have at least $\binom{n}{2} + 2^{n-1}$ inequalities. Therefore, any algorithm that computes such a representation must add at least $\binom{n}{2} + 2^{n-1} - n - n \cdot \binom{n-1}{2}$ inequalities to $\mathcal{O}$, which is super-polynomial in the size of $\mathcal{O}$. Unsurprisingly, the tight closure of $\mathcal{O}$ does not yield its integer hull (it only adds $x_e \leq 1$ for each x_e). □

Note that the above theorem does not rule out a polynomial-time algorithm for LINRF($\mathbb{Z}$), for SLC loops in which the transition polyhedron $\mathcal{Q}$ is octagonal, or where the condition polyhedron is octagonal and the update is linear with integer coefficients. It just rules out an algorithm that is based on computing the integer hull of the polyhedra. However, the coNP-hardness proof of Sec. 3.1 could be also carried out by a reduction from 3SAT that produces an SLC loop where the condition is octagonal and the update is linear with integer coefficients—so at least for this class there is, presumably, no polynomial solution. This reduction can be found in the technical report [8].

4.4 Strongly polynomial cases

Polynomial-time algorithms for LINRF($\mathbb{Q}$) [3, 36, 38] inherit their complexity from that of LP. While it is known that LP can be solved by a polynomial-time algorithm, it is an open problem whether it has a *strongly polynomial* algorithm. Such an algorithm should perform a number of elementary arithmetic operations polynomial in the *dimensions* of the input matrix instead of its bit-size (which accounts for the size of the matrix entries), and such operations should be performed on numbers of size which is polynomial to the input bit-size. However, there are some cases for which LP is known to have a strongly polynomial algorithm. We first use these cases to define classes of SLC loops for which LINRF($\mathbb{Q}$) has a strongly polynomial algorithm, which we then use to show that LINRF($\mathbb{Z}$) has a strongly polynomial algorithm for some corresponding classes of SLC loops. Our results are based on the following result by Tardos [44] (quoted from [41, p. 196]).

THEOREM 4.17 (Tardos). *There exists an algorithm which solves a given rational LP problem* $\max\{\mathbf{c}\cdot\mathbf{x} \mid A\mathbf{x} \leq \mathbf{b}\}$ *with at most* $P(size(A))$ *elementary arithmetic operations on numbers of size polynomially bounded by* $size(A, \mathbf{b}, \mathbf{c})$, *for some polynomial* P.

Note that the number of arithmetic operations required by the LP algorithm only depends on the bit-size of A. Clearly, if we restrict the LP problem to cases in which the bit-size of the entries of A is bounded by a constant, then $size(A)$ depends only on its dimensions, and we get a strongly polynomial time algorithm. In particular we can state the following.

COROLLARY 4.18. *There exists a strongly polynomial algorithm to solve an LP problem* $\max\{\mathbf{c}\cdot\mathbf{x} \mid A\mathbf{x} \leq \mathbf{b}\}$ *where the entries of* A *are* $\{0, \pm 1, \pm 2\}$.

We can use this to show that LINRF($\mathbb{Q}$) can sometimes be implemented with strongly polynomial complexity. To do this, we use the Podelski-Rybalchenko formulation of the procedure [38], slightly modified to require that the LRF decreases at least by 1 instead of by some $\delta > 0$.

THEOREM 4.19 (Podelski-Rybalchenko). *Given an SLC loop with a transition polyhedron* $\mathcal{Q} \subseteq \mathbb{Q}^{2n}$, *specified by* $A''\mathbf{x}'' \leq \mathbf{c}''$, *let* $A'' = (A\ A')$ *where each* A *and* A' *has* n *columns and* m *rows, and let* $\vec{\mu}, \vec{\eta}$ *be row vectors of different* m *rational variables each. A LRF for* $\mathcal{Q}$ *exists iff there is a (rational) solution to the following set of constraints*

$$\vec{\mu}, \vec{\eta} \geq \mathbf{0}^T, \quad \text{(18a)} \qquad \vec{\eta}\cdot(A + A') = \mathbf{0}^T, \quad \text{(18d)}$$
$$\vec{\mu}\cdot A' = \mathbf{0}^T, \quad \text{(18b)} \qquad \vec{\eta}\cdot\mathbf{c}'' \leq -1. \quad \text{(18e)}$$
$$(\vec{\mu} - \vec{\eta})\cdot A = \mathbf{0}^T, \quad \text{(18c)}$$

THEOREM 4.20. *The* LINRF($\mathbb{Q}$) *problem is decidable in strongly polynomial time for SLC loops specified by* $A''\mathbf{x}'' \leq \mathbf{c}''$ *where the coefficients of* A'' *are from* $\{0, \pm 1\}$.

Proof. First observe that, in Th. 4.19, when the matrix A'' has only entries from $\{0, \pm 1\}$, then all coefficients in the constraints (18a–18d) are from $\{0, \pm 1, \pm 2\}$. Moreover, the number of inequalities and variables in (18a–18d) is polynomial in the dimensions of A''. Now let us modify the Podelski-Rybalchenko procedure such that instead of testing for feasibility of the constraints (18a–18e), we consider the minimization of $\vec{\eta}\cdot\mathbf{c}''$ under the other constraints (18a–18d). Clearly, this answers the same question since: (18a–18e) is feasible, iff the minimization problem is unbounded, or the minimum is negative. This brings the problem to the form required by Cor. 4.18 and yields our result. □

COROLLARY 4.21. *The* LINRF($\mathbb{Z}$) *is decidable in strongly polynomial time for SLC loops, specified by* $A''\mathbf{x}'' \leq \mathbf{c}''$, *that are covered by any of the special cases of secs. 4.1 and 4.2 and the entries of* A'' *are from* $\{0, \pm 1\}$.

Proof. In the cases of Sec. 4.1, the transition polyhedron is guaranteed to be integral. In the $PTVPI$ case of Sec. 4.2: (1) the integer hull can be computed using Harvey's procedure, which is strongly polynomial in this case since the entries of A are from $\{0, \pm 1\}$. This can be done also using the tight closure of 2-dimensional octagons; and (2) the $TVPI$ constraints that we add when computing the integer hull have coefficients from $\{0, \pm 1\}$, and the number of such constraints is polynomially bounded by the number of the original inequalities. Thus, by Th. 4.20, we can apply a strongly polynomial-time algorithm for LINRF($\mathbb{Q}$). □

4.5 Multipath loops

Recall that a linear function ρ is a LRF for an MLC loop with transition polyhedra $\mathcal{Q}_1, \ldots, \mathcal{Q}_k$, iff it is a LRF for each $\mathcal{Q}_i$. Thus, if we have the set of $LRFs$ for each $\mathcal{Q}_i$, we can simply take the intersection and obtain the set of $LRFs$ for $\mathcal{Q}_1, \ldots, \mathcal{Q}_k$. In the Podelski-Rybalchenko procedure, the set of solutions for the inequalities (18a–18e) defines the set of $LRFs$ for the corresponding SLC loop as follows.

LEMMA 4.22. *Given an SLC loop with a transition polyhedron* $\mathcal{Q}$, *specified by* $A''\mathbf{x}'' \leq \mathbf{c}''$, *let* $\Delta(\vec{\mu}, \vec{\eta}, A'', c'')$ *be the conjunction of (18a–18e). Then,* $\rho(\mathbf{x}) = \vec{\lambda}\cdot\mathbf{x} + \lambda_0$ *is a LRF for* $\mathcal{Q}$ *iff* $\Delta(\vec{\mu}, \vec{\eta}, A'', c'')$ *has a solution such that* $\vec{\lambda} = \vec{\eta}\cdot A'$ *and* $\lambda_0 \geq \vec{\mu}\cdot\mathbf{c}''$.

The following lemma shows how to compute, using the above lemma, the intersection of sets of $LRFs$ for several transition polyhedra, and thus obtain the set of $LRFs$ for a given MLC loop. (a very similar statement appears in [22, Lemma 3]).

LEMMA 4.23. *Given an MLC loop with transition polyhedra* $\mathcal{Q}_1, \ldots, \mathcal{Q}_k$, *each specified by* $A''_i\mathbf{x}'' \leq \mathbf{c}''_i$, *let* $\Delta(\vec{\mu}_i, \vec{\eta}_i, A''_i, c''_i)$ *be the constraints (18a–18e) for the* i*-th path, and* $(\lambda_0, \vec{\lambda})$ *be* $n+1$ *rational variables. Then, there is a LRF for* $\mathcal{Q}_1, \ldots, \mathcal{Q}_k$, *iff the following is feasible (over the rationals)*

$$\bigwedge_{i=1}^{k} \Delta(\vec{\mu}_i, \vec{\eta}_i, A''_i, c''_i) \wedge \vec{\lambda} = \vec{\eta}_i\cdot A'_i \wedge \lambda_0 \geq \vec{\mu}_i\cdot\mathbf{c}''_i \qquad (19)$$

Moreover, the values of $(\lambda_0, \vec{\lambda})$ *in the solutions of* (19) *define the set of all LRFs for* $\mathcal{Q}_1, \ldots, \mathcal{Q}_k$.

Proof. Immediate by Lemma 4.22, noting that for each i the constraints $\Delta(\vec{\mu}_i, \vec{\eta}_i, A''_i, c''_i)$ use different $\vec{\mu}_i$ and $\vec{\eta}_i$, while $(\lambda_0, \vec{\lambda})$ are the same for all i. □

COROLLARY 4.24. *The* LINRF($\mathbb{Q}$) *problem for MLC loops is PTIME-decidable.*

Proof. The size of the set of inequalities (19) is polynomial in the size of the input MLC loop, and checking if it has a rational solution can be done in polynomial time. □

COROLLARY 4.25. *The* LINRF($\mathbb{Z}$) *problem for* MLC *loops is PTIME-decidable when each path corresponds to one of the special cases, for* SLC *loops, discussed in secs. 4.1 and 4.2.*

Proof. Immediate, since if the transition polyhedra are integral, LINRF($\mathbb{Z}$) and LINRF($\mathbb{Q}$) are equivalent. □

EXAMPLE 4.26. Consider an MLC loop with the following two paths: Loop (1) of Sec. 1; and the loop of Ex. 4.12. Applying LINRF($\mathbb{Q}$) (as in Lemma 4.23) does not find a LRF since both paths do not terminate when the variables range over $\mathbb{Q}$. If we first compute the integer hull of both paths, LINRF($\mathbb{Q}$) finds the LRF $f(x_1, x_2) = 3x_1+x_2-2$. Note that the integer hull of the first path is computable in polynomial-time since the condition is $PTVPI$ and the update is linear with integer coefficients. That of the second path is also computable in polynomial-time as in Ex. 4.12.

5. Prototype Implementation

The different algorithms presented in this paper, both for the general case and the special PTIME cases, have been implemented. The tool receives as input an MLC loop in constraints representation, and allows applying LINRF($\mathbb{Z}$) or LINRF($\mathbb{Q}$). It can be tried out via `http://www.loopkiller.com/irankfinder`, where all examples of this paper are also available. The implementation includes the algorithms of Lemmas 3.19 and 4.23. By default it uses the second one since the first one requires generating the generator representation of the transition polyhedron, which is exponential.

Computing the integer hull of a polyhedron, in the case of LINRF($\mathbb{Z}$), is done by first decomposing its set of inequalities into independent sets, and then computing the integer hull of each set separately. Each set of inequalities is first matched against one of the PTIME cases of secs. 4.1 and 4.2. If this matching fails, it computes the integer hull using Hartmann's algorithm [28] as explained by Charles et al. [18]. Note that this algorithm supports only bounded polyhedra, the integer hull of an unbounded polyhedron is computed by considering a corresponding bounded one [41, Th. 16.1, p. 231]. In addition, for octagonal relations, it gives the possibility of computing the tight closure instead of the integer hull. As we have seen in Sec. 4.3, when this option is used, completeness of LINRF($\mathbb{Z}$) is not guaranteed. The Parma Polyhedra Library [5] is used for converting between generator and constraints representations, solving (mixed) LP problems, etc.

6. Related work

There are several works [3, 20, 36, 38, 42] that directly address the LINRF($\mathbb{Q}$) problem for SLC or MLC loops. In all these works, the underlying techniques allow synthesizing $LRFs$ and not only deciding if one exists. The common observation to all these works is that synthesising $LRFs$ can be done by inferring the implied inequalities of a given polyhedron (the transition polyhedron of the loop), in particular inequalities like conditions (4) and (5) of Def. 2.3 that define a LRF. Regarding completeness, all these methods are complete for LINRF($\mathbb{Q}$) but not for LINRF($\mathbb{Z}$). They can also be used to approximate LINRF($\mathbb{Z}$) by relaxing the loop such that its variables range over $\mathbb{Q}$ instead of $\mathbb{Z}$, thus sacrificing completeness. All these methods have a corresponding PTIME algorithm. Exceptions in this line of research are the work of Bradley et al. [13] and Cook et al. [22] that directly address the LINRF($\mathbb{Z}$) problem for MLC loops.

Sohn and Van Gelder [42] considered MLC loops with variables ranging over $\mathbb{N}$. These are abstractions of loops from logic programs. The loops were, in fact, relaxed from $\mathbb{N}$ to $\mathbb{Q}_+$ before seeking a LRF, however, this is not explicitly mentioned. The main observation is that the duality theorem of LP [41, p. 92] can be used to infer inequalities that are implied by the transition polyhedron. The authors also mention that this was observed before by Lassez [33] in the context of solving CLP($\mathbb{R}$) queries. Completeness was not addressed in this work, and the PTIME complexity was mentioned but not formally addressed. Later, Mesnard and Serebrenik [36] formally proved that the techniques of Sohn and Van Gelder [42] provide a complete PTIME method for LINRF($\mathbb{Q}$), also for the case of MLC loops. They pointed out the incompleteness for LINRF($\mathbb{Z}$).

Probably the most popular work on the synthesis of $LRFs$ is the one of Podelski and Rybalchenko [38]. They also observed the need for deriving inequalities implied by the transition polyhedron, but instead of using the duality theorem of LP they used the affine form of Farkas' lemma [41, p. 93]. Completeness was claimed, and the statement did not make it clear that the method is complete for LINRF($\mathbb{Q}$) but not for LINRF($\mathbb{Z}$). This was clarified, however, in the PhD thesis of Rybalchenko [40].

Bagnara et al. [6] proved that the methods of Sohn and Van Gelder [36] and Podelski and Rybalchenko [38] are actually equivalent, i.e., they compute the same set of $LRFs$. They also showed that the method of Podelski and Rybalchenko can, potentially, be more efficient since it requires solving rational constraints systems with fewer variables and constraints.

The earliest appearances of a solution based on Farkas' Lemma, that we know of, are by Colón and Sipma [20], in the context of termination analysis, and by Feautrier [25], in the context of automatic parallelization of computations. Colón and Sipma did not claim that the problem can be solved in polynomial time, and indeed their implementation seems to have exponential complexity since they use generators and polars, despite the similarity of the underlying theory to that of [38]. Completeness was claimed, however it was not explicitly mentioned that the variables range over $\mathbb{Q}$ and not $\mathbb{Z}$.

Feautrier [25] described scheduling of computations that can be described by recursive equations. An abstraction to a form similar to an MLC loop allowed him to compute a so-called *schedule*, which is essentially a ranking function, but used backwards, since the computations at the bottom of the recursion tree are to be completed first.

Cook et al. [22] observed that the Farkas-lemma based solution is complete for LINRF($\mathbb{Z}$) when the input MLC loop is specified by integer polyhedra. They also mention that any polyhedron can be converted to an integer one, and that this might increase its size exponentially. Unlike our work, they do not address PTIME cases or the complexity of LINRF($\mathbb{Z}$). In fact, the main issue in that work is the synthesis of ranking functions for bit-victors relations.

Bradley et al. [13] directly addressed the LINRF($\mathbb{Z}$) problem for MLC loops, and stated that the methods of Colón and Sipma [20] and Podelski and Rybalchenko [38] are not complete for LINRF($\mathbb{Z}$). Their technique is based on the observation that if there is a LRF, then there exists one in which each coefficient λ_i has a value in the interval $[-1, 1]$, and moreover with denominators that are power of 2. Using this observation, they recursively search for the coefficients starting from a region defined by a hyperrectangle in which each λ_i is in the interval $[-1, 1]$. Given a hyperrectangle, the algorithm first checks if one of its corners defines a LRF, in which case it stops. Otherwise, the region is either pruned (if it can be verified that it contains no solution), or divided into smaller regions for recursive search. Testing if a region should be pruned is done by checking the satisfiability of a possibly exponential (in the number of variables) number of Presburger formulas. The algorithm will find a LRF if exists, but it might not terminate if no LRF exists. To make it practical, it is parametrized by the search depth, thus sacrificing completeness. It is interesting to note that the search-depth parameter in their algorithm actually bounds the bit-size of the LRF coefficients. Our Cor. 3.21 shows that it is possible to deterministically bound this depth, that turning their algorithm into a complete one, though still exponential.

Codish et al. [19] studied the synthesis of $LRFs$ for SLC loops with *size-change* constraints (i.e., of the form $x_i \geq x'_j + c$ where $c \in \{0, 1\}$), and *monotonicity* constraints (i.e., of the form $X \geq Y + c$, where X and Y are variables or primed variables, and $c \in \{0, 1\}$). In both cases the variables ranged over $\mathbb{N}$. For size-change constraints, they proved that the loop terminates iff a LRF exists, moreover, such function has the form $\sum \lambda_i \cdot x_i$ with $\lambda_i \in \{0, 1\}$. For the case of monotonicity constraints, they proved that the loop terminates iff a LRF exists for the *balanced* version of the loop, and has the form $\sum \lambda_i \cdot x_i$ with $\lambda_i \in \{0, \pm 1\}$. Intuitively, a balanced loop includes $x'_i \geq x'_j + c$ iff it includes $x_i \geq x_j + c$. They showed how to balance the loop while preserving its termination behavior. Recently, Bozga et al. [10] presented similar results for SLC loops defined by octagonal relations.

Bradley et al. [12] extended the work of Colón and Sipma [20] and searched *lexicographic* $LRFs$. In [14, 15] they considered multipath loops with polynomial transitions and the synthesis of lexicographic polynomial ranking functions, where the notion of ranking functions was also relaxed to functions that *eventually* decrease. Cousot [23] used Lagrangian relaxation for inferring possibly non-linear ranking functions. In the linear case, Lagrangian relaxation is similar to the affine form of Farkas' lemma.

Alias et al. [3] again rediscovered the Farkas-lemma based solution for LINRF($\mathbb{Q}$), or rather "ported" it from the former work by Feautrier, but this time for termination and cost analysis. Like [12], they construct lexicographic $LRFs$, however, they do it for programs with an arbitrary control-flow graph, and they prove completeness of their procedure. Their goal was to use these functions to derive cost bounds (like a bound on the worst-case number of transitions in terms of the initial state); this bound is (when it can be found) a polynomial, whose degree is at most the dimension of the (co-domain of the) lexicographic ranking function. Alias et al.'s construction produces a function of minimum dimension. They, too, have relaxed the problem from integers to rationals and failed to state that their completeness results depend on this relaxation.

Decidability and complexity of termination (in general, not necessarily with $LRFs$) of SLC and MLC loops has been intensively studied for different classes of constraints. For SLC loops, Tiwari [45] proved that the problem is decidable when the update is linear and the variables range over $\mathbb{R}$. Braverman [16] proved that this holds also for $\mathbb{Q}$, and for the homogeneous case it holds for $\mathbb{Z}$. Both considered universal termination. Also, in both cases they allow the use of strict inequalities in the condition. Ben-Amram et al. [9] showed that the termination of SLC loops is at least EXPSPACE-hard, and that the problem is undecidable for some extensions that introduce a simple form of non-linearity; and also for SLC loops in which the use of a single irrational coefficient is allowed. See these works for references to additional results on the decidability of termination in other types of loops.

7. Concluding remarks

We have studied the Linear Ranking problem for single-path and multipath linear constraint loops and observed the difference between the LINRF($\mathbb{Q}$) problem, where variables range over the rationals, and the LINRF($\mathbb{Z}$) problem, where variables only take integer values. In practice, the latter is more common, but the complexity of the problem has not been studied before; the common approach has been to relax the problem to the rationals, where complete, polynomial-time decision procedures have been known.

We have confirmed that LINRF($\mathbb{Z}$) is a harder problem, proving it to be coNP-complete. On a positive note, this shows that there *is* a complete solution, even if exponential-time. We further showed that some special cases of importance do have a PTIME solution.

The latter results arise from a proof that for integer polyhedra, LINRF($\mathbb{Z}$) and LINRF($\mathbb{Q}$) are equivalent. Interestingly, this is not the case for termination in general. For example, the transition polyhedron of the loop "$while\ x \geq 0\ do\ x' = 10 - 2x$" is integral; the loop terminates when the variables range over $\mathbb{Z}$ but does not terminate when they range over $\mathbb{Q}$, specifically for $x = 3\frac{1}{3}$. Note that this loop does not have a LRF over the integers.

A more general notion of ranking function applies to an arbitrary control-flow graph with transitions specified by source and target nodes as well as linear constraints on the values of variables. In this setting, one seeks to associate a (possibly different) affine function ρ_ν with each node ν, so that on a transition from ν to ν' we have $\rho_\nu(\mathbf{x}) > \rho_{\nu'}(\mathbf{x}')$. Such functions can be found by LP, a procedure complete over the rationals, using a simple extension of the solution for the loops we have discussed [3, 36]. The considerations regarding the complexity of the corresponding problem over integers are essentially the same as those we have presented, and we preferred to use the simpler model for clearer presentation.

In all examples that we have discussed in this paper, when a loop has a LRF over $\mathbb{Z}$ but not over $\mathbb{Q}$, then the loop did not terminate over $\mathbb{Q}$. This is, however, not the case in general. A counter-example can be constructed by combining (i.e., executing simultaneously) the loop of Ex. 3.6 and Loop (1) of Sec. 1.

In the context of complexity (cost) analysis, there is a special interest in $LRFs$ that decrease at least by 1 in each iteration, since they bound the number of iterations of a given loop. In order to get tight bounds, even if $\mathcal{Q}$ has a LRF it might be worthwhile to compute one for $I(\mathcal{Q})$. To see this, let us add $4x_1 \geq 3$ to the condition of Loop (1) in Sec. 1. Then, both $\mathcal{Q}$ and $I(\mathcal{Q})$ have $LRFs$. For $I(\mathcal{Q})$ the most tight one (under the requirement to decrease by at least 1) is $f_1(x_1, x_2) = x_1 + x_2 - 1$, while for $\mathcal{Q}$ it is $f_2(x_1, x_2) = 2x_1 + 2x_2 - 2$. Hence, a better bound is obtained using $I(\mathcal{Q})$. The same observation applies to loop parallelization: the functions' value gives the schedule's *latency* (depth of the computation tree) and a lower value is preferable.

Acknowledgments

We thank Alain Darte for a helpful discussion. The work of Samir Genaim was funded in part by the EU project ICT-231620 *HATS*, and the Spanish projects TIN-2008-05624 *DOVES* and TIN-2012-38137 *VIVAC*.

References

[1] E. Albert, P. Arenas, S. Genaim, G. Puebla, and D. Zanardini. Costa: Design and implementation of a cost and termination analyzer for java bytecode. In F. S. de Boer, M. M. Bonsangue, S. Graf, and W. P. de Roever, editors, *Formal Methods for Components and Objects, FMCO'07*, volume 5382 of *LNCS*, pages 113–132. Springer, 2007.

[2] E. Albert, P. Arenas, S. Genaim, and G. Puebla. Closed-form upper bounds in static cost analysis. *J. Autom. Reasoning*, 46(2):161–203, 2011.

[3] C. Alias, A. Darte, P. Feautrier, and L. Gonnord. Multi-dimensional rankings, program termination, and complexity bounds of flowchart programs. In R. Cousot and M. Martel, editors, *Static Analysis Symposium, SAS'10*, volume 6337 of *LNCS*, pages 117–133. Springer, 2010.

[4] R. Bagnara, P. M. Hill, and E. Zaffanella. An improved tight closure algorithm for integer octagonal constraints. In F. Logozzo, D. Peled, and L. D. Zuck, editors, *Verification, Model Checking, and Abstract Interpretation, VMCAI'08*, volume 4905 of *LNCS*, pages 8–21. Springer, 2008.

[5] R. Bagnara, P. M. Hill, and E. Zaffanella. The parma polyhedra library: Toward a complete set of numerical abstractions for the analysis and verification of hardware and software systems. *Sci. Comput. Program.*, 72(1-2):3–21, 2008.

[6] R. Bagnara, F. Mesnard, A. Pescetti, and E. Zaffanella. A new look at the automatic synthesis of linear ranking functions. *Inf. Comput.*, 215: 47–67, 2012.

[7] A. M. Ben-Amram. Size-change termination with difference constraints. *ACM Trans. Program. Lang. Syst.*, 30(3), 2008.

[8] A. M. Ben-Amram and S. Genaim. On the linear ranking problem for integer linear-constraint loops. *CoRR*, abs/1208.4041, 2012.

[9] A. M. Ben-Amram, S. Genaim, and A. N. Masud. On the termination of integer loops. In V. Kuncak and A. Rybalchenko, editors, *Verification, Model Checking, and Abstract Interpretation, VMCAI'12*, volume 7148 of *LNCS*, pages 72–87. Springer, 2012.

[10] M. Bozga, R. Iosif, and F. Konecný. Deciding conditional termination. In C. Flanagan and B. König, editors, *Tools and Algorithms for the Construction and Analysis of Systems, TACAS'12*, volume 7214 of *LNCS*, pages 252–266. Springer, 2012.

[11] L. Bozzelli and S. Pinchinat. Verification of gap-order constraint abstractions of counter systems. In V. Kuncak and A. Rybalchenko, editors, *Verification, Model Checking, and Abstract Interpretation, VMCAI'12*, volume 7148 of *LNCS*, pages 88–103. Springer, 2012.

[12] A. R. Bradley, Z. Manna, and H. B. Sipma. Linear ranking with reachability. In K. Etessami and S. K. Rajamani, editors, *Computer Aided Verification, CAV'05*, volume 3576 of *LNCS*, pages 491–504. Springer, 2005.

[13] A. R. Bradley, Z. Manna, and H. B. Sipma. Termination analysis of integer linear loops. In M. Abadi and L. de Alfaro, editors, *Concurrency Theory, CONCUR 2005*, volume 3653 of *LNCS*, pages 488–502. Springer, 2005.

[14] A. R. Bradley, Z. Manna, and H. B. Sipma. The polyranking principle. In L. Caires, G. F. Italiano, L. Monteiro, C. Palamidessi, and M. Yung, editors, *International Colloquium on Automata, Languages and Programming, ICALP'05*, volume 3580 of *LNCS*, pages 1349–1361. Springer, 2005.

[15] A. R. Bradley, Z. Manna, and H. B. Sipma. Termination of polynomial programs. In R. Cousot, editor, *Verification, Model Checking, and Abstract Interpretation, VMCAI'05*, volume 3385 of *LNCS*, pages 113–129. Springer, 2005.

[16] M. Braverman. Termination of integer linear programs. In T. Ball and R. B. Jones, editors, *Computer Aided Verification, CAV'06*, volume 4144 of *LNCS*, pages 372–385. Springer, 2006.

[17] M. Bruynooghe, M. Codish, J. P. Gallagher, S. Genaim, and W. Vanhoof. Termination analysis of logic programs through combination of type-based norms. *ACM Trans. Program. Lang. Syst.*, 29(2), 2007.

[18] P. J. Charles, J. M. Howe, and A. King. Integer polyhedra for program analysis. In A. V. Goldberg and Y. Zhou, editors, *Algorithmic Aspects in Information and Management, AAIM'09*, volume 5564 of *LNCS*, pages 85–99. Springer, 2009.

[19] M. Codish, V. Lagoon, and P. J. Stuckey. Testing for termination with monotonicity constraints. In M. Gabbrielli and G. Gupta, editors, *International Conference on Logic Programming, ICLP'05*, volume 3668 of *LNCS*, pages 326–340. Springer, 2005.

[20] M. Colón and H. Sipma. Synthesis of linear ranking functions. In T. Margaria and W. Yi, editors, *Tools and Algorithms for the Construction and Analysis of Systems, TACAS'01*, volume 2031 of *LNCS*, pages 67–81. Springer, 2001.

[21] B. Cook, A. Podelski, and A. Rybalchenko. Termination proofs for systems code. In M. I. Schwartzbach and T. Ball, editors, *Programming Language Design and Implementation, PLDI'06*, pages 415–426. ACM, 2006.

[22] B. Cook, D. Kroening, P. Rümmer, and C. M. Wintersteiger. Ranking function synthesis for bit-vector relations. In J. Esparza and R. Majumdar, editors, *Tools and Algorithms for the Construction and Analysis of Systems, 16th International Conference, TACAS'10*, volume 6015 of *LNCS*, pages 236–250. Springer, 2010.

[23] P. Cousot. Proving program invariance and termination by parametric abstraction, lagrangian relaxation and semidefinite programming. In R. Cousot, editor, *Verification, Model Checking, and Abstract Interpretation, VMCAI'05*, volume 3385 of *LNCS*, pages 1–24, 2005.

[24] A. Darte. Understanding loops: The influence of the decomposition of Karp, Miller, and Winograd. In *Formal Methods and Models for Codesign, MEMOCODE'10*, pages 139–148. IEEE Computer Society, 2010.

[25] P. Feautrier. Some efficient solutions to the affine scheduling problem. I. one-dimensional time. *International Journal of Parallel Programming*, 21(5):313–347, 1992.

[26] M. R. Garey and D. S. Johnson. *Computers and Intractability*. W.H. Freeman and Co., New York, 1979.

[27] J. Giesl, R. Thiemann, P. Schneider-Kamp, and S. Falke. Automated termination proofs with aprove. In V. van Oostrom, editor, *Rewriting Techniques and Applications, RTA'04*, volume 3091 of *LNCS*, pages 210–220. Springer, 2004.

[28] M. E. Hartmann. *Cutting Planes and the Complexity of the Integer Hull*. PhD thesis, School of Operations Research and Industrial Engineering, Cornell University, 1988.

[29] W. Harvey. Computing two-dimensional integer hulls. *SIAM J. Comput.*, 28(6):2285–2299, 1999.

[30] W. Harvey and P. J. Stuckey. A unit two variable per inequality integer constraint solver for constraint logic programming. In *Australasian Computer Science Conference, ACSC'97*, pages 102–111, 1997.

[31] R. M. Karp. Reducibility among combinatorial problems. In R. E. Miller and J. W. Thatcher, editors, *Complexity of Computer Computations*, pages 85–103. Plenum Press, New York, 1972.

[32] R. M. Karp and C. H. Papadimitriou. On linear characterizations of combinatorial optimization problems. In *Symp. on Foundations of Computer Science, FOCS'80*, pages 1–9. IEEE Computer Society, 1980.

[33] J.-L. Lassez. Querying constraints. In *Symposium on Principles of Database Systems*, pages 288–298. ACM Press, 1990.

[34] C. S. Lee, N. D. Jones, and A. M. Ben-Amram. The size-change principle for program termination. In C. Hankin and D. Schmidt, editors, *Symposium on Principles of Programming Languages, POPL'01*, pages 81–92, 2001.

[35] N. Lindenstrauss and Y. Sagiv. Automatic termination analysis of Prolog programs. In L. Naish, editor, *International Conference on Logic Programming, ICLP'97*, pages 64–77. MIT Press, 1997.

[36] F. Mesnard and A. Serebrenik. Recurrence with affine level mappings is p-time decidable for clp(r). *TPLP*, 8(1):111–119, 2008.

[37] A. Miné. The octagon abstract domain. *Higher-Order and Symbolic Computation*, 19(1):31–100, Mar. 2006.

[38] A. Podelski and A. Rybalchenko. A complete method for the synthesis of linear ranking functions. In B. Steffen and G. Levi, editors, *Verification, Model Checking, and Abstract Interpretation, VMCAI'04*, volume 2937 of *LNCS*, pages 239–251. Springer, 2004.

[39] P. Z. Revesz. Tightened transitive closure of integer addition constraints. In V. Bulitko and J. C. Beck, editors, *Symposium on Abstraction, Reformulation, and Approximation, SARA'09*, 2009.

[40] A. Rybalchenko. *Temporal Verification with Transition Invariants*. PhD thesis, Universität des Saarlandes, 2004.

[41] A. Schrijver. *Theory of Linear and Integer Programming*. John Wiley and Sons, New York, 1986.

[42] K. Sohn and A. V. Gelder. Termination detection in logic programs using argument sizes. In D. J. Rosenkrantz, editor, *Symposium on Principles of Database Systems*, pages 216–226. ACM Press, 1991.

[43] F. Spoto, F. Mesnard, and É. Payet. A termination analyzer for java bytecode based on path-length. *ACM Trans. Program. Lang. Syst.*, 32 (3), 2010.

[44] Éva. Tardos. A strongly polynomial algorithm to solve combinatorial linear programs. *Operations Research*, 34:250–256, 1986.

[45] A. Tiwari. Termination of linear programs. In R. Alur and D. Peled, editors, *Computer Aided Verification, CAV'04*, volume 3114 of *LNCS*, pages 387–390. Springer, 2004.

Advanced Automata Minimization

Lorenzo Clemente
LaBRI, University of Bordeaux I
lorenzo.clemente@labri.fr

Richard Mayr
University of Edinburgh
homepages.inf.ed.ac.uk/rmayr

Abstract

We present an efficient algorithm to reduce the size of nondeterministic Büchi word automata, while retaining their language. Additionally, we describe methods to solve PSPACE-complete automata problems like universality, equivalence and inclusion for much larger instances (1-3 orders of magnitude) than before. This can be used to scale up applications of automata in formal verification tools and decision procedures for logical theories.

The algorithm is based on new transition pruning techniques. These use criteria based on combinations of backward and forward trace inclusions. Since these relations are themselves PSPACE-complete, we describe methods to compute good approximations of them in polynomial time.

Extensive experiments show that the average-case complexity of our algorithm scales quadratically. The size reduction of the automata depends very much on the class of instances, but our algorithm consistently outperforms all previous techniques by a wide margin. We tested our algorithm on Büchi automata derived from LTL-formulae, many classes of random automata and automata derived from mutual exclusion protocols, and compared its performance to the well-known automata tool GOAL [34].

Categories and Subject Descriptors D.2.4 [*Software Verification*]: Model checking; F.1.1 [*Models of Computation*]: Automata

General Terms Automata minimization, inclusion checking

Keywords Büchi automata, simulation, minimization

1. Introduction

Nondeterministic Büchi automata are an effective way to represent and manipulate ω-regular languages, since they are closed under boolean operations. They appear in many automata-based formal software verification methods, as well as in decision procedures for logical theories. For example, in LTL software model checking [13, 22], temporal logic specifications are converted into Büchi automata. In other cases, different versions of a program (obtained by abstraction or refinement of the original) are translated into automata whose languages are then compared. Testing the conformance of an implementation with its requirements specification thus reduces to a language inclusion or language equivalence problem. Another application of Büchi automata in software engineering is program termination analysis by the size-change termination method [15, 26]. Via an abstraction of the effect of program operations on data, the termination problem can often be reduced to a language inclusion problem about two derived Büchi automata.

Our goal is to improve the efficiency and scalability of automata-based formal software verification methods. We consider efficient algorithms for the minimization of automata, in the sense of obtaining a smaller automaton with the same language, though not necessarily with the absolute minimal possible number of states. (And, in general, the minimal automaton for a language is not even unique.) The reason to perform minimization is that the smaller minimized automaton is more efficient to handle in a subsequent computation. Thus there is an algorithmic tradeoff between the effort for minimization and the complexity of the problem later considered for this automaton. If only computationally easy questions are asked (e.g., reachability/emptiness; solvable in Logspace/PTIME) then extensive minimization usually does not pay off. Instead, the main applications are the following:

1. Computationally hard automata problems like universality, equivalence, and inclusion. These are PSPACE-complete [25], but many practically efficient methods have been developed [3, 4, 6, 10, 11, 15, 16, 29]. Still, these all have exponential time complexity and do not scale well. Typically they are applied to automata with 15–100 states (unless the automaton has a particularly simple structure). Thus, one should first minimize the automata before applying these exponential-time methods. A good minimization algorithm makes it possible to solve much larger instances. Even better, many instances of the PSPACE-complete universality, equivalence, and inclusion problems can already be solved in the *polynomial time* minimization algorithm (e.g., by reducing the automaton to the trivial universal automaton), so that the complete *exponential time* methods only need to be invoked in a small minority of instances.
2. Cases where the size of an automaton strongly affects the complexity of an algorithm. In LTL model checking [22] one searches for loops in a graph that is the *product* of a large system specification with an automaton derived from an LTL-formula. Smaller automata often make this easier, though in practice it also depends on the degree of nondeterminism [30].
3. Procedures that combine and modify automata repeatedly. Model checking algorithms and automata-based decision procedures for logical theories compute automata products, unions, complements, projections, etc., and thus the sizes of automata grow rapidly. Thus, it is important to intermittently minimize the automata to keep their size manageable, e.g., [27].

In general, finding an automaton with the minimal number of states for a given language is computationally hard; even deciding whether a given automaton is minimal is already PSPACE-complete [23]. Thus much effort has been devoted to finding methods for partial minimization [8, 13, 14, 24]. Simulation preorders played a central role in these efforts, because they provide PTIME-

POPL'13, January 23–25, 2012, Rome, Italy.

computable under-approximations of trace inclusions. However, the quality of the approximation is insufficient in many practical examples. Multipebble simulations [12] yield coarser relations by allowing the Duplicator player to hedge her bets in the simulation game, but they are not easily computable in practice.

1. We present methods for transition pruning, i.e., removing transitions from automata without changing their language. The idea is that certain transitions can be removed, because other 'better' transitions remain. The 'better' criterion relies on combinations of forward and backward simulations and trace inclusions. We provide a complete picture which combinations are correct to use for pruning. Moreover, the pruned transitions can be removed 'in parallel' (i.e., without re-computing the simulations and trace inclusions after every change), which makes the method efficient and practical.
2. We present an efficient practical method to compute good under-approximations of trace inclusions, by introducing *lookahead simulations*. While it is correct to use full trace inclusions and maximal-pebble multipebble simulations in our minimization methods, these are not easily computed (PSPACE-hard). However, lookahead simulations are PTIME-computable, and it is correct to use them instead of the more expensive trace inclusions and multipebble simulations. Lookahead itself is a classic concept in parsing and many other areas, but it can be defined in many different variants. Our contribution is to identify and formally describe the lookahead-variant for simulation preorders that gives the optimal compromise between efficient computability and maximizing the sizes of the relations.[1] Practical degrees of lookahead range from 4 to 25, depending on the size and shape of the automata. Our experiments show that even moderate lookahead helps considerably in obtaining good approximations of trace-inclusions and multipebble simulations.
3. We show that variants of the *polynomial time* minimization algorithm can solve most instances of the PSPACE-complete language inclusion problem. Thus, the complete *exponential time* methods of [3, 4, 6, 10, 11, 15, 16] need only be invoked in a minority of the cases. This allows to scale language inclusion testing to much larger instances (e.g., automata with ≥ 1000 states) which are beyond traditional methods.
4. We performed extensive tests of our algorithm on automata of up-to 20000 states. These included random automata according to the Tabakov-Vardi model [33], automata obtained from LTL formulae, and real-world mutual exclusion protocols. The empirically determined average-case time complexity on random automata is quadratic, while the (never observed) worst-case complexity is $O(n^4)$. The worst-case space complexity is quadratic. Our algorithm always minimizes better, on average, than all previously available practical methods. However, the exact advantage varies, depending on the type of instances; cf. Section 7. For example, consider random automata with 100–1000 states, binary alphabet and varying transition density *td*. Random automata with $td = 1.4$ cannot be minimized much by *any method*. The only effect is achieved by the trivial removal of dead states which, on average, yields automata of 78% of the original size. On the other hand, for $td = 1.8, \ldots, 2.2$, the best previous minimization methods yielded automata of 85%–90% of the original size on average, while our algorithm yielded automata of 3%–15% of the original size on average.

While we present our methods in the framework of Büchi automata, they directly carry over to the simpler case of finite-word automata.

[1] A thorough literature search showed that this has never been formally described so far.

2. Preliminaries

A *non-deterministic Büchi Automaton (BA)* $\mathcal{A}$ is a tuple $(\Sigma, Q, I, F, \delta)$ where Σ is a finite alphabet, Q is a finite set of states, $I \subseteq Q$ is the set of *initial* states, $F \subseteq Q$ is the set of *accepting* states, and $\delta \subseteq Q \times \Sigma \times Q$ is the transition relation. We write $p \xrightarrow{\sigma} q$ for $(p, \sigma, q) \in \delta$. A transition is *transient* iff any path can contain it at most once. To simplify the presentation, we assume that automata are *forward and backward complete*, i.e., for any state $p \in Q$ and symbol $\sigma \in \Sigma$, there exist states $q_0, q_1 \in Q$ s.t. $q_0 \xrightarrow{\sigma} p \xrightarrow{\sigma} q_1$. Every automaton can be converted into an equivalent complete one by adding at most two states and a linear number of transitions.[2] A state is *dead* iff either it is not reachable from an initial state, or it cannot reach an accepting loop. In our simplification techniques, we always remove dead states.

A Büchi automaton $\mathcal{A}$ describes a set of infinite words (its language), i.e., a subset of Σ^ω. An *infinite trace* of $\mathcal{A}$ on a word $w = \sigma_0\sigma_1 \cdots \in \Sigma^\omega$ (or *w-trace*) *starting* in a state $q_0 \in Q$ is an infinite sequence of transitions $\pi = q_0 \xrightarrow{\sigma_0} q_1 \xrightarrow{\sigma_1} \cdots$. By $\pi[0..i]$ we denote the finite prefix $\pi = q_0 \xrightarrow{\sigma_0} \cdots \xrightarrow{\sigma_{i-1}} q_i$, and by $\pi[i..]$ the infinite suffix $q_i \xrightarrow{\sigma_i} q_{i+1} \xrightarrow{\sigma_{i+1}} \cdots$. Finite traces starting in q_0 and *ending* in a state $q_m \in Q$ are defined similarly. A finite or infinite trace is *initial* iff it starts in an initial state $q_0 \in I$; if it is infinite, then it is *fair* iff $q_i \in F$ for infinitely many i. The *language of* $\mathcal{A}$ is $\mathcal{L}(\mathcal{A}) = \{w \in \Sigma^\omega \mid \mathcal{A}$ has an infinite, initial and fair trace on $w\}$.

Language inclusion. When automata are viewed as a finite representation for languages, it is natural to ask whether two different automata represent the same language, or, more generally, to compare these languages for inclusion. Formally, for two automata $\mathcal{A} = (\Sigma, Q_\mathcal{A}, I_\mathcal{A}, F_\mathcal{A}, \delta_\mathcal{A})$ and $\mathcal{B} = (\Sigma, Q_\mathcal{B}, I_\mathcal{B}, F_\mathcal{B}, \delta_\mathcal{B})$ we write $\mathcal{A} \subseteq \mathcal{B}$ iff $\mathcal{L}(\mathcal{A}) \subseteq \mathcal{L}(\mathcal{B})$ and $\mathcal{A} \approx \mathcal{B}$ iff $\mathcal{L}(\mathcal{A}) = \mathcal{L}(\mathcal{B})$. The *language inclusion/equivalence problem* consists in determining whether $\mathcal{A} \subseteq \mathcal{B}$ or $\mathcal{A} \approx \mathcal{B}$ holds, respectively. For general non-deterministic automata, language inclusion and equivalence are PSPACE-complete [25] (which entails that, under standard theoretic-complexity assumptions, they admit no efficient deterministic algorithm). Therefore, one considers suitable under-approximations.

Definition A preorder $\sqsubseteq$ on $Q_\mathcal{A} \times Q_\mathcal{B}$ is *good for inclusion* (GFI) iff the following holds: If $\forall q \in I_\mathcal{A} \exists q' \in I_\mathcal{B} \cdot q \sqsubseteq q'$, then $\mathcal{A} \subseteq \mathcal{B}$.

In other words, GFI preorders give a sufficient condition for inclusion, by matching initial states of $\mathcal{A}$ with initial states of $\mathcal{B}$. (They are not necessary for inclusion since there are several initial states.) Moreover, if computing a GFI preorder is efficient, than also inclusion can be established efficiently. Finally, if a preorder is GFI, then all smaller preorders are GFI too, i.e., GFI is $\subseteq$-downward closed.

Quotienting. Another interesting problem is how to simplify an automaton while preserving its semantics, i.e., its language. Generally, one tries to reduce the number of states/transitions. This is useful because the complexity of decision procedures usually depends on the size of the input automata.

A classical operation for reducing the number of states of an automaton is that of quotienting, where states of the automaton are identified according to a given equivalence, and transitions are projected accordingly. Since in practice we obtain quotienting equivalences from suitable preorders, we directly define quotienting w.r.t. a preorder. Formally, fix a BA $\mathcal{A} = (\Sigma, Q, I, F, \delta)$ and a preorder $\sqsubseteq$ on Q, with induced equivalence $\equiv = \sqsubseteq \cap \sqsupseteq$. Given a state $q \in Q$, we denote by $[q]$ its equivalence class w.r.t. $\equiv$, and, for a set of states $P \subseteq Q$, $[P]$ is the set of equivalence classes $[P] = \{[p] \mid p \in P\}$.

[2] For efficiency reasons, our implementation works directly on incomplete automata.

Definition The *quotient* of $\mathcal{A}$ by $\sqsubseteq$ is $\mathcal{A}/\sqsubseteq = (\Sigma, [Q], [I], [F], \delta')$, where $\delta' = \{([q_1], \sigma, [q_2]) \mid \exists q_1' \in [q_1], q_2' \in [q_2] \cdot (q_1', \sigma, q_2') \in \delta\}$, i.e., transitions are induced element-wise.

Clearly, every trace $q_0 \xrightarrow{\sigma_0} q_1 \xrightarrow{\sigma_1} \cdots$ in $\mathcal{A}$ immediately induces a corresponding trace $[q_0] \xrightarrow{\sigma_0} [q_1] \xrightarrow{\sigma_1} \cdots$ in $\mathcal{A}/\sqsubseteq$, which is fair/initial if the former is fair/initial, respectively. Consequently, $\mathcal{A} \subseteq \mathcal{A}/\sqsubseteq$ for *any* preorder $\sqsubseteq$. If, additionally, $\mathcal{A}/\sqsubseteq \subseteq \mathcal{A}$, then we say that the preorder $\sqsubseteq$ is good for quotienting (GFQ).

Definition A preorder $\sqsubseteq$ is *good for quotienting* iff $\mathcal{A}/\sqsubseteq \approx \mathcal{A}$.

Like GFI preorders, also GFQ preorders are downward closed (since a smaller preorder is quotienting "less"). Therefore, we are interested in efficiently computable GFI/GFQ preorders. A classical example is given by *simulation relations*.

Simulation relations. Basic forward simulation is a binary relation on the states of $\mathcal{A}$; it relates states whose behaviors are step-wise related, which allows one to reason about the internal structure of automaton $\mathcal{A}$— i.e., *how* a word is accepted, and not just *whether* it is accepted. Formally, simulation between two states p_0 and q_0 can be described in terms of a game between two players, Spoiler and Duplicator, where the latter wants to prove that q_0 can step-wise mimic any behavior of p_0, and the former wants to disprove it. The game starts in the initial configuration (p_0, q_0). Inductively, given a game configuration (p_i, q_i) at the i-th round of the game, Spoiler chooses a symbol $\sigma_i \in \Sigma$ and a transition $p_i \xrightarrow{\sigma_i} p_{i+1}$. Then, Duplicator responds by choosing a matching transition $q_i \xrightarrow{\sigma_i} q_{i+1}$, and the next configuration is (p_{i+1}, q_{i+1}). Since the automaton is assumed to be complete, the game goes on forever, and the two players build two infinite traces $\pi_0 = p_0 \xrightarrow{\sigma_0} p_1 \xrightarrow{\sigma_1} \cdots$ and $\pi_1 = q_0 \xrightarrow{\sigma_0} q_1 \xrightarrow{\sigma_1} \cdots$. The winning condition depends on the type of simulation, and different types have been considered depending on whether one is interested in GFQ or GFI relations. Here, we consider *direct* [10], *delayed* [14] and *fair simulation* [21]. Let $x \in \{\mathrm{di}, \mathrm{de}, \mathrm{f}\}$. Duplicator wins the play if $C^x(\pi_0, \pi_1)$ holds, where

$$C^{\mathrm{di}}(\pi_0, \pi_1) \iff \forall (i \geq 0) \cdot p_i \in F \implies q_i \in F \quad (1)$$

$$C^{\mathrm{de}}(\pi_0, \pi_1) \iff \forall (i \geq 0) \cdot p_i \in F \implies \exists (j \geq i) \cdot q_j \in F \quad (2)$$

$$C^{\mathrm{f}}(\pi_0, \pi_1) \iff \text{if } \pi_0 \text{ is fair, then } \pi_1 \text{ is fair} \quad (3)$$

Intuitively, direct simulation requires that accepting states are matched immediately (the strongest condition), while in delayed simulation Duplicator is allowed to accept only after a finite delay. In fair simulation (the weakest condition), Duplicator must visit accepting states only if Spoiler visits infinitely many of them. Thus, $C^{\mathrm{di}}(\pi_0, \pi_1)$ implies $C^{\mathrm{de}}(\pi_0, \pi_1)$, which, in turn, implies $C^{\mathrm{f}}(\pi_0, \pi_1)$.

We define x-simulation relation $\sqsubseteq^x \subseteq Q \times Q$ by stipulating that $p_0 \sqsubseteq^x q_0$ iff Duplicator has a winning strategy in the x-simulation game, starting from configuration (p_0, q_0); clearly, $\sqsubseteq^{\mathrm{di}} \subseteq \sqsubseteq^{\mathrm{de}} \subseteq \sqsubseteq^{\mathrm{f}}$. Simulation between states in different automata $\mathcal{A}$ and $\mathcal{B}$ can be computed as a simulation on their disjoint union. All these simulation relations are GFI preorders which can be computed in polynomial time [10, 14, 20]; moreover, direct and delayed simulation are GFQ [14], but fair simulation is not [21].

Lemma 2.1 ([10, 14, 20, 21])**.** *For $x \in \{\mathrm{di}, \mathrm{de}, \mathrm{f}\}$, x-simulation $\sqsubseteq^x$ is a PTIME, GFI preorder, and, for $y \in \{\mathrm{di}, \mathrm{de}\}$, $\sqsubseteq^y$ is also GFQ.*

Trace inclusions. While simulations are efficiently computable, their use is often limited by their size, which can be much smaller than other GFI/GFQ preorders. One such example of coarser GFI/GFQ preorders is given by *trace inclusions*, which are obtained through a modification of the simulation game, as follows.

In simulation games, the players build two paths π_0, π_1 by choosing single transitions in an alternating fashion; Duplicator moves by knowing only the next 1-step move of Spoiler. We can obtain coarser relations by allowing Duplicator a certain amount of *lookahead* on Spoiler's moves. In the extremal case of ω-lookahead, i.e., where Spoiler has to reveal her whole path in advance, we obtain trace inclusions.

Analogously to simulations, we define direct, delayed, and fair trace inclusion, as binary relations on Q. For $x \in \{\mathrm{di}, \mathrm{de}, \mathrm{f}\}$, *x-trace inclusion* holds between p and q, written $p \subseteq^x q$ iff, for every word $w = \sigma_0\sigma_1 \cdots \in \Sigma^\omega$, and for every infinite w-trace $\pi_0 = p_0 \xrightarrow{\sigma_0} p_1 \xrightarrow{\sigma_1} \cdots$ starting at $p_0 = p$, there exists an infinite w-trace $\pi_1 = q_0 \xrightarrow{\sigma_0} q_1 \xrightarrow{\sigma_1} \cdots$ starting at $q_0 = q$, s.t. $C^x(\pi_0, \pi_1)$. All these trace inclusions are GFI preorders subsuming the corresponding simulation, i.e., $\sqsubseteq^x \subseteq \subseteq^x$ (since Duplicator has more power in the trace inclusion game); also, $\subseteq^{\mathrm{di}}$ is a subset of $\subseteq^{\mathrm{de}}$, which, in turn, is a subset of $\subseteq^{\mathrm{f}}$. Regarding quotienting, $\subseteq^{\mathrm{di}}$ is GFQ (like $\sqsubseteq^{\mathrm{di}}$; this follows from [12]), while $\subseteq^{\mathrm{f}}$ is not, since it is coarser than fair simulation, which is not GFQ [21]. While delayed simulation $\sqsubseteq^{\mathrm{de}}$ is GFQ, delayed trace inclusion $\subseteq^{\mathrm{de}}$ is not GFQ [8].

Lemma 2.2. *For $x \in \{\mathrm{di}, \mathrm{de}, \mathrm{f}\}$, x-trace inclusion $\subseteq^x$ is a GFI preorder. Moreover, $\subseteq^{\mathrm{di}}$ is a GFQ preorder.*

Finally, though $\sqsubseteq^{\mathrm{de}}$ and $\subseteq^{\mathrm{di}}$ are incomparable, there exists a common generalization included in $\subseteq^{\mathrm{de}}$ called *delayed fixed-word simulation* which is GFQ [8].[3]

Backward simulation and trace inclusion. Yet another way of obtaining GFQ/GFI preorders is to consider variants of simulation/trace inclusion which go backwards in time. *Backward simulation* $\sqsubseteq^{\mathrm{bw}}$ ([32], where it is called *reverse simulation*) is defined like ordinary simulation, except that transitions are taken backwards: From configuration (p_i, q_i), Spoiler selects a transition $p_{i+1} \xrightarrow{\sigma_i} p_i$, Duplicator replies with a transition $q_{i+1} \xrightarrow{\sigma_i} q_i$, and the next configuration is (p_{i+1}, q_{i+1}). Let π_0 and π_1 be the two infinite backward traces built in this way. The corresponding winning condition considers both accepting and initial states:

$$C^{\mathrm{bw}}(\pi_0, \pi_1) \iff \forall (i \geq 0) \cdot \begin{cases} p_i \in F \implies q_i \in F, \text{ and} \\ p_i \in I \implies q_i \in I \end{cases} \quad (4)$$

$\sqsubseteq^{\mathrm{bw}}$ is an efficiently computable GFQ preorder [32] incomparable with forward simulations. It can be used to establish language inclusion by matching final states of $\mathcal{A}$ with final states of $\mathcal{B}$ (dually to forward simulations); in this sense, it is GFI.

Lemma 2.3 ([32])**.** *Backward sim. is a PTIME GFQ/GFI preorder.*

The corresponding notion of *backward trace inclusion* $\subseteq^{\mathrm{bw}}$ is defined as follows: $p \subseteq^{\mathrm{bw}} q$ iff, for every finite word $w = \sigma_0\sigma_1 \cdots \sigma_{m-1} \in \Sigma^*$, and for every initial, finite w-trace $\pi_0 = p_0 \xrightarrow{\sigma_0} p_1 \xrightarrow{\sigma_1} \cdots \xrightarrow{\sigma_{m-1}} p_m$ ending in $p_m = p$, there exists an initial, finite w-trace $\pi_1 = q_0 \xrightarrow{\sigma_0} q_1 \xrightarrow{\sigma_1} \cdots \xrightarrow{\sigma_{m-1}} q_m$ ending in $q_m = q$, s.t., for any $i \geq 0$, if $p_i \in F$, then $q_i \in F$. Note that backward trace inclusion deals with *finite traces* (unlike forward trace inclusions), which is due to the asymmetry between past and future in ω-automata. Clearly, $\sqsubseteq^{\mathrm{bw}} \subseteq \subseteq^{\mathrm{bw}}$; we observe that even $\subseteq^{\mathrm{bw}}$ is GFQ/GFI.

Theorem 2.4. *Backward trace inclusion is a GFQ/GFI preorder.*

Proof. We first prove that $\subseteq^{\mathrm{bw}}$ is GFQ. Let $\sqsubseteq := \subseteq^{\mathrm{bw}}$. Let $w = \sigma_0\sigma_1 \cdots \in \mathcal{L}(\mathcal{A}/\sqsubseteq)$, and we show $w \in \mathcal{L}(\mathcal{A})$. There exists an initial, infinite and fair w-trace $\pi = [q_0] \xrightarrow{\sigma_0} [q_1] \xrightarrow{\sigma_1} \cdots$. For $i \geq 0$, let $w_i = \sigma_0\sigma_1 \cdots \sigma_i$ (with $w_{-1} = \varepsilon$), and let $\pi[0..i]$ be the w_{i-1}-trace

[3] Delayed fixed-word simulation is defined as a variant of simulation where Duplicator has ω-lookahead only on the input word w, and *not* on Spoiler's actual w-trace π_0; that it subsumes $\subseteq^{\mathrm{di}}$ is non-trivial.

prefix of π. For any $i \geq 0$, we build by induction an initial, finite w_{i-1}-trace π_i ending in q_i (of length i) visiting at least as many accepting states as $\pi[0..i]$ (and at the same time $\pi[0..i]$ does).

For $i = 0$, just take the empty ε-trace $\pi_0 = q_0$. For $i > 0$, assume that an initial w_{i-2}-trace π_{i-1} ending in q_{i-1} has already been built. We have the transition $[q_{i-1}] \xrightarrow{\sigma_{i-1}} [q_i]$ in $\mathcal{L}(\mathcal{A}/\sqsubseteq)$. There exist $\hat{q} \in [q_{i-1}]$ and $\hat{q}' \in [q_i]$ s.t. we have a transition $\hat{q} \xrightarrow{\sigma_{i-1}} \hat{q}'$ in $\mathcal{A}$. W.l.o.g. we can assume that $\hat{q}' = q_i$, since $[q_i] = [\hat{q}']$. By $q_{i-1} \subseteq^{\mathsf{bw}} \hat{q}$, there exists an initial, finite w_{i-2}-trace π' ending in $\hat{q}$. By the definition of backward inclusion, π' visits at least as many accepting states as π_{i-1}, which, by inductive hypothesis, visits at least as many accepting states as $\pi[0..i-1]$. Therefore, $\pi_i := \pi' \xrightarrow{\sigma_{i-1}} q_i$ is an initial, finite w_{i-1}-trace ending in q_i. Moreover, if $[q_i] \in F'$, then, since backward inclusion respects accepting states, $[q_i] \subseteq F$, hence $q_i \in F$, and, consequently, π_i visits at least as many accepting states as $\pi[0..i]$. Since π is fair, the finite, initial traces $\pi_0, \pi_1, \cdots$ visit unboundedly many accepting states. Since $\mathcal{A}$ is finitely branching, by König's Lemma there exists an initial, infinite and fair w-trace π_ω. Therefore, $w \in \mathcal{L}(\mathcal{A})$.

We now prove that $\subseteq^{\mathsf{bw}}$ is GFI. Let $\mathcal{A}$ and $\mathcal{B}$ be two automata. For backward notions, we require that every accepting state in $\mathcal{A}$ is in relation with an accepting state in $\mathcal{B}$. Let $w = \sigma_0\sigma_1 \cdots \in \mathcal{L}(\mathcal{A})$, and let $\pi_0 = p_0 \xrightarrow{\sigma_0} p_1 \xrightarrow{\sigma_0} \cdots$ be an initial and fair w-path in $\mathcal{A}$. Since π_0 visits infinitely many accepting states, and since each such state is $\subseteq^{\mathsf{bw}}$-related to an accepting state in $\mathcal{B}$, by using the definition of $\subseteq^{\mathsf{bw}}$ it is possible to build in $\mathcal{B}$ longer and longer finite initial traces in $\mathcal{B}$ visiting unboundedly many accepting states. Since $\mathcal{B}$ is finitely branching, by König's Lemma there exists an infinite, initial and fair w-trace π_ω in $\mathcal{B}$. Thus, $w \in \mathcal{L}(\mathcal{B})$. □

3. Transition Pruning Minimization Techniques

While quotienting-based minimization techniques reduce the number of states by merging them, we explore an alternative method which prunes (i.e., removes) transitions. The intuition is that certain transitions can be removed from an automaton without changing its language when other 'better' transitions remain.

Definition Let $\mathcal{A} = (\Sigma, Q, I, F, \delta)$ be a BA and let P a transitive, asymmetric relation on δ. The *pruned automaton* is defined as $Prune(\mathcal{A}, P) := (\Sigma, Q, I, F, \delta')$, with $\delta' = \{(p,\sigma,r) \in \delta \mid \nexists (p',\sigma',r') \in \delta \cdot (p,\sigma,r) P (p',\sigma',r')\}$.

By the assumptions on P, the pruned automaton $Prune(\mathcal{A}, P)$ is uniquely defined. Notice that transitions are removed 'in parallel'. Though P might depend on δ, P is *not* re-computed even if the removal of a single transition changes δ. This is important because computing P may be expensive. Since removing transitions cannot introduce new words in the language, $Prune(\mathcal{A}, P) \subseteq \mathcal{A}$. When also the converse inclusion holds (so the language is preserved), we say that P is *good for pruning* (GFP), i.e., P is GFP iff $Prune(\mathcal{A}, P) \approx \mathcal{A}$. Clearly, GFP is $\subseteq$-downward closed (like GFI and GFQ).

We study GFP relations obtained by comparing the endpoints of transitions over the same input symbol. Formally, given two binary relations $R_b, R_f \subseteq Q \times Q$, we define

$$P(R_b, R_f) = \{((p,\sigma,r),(p',\sigma,r')) \mid pR_bp' \text{ and } rR_fr'\}$$

$P(\cdot,\cdot)$ is monotone in both arguments. In the following, we explore which state relations R_b, R_f induce GFP relations $P(R_b, R_f)$.

It has long been known that $P(id, \sqsubset^{\mathsf{di}})$ and $P(\sqsubset^{\mathsf{bw}}, id)$ are GFP (see [7] where the removed transitions are called 'little brothers'). Moreover, even the relation $R_t(\subset^{\mathsf{f}}) := P(id, \sqsubset^{\mathsf{di}}) \cup \{((p,\sigma,r),(p,\sigma,r')) \mid (p,\sigma,r') \text{ is transient and } r \subset^{\mathsf{f}} r'\}$ is GFP [32], i.e., strict fair trace inclusion suffices if the remaining transition can only be used once. However, in general, $P(id, \subset^{\mathsf{f}})$ is not GFP. Moreover, even if only transient transitions are compared/pruned, $P(\sqsubset^{\mathsf{bw}}, \subset^{\mathsf{f}})$ is not GFP; cf. Fig. 2.

$R_b \backslash R_f$	id	$\sqsubset^{\mathsf{di}}$	$\subset^{\mathsf{di}}$	$\sqsubset^{\mathsf{de}}$	$\sqsubset^{\mathsf{f}}$
id	×	✓	✓	×	×
$\sqsubset^{\mathsf{bw}}$	✓	✓	✓	×	×
$\subset^{\mathsf{bw}}$	✓	✓	×	×	×

Figure 1. GFP relations $P(R_b, R_f)$

Theorem 3.1. *For every asymmetric and transitive relation $R \subseteq \subseteq^{\mathsf{di}}$, $P(id, R)$ is GFP.*

Proof. Let $\mathcal{A}' = Prune(\mathcal{A}, P(id, R))$. We show $\mathcal{A} \subseteq \mathcal{A}'$. If $w = \sigma_0\sigma_1 \cdots \in \mathcal{L}(\mathcal{A})$ then there exists an infinite fair initial trace $\hat{\pi}$ on w in $\mathcal{A}$. We show $w \in \mathcal{L}(\mathcal{A}')$.

We call a trace $\pi = q_0 \xrightarrow{\sigma_0} q_1 \xrightarrow{\sigma_1} \cdots$ on w in $\mathcal{A}$ *i-good* if it does not contain any transition $q_j \xrightarrow{\sigma_j} q_{j+1}$ for $j < i$ s.t. there exists an $\mathcal{A}$ transition $q_j \xrightarrow{\sigma_j} q'_{j+1}$ with $q_{j+1} R q'_{j+1}$ (i.e., no such transition is used within the first i steps). Since $\mathcal{A}$ is finitely branching, for every state and symbol there exists at least one R-maximal successor that is still present in $\mathcal{A}'$, because R is asymmetric and transitive. Thus, for every i-good trace π on w there exists an $(i+1)$-good trace π' on w s.t. π and π' are identical on the first i steps and $\mathcal{C}^{\mathsf{di}}(\pi, \pi')$, because $R \subseteq \subseteq^{\mathsf{di}}$. Since $\hat{\pi}$ is an infinite fair initial trace on w (which is trivially 0-good), there exists an infinite initial trace $\tilde{\pi}$ on w that is i-good for every i and $\mathcal{C}^{\mathsf{di}}(\hat{\pi}, \tilde{\pi})$. Moreover, $\tilde{\pi}$ is a trace in $\mathcal{A}'$. Since $\hat{\pi}$ is fair and $\mathcal{C}^{\mathsf{di}}(\hat{\pi}, \tilde{\pi})$, $\tilde{\pi}$ is an infinite fair initial trace on w that is i-good for every i. Therefore $\tilde{\pi}$ is a fair initial trace on w in $\mathcal{A}'$ and thus $w \in \mathcal{L}(\mathcal{A}')$. □

Theorem 3.2. *For every asymmetric and transitive relation $R \subseteq \subseteq^{\mathsf{bw}}$, $P(R, id)$ is GFP.*

Proof. Let $\mathcal{A}' = Prune(\mathcal{A}, P(R, id))$. We show $\mathcal{A} \subseteq \mathcal{A}'$. If $w = \sigma_0\sigma_1 \cdots \in \mathcal{L}(\mathcal{A})$ then there exists an infinite fair initial trace $\hat{\pi}$ on w in $\mathcal{A}$. We show $w \in \mathcal{L}(\mathcal{A}')$.

We call a trace $\pi = q_0 \xrightarrow{\sigma_0} q_1 \xrightarrow{\sigma_1} \cdots$ on w in $\mathcal{A}$ *i-good* if it does not contain any transition $q_j \xrightarrow{\sigma_j} q_{j+1}$ for $j < i$ s.t. there exists an $\mathcal{A}$ transition $q'_j \xrightarrow{\sigma_j} q_{j+1}$ with $q_j R q'_j$ (i.e., no such transition is used within the first i steps).

We show, by induction on i, the following property (P): For every i and every initial trace π on w in $\mathcal{A}$ there exists an initial i-good trace π' on w in $\mathcal{A}$ s.t. π and π' have identical suffixes from step i onwards and $\mathcal{C}^{\mathsf{di}}(\pi, \pi')$.

The base case $i = 0$ is trivial with $\pi' = \pi$. For the induction step there are two cases. If π is $(i+1)$-good then we can take $\pi' = \pi$. Otherwise there exists a transition $q'_i \xrightarrow{\sigma_i} q_{i+1}$ with $q_i R q'_i$. Without restriction (since $\mathcal{A}$ is finite and R is asymmetric and transitive) we assume that q'_i is R-maximal among the σ_i-predecessors of q_{i+1}. In particular, the transition $q'_i \xrightarrow{\sigma_i} q_{i+1}$ is present in $\mathcal{A}'$. Since $R \subseteq \subseteq^{\mathsf{bw}}$, there exists an initial trace π'' on w that has suffix $q'_i \xrightarrow{\sigma_i} q_{i+1} \xrightarrow{\sigma_{i+1}} q_{i+2} \cdots$ and $\mathcal{C}^{\mathsf{di}}(\pi, \pi'')$. Then, by induction hypothesis, there exists an initial i-good trace π' on w that has suffix $q'_i \xrightarrow{\sigma_i} q_{i+1} \xrightarrow{\sigma_{i+1}} q_{i+2} \cdots$ and $\mathcal{C}^{\mathsf{di}}(\pi'', \pi')$. Since q'_i is R-maximal among the σ_i-predecessors of q_{i+1} we obtain that π' is also $(i+1)$-good. Moreover, π' and π have identical suffixes from step $i+1$ onwards. Finally, by $\mathcal{C}^{\mathsf{di}}(\pi, \pi'')$ and $\mathcal{C}^{\mathsf{di}}(\pi'', \pi')$, we obtain $\mathcal{C}^{\mathsf{di}}(\pi, \pi')$.

Given the infinite fair initial trace $\hat{\pi}$ on w in $\mathcal{A}$, it follows from property (P) and König's Lemma that there exists an infinite initial trace $\hat{\pi}$ on w that is i-good for every i and $C^{\text{di}}(\hat{\pi},\tilde{\pi})$. Therefore $\tilde{\pi}$ is an infinite fair initial trace on w in $\mathcal{A}'$ and thus $w \in \mathcal{L}(\mathcal{A}')$. □

Theorem 3.3. *If $\mathcal{A} = \mathcal{A}/\sqsubseteq^{\text{bw}}$ then $P(\sqsubset^{\text{bw}},\subseteq^{\text{di}})$ is GFP.*

Proof. Let $\mathcal{A}' = Prune(\mathcal{A},P(\sqsubset^{\text{bw}},\subseteq^{\text{di}}))$. We show $\mathcal{A} \subseteq \mathcal{A}'$. Let $w = \sigma_0\sigma_1\cdots \in \mathcal{L}(\mathcal{A})$. Then there exists an infinite fair initial trace $\hat{\pi}$ on w in $\mathcal{A}$. We show $w \in \mathcal{L}(\mathcal{A}')$.

We call a trace $\pi = q_0 \xrightarrow{\sigma_0} q_1 \xrightarrow{\sigma_1} \cdots$ on w start-maximal iff it is initial and there does not exist any trace $\pi' = q_0' \xrightarrow{\sigma_0} q_1' \xrightarrow{\sigma_1} \cdots$ on w s.t. $C^{\text{di}}(\pi,\pi')$ and $q_0 \sqsubset^{\text{bw}} q_0'$. We call a trace $\pi = q_0 \xrightarrow{\sigma_0} q_1 \xrightarrow{\sigma_1} \cdots$ on w *i-good* iff it is start-maximal and π does not contain any transition $q_j \xrightarrow{\sigma_j} q_{j+1}$ for $j < i$ s.t. there exists an $\mathcal{A}$ transition $q_j \xrightarrow{\sigma_j} q_{j+1}'$ with $q_{j+1} \sqsubset^{\text{bw}} q_{j+1}'$ and there exists an infinite trace $\pi'[j+1..]$ from q_{j+1}' with $C^{\text{di}}(\pi[j+1..],\pi'[j+1..])$.

Since $\mathcal{A}$ is finite, there are $\sqsubset^{\text{bw}}$-maximal elements among those finitely many successors of every state q_j from which there exists an infinite trace $\pi'[j+1..]$ with $C^{\text{di}}(\pi[j+1..],\pi'[j+1..])$. Thus, for every infinite i-good trace π on w there exists an $(i+1)$-good trace π' on w s.t. π and π' are identical on the first i steps and $C^{\text{di}}(\pi,\pi')$.

Since there is an infinite fair initial trace $\hat{\pi}$ on w, there also exists a start-maximal, and thus 0-good, fair initial trace on w, because $\sqsubset^{\text{bw}}$ has maximal elements. Then it follows from the property above that there exists an infinite initial trace $\tilde{\pi}$ on w that is i-good for every i and $C^{\text{di}}(\hat{\pi},\tilde{\pi})$. In particular, this implies that $\tilde{\pi}$ is fair. So $\tilde{\pi}$ is an infinite fair initial trace on w that is i-good for every i.

Let now $\tilde{\pi} = q_0 \xrightarrow{\sigma_0} q_1 \xrightarrow{\sigma_1} \cdots$. We show that $\tilde{\pi}$ is also possible in $\mathcal{A}'$ by assuming the opposite and deriving a contradiction. Suppose that $\tilde{\pi}$ contains a transition $q_j \xrightarrow{\sigma_j} q_{j+1}$ that is not present in $\mathcal{A}'$. Then there must exist a transition $q_j' \xrightarrow{\sigma_j} q_{j+1}'$ in $\mathcal{A}'$ s.t. $q_j \sqsubset^{\text{bw}} q_j'$ and $q_{j+1} \subseteq^{\text{di}} q_{j+1}'$. We cannot have $j = 0$, because in this case $\tilde{\pi}$ would not be start-maximal and thus not even 1-good. So we get $j \geq 1$. Since $q_j \sqsubset^{\text{bw}} q_j'$ and $q_{j-1} \xrightarrow{\sigma_{j-1}} q_j$ there must exist a state q_{j-1}' s.t. $q_{j-1}' \xrightarrow{\sigma_{j-1}} q_j'$ and $q_{j-1} \sqsubseteq^{\text{bw}} q_{j-1}'$. In particular, $q_x \in F \Rightarrow q_{x+1}' \in F$ for $x \in \{j-1, j\}$. By $\mathcal{A} = \mathcal{A}/\sqsubseteq^{\text{bw}}$ we obtain that either $q_{j-1} = q_{j-1}'$ or $q_{j-1} \sqsubset^{\text{bw}} q_{j-1}'$. The first case would imply that π' is not j-good, because $q_{j+1} \subseteq^{\text{di}} q_{j+1}'$, and thus yield a contradiction. Therefore, we must have $q_{j-1} \sqsubset^{\text{bw}} q_{j-1}'$. We cannot have $j-1 = 0$, because in this case π' would not be start-maximal and thus not even 1-good. So we get $j-1 \geq 1$. The whole argument above repeats with $j-1, j-2, j-3, \ldots$ substituted for j until we get a contradiction or 0 is reached. Reaching 0 also yields a contradiction to start-maximality of $\tilde{\pi}$, as above. Therefore $\tilde{\pi}$ is a fair initial trace on w in $\mathcal{A}'$ and thus $w \in \mathcal{L}(\mathcal{A}')$. □

Theorem 3.4. *$P(\subseteq^{\text{bw}},\sqsubset^{\text{di}})$ is GFP.*

Proof. Let $\mathcal{A}' = Prune(\mathcal{A},P(\subseteq^{\text{bw}},\sqsubset^{\text{di}}))$. We show $\mathcal{A} \subseteq \mathcal{A}'$. Let $w = \sigma_0\sigma_1\cdots \in \mathcal{L}(\mathcal{A})$. Then there exists an infinite fair initial trace $\hat{\pi}$ on w in $\mathcal{A}$. We show $w \in \mathcal{L}(\mathcal{A}')$.

Given some infinite initial trace $\pi = q_0 \xrightarrow{\sigma_0} q_1 \xrightarrow{\sigma_1} \cdots$ on w, we call it i-good iff its first i transitions are also possible in $\mathcal{A}'$.

We now show, by induction on i, the following property (P): For every infinite initial trace $\pi = q_0 \xrightarrow{\sigma_0} q_1 \xrightarrow{\sigma_1} \cdots$ on w and every $i \geq 0$, there exists an infinite initial trace $\pi' = q_0' \xrightarrow{\sigma_0} q_1' \xrightarrow{\sigma_1} \cdots$ on w that is i-good and $C^{\text{di}}(\pi,\pi')$ and $\forall j \geq i.\, q_j \sqsubseteq^{\text{di}} q_j'$.

The base case $i = 0$ is trivially true with $\pi' = \pi$. For the induction step consider an infinite initial trace $\pi = q_0 \xrightarrow{\sigma_0} q_1 \xrightarrow{\sigma_1} \cdots$ on w. By induction hypothesis, there exists an infinite initial trace $\pi^1 = q_0^1 \xrightarrow{\sigma_0} q_1^1 \xrightarrow{\sigma_1} \cdots$ on w that is i-good and $C^{\text{di}}(\pi,\pi^1)$ and $\forall j \geq i.\, q_j \sqsubseteq^{\text{di}} q_j^1$.

If π^1 is $(i+1)$-good then we are done. Otherwise, the transition $q_i^1 \xrightarrow{\sigma_i} q_{i+1}^1$ is not present in $\mathcal{A}'$. Since $\mathcal{A}' = Prune(\mathcal{A},P(\subseteq^{\text{bw}},\sqsubset^{\text{di}}))$, there must exist a transition $q_i^2 \xrightarrow{\sigma_i} q_{i+1}^2$ in $\mathcal{A}'$ s.t. $q_i^1 \subseteq^{\text{bw}} q_i^2$ and $q_{i+1}^1 \sqsubset^{\text{di}} q_{i+1}^2$. It follows from the definitions of $\subseteq^{\text{bw}}$ and $\sqsubset^{\text{di}}$ that there exists an infinite initial trace $\pi^2 = q_0^2 \xrightarrow{\sigma_0} q_1^2 \xrightarrow{\sigma_1} \cdots$ on w s.t. $C^{\text{di}}(\pi^1,\pi^2)$, $q_{i+1}^1 \sqsubset^{\text{di}} q_{i+1}^2$ and $\forall j \geq i+1.\, q_j^1 \sqsubseteq^{\text{di}} q_j^2$. (This last property uses the fact that $\sqsubseteq^{\text{di}}$ propagates forward. Direct trace inclusion $\subseteq^{\text{di}}$ does not suffice.) By induction hypothesis, there exists an infinite initial trace $\pi^3 = q_0^3 \xrightarrow{\sigma_0} q_1^3 \xrightarrow{\sigma_1} \cdots$ on w that is i-good and $C^{\text{di}}(\pi^2,\pi^3)$ and $\forall j \geq i.\, q_j^2 \sqsubseteq^{\text{di}} q_j^3$. By transitivity we obtain $C^{\text{di}}(\pi^1,\pi^3)$, $q_{i+1}^1 \sqsubset^{\text{di}} q_{i+1}^3$ and $\forall j \geq i+1.\, q_j^1 \sqsubseteq^{\text{di}} q_j^3$.

If π^3 is $(i+1)$-good then we are done. Otherwise, the argument of the above paragraph repeats and we obtain an infinite initial trace $\pi^5 = q_0^5 \xrightarrow{\sigma_0} q_1^5 \xrightarrow{\sigma_1} \cdots$ on w that is i-good and $C^{\text{di}}(\pi^3,\pi^5)$, that $q_{i+1}^3 \sqsubset^{\text{di}} q_{i+1}^5$ and $\forall j \geq i+1.\, q_j^3 \sqsubseteq^{\text{di}} q_j^5$. This process cannot repeat infinitely often, because this would imply an infinite strictly increasing $\sqsubset^{\text{di}}$-chain q_{i+1}^{2x+1} for $x = 0,1,2,\ldots$, which is impossible in finite automata. Therefore, for some finite index x, we obtain an infinite initial trace $\pi^x = q_0^x \xrightarrow{\sigma_0} q_1^x \xrightarrow{\sigma_1} \cdots$ on w that is $(i+1)$-good and, by transitivity, $C^{\text{di}}(\pi,\pi^x)$ and $\forall j \geq i+1.\, q_j \sqsubseteq^{\text{di}} q_j^x$. Thus π^x is the trace π' that we were looking for.

Given the infinite fair initial trace $\hat{\pi}$ on w in $\mathcal{A}$, it follows from property (P) and König's Lemma that there exists an infinite initial trace $\tilde{\pi}$ on w that is i-good for every i and $C^{\text{di}}(\hat{\pi},\tilde{\pi})$. Therefore $\tilde{\pi}$ is an infinite fair initial trace on w in $\mathcal{A}'$ and thus $w \in \mathcal{L}(\mathcal{A}')$. □

Theorem 3.4 implies that $P(\sqsubset^{\text{bw}},\sqsubset^{\text{di}})$ is GFP, but $P(\subset^{\text{bw}},\subset^{\text{di}})$ is not; see Figure 2. Moreover, $P(id,\sqsubset^{\text{de}})$ is not GFP (even if $\mathcal{A} = \mathcal{A}/\sqsubseteq^{\text{de}}$); see Figure 2.

The quotienting and transition pruning techniques described above use intricate combinations of backward and forward simulations (and more general trace inclusions). In particular, they subsume previous attempts to combine backward and forward simulations for automata minimization by *mediated preorder* [5] (but not vice-versa). Mediated preorder is defined as the largest fragment $M \subseteq \sqsubseteq^{\text{di}} \circ (\sqsubseteq^{\text{bw}})^{-1}$ s.t. $M \circ \sqsubseteq^{\text{di}} \subseteq M$. In particular, M is a preorder that is GFQ. However, an automaton $\mathcal{A}$ that has been minimized by the techniques described above cannot be further reduced by mediated preorder. First we have $\mathcal{A} = \mathcal{A}/\sqsubseteq^{\text{bw}} = \mathcal{A}/\sqsubseteq^{\text{di}}$ by repeated quotienting. Second, there cannot exist any distinct states x,y in $\mathcal{A}$ s.t. $(x \sqsubseteq^{\text{di}} y \wedge x \sqsubseteq^{\text{bw}} y)$ by the pruning techniques above (used with simulations as approximations for trace inclusions) and the removal of dead states. Under these conditions, quotienting with mediated preorder has no effect, as the following theorem shows.

Theorem 3.5. *Let $\mathcal{A}$ be an automaton s.t. (1) $\mathcal{A} = \mathcal{A}/\sqsubseteq^{\text{bw}} = \mathcal{A}/\sqsubseteq^{\text{di}}$ and (2) $x \sqsubseteq^{\text{di}} y \wedge x \sqsubseteq^{\text{bw}} y \Rightarrow x = y$. Then $\mathcal{A} = \mathcal{A}/M$.*

Proof. We show that $xMy \wedge yMx \Rightarrow x = y$ which implies $\mathcal{A} = \mathcal{A}/M$.

Let xMy and yMx. By definition of M there exist mediators z s.t. $x \sqsubseteq^{\text{di}} z$ and $y \sqsubseteq^{\text{bw}} z$, and w s.t. $x \sqsubseteq^{\text{bw}} w$ and $y \sqsubseteq^{\text{di}} w$. Since $M \circ \sqsubseteq^{\text{di}} \subseteq M$ we have xMw. Thus there exists a mediator k s.t. $x \sqsubseteq^{\text{di}} k$ and $w \sqsubseteq^{\text{bw}} k$. By transitivity of $\sqsubseteq^{\text{bw}}$ we also have $x \sqsubseteq^{\text{bw}} k$. By (2) we get $x = k$. Thus $x \sqsubseteq^{\text{bw}} w$ and $w \sqsubseteq^{\text{bw}} x$. By (1) we get $x = w$. Thus $y \sqsubseteq^{\text{di}} w = x \sqsubseteq^{\text{di}} z$ and by transitivity $y \sqsubseteq^{\text{di}} z$. Moreover, $y \sqsubseteq^{\text{bw}} z$ as above. By (2) we get $z = y$. Thus $x \sqsubseteq^{\text{di}} z = y$ and $y \sqsubseteq^{\text{di}} w = x$. By (1) we get $x = y$. □

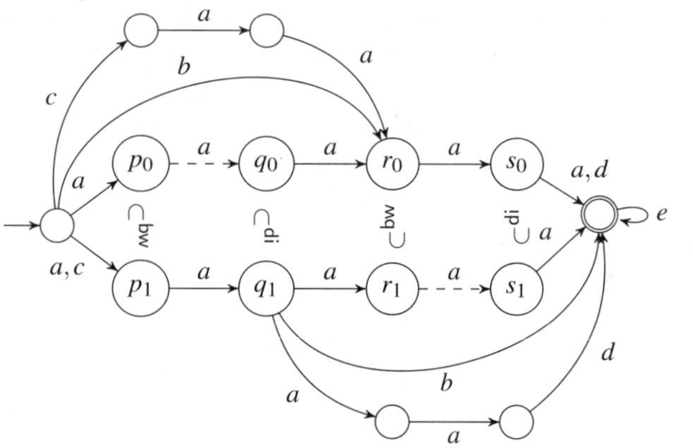

(a) $P(\subset^{\mathrm{bw}}, \subset^{\mathrm{di}})$ is not GFP: If the dashed transitions $p_0 \xrightarrow{a} q_0$ and $r_1 \xrightarrow{a} s_1$ are removed, then $a^5 e^\omega$ is no longer accepted. Note that $\mathcal{A} = \mathcal{A}/\subseteq^{\mathrm{bw}} = \mathcal{A}/\subseteq^{\mathrm{di}}$. (This example even holds for $\prec^{k\text{-bw}}, \prec^{k\text{-di}}$ and $k = 3$; cf. Section 4).

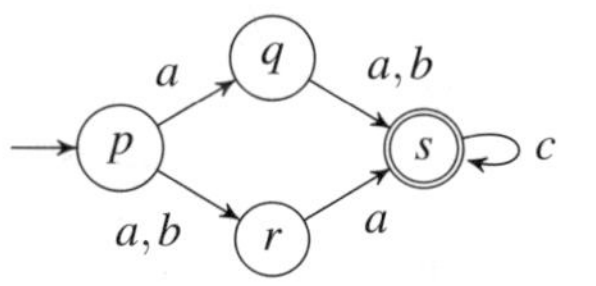

(b) GFP is not closed under union: Pruning automaton $\mathcal{A}$ with $P(id, \sqsubset^{\mathrm{di}}) \cup P(\sqsubset^{\mathrm{bw}}, id)$ would remove the transitions $p \xrightarrow{a} r$ and $q \xrightarrow{a} s$, and thus aac^ω would no longer be accepted.

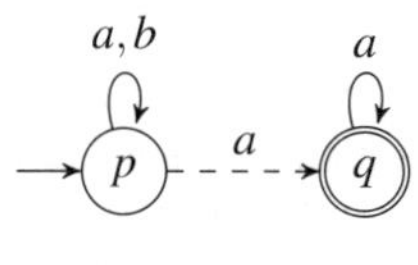

(c) $P(id, \sqsubset^{\mathrm{de}})$ is not GFP: We have $q \sqsubset^{\mathrm{de}} p$, but removing the dashed transition $p \xrightarrow{a} q$ makes the language empty, even though $\mathcal{A} = \mathcal{A}/\sqsubseteq^{\mathrm{de}}$.

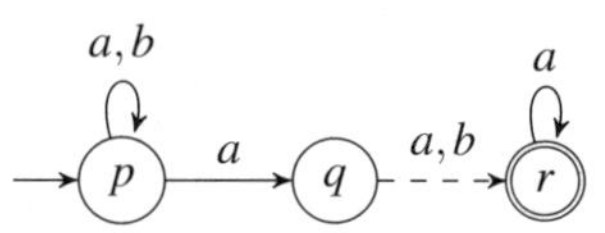

(d) $P(\sqsubset^{\mathrm{bw}}, \subset^{\mathrm{f}})$ is not GFP: In the automaton above, both transitions $p \xrightarrow{a} q$ and $q \xrightarrow{a} r$ are transient. Moreover, $r \subset^{\mathrm{f}} q$ (even $r \sqsubset^{\mathrm{de}} q$) and $q \sqsubset^{\mathrm{bw}} p$. However, removing the smaller transition $q \xrightarrow{a} r$ changes the language, since a^ω is no longer accepted. Thus, $P(\sqsubset^{\mathrm{bw}}, \subset^{\mathrm{f}})$ is not GFP even when one restricts to comparing/pruning only transient transitions (unlike $P(id, \subset^{\mathrm{f}})$).

Figure 2. Pruning counterexamples.

4. Lookahead Simulations

While trace inclusions are theoretically appealing as GFQ/GFI preorders coarser than simulations, it is not feasible to use them in practice, because they are too hard to compute (even their membership problem is PSPACE-complete). As a first attempt at achieving a better trade-off between complexity and size we recall *multipebble simulations* [12], which are obtained by providing Duplicator with several pebbles, instead of one. However, computing multipebble simulations is not feasible in practice either, on automata of nontrivial size. Therefore, we explore yet another way of obtaining good under-approximations of trace inclusion: We introduce *lookahead simulations*, which are obtained by providing Duplicator with a limited amount of information about Spoiler's future moves. While lookahead itself is a classic concept (e.g., in parsing) it can be defined in several different ways in the context of adversarial games like in simulation. We compare different variants for computational efficiency and approximation quality.

***k*-pebble simulation.** Simulation preorder can be generalized by allowing Duplicator to control several pebbles instead of just one. In k-pebble simulation, $k > 0$, Duplicator's position is a set of at most k states (while Spoiler still controls exactly 1 state), which allows Duplicator to 'hedge her bets' in the simulation game. The direct, delayed, fair and backward winning conditions can be generalized to the multipebble framework [12]. For $x \in \{\mathrm{di}, \mathrm{de}, \mathrm{f}, \mathrm{bw}\}$ and $k > 0$, k-pebble x-simulation is coarser than x-simulation and it implies x-containment; by increasing k, one can control the quality of the approximation to trace inclusion. Direct, delayed, fair and backward k-pebble simulations are not transitive in general, but their transitive closures are GFI preorders; the direct, delayed and backward variants are also GFQ. However, computing k-pebble simulations is infeasible, even for modest values for k. In fact, for a BA with n states, computing k-pebble simulation requires solving a game of size $n \cdot n^k$. Even in the simplest case of $k = 2$ this means at least cubic space, which is not practical for large n. For this reason, we consider a different way to extend Duplicator's power, i.e., by using *lookahead* on the moves of Spoiler.

***k*-step simulation.** We generalize simulation by having the players select sequences of transitions of length $k > 0$ instead of single transitions: This gives Duplicator more information, and thus yields a larger simulation relation. In general, k-step simulation and k-pebble simulation are incomparable, but k-step simulation is strictly contained in n-pebble simulation. However, the rigid use of lookahead in big-steps causes at least two issues: 1) For a BA with n states, we need to store only n^2 configurations (p, q) (which is much less than k-pebble simulation). However, in *every round* we have to explore up-to d^k different moves for each player (where d is the maximal out-degree of the automaton). In practice (e.g., $d = 4$, $k = 12$) this is still too large. 2) Duplicator's lookahead varies between 1 and k, depending where she is in her response to Spoiler's long move. Thus, Duplicator might lack lookahead where it is most needed, while having a large lookahead in other situations where it is not useful. In the next notion, we attempt at ameliorating this.

***k*-continuous simulation.** Duplicator is continuously kept informed about Spoiler's next k moves, i.e., she always has lookahead k. Formally, a configuration of the simulation game consists in a pair (ρ_i, q_i), where ρ_i is the sequence of the next $k-1$ moves from p_i that Spoiler has already committed to. In every round of the game, Spoiler reveals another move k steps in the future, and then makes the first of her announced k moves, to which Duplicator responds as usual. A pair of states (p, q) is in k-continuous simulation if Duplicator can win this game from every configuration (ρ, q), where ρ is a sequence of $k-1$ moves from p. ($k = 1$ is ordinary simulation.) k-continuous simulation is strictly contained in n-pebble simulation (but incomparable with k-pebble simulation), and larger than k-step simulation. While this is arguably the strongest way of giving lookahead to Duplicator, it requires storing $n^2 \cdot d^{k-1}$ configurations, which is infeasible for nontrivial n and k (e.g., $n = 10000$, $d = 4$, $k = 12$).

***k*-lookahead simulation.** We introduce k-lookahead simulation as an optimal compromise between k-step and k-continuous simulation. Intuitively, we put the lookahead under Duplicator's control, who can choose at each round how much lookahead she needs (up to k). Formally, configurations are pairs (p_i, q_i) of states. In every round of the game, Spoiler chooses a sequence of k consecutive transitions $p_i \xrightarrow{\sigma_i} p_{i+1} \xrightarrow{\sigma_{i+1}} \cdots \xrightarrow{\sigma_{i+k-1}} p_{i+k}$. Duplicator then chooses a number $1 \leq m \leq k$ and responds with a matching sequence of m transitions $q_i \xrightarrow{\sigma_i} q_{i+1} \xrightarrow{\sigma_{i+1}} \cdots \xrightarrow{\sigma_{i+m-1}} q_{i+m}$. The remaining $k - m$ moves of Spoiler are forgotten, and the next round of the game starts at (p_{i+m}, q_{i+m}). In this way, the players build two infinite traces π_0 from p_0 and π_1 from q_0. Backward simulation is defined similarly with backward transitions. For acceptance condition $x \in \{\mathrm{di}, \mathrm{de}, \mathrm{f}, \mathrm{bw}\}$, Duplicator wins this play if $C^x(\pi_0, \pi_1)$ holds.

Definition Two states (p_0, q_0) are in *k-lookahead x-simulation*, written $p_0 \sqsubseteq^{k\text{-}x} q_0$, iff Duplicator has a winning strategy in the above game.

Since $\sqsubseteq^{k\text{-}x}$ is not transitive (unless $k = 1$) [2], we denote its transitive closure, which is a preorder, by $\preceq^{k\text{-}x}$, and its asymmetric restriction by $\prec^{k\text{-}x} = \preceq^{k\text{-}x} \setminus (\preceq^{k\text{-}x})^{-1}$.

Lookahead simulation offers the optimal trade-off between k-step and k-continuous simulation. Since the lookahead is discarded at each round, k-lookahead simulation is (strictly) included in k-continuous lookahead (where the lookahead is never discarded). However, this has the benefit of only requiring to store n^2 configurations, which makes computing lookahead simulation space-efficient. On the other side, when Duplicator always chooses a maximal reply $m = k$ we recover k-step simulation, which is thus included in k-lookahead simulation. Moreover, thanks to the fact that Duplicator controls the lookahead, most rounds of the game can be solved without ever reaching the maximal lookahead k: 1) for a fixed attack by Spoiler, we only consider Duplicator's responses for small $m = 1, 2, \ldots, k$ until we find a winning one, and 2) also Spoiler's attacks can be built incrementally since, if she loses for some lookahead h, then she also loses for $h' > h$. In practice, this greatly speeds up the computation, and allows us to use lookaheads in the range 4-25, depending on the size and structure of the automata; see Section 7 for the experimental evaluation and benchmark against the GOAL tool [34].

k-lookahead simulation can also be expressed as a restriction of n-pebble simulation, where Duplicator is allowed to split pebbles maximally (thus n-pebbles), but after a number $m \leq k$ rounds (where m is chosen dynamically by Duplicator) she has to discard all but one pebble. Then, Duplicator is allowed to split pebbles maximally again, etc. Thus, k-lookahead simulation is contained in n-pebble simulation, though it is generally incomparable with k-pebble simulation.

Direct, delayed, fair and backward k-lookahead simulation have a fixed-point characterization expressible in μ-calculus [2], which can be useful for a symbolic implementation. However, our current algorithm computes them with an explicit-state representation.

5. Automata Minimization

We minimize automata by transition pruning and quotienting. While trace inclusions would be an ideal basis for such techniques, they (i.e., their membership problems) are PSPACE-complete. Instead, we use lookahead simulations as efficiently computable under-approximations; in particular, we use

- $\preceq^{k\text{-di}}$ in place of direct trace inclusion $\subseteq^{\mathrm{di}}$ (which is GFQ [12]).
- $\preceq^{k\text{-de}}$ in place of n-pebble delayed simulation (GFQ [12]).
- $\preceq^{k\text{-f}}$ in place of fair trace inclusion $\subseteq^{\mathrm{f}}$ (which is GFI).
- $\preceq^{k\text{-bw}}$ in place of backward trace inclusion $\subseteq^{\mathrm{bw}}$ (which is GFQ by Theorem 2.4).

For pruning, we apply the results of Section 3 and the substitutions above to obtain the following GFP relations:

$$P(id, \prec^{k\text{-di}}), P(\prec^{k\text{-bw}}, id), P(\sqsubset^{\mathrm{bw}}, \preceq^{k\text{-di}}), P(\preceq^{k\text{-bw}}, \sqsubset^{\mathrm{di}}), R_t(\prec^{k\text{-f}})$$

For quotienting, we employ delayed $\preceq^{k\text{-de}}$ and backward $\preceq^{k\text{-bw}}$ k-lookahead simulations (which are GFQ). Below, we describe two possible ways to combine our simplification techniques: *Heavy-k* and *Light-k* (which are parameterized by the lookahead value k).

Heavy-k. We advocate the following minimization procedure, which repeatedly applies all the techniques described in this paper until a fixpoint is reached: 1) Remove dead states. 2) Prune transitions w.r.t. the GFP relations above (using lookahead k). 3) Quotient w.r.t. $\preceq^{k\text{-de}}$ and $\preceq^{k\text{-bw}}$. The resulting simplified automaton cannot be further reduced by any of these techniques. In this sense, it is a local minimum in the space of automata. Applying the techniques in a different order might produce a different local minimum, and, in general, there does not exist an optimal order that works best in every instance. In practice, the order is determined by efficiency considerations and easily computable operations are used first [1, 2].

Remark While quotienting with ordinary simulation is idempotent, in general this is not true for lookahead simulations, because these relations are not preserved under quotienting (unlike ordinary simulation). Moreover, quotienting w.r.t. forward simulations does not preserve backward simulations, and vice-versa. Our experiments showed that repeatedly and alternatingly quotienting w.r.t. $\preceq^{k\text{-de}}$ and $\preceq^{k\text{-bw}}$ (in addition to our pruning techniques) yields the best minimization effect.

The Heavy-k procedure *strictly subsumes* all simulation-based automata minimization methods described in the literature (removing dead states, quotienting, pruning of 'little brother' transitions, mediated preorder), except for the following two: 1) The *fair simulation minimization* of [19] works by tentatively merging fair simulation equivalent states and then checking if this operation preserved the language. (In general, fair simulation is not GFQ.) It subsumes quotienting with $\sqsubseteq^{\mathrm{de}}$ (but not $\preceq^{k\text{-de}}$) and is implemented in GOAL [34]. We benchmarked our methods against it and found Heavy-k to be much better in both effect and efficiency; cf Section 7. 2) The GFQ *jumping-safe preorders* of [8, 9] are incomparable to the techniques described in this paper. If applied in addition to Heavy-k, they yield a very modest extra minimization effect.

Light-k. This procedure is defined purely for comparison reasons. It demonstrates the effect of the lookahead k in a single quotienting operation and works as follows: Remove all dead states and then quotient w.r.t. $\preceq^{k\text{-de}}$. Although Light-k achieves much less than Heavy-k, it is not necessarily faster. This is because it uses the more expensive to compute relation $\preceq^{k\text{-de}}$ directly, while Heavy-k applies other cheaper (pruning) operations first and only then computes $\preceq^{k\text{-de}}$ on the resulting smaller automaton.

6. Language Inclusion Checking

The language inclusion problem $\mathcal{A} \subseteq \mathcal{B}$ is PSPACE-complete [25]. It can be solved via complementation of $\mathcal{B}$ [31, 34] and, more efficiently, by rank-based ([17] and references therein) or Ramsey-based methods [3, 4, 15, 16], or variants of Piterman's construction [29, 34]. Since these all have *exponential* time complexity, it helps significantly to first minimize the automata in a preprocessing step. Better minimization techniques, as described in the previous sections, make it possible to solve significantly larger instances. However, our simulation-based techniques can not only be used in preprocessing, but actually solve most instances of the inclusion problem *directly*. This is significant, because simulation scales *polynomially* (quadratic average-case complexity; cf. Section 7).

6.1 Inclusion-preserving minimization

Inclusion checking algorithms generally benefit from language-preserving minimization preprocessing (cf. Sec. 5). However, preserving the languages of $\mathcal{A}$ and $\mathcal{B}$ in the preprocessing is not actually necessary. A preprocessing on $\mathcal{A}, \mathcal{B}$ is said to be *inclusion-preserving* iff it produces automata $\mathcal{A}', \mathcal{B}'$ s.t. $\mathcal{A} \subseteq \mathcal{B} \iff \mathcal{A}' \subseteq \mathcal{B}'$ (regardless of whether $\mathcal{A} \approx \mathcal{A}'$ or $\mathcal{B} \approx \mathcal{B}'$). In the following, we consider two inclusion-preserving preprocessing steps.

***Simplify* $\mathcal{A}$.** In theory, the problem $\mathcal{A} \subseteq \mathcal{B}$ is only hard in $\mathcal{B}$, but polynomial in the size of $\mathcal{A}$. However, this is only relevant if one actually constructs the exponential-size complement of $\mathcal{B}$, which is of course to be avoided. For polynomial simulation-based algorithms it is crucial to also minimize $\mathcal{A}$. The idea is to remove transitions in $\mathcal{A}$ which are 'covered' by better transitions in $\mathcal{B}$.

Definition Given $\mathcal{A} = (\Sigma, Q_\mathcal{A}, I_\mathcal{A}, F_\mathcal{A}, \delta_\mathcal{A})$, $\mathcal{B} = (\Sigma, Q_\mathcal{B}, I_\mathcal{B}, F_\mathcal{B}, \delta_\mathcal{B})$, let $P \subseteq \delta_\mathcal{A} \times \delta_\mathcal{B}$ be a relation for comparing transitions in $\mathcal{A}$ and $\mathcal{B}$. The pruned version of $\mathcal{A}$ is $Prune(\mathcal{A},\mathcal{B},P) := (\Sigma, Q_\mathcal{A}, I_\mathcal{A}, F_\mathcal{A}, \delta')$ with $\delta' = \{(p,\sigma,r) \in \delta_\mathcal{A} \mid \nexists (p',\sigma',r') \in \delta_\mathcal{B}.\, (p,\sigma,r)P(p',\sigma',r')\}$.

$\mathcal{A} \subseteq \mathcal{B}$ implies $Prune(\mathcal{A},\mathcal{B},P) \subseteq \mathcal{B}$ (since $Prune(\mathcal{A},\mathcal{B},P) \subseteq \mathcal{A}$). When also the other direction holds (so pruning is inclusion-preserving), we say that P is *good for $\mathcal{A},\mathcal{B}$-pruning*, i.e., when $\mathcal{A} \subseteq \mathcal{B} \iff Prune(\mathcal{A},\mathcal{B},P) \subseteq \mathcal{B}$. Intuitively, pruning is correct when the removed edges do not allow $\mathcal{A}$ to accept any word which is not already accepted by $\mathcal{B}$. In other words, if there is a counter example to inclusion in $\mathcal{A}$, then it can even be found in $Prune(\mathcal{A},\mathcal{B},P)$. As in Sec. 3, we compare transitions by looking at their endpoints: For state relations $R_b, R_f \subseteq Q_\mathcal{A} \times Q_\mathcal{B}$, let $P(R_b,R_f) = \{((p,\sigma,r),(p',\sigma',r')) \mid pR_bp' \wedge rR_fr'\}$.

Since inclusion-preserving pruning does not have to respect the language, we can use much weaker (i.e., coarser) relations for comparing endpoints. Let $\subseteq^{\text{bw-}}$ be the variant of $\subseteq^{\text{bw}}$ where accepting states are not taken into consideration.

Theorem 6.1. *$P(\subseteq^{\text{bw-}}, \subseteq^{\text{f}})$ is good for $\mathcal{A},\mathcal{B}$-pruning.*

Proof. Let $P = P(\subseteq^{\text{bw-}}, \subseteq^{\text{f}})$. One direction is trivial. For the other direction, by contraposition, assume $Prune(\mathcal{A},\mathcal{B},P) \subseteq \mathcal{B}$, but $\mathcal{A} \not\subseteq \mathcal{B}$. There exists a $w \in \mathcal{L}(\mathcal{A})$ s.t. $w \notin \mathcal{L}(\mathcal{B})$. There exists an initial fair trace $\pi = q_0 \xrightarrow{\sigma_0} q_1 \xrightarrow{\sigma_1} \cdots$ on w in $\mathcal{A}$. There are two cases.

1. π does not contain any transition $q_i \xrightarrow{\sigma_i} q_{i+1}$ that is not present in $Prune(\mathcal{A},\mathcal{B},P)$. Then π is also an initial fair trace on w in $Prune(\mathcal{A},\mathcal{B},P)$, and thus we obtain $w \in \mathcal{L}(Prune(\mathcal{A},\mathcal{B},P))$ and $w \in \mathcal{L}(\mathcal{B})$. Contradiction.
2. π contains a transition $q_i \xrightarrow{\sigma_i} q_{i+1}$ that is not present in $Prune(\mathcal{A},\mathcal{B},P)$. Therefore there exists a transition $q'_i \xrightarrow{\sigma_i} q'_{i+1}$ in $\mathcal{B}$ s.t. $q_i \subseteq^{\text{bw-}} q'_i$ and $q_{i+1} \subseteq^{\text{f}} q'_{i+1}$. Thus there exists an initial fair trace on w in $\mathcal{B}$ and thus $w \in \mathcal{L}(\mathcal{B})$. Contradiction. □

We can approximate $\subseteq^{\text{bw-}}$ with (the transitive closure of) a corresponding k-lookahead simulation $\sqsubseteq^{k\text{-bw-}}$, which is defined as $\sqsubseteq^{k\text{-bw}}$, except that only initial states are considered, i.e., the winning condition is $\mathcal{C}^{\text{bw-}}(\pi_0,\pi_1) \iff \forall (i \geq 0) \cdot p_i \in I \implies q_i \in I$. Let $\preceq^{k\text{-bw-}}$ be the transitive closure of $\sqsubseteq^{k\text{-bw-}}$. Since GFP is $\subseteq$-downward closed and $P(\cdot,\cdot)$ is monotone, we get this corollary.

Corollary 6.2. *$P(\preceq^{k\text{-bw-}}, \preceq^{k\text{-f}})$ is good for $\mathcal{A},\mathcal{B}$-pruning.*

***Simplify* $\mathcal{B}$.** Let $\mathcal{A} \times \mathcal{B}$ be the synchronized product of $\mathcal{A}$ and $\mathcal{B}$. The idea is to remove states in $\mathcal{B}$ which cannot be reached in $\mathcal{A} \times \mathcal{B}$. Let R be the set of states in $\mathcal{A} \times \mathcal{B}$ reachable from $I_\mathcal{A} \times I_\mathcal{B}$, and let $X \subseteq Q_\mathcal{B}$ be the projection of R to the $\mathcal{B}$-component. We obtain $\mathcal{B}'$ from $\mathcal{B}$ by removing all states $\notin X$ and their associated transitions. Although $\mathcal{B}' \not\approx \mathcal{B}$, this operation is clearly inclusion-preserving.

6.2 Jumping fair simulation as a better GFI relation

We further generalize the GFI preorder $\preceq^{k\text{-f}}$ by allowing Duplicator even more freedom. The idea is to allow Duplicator to take *jumps* during the simulation game (in the spirit of [9]). For a preorder $\leq$ on Q, in the game for *$\leq$-jumping k-lookahead simulation* Duplicator is allowed to jump to $\leq$-larger states before taking a transition. Thus, a Duplicator's move is of the form $q_i \leq q'_i \xrightarrow{\sigma_i} q_{i+1} \leq q'_{i+1} \xrightarrow{\sigma_{i+1}} \cdots \xrightarrow{\sigma_{i+m-1}} q_{i+m}$, and she eventually builds an infinite $\leq$-jumping trace. We say that this trace is *accepting* at step i iff $\exists q''_i \in F.\, q_i \leq q''_i \leq q'_i$, and *fair* iff it is accepting infinitely often. As usual, *$\leq$-jumping k-lookahead fair simulation* holds iff Duplicator wins the corresponding game, with the fair winning condition lifted to jumping traces.

Not all preorders $\leq$ induce GFI jumping simulations. The preorder $\leq$ is called *jumping-safe* [9] if, for every word w, there exists a $\leq$-jumping initial fair trace on w iff there exists an initial fair non-jumping one. Thus, jumping-safe preorders allows to convert jumping traces into non-jumping ones. Consequently, for a jumping-safe preorder $\leq$, $\leq$-jumping k-lookahead fair simulation is GFI.

One can prove that $\subseteq^{\text{bw}}$ is jumping-safe, while $\subseteq^{\text{bw-}}$ is not. We even improve $\subseteq^{\text{bw}}$ to a slightly more general jumping-safe relation $\subseteq^{\text{bw-c}}$, by only requiring that Duplicator visits at least as many accepting states as Spoiler does, but not necessarily at the same time. Formally, $p_m \subseteq^{\text{bw-c}} q_m$ iff, for every initial w-trace $\pi_0 = p_0 \xrightarrow{\sigma_0} p_1 \xrightarrow{\sigma_1} \cdots \xrightarrow{\sigma_{m-1}} p_m$, there exists an initial w-trace $\pi_1 = q_0 \xrightarrow{\sigma_0} q_1 \xrightarrow{\sigma_1} \cdots \xrightarrow{\sigma_{m-1}} q_m$, s.t. $|\{i \mid p_i \in F\}| \leq |\{i \mid q_i \in F\}|$.

Theorem 6.3. *The preorder $\subseteq^{\text{bw-c}}$ is jumping-safe.*

Proof. Since $\subseteq^{\text{bw-c}}$ is reflexive, the existence of an initial fair trace on w directly implies the existence of a $\subseteq^{\text{bw-c}}$-jumping initial fair trace on w.

Now, we show the reverse implication. Given two initial $\subseteq^{\text{bw-c}}$-jumping traces on w $\pi_0 = p_0 \subseteq^{\text{bw-c}} p'_0 \xrightarrow{\sigma_0} p_1 \subseteq^{\text{bw-c}} p'_1 \xrightarrow{\sigma_1} \cdots$ and $\pi_1 = q_0 \subseteq^{\text{bw-c}} q'_0 \xrightarrow{\sigma_0} q_1 \subseteq^{\text{bw-c}} q'_1 \xrightarrow{\sigma_1} \cdots$ we define $\mathcal{C}^c_j(\pi_0,\pi_1)$ iff $|\{i \leq j \mid \exists p''_i \in F.\, p_i \subseteq^{\text{bw-c}} p''_i \subseteq^{\text{bw-c}} p'_i\}| \leq |\{i \leq j \mid \exists q''_i \in F.\, q_i \subseteq^{\text{bw-c}} q''_i \subseteq^{\text{bw-c}} q'_i\}|$. We say that an initial $\subseteq^{\text{bw-c}}$-jumping trace on w is *i-good* iff it does not jump within the first i steps.

We show, by induction on i, the following property (P): For every i and every infinite $\subseteq^{\text{bw-c}}$-jumping initial trace $\pi = p_0 \subseteq^{\text{bw-c}} p'_0 \xrightarrow{\sigma_0} p_1 \subseteq^{\text{bw-c}} p'_1 \xrightarrow{\sigma_1} \cdots$ on w there exists an initial i-good trace $\pi^i = q_0 \xrightarrow{\sigma_0} q_1 \xrightarrow{\sigma_1} \cdots \xrightarrow{\sigma_i} q_i \cdots$ on w s.t. $\mathcal{C}^c_i(\pi,\pi^i)$ and the suffixes of the traces are identical, i.e., $q_i = p_i$ and $\pi[i..] = \pi^i[i..]$.

For the case base $i = 0$ we take $\pi^0 = \pi$. Now we consider the induction step. By induction hypothesis we get an initial i-good trace π^i s.t. $\mathcal{C}^c_i(\pi,\pi^i)$ and $q_i = p_i$ and $\pi[i..] = \pi^i[i..]$. If π^i is $(i+1)$-good then we can take $\pi^{i+1} = \pi^i$. Otherwise, π^i contains a step $q_i \subseteq^{\text{bw-c}} q'_i \xrightarrow{\sigma_i} q_{i+1}$. First we consider the case where there exists a $q''_i \in F$ s.t. $q_i \subseteq^{\text{bw-c}} q''_i \subseteq^{\text{bw-c}} q'_i$. (Note that the i-th step in π^i can count as accepting in $\mathcal{C}^c$ because $q''_i \in F$, even if q_i and q'_i are not accepting.) By def. of $\subseteq^{\text{bw-c}}$ there exists an initial trace π'' on a prefix of w that ends in q''_i and visits accepting states at least as often as the non-jumping prefix of π^i that ends in q_i. Again by definition of $\subseteq^{\text{bw-c}}$ there exists an initial trace π' on a prefix of w that ends in q'_i and visits accepting states at least as often as π''. Thus π' visits accepting states at least as often as the *jumping* prefix of π^i that ends in q'_i (by the definition of $\mathcal{C}^c$). By composing the traces we get $\pi^{i+1} = \pi'(q'_i \xrightarrow{\sigma_i} q_{i+1})\pi^i[i+1..]$. Thus π^{i+1} is an $(i+1)$-good initial trace on w and $\pi[i+1..] = \pi^i[i+1..] = \pi^{i+1}[i+1..]$ and $\mathcal{C}^c_{i+1}(\pi^i,\pi^{i+1})$ and $\mathcal{C}^c_{i+1}(\pi,\pi^{i+1})$. The other case where there is no $q''_i \in F$ s.t. $q_i \subseteq^{\text{bw-c}} q''_i \subseteq^{\text{bw-c}} q'_i$ is similar, but simpler.

Let π be an initial $\subseteq^{\text{bw-c}}$-jumping fair trace on w. By property (P) and König's Lemma there exists an infinite initial non-jumping fair trace π' on w. Thus $\subseteq^{\text{bw-c}}$ is jumping-safe. □

As a direct consequence, $\subseteq^{\text{bw-c}}$-jumping k-lookahead fair simulation is GFI. Since $\subseteq^{\text{bw-c}}$ is difficult to compute, we approximate it by a corresponding lookahead-simulation $\sqsubseteq^{k\text{-bw-c}}$ which, in the same spirit, counts and compares the number of visits to accepting states in every round of the k-lookahead backward simulation game. Let $\preceq^{k\text{-bw-c}}$ be the transitive closure of $\sqsubseteq^{k\text{-bw-c}}$.

Corollary 6.4. *$\preceq^{k\text{-bw-c}}$-jumping k-lookahead fair sim. is GFI.*

6.3 Advanced inclusion checking algorithm

Given these techniques, we propose the following algorithm for inclusion checking $\mathcal{A} \subseteq \mathcal{B}$.

(1) Use the Heavy-k procedure to minimize $\mathcal{A}$ and $\mathcal{B}$, and additionally apply the inclusion-preserving minimization techniques from Sec. 6. Lookahead simulations are computed not only on $\mathcal{A}$ and $\mathcal{B}$, but also *between* them (i.e., on their disjoint union). Since they are GFI, we check whether they already witness inclusion. Since many simulations are computed between partly minimized versions of $\mathcal{A}$ and $\mathcal{B}$, this witnesses inclusion much more often than checking fair simulation between the original versions. This step either stops showing inclusion, or produces smaller inclusion-equivalent automata $\mathcal{A}', \mathcal{B}'$.

(2) Check the GFI $\preceq^{k\text{-bw-c}}$-jumping k-lookahead fair simulation from Sec. 6.2 between $\mathcal{A}'$ and $\mathcal{B}'$, and stop if the answer is yes.

(3) If inclusion was not established in steps (1) or (2) then try to find a counterexample to inclusion. This is best done by a Ramsey-based method (optionally using simulation-based subsumption techniques), e.g., [1, 4]. Use a small timeout value, since in most non-included instances there exists a very short counterexample. Stop if a counterexample is found.

(4) If steps (1)-(3) failed (rare in practice), use any complete method, (e.g., Rank-based, Ramsey-based or Piterman's construction) to check $\mathcal{A}' \subseteq \mathcal{B}'$. At least, it will benefit from working on the smaller instance $\mathcal{A}', \mathcal{B}'$ produced by step (1).

Note that steps (1)-(3) take polynomial time, while step (4) takes exponential time. (For the latter, we recommend the improved Ramsey method of [1, 4] and the on-the-fly variant of Piterman's construction [29] implemented in GOAL [34].) This algorithm allows to solve much larger instances of the inclusion problem than previous methods [3, 4, 15–17, 29, 31, 34], i.e., automata with 1000-20000 states instead of 10-100 states; cf. Section 7.

7. Experiments

We test the effectiveness of Heavy-k minimization on Tabakov-Vardi random automata [33], on automata derived from LTL formulae, and on automata derived from mutual exclusion protocols, and compare it to the best previously available techniques implemented in GOAL [34]. A scalability test shows that Heavy-k has quadratic average-case complexity and it is vastly more efficient than GOAL. Furthermore, we test our methods for language inclusion on large instances and compare their performance to previous techniques. Due to space limitations, we only give a summary of the results, but all details and the runnable tools are available [2]. Unless otherwise stated, the experiments were run with Java 6 on Intel Xeon X5550 2.67GHz and 14GB memory.

Random automata. The Tabakov-Vardi model [33] generates random automata according to the following parameters: the number of states n, the size of the alphabet $|\Sigma|$, the transition density td (number of transitions, relative to n and $|\Sigma|$) and the acceptance density ad (percentage of accepting states). Apart from this, they do not have any special structure, and thus minimization and language inclusion problem are harder for them than for automata from other sources (see below). Random automata provide general reproducible test cases, on average. Moreover, they are the only test cases that are guaranteed to be unbiased towards any particular method. Thus, it is a particular sign of quality if a method performs well even on these hard cases.

The inherent difficulty of the minimization problem, and thus also the effectiveness of minimization methods, depends strongly on the class of random automata, i.e., on the parameters listed above. Thus, one needs to compare the methods over the whole range, not just for one example. Variations in ad do not affect Heavy-k much [2], but very small values make minimization harder for the other methods. By far the most important parameter is td. The following figure shows typical results. We take $n = 100$, $|\Sigma| = 2$, $ad = 0.5$ and the range of $td = 1.0, 1.1, \ldots, 3.0$. For each td we created 300 random automata, minimized them with different methods, and plotted the resulting average number of states after minimization. Each curve represents a different method: RD (just remove dead states), Light-1, Light-12, Heavy-1, and Heavy-12 and GOAL. The GOAL curve shows the best effort of all previous techniques (as implemented in GOAL), which include RD, quotienting with backward and forward simulation, pruning of little brother transitions and the fair simulation minimization of [19] (which subsumes quotienting with delayed simulation).

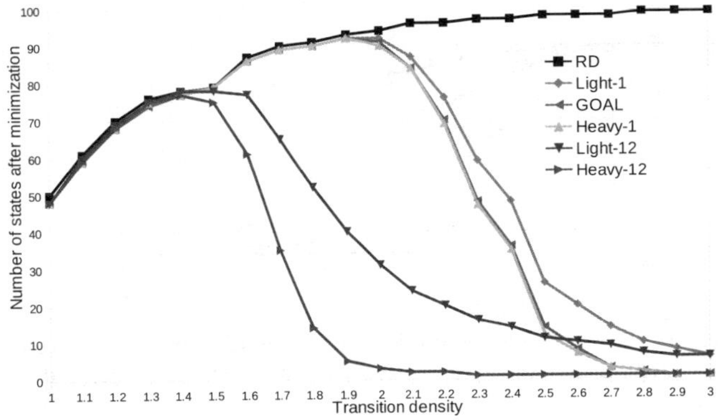

Sparse automata with low td have more dead states. For $td \leq 1.4$ no technique except RD has any significant effect. GOAL minimizes just slightly worse than Heavy-1 but it is no match for our best techniques. Heavy-12 vastly outperforms all others, particularly in the interesting range between 1.4 and 2.5. Moreover, the minimization of GOAL (in particular the fair simulation minimization of [19]) is very slow. For GOAL, the average minimization time per automaton varies between 39s (at $td = 1.0$) and 612s (maximal at $td = 2.9$). In contrast, for Heavy-12, the average minimization time per automaton varies between 0.012s (at $td = 1.0$) and 1.482s (max. at $td = 1.7$). So Heavy-12 minimizes not only much better, but also at least 400 times faster than GOAL (see also the scalability test).

For $td \geq 2.0$, Heavy-12 yields very small automata. Many of these are even universal, i.e., with just one state and a universal loop. However, this frequent universality is *not* due to trivial reasons (otherwise simpler techniques like Light-1 and GOAL would also recognize this). Consider the following question: Given Tabakov-Vardi random automata with parameters n, $|\Sigma|$ and td, what is the probability $U(n, |\Sigma|, td)$ that every state has at least one outgoing transition for every symbol in Σ? (Such an automaton would be trivially universal if $ad = 1$.)

Theorem 7.1. *$U(n,|\Sigma|,td) = (\alpha(n,T)/\beta(n,T))^{|\Sigma|}$, with $T = n \cdot td$, $\alpha(n,T) = \sum_{m=n}^{n^2} \binom{m-n}{T-n} \sum_{i=0}^{n} (-1)^i \binom{n}{i} \binom{m-in-1}{n-1}$ and $\beta(n,T) = \binom{n^2}{T}$*

Proof. For each symbol in Σ there are $T = n \cdot td$ transitions and n^2 possible places for transitions, described as a grid. $\alpha(n,T)$ is the number of ways T items can be placed onto an $n \times n$ grid s.t. every row contains ≥ 1 item, i.e., every state has an outgoing transition. $\beta(n,T)$ is the number of possibilities without this restriction, which is trivially $\binom{n^2}{T}$. Since the Tabakov-Vardi model chooses transitions for different symbols independently, we have $U(n,|\Sigma|,td) = (\alpha(n,T)/\beta(n,T))^{|\Sigma|}$. It remains to compute $\alpha(n,T)$. For the i-th row let $x_i \in \{1,\ldots,n\}$ be the maximal column containing an item. The remaining $T-n$ items can only be distributed to lower columns. Thus $\alpha(n,T) = \sum_{x_1,\ldots,x_n} \binom{(\sum x_i)-n}{T-n}$. With $m = \sum x_i$ and a standard dice-sum problem from [28] the result follows. □

For $n = 100$, $|\Sigma| = 2$ we obtain the following values for $U(n,|\Sigma|,td)$: 10^{-15} for $td = 2.0$, $2.9 \cdot 10^{-5}$ for $td = 3.0$, 0.03 for $td = 4.0$, 0.3 for $td = 5.0$, 0.67 for $td = 6.0$, and 0.95 for $td = 8.0$. So this transition saturation effect is negligible in our tested range with $td \leq 3.0$.

While Heavy-12 performs very well, an even smaller lookahead can already be sufficient for a good minimization. However, this depends very much on the density td of the automata. The following chart shows the effect of the lookahead by comparing Heavy-k for varying k on different classes of random automata with different density $td = 1.6, 1.7, 1.8, 1.9, 2.0$. We have $n = 100$, $|\Sigma| = 2$ and $ad = 0.5$, and every point is the average of 1000 automata.

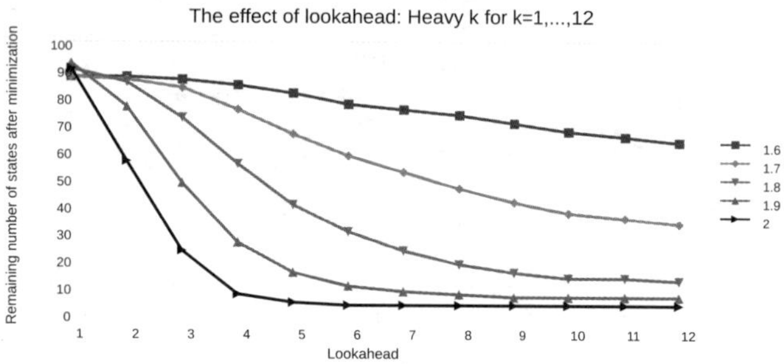

The big advantage of Heavy-12 over Light-12 is due to the pruning techniques. However, these only reach their full potential at higher lookaheads (thus the smaller difference between Heavy-1 and Light-1). Indeed, the simulation relations get much denser with higher lookahead k. We consider random automata with $n = 100$, $|\Sigma| = 2$ and $td = 1.8$ (a nontrivial case; larger td yield larger simulations). We let $ad = 0.1$ (resp. $ad = 0.9$), and plot the size of fair, delayed, direct, and backward simulation as k increases from 1 to 12. Every point is the average of 1000 automata.

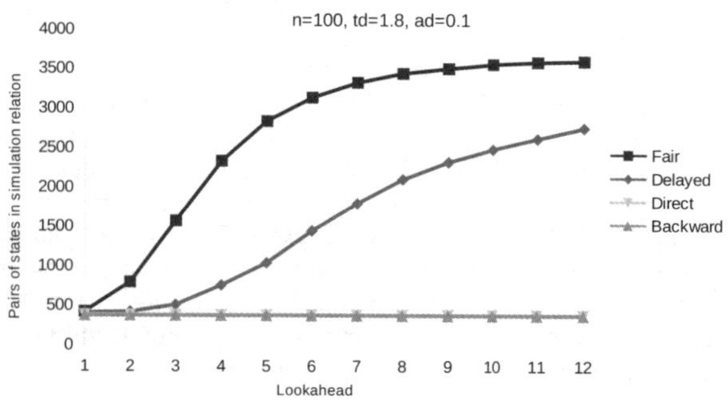

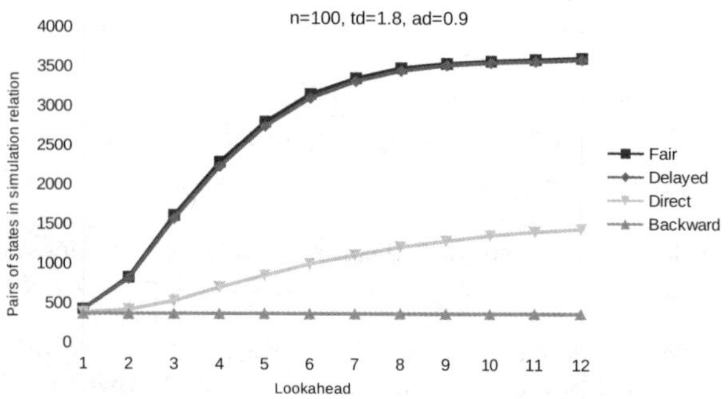

Fair/delayed simulation is not much larger than direct simulation for $k = 1$, but they benefit strongly from higher k. Backward simulation increases only slightly (e.g., from 365 to 381 pairs for $ad = 0.9$). Initially, it seems as if backward/direct simulation does not benefit from higher k if ad is small (on random automata), but this is wrong. Even random automata get less random during the Heavy-k minimization process, making lookahead more effective for backward/direct simulation. Consider the case of $n = 300$, $td = 1.8$ and $ad = 0.1$. Initially, the average ratio $|\preceq^{\text{12-di}}|/|\preceq^{\text{1-di}}|$ is 1.00036, but after quotienting with $\preceq^{\text{12-de}}$ this ratio is 1.103.

LTL. For model checking [22], LTL-formulae are converted into Büchi automata. This conversion has been extensively studied and there are many different algorithms which try to construct the smallest possible automaton for a given formula (see references in [34]). It should be noted however, that LTL is designed for human readability and does not cover the full class of ω-regular languages. Moreover, Büchi Store [35] contains handcrafted automata for almost every human-readable LTL-formula and none of these automata has more than 7 states. Still, since many people are interested in LTL to automata conversion, we tested how much our minimization algorithm can improve upon the best effort of previous techniques. For LTL model checking, the size of the automata is not the only criterion [30], since more non-determinism also makes the problem harder. However, our transition pruning techniques only make an automaton 'more deterministic'.

Using a function of GOAL, we created 300 random LTL-formulae of nontrivial size: length 70, 4 predicates and probability weights 1 for boolean and 2 for future operators. We then converted these formulae to Büchi automata and minimized them with GOAL. Of the 14 different converters implemented in GOAL we chose LTL2BA [18] (which is also used by the SPIN model checker [22]), since it was the only one which could handle such large formulae. (The second best was COUVREUR which succeeded on 90% of the instances, but produced much larger automata than LTL2BA. The other converters ran out of time (4h) or memory (14GB) on most instances.) We thus obtained 300 automata and minimized them with GOAL. The resulting automata vary significantly in size from 1 state to 1722 states [2].

Then we tested how much *further* these automata could be reduced in size by our Heavy-12 method [2]. In summary, 82% of the automata could be further reduced in size. The average number of states declined from 138 to 78, and the average number of transitions from 3102 to 1270. Since larger automata have a disproportionate effect on averages, we also computed the average reduction ratio per automaton, i.e., $(1/300)\sum_{i=1}^{300} newsize_i/oldsize_i$. (Note the difference between the average ratio and the ratio of averages.) The average ratio was 0.76 for states and 0.68 for transitions. The computation times for minimization vary a lot due to different automata sizes (average 122s), but were always less than the time used by the LTL to automata translation. If one only considers the 150 automata above median size (30 states) then the results are even stronger. 100% of these automata could be further reduced in size. The average number of states declined from 267 to 149, and the average number of transitions from 6068 to 2435. The average reduction ratio was 0.65 for states and 0.54 for transitions. To conclude, our minimization can significantly improve the quality of LTL to automata translation with a moderate overhead.

Mutual exclusion protocols. We consider automata derived from mutual exclusion protocols. The protocols were described in a language of guarded commands and automatically translated into Büchi automata, whose size is given in the column 'Original'. By row, the protocols are Bakery.1, Bakery.2, Fischer.3.1, Fischer.3.2, Fischer.2, Phils.1.1, Phils.2 and Mcs.1.2. We minimize these automata with GOAL and with our Heavy-12 method and describe the sizes of the resulting automata and the runtime in subsequent columns (Java 6 on Intel i7-740, 1.73 GHz). In some instances GOAL ran out of time (2h) or memory (14GB).

Original		GOAL		Time	Heavy-12		Time
Trans.	States	Tr.	St.	GOAL	Tr.	St.	Heavy-12
2597	1506	N/A	N/A	$> 2h$	696	477	6.17s
2085	1146	N/A	N/A	$> 2h$	927	643	9.04s
1401	638	14	10	15.38s	14	10	1.16s
3856	1536	212	140	4529s	96	70	5.91s
67590	21733	N/A	N/A	oom(14GB)	316	192	325.76s
464	161	362	134	540.3s	359	134	11.51s
2350	581	284	100	164.2s	225	97	4.04s
21509	7968	108	69	2606.7s	95	62	48.18s

Scalability. We test the scalability of Heavy-12 minimization by applying it to Tabakov-Vardi random automata of increasing size but fixed *td*, *ad* and Σ. We ran four separate tests with $td = 1.4, 1.6, 1.8$ and 2.0. In each test we fixed $ad = 0.5$, $|\Sigma| = 2$ and increased the number of states from $n = 50$ to $n = 1000$ in increments of 50. For each parameter point we created 300 random automata and minimized them with Heavy-12. We analyze the average size of the minimized automata in percent of the original size n, and how the average computation time increases with n.

For $td = 1.4$ the average size of the minimized automata stays around 77% of the original size, regardless of n. For $td = 1.6$ it stays around 65%. For $td = 1.8$ it *decreases* from 28% at $n = 50$ to 2% at $n = 1000$. For $td = 2.0$ it *decreases* from 8% at $n = 50$ to $< 1\%$ at $n = 1000$ [2]. Note that the lookahead of 12 did *not change* with n. Surprisingly, larger automata do not require larger lookahead for a good minimization.

We plot the average computation time (measured in ms) in n and then compute the optimal fit of the function $time = a * n^b$ to the data by the least-squares method, i.e., this computes the parameters a and b of the function that most closely fits the experimental data. The important parameter is the exponent b. For $td = 1.4, 1.6, 1.8, 2.0$ we obtain $0.018 * n^{2.14}$, $0.32 * n^{2.39}$, $0.087 * n^{2.05}$ and $0.055 * n^{2.09}$, respectively. Thus, the average-case complexity of Heavy-12 scales (almost) quadratically. This is especially surprising given that Heavy-12 does not only compute one simulation relation but potentially many simulations until the repeated minimization reaches a fixpoint. Quadratic complexity is the very best one can hope for in any method that explicitly compares states/transitions by simulation relations, since the relations themselves are of quadratic size. Lower complexity is only possible with pure partition refinement techniques (e.g., bisimulation, which is $O(n \log n)$), but these achieve even less minimization than quotienting with direct simulation (i.e., next to nothing on hard instances).

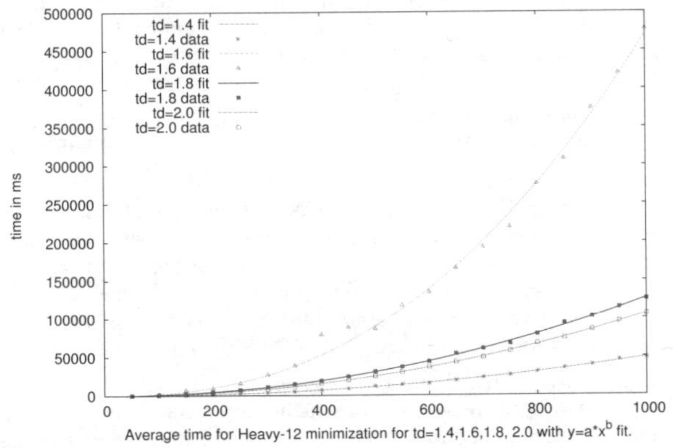

Average time for Heavy-12 minimization for td=1.4,1.6,1.8, 2.0 with $y=a^*x^b$ fit.

The computation time of Heavy-k depends on the class of automata, i.e., on the density *td*, as the scalability test above shows. Moreover, it also depends on k. The following graph shows the average computation time of Heavy-k on automata of size 100 and varying *td* and k. The most difficult cases are those where minimization is possible (and thus the alg. does not give up quickly), but does not massively reduce the size of the instance. For Heavy-k, this peak is around $td = 1.6, 1.7$ (like in the scalability test).

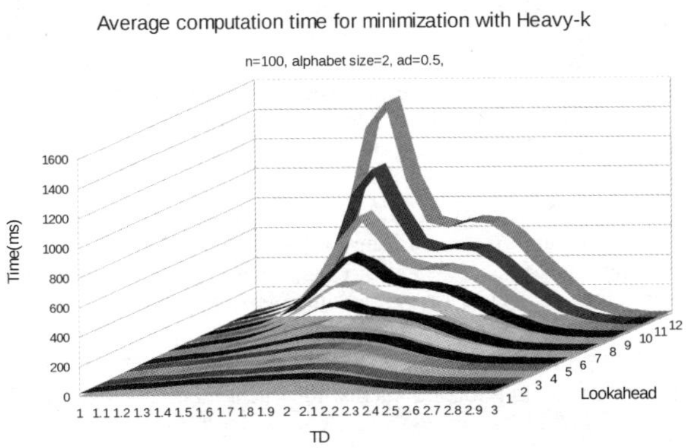

Language Inclusion Checking. We test the language inclusion checking algorithm of Section 6.3 (with lookahead up-to 15) on nontrivial instances and compare its performance to previous techniques like ordinary fair simulation checking and the best effort of GOAL (which uses simulation-based minimization followed by an on-the-fly variant of Piterman's construction [29, 34]). In this test we use only the polynomial time steps (1)-(3) of our algorithm, thus it may fail in some instances. We consider pairs of Tabakov-Vardi random automata with 1000 states each, $|\Sigma| = 2$ and $ad = 0.5$. For each separate case of $td = 1.6, 1.8$ and 2.0, we create 300 such automata pairs and check if language inclusion holds. (For $td < 1.6$ inclusion rarely holds, except trivially if one automaton has empty language. For $td > 2$ inclusion often holds but is easier to prove.)

For $td = 1.6$ our algorithm solved 294 of 300 instances (i.e., 98%): 45 included (16 in step (1) and 29 in step (2)), 249 non-included (step (3)), and 6 failed. Average computation time 1167s. Ordinary fair simulation solved only 13 included instances. GOAL (timeout 60min, 14GB memory) solved only 13 included instances (the same 13 as fair simulation) and 155 non-included instances.

For $td = 1.8$ our algorithm solved 297 of 300 instances (i.e., 99%): 104 included (103 in step (1) and 1 in step (2)) and 193 non-included (step (3)) and 3 failed. Average computation time 452s. Ordinary fair simulation solved only 5 included instances. GOAL (timeout 30min, 14GB memory) solved only 5 included instances (the same 5 as fair simulation) and 115 non-included instances.

For $td = 2.0$ our algorithm solved every instance: 143 included (shown in step (1)) and 157 non-included (step (3)). Average computation time 258s. Ordinary fair simulation solved only 1 of the 143 included instances. GOAL (timeout 30min, 14GB memory) solved only 1 of 143 included instances (the same one as fair simulation) and 106 of 157 non-included instances.

8. Conclusion and Future Work

Our automata minimization techniques perform significantly better than previous methods. In particular, they can be applied to solve PSPACE-complete automata problems like language inclusion for much larger instances. While we presented our methods in the context of Büchi automata, most of them trivially carry over to the simpler case of automata over finite words. Future work includes more efficient algorithms for computing lookahead simulations, either along the lines of [20] for normal simulation, or by using symbolic representations of the relations. Moreover, we are applying similar techniques to minimize tree-automata.

References

[1] RABIT tool: www.languageinclusion.org/doku.php?id=tools.

[2] L. Clemente and R. Mayr. Advanced Automata Minimization. Tech. Rep. EDI-INF-RR-1414, U. of Edinburgh (2012), arXiv:1210.6624 http://www.inf.ed.ac.uk/publications/report/1414.html.

[3] P. Abdulla, Y.-F. Chen, L. Clemente, L. Holik, C.-D. Hong, R. Mayr, and T. Vojnar. Simulation Subsumption in Ramsey-Based Büchi Automata Universality and Inclusion Testing. In T. Touili, B. Cook, and P. Jackson, editors, *Computer Aided Verification*, volume 6174 of *LNCS*, pages 132–147, 2010. ISBN 978-3-642-14294-9. doi: 10.1007/978-3-642-14295-6_14. URL http://dx.doi.org/10.1007/978-3-642-14295-6_14.

[4] P. Abdulla, Y.-F. Chen, L. Clemente, L. Holik, C.-D. Hong, R. Mayr and T. Vojnar. Advanced Ramsey-based Büchi Automata Inclusion Testing. In J.-P. Katoen and B. König, editors, *International Conference on Concurrency Theory*, volume 6901 of *LNCS*, pages 187–202, Sept. 2011.

[5] P. A. Abdulla, Y.-F. Chen, L. Holík, and T. Vojnar. Mediating for reduction (on minimizing alternating Büchi automata). In *FSTTCS*, volume 4 of *LIPIcs*, pages 1–12. Schloss Dagstuhl - Leibniz-Zentrum fuer Informatik, 2009.

[6] P. A. Abdulla, Y.-F. Chen, L. Holik, R. Mayr, and T. Vojnar. When Simulation Meets Antichains. In *Tools and Algorithms for the Construction and Analysis of Systems*, volume 6015 of *LNCS*, 2010. URL http://hal.inria.fr/inria-00460294/en/.

[7] D. Bustan and O. Grumberg. Simulation-based minimization. *ACM Trans. Comput. Logic*, 4:181–206, April 2003. ISSN 1529-3785. doi: http://doi.acm.org/10.1145/635499.635502. URL http://doi.acm.org/10.1145/635499.635502.

[8] L. Clemente. Büchi Automata Can Have Smaller Quotients. In L. Aceto, M. Henzinger, and J. Sgall, editors, *ICALP*, volume 6756 of *LNCS*, pages 258–270. 2011. ISBN 978-3-642-22011-1. doi: 10.1007/978-3-642-22012-8_20. URL http://arxiv.org/pdf/1102.3285.

[9] L. Clemente. *Generalized Simulation Relations with Applications in Automata Theory*. PhD thesis, University of Edinburgh, 2012.

[10] D. L. Dill, A. J. Hu, and H. Wont-Toi. Checking for Language Inclusion Using Simulation Preorders. In *Computer Aided Verification*, volume 575 of *LNCS*. Springer-Verlag, 1991. doi: 10.1007/3-540-55179-4_25. URL http://dx.doi.org/10.1007/3-540-55179-4_25.

[11] L. Doyen and J.-F. Raskin. Antichains Algorithms for Finite Automata. In *Tools and Algorithms for the Construction and Analysis of Systems*, volume 6015 of *LNCS*, pages 2–22. Springer-Verlag, 2010.

[12] K. Etessami. A Hierarchy of Polynomial-Time Computable Simulations for Automata. In *International Conference on Concurrency Theory*, volume 2421 of *LNCS*, pages 131–144. Springer-Verlag, 2002. doi: 10.1007/3-540-45694-5_10. URL http://dx.doi.org/10.1007/3-540-45694-5_10.

[13] K. Etessami and G. Holzmann. Optimizing Büchi Automata. In *International Conference on Concurrency Theory*, volume 1877 of *LNCS*, pages 153–168. Springer-Verlag, 2000.

[14] K. Etessami, T. Wilke, and R. A. Schuller. Fair Simulation Relations, Parity Games, and State Space Reduction for Büchi Automata. *SIAM J. Comput.*, 34(5):1159–1175, 2005. doi: 10.1137/S0097539703420675. URL http://epubs.siam.org/sam-bin/dbq/article/42067.

[15] S. Fogarty and M. Vardi. Büchi Complementation and Size-Change Termination. In S. Kowalewski and A. Philippou, editors, *Tools and Algorithms for the Construction and Analysis of Systems*, volume 5505 of *LNCS*, pages 16–30. 2009. doi: 10.1007/978-3-642-00768-2_2. URL http://dx.doi.org/10.1007/978-3-642-00768-2_2.

[16] S. Fogarty and M. Y. Vardi. Efficient Büchi Universality Checking. In *Tools and Algorithms for the Construction and Analysis of Systems*, pages 205–220, 2010.

[17] S. Fogarty, O. Kupferman, M. Y. Vardi, and T. Wilke. Unifying Büchi Complementation Constructions. In M. Bezem, editor, *Computer Science Logic*, volume 12 of *LIPIcs*, pages 248–263. Schloss Dagstuhl–Leibniz-Zentrum fuer Informatik, 2011. doi: http://dx.doi.org/10.4230/LIPIcs.CSL.2011.248.

[18] P. Gastin and D. Oddoux. Fast LTL to Büchi automata translation. In *CAV*, volume 2102 of *LNCS*, pages 53–65. Springer, 2001.

[19] S. Gurumurthy, R. Bloem, , and F. Somenzi. Fair simulation minimization. In *CAV*, volume 2404 of *LNCS*, pages 610–624. Springer, 2002.

[20] M. R. Henzinger, T. A. Henzinger, and P. W. Kopke. Computing simulations on finite and infinite graphs. In *Foundations of Computer Science*, FOCS '95, Washington, DC, USA, 1995. IEEE Computer Society. ISBN 0-8186-7183-1. URL http://portal.acm.org/citation.cfm?id=796255.

[21] T. A. Henzinger, O. Kupferman, and S. K. Rajamani. Fair Simulation. *Information and Computation*, 173: 64–81, 2002. doi: 10.1006/inco.2001.3085. URL http://dx.doi.org/10.1006/inco.2001.3085.

[22] G. Holzmann. *The SPIN Model Checker*. Addison-Wesley, 2004.

[23] T. Jiang and B. Ravikumar. Minimal NFA Problems are Hard. In J. Albert, B. Monien, and M. Artalejo, editors, *ICALP*, volume 510 of *LNCS*, pages 629–640. 1991. doi: 10.1007/3-540-54233-7_169.

[24] S. Juvekar and N. Piterman. Minimizing Generalized Büchi Automata. In *Computer Aided Verification*, volume 4414 of *LNCS*, pages 45–58. Springer-Verlag, 2006. doi: 10.1007/11817963_7. URL http://dx.doi.org/10.1007/11817963_7.

[25] O. Kupferman and M. Vardi. Verification of Fair Transition Systems. In *Computer Aided Verification*, volume 1102 of *LNCS*, pages 372–382. Springer-Verlag, 1996. URL http://citeseer.ist.psu.edu/viewdoc/summary?doi=10.1.1.29.9654.

[26] C. S. Lee, N. D. Jones, and A. M. Ben-Amram. The size-change principle for program termination. POPL '01, pages 81–92, 2001. doi: http://doi.acm.org/10.1145/360204.360210.

[27] J. Leroux and G. Point. TaPAS: The Talence Presburger Arithmetic Suite. In *Proceedings of the 15th International Conference on Tools and Algorithms for the Construction and Analysis of Systems (TACAS)*, volume 5505 of *LNCS*. Springer, 2009.

[28] I. Niven. *Mathematics of Choice*. The Mathematical Association of America, 1965.

[29] N. Piterman. From nondeterministic Büchi and Streett automata to deterministic parity automata. In *LICS*, pages 255–264. IEEE, 2006.

[30] R. Sebastiani and S. Tonetta. More deterministic vs. smaller Büchi automata for efficient LTL model checking. In *Correct Hardware Design and Verification Methods*, volume 2860 of *LNCS*, 2003.

[31] A. P. Sistla, M. Y. Vardi, and P. Wolper. The complementation problem for Büchi automata with applications to temporal logic. *Theor. Comput. Sci.*, 49:217–237, Jan. 1987. ISSN 0304-3975. doi: 10.1016/0304-3975(87)90008-9. URL http://dx.doi.org/10.1016/0304-3975(87)90008-9.

[32] F. Somenzi and R. Bloem. Efficient Büchi Automata from LTL Formulae. In *Computer Aided Verification*, volume 1855 of *LNCS*, pages 248–263. Springer-Verlag, 2000. doi: 10.1007/10722167_21. URL http://dx.doi.org/10.1007/10722167_21.

[33] D. Tabakov and M. Vardi. Model Checking Büchi Specifications. In *LATA*, volume Report 35/07. Research Group on Mathematical Linguistics, Universitat Rovira i Virgili, Tarragona, 2007.

[34] Y.-K. Tsay, Y.-F. Chen, M.-H. Tsai, W.-C. Chan, and C.-J. Luo. GOAL extended: Towards a research tool for omega automata and temporal logic. In C. Ramakrishnan and J. Rehof, editors, *Tools and Algorithms for the Construction and Analysis of Systems*, volume 4963 of *LNCS*, pages 346–350. 2008. ISBN 978-3-540-78799-0. URL http://dx.doi.org/10.1007/978-3-540-78800-3_26.

[35] Y.-K. Tsay, M.-H. Tsai, J.-S. Chang, and Y.-W. Chang. Büchi store: An open repository of Büchi automata. In P. Abdulla and K. Leino, editors, *Tools and Algorithms for the Construction and Analysis of Systems*, volume 6605 of *LNCS*, pages 262–266. 2011. ISBN 978-3-642-19834-2. URL http://dx.doi.org/10.1007/978-3-642-19835-9_23. 10.1007/978-3-642-19835-9_23.

Automating Relatively Complete Verification of Higher-Order Functional Programs

Hiroshi Unno
University of Tsukuba
uhiro@cs.tsukuba.ac.jp

Tachio Terauchi
Nagoya University
terauchi@is.nagoya-u.ac.jp

Naoki Kobayashi
University of Tokyo
koba@is.s.u-tokyo.ac.jp

Abstract

We present an automated approach to relatively completely verifying safety (i.e., reachability) property of higher-order functional programs. Our contribution is two-fold. First, we extend the refinement type system framework employed in the recent work on (incomplete) automated higher-order verification by drawing on the classical work on relatively complete "Hoare logic like" program logic for higher-order procedural languages. Then, by adopting the recently proposed techniques for solving constraints over quantified first-order logic formulas, we develop an automated type inference method for the type system, thereby realizing an automated relatively complete verification of higher-order programs.

Categories and Subject Descriptors D.2.4 [*Software Engineering*]: Software/Program Verification; F.3.1 [*Logics and Meaning of Programs*]: Specifying and Verifying and Reasoning about Programs

Keywords Relative Completeness, Higher-Order Programs, Software Model Checking, Type Inference

1. Introduction

Recently, motivated by the success of *software model checkers* [12] for the automated verification of first-order programs, researchers have proposed "model checkers" for the automated verification of higher-order programs [13, 18, 23, 26, 27]. Interestingly, they have all been formulated as a form of refinement type inference.[1]

The refinement type systems employed in the automated higher-order program verification have some important differences from the ones from the original, non-automated approaches like DML [30], making them more amenable to automation (such as the lack of implicit Π types). But, they follow the non-automated ones in that the types embed first-order logic (FOL) formulas, called *refinement predicates*, over program values (as in dependent types) that are used to express and enforce detailed properties of the program.

For example, consider the OCaml program shown in Figure 1. Here, * denotes a non-deterministic choice. Given an integer argument i to main, the program recursively calls app non-deterministically to apply the closure check i to $i + j$ where j is the number of times the then branch is taken in app. The program is safe in that assert false is unreachable for any argument i. The program is difficult to verify via first-order program verification methods because of the higher-order recursive function app.

```
let rec app x f = if * then app (x+1) f
                  else f x in
let check x y = if x <= y then ()
                else assert false in
let main i = app i (check i)
```

Figure 1. A simple higher-order program.

Recent advances in higher-order program verification have enabled automated verification of such programs via refinement type inference. For the program above, the following refinement types may be automatically inferred to verify its safety.[2]

$$\begin{aligned}\texttt{app} &: x{:}\texttt{int} \to f{:}(\{u{:}\texttt{int} \mid u \geq x\} \to \texttt{unit}) \to \texttt{unit}\\ \texttt{check} &: x{:}\texttt{int} \to y{:}\{u{:}\texttt{int} \mid u \geq x\} \to \texttt{unit}\\ \texttt{main} &: i{:}\texttt{int} \to \texttt{unit}\end{aligned}$$

The type of app expresses the fact that the function takes an integer argument x, and a function-type argument f which takes an integer at least as large as x. The type of check says that it takes integers x and y such that $x \leq y$. And, the type of main says that it takes any integer argument.

The refinement type systems underlying the verifiers are sound, that is, they only type safe programs. However, they are incomplete in that there are safe programs that they cannot type. Indeed, the only known positive result is for the class of the finite domain base-type data programs, which can be verified completely by a refinement type system augmented with intersection types [16, 17]. The situation is in stark contrast to that of automated first-order program verification [12] where the underlying program logic, such as the Hoare logic, is relatively complete.

For example, none of the refinement type systems proposed for automated higher-order program verification can type and verify the program shown in Figure 2, even though the program is only a small modification of the one from Figure 1: it simply switches the order of app's arguments. Nor, are they able to type and verify the program shown in Figure 3, which uses the function succ to successively build closures to pass integers larger than i to check i. The program is untypable even if we were allowed to change the order of the function arguments.

We note that this is an incompleteness at the level of the program logic (i.e., refinement type system) and not the verification algorithm (i.e., type inference algorithm). That is, there exist no types within the refinement type system that can type the program,

[1] In fact, the equivalence of model checking and refinement type inference has been shown for the finite domain base-type data case [16, 17].

[2] The type syntax is borrowed from Augustsson [1].

POPL'13, January 23–25, 2013, Rome, Italy.

```
let rec app f x = if * then app f (x+1)
                  else f x in
let check x y = if x <= y then ()
                else assert false in
let main i = app (check i) i
```

Figure 2. A variant of Figure 1.

```
let rec app3 f g = if * then app3 (succ f) g
                   else g f in
let app x f = f x in
let succ f x = f (x + 1) in
let check x y = if x <= y then ()
                else assert false in
let main i = app3 (check i) (app i)
```

Figure 3. Another variant of Figure 1.

let alone inferable ones. While higher-order program verification is in general undecidable, like the first-order program verification is, it would be desirable to have a relatively complete reasoning framework that would serve as the basis of verification algorithms, as the Hoare logic does for first-order programs.

To this end, this paper presents an automated approach to a relatively complete verification of higher-order programs. First, we present an extension to the refinement type system such that the resulting refinement type system is relatively complete. The extension is inspired by the classical work on relatively complete program logic for higher-order procedural languages by German et al. [6, 7] (also, [8]) who showed that relative completeness is achievable while avoiding the explicit use of functions as data so as to maintain a "Hoare logic like" control-data separation.

However, their proof of relative completeness does use encoding of functions as base-type data, and we rely on the same technique for our relative completeness proof. Moreover, to hide the use of functions as data from the program logic, they introduce quantifiers that the client verifier must appropriately instantiate. (To the best of our knowledge, no actual verifier was built based on their program logic.) Therefore, as our second contribution, we show a type inference method that extends the first-order logic constraint solving of the previous automated refinement type inference systems to quantified reasoning by leveraging recent advances on a related problem [4, 9, 24].

In summary, the paper's contributions are as follows.

- A refinement type system that is relatively complete for safety verification of higher-order functional programs.
- A type inference algorithm for the refinement type system.

In the next section, we give an informal overview of the main ideas.

On incompleteness of the inference: The type inference algorithm that we propose is, of course, incomplete in that it is not able to decide the typability of all programs. This is expected because safety verification is undecidable in general. Instead, our contribution is a type system that is complete relative to a hypothetical theorem prover complete for first-order arithmetic, and a novel inference algorithm that is able to automatically verify a non-trivial subset of the programs that were not possible to verify with the previous automated approaches.

2. Informal Overview

We informally describe the incompleteness issue by showing how the existing approaches [13, 18, 23, 26, 27] fail to type the programs shown in Figures 2 and 3.

First, let us try to type Figure 2. Here, the goal is to show that `main` can be given the type $i\!:\!\texttt{int} \to \texttt{unit}$, that is, `main` is safe to be called with any integer i. (For a base type B, we often abbreviate the refinement type $\{u\!:\!B \mid \top\}$ as B. E.g., $\texttt{int} = \{u\!:\!\texttt{int} \mid \top\}$.) Therefore, we try to type the body of `main` under the assumption that the type of `i` is $\{u\!:\!\texttt{int} \mid \top\}$. The most precise type for the partial application `check i` is $y\!:\!\{u\!:\!\texttt{int} \mid u \geq \texttt{i}\} \to \texttt{unit}$ (i.e., functions that can take any integer at least as large as `i`), and the most precise type for `i` is $\{u\!:\!\texttt{int} \mid u = \texttt{i}\}$ (i.e., integers equal to `i`). (Intuitively, $\{u\!:\!B \mid \theta\}$ expresses values of the base type B satisfying the refinement predicate θ, and $x : \tau \to \sigma$ expresses functions that return a value of the type $\sigma[e/x]$ when given the argument e of the type τ.)

We show that the type systems fail to give the higher-order function `app` a sufficiently precise type to verify the program's safety. The type of `app` must be of the form

$$f\!:\!(\{u\!:\!\texttt{int} \mid \theta\} \to \texttt{unit}) \to x\!:\!\{u\!:\!\texttt{int} \mid \phi\} \to \texttt{unit}$$

where the refinement predicates θ and ϕ are FOL formulas in the theory of base-type data.[3] In addition, as discussed below, to prevent degenerate types, the refinement type systems enforce an important *well-formedness* condition that restricts the variables that can appear free in a refinement predicate. (Here, θ and ϕ are restricted so that $fv(\theta) \subseteq \{u\}$ and $fv(\phi) \subseteq \{f, u\}$, where $fv(\theta)$ denotes the free variables of θ.)

From the application `f x` in the body of `app`, the type system asserts that $\phi \Rightarrow \theta$, that is, `f` must be safe to be given the argument `x`. In the body of `main`, `app` is applied to `check i` and `i`, and the type system asserts that the type of `check i` is a subtype of $\{u\!:\!\texttt{int} \mid \theta\} \to \texttt{unit}$ and the type of `i` is a subtype of $\{u\!:\!\texttt{int} \mid \phi\}$. This leads to the constraints $u = \texttt{i} \Rightarrow \phi$ and $\theta \Rightarrow u \geq \texttt{i}$, accurately expressing the fact that `i` is passed as the second argument to `app` and that the first argument to `app` (i.e., `check i`) expects a value at least as large as `i`.

A solution to the set of constraints is $\theta \equiv u \geq \texttt{i}$ and $\phi \equiv u = \texttt{i}$, but this is degenerate because `main`'s variable `i` would appear in `app`'s type. (Recall that θ, ϕ are refinement predicates of `app`'s type.) Intuitively, it means that the function `app` could "see" values from a specific context of its use (i.e., `main`). Indeed, as remarked above, the refinement type systems disallow such degenerate types via the well-formedness condition, and only allow θ, ϕ such that $fv(\theta) \subseteq \{u\}$ and $fv(\phi) \subseteq \{f, u\}$. That is, the refinement predicates are allowed to only mention the variables in their respective scopes. Consequently, the program is (conservatively) rejected as untypable. It is worth noting that the program of Figure 1 does not have this issue as `app`'s arguments are conveniently ordered so that `app`'s function-type argument could depend on the base-type argument to allow the following sufficiently precise type:

$$x\!:\!\texttt{int} \to f\!:\!(\{u\!:\!\texttt{int} \mid u \geq x\} \to \texttt{unit}) \to \texttt{unit}$$

Unfortunately, as exemplified by Figure 3, the incompleteness issue is not just a matter of choosing the right order of function arguments. Here, the program is untypable even if we were allowed to change the order of the arguments, and the untypability comes from not being able to give a precise enough type to `app3`. Ideally, we would like to express via `app3`'s type the fact that `g` is safe when applied to `f` (and also when applied to $\texttt{succ}^j$ `f` for any $j > 0$). But, this requires a type that is parametric in `f` and `g`'s behavior, and that cannot be given because the only parameters of `app3` are `f` and `g`, and they are both function-type arguments. Note that refinement predicates of the form "`g` is safe to be called with `f`" are prohibited as they are required to be FOL formulas over the base-type data.

[3] We could also give non-$\top$ refinement predicates to `unit`, but it does not affect the example.

2.1 Our Approach

Our approach to solving the incompleteness issue is inspired by the research on relatively complete program logic for higher-order procedural languages [6–8]. The main idea is to add extra *dummy* base-type parameters that are *instantiated* appropriately so that the refinement type of a higher-order function can depend on the parameters.

For example, for the program of Figure 2, we add an extra base-type parameter a to app and obtain the following program.

```
let rec app a f x = if * then app[a] f (x+1)
                    else f x in
let check x y = if x <= y then ()
                else assert false in
let main i = app[i] (check i) i
```

Here, for clarity, the parameter passings for the extra parameters are written as quantifier instantiations, but they may be understood as ordinary function applications (e.g., app[a] is app a). With the addition of the extra parameter, it becomes possible for the existing refinement type systems designed for automated verification to type and verify the program. For example, the following types are sufficient for typing the program.

$$\begin{aligned} \texttt{app} &: a{:}\texttt{int} \to f{:}(\tau \to \texttt{unit}) \to x{:}\tau \to \texttt{unit} \\ \texttt{check} &: x{:}\texttt{int} \to y{:}\{u{:}\texttt{int} \mid u \geq x\} \to \texttt{unit} \\ \texttt{main} &: i{:}\texttt{int} \to \texttt{unit} \end{aligned}$$

where $\tau = \{u{:}\texttt{int} \mid u \geq a\}$. Note that the extra parameter a is used to parametrize f's behavior in the type of app.

There is a simple rule to adding extra parameters that can be shown to be sufficient for relative completeness: *add one just before each function-type argument.* Following the rule, for example, the program of Figure 3 is translated as follows.

```
let rec app3 a f b g =
          if * then (app3[a] (succ[a] f))[a] g
          else g[a] f in
let succ b f x = f (x + 1) in
let check x y = if x <= y then ()
                else assert false in
let app x a f = f x in
let main i = (app3[i] (check i))[i] (app i)
```

And, it can be shown that the resulting program is typable, for example, by the following types.

$$\begin{aligned} \texttt{app3} &: a{:}\texttt{int} \to f{:}\tau_1 \to b{:}\texttt{int} \to g{:}\tau_2 \to \texttt{unit} \\ \texttt{app} &: \\ & x{:}\texttt{int} \to a{:}\texttt{int} \to f{:}(\{u{:}\texttt{int} \mid u \geq x\} \to \texttt{unit}) \to \texttt{unit} \\ \texttt{succ} &: b{:}\texttt{int} \to f{:}(\sigma \to \texttt{unit}) \to x{:}\sigma \to \texttt{unit} \\ \texttt{check} &: x{:}\texttt{int} \to y{:}\{u{:}\texttt{int} \mid u \geq x\} \to \texttt{unit} \\ \texttt{main} &: i{:}\texttt{int} \to \texttt{unit} \end{aligned}$$

where $\sigma = \{u{:}\texttt{int} \mid u \geq b\}$, $\tau_1 = \{u{:}\texttt{int} \mid u \geq a\} \to \texttt{unit}$, and $\tau_2 = c{:}\texttt{int} \to \tau_1 \to \texttt{unit}$.

However, the rule does not answer how the extra parameters should be instantiated. (In the above, we seem to have magically conjured the appropriate instantiations i and a!) Indeed, an analogous rule was first discovered by German, Clarke, and Halpern [6, 7] in their work on a relatively complete program logic for higher-order procedural languages, and their proof of relative completeness relies on the fact that, with an expressive theory of the base-type data domain (such as Peano arithmetic), one can encode each function closure as a base-type data expression so that the extra parameters can be instantiated by the base-type data representation of the corresponding function-type argument. However, explicitly instantiating the extra parameters by such encoded expressions and forcing the client verifier to reason about them is impractical.

$$\begin{aligned} d &::= d \cup \{F\,\overrightarrow{x} = e\} \mid \emptyset \\ e &::= x \mid F \mid c \mid \texttt{let}\ x = e_1\ \texttt{in}\ e_2 \mid e\ x \\ &\mid\ \ \texttt{if} * \texttt{then}\ e_1\ \texttt{else}\ e_2 \end{aligned}$$

Figure 4. The syntax of the simple functional language.

Therefore, they proposed to leave the instantiations unspecified in the program logic so that the task of finding sufficient instantiations is left to (the FOL theorem prover of) the client verifier.

Following the idea, for example, the program of Figure 2 is translated as follows by introducing fresh variables v1 and v2.

```
let rec app a f x = if * then app[v1] f (x+1)
                    else f x in
let check x y = if x <= y then ()
                else assert false in
let main i = app[v2] (check i) i
```

Then, the refinement type inference problem is reduced to the problem of finding appropriate instantiations for v1 and v2 along with the types for the program. For this, we extend the FOL constraint solving used in the previous work on refinement type inference with quantified reasoning over *template* expressions [4, 9, 24]. Concretely, in Section 4, we show how the counterexample-guided refinement type inference [18, 26] can be extended in this way to infer appropriate instantiations as well as types.

2.2 Paper Organization

The rest of the paper is organized as follows. Section 3 presents the refinement type system along with the target functional language, and proves its relative completeness under the extra parameter addition strategy. Section 4 presents the type inference algorithm. Section 5 presents the preliminary experience with the type inference algorithm, implemented as an extension to the higher-order software model checker (i.e., refinement type inference system) MoCHi [18]. Section 6 discusses related work, and Section 7 concludes. The extended report [28] contains the omitted materials.

3. Language and Type System

We formalize the target programming language. Figure 4 shows the syntax. The language is essentially the simply-typed lambda calculus with recursion and primitives for integer arithmetic operations. For simplicity the only base-type data in this language is integers, but other base types and their operations can be encoded in the standard way: for example, true $= 1$ and false $= 0$.

A *program*, d, is a finite set of function definitions, $F\,\overrightarrow{x} = e$, defining a function named F with the formal parameters $\overrightarrow{x}$ and the body e. The notation $\overrightarrow{a}$ denotes a possibly empty sequence. The functions are mutually recursive in that the body of a function may refer to other functions, including itself. Each function is closed except for the free function names (i.e., functions are lambda lifted [15]). We also assume that d contains a function named main that only takes base-type (i.e., integer) arguments.

Expressions, e, comprise non-deterministic branches, let expressions, constants c, function names F, variables x, and (constant or user-defined function) applications $e\ x$. Constants include integer constants such as $-1, 0, 1, 2$, and integer operations such as $+$ and $\leq$ (recall that we model booleans via integers). We assume that there are unary constant operators named assert and assume.

We restrict expressions to be in continuation passing style (CPS) so that they are non-returning, except when they occur let-bound (i.e., occurs as e_1 in $\texttt{let}\ x = e_1\ \texttt{in}\ e_2$). By contrast, let-bound expressions are restricted to be non-CPS (i.e., value returning) expressions, which are total applications of constant operators including the assume and assertion expressions $\texttt{assume}\ x$ and $\texttt{assert}\ x$, and

$$\begin{array}{ll}
\texttt{let}\ x = e_1\ \texttt{in}\ e_2 \rightarrow_d e_2[e_3/x] & \text{where } e_1 \Downarrow e_3\\
\texttt{let}\ x = \texttt{assert}\ 1\ \texttt{in}\ e \rightarrow_d e[1/x] & \\
\texttt{let}\ x = \texttt{assert}\ i\ \texttt{in}\ e \rightarrow_d \mathsf{fail} & \text{where } i \neq 1\\
\texttt{let}\ x = \texttt{assume}\ 1\ \texttt{in}\ e \rightarrow_d e[1/x] & \\
\texttt{let}\ x = \texttt{assume}\ i\ \texttt{in}\ e \rightarrow_d \mathsf{safe} & \text{where } i \neq 1\\
\texttt{if} * \texttt{then}\ e_1\ \texttt{else}\ e_2 \rightarrow_d e_1 & \\
\texttt{if} * \texttt{then}\ e_1\ \texttt{else}\ e_2 \rightarrow_d e_2 & \\
F\ \overrightarrow{e} \rightarrow_d e'[\overrightarrow{e}/\overrightarrow{x}] & \text{where } F\ \overrightarrow{x} = e' \in d
\end{array}$$

Figure 5. The reduction rules.

partial applications (of user-defined functions). We restrict constant operator applications to be total. CPS/A-normal-form-style is used for simplicity. Direct-style syntax can be supported by CPS conversion.

The rest of the syntax is straightforward. As usual, applications associate to the left so that $e_0\, e_1\ e_2 = (e_0\, e_1)\ e_2$. We write $e_0\ \overrightarrow{e}$ for the series of applications $e_0\ e_1\ e_2\ \ldots\ e_n$ where $\overrightarrow{e} = e_1, e_2, \ldots, e_n$. We write $e_1; e_2$ for $\texttt{let}\ x = e_1\ \texttt{in}\ e_2$ such that $x \notin \mathit{fv}(e_2)$, where $\mathit{fv}(e)$ denotes the free variables of e. Without loss of generality, we assume that bound variables are distinct. Note that, while the language only has non-deterministic branches, a conditional branch $\texttt{if}\ x\ \texttt{then}\ e_1\ \texttt{else}\ e_2$ can be encoded as

$$\texttt{if} * \texttt{then}\ \texttt{assume}\ x; e_1\ \texttt{else}\ \texttt{let}\ y = \neg x\ \texttt{in}\ \texttt{assume}\ y; e_2$$

which is equivalent for assertion safety.

We define the operational semantics of the language as a small-step reduction relation from states to states. A *state* is a run-time expression e that extends the source expressions with non-variable arguments at function applications, a special failure state fail, and a special safe state safe. (We overload the symbol e to range over run-time expressions when it is clear from the context.)

The reduction relation $\rightarrow_d$ is defined by the rules shown in Figure 5. Here, $e \Downarrow e'$ denotes the evaluation of the value returning expression e to the *value* e', and is defined as $F\ \overrightarrow{e} \Downarrow F\ \overrightarrow{e}$ and $c\ \overrightarrow{e} \Downarrow [\![c]\!](\overrightarrow{e})$ where $[\![c]\!]$ is the relation denoting the semantics of a non-assume/assert constant c, so that, for example $[\![+]\!](i, j) = i + j$ for integers i and j. (An integer constant is represented by a 0-ary constant.) We let partial applications (i.e., $F\ \overrightarrow{e}$) represent function closures. Formally, a value is either an integer constant or a function closure.

The semantics of a program d is defined as a series of reductions starting from an initial state $e_{\texttt{main}}[\overrightarrow{i}/\overrightarrow{x}]$ where $\texttt{main}\ \overrightarrow{x} = e_{\texttt{main}} \in d$ and $\overrightarrow{i}$ are integer arguments for main (i.e., $|\overrightarrow{i}| = |\overrightarrow{x}|$). Note that, because of CPS, reductions only occur at the top level. We write $e \rightarrow_d^* e'$ for zero or more reductions from e to e'. We say that a program is *(assertion) safe* if its evaluation does not cause an assertion failure, that is, if $e_{\texttt{main}}[\overrightarrow{i}/\overrightarrow{x}] \not\rightarrow_d^* \mathsf{fail}$ for any arguments $\overrightarrow{i}$ of main.

We assume that a program is typed under the standard simple type system whose type grammar is shown below.

$$s ::= \star \mid \texttt{int} \mid s \rightarrow s'$$

Here, the type $\star$ represents the type of a CPS expression. For each expression e in the program, we write $\mathit{sty}(e)$ to denote its simple type.

The typability in the simple type system assures that the program does not "get stuck", for example, by trying to use an integer as a function, but it does not guarantee its safety. Therefore, a program either runs forever safely (due to CPS, a program cannot return), stops safely in the state safe by reaching a false assume, or aborts with an assertion failure. The typing rules for the simple type system are standard and are deferred to the extended report [28].

$$\tau, \sigma \quad ::= \quad \star \mid \{u \mid \theta\} \mid x{:}\sigma \rightarrow \tau$$

Figure 6. The syntax of refinement types.

$$\frac{\mathit{sty}(x) = \texttt{int}}{\Gamma \vdash x : \{u \mid u = x\}}\ \textbf{Vb} \qquad \frac{\mathit{sty}(\kappa) \in \rightarrow}{\Gamma \vdash \kappa : \Gamma(\kappa)}\ \textbf{Vf}$$

$$\frac{}{\Gamma \vdash c : \mathit{ty}(c)}\ \textbf{Cst} \qquad \frac{\Gamma \vdash e_1 : \sigma \quad \Gamma, x{:}\sigma \vdash e_2 : \star}{\Gamma \vdash \texttt{let}\ x = e_1\ \texttt{in}\ e_2 : \star}\ \textbf{Let}$$

$$\frac{\Gamma \vdash e : y{:}\sigma \rightarrow \tau \quad \Gamma \vdash x : \sigma}{\Gamma \vdash e\, x : \tau[x/y]}\ \textbf{App}$$

$$\frac{\Gamma \vdash e_1 : \star \quad \Gamma \vdash e_2 : \star}{\Gamma \vdash \texttt{if} * \texttt{then}\ e_1\ \texttt{else}\ e_2 : \star}\ \textbf{If}$$

$$\frac{\Gamma \vdash e : \sigma \quad \Gamma \vdash \sigma \leq \tau \quad \mathit{fv}(\tau) \subseteq \mathit{dom}(\Gamma)}{\Gamma \vdash e : \tau}\ \textbf{Sub}$$

Figure 7. The typing rules.

3.1 Refinement Type System

We present a refinement type system for the language. First, we present a sound but incomplete refinement type system without the extra parameter addition, and then introduce the extra parameter addition as an extension in Section 3.2. The (incomplete) refinement type system is not significantly different from the ones proposed previously for automated verification [13, 18, 23, 26, 27] (e.g., it can be obtained by removing intersection types from [18, 26][4]).

Figure 6 shows the syntax of refinement types. Here, $\{u \mid \theta\}$ is a *refinement base (i.e., integer) type* that refines an integer by the refinement predicate θ which is a FOL arithmetic formula over the base (i.e., integer) type variables.[5] We sometimes abbreviate $\{u \mid \theta\}$ as $\texttt{int}$ when θ is a tautology (e.g., $\{u \mid \top\} = \texttt{int}$). Intuitively, $\{u \mid \theta\}$ denotes the type of integers u satisfying the formula θ.

The type $x : \sigma \rightarrow \tau$ is a *dependent function type*, consisting of the argument type σ and the return type τ. Intuitively, $x : \sigma \rightarrow \tau$ denotes the type of a function (or a constant operation) that returns a value of the type $\tau[y/x]$ when applied to an argument y of the type σ. As usual, $\rightarrow$ associates to the right.

The type $\{x \mid \theta\}$ binds x in θ. Likewise, $x{:}\sigma \rightarrow \tau$ binds x in τ (but not in σ). That is,

$$\begin{array}{l}
\mathit{fv}(\{x \mid \theta\}) = \mathit{fv}(\theta) \setminus \{x\}\\
\mathit{fv}(x{:}\sigma \rightarrow \tau) = \mathit{fv}(\sigma) \cup (\mathit{fv}(\tau) \setminus \{x\})
\end{array}$$

We sometimes abbreviate $x : \sigma \rightarrow \tau$ as $\sigma \rightarrow \tau$ when x does not occur free in τ. (It actually suffices to limit x to occur free in τ only if x is a base type argument because refinement predicates are restricted to be over the base-type variables.) Types are equivalent up to renaming of bound variables.

The *simple-type shape* of σ, $\mathit{tshape}(\sigma)$, is defined as follows:

$$\begin{array}{ll}
\mathit{tshape}(\{u \mid \theta\}) = \texttt{int} & \mathit{tshape}(\star) = \star\\
\mathit{tshape}(x{:}\sigma \rightarrow \tau) = \mathit{tshape}(\sigma) \rightarrow \mathit{tshape}(\tau) &
\end{array}$$

[4] While intersection types are not needed for relative completeness, they compromise neither soundness nor completeness, and sometimes aid the verification in practice. The implementation shown in Section 5 supports intersection types.

[5] The full theory of Peano arithmetic is needed for relative completeness, but any subset (e.g., the quantifier-free theory of linear arithmetic) is sufficient for soundness.

$$\frac{\Gamma \vdash \sigma_2 \leq \sigma_1 \quad \Gamma, x:\sigma_2 \vdash \tau_1 \leq \tau_2}{\Gamma \vdash x{:}\sigma_1 \to \tau_1 \leq x{:}\sigma_2 \to \tau_2}\ \textbf{Sf}$$

$$\frac{}{\Gamma \vdash \star \leq \star}\ \textbf{Sc} \qquad \frac{u \notin fv([\![\Gamma]\!]) \quad ([\![\Gamma]\!] \wedge \theta_1) \Rightarrow \theta_2}{\Gamma \vdash \{u \mid \theta_1\} \leq \{u \mid \theta_2\}}\ \textbf{Sb}$$

Figure 8. The subtyping rules.

Figure 7 shows the typing rules. The judgements for the expressions are of the form $\Gamma \vdash e : \tau$ where Γ is a *type environment* mapping variables and function names to types.

We discuss each typing rule. **Vb** types base-type variables. Note that the rule ignores the environment. Expressibility is not reduced, however, because the assumption about x in the environment gets discharged at subtyping. **Vf** types function-type variables and function names by looking up the environment. Here, $\to$ denotes the set of simple function types. (We use the meta variable κ to range over both variables and function names.) **Cst** types constants. Here, $ty(c)$ denotes the pre-assigned type of the constant c such that

$$ty(\texttt{assume}) = x{:}\texttt{int} \to \{u \mid x = 1 \wedge u = 1\}$$
$$ty(\texttt{assert}) = x{:}\{u \mid u = 1\} \to \{u \mid u = 1\}$$

and $ty(c)$ is the *precise* type for a non-assume/assert constant c (e.g., $ty(+) = x : \texttt{int} \to y{:}\texttt{int} \to \{u \mid u = x + y\}$).[6] **Let** is self-explanatory. **App** types applications. Here, $\tau[x/y]$ is the usual capture-avoiding substitution. **If** types branch expressions.

Sub is the subsumption rule. The subtyping relation is defined in Figure 8. In **Sb**, $[\![\Gamma]\!]$ is the FOL formula denoting the assumptions about the base-type variables in Γ, and is defined as follows.

$$[\![\Gamma]\!] = \bigwedge\nolimits_{x:\{u|\theta\}\in\Gamma} \theta[x/u]$$

Like the *rule of consequence* of the Hoare logic [10], **Sb** asks the client verifier (i.e., the type inference system) to decide the validity of arbitrary FOL arithmetic formulas. As expected, our completeness result is *relative* to the hypothetical completeness of deciding this. In verification practice, one may settle for incomplete theorem proving or a decidable theory subset to make type checking decidable.[7]

Sub enforces *well-formedness* of the introduced type by asserting that its free variables appear bound in the environment. As shown below, the top-level types (i.e., the types of the recursive functions) are required not to contain free variables.

DEFINITION 3.1 (Well-formed type). *We say that a type is* closed *if it has no free variables. Let Δ be a top-level type environment mapping function names to types. We say that σ is a* well-formed type *for F if σ is closed and $tshape(\sigma) = sty(F)$. We say that Δ is a* well-formed top-level type environment *if $\Delta(F)$ is well-formed for each F.*

Let us write $\overrightarrow{x{:}\sigma} \to \tau$ to abbreviate the function type $x_1{:}\sigma_1 \to \dots \to x_n{:}\sigma_n \to \tau$ where $\overrightarrow{x{:}\sigma} = x_1 : \sigma_1, \dots, x_n : \sigma_n$. We define the notion of a well-typed program.

DEFINITION 3.2 (Well-typed program). *We write $\Delta \vdash d$ if the following conditions hold.*

(1) Δ is a well-formed top-level type environment.

(2) For each function $F\ \vec{x} = e \in d$, we have $\Delta, \overrightarrow{x{:}\sigma} \vdash e : \star$ where $\Delta(F) = \overrightarrow{x{:}\sigma} \to \star$.

(3) $\Delta(\texttt{main})$ is of the form $\overrightarrow{x{:}\mathit{int}} \to \star$. (I.e., the refinement predicates for the arguments of main *are all $\top$.)*

A program d is said to be well-typed (equivalently, typable) if there exists Δ such that $\Delta \vdash d$.

The condition (2) says that Δ contains fixed-point types for the recursive functions comprising d, and (3) says that main is safe to be called with any arguments (recall that main is a function over integer arguments).

The type system is sound in that it ensures that a well-typed program does not cause an assertion failure.

THEOREM 3.3 (Soundness). *If $\Delta \vdash d$ then d is safe.*

The theorem follows from the soundness of the refinement type system extended with extra parameter additions (Theorem 3.6).

EXAMPLE 3.4. Let the program d_1 consist of the following functions.

```
app x f = if * then app (x + 1) f else f x
check x y = if * then assume (x ≤ y); check x y
                 else assume ¬(x ≤ y); assert 0; check x y
main i = app i (check i)
```

The program is the one from Figure 1 translated into the target language. (We elide A-normalization for readability.) Let Δ be the following type environment.

$$\Delta(\texttt{app}) = x{:}\texttt{int} \to f{:}(\{u \mid u \geq x\} \to \star) \to \star$$
$$\Delta(\texttt{check}) = x{:}\texttt{int} \to y{:}\{u \mid u \geq x\} \to \star$$
$$\Delta(\texttt{main}) = i{:}\texttt{int} \to \star$$

It is routine to check that $\Delta \vdash d_1$. Therefore, d_1 is typable and is safe.

Next, consider d_2 shown below.

```
app f x = if * then app f (x + 1) else f x
check x y = if * then assume (x ≤ y); check x y
                 else assume ¬(x ≤ y); assert 0; check x y
main i = app (check i) i
```

The program is a translation of the program from Figure 2. The program is safe but untypable (as remarked in Section 2, also under the previous refinement type systems [13, 18, 23, 26, 27]). Note that we cannot simply assign app the type $\Delta(\texttt{app})$ from the above but with the order of x and f reversed so that

$$f{:}(\{u \mid u \geq x\} \to \star) \to x{:}\texttt{int} \to \star$$

The type is not closed and therefore is not a well-formed top-level type (cf. Definition 3.1). The well-formedness condition forces the refinement predicates to only refer to the values passed earlier. Well-formedness is not a superficial restriction: In the presence of higher-order functions and function closures (i.e., partial applications), we cannot generally determine "up front" in the program logic what will be passed later to a closure.

The issue is apparent in the following program d_3, which is a translation of Figure 3.

```
app3 f g = if * then app3 (succ f) g else g f
app x f = f x
succ f x = f (x + 1)
check x y = if * then assume (x ≤ y); check x y
                 else assume ¬(x ≤ y); assert 0; check x y
main i = app3 (check i) (app i)
```

As remarked in Section 2, the program is safe but untypable, even if we were allowed to change the order of the function arguments. Here, it is not possible to determine what will be passed to the

[6] See the extended report [28] for the definition of a precise constant type. Also, non-precise but *sound* constant types, that over-approximate the actual semantics, are sufficient for soundness.

[7] Also, type checking being decidable is different from type inference (i.e., typability) being decidable. The previous research has proposed various incomplete inference approaches [13, 18, 23, 26, 27].

$$\frac{\Gamma \vdash_\forall e : \forall x{:}\sigma.\tau \quad \Gamma \vdash_\forall o : \sigma \quad o \in \mathit{pureExps}}{\Gamma \vdash_\forall e : \tau[o/x]}\ \textbf{Inst}$$

$$\frac{\Gamma \vdash_\forall \sigma_2 \leq \sigma_1 \quad \Gamma, x{:}\sigma_2 \vdash_\forall \tau_1 \leq \tau_2}{\Gamma \vdash_\forall \forall x{:}\sigma_1.\tau_1 \leq \forall x{:}\sigma_2.\tau_2}\ \textbf{S}\forall$$

Figure 9. Additional typing rules.

closures $\mathtt{succ}^j\ f$ without some non-trivial program reasoning (i.e., i captured in g added the number of times app3's then branch is taken before the else branch is reached). In effect, the idea of the extra parameter addition for relative completeness is to delegate such tasks to the client verifier.

3.2 Extra Parameters for Relative Completeness

As shown in Example 3.4 (also Section 2), the refinement type system is incomplete by itself. While a complete checking of safety is clearly undecidable as the language allows arbitrary integer operations, we would like to make the refinement type system be complete relative to an oracle that could decide the FOL implications discharged at the subtyping rule **Sb**.

Rather than formulating the extra parameter addition as a program translation as done in Section 2, here, we present it as a type system extension in the form of universally quantified types. This is expositionally convenient, because extra parameters can be represented as universally bound variables so that they can be easily distinguished from ordinary parameters.

We extend the grammar of refinement types with universally quantified types as follows.

$$\tau, \sigma ::= \ldots \mid \forall x{:}\sigma.\tau$$

In $\forall x{:}\sigma.\tau$, x is a binding occurrence and may occur free in τ (i.e., $\mathit{fv}(\forall x{:}\sigma.\tau) = \mathit{fv}(\sigma) \cup (\mathit{fv}(\tau) \setminus \{x\})$). Intuitively, it expresses the function type $x{:}\sigma \to \tau$ such that x is an extra parameter. We define $\mathit{tshape}(\forall x{:}\sigma.\tau) = \mathit{tshape}(\tau)$.

We extend the type system with the quantifier instantiation and the subtyping rules shown in Figure 9. Here, *pureExps* is the set of side-effect-free integer-type expressions defined by the grammar

$$o ::= x \mid c\,\overrightarrow{o}$$

where x is an integer-type variable and $c\,\overrightarrow{o}$ is a total application of a non-assume/assert constant.[8] Therefore, **Inst** allows instantiation with any in-scope side-effect-free integer-type expression having the requested type. **S**$\forall$ is analogous to the subtyping rule for function types (i.e., **Sf**). To distinguish, we write $\vdash_\forall$ for the type judgements of the extended type system. All the rules from Figure 7 and Figure 8 are assumed to be included in $\vdash_\forall$ (with $\vdash$ replaced by $\vdash_\forall$).

The well-formedness definition is also retained from the pre-extension (cf. Definition 3.1). Therefore, for example, both

$$x{:}\mathtt{int} \to (\{u \mid u = 0\} \to \star) \to \star$$
$$x{:}\mathtt{int} \to \forall y{:}\mathtt{int}.(\{u \mid u = y\} \to \star) \to \star$$

are well-formed refinement types for F such that $\mathit{sty}(F) = \mathtt{int} \to (\mathtt{int} \to \star) \to \star$.

Let γ be a disjoint union of variable bindings $x : \sigma$ or *universal quantifier bindings* $\forall x{:}\sigma$. The type abbreviation $\overrightarrow{\gamma} \to \tau$ is defined as follows.

$$\overrightarrow{\gamma} \to \tau = \begin{cases} \tau & \text{if } \overrightarrow{\gamma} = \varepsilon \\ \forall x{:}\sigma.\tau_1 & \text{if } \overrightarrow{\gamma} = \forall x{:}\sigma, \overrightarrow{\gamma_1} \text{ and } \overrightarrow{\gamma_1} \to \tau = \tau_1 \\ x{:}\sigma \to \tau_1 & \text{if } \overrightarrow{\gamma} = x{:}\sigma, \overrightarrow{\gamma_1} \text{ and } \overrightarrow{\gamma_1} \to \tau = \tau_1 \end{cases}$$

[8] We extend the typing rules to (non-A-normal-form) side-effect-free integer-type expressions in the obvious way. See the extended report [28].

(Note that this subsumes the $\overrightarrow{x{:}\sigma} \to \tau$ abbreviation introduced earlier.) Let $\langle\overrightarrow{\gamma}\rangle$ be the sequence $\overrightarrow{\gamma}$ with each universal quantifier binding $\forall x : \sigma$ replaced with the variable binding $x : \sigma$. That is, $\langle\varepsilon\rangle = \varepsilon$, and $\langle x{:}\sigma, \overrightarrow{\gamma}\rangle = \langle\forall x{:}\sigma, \overrightarrow{\gamma}\rangle = x{:}\sigma, \langle\overrightarrow{\gamma}\rangle$.

We extend the notion of well-typed program to accommodate universal quantifier bindings.

DEFINITION 3.5 (Well-typed program – Extended). *We write $\Delta \vdash_\forall d$ if the following conditions hold.*

(1) Δ is a well-formed top-level type environment.
(2) For each function $F\,\overrightarrow{x} = e \in d$, we have $\Delta, \langle\overrightarrow{\gamma}\rangle \vdash_\forall e : \star$ where $\Delta(F) = \overrightarrow{\gamma} \to \star$.
(3) $\Delta(\mathtt{main})$ is of the form $\overrightarrow{x : \mathtt{int}} \to \star$.

A program d is said to be well-typed if $\exists\Delta.\Delta \vdash_\forall d$.

Note that the only differences from Definition 3.2 are $\overrightarrow{\gamma} \to \star$ and $\langle\overrightarrow{\gamma}\rangle$ in (2) which allow universal quantifiers in the type of the functions. Also, note that the well-formedness condition now allows the refinement predicates to refer to the universally quantified variables in their scope.

We state the soundness of the extended refinement type system.

THEOREM 3.6 (Soundness – Extended). *If $\Delta \vdash_\forall d$ then d is safe.*

The proof is standard [23, 27, 29] and is deferred to the extended report [28].

As remarked in Section 2, for relative completeness, it suffices to limit the position of extra parameters (i.e., universal quantifiers) to one before each function-type parameter. To this end, we define $\mathit{ushape}(\sigma)$ to be a simple type such that, for a function of the simple type $\mathit{ushape}(\sigma)$, σ has just the sufficient extra parameters. Formally, $\mathit{ushape}(\sigma)$ is defined by the rules below.

$$\frac{}{\mathit{ushape}(\{u \mid \theta\}) = \mathtt{int}} \qquad \frac{}{\mathit{ushape}(\star) = \star}$$

$$\frac{\mathit{tshape}(\sigma) = \mathtt{int}}{\mathit{ushape}(x{:}\sigma \to \tau) = \mathit{ushape}(\sigma) \to \mathit{ushape}(\tau)}$$

$$\frac{\mathit{tshape}(\sigma') = \mathtt{int} \quad \mathit{tshape}(\sigma) \in \to}{\mathit{ushape}(\forall y{:}\sigma'.x{:}\sigma \to \tau) = \mathit{ushape}(\sigma) \to \mathit{ushape}(\tau)}$$

Note that $\mathit{ushape}(\sigma)$ is defined only for σ that has one extra parameter just before a function-type parameter. Also, for σ such that $\mathit{ushape}(\sigma)$ is defined, we have $\mathit{ushape}(\sigma) = \mathit{tshape}(\sigma)$. We are now ready to state the relative completeness theorem, which says that if a program is safe then it can be typed with extra parameter additions (even when their positions are restricted to the pattern above).

THEOREM 3.7 (Relative Completeness). *If d is safe, then there exists Δ such that $\Delta \vdash_\forall d$ and $\mathit{ushape}(\Delta(F)) = \mathit{sty}(F)$ for each $F\,\overrightarrow{x} = e \in d$.*

We defer the proof to the extended report [28]. The proof adopts the ideas from the work on relatively complete program logics for higher-order procedural languages [6–8] that instantiate the extra parameters by the base-type encoding of the function closures. It is worth noting that, as a corollary of Theorem 3.7, it follows that the refinement type system is relatively complete for first-order programs (i.e., programs without function-type parameters) even without the extra parameter extension.

EXAMPLE 3.8. We show how $\vdash_\forall$ types d_2 and d_3 from Example 3.4. First, we have $\Delta_2 \vdash_\forall d_2$ where

$$\begin{aligned} &\Delta_2(\mathtt{app}) = \\ &\quad \forall a{:}\mathtt{int}.f{:}(\{u \mid u \geq a\} \to \star) \to x{:}\{u \mid u \geq a\} \to \star \\ &\Delta_2(\mathtt{check}) = x{:}\mathtt{int} \to y{:}\{u \mid u \geq x\} \to \star \\ &\Delta_2(\mathtt{main}) = i{:}\mathtt{int} \to \star \end{aligned}$$

Note that the types correspond to the ones used to type Figure 2 in Section 2.1. Also, note that $\mathit{ushape}(\Delta_2(\texttt{app})) = \mathit{sty}(\texttt{app})$, $\mathit{ushape}(\Delta_2(\texttt{check})) = \mathit{sty}(\texttt{check})$, and $\mathit{ushape}(\Delta_2(\texttt{main})) = \mathit{sty}(\texttt{main})$. It is easy to see that check can be given the type $\Delta_2(\texttt{check})$. We show that app can be given the type $\Delta_2(\texttt{app})$. We type the body of app under the type environment $\Delta_2, a : \texttt{int}, f : \{u \mid u \geq a\} \to \star, x : \{u \mid u \geq a\}$. Therefore, the application $f\ x$ type-checks to give the type $\star$. To type the other branch, app $f\ (x+1)$, we instantiate $\Delta_2(\texttt{app})$ with a at app to give the type

$$f{:}(\{u \mid u \geq a\} \to \star) \to x{:}\{u \mid u \geq a\} \to \star$$

The type is then used to give the application app f the type $x : \{u \mid u \geq a\} \to \star$, which in turn gives the branch the type $\star$. Finally, main can be given the type $\Delta_2(\texttt{main})$ by instantiating $\Delta_2(\texttt{app})$ with i.

Likewise, let Δ_3 be the following type environment.

$$\begin{aligned}
&\Delta_3(\texttt{app3}) = \forall a{:}\texttt{int}.f{:}\tau_1 \to \forall b{:}\texttt{int}.g{:}\tau_2 \to \star\\
&\Delta_3(\texttt{app}) = x{:}\texttt{int} \to \forall a{:}\texttt{int}.f{:}(\{u \mid u \geq x\} \to \star) \to \star\\
&\Delta_3(\texttt{succ}) = \forall b{:}\texttt{int}.f{:}(\sigma \to \star) \to x{:}\sigma \to \star\\
&\Delta_3(\texttt{check}) = x{:}\texttt{int} \to y{:}\{u \mid u \geq x\} \to \star\\
&\Delta_3(\texttt{main}) = i{:}\texttt{int} \to \star
\end{aligned}$$

such that $\tau_1 = \{u \mid u \geq a\} \to \star$, $\tau_2 = \forall c : \texttt{int}.\tau_1 \to \star$, and $\sigma = \{u \mid u \geq b\}$. Note that $\mathit{ushape}(F) = \mathit{sty}(\Delta_3(F))$ for each F = app3, app, succ, check, and main. We show that $\Delta_3 \vdash_\forall d_3$ by following the same instantiation scheme used to type Figure 3 in Section 2.1. We type the then branch of app3 by instantiating app3 and succ with a, and instantiating the resulting app3 (succ f) with a (or with an arbitrary side-effect-free integer-type expression, because b does not appear free in its scope in $\Delta_3(\texttt{app3})$). The else branch can be typed by instantiating g with an arbitrary side-effect-free integer-type expression (because c does not appear free in its scope in $\Delta_3(\texttt{app3})$). Then, to type main, we instantiate app3 with i, and instantiate app3 (check i) with an arbitrary side-effect-free integer-type expression.

The examples show that instantiating via simple expressions are often sufficient for verifying safety, and not all quantifiers may even be needed. (Contrast this with the instantiation via Gödel numbering used in the proof of Theorem 3.7.[9]) We take advantage of the observation in the type inference method described in Section 4.

4. Type Inference

The type inference framework is based on, and extends the recent work on the counterexample-guided approach to refinement type inference [18, 26] (but, the idea may be adopted to extend the back-end of other refinement type inference systems like [13, 27]). To allow smooth adoption and use the existing type inference algorithms mostly as a blackbox, we implement the extra parameter addition as a program translation as in Section 2, instead of modifying the underlying type system to model it by universally quantified types as in Section 3.2.

Figure 10 shows the overview of the type inference process. In Step 1, we translate the given program by adding extra parameters as done in Section 2. Here, we maintain and use a *parameter substitution* for instantiating the extra parameters. We initialize the instantiation expressions to arbitrary constants (e.g., 0), and then perform a counterexample-guided refinement type inference over the translated program.

Following the counterexample-guided abstraction refinement (CEGAR) scheme popularized in model checking [3, 12], in the counterexample-guided refinement type inference, we maintain a set of *candidate* refinement types (or the refinement predicates that comprise them). Then, we try to find a type assignment for the program within the candidates via the standard fixed-point type inference process (Step 2 in Figure 10). The fixed-point type inference uses an automated FOL theorem prover, such as a SMT solver, to decide the FOL implications discharged at the subtyping rule **Sb**. We refer interested readers to the previous work [18, 26] for details.

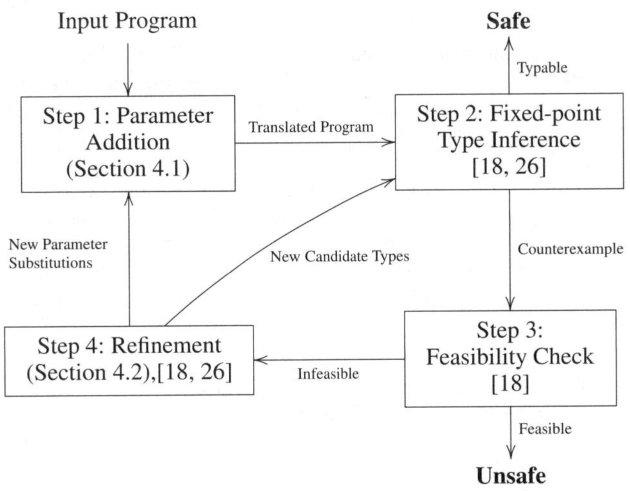

Figure 10. The type inference overview.

A *counterexample* is generated when the candidates are found insufficient, and we analyze the reason for the failure to either validate the counterexample (Step 3), or update the candidate types or the parameter substitution to eliminate the spurious counterexample (Step 4). In the refinement step, the previous work [18, 26] only generated new candidate types (i.e., the arrow from Step 4 to Step 2). But, because of the incompleteness of the underlying type system, some spurious counterexamples are impossible to refute by just adding new candidate types. *The key component of our new type inference method is generating new parameter substitutions in such a situation* (i.e., the arrow from Step 4 to Step 1).

Then, the CEGAR process is repeated with the updated candidate types or the updated parameter substitutions. The former case is identical to the previous work, and in the latter case, we repeat from Step 1 to re-translate the program with the updated parameter instantiations.

4.1 Adding Extra Parameters

We add an extra parameter just before each function-type parameter. Also, we assign a unique label to each sub-expression of the program where a parameter instantiation occurs. (Note that such places are syntactically determined.) Let L be the set of the labels and $\mathit{bvs}(\ell)$ denote the base-type variables that can occur free in the scope of the sub-expression with the label $\ell \in L$.

The type inference process maintains the *parameter substitution* P that maps each ℓ to a side-effect-free integer-type expression o such that $\mathit{fv}(o) \subseteq \mathit{bvs}(\ell)$. We use $P(\ell)$ as the instantiation expression at ℓ. We restrict the range of P, and therefore, the instantiation expressions, to linear arithmetic expressions. That is, $P(\ell)$ is restricted to be of the form

$$c_0 + c_1 x_1 + \cdots + c_n x_n$$

where $\mathit{bvs}(\ell) = \{x_1, \ldots, x_n\}$ and $c_0, \ldots, c_n$ are integer constants. This is an important design choice motivated both by the desire to minimize the complexity of the type inference, and also by the ob-

[9] This can be seen as a difference between just checking safety and expressing the precise semantics as weakest preconditions.

servation that sufficient instantiations tend to be simple expressions in practice (cf. Example 3.8).

The parameter substitution P may be initialized arbitrarily, for example, $P(\ell) = 0$ for all ℓ. We translate the input program by adding the extra parameters to the function definitions and replacing each instantiation site e with the application $e\,P(\ell)$ where ℓ is the label of e.

EXAMPLE 4.1. Recall the program d_2 in Example 3.4. We add an extra parameter a just before the function-type parameter f of `app`. Let ℓ_1 and ℓ_2 be the labels of the occurrences of `app` in the body of `app` and `main` respectively. We have $L = \{\ell_1, \ell_2\}$, $bvs(\ell_1) = \{a, x\}$, and $bvs(\ell_2) = \{i\}$. Suppose that the parameter substitution is $P = \{\ell_1 \mapsto a, \ell_2 \mapsto i\}$. Then, d_2 is translated to the program d_P shown below.

```
app a f x = if * then app a f (x + 1) else f x
check x y = if * then assume (x ≤ y); check x y
                  else assume ¬(x ≤ y); assert 0; check x y
main i = app i (check i) i
```

4.2 Counterexample-Guided Refinement

In MoCHi [18], a counterexample is a *straightline higher-order program* (SHP) that is untypable with the current candidate types. SHP is defined to be a recursion-free slice of the target program obtained by copying functions and removing branches so that it contains no branches and every function occurrence is "linear" (i.e., each function is called only once).[10] Intuitively, a counterexample corresponds to the (abstract) program path taken to reach the assertion failure.

We check if the counterexample SHP is feasible. This part is identical to the previous work [18] and is done by symbolically evaluating the SHP. If it is feasible, then the program is determined unsafe and we are done. Otherwise, we attempt to infer refinement types for the SHP. If the SHP is found typable, then the inferred refinement types (or the refinement predicates embedded therein) are added to the candidates and the CEGAR iteration returns to the fixed-point type inference phase (i.e., Step 2 of Figure 10).

We infer types for counterexamples by using the techniques from the previous work [18, 26, 27] that reduce the inference problem to solving constraints over FOL formulas and *predicate variables* such that the predicate variables serve as placeholders of the refinement predicates to be inferred. We refer to the previous work for details.

EXAMPLE 4.2. Given d_P from Example 4.1, MoCHi may generate the SHP d_S shown below.

```
app1 a f x = app2 a f (x + 1)
app2 a f x = f x
check x y = assume ¬(x ≤ y); assert 0
main i = app1 i (check i) i
```

Note that d_S is recursion-free and linear. The SHP is typable and MoCHi may infer refinement types Δ such that

$$\begin{array}{l}\Delta(\texttt{app1}) = \Delta(\texttt{app2}) = \\ \quad a{:}\texttt{int} \to f{:}(\{u \mid u \geq a\} \to \star) \to x{:}\{u \mid u \geq a\} \to \star \\ \Delta(\texttt{check}) = x{:}\texttt{int} \to y{:}\{u \mid u \geq x\} \to \star \\ \Delta(\texttt{main}) = i{:}\texttt{int} \to \star\end{array}$$

Note that $\Delta \vdash d_S$.

As remarked above, because of the incompleteness of the underlying type system (i.e., $\vdash$), sometimes, a counterexample that is detected to be infeasible is also found untypable. (The feasibility check is actually relatively complete.) In such a situation, we infer a new parameter substitution P_R for the SHP so that the SHP with each of its instantiation site ℓ instantiated with $P_R(\ell)$ is typable. Then, we update the parameter substitution with P_R, that is, we set $P := P_R \cup P|_{L \setminus L_{\text{SHP}}}$ where L_{SHP} is the labels of the SHP. And, the CEGAR process returns to the parameter addition phase to re-translate the program (i.e., Step 1 of Figure 10).

The parameter substitution inference proceeds as follows. First, we assign labels to the SHP such that every copy of a subexpression gets the same label as the one in the original. (Note that because of function copying, the same expression in the original program can have multiple copies in the SHP.) Next, we introduce a *parameter substitution template*, P_T, that maps each $\ell \in L_{\text{SHP}}$ to a linear arithmetic expression template $p_0 + p_1 x_1 + \cdots + p_n x_n$, where $bvs(\ell) = \{x_1, \ldots, x_n\}$ and $p_0, \ldots, p_n$ are fresh integer variables. This, in turn, induces a SHP *template* that has $P_T(\ell)$ as the instantiation expression at each $\ell \in L_{\text{SHP}}$.

Now, the problem of inferring P_R is reduced to that of inferring an appropriate integer substitution for the integer variables $\overrightarrow{p}$ in the template. We reduce the problem to constraint solving by generating a FOL constraint over $\overrightarrow{p}$ of the form $\forall \overrightarrow{x}.\theta$ (for some non-linear FOL formula θ over the variables $\overrightarrow{p}$ and $\overrightarrow{x}$). That is, the SHP is typable with the instantiation expression $P_T(\ell)\rho$ at each ℓ iff $(\forall \overrightarrow{x}.\theta)\rho$ holds where ρ is a substitution that maps $\overrightarrow{p}$ to integer constants. Although the problem of solving quantified integer non-linear FOL constraints is undecidable in general, the recently proposed constraint solving techniques based on Farkas' lemma [4, 9, 24] have shown effective for our application in many cases. We describe the constraint generation process in Section 4.2.1 and the constraint solving process in Section 4.2.2.

4.2.1 Constraint Generation

The constraint generation algorithm is essentially the same as the ones from the previous work [18, 26, 27] used for candidate type inference. We give a brief review of the algorithm. For each function in the program, we prepare type templates containing predicate variables that serve as placeholders of the refinement predicates to be inferred. Then, we generate constraints over the predicate variables in the standard way. That is, we apply the typing rules to the SHP but restricting the application of the subsumption rule **Sub** to just the argument position of function applications (cf. Section 3.1). This generates constraints over the type templates, which, in turn, reduce to Horn-clause-like constraints over the predicate variables. (See the extended report [28] for the formal definition of the constraint generation rules.) Because SHP is recursion-free and linear, the generated Horn clauses are non-recursive, and we can obtain an equivalent FOL formula.

EXAMPLE 4.3. Consider the SHP d'_S shown below, which is equivalent to d_S from Example 4.2 except that the extra parameter of `app1` is instantiated by 0 instead of i.

```
app1 a f x = app2 a f (x + 1)
app2 a f x = f x
check x y = assume ¬(x ≤ y); assert 0
main i = app1 0 (check i) i
```

It is easy to see that the counterexample d'_S is infeasible (i.e., is safe), and MoCHi is also able to detect the infeasibility. However, d'_S is untypable with the underlying type system $\vdash$ because of the inappropriate instantiation expression.

To infer a new instantiation expression, we prepare the parameter substitution template P_T for the instantiation sites of d'_S, and

[10] [26] defines a counterexample to be simply a currently-untypable recursion-free program slice (i.e., possibly containing branches and non-linearity), but uses linear intersection types to obtain a similar effect.

from it, obtain the SHP template d_T shown below.

$$\begin{array}{l}
\texttt{app1}\ a\ f\ x = \texttt{app2}\ (p_0 + p_1 a + p_2 x)\ f\ (x+1) \\
\texttt{app2}\ a\ f\ x = f\ x \\
\texttt{check}\ x\ y = \texttt{assume}\ \neg(x \leq y);\ \texttt{assert}\ 0 \\
\texttt{main}\ i = \texttt{app1}\ (p_3 + p_4 i)\ (\texttt{check}\ i)\ i
\end{array}$$

where $p_0, \ldots, p_4$ are free integer variables. Next, we generate the constraints by preparing the type template Δ such that

$$\begin{array}{l}
\Delta(\texttt{app1}) = \\
a{:}\{u \mid P_1(u)\} \to (\{u \mid P_2(a,u)\} \to \star) \to \{u \mid P_3(a,u)\} \to \star \\
\Delta(\texttt{app2}) = \\
a{:}\{u \mid P_4(u)\} \to (\{u \mid P_5(a,u)\} \to \star) \to \{u \mid P_6(a,u)\} \to \star \\
\Delta(\texttt{check}) = x{:}\{u \mid P_7(u)\} \to y{:}\{u \mid P_8(x,u)\} \to \star \\
\Delta(\texttt{main}) = i{:}\texttt{int} \to \star
\end{array}$$

This generates the following non-recursive set of Horn-clause-like constraints on the predicate variables $P_1, \ldots, P_8$.

$$\begin{array}{ll}
\forall a, x. P_1(a) \wedge P_3(a,x) \Rightarrow P_4(p_0 + p_1 a + p_2 x) & \\
\forall a, x, u. P_1(a) \wedge P_3(a,x) \wedge P_5(p_0 + p_1 a + p_2 x, u) \Rightarrow P_2(a,u) & \\
\forall a, x. P_1(a) \wedge P_3(a,x) \Rightarrow P_6(p_0 + p_1 a + p_2 x, x+1) & \\
\forall a, x, u. P_4(a) \wedge P_6(a,x) \Rightarrow P_5(a,x) & \\
\forall x, y. P_7(x) \wedge P_8(x,y) \Rightarrow x \leq y & \\
\forall i. \top \Rightarrow P_1(p_3 + p_4 i) & \forall i. \top \Rightarrow P_7(i) \\
\forall i, u. P_2(p_3 + p_4 i, u) \Rightarrow P_8(i,u) & \forall i. \top \Rightarrow P_3(p_3 + p_4 i, i)
\end{array}$$

Systematically simplifying the constraints by computing the least solutions for the predicate variables in a bottom-up manner, we obtain an equisatisfiable FOL formula on the variables $p_0, \ldots, p_4$ shown below.

$$\begin{array}{l}
\forall x, y, z. \\
\quad p_4 x = p_4 z \wedge p_1 p_4 x + p_2 z = (p_1 p_4 + p_2)(y-1) \Rightarrow x \leq y
\end{array}$$

4.2.2 Constraint Solving

The constraint generation process above returns a constraint of the form $\forall \overrightarrow{x}.\theta$, where θ is a quantifier-free non-linear FOL formula over the variables $\overrightarrow{p}$ and $\overrightarrow{x}$. (More precisely, θ is linear over $\overrightarrow{x}$ with coefficients over $\overrightarrow{p}$.)[11] The goal of the constraint solving phase is to find an assignment ρ for $\overrightarrow{p}$ satisfying $\forall \overrightarrow{x}.\theta$.

We solve the constraints by adopting Gulwani et al.'s approach [9]. We give a brief overview of the idea. First, we use Farkas' lemma to remove the universal quantifications in the constraint $\forall \overrightarrow{x}.\theta$, and obtain a constraint of the form $\exists \overrightarrow{r}.\phi$, where ϕ is a quantifier-free non-linear FOL formula on the variables $\overrightarrow{p}$ and $\overrightarrow{r}$. Then, we translate the constraint to a SAT formula by modeling integer variables as bit-vectors and integer operations such as addition, multiplication, and comparison as boolean operations. Finally, we use a state-of-the-art SAT solver to find a substitution ρ for $\overrightarrow{p}$ and $\overrightarrow{r}$ that satisfies ϕ.

We describe the approach in a more detail. Given a universally quantified constraint $\forall \overrightarrow{x}.\theta$, we convert θ to an equivalent formula of the form $\bigwedge_i \theta_i$, where each θ_i is of the form $\neg(\bigwedge_{j=1,\ldots,m_i} e_{i,j} \geq 0)$ such that each $e_{i,j} \geq 0$ is a linear inequality on $\overrightarrow{x}$ with polynomials on $\overrightarrow{p}$ as coefficients. We translate each θ_i by applying Farkas' lemma.

THEOREM 4.4 (Farkas' lemma). *Consider the following system of inequalities over real-valued variables $x_1, \ldots, x_n$.*

$$\begin{bmatrix}
c_{1,0} & + & c_{1,1}x_1 & + & \ldots & + & c_{1,n}x_n & \geq 0 \\
\vdots & & \vdots & & & & \vdots & \\
c_{m,0} & + & c_{m,1}x_1 & + & \ldots & + & c_{m,n}x_n & \geq 0
\end{bmatrix}$$

The system is unsatisfiable iff there exist non-negative reals $r_0, r_1, \ldots, r_m$ such that

- $r_0 + r_1 c_{1,0} + \cdots + r_m c_{m_0} = -1$, *and*
- $r_1 c_{1,j} + \cdots + r_m c_{m_j} = 0$ *for each* $j = 1, \ldots, n$.

Farkas' lemma is incomplete for integers because the "only if" direction does not always hold. (Trivially, the "if" direction holds even for integers.) The incompleteness, however, has not affected the experiments in Section 5. (See Section 4.3 for the list of limitations with our approach.)

EXAMPLE 4.5. Recall the constraints generated from the SHP template d_T in Example 4.3. We translate the constraints to the equivalent form below.

$$\forall x, y, z. \quad \neg \left(\begin{array}{rrrrl}
 & p_4 x & & -p_4 z & \geq 0 \wedge \\
 & -p_4 x & & +p_4 z & \geq 0 \wedge \\
p_1 p_4 + p_2 & +p_1 p_4 x & -(p_1 p_4 + p_2) y & +p_2 z & \geq 0 \wedge \\
-p_1 p_4 - p_2 & -p_1 p_4 x & +(p_1 p_4 + p_2) y & -p_2 z & \geq 0 \wedge \\
-1 & +x & -y & & \geq 0
\end{array} \right)$$

Applying Farkas' lemma, the constraint is further translated to the following form.

$$\begin{array}{l}
\exists r_0, r_1, r_2, r_3, r_4 \geq 0. \\
\quad r_0 + (p_1 p_4 + p_2)(r_3 - r_4) - r_5 = -1 \wedge \\
\quad p_4(r_1 - r_2) + p_1 p_4 (r_3 - r_4) + r_5 = 0 \wedge \\
\quad -(p_1 p_4 + p_2)(r_3 - r_4) - r_5 = 0 \wedge \\
\quad -p_4(r_1 - r_2) + p_2(r_3 - r_4) = 0
\end{array}$$

We reduce the constraints to SAT by modeling integers as bit-vectors, and apply SAT solving to find a satisfying assignment. A possible solution is

$$\begin{array}{l}
p_0 = 0,\ p_1 = 1,\ p_2 = 0,\ p_3 = 0,\ p_4 = 1 \\
r_0 = 1,\ r_1 = 0,\ r_2 = 0,\ r_3 = 0,\ r_4 = 1,\ r_5 = 1
\end{array}$$

And from the solution, we obtain the substitution

$$\rho = \{p_0 \mapsto 0, p_1 \mapsto 1, p_2 \mapsto 0, p_3 \mapsto 0, p_4 \mapsto 1\}$$

Note that applying the inferred parameter substitution ρ to d_T results in the program equivalent to d_S from Example 4.2. Finally, we update the parameter substitution P via $P_T\rho$ to translate the input program, which results in the program d_P from Example 4.1, and is typable by the underlying type system. While the example only require a variable as the instantiation expression, this is not the case in general (even when the instantiations are restricted to linear arithmetic expressions). Section 5 shows examples needing non-variable instantiation expressions.

We use the iterative approach of Gulwani et al. [9] to model integers as bit-vectors: we start with a low number of bits, and gradually increase the number of bits until a solution is found. Because of the incompleteness limitation, it is possible that a solution is not found even though the process is given an infeasible SHP. (cf. Section 4.3.) Section 5 shows heuristics for coping with the issue.

New candidate types with new parameter substitutions It is often desirable to infer new candidate types along with the new parameter substitutions. For instance, in Example 4.5, rather than returning to Step 1 of Figure 10 after the updated parameter substitution $P_T\rho$ is inferred, it is better to infer candidate types for the translated counterexample SHP $d_T\rho$ so that the counterexample is immediately eliminated from the future CEGAR iterations.

Inferring parameter substitution for prior counterexamples For simplicity, we have shown how to infer a parameter substitution for one counterexample SHP. In practice, it is better to record the counterexamples that have been encountered (or, the constraints

[11] We assume that constant types only embed quantifier-free linear arithmetic refinement predicates.

generated from them), so that the inferred parameter substitution is able to also refute the past counterexamples. This can be done by a minor modification to the algorithm because constraints from multiple counterexamples simply add up as conjunctions. We take this approach in the implementation described in Section 5.

4.3 Limitations

Our type inference algorithm is incomplete as it is not able to decide the typability of all programs. This is expected because the underlying problem (i.e., safety verification) is undecidable. Here, we list the source of incompleteness.

(1) Like the predicate abstraction in first-order software model checking [12], we restrict the refinement predicates to an efficiently decidable first-order theory, such as the quantifier-free theory of linear arithmetic. Consequently, there are programs, even ones that are first-order, that we cannot verify. Also, predicate discovery uses various heuristics such as interpolation, and is in general incomplete even for the theory subset (but, there are approaches to make this part complete [14]).

(2) As remarked in Section 4.1, we restrict instantiation expressions to linear arithmetic expressions. While this has been sufficient for many cases, as we show in Section 5, there are programs that we cannot verify because of the restriction.[12] (But, as we show there, simple heuristics can often be used to handle such cases.)

(3) The parameter substitution inference is invoked only when the counterexample is untypable with the current substitutions, because otherwise it may simply infer the same substitutions. For some programs, the parameter substitution inference becomes forever blocked because the program generates infinitely many counterexamples each of which can be refuted by just updating the candidate types.[13] (See Section 5 for an example.)

(4) As remarked in Section 4.2.2, Farkas' lemma is incomplete for integers.

5. Implementation and Experiments

We have implemented a prototype of the type inference algorithm as an extension to the higher-order model checker MoCHi [18]. It takes (direct-style and CPS) OCaml programs. We use CVC3 [2] for the SAT-based non-linear constraint solving described in Section 4.2.2. A web interface of the implementation and the benchmark programs from the experiments are available online [28].

We ran experiments on small but representative higher-order programs. Table 1 summarizes the results. The column S is the size measured in the number of words in the program. O is the largest order of the functions in the program. (Base-type values are order-0, and order-n functions only take arguments of order less than n.) The column $|\overrightarrow{p}|$ is the total number of the variables $\overrightarrow{p}$ that occur in the range of the parameter substitution template P_T (cf. Section 4.2). #E is the number of extra parameters added before each function-type parameter. (#E $>$ 1 is used in the heuristics described below.) #I is the number of CEGAR iterations. The column T is the running time in seconds, and P/T is the fraction of the running time spent on the parameter substitution inference. NV marks the programs that required non-variable instantiation expressions. The experiments were conducted on a machine with Intel Xeon E5620 2.4GHz CPU and 4GB RAM.

Note that the programs are higher-order (i.e., O $>$ 1). The programs are safe, but none of them can be verified by the previous

[12] The limitation is also linked with (1) above, because allowing more complex instantiations has no benefit when the underlying theorem prover cannot decide formulas embedding them.

[13] This is an instance of a more general issue with the parameter substitution inference not inferring sufficiently general substitutions.

program	S	O	$\lvert\overrightarrow{p}\rvert$	#E	#I	T	P/T	NV
d_2	40	2	3	1	2	0.43s	40%	
d_3	56	3	10	1	3	1.76s	68%	
`fhnhn`	26	2	2	1	1	0.15s	12%	
`repeat-add`	51	2	5	1	3	1.05s	7%	
`app-leq`	29	2	2	1	1	0.26s	41%	✓
`app-lin-ord2`	37	2	2	1	1	0.22s	38%	✓
`app-lin-ord3`	45	3	6	1	1	0.96s	84%	✓
`app-succ`	50	2	5	1	2	0.36s	37%	
`app-succ0`	50	2	5	–	–	—	—%	
`a-test-upd`	80	2	9	2	7	2.06s	32%	
`a-checksum`	76	2	6	2	8	3.38s	29%	
`a-max`	78	2	8	1	4	7.32s	26%	
`l-forall-leq`	69	2	8	1	2	2.68s	51%	
`l-len-append`	126	2	22	1	2	0.73s	35%	✓
`l-isort`	170	2	39	–	–	—	—%	

Table 1. Experiment results.

refinement type systems proposed for automated higher-order program verification [13, 18, 23, 26, 27]. We describe each program.

- d_2 and d_3 are from Example 3.4.
- `fhnhn` compares the return value of two function arguments:

```
let f x y = assert (x () = y ()) in
let h x () = x in let main n = f (h n) (h n)
```

- `repeat-add` makes the closure `add n` for some `n` ≥ 0, applies it to 0 for `k`-times for some `k` > 0, and asserts that the result is not less than `n`:

```
let add x1 x2 = x1 + x2 in
let rec repeat f k x = if k <= 0 then x
                       else f (repeat f (k - 1) x) in
let main n k =
  if n >= 0 && k > 0 then
    assert (repeat (add n) k 0 >= n)
```

- `app-leq` (resp. `app-lin-ord2`) is the program below with `e` $\equiv$ `(a<=b)` (resp. `e` $\equiv$ `(4*a+2*b)`).

```
let app f x = f x in
let check x y = assert (x = y) in
let main a b = app (check e) e
```

- `app-lin-ord3` is `app-lin-ord2` "lifted" one order higher.
- `app-succ` calls `check` i i for some non-deterministically-chosen $i \geq$ `n`:

```
let succ f x = f (x + 1) in
let rec app f x =
  if * then app (succ f) (x - 1) else f x in
let check x y = assert (x = y) in
let main n = app (check n) n
```

- `app-succ0` is `app-succ` with `n` in the body of `main` fixed to 0.
- In `a-xxx`, we model and check array manipulating programs. We model an array as the pair consisting of its size and the function that maps indices to the array elements:

```
let make_array n =
  (n, fun i -> assert (0 <= i && i < n); 0)
let upd (n, ar) i x =
  assert (0 <= i && i < n);
  (n, fun j -> if j = i then x else ar j)
```

The array benchmarks extend the ones from the previous work [18] that demonstrate the application of higher-order program verification to the verification of data structure properties.

- `a-test-upd` tests array updates. It creates an array of size `n` and updates the `i`-th element to `x` for some `i` $\in \{0, \ldots, \mathtt{n}-1\}$. The program then reads the element and checks that the result is equal to `x` as expected:

```
let test (n, ar) i x = assert (ar i = x) in
let main n i x =
  if 0 <= i && i < n then
    test (upd (make_array n) i x) i x
```

Note that the program also checks for array bounds violation.

- `a-checksum` creates an array of size 2, updates the first and the second elements to `a` and `b` respectively, and asserts that the sum of the two array elements equals `a` + `b`:

```
let checksum (n, ar) x =
  assert ((ar 0) + (ar 1) = x) in
let main a b =
  checksum
    (upd (upd (make_array 2) 0 a) 1 b) (a + b)
```

- `a-max` creates an array of size `n` whose elements are from the set $\{0, \ldots, \mathtt{x}\}$ where $\mathtt{x} > 0$, computes the maximum element `m` of the array, and asserts that $\mathtt{m} \leq \mathtt{x}$.

- The programs `l-xxx` model and check list operations. We model a list by a pair of its length and a function from a non-negative integer i to the i-th element. We model the core list operations as follows:

```
let nil = (0, fun i -> assert false)
let cons a (len, l) =
  (len + 1, fun i -> if i=0 then a else l (i-1))
let hd (len, l) = l 0
let tl (len, l) = (len - 1, fun i -> l (i + 1))
let is_nil (len, l) = len=0
```

- `l-forall-leq` creates a list of the length `n` whose `i`-th element is `n` − `i`, and asserts that $\mathtt{x} \leq \mathtt{n}$ holds for all element `x` of the list.

- `l-len-append` appends two lists of the length `len1` and `len2`, computes the length of the resulting list, and asserts that it is not greater than `len1` + `len2`.

- `l-isort` creates a list, sorts the list via an insertion sort, and then checks that the result is actually sorted.

The implementation was able to successfully verify the programs by automatically inferring appropriate extra parameter substitutions, except for `app-succ0` and `l-isort`. Before we discuss the reason for failure on these two, we describe the heuristic that was needed for verifying `a-test-upd` and `a-checksum`.

Recall that we limit instantiation expressions to linear arithmetic expressions. With this restriction, it can be shown that `a-test-upd` and `a-checksum` (and also `l-isort`) are actually untypable when we are allowed to add only one extra parameter before a function-type parameter.[14] However, `a-test-upd` and `a-checksum` can be typed if we are allowed to add two extra parameters before a function-type parameter, even with the linear-instantiation-expression restriction. (Note that #E is 2 for these programs in Table 1.)

For instance, in `a-checksum`, to show the safety of the call to `checksum`, we need to infer the property that the second argument equals the sum of the first and the second elements of the function-encoded array passed as the first argument. Because the two elements of the array are independent (i.e., the arguments `a` and `b` of `main`), it is not possible to express such a fact via a refinement type with just one (linearly instantiatable) extra parameter. Nonetheless, the property can be expressed even under the linear-instantiation-expression restriction by using two extra parameters. For example, the following type is sufficient:

$$\forall a{:}\mathtt{int}.\forall b{:}\mathtt{int}.\\ (\mathtt{int} \times (x{:}\mathtt{int} \to \{u \mid \theta\})) \to \{u \mid u = a + b\} \to \star$$

where $\theta \equiv (x = 0 \Rightarrow u = a) \wedge (x = 1 \Rightarrow u = b)$, and $\times$ is the pair type constructor. We use a simple heuristic to progressively increase the number of extra parameters that are added before each function-type parameter: we increment the number by one when the parameter substitution inference fails to find a solution to the constraints, with some pre-defined threshold on the number of bits used in the bit-vector modeling (cf. Section 4.2.2). With the heuristic, the implementation was able to verify `a-test-upd` and `a-checksum`. Note that the increased extra parameter heuristic is sound because the soundness theorem (Theorem 3.6) holds for any pattern of extra parameter additions.

The program `l-isort` remains untypable even with the heuristic. In fact, it can be shown that no finite number of extra parameter additions can type the program when the instantiation expressions are restricted to be linear.

The implementation fails to verify `app-succ0` for a different reason. To verify the program, we need to infer the following type for `app` with the extra parameter i.

$$\forall i{:}\mathtt{int}.f{:}(\{u \mid u = i\} \to \star) \to x{:}\{u \mid u = i\} \to \star$$

However, each counterexample SHP generated from `app-succ0` is actually typable by assigning (the copies of) `app` the types of the following form whose refinement predicates do not mention the extra parameter:

$$\forall i{:}\mathtt{int}.f{:}(\{u \mid u = c\} \to \star) \to x{:}\{u \mid u = c\} \to \star$$

where c is some integer constant. Therefore, the type inference system generates infinitely many counterexample SHPs that are refuted by the types of the above form each time, and the parameter substitution inference is never invoked to infer the necessary type that uses the extra parameter. We leave the issue for future work.

6. Related Work

6.1 Refinement Type Systems

The relatively complete refinement type system of this paper can be seen as DML [30] but with quantifiers (i.e., introduction of Π types) restricted to one before each function-type parameter. Hence, our result shows that DML is actually relatively complete (even when the quantification pattern is restricted). In relation to DML, this paper's contribution is in actually proving relative completeness, and in proposing an automated type inference method.

The previous refinement type systems proposed for automated higher-order program verification [13, 18, 23, 26, 27] lack relative completeness, except for the case when the base-type data domain is finite [16, 17]. We have shown how the type inference systems underlying the verifiers may be extended to attain relative completeness.

6.2 Hoare Logic for Higher-order Languages

There is a long line of research on relatively complete Hoare logic like proof systems for higher-order functional (or procedural) languages. One way to achieve relative completeness is to have a higher-order logic as the *interpretation* logic (i.e., the logic for the

[14] Note that the relative completeness theorem (Theorem 3.7) assumes that arbitrary side-effect-free integer-type expressions can be used for instantiation.

data part) so that the formulas can directly refer to higher-order functions as data (see, e.g., [5, 11, 21, 22]). However, such an approach is difficult to automate as the client verifier must rely on a higher-order logic theorem prover. The dilemma is similar to that arising from explicitly encoding functions as base-type data in the program logic.

The approach of using base-type encoding of functions to achieve relative completeness was first proposed by German et al. [6, 7]. (A similar approach is taken in [8].) Crucial to their approach is the idea of avoiding the explicit encoding in the program logic via quantification, allowing the client verifier to choose appropriate quantifier instantiations. To our knowledge, no actual verifier was built based on their program logic.

The encoding approach is also used in a recent work on relatively complete dependent (refinement) type system [19] where a DML-like type system is extended with linear intersection types, and is shown sound and relatively complete (for terminating programs). Their type system is designed for a type-based complexity analysis, and the paper does not discuss automated verification.

6.3 Quantified First-order Logic Constraint Solving

Our type inference method utilizes an algorithm for deciding the validity a FOL formula of the form $\exists\overrightarrow{x}.\forall\overrightarrow{y}.\theta$ where θ is a quantifier-free arithmetic formula over the variables $\overrightarrow{x}$ and $\overrightarrow{y}$, and if valid, finding appropriate instantiations for $\overrightarrow{x}$ so that the formula can be reduced to $\forall\overrightarrow{y}.\theta[\overrightarrow{e}/\overrightarrow{x}]$.

The problem is studied in the context of *constraint-based* (or, *template-based*) program verification [4, 9, 24] where the existentially quantified variables are used to represent the unknowns in the invariant template. The technique has found wide applicability, including hybrid system verification [20] and program synthesis [25]. Our work adds higher-order program verification to the list.

7. Conclusion

We have presented an automated approach to a relatively complete verification of higher-order functional programs. Our work extends the recent research on refinement type inference for automated program verification. We have extended the underlying refinement type system by adopting the classical result on relatively complete Hoare logic like proof systems for higher-order procedural languages, which shows that certain extra base-type parameter additions are sufficient for relative completeness. Then, we have extended the type inference system by utilizing the techniques from the recent work on quantified FOL constraint solving over template expressions to infer appropriate instantiations for the extra base-type parameters.

Acknowledgments We thank the anonymous reviewers for useful comments. This work is partially supported by Kakenhi 23220001 and 23700026.

References

[1] L. Augustsson. Cayenne - a language with dependent types. In *ICFP*, pages 239–250, 1998.

[2] C. Barrett and C. Tinelli. CVC3. In *CAV*, pages 298–302, 2007.

[3] E. M. Clarke, O. Grumberg, S. Jha, Y. Lu, and H. Veith. Counterexample-guided abstraction refinement. In *CAV*, pages 154–169, 2000.

[4] M. Colón, S. Sankaranarayanan, and H. Sipma. Linear invariant generation using non-linear constraint solving. In *CAV*, pages 420–432, 2003.

[5] W. Damm and B. Josko. A sound and relatively* complete Hoare-logic for a language with higher type procedures. *Acta Inf.*, 20:59–101, 1983.

[6] S. M. German, E. M. Clarke, and J. Y. Halpern. Reasoning about procedures as parameters. In *Logic of Programs*, pages 206–220, 1983.

[7] S. M. German, E. M. Clarke, and J. Y. Halpern. Reasoning about procedures as parameters in the language L4. *Inf. Comput.*, 83(3):265–359, 1989.

[8] A. Goerdt. A Hoare calculus for functions defined by recursion on higher types. In *Logic of Programs*, pages 106–117, 1985.

[9] S. Gulwani, S. Srivastava, and R. Venkatesan. Program analysis as constraint solving. In *PLDI*, pages 281–292, 2008.

[10] C. A. R. Hoare. An axiomatic basis for computer programming. *Commun. ACM*, 12(10):576–580, 1969.

[11] K. Honda, M. Berger, and N. Yoshida. Descriptive and relative completeness of logics for higher-order functions. In *ICALP (2)*, pages 360–371, 2006.

[12] R. Jhala and R. Majumdar. Software model checking. *ACM Comput. Surv.*, 41(4), 2009.

[13] R. Jhala, R. Majumdar, and A. Rybalchenko. HMC: Verifying functional programs using abstract interpreters. In *CAV*, pages 470–485, 2011.

[14] R. Jhala and K. L. McMillan. A practical and complete approach to predicate refinement. In *TACAS*, pages 459–473, 2006.

[15] T. Johnsson. Lambda lifting: Transforming programs to recursive equations. In *FPCA*, pages 190–203, 1985.

[16] N. Kobayashi. Types and higher-order recursion schemes for verification of higher-order programs. In *POPL*, pages 416–428, 2009.

[17] N. Kobayashi and C.-H. L. Ong. A type system equivalent to the modal mu-calculus model checking of higher-order recursion schemes. In *LICS*, pages 179–188, 2009.

[18] N. Kobayashi, R. Sato, and H. Unno. Predicate abstraction and CEGAR for higher-order model checking. In *PLDI*, pages 222–233, 2011.

[19] U. D. Lago and M. Gaboardi. Linear dependent types and relative completeness. In *LICS*, pages 133–142, 2011.

[20] J. Liu, N. Zhan, and H. Zhao. Computing semi-algebraic invariants for polynomial dynamical systems. In *EMSOFT*, pages 97–106, 2011.

[21] E.-R. Olderog. Correctness of programs with Pascal-like procedures without global variables. *Theor. Comput. Sci.*, 30:49–90, 1984.

[22] B. Reus and T. Streicher. Relative completeness for logics of functional programs. In *CSL*, pages 470–480, 2011.

[23] P. M. Rondon, M. Kawaguchi, and R. Jhala. Liquid types. In *PLDI*, pages 159–169, 2008.

[24] S. Sankaranarayanan, H. B. Sipma, and Z. Manna. Constraint-based linear-relations analysis. In *SAS*, pages 53–68, 2004.

[25] S. Srivastava, S. Gulwani, and J. S. Foster. From program verification to program synthesis. In *POPL*, pages 313–326, 2010.

[26] T. Terauchi. Dependent types from counterexamples. In *POPL*, pages 119–130, 2010.

[27] H. Unno and N. Kobayashi. Dependent type inference with interpolants. In *PPDP*, pages 277–288, 2009.

[28] H. Unno, T. Terauchi, and N. Kobayashi. Automating relatively complete verification of higher-order functional programs, 2012. `http://www.kb.is.s.u-tokyo.ac.jp/~uhiro/relcomp`.

[29] A. K. Wright and M. Felleisen. A syntactic approach to type soundness. *Inf. Comput.*, 115(1):38–94, 1994.

[30] H. Xi and F. Pfenning. Dependent types in practical programming. In *POPL*, pages 214–227, 1999.

Abstraction and Invariance for Algebraically Indexed Types

Robert Atkey Patricia Johann
University of Strathclyde
{Robert.Atkey,Patricia.Johann}@strath.ac.uk

Andrew Kennedy
Microsoft Research Cambridge
akenn@microsoft.com

Abstract

Reynolds' relational parametricity provides a powerful way to reason about programs in terms of invariance under changes of data representation. A dazzling array of applications of Reynolds' theory exists, exploiting invariance to yield "free theorems", non-inhabitation results, and encodings of algebraic datatypes. Outside computer science, invariance is a common theme running through many areas of mathematics and physics. For example, the area of a triangle is unaltered by rotation or flipping. If we scale a triangle, then we scale its area, maintaining an invariant relationship between the two. The transformations under which properties are invariant are often organised into groups, with the algebraic structure reflecting the composability and invertibility of transformations.

In this paper, we investigate programming languages whose types are indexed by algebraic structures such as groups of geometric transformations. Other examples include types indexed by principals–for information flow security–and types indexed by distances–for analysis of analytic uniform continuity properties. Following Reynolds, we prove a general Abstraction Theorem that covers all these instances. Consequences of our Abstraction Theorem include free theorems expressing invariance properties of programs, type isomorphisms based on invariance properties, and non-definability results indicating when certain algebraically indexed types are uninhabited or only inhabited by trivial programs. We have fully formalised our framework and most examples in Coq.

Categories and Subject Descriptors D.1.1 [*Programming techniques*]: Applicative (functional) programming; D.2.4 [*Software Engineering*]: Software/Program Verification; D.3.3 [*Programming Languages*]: Language Constructs and Features—Data types and structures

General Terms Languages, Theory, Types

Keywords parametricity, units of measure, dimensional analysis, invariance, computational geometry, information flow, metric types, uniform continuity

1. Introduction

The best way we know of describing the semantics of parametric polymorphism is *relational parametricity*, whose central result is Reynolds' Abstraction Theorem [18]. Its striking consequences include the well-known "free theorems" for polymorphic types [22], non-inhabitation results, and precise correspondences between System F encodings and algebraic datatypes [16], abstract data types, and, most recently, higher-order encodings of binder syntax [2].

Relational parametricity is in essence a principle of *invariance*: the behaviour of polymorphic code is invariant under changes of data representation. For example, the type $\forall\alpha.\mathtt{list}\langle\alpha\rangle \rightarrow \mathtt{list}\langle\alpha\rangle$ tells us that any transformation applied to elements of the input list will be reflected by the same transformation applied to elements of the result. Invariance results also abound in mathematics and physics. The area of a triangle is invariant with respect to isometries of the Euclidean plane; the determinant of a matrix is invariant under changes of basis; and Newton's laws are the same in all inertial frames. Typically, the transformations under which invariants are preserved have interesting structure: for example, translations in the Euclidean plane form an abelian group.

Inspired by this connection, we study type systems that capture rich invariants in types indexed by attributes with algebraic structure. For example, in computational geometry, points in the plane can be indexed by attributes representing affine transformations; in information-flow security, computations can be indexed by principals; in differential privacy, types can be indexed by 'distance'. Types that are polymorphic over such indices induce invariance properties and abstraction barriers beyond those introduced by their unindexed versions, as we shall illustrate. This generalises previous work by the third author on types parameterized by units of measure, whose invariance properties relate to changes of units, or *scaling* [13].

Invariance To illustrate type-induced invariance properties, consider two-dimensional geometry. In a conventional type system, a function areaTri that computes the area of a triangle might be assigned the type: $\mathtt{vec} \times \mathtt{vec} \times \mathtt{vec} \rightarrow \mathtt{real}$. But in our proposed system we can assign it the following more expressive polymorphic type:

$$\text{areaTri} : \forall t{:}\mathsf{T}_2.\mathtt{vec}\langle t\rangle \times \mathtt{vec}\langle t\rangle \times \mathtt{vec}\langle t\rangle \rightarrow \mathtt{real}$$

This type expresses the fact that if each of the arguments to areaTri is translated by the same vector, then the result remains the same, that is, it is *invariant* under translation. Formally, for any vector $\vec{t}$,

$$\text{areaTri}\ (\vec{t}+\vec{v_1}, \vec{t}+\vec{v_2}, \vec{t}+\vec{v_3}) = \text{areaTri}\ (\vec{v_1}, \vec{v_2}, \vec{v_3})$$

Transformations typically *compose* in various ways, and the compositions satisfy algebraic laws. For example, we can assign a function that computes the area of a circle given its radius the following polymorphic type:

$$\text{areaCircle} : \forall s{:}\mathsf{GL}_1.\mathtt{real}\langle s\rangle \rightarrow \mathtt{real}\langle s\cdot s\rangle$$

This captures the fact that the area of a circle varies as the square of its radius, i.e., $\text{areaCircle}(kr) = k^2 \cdot \text{areaCircle}(r)$ for any $k \neq 0$ (the 'sorts' T_2 and GL_1 will be explained later). Here, s can be interpreted as the *units of measure* of the argument to areaCircle, and '$\cdot$' composes units using the product. We can also add an

POPL'13, January 23–25, 2013, Rome, Italy.

inverse operation and identity unit of measure 1, and then impose the algebraic laws of abelian groups. This permits identification of, for example, $\mathtt{real}\langle s \cdot s^{-1} \rangle$ with the type $\mathtt{real}\langle 1 \rangle$ of dimensionless constants.

Abstraction In his original paper on parametricity, Reynolds asserted that *type structure is a syntactic discipline for enforcing levels of abstraction*. We see something analogous here: if all primitive operations are given types that reflect their behaviour under translation, then there is no way to 'break' this property. For example, there is no way that areaTri can depend on the actual coordinates of its inputs. Furthermore, the distinction between points and vectors that is often enforced through abstract data types [7] is captured here by indices instead. For example, the operation that takes two points and computes their vector difference can be assigned the type $\forall t{:}\mathsf{T}_2.\mathtt{vec}\langle t \rangle \times \mathtt{vec}\langle t \rangle \rightarrow \mathtt{vec}\langle 0 \rangle$, reflecting the invariance of the result (a pure vector) under translations of the point arguments. As a result through types alone we can, in essence, derive so-called *coordinate-free* geometry [15].

The invariance properties discussed above can be seen as "free theorems" [22], but the abstraction afforded by polymorphic indexed types can also induce interesting type *isomorphisms*. The type of areaCircle above is in fact isomorphic to $\mathtt{real}\langle 1 \rangle$. A moment's thought reveals why: what possible unary functions can be constructed whose outputs scale as the square of the scaling of their inputs? Answer: just those functions of the form $\lambda x.kx^2$ for some constant k. In this case, of course, we expect that $k = \pi$.

Relational parametricity To derive such invariance and abstraction properties of types, we adopt the techniques of relational parametricity. Over an underlying index-erasure semantics we construct binary relations parameterised by an environment ρ that describes how values of primitive type are related according to their indices. For example, values v and w of type $\mathtt{real}\langle s \rangle$ are related when v "scales to" w according to an interpretation of s (i.e., $w = \rho(s) \cdot v$). Values of polymorphic type are related exactly when they are related for all possible interpretations of the quantified variable. For example, values v and w of type $\forall t{:}\mathsf{T}_2.\mathtt{vec}\langle t \rangle \rightarrow \mathtt{vec}\langle t \rangle$ are related when they are related at type $\mathtt{vec}\langle t \rangle \rightarrow \mathtt{vec}\langle t \rangle$ for all translations $\vec{t} \in \mathrm{T}_2$ associated with t.

As it happens, the relational interpretations given above are functional, relating one value uniquely to another. Other applications make use of primitive relations that are not simple functions. For example, in a type system in which the index in $\mathtt{real}\langle s \rangle$ is interpreted not as a unit of measure, but as a measure of *closeness*, two values x and y of this type are related if $|x - y| < \rho(s)$ for a positive real number $\rho(s)$. Rather beautifully, the standard notion of uniform continuity can then be expressed as $\forall \epsilon{:}\mathsf{R}^{>0}.\ \exists \delta{:}\mathsf{R}^{>0}.\ \mathtt{real}\langle \delta \rangle \rightarrow \mathtt{real}\langle \epsilon \rangle$.

Motivations Our motivations for studying algebraically indexed types are threefold. First, we believe that, as with units of measure [14], practical programming language extensions will follow. For example, in computational geometry and graphics, attributes on points, vectors, and other geometric types could be used to prevent the mixing of different coordinate systems, or 'frames'. Second, type-based static analyses can be based on indexed types, for example, in effect systems [4], and, more speculatively, in continuity analysis [8]. Finally, we believe that expressing algebraic invariants through types has the potential to offer slick proof techniques for mechanized mathematics. Harrison has applied the invariance properties of geometric primitives to create elegant proofs in geometry, based on 'without loss of generality' principles [10]. The invariance properties are expressed and propagated using ad-hoc tactics; our types offer a more principled means of achieving the same end, and the 'wlog' principle itself is expressed through type isomorphisms.

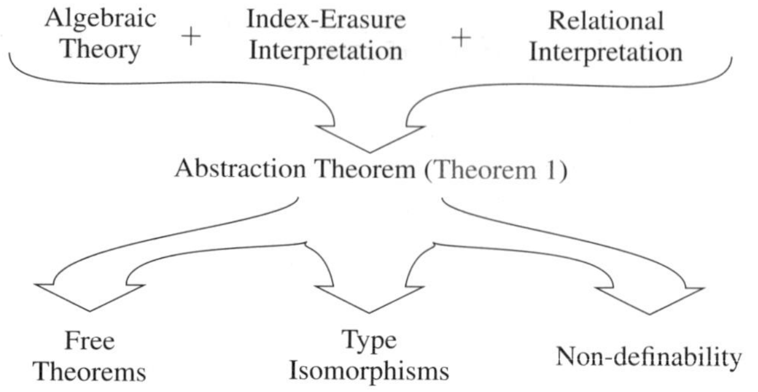

Figure 1. Summary of the Paper

We follow the mantra *semantics first, syntax later* in studying types with algebraic structure. We have not yet built a practical programming language that supports algebraically indexed types; nor have we designed type checking, type inference, or static analysis algorithms. But when we do so, the semantics will guide us. The fact that zero is polymorphic in units of measure (it can be given type $\forall u.\mathtt{real}\langle u \rangle$) whereas other constants are dimensionless (having type $\mathtt{real}\langle 1 \rangle$) is justified by the invariance properties induced by the types: zero is invariant under scaling, other constants are not. For less trivial constants and operations, the appropriate types are not so apparent, as we shall see, but invariance properties expressed by the semantics guide us in assigning appropriate types. Semantics does not lie!

1.1 Contributions

This paper makes the following specific contributions:

- We present a collection of compelling examples of algebraically indexed types, including a novel type system for geometry, a refined type system for information flow based on logic, and a simple type system with distance-indexed types.
- We formulate a type system that can either be used as a programming language in its own right, or as the target of type-based analyses. The type system consists of the usual type constructors together with a collection of indexed primitive types, universal and existential quantification over the indices, and a multi-sorted equational theory for indices.
- We describe a relational semantics for the type system and prove an analogue of Reynolds' Abstraction Theorem, for a given *model* of index sorts and relational interpretation of primitive types. We prove that the semantics soundly approximates contextual equivalence.
- For each of our main examples we deduce free theorems that are consequences of our Abstraction Theorem, prove specific non-definability results, and derive interesting type isomorphisms. For a large class of first-order types we give a general method for constructing suitable models to prove non-definability results. Figure 1 illustrates the central position of our analogue of Reynolds' Abstraction Theorem (Theorem 1) in these results.

We improve on the earlier semantics of units of measure [13] in a number of ways. By extending the language of units with an 'absolute value' operation, we can give more precise types and obtain more general invariance properties. The relational interpretation for units is both simpler and more flexible, and we derive slicker proofs of non-definability, and new results. Our notion of type isomorphism is stronger than before, being based on contextual equivalence.

We have fully formalised our framework and most examples in Coq, using strongly-typed term representations throughout [3]. The formalisation is available from
`https://github.com/bobatkey/algebraically-indexed-types`

1.2 Structure of paper

Our paper is structured as follows. In Section 2 we present an extended case study of two-dimensional geometry, with semi-formal description of types and results. In Section 3 we describe fully formally a general framework for algebraically-indexed types, and prove the Abstraction Theorem and soundness for semantic equivalence. Section 4 presents a number of applications of the theory to 2-d geometry, including free theorems, type isomorphisms and non-definability. Section 5 develops a more general technique for proving non-definability results. Section 6 presents the application of algebraically indexed types to information flow security, and Section 7 applies it to types indexed by distances. Finally, Section 8 discusses related work and future plans.

2. Geometry via Algebraically Indexed Types

We motivate our investigation of algebraically indexed types and their relational interpretations by developing a novel type system for programs that manipulate two-dimensional geometric data. Geometry is rich with operations that are invariant under transformation: affine operations are invariant under change of origin (Section 2.3), vector space operations are invariant under change of basis, and dot product is invariant under orthogonal changes of basis (Section 2.4). On the other hand, some geometric operations are interestingly variant under transformation. For example, cross products vary with scalings of the plane (Section 2.5). We incorporate (in)variance information about geometric primitives into type systems via algebraically indexed types.

2.1 Origin Invariance and Representation Independence

The basic data structure used in programs that manipulate geometric data is the n-tuple of numbers. In the 2-dimensional case, tuples $\vec{v} = (x, y)$ serve double duty, representing both *points*—offsets from some origin—and *vectors*—offsets in their own right. Despite their common representation, points and vectors are very different, and distinguishing between them is the key feature of *affine geometry* (see, for example, Chapter 2 of Gallier's book [9]). Nevertheless, computational geometry libraries traditionally either leave it to the programmer to maintain the distinction between points and vectors, or else use different abstract types for points and vectors to enforce it. In this paper we investigate a more sophisticated approach based on types indexed by change of origin transformations.

This approach regards the difference between points and vectors as a change of data representation. For example, if $(0, 0)$ and $(10, 20)$ are two origins, then the tuple $(1, 1)$ with respect to $(0, 0)$ and the tuple $(11, 21)$ with respect to $(10, 20)$ represent *the same point* because they have the same displacement from these two origins, respectively. This suggests that programs that manipulate points should be invariant with respect to changes of origin. Programs that manipulate vectors, on the other hand, should not be invariant under change of origin. Different vectors represent different offsets, and the vector $(0, 0)$ always represents the zero offset.

Invariance under change of representation immediately recalls Reynolds' fable about two professors teaching the theory of complex numbers [18]. One professor represents complex numbers using rectangular coordinates ($x+iy$), while the other represents them using polar coordinates ($\alpha \cos\theta + i\alpha \sin\theta$). Happily, after learning the basic operations on complex numbers in the two representations, the two classes can interact because the theory of complex numbers is invariant under the choice of representation. Reynolds formalises the idea of invariance under changes of representation as preservation of relations. For example, if a binary relation R relates the rectangular and polar representations of complex numbers, then a program that manipulates complex numbers at a level of abstraction above their specific representation should preserve R.

Reynolds' relational approach can be applied in the geometric setting to show how quantifying over all changes of origin ensures the invariance of programs under any particular choice of origin. For this, we first define a family of binary relations on $\mathbb{R}^2$ that is indexed by changes of origin. Changes of origin are represented by vectors in $\mathbb{R}^2$, and form a group T_2 of translations under addition. The T_2-indexed family of binary relations $\{R_{\vec{t}} \subseteq \mathbb{R}^2 \times \mathbb{R}^2\}_{\vec{t} \in \mathrm{T}_2}$ is then defined by $R_{\vec{t}} = \{(\vec{v}, \vec{v'}) \mid \vec{v'} = \vec{v} + \vec{t}\}$. We then consider a function f that takes as input two tuples in $\mathbb{R}^2$ and returns a single tuple in $\mathbb{R}^2$. We intend that the tuples all represent points with respect to the same origin, and that f is invariant under the choice of origin. Reynolds' relational approach formalises this intention precisely. For any $\vec{t} \in \mathrm{T}_2$:

$$\forall (\vec{v_1}, \vec{v_1'}) \in R_{\vec{t}}, (\vec{v_2}, \vec{v_2'}) \in R_{\vec{t}}. (f(\vec{v_1}, \vec{v_2}), f(\vec{v_1'}, \vec{v_2'})) \in R_{\vec{t}} \quad (1)$$

Unfolding the definition of $R_{\vec{t}}$ gives the equivalent formulation, again for all $\vec{t} \in \mathrm{T}_2$:

$$\forall \vec{v_1}, \vec{v_2}.\ f(\vec{v_1} + \vec{t}, \vec{v_2} + \vec{t}) = f(\vec{v_1}, \vec{v_2}) + \vec{t}. \quad (2)$$

Thus, Reynolds' preservation of relations, when instantiated with the family of relations $\{R_{\vec{t}}\}$, yields exactly the geometric property of invariance under change of origin.

2.2 A Type System for Change of Origin Invariance

Reynolds also showed how a type discipline can be used to establish that (the denotational interpretations of) programs preserve relations. For Reynolds, the type discipline of interest was that of the polymorphic λ-calculus, which supports the construction of new types by universal quantification over types. In terms of relations, Reynolds interprets universal quantification over types as quantification over binary relations between denotations of types. By contrast, in our statements of geometric invariance in Section 2.1 we did not quantify over all relations, but instead quantified over all changes of origin and used a specific choice of origin to select a relation from the family $\{R_{\vec{t}}\}$. This suggests introducing quantification over changes of origin into the language of types. We use the notation $\forall t{:}\mathsf{T}_2.A$ for quantification over all 2-dimensional translations (i.e., choices of origin) t, and refer to T_2 as the *sort* of t. Note the difference in fonts used to distinguish the semantic group T_2 from the syntactic sort T_2. We use a similar convention below, too.

Since the sort T_2 represents an abelian group, we can combine its elements using the usual group operations. We write operations additively, using $e_1 + e_2$ for the group operation, $-e$ for inverse and 0 for the unit. We also regard expressions built from variables and the group operations up to the abelian group axioms. For example, we regard $e_1 + (e_2 + e_3)$ and $(e_1 + e_2) + e_3$ as equivalent.

Our language of types includes the unit type `unit` and, for all types A and B, the function type $A \to B$, the sum type $A + B$, and the tuple type $A \times B$. We also assume a primitive type `real`, used to represent scalars. Although tuples of real numbers represent points and vectors in geometric applications, we cannot express this via the type `real` $\times$ `real`. Indeed, two elements of type `real` are related if and only if they are equal and, by Reynolds' interpretation of tuple types, two elements of `real` $\times$ `real` are also related if and only if they are equal. But since this does not give the correct relational interpretations for points and vectors, we introduce a new type $\mathtt{vec}\langle e\rangle$, indexed by expressions e of sort T_2, to represent them. The index e represents the displacement by change of origin of a point of this type. Although we have taken pains to distinguish geometric points and vectors, we use the name `vec` for both to recall the computer science notion of vector as a homogeneous sequence of values with a known length (in this case, 2).

As is standard for parametricity, every type has two interpretations: an index-erasure interpretation that ignores the indexing expression, and a relational interpretation as a binary relation on the index-erasure interpretation. We denote the index-erasure and relational interpretations with the notations $\lfloor\cdot\rfloor$ and $[\![\cdot]\!]$ respectively. To give such interpretations for the types $\texttt{vec}\langle e\rangle$ and $\forall t{:}\mathsf{T}_2.A$, we assume for now that we can map each expression e of sort T_2 to an element $[\![e]\!]\rho$ of the group T_2 using some environment ρ that interprets e's free variables. The index-erasure and relational interpretations of $\texttt{vec}\langle e\rangle$ are:

$$\begin{aligned}\lfloor\texttt{vec}\langle e\rangle\rfloor &= \mathbb{R}^2\\ [\![\texttt{vec}\langle e\rangle]\!]\rho &= R_{[\![e]\!]\rho} = \{(\vec{v},\vec{v'}) \mid \vec{v'} = \vec{v} + [\![e]\!]\rho\}\end{aligned}$$

The index-erasure and relational interpretations of $\forall t{:}\mathsf{T}_2.A$ are:

$$\begin{aligned}\lfloor\forall t{:}\mathsf{T}_2.A\rfloor &= \lfloor A\rfloor\\ [\![\forall t{:}\mathsf{T}_2.A]\!]\rho &= \bigcap\{[\![A]\!](\rho,\vec{t}) \mid \vec{t}\in \mathrm{T}_2\}\end{aligned}$$

The index-erasure and relational interpretations are given formally in Sections 3.3 and 3.4.

At the end of Section 2.1 we considered functions $f : \mathbb{R}^2 \times \mathbb{R}^2 \to \mathbb{R}^2$ that preserve all changes of origin. This property of f can be expressed in terms of types by $f : \forall t{:}\mathsf{T}_2.\ \texttt{vec}\langle t\rangle \times \texttt{vec}\langle t\rangle \to \texttt{vec}\langle t\rangle$. Spelling out the relational interpretation of this type using the definitions above and the standard relational interpretations for tuple and function types, we recover Statement 2 exactly.

2.3 Affine and Vector Operations

Invariance under change of origin is the key feature of affine geometry, whose central operation is the affine combination of points: $\lambda_1\vec{v_1} + \lambda_2\vec{v_2}$, where $\lambda_1 + \lambda_2 = 1$. Geometrically, this can be interpreted as describing all the points on the unique line through the points represented by $\vec{v_1}$ and $\vec{v_2}$ (assuming $\vec{v_1} \neq \vec{v_2}$). We add affine combination of points to our calculus as follows:

$$\begin{aligned}&\mathrm{affComb} : \forall t{:}\mathsf{T}_2.\ \texttt{vec}\langle t\rangle \to \texttt{real} \to \texttt{vec}\langle t\rangle \to \texttt{vec}\langle t\rangle\\ &\lfloor\mathrm{affComb}\rfloor\ \vec{v_1}\ r\ \vec{v_2} = (1-r)\vec{v_1} + r\vec{v_2}\end{aligned}$$

It can be verified by hand that the index-erasure interpretation $\lfloor\mathrm{affComb}\rfloor$ is invariant under all changes of origin, as dictated by its type.

Example 1. The evaluation of quadratic Bézier curves (Bézier curves with two endpoints and a single control point) can be expressed using the affine combination primitive as follows:

$$\begin{aligned}&\mathrm{quadB\acute{e}zier} : \forall t{:}\mathsf{T}_2.\ \texttt{vec}\langle t\rangle{\to}\texttt{vec}\langle t\rangle{\to}\texttt{vec}\langle t\rangle{\to}\texttt{real}{\to}\texttt{vec}\langle t\rangle\\ &\mathrm{quadB\acute{e}zier}\ [t]\ p_0\ p_1\ p_2\ s =\\ &\quad \mathrm{affComb}\ [t]\ (\mathrm{affComb}\ [t]\ p_0\ s\ p_1)\ s\ (\mathrm{affComb}\ [t]\ p_1\ s\ p_2)\end{aligned}$$

For two endpoints p_0 and p_2, a control point p_1, and $s \in [0,1]$, an application quadBézier $p_0\ p_1\ p_2\ s$ gives the point on the curve at "time" s. The type of quadBézier immediately tells us that it preserves all changes of origin.

The obvious type for vector addition is $(+) : \texttt{vec}\langle 0\rangle \to \texttt{vec}\langle 0\rangle \to \texttt{vec}\langle 0\rangle$. But we can reflect the fact that $(+)$ is not invariant under change of origin by giving it a more precise type that reflects how it varies with change of origin:

$$(+) : \forall t_1, t_2{:}\mathsf{T}_2.\ \texttt{vec}\langle t_1\rangle \to \texttt{vec}\langle t_2\rangle \to \texttt{vec}\langle t_1 + t_2\rangle$$

Intuitively, this type says that if the first input vector has been displaced by t_1 and the second by t_2, then their sum is displaced by $t_1 + t_2$. We can also negate vectors, yielding a vector which points in the opposite direction. Negation negates translation arguments:

$$\mathrm{negate} : \forall t{:}\mathsf{T}_2.\ \texttt{vec}\langle t\rangle \to \texttt{vec}\langle -t\rangle$$

Finally, with the primitive operations of addition and negation of vectors we can define the derived operation of subtraction:

$$\begin{aligned}&(-) : \forall t_1, t_2{:}\mathsf{T}_2.\ \texttt{vec}\langle t_1\rangle \to \texttt{vec}\langle t_2\rangle \to \texttt{vec}\langle t_1 - t_2\rangle\\ &(-)\ [t_1]\ [t_2]\ p_1\ p_2 = p_1 + \mathrm{negate}\ p_2\end{aligned}$$

Given two points that are invariant with respect to the same change of origin—i.e., two values of type $\texttt{vec}\langle t\rangle$—we can use subtraction to compute their offset:

$$\begin{aligned}&\mathrm{offset} : \forall t{:}\mathsf{T}_2.\ \texttt{vec}\langle t\rangle \to \texttt{vec}\langle t\rangle \to \texttt{vec}\langle 0\rangle\\ &\mathrm{offset}\ [t]\ p_1\ p_2 = p_1 - p_2\end{aligned}$$

The result is a vector expressed with respect to the null change of origin: note how the algebraic structure on the indexing theory induces type equalities that can be used to simplify the type of the result of offset from $\texttt{vec}\langle t-t\rangle$ to $\texttt{vec}\langle 0\rangle$. The type of $(+)$ can also be specialised to the case of moving a point by a vector:

$$\begin{aligned}&\mathrm{moveBy} : \forall t{:}\mathsf{T}_2.\ \texttt{vec}\langle t\rangle \to \texttt{vec}\langle 0\rangle \to \texttt{vec}\langle t\rangle\\ &\mathrm{moveBy}\ [t]\ p\ v = p + v\end{aligned}$$

The types we assign to the remaining vector space primitives, namely $0 : \texttt{vec}\langle 0\rangle$ for the zero vector and $(*) : \texttt{real} \to \texttt{vec}\langle 0\rangle \to \texttt{vec}\langle 0\rangle$ for multiplication by a scalar, do not describe any interesting effects on translations.

Example 2. The vector space operators and the properties that follow from their types allow us to establish a useful type isomorphism. Consider functions with types following the schema:

$$\tau_n \stackrel{def}{=} \forall t{:}\mathsf{T}_2.\ \underbrace{\texttt{vec}\langle t\rangle \to \ldots \to \texttt{vec}\langle t\rangle}_{n+1 \text{ times}} \to \texttt{real}$$

Just by looking at the types τ_n, we know that their inhabitants will be invariant under change of origin because of the quantification over all t in T_2. So we may as well choose one of the input points as the origin and assume that all the other points are defined with respect to it. This formalises the common mathematical practice of stating that "without loss of generality" we can take some point in a description of a problem to be the origin provided the problem statement is invariant under translation. Each type τ_n is isomorphic to the corresponding type σ_n:

$$\sigma_n \stackrel{def}{=} \underbrace{\texttt{vec}\langle 0\rangle \to \ldots \texttt{vec}\langle 0\rangle}_{n \text{ times}} \to \texttt{real}$$

We demonstrate these isomorphisms formally in Section 4, in the more general setting of types indexed by abelian groups.

Example 3. So far we have emphasised the derivation of properties, or "free theorems", of programs from their types. But using more refined relational interpretations of types we can also show that certain types are uninhabited. For example, the type $\forall t{:}\mathsf{T}_2.\ \texttt{vec}\langle t+t\rangle \to \texttt{vec}\langle t\rangle$ has no inhabitants. Intuitively, this is because we cannot remove the extra t in $\texttt{vec}\langle t+t\rangle$ using the vector operations. We formalise this non-definability result in Section 5 using a specialised relational interpretation.

2.4 Change of Basis Invariance

Although vector addition, negation, and scaling are not invariant under change of origin, they are invariant under change of basis. As with origin invariance, we can express basis invariance as preservation of relations indexed by changes of basis. Change of basis is achieved by applying an invertible linear map, and the collection of all such maps on $\mathbb{R}^2$ forms the *General Linear* group GL_2, which we represent in our language by a new indexing sort GL_2 with (non-abelian) group structure that we will write multiplicatively. We then extend $\texttt{vec}$ to allow indices of sort GL_2, as well as T_2, so that $\texttt{vec}\langle B, t\rangle$ is a vector that varies with change of basis B

$$
\begin{array}{rcl}
0 & : & \forall s{:}\mathsf{GL}_1.\ \mathtt{real}\langle s\rangle \\
1 & : & \mathtt{real}\langle 1\rangle \\
(+) & : & \forall s{:}\mathsf{GL}_1.\ \mathtt{real}\langle s\rangle \rightarrow \mathtt{real}\langle s\rangle \rightarrow \mathtt{real}\langle s\rangle \\
(-) & : & \forall s{:}\mathsf{GL}_1.\ \mathtt{real}\langle s\rangle \rightarrow \mathtt{real}\langle s\rangle \rightarrow \mathtt{real}\langle s\rangle \\
(*) & : & \forall s_1, s_2{:}\mathsf{GL}_1.\ \mathtt{real}\langle s_1\rangle \rightarrow \mathtt{real}\langle s_2\rangle \rightarrow \mathtt{real}\langle s_1 s_2\rangle \\
(/) & : & \forall s_1, s_2{:}\mathsf{GL}_1.\ \mathtt{real}\langle s_1\rangle \rightarrow \mathtt{real}\langle s_2\rangle \\
 & & \quad \rightarrow \mathtt{real}\langle s_1 s_2^{-1}\rangle + \mathtt{unit} \\
\mathrm{abs} & : & \forall s{:}\mathsf{GL}_1.\ \mathtt{real}\langle s\rangle \rightarrow \mathtt{real}\langle |s|\rangle
\end{array}
$$

Figure 2. Operations on scaled real numbers

and change of origin t. Formally, the index-erasure and relational semantics of $\mathtt{vec}\langle B, t\rangle$ are given by:

$$
\begin{array}{rcl}
\lfloor \mathtt{vec}\langle e_B, e_t\rangle \rfloor & = & \mathbb{R}^2 \\
[\![\mathtt{vec}\langle e_B, e_t\rangle]\!]\rho & = & \{(\vec{v}, \vec{v}') \mid \vec{v}' = ([\![e_B]\!]\rho)\vec{v} + [\![e_t]\!]\rho\}
\end{array}
$$

Affine Geometry An *affine transformation* is an invertible linear map together with a translation. We can assign types to all the primitive affine and vector space operations indicating how they they behave with respect to affine transformations:

$$
\begin{array}{rcl}
\mathrm{affComb} & : & \forall B{:}\mathsf{GL}_2, t{:}\mathsf{T}_2. \\
 & & \quad \mathtt{vec}\langle B, t\rangle \rightarrow \mathtt{real} \rightarrow \mathtt{vec}\langle B, t\rangle \rightarrow \mathtt{vec}\langle B, t\rangle \\
(+) & : & \forall B{:}\mathsf{GL}_2, t_1, t_2{:}\mathsf{T}_2. \\
 & & \quad \mathtt{vec}\langle B, t_1\rangle \rightarrow \mathtt{vec}\langle B, t_2\rangle \rightarrow \mathtt{vec}\langle B, t_1 + t_2\rangle \\
\mathrm{negate} & : & \forall B{:}\mathsf{GL}_2, t{:}\mathsf{T}_2.\ \mathtt{vec}\langle B, t\rangle \rightarrow \mathtt{vec}\langle B, -t\rangle \\
0 & : & \forall B{:}\mathsf{GL}_2.\ \mathtt{vec}\langle B, 0\rangle \\
(*) & : & \forall B{:}\mathsf{GL}_2.\ \mathtt{real} \rightarrow \mathtt{vec}\langle B, 0\rangle \rightarrow \mathtt{vec}\langle B, 0\rangle
\end{array}
$$

Euclidean Geometry Euclidean geometry extends affine geometry with the *dot product*, or *inner product*, operation of two vectors. The dot product is defined by $(x_1, y_1) \cdot (x_2, y_2) = x_1 x_2 + y_1 y_2$. To assign it a type we note that, although dot product is not invariant under GL_2 or T_2, it is invariant under the subgroup O_2 of GL_2 of *orthogonal* linear transformations, i.e., the subgroup of invertible linear maps whose matrix representations' transposes are equal to their inverses. We thus introduce a new sort O_2 of orthogonal transformations, and overload the multiplicative group operations for inhabitants of O_2. Further assuming an injection ι_O that takes $e : \mathsf{O}_2$ to $\iota_O(e) : \mathsf{GL}_2$ we assign dot product this type:

$$
(\cdot) : \forall O{:}\mathsf{O}_2.\ \mathtt{vec}\langle \iota_O O, 0\rangle \rightarrow \mathtt{vec}\langle \iota_O O, 0\rangle \rightarrow \mathtt{real}
$$

The cross product of two vectors is defined on coordinate representations as $(x_1, y_1) \times (x_2, y_2) = x_1 y_2 - x_2 y_1$. Geometrically, the cross product is the signed area of the parallelogram described by the pair of input vectors. Under change of basis by an invertible linear transformation B, the cross product of two vectors varies with the determinant of B. This corresponds to scaling the plane by the change of basis transformation, so we augment our calculus with a new sort GL_1 of scale factors (i.e., 1-dimensional invertible linear maps). Semantically, GL_1 ranges over the non-zero real numbers and forms an abelian group which we write multiplicatively. We also add two new operations: determinant, $\det B$, which takes an inhabitant of GL_2 to its determinant in GL_1, and absolute value, $|e|$, which takes scaling factors to scaling factors. We also refine the type `real` of real numbers so that it is indexed by the sort GL_1: $\mathtt{real}\langle e\rangle$. The old type `real` is then just $\mathtt{real}\langle 1\rangle$, and the full collection of operations on real numbers indexed by scaling factors is shown in Figure 2. We can thus assign cross product the type:

$$
(\times) : \forall B{:}\mathsf{GL}_2.\ \mathtt{vec}\langle B, 0\rangle \rightarrow \mathtt{vec}\langle B, 0\rangle \rightarrow \mathtt{real}\langle \det B\rangle
$$

Since the absolute value of the determinant of an orthogonal transformation is always 1, we assume $|\det(\iota_O O)| = 1$ to hold for any $O \in \mathsf{O}_2$.

Example 4. We can use the operations of this subsection to compute the area of a triangle. We have:

$$
\begin{array}{l}
\mathrm{area} : \forall B{:}\mathsf{GL}_2, t{:}\mathsf{T}_2. \\
\qquad \mathtt{vec}\langle B, t\rangle \rightarrow \mathtt{vec}\langle B, t\rangle \rightarrow \mathtt{vec}\langle B, t\rangle \rightarrow \mathtt{real}\langle |\det B|\rangle \\
\mathrm{area}\ [B]\ [t]\ p_1\ p_2\ p_3 = \frac{1}{2} * \mathrm{abs}\,((p_2 - p_1) \times (p_3 - p_1))
\end{array}
$$

The calculation is performed in several steps, each of which removes some of the symmetry described by the type of area. First, the two offset vectors $p_2 - p_1$ and $p_3 - p_1$ are computed. These operations remove the effect of translations on the result in exactly the same way as the type isomorphism in Example 2. Next, we compute the cross product of the two vectors, which gives the area of the parallelogram described by the sides of the triangle and has type $\mathtt{real}\langle \det B\rangle$. This removes some of the symmetry due to invertible linear maps, but the cross product still varies with the sign of the determinant. We remove this symmetry as well using abs. This gives a value of type $\mathtt{real}\langle |\det B|\rangle$ which we multiply by $\frac{1}{2}$ to recover the area of the triangle rather than that of the whole parallelogram. If we specialise area to just orthogonal transformations, the assumption $|\det(\iota_O O)| = 1$ gives the following type:

$$
\begin{array}{l}
\mathrm{area} : \forall O{:}\mathsf{O}_2, t{:}\mathsf{T}_2. \\
\qquad \mathtt{vec}\langle \iota_O O, t\rangle \rightarrow \mathtt{vec}\langle \iota_O O, t\rangle \rightarrow \mathtt{vec}\langle \iota_O O, t\rangle \rightarrow \mathtt{real}\langle 1\rangle
\end{array}
$$

This type shows that the area of a triangle is invariant under orthogonal transformations and translations. Combinations of such transformations are *isometries*, i.e., distance preserving maps.

2.5 Scale Invariance and Dimensional Analysis

Indexing types by scaling factors brings us to the original inspiration for the current work: Kennedy's interpretation of his units of measure type system via scaling invariance [13]. Kennedy shows how interpreting types in terms of scaling invariance brings the techniques of dimensional analysis to bear on programming. The types of the real number arithmetic operations in Figure 2 are exactly the types Kennedy assigns in his units of measure system, except for that of the absolute value operation. Semantically, our type indexes by non-zero scaling factors, whereas Kennedy's indexes by strictly positive ones.

In our two-dimensional setting we can add to Kennedy's one-dimensional scaling invariance an operation ι_1 that, semantically, takes scale factors in GL_1 to invertible linear maps in GL_2, i.e., takes numbers s to matrices $\left(\begin{smallmatrix} s & 0 \\ 0 & s \end{smallmatrix}\right)$. This operation satisfies the equation $\det(\iota_1 s) = s^2$, indicating that scaling the plane by s in both directions scales areas by s^2.

Example 5. Just as we specialised the type of the area function to orthogonal transformations in Example 4, we can also specialise area's type to scaling transformations. This yields the type:

$$
\begin{array}{l}
\mathrm{area} : \forall s{:}\mathsf{GL}_1, t{:}\mathsf{T}_2. \\
\qquad \mathtt{vec}\langle \iota_1 s, t\rangle \rightarrow \mathtt{vec}\langle \iota_1 s, t\rangle \rightarrow \mathtt{vec}\langle \iota_1 s, t\rangle \rightarrow \mathtt{real}\langle s^2\rangle
\end{array}
$$

As expected, the area of a triangle varies with the square of scalings of the plane, and this is reflected in the type.

Linear maps of the form $\left(\begin{smallmatrix} s & 0 \\ 0 & s \end{smallmatrix}\right)$, as generated by ι_1, commute with all other invertible linear maps. We thus require $(\iota_1 s)B = B(\iota_1 s)$ to hold. The scaling maps $\left(\begin{smallmatrix} s & 0 \\ 0 & s \end{smallmatrix}\right)$ are precisely the elements of GL_2 that commute with all others; these form the *centre* of GL_2. If we keep track of scalings, then we can assign the more precise types to scalar multiplication and dot product. These are shown in Figure 3, which summarises the most general types of all the vector operations that we have described.

$$
\begin{aligned}
0 &: \forall B{:}\mathsf{GL}_2.\ \mathtt{vec}\langle B, 0\rangle \\
(+) &: \forall B{:}\mathsf{GL}_2, t_1, t_2{:}\mathsf{T}_2. \\
&\quad \mathtt{vec}\langle B, t_1\rangle \to \mathtt{vec}\langle B, t_2\rangle \to \mathtt{vec}\langle B, t_1 + t_2\rangle \\
\text{negate} &: \forall B{:}\mathsf{GL}_2, t{:}\mathsf{T}_2.\ \mathtt{vec}\langle B, t\rangle \to \mathtt{vec}\langle B, -t\rangle \\
(*) &: \forall s{:}\mathsf{GL}_1, B{:}\mathsf{GL}_2. \\
&\quad \mathtt{real}\langle s\rangle \to \mathtt{vec}\langle B, 0\rangle \to \mathtt{vec}\langle \iota_1(s)B, 0\rangle \\
\text{affComb} &: \forall B{:}\mathsf{GL}_2, t{:}\mathsf{T}_2. \\
&\quad \mathtt{vec}\langle B, t\rangle \to \mathtt{real}\langle 1\rangle \to \mathtt{vec}\langle B, t\rangle \to \mathtt{vec}\langle B, t\rangle \\
(\cdot) &: \forall s{:}\mathsf{GL}_1, O{:}\mathsf{O}_2.\ \mathtt{vec}\langle \iota_1(s)\iota_O(O), 0\rangle \to \\
&\quad \mathtt{vec}\langle \iota_1(s)\iota_O(O), 0\rangle \to \mathtt{real}\langle s^2\rangle \\
(\times) &: \forall B{:}\mathsf{GL}_2.\ \mathtt{vec}\langle B, 0\rangle \to \mathtt{vec}\langle B, 0\rangle \to \mathtt{real}\langle \det B\rangle
\end{aligned}
$$

Figure 3. Operations on vectors

Example 6. With the operations in Figure 2, it is not possible to write a term with the following type that is not constantly zero:

$$\forall s{:}\mathsf{GL}_2.\ \mathtt{real}\langle s^2\rangle \to \mathtt{real}\langle s\rangle$$

This was shown by Kennedy for his units of measure system [13]. In particular, it is not possible to write a square root function with the above type. The non-definability of square root is similar to the uninhabitation of the type in Example 3.

In Section 4.3 we revisit Kennedy's result and show that even if we add square root as a primitive operation—with the type above—then it is still not possible to construct the cube root function. The non-definability of cube root is related to the impossibility of trisecting an arbitrary angle by ruler and compass constructions.

3. A General Framework

We now present our framework for algebraically indexed types and its relational interpretation. We define the syntax of algebraically indexed types (Section 3.1) and a syntax for terms in a general programming language for algebraically indexed types (Section 3.2). We give an index-erasure semantics to types and terms (Section 3.3), and based on this semantics define notions of contextual equivalence and type isomorphism. We then introduce a relational semantics for types parameterised by an appropriate 'model' of the algebraic theory (Section 3.4), prove the central Abstraction Theorem and use the relational semantics to define a notion of semantic equivalence that soundly approximates contextual equivalence (Section 3.5).

We will use a type system for affine geometry as a running example throughout, so that by the end of the section we have prepared enough syntactic and semantic gadgets to let us prove invariance and abstraction properties for geometric examples in Section 4.

3.1 Algebraically-Indexed Types

The index expressions and types of an instantiation of our general framework are derived from the following data:

1. A collection *Sort* of index sorts. We use the meta-syntactic variables $s, s_1, s_2, \ldots$ for arbitrary sorts taken from *Sort*.
2. A collection *IndexOp* of index operations, with a function $\text{opArity} : \mathit{IndexOp} \to \mathit{Sort}^* \times \mathit{Sort}$. (We use the notation A^* to denote the set of lists of elements of some set A.)
3. A collection *PrimType* of primitive types, with a function $\text{tyArity} : \mathit{PrimType} \to \mathit{Sort}^*$, describing the sorts of the arguments of each primitive type.

Example (Geometry: syntax)**.** The two-dimensional geometry system has a sort for each of the geometric groups mentioned in Section 2, so $\mathit{Sort} = \{\mathsf{T}_2, \mathsf{GL}_2, \mathsf{O}_2, \mathsf{GL}_1\}$. We have additive group structure on T_2, multiplicative group structure on GL_1, GL_2, and O_2, injections from O_2 and GL_1 into GL_2, determinant, and absolute value. Thus, $\mathit{IndexOp} = \{0, +, -, 1_G, - \cdot_G -, -^{-1_G}, \iota_O, \iota_1, \det, |\cdot|\}$, where $G \in \{\mathsf{GL}_1, \mathsf{GL}_2, \mathsf{O}_2\}$, and

$$
\begin{array}{ll}
\text{opArity}(0) = ([], \mathsf{T}_2) & \text{opArity}(1_G) = ([], G) \\
\text{opArity}(+) = ([\mathsf{T}_2, \mathsf{T}_2], \mathsf{T}_2) & \text{opArity}(\cdot_G) = ([G, G], G) \\
\text{opArity}(-) = ([\mathsf{T}_2], \mathsf{T}_2) & \text{opArity}(^{-1_G}) = ([G], G) \\
\text{opArity}(\iota_O) = ([\mathsf{O}_2], \mathsf{GL}_2) & \text{opArity}(\iota_1) = ([\mathsf{GL}_1], \mathsf{GL}_2) \\
\text{opArity}(\det) = ([\mathsf{GL}_2], \mathsf{GL}_1) & \text{opArity}(|\cdot|) = ([\mathsf{GL}_1], \mathsf{GL}_1)
\end{array}
$$

The intended interpretations of the top three pairs of operations are group unit, group combination and group negation, respectively. When we discuss equational theories on index expressions in Section 3.1.2 we will impose the (abelian) group laws. For this example, we also have $\mathit{PrimType} = \{\mathtt{vec}, \mathtt{real}\}$, with $\text{tyArity}(\mathtt{vec}) = [\mathsf{GL}_2, \mathsf{T}_2]$ and $\text{tyArity}(\mathtt{real}) = [\mathsf{GL}_1]$. □

We assume a countably infinite collection of index variable names i, i_1, i_2, *etc. Index contexts* $\Delta = i_1{:}s_1, \ldots, i_n{:}s_n$ are lists of variable/sort pairs such that all the variable names are distinct. The rules in Figure 4 generate two judgements: well-sorted index expressions $\Delta \vdash e : s$ and well-indexed types $\Delta \vdash A$ type. Since index variables may appear in types, types are judged to be well-indexed with respect to an index context Δ. The rules for well-sorted index expressions are particularly simple: either an index expression is a variable that appears in the context (rule IVAR), or it is an application of an index operation taken from *IndexOp* to other index expressions (rule IOP). The rules for well-indexed types include the usual ones for the simply-typed λ-calculus with unit, sum and tuple types (rules TYUNIT, TYARR, TYTUPLE and TYSUM). We use `bool` as an abbreviation for `unit` + `unit`. The rule TYPRIM forms, from a primitive type `X` and appropriately sorted index expressions $e_1, \ldots, e_n$, the well-indexed type $\mathtt{X}\langle e_1, \ldots, e_n\rangle$. The rule TYFORALL forms universally quantified types, where the universal quantification ranges over all index expressions of some sort. Existential types, formed using the TYEX rule, allow for abstraction by hiding.

3.1.1 Substitution of Index Expressions

It is convenient to express substitution of index expressions in terms of simultaneous substitutions. Given a pair of index contexts Δ and $\Delta' = i_1{:}s_1, \ldots, i_n{:}s_n$, a (simultaneous) *substitution* $\Delta \vdash \sigma \Rightarrow \Delta'$ is a sequence of expressions $\sigma = (e_1, \ldots, e_n)$ such that $\Delta \vdash e_j : s_j$ for all $1 \le j \le n$. Given a substitution $\Delta \vdash \sigma = (e_1, \ldots, e_n) \Rightarrow \Delta'$ and a variable $i_j{:}s_j$ in Δ', we write $\sigma(i_j)$ for the index expression e_j. We write $\Delta \Rightarrow \Delta'$ for the set of all substitutions σ such that $\Delta \vdash \sigma \Rightarrow \Delta'$. We can think of any sequence of sorts as an index context. In particular, we will make use of substitutions of the form $\Delta \vdash \sigma \Rightarrow \text{tyArity}(\mathtt{X})$, since these are exactly sequences of index arguments suitable for the primitive type `X`. By further abuse of notation, we write $\Delta \Rightarrow \text{tyArity}(\mathtt{X})$ for the set of all substitutions σ such that $\Delta \vdash \sigma \Rightarrow \text{tyArity}(\mathtt{X})$.

For a substitution $\Delta \vdash \sigma \Rightarrow \Delta'$, where $\Delta' = i_1{:}s_1, \ldots, i_n{:}s_n$, and a variable/sort pair $i{:}s$ such that i does not appear in either Δ or Δ', we can form the *lifted* substitution $\Delta, i{:}s \vdash \sigma_{i:s} = (\sigma(i_1), \ldots, \sigma(i_n), i) \Rightarrow \Delta', i{:}s$. Application of a substitution $\Delta \vdash \sigma \Rightarrow \Delta'$ to a well-sorted index expression $\Delta' \vdash e : s$ yields a well-sorted index expression $\Delta \vdash \sigma^* e : s$. The expression $\sigma^* e$ is defined on variables as $\sigma^* i \stackrel{def}{=} \sigma(i)$, and on operation symbols as $\sigma^*(\mathtt{f}(e_1, \ldots, e_n)) \stackrel{def}{=} \mathtt{f}(\sigma^* e_1, \ldots, \sigma^* e_n)$. Given $\Delta' \vdash A$ type, we have $\Delta \vdash \sigma^* A$ type. The key clauses defining $\sigma^* A$ are for

Well-sorted index expressions

$$\frac{i:s \in \Delta}{\Delta \vdash i : s}\text{IVAR} \qquad \frac{\mathtt{f} \in \mathit{IndexOp} \quad \mathrm{opArity}(\mathtt{f}) = ([s_1,\ldots,s_n], s) \quad \{\Delta \vdash e_j : s_j\}_{1\le j\le n}}{\Delta \vdash \mathtt{f}(e_1,\ldots,e_n) : s}\text{IOP}$$

Well-indexed types

$$\frac{\mathtt{X} \in \mathit{PrimType} \quad \mathrm{tyArity}(\mathtt{X}) = [s_1,\ldots,s_n] \quad \{\Delta \vdash e_j : s_j\}_{1\le j\le n}}{\Delta \vdash \mathtt{X}\langle e_1,\ldots,e_n\rangle \ \mathsf{type}}\text{TYPRIM} \qquad \frac{}{\Delta \vdash \mathtt{unit}\ \mathsf{type}}\text{TYUNIT} \qquad \frac{\Delta \vdash A\ \mathsf{type} \quad \Delta \vdash B\ \mathsf{type}}{\Delta \vdash A \to B\ \mathsf{type}}\text{TYARR}$$

$$\frac{\Delta \vdash A\ \mathsf{type} \quad \Delta \vdash B\ \mathsf{type}}{\Delta \vdash A \times B\ \mathsf{type}}\text{TYTUPLE} \qquad \frac{\Delta \vdash A\ \mathsf{type} \quad \Delta \vdash B\ \mathsf{type}}{\Delta \vdash A + B\ \mathsf{type}}\text{TYSUM} \qquad \frac{\Delta, i{:}s \vdash A\ \mathsf{type}}{\Delta \vdash \forall i{:}s.A\ \mathsf{type}}\text{TYFORALL} \qquad \frac{\Delta, i{:}s \vdash A\ \mathsf{type}}{\Delta \vdash \exists i{:}s.A\ \mathsf{type}}\text{TYEX}$$

Figure 4. Index expressions and types

primitive types and the universal and existential quantifiers:

$$\sigma^*(\mathtt{X}\langle e_1,\ldots,e_n\rangle) \stackrel{def}{=} \mathtt{X}\langle \sigma^* e_1,\ldots,\sigma^* e_n\rangle$$
$$\sigma^*(\forall i{:}s.A) \stackrel{def}{=} \forall i{:}s.\sigma^*_{i:s}A \qquad \sigma^*(\exists i{:}s.A) \stackrel{def}{=} \exists i{:}s.\sigma^*_{i:s}A$$

The *identity* substitution $\Delta \vdash \mathrm{id}_\Delta \Rightarrow \Delta$ is $\mathrm{id}_\Delta = (i_1,\ldots,i_n)$ where $\Delta = i_1{:}s_1,\ldots,i_n{:}s_n$. The *composition* of two substitutions $\Delta \vdash \sigma \Rightarrow \Delta'$ and $\Delta' \vdash \sigma' \Rightarrow \Delta''$, where $\sigma' = (e'_1,\ldots,e'_n)$, is defined as $\Delta \vdash \sigma' \circ \sigma \stackrel{def}{=} (\sigma^* e'_1,\ldots,\sigma^* e'_n) \Rightarrow \Delta''$. Given a context $\Delta = i_1{:}s_1,\ldots,i_n{:}s_n$, and a variable/sort pair $i{:}s$ such that i does not appear in Δ, we define the *projection* substitution $\Delta, i{:}s \vdash \pi_{i:s} \Rightarrow \Delta$ as $\pi_{i:s} = (i_1,\ldots,i_n)$.

3.1.2 Index Expression Equality and Type Equality

Much of the power of indexing types by the expressions of an algebraic theory comes from the equations of the theory. For example, in Section 2 the types $\mathtt{vec}\langle B, t_1+t_2\rangle$ and $\mathtt{vec}\langle B, t_2+t_1\rangle$ are considered equal by the type system because $+$ is commutative. In the general framework, the equations between types are derived from a set *IndexAx* of axioms $\Delta \vdash e \stackrel{ax}{\equiv} e' : s$ that are well-sorted, in the sense that both $\Delta \vdash e : s$ and $\Delta \vdash e' : s$ hold.

Given a set *IndexAx* of axioms, we generate the equality judgment between index expressions $\Delta \vdash e \equiv e' : s$ by a set of rules. The following rule lets us use substitution instances of axioms:

$$\frac{(\Delta' \vdash e \stackrel{ax}{\equiv} e' : s) \in \mathit{IndexAx} \qquad \Delta \vdash \sigma \Rightarrow \Delta'}{\Delta \vdash \sigma^* e \equiv \sigma^* e' : s}$$

We also assume the standard congruence, reflexivity, symmetry and transitivity rules for the equality judgment.

Example (Geometry: axioms). In Section 2 we assumed various equational axioms for indexing expressions standing for elements of geometric groups. Assuming the abelian group axioms for translations we can formalise this in our framework:

$$t : \mathsf{T}_2 \vdash t + 0 \stackrel{ax}{\equiv} t : \mathsf{T}_2$$
$$t_1, t_2, t_3 : \mathsf{T}_2 \vdash t_1 + (t_2 + t_3) \stackrel{ax}{\equiv} (t_1 + t_2) + t_3 : \mathsf{T}_2$$
$$t : \mathsf{T}_2 \vdash t + (-t) \stackrel{ax}{\equiv} 0 : \mathsf{T}_2$$
$$t_1, t_2 : \mathsf{T}_2 \vdash t_1 + t_2 \stackrel{ax}{\equiv} t_2 + t_1 : \mathsf{T}_2$$

Similarly, the sort of scale factors GL_1 forms an abelian group under multiplication, and the sorts GL_2 and O_2 form (non-abelian) multiplicative groups, so we assume the appropriate axioms. We also assume that the operations ι_O, ι_1, det and $|\cdot|$ are group homomorphisms, and that expressions of the form $\iota_1(s)$ commute with group multiplication in the sort GL_2. The absolute value of the determinant of an orthgonal transformation is always 1, so we also assume $|\det(\iota_O O)| \stackrel{ax}{\equiv} 1$. Similarly, scaling maps have a determinant expressible in terms of other operations: $\det(\iota_1(s)) \stackrel{ax}{\equiv} s \cdot s$. We also assume the axiom $|s^2| \stackrel{ax}{\equiv} s^2$. □

The equality judgment $\Delta \vdash e \equiv e' : s$ on index expressions generates the equality judgment $\Delta \vdash A \equiv B$ type on types. The basic rule generating equality judgments on types equates applications of primitive types if their arguments are equal:

$$\frac{\{\Delta \vdash e_j \equiv e'_j : s_j\}_{1\le j\le n}}{\Delta \vdash \mathtt{X}\langle e_1,\ldots,e_n\rangle \equiv \mathtt{X}\langle e'_1,\ldots,e'_n\rangle\ \mathsf{type}}$$

The rest of the rules for equality on types ensure that it is a congruence relation and an equivalence relation.

The substitutions $\Delta \vdash \sigma \Rightarrow \Delta'$ and $\Delta \vdash \sigma' \Rightarrow \Delta'$ are defined to be equal, and written $\Delta \vdash \sigma \equiv \sigma' \Rightarrow \Delta'$, if their component expressions are equal in the context Δ: i.e., if $\Delta \vdash e_j \equiv e'_j : s_j$, for all j.

3.2 Well-typed terms

We now present the rules for well-typed terms over the collection of types we defined in Section 3.1.

Well-typed terms are defined with respect to well-indexed typing contexts, which are in turn defined with respect to an index context. Well-indexed typing contexts with respect to an index context Δ are sequences of variable/type pairs with no repeated variable names such that each type is well-indexed with respect to Δ. Formally, well-indexed typing contexts are given by

$$\frac{}{\Delta \vdash \epsilon\ \mathsf{ctxt}} \qquad \frac{\Delta \vdash \Gamma\ \mathsf{ctxt} \quad \Delta \vdash A\ \mathsf{type} \quad x \notin \Gamma}{\Delta \vdash \Gamma, x : A\ \mathsf{ctxt}}$$

Application of substitutions extends to typing contexts by applying the substitution to each type.

Well-typed terms are defined with respect to an index context Δ and a type context $\Delta \vdash \Gamma$ ctxt. The judgment $\Delta; \Gamma \vdash M : A$ is defined in Figure 5. The equational theory on types is incorporated into the type system via the rule TYEQ, which allows a term that has type A to also have any equal type B as well.

For any particular theory we assume that there is a closed typing context Γ_{ops} that describes the types of the primitive operations.

Example (Geometry: operations). For geometry Γ_{ops} would collect together the types of primitive operations as listed in Figure 2 and Figure 3. □

3.3 Index-Erasure Semantics

Having defined the syntax of algebraically indexed types and terms, we turn to their denotational interpretation. We first define an *index-erasure* interpretation of types and terms that interprets every well-indexed type as a set, ignoring the indexing expressions, and which

$$\frac{\Delta \vdash \Gamma\ \mathsf{ctxt} \qquad x : A \in \Gamma}{\Delta;\Gamma \vdash x : A}\ \textsc{Var} \qquad \frac{\Delta;\Gamma \vdash M : A \qquad \Delta \vdash A \equiv B\ \mathsf{type}}{\Delta;\Gamma \vdash M : B}\ \textsc{TyEq} \qquad \frac{\Delta \vdash \Gamma\ \mathsf{ctxt}}{\Delta;\Gamma \vdash * : 1}\ \textsc{Unit}$$

$$\frac{\Delta;\Gamma \vdash M : A \qquad \Delta;\Gamma \vdash N : B}{\Delta;\Gamma \vdash (M,N) : A \times B}\ \textsc{Pair} \qquad \frac{\Delta;\Gamma \vdash M : A \times B}{\Delta;\Gamma \vdash \pi_1 M : A}\ \textsc{Proj1} \qquad \frac{\Delta;\Gamma \vdash M : A \times B}{\Delta;\Gamma \vdash \pi_2 M : B}\ \textsc{Proj2} \qquad \frac{\Delta;\Gamma \vdash M : A}{\Delta;\Gamma \vdash \mathrm{inl}\ M : A + B}\ \textsc{Inl}$$

$$\frac{\Delta;\Gamma \vdash M : B}{\Delta;\Gamma \vdash \mathrm{inr}\ M : A + B}\ \textsc{Inr} \qquad \frac{\Delta;\Gamma \vdash M : A + B \quad \Delta;\Gamma, x : A \vdash N_1 : C \quad \Delta;\Gamma, y : B \vdash N_2 : C}{\Delta;\Gamma \vdash \mathrm{case}\ M\ \mathrm{of}\ \mathrm{inl}\ x.N_1; \mathrm{inr}\ y.N_2 : C}\ \textsc{Case} \qquad \frac{\Delta;\Gamma, x : A \vdash M : B}{\Delta;\Gamma \vdash \lambda x.M : A \to B}\ \textsc{Abs}$$

$$\frac{\Delta;\Gamma \vdash M : A \to B \qquad \Delta;\Gamma \vdash N : A}{\Delta;\Gamma \vdash MN : B}\ \textsc{App} \qquad \frac{\Delta, i{:}s; \pi^*_{i:s}\Gamma \vdash M : A}{\Delta;\Gamma \vdash \Lambda i.M : \forall i{:}s.A}\ \textsc{UnivAbs} \qquad \frac{\Delta;\Gamma \vdash M : \forall i{:}s.A \qquad \Delta \vdash e : s}{\Delta;\Gamma \vdash M[e] : (\mathrm{id}_\Delta, e)^* A}\ \textsc{UnivApp}$$

$$\frac{\Delta;\Gamma \vdash M : (\mathrm{id}_\Delta, e)^* A \qquad \Delta \vdash e : s \qquad \Delta, i{:}s \vdash A\ \mathsf{type}}{\Delta;\Gamma \vdash \langle [e], M\rangle : \exists i{:}s.A}\ \textsc{ExPack} \qquad \frac{\Delta;\Gamma \vdash M : \exists i{:}s.A \quad \Delta, i{:}s; \pi^*_{i:s}\Gamma, x : A \vdash N : \pi^*_{i:s}B}{\Delta;\Gamma \vdash \mathrm{let}\langle [i], x\rangle = M\ \mathrm{in}\ N : B}\ \textsc{ExUnpack}$$

Figure 5. Well-typed terms

interprets open terms as functions that map environments to final values.

Interpretation of Types. The defining feature of the index erasure interpretation is that semantics of a well-indexed type $\mathtt{X}\langle e_1, \ldots, e_n\rangle$ is determined solely by the primitive type $\mathtt{X}$ and not by the index expressions $e_1, \ldots, e_n$. We thus assume each primitive type $\mathtt{X} \in \mathit{PrimType}$ is assigned a set $\lfloor \mathtt{X} \rfloor$ and extend this assignment to well-indexed types by induction on the type structure:

$$\begin{array}{ll}
\lfloor \mathtt{unit} \rfloor \stackrel{def}{=} \{*\} & \lfloor A + B \rfloor \stackrel{def}{=} \lfloor A \rfloor + \lfloor B \rfloor \\
\lfloor A \times B \rfloor \stackrel{def}{=} \lfloor A \rfloor \times \lfloor B \rfloor & \lfloor \mathtt{X}\langle e_1, \ldots, e_n\rangle \rfloor \stackrel{def}{=} \lfloor \mathtt{X} \rfloor \\
\lfloor A \to B \rfloor \stackrel{def}{=} \lfloor A \rfloor \to \lfloor B \rfloor & \lfloor \forall i{:}s.A \rfloor \stackrel{def}{=} \lfloor A \rfloor \\
 & \lfloor \exists i{:}s.A \rfloor \stackrel{def}{=} \lfloor A \rfloor
\end{array}$$

(We will overload the notation $\lfloor \cdot \rfloor$ for all index-erasure interpretations, and reserve notation $[\![\cdot]\!]$ for the index-observing relational semantics defined later.)

The index-erasure interpretation completely ignores index expressions and quantifiers, and type equality is defined as an extension of index equality. Therefore, it is straightforward to prove that equal types have equal denotations when interpreted in the index-erasure semantics, and that substitution of index terms has no effect on the index-erasure interpretation of types:

Lemma 1. *1. If $\Delta \vdash A \equiv B$ type then $\lfloor A \rfloor = \lfloor B \rfloor$; and*
2. If $\Delta' \vdash A$ type and $\Delta \vdash \sigma \Rightarrow \Delta'$, then $\lfloor \sigma^* A \rfloor = \lfloor A \rfloor$.

Interpretation of Terms. We assign an index-erasure semantics to any well-indexed typing context $\Delta \vdash \Gamma$ ctxt by induction: $\lfloor \epsilon \rfloor = \{*\}$ and $\lfloor \Gamma, x : A \rfloor = \lfloor \Gamma \rfloor \times \lfloor A \rfloor$. For a well-typed term $\Delta;\Gamma \vdash M : A$, we define the *erasure interpretation* as a function $\lfloor M \rfloor : \lfloor \Gamma \rfloor \to \lfloor A \rfloor$ that completely ignores the indexing information. In light of Lemma 1, we do this directly on the syntax of well-typed terms, rather than on typing derivations. The definition of $\lfloor M \rfloor$ is completely standard, except for the clauses for universal and existential types:

$$\begin{array}{ll}
\lfloor \Lambda i.\, M \rfloor \eta \stackrel{def}{=} \lfloor M \rfloor \eta & \lfloor M[e] \rfloor \eta \stackrel{def}{=} \lfloor M \rfloor \eta \\
\lfloor \langle [e], M\rangle \rfloor \eta \stackrel{def}{=} \lfloor M \rfloor \eta & \\
\lfloor \mathrm{let}\langle [i], x\rangle = M\ \mathrm{in}\ N \rfloor \eta \stackrel{def}{=} \lfloor N \rfloor (\eta, \lfloor M \rfloor \eta) &
\end{array}$$

For any particular theory we assume that there is an interpretation of the primitive operations $\eta_{ops} \in \lfloor \Gamma_{ops} \rfloor$.

Example (Geometry: interpretation)**.** The two-dimensional geometry instantiation of the general framework uses the assignment $\lfloor \mathtt{vec} \rfloor = \mathbb{R}^2$ and $\lfloor \mathtt{real} \rfloor = \mathbb{R}$. We assume that η_{ops} gives the usual interpretation to scalar and vector operations from Figure 2 and Figure 3. □

Contextual Equivalence. We use our index-erasure semantics to define when a pair of terms are contextually equivalent with respect to syntactically defined contexts, following Hofmann [11]. Given an index context $\Delta = i_1{:}s_1, \ldots, i_n{:}s_n$, we write $\forall\Delta.A$ for $\forall i_1{:}s_1. \ldots \forall i_n{:}s_n.A$, and similarly for $\Lambda\Delta.M$ and $\lambda\Gamma.M$.

Definition 1 (Contextual Equivalence)**.** *Two terms $\Delta;\Gamma_{ops},\Gamma \vdash M_1, M_2 : A$ are* contextually equivalent*, written $\Delta;\Gamma \vdash M_1 \approx M_2 : A$, if for all contexts $\cdot;\Gamma_{ops} \vdash C : (\forall\Delta.\Gamma \to A) \to \mathtt{bool}$, it is the case that $\lfloor C\ (\Lambda\Delta.\lambda\Gamma.M_1) \rfloor\, \eta_{ops} = \lfloor C\ (\Lambda\Delta.\lambda\Gamma.M_2) \rfloor\, \eta_{ops}$.*

Type Isomorphism. We say that well-indexed types $\Delta \vdash A$ type and $\Delta \vdash B$ type are isomorphic, and write $\Delta \vdash A \cong B$, if there exist maps between them that are mutually inverse with respect to contextual equivalence, i.e., if there are terms $\Delta \vdash I : A \to B$ and $\Delta \vdash J : B \to A$ such that $\Delta; x : A \vdash J(I(x)) \approx x : A$ and $\Delta; y : B \vdash I(J(y)) \approx y : B$. That $\cong$ is a congruence with respect to the type formation rules of Figure 4 is straightforward. We can also derive isomorphisms that are independent of the indexing theory, such as $\Delta \vdash A \times B \cong B \times A$, and $\Delta \vdash \forall i{:}s.(A \to B) \cong A \to \forall i{:}s.B$ for i not free in A.

3.4 The Relational Interpretation of Types

The relational semantics of the well-indexed type $\Delta \vdash A$ type is a binary relation on the index-erasure interpretation of A. We write $\mathrm{Rel}(X)$ for the set of binary relations $R \subseteq X \times X$ on the set X.

For the unit, tuple, sum and function types we define the relational interpretation as a standard logical relation. The relational interpretations of primitive types with index arguments and the universally quantified types require an interpretation of index contexts.

An *index environment* ρ assigns to each index variable $i : s$ in the context Δ a value drawn from an interpretation of the sort s that soundly models the equational theory associated with s. We call such an interpretation a *model*: it assigns to each index operation in the equational theory a corresponding operation in the interpretation, so that index expressions can be interpreted by recursion on their structure.

For example, the sort T_2 of translations can be modelled by any abelian group. An obvious candidate here is the additive group over

$\mathbb{R}^2$, which we will use to obtain invariance under translation; but we could use the additive group $\mathbb{Q}$, or even a finite group such as the two-element group $\mathbb{Z}_2$.

Models. A *model* assigns to each sort $s \in \mathit{Sort}$ a carrier set $[\![s]\!]$, and assigns to each operation $\mathtt{f} \in \mathit{IndexOp}$ with $\mathrm{opArity}(\mathtt{f}) = ([s_1, \ldots, s_n], s)$, a function $[\![\mathtt{f}]\!] : [\![s_1]\!] \times \cdots \times [\![s_n]\!] \to [\![s]\!]$.

An index context $\Delta = (i_1{:}s_1, \ldots, i_n{:}s_n)$ is interpreted as cartesian product, i.e., $[\![\Delta]\!] \stackrel{def}{=} [\![s_1]\!] \times \cdots \times [\![s_n]\!]$. For each well-sorted index expression $\Delta \vdash e : s$, we assign a function $[\![e]\!] : [\![\Delta]\!] \to [\![s]\!]$ by recursion on the structure of e:

$$[\![i]\!]\rho \stackrel{def}{=} \rho(i) \qquad [\![\mathtt{f}(e_1, \ldots, e_n)]\!]\rho \stackrel{def}{=} [\![\mathtt{f}]\!]([\![e_1]\!]\rho, \ldots, [\![e_n]\!]\rho)$$

Finally, a model must be sound, that is, for each axiom $\Delta \vdash e \stackrel{ax}{\equiv} e' : s \in \mathit{IndexAx}$, we have $[\![e]\!] = [\![e']\!]$.

Example (Geometry: affine model)**.** We define the model of the indexing theory for the two-dimensional geometry example as follows. Each of the sorts is interpreted just as its semantic counterpart:

$$[\![\mathsf{T}_2]\!] = \mathrm{T}_2 \quad [\![\mathsf{GL}_2]\!] = \mathrm{GL}_2 \quad [\![\mathsf{O}_2]\!] = \mathrm{O}_2 \quad [\![\mathsf{GL}_1]\!] = \mathrm{GL}_1$$

Each of the index operations (e.g., the group structure and determinant) is interpreted by the intended semantic operation, and clearly satisfies the axioms in Example 3.1.2. □

Given $\rho \in [\![\Delta]\!]$ and a substitution $\Delta \vdash \sigma \Rightarrow \Delta'$ with $\sigma = (e_1, \ldots, e_n)$, we can derive the composed index environment $\rho \circ \sigma \in [\![\Delta']\!]$ as $\rho \circ \sigma \stackrel{def}{=} ([\![e_1]\!]\rho, \ldots, [\![e_n]\!]\rho)$.

Relational interpretation of primitive types. Having fixed a model we next choose a relational interpretation of primitive types: for each each primitive type $\mathtt{X}$, its relational interpretation is parameterised by elements from the model: $[\![\mathtt{X}]\!] : [\![\mathrm{tyArity}(\mathtt{X})]\!] \to \mathrm{Rel}(\lfloor \mathtt{X} \rfloor)$.

Example (Geometry: change of basis interpretation)**.** Given the model of geometric groups described above, for the relational interpretation of $\mathtt{vec}\langle B, t\rangle$ and $\mathtt{real}\langle s\rangle$, we use $[\![\mathtt{vec}]\!](B, \vec{t}) = \{(\vec{v}, B\vec{v} + \vec{t}) \mid \vec{v} \in \mathbb{R}^2\}$ and $[\![\mathtt{real}]\!](k) = \{(x, kx) \mid x \in \mathbb{R}\}$. □

Relational interpretation of types. We assign a relational interpretation to all well-indexed types $\Delta \vdash A$ type by induction on their derivations, parameterised by index environments $\rho \in [\![\Delta]\!]$:

$$\begin{array}{rcl}
[\![\mathtt{unit}]\!]\rho & \stackrel{def}{=} & \{(*, *)\} \\
[\![\mathtt{X}\langle e_1, \ldots, e_n\rangle]\!]\rho & \stackrel{def}{=} & [\![\mathtt{X}]\!]([\![e_1]\!]\rho, \ldots, [\![e_n]\!]\rho) \\
[\![A \to B]\!]\rho & \stackrel{def}{=} & [\![A]\!]\rho \mathrel{\widehat{\to}} [\![B]\!]\rho \\
[\![A \times B]\!]\rho & \stackrel{def}{=} & [\![A]\!]\rho \mathrel{\widehat{\times}} [\![B]\!]\rho \\
[\![A + B]\!]\rho & \stackrel{def}{=} & [\![A]\!]\rho \mathrel{\widehat{+}} [\![B]\!]\rho \\
[\![\forall i{:}s.A]\!]\rho & \stackrel{def}{=} & \bigcap\{[\![A]\!](\rho, m) \mid m \in [\![s]\!]\} \\
[\![\exists i{:}s.A]\!]\rho & \stackrel{def}{=} & \bigcup\{[\![A]\!](\rho, m) \mid m \in [\![s]\!]\}
\end{array}$$

In this definition, the relational interpretation of an application of a primitive type $[\![\mathtt{X}\langle e_1, \ldots, e_n\rangle]\!]\rho$ is built from the relational interpretation of the primitive type, $[\![\mathtt{X}]\!]$, and the interpretation of the index terms $e_1, \ldots, e_n$ in the index environment ρ. Universal and existential quantification are interpreted by the set-theoretic intersection and union, respectively, over all extensions of the index environment.

We have also used the following standard constructions on binary relations: if $R \in \mathrm{Rel}(X)$ and $S \in \mathrm{Rel}(Y)$, then $R \mathrel{\widehat{\to}} S \in \mathrm{Rel}(X \to Y)$ is $\{(f_1, f_2) \mid \forall (a_1, a_2) \in R.\ (f_1 a_1, f_2 a_2) \in S\}$, and $R \mathrel{\widehat{\times}} S \in \mathrm{Rel}(X \times Y)$ is $\{((a_1, b_1), (a_2, b_2)) \mid (a_1, a_2) \in R \wedge (b_1, b_2) \in S\}$, and $R \mathrel{\widehat{+}} S \in \mathrm{Rel}(X + Y)$ is $\{(\mathrm{inl}\, x, \mathrm{inl}\, x') \mid (x, x') \in R\} \cup \{(\mathrm{inr}\, y, \mathrm{inr}\, y') \mid (y, y') \in S\}$.

The following lemma states that the relational interpretation of types that we have defined in this section behaves well: the first part of the lemma states that two types that are judgmentally equal are given equal relational interpretations, and the second part states that substitution of index expressions in types can be interpreted by the composition of index environments with substitutions.

Lemma 2. *1. If $\Delta \vdash A \equiv B$ type, then $[\![A]\!] = [\![B]\!]$;*
2. If $\Delta' \vdash A$ type then for all $\Delta \vdash \sigma \Rightarrow \Delta'$ and $\rho \in [\![\Delta]\!]$, $[\![\sigma^* A]\!]\rho = [\![A]\!](\rho \circ \sigma)$.

Note that the equations in both parts of Lemma 2 are well-typed by virtue of the corresponding parts of Lemma 1.

3.5 The Abstraction Theorem and Semantic Equivalence

Our main result (Theorem 1) is that the index-erasure semantics of every well-typed term is related to itself in the relational interpretation of its type: this is the Abstraction Theorem for every instantiation of our general framework.

The Abstraction Theorem. We now state the Abstraction Theorem for well-typed terms. To state and prove this theorem for open terms, we extend the relational interpretation of types to typing contexts. The relational interpretation of contexts is defined by:

$$[\![\epsilon]\!]\rho \stackrel{def}{=} \{(*, *)\} \qquad [\![\Gamma, x : A]\!]\rho \stackrel{def}{=} [\![\Gamma]\!]\rho \mathrel{\widehat{\times}} [\![A]\!]\rho$$

The relational interpretation of contexts inherits from the relational interpretation of types the property of interpreting the application of substitutions as composition:

Lemma 3. *If $\Delta' \vdash \Gamma$ ctxt and $\Delta \vdash \sigma \Rightarrow \Delta'$, then for all $\rho \in [\![\Delta]\!]$, we have $[\![\sigma^* \Gamma]\!]\rho = [\![\Gamma]\!](\rho \circ \sigma)$.*

Given a particular choice of model and relational interpretation of primitive types, we can then prove the following.

Theorem 1 (Abstraction)**.** *If $\Delta; \Gamma \vdash M : A$, then for all $\rho \in [\![\Delta]\!]$ and $\eta_1, \eta_2 \in \lfloor \Gamma \rfloor$ such that $(\eta_1, \eta_2) \in [\![\Gamma]\!]\rho$, we have $(\lfloor M \rfloor \eta_1, \lfloor M \rfloor \eta_2) \in [\![A]\!]\rho$.*

Proof. By induction on the typing derivation, making use of Lemma 2 (part 1) for rule TyEq, Lemma 2 (part 2) for rules UnivApp and ExPack, and Lemma 3 for rules UnivAbs and ExUnpack. The details can be found in the Coq development. □

Semantic equivalence of terms is defined in terms of the relational interpretation. As a consequence of Theorem 1, semantic equivalence is a sound approximation of contextual equivalence.

Let Γ_{ops} be the context of primitive operations and η_{ops} its interpretation Fix a model and relational interpretation of primitive types so that $(\eta_{ops}, \eta_{ops}) \in [\![\Gamma_{ops}]\!]*$.

Definition 2 (Semantic equivalence)**.** *Two terms $\Delta; \Gamma_{ops}, \Gamma \vdash M_1, M_2 : A$ are* semantically equal*, written $\Delta; \Gamma \models M_1 \sim M_2 : A$, if for all $\rho \in [\![\Delta]\!]$, and all $(\eta_1, \eta_2) \in [\![\Gamma]\!]\rho$, we have $(\lfloor M_1 \rfloor (\eta_{ops}, \eta_1), \lfloor M_2 \rfloor (\eta_{ops}, \eta_2)) \in [\![A]\!]\rho$.*

Theorem 2 (Soundness)**.** *If $\Delta; \Gamma \models M_1 \sim M_2 : A$ then $\Delta; \Gamma \vdash M_1 \approx M_2 : A$.*

4. Geometric Consequences of Abstraction

We now instantiate our general framework with the indexing theory of Section 2, and present more general and formally-justified free theorems, type isomorphisms, and non-definability results. For the free theorems and isomorphisms, we use the model and relational interpretation of primitive types described in Section 3.4, namely that of affine transformations for vectors and scaling for scalars.

4.1 Free Theorems

Consider the type of the triangle area function from Example 4:

$$\begin{aligned}\text{area} : \forall B{:}\mathsf{GL}_2, t{:}\mathsf{T}_2.\\ \mathtt{vec}\langle B,t\rangle \to \mathtt{vec}\langle B,t\rangle \to \mathtt{vec}\langle B,t\rangle \to \mathtt{real}\langle|\det B|\rangle\end{aligned}$$

By Theorem 1, we can derive the following free theorem. For all $B \in \mathrm{GL}_2$, $\vec{t} \in \mathrm{T}_2$, and $\vec{x}, \vec{y}, \vec{z} \in \mathbb{R}^2$, we have

$$|\det B|(\lfloor\text{area}\rfloor\ \vec{x}\ \vec{y}\ \vec{z}) = \lfloor\text{area}\rfloor\ (B\vec{x}+\vec{t})\ (B\vec{y}+\vec{t})\ (B\vec{z}+\vec{t})$$

Thus, directly from the type of the area function, we can see that its index-erasure semantics is (a) invariant under translations, and (b) if the inputs are subjected to a linear transformation B, the output varies with the absolute value of the determinant of B.

4.2 Type Isomorphisms

Types indexed by abelian groups induce a particularly rich theory of type isomorphisms; previous work on units of measure [13] relates these to Buckingham's theorem from dimensional analysis. Here we consider the additive abelian groups of translations and the multiplicative abelian group of scalings.

Translations Consider first the group T_2 of translations from Section 2.2 and Section 2.3.

Example 7 (Geometry: wlog)**.** We prove that

$$\Delta, B{:}\mathsf{GL}_2 \vdash (\forall t{:}\mathsf{T}_2.\mathtt{vec}\langle B,t\rangle \to \mathtt{vec}\langle B,t\rangle) \cong \mathtt{vec}\langle B,0\rangle.$$

Let

$$\begin{aligned}X &\stackrel{def}{=} \forall t{:}\mathsf{T}_2.\mathtt{vec}\langle B,t\rangle \to \mathtt{vec}\langle B,t\rangle \quad\text{and}\quad Y \stackrel{def}{=} \mathtt{vec}\langle B,0\rangle\\ I &\stackrel{def}{=} \lambda f{:}X.f\ [0]\ (0\ [B])\\ J &\stackrel{def}{=} \lambda v{:}Y.\Lambda t{:}\mathsf{T}_2.\lambda w{:}\mathtt{vec}\langle B,t\rangle.v + [B,0,t]w\end{aligned}$$

Unfolding definitions gives that $\lfloor I(J(v))\rfloor\,(\eta_{ops}, \vec{v}) = \vec{v} + \vec{0}$ for any $\vec{v} \in \mathbb{R}^2$. Because $\vec{0}$ is the identity for vector addition it follows that $\Delta, B{:}\mathsf{GL}_2; v{:}Y \vdash I(J(v)) \approx v : Y$. To show $\Delta, B{:}\mathsf{GL}_2; f{:}X \vdash J(I(f)) \approx f : X$ we appeal to Theorem 2 and reason using the relational semantics. It suffices to show $\Delta, B{:}\mathsf{GL}_2; f{:}X \models J(I(f)) \sim f : X$; that is, given $\rho \in [\![\Delta, B{:}\mathsf{GL}_2]\!]$, for any f and f' with $(f, f') \in [\![X]\!]\rho$, it is the case that $(\lfloor J(I(f))\rfloor\,(\eta_{ops}, f), f') \in [\![X]\!]\rho$. Expanding the premise, we have

$$\forall \vec{t} \in \mathbb{R}^2, \forall \vec{v} \in \mathbb{R}^2, f'(\rho(B)\vec{v} + \vec{t}) = \rho(B)(f(\vec{v})) + \vec{t} \qquad (3)$$

Expanding the conclusion, we have to show that for any $\vec{t_0} \in \mathbb{R}^2$ and $\vec{v_0} \in \mathbb{R}^2$, it is the case that $f'(\rho(B)\vec{v_0} + \vec{t_0}) = \rho(B)(\vec{v_0} + f(0)) + \vec{t_0}$. By instantiating Equation 3 with $\vec{v} = \vec{0}$ and $\vec{t} = \rho(B)\vec{v_0} + \vec{t_0}$ and applying a little algebra we obtain this result. □

We can generalise this isomorphism substantially, proving that for any quantifier-free type A, the type $\forall t{:}\mathsf{T}_2.\mathtt{vec}\langle B,t\rangle \to A$ is isomorphic to $A[0/t]$, where $A[0/t]$ denotes substitution of the identity translation 0 for index variable t in type A. This isomorphism formalises the equivalence between *coordinate-free* geometry, expressed by a polymorphic type whose first argument can be thought of as the *origin* with respect to which A is specified, and a *coordinate-based* geometry, expressed by the type $A[0/t]$, in which the origin is fixed at $(0, 0)$. It is sometimes said that an affine space is a vector space that has forgotten its origin; we have captured this in a type isomorphism.

Lemma 4. *Suppose that* $\Delta, B{:}\mathsf{GL}_2, t{:}\mathsf{T}_2 \vdash A$ type*,* A *contains no quantifiers and every occurrence of* vec *is of the form* $\mathtt{vec}\langle B,?\rangle$*. Then*

$$\Delta, B{:}\mathsf{GL}_2 \vdash (\forall t{:}\mathsf{T}_2.\mathtt{vec}\langle B,t\rangle \to A) \cong A[0/t]$$

Proof. Let

$$\begin{aligned}X &\stackrel{def}{=} \forall t{:}\mathsf{T}_2.\mathtt{vec}\langle B,t\rangle \to A \quad\text{and}\quad Y \stackrel{def}{=} A[0/t]\\ I &\stackrel{def}{=} \lambda f{:}X.f\ [0]\ (0\ [B])\\ J &\stackrel{def}{=} \lambda y{:}Y.\Lambda t.\lambda v{:}\mathtt{vec}\langle B,t\rangle.\uparrow_A^{t:v}(y)\end{aligned}$$

where terms

$$\begin{aligned}&\Delta, B{:}\mathsf{GL}_2, t{:}\mathsf{T}_2; v{:}\mathtt{vec}\langle B,t\rangle \vdash \uparrow_A^{t:v} : A[0/t] \to A\\ &\Delta, B{:}\mathsf{GL}_2, t{:}\mathsf{T}_2; v{:}\mathtt{vec}\langle B,t\rangle \vdash \downarrow_A^{t:v} : A \to A[0/t]\\ &\Delta, B{:}\mathsf{GL}_2, t{:}\mathsf{T}_2; v{:}\mathtt{vec}\langle B,t\rangle \vdash \uparrow_e^{t:v} : \mathtt{vec}\langle B, e[0/t]\rangle \to \mathtt{vec}\langle B,e\rangle\\ &\Delta, B{:}\mathsf{GL}_2, t{:}\mathsf{T}_2; v{:}\mathtt{vec}\langle B,t\rangle \vdash \downarrow_e^{t:v} : \mathtt{vec}\langle B,e\rangle \to \mathtt{vec}\langle B, e[0/t]\rangle\end{aligned}$$

are defined by induction over the structure of A and e. For brevity we omit types on binders; also note that the omitted cases for $\downarrow_A^{t:v}$ have definition symmetric to $\uparrow_A^{t:v}$:

$$\begin{aligned}&\uparrow_{\mathtt{unit}}^{t:v} = \lambda x.x \qquad \uparrow_{\mathtt{real}\langle e\rangle}^{t:v} = \lambda x.x\\ &\uparrow_{A_1\times A_2}^{t:v} = \lambda p.(\uparrow_{A_1}^{t:v}(\pi_1 p), \uparrow_{A_2}^{t:v}(\pi_2 p))\\ &\uparrow_{A_1+A_2}^{t:v} = \lambda x.\text{case } x \text{ of inl } y.\text{inl}(\uparrow_{A_1}^{t:v} y); \text{inr } y.\text{inr}(\uparrow_{A_2}^{t:v} y)\\ &\uparrow_{A_1\to A_2}^{t:v} = \lambda f.\lambda x.\uparrow_{A_2}^{t:v}(f(\downarrow_{A_1}^{t:v} x))\end{aligned}$$

$$\begin{aligned}\uparrow_{\mathtt{vec}\langle B,e\rangle}^{t:v} &= \lambda x.\downarrow_e^{t:v}(x) & \downarrow_{\mathtt{vec}\langle B,e\rangle}^{t:v} &= \lambda x.\uparrow_e^{t:v}(x)\\ \uparrow_0^{t:v} &= \lambda w.w & \downarrow_0^{t:v} &= \lambda w.w\\ \uparrow_{e_1+e_2}^{t:v} &= \lambda w.\uparrow_{e_1}^{t:v}(\uparrow_{e_2}^{t:v}(w)) & \downarrow_{e_1+e_2}^{t:v} &= \lambda w.\downarrow_{e_1}^{t:v}(\downarrow_{e_2}^{t:v}(w))\\ \uparrow_{-e}^{t:v} &= \lambda w.\downarrow_e^{t:v}(w) & \downarrow_{-e}^{t:v} &= \lambda w.\uparrow_e^{t:v}(w)\\ \uparrow_t^{t:v} &= \lambda w.w + v & \downarrow_t^{t:v} &= \lambda w.w + (\text{negate}\, v)\\ \uparrow_{t'}^{t:v} &= \lambda w.w \quad (t' \neq t) & \downarrow_{t'}^{t:v} &= \lambda w.w \quad (t' \neq t)\end{aligned}$$

Unfolding definitions, we deduce that

$$\lfloor I(J(y))\rfloor\,(\eta_{ops}, y) = \lfloor\uparrow_A^{t:v}\rfloor\,(\eta_{ops}, \vec{0})(y)$$

for any $y \in \lfloor A[0/t]\rfloor$. It's easy to prove by induction on A that $\lfloor\uparrow_A^{t:v}\rfloor\,(\eta_{ops}, \vec{0})(y) = y$, and so $\Delta, B{:}\mathsf{GL}_2; y{:}Y \vdash I(J(y)) \approx y : Y$ follows.

For the opposite direction of the isomorphism, we appeal to Theorem 2 and so it suffices to show $\Delta, B{:}\mathsf{GL}_2; f{:}X \models J(I(f)) \sim f : X$; that is, given $\rho \in [\![\Delta, B{:}\mathsf{GL}_2]\!]$, for any f and f' with $(f, f') \in [\![X]\!]\rho$, it is the case that $(\lfloor J(I(f))\rfloor\,(\eta_{ops}, f), f') \in [\![X]\!]\rho$. Expanding the premise, we have

$$\forall \vec{t} \in \mathbb{R}^2, \forall \vec{v} \in \mathbb{R}^2, (f(\vec{v}), f'(\rho(B)\vec{v} + \vec{t})) \in [\![A]\!](\rho, \vec{t}) \qquad (4)$$

Expanding the conclusion, we have to show for any $\vec{t_0} \in \mathbb{R}^2$ and $\vec{v_0} \in \mathbb{R}^2$, it is the case that $(\lfloor J(I(f))\rfloor\,(\eta_{ops}, f)(\vec{v_0}), f'(\rho(B)\vec{v_0} + \vec{t_0})) \in [\![A]\!](\rho, \vec{t_0})$. Unfolding the definitions of J and I and expanding the erasure semantics, this amounts to showing that

$$\forall \vec{t_0}, \vec{v_0} \in \mathbb{R}^2, (\lfloor\uparrow_A^{t:v}\rfloor\,(\eta_{ops}, \vec{v_0})(f\,\vec{0}), f'(\rho(B)\vec{v_0} + \vec{t_0})) \in [\![A]\!](\rho, \vec{t_0}).$$

In order to make progress we prove first by induction on A that for any $\vec{v}$ and $\vec{w}$, the meaning of $\uparrow_A^{t:v}$ can be characterized by

$$\begin{aligned}&(\lfloor\uparrow_A^{t:v}\rfloor\,(\eta_{ops}, \vec{v})(x), y) \in [\![A]\!](\rho, \vec{w})\\ &\qquad\Leftrightarrow (x, y) \in [\![A]\!](\rho, \rho(B)\vec{v} + \vec{w})\end{aligned}$$

Thus our goal becomes

$$\forall \vec{t_0}, \vec{v_0} \in \mathbb{R}^2, (f\,\vec{0}, f'(\rho(B)\vec{v_0} + \vec{t_0})) \in [\![A]\!](\rho, \rho(B)\vec{v_0} + \vec{t_0}).$$

This is obtained immediately by instantiating Equation 4 with $\vec{v} = \vec{0}$ and $\vec{t} = \rho(B)\vec{v_0} + \vec{t_0}$. □

Example 2 and Example 7 are special cases of this isomorphism. Another instance is the type of vector addition:

$$\begin{aligned}
&\forall B{:}\mathsf{GL}_2, t_1, t_2{:}\mathsf{T}_2.\mathtt{vec}\langle B,t_1\rangle \to \mathtt{vec}\langle B,t_2\rangle \to \mathtt{vec}\langle B,t_1{+}t_2\rangle \\
\cong\quad &\forall B{:}\mathsf{GL}_2, t_1{:}\mathsf{T}_2.\mathtt{vec}\langle B,t_1\rangle \to \mathtt{vec}\langle B,t_1\rangle \quad \text{(by Lemma 4)} \\
&\cong\quad \forall B{:}\mathsf{GL}_2.\mathtt{vec}\langle B,0\rangle \quad \text{(by Lemma 4)} \\
&\cong\quad \mathtt{unit} \quad \text{(by Theorem 1)}
\end{aligned}$$

In other words, the vector addition operation is the only inhabitant of its type!

Scalings For the group GL_1 of scalings we can treat a real-valued argument to a function as a unit of measure with which to scale the result. Although the argument might be zero, and this cannot be used for scaling, we still can obtain the following slightly more complicated isomorphism:

$$\forall s{:}\mathsf{GL}_1.\mathtt{real}\langle s\rangle \to A \quad\cong\quad A[1/s] \times \forall s{:}\mathsf{GL}_1.A \qquad (5)$$

The type of areaCircle from the introduction is one instance:

$$\begin{aligned}
&\forall s{:}\mathsf{GL}_1.\mathtt{real}\langle s\rangle \to \mathtt{real}\langle s^2\rangle \\
\cong\quad &\mathtt{real}\langle 1\rangle \times (\forall s{:}\mathsf{GL}_1.\mathtt{real}\langle s^2\rangle) \quad \text{(by Equation 5)} \\
\cong\quad &\mathtt{real}\langle 1\rangle \times \mathtt{unit} \quad \text{(by Theorem 1)} \\
\cong\quad &\mathtt{real}\langle 1\rangle \quad \text{(trivially)}
\end{aligned}$$

4.3 Non-definability

To prove non-definability results, the model and relational interpretation used in the previous two sections are not sufficient. This is true even for simple scalars with invariance under scaling. Consider the type $\forall s{:}\mathsf{GL}_1.\mathtt{real}\langle s^2\rangle \to \mathtt{real}\langle s\rangle$. There are many functions $f : \mathbb{R} \to \mathbb{R}$ that satisfy its relational interpretation, i.e., for which $f(k^2 \cdot x) = k \cdot f(x)$ for any $k \neq 0$. Consider

$$f(x) = \begin{cases} \sqrt{x} & \text{if } x > 0 \\ 0 & \text{otherwise} \end{cases}$$

for instance. Yet this type contains only the constant zero function, a fact that we can prove using a surprisingly simple model!

Example 8. If $\Gamma_{ops} \vdash f : \forall s{:}\mathsf{GL}_1.\ \mathtt{real}\langle s^2\rangle \to \mathtt{real}\langle s\rangle$ then $\lfloor f\rfloor = \lambda x.0$. To show this, take the model

$$\begin{aligned}
&[\![\mathsf{GL}_1]\!] \stackrel{def}{=} \{0,1\} \qquad [\![1]\!] \stackrel{def}{=} 0 \qquad [\![^{-1}]\!] \stackrel{def}{=} \mathrm{id} \\
&[\![\cdot]\!] \stackrel{def}{=} \lambda(x,y).(x+y) \bmod 2 \qquad [\![|-|]\!] \stackrel{def}{=} \mathrm{id},
\end{aligned}$$

in other words, the additive abelian group $(\mathbb{Z}_2, +)$. Now set

$$[\![\mathtt{real}]\!](z) = \begin{cases} \Delta_{\mathbb{R}} & \text{if } z = 0 \\ \{(0,0)\} & \text{if } z = 1 \end{cases}$$

It's easy to check that $(\eta_{ops}, \eta_{ops}) \in [\![\Gamma_{ops}]\!]*$.

We think of z as tracking whether or not exponents on scale parameters are divisible by 2: all the primitive operations in Figure 2 produce results with even exponents if their inputs have even exponents. But the type under consideration here does not.

By Theorem 1 we have that $(f,f) \in [\![\forall s{:}\mathsf{GL}_1.\ \mathtt{real}\langle s^2\rangle \to \mathtt{real}\langle s\rangle]\!]*$. Expanding the definitions, this means that for any $z \in [\![\mathsf{GL}_1]\!]$ and any $(x,y) \in [\![\mathtt{real}]\!]((z+z) \bmod 2)$, it is the case that $(f(x), f(y)) \in [\![\mathtt{real}]\!](z)$. Set $z = 1$. Then we have that if $x = y$ then $f(x) = f(y) = 0$. □

The particular model and relational interpretation used here is devised only to rule out the 'square root type' (it does not rule out a 'cube root type', for instance); nevertheless, it is possible to devise craftier interpretations that serve up both invariance and more general non-definability results. For example, we can set

$$\begin{aligned}
&[\![\mathsf{GL}_1]\!] \stackrel{def}{=} \mathrm{GL}_1 \times \mathbb{Q} \qquad [\![\cdot]\!] \stackrel{def}{=} (\cdot, +) \qquad [\![1]\!] \stackrel{def}{=} (1,0) \\
&[\![^{-1}]\!] \stackrel{def}{=} (^{-1}, -) \qquad [\![|\cdot|]\!] \stackrel{def}{=} (|\cdot|, \mathrm{id})
\end{aligned}$$

and

$$[\![\mathtt{real}]\!](k,q) = \begin{cases} \{(x, kx) \mid x \in \mathbb{R}\} & \text{if } q \in \mathbb{Z} \\ \{(0,0)\} & \text{otherwise} \end{cases}$$

Example 9. Suppose we extend the operations Γ_{ops} of Figure 2 and corresponding η_{ops} with a square root operation typed by

$$\mathrm{sqrt} : \forall s{:}\mathsf{GL}_1.\mathtt{real}\langle s^2\rangle \to \mathtt{real}\langle s\rangle.$$

If $\Gamma_{ops} \vdash f : \forall s{:}\mathsf{GL}_1.\ \mathtt{real}\langle s^3\rangle \to \mathtt{real}\langle s\rangle$ then $\lfloor f\rfloor = \lambda x.0$. To show this, take the model

$$[\![\mathsf{GL}_1]\!] \stackrel{def}{=} \mathbb{Q} \quad [\![\cdot]\!] \stackrel{def}{=} + \quad [\![1]\!] \stackrel{def}{=} 0 \quad [\![^{-1}]\!] \stackrel{def}{=} - \quad [\![|\cdot|]\!] \stackrel{def}{=} \mathrm{id},$$

in other words, the additive abelian group $(\mathbb{Q}, +)$. Now set

$$[\![\mathtt{real}]\!](q) = \begin{cases} \Delta_{\mathbb{R}} & \text{if } \exists n, 2^n q \in \mathbb{Z} \\ \{(0,0)\} & \text{otherwise} \end{cases}$$

It's easy to check that $(\eta_{ops}, \eta_{ops}) \in [\![\Gamma_{ops}]\!]*$.

Here, q is tracking the exponents on scale parameters, with $[\![\mathtt{real}]\!](q)$ relating only zero to itself unless the denominator of q is a power of two (a so-called *dyadic* number). Applying the Abstraction Theorem and expanding, we have that for any $q \in \mathbb{Q}$ and any $(x,y) \in [\![\mathtt{real}]\!](3q)$, it is the case that $(f(x), f(y)) \in [\![\mathtt{real}]\!](q)$. Set $q = \frac{1}{3}$. Then we have that if $x = y$ then $f(x) = f(y) = 0$. □

5. Non-definability for the General Framework

The non-definability results in the previous section required the use of specially crafted models and relational interpretations. It is reasonable to ask whether or not there is a general method for constructing suitable models and relational interpretations to prove non-definability results. In this section, we show that this is possible for a large class of first-order types in any instance of our general framework.

In Example 8, we showed that the type $\forall s{:}\mathsf{GL}_1.\ \mathtt{real}\langle s^2\rangle \to \mathtt{real}\langle s\rangle$ only has trivial inhabitants. Intuitively, this is because the index of the result type (s) cannot be obtained from the index of the input type (s^2) using the abelian group operations and axioms. This observation can be used to give a sufficient condition for non-inhabitation for types of the form:

$$\forall i_1{:}s_1, \ldots, i_m{:}s_m.\ \mathtt{X}\langle e_1\rangle \to \ldots \to \mathtt{X}\langle e_n\rangle \to \mathtt{X}\langle e\rangle$$

Roughly speaking, if this type is inhabited, then it must be the case that the index expression e can be generated from the set of index expressions $\{e_1, ..., e_n\}$.

We assume that we are working with an instantiation of the general framework from Section 3 with a closed typing context Γ_{ops} describing the types of the primitive operations and a chosen index-erasure semantics. We will use a special relational interpretation built from the syntax of the indexing expressions to prove our general non-definability result. For simplicity, we assume that there is only one primitive type, $\mathtt{X}$, but the technique we describe here extends to the general case. We also assume that $\lfloor\mathtt{X}\rfloor$ is non-empty.

To state our general non-definability condition, we need to define the set of index expressions generated by some finite set of index expressions. Given a set S of index expressions that are all well-indexed in some index context Δ, we define $\mathrm{Gen}_0(S)$ to be the set of expressions that are built from the elements of S and the primitive index operations. To account for the equations between indexing terms, we close under index expression equivalence to get the set $\mathrm{Gen}(S) = \{e \mid \exists s.\ \exists e' \in \mathrm{Gen}_0(S).\ \Delta \vdash e \equiv e' : s\}$. Now a type is *well-generated* if it is closed and of the form:

$$\forall i_1{:}s_1, \ldots, i_m{:}s_m.\ \mathtt{X}\langle e_1\rangle \to \ldots \to \mathtt{X}\langle e_n\rangle \to \mathtt{X}\langle e\rangle$$

and $e \in \mathrm{Gen}(\{e_1, ..., e_n\})$.

Theorem 3. *Assume that the members of Γ_{ops} are all of well-generated types. If there exists an M with typing:*

$$\Gamma_{ops} \vdash M : \forall i_1{:}s_1, ..., i_m{:}s_m.\ \mathtt{X}\langle e_1\rangle \to ... \to \mathtt{X}\langle e_n\rangle \to \mathtt{X}\langle e\rangle$$

then $e \in \mathrm{Gen}(\{e_1, ..., e_n\})$.

This theorem is usually applied in the contrapositive: if $e \notin \mathrm{Gen}(\{e_1, ..., e_n\})$ then no such M can exist. Note that if Γ_{ops} contains operations corresponding to each of the index-level operations (as, for example, in Figure 2), then this theorem yields a characterisation of definable terms, since the construction of e from $e_1, ..., e_n$ can be replicated at the term level.

Proof. Let $\Delta = i_1{:}s_1, ..., i_m{:}s_m$ be the index context constructed from the universally quantified type variables in the type of M. To interpret the index expressions, we use the free model over the variables in Δ constructed from the syntax. This model assigns to each sort s the set $\{e \mid \Delta \vdash e : s\}/{\equiv}$ of index expressions quotiented by index expression equality. Index operations are interpreted by the corresponding syntactic operation on equivalence classes: $[\![\mathtt{f}]\!]([e_1], ..., [e_n]) = [\mathtt{f}(e_1, ..., e_n)]$.

We take the relational interpretation of the primitive type X as:

$$[\![\mathtt{X}]\!](e) = \{(x, x) \mid x \in \lfloor \mathtt{X} \rfloor \wedge e \in \mathrm{Gen}(\{e_1, ..., e_n\})\}$$

It is straightforward to check that for any index-erasure interpretation of the primitive operations $\eta_{ops} \in \Gamma_{ops}$, we have $(\eta_{ops}, \eta_{ops}) \in [\![\Gamma_{ops}]\!]*$ because all members of Γ_{ops} have well-generated types. Hence, by Theorem 1, we know that for all terms (i.e., elements of the free model over Δ) $e'_1{:}s_1, ..., e'_m{:}s_m$:

$$\begin{array}{l}\forall (x_1, x'_1) \in [\![\mathtt{X}\langle e_1\rangle]\!](e'_1, ..., e'_m), ..., \\ \quad (x_n, x'_n) \in [\![\mathtt{X}\langle e_n\rangle]\!](e'_1, ..., e'_m). \\ \quad (\lfloor M \rfloor\ \eta_{ops}\ x_1 \ldots x_n, \lfloor M \rfloor\ \eta_{ops}\ x'_1 \ldots x'_n) \in [\![\mathtt{X}\langle e\rangle]\!](e'_1, ..., e'_m)\end{array}$$

By setting $e'_j = i_j$, and using an arbitrary element $x \in \lfloor \mathtt{X} \rfloor$ (which we have assumed non-empty), we have, for all k, $(x, x) \in [\![\mathtt{X}\langle e_k\rangle]\!](i_1, ..., i_m)$ since each e_k is a member of the set we are using to generate terms. Now $(\lfloor M \rfloor\ \eta_{ops}\ x...x, \lfloor M \rfloor\ \eta_{ops}\ x...x) \in [\![\mathtt{X}]\!](e)$ and so $e \in \mathrm{Gen}(\{e_1, ..., e_n\})$. □

Application to Example 3 Theorem 3 can be directly applied to show that the type $\forall t{:}\mathsf{T}_2.\ \mathtt{vec}\langle t + t\rangle \to \mathtt{vec}\langle t\rangle$ has no inhabitants. The free model over the single index variable t is (isomorphic to) the integers, and the sub-model generated by the index expression $t + t$ corresponds to the even integers. The result now follows simply because 1 (i.e., the interpretation of t) is not an even number.

Abelian Group Indexed Types Kennedy [13] has given a general characterisation of definability at first-order in the case of abelian group indexing in terms of integer solutions to a set of linear equations. Specialising Theorem 3 to the case of abelian group indexing yields Kennedy's characterisation.

Polymorphic Constants Theorem 3 does not apply in the case when we have polymorphic constants. This is the case with the polymorphic $0 : \forall s{:}\mathsf{GL}_1.\ \mathtt{real}\langle s\rangle$ in Figure 2. Theorem 3 does not apply because the index expression s is not generated by the empty set: 0's type is not well-generated. Nevertheless, it is easy to adapt the proof of Theorem 3 to handle a polymorphic constant like 0 by setting the relational interpretation of X to be:

$$[\![X]\!](e) = \{(x, x) \mid x \in \lfloor \mathtt{X} \rfloor \wedge (x = 0 \vee e \in \mathrm{Gen}(\{e_1, ..., e_n\}))\}$$

The conclusion of the theorem now states that either we have $e \in \mathrm{Gen}(\{e_1, ..., e_n\})$ *or* $\lfloor M \rfloor$ is the constant 0 function. This extended theorem can now be used to give an alternative proof for Example 8. As this example illustrates, there may be many different models that can be used to prove a non-definability result.

Adding Index Operations Theorem 3 also does not directly apply in the case of Example 9, again because assumption that the types of the primitive operations are all well-generated is not satisfied. In this case, the assumed square root operation has type $\forall s{:}\mathsf{GL}_1.\ \mathtt{real}\langle s^2\rangle \to \mathtt{real}\langle s\rangle$, and as we observed at the start of this section, s is not in the set generated by s^2. However, to enable the application of the theorem, we can assume an additional index operation $-^{1/2}$, acting like square root at the index level. Now the free model produced in the proof of the theorem is isomorphic to the dyadic numbers with addition and halving, and the generated sub-model consists of the dyadic rationals of the form $\frac{3k}{2^n}$. Again there is a diversity of models that can be used to prove a single non-definability result.

6. Logical Information Flow

We now apply our general framework to types that are indexed by logical propositions. By including a primitive type that represents logical truth, we can recover–through a construction due to Tse and Zdancewic [21]–strong information flow properties of programs. As a result of our general framework being parameterised by the choice of equational theory, we can alter the logic that we use for reasoning about type equality, and hence alter the information flow properties of the system.

We first recall the concept of information flow. A function $f : A \times B \to C$ is said to not allow information to flow from its second argument to the output if for all $b, b' \in B$ and all $a \in A$, $f(a, b) = f(a, b')$. If we think of the B argument as representing high-security information, then we have stated that f does not allow the high-security input to flow to the low security output. Information flow can be seen as a kind of invariance property of programs, and so our relational interpretation of types is well tailored to proving this kind of property.

As described by Sabelfeld and Sands [19], information flow can be captured semantically by partial equivalence relations (PERs). Abadi, Banerjee, Heintze and Riecke [1] built a *Core Calculus for Dependency*, using a type system based around a security level indexed monad $T_l A$, using PERs to prove the information flow properties. Tse and Zdancewic [21] translated Abadi *et al.*'s calculus into System F[1] translating the monadic type $T_l A$ to $\alpha_l \to A$ for some free type variable α_l, and using Reynolds' Abstraction Theorem to prove information flow properties. For example, if the type variable α_H represents high-level information, then the non-interference property of the function f could be expressed by the System F type $A \to (\alpha_H \to B) \to C$. If a program cannot generate a value of type α_H, then it cannot access the value of B, and hence is insensitive to the actual value. Relationships between security levels are captured by postulating functions $\alpha_{l_1} \to \alpha_{l_2}$ whenever l_1 is a lower security level than l_2.

Using algebraic indexing, we refine Tse and Zdancewic's translation by replacing each type variable α_l with a primitive type $\mathtt{T}\langle\phi_l\rangle$ of representations of the truth of a logical proposition ϕ_l that stands for the security level l. The relationships between security levels are now replaced by logical entailment, so we only have functions of type $\mathtt{T}\langle\phi_{l_1}\rangle \to \mathtt{T}\langle\phi_{l_2}\rangle$ when ϕ_{l_1} entails ϕ_{l_2}. We instantiate our general relational framework to interpret $\mathtt{T}\langle\phi\rangle$ as the identity rela-

[1] Tse and Zdancewic's translation did not satisfy all the properties that they claimed, as pointed out by Shikuma and Igarashi [20]. However, this problem is not relevant to our discussion here.

tion if ϕ is true and the empty relation if ϕ is false. We shall see that this recovers the information flow properties of Abadi *et al.* and Tse and Zdancewic.

Instantiation of the General Framework We assume a single indexing sort prop and assume the operations and equations of boolean algebra. Thus we have constants $\top$, $\bot$ and binary operators $\wedge$, $\vee$ with the axioms of a bounded lattice, and a unary complementation operator $\neg$. We will use ϕ, ψ to stand for index expressions of sort prop. We use an equational presentation of boolean algebras to fit with our general framework, but note that we can define an order on index expressions as $\phi \leq \psi$ when $\phi = \phi \wedge \psi$.

We have a single primitive type T, with $\text{tyArity}(\mathtt{T}) = [\mathsf{prop}]$ and index-erasure semantics $\lfloor \mathtt{X} \rfloor = \{*\}$. Thus values of type $\mathtt{T}\langle\phi\rangle$ have no run-time content; their only meaning is given by the relational semantics. For the model of the indexing theory, we take an arbitrary boolean algebra L. The relational interpretation of the truth representation type is $[\![\mathtt{T}]\!](x) = \{(*,*) \mid x = \top\}$, where $\top$ is the top element of the boolean algebra L. The primitive operations Γ_{Log} reflect logical consequence:

$$\text{truth} : \mathtt{T}\langle\top\rangle \qquad \text{and} : \forall p, q{:}\mathsf{prop}.\ \mathtt{T}\langle p\rangle \to \mathtt{T}\langle q\rangle \to \mathtt{T}\langle p \wedge q\rangle$$
$$\text{up} : \forall p, q{:}\mathsf{prop}.\ \mathtt{T}\langle p \wedge q\rangle \to \mathtt{T}\langle p\rangle$$

The combination of the TYEQ rule and the primitive up operation allow for logical entailment to be reflected in programs: if we have $\phi \leq \psi$ and $M : \mathtt{T}\langle\phi\rangle$ then up $M : \mathtt{T}\langle\psi\rangle$. Each of the primitive operations has a trivial interpretation, due to the index-erasure interpretation of $\mathtt{T}\langle\phi\rangle$ as a one-element set, giving an environment $\eta_{Log} \in \lfloor\Gamma\rfloor$. Less trivially, we have this lemma:

Lemma 5. $(\eta_{Log}, \eta_{Log}) \in [\![\Gamma_{Log}]\!]*$.

Information Flow We think of logical expressions as "composite principals". That is, propositional variables representing atomic principals that are combined using the logical connectives. We interpret "truth" for principals as stating that a principal is true when satisfied with the current state of affairs. Thus a relationship $\phi \leq \psi$ indicates that satisfaction of the composite principal ϕ implies satisfaction of the composite principal ψ. In terms of security levels, the ordering is reversed: if a high security principal is satisfied, then all of their subordinates must also be satisfied.

We adapt Tse and Zdancewic's translation of Abadi *et al.*'s monadic type to our setting. We define a type abbreviation $T_\phi A = \mathtt{T}\langle\phi\rangle \to A$, where A is a type and ϕ is an expression of sort prop. For every ϕ, we can endow the types $T_\phi-$ with the structure of a monad. This is due to the fact that it is an instance of the "environment" (or "reader") monad [12]. We read the types $T_\phi A$ as data of type A "protected" by the principal ϕ.

As a consequence of the relational interpretation given above, it follows that if we have an index expression ϕ that is interpreted as some value other than $\top$ in an index environment ρ, then for all $x, x' \in \lfloor T_\phi\mathtt{bool}\rfloor$, we have $(x, x') \in [\![T_\phi\mathtt{bool}]\!]\rho$. Thus if a principal is dissatisfied (i.e., $\phi \neq \top$), then data protected by this principal is indistinguishable from any other data, and a program cannot get access to the exact value. From this observation, and Theorem 1, we obtain the following information flow result:

Theorem 4. *Let ϕ and ψ be index expressions of sort* prop *in some indexing context Δ, such that $\psi \not\leq \phi$. Then for all terms:*

$$\Delta; \Gamma_{Log}, \Gamma \vdash M : T_\phi\mathtt{bool} \to T_\psi\mathtt{bool}$$

and all terms N_1, N_2 of type $T_\phi\mathtt{bool}$, $M\ N_1 \overset{ctx}{\approx} M\ N_2$. Thus there is no information flow from M's input to its output.

Note that if $\psi \leq \phi$, then it is always possible to write the identity function with this type, using the up operation. The theorem also holds if we move to logics other than boolean logic. For example, if our equational theory models intuitionistic logic by taking the axioms of Heyting algebras, then the same non-flow property for programs of type $T_{p\vee\neg p}\mathtt{bool} \to T_\top\mathtt{bool}$ holds, due to the lack of excluded middle. If we take linear logic, then programs of type $T_{p\otimes p}\mathtt{bool} \to T_p\mathtt{bool}$ have no information flow from their input, due to non-provability of $p \vdash p \otimes p$.

7. Distance-Indexed Types

The type system for geometry we discussed in Section 2 and Section 4 made use of a relational interpretation of primitive types that relates pairs of elements by some transformation if applying the transformation to the first element of a pair yields the second. Thus, the free theorems that we derived directly take the form of "invariance" properties, where some equation holds between two terms. In this section, we examine another instantiation of our general framework that relates values when they are within a certain distance. The free theorems that we obtain inform us of the effect that programs have on the distances between values. For example, a program M of type:

$$\forall\epsilon_1, \epsilon_2{:}\mathsf{R}^{>0}.\ \mathtt{real}\langle\epsilon_1\rangle \to \mathtt{real}\langle\epsilon_2\rangle \to \mathtt{real}\langle\epsilon_1 + \epsilon_2\rangle$$

must satisfy the property that for all $\epsilon_1, \epsilon_2 > 0$ and $x, x', y, y' \in \mathbb{R}$:

$$\text{if } |x - x'| < \epsilon_1 \text{ and } |y - y'| < \epsilon_2 \text{ then}$$
$$|\lfloor M\rfloor\ \eta_{Met}\ x\ y - \lfloor M\rfloor\ \eta_{Met}\ x'\ y'| < \epsilon_1 + \epsilon_2$$

Instantiation of the General Framework We assume a single indexing sort $\mathsf{R}^{>0}$ to represent positive, non-zero real numbers. For the index operations, we assume the operations min, max, + and multiplication by constant reals. There is a single primitive type $\mathtt{real}$ with $\text{tyArity}(\mathtt{real}) = [\mathsf{R}^{>0}]$. The primitive operations Γ_{Met} are as follows, where c stands for arbitrary real-valued constants:

$$\begin{aligned}
\underline{c} &: \forall\epsilon{:}\mathsf{R}^{>0}.\ \mathtt{real}\langle\epsilon\rangle \\
(+) &: \forall\epsilon_1, \epsilon_2{:}\mathsf{R}^{>0}.\ \mathtt{real}\langle\epsilon_1\rangle \to \mathtt{real}\langle\epsilon_2\rangle \to \mathtt{real}\langle\epsilon_1 + \epsilon_2\rangle \\
(-) &: \forall\epsilon_1, \epsilon_2{:}\mathsf{R}^{>0}.\ \mathtt{real}\langle\epsilon_1\rangle \to \mathtt{real}\langle\epsilon_2\rangle \to \mathtt{real}\langle\epsilon_1 + \epsilon_2\rangle \\
\underline{c}* &: \forall\epsilon{:}\mathsf{R}^{>0}.\ \mathtt{real}\langle\epsilon\rangle \to \mathtt{real}\langle c\epsilon\rangle \\
\text{up} &: \forall\epsilon_1, \epsilon_2{:}\mathsf{R}^{>0}.\ \mathtt{real}\langle\epsilon_1\rangle \to \mathtt{real}\langle\max(\epsilon_1, \epsilon_2)\rangle
\end{aligned}$$

We assume that the index-erasure semantics of the $\mathtt{real}$ type is just the set $\mathbb{R}$, so all except the last operation have straightforward interpretations. The up operation is interpreted just as the identity function. The index-erasure interpretations of the primitive operations are collected together into an environment $\eta_{Met} \in \lfloor\Gamma_{Met}\rfloor$.

For the relational intepretation we construct a model of the indexing theory by interpreting $\mathsf{R}^{>0}$ with strictly positive real numbers. We set $[\![\mathtt{real}]\!](\epsilon) = \{(x, x') \mid |x - x'| < \epsilon\}$.

Lemma 6. $(\eta_{Met}, \eta_{Met}) \in [\![\Gamma_{Met}]\!]*$.

Uniform continuity Using existential types, the standard ϵ-δ definition of *uniform* continuity can be expressed as $\forall\epsilon{:}\mathsf{R}^{>0}.\ \exists\delta{:}\mathsf{R}^{>0}.\ \mathtt{real}\langle\delta\rangle \to \mathtt{real}\langle\epsilon\rangle$. For any program M of this type, Theorem 1 gives a free theorem that is exactly uniform continuity:

$$\forall\epsilon{>}0.\exists\delta{>}0.\forall x, x'.|x{-}x'|{<}\delta \Rightarrow |\lfloor M\rfloor\ \eta_{Met}\ x{-}\lfloor M\rfloor\ \eta_{Met}\ x'|{<}\epsilon$$

This definition differs from the ϵ-δ definition of (regular) continuity by the order of quantification: there, $\forall x$ comes before $\exists\delta$, so the distance δ may depend on x. We suspect that to express standard continuity as a type would require some form of type dependency. Chaudhuri, Gulwani and Lublinerman [8] have given a program logic based approach to verifying the continuity of programs.

Function Sensitivity A type system with a relational interpretation that tracks distances between values has been investigated by Reed and Pierce [17] in the setting of differential privacy. Their system uses a linear type discipline to ensure that all programs are c-sensitive (i.e., the distance between the outputs is no greater than c times the distance between the inputs, for some constant c). We can express their central concept of c-sensitivity (for functions on the reals) as an algebraically indexed type: $\forall \epsilon{:}\mathsf{R}^{>0}.\ \mathtt{real}\langle\epsilon\rangle \rightarrow \mathtt{real}\langle\frac{1}{c}\epsilon\rangle$. Investigating the precise connection between their system and ours is left to future work.

8. Discussion

We presented a general framework for algebraically indexed types and instantiated it to yield novel type systems for geometry, logical information flow and distance-indexed types. Our framework further demonstrates the power of relational reasoning about typed programs. From Theorem 1, we derived interesting free theorems, type isomorphisms and non-definability results. We conclude with some observations and suggestions for further work.

Further Applications and Extensions We have covered several applications of algebraically indexed types in this paper, but there are undoubtedly many more. Geometry for dimensions greater than two is an obvious candidate, as are systems that are invariant under different geometric groups (e.g., the Poincaré group for relativity). Mathematical Physics is particularly rich in theories that have some notion of invariance, and it will be exciting to pin down the precise connections between these and type systems for which an Abstraction Theorem holds. Cardelli and Gardner describe a process calculus that builds in 3D affine geometry [6], proving that process behaviour is invariant under affine transformations. Distinguishing points from vectors provides the appropriate abstraction barrier, and the geometric group is determined by inspecting term syntax. It would be interesting to recast their language in terms of our indexed types to obtain purely type-based invariance theorems.

Geometric theorem proving is another application. Harrison [10] comments on the pervasiveness of invariance properties in this area. Programs in our framework automatically satisfy invariance properties, removing the need for *ad hoc* proofs of these facts.

Type and effect analyses use types indexed by effect annotations with algebraic structure (e.g., sets of read/write effect labels with an idempotent monoid structure). Benton *et al.* have used relational interpretations to prove effect-dependent equivalences [4]. An extension of our framework with type-indexed types should be able to express their effect-indexed monads and prove their equivalences.

Extending our framework with type dependency would also allow for further applications. For example, we could consider a type of lists of length n, indexed by elements of the permutation group S_n. Bernardy *et al.* have presented a general framework for relational reasoning and an Abstraction Theorem for dependent types [5]. However, they work with pure type systems, which define type equality via untyped rewriting, so it is not immediately obvious how to integrate arbitrary equational theories into their framework.

Semantic Equality In general, the semantic equality in Definition 2 is not an equivalence relation. If the interpretations of all primitive types are partial equivalence relations then semantic equality is indeed an equivalence relation. However, this excludes the geometry and distance-indexed examples. More generally, we can consider relational interpretations that are *difunctional*. (A relation is difunctional if whenever (x, y), (x', y') and (x, y') are in the relation then so is (x', y).) Difunctionality is weaker than being a PER, but still suffices to prove that semantic equality is an equivalence relation. Hofmann [11] has used difunctional relations in the setting of effect analyses. Difunctionality covers all our examples except distance-indexed types. Note that for both PERs and difunctional relations we need to close the relational interpretation of existential types under the appropriate property to ensure that all types are interpreted as PERs/difunctional relations. For distance-indexed types it is possible that a new notion of equivalence based on closeness is required.

Acknowledgements

The authors would like to thank Nick Benton, Kenneth MacKenzie, John Reppy and Martin Will for illuminating discussions on geometry and types. Atkey and Johann were supported by EPSRC grant EP/G068917/1.

References

[1] M. Abadi, A. Banerjee, N. Heintze, and J. G. Riecke. A Core Calculus of Dependency. Proceedings, POPL, pp.147-160, 1999.

[2] R. Atkey. Syntax for Free: Representing Syntax with Binding Using Parametricity. Proceedings, TLCA, pp. 35-49, 2009.

[3] N. Benton, C.-K. Hur, A. J. Kennedy, C. McBride. Strongly Typed Term Representations in Coq. *Journal of Automated Reasoning* 49(2), pp. 141-159, 2012.

[4] N. Benton, A. Kennedy, M. Hofmann, L. Beringer. Reading, Writing and Relations. Proceedings, APLAS, pp. 114-130, 2006.

[5] J.-P. Bernardy, P. Jansson, R. Paterson. Proofs for Free: Parametricity for Dependent Types. *Journal of Functional Programming* 22(2), pp. 107-152, 2012.

[6] L. Cardelli, P. Gardner. Processes in Space. *Programs, Proofs, Processes*: Proceedings, CiE, pp. 78-87, 2010.

[7] Computational Geometry Algorithms Library (CGAL): User and Reference Manual. Available at `http://www.cgal.org`.

[8] S. Chaudhuri, S. Gulwani, and R. Lublinerman. Continuity Analysis of Programs. Proceedings, POPL, pp. 57-70, 2010.

[9] J. Gallier. *Geometric Methods and Applications For Computer Science and Engineering*. Springer, 2011.

[10] J. Harrison. Without Loss of Generality. Proceedings, TPHOLs, pp. 43-59, 2009.

[11] M. Hofmann. Correctness of Effect-based Program Transformations. Formal Logical Methods for System Security and Correctness, pp. 149-173, 2008.

[12] M. P. Jones. Functional Programming with Overloading and Higher-Order Polymorphism. Proceedings, AFP, pp. 97-136, 1995.

[13] A. J. Kennedy. Relational Parametricity and Units of Measure. Proceedings, POPL, pp. 442-455, 1997.

[14] A. J. Kennedy. Types for Units-of-Measure: Theory and Practice. Central European Functional Programming school (CEFP), pp. 268–305, LNCS vol. 6299, 2010.

[15] S. Mann, N. Litke, T. DeRose. A Coordinate Free Geometry ADT. Technical Report CS-97-15, University of Waterloo, 1997.

[16] A. M. Pitts. Parametric Polymorphism and Operational Equivalence. *Mathematical Structures in Computer Science* 10(3), pp. 321-359, 2000.

[17] J. Reed and B. C. Pierce. Distance Makes the Types Grow Stronger. Proceedings, ICFP, pp. 157-169, 2010.

[18] J. C. Reynolds. Types, Abstraction and Parametric Polymorphism. *Information Processing* 83, pp. 513-523, 1983.

[19] A. Sabelfeld and D. Sands. A PER Model of Secure Information Flow in Sequential Programs. *Higher-Order and Symbolic Computation* 14 (1), pp. 59-91, 2001.

[20] N. Shikuma and A.Igarahsi. Proving Noninterference by a Fully Complete Translation to the Simply Typed lambda-calculus. *Logical Methods in Computer Science* 4(3), 2008.

[21] S. Tse and S. Zdancewic. Translating Dependency into Parametricity. Proceedings, ICFP, pp. 115-125, 2004.

[22] P. Wadler. Theorems for Free!. Proceedings, FPCA, pp. 347-359, 1989.

Static and Dynamic Semantics of NoSQL Languages

Véronique Benzaken[1] Giuseppe Castagna[2] Kim Nguyễn[1] Jérôme Siméon[3]

[1]LRI, Université Paris-Sud, Orsay, France,
[2]CNRS, PPS, Université Paris Diderot, Sorbonne Paris Cité, Paris, France
[3]IBM Watson Research, Hawthorne, NY, USA

Abstract

We present a calculus for processing semistructured data that spans differences of application area among several novel query languages, broadly categorized as "NoSQL". This calculus lets users define their own operators, capturing a wider range of data processing capabilities, whilst providing a typing precision so far typical only of primitive hard-coded operators. The type inference algorithm is based on semantic type checking, resulting in type information that is both precise, and flexible enough to handle structured and semistructured data. We illustrate the use of this calculus by encoding a large fragment of Jaql, including operations and iterators over JSON, embedded SQL expressions, and co-grouping, and show how the encoding directly yields a typing discipline for Jaql as it is, namely without the addition of any type definition or type annotation in the code.

Categories and Subject Descriptors D.3.1 [*Programming Languages*]: Formal Definitions and Theory; F.3.2 [*Logics and Meanings of Programs*]: Semantics of Programming Languages—Operational semantics; F.3.3 [*Logics and Meanings of Programs*]: Studies of Program Constructs—Type structure; H.3.3 [*Information Storage and Retrieval*]: Information Search and Retrieval—Query formulation

Keywords NoSQL, BigData Analytics, Jaql, Cloud Computing, Type Inference.

1. Introduction

The emergence of Cloud computing, and the ever growing importance of data in applications, has given birth to a whirlwind of new data models [17, 22] and languages. Whether they are developed under the banner of "NoSQL" [28, 33], for BigData Analytics [6, 16, 26], for Cloud computing [4], or as domain specific languages (DSL) embedded in a host language [19, 25, 30], most of them share a common subset of SQL and the ability to handle semistructured data. While there is no consensus yet on the precise boundaries of this class of languages, they all share two common traits: *(i)* an emphasis on sequence operations (*eg*, through the popular MapReduce paradigm) and *(ii)* a lack of types for both data and programs (contrary to, say, XML programming or relational databases where data schemas are pervasive). In [19, 20], Meijer argues that such languages can greatly benefit from formal foundations, and suggests comprehensions [8, 31, 32] as a unifying model. Although we agree with Meijer for the need to provide unified, formal foundations to those new languages, we argue that such foundations should account for novel features critical to various application domains that are not captured by comprehensions. Also, most of those languages provide limited type checking, or ignore it altogether. We believe type checking is essential for many applications, with usage ranging from error detection to optimization. But we understand the designers and programmers of those languages who are averse to any kind of type definition or annotation. In this article, we propose a calculus which is expressive enough to capture languages that go beyond SQL or comprehensions. We show how the calculus adapts to various data models while retaining a precise type checking that can exploit in a flexible way limited type information, information that is deduced directly from the structure of the program even in the absence of any explicit type declaration or annotation.

Example. We use Jaql [6, 16], a language over JSON [17] developed for BigData analytics, to illustrate how our proposed calculus works. Our reason for using Jaql is that it encompasses all the features found in the previously cited query languages and includes a number of original ones, as well. Like Pig [26] it supports sequence iteration, filtering, and grouping operations on non-nested queries. Like AQL [4] and XQuery [7], it features nested queries. Furthermore, Jaql uses a rich data model that allows arbitrary nesting of data (it works on generic sequences of JSON records whose fields can contain other sequences or records) while other languages are limited to flat data models, such as AQL whose data-model is similar to the standard relational model used by SQL databases (tuples of scalars and of lists of scalars). Lastly, Jaql includes SQL as an embedded sub-language for relational data. For these reasons, although in the present work we focus almost exclusively on Jaql, we believe that our work can be adapted without effort to a wide array of sequence processing languages.

The following Jaql program illustrates some of those features. It performs co-grouping [26] between one JSON input, containing information about departments, and one relational input containing information about employees. The query returns for each department its name and id, from the first input, and the number of high-income employees from the second input. A SQL expression is used to select the employees with income above a given value, while a Jaql filter is used to access the set of departments and the elements of these two collections are processed by the group expression (in Jaql "$" denotes the current element).

```
group
  (depts -> filter each x (x.size > 50))
       by g = $.depid  as ds,
  (SELECT * FROM employees WHERE income > 100)
       by g = $.dept as es
into { dept: g,
       deptName: ds[0].name,
       numEmps: count(es) };
```

The query blends Jaql expressions (*eg*, `filter` which selects, in the collection `depts`, departments with a `size` of more than 50 employees, and the grouping itself) with a SQL statement (select-

This work was partially supported by the ANR TYPEX project n. ANR-11-BS02-007 and by a visiting researcher grant of "Fondation Digiteo".

POPL '13, January 23–25, 2013, Rome, Italy.

ing employees in a relational table for which the salary is more than 100). Relations are naturally rendered in JSON as collections of records. In our example, one of the key difference is that field access in SQL requires the field to be present in the record, while the same operation in Jaql does not. Actually, field selection in Jaql is very expressive since it can be applied also to collections with the effect that the selection is recursively applied to the components of the collection and the collection of the results returned, and similarly for `filter` and other iterators. In other words, the expression `filter each x (x.size > 50)` above will work as much when `x` is bound to a record (with or without a `size` field: in the latter case the selection returns `null`), as when `x` is bound to a collection of records or of arbitrary nested collections thereof. This accounts for the semistructured nature of JSON compared to the relational model. Our calculus can express both, in a way that illustrates the difference in both the dynamic semantics and static typing.

In our calculus, the selection of all records whose *mandatory* field `income` is greater than 100 is defined as:

```
let Sel =
     `nil => `nil
   | ({income: x, .. } as y , tail) =>
        if x > 100 then (y,Sel(tail)) else Sel(tail)
```

(collections are encoded as lists *à la* Lisp) while the filtering among records or arbitrary nested collections of records of those where the (optional) `size` field is present and larger than 50 is:

```
let Fil =
     `nil => `nil
   | ({size: x, .. } as y,tail) =>
          if x > 50 then (y,Fil(tail)) else Fil(tail)
   | ((x,xs),tail) =>   (Fil(x,xs),Fil(tail))
   | (_,tail) => Fil(tail)
```

The terms above show nearly all the basic building blocks of our calculus (only composition is missing), building blocks that we dub *filters*. Filters can be defined recursively (*eg*, `Sel(tail)` is a recursive call); they can perform pattern matching as found in functional languages (the filter $p \Rightarrow f$ executes f in the environment resulting from the matching of pattern p); they can be composed in alternation ($f_1|f_2$ tries to apply f_1 and if it fails it applies f_2), they can spread over the structure of their argument (*eg*, (f_1,f_2) —of which `(x,Sel(tail))` is an instance— requires an argument of a product type and applies the corresponding f_i component-wise).

For instance, the filter `Fil` scans collections encoded as lists *à la* Lisp (*ie*, by right associative pairs with `` `nil `` denoting the empty list). If its argument is the empty list, then it returns the empty list; if it is a list whose head is a record with a `size` field (and possibly other fields matched by "`..`"), then it captures the whole record in `y`, the content of the field in `x`, the tail of the list in `tail`, and keeps or discards `y` (*ie*, the record) according to whether `x` (*ie*, the field) is larger than 50; if the head is also a list, then it recursively applies both on the head and on the tail; if the head of the list is neither a list, nor a record with a size field, then the head is discarded. The encoding of the whole grouping query is given in Section 5.1.

Our aim is not to propose yet another "NoSQL/cloud computing/bigdata analytics" query language, but rather to show how to *express* and *type* such languages via an encoding into our core calculus. Each such language can in this way preserve its execution model but obtain for free a formal semantics, a type inference system and, as it happens, a prototype implementation. The type information is deduced via the encoding (without the need of *any* type annotation) and can be used for early error detection and debugging purposes. The encoding also yields an executable system that can be used for rapid prototyping. Both possibilities are critical in most typical usage scenarios of these languages, where deployment is very expensive both in time and in resources. As observed by Meijer [19] the advent of big data makes it more important than ever for programmers (and, we add, for language and system designers) to have a single abstraction that allows them to process, transform, query, analyze, and compute across data presenting utter variability both in volume and in structure, yielding a "mind-blowing number of new data models, query languages, and execution fabrics" [19] . The framework we present here, we claim, encompasses them all. A long-term goal is that the compilers of these languages could use the type information inferred from the encoding and the encoding itself to devise further optimizations.

Types. Pig [26], Jaql [16, 27], AQL [4] have all been conceived by considering just the map-reduce execution model. The type (or, schema) of the manipulated data did not play any role in their design. As a consequence these languages are untyped and, when present, types are optional and clearly added as an afterthought. Differences in data model or type discipline are particularly important when embedded in a host language (since they yield the so-called impedance mismatch). The reason why types were/are disregarded in such languages may originate in an alleged tension between type inference and heterogeneous/semistructured data: on the one hand these languages are conceived to work with collections of data that are weakly or partially structured, on the other hand current languages with type inference (such as Haskell or ML) can work only on homogeneous collections (typically, lists of elements of the same type).

In this work we show that the two visions can coexist: we type data by semantic subtyping [15], a type system conceived for semi-structured data, and describe computations by our *filters* which are untyped combinators that, thanks to a technique of weak typing introduced in [10], can polymorphically type the results of data query and processing with a high degree of precision. The conception of *filters* is driven by the schema of the data rather than the execution model and we use them (i) to capture and give a uniform semantics to a wide range of semi structured data processing capabilities, (ii) to give a type system that encompasses the types defined for such languages, if any, notably Pig, Jaql and AQL (but also XML query and processing languages: see Section 5.1), (iii) to infer the precise result types of queries written in these languages *as they are* (so without the addition of any explicit type annotation/definition or new construct), and (iv) to show how minimal extensions/modifications of the current syntax of these languages can bring dramatic improvements in the precision of the inferred types.

The types we propose here are extensible record types and heterogeneous lists whose content is described by regular expressions on types as defined by the following grammar:

Types	t	$::=$	v	(singleton)
		$\mid$	$\{\ell{:}t, \ldots, \ell{:}t\}$	(closed record)
		$\mid$	$\{\ell{:}t, \ldots, \ell{:}t, ..\}$	(open record)
		$\mid$	$[r]$	(sequences)
		$\mid$	`int` $\mid$ `char`	(base)
		$\mid$	`any` $\mid$ `empty` $\mid$ `null`	(special)
		$\mid$	$t \vert t$	(union)
		$\mid$	$t \backslash t$	(difference)
Regexp	r	$::=$	$\varepsilon \mid t \mid r* \mid r+ \mid r? \mid r\,r \mid r \vert r$	

where ε denotes the empty word. The semantics of types can be expressed in terms of sets of *values* (values are either constants —such as `1`, `2`, `true`, `false`, `null`, `'1'`, the latter denoting the character `1`—, records of values, or lists of values). So the singleton type v is the type that contains just the value v (in particular `null` is the singleton type containing the value `null`). The closed record type `{a:int, b:int}` contains all record values with exactly two fields `a` and `b` with integer values, while the open record type `{a:int, b:int, ..}` contains all record values with *at least* two fields `a` and `b` with integer values. The sequence type $[r]$ is the set of all sequences whose content is described by the *regular expression* r; so, for example [char*] contains all sequences of characters (we will use string to denote this type and the standard double quote notation to denote its values) while [({a:int} {a:int})+] denotes nonempty lists of even length containing record values of type {a:int}. The union type $s|t$ contains all the values of s and of t, while the difference type $s\backslash t$ contains all the values of s that are not in t. We shall use bool as an abbreviation of the union of the two singleton types containing true and false: 'true|'false. any and empty respectively contain all and no values. Recursive type definitions are also used (see Section 2.2 for formal details).

These types can express all the types of Pig, Jaql and AQL, all XML types, and much more. So for instance, AQL includes only homogeneous lists of type t, that can be expressed by our types as [t*]. In Jaql's documentation one can find the type [long(value=1), string(value="a"), boolean*] which is the type of arrays whose first element is 1, the second is the string "a" and all the other are booleans. This can be easily expressed in our types as [1 "a" bool*]. But while Jaql only allows a limited use of regular expressions (Kleene star can only appear in tail position) our types do not have such restrictions. So for example [char* '@' char* '.' (('f' 'r')|('i' 't'))] is the type of all strings (*ie*, sequences of chars) that denote email addresses ending by either .fr or .it. We use some syntactic sugar to make terms as the previous one more readable (*eg*, [.* '@' .* ('.fr'|'.it')]). Likewise, henceforth we use {a?:t} to denote that the field a of type t is optional; this is just syntactic sugar for stating that either the field is undefined or it contains a value of type t (for the formal details of this encoding see the full version of this work available on line).

Coming back to our initial example, the filter Fil defined before expects as argument a collection of the following type:

```
type Depts = [ ( {size?: int, ..} | Depts )* ]
```

that is a, possibly empty, arbitrary nested list of records with an optional size field of type int: notice that it is important to specify the optional field and its type since a size field of a different type would make the expression x > 50 raise a run-time error. This information is deduced just from the *structure* of the filter (since Fil does not contain any type definition or annotation).

We define a type inference system that rejects any argument of Fil that has not type Depts, and deduces for arguments of type [({size: int, addr: string}| {sec: int} | Depts)+] (which is a subtype of Depts) the result type [({size: int, addr: string}|Depts)*] (so it does not forget the field addr but discards the field sec, and by replacing * for + recognizes that the test may fail).

By encoding primitive Jaql operations into a formal core calculus we shall provide them a formal and clean semantics as well as precise typing. So for instance it will be clear that applying the following dot selection [[{a:3}] {a:5, b:true}].a the result will be [[3] 5] and we shall be able to deduce that _.a applied to arbitrary nested lists of records with an optional integer a field (*ie*, of type t = {a?:int} | [t*]) yields arbitrary nested lists of int or null values (*ie*, of type u = int | null | [u*]).

Finally we shall show that if we accept to extend the current syntax of Jaql (or of some other language) by some minimal filter syntax (*eg*, the pattern filter) we can obtain a huge improvement in the precision of type inference.

Contributions. The main contribution of this work is the definition of a calculus that encompasses structural operators scattered over NoSQL languages and that possesses some characteristics that make it unique in the swarm of current semi-structured data processing languages. In particular it is parametric (though fully embeddable) in a host language; it uniformly handles both width and deep nested data recursion (while most languages offer just the former and limited forms of the latter); finally, it includes first-class arbitrary deep composition (while most languages offer this operator only at top level), whose power is nevertheless restrained by the type system.

An important contribution of this work is that it directly compares a programming language approach with the tree transducer one [13]. Our calculus implements transformations typical of top-down tree transducers but has several advantages over the transducer approach: (1) the transformations are expressed in a formalism immediately intelligible to any functional programmer; (2) our calculus, in its untyped version, is Turing complete; (3) its transformations can be statically typed (at the expenses of Turing completeness) without any annotation yielding precise result types (4) even if we restrict the calculus only to well-typed terms (thus losing Turing completeness), it still is strictly more expressive than well-known and widely studied deterministic top-down tree transducer formalisms.

The technical contributions are (i) the proof of Turing completeness for our formalism, (ii) the definition of a type system that copes with records with computable labels (iii) the definition of a static type system for filters and its correctness, (iv) the definition of a static analysis that ensures the termination (and the proof thereof) of the type inference algorithm with complexity bounds expressed in the size of types and filters and (iv) the proof that the terms that pass the static analysis form a language strictly more expressive than top-down tree transducers.

Outline. In Section 2 we present the syntax of the three components of our system. Namely, a minimal set of *expressions*, the calculus of *filters* used to program user-defined operators or to encode the operators of other languages, and the core *types* in which the types we just presented are to be encoded. Section 3 defines the operational semantics of filters and a declarative semantics for operators. The type system as well as the type inference algorithm are described in Section 4. In Section 5 we present how to handle a large subset of Jaql. Section 6 reports on some subtler design choices of our system and compare with related work. For space constraints, proofs, secondary results, encodings, some formal definitions (in particular the definition of the static analysis for termination and the interpretation of record values as *quasi-constant* functions), and further extensions can be found only in the full version available online.

2. Syntax

In this section we present the syntax of the three components of our system: a minimal set of *expressions*, the calculus of *filters* used to program user-defined operators or to encode the operators of other languages, and the core *types* in which the types presented in the introduction are to be encoded.

The core of our work is the definition of filters and types. The key property of our development is that filters can be grafted to any host language that satisfies minimal requirements, by simply adding filter application to the expressions of the host language. The minimal requirements of the host language for this to be possible are quite simple: it must have constants (typically for types int, char, string, and bool), variables, and either pairs or record values (not necessarily both). On the static side the host language must have at least basic and products types and be able to assign a type to expressions in a given type environment (*ie*, under some typing assumptions for variables). By the addition of filter applications, the host language can acquire or increase the capability to define polymorphic user-defined iterators, query and processing expressions, and be enriched with a powerful and precise type system.

2.1 Expressions

In this work we consider the following set of expressions

Definition 1 (expressions).

Exprs e ::=		
	c	(constants)
|	x	(variables)
|	(e, e)	(pairs)
|	$\{e{:}e, ..., e{:}e\}$	(records)
|	$e + e$	(record concatenation)
|	$e \setminus \ell$	(field deletion)
|	$\mathsf{op}(e, ..., e)$	(built-in operators)
|	$f e$	(filter application)

where f ranges over *filters* (defined later on), c over generic constants, and ℓ over *string* constants.

Intuitively, these expressions represent the syntax supplied by the host language —though only the first two and one of the next two are really needed— that we extend with (the missing expressions and) the expression of filter application. Expressions are formed by constants, variables, pairs, records, and operation on records: record concatenation gives priority to the expression on the right. So if in $r_1 + r_2$ both records contains a field with the same label, it is the one in r_2 that will be taken, while field deletion does not require the record to contain a field with the given label (though this point is not important). The metavariable op ranges over operators as well as functions and other constructions belonging to or defined by the host language. Among expressions we single out a set of *values*, intuitively the results of computations, that are formally defined as follows:

$$v \quad ::= \quad c \mid (v, v) \mid \{\ell{:}v;\ \ldots;\ \ell{:}v\}$$

We use `"foo"` for character string constants, `'c'` for characters, `1 2 3 4 5` and so on for integers, and backquoted words, such as `` `foo ``, for atoms (*ie*, user-defined constants). We use three distinguished atoms `` `nil ``, `` `true ``, and `` `false ``. Double quotes can be omitted for strings that are labels of record fields: thus we write `{name:"John"}` rather than `{"name":"John"}`. Sequences (*aka*, heterogeneous lists, ordered collections, arrays) are encoded *à la LISP*, as nested pairs where the atom `` `nil `` denotes the empty list. We use $[e_1\ \ldots\ e_n]$ as syntactic sugar for $(e_1, \ldots, (e_n, \text{`nil})\ldots)$.

2.2 Types

Definition 2 (types).

Types t ::=		
	b	(basic types)
|	v	(singleton types)
|	(t,t)	(products)
|	$\{\ell{:}t, \ldots, \ell{:}t\}$	(closed records)
|	$\{\ell{:}t, \ldots, \ell{:}t, ..\}$	(open records)
|	$t \vert t$	(union types)
|	$t \& t$	(intersection types)
|	$\neg t$	(negation type)
|	`empty`	(empty type)
|	`any`	(any type)
|	$\mu T.t$	(recursive types)
|	T	(recursion variable)
|	$\mathsf{Op}(t, ..., t)$	(foreign type calls)

where every recursion is guarded, that is, every type variable is separated from its binder by at least one application of a type constructor (*ie*, products, records, or Op).

Most of these types were already explained in the introduction. We have basic types (`int`, `bool`, ...) ranged over by b and singleton types v denoting the type that contains only the value v. Record types come in two flavors: closed record types whose values are records with exactly the fields specified by the type, and open record types whose values are records with *at least* the fields specified by the type. Product types are standard and we have a complete set of type connectives, that is, finite unions, intersections and negations. We use `empty`, to denote the type that has no values and `any` for the type of all values (sometimes denoted by "_" when used in patterns). We added a term for recursive types, which allows us to encode both the regular expression types defined in the introduction and, more generally, the recursive type definitions we used there. Finally, we use Op (capitalized to distinguish it from expression operators) to denote the host language's *type* operators (if any). Thus, when filter applications return values whose type belongs just to the foreign language (*eg*, a list of functions) we suppose the typing of these functions be given by some type operators. For instance, if succ is a user defined successor function, we will suppose to be given its type in the form Arrow(`int`,`int`) and, similarly, for its application, say apply(succ,3) we will be given the type of this expression (presumably `int`). Here Arrow is a type operator and apply an expression operator.

The denotational semantics of types as sets of values, that we informally described in the introduction, is at the basis of the definition of the subtyping relation for these types. We say that a type t_1 is a subtype of a type t_2, noted $t_1 \leq t_2$, if and only if the set of values denoted by t_1 is contained (in the set-theoretic sense) in the set of values denoted by t_2. For the formal definition and the decision procedure of this subtyping relation the reader can refer to the work on semantic subtyping [15].

2.3 Patterns

Filters are our core untyped operators. All they can do are three different things: (1) they can structurally decompose and transform the values they are applied to, or (2) they can be sequentially composed, or (3) they can do pattern matching. In order to define filters, thus, we first need to define patterns.

Definition 3 (patterns).

Patterns p ::=		
	t	(type)
|	x	(variable)
|	(p,p)	(pair)
|	$\{\ell{:}p, \ldots, \ell{:}p\}$	(closed rec)
|	$\{\ell{:}p, \ldots, \ell{:}p, ..\}$	(open rec)
|	$p \vert p$	(or/union)
|	$p \& p$	(and/intersection)

where the subpatterns forming pairs, records, and intersections have distinct capture variables, and those forming unions have the same capture variables.

Patterns are essentially types in which capture variables (ranged over by x, y, ...) may occur in every position that is not under a negation or a recursion. A pattern is used to match a value. The matching of a value v against a pattern p, noted v/p, either fails (noted Ω) or it returns a substitution from the variables occurring in the pattern, into values. The substitution is then used as an environment in which some expression is evaluated. If the pattern is a type, then the matching fails if and only if the pattern is matched against a value that does not have that type, otherwise it returns the empty substitution. If it is a variable, then the matching always succeeds and returns the substitution that assigns the matched value to the variable. The pair pattern (p_1,p_2) succeeds if and only if it is matched against a pair of values and each sub-pattern succeeds on the corresponding projection of the value (the union of the two substitutions is then returned). Both record patterns are similar to the product pattern with the specificity that in the open record pattern ".." matches all the fields that are not specified in the pattern. An intersection pattern $p_1\&p_2$ succeeds if and only if both patterns succeed (the union of the two substitutions is then returned). The union pattern $p_1|p_2$ first tries to match the pattern p_1 and if it fails it tries the pattern p_2.

For instance, the pattern $(\texttt{int\&}x,y)$ succeeds only if the matched value is a pair of values (v_1, v_2) in which v_1 is an integer —in which case it returns the substitution $\{x/v_1, y/v_2\}$— and fails otherwise. Finally notice that the notation "p `as` x" we used in the examples of the introduction, is syntactic sugar for $p\&x$.

This informal semantics of matching (see [15] for the formal definition) explains the reasons of the restrictions on capture variables in Definition 3: in intersections, pairs, and records all patterns must be matched and, thus, they have to assign distinct variables, while in union patterns just one pattern will be matched, hence the same set of variables must be assigned, whichever alternative is selected.

The strength of patterns is their connections with types and the fact that the pattern matching operator can be typed *exactly*. This is entailed by the following theorems (both proved in [15]):

Theorem 4 (Accepted type [15]). *For every pattern p, the set of all values v such that $v/p \neq \Omega$ is a type. We call this set the* accepted type *of p and note it by $\langle p \rangle$.*

The fact that the exact set of values for which a matching succeeds is a type is not obvious. It states that for every pattern p there exists a syntactic type produced by the grammar in Definition 2 whose semantics is exactly the set of all and only values that are matched by p. The existence of this syntactic type, which we note $\langle p \rangle$, is of utmost importance for a precise typing of pattern matching. In particular, given a pattern p and a type t contained in (*ie*, subtype of) $\langle p \rangle$, it allows us to compute the *exact* type of the capture variables of p when it is matched against a value in t:

Theorem 5 (Type environment [15]). *There exists an algorithm that for every pattern p, and $t \leq \langle p \rangle$ returns a type environment $t/p \in$ **Vars**$(p) \rightarrow$ **Types** such that $(t/p)(x) = \{(v/p)(x) \mid v : t\}$.*

2.4 Filters

Definition 6 (filters). A *filter* is a term generated by:

Filters	f	::=	e	(expression)
		|	$p \Rightarrow f$	(pattern)
		|	(f,f)	(product)
		|	$\{\ell{:}f, \ldots, \ell{:}f\,,..\}$	(record)
		|	$f\|f$	(union)
		|	$\mu X.f$	(recursion)
		|	Xa	(recursive call)
		|	$f;f$	(composition)
		|	o	(declarative operators)
Operators	o	::=	`groupby` f	(filter grouping)
		|	`orderby` f	(filter ordering)
Arguments	a	::=	x	(variables)
		|	c	(constants)
		|	(a,a)	(pairs)
		|	$\{\ell{:}a, \ldots, \ell{:}a\}$	(record)

such that for every subterm of the form $f;g$, no recursion variable is free in f.

Filters are like transducers, that when applied to a value return another value. However, unlike transducers they possess more "programming-oriented" constructs, like the ability to test an input and capture subterms, recompose an intermediary result from captured values and a composition operator. We first describe informally the semantics of each construct.

The expression filter e always returns the value corresponding to the evaluation of e (and discards its argument). The filter $p \Rightarrow f$ applies the filter f to its argument in the environment obtained by matching the argument against p (provided that the matching does not fail). This rather powerful feature allows a filter to perform two critical actions: *(i)* inspect an input with regular pattern-matching before exploring it and *(ii)* capture part of the input that can be reused during the evaluation of the subfilter f. If the argument application of f_i to v_i returns v'_i then the application of the product filter (f_1,f_2) to an argument (v_1, v_2) returns (v'_1, v'_2); otherwise, if any application fails or if the argument is not a pair, it fails. The record filter is similar: it applies to each specified field the corresponding filter and, as stressed by the "`..`", leaves the other fields unchanged; it fails if any of the applications does, or if any of the specified fields is absent, or if the argument is not a record. The filter $f_1|f_2$ returns the application of f_1 to its argument or, if this fails, the application of f_2. The semantics of a recursive filter is given by standard unfolding of its definition in recursive calls. The only real restriction that we introduce for filters is that recursive calls can be done only on arguments of a given form (*ie*, on arguments that have the form of values where variables may occur). This restriction in practice amounts to forbid recursive calls on the result of another recursively defined filter (all other cases can be easily encoded). The reason of this restriction is technical, since it greatly simplifies the analysis of Section 4.4 (which ensures the termination of type inference) without hampering expressiveness: filters are Turing complete even with this restriction (see Theorem 7). Filters can be composed: the filter $f_1;f_2$ applies f_2 to the result of applying f_1 to the argument and fails if any of the two does. The condition that in every subterm of the form $f;g$, f does not contain free recursion variables is not strictly necessary. Indeed, we could allow such terms. The point is that the analysis for the termination of the typing would then reject all such terms (apart from trivial ones in which the result of the recursive call is not used in the composition). But since this restriction *does not* restrict the expressiveness of the calculus (Theorem 7 proves Turing completeness with this restriction), then the addition of this restriction is just a design (rather than a technical) choice: we prefer to forbid the programmer to write recursive calls on the left-hand side of a composition, than systematically reject all the programs that use them in a non-trivial way.

Finally, we singled out some specific filters (specifically, we chose `groupby` and `orderby`) whose semantics is generally specified in a declarative rather than operational way. These do not bring any expressive power to the calculus (the proof of Turing completeness, Theorem 7, does not use these declarative operators) and actually they can be encoded by the remaining filters, but it is interesting to single them out because they yield either simpler encodings or more precise typing.

3. Semantics

The operational semantics of our calculus is given by the reduction semantics for filter application and for the record operations. Since the former is the only novelty of our work, we save space and omit the latter, which are standard anyhow.

We define a big step operational semantics for filters. The definition is given by the inference rules in Figure 1 for judgments of the form $\delta;\gamma \vdash_{eval} f(a) \rightsquigarrow r$ and describes how the evaluation of the application of filter f to an argument a in an environment γ yields an object r where r is either a value or Ω. The latter is a special value which represents a runtime error: it is raised by the rule **(error)** either because a filter did not match the form of its argument (*eg*, the argument of a filter product was not a pair) or because some pattern matching failed (*ie*, the side condition of **(patt)** did not hold). Notice that the argument a of a filter is always a value v unless the filter is the unfolding of a recursive

(expr) $$\frac{}{\delta;\gamma \vdash_{eval} e(v) \rightsquigarrow r} \quad r = \mathtt{eval}(\gamma, e)$$

(prod) $$\frac{\delta;\gamma \vdash_{eval} f_1(v_1) \rightsquigarrow r_1 \quad \delta;\gamma \vdash_{eval} f_2(v_2) \rightsquigarrow r_2}{\delta;\gamma \vdash_{eval} (f_1,f_2)(v_1,v_2) \rightsquigarrow (r_1,r_2)} \quad \text{if } r_1 \neq \Omega \text{ and } r_2 \neq \Omega$$

(patt) $$\frac{\delta;\gamma\,,\, v/p \vdash_{eval} f(v) \rightsquigarrow r}{\delta;\gamma \vdash_{eval} (p \Rightarrow f)(v) \rightsquigarrow r} \quad \text{if } v/p \neq \Omega$$

(comp) $$\frac{\delta;\gamma \vdash_{eval} f_1(v) \rightsquigarrow r_1 \quad \delta;\gamma \vdash_{eval} f_2(r_1) \rightsquigarrow r_2}{\delta;\gamma \vdash_{eval} (f_1;f_2)(v) \rightsquigarrow r_2} \quad \text{if } r_1 \neq \Omega$$

(union1) $$\frac{\delta;\gamma \vdash_{eval} f_1(v) \rightsquigarrow r_1}{\delta;\gamma \vdash_{eval} (f_1|f_2)(v) \rightsquigarrow r_1} \quad \text{if } r_1 \neq \Omega$$

(union2) $$\frac{\delta;\gamma \vdash_{eval} f_1(v) \rightsquigarrow \Omega \quad \delta;\gamma \vdash_{eval} f_2(v) \rightsquigarrow r_2}{\delta;\gamma \vdash_{eval} (f_1|f_2)(v) \rightsquigarrow r_2}$$

(rec) $$\frac{\delta, (X \mapsto f);\gamma \vdash_{eval} f(v) \rightsquigarrow r}{\delta;\gamma \vdash_{eval} (\mu X.f)(v) \rightsquigarrow r}$$

(rec-call) $$\frac{\delta;\gamma \vdash_{eval} (\delta(X))(a) \rightsquigarrow r}{\delta;\gamma \vdash_{eval} (Xa)(v) \rightsquigarrow r}$$

(error) $$\frac{}{\delta;\gamma \vdash_{eval} f(a) \rightsquigarrow \Omega} \quad \text{if no other rule applies}$$

(recd) $$\frac{\delta;\gamma \vdash_{eval} f_1(v_1) \rightsquigarrow r_1 \quad \cdots \quad \delta;\gamma \vdash_{eval} f_n(v_n) \rightsquigarrow r_n}{\delta;\gamma \vdash_{eval} \{\ell_1{:}f_1, ..., \ell_n{:}f_n\, ,..\}(\{\ell_1{:}v_1, ..., \ell_n{:}v_n, ..., \ell_{n+k}{:}v_{n+k}\}) \rightsquigarrow \{\ell_1{:}r_1, ..., \ell_n{:}r_n, ..., \ell_{n+k}{:}v_{n+k}\}} \quad \text{if } \forall i, r_i \neq \Omega$$

Figure 1. Dynamic semantics of filters

call, in which case variables may occur in it (*cf.* rule **rec-call**). Environment δ is used to store the body of recursive definitions.

The semantics of filters is quite straightforward and inspired by the semantics of patterns. The *expression* filter discards its input and evaluates (rather, asks the host language to evaluate) the expression e in the current environment (**expr**). It can be thought of as the right-hand side of a branch in a `match_with` construct.

The *product* filter expects a pair as input, applies its sub-filters component-wise and returns the pair of the results (**prod**). This filter is used in particular to express sequence mapping, as the first component f_1 transforms the element of the list and f_2 is applied to the tail. In practice it is often the case that f_2 is a recursive call that iterates on arbitrary lists and stops when the input is `‘nil`. If the input is not a pair, then the filter fails (rule (**error**) applies).

The *record* filter expects as input a record value with *at least* the same fields as those specified by the filter. It applies each sub-filter to the value in the corresponding field leaving the contents of other fields unchanged (**recd**). If the argument is not a record value or it does not contain all the fields specified by the record filter, or if the application of any subfilter fails, then the whole application of the record filter fails.

The *pattern* filter matches its input value v against the pattern p. If the matching fails so the filter does, otherwise it evaluates its sub-filter in the environment augmented by the substitution v/p (**patt**).

The *alternative* filter follows a standard first-match policy: If the filter f_1 succeeds, then its result is returned (**union-1**). If f_1 fails, then f_2 is evaluated against the input value (**union-2**). This filter is particularly useful to write the alternative of two (or more) *pattern* filters, making it possible to conditionally continue a computation based on the shape of the input.

The *composition* allows us to pass the result of f_1 as input to f_2. The composition filter is of paramount importance. Indeed, without it, our only way to iterate (deconstruct) an input value is to use a *product* filter, which always rebuilds a pair as result.

Finally, a *recursive* filter is evaluated by recording its body in δ and evaluating it (**rec**), while for a *recursive call* we replace the recursion variable by its definition (**rec-call**).

This concludes the presentation of the semantics of non-declarative filters (*ie*, without groupby and orderby). These form a Turing complete formalism (complete proof in the full version):

Theorem 7 (Turing completeness). *The language formed by constants, variables, pairs, equality, and applications of non-declarative filters is Turing complete.*

Proof (sketch). We can encode untyped call-by-value λ-calculus by first applying continuation passing style (CPS) transformations and encoding CPS term reduction rules and substitutions via filters. Thanks to CPS we eschew the restrictions on composition. □

To conclude the presentation of the semantics we have to define the semantics of groupby and orderby. We prefer to give the semantics in a declarative form rather than operationally in order not to tie it to a particular order (of keys or of the execution):

Groupby: `groupby` f applied to a sequence $[v_1 \ldots v_m]$ reduces to a sequence $[\,(k_1,l_1)\ldots(k_n,l_n)\,]$ such that:

1. $\forall i,\ 1 \leq i \leq m,\ \exists j,\ 1 \leq j \leq n,$ s.t. $k_j = f(v_i)$
2. $\forall j,\ 1 \leq j \leq n,\ \exists i,\ 1 \leq i \leq m,$ s.t. $k_j = f(v_i)$
3. $\forall j,\ 1 \leq j \leq n,\ l_j$ is a sequence: $[\,v_1^j \ldots v_{n_j}^j]$
4. $\forall j,\ 1 \leq j \leq n, \forall k,\ 1 \leq k \leq n_j,\ f(v_k^j) = k_j$
5. $k_i = k_j \Rightarrow i = j$
6. $l_1, \ldots, l_n$ is a partition of $[v_1 \ldots v_m\,]$

Orderby: `orderby` f applied to $[v_1 \ldots v_n]$ reduces to $[v_1' \ldots v_n']$ such that:

1. $[v_1' \ldots v_n']$ is a permutation of $[v_1 \ldots v_n]$,
2. $\forall i, j$ s.t. $1 \leq i \leq j \leq n, f(v_i) \leq f(v_j)$

Since the semantics of both operators is deeply connected to a notion of equality and order on values of the host language, we give them as "built-in" operations. However we will illustrate how our type algebra allows us to provide very precise typing rules, specialized for their particular semantics. It is also possible (see full version) to encode co-grouping (or `groupby` on several input sequences) with a combination of `groupby` and filters.

Syntactic sugar. The reader may have noticed that the productions for expressions (Definition 1) do not define any destructor (*eg*, projections, label selection, ...), just constructors. The reason is that destructors, as well as other common expressions, can be encoded by filter applications:

$e.\ell$	$\stackrel{\text{def}}{=}$	$(\{\ell{:}x\,,..\} \Rightarrow x)e$
$\mathtt{fst}(e)$	$\stackrel{\text{def}}{=}$	$((x,\mathbf{any}) \Rightarrow x)e$
$\mathtt{snd}(e)$	$\stackrel{\text{def}}{=}$	$((\mathbf{any},x) \Rightarrow x)e$
$\mathtt{let}\ p = e_1\ \mathtt{in}\ e_2$	$\stackrel{\text{def}}{=}$	$(p \Rightarrow e_2)e_1$
$\mathtt{if}\ e\ \mathtt{then}\ e_1\ \mathtt{else}\ e_2$	$\stackrel{\text{def}}{=}$	$(\text{‘}\mathtt{true} \Rightarrow e_1 \mid \text{‘}\mathtt{false} \Rightarrow e_2)e$
$\mathtt{match}\ e\ \mathtt{with}\ p_1 \Rightarrow e_1 \mid \ldots \mid p_n \Rightarrow e_n$	$\stackrel{\text{def}}{=}$	$(p_1 \Rightarrow e_1 \mid \ldots \mid p_n \Rightarrow e_n)e$

These are just a possible choice, but others are possible. For instance in Jaql dot selection is overloaded: when $\_.\ell$ is applied to a record, Jaql returns the content of its ℓ field; if the field is absent or the argument is `null`, then Jaql returns `null` and fails if the argument is not a record; when applied to a list ('array' in Jaql terminology) it recursively applies to all the elements of the list. So Jaql's "$\_.\ell$" is precisely defined as

$$\mu X.(\{\ell{:}x\,,..\} \Rightarrow x \mid (\{..\}|\mathtt{null}) \Rightarrow \mathtt{null} \mid (h,t) \Rightarrow (Xh,Xt))$$

Besides the syntactic sugar above, in the next section we will use $t_1 + t_2$ to denote the record type formed by all field types in t_2 and all the field types in t_1 whose label is not already present in t_2. Similarly $t \setminus \ell$ will denote the record types formed by all field types in t apart from the one labeled by ℓ, if present. Finally, we will also use for expressions, types, and patterns the syntactic sugar for lists used in the introduction. So, for instance, $[p_1\ p_2\ \ldots\ p_n]$ is matched by lists of n elements provided that their i-th element matches p_i.

4. Type inference

The type inference system assign types to *expressions*. Variables, constants, and pairs are typed by standard rules, while we suppose that the typing of foreign expressions is provided by the host language.[1] So we omit the corresponding rules (they can be found in the full version). The core of our type system starts with records.

4.1 Typing of records

The typing of records is novel and challenging because record expressions may contain string *expressions* in label position, such as in $\{e_1\texttt{:}e_2\}$, while in all type systems for record we are aware of, labels are never computed. It is difficult to give a type to $\{e_1\texttt{:}e_2\}$ since, in general, we do not statically know the value that e_1 will return, and which is required to form a record type. All we can (and must) ask is that this value will be a string. To type a record expression $\{e_1\texttt{:}e_2\}$, thus, we distinguish two cases according to whether the type t_1 of e_1 is finite (*ie*, it contains only finitely many values, such as, say, `Bool`) or not. If a type is finite, (finiteness of regular types seen as tree automata can be decided in polynomial time [11]), then it is possible to write it as a finite union of values (actually, of singleton types). So consider again $\{e_1\texttt{:}e_2\}$ and let t_1 be the type of e_1 and t_2 the type of e_2. First, t_1 must be a subtype of `string` (since record labels are strings). So if t_1 is finite it can be expressed as $\ell_1|\cdots|\ell_n$ which means that e_1 will return the string ℓ_i for some $i \in [1..n]$. Therefore $\{e_1\texttt{:}e_2\}$ will have type $\{\ell_i : t_2\}$ for some $i \in [1..n]$ and, thus, the union of all these types, as expressed by the rule [RCD-FIN] below. If t_1 is infinite instead, then all we can say is that it will be a record with some (unknown) labels, as expressed by rule [RCD-INF].

[RCD-FIN]
$$\frac{\Gamma \vdash e : \ell_1|\cdots|\ell_n \qquad \Gamma \vdash e' : t}{\Gamma \vdash \{e\texttt{:}e'\} : \{\ell_1\texttt{:}t\}|\cdots|\{\ell_n\texttt{:}t\}}$$

[RCD-INF]
$$\frac{\Gamma \vdash e : t \qquad \Gamma \vdash e' : t'}{\Gamma \vdash \{e\texttt{:}e'\} : \{..\}} \quad \begin{array}{c} t \leq \texttt{string} \\ t \text{ is infinite} \end{array}$$

[RCD-MUL]
$$\frac{\Gamma \vdash \{e_1\texttt{:}e'_1\} : t_1 \quad \cdots \quad \Gamma \vdash \{e_n\texttt{:}e'_n\} : t_n}{\Gamma \vdash \{e_1\texttt{:}e'_1, \ldots, e_n\texttt{:}e'_n\} : t_1 + \cdots + t_n}$$

[RCD-CONC]
$$\frac{\Gamma \vdash e_1 : t_1 \quad \Gamma \vdash e_2 : t_2}{\Gamma \vdash e_1 + e_2 : t_1 + t_2} \quad \begin{array}{c} t_1 \leq \{..\} \\ t_2 \leq \{..\} \end{array}$$

[RCD-DEL]
$$\frac{\Gamma \vdash e : t}{\Gamma \vdash e \setminus \ell : t \setminus \ell} \; t \leq \{..\}$$

Records with multiple fields are handled by the rule [RCD-MUL] which "merges" the result of typing single fields by using the type operator $+$ as defined in ℂDuce [5, 14], which is a right-priority record concatenation defined to take into account undefined and unknown fields: for instance, $\{a\texttt{:int}, b\texttt{:int}\} + \{a?\texttt{:bool}\} = \{a\texttt{:int|bool}, b\texttt{:int}\}$; unknown fields in the right-hand side may override known fields of the left-hand side, which is why, for instance, we have $\{a\texttt{:int}, b\texttt{:bool}\} + \{b\texttt{:int},..\} = \{b\texttt{:int},..\}$; likewise, for every record type t (*ie*, for every t subtype of $\{..\}$) we have $t + \{..\} = \{..\}$. Finally, [RCD-CONC] and [RCD-DEL] deal with record concatenation and field deletion, respectively, in a straightforward way: the only constraint is that all expressions must have a record type (*ie*, the constraints of the form $\ldots \leq \{..\}$). See the full version for formal definitions of all these type operators.

Notice that these rules do not ensure that a record will not have two fields with the same label, which is a run-time error. Detecting such an error needs sophisticated type systems (*eg*, dependent types) beyond the scope of this work. This is why in the rule [RCD-MUL] we used type operator "+" which, in case of multiple occurring labels, since records are unordered, corresponds to randomly choosing one of the types bound to these labels: if such a field is selected, it would yield a run-time error, so its typing can be ambiguous. We can fine tune the rule [RCD-MUL] so that when all the t_i are finite unions of record types, then we require to have pairwise disjoint sets of labels; but since the problem would still persist for infinite types we prefer to retain the current, simpler formulation.

4.2 Typing of filter application

Filters are not first-class: they can be applied but not passed around or computed. Therefore we do not assign types to filters but, as for any other expression, we assign types to *filter applications*. The typing rule for filter application

[FILTER-APP]
$$\frac{\Gamma \vdash e : t \qquad \Gamma ; \varnothing ; \varnothing \vdash_{\mathit{fil}} f(t) : s}{\Gamma \vdash f e : s}$$

relies on an auxiliary deduction system for judgments of the form $\Gamma ; \Delta ; M \vdash_{\mathit{fil}} f(t) : s$ that states that if in the environments Γ, Δ, M (explained later on) we apply the filter f to a value of type t, then it will return a result of type s.

To define this auxiliary deduction system, which is the core of our type analysis, we first need to define $\wr f \int$, the type accepted by a filter f. Intuitively, this type gives a necessary condition on the input for the filter not to fail:

Definition 8 (Accepted type). Given a filter f, the *accepted type* of f, written $\wr f \int$ is the set of values defined by:

$$\begin{array}{lcl} \wr e \int & = & \texttt{any} \\ \wr p \Rightarrow f \int & = & \wr p \int \,\&\, \wr f \int \\ \wr f_1 | f_2 \int & = & \wr f_1 \int | \wr f_2 \int \\ \wr (f_1,f_2) \int & = & (\wr f_1 \int , \wr f_2 \int) \\ \wr f_1 ; f_2 \int & = & \wr f_1 \int \end{array} \qquad \begin{array}{lcl} \wr X a \int & = & \texttt{any} \\ \wr \mu X.f \int & = & \wr f \int \\ \wr \texttt{groupby}\ f \int & = & \texttt{[any*]} \\ \wr \texttt{orderby}\ f \int & = & \texttt{[any*]} \end{array}$$
$$\wr \{\ell_1\texttt{:}f_1,.., \ell_n\texttt{:}f_n,..\} \int = \{\ell_1\texttt{:} \wr f_1 \int ,.., \ell_n\texttt{:} \wr f_2 \int ,..\}$$

It is easy to show that an argument included in the accepted type is a necessary (but not sufficient, because of the cases for composition and recursion) condition for the evaluation of a filter not to fail:

Lemma 9. *Let f be a filter and v be a value such that $v \notin \wr f \int$. For every γ, δ, if $\delta;\gamma \vdash_{\mathit{eval}} f(v) \rightsquigarrow r$, then $r \equiv \Omega$.*

The last two auxiliary definitions we need are related to product and record types. In the presence of unions, the most general form for a product type is a finite union of products (since intersections distribute on products). For instance consider the type

$$\texttt{(int,int)|(string,string)}$$

This type denotes the set of pairs for which either both projections are `int` or both projections are `string`. A type such as

$$\texttt{(int|string,int|string)}$$

is less precise, since it also allows pairs whose first projection is an `int` and second projection is a `string` and *vice versa*. We see that it is necessary to manipulate finite unions of products (and similarly for records), and therefore, we introduce the following notations:

[1] Notice that our expressions, whereas they include *filter* applications, do not include applications of expressions to expressions. Therefore if the host language provides function definitions, then the applications of the host language must be dealt as foreign expressions, as well (*cf.* `apply` in §2.2).

Lemma 10 (Product decomposition). *Let* $t \in$ **Types** *such that* $t \leq$ (any,any)*. A* product decomposition *of* t*, denoted by* $\boldsymbol{\pi}(t)$ *is a set of types:*

$$\boldsymbol{\pi}(t) = \{(t_1^1,t_2^1), \ldots, (t_1^n,t_2^n)\}$$

such that $t = \bigvee_{t_i \in \boldsymbol{\pi}(t)} t_i$*. For a given product decomposition, we say that* n *is the* rank *of* t*, noted* $\texttt{rank}(t)$*, and use the notation* $\boldsymbol{\pi}_i^j(t)$ *for the type* t_i^j*.*

There exist several suitable decompositions whose details are out of the scope of this article. We refer the interested reader to [14] and [21] for practical algorithms that compute such decompositions for any subtype of (any,any) or of {..}. These notions of decomposition, rank and projection can be generalized to records:

Lemma 11 (Record decomposition). *Let* $t \in$ **Types** *such that* $t \leq$ {..}*. A* record decomposition *of* t*, denoted by* $\boldsymbol{\rho}(t)$ *is a finite set of types* $\boldsymbol{\rho}(t)=\{r_1, \ldots, r_n\}$ *where each* r_i *is either of the form* $\{\ell_1^i{:}t_1^i, \ldots, \ell_{n_i}^i{:}t_{n_i}^i\}$ *or of the form* $\{\ell_1^i{:}t_1^i, \ldots, \ell_{n_i}^i{:}t_{n_i}^i, ..\}$ *and such that* $t = \bigvee_{r_i \in \boldsymbol{\rho}(t)} r_i$*. For a given record decomposition, we say that* n *is the* rank *of* t*, noted* $\texttt{rank}(t)$*, and use the notation* $\boldsymbol{\rho}_\ell^j(t)$ *for the type of label* ℓ *in the* j^{th} *component of* $\boldsymbol{\rho}(t)$*.*

In our calculus we have three different sets of variables. The set **Vars** of term variables, ranged over by $x, y, \ldots$, introduced in patterns and used in expressions and in arguments of calls of recursive filters. The set **RVars** of term recursion variables, ranged over by $X, Y, \ldots$ and that are used to define recursive filters. The set **TVars** of type recursion variables, ranged over by $T, U, \ldots$ used to define recursive types. In order to use them we need to define three different environments: Γ : **Vars** $\to$ **Types** denoting *type environments* that associate term variables with their types; Δ : **RVars** $\to$ **Filters** denoting *definition environments* that associate each filter recursion variable with the body of its definition; M : **RVars** $\times$ **Types** $\to$ **TVars** denoting *memoization environments* which record that the call of a given recursive filter on a given type yielded the introduction of a fresh recursion type variable. Our typing rules, thus work on judgments of the form $\Gamma\,;\Delta\,;M \vdash f(t) : t'$ stating that applying f to an expression of type t in the environments Γ, Δ, M yields a result of type t'. This judgment can be derived with the set of rules given in Figure 2.

These rules are straightforward, when put side by side with the dynamic semantics of filters, given in Section 3. It is clear that this type system simulates *at the level of types* the computations that are carried out by filters on values at runtime. For instance, rule [FIL-EXPR] calls the typing function of the host language to determine the type of an expression e. Rule [FIL-PROD] applies a product filter recursively on the first and second projection for each member of the product decomposition of the input type and returns the union of all result types. Rule [FIL-REC] for records is similar, recursively applying sub-filters label-wise for each member of the record decomposition and returning the union of the resulting record types. As for the pattern filter (rule [FIL-PAT]), its subfilter f is typed in the environment augmented by the mapping t/p of the input type against the pattern (*cf.* Theorem 5). The typing rule for the union filter, [FIL-UNION] reflects the first match policy: when typing the second branch, we know that the first was not taken, hence that at runtime the filtered value will have a type that is in t but not in $\wr f_1 \int$. Notice that this is *not* ensured by the definition of accepted type — which is a rough approximation that discards grosser errors but, as we stressed right after its definition, is not sufficient to ensure that evaluation of f_1 will not fail— but by the type system itself: the premises *check* that $f_1(t_1)$ is well-typed which, by induction, implies that f_1 will never fail on values of type t_1 and, ergo, that these values will never reach f_2. Also, we discard from the output type the contribution of the branches that cannot be taken, that is, branches whose accepted type have an empty intersection with the input type t. Composition (rule [FIL-COMP]) is straightforward. In this rule, the restriction that f_1 is a filter with no open recursion variable ensures that its output type s is also a type without free recursion variables and, therefore, that we can use it as input type for f_2. The next three rules work together. The first, [FIL-FIX] introduces for a recursive filter a fresh recursion variable for its output type. It also memoize in Δ that the recursive filter X is associated with a body f and in M that for an input filter X and an input type t, the output type is the newly introduced recursive type variable. When dealing with a recursive call X two situations may arise. One possibility is that it is the first time the filter X is applied to the input type t. We therefore introduce a fresh type variable T and recurse, replacing X by its definition f. Otherwise, if the input type has already been encountered while typing the filter variable X, we can return its memoized type, a type variable T. Finally, Rule [FIL-ORDBY] and Rule [FIL-GRPBY] handle the special cases of groupby and orderby filters. Their typing is explained in the following section.

4.3 Typing of orderby and groupby

While the "structural" filters enjoy simple, compositional typing rules, the ad-hoc operations orderby and groupby need specially crafted rules. Indeed it is well known that when transformation languages have the ability to compare data values type-checking (and also type inference) becomes undecidable (*eg*, see [2, 3]). We therefore provide two typing approximations that yield a good compromise between precision and decidability. First we define an auxiliary function over sequence types:

Definition 12 (Item set). Let $t \in$ **Types** such that $t \leq$ [any*]. The *item set* of t denoted by $\texttt{item}(t)$ is defined by:

$$\begin{array}{lll} \texttt{item}(\texttt{empty}) & = \varnothing & \\ \texttt{item}(t) & = \texttt{item}(t\&(\texttt{any},\texttt{any})) & \text{if } t \not\leq (\texttt{any},\texttt{any}) \\ \texttt{item}(\bigvee_{1\leq i\leq \texttt{rank}(t)} (t_i^1,t_i^2)) & = \bigcup_{1\leq i\leq \texttt{rank}(t)} (\{t_i^1\} \cup \texttt{item}(t_i^2)) & \end{array}$$

The first and second line in the definition ensure that item() returns the empty set for sequence types that are not products, namely for the empty sequence. The third line handles the case of non-empty sequence type. In this case t is a finite union of products, whose first components are the types of the "head" of the sequence and second components are recursively the types of the tails. Note also that this definition is well-founded. Since types are regular trees the number of distinct types accumulated by item() is finite. We can now defined typing rules for the orderby and groupby operators.

orderby f: The orderby filter uses its argument filter f to compute a key from each element of the input sequence and then returns the same sequence of elements, sorted with respect to their key. Therefore, while the types of the elements in the result are still known, their order is lost. We use item() to compute the output type of an orderby application:

$$\text{OrderBy}(t) = \texttt{[}(\bigvee_{t_i \in \texttt{item}(t)} t_i) * \texttt{]}$$

groupby f: The typing of orderby can be used to give a rough approximation of the typing of groupby as stated by rule [FIL-GRPBY]. In words, we obtain a list of pairs where the key component is the result type of f applied to the items of the sequence, and use OrderBy to shuffle the order of the list. A far more precise typing of groupby that keeps track of the relation between list elements and their images via f is given in the full version.

4.4 Soundness, termination, and complexity

The soundness of the type inference system is given by the property of subject reduction for filter application

[FIL-EXPR]

$$\frac{}{\Gamma\,;\Delta\,;M \vdash_{\mathit{fil}} e(t) : \mathtt{type}(\Gamma, e,)}$$

[FIL-PAT]

$$\frac{\Gamma \cup t/p\,;\Delta\,;M \vdash_{\mathit{fil}} f(t) : s}{\Gamma\,;\Delta\,;M \vdash_{\mathit{fil}} p \Rightarrow f(t) : s}\; t \leq \wr p \int \mathbin{\&} \wr f \int$$

[FIL-PROD]

$$\frac{i{=}1..\mathtt{rank}(t),\ j{=}1,2 \qquad \Gamma\,;\Delta\,;M \vdash_{\mathit{fil}} f_j(\boldsymbol{\pi}^i_j(t)) : s^i_j}{\Gamma\,;\Delta\,;M \vdash_{\mathit{fil}} (f_1,f_2)(t) : \bigvee_{i=1..\mathtt{rank}(t)} (s^i_1,s^i_2)}$$

[FIL-REC]

$$\frac{i{=}1..\mathtt{rank}(t),\ j{=}1..m \qquad \Gamma\,;\Delta\,;M \vdash_{\mathit{fil}} f_j(\boldsymbol{\rho}^i_{\ell_j}(t)) : s^i_j}{\Gamma\,;\Delta\,;M \vdash_{\mathit{fil}} \{\ell_1{:}f_1,\ldots,\ell_m{:}f_m\,,..\}(t) : \bigvee_{i=1..\mathtt{rank}(t)} \{\ell_1{:}s^i_1,\ldots,\ell_m{:}s^i_m\,,..\}}$$

[FIL-UNION]

$$\frac{i = 1,2 \quad \Gamma\,;\Delta\,;M \vdash_{\mathit{fil}} f_i(t_i) : s_i}{\Gamma\,;\Delta\,;M \vdash_{\mathit{fil}} f_1|f_2(t) : \bigvee_{\{i|s_i \neq \mathtt{empty}\}} s_i}\; \begin{array}{l} t \leq \wr f_1 \int | \wr f_2 \int \\ t_1 = t\mathbin{\&} \wr f_1 \int \\ t_2 = t\mathbin{\&}\neg \wr f_1 \int \end{array}$$

[FIL-COMP]

$$\frac{\Gamma\,;\Delta\,;M \vdash_{\mathit{fil}} f_1(t) : s \qquad \Gamma\,;\Delta\,;M \vdash_{\mathit{fil}} f_2(s) : s'}{\Gamma\,;\Delta\,;M \vdash_{\mathit{fil}} f_1;f_2(t) : s'}$$

[FIL-FIX]

$$\frac{\Gamma\,;\Delta,(X \mapsto f)\,;M,((X,t) \mapsto T) \vdash_{\mathit{fil}} f(t) : s}{\Gamma\,;\Delta\,;M \vdash_{\mathit{fil}} (\boldsymbol{\mu}X.f)(t) : \boldsymbol{\mu}T.s}\; T \text{ fresh}$$

[FIL-CALL-NEW]

$$\frac{\Gamma\,;\Delta\,;M,((X,t) \mapsto T) \vdash_{\mathit{fil}} \Delta(X)(t) : t'}{\Gamma\,;\Delta\,;M \vdash_{\mathit{fil}} (Xa)(s) : \boldsymbol{\mu}T.t'}\; \begin{array}{c} t = \mathtt{type}(\Gamma, a) \\ (X,t) \notin \mathit{dom}(M) \\ T \text{ fresh} \end{array}$$

[FIL-CALL-MEM]

$$\frac{}{\Gamma\,;\Delta\,;M \vdash_{\mathit{fil}} (Xa)(s) : M(X,t)}\; \begin{array}{c} t = \mathtt{type}(\Gamma, a) \\ (X,t) \in \mathit{dom}(M) \end{array}$$

[FIL-ORDBY]

$$\frac{\forall t_i \in \mathtt{item}(t) \quad \Gamma\,;\Delta\,;M \vdash_{\mathit{fil}} f(t_i) : s_i}{\Gamma\,;\Delta\,;M \vdash_{\mathit{fil}} (\mathtt{orderby}\ f)(t) : \mathsf{OrderBy}(t)}\; \begin{array}{l} t \leq \mathtt{[any*]} \\ \bigvee_i s_i \text{ is ordered} \end{array}$$

[FIL-GRPBY]

$$\frac{\forall t_i \in \mathtt{item}(t) \quad \Gamma\,;\Delta\,;M \vdash_{\mathit{fil}} f(t_i) : s_i}{\Gamma\,;\Delta\,;M \vdash_{\mathit{fil}} (\mathtt{groupby}\ f)(t) : \mathtt{[}((\bigvee_i s_i),\mathsf{OrderBy}(t))\mathtt{*]}}\; t \leq \mathtt{[any*]}$$

Figure 2. Type inference algorithm for filter application

Theorem 13 (subject reduction). *If* $\varnothing\,;\varnothing\,;\varnothing \vdash_{\mathit{fil}} f(t) : s$, *then for all* $v : t$, $\varnothing;\varnothing \vdash_{\mathit{eval}} f(v) \rightsquigarrow r$ *implies* $r : s$.

whose proof is given in the full version. It is easy to write a filter for which the type inference algorithm, that is the deduction of $\vdash_{\text{fil}}$, does not terminate: $\boldsymbol{\mu}X.x \Rightarrow X(x,x)$. The deduction of $\Gamma\,;\Delta\,;M \vdash_{\mathit{fil}} f(t) : s$ simulates an (abstract) execution of the filter f on the type t. Since filters are Turing complete, then in general it is not possible to decide whether the deduction of $\vdash_{\text{fil}}$ for a given filter f will terminate for every input type t. For this reason we define a static analysis *Check*(f) for filters that ensures that if f passes the analysis, then for every input type t the deduction of $\Gamma\,;\Delta\,;M \vdash_{\mathit{fil}} f(t) : s$ terminates. For space reasons the formal definition of *Check*(f) is available in only the full version, but its behavior can be easily explained. Imagine that a recursive filter f is applied to some input type t. The algorithm tracks all the recursive calls occurring in f; next it performs one step of reduction of each recursive call by unfolding the body; finally it checks in this unfolding that if a variable occurs in the argument of a recursive call, then it is bound to a type that is a subtree of the original type t. In other words, the analysis verifies that in the execution of the derivation for $f(t)$ every call to s/p for some type s and pattern p always yields a type environment where variables used in recursive calls are bound to subtrees of t. This implies that the rule [FIL-CALL-NEW] will always memoize for a given X, types that are obtained from the arguments of the recursive calls of X by replacing their variables with a subtree of the original type t memoized by the rule [FIL-FIX]. Since t is regular, then it has finitely many distinct subtrees, thus [FIL-CALL-NEW] can memoize only finitely many distinct types, and therefore the algorithm terminates.

More precisely, the analysis proceeds in two passes. In the first pass the algorithm tracks all recursive filters and for each of them it (i) marks the variables that occur in the arguments of its recursive calls, (ii) assigns to each variable an abstract identifier representing the subtree of the input type to which the variable will be bound at the initial call of the filter, and (iii) it returns the set of all types obtained by replacing variables by the associated abstract identifier in each argument of a recursive call. The last set intuitively represents all the possible ways in which recursive calls can shuffle and recompose the subtrees forming the initial input type. The second phase of the analysis first abstractly reduces by one step each recursive filter by applying it on the set of types collected in the first phase of the analysis and then checks whether, after this reduction, all the variables marked in the first phase (*ie*, those that occur in arguments of recursive calls) are still bound to subtrees of the initial input type: if this checks fails, then the filter is rejected.

It is not difficult to see that the type inference algorithm converges if and only if for every input type there exists a integer n such that after n recursive calls the marked variables are bound only to subtrees of the initial input type (or to something that does not depend on it, of course). Since deciding whether such an n exists is not possible, our analysis checks whether for all possible input types a filter satisfies it for $n{=}1$, that is to say, that at every recursive call its marked variables satisfy the property; otherwise it rejects the filter.

Theorem 14 (Termination). *If Check*(f), *then for every type t the deduction of* $\Gamma\,;\varnothing\,;\varnothing \vdash_{\mathit{fil}} f(t) : s$ *is in 2-EXPTIME. Furthermore, if t is given as a non-deterministic tree automaton (NTA) then* $\Gamma\,;\varnothing\,;\varnothing \vdash_{\mathit{fil}} f(t) : s$ *is in EXPTIME, where the size of the problem is* $|f| \times |t|$.

This complexity result is in line with those of similar formalisms. For instance in [18], it is shown that type-checking non deterministic top-down tree transducers is in EXPTIME when the input and output types are given by a NTA.

All filters defined in this article pass the analysis. As an example consider the filter `rotate` that applied to a list returns the same list with the first element moved to the last position (and the empty list if applied to the empty list):

$$\boldsymbol{\mu}X.\ (\ (x,(y,z)) \Rightarrow (y,X(x,z)) \quad | \quad w \Rightarrow w\ )$$

The analysis succeeds on this filter. If we denote by ι_x the abstract subtree bound to the variable x, then the recursive call will be executed on the abstract argument (ι_x,ι_z). So in the unfolding of the recursive call x is bound to ι_x, whereas y and z are bound to two distinct subtrees of ι_z. The variables in the recursive call, x and z, are thus bound to subtrees of the original tree (even though the argument of the recursive call is *not* a subtree of the original tree), therefore the filter is accepted . In order to appreciate the precision of the inference algorithm consider the type `[int+ bool+]`, that is, the type of lists formed by some integers (at least one) followed by some booleans (at least one). For the application of `rotate` to an argument of this type our algorithm *statically* infers the most precise type, that is, `[int* bool+ int]`. If we apply it once more the inferred type is `[int* bool+ int int]|[bool* int bool]`.

Generic filters are Turing complete. However, requiring that *Check*() holds —meaning that the filter is typeable by our system— restricts the expressive power of our filters by preventing them from *recomposing* a new value before doing a recursive call. For instance, it is not possible to typecheck a filter which reverses the elements of a sequence. Determining the exact class of transformations that typeable filters can express is challenging. However it is possible to show (see the full version for the proof) that typeable filters are strictly more expressive than top-down tree transducers with regular look-ahead, a formalism for tree transformations introduced in [13]. For an intuition of this result consider the tree:

$$a(u_1(\ldots(u_n()))v_1(\ldots(v_m())))$$

that is, a tree whose root is labeled a with two children, each being a monadic tree of height n and m, respectively. It is not possible to write a top-down tree transducer with regular look-ahead that creates the tree

$$a(u_1(\ldots(u_n(v_1(\ldots v_m()))))))$$

which is just the concatenation of the two children of the root, seen as sequences, a transformation that can be easily programmed by typeable filters. The key difference in expressive power comes from the fact that filters are evaluated with an *environment* that binds capture variables to sub-trees of the input. This feature is essential to encode sequence concatenation and sequence flattening —two pervasive operations when dealing with sequences— that cannot be expressed by top-down tree transducers with regular look-ahead.

5. Jaql

In this Section, we show how filters can be used to capture some popular languages for processing data on the Cloud. We consider Jaql [16], a query language for JSON developed by IBM. We give translation rules from a subset of Jaql into filters.

Definition 15 (Jaql expressions). We use the following simplified grammar for Jaql (where we distinguish simple expressions, ranged over by e, from "core expressions" ranged over by k).

```
e ::= c                                            (constants)
    | x                                            (variables)
    | $                                            (current value)
    | [e, ..., e]                                  (arrays)
    | { e:e, ..., e:e }                            (records)
    | e.l                                          (field access)
    | op(e, ...,e)                                 (function call)
    | e -> k                                       (pipe)
k ::= filter (each x )? e                          (filter)
    | transform (each x)? e                        (transform)
    | expand ((each x)? e)?                        (expand)
    | group ((each x)? by x=e (as x)?)? into e     (grouping)
```

In order to ease the presentation we extend our syntax by adding "filter definitions" (already informally used in the introduction) to filters and "filter calls" to expressions:

$$e ::= \texttt{let filter } F[F_1,\ldots,F_n] = f \texttt{ in } e \quad \textbf{(filter defn.)}$$
$$f ::= F[f,\ldots,f] \quad \textbf{(call)}$$

where F ranges over *filter names*. The mapping for most of the language we consider rely on the following built-in filters.

```
let filter Filter [F] = μX.
      `nil ⇒ `nil
    | ((x, xs),tl) ⇒ (X(x, xs),X(tl))
    | (x,tl) ⇒ Fx ;(`true ⇒ (x, X(tl))|`false ⇒ X(tl))

let filter Transform [F] = μX.
      `nil ⇒ `nil
    | ((x, xs),tl) ⇒ (X(x, xs),X(tl))
    | (x,tl) ⇒ (Fx, X(tl))

let filter Expand = μX.
      `nil ⇒ `nil
    | (`nil,tl) ⇒ X(tl)
    | ((x, xs),tl) ⇒ (x,X(xs, tl))
```

Jaql expressions are mapped to our expressions as follows (where $ is a distinguished expression variable interpreting Jaql's $):

$$\begin{array}{lcl}
\llbracket \mathtt{c} \rrbracket & = & c \\
\llbracket x \rrbracket & = & x \\
\llbracket \$ \rrbracket & = & \$ \\
\llbracket \{e_1 : e'_1, \ldots, e_n : e'_n\} \rrbracket & = & \{\llbracket e_1 \rrbracket : \llbracket e'_1 \rrbracket, \ldots, \llbracket e_n \rrbracket : \llbracket e'_n \rrbracket\} \\
\llbracket e.\mathtt{l} \rrbracket & = & \llbracket e \rrbracket .l \\
\llbracket \mathsf{op}(e_1, \ldots, e_n) \rrbracket & = & \mathsf{op}(\llbracket e_1 \rrbracket, \ldots, \llbracket e_n \rrbracket) \\
\llbracket [e_1, \ldots, e_n] \rrbracket & = & (\llbracket e_1 \rrbracket, \ldots (\llbracket e_n \rrbracket, \texttt{`nil}) \ldots) \\
\llbracket e \texttt{ -> } k \rrbracket & = & \llbracket e \rrbracket ; \llbracket k \rrbracket_{\mathsf{F}}
\end{array}$$

Jaql core expressions are mapped to filters as follows:

$$\begin{array}{lcl}
\llbracket \texttt{filter } e \rrbracket_{\mathsf{F}} & = & \llbracket \texttt{filter each } \$\, e \rrbracket_{\mathsf{F}} \\
\llbracket \texttt{filter each } x\, e \rrbracket_{\mathsf{F}} & = & \texttt{Filter } [x \Rightarrow \llbracket e \rrbracket] \\
\llbracket \texttt{transform } e \rrbracket_{\mathsf{F}} & = & \llbracket \texttt{transform each } \$\, e \rrbracket_{\mathsf{F}} \\
\llbracket \texttt{transform each } x\, e \rrbracket_{\mathsf{F}} & = & \texttt{Transform } [x \Rightarrow \llbracket e \rrbracket] \\
\llbracket \texttt{expand each } x\, e \rrbracket_{\mathsf{F}} & = & \llbracket \texttt{expand} \rrbracket_{\mathsf{F}} ; \llbracket \texttt{transform each } x\, e \rrbracket_{\mathsf{F}} \\
\llbracket \texttt{expand} \rrbracket_{\mathsf{F}} & = & \texttt{Expand} \\
\llbracket \texttt{group into } e \rrbracket_{\mathsf{F}} & = & \llbracket \texttt{group by } y\texttt{=true into } e \rrbracket_{\mathsf{F}} \\
\llbracket \texttt{group by } y\texttt{=}e_1 \texttt{ into } e_2 \rrbracket_{\mathsf{F}} & = & \llbracket \texttt{group each } \$ \texttt{ by } y\texttt{=}e_1 \texttt{ into } e_2 \rrbracket_{\mathsf{F}}
\end{array}$$

$$\llbracket \texttt{group each } x \texttt{ by } y\texttt{=}e_1 \texttt{ into } e_2 \rrbracket_{\mathsf{F}} = \llbracket \texttt{group each } x \texttt{ by } y = e_1 \texttt{ as } \$ \texttt{ into } e_2 \rrbracket_{\mathsf{F}}$$

$$\llbracket \texttt{group each } x \texttt{ by } y = e_1 \texttt{ as } g \texttt{ into } e_2 \rrbracket_{\mathsf{F}} = \texttt{groupby } x \Rightarrow \llbracket e_1 \rrbracket \texttt{; Transform } [(y,g) \Rightarrow \llbracket e_2 \rrbracket]$$

This translation defines the (first, in our knowledge) formal semantics of Jaql. Such a translation is *all* that is needed to define the semantics of a NoSQL language and, as a bonus, endow it with the type inference system we described *without requiring any modification of the original language*. No further action is demanded since the machinery to exploit it is all developed in this work.

As for typing, every Jaql expression is encoded into a filter for which type-checking is ensured to terminate: *Check*() holds for `Filter[]`, `Transform[]`, and `Expand` (provided it holds also for their arguments) since they only perform recursive calls on recombinations of subtrees of their input; by its definition, the encoding does not introduce any new recursion and, hence, it always yields a composition and application of filters for which *Check*() holds.

5.1 Examples

To show how we use the encoding, let us encode the example of the introduction. For the sake of the concision we will use filter definitions (rather than expanding them in details). We use `Fil` and `Sel` defined in the introduction, `Expand` and `Transform[]` defined at the beginning of the section, the encoding of Jaql's field selection as defined in Section 3, and finally `Head` that returns the first element of a sequence and a family of recursive filters `Rgrp`i with $i \in \mathbb{N}^+$ both defined below:

```
let filter Head = `nil => null | (x,xs) => x

let filter Rgrpi = `nil => `nil
                 | ((i,x),tail) => (x , Rgrpi tail)
                 | _ => Rgrpi tail
```

Then, the query in the introduction is encoded as follows

```
[employees depts];
[Sel Fil];
[Transform[x =>(1,x)]  Transform[x =>(2,x)]];
Expand;
groupby ( (1,$)=>$.dept | (2,$)=>$.depid );
Transform[(g,1)=>(
          [(1; Rgrp1) (1; Rgrp2)];
          [es ds] =>
                 { dept: g,
                   deptName: (ds ; Head).name),
                   numEmps: count(es) } )]
```

In words, we perform the selection on employees and filter the departments (lines 1-2); we tag each element by 1 if it comes from employees, and by 2 if it comes from departments (line 3); we merge the two collections (line 4); we group the heterogeneous list according to the corresponding key (line 5); then for each element of the result of grouping we capture in g the key (line 6), split the group into employees and depts (line 7), capture each subgroup into the corresponding variable (*ie*, `es` and `ds`) (line 8) and return the expression specified in the query after the "`into`" (lines 8-10). The general definition of the encoding for the co-grouping can be found in the full version.

Let us now illustrate how the above composition of filters is typed. Consider an instance where:

- `employees` has type `[` *Remp*`* ]`, where *Remp* ≡ `{ dept: int, income:int, ..}`
- `depts` has type `[ (`*Rdep* `|` *Rbranch*`)* ]`, where *Rdep* ≡ `{depid:int, name: string, size: int}` *Rbranch* ≡ `{brid:int, name: string}` (this type is a subtype of `Dept` as defined in the introduction)

The global input type is therefore (line 1)

`[ [` *Remp*`* ] [ (`*Rdep* `|` *Rbranch*`)* ] ]`

which becomes, after selection and filtering (line 2)

`[ [` *Remp*`* ] [` *Rdep*`* ] ]`

(note how all occurrences of *Rbranch* are ignored by `Fil`). Tagging with an integer (line 3) and flattening (line 4) yields

`[ (1,`*Remp*`)* (2,`*Rdep*`)* ]`

which illustrates the precise typing of products coupled with singleton types (*ie*, `1` instead of `int`). While the `groupby` (line 5) introduces an approximation the dependency between the tag and the corresponding type is kept

`[ (int, [ ((1,`*Remp*`) | (2,`*Rdep*`) )+ ]) * ]`

Lastly the transform is typed exactly, yielding the final type

`[ {dept:int, deptName:string|null, numEmps:int }* ]`

Note how `null` is retained in the output type (since there may be employees without a department, then `Head` may be applied to an empty list returning `null`, and the selection of `name` of `null` returns `null`). For instance suppose to pipe the Jaql grouping defined in the introduction into the following Jaql expression, in order to produce a printable representation of the records of the result

```
transform each x (
 (x.deptName)@":"@(to_string x.dep)@":"@(x.numEmps))
```

where `@` denotes string concatenation and `to_string` is a conversion operator (from any type to string). The composition is ill-typed for three reasons: the field `dept` is misspelled as `dep`, `x.numEmps` is of type `int` (so it must be applied to `to_string` before concatenation), and the programmer did not account for the fact that the value stored in the field `deptName` may be `null`. The encoding produces the following lines to be appended to the previous code:

```
12 Transform[ x =>
13  (x.deptName)@":"@(to_string x.dep)@":"@(x.numEmps)]
```

in which all the three errors are detected by our type system. A subtler example of error is given by the following alternative code

```
12 Transform[
13   { dept : d, deptName: n&String, numEmps: e } =>
14       n @ ":" @ (to_string d) @ ":" @ (to_string e)
15  | { deptName: null, .. } => ""
16  | _ => "Invalid department" ]
```

which corrects all the previous errors but adds a new one since, as detected by our type system, the last branch can be never selected. As we can see, our type-system ensures soundness, forcing the programmer to handle exceptional situations (as in the `null` example above) but is also precise enough to detect that some code paths can never be reached.

In order to focus on our contributions we kept the language of types and filters simple. However there already exists several contributions on the types and expressions used here. Two in particular are worth mentioning in this context: recursive patterns and XML.

Definition 3 defines patterns inductively but, alternatively, we can consider the (possibly infinite) regular trees *coinductively* generated by these productions and, on the lines of what is done in ℂDuce, use the recursive patterns so obtained to encode regular expressions patterns (see [5]). Although this does not enhance expressiveness, it greatly improves the writing of programs since it makes it possible to capture distinct subsequences of a sequence by a single match. For instance, when a sequence is matched against a pattern such as `[ (int as x | bool as y | _)* ]`, then `x` captures (the list of) all integer elements (capture variables in regular expression patterns are bound to lists), `y` captures all Boolean elements, while the remaining elements are ignored. By such patterns, co-grouping can be encoded without the `Rgrp`. For instance, the transform in lines 6-11 can be more compactly rendered as:

```
6  Transform[(g,[ ((1,es)|(2,ds))* ]) =>
7                  { dept: g,
8                    deptName: (ds;Head).name,
9                    numEmps: count(es) }]
```

For what concerns XML, the types used here were originally defined for XML, so it comes as a no surprise that they can seamlessly express XML types and values. For example ℂDuce uses the very same types used here to encode both XML types and elements as triples, the first element being the tag, the second a record representing attributes, and the third a heterogeneous sequence for the content of the element. Furthermore, we can adapt the results of [10] to encode forward XPath queries in filters. Therefore, it requires little effort to use the filters presented here to encode languages such as JSONiq [28] designed to integrate JSON and XML, or to precisely type regular expressions, the import/export of XML data, or XPath queries embedded in Jaql programs. The description of these encodings can be found in the long version of this article, where we also argue that it is better to extend NoSQL languages with XML primitives directly derived from our system rather than to use our system to encode languages such as JSONiq. As a matter of fact, existing approaches tend to juxtapose XML and JSON operators thus yielding to stratified (*ie*, not tightly integrated) systems which have several drawbacks (*eg*, JSONiq does not allow XML nodes to contain JSON objects and arrays). Such restrictions are absent from our approach since both XML and JSON operators are encoded in the same basic building blocks and, as such, can be freely nested and combined.

5.2 Extensions

Hitherto we used filters only to encode primitive operators of some NoSQL languages, in particular Jaql. However, it is possible to *add* filters to other languages, so as to have user-defined operators typed as precisely as primitive ones. From a linguistic point of view this is a no-brainer: it suffices to add filter application to the expressions of the host language. However, such an extension can be problematic from a computational viewpoint, since it may disrupt the execution model, especially for what concerns aspects of parallelism and distribution. A good compromise is to add only filters that have "local" effects, which can already bring dramatic increases in expressiveness and type precision without disrupting the distributed compilation model. For instance, one can add just pattern and union filters as in the following (extended) Jaql program:

```
transform ( {a:x,..} as y => {y.*, sum:x+x} | y => y )
```

(with the convention that a filter occurring as an expression denotes its application to the current argument `$`). With this syntax, our inference system is able to deduce that feeding this expression with an argument of type `[{a?:int, c:bool}*]` returns a result of type `[({a:int, c:bool, sum:int} | {c:bool})*]`. This precision comes from the capacity of our inference system to discriminate between the two branches of the filter and deduce that a `sum` field will be added only if the `a` field is present. Similarly by using pattern matching in a Jaql "`filter`" expression, we can deduce that `filter ( int => true | _ => false )` fed with any sequence of elements always returns a (possibly empty) list of integers. An even greater precision can be obtained for grouping expressions when the generation of the key is performed by a filter that discriminates on types: the result type can keep a precise correspondence between keys and the corresponding groups.

6. Commentaries

Finally, let us explain some subtler design choices for our system.

Filter design: The reader may wonder whether products and record *filters* are really necessary since, at first sight, the filter (f_1,f_2) could be encoded as $(x, y) \Rightarrow (f_1x, f_2y)$ and similarly for records. The point is that f_1x and f_2y are expressions —and thus their pair is a filter— only if the f_i's are closed (*ie*, without free term recursion variables). Without an explicit product filter it would not be possible to program a filter as simple as the identity map, $\mu X.$`'nil` $\Rightarrow$ `'nil`$|(h, t) \Rightarrow (h,Xt)$ since Xt is not an expression (X is a free term recursion variable). Similarly, we need an explicit record filter to process recursively defined record types such as $\mu X.$(`{head:int, tail:`X`}`|`'nil`).

Likewise, one can wonder why we put in filters only the "open" record variant that copy extra fields and not the closed one. The reason is that if we want a filter to be applied only to records with exactly the fields specified in the filter, then this can be simply obtained by a pattern matching. So the filter $\{\ell_1\mathtt{:}f_1, \ldots, \ell_n\mathtt{:}f_n\}$ (*ie*, without the trailing "`..`") can be simply introduced as syntactic sugar for $\{\ell_1\mathtt{:any}, \ldots, \ell_n\mathtt{:any}\} \Rightarrow \{\ell_1\mathtt{:}f_1, \ldots, \ell_n\mathtt{:}f_n\ \mathtt{,..}\}$

Constructors: The syntax for constructing records and pairs is exactly the same in patterns, types, expressions, and filters. The reader may wonder why we did not distinguish them by using, say, $\times$ for product types or $=$ instead of `:` in record values. This, combined with the fact that values and singletons have the same syntax, is a critical design choice that greatly reduces the confusion in these languages, since it makes it possible to have a unique representation for constructions that are semantically equivalent. Consider for instance the pattern $(x,(3,$`'nil`$))$. With our syntax $(3,$`'nil`$)$ denotes both the product type of two singletons 3 and `'nil`, or the value $(3,$`'nil`$)$, or the singleton that contains this value. According to the interpretation we choose, the pattern can then be interpreted as a pattern that matches a product or a pattern that matches a value. If we had differentiated the syntax of singletons from that of values (*eg*, $\{v\}$) and that of pairs from products, then the pattern above could have been written in five different ways. The point is that they all would match exactly the same sets of values, which is why we chose to have the same syntax for all of them.

Record types: In order to type records with computed labels we distinguished two cases according to whether the type of a record label is finite or not. Although such a distinction is simple, it is not unrealistic. Labels with singleton types cover the (most common) case of records with statically fixed labels. The dynamic choice of a label from a statically known list of labels is a usage pattern seen in JavaScript when building an object which must conform to some interface based on a run-time value. Labels with infinite types cover the fairly common usage scenario in which records are used as dictionaries: we deduce for the expression computing the label the type `string`, thus forcing the programmer to insert some code that checks that the label is present before accessing it.

The rationale behind the typing of records was twofold. First and foremost, in this work we wanted to avoid type annotations at all costs (since there is not even a notion of schema for JSON records and collections —only the notion of basic type is defined— we cannot expect the Jaql programmer to put any kind of type information in the code). More sophisticated type systems, such as dependent types, would probably preclude type reconstruction: dependent types need a lot of annotations and this does not fit our requirements. Second, we wanted the type-system to be simple yet precise. Making the finite/infinite distinction increases typing precision at no cost (we do not need any extra machinery since we already have singleton types). Adding heuristics or complex analysis just to gain some precision on records would have blurred the main focus of our article, which is not on typing records but on typing *transformations* on records. We leave such additions for future work.

Record polymorphism: The type-oriented reader will have noticed that we do not use row variables to type records, and nevertheless we have a high degree of polymorphism. Row variables are useful to type functions or transformations since they can keep track of record fields that are not modified by the transformation. In this setting we do not need them since we do not type transformations (*ie*, filters) but just the application of transformations (filters are not first-class terms). We have polymorphic typing via filters (see how the first example given in Section 5.2 keeps track of the `c` field) and therefore open records suffice.

Related work: In the (nested) relational (and SQL) context, many works have studied the integration of (nested)-relational algebra or SQL into general purpose programming languages. Among the first attempts was the integration of the relational model in Pascal [29] or in Smalltalk [12]. Also, monads or comprehensions [8, 31, 32] have been successfully used to design and implement query languages including a way to embed queries within host languages. Significant efforts have been done to equip those languages with type systems and type checking disciplines [1, 9, 23, 24] and more recently [25] for integration and typing aspects. However, these approaches only support homogeneous sequences of records in the context of specific classes of queries (practically equivalent to a nested relational algebra or calculus), they do not account for records with computable labels, and therefore they are not easily transposable to a setting where sequences are heterogeneous, data are semi-structured, and queries are much more expressive.

While the present work is inspired and stems from previous works on the XML iterators, targeting NoSQL languages made the filter calculus presented here substantially different from the one of [10, 21] (dubbed XML filters in what follows), as well in syntax as in dynamic and static semantics. In [10] XML filters behave as some kind of top-down tree transducers, termination is enforced by heavy syntactic restrictions, and a *less* constrained use of the composition makes type inference challenging and requires sometimes cumbersome type annotations. While XML filters are allowed to operate by composition on the *result* of a recursive call (and, thus, simulate bottom-up tree transformations), the absence of explicit arguments in recursive calls makes programs understandable only to well-trained programmers. In contrast, the main focus of the current work was to make programs immediately intelligible to any functional programmer and make filters effective for the typing of sequence transformations: sequence iteration, element filtering, one-level flattening. The last two are especially difficult to write with XML filters (and require type annotations). Also, the integration of filters with record types (absent in [10] and just sketched in [21]) is novel and much needed to encode JSON transformations.

7. Conclusion

Our work addresses two very practical problems, namely the typing of NoSQL languages and a comprehensive definition of their semantics. These languages add to list comprehension and SQL operators the ability to work on heterogeneous data sets and are based on JSON (instead of tuples). Typing precisely each of these features using the best techniques of the literature would probably yield quite a complex type-system (mixing row polymorphism for records, parametric polymorphism, some form of dependent typing,...) and we are skeptical that this could be achieved without using any explicit type annotation. Therefore we explored the formalization of these languages from scratch, by defining a calculus and a type system. The thesis we defended is that all operations typical of current NoSQL languages, as long as they operate structurally (*ie*, without resorting on term equality or relations), amount to a combination of more basic bricks: our filters. On the structural side, the claim is that combining recursive records and pairs by unions, intersections, and negations suffices to capture all possible structuring of data, covering a palette ranging from comprehensions, to heterogeneous lists mixing typed and untyped data, through regular expressions types and XML schemas. Therefore, our calculus not only provides a simple way to give a formal semantics to, reciprocally compare, and combine operators of different NoSQL languages, but also offers a means to equip these languages, in they current definition (*ie*, without any type definition or annotation), with precise type inference. This type inference yields and surpasses in precision systems using parametric polymorphism and row variables. The price to pay is that *transformations* are not first class: we do not type filters but just their applications. However, this seems an advantageous deal in the world of NoSQL languages where "selects" are never passed around (at least, not explicitly), but early error detection is critical, especially in the view of the cost of code deployment.[2]

The result are filters, a set of untyped terms that can be easily included in a host language to complement in a typeful framework existing operators with user-defined ones. The requirements to include filters into a host language are so minimal that every modern typed programming language satisfies them. The interest resides not in the fact that we can add filter applications to any language, rather that filters can be used to define a smooth integration of calls to domain specific languages (*eg*, SQL, XPath, Pig, Regex) into general purpose ones (*eg*, Java, C#, Python, OCaml) so as both can share the same set of values and the same typing discipline. Likewise, even though filters can provide a prototyping platform for queries, they cannot currently be used as a final compilation stage for NoSQL languages: their operations rely on a Lisp-like encoding of sequences and this makes the correspondence with optimized bulk operations on lists awkward. Whether we can derive an efficient compilation from filters to map-reduce (recovering the bulk semantics of the high-level language) is a challenging open question. Future plans include practical experimentation of our technique: we intend to benchmark our type analysis against existing collections of Jaql programs, gauge the amount of code that is ill typed and verify on this how frequently the programmer adopted defensive programming to cope with the potential type errors.

References

[1] A. Albano, G. Ghelli, and R. Orsini. Fibonacci: A programming language for object databases. *The VLDB Journal*, 4:403–444, 1995.

[2] N. Alon, T. Milo, F. Neven, D. Suciu, and V. Vianu. XML with data values: typechecking revisited. In *PODS '01*. ACM, 2001.

[2] Only filter-encoded operators are not first class: if the host language provides, say, higher-order functions, then they stay higher-order and are typed by embedding the host type system, if any, via "foreign type calls".

[3] N. Alon, T. Milo, F. Neven, D. Suciu, and V. Vianu. Typechecking XML views of relational databases. *ACM Trans. Comput. Logic*, 4:315–354, July 2003.

[4] A. Behm *et al.* Asterix: towards a scalable, semistructured data platform for evolving-world models. *DAPD*, 29(3):185–216, 2011.

[5] V. Benzaken, G. Castagna, and A. Frisch. CDuce: an XML-friendly general purpose language. In *ICFP '03*. ACM, 2003.

[6] K. Beyer *et al.* Jaql: A scripting language for large scale semistructured data analysis. *PVLDB*, 4(12):1272–1283, 2011.

[7] S. Boag, D. Chamberlain, M. F. Fernández, D. Florescu, J. Robie, and J. Siméon. XQuery 1.0: An XML query language, W3C rec., 2007.

[8] P. Buneman, L. Libkin, D. Suciu, V. Tannen, and L. Wong. Comprehension syntax. *SIGMOD Record*, 23(1):87–96, 1994.

[9] P. Buneman, R. Nikhil, and R. Frankel. A Practical Functional Programming System for Databases. In *Proc. Conference on Functional Programming and Architecture*. ACM, 1981.

[10] G. Castagna and K. Nguyễn. Typed iterators for XML. In *ICFP '08*. ACM, 2008.

[11] H. Comon, M. Dauchet, R. Gilleron, F. Jacquemard, C. Löding, D. Lugiez, S. Tison, and M. Tommasi. Tree automata techniques and applications. http://www.grappa.univ-lille3.fr/tata, 2007.

[12] G. Copeland and D. Maier. Making Smalltalk a database system. In *ACM SIGMOD Conf.*, 1984.

[13] J. Engelfriet. Top-down tree transducers with regular look-ahead. *Mathematical Systems Theory*, 10(1):289–303, Dec. 1976.

[14] A. Frisch. *Théorie, conception et réalisation d'un langage de programmation adapté à XML*. PhD thesis, Université Paris 7 Denis Diderot, 2004.

[15] A. Frisch, G. Castagna, and V. Benzaken. Semantic subtyping: Dealing set-theoretically with function, union, intersection, and negation types. *Journal of the ACM*, 55(4):1–64, 2008.

[16] Jaql. `http://code.google.com/p/jaql`.

[17] JavaScript Object Notation (JSON). `http://json.org/`.

[18] W. Martens and F. Neven. Typechecking top-down uniform unranked tree transducers. In *ICDT '03*. Springer, 2002.

[19] E. Meijer. The world according to LINQ. *ACM Queue*, 9(8):60, 2011.

[20] E. Meijer and G. Bierman. A co-relational model of data for large shared data banks. *Communications of the ACM*, 54(4):49–58, 2011.

[21] K. Nguyễn. *Language of Combinators for XML: Conception, Typing, Implementation*. PhD thesis, Université Paris-Sud 11, 2008.

[22] Odata. `http://www.odata.org/`.

[23] A. Ohori and P. Buneman. Type Inference in a Database Programming Language. In *LISP and Functional Programming*, 1988.

[24] A. Ohori, P. Buneman, and V. Tannen. Database Programming in Machiavelli –a Polymorphic Language with Static Type Inference. In *ACM SIGMOD Conf.*, 1989.

[25] A. Ohori and K. Ueno. Making standard ML a practical database programming language. In *ICFP '11*, 2011.

[26] C. Olston, B. Reed, U. Srivastava, R. Kumar, and A. Tomkins. Pig latin: a not-so-foreign language for data processing. In *ACM SIGMOD Conf.*, 2008.

[27] F. Özcan *et al.* Emerging trends in the enterprise data analytics: connecting Hadoop and DB2 warehouse. In *ACM SIGMOD Conf.*, 2011.

[28] J. Robie (editor). JSONiq. `http://jsoniq.org`.

[29] J. Schmidt and M. Mall. Pascal/R Report. Technical Report 66, Fachbereich Informatik, université de Hamburg, 1980.

[30] Squeryl: A Scala ORM and DSL for talking with Databases with minimum verbosity and maximum type safety. `http://squeryl.org/`.

[31] V. Tannen, P. Buneman, and L. Wong. Naturally embedded query languages. In *ICDT*, pages 140–154, 1992.

[32] P. Trinder and P. Wadler. Improving list comprehension database queries. In *4th IEEE Region 10 Conference (TENCON)*, 1989.

[33] Unql. `http://www.unqlspec.org/`.

Quantitative Abstraction Refinement *

Pavol Černý Thomas A. Henzinger Arjun Radhakrishna
IST Austria

Abstract

We propose a general framework for abstraction with respect to quantitative properties, such as worst-case execution time, or power consumption. Our framework provides a systematic way for counter-example guided abstraction refinement for quantitative properties. The salient aspect of the framework is that it allows anytime verification, that is, verification algorithms that can be stopped at any time (for example, due to exhaustion of memory), and report approximations that improve monotonically when the algorithms are given more time.

We instantiate the framework with a number of quantitative abstractions and refinement schemes, which differ in terms of how much quantitative information they keep from the original system. We introduce both state-based and trace-based quantitative abstractions, and we describe conditions that define classes of quantitative properties for which the abstractions provide over-approximations. We give algorithms for evaluating the quantitative properties on the abstract systems. We present algorithms for counter-example based refinements for quantitative properties for both state-based and segment-based abstractions. We perform a case study on worst-case execution time of executables to evaluate the anytime verification aspect and the quantitative abstractions we proposed.

Categories and Subject Descriptors D.2.4 [*Software/Program Verification*]

General Terms Theory, Verification

Keywords abstraction, refinement, quantitative analysis

1. Introduction

The quantitative analysis of systems is gaining importance due to the spread of embedded systems with requirements on resource consumption and timeliness of response. Quantitative analyses have been proposed for properties such as worst-case execution time (see [19] for a survey), power consumption (pioneered in [17]), and prediction of cache behavior for timing analysis (see, for example, [9]).

Anytime algorithms (see [1]) are algorithms that generate imprecise answers quickly and proceed to construct progressively better approximate solutions over time, eventually finding the correct solution. Anytime algorithms are useful in verification, as they offer a way to deal with the state-space explosion problem — if the algorithm is terminated early, for example due to memory exhaustion, it is still able to report an approximation of the desired result. The term *anytime verification* has been proposed [16] recently in the context of verifying boolean properties, as a way to get (non-quantifiably) better estimates on whether a property holds for a system. The anytime concept, however, is particularly well-suited in the context of *quantitative* verification. In this context, abstraction gives a quantitative over-approximation of the quantitative answer to a verification question, and it is natural to require the anytime property: the more time the verification run is given, the (quantifiably) better the over-approximation of the correct answer should be. We implement this anytime property for quantitative verification through an abstraction refinement scheme that monotonically improves the answer. For instance, abstraction refinement may compute increasingly better approximations of power consumption of a system.

We propose a framework for abstraction and abstraction refinement for quantitative properties that is suitable for anytime verification. We explain the motivation and intuition behind the framework using the following example.

Motivating example. Consider the problem of estimating the worst-case execution time (WCET) of the program in Figure 1. We assume an idealized situation where the performance is affected mostly by the cache behavior. Let each program statement have a cost depending on whether it accesses only the cache (or no memory at all), for a cost of 1, or main memory for a cost of 25. we assume that the program variables `i,a,v` are mapped to different cache entries, while `b` and `c` are mapped to the same entry (different from the entries for the other variables). We consider abstractions that abstract only the cache (not the program). The cache is abstracted by an *abstract cache* with a smaller number of entries (accesses to the entries not tracked in the abstract cache are always considered to be a cache miss). Let us start the analysis with an abstract cache of size 2 which caches variables `i` and `v`. In the abstract system (i.e., the original program composed with the abstract cache), the worst-case trace has `v` equal to 1, and the program accesses the (uncached) variable `a` 16 times. The analysis then uses this trace to refine the abstraction. The refinement extends the cache to include the cache entry for `a`. The worst-case execution then has v equal to 2, and it has 8 accesses to `b`. The analysis now refines the abstraction by extending the cache with an entry for `b`.

```
a,b,c,i,v: int; input v;
if (v == 1)
 for (i=0;i<16;i++) read(a);
else if(v == 2)
 for (i=0;i<16;i++)
  if (i mod 2 = 0) read(b);
else
 for (i=0;i<16;i++)
  if (i mod 4 = 0) read(c);
```

Figure 1: Example 1

* This research was supported in part by the European Research Council (ERC) Advanced Investigator Grant QUAREM and by the Austrian Science Fund (FWF) project S11402-N23.

POPL'13, January 23–25, 2013, Rome, Italy.

The WCET estimate is thus tightened, until either the highest-cost trace corresponds to a real execution (and thus the WCET estimate is precise), or the analysis runs out of resources and reports the computed over-approximation.

Abstraction for quantitative properties. Our model of systems is weighted transition systems. We provide a way of formalizing quantitative properties of systems which capture important properties studied in literature, including *limit-average*, *discounted-sum*, and boolean properties such as safety and liveness. The framework makes it possible to investigate quantitative versions of the boolean properties: for instance, for safety one could ask not only if an error state is reached, but also how often it is reached. We focus on properties that admit a linear trace that maximizes (or minimizes) the value of the quantitative property. Such a trace is called the *extremal trace* (ext-trace for short).

We present two types of quantitative abstraction schemes. The first is *state-based*, that is, the elements of the abstract domain correspond to sets of states. The second is *segment-based*, that is, the elements of the abstract domain correspond to sets of trace segments.

State-based quantitative abstractions. The abstraction scheme $ExistMax$ is state-based. It is a direct extension of predicate abstraction, where each abstract state corresponds to an equivalence class of concrete states. In addition, with each abstract state, $ExistMax$ stores the maximum weight of the corresponding concrete states. We give conditions for the class of quantitative properties for which $ExistMax$ is a *monotonic over-approximation* (that is, it provides better estimates as the underlying equivalence relation on states is refined). This class includes all the quantitative properties mentioned above. However, we show that there are naturally defined properties for which $ExistMax$ is not a monotonic over-approximation. This is in contrast to the abstraction refinement of boolean properties (in the boolean case, we do not get less precise invariants if we add more predicates).

Segment-based quantitative abstractions. We introduce a number of segment-based abstraction schemes. A *segment* is a (finite or infinite) sequence of states that is a consecutive subsequence of an execution trace. As the quantitative properties we consider accumulate quantities along (infinite) traces, it is natural, and advantageous, to consider abstract domains whose elements correspond to sets of segments, not sets of states. This is similar to termination and liveness analysis using transition predicates [14], and their generalizations to segment covers [7]. We build upon these approaches to develop our quantitative abstractions. The $PathBound$ abstraction scheme stores with each abstract state t (representing a set of segments) (i) $minp(t)$, the length of a shortest finite segment in t, (ii) $maxp(t)$, the length of the longest finite segment in t, (iii) $hasInfPath(t)$ a bit that is true if t contains a segment of infinite length, and (iv) $val(t)$, a summary value of the weights of the states. Defining $val(t)$ as the maximal weight of a state occurring in one of the segments in t makes $PathBound$ a sound over-approximation for a general class of quantitative properties. To get better approximations for particular quantitative properties $val(t)$ can be a different summary of the weights. For instance, we specialized $PathBound$ to limit average by storing not the maximal occurring value, but the maximal average of values along a segment.

In order to compare state-based and segment-based abstractions, let us consider the limit-average property applied to a program with a simple `for` loop for which the loop bound is statically known to be 10. Let us assume that the cost of the operations inside the loop is much greater than the cost of the operations outside the loop. Now consider the state-based abstraction $ExistMax$ with an abstract state t that groups together all states whose control location is in the `for` loop. In the $ExistMax$ abstraction, this abstract state has a self-loop. Analyzing the abstract system would conclude that the highest-cost trace is the one which loops forever in t. This would be a very imprecise result, as the concrete traces all leave the loop after 10 iterations. To correct for this, the loop would have to be unrolled 10 times, using 10 counterexample-guided refinement steps. On the other hand, consider the $PathBound$ abstraction, with an abstract state t representing all the segments in the loop. For t, $hasInfPath(t)$ is false and $maxp(t) = 10$, allowing immediately for more precise estimates.

The $PathBound$ abstraction scheme is a sound abstraction in the sense that the quantitative value we obtain by analyzing the abstract system over-approximates the value for the concrete system. As in $ExistMax$, this holds for a large class of quantitative properties. However, we show that $PathBound$ is not a monotonic over-approximation even for standard quantitative properties such as the limit-average property in the sense that after refinement of the abstract states, we may get worse estimates. We therefore present a hierarchical generalization of $PathBound$ called $HPathBound$. In $PathBound$, each abstract state represents a set of segments, and stores some quantitative characteristics (such as $minp$, $maxp$) of that set. In order to compute better estimates of these quantitative characteristics, one can perform another level of refinement, within abstract states. This leads to the idea of a hierarchical abstraction. It is particularly useful for software, which already has a hierarchical structure in many cases (e.g., nested loops, function calls). This approach corresponds to the (multi-level) abstract inductive segment cover of [7, Section 16.1].

Refinement of state-based abstractions for quantitative properties. For the state-based abstraction scheme $ExistMax$, we give an algorithm for counterexample-guided abstraction refinement (CEGAR) for quantitative properties. The algorithm is based on the classical CEGAR algorithm [2], which we extend to the quantitative case. In the classical CEGAR loop, the counterexample to be examined is chosen using heuristics. For quantitative properties, it is clear that an extremal counterexample trace (the ext-trace) should be chosen for refinement. The reason is that if the ext-trace does not correspond to a real trace, then a refinement which does not eliminate this trace would have the same value as the previous abstract system.

Refinement of segment-based abstractions for quantitative properties. We propose a refinement algorithm for the segment-based abstraction $HPathBound$. We chose $HPathBound$ because, as discussed above, it is particularly suitable for software, and it is a monotonic over-approximation for a large set of quantitative properties. An abstract counterexample for $HPathBound$ is a hierarchical trace. Given an extremal abstract counterexample which does not correspond to a concrete counterexample, the abstract counterexample is traversed, similarly as in the classical CEGAR algorithm, until an abstract segment that provides values that are too "pessimistic" (e.g., $maxp$ and val values which cannot be achieved in the concrete system by a concretization of the abstract counterexample) is found. This abstract segment is then refined. Note that the fact that the counterexample is hierarchic gives freedom to the traversal algorithm — at each step, it can decide whether or not to descend one level lower and to find a mismatch between a concrete and abstract execution there.

Experimental results In order to evaluate the proposed abstraction schemes, both state-based and segment-based, we performed a case study on worst-case execution time analysis of x86 executables. We focused on one aspect, the cache behavior analysis, and in particular, on estimating the rate of cache misses over the course of the worst-case execution. In order to abstract the cache, we used the abstractions introduced in [9]. To the best of our knowledge, this is the first work on automated refinement for these abstractions.

We implemented two abstraction schemes: the state-based $ExistMax$ and the segment-based $HPathBound$. We performed the case study on our own (small) examples, and on some of the benchmarks collected in [11]. The experiments show that we obtain more precise quantitative results as the abstraction is refined, for example, by having a larger abstract cache. Furthermore, we show that using the segment-based abstraction $HPathBound$ enables scaling up. This is due to the fact that in the presence of loops, the $HPathBound$ abstraction can quickly obtain good over-approximations if it can statically over-approximate loop bounds, whereas the $ExistMax$ abstraction would have to unroll the loop many times to get comparable results. Similarly to the $ExistMax$ case, the experiments show that we obtain more precise quantitative results as the $HPathBound$ abstraction is (hierarchically) refined by computing better estimates for loop bounds. The running time of the analysis was under 35 seconds in all cases.

Related work. The theory of abstractions for programs was introduced in [5]. We build on the transition predicates of [14] and segment covers of [7] to construct our quantitative abstractions. The CEGAR algorithm was introduced in [2] and is widely used. Automated abstraction refinement for transition predicates was presented in [4]. To the best of our knowledge, CEGAR-like algorithms for quantitative properties have not yet been studied.

However, quantitative abstractions and refinements have been introduced for *stochastic* systems [8, 12, 13], where the need for quantitative reasoning arises because of stochasticity. They are mainly directed towards the estimation of expected values, and the algorithms reflect this fact. The probabilistic work does not aim at handling accumulative properties like the limit-average property.

Abstractions (but not CEGAR-like algorithms) have been proposed for certain quantitative properties of non-probabilistic systems, such as cache abstractions for WCET analysis [9]. WCET analysis using interval abstraction was performed in [15].The power consumption analysis of software based on the costs of single instructions were presented in [17]. Our WCET analysis of executables based on quantitative abstraction refinement could be adapted for power consumption analysis using these models.

2. Quantitative properties

A *weighted transition system* (WTS) is defined by a tuple $S = (Q, \delta, \varrho, q_\iota)$, with a (finite or infinite) set of states Q, a transition set $\delta \subseteq Q \times Q$, weight function $\varrho : Q \to \mathbb{R}$, and an initial state $q_\iota \in Q$. Let $\mathcal{S}$ denote the set of all WTSs and let $\mathcal{S}(\mathcal{Q}) \subseteq \mathcal{S}$ be the set of all WTSs with a set of states Q such that $Q \subseteq \mathcal{Q}$. We assume that $\forall q \in Q : \exists q' : (q, q') \in \delta$. System S_1 in Figure 2 is an example of a WTS.

A *trace* of a WTS S is an infinite sequence $\pi = q_0 q_1 \ldots$ with $q_0 = q_\iota$, and $\forall i \geq 0 : (q_i, q_{i+1}) \in \delta$. The set of all traces of S is denoted by $\Pi(S)$. We extend the weight function ϱ to traces as $\varrho(q_0 q_1 \ldots) = r_0 r_1 \ldots \in \mathbb{R}^\omega$ where $r_i = \varrho(q_i)$, and to sets of traces as $\varrho(T) = \{w \mid \exists \pi \in T : w = \varrho(\pi)\}$.

A trace $\pi = q_0 q_1 \ldots$ is *memoryless* if for all $i, j \geq 0$, we have $q_i = q_j \to (q_{i+1} = q_{j+1})$. For instance, system S_1 in Figure 2 has two memoryless traces, a trace π_1 with $\varrho(\pi_1) = (1\ 10\ 4\ 3\ 1\ 1\ 1)^\omega$, and a trace π_2 with $\varrho(\pi_2) = (1\ 10\ 4\ 3\ 1\ 1\ 1\ 1)^\omega$.

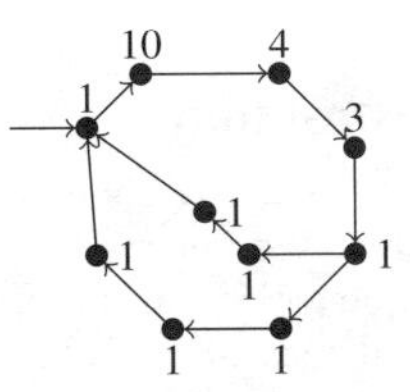

Figure 2: System S_1

A *quantitative property* $f : \mathcal{S} \to \mathbb{R}$ is defined using two functions: a *trace value* function f_t and a *system value* function f_s. The trace value function $f_t : \mathbb{R}^\omega \to \mathbb{R}$ summarizes a single trace of the system. The system value functions $f_s : 2^\mathbb{R} \to \mathbb{R}$ summarizes the set of f_t values of all traces of the system. We then have $f(S) = f_s(\{f_t(r) \mid \exists \pi \in \Pi(S) : \varrho(\pi) = r\})$. We extend f_t to $2^{\mathbb{R}^\omega}$ by letting $f_t(T) = \{f_t(r) \mid r \in T\}$. Hence, we have that $f(S) = f_s(f_t(\varrho(\Pi(S))))$.

We present a number of common quantitative properties below. We also model some classical boolean properties in our framework. First, we give examples of trace value functions:

Limit-average. The limit-average trace value function measures the maximal long-term average weight over a trace. The function $limavg : \mathbb{R}^\omega \to \mathbb{R}$ is defined by $limavg(r_0 r_1 \ldots) = \liminf_{i\to\infty} \frac{1}{i} \cdot \sum_{k=0}^{i-1} r_k$. For the trace π_1 of S_1, the value $limavg(\varrho(\pi_1)) = \frac{21}{7} = 3$.

Discounted-sum. The discounted-sum trace value function accumulates the weights over a trace where weights occurring further along the trace are discounted by a factor $\lambda \in (0, 1)$. Formally, the function $disc_\lambda(r_0 r_1 \ldots) = \sum_{i=0}^{\infty} \lambda^i \cdot r_i$.

Safety and quantitative safety. The classical safety property is defined by a set of unsafe states U, and a trace is safe if it never visits a state in U. To model a safety property, we assign the weight 1 to each state in U and the weight 0 to all other states. The safety trace value function is defined as $safety(r_0 r_1 \ldots) = \sup r_i$. Now, for any trace π, we have $safety(\varrho(\pi)) = 0$ if and only if π is safe. Note that this modeling of safety is still boolean, because the trace value can only be either 0 or 1. In some applications, a more quantitative view might be useful. Consider $safety_\lambda$ defined by $safety_\lambda(r_0 r_1 \ldots) = \lim_{n\to\infty} \sum_{k=1}^{n-1} \lambda^k \cdot r_k$ (discounted sum of the number of 1's in the run). For a safe trace π, we still have that $safety_\lambda(\varrho(\pi)) = 0$. However, for an unsafe trace, $safety_\lambda(\varrho(\pi))$ gives a more fine-grained picture: it measures how early and often the bad states are visited.

Liveness and quantitative liveness. The liveness property is defined by a set of Büchi (live) states L, and a trace is live if it visits states in L infinitely often. To model a liveness property, we assign weight 0 to each state in L and weight 1 to all other states. The trace value function $live(r_0 r_1 \ldots) = \liminf_{i\to\infty} r_i$. This function is faithful to the liveness property, i.e, $live(\varrho(\pi)) = 0$ if and only if the trace is live. As in the safety case, we can get a finer view of liveness by measuring how often states in L are visited. We do it by letting $live(r_0 r_1 \ldots) = \liminf_{i\to\infty} \frac{1}{i} \cdot \sum_{k=0}^{i-1} r_i$.

Second, we give examples of standard system value functions.

- *Supremum and Infimum.* Intuitively, the supremum and infimum functions measure the worst-case and best-case traces in the system.
- *Threshold.* The threshold function checks if any of the values in the given set are above or below given thresholds. Formally, $threshold_u(R) = 1$ if $\exists r \in R : r \geq u$, and $threshold_u(R) = 0$ otherwise.

Any combination of a trace value function and a system value function defines a quantitative property. In this paper, we implicitly assume that the system value function for any quantitative property is sup unless otherwise mentioned.

A trace π is an *extremal counterexample trace* (or ext-trace for short) if $f(S) = f_s(\{f_t(\varrho(\pi))\})$. We restrict ourselves to a class of quantitative properties that admit *memoryless extremal counterexample traces*, i.e., every system S has a extremal counterexample trace that is memoryless. Formally, f is *memoryless* if and only if $\forall S \in \mathcal{S} : \exists \pi \in \Pi(S) : f(S) = f_s(\{f_t(\varrho(\pi))\})$. Note that all properties mentioned above are memoryless.

3. State-based quantitative abstractions

A *quantitative abstraction* $C = (\mathcal{S}^C, f^C, \alpha^C)$ is triple consisting of a set of abstract systems $\mathcal{S}^C$, an abstract quantitative property $f^C : \mathcal{S}^C \to \mathbb{R}$ and an abstraction function $\alpha^C : \mathcal{S} \to \mathcal{S}^C$. A quantitative abstraction C is an *over-approximation* of f, if for all $S \in \mathcal{S}, f^C(\alpha^C(S)) \geq f(S)$.

3.1 *ExistMax* abstraction.

In this section, we present a quantitative abstraction technique based on state abstractions. In this case, the abstract system is a WTS whose states are sets of states of the concrete systems. In particular, our abstraction scheme *ExistMax* is a direct extension of the classical predicate abstraction. Compared to predicate abstraction, *ExistMax* additionally stores, with each abstract state, the maximum weight occurring in the set of corresponding concrete states. The name *ExistMax* refers to transitions abstracted existentially, and that the weights abstracted by maxima.

ExistMax is a state based abstraction scheme: a family of quantitative abstractions parameterized by equivalence relations on $\mathcal{Q}$. Given an equivalence relation $\approx \subseteq \mathcal{Q} \times \mathcal{Q}$, the quantitative abstraction $ExistMax_{\approx} = (\mathcal{S}^{em}, f^{em}, \alpha^{em}_{\approx})$ has (a) $\mathcal{S}^{em} = \mathcal{S}(2^{\mathcal{Q}})$, (i.e., abstract states are set of concrete states), (b) $f^{em} = f$ as the abstract quantitative property, and (c) for a WTS $S = (Q, \delta, \varrho, q_\iota)$ we have that the abstract system $\alpha^{em}_{\approx}(S)$ is a WTS $S^{em} = (Q^{em}, \delta^{em}, \varrho^{em}, t^{em}_\iota)$ where:

- Q^{em} are equivalence classes of $\approx$ that contain states from Q;
- $(t_1, t_2) \in \delta^{em} \Leftrightarrow \exists q_1 \in t_1, q_2 \in t_2 : (q_1, q_2) \in \delta$;
- $\varrho(t) = \sup\{d \mid \exists q \in t : \varrho(q) = d\}$; and
- t^{em}_ι is the equivalence class in Q^{em} that contains q_ι.

Intuitively, $\alpha^{em}(S)$ is an existential abstraction and ϱ^{em} maps an abstract state to the maximum weight of the corresponding concrete state.

Example 1. *Consider again the system S_1 from Figure 2, and the equivalence relation $\approx$, whose two equivalence classes (indicated by the dashed shapes) are shown in the upper part of Figure 3. The abstract system $S^{em} = \alpha^{em}_{\approx}(S_1)$ is in the lower part of Figure 3. We have $limavg^{em}(\alpha^{em}_{\approx}(S^{em})) = 10$, due to a self-loop on the abstract node with weight* 10.

3.1.1 Over-approximation and monotonicity.

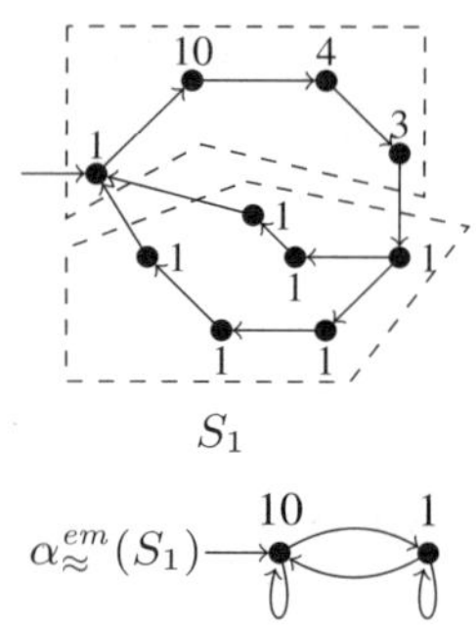

Fig. 3: *ExistMax* abs.

We characterize the quantitative properties for which *ExistMax* is an over-approximation, and for which monotonicity of refinements holds, i.e., where refinement of the abstraction leads to tighter approximations of the system value.

We borrow the classical notion of refinement for abstractions. An equivalence relation $\equiv$ is a *refinement* of an equivalence relation $\approx$ if and only if every equivalence class of $\equiv$ is a subset of an equivalence class of $\approx$.

We define the following quasi-orders:

- let $\leq_p \subseteq \mathbb{R}^\omega \times \mathbb{R}^\omega$ be defined by: $r^1_0 r^1_1 \ldots \leq_p r^2_0 r^2_1 \ldots$ if and only if $\forall i : r^1_i \leq r^2_i$, and
- let $\sqsubseteq \subseteq 2^{\mathbb{R}} \times 2^{\mathbb{R}}$ be defined by: for $U, U' \subseteq \mathbb{R}$, we have $U \sqsubseteq U'$ iff $\sup U \leq \sup U'$.

A quantitative property f is $(\leq_p, \sqsubseteq)$*-monotonic* if $\forall r, r' \in \mathbb{R}^\omega : r \leq_p r' \implies f_t(r) \leq f_t(r')$ and $\forall U, U' \in 2^{\mathbb{R}} : U \sqsubseteq U' \implies f_s(U) \leq f_s(U')$.

ExistMax is a *monotonic over-approximation* for a quantitative property f, if (a) *ExistMax* is an over-approximation for f, and (b) if for all $S \in \mathcal{S}(\mathcal{Q})$, and for all equivalence relations $\equiv$ and $\approx$ on $\mathcal{Q}$, such that $\equiv$ is a refinement of $\approx$, we have that $f^{em}(\alpha^{em}_{\equiv}(S)) \leq f^{em}(\alpha^{em}_{\approx}(S))$.

Theorem 2. *If f is $(\leq_p, \sqsubseteq)$-monotonic quantitative property, then ExistMax is a monotonic over-approximation of f.*

Proof. We first prove the monotonicity property of *ExistMax*. The over-approximation property follows naturally as follows. For any system S, we have $S = \alpha^{em}_{id}(S)$ where id is the identity relation. As id is a refinement of any equivalence relation $\approx$, by monotonicity it follows that $f(S) = f^{em}(\alpha^{em}_{id}(S)) \leq f^{em}(\alpha^{em}_{\approx}(S))$.

Let S be a system in $\mathcal{S}(\mathcal{Q})$, and let $\equiv$ and $\approx$ be equivalence relations on $\mathcal{Q}$. Let $\alpha_{\approx}(S) = (Q^1, \delta^1, \varrho^1, q^1_\iota)$ and $\alpha_{\equiv}(S) = (Q^2, \delta^2, \varrho^2, q^2_\iota)$ be *ExistMax* abstractions of S, where $\equiv$ is a refinement of $\approx$. Furthermore, let f defined by f_t and f_s be $(\leq_p, \sqsubseteq)$-monotonic. For each equivalence class t of $\equiv$, let $t^\sharp$ be the unique equivalence class of $\approx$ for which $t \subseteq t^\sharp$. The class $t^\sharp$ is guaranteed to exist as $\equiv$ is a refinement of $\approx$. Furthermore, by the definition of *ExistMax*, we have that: (a) $\varrho^1(t) \leq \varrho^2(t^\sharp)$, and (b) $(t_1, t_2) \in \delta^1 \implies (t^\sharp_1, t^\sharp_2) \in \delta^2$. Therefore, for any trace $\pi = t_0 t_1 \ldots$ of $\alpha_{\equiv}(S)$, there exists a trace $\pi^\sharp = t^\sharp_0 t^\sharp_1 \ldots$ of $\alpha_{\approx}(S)$ such that: $\varrho^1(t_0)\varrho^1(t_1)\ldots \leq_p \varrho^2(t^\sharp_0)\varrho^2(t^\sharp_1)\ldots$. By $\leq_p$-monotonicity of f_t, we get $f_t(\varrho(\pi)) \leq f_t(\varrho(\pi^\sharp))$. Hence, for each $w \in f_t(\varrho(\Pi(\alpha_{\equiv}(S))))$, there exists $w^\sharp \in f_t(\varrho(\Pi(\alpha_{\approx}(S))))$ with $w \leq w^\sharp$. This, in turn, gives us $f_t(\varrho(\Pi(\alpha_{\equiv}(S)))) \sqsubseteq f_t(\varrho(\Pi(\alpha_{\equiv}(S))))$. Hence, by $\sqsubseteq$-monotonicity of f_s, we get $f_s(f_t(\varrho(\Pi(\alpha_{\equiv}(S))))) \leq f_s(f_t(\varrho(\Pi(\alpha_{\approx}(S)))))$, or equivalently, $f(\alpha_{\equiv}(S)) \leq f(\alpha_{\approx}(S))$. This proves the required theorem. as $f = f^{em}$. □

It is easy to show that safety, liveness, limit average, and discounted sum are $(\leq_p, \sqsubseteq)$-monotonic. The following proposition is a direct consequence.

Proposition 3. *ExistMax is a monotonic over-approximation for the limit-average, discounted-sum, safety, and liveness properties.*

Example 4. *We describe a property for which ExistMax is not a monotonic over-approximation. Let f be defined by $f_t(r) = \sup_{i,j \geq 0}(r_i - r_j)$ and $f_s(U) = \sup U$. The property f can be used to measure the variance in resource usage (where the usage in each step is given by the weight) during the execution of a program. Consider the system in Figure 4 and the ExistMax abstraction with abstract states given by the rectangles (the nodes outside the dotted boxes are each in a separate singleton equivalence classes) . Property f has value 2 on the abstract system due to the trace $A \rightarrow B \rightarrow C$ having maximal and minimal weights as 5 and 3 (under ExistMax abstract state A, B, and C have weights 5, 3, and 3 respectively). Refining the abstraction by completely splitting state B increases f to 4. Refining further by splitting both states A and C decreases f to 3 which is the true value of the concrete system. The sequence of refinements show that for property f, the ExistMax abstraction is neither an over-approximation (as the first abstract system has value 2 which is less than 3, the value of the concrete system), nor monotonic (as the sequence of values 2, 4 and 3 obtained through subsequent refinements first increase and then decrease).*

3.1.2 Evaluating quantitative properties on *ExistMax* abstractions.

Recall $f^{em} = f$ for *ExistMax* abstractions. To evaluate f^{em} (and obtain an *ext*-trace for refinement), any algorithm for finding *ext*-traces for the quantitative property f suffices. Standard algorithms exist when f is one of safety, liveness, discounted-sum, and limit-average properties. For limit-average, we use the classical Howard's policy iteration.

4. Segment-based quantitative abstractions

In this section, we present quantitative abstractions where elements of the abstract domain correspond to sets of trace segments.

Segments. A *segment* is a finite or infinite sequence of states in $\mathcal{Q}$. Let $\mathcal{Q}^*$ be the set of all finite segments, $\mathcal{Q}^\infty$ the set of all infinite segments, and let $\mathcal{Q}^{*\infty} = \mathcal{Q}^* \cup \mathcal{Q}^\infty$ be the set of all finite and infinite segments. Given a segment σ, let $|\sigma|$ denote the length of the segment (the range of $|.|$ is thus $\mathbb{N} \cup \{\infty\}$). Given two segments σ_1 and σ_2 in $\mathcal{Q}^{*\infty}$ we write $\sigma_1\sigma_2$ for their concatenation, with $\sigma_1\sigma_2 = \sigma_1$, if σ_1 is in $\mathcal{Q}^{\infty}$. Also, we the notation $last(\sigma_1)$ and $first(\sigma_2)$ to represent the last state of a finite segment σ_1 and the first state of a segment σ_2.

We dub a nonempty set of segments a *SegmentSet*. We define the following operations and relations on SegmentSets and sets of SegmentSets.

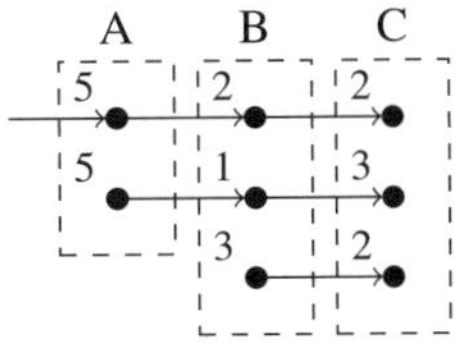

Fig. 4: Non-monotonic refinements

- For SegmentSets T_1 and T_2, we have $T_1 \Subset T_2$ if $T_1 \subseteq \{w \mid \exists x \in \mathcal{Q}^*, \exists y \in \mathcal{Q}^{*\infty} : xwy \in T\}$, that is, all segments from T_1 occur as sub-segments of segments in T_2.
- For a set of SegmentSets $\mathcal{T}$, we define $\biguplus\mathcal{T}$ to be set of segments which can be obtained by concatenation of segments contained in SegmentSets in $\mathcal{T}$. Formally, $\biguplus\mathcal{T} = \{\sigma_0\sigma_1\ldots\sigma_n \mid \exists T_0, T_1 \ldots T_n : (\forall i : 0 \leq i \leq n \implies \sigma_i \in T_i)\} \cup \{\sigma_0\sigma_1\ldots \mid \exists T_0, T_1 \ldots : (\forall i : 0 \leq i \to \sigma_i \in T_i)\}$.
- A set of SegmentSets $\mathcal{T}$ *covers* a SegmentSet T if and only if
  - for all $T_i \in \mathcal{T}$, we have $T_i \Subset T$, and
  - $T \subseteq \biguplus\mathcal{T}$.

Note that for a WTS S, the set of all its traces $\Pi(S)$ is a SegmentSet. We call $\mathcal{T}$ a *segment cover* of a system S if and only if $\mathcal{T}$ covers $\Pi(S)$. For example, the two SegmentSets T_1 and T_2 in Figure 5 form a segment cover of the system in Figure 2. It is easy to see that all traces of S are covered by segments in T_1 and T_2. Our notion of segment cover corresponds to the inductive trace segment cover from [7] with height 1. The notion of the segment cover plays the same role in segment-based abstractions as the equivalence relation on states plays in state-based abstractions.

4.1 *PathBound* abstraction.

PathBound is a segment-based abstraction scheme: a family of quantitative abstractions parameterized by sets of SegmentSets on $\mathcal{Q}$. Given a set of SegmentSets $\mathcal{T}$, the quantitative abstraction $PathBound_{\mathcal{T}}$ is defined by $(\mathcal{S}^{pb}_{\mathcal{T}}, f^{pb}, \alpha^{pb}_{\mathcal{T}})$. We now define each element of the triple.

Abstract systems $\mathcal{S}^{pb}_{\mathcal{T}}$. An abstract system in $\mathcal{S}^{pb}_{\mathcal{T}}$ is a tuple $(R, \delta_R, val, minp, maxp, hasInfPath, R_0)$, where R is $\mathcal{T}$, δ_R is a transition relation, and R_0 is the set of initial states. The type of val, $minp$ and $maxp$ functions is $R \to \mathbb{R}$ and the type of $hasInfPath$ is $R \to \mathbb{B}$. Their intuitive meaning is given below. The systems in $\mathcal{S}^{pb}_{\mathcal{T}}$ are called *pb-systems*.

Abstraction $\alpha^{pb}_{\mathcal{T}}$. The partial abstraction function $\alpha^{pb}_{\mathcal{T}}$ is defined as follows. For a WTS S, if $\mathcal{T}$ is not a segment cover of $\Pi(S)$, then the value $\alpha^{pb}_{\mathcal{T}}(S)$ is undefined. Otherwise, given $S = (Q, \delta, \varrho, q_\iota)$, let $\alpha^{pb}_{\mathcal{T}}(S) = S^{pb} \in \mathcal{S}^{pb}$ where $S^{pb} = (Q^{pb}, \delta^{pb}, val, minp, maxp, hasInfPath, Q^{pb}_0)$ and

- Q^{pb} is $\mathcal{T}$
- $(T_1, T_2) \in \delta^{pb}$ if $\exists \sigma_1 \in T_1, \sigma_2 \in T_2$, such that σ_1 is a finite segment in $\mathcal{Q}^*$, $(last(\sigma_1), first(\sigma_2)) \in \delta$.
- $val(T) = \max\{\varrho(q) \mid \exists \sigma \in T \text{ and } q \text{ occurs in } \sigma\}$, i.e., $val(T)$ is the maximal weight of a state occurring in one of the segments in T
- $minp(T) = \min\{|\sigma| \mid \sigma \in T \text{ is a finite segment}\}$ if T contains a finite segment, and is ∞ otherwise.
- $maxp(T) = \max\{|\sigma| \mid \sigma \in T \text{ is a finite segment}\}$, if T contains a finite segment, and is ∞ otherwise.
- $hasInfPath(T) = true$ iff $T \cap \mathcal{Q}^{\infty} \neq \emptyset$, i.e., $hasInfPath(T)$ is true if and only if T contains an infinite segment,

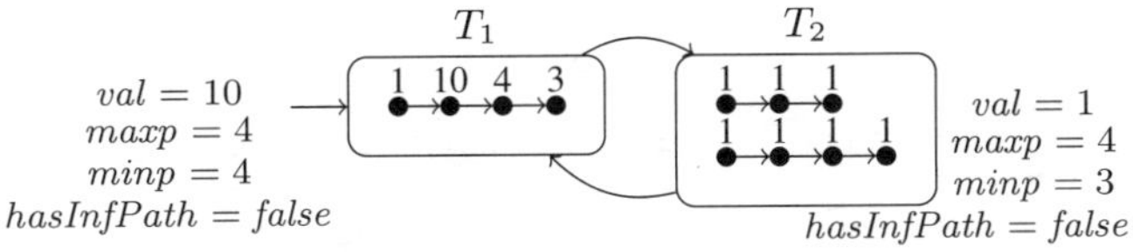

Figure 5: $PathBound$ abstraction of S_1

- Q^{pb}_0 contains a set T in $\mathcal{T}$ iff T contains a segment whose first state is q_ι. As $\mathcal{T}$ is a segment cover of S, we have that Q^{pb}_0 is non-empty.

A *pb-trace* ρ of a pb-system S^{α} is either (a) a finite sequence $T_0T_1\ldots T_n$ such that $T_0 \in Q^{pb}_0$, $hasInfPath(T_n)$, and $\forall i : 0 \leq i < n : (T_i, T_{i+1}) \in \delta^{pb}$, or (b) an infinite sequence $T_0T_1\ldots$ with $T_0 \in Q^{pb}_0$, and $\forall i \geq 0 : (T_i, T_{i+1}) \in \delta^{pb}$. The set of all pb-traces of S^{α} is denoted by $\Pi^{pb}(S^{\alpha})$.

Example 5. *Recall the system S_1 from Figure 2. Consider a segment cover $\mathcal{T} = \{T_1, T_2\}$ of $\Pi(S)$ depicted in Figure 5. T_1 and T_2 can now act as abstract states, with the values $val, minp, maxp$, and $hasInfPath$ given in Figure 5.*

Abstract quantitative property f^{pb}. In order to define the abstract quantitative property f^{pb}, we will need the following notions.

Let us fix a system $S = (Q, \delta, \varrho, q_\iota)$. Let us also fix a set $\mathcal{T}$ of SegmentSets, such that $\mathcal{T}$ is a segment cover for S. Let $\alpha^{pb}_{\mathcal{T}}(S) = S^{\alpha} = (Q^{pb}, \delta^{pb}, val, minp, maxp, hasInfPath, Q^{pb}_0)$ be a $PathBound$ abstraction of S for $\mathcal{T}$.

We now define a function B that for a given pb-trace ρ returns a set of possible sequences of weights that correspond to ρ. The function $B : \Pi(S^{\alpha}) \to 2^{\mathbb{R}^{\omega}}$ is defined as follows. The set $B(\rho)$ contains a sequence:

- $w_0^{n_0} w_1^{n_1} \ldots w_n^{\infty}$ in $\mathbb{R}^{\omega}$ iff ρ is a finite pb-trace $T_0T_1T_2\ldots T_n$, such that (a) $\forall i$ such that $0 \leq i \leq n$, we have $w_i = val(T_i)$, and (b) $\forall i$ such that $0 \leq i < n$, we have $minp(T_i) \leq n_i \leq maxp(T_i)$ and $0 < n_i \neq \infty$.
- $w_0^{n_0} w_1^{n_1} \ldots$ in $\mathbb{R}^{\omega}$ iff ρ is an infinite pb-trace $T_0T_1 \in \Pi^{pb}(S^{\alpha})$ such that (a) $\forall i \geq 0 : w_i = val(T_i)$, and (b) $\forall i \geq 0 : minp(T_i) \leq n_i \leq maxp(T_i) \wedge 0 < n_i \neq \infty$.

Let f be a quantitative property defined by a trace value function f_t and a system value function f_s. We are now able to define the abstract quantitative property f^{pb} by $f^{pb}(S^{\alpha}) = f_s(f_t((\bigcup_{\rho \in \Pi^{pb}} B(\rho))))$.

Example 6. *Recall again the system S_1 from Figure 2 and the abstract cover described in Example 5. Consider the abstraction $\alpha^{pb}_{\mathcal{T}}(S_1)$ (the abstract system is depicted in Figure 5). There is only one pb-trace ρ of the abstract system, and we have $\rho = (T_1T_2)^{\omega}$. Let us assume that the quantitative property we are interested in is the limit average quantitative property. We get that $B(\rho) = \{(10\ 10\ 10\ 10\ 1\ 1\ 1)^{\omega}, (10\ 10\ 10\ 10\ 1\ 1\ 1)^{\omega}\}$. We therefore obtain $f^{pb}(\alpha^{pb}_{\mathcal{T}}(S_1)) = (10 \cdot 4 + 1 \cdot 3)/(4+3) = \frac{43}{7}$, as the maximum value is achieved if the execution stays at the more costly abstract state T_1 as much as possible ($maxp(T_1)$ times), and at the less costly abstract state T_2 as little as possible ($minp(T_2)$ times).*

4.1.1 Over-approximation and monotonicity

The following theorem states that the abstraction scheme $PathBound$ is an over-approximation for a large class of quantitative properties.

Theorem 7. *PathBound abstraction scheme is an over-approximation for a quantitative property f if f is $(\leq_P, \sqsubseteq)$-monotonic.*

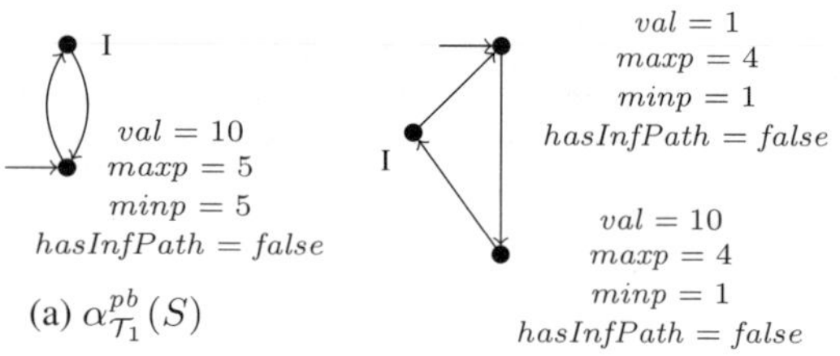

(a) $\alpha^{pb}_{\mathcal{T}_1}(S)$

(b) $\alpha^{pb}_{\mathcal{T}_2}(S)$

Figure 7: Abstractions of system S_2

A set of SegmentSets $\mathcal{T}_1$ *refines* a set of SegmentSets $\mathcal{T}_2$ iff for all $T \in \mathcal{T}_2$, there exists a set of SegmentSets $\mathcal{T}$, such that $\mathcal{T} \subseteq \mathcal{T}_1$, and $\mathcal{T}$ covers T.

$PathBound$ is a *monotonic over-approximation* for a quantitative property f, if (a) $PathBound$ is an over-approximation for f, and (b) if for all $S \in \mathcal{S}(\mathcal{Q})$, and for all sets $\mathcal{T}_1$ and $\mathcal{T}_2$ of SegmentSets such that (a) $\mathcal{T}_1$ covers $\Pi(S)$, (b) $\mathcal{T}_2$ covers $\Pi(S)$, and (c) $\mathcal{T}_2$ is a refinement of $\mathcal{T}_1$, we have that $f^{pb}(\alpha^{pb}_{\mathcal{T}_2}(S)) \leq f^{pb}(\alpha^{pb}_{\mathcal{T}_1}(S))$.

The abstraction $PathBound$ is not a monotonic approximation in general even for quantitative properties that are $(\leq_p, \sqsubseteq)$-monotonic. We show this by constructing a counterexample (see Example 10) for which the abstraction is not a monotonic approximation for the limit-average property.

4.2 State-equivalence induced segment-based abstraction

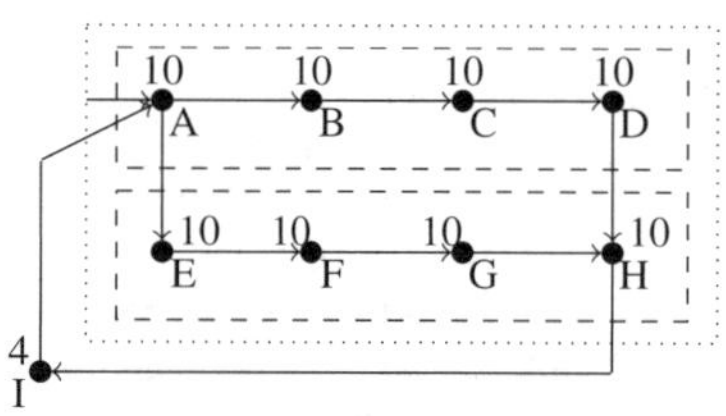

Figure 6: System S_2

Given an equivalence relation on states, we can define a set of SegmentSets. Let $S = (Q, \delta, \varrho, q_\iota)$ be a WTS, and let $\approx$ be an equivalence relation on states in $\mathcal{Q}$. Given an equivalence class e of $\approx$, we can define a corresponding SegmentSet T_e as follows. First, let T'_e be the set of (finite or infinite) segments σ such that all states q that occur in σ are in e. Now we define T_e as the set of maximal segments in T'_e. A segment σ is *maximal* in T_e iff (a) σ is in T'_e; (b) there is a transition $(q_b, first(\sigma)) \in \delta$ such that $q_b \notin e$; and (c) either $\sigma \in \mathcal{Q}^\infty$ or there is a transition $(last(\sigma), q_f) \in \delta$ such that $q_f \notin e$. Let $\mathcal{T}_\approx$ be a set of SegmentSets defined by $\{T_e \mid e \text{ is an equivalence class of } \approx\}$.

Example 8. *Consider again the system S_1 in Figure 2, and the equivalence relation $\approx$ on its states given by the dashed shapes in Figure 3. The SegmentSets we get from the equivalence classes are given by the nodes T_1 and T_2 in Figure 5. The set of these SegmentSets is $\mathcal{T}_\approx$. As calculated in Example 6, the value for the abstract system (for the limit-average objective) given by $PathBound_{\mathcal{T}_\approx}$ is $\frac{43}{7}$. Note that this is better (more precise) than the value given by the $ExistMax$ abstraction defined by the same equivalence relation $\approx$. As calculated in Example 1, the value given by $ExistMax$ is 10.*

Given an equivalence relation $\approx$ on states, the abstraction $PathBound_{\mathcal{T}_\approx}$ gives a better over-approximation for limit-average objective than the $ExistMax_\approx$.

Proposition 9. *Let f be a $(\leq_p, \sqsubseteq)$-monotonic quantitative property. Let $\approx$ be an equivalence relation on $\mathcal{Q}$ and consider the two abstraction schemes $PathBound_{\mathcal{T}_\approx} = (\mathcal{S}^{pb}, f^{pb}, \alpha^{pb}_{\mathcal{T}_\approx})$ and $ExistMax_\approx = (\mathcal{S}^{em}, f^{em}, \alpha^{em}_\approx)$ parameterized by $\approx$. Then, for all $S \in \mathcal{S}(\mathcal{Q})$, $f^{pb}(\alpha^{pb}_{\mathcal{T}_\approx}(S)) \leq f^{em}(\alpha^{em}_\approx(S))$.*

We observe that if $\approx_2$ is a refinement $\approx_1$, then $\mathcal{T}_{\approx_2}$ is a refinement $\mathcal{T}_{\approx_1}$. However, we show an example system where the over-approximation computed using the $\mathcal{T}_{\approx_2}$ abstraction is worse (less precise) than the over-approximation computed using the $\mathcal{T}_{\approx_1}$. This means that, in general, $PathBound$ is not a monotonic over-approximation for $(\leq_p, \sqsubseteq)$-monotonic quantitative properties.

Example 10. *Consider the system S_2 in Figure 6. Consider an equivalence relation $\approx$ on states given by the dotted rectangle in the figure (that is all states except the state I are equivalent to each other). This equivalence relation defines a set $\mathcal{T}_1$ of SegmentSets. The resulting abstract system $\alpha^{pb}_{\mathcal{T}_1}(S)$ is in Figure 7 (a). Note that in Figure 7 (a), the node for which the values of $maxp$, $minp$, etc. are given corresponds to the dotted rectangle in Figure 6, the other node in the abstract system corresponds to the singleton segment of length one generated from the singleton equivalence class of the node I of system S_2. Consider now a refinement of $\approx$ where the equivalence class of the dotted rectangle is split into two equivalence classes given by the dashed rectangles. The new equivalence relation defines a set $\mathcal{T}_2$ of SegmentSets. The abstract system in Figure 7 (b) results from a refinement where the equivalence class of the dotted rectangle is split into two equivalence classes given by the dashed rectangles. The resulting abstract system $\alpha^{pb}_{\mathcal{T}_2}(S)$ is in Figure 7 (b).*

Let us now assume that the abstract quantitative objective is $limavg$. The value we get for system $\alpha^{pb}_{\mathcal{T}_1}(S)$ is $((10 \cdot 5 + 4 \cdot 1)/6) = 9$. The value we get for its refinement $\alpha^{pb}_{\mathcal{T}_2}(S)$ is $((10 \cdot 4 + 10 \cdot 4 + 4 \cdot 1)/9) = \frac{84}{9} > 9$. This shows that the estimate is worse (less precise) for the refinement $\alpha^{pb}_{\mathcal{T}_2}(S)$ than for $\alpha^{pb}_{\mathcal{T}_1}(S)$.

4.3 Specialization of $PathBound$ abstraction for the limit-average quantitative property

We presented a general definition of the $PathBound$ abstraction which is an over-approximation for a large class of quantitative properties. We now specialize the $PathBound$ abstraction for the limit-average property by introducing sound optimizations.

We define the limit-average $PathBound$-abstraction (denoted by $PathBoundLA$) scheme as $(\mathcal{S}^{pba}, f^{pba}, \alpha^{pba}_{\mathcal{T}})$. Let S be a system and let $S^{pb} = \alpha^{pb}_{\mathcal{T}}(S) = (Q^{pb}, \delta^{pb}, val, minp, maxp, hasInfPath, Q^{pb}_0)$ be a $PathBound$ abstraction of S. Furthermore, we fix f to be the limit-average property, i.e., $f_t = limavg$ and $f_s = \sup$ for the remainder of this subsection. We have that $S^{pba} = \alpha^{pba}_{\mathcal{T}}(S) = (Q^{pb}, \delta^{pb}, val^{pba}, minp, maxp, hasInfPath)$ is a pb-system similar to $\alpha^{pb}_{\mathcal{T}}(S)$. In the $PathBoundLA$ abstraction scheme, we have the following differences:

- $val^{pba}(T) = \max\{\sup_{\sigma \in (T \cap \mathcal{Q}^*)} \frac{\sum_{s \in \sigma} \varrho(s)}{|\sigma|}, \sup_{\sigma \in (T \cap \mathcal{Q}^\infty)} limavg(\sigma)\}$. Here, we let the value of an abstract SegmentSet T be the supremum of the average weight of the segments in T, rather than the maximum weight occurring in T. Note that if $T \subseteq \mathcal{Q}^\infty$, we have $val^{pba}(T) = \sup(limavg(\varrho(T)))$.
- The abstract quantitative property f^{pba} is defined in the same way as f^{pb} (at the beginning of Section 4), except that the definition of $B : \Pi(S^\alpha) \to 2^{\mathbb{R}^\omega}$ we have that:
  - $w_0^{n_0} w_1^{n_1} \ldots \in B(\rho)$ if and only if $\rho = T_0 T_1 \ldots$ with $w_i = val^{pba}(T_i) \wedge 0 < n_i < \infty \wedge n_i \in \{minp(T_i), maxp(t_i)\}$.
  - $w_0^{n_0} w_1^{n_1} \ldots w_n^\infty \in B(\rho)$ if and only if $\forall 0 \leq i \leq n$: $w_i = val^{pba}(T_i) \wedge (i < n \implies 0 < n_i < \infty \wedge n_i \in \{minp(T_i), maxp(t_i)\})$.

The above differences between the *PathBoundLA* and *PathBound* can be summarized as follows: (a) the value summarization function for each SegmentSet can be average instead of maximum, and (b) more crucially (from a practical point of view), the evaluation of the abstract property on a pb-system can be done by considering only the lengths of the longest and shortest finite paths of an SegmentSet, rather than considering all lengths between them. This is because limit-average is a memoryless property.

The following theorem states that *PathBoundLA* provides a better approximations of the limit-average property than *PathBound*.

Theorem 11. *Given a system S and an segment cover $\mathcal{T}$ of $\Pi(S)$ and f being the limit-average property, we have*

$$f(S) \le f^{pba}(\alpha_{\mathcal{T}}^{pba}(S)) \le f^{pb}(\alpha_{\mathcal{T}}^{pb}(S))$$

Example 12. *Consider again the system S_1 from Figure 2, and the SegmentSets T_1 and T_2 from Figure 5. In PathBoundLA abstraction, we have $val(T_1) = (10+1+4+3)/4 = 18/4$ (while the other values for T_1 are as in Figure 5). For $val(T_2)$, we have $val(T_2) = (1+1+1)/3 = 1$. The value of the system is $f^{pba}(\alpha_{\mathcal{T}}(S_1)) = (18+3)/7 = 3$. Recall that for PathBound abstraction, the value f^{pb} for S_1 was calculated in Example 6 to be $\frac{43}{7}$. For PathBoundLA abstraction, we thus get a better approximation than in the PathBound abstraction.*

Evaluating limit-averages on pb-abstract systems. Minimum-mean cycle algorithms compute the limit-average value for a graph with weights on edges. Therefore, from a pb-system, we construct a graph which has weights and lengths on edges, rather than nodes. Intuitively, we consider the graph with edges of the pb-system being the nodes. There are two edges between the node (T_1, T) and (T, T_2): one of weight $maxp(T) \times val(T)$ and length $maxp(T)$, and another of weight $minp(T) \times val(T)$ and length $minp(T)$. The node (T_1, T) has the self-loop of weight $val(T)$ and length 1, if $hasInfPath(T)$ is true. We denote this graph by $S^{\dagger}$.

Howard's policy iteration was extended in [3] to compute the limit-average values in graphs where edges have both weight and length, as is the case of $S^{\dagger}$. Howard's policy iteration works by picking a policy (that maps states to successors) and improves the policy as long as possible. Each improvement takes linear time, but only an exponential upper-bound is known on the number of improvements required. However, a number of reports state that only linear number of improvements are required for most cases in practice [3].

5. Generalizations of *PathBound* abstractions

In this section, we present two generalizations of the *PathBound* abstraction scheme. The first one generalizes *PathBound* by considering different summaries of SegmentSets rather than set of properties $\{minp, maxp, val, hasInfPath\}$. The second one generalizes *PathBound* by allowing inductive fixed-point style computations of properties.

5.1 Generalized segment-based abstraction

Let S be a WTS, and let $\mathcal{T}$ be a segment over of $\Pi(S)$. In the *PathBoundLA* abstraction from Section 4.3, we used the values of $maxp$, $minp$, $hasInfPath$, and val^{pba} to abstract SegmentSets in $\mathcal{T}$. The abstract values are in turn used to compute an over-approximation of the limit-average property for S. In this subsection, we provide a generic segment-based abstraction scheme for any set of properties.

More specifically, let us assume that we have a set $\mathcal{P}$ of quantitative properties, a set $\mathcal{T}$ of SegmentSets that is a segment cover of a segment set T. We provide a generic technique to answer the following question: if we know the values of quantitative properties in $\mathcal{P}$ on all SegmentSets in $\mathcal{T}$, can we compute the values of quantitative properties in $\mathcal{P}$ on SegmentSet T?

We need to extend notation in two ways: (a) We will use quantitative properties f defined by f_t and f_s for both finite and infinite traces. The type of f_t will thus be $\mathbb{R}^{\omega} \cup \mathbb{R}^* \to \mathbb{R}$; and (b) We will evaluate quantitative properties on a SegmentSet T (instead of a WTS) by letting $f(T) = f_s(\{f_t(\varrho(\pi)) \mid \pi \in T\})$.

Fix an arbitrary WTS $S = (Q, \delta, \varrho, q_\iota)$. Consider an arbitrary set of SegmentSets $\mathcal{T} = \{T_0, T_1, \ldots, T_n\}$, where all segments are sequences of states from Q. We define the set of *valid segments* generated by $\mathcal{T}$ as $\biguplus^{\delta} \mathcal{T} = \{\sigma_0 \ldots \sigma_n \mid \forall j : \sigma_j \in \bigcup \mathcal{T} \wedge \forall j < n : (last(\sigma_j), first(\sigma_{j+1})) \in \delta\} \cup \{\sigma_0 \ldots \mid \forall j : \sigma_j \in \bigcup \mathcal{T} \wedge \forall j \ge 0 : (last(\sigma_j), first(\sigma_{j+1})) \in \delta\}$ where $first(\sigma)$ and $last(\sigma)$ denote the first and last states of a segment. Intuitively, the set $\biguplus^{\delta} \mathcal{T}$ is the set of segments generated by $\mathcal{T}$ where the transition relation of the system S holds at the sub-segment boundaries.

Let $\mathcal{T} = \{T_1, \ldots, T_n\}$ be a cover of the SegmentSet T (not necessarily $\Pi(S)$). Note that $\biguplus^{\delta} \mathcal{T}$ can be a proper subset of T, i.e., $T \subseteq \biguplus \mathcal{T}$, but $\biguplus^{\delta} \mathcal{T} \subsetneq T$. We call the SegmentSet $T \cap \biguplus^{\delta} \mathcal{T}$ the *strengthening* of the SegmentSet T by $\mathcal{T}$ and δ. Our question thus becomes: provided that we know the values of quantitative properties in $\mathcal{P}$ on all SegmentSets in $\mathcal{T}$, can we compute the values of quantitative properties in $\mathcal{P}$ on the strengthening of the SegmentSet T by $\mathcal{T}$ and δ, i.e. on $T \cap \biguplus^{\delta} \mathcal{T}$?

Abstract SegmentSet and property domains. Let $\langle SEG, \subseteq \rangle$ be the set of all SegmentSets partially ordered by the subset relation, and let $\langle \mathcal{L}, \preceq \rangle$ be a lattice. The lattice serves as an abstract domain for describing SegmentSets. Elements of L can be for instance syntactical objects, such as formulas in a logic. Let $\langle SEG, \subseteq \rangle \underset{\alpha^{SEG}}{\overset{\gamma^{SEG}}{\leftrightarrows}} \langle \mathcal{L}, \preceq \rangle$ be a Galois connection (see [6]). We call the domain $\langle \mathcal{L}, \preceq \rangle$ the *abstract SegmentSet domain* and each element $\phi \in \mathcal{L}$ an *abstract SegmentSet*.

A *property set* $\mathcal{P}$ is a tuple $\langle \langle f_1^l, \ldots f_n^l \rangle, \langle f_1^u, \ldots f_m^u \rangle \rangle$ where (a) all f_i^l's are quantitative properties where $f_s = \inf$; and (b) all f_i^u's are quantitative properties where $f_s = \sup$. We define the corresponding property domain $\mathcal{D}_{\mathcal{P}} = \langle (\mathbb{R}^n \times \mathbb{R}^m), \sqsubseteq_{\mathcal{P}} \rangle$ to be the abstract domain where $((a_1^l, \ldots, a_n^l), (a_1^u, \ldots, a_n^u)) \sqsubseteq ((b_1^l, \ldots, b_n^l), (b_1^u, \ldots, b_n^u))$ if and only if all $a_i^l \ge b_i^l$ and $a_i^u \le b_i^u$. We write $\mathcal{P}(T)$ for $((f_1^l(T), \ldots, f_n^l(T)), (f_1^u(T), \ldots, f_n^u(T)))$.

Example 13. *The property set $\mathcal{P}^{LA} = \langle \langle minp \rangle, \langle maxp, val^{pba}, hasInfPath \rangle$ is a property set. For example, $minp(T) = \inf(\{|\sigma| \mid \sigma \in T\})$ and $hasInfPath(T) = \sup(\{hasInfPath_t(\sigma) \mid \sigma \in T\})$ where $hasInfPath_t(\sigma)$ is 1 if $|\sigma| = \infty$ and 0 otherwise.*

It is easy to see that a Galois connection $\langle SEG, \subseteq \rangle \underset{\alpha^{\mathcal{P}}}{\overset{\gamma^{\mathcal{P}}}{\leftrightarrows}} \langle \mathcal{D}_{\mathcal{P}}, \sqsubseteq_{\mathcal{P}} \rangle$ can be defined by letting $\alpha^{\mathcal{P}}(T) = \mathcal{P}(T)$ and $\gamma^{\mathcal{P}}(P) = \bigcup\{T \mid \mathcal{P}(T) \sqsubseteq P\}$. Intuitively, $((l_1, \ldots, l_n), (u_1, \ldots, u_n)) \in \mathcal{P}(T)$ represents the largest SegmentSet T that respects the lower and upper bounds placed by P, i.e., $f_i^l(T) \ge l_i \wedge f_j^u(T) \le u_j$. We call $\mathcal{D}_{\mathcal{P}}$ the *property bound domain* and an individual $P \in \mathcal{D}_{\mathcal{P}}$ a *property bound*.

Let $\langle \mathcal{L} \times \mathcal{D}_{\mathcal{P}}, \le \rangle$, where $\le$ is $\preceq \times \sqsubseteq_{\mathcal{P}}$, be the product of $\langle \mathcal{L}, \preceq \rangle$ and $\langle \mathcal{D}_{\mathcal{P}}, \sqsubseteq_{\mathcal{P}} \rangle$. We call $\mathcal{L} \times \mathcal{D}_{\mathcal{P}}$ the domain of abstract bound pairs and each element (written as $\phi \wedge P$) an abstract bound pair. Let $\langle SEG, \subseteq \rangle \underset{\alpha}{\overset{\gamma}{\leftrightarrows}} \langle \mathcal{L} \times \mathcal{D}_{\mathcal{P}}, \preceq \times \sqsubseteq_{\mathcal{P}} \rangle$ be a Galois connection naturally defined for the product of abstract domains, where $\alpha(T) = (\alpha^{SEG}(T), \alpha^{\mathcal{P}}(T))$, and $\gamma(\phi, P) = \gamma^{SEG}(\phi) \cap \gamma^{\mathcal{P}}(P)$. Intuitively, the element $\phi \wedge P$ represents a SegmentSet that is contained in ϕ and respects the property bounds P. We identity abstract segments $\phi \in \mathcal{L}$ with the abstract bound pair in $\phi \wedge \top$

where $\top = ((-\infty, \dots, -\infty), (\infty, \dots, \infty))$, i.e., there are no bounds on any of the properties in $\mathcal{P}$.

Example 14. *Let $\mathcal{L} = SEG$, i.e., the abstract SegmentSets are the same as concrete SegmentSets. Note that this assumption is to simplify the example. It would be more natural to use syntactical objects (e.g. formulas in some logic) for $\mathcal{L}$. Consider $\mathcal{D}_{\mathcal{P}}^{LA}$ for the property bound domain defined in Example 13. An example of an element in $\mathcal{L} \times \mathcal{D}_{\mathcal{P}}^{LA}$ is $T_1 \wedge ((4), (4, \frac{18}{4}, 0))$ where T_1 is from Example 12. Here, $((4), (4, \frac{18}{4}, 0))$ represent bounds on values of properties $((minp), (maxp, val^{pba}, hasInfPath))$. Note that $T_1 \wedge ((4), (4, \frac{18}{4}, 0))$ contains exactly the same information that PathBoundLA stores about a SegmentSet.*

Evaluating quantitative properties on abstract SegmentSets. In what follows, we fix a WTS S, and a segment cover $\mathcal{T} = \{T_1, T_2, \dots, T_{|\mathcal{T}|}\}$ of $T = \Pi(S)$. Let K be the interval $[1..|\mathcal{T}|]$. Given an abstract bound pair domain $\langle \mathcal{L} \times \mathcal{D}_{\mathcal{P}}, \preceq \times \sqsubseteq_{\mathcal{P}} \rangle$, where f is a property in $\mathcal{P}$, we can perform the computation of $f(T \cap \biguplus^{\delta} \mathcal{T})$ in the abstract domain. For this computation, the abstract bound pair domain needs to support the following additional operations.

Let $\phi \wedge P$ be an abstract bound pair, and $\Phi = \{\phi_1 \wedge P_1, \dots, \phi_{|\mathcal{T}|} \wedge P_{|\mathcal{T}|}\}$ be a set of abstract bound pairs. The abstract bound pairs domain $\langle \mathcal{L} \times \mathcal{D}_{\mathcal{P}}, \preceq \times \sqsubseteq_{\mathcal{P}} \rangle$ is an *inductive domain* if it supports the following operations in addition to the standard lattice operations.

- *Transition check.* This operation checks for two abstract SegmentSets, whether a segment from the first can be validly followed by a segment from the second. Formally, $TrCheck_{\phi}(\phi_i, \phi_j)$ is true if and only if there is validly generated segment σ, i.e., $\sigma \in \gamma(\phi) \cap \biguplus^{\delta} \{\gamma(\phi_i) \mid i \in K\}$, where $\sigma = \sigma' \sigma_i \sigma_j \sigma''$ such that (a) $\sigma_i \in \gamma(\phi_i) \wedge \sigma_j \in \gamma(\phi_j)$, and (b) σ' and σ'' are also validly generated.
- *Reduce Property Bounds.* Given an abstract SegmentSet ϕ, compute (an over-approximation) of the property bounds on ϕ. Formally, $ReduceBound(\phi)$ returns $\phi \wedge P^*$ such that $\gamma(\phi \wedge P^*) \supseteq \gamma(\phi)$.
- *Property computation.* Given only the bounds P_i on abstract SegmentSets ϕ_i and the values $TrCheck_{\phi}(\phi_i, \phi_j)$, $PropComp$ computes (an over-approximation) of the property bounds on the abstract segment $\phi \wedge P$. Formally, given $\delta^{gpb} = \{(i,j) \mid TrCheck_{\phi}(\phi_i, \phi_j) = true\}$, and the values P_i for all i, the function $PropComp(\phi, \delta^{gpb}, \langle P_1 \dots P_{|\mathcal{T}|} \rangle)$ outputs $\phi^* \wedge P^*$ such that $\phi^* \wedge P^* \geq (\phi \wedge \top) \wedge \alpha(\biguplus^{\delta} \{\gamma(\phi_i \wedge P_i) \mid i \in K\})$. Note that we sometimes abuse the notation and write $PropComp(\phi, \{\phi_1 \wedge P_1, \dots, \phi_{|\mathcal{T}|} \wedge P_{|\mathcal{T}|}\})$ instead of $PropComp(\phi, \delta^{gpb}, \langle P_1 \dots P_{|\mathcal{T}|} \rangle_i)$.

Example 15. *Continuing from Example 14, i.e., $\mathcal{L} = SEG$ and the system under consideration is S_1 from Figure 5.*

- *$TrCheck_{\Pi(S)}(T_1, T_2)$ can be as precise as the transition relation of PathBoundLA, i.e, $(T_1, T_2) \in \delta^{pba} \Leftrightarrow TrCheck_{\Pi(S)}(T_1, T_2)$. Suppose $\sigma_1 \in T_1$ and $\sigma_2 \in T_2$. We have that σ_1 can be followed by σ_2 if and only if $(last(\sigma_1), first(\sigma_2)) \in \delta$. This is the condition that defines $(T_1, T_2) \in \delta^{pb}$.*
- *If we take $ReduceBound(T_2)$ to be precise (and computationally expensive) procedure that concretizes abstract states, it can return $T_2 \wedge ((3), (4, 1, 0))$, i.e., it computes (an over-approximation) of the information stored for the particular SegmentSetT_2.*
- *$PropComp(\Pi(S), \{T_1 \wedge P_1, T_2 \wedge P_2\})$ (where $P_1 = ((4), (4, \frac{18}{4}, 0))$ and $P_2 = ((3), (4, 1, 0))$) computes an over-approximation of $\mathcal{P}(\Pi(S))$ by computing on abstract states. If $PropComp$ is defined using the same approach as the B and f^{pba} definitions from Section 4.3, it returns $((4), (\infty, 3, 1))$. Here, $val^{pba}(\Pi(S))$ is 3, $minp = 4$, and $maxp$ and $hasInfPath$ are over-approximated to the largest possible values.*

Remark 16. *Note that in the arguments of PropComp, we do not require P_i to be equal to $\mathcal{P}(\phi_i)$. In fact, even in the case where P_i is a $\sqsubseteq_{\mathcal{P}}$-over-approximation of $\mathcal{P}(\phi_i)$, the procedure PropComp is required to produce a valid $\sqsubseteq_{\mathcal{P}}$-over-approximation of the $\mathcal{P}$ value of $\gamma(\phi) \cap \biguplus^{\delta} \{\gamma(\phi_i) \mid i \in K\}$.*

We call an abstract bound pair domain *effective* if: (a) each of the operations $ReduceBound$, $TrCheck$, and $PropComp$ can be computed effectively, i.e., by a terminating procedure; and (b) $ReduceBound$ and $PropComp$ are monotonic, i.e., giving more precise inputs produces more precise outputs. Formally, (a) $\phi \preceq \phi' \implies ReduceBound(\phi) \leq ReduceBound(\phi')$; (b) $(\phi \preceq \phi' \wedge \forall i \in K : P_i \sqsubseteq P_i' \wedge \phi_i \preceq \phi_i') \implies PropComp(\phi, \{\phi_1 \wedge P_1, \dots, \phi_{|\mathcal{T}|} \wedge P_{|\mathcal{T}|}\}) \leq PropComp(\phi, \{\phi_1 \wedge P_1', \dots, \phi_{|\mathcal{T}|} \wedge P_{|\mathcal{T}|}'\})$; and (c) $(\phi_1^1 \wedge P_1^1 \leq \phi_1 \wedge P_1) \wedge (\phi_1^2 \wedge P_1^2 \leq \phi_1 \wedge P_1) \implies PropComp(\phi, \{\phi_1^1 \wedge P_1^1, \phi_1^2 \wedge P_1^2, \phi_2 \wedge P_2, \dots, \phi_{|\mathcal{T}|} \wedge P_{|\mathcal{T}|}\}) \leq PropComp(\phi, \{\phi_1 \wedge P_1, \phi_2 \wedge P_2, \dots, \phi_{|\mathcal{T}|} \wedge P_{|\mathcal{T}|}\})$.

We can now generalize $PathBound$ abstraction scheme by letting the summaries of SegmentSets be the set of values of properties from any effectively inductive quantitative property set. Intuitively, given a WTS S, and a property set $\mathcal{P}$, the $PathBound[\mathcal{L} \times \mathcal{D}_{\mathcal{P}}]$ abstraction stores with each SegmentSet T in the cover of $\Pi(S)$ the values $\alpha^{SEG}(T) \wedge \mathcal{P}(T)$. To compute the value of the abstract system, the procedures $ReduceBound$, $TrCheck$, and $PropComp$ are used.

Formally, $PathBound[\mathcal{L} \times \mathcal{D}_{\mathcal{P}}]_{\mathcal{T}} = \langle \mathcal{S}[\mathcal{L} \times \mathcal{D}_{\mathcal{P}}], \alpha[\mathcal{L} \times \mathcal{D}_{\mathcal{P}}]_{\mathcal{T}}, f[\mathcal{L} \times \mathcal{D}_{\mathcal{P}}] \rangle$ is defined as:

- $\alpha[\mathcal{L} \times \mathcal{D}_{\mathcal{P}}]_{\mathcal{T}}(S) = \langle \phi, \langle \phi_1, \dots, \phi_{|\mathcal{T}|} \rangle, \delta^{gpb} \rangle$ where (a) $\phi = \alpha^{SEG}(\Pi(S))$; (b) $\phi_i = \alpha^{SEG}(T_i)$; and (c) $(i,j) \in \delta^{gpb}$ if and only if $TrCheck_{\phi}(\phi_i, \phi_j)$ returns true.
- $f[\mathcal{L} \times \mathcal{D}_{\mathcal{P}}]$ is computed as the value of f in P^* where $\phi^* \wedge P^* = PropComp(\phi, \delta^{gpb}, \langle ReduceBound(\phi_1), \dots, ReduceBound(\phi_{|\mathcal{T}|}) \rangle) \wedge ReduceBound(\phi)$.

Precise abstractions. In the $ExistMax$ case, if the abstraction function does not lose any information, i.e., if the equivalence relation used is the identity relation, the abstract system value is the same as the concrete system value. We give the conditions when an segment-based abstraction does not lose any information either.

Intuitively, we want the property computation for a SegmentSet T from a cover $\mathcal{T} = \{T_1, \dots T_n\}$ to be accurate when T is exactly covered by $\mathcal{T}$, i.e, $T = \biguplus^{\delta} \mathcal{T}$.

An quantitative property set is *precisely inductive* if there exists a $PropComp$ procedure which produces the output $(\phi, \mathcal{P}(\phi))$ when the following hold: (a) $P_i = \mathcal{P}(\gamma(\phi_i))$, and (b) $\gamma(\phi) = \biguplus^{\delta} \{\gamma(\phi_i) \mid i \in K\}$.

Example 17. *The limit-average property is not precisely inductive, i.e., by knowing only the limit-average value of the subsegments of a segment, we cannot estimate the limit-average accurately without knowing the length of the subsegments. However, strengthening it to the property set $\langle \langle minp \rangle, \langle maxp, limavg, hasInfPath \rangle \rangle$ makes it precisely inductive.*

5.2 Hierarchical segment-based abstraction

Effective abstract bound pair domains allow computation of property bounds for a whole set of properties on a SegmentSet from the property bounds on each element of the cover. For example, if $\mathcal{T}$ covers T, the four properties $minp$, $maxp$, val, $hasInfPath$ of SegmentSets in $\mathcal{T}$ are used to compute not only the $limavg$, but also the $maxp$, $minp$, and $hasInfPath$ values of the SegmentSet T

too. This leads to the possibility of computing these properties hierarchically for a multi-level trace segment cover.

An *inductive trace segment cover* [7] $\mathcal{C}$ is a finite rooted-tree where the nodes are labelled with abstract bound pairs such that for every non-leaf node labelled with SegmentSet $\phi \wedge P$, and $\phi_1 \wedge P_1, \ldots, \phi_n \wedge P_n$ the set of labels of its children, $\{\gamma(\phi_1 \wedge P_1), \ldots, \gamma(\phi_n \wedge P_n)\}$ is a segment cover of $\gamma(\phi \wedge P)$. An inductive trace segment cover $\mathcal{C}$ *inductively covers* a SegmentSet T if $T \subseteq \gamma(root(\mathcal{C}))$. Similarly, $\mathcal{C}$ inductively covers a system S if $\Pi(S) \subseteq \gamma(root(\mathcal{C}))$.

We can now introduce an abstraction scheme $HPathBound[\mathcal{L} \times \mathcal{D}_\mathcal{P}]_\mathcal{C} = \langle S^{hpb}[\mathcal{L} \times \mathcal{D}_\mathcal{P}], \alpha^{hpb}[\mathcal{L} \times \mathcal{D}_\mathcal{P}]_\mathcal{C}, f^{hpb}[\mathcal{L} \times \mathcal{D}_\mathcal{P}]\rangle$ parameterized by an abstract bound pair domain $\mathcal{L} \times \mathcal{D}_\mathcal{P}$, and an abstract inductive trace segment cover $\mathcal{C}$. Intuitively, $HPathBound$ stores for each internal node a of $\mathcal{C}$, a $PathBound[\mathcal{L} \times \mathcal{D}_\mathcal{P}]_{\mathcal{T}(a)}$ abstraction $\langle label(a), \mathcal{T}(a), \delta^{gpb}\rangle$. The abstract trace segment cover $\mathcal{T}(a)$ for this abstraction is the labels of the set $children(a)$.

Abstract hierarchical traces. We fix an abstract bound pair domain $\mathcal{L} \times \mathcal{P}_\mathcal{D}$. An *abstract hierarchical trace* $\psi = \langle(\phi_0 \wedge P_0)(\phi_1 \wedge P_1)\ldots, sub_\psi\rangle$ consists of (a) a finite or infinite sequence of abstract bound pairs; and (b) a partial function sub_π from $\mathbb{N}$ to hierarchical traces.

The concrete traces $\gamma(\psi)$ corresponding to a given abstract trace $\psi = \langle(\phi_0 \wedge P_0)(\phi_1 \wedge P_1)\ldots, sub_\psi\rangle$ are defined as $\{\sigma_0\sigma_1\ldots | \forall i : \sigma_i \in \gamma(\phi_i \wedge P_i) \wedge sub_\psi(i) \neq \bot \implies \sigma_i \in \gamma(sub_\psi(i))\}$. Intuitively, a concrete trace of an abstract hierarchical trace ψ is made of segments σ_i from $\phi_i \wedge P_i$, with the additional condition that $\sigma_i \in sub_\psi(i)$ if $sub_\psi(i)$ is defined.

Given a property set $\mathcal{P}$, an effective abstract bound pair domain, and an inductive trace segment cover $\mathcal{C}$ of system S, we inductively compute property bounds (and hence, abstract system values) using Algorithm 1. The algorithm is based on the inductive proof method presented in [7]. It can be rewritten as a fixed-point computation in

Algorithm 1 Inductive Property Computation (InductiveCompute)

Input: WTS S,
Effective abstract bound pair domain $\mathcal{L} \times \mathcal{D}_\mathcal{P}$,
Abstract Inductive Segment Cover $\mathcal{C}$ (labelled from $\mathcal{L} \times \mathcal{D}_\mathcal{P}$),
Output: abstract bound pair $\phi^* \wedge P^*$ such that $(\phi^* \wedge P^*) \geq \mathcal{P}(label(root(\mathcal{C})))$

```
(φ ∧ P) ← label(root(C))
if root(C) has no children then
    return (φ ∧ P) ∧ (ReduceBound(φ ∧ P))
else
    subTrees ← top level sub-trees of C
    return (φ ∧ P) ∧ PropComp(φ ∧ P, {InductiveCompute(C′) | C′ ∈ subTrees})
```

the lattice $\mathcal{C} \to \mathcal{L} \times \mathcal{D}_\mathcal{P}$ of maps from $nodes(\mathcal{C})$ to $\mathcal{L} \times \mathcal{D}_\mathcal{P}$ (the lattice ordered point-wise by $(\preceq, \sqsubseteq_\mathcal{P})$). At the final line in Algorithm 1, the value of $\mathcal{C}$ will be the least fixed-point of the function which replaces each node in $\mathcal{C}$ with a best approximation obtained from among the current value of the node, and (a) $ReduceBound$ applied on the node if it is a leaf node, or (b) $PropComp$ applied on the node and its children if it is an internal node.

Monotonicity. We define refinements of $HPathBound$ abstractions using refinement steps. Let $\mathcal{C}$ be an inductive trace segment cover and let a be a non-root node in $\mathcal{C}$, b be its parent, $\mathcal{C}(a)$ be the sub-tree of $\mathcal{C}$ rooted at b, and $\phi \wedge P$ and $\phi^b \wedge P^b$ the labels of a and b. A *one-step refinement* of $\mathcal{C}$ is one of the following:

- Horizontal refinement. Let ϕ_1 and ϕ_2 be such that $\gamma(\phi \wedge P) = \gamma(\phi_1 \wedge P_1) \cup \gamma(\phi_2 \wedge P_2)$. Let $\mathcal{C}(a)[label(a) \leftarrow \phi_1 \wedge P_1]$ and $\mathcal{C}(a)[label(a) \leftarrow \phi_2 \wedge P_2]$ be the tree $\mathcal{C}(a)$ with $\phi \wedge P$ replaced by $\phi_1 \wedge P_1$ and $\phi_2 \wedge P_2$, respectively. Let the tree $\mathcal{C}'$ be obtained by detaching $\mathcal{C}(a)$ from p and then attaching $\mathcal{C}(a)[label(a) \leftarrow \phi_1 \wedge P_1]$ and $\mathcal{C}(a)[label(a) \leftarrow \phi_2 \wedge P_2]$ to p. Then $\mathcal{C}'$ is a *one-step horizontal refinement* of $\mathcal{C}$.
- Vertical splitting refinement. Suppose $\{\gamma(\phi_1 \wedge P_1), \ldots \gamma(\phi_n \wedge P_n)\}$ cover $\phi \wedge P$ and that a does not have any children. Suppose $\mathcal{C}'$ is obtained from $\mathcal{C}$ by adding the children with labels $\phi_1 \wedge P_1, \ldots, \phi_n \wedge P_n$ to a. Then, $\mathcal{C}'$ is a *one-step vertical splitting refinement* of $\mathcal{C}$.
- Vertical joining refinement. Suppose that b has no grandchildren, and let $(\phi^b \wedge P^b) \leq PropComp(\phi \wedge P, children(b), \delta)$ and $\forall c \in children(b) : c) \leq ReduceBound(c))$. If $\mathcal{C}'$ is the tree obtained by removing all the children of b in $\mathcal{C}$, then $\mathcal{C}'$ is a *one-step vertical joining refinement* of $\mathcal{C}$.
- Downward strengthening refinement. Suppose $\gamma(\phi') \subseteq \gamma(\phi)$ and $\phi^b \wedge P^b \subseteq \biguplus^\delta\{\gamma(\psi) \mid \psi \in ((children(b) \setminus \{\phi \wedge P\}) \cup \{\phi' \wedge P'\})\}$. Let $\mathcal{C}'$ be the tree obtained by replacing $\mathcal{C}(a)$ by $\mathcal{C}(a)[label(a) \leftarrow \phi' \wedge P']$. Then, $\mathcal{C}'$ is a *one-step downward strengthening refinement* of $\mathcal{C}$.
- Upward strengthening refinement. Suppose that $\phi' \wedge P'$ is such that $\biguplus^\delta\{\gamma(\psi) \mid \psi \in children(b)\} \subseteq \gamma(\phi' \wedge P') \subseteq \gamma(\phi^b \wedge P^b)$. If $\mathcal{C}'$ is obtained from $\mathcal{C}$ by replacing $\phi^b \wedge P^b$ with $\phi' \wedge P'$, then $\mathcal{C}'$ is a *one-step upward strengthening refinement* of $\mathcal{C}$.

A $\mathcal{C}_n$ is a *refinement* of $\mathcal{C}_0$ if there exists a sequence $\mathcal{C}_1, \mathcal{C}_2, \ldots, \mathcal{C}_{n-1}$ such that $\mathcal{C}_i$ is a one-step refinement of $\mathcal{C}_{i-1}$ for all i such that $n \geq i > 0$.

$HPathBound[\mathcal{L} \times \mathcal{D}_\mathcal{P}]$ is *monotonic* if for all systems S and abstract inductive trace segment covers $\mathcal{C}$ and $\mathcal{C}'$ of S, if $\mathcal{C}'$ is a refinement of $\mathcal{C}$, then abstract value $f^{hpb}[\mathcal{L} \times \mathcal{D}_\mathcal{P}](\alpha^{hpb}[\mathcal{L} \times \mathcal{D}_\mathcal{P}]_{\mathcal{C}'}(S)) \leq f^{hpb}[\mathcal{L} \times \mathcal{D}_\mathcal{P}](\alpha^{hpb}[\mathcal{L} \times \mathcal{D}_\mathcal{P}]_\mathcal{C}(S))$.

Theorem 18. *If f is a property such that $f_s = \sup$, and the inductive property set $\mathcal{P}$ contains f, and $\mathcal{L} \times \mathcal{D}_\mathcal{P}$ is effectively inductive, $HPathBound[\mathcal{L} \times \mathcal{D}_\mathcal{P}]$ is monotonic for f.*

Intuitively, the theorem holds as every one-step refinement preserves the information about the property-bounds of nodes from the previous iteration. For all one-step refinements other than the vertical joining refinements, the monotonicity follows from the monotonicity of $PropComp$ and $ReduceBound$. For vertical splitting one-step refinements, the monotonicity holds as all the information that can be generated from the deleted children is already present in the parent node.

5.3 $HPathBound$ abstractions for control-flow graphs

A control-flow graph of a program written in a high-level language is contains many structures like loops and function calls. The traces of transition systems produced from such programs are structured. This opens the possibility of using hierarchical segment-based abstractions to analyze them.

Control-flow graphs and Programs. Following, e.g., [4], we abstract away from the syntax of a concrete programming language, and model programs as graphs whose nodes correspond to program locations. Here we assume simple programs with inlined function calls (this implies that there are no recursive functions).

Let V be a set of variables and let $D(V)$ be the combined range of variables in V. A *control-flow graph* (CFG) is a tuple of $\langle L, V, \Delta, \psi : \Delta \to 2^{D(V) \times D(V)}\rangle$ where L is a finite set of control locations, Δ is a transition relation, V is a set of variables, and ψ is a function from Δ to assertions over program variables V and their primed versions V'. The primed variables V' refer to the values of the variables after executing the transition. We assume that V contains a special variable wt ranging over $\mathbb{R}$ which denotes the weight of a particular state.

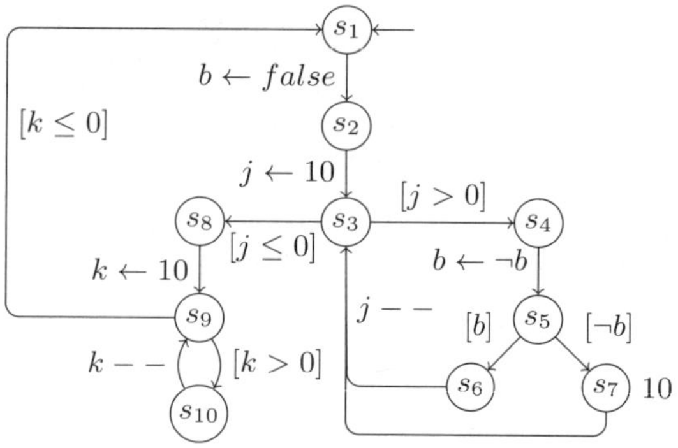

Figure 9: An example CFG

Given a CFG C, a corresponding transition system can be generated (with state-space $L \times D(V)$) in a standard way. We add the weight function $\varrho(l, d) = w$, where w is the value of the special variable wt in d, to turn the transition system into a WTS.

We assume the following about the CFG (these assumptions are valid for CFGs generated for programs in most programming languages): (a) *Reducibility.* In the graph (L, Δ), every maximal strongly connected component has a single entry and exit point, i.e., if $G \subseteq L$ is a maximal strongly connected component, there exists a node l_G such that $(l, l') \in \Delta \cap ((L \setminus G) \times G) \implies l' = l_G \wedge (l, l') \in \Delta \cap (G \times (L \setminus G)) \implies l = l_G$; (b) *Recursive reducibility.* Suppose $G \subseteq L$ is a maximal strongly connected component. The graph $(G, \Delta \cap (G \times (G \setminus \{l_G\}))$ is also reducible. Intuitively, the above conditions imply that loops in the CFG are single-entry and single-exit, and that they are nested.

```
while(true)
 b = false;
 j = 10;
 while j > 0
   b = not b;
   if b costlyOp;
   j--
 k = 10;
 while (k>0) k--
```

Figure 8: Prg

A *hierarchical control-flow graph* (HCFG) is a graph $\langle \mathcal{H}, \Delta \subseteq \mathcal{H} \times \mathcal{H}, h_i \rangle$ where each node $h \in \mathcal{H}$ is either a control-flow location, or a hierarchical control-flow graph. We call the first kind of nodes, *abstract state nodes* and the second kind of nodes *subgraph nodes.*

Any recursively reducible CFG C can be converted into a HCFG H of a special form using a standard algorithm on reducible graphs. In this special form, H and all sub-HCFGs occurring in H have the following property: either they are acyclic, or they have a single node with a self-loop on itself. Note that each loop of a program will correspond to such sub-HCFG. In what follows, we assume that all our HCFGs are of this special form.

Example 19. *Consider the example CFG shown in Figure 9 (generated from program in Figure 8). The equivalent HCFG of the special form to this CFG is shown in Figure 10. The statements on the transitions in Figure 10 are omitted for the sake of clarity. Each of the dotted boxes represent a HCFG. Intuitively, each loop has been separated out into an acyclic CFG containing the loop body and a single self-loop CFG.*

Inductive trace segment covers can be derived from HCFGs. In particular, every HCFG H represents a unique inductive trace segment cover $\mathcal{C}(H)$. Intuitively, the root of the inductive trace segment cover is the set of all traces of H, and the children of the root node are either (a) $\mathcal{C}(H')$ if H' is a subgraph node of H, and (b) $\{S\}$ if S is a abstract state node of H where $\{S\}$ is the SegmentSet containing all segments of length 1 with states in S. From now on, we use HCFGs and abstract inductive trace segment covers interchangeably.

Example 20. *Consider the program in Figure 8. Its CFG is in Figure 9 and the corresponding HCFG is in Figure 10. We use regular expressions over control locations as our abstract SegmentSet domain $\mathcal{L}$. The regular expressions have their intuitive meaning. For example, (a) the expression $s_1 s_2$ represents all segments $q_1 q_2$ such that the control location of q_1 (resp. q_2) is s_1 (resp. s_2); and (b) the expression $(s_1 s_2)^*$ represents the set of segments obtained by concatenation of segments from $s_1 s_2$.*

The HCFG corresponds to the following inductive trace segment cover $\mathcal{C}$ of the traces generated by the CFG. The root of $\mathcal{C}$ is the expression $H = (s_1 s_2 s_3 (s_4 s_5 (s_6 + s_7) s_3)^* s_8 s_9 (s_{10} s_9)^*)^*$. Its only child is $F = s_1 s_2 s_3 (s_4 s_5 (s_6 + s_7) s_3)^* s_8 s_9 (s_{10} s_9)^*$. The children of F are $\{C_B, L_1, C_M, L_2\}$ where $C_B = s_1 s_2 s_3$, $L_1 = (s_4 s_5 (s_6 + s_7) s_3)^*$, $C_M = s_8 s_9$, and $L_2 = (s_{10} s_9)^*$. Of these, only L_1 and L_2 are non-leaf nodes having one child each $C_{L_1} = s_4 s_5 (s_6 + s_7) s_3$ and $C_{L_2} = s_{10} s_9$, respectively.

Evaluating $limavg$ **for** $HPathBound$ **abstractions induced by HCFGs.** Let H be a HCFG of a special form. We compute the values $maxp$, $minp$, val^{pba}, and $hasInfPath$ using the technique of computing loop bounds. We consider a the domain of abstract bound pairs with elements of the form $\phi \wedge P$ as before.

Suppose H is a HCFG with a single node and a self-loop. Furthermore, let $\phi \wedge P$ be the corresponding abstract SegmentSet property bound in $\mathcal{C}(H)$, and let $\{\phi_1 \wedge P_1, \ldots, \phi_n \wedge P_n\}$ be its children. Let segment σ be in $\gamma(\phi \wedge P) \cap \biguplus^{\delta} \{\gamma(\phi_1 \wedge P_1), \ldots, \gamma(\phi_n \wedge P_n)\}$. Let $iters(\sigma) \subseteq \mathbb{N}$ where $n \in iters(\sigma)$ if and only if there exist $\sigma_0, \ldots, \sigma_{n-1}$ such that $\forall j < n. \exists i : \sigma_j \in \gamma(\phi_i \wedge P_i)$. Let $Iters(H) = \bigcup iters(\sigma)$ for all such σ. We define the *upper loop bound* (resp. *lower loop bound*), denoted by $ulb(H)$ (resp. $llb(H)$) as the value $\sup Iters(H)$ (resp. $\inf Iters(H)$). Note that there exists techniques to compute loop bounds using for example relational abstractions and ranking functions, see for example [10], and references therein.

Now, given the values of $maxp$, $minp$, val^{pba}, and $hasInfPath$ of subgraphs of an HCFG H, we inductively compute the value of the properties for H as follows:

- If H is a single node with no self-loop, i.e., an abstract state node, we have $maxp(H) = minp(H) = 1$, $val^{pba}(H) = \varrho(H)$, and $hasInfPath(H) = false$.
- If H is acyclic, we construct the following graph $H^\dagger$ as in Section 4.3, i.e., edges of H correspond to nodes of $H^\dagger$, and every node of H corresponds to two edges of weights (resp. lengths) $maxp(H') \cdot val^{pba}(H')$ and $maxp(H') \cdot val^{pba}(H')$ (resp. $maxp(H')$ and $minp(H')$). Now, $maxp(H)$ and $minp(H)$ are equal to the length of the longest and shortest paths in $H^\dagger$. Also, $hasInfPath(H) = true$ if and only if there is a node H' in H with $hasInfPath(H') = 1$. The value $val^{pba}(H)$ can be evaluated using Howard's policy iteration as in Section 4.3.
- If H is a single node with a self-loop, there is only one subgraph of H (say H'). We have $maxp(H) = ulb(H) \cdot maxp(H')$, $llb(H) \cdot minp(H')$, $val^{pba}(H) = val^{pba}(H')$, and $hasInfPath(H) = hasInfPath(H') \vee ulb(H) = \infty$.

Thus for such an HCFG, we can evaluate the limit-average value by using the inductive evaluation scheme from Section 5.2, i.e., using the values $minp$, $maxp$, val^{pba} and $hasInfPath$, we can inductively compute the limit-average values for an HCFG.

Example 21. *Consider the HCFG in Figure 10 and its inductive cover $\mathcal{C}$ from Example 20. We will illustrate a few steps of the inductive computation of the properties on $\mathcal{C}$. Fix $\mathcal{P} = \langle\langle minp \rangle, \langle maxp, val^{pba}, hasInfPath \rangle\rangle$.*

Let us start for the leaves of $\mathcal{C}$, i.e., $C_B = s_1 s_2 s_3$, $C_M = s_8 s_9$, $C_{L1} = s_4 s_5 (s_6 + s_7) s_3$, and $C_{L2} = s_{10} s_9$. Now, we can compute $minp$ and $maxp$ for these as the shortest and longest paths in the corresponding HCFGs. Furthermore, the $hasInfPath$ values for each of these is 0 as all of these CFGs are acyclic. The val^{pba} of

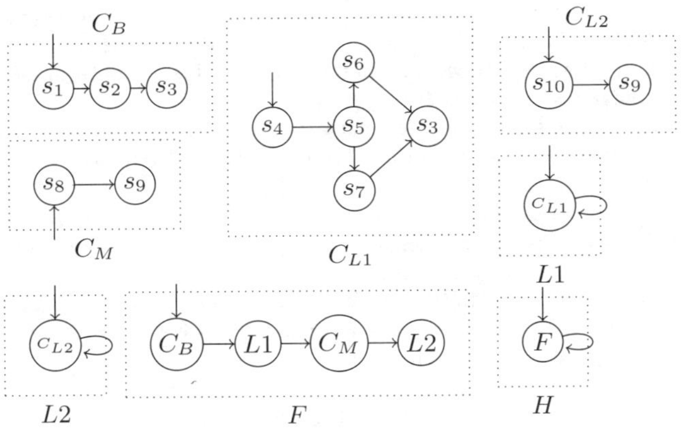

Figure 10: HCFG of a program

all the leaves except C_{L1} is 0 as the weights of all nodes except s_7 are 0. For C_{L1}, the val^{pba} can be computed to be $\frac{10}{4}$. Therefore, $ReduceBound(C_B) = ((3),(3,0,0))$, $ReduceBound(C_M) = ((2),(2,0,0))$, $P_1 = ReduceBound(C_{L1}) = ((4),(4,\frac{10}{4},0))$, and $P_2 = ReduceBound(C_{L2}) = ((2),(2,0,0))$.

Now, the nodes $L_1 = C_{L1}^*$ and $L_2 = C_{L2}^*$ have the children $\{C_{L1}\}$ and $\{C_{L2}\}$ respectively. The PropComp procedure has to now compute the properties $\mathcal{P}(L_1)$ using P_{L1}. However, note that the domain $\mathcal{L}$ does not give methods to compute loop-bounds (see Example 22 for a refinement of the domain $\mathcal{L}$ which can compute loop-bounds). Therefore, assuming ulb and llb for the loops are 0 and ∞ respectively, we get the values $\mathcal{P}(L_1) \leq P_{L1} = ((0),(\infty,\frac{10}{4},1))$ and $\mathcal{P}(L_2) \leq P_{L2} = ((0),(\infty,0,1))$.

Proceeding similarly, we get the estimates for $\mathcal{P}(F) \leq P_F = ((5),(\infty,\frac{10}{4},1))$ and $\mathcal{P}(H) \leq P_H = ((0),(\infty,\frac{10}{4},1))$. Intuitively, this corresponds to a counterexample that ends with an infinite loop in L1 that contains the costly operation.

6. Quantitative refinements

In this section, we present quantitative refinement algorithms for the state-based and segment-based abstraction schemes.

6.1 Algorithmic Refinement of $ExistMax$ abstractions

For the state-based abstraction scheme $ExistMax$, we give an algorithm for counterexample-guided abstraction refinement (CEGAR) for quantitative properties. The algorithm is based on the classical CEGAR algorithm [2], which we extend to the quantitative case. Here (as in [2]), we assume that the concrete system is finite-state, and obtain a sound and complete algorithm. In the infinite-state case, the algorithm is sound, but incomplete.

Let $S = (Q, \delta, \rho, q_\iota)$, let f be a $(\preceq_p, \sqsubseteq)$-monotonic quantitative property that admits memoryless extremal counterexamples (as stated in Section 2, we restrict ourselves to these properties), and let $\approx_1$ be an equivalence relation on Q. Let us further assume that $S^\alpha = (Q^\alpha, \delta^\alpha, \rho^\alpha, q_\iota^\alpha)$ is the result of applying the $ExistMax$ abstraction parameterized by $\approx_1$ on S. Let ρ_{ext} be the memoryless counterexample of S^α which realizes the value $f(S^\alpha)$.

Algorithm 2 is a refinement procedure for $ExistMax$ abstractions. Its input consists of the concrete and abstract systems, the equivalence relation that parameterizes the abstraction, the quantitative property, and the extremal trace ρ_{ext}. As the extremal counterexample is memoryless, it is of the shape $H_1 \ldots H_k(H_{k+1} \ldots H_n)^\omega$. The output of the algorithm is either a concrete counterexample (if one corresponding to ρ_{ext} exists), or a refined equivalence relation (which can be used to produce a new abstract system).

Let us consider a set of traces $\gamma(\rho_{ext})$ of the system S that correspond to an abstract memoryless trace $\rho_{ext} = H_1 \ldots H_k(H_{k+1} \ldots H_n)^\omega$. The first observation is that checking whether a concrete counterexample exists, i.e., whether $\gamma(\rho_{ext})$ is non-empty, can be done by checking whether a finite abstract trace ρ_u corresponds to a concrete trace. The finite abstract trace ρ_u can be obtained by unwinding the loop part of ρ_{ext} m number of times, where m is the size of the smallest abstract state in the loop part of ρ_{ext}, or formally, $m \leftarrow \min\{|H_i| \mid k+1 \leq i \leq n\}$ (line 1). This result can easily be adapted from [2] to the quantitative case.

Algorithm 2 Refinement for $ExistMax$

Input: WTS $S = (Q, \delta, \rho, q_\iota)$, quant. prop. f, eq. rel. $\approx_1$,
abstract WTS $S^\alpha = (Q^\alpha, \delta^\alpha, \rho^\alpha, q_\iota^\alpha)$,
abstract counterexample $\rho_{ext} = H_1 \ldots H_k(H_{k+1} \ldots H_n)^\omega$
Output: refined eq. rel. $\approx_2$
or a concrete counterex. $tecx$

1: $m \leftarrow \min\{|\gamma(H_i)| \mid k+1 \leq i \leq n\}$
2: $\rho_u \leftarrow$ unwind(ρ_{ext}, m, k, n)
   {we have $\rho_u = G_1 \ldots G_{k+(n-k)\cdot m}$}
3: $R_1 \leftarrow \gamma(\sigma_1) \cap \{q_\iota\}$
4: $i \leftarrow 1$
5: **while** $R_i \neq \emptyset \wedge i < (k + (n-k)\cdot m)$ **do**
6: $\quad R_{i+1} \leftarrow post(R_i, \rho^\alpha(G_{i+1})) \cap \gamma(G_{i+1})$
7: $\quad i \leftarrow i + 1$
8: **if** $R_{i-1} \neq \emptyset$ **then**
9: $\quad$ **return** counterEx$(R_0, \ldots, R_{i-1})$
10: **else**
11: $\quad U \leftarrow \{s \in \gamma(R_{i-1}) \mid \exists s' \in \gamma(G_i) : \delta_S(s,s') \wedge \rho(s') = \rho^\alpha(G_i)\}$
12: $\quad$ **return** refine$(\approx_1, G_{i-1}, U)$

Lines 3 to 7 traverse the finite abstract trace ρ_u, and at each step maintain the set of states that are reachable form the initial state along a path corresponding to ρ_u. (The $post$ operator in line 6 takes as input a set of concrete states L and a weight w, and returns all the successors of states in L that have weight w.)

If the traversal finishes because at i-th step the set R_i is empty, then the algorithm refines the equivalence relation $\approx_1$ by splitting the equivalence class given by G_{i-1} into U and $G_{i-1} \setminus U$ (line 11). The set U contains those states that have a transition (corresponding to a transition in ρ_u) to a state with weight $\rho^\alpha(G_i)$. The intersection $U \cap R_{i-1}$ is empty, because R_i is empty. Thus separating U leads to eliminating the counterexample from the abstract system.

If the traversal finishes a pass over the whole trace ρ_u, it can construct a concrete counterexample using sets of states $R_0, \ldots, R_{i-1}$ (line 9).

We have thus extended the classical CEGAR algorithm [2] to the quantitative case. The extension is simple, the main difference is in taking into account the weights in lines 6 and 11.

6.2 Algorithmic Refinement of $HPathBound$ abstractions

In this subsection, we describe an algorithmic technique for refinement of segment-based abstractions. We assume that the abstract bound pair domain is precisely inductive.

We assume that the extremal counter-example from the evaluation of a $HPathBound$ abstraction is returned as a abstract hierarchical trace $\psi = \langle(\phi_0 \wedge P_0)(\phi_1 \wedge P_1) \ldots (\phi_k \wedge P_k)((\phi_{k+1} \wedge P_{k+1}) \ldots (\phi_n \wedge P_n))^\omega, sub_\psi\rangle$. Note that we can assume a lasso-shaped counter-example due to the memoryless property of the quantitative properties we consider. Furthermore, without loss of generality we also assume that every leaf in the abstract trace segment cover is composed of segments of length 1.

The basic structure of the refinement algorithm is same as in $ExistMax$. However, the main difference is in the $post$ operator.

For hierarchical traces, we define a non-deterministic *post* operator in Algorithm 3. Intuitively, the algorithm non-deterministically chooses a level of the hierarchical trace to perform the analysis. First, given a hierarchical trace of length 1, *post* operator computes (Lines 3 and 4) the set $\gamma(\phi_0 \wedge P_0) \circ \delta = \{q\sigma \mid \sigma \in \gamma(\phi_0 \wedge P_0) \wedge (q, \mathit{first}(\sigma)) \in \delta\}$. Then, it computes the top-level post set R^* of states reachable from R using the segments from $\gamma(\phi_0 \wedge P_0) \circ \delta$. Now, non-deterministically (Line 5) it chooses whether to descend into the next level of the hierarchy. If it decides to, the set of post states $R^\dagger$ is computed from the levels below, and then the strengthening of R^* by $R^\dagger$, i.e., $R^* \cap R^\dagger$ is returned.

Assume that the *post* computation is done at a particular level, i.e., the level below is not used. Intuitively, this means that all the segments in $\phi_0 \wedge P_0$ are assumed to be valid segments, and the property bounds are assumed to be tight, i.e., the part of the counter-example corresponding to $\phi_0 \wedge P_0$ is considered non-spurious. Note that in the case where the algorithm always descends to the lowest level, the set returned is exactly the set of states reachable using segments in $\gamma(\psi) \circ \delta$. We also remark that nondeterminism in Algorithm 3 can be instantiated in a manner suitable for a particular domain.

Algorithm 3 Counterexample analysis for *HPathBound*

Input: Hierarchical trace $\psi = \langle(\phi_0 \wedge P_0)\ldots(\phi_k \wedge P_k), sub_\psi\rangle$, Concrete set of states R,
Output: Over-approximation of states reachable through segments in $\gamma(\psi)$.

1: **if** $n > 1$ **then**
2:     **return** $post(\langle(\phi_1 \wedge P_1)\ldots(\phi_n \wedge P_n), sub_\psi\rangle, post(\langle\phi_0 \wedge P_0, sub_\psi\rangle, R))$
3: $T \leftarrow \gamma(\phi_0 \wedge P_0) \circ \delta$
4: $R^* \leftarrow \{q' \mid \exists q\sigma q' \in T : q \in R\}$
5: **if** $*$ **then**
6:     **if** $sub_\psi(0) \neq \bot$ **then**
7:         $R^\dagger \leftarrow post(sub_\psi(0), R)$
8: **else**
9:     $R^\dagger \leftarrow R^*$
10: **return** $(R^* \cap R^\dagger, R^*, R^\dagger)$

Let $\mathcal{C}$ be the inductive trace segment cover and let $\psi = \langle(\phi_0 \wedge P_0)(\phi_1 \wedge P_1)\ldots(\phi_k \wedge P_k)((\phi_{k+1} \wedge P_{k+1})\ldots(\phi_n \wedge P_n))^\omega, sub_\psi\rangle$ be the extremal abstract trace. The abstraction refinement procedure *hAbsRefine*$(\mathcal{C}, \psi, R_0)$ proceeds similarly to Algorithm 2 as follows:

- The abstract hierarchical trace ψ is unwound m number of times, where $m = \min\{|\gamma(\phi_i \wedge P_i)| \mid i \in \{k+1, \ldots, n\}\}$;
- Let R_0 be the set of concrete initial states. For each abstract SegmentSet property pair $\phi_i \wedge P_i$ in the unwound trace, we compute $(R_{i+1}, R^*, R^\dagger) = post(\langle\phi_i \wedge P_i, sub_\psi\rangle, R_i)$;
- If at any step $R_{i+1} = \emptyset$, we refine the inductive trace segment cover $\mathcal{C}$ using set R_i and $\langle\phi_i, sub_\rho\rangle$ as *hRefine*$(R_i, \langle\phi_i, sub_\rho\rangle)$ (explained below). Otherwise, return any concrete counter-example constructed from the set $\{R_0, R_1, \ldots\}$.

We describe the computation of *hRefine*$(R_i, \langle\phi_i \wedge P_i, sub_\rho\rangle)$ when $post(\langle\phi_i, sub_\rho\rangle, R_i) = \emptyset$: during the computation $post(\langle\phi_i, sub_\rho\rangle, R_i)$ (execution of Algorithm 3) we have at least one of the following cases based on the values of R^* and $R^\dagger$. First, we define $T_R = \{\sigma \mid \exists q \in R(r, \mathit{first}(\sigma)) \in \delta \wedge \sigma \in \gamma(\phi_i \wedge P_i)\}$ and $T_R^{below} = \{\sigma \mid \exists r \in R.(r, \mathit{first}(\sigma)) \in \delta \wedge \sigma \in \gamma(sub_\psi(i))\}$. Intuitively, T_R is the set of concrete segments from R in $\phi_i \wedge P_i$, and T_R^{below} is the set of concrete segments from R generated from the hierarchical levels under $\phi_i \wedge P_i$. We have one of the following options:

- $R^* = \emptyset \wedge R^\dagger = \emptyset$. In this case, the refinement returned is *hAbsRefine*$(\mathcal{C}, \langle sub_\rho(i), sub_\rho\rangle, R)$, i.e., we run the abstraction refinement procedure on the lower level, starting from the concrete set of states R.
- $R^* = \emptyset$. In this case, we perform a horizontal refinement to separate the sets T_R and $T \setminus T_R$, i.e., the node labelled $\phi_i \wedge P_i$ is split into $\phi^A \wedge P^A$ and $\phi^B \wedge P^B$ where $\gamma(\phi^A \wedge P^A) \cup \gamma(\phi^B \wedge P^B) = \gamma(\phi_i \wedge P_i)$ and $T_R \subseteq \gamma(\phi^A \wedge P^A) \wedge T_R \cap \gamma(\phi^B \wedge P_B) = \emptyset$. Intuitively, we are separating segments in $\phi_i \wedge P_i$ that are from R from those that are not from R.
- $R^* \neq \emptyset \wedge R^* \cap R^\dagger = \emptyset$. In this case, we perform multiple simultaneous refinements. The segment sets which need to be distinguished from each other are $T \setminus (T_R \cup T_R^{below})$, T_R and T_R^{below}. Intuitively, we are trying to separate the segments in $\gamma(\phi_i \wedge P_i)$ that (a) do not start from R (i.e., $T \setminus (T_R \cup T_R^{below})$), (b) those that start from R and are validly generated from the levels below (i.e., T_R^{below}); and (c) those that do start from R and are not validly generated from the levels below (i.e., T_R). Formally, let $\phi^A \wedge P^A$, $\phi^B \wedge P^B$, and $\phi^C \wedge P^C$ be such that:
  - $T \subseteq \gamma(\phi^A \wedge P^A) \cup \gamma(\phi^B \wedge P^B) \cup \gamma(\phi^C \wedge P^C)$;
  - $T_R \subseteq \gamma(\phi^A \wedge P^A) \wedge T_R^{below} \cap \gamma(\phi^A \wedge P^A) = \emptyset$;
  - $T_R^{below} \subseteq \gamma(\phi^B \wedge P^B) \wedge T_R \cap \gamma(\phi^B \wedge P^B) = \emptyset$; and
  - $(T_R \cup T_R^{below}) \cap \gamma(\phi^C \wedge P^C) = \emptyset$.

  First, we do a horizontal refinement splitting the node $\phi_i \wedge P_i$ into $\phi^A \wedge P^A$, $\phi^B \wedge P^B$, and $\phi^C \wedge P^C$. Second, in the subtree rooted at $\phi^A \wedge P^A$, the levels below contains the information that T_R is infeasible, but the root does not. So, we perform upward strengthening refinements till the root contains the same information. Third, in the subtree rooted at $\phi^B \wedge P^B$, the root contains the information that T_R^{below} is infeasible, but the levels below do not. So, we perform either (a) downward strengthening refinements till the levels below contain the same information; or (b) vertical joining refinements till there are no levels below. Note that if one of $\phi^A \wedge P^A$, $\phi^B \wedge P^B$, or $\phi^B \wedge P^B$ is empty, we omit it.

Example 22. *Consider the HCFG H and the corresponding abstract trace segment cover $\mathcal{C}$ from Example 21. We now show some examples of hierarchical counter-example guided refinements for computing the limit-average value.*

We work in a more powerful refined domain than in Example 21, one that allows computation of loop bounds. Let $\mathcal{L}$ be the domain of regular expressions over HCFG's along with a relation between the values of the variables in the initial and final states. For example, the expression $((s_4 s_5(s_6 + s_7)s_3, b' = \neg b)$ represents the set of segments which match $s_4 s_5(s_6 + s_7)s_3$ and have the value of b is the last state is negation of the value of b in the first state.

Let us first start with abstract trace segment cover $\mathcal{C}$ from 21. A part of the abstract extremal trace generated from $\mathcal{C}$ will be $\langle L_1, sub\rangle$ where (a) $sub(1) = \langle(C_{L1})^\omega, sub'\rangle$, where (b) $sub'(i) = s_4 s_5 s_7 s_3$ for all $i \geq 1$. We will illustrate two refinement steps that might occur:

- *Suppose during the refinement process we are computing $post(\langle L_1, sub'\rangle, R)$ where R is the set of states at location s_3 with $j = 0$. Now, we can perform the analysis either at the top level or at the lower level:*
  - *At the top level, we get the post states to be R^* where the control location of a state is in s_3.*
  - *At the lower level, we get the post states to be $R^\dagger = \emptyset$ as the transition from s_3 to s_4 is disabled due to j being 0.*

  Therefore, we need to refine the abstract SegmentSet $s_4 s_5(s_6 + s_7)s_3$. One possible valid refinement is to strengthen the set $s_4 s_5(s_6 + s_7)s_3$ to $s_4 s_5(s_6 + s_7)s_3, j > 0 \wedge j' = j - 1$. Using this strengthened set, we can compute that the upper and lower loop bounds for L_1 are 10. This leads to a improvement in the *value of the system as now, there is no infinite path in the high value segment L_1. The new value of the system is $\frac{20}{9}$.*

- *Suppose during the refinement process we are computing $post(\langle L_1 \wedge P, sub' \rangle, R)$ where P bounds the limit-average of segments in L_1 to $\frac{10}{4}$, R is the set of states at location s_3 with $b = true$. Again, performing the analysis at top level produces $R^* = \{s_7\}$, but the lower level produces $R^\dagger$ where $R^\dagger = \emptyset$. Therefore, we can to refine the abstract SegmentSet $s_4 s_5 (s_6 + s_7) s_3$ and one possible refinement is a horizontal split into $s_4 s_5 s_6 s_3, b = true \wedge b' = false$ and $s_4 s_5 s_7 s_3, b = false \wedge b' = true$. Performing this refinement reduces the value of L_1 to $\frac{20}{9}$ and hence, by upward strengthening the value of the whole system to $\frac{20}{9}$.*

7. Case study: WCET analysis

We present a case study to demonstrate anytime verification, and to evaluate $ExistMax$ and hierarchical $PathBound$ abstractions. Worst-case execution time (WCET) estimation is an important part of verifying real-time systems. We only study one aspect, i.e., cache behavior prediction. In a processor, clock cycles needed for an instruction can vary by factors of 10-100 based on cache hits vs misses. Assuming the worst-case for all instructions leads to bad WCET estimates. Abstract domains for cache behavior prediction are well studied (e.g., [9, 18]). However, we know of no work on automated refinement for these abstractions. Note that this case study and the accompanying implementation is not a complete WCET analysis tool, but a prototype used to illustrate the quantitative abstraction refinement approach. Our intention is just to evaluate the anytime aspect of our approach.

We estimate WCET using the limit-average property. Intuitively, we put the whole program in a nonterminating loop. The limit-average then corresponds to the average cost of an instruction in the worst-case execution of a loop. (For a terminating program, it is the execution of the artificial outer loop.) WCET is estimated by multiplying the limit-average values with (an over-approximation of) the length of the longest trace. We report limit-average values instead of WCETs.

The cache model and the abstract domain used are from [9]. Multiple abstract domains are possible based on the tracked locations. If no set is tracked, every memory access is deemed a cache-miss; whereas the invariant computation is very expensive in the domain which tracks all cache-sets. Here, we start from the empty cache and refine by tracking more cache-sets as necessary.

7.1 Implementation details

We implemented a WCET analyzer based on the presented techniques in a tool QUART that analyzes x86 binaries.

Static analysis. We analyze the binary and produce the control flow graph. Instructions in the program may operate on non-constant addresses (for example, array indexing leads to variable offsets from a fixed address). However, if the exact addresses cannot be computed statically, we perform no further analysis and assume that the memory access is a cache miss. This restriction comes from the cache abstract domain we use from [9].

Worst-case computation. In the resulting graph, we annotate states with invariants from the current cache abstract domain. From the invariants, we compute costs of each transition (we use costs of 1 and 25 cycles for cache-hits and cache-misses, respectively). We then find the worst-case using techniques of Section 3 and Section 4.3 to find a the worst-case limit-average value. Furthermore, we implemented the extension of the algorithm to graphs with both edge weights and edge lengths [3].

Refinement. We analyze worst-case counter-example ext:

Feasibility analysis. We first check if ext is a valid program execution (ignoring the cache) using a custom symbolic execution computation. If ext is not a valid execution, we refine the abstract graph using standard CEGAR techniques.

Cache Analysis. If ext is valid, we compute the concrete cache states for it. If the concrete value obtained is the same as that of ext, we return the concrete trace.

Refinement heuristic. Otherwise, of all locations accessed in the loop of ext, we find the one with most abstract cache misses which are concrete cache hits. The current cache abstract domain is refined by additionally tracking this location.

Fall-back refinement. If all the locations accessed in ext are already being tracked, we use Algorithm 2 and the algorithm given by $hAbsRefine$ to do the refinement.

Example	Step	Value	Time (ms)	Tracked
Basic Example	0	14.14	1240	
	1	6.50	2102	i
	2	4.87	2675	a
	3	4.75	3275	b
	4	1.27	3864	c
	5	1.03	4631	v
Binary search	0	15.77	908	
	1	11.15	1130	m
	2	8.23	1369	r
	3	5.0	1707	l
	4	3.76	1895	s
	5	3.0	2211	a[$\frac{(N-1)}{2}$]
	6	2.97	2527	a[$\frac{(N-3)}{4}$]
	7	2.85	3071	a[$\frac{(3N-1)}{4}$]
Polynomial Eval.	0	15.49	524	
	1	8.13	759	i
	2	4.45	1025	val
	3	2.95	1237	x
GCD	0	13.76	289	
	1	9.47	399	inp2
	2	6.65	472	inp1
	3	6.33	536	temp

Table 1: $ExistMax$ abstraction results

7.2 Evaluation of $ExistMax$ abstraction

For evaluating the $ExistMax$ abstraction and refinement methods, we consider binaries for five (small) C programs, including the example from the introduction (called Basic example in the table). The results are in Table 1. For each example program, the table contains lines, with each corresponding to a refinement step. For each refinement step we report the current estimate for the limit-average value, the running time for the analysis (cumulative; in milliseconds) and in case the refinement enlarged the abstract cache, we also show what new memory locations correspond to the entries in the abstract cache. In each case, the over-approximated limit-average value decreases monotonically as the tool is given more time.

```
while(true)
 input(s);
 l = 0; r = N - 1;
 do {
  m = l + r / 2;
  if(s > a[m])
   l = m + 1;
  else
   r = m - 1;
 } while(l <= r
     ∧ a[m] != s)
```

Figure 11: Bin. Search

Binary search. We analyze a procedure (Figure 11) that repeatedly performs binary search for different inputs on a given array. We start with the empty abstract cache domain and all behaviors have high values (with worst-case value 15.77). In the ext-trace, variable `m`, accessed 4 times every iteration of the inner loop, causes most spurious cache misses.

Using the *Refinement heuristic* we heuristically choose the location of `m` is additionally tracked in the cache abstract domain reducing the value to 11.15. Indices `l`, `r` and the input `s` are the next most frequently used, and are added subsequently to the cache abstract domain. More importantly, the most used array elements are added in order. During binary search, the element at position $N/2$ is accessed always, and the elements at $N/4$ and $3N/4$ half the times, and so on. The refinements obtained add these array elements in order. This illustrates the anytime aspect: refinement can be stopped at any point to obtain an over-approximation of the value.

7.3 Evaluation of the hierarchical $PathBound$ abstraction

For evaluating the $PathBound$ abstraction refinement procedure, we picked 4 benchmarks from the collection of WCET benchmarks in [11]. These benchmarks were larger than the ones for the $ExistMax$ evaluation with around 150-400 lines of code each. The benchmarks we picked included a simple program which scanned a matrix and counted elements, matrix multiplication, and two versions of discrete-cosine transformations.

Bench mark	Step	Value	Time (ms)
cnt	0	8.74	1810
	3	8.64	6349
	4	4.08	8298
matmult	0	8.73	4669
	2	8.71	15660
	5	8.71	30408
	6	4.17	35676
fdct	0	6.88	2142
	1	1.94	4274
	2	1.76	6685
jfdctint	0	6.95	3095
	1	3.35	5759
	2	1.89	8674
	3	1.57	11809

Table 2: $PathBound$ abstraction results

We used the hierarchical $PathBound$ abstraction-refinement algorithm, i.e., the algorithm given by *hRefine*. We note that we do not perform any cache refinements. Nevertheless, the hierarchical aspect of hierarchical $PathBound$ abstraction was evaluated, as three of the benchmarks contained a number of nested loops. The challenge addressed was to obtain good (and monotonically decreasing) estimates on WCET, as the abstraction is refined.

We summarize the results in Table 2. For each example program, the table contains a number of lines, with each line corresponding to a refinement step. For each refinement step we show the current estimate for the limit-average value, and the running time for the analysis (cumulative; in milliseconds). As it can be seen, the limit-average values monotonically decrease with longer execution time. It should be noted that for most of these programs, to obtain similar values with the $ExistMax$ approach, one would need to perform a large number (in thousands) of counter-example guided refinements (as the nested loops would have to be unrolled).

8. Conclusion

Summary. This paper makes four main contributions. First, we present a general framework for abstraction and refinement with respect to quantitative system properties. Refinements for quantitative abstractions have not been studied before.Second, we propose both state-based and segment-based quantitative abstraction schemes. Quantitative segment-based abstractions are entirely novel, to the best of our knowledge. Third, we present algorithms for the automated refinement of quantitative abstractions, achieving the monotonic over-approximation property that enables anytime verification. Fourth, we implement refinement algorithms for WCET analysis of executables, in order to demonstrate the anytime verification property of our analysis, and to investigate trade-offs between the proposed abstractions.

Future work. There are several directions for future work. The first is to perform larger-scale case studies, for instance for worst-case execution time analysis, with more realistic architecture models. Second, quantitative abstraction can aid partial-program synthesis, as quantitative reasoning is necessary if the goal is not to synthesize any program, but rather the best performing program according to quantitative measures such as performance or robustness. Furthermore, the anytime verification property of the refinements we proposed can lead to *anytime synthesis* methods, that is, methods that would synthesize correct programs, and refine these into more optimized versions if given more time.

References

[1] M. Boddy. Anytime problem solving using dynamic programming. In *AAAI*, pages 738–743, 1991.

[2] E. Clarke, O. Grumberg, S. Jha, Y. Lu, and H. Veith. Counterexample-guided abstraction refinement for symbolic model checking. *J. ACM*, 50(5):752–794, 2003.

[3] J. Cochet-Terrasson, G. Cohen, S. Gaubert, M. McGettrick, and J.-P. Quadrat. Numerical computation of spectral elements in max-plus algebra, 1998.

[4] B. Cook, A. Podelski, and A. Rybalchenko. Abstraction refinement for termination. In *SAS*, pages 87–101, 2005.

[5] P. Cousot and R. Cousot. Abstract interpretation: A unified lattice model for static analysis of programs by construction or approximation of fixpoints. In *POPL*, pages 238–252, 1977.

[6] P. Cousot and R. Cousot. Systematic design of program analysis frameworks. In *POPL*, pages 269–282, 1979.

[7] P. Cousot and R. Cousot. An abstract interpretation framework for termination. In *POPL*, pages 245–258, 2012.

[8] L. de Alfaro and P. Roy. Magnifying-lens abstraction for Markov decision processes. In *CAV*, pages 325–338, 2007.

[9] C. Ferdinand, F. Martin, R. Wilhelm, and M. Alt. Cache behavior prediction by abstract interpretation. *Sci. Comput. Program.*, 35(2):163–189, 1999.

[10] S. Gulwani and F. Zuleger. The reachability-bound problem. In *PLDI*, pages 292–304, 2010.

[11] J. Gustafsson, A. Betts, A. Ermedahl, and B. Lisper. The mälardalen WCET benchmarks: Past, present and future. In *WCET*, pages 136–146, 2010.

[12] H. Hermanns, B. Wachter, and L. Zhang. Probabilistic CEGAR. In *CAV*, pages 162–175, 2008.

[13] M. Kattenbelt, M. Kwiatkowska, G. Norman, and D. Parker. Abstraction refinement for probabilistic software. In *VMCAI*, pages 182–197, 2009.

[14] A. Podelski and A. Rybalchenko. Transition predicate abstraction and fair termination. In *POPL*, pages 132–144, 2005.

[15] A. Prantl, M. Schordan, and J. Knoop. TuBound - a conceptually new tool for worst-case execution time analysis. In *WCET*, 2008.

[16] N. Shankar. A tool bus for anytime verification. Usable Verification, 2010.

[17] V. Tiwari, S. Malik, and A. Wolfe. Power analysis of embedded software: a first step towards software power minimization. In *ICCAD*, pages 384–390, 1994.

[18] R. Wilhelm, S. Altmeyer, C. Burguière, D. Grund, J. Herter, J. Reineke, B. Wachter, and S. Wilhelm. Static timing analysis for hard real-time systems. In *VMCAI*, pages 3–22, 2010.

[19] R. Wilhelm, J. Engblom, A. Ermedahl, N. Holsti, S. Thesing, D. Whalley, G. Bernat, C. Ferdinand, R. Heckmann, T. Mitra, F. Mueller, I. Puaut, P. Puschner, J. Staschulat, and P. Stenström. The worst-case execution-time problem - overview of methods and survey of tools. *ACM Trans. Embedded Comput. Syst.*, 7(3), 2008.

Inductive Data Flow Graphs

Azadeh Farzan Zachary Kincaid
University of Toronto

Andreas Podelski
University of Freiburg

Abstract

The correctness of a sequential program can be shown by the annotation of its control flow graph with inductive assertions. We propose *inductive data flow graphs*, data flow graphs with incorporated inductive assertions, as the basis of an approach to verifying concurrent programs. An inductive data flow graph accounts for a set of dependencies between program actions in interleaved thread executions, and therefore stands as a representation for the set of concurrent program traces which give rise to these dependencies. The approach first constructs an inductive data flow graph and then checks whether all program traces are represented. The size of the inductive data flow graph is polynomial in the number of data dependencies (in a sense that can be made formal); it does not grow exponentially in the number of threads unless the data dependencies do. The approach shifts the burden of the exponential explosion towards the check whether all program traces are represented, i.e., to a combinatorial problem (over finite graphs).

Categories and Subject Descriptors D.2.4 [*Software/Program Verification*]: Correctness Proofs; F.3.1 [*Logics and Meanings of Programs*]: Specifying, Verifying and Reasoning about Programs

General Terms Languages, Verification

Keywords Concurrency, Verification, Static Analysis

1. Introduction

The success of the two main approaches to algorithmic verification is well established for their intended target domains:

- static analysis for the verification of sequential programs [9],
- model checking for the verification of finite-state concurrent protocols [8].

This paper addresses the algorithmic verification of concurrent programs. Considerable progress has been made with approaches that, depending on terminology, extend static analysis to concurrent control or extend model checking to general data domains [3, 11–13, 17, 22, 27]. Each of these approaches provides a different angle of attack to circumvent the same fundamental issue: *the space required to prove the correctness of a concurrent program grows exponentially in the number of its threads.*

We propose *inductive data flow graphs (iDFGs)*, data flow graphs with incorporated inductive assertions, as the basis of an approach to verifying concurrent programs. An iDFG accounts for a set of dependencies between data operations in interleaved thread executions, and therefore stands as a representation for the set of concurrent program traces which give rise to these dependencies. The approach first constructs an iDFG and then checks whether all program traces are represented. The size of an iDFG is polynomial in the number of data dependencies (in a sense that can be made formal); it does not grow exponentially in the number of threads unless the data dependencies do. Intuitively, this succinctness is possible because iDFGs represent only the *data flow* of the program, and abstract away control features that are irrelevant to the proof. The approach shifts the burden of the exponential explosion towards the check whether all program traces are represented, which is a combinatorial problem (over finite graphs).

There are several directions in which one can explore the practical potential of the approach. This is not the focus of this paper. The focus in this paper is to introduce the approach and to investigate its formal foundation.

We will next explain in what sense our approach relies on the respective strength of both static analysis and model checking.

In static analysis, techniques have been developed that are successful in finding solutions to fixpoint equations, namely by solving them over *abstract domains*. In the settings where the elements of the abstract domain denote state predicates, static analysis amounts to establishing a Floyd-Hoare annotation of the control flow graph of the program. The validity of the fixpoint equation translates to the inductiveness of the annotation, i.e., the validity of the Hoare triple at each node of the control flow graph. To establish the validity (of the solution for the fixpoint equation/of the Hoare triples), the Floyd-Hoare annotation of the control flow graph has to be stored. This becomes an obstacle for the naive approach to apply static analysis to a concurrent program. The naive approach is to *flatten* the concurrent program, i.e., transform it to a non-deterministic sequential program whose executions include *all* interleaved executions of the concurrent program. The size of the control flow graph of the flattened program grows exponentially with the number of threads.

One motivation behind the work in this paper is the question whether static analysis—with the techniques that are well established for sequential programs [4]—can be put into work for concurrent programs. Our approach does not aim at improving those techniques (for constructing abstract domains, widening, strengthening loop invariants, etc.) but, instead, relies on them. The question is whether the output of the static analysis applied to interleaved executions of the threads of a concurrent program can be assembled (and used) in a space-efficient way. The answer we propose lies in iDFGs.

In model checking, techniques have been developed that are successful for the exhaustive exploration of the finite, though exponentially large state space of concurrent protocols. Model checking is a combinatorial problem that is "easy" in the sense that it can be reduced to search, and therefore can be solved in PSPACE. Our

POPL'13, January 23–25, 2013, Rome, Italy.

approach relies on the efficiency of space exploration techniques as used in model checking for checking whether all program traces are represented by a given iDFG. The check solves a problem which is directly related to model checking, and inherits its theoretical complexity bound; i.e., the check can be implemented in polynomial space (polynomial in the number of threads of the given concurrent program).

We will next explain how the concept of *data dependencies* in connection with *Hoare triples* leads to iDFGs.

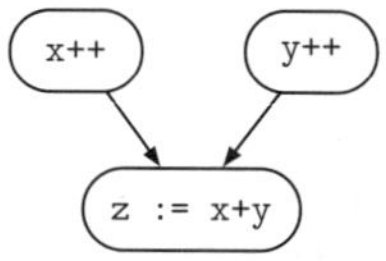

Assume trace τ is composed of three actions `a1: x++`, `a2: y++`, and `a3: z:=x+y` (possibly from different threads of a concurrent program). The two edges in the graph to the right express the data dependencies in τ. Conceptually, the graph represents the set of all traces that preserve the data dependencies expressed by its edges. Such traces contain the three actions in an order that complies with the two edges (i.e., `a1` and `a2` must occur before `a3`); they can contain additional actions as long as these actions do not modify the value of `x`, `y`, or `z`. All such traces have the same behavior, which formally means that they satisfy the same set of pre/postcondition pairs. Now, in the setting of verification where correctness is defined by one particular pre/postcondition pair, we would like to have a more targeted sense of data dependencies (and thus a means to define a more targeted set of traces).

As an example, we take the pre/postcondition pair that defines the correctness of the trace τ in the Hoare triple below:

$$\{\texttt{x} \geq 0 \wedge \texttt{y} \geq 0\}\ \texttt{x++}\ ;\ \texttt{y++}\ ;\ \texttt{z:=x+y}\ \{\texttt{z} > 0\}.$$

The *essence* of a possible correctness proof for τ consists of the three Hoare triples below.

$$\begin{array}{lll} \{\texttt{x} > 0 \wedge \texttt{y} > 0\} & \texttt{z:=x+y} & \{\texttt{z} > 0\} \\ \{\texttt{y} \geq 0\} & \texttt{y++} & \{\texttt{y} > 0\} \\ \{\texttt{x} \geq 0\} & \texttt{x++} & \{\texttt{x} > 0\} \end{array} \qquad (1)$$

In addition to the three *essential* Hoare triples, the correctness proof contains the two *stability* Hoare triples below, which state the invariance ("stability") of an assertion under an action.

$$\begin{array}{lll} \{\texttt{y} \geq 0\} & \texttt{x++} & \{\texttt{y} \geq 0\} \\ \{\texttt{x} > 0\} & \texttt{y++} & \{\texttt{x} > 0\} \end{array}$$

We obtain the two Hoare triples below by taking the sequential composition of Hoare triples that appear above.

$$\begin{array}{lll} \{\texttt{x} \geq 0\} & \texttt{x++}\ ;\ \texttt{y++} & \{\texttt{x} > 0\} \\ \{\texttt{y} \geq 0\} & \texttt{x++}\ ;\ \texttt{y++} & \{\texttt{y} > 0\} \end{array}$$

To obtain a correctness proof for τ, we apply the conjunction rule to these two Hoare triples and then sequentially compose with the Hoare triple for `z:=x+y` in (1).

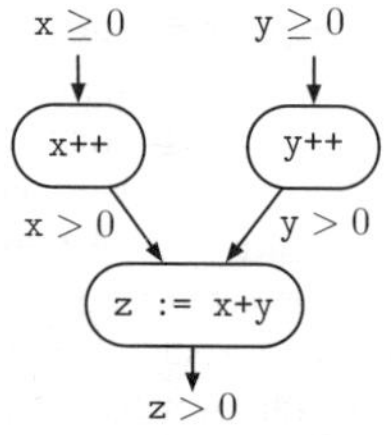

The iDFG to the right is constructed from the correctness proof for the trace τ. The annotation of edges with assertions corresponds to the three Hoare triples in (1) which form the essence of the correctness proof.

We consider the iDFG to be a representation the set of all traces such that the three Hoare triples in (1) form the essence of a possible correctness proof (all other axioms used in the correctness proof are stability Hoare triples). By definition, all traces in this set are correct. The set contains the trace τ. We next give more examples of traces in the set.

If we permute the actions `a1` and `a2` in the trace τ, the resulting trace τ' lies in the set: the essence of the correctness proof for τ' is the three Hoare triples in (1); the other Hoare triples in the correctness proof for τ' state the stability of $\texttt{x} \geq 0$ under the action `y++` and the stability of $\texttt{y} > 0$ under the action `x++`.

If we add actions to the trace τ (or to the trace τ') and the assertion at each position with an added action is stable under the added action, then the new trace lies in the set: the essence of its correctness proof are the Hoare triples in (1); the new Hoare triples in the correctness proof are stability Hoare triples.

The edges in an iDFG explicitly formulate ordering constraints on the actions in a trace (as in the example above). We will next illustrate that the assertion labels of edges implicitly define additional ordering constraints.

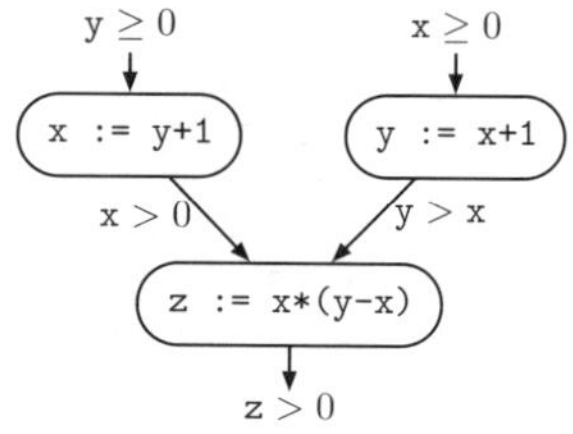

The iDFG shown to the right can be constructed from the correctness proof for the trace composed of the actions `b1: x:=y+1`, `b2: y:=x+1`, and `b3: z:=x*(y-x)` (correctness is defined as above, through the same pre/postcondition pair). The assertions labeling the two edges are $\texttt{x} > 0$ and $\texttt{y} > \texttt{x}$. The assertion $\texttt{x} > 0$ is stable under the action `b2` (the Hoare triple $\{\texttt{x} > 0\}$ `y:=x+1` $\{\texttt{x} > 0\}$ holds). However, the assertion $\texttt{y} > \texttt{x}$ is not stable under the action `b1` (the Hoare triple $\{\texttt{y} > \texttt{x}\}$ `x:=y+1` $\{\texttt{y} > \texttt{x}\}$ does not hold). This means that the action `b2` may come after the action `b1`, but not vice versa. That is, the trace `b1.b2.b3` lies in the set of traces represented by the iDFG, but the trace `b2.b1.b3` does not. Note that the trace `b1.b2.b3` is correct but the trace `b2.b1.b3` is not.

We use iDFGs as the basis of an algorithm to verify concurrent programs (see also Figure 3). The algorithm iteratively picks a program trace, applies a static analysis to the program trace, uses the output of the static analysis to *construct* an iDFG, *merges* the new iDFG with the one constructed so far, and *checks* whether the set of traces that is represented by the resulting iDFG includes all program traces. If this is the case, the iteration stops; the program is proven correct.

In Section 2 we will see examples in the context of concurrent programs. Sections 3 to 7 then present the individual conceptual and technical contributions of our work:

- the concept of iDFGs as a representation of a set of interleavings of thread executions, and the characterization of program correctness by an iDFG (Section 3),
- the reduction of the *check* of program correctness, given a program and an iDFG, to a combinatorial problem in PSPACE (Section 4),
- the formalization of a measure of data complexity and the proof that iDFGs can be polynomial in this measure (Section 5),
- a verification algorithm (Section 6), and
- the proof that the algorithm constructs a polynomial-size iDFG under the assumption that the underlying static analysis provides the required inductive assertions (Section 7).

2. Examples

In this section, we use a few simple examples of concurrent programs to illustrate iDFGs.

Lamport's Bakery Algorithm

The code below implements a version of Lamport's mutual exclusion protocol for two threads [24]. The integer variables `n1` and `n2` (the *tickets*) are initially set to 0, the boolean variables `e1` and `e2` to *false*. We use the notation `[exp]` for *assume* statements ("`if(exp)`

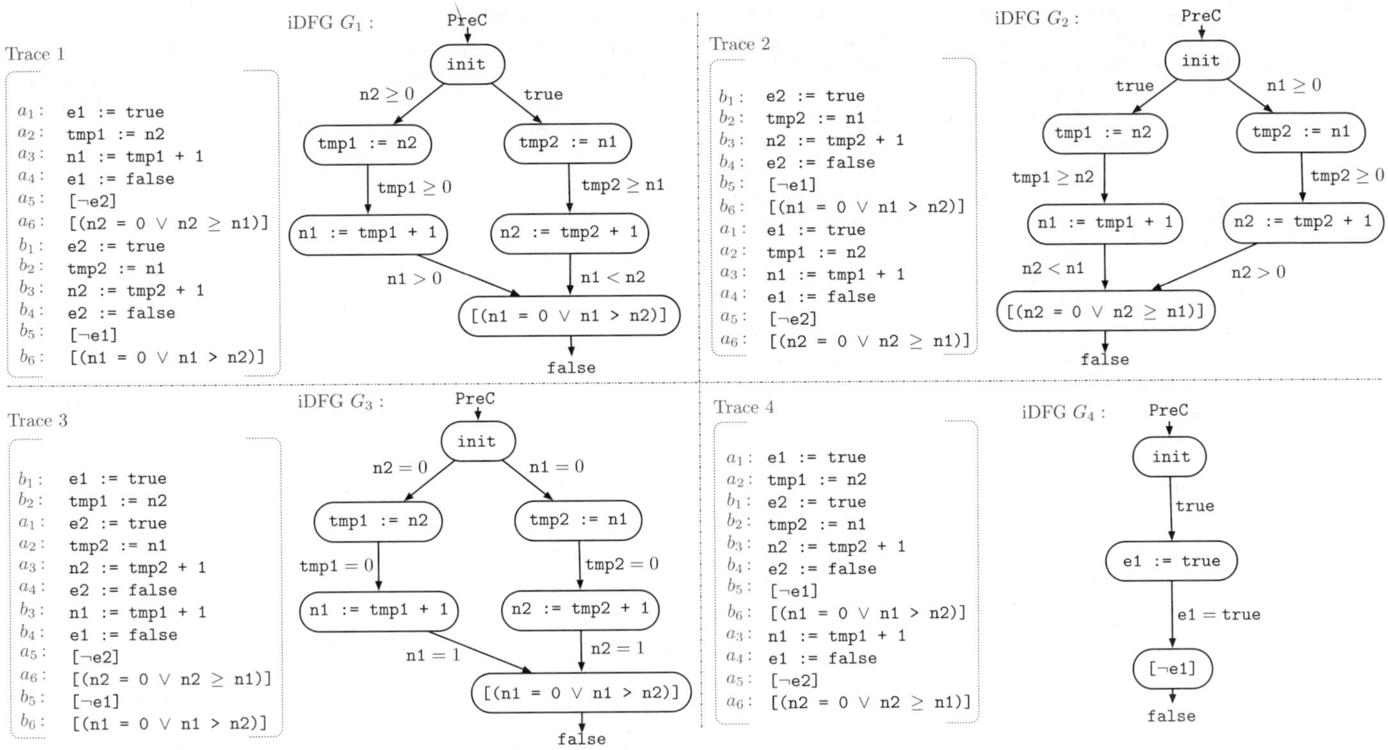

Figure 1. Four traces of the Bakery algorithm and their corresponding iDFGs. The four iDFGs constitute a proof of the correctness of the mutual exclusion property. Correctness here means: every trace that violates mutual exclusion is infeasible, i.e., has postcondition *false*. The precondition `PreC` is $\texttt{n1} = \texttt{n2} = 0 \land \texttt{e1} = \texttt{e2} = \texttt{false}$. The action `init` is a dummy label of the initial node in an iDFG.

`then skip else block`"). Thread B cannot enter its critical section unless either $\texttt{n1} = 0$ (Thread A has not asked to enter the critical section) or $\texttt{n1} < \texttt{n2}$ (Thread A has asked but it has done so after Thread B). Symmetrically for Thread A, except if there is a tie ($\texttt{n1} = \texttt{n2}$), Thread A has priority over Thread B to enter its critical section first. We break the ticket acquisition statement (`n1 := n2 + 1`) into two statements `tmp1 := n2` and `n1 := tmp1 + 1` to reflect the possibility of the update happening non-atomically (we treat individual program statements as atomic). The flag `e1` (initially `false`) is used to communicate that Thread A is *entering* (that is, it is in the process of acquiring its ticket). The flag `e2` is used similarly for Thread B.

Thread A

```
a1: e1 := true
a2: tmp1 := n2
a3: n1 := tmp1 + 1
a4: e1 := false
a5: [¬e2]
a6: [(n2 = 0 ∨ n2 ≥ n1)]
    // critical section
a7: n1 := 0
```

Thread B

```
b1: e2 := true
b2: tmp2 := n1
b3: n2 := tmp2 + 1
b4: e2 := false
b5: [¬e1]
b6: [(n1 = 0 ∨ n1 > n2)]
    // critical section
b7: n2 := 0
```

We wish to verify that this protocol guarantees mutual exclusion: only one thread at a time can be in its critical section. Each trace leading to a state where both threads are in their critical sections (after executing a_6 respectively b_6) must be infeasible (i.e., there exists no initial state that has an execution along the trace) or, equivalently, must have the postcondition `false`.

Trace 1 in Figure 1 is a run of Bakery where first Thread A runs until it enters its critical section and then Thread B runs until it enters its critical section. The iDFG G_1 in Figure 1 expresses the essence of the proof that Trace 1 is infeasible. This graph should be read from bottom to top, and should be thought of as backwards proof argument, along the lines of the following dialogue between *Student* and Teacher:

> *Why is Trace 1 infeasible?* – Thread B can not execute the statement b_6. – *Why not?* – When Thread B tries to execute b_6, $\texttt{n1} > 0$ (Thread A has a ticket) and $\texttt{n1} < \texttt{n2}$ (Thread A's ticket is smaller than Thread B's ticket).
>
> The dialogue then bifurcates:
>
> - *Why is* $\texttt{n1} > 0$ *at* b_6? – Thread A executes `n1:=tmp1+1` at a_3 when $\texttt{tmp1} \geq 0$. – *But what about everything that happens between* a_3 *and* b_6? – Irrelevant. Nothing between a_3 and b_6 can change the fact that $\texttt{n1} > 0$. – *Why is* $\texttt{tmp1} \geq 0$ *at* a_3? – ...
> - *Why is* $\texttt{n1} < \texttt{n2}$ *at* b_6? – ...

The iDFG G_1 in Figure 1 keeps account of the relevant details of the trace (e.g., the edge labeled $\texttt{n1} > 0$ represents that a_3 must be executed before b_6, and nothing executed between a_3 and b_6 may change the fact that $\texttt{n1} > 0$). It abstracts away irrelevant details of the trace (e.g., the ordering between a_2 and b_2). The iDFG represents the set of traces which are infeasible for essentially the same reason as Trace 1 (i.e., which have essentially the same Hoare triples in the proof that the postcondition is `false`). The traces in the set can be obtained from Trace 1 by reordering actions or by inserting actions that are irrelevant for the proof (they leave the corresponding assertion stable). Informally, the set contains *all traces where Thread B enters its critical section while Thread A has a smaller (nonzero) ticket.*

Every trace that violates mutual exclusion falls into one of four scenarios, each scenario being exemplified by a trace in Figure 1. The scenarios are: (Trace 1) Thread B attempts to enter its critical section when Thread A has a smaller ticket, (Trace 2) the symmetric scenario where Thread A attempts to enter its critical section when Thread B has a smaller ticket, (Trace 3) Thread B attempts to enter its critical section when Thread A and B have the same ticket (recalling that Thread A has priority in this situation), (Trace 4) Thread B enters its critical section without waiting for Thread A to receive its ticket. The iDFGs $G_1,\ldots, G_4$ express the essence of the proof of the infeasibility of each trace that falls into the corresponding scenario. Together, they form a proof of the correctness of Bakery. This is because each trace of Bakery falls into one of the four scenarios; formally, it lies in one of the four sets represented by $G_1,\ldots, G_4$ (which one can check with the algorithm of Section 4). Note that there is no need for a new iDFG for the trace symmetric to Trace 4. The corresponding scenario is accounted for by the scenario of Trace 3. This asymmetry is due to the asymmetry of the protocol (Thread A has priority over Thread B if they have the same ticket).

Increment Example

We use a simple program with a parametrized number of threads to illustrate the exponential succinctness of data flow graphs. The program has one global variable `x` (initially `0`) and is composed of a thread that asserts $\texttt{x} \leq 0$ and a parametrized number N of threads that each increment `x` once.

Thread 0	Thread 1		Thread N
a_0: `assert(x ≤ N)`	a_1: `x++`	...	a_N: `x++`

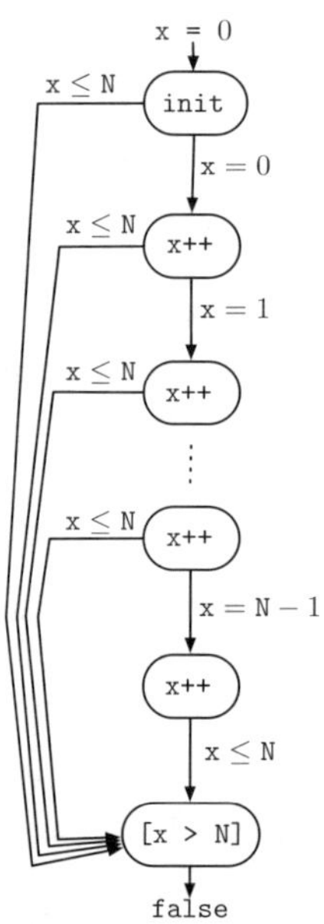

The program is *safe* (the `assert` never fails) if $\texttt{x} \leq \texttt{N}$ is an invariant. Formally, the correctness of the program means that each trace containing the assume statement `[x>N]` is infeasible, i.e., has postcondition `false`. The iDFG shown on the right is a proof of the correctness of the program. Its size *linear* in N. As one can check algorithmically (Section 4), the set of traces it represents contains all program traces. Thus, it is a proof of the correctness of the program.

The program is based on an example that was used in [29] to illustrate the need for auxiliary variables in compositional proof rules. The program is a challenge for many existing approaches. We ran experiments, for example, with the tool THREADER [17], which generates Owicki-Gries type proofs and rely-guarantee type proofs, and with the tool SLAB [12], which uses abstraction-refinement using Craig interpolation with slicing. In both tools, the space used for the proof grows exponentially in N.

If we consider the increment actions of each thread as pairwise distinct (i.e., the program has N actions instead of just one), then we can give a correctness proof in the form of an iDFG of size *quadratic* in N. The graph can be depicted as an $(N+1)\times N$ matrix of vertices. Each column i contains N vertices labeled with the increment action of the i-th thread (plus the vertex labeled `[x>N]`). Each vertex in row j has an edge to every vertex in row $j + 1$. The set represented by this iDFG thus contains traces with more than one occurrences of the increment action of the same thread (for example, the traces corresponding to a column). These traces do not correspond to a path in the control flow graph but they are correct. This illustrates the point that a set of correct traces can represented more compactly if it is larger.

Ticket Algorithm

In the parametrized version of the ticket algorithm [1] depicted below, the statement at line $\ell_{1,i}$ (for $i \in [1, N]$) indicates an atomic operation that increments `t` after assigning its current value to `mi`. Initially `s = t = 0`. The algorithm is a challenge for many existing approaches to concurrent program verification in that, as with the increment example, the space used for the proof will grow exponentially in N.

Thread 1		Thread N
$\ell_{1,1}$: `m1 := t++` $\ell_{1,2}$: `[m1 ≤ s]` `// critical section` $\ell_{1,3}$: `s := s + 1`	...	$\ell_{N,1}$: `mN := t++` $\ell_{N,2}$: `[mN ≤ s]` `// critical section` $\ell_{N,3}$: `s := s + 1`

We can give a correctness proof in the form of an iDFG of *quadratic* size in N. It is related to the one for the increment example. We present its construction (for $N = 3$) as an example in Section 6.

3. Inductive Data Flow Graphs (iDFGs)

We will first introduce the notation needed to define the correctness of programs. We then introduce the notion of inductive data flow graphs and use it to characterize program correctness.

To abstract away from the specifics of a programming language and from the specifics of a program analysis and verification environment, we use a very general setup. A program is given as an edge-labeled graph $\mathcal{P} = \langle \mathsf{Loc}, \delta\rangle$ (the *control flow graph*) where the edge labels are taken from the set $\mathsf{Actions}$ (a given set of *actions*); i.e., $\delta \subseteq \mathsf{Loc}\times\mathsf{Actions}\times\mathsf{Loc}$. We say that the edge between the two vertices (*locations*) ℓ and ℓ' is labeled by the action a if $(\ell, a, \ell') \in \delta$.

The program $\mathcal{P} = \langle \mathsf{Loc}, \delta\rangle$ can be defined as the *parallel composition* of a number N of programs $\mathcal{P}_1 = \langle \mathsf{Loc}_1, \delta_1\rangle, \ldots, \mathcal{P}_N = \langle \mathsf{Loc}_N, \delta_N\rangle$ (we will say that $\mathcal{P}_1, \ldots, \mathcal{P}_N$ are the *threads* of the program $\mathcal{P}$). Its set of locations is the Cartesian product of the sets of thread locations, i.e., $\mathsf{Loc} = \mathsf{Loc}_1 \times\cdots\times \mathsf{Loc}_N$. Each edge (ℓ_i, a_i, ℓ_i') in the i-th thread $\mathcal{P}_i$ gives rise to an edge (ℓ, a_i, ℓ') in the program $\mathcal{P}$; the edge is labeled by the same action a_i and goes from the location $\ell = (\ell_1, \ldots, \ell_i, \ldots, \ell_N)$ to the location $\ell' = (\ell_1, \ldots, \ell_i', \ldots, \ell_N)$ (i.e., only the i-th component can change). In algorithms that take $\mathcal{P}_1, \ldots, \mathcal{P}_N$ as the input, the control flow graph for the program $\mathcal{P}$ is generally not constructed explicitly.

We assume a set Φ of *assertions*. Each assertion φ is a first-order logic formula over a given vocabulary that includes a set Var of variables (the *program variables*). We assume that the set of assertions comes with a binary relation, the *entailment* relation.

Each action a comes with a binary relation between assertions (the set of its *precondition/postcondition pairs*). We say that the Hoare triple $\{\varphi_{\mathsf{pre}}\}\ a\ \{\varphi_{\mathsf{post}}\}$ is valid if the binary relation for the action a holds between the assertions φ_{pre} and φ_{post}.

It is useful to suppose that we have actions that correspond to *assume* statements. That is, for every assertion ψ we have an action $[\psi]$ such that the Hoare triple $\{\varphi_{\mathsf{pre}}\}\ [\psi]\ \{\varphi_{\mathsf{post}}\}$ is valid if the assertion φ_{post} is entailed by the conjunction $\psi \wedge \varphi_{\mathsf{pre}}$.

A *trace* τ is a sequence of actions, say $\tau = a_1 \ldots a_n$. We extend the validity of Hoare triples to traces in the canonical way. The Hoare triple $\{\varphi_{\mathsf{pre}}\}\ \tau\ \{\varphi_{\mathsf{post}}\}$ is valid for the empty trace ε if φ_{pre} entails φ_{post}. It is valid for the trace $\tau = a_1 \ldots a_n$ if each of the Hoare triples $\{\varphi_{\mathsf{pre}}\}\ a_1\ \{\varphi_1\}, \ldots, \{\varphi_{n-1}\}\ a\ \{\varphi_{\mathsf{post}}\}$ is valid. Later, when we formulate algorithms, we will abstract away from the specific procedure (static analysis, interpolant generation, ...) used to construct the sequence of intermediate assertions $\varphi_1, \ldots, \varphi_{n-1}$.

To define the correctness of the program $\mathcal{P}$, we need to define its set of *program traces*. We assume that the control flow graph of the program $\mathcal{P}$ comes with an *initial* location ℓ_0 and a set F of *final* locations. We say that the trace τ is a program trace of $\mathcal{P}$ if τ labels a path between the initial and a final location. Not every such path corresponds to a possible execution of the program. The set of program traces is generally not prefix-closed.

We say that the program $\mathcal{P}$ is *correct* w.r.t. to the pre/postcondition pair $(\varphi_{\mathsf{pre}}, \varphi_{\mathsf{post}})$ if the Hoare triple $\{\varphi_{\mathsf{pre}}\}\ \tau\ \{\varphi_{\mathsf{post}}\}$ is valid for every program trace τ of $\mathcal{P}$. We will later characterize program correctness in terms of the notion that we introduce next.

Definition 3.1 (Inductive Data Flow Graph, iDFG) An *inductive data flow graph* (iDFG)

$$G = \langle V, E, \varphi_{\mathsf{pre}}, \varphi_{\mathsf{post}}, v_0, V_{\mathsf{final}} \rangle$$

consists of a vertex-labeled edge-labeled graph $\langle V, E \rangle$, an assertion φ_{pre} (the *precondition*), an assertion φ_{post} (the *postcondition*), a vertex $v_0 \in V$ (the *initial vertex*), and the subset of vertices $V_{\mathsf{final}} \subseteq V$ (the set of *final vertices*).

- Vertices are labeled by actions. We use $\mathsf{act}(v)$ to denote the action that labels v. The initial vertex v_0 has a dummy label: the special action `init` which has the same Hoare triples as `skip`, i.e., $\{\varphi\}$ `init` $\{\varphi'\}$ holds if φ entails φ'.
- Edges are labeled by assertions, i.e., $E \subseteq V \times \Phi \times V$. We require that the initial vertex v_0 has no incoming edges. We will use the notation $v \xrightarrow{\varphi} v'$ to denote an edge from v to v' labeled by the assertion φ.
- The labeling of edges with assertions is *inductive*, i.e., for every vertex v labeled with, say, the action a, the Hoare triple $\{\psi\}\ a\ \{\psi'\}$ holds for assertions ψ and ψ' chosen as follows.
  - If v is the initial vertex (i.e., $v = v_0$), then ψ is the precondition φ_{pre}; otherwise, ψ is the conjunction of the assertions labeling the incoming edges to v.
  - If v is a final vertex (i.e., $v \in V_{\mathsf{final}}$), then ψ' is the conjunction of the postcondition φ_{post} and the assertions labeling the outgoing edges of v; otherwise ψ' is just the conjunction of the assertions labeling the outgoing edges of v. ⌟

Remark 3.2 If the initial vertex of the iDFG G is a final vertex, then the precondition of G entails its postcondition (formally, if $v_0 \in V_{\mathsf{final}}$ then $\varphi_{\mathsf{pre}} \models \varphi_{\mathsf{post}}$). ⌟

We will use an iDFG G as a representation of a set of traces $[\![G]\!]$ (the *denotation* of G). The set $[\![G]\!]$ consists of those traces τ for which G can be used—in a prescribed way—to justify the correctness of τ (in this paper, whenever the context is given by an iDFG G, the term *correctness* refers to the pre/postcondition pair of G). We will next use an example to explain how one uses an iDFG G to justify the correctness of a trace τ, i.e., how one derives that $\tau \in [\![G]\!]$.

Consider the iDFGs $G_0, \ldots, G_4$ in Figure 2 (which all have the same precondition, $\varphi_{\mathsf{pre}} = \mathtt{x} \geq 0 \land \mathtt{y} \geq 0$, but different postconditions), the trace $\tau_0 =$ x++.y++.z:=x+y, and its prefix traces $\tau_1 =$ x++.y++, $\tau_2 =$ x++, and $\tau_3 = \varepsilon$. We will derive $\tau_0 \in [\![G_0]\!]$ via $\tau_3 \in [\![G_3]\!]$, $\tau_2 \in [\![G_1]\!]$, and $\tau_1 \in [\![G_1]\!]$ in one derivation branch and via $\tau_3 \in [\![G_4]\!]$, $\tau_2 \in [\![G_4]\!]$, and $\tau_1 \in [\![G_2]\!]$ in the other.

By Remark 3.2, the precondition of G_3 entails its postcondition, so we can use G_3 to justify the *correctness* of the empty trace w.r.t. the specification of G_3 (i.e., the validity of $\{\varphi_{\mathsf{pre}}\}\ \varepsilon\ \{\mathtt{x} \geq 0\}$). Thus, $\tau_3 \in [\![G_3]\!]$.

The iDFG G_1 has the postcondition $\mathtt{x} > 0$. The trace τ_2 is of the form $\tau_2 = \tau_3$.x++. We have already used G_3 to justify that τ_3 has the postcondition $\mathtt{x} \geq 0$. Since, by the inductiveness of G_1, the Hoare triple $\{\mathtt{x} \geq 0\}$ x++ $\{\mathtt{x} > 0\}$ is valid, we can use G_1 to justify the correctness of τ_2 (w.r.t. the postcondition $\mathtt{x} > 0$). Thus, $\tau_2 \in [\![G_1]\!]$.

The trace τ_1 is of the form $\tau_1 = \tau_2$.y++. We have already used G_1 to justify that τ_2 has the postcondition $\mathtt{x} > 0$. The iDFG G_1 has the postcondition $\mathtt{x} > 0$ which is *stable* under the action y++, i.e., $\{\mathtt{x} > 0\}$ y++ $\{\mathtt{x} > 0\}$ is valid. Taken together, this means that we can use G_1 also to justify the correctness of τ_1 (w.r.t. the postcondition $\mathtt{x} > 0$). Thus, $\tau_1 \in [\![G_1]\!]$.

We use G_2 to justify the correctness of τ_1 (now w.r.t. the postcondition $\mathtt{y} > 0$). In three steps that are similar but not symmetric to the previous one, we derive (1) $\varepsilon \in [\![G_4]\!]$ (by Remark 3.2), (2) $\tau_2 \in [\![G_4]\!]$ (because $\tau_2 = \varepsilon$.x++ and the postcondition of G_4 is stable under the action x++, i.e., $\{\mathtt{y} \geq 0\}$ y++ $\{\mathtt{y} \geq 0\}$), and (3) $\tau_1 \in [\![G_2]\!]$ ($\tau_1 = \tau_2$.y++ and, by the inductiveness of G_1, $\{\mathtt{y} \geq 0\}$ x++ $\{\mathtt{y} > 0\}$ is valid).

The trace τ_0 is of the form $\tau_0 = \tau_1$.z:=x+y. We can use G_1 and G_2 *together* to justify that τ_1 has the postcondition $\mathtt{x} > 0 \land \mathtt{y} > 0$ which is the *conjunction* of the postconditions of G_1 resp. G_2. Since, by the inductiveness of G_0, $\{\mathtt{x} > 0 \land \mathtt{y} > 0\}$ z:=x+y $\{\mathtt{z} > 0\}$ is valid, we can use G_0 to justify the correctness of τ_0 (w.r.t. the postcondition $\mathtt{z} > 0$). Thus, $\tau_0 \in [\![G_0]\!]$.

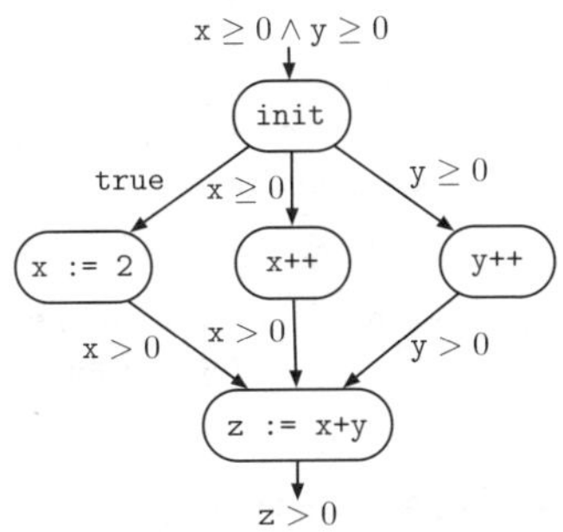

In the derivation above, the iDFGs G_1 and G_2 corresponding to the two incoming edges to the final node of G_0 are treated in *conjunction*: one derives that the prefix τ_1 of τ_0 lies in $[\![G_1]\!]$ *and* in $[\![G_2]\!]$. We next illustrate that the notion of iDFGs also provides a concept of *disjunction*. In the iDFG G_0' to the right, two of the three incoming edges to the final node are labeled with the same assertion, namely $\mathtt{x} > 0$. The two iDFGs corresponding to the two edges are G_1 and G_1', where G_1 is as before and G_1' is the iDFG whose final node is the new node (labeled with the action x:=2). Both, G_1 and G_1', have the postcondition $\mathtt{x} > 0$. They are treated in *disjunction*: in order to derive $\tau_0 \in [\![G_0']\!]$, one can derive that τ_1 lies in $[\![G_1]\!]$ *or* in $[\![G_1']\!]$. As a consequence, we can derive not only $\tau_0 \in [\![G_0']\!]$ (via $\tau_1 \in [\![G_1]\!]$) but also $\tau_0' \in [\![G_0']\!]$ where $\tau_0' =$ x:=2.y++.z:=x+y (via $\tau_1' \in [\![G_1']\!]$ where $\tau_1' =$ x:=2.y++).

The examples above illustrate how one can use an iDFG G to justify the correctness of a trace τ and derive $\tau \in [\![G]\!]$. The definition below generalizes the examples.

Definition 3.3 (Denotation of an iDFG, $[\![G]\!]$) We define when a trace τ lies in the denotation of an iDFG G, formally

$$\tau \in [\![G]\!]$$

by induction over the construction of the trace τ. The empty trace $\tau = \varepsilon$ lies in $[\![G]\!]$ iff $v_0 \in V_{\mathsf{final}}$. The trace $\tau = \tau'.a$ obtained by attaching the action a at the end of the trace τ' lies in the denotation of an iDFG G of the form

$$G = \langle V, E, \varphi_{\mathsf{pre}}, \varphi_{\mathsf{post}}, v_0, V_{\mathsf{final}} \rangle$$

if either:

- the postcondition of G is *stable* under the action a and the trace τ' lies in the denotation of G, i.e.,

$$\{\varphi_{\mathsf{post}}\}\ a\ \{\varphi_{\mathsf{post}}\} \text{ and } \tau' \in [\![G]\!]$$

or

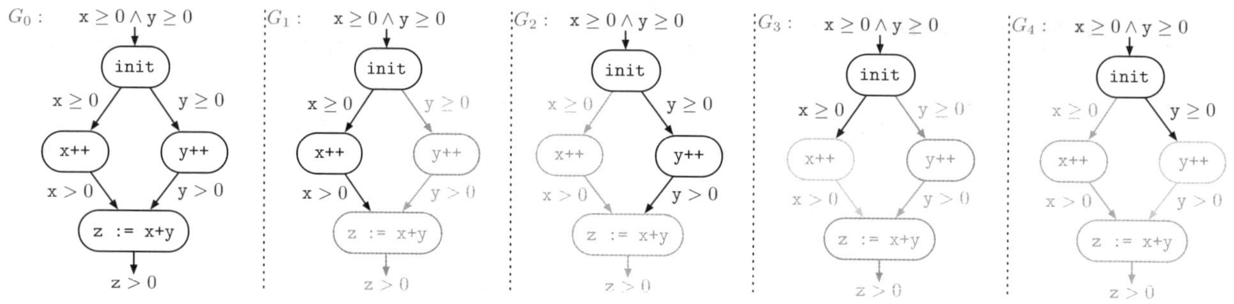

Figure 2. Example iDFGs used to illustrate Definition 3.3. The five iDFGs differ in the postcondition φ_{post} and the set of final vertices V_{final}. In each iDFG, V_{final} consists of the vertex with a *dangling* outgoing edge (the edge has no target or its target lies in the gray part of the graph), and φ_{post} is the assertion labeling that edge. For example, the final vertex of G_1 is the vertex labeled with the action x++ and φ_{post} is $\mathtt{x} > 0$; the final node of G_3 is the initial vertex and φ_{post} is $\mathtt{x} \geq 0$.

- one of the final vertices $v_f \in V_{\text{final}}$ is labeled by the action a, and:
  - the assertions $\varphi_1, \ldots, \varphi_n$ are the labels of the incoming edges of the final vertex v_f, i.e.,

$$\{\varphi_1, \ldots, \varphi_n\} = \{\psi \mid v \xrightarrow{\psi} v_f\},$$

  - for each $i = 1, \ldots, n$, the trace τ' lies in the denotation of the iDFG G_i which we obtain from G by taking the assertion φ_i for the postcondition and the set of vertices V_i (defined below) for the set of final vertices, i.e.,

$$G_i = \langle V, E, \varphi_{\text{pre}}, \varphi_i, v_0, V_i \rangle$$

  where V_i is the set of vertices that have an outgoing edge labeled with the assertion φ_i to the final vertex v_f, i.e.,

$$V_i = \{v \mid v \xrightarrow{\varphi_i} v_f\}.$$ ⌟

Remark 3.4 An alternative, equivalent definition of the denotation of an iDFG is based on fixpoints. Given the iDFG G as above, we define a monotone function

$$F : (V \to 2^{\text{Actions}^*}) \to (V \to 2^{\text{Actions}^*})$$

over the complete lattice $V \to 2^{\text{Actions}^*}$ as follows:

$$F(L)(v_0) = \{\varepsilon\}$$

and for all $v \neq v_0$,

$$F(L)(v) = \bigcap_{\{\varphi \mid \exists u \in V. u \xrightarrow{\varphi} v\}} \bigcup_{\{u \mid u \xrightarrow{\varphi} v\}} L(u).Stable(\varphi)^*.\mathsf{act}(v)$$

where

$$Stable(\varphi) = \{a \in \mathsf{Actions} \mid \{\varphi\}\ a\ \{\varphi\}\}$$

We use L_0 to denote the least fixpoint of F. The denotation of G can be equivalently defined as below.

$$[\![G]\!] = \bigcup_{v \in V_{\text{final}}} L_0(v).Stable(\varphi_{\text{post}})^*$$ ⌟

The following observation, a direct consequence of Definition 3.3, relates the correctness of a trace with the denotation of an iDFG.

Remark 3.5 Let $G = \langle V, E, \varphi_{\text{pre}}, \varphi_{\text{post}}, v_0, V_{\text{final}} \rangle$ be an iDFG. Then for any $\tau \in [\![G]\!]$, the Hoare triple $\{\varphi_{\text{pre}}\}\ \tau\ \{\varphi_{\text{post}}\}$ holds. ⌟

Since we defined that the program $\mathcal{P}$ is correct w.r.t. the pre/postcondition pair $(\varphi_{\text{pre}}, \varphi_{\text{post}})$ if the Hoare triple $\{\varphi_{\text{pre}}\}\ \tau\ \{\varphi_{\text{post}}\}$ is valid for every program trace, the above observation gives immediately rise to a characterization of program correctness.

Theorem 3.6 (Program correctness via iDFG) A program $\mathcal{P}$ is correct w.r.t. the precondition φ_{pre} and the postcondition φ_{post} if there exists an iDFG G with precondition φ_{pre} and postcondition φ_{post} such that every program trace of the program $\mathcal{P}$ lies in the denotation of the iDFG G:

$$\{\text{program traces of } \mathcal{P}\} \subseteq [\![G]\!].$$ ⌟

We say that G is a proof for $\mathcal{P}$ if the above inclusion holds. In the next sections, we will investigate how one can algorithmically check the inclusion for a given program and a given iDFG, and how one can construct an iDFG.

4. Checking iDFGs

In order to show that a given iDFG G is a proof for a given program $\mathcal{P}$, we need to check the condition that every program trace of $\mathcal{P}$ lies in the denotation of G. We will reduce this check to an inclusion problem between two automata.

The set of program traces of the program $\mathcal{P}$ is the set of labelings of paths between the initial location ℓ_0 and a final location $\ell \in F$ in the control flow graph of the program $\mathcal{P}$ (as mentioned previously, not every such path corresponds to a possible execution of the program). Thus, the set of program traces is a *regular language* over the alphabet Actions, the set of actions. It is recognized by the program $\mathcal{P}$ viewed as an automaton. Its set of states is Loc, the set of program locations. Its transition are the edges $\ell_1 \xrightarrow{a} \ell_2$ (state ℓ_1 goes to state ℓ_2 upon reading letter a). The initial state is the initial location ℓ_0 and the set of final states is the set F of final locations. We use $\mathcal{L}(\mathcal{A})$ to denote the language recognized by the automaton $\mathcal{A}$. We thus have

$$\{\text{program traces of } \mathcal{P}\} = \mathcal{L}(\mathcal{P}).$$

We will next transform an iDFG G into an *alternating finite automaton*. Alternating finite automata [6, 7] or AFA are a generalization of NFA. This generalization is easily understood if one views the generalization from DFA to NFA as follows. The value of the deterministic successor function is generalized from a single successor state to a disjunction of states, and the initial state is generalized to be a disjunction of states. The NFA associates with any word a Boolean expression (in fact, a disjunction of states) obtained by repeatedly rewriting the initial formula using the successor function, and accepts if that Boolean expression evaluates to *true* under the assignment that sends final states to *true* and non-final states to *false*. The generalization to AFA is then very natural: one allows a general Boolean expression over states for the image of the successor function and for the initial condition.

From data flow graph G to alternating finite automaton $\mathcal{A}_G$. Given the data flow graph $G = \langle V, E, \varphi_{\mathsf{pre}}, \varphi_{\mathsf{post}}, v_0, V_{\mathsf{final}} \rangle$, we define the AFA $\mathcal{A}_G = \langle \Sigma, Q, \delta, q_0, Q_{\mathsf{final}} \rangle$ where

- $\Sigma = \mathsf{Actions}$
- $Q = \{(\psi, v) \mid \exists v' \in V.\ v \xrightarrow{\psi} v'\} \cup \{(\varphi_{\mathsf{post}}, v_{\mathsf{f}}) \mid v_{\mathsf{f}} \in V_{\mathsf{final}}\}$
- $\delta((\psi, v), a) = \mathit{skip}((\psi, v), a) \vee \mathit{step}((\psi, v), a)$ where

$$\mathit{skip}((\psi, v), a) = \begin{cases} (\psi, v) & \text{if } \{\psi\}\ a\ \{\psi\} \\ \mathit{false} & \text{otherwise} \end{cases}$$

$$\mathit{step}((\psi, v), a) = \begin{cases} \bigwedge_{\{\varphi \mid v' \xrightarrow{\varphi} v\}} \bigvee_{\{v' \mid v' \xrightarrow{\varphi} v\}} (\varphi, v') & \text{if } \mathsf{act}(v) = a \\ \mathit{false} & \text{otherwise} \end{cases}$$

- $q_0 = \bigvee_{v_{\mathsf{f}} \in V_{\mathsf{final}}} (\varphi_{\mathsf{post}}, v_{\mathsf{f}})$
- $Q_{\mathsf{final}} = \{(\psi, v) \in Q \mid v = v_0\}$.

The observation below is immediate by the fact that the construction of $\mathcal{A}_G$ mimics the definition of the denotation of G. We write L^{rev} for the reversal of the language L.

Remark 4.1 The set of traces denoted by G is the reverse of the language recognized by $\mathcal{A}_G$, i.e., $[\![G]\!] = \mathcal{L}(\mathcal{A}_G)^{\mathit{rev}}$. ⌟

We can now reformulate Theorem 3.6 from the previous section. The check whether a given language is included in the reversal of the language of a given AFA can bypass the construction of the reversal of the AFA (because we can reverse the program traces instead).

Theorem 4.2 (Checking program correctness via an iDFG) A program $\mathcal{P}$ is correct w.r.t. the precondition φ_{pre} and the postcondition φ_{post} if there exists an iDFG G with precondition φ_{pre} and postcondition φ_{post} such that the language inclusion

$$\mathcal{L}(\mathcal{P}) \subseteq \mathcal{L}(\mathcal{A}_G)^{\mathit{rev}}$$

holds for the program automaton of $\mathcal{P}$ and the alternating finite automaton $\mathcal{A}_G$ derived from the iDFG G. ⌟

The theorem above expresses that we can shift the burden of having to deal with the exponential size of the control flow graph of a concurrent program $\mathcal{P}$ defined by the parallel composition of N threads to a combinatorial problem over finite graphs (and thus to a place where *it hurts less*, in comparison to a setting where one has to deal with data). We can view the problem as a finite-state model checking problem since it is equivalent to the satisfaction of a linear time property (a regular safety property defined by the AFA) by a finite-state model (the control flow graph of $\mathcal{P}$). It is a classical result that this problem can be solved in polynomial space.

Theorem 4.3 (PSPACE) The problem of checking whether an iDFG G is a proof for a program $\mathcal{P}$ given as the parallel composition of N threads, (i.e., checking whether all program traces of $\mathcal{P}$ are included in the denotation of G) is PSPACE (in the number N of threads). ⌟

5. Succinctness of iDFGs

In this section, we justify our claim that iDFGs are succinct proof objects. We introduce *localized proofs* in order to define a measure of the difficulty of proving that given program $\mathcal{P}$ satisfies a specification $(\varphi_{\mathsf{pre}}, \varphi_{\mathsf{post}})$; we call this measure the *data complexity* of $\mathcal{P}$ (with respect to $(\varphi_{\mathsf{pre}}, \varphi_{\mathsf{post}})$). We prove that if there exists a "small" proof of correctness for a program (i.e., if the program has low data complexity), then there exists a small iDFG proof.

It is easy to construct an iDFG proof from a control flow graph with a Floyd annotation by replacing edges with vertices, and vertices with edges. This construction proves the completeness of our proof rule (relative to the completeness of Floyd/Hoare proofs), but it leaves something to be desired: for a concurrent program $\mathcal{P}$, the iDFG resulting from this construction is of the same size as the control flow graph for $\mathcal{P}$, which is exponential in the number of threads in $\mathcal{P}$. In the rest of this section, we develop a characterization of when it is possible to prove that small iDFG proofs exist.

Consider the increment example from Section 2. There is an intuitive sense in which it is easy to prove that this program is correct because, although the size of the control flow graph for increment is exponential in the number of threads, the number of distinct assertions in the labeling of the control flow graph as required by a Floyd/Hoare proof is linear (the assertions appearing in the Floyd annotation are the ones of the form $x = i$, for $i \in [1, N]$). Following this example, a first attempt at defining a measure of the inherent difficulty of proving a program correct w.r.t. a specification may be "the minimal number of assertions in a Floyd/Hoare proof of the property." This definition fails a natural requirement for such a measure, which is that if the threads have no shared data (disjoint parallelism), then their parallel composition should have a small proof. It is for this reason that we introduce the concept of *localized proofs*. We first explain the intuition behind localized proofs, and then give their formal definition.

Localized proofs are a way of exposing "how compositional" a Floyd/Hoare proof is, while avoiding syntactic issues common to practical compositional proof methods such as auxiliary variables in Owicki-Gries or Rely/Guarantee. A localized proof essentially splits each assertion in the Floyd annotation of the control flow graph of $\mathcal{P}$ into a global assertion and a set of local assertions (local for a thread). The total number of distinct assertions (both global and local) can then be seen as a measure of the inherent complexity of the proof. The intuition behind this view comes from the idea of transforming a succinct proof (in some other framework, e.g., Owicki-Gries) to a Floyd/Hoare proof for the product program. In performing this transformation, assertions from the succinct proof will be replicated several times: an assertion attached to the control location ℓ of some thread $\mathcal{P}_i$ will appear as a conjunct in each assertion attached to a location of the control flow graph of $\mathcal{P}$ where thread $\mathcal{P}_i$ is at ℓ, i.e., a location of the form $(\ell_1, \ldots, \ell_i, \ldots, \ell_N)$ where $\ell_i = \ell$.

Definition 5.1 (Localized proof) Given a concurrent program $\mathcal{P}$ defined by the parallel composition of N threads $\mathcal{P}_1, \ldots, \mathcal{P}_N$ and a pre/postcondition pair $(\varphi_{\mathsf{pre}}, \varphi_{\mathsf{post}})$, a *localized proof*

$$\iota = \langle \iota_0, \iota_1, \ldots, \iota_N \rangle$$

is as a tuple of annotations (i.e., mappings from locations of the control flow graph of $\mathcal{P}$ to assertions) where each assertion $\iota_0(\ell)$ ("the global assertion at ℓ") may refer to global and local variables but each assertion $\iota_i(\ell)$ may refer only to the local variables of thread $\mathcal{P}_i$.

1. If the edge (ℓ, a, ℓ') labeled by the action a from the location ℓ to the location ℓ' in the control flow graph of $\mathcal{P}$ is induced by the edge (ℓ_k, a, ℓ'_k) of the thread $\mathcal{P}_k$ (i.e., if $\ell = (\ell_1, \ldots, \ell_N)$ and $\ell' = (\ell'_1, \ldots, \ell'_N)$ then $\ell_i = \ell'_i$ for $i \neq k$), then the Hoare triple
$$\{\iota_0(\ell) \wedge \iota_k(\ell)\}\ a\ \{\iota_0(\ell') \wedge \iota_k(\ell')\}$$
is valid and for all $i > 0$ different from k, the local assertion is the same for location ℓ and location ℓ'; i.e., $\iota_i(\ell) = \iota_i(\ell')$ for $i \neq k$.
2. The assertions at the initial location are entailed by the precondition; i.e., $\varphi_{\mathsf{pre}} \models \iota_i(\ell_0)$ for $i = 0, 1, \ldots, N$.
3. Every final location is annotated with the same tuple of assertions and their conjunction entails the postcondition; i.e., there

exist $\varphi_0, \varphi_1, \ldots, \varphi_N$ such that $\iota(\ell) = \langle \varphi_0, \varphi_1, \ldots, \varphi_N \rangle$ for all final locations ℓ and $\varphi_0 \wedge \varphi_1 \wedge \cdots \wedge \varphi_N \models \varphi_{\mathsf{post}}$. ⌟

A localized proof can be viewed as a particular presentation of the Floyd/Hoare proof that labels each location ℓ with the conjunction of the global assertion and all local assertions for location ℓ.

In a degenerate case of a localized proof, the local annotations $\iota_1, \cdots, \iota_N$ are all trivial; i.e., $\iota_i(\ell) = \mathit{true}$ for each location ℓ of $\mathcal{P}$ and for $i = 1, \ldots, N$. In this case, the whole assertion for location ℓ in a Floyd/Hoare proof is put into the global assertion $\iota_0(\ell)$ of the localized proof.

The size of a localized proof $\iota = \langle \iota_0, \iota_1, \ldots, \iota_N \rangle$ is the number of distinct assertions appearing in ι. Formally,

$$\mathsf{size}(\iota) = \sum_{i \in [1,N]} |\mathsf{Actions}_i| \cdot |\mathrm{rng}(\iota_0)| \cdot |\mathrm{rng}(\iota_i)|$$

where $\mathrm{rng}(\iota)$ denotes the range of the annotation ι, and $\mathsf{Actions}_i$ is the set of actions in the i-th thread $\mathcal{P}_i$.

Example 5.2 Consider the following simple example program, consisting of N threads, which each increment a local variable $\mathtt{t_i}$ before storing that value in a global variable $\mathtt{x}$:

Thread 1: $\mathtt{t_1{+}{+};\ x{:=}t_1}$

$\vdots$

Thread N: $\mathtt{t_N{+}{+};\ x{:=}t_N}$

In the Hoare proof that this program satisfies the specification $\varphi_{\mathsf{pre}} : \mathtt{x} = \mathtt{t_1} = \ldots = \mathtt{t_N} = 0 / \varphi_{\mathsf{post}} : \mathtt{x} = 1$, a distinct assertion is required for each combination of values for the $\mathtt{t_i}$ and $\mathtt{x}$ variables (except the combination where $\mathtt{x} = 1$ and each $\mathtt{t_i} = 0$). The total number of such assertions is $2^{N+1} - 1$. In the *localized* Hoare proof, ι_i assigns $\mathtt{t_i} = 1$ to every location after thread i executes $\mathtt{t_i{+}{+}}$ and $\mathtt{t_i} = 0$ to every other location. The global annotation ι_0 assigns $\mathtt{x} = 1$ to every location where some thread has executed $\mathtt{x{:=}t_i}$ and $\mathtt{x} = 0$ to every other location. The size of this localized proof is $\sum_{i \in [1,N]} 2 \cdot 2 \cdot 2 = 8N$. ⌟

Definition 5.3 (Data complexity) Given a pre/postcondition pair $(\varphi_{\mathsf{pre}}, \varphi_{\mathsf{post}})$, the *data complexity* of a program $\mathcal{P}$ is the minimum size of a localized proof that $\mathcal{P}$ satisfies the specification $(\varphi_{\mathsf{pre}}, \varphi_{\mathsf{post}})$. ⌟

We can now state the main result of this section.

Theorem 5.4 (Size of iDFG proofs) Given the pre/postcondition pair $(\varphi_{\mathsf{pre}}, \varphi_{\mathsf{post}})$, if a proof for the program $\mathcal{P}$ exists, then there exists a proof for $\mathcal{P}$ in the form of an iDFG whose size is polynomial in the data complexity of $\mathcal{P}$. ⌟

Proof. Let $\varphi_{\mathsf{pre}}, \varphi_{\mathsf{post}}$ be a specification, $\mathcal{P} = \langle \mathsf{Loc}, \delta \rangle$ be a program obtained as the parallel composition of N threads $\mathcal{P}_1, \ldots, \mathcal{P}_N$, and $\iota = \langle \iota_0, \iota_1, \ldots, \iota_N \rangle$ be a localized proof of minimum size that $\mathcal{P}$ satisfies $\varphi_{\mathsf{pre}} / \varphi_{\mathsf{post}}$. We construct an iDFG

$$G = \langle V, E, \varphi_{\mathsf{pre}}, \varphi_{\mathsf{post}}, v_0, V_{\mathsf{final}} \rangle$$

that proves that $\mathcal{P}$ satisfies the specification $\varphi_{\mathsf{pre}} / \varphi_{\mathsf{post}}$.

The set of vertices of G consists of the *initial* vertex v_0, *regular* vertices, and *final* vertices.

$$V = \{v_0\} \cup V_{\mathsf{regular}} \cup V_{\mathsf{final}}$$

The regular vertices are defined as:

$$V_{\mathsf{regular}} = \{\langle a, \iota_0(\ell), \iota_i(\ell) \rangle \mid i \in [1, N], \exists \ell'.(\ell, a, \ell') \in \delta_i\},$$

where for any $i \in [1, N]$, δ_i denotes the set of edges due to thread $\mathcal{P}_i$. The final vertices are defined as:

$$V_{\mathsf{final}} = \{\langle a, \iota_0(\ell), \iota_1(\ell), \ldots, \iota_N(\ell) \rangle \mid (\ell, a, \ell') \in \delta, \ell' \in F\}$$

where F denotes the set of final locations of $\mathcal{P}$. The labeling act of a vertex v with an action is as one expects.

The construction of the set of edges of G uses two auxiliary functions: the function in maps each vertex v to a set of assertions that will label the incoming edges to v, and the function pre maps each vertex to an assertion that can be thought of as its precondition.

$$\begin{aligned}
&\mathsf{in}(v_0) = \emptyset \\
&\mathsf{in}(\langle a, \varphi, \varphi_i \rangle) = \{\varphi, \varphi_i\} \\
&\mathsf{in}(\langle a, \varphi_0, \varphi_1, \ldots, \varphi_N \rangle) = \{\varphi_0, \varphi_1, \ldots, \varphi_N\} \\
&\mathsf{pre}(v_0) = \varphi_{\mathsf{pre}} \\
&\mathsf{pre}(\langle a, \varphi, \varphi_i \rangle) = \varphi \wedge \varphi_i \\
&\mathsf{pre}(\langle a, \varphi_0, \varphi_1, \ldots, \varphi_N \rangle) = \varphi_0 \wedge \varphi_1 \wedge \cdots \wedge \varphi_N
\end{aligned}$$

The set of edges is defined as

$$\begin{aligned}
E = \{u \xrightarrow{\varphi} v \mid\ & u, v \in V, u \notin V_{\mathsf{final}}, \varphi \in \mathsf{in}(v), \text{and} \\
& \{\psi\}\ a\ \{\varphi\} \text{ for } \psi = \mathsf{pre}(u) \text{ and } a = \mathsf{act}(u)\}
\end{aligned}$$

This completes our definition of G. It is easy to check that the labeling of the edges of G with assertions φ is inductive. We now argue that the number of vertices of G is linear in the size of the localized proof ι (and therefore the size of G is polynomial). A regular vertex is a triple of an action, a global assertion, and a local assertion. Hence the number of regular vertices is at most $\mathsf{size}(\iota)$. A final vertex corresponds to a location ℓ that has an edge to a final location ℓ' in $\mathcal{P}$. According to the definition of a localized proof, $\iota(\ell)$ can vary from $\iota(\ell')$ only in two components (the global assertion and one of the local assertions), and every final location is annotated with the same tuple of assertions, i.e., $\iota(\ell')$. Hence, the number of final vertices is at most $\mathsf{size}(\iota)$.

In order to prove that every program trace τ of $\mathcal{P}$ belongs to $[\![G]\!]$, we prove the lemma below; here, the notation $G/(v, \varphi)$ refers to the iDFG obtained from G by making v the (unique) final vertex and φ the postcondition, for a vertex v of G and an assertion φ.

$$G/(v, \varphi) = \langle V, E, \varphi_{\mathsf{pre}}, \varphi, v_0, \{v\} \rangle$$

Lemma 5.5 For any path $\ell_0 a_0 \cdots a_{n-1} \ell_n$ in $\mathcal{P}$ of length $n \geq 0$ (starting at the initial location ℓ_0 and leading to the location ℓ_n), there exists a tuple of non-final vertices $\langle u_0, u_1, \ldots, u_N \rangle$ such that

$$a_0 \cdots a_{n-1} \in [\![G/(u_i, \iota_i(\ell_n))]\!]$$

for $i = 0, 1, \ldots, N$. ⌟

Before we prove this lemma, we show why it implies that every trace of $\mathcal{P}$ belongs to $[\![G]\!]$. Suppose τ is a trace of $\mathcal{P}$. Then there exists a path $\ell_0 a_0 \cdots a_{n-1} \ell_n a_n \ell_{n+1}$ such that $a_0 \cdots a_n = \tau$ and ℓ_{n+1} is a final location. By the lemma, there exists some $u_0, u_1, \ldots, u_N$ such that $a_0 \cdots a_{n-1} \in [\![G/(u_i, \iota_i(\ell_n))]\!]$ for all $i = 0, 1, \ldots, N$. Let $u_{\mathsf{f}} = \langle a_n, \iota_0(\ell_n), \iota_1(\ell_n), \ldots, \iota_N(\ell_n) \rangle$. Then it follows from the construction of E that $u_i \xrightarrow{\iota_i(\ell_n)} u_{\mathsf{f}} \in E$ for all $i = 0, 1, \ldots, N$, and thus that $\tau = a_0 \cdots a_{n-1} a_n \in [\![G]\!]$.

Now we prove the lemma by induction on the length n of paths in $\mathcal{P}$. The base case $n = 0$ is trivial: we may set each of $u_0, u_1, \ldots, u_N$ to be the initial vertex v_0.

For the induction step, suppose that $\ell_0 a_0 \cdots a_{n-1} \ell_n a_n \ell_{n+1}$ is a path in $\mathcal{P}$ and that there exists $u'_0, u'_1, \cdots, u'_N$ such that $a_0 \cdots a_{n-1}$ belongs to $[\![G/(u'_i, \iota_i(\ell_n))]\!]$ for all $i \in [0, N]$. Let $k \in [1, N]$ be the index of the thread that executes the last action a_n. We distinguish two cases:

For $i \neq k$, we may take $u_i = u'_i$. By the induction hypothesis, $a_0 \cdots a_{n-1} \in [\![G/(u'_i, \iota_i(\ell_n))]\!]$. By condition 1 of Definition 5.1, $\iota_i(\ell_n) = \iota_i(\ell_{n+1})$, so $a_0 \cdots a_{n-1} \in [\![G/(u'_i, \iota_i(\ell_{n+1}))]\!]$. Since $\iota_i(\ell_{n+1})$ is stable under the action a_n (since a_n is executed by thread $k \neq i$), it follows that $a_0 \cdots a_{n-1} a_n \in [\![G/(u'_i, \iota_i(\ell_{n+1}))]\!]$.

For $i = k$, we make take $u_i = \langle a_n, \iota_0(\ell_n), \iota_k(\ell_n)\rangle$. By the definition of E, we have:

$$u'_0 \xrightarrow{\iota_0(\ell_n)} u_i \in E \quad \text{and} \quad u'_k \xrightarrow{\iota_k(\ell_n)} u_i \in E.$$

Since (by the induction hypothesis), $a_0 \cdots a_{n-1}$ is in both $[\![G/(u'_0, \iota_0(\ell_n))]\!]$ and $[\![G/(u'_i, \iota_i(\ell_n))]\!]$, we have the desired result: $a_0 \cdots a_{n-1} a_n \in [\![G/(u_i, \iota_k(\ell_{n+1}))]\!]$. We still need to choose a vertex of G that we take for u_0. We take the same vertex that we took for u_i. The same argument as above shows that $a_0 \cdots a_{n-1} a_n \in [\![G/(u_i, \iota_0(\ell_{n+1}))]\!]$.

□

The proof shows that the number of nodes of G is linear in the data complexity. In the extreme case of *disjoint parallelism* (a concurrent program composed of N threads with no shared data) there exists a localized proof without global assertion (formally, each global assertion is *true*.) In this case, the iDFG constructed in the proof of Theorem 5.4 is essentially the collection of local proofs as in an Owicki-Gries style proof (the local proofs are connected via edges from the initial vertex v_0). Its vertices correspond to pairs consisting of an action and a local assertion. Hence, the number of its vertices is linear in N.

A special case of this theorem is a concurrent program in a parametrized number N of threads that has a localized proof where the number of global assertions (i.e., the size of $rng(\iota_0)$) grows linearly in N, and the number of actions and local assertions (i.e., the size of $rng(\iota_i)$) is constant. The increment example from Section 2 falls into this case. The iDFG constructed in the proof of Theorem 5.4 has $O(N)$ vertices (as does the one we constructed manually in Section 2). In Section 2, we also hinted at the iDFG (with $O(N^2)$ vertices) for the case where we rename apart the action `x++` in each thread. This case illustrates the motivation to use the number of actions as a parameter for the data complexity (which becomes quadratic in N in this case).

In the case of the Ticket algorithm, not only the number of global assertions, but also the number of local assertions grows linearly in N. Therefore, the data complexity is quadratic in N. Indeed, the iDFG we will construct in Section 6 has $O(N^2)$ vertices.

6. Verification Algorithm

In this section, we develop an iDFG-based algorithm for verifying concurrent programs. Given a program $\mathcal{P}$ and a pre/postcondition pair $(\varphi_{\mathsf{pre}}, \varphi_{\mathsf{post}})$, the goal of this algorithm is to either:

- construct a proof for $\mathcal{P}$ in the form of an iDFG G, or
- return a counterexample, i.e., a program trace τ such that the Hoare triple $\{\varphi_{\mathsf{pre}}\}\ \tau\ \{\varphi_{\mathsf{post}}\}$ does not hold.

We use Figure 3 to explain the basic idea behind the algorithm. The algorithm starts by picking a program trace τ. If the trace does not satisfy the Hoare triple $\{\varphi_{\mathsf{pre}}\}\ \tau\ \{\varphi_{\mathsf{post}}\}$, then the program is not correct with respect to the given specification. If it does, then τ is abstracted into an iDFG G_τ.

The algorithm maintains an iDFG G that represents a set of traces proven correct (initially, this set is empty). The iDFG G is updated by merging it with G_τ. If the resulting iDFG contains every program trace, then G is a proof for the program. If not, then the algorithm keeps generating traces and updating G until either a proof or a counterexample is found.

In component (d), we check whether an iDFG G is a proof for $\mathcal{P}$, which means checking the inclusion $\mathcal{L}(\mathcal{P}) \subseteq [\![G]\!]$; we discussed how to accomplish this in Section 4. The failure of the inclusion check means that there is a trace τ in the difference between the two sets, $\mathcal{L}(\mathcal{P}) \setminus [\![G]\!]$. By choosing such a trace in component (a),

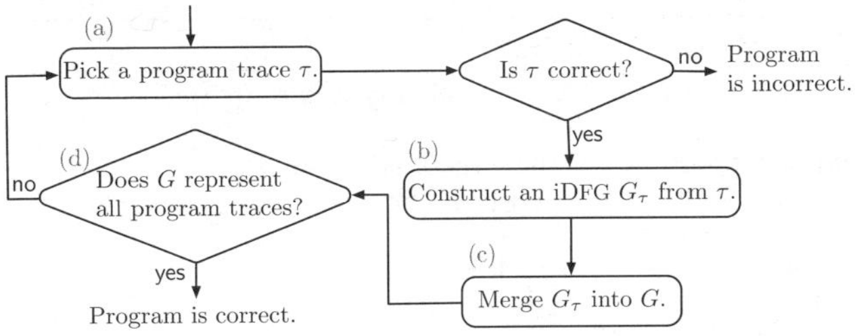

Figure 3. Verification algorithm based on inductive data flow graphs (iDFGs). Initially G is empty.

we ensure progress of the algorithm (i.e., after each iteration, G denotes a larger set of correct traces). In what follows, we discuss the remaining components (b) and (c). We will explain how an iDFG G_τ is constructed from a trace τ (Section 6.1) and how iDFG G is updated by merging it with G_τ (Section 6.2). Finally, we present the full algorithm in Section 6.3.

6.1 Constructing an iDFG from a trace

We will present an algorithm that, given a trace τ and a pre/postcondition pair $(\varphi_{\mathsf{pre}}, \varphi_{\mathsf{post}})$ such that the Hoare triple $\{\varphi_{\mathsf{pre}}\}\ \tau\ \{\varphi_{\mathsf{post}}\}$ holds, constructs an iDFG G_τ (with the same pre/postcondition pair) whose denotation contains τ. By Remark 3.5, G_τ is a proof for the correctness of τ, i.e., for the validity of the Hoare triple $\{\varphi_{\mathsf{pre}}\}\ \tau\ \{\varphi_{\mathsf{post}}\}$.

This algorithm uses an auxiliary procedure Interpolate. Given a trace τ which ends in the action a, i.e., $\tau = \tau'.a$ and which is correct for a given pair of assertions $(\varphi_{\mathsf{pre}}, \varphi_{\mathsf{post}})$, i.e.,

$$\{\varphi_{\mathsf{pre}}\}\ \tau'.a\ \{\varphi_{\mathsf{post}}\},$$

the call of the auxiliary procedure $\mathsf{Interpolate}(\varphi_{\mathsf{pre}}, \tau, a, \varphi_{\mathsf{post}})$ returns an intermediate assertion ψ such that

$$\{\varphi_{\mathsf{pre}}\}\ \tau'\ \{\psi\} \text{ and } \{\psi\}\ a\ \{\varphi_{\mathsf{post}}\}.$$

The auxiliary procedure Interpolate is always applied to a finite program trace, which is effectively a very simple sequential program. This means that it can be implemented by one form or another of static analysis applied backwards to this sequential program (that consists just of the trace τ). One can leverage the power of existing static analysis methods such as apply a backwards transformer in some abstract domain, Craig interpolation, weakest precondition computation, among others to construct iDFGs [9].

Intuitively, the procedure $\mathsf{construct\text{-}idfg}(\tau, \varphi, \varphi')$ takes the trace τ and detects what actions in τ and what ordering constraints embodied in τ are irrelevant (for attaining the postcondition φ'). This is accomplished by leveraging the Interpolate procedure as follows:

- If $\mathsf{Interpolate}(\varphi, \tau', a, \varphi')$ returns the postcondition φ' (and thus, the postcondition φ' is stable w.r.t. the action a (i.e., $\{\varphi'\}\ a\ \{\varphi'\}$), and therefore a is irrelevant.
- Otherwise, if $\mathsf{Interpolate}(\varphi, \tau', a, \varphi')$ returns a proper conjunction $\psi_1 \wedge \cdots \wedge \psi_k$, then each assertion $\psi_1, \ldots,$ or ψ_k can be attained as postcondition for the prefix trace τ' *in parallel* (as opposed to in sequential order).

One possibility to maximize parallelism is to have Interpolate return formulae in conjunctive normal form. The particular strategy to break the intermediate assertions into conjuncts does not matter for the correctness of the overall algorithm.

Note that construct-idfg produces acyclic iDFGs without disjunctions (no vertex has multiple incoming edges labeled with the same assertion). Disjunctions and cycles will be produced by the *merge* procedure that we will discuss in Section 6.2.

Algorithm construct-idfg$(\tau, \varphi, \varphi')$

Input: trace τ and a pair of assertions (φ, φ') such that $\{\varphi\}\ \tau\ \{\varphi'\}$
Output: proof for τ in the form of an iDFG G_τ
(i.e., G_τ has the pre/postcondition pair (φ, φ') and $\tau \in [\![G_\tau]\!]$)
  if $\tau = \varepsilon$ **then**
    return $G_\tau = \langle\{v_0\}, \emptyset, \varphi, \varphi', v_0, \{v_0\}\rangle$
  else
    $\tau = \tau'.a$ for some trace τ' and action a
    $\psi \leftarrow$ Interpolate$(\varphi, \tau', a, \varphi')$
    if $\psi = \varphi'$ **then**
      return construct-idfg$(\tau', \varphi, \varphi')$
    else
      $\psi = \psi_1 \wedge \cdots \wedge \psi_k$
      $v \leftarrow$ fresh vertex with label a (i.e., act$(v) = a$)
      parallel for $i = 1, \ldots, k$ **do**
        $\langle V_i, E_i, \varphi, \psi_i, v_0, V^i_{\mathsf{final}}\rangle \leftarrow$ construct-idfg(τ', φ, ψ_i)
      end parallel for
      $V \leftarrow \{v\} \cup \bigcup_{i=1,\ldots,k} V_i$
      $E \leftarrow \bigcup_{i=1,\ldots,k}(E_i \cup \{u \xrightarrow{\psi_i} v \mid u \in V^i_{\mathsf{final}}\})$
      return $G_\tau = \langle V, E, \varphi, \varphi', v_0, \{v\}\rangle$
    end if
  end if

Example 6.1 We will demonstrate the algorithm by applying it to Trace 1 of Bakery, pictured in Figure 1(a). The precondition is $\texttt{PreC} = \texttt{n1} = \texttt{n2} = 0 \wedge \neg\texttt{e1} \wedge \neg\texttt{e2}$ and the postcondition is $\texttt{false}$. We use τ to denote Trace 1 and τ_1 to denote the prefix of τ obtained by removing last action b_6.

For this example, we use the Craig interpolation feature of MathSAT5 [16] to implement Interpolate. The first call to Interpolate in construct-idfg yields the following interpolant:

$$\text{Interpolate}(\texttt{PreC}, \tau_1, b_6, \texttt{false}) = \texttt{n1} > 0 \wedge \texttt{n1} < \texttt{n2}$$

Intuitively, the order in which the two assertions $\texttt{n1} > 0$ and $\texttt{n1} < \texttt{n2}$ are enforced is irrelevant, as long as both are enforced before b_6 is executed. This is reflected by how the execution of construct-idfg proceeds, namely by calling

$$\text{construct-idfg}(\tau_1, \texttt{PreC}, \texttt{n1} > 0)$$

and

$$\text{construct-idfg}(\tau_1, \texttt{PreC}, \texttt{n1} < \texttt{n2})$$

in parallel. The two calls correspond, respectively, to the left and the right branch of the iDFG (c) in Figure 1.

In order to illustrate how construct-idfg suppresses irrelevant actions, we will continue and follow the execution of the call

$$\text{construct-idfg}(\tau_1, \texttt{PreC}, \texttt{n1} > 0).$$

We use τ_2 to denote the prefix of τ_1 obtained by removing last action, which is $[\neg\texttt{e1}]$. The action $[\neg\texttt{e1}]$ is irrelevant in the sense that it is not needed to enforce the postcondition $\texttt{n1} > 0$. This is established by construct-idfg when the next interpolant along this branch is computed:

$$\text{Interpolate}(\texttt{PreC}, \tau_2, [\neg\texttt{e1}], \texttt{n1} > 0) = \texttt{n1} > 0$$

Since the computed interpolant is the same as the postcondition, construct-idfg enters the **then** branch of the conditional and proceeds to the call

$$\text{construct-idfg}(\tau_2, \texttt{PreC}, \texttt{n1} > 0).$$

The algorithm continues to suppress irrelevant actions in this way, going backwards along τ_2 until it comes to the first action under which $\texttt{n1} > 0$ is not stable, which is $a_3 : \texttt{n1 := tmp1 + 1}$. This action becomes the next vertex along the n1>0 branch of the iDFG in Figure 1(a). ⌟

The essential property of construct-idfg is that it constructs an iDFG proof of the correctness of a trace with respect to a given pre/postcondition. This is expressed in the following lemma.

Lemma 6.2 Let τ be a trace that is correct with respect to the pre/postconditions φ/φ', and let G_τ = construct-idfg$(\tau, \varphi, \varphi')$. Then $\tau \in [\![G_\tau]\!]$. ⌟

6.2 Merging iDFGs

Our merge operator $G_1 \mathbin{/\!\!\!\backslash\!\!\!\backslash} G_2$ can be thought of as a three step process: in the first step, we construct the disjoint union of G_1 and G_2; in the second step, *completion*, we saturate this iDFG by adding edges that do not violate the inductiveness property for iDFGs; in the third step, *reduction*, we collapse "equivalent" vertices.

We begin with a declarative definition for what it means for an iDFG to be complete (i.e., edge-saturated).

Definition 6.3 (Complete) An iDFG $G = \langle V, E, \varphi, \varphi', v_0, V_{\mathsf{final}}\rangle$ is *complete* if:

- For any $v \in V$ with such that $\{\mathsf{pre}(v)\}\ \mathsf{act}(v)\ \{\varphi'\}$ holds, $v \in V_{\mathsf{final}}$
- For any $u, v \in V$, and any φ such that v has an incoming edge labeled φ and $\{\mathsf{pre}(u)\}\ \mathsf{act}(u)\ \{\varphi\}$ holds, $u \xrightarrow{\varphi} v \in E$

where

$$\mathsf{pre}(v) = \begin{cases} \varphi & \text{if } v = v_0 \\ \bigwedge_{u \xrightarrow{\varphi} v \in E} \varphi & \text{otherwise} \end{cases}$$

⌟

Completion plays an essential role in the construction of iDFG proofs for programs. It is essential for producing proofs of programs that contain loops. Note that, as we mentioned in Section 6.1, the construct-idfg procedure does not introduce any disjunctions. Disjunctions are essential for capturing program behaviour produced by loops. The completion process can introduce these necessary disjunctions.

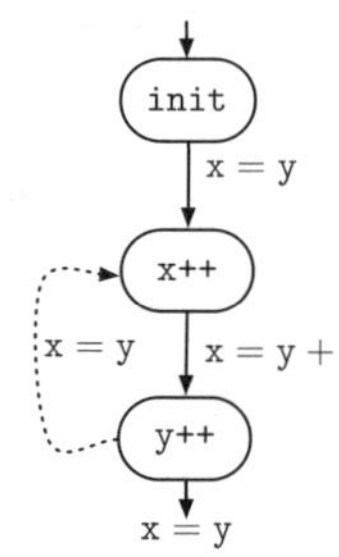

For example consider the following simple program and its specification: `{x = y} while(*): x++; y++ {x = y}` The iDFG pictured to the right proves that this program satisfies the specification. The subgraph consisting only of the solid arrows can be generated by construct-idfg from a sample trace of the program `x++.y++`. The remaining dotted edge is added to the iDFG by the completion procedure (since `x++` has an incoming edge labeled $x = y$ and the Hoare triple $\{\mathsf{pre}(\texttt{y++})\}\ \texttt{y++}\ \{x = y\}$ holds). This generalizes the iDFG so that it proves the correctness of *any number* of iterations of the loop rather than a single iteration.

The following is a declarative definition for what it means for an iDFG to be reduced (i.e., vertex-minimal)

Definition 6.4 (Reduced) An iDFG $G = \langle V, E, \varphi, \varphi', v_0, V_{\mathsf{final}}\rangle$ is *reduced* if there exist no distinct $u, v \in V$ such that $\mathsf{act}(u) = \mathsf{act}(v)$ and the set of assertions labeling the incoming edges to u and v are the same (i.e., $\{\varphi \mid \exists w. w \xrightarrow{\varphi} v \in E\} = \{\varphi \mid \exists w. w \xrightarrow{\varphi} u \in E\}$). ⌟

There is an algorithm that, given an arbitrary iDFG G, constructs a reduced complete iDFG $rc(G)$ such that $[\![rc(G)]\!]$ contains

$[\![G]\!]$. We call $rc(G)$ the *reduced completion of* G. This is stated formally in the following proposition:

Proposition 6.5
For every iDFG $G = \langle V, E, \varphi_{\mathsf{pre}}, \varphi_{\mathsf{post}}, v_0, V_{\mathsf{final}}\rangle$, there is a reduced, complete iDFG $rc(G)$ that can be computed from G in $O(|V| \cdot |E|)$ time and such that the precondition of $rc(G)$ is φ_{pre}, the postcondition of $rc(G)$ is φ_{post}, and $[\![G]\!] \subseteq [\![rc(G)]\!]$. ┘

Proof. For any vertex v, we define

$$\mathsf{in}(v) = \{\varphi \mid \exists u. u \xrightarrow{\varphi} v \in G\}$$

We define $rc(G) = \langle V', E', \varphi_{\mathsf{pre}}, \varphi_{\mathsf{post}}, v_0, V'_{\mathsf{final}}\rangle$, where

$$\begin{aligned} V' &= \{v_0\} \cup \{\langle \mathsf{act}(v), \mathsf{in}(v)\rangle \mid v \in V \setminus \{v_0\}\} \\ E' &= \{\langle a, \Psi\rangle \xrightarrow{\varphi} \langle a', \Psi'\rangle \mid \varphi \in \Psi' \wedge \{\textstyle\bigwedge \Psi\}\ a\ \{\varphi\}\} \\ &\quad \cup \{v_0 \xrightarrow{\varphi} \langle a', \Psi'\rangle \mid \varphi \in \Psi' \wedge \{\varphi_{\mathsf{pre}}\}\ a\ \{\varphi\}\} \end{aligned}$$

and

$$V'_{\mathsf{final}} = \begin{cases} \{v_0\} \cup \{\langle \mathsf{act}(v), \mathsf{in}(v)\rangle \mid v \in V_{\mathsf{final}}\} & \text{if } \varphi_{\mathsf{pre}} \Rightarrow \varphi_{\mathsf{post}} \\ \{\langle \mathsf{act}(v), \mathsf{in}(v)\rangle \mid v \in V_{\mathsf{final}}\} & \text{otherwise} \end{cases}$$

It is easy to check that $rc(G)$ is well-defined. The machinery required to prove that $[\![G]\!] \subseteq [\![rc(G)]\!]$ is presented in Section 7. □

Finally, we describe our merge operation. The merge operator $G_1 \curlywedge G_2$ functions by forming the disjoint union of G_1 and G_2, and then taking the reduced completion of the resulting iDFG. Formally, we define merge as follows:

Definition 6.6 Given two iDFGs $G_1 = \langle V_1, E_1, \varphi, \varphi', v_0, V^1_{\mathsf{final}}\rangle$ and $G_2 = \langle V_2, E_2, \varphi, \varphi', v_0, V^2_{\mathsf{final}}\rangle$, their *merge*, $G_1 \curlywedge G_2$ is defined to be the iDFG

$$G_1 \curlywedge G_2 = rc(\langle V^{\curlywedge}, E^{\curlywedge}, \varphi, \varphi', v_0, V^{\curlywedge}_{\mathsf{final}}\rangle)$$

where $V^{\curlywedge} = V_1 \cup V_2$, $E^{\curlywedge} = E_1 \cup E_2$, $V^{\curlywedge}_{\mathsf{final}} = V^1_{\mathsf{final}} \cup V^2_{\mathsf{final}}$, and $\mathsf{act}(v)$ is defined in the obvious way. For simplicity, this definition assumes that the initial vertex of G is also the initial vertex of G' and that otherwise their vertices are disjoint. ┘

Applying the rc operator in the merge plays an essential role in reducing the size of iDFG proofs. For example, the iDFG proof for the Ticket example from Section 2 would require $O(N!)$ vertices without applying the rc operator (see Example 6.9).

The progress of our algorithm depends on the following lemma concerning the merge operator:

Lemma 6.7 Let G_1 and G_2 be two iDFGs. We have

$$[\![G_1]\!] \cup [\![G_2]\!] \subseteq [\![G_1 \curlywedge G_2]\!].$$

┘

An example of the merge operator appears in Figure 4: part (c) is the merge of parts (a) and (b). Notice that (c) proves that the trace

```
m1=t++.m3=t++.[m3 <= s]
```

is infeasible (starting from the precondition $\mathtt{s} = \mathtt{t} = 0$), even though this fact is not proved by (a) or (b).

6.3 Putting it all together

We are now ready to present a formal description of our verification algorithm. The last component of this algorithm that has not already been described is the initialization of G. If φ_{pre} implies φ_{post} (or equivalently, the Hoare triple $\{\varphi_{\mathsf{pre}}\}\ \varepsilon\ \{\varphi_{\mathsf{post}}\}$ holds), then G is initialized to an iDFG with a single vertex that is both initial and final (and therefore, $[\![G]\!] = \{\varepsilon\}$). Otherwise, G is initialized to an iDFG that has no final vertices (and therefore, $[\![G]\!] = \emptyset$).

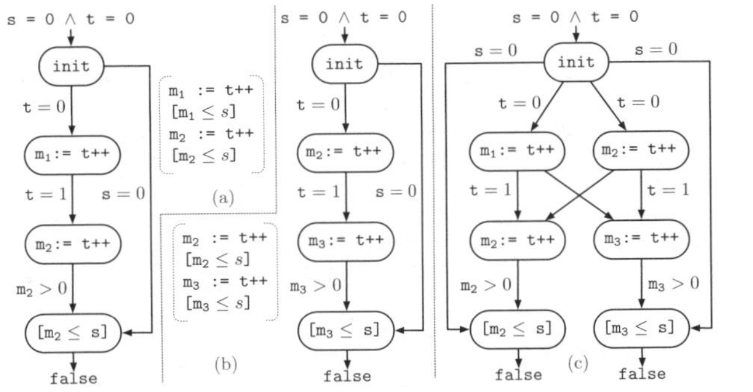

Figure 4. Intermediate iDFGs for the Ticket algorithm

Algorithm Verification algorithm

Input: Program $\mathcal{P}$, precondition φ_{pre}, postcondition φ_{post}
Output: Yes if $\mathcal{P}$ is correct w.r.t. the specification; No otherwise.
  if φ_{pre} entails φ_{post} **then**
    $G := \langle v_0, \emptyset, \varphi_{\mathsf{pre}}, \varphi_{\mathsf{post}}, v_0, \{v_0\}\rangle$
  else
    $G := \langle v_0, \emptyset, \varphi_{\mathsf{pre}}, \varphi_{\mathsf{post}}, v_0, \emptyset\rangle$
  end if
  while $\mathcal{L}(\mathcal{P}) \not\subseteq [\![G]\!]$ **do**
    Let $\tau \in \mathcal{L}(\mathcal{P}) \setminus [\![G]\!]$
    if the Hoare triple $\{\varphi_{\mathsf{pre}}\}\ \tau\ \{\varphi_{\mathsf{post}}\}$ holds **then**
      $G_\tau := \mathsf{construct\text{-}idfg}(\tau, \varphi_{\mathsf{pre}}, \varphi_{\mathsf{post}})$
      $G := G \curlywedge G_\tau$
    else
      return No (with counter-example τ)
    end if
  end while
  return Yes

As a direct consequence of Lemmas 6.2 and 6.7, we can state the following progress property of the verification algorithm:

Proposition 6.8 (Progress) If G_i and G_{i+1} are the iDFGs constructed by the verification algorithm in (respectively) the round i and round $(i + 1)$, then we have $[\![G_i]\!] \subset [\![G_{i+1}]\!]$ (the inclusion is strict). ┘

We conclude this section with an example run of the verification algorithm on the Ticket algorithm mentioned in Section 2.

Example 6.9 We consider the 3-thread instance of the Ticket mutual exclusion algorithm, which runs three copies of the thread below in parallel (where i is substituted for the thread id).

Thread i

```
ℓi,1 :  mi := t++
ℓi,2 :  [mi ≤ s]
        // critical section
ℓi,3 :  s := s + 1
```

The first two rounds of the verification algorithm are depicted in Figure 4. Since the property of interest is mutual exclusion, we take the traces of this program to be the ones that end with (at least) two threads inside their critical section, and prove that the program meets the specification with precondition $\mathtt{s} = 0 \wedge \mathtt{t} = 0$ and postcondition $\mathtt{false}$ (i.e., every trace violating mutual exclusion is infeasible).

The algorithm begins with the empty iDFG, $G_\emptyset$. The first program trace τ_1 that we select in $\mathcal{L}(\mathcal{P}) \setminus [\![G_\emptyset]\!]$ is depicted in Figure 4(a) along with an iDFG proof for τ_1, as constructed by $\mathsf{construct\text{-}idfg}$. We call this iDFG G_1.

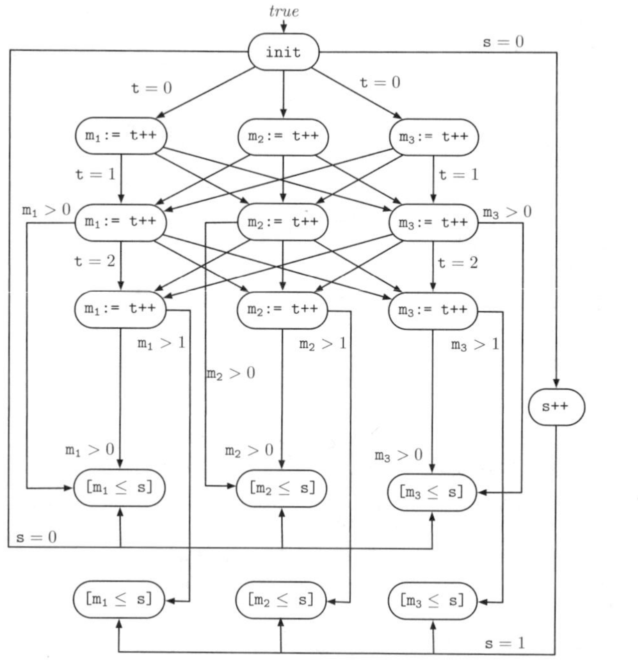

Figure 5. Correctness proof of the Ticket algorithm. Note that the post-conditions (all `false`) have been removed from the figure to keep it clean. In a complete version of this figure all 6 nodes with labels $[\mathtt{m_i} \leq \mathtt{s}]$ have a dangling arrow with a label `false`.

On the next iteration of the loop, we select the trace τ_2 depicted in part Figure 4(b), and merge its corresponding iDFG proof (called G_{τ_2}) with G_1 to form G_2 pictured in Figure 4(c). Since $[\![G_2]\!]$ does not cover every program trace (i.e., $\mathcal{L}(\mathcal{P}) \not\subseteq \mathcal{L}(G_2)$), the algorithm continues the loop. After four more iterations, the algorithm will terminate after all traces that violate mutual exclusion have been proved to be infeasible. The iDFG that is constructed by this algorithm is depicted in Figure 5.

The intuition for the iDFG in Figure 5 can be used to construct a proof for the Ticket mutual exclusion algorithm for any number of threads. For any such iDFG proof, the number of vertices is quadratic in the number of threads. ⌟

7. Properties of the Verification Algorithm

We will now investigate the properties of the verification algorithm. In particular, we prove that the algorithm is sound, that it is complete (under the assumption that the auxiliary procedure Interpolate returns the right assertions), and that its time and space complexity is polynomial in the data complexity of the input program and specification (again, under the assumption about Interpolate). We will also introduce some technical machinery required to prove these results. We begin with soundness (if the algorithm returns a result, then the result is correct), which is a direct consequence of Theorem 3.6.

Theorem 7.1 (Soundness) If the verification algorithm returns Safe, $\mathcal{P}$ satisfies the given specification. If it returns Unsafe, the program does not satisfy the given specification. ⌟

We now move on to our completeness result. No algorithm exists that is complete in the strong sense (due to the halting problem). Instead, we show that the verification algorithm is complete in the sense that, if a there exists a safety proof for a program, then the algorithm will find one *under the assumption that Interpolate produces the right assertions*. We formalize this by assuming that Interpolate is a nondeterministic procedure that may return any valid interpolant, and showing that the following holds:

Theorem 7.2 (Completeness) If a program has a Hoare safety proof, then there exists a run of the verification algorithm that terminates with a Safe result. ⌟

In fact, we can strengthen this completeness theorem and give bounds on the time and space required by the verification algorithm:

Theorem 7.3 (Complexity) If a program $\mathcal{P}$ has a Hoare proof that it satisfies a specification $\varphi_{\mathsf{pre}}/\varphi_{\mathsf{post}}$, then there exists a run of the verification algorithm that terminates with an iDFG of size polynomial in the data complexity of $\mathcal{P}$ (w.r.t. $\varphi_{\mathsf{pre}}/\varphi_{\mathsf{post}}$). Moreover, the number of iterations of the main loop of the algorithm required to produce this proof is polynomial in the data complexity. ⌟

The proof of this theorem requires some technical machinery, which will be presented in the following. However, we present some early intuition on the proof for readers that wish to skip the technical details in the remainder of this section. We assume that we are given a proof presented as an iDFG G_0 (the size of which we may assume is polynomial in the data complexity, by Theorem 5.4). Given any trace τ, there is a substructure of G_0 that corresponds to τ (roughly speaking, this structure corresponds to the accepting run of τ through the AFA corresponding to G_0). Under the assumption that Interpolate produces the assertions corresponding to this structure, construct-idfg($\tau, \varphi_{\mathsf{pre}}, \varphi_{\mathsf{post}}$) produces this structure exactly. Intuitively, this is a way of reasoning about why the appropriate assertions exist for Interpolate to produce. We can show that G_0 is "covered" by finitely many such substructures, so that the algorithm will terminate in finite time with a proof that is "essentially the same" as G_0.

Proofs

We now present the technical machinery required to prove Theorem 7.3. The main concept we introduce here is *iDFG embeddings*, which is a structural relationship between iDFGs. We say that an iDFG G embeds into G' if G can be mapped onto a subgraph of G' in a way that is, in some sense, "tight". Formally, we define an iDFG embedding as follows:

Definition 7.4 (Embedding) Given iDFGs

$$G = \langle V, E, \varphi_{\mathsf{pre}}, \varphi_{\mathsf{post}}, v_0, V_{\mathsf{final}} \rangle$$

and

$$G' = \langle V', E', \varphi_{\mathsf{pre}}, \varphi_{\mathsf{post}}, v_0', V_{\mathsf{final}}' \rangle$$

sharing the same precondition and postcondition, we say that a map $h : V \to V'$ is an *embedding* if the following hold:

- $\forall v \in V$, $\mathsf{act}(v) = \mathsf{act}(h(v))$ and
$$\{\varphi \mid \exists u.u \xrightarrow{\varphi} v \in E\} = \{\varphi \mid \exists u.u \xrightarrow{\varphi} h(v) \in E'\}$$
- $h(v_0) = v_0'$
- $\forall v \in V_{\mathsf{final}}, h(v) \in V_{\mathsf{final}}'$
- $\forall u \xrightarrow{\varphi} v \in E, h(u) \xrightarrow{\varphi} h(v) \in E'$

If such an embedding exists, we say that G *embeds* into G'. ⌟

The main property of interest concerning embeddings is the following lemma:

Lemma 7.5 If G and G' are iDFGs such that G embeds into G', then $[\![G]\!] \subseteq [\![G']\!]$. ⌟

The key idea of our completeness theorem is that we can use a given iDFG proof G_0 as an oracle to guide the interpolation procedure, so that construct-idfg$(\tau, \varphi_{\text{pre}}, \varphi_{\text{post}})$ will yield an iDFG representing some substructure of the target proof G_0 (i.e., an iDFG that embeds into G_0). Formally,

Lemma 7.6 For any iDFG $G = \langle V, E, \varphi_{\text{pre}}, \varphi_{\text{post}}, v_0, V_{\text{final}} \rangle$ and any trace $\tau \in [\![G]\!]$, there is a run of construct-idfg$(\tau, \varphi_{\text{pre}}, \varphi_{\text{post}})$ that produces an iDFG G_τ such that G_τ embeds into G. ⌟

Our proof of Theorem 7.2 is based on being able to maintain a loop invariant that G embeds into some target proof G_0. In order to prove this invariant, we must show that if G and G' embed into some target proof G_0, then $G \curlywedge G'$ also embeds into G_0. Formally, we have the following:

Lemma 7.7 For any iDFGs G and G' sharing the same precondition and postcondition, both G and G' embed into $G \curlywedge G'$. For any complete iDFG G_0 such that G and G' both embed into G_0, $G \curlywedge G'$ embeds into G_0[1]. ⌟

We are now ready to provide a sketch of the proof of Theorem 7.3. In fact, we will prove a stronger (by Theorem 5.4) result: for any reduced, complete iDFG G_0 such that $\mathcal{L}(\mathcal{P}) \subseteq [\![G_0]\!]$, there exists a run of the verification algorithm that terminates with an iDFG G such that $\mathcal{L}(\mathcal{P}) \subseteq [\![G]\!]$ and such that G embeds into G_0 (since G and G_0 are reduced and complete, the fact that G embeds into G_0 implies that G is no larger than G_0). Moreover, regardless of how traces are chosen from $\mathcal{L}(\mathcal{P}) \setminus [\![G]\!]$, the algorithm will terminate in at most $|V_0|$ iterations, where $|V_0|$ is the number of vertices in G_0.

The proof is by induction: we assume that at the start of the iteration of the loop, G embeds into G_0, and prove that there is an execution of the loop body such that the number of vertices in G increases and such that G still embeds into G_0 at the end of the loop.

Let $\tau \in \mathcal{L}(\mathcal{P}) \setminus [\![G]\!]$. Since G_0 is a safety proof, we must have $\tau \in \mathcal{L}(G_0)$. By Lemma 7.6, there exists a run of construct-idfg$(\tau, \varphi_{\text{pre}}, \varphi_{\text{post}})$ that produces an iDFG G_τ that embeds into G_0. We let $G' = G \curlywedge G_\tau$ be the iDFG at the end of the loop. The invariant that G' embeds into G_0 is ensured by Lemma 7.7. The condition that G' has more vertices than G is ensured by the fact that G_τ embeds into G', but not G (since that would contradict $\tau \notin [\![G]\!]$).

8. Related Work

Concurrent Program Verification. As mentioned above, existing approaches to the algorithmic verification of concurrent programs, e.g. [11, 12, 17, 20], provide a different angle of attack at the same fundamental issue: the exponential space complexity (exponential in the number of threads). None of these approaches shifts the burden of the exponential growth of space towards a combinatorial problem (over finite graphs). The practical potential of these approaches is demonstrated on a selection of practical examples. None of the approaches investigates the question whether there are assumptions under which the space complexity is polynomial. The exponential cost of space is not an issue that occurs just in theory. We observe the exponential curve, e.g., when we run THREADER [17] and SLAB [12] on the ticket algorithm and the program Increment (see Section 2). These are two concurrent programs (parametrized in the number n of threads) where our approach comes with a formal guarantee for polynomial space consumption.

[1] This proposition establishes that $G \curlywedge G'$ is a coproduct in the category of reduced complete iDFGs, where the morphisms are embeddings.

All the approaches mentioned above are based on abstraction. The construction of an iDFG from a trace can be viewed as an abstraction of the trace. It is interesting to compare the two concepts of abstraction. In the setting of the above-mentioned approaches, if an abstraction is *too coarse*, it introduces spurious errors. In our setting, it is desirable to abstract a trace aggressively (in order to obtain a succinct iDFG that denotes a large set of traces). This is because iDFG's are used to represent *correct* behaviours rather than program behaviours. More over-approximation leads to a larger set of correct traces.

Compositional Proof Rules. Our notion of inductive data flow graph bears similarities with Owicki-Gries style proof rules and other compositional proof rules for concurrent programs (e.g., the use of local assertions, of conjunction, of stability) [2]. Compositionality is often thought of as the only way to go for polynomial-sized proofs (in the number of threads). Our approach to algorithmic verification can be viewed as the automation of a *non-compositional* proof rule (the proof rule is obtained by reformulating the characterization of program correctness in Theorem 3.6). However, one can view sets of traces as *semantics-based* modules (as opposed to modules based on the syntactic construction of programs). These modules capture the intuitive notion of scenarios. The composition of modules is set union.

Thread-Modular Verification. The thread-modular approach to verification [15] achieves modularity at the expense of giving up completeness. In fact, the approach is complete exactly for the class of programs whose correctness can be proven in Owicki-Gries style proofs without auxiliary variables [10, 25]. Our approach, in contrast, is motivated by combining the goal of full (relative) completeness with space efficiency.

Data Flow Graphs. Variations of data flow graphs have a long history within the compilers community, both as a means for exposing parallelism in sequential code for parallelizing compilers [14, 23], and as a data structure for use in sparse dataflow analysis [21, 31]. Our use of DFGs is closer to this first line of work: construct-idfg can be seen as a procedure that exposes the parallelism in a single example trace. For a parallelizing compiler to be correct, parallelization must preserve the behaviour of the sequential code; the correctness of construct-idfg depends on the much weaker condition that a proof argument is preserved.

More recently, DFGs have been used for invariant generation in both concurrent [13] and sequential [28] settings. The work of [13] is particularly relevant: it uses data flow graphs to generate numerical invariants for parameterized concurrent programs. These invariants can be used to prove safety properties, but if the invariants are too weak to prove a property of interest, a false alarm is reported. Our verification algorithm produces no false alarms, and can provide a counter-example for properties that fail. Moreover, the inductive DFGs presented in this paper are capable of expressing proofs that cannot be represented using the (variable-labeled, rather than assertion-labeled) DFGs used in [13] (i.e., every DFG proof in [13] corresponds to an iDFG, but some iDFG's do not correspond to DFG proofs).

Trace Abstraction. The work in [18, 19] presents an automata-theoretic approach to the analysis and verification of sequential and recursive programs. The present paper continues this line of work and extends it to concurrent programs. Another form of trace abstraction appears in the work on trace covers and trace partitioning [5, 26, 30]. There, the general goal is to obtain to obtain more precision by targeting the static analysis to specific subsets of program traces. In contrast, in our work, the subsets of program traces are defined by the iDFGs (which are constructed via the static analysis of a single trace).

9. Conclusion and Future Work

In this paper, we have introduced a new approach for the verification of concurrent programs. The approach succeeds in putting the well-established static analysis techniques for sequential programs to work, namely by assembling the output of the static analysis applied to interleaved executions in a space-efficient way. We formalize under what assumptions the space efficiency can be guaranteed. For fundamental reasons, we cannot avoid the exponential explosion in the number of threads but we can shift its burden to a combinatorial problem over finite graphs ("to a place where it hurts less").

The approach has an interesting practical potential. The focus in this paper was to introduce the approach and to investigate its formal foundation. There are several directions in which one can explore the practical potential of the approach. This should be the focus of future work.

The most critical operation is perhaps the construction of an iDFG from a given trace τ of the program (construct-idfg). In Section 6.1, we already hinted at several directions for practical optimizations. We need to develop and evaluate these optimizations for practical examples.

The operation construct-idfg depends on the static analysis that is applied to the trace (as a special case of a sequential program). The abstract values generated by the static analysis are used to extract single conjuncts for the labeling of an iDFG with inductive assertions. One possible research direction for practical implemetation of construct-idfg is to design a procedure that heuristically splits formulae into "independent" clauses that can be achieved in parallel (for use in the current Interpolate procedure). Another direction is to develop a Craig interpolation procedure that can generate the branching structure of an iDFG directly from a resolution proof.

References

[1] G. R. Andrews. *Concurrent programming - principles and practice*. Benjamin/Cummings, 1991. ISBN 978-0-8053-0086-4.

[2] K. R. Apt, F. S. de Boer, and E. R. Olderog. *Verification of Sequential and Concurrent Programs*. Springer-Verlag, 2009. ISBN 978-1-84882-744-8.

[3] J. Berdine, T. Lev-Ami, R. Manevich, G. Ramalingam, and M. Sagiv. Thread quantification for concurrent shape analysis. In *CAV*, volume 5123 of *LNCS*, pages 399–413. Springer Berlin / Heidelberg, 2008.

[4] B. Blanchet, P. Cousot, R. Cousot, J. Feret, L. Mauborgne, A. Miné, D. Monniaux, and X. Rival. A static analyzer for large safety-critical software. In *PLDI*, pages 196–207, 2003.

[5] F. Bourdoncle. Abstract interpretation by dynamic partitioning. *Journal of Functional Programming*, 2(04):407–435, 1992.

[6] J. Brzozowski and E. Leiss. On equations for regular languages, finite automata, and sequential networks. *Theoretical Computer Science*, 10 (1):19 – 35, 1980.

[7] A. K. Chandra, D. C. Kozen, and L. J. Stockmeyer. Alternation. *J. ACM*, 28(1):114–133, Jan. 1981.

[8] E. M. Clarke and E. A. Emerson. Design and synthesis of synchronization skeletons using branching-time temporal logic. In *Logic of Programs*, pages 52–71, 1981.

[9] P. Cousot and R. Cousot. Abstract interpretation: A unified lattice model for static analysis of programs by construction or approximation of fixpoints. In *POPL*, pages 238–252, 1977.

[10] R. Cousot. *Fondements des méthodes de preuve d'invariance et de fatalité de programmes parallèles*. les-Nancy, 1985.

[11] A. F. Donaldson, A. Kaiser, D. Kroening, and T. Wahl. Symmetry-aware predicate abstraction for shared-variable concurrent programs. In *CAV*, pages 356–371, 2011.

[12] K. Dräger, A. Kupriyanov, B. Finkbeiner, and H. Wehrheim. Slab: a certifying model checker for infinite-state concurrent systems. In *TACAS*, pages 271–274, 2010.

[13] A. Farzan and Z. Kincaid. Verification of parameterized concurrent programs by modular reasoning about data and control. In *POPL*, pages 297–308, 2012.

[14] J. Ferrante, K. J. Ottenstein, and J. D. Warren. The program dependence graph and its use in optimization. *ACM Trans. Program. Lang. Syst.*, 9(3):319–349, 1987.

[15] C. Flanagan and S. Qadeer. Thread-modular model checking. In *SPIN*, pages 213–224, 2003.

[16] A. Griggio. A Practical Approach to Satisfiability Modulo Linear Integer Arithmetic. *JSAT*, 8:1–27, January 2012.

[17] A. Gupta, C. Popeea, and A. Rybalchenko. Predicate abstraction and refinement for verifying multi-threaded programs. In *POPL*, pages 331–344, 2011.

[18] M. Heizmann, J. Hoenicke, and A. Podelski. Refinement of trace abstraction. In *SAS*, pages 69–85, 2009.

[19] M. Heizmann, J. Hoenicke, and A. Podelski. Nested interpolants. In *POPL*, pages 471–482, 2010.

[20] T. A. Henzinger, R. Jhala, R. Majumdar, and S. Qadeer. Thread-modular abstraction refinement. In *CAV*, pages 262–274, 2003.

[21] R. Johnson and K. Pingali. Dependence-based program analysis. In *PLDI*, pages 78–89, 1993.

[22] V. Kahlon, S. Sankaranarayanan, and A. Gupta. Semantic reduction of thread interleavings in concurrent programs. In *TACAS*, pages 124–138, 2009.

[23] D. J. Kuck, R. H. Kuhn, D. A. Padua, B. Leasure, and M. Wolfe. Dependence graphs and compiler optimizations. In *POPL*, pages 207–218, 1981.

[24] L. Lamport. A new solution of Dijkstra's concurrent programming problem. *Commun. ACM*, 17(8):453–455, 1974.

[25] A. Malkis. *Cartesian abstraction and verification of multithreaded programs*. PhD thesis, University of Freiburg, 2010.

[26] L. Mauborgne and X. Rival. Trace partitioning in abstract interpretation based static analyzers. In *ESOP*, page 520, 2005.

[27] A. Miné. Static analysis of run-time errors in embedded critical parallel C programs. In *ESOP*, pages 398–418, 2011.

[28] H. Oh, K. Heo, W. Lee, W. Lee, and K. Yi. Design and implementation of sparse global analyses for C-like languages. In *PLDI*, pages 229–238, 2012.

[29] S. Owicki and D. Gries. Verifying properties of parallel programs: an axiomatic approach. *Commun. ACM*, 19:279–285, May 1976.

[30] A. Venet. Abstract cofibered domains: application to the alias analysis of untyped programs. In *SAS*, pages 366–382, 1996.

[31] D. Weise, R. F. Crew, M. Ernst, and B. Steensgaard. Value dependence graphs: representation without taxation. In *POPL*, pages 297–310, 1994.

Abstract Conflict Driven Learning

Vijay D'Silva
Department of Computer Science
University of California, Berkeley
vijayd@eecs.berkeley.edu

Leopold Haller
Department of Computer Science
Oxford University
leopold.haller@cs.ox.ac.uk

Daniel Kroening
Department of Computer Science
Oxford University
daniel.kroening@cs.ox.ac.uk

Abstract

Modern satisfiability solvers implement an algorithm, called Conflict Driven Clause Learning, which combines search for a model with analysis of conflicts. We show that this algorithm can be generalised to solve the lattice-theoretic problem of determining if an additive transformer on a Boolean lattice is always bottom. Our generalised procedure combines overapproximations of greatest fixed points with underapproximations of least fixed points to obtain more precise results than computing fixed points in isolation. We generalise implication graphs used in satisfiability solvers to derive underapproximate transformers from overapproximate ones. Our generalisation provides a new method for static analyzers that operate over non-distributive lattices to reason about properties that require disjunction.

Categories and Subject Descriptors F.3 [*Logics and Meanings of Programs*]: Specifying and Verifying and Reasoning about Programs

Keywords Satisfiability, Conflict Driven Clause Learning, Lattices

1. The Algebraic Essence of Satisfiability Solvers

The performance of solvers for the Boolean satisfiability problem (SAT) has improved at an exponential rate in the last decade. Several factors contribute to these improvements including and elegant algorithm, efficient, architecture-aware implementations of data structures, and heuristics that exploit the non-adversarial nature of practical problem instances. A recent survey of these developments by Malik and Zhang [21] concludes with the following question:

> *"Given its theoretical hardness, the practical success of* SAT *has come as a surprise to many in the computer science community. [...] Can we take these lessons to other problems and domains?"*

This paper presents an approach to instantiating the Conflict Driven Clause Learning algorithm (CDCL) in SAT solvers on new problems. We introduce a lattice-theoretic generalisation of Boolean satisfiability. The *bottom-everywhere problem* is to determine if a function on a lattice maps all elements of the lattice to bottom. Instances of the bottom-everywhere problem include satisfiability for formulae in propositional logic and quantifier-free first order theories, source to target reachability in transition systems, language emptiness for automata, and assertion violation in programs. We show that CDCL solves an instance of the bottom-everywhere problem for certain functions on finite, powerset lattices.

The contribution of this paper is *Abstract Conflict Driven Clause Learning* (ACDCL), a strict, mathematical generalisation of CDCL to lattice-based abstractions. We show that CDCL is a specific technique to combine overapproximations of a greatest fixed point with underapproximations of a least fixed point. We provide a correctness argument for ACDCL under general, lattice-theoretic conditions. These conditions are satisfied by abstract domains used in practice and lead to a new family of analysis procedures. Our work also enables a new understanding of CDCL, discussed next.

Abstract Interpretation Perspectives of CDCL

Many existing lattices used in static analysis lack negation, have meet operations that precisely model conjunction, and join operations that overapproximate disjunction. Precision loss due to joins is often eliminated by enriching a domain or analysis with disjunction. Such enrichment may suffer from *case explosion*, meaning that the number of disjunctive cases to be considered grows infeasibly large as the analysis progresses.

We show that the main data structure in a SAT solver, called a partial assignment, represents elements of a well known abstract domain, and that constraint propagation in SAT solvers is fixed point iteration in this domain. SAT solvers compute fixed points in non-Boolean abstract domains. The conceptual insight of this paper is that learning techniques used by SAT solvers can be viewed as synthesising an abstract transformer for negation. The combination of precise conjunction in the partial assignments domain with imprecise negation provided by learning allow a solver to reason indirectly about disjunction without enumerating cases. We show that abstract domains used in practice satisfy the conditions required to support learning.

A second insight of this paper is that the implication graph construction in SAT solvers is a technique for constructing an underapproximate transformer starting from an overapproximation. An abstract transformer can be viewed as a directed graph in which edges represent transformer application. The inverted graph represents a dual transformer and sets of vertices approximate applications of this dual transformer. In a SAT solver, the graph represents a deduction transformer and its inverse represents an abduction transformer. When lifted to programs, we can start with an overapproximate postcondition transformer and derive an underapproximate precondition transformer.

The insights above have practical ramifications, which we have demonstrated with two practical instantiations of ACDCL. We have instantiated ACDCL with the interval abstract domain to analyse C programs that manipulate floating point variables [14]. Our analyser is more precise that a standard static analyser and more efficient than an SMT solver, if either is run in isolation. We have also instantiated ACDCL in the MathSAT framework to derive an SMT solver for

POPL'13, January 23–25, 2013, Rome, Italy.

floating point logic [17]. In both cases, our instantiations avoid case explosion experienced by several competing tools.

Contribution and Content

This paper presents *Abstract Conflict Driven Learning* (ACDL), a procedure for reasoning about functions on Boolean lattices by operating on non-Boolean lattices. Our goal is to present an account of ACDCL that reveals its generality and to present correctness arguments that apply to all instantiations of ACDCL. Towards this end, we make the contributions below.

1. The bottom-everywhere problem, a lattice-theoretic problem which encompasses satisfiability of logical formulae, reachability in transition systems, and assertion violation in programs.
2. A view of CDCL as a procedure for solving a specific instance of the bottom-everywhere problem.
3. A generalisation of CDCL to solve the bottom-everywhere problem by combining greatest fixed point and least fixed point computation.
4. A novel technique for deriving underapproximate transformers from overapproximate transformers, based on a generalisation of implication graphs to abstract domains.
5. Lattice-theoretic soundness and completeness arguments that apply to all instances of ACDCL.

The paper is organised as follows: We introduce the bottom-everywhere problem in Section 2 and discuss several instances of this problem. We apply abstract interpretation to derive over- and underapproximate solutions to the bottom-everywhere problem in Section 3, and combine these approximations in Sections 4 and 5. The generalisation of implication graphs to abstract domains is discussed and illustrated in Section 6.

2. The Bottom-Everywhere Problem

We introduce the bottom-everywhere problem and show that satisfiability of formulae and error reachability in transition systems are instances of this problem. Subsequent sections lift CDCL to solve this problem.

Lattice-Theoretic Terminology A lattice is called *bounded* if it has a greatest element, called *top* and denoted $\top$, and has a least element called *bottom* and denoted $\bot$. A function f on a complete lattice L is *additive* if $f(x \sqcup y) = f(x) \sqcup f(y)$ and is *completely additive* if $f(\bigsqcup X) = \bigsqcup f(X)$. A completely additive function maps $\bot$ to $\bot$. The dual notions are called multiplicative and completely multiplicative. The function f is *reductive* if $f(x) \sqsubseteq x$ for all x and is *extensive* if $f(x) \sqsupseteq x$ for all x. A function is *idempotent* if $f(f(x)) = f(x)$ for all x. A *transformer* is a monotone function on a lattice. An *upper closure* is an idempotent and extensive transformer, and a *lower closure* is an idempotent and reductive transformer. The *pointwise order* $f \sqsubseteq g$ between functions from a set to a poset holds if $f(x) \sqsubseteq g(x)$ holds for all x. The *pointwise meet* of f and g, denoted $f \sqcap g$, where both functions map into a lattice is defined as $\lambda x.\ f(x) \sqcap g(x)$. The pointwise join is similarly defined. The set of transformers on a complete lattice form a complete lattice under the pointwise order. The *De Morgan dual* of a function f on a Boolean lattice is $\tilde{f} \mathrel{\hat{=}} \neg \circ f \circ \neg$. We require the following property of De Morgan duals.

Proposition 1. *If f is a completely additive, reductive function on a powerset lattice, $\tilde{f}$ is a completely multiplicative, extensive function.*

The least fixed point of a transformer f on a complete lattice is denoted $\mathsf{lfp}(f)$ and the greatest fixed point is denoted $\mathsf{gfp}(f)$.

2.1 Bottom and Top Everywhere

The material below is new.

Definition 2. *A function f on a bounded lattice is* bottom-everywhere *if $f(x) = \bot$ for all x. The bottom-everywhere problem is to determine if a function on a lattice is bottom-everywhere.*

A *non-bottom witness* is an element a such that $f(a)$ is not bottom. A non-bottom witness a is minimal if no $b \sqsubset a$ is a non-bottom witness. The *top-everywhere* property and *top-everywhere problem* are similarly defined. The dual notions for the top-everywhere problem are a non-top witness and a maximal non-top witness.

In this paper, we consider the bottom-everywhere problem for completely additive, reductive functions on powerset lattices.

Lemma 3. *A completely additive, reductive function on a powerset lattice is a lower closure.*

Proof. Consider a function $f : \mathscr{P}(S) \to \mathscr{P}(S)$. For each x in S, $f(\{x\})$ is either $\emptyset$ or is $\{x\}$, because f is reductive. Since f is completely additive, $f(X)$ equals $\bigcup f(X)$ for every subset X of S. In particular, $f(X)$ equals $\{x \in X \mid f(\{x\}) \neq \emptyset\}$. It follows that $f(f(X))$ equals $f(X)$. □

Due to Lemma 3 we abbreviate 'completely additive, reductive function' to 'additive closure' for the rest of the paper. Theorem 4 below is a consequence of Lemma 3. It is straightforward to prove but the fixed point view is valuable because an abstraction of a lower closure may not be idempotent, in which case iterating a transformer in the abstract yields strictly more precision than applying it once.

Theorem 4. *The following statements are equivalent for a completely additive, reductive function f on a powerset lattice.*

1. *f is bottom-everywhere.*
2. *$\mathsf{gfp}(f)$ is bottom.*
3. *$\tilde{f}$ is top-everywhere.*
4. *$\mathsf{lfp}(\tilde{f})$ is top.*

The implication from 1 to 2 is straightforward, while the implication 2 to 1 holds because f is a lower closure. The equivalence of 1 and 3 follows by negation and of 3 and 4 due to the closure property and complementation of fixed points.

Next, we show that two well-known problems, satisfiability and error reachability, can be reduced to the bottom-everywhere problem. Neither reduction is mathematically surprising but allows us to think of decision problems rather than function problems.

2.2 Unsatisfiability as Bottom Everywhere

Let *Struct* be a set of structures and *Form* be a set of formulae, and $\models \subseteq \mathit{Struct} \times \mathit{Form}$ be a satisfaction relation between structures and formulae. If (σ, φ) is in $\models$, we write $\sigma \models \varphi$, and say σ *satisfies* φ, or that σ *is a model of* φ. The details of the structures and the formulae are not relevant for the formalisation. A formula φ is *satisfiable over Struct* if some σ in *Struct* satisfies φ, and is *unsatisfiable* over *Struct* otherwise. We drop the qualifier "over *Struct*". The *satisfiability problem* is to determine if a given formula φ is satisfiable.

We formulate satisfiability in terms of a transformer. The *domain* of structures is $(\mathscr{P}(\mathit{Struct}), \subseteq, \cup, \cap)$. The *model transformer* $\mathit{mod}_\varphi : \mathscr{P}(\mathit{Struct}) \to \mathscr{P}(\mathit{Struct})$ maps a set of structures to the subset containing only models of φ.

$$\mathit{mod}_\varphi(S) \mathrel{\hat{=}} \{\sigma \in S \mid \sigma \models \varphi\}$$

Properties of φ can be expressed as properties of mod_φ. The set of models of φ is $\mathit{mod}_\varphi(\mathit{Struct})$ and φ is unsatisfiable exactly if $\mathit{mod}_\varphi(\mathit{Struct})$ is empty. Observe that mod_φ is completely additive and reductive, hence it is in the scope of problems we consider.

We denote the function $(\neg \circ \mathit{mod}_\varphi \circ \neg)$ as ucmod_φ and call ucmod_φ the *conflict transformer*. The conflict transformer ucmod_φ adds to any set of structures all countermodels of φ. The set of countermodels of φ is $ucmod_\varphi(\emptyset)$ and φ is unsatisfiable exactly if $ucmod_\varphi(\emptyset)$ contains all structures. Observe that $ucmod_\varphi$ is completely multiplicative and extensive.

Theorem 5. *A formula φ is unsatisfiable exactly if mod_φ is bottom-everywhere.*

A non-bottom witness for mod_φ is a set of structures that contains a model of φ. A minimal non-bottom witness is a singleton set containing a model of φ. A non-top witness for $ucmod_\varphi$ is a set of structures strictly contained in $Struct$ that excludes some models of φ. A maximal non-top witness for $ucmod_\varphi$ is a set that contains all structures except one model of φ.

We define two logics for use in examples.

Propositional Logic Let $Prop$ be a finite set of propositional variables. The set of *literals* is $Lit \mathrel{\hat{=}} \{p, \neg p \mid p \in Prop\}$, containing a variable or its negation. A *clause* is a disjunction of literals and a CNF *formula* is a conjunction of clauses. As is common in the SAT literature, we view clauses as sets of literals and formulae as sets of clauses. The set of truth values is $\mathbb{B} \mathrel{\hat{=}} \{\mathsf{t}, \mathsf{f}\}$. Literals, formulae and clauses are interpreted over functions $Asg \mathrel{\hat{=}} Prop \to \mathbb{B}$, from variables to truth values, and are called *propositional assignments*. The entailment relation $\models$ is defined as follows. For each assignment σ and literal l, $\sigma \models l$ exactly if $\sigma(l) = \mathsf{t}$ if l is a variable, and $\sigma(l) = \mathsf{f}$ if l is the negation of a variable. For each clause C, $\sigma \models C$ exactly if $\sigma \models l$ for some literal l in C. For a CNF formula φ, we say $\sigma \models \varphi$ if $\sigma \models C$ for every clause C in φ.

Inequality Logic Inequality logic can express order between variables. Let $Vars$ be a set of first-order variables. The set of difference predicates is $\{x < y \mid x, y \in Vars\}$. The set of inequality literals contains all difference predicates and their negations. We interpret difference formulae over integers. The set of structures $Struct \mathrel{\hat{=}} Vars \to \mathbb{Z}$ consists of functions from variables to integers. A structure σ satisfies a predicate $x < y$ if the inequality $\sigma(x) < \sigma(y)$ holds. For formulae, the entailment relation $\models$ is defined as expected.

2.3 Feasible Traces via Bottom Everywhere

Let $M = (S, T)$ be a transition system where S is a set of states and $T \subseteq S \times S$ is a transition relation. Let S^+ be the set of non-empty sequences of states. A trace is a sequence $\tau = \tau_0, \ldots, \tau_{n-1}$ satisfying that every (τ_i, τ_{i+1}) is a valid transition. A state t is reachable from s if there exists a trace starting in s and ending in t. Given sets of states P and Q, the *feasible trace problem* is to determine if there exists a trace from a state in P to a state in Q.

We formulate the feasible trace problem as a bottom-everywhere problem. The *domain of sequences* is $\mathscr{P}(S^+)$. The *feasible trace transformer* $trace_{P,Q} : \mathscr{P}(S^+) \to \mathscr{P}(S^+)$ maps a set of non-empty sequences of states to the subset containing only traces that start from a state in P and reach a state in Q. We assume τ_n is the last state of τ below.

$$trace_{P,Q}(X) \mathrel{\hat{=}} \{\tau \in X \mid \tau \text{ is a trace}, \tau_0 \in P, \tau_n \in Q\}$$

The set of traces from P to Q has several fixed point characterisations, consolidated by Cousot [6]. Once again, the function $trace_{P,Q}$ is completely additive and reductive.

We denote the function $(\neg \circ trace_{P,Q} \circ \neg)$ as $uctrace_{P,Q}$, and call it the *countertrace transformer*. The set $uctrace_{P,Q}(X)$ contains the set X, as well as all sequences that are not traces, all sequences that start in P but do not lead to Q and all sequences that end in Q but do not start in P.

Theorem 6. *Given a transition system, and sets of states P and Q, there is no trace from P to Q exactly if $trace_{P,Q}$ is bottom-everywhere.*

A non-bottom witness for $trace_{P,Q}$ is a set of sequences containing a trace from P to Q. A minimal non-bottom witness is a singleton set containing a feasible trace from P to Q. A non-top witness for $uctrace_{P,Q}$ is a set of sequences that excludes a trace from P to Q. A maximal non-top witness contains all sequences except one trace from P to Q.

The view of feasible traces as bottom-everywhere lifts to reachability and assertion checking in programs. The definition of the set of traces of a program is well-known and is not recalled here. We directly apply the procedures developed in this paper to reason about programs.

2.4 Reachable States via Bottom Everywhere

We consider reachability problems defined in terms of states rather than over traces. We make such a distinction because the details of lifting CDCL are different for trace-based abstractions and for state-based abstractions. The material recalled here is also required to distinguish CDCL from Cousot's forward-backward iteration [7].

Let $M = (S, T)$ be a transition system where S is a set of states and $T \subseteq S \times S$ is a transition relation. The concrete lattice of states is $\mathscr{P}(S)$. Recall that a transition system defines the two transformers below.

$$post(X) \mathrel{\hat{=}} \{t \in S \mid (s,t) \text{ is in } T \text{ and } s \text{ is in } X\}$$
$$pre(X) \mathrel{\hat{=}} \{s \in S \mid (s,t) \text{ is in } T \text{ and } t \text{ is in } X\}$$

The sets of forward and backward reachable states have standard fixed point characterisations, recalled below. Forward-backward reachable states consist of pairs (X, Y) such that every state in X reaches some state in Y and vice-versa. When applied in an abstract domain, this kind of iteration yields strictly more information than forward analysis or backward analysis in isolation.

$$freach_{P,Q}(X) \mathrel{\hat{=}} X \cap [\mathsf{lfp}\, x.\ (P \cup post(x))] \cap Q$$
$$breach_{P,Q}(X) \mathrel{\hat{=}} X \cap [\mathsf{lfp}\, x.\ (Q \cup pre(x))] \cap P$$
$$fbreach_{P,Q}(X, Y) \mathrel{\hat{=}} [\mathsf{lfp}\, x.\ (P \cap Y) \cup post(x),\ \mathsf{lfp}\, x.\ (Q \cap X) \cup pre(x)]$$

The functions $freach_{P,Q}$ and $breach_{P,Q}$ above are completely additive and reductive. The function $fbreach_{P,Q}$ is completely additive (see Chapter 22 of Cousot's notes [7] for a proof). To see that $fbreach_{P,Q}$ is not reductive, consider $fbreach_{P,Q}(P, Q)$, which will contain the states reachable from P and Q respectively. Component-wise intersection can be used to make the function $fbreach_{P,Q}$ reductive.

Theorem 7. *The following are equivalent, given a transition system and sets of states P and Q.*

1. *No state in Q is reachable from a state in P.*
2. *$freach_{P,Q}$ is bottom-everywhere.*
3. *$breach_{P,Q}$ is bottom-everywhere.*
4. *$fbreach_{P,Q}$ is bottom-everywhere.*

The proof of the first three statements is straightforward. The proof of equivalence to 4 is due to Cousot [7]. A minimal non-bottom witness for $freach_{P,Q}$ is a state in Q that is reachable from P. A minimal non-bottom witness for $breach_{P,Q}$ is a state in P from which a state in Q is reachable.

The function $(\neg \circ freach_{P,Q} \circ \neg)$ maps a set of states X to a set containing X and states that are not reachable from P and states not in Q. Observe that such a function can directly be computed by computing a fixed point using the function $\neg \circ post \circ \neg$. The same applies for $breach_{P,Q}$ and the function $\neg \circ pre \circ \neg$. These dual functions have been implemented in model checkers and used to compute fixed points. Henzinger et al. [19] discuss temporal properties that can be checked with these fixed points, and Cousot and Cousot [11] combine these fixed points with abstraction.

Note that the functions *fbreach*$_{P,Q}$ and $(\neg \circ$ *fbreach*$_{P,Q} \circ \neg)$ are different. Intuitively, forward-backward iteration exploits a temporal duality between forwards and backwards analysis. In contrast, ACDCL will exploit a different duality between functions and their De Morgan duals.

3. Abstract Procedures for Bottom-Everywhere

In this section, we apply abstraction to the bottom-everywhere problem. If an overapproximation of a function f on $\mathscr{P}(S)$ is bottom-everywhere, the function f is also bottom-everywhere. If an underapproximation of the dual function $\tilde{f}$ is top-everywhere, the function $\tilde{f}$ is also top-everywhere. We now highlight the overapproximate and underapproximate analysis present in SAT solvers and model checkers. We begin by recalling abstract interpretation.

Abstract Interpretation The key idea of abstract interpretation is to characterise solutions to a problem by a fixed point and derive approximate solutions by fixed point approximation. For convenience, we work in the Galois connection framework. Cousot and Cousot [10] extensively discuss generalisations. These generalisations are required to analyse theories such as linear arithmetic because the lattice of polyhedra is not complete, and for analysis of automata, and trace-based abstractions.

A *Galois connection* between posets $(C, \preccurlyeq)$ and $(A, \sqsubseteq)$, written $C \underset{\alpha}{\overset{\gamma}{\leftrightarrows}} A$, is a pair of monotone functions $\alpha : C \to A$ and $\gamma : A \to C$ satisfying that $\alpha(x) \sqsubseteq y$ holds exactly if $x \preccurlyeq \gamma(y)$ does. The lattice C is called the *concrete domain* and A is called the *abstract domain*. Monotone functions on C are called *concrete transformers* and those on A are called *abstract transformers*. An abstract transformer $fo : A \to A$ *soundly approximates* $f : C \to C$ if the pointwise order $f \circ \gamma \preccurlyeq \gamma \circ fo$ holds.

If $(C, \subseteq)$ is a powerset lattice, an abstract domain $(A, \sqsubseteq)$ is called an overapproximation because it satisfies $x \subseteq \gamma(\alpha(x))$ for all x. If $(A, \sqsupseteq)$ is an abstract domain of $(C, \supseteq)$ it is called an underapproximation of $(C, \subseteq)$ because it satisfies $x \supseteq \gamma(\alpha(x))$. A sound abstract transformer on an overapproximation is called a sound overapproximation and one on an underapproximation is called a sound underapproximation.

The next two notions formalise precision of an approximation. A Galois connection implies there is a maximally precise approximation $\alpha \circ f \circ \gamma$, called the *best abstract transformer*. An abstract transformer fo approximating f is *γ-complete at a* if $f(\gamma(a)) = \gamma(fo(a))$, and is *$\gamma$-complete* if it is γ-complete at every a. If an abstract transformer fo is γ-complete at a, no precision is lost. For example, if *post* is a concrete successor transformer and *apost* is a sound abstraction that is γ-complete at an abstract state a, every abstract transition from a also exists in the concrete. In other words, there are no spurious transitions. Giacobazzi and Quintarelli [16] discuss γ-completeness in detail.

Parametric Fixed Points We require the notion of a fixed point above (or below) an element. Let $f : L \to L$ be a monotone function on a complete lattice and a be an element of L. The *greatest fixed point below a* denoted $\mathsf{gfp}_a(f)$ is the greatest fixed point of the function $\lambda x. f(x \sqcap a)$. The *least fixed point above a* denoted $\mathsf{lfp}_a(f)$ is the least fixed point of the function $\lambda x. f(x \sqcup a)$. The *parametric fixed point* functions below map an element x of L to the least fixed point above x and greatest fixed point below x, respectively.

$$\mathsf{plfp}(f) \mathrel{\hat{=}} \lambda x.\mathsf{lfp}_x(f) \qquad \mathsf{pgfp}(f) \mathrel{\hat{=}} \lambda x.\mathsf{gfp}_x(f)$$

Extrapolation and Interpolation We use the terms extrapolation and interpolation for techniques used to accelerate fixed point computation. Figuratively, extrapolation operators move upwards or downwards from an element in a lattice, as illustrated in Figure 1. Interpolation operators move between elements.

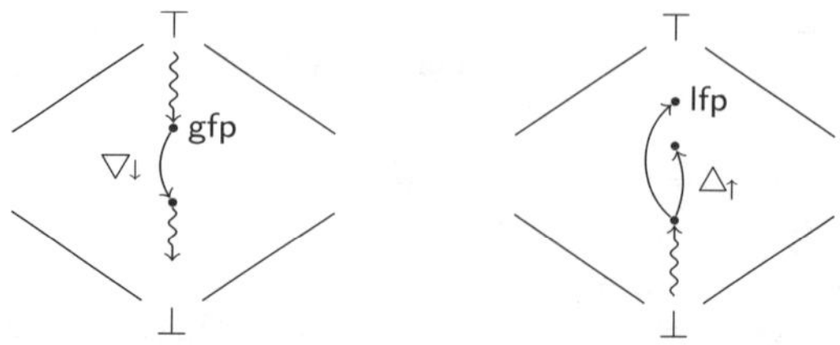

Figure 1. Downwards extrapolation to underapproximate a greatest fixed point, and upwards interpolation to underapproximate a least fixed point. The two operations are not dual.

Let L be a lattice. An *upwards extrapolation* $\nabla_{\uparrow} : L \to L$ is a unary *extensive* function. We write $\nabla_{\uparrow} a$ for the application $\nabla_{\uparrow}(a)$. The dual notion of a *downwards extrapolation* $\nabla_{\downarrow} : L \to L$ is a unary *reductive* function. The definitions above are based on (but not identical to) those for widening operators without a well-foundedness requirement [10].

A *downwards interpolation* is a binary function $\triangle_{\downarrow} : L \times L \to L$ satisfying that for all x and y in L, the inequality $x \sqsupseteq y$ implies the inequality $x \sqsupseteq \triangle_{\downarrow}(x, y) \sqsupseteq y$. We write interpolation application as $x \triangle_{\downarrow} y$. The standard definition of a *narrowing operator* extends downwards interpolation with a well-foundedness condition. The notions of *upwards interpolation* and dual narrowing, both denoted $\triangle_{\uparrow}$, are dually defined. Note that extrapolation and interpolation are not dual operations, just as widening and narrowing are not dual. Though interpolation is self-dual, we distinguish between upwards and downwards interpolation based on whether the operator is used in a least or greatest fixed point computation.

Downset Completion Downset completion is an operation that enriches an abstraction with disjunction [9]. Consider an abstraction $(A, \sqsubseteq, \sqcup, \sqcap)$ of a powerset lattice $\mathscr{P}(S)$ with concretisation γ. The abstraction A *is disjunctive* if $\gamma(a \sqcup b) = \gamma(a) \cup \gamma(b)$.

A subset Q of A is *downwards closed* if for every x in Q and y in A, $y \sqsubseteq x$ implies that y is in Q. A downwards-closed set is called a *downset*. The smallest downset containing Q is denoted $Q{\downarrow}$, and the downset of a singleton set $\{x\}$ is denoted $x{\downarrow}$. In examples, we denote a downset as the set of its maximal elements. We omit a general discussion of when such a representation is possible. The *downset lattice* over A, written $(\mathscr{D}(A), \subseteq, \cap, \cup)$, is the set of downsets of A ordered by inclusion. Downsets strictly generalise powersets because the downset lattice with respect to the identity relation is isomorphic to $\mathscr{P}(S)$.

The *downset completion* of A is the lattice $\mathscr{D}(A)$ with the abstraction and concretisation functions below. In contrast to the standard treatment, we use downsets as underapproximating abstractions.

$$\gamma_{\mathscr{D}(A)} : \mathscr{D}(A) \to \mathscr{P}(S) \qquad \gamma_{\mathscr{D}(A)}(Q) \mathrel{\hat{=}} \bigcup\{\gamma(x) \mid x \in Q\}$$
$$\alpha_{\mathscr{D}(A)} : \mathscr{P}(S) \to \mathscr{D}(A) \qquad \alpha_{\mathscr{D}(A)}(P) \mathrel{\hat{=}} \{x \mid \gamma(x) \subseteq P\}$$

Consult [9] for proofs that the pairs of functions above form Galois connections and that the domains are disjunctive.

3.1 Abstract Bottom-Everywhere

We apply abstract interpretation to determine if a function is bottom-everywhere. Let $(O, \sqsubseteq, \sqcup, \sqcap)$ be an abstract domain in a Galois connection with $(\mathscr{P}(S), \subseteq, \cup, \cap)$. We denote the abstraction and concretisation functions as α_O and γ_O. We assume that $\gamma_O(\bot)$ is the empty set.

Let $fo : O \to O$ be a sound abstraction of a completely additive, reductive function f. If $\mathsf{gfp}(fo)$ concretises to $\bot$, the function f is bottom-everywhere. If $\mathsf{gfp}(fo)$ does not concretise to $\bot$, we do not know if f is bottom-everywhere, due to imprecision in the transformer. This intuition is stated below and the proof follows from the basic soundness results of abstract interpretation.

Theorem 8. *If f a completely additive, reductive function on a powerset lattice, $fo : O \to O$ is a sound overapproximation of f, and* $\mathsf{gfp}(fo)$ *is $\bot$, the function f is bottom-everywhere.*

If we know that fo is γ-complete at some element a, we can determine, despite working in an abstraction, that f is not bottom-everywhere. Since fo only has to be γ-complete at a single element, the lattice and transformer may still be imprecise.

Proposition 9. *If fo is γ-complete at a and $\gamma(fo(a))$ is not $\bot$, f is not bottom-everywhere.*

The procedure Abstract-non-$\bot$ below takes as input an overapproximate transformer fo, an abstract element o and a downwards extrapolation operator $\nabla\downarrow$. In addition, a procedure to check emptiness $\gamma(o) = \emptyset$ is required together with a sufficient criterion for γ-completeness of fo. The procedure attempts to determine if fo is bottom on all elements below o in the lattice. The output is a pair with the first element being either $\bot$, not $\bot$ or unknown, and the second element representing the last lattice element obtained.

If $\mathsf{pgfp}(fo)(o)$ concretises to $\bot$, the function f is bottom on elements below $\gamma_O(o)$. If fo is not bottom on the fixed point o' and is γ-complete at o', we know f is not bottom-everywhere. Neither condition above may hold due to imprecision in the transformer or domain. In this case, downwards extrapolation is used to check if fo is also bottom on elements below the fixed point. Unlike standard applications of widening, downwards extrapolation is applied here to improve precision.

Algorithm 1: Abstract Search for a Non-$\bot$ Witness

```
Abstract-non-⊥(fo : O → O, ∇↓ : O → O, o : O)
    repeat
        o' ← o
        o ← o ⊓ fo(o)
    until o = o' or γ(o) = ∅
    if γ(o) = ∅ then return (⊥, o')
    if fo satisfies γ-completeness criterion at o then
        return (not ⊥, o)
    d ← ∇↓o
    if d = o then return (unknown, d)
    return Abstract-non-⊥(fo, ∇↓, d)
```

Model Search in SAT Solvers

We show that the procedure in Algorithm 1 generalises *model search* in SAT solvers. The abstract lattice contains *partial assignments*, the abstract transformer is called the *unit rule*, the greatest fixed point computation $\mathsf{pgfp}(fo)$ is *Boolean Constraint Propagation* (BCP) and downwards extrapolation is implemented by *decisions*. We briefly elaborate on these points. Further details are in [13].

A partial assignment maps each variable to true, false, or unknown. The set of partial assignments $PAsg \mathrel{\hat{=}} (Vars \to \{\mathsf{true}, \mathsf{false}, \top\}) \cup \{\bot\}$ consists of partial assignments and a unique element $\bot$. In implementations of SAT solvers, the state $\bot$ is indicated by a special conflict flag. Partial assignments form a lattice with respect to the natural pointwise order and are equivalent to the constants lattice or the Cartesian abstraction for Boolean valued variables. The element $\top$ represents a partial assignment in which all variables have undefined values, and $\bot$ represents the empty set. The concretisation function $\gamma : PAsg \to \mathscr{P}(Asg)$ maps $\bot$ to $\emptyset$, and $\pi \neq \bot$ to the set defined below.

$$\gamma(\pi) \mathrel{\hat{=}} \{\sigma \mid \text{ for all } x \in Vars, \pi(x) \neq \top \text{ implies } \pi(x) = \sigma(x)\}$$

Propositional solvers deduce properties about a formula using the unit rule. The unit rule asserts that if a partial assignment is defined on all but one literals in a clause and does not satisfy those literals, it must satisfy the remaining literal to satisfy the formula. For a propositional literal l, we write $\pi \models l$ if $l = x$ and $\pi(x) = \mathsf{t}$ or if $l = \neg x$ and $\pi(x) = \mathsf{f}$. Lattice-theoretically, the unit rule for a clause is a decreasing transformer on the lattice of partial assignments.

$$Unit_C(\pi) \mathrel{\hat{=}} \begin{cases} \bot & \text{for all } l \in C.\ \pi \models \neg l \\ \pi \sqcap \{x \mapsto \mathsf{t}\} & C = C' \cup \{x\}, \pi(x) = \top \text{ and} \\ & \text{for all } l \in C'.\ \pi \models \neg l \\ \pi \sqcap \{x \mapsto \mathsf{f}\} & C = C' \cup \{\neg x\}, \pi(x) = \top \text{ and} \\ & \text{for all } l \in C'.\ \pi \models \neg l \\ \pi & \text{otherwise} \end{cases}$$

Moreover, $Unit_C$ can be characterised as the best abstract transformer for the model transformer mod_C. The unit rule extends to formulae in CNF by taking the pointwise meet of unit rules for each clause in the formula.

$$Unit_\varphi \mathrel{\hat{=}} \bigsqcap_{C \in \varphi} Unit_C$$

Boolean Constraint Propagation (BCP) repeatedly applies the unit rule and computes the fixed point $\mathsf{gfp}(Unit_\varphi)$. A solver makes a *decision* by assuming that some variable, which is unknown in a partial assignment, has a definite value. Mathematically, a decision maps a partial assignment π to $\pi[x \mapsto v]$, where x is unknown in π and v is a truth value. Observe that decisions are applications of a downward extrapolation operator $\nabla_\downarrow : PAsg \to PAsg$. If all variables are assigned to t or f in π, then $\nabla_\downarrow \pi = \pi$. Otherwise, $\nabla_\downarrow \pi$ is $\pi[x \mapsto \mathsf{t}]$ or $\pi[x \mapsto \mathsf{f}]$ for some x such that $\pi(x) = \top$.

Consider the conditionals in Abstract-non-$\bot$. If BCP starts from $\top$ and leads to $\bot$, the formula is unsatisfiable, as returned by the first conditional. A SAT solver terminates if it finds a satisfying assignment. Since assignments are partial assignments, the unit rule applies to them. Observe that $Unit_\varphi(\pi)$ for an assignment is $\bot$ if π does not satisfy φ and is π otherwise. More generally, $\gamma(Unit_\varphi(\pi))$ equals $mod_\varphi(\gamma(\pi))$, so finding a satisfying assignment is a sufficient condition for γ-completeness. Another sufficient condition is that at least one literal in each clause is satisfied by the current partial assignment.

To summarise, the algorithmic content of model search in a SAT solver is an instance of Abstract-non-$\bot$ where $O = PAsg$, $\nabla_\downarrow$ is propositional decision making, fo is given by $Unit_\varphi$ and the γ-completeness check tests whether all variables have been assigned to t or f. Several heuristics and carefully implemented data structures are required to achieve high performance with BCP, but these aspects correspond to optimising the fixed point iteration and abstract domain implementation.

Model Search for Inequalities

We instantiate Abstract-non-$\bot$ for reasoning about inequality formulae. Let Lit be the set of inequality literals. We introduce an inequality abstract domain, which contains only conjunctions of inequalities. Specifically, each element of $(Ineq, \supseteq, \cup, \cap)$, where $Ineq = \mathscr{P}(Lit)$ represents a conjunction of inequalities. We use the superset order because a larger set of constraints represents more constraints and has fewer models. The join is intersection of sets of constraints and meet is union. The empty set represents true and the set of all inequalities is one representation of false. Observe that false has multiple representations because every set containing a predicate and its negation is equivalent to false.

Recall that the concrete domain of structures was $\mathscr{P}(Vars \to \mathbb{Z})$. The concretisation function $\gamma_{Ineq} : Ineq \to \mathscr{P}(Vars \to \mathbb{Z})$ maps a set of constraints to their models.

$$\gamma_{Ineq}(\pi) \mathrel{\hat=} \{\sigma \mid \sigma \models P, \text{ for every } P \text{ in } \pi\}$$

We use an example due to McMillan et al. [23] to illustrate Abstract-non-$\bot$ on an inequality formula.

$$\varphi \mathrel{\hat=} (a < b) \wedge (a < c) \wedge (b < d \vee c < d) \wedge (d < a)$$

As with propositional logic, we will use the best abstract transformer for a clause, but construct the transformer for a formula in the abstract.

$$amod_\varphi \mathrel{\hat=} \bigsqcap_{C \in \varphi} \alpha_{Ineq} \circ mod_C \circ \gamma_{Ineq}$$

We apply Abstract-non-$\bot$ to check satisfiability of φ. The sets below represent the evaluation of each clause in the abstract domain.

$$\begin{aligned} amod_\varphi(\emptyset) &= \{a < b\} \cup \{a < c\} \cup \emptyset \cup \{d < a\} \\ &= \{a < b, a < c, d < a\} = \pi \\ amod_\varphi(\pi) &= \pi \cup \{d < b, d < c\} \\ &\quad \cup (amod_{b<d}(\pi) \cap amod_{c<d}(\pi)) \\ &= Lit \end{aligned}$$

The second step above requires explanation. The best abstract transformer for the singleton clauses when applied to π has the effect of computing the transitive closure of constraints in π. Due to $(a < b)$ and $(d < a)$, the inequality $(d < b)$ is added to π. The conjunction of π with $b < d$, represented by $amod_{b<d}(\pi)$, is unsatisfiable, as is the conjunction of π with $c < d$. The best representation of an unsatisfiable conjunction is the set of all constraints.

Compare the calculation above to solving the same formula with DPLL(T). In DPLL(T), a propositional variable would have been introduced for each predicate, and two solvers, one for propositional logic and one for inequalities would have been required to solve the formula. By instantiating Abstract-non-$\bot$, we can solve the formula using only the abstract domain, which plays the role of a theory solver, and without introducing extra variables. This difference becomes important for large formulae and is the motivation for techniques like *natural domain* SMT [5].

The generalised DPLL technique of McMillan et al. [23], referred to as GDPLL, also solves this formula without introducing propositional variables. Unlike ACDCL, GDPLL makes decisions and uses the shadow rule for conflict analysis to solve the formula.

An instantiation of Abstract-non-$\bot$ over *Ineq* may use *amod* as defined above for *fo*, a decision operator $\triangledown_\downarrow : Ineq \to Ineq$ such that $\triangledown_\downarrow Ineq = Ineq$ and otherwise $\triangledown_\downarrow \pi = \pi \cup \{x < y\}$ such that $x < y$ is not in π. The γ-completeness check for an element π can be performed by determining whether for every clause $C \in \varphi$, the intersection $\pi \cap C$ is non-empty. The check for $\gamma(o)$ being empty amounts to detecting a conjunction of unsatisfiable constraints. If constraints are represented as directed graphs, the emptiness check is implemented by cycle detection.

Feasible Traces The automata-theoretic approach to the feasible traces problem is to construct an automaton representing the traces of a system and the negation of a correctness property, and check if the language of this automaton is empty. This approach can be viewed as indirectly computing the greatest fixed point of $trace_{P,Q}$, where P represents the set of initial states of a system, and Q represents states that violate a property.

3.2 Abstract Top-Everywhere

CDCL is distinguished from several procedures that combine dual reasoning because the procedure used to reason about the top-everywhere problem *is not dual* to Abstract-non-$\bot$. Let $(U, \geqslant, \vee, \wedge)$ be an abstract domain that underapproximates $(\mathscr{P}(S), \subseteq, \cup, \cap)$ with functions α_U and γ_U. We assume that $\gamma_U(\top)$ is S. Let $\tilde{fu} : U \to U$ be a sound abstraction of a completely multiplicative, extensive function $\tilde{f}$, where f is completely additive and reductive. If $\mathsf{lfp}(\tilde{fu})$ concretises to $\top$, then the function f is bottom-everywhere.

The procedure Abstract-non-$\top$ computes an underapproximation of a least fixed point using the upwards interpolation operator $\triangle_\uparrow$. Correctness follows directly from known theorems in abstract interpretation and it suffices for us to discuss instantiations of this procedure.

Algorithm 2: Abstract non-$\top$

```
Abstract-non-⊤(f̃u : U → U, △↑ : U × U → U, u : U)
    c ← u △↑ (u ⊔ f̃u(u))
    if γ(c) = ⊤ then return (⊤, c)
    if f̃u satisfies γ-completeness criterion at c then
        return (not ⊤, c)
    if c = u then return (unknown, c)
    return Abstract-non-⊤(f̃u, △↑, c)
```

Conflict Analysis in SAT Solvers

We now show that conflict analysis in SAT solvers is an instance of Abstract-non-$\top$. Consider the downset completion $(\mathscr{D}(PAsg), \subseteq)$ of partial assignments treated as an underapproximation. That is, every set of truth assignments is underapproximated by a set of partial assignments. Conflict minimisation [26] is a technique used by SAT solvers to generalise the reason behind a partial assignment leading to a conflict. Minimisation techniques replace a partial assignment π with partial assignments from which π can be derived by the unit rule. There may not be a unique partial assignment from which π is derived, so downsets of partial assignments have to be considered. We define a transformer for conflict minimisation below.

$$\begin{aligned} &minimise_\varphi : \mathscr{D}(PAsg) \to \mathscr{D}(PAsg) \\ &minimise_\varphi(Q) \mathrel{\hat=} Q \cup \{\pi \mid Unit_C(\pi) \in Q \text{ for some } C \in \varphi\} \end{aligned}$$

Conflict minimisation can dually be viewed as restricted application of resolution.

Example 1. Consider a formula $\varphi \mathrel{\hat=} \theta \wedge (x \vee \neg y) \wedge (\neg x \vee y)$ and a partial assignment $\pi = \{x \mapsto \mathsf{true}, y \mapsto \mathsf{true}\}$ such that $\mathsf{pgfp}(Unit_\varphi)(\pi)$ is $\bot$. Since y can be derived by the unit rule if x is true and x can be derived if y is true, we have $minimise_\varphi(\pi) = \{\{x \mapsto \mathsf{true}\}, \{y \mapsto \mathsf{true}\}\}$. ◁

There may be many ways to minimise a conflict but generating all minimisations exhausts solver memory. To avoid representing sets of conflicts, a SAT solver usually chooses one conflict. In Example 1, each set in $\Pi = \{\{x \mapsto \mathsf{true}\}, \{y \mapsto \mathsf{true}\}\}$ can be used. We model this step with a choice function $choice : \mathscr{D}(PAsg) \times \mathscr{D}(PAsg) \to \mathscr{D}(PAsg)$. The choice function ensures that the effort of generalising a conflict is not lost, and satisfies $\Pi \sqsubseteq choice(\Pi, \Pi') \sqsubseteq \Pi'$, where Π and Π' are downsets. Observe that *choice* is an upwards interpolation.

We emphasise that the soundness of the procedures in this section follows from standard results in abstract interpretation.

Over programs, instances of Abstract-non-$\top$ are procedures that underapproximate least fixed point computations. For example, the set of all counterexamples leading to an error can be defined by a least fixed point. Counterexample analysis techniques usually underapproximate this set by heuristically choosing one, or some subset of counterexamples.

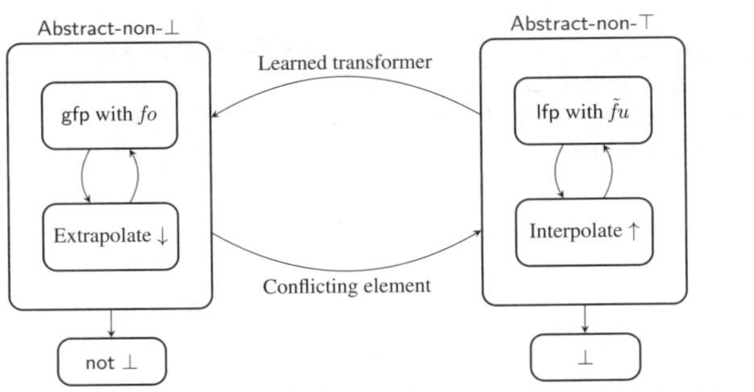

Figure 2. Abstract Conflict Driven Learning

4. Abstract Conflict Driven Learning

The procedures in the previous section were treated separately. The CDCL algorithm in modern solvers combines Abstract-non-$\bot$ and Abstract-non-$\top$ as summarised in Figure 2. Rather than return unknown from Abstract-non-$\bot$, information from the fixed point computation drives Abstract-non-$\top$. If Abstract-non-$\top$ produces inconclusive results, Abstract-non-$\bot$ can still "learn" information about the conflict for the greatest fixed point computation. This section makes this combination precise.

The *Abstract Conflict Driven Learning* procedure (ACDL) is shown in Algorithm 3. The procedures alternates runs of Abstract-non-$\bot$ and Abstract-non-$\top$. Communication between the two procedures is achieved using two functions, $\tilde{fou}$ and $learn$. Conflicting elements are transferred from Abstract-non-$\bot$ to Abstract-non-$\top$ using a function $\tilde{fou}$. We require that this function soundly underapproximates $\tilde{f}$, i.e., that $\tilde{f} \circ \gamma_O \subseteq \gamma_U \circ \tilde{fou}$. A natural choice for this transformer is to compute the composition $\alpha_U \circ \gamma_O$, which maps an abstract element in O to its best underappproximation in U. In the other direction, a transformer is learnt, as discussed below.

Algorithm 3: Abstract Conflict Driven Learning

ACDL($fo : O \to O,\ \nabla_{\downarrow} : O \to O,$
  $\tilde{fu} : U \to U,\ \Delta_{\uparrow} : U \times U \to U,$
  $\tilde{fou} : O \to U,\ learn : U \to (O \to O)$)
loop
  $(s, o) \leftarrow$ Abstract-non-$\bot$(fo, $\top$, $\nabla_{\downarrow}$)
  if $s \neq \bot$ **then return** (s, o)
  $u \leftarrow \tilde{fou}(o)$
  $(s, u) \leftarrow$ Abstract-non-$\top$($\tilde{fu}$, u, $\Delta_{\uparrow}$)
  if $s = \top$ **then return** $(\bot, u)$
  $fo \leftarrow fo \sqcap learn(u)$

Best Learning Transformer If Abstract-non-$\bot$ derives $\bot$ starting from o, to determine if f is bottom at a concrete element c, it suffices to check if f is bottom at $c \cap \neg\gamma_O(o)$, because f is reductive. If Abstract-non-$\bot$ is invoked on an abstract element a, it suffices to check if fo is bottom on elements below $\alpha_O(\neg\gamma_O(o) \cap \gamma_O(a))$. The procedure Abstract-non-$\top$ is used to generalise an element that leads to a conflict but it operates in an underapproximating domain. Thus, we need to learn information about overapproximate elements after generalising within an underapproximation.

The *best learning transformer* is a function that takes elements u and o and subtracts u from o.

$$learn : U \times O \to O \quad learn_u(o) \mathrel{\hat{=}} \alpha_O(\gamma_O(o) \cap \neg\gamma_U(u))$$

Theorem 10. *Let fo be a sound overapproximation of a completely additive, reductive transformer f and let $\tilde{fu}$ be a sound underapproximation of the De Morgan dual $\tilde{f}$ of f. If* pgfp$(fo)(o)$ *represents the empty set, then the transformer*

$$fo \sqcap learn_u, \text{ where } u \text{ is } \mathsf{plfp}(\tilde{fu})(\alpha_U(\gamma_O(o)))$$

is a sound overapproximation of f.

Theorem 10 strictly generalises the notion of learning from SAT solvers to every instance of the bottom-everywhere problem.

We give an example of a simple, sound learning procedure supported by all lattices. An element that leads to $\bot$ is *tabu*, in the sense of tabu search. Tabu learning defines a sound learning transformer $Tabu : U \times O \to O$.

$$Tabu_u(o) \mathrel{\hat{=}} \begin{cases} \bot & \text{if } \gamma(o) \subseteq \gamma(u) \\ o & \text{otherwise} \end{cases}$$

The tabu rule checks whether search has entered a region that is known to map to $\bot$.

Theorem 11 (Soundness)**.** *If* ACDL *returns* not $\bot$, *then f is not bottom everywhere. If it returns $\bot$, then f is bottom everywhere.*

Proof. Assume the algorithm returns not $\bot$. Then Abstract-non-$\bot$ returned (not $\bot, o$). Then fo is γ-complete at o, $\gamma_O(o) \neq \bot$ and $fo(o) = o$. By γ-completeness, we then conclude that f is not bottom at $\gamma_O(o)$.

Assume the algorithm returns $\bot$. Then Abstract-non-$\top$ returned $\top$. We denote by u the initial value of u in Abstract-non-$\top$, and by u' the return value with $\gamma_U(u') = \top$. It is an invariant of the algorithm that fo is a sound overapproximation of f. Hence, whenever Abstract-non-$\bot$ returns $(\bot, o)$ it holds that $f(\gamma_O(o)) = \bot$. It holds that $u = \alpha_U \circ \gamma_O(o)$ for such an o. By duality, we have that $\tilde{f}(\bot) \supseteq \gamma_O(o) \supseteq \gamma_U(u)$. Abstract-non-$\top$ returns $u' \sqsupseteq u$ such that $\gamma_U(u') = \top$. By soundness of abstract interpretation it holds that $\gamma_U(u') = \tilde{f}(\gamma_U(u)) = \top$. Since $\tilde{f}$ is an upper closure operator with $\tilde{f}(\bot) \supseteq \gamma_U(u)$ and $\tilde{f}(\gamma_U(u)) = \top$, it follows by idempotence that $\tilde{f}(\bot) = \top$. Dually, it follows that $f(\top) = \bot$. Therefore, f is bottom everywhere. □

5. Abstract Conflict Driven Clause Learning

The previous section showed that the notion of learning is very general. Clause learning is a specific form of learning in which abstract transformers are implicitly represented by clauses. Since model search in SAT solvers is driven by the unit rule, clause learning can be viewed as learning unit rule transformers. We present a generalised unit rule that lifts clause learning to richer lattices. Abstract Conflict Driven Clause Learning (ACDCL) is a strict generalisation of the CDCL algorithm in SAT solvers. In § 3, we demonstrate that propositional solvers operates over the overapproximate partial assignments domain $PAsg$ and its underapproximate downset completion $\mathscr{D}(PAsg)$. We present ACDCL as a variant of the ACDL procedure presented in the previous section operating over an overapproximation O and its downset completion $\mathscr{D}(O)$.

5.1 Generalising Clause Learning

To understand the lattice-theoretic essence of clause learning, it is useful to compare the unit rule with tabu learning. Consider a clause $C = p \vee \neg q$ and the partial assignment $\pi = \{p \mapsto \mathsf{f}, q \mapsto \mathsf{t}\}$, which contains no satisfying assignment to C. Consider π' strictly greater than π. We have that $Tabu_\pi(\pi') = \pi'$. However, if π' is the partial assignment $\{p \mapsto \mathsf{false}\}$, by unit rule application we have $Unit_C(\pi') = \{p \mapsto \mathsf{false}, q \mapsto \mathsf{false}\}$. The tabu rule only drives search away from elements where f is bottom. In contrast, if f is

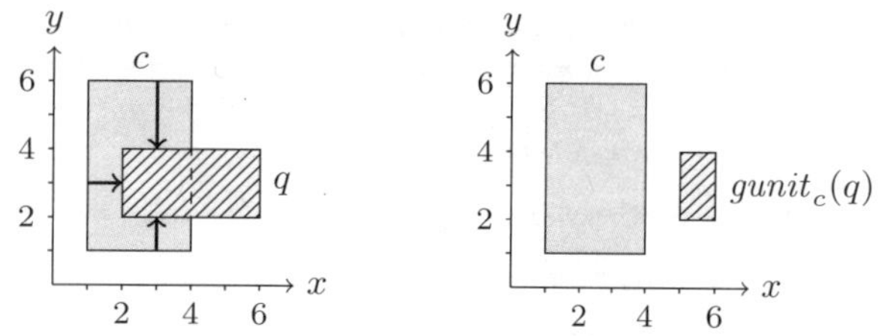

Figure 3. Generalised unit rule $gunit_c$ for intervals

"almost bottom" on π', the unit rule drives the search away from the part of π' that leads to bottom.

Example 2. We illustrate a generalised unit rule for the abstract domain of intervals over integers. Assume an abstract transformer fo is $\bot$ on the interval c in Figure 3. We design a generalised unit rule that maps the shaded interval q in the figure to the interval $gunit_c(q)$, which drives the search to the portion of q not known to lead to $\bot$. In what follows, we write an interval constraint such as $5 \le x \le 7 \wedge -\infty \le y \le \infty$ as $\{x \mapsto [5,7]\}$.

The complement of the interval $c = \{x \mapsto [1,4], y \mapsto [1,6]\}$ is not an interval. However, c is the intersection of the one-way infinite intervals $\{x \mapsto [1,\infty]\}$, $\{x \mapsto [-\infty,4]\}$, $\{y \mapsto [1,\infty]\}$ and $\{y \mapsto [-\infty,6]\}$. The complement of each of these intervals is an interval, and the set of complements can be viewed as a clause containing $\{x \mapsto [-\infty,0]\}$, $\{x \mapsto [5,\infty]\}$, $\{y \mapsto [-\infty,0]\}$ and $\{y \mapsto [7,\infty]\}$. The meet of $q = \{x \mapsto [2,6], y \mapsto [2,4]\}$ with each element of this generalised clause is bottom for all elements except $\{x \mapsto [5,\infty]\}$, so we only consider $\{x \mapsto [5,6]\}$. In this way, we generalise the propositional unit rule to new domains. $\lhd$

We point out the similarities to the propositional unit rule. Every interval is the intersection of one-way infinite intervals, just as a partial assignment is the conjunction of literals. One-way infinite intervals, like propositional literals, have complements. The complement of a partial assignment is a clause, and the complement of an interval can be represented as the disjunction of one-way infinite intervals. The rest of this section lifts the unit rule to new domains.

Complementable Decompositions This section deals with decompositions of lattice elements into elements which cannot be further decomposed, called *irreducibles*. An element m is *meet irreducible* if $x \sqcap y = m$ implies that $x = m$ or $y = m$. The set of meet irreducibles of a lattice A is $\mathcal{M}_A$. A function $mdc : A \to \mathscr{P}(\mathcal{M}_A)$ is a *meet decomposition* if, for all a, the set $mdc(a)$ is finite, and $\bigsqcap mdc(a) = a$. A meet decomposition is *irredundant*, if for any $a \in A$ and $b \in mdc(a)$ it holds that $\bigsqcap mdc(a) \setminus \{a\} \neq a$. Most abstract domains used in practice have an obvious unique irredundant meet decomposition (e.g., partial assignments decompose into partial assignments with only one variable taking a Boolean value, intervals and octagons decompose into sets of half-spaces). A number of examples of possible abstract domains with complementable decompositions are given in Figure 4. Complementable decompositions are not limited to numeric abstractions. For example, the depicted control-flow abstraction abstractly represents a set of traces in terms of control-flow branches.

An element a of an abstract domain A has a *precise complement* if there exists an element $\overline{a}$ such that $\gamma(a) = \neg\gamma(\overline{a})$. A has *complementable meet irreducibles* if every element $m \in \mathcal{M}_A$ has a precise complement $\overline{m} \in \mathcal{M}_A$. A domain A admits *complementable meet decompositions* if A has complementable meet irreducibles and a meet decomposition.

Generalised Unit Rule An abstraction A with complementable meet decompositions admits a generalised unit rule $gunit : A \times A \to A$. In contrast to the propositional unit rule, which is defined with respect to a clause, we define the generalisation with respect to elements that lead to $\bot$. This is only a difference of presentation, since the negation of a clause is a partial assignment on which $Unit_\varphi$ is bottom.

$$gunit_c(a) \mathrel{\hat{=}} \begin{cases} \bot & \text{for all } m \in mdc(c).\ a \sqsubseteq m \\ a \sqcap \overline{n} & mdc(c) = M \cup \{n\} \\ & \text{and for all } m \in M.\ a \sqsubseteq m \\ a & \text{otherwise} \end{cases}$$

If $gunit_c(a)$ returns $a \sqcap \overline{n}$ as above, we call $\overline{n}$ a *unit irreducible*. The transformer $gunit$ can be lifted to a learning transformer $gunit : O \times U \to O$, where $U = \mathscr{D}(O)$. For a downwards-closed set S, we define $gunit_S \mathrel{\hat{=}} \bigsqcap_{c \in S} gunit_c$. We skip the proof that $gunit$ is a sound learning transformer. We instantiate abstract conflict driven learning with $gunit$ to derive *Abstract Conflict Driven Clause Learning*.

5.2 An Abstract Backjumping Algorithm

Abstract conflict driven learning is sound. To achieve completeness, we need to ensure that learning drives the Abstract-non-$\bot$ procedure to explore new regions of the abstract lattice. The abstract backjumping algorithm appearing next generalises the backjumping search of propositional CDCL. The abstract procedure in Algorithm 4 operates over an overapproximate domain O with complementable decompositions, and its underapproximate downset completion $\mathscr{D}(O)$. Learning refines the transformer fo with the generalised unit rule $gunit$.

Algorithm 4: Backjumping and Clause Learning

ACDCL(fo: $O \to O$,
    $\nabla_\downarrow: O \to O$,
    $\tilde{fu}$: $\mathscr{D}(O) \to \mathscr{D}(O)$,
    $\triangle_\uparrow$: $\mathscr{D}(O) \times \mathscr{D}(O) \to \mathscr{D}(O)$)
  Initialize $\rho \in O^*$ to singleton sequence $\top_O$
  repeat
    $(s, \rho) \leftarrow$ Abstract-non-$\bot^*$(fo, ρ, $\nabla_\downarrow$)
    if $s \neq \bot$ **then return** $(s, \bigsqcap \rho)$
    $u \leftarrow \{\bigsqcap \rho\}$
    $(s, \{c\}) \leftarrow$ Abstract-non-$\top$($\tilde{fu}$, u, $\triangle_\uparrow$)
    $l \leftarrow gunit_c$
    $\rho \leftarrow$ backjump(l, fo, ρ)
    $fo \leftarrow fo \sqcap l$
  until ρ *is empty*
  return not $\bot$

Abstract-non-$\bot^*$($fo : O \to O$, $\nabla_\downarrow : O \to O$, $\rho : O^*$)
  $o \leftarrow \bigsqcap \rho$
  repeat
    $o' \leftarrow o$; $o \leftarrow fo(o) \sqcap o$
  until $o = o'$ *or* $\gamma(o) = \emptyset$
  if $\gamma(o) = \emptyset$ **then return** $(\bot, \rho)$
  $\rho \leftarrow \rho \cdot o$
  if *fo satisfies γ-completeness criterion at o* **then**
    return (not $\bot$, ρ)
  $d \leftarrow \nabla_\downarrow o$
  if $d = o$ **then return** (unknown,o)
  return Abstract-non-$\bot^*$(fo, $\rho \cdot d$, $\nabla_\downarrow$)

The algorithm uses a modification of Abstract-non-$\bot$ to record transformer application on a stack ρ. Concatenation of two stacks

	INTERVALS	OCTAGONS	EQUALITY
Concrete Domain	$\mathscr{P}(V \to \mathbb{Z})$	$\mathscr{P}(V \to \mathbb{Z})$	$\mathscr{P}(V \to \mathbb{Z})$
Abstract Elements	$(l \leq x \leq u, \ldots)$	$(\pm x \pm y < c, \ldots)$	$(x = y, w \neq z, \ldots)$
Meet Irreducibles	$(x \leq 4)$	$(x + y < 1)$	$(x \neq y)$
Complemented Irreducible	$(5 \leq x)$	$(-x - y < 0)$	(x = y)
	ARRAY ABSTRACTION	SET ABSTRACTION	CONTROL-FLOW ABSTRACTION
Concrete	$\mathscr{P}(V \to (\mathbb{N} \to \mathbb{Z}))$	$\mathscr{P}((V \to D) \times (SV \to \mathscr{P}(D))$	$\mathscr{P}(\mathit{Traces})$
Abstract Elements	$(x \preceq \lambda i.c_x, y \not\preceq \lambda i.c_y, \ldots)$	$(x \in S, y \notin R, \ldots)$	$(l_i \to \texttt{else}, \ldots)$
Meet Irreducibles	$x \preceq \lambda i.4$	$x \in Q$	$(l_1 \to \texttt{else})$
Complemented Irreducibles	$x \not\preceq \lambda i.4$	$x \notin Q$	$(l_1 \to \texttt{if})$

Figure 4. Complementable Decompositions. The set V represents program variables.

ρ and ρ' is denoted by $\rho \cdot \rho'$. The difference to Abstract-non-$\bot$ is that after learning backjumping resets the procedure to a state before the element that is negated by the learning transformer. A call to backjump(l, fo, ρ) returns a non-empty prefix ρ' of ρ such that $\gamma(fo'(\bigsqcap \rho')) \neq \bot$ where $fo' = l \sqcap fo$. If no such prefix exists, the empty sequence is returned, indicating that fo is bottom-everywhere.

Progress and Precision If we disregard extensions such as restarts and forgets, propositional CDCL never generates the same clause twice. The number of clauses over a fixed set of literals is finite, so a CDCL solver makes constant progress and necessarily terminates. The procedure ACDCL makes *progress* if each iteration of the outer loop decreases some well-founded order. CDCL solvers do not return unknown. Decisions refine partial assignments until either $\bot$ or a satisfying assignment is obtained.

In propositional solvers, decisions are made by computing a greatest lower bound between the current element and a meet irreducible, that is, a partial assignment in which only one variable is not $\top$. Decisions never directly cause a conflict. We generalise these conditions below. A *meet irreducible extrapolation* is a downwards extrapolation operator $\nabla_{\downarrow} : O \to O$ satisfying two conditions.

1. $\nabla_{\downarrow} o$ equals $o \sqcap m$ for some meet-irreducible m.
2. If $\gamma_O(o)$ is not $\bot$, $\gamma_O(\nabla_{\downarrow} o)$ is not $\bot$.

The precision requirement given next ensures that a sequence of decisions eventually leads to an abstract element that can be analysed without loss of precision. A meet-irreducible extrapolation is *precise* if whenever o is equal to $\nabla_{\downarrow} o$, the function fo is γ-complete at o with respect to f.

The progress condition in a propositional solver is that learning causes model search to deduce new information. The generalised notion we use is that of *asserting backjumps*, which ensures that the procedure navigates away from the element that most recently led to $\bot$. A backjump function is *asserting* if whenever backjump(l, fo, ρ) returns ρ', then ρ' is the empty sequence or $l(\bigsqcap \rho')$ is strictly smaller than $\bigsqcap \rho'$. This condition ensures that backjumping drives the search into a new part of the search space.

Lemma 12. *In some non-final iteration of the* ACDCL *main loop, let ρ and ρ' be, respectively, the stack before and after backjumping. If the backjumping function is asserting, then after learning, it holds that $fo(\bigsqcap \rho')$ and $\bigsqcap \rho$ are incomparable.*

Proof. Let o and o' be, respectively, $\bigsqcap \rho$ and $\bigsqcap \rho'$, and let $\{c\}$ be the element returned by Abstract-non-$\top$. It holds that $c \sqsupseteq o$. Let $gunit_c(o') = o' \sqcap \overline{m}$ where $\overline{m}$ is the unit irreducible and therefore after learning $fo(o') \sqsubseteq \overline{m}$. It holds that $m \sqsupseteq c$ and therefore also $m \sqsupseteq o$.

We now show that $fo(o')$ and o are not ordered. Assume for a contradiction that $fo(o') \sqsubseteq o$. Then it holds that $fo(o') \sqsubseteq m$. Since we also know that $fo(o') \sqsubseteq \overline{m}$ it must hold that $\gamma(fo(o')) = \emptyset$. This violates the condition that the backjumping function returns a non-conflicting prefix ρ'. Therefore $fo(o') \not\sqsubseteq o$. Now assume for a contradiction that $o \sqsubseteq fo(o')$. Then $o \sqsubseteq \overline{m}$, and from $o \sqsubseteq c$ we can derive $o \sqsubseteq m$ and consequently $\gamma(o) = \bot$. This is not possible because Abstract-non-$\bot^*$ never returns a trail representing the empty set. We have shown that o and $fo(o')$ are incomparable. $\square$

Analogous to the case of propositional SAT, asserting backjumps can be implemented using a meet-irreducible extrapolation operator. We informally sketch the reason: Let ρ be the stack $\rho_1 \ldots \rho_k(\rho_k \sqcap m)$ during a run of the procedure such that the last element $(\rho_k \sqcap m)$ is derived by applying a meet-irreducible extrapolation operator. If we can determine that $f(\gamma_O(\bigsqcap \rho)) = \emptyset$, we may refine fo by learning the transformer $gunit_{\bigsqcap \rho}$. Backjumping to $\rho_1 \ldots \rho_k$ and then applying $gunit_{\bigsqcap \rho}$ yields the element $\rho_k \sqcap \overline{m}$, which drives the search to a new region.

Theorem 13 (Relative Completeness)**.** *If the downwards extrapolation $\nabla_{\downarrow}$ is precise, and* ACDCL$(fo, \nabla_{\downarrow}, \tilde{fu}, \triangle_{\uparrow})$ *terminates, the result is $\bot$ or* not $\bot$.

Proof. We prove by contradiction. If unknown is returned, Abstract-non-$\bot$ returned (unknown, o), which is only possible if $\nabla_{\downarrow} o$ equals o. Since $\nabla_{\downarrow}$ is precise, we know that fo is γ-complete at o. This is impossible because not $\bot$ would have been returned. $\square$

Theorem 14 (Termination)**.** *If O is finite and backjumps are asserting, then* ACDCL *makes progress.*

Proof. The procedures Abstract-non-$\bot$ and Abstract-non-$\top$ terminate over finite lattices. To prove the theorem, we assume that the outer loop of ACDCL is non-terminating and derive a contradiction.

Let r be the last element of the sequence ρ at the beginning of an arbitrary iteration of the main loop of ACDCL. Since the lattice is finite, we can reason using well-founded induction. We show that backjumping eventually resets the stack to a prefix whose last element is $b \sqsupset r$.

Base step: Assume r is an atom, meaning every r' that satisfies $r' \sqsubset r$ also satisfies $r' = \bot$. Then the Abstract-non-$\top$ step will be initialised with $\{r\}$, and will return an element $c \sqsupseteq r$. Therefore, it holds that after learning, $fo(r) = \bot$. Backjumping therefore necessarily returns to an element $b \sqsupset r$ in order to satisfy the condition that after a backjump $fo(b) \neq \bot$.

Induction step: Assume that for all $r' \sqsubset r$, the induction hypothesis holds. Assume for a contradiction that backjumping never jumps to an element greater than r. Then r is the target of a backjump infinitely often. Then it must be the case that in two subsequent iterations i_1 and i_2, Abstract-non-$\bot^*$ returns a stack with the same final conflicting element c such that r is the target of the corresponding backjump in both cases. After the first such backjump, we have by Lemma 12 that *fo* immediately infers an element $a \sqsubset r$ such that a and c are unordered. Specifically, a is not greater than c. Therefore, any subsequent call to Abstract-non-$\bot^*$ returns a stack with a last element that is smaller than a, and therefore different from c. This contradicts the above, which states that i_2 backtracks from c.

This completes the proof. It therefore holds that, in an infinite run, backtracking will eventually return an element strictly greater than $\top$. This is impossible, hence all runs of ACDCL terminate. □

Though we only show termination for finite lattices, the termination of CDCL is usually non-trivial to argue. When applied to decidable logics that involve infinite lattices (such as linear arithmetic), specific details of the theory, the transformers and acceleration techniques must be used to prove termination. It is not clear that there are general termination arguments for infinite lattices. Ascending and descending chain conditions are not enough because of the alternation of the two procedures and the use of decisions and choice, which also operate on infinite sets.

6. Abstract Implication Graphs

The design of underapproximate transformers, such as $\tilde{fu}$, is a challenging problem that has received less attention than the design of overapproximate transformers. SAT solvers use *fo* applications to construct an implication graph, and use this graph to derive $\tilde{fu}$. We now generalise implication graphs to other domains.

Implication Graphs as Transformer Abstractions Consider a proof rule that when applied to antecedents $a_1, \ldots, a_n$ yields the consequent c. If we view antecedents and consequents as elements of an abstract domain, we can formalise a proof rule as a transformer *fo* that satisfies $fo(\bigsqcap\{a_1, \ldots, a_n\}) \sqsubseteq c$. Implication graphs provide a means to derive antecedents from consequents thereby implementing an abduction transformer.

Recall that $\mathcal{M}_O$ is the set of meet irreducibles of O. An *implication edge* is a directed hyperedge in $E_\mathcal{I} \mathrel{\hat=} \mathscr{P}(\mathcal{M}_O) \times \mathcal{M}_O$. We order implication edges so that $E_1 \preceq E_2$ means E_1 requires weaker antecedents than E_2 to derive stronger consequents. Define $(M_1, m_1) \preceq (M_2, m_2)$ to hold if $m_1 \sqsubseteq m_2$ and for every m'_1 in M_1 there exists m'_2 in M_2 satisfying $m'_1 \sqsupseteq m'_2$. An *implication graph* G is an upwards-closed set of implication edges and the *domain of implication graphs* $\mathcal{I} \mathrel{\hat=} (\mathscr{U}(E_\mathcal{I}), \supseteq, \cup, \cap)$ contains implication graphs with the supserset order. In practice, an upwards-closed set is represented by its minimal elements.

Figure 5 contains examples of implication graphs. All incoming edges to a node represent one hyperedge and each hyperedge represents its upwards-closure. A hyperedge of the form $(\{\}, m)$ is depicted by m.

An implication graph represents an abstraction of a transformer, as shown below. Assume below that *fo* is a reductive transformer. Let $(Red_O, \sqsubseteq)$ be the lattice of reductive transformers on O with the pointwise order. Define two functions $\alpha_\mathcal{I} : Red_O \to \mathcal{I}$ and $\gamma_\mathcal{I} : \mathcal{I} \to Red_O$ below.

$$\alpha_\mathcal{I}(f) \mathrel{\hat=} \{(M, m) \in E_\mathcal{I} \mid f(\bigsqcap M) \sqsubseteq m\}$$

$$\gamma_\mathcal{I}(I) \mathrel{\hat=} \lambda o. \bigsqcap\{m \mid \exists (M, m) \in I.\ \bigsqcap M \sqsupseteq o\}$$

Proposition 15. *The functions $\alpha_\mathcal{I}$ and $\gamma_\mathcal{I}$ form a Galois connection.*

Example 3. We illustrate the application graph construction for reachability analysis of a program with the interval abstract domain. The problem is to determine if the location $\lightning$ is reachable in the flow graph in Figure 6. An implication graph derived by applying abstract successor transformers is shown alongside.

The label DL0, denotes *decision level 0*, which contains meet irreducibles that are deduced without making assumptions. These represent facts obtained by a run of a static analyser. Due to imprecision, the error is reachable in the abstract.

Suppose we apply downwards extrapolation to force the constraint $a \leq -42$ at the location n_1. This constraint is shaded in the figure. If we continue static analysis with this assumption, we conclude that $\lightning$ is unreachable. The facts required to arrive at this conclusion are shown in the implication graph in the figure. ◁

Extracting Dual Transformers We now show how conflict analysis can be viewed as construction of a dual transformer from an implication graph. The dual transformer maps a set of consequences C to the set of antecedents A from which we could have derived C. The *dual implication transformer* defined by an implication graph I is $\tilde{fu}_I : \mathscr{D}(O) \to \mathscr{D}(O)$ below.

$$\tilde{fu}_I(C) \mathrel{\hat=} C \cup \{q \sqcap (\bigsqcap M) \mid q \sqcap m \in C \wedge (M, m) \in I\}$$

Theorem 16. *If the implication graph I represents an overapproximation of fo, the transformer $\tilde{fu}_I$ underapproximates $\tilde{f}$.*

Proof. Consider an implication graph I that overapproximates the transformer *fo* and a downwards closed set $C \subseteq O$. We prove the inequality $\gamma_{\mathscr{D}(O)} \circ \tilde{fu}_I(C) \subseteq \tilde{f} \circ \gamma_{\mathscr{D}(O)}(C)$.

We show that $fo(c)$ is in C for all c in $\tilde{fu}_I(C)$. Consider c in $\tilde{fu}_I(C)$. If c is in C, we have that $fo(c)$ is in C because *fo* is reductive and C is downwards-closed. If c is in $\tilde{fu}_I(C) \setminus C$, c is, by definition of the form $c = q \sqcap (\bigsqcap M)$, where $q \sqcap m$ is in C for some (M, m) in I. Since I soundly approximates *fo*, we have that $fo(\bigsqcap M) \sqsubseteq m$, and as a consequence also that $fo(c) = fo(q \sqcap (\bigsqcap M)) \sqsubseteq q \sqcap m$. Since C is downwards closed and $q \sqcap m$ is in C it holds that $c \in C$. We have shown that $\{fo(c) \mid c \in \tilde{fu}_I(C)\}$ is contained in C.

The soundness of *fo* implies that the downwards-closure of $\bigcup\left\{f(\gamma_O(c)) \mid c \in \tilde{fu}_I(C)\right\}$ is contained in the downwards closure of $\left\{\gamma_O(c) \mid c \in \tilde{fu}_I(C)\right\}$. We can rewrite the above condition as $f \circ \gamma_{\mathscr{D}(O)} \circ \tilde{fu}_I \subseteq \gamma_{\mathscr{D}(O)}$, where $\subseteq$ is the pointwise lifting of the subset order. The functions $(f, \tilde{f})$ form a Galois connection, due to which, the inequality $f \circ \gamma_{\mathscr{D}(O)} \circ \tilde{fu}_I \subseteq \gamma_{\mathscr{D}(O)}$ is equivalent to $\gamma_{\mathscr{D}(O)} \circ \tilde{fu}_I \subseteq \tilde{f} \circ \gamma_{\mathscr{D}(O)}$. Thus, $\tilde{fu}_I$ underapproximates $\tilde{f}$. □

Example 4. Consider the interval implication graph I shown in Figure 5, consisting of the following hyperedges.

$$\{(\emptyset, y \geq 5), (\emptyset, x \leq 2), (\{y \geq 5\}, x \geq 6), (\{x \geq 6, x \leq 2\}, \bot)\}$$

We compute a least fixed point over $\tilde{fu}_I$, and represent downwards-closed sets by their maximal elements.

$$C_0 = \tilde{fu}_I(\bot) = \{(x \geq 6, x \leq 2)\}$$
$$C_1 = \tilde{fu}_I(C_0) = C_0 \cup \{\{(y \geq 5, x \leq 2), (x \geq 6)\}\}$$
$$C_2 = \tilde{fu}_I(C_1) = C_1 \cup \{\top\} = \top$$

It follows that the formula is unsatisfiable. This fixed point computation, in which meet irreducibles are replaced by their explanations, is similar to conflict analysis in SAT solvers. ◁

Generalising Implication Graphs We briefly discuss implication graph generalisation. See [17] for a more algorithmic discussion. In propositional CDCL, meet irreducibles are of the form $\{x \mapsto v\}$ where v is t or f. Meet irreducible partial assignments are incomparable. In more general lattices, such as intervals, there is an order on meet irreducibles. The order on meet irreducibles represents implications that follow from theory axioms. This order

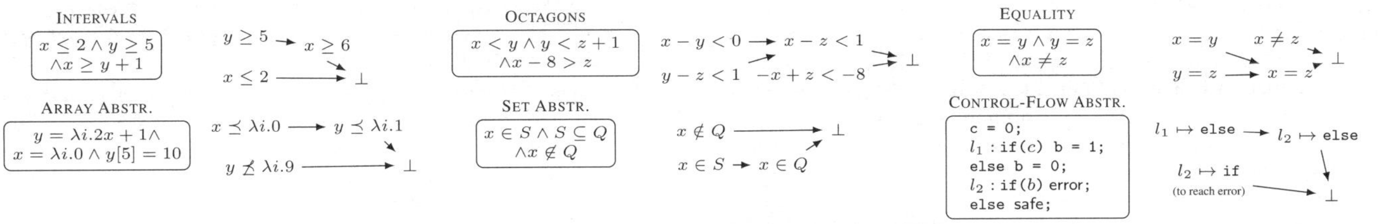

Figure 5. Abstract Implication Graphs

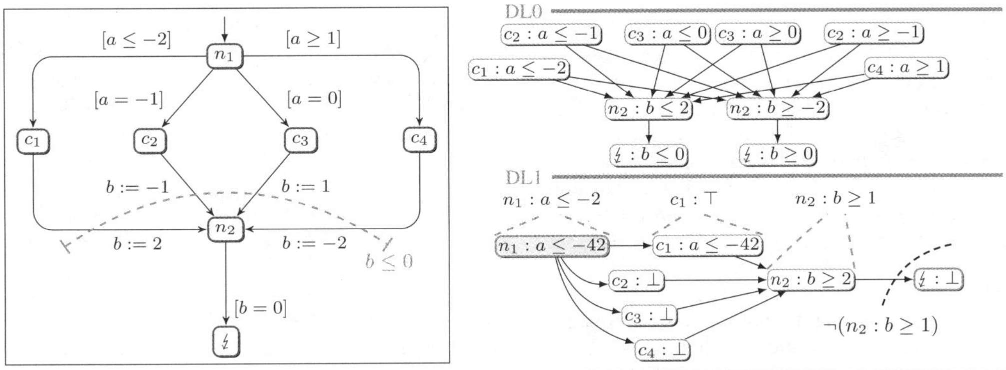

Figure 6. Implication Graph for Reachability of the Program Location Marked with ↯

can be used to generalise implication graphs to derive more useful dual transformers.

Example 5. We illustrate implication graph generalisation on the example in Figure 6. Computing $\tilde{fu}_I$ for the graph I depicted leads to a sound transformer. Using this transformer one can find, for example, that $n_2 : b \ge 2$ is sufficient to deduce a conflict.

There is a more general graph that still allows deduction of unreachability of ↯: The constraint on the node $n_2 : b \ge 2$ can be weakened to obtain $n_2 : b \ge 1$. Likewise, $c_1 : a \le -42$ and $n_1 : a \le -42$ can be generalised, respectively, to $c_1 : \top$ and $n_1 : a \le -2$. Computing $\tilde{fu}_{I'}$ over the resulting graph I' allows one to find that $n_2 : b \ge 1$ is sufficient to deduce a conflict. By generalising the graph, we can derive more general conditions under which a location is unreachable.

Learning allows us to negate this condition and discover that the flow graph always satisfies $n_2 : b \le 0$ because the variable b is in the interval $[-1, -2]$ at the location n_2. We can now prove that ↯ is unreachable without any assumptions. We note that ACDCL instantiated in this way over programs is a method to dynamically discover a trace partitioning [25]. ◁

7. Related Work

A survey of the literature on combining logical solvers and abstract interpreters is beyond the scope of this paper. We limit ourselves to discussing extensions of CDCL solvers to richer problems.

The DPLL(T) architecture, also called *lazy* SMT combines a SAT solver with a solver for the conjunctive fragment of a theory, to determine satisfiability of quantifier-free formulae in a theory [15]. In the original lazy SMT architecture, decisions and learning take place in the propositional solver, which may cause theory facts to be enumerated. *Splitting on demand* allows new theory facts to be encoded by propositional variables and added to a formula [2]. ACDCL is an alternative to lazy SMT in which all reasoning happens directly in a fragment of the theory, and no propositional solver is required. See [3] for a theoretical and empirical comparison of ACDCL and DPLL(T).

Other approaches that jettison a propositional solver in favour of making decisions and learning directly in a theory include *natural-domain* SMT [5], *generalised* DPLL [23] and theory specific solutions for equality [1], and integer linear arithmetic [20] using the cutting-planes proof system. ACDCL is one recipe for generalising CDCL to new domains. The details of the decision and learning operations have to be designed anew for each theory, but the algorithm used by the solver, and its soundness and relative-completeness follow from our work. In separate work, we have instantiated ACDCL to derive an SMT solver for floating-point logic and shown that this solver performs better than using a propositional encoding [17], and better than DPLL(T) [17].

SMT solvers use the *Nelson-Oppen* and *Delayed Theory Combination* methods to combine solvers for different theories. Abstract interpretation is a modular framework, which allows abstract domains to be combined in several different ways [8]. The *Nelson-Oppen* method and DPLL(T) have recently been shown to be instances of more general product constructions in abstract interpretation [3, 12]. These product constructions lift to instantiations of ACDCL: if ACDCL can be instantiated over domains O_1 and O_2, it can be instantiated over the cardinal product $O_1 \times O_2$.

Our work allows CDCL to be lifted to verification problems. We have instantiated ACDCL with the interval abstract domain to analyse the bounds of variables in programs with floating-point variables [14]. *Lazy annotation with interpolants* [22] lifts CDCL to programs, and uses an SMT solver to implement constraint propagation, and Craig interpolation for learning. We work with abstract domains, and do not assume the domain is closed under Boolean operations, or that it supports interpolation. *Satisfiability Modulo Path Programs* [18] lifts DPLL(T) to programs by combining a SAT solver and an abstract interpreter, and Stålmarck's method has been lifted to programs in [28].

Our work provides an abstract interpretation view of CDCL, which we extended to other procedures in [13], and to DPLL(T) in [3]. An account of Stålmarck's method is given in [27], and [24] contains a transition system view of CDCL.

A natural question is whether ACDCL is a form of Counter-Example Guided Abstraction Refinement (CEGAR) [4]. CEGAR uses non-$\bot$ witnesses to construct a new domain and new transformers. ACDCL implements proof-guided transformer refinement and makes progress when no non-$\bot$ witness is found. ACDCL never changes the domain, and this immutability is crucial for efficiency, because the implementations of the abstract domain and transformers can be highly optimised.

8. Conclusion

In this paper, we applied abstract interpretation to study the Conflict Driven Clause Learning algorithm (CDCL) implemented by contemporary SAT solvers. We showed that CDCL can be understood as a lattice-theoretic approximation algorithm that combines overapproximations of greatest fixed points and underapproximations of least fixed points to determine properties of a function on a Boolean lattice. Our generalised Abstract Conflict Driven Clause Learning (ACDCL) procedure and its correctness proofs rely on properties enjoyed by the data structures in SAT solvers as well as by abstract domains used in practice.

In separate work, we have instantiated ACDCL to derive an SMT solver and a program analyser and obtained positive results. Problems to investigate in future instantiations include satisfiability in theories of weak arithmetic, assertion checking with relational abstract domains, and nullness of pointers. A second family of problems is to design non-Boolean abstractions of states and traces so that ACDCL can be applied to model checking problems, and to determine emptiness of non-deterministic automata over finite and infinite words.

We opened the paper by recalling a question posed by Malik and Zhang about whether the lessons from the success of SAT solvers lift to other domains. We believe that our work contributes a mathematical answer to this question that applies to algorithmic issues. Our work does not explain or provide a means to lift the heuristics used by SAT solvers to new problems. We conjecture that heuristics to boost efficiency of constraint propagation are closely related to those for exploiting sparsity in program analysis. It is our hope that future work will provide a framework for understanding these connections and for lifting engineering techniques in SAT solvers to new problem domains.

Acknowledgments

This work was supported by the Toyota Motor Corporation, ERC project 280053, EPSRC project EP/H017585/1, and the FP7 STREP PINCETTE. Vijay D'Silva was supported by a Microsoft Research PhD Scholarship.

We thank the abstract interpretation community, in particular Patrick and Radhia Cousot, for their support and encouragement of this work. Vijay D'Silva thanks Heejong Lee and Wonchan Lee for their diligence in an independent project, which allowed him time for this one.

References

[1] B. Badban, J. van de Pol, O. Tveretina, and H. Zantema. Generalizing DPLL and satisfiability for equalities. *Information and Computation*, 205(8):1188–1211, 2007.

[2] C. Barrett, R. Nieuwenhuis, A. Oliveras, and C. Tinelli. Splitting on demand in SAT modulo theories. In *Proc. of Logic for Programming, Artificial Intelligence, and Reasoning*, pages 512–526, 2006.

[3] M. Brain, V. D'Silva, L. Haller, A. Griggio, and D. Kroening. An abstract interpretation of DPLL(T). In *Proc. of Verification, Model Checking and Abstract Interpretation*, 2013. To appear.

[4] E. Clarke, O. Grumberg, S. Jha, Y. Lu, and H. Veith. Counterexample-guided abstraction refinement for symbolic model checking. *J. of the ACM*, 50:752–794, 2003.

[5] S. Cotton. Natural domain SMT: A preliminary assessment. In *Proc. of Formal Modeling and Analysis of Timed Systems*, pages 77–91, 2010.

[6] P. Cousot. Constructive design of a hierarchy of semantics of a transition system by abstract interpretation. *Theoretical Computer Science*, 277(1-2):47–103, Apr. 2002.

[7] P. Cousot. Abstract interpretation. MIT course 16.399, Feb.–May 2005.

[8] P. Cousot and R. Cousot. Systematic design of program analysis frameworks. In *Proc. of Principles of Programming Languages*, pages 269–282, 1979.

[9] P. Cousot and R. Cousot. Abstract interpretation and application to logic programs. *Journal of Logic Programming*, 13:103–179, 1992.

[10] P. Cousot and R. Cousot. Abstract interpretation frameworks. *Journal of Logic and Computation*, 2(4):511–547, Aug. 1992.

[11] P. Cousot and R. Cousot. Refining model checking by abstract interpretation. *Automated Software Engineering*, 6(1):69–95, 1999.

[12] P. Cousot, R. Cousot, and L. Mauborgne. The reduced product of abstract domains and the combination of decision procedures. In *Proc. of Foundations of Software Science and Computational Structures*, pages 456–472, 2011.

[13] V. D'Silva, L. Haller, and D. Kroening. Satisfiability solvers are static analysers. In *Proc. of Static Analysis Symposium*, pages 317–333, 2012.

[14] V. D'Silva, L. Haller, D. Kroening, and M. Tautschnig. Numeric bounds analysis with conflict-driven learning. In *Proc. of Tools and Algorithms for the Construction and Analysis of Systems*, pages 48–63, 2012.

[15] H. Ganzinger, G. Hagen, R. Nieuwenhuis, A. Oliveras, and C. Tinelli. DPLL(T): Fast decision procedures. In *Proc. of Computer Aided Verification*, pages 175–188, 2004.

[16] R. Giacobazzi and E. Quintarelli. Incompleteness, counterexamples, and refinements in abstract model-checking. In *Proc. of Static Analysis Symposium*, pages 356–373, 2001.

[17] L. Haller, A. Griggio, M. Brain, and D. Kroening. Deciding floating-point logic with systematic abstraction. In *Proc. of Formal Methods in Computer-Aided Design*, pages 131–140, 2012.

[18] W. R. Harris, S. Sankaranarayanan, F. Ivančić, and A. Gupta. Program analysis via satisfiability modulo path programs. In *Proc. of Principles of Programming Languages*, pages 71–82, 2010.

[19] T. A. Henzinger, O. Kupferman, and S. Qadeer. From pre-historic to post-modern symbolic model checking. *Formal Methods in Systems Design*, 23(3):303–327, Nov. 2003.

[20] D. Jovanovic and L. M. de Moura. Cutting to the chase - solving linear integer arithmetic. In *Proc. of Automated Deduction*, pages 338–353, 2011.

[21] S. Malik and L. Zhang. Boolean satisfiability: From theoretical hardness to practical success. *Communications of the ACM*, 52:76–82, Aug. 2009.

[22] K. L. McMillan. Lazy annotation for program testing and verification. In *Proc. of Computer Aided Verification*, pages 104–118, 2010.

[23] K. L. McMillan, A. Kuehlmann, and M. Sagiv. Generalizing DPLL to richer logics. In *Proc. of Computer Aided Verification*, pages 462–476, 2009.

[24] R. Nieuwenhuis, A. Oliveras, and C. Tinelli. Solving SAT and SAT modulo theories: From an abstract Davis–Putnam–Logemann–Loveland procedure to DPLL(T). *JACM*, 53:937–977, 2006.

[25] X. Rival and L. Mauborgne. The trace partitioning abstract domain. *ACM Transactions on Programming Languages and Systems*, 29, 2007.

[26] N. Sörensson and A. Biere. Minimizing learned clauses. In *Proc. of Theory and Applications of Satisfiability Testing*, pages 237–243, 2009.

[27] A. Thakur and T. Reps. A Generalization of Stålmarck's Method. In *Proc. of Static Analysis Symposium*, pages 334–351, 2012.

[28] A. Thakur and T. Reps. A method for symbolic computation of abstract operations. In *Proc. of Computer Aided Verification*. Springer, 2012.

The $\lambda\bar{\lambda}$-calculus

A dual calculus for unconstrained strategies

Alexis Goyet

Univ Paris Diderot, Sorbonne Paris Cité,
PPS, UMR 7126, CNRS,
F-75205 Paris, France
alexis.goyet@pps.univ-paris-diderot.fr

Abstract

We present a calculus which combines a simple, CCS-like representation of finite behaviors, with two dual binders λ and $\bar{\lambda}$. Infinite behaviors are obtained through a syntactical fixed-point operator, which is used to give a translation of λ-terms. The duality of the calculus makes the roles of a function and its environment symmetrical. As usual, the environment is allowed to call a function at any given point, each time with a different argument. Dually, the function is allowed to answer any given call, each time with a different behavior. This grants terms in our language the power of functional references.

The inspiration for this language comes from game semantics. Indeed, its normal forms give a simple concrete syntax for finite strategies, which are inherently non-innocent. This very direct correspondence allows us to describe, in syntactical terms, a number of features from game semantics. The fixed-point expansion of translated λ-terms corresponds to the generation of infinite plays from the finite views of an innocent strategy. The syntactical duality between terms and co-terms corresponds to the duality between Player and Opponent. This duality also gives rise to a Böhm-out lemma.

The paper is divided into two parts. The first one is purely syntactical, and requires no background in game semantics. The second describes the fully abstract game model.

Categories and Subject Descriptors I.1.3 [*Languages and Systems*]

Keywords Game semantics, Lambda-calculus

1. Introduction

Game semantics has proven to be a very effective tool as both a precise and insightful model of languages. It was used to give models for many languages [1, 2, 14, 15, 19], and has otherwise been the inspiration for many analyses [11, 17, 18]. This sustained interest has also made game semantics a subject of investigation, this time not as a tool, but for itself. In particular, recently, a growing body of work [6, 7, 16] is proposing syntaxes derived from game semantics. But why reverse the roles, and invent a new language for a semantics? One answer is that an interesting model has its own coherent structure, which may not be present in the initial object. In the case of game semantics, the model uses a notion of interaction history which both the program and its environment access in a symmetrical way. This gives a precision level which was in fact too high for the first language modeled: the purely functional PCF [2, 14, 19]. This led to the definition of the *innocence* and *visibility* conditions (following the presentation in [14]), which force the strategy to depend only on a subset of the interaction history. This restriction introduces an asymmetry between the information available to the Player and the Opponent, corresponding to the asymmetry between a function and its argument. Thus the duality of the unconstrained model is not visible in the language's syntax. Later, it was shown [1] that non-innocent, non-visible strategies give a fully abstract model for a functional language extended with higher order references. Additionally, removing the *bracketing* condition, which is also present in [14], yields a language with non-local control [15]. This correspondence between different restrictions in the model and well known language features is remarkable. But the languages presented in the cited works, because they contain the λ-calculus as a sub-language, still do not exhibit the duality that we seek. In the case of [1] for example, the set of all strategies is built by factorization: a single "memory cell" strategy is added beside innocent ones. In comparison, our approach does not give a special role to innocent strategies; instead, we use *finite* strategies, which are inherently non-innocent, as our building blocks. The set of finite strategies is self-dual, and it is compact in the set of all strategies.

Syntactically, this leads to a very direct relationship between the model and the terms of our syntax. Indeed, η-long normal forms can be seen as a concrete syntax for finite strategies. The syntax dualizes that of λ-calculus, by adding a $\bar{\lambda}$ binder for *co-variables*. Together, λ and $\bar{\lambda}$ bindings correspond to the game notion of *justification*, which is itself symmetrical between the Player and the Opponent. In the λ-calculus, an occurrence of a variable x represents a call to an argument which was received at a previous point in the history; this point being represented by the binder λx. In the $\lambda\bar{\lambda}$-calculus, in addition, an occurrence of a co-variable u represents an incoming call to an argument which was *passed* at a previous point, represented by $\bar{\lambda}u$.

The calculus is endowed with a confluent set of reduction rules. The base language, which does not include fixed-point, is strongly normalizing. The model is given in a framework of game semantics, which we take as simple as possible. For this purpose, we choose types built from $\bot$ and the operators $\times$ and $\Rightarrow$ only; therefore we do not make the usual distinction between "questions" and "answers" moves (which are used when modeling base types other than $\bot$), and thus no bracketing condition is defined. We

POPL'13, January 23–25, 2013, Rome, Italy.

also do not impose determinism, and include odd-length plays in strategies. The language is fully abstract for this semantics. The expressive power of the language is illustrated by a translation of the λ-calculus (section 5), and a coding for a memory-cell (section 6.3). An implementation of the language is available [10].

We start with a very simple example, which is the translation, in our language, of the identity:

$$\begin{aligned} &\mathrm{tr}(\lambda y.y) \\ = \ &\bar{\lambda} u.u\_\nu\alpha.\lambda y.y\_u\_\alpha \\ \to^* \ &(\bar{\lambda} u.u\_\lambda y.y\_\bar{\epsilon}) + \sigma \end{aligned}$$

Details about this translation, and the syntactical fixed-point operator $\nu\alpha$, are given in section 5. The "+" operator is a non-deterministic sum; but for now we will focus on the expression on its left-hand side. We can see that the connectors of the initial λ-term are still present in this expression. Indeed, here the translation can be seen as a decoration of the initial term, with the following meaning: "Name u this function. If the environment calls u, it will pass it an argument; name it y, then call y.". All the connectors present in that expression are unary, meaning it could be written $\bar{\lambda} u.(u\_(\lambda y.(y\_(\bar{\epsilon}))))$. The notation "_", which is automatic after an occurrence of a variable y, or of a *co-variable* u, represents sequentiality, in the spirit of the CCS (or π-calculus) notation "$\cdot$". By itself, the behavior of the expression $\bar{\lambda} u.u\_\lambda y.y\_\bar{\epsilon}$ only approximates that of the λ-term $\lambda y.y$. This is because the last constructor, $\bar{\epsilon}$, signifies that the interaction stops. A better approximation can be obtained:

$$\begin{aligned} &\mathrm{tr}(\lambda y.y) \\ \to^* \ &(\bar{\lambda} u.u\_\lambda y.y\_u\_\lambda y.y\_\bar{\epsilon}) + \sigma' \end{aligned}$$

Here the expression $\bar{\lambda} u.u\_\lambda y.y\_u\_\lambda y.y\_\bar{\epsilon}$ will react to the environment call u not once, but twice in a row, and in the same way (by calling the argument y it just received). This means that it will have the same behavior as (the translation of) the λ-term $\lambda y.y$ when interacting with (the translation of) the environment $\lambda x.(x\ (x\ c))\ []$; each occurrence of x in the environment corresponding to an occurrence of u. On the other hand, the expression $\bar{\lambda} u.u\_\lambda y.y\_\bar{\epsilon}$ would have stopped reacting after the first call of x. The translation of $\lambda y.y$ can be co-inductively expanded to produce interactions of any length, answering the query u as many times as necessary, and always with the same behavior. This corresponds, in game semantics, to the condition of *innocence* for strategies, which essentially stipulates that any queries must be answered as if it was the first of its kind. This corresponds to the inability of the program to remember the previous calls, and thus to the absence of references. Terms of the $\lambda\bar{\lambda}$-calculus, on the other hand, do have the power of references, as we will see on our next example:

$$\text{new } r;\ r := \text{false};\ (M\ N) \qquad \text{where :}$$

$$\begin{aligned} M &= \lambda x.\lambda c.(\text{if } x \text{ then } (\text{if } x \text{ then diverge else } c) \text{ else diverge}) \\ N &= r := (\text{not } !r);\ !r \end{aligned}$$

Note here that the use of references in N is necessary for the interaction to reach the sub-term c of M. Indeed, a context with an innocent behavior would not be able to separate M from the program "diverge". When M calls x for the first time, N reacts as the boolean true; M then calls x a second time, and N reacts as the boolean false; finally M calls c. If N had reacted the same way twice (which it would be forced to do if it did not contain references), M would have diverged. We will present in our language an interaction similar to that of M and N. This requires a few adaptations. First, instead of booleans, which are absent in our setting, we will use the type $(\bot \times \bot) \Rightarrow \bot$ (with the behavior of $\lambda x.\lambda y.x$ representing the value true, and $\lambda x.\lambda y.y$ representing false). Thus, instead of M, we will consider the λ-term M_1:

$$M_1 = \lambda x.\lambda c.(x\ (x\ \Omega\ c)\ \Omega)$$

Additionally, the behaviors of M, M_1 and N are infinite, whereas, as we saw in our first example, terms in our syntax more naturally represent finite behaviors. For example, N reacts as true, then false, then true, etc; but the term we will give will only react to the first two queries. We now consider the interpretation of M_1 as a strategy. The picture below shows a *play* of this strategy , in the usual graphical representation; note that the labeling (x, x, and c) is not part of the play.

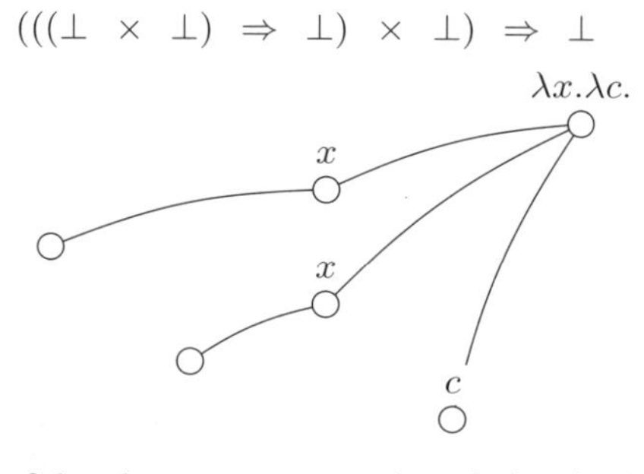

The moves of the play are represented as circles, in chronological order from top to bottom. The first move is the initial query made by the environment (the Opponent); M_1 (the Player) reacts by playing a move labeled by x; the Opponent then plays one of two possible moves in the product $\bot \times \bot$; M_1 plays x again; the Opponent this time chooses the second possibility; M_1 finally plays c. The two possible moves in $\bot \times \bot$ correspond to calls to either the first or the second argument passed to x by M_1 (simulating a value of either true or false for x). In the same way, the position of the moves labeled by x or c correspond to M_1 calling either its first argument (x) or its second one (c). In both cases, the move is placed under the occurrence of $\bot$ corresponding to the return type of x or c. This illustrates how the strategy contains all the information of the term. In general, the positions of the moves are not enough, and the *justification pointers* are also required; here they are represented as arcs between moves. We now give a more detailed labeling of the play, using syntactic elements from our language:

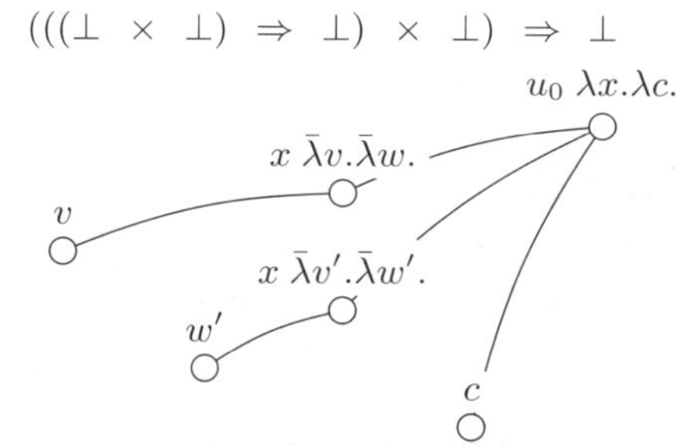

The label for each move consists of a name, followed by zero or more binders. In this representation, all moves are labeled by a name, and all justification pointers correspond to the link between a name and its binder (the same could have been done with the λ-calculus syntax, but only for Player moves). When there is more than one binder (for example, in the label "$x\ \bar{\lambda} v.\bar{\lambda} w.$"), they distinguish between available moves which could be justified by the current one (here either v or w). This gives a syntactical representation of the position in the arena (with v and w corresponding to the simulated value true and false for x). Again, the same could be said when labeling with the λ-calculus syntax, but only for Player moves. The syntax is dual; on one hand are *variables* x, c, which label Player moves, and binders $\lambda x, \lambda y$; on the other hand, *co-variables* u_0, v, w, which label Opponent moves, and their binders $\bar{\lambda} u_0, \bar{\lambda} v, \bar{\lambda} w$. This labeling can be obtained in a systematic way, given a choice of names for every moves. Notice that here we chose similar names v, w and v', w' for moves at the same position in the arena; but they are indeed different moves, distinguished by their justifier. For example, the move following $x\ \bar{\lambda}v'.\bar{\lambda}w'.$ could have been justified by $x\ \bar{\lambda}v.\bar{\lambda}w.$, in which case its label would be w, resulting in a different play. This new syntax can be used to directly represent plays; for example, the above example is denoted by:

$$\sigma_1 = \bar{\lambda}u_0.u_0\_\lambda x.\lambda c.x\_\bar{\lambda}v.\bar{\lambda}w.v\_x\_\bar{\lambda}v'.\bar{\lambda}w'.w'\_c\_\bar{\epsilon}$$

Note that the alternation between Player and Opponent moves is marked by a "_", and that the sequence ends with $\bar{\epsilon}$, which denotes the empty Opponent strategy (it has a dual, ϵ). This is a valid *co-term* in the syntax of the $\lambda\bar{\lambda}$-calculus; its interpretation is the smallest strategy containing the play in question (and its prefixes). In a sense, a strategy such as this one is passive: it waits for the Opponent to make the first move. In this work we are also interested in strategies in which the Player acts first; these *Player-starting strategies* are used to interpret *terms* in the $\lambda\bar{\lambda}$-calculus. To illustrate, we modify σ_1 by removing the initial move; this yields the term ϕ_1:

$$\phi_1 = \lambda x.\lambda c.x\_\bar{\lambda}v.\bar{\lambda}w.v\_x\_\bar{\lambda}v'.\bar{\lambda}w'.w'\_c\_\bar{\epsilon}$$

We now give an (Opponent-starting) strategy on the arena corresponding to the type $(\bot \times \bot) \Rightarrow \bot$:

$$\sigma_2 = \bar{\lambda}u.u\_\lambda y.\lambda z.y\_u\_\lambda y'.\lambda z'.z'\_\bar{\epsilon}$$

This co-term approximates, in our setting, the behavior of the program N: it reacts to the initial query u by calling y (thus behaving as $\lambda y.\lambda z.y$, which represents true), then reacts to the second occurrence of u by calling z' (behaving as $\lambda y'.\lambda z'.z'$, which represents false). As we mentioned before, this is only an approximation, in the sense that a third query u would be met with no reaction (this could be made more obvious by replacing $\bar{\epsilon}$ in σ_2 by u_ϵ; the obtained co-term being observationally equivalent to σ_2). Note that σ_1 was also an approximation of the strategy of M_1; this is because σ_1 and σ_3 represent finite strategies, whereas any innocent non-empty strategy contains infinite plays. For example, the strategy of M_1 will keep reacting to its initial move as many time as necessary; whereas σ_1 will only react to u_0 once. We can now represent the interaction of M and N, as the interaction of ϕ_1 and σ_2:

$$\begin{aligned} \phi_1 &= \lambda x.\lambda c.x\_\bar{\lambda}v.\bar{\lambda}w.v\_x\_\bar{\lambda}v'.\bar{\lambda}w'.w'\_c\_\bar{\epsilon} \\ \sigma_2 &= \bar{\lambda}u.\quad u\_\lambda y.\lambda z\ .y\_u\_\lambda y'.\lambda z'\ .z'\ \_\bar{\epsilon} \end{aligned}$$

$$\phi_1 \lhd \sigma_2 \to^* \lambda c.c\_\bar{\epsilon} \qquad\qquad \lambda x.\lambda c.\epsilon \lhd \sigma_2 \to^* \lambda c.\epsilon$$

The interaction operator in $\lambda\bar{\lambda}$-calculus is denoted by $\lhd$. It connects a term and a co-term; the result is a term. As indicated above, $\phi_1 \lhd \sigma_2$ reduces to $\lambda c.c\_\bar{\epsilon}$. Before we give more details about the reduction, notice that ϕ_1 and σ_2 are essentially dual; and that the connectors of ϕ_1 which are not mirrored in σ_2 are precisely those appearing in the result of the interaction. This is a fundamental property of the language: a normal branch and its dual will eliminate each other (without blocking) when interacting. Moreover, because this dual always exists, for any term representing a play (as does ϕ_1) we immediately have a context which will reach the end of this play (here σ_2). This can be seen as a form of "Böhm-out" lemma for the language. In this example, we obtain a separator between ϕ_1 and a term of the same type, $\lambda x.\lambda c.\epsilon$, which simply diverges (in that it plays no moves). The reduction rules of the language are given in section 4; additionally, the full reduction of $\phi_1 \lhd \sigma_2$ is given in the appendix A. We simply illustrate below two of the main points of the rules:

$$\begin{aligned} (\lambda x.\phi) \lhd (\bar{\lambda}u.\sigma) &\to^* \overset{(x,u)}{\nabla}.(\phi \lhd \sigma) \\ \overset{(x,u)}{\nabla}.(x\_\sigma \lhd u\_\phi) &\to^* \overset{(x,u)}{\nabla}.(\phi \lhd \sigma) \end{aligned}$$

The operator $\overset{(x,u)}{\nabla}$, which is created when the dual binders λx and $\bar{\lambda}u$ are eliminated, is called *connection*. It binds both x and u in $\phi \lhd \sigma$. This first reduction holds for any term ϕ and co-term σ (provided that x is not free in σ and u is not free in ϕ). The second shows how x and u are also eliminated together, once they are connected by the operator ∇. This reduction holds for any term ϕ and co-term σ, provided that σ can be put in a certain form, for example v_ϕ'.

The paper is divided into two parts. The first part, which does not require any background in game semantics, describes the language from a syntactical point of view: its syntax, in section 2, the typing system, in section 3, its reduction rules, in section 4, and its extension by a fixed-point operator, in section 5. A comparison with other languages, in section 6, and a Böhm-out lemma, in section 7 are also included.

In the second part we describes the game model. We define basic operations on games and plays in section 8; we give the semantics of the language in section 9, and list its main properties, including full abstraction, in section 10. We expand on the notion of *view*, and its link to history access control, in section 11. Section 12 discusses future works, and in section 13 we conclude.

2. Syntax

We assume two (disjoint) infinite sets of names: variables, denoted by $x, y, z, \cdots$ and *co-variables*, denoted by $u, v, w, \cdots$.

$$\begin{array}{lclclclclclcl} \phi,\psi & := & \epsilon & \mid & \lambda x.\phi & \mid & x\_\sigma & \mid & \phi+\psi & \mid & \phi\lhd\tau & \mid & \overset{L}{\nabla}^{S}.\phi \\ \sigma,\tau & := & \bar{\epsilon} & \mid & \bar{\lambda}u.\sigma & \mid & u\_\phi & \mid & \sigma+\tau & \mid & \sigma\lhd\tau & & \end{array}$$

where L is a set of pairs of the form (x, u), called *links*, and S is a stack of co-variables. The first line defines a syntax of *terms*, the second a syntax of *co-terms*; each constructor except $\overset{L}{\nabla}^{S}$ and $\lhd$ has a dual. We use the notations $\lambda\vec{x}.\phi$ for $\lambda x_1.\cdots\lambda x_n.\phi$ (and dually for $\bar{\lambda}\vec{u}$) and $\vec{v}$ for the stack $v_1\cdot\cdots\cdot v_n$. The construction $\overset{(x_i,u_i)_i}{\nabla}^{\vec{v}}.\phi$, called *connection*, binds all the x_i, u_i and v_j in ϕ. The constructors λx and $\bar{\lambda}u$ are also binders. We note $\mathrm{FN}(\phi)$ the free names of ϕ (and dually for $\mathrm{FN}(\sigma)$). We improperly write $x \in L$ when $(x, u) \in L$ for some u; and dually for $u \in L$. Finally, unary operators take precedence over binary operators.

3. Typing

Types are of the form $T := 1 \mid \bot \mid T \times T \mid \neg T$ (in the examples of the introduction, we wrote $A \Rightarrow \bot$ for $\neg A$). Sequents are of two forms: $\Gamma \mid \phi : A \vdash \mid \Delta$, and $\Gamma \mid \vdash \sigma : A \mid \Delta$. In both cases, the environment Γ is a set of the form $(x_i : \neg A_i)_i$ (and dually for Δ). The typing rules are given in fig 1. As mentionned in section 10, the translation from λ-calculus preserves types, modulo the equivalence $(A \times B) \Rightarrow C \approx A \Rightarrow B \Rightarrow C$. In particular the co-term $\bar{\lambda}u.u\_\lambda y.y\_\bar{\epsilon}$, seen in the introduction, shares the type of the identity $\lambda y.y$, which it approximates:

$$\dfrac{\dfrac{\dfrac{\dfrac{\overline{y:\bot \mid \bar{\epsilon}:1 \vdash \ \mid u:\bot\Rightarrow\bot}}{y:\bot \mid y\_\bar{\epsilon}:1 \vdash \ \mid u:\bot\Rightarrow\bot}}{\mid \lambda y.y\_\bar{\epsilon}:\bot \vdash \ \mid u:\bot\Rightarrow\bot}}{\mid \ \vdash u\_\lambda y.y\_\bar{\epsilon}:1 \mid u:\bot\Rightarrow\bot}}{\mid \ \vdash \bar{\lambda}u.u\_\lambda y.y\_\bar{\epsilon}:\bot\Rightarrow\bot \mid}$$

4. Reduction rules

We define below an equivalence relation $\equiv$ on terms and co-terms, and in Figure 2 we define a "base" reduction relation. In this figure,

$$\frac{}{\Gamma \mid \epsilon : A \vdash \ \mid \Delta} \qquad \frac{}{\Gamma \mid \ \vdash \bar{\epsilon} : 1 \mid \Delta}$$

$$\frac{\Gamma, x : A \mid \phi : B \vdash \ \mid \Delta}{\Gamma \mid \lambda x.\phi : A \times B \vdash \ \mid \Delta} \qquad \frac{\Gamma \mid \ \vdash \sigma : B \mid u : A, \Delta}{\Gamma \mid \ \vdash \bar{\lambda} u.\sigma : A \times B \mid \Delta}$$

$$\frac{\Gamma, x : \neg(A \times B) \mid \ \vdash \sigma : A \mid \Delta}{\Gamma, x : \neg(A \times B) \mid x\_\sigma : B \vdash \ \mid \Delta} \qquad \frac{\Gamma \mid \phi : A \vdash \ \mid u : \neg A, \Delta}{\Gamma \mid \ \vdash u\_\phi : 1 \mid u : \neg A, \Delta}$$

$$\frac{\Gamma \mid \phi : A \vdash \ \mid \Delta \qquad \Gamma \mid \psi : A \vdash \ \mid \Delta}{\Gamma \mid \phi + \psi : A \vdash \ \mid \Delta} \qquad \frac{\Gamma \mid \ \vdash \sigma : A \mid \Delta \qquad \Gamma \mid \ \vdash \tau : A \mid \Delta}{\Gamma \mid \ \vdash \sigma + \tau : A \mid \Delta}$$

$$\frac{\Gamma \mid \phi : A \times B \vdash \ \mid \Delta \qquad \Gamma \mid \ \vdash \sigma : A \mid \Delta}{\Gamma \mid \phi \triangleleft \sigma : B \vdash \ \mid \Delta} \qquad \frac{\Gamma \mid \ \vdash \sigma : A \mid \Delta \qquad \Gamma \mid \ \vdash \tau : B \mid \Delta}{\Gamma \mid \ \vdash \sigma \triangleleft \tau : A \times B \mid \Delta}$$

$$\frac{\Gamma, \vec{x} : L \mid \phi : S \times A \vdash \ \mid \ \vec{v} : S,\ \vec{u} : L, \Delta}{\Gamma \mid \stackrel{(x_i,u_i)_i}{\nabla}{}^{\vec{v}}.\phi : A \vdash \ \mid \Delta}$$

Figure 1. Typing rules.

$\sigma_{\mathrm{g}}, \tau_{\mathrm{g}}$ denote *guarded* co-terms, i.e. co-terms of the form $\bar{\epsilon}$ or u_ϕ. We then define the relation $\to$ as the composition $\equiv \circ \to_b \circ \equiv$. Moreover, by convention, $\to^*$ will denote the union of $\equiv$ and of the transitive closure of $\to$. The relation $\equiv$ is the smallest context-closed equivalence relation such that:

- It includes $\equiv_\alpha$ (α-renaming).
- It makes the operator $+$ commutative and associative, with neutral element ϵ or $\bar{\epsilon}$ (depending on the polarity).[1]
- It makes all operators distribute over $+$; for example:

$$\lambda x.(\phi + \psi) \equiv \lambda x.\phi + \lambda x.\psi$$

- It contains the following three rules:

$$\begin{array}{rcl} \epsilon \triangleleft \sigma & \equiv & \epsilon \\ \stackrel{L}{\nabla}{}^{S}.\epsilon & \equiv & \epsilon \\ \stackrel{L_1}{\nabla}{}^{S_1}.\stackrel{L_2}{\nabla}{}^{S_2}.\phi & \equiv & \stackrel{L_1 \cup L_2}{\nabla}{}^{S_2 \cdot S_1}.\phi \end{array}$$

Note how, in the last rule, the stacks S_1 and S_2 are concatenated with S_2, the closest to ϕ, first.

A term (or co-term) in normal form exactly when it does not contain the operators $\triangleleft$ or ∇. If additionally it does not contain the operator $+$, it is said to be a *normal branch*. For example, all the terms and co-terms named in the introduction are in normal form; and all are normal branches, except σ_3, which contains a connector $+$. The main properties of the language are listed in section 10, after its extension with fixed-points in section 5. But already we can note a property which is specific to the language without fixed-point:

$$\begin{array}{rcll} \phi \triangleleft \bar{\lambda}\vec{u}.\sigma_{\mathrm{g}} & \to_b & \nabla^{\vec{u}}.(\phi \triangleleft \sigma_{\mathrm{g}}) & u_i \notin \mathrm{FN}(\phi) \\ \lambda x.\phi \triangleleft \sigma_{\mathrm{g}} & \to_b & \lambda x.(\phi \triangleleft \sigma_{\mathrm{g}}) & x \notin \mathrm{FN}(\sigma_{\mathrm{g}}) \\ x\_\sigma \triangleleft \tau_{\mathrm{g}} & \to_b & x\_(\sigma \triangleleft \tau_{\mathrm{g}}) & \\ & & & \\ \bar{\lambda}u.\sigma \triangleleft \tau & \to_b & \bar{\lambda}u.(\sigma \triangleleft \tau) & u \notin \mathrm{FN}(\tau) \\ \sigma_{\mathrm{g}} \triangleleft \bar{\lambda}v.\tau & \to_b & \bar{\lambda}v.(\sigma_{\mathrm{g}} \triangleleft \tau) & v \notin \mathrm{FN}(\sigma_{\mathrm{g}}) \\ u\_\phi \triangleleft v\_\psi & \to_b & u\_(\phi \triangleleft v\_\psi) + v\_(\psi \triangleleft u\_\phi) & \\ & & & \\ \stackrel{L}{\nabla}{}^{u \cdot S}.\lambda x.\phi & \to_b & \stackrel{(x,u),L}{\nabla}{}^{S}.\phi & x \notin L, u \notin L \\ \stackrel{L}{\nabla}.\lambda x.\phi & \to_b & \lambda x.\ \stackrel{L}{\nabla}.\phi & x \notin L \\ & & & \\ \stackrel{L}{\nabla}{}^{S}.x\_\bar{\lambda}\vec{v}.u\_\phi & \to_b & \stackrel{L}{\nabla}{}^{\vec{v} \cdot S}.\phi & (x,u) \in L \\ \stackrel{L}{\nabla}{}^{S}.x\_\bar{\lambda}\vec{v}.w\_\phi & \to_b & \epsilon & (x,u) \in L \\ \stackrel{L}{\nabla}{}^{S}.x\_\bar{\lambda}\vec{v}.\bar{\epsilon} & \to_b & \epsilon & (x,u) \in L \\ & & & \\ \stackrel{L}{\nabla}{}^{\vec{u}}.x\_\bar{\lambda}\vec{v}.w\_\phi & \to_b & x\_\bar{\lambda}\vec{v}.\bar{\lambda}\vec{u}.w\_\ \stackrel{L}{\nabla}.\phi & x \notin L, w \notin L \\ \stackrel{L}{\nabla}{}^{\vec{u}}.x\_\bar{\lambda}\vec{v}.w\_\phi & \to_b & x\_\bar{\lambda}\vec{v}.\bar{\lambda}\vec{u}.\bar{\epsilon} & x \notin L, w \in L \\ \stackrel{L}{\nabla}{}^{\vec{u}}.x\_\bar{\lambda}\vec{v}.\bar{\epsilon} & \to_b & x\_\bar{\lambda}\vec{v}.\bar{\lambda}\vec{u}.\bar{\epsilon} & x \notin L \end{array}$$

Figure 2. Reduction rules.

Proposition 1. *The $\lambda\bar{\lambda}$-calculus, as defined in section 2, equipped with the reduction $\to$, is strongly normalizing.*

Proof. Each rule in Figure 2 has the effect of reducing the size of a term or co-term to which a connector $\triangleleft$ or ∇ is applied; thus pushing those connectors toward the leaves of the syntactic tree. Additionally, consider a non-normal term (or co-term) which contains only one connector $\triangleleft$ or ∇, and no connector $+$. Then there is one (and only one) reduction rule which applies. Together with the equivalence rules which apply to the operator $+$, this proves by induction that the reduction only terminates on normal forms. □

5. Fixed-point and innocent expansion

In game semantics, strategies naturally represent programs with the power of functional references. To obtain the behaviors of purely functional programs, this power must be limited, using conditions called *innocence* and *visibility*. Innocence states that, for a given query of the environment, the program must always react in the same way (the formal definition is recalled in section 11). In this section, we will see how translated λ-terms generate this infinite number of identical reaction through fixed-point expansion.

[1] This is correct in the setting of this work, where a well-typed term of the form $\sigma + \bar{\epsilon}$ is such that σ is of type 1. However, in an untyped setting one should restrict $\sigma + \bar{\epsilon} \equiv \sigma$ to be true only if σ is guarded. This restriction is not necessary for ϵ.

We extend the syntax with additional constructions and an additional rule, shown below. The new fixed-point names are ranged over by α, β and their variants. They appear in the environment as distinguished variables:

$$\frac{\Gamma, \alpha^u : \neg A \mid \phi : A \vdash \; \mid u : \neg A, \Delta}{\Gamma \mid \; \vdash u\_\nu\alpha.\phi : 1 \mid u : \neg A, \Delta}$$

$$\frac{}{\Gamma, \alpha^u : \neg A \mid \; \vdash u\_\alpha : 1 \mid u : \neg A, \Delta}$$

$$\nu\alpha.\phi \rightarrow_b \phi[\alpha \backslash \nu\alpha.\phi]$$

The new reduction rule extends the "base" reduction $\rightarrow_b$ defined in Figure 2, and thus extends the reduction relation $\rightarrow$. The typing ensures that a fixed-point name α is always "guarded" by the same co-variable u.

We now define a syntactical "innocent lifting" Inn, which takes a term ϕ, and returns co-term $\bar\lambda u.u\_\psi$, in which u_ϕ occurs at every possible position in ψ.

$$\begin{array}{rcll}
\mathrm{Inn}(\phi) & = & \bar\lambda u.u_\nu\alpha.\mathrm{Inn}^{\alpha,u}(\phi) & u, \alpha \notin \mathrm{FN}(\phi) \\
\mathrm{Inn}^{\alpha,u}(\bar\epsilon) & = & u_\alpha & \\
\mathrm{Inn}^{\alpha,u}(v_\phi) & = & u_\alpha \triangleleft v_\mathrm{Inn}^{\alpha,u}(\phi) & \\
(\cdots) & & &
\end{array}$$

The omitted rules in this definition stipulate that $\mathrm{Inn}^{\alpha,u}$ "passes through" every other operator; for example, $\mathrm{Inn}^{\alpha,u}(\lambda x.\phi) = \lambda x.\mathrm{Inn}^{\alpha,u}(\phi)$, and $\mathrm{Inn}^{\alpha,u}(\sigma + \tau) = \mathrm{Inn}^{\alpha,u}(\sigma) + \mathrm{Inn}^{\alpha,u}(\tau)$. Note that the operation Inn applies only to terms, while $\mathrm{Inn}^{\alpha,u}$ (for a given α) applies to both terms and co-terms (and preserves polarity). As an example, consider the effect of Inn on the term $\lambda x.x$:

$$\begin{array}{rl}
 & \mathrm{Inn}(\lambda x.x_\bar\epsilon) \\
= & \bar\lambda u.u_\nu\alpha.\mathrm{Inn}^{\alpha,u}(\lambda x.x_\bar\epsilon) \\
= & \bar\lambda u.u_\nu\alpha.\lambda x.x_u_\alpha \\
\rightarrow & \bar\lambda u.u_\lambda x.x_u_\nu\alpha.\lambda x.x_u_\alpha \\
\rightarrow^* & \bar\lambda u.u_\lambda x.x_u_\lambda x.x_u_\lambda x.x_u_\cdots
\end{array}$$

This transforms the finite behavior of of the $\lambda\bar\lambda$-term $\lambda x.x\_\bar\epsilon$ into an infinite behavior, which reacts to the initial query u as many times as needed. Without the fixed-point, finite terms in our syntax could only describe finite behaviors (with the exception of the infinite behaviors due to lack of η-expansion).

The operation Inn allows us to define a translation tr from the λ-calculus to the $\lambda\bar\lambda$-calculus:

$$\begin{array}{rcl}
\mathrm{tr}(M) & = & \mathrm{Inn}([M]) \\
{[MN]} & = & [M] \triangleleft \mathrm{Inn}([N]) \\
{[\lambda x.M]} & = & \lambda x.[M] \\
{[x]} & = & x_\bar\epsilon \\
{[\Omega]} & = & \epsilon
\end{array}$$

Note the initial innocent lifting, which makes this translations return an Opponent-starting strategy.

The correction of this translation (with respect to the semantics of the $\lambda\bar\lambda$-calculus, and of the λ-calculus in a comparable setting) is stated in section 10.4. In particular, this translation preserves the type, modulo the equivalence $(A \times B) \Rightarrow C \approx A \Rightarrow B \Rightarrow C$ (which corresponds to an equality of the corresponding arenas). It does not, however, send normal forms to normal forms. On the contrary, the translation of any λ-term (except Ω) has an infinite reduction path (as in the above example). But, if the λ-term was normal, this reduction path consists exclusively of fixed-point expansion. As long as the guard condition (imposed by typing) is respected for all occurrences of $\nu\alpha$ and α, this expansion is well behaved: it will always produce a move u in one reduction. This prompts the definition of *pseudo-normal* terms (and co-terms), which may contain any connectors of the extended language, except $\triangleleft$ and $\triangledown$.

We give two examples of the translation's action. The first is $\mathrm{tr}(\lambda x.x)$, which is simply $\mathrm{Inn}(\lambda x.x\_\bar\epsilon)$, which we have already seen. A more complete example is given by the once η-expanded identity:

$$\begin{array}{rl}
 & \mathrm{tr}(\lambda x.\lambda y.xy) \\
= & \mathrm{Inn}(\lambda x.\lambda y.(x_\bar\epsilon \triangleleft \mathrm{Inn}(y_\bar\epsilon))) \\
= & \mathrm{Inn}(\lambda x.\lambda y.(x_\bar\epsilon \triangleleft \bar\lambda v.v_\nu\beta.y_v_\beta)) \\
\rightarrow & \mathrm{Inn}(\lambda x.\lambda y.(x_\bar\lambda v.v_\nu\beta.y_v_\beta)) \\
= & \bar\lambda u.u_\nu\alpha.\lambda x.\lambda y.(x_\bar\lambda v.(u_\alpha \triangleleft v_\nu\beta.y_(u_\alpha \triangleleft v_\beta))) \\
\rightarrow^* & \bar\lambda u.u_\lambda x.\lambda y.x_\bar\lambda v. \\
 & \quad ((u_\lambda x.\lambda y.x_\cdots) \triangleleft (v_y_((u_\cdots) \triangleleft (v_\cdots))))
\end{array}$$

Notice the sequence "v_y_u", which illustrates that the co-term is ready to react to u in every branch of the co-term. Terms whose strategy correspond to a program without effect can be described directly as a sub-language of the $\lambda\bar\lambda$-calculus, as described in section 10.4.

6. Comparison with other languages

6.1 The π-calculus and similar languages

There are many similarities between the $\lambda\lambda$-calculus and the π-calculus, essentially in the behavior of terms without binders λ or $\bar\lambda$. For example, the following reductions are very similar (here σ is supposed to be of a certain form, for example v_ϕ'):

$$\begin{array}{llcl}
\lambda\bar\lambda\text{-calculus:} & \overset{(x,u)}{\triangledown}.(x_\sigma \triangleleft u_\phi) & \rightarrow^* & \overset{(x,u)}{\triangledown}.(\phi \triangleleft \sigma) \\
\pi\text{-calculus:} & \nu x.(x().Q \mid \bar{x}\langle\rangle.P) & \rightarrow^* & \nu x.(Q \mid P)
\end{array}$$

In $\nu x.(x().Q \mid \bar{x}\langle\rangle.P)$, two processes, $x().Q$ and $\bar{x}\langle\rangle.P$, interact along a shared private channel x, whose scope is restricted by νx. The input $x()$ and the output $x\langle\rangle$ must occur before P and Q can interact with the outside world. The same description applies to $\overset{(x,u)}{\triangledown}.(x\_\sigma \triangleleft u\_\phi)$: the input x and the output u form a private channel, restricted by $\overset{(x,u)}{\triangledown}$, and the two processes x_σ and u_ϕ interact along this channel.

As can been seen on this example, a lifting by x or u corresponds to an action of arity zero ($x()$ or $\bar{x}\langle\rangle$): no information beyond the action itself is transmitted. In that sense, the $\lambda\bar\lambda$-calculus seems closer to a simpler language, such as CCS. There are other similarities with this language: the notion of recursive process definition in CCS ($A \overset{\mathrm{def}}{=} P$, where P may contain A) is closer to our syntactic fixed-point construction ($\nu\alpha$) than to the replication "!" of the π-calculus (note that in our language, $\nu\alpha$ denote a syntactical fixed-point, and not a restriction as in π-calculus). Additionally, the operator "+" in CCS is similar to ours.

Other aspects of the $\lambda\bar\lambda$-calculus bring it closer to the fusion calculus [21]. This language introduces "fusion" actions which link pairs of names, and shows a complete symmetry between the input and the output; whereas the π-calculus gives a special role to an input of the form $x(y).P$, which binds y in P (when the output $\bar{x}\langle y\rangle.Q$ does not bind y in Q). The fusion calculus is more effective at representing shared state between processes, and strong reduction strategies involving reduction under abstraction; both of which require elaborate encoding in the π-calculus. These two strength are also present in the $\lambda\bar\lambda$-calculus, which represent non-innocent strategies (corresponding to programs with shared states), and allows reduction inside any context (in particular, this allows reduction under abstraction in the image of a λ-term by the translation seen in section 5).

But, just as the π-calculus, the expressivity of the fusion calculus depends on actions which send and receive channel names; whereas our language relies on its system of binders: λ, $\bar\lambda$ and $\triangledown$.

In particular, this means that we have no extrusion, which makes reasoning on scopes much simpler. Additionally, in the fusion calculus, the fusions are represented as a global equivalence relation on names, which is independent from the scope operator. In comparison, our notion of links is local and represented with binders.

6.2 The $\bar{\lambda}\nu\tilde{\mu}$-calculus

We briefly mention this language, described in [8] as an other example of a syntactic duality between programs and their environments, with two dual binders: the μ and $\tilde{\mu}$. But the similarity is only superficial. In the $\bar{\lambda}\mu\tilde{\mu}$-calculus, when a term, starting with a μ, and an *environment*, starting with a $\tilde{\mu}$, interact, the two dual binders do not fusion in a single symmetric step as would λ and $\bar{\lambda}$. Instead, such an interaction is a critical pair, in which either the μ or the $\tilde{\mu}$ may be eliminated; and the choice between those two possibility correspond to either call-by-value or call-by-name disciplines. In general, the duality in this language is a tool to study CBV and CBN, whereas in our language, there are no critical pairs, and the object of study is the power of effects.

6.3 Languages with references

There are many differences between the $\lambda\bar{\lambda}$-calculus and languages with references, in particular the one presented in [1], which is a simply typed λ-calculus extended with reference types. Our language allows reduction under any context, and that the reduction is confluent, when the language in [1] uses an abstract machine with a store. Additionally, in this work the power of references is obtained by duality, and not by factorization via a memory-cell strategy.

The expressive power of the two languages can be compared by considering their semantics. Aside from the differences in the chosen setting (integer types, and the family construction for call-by-value behavior, are not used here), the strategies represented in [1] and in this work are the same, with one distinction. This difference concerns strategies which are not *single-threaded*. These are represented in the $\lambda\bar{\lambda}$-calculus, but not in the language described in [1]. Single-threaded strategies only differ from others in that their reaction to initial moves must always be the same. This appears clearly in the difference, in the introduction's example, between $\text{new } r;\ r := \text{true};\ (M\ N)$ and $\phi_1 \lhd \sigma_2$. In the first case, for N to behave differently on its second call, a reference r must be defined *before* the application $(M\ N)$. If r was declared inside N, this behavior would not be possible, as it is not a single-threaded strategy. On the other hand, this same behavior is directly represented by σ_2.

More directly, a simple memory-cell strategy can be expressed in the $\lambda\bar{\lambda}$-calculus. We start with an example in a language with references:

$$\text{new } r;\ r := c_1;\ r := c_2;\ !r$$

This program behaves as c_2. We represent this program in our setting as the interaction of the term ϕ_3, defined as the translation of a λ-term, with a co-term "cell" which represents the memory-cell, and will be defined later.

$$\phi_3 = \text{tr}(\lambda r_{\text{write}}.\lambda r_{\text{read}}.(r_{\text{write}}\ (c_1)\ (r_{\text{write}}\ (c_2)\ (r_{\text{read}}))))$$
$$\phi_3 \lhd \text{cell} \to^* c_2\_\bar{\epsilon}$$

Here ϕ_3 receives two variables, r_{write} and r_{read}. These correspond to the read and write methods of the reference; both are provided by "cell". The write method takes two arguments: a value, and a co-term representing the rest of the program. Here we can see two successive writes, one with value c_1, and one with value c_2; followed by a read. We now give the memory cell co-term:

$$\begin{aligned}\text{cell} = {}&\bar{\lambda}\text{write}.\bar{\lambda}\text{read}.\text{write}\_\nu\alpha.\lambda\text{val}.\lambda k.k\_\\ &(\text{write}\_\alpha + \text{read}\_\nu\beta.\text{val}\_(\text{read}\_\beta + \text{write}\_\alpha))\end{aligned}$$

The two co-variables "write" and "read", are the methods mentioned above. When the write method is called, it takes a variable "val", the value, and k, which is immediately called (this gives the hand back to the calling term). If a call to "read" immediately follows, the memory cell reacts by calling "val". To show how the strategy answers to a read after two successive writes, we apply one step of fixed-point expansion to the co-term:

$$\begin{aligned}\text{cell} \to {}&\bar{\lambda}\text{write}.\bar{\lambda}\text{read}.\text{write}\_\lambda\text{val}.\lambda k.k\_\\ &(\quad \text{read}\_\nu\beta.\text{val}\_\text{read}\_\beta\\ &\ + \text{write}\_\nu\alpha.\lambda\text{val}'.\lambda k'.k'\_(\quad \text{write}\_\alpha\\ &\qquad\qquad\qquad + \text{read}\_\nu\beta'.\text{val}'\_\text{read}\_\beta'))\end{aligned}$$

Here we have also applied α-renaming to val, k and β. This shows that, after two consecutive calls to "write", the co-term will answer any call to "read" by calling the new variable val$'$. Note that the other branch of the co-term, "read_val_β", will be discarded as soon as the Opponent makes the second call to "write". To show that $\phi_3 \lhd \text{cell}$ indeed reduces to $c_2\_\bar{\epsilon}$, we give ϕ_3', which is the relevant branch of ϕ_3 (more precisely, ϕ_3' is a term in normal branch form, which is a sub-term of some expansion of ϕ_3).

$$\begin{aligned}\phi_3' = {}&\lambda r_{\text{write}}.\lambda r_{\text{read}}.r_{\text{write}}\_\bar{\lambda}v.\bar{\lambda}u.u\_\\ &\qquad r_{\text{write}}\_\bar{\lambda}v'.\bar{\lambda}u'.u'\_r_{\text{read}}\_v'\_c_2\_\bar{\epsilon}\end{aligned}$$
$$\phi_3' \lhd \text{cell} \ \to^*\ \overset{L}{\nabla}.c_2\_\bar{\epsilon} \ \to\ c_2\_\bar{\epsilon}$$

where L is:

$$\{(r_{\text{write}}, \text{write}), (r_{\text{read}}, \text{read}), (\text{val}, v), (k, u), (\text{val}', v'), (k', u')\}$$

7. Duality and the Böhm-out lemma

The most prominent feature of our language is the duality between terms and co-terms. This duality is the syntactical representation of the symmetry between the Player and the Opponent in game semantics; in particular, it shows that any action taken by the Opponent can be matched by the Player. This allows a (non-innocent) strategy to "follow", and thus to recognize any possible play; which is why, in game semantics, the existence of a separator between two different strategies is immediate. Syntactically, this translates to the following, which is a form of "Böhm-out" lemma for the $\lambda\bar{\lambda}$-calculus, and will provide us with separators when proving full abstraction in section 10.

We first define the *dual* of a normal branch, which is obtained by replacing each constructor with its dual, and each variable x or covariable u with a new co-variable or variable, typically denoted by $\bar{x}$ or $\bar{u}$ (respectively). We write $\phi[]$ or $\sigma[]$ for contexts which are terms or co-terms.

Lemma 2. *For any term of the form $\phi[\phi']$, where $\phi[\epsilon]$ is a closed normal branch, and any co-term of the form $\sigma[\sigma'_{\text{g}}]$, where $\sigma[\bar{\epsilon}]$ is the dual of $\phi[\epsilon]$,*

$$\phi[\phi'] \lhd \sigma[\sigma'_{\text{g}}] \ \to^*\ \overset{L}{\nabla}.(\phi' \lhd \sigma'_{\text{g}})$$

for some set of links L.

Dually, for any co-term of the form $\sigma[\phi']$, where $\sigma[\epsilon]$ is a closed normal branch, and any term of the form $\phi[\sigma'_{\text{g}}]$, where $\phi[\bar{\epsilon}]$ is the dual of $\sigma[\epsilon]$,

$$\sigma[\phi'] \lhd \phi[\sigma'_{\text{g}}] \ \to^*\ \overset{L}{\nabla}.(\phi' \lhd \sigma'_{\text{g}})$$

for some set of links L.

To illustrate, consider the following:

$$\phi_1' = \lambda x.x\_\bar{\lambda}v.\bar{\lambda}w.v\_x\_\bar{\lambda}v'.\bar{\lambda}w'.w'\_c\_\bar{\epsilon}$$
$$\sigma_2 = \bar{\lambda}u.u\_\lambda y.\lambda z\ .y\_u\_\lambda y'.\lambda z'\ .z'\ \_\bar{\epsilon}$$

$$\phi_1' \lhd \sigma_2 \ \to^*\ \overset{L}{\nabla}.(c\_\bar{\epsilon} \lhd \bar{\epsilon}) \ \to^*\ c\_\bar{\epsilon}$$

where $L = \{(x, u), (y, v), (z, w), (y', v'), (z', w')\}$; note that to obtain this form, the equivalence $\overset{L_1}{\nabla} \cdot \overset{L_2}{\nabla} \cdot\phi \equiv \overset{L_1 \cup L_2}{\nabla} \cdot\phi$ needs to be used. This example is taken from the introduction (with the modification that c is free in ϕ_1', whereas ϕ_1 was a closed term in the introduction; this makes the application of the lemma more direct). To make the duality obvious, σ_2 can be rewritten as:

$$\sigma_2 =_\alpha \bar{\lambda}\bar{x}.\bar{x}\_\lambda\bar{v}.\lambda\bar{w}.\bar{v}\_\bar{x}\_\lambda\bar{v}'.\lambda\bar{w}'.\bar{w}'\_\bar{\epsilon}$$

In which case the value of L is $\{(x, \bar{x}), (\bar{v}, v), (\bar{w}, w), (\bar{v}', v'), (\bar{w}', w')\}$, linking each variable or co-variable of ϕ_1' to its dual.

8. Game semantics

8.1 Arenas and strategies

The following definitions are those of the standard Hyland-Ong game semantics [14], but with the following simplifications: no distinction is made between questions and answers (and therefore there is no bracketing condition); there is no condition of determinism; and we allow odd-length plays in strategies[2]. These games can be equipped with a structure of CCC (Cartesian Closed Category) [14].

An *arena* A is a triple $\langle M_A, \lambda_A, \vdash_A\rangle$ where

- M_A is a finite set of *moves*, called the *alphabet of* A.
- $\lambda_A : M_A \to \{P, O\}$ is a *polarity*, or *labeling* function on M_A; P denotes a Player move, and O an Opponent move.
- $\vdash_A$ is an *enabling* relation on $M_A \times M_A$, giving a forest structure on M_A, and satisfying:
  - $a \vdash_A b \Rightarrow \lambda_A(a) \neq \lambda_A(b)$
  - $(\nexists b,\ b \vdash_A a) \Rightarrow \lambda_A(a) = O$

  In the second case, a is said to be *initial*.

The basic arenas 1 and $\perp$ are the arenas with zero and one move, respectively.

Given arenas A and B, one can build $A \times B$:

- $M_{A\times B} = M_A + M_B$;
- $\lambda_{A\times B} = [\lambda_A, \lambda_B]$ (the co-pairing in $\mathtt{Set}$);
- $a \vdash_{A\times B} b$ iff $a \vdash_A b$ or $a \vdash_B b$.

As well as $A \Rightarrow B$:

- $M_{A\Rightarrow B} = M_A + M_B$;
- $\lambda_{A\Rightarrow B} = [-\lambda_A, \lambda_B]$;
- $b \vdash_{A\Rightarrow B} a$ iff $b \vdash_B a$, or $b \vdash_A a$, or b is initial in B and a is initial in A.

We are now able to give an interpretation $[\![A]\!]$, in the obvious way, for any type A as defined in section 3. For the sake of simplicity, we will in general confuse A and $[\![A]\!]$. A *legal play* s on an arena A is a sequence of moves of A, of alternating polarities, equipped with *justification pointers*: any occurrence b of a move in s must point to an occurrence of a move a earlier in s, with $a \vdash_A b$; with the exceptions of initial moves, which have no pointer. The set of legal plays on A is written P_A. We will also use the relaxed notion of *plays*, which imposes no condition on the justification pointers. A *strategy* on A is a prefix-closed set of legal plays on A. A strategy is *finite* if all its plays are of finite length.

8.2 Player-starting arenas and strategies

The arenas defined above may be called *Opponent-starting arenas*, because of the polarity of initial moves. We define dually the *Player-starting arenas*, and note $(\cdot)^*$ the operator which reverses polarity.

[2] Allowing odd-length plays improves the symmetry between Player and Opponent, and avoids some technicalities. The cost is that two strategies differing only on odd-length plays will be observationally equivalent.

8.3 Operations on plays

We now give basic operators on sets of plays. If s is a Player-starting play and m is an Opponent move, we define the concatenation, or *lifting* $m \cdot s$ as the sequence $m \cdot s$ where m justifies every move which was unjustified in s; and dually if the polarity of m and s are reversed (here we leave arenas implicit for simplicity). A *thread* of a play s is a sub-sequence of moves of s which are all hereditarily justified by the same initial move. In the following definitions, $\boldsymbol{\phi}$ denotes a Player-starting strategy, $\boldsymbol{\sigma}$ and $\boldsymbol{\tau}$ Opponent-starting strategies, M an alphabet, s a play, and A, B and X_1, X_2 denote arenas (we use bold letters $\boldsymbol{\phi}, \cdots$ for strategies, to distinguish them from elements of the syntax).

- Prefixes: $\mathrm{Prefixes}(s)$ is the set of prefixes of the play s. This extends to sets of plays.
- Thread: $\mathrm{Thread}(s)$ is the play obtained by keeping only the moves of s which are hereditarily justified by the first move of s.
- Hiding: $\upharpoonright_A(s)$ is obtained by removing in s any move not in M_A; this may leave some moves in s without a pointer.[3]
- Interleaving (merging): $\mathrm{Merge}(\boldsymbol{\phi}, \boldsymbol{\sigma}) = \{s \in P_{A\Rightarrow B} \mid s\upharpoonright_{A^*} \in \boldsymbol{\phi},\ s\upharpoonright_B \in \boldsymbol{\sigma}\}$, where A^* is the Player-starting arena of $\boldsymbol{\phi}$, and B is the arena of $\boldsymbol{\sigma}$. Similarly, $\mathrm{Merge}(\boldsymbol{\sigma}, \boldsymbol{\tau}) = \{s \in P_{A\times B} \mid s\upharpoonright_A \in \boldsymbol{\sigma},\ s\upharpoonright_B \in \boldsymbol{\tau}\}$, where A is the arena of $\boldsymbol{\sigma}$, and B is the arena of $\boldsymbol{\tau}$.
- Renaming: $\mathrm{Rename}_{A_1\backslash A_2}(s) = s[M_{A_1}\backslash M_{A_2}]$, the renaming of moves in s, for two isomorphic arenas A_1, A_2. This extends to strategies (both Player and Opponent-starting).
- Connection: Let $\boldsymbol{\phi}$ be a Player-starting strategy on the Player-starting arena $((A \times C_2) \Rightarrow (B \times C_1))^*$, where C_1 and C_2 are isomorphic; then $\mathrm{Connection}_{C_2,C_1}(\boldsymbol{\phi}) = \mathrm{Prefixes}(\{s\upharpoonright_{(A\Rightarrow B)^*} \mid s \in \boldsymbol{\phi},\ s\upharpoonright_{C_2} \approx s\upharpoonright_{C_1}\})$.[4]
- Detach: $\mathrm{Detach}_A(s)$ is obtained by removing the justification pointers of each move m in s such that m is initial in A. This extends to sets of plays.

9. Semantics

The types are interpreted as Opponent-starting arenas, as seen in section 8.1. The interpretation for an environment $\Gamma = (x_i : \neg A_i)_i$ is that of the type $A_1 \times \cdots \times A_n$; and similarly for a co-environment Δ. A typing of the form $\Gamma \mid\vdash \sigma : A \mid \Delta$ is interpreted as an Opponent-starting strategy $[\![\sigma]\!]$ on the Opponent-starting arena $\Gamma \Rightarrow (A \times \Delta)$. A typing of the form $\Gamma \mid \phi : A \vdash \mid \Delta$ is interpreted as a Player-starting strategy $[\![\phi]\!]$, on the Player-starting arena $(\Delta \Rightarrow (\Gamma \times A))^*$. In the following definitions, we use the notations of the typing rule corresponding to each case. In some instances, indices are added to distinguish isomorphic sub-arenas.

- $[\![u\_\phi]\!]$: We note $((\Delta \times (A_2 \Rightarrow \perp_2)) \Rightarrow (\Gamma \times A))^*$ the Player-starting arena of $[\![\phi]\!]$ in the following:

  $$[\![u\_\phi]\!] = \mathrm{Detach}_{\Delta\times(A_2\Rightarrow\perp_2)}(\mathrm{Prefixes}(\{q_2 \cdot s \mid s \in \mathrm{Rename}_{A\backslash A_2}([\![\phi]\!])\}))$$

[3] This differs slightly from the usual definition of hiding, in which some of the moves which loose their pointer gain a new one (if a move which hereditarily justifies it still exists).

[4] We close by prefixes here because the condition $s\upharpoonright_{C_1} \approx s\upharpoonright_{C_2}$ rejects odd-length plays.

where q_2 is the only (Opponent) move of $\bot_2$. The resulting strategy plays on $\Gamma \Rightarrow (\Delta \times (A_2 \Rightarrow \bot_2))$.

We started with this construction, as it is the most representative of the specificity of the language. The strategy $[\![\phi]\!]$ is lifted by an Opponent move q_2. But instead of this move being a fresh one, it is the initial move in the arena corresponding to the type of the co-variable u. Recall that this type is necessarily a negation form, guaranteeing the existence and uniqueness of q_2. The moves of A occurring in $[\![\phi]\!]$ are also renamed to their counterparts in A_2, which is the copy of A, contained in the co-environment, and specific to u; this hides A from the outside. Intuitively, this means that we build plays on $A_2 \Rightarrow \bot_2$ by playing the first move (q_2), then by using an existing play on A. We also need to fix the pointer structure, which otherwise would show the initial moves of Δ as having a justifier, itself justified by q_2. In fact, the resulting strategy will only play in Δ if it already played q_2 followed by some Player move; but the arrival type is more liberal, and would have allowed moves in Δ to be played immediately. To reflect this, we "detach" the moves which are initial in Δ, showing that they did not need any justification (the same is done for the initial moves of $A_2 \Rightarrow \bot_2$, i.e. for q_2).

- $[\![x\_\sigma]\!]$: We note $(\Gamma \times (A_2 \times B_2 \Rightarrow \bot_2)) \Rightarrow (A \times \Delta)$ the arena of $[\![\sigma]\!]$ in the following:

  $$\begin{aligned}[\![x\_\sigma]\!] = \mathrm{Detach}_{\Gamma\times(A_2\times B_2\Rightarrow\bot_2)}(\mathrm{Prefixes}(\\ \{q_2\cdot s \in P_{(\Delta\Rightarrow(\Gamma\times((A_2\times B_2)\Rightarrow\bot_2)\times B))^*} \mid \\ s\restriction_{(\Delta\Rightarrow(\Gamma\times(A_2\times B_2)\Rightarrow\bot_2))^*} \in \mathrm{Rename}_{A\backslash A_2}([\![\sigma]\!]),\\ s\restriction_B \approx \mathrm{Thread}(q_2\cdot s)\restriction_{B_2}\}))\end{aligned}$$

  where q_2 is the only (Player) move of the Player-starting arena ${\bot_2}^*$. The resulting strategy plays on:

  $$(\Delta \Rightarrow (\Gamma \times (A_2 \times B_2 \Rightarrow \bot_2) \times B))^*$$

  This construction is very similar to the previous one, but must support partial application (note that in u_ϕ, the types of u and ϕ must match, whereas in x_σ, the match is only partial, leaving B out). This translates to "copycat" moves between two copies of B: the first one (noted B_2) was already present in the environment as part of the type of x; while a new one (noted simply B) is introduced by the construction. The introduction of this new copy is done when we pick plays in $P_{(\Delta\Rightarrow(\Gamma\times((A_2\times B_2)\Rightarrow\bot_2)\times B))^*}$, while the copycat behavior is enforced by the condition $s\restriction_{B_2} \approx s\restriction_B$. Only moves in the current thread, that are hereditarily justified by the new occurrence of q_2, are copied in this way. Thus, as in the previous construction of $[\![u\_\phi]\!]$, we are extending the behavior of the strategy in the arena corresponding to a given variable (or co-variable) name, by adding a single new thread, which is initiated with the negation move specific to that name.

- $[\![\sigma \lhd \tau]\!]$: We note $\Gamma \Rightarrow (A \times \Delta)$ the arena of $[\![\sigma]\!]$, and $\Gamma' \Rightarrow (B \times \Delta')$ the arena of $[\![\tau]\!]$ in the following:

  $[\![\sigma \lhd \tau]\!] = \mathrm{Rename}_{\Delta'\backslash\Delta}(\mathrm{Rename}_{\Gamma'\backslash\Gamma}(\mathrm{Merge}([\![\sigma]\!], [\![\tau]\!])))$

  Note the identification of the environments and co-environments of the two strategies.

- $[\![\phi \lhd \sigma]\!]$: We note $(\Delta \Rightarrow (\Gamma \times A \times B))^*$ the Player-starting arena of $[\![\phi]\!]$, and $(\Gamma' \Rightarrow (A' \times \Delta')$ the arena of $[\![\sigma]\!]$ in the following:

  $$\begin{aligned}[\![\phi \lhd \sigma]\!] = \mathrm{Rename}_{\Delta'\backslash\Delta}(\mathrm{Rename}_{\Gamma'\backslash\Gamma}(\\ \mathrm{Connection}_{A,A'}(\mathrm{Merge}([\![\phi]\!], [\![\sigma]\!]))))\end{aligned}$$

  This is similar to the previous construction, but with the addition of the implicit "connection" between the two strategies (on the shared type A). The remaining constructions are all straightforward.

- $[\![\overset{L}{\nabla}{}^S(\phi)]\!]$: We note $((S_2 \times L_2 \times \Delta) \Rightarrow (\Gamma \times L \times S \times A))^*$ the Player-starting arena of $[\![\phi]\!]$ in the following:

  $[\![\overset{L}{\nabla}{}^S(\phi)]\!] = \mathrm{Connection}_{S\times L, S_2\times L_2}([\![\phi]\!])$

- $[\![\lambda x.\phi]\!] = [\![\phi]\!]$. Here the type changes, but neither its interpretation nor the strategy.
- $[\![\bar{\lambda} u.\sigma]\!] = [\![\sigma]\!]$.
- $[\![\phi + \psi]\!] = [\![\phi]\!] \cup [\![\psi]\!]$.
- $[\![\sigma + \tau]\!] = [\![\sigma]\!] \cup [\![\tau]\!]$.
- $[\![\epsilon]\!]$ is the empty Player-starting strategy.
- $[\![\bar{\epsilon}]\!]$ is the empty strategy.
- $[\![\nu\alpha.\phi]\!]$: In section 5, we defined the syntactical "innocent lifting" using the fixed-point. This is coherent with the syntax-driven approach of this work. But in the semantics, it is more natural to proceed in the other direction. We will thus define a semantic operation, the *innocent lifting* $\mathrm{Innocent}(\phi)$. It is the set of plays s such that all threads of s, seen as separate plays, are in $q \cdot \phi$, where q is a fresh move; and it can be shown that $[\![\mathrm{Inn}(\phi)]\!] = \mathrm{Innocent}([\![\phi]\!])$. The result is a strategy which satisfies a form of weak innocence: it always reacts the same way to the query q (the initial "lifting" move). This is close to the usual definition of "single threaded" strategies. The difference is that single threaded strategies may have more than one initial move; and are "weakly innocent" for each of these.[5] We now use $\mathrm{Innocent}([\![\phi]\!])$ as the basis for the definition of $[\![\nu\alpha.\phi]\!]$. On one hand, the strategy $\mathrm{Innocent}([\![\phi]\!])$ reacts to its initial move as many time as asked, by behaving as ϕ; on the other hand, it contains moves corresponding to the distinguished variable α. A $\mathrm{Connection}$ operation is used to link these two types of moves. Formally, we note $(\Delta \Rightarrow (A_1 \times A_2 \times \Gamma))^*$ the Player-starting arena of $[\![\phi]\!]$ in:

  $$\begin{aligned}[\![\nu\alpha.\phi]\!] = \mathrm{Connection}_{A_1\Rightarrow\bot_1, A_2\Rightarrow\bot_2}(\mathrm{Prefixes}(\\ \{q_2\cdot s \in P_{(((A_1\Rightarrow\bot_1)\times\Delta)\Rightarrow(\Gamma\times(A_2\Rightarrow\bot_2)\times A))^*} \mid \\ s\restriction(((A_1 \Rightarrow \bot_1) \times \Delta) \Rightarrow (\Gamma \times (A_2 \Rightarrow \bot_2)))^* \\ \in \mathrm{Innocent}([\![\phi]\!]),\\ s\restriction A \approx \mathrm{Thread}(q_2\cdot s)\restriction A_2\}\end{aligned}$$

  where q_2 is the only move in ${\bot_2}^*$. In addition to the operations $\mathrm{Connection}$ and $\mathrm{Innocent}$, this definition uses elements of the definition of $[\![x\_\sigma]\!]$, with the move corresponding to α as the lifting move (q_2); thus prompting the strategy to start acting as ϕ a first time.

- $[\![\alpha]\!]$: We do not write the definition of $[\![\alpha]\!]$, which is identical to that of a standard variable call.

Lemma 3. *These definitions are correct, i.e. each of the above constructions defines a strategy or Player-starting strategy on the appropriate arena or Player-starting arena.*

10. Properties

We have now seen two versions of the $\lambda\bar{\lambda}$-calculus, and their respective semantics; we will now list their main properties. When a distinction between the two languages is needed, we will refer to the syntax described in section 2 as the *base* language, while the *extended* language includes the fixed-point.

[5] These strategies are captured by co-terms of the form $\mathrm{Inn}(\phi_1) \lhd \cdots \lhd \mathrm{Inn}(\phi_n)$, where Inn is a syntactic operation defined later in the same section.

10.1 Subject reduction

Lemma 4. *If ϕ is a term in the extended $\lambda\bar{\lambda}$-calculus such that $\Gamma \mid \phi : A \vdash \ \mid \Delta$ and $\phi \to^* \psi$, then $\Gamma \mid \psi : A \vdash \ \mid \Delta$.*
The dual also holds.

10.2 Confluence

Theorem 5. *The reduction relation $\to$ for the extended $\lambda\bar{\lambda}$-calculus is confluent, i.e, for any term ϕ, we have:*

$$(\phi \to^* \psi_1 \ \wedge \ \phi \to^* \psi_2) \ \Rightarrow \ \exists \psi, \psi_1 \to^* \psi \ \wedge \ \psi_2 \to^* \psi$$

The dual also holds.

Proof. The proof follows the pattern of a proof of the confluence of λ-calculus as described [4]. We define a new relation $\Longrightarrow$ which corresponds to multiple parallel applications of the reduction $\to$ inside a term (or co-term). This relation verifies the Church-Rosser property, and its transitive closure is equal to $\to^*$. □

10.3 Reduction soundness

Proposition 6. *The reduction $\to$ for the extended $\lambda\bar{\lambda}$-calculus is sound:*
$\phi \to \psi \ \Rightarrow \ [\![\phi]\!] = [\![\psi]\!]$ *and* $\phi \equiv \psi \ \Rightarrow \ [\![\phi]\!] = [\![\psi]\!]$
The dual also holds.

Proof. As an illustration, we detail the case of the rule:

$$\overset{L,(x,u)}{\nabla}{}^{S}.x\_\bar{\lambda}\vec{v}.u\_\phi \ \to \ \overset{L,(x,u)}{\nabla}{}^{\vec{v}\cdot S}.\phi$$

To make the notations more compact, we will write AB for $A \times B$, and $\neg(A_1B_1)$ (for example) for $(A_1B_1) \Rightarrow \bot_1$; moreover $[\![\phi]\!] : A^*$ will mean that ϕ plays on A^* (and similarly for $[\![\sigma]\!] : A$).
We start from the right-hand side of the rule:
$[\![\phi]\!] : ((A_4S_4L_4\neg(A_3S_3B_3)) \Rightarrow (L\neg(A_2S_2B_2)ASB))^*$
$[\![\overset{L,(x,u)}{\nabla}{}^{\vec{v}\cdot S}.\phi]\!] : B^* =$
$\quad \mathrm{Connection}_{A_4S_4L_4\neg(A_3S_3B_3)\ ,\ ASL\neg(A_2S_2B_2)}([\![\phi]\!])$
(The type of $\vec{v}$ is A, while x and u have type $\neg(ASB)$).
Consider now the left-hand side:
$[\![u\_\phi]\!] : (L\neg(A_2S_2B_2)) \Rightarrow (A_4S_4L_4\neg(A_3S_3B_3))$
$\quad = \mathrm{Detach}_{A_4S_4L_4\neg(A_3S_3B_3)}(\mathrm{Prefixes}($
$\quad\quad \{q_3 \cdot s \in \mathrm{Rename}_{ASB\backslash A_3S_3B_3}([\![\phi]\!])))$
$[\![x\_\bar{\lambda}\vec{v}.u\_\phi]\!] : ((S_4L_4\neg(A_3S_3B_3)) \Rightarrow (L\neg(A_2S_2B_2)S_5B_5))^*$
$\quad = \mathrm{Detach}_{L\neg(A_2S_2B_2)}(\mathrm{Prefixes}($
$\quad\quad \{q_2 \cdot s \in P_{((S_4L_4\neg(A_3S_3B_3))\Rightarrow(L\neg(A_2S_2B_2)S_5B_5))^*}$
$\quad\quad s \restriction_{((S_4L_4\neg(A_3S_3B_3))\Rightarrow(L\neg(A_2S_2B_2)))^*}$
$\quad\quad\quad \in \mathrm{Rename}_{A_4\backslash A_2}([\![u\_\phi]\!]),$
$\quad\quad s \restriction_{S_5B_5} \approx \mathrm{Thread}(s) \restriction_{S_2B_2} \}))$
$[\![\overset{L,(x,u)}{\nabla}{}^{S}.x\_\bar{\lambda}\vec{v}.u\_\phi]\!] : {B_5}^* =$
$\quad \mathrm{Connection}_{S_4L_4\neg(A_3S_3B_3)\ ,\ S_5L\neg(A_2S_2B_2)}([\![x\_\bar{\lambda}\vec{v}.u\_\phi]\!])$

The semantic constructions on each side of the rule send plays of $[\![\phi]\!]$ to sets of plays in either $[\![\overset{L,(x,u)}{\nabla}{}^{S}.x\_\bar{\lambda}\vec{v}.u\_\phi]\!]$ or $[\![\overset{L,(x,u)}{\nabla}{}^{\vec{v}\cdot S}.\phi]\!]$. Let s be a play of $[\![\phi]\!]$; we can assume that its image in the left-hand side is not obtained from any of its strict prefixes (this amounts to say that the conditions of the type "$s' \restriction_{C_1} \approx s' \restriction_{C_2}$" are respected). The moves of B in s are renamed to B_3, which must match moves in B_2, some of which must match moves in B_5, the target arena. The moves of B_3 which will in the end be matched in B_5 are exactly those in the first thread of plays in $[\![u\_\phi]\!]$, i.e., those justified by the new occurrence of q_3 introduced by the lifting. These are exactly those which originated in B (those originally from B_3 are justified by a later occurrence of q_3, which has been "detached"). These transformations preserve relative order and relative justification. Additionally, initial moves in a copy of B which gain a justifier (q_2 or q_3) through lifting are again initial in the image of s, as both q_2 and q_3 are absent from it. We now compare with the image of s by the syntactic construction of the right-hand side. This image too contains only moves of B which appeared in s, and also preserves the justification structure and the relative order of these moves. Under our assumption (that the image of s in the left-hand side was maximal among its prefixes), all the moves of B appearing in s appear in its left-hand side image. From this it can be deduced that in s, the moves of A and A_4, S and S_4 and $L\neg(A_2S_2B_2)$ and $L_4\neg(A_3S_3B_3)$ match, by tracking the behavior of s in the copies of A, S and L as we did for B. Therefore all the moves of B in s also appear in the image of s in the right-hand side, and thus the two images coincide. □

10.4 Translation from λ-calculus

Lemma 7. *The translation tr defined in section 5 is correct: given a simply typed λ-term M whose type contains only $\bot$ as base type, we have:*

$$[\![\mathrm{tr}(M)]\!] \ = \ [\![M]\!]_\lambda$$

Where $[\![\cdot]\!]_\lambda$ is, for example, the semantics of M as a PCF term as seen in [14]; and all moves in $[\![\mathrm{tr}(M)]\!]$ are taken to be questions.

Innocent strategies can also be described directly as the co-terms written in the following syntax:

$$\begin{array}{lclclclclcl} \phi, \psi & := & \epsilon & \mid & \lambda x.\phi & \mid & x\_\sigma & \mid & \phi + \psi & \mid & \phi \lhd \sigma \\ \sigma, \tau & := & \bar{\epsilon} & \mid & \multicolumn{3}{c}{\mathrm{Inn}(\phi)} & \mid & \sigma + \tau & \mid & \sigma \lhd \tau \end{array}$$

This intuitively builds strategies which are "weakly innocent" for every query. Notice that co-variables do not appear explicitly in this syntax.

Lemma 8. *For any co-term σ in the above syntax, $[\![\sigma]\!]$ is innocent.*

The definition of innocence is recalled at the beginning of section 11. In the above lemma we did not mention terms, to stay in the framework of the standard notion of (Opponent-starting) strategies. But innocence obviously extends to Player-starting strategies, and the syntax above is one way of defining such an extension.

10.5 Full abstraction

As is the case in other works, including [1], definability is obtained by compactness: the set of finite strategies is compact in the set of all strategies, for the order $\subseteq$ (the inclusion). In the following, we distinguish A and $\mathbf{A} = [\![A]\!]$.

Lemma 9 (Definability). *For any finite strategy $\boldsymbol{\sigma}$ on the arena $\mathbf{A}$, there exists a closed normal co-term σ of type A such that $[\![\sigma]\!] = \boldsymbol{\sigma}$.*
The dual also holds.

Proof. The co-term σ is obtained using the systematic labeling of plays which we sketched in the introduction. Each maximal-length play of the strategy can be represented in this way; the obtained co-terms are in finite number (arenas in our setting have finitely many positions, making any strategy a finitely-branching tree), and their sum, by the operator $+$, represents the full strategy. □

Note that construction does not use fixed-points. The tight connection between terms and strategies is illustrated by the following proposition:

Proposition 10. *For any well-typed term ϕ in the extended $\lambda\bar{\lambda}$-calculus, for any finite play s,*

$$s \in [\![\phi]\!] \ \Leftrightarrow \ \exists \phi_b, \phi' \ \phi \to^* \phi_b + \phi' \ \wedge \ s \in [\![\phi_b]\!]$$

where ϕ_b is a normal branch. The dual also holds.

Proof. This is a consequence of the construction ϕ_∞ used in the proof of full abstraction. □

We now define the observational equivalence, as well as an equivalence relation on strategies:

Definition 11. *Two terms ϕ and ψ are said to be observationally equivalent, noted $\phi \sim \psi$, if, for any context $C[]$, and any variable c:*

$$C[\phi] \to^* c\_\bar{\epsilon} + \phi' \quad \Leftrightarrow \quad C[\psi] \to^* c\_\bar{\epsilon} + \psi'$$

for some ϕ' and ψ'.

The dual $\sigma \sim \tau$ is defined similarly.

Definition 12. *For two strategies $\boldsymbol{\phi}$ and $\boldsymbol{\psi}$, we write $\boldsymbol{\phi} \approx_{\mathrm{PE}} \boldsymbol{\psi}$ when their sets of Player-ending plays are equal.*

Theorem 13 (Full abstraction). *For any terms ϕ, ψ of the same type in the extended $\lambda\bar{\lambda}$-calculus,*

$$\phi \sim \psi \Leftrightarrow [\![\phi]\!] \approx_{\mathrm{PE}} [\![\psi]\!]$$

The dual also holds.

Proof. To prove this, we define (potentially) infinite terms ϕ_∞ and ψ_∞, and prove that both $\phi \sim \psi$ and $[\![\phi]\!] \approx_{\mathrm{PE}} [\![\psi]\!]$ are equivalent to $\phi_\infty \equiv \psi_\infty$. We first show that, for any well-typed term ϕ, and any $n \in \mathbb{N}$, there exists ϕ_n with $\phi \to^* \phi_n$, such that ϕ_n is in normal form "up to depth n", except for non-normal sub-terms whose interpretation is the empty strategy. This is proven by induction on terms and co-terms, using properties of normal-branch contexts (of which Lemma 2 is an example). From ϕ_n we build ϕ'_n, in which sub-terms with empty interpretations have been replaced by ϵ, then sub-coterms of the form u_ϵ have been replaced by $\bar{\epsilon}$. The sequence $(\phi'_n)_n$ has a limit, and ϕ_∞ is defined as the η-expansion of this limit. This (potentially) infinite term ϕ_∞ directly represents the strategy $[\![\phi]\!]$ (up to $\approx_{\mathrm{PE}}$), similarly to what was seen in the introduction for finite strategies. □

11. History access control and the notion of view

In game semantics, the condition of innocence restricts the information and actions available to a strategy, by limiting it's access of the history to a specific sub-sequence called the *view*. In this section, we will show how the description of innocence as a fixed-point expansion (seen in section 5) gives a direct syntactic representation of views. This new notion is more general, and allows to define a more precise history access control.

We start by recalling the standard definition of the view. Let s be an Opponent-starting play of odd-length in the following:

- If s is of the form $s' \cdot a$, where a is an initial Opponent move, then $\mathrm{view}(s) = a$.
- If s is of the form $s' \cdot a \cdot s'' \cdot b$, where b is justified by a, then $\mathrm{view}(s) = \mathrm{view}(s') \cdot a \cdot b$, where b is justified by a.

An Opponent-starting strategy $\boldsymbol{\sigma}$ satisfies the *visibility condition* if, for all plays $s \cdot a \in \boldsymbol{\sigma}$ where a is a Player move, the justifier of a in that play is in $\mathrm{view}(s)$. Finally, if $\boldsymbol{\sigma}$ satisfies the visibility condition, it is called *innocent* if its behavior depends only on the current view, i.e.: if s, s' are even-length Opponent-starting plays, $s \cdot a \cdot b \in \boldsymbol{\phi}$, $s' \cdot b \in P(A)$ and $\mathrm{view}(s \cdot a) = \mathrm{view}(s' \cdot a)$, then $s' \cdot a \cdot b \in \boldsymbol{\sigma}$ (where A is the arena of $\boldsymbol{\sigma}$).

The behavior of an innocent strategy is characterized by the set of its views. The generation of the full strategy from this set is exactly the process of innocent expansion. Taking the simple example of $\mathrm{tr}(\lambda x.x)$, the only view of the strategy corresponds to $\bar{\lambda} u.u\_\lambda x.x$. In the case of $\mathrm{tr}(\lambda x.\lambda y.xy)$, there are two views, $\bar{\lambda} u.u\_\lambda x.\lambda y.x\_\bar{\epsilon}$ and $\bar{\lambda} u.u\_\lambda x.\lambda y.x\_\bar{\lambda} v.v\_y\_\bar{\epsilon}$. These can be seen as the states of the program, and the Opponent moves as the transitions between the states. For example, the Opponent move v is a transition from the first to the second view of $\mathrm{tr}(\lambda x.\lambda y.xy)$; this transition leads to a view which extends the previous one. On the other hand, if the Opponent plays the move u from the second view, it forces a transition back to the first view. This second case, in which a transition goes back to a previous state, is exactly represented by the occurrences of u_α in the translated term:

$$\bar{\lambda} u.u\_\nu\alpha.\lambda x.\lambda y.(x\_\bar{\lambda} v.\nu\beta.(u\_\alpha \triangleleft v\_y\_(u\_\alpha \triangleleft \beta)))$$

The occurrences of u_α can be seen as a "goto" instructions which points back to the binder $\nu\alpha$. In the above, there are three such transitions: from the first view to itself, along u, from the second view to itself, along v, and finally from the second view to the first, along u. When adding the "forward" transitions, this equips the co-term with a structure resembling an automaton. The difference with an actual automaton is that the "alphabet" (the set of co-variable names) is infinite. Syntactically, fixed-points expansion may duplicate binders, increasing the number of available names. Additionally, when a transition goes back to a previous state, it opens a new copy of the program. A subsequent Opponent move may jump between copies, in addition to jumping backward or extending the current view. For example, $\mathrm{tr}(\lambda x.\lambda y.xy)$ contains the following play:

$$\bar{\lambda} u.u\_\lambda x.\lambda y.x\_\bar{\lambda} v.v\_y\_u\_\lambda x'.\lambda y'.x'\_\bar{\lambda} v'.v\_y\_\bar{\epsilon}$$

Here the second occurrence of v illustrates such a jump. The first copy here corresponds to $\bar{\lambda} u.u\_\lambda x.\lambda y.x\_v\_y\_\bar{\epsilon}$, and the second copy, opened by the second occurrence of u, corresponds to "$u\_\lambda x'.\lambda y'.x'\_\bar{\lambda} v'$". Notice that, when the Opponent plays the second occurrence of v, this move cannot extend the current view at this point, nor jump back in that view; it has to jump to the (still opened) first view, where the binder $\bar{\lambda} v$ lies. Syntactically, the fact that a backward jump keeps the old view opened is due to the presence of "$\triangleleft$" (instead of $+$) in the definition of Inn.

We now formalize the notion of syntactic view. Let ϕ be a term in the extended $\lambda\bar{\lambda}$-calculus; let ϕ' be the term obtained by removing all $\nu\alpha.$ and α in ϕ (the occurrences of a α being replaced by ϵ). If ϕ' is a normal term, then its branches are called the *generalized views* of ϕ. The generalized views of a co-term σ are defined dually.

The set of generalized views of a normal term (or co-term) determines its level of access to the history of the interaction. Every transition between views which is due to an occurrence α prevents the program to "follow" the transition, and to distinguish this play from a shorter one. In the previous example, this means that the program cannot distinguish between an interaction history containing only one move u, or two successive moves u. In this example, the restriction of information corresponds to the innocence of $\mathrm{tr}(\lambda x.\lambda y.xy)$. This is not the case for the co-term cell defined in section 6.3. This co-term is not innocent (it reacts differently to different calls to the co-variable read), but it is imposed a form of history access control; in particular, it cannot distinguish between two occurrences of read if a write does not occur between the two. This behavior can be seen as form of "conditional innocence" for the co-variable read.

12. Future work: toward better static control of effects

Section 5 gives a blueprint to write static program specifications in the $\lambda\bar{\lambda}$-calculus. In this section, we used the fixed-point $\nu\alpha$ to define a construction Inn. We then defined a syntax of terms and co-terms, which includes this new construction, but does not include the covariables u and their binder $\bar{\lambda}u$. This forces elements of this syntax to conform to a certain discipline, set by the definition of Inn. In this example, it was merely to regain the well known behavior of innocent strategies. But this method can be generalized. In the previous section, we saw that the fixed-point allows us to describe history access control in a flexible way. We used cell as an example of a strategy obeying a discipline other than innocence. The blueprint of section 5 could be used to formalize this notion of "conditional innocence", and give a syntax of terms which are guaranteed to respect it.

This method could also be used to give syntaxes corresponding to classes of strategies described in other works. For example, in [11], operators are defined on games, corresponding to granting either the Player or the Opponent the right to backtrack in the history. The composition of these operators builds the innocent strategies. But taken separately each operator describes a new discipline. Additionally, the modular approach of this work may benefit from a syntactical description. Another example is given by the *cellular* strategies [12], which were inspired by *cellular terms* [20], used in decidability results. These strategies obey a very specific discipline. Their actions (the available Player moves) are restricted according to a first notion of view, which is more strict than in the case of innocence; but their available information depends on another notion of view, which is more lax than for innocence. These interaction of such strategies exhibits certain properties; in particular, it does not require a referee. Because they are not innocent, they correspond to programs with effects, but with important restrictions.

The examples above come from theoretical works. But we believe that the ability to define meaningful constraints on behaviors with effect can have more practical applications; and that this approach could provide syntaxes which allow some of the power of effects, but still guarantee safety properties.

13. Conclusion

We have presented a language, which very directly reflects the structure of game semantics. This has allowed us to give a syntactic account of many key concepts of the model. We have shown that the implicit repetitions in innocent strategies could be seen as a fixed-point expansion. On translated λ-terms, we have recognized views in the syntactic branches, and seen that the transitions between these views were made explicit by the structure of pointers given by the $\nu\alpha$ and α (the fixed-point). This immediately gave a generalization of views, as a flexible way to express history access control. Beyond innocence, we have seen that the power of effects is obtained by dualization of the λ-calculus; in other words, that this power corresponds to a symmetric access to the history, for the Player and the Opponent. This naturally leads to the obtention of separators through duality: any normal branch can be "matched" by its dual, giving a form of Böhm-out lemma. Finally, we have argued that our language gives an interesting method of constraining effects, without forbidding them entirely; which could lead to better static control of effects.

References

[1] S. Abramsky, K. Honda, and G. McCusker. A fully abstract game semantics for general references. In *Logic in Computer Science, 1998. Proceedings. Thirteenth Annual IEEE Symposium on*, pages 334–344. IEEE, 1998.

[2] S. Abramsky, R. Jagadeesan, and P. Malacaria. Full abstraction for pcf. *Information and Computation*, 163(2):409–470, 2000.

[3] S. Abramsky and G. McCusker. Linearity, sharing and state: a fully abstract game semantics for idealized algol with active expressions. In *Algol-like languages*. Citeseer, 1997.

[4] H.P. Barendregt. *The lambda calculus: its syntax and semantics*, volume 103. North Holland, 1984.

[5] M. Basaldella and C. Faggian. Ludics with repetitions (exponentials, interactive types and completeness). In *Logic In Computer Science, 2009. LICS'09. 24th Annual IEEE Symposium on*, pages 375–384. IEEE, 2009.

[6] M. Churchill and J. Laird. A logic of sequentiality. In *Computer Science Logic*, pages 215–229. Springer, 2010.

[7] M. Churchill, J. Laird, and G. McCusker. Imperative programs as proofs via game semantics. In *Logic in Computer Science (LICS), 2011 26th Annual IEEE Symposium on*, pages 65–74. IEEE, 2011.

[8] P.L. Curien and H. Herbelin. The duality of computation. In *ACM sigplan notices*, volume 35, pages 233–243. ACM, 2000.

[9] P.L. Curien and H. Herbelin. Abstract machines for dialogue games. *Arxiv preprint arXiv:0706.2544*, 2007.

[10] A. Goyet. The $\lambda\bar{\lambda}$-calculus, implementation manual. `http://www.pps.univ-paris-diderot.fr/~agoyet/llbc`.

[11] R. Harmer, M. Hyland, and P.A. Mellies. Categorical combinatorics for innocent strategies. In *Logic in Computer Science, 2007. LICS 2007. 22nd Annual IEEE Symposium on*, pages 379–388. IEEE, 2007.

[12] Russ Harmer. Cellular strategies and innocent interaction. Draft.

[13] H. Herbelin. Games and weak-head reduction for classical pcf. *Typed Lambda Calculi and Applications*, pages 214–230, 1997.

[14] J.M.E. Hyland and C.H.L. Ong. On full abstraction for pcf: I, II, and III. *Information and computation*, 163(2):285–408, 2000.

[15] J. Laird. Full abstraction for functional languages with control. In *Logic in Computer Science, 1997. LICS'97. Proceedings., 12th Annual IEEE Symposium on*, pages 58–67. IEEE, 1997.

[16] J. Longley. Some programming languages suggested by game models. *Electronic Notes in Theoretical Computer Science*, 249:117–134, 2009.

[17] P.A. Mellies. Asynchronous games 2: the true concurrency of innocence. *CONCUR 2004-Concurrency Theory*, pages 448–465, 2004.

[18] P.A. Melliès and N. Tabareau. Resource modalities in tensor logic. *Annals of Pure and Applied Logic*, 161(5):632–653, 2010.

[19] H. Nickau. Hereditarily sequential functionals. *Logical Foundations of Computer Science*, pages 253–264, 1994.

[20] Vincent Padovani. Decidability of All Minimal Models. `http://hal.archives-ouvertes.fr/hal-00741219`, 2012.

[21] J. Parrow and B. Victor. The fusion calculus: Expressiveness and symmetry in mobile processes. In *Logic in Computer Science, 1998. Proceedings. Thirteenth Annual IEEE Symposium on*, pages 176–185. IEEE, 1998.

A. A complete reduction example

In Figure 3, we show the complete reduction of one of the examples of the introduction: the term $\phi_1 \lhd \sigma_2$. This figure was obtained as an output of the implementation which is available at [10].

$$
\begin{array}{ll}
 & \lambda x.\lambda c.x\_\bar\lambda v.\bar\lambda w.v\_x\_\bar\lambda v'.\bar\lambda w'.w'\_c\_\bar\epsilon \triangleleft \bar\lambda u.u\_\lambda y.\lambda z.y\_u\_\lambda y'.\lambda z'.z'\_\bar\epsilon \\
\to & \triangledown^{u}.(\lambda x.\lambda c.x\_\bar\lambda v.\bar\lambda w.v\_x\_\bar\lambda v'.\bar\lambda w'.w'\_c\_\bar\epsilon \triangleleft u\_\lambda y.\lambda z.y\_u\_\lambda y'.\lambda z'.z'\_\bar\epsilon) \\
\to & \triangledown^{u}.\lambda x.(\lambda c.x\_\bar\lambda v.\bar\lambda w.v\_x\_\bar\lambda v'.\bar\lambda w'.w'\_c\_\bar\epsilon \triangleleft u\_\lambda y.\lambda z.y\_u\_\lambda y'.\lambda z'.z'\_\bar\epsilon) \\
\to & \overset{(x,u)}{\triangledown}.(\lambda c.x\_\bar\lambda v.\bar\lambda w.v\_x\_\bar\lambda v'.\bar\lambda w'.w'\_c\_\bar\epsilon \triangleleft u\_\lambda y.\lambda z.y\_u\_\lambda y'.\lambda z'.z'\_\bar\epsilon) \\
\to & \overset{(x,u)}{\triangledown}.\lambda c.(x\_\bar\lambda v.\bar\lambda w.v\_x\_\bar\lambda v'.\bar\lambda w'.w'\_c\_\bar\epsilon \triangleleft u\_\lambda y.\lambda z.y\_u\_\lambda y'.\lambda z'.z'\_\bar\epsilon) \\
\to & \lambda c.\overset{(x,u)}{\triangledown}.(x\_\bar\lambda v.\bar\lambda w.v\_x\_\bar\lambda v'.\bar\lambda w'.w'\_c\_\bar\epsilon \triangleleft u\_\lambda y.\lambda z.y\_u\_\lambda y'.\lambda z'.z'\_\bar\epsilon) \\
\to & \lambda c.\overset{(x,u)}{\triangledown}.x\_(\bar\lambda v.\bar\lambda w.v\_x\_\bar\lambda v'.\bar\lambda w'.w'\_c\_\bar\epsilon \triangleleft u\_\lambda y.\lambda z.y\_u\_\lambda y'.\lambda z'.z'\_\bar\epsilon) \\
\to & \lambda c.\overset{(x,u)}{\triangledown}.x\_\bar\lambda v.(\bar\lambda w.v\_x\_\bar\lambda v'.\bar\lambda w'.w'\_c\_\bar\epsilon \triangleleft u\_\lambda y.\lambda z.y\_u\_\lambda y'.\lambda z'.z'\_\bar\epsilon) \\
\to & \lambda c.\overset{(x,u)}{\triangledown}.x\_\bar\lambda v.\bar\lambda w.(v\_x\_\bar\lambda v'.\bar\lambda w'.w'\_c\_\bar\epsilon \triangleleft u\_\lambda y.\lambda z.y\_u\_\lambda y'.\lambda z'.z'\_\bar\epsilon) \\
\to & \lambda c.\overset{(x,u)}{\triangledown}.x\_\bar\lambda v.\bar\lambda w.(v\_(x\_\bar\lambda v'.\bar\lambda w'.w'\_c\_\bar\epsilon \triangleleft u\_\lambda y.\lambda z.y\_u\_\lambda y'.\lambda z'.z'\_\bar\epsilon) + u\_(\lambda y.\lambda z.y\_u\_\lambda y'.\lambda z'.z'\_\bar\epsilon \triangleleft v\_x\_\bar\lambda v'.\bar\lambda w'.w'\_c\_\bar\epsilon)) \\
\equiv & \lambda c.(\overset{(x,u)}{\triangledown}.x\_\bar\lambda v.\bar\lambda w.v\_(x\_\bar\lambda v'.\bar\lambda w'.w'\_c\_\bar\epsilon \triangleleft u\_\lambda y.\lambda z.y\_u\_\lambda y'.\lambda z'.z'\_\bar\epsilon) + \overset{(x,u)}{\triangledown}.x\_\bar\lambda v.\bar\lambda w.u\_(\lambda y.\lambda z.y\_u\_\lambda y'.\lambda z'.z'\_\bar\epsilon \triangleleft v\_x\_\bar\lambda v'.\bar\lambda w'.w'\_c \\
\to & \lambda c.(\epsilon + \overset{(x,u)}{\triangledown}.x\_\bar\lambda v.\bar\lambda w.u\_(\lambda y.\lambda z.y\_u\_\lambda y'.\lambda z'.z'\_\bar\epsilon \triangleleft v\_x\_\bar\lambda v'.\bar\lambda w'.w'\_c\_\bar\epsilon)) \\
\equiv & \lambda c.\overset{(x,u)}{\triangledown}.x\_\bar\lambda v.\bar\lambda w.u\_(\lambda y.\lambda z.y\_u\_\lambda y'.\lambda z'.z'\_\bar\epsilon \triangleleft v\_x\_\bar\lambda v'.\bar\lambda w'.w'\_c\_\bar\epsilon) \\
\to & \lambda c.\overset{(x,u)}{\triangledown}{}^{v\cdot w}.(\lambda y.\lambda z.y\_u\_\lambda y'.\lambda z'.z'\_\bar\epsilon \triangleleft v\_x\_\bar\lambda v'.\bar\lambda w'.w'\_c\_\bar\epsilon) \\
\to & \lambda c.\overset{(x,u)}{\triangledown}{}^{v\cdot w}.\lambda y.(\lambda z.y\_u\_\lambda y'.\lambda z'.z'\_\bar\epsilon \triangleleft v\_x\_\bar\lambda v'.\bar\lambda w'.w'\_c\_\bar\epsilon) \\
\to & \lambda c.\overset{(y,v)(x,u)}{\triangledown}{}^{w}.(\lambda z.y\_u\_\lambda y'.\lambda z'.z'\_\bar\epsilon \triangleleft v\_x\_\bar\lambda v'.\bar\lambda w'.w'\_c\_\bar\epsilon) \\
\to & \lambda c.\overset{(y,v)(x,u)}{\triangledown}{}^{w}.\lambda z.(y\_u\_\lambda y'.\lambda z'.z'\_\bar\epsilon \triangleleft v\_x\_\bar\lambda v'.\bar\lambda w'.w'\_c\_\bar\epsilon) \\
\to & \lambda c.\overset{(z,w)(y,v)(x,u)}{\triangledown}.(y\_u\_\lambda y'.\lambda z'.z'\_\bar\epsilon \triangleleft v\_x\_\bar\lambda v'.\bar\lambda w'.w'\_c\_\bar\epsilon) \\
\to & \lambda c.\overset{(z,w)(y,v)(x,u)}{\triangledown}.y\_(u\_\lambda y'.\lambda z'.z'\_\bar\epsilon \triangleleft v\_x\_\bar\lambda v'.\bar\lambda w'.w'\_c\_\bar\epsilon) \\
\to & \lambda c.\overset{(z,w)(y,v)(x,u)}{\triangledown}.y\_(u\_(\lambda y'.\lambda z'.z'\_\bar\epsilon \triangleleft v\_x\_\bar\lambda v'.\bar\lambda w'.w'\_c\_\bar\epsilon) + v\_(x\_\bar\lambda v'.\bar\lambda w'.w'\_c\_\bar\epsilon \triangleleft u\_\lambda y'.\lambda z'.z'\_\bar\epsilon)) \\
\equiv & \lambda c.(\overset{(z,w)(y,v)(x,u)}{\triangledown}.y\_u\_(\lambda y'.\lambda z'.z'\_\bar\epsilon \triangleleft v\_x\_\bar\lambda v'.\bar\lambda w'.w'\_c\_\bar\epsilon) + \overset{(z,w)(y,v)(x,u)}{\triangledown}.y\_v\_(x\_\bar\lambda v'.\bar\lambda w'.w'\_c\_\bar\epsilon \triangleleft u\_\lambda y'.\lambda z'.z'\_\bar\epsilon)) \\
\to & \lambda c.(\epsilon + \overset{(z,w)(y,v)(x,u)}{\triangledown}.y\_v\_(x\_\bar\lambda v'.\bar\lambda w'.w'\_c\_\bar\epsilon \triangleleft u\_\lambda y'.\lambda z'.z'\_\bar\epsilon)) \\
\equiv & \lambda c.\overset{(z,w)(y,v)(x,u)}{\triangledown}.y\_v\_(x\_\bar\lambda v'.\bar\lambda w'.w'\_c\_\bar\epsilon \triangleleft u\_\lambda y'.\lambda z'.z'\_\bar\epsilon) \\
\to & \lambda c.\overset{(z,w)(y,v)(x,u)}{\triangledown}.(x\_\bar\lambda v'.\bar\lambda w'.w'\_c\_\bar\epsilon \triangleleft u\_\lambda y'.\lambda z'.z'\_\bar\epsilon) \\
\to & \lambda c.\overset{(z,w)(y,v)(x,u)}{\triangledown}.x\_(\bar\lambda v'.\bar\lambda w'.w'\_c\_\bar\epsilon \triangleleft u\_\lambda y'.\lambda z'.z'\_\bar\epsilon) \\
\to & \lambda c.\overset{(z,w)(y,v)(x,u)}{\triangledown}.x\_\bar\lambda v'.(\bar\lambda w'.w'\_c\_\bar\epsilon \triangleleft u\_\lambda y'.\lambda z'.z'\_\bar\epsilon) \\
\to & \lambda c.\overset{(z,w)(y,v)(x,u)}{\triangledown}.x\_\bar\lambda v'.\bar\lambda w'.(w'\_c\_\bar\epsilon \triangleleft u\_\lambda y'.\lambda z'.z'\_\bar\epsilon) \\
\to & \lambda c.\overset{(z,w)(y,v)(x,u)}{\triangledown}.x\_\bar\lambda v'.\bar\lambda w'.(w'\_(c\_\bar\epsilon \triangleleft u\_\lambda y'.\lambda z'.z'\_\bar\epsilon) + u\_(\lambda y'.\lambda z'.z'\_\bar\epsilon \triangleleft w'\_c\_\bar\epsilon)) \\
\equiv & \lambda c.(\overset{(z,w)(y,v)(x,u)}{\triangledown}.x\_\bar\lambda v'.\bar\lambda w'.w'\_(c\_\bar\epsilon \triangleleft u\_\lambda y'.\lambda z'.z'\_\bar\epsilon) + \overset{(z,w)(y,v)(x,u)}{\triangledown}.x\_\bar\lambda v'.\bar\lambda w'.u\_(\lambda y'.\lambda z'.z'\_\bar\epsilon \triangleleft w'\_c\_\bar\epsilon)) \\
\to & \lambda c.(\epsilon + \overset{(z,w)(y,v)(x,u)}{\triangledown}.x\_\bar\lambda v'.\bar\lambda w'.u\_(\lambda y'.\lambda z'.z'\_\bar\epsilon \triangleleft w'\_c\_\bar\epsilon)) \\
\equiv & \lambda c.\overset{(z,w)(y,v)(x,u)}{\triangledown}.x\_\bar\lambda v'.\bar\lambda w'.u\_(\lambda y'.\lambda z'.z'\_\bar\epsilon \triangleleft w'\_c\_\bar\epsilon) \\
\to & \lambda c.\overset{(z,w)(y,v)(x,u)}{\triangledown}{}^{v'\cdot w'}.(\lambda y'.\lambda z'.z'\_\bar\epsilon \triangleleft w'\_c\_\bar\epsilon) \\
\to & \lambda c.\overset{(z,w)(y,v)(x,u)}{\triangledown}{}^{v'\cdot w'}.\lambda y'.(\lambda z'.z'\_\bar\epsilon \triangleleft w'\_c\_\bar\epsilon) \\
\to & \lambda c.\overset{(y',v')(z,w)(y,v)(x,u)}{\triangledown}{}^{w'}.(\lambda z'.z'\_\bar\epsilon \triangleleft w'\_c\_\bar\epsilon) \\
\to & \lambda c.\overset{(y',v')(z,w)(y,v)(x,u)}{\triangledown}{}^{w'}.\lambda z'.(z'\_\bar\epsilon \triangleleft w'\_c\_\bar\epsilon) \\
\to & \lambda c.\overset{(z',w')(y',v')(z,w)(y,v)(x,u)}{\triangledown}.(z'\_\bar\epsilon \triangleleft w'\_c\_\bar\epsilon) \\
\to & \lambda c.\overset{(z',w')(y',v')(z,w)(y,v)(x,u)}{\triangledown}.z'\_(\bar\epsilon \triangleleft w'\_c\_\bar\epsilon) \\
\equiv & \lambda c.\overset{(z',w')(y',v')(z,w)(y,v)(x,u)}{\triangledown}.z'\_w'\_c\_\bar\epsilon \\
\to & \lambda c.\overset{(z',w')(y',v')(z,w)(y,v)(x,u)}{\triangledown}.c\_\bar\epsilon \\
\to & \lambda c.c\_\bar\epsilon
\end{array}
$$

Figure 3. A complete reduction example.

The Geometry of Types

Ugo Dal Lago Barbara Petit
Università di Bologna & INRIA
{dallago,petit}@cs.unibo.it

Abstract

We show that time complexity analysis of higher-order functional programs can be effectively reduced to an arguably simpler (although computationally equivalent) verification problem, namely checking first-order inequalities for validity. This is done by giving an efficient inference algorithm for linear dependent types which, given a PCF term, produces in output both a linear dependent type and a cost expression for the term, together with a set of proof obligations. Actually, the output type judgement is derivable *iff* all proof obligations are valid. This, coupled with the already known *relative completeness* of linear dependent types, ensures that no information is lost, i.e., that there are no false positives or negatives. Moreover, the procedure reflects the difficulty of the original problem: simple PCF terms give rise to sets of proof obligations which are easy to solve. The latter can then be put in a format suitable for automatic or semi-automatic verification by external solvers. Ongoing experimental evaluation has produced encouraging results, which are briefly presented in the paper.

Categories and Subject Descriptors F.3.2 [*Logics And Meanings Of Programs*]: Semantics of Programming Languages—Program Analysis; F.3.1 [*Logics And Meanings Of Programs*]: Specifying and Verifying and Reasoning about Programs

General Terms Performance, Theory, Verification

Keywords Functional Programming, Higher-order Types, Linear Logic, Resource Consumption, Complexity Analysis

1. Introduction

One of the most crucial non-functional properties of programs is the amount of resources (like time, memory and power) they need when executed. Deriving upper bounds on the resource consumption of programs is crucial in many cases, but is in fact an undecidable problem as soon as the underlying programming language is non-trivial. If the units of measurement in which resources are measured become concrete and close to the physical ones, the problem becomes even more complicated, given the many transformation and optimisation layers programs are applied to before being executed. A typical example is the one of WCET techniques adopted in real-time systems [29], which do not only need to deal with how many machine instructions a program corresponds to, but also with how much time each instruction costs when executed by possibly complex architectures (including caches, pipelining, etc.), a task which is becoming even harder with the current trend towards multicore architectures.

A different approach consists in analysing the *abstract* complexity of programs. As an example, one can take the number of instructions executed by the program as a measure of its execution time. This is of course a less informative metric, which however becomes more accurate if the actual time complexity *of each instruction* is kept low. One advantage of this analysis is the independence from the specific hardware platform executing the program at hand: the latter only needs to be analysed once. A variety of verification techniques have been employed in this context, from abstract interpretation [20] to type systems [23] to program logics [3] to interactive theorem proving[1].

Among the many type-based techniques for complexity analysis, a recent proposal consists in going towards systems of *linear dependent types*, as suggested by Marco Gaboardi and the first author [11]. In linear dependent type theories, a judgement has the form $\vdash_{\mathrm{I}} t : \sigma$, where σ is the type of t and I is its *cost*, an estimation of its time complexity. In this paper, we show that the problem of checking, given a PCF term t and I, whether $\vdash_{\mathrm{I}} t : \sigma$ holds can be efficiently reduced to the one of checking the truth of a set of proof obligations, themselves formulated in the language of a *first-order* equational program. Interestingly, simple λ-terms give rise to simple equational programs. In other words, linear dependent types are not only a sound and *relatively* complete methodology for inferring *time* bounds of programs [11, 13]: they also allow to reduce complexity analysis to an arguably simpler (although computationally equivalent) problem which is much better studied and for which a variety of techniques and concrete tools exist [6]. Noticeably, the bounds one obtains this way translate to bounds on the number of steps performed by evaluation machines for the λ-calculus, which means that the induced metrics are not too abstract after all. The type inference algorithm is described in Section 4.

The scenario, then, becomes similar to the one in Floyd-Hoare program logics for imperative programs, where completeness holds [9] (at least for the simplest idioms [7]) *and* weakest preconditions can be generated automatically (see, e.g., [3]). A benefit of working with functional programs is that type inference — the analogue of generating WPs — can be done compositionally without the need of guessing invariants.

Linear dependent types are simple types annotated with some *index terms*, i.e. first-order terms reflecting the value of data flowing inside the program. Type inference produces in output a type derivation, a set of inequalities (which should be thought of as proof obligations) and an equational program $\mathcal{E}$ giving meaning to function symbols appearing in index terms (see Figure 1). A natural thing to do once $\mathcal{E}$ and the various proof obligations are available is to try to solve them automatically, as an example through SMT solvers. If automatically checking the inequalities for truth does not

[1] A detailed discussion with related work is in Section 6.

POPL'13, January 23–25, 2013, Rome, Italy.

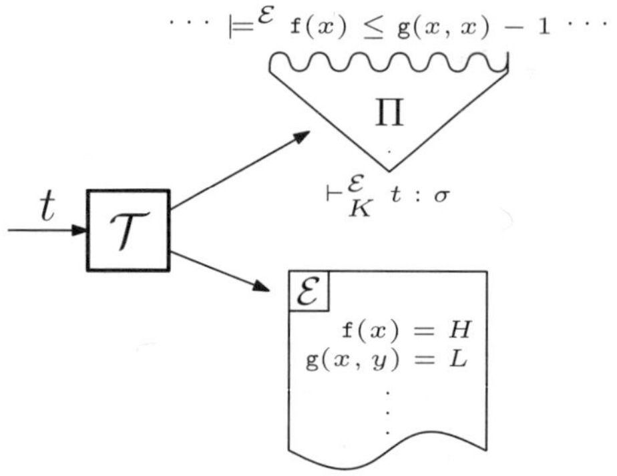

Figure 1. General scheme of the type inference algorithm.

succeed (which must happen, in some cases), one can anyway find useful information in the type derivation, as it tells you precisely *which* data every symbol corresponds to. We elaborate on this issue in Section 5.

But where does linear dependency come from? Linear dependent types can be seen as a way to turn Girard's geometry of interaction (or, equivalently, AJM games [1]) into a type system for the λ-calculus: the equational program one obtains as a result of type inference of a term t is nothing but as a description of a token machine [14] for t. In presence of linear dependency, any term which can possibly be duplicated, can receive different, although uniform, types, similarly to what happens in BLL [19]. As such, this form of dependency is significantly simpler than the one of, e.g., the calculus of inductive constructions.

2. Linear Dependency at a Glance

Traditionally, type systems carry very little information about the *value* of data manipulated by programs, instead focusing on their *nature*. As an example, all (partial recursive) functions from natural numbers to natural numbers can be typed as $\mathtt{Nat} \Rightarrow \mathtt{Nat}$ in the λ-calculus with natural numbers and higher-order recursion, also known as PCF [26]. This is not an intrinsic limit of the type-based analysis of programs, however: much richer type disciplines have flourished in the last twenty years [4, 15, 22]. All of them guarantee stronger properties for typable programs, the price being a more complicated type language and computationally more difficult type inference and checking problems. As an example, sized types [22] are a way to ensure termination of functional programs based on size information. In systems of sized types, a program like

$$t = \lambda x.\lambda y.\mathrm{add}\ (\mathrm{add}\ x\ y)\ (\mathrm{succ}\ y)$$

can be typed as $\mathtt{Nat}_a \Rightarrow \mathtt{Nat}_b \Rightarrow \mathtt{Nat}_{a+2b+1}$, and in general as $\mathtt{Nat}_a \Rightarrow \mathtt{Nat}_b \Rightarrow \mathtt{Nat}_{\mathrm{I}}$, where $\mathrm{I} \geqslant a + 2b + 1$. In other words, the PCF type Nat is refined into $\mathtt{Nat}_{\mathrm{I}}$ (where I is an arithmetical expression) whose semantics is the set of all natural numbers smaller or equal to I, i.e. the interval $[0, \mathrm{I}] \subseteq \mathbb{N}$. The role of size information is to ensure that all functions terminate, and this is done by restricting the kind of functions of which one is allowed to form fixpoints. Sized types are nonlinear: arguments to functions can be freely duplicated. Moreover, the size information is only approximate, since the expression labelling base types is only an *upper* bound on the size of typable values.

Linear dependent types can be seen as a way to inject precision and linearity into sized types. Indeed, t receives the following type in dℓPCF$_\mathsf{V}$ [13]:

$$\mathtt{Nat}[0, a] \overset{c<\mathrm{I}}{\multimap} \mathtt{Nat}[0, b] \overset{d<\mathrm{J}}{\multimap} \mathtt{Nat}[0, a + 2b + 1]. \quad (1)$$

As one can easily realise, $\mathtt{Nat}[\mathrm{K}, \mathrm{H}]$ is the type of all natural numbers in the interval $[\mathrm{K}, \mathrm{H}] \subseteq \mathbb{N}$. Moreover, $\sigma \overset{b<\mathrm{J}}{\multimap} \tau$ is the type of *linear* functions from σ to τ which can be copied by the environment J times. The J copies of the function have types obtained by substituting $0, \ldots, \mathrm{J} - 1$ for b in σ and τ. This is the key idea behind linear dependency. The type (1) is imprecise, but can be easily turned into

$$\mathtt{Nat}[a, a] \overset{c<\mathrm{I}}{\multimap} \mathtt{Nat}[b, b] \overset{d<\mathrm{J}}{\multimap} \mathtt{Nat}[a + 2b + 1, a + 2b + 1], \quad (2)$$

itself a type of t. In the following, the singleton interval type $\mathtt{Nat}[\mathrm{K}, \mathrm{K}]$ is denoted simply as $\mathtt{Nat}[\mathrm{K}]$.

Notice that linear dependency is not exploited in (2), e.g., d does not appear free in $\mathtt{Nat}[b]$ nor in $\mathtt{Nat}[a + 2b + 1]$. Yet, (2) precisely captures the functional behaviour of t. If d does not appear free in σ nor in τ, then $\sigma \overset{d<\mathrm{I}}{\multimap} \tau$ can be abbreviated as $\sigma \overset{\mathrm{I}}{\multimap} \tau$. Linear dependency becomes necessary in presence of higher-order functions. Consider, as another example, the term

$$u = \lambda x.\lambda y.\ \mathtt{ifz}\ y\ \mathtt{then}\ \underline{0}\ \mathtt{else}\ xy$$

u has simple type $(\mathtt{Nat} \Rightarrow \mathtt{Nat}) \Rightarrow \mathtt{Nat} \Rightarrow \mathtt{Nat}$. One way to turn it into a linear dependent type is the following

$$(\mathtt{Nat}[a] \overset{\mathrm{H}}{\multimap} \mathtt{Nat}[\mathrm{I}]) \overset{\mathrm{K}}{\multimap} \mathtt{Nat}[a] \overset{\mathrm{L}}{\multimap} \mathtt{Nat}[\mathrm{J}], \quad (3)$$

where J equals 0 when $a = 0$ and J equals I otherwise. Actually, u has type (3) *for every* I and J, provided the two expressions are in the appropriate relation. Now, consider the term

$$v = (\lambda x.\lambda y.(x\ \mathrm{pred}\ (x\ \mathrm{id}\ y)))\ u.$$

The same variable x is applied to the identity id and to the predecessor pred. Which type should we give to the variable x and to u, then? If we want to preserve precision, the type should reflect *both* uses of x. The right type for u is actually the following

$$(\mathtt{Nat}[a] \overset{1}{\multimap} \mathtt{Nat}[\mathrm{I}]) \overset{c<2}{\multimap} \mathtt{Nat}[a] \overset{1}{\multimap} \mathtt{Nat}[\mathrm{J}], \quad (4)$$

where both I and J evaluate to a if $c = 0$ and to $a - 1$ otherwise. If id is replaced by succ in the definition of v, then (4) becomes even more complicated: the first "copy" of J is fed not with a but with either 0 or $a + 1$.

Linear dependency precisely consists in allowing different copies of a term to receive types which are indexed differently (although having the same "functional skeleton") and to represent all of them in compact form. This is in contrast to, e.g., intersection types, where the many different ways a function uses its argument could even be structurally different. This, as we will see in Section 3, has important consequences on the kind of completeness results one can hope for: if the language in which *index terms* are written is sufficiently rich, then the obtained system is complete in an intensional sense: a precise type can be given to *every* terminating *t having type* $\mathtt{Nat} \Rightarrow \mathtt{Nat}$.

Noticeably, linear dependency allows to get precise information about the functional behaviour of programs without making the language of types too different from the one of simple types (e.g., one does not need to quantify over index variables, as in sized types). The price to pay, however, is that types, and especially higher-order types, need to be *context aware*: when you type u as a subterm of v (see above) you need to know which arguments u will be applied to. Despite this, a genuinely compositional type inference procedure can actually be designed and is the main technical contribution of this paper.

2.1 Linearity, Abstract Machines and the Complexity of Evaluation

Why dependency, but specially *linearity*, are so useful for complexity analysis? Actually, typing a term using linear dependent types requires finding an upper bound to the number of times each value is copied by its environment, called its *potential*. In the term v from the example above, the variable x is used twice, and accordingly one finds $c < 2$ in (4). Potentials of higher-order values occurring in a term are crucial parameters for the complexity of evaluating the term by abstract mechanisms [10]. The following is an hopefully convincing (but necessarily informal) discussion about why this is the case.

Configurations of abstract machines for the λ-calculus (like Friedman and Felleisen's CEK and Krivine's KAM) can be thought of as being decomposable into two distinct parts:

- First of all, there are *duplicable* entities which are either copied entirely or turned into non-duplicable entities. This includes, in particular, terms in so-called environments. Each (higher-order) duplicable entity is a subterm of the term the computation started from.
- There are *non-duplicable* entities that the machine uses to look for the next redex to be fired. Typically, these entities are the current term and (possibly) the stack. The essential feature of non-duplicable entities is the fact that they are progressively "consumed" by the machine: the search for the next redex somehow consists in traversing the non-duplicable entities until a redex is found *or* a duplicable entity needs to be turned into a non-duplicable one.

As an example, consider the process of evaluating the PCF term

$$(\lambda f.\, \texttt{ifz}\ (f\,\underline{0})\ \texttt{then}\ \underline{0}\ \texttt{else}\ f(f\,\underline{0}))((\lambda x.\lambda y.\mathrm{add}\,x\,y)\ \underline{3})$$

by an appropriate generalisation of the CEK, see Figure 2. Initially, the whole term is non-duplicable. By travelling into it, the machine finds a first redex u; at that point, $\underline{3}$ becomes duplicable. The obtained closure itself becomes part of the environment ξ, and the machine looks into the body of t, ending up in an occurrence of f, which needs to be replaced by a copy of $\xi(f)$. After an *instantiation step*, a new non-duplicable entity $\xi(f)$ indeed appears. Note that, by an easy combinatorial argument, the number of machine steps necessary to reach f is at most (proportional to) the size of the starting term tu, since reaching f requires consuming non-duplicable entities which can only be created through instantiations. After a copy of $\xi(f)$ becomes non-duplicable, some additional "nonduplicable fuel" becomes available, but not too much: $\lambda y.\mathrm{add}\,x\,y$ is after all a subterm of the initial term.

The careful reader should already have guessed the moral of this story: when analysing the time complexity of evaluation, we could limit ourselves to counting how many *instantiation steps* the machine performs (as opposed to counting *all* machine steps). We claim, on the other hand, that the number of instantiation steps *equals* the sum of potentials of all values appearing in the initial term, something that can be easily inferred from the kind of precise linear typing we were talking about at the beginning of this section.

Summing up, once a dependently linear type has been attributed to a term t, the time complexity of evaluating t can be derived somehow for free: not only an expression bounding the number of instantiation steps performed by an abstract machine evaluating t can be derived, but it is part of the underlying type derivation, essentially. As a consequence, reasoning (automatically or not) about it can be done following the structure of the program.

3. Programs and Types, Formally

In this section, we present some details of dℓPCF, a system of *linear dependent* types for PCF [26]. Two versions exist: dℓPCF$_\mathsf{N}$ and dℓPCF$_\mathsf{V}$, corresponding to *call-by-name* and *call-by-value* evaluation of terms, respectively. The two type systems are different, but the underlying idea is basically the same. We give here the details of the CBV version [13], which better corresponds to widespread intuitions about evaluation, but also provide some indications about the CBN setting [11].

3.1 Terms and Indexes

Terms are given by the usual PCF grammar:

$$s,t,u ::= x \;\big|\; \underline{\mathtt{n}} \;\big|\; t\,u \;\big|\; \lambda x.t \;\big|\; \mathtt{p}(t) \;\big|\; \mathtt{s}(t)$$
$$\mathtt{fix}\,x.t \;\big|\; \mathtt{ifz}\ t\ \mathtt{then}\ u\ \mathtt{else}\ s.$$

A *value* (denoted by v, w etc.) is either a primitive integer $\underline{\mathtt{n}}$, or an abstraction $\lambda x.t$, or a fixpoint $\mathtt{fix}\,x.t$. In addition to the usual terms of the λ-calculus, there are a fixpoint construction, primitive natural numbers with predecessor and successor, and conditional branching with a test for zero. For instance, a simple program computing addition is the following:

$$\mathrm{add} \;=\; \mathtt{fix}\,x.\ \lambda y.\lambda z.\ \mathtt{ifz}\ y\ \mathtt{then}\ z\ \mathtt{else}\ \mathtt{s}(x\ (\mathtt{p}(y))\ z)\ .$$

3.1.1 Language of Indexes

As explained informally in Section 2, a type in dℓPCF consists in an annotation of a PCF type, where the annotation consists in some *indexes*. The latter are parametrised by a set of index variables $\mathcal{V} = \{a, b, c, \dots\}$ and an untyped signature Θ of *function symbols*, denoted by f, g, h, etc. We assume Θ contains at least the arithmetic symbols $+$, $-$, 0 and 1, and we write $\underline{n}$ for $1 + \cdots + 1$ (n times). Indexes are then constructed by the following grammar:

$$\mathrm{I},\mathrm{J},\mathrm{K} ::= a \;\big|\; \mathrm{f}(\mathrm{I}_1,\dots,\mathrm{I}_n) \;\big|\; \sum_{a<\mathrm{I}} \mathrm{J} \;\big|\; \bigtriangleup_{a}^{\mathrm{I},\mathrm{J}}\mathrm{K},$$

where n is the arity of f in Θ. Free and bound index variables are defined as usual, taking care that all free occurrences of a in J are bound in both $\sum_{a<\mathrm{I}} \mathrm{J}$ and $\bigtriangleup_{a}^{\mathrm{I},\mathrm{K}}\mathrm{J}$. The substitution of a variable a by J in I is written $\mathrm{I}\{\mathrm{J}/a\}$. Given an *equational program* $\mathcal{E}$ attributing a *meaning* in $\mathbb{N}^n \rightharpoonup \mathbb{N}$ to some symbols of arity n, and a *valuation* ρ mapping index variables to $\mathbb{N}$, the *semantics* $[\![\mathrm{I}]\!]_\rho^{\mathcal{E}}$ of an index I is either a natural number or undefined. Let us describe how we interpret the last two constructions, namely *bounded sums* and *forest cardinalities*.

Bounded sums have the usual meaning: $\sum_{a<\mathrm{I}} \mathrm{J}$ is simply the sum of all possible values of J with a taking the values from 0 up to I, excluded. Describing the meaning of forest cardinalities, on the other hand, requires some effort. Informally, the index $\bigtriangleup_{a}^{\mathrm{I},\mathrm{J}}\mathrm{K}$ counts the number of nodes in a forest composed of J trees described using K. Each node in the forest is (uniquely) identified by a natural number, starting from I and visiting the tree in pre-order. The index K has the role of describing the number of children of each forest node, e.g. the number of children of the node 0 is $\mathrm{K}\{0/a\}$. Consider the following forest comprising two trees:

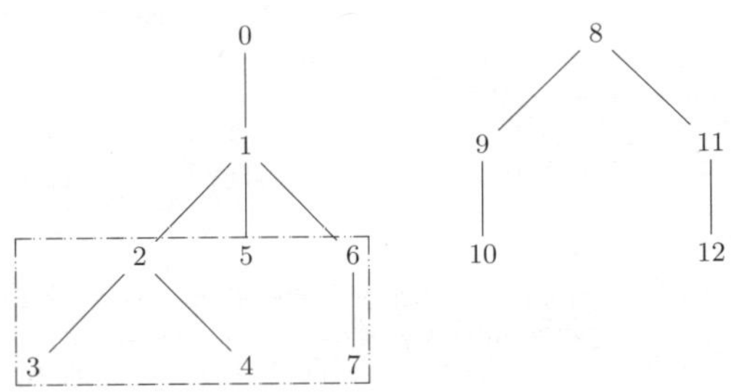

and consider an index K with a free index variable a such that $\mathrm{K}\{1/a\} = 3$; $\mathrm{K}\{\underline{n}/a\} = 2$ for $n \in \{2, 8\}$; $\mathrm{K}\{\underline{n}/a\} = 1$ when $n \in$

$$t = \lambda f.\, \mathtt{ifz}\,(f\,\underline{0})\ \mathtt{then}\ \underline{0}\ \mathtt{else}\ f(f\,\underline{0}); \qquad u = (\lambda x.\lambda y.\mathrm{add}\,x\,y)\,\underline{3}; \qquad \xi = f \mapsto \langle\, \lambda y.\mathrm{add}\,x\,y\,;\, x \mapsto \langle \underline{3} \rangle \rangle.$$

$$\begin{array}{lll}
\langle\, tu \,\rangle \star \diamond & \succ & \langle\, t \,\rangle \star \mathsf{arg}\langle\, u \,\rangle \cdot \diamond \\
& \succ & \langle\, u \,\rangle \star \mathsf{fun}\langle\, t \,\rangle \cdot \diamond \\
& \succ & \langle\, \lambda x.\lambda y.\mathrm{add}\,x\,y \,\rangle \star \mathsf{arg}\langle\, \underline{3} \,\rangle \cdot \mathsf{fun}\langle\, t \,\rangle \cdot \diamond \\
& \succ^* & \langle\, \lambda y.\mathrm{add}\,x\,y\,;\, x \mapsto \langle \underline{3} \rangle \rangle \star \mathsf{fun}\langle\, t \,\rangle \cdot \diamond \\
& \succ & \langle\, \mathtt{ifz}\,(f\,\underline{0})\ \mathtt{then}\ \underline{0}\ \mathtt{else}\ f(f\,\underline{0})\,;\, \xi \,\rangle \star \diamond \\
& \succ & \langle\, f\,\underline{0}\,;\, \xi \,\rangle \star \mathsf{fork}\langle \underline{0}\,;\, f(f\,\underline{0})\,;\, \xi \rangle \cdot \diamond \\
& \succ & \langle\, f\,;\, \xi \,\rangle \star \mathsf{arg}\langle\, \underline{0}\,;\, \xi \,\rangle \cdot \mathsf{fork}\langle \underline{0}\,;\, f(f\,\underline{0})\,;\, \xi \rangle \cdot \diamond \\
& \succ & \langle\, \lambda y.\mathrm{add}\,x\,y\,;\, x \mapsto \langle \underline{3} \rangle \rangle \star \mathsf{arg}\langle\, \underline{0}\,;\, \xi \,\rangle \cdot \mathsf{fork}\langle \underline{0}\,;\, f(f\,\underline{0})\,;\, \xi \rangle \cdot \diamond \\
& \succ^* & \langle\, \mathrm{add}\,x\,y\,;\, (y \mapsto \langle \underline{0}\,;\, \xi \rangle, x \mapsto \langle \underline{3} \rangle) \,\rangle \star \mathsf{fork}\langle \underline{0}\,;\, f(f\,\underline{0})\,;\, \xi \rangle \cdot \diamond \\
& \succ^* & \langle\, \underline{3} \,\rangle \star \mathsf{fork}\langle \underline{0}\,;\, f(f\,\underline{0})\,;\, \xi \rangle \cdot \diamond \\
& \succ & \langle\, f(f\,\underline{0})\,;\, \xi \,\rangle \star \diamond \\
& \succ & \langle\, f\,;\, \xi \,\rangle \star \mathsf{arg}\langle\, f\,\underline{0}\,;\, \xi \,\rangle \cdot \diamond \\
& \succ & \langle\, \lambda y.\mathrm{add}\,x\,y\,;\, x \mapsto \langle \underline{3} \rangle \rangle \star \mathsf{arg}\langle\, f\,\underline{0}\,;\, \xi \,\rangle \cdot \diamond \\
& \succ & \langle\, f\,\underline{0}\,;\, \xi \,\rangle \star \mathsf{fun}\langle\, \lambda y.\mathrm{add}\,x\,y\,;\, x \mapsto \langle \underline{3} \rangle \rangle \cdot \diamond \\
& \succ^* & \langle\, \underline{3} \,\rangle \star \mathsf{fun}\langle\, \lambda y.\mathrm{add}\,x\,y\,;\, x \mapsto \langle \underline{3} \rangle \rangle \cdot \diamond \\
& \succ^* & \langle\, \underline{6} \,\rangle \star \diamond
\end{array}$$

Figure 2. Evaluation of a term in the $\mathsf{CEK}_{\mathsf{PCF}}$ abstract machine.

$\{0, 6, 9, 11\}$; and $\mathrm{K}\{\underline{n}/a\} = 0$ when $n \in \{3, 4, 7, 10, 12\}$. That is, K describes the number of children of each node. Then $\triangle_a^{0,2}\,\mathrm{K} = 13$ since it takes into account the entire forest; $\triangle_a^{0,1}\,\mathrm{K} = 8$ since it takes into account only the leftmost tree; $\triangle_a^{8,1}\,\mathrm{K} = 5$ since it takes into account only the second tree of the forest; finally, $\triangle_a^{2,3}\,\mathrm{K} = 6$ since it takes into account only the three trees (as a forest) within the dashed rectangle.

One may wonder what is the role of forest cardinalities in the type system. Actually, they play a crucial role in the treatment of recursion, where the unfolding of recursive calls produces a tree-like structure whose size is just the number of times the (recursively defined) function will be used *globally*.

Notice that $[\![\mathrm{I}]\!]_\rho^{\mathcal{E}}$ is undefined whenever the equality between I and any natural number cannot be derived from the underlying equational program. In particular, a forest cardinality may be undefined even if all its subterms are defined: as an example $\mathrm{I} = \triangle_a^{0,1}\,1$ has no value, because the corresponding tree consists of an infinite descending chain and its cardinality is infinite. By the way I is the index term describing the structure of the recursive calls induced by the program $\mathtt{fix}\ x.x$.

3.1.2 Semantic Judgements

A *constraint* is an inequality on indexes. A constraint $\mathrm{I} \leqslant \mathrm{J}$ is *valid* for ρ and $\mathcal{E}$ when both $[\![\mathrm{I}]\!]_\rho^{\mathcal{E}}$ and $[\![\mathrm{J}]\!]_\rho^{\mathcal{E}}$ are defined, and $[\![\mathrm{I}]\!]_\rho^{\mathcal{E}} \leqslant [\![\mathrm{J}]\!]_\rho^{\mathcal{E}}$. As usual, we can derive a notion of equality and strict inequality from $\leqslant$. A *semantic judgement* is of the form

$$\phi; \Phi \vDash_{\mathcal{E}} \mathrm{I} \leqslant \mathrm{J},$$

where Φ is a set of constraints and ϕ is the set of free index variables in Φ, I and J. These semantic judgements are used as axioms in the typing derivations of $\mathsf{d}\ell\mathsf{PCF}$, and the set of constraints Φ, called the *index context*, contains *mainly* some indications of bounds for the free index variables (such as $a < \mathrm{K}$). Such a judgement is valid when, for every valuation $\rho : \phi \to \mathbb{N}$, if all constraints in Φ are valid for $\mathcal{E}$ and ρ then so is $\mathrm{I} \leqslant \mathrm{J}$.

3.2 Types

Remember that $\mathsf{d}\ell\mathsf{PCF}$ is aimed at controlling the complexity of programs. The time complexity *of the evaluation* is thus analysed statically, while typing the term at hand. The grammar for types distinguishes the subclass of *linear types*, which correspond to *non-duplicable* terms (see Section 2.1), and the one of *modal types*, for *duplicable* terms. In $\mathsf{d}\ell\mathsf{PCF}_\mathsf{V}$, they are defined as follows:

$$\begin{array}{lcll}
A, B & ::= & \sigma \multimap \tau; & \text{linear types} \\
\sigma, \tau & ::= & [a < \mathrm{I}] \cdot A \;\big|\; \mathtt{Nat}[\mathrm{I}, \mathrm{J}]. & \text{modal types}
\end{array}$$

Indeed, CBV evaluation only duplicates values. If such a value has an arrow type, then it is a function (either an abstraction or a fixpoint) that can potentially increase the complexity of the whole program if we duplicate it. Hence we need a bound on the number of times we instantiate it if we want to keep the overall complexity under control. This bound, call the *potential* of the value, is represented by I in the type $[a < \mathrm{I}] \cdot (\sigma \multimap \tau)$ (also written $\sigma \overset{a<\mathrm{I}}{\multimap} \tau$). As explained in Section 2, $\mathtt{Nat}[\mathrm{I}, \mathrm{J}]$ is the type of programs evaluating to a natural number in the closed interval $[\mathrm{I}, \mathrm{J}]$. The potential of natural number values is not specified, as they can be freely duplicated along CBV evaluation.

3.2.1 Summing types

Intuitively, the modal type $\sigma \equiv [a < \mathrm{I}] \cdot A$ is assigned to terms that can be copied I times, the kth copy being of type $A\{\underline{k} - 1/a\}$. For those readers who are familiar with Linear Logic, σ can be thought of as representing the type $A\{0/a\} \otimes \cdots \otimes A\{\mathrm{I} - 1/a\}$.

In the typing rules we are going to define, modal types need to be manipulated in an algebraic way. For this reason, two operations on modal types are required. The first one is a binary operation $\uplus$ on modal types. Suppose that $\sigma \equiv [a < \mathrm{I}] \cdot A\{a/c\}$ and that $\tau \equiv [a < \mathrm{J}] \cdot A\{\mathrm{I} + a/c\}$. In other words, σ consists of the first I instances of A, i.e. $A\{0/c\} \otimes \cdots \otimes A\{\mathrm{I} - 1/c\}$, while τ consists of the next J instances of A, i.e. $A\{\mathrm{I} + 0/c\} \otimes \cdots \otimes A\{\mathrm{I} + \mathrm{J} - 1/c\}$. Their *sum* $\sigma \uplus \tau$ is naturally defined as a modal type consisting of the first $\mathrm{I} + \mathrm{J}$ instances of A, i.e. $[c < \mathrm{I} + \mathrm{J}] \cdot A$. Furthermore, $\mathtt{Nat}[\mathrm{I}, \mathrm{J}] \uplus \mathtt{Nat}[\mathrm{I}, \mathrm{J}]$ is just $\mathtt{Nat}[\mathrm{I}, \mathrm{J}]$. A bounded sum operator on modal types can be defined by generalising the idea above: suppose that

$$\sigma = [b < \mathrm{J}] \cdot A \left\{ b + \sum_{d<a} \mathrm{J}\{d/a\}/c \right\}.$$

Then its *bounded sum* $\sum_{a<\mathrm{I}} \sigma$ is just $[c < \sum_{a<\mathrm{I}} \mathrm{J}] \cdot A$. Finally, $\sum_{a<\mathrm{I}} \mathtt{Nat}[\mathrm{J}, \mathrm{K}] = \mathtt{Nat}[\mathrm{J}, \mathrm{K}]$, provided a does not occur free in J nor in K.

3.2.2 Subtyping

Central to $\mathsf{d}\ell\mathsf{PCF}$ is the notion of subtyping. An inequality relation $\sqsubseteq$ between (linear or modal) types can be defined using the

$$\frac{\phi;\Phi\models_{\mathcal{E}}\mathrm{K}\leqslant\mathrm{I}\qquad\phi;\Phi\models_{\mathcal{E}}\mathrm{J}\leqslant\mathrm{H}}{\phi;\Phi\vdash_{\mathcal{E}}\mathtt{Nat}[\mathrm{I},\mathrm{J}]\sqsubseteq\mathtt{Nat}[\mathrm{K},\mathrm{H}]}\qquad\frac{\phi;\Phi\vdash_{\mathcal{E}}\varrho\sqsubseteq\sigma\qquad\phi;\Phi\vdash_{\mathcal{E}}\tau\sqsubseteq\xi}{\phi;\Phi\vdash_{\mathcal{E}}\sigma\multimap\tau\sqsubseteq\varrho\multimap\xi}$$

$$\frac{(a,\phi);(a<\mathrm{J},\Phi)\vdash_{\mathcal{E}}A\sqsubseteq B\qquad\phi;\Phi\models_{\mathcal{E}}\mathrm{J}\leqslant\mathrm{I}}{\phi;\Phi\vdash_{\mathcal{E}}[a<\mathrm{I}]\cdot A\sqsubseteq[a<\mathrm{J}]\cdot B}$$

Figure 3. Subtyping derivation rules of dℓPCF$_\mathsf{V}$.

formal system in Fig. 3. This relation corresponds to lifting index inequalities to the type level. As defined here, $\sqsubseteq$ is a pre-order (i.e. a reflexive and transitive relation), which allows to cope with approximations in the typed analysis of programs. However, in the type inference algorithm we will present in the next section only the symmetric closure $\equiv$ of $\sqsubseteq$, called *type equivalence* will be used. This ensures that the type produced by the algorithm is *precise*.

3.2.3 Typing

A typing judgement is of the form

$$\phi;\Phi;\Gamma\vdash^{\mathcal{E}}_{\mathrm{K}} t:\tau,$$

where K is the *weight* of t, that is (informally) the maximal number of substitutions involved in the CBV evaluation of t (including the potential substitutions by t itself in its evaluation context). The index context Φ is as in a semantic judgement (see Section 3.1.2), and Γ is a (term) context assigning a modal type to (at least) each free variable of t. Both sums and bounded sums are naturally extended from modal types to contexts (with, for instance, $\{x:\sigma;y:\tau\}\uplus\{x:\varrho,z:\xi\}=\{x:\sigma\uplus\varrho;y:\tau;z:\xi\}$). There might be free index variables in Φ,Γ,τ and K, all of them from ϕ. Typing judgements can be derived from the rules of Figure 4.

Observe that, in the typing rule for the abstraction ($\multimap$), I represents the number of times the value $\lambda x.t$ can be copied. Its weight (that is, the number of substitutions involving $\lambda x.t$ or one of its subterms) is then I plus, for each of these copies, the weight of t. In the typing rule (*App*), on the other hand, t is used once as a function, without been copied. Its potential needs to be at least 1. The typing rule for the fixpoint is arguably the most complicated one. As a first approximation, assume that only one copy of $\mathtt{fix}\,x.t$ will be used (that is, $\mathrm{K}\equiv 1$ and a does not occur free in B). To compute the weight of $\mathtt{fix}\,x.t$, we need to know the number of times t will be copied during the evaluation, that is the number of nodes in the tree of its recursive calls. This tree is described by the index I (as explained in Section 3.1.1), since each occurrence of x in t stands for a recursive call. It has $\mathrm{H}=\triangle_b^{0,1}\,\mathrm{I}$ nodes. At each node b of this tree, there is a copy of t in which the ath occurrence of x will be replaced by the ath son of b, i.e. by $b+1+\triangle_b^{b+1,a}\,\mathrm{I}$. The types thus have to correspond, which is what the second premise of this rule prescribes. Now if $\mathtt{fix}\,x.t$ is in fact aimed at being copied $\mathrm{K}\geqslant 0$ times, then all the copies of t are represented by a forest of K trees described by I.

For the sake of simplicity, we present here the type system with an explicit subsumption rule. The latter allows to relax any bound in the types (and the weight), thereby loosing some precision in the information provided by the typing judgement. However, we could alternatively replace this rule by relaxing the premises of all the other ones (which corresponds to the presentation of the type system given in [13], or in [11] for dℓPCF$_\mathsf{N}$). Restricting subtyping to type equivalence amounts to considering types up to index equality in the type system of Figure 4 without the rule (*Subs*) — this is what we do in the type inference algorithm in Section 4. In this case we say that the typing judgements are *precise*:

DEFINITION 3.1. *A derivable judgement* $\phi;\Phi;\Gamma\vdash^{\mathcal{E}}_{\mathrm{I}} t:\sigma$ *is* precise *if*

$$\phi;\Phi;\Delta\vdash^{\mathcal{E}}_{\mathrm{J}} t:\tau \textit{ is derivable}\quad\Longrightarrow\quad\begin{cases}\phi;\Phi\vdash_{\mathcal{E}}\Delta\sqsubseteq\Gamma\\ \phi;\Phi\vdash_{\mathcal{E}}\sigma\sqsubseteq\tau\\ \phi;\Phi\models_{\mathcal{E}}\mathrm{I}\leqslant\mathrm{J}\end{cases}$$

3.2.4 Call-by-value vs. Call-by-name

In dℓPCF$_\mathsf{N}$, the syntax of terms and of indexes is the same as in dℓPCF$_\mathsf{V}$, but the language of types differs:

$$\begin{array}{rcll} A,B & := & \sigma\multimap A \;\big|\; \mathtt{Nat}[\mathrm{I},\mathrm{J}]; & \text{linear types}\\ \sigma,\tau & := & [a<\mathrm{I}]\cdot A. & \text{modal types}\end{array}$$

Modal types still represent duplicable terms, except that now not only values but any argument to functions can be duplicated. So modal types only occur in negative position in arrow types. In the same way, one can find them in the *context* of any typing judgement,

$$\phi;\Phi;x_1:\sigma_1,\ldots,x_n:\sigma_n\vdash^{\mathcal{E}}_{\mathrm{K}} t:A.$$

When a term is typed, it is *a priori* not duplicable, and its type is linear. It is turned into a duplicable term when it holds the argument position in an application. As a consequence, the typing rule (*App*) becomes the most "expansive" one (for the weight) in dℓPCF$_\mathsf{N}$: the whole context used to type the argument has to be duplicated, whereas in dℓPCF$_\mathsf{V}$ this duplication of context is "anticipated" in the typing rules for values.

The readers who are familiar with linear logic, could have noted that if we replace modal types by banged types (and we remove all annotations with indexes), then dℓPCF$_\mathsf{N}$ corresponds to the target fragment of the CBN translation from simply-typed λ-calculus to LL, and dℓPCF$_\mathsf{V}$ to the target of the CBV translation [25].

In dℓPCF$_\mathsf{N}$, the weight K of a typing judgement represents the maximal number of substitutions that may occur in the CBN evaluation of t. We do not detail the typing rules of dℓPCF$_\mathsf{N}$ here (they can be found in [11]). However, an important remark is that in dℓPCF$_\mathsf{N}$, just like in dℓPCF$_\mathsf{V}$, some semantic judgements can be found in the axioms of a typing derivation, and every typing rule is reversible (except subsumption). The type inference algorithm for dℓPCF$_\mathsf{V}$ that we present in Section 4 can be easily adapted to dℓPCF$_\mathsf{N}$.

3.3 Abstract Machines

The evaluation of PCF terms can be simulated through an extension KAM$_\mathsf{PCF}$ of Krivine's abstract machine [24] (for CBN evaluation) or through an extension CEK$_\mathsf{PCF}$ of Felleisen and Friedman's CEK machine [16] (for CBV evaluation).

Both these machines have states in the form of *processes*, that are pairs of a *closure* (i.e. a term with an environment defining its free variables) and a *stack*, representing the evaluation context. In the KAM$_\mathsf{PCF}$, these objects are given by the following grammar:

$$\begin{array}{lrcl} \text{Closures:} & \mathsf{c} & := & \langle t\,;\,\xi\rangle;\\ \text{Environment:} & \xi & := & \{x_1\mapsto\mathsf{c}_1;\cdots;x_k\mapsto\mathsf{c}_k\};\\ \text{Stacks:} & \pi & := & \diamond \;\big|\; \mathsf{arg}\langle t\,;\,\xi\rangle\cdot\pi \;\big|\; \mathsf{s}\cdot\pi \;\big|\; \mathsf{p}\cdot\pi\\ & & & \big|\; \mathsf{fork}\langle t\,;\,u\,;\,\xi\rangle\cdot\pi;\\ \text{Processes:} & P & := & \mathsf{c}\star\pi.\end{array}$$

When the environment is empty, we may use the notation $\langle t\rangle$ instead of $\langle t\,;\,\varnothing\rangle$ for closures. The evaluation rules of the KAM$_\mathsf{PCF}$ are given in Figure 5. The fourth evaluation rule is said to be an *instantiation step*: the value of a variable x is replaced by the term x maps to in the underlying environment ξ.

The CEK$_\mathsf{PCF}$, which performs CBV evaluation, is slightly more complex: within closures, the *value closures* are those whose first

$$\frac{}{\phi;\Phi;\Gamma,x:\sigma\vdash^{\mathcal{E}}_{0} x:\sigma}(Ax)\qquad\frac{\phi;\Phi;\Gamma\vdash^{\mathcal{E}}_{\mathrm{I}} t:\sigma\qquad \phi;\Phi\vdash_{\mathcal{E}}\Delta\sqsubseteq\Gamma\qquad \phi;\Phi\vdash_{\mathcal{E}}\sigma\sqsubseteq\tau\qquad \phi;\Phi\models_{\mathcal{E}}\mathrm{I}\leqslant\mathrm{J}}{\phi;\Phi;\Delta\vdash^{\mathcal{E}}_{\mathrm{J}} t:\tau}(Subs)$$

$$\frac{(a,\phi);(a<\mathrm{I},\Phi);\Gamma,x:\sigma\vdash^{\mathcal{E}}_{\mathrm{K}} t:\tau}{\phi;\Phi;\sum_{a<\mathrm{I}}\Gamma\vdash^{\mathcal{E}}_{\mathrm{I}+\sum_{a<\mathrm{I}}\mathrm{K}}\lambda x.t:[a<\mathrm{I}]\cdot\sigma\multimap\tau}(\multimap)\qquad\frac{\phi;\Phi;\Gamma\vdash^{\mathcal{E}}_{\mathrm{K}} t:[a<1]\cdot\sigma\multimap\tau\qquad \phi;\Phi;\Delta\vdash^{\mathcal{E}}_{\mathrm{H}} u:\sigma\{0/a\}}{\phi;\Phi;\Gamma\uplus\Delta\vdash^{\mathcal{E}}_{\mathrm{K}+\mathrm{H}} tu:\tau\{0/a\}}(App)$$

$$\frac{\phi;\Phi;\Gamma\vdash^{\mathcal{E}}_{\mathrm{M}} t:\mathtt{Nat}[\mathrm{J},\mathrm{K}]\qquad \phi;(\mathrm{J}\leqslant 0,\Phi);\Delta\vdash^{\mathcal{E}}_{\mathrm{N}} u:\tau\qquad \phi;(\mathrm{K}\geqslant 1,\Phi);\Delta\vdash^{\mathcal{E}}_{\mathrm{N}} s:\tau}{\phi;\Phi;\Gamma\uplus\Delta\vdash^{\mathcal{E}}_{\mathrm{M}+\mathrm{N}}\ \mathtt{ifz}\ t\ \mathtt{then}\ u\ \mathtt{else}\ s:\tau}(If)$$

$$\frac{}{\phi;\Phi;\Gamma\vdash^{\mathcal{E}}_{0}\underline{\mathtt{n}}:\mathtt{Nat}[\underline{n},\underline{n}]}(n)\qquad\frac{\phi;\Phi;\Gamma\vdash^{\mathcal{E}}_{\mathrm{M}} t:\mathtt{Nat}[\mathrm{I},\mathrm{J}]}{\phi;\Phi;\Gamma\vdash^{\mathcal{E}}_{\mathrm{M}}\mathtt{s}(t):\mathtt{Nat}[\mathrm{I}+1,\mathrm{J}+1]}(s)\qquad\frac{\phi;\Phi;\Gamma\vdash^{\mathcal{E}}_{\mathrm{M}} t:\mathtt{Nat}[\mathrm{I},\mathrm{J}]}{\phi;\Phi;\Gamma\vdash^{\mathcal{E}}_{\mathrm{M}}\mathtt{p}(t):\mathtt{Nat}[\mathrm{I}-1,\mathrm{J}-1]}(p)$$

$$\frac{(b,\phi);(b<\mathrm{H},\Phi);\Gamma,x:[a<\mathrm{I}]\cdot A\vdash^{\mathcal{E}}_{\mathrm{J}} t:[a<1]\cdot B\qquad (a,b,\phi);(a<\mathrm{I},b<\mathrm{H},\Phi)\vdash_{\mathcal{E}} B\{0/a\}\{\bigcirc\!\!\!\!\triangle_{b}^{b+1,a}\,\mathrm{I}+b+1/b\}\sqsubseteq A}{\phi;\Phi;\sum_{b<\mathrm{H}}\Gamma\vdash^{\mathcal{E}}_{\mathrm{H}+\sum_{b<\mathrm{H}}\mathrm{J}}\ \mathtt{fix}\ x.t:[a<\mathrm{K}]\cdot B\{0/a\}\{\bigcirc\!\!\!\!\triangle_{b}^{0,a}\,\mathrm{I}/b\}}(Fix)$$

(where $\mathrm{H}=\bigcirc\!\!\!\!\triangle_{b}^{0,\mathrm{K}}\,\mathrm{I}$)

Figure 4. Typing rules of dℓPCF$_{\mathsf{V}}$.

component is a value: $\mathsf{v} := \langle v\,;\,\xi\rangle$ (remember that a *value* v is of the form $\underline{\mathtt{n}}$, $\lambda x.t$ or $\mathtt{fix}\ x.t$). Moreover, environments assign only value closures to variables:

$$\xi \ :=\ \{x_1\mapsto \mathsf{v}_1;\cdots;x_k\mapsto\mathsf{v}_k\}.$$

The grammar for stacks is the same, with one additional construction $(\mathsf{fun}(\mathsf{v})\cdot\pi)$ that is used to encapsulate a function (lambda abstraction or fixpoint) while its argument is computed. Indeed, the latter cannot be substituted for a variable if it is not a value. Evaluation rules for processes are the same as the ones in Figure 5, except that the second and the third ones are replaced by the following:

$$\begin{array}{llcll}
\mathsf{v}\ \star & \mathsf{arg}(\mathsf{c})\cdot\pi & \succ & \mathsf{c} & \star\ \mathsf{fun}(\mathsf{v})\cdot\pi\\
\mathsf{v}\ \star & \mathsf{fun}\langle\lambda x.t\,;\,\xi\rangle\cdot\pi & \succ & \langle t\,;\,x\mapsto\mathsf{v}\cdot\xi\rangle\ \star & \pi\\
\mathsf{v}\ \star & \mathsf{fun}\langle\mathtt{fix}\ x.t\,;\,\xi\rangle\cdot\pi & \succ & & \\
 & & & \langle t\,;\,x\mapsto\langle\mathtt{fix}\ x.t\,;\,\xi\rangle\cdot\xi\rangle & \star\ \mathsf{arg}(\mathsf{v})\cdot\pi
\end{array}$$

An example of the evaluation of a term by the CEK$_{\mathsf{PCF}}$ can be found in Figure 2.

We say that a term t *evaluates* to u in an abstract machine when $\langle t\rangle\star\diamond\succ\langle u\,;\,\xi\rangle\star\diamond$. Observe that if t is a closed term, then u is necessarily a value. We write $t\Downarrow^{n}_{\mathsf{N}} u$ whenever the KAM$_{\mathsf{PCF}}$ evaluates t to u in exactly n steps, and $t\Downarrow^{n}_{\mathsf{V}} u$ when the same holds for the CEK$_{\mathsf{PCF}}$ (we may also omit the exponent n when the number of steps is not relevant).

Abstract Machines and Weight. The *weight* of a typable term was informally presented as the number of instantiation steps in its evaluation. Abstract machines enable a more precise formulation of this idea:

FACT 1. *1. If $t\Downarrow_{\mathsf{N}} u$, and $\vdash^{\mathcal{E}}_{\mathrm{I}} t:A$ is derivable in dℓPCF$_{\mathsf{N}}$, then $[\![\mathrm{I}]\!]^{\mathcal{E}}$ is an upper bound for the number of instantiation steps in the evaluation of t by the KAM$_{\mathsf{PCF}}$.*
2. If $t\Downarrow_{\mathsf{V}} u$, and $\vdash^{\mathcal{E}}_{\mathrm{I}} t:[a<1]\cdot A$ is derivable in dℓPCF$_{\mathsf{V}}$, then $[\![\mathrm{I}]\!]^{\mathcal{E}}$ is an upper bound for the instantiation steps in the evaluation of t by the CEK$_{\mathsf{PCF}}$.

This can be shown by extending the notion of weight and of typing judgement to stacks and processes [11, 13], and is the main ingredients for proving Intensional Soundness (see Section 3.4).

3.4 Key Properties

In this section we briefly recall the main properties of dℓPCF, arguing for its relevance as a methodology for complexity analysis. We give the results for dℓPCF$_{\mathsf{V}}$, but they also hold for dℓPCF$_{\mathsf{N}}$ (all proofs can be found in [11, 13]).

The Subject Reduction Property guarantees as usual that typing is correct with respect to term reduction, but specifies also that the weight of a term cannot increase along reduction:

PROPOSITION 3.1 (Subject Reduction). *For any PCF-terms t,u, if $\phi;\Phi;\varnothing\vdash^{\mathcal{E}}_{\mathrm{I}} t:\tau$ is derivable in dℓPCF$_{\mathsf{V}}$, and if $t\to u$ in* CBV, *then $\phi;\Phi;\varnothing\vdash^{\mathcal{E}}_{\mathrm{J}} u:\tau$ is also derivable for some J such that $\phi;\Phi\models_{\mathcal{E}}\mathrm{J}\leqslant\mathrm{I}$.*

As a consequence, the weight does not tell us much about the number of reduction steps bringing a (typable) term to its normal form. So-called *Intensional Soundness*, on the other hand, allows to deduce some sensible information about the time complexity of evaluating a typable PCF program *by an abstract machine* from its dℓPCF typing judgement.

PROPOSITION 3.2 (Intensional Soundness). *For any term t, if $\vdash^{\mathcal{E}}_{\mathrm{K}} t:\mathtt{Nat}[\mathrm{I},\mathrm{J}]$ is derivable in dℓPCF$_{\mathsf{V}}$, then t evaluates to $\underline{\mathtt{n}}$ in k steps in the CEK$_{\mathsf{PCF}}$, with $[\![\mathrm{I}]\!]^{\mathcal{E}}\leqslant n\leqslant[\![\mathrm{J}]\!]^{\mathcal{E}}$ and $k\leqslant|t|\cdot([\![\mathrm{K}]\!]^{\mathcal{E}}+1)$.*

Intensional Soundness guarantees that the evaluation of any program typable in dℓPCF takes (at most) a number of steps directly proportional to both its syntactic size and its weight. A similar theorem holds when t has a functional type: if, as an example, the type of t is $\mathtt{Nat}[a]\overset{1}{\multimap}\mathtt{Nat}[\mathrm{J}]$, then K is parametric on a and $(|t|+2)\cdot([\![\mathrm{K}]\!]^{\mathcal{E}}+1)$ is an upper bound on the complexity of evaluating t when fed with any integer a.

But is dℓPCF powerful enough to type natural complexity bounded programs? Actually, it is as powerful as PCF itself, since any PCF type derivation can be turned into a dℓPCF one (for an expressive enough equational program), as formalised by the type inference algorithm (Section 4). We can make this statement even more precise for terms of base or first order type, provided two conditions are satisfied:

- On the one hand, the equational program $\mathcal{E}$ needs to be *universal*, meaning that every partial recursive function is representable by some index term. This can be guaranteed, as an example, by the presence of a universal program in $\mathcal{E}$.
- On the other hand, all *true* statements in the form $\phi;\Phi\models_{\mathcal{E}}\mathrm{I}\leqslant\mathrm{J}$ must be "available" in the type system for completeness to hold. In other words, one cannot assume that those judgements are derived in a given (recursively enumerable) formal system, because this would violate Gödel's Incompleteness Theorem. In fact, in dℓPCF completeness theorems are *relative* to an oracle for the truth of those assumptions, which is precisely what happens in Floyd-Hoare logics [9].

$$
\begin{array}{ccccccc}
\langle tu\,;\,\xi\rangle & \star & \pi & \succ & \langle t\,;\,\xi\rangle & \star & \mathsf{arg}\langle u\,;\,\xi\rangle\cdot\pi \\
\langle \lambda x.t\,;\,\xi\rangle & \star & \mathsf{arg}(\mathsf{c})\cdot\pi & \succ & \langle t\,;\,(x\mapsto\mathsf{c})\cdot\xi\rangle & \star & \pi \\
\langle\, \mathtt{fix}\,x.t\,;\,\xi\rangle & \star & \pi & \succ & \langle t\,;\,(x\mapsto\langle\,\mathtt{fix}\,x.t\,;\,\xi\rangle)\cdot\xi\rangle & \star & \pi \\
\langle x\,;\,\xi\rangle & \star & \pi & \succ & \xi(x) & \star & \pi \\
\langle\, \mathtt{ifz}\,t\,\mathtt{then}\,u\,\mathtt{else}\,s\,;\,\xi\rangle & \star & \pi & \succ & \langle t\,;\,\xi\rangle & \star & \mathsf{fork}\langle u\,;\,s\,;\,\xi\rangle\cdot\pi \\
\langle \underline{0}\,;\,\xi'\rangle & \star & \mathsf{fork}\langle t\,;\,u\,;\,\xi\rangle\cdot\pi & \succ & \langle t\,;\,\xi\rangle & \star & \pi \\
\langle \underline{\mathtt{n+1}}\,;\,\xi'\rangle & \star & \mathsf{fork}\langle t\,;\,u\,;\,\xi\rangle\cdot\pi & \succ & \langle u\,;\,\xi\rangle & \star & \pi \\
\langle \mathtt{s}(t)\,;\,\xi\rangle & \star & \pi & \succ & \langle t\,;\,\xi\rangle & \star & \mathsf{s}\cdot\pi \\
\langle \mathtt{p}(t)\,;\,\xi\rangle & \star & \pi & \succ & \langle t\,;\,\xi\rangle & \star & \mathsf{p}\cdot\pi \\
\langle \underline{\mathtt{n}}\,;\,\xi\rangle & \star & \mathsf{s}\cdot\pi & \succ & \langle \underline{\mathtt{n+1}}\rangle & \star & \pi \\
\langle \underline{\mathtt{n}}\,;\,\xi\rangle & \star & \mathsf{p}\cdot\pi & \succ & \langle \underline{\mathtt{n-1}}\rangle & \star & \pi
\end{array}
$$

Figure 5. $\mathsf{KAM}_{\mathsf{PCF}}$ evaluation rules.

PROPOSITION 3.3 (Relative Completeness). *If* $\mathcal{E}$ *is universal, then for any* PCF *term* t,

1. *if* $t \Downarrow_{\mathsf{V}}^{k} \underline{\mathtt{m}}$, *then* $\vdash_{\underline{k}}^{\mathcal{E}} t : \mathtt{Nat}[\underline{m}]$ *is derivable in* $\mathsf{d}\ell\mathsf{PCF}_{\mathsf{V}}$.
2. *if, for any* $n \in \mathbb{N}$, *there exist* k_n, m_n *such that* $t\,\underline{\mathtt{n}} \Downarrow_{\mathsf{V}}^{k_n} \underline{\mathtt{m_n}}$, *then there exist* I *and* J *such that*

$$a; \varnothing; \varnothing \vdash_{\mathrm{I}}^{\mathcal{E}} t : [b < 1] \cdot (\mathtt{Nat}[a] \multimap \mathtt{Nat}[\mathrm{J}])$$

is derivable in $\mathsf{d}\ell\mathsf{PCF}_{\mathsf{V}}$, *with* $\models_{\mathcal{E}} \mathrm{J}\{\underline{n}/a\} = \underline{m_n}$ *and* $\models_{\mathcal{E}} \mathrm{I}\{\underline{n}/a\} \leqslant \underline{k_n}$ *for all* $n \in \mathbb{N}$.

The careful reader should have noticed that there is indeed a gap between the lower bound provided by completeness and the upper bound provided by soundness: this is indeed the reason why our complexity analysis is only meaningful in an asymptotic sense. Sometimes, however, programs with the same asymptotic behavior *can* indeed be distinguished, e.g. when their size is small relative to the constants in their weight.

In the next section, we will see how to make a concrete use of Relative Completeness. Indeed, we will describe an algorithm that, given a PCF term, returns a $\mathsf{d}\ell\mathsf{PCF}$ judgement $\vdash_{\mathrm{K}}^{\mathcal{E}} t : \tau$ for this term, where $\mathcal{E}$ is equational program that is not *universal*, but expressive enough to derive the typing judgement. To cope with the "relative" part of the result (i.e., the very strong assumption that every *true* semantic judgement must be available), the algorithm also returns a set of *side conditions* that have to be checked. These side conditions are in fact semantic judgements that act as axioms (of instances of the subsumption rule) in the typing derivation.

4. Relative Type Inference

Given on the one hand soundness and relative completeness of $\mathsf{d}\ell\mathsf{PCF}$, and on the other undecidability of complexity analysis for PCF programs, one may wonder whether looking for a type inference procedure makes sense at all. As stressed in the Introduction, we will not give a type inference algorithm *per se*, but rather reduce type inference to the problem of checking the validity of a set of inequalities modulo an equational program (see Figure 1). This is the reason why we can only claim type inference to be algorithmically solvable in a *relative* sense, i.e. assuming the existence of an oracle for proof obligations.

Why is solving relative type inference useful? Suppose you have a program $t : \mathtt{Nat} \Rightarrow \mathtt{Nat}$ and you want to prove that it works in a number of steps bounded by a polynomial $p : \mathbb{N} \to \mathbb{N}$ (e.g., $p(x) = 4 \cdot x + 7$). You could of course proceed by building a $\mathsf{d}\ell\mathsf{PCF}$ type derivation for t by hand, or even reason directly on the complexity of t. Relative type inference simplifies your life: it outputs an equational program $\mathcal{E}$, a *precise* type derivation for t whose conclusion is $a; \varnothing; \varnothing \vdash_{\mathrm{I}}^{\mathcal{E}} t : \mathtt{Nat}[a] \overset{1}{\multimap} \mathtt{Nat}[\mathrm{J}]$ and a set $\mathcal{I}$ of inequalities on the same signature as the one of $\mathcal{E}$. Your original problem, then, is reduced to verifying $\models^{\mathcal{E}} \mathcal{I} \cup \{\mathrm{I} \leqslant p(a)\}$. This is arguably an easier problem than the original one: first of all, it has nothing to do with complexity analysis but is rather a problem about the *value* of arithmetical expressions. Secondly it only deals with first-order expressions.

4.1 An Informal Account

From the brief discussion in Section 2, it should be clear that devising a compositional type inference procedure for $\mathsf{d}\ell\mathsf{PCF}$ is nontrivial: the type one assigns to a subterm heavily depends on the ways the rest of the program uses the subterm. The solution we adopt here consists in allowing the algorithm to return *partially unspecified* equational programs: $\mathcal{E}$ as produced in output by $\mathcal{T}$ gives meaning to all the symbols in the output type derivation *except* those occurring in negative position in its conclusion.

To better understand how the type inference algorithm works, let us consider the following term t:

$$uv = (\lambda x.\lambda y.x(xy))(\lambda z.\mathtt{s}(z)).$$

The subterm u can be given type $(\mathtt{Nat} \Rightarrow \mathtt{Nat}) \Rightarrow \mathtt{Nat} \Rightarrow \mathtt{Nat}$ in PCF, while v has type $\mathtt{Nat} \Rightarrow \mathtt{Nat}$. This means t as a whole has type $\mathtt{Nat} \Rightarrow \mathtt{Nat}$ and computes the function $x \mapsto 2 \cdot x$. The type inference algorithm proceeds by giving types to u and to v separately, then assembling the two into one. Suppose we start with v. The type inference algorithm refines $\mathtt{Nat} \Rightarrow \mathtt{Nat}$ into $\sigma = \mathtt{Nat}[\mathrm{f}(a,b)] \overset{b<\mathrm{h}(a)}{\multimap} \mathtt{Nat}[\mathrm{g}(a,b)]$ and the equational program $\mathcal{A}_v$, which gives meaning to g in terms of f:

$$\mathrm{g}(a,b) = \mathrm{f}(a,b) + 1.$$

Observe how both f and h are not specified in $\mathcal{A}_v$, because they appear in *negative* position in σ: $\mathrm{f}(a,b)$ intuitively corresponds to the argument(s) v will be applied to, while $\mathrm{h}(a)$ is the number of times v will be used. Notice that everything is parametrised on a, which is something like a global parameter that will later be set as the input to t. The function u, on the other hand, is given type

$$(\mathtt{Nat}[\mathrm{p}(a,b,c)] \overset{c<\mathrm{j}(a,b)}{\multimap} \mathtt{Nat}[\mathrm{q}(a,b,c)]) \overset{b<\mathrm{k}(a)}{\multimap} \mathtt{Nat}[\mathrm{l}(a,b,c)] \overset{c<\mathrm{m}(a,b)}{\multimap} \mathtt{Nat}[\mathrm{n}(a,b,c)].$$

The newly introduced function symbols are subject to the following equations:

$$\begin{aligned}
\mathrm{j}(a,b) &= 2 \cdot \mathrm{m}(a,b);\\
\mathrm{n}(a,b,c) &= \mathrm{q}(a,b,2c);\\
\mathrm{p}(a,b,2c) &= \mathrm{q}(a,b,2c+1);\\
\mathrm{p}(a,b,2c+1) &= \mathrm{l}(a,b,2c).
\end{aligned}$$

Again, notice that some functions are left unspecified, namely l, m, q and k. Now, a type for uv can be found by just combining the types for u and v, somehow following the typing rule for applications. First of all, the number of times u needs to be copied is set to 1 by the equation $\mathrm{k}(a) = 1$. Then, the matching symbols of u and v are defined one in terms of the others:

$$\mathrm{q}(a,0,b) = \mathrm{g}(a,b);$$
$$\mathrm{f}(a,b) = \mathrm{p}(a,0,b);$$
$$\mathrm{h}(a) = \mathrm{j}(a,0).$$

This is the last step of type inference, so it is safe to stipulate that $\mathrm{m}(a,0) = 1$ and that $\mathrm{l}(a,0,c) = a$, thus obtaining a fully specified equational program $\mathcal{E}$ and the following type τ for t:

$$\mathtt{Nat}[a] \overset{c<1}{\multimap} \mathtt{Nat}[\mathrm{n}(a,0,c)].$$

As an exercise, the reader can verify that the equational program above allows to verify that $\mathrm{n}(a,0,0) = a+2$, and that

$$a;\varnothing;\varnothing \vdash_2^{\mathcal{E}} t : \tau.$$

4.2 Preliminaries

Before embarking on the description of the type inference algorithms, some preliminary concepts and ideas need to be introduced, and are the topic of this section.

4.2.1 Getting Rid of Subsumption

The type inference algorithm takes in input a PCF term t, and returns a typing judgement $\mathcal{J}$ for t, together with a set $\mathscr{R}$ of so-called *side conditions*. We will show below that $\mathcal{J}$ is derivable *iff* all the side conditions in $\mathscr{R}$ are valid. Moreover, in this case $\mathcal{J}$ is *precise* (see Definition 3.1): all occurrences of the base type $\mathtt{Nat}[\mathrm{I},\mathrm{J}]$ are in fact of the form $\mathtt{Nat}[\mathrm{I}]$, and the weight and all potentials H occurring in a sub-type $[a<\mathrm{H}]\cdot A$ are kept as low as possible. Concretely, this means that there is a derivation for $\mathcal{J}$ in which the subsumption rule is restricted to the following form:

$$\frac{\phi;\Phi;\Gamma \vdash_{\mathrm{I}}^{\mathcal{E}} t:\sigma \qquad \begin{array}{l}\phi;\Phi \vdash_{\mathcal{E}} \Delta \equiv \Gamma \\ \phi;\Phi \vdash_{\mathcal{E}} \sigma \equiv \tau \\ \phi;\Phi \models_{\mathcal{E}} \mathrm{I} = \mathrm{J}\end{array}}{\phi;\Phi;\Delta \vdash_{\mathrm{J}}^{\mathcal{E}} t:\tau}$$

The three premises on the right boil down to a set of semantic judgements of the form $\{\phi;\Phi \models_{\mathcal{E}} \mathrm{K}_i = \mathrm{H}_i\}$ (see Figure 3), where the K_i's are indexes occurring in σ or Δ (or I itself) and the H_i's occur in τ or Γ (or are J itself). If the equalities $\mathrm{K}_i = \mathrm{H}_i$ can all be derived from $\mathcal{E}$, then the three premises on the right are equivalent to the conjunction (on i) of the following properties:

$$\text{“}[\![\mathrm{H}_i]\!]_\rho^{\mathcal{E}} \text{ is defined for any } \rho:\phi\to\mathbb{N} \text{ satisfying } \Phi\text{”}$$

(see Section 3.1.2). Given $\mathcal{E}$, this property (called a *side condition*) is denoted by $\phi;\Phi \models \mathrm{H}_i\downarrow$. Actually the type inference algorithm does *not* verify any semantic or subtyping judgement coming from (instances of) the subsumption rule. Instead, it turns all index equivalences $\mathrm{H}_i = \mathrm{K}_i$ into rewriting rules in $\mathcal{E}$, and put all side conditions $\phi;\Phi \models \mathrm{H}_i\downarrow$ in $\mathscr{R}$. If every side condition in $\mathscr{R}$ is true for $\mathcal{E}$, we write $\mathcal{E} \Vdash \bigwedge\mathscr{R}$. Informally, this means that all subsumptions assumed by the algorithm are indeed valid.

4.2.2 Function Symbols

Types and judgements manipulated by our type inference algorithm have a very peculiar shape. In particular, not every index term is allowed to appear in types, and this property will be crucial when showing soundness and completeness of the algorithm itself:

DEFINITION 4.1 (Primitive Types). *A type is* primitive for ϕ *when it is on the form* $\mathtt{Nat}[\mathrm{f}(\phi)]$, *or* $A \multimap B$ *with* A *and* B *primitive for* ϕ, *or* $[a<\mathrm{f}(\phi)]\cdot A$ *with* $a\notin\phi$ *and* A *primitive for* $a;\phi$. *A type is said to be* primitive *when it is primitive for some* ϕ.

As an example, a primitive type for $\phi = a;b$ is

$$\mathtt{Nat}[\mathrm{f}(a,b,c)] \overset{c<\mathrm{g}(a,b)}{\multimap} \mathtt{Nat}[\mathrm{h}(a,b,c)].$$

Informally, then, a type is primitive when the only allowed index terms are function symbols (with the appropriate arity).

4.2.3 Equational Programs

The equational program our algorithm constructs is in fact a *rewriting program*: every equality corresponds to the (partial) definition of a function symbol, and we may write it $\mathrm{f}(a_1,\ldots,a_k) := \mathrm{J}$ (where all free variables of J are in $\{a_1,\ldots,a_k\}$). If there is no such equation in the rewriting program, we say that f is *unspecified*.

An equational program $\mathcal{E}$ is *completely specified* if it allows to deduce a precise meaning (namely a partial recursive function) for each symbol of its underlying signature (written $\Sigma_{\mathcal{E}}$), i.e. none of the symbols in $\Sigma_{\mathcal{E}}$ are unspecified. In other words: a completely specified equational programs has only one *model*. On the other hand, a *partially specified* equational program (i.e. a program where symbols can possibly be unspecified) can have many models, because partial recursive functions can be assigned to unspecified function symbols in many different ways, all of them consistent with its equations. Up to now, we only worked with completely specified programs, but allowing the possibility to have unspecified symbols is crucial for being able to describe the type inference algorithm in a simple way. In the following, $\mathcal{E}$ and $\mathcal{F}$ denote completely specified equational programs, while $\mathcal{A}$ and $\mathcal{B}$ denote rewriting programs that are only partially specified.

DEFINITION 4.2 (Model of a Rewriting Program). *An* interpretation μ *of* $\mathcal{A}$ *in* $\mathcal{E}$ *is simply a map from unspecified symbols of* $\mathcal{A}$ *to indexes on the signature* $\Sigma_{\mathcal{E}}$, *such that if* f *has arity* n, *then* $\mu(\mathrm{f})$ *is a term in* $\Sigma_{\mathcal{E}}$ *with free variables from* $\phi_{\mathrm{f}} = \{a_1,\ldots,a_n\}$. *When such an interpretation is defined, we say that* $\mathcal{E}$ *is a* model *of* $\mathcal{A}$, *and we write* $\mu:\mathcal{E}\models\mathcal{A}$.

Notice that such an interpretation can naturally be extended to arbitrary index terms on the signature $\Sigma_{\mathcal{A}}$, and we assume in the following that a rewriting program and its model have disjoint signatures.

DEFINITION 4.3 (Validity in a Model). *Given* $\mu:\mathcal{E}\models\mathcal{A}$, *we say that a semantic judgement* $\phi;\Phi \models_{\mathcal{A}} \mathrm{I}\leqslant\mathrm{J}$ *is* valid in the model *(notation:* $\phi;\Phi \models_{\mu} \mathrm{I}\leqslant\mathrm{J}$*) when* $\phi;\Phi \models_{\mathcal{F}} \mathrm{I}\leqslant\mathrm{J}$ *where* $\mathcal{F} = \mathcal{A}\cup\mathcal{E}\cup\{\mathrm{f}(\phi_{\mathrm{f}}) := \mu(\mathrm{f}) \mid \mathrm{f} \text{ is unspecified in } \mathcal{A}\}$. *This definition is naturally extended to side conditions (with* $\mu \Vdash \bigwedge\mathscr{R}$ *standing for* $\mathcal{F}\Vdash\bigwedge\mathscr{R}$*).*

Please note that if $\mathcal{A}$ is a completely specified rewriting program, then any model $\mu:\mathcal{E}\models\mathcal{A}$ has an interpretation μ with an empty domain, and $\mu\Vdash\bigwedge\mathscr{R}$ iff $\mathcal{A}\Vdash\bigwedge\mathscr{R}$ (still assuming that $\Sigma_{\mathcal{A}}$ and $\Sigma_{\mathcal{E}}$ are disjoint).

As already mentioned, the equational programs handled by our type inference algorithm are not necessarily completely specified. Function symbols which are not specified are precisely those occurring in "negative position" in the judgement produced in output. This invariant will be very useful and is captured by the following definition:

DEFINITION 4.4 (Positive and Negative Symbols). *Given a primitive type* τ, *the sets of its* positive *and* negative *symbols (denoted* *by τ^+ and τ^- respectively) are defined inductively by*

$$\mathtt{Nat}[\mathrm{i}(\phi)]^+ = \{\mathrm{i}\};$$
$$\mathtt{Nat}[\mathrm{i}(\phi)]^- = \varnothing;$$
$$[a < \mathrm{h}(\phi)] \cdot (\sigma \multimap \tau)^+ = \sigma^- \cup \tau^+;$$
$$[a < \mathrm{h}(\phi)] \cdot (\sigma \multimap \tau)^-; = \{\mathrm{h}\} \cup \sigma^+ \cup \tau^-.$$

Then the set of positive *(resp.* negative*) symbols of a judgement $\phi; \Phi; (x_i : \sigma_i)_{i \leqslant n} \vdash^{\mathcal{E}}_{\mathrm{I}} t : \tau$ is the union of all negative (resp. positive) symbols of the σ_i's and all positive (resp. negative) symbols of τ.*

Polarities in $\{+, -\}$ are indicated with symbols like p, q. Given such a p, the opposite polarity is $\neg p$.

DEFINITION 4.5 (Specified Symbols, Types and Judgments). *Given a set of function symbols $\mathcal{S}$, a symbol* f *is said to be* $(\mathcal{S}, \mathcal{A})$-specified *when there is a rule $\mathrm{f}(\phi) := \mathrm{J}$ in $\mathcal{A}$ such that any function symbol appearing in* J *is either* f *itself, or in $\mathcal{S}$, or a symbol that is $(\mathcal{S} \cup \{\mathrm{f}\}, \mathcal{A} \backslash \{\mathrm{f}(\phi) := \mathrm{J}\})$-specified. Remember that when there is no rule $\mathrm{f}(\phi) := \mathrm{J}$ in $\mathcal{A}$ the symbol* f *is* unspecified *in $\mathcal{A}$. A primitive type σ is said to be* $(p, \mathcal{S}, \mathcal{A})$-specified *when all function symbols in σ^p are $(\mathcal{S}, \mathcal{A})$-specified and all symbols in $\sigma^{\neg p}$ are unspecified. A judgement $\phi; \Phi; \Gamma \vdash^{\mathcal{A}}_{\mathrm{I}} t : \tau$ is* correctly specified *when τ and all types in Γ are primitive for ϕ, and τ is $(+, \mathcal{N}, \mathcal{A})$-specified, and all types in Γ are $(-, \mathcal{N}, \mathcal{A})$-specified, and all function symbols in* I *are $(\mathcal{N}, \mathcal{A})$-specified where $\mathcal{N}$ is the set of negative symbols of the judgement.*

In other words, a judgement is correctly specified if the underlying equational program (possibly recursively) defines all symbols in positive position depending on those in negative position.

4.3 The Structure of the Algorithm

The type inference algorithm receives in input a PCF term t and returns a dℓPCF judgement $\varnothing \vdash^{\mathcal{E}}_{\mathrm{K}} t : \tau$ for it, together with a set of side conditions $\mathscr{R}$. We will prove that it is *correct*, in the sense that the typing judgement is derivable *iff* the side conditions hold. The algorithm proceeds as follows:

1. Compute d_{PCF}, a PCF type derivation for t;
2. Proceeding by structural induction on d_{PCF}, construct a dℓPCF derivation for t (call it d_{v}) and the corresponding set of side conditions $\mathscr{R}$;
3. Returns $\mathscr{R}$ and the conclusion of d_{v}.

The *skeleton* $(\!\lbrack\sigma\rbrack\!)$ (or $(\!\lbrack A\rbrack\!)$) of a modal type σ (*resp.* of a linear type A) is obtained by erasing all its indexes (and its bounds $[a < \mathrm{I}]$). The *skeleton* of a dℓPCF derivation is obtained by replacing each type by its skeleton, and erasing all the subsumption rules. In PCF the type inference problem is decidable, and Step 1 raises no difficulty: actually, one could even assume that the type d_{PCF} attributes to t is principal. The core of the algorithm is of course Step 2. In Section. 4.5 we define a recursive algorithm GEN that build d_{v} and $\mathscr{R}$ by annotating d_{PCF}. The algorithm GEN itself relies on some auxiliary algorithms, which will be described in Section 4.4 below.

All algorithms we will talk about have the ability to generate fresh variables and function symbols. Strictly speaking, then, they should take a counter (or anything similar) as a parameter, but we elide this for the sake of simplicity. Also, we assume the existence of a function $\alpha(\phi; T)$ that, given a set of index variables ϕ and a PCF type T, returns a modal type τ primitive for ϕ, containing only fresh function symbols, and such that $(\!\lbrack\tau\rbrack\!) = T$.

4.4 Auxiliary Algorithms and Linear Logic

The design of systems of linear dependent types such as dℓPCF$_{\mathsf{V}}$ and dℓPCF$_{\mathsf{N}}$ is strongly inspired by BLL, itself a restriction of linear logic. Actually, the best way to present the type inference algorithm consists in first of all introducing four auxiliary algorithms, each corresponding to a principle regulating the behaviour of the exponential connectives in linear logic. Notice that these auxiliary algorithms are the main ingredients of both dℓPCF$_{\mathsf{V}}$ and dℓPCF$_{\mathsf{N}}$ type inference. Consistently to what we have done so far, we will prove and explain them with dℓPCF$_{\mathsf{V}}$ in mind. All the auxiliary algorithm we will talk about in this section will take a tuple of dℓPCF$_{\mathsf{V}}$ types as first argument; we assume that all of them have the same skeleton and, moreover, that all index terms appearing in them are pairwise distinct.

Dereliction. Dereliction is the following principle: any duplicable object (say, of type $!A$) can be made linear (of type A), that is to say $!A \to A$. In dℓPCF, being duplicable means having a modal type, which also contains some quantitative information, namely how many times the object can be duplicated, at most. In dℓPCF$_{\mathsf{V}}$, dereliction can be simply seen as the principle $[a < 1] \cdot A \to A\{0/a\}$, and is implicitly used in the rules (*App*) and (*Fix*). Along the type inference process, as a consequence, we often need to create "fresh instances" of dereliction in the form of pairs of types being in the correct semantic relation. This is indeed possible:

LEMMA 4.1. *There is an algorithm* DER *such that given two types τ (primitive for ϕ) and σ (primitive for a, ϕ) of the same skeleton,* $\mathrm{DER}((\sigma, \tau); a; \phi; \Phi; p) = (\mathcal{A}, \mathscr{R})$ *where:*

1. *for every $\mathcal{E} \supseteq \mathcal{A}$, if $\mathcal{E} \Vdash \bigwedge \mathscr{R}$ then $\phi; \Phi \vdash_{\mathcal{E}} \sigma\{0/a\} \equiv \tau$;*
2. *whenever $\phi; \Phi \vdash_{\mathcal{E}} \varrho\{0/a\} \equiv \xi$ where $(\!\lbrack\varrho\rbrack\!) \equiv (\!\lbrack\sigma\rbrack\!)$, there is $\mu : \mathcal{E} \models \mathcal{A}$ such that $\phi; \Phi \vdash_{\mu} \sigma\{0/a\} \equiv \varrho\{0/a\}$, $\phi; \Phi \vdash_{\mu} \tau \equiv \xi$, and $\mu \Vdash \bigwedge \mathscr{R}$;*
3. *σ is $(p, \tau^p, \mathcal{A})$-specified and τ is $(\neg p, \sigma^{\neg p}, \mathcal{A})$-specified.*

The algorithm DER works by recursion on the PCF type $(\!\lbrack\sigma\rbrack\!)$ and has thus linear complexity in $|(\!\lbrack\sigma\rbrack\!)|$. The proof of Lemma 4.1 (see [12]), as a consequence, proceeds by induction on the structure of $(\!\lbrack\sigma\rbrack\!)$.

Contraction. Another key principle in linear logic is contraction, according to which two copies of a duplicable object can actually be produced, $!A \to !A \otimes !A$. Contraction is used in binary rules like (*App*) or (*If*), in the form of the operator $\uplus$. This time, we need an algorithm CTR which takes *three* linear types A, B and C (all of them primitive for (a, ϕ)) and turn them into an equational program and a set of side conditions:

$$\mathrm{CTR}((A, B, C); (\mathrm{I}, \mathrm{J}); a; \phi; \Phi; p) = (\mathcal{A}, \mathscr{R}).$$

The parameters I and J are index terms capturing the number of times B and C can be copied. A Lemma akin to 4.1 can indeed be proved about CTR. In particular, for any $\mathcal{E} \supseteq \mathcal{A}$, if $\mathcal{E} \Vdash \bigwedge \mathscr{R}$ then

$$\phi; \Phi \vdash_{\mathcal{E}} [a < \mathrm{I} + \mathrm{J}] \cdot A \equiv ([a < \mathrm{I}] \cdot D) \uplus ([a < \mathrm{J}] \cdot E) \quad (5)$$

for some D and E such that $\phi; \Phi, a < \mathrm{I} \vdash_{\mathcal{E}} D \equiv B$ and $\phi; \Phi, a < \mathrm{J} \vdash_{\mathcal{E}} E \equiv C$.

Digging. In linear logic, any duplicable object having type $!A$ can be turned into an object of type $!!A$, namely an object which is the duplicable version of a duplicable object. Digging is the principle according to which this transformation is possible, namely $!A \to !!A$. At the quantitative level, this corresponds to splitting a bounded sum into its summands. This is used in the typing rules for functions, ($\multimap$) and (*Fix*).

The auxiliary algorithm corresponding to the digging principle takes two linear types and builds, as usual, a rewriting program and a set of side conditions capturing the fact that the first of the two types is the bounded sum of the second:

$$\mathrm{DIG}((A, B); (\mathrm{I}, \mathrm{J}); \phi; (a, b); \Phi; p) = (\mathcal{A}, \mathscr{R}).$$

The correctness of DIG can again be proved similarly to what we did in Lemma 4.1, the key statement being that for every $\mathcal{E} \supseteq \mathcal{A}$ such that $\mathcal{E} \Vdash \bigwedge \mathscr{R}$, the following must hold

$$\phi; \Phi \vdash_{\mathcal{E}} [b < \sum_{a<\mathrm{I}} \mathrm{J}] \cdot A \equiv \sum_{a<I} [b < J] \cdot C$$

for some C such that $\phi; \Phi, a < \mathrm{I}, b < \mathrm{J} \vdash_{\mathcal{E}} C \equiv B$.

Weakening. Weakening means that duplicable objects can also be erased, even when the underlying index is 0. Weakening is useful in the rules (*Ax*) and (*n*). Once a fresh dℓPCF$_\mathsf{V}$ type A is produced, the only thing we need to do is to produce an equational program $\mathcal{A}$ specifying (in an arbitrary way) the symbols in A^p, this way preserving the crucial invariants about the equational programs manipulated by the algorithm. Formally, it means that there is an algorithm WEAK such that

$$\mathrm{WEAK}(A; \phi; a; p) = \mathcal{A},$$

where A is $(p, \varnothing, \mathcal{A})$-specified Observe how no sets of constraints is produced in output by WEAK, contrarily to DER, CTR, and DIG.

4.5 The Type Inference Procedure

In this section, we will describe the core of our type inference algorithm. This consists in a recursive algorithm GEN which decorates a PCF type derivation d_{PCF}, producing in output a dℓPCF judgement, together with an equational program and a set of side conditions. In order to correctly create fresh symbols and to format side conditions properly, the main recursive function GEN also receives a set of index variables ϕ and a set of constraints Φ in input. Thus, it has the following signature:

$$\mathrm{GEN}(\phi; \Phi; d_{\mathsf{PCF}}) \quad = \quad (\Gamma \vdash_{\mathrm{I}} t : \tau; \mathcal{A}; \mathscr{R}).$$

We will prove that the the output of GEN satisfies the following two invariants:

- *Decoration.* d_{PCF} has conclusion $(\!|\Gamma|\!) \vdash t : (\!|\tau|\!)$.
- *Polarity.* $\phi; \Phi; \Gamma \vdash_{\mathrm{I}}^{\mathcal{A}} t : \tau$ is correctly specified (see Definition 4.5).

The algorithm GEN proceeds by inspecting d_{PCF} in an inductive manner. It first annotates the types in the conclusion judgement with fresh function symbols to get a dℓPCF judgement $\mathcal{J}$. Then a recursive call is performed on the immediate sub-derivations of d_{PCF}, this way obtaining some dℓPCF typing judgement $\mathcal{J}_i$. Finally GEN generates, calling the auxiliary algorithms, the equations on function symbols that allow to derive $\mathcal{J}$ from the $\mathcal{J}_i$'s, The equations are written in $\mathcal{A}$, and the required assumptions of index convergence in $\mathscr{R}$.

Decoration and Polarity are the invariants of the algorithm GEN. In particular, the auxiliary algorithms are always called with the appropriate parameters, this way enforcing Polarity.

The algorithm computing GEN proceeds by case analysis on d_{PCF}. We give some cases here, the other ones are developed in [12].

- Suppose that d_{PCF} is

$$\frac{}{y_1 : U_1, \ldots, y_k : U_k \vdash \underline{\mathrm{n}} : \mathtt{Nat}}$$

For each i, let $B_i = \alpha(\phi; U_i)$ and $\mathcal{A}_i = \mathrm{WEAK}(B_i; \phi; b_i; -)$ (where all the b_i's are fresh). Let $\mathrm{i}(\phi)$ be a fresh function symbol. Then return $(\Gamma \vdash_0 \underline{\mathrm{n}} : \mathtt{Nat}[\mathrm{i}(\phi)]; \mathcal{A}; \varnothing)$ where the h_i's are fresh symbols and

$$\mathcal{A} = \bigcup_i (\mathcal{A}_i \cup \{\mathrm{h}_i(\phi) := 0\}) \cup \{\, \mathrm{i}(\phi) := \underline{n} \,\};$$

$$\Gamma = \{y_i : [b_i < \mathrm{h}_i(\phi)] \cdot B_i\}_{1 \leqslant i \leqslant k}.$$

- If d_{PCF} is on the form

$$\frac{e^1_{\mathsf{PCF}} : \Pi \vdash t : U \Rightarrow T \quad e^2_{\mathsf{PCF}} : \Pi \vdash u : U}{\Pi \vdash t\,u : T}$$

let $(\Gamma_1 \vdash_{\mathrm{K}} t : [a < \mathrm{f}(\phi)] \cdot (\sigma_1 \multimap \sigma_2); \mathcal{A}_1; \mathscr{R}_1) = \mathrm{GEN}(\phi; \Phi; e^1_{\mathsf{PCF}})$, and $(\Gamma_2 \vdash_{\mathrm{H}} u : \tau; \mathcal{A}_2; \mathscr{R}_2) = \mathrm{GEN}(\phi; \Phi; e^2_{\mathsf{PCF}})$. Let $(\mathcal{B}, \mathscr{S}) = \mathrm{DER}((\sigma_1, \tau); a; \phi; \Phi; +)$. We then annotate T: let $\tau_2 = \alpha(\phi; T)$, and let $(\mathcal{C}, \mathscr{U}) = \mathrm{DER}((\sigma_2, \tau_2); a; \phi; \Phi; -)$. Then we build a context equivalent to $\Gamma_1 \uplus \Gamma_2$: by the decoration property, Γ_1 and Γ_2 have the same skeleton Π, so for any $y : [b_y < \mathrm{i}_y(\phi)] \cdot B_y$ in Γ_1, there is some $y : [b_y < \mathrm{j}_y(\phi)] \cdot C_y$ in Γ_2 (possibly after some α-conversion). Then let $A_y = \alpha((b_y, \phi); (\!|B_y|\!))$, and $(\mathcal{A}_y; \mathscr{R}_y) = \mathrm{CTR}((A_y, B_y, C_y); (\mathrm{i}_y(\phi), \mathrm{j}_y(\phi)); b_y; \phi; \Phi; -)$. There are $\Delta_i \equiv \Gamma_i$ (for $i = 1, 2$) such that $\phi; \Phi \vdash_{\mathcal{E}} \{y : [b_y < \mathrm{i}_y(\phi) + \mathrm{j}_y(\phi)] \cdot A_y\}_y \equiv \Delta_1 \uplus \Delta_2$, for every $\mathcal{E} \supseteq \bigcup_y \mathcal{A}_y$ such that $\mathcal{E} \Vdash \bigwedge(\bigcup_y \mathscr{R}_y)$. Thus, let h_y's be fresh symbols and return $(\Delta \vdash_{\mathrm{K+H}} t\,u : \tau_2; \mathcal{A}; \mathscr{R})$ in output, where

$$\mathscr{R} = \mathscr{R}_1 \cup \mathscr{R}_2 \cup \mathscr{S} \cup \mathscr{U} \cup \bigcup_y (\mathscr{R}_y \cup \{\phi; \Phi \vDash \mathrm{i}_y(\phi) + \mathrm{j}_y(\phi) \downarrow\});$$

$$\mathcal{A} = \mathcal{A}_1 \cup \mathcal{A}_2 \cup \mathcal{B} \cup \mathcal{C} \cup \{\mathrm{f}(\phi) := 1\} \cup \bigcup_y (\mathcal{A}_y \cup \{\mathrm{h}_y(\phi) := \mathrm{i}_y(\phi) + \mathrm{j}_y(\phi)\});$$

$$\Delta = \{y : [b_y < \mathrm{h}_y(\phi)] \cdot A_y\}_y.$$

- Assume that d_{PCF} is

$$\frac{e_{\mathsf{PCF}} : \Pi, x : U \vdash t : T}{\Pi \vdash \lambda x.t : U \Rightarrow T}$$

Let a be a fresh index variable, and $\mathrm{i}(\phi)$ be a fresh function symbol, and compute $(\Gamma, x : \sigma \vdash_{\mathrm{K}} t : \tau; \mathcal{B}; \mathscr{S}) = \mathrm{GEN}(e_{\mathsf{PCF}}, (a, \phi), (a < \mathrm{i}(\phi), \Phi))$. We build a context equivalent to $\sum_{a<\mathrm{i}(\phi)} \Gamma$: for every $y : [b_y < \mathrm{j}_y(a, \phi)] \cdot B_y \in \Gamma$, let $A_y = \alpha((b_y, \phi); (\!|B_y|\!))$, let $\mathrm{h}_y(\phi)$ be a fresh symbol, and let $(\mathcal{A}_y, \mathscr{R}_y)$ be $\mathrm{DIG}((A_y, B_y); (\mathrm{i}(\phi), \mathrm{j}_y(a, \phi)); \phi; (a, b_y); \Phi; -)$. Then return

$$(\Delta \vdash_{\mathrm{i}(\phi) + \sum_{a<\mathrm{i}(\phi)} \mathrm{K}} \lambda x.t : [a < \mathrm{i}(\phi)] \cdot (\sigma \multimap \tau); \mathcal{A}; \mathscr{R})$$

where

$$\mathscr{R} = \mathscr{S} \cup \bigcup_y (\mathscr{R}_y \cup \{\phi; \Phi \vDash_{\mathcal{E}} \sum_{a<\mathrm{i}(\phi)} \mathrm{j}_y(a, \phi) \downarrow\});$$

$$\mathcal{A} = \mathcal{B} \cup \cup_y (\mathcal{A}_y \cup \{\mathrm{h}_y(\phi) := \sum_{a<\mathrm{i}(\phi)} \mathrm{j}_y(a, \phi)\});$$

$$\Delta = \{y : [b_y < \mathrm{h}_y(\phi)] \cdot A_y\}_y.$$

LEMMA 4.2. *For every ϕ, Φ, and every* PCF *derivation d_{PCF}, the output of* $\mathrm{GEN}(\phi; \Phi; d_{\mathsf{PCF}})$ *satisfies Decoration and Polarity.*

4.6 Correctness

The algorithm we have just finished describing needs to be proved sound and complete with respect to dℓPCF$_\mathsf{V}$ typing. As usual, this is not a trivial task. Moreover, linear dependent types have a semantic nature which makes the task of formulating (if not proving) the desired results even more challenging.

4.6.1 Soundness

A type inference procedure is *sound* when the inferred type can actually be derived by way of the type system at hand. As already remarked, GEN outputs an equational program $\mathcal{A}$ which possibly contains unspecified symbols and which, as a consequence, cannot be exploited in typing. Moreover, the role of the set of proof obligations in $\mathscr{R}$ may be unclear at first. Actually, soundness holds for *every* completely specified $\mathcal{E} \supseteq \mathcal{A}$ which makes the proof obligations in $\mathscr{R}$ true:

THEOREM 4.3 (Soundness). *If d_{PCF} is a* PCF *derivation for t, then for any ϕ and Φ,* GEN$(\phi;\Phi;d_{\mathsf{PCF}}) = (\Gamma \vdash_{\mathrm{I}} t : \tau; \mathcal{A}; \mathscr{R})$ *where $\phi;\Phi;\Gamma \vdash^{\mathcal{A}}_{\mathrm{I}} t : \tau$ is correctly specified and for any $\mathcal{E} \supseteq \mathcal{A}$,*

$$\mathcal{E} \Vdash \bigwedge \mathscr{R} \quad \Longrightarrow \quad \phi;\Phi;\Gamma \vdash^{\mathcal{E}}_{\mathrm{I}} t : \tau \textit{ is derivable and precise.}$$

Soundness can be proved by induction on the structure of d_{PCF}, exploiting auxiliary results like Lemma 4.1.

4.6.2 Completeness

But are we sure that *at least* one type derivation can be built from the outcome of GEN *if* one such type derivation exists? Again, it is nontrivial to formulate the fact that this is actually the case.

THEOREM 4.4 (Completeness). *If $\phi;\Phi;\Delta \vdash^{\mathcal{E}}_{\mathrm{J}} t : \sigma$ is a precise* dℓPCF$_{\mathsf{V}}$ *judgement derivable by d_{v}, then* GEN$(\phi;\Phi;(\!|d_{\mathsf{v}}|\!))$ *is of the form $(\Gamma \vdash_{\mathrm{I}} t : \tau; \mathcal{A}; \mathscr{R})$, and there is $\mu : \mathcal{E} \models \mathcal{A}$ such that $\mu \Vdash \bigwedge \mathscr{R}$.*

Completeness can be proved by an induction on the structure of d_{v}; its statement, however, needs to be appropriately enriched for induction to work. Again, results like Lemma 4.1 greatly help here: Point 2 states completeness of DER, and the latter is called by GEN many times.

A direct consequence of Soundness and Completeness (and the remark on Definition 4.3) is the following:

COROLLARY 4.5. *If a closed term t is typable in* PCF *with type* Nat *and a derivation d_{PCF}, then*

$$\mathrm{GEN}(\varnothing;\varnothing;d_{\mathsf{PCF}}) \;=\; (\vdash_{\mathrm{I}} t : \mathtt{Nat}[\mathrm{f}]; \mathcal{E}; \mathscr{R})$$

and t is typable in dℓPCF$_{\mathsf{V}}$ *iff $\mathcal{E} \Vdash \bigwedge \mathscr{R}$.*

5. Type Inference at Work

The type inference algorithm presented in the previous section has been implemented in OCAML[2]. Programs, types, equational programs and side conditions become values of appropriately defined inductive data structures in OCAML, while the functional nature of the latter makes the implementation effort easier. This section is devoted to discussing the main issues we have faced along the process, which is still ongoing.

The core of our implementation is an OCAML function called `CheckBound`. Taking a closed term t having PCF type T in input, `CheckBound` returns a typing derivation d_{v}, an equational program $\mathcal{E}$ and a set of side conditions $\mathscr{R}$. The conclusion of d_{v} is a dℓPCF typing judgement for the input term. If T is a first-order type, then the produced judgement is derivable *iff* all the side conditions in $\mathscr{R}$ are valid. To do so, `CheckBound` calls (an implementation of) GEN on t and a context ϕ consisting of n unconstrained index variables, where n is the arity of t. This way, `CheckBound` obtains $\mathcal{A}$ and $\mathscr{R}$ as results, and then proceeds as follows:

- If T is `Nat`, then $\mathcal{A}$ is already completely specified and Corollary 4.5 ensures that we already have what we need.
- If T has a strictly positive arity, then some of the symbols in $\mathcal{A}$ are unspecified, and appropriate equations for them need to be added to $\mathcal{A}$. Take for instance a term s of type `Nat` $\Rightarrow$ `Nat`. `CheckBound`(s) returns $\mathcal{A}$, $\mathscr{R}$, and a typing judgement of the form

$$a;\varnothing;\varnothing \vdash^{\mathcal{A}}_{\mathrm{K}} t : \mathtt{Nat}[\mathrm{g}(a,b)] \overset{b<\mathrm{f}(a)}{\multimap} \mathtt{Nat}[\mathrm{j}(a,b)],$$

where j is a positive symbol while f and g are negative, thus unspecified in $\mathcal{A}$. $\mathcal{A}$ can be appropriately "completed" by adding the equations $\mathrm{f}(a) := \underline{1}$ and $\mathrm{g}(a,b) := a$ to it. This way, we are insisting on the behaviour of t when fed with *any* natural number (represented by a) and when the environment needs t only once.

How about complexity analysis? Actually, we are already there: the problem of proving the number of machine reduction steps needed by t to be at most $p : \mathbb{N} \to \mathbb{N}$ (where p is, e.g. a polynomial) becomes the problem of checking $\mathcal{E} \Vdash \bigwedge \mathscr{S}$ where $\mathcal{E}$ is the appropriate completion of $\mathcal{A}$, and $\mathscr{S}$ is $\mathscr{R} \cup \{(\mathrm{K}+1)(|t|+2) \leqslant p(a)\}$ (Proposition 3.2).

Simplifying Equations. Equational programs obtained in output from `CheckBound` contains many equations which are trivial (such as $\mathrm{f}(a) := \underline{n}$ or $\mathrm{f}(a) := \mathrm{g}(a)$), and as such can be eliminated. Moreover, instances of forest cardinalities and bounded sums can sometime be greatly simplified. As an example, $\sum_{a<\underline{0}} \mathrm{J}$ can always be replaced by $\underline{0}$. This allows, in particular, to turn $\mathcal{A}$ into a set of fewer and simpler rules, thus facilitating the next phase.

A basic simplification procedure has already been implemented, and is called by `CheckBound` on the output of GEN. However, automatically treating the equational program by an appropriate prover would of course be desirable. For this purpose, the possibility for `CheckBound` to interact with MAUDE [8], a system supporting equational and rewriting logic specification, is currently investigated.

Checking Side Conditions. As already stressed, once `CheckBound` has produced a pair $(\mathcal{A}, \mathscr{R})$, the task we started from, namely complexity analysis of t, is not finished, yet: checking proof obligations in $\mathscr{R}$ is as undecidable as analysing the complexity of t directly, since most of the obligations in $\mathscr{R}$ are termination statements anyway. There is an important difference, however: statements in $\mathscr{R}$ are written in a language (the first-order equational logic) which is more amenable to be treated by already existing automatic and semi-automatic tools.

Actually, the best method would be to first call as many existing automatic provers as possible on the set of side conditions, then asking the programmer to check those which cannot be proved automatically by way of an interactive theorem prover. For this purpose, we have implemented an algorithm translating a pair in the form $(\mathcal{A}, \mathscr{R})$ into a WHY3 theory [6].

6. Related Work

Complexity analysis of higher-order programs has been the object of many studies. We can for example mention the proposals for type systems for the λ-calculus which have been shown to correspond in an *extensional sense* to, e.g. polynomial time computable functions. Many of them can be seen as static analysis methodologies: once a program is assigned a type, an upper bound to its time complexity is relatively easy to be synthesised. The problem with these systems, however, is that they are usually very weak from an *intentional* point of view, since the class of typable programs is quite restricted compared to the class of all terms working within the prescribed resource bounds.

More powerful static analysis methodologies can actually be devised. All of them, however, are either limited to very specific forms of resource bounds or to a peculiar form of higher-order functions or else they do not get rid of higher-order as the underlying logic. Consider, as an example, one of the earliest work in this direction, namely Sands's system of cost closures [27]: the class of programs that can be handled includes the full lazy λ-calculus, but the way complexity is reasoned about remains genuinely higher-order, being based on closures and contexts. In Benzinger's framework [5] higher-order programs are translated into higher-order equations,

[2] the source code is available at `http://lideal.cs.unibo.it`.

and the latter are turned into first-order ones; both steps, and in particular the second one, are not completeness-preserving. Recent works on amortised resource analysis are either limited to first-order programs [21] or to linear bounds [23]. A recent proposal by Amadio and Régis-Gianas [2] allows to reason on the the cost of higher-order functional programs by way of so-called cost-annotations, being sure that the actual behaviour of compiled code somehow reflects the annotation. The logic in which cost annotations are written, however, is a *higher-order* Hoare logic. None of the proposed systems, on the other hand, are known to be (relatively) complete in the sense we use here.

Ghica's slot games [17] are maybe the work which is closest to ours, among the many in the literature. Slot Games are simply ordinary games in the sense of game semantics, which are however instrumented so as to reflect not only the observable behaviour of (higher-order) programs, but also their performance. Indeed, slot games are fully abstract with respect to an operational theory of improvements due do Sands [28]: this can be seen as the counterpart of our relative completeness theorem. An aspect which has not been investigated much since Ghica's proposal is whether slot games provides a way to perform actual verification of programs, maybe via some form of model checking. As we have already mentioned, linear dependency can be seen as a way to turn games and strategies into types, so one can see the present work also as an attempt to keep programs and strategies closer to each other, this way facilitating verification. Another recent work which seems to be quite close to ours is Geometry of Synthesis, in particular when the latter takes the form of type inference [18].

7. Conclusions

A type inference procedure for $\mathsf{d}\ell\mathsf{PCF}$ has been introduced which, given a PCF term, reduces the problem of finding a type derivation for it to the one of solving proof obligations on an equational program, itself part of the output. Truth of the proof obligations correspond to termination of the underlying program. Any type derivation in $\mathsf{d}\ell\mathsf{PCF}$ comes equipped with an expression bounding the complexity of evaluating the underlying program. Noticeably, proof obligations and the related equational program can be obtained in polynomial time in the size of the input PCF program.

The main contribution of this paper consists in having shown that linear dependency is not only a very powerful tool for the analysis of higher-order functional programs, but is also a way to effectively and efficiently turn a complex problem (that of evaluating the time complexity of an higher-order program) into a much easier one (that of checking a set of proof obligations for truth).

Although, as explained in Section 5, experimental evaluation shows that proof obligations can potentially be handled by modern tools, much remains to be done about the technical aspects of turning proof obligations into a form which is suitable to automatic or semi-automatic solving. Actually, many different tools could conceivably be of help here, each of them requiring a specific input format. This implies, however, that the work described in this paper, although not providing a fully-fledged out-of-the-box methodology, has the merit of allowing to factor a complex non-well-understood problem into a much-better-studied problem, namely verification of first-order inequalities on the natural numbers.

References

[1] Abramsky, S., Jagadeesan, R., Malacaria, P.: Full abstraction for PCF. I & C 163(2), 409–470 (2000)

[2] Amadio, R.M., Régis-Gianas, Y.: Certifying and reasoning on cost annotations of functional programs. CoRR abs/1110.2350 (2011)

[3] de Bakker, J.W.: Mathematical Theory of Program Correctness. Prentice-Hall (1980)

[4] Barthe, G., Grégoire, B., Riba, C.: Type-based termination with sized products. In: CSL 2008. LNCS, vol. 5213, pp. 493–507. Springer (2008)

[5] Benzinger, R.: Automated higher-order complexity analysis. Theor. Comput. Sci. 318(1-2), 79–103 (2004)

[6] Bobot, F., Filliatre, J.C., Marché, C., Paskevich, A.: Why3: Shepherd your herd of provers. In: First International Workshop on Intermediate Verification Languages. pp. 53–64 (2011)

[7] Clarke, E.M.: Programming language constructs for which it is impossible to obtain good hoare axiom systems. J. ACM 26(1), 129–147 (1979)

[8] Clavel, M., Durán, F., Eker, S., Lincoln, P., Mart´i-Oliet, N., Meseguer, J., Talcott, C.: The Maude 2.0 system. In: RTA 2003. LNCS, vol. 2706, pp. 76–87 (2003)

[9] Cook, S.A.: Soundness and completeness of an axiom system for program verification. SIAM J. on Computing 7, 70–90 (1978)

[10] Dal Lago, U.: Context semantics, linear logic and computational complexity. In: LICS 2006. pp. 169–178 (2006)

[11] Dal Lago, U., Gaboardi, M.: Linear dependent types and relative completeness. In: LICS 2011. pp. 133–142 (2011)

[12] Dal Lago, U., Petit, B.: The geometry of types (long version) (2012), available at `http://arxiv.org/abs/1210.6857`

[13] Dal Lago, U., Petit, B.: Linear dependent types in a call-by-value scenario. In: ACM PPDP 2012. pp. 115–126 (2012)

[14] Danos, V., Regnier, L.: Reversible, irreversible and optimal lambda-machines. Theor. Comput. Sci. 227(1-2), 79–97 (1999)

[15] Denney, E.: Refinement types for specification. In: IFIP-PROCOMET. pp. 148–166 (1998)

[16] Felleisen, M., Friedman, D.P.: Control operators, the SECD-machine and the λ-calculus. Tech. Rep. 197, Computer Science Department, Indiana University (1986)

[17] Ghica, D.R.: Slot games: a quantitative model of computation. In: ACM POPL 2005. pp. 85–97 (2005)

[18] Ghica, D.R., Smith, A.: Geometry of synthesis III: resource management through type inference. In: ACM POPL 2011. pp. 345–356 (2011)

[19] Girard, J.Y., Scedrov, A., Scott, P.: Bounded linear logic. Theor. Comp. Sci. 97(1), 1–66 (1992)

[20] Gulwani, S.: Speed: Symbolic complexity bound analysis. In: CAV. pp. 51–62 (2009)

[21] Hoffmann, J., Aehlig, K., Hofmann, M.: Multivariate Amortized Resource Analysis. In: ACM POPL 2011. pp. 357–370 (2011)

[22] Hughes, J., Pareto, L., Sabry, A.: Proving the correctness of reactive systems using sized types. In: ACM POPL 1996. pp. 410–423 (1996)

[23] Jost, S., Hammond, K., Loidl, H.W., Hofmann, M.: Static determination of quantitative resource usage for higher-order programs. In: ACM POPL 2010. Madrid, Spain (2010)

[24] Krivine, J.L.: A call-by-name lambda-calculus machine. Higher-Order and Symbolic Computation 20(3), 199–207 (2007)

[25] Maraist, J., Odersky, M., Turner, D.N., Wadler, P.: Call-by-name, call-by-value, call-by-need and the linear lambda calculus. Electr. Notes Theor. Comput. Sci. 1, 370–392 (1995)

[26] Plotkin, G.D.: LCF considerd as a programming language. Theor. Comp. Sci. 5, 225–255 (1977)

[27] Sands, D.: Complexity analysis for a lazy higher-order language. In: ESOP 1990. LNCS, vol. 432, pp. 361–376 (1990)

[28] Sands, D.: Operational theories of improvement in functional languages (extended abstract). In: Functional Programming. pp. 298–311 (1991)

[29] Wilhelm, R., Engblom, J., Ermedahl, A., Holsti, N., Thesing, S., Whalley, D., Bernat, G., Ferdinand, C., Heckmann, R., Mitra, T., Mueller, F., Puaut, I., Puschner, P., Staschulat, J., Stenstrom, P.: The worst case execution time problem - overview of methods and survey of tools. ACM Trans. Embed. Comput. Syst. (2008)

Universal Properties of Impure Programming Languages

Sam Staton

Computer Laboratory, University of Cambridge

Paul Blain Levy

School of Computer Science, University of Birmingham

Abstract

We investigate impure, call-by-value programming languages. Our first language only has variables and let-binding. Its equational theory is a variant of Lambek's theory of multicategories that omits the commutativity axiom.

We demonstrate that type constructions for impure languages — products, sums and functions — can be characterized by universal properties in the setting of 'premulticategories', multicategories where the commutativity law may fail. This leads us to new, universal characterizations of two earlier equational theories of impure programming languages: the premonoidal categories of Power and Robinson, and the monad-based models of Moggi. Our analysis thus puts these earlier abstract ideas on a canonical foundation, bringing them to a new, syntactic level.

Categories and Subject Descriptors F.3.2 [*Semantics of Programming Languages*]

Keywords Multicategories, Premonoidal categories, Monads

1. Introduction

In this paper we introduce a new equational account of impure programs. This account is analogous to the $\beta\eta$-equality for the pure typed λ-calculus. It provides a simple reasoning tool that is justified both syntactically and semantically, by compositional interpretations in a variety of models. It is given a canonical status through universal properties and representability.

Let us stress that the $\beta\eta$-equality of the pure λ-calculus is not appropriate in the impure setting under the call-by-value semantics. For instance, if M has side effects then the η-law for products does not hold: $M \not\equiv \langle \#1\, M, \#2\, M\rangle$. For this reason, the categorical notion of product does not immediately apply to call-by-value programming languages.

1.1 An equational account of let-binding: premulticategories

To move to the impure setting, we must reassess the nature of substitution, which we do by introducing the new notion of *premulticategory* (§2). In the $\beta\eta$-equality of a pure λ-calculus, substitution is essential (e.g. $(\lambda x.M)\,N \equiv M[{}^{N}\!/_{x}]$). In a call-by-value language, substitution is more intricate. The Standard ML expression

$$\texttt{let val}\ x = N\ \texttt{in}\ M\ \texttt{end}$$

is (in some sense) equivalent to $M[{}^{N}\!/_{x}]$ in the pure fragment of ML, whereas in the general it means 'evaluate N, call the result x, and continue as M'. This sequencing plays a fundamental role, and it forms the basis of our definition of premulticategory.

Our starting point is a language with at least two typing rules

$$\frac{-}{x{:}\,A \vdash x : A} \qquad \frac{\Delta \vdash t : A \qquad \Gamma, x{:}\,A, \Gamma' \vdash u : B}{\Gamma, \Delta, \Gamma' \vdash \texttt{let val}\ x = t\ \texttt{in}\ u\ \texttt{end} : B}$$

and satisfying three equations

$$\texttt{let val}\ x{=}x\ \texttt{in}\ t\ \texttt{end} \equiv t \qquad \texttt{let val}\ x{=}t\ \texttt{in}\ x\ \texttt{end} \equiv t\ \ (x \notin \mathrm{fv}(t))$$

$$\begin{aligned}&\texttt{let val}\ x = t\ \texttt{in let val}\ y = u\ \texttt{in}\ v\ \texttt{end end}\\ \equiv\ &\texttt{let val}\ y = (\texttt{let val}\ x = t\ \texttt{in}\ u\ \texttt{end})\ \texttt{in}\ v\ \texttt{end} \quad (x \notin \mathrm{fv}(v)).\end{aligned}$$

Any reasonable call-by-value programming language will have an analogue of `let val`. Roughly speaking it is the essence of A-Normal Form and Single-Static-Assignment (e.g. [10]).

It is often helpful to understand a term in context $\Gamma \vdash t : A$ as a generalized function which takes a valuation for the context Γ and returns a result of type A. If we thus draw a term graphically

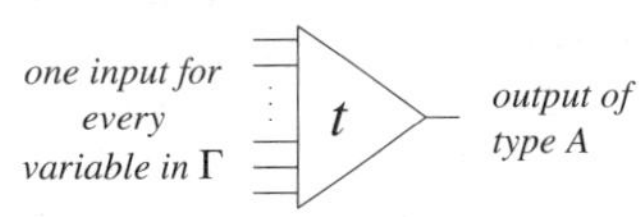

then we can understand `let val` as composition of functions, and a single variable is just a wire. The third law says

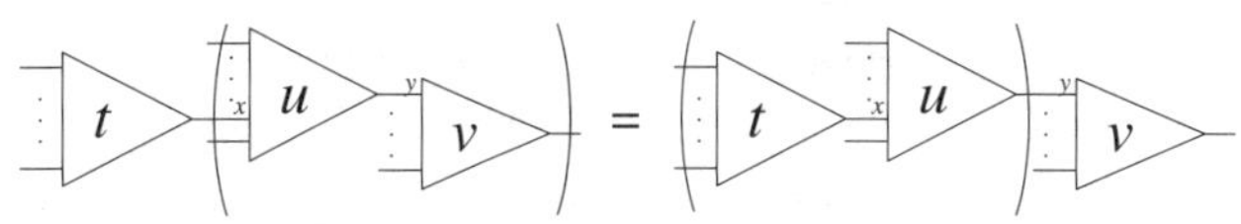

The three laws are thus the laws of identity and associativity for composing multivariate functions. The classical theory of multicategories also proposes a commutativity law:

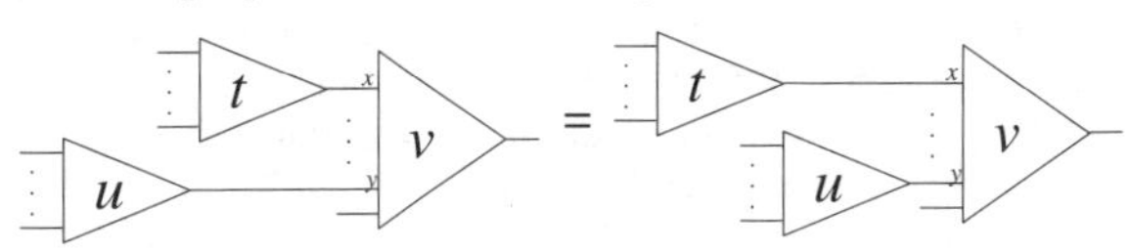

$$\begin{aligned}&\texttt{let val}\ x = t\ \texttt{in let val}\ y = u\ \texttt{in}\ v\ \texttt{end end} \quad (x \notin \mathrm{fv}(u),\\ \equiv\ &\texttt{let val}\ y = u\ \texttt{in let val}\ x = t\ \texttt{in}\ v\ \texttt{end end} \qquad y \notin \mathrm{fv}(t))\end{aligned}$$

This law does not hold for impure programs: consider the case where $t \stackrel{\text{def}}{=}$ `print "hello "` and $u \stackrel{\text{def}}{=}$ `print "world"`. Our equational theory of `let val` is thus a non-commutative variant of multicategories, which we call 'premulticategories' (§2).

(Jeffrey [18] resolves the inaccuracy of the graphical calculus by introducing special control arrows.)

POPL'13, January 23–25, 2013, Rome, Italy.

1.2 First class types via representability

We argue that type and term constructions should be defined in the context of the simple language with `let val`, in a canonical and universal way. To this end, we give universal properties for products (§3), sums (§4) and call-by-value functions (§6) in impure languages. One important consequence of universal properties is that although there may be many isomorphic implementations of (say) a product type, there is exactly one isomorphism between any two implementations, which means that there is a canonical way to translate between them.

We focus on product types for now, but we will later deal with sum types and function types. The concept of 'product' is already present in the little language with `let val`, for we can describe terms '$\Gamma, x{:}\,(A \times B) \vdash t : C$' as terms $\Gamma, x_1{:}\,A, x_2{:}\,B \vdash t' : C$. The principle of representability says that this concept determines the product types, if they exist. Concretely, representability requires that there is a term

$$x{:}\,A, y{:}\,B \vdash \langle x, y\rangle : A \times B$$

which is universal in the following sense. The term induces a family of functions between sets:

$$P_{\Gamma,C} : \{t \mid \Gamma, z{:}\,A \times B \vdash t : C\} \to \{u \mid \Gamma, x{:}\,A, y{:}\,B \vdash u : C\}$$

where $P_{\Gamma,C}(t) \stackrel{\text{def}}{=} \texttt{let val}\ z = \langle x, y\rangle\ \texttt{in}\ t\ \texttt{end}$, and this family of functions is required to be a natural family of bijections. The bijectivity condition means that each $P_{\Gamma,C}$ has an inverse, in other words that there is an assignment

$$\frac{\Gamma, x{:}\,A, y{:}\,B \vdash u : C}{\Gamma, z{:}\,A \times B \vdash P^{-1}_{\Gamma,C}(u) : C}$$

satisfying some equations. In Standard ML, we can define $P^{-1}_{\Gamma,C}$ by pattern matching: let $P^{-1}_{\Gamma,C}(u) \stackrel{\text{def}}{=} \texttt{let val}\ \langle x, y\rangle = z\ \texttt{in}\ u\ \texttt{end}$.

The technique of representability is syntactic, in that it suggests constructors and destructors for product types. It is also semantic, because it only determines the types up-to unique isomorphism of types. It gives a universal property: there is a unique isomorphism between any two implementations.

The principle of representability is a fundamental idea in abstract mathematics. Hermida [14] gives an account of representability for multicategories. One of our main technical contributions is to develop the theory of representability in the non-commutative setting of premulticategories (§7) and to demonstrate its relevance to the principles of programming languages (§3–6).

1.3 Explaining monads and premonoidal categories

Two important precursors to this work are Moggi's work on monads [29, 30] and the line of work on premonoidal categories and Freyd categories [12, 33, 34] begun by Power and Robinson. This earlier work has been very influential in programming languages research. Our criticism of it is that its analysis of impure computation is inextricably tied with its treatment of types. Using premonoidal categories, we show that impure computation can be separated from types in these models (§8).

Moggi's notion of λ_C-model [29, Def. 2.6] is defined in terms of strong monads. It axiomatizes in one fell swoop the structure of impure programming languages with product types and function types.

One of the contributions of Power and Robinson's work [33] is to decouple the function types from Moggi's notion of λ_C-model. They do this by directly axiomatizing categorical structures of 'computations' which they call premonoidal categories. This is in contrast to Moggi's development which centres around monads on a category of 'values'. The notion of premonoidal category axiomatizes (again, in one fell swoop) the structure of impure languages with product types. Freyd categories adjoin the distinction between computations and values to the theory of premonoidal categories.

In this paper we isolate the principles of impure computation from type structure by introducing the notion of premulticategory and the related notion of Freyd multicategory, a premulticategory with a distinguished class of values. Our main theorems recover the earlier constructions by using universal properties to introduce type structure to this framework:

- A premonoidal category [33] is a premulticategory with products (Theorem 26);
- A Freyd category [33, 34] is a Freyd multicategory with products (Proposition 33).
- A λ_C-model [29] is a Freyd multicategory with products and function spaces (§8.3).

Coherence from representability. We now give a more technical summary of the connections between premonoidal categories and premulticategories. In a programming language, the types

$$(A * B) * C \qquad \text{and} \qquad A * (B * C) \tag{1}$$

are not identical but they are isomorphic in a canonical way. In the approach of Power and Robinson, the isomorphism between the two types (1) is *given* as part of the data for a premonoidal category [33]. This 'coherence' approach has proved extremely successful in many areas of mathematics, but it appears several steps away from programming language syntax. In our work, the isomorphism (1) does not need to be given: instead, it can be *derived* from the universal property of products. This is a non-commutative version of Hermida's result [14]: to give a monoidal category is to give a multicategory with tensor products.

The situation is actually more complicated. Power and Robinson require that the given isomorphism (1) is 'central', which informally means that it doesn't matter when it is executed. Although this requirement is reasonable from a pragmatic point of view, it does not seem to arise from a requirement of higher category theory: premonoidal categories do not seem to be pseudomonoids in a monoidal bicategory. This problem is remedied by our representability result, which provides a principled explanation of the centrality requirements in premonoidal categories.

In summary, whereas the original definition of premonoidal category is several steps away from programming language syntax, our new characterization essentially *is* programming language syntax. This is because rather than axiomatizing everything in one fell swoop, we characterize type constructions as universal properties over a basic framework for impure computation.

2. A basic equational account of impure programs: premulticategories

We begin by analyzing the basic structure of an impure programming language with variables and let-binding. The equations which we propose are three of the four equations of multicategories.

Recall that an ordinary category comprises a collection of objects, a collection of morphisms between the objects, a selection of identity morphisms, and an associative composition operation. Roughly speaking, a premulticategory is similar except that the morphisms do not go from one object to another. Rather, they go from a context Γ to an object A. This is a natural way to study typed programming languages, since a program in a context Γ has a type A.

At this stage, we do not ask for the objects to be closed under operations (product types, unit types) nor for any special morphisms (printing, arithmetic). Nonetheless we certainly do not forbid these things at this stage: a premulticategory can have more content than the basic structural requirements.

As well as the syntactic examples of premulticategories that arise from programming languages, we have more concrete examples coming from set theory, pointed sets, and we explain how a strong monad gives rise to a premulticategory.

2.1 Definitions: premulticategories and centrality

Notational convention. Informally, the language of premulticategories can be thought of as a language for terms in context. Formally, a morphism $\Gamma \to A$ goes from a list Γ of objects to an object. We introduce the following informal convention. We will often write a list (A, B, C) annotated with variables $(x : A, y : B, z : C)$. This allows us to informally index the list using variables rather than numbers, e.g. we can write y for the second element of the list. By doing this we can reason about concatenated lists without fumbling with arithmetic on indices. In everything we do, the informal variables can be translated into numbers at the expense of readability.

The cornerstone of this paper is the following definition of premulticategory. This is a non-commutative version of 'multicategory', an idea first extensively investigated by Lambek [21].

Definition 1. A *premulticategory* is given by the following data.

- A collection of objects, ranged over by A, B etc.
- For each list of objects Γ and each object A a collection of morphisms $\Gamma \to A$ is given. If $t : \Gamma \to A$ then we write $\Gamma \vdash t : A$.
- *Identity morphisms:* For each object A a morphism $\mathrm{id}_A\colon (A) \to A$ must be given. We notate this requirement informally as a rule:

$$\frac{}{x\colon A \vdash x : A}$$

- *Composition:* Given a morphism $t\colon \Delta \to A$ and morphism $u\colon (\Gamma, A, \Gamma') \to B$, if the length of Γ is i then a morphism $(u \circ_i t) : (\Gamma, \Delta, \Gamma') \to B$ must be given. We notate this requirement informally as a rule:

$$\frac{\Delta \vdash t : A \qquad \Gamma, x\colon A, \Gamma' \vdash u : B}{\Gamma, \Delta, \Gamma' \vdash t \rightsquigarrow x.\, u : B}$$

  The notation $(t \rightsquigarrow x.u)$ can be understood as shorthand for `let val` x `=` t `in` u `end`: "execute t, bind the result to x, and continue as u".

The data is subject to the following equations.

- Identity laws.

$$\frac{\Gamma, x\colon A, \Gamma' \vdash t : B}{\Gamma, x\colon A, \Gamma' \vdash x \rightsquigarrow x.\, t \equiv t : B} \qquad \frac{\Gamma \vdash t : A}{\Gamma \vdash t \rightsquigarrow x.\, x \equiv t : A}$$

  In case the notation is unclear: the first law means that for any morphism $t\colon (\Gamma, A, \Gamma') \to B$, the composite of id_A with t at position i (where i is the length of Γ) is equal to t.
- Associativity law:

$$\frac{\Gamma_3 \vdash t : A \qquad \Gamma_2, x\colon A, \Gamma_2' \vdash u : B \qquad \Gamma_1, y\colon B, \Gamma_1' \vdash v : C}{\Gamma_1, \Gamma_2, \Gamma_3, \Gamma_2', \Gamma_1' \vdash (t \rightsquigarrow x.\, u) \rightsquigarrow y.\, v \equiv t \rightsquigarrow x.\, (u \rightsquigarrow y.\, v) : C}$$

  More formally this law is notated $v \circ_i (u \circ_j t) = (v \circ_i u) \circ_{i+j} t$, where i is the length of Γ_1 and j is the length of Γ_2.

Commutativity and centrality. In general, given morphisms $t\colon \Gamma_1 \to A$ and $u\colon \Gamma_2 \to B$, we say that t *commutes with* u if it doesn't matter which order t and u are executed. To be precise, t commutes with u if the following equations hold (for all v):

$$\frac{\Delta_1, x\colon A, \Delta_2, y\colon B, \Delta_3 \vdash v : C}{\Delta_1, \Gamma_1, \Delta_2, \Gamma_2, \Delta_3 \vdash t \rightsquigarrow x.\, u \rightsquigarrow y.\, v \equiv u \rightsquigarrow y.\, t \rightsquigarrow x.\, v : C}$$

$$\frac{\Delta_1, y\colon B, \Delta_2, x\colon A, \Delta_3 \vdash v : C}{\Delta_1, \Gamma_2, \Delta_2, \Gamma_1, \Delta_3 \vdash t \rightsquigarrow x.\, u \rightsquigarrow y.\, v \equiv u \rightsquigarrow y.\, t \rightsquigarrow x.\, v : C}$$

If t commutes with all u, then we say that t is *central*. In other words, t is central if it doesn't matter when it is executed. A premulticategory is a *multicategory* if all morphisms are central. (Lambek [21] calls this the axiom of commutativity.)

2.2 Examples of premulticategories

Multicategories have attracted significant recent interest in category theory, logic and algebra (e.g. [7, 14, 15, 22]), and in the semantics of continuation-passing [27] and of state [26, 35]. Premulticategories have not been studied before, to our knowledge.

First simple example: multicategory of sets. We begin by describing the multicategory of sets, but let us first set up some notation. Given a list Γ of sets, we write $\prod\Gamma$ for the product of those sets. For instance, $\prod(A, B, C) = \{(a, b, c) \mid a \in A, b \in B, c \in C\}$. If we view Γ as a context, then $\prod\Gamma$ is the set of valuations for that context.

In the multicategory of sets, the objects are sets, and a morphism $\Gamma \to A$ is a function $\prod\Gamma \to A$. Thus a morphism $\Gamma \to A$ is something which assigns a result in A to every valuation of Γ. The identity morphisms are the identity functions. Composition is by composition of functions: given morphisms $t\colon \Delta \to A$ and $u\colon (\Gamma, x\colon A, \Gamma') \to B$ and given valuations $\vec{a} \in \prod\Gamma$, $\vec{b} \in \prod\Delta$, $\vec{c} \in \prod\Gamma'$, let $(t \rightsquigarrow x.\, u)(\vec{a}, \vec{b}, \vec{c}) \stackrel{\text{def}}{=} u(\vec{a}, t(\vec{b}), \vec{c})$. This is a multicategory: all morphisms are central.

Second simple example: multicategory of pointed sets. In the multicategory of pointed sets, the objects are sets A equipped with a distinguished element $\bot_A$. A morphism $t\colon \Gamma \to A$ is a function $t\colon \prod\Gamma \to A$ that is strict in each argument: if $\vec{a} \in \prod\Gamma$ is such that $a_i = \bot$ for some i, then $t(\vec{a}) = \bot_A$. Identities and composition are as in the multicategory of sets; it is easy to check that these yield functions that are strict in each argument. All morphisms are central.

Third simple example: premulticategory of 'stateful' functions. Let S be a fixed set, thought of as a set of states. We form a premulticategory whose objects are sets and where a morphism $\Gamma \to A$ is a function $(\prod\Gamma) \times S \to A \times S$. The idea is that a 'stateful' function takes as an argument a valuation of its context and also an initial state; it returns a result and also a final state.

Composition is defined as follows. Given $t\colon \Delta \to A$ and $u\colon (\Gamma, x\colon A, \Gamma') \to B$ and given valuations $\vec{a} \in \prod\Gamma$, $\vec{b} \in \prod\Delta$, $\vec{c} \in \prod\Gamma'$ and an element $s \in S$, let $(t \rightsquigarrow x.\, u)(\vec{a}, \vec{b}, \vec{c}, s) \stackrel{\text{def}}{=} u(\vec{a}, a, \vec{c}, s')$ where $(a, s') = t(\vec{b}, s)$. This premulticategory is not a multicategory unless S has at most one element. The central morphisms $t\colon \Gamma \to A$ are the functions that do not change the state, i.e. for each valuation $\vec{a} \in \prod\Gamma$ there is an element $t_1(\vec{a})$ of A such that for all states $s \in S$ we have $t(\vec{a}, s) = (t_1(\vec{a}), s)$.

Connection with programming languages. Well-typed terms of a programming language such as Standard ML form a premulticategory, modulo observational equivalence. Composition $(t \rightsquigarrow x.\, u)$ amounts to the ML syntax `let val` x `=` t `in` u `end`. The identity and associativity laws are simple observational equations under this interpretation. Not all morphisms are central. For instance

$$\begin{aligned} &\mathsf{print}\ \text{"hello"} \rightsquigarrow x.\, \mathsf{print}\ \text{" world"} \rightsquigarrow y.\, (x, y) \\ &\quad \not\equiv \mathsf{print}\ \text{"world"} \rightsquigarrow x.\, \mathsf{print}\ \text{" hello"} \rightsquigarrow y.\, (x, y). \end{aligned}$$

Connection with deductive systems. As Lambek observed [21], multicategories are closely related to deductive systems such as the sequent calculus. The identity morphisms correspond to the axiom, and composition corresponds to cut. The identity and associativity laws provide a starting point for a cut-elimination procedure. However, whereas the commutativity axiom plays a natural role in equivalence of proofs, we are rejecting it in the context of programming languages. Moreover, we are not interested in cut elimination, since cut/sequencing plays a crucial role. For instance, we cannot eliminate sequencing from the following program without changing its meaning.

$$(\mathsf{print}\ \text{"Enter your name:"}) \rightsquigarrow x.\,\mathsf{readline} \rightsquigarrow y.\,\mathsf{print}\ \text{"Hello "}\hat{}\,y$$

Connection with algebra. The words 'commutativity' and 'centrality' are used by analogy with algebra. Let $(M, \cdot, e)$ be a monoid, i.e. a set with an associative binary operation $\cdot$ and unit e. We can build a premulticategory from M: it has one object $*$ and a morphism $\Gamma \to *$ for each element of M. The identity morphism is e and composition $m \rightsquigarrow x.n$ is monoid multiplication, $m \cdot n$.

A morphism m in this premulticategory is central if and only if it is central in the usual algebraic sense: $\forall n.\, m \cdot n = n \cdot m$. The premulticategory is a multicategory if and only if the monoid is commutative: $\forall m, n.\, m \cdot n = n \cdot m$.

This is a simple motivating example. Let Σ be an alphabet, and let Σ^* be the monoid of strings over the alphabet. The unit is the empty string and multiplication is concatenation. When we think of this as a premulticategory, we can think of the object $*$ as the `unit` type in ML, and we can think of elements s of the monoid Σ^* as commands $\Gamma \vdash \mathsf{output}\, s : *$, with the equation

$$\Gamma \vdash (\mathsf{output}\, s \rightsquigarrow x.\,\mathsf{output}\, t) \equiv \mathsf{output}\,(st) : *.$$

Examples from monads. Moggi proposed monads as models of impure programming languages [30]. Let-binding plays a key role in his metalanguage. This can be explained by noting that every strong monad induces a premulticategory. Examples of monads on the category of sets include the state monad $(S \Rightarrow ((-) \times S))$, the continuations monad $((-) \Rightarrow R) \Rightarrow R$, and the exceptions monad $((-) \uplus E)$. All of these computational effects can be accommodated in premulticategories.

Recall that a monad on the (ordinary) category of sets is given by an assignment of a set $T(A)$ to each set A, a family of functions $\eta_A : A \to T(A)$ and an assignment from functions $f : A \to T(A)$ to functions $f^* : T(A) \to T(B)$, all satisfying some axioms. Given a monad T, we can define a 'Kleisli' premulticategory of T-functions. The objects are sets, and a morphism $\Gamma \to A$ is a function $\prod\Gamma \to T(A)$. The identities are defined using η. Composition is defined as follows: given $t : \Delta \to A$ and $u : (\Gamma, x : A, \Gamma') \to B$ and valuations $\vec{a} \in \prod\Gamma$, $\vec{b} \in \prod\Delta$, $\vec{c} \in \prod\Gamma'$, let

$$(t \rightsquigarrow x.\,u)(\vec{a}, \vec{b}, \vec{c}) \stackrel{\text{def}}{=} u^*(str(\vec{a}, t(\vec{b}), \vec{c}))$$

where $str : \prod(\Gamma, T(A), \Gamma') \to T(\prod(\Gamma, A, \Gamma'))$ is a *strength* which is uniquely defined for any set-theoretic monad [30, Prop. 3.4]. This construction can be carried out for any strong monad on a symmetric monoidal category.

The Kleisli premulticategory induced by a monad is a multicategory if and only if the monad is commutative in the sense of [19]. Commutative monads have special relevance in the study of linear logic (e.g. [4, 16]).

Any monoid $(M, \cdot, e)$ induces a monad $M \times (-)$ on the category of sets. The premulticategory induced by the monoid embeds in the Kleisli premulticategory induced by its monad, and the three notions of commutativity for monoids, monads and premulticategories coincide in this situation.

While many notions of computation can be described by monads, there is a difference between premulticategories and monads: a strong monad cannot be defined without having a product structure and a construction T. We argue that these constructions on types ($\times$ and T) have nothing to do with impure computation. In Section 8.3 we show that these constructions ($\times$ and T) have universal properties when they exist, so that they need not be specified at all.

2.3 Structural laws

Our language for premulticategories doesn't have any structural laws. In a composite $t \rightsquigarrow x.\,u$, there is a linearity constraint: the variables in t must be distinct from the variables in u (except for x). Moreover, the context cannot necessarily be reordered. There are many situations in programming languages where non-linearity is essential, and so we now explain how to introduce the structural laws into the theory of premulticategories.

If $\Gamma = (A_1, \ldots, A_m)$ and $\Delta = (B_1, \ldots, B_n)$ are lists of objects then we define a *renaming* $f : \Gamma \to \Delta$ to be a function $m \to n$ such that $A_i = B_{f(i)}$ for $i \le m$. Renamings compose as functions. (See also e.g. [9, §II.1].)

Definition 2. A premulticategory is *cartesian* when for every morphism $t : \Gamma_1 \to A$ and every renaming $f : \Gamma_1 \to \Gamma_2$ a morphism $t[f] : \Gamma_2 \to A$ is given,

$$\frac{\Gamma_1 \vdash t : A}{\Gamma_2 \vdash t[f] : A}\ (f : \Gamma_1 \to \Gamma_2)$$

such that $t[\mathrm{id}_\Gamma] = t$ and $t[f; g] = (t[f])[g]$ when both sides are defined, and satisfying the rule

$$\frac{\Delta_1 \vdash t : A \qquad \Gamma_1, x : A, \Gamma_1' \vdash u : B}{\Gamma_2, \Delta_2, \Gamma_2' \vdash (t \rightsquigarrow x.\,u)[g_1 \backslash f / g_2] \equiv t[f] \rightsquigarrow x.\,u[g_1 \backslash \mathrm{id}_A / g_2] : B}$$

for any $f : \Delta_1 \to \Delta_2$, $g_1 : \Gamma_1 \to (\Gamma_2, \Gamma_2')$ and $g_2 : \Gamma_1' \to (\Gamma_2, \Gamma_2')$, where the renamings $(g_1 \backslash f / g_2) : (\Gamma_1, \Delta, \Gamma_1') \to (\Gamma_2, \Delta_2, \Gamma_2')$ and $(g_1 \backslash \mathrm{id}_A / g_2) : (\Gamma_1, x : A, \Gamma_1') \to (\Gamma_2, x : A, \Gamma_2')$ are defined in the obvious way.

Special kinds of renaming correspond to the classical structural laws. The bijective renamings of the form $(\Gamma, x : A, y : B, \Gamma') \to (\Gamma, y : B, x : A, \Gamma')$ determine the exchange laws; the injective renamings of the form $\mathsf{wk}_x : (\Gamma, \Gamma') \to (\Gamma, x : A, \Gamma')$ determine the weakening laws; and the surjective renamings of the form $\mathsf{ctrct}_x^{y,z} : (\Gamma, y : A, z : A, \Gamma') \to (\Gamma, x : A, \Gamma')$ determine the contraction laws. All renamings can be built from morphisms of these three kinds (e.g. [6, 20]). We can work with a subset of the structural laws by focusing on a particular well-behaved class of renamings:

Definition 3 (c.f. [22], Def 2.2.21)**.** A premulticategory is *symmetric* when for every morphism $t : \Gamma_1 \to A$ and every bijective renaming $f : \Gamma_1 \to \Gamma_2$ a morphism $t[f] : \Gamma_2 \to A$ is given such that the rules in Definition 2 are satisfied.

(We emphasize that 'symmetric' and 'commutative' are not synonyms.)

In a cartesian premulticategory, some morphisms interact particularly well with the renaming structure (c.f. [12]). We say that a morphism $t : \Delta \to A$ is *discardable* if, for all $u : (\Gamma, \Gamma') \to B$,

$$\Gamma, \Delta, \Gamma' \vdash t \rightsquigarrow x.\,(u[\mathsf{wk}_x]) \equiv u[\mathsf{wk}_\Delta] : B$$

and $t : \Delta \to A$ is *copyable* if, for all $u : (\Gamma, y : A, z : A, \Gamma') \to B$,

$$\Gamma, \Delta, \Gamma' \vdash t \rightsquigarrow x.\,(u[\mathsf{ctrct}_x^{y,z}]) \equiv (t \rightsquigarrow y.\,t \rightsquigarrow z.\,u)[\mathsf{ctrct}_\Delta^{\Delta,\Delta}] : B.$$

Definition 4. A *cartesian multicategory* is a cartesian premulticategory in which every morphism is central, discardable and copyable.

(Various authors have investigated general categorical frameworks that include symmetric multicategories, cartesian multicategories, and many more elaborate examples [5, 7, 15, 22], but those frameworks are based on simultaneous substitution and do not seem to work well for premulticategories.)

3. Product types and tensor products

In the previous section we introduced an equational theory for programs with let-binding. We did this without making any assumptions about the type constructions in the language.

We now explain what it means for a language to have product/record types. We do this by using the universal property of tensor products, which is well understood for multicategories [14]. This universal property has the immediate consequence that any two implementations of the product type are canonically isomorphic. In this sense, 'having products' is seen as a property and not additional structure. (We discuss a limitation of this view in §5.2.)

In this section and in the following two sections on sums and functions we will deal with particular concepts. In Section 7 we provide general notions of representability and show that these particular concepts are instances of the general notions.

3.1 Tensor products: definition

Consider a list $\Delta = (A_1, \ldots, A_n)$ of objects in a premulticategory. The list Δ can be thought of as a specification for a product type $(A_1 * \ldots * A_n)$. The list is not actually a product type because it is not actually an object. A tensor product for Δ is a single object that represents it.

Definition 5. A *tensor product* for a list of objects $\Delta = (A_1, .., A_n)$ is an object $\otimes\Delta$ together with a morphism $\Delta \to \otimes\Delta$, which we notate

$$\overline{x_1{:}\, A_1, \ldots, x_n{:}\, A_n \vdash \langle x_1, \ldots, x_n \rangle : \otimes\Delta}$$

together with an operation on morphisms

$$\frac{\Gamma, x_1{:}\, A_1, \ldots, x_n{:}\, A_n, \Gamma' \vdash t : B}{\Gamma, y{:}\, \otimes\Delta, \Gamma' \vdash y \twoheadleftarrow \langle x_1 \ldots x_n \rangle.\, t : B} \tag{2}$$

for each pair of lists Γ, Γ' and each object B. The notation $y \twoheadleftarrow \langle x_1 \ldots x_n \rangle.\, t$ should be understood as pattern matching a variable of product type into its components $x_1 \ldots x_n$, binding them in t.

We require the morphism $\Delta \to \otimes\Delta$ to be central (that is, $\langle x_1..x_n \rangle \rightsquigarrow y.\, t \rightsquigarrow z.\, u \equiv t \rightsquigarrow z.\, \langle x_1..x_n \rangle \rightsquigarrow y.\, u$) and we impose the following two conditions:

$$\frac{\Gamma, x_1{:}\, A_1, \ldots, x_n{:}\, A_n, \Gamma' \vdash t : B}{\Gamma, x_1{:}\, A_1, \ldots, x_n{:}\, A_n, \Gamma' \vdash \langle \vec{x} \rangle \rightsquigarrow y.\, (y \twoheadleftarrow \langle \vec{x} \rangle.\, t) \equiv t : B}$$

$$\frac{\Gamma, y{:}\, \otimes\Delta, \Gamma' \vdash u : B}{\Gamma, y{:}\, \otimes\Delta, \Gamma' \vdash y \twoheadleftarrow \langle x_1, \ldots, x_n \rangle.\, (\langle x_1, \ldots, x_n \rangle \rightsquigarrow y.\, u) \equiv u : B}$$

The first equation says that if we form a tuple and then extract its elements, nothing happens. The second equation says that if we extract the elements of tuple and then build the tuple again, nothing happens.

In Section 7.2.2 we will explain how this definition amounts to representability in a more abstract sense.

3.2 Examples of tensors

In the multicategory of sets, every list of objects has a tensor product. The tensor product of a list Δ is the product set $\prod\Delta$, that is, the set of valuations for Δ. The universal morphism $\Delta \to \otimes\Delta$ is the identity function. Essentially the same representation works in the premulticategory of stateful functions and the premulticategory of arising from a monad on the category of sets.

Recall that a pointed set is a set A equipped with a chosen element $\bot_A \in A$. In the multicategory of pointed sets, every list $\Delta = (A_1, \ldots, A_n)$ has a tensor product given by the 'smash product', which is a quotient of the free pointed set on the product of Δ,

$$\otimes\Delta = (\{\bot_{\otimes\Delta}\} \cup \textstyle\prod\Delta)/_{\sim}$$

where $\sim$ is generated by $\bot_{\otimes\Delta} \sim (a_1, \ldots, \bot_{A_i}, \ldots, a_n)$.

Pointed sets are a simple algebraic theory. More generally, one can build a multicategory from *any* algebraic theory, with algebras as objects and multilinear maps as morphisms. A famous example is the of multicategory of vector spaces which also has tensor products. A well-known characterization theorem says that, for a given algebraic theory, the multicategory of algebras has tensor products if and only the corresponding free-algebra monad is commutative (c.f. [25]).

Connection with programming languages. The syntax for tensor products is very similar to the syntax in ML. In Standard ML, the object $\otimes\Delta$ would be written $(A_1 * \ldots * A_n)$, and the assignment $y \twoheadleftarrow \langle x_1, \ldots, x_n \rangle.\, t$ is written as follows:

$$\texttt{let val}\,(x_1, \ldots, x_n) = y\,\texttt{in}\,t\,\texttt{end}.$$

The centrality of the universal morphism and the two equations are straightforward observational equivalences. Thus we can build a premulticategory with all tensor products whose objects are types and whose morphisms are terms in context modulo observational equivalence.

If the empty list $()$ has a tensor product $\otimes()$ then this behaves like the `unit` type in ML. For instance, the sequencing notation $(t\,;u)$ can be understood as shorthand for $t \rightsquigarrow x.\, x \twoheadleftarrow \langle\rangle.\, u$.

A convenient programming practice is to write tuples with terms in the components. By fixing a left-to-right order of evaluation, we have the following derived typing rule:

$$\frac{\Gamma_1 \vdash t_1 : A_1 \quad \ldots \quad \Gamma_n \vdash t_n : A_n}{\Gamma_1..\Gamma_n \vdash \langle t_1..t_n \rangle \stackrel{\text{def}}{=} t_1 \rightsquigarrow x_1 \ldots t_n \rightsquigarrow x_n.\, \langle x_1..x_n \rangle : \otimes\Delta} \tag{3}$$

Connection with logic. The rule for matching (2) is the left rule for tensor products in the sequent calculus presentation of linear logic. The right rule of the sequent calculus looks like the derived rule (3) although there is nothing canonical about it in the non-commutative setting: the order of evaluation of $t_1 \ldots t_n$ matters unless they are central.

3.3 Basic first results

We now state some basic results that can be derived from the definition of tensor product. They are instances of general results in Section 7.2.

Proposition 6. *Matching associates and commutes with composition:*

$$\frac{\Gamma_1, \Delta, \Gamma_1' \vdash t : B \qquad \Gamma_2, z{:}\, B, \Gamma_2' \vdash u : C}{\Gamma_2, \Gamma_1, y{:}\, \otimes\Delta, \Gamma_1', \Gamma_2' \vdash (y \twoheadleftarrow \langle \vec{x} \rangle.\, t) \rightsquigarrow z.\, u \equiv y \twoheadleftarrow \langle \vec{x} \rangle.\, (t \rightsquigarrow z.\, u) : C}$$

$$\frac{\Gamma_1 \vdash t : B \qquad \Gamma_2, \Delta, z{:}\, B, \Gamma_2' \vdash u : C}{\Gamma_2, y{:}\, \otimes\Delta, \Gamma_1, \Gamma_2' \vdash y \twoheadleftarrow \langle \vec{x} \rangle.\, (t \rightsquigarrow z.\, u) \equiv t \rightsquigarrow z.\, (y \twoheadleftarrow \langle \vec{x} \rangle.\, u) : C}$$

Proposition 7. *For any list $\Delta = (x_1{:}\, A_1, \ldots, x_n{:}\, A_n)$ of objects, any object R and any morphism $r{:}\, \Delta \to R$ there is a unique morphism $t{:}\, (y{:}\, \otimes\Delta) \to R$ such that $\langle x_1, \ldots, x_n \rangle \rightsquigarrow y.\, t \equiv r$. The unique morphism t is central if r is central.*

As a corollary of this result we achieve our main theorem:

Theorem 8. *Tensor products are unique up to unique isomorphism, and the unique mediating isomorphisms are central.*

In other words, there is a canonical way to translate between any two implementations of product types.

4. Sums and labelled variants

In the previous section we demonstrated that products can be given a universal property in a model of an impure programming language. In this section we show that sum types (labelled variants) can also be given a universal property in a similar way.

4.1 Definitions: constructor contexts and sums

We fix an infinite set of 'constructors'. A *constructor context* is a finite partial function from constructors to objects of a premulticategory. A *sum* for a constructor context Δ is an object $\oplus\Delta$ and a family of morphisms $\{\Delta(\mathrm{c}) \to \oplus\Delta\}_{\mathrm{c}\in dom(\Delta)}$:

$$\frac{}{x{:}\,\Delta(\mathrm{c}) \vdash \mathrm{c}(x) : \oplus\Delta}\;(\mathrm{c} \in dom(\Delta))$$

that is universal in the sense that each morphism is central and there is an operation on morphisms

$$\frac{\Gamma, x_{\mathrm{c}}{:}\,\Delta(\mathrm{c}), \Gamma' \vdash t_{\mathrm{c}} : A \quad (\mathrm{c} \in dom(\Delta))}{\Gamma, y{:}\oplus\Delta, \Gamma' \vdash \mathsf{match}\, y\, \mathsf{as}\, (\mathrm{c}(x_{\mathrm{c}}) \Rightarrow t_{\mathrm{c}})_{\mathrm{c}\in dom(\Delta)} : A}$$

subject to the following equations:

$$\frac{\Gamma, x_{\mathrm{c}}{:}\,\Delta(\mathrm{c}), \Gamma' \vdash t_{\mathrm{c}} : A \quad (\mathrm{c} \in dom(\Delta))}{\Gamma, x_{\mathrm{d}}{:}\,\Delta(\mathrm{d}), \Gamma' \vdash \mathrm{d}(x_{\mathrm{d}}) \rightsquigarrow y.\, \mathsf{match}\, y\, \mathsf{as}\, \big(\mathrm{c}(x_{\mathrm{c}}) \Rightarrow t_{\mathrm{c}}\big)_{\mathrm{c}} \equiv t_{\mathrm{d}} : A}$$

$$\frac{\Gamma, y{:}\oplus\Delta, \Gamma' \vdash t : A}{\Gamma, y{:}\oplus\Delta, \Gamma' \vdash \mathsf{match}\, y\, \mathsf{as}\, \big(\mathrm{c}(x_{\mathrm{c}}) \Rightarrow (\mathrm{c}(x_{\mathrm{c}}) \rightsquigarrow y.\, t)\big)_{\mathrm{c}} \equiv t : A}$$

4.2 Examples of sums

Sums in set-theoretic premulticategories. The multicategory of sets has sets as objects and multivariate functions as morphisms. Sums of constructor contexts are given by disjoint unions:

$$\oplus\Delta \overset{\text{def}}{=} \{(\mathrm{c}, a) \mid a \in \Delta(\mathrm{c})\}.$$

The universal maps take $a \in \Delta(\mathrm{c})$ to $(\mathrm{c}, a) \in \oplus\Delta$. A similar analysis works for stateful functions and for the premulticategory arising from a monad on a distributive category.

In the multicategory of pointed sets, the objects are sets A equipped with an element $\bot_A$, and the morphisms are multivariate functions that are strict in each argument. This multicategory also has sums of constructor contexts, given by a coalesced sum:

$$\oplus\Delta \overset{\text{def}}{=} (\{(\mathrm{c}, a) \mid a \in \Delta(\mathrm{c})\} \uplus \bot_{\oplus\Delta})/_{\sim} \quad \text{where } \bot_{\oplus\Delta} \sim (\mathrm{c}, \bot_{\Delta(\mathrm{c})}).$$

Connections with programming languages. In ML-like languages, variant types must be declared. Given a constructor context $\Delta = (\mathrm{c}_1{:}\,A_1, \dots, \mathrm{c}_n{:}\,A_n)$, we would expect an ML definition

$$\texttt{datatype}\ \oplus\Delta\ =\ \mathrm{c}_1 : A_1 \mid \dots \mid \mathrm{c}_n : A_n.$$

The universal family of morphisms can be combined with composition to yield the more familiar term formation for constructors:

$$\frac{\Gamma \vdash t : \Delta(\mathrm{c})}{\Gamma \vdash \mathrm{c}(t) \overset{\text{def}}{=} t \rightsquigarrow x.\, \mathrm{c}(x) : A}\;(\mathrm{c} \in dom(\Delta))$$

The equations in the definition are straightforward observational equivalences in a programming language.

4.2.1 Basic first results

We state some basic properties that can be derived from the definition of sums. They are instances of general results in Section 7.2.

Proposition 9. *Matching associates and commutes with composition:*

$$\frac{\Gamma_1, x_{\mathrm{c}}{:}\,\Delta(\mathrm{c}), \Gamma_1' \vdash t_{\mathrm{c}} : A\ (\mathrm{c} \in dom(\Delta)) \quad \Gamma_2, z{:}\,A, \Gamma_2' \vdash u : B}{\begin{array}{r}\Gamma_2, \Gamma_1, y{:}\oplus\Delta, \Gamma_1', \Gamma_2' \vdash \mathsf{match}\, y\, \mathsf{as}\, (\mathrm{c}(x_{\mathrm{c}}) \Rightarrow (t_{\mathrm{c}} \rightsquigarrow z.\, u))_{\mathrm{c}} \\ \equiv\ (\mathsf{match}\, y\, \mathsf{as}\, (\mathrm{c}(x_{\mathrm{c}}) \Rightarrow t_{\mathrm{c}})_{\mathrm{c}}) \rightsquigarrow z.\, u : B\end{array}}$$

$$\frac{\Gamma_1 \vdash t : A \qquad \Gamma_2, x_{\mathrm{c}}{:}\,\Delta(\mathrm{c}), z{:}\,A, \Gamma_2' \vdash u_{\mathrm{c}} : B \quad (\mathrm{c} \in dom(\Delta))}{\begin{array}{r}\Gamma_2, y{:}\oplus\Delta, \Gamma_1, \Gamma_2' \vdash \mathsf{match}\, y\, \mathsf{as}\, (\mathrm{c}(x_{\mathrm{c}}) \Rightarrow (t \rightsquigarrow z.\, u_{\mathrm{c}}))_{\mathrm{c}} \\ \equiv\ t \rightsquigarrow z.\, (\mathsf{match}\, y\, \mathsf{as}\, (\mathrm{c}(x_{\mathrm{c}}) \Rightarrow u_{\mathrm{c}})_{\mathrm{c}}) : B\end{array}}$$

Proposition 10. *For any constructor context Δ, any object R and any family of morphisms $\{r_{\mathrm{c}}{:}\,(x{:}\,\Delta(\mathrm{c})) \to R\}_{\mathrm{c}\in dom(\Delta)}$, there is a unique morphism $t{:}\,(y{:}\oplus\Delta) \to R$ such that for all $\mathrm{c} \in dom(\Delta)$,*

$$x{:}\,\Delta(\mathrm{c}) \vdash \mathrm{c}(x) \rightsquigarrow y.\, t \equiv r_{\mathrm{c}} : R.$$

The mediating morphism t is central if each r_{c} is central.

In consequence, sums are unique up to unique isomorphism, and the unique mediating isomorphisms are central.

5. On values and Freyd multicategories

In impure programming languages it is usually necessary to identify a class of values among the class of all programs. For instance, in an impure functional programming language, the most natural evaluation strategy for function application is call-by-value: expressions are reduced to values before they are passed as arguments.

We have proposed to understand a program as a morphism in a premulticategory. To accommodate values, we must identify a class of morphisms which are the values. We call this structure a 'Freyd multicategory'. The idea of distinguishing between values and computations is long-established in the categorical study of semantics, stemming from Moggi's distinction between ordinary morphisms and Kleisli morphisms [30], running through the work on premonoidal categories (e.g. [18, 32, 33]) and Freyd categories [24, 34]. The distinction between values and computations also arises in 'arrows' in functional programming [2, 3, 17] and forms the basis of recent syntactic systems (e.g. [8, 23, 28]). The idea of identifying a class of values also plays a crucial technical role from the perspective of morphisms between premulticategories with tensor products.

5.1 Morphisms of premulticategories

If premulticategories represent programming languages, then a morphism between them is a compositional translation.

Definition 11. Let $\mathcal{C}$ and $\mathcal{D}$ be premulticategories. A morphism $F : \mathcal{C} \to \mathcal{D}$ is given by an assignment of an object FA of $\mathcal{D}$ to each object A of $\mathcal{C}$, and an assignment of a morphism $Ff : F\Gamma \to FB$ in $\mathcal{D}$ to each morphism $f{:}\,\Gamma \to B$ in $\mathcal{C}$, such that identities and composition are preserved.

Our running example concerns the two-element monoid $S_2 = (\{\mathtt{flip}, e\}, \cdot, e)$ where $\mathtt{flip} \cdot \mathtt{flip} = e$. As explained in Section 2.2, the monad $S_2 \times (-)$ on the category of sets induces a Kleisli premulticategory $\mathcal{C}$ whose objects are sets and where a morphism $\Gamma \to B$ is a function $\prod \Gamma \to S_2 \times B$. It can be thought of as a semantics for a simple programming language with a command `flip` that flips the contents of a bit of memory.

We also consider the premulticategory $\mathcal{D}$ of stateful functions (§2.2) with two states $Bool = \{\mathrm{True}, \mathrm{False}\}$. The objects of $\mathcal{D}$ are sets and the morphisms $\Gamma \to B$ are functions $\prod \Gamma \times Bool \to B \times Bool$.

There is a morphism of multicategories $F{:}\,\mathcal{C} \to \mathcal{D}$ that is identity on objects and takes a morphism $f : \Gamma \to B$ in $\mathcal{C}$ to the stateful function given by $(Ff)(\vec{a}, s) = (b, s \text{ xor } s')$ where $f(\vec{a}) = (b, s')$, i.e., interpreting the command `flip` as an instruction that flips the state. This can be understood as arising from a monad morphism $(S_2 \times -) \to (- \times Bool)^{Bool}$.

5.2 Discussion: Preservation of tensors

We now investigate what it means for a morphism of premulticategories to preserve tensor products. Since tensor products have a universal property we would expect preservation of tensors to be a property rather than extra structure.

Given a list $\Delta = (A_1, \ldots, A_n)$ of objects of $\mathcal{V}$ and a tensor product $r: \Delta \to R$, we say that a morphism $F: \mathcal{C} \to \mathcal{D}$ preserves the tensor if Fr is also a tensor.

Proposition 12. *Let $F : \mathcal{C} \to \mathcal{D}$ be a morphism between premulticategories, where $\mathcal{C}$ has tensor products. The following are equivalent:*

1. *F preserves every tensor product.*
2. *F preserves central isomorphisms, and every list of objects in $\mathcal{C}$ has a tensor product that is preserved by F.*

The issue here is that there may be many different tensors for a given list of objects, all related by canonical central isomorphisms. If F preserves central isomorphisms, e.g. if $\mathcal{D}$ is is a multicategory, then the equivalence of items 1 and 2 allows us to check that F preserves all tensor products by checking that one chosen tensor product is preserved.

To illustrate this, let us return to our example of the Kleisli premulticategory $\mathcal{C}$ and the premulticategory $\mathcal{D}$ of stateful functions. The premulticategory $\mathcal{C}$ is actually a multicategory, since e and `flip` commute. The morphism $F : \mathcal{C} \to \mathcal{D}$ does not preserve centrality, because $F(\texttt{flip}, \mathrm{id}) : () \to 1$ is not central in $\mathcal{D}$.

This example also illustrates the complications involved with preservation of tensor products in the non-commutative setting. In $\mathcal{C}$, every list Δ has a tensor product given by $(e, \mathrm{id}): \Delta \to \prod \Delta$. This is a reasonable implementation of the tensor product from the programming language perspective. This tensor product is preserved by the morphism $F : \mathcal{C} \to \mathcal{D}$ into the premulticategory of stateful functions. However, the structure $(\texttt{flip}, \mathrm{id}): \Delta \to \prod \Delta$ also happens to be a tensor product of the list Δ in $\mathcal{C}$. This tensor product is not preserved by the morphism $F: \mathcal{C} \to \mathcal{D}$, because $F(\texttt{flip}, \mathrm{id})$ is not central in $\mathcal{D}$.

In the example, informally, $(\texttt{flip}, \mathrm{id})$ is central in $\mathcal{C}$ by accident: it would have been better to explicitly designate (e, id) as a value and $(\texttt{flip}, \mathrm{id})$ as a non-value. We could then require this special class of central 'value' morphisms to be used for the representations for tensors, and we could require this class of value morphisms to be preserved by morphisms of premulticategories.

Before we make this formal, we briefly consider another way to resolve the situation: we could remove the requirement that the representing morphism $\Delta \to \otimes\Delta$ be central. This is difficult to motivate from a pragmatic perspective. Moreover from the mathematical perspective it is badly behaved, because the induced family of associativity morphisms $\alpha_{A,B,C} : \otimes(\otimes(A, B), C) \to \otimes(A, \otimes(B, C))$ is not natural and moreover does not support a coherence result: the pentagon diagram does not commute (see §8).

5.3 Definition: Freyd multicategory

Informally, a Freyd multicategory is a premulticategory that is equipped with data about which morphisms are values.

Formally, a Freyd multicategory is a morphism $return: \mathcal{V} \to \mathcal{C}$ from a multicategory $\mathcal{V}$ to a premulticategory $\mathcal{C}$ such that $\mathcal{V}$ and $\mathcal{C}$ have the same objects and $return$ is identity on objects and preserves centrality. The idea is that morphisms in $\mathcal{V}$ are values, morphisms in $\mathcal{C}$ are computations, and $return(v)$ is the computation that immediately returns v. We do not require $return$ to be injective on morphisms, although it often will be in practice.

We notate Freyd multicategories by introducing a special judgement $\Gamma \vdash_{\mathcal{V}} v : A$ of values (morphisms in $\mathcal{V}$) and a rule

$$\frac{\Gamma \vdash_{\mathcal{V}} v : A}{\Gamma \vdash return(v) : A}$$

describing the morphism $return: \mathcal{V} \to \mathcal{C}$. The functoriality of $return$ is expressed by the following equations:

$$\frac{}{x{:}\, A \vdash x \equiv return(x) : A}$$

$$\frac{\Delta \vdash_{\mathcal{V}} v : A \qquad \Gamma, x{:}\, A, \Gamma' \vdash_{\mathcal{V}} w : B}{\Gamma, \Delta, \Gamma' \vdash return(v \rightsquigarrow x.\, w) \equiv return(v) \rightsquigarrow x.\, return(w) : B}$$

We also have the two equations stating that values are central among all morphisms (§2.1).

Because $\mathcal{V}$ is a multicategory and $\mathcal{V} \to \mathcal{C}$ preserves centrality then we can understand $return(v) \rightsquigarrow x.\, t$ as an explicit substitution of the value v for x in t. In the syntax, we can textually substitute $t\{v/x\}$ as shorthand for $return(v) \rightsquigarrow x.\, t$. (Note that this implicit substitution is only an informal convention, whereas it is genuine syntax in the explicit substitutions of Abadi et al. [1].)

A *morphism of Freyd multicategories*

$$(F_1, F_2) : (\mathcal{V} \xrightarrow{return} \mathcal{C}) \longrightarrow (\mathcal{V}' \xrightarrow{return'} \mathcal{C}')$$

is a pair of morphisms between premulticategories ($F_1: \mathcal{V} \to \mathcal{V}'$, $F_2: \mathcal{C} \to \mathcal{C}'$) such that $return' \circ F_1 = F_2 \circ return$.

5.3.1 Examples of Freyd multicategories

Recall that the premulticategory of stateful functions has sets as objects and stateful functions as morphisms. A stateful function $\Gamma \to A$ is an ordinary function $(\prod \Gamma) \times S \to A \times S$, where S is a fixed set of states. In this context we let our multicategory of values be the multicategory of sets and pure (stateless) functions, and $return: \mathcal{V} \to \mathcal{C}$ is the evident inclusion morphism, which is faithful provided S is not empty.

Given a monad T, recall that the associated Kleisli premulticategory has sets as objects and morphisms $\Gamma \to A$ are ordinary functions $(\prod \Gamma) \to T(A)$. In this context we let our multicategory of values be the category of sets and pure functions. The morphism $return: \mathcal{V} \to \mathcal{C}$ is defined by the unit of the monad.

We can now revisit our morphism $\mathcal{C} \to \mathcal{D}$ from the Kleisli premulticategory induced by the monad $(S_2 \times -)$ to the premulticategory of stateful functions (§5.2). In both cases, the value multicategory is the multicategory of sets and pure functions, and $(\mathrm{Id}, F) : \mathcal{C} \to \mathcal{D}$ is a morphism of Freyd multicategories.

5.3.2 Tensors and sums in Freyd multicategories

We define a *Freyd multicategory with tensors/sums* to be a Freyd multicategory $return: \mathcal{V} \to \mathcal{C}$ in which $\mathcal{V}$ has tensors/sums and $return$ preserves them. This makes sense because $return$ preserves centrality.

We say that a morphism of Freyd multicategories $(F_1, F_2) : (\mathcal{V} \to \mathcal{C}) \to (\mathcal{V}' \to \mathcal{C}')$ preserves tensors (resp. sums) if F_1 preserves tensors (resp. sums). To illustrate, we return to our motivating example: the morphism from the Freyd multicategory induced by the monad $(S_2 \times -)$ to the Freyd multicategory of stateful functions. This does preserves tensors.

As an aside we remark that, from the syntactic point of view, it is slightly unnatural to ask for $\mathcal{V}$ to have tensors/sums. For tensors, although it is usual to consider the representing maps $\langle v_1, \ldots, v_n \rangle$ as values, it is less common to consider the pattern matching syntax $x \twoheadleftarrow \langle \vec{y} \rangle.\, v$ as a value expression. Levy [24] coined the phrase 'complex value' for this situation. Our framework provides us with an option for describing tensors with*out* using complex values, by asking $\mathcal{C}$ to have tensors and for the representing maps to come from $\mathcal{V}$, without asking for $\mathcal{V}$ to have tensors. Using implicit substitution, we would have a more familiar grammar for values:

$$v ::= \langle v_1, \ldots, v_n \rangle \mid X[v] \mid \ldots$$

Notice that these maps in $\mathcal{V}$ are not uniquely determined unless the functor $\mathit{return}: \mathcal{V} \to \mathcal{C}$ is injective on morphisms. Moreover, two such representations are not necessarily isomorphic in $\mathcal{V}$.

5.3.3 Structural laws

We can also speak of symmetric Freyd multicategories, which are Freyd multicategories $\mathit{return}: \mathcal{V} \to \mathcal{C}$ such that $\mathcal{V}$ and $\mathcal{C}$ are symmetric (Def. 3) and return preserves the renaming structure:

$$\frac{\Gamma_1 \vdash_{\mathcal{V}} v : A}{\Gamma_2 \vdash \mathit{return}(v[f]) \equiv (\mathit{return}(v))[f] : A} \quad (f : \Gamma_1 \xrightarrow{\cong} \Gamma_2)$$

We say that a Freyd multicategory $\mathit{return}: \mathcal{V} \to \mathcal{C}$ is *cartesian* when $\mathcal{V}$ is cartesian as a multicategory (Def. 4), $\mathcal{C}$ is cartesian as a premulticategory (Def. 2), and return preserves the renaming structure. All the examples in Section 5.3.1 are cartesian.

6. Function spaces

We have introduced an equational theory for impure programs (§2) and shown that product and sum types can be characterized by universal properties (§3, 4). We now characterize call-by-value function types by a universal property.

We characterize function types in the context of Freyd multicategories (§5.3) by retracing the steps taken by Power and Thielecke [34]. The key point is that first-class call-by-value functions can delay computations. For instance, in ML the expression

```
fn x => (print "testing" ; 3)
```

does not immediately print: it will only print when applied to an argument. We use Freyd multicategories to distinguish between computations, which can be delayed, and values, which cannot be delayed.

In what follows we will assume that our premulticategories are symmetric, in the sense of Section 2.3. This means that objects in contexts can be reordered. It is clumsy to work with function spaces without this assumption.

6.1 Definition: function spaces

We define the concept of function space in the setting of a symmetric Freyd multicategory (§5.3): a symmetric multicategory $\mathcal{V}$ (values), a symmetric premulticategory $\mathcal{C}$ (computations) and an identity-on-objects morphism of symmetric premulticategories $\mathit{return}: \mathcal{V} \to \mathcal{C}$ such that each $\mathit{return}(v)$ is central.

Let Δ be a list of objects and let A be an object. We will define what it means for the Freyd multicategory to have a function space $(\Delta \Rightarrow A)$. The idea is that the 'inhabitants' of the function space are functions that take a valuation of the context Δ and return a result of type A, perhaps with some side-effects along the way. When Δ is empty then the object $(\Delta \Rightarrow A)$ behaves like a space of delayed computations, like Moggi's monadic type constructor.

We do not have the currying isomorphism in a call-by-value language, and unless the Freyd multicategory has all tensor products we cannot accurately express n-ary functions in terms of unary functions.

Definition 13. A symmetric Freyd multicategory $\mathit{return}: \mathcal{V} \to \mathcal{C}$ has *function spaces* if for every list $\Delta = (x_1 : A_1, \ldots, x_n : A_n)$ and every object B there is an object $(\Delta \Rightarrow B)$ and a morphism $(\Delta \Rightarrow B, \Delta) \to B$ (not necessarily central):

$$\frac{}{f : \Delta \Rightarrow B, x_1 : A_1, \ldots, x_n : A_n \vdash f(\vec{x}) : B}$$

together with an operation on morphisms:

$$\frac{\Gamma, \Delta \vdash t : B}{\Gamma \vdash_{\mathcal{V}} \lambda(\Delta) t : (\Delta \Rightarrow B)} \quad (4)$$

subject to the following equations:

$$\frac{\Gamma, \Delta \vdash t : B}{\Gamma, \Delta \vdash \mathit{return}(\lambda(\vec{x})t) \rightsquigarrow f.\, f(\vec{x}) \equiv t : B}$$

$$\frac{\Gamma \vdash_{\mathcal{V}} v : \Delta \Rightarrow B}{\Gamma \vdash_{\mathcal{V}} \lambda(\vec{x}).\, (\mathit{return}(v) \rightsquigarrow f.\, f(\vec{x})) \equiv v : \Delta \Rightarrow B}$$

We work up to α-equivalence — we consider variables to be informal notation for indices in lists.

6.2 Examples of function spaces

Set theoretic examples. The Freyd multicategory of sets has $\mathcal{V} = \mathcal{C}$ as the multicategory with sets as objects and multivariate functions as morphisms. The function space $(\Delta \Rightarrow B)$ is the set of functions $(\prod \Delta) \to B$. The representing map is the evaluation function, which takes a function and a valuation and evaluates that function.

Recall that the Freyd multicategory of stateful functions has $\mathcal{V}$ as the multicategory of sets and functions and $\mathcal{C}$ as the premulticategory of sets and stateful functions. The function space $(\Delta \Rightarrow B)$ is the set of all stateful functions $\Delta \to B$. Notice that, in particular, the function space $(() \Rightarrow B)$ is the state monad $(S \to B \times S)$.

Given a monad T on the category of sets, recall that the corresponding Freyd multicategory has $\mathcal{V}$ as the multicategory of sets and functions and $\mathcal{C}$ as a premulticategory of sets and Kleisli functions. The function space $(\Delta \Rightarrow B)$ is the set of all functions $(\prod \Delta) \to T(B)$. In particular, the function space $(() \Rightarrow B)$ is isomorphic to the monad T.

Connection to programming languages. The connection with programming languages is hopefully clear. The two equations are variants of the β and η equations which are straightforward observational equivalences in all higher-typed languages. We suggest the following syntactic sugar: let

$$f(t_1, \ldots, t_n) \stackrel{\text{def}}{=} t_1 \rightsquigarrow x_1 \ldots t_n \rightsquigarrow x_n.\, f(\vec{x}). \quad (5)$$

In this 'call-by-value' semantics, expressions are reduced before being passed as arguments.

We certainly have not captured exactly observational equivalence. That is not our aim. Our aim is to identify an equational theory that holds in all good models. Our equations hold in syntactic models and also in more semantic models which are not fully abstract but which are nonetheless useful.

Connections with proof theory. Let us briefly investigate the extent to which the Curry-Howard correspondence is relevant in the call-by-value setting. The rule for λ-abstraction (4) is essentially the right implication rule of the sequent calculus. The syntactic sugar (5) leads to the left rule for implication:

$$\frac{\Gamma \vdash t_1 : A_1 \quad \ldots \quad \Gamma \vdash t_n : A_n \qquad \Gamma, y : B \vdash u : C}{\Gamma, f : (A_1, \ldots, A_n) \Rightarrow B \vdash f(t_1, \ldots, t_n) \rightsquigarrow y.\, u : C}$$

which is clearly not canonical, because it depends on the order of $t_1, \ldots, t_n$. In fact, the explicit let-binding helps us to distinguish different proofs. For example, consider the following two terms:

$$f : A \Rightarrow B, x : A \vdash \mathit{return}(\lambda(y : C).\, (f(x))) : C \Rightarrow B$$
$$f : A \Rightarrow B, x : A \vdash (f(x)) \rightsquigarrow w.\, \mathit{return}(\lambda(y : C).\, w) : C \Rightarrow B$$

If $(f(x))$ is a value, which is an assumption that the language is pure, then these terms are equal. Without this assumption, these are two distinct terms which correspond to two different sequent calculus proofs, as first observed by Herbelin [13].

7. Representability in general

The last two technical sections of this article place our work on a secure abstract foundation.

Throughout this article we have spoken of representability and universal properties on the understanding that these concepts lend a canonical status to various constructions. We now provide a general notion of representability that accounts for the constructions that we have introduced: products, sums and function spaces.

For an ordinary category $\mathcal{C}$ there are two notions of representability that are dual to each other: we can speak of representability for a covariant functor $\mathcal{C} \to \mathbf{Set}$ and of representability for a contravariant functor $\mathcal{C}^{\mathrm{op}} \to \mathbf{Set}$. The covariant notion of representability allows us to describe colimits, and the contravariant notion allows us to describe limits.

The situation is more sophisticated with multicategories, for there is no reasonable notion of 'dual' for multicategories. Thus we must treat the two variances differently. We do this by considering representability for left and right modules of (pre)multicategories.

Very informally, we may say that a left or right module specifies a concept – a concept like product, sum or function. A representation for the module is a first class type that represents the concept.

Throughout this section we work with symmetric premulticategories. This means that we can reorder the contexts, which makes the notation easier.

7.1 Left modules and left representability

We introduce a notion of left module and of representability for premulticategories. This general notion specializes to our characterization of function types.

7.1.1 Definitions and first results

Given a symmetric premulticategory $\mathcal{C}$ we define a *left module* M to be an assignment of a set $M(\Gamma)$ to each list Γ of objects, together with a family of functions

$$\mu_{\Gamma,A,\Delta,\Gamma'} : \mathcal{C}(\Delta;A) \times M(\Gamma,A,\Gamma') \to M(\Gamma,\Delta,\Gamma')$$

satisfying two conditions. We write $\Gamma \vdash_M t$ when $t \in M(\Gamma)$, and we write

$$\frac{\Delta \vdash t : A \qquad \Gamma, x{:}\,A, \Gamma' \vdash_M u}{\Gamma, \Delta, \Gamma' \vdash_M t \overset{M}{\rightsquigarrow} x.\,u}$$

for $\mu_{\Gamma,A,\Delta,\Gamma'}(t,u)$. The two conditions are

$$\frac{\Gamma, x{:}\,A, \Gamma' \vdash_M t}{\Gamma, x{:}\,A, \Gamma' \vdash_M x \overset{M}{\rightsquigarrow} x.\,t \equiv t} \qquad \text{(LM1)}$$

$$\frac{\Gamma_3 \vdash t : A \quad \Gamma_2, x{:}\,A, \Gamma_2' \vdash u : B \quad \Gamma_1, y{:}\,B, \Gamma_1' \vdash_M v}{\Gamma_1, \Gamma_2, \Gamma_3, \Gamma_2', \Gamma_1' \vdash_M t \overset{M}{\rightsquigarrow} x.\,(u \overset{M}{\rightsquigarrow} y.\,v) \equiv (t \rightsquigarrow x.\,u) \overset{M}{\rightsquigarrow} y.\,v} \qquad \text{(LM2)}$$

Representations of left modules. For a fixed object R, we can understand $\mathcal{C}(-;R)$ as a left module.

Definition 14. Let M be a left module for a symmetric premulticategory $\mathcal{C}$. A *representation* of M is an object R of $\mathcal{C}$ together with an isomorphism of left modules:

$$\{\mathcal{C}(\Gamma;R) \cong M(\Gamma)\}_\Gamma$$

(An isomorphism of left modules is a family of bijections that respects the left module structure.)

A representation is always determined by an object R and an element of $M(R)$. To show this, we use the following variant of the Yoneda lemma. (Technically this can be seen an instance of the Yoneda lemma for ordinary categories.)

Proposition 15. *Let M be a left module for a symmetric premulticategory $\mathcal{C}$ and let R be an object. To give a left module morphism $\{\mathcal{C}(\Gamma;R) \to M(\Gamma)\}_\Gamma$ is to give an element of $M(R)$.*

In more detail, given an object R and an element $r \in M(R)$ we have a family of functions $(R,r)_\Gamma : \mathcal{C}(\Gamma;R) \to M(\Gamma)$ given by $(R,r)_\Gamma(t) \overset{\mathrm{def}}{=} t \overset{M}{\rightsquigarrow} x.\,r$:

$$\frac{\Gamma \vdash t : R}{\Gamma \vdash_M t \overset{M}{\rightsquigarrow} x.\,r} \qquad (\text{using} \quad x{:}\,R \vdash_M r).$$

Conversely, given a left module morphism, i.e. a family of functions $\{\phi_\Gamma{:}\,\mathcal{C}(\Gamma;R) \to M(\Gamma)\}_\Gamma$ that respects the left module structure, we recover an element $\phi_R(\mathrm{id}_R)$ of $M(R)$. Proposition 15 says that these two constructions are mutually inverse.

Corollary 16. *Let M be a left module of a symmetric premulticategory. The following data are equivalent.*

- *A representation for M (Def. 14).*
- *An object R and an element $r \in M(x{:}\,R)$ together with a family of functions $\rho_\Gamma : M(\Gamma) \to \mathcal{C}(\Gamma;R)$ notated*

$$\frac{\Gamma \vdash_M t}{\Gamma \vdash \rho t : R}$$

satisfying the following conditions:

$$\frac{\Gamma \vdash_M t}{\Gamma \vdash_M (\rho t) \overset{M}{\rightsquigarrow} x.\,r \equiv t} \qquad \frac{\Gamma \vdash t : R}{\Gamma \vdash \rho(t \overset{M}{\rightsquigarrow} x.\,r) \equiv t : R} \qquad \text{(LR1–2)}$$

Uniqueness of representations.

Proposition 17. *If $(R, r \in M(x{:}\,R))$ is a representation of M and $a \in M(y{:}\,A)$ then there is a unique morphism $t{:}\,(y{:}\,A) \to R$ such that $y{:}\,A \vdash_M a \equiv t \overset{M}{\rightsquigarrow} x.\,r$. In consequence, representations are unique up to unique isomorphism.*

7.1.2 Example: function spaces

In Section 6 we defined a notion of function space for Freyd multicategories *return*: $\mathcal{V} \to \mathcal{C}$. Given a context Δ and an object B, we define a module M for $\mathcal{V}$ as follows:

$$M(\Gamma) \overset{\mathrm{def}}{=} \mathcal{C}(\Gamma, \Delta; B).$$

The module structure μ is defined in terms of the premulticategory structure of $\mathcal{C}$:

$$\frac{\Gamma_2 \vdash_{\mathcal{V}} v : A \qquad \Gamma_1, x{:}\,A, \Gamma_1' \vdash_M u}{\Gamma_1, \Gamma_2, \Gamma_1' \vdash_M (v \overset{M}{\rightsquigarrow} x.\,u) \overset{\mathrm{def}}{=} (\mathit{return}(v) \rightsquigarrow x.\,u)}$$

The two conditions LM1–2 are immediately verified.

The data for a left representation is exactly the data for a function space $(\Delta \Rightarrow B)$. The axioms LR1–2 are exactly the axioms for function spaces in Section 6.1.

7.1.3 Centrality in terms of module morphisms

We briefly remark that left modules provide a more abstract account of centrality. Recall that a morphism t is central if it commutes with all morphisms: for all u and v, $t \rightsquigarrow x.\,u \rightsquigarrow y.\,v \equiv u \rightsquigarrow y.\,t \rightsquigarrow x.\,v$. This can be explained in a more abstract way as follows. Every morphism $t{:}\,\Delta \to A$ determines a family of functions between sets of morphisms:

$$(t \rightsquigarrow x.\,-) : \mathcal{C}(\Gamma, x{:}\,A; B) \to \mathcal{C}(\Gamma, \Delta; B)$$

The domain and codomain have an obvious left module structure, and the morphism t is central if and only if this family of functions is a left module morphism for all B.

7.2 Right modules and right representability

We now provide a notion of right module, which is an account of composing on the right. The induced notion of representability accounts for the product and sum types that we introduced in Sections 3 and 4.

7.2.1 Definitions and first results

Given a symmetric premulticategory $\mathcal{C}$ we define a *right module* M to be an assignment of a set $M(\Gamma; A)$ to each list Γ and each object A, together with for each B the structure of a left module (§7.1.1)

$$\mu_{\Gamma,A,\Delta,\Gamma';B} : \mathcal{C}(\Delta; A) \times M(\Gamma, A, \Gamma'; B) \to M(\Gamma, \Delta, \Gamma'; B)$$

and also a family of functions

$$\bar{\mu}_{\Gamma,\Delta,A,\Gamma';B} : M(\Delta; A) \times \mathcal{C}(\Gamma, A, \Gamma'; B) \to M(\Gamma, \Delta, \Gamma'; B)$$

satisfying three conditions. We use the following notation: we write $\Gamma \vdash_M t : A$ if $t \in M(\Gamma; A)$, and we write

$$\frac{\Delta \vdash t : A \quad \Gamma, x{:}A, \Gamma' \vdash_M u : B}{\Gamma, \Delta, \Gamma' \vdash_M t \overset{M}{\leadsto} x.\, u : B} \qquad \frac{\Delta \vdash_M t : A \quad \Gamma, x{:}A, \Gamma' \vdash u : B}{\Gamma, \Delta, \Gamma' \vdash_M t \overset{M}{\leadsto} x.\, u : B}$$

for $\mu_{\Gamma,A,\Delta,\Gamma';B}(t, u)$ and $\bar{\mu}_{\Gamma,A,\Delta,\Gamma';B}(t, u)$ respectively. The three conditions (in addition to LM1 and LM2) are

$$\frac{\Gamma \vdash_M t : A}{\Gamma \vdash_M t \overset{M}{\leadsto} x.\, x \equiv t : A} \tag{RM1}$$

$$\frac{\Gamma_3 \vdash_M t : A \quad \Gamma_2, x{:}A, \Gamma_2' \vdash u : B \quad \Gamma_1, y{:}B, \Gamma_1' \vdash v : C}{\Gamma_1, \Gamma_2, \Gamma_3, \Gamma_2', \Gamma_1' \vdash_M (t \overset{M}{\leadsto} x.\, u) \overset{M}{\leadsto} y.\, v \equiv t \overset{M}{\leadsto} x.\, (u \leadsto y.\, v) : C} \tag{RM2}$$

$$\frac{\Gamma_3 \vdash t : A \quad \Gamma_2, x{:}A, \Gamma_2' \vdash_M u : B \quad \Gamma_1, y{:}B, \Gamma_1' \vdash v : C}{\Gamma_1, \Gamma_2, \Gamma_3, \Gamma_2', \Gamma_1' \vdash_M (t \overset{M}{\leadsto} x.\, u) \overset{M}{\leadsto} y.\, v \equiv t \overset{M}{\leadsto} x.\, (u \overset{M}{\leadsto} y.\, v) : C} \tag{RM3}$$

The last condition, RM3, specifies that the left (μ) and right ($\bar{\mu}$) structures associate with each other. Technically, our notion of right module can be seen as an instance of a general concept in locally indexed category theory and the self construction (see [23, §9.3.4, §9.3.6]).

Representations of right modules. For a fixed object R, the assignment $M(\Gamma; A) = \mathcal{C}(\Gamma, R; A)$ can be made into a right module in a straightforward way.

Definition 18. Let M be a right module for a premulticategory $\mathcal{C}$. A *representation of* M is an object R of $\mathcal{C}$ together with an isomorphism of right modules

$$\{\mathcal{C}(\Gamma, R; A) \cong M(\Gamma; A)\}_{\Gamma,A}$$

(An isomorphism of right modules is a family of bijections that respects the right module structure — that is, both μ and $\bar{\mu}$.)

A representation is always determined by an object R and an element of $M(R)$. This follows from a new variant of the Yoneda lemma, for which we need the following definition.

Definition 19. Let M be a right module for a premulticategory. An element $t \in M(\Gamma_1; A)$ is *central* if it satisfies the following equations:

$$\frac{\Gamma_2 \vdash u : B \quad \Delta_1, x{:}A, \Delta_2, y{:}B, \Delta_3 \vdash v : C}{\Delta_1, \Gamma_1, \Delta_2, \Gamma_2, \Delta_3 \vdash_M t \overset{M}{\leadsto} x.\, (u \leadsto y.\, v) \equiv u \overset{M}{\leadsto} y.\, (t \overset{M}{\leadsto} x.\, v) : C}$$

$$\frac{\Gamma_2 \vdash u : B \quad \Delta_1, y{:}B, \Delta_2, x{:}A, \Delta_3 \vdash v : C}{\Delta_1, \Gamma_2, \Delta_2, \Gamma_1, \Delta_3 \vdash_M t \overset{M}{\leadsto} x.\, (u \leadsto y.\, v) \equiv u \overset{M}{\leadsto} y.\, (t \overset{M}{\leadsto} x.\, v) : C}$$

Proposition 20. *Let M be a right module of a symmetric premulticategory $\mathcal{C}$ and let R be an object. To give a right module morphism $\{\mathcal{C}(\Gamma, R; A) \to M(\Gamma; A)\}_{\Gamma,A}$ is to give a central element in $M((); R)$.*

Corollary 21. *Let M be a right module of a symmetric premulticategory. The following data are equivalent.*

- *A representation for M (Def. 18).*
- *An object R and a central element $r \in M((); R)$ together with a family of functions $\rho_{\Gamma,A} : M(\Gamma; A) \to \mathcal{C}(\Gamma, R; A)$ notated*

$$\frac{\Gamma \vdash_M t : A}{\Gamma, x{:}R \vdash \rho(x, t) : A}$$

satisfying the following conditions:

$$\frac{\Gamma \vdash_M t : A}{\Gamma \vdash_M r \overset{M}{\leadsto} x.\, \rho(x, t) \equiv t : A} \tag{RR1}$$

$$\frac{\Gamma, x{:}R \vdash t : A}{\Gamma, x{:}R \vdash \rho(x, r \overset{M}{\leadsto} x.\, t) \equiv t : A} \tag{RR2}$$

Uniqueness of representations.

Proposition 22. *If $(R, r \in M((), R))$ is a representation of M and $a \in M((); A)$ then there is a unique morphism $t{:}\,(x{:}\,R) \to A$ in $\mathcal{C}$ such that $- \vdash_M r \overset{M}{\leadsto} x.\, t \equiv a : A$. If a is central then so is t.*

In consequence, representations are unique up to unique isomorphism and the unique mediating isomorphism is central.

7.2.2 Examples: products and sums

- Given a list Δ, define a right module M_Δ by

$$M_\Delta(\Gamma; A) \overset{\text{def}}{=} \mathcal{C}(\Gamma, \Delta; A).$$

  A representation for M_Δ is a tensor product $\otimes\Delta$ in the sense of Section 3.1.

- Given a constructor context Δ (§4.1), define a right module M^Δ by $M^\Delta(\Gamma; A) \overset{\text{def}}{=} \prod_{c \in dom(\Delta)} \mathcal{C}(\Gamma, \Delta(c); A)$. A representation for M^Δ is a sum $\oplus\Delta$ in the sense of Section 4.1.

8. Premonoidal categories and monads

In Section 2 we defined premulticategories as a notion of model for an impure programming language with variables and let-binding. We argue that this is the primitive setting for studying call-by-value impure programming languages.

In Sections 3 and 4 we showed that products and sums can be characterized by a universal property, which means that they are unique up to unique isomorphism. In Section 6 we provided a similar universal property for function spaces.

We now justify our work by showing that it subsumes earlier axiomatizations of call-by-value programming languages: the premonoidal and Freyd categories of Power and Robinson [33] and the monadic models of Moggi [30].

- We show that a premonoidal category is essentially the same thing as a premulticategory with tensor products.
- We show that a Freyd category is essentially the same thing as a cartesian Freyd multicategory with tensor products.
- We show that a strong monad on a category with finite products is essentially the same thing as a cartesian Freyd multicategory with tensor products and function types with empty domain.
- We show that a λ_C-model is essentially the same thing as a cartesian Freyd multicategory with tensor products and all function types.

The last three facts can be deduced from the first one by building on earlier work by Levy, Power and Thielecke [24].

8.1 Premonoidal categories

We now recall the notion of premonoidal category. Before we begin, we give some concrete examples. The category of sets and functions is a premonoidal category, with the product of sets forming a premonoidal structure. Indeed, any monoidal category is a premonoidal category. But the motivating example is the Kleisli category for a monad. Let T be a monad on the category of sets. Recall that the Kleisli category of T has objects sets and that morphisms $A \to B$ are functions $A \to T(B)$. The product of sets induces a premonoidal structure on this Kleisli category which is typically not monoidal.

In Section 8.2 we will show how to convert a premulticategory to a premonoidal category. This will suggest a premonoidal category built from the syntax of a programming language.

Our definition of premonoidal category is streamlined by taking things up a level: we take advantage of a multicategory whose objects are themselves categories. We start by defining strict premonoidal categories, and move gradually to premonoidal categories.

8.1.1 A multicategory of categories

We organize the collection of all ordinary categories into a symmetric multicategory $\mathbf{Cat}_{\mathrm{m}}$. The objects of the multicategory $\mathbf{Cat}_{\mathrm{m}}$ are themselves ordinary categories, and so our contexts Γ are lists of categories. A morphism $F : \Gamma \to \mathcal{A}$ in $\mathbf{Cat}_{\mathrm{m}}$ is defined to be a mapping that is functorial in each argument. For instance, if $\Gamma = (\mathcal{B}, \mathcal{C})$ then for each pair of objects B and C, respectively from $\mathcal{B}$ and $\mathcal{C}$, an object $F(B,C)$ of $\mathcal{A}$ must be given, and this must extend to families of functors $F(-,C) : \mathcal{B} \to \mathcal{A}$ and $F(B,-) : \mathcal{C} \to \mathcal{A}$ (but not necessarily a functor $\mathcal{B} \times \mathcal{C} \to \mathcal{A}$).

This multicategory has tensor products [11] and this structure has been used in various areas, from rewriting theory [36] to bunched implications [31, Ex. 14].

8.1.2 Strict premonoidal categories

Before turning to premonoidal categories in general, we define strict premonoidal categories. A strict premonoidal category [33] is a monoid in the multicategory $\mathbf{Cat}_{\mathrm{m}}$. A monoid in a multicategory is an object $\mathcal{A}$ with morphisms $- \vdash i : \mathcal{A}$ and $x{:}\mathcal{A}, y{:}\mathcal{A} \vdash x \odot y : \mathcal{A}$ satisfying the monoid laws:

$$\begin{gathered} y{:}\mathcal{A} \vdash i \rightsquigarrow x.\, x \odot y \equiv y : \mathcal{A} \qquad x{:}\mathcal{A} \vdash i \rightsquigarrow y.\, x \odot y \equiv x : \mathcal{A} \\ x, y, z : \mathcal{A} \vdash x \odot y \rightsquigarrow w.\, w \odot z \equiv y \odot z \rightsquigarrow w.\, x \odot w : \mathcal{A}. \end{gathered} \tag{6}$$

In $\mathbf{Cat}_{\mathrm{m}}$, the morphism $i : () \to \mathcal{A}$ is the same thing as an object of the category $\mathcal{A}$. The construction $\odot : (\mathcal{A}, \mathcal{A}) \to \mathcal{A}$ is not a functor $\mathcal{A} \times \mathcal{A} \to \mathcal{A}$ from the product of categories, but rather a construction that is functorial in each argument.

8.1.3 Central morphisms

Just as central morphisms play a crucial role in premulticategories, they also play an important role in the theory of premonoidal categories.

We begin by recalling that a *binoidal category* [33] is a category $\mathcal{A}$ together with a morphism $\odot : (\mathcal{A}, \mathcal{A}) \to \mathcal{A}$ in the multicategory $\mathbf{Cat}_{\mathrm{m}}$. For each object C and each morphism $f{:}A \to B$ we have morphisms $(f \odot C) : A \odot C \to B \odot C$ and $(C \odot f) : C \odot A \to C \odot B$. Given morphisms $f{:}A \to B$, $g{:}C \to D$ in $\mathcal{A}$ we thus have two morphisms $A \odot C \to B \odot D$:

$$A \odot C \xrightarrow{f \odot C} B \odot C \xrightarrow{B \odot g} B \odot D \qquad A \odot C \xrightarrow{A \odot g} A \odot D \xrightarrow{f \odot D} B \odot D$$

If these are equal, we say that f and g commute. A morphism in a binoidal category is *central* if it commutes with all morphisms.

8.1.4 Premonoidal categories

In the multicategory $\mathbf{Cat}_{\mathrm{m}}$ the sets of morphisms $(\mathcal{A}_1 \ldots \mathcal{A}_n) \to \mathcal{B}$ can themselves be considered as categories. Given morphisms $F, G : (\mathcal{A}_1 \ldots \mathcal{A}_n) \to \mathcal{B}$, a 2-cell $\alpha{:}F \to G$ comprises a family of morphisms $\alpha_{\vec{A}}{:}F(\vec{A}) \to G(\vec{A})$ in $\mathcal{B}$ indexed by lists of objects $(A_1 \ldots A_n)$ from categories $\mathcal{A}_1 \ldots \mathcal{A}_n$ respectively, that is natural in each argument. With this in mind, we can weaken (6) by replacing the equalities with central natural isomorphisms.

Definition 23 ([33]). A *premonoidal category* is a binoidal category $(\mathcal{A}, \odot : (\mathcal{A}, \mathcal{A}) \to \mathcal{A})$ with an object i and central natural isomorphisms

$$\lambda_y : i \odot y \cong y \qquad \rho_x : x \odot i \cong x \qquad \alpha_{x,y,z} : (x \odot y) \odot z \cong x \odot (y \odot z)$$

that make the following triangle and pentagon laws hold:

$$(i \odot x) \odot y \xrightarrow{\alpha_{i,x,y}} i \odot (x \odot y) \xrightarrow{\lambda_{x \odot y}} x \odot y \;=\; (i \odot x) \odot y \xrightarrow{(\lambda_x \odot y)} x \odot y$$

$$(x \odot y) \odot i \xrightarrow{\alpha_{x,y,i}} x \odot (y \odot i) \xrightarrow{x \odot \rho_y} x \odot y \;=\; (x \odot y) \odot i \xrightarrow{\rho_{x \odot y}} x \odot y$$

$$((wx)y)z \xrightarrow{(\alpha_{w,x,y}) \odot z} (w(xy))z \xrightarrow{\alpha_{w,x \odot y,z}} w((xy)z) \xrightarrow{w \odot \alpha_{x,y,z}} w(x(yz)) \;=\; ((wx)y)z \xrightarrow{\alpha_{w \odot x,y,z}} (wx)(yz) \xrightarrow{\alpha_{w,x,y \odot z}} w(x(yz))$$

Note that while the centrality of λ, ρ, and α is reasonable from a pragmatic perspective, it is ad hoc in that it does not come from the analysis of $\mathbf{Cat}_{\mathrm{m}}$ as a 2-multicategory.

8.1.5 Coherence

The definition of premonoidal category is not based on universal properties and so, a priori, there is nothing canonical about λ, ρ and α. A canonical status is given by the coherence theorem (Proposition 25) which characterizes the morphisms that can be built from λ, ρ and α.

Definition 24. Let $\mathbb{A}$ be a set. An *object-string* is generated from the grammar

$$S, T ::= i \mid (S \odot T) \mid A \quad (A \in \mathbb{A}).$$

such that each element of the set $\mathbb{A}$ appears exactly once. An *isomorphism-string* between object-strings, $f : S \to T$, is a string that is built using composition, $\odot$, λ, ρ, α and their inverses, subject to the obvious well-formedness condition.

Proposition 25 ([33]). *Let S and T be object-strings. All isomorphism strings $f, g : S \cong T$ are equal when interpreted in any premonoidal category.*

Coherence theorems like this form an important part of the category theory literature. Nonetheless we contend that it is more desirable that the structure arises a priori from universal properties, which is the content of our main theorem (Theorem 26). For one thing, the universal properties place the structure closer to programming language syntax.

8.2 Main theorem

Our main theorem provides a connection between premulticategories with tensor products and premonoidal categories. It is a variation of the established connection between multicategories with tensor products and monoidal categories [14, 22].

Theorem 26. *Let $\mathbb{A}$ be a set. The following data are equivalent.*

1. *A premulticategory with tensor products whose objects are $\mathbb{A}$.*
2. *A premonoidal category whose objects are $\mathbb{A}$.*

This section is devoted to the proof of this theorem. We begin with the following straightforward property of tensor products in premulticategories.

Proposition 27. *A premulticategory has all tensor products if and only if it has tensor products of the empty list and of every two element list.*

Of course, it is sometime useful to have explicit n-ary product types, but the universal property tells us that any two implementations are canonically isomorphic.

From a premulticategory to a premonoidal category. Given a premulticategory $\mathcal{C}$ with tensor products, we define a premonoidal category. A morphism $f: A \to B$ in the premonoidal category is a morphism $f:(A) \to B$ in $\mathcal{C}$. Composition and identities are immediately derived from the premulticategory too.

The unit of the premonoidal structure is $\otimes()$, and the premonoidal tensor $A \odot C$ is the tensor product $\otimes(A, C)$ in the premulticategory. This can be made into a binoidal structure: given $x{:}\,A \vdash f : B$ and $y{:}\,C \vdash g : D$, let

$$f \odot C \stackrel{\text{def}}{=} z{:}\otimes(A,C) \vdash z \twoheadleftarrow \langle x,y\rangle.\, f \leadsto x'.\langle x',y\rangle : \otimes(B,C)$$

$$A \odot g \stackrel{\text{def}}{=} z{:}\otimes(A,C) \vdash z \twoheadleftarrow \langle x,y\rangle.\, g \leadsto y'.\langle x,y'\rangle : \otimes(A,D)$$

One verifies that this structure is functorial (preserves composition and identities) by some algebraic manipulation using the axioms for premulticategories, which we omit for brevity.

Having the binoidal structure in place we can note that the two notions of centrality are related:

Proposition 28. *A morphism $f:(A) \to B$ in a premulticategory is central (§2.1) if and only if it is central in the induced binoidal category (§8.1.3).*

(This is deduced by algebraic manipulation.)

The coherence isomorphisms in the premonoidal category are defined by

$$\lambda_B \stackrel{\text{def}}{=} z{:}\,(\otimes(\otimes(),B)) \vdash z \twoheadleftarrow \langle x,y\rangle.\, x \twoheadleftarrow \langle\rangle.\, y : B$$

$$\rho_A \stackrel{\text{def}}{=} z{:}\,(\otimes(A,\otimes())) \vdash z \twoheadleftarrow \langle x,y\rangle.\, y \twoheadleftarrow \langle\rangle.\, x : A$$

$$\alpha_{A,B,C} \stackrel{\text{def}}{=} xyz{:}\,(\otimes(\otimes(A,B),C)) \vdash$$
$$xyz \twoheadleftarrow \langle xy,z\rangle.\, xy \twoheadleftarrow \langle x,y\rangle.\langle x,\langle y,z\rangle\rangle : (\otimes(A,\otimes(B,C)))$$

Again, some algebraic manipulation is needed to show that these morphisms are isomorphisms, that they are central, that they are natural, and that they satisfy the coherence diagrams.

From a premonoidal category to a premulticategory. We begin with some remarks about contexts in a premonoidal category. A list of objects determines an object $|\Gamma|$ of the premonoidal category:

$$|A_1, A_2, A_3, \ldots, A_n| \stackrel{\text{def}}{=} ((((A_1 \odot A_2) \odot A_3) \cdots \odot A_n) \odot I.$$

In particular, $|\varnothing| = I$ and $|A| = A \odot I$. We often need to concatenate lists. The coherence result (Prop. 25) gives us a canonical central isomorphism between $|\Gamma, \Delta|$ and $|\Gamma| \odot |\Delta|$. (The objects are typically not identical.)

Given a premonoidal category, we define a premulticategory with the same objects. A morphism $\Gamma \to A$ in the premulticategory is a morphism $|\Gamma| \to A$ in the premonoidal category. The identity morphisms $(A) \to A$ in the premulticategory are the right identity isomorphisms $A \odot I \to A$ in the premonoidal category. For composition, given $t{:}\,|\Delta| \to A$ and $u{:}\,|\Gamma, x{:}\,A, \Gamma'| \to B$ we let $(t \leadsto x.\,u)$ be the following composite:

$$|\Gamma, \Delta, \Gamma'| \cong (|\Gamma| \odot |\Delta|) \odot |\Gamma'| \xrightarrow{(|\Gamma|\odot t)\odot|\Gamma'|} (|\Gamma| \odot A) \odot |\Gamma'|$$
$$\cong |\Gamma, A, \Gamma'| \xrightarrow{u} B$$

where the unlabelled isomorphisms are the canonical coherence isomorphisms in the premonoidal category.

The identity and associativity laws for premulticategories follow from the centrality and canonicity of the coherence isomorphisms.

Proposition 29. *A morphism $t{:}\,|\Gamma| \to A$ in a premonoidal category is central in the premonoidal category if and only if it is central in the induced premulticategory.*

The tensor product of the premulticategory is straightforward: for any list Δ, let $\otimes\Delta \stackrel{\text{def}}{=} |\Delta|$. The universal morphism $\Delta \to |\Delta|$ is the identity morphism. Given $t{:}\,|\Gamma, \Delta, \Gamma'| \to B$ we let

$$y \twoheadleftarrow \langle\vec{x}\rangle.\, t \stackrel{\text{def}}{=} |\Gamma, y{:}\otimes\Delta, \Gamma'| \cong |\Gamma, \Delta, \Gamma'| \xrightarrow{t} B.$$

Again, the unlabelled isomorphism is the canonical coherence isomorphism. The two laws for tensor products follow from the centrality and canonicity of the coherence isomorphisms.

Equivalence. In the statement of Theorem 26, when we say that the two notions are equivalent, we do not mean that they are exactly the same. Rather, we mean that if we begin with a premulticategory $\mathcal{C}$, build a premonoidal category, and then recover a premulticategory from the premonoidal category, we recover a premulticategory that is canonically isomorphic to $\mathcal{C}$. Conversely, if we begin with a premonoidal category $\mathcal{C}$, and then build a premulticategory out of it, and then recover a premonoidal category from the premulticategory, we recover a premonoidal category that is isomorphic to $\mathcal{C}$. In this sense, the two notions are equivalent.

This concludes our proof of Theorem 26.

8.3 Corollaries of the main theorem

We conclude this paper by building on the main theorem (Theorem 26) to recover new universal characterizations of various models from the literature.

Structural laws. Power and Robinson [33] define a *symmetric premonoidal category* to be a premonoidal category with a central natural isomorphism $\{s_{A,B}{:}\,A \odot B \to B \odot A\}_{A,B}$ satisfying coherence conditions.

Proposition 30. *To give a symmetric premonoidal category is to give a symmetric premulticategory (Def. 3) with tensor products.*

Sums and predistributive categories. Power and Robinson [33] define a *predistributive category* to be a premonoidal category with finite coproducts in which the functors $A \odot (-)$ and $(-) \odot A$ preserve finite coproducts for all objects A.

Proposition 31. *To give a predistributive category is to give a premulticategory with all tensor products and sums (§4).*

Multicategories and monoidal categories. We turn to the well-known representation theorem for multicategories [14, 22]. Recall that a multicategory is a premulticategory in which all morphisms are central (§2.1). Similarly, a monoidal category is a premonoidal category (§8.1.4) in which all morphisms are central (§8.1.3).

Proposition 32 (c.f. [14])**.**

1. *A premulticategory with tensor products is a multicategory if and only if the corresponding premonoidal category is a monoidal category.*
2. *To give a symmetric multicategory (Def. 3) with tensor products is to give a symmetric monoidal category.*
3. *To give a cartesian multicategory (Def. 4) with tensor products is to give a category with finite products.*

Freyd multicategories and Freyd categories. We now connect our analysis of values (§5) with the notion of Freyd category [23, 24, 34]. A Freyd category is defined to be an identity-on-objects premonoidal functor $\mathcal{V} \to \mathcal{C}$ from a category $\mathcal{V}$ with cartesian products to a premonoidal category $\mathcal{C}$.

Proposition 33. *To give a Freyd category is to give a cartesian Freyd multicategory (§5.3.3) that has tensor products (§5.3.2).*

Strong monads and function spaces. We now use the known connections between closed Freyd categories and monads [24, 34] to provide a universal characterization for Moggi's monads in computation [30] .

Proposition 34. *Let $\mathcal{V}$ be a symmetric multicategory with all tensors. Let $Mon(\mathcal{V})$ be the corresponding symmetric monoidal category (Proposition 32). The following data are equivalent:*

1. *A strong monad on $Mon(\mathcal{V})$.*
2. *A symmetric Freyd multicategory $\mathcal{V} \to \mathcal{C}$ that has function spaces with empty domain $(() \Rightarrow A)$ (§6.1).*

Proof outline. From 1 to 2, let $\mathcal{C}$ be the Kleisli premulticategory for the monad (§2.2). From 2 to 1, a monad on $\mathcal{V}$ is given by the construction $T(A) \stackrel{\text{def}}{=} (() \Rightarrow A)$. □

Moggi [29] models a call-by-value functional programming language by a λ_C-model, which is a strong monad on a category with products and with certain 'Kleisli' function spaces. We now give this a universal status by exhibiting an equivalent definition using premulticategories.

Proposition 35. *Let $\mathcal{V}$ be a cartesian multicategory with tensor products. Let $Mon(\mathcal{V})$ be the corresponding category with finite products (Proposition 32). The following data are equivalent.*

1. *A λ_C-model structure for $Mon(\mathcal{V})$.*
2. *A cartesian Freyd multicategory $\mathcal{V} \to \mathcal{C}$ with tensor products and function spaces.*

9. Concluding remarks

We have given universal properties for type constructions in impure programming languages: products, sums, and function spaces. We have done this using the novel notion of premulticategory, which is a basic equational account of impure computation. We have shown that monads and premonoidal categories can be understood from this point of view and hence given a canonical status.

Acknowledgments

S Staton partly supported by the Isaac Newton Trust and ERC Grant ECSYM. PB Levy supported by EPSRC Advanced Research Fellowship EP/E056091/1.

References

[1] M. Abadi, L. Cardelli, P.-L. Curien, and J.-J. Lévy. Explicit substitutions. *J. Funct. Program.*, 1(4):375–416, 1991.

[2] T. Altenkirch, J. Chapman, and T. Uustalu. Monads need not be endofunctors. In *FOSSACS'10*, pages 297–311, 2010.

[3] R. Atkey. What is a categorical model of arrows? In *Proc. MSFP'08*, pages 19–37, 2011.

[4] P. N. Benton and P. Wadler. Linear logic, monads and the lambda calculus. In *Proc. LICS'96*, pages 420–431, 1996.

[5] A. Burroni. T-categories (catégories dans un triple). *Cahiers Topologie Géom. Différentielle*, 12(3):215–312, 1971.

[6] A. Burroni. Higher dimensional word problem. In *Proc. CTCS'91*, pages 94–105, 1991.

[7] P.-L. Curien. Operads, clones, and distributive laws. In *Operads and Universal Algebra*, 2010.

[8] J. Egger, R. E. Møgelberg, and A. Simpson. Enriching an effect calculus with linear types. In *Proc. CSL'09*, pages 240–254, 2009.

[9] M. P. Fiore. Semantic analysis of normalisation by evaluation for typed lambda calculus. In *Proc. PPDP'02*, pages 26–37, 2002.

[10] C. Flanagan, A. Sabry, B. F. Duba, and M. Felleisen. The essence of compiling with continuations. In *Proc. PLDI'93*, pages 237–247, 1993.

[11] F. Foltz, C. Lair, and G. M. Kelly. Algebraic categories with few monoidal biclosed structures or none. *J. Pure and Applied Algebra*, 17:171–177, 1980.

[12] C. Führmann. Direct models of the computational lambda-calculus. In *Proc. MFPS XV*, pages 147–172, 1999.

[13] H. Herbelin. A lambda-calculus structure isomorphic to Gentzen-style sequent calculus structure. In *Proc. CSL'94*, pages 61–75, 1994.

[14] C. Hermida. Representable multicategories. *Advances in Mathematics*, 151:164–225, 2000.

[15] M. Hyland. Multicategories in and around algebra and logic. Invited talk, TACL'09. Slides available from the author's home page, 2009.

[16] B. Jacobs. Semantics of weakening and contraction. *Annals of Pure and Applied Logic*, 69(1):73 – 106, 1994.

[17] B. Jacobs and I. Hasuo. Freyd is Kleisli, for arrows. In *Proc. MSFP'06*, 2006.

[18] A. Jeffrey. Premonoidal categories and a graphical view of programs. Unpublished, 1997.

[19] A. Kock. Monads on symmetric monoidal closed categories. *Archiv der Math.*, 21:1–10, 1970.

[20] Y. Lafont. Towards an algebraic theory of Boolean circuits. *J. Pure Appl. Algebra*, 184(2–3):257–310, 2003.

[21] J. Lambek. Deductive systems and categories II. In *Category theory, homology theory and their applications*, volume 86 of *LNM*, pages 76–122. Springer, 1969.

[22] T. Leinster. *Higher operads, higher categories*. CUP, 2004.

[23] P. B. Levy. *Call-by-push-value*. Springer, 2004.

[24] P. B. Levy, J. Power, and H. Thielecke. Modelling environments in call-by-value programming languages. *Inform. Comput.*, 2003.

[25] F. Linton. Autonomous equational categories. *Indiana Univ. Math. J.*, 15:637–642, 1966.

[26] G. McCusker. A fully abstract relational model of syntactic control of interference. In *Proc. CSL'02*, pages 247–261, 2002.

[27] P. Melliès and N. Tabareau. Linear continuations and duality. `hal.archives-ouvertes.fr/hal-00339156`, 2008.

[28] R. E. Møgelberg and S. Staton. Linearly-used state in models of call-by-value. In *CALCO'11*, pages 298–313, 2011.

[29] E. Moggi. Computational lambda-calculus and monads. In *LICS'89*, pages 14–23, 1989.

[30] E. Moggi. Notions of computation and monads. *Inform. Comput.*, 93 (1), 1991.

[31] P. W. O'Hearn. On bunched typing. *J. Funct. Program.*, 13(4):747–796, 2003.

[32] J. Power. Premonoidal categories as categories with algebraic structure. *Theor. Comput. Sci.*, 278(1–2):303–321, 2002.

[33] J. Power and E. Robinson. Premonoidal categories and notions of computation. *Math. Struct. Comput. Sci.*, 7(5):453–468, 1997.

[34] J. Power and H. Thielecke. Closed Freyd- and kappa-categories. In *Proc. ICALP'99*, 1999.

[35] U. S. Reddy. Global state considered unnecessary: An introduction to object-based semantics. *Lisp and Symbolic Computation*, 9(1):7–76, 1996.

[36] J. G. Stell. Modelling term rewriting systems by sesqui-categories. Technical Report TR94-02, Keele University, 1994.

The Power of Parameterization in Coinductive Proof

Chung-Kil Hur
Microsoft Research
gil@microsoft.com

Georg Neis
MPI-SWS & Saarland University
neis@mpi-sws.org

Derek Dreyer
MPI-SWS
dreyer@mpi-sws.org

Viktor Vafeiadis
MPI-SWS
viktor@mpi-sws.org

Abstract

Coinduction is one of the most basic concepts in computer science. It is therefore surprising that the commonly-known lattice-theoretic accounts of the principles underlying coinductive proofs are lacking in two key respects: they do not support *compositional* reasoning (*i.e.,* breaking proofs into separate pieces that can be developed in isolation), and they do not support *incremental* reasoning (*i.e.,* developing proofs interactively by starting from the goal and generalizing the coinduction hypothesis repeatedly as necessary).

In this paper, we show how to support coinductive proofs that are both compositional and incremental, using a dead simple construction we call the *parameterized greatest fixed point*. The basic idea is to parameterize the greatest fixed point of interest over the *accumulated knowledge* of "the proof so far". While this idea has been proposed before, by Winskel in 1989 and by Moss in 2001, neither of the previous accounts suggests its general applicability to improving the state of the art in interactive coinductive proof.

In addition to presenting the lattice-theoretic foundations of parameterized coinduction, demonstrating its utility on representative examples, and studying its composition with "up-to" techniques, we also explore its mechanization in proof assistants like Coq and Isabelle. Unlike traditional approaches to mechanizing coinduction (*e.g.,* Coq's `cofix`), which employ *syntactic* "guardedness checking", parameterized coinduction offers a *semantic* account of guardedness. This leads to faster and more robust proof development, as we demonstrate using our new Coq library, *Paco*.

Categories and Subject Descriptors D.3.1 [*Programming Languages*]: Formal Definitions and Theory; F.4.1 [*Mathematical Logic and Formal Languages*]: Mathematical Logic

Keywords Coinduction, simulation, parameterized greatest fixed point, compositionality, lattice theory, interactive theorem proving

1. Introduction

Coinduction is one of the most basic concepts in computer science. Coinductive proofs, especially those based on *simulation* arguments, are relevant in many settings where one wishes to model infinitary properties or recursive behaviors [13, 18]. It is therefore surprising that the commonly-known lattice-theoretic accounts of the principles underlying coinductive proofs are lacking in two key respects: they do not support *compositional* reasoning (*i.e.,* breaking proofs into separate pieces that can be developed in isolation), and they do not support *incremental* reasoning (*i.e.,* developing proofs interactively by starting from the goal and generalizing the coinduction hypothesis repeatedly as necessary).

The Trouble with Compositionality. Consider, for instance, two possibly non-terminating, mutually recursive but loosely coupled functions, f and g, which we would like to show equivalent to another pair of recursive functions, f' and g'. Ideally, we should be able to reason about each function separately. That is, we should be able to prove that $f \simeq f'$ entails $g \simeq g'$, and similarly that $g \simeq g'$ entails $f \simeq f'$, and somehow derive from those two entailments that $(f, g) \simeq (f', g')$. The problem, however, is that this type of circular reasoning (aka "rely-guarantee"-style reasoning) is unsound in general. For example, if $f = g$ and $f' = g'$, then we would be able to derive $f \simeq f'$ from a tautology.

One way to avoid this kind of unsound circularity is by placing a syntactic *guardedness* restriction on the proofs of each of the entailments, ensuring that their hypotheses are only used after the definitions of the functions in their conclusions have been unfolded. This is the approach taken, for instance, by Coq's `cofix` tactic for coinduction [3]. Unfortunately, the limitation of using a *syntactic* criterion is that it is inherently non-compositional: it requires one to have access to the *proof* of each of the component entailments in order to determine whether the whole coinductive argument is valid. Moreover, as we explain in more detail in Section 7.3, the syntactic nature of guardedness checking makes proof checking severely inefficient and interacts poorly with other tactics. What we would really like instead is a more *semantic* account of guardedness checking, by which the guardedness condition is reflected directly in the statement of the entailment being proved, rather than being relegated to a syntactic property of the proof itself.

The Desire for Incrementality. Consider the transition system shown in Figure 1, and suppose we want to show that there is an infinite path starting from node a.

Let us first try to imitate a model checker and explore all paths starting from a in a depth-first fashion. For the first step, there is only one choice: the edge $a \to b$. Then at b, we have two choices. Perhaps we can try $b \to c$, but this will soon lead to a dead end, at which point we will have to backtrack. So let us follow the edge $b \to d$ instead. Then, we follow $d \to b$ and we are back to a node we have already visited. We have discovered a cycle, and thus an infinite path, reachable from a.

Now let us try to do the same proof formally. The set of nodes from which infinite paths emanate can be defined as the greatest fixed point $inf \stackrel{\text{def}}{=} \nu\, step$ of the following monotone function:

$$step(X) \stackrel{\text{def}}{=} \{x \in \mathsf{Node} \mid \exists y \in X.\, x \to y\}$$

Our goal then is to show that $a \in inf$. Of course, in this small example, we could just compute inf directly by iteration and then

This research was carried out primarily while the first author was a post-doctoral researcher at MPI-SWS. The second author is currently funded by a Google European Doctoral Fellowship.

POPL'13, January 23–25, 2013, Rome, Italy.
Copyright © 2013 ACM 978-1-4503-1832-7/13/01...$10.00

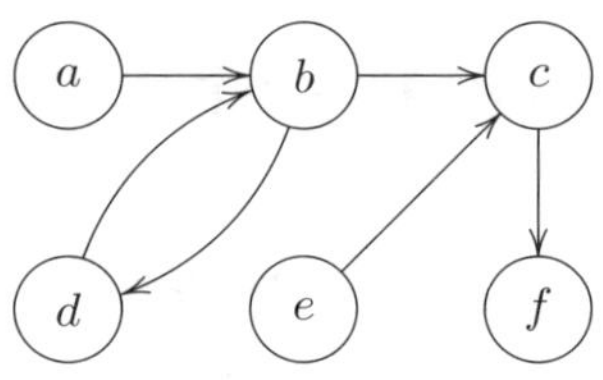

Node($=x$)	$\mathrm{G}_{step}(\{x\})$
a	$\{a, b, d\}$
b	$\{a, b, d\}$
c	$\{a, b, d, e\}$
d	$\{a, b, d\}$
e	$\{a, b, d\}$
f	$\{a, b, c, d, e\}$

Figure 1. A simple transition system and tabulation of G_{step}.

check if a is in it, but suppose we do not want to do this because in practice the transition system may be huge or even infinite.

Instead, we may employ Tarski's fixed-point theorem [22], which says that, to show $a \in inf$, it suffices to find a set of nodes X such that $a \in X$ and $\forall x \in X.\ \exists y \in X.\ x \to y$. For the given transition system, a possible such set is $X = \{a, b, d\}$, which corresponds to the set of nodes that we followed to exhibit the cycle earlier. The problem, however, is that this proof is rather different from the "model checking" one, and actually more difficult because it forces us to figure out what X is up front. What we would really like is a way to prove our goal by incrementally expanding the coinduction hypothesis from $\{a\}$ to $\{a, b\}$ to $\{a, b, d\}$ as we explore the transition system and see what nodes are reachable from a. The validity of such an approach is intuitively obvious, but what is the general lattice-theoretic proof principle that justifies it?

Contributions. In this paper, we show how to support coinductive proofs that are *both compositional and incremental*, using a dead simple construction we call the *parameterized greatest fixed point*. The basic idea is to parameterize the greatest fixed point of interest over the *accumulated knowledge* of "the proof so far".

Neither the idea nor the construction behind it is an original invention of ours *per se*. In 1989, Winskel [23] proposed the same idea for supporting "local model checking" in the modal μ-calculus. (His construction, which is slightly different from ours, supports incrementality but not compositionality—in our sense of the word—but it is straightforward to repurpose his core "reduction lemma" to derive a compositional version of his construction.) Independently, in 2001, Moss [14] presented a construction that *is* essentially the same as ours, albeit in a more abstract categorical setting. However, neither of these prior accounts suggests the general applicability of the parameterized greatest fixed point to improving the state of the art in interactive coinductive proof.

Our goal in the present paper is to popularize the idea of parameterized coinduction and explore its potential as a practically useful tool. More specifically, we make the following contributions:

- We present the parameterized greatest fixed point in simple lattice-theoretic terms, and show that it validates several useful principles for compositional, incremental proofs (Section 2). We give representative examples to illustrate the utility of these proof principles (Sections 2 and 3).
- We show how parameterized coinduction is complementary to the traditional approach to simplifying simulation proofs via *"up-to" techniques*, and we develop the basic theory of how these approaches compose (Section 4).
- We explore the issues that arise in the *mechanization* of parameterized coinduction in existing interactive theorem provers like Coq and Isabelle (Section 5). Fortunately, several of these issues can be resolved through variations on a somewhat esoteric technique called *Mendler-style recursion* (Section 6).
- We describe *Paco* (pronounced "pah-ko"), a new Coq library we have developed for parameterized coinduction. Compared to Coq's existing `cofix` tactic, Paco enables faster and more robust proof development, thanks to its support for *semantic*, rather than syntactic, guardedness checking (Section 7).

Finally, we conclude the paper in Section 8 with a detailed discussion of related work.

The technical development of this paper has been formalized in the Coq proof assistant. That formalization, together with a tutorial for our Coq library, Paco, is available from the Paco website:

`http://plv.mpi-sws.org/paco/`

2. Parameterized Coinduction

Let us begin by reviewing the basic lattice theory underlying coinductive definitions and their associated standard proof principles.

Consider a complete lattice $(C, \sqsubseteq, \sqcap, \sqcup, \top, \bot)$, and a monotone (*i.e.*, order-preserving) function $f \in C \xrightarrow{\text{mon}} C$. Strictly speaking, for generality, we do not require $\sqsubseteq$ to be antisymmetric, and we write $\equiv$ for the intersection of $\sqsubseteq$ and $\sqsupseteq$ (its inverse), which corresponds to $=$ if we have antisymmetry. We say that r is a *prefixed point* of f if $f(r) \sqsubseteq r$, and r is a *postfixed point* of f if $r \sqsubseteq f(r)$. Further, we write μf for f's least fixed point and νf for its greatest fixed point, which by Tarski's fixed-point theorem [22] is equal to the join of all postfixed points of f:

$$\nu f \;\equiv\; \bigsqcup \{r \in C \mid r \sqsubseteq f(r)\}$$

Tarski's Principle. We are concerned with proving statements of the form $x \sqsubseteq \nu f$. From Tarski's theorem we directly get that postfixed points are included in the greatest fixed point:

$$x \sqsubseteq f(x) \implies x \sqsubseteq \nu f \qquad \text{(TARSKI)}$$

To prove that $x \sqsubseteq \nu f$ when $x \not\sqsubseteq f(x)$ using this principle, we have to determine a postfixed point of f larger than x up front:

$$x \sqsubseteq \nu f \iff \exists r.\ x \sqsubseteq r \land r \sqsubseteq f(r)$$

This is clearly inconvenient for doing interactive proofs, as it forces one to construct the coinduction hypothesis r up front, instead of allowing r to be generated naturally in the course of the proof. Recall that in the example of the introduction, although we were only interested in showing that $a \in \nu\, step$, we had to pick $r := \{a, b, d\}$ up front. In large proofs, this quickly becomes a big problem. For example, the ClightTSO-Csharpminor simulation proof in the CompCertTSO verified compiler [20] requires a simulation relation r that comprises 69 cases, most of which tediously relate intermediate execution states.

Strong Coinduction. Second, there is a slight variant of (TARSKI), sometimes called the *strong coinduction principle* [4]:

Lemma 1 (Strong coinduction). $x \sqsubseteq \nu f \iff x \sqsubseteq f(x \sqcup \nu f)$.

Proof. First, we have $\nu f \equiv f(\nu f) \sqsubseteq f(x \sqcup \nu f)$ (†). The ($\Longrightarrow$) direction follows directly from (†). For the ($\Longleftarrow$) direction: from $x \sqsubseteq f(x \sqcup \nu f)$ and (†), we get $x \sqcup \nu f \sqsubseteq f(x \sqcup \nu f)$, *i.e.*, $x \sqcup \nu f$ is a postfixed point of f. So, from (TARSKI), $x \sqsubseteq x \sqcup \nu f \sqsubseteq \nu f$. □

This principle is "strong" in the sense that it is complete, but it still does not offer us a very useful interactive proof technique. The problem arises if in the course of proving that $x \sqsubseteq f(x \sqcup \nu f)$, we ever need to generalize the coinduction hypothesis by adding some y to it. The only recourse the strong coinduction principle gives us at this point (if we want to continue interactively with the proof) is to show that $y \sqsubseteq \nu f$. But of course the proof of that may cycle around, forcing us to prove that $x \sqsubseteq \nu f$, in which case we are stuck. We are therefore forced to restart the proof, generalizing the coinduction hypothesis to $x \sqcup y$, *i.e.*, showing that $x \sqcup y \sqsubseteq \nu f$.

Parameterized Coinduction. Our *parameterized coinduction* principle gives us a way to avoid restarting the proof by making explicit the idea of *accumulated knowledge*. In the course of the proof, we remember the things that we have already claimed are $\sqsubseteq \nu f$ and we can treat those as assumed knowledge in *guarded* subproofs (where guardedness is enforced semantically, not syntactically).

Formally, the idea is that instead of dealing with νf directly, we deal instead with some G_f that is parameterized by accumulated knowledge. That is, $\mathrm{G}_f \in C \xrightarrow{\text{mon}} C$, and intuitively, $\mathrm{G}_f(x)$ represents our "goal" of proving that something is in νf, under accumulated (or assumed) knowledge x.

Definition 1 (Parameterized greatest fixed point).
We define $\mathrm{G} \in (C \xrightarrow{\text{mon}} C) \xrightarrow{\text{mon}} (C \xrightarrow{\text{mon}} C)$:

$$\mathrm{G}_f(x) \stackrel{\text{def}}{=} \nu y.\ f(x \sqcup y)$$

Here, and elsewhere, we write $\nu y.a$ for $\nu(\lambda y.a)$. Note that the fixed point in the definition exists because $\lambda y.\ f(x \sqcup y)$ is monotone for monotone f. The monotonicity of G and G_f is easy to check.

One way of understanding G is pictorially. In the transition system from the introduction, $\mathrm{G}_{step}(X)$ describes the set of nodes that either have an infinite path (*i.e.,* are in ν *step*), or else have a *non-empty* path leading to a node in X.[1] To illustrate, Figure 1 lists the set $\mathrm{G}_{step}(\{x\})$ for each node x.

Incrementality of Parameterized Coinduction. We begin with the trivial observation that the parameterized greatest fixed point coincides with the standard one if no knowledge has been accumulated.

Lemma 2 (Initialize). $\nu f \equiv \mathrm{G}_f(\bot)$.

Further, by simply unfolding the fixed point, we obtain the following analogue of the strong coinduction principle mentioned previously (Lemma 1), except that this version can be stated directly as an equality on the parameterized greatest fixed point:

Lemma 3 (Unfold). $\mathrm{G}_f(x) \equiv f(x \sqcup \mathrm{G}_f(x))$.

What G_f allows us to do in addition, that νf does not support, is to accumulate knowledge in the following sense:

Theorem 4 (Accumulate). $y \sqsubseteq \mathrm{G}_f(x) \iff y \sqsubseteq \mathrm{G}_f(x \sqcup y)$.

Proof. The $(\Longrightarrow)$ direction follows straight from the monotonicity of G_f. In the $(\Longleftarrow)$ direction, assume $y \sqsubseteq \mathrm{G}_f(x \sqcup y)$ (*). Then,

$$\begin{aligned}\mathrm{G}_f(x \sqcup y) &\equiv f(x \sqcup y \sqcup \mathrm{G}_f(x \sqcup y)) && \text{fixed point equation}\\ &\sqsubseteq f(x \sqcup \mathrm{G}_f(x \sqcup y)) && f \text{ monotone and (*)}\\ &\equiv (\lambda z.\ f(x \sqcup z))\,(\mathrm{G}_f(x \sqcup y))\end{aligned}$$

Therefore, as $\mathrm{G}_f(x \sqcup y)$ is a postfixed point of $\lambda y.f(x \sqcup y)$, we obtain from (TARSKI) that $\mathrm{G}_f(x \sqcup y) \sqsubseteq \mathrm{G}_f(x)$, which together with (*) entails $y \sqsubseteq \mathrm{G}_f(x)$, as required. □

Compositionality of Parameterized Coinduction. Our construction also admits a clean compositional rule for combining proofs in the circular rely-guarantee style [8]:

$$\frac{g_1 \sqsubseteq \mathrm{G}_f(r_1) \qquad r_1 \sqsubseteq r \sqcup g_2 \qquad g_2 \sqsubseteq \mathrm{G}_f(r_2) \qquad r_2 \sqsubseteq r \sqcup g_1}{g_1 \sqcup g_2 \sqsubseteq \mathrm{G}_f(r)} \quad \text{(COMPOSE)}$$

The rule says that we can prove g_1 and g_2 are "correct" under assumptions r by proving that g_1 is correct under the additional assumption that g_2 is correct and similarly that g_2 is correct under the additional assumption that g_1 is. In essence, this rule is sound because $\mathrm{G}_f(r)$ allows the use of the assumptions r only within a guarded context.

[1] The fact that the paths to nodes in x must be non-empty is what ensures that x can be used as an assumption only within guarded contexts.

Although we have motivated the desire for compositionality separately from the desire for incrementality, it turns out that this (COMPOSE) rule is equivalent to the accumulation theorem (Theorem 4), which we have already proved, and in fact the two principles are *interderivable* under no assumptions about how G_f is defined (aside from the fact that it is monotone).

To see this, let us first derive (COMPOSE) from Theorem 4. Assuming the premises of (COMPOSE) hold, it is clear by monotonicity of G_f that $g_1 \sqsubseteq \mathrm{G}_f(r \sqcup g_1 \sqcup g_2)$ and $g_2 \sqsubseteq \mathrm{G}_f(r \sqcup g_1 \sqcup g_2)$, so $g_1 \sqcup g_2 \sqsubseteq \mathrm{G}_f(r \sqcup g_1 \sqcup g_2)$. By Theorem 4, $g_1 \sqcup g_2 \sqsubseteq \mathrm{G}_f(r)$ as desired. Conversely, we can derive Theorem 4 from (COMPOSE). As before, the $(\Longrightarrow)$ direction follows straight from the monotonicity of G_f. In the $(\Longleftarrow)$ direction, assume $y \sqsubseteq \mathrm{G}_f(x \sqcup y)$. Then, instantiate (COMPOSE) with $g_1 = g_2 = y$, $r = x$, and $r_1 = r_2 = x \sqcup y$. The conclusion yields $y \equiv y \sqcup y \sqsubseteq \mathrm{G}_f(x)$ as desired.

A Simple Application of Parameterized Coinduction. We now return to the "model checking" example presented in the introduction, and show how to use parameterized coinduction to prove $a \in \mathit{inf}$ incrementally. Here, we instantiate the principle with the powerset lattice on states of the transition system. Thus, showing $x \in S$ is equivalent to showing $\{x\} \sqsubseteq S$ in this lattice.

$$\begin{aligned}& a \in \mathit{inf} = \nu\ \mathit{step} &&\\ \iff\ & a \in \mathrm{G}_{step}(\emptyset) && \text{initialize}\\ \iff\ & \exists y \in \mathrm{G}_{step}(\emptyset).\ a \to y && \text{unfold}\\ \Longleftarrow\ & b \in \mathrm{G}_{step}(\emptyset) && \text{pick } y := b\\ \iff\ & b \in \mathrm{G}_{step}(\{b\}) && \text{accumulate}\\ \iff\ & \exists y \in \{b\} \cup \mathrm{G}_{step}(\{b\}).\ b \to y && \text{unfold}\\ \Longleftarrow\ & d \in \{b\} \cup \mathrm{G}_{step}(\{b\}) && \text{pick } y := d\\ \iff\ & d \in \mathrm{G}_{step}(\{b\}) && \text{since } d \neq b\\ \iff\ & \exists y \in \{b\} \cup \mathrm{G}_{step}(\{b\}).\ d \to y && \text{unfold}\\ \Longleftarrow\ & b \in \{b\} \cup \mathrm{G}_{step}(\{b\}) && \text{pick } y := b \quad \square\end{aligned}$$

As you can see, we can perform the same incremental proof as when "model checking" the example. Note that in the proof we do not necessarily have to accumulate the visited nodes at every step, but rather only when we think that their addition to the accumulated knowledge will be useful in the remainder of the proof.

With the same example, we can also illustrate a simple use of compositionality. We can easily establish:

$$\begin{aligned}& b \in \mathrm{G}_{step}(\{d\}) && \text{by unfolding \& picking } y := d\\ & d \in \mathrm{G}_{step}(\{b\}) && \text{by unfolding \& picking } y := b\end{aligned}$$

Thus, by (COMPOSE), $\{b, d\} \subseteq \mathrm{G}_{step}(\emptyset) = \mathit{inf}$.

Full Characterization of G_f. Finally, we observe that Lemma 3 and Theorem 4 uniquely determine G_f up to $\equiv$.

Proposition 5. For any G' such that (i) $\forall x.\ \mathrm{G}'(x) \equiv f(x \sqcup \mathrm{G}'(x))$ and (ii) $\forall x, y.\ y \sqsubseteq \mathrm{G}'(x \sqcup y) \implies y \sqsubseteq \mathrm{G}'(x)$, we have $\mathrm{G}' \equiv \mathrm{G}_f$.

Proof. Given x, $\mathrm{G}'(x) \sqsubseteq \mathrm{G}_f(x)$ follows by (TARSKI) from assumption (i). To show $\mathrm{G}_f(x) \sqsubseteq \mathrm{G}'(x)$, it suffices by (ii) to show $\mathrm{G}_f(x) \sqsubseteq \mathrm{G}'(x \sqcup \mathrm{G}_f(x))$, which, after unfolding on the left and rewriting using (i) on the right, follows by monotonicity of f. □

3. A Simulation Example

In this section, we illustrate parameterized coinduction on a slightly larger example that demonstrates the practical motivation for a compositional, incremental coinduction principle.

Consider the two recursive programs f and g shown in Figure 2. These programs continually poll the user for a new (numerical) input, compute the double of the sum of all inputs seen so far,

```
restart ≝ fix restart(f). λn.
        if n > 0 then (output n; restart f (n − 1)) else f 0
f ≝ fix f(n).
        let v = (output n; input()) ∗ 2 in
        (if v ≠ 0 then f else restart f) (v + n)
g ≝ fix g(m).
        output (2 ∗ m);
        let v = input() in
        if v = 0 then restart g (2 ∗ m) else g (v + m)
```

Figure 2. Recursive programs in the simulation example.

$$
\begin{array}{lll}
v & ::= \underline{n} \mid \mathsf{fix}\, f(x).\, e & \oplus ::= + \mid - \mid * \mid = \mid \neq \mid > \mid \geq \\
e & ::= x \mid v \mid e_1 \oplus e_2 \mid e_1\ e_2 \mid \mathsf{if}\ e_0\ \mathsf{then}\ e_1\ \mathsf{else}\ e_2 \mid \mathsf{input}() \mid \mathsf{output}\ e & \\
K & ::= e \oplus \bullet \mid \bullet \oplus v \mid e\ \bullet \mid \bullet\ v \mid \mathsf{if}\ \bullet\ \mathsf{then}\ e_1\ \mathsf{else}\ e_2 \mid \mathsf{output}\ \bullet & \\
q & ::= \tau \mid \mathsf{in}\ n \mid \mathsf{out}\ n &
\end{array}
$$

$$
\begin{array}{rcll}
\lambda x.\, e & \stackrel{\text{def}}{=} & \mathsf{fix}\, f(x).\, e & \text{where } f \notin \mathrm{fv}(e) \\
\mathsf{let}\ x = e_1\ \mathsf{in}\ e_2 & \stackrel{\text{def}}{=} & (\lambda x.\, e_2)\ e_1 & \\
e_1; e_2 & \stackrel{\text{def}}{=} & \mathsf{let}\ x = e_1\ \mathsf{in}\ e_2 & \text{where } x \notin \mathrm{fv}(e_2) \\
\underline{n_1} \oplus \underline{n_2} & \to & \underline{n_1 \oplus n_2} & \\
\mathsf{if}\ \underline{n}\ \mathsf{then}\ e_1\ \mathsf{else}\ e_2 & \to & e_1 & \text{where } n \neq 0 \\
\mathsf{if}\ \underline{0}\ \mathsf{then}\ e_1\ \mathsf{else}\ e_2 & \to & e_2 & \\
(\mathsf{fix}\, f(x).\, e)\ v & \to & e[(\mathsf{fix}\, f(x).\, e)/f, v/x] & \\
\mathsf{input}() & \xrightarrow{\mathsf{in}\ n} & \underline{n} & \\
\mathsf{output}\ \underline{n} & \xrightarrow{\mathsf{out}\ n} & \underline{0} & \\
K[e] & \xrightarrow{q} & K[e'] & \text{where } e \xrightarrow{q} e'
\end{array}
$$

Figure 3. Syntax and semantics of a tiny programming language.

and report the current value of the sum. If at any point, the user provides zero as an input, then the programs count down to zero, and start again. The two programs differ in the representation of the double of the sum, as well as in their programming style (as the programmer responsible for f followed a somewhat peculiar coding style). Nevertheless, it should be relatively straightforward to see that $\mathsf{g}(\underline{m})$ is equivalent to $\mathsf{f}(\underline{2m})$.

Formally, these programs are written in the minimal programming language defined in Figure 3. This is a standard call-by-value λ-calculus with integers, recursion, primitives for inputting and outputting integer values, and a right-to-left evaluation order for applications and arithmetic operations. We give its operational semantics as a labelled transition system, $e \xrightarrow{q} e'$, with the labels recording numerical inputs and outputs. We follow the standard convention of writing $\to$ instead of $\xrightarrow{\tau}$ for internal transitions.

For this language, we can define (weak) similarity as the greatest fixed point of the following function on expression relations:

$$
\begin{aligned}
sim(R) \stackrel{\text{def}}{=} \{(e_1, e_2) \mid\ & \\
& (\forall v.\, e_1 = v \implies e_2 \overset{\tau}{\rightsquigarrow} v) \\
& \wedge (\forall q, e_1'.\, e_1 \xrightarrow{q} e_1' \implies \exists e_2'.\, e_2 \overset{q}{\rightsquigarrow} e_2' \wedge R(e_1', e_2'))\}
\end{aligned}
$$

where $\overset{\tau}{\rightsquigarrow}$ is equal to $\to^*$ (the reflexive-transitive closure of $\to$), and $\overset{q}{\rightsquigarrow}$ is equal to $\to^* \xrightarrow{q}$ for $q \neq \tau$. If e_1 is a value, we require e_2 to evaluate to the same value; otherwise, if e_1 reduces to some e_1', we require that e_2 can match that execution step and end up in a R-related state.[2] Note that we are working with the powerset lattice $\mathcal{P}(\mathsf{exp} \times \mathsf{exp})$ where $\sqsubseteq\, = \,\subseteq, \sqcup = \cup, \sqcap = \cap$, and $\bot = \emptyset$.

[2] We chose this simulation definition for simplicity. We can also handle more elaborate definitions that result in coarser equivalences for values of function type.

Our goal is to show that $\mathsf{g}(\underline{m})$ simulates $\mathsf{f}(\underline{2m})$, that is:

$$R_0 := \{(\mathsf{f}(\underline{2m}), \mathsf{g}(\underline{m})) \mid m \in \mathbb{Z}\} \subseteq \nu sim$$

While this might appear trivial, proving this formally using Tarski's coinduction principle is extemely laborious. We have to come up with a "simulation relation" R containing all the intermediate execution steps of f and g appropriately matched: just before the output, just after the output, just before the input, just after the input, just before the evaluation of the condition, just after the evaluation of the condition, just after the choice of the condition, and so on. In total, there are 16 cases. This relation must be fully defined before we can even start the proof.

We remark that up-to techniques [18, 17], the standard toolbox for simplifying simulation proofs, while very helpful in many cases, are of limited use in this example. As the programs strictly alternate internal and external execution steps, the "up to reduction" technique can reduce the cases only by a factor of two. Similarly, the "up to context" technique does not help us relate the intermediate states of the calls to f and g because the two functions have rather different internal structure. (It does, however, help in reasoning about restart, as we will see in Section 4.)

3.1 Proof Sketch using Parameterized Coinduction

We now show how to apply parameterized coinduction in order to avoid the explicit, manual generalization of the coinduction hypothesis that is required with Tarski's principle. First, let us introduce the following shorthand:

$$
\begin{aligned}
f\!f(v) &\stackrel{\text{def}}{=} (\mathsf{if}\ v \neq \underline{0}\ \mathsf{then\ f\ else\ restart\ f})\ (v + \underline{2m}) \\
gg(v) &\stackrel{\text{def}}{=} \mathsf{if}\ v = \underline{0}\ \mathsf{then\ restart\ g}\ (\underline{2} * \underline{m})\ \mathsf{else}\ \mathsf{g}(v + \underline{m})
\end{aligned}
$$

We will now prove $R_0 \subseteq \mathrm{G}_{sim}(\emptyset)$, which by Lemma 2, $\equiv \nu sim$.
Step 1. By applying Theorem 4 followed by Lemma 3, we get as our goal:

$$R_0 \subseteq sim(\emptyset \cup R_0 \cup \mathrm{G}_{sim}(\emptyset \cup R_0)) = sim(R_0 \cup \mathrm{G}_{sim}(R_0))$$

This reduces to showing

$$\exists e_2'.\ \mathsf{g}(\underline{m}) \to^* e_2' \wedge (e_1', e_2') \in R_0 \cup \mathrm{G}_{sim}(R_0)$$

where $e_1' = (\mathsf{let\ v} = (\mathsf{output}\ \underline{2m};\ \mathsf{input}()) * \underline{2}\ \mathsf{in}\ f\!f(\mathsf{v}))$.
We pick $e_2' = (\mathsf{output}\ \underline{2m};\ \mathsf{let\ v} = \mathsf{input}()\ \mathsf{in}\ gg(\mathsf{v}))$ and proceed to show $(e_1', e_2') \in \mathrm{G}_{sim}(R_0)$.
Step 2. We now unfold the fixed point (Lemma 3) to get as our goal $(e_1', e_2') \in sim(R_0 \cup \mathrm{G}_{sim}(R_0))$, which means showing

$$\exists e_2''.\ e_2' \to^* \xrightarrow{\mathsf{out}\ 2m} e_2'' \wedge (e_1'', e_2'') \in R_0 \cup \mathrm{G}_{sim}(R_0)$$

where $e_1'' = (\mathsf{let\ v} = (\underline{0};\ \mathsf{input}()) * \underline{2}\ \mathsf{in}\ f\!f(\mathsf{v}))$. Now, we pick $e_2'' = (\underline{0};\ \mathsf{let\ v} = \mathsf{input}()\ \mathsf{in}\ gg(\mathsf{v}))$ and proceed to show $(e_1'', e_2'') \in \mathrm{G}_{sim}(R_0)$.
Next Steps. Further steps using Lemma 3 eventually lead us to a point where we have to prove the following two inclusions:

$$(\mathsf{f}(\underline{2v + 2m}), \mathsf{g}(\underline{v + m})) \in R_0 \cup \mathrm{G}_{sim}(R_0)$$
$$(\mathsf{restart\ f}\ \underline{2m},\ \mathsf{restart\ g}\ \underline{2m}) \in R_0 \cup \mathrm{G}_{sim}(R_0).$$

Regarding the former, we observe that the terms are related by R_0 and so we are done. Regarding the latter, we proceed as follows to show that they are related by $\mathrm{G}_{sim}(R_0)$.
Accumulation Step. We realize that (i) we have to increase the knowledge R_0 because restart calls itself recursively, and (ii) that before doing so we should generalize the goal to:

$$R_1 := \{(\mathsf{restart\ f}\ \underline{n},\ \mathsf{restart\ g}\ \underline{n}) \mid n \in \mathbb{Z}\} \subseteq \mathrm{G}_{sim}(R_0)$$

To this, we now apply the accumulating principle (Theorem 4) and get as our new goal:

$$R_1 \subseteq \mathrm{G}_{sim}(R_0 \cup R_1)$$

Final Steps. We proceed in the same manner as earlier, using Lemma 3 to step through the code of restart. When arriving at the recursive call in the then-branch, we use the new R_1 part of the coinduction hypothesis and are done. When reasoning about the else-branch, on the other hand, we conclude by appeal to the original R_0 part, which fortunately is still around. □

The benefit of our approach over the traditional Tarski approach here is that the simulation relation does not have to be defined up front. Instead, the intermediate goals and the quantifier instantiations can be generated automatically by an interactive theorem prover using simple tactics. The details for achieving this will be presented in Section 5.

3.2 Decomposing the Proof

Since parameterized coinduction also supports compositionality, we can factor out the reasoning about restart from the previous proof into a separate generic lemma that may then be reused in other proofs.

Lemma 6 (Restart)**.** For all values f_1 and f_2, we have:

$$\{(\mathsf{restart}\ f_1\ \underline{n},\ \mathsf{restart}\ f_2\ \underline{n}) \mid n \in \mathbb{Z}\} \subseteq \mathrm{G}_{sim}(\{(f_1\ \underline{0}, f_2\ \underline{0})\})$$

Its proof follows straightforwardly from the fact that restart applies its function argument only to $\underline{0}$.

Instead of proving the previous goal $R_0 \subseteq \mathrm{G}_{sim}(\emptyset)$ directly, it now suffices to prove the following:

Lemma 7. $R_0 \subseteq \mathrm{G}_{sim}(R_1)$

Then $R_0 \subseteq \mathrm{G}_{sim}(\emptyset)$ is obtained from Lemmas 6 and 7 by rule (COMPOSE) (using empty initial assumptions). The proof of Lemma 7 follows the same structure as the one sketched for $R_0 \subseteq \mathrm{G}_{sim}(\emptyset)$, except that we are done after performing what were called above the "Next Steps".

Remark. Without G_{sim} we cannot split the proof into separate lemmas about restart and about f and g. For example, while we can prove the following statements:

$$R_0 \subseteq \nu\, sim \implies R_1 \subseteq \nu\, sim$$
$$R_1 \subseteq \nu\, sim \implies R_0 \subseteq \nu\, sim$$

we cannot combine the two to derive $R_0 \subseteq \nu\, sim$. This requires a sound form of circular reasoning, such as the one provided by the (COMPOSE) rule.

4. Combination with Up-To Techniques

The incremental proof sketched in the previous section, despite being a huge improvement over the one based on (TARSKI), is still quite tedious to do (at least on paper). Most of the proof involved trivally stepping through f and g. Doing so for f and g is arguably necessary, because their structure is quite different, but for the proof of Lemma 6 about restart, where the structure is identical, it seems unnecessary. In this section, we will see that with a bit of additional theory, this tedium can be avoided as well.

In traditional (bi-)simulation proofs, people often employ simplification techniques known as *up-to functions* [19, 17]. Intuitively, an up-to function maps an element $r \in C$ to an element r^* (typically larger than r) that is still valid as a coinduction hypothesis for proving $r \sqsubseteq \nu f$.

Definition 2. $(-)^* \in C \xrightarrow{\text{mon}} C$ is a *sound up-to function* for $f \in C \xrightarrow{\text{mon}} C$ iff $r \sqsubseteq f(r^*)$ implies $r \sqsubseteq \nu f$ for all $r \in C$.

The standard definition (*e.g.*, [17]) does not require $(-)^*$ to be monotone, but this is a very natural condition, which holds of all up-to functions in the literature that we are aware of, and is needed for taking fixed points involving $(-)^*$.

This raises the question: is parameterized coinduction compatible with the use of up-to functions? Fortunately, the answer is yes. To see how up-to functions and parameterized coinduction can be combined, we observe that sound up-to functions respect the greatest fixed point:

Lemma 8. If $(-)^*$ is a sound up-to function for $f \in C \xrightarrow{\text{mon}} C$, then:

$$\nu f^* \sqsubseteq \nu f \quad \text{where} \quad f^* \stackrel{\text{def}}{=} \lambda r.\ f(r^*)$$

Proof. We have $\nu f^* \sqsubseteq f^*(\nu f^*) = f((\nu f^*)^*)$, which by Definition 2 implies $\nu f^* \sqsubseteq \nu f$. □

Thus, to prove $x \sqsubseteq \nu f$ using parameterized coinduction, we can instead show $x \sqsubseteq \mathrm{G}_{f^*}(\bot)$ for any sound up-to function $(-)^*$.

How does this interact with compositionality? Suppose we have two separate proofs using two up-to functions $\star$ and $\circ$:

$$x \sqsubseteq \mathrm{G}_{f^\star}(y \sqcup r) \quad \text{and} \quad y \sqsubseteq \mathrm{G}_{f^\circ}(x \sqcup r)$$

If $f^\star$ and f° happen to be equal, then we can combine the proofs using (COMPOSE) as expected. However, in general $(-)^\star$ and $(-)^\circ$ might be two arbitrarily different up-to functions, and thus we may not be able to apply the composition rule.

Fortunately, there is a solution to this dilemma if we confine ourselves to *respectful* up-to functions:

Definition 3. $(-)^* \in C \xrightarrow{\text{mon}} C$ is a *respectful up-to function* for $f \in C \xrightarrow{\text{mon}} C$ iff for any $r, s \in C$ the following holds:[3]

$$r \sqsubseteq s \wedge r \sqsubseteq f(s) \implies r^* \sqsubseteq f(s^*)$$

Lemma 9. If $(-)^*$ is a respectful up-to function for f, then it is also a sound one. (The proof follows that in [17].)

Respectfulness, although stronger than soundness, is still satisfied by most up-to functions of interest, and, crucially, has better compositionality properties. In particular:

Proposition 10.

1. $\mathrm{id} \stackrel{\text{def}}{=} (\lambda x.\ x)$ is a respectful up-to function for any f.
2. If u and u' are respectful up-to functions for f, then so is $u \circ u'$.
3. If each element of a set X is a respectful up-to function for f, then so is $\bigsqcup X$.[4]

We can thus define the greatest respectful up-to function for a given $f \in C \xrightarrow{\text{mon}} C$:

$$f^\dagger \stackrel{\text{def}}{=} \bigsqcup\{u \in C \xrightarrow{\text{mon}} C \mid u \text{ is a respectful up-to function for } f\}$$

Using Proposition 10.3, it is easy to show that $(-)^\dagger$ is a respectful up-to function, and that it is the greatest such. Moreover, we have:

Lemma 11. If $(-)^*$ is a respectful up-to function for f, then:

$$\mathrm{G}_{f^*} \sqsubseteq \mathrm{G}_{f^\dagger}$$

Proof. Follows from monotonicity of G and $(-)^* \sqsubseteq (-)^\dagger$. □

Now, using Lemma 11, we can bring the two proofs from above to a "common denominator",

$$x \sqsubseteq \mathrm{G}_{f^\dagger}(y \sqcup r) \quad \text{and} \quad y \sqsubseteq \mathrm{G}_{f^\dagger}(x \sqcup r),$$

and then compose them to get $x \sqcup y \sqsubseteq \mathrm{G}_{f^\dagger}(r)$.

[3] As with the definition of a sound up-to function, Sangiorgi [17] does not assume monotonicity of $(-)^*$, but here he requires a slightly weaker property: $r \sqsubseteq s \wedge r \sqsubseteq f(s) \implies r^* \sqsubseteq s^*$.

[4] Here and elsewhere, we treat a function space $A \to C$ as the complete lattice obtained by canonically lifting C pointwise.

$$\frac{(e,e') \in r}{(e,e') \in r^{\text{ctx}}}\ (\text{INCL}) \qquad \frac{}{(e,e) \in r^{\text{ctx}}}\ (\text{REFL})$$

$$\frac{(e,e') \in r \qquad (e_1,e_1') \in r \qquad (e_2,e_2') \in r}{(\mathsf{if}\ e\ \mathsf{then}\ e_1\ \mathsf{else}\ e_2, \mathsf{if}\ e'\ \mathsf{then}\ e_1'\ \mathsf{else}\ e_2') \in r^{\text{ctx}}}\ (\text{IF})$$

$$\frac{\forall v. \begin{pmatrix} e_1[v/x, \mathsf{fix}\, f(x).\, e_1/f], \\ e_1'[v/x', \mathsf{fix}\, f'(x').\, e_1'/f'] \end{pmatrix} \in r \qquad (e_2,e_2') \in r}{((\mathsf{fix}\, f(x).\, e_1)\ e_2, (\mathsf{fix}\, f'(x').\, e_1')\ e_2') \in r^{\text{ctx}}}\ (\text{APPV})$$

Figure 4. A respectful up-to function.

Actually, since the greatest respectful up-to function is so powerful, we see no point in ever stating a proof component's contribution involving a different respectful up-to function. In other words: state your goal in terms of the greatest one. The following properties enable the use of zero or more particular respectful up-to functions inside the proof of such a goal:

Lemma 12. If $(-)^*$ is a respectful up-to function for f, then for any $r \in C$:

1. $r \sqsubseteq r^\dagger$
2. $(r^\dagger)^* \sqsubseteq r^\dagger$

Proof. Follows from Proposition 10.1 and 10.2, respectively. □

We remark that the greatest respectful up-to function also allows us to use up-to reasoning at any point in a proof by parameterized coinduction (not just after unfolding).

Theorem 13. $G_{f^\dagger}(r) \equiv (G_{f^\dagger}(r))^\dagger$

Proof. The ($\sqsubseteq$) direction holds by Lemma 12.1. The ($\sqsupseteq$) direction is more complicated. By (TARSKI) it suffices to show $G_{f^\dagger}(r)^\dagger \sqsubseteq f((r \sqcup G_{f^\dagger}(r)^\dagger)^\dagger)$. This follows from Lemma 12.2 if we can show $G_{f^\dagger}(r)^\dagger \sqsubseteq f((r \sqcup G_{f^\dagger}(r)^\dagger)^{\dagger\dagger})$. By respectfulness in turn it suffices to show $G_{f^\dagger}(r) \sqsubseteq (r \sqcup G_{f^\dagger}(r)^\dagger)^\dagger$ and $G_{f^\dagger}(r) \sqsubseteq f((r \sqcup G_{f^\dagger}(r)^\dagger)^\dagger)$. Both are not hard to show using Lemma 12.1 and, for the second, monotonicity of f and $(-)^\dagger$. □

Simulation Example. We return to the simulation example presented in Section 3, and show how to apply an "up to context" technique in order to simplify the proof.

To reason up to contexts, one usually defines a context closure operation. We could do this here as well, but, in combination with $(-)^\dagger$, we can get away with something simpler: Figure 4 defines a function $(-)^{\text{ctx}} \in \mathcal{P}(\mathsf{exp}^2) \to \mathcal{P}(\mathsf{exp}^2)$. It is straightforward to verify that this is a respectful up-to function for *sim* (the proof can be found in our Coq formalization). Observe, however, that the definition is not recursive and thus $(-)^{\text{ctx}}$ only adds *atomic* contexts (*i.e.*, contexts whose definition does not involve any form of recursion); we will see in a moment how we can nevertheless get the full power of a proper context closure operation.

The final rule (APPV) is the case for function application. As $\nu\, sim$ relates values only if they are identical, the simpler rule—$\{$if $(e_1, e_1') \in r$ and $(e_2, e_2') \in r$ then $(e_1\, e_2,\ e_1'\, e_2') \in r^{\text{ctx}}\}$—while sound, is useless because the first assumption requires e_1 and e_1' to evaluate to syntactically the same function. Therefore, APPV requires the functions to be already values, and checks that their bodies are related whenever the functions are applied to the same arguments. Finally, note that the following rule can be derived from APPV:

$$\frac{(e_1,e_1') \in r \qquad (e_2,e_2') \in r}{(e_1; e_2,\ e_1'; e_2') \in r^{\text{ctx}}}\ (\text{SEQ})$$

With the help of this up-to function we will now prove the same two lemmas as before (Lemmas 6 and 7), except that we replace G_{sim} by $G_{sim^\dagger}$.

Lemma 14. For all values f_1 and f_2, we have:

$$\{(\mathsf{restart}\ f_1\ \underline{n},\ \mathsf{restart}\ f_2\ \underline{n}) \mid n \in \mathbb{Z}\} \subseteq G_{sim^\dagger}(\{(f_1\ \underline{0}, f_2\ \underline{0})\})$$

Lemma 15. $R_0 \subseteq G_{sim^\dagger}(R_1)$.

Proof of Lemma 14. As in Section 3, we apply the accumulation principle and reason about the first two steps of execution with the help of Lemma 12.1. Then we obtain the following proof obligation:

$$(e_1,\ e_2) \in (R \cup G_{sim^\dagger}(R))^\dagger$$

where:

$$e_i := \mathsf{if}\ \underline{n} > 0\ \mathsf{then}\ (\mathsf{output}\ \underline{n}; \mathsf{restart}\ f_i\ (\underline{n} - \underline{1}))\ \mathsf{else}\ f_i\ \underline{0}$$
$$R := \{(\mathsf{restart}\ f_1\ \underline{n},\ \mathsf{restart}\ f_2\ \underline{n}) \mid n \in \mathbb{Z}\} \cup \{(f_1\ \underline{0}, f_2\ \underline{0})\}$$

At this point, since $(-^\dagger)^{\text{ctx}} \sqsubseteq (-)^\dagger$ by Lemma 12.2, we may apply one of the rules from Figure 4 in order to simplify this goal. We pick IF and hence it remains to show the following three:

1. $(\underline{n} > 0,\ \underline{n} > 0) \in (R \cup G_{sim^\dagger}(R))^\dagger$
2. $((\mathsf{output}\ \underline{n}; \mathsf{restart}\ f_1\ (\underline{n} - \underline{1})),$
   $(\mathsf{output}\ \underline{n}; \mathsf{restart}\ f_2\ (\underline{n} - \underline{1}))) \in (R \cup G_{sim^\dagger}(R))^\dagger$
3. $(f_1\ \underline{0}, f_2\ \underline{0}) \in (R \cup G_{sim^\dagger}(R))^\dagger$

Now, by the *same argument*, we may apply another of these rules in each case. So, effectively, we can apply an arbitrary number of rules and thus did not lose any power by defining $(-)^{\text{ctx}}$ in terms of atomic contexts only.

(1) is solved by rule REFL, and (3) is solved by Lemma 12.1 since the terms are related by R. To show (2), we first apply rules SEQ and REFL, and then use Lemma 12.1 to reduce the goal to:

$$(\mathsf{restart}\ f_1\ (\underline{n} - \underline{1}),\ \mathsf{restart}\ f_2\ (\underline{n} - \underline{1})) \in G_{sim^\dagger}(R)$$

This is easily shown by unfolding (Lemma 3), performing a step of computation, which converts the two instances of $\underline{n} - \underline{1}$ to $\underline{n-1}$, and then concluding once again with Lemma 12.1.

The attentive reader may have noticed that we never seem to need rule INCL. Indeed, this is a side effect of reasoning via Lemma 12. Nevertheless, the rule is necessary: without it, $(-)^{\text{ctx}}$ would not be respectful. □

Proof of Lemma 15. Here, reasoning up to contexts seems not to buy us anything, so we just derive the goal from our old proof (Lemma 7) via Lemma 11. □

Finally, we can, as before, use (COMPOSE) to deduce that $R_0 \subseteq G_{f^\dagger}(\emptyset)$. By Lemmas 2, 8 and 9, this implies $R_0 \subseteq \nu f$.

5. Mechanizing Parameterized Coinduction

In this section, we discuss at a high level the issues raised by formalizing our parameterized coinduction principle from Section 2 in a proof assistant such as Isabelle/HOL or Coq. Details about our Coq implementation, as well as examples using it, follow in Section 7.

To establish some common terminology, we say that a *predicate* of arity n is a (dependent) function of type

$$\Pi a_1{:}A_1.\ \Pi a_2{:}A_2(a_1).\ \ldots \Pi a_n{:}A_n(a_1, \ldots, a_{n-1}).\ S$$

where the sort S is impredicative (`Prop` in Coq, `bool` in Isabelle). If instead the sort S is predicative (`Type` in Coq, or `Set` in Agda), we call such objects *indexed sets*.

Predicates are normally used for writing "proofs" (whose computational meaning is not of interest), whereas indexed sets are used for writing "programs" (whose computational meaning is their main point of interest), and of these two actually only *predicates* form complete lattices. Therefore, in this paper, whose main focus is on coinductive *proofs*, we shall largely ignore indexed sets, and only briefly discuss them in Section 8.

There are two ways in which a formalization can be done, namely what we call the *external* and the *internal* approach. They differ in the way in which the parameterized greatest fixed point is constructed.

- The *external approach* develops a library of complete lattices that uses Tarski's construction for greatest fixed points, and then uses that library to define G. Defining such a library, however, requires impredicative quantification, and so this approach only works for Isabelle and Coq, but not Agda.
- The *internal approach* defines G directly using the proof assistant's primitive mechanism for defining coinductive types (*e.g.*, Coq's **CoInductive** or Agda's ∞ constructor). In Isabelle/HOL and related systems, where coinductive types/relations are not primitive, one must instead follow the external approach.

In Coq, where both approaches are applicable, the internal approach, besides being more direct, is also easier to use because Coq's automation works much better there. The main problem is that in the external approach, Coq's automation tactics do not know how to unfold the lattice-theoretic constructs, and so the user has to instruct Coq manually to do so.

We now discuss the two approaches in more detail.

The External Approach. In this approach, one defines a generic library of complete lattices and greatest fixed points of arbitrary monotone endofunctions, and uses that to construct G and prove its properties. The library can then be instantiated to the application domain at hand.

This approach is arguably as general and modular as it gets, and works quite well for both Coq and Isabelle/HOL. The Isabelle implementation is actually simpler: Isabelle already has a complete lattice theory, which only needs to be extended with our parameterized coinduction.

To apply the library definitions and lemmas to arbitrary predicates, one has to prove that `Prop` (in Coq, or `bool` in Isabelle) forms a complete lattice and that the space of (dependent) functions to a complete lattice forms again a complete lattice (the pointwise lifting). Using *type classes* (in Isabelle or Coq) or *canonical structures* (only in Coq), one can easily arrange that the appropriate lattice structure for a given predicate is automatically inferred.

The Internal Approach. As mentioned above, the internal approach depends on having primitive support for coinductive types, but if it is available, it can be more a convenient option. However, the applicability of the internal approach is somewhat limited for two further reasons:

1. The "only" objects that one can define with the primitive coinductive definition mechanism are predicates (and indexed sets). Hence, this approach does not work for arbitrary complete lattices. However, it is still very useful in practice, because (*i*) predicates are already quite expressive, and (*ii*) we found a clever trick that enables us to extend this approach to *refined* predicates, explained in detail in Section 6.2.
2. Moreover, the predicates themselves must have a certain syntactic form: all recursive uses of a (co-)inductively defined object in its definition must be *strictly positive*, *i.e.*, roughly speaking, not occur on the left of an arrow. While this syntactic condition is overly restrictive for predicates, it is important for ensuring consistency in the case of indexed sets, and is thus imposed for uniformity on all coinductive definitions.

What does this entail for the formalization? Consider the powerset lattice from Section 3. It satisfies condition (1) above (*i.e.*, it is a predicate type), but condition (2) prevents one from parameterizing the definition of G_f over f. Recall its definition:

$$\mathrm{G} \in (\mathcal{P}(\mathsf{exp}^2) \xrightarrow{\text{mon}} \mathcal{P}(\mathsf{exp}^2)) \xrightarrow{\text{mon}} (\mathcal{P}(\mathsf{exp}^2) \xrightarrow{\text{mon}} \mathcal{P}(\mathsf{exp}^2))$$
$$\mathrm{G}_f(x) \stackrel{\text{def}}{=} \nu y.\ f(x \sqcup y)$$

This can be translated into Coq as follows:

```
Definition erel :=  exp → exp → Prop.
CoInductive G (f: erel → erel) (fM: monotonic f)
          (x: erel) (e1 e2: exp) : Prop :=
  | G_fold (IN: f (x ⊔ G f fM x) e1 e2). (* REJECTED *)
```

This definition, however, is rejected because it violates strict positivity: in the type of the constructor argument `IN`, `G` occurs in the argument of a function application, where the function, `f`, is a variable. This is forbidden, intuitively because `f` could be instantiated to a function that uses its argument on the left side of an arrow.

Fortunately, there is a simple—but clever—trick that lets us work around the strict positivity requirement as long as the function in question (here: $\lambda y. f(x \sqcup y)$) is monotone. This trick is based on *Mendler-style recursion* and explained in Section 6.1. Consequently, in the internal approach, we can also define a library for parameterized greatest fixed points of arbitrary monotone predicates up to some fixed arity—see Section 7.4.

6. Mendler-Style Recursion to the Rescue!

Mendler [12] proposed a strongly normalizing calculus featuring an unusual treatment of inductive and coinductive types. In this section, we show how recursion in the Mendler style can be used to address the two issues mentioned in Section 5 that come up when mechanizing parameterized greatest fixed points following the internal approach.

We first review the idea of Mendler-style recursion in the setting of complete lattices and show how it can be employed to overcome Coq's strict positivity restriction in the case of predicates. This observation is not novel, and has been made before by Matthes [11].

Second, we generalize this theory in a way that yields a method for defining fixed points in complete *sub*lattices. In the internal approach, this enables us to define *refined* predicates coinductively, while, in the external approach, it aids in avoiding dealing with dependent types. As far as we can tell, both the generalization of the theory and its application to mechanization are new.

6.1 Strict Positivization

A convenient way to view Mendler's fixed point constructions is as ordinary fixed points of *monotonized* functions. Given a function $g \in C \to C$ (where C is a complete lattice), there are two canonical ways of adapting this function slightly to make it monotone:

Definition 4 (Monotonizations)**.** We define $\lfloor g \rfloor, \lceil g \rceil \in C \xrightarrow{\text{mon}} C$:

$$\lfloor g \rfloor \stackrel{\text{def}}{=} \lambda x.\ \bigsqcap\{g(y) \mid y \sqsupseteq x\}$$
$$\lceil g \rceil \stackrel{\text{def}}{=} \lambda x.\ \bigsqcup\{g(y) \mid y \sqsubseteq x\}$$

Their monotonicity is easy to see, given that for $x \sqsubseteq x'$ we have:

$$\{g(y) \mid y \sqsupseteq x\} \supseteq \{g(y) \mid y \sqsupseteq x'\}$$
$$\text{and} \quad \{g(y) \mid y \sqsubseteq x\} \subseteq \{g(y) \mid y \sqsubseteq x'\}.$$

It is also easy to verify that both $\lfloor - \rfloor$ and $\lceil - \rceil$ form a Galois connection with the canonical embedding of $C \xrightarrow{\text{mon}} C$ in $C \to C$, in the way depicted in Figure 5. This means that

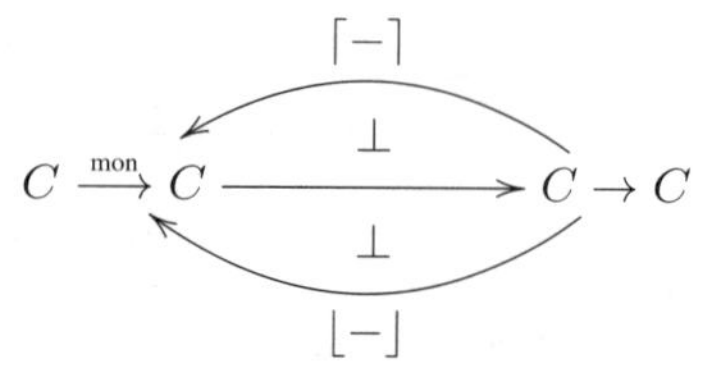

Figure 5. Monotonization operators and their Galois connections.

- $\forall f \in C \xrightarrow{\text{mon}} C.\ f \sqsubseteq \lfloor g \rfloor \iff f \sqsubseteq g$
  i.e., $\lfloor g \rfloor$ is the greatest monotone function below g, and
- $\forall f \in C \xrightarrow{\text{mon}} C.\ \lceil g \rceil \sqsubseteq f \iff g \sqsubseteq f$
  i.e., $\lceil g \rceil$ is the least monotone function above g,

and thus $\lfloor g \rfloor \sqsubseteq g \sqsubseteq \lceil g \rceil$ (which explains our choice of notation). Now, if g is already monotone, then all three are equivalent, and consequently so are their least and greatest fixed points:

Proposition 16. If $g \in C \xrightarrow{\text{mon}} C$, then $\lfloor g \rfloor \equiv g \equiv \lceil g \rceil$, and hence $\mu\lfloor g \rfloor \equiv \mu g \equiv \mu\lceil g \rceil$ and $\nu\lfloor g \rfloor \equiv \nu g \equiv \nu\lceil g \rceil$.

So why is this interesting at all? The point is that monotonizing an already monotone function using $\lceil - \rceil$ yields the same function in a form that translates to a strictly positive one in Coq. To see this, let us apply it to the definition of G that we attempted at the end of the previous section.

Given a monotone function f, there are actually two ways to apply Proposition 16 to $\mathrm{G}_f(x)$. In the first, we "monotonize" f:

$$\mathrm{G}_f(x) \equiv \mathrm{G}_{\lceil f \rceil}(x) = \nu z.\ \bigsqcup\{f(y) \mid y \sqsubseteq x \sqcup z\}$$

In the second, we "monotonize" $\lambda z.\ f(x \sqcup z)$:

$$\mathrm{G}_f(x) = \nu z.\ f(x \sqcup z) \equiv \nu z.\ \bigsqcup\{f(x \sqcup y) \mid y \sqsubseteq z\}$$

Hence we have two possible definitions of G in Coq:

```
CoInductive G (f: erel → erel)
        (x: erel) (e1 e2: exp) : Prop :=
| G_fold y (LE: y ⊆ x ∪ G f x) (IN: f y e1 e2).
```

```
CoInductive G (f: erel → erel)
        (x: erel) (e1 e2: exp) : Prop :=
| G_fold y (LE: y ⊆ G f x) (IN: f (x ∪ y) e1 e2).
```

Note the similarity to the rejected definition in the previous section and the absence of the `fM` assumption. These new definitions are well-formed for arbitrary functions f (not necessarily monotone), and dropping `fM` makes them more convenient to work with. Of course, we need to assume monotonicity in statements about `G` then instead. We prefer the first definition, because then monotonicity of f is required only for unfolding G_f (the $\sqsubseteq$ direction of Lemma 3) and is not needed for the accumulation theorem (Theorem 4).

We remark that this trick of monotonizing functions that are already monotone in order to obtain a strictly positive form applies to inductive predicates (defined using Coq's `Inductive` command) as well, but we do not exploit that observation in this development.

6.2 Fixed Points in Sublattices

The Problem. Recall that, in the internal approach, (co-)inductive definitions are limited to predicates and indexed sets. Here we show how to broaden this to *refined* predicates.

By refined predicates, we mean objects whose type has the form

$$\{x : \Pi a_1{:}A_1.\ \ldots \Pi a_n{:}A_n(a_1,\ldots,a_{n-1}).\ \mathtt{Prop} \mid P(x)\},$$

i.e., a regular predicate type refined by some property P. This is best illustrated with an example. Imagine we want to define the greatest fixed point of a function

$$f \in (\mathcal{P}(\mathsf{exp}^2) \to \mathcal{P}(\mathsf{exp}^2)) \xrightarrow{\text{mon}} (\mathcal{P}(\mathsf{exp}^2) \to \mathcal{P}(\mathsf{exp}^2)).$$

We can easily do this using Coq's **CoInductive** mechanism since $\mathcal{P}(\mathsf{exp}^2) \to \mathcal{P}(\mathsf{exp}^2)$ is naturally expressed as a predicate type (we may have to bring f into strictly positive form, of course). Now imagine we want to define the greatest fixed point of a different function

$$g \in (\mathcal{P}(\mathsf{exp}^2) \xrightarrow{\text{mon}} \mathcal{P}(\mathsf{exp}^2)) \xrightarrow{\text{mon}} (\mathcal{P}(\mathsf{exp}^2) \xrightarrow{\text{mon}} \mathcal{P}(\mathsf{exp}^2)).$$

Note that the complete lattice $\mathcal{P}(\mathsf{exp}^2) \xrightarrow{\text{mon}} \mathcal{P}(\mathsf{exp}^2)$ cannot be expressed as a predicate type due to the restriction of the function space. Instead, it can be seen as a refined predicate type (where P is monotonicity).

In the external approach, there is no problem: we can define the complete lattice structure for this type, then use that to write down the faithful definition of g, prove that it is monotone, and finally just apply the greatest fixed point operator to it. But in the internal approach, this is not possible. The best we can do there, so it seems, is take the greatest fixed point in the unrestricted function space. However, (i) this assumes that g is well-defined and monotone in the larger space, and (ii) even if that fixed point exists, it will not necessarily be the desired one.

The Solution. Our solution is as follows: we do indeed take the greatest fixed point in the unrestricted space, but only after modifying the function in a way that ensures (i) that it is well-defined and monotone, and (ii) that the result actually coincides with the desired greatest fixed point in the original restricted space. The math behind this is a generalization of what we saw in Section 6.1, and is basically stated in terms of an arbitrary complete lattice and an arbitrary complete sublattice thereof that preserves meets and/or joins.

Because the theory is so general, it could actually also be used in the external approach, where the (non-negligible) benefit would be avoiding to work with (dependent) subset types.

The Theory. Consider two complete lattices B and C. We are interested in the scenario where there exists an embedding of B in C, in the following sense:

Definition 5. A function $i \in B \to C$ is an *embedding* of B in C, written $i : B \hookrightarrow C$, iff $\forall b, b' \in B.\ b \sqsubseteq_B b' \iff i(b) \sqsubseteq_C i(b')$.

(Note that this implies injectivity.) In the case where B is a complete sublattice of C, the canonical injection from B to C constitutes such an embedding.

With the help of an embedding, we can now define generalized versions of the monotonization operators from Section 6.1:

Definition 6 (Generalized Monotonizations)**.** For $i : B \hookrightarrow C$ and a function $g \in B \to B$ we define $\lfloor g \rfloor_i, \lceil g \rceil^i \in C \xrightarrow{\text{mon}} C$:

$$\begin{aligned} \lfloor g \rfloor_i &\stackrel{\text{def}}{=} \lambda x.\ \bigsqcap\{i(g(y)) \mid y \in B \wedge i(y) \sqsupseteq x\} \\ \lceil g \rceil^i &\stackrel{\text{def}}{=} \lambda x.\ \bigsqcup\{i(g(y)) \mid y \in B \wedge i(y) \sqsubseteq x\} \end{aligned}$$

Now, if i preserves meets and joins (*e.g.*, because C is a function space with a pointwise ordering and B its restriction to monotone functions), then the Galois connections from earlier generalize as well. And, if moreover g is monotone, then the least and greatest fixed points of g, $\lfloor g \rfloor_i$ and $\lceil g \rceil^i$ coincide modulo the embedding.

Proposition 17. If $\forall X.\ i(\bigsqcap X) \equiv \bigsqcap(i(X))$, the following hold for any $f \in C \xrightarrow{\text{mon}} C$ and $g \in B \to B$:

1. $f \sqsubseteq \lfloor g \rfloor_i \iff |f|_i \sqsubseteq g$, for $|f|_i \stackrel{\text{def}}{=} \bigsqcap\{y \mid i(y) \sqsupseteq f(i(x))\}$.
2. If g is monotone, then $\mu\lfloor g \rfloor_i \equiv i(\mu g)$ and $\nu\lfloor g \rfloor_i \equiv i(\nu g)$.

Proposition 18. If $\forall X.\ i(\bigsqcup X) \equiv \bigsqcup(i(X))$, the following hold for any $f \in C \xrightarrow{\text{mon}} C$ and $g \in B \to B$:

1. $\lceil g \rceil^i \sqsubseteq f \iff g \sqsubseteq |f|^i$, for $|f|^i \stackrel{\text{def}}{=} \bigsqcup\{y \mid i(y) \sqsubseteq f(i(x))\}$.
2. If g is monotone, then $\mu\lceil g \rceil^i \equiv i(\mu g)$ and $\nu\lceil g \rceil^i \equiv i(\nu g)$.

Finally, observe that the results in Section 6.1 are merely a special case of the results presented here, namely where $B = C$ and $i = \text{id}$, in which case $\lfloor - \rfloor_i = \lfloor - \rfloor$, $\lceil - \rceil^i = \lceil - \rceil$, and $|-|^i = |-|_i = \text{id}$.

The Example. To see what this looks like in practice, let us return to the example g from the beginning. Since $\mathcal{P}(\mathsf{exp}^2) \xrightarrow{\text{mon}} \mathcal{P}(\mathsf{exp}^2)$ is a complete sublattice of $\mathcal{P}(\mathsf{exp}^2) \to \mathcal{P}(\mathsf{exp}^2)$, we have by Propositions 17 and 18 (for the canonical injection i):

$$\nu g \equiv \nu\lfloor g \rfloor_i \equiv \nu\lceil g \rceil^i$$

We can now mechanize either $\lfloor g \rfloor_i$ or $\lceil g \rceil^i$. Because $\lceil - \rceil^i$ has the added benefit of yielding a strictly positive form (even if g does not have one), we pick the latter. To see how this translates into Coq, note that

$$\lceil g \rceil^i \in (\mathcal{P}(\mathsf{exp}^2) \to \mathcal{P}(\mathsf{exp}^2)) \xrightarrow{\text{mon}} \mathcal{P}(\mathsf{exp}^2) \to \mathcal{P}(\mathsf{exp}^2)$$
$$\lceil g \rceil^i = \lambda x.\ \bigsqcup\{i(g(y)) \mid y \in \mathcal{P}(\mathsf{exp}^2) \xrightarrow{\text{mon}} \mathcal{P}(\mathsf{exp}^2) \wedge i(y) \sqsubseteq x\}$$

and that $\nu\lceil g \rceil^i$, by unfolding, is equal to:

$$\bigsqcup\{i(g(y)) \mid y \in \mathcal{P}(\mathsf{exp}^2) \xrightarrow{\text{mon}} \mathcal{P}(\mathsf{exp}^2) \wedge i(y) \sqsubseteq \nu\lceil g \rceil^i\}$$

Accordingly, we write:

```
CoInductive nu_g (r: erel) (e1 e2: exp): Prop :=
  nu_g_fold (y: erel → erel) (yM: monotonic y)
        (LE: ∀r', y r' ⊆ nu_g r') (IN: g y yM e1 e2).
```

Here, `g y yM e1 e2` may look a bit different, depending on how g is defined (if it is not defined explicitly, one can just inline it here).

Similar to the first part, and as is evident from the theory, all this applies to induction (*i.e.,* least fixed points) as well.

Remark. The type that we used for illustration,

$$(\mathcal{P}(\mathsf{exp}^2) \xrightarrow{\text{mon}} \mathcal{P}(\mathsf{exp}^2)) \xrightarrow{\text{mon}} (\mathcal{P}(\mathsf{exp}^2) \xrightarrow{\text{mon}} \mathcal{P}(\mathsf{exp}^2)),$$

is highly reminiscent of one that occurs in the meta-theory of *Relation Transition Systems (RTS)* [7], a new kind of semantic model that we recently introduced for compositional reasoning about program equivalences in higher-order stateful languages. Reasoning using this method feels very much like a regular bisimulation argument: to show the equivalence of two functions, one has to construct a "local knowledge" relating them and then prove its "consistency". In our mechanized RTS proofs, we found that explicitly defining this local knowledge up front was quite a painful experience, for essentially the same reasons as defining the Tarski-style simulation relation was painful in the example in Section 3.

It turns out that being a consistent local knowledge can be expressed as being a postfixed point of a certain monotone function of basically the above type:

$$(\mathcal{P}(\mathsf{exp}^2) \xrightarrow{\text{mon}} \mathcal{P}(\mathsf{exp}^2)) \xrightarrow{\text{mon}} (\mathcal{P}(\mathsf{exp}^2) \xrightarrow{\text{mon}} \mathcal{P}(\mathsf{exp}^2))$$

By following the internal approach and using the trick presented here, we were able to bring the benefits of parameterized coinduction to our RTS framework, while keeping changes to existing definitions to a minimum.

7. Coq Implementation and Evaluation

In this section, we discuss our implementation of parameterized coinduction in Coq, and compare it to other approaches, most notably Coq's builtin `cofix` tactic.

Technique	Lines	Proof (s)	Qed (s)	Composes?
Tarski	74	8.5	3.5	no
Coq's `cofix` (§7.3)	8	7.9	14.0	no
Internal (§7.1)	8	8.6	5.1	yes
External (§7.2)	8	11.8	4.3	yes

Table 1. Comparison of the mechanization approaches

For a fair comparison, we have carried out the simulation proof of the example from Section 3 using a number of different approaches, and show the results in Table 1. In each case, we report: (a) the number of lines of proof and auxiliary lemmas/definitions, not counting the lines of generic library lemmas and tactics as these can be defined once and for all; (b) the time taken to execute the corresponding proof script; and (c) the time taken to check (`Qed`) that the constructed proof object (from running the script) is valid.

Tarski: Explicitly define a simulation relation, prove that it is valid (*i.e.,* a postfixed point of *sim*), and then apply (TARSKI). This requires by far the most human effort, which is partially reflected in lines of code needed to define the simulation relation; the proof itself is quite short, and hence `Qed`-checking is fast.

Cofix: Use Coq's builtin `cofix` tactic to simulate an incremental proof. We shall discuss this approach in detail in Section 7.3, but for the moment we remark that proof checking (the Qed column) for `cofix` is significantly slower than for all the other approaches, and can become a serious usability bottleneck in larger examples.

Internal: Use a direct encoding of G_{sim} following the internal approach described in Section 5. (See Section 7.1 for the details.)

External: Use a library-based definition of G_{sim} following the external approach. (See Section 7.2 for the details.)

Among these approaches, it is quite clear that the internal and external approaches are roughly equivalent, with the internal approach being somewhat more efficient by virtue of using primitive definitions, and avoiding the use of clever inference during type checking (namely, canonical structures or type classes) that the external approach requires. The two are much faster than the `cofix` approach. Moreover, they enable compositional proof developments, unlike the other two approaches.

7.1 Internal Implementation of Parameterized Coinduction

We now show what the internal approach to mechanizing parameterized coinduction (discussed in Section 5) looks like in practice, by applying it to the example from Section 3.

For the sake of a sharper contrast with the external approach, we do not parameterize G (which we could, with the help of the trick from Section 6.1), but directly define G_{sim}:

```
CoInductive psimil r (e1 e2 : exp) : Prop := psimil_fold
 (VAL: ∀v : val, e1 = v → e2 ⇝τ v)
 (EXP: ∀q e1', e1 →q e1' →
     ∃ e2', e2 ⇝q e2' ∧ (psimil r e1' e2' ∨ r e1' e2')).
```

Observe how `psimil r` corresponds to $G_{sim}(r)$. Next, we prove the following accumulation property, which we could in principle instrument Coq to generate and prove automatically.

```
Theorem psimil_acc : ∀l r,
 (∀ r', r ⊆ r' → l ⊆ r' → l ⊆ psimil r') →
 l ⊆ psimil r.
```

This is a variant of the ($\Longleftarrow$) direction of Theorem 4 in "Mendler form", which avoids the explicit join operation and is thus a bit more convenient to use interactively than its simpler counterpart. Also, note that the unfold property (Lemma 3) is implicit in the definition of psimil, and that we do not need to state Lemma 2 either, because we simply work with $G_{sim}(\bot)$ directly.

We can now already state and prove the example from Section 3:

```
Theorem fg_simulated :
  ∀ n m (EQ: n = 2 * m), psimil bot2 (f @ n) (g @ m).
Proof.
  pcofix CIH using psimil_acc.
  intros; subst; do 6 psimil_step 1; do 2 psimil_step 0.
  destruct m0; psimil_step 2; [|eauto].
  left; fold restart f g; generalize (m+(m+0)).
  pcofix CIH' using psimil_acc.
  intros; do 3 psimil_step 1.
  destruct n; psimil_step 1; [eauto|].
  do 3 psimil_step 1; eauto.
Qed.
```

In this proof script, all tactics except psimil_step and pcofix are standard (*i.e.*, part of Coq). The former matches one step of e_1 with n steps of e_2. The latter assists in applying parameterized coinduction: pcofix rewrites the goal to a form suitable for applying the accumulation theorem, applies the theorem, and then simplifies the result. For instance, at the beginning of the proof (when the goal is simply the theorem statement), applying psimil_acc directly is not possible, because Coq cannot figure out how to instantiate its l parameter. Hence we invoke pcofix, which first transforms the goal into the following equivalent statement:

```
(fun x y ⇒ ∃n m, f @ n = x ∧ g @ m = y ∧ n = 2 * m)
⊑ psimil bot2
```

After that, it applies psimil_acc (its argument), which now matches the goal, and finally pcofix simplifies the resulting proof state so that the user never sees this explicit function expression:

```
r : exp → exp → Prop
CIH : ∀n m, n = 2 * m → r (f @ n) (g @ m)
------------------------------------------------
∀ n m, n = 2 * m → psimil r (f @ n) (g @ m)
```

Note that the new goal essentially also appears as the coinduction hypothesis CIH, except that psimil has been removed, and so the hypothesis is "semantically guarded."

The second use of pcofix corresponds to the "Accumulation Step" of the proof sketch, and results in the following proof state:

```
r : exp → exp → Prop
CIH : ∀n m, n = 2 * m → r (f @ n) (g @ m)
CIH' : ∀n, r ((restart @ f) @ n) ((restart @ g) @ n)
------------------------------------------------
∀ n, psimil r ((restart @ f) @ n) ((restart @ g) @ n)
```

It essentially added the additional assumption CIH', but to achieve this, it had quite some cleaning up to do internally: after applying the accumulation theorem, a new r' (greater than r) had been introduced, so pcofix used transitivity of ⊑ to convert all existing hypotheses involving r into statements about r', which it then finally renamed to r again.

Although we have demonstrated the use of our pcofix tactic on one example, it is not tailored to this particular example—rather, it is a general tactic that applies to arbitrary coinductive predicates. It is implemented in Ltac with the help of the **hpattern** [6] library for handling dependent types.

7.2 External Implementation of Parameterized Coinduction

We implement G from Section 2 using a complete lattice library that provides a type of complete lattices (cola) and operations such as gfp, ⊑, ⊔ (all with the obvious meaning):

```
Definition G {C : cola} (f : C → C) (x : C) :=
  gfp (fun y ⇒ f (x ⊔ y)).
```

Next, we prove Lemma 3 (here as two separate lemmas) and (the interesting direction of) the accumulation property (Theorem 4, again expressed in Mendler-style to make it easier to use). Like before, there is no point in defining $\nu\, sim$ explicitly and proving Lemma 2, because we can just work with $G_{sim}(\bot)$ directly.

```
Lemma G_fold: ∀(C:cola) (f:C → C), monotone f →
  ∀ r: C, f (G f r ⊔ r) ⊑ G f r.
Lemma G_unfold: ∀(C:cola) (f:C → C), monotone f →
  ∀ r: C, G f r ⊑ f (G f r ⊔ r).
Theorem G_acc: ∀(C:cola) (f:C → C), monotone f →
  ∀ l r, (∀ r', r ⊑ r' → l ⊑ r' → l ⊑ G f r') →
  l ⊑ G f r.
```

To use this library, we simply define the generating function sim.

```
Inductive sim r (e1 e2: exp) : Prop := sim_fold
  (VAL: ∀v : val, e1 = v → e2 ~τ~> v)
  (EXP: ∀q e1', e1 -q-> e1' → ∃e2', e2 ~q~> e2' ∧ r e1' e2').
```

Then G sim corresponds to G_{sim}, where the implicit argument C:cola is automatically inferred from the type of sim with the help of Coq's canonical structure mechanism.

The statement of the example from Section 3 is the same as in the internal implementation (fg_simulated above), except that psimil is replaced by (G sim). In the corresponding proof script, the argument to the pcofix tactic changes from psimil_acc to (G_acc sim). Similarly, the psimil_step tactic is replaced by one that applies (G_fold sim) instead of psimil_fold.

7.3 Coq's cofix

Coq's standard coinduction principle is rather syntactic and thus quite different from the Tarski principle. It basically works as follows: to show $x \sqsubseteq \nu f$, one invokes Coq's builtin cofix tactic, which adds the very same proposition as an assumption to the local context. Being an ordinary assumption, it can be used at any point in the proof script. However, once the proof is finished, Coq runs a syntactic check on the proof term and accepts it only if the use of the coinductive assumption is guarded [3].

It is possible, although not well known, that one can nest uses of cofix and thereby achieve a form of incremental (albeit non-compositional) coinduction. For example, if we take the proof script from Section 7.1 and simply replace the two occurrences of "pcofix CIH['] using psimil_acc" with "cofix CIH[']", we obtain a valid proof!

Despite its surprising usefulness in allowing a form of accumulation, Coq's cofix approach to coinductive proofs has several important drawbacks due to its syntactic nature:[5]

- It is non-compositional. Inside a proof via cofix, the use of normal lemmas involving the coinduction hypothesis is not permitted by guardedness checking, because they are treated opaquely. One can of course mark these lemmas as transparent (thereby further slowing down proof checking), but this does not yield proper compositionality: from the *statements* of the transparent lemmas alone, one cannot know whether their proofs can be composed together to yield a valid proof.[6]
- It is inefficient. Guardedness checking can be very slow, mainly because it has to reduce proof terms to normal forms, which may be huge. This problem is already apparent from Table 1 and

[5] Another critique of Coq's syntactic guardedness checking can be found in Barthe et al. [2].

[6] One way to think of this is by the following analogy. Our (COMPOSE) rule corresponds to the rely-guarantee parallel composition rule [8], whereas transparent lemma application within a cofix-proof corresponds to the earlier non-compositional Owicki-Gries rule [15] with the syntactic non-interference side condition.

becomes aggravated in larger developments. In our accompanying Coq code, we provide an example from an earlier project, where proof checking takes 192 seconds due to `cofix`. Replacing `cofix` with `pcofix` reduces this to 40 seconds.

- It is not at all user-friendly. The user interface does not indicate when exactly in a proof it is safe to use the coinductive assumption. Coq provides a designated command for explicitly checking guardness, but, due to the previous issue, its repeated use during the proof is often impractical.
- It interacts poorly with builtin automation tactics. They do not know about guardedness and hence very frequently produce incorrect "proofs". Usually this happens because automation applies constructors and hypotheses in the wrong order, solving the goal but causing the proof to be rejected later by the guardedness checker. To make matters worse, as a consequence of the two previous issues, it is very painful to debug such situations. Consequently, one has to be extremely careful when using automation.

  As a demonstration of automation leading to a dead end, consider the following code:

```
Definition monotone0 (f: Prop → Prop) :=
  ∀ (p q: Prop), f p → (p → q) → f q.
CoInductive A f: Prop :=
  foldA (p: Prop) (LE: p → A f) (IN: f (f p)).

Goal ∀(f: Prop → Prop) (MON: monotone0 f),
  ∀p: Prop, (p → f (f p)) → p → A f.
Proof.
  cofix CIH; intros; eapply foldA; eauto.
Qed. (* REJECTED *)
```

  Here, although we explicitly apply the constructor (`foldA`) first, `eauto` somehow manages to construct an invalid proof term. We can obtain a proper proof by manually applying the coinduction hypothesis before letting `eauto` take over (this is the result of trial and error):

```
cofix CIH; intros; eapply foldA; [apply CIH|]; eauto.
```

  Alternatively, we can just do the proof using our `pcofix` tactic instead of `cofix` (where `A_acc` is the corresponding accumulation lemma):

```
pcofix CIH using A_acc; eauto using foldA.
```

7.4 Paco: A Coq Library for Parameterized Coinduction

In order to make parameterized coinduction more easily applicable, we have built the Coq library *Paco* (standing for *pa*rameterized *co*induction). Paco contains internal implementations of parameterized coinduction for predicates of arity up to 15, with $\text{paco}\{n\}\ f$ standing for G_f for any monotone function f from predicates of arity n to predicates of arity n.

Besides the `pcofix` tactic that we have already seen in Section 7.1, the library provides tactics for folding (`pfold`) and unfolding (`punfold`) the definition of G_f, for proving monotonicity of predicates (`pmonauto`) and for simplifying hypotheses by reducing occurrences of $r \sqcup \bot$ to r (`pclearbot`). It also provides multiplication lemmas ($\text{paco}\{n\}$`_mult`) of the form $G_f(G_f(r)) \sqsubseteq G_f(r)$. These follow easily from Theorem 4 and monotonicity of G_f, and show that "doubly guarded" assumptions r are also simply guarded. We have found these multiplication lemmas useful for composing parameterized coinduction proofs.

To illustrate the use of our library, we build on the example of the introduction. We represent a graph by a type of nodes and a relation, R, characterizing the edges between nodes:

```
Variables (Node: Type) (R: Node → Node → Prop).
```

We now define infinite paths using parameterized coinduction. (We write `paco1` and `bot1` as the predicate is unary.)

```
Inductive step (X: Node → Prop) (x: Node) : Prop :=
 | step_intro : ∀y, R x y → X y → step X x.
Hint Constructors step.
Definition infpath := paco1 step bot1.
```

We also prove monotonicity of `step`, and register the corresponding lemma in the `paco` hint database that is used by `punfold`.

```
Lemma step_mon : monotone1 step. Proof. pmonauto. Qed.
Hint Resolve step_mon : paco.
```

Further, we define the predicate `path n x` to say that there exists an outgoing path of length `n` from node `x`.

```
Fixpoint path n x := match n with
  | O ⇒ True
  | S n ⇒ ∃y, R x y ∧ path n y
 end.
```

Then we can establish that if an infinite path emanates from x, then so do paths of length n, for any n. This is proved by induction on n and unfolding and inverting the definition of infinite paths.

```
Goal ∀n x, infpath x → path n x.
Proof.
  induction n; intros; simpl; auto.
  punfold H; inversion H; pclearbot; eauto.
Qed.
```

This shows that Paco-style coinductive definitions can, after unfolding, be inverted just as native Coq coinductive definitions can.

We move on to a more interesting property involving transitive closure that was suggested to us by an anonymous reviewer. The goal is to prove that if there is a predicate P holding of a node x in a graph and that whenever P holds of a node there is a non-empty path at the end of which P holds again, then there is an infinite path starting from x. The infinite path can be constructed by concatenating these non-empty paths, which is formally done by an inner induction inside a coinductive proof.

```
Goal ∀(P: Node → Prop),
     (∀ x, P x → ∃y, clos_trans_1n _ R x y ∧ P y) →
     ∀ x, P x → infpath x.
Proof.
  pcofix CIH; intros P M x Px.
  destruct (M _ Px) as (y & C & Py); clear Px.
  induction C; pfold; eauto.
Qed.
```

Using Paco, the proof is straightforward: `destruct` instantiates the second assumption and destructs the existential quantifier to expose the transitive closure, upon which an induction is later performed, whereas `clear Px` simply forgets `Px` to avoid confusing the later automation. Moreover, `pcofix` ensures that the coinductive hypothesis `CIH` is used in a semantically guarded way by construction, thereby placing no further restrictions on the proof. In contrast, carrying out this proof using Coq's builtin `cofix` tactic is surprisingly difficult because the inner inductive proof turns out to violate Coq's conservative syntactic notion of guardedness, thus necessitating ugly workarounds.

8. Discussion and Related Work

In this section, we compare to some related forms of incremental coinduction that have appeared in the literature, including the earlier versions of our construction due to Winskel [23] and Moss [14]. We conclude with some thoughts about Coq.

Local Model Checking and the "Reduction Lemma". To our knowledge, the earliest account of the parameterized greatest fixed point is in a 1989 paper by Winskel [23]. That paper, building on prior work of Larsen [10] and Stirling and Walker [21], is focused on the specific problem of "local model checking" in the modal μ-calculus—*i.e.,* deciding whether a particular state or process in a labelled transition system satisfies some recursively-defined assertion. However, in the course of attacking this specific problem, Winskel presents a generally useful construction (on power sets, but easily generalizable to lattices) that, with hindsight, we can analyze and appreciate in a more abstract way.

Winskel's key innovation is a parameterized recursive assertion, which he writes as $\nu X\{\vec{r}\}A$. One can understand this assertion as representing the greatest fixed point $\nu X.A$ under the "accumulated knowledge" $\vec{r}$, but where—and this is the key difference from our parameterized greatest fixed point—the use of the accumulated knowledge is *not guarded*. Winskel correspondingly provides the following rules for checking recursive assertions incrementally (where $p \vdash A$ denotes that process p satisfies assertion A):

$$\frac{p \in \{\vec{r}\}}{p \vdash \nu X\{\vec{r}\}A} \qquad \frac{p \notin \{\vec{r}\} \quad p \vdash A[\nu X\{p,\vec{r}\}A/X]}{p \vdash \nu X\{\vec{r}\}A}$$

Due to the *un*-guardedness embodied by the first of these rules, Winskel's parameterized ν-assertion does not support compositional reasoning along the lines of our COMPOSE rule. In particular, from $p \vdash \nu X\{q,\vec{r}\}A$ and $q \vdash \nu X\{p,\vec{r}\}A$, one cannot conclude that $p \vdash \nu X\{\vec{r}\}A$ or $q \vdash \nu X\{\vec{r}\}A$, since the premises hold trivially if $p = q$. Interestingly, a subsequent paper by Andersen, Stirling and Winskel [1], building on Winskel's parameterized ν-assertions, presents a "compositional proof system" for the modal μ-calculus, but they mean "compositional"—an admittedly overloaded term—in a very different sense from us (their "compositional" concerns the structure of *processes*).

Our parameterized greatest fixed point may be understood as a guarded version of Winskel's. Formally, Winskel's model of $\nu X\{\vec{r}\}A$ is synonymous with $\nu X.(\{\vec{r}\} \cup A)$. In the notation of our paper, this suggests the following alternative to our $\mathrm{G}_f(x)$:

$$W_f(x) \stackrel{\text{def}}{=} \nu z.\ x \sqcup f(z)$$

The connection to $\mathrm{G}_f(x)$, provable using a few straightforward applications of Tarski's principle, is then very simple:

$$\begin{aligned} W_f(x) &\equiv x \sqcup \mathrm{G}_f(x) \\ \mathrm{G}_f(x) &\equiv f(W_f(x)) \end{aligned}$$

For the purpose of proving soundness of local model checking, the lack of guardedness in $W_f(x)$ was not an issue, but for compositional proof development it is.

That said, the key technical result that Winskel employs in order to prove soundness of his local model checking algorithm, namely a "reduction lemma" due to Kozen [9], is in fact interderivable with our Theorem 4. The reduction lemma states, for monotone f:

$$y \sqsubseteq \nu f \iff y \sqsubseteq f(W_f(y))$$

To see the connection with Theorem 4, first observe that since $f(W_f(y)) \equiv G_f(y)$, the reduction lemma can be restated as:

$$y \sqsubseteq \nu f \iff y \sqsubseteq G_f(y)$$

And since $\nu f \equiv \mathrm{G}_f(\bot)$, the lemma can thus be seen as an instantiation of Theorem 4 where $x := \bot$. At the same time, Theorem 4 can also be seen as an instantiation of the reduction lemma! Specifically, if (given x) we instantiate the reduction lemma's f with $f(x \sqcup -)$, it yields

$$y \sqsubseteq \nu z.\ f(x \sqcup z) \iff y \sqsubseteq \nu z.\ f(x \sqcup y \sqcup z)$$

This is precisely Theorem 4.

Incremental Coinduction. In 2010, Popescu and Gunter [16] proposed a proof system for incremental coinduction, tailored towards bisimilarity in a process calculus, and they established the soundness of their system by a global, monolithic argument. Their judgment $\theta \vdash \theta'$ corresponds precisely to $\theta' \sqsubseteq \theta \sqcup \mathrm{G}_f(\theta)$ (where f is the generating function of their process bisimilarity). This suggests that our/Winskel's lattice-theoretic account of parameterized coinduction might (a) offer a simpler alternative proof of their logic's soundness, and (b) support a shallow embedding of their logic in Isabelle/HOL, which is much more efficient than a deep embedding since it reuses the proof assistant's underlying infrastructure. Finally, we note that because their proof system (like Winskel's) does not offer a way of expressing guarded entailments, it does not admit a circular compositional rule, such as (COMPOSE).

Circular Coinduction. Rather than developing a custom proof system, another approach to incremental coinduction that has been tried is to engineer a tactic that builds the full simulation relation on the fly as the interactive proof progresses [5]. The idea is to use a unification metavariable during the proof and try to show that $R_0 \subseteq ?r$ and $?r \subseteq f(?r)$. To solve the first goal, we set $?r := R_0 \cup ?r'$, where $?r'$ is a fresh metavariable. Each time we later encounter a goal $R_0' \subseteq R_0 \cup ?r'$, where $R_0' \not\subseteq R_0$, we instantiate $?r' := R_0' \cup ?r''$, where $?r''$ is another fresh metavariable, and proceed. If this exploration phase ever terminates, then at the end there should be one uninstantiated $?r^{(n)}$ metavariable left, which we can instantiate to the empty relation, $\emptyset$. In this way, we will have constructed a valid postfixed point of f incrementally, and Coq can thus conclude that $R_0 \subseteq \nu f$.

Under this approach, even if the construction of the simulation relation can be done incrementally using clever tactics, the whole simulation has to eventually be constructed. As a result, this approach does not support compositional reasoning.

Coen's Principle. Isabelle's standard library (theory `Inductive`) contains an interesting coinduction principle for sets attributed to Martin Coen. Generalized to complete lattices, it reads:

$$x \sqsubseteq f(\mu y.\ f(y) \sqcup x \sqcup \nu f) \implies x \sqsubseteq \nu f \qquad \text{(COEN)}$$

This principle is strictly less useful than our parameterized coinduction. While it lets us remember the initial x for as many unfoldings of νf as desired, it does not let us accumulate further knowledge during the proof, nor does it support compositional reasoning. Interestingly, if we change the least fixed point into a greatest one, then the result, $f(\nu y.\ f(y) \sqcup x \sqcup \nu f)$, is equivalent to our G_f.

Parametric Corecursion. Moss [14] first introduced the construction that we use in this paper in a categorical setting, calling it parametric corecursion and proving an analogue of Theorem 4. He was chiefly concerned with defining elements of coinductive sets, rather than constructing proofs of coinductive predicates, and thus did not observe the compositionality of this simple construction nor its practical utility in mechanized theorem proving. More specifically, in his work, given sets X and Y of variables, a function of type $X \to \mathrm{G}_f(Y)$ models a set of equations of the form $\{\, x = \phi_x(Y)\,\}_{x \in X}$, where $\mathrm{G}_f(Y)$ is the coinductive set defined by the functor $f(Y + (-))$ (which corresponds to our G_f constructor) and ϕ_x's are formulae of some particular form related to f. Then, given a set of recursive equations of type $X \to \mathrm{G}_f(X + Y)$, the variant of Theorem 4 gives its solution for X, which is a set of non-recursive equations of type $X \to \mathrm{G}_f(Y)$. In particular, when Y is the empty set, $X \to \mathrm{G}_f(\emptyset)$ determines elements of $\mathrm{G}_f(\emptyset)$, the final coalgebra of f (*i.e.,* the coinductive set defined by f).

Below, we present an example showing that this construction can be useful for programming (guarded) corecursive functions. Take `pcotree` to be the set of parameterized infinite binary trees with nodes containing natural numbers, defined as follows:

```
CoInductive pcotree (R: Type) : Type :=
| tcons (a: nat) (tl: pcotree R + R) (tr: pcotree R + R).
```

We can then define the coiterator combinator `coitr` of the following type using the construction above (see the website for details):

```
coitr: ∀L R, (L → cotree (L + R)) → L → cotree R
```

Now we define the infinite tree `fliptree` containing 1 on every left child and 2 on every right child, depicted below:

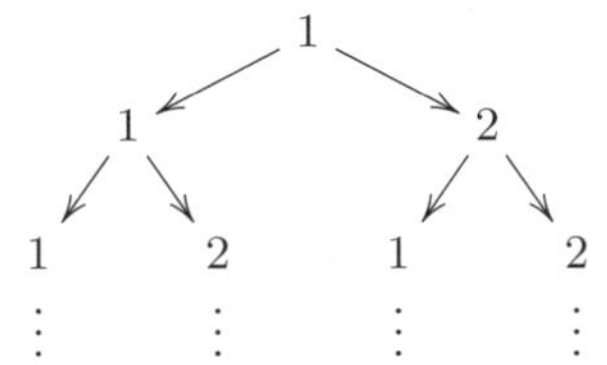

Using `coitr`, we can write the corecursive definition of `fliptree` without using **CoFixpoint**, thus avoiding guardedness checking:

```
Definition fliptree : cotree False :=
  coitr (fun onetree ⇒ tcons 1
    (inr (inl onetree))
    (inl (coitr (fun twotree ⇒ tcons 2
          (inr (inr (inl onetree)))
          (inr (inl twotree))) I))) I.
```

Nice as these examples are, we believe that the more important use of Moss's categorical construction is in building *proofs* incrementally and compositionally using tactics, as we have sought to demonstrate in this paper.

Application to Agda. We remark that the direct internal approach also works for Agda and Coq's indexed sets, because Lemmas 2–3 and Theorem 4 can be generalized to a lattice where the greatest fixed point $G_f(x)$ exists for a particular f (*i.e.,* it does not have to exist for all f as in a complete lattice). We can easily show that indexed sets form (non-complete) lattices, as they have a natural order, finite products and coproducts. Also, for a strictly positive function f, we can define $G_f(x)$ using Agda's ∞ constructor (or Coq's **CoInductive**), which gives a greatest fixed point of f on this lattice, and we can thus reason about statements of the form $y \sqsubseteq G_f(x)$ using our principle. In this setting, however, we cannot use Mendler-style recursion because it requires impredicative quantification.

Coinduction vs Induction in Coq. It is instructive to contrast Coq's support for induction and coinduction. In both cases, Coq provides a built-in (co-)recursion combinator that comes with a syntactic guardedness condition. As we have seen in Section 7.3, it is possible (but quite inconvenient) to use corecursion directly inside a proof via the `cofix` tactic.

For each inductively defined type, Coq additionally generates induction lemmas (proved using the aforementioned recursion combinator), which semantically enforce guardedness. These lemmas can conveniently be applied using the `induction` tactic, rendering the use of the low-level recursion combinator inside proofs unnecessary for most users.

For coinductively defined types, however, Coq does not generate any lemmas, nor does it provide a "`coinduction`" tactic analogous to its `induction` tactic. Our work can be seen as filling this gap by providing lemmas such as `G_unfold` and `G_acc` and the tactic `pcofix`. It is also worth pointing out that, unlike the Coq-generated principles for induction, ours are *complete*: whatever can be proved using `cofix` can also be proved using `G_acc` & co.

Acknowledgements

We would like to give special thanks to Deepak Garg for alerting us to the connection with Winskel's work. We would also like to thank Andreas Abel, Fritz Henglein, Neel Krishnaswami, Andy Pitts, and Glynn Winskel for helpful discussions, as well as the anonymous reviewers for their constructive feedback.

References

[1] H. R. Andersen, C. Stirling, and G. Winskel. A compositional proof system for the modal μ-calculus. In *LICS*, pages 144–153. IEEE Computer Society, 1994.

[2] G. Barthe, M. J. Frade, E. Giménez, L. Pinto, and T. Uustalu. Type-based termination of recursive definitions. *Mathematical Structures in Comp. Sci.*, 14(1):97–141, Feb. 2004.

[3] E. Giménez. Codifying guarded definitions with recursive schemes. In *Types for Proofs and Programs*, volume 996 of *LNCS*, pages 39–59. Springer, 1995.

[4] A. D. Gordon. Bisimilarity as a theory of functional programming. *Theoretical Computer Science*, 228(1-2):5–47, 1999.

[5] D. Hausmann, T. Mossakowski, and L. Schroeder. Iterative circular coinduction for CoCasl in Isabelle/HOL. In *FASE*, volume 3442 of *LNCS*, pages 341–356. Springer, 2005.

[6] C.-K. Hur. Heq: a Coq library for heterogeneous equality, 2010. Presented at Coq-2 workshop.

[7] C.-K. Hur, D. Dreyer, G. Neis, and V. Vafeiadis. The marriage of bisimulations and Kripke logical relations. In *POPL*, 2012.

[8] C. B. Jones. Specification and design of (parallel) programs. In *IFIP Congress*, pages 321–332, 1983.

[9] D. Kozen. Results on the propositional μ-calculus. *Theor. Comput. Sci.*, 27:333–354, 1983.

[10] K. G. Larsen. Proof systems for Hennessy-Milner logic with recursion. In *CAAP*, volume 299 of *LNCS*, pages 215–230. Springer, 1988.

[11] R. Matthes. Recursion on nested datatypes in dependent type theory. In *Computability in Europe (CiE)*, volume 5028 of *LNCS*, pages 431–446. Springer, 2008.

[12] N. P. Mendler. Inductive types and type constraints in the second-order lambda calculus. *Annals of Pure and Applied Logic*, 51(1-2):159 – 172, 1991.

[13] R. Milner. *Communicating and Mobile Systems: The Pi-Calculus*. Cambridge University Press, 1999.

[14] L. S. Moss. Parametric corecursion. *Theor. Comput. Sci.*, 260(1-2):139–163, June 2001.

[15] S. S. Owicki and D. Gries. An axiomatic proof technique for parallel programs. *Acta Informatica*, 6:319–340, 1976.

[16] A. Popescu and E. L. Gunter. Incremental pattern-based coinduction for process algebra and its Isabelle formalization. In *FOSSACS*, pages 109–127, 2010.

[17] D. Sangiorgi. On the bisimulation proof method. *Mathematical Structures in Comp. Sci.*, 8(5):447–479, Oct. 1998.

[18] D. Sangiorgi. *Introduction to Bisimulation and Coinduction*. Cambridge University Press, 2011.

[19] D. Sangiorgi and J. Rutten. *Advanced Topics in Bisimulation and Coinduction*. Cambridge Tracts in Theoretical Computer Science. Cambridge University Press, 2011.

[20] J. Ševčík, V. Vafeiadis, F. Zappa Nardelli, S. Jagannathan, and P. Sewell. Relaxed-memory concurrency and verified compilation. In *POPL*, 2011.

[21] C. Stirling and D. Walker. Local model checking in the modal mu-calculus. In *TAPSOFT, Vol.1 (CAAP)*, volume 351 of *LNCS*, pages 369–383. Springer, 1989.

[22] A. Tarski. A lattice-theoretical fixpoint theorem and its applications. *Pacific J. Math.*, 5(2):285–309, 1955.

[23] G. Winskel. A note on model checking the modal ν-calculus. In *ICALP*, volume 372 of *LNCS*, pages 761–772. Springer, 1989.

Meta-Theory à la Carte

Benjamin Delaware
University of Texas at Austin
bendy@cs.utexas.edu

Bruno C. d. S. Oliveira
National University of Singapore
oliveira@comp.nus.edu.sg

Tom Schrijvers
Universiteit Gent
tom.schrijvers@ugent.be

Abstract

Formalizing meta-theory, or proofs about programming languages, in a proof assistant has many well-known benefits. Unfortunately, the considerable effort involved in mechanizing proofs has prevented it from becoming standard practice. This cost can be amortized by reusing as much of existing mechanized formalizations as possible when building a new language or extending an existing one. One important challenge in achieving reuse is that the inductive definitions and proofs used in these formalizations are closed to extension. This forces language designers to cut and paste existing definitions and proofs in an ad-hoc manner and to expend considerable effort to patch up the results.

The key contribution of this paper is the development of an induction technique for extensible Church encodings using a novel reinterpretation of the universal property of folds. These encodings provide the foundation for a framework, formalized in Coq, which uses type classes to automate the composition of proofs from modular components. This framework enables a more structured approach to the reuse of meta-theory formalizations through the composition of modular inductive definitions and proofs.

Several interesting language features, including binders and general recursion, illustrate the capabilities of our framework. We reuse these features to build fully mechanized definitions and proofs for a number of languages, including a version of mini-ML. Bounded induction enables proofs of properties for non-inductive semantic functions, and mediating type classes enable proof adaptation for more feature-rich languages.

Categories and Subject Descriptors D.3.1 [*Programming Languages*]: Formal Definitions and Theory—Semantics

Keywords Modular Mechanized Meta-Theory, Extensible Church Encodings, Coq

1. Introduction

With their POPLMARK challenge, Aydemir et al. [3] identified *representation of binders*, *complex inductions*, *experimentation*, and *reuse of components* as key challenges in mechanizing programming language meta-theory. While progress has been made, for example on the representation of binders, it is still difficult to reuse components, including language definitions and proofs.

The current approach to reuse still involves copying an existing formalization and adapting it manually to incorporate new features. An extreme case of this copy-&-adapt approach can be found in Leroy's three person-year verified compiler project [22], which consists of eight intermediate languages in addition to the source and target languages, many of which are minor variations of each other. Due to the crosscutting impact of new features, the adaptation of existing features is unnecessarily labor-intensive. Moreover, from a software/formalization management perspective a proliferation of copies is obviously a nightmare. Typical formalizations present two important challenges to providing reuse:

1. **Extensibility:** Conventional inductive definitions and proofs are *closed* to extension and cannot simply be imported and extended with new constructors and cases. This is a manifestation of the well-known *Expression Problem* (EP) [45].
2. **Modular reasoning:** Reasoning with modular definitions requires reasoning about partial definitions and composing partial proofs to build a complete proof. However, conventional induction principles which are the fundamental reasoning techniques in most theorem provers only work for complete definitions.

The lack of reuse in formalizations is somewhat surprising, because proof assistants such as Coq and Agda have powerful modularity constructs including *modules* [26], *type classes* [17, 42, 46] and expressive forms of *dependent types* [11, 34]. It is reasonable to wonder whether these language constructs can help to achieve better reuse. After all, there has been a lot of progress in addressing extensibility [14, 30, 32, 43] issues in general-purpose languages using advanced type system features – although not a lot of attention has been paid to modular reasoning.

This paper presents MTC, a framework for defining and reasoning about extensible inductive datatypes. The framework is implemented as a Coq library which enables modular mechanized meta-theory by allowing language features to be defined as reusable components. Using MTC, language developers can leverage existing efforts to build new languages by developing new and interesting features and combining them with previously written components.

The solution to extensibility in MTC was partly inspired by the popular "Data types à la Carte" (DTC) [43] technique. However, DTC fundamentally relies on a type-level fixpoint definition for building modular data types, which cannot be encoded in Coq. MTC solves this problem by using (extensible) *Church encodings* of data types [30, 34, 35]. These encodings allow DTC-style modular data types to be defined in the restricted Coq setting. Another difference between DTC and MTC is the use of Mendler-style folds and algebras instead of conventional folds to express modular definitions. The advantage of Mendler-style folds [44] and algebras is that they offer explicit control over the evaluation order, which is important when modeling semantics of programming languages. MTC employs similar techniques to solve extensibility problems in proofs and *inductively defined predicates*.

MTC's solution to modular reasoning uses a novel reinterpretation of the *universal property* of folds. Because MTC relies on

POPL'13, January 23–25, 2013, Rome, Italy.

folds, the proof methods used in the *initial algebra semantics of data types* [16, 27] offer an alternative to structural induction. With some care, universal properties can be exploited to adapt these techniques to modular Church encodings. In addition to enabling modular reasoning about extensible inductive datatypes, universal properties also overcome some theoretical issues related to Church encodings in the Calculus of (Inductive) Constructions [34, 35].

MTC also supports ubiquitous higher-order language features such as binders and general recursion. Binders are modeled with a *parametric HOAS* [8] representation (a first-order representation would be possible too). Because these features require general recursion, they cannot be defined inductively using folds. To support these non-inductive features MTC uses a variation of mixins [10]. Mixins are closely related to Mendler-style folds, but they allow uses of general recursion, and can be modeled on top of Mendler-style Church encodings using a bounded fixpoint combinator.

To illustrate the utility of MTC, we present a case study modularizing several orthogonal features of a variant of mini-ML [9]. The case study illustrates how various features and partial *type soundness* proofs can be modularly developed and verified and later composed to assemble complete languages and proofs.

1.1 Contributions

The main contribution of our work is a novel approach to defining and reasoning about extensible inductive datatypes. MTC is a Coq framework for building reusable components that implements this approach to modular mechanized meta-theory.

More technically this paper makes the following contributions:

- **Extensibility Techniques for Mechanization:** The paper provides a solution to the EP and an approach to extensible mechanization of meta-theory in the restricted type-theoretic setting of Coq. This solution offers precise control over the evaluation order by means of Mendler folds and algebras. Mixins are used to capture ubiquitous higher-order features, like PHOAS binders and general recursion.
- **Non-Axiomatic Reasoning for Church Encodings:** The paper reinterprets the universal property of folds to recover induction principles for Mendler-style Church encodings. This allows us to avoid the axioms used in earlier approaches and preserves Coq's strong normalization.
- **Modular Reasoning:** The paper presents modular reasoning techniques for modular components. It lifts the recovered induction principle from individual inductive features to compositions, while induction over a bounded step count enables modular reasoning about non-inductive higher-order features modeled with mixins.

MTC is implemented in the Coq proof assistant and the code is available at `http://www.cs.utexas.edu/~bendy/MTC`. Our implementation minimizes the user's burden for adding new features by automating the boilerplate with type classes and default tactics. Moreover, the framework already provides modular components for mini-ML as a starting point for new language formalizations. We also provide a complimentary Haskell implementation of the computational subset of code used in this paper.

1.2 Code and Notational Conventions

While all the code underlying this paper has been developed in Coq, the paper adopts a terser syntax for its code fragments. For the computational parts, this syntax exactly coincides with Haskell syntax, while it is an extrapolation of Haskell syntax for proof-related concepts. The Coq code requires the impredicative-set option.

2. Extensible Semantics in MTC

This section shows MTC's approach to extensible and modular semantic components in the restrictive setting of Coq. The approach is partly inspired by the DTC solution to the Expression Problem in Haskell, in particular its composition mechanisms for extensible inductive definitions. MTC differs from DTC in two important ways. Firstly, it uses Church encodings to avoid the termination issues of DTC's generally recursive definitions. Secondly, it uses Mendler-style folds instead of conventional folds to provide explicit control over evaluation order.

2.1 Data Types à la Carte

This subsection reviews the core ideas of DTC. DTC represents the shape of a particular data type as a *functor*. That functor uses its type parameter a for inductive occurrences of the data type, leaving the data type definition open. $Arith_F$ is an example functor for a simple arithmetic expression language with literals and addition.

$$\mathbf{data}\ Arith_F\ a = Lit\ Nat \mid Add\ a\ a$$

The explicitly recursive definition $Fix_{DTC}\ f$ closes the open recursion of a functor f.

$$\mathbf{data}\ Fix_{DTC}\ f = In\ (f\ (Fix_{DTC}\ f))$$

Applying Fix_{DTC} to $Arith_F$ builds the data type for arithmetic expressions.

$$\mathbf{type}\ Arith = Fix_{DTC}\ Arith_F$$

Functions over $Fix_{DTC}\ f$ are expressed as folds of f-algebras.

$$\begin{aligned}&\mathbf{type}\ Algebra\ f\ a = f\ a \to a\\ &fold_{DTC} :: Functor\ f \Rightarrow Algebra\ f\ a \to Fix_{DTC}\ f \to a\\ &fold_{DTC}\ alg\ (In\ fa) = alg\ (fmap\ (fold_{DTC}\ alg)\ fa)\end{aligned}$$

For example, the evaluation algebra of $Arith_F$ is defined as:

$$\begin{aligned}&\mathbf{data}\ Value = I\ Int \mid B\ Bool\\ &eval_{Arith} :: Algebra\ Arith_F\ Value\\ &eval_{Arith}\ (Lit\ n) = I\ n\\ &eval_{Arith}\ (Add\ (I\ v_1)\ (I\ v_2)) = I\ (v_1 + v_2)\end{aligned}$$

Note that the recursive occurrences in $eval_{Arith}$ are of the same type as the result type $Value$.[1] In essence, folds process the recursive occurrences so that algebras only need to specify how to combine the values (for example v_1 and v_2) resulting from evaluating the subterms. Finally, the overall evaluation function is:

$$\begin{aligned}&[\![\cdot]\!] :: Fix_{DTC}\ Arith_F \to Value\\ &[\![\cdot]\!] = fold_{DTC}\ eval_{Arith}\end{aligned}$$

$$\begin{aligned}&> [\![(Add\ (Lit\ 1)\ (Lit\ 2))]\!]\\ &3\end{aligned}$$

Unfortunately, DTC's two uses of general recursion are not permitted in Coq. Coq does not accept the type-level fixpoint combinator $Fix_{DTC}\ f$ because it is not strictly positive. Coq similarly disallows the $fold_{DTC}$ function because it is not structurally recursive.

2.2 Recursion-Free Church Encodings

MTC encodes data types and folds with Church encodings [6, 35], which are recursion-free. Church encodings represent (least) fixpoints and folds as follows:

$$\begin{aligned}&\mathbf{type}\ Fix\ f = \forall a. Algebra\ f\ a \to a\\ &fold :: Algebra\ f\ a \to Fix\ f \to a\\ &fold\ alg\ fa = fa\ alg\end{aligned}$$

[1] Boolean values are not needed yet, but they are used later in this section.

Both definitions are non-recursive and can be encoded in Coq (although we need to enable impredicativity for certain definitions). Since Church encodings represent data types as folds, the definition of *fold* is trivial: it applies the folded $Fix\ f$ data type to the algebra.

Example Church encodings of $Arith_F$'s literals and addition are given by the *lit* and *add* functions:

$$\begin{array}{l} lit :: Nat \to Fix\ Arith_F \\ lit\ n = \lambda alg \to alg\ (Lit\ n) \\ add :: Fix\ Arith_F \to Fix\ Arith_F \to Fix\ Arith_F \\ add\ e_1\ e_2 = \lambda alg \to alg\ (Add\ (fold\ alg\ e_1)\ (fold\ alg\ e_2)) \end{array}$$

The evaluation algebra and evaluation function are defined as in DTC, and expressions are evaluated in much the same way.

2.3 Lack of Control over Evaluation

Folds are structurally recursive and therefore capture *compositionality* of definitions, a desirable property of semantics. A disadvantage of the standard fold encoding is that it does not provide the implementer of the algebra with explicit control of evaluation. The fold encoding reduces all subterms; the only freedom in the algebra is whether or not to use the result.

Example: Modeling* if *expressions As a simple example that illustrates the issue of lack of control over evaluation consider modeling **if** expressions and their corresponding semantics. The big-step semantics of **if** expressions is:

$$\frac{[\![e_1]\!] \leadsto \mathbf{true} \qquad [\![e_2]\!] \leadsto v_2}{[\![\ \mathbf{if}\ e_1\ e_2\ e_3]\!] \leadsto v_2} \qquad \frac{[\![e_1]\!] \leadsto \mathbf{false} \qquad [\![e_3]\!] \leadsto v_3}{[\![\ \mathbf{if}\ e_1\ e_2\ e_3]\!] \leadsto v_3}$$

Using our framework of Church encodings, we could create a modular feature for boolean expressions such as **if** expressions and boolean literals as follows:

$$\mathbf{data}\ Logic_F\ a = If\ a\ a\ a \mid BLit\ Bool \quad \text{-- Boolean functor}$$

$$\begin{array}{l} eval_{Logic} :: Algebra\ Logic_F\ Value \\ eval_{Logic}\ (If\ v_1\ v_2\ v_3) = \mathbf{if}\ (v_1 \equiv B\ True)\ \mathbf{then}\ v_2\ \mathbf{else}\ v_3 \\ eval_{Logic}\ (BLit\ b) \qquad = B\ b \end{array}$$

However, an important difference with the big-step semantics above is that $eval_{Logic}$ cannot control where evaluation happens. All it has in hand are the values v_1, v_2 and v_3 that result from evaluation. While this difference is not important for simple features like arithmetic expressions, it does matter for **if** expressions.

Semantics guides the development of implementations. Accordingly, we believe that it is important that a semantic specification does not rely on a particular evaluation strategy (such as laziness). This definition of $eval_{Logic}$ might be reasonable in a lazy meta-language like Haskell (which is the language used by DTC), but it is misleading when used as a basis for an implementation in a strict language like ML. In a strict language $eval_{Logic}$ is clearly not a desirable definition because it evaluates both branches of the **if** expression. Aside from the obvious performance drawbacks, this is the wrong thing to do if the object language features, for example, non-termination. Furthermore, this approach can be quite brittle: in more complex object languages using folds and laziness can lead to subtle semantic issues [4].

2.4 Mendler-style Church Encodings

To express semantics in a way that allows explicit control over evaluation and does not rely on the evaluation semantics of the meta-language, MTC adapts Church encodings to use Mendler-style algebras and folds [44] which make recursive calls explicit.

$$\mathbf{type}\ Algebra_M\ f\ a = \forall r.(r \to a) \to f\ r \to a$$

A Mendler-style algebra differs from a traditional f-algebra in that it takes an additional argument $(r \to a)$ which corresponds to recursive calls. To ensure that recursive calls can only be applied structurally, the arguments that appear at recursive positions have a polymorphic type r. The use of this polymorphic type r prevents case analysis, or any other type of inspection, on those arguments. Using $Algebra_M\ f\ a$, Mendler-style folds and Mendler-style Church encodings are defined as follows:

$$\begin{array}{l} \mathbf{type}\ Fix_M\ f = \forall a.Algebra_M\ f\ a \to a \\ fold_M :: Algebra_M\ f\ a \to Fix_M\ f \to a \\ fold_M\ alg\ fa = fa\ alg \end{array}$$

Mendler-style folds allow algebras to state their recursive calls explicitly. As an example, the definition of the evaluation of **if** expressions in terms of a Mendler-style algebra is:

$$\begin{array}{l} eval_{Logic} :: Algebra_M\ Logic_F\ Value \\ eval_{Logic}\ [\![\cdot]\!]\ (BLit\ b) \qquad = B\ b \\ eval_{Logic}\ [\![\cdot]\!]\ (If\ e_1\ e_2\ e_3) = \mathbf{if}\ ([\![e_1]\!] \equiv B\ True)\ \mathbf{then}\ [\![e_2]\!] \\ \qquad\qquad\qquad\qquad\qquad\qquad\qquad\qquad \mathbf{else}\ \ [\![e_3]\!] \end{array}$$

Note that this definition allows explicit control over the evaluation order just like the big-step semantics definition. Furthermore, like the fold-definition, $eval_{Logic}$ enforces compositionality because all the algebra can do to e_1, e_2 or e_3 is to apply the recursive call $[\![\cdot]\!]$.

2.5 A Compositional Framework for Mendler-style Algebras

DTC provides a convenient framework for composing conventional fold algebras. MTC provides a similar framework, but for Mendler-style algebras instead of f-algebras. In order to write modular proofs, MTC regulates its definitions with a number of laws.

Modular Functors Individual features can be modularly defined using functors, like $Arith_F$ and $Logic_F$. Functors are composed with the $\oplus$ operator:

$$\mathbf{data}\ (\oplus)\ f\ g\ a = Inl\ (f\ a) \mid Inr\ (g\ a)$$

$Fix_M\ (Arith_F \oplus Logic_F)$ represents a data type isomorphic to:

$$\begin{array}{l} \mathbf{data}\ Exp = Lit\ Nat \mid Add\ Exp\ Exp \\ \qquad\qquad \mid If\ Exp\ Exp\ Exp \mid BLit\ Bool \end{array}$$

Modular Mendler Algebras A type class is defined for every semantic function. For example, the evaluation function has the following class:

$$\mathbf{class}\ Eval\ f\ \mathbf{where}\ eval_{alg} :: Algebra_M\ f\ Value$$

In this class $eval_{alg}$ represents the evaluation algebra of a feature f.

Algebras for composite functor are built from feature algebras:

$$\begin{array}{l} \mathbf{instance}\ (Eval\ f, Eval\ g) \Rightarrow Eval\ (f \oplus g)\ \mathbf{where} \\ \quad eval_{alg}\ [\![\cdot]\!]\ (Inl\ fexp) = eval_{alg}\ [\![\cdot]\!]\ fexp \\ \quad eval_{alg}\ [\![\cdot]\!]\ (Inr\ gexp) = eval_{alg}\ [\![\cdot]\!]\ gexp \end{array}$$

Overall evaluation can then be defined as:

$$\begin{array}{l} eval :: Eval\ f \Rightarrow Fix_M\ f \to Value \\ eval = fold_M\ eval_{alg} \end{array}$$

In order to avoid the repeated boilerplate of defining a new type class for every semantic function and corresponding instance for $\oplus$, MTC defines a single generic Coq type class, *FAlg*, that is indexed by the name of the semantic function. This class definition can be found in Figure 3 and subsumes all other algebra classes found in this paper. The paper continues to use more specific classes to make a gentler progression for the reader.

Injections and Projections of Functors Figure 1 shows the multi-parameter type class $\prec:$. This class provides a means to lift or inject (inj) (sub)functors f into larger compositions g and project (prj) them out again. The inj_prj and prj_inj laws relate the

```
class f ≺: g where
  inj      :: f a → g a
  prj      :: g a → Maybe (f a)
  inj_prj :: prj ga = Just fa → ga = inj fa   -- law
  prj_inj :: prj ∘ inj = Just                  -- law
instance (f ≺: g) ⇒ f ≺: (g ⊕ h) where
  inj fa        = Inl (inj fa)
  prj (Inl ga) = prj ga
  prj (Inr ha) = Nothing
instance (f ≺: h) ⇒ f ≺: (g ⊕ h) where
  inj fa        = Inr (inj fa)
  prj (Inl ga) = Nothing
  prj (Inr ha) = prj ha
instance f ≺: f where
  inj fa = fa
  prj fa = Just fa
```

Figure 1. Functor subtyping.

injection and projection methods in the $\prec:$ class, ensuring that the two are effectively inverses. The idea is to use the type class resolution mechanism to encode (coercive) subtyping between functors. In Coq this subtyping relation can be nicely expressed because Coq type classes [42] perform a backtracking search for matching instances. Hence, highly overlapping definitions like the first and second instances are allowed. This is a notable difference to Haskell's type classes, which do not support backtracking. Hence, DTC's Haskell solution has to provide a biased choice that does not accurately model the expected subtyping relationship.

The in_f function builds a new term from the application of f to some subterms.

```
in_f :: f (Fix_M f) → Fix_M f
in_f fexp = λalg → alg (fold_M alg) fexp
```

Smart constructors are built using in_f and inj as follows:

```
inject :: (g ≺: f) ⇒ g (Fix_M f) → Fix_M f
inject gexp = in_f (inj gexp)

lit :: (Arith_F ≺: f) ⇒ Nat → Fix_M f
lit n = inject (Lit n)

blit :: (Logic_F ≺: f) ⇒ Bool → Fix_M f
blit b = inject (BLit b)

cond :: (Logic_F ≺: f)
     ⇒ Fix_M f → Fix_M f → Fix_M f → Fix_M f
cond c e1 e2 = inject (If c e1 e2)
```

Expressions are built with the smart constructors and used by operations like evaluation:

```
exp :: Fix_M (Arith_F ⊕ Logic_F)
exp = cond (blit True) (lit 3) (lit 2)

> eval exp
3
```

The out_f function exposes the toplevel functor again:

```
out_f :: Functor f ⇒ Fix_M f → f (Fix_M f)
out_f exp = fold_M (λrec fr → fmap (in_f ∘ rec) fr) exp
```

We can pattern match on particular features using prj and out_f:

```
project :: (g ≺: f, Functor f) ⇒
  Fix_M f → Maybe (g (Fix_M f))
project exp = prj (out_f exp)
isLit :: (Arith_F ≺: f, Functor f) ⇒ Fix_M f → Maybe Nat
isLit exp = case project exp of
  Just (Lit n) → Just n
  Nothing      → Nothing
```

2.6 Extensible Semantic Values

In addition to modular language features, it is also desirable to have modular result types for semantic functions. For example, it is much cleaner to separate natural number and boolean values along the same lines as the $Arith_F$ and $Logic_F$ features. To easily achieve this extensibility, we make use of the same sorts of extensional encodings as the expression language itself:

```
data NVal_F a = I Nat
data BVal_F a = B Bool
data Stuck_F a = Stuck

vi :: (NVal_F ≺: r) ⇒ Nat → Fix_M r
vi n = inject (I n)

vb :: (BVal_F ≺: r) ⇒ Bool → Fix_M r
vb b = inject (B b)

stuck :: (Stuck_F ≺: r) ⇒ Fix_M r
stuck = inject Stuck
```

Besides constructors for integer (vi) and boolean (vb) values, we also include a constructor denoting stuck evaluation ($stuck$).

To allow for an extensible return type r for evaluation, we need to parametrize the $Eval$ type class in r:

```
class Eval f r where
  eval_alg :: Algebra_M f (Fix_M r)
```

Projection is now essential for pattern matching on values:

```
instance (Stuck_F ≺: r, NVal_F ≺: r, Functor r) ⇒
  Eval Arith_F r where
    eval_alg ⟦·⟧ (Lit n)      = vi n
    eval_alg ⟦·⟧ (Add e1 e2) =
      case (project ⟦e1⟧, project ⟦e2⟧) of
        (Just (I n1), (Just (I n2))) → vi (n1 + n2)
        _                            → stuck
```

This concludes MTC's support for extensible inductive data types and functions. To cater to meta-theory, MTC must also support reasoning about these modular definitions.

3. Reasoning with Church Encodings

While Church encodings are the foundation of extensibility in MTC, Coq does not provide induction principles for them. It is an open problem to do so without resorting to axioms. MTC solves this problem with a novel axiom-free approach based on adaptations of two important aspects of folds discussed by Hutton [19].

3.1 The Problem of Church Encodings and Induction

Coq's own original approach [35] to inductive data types was based on Church encodings. It is well-known that Church encodings of inductive data types have problems expressing induction principles such as A_{ind}, the induction principle for arithmetic expressions.

```
A_ind :: ∀P :: (Arith → Prop).
         ∀H_l :: (∀n.P (Lit n)).
         ∀H_a :: (∀a b.P a → P b → P (Add a b)).
         ∀a.P a
A_ind P H_l H_a e =
  case e of Lit n → H_l n
    Add x y      → H_a a b (A_ind P H_l H_a x)
                           (A_ind P H_l H_a y)
```

The original solution to this problem in Coq involved axioms for induction, which endangered strong normalization of the calculus (among other problems). This was the primary motivation for the creation of the *calculus of inductive constructions* [34] with built-in inductive data types.

Why exactly are proofs problematic for Church encodings, where inductive functions are not? After all, a Coq proof is essentially a function that builds a proof term by induction over a data type. Hence, the Church encoding should be able to express a proof as a fold with a *proof algebra* over the data type, in the same way it represents other functions.

The problem is that this approach severely restricts the propositions that can be proven. Folds over Church encodings are destructive, so their result type cannot depend on the term being destructed. For example, it is impossible to express the proof for *type soundness* because it performs induction over the expression e mentioned in the type soundness property.

$$\forall e.\Gamma \vdash e : t \rightarrow \Gamma \vdash [\![e]\!] : t$$

This restriction is a showstopper for the semantics setting of this paper, as it rules out proofs for most (if not all) theorems of interest. Supporting reasoning about semantic functions requires a new approach that does not suffer from this restriction.

3.2 Type Dependency with Dependent Products

Hutton's first aspect of *folds* is that they become substantially more expressive with the help of tuples. The dependent products in Coq take this observation one step further. While an f-algebra cannot refer to the original term, it can simultaneously build a copy e of the original term and a proof that the property $P\ e$ holds for the new term. As the latter depends on the former, the result type of the algebra is a dependent product $\Sigma\ e.P\ e$. A generic algebra can exploit this expressivity to build a poor-man's induction principle, e.g., for the $Arith_F$ functor:

$$\begin{array}{l} A^2_{ind} :: \forall P :: (Fix_M\ Arith_F \rightarrow Prop). \\ \quad\quad \forall H_l :: (\forall n.P\ (lit\ n)). \\ \quad\quad \forall H_a :: (\forall a\ b.P\ a \rightarrow P\ b \rightarrow P\ (add\ a\ b)). \\ \quad\quad Algebra\ Arith_F\ (\Sigma\ e.P\ e) \\ A^2_{ind}\ P\ H_l\ H_a\ e = \\ \quad \mathbf{case}\ e\ \mathbf{of} \\ \quad\quad Lit\ n \quad\ \rightarrow \exists\ (lit\ n)\ (H_l\ n) \\ \quad\quad Add\ x\ y \rightarrow \exists\ (add\ (\pi_1\ x)\ (\pi_1\ y))\ (H_a\ (\pi_1\ x)\ (\pi_1\ y) \\ \quad\quad\quad\quad\quad\quad\quad\quad\quad\quad\quad\quad\quad\quad\quad\quad (\pi_2\ x)\ (\pi_2\ y)) \end{array}$$

Provided with the necessary proof cases, A^2_{ind} can build a specific proof algebra. The corresponding proof is simply a fold over a Church encoding using this proof algebra.

Note that since a proof is not a computational object, it makes more sense to use regular algebras than Mendler algebras. Fortunately, regular algebras are compatible with Mendler-based Church encodings as the following variant of $fold'_M$ shows.

$$\begin{array}{l} fold'_M :: Functor\ f \Rightarrow Algebra\ f\ a \rightarrow Fix_M\ f \rightarrow a \\ fold'_M\ alg = fold_M\ (\lambda rec \rightarrow alg \circ fmap\ rec) \end{array}$$

3.3 Term Equality with the Universal Property

Of course, the dependent product approach does not directly prove a property of the original term. Instead, given a term, it builds a new term and a proof that the property holds for the new term. In order to draw conclusions about the original term from the result, the original and new term must be equal.

Clearly the equivalence does not hold for arbitrary terms that happen to match the type signatures $Fix_M\ f$ for Church encodings and $Algebra\ f\ (\Sigma\ e.P\ e)$ for proof algebras. Statically ensuring this equivalence requires additional *well-formedness conditions* on both. These conditions formally capture our notion of Church encodings and proofs algebras.

3.3.1 Well-Formed Proof Algebras

The first requirement, for algebras, states that the new term produced by application of the algebra is equal to the original term.

$$\forall alg :: Algebra\ f\ (\Sigma\ e.P\ e).\pi_1 \circ alg = in_f \circ fmap\ \pi_1$$

This constraint is encoded in the typeclass for proof algebras, $PAlg$. It is easy to verify that A^2_{ind} satisfies this property. Other proof algebras over $Arith_F$ can be defined by instantiating A^2_{ind} with appropriate cases for H_l and H_a. In general, well-formedness needs to be proven only once for any data type and induction algebra.

3.3.2 Well-Formed Church Encodings

Well-formedness of proof algebras is not enough because a proof is not a single application of an algebra, but rather a $fold'_M$ of it. So the $fold'_M$ used to build a proof must be a *proper* $fold'_M$. As the Church encodings represent inductive data types as their folds, this boils down to ensuring that the Church encodings are well-formed.

Hutton's second aspect of folds formally characterizes the definition of a fold using its *universal property*:

$$h = fold'_M\ alg \Leftrightarrow h \circ in_f = alg\ h$$

In an initial algebra representation of an inductive data type, there is a single implementation of $fold'_M$ that can be checked once and for all for the universal property. In MTC's Church-encoding approach, every term of type $Fix_M\ f$ consists of a separate $fold'_M$ implementation that must satisfy the universal property. Note that this definition of the universal property is for a $fold'_M$ using a traditional algebra. As the only concern is the behavior of proof algebras (which are traditional algebras) folded over Church encodings, this is a sufficient characterization of well-formedness. Hinze [18] uses the same characterization for deriving Church numerals.

Fortunately, the left-to-right implication follows trivially from the definitions of $fold'_M$ and in_f, independent of the particular term of type $Fix_M\ f$. Thus, the only hard well-formedness requirement for a Church-encoded term e is that it satisfies the right-to-left implication of the universal property.

$$\begin{array}{l} \mathbf{type}\ UP\ f\ e = \\ \quad \forall a\ (alg :: Algebra_M\ f\ a)\ (h :: Fix_M\ f \rightarrow a). \\ \quad\quad (\forall e'.h\ (in_f\ e') = alg\ h\ e') \rightarrow h\ e = fold'_M\ alg\ e \end{array}$$

This property is easy to show for any given smart constructor. MTC actually goes one step further and redefines its smart constructors in terms of a new in_f, that only builds terms with the universal property:

$$in'_f :: Functor\ f \Rightarrow f\ (\Sigma\ e.UP\ f\ e) \rightarrow \Sigma\ e.UP\ f\ e$$

about Church-encoded terms built from these smart-*er* constructors, as all of the nice properties of initial algebras hold for these terms and, importantly, these properties provide a handle on reasoning about these terms.

Two known consequences of the universal property are the famous *fusion* law, which describes the composition of a fold with another computation,

$$h \circ alg_1 = alg_2 \circ fmap\ h \quad \Rightarrow \quad h \circ fold'_M\ alg_1 = fold'_M\ alg_2$$

and the lesser known *reflection* law,

$$fold'_M\ in_f = id$$

3.3.3 Soundness of Input-Preserving Folds

Armed with the two well-formedness properties, we can prove the key theorem for building inductive proofs over Church encodings:

Theorem 3.1. *Given a functor f, property P, and a well-formed P-proof algebra alg, for any Church-encoded f-term e with the universal property, we can conclude that $P\ e$ holds.*

Proof. Given that $fold'_M\ alg\ e$ has type $\Sigma\ e'.P\ e'$, we have that $\pi_2\ (fold'_M\ alg\ e)$ is a proof for $P\ (\pi_1\ (fold'_M\ alg\ e))$. From that the lemma is derived as follows:

$$
\begin{array}{l}
P\ (\pi_1\ (fold'_M\ alg\ e)) \\
\Longrightarrow\ \{\text{-well-founded algebra and fusion law -}\} \\
P\ (fold'_M\ in_f\ e) \\
\Longleftrightarrow\ \{\text{-reflection law -}\} \\
P\ e
\end{array}
$$

□

Theorem 3.1 enables the construction of a statically-checked proof of correctness as an input-preserving fold of a proof algebra. This provides a means to achieve our true goal: modular proofs for extensible Church encodings.

4. Modular Proofs for Extensible Church Encodings

The aim of modularity in this setting is to first write a separate proof for every feature and then compose the individual proofs into an overall proof for the feature composition. These proofs should be independent from one another, so that they can be reused for different combinations of features.

Fortunately, since proofs are essentially folds of proof algebras, all of the reuse tools developed in Section 2 apply here. In particular, composing proofs is a simple matter of combining proof algebras with $\oplus$. Nevertheless, the transition to modular components does introduce several wrinkles in the reasoning process.

4.1 Algebra Delegation

Due to injection, propositions range over the abstract (super)functor f of the component composition. The signature of A^2_{ind}, for example, becomes:

$$
\begin{array}{l}
A^2_{ind} :: \forall f. Arith_F \prec: f \Rightarrow \\
\quad \forall P :: (Fix_M\ f \rightarrow Prop). \\
\quad \forall H_l :: (\forall n. P\ (lit\ n)). \\
\quad \forall H_a :: (\forall a\ b. P\ a \rightarrow P\ b \rightarrow P\ (add\ a\ b)). \\
\quad Algebra\ Arith_F\ (\Sigma\ e. P\ e)
\end{array}
$$

Consider building a proof of

$$\forall e. typeof\ e = Just\ nat \rightarrow \exists\ m :: nat. eval\ e = vi\ m$$

using A^2_{ind}. Then, the first proof obligation is

$$typeof\ (lit\ n) = Just\ nat \rightarrow \exists\ m :: nat. eval\ (lit\ n) = vi\ m$$

While this appears to follow immediately from the definition of $eval$, recall that $eval$ is a fold of an abstract algebra over f and is thus opaque. To proceed, we need the additional property that this f-algebra delegates to the $Arith_F$-algebra as expected:

$$\forall r\ (rec :: r \rightarrow Nat). eval_{alg}\ rec \circ inj = eval_{alg}\ rec$$

This delegation behavior follows from our approach: the intended structure of f is a $\oplus$-composition of features, and $\oplus$-algebras are intended to delegate to the feature algebras. We can formally capture the delegation behavior in a type class that serves as a precondition in our modular proofs.

```
class (Eval f, Eval g, f ≺: g) ⇒
  WF_Eval f g where
  wf_eval_alg :: ∀r (rec :: r → Nat) (e :: f r).
    eval_alg rec (inj e :: g r) =
    eval_alg rec e
```

```
instance (Eval f, Eval g, Eval h, WF_Eval f g) ⇒
  WF_Eval (f ≺: g ⊕ h)
instance (Eval f, Eval g, Eval h, WF_Eval f h) ⇒
  WF_Eval (f ≺: g ⊕ h)
instance (Eval f) ⇒ WF_Eval f f
```

Figure 2. *WF_Eval* instances.

MTC provides the three instances of this class in Figure 2, one for each instance of $\prec:$, allowing Coq to automatically build a proof of well-formedness for every composite algebra.

4.1.1 Automating Composition

A similar approach is used to automatically build the definitions and proofs of languages from pieces defined by individual features. In addition to functor and algebra composition, the framework derives several important reasoning principles as type class instances, similarly to *WF_Eval*. These include the *DistinctSubFunctor* class, which ensures that injections from two different subfunctors are distinct, and the *WF_Functor* class that ensures that *fmap* distributes through injection.

Figure 3 provides a summary of all the classes defined in MTC, noting whether the base instances of a particular class are provided by the user or inferred with a default instance. Importantly, instances of all these classes for feature compositions are built automatically, analogously to the instances in Figure 2.

4.2 Extensible Inductive Predicates

Many proofs appeal to rules which define a predicate for an important property. In Coq these predicates are expressed as inductive data types of kind *Prop*. For instance, a soundness proof makes use of a judgment about the well-typing of values.

```
data WTValue :: Value → Type → Prop where
  WTNat  :: ∀n. WTValue (I n) TNat
  WTBool :: ∀b. WTValue (B b) TBool
```

When dealing with a predicate over extensible inductive data types, the set of rules defining the predicate must be extensible as well. Extensibility of these rules is obtained in much the same way as that of inductive data types: by means of Church encodings. The important difference is that logical relations are indexed data types: e.g., *WTValue* is indexed by a value and a type. This requires functors indexed by values x of type i. For example, $WTNat_F\ v\ t$ is the corresponding indexed functor for the extensible variant of *WTNat* above.

```
data WTNat_F :: v → t → (WTV :: (v, t) → Prop)
                           → (v, t) → Prop
  where WTNat :: ∀n.(NVal_F ≺: v, Functor v,
                     NTyp_F ≺: t, Functor t)
            ⇒ WTNat_F v t WTV (vi n, tnat)
```

This index is a pair (v, t) of a value and a type. As object-language values and types are themselves extensible, the corresponding meta-language types v and t are parameters of the *WTNat* functor.

To manipulate extensible logical relations, we need indexed algebras, fixpoints and operations:

```
type iAlg i (f :: (i → Prop) → (i → Prop)) a
  = ∀x :: i.f a x → a x
type iFix i (f :: (i → Prop) → (i → Prop)) (x :: i)
  = ∀a :: i → Prop.iAlg f a → a x ...
```

As these indexed variants are meant to construct logical relations, their parameters range over *Prop* instead of *Set*. Fortunately,

Class Definition	Description
class $Functor\ f$ **where** $fmap :: (a \to b) \to (f\ a \to f\ b)$ $fmap\_id :: fmap\ id = id$ $fmap\_fusion :: \forall g\ h.$ $fmap\ h \circ fmap\ g = fmap\ (h \circ g)$	**Functors** Supplied by the user
class $f \prec: g$ **where** $inj :: f\ a \to g\ a$ $prj :: g\ a \to Maybe\ (f\ a)$ $inj\_prj :: prj\ ga = Just\ fa \to$ $ga = inj\ fa$ $prj\_inj :: prj \circ inj = Just$	Functor Subtyping Inferred
class $(Functor\ f, Functor\ g, f \prec: g) \Rightarrow$ $WF\_Functor\ f\ g$ **where** $wf\_functor :: \forall a\ b\ (h :: a \to b).$ $fmap\ h \circ inj = inj \circ fmap\ h$	Functor Delegation Inferred
class $(Functor\ h, f \prec: h, g \prec: h) \Rightarrow$ $DistinctSubFunctor\ f\ g\ h$ **where** $inj\_discriminate :: \forall a\ (fe :: f\ a)$ $(ge :: g\ a). inj\ fe \neq inj\ ge$	Functor Discrimination Inferred
class $FAlg\ name\ t\ a\ f$ **where** $f\_algebra : Mixin\ t\ f\ a$	**Function Algebras** Supplied by the user
class $(f \prec: g, FAlg\ n\ t\ a\ f, FAlg\ n\ t\ a\ g) \Rightarrow$ $WF\_FAlg\ n\ t\ a\ f\ g$ **where** $wf\_algebra :: \forall rec\ (fa :: f\ t).$ $f\_algebra\ rec\ (inj\ fa) =$ $f\_algebra\ rec\ fa$	Algebra Delegation Inferred
class $(Functor\ f, Functor\ g, f \prec: g) \Rightarrow$ $PAlg\ name\ f\ g\ a$ **where** $p\_algebra :: Algebra\ f\ a$ $proj\_eq :: \forall e.\pi_1\ (p\_algebra\ e) =$ $in_f\ (inj\ (fmap\ \pi_1\ e))$	**Proof Algebras** Supplied by the User

Figure 3. Type classes provided by MTC

this shift obviates the need for universal properties for $iFix$-ed values: it does not matter *how* a logical relation is built, but simply that it exists. Analogues to $WF\_Functor$, $WF\_Algebra$, and $DistinctSubFunctor$ are similarly unnecessary.

4.3 Case Study: Soundness of an Arithmetic Language

Here we briefly illustrate modular reasoning with a case study proving soundness for the $Arith_F \oplus Logic_F$ language.

The previously defined $eval$ function captures the operational semantics of this language in a modular way and reduces an expression to a $NVal_F \oplus BVal_F \oplus Stuck_F$ value. Its type system is similarly captured by a modularly defined type-checking function $typeof$ that *maybe* returns a $TNat_F \oplus TBool_F$ type representation:

$$\textbf{data}\ TNat_F\ t = TNat$$
$$\textbf{data}\ TBool_F\ t = TBool$$

For this language soundness is formulated as:

Theorem $soundness$ ::
$\forall e\ t\ env, typeof\ e = Just\ t \to WTValue\ (eval\ e\ env)\ t$

The proof of this theorem is a fold of a proof algebra over the expression e which delegates the different cases to separate proof algebras for the different features. A summary of the most noteworthy aspects of these proofs follows.

Sublemmas The modular setting requires every case analysis to be captured in a sublemma. Because the superfunctor is abstract, the cases are not known locally and must be handled in a distributed fashion. Hence, modular lemmas built from proof algebras are not just an important tool for reuse in MTC – they are the main method of constructing extensible proofs.

Universal Properties Everywhere Universal properties are key to reasoning, and should thus be pervasively available throughout the framework. MTC has more infrastructure to support this.

As an example of their utility when constructing a proof, we may wish to prove a property of the extensible return value of an extensible function. Consider the $Logic_F$ case of the soundness proof: given that $typeof\ (If\ c\ e_1\ e_2) = Some\ t_1$, we wish to show that $WTValue\ (eval\ (If\ c\ e_1\ e_2))\ t_1$. If c evaluates to $false$, we need to show that $WTValue\ e_2\ t_1$.

Since $If\ c\ e_1\ e_2$ has type t_1, the definition of $typeof$ says that e_1 has type t_1:

```
typeof_alg rec (If c e1 e2) =
  case project (rec c) of
    Just TBool →
      case (rec e1, rec e2) of
        (Just t1, Just t2) →
          if eq_type t1 t2 then Just t1 else Nothing
        _                 → Nothing
    Nothing → Nothing
```

In addition, the type equality test function, eq_{type}, says that e_1 and e_2 have the same type: $eq_{type}\ t_1\ t_2 = true$. We need to make use of a sublemma showing that $\forall t_1\ t_2.\ eq_{type}\ t_1\ t_2 = true \to t_1 = t_2$. As we have seen, in order to do so, the universal property must hold for $typeof\ \ e_1$. This is easily accomplished by packaging a proof of the universal property alongside t_1 in the $typeof$ function.

Using universal properties is so important to reasoning that this packaging should be the default behavior, even though it is computationally irrelevant. Thankfully, packaging becomes trivial with the use of smarter constructors. These constructors have the additional advantage over standard smart constructors of being injective: $lit\ j = lit\ k \to j = k$, an important property for proving inversion lemmas. The proof of injectivity requires that the subterms of the functor have the universal property, established by the use of in'_f. To facilitate this packaging, we provide a type synonym that can be used in lieu of Fix_M in function signatures:

$$\textbf{type}\ UP_F\ f = Functor\ f \Rightarrow \Sigma\ e.(UP\ f\ e)$$

Furthermore, the universal property should hold for any value subject to proof algebras, so it is convenient to include the property in all proof algebras. MTC provides a predicate transformer, UP_P, that captures this and augments induction principles accordingly.

$$UP_P :: Functor\ f \Rightarrow$$
$$(P :: \forall e.UP\ f\ e \to Prop) \to (e :: Fix_M\ f) \to \Sigma\ e.(P\ e)$$

Equality and Universal Properties While packaging universal properties with terms enables reasoning, it does obfuscate equality of terms. In particular, two UP_F terms t and t' may share the same underlying term (i.e., $\pi_1\ t = \pi_1\ t'$), while their universal property proof components are different.[2]

This issue shows up in the definition of the typing judgment for values. This judgment needs to range over $UP_F\ f_v$ values and $UP_F\ f_t$ types (where f_v and f_t are the value and type functors), because we need to exploit the injectivity of $inject$ in our inversion lemmas. However, knowing $WTValue\ v\ t$ and $\pi_1\ t = \pi_1\ t'$ no longer necessarily implies $WTValue\ v\ t'$ because t and t' may have distinct proof components. To solve this, we make use of two auxiliary lemmas $WTV_{\pi_1,v}$ and $WTV_{\pi_1,t}$ that establish the implication:

[2] Actually, as proofs are opaque, we cannot tell if they are equal.

Theorem $WTV_{\pi_1,v}\ (i :: WTValue\ v\ t) =$
$\quad \forall v'.\pi_1\ v = \pi_1\ v' \rightarrow WTValue\ v'\ t$

Theorem $WTV_{\pi_1,t}\ (i :: WTValue\ v\ t) =$
$\quad \forall t'.\pi_1\ t' = \pi_1\ t' \rightarrow WTValue\ v\ t'$

Similar lemmas are used for other logical relations. Features which introduce new rules need to also provide proofs showing that they respect this "safe projection" property.

5. Higher-Order Features

Binders and general recursion are ubiquitous in programming languages, so MTC must support these sorts of higher-order features. The untyped lambda calculus demonstrates the challenges of implementing both these features with extensible Church encodings.

5.1 Encoding Binders

To encode binders we use a *parametric HOAS* (PHOAS) [8] representation. PHOAS allows binders to be expressed as functors, while still preserving all the convenient properties of HOAS.

$Lambda_F$ is a PHOAS-based functor for a feature with function application, abstraction and variables. The PHOAS style requires $Lambda_F$ to be parameterized in the type v of variables, in addition to the usual type parameter r for recursive occurrences.

$$\mathbf{data}\ Lambda_F\ v\ r = Var\ v \mid App\ r\ r \mid Lam\ (v \rightarrow r)$$

As before, smart constructors build extensible expressions:

$$\begin{aligned}
&var :: (Lambda_F\ v \prec: f) \Rightarrow v \rightarrow Fix_M\ f \\
&var\ v = inject\ (Var\ v) \\
&app :: (Lambda_F\ v \prec: f) \Rightarrow Fix_M\ f \rightarrow Fix_M\ f \rightarrow Fix_M\ f \\
&app\ e_1\ e_2 = inject\ (App\ e_1\ e_2) \\
&lam :: (Lambda_F\ v \prec: f) \Rightarrow (v \rightarrow Fix_M\ f) \rightarrow Fix_M\ f \\
&lam\ f = inject\ (Lam\ f)
\end{aligned}$$

5.2 Defining Non-Inductive Evaluation Algebras

Defining an evaluation algebra for the $Lambda_F$ feature presents additional challenges. Evaluation of the untyped lambda-calculus can produce a closure, requiring a richer value type than before:

$$\begin{aligned}
&\mathbf{data}\ Value = \\
&\quad Stuck \mid I\ Nat \mid B\ Bool \mid Clos\ (Value \rightarrow Value)
\end{aligned}$$

Unfortunately, Coq does not allow such a definition, as the closure constructor is not strictly positive (recursive occurrences of $Value$ occur both at positive and negative positions). Instead, a closure is represented as an expression to be evaluated in the context of an environment of variable-value bindings. The environment is a list of values indexed by variables represented as natural numbers Nat.

$$\mathbf{type}\ Env\ v = [v]$$

The modular functor $Closure_F$ integrates closure values into the framework of extensible values introduced in Section 2.6.

$$\begin{aligned}
&\mathbf{data}\ Closure_F\ f\ a = Clos\ (Fix_M\ f)\ (Env\ a) \\
&closure :: (Closure_F\ f \prec: r) \Rightarrow \\
&\qquad Fix_M\ f \rightarrow Env\ (Fix_M\ r) \rightarrow Fix_M\ r \\
&closure\ mf\ e = inject\ (Clos\ mf\ e)
\end{aligned}$$

A first attempt at defining evaluation is:

$$\begin{aligned}
&eval_{Lambda} :: \quad (Closure_F\ f \prec: r, Stuck_F \prec: r, Functor\ r) \Rightarrow \\
&\qquad Algebra_M\ (Lambda_F\ Nat)\ (Env\ (Fix_M\ r) \rightarrow Fix_M\ r) \\
&eval_{Lambda}\ [\![\cdot]\!]\ exp\ env = \\
&\quad \mathbf{case}\ exp\ \mathbf{of} \\
&\qquad Var\ index \rightarrow env\ !!\ index \\
&\qquad Lam\ f \qquad \rightarrow closure\ (f\ (length\ env))\ env \\
&\qquad App\ e_1\ e_2 \rightarrow \\
&\qquad\quad \mathbf{case}\ project\ \$\ [\![e_1]\!]\ env\ \mathbf{of} \\
&\qquad\qquad Just\ (Clos\ e_3\ env') \rightarrow [\![e_3]\!]\ ([\![e_2]\!]\ env : env') \\
&\qquad\qquad _ \qquad\qquad\qquad\quad \rightarrow stuck
\end{aligned}$$

The function $eval_{Lambda}$ instantiates the type variable v of the $Lambda_F\ v$ functor with a natural number Nat, representing an index in the environment. The return type of the Mendler algebra is now a function that takes an environment as an argument. In the variable case there is an index that denotes the position of the variable in the environment, and $eval_{Lambda}$ simply looks up that index in the environment. In the lambda case $eval_{Lambda}$ builds a closure using f and the environment. Finally, in the application case, the expression e_1 is evaluated and analyzed. If that expression evaluates to a closure then the expression e_2 is evaluated and added to the closure's environment (env'), and the closure's expression e_3 is evaluated under this extended environment. Otherwise e_1 does not evaluate to a closure, and evaluation is stuck.

Unfortunately, this algebra is ill-typed on two accounts. Firstly, the lambda binder function f does not have the required type $Nat \rightarrow Fix_M\ f$. Instead, its type is $Nat \rightarrow r$, where r is universally quantified in the definition of the $Algebra_M$ algebra. Secondly, and symmetrically, in the App case, the closure expression e_3 has type $Fix_M\ f$ which does not conform to the type r expected by $[\![\cdot]\!]$ for the recursive call.

Both these symptoms have the same problem at their root. The Mendler algebra enforces inductive (structural) recursion by hiding that the type of the subterms is $Fix_M\ f$ using universal quantification over r. Yet this information is absolutely essential for evaluating the binder: we need to give up structural recursion and use general recursion instead. This is unsurprising, as an untyped lambda term can be non-terminating.

5.3 Non-Inductive Semantic Functions

Mixin algebras refine Mendler algebras with a more revealing type signature.

$$\mathbf{type}\ Mixin\ t\ f\ a = (t \rightarrow a) \rightarrow f\ t \rightarrow a$$

This algebra specifies the type t of subterms, typically $Fix_M\ f$, the overall expression type. With this mixin algebra, $eval_{Lambda}$ is now well-typed:

$$\begin{aligned}
&eval_{Lambda} :: (Closure_F\ e \prec: v, Stuck_F \prec: v) \Rightarrow \\
&\quad Mixin\ (Fix_M\ e)\ (Lambda_F\ Nat) \\
&\quad (Env\ (Fix_M\ v) \rightarrow Fix_M\ v)
\end{aligned}$$

Mixin algebras have an analogous implementation to $Eval$ as type classes, enabling all of MTC's previous composition techniques.

$$\begin{aligned}
&\mathbf{class}\ Eval_X\ f\ g\ r\ \mathbf{where} \\
&\quad eval_{xalg} :: Mixin\ (Fix_M\ f)\ g\ (Env\ (Fix_M\ r) \rightarrow Fix_M\ r) \\
&\mathbf{instance}\ (Stuck_F \prec: r, Closure_F\ f \prec: r, Functor\ r) \Rightarrow \\
&\qquad\qquad Eval_X\ f\ (Lambda_F\ Nat)\ r\ \mathbf{where} \\
&\quad eval_{xalg} = eval_{Lambda}
\end{aligned}$$

Although the code of $eval_{Lambda}$ still appears generally recursive, it is actually *not* because the recursive calls are abstracted as a parameter (like with Mendler algebras). Accordingly, $eval_{Lambda}$ does not raise any issues with Coq's termination checker. Mixin algebras resemble the *open recursion* style which is used to model inheritance and mixins in object-oriented languages [10]. Still, Mendler encodings only accept Mendler algebras, so using mixin algebras with Mendler-style encodings requires a new form of fold.

In order to overcome the problem of general recursion, the open recursion of the mixin algebra is replaced with a bounded inductive fixpoint combinator, *boundedFix*, that returns a default value if the evaluation does not terminate after n recursion steps.

$$\begin{array}{l} \mathit{boundedFix} :: \forall f\ a.\mathit{Functor}\ f \Rightarrow \mathit{Nat} \rightarrow a \rightarrow \\ \qquad\qquad \mathit{Mixin}\ (\mathit{Fix}_M\ f)\ f\ a \rightarrow \mathit{Fix}_M\ f \rightarrow a \\ \mathit{boundedFix}\ n\ \mathit{def}\ \mathit{alg}\ e = \\ \quad \textbf{case}\ n\ \textbf{of} \\ \qquad 0 \rightarrow \mathit{def} \\ \qquad m \rightarrow \mathit{alg}\ (\mathit{boundedFix}\ (m-1)\ \mathit{def}\ \mathit{alg})\ (\mathit{out}_f\ e) \end{array}$$

The argument e is a Mendler-encoded expression of type $\mathit{Fix}_M\ f$. *boundedFix* first uses out_f to unfold the expression into a value of type $f\ (\mathit{Fix}_M\ f)$ and then applies the algebra to that value recursively. In essence *boundedFix* can define *generally* recursive operations by case analysis, since it can inspect values of the recursive occurrences. The use of the bound prevents non-termination.

Bounded Evaluation Evaluation can now be modularly defined as a bounded fixpoint of the mixin algebra Eval_X. The definition uses a distinguished bottom value, $\bot$, that represents a computation which does not finish within the given bound.

$$\begin{array}{l} \textbf{data}\ \bot_F\ a = \mathit{Bot} \\ \bot = \mathit{inject}\ \mathit{Bot} \\ \mathit{eval}_X :: (\mathit{Functor}\ f, \bot_F \prec: r, \mathit{Eval}_X\ f\ f\ r) \Rightarrow \\ \quad \mathit{Nat} \rightarrow \mathit{Fix}_M\ f \rightarrow \mathit{Env} \rightarrow \mathit{Fix}_M\ r \\ \mathit{eval}_X\ n\ e\ \mathit{env} = \mathit{boundedFix}\ n\ (\backslash\_ \rightarrow \bot)\ \mathit{eval}_{xalg}\ e\ \mathit{env} \end{array}$$

5.4 Backwards compatibility

The higher-order PHOAS feature has introduced a twofold change to the algebras used by the evaluation function:

1. eval_X uses mixin algebras instead of Mendler algebras.
2. eval_X now expects algebras over a parameterized functor.

The first change is easily accommodated because Mendler algebras are compatible with mixin algebras. If a non-binder feature defines evaluation in terms of a Mendler algebra, it does not have to define a second mixin algebra to be used alongside binder features. The *mendlerToMixin* function automatically derives the required mixin algebra from the Mendler algebra.

$$\begin{array}{l} \mathit{mendlerToMixin} :: \mathit{Algebra}_M\ f\ a \rightarrow \mathit{Mixin}\ (\mathit{Fix}_M\ g)\ f\ a \\ \mathit{mendlerToMixin}\ \mathit{alg} = \mathit{alg} \end{array}$$

This conversion function can be used to adapt evaluation for the arithmetic feature to a mixin algebra:

$$\begin{array}{l} \textbf{instance}\ \mathit{Eval}\ \mathit{Arith}_F\ f \Rightarrow \mathit{Eval}_X\ f\ \mathit{Arith}_F\ r\ \textbf{where} \\ \quad \mathit{eval}_{xalg}\ [\![\cdot]\!]\ e\ \mathit{env} = \\ \qquad \mathit{mendlerToMixin}\ \mathit{evalAlgebra}\ (\mathit{flip}\ [\![\cdot]\!]\ \mathit{env})\ e \end{array}$$

The algebras of binder-free features can be similarly adapted to build an algebra over a parametric functor. Figure 4 summarizes the hierarchy of algebra adaptations. Non-parameterized Mendler algebras are the most flexible because they can be adapted and reused with both mixin algebras and parametric superfunctors. They should be used by default, only resorting to mixin algebras when necessary.

6. Reasoning with Higher-Order Features

The switch to a bounded evaluation function over parameterized Church encodings requires a new statement of soundness.

$$\begin{array}{l} \textbf{Theorem}\ \mathit{soundness}_X :: \forall f\ f_t\ \mathit{env}\ t\ \Gamma\ n. \\ \forall e_1 :: \mathit{Fix}_M\ (f\ (\mathit{Maybe}\ (\mathit{Fix}_M\ f_t))). \\ \forall e_2 :: \mathit{Fix}_M\ (f\ \mathit{Nat}). \end{array}$$

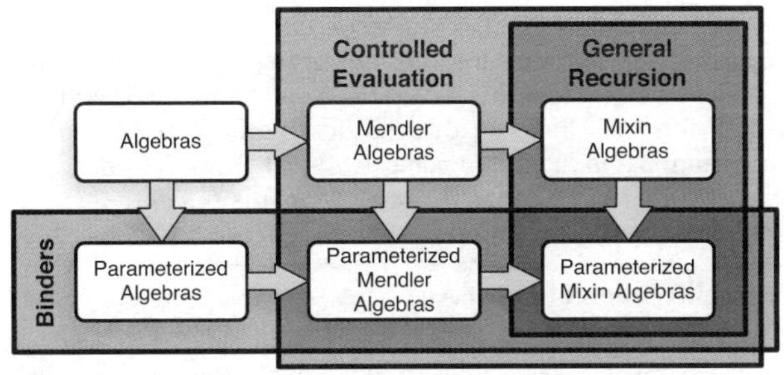

Figure 4. Hierarchy of Algebra Adaptation

$$\begin{array}{l} \Gamma \vdash e_1 \equiv e_2 \rightarrow \mathit{WF\_Environment}\ \Gamma\ \mathit{env} \rightarrow \\ \mathit{typeof}\ e_1 = \mathit{Just}\ t \rightarrow \mathit{WTValue}\ (\mathit{eval}_X\ n\ e_2\ \mathit{env})\ t \end{array}$$

The proof of $\mathit{soundness}_X$ features two substantial changes to the proof of *soundness* from Section 4.3.

6.1 Proofs over Parametric Church Encodings

The statement of $\mathit{soundness}_X$ uses two instances of the same PHOAS expression $e :: \forall v.\mathit{Fix}_M\ (f\ v)$. The first, e_1, instantiates v with the appropriate type for the typing algebra, while e_2 instantiates v for the evaluation algebra.

In recursive applications of $\mathit{soundness}_X$, the connection between e_1 and e_2 is no longer apparent. As they have different types, Coq considers them to be distinct, so case analysis on one does not convey information about the other. Chlipala [8] shows how the connection can be retained with the help of an auxiliary equivalence relation $\Gamma \vdash e_1 \equiv e_2$, which uses the environment Γ to keep track of the current variable bindings. The top-level application, where the common origin of e_1 and e_2 is apparent, can easily supply a proof of this relation. By induction on this proof, recursive applications of $\mathit{soundness}_X$ can then analyze e_1 and e_2 in lockstep. Figure 5 shows the rules for determining equivalence of lambda expressions.

$$\frac{(x, x') \in \Gamma}{\Gamma \vdash \mathit{var}\ x \equiv \mathit{var}\ x'}\ (\text{EQV-VAR}) \qquad \frac{\Gamma \vdash e_1 \equiv e_1' \qquad \Gamma \vdash e_2 \equiv e_2'}{\Gamma \vdash \mathit{app}\ e_1\ e_2 \equiv \mathit{app}\ e_1'\ e_2'}\ (\text{EQV-APP})$$

$$\frac{\forall x x'.(x, x'), \Gamma \vdash f(x) \equiv f'(x')}{\Gamma \vdash \mathit{lam}\ f \equiv \mathit{lam}\ f'}\ (\text{EQV-ABS})$$

Figure 5. Lambda Equivalence Rules

6.2 Proofs for Non-Inductive Semantics Functions

Proofs for semantic functions that use *boundedFix* proceed by induction on the bound. Hence, the reasoning principle for mixin-based bounded functions f is in general: provided a base case $\forall e, P(f\ 0\ e)$, and inductive case $\forall n\ e, (\forall e', P(f\ n\ e')) \rightarrow \forall e, P(f\ (n+1)\ e)$ hold, $\forall n\ e, P(f\ n\ e)$ also holds.

In the base case of $\mathit{soundness}_X$, the bound has been reached and eval_X returns $\bot$. The proof of this case relies on adding to the *WTValue* judgment the WF-BOT rule stating that every type is inhabited by $\bot$.

$$\frac{}{\vdash \bot : T}\ (\text{WF-BOT})$$

Hence, whenever evaluation returns $\bot$, soundness trivially holds.

The inductive case is handled by a proof algebra whose statement includes the inductive hypothesis provided by the induction on the bound: $\mathit{IH} :: \forall n\ e, (\forall e', P(f\ n\ e')) \rightarrow P(f\ (n+1)\ e)$. The $\mathit{App}\ e_1\ e_2$ case of the soundness theorem illustrates the reason for including *IH* in the statement of the proof algebra. After using the induction hypothesis to show that $eval_X\ e_1\ env$ produces a well-formed closure $Clos\ e_3\ env'$, we must then show that evaluating e_3 under the $(eval_X\ e_2\ env) : env'$ environment is also well-formed. However, e_3 is not a subterm of $App\ e_1\ e_2$, so the conventional induction hypothesis for subterms does not apply. Because $eval_X\ e_3\ ((eval_X\ e_2\ env) : env')$ is run with a smaller bound, the bounded induction hypothesis IH can be used.

6.3 Proliferation of Proof Algebras

In order to incorporate non-parametric inductive features in the $soundness_X$ proof, existing proof algebras for those features need to be adapted. To cater to the four possible proof signatures of soundness (one for each definition of $[\![\cdot]\!]$), a naive approach requires four different proof algebras for an inductive non-parametric feature.[3] This is not acceptable, because reasoning about a feature's soundness should be independent of how a language adapts its evaluation algebra. Hence, MTC allows features to define a single proof algebra, and provides the means to adapt and reuse that proof algebra for the four variants. These proof algebra adaptations rely on *mediating type class instances* which automatically build an instance of the new proof algebra from the original proof algebra.

6.3.1 Adapting Proofs to Parametric Functors

Adapting a proof algebra over the expression functor to one over the indexed functor for the equivalence relation first requires a definition of equivalence for non-parametric functors. Fortunately, equivalence for any such functor f_{np} can be defined generically:

$$\frac{\Gamma \vdash \overline{a} \equiv \overline{b}}{\Gamma \vdash inject(C\ \overline{a}) \equiv inject(C\ \overline{b})} \quad (\textrm{EQV-NP})$$

EQV-NP states that the same constructor C of f_{np}, applied to equivalent subterms $\bar{a}$ and $\bar{b}$, produces equivalent expressions.

The mediating type class adapts f_{np} proofs of propositions on two instances of the same PHOAS expression, like soundness, to proof algebras over the parametric functor.

$$\textbf{instance}\ (PAlg\ N\ P\ f_{np}) \Rightarrow iPAlg\ N\ P\ (\textrm{EQV-NP}\ f_{np})$$

This instance requires a small concession: proofs over f_{np} have to be stated in terms of two expressions with distinct superfunctors f and f' rather than two occurrences of the same expression. Induction over these two expressions requires a variant of $PAlg$ for pairs of fixpoints.

6.3.2 Adapting Proofs to Non-Inductive Semantic Functions

To be usable regardless of whether $fold_M$ or $boundedFix$ is used to build the evaluation function, an inductive feature's proof needs to reason over an abstract fixpoint operator and induction principle. This is achieved by only considering a single step of the evaluation algebra and leaving the recursive call abstract:

$$
\begin{array}{l}
\textbf{type}\ soundness\ e\ tp\ ev = \\
\quad \forall env\ t.tp\ (out_f\ (\pi_1\ e)) = Just\ t \rightarrow \\
\qquad WTValue\ (ev\ (out\_t'\ (\pi_1\ e))\ env)\ t) \\
\textbf{type}\ soundness_{alg}\ rec_t\ rec_e \\
\quad (typeof_{alg} :: Mixin\ (Fix_M\ f)\ f\ (Maybe\ (Fix_M\ t)) \\
\quad (eval_{alg} :: Mixin\ (Fix_M\ f)\ f\ (Env\ (Fix_M\ r) \rightarrow Fix_M\ r)) \\
\quad (e :: Fix_M\ f)\ (e\_UP' :: UP\ e) = \\
\qquad \forall IHc :: (\forall e'. \\
\qquad\quad soundness\ e'\ (typeof_{alg}\ rec_t)\ (eval_{alg}\ rec_e) \rightarrow \\
\qquad\quad soundness\ e'\ rec_t\ rec_e). \\
\qquad soundness\ e\ (typeof_{alg}\ rec_t)\ (eval_{alg}\ rec_e)
\end{array}
$$

The hypothesis IHc is used to relate calls of rec_e and rec_t to applications of $eval_{alg}$ and $typeof_{alg}$.

A mediating type class instance again lifts a proof algebra with this signature to one that includes the Induction Hypothesis generated by induction on the bound of $boundedFix$.

$$\textbf{instance}\ (PAlg\ N\ P\ E) \Rightarrow iPAlg\ N\ (IH \rightarrow P)\ E$$

7. Case Study

As a demonstration of the MTC framework, we have built a set of five reusable language features and combined them into a mini-ML [9] variant. The study also builds five other languages from these features.[4] Figure 6 presents the syntax of the expressions, values, and types provided by the features; each line is annotated with the feature that provides that set of definitions.

The Coq files that implement these features average roughly 1100 LoC and come with a typing and evaluation function in addition to soundness and continuity proofs. Each language needs on average only 100 LoC to build its semantic functions and soundness proofs from the files implementing its features. The framework itself consists of about 2500 LoC.

Expressions	Feature
e ::= $\mathbb{N}$ | e + e	*Arith*
| $\mathbb{B}$ | **if** e **then** e **else** e	*Bool*
| **case** e **of** { **z** ⇒ e ; **S** n ⇒ e}	*NatCase*
| **lam** x : T.e | e e | x	*Lambda*
| **fix** x : T.e	*Recursion*

Values	Feature
V ::= $\mathbb{N}$	*Arith*
| $\mathbb{B}$	*Bool*
| **closure** e $\overline{\textrm{V}}$	*Lambda*

Types	Feature
T ::= **nat**	*Arith*
| bool	*Bool*
| T → T	*Lambda*

Figure 6. mini-ML expressions, values, and types

The generic soundness proof, reused by each language, relies on a proof algebra to handle the case analysis of the main lemma. Each case is handled by a sub-algebra. These sub-algebras have their own set of proof algebras for case analysis or induction over an abstract superfunctor. The whole set of dependencies of a top-level proof algebra forms a *proof interface* that must be satisfied by any language which uses that algebra.

Such proof interfaces introduce the problem of *feature interactions* [5], well-known from modular component-based frameworks. In essence, a feature interaction is functionality (e.g., a function or a proof) that is only necessary when two features are combined. An example from this study is the inversion lemma which states that values with type **nat** are natural numbers: ⊢ x : **nat** → x :: $\mathbb{N}$. The *Bool* feature introduces a new typing judgment, WT-BOOL for boolean values. Any language which includes both these features must have an instance of this inversion for WT-BOOL. Our modular approach supports feature interactions by capturing them in type classes. A missing case, like for WT-BOOL, can then be easily added as a new instance of that type class, without affecting or overriding existing code.

In the case study, feature interactions consist almost exclusively of inversion principles for judgments and the projection principles of Section 4.3. Thankfully, their proofs are relatively straightforward and can be dispatched by tactics hooked into the type class inference algorithm. These tactics help minimize the number of interaction type class instances, which could otherwise easily grow exponentially in the number of features.

[3] Introducing type-level binders would further compound the situation with four possible signatures for the *typeof* algebra.

[4] Also available at `http://www.cs.utexas.edu/~bendy/MTC`

8. Related Work

This section discusses related work.

Modular Reasoning There is little work on mechanizing modular proofs for extensible components. An important contribution of our work is how to use *universal properties* to provide modular reasoning techniques for encodings of inductive data types that are compatible with theorem provers like Coq. Old versions of Coq, based on the *calculus of constructions* [11], also use Church encodings to model inductive data types [35]. However, the inductive principles to reason about those encodings had to be axiomatized, which endangered strong normalization of the calculus. The *calculus of inductive constructions* [34] has inductive data types built-in and was introduced to avoid the problems with Church encodings. MTC returns to Church encodings to allow extensibility, but does not use standard, closed induction principles. It instead uses a reasoning framework based on universal properties which allow modular reasoning without axioms in Coq.

Extensibility Our approach to extensibility combines and extends ideas from existing solutions to the expression problem. The type class infrastructure for (Mendler-style) f-algebras is inspired by DTC [14, 43]. However the type-level fixpoints that are central to DTC cannot be used in Coq because of their use of general recursion. To avoid general recursion, MTC encodes *least-fixpoints* with Church encodings [6, 35]. Church encodings have inspired other solutions to the expression problem (especially in object-oriented languages) [30–32]. Those solutions do not use f-algebras: instead, they use an isomorphic representation called *object algebras* [31]. Object algebras are a better fit for languages where records are the main structuring construct (such as OO languages). MTC differs from previous approaches by using Mendler-style f-algebras instead of conventional f-algebras or object algebras. Unlike previous solutions to the expression problem, which focus only on the extensibility aspects of implementations, MTC also deals with modular reasoning and extensibile inductively defined predicates.

Mechanized Meta-Theory and Reuse Several ad-hoc tool-based approaches provide reuse, but none is based on a proof assistant's modularity features alone. The Tinkertype project [23] is a framework for modularly specifying formal languages. It was used to format the language variants used in Pierce's "Types and Programming Languages" [37], and to compose traditional pen-and-paper proofs. The Ott tool [41] allows users to write definitions and theorem statements in an ASCII format designed to mirror pen-and-paper formalizations. These are then automatically translated to definitions in either LaTeX or a theorem prover and proofs and functions are then written using the generated definitions.

Both Boite [7] and Mulhern [29] consider how to extend existing inductive definitions and reuse related proofs in the Coq proof assistant. Both their techniques rely on external tools which are no longer available and have users write extensions with respect to an existing specification. As such, features cannot be checked independently or easily reused with new specifications. In contrast, our approach is fully implemented within Coq and allows for independent development and verification of features.

Delaware et al. [13] applied product-line techniques to modularizing mechanized meta-theory proofs. As a case study, they built type safety proofs for a family of extensions to Featherweight Java from a common base of features. Importantly, composition of these features was entirely manual, as opposed to the automated composition developed here.

Concurrently with our development of MTC, Schwaab et al. have been working on modularizing meta-theory in Agda [40]. While MTC uses Church encodings to encode extensible datatypes, their approach achieves extensibility by using universes which can be lifted to the type level. Encodings and their associated proofs can be modified to derive new languages.

Transparency One long-standing criticism of mechanized meta-theory has been that it interferes with adequacy, i.e. convincing users that the proven theorem is in fact the desired one [39]. Certainly the use of PHOAS can complicate the transparency of mechanized definitions. The $soundness_X$ theorem, for example, uses a more complicated statement than the pen-and-paper version because PHOAS requires induction over the equivalence relation. Modular inductive datatypes have the potential for exacerbating transparency concerns, as the encodings are distributed over different components. Combining a higher-level notation provided by a tool like Ott with the composition mechanisms of MTC is an interesting direction for future work. Such a higher-level notation could help with transparency; while MTC's composition mechanisms could help with generating modular code for Ott specifications.

Binding To minimize the work involved in modeling binders, MTC provides reusable binder components. The problem of modeling binders has previously received a lot of attention. Some proof assistants and type theories address this problem with better support for names and abstract syntax [36, 38]. In general-purpose proof assistants like Coq, however, such support is not available. A popular approach, widely used in Coq formalizations, is to use mechanization-friendly first-order representations of binders such as the *locally nameless* approach [1]. This involves developing a number of straightforward, but tedious infrastructure lemmas and definitions for each new language. Such tedious infrastructure can be automatically generated [2] or reused from data type-generic definitions [21]. However this typically requires additional tool support. A higher-order representation like PHOAS [8] avoids most infrastructure definitions. While we have developed PHOAS-based binders in MTC, it supports first-order representations as well.

Semantics and Interpreters While the majority of semantics formalization approaches use inductively defined predicates, we propose an approach based on interpreters. Of course, MTC supports standard approaches as well.

A particularly prominent line of work based on interpreters is that of using *monads* to structure semantics. Moggi [28] pioneered monads to model computation effects and structure denotation semantics. Liang et al. [25] introduced *monad transformers* to compose multiple monads and build modular interpreters. Jaskelioff et al. [20] used an approach similar to DTC in combination with monads to provide modular implementation of mathematical operational semantics. Our work could benefit from using monads to model more complex language features. However, unlike previous work, we also have to consider modular reasoning. Monads introduce important challenges in terms of modular reasoning. Only very recently have some modular proof techniques for reasoning about monads have been introduced [15, 33]. While these are good starting points, it remains to be seen whether these techniques are sufficient to reason about suitably generalized modular statements like soundness.

Mechanization of interpreter-based semantics clearly poses its own challenges. Yet, it is highly relevant as it bestows the high degree of confidence in correctness directly on the executable artifact, rather than on an intermediate formulation based on inductively defined relations. The only similar work in this direction, developed concurrently to our own, is that of Danielsson [12]. He uses the *partiality monad*, which fairly similar to our bounded fixpoint, to formalize semantic interpreters in Agda. He argues that this style is more easily understood and more obviously deterministic and computable than logical relations. Unlike us, Danielsson does not consider modularization of definitions and proofs.

9. Conclusion

Formalizing meta-theory can be very tedious. For larger programming languages the required amount of work can be overwhelming.

We propose a new approach to formalizing meta-theory that allows *modular* development of language formalizations. By building on existing solutions to modularity problems in conventional programming languages, MTC allows modular definitions of language components. Furthermore, MTC supports modular reasoning about these components. Our approach enables reuse of modular inductive definitions and proofs that deal with standard language constructs, allowing language designers to focus on the interesting constructs of a language.

This paper addresses many, but obviously not all, of the fundamental issues for providing a formal approach to modular semantics. We will investigate further extensions of our approach, guided by the formalization of larger and more complex languages on top of our modular mini-ML variant. A particularly challenging issue we are currently considering of is the pervasive impact of new side-effecting features on existing definitions and proofs. We believe that existing work on modular *monadic* semantics [20, 24, 25] is a good starting point to overcome this hurdle.

Acknowledgements We would like to especially thank William Cook for his help in structuring the presentation of this work. Further thanks to Don Batory, Twan van Laarhoven and the reviewers for their comments and suggestions. This work was supported by the National Science Foundation under Grant CCF 0724979.

References

[1] B. E. Aydemir, A. Charguéraud, B. C. Pierce, R. Pollack, and S. Weirich. Engineering Formal Metatheory. In *POPL '08*, 2008.

[2] B. E. Aydemir and S. Weirich. LNgen: Tool Support for Locally Nameless Representations, 2009. Unpublished manuscript.

[3] B.E. Aydemir et al. Mechanized Metatheory for the Masses: The PoplMark Challenge. In *TPHOLs'05*, 2005.

[4] P. Bahr. Evaluation à la carte: Non-strict evaluation via compositional data types. In *Proceedings of the 23rd Nordic Workshop on Programming Theory*, NWPT '11, pages 38–40, 2011.

[5] D. Batory, J. Kim, and P. Höfner. Feature interactions, products, and composition. In *GPCE*, 2011.

[6] C. Böhm and A. Berarducci. Automatic synthesis of typed lambda-programs on term algebras. *Theor. Comput. Sci.*, 39, 1985.

[7] O. Boite. Proof reuse with extended inductive types. In *Theorem Proving in Higher Order Logics*, pages 50–65, 2004.

[8] A. Chlipala. Parametric higher-order abstract syntax for mechanized semantics. In *ICFP'08*, 2008.

[9] D. Clément, T. Despeyroux, G. Kahn, and J. Despeyroux. A Simple Applicative Language: mini-ML. In *LFP '86*, 1986.

[10] W. R. Cook. *A denotational semantics of inheritance*. PhD thesis, Providence, RI, USA, 1989. AAI9002214.

[11] T. Coquand and Gérard Huet. The calculus of constructions. Technical Report RR-0530, INRIA, May 1986.

[12] N. A. Danielsson. Operational semantics using the partiality monad. In *ICFP'12*, 2012.

[13] B. Delaware, W. R. Cook, and D. Batory. Product lines of theorems. In *OOPSLA '11*, 2011.

[14] L. Duponcheel. Using catamorphisms, subtypes and monad transformers for writing modular functional interpreters., 1995.

[15] J. Gibbons and R. Hinze. Just do it: simple monadic equational reasoning. In *ICFP '11*, 2011.

[16] J. A. Goguen, J. W. Thatcher, E. G. Wagner, and J. B. Wright. Initial algebra semantics and continuous algebras. *J. ACM*, 24(1), Jan. 1977.

[17] G. Gonthier, B. Ziliani, A. Nanevski, and D. Dreyer. How to make ad hoc proof automation less ad hoc. In *ICFP '11*, 2011.

[18] R. Hinze. Church numerals, twice! *JFP*, 15(1):1–13, 2005.

[19] G. Hutton. A tutorial on the universality and expressiveness of fold. *J. Funct. Program.*, 9(4):355–372, 1999.

[20] M. Jaskelioff, N. Ghani, and G. Hutton. Modularity and implementation of mathematical operational semantics. *Electron. Notes Theor. Comput. Sci.*, 229(5), March 2011.

[21] G. Lee, B. C. d. S. Oliveira, S. Cho, and K. Yi. Gmeta: A generic formal metatheory framework for first-order representations. In *ESOP 2012*, 2012.

[22] X. Leroy. Formal verification of a realistic compiler. *Communications of the ACM*, 52(7), 2009.

[23] M. Y. Levin and B. C. Pierce. Tinkertype: A language for playing with formal systems. *Journal of Functional Programming*, 13(2), March 2003.

[24] S. Liang and P. Hudak. Modular denotational semantics for compiler construction. In *ESOP '96*, 1996.

[25] S. Liang, P. Hudak, and M. Jones. Monad transformers and modular interpreters. In *POPL '95*, 1995.

[26] D. MacQueen. Modules for standard ML. In *LFP '84*, 1984.

[27] G. Malcolm. *Algebraic Data Types and Program Transformation*. PhD thesis, Rijksuniversiteit Groningen, September 1990.

[28] E. Moggi. Notions of computation and monads. *Inf. Comput.*, 93(1), July 1991.

[29] A. Mulhern. Proof weaving. In *WMM '06*, September 2006.

[30] B. C. d. S. Oliveira. Modular visitor components. In *ECOOP'09*, 2009.

[31] B. C. d. S. Oliveira and W. R. Cook. Extensibility for the masses: Practical extensibility with object algebras. In *ECOOP'12*, 2012.

[32] B. C. d. S. Oliveira, R. Hinze, and A. Löh. Extensible and modular generics for the masses. In *Trends in Functional Programming*, 2006.

[33] B. C. d. S. Oliveira, T. Schrijvers, and W. R. Cook. Effectiveadvice: disciplined advice with explicit effects. In *AOSD '10*, 2010.

[34] C. Paulin-Mohring. Inductive definitions in the system Coq - rules and properties. In *TLCA '93*, 1993.

[35] F. Pfenning and C. Paulin-Mohring. Inductively defined types in the calculus of constructions. In *MFPS V*, 1990.

[36] F. Pfenning and C. Schürmann. System description: Twelf - a meta-logical framework for deductive systems. In *CADE '99*, 1999.

[37] B. C. Pierce. *Types and Programming Languages*. MIT Press, 2002.

[38] A. M. Pitts. Nominal logic, a first order theory of names and binding. *Inf. Comput.*, 186(2):165–193, 2003.

[39] Robert Pollack. How to believe a machine-checked proof. In *Twenty Five Years of Constructive Type Theory*, 1998.

[40] Christopher Schwaab and Jeremy G. Siek. Modular type-safety proofs using dependant types. *CoRR*, abs/1208.0535, 2012.

[41] Peter Sewell et al. Ott: effective tool support for the working semanticist. In *ICFP '07*, 2007.

[42] M. Sozeau and N. Oury. First-class type classes. In *TPHOLs '08*, 2008.

[43] W. Swierstra. Data types à la carte. *J. Funct. Program.*, 18(4), 2008.

[44] T. Uustalu and V. Vene. Coding recursion a la Mendler. In *WGP '00*, pages 69–85, 2000.

[45] P. Wadler. The Expression Problem. Email, November 1998. Discussion on the Java Genericity mailing list.

[46] P. Wadler and S. Blott. How to make ad-hoc polymorphism less ad hoc. In *POPL '89*, pages 60–76, 1989.

A Theorem Prover for Boolean BI

Jonghyun Park Jeongbong Seo Sungwoo Park

Department of Computer Science and Engineering
Pohang University of Science and Technology (POSTECH)
Republic of Korea
{parjong,baramseo,gla}@postech.ac.kr

Abstract

While separation logic is acknowledged as an enabling technology for large-scale program verification, most of the existing verification tools use only a fragment of separation logic that excludes separating implication. As the first step towards a verification tool using full separation logic, we develop a nested sequent calculus for Boolean BI (Bunched Implications), the underlying theory of separation logic, as well as a theorem prover based on it. A salient feature of our nested sequent calculus is that its sequent may have not only smaller child sequents but also multiple parent sequents, thus producing a graph structure of sequents instead of a tree structure. Our theorem prover is based on backward search in a refinement of the nested sequent calculus in which weakening and contraction are built into all the inference rules. We explain the details of designing our theorem prover and provide empirical evidence of its practicality.

Categories and Subject Descriptors F.4.1 [*Mathematical Logic*]: Mechanical theorem proving, Proof theory

General Terms Verification

Keywords Separation logic, Boolean BI, Theorem prover, Nested sequent calculus

1. Introduction

1.1 Separation logic

Separation logic [36] is an extension of Hoare logic which facilitates reasoning about programs using mutable data structures. As it is acknowledged as an enabling technology for large-scale program verification [7, 31, 38], researchers have developed automated verification tools that use separation logic as their foundational theory. Examples of such tools include Smallfoot [4], Space Invader [15], THOR [30], SLAyer [6], HIP [33], VeriFast [26], jStar [14], and Xisa [13]. The active development of such tools attests to the importance of local reasoning in program verification, which is precisely the key feature that separation logic intends to support.

All the aforementioned tools, however, use not full separation logic but only a decidable fragment by Berdine *et al.* [3] or its extension. Specifically separation logic features two new logical connectives, separating conjunction $\star$ and separating implication $-\!\!\star$, but this decidable fragment includes only separating conjunction. Lack of separating implication implies that for any program performing heap mutation or allocation, there is no support for backward reasoning by weakest precondition generation, an essential requirement for any complete program verification system (see Ishtiaq and O'Hearn [25]). Thus, while very effective in their respective application domains, these tools allow only forward reasoning based on symbolic execution as in [5] and fail to demonstrate the full potential of separation logic in program verification.

Omitting separating implication is not a deliberate decision. Rather it is an inevitable decision due to the availability of no theorem prover for full separation logic. Berdine *et al.* [5] suggest that such a theorem prover is highly desirable and can evolve into a complete program verification system based on separation logic:

> *This incompleteness could be dealt with if we instead used the backwards-running weakest preconditions of Separation Logic. Unfortunately, there is no existing automatic theorem prover which can deal with the form of these assertions (which use quantification and the separating implication $-\!\!\star$). If there were such a prover, we would be eager consumers of it.*

Still, however, there is no practical theorem prover for full separation logic.

Our long-term goal is to develop a theorem prover for full separation logic and incorporate it into a program verification system supporting backward reasoning. The first step is then to study Boolean BI, the underlying theory of separation logic.

1.2 Boolean BI

Boolean BI is a substructural logic which belongs to the family of the logic of BI (Bunched Implications) of O'Hearn and Pym [34]. It inherits additive connectives from classical propositional logic, thus retaining the convenience of classical reasoning. It is also particularly suitable for reasoning about local resources because of multiplicative connectives inherited from intuitionistic linear logic. Like other members in the family, Boolean BI allows us to consider free combinations of these additive connectives and multiplicative connectives, giving rise to an unusual form of contexts called bunches: trees whose internal nodes specify whether subtrees are combined additively or multiplicatively. We obtain separation logic as a model for Boolean BI based on a monoid of heaps.

While theoretical work on Boolean BI is maturing with recent discoveries of its undecidability [11, 29], there is still no practical theorem prover for Boolean BI. The display calculus for Boolean BI by Brotherston [10], which draws on the framework of display logic by Belnap [1], has the cut elimination property and thus can be easily turned into a theorem prover, but developing a practical proof search strategy on top of it does not seem to be easy because of the complexity due to its display rules [9]. In order to develop

POPL'13, January 23–25, 2013, Rome, Italy.

a practical theorem prover for Boolean BI and hence also for full separation logic, we choose to develop another proof theory that directly reflects the characteristics of Boolean BI and lends itself well to proof search. This paper presents such a proof theory for Boolean BI as well as a theorem prover based on it.

1.3 Contribution

We present a *nested sequent calculus* $\mathbf{S_{BBI}}$ for Boolean BI. Unlike in typical nested sequent calculi [12, 22–24, 27], its sequent may have not only smaller child sequents but also multiple parent sequents, thus producing a graph structure of sequents instead of a tree structure. The use of nested sequents is necessary because of the presence of intuitionistic multiplicative conjunction in a classical setting. The use of a graph structure of sequents is necessary because of the interaction between multiplicative implication and classical negation. As in typical multi-conclusioned sequent calculi for classical logic, we use multisets of formulas not only for antecedents but also for succedents of a sequent. Thus sequents in $\mathbf{S_{BBI}}$ do not use bunches, which are supplanted by new structural connectives specifying a graph structure of sequents. $\mathbf{S_{BBI}}$ has the cut elimination property and is sound and complete with respect to the Kripke semantics for Boolean BI.

Our theorem prover for Boolean BI is based on backward proof search in another nested sequent calculus $\mathbf{CS_{BBI}}$ which is obtained from $\mathbf{S_{BBI}}$ by building weakening and contraction into all the inference rules. In conjunction with a graph structure of sequents, the structural rules in $\mathbf{CS_{BBI}}$ make it particularly challenging to devise a practical proof search strategy, even if it is based on backward proof search. We deal with an explosion in the search space due to the structural rules, which can be applied indefinitely and exponentially increase the search space, by prioritizing their applications. We find that our theorem prover is reasonably fast in proving typical formulas of Boolean BI. To the best of our knowledge, our theorem prover is the first theorem prover for Boolean BI.

1.4 Organization of the paper

Section 2 gives preliminaries on Boolean BI. Section 3 presents the nested sequent calculus $\mathbf{S_{BBI}}$ and the satisfaction relation for its sequents. Section 4 proves the cut elimination property of $\mathbf{S_{BBI}}$, and Section 5 proves the soundness and completeness of $\mathbf{S_{BBI}}$ with respect to the satisfaction relation as well as the Kripke semantics for Boolean BI. Section 6 reviews the display calculus for Boolean BI by Brotherston [10] and shows that $\mathbf{S_{BBI}}$ is an optimization of the display calculus. Section 7 presents the nested sequent calculus $\mathbf{CS_{BBI}}$. Section 8 describes the backward search strategy in our theorem prover and presents experimental results. Section 9 discusses related work and Section 10 concludes. Our theorem prover (with an online demo) and accompanying technical report are available at `http://pl.postech.ac.kr/BBI/`.

2. Preliminaries on Boolean BI

Formulas in Boolean BI extend classical propositional logic with multiplicative connectives from linear logic:

$$\text{formula } A \ ::= \ P \mid \bot \mid \neg A \mid A \vee A \mid \mathsf{I} \mid A \star A \mid A \mathrel{-\!\!\star} A$$

P denotes an atomic formula drawn from a set V. I is the multiplicative unit. $A \star B$ is a multiplicative conjunction and $A \mathrel{-\!\!\star} B$ is a multiplicative implication. We define $\top$ as $\neg\bot$, $A \wedge B$ as $\neg(\neg A \vee \neg B)$, and $A \to B$ as $\neg A \vee B$. We use conventional precedence rules for logical connectives: $\neg > \wedge, \star > \vee > \to, \mathrel{-\!\!\star}$.

The Kripke semantics of Boolean BI [17] uses a non-deterministic commutative monoid on a set U. Assume a binary operator $\circ : U \times U \to \mathcal{P}(U)$ and a unit element $e \in U$ (where $\mathcal{P}(U)$ denotes the power set of U). We extend $\circ$ to a binary operator on $\mathcal{P}(U)$ such that $U_1 \circ U_2 = \cup\{w_1 \circ w_2 \mid w_1 \in U_1, w_2 \in U_2\}$. A non-deterministic commutative monoid is a triple $\langle U, \circ, e\rangle$ which satisfies the following conditions:

$$\begin{array}{rl}
\text{(neutrality)} & \forall w \in U.\ w \circ e = \{w\} \\
\text{(commutativity)} & \forall w_1, w_2 \in U.\ w_1 \circ w_2 = w_2 \circ w_1 \\
\text{(associativity)} & \forall w_1, w_2, w_3 \in U.\ w_1 \circ (w_2 \circ w_3) = \\
& \qquad (w_1 \circ w_2) \circ w_3
\end{array}$$

$$\begin{array}{rll}
w, \rho \models P & \text{iff.} & w \in \rho(P) \\
w, \rho \models \bot & \text{iff.} & \text{never} \\
w, \rho \models \neg A & \text{iff.} & w, \rho \not\models A \\
w, \rho \models A \vee B & \text{iff.} & w, \rho \models A \text{ or } w, \rho \models B \\
w, \rho \models \mathsf{I} & \text{iff.} & w = e \\
w, \rho \models A \star B & \text{iff.} & \exists w_1, w_2 \in U \text{ such that } w \in w_1 \circ w_2 \\
& & \text{and } w_1, \rho \models A \text{ and } w_2, \rho \models B \\
w, \rho \models A \mathrel{-\!\!\star} B & \text{iff.} & \forall w_1 \in U.\ w_1, \rho \models A \text{ implies} \\
& & \forall w_2 \in w \circ w_1.\ w_2, \rho \models B
\end{array}$$

Figure 1. Satisfaction relation $w, \rho \models A$ for formulas

$$\begin{array}{ll}
\text{(Axiom 1)} & \vdash A \to \mathsf{I} \star A \\
\text{(Axiom 2)} & \vdash \mathsf{I} \star A \to A \\
\text{(Axiom 3)} & \vdash A \star B \to B \star A \\
\text{(Axiom 4)} & \vdash A \star (B \star C) \to (A \star B) \star C
\end{array}$$

$$\frac{\vdash A_1 \to A_2 \quad \vdash B_1 \to B_2}{\vdash (A_1 \star B_1) \to (A_2 \star B_2)} \star H$$

$$\frac{\vdash (A \star B) \to C}{\vdash A \to (B \mathrel{-\!\!\star} C)} \mathrel{-\!\!\star} H_1 \qquad \frac{\vdash A \to (B \mathrel{-\!\!\star} C)}{\vdash (A \star B) \to C} \mathrel{-\!\!\star} H_2$$

Figure 2. Axioms and inference rules for multiplicative connectives in the Hilbert system for Boolean BI

Given a non-deterministic commutative monoid $\langle U, \circ, e\rangle$ and a valuation $\rho : V \to \mathcal{P}(U)$ of atomic formulas, we obtain the Kripke semantics of Boolean BI from the satisfaction relation $w, \rho \models A$ for formulas given in Figure 1. The satisfaction relation $w, \rho \models A$ is defined inductively on the structure of formula A. A formula A is valid, written $\models A$, if $w, \rho \models A$ holds for any element w and valuation ρ.

The Hilbert system for Boolean BI [35] uses a judgment $\vdash A$ and is obtained by extending classical propositional logic with axioms and inference rules for multiplicative connectives given in Figure 2. An induction on the structure of the proof of $\vdash A$ proves the soundness of the Hilbert system with respect to the Kripke semantics of Boolean BI. Galmiche and Larchey-Wendling [17] prove that the Hilbert system is also complete with respect to the Kripke semantics of Boolean BI.

Theorem 2.1. *$\models A$ if and only if $\vdash A$.*

3. Nested sequent calculus $\mathbf{S_{BBI}}$ for Boolean BI

This section presents the nested sequent calculus $\mathbf{S_{BBI}}$ for Boolean BI. We first explain the definition of sequents in $\mathbf{S_{BBI}}$. Then we present the satisfaction relation for sequents and the inference rules of $\mathbf{S_{BBI}}$.

3.1 Nested sequents

A sequent in $\mathbf{S_{BBI}}$ represents a graph structure whose nodes store sequents in classical logic. A node can have multiple parent nodes

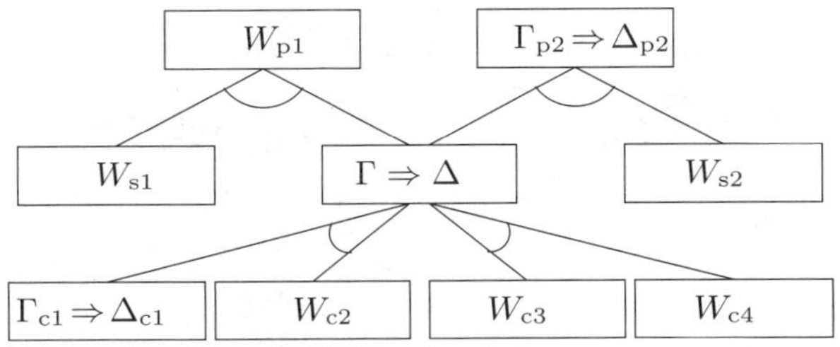

Figure 3. An example of a graph structure of nodes in $\mathbf{S_{BBI}}$ (p for parent, c for child, s for sibling)

as well as multiple child nodes, but the following two relations should always hold:

1. A node can have multiple parent nodes, but each parent node determines a unique sibling node. Hence no node can have two parent nodes with the same sibling node.
2. A node can have multiple child nodes, but each child node determines another unique child node. Hence we can divide all child nodes into groups of two sibling nodes.

Formally a sequent W describes a graph structure with respect to a certain node in it, which we refer to as the *reference node*. It consists of a truth context and a falsehood context. A truth context contains *node states* which are either true formulas specific to the reference node or descriptions of its relation to child, sibling, and parent nodes; a falsehood context contains false formulas specific to the reference node:

$$\begin{array}{rrcl} \text{sequent} & W & = & \Gamma \Rightarrow \Delta \\ \text{truth context} & \Gamma & ::= & \cdot \mid \Gamma; S \\ \text{falsehood context} & \Delta & ::= & \cdot \mid \Delta; A \\ \text{node state} & S & ::= & A \mid \emptyset_{\mathsf{m}} \mid W, W \mid W\langle\!\langle W \rangle\!\rangle \end{array}$$

We use truth contexts and falsehood contexts as unordered sets and do not use an additive zero (like $\emptyset_{\mathsf{a}}$ in the definition of bunches). $\emptyset_{\mathsf{m}}$ is a special node state which corresponds to the unit element of the monoid in the Kripke semantics of Boolean BI. A *multiplicative pair* W, W' asserts the existence of a pair of child nodes which are reference nodes of W and W'. An *adjoint pair* $W\langle\!\langle W' \rangle\!\rangle$ asserts the existence of a sibling node and a common parent node which are reference nodes of W and W', respectively. Note that a sequent in $\mathbf{S_{BBI}}$ reverts to a sequent in classical logic if we leave only true formulas in its truth context.

The use of adjoint pairs implies that we can describe the same graph structure of nodes using different sequents by changing the reference node. As an example, consider the graph structure in Figure 3 where lines denote parent-child relations and arcs denote sibling relations. We let $\Gamma' = W_{\mathrm{s1}}\langle\!\langle W_{\mathrm{p1}} \rangle\!\rangle; (W_{\mathrm{c3}}, W_{\mathrm{c4}})$. Then the following three sequents describe the same graph structure in Figure 3, but all use different reference nodes (top right, center, and bottom left):

$$\begin{array}{c} \Gamma_{\mathrm{p2}}; (\Gamma; \Gamma'; (\Gamma_{\mathrm{c1}} \Rightarrow \Delta_{\mathrm{c1}}, W_{\mathrm{c2}}) \Rightarrow \Delta, W_{\mathrm{s2}}) \Rightarrow \Delta_{\mathrm{p2}} \\ \Gamma; \Gamma'; (\Gamma_{\mathrm{c1}} \Rightarrow \Delta_{\mathrm{c1}}, W_{\mathrm{c2}}); W_{\mathrm{s2}}\langle\!\langle \Gamma_{\mathrm{p2}} \Rightarrow \Delta_{\mathrm{p2}} \rangle\!\rangle \Rightarrow \Delta \\ \Gamma_{\mathrm{c1}}; W_{\mathrm{c2}}\langle\!\langle \Gamma; \Gamma'; W_{\mathrm{s2}}\langle\!\langle \Gamma_{\mathrm{p2}} \Rightarrow \Delta_{\mathrm{p2}} \rangle\!\rangle \Rightarrow \Delta \rangle\!\rangle \Rightarrow \Delta_{\mathrm{c1}} \end{array}$$

$\mathbf{S_{BBI}}$ provides two inference rules which convert a sequent into another equivalent sequent by changing the reference node.

Our definition of sequents in $\mathbf{S_{BBI}}$ embodies the principle of proof by contradiction from classical logic: a proof of a sequent means that its truth and falsehood contexts together lead to a logical contradiction. This departure from the standard interpretation of sequents for classical logic (in which the conjunction of antecedents implies the disjunction of succedents) is intentional, as the principle of proof by contradiction guides the development of both the satisfaction relation and the rules for $\mathbf{S_{BBI}}$.

3.2 Satisfaction relation for sequents

Given a non-deterministic commutative monoid $\langle U, \circ, e \rangle$ and a valuation $\rho : V \rightarrow \mathcal{P}(U)$ of atomic formulas, we can define the satisfaction relation $w, \rho \models_{\mathcal{W}} W$ for sequents. It uses another satisfaction relation $w, \rho \models_{\mathcal{S}} S$ for node states and the satisfaction relation $w, \rho \models A$ for formulas:

$$w, \rho \models_{\mathcal{W}} \Gamma \Rightarrow \Delta \quad \text{iff.} \quad \begin{cases} \forall S \in \Gamma.\ w, \rho \models_{\mathcal{S}} S \\ \forall A \in \Delta.\ w, \rho \not\models A \end{cases}$$

The satisfaction relation $w, \rho \models_{\mathcal{S}} S$ for node states is defined as follows:

$$\begin{array}{rll} w, \rho \models_{\mathcal{S}} A & \text{iff.} & w, \rho \models A \\ w, \rho \models_{\mathcal{S}} \emptyset_{\mathsf{m}} & \text{iff.} & w = e \\ w, \rho \models_{\mathcal{S}} W_1, W_2 & \text{iff.} & \exists w_1, w_2 \in U \text{ such that } w \in w_1 \circ w_2 \\ & & \text{and } w_1, \rho \models_{\mathcal{W}} W_1 \text{ and } w_2, \rho \models_{\mathcal{W}} W_2 \\ w, \rho \models_{\mathcal{S}} W_1\langle\!\langle W_2 \rangle\!\rangle & \text{iff.} & \exists w_1, w_2 \in U \text{ such that } w_2 \in w \circ w_1 \\ & & \text{and } w_1, \rho \models_{\mathcal{W}} W_1 \text{ and } w_2, \rho \models_{\mathcal{W}} W_2 \end{array}$$

Note that the satisfaction relation for multiplicative formulas can be rewritten in terms of the satisfaction relation for node states as follows:

- $w, \rho \models \mathsf{I}$ iff. $w, \rho \models_{\mathcal{S}} \emptyset_{\mathsf{m}}$.
- $w, \rho \models A \star B$ iff. $w, \rho \models_{\mathcal{S}} (A \Rightarrow \cdot), (B \Rightarrow \cdot)$.
- $w, \rho \models A \mathrel{-\!\!\star} B$ iff. $w, \rho \not\models_{\mathcal{S}} (A \Rightarrow \cdot)\langle\!\langle \cdot \Rightarrow B \rangle\!\rangle$.

If $w, \rho \not\models_{\mathcal{W}} W$ holds for any element w and valuation ρ, we say that W is unsatisfiable and write $\not\models_{\mathcal{W}} W$.

3.3 Nested sequent calculus $\mathbf{S_{BBI}}$

Figure 4 shows the nested sequent calculus $\mathbf{S_{BBI}}$ for Boolean BI. The inference rules are divided into three groups: structural rules, traverse rules, and logical rules. We read every rule from the conclusion to the premise.

A structural rule makes a change to the sequent in the conclusion, but does not change the reference node. The rules $\mathit{WL}_{\mathcal{S}}$, $\mathit{WR}_{\mathcal{S}}$, $\mathit{CL}_{\mathcal{S}}$, and $\mathit{CR}_{\mathcal{S}}$ are weakening and contraction rules. The rules $\mathit{EC}_{\mathcal{S}}$ and $\mathit{EA}_{\mathcal{S}}$ rewrite a node state according to commutativity and associativity of sequents, respectively. Note that associativity of sequents does not use $(W_1, W_2), W_3$ and $W_1, (W_2, W_3)$, both of which are syntactically ill-formed. The rule $\emptyset_{\mathsf{m}}\mathit{U}_{\mathcal{S}}$ creates a new child node with a special form of sequent $\emptyset_{\mathsf{m}} \Rightarrow \cdot$, which can be absorbed back into the parent node by the rule $\emptyset_{\mathsf{m}}\mathit{D}_{\mathcal{S}}$. Intuitively $\emptyset_{\mathsf{m}} \Rightarrow \cdot$ describes an empty node whose sibling node can be identified with its parent node.

A traverse rule changes the reference node without changing parent-child or sibling relations between nodes. The rules $\mathit{TC}_{\mathcal{S}}$ and $\mathit{TP}_{\mathcal{S}}$ promote the left child node (corresponding to $\Gamma_{\mathrm{c1}} \Rightarrow \Delta_{\mathrm{c1}}$) and the parent node (corresponding to $\Gamma_{\mathrm{p}} \Rightarrow \Delta_{\mathrm{p}}$), respectively, as the new reference node. In conjunction with the rule $\mathit{EC}_{\mathcal{S}}$, the two traverse rules enable us to designate an arbitrary node as the reference node because every pair of nodes can be connected only via parent-child relations. The following example shows how to promote the sibling node as the reference node:

$$\dfrac{\dfrac{\dfrac{\Gamma_{\mathrm{s}}; (\Gamma \Rightarrow \Delta)\langle\!\langle \Gamma_{\mathrm{p}} \Rightarrow \Delta_{\mathrm{p}} \rangle\!\rangle \Rightarrow \Delta_{\mathrm{s}}}{\Gamma_{\mathrm{p}}; (\Gamma_{\mathrm{s}} \Rightarrow \Delta_{\mathrm{s}}), (\Gamma \Rightarrow \Delta) \Rightarrow \Delta_{\mathrm{p}}}\,\mathit{TC}_{\mathcal{S}}}{\Gamma_{\mathrm{p}}; (\Gamma \Rightarrow \Delta), (\Gamma_{\mathrm{s}} \Rightarrow \Delta_{\mathrm{s}}) \Rightarrow \Delta_{\mathrm{p}}}\,\mathit{EC}_{\mathcal{S}}}{\Gamma; (\Gamma_{\mathrm{s}} \Rightarrow \Delta_{\mathrm{s}})\langle\!\langle \Gamma_{\mathrm{p}} \Rightarrow \Delta_{\mathrm{p}} \rangle\!\rangle \Rightarrow \Delta}\,\mathit{TP}_{\mathcal{S}}$$

A logical rule focuses on a principal formula in the reference node. If the sequent already expresses a logical contradiction, it

Structural rules:

$$\frac{\Gamma \Rightarrow \Delta}{\Gamma; S \Rightarrow \Delta}\ WL_S \qquad \frac{\Gamma \Rightarrow \Delta}{\Gamma \Rightarrow \Delta; A}\ WR_S \qquad \frac{\Gamma; S; S \Rightarrow \Delta}{\Gamma; S \Rightarrow \Delta}\ CL_S \qquad \frac{\Gamma \Rightarrow \Delta; A; A}{\Gamma \Rightarrow \Delta; A}\ CR_S \qquad \frac{\Gamma; W', W \Rightarrow \Delta}{\Gamma; W, W' \Rightarrow \Delta}\ EC_S$$

$$\frac{\Gamma; W_1, (W_2, W_3 \Rightarrow \cdot) \Rightarrow \Delta}{\Gamma; (W_1, W_2 \Rightarrow \cdot), W_3 \Rightarrow \Delta}\ EA_S \qquad \frac{\Gamma_1; (\Gamma_2 \Rightarrow \Delta_2), (\emptyset_{\mathsf{m}} \Rightarrow \cdot) \Rightarrow \Delta_1}{\Gamma_1; \Gamma_2 \Rightarrow \Delta_1; \Delta_2}\ \emptyset_{\mathsf{m}}U_S \qquad \frac{\Gamma_1; \Gamma_2 \Rightarrow \Delta_1; \Delta_2}{\Gamma_1; (\Gamma_2 \Rightarrow \Delta_2), (\emptyset_{\mathsf{m}} \Rightarrow \cdot) \Rightarrow \Delta_1}\ \emptyset_{\mathsf{m}}D_S$$

Traverse rules:

$$\frac{\Gamma_{\mathsf{c}1}; (\Gamma_{\mathsf{c}2} \Rightarrow \Delta_{\mathsf{c}2})\langle\!\langle \Gamma \Rightarrow \Delta \rangle\!\rangle \Rightarrow \Delta_{\mathsf{c}1}}{\Gamma; (\Gamma_{\mathsf{c}1} \Rightarrow \Delta_{\mathsf{c}1}), (\Gamma_{\mathsf{c}2} \Rightarrow \Delta_{\mathsf{c}2}) \Rightarrow \Delta}\ TC_S \qquad \frac{\Gamma_{\mathsf{p}}; (\Gamma \Rightarrow \Delta), (\Gamma_{\mathsf{s}} \Rightarrow \Delta_{\mathsf{s}}) \Rightarrow \Delta_{\mathsf{p}}}{\Gamma; (\Gamma_{\mathsf{s}} \Rightarrow \Delta_{\mathsf{s}})\langle\!\langle \Gamma_{\mathsf{p}} \Rightarrow \Delta_{\mathsf{p}} \rangle\!\rangle \Rightarrow \Delta}\ TP_S$$

(p for parent, c for child, s for sibling)

Logical rules:

$$\frac{}{A \Rightarrow A}\ Init_S \qquad \frac{}{\bot \Rightarrow \cdot}\ \bot L_S \qquad \frac{\Gamma \Rightarrow \Delta}{\Gamma \Rightarrow \Delta; \bot}\ \bot R_S \qquad \frac{\Gamma \Rightarrow \Delta; A}{\Gamma; \neg A \Rightarrow \Delta}\ \neg L_S \qquad \frac{\Gamma; A \Rightarrow \Delta}{\Gamma \Rightarrow \Delta; \neg A}\ \neg R_S \qquad \frac{\Gamma_1; A \Rightarrow \Delta_1 \quad \Gamma_2; B \Rightarrow \Delta_2}{\Gamma_1; \Gamma_2; A \vee B \Rightarrow \Delta_1; \Delta_2}\ \vee L_S$$

$$\frac{\Gamma \Rightarrow \Delta; A; B}{\Gamma \Rightarrow \Delta; A \vee B}\ \vee R_S \qquad \frac{\Gamma; \emptyset_{\mathsf{m}} \Rightarrow \Delta}{\Gamma; \mathsf{I} \Rightarrow \Delta}\ \mathsf{I}L_S \qquad \frac{}{\emptyset_{\mathsf{m}} \Rightarrow \mathsf{I}}\ \mathsf{I}R_S \qquad \frac{\Gamma; (A \Rightarrow \cdot), (B \Rightarrow \cdot) \Rightarrow \Delta}{\Gamma; A \star B \Rightarrow \Delta}\ \star L_S$$

$$\frac{\Gamma_1 \Rightarrow \Delta_1; A \quad \Gamma_2 \Rightarrow \Delta_2; B}{(\Gamma_1 \Rightarrow \Delta_1), (\Gamma_2 \Rightarrow \Delta_2) \Rightarrow A \star B}\ \star R_S \qquad \frac{\Gamma_1 \Rightarrow \Delta_1; A \quad \Gamma_2; B \Rightarrow \Delta_2}{(\Gamma_1 \Rightarrow \Delta_1)\langle\!\langle \Gamma_2 \Rightarrow \Delta_2 \rangle\!\rangle; A \mathrel{-\!\!\star} B \Rightarrow \cdot}\ {-\!\!\star}L_S \qquad \frac{\Gamma; (A \Rightarrow \cdot)\langle\!\langle \cdot \Rightarrow B \rangle\!\rangle \Rightarrow \Delta}{\Gamma \Rightarrow \Delta; A \mathrel{-\!\!\star} B}\ {-\!\!\star}R_S$$

Figure 4. Nested sequent calculus $\mathbf{S_{BBI}}$ for Boolean BI

completes the proof without generating a premise. All the rules from $Init_S$ to $\vee R_S$ are from classical propositional logic. The rule $Init_S$ expresses the principle of proof by contradiction. The rules $\mathsf{I}L_S$ and $\mathsf{I}R_S$ use the fact that I is true only in an empty node which $\emptyset_{\mathsf{m}}$ describes. The rules $\star L_S$ and $\star R_S$ are based on the following interpretation of multiplicative conjunction $\star$:

$$\begin{array}{lll} w, \rho \models A \star B & \text{iff.} & \exists w_1, w_2 \in U \text{ such that } w \in w_1 \circ w_2 \\ & & \text{and } w_1, \rho \models A \text{ and } w_2, \rho \models B \\ w, \rho \not\models A \star B & \text{iff.} & \forall w_1, w_2 \in U.\ w \in w_1 \circ w_2 \text{ implies} \\ & & w_1, \rho \not\models A \text{ or } w_2, \rho \not\models B \end{array}$$

The rule $\star L_S$ creates ($\exists$) two fresh child nodes (corresponding to w_1 and w_2) where A and B are true, respectively, which explains why we need to use nested sequents. The rule $\star R_S$ chooses ($\forall$) two existing child nodes (corresponding to w_1 and w_2) which are described by $\Gamma_1 \Rightarrow \Delta_1$ and $\Gamma_2 \Rightarrow \Delta_2$. The rules ${-\!\!\star}L_S$ and ${-\!\!\star}R_S$ are based on the following interpretation of multiplicative implication ${-\!\!\star}$:

$$\begin{array}{lll} w, \rho \models A \mathrel{-\!\!\star} B & \text{iff.} & \forall w_1 \in U.\ w_1, \rho \models A \text{ implies} \\ & & \forall w_2 \in w \circ w_1.\ w_2, \rho \models B \\ w, \rho \not\models A \mathrel{-\!\!\star} B & \text{iff.} & \exists w_1, w_2 \in U \text{ such that } w_2 \in w \circ w_1 \\ & & \text{and } w_1, \rho \models A \text{ and } w_2, \rho \not\models B \end{array}$$

The rule ${-\!\!\star}L_S$ chooses ($\forall$) existing sibling and parent nodes (corresponding to w_1 and w_2) which are described by $\Gamma_1 \Rightarrow \Delta_1$ and $\Gamma_2 \Rightarrow \Delta_2$. The rule ${-\!\!\star}R_S$ creates ($\exists$) a fresh sibling node (corresponding to w_1) where A is true and a fresh parent node (corresponding to w_2) where B is false, which explains why we need to allow multiple parent nodes.

Figure 5 shows an example of proving $A \to (A \star B) \vee (A \star \neg B)$ in $\mathbf{S_{BBI}}$. The formula means that every node can have an adjacent node in which either B or $\neg B$ is true. First we apply the rule $\emptyset_{\mathsf{m}}U_S$ to create an empty node, described by $\emptyset_{\mathsf{m}} \Rightarrow \cdot$, in which we later mix assumptions of B and $\neg B$ to produce a logical contradiction:

$$(A \Rightarrow \cdot), (\emptyset_{\mathsf{m}} \Rightarrow \cdot) \Rightarrow A \star B; A \star \neg B$$

Then we extend the truth context of the empty node with a node state S describing the current relation with its sibling and parent nodes:

$$(A \Rightarrow \cdot), (\emptyset_{\mathsf{m}}; S \Rightarrow \cdot) \Rightarrow A \star B; A \star \neg B$$

Here we promote the empty node as the reference node to generate S and apply the contraction rule CL_S to duplicate S. After isolating the sequent for the empty node and adding B to its falsehood context, we consume S in $\emptyset_{\mathsf{m}}; S \Rightarrow B$ (by the rule TP_S) to restore

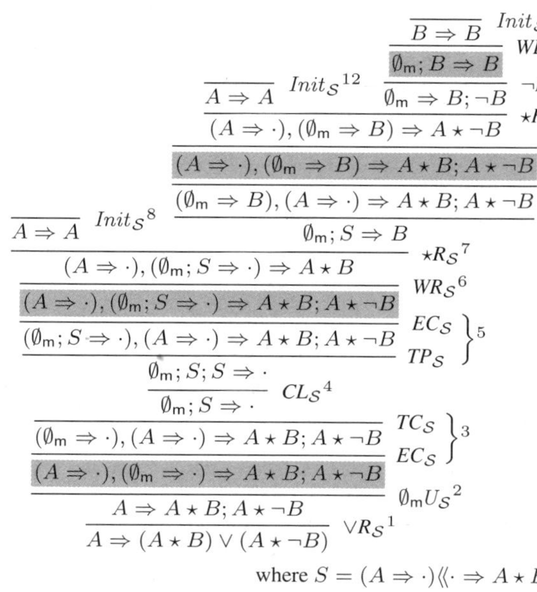

Figure 5. A proof of $A \Rightarrow (A \star B) \vee (A \star \neg B)$ in $\mathbf{S_{BBI}}$. We number all proof steps for comparison with Figure 6.

the previous relation between the empty node and its sibling and parent nodes:

$$(A \Rightarrow \cdot), (\emptyset_{\mathsf{m}} \Rightarrow B) \Rightarrow A \star B; A \star \neg B$$

Finally we add B to the truth context and produce a logical contradiction:

$$\emptyset_{\mathsf{m}}; B \Rightarrow B$$

4. Cut elimination in $\mathbf{S_{BBI}}$

We state the cut elimination property of $\mathbf{S_{BBI}}$ as follows:[1]

Theorem 4.1 (Cut elimination).
If $\Gamma \Rightarrow \Delta; C$ *and* $\Gamma'; C \Rightarrow \Delta'$, *then* $\Gamma; \Gamma' \Rightarrow \Delta; \Delta'$.

[1] Strictly speaking, Theorem 4.1 states only the admissibility of the cut rule. The cut elimination property, however, immediately follows as a corollary and we refer to Theorem 4.1 as the cut elimination theorem.

Section 6 gives an indirect proof of Theorem 4.1 which exploits the cut elimination property of the display calculus for Boolean BI [10]. Here we give a sketch of a direct proof which is inspired by the proof of cut elimination in original display logic [1].

The main complication in proving Theorem 4.1 is that the two contraction rules CL_S and CR_S duplicate a node state or a formula in their premise. In conjunction with the traverse rules, these contraction rules can produce copies of the cut formula C in different (smaller) sequents within the same sequent, as in:

$$\Gamma; (\Gamma_1; C^{n_1} \Rightarrow \Delta_1), W_1; (\Gamma_2; C^{n_2} \Rightarrow \Delta_2), W_2 \Rightarrow \Delta$$

Here C^n means a truth context containing n copies of C. To represent such a sequent containing smaller sequents with copies of the cut formula, we introduce the following definitions:

$$\begin{array}{rrcl} \text{partial sequent} & \omega & ::= & [] \mid [;\gamma \Rightarrow] \mid \Gamma;\gamma \Rightarrow \Delta \\ \text{partial truth context} & \gamma & ::= & \sigma \mid \sigma;\gamma \\ \text{partial node state} & \sigma & ::= & \omega, W \mid W, \omega \mid \omega, \omega \mid \\ & & & \omega\langle\langle W \rangle\rangle \mid W\langle\langle \omega \rangle\rangle \mid \omega\langle\langle \omega \rangle\rangle \end{array}$$

A partial sequent is a sequent with one or more holes in it; similarly partial truth contexts and partial node states contain one or more holes. We write $\omega[W_1]\cdots[W_n]$ for the sequent obtained by filling holes in ω with sequents $W_1, \cdots, W_n$ in that order; we define $\gamma[W_1]\cdots[W_n]$ and $\sigma[W_1]\cdots[W_n]$ in a similar way:

$$\omega[W_1]\cdots[W_n] = \begin{cases} W_1 & \text{where } \omega = [], n = 1 \\ \Gamma_1; \gamma[W_2]\cdots[W_n] \Rightarrow \Delta_1 & \text{where } \omega = [;\gamma \Rightarrow], \\ & \quad n > 1, W_1 = \Gamma_1 \Rightarrow \Delta_1 \\ \Gamma; \gamma[W_1]\cdots[W_n] \Rightarrow \Delta & \text{where } \omega = \Gamma; \gamma \Rightarrow \Delta \end{cases}$$

Note that $[;\gamma \Rightarrow]$ uses the first sequent to describe the reference node and remaining sequents to fill the holes in γ.

The proof of Theorem 4.1, which is inspired by the proof of cut elimination in display logic [1], proceeds by proving the following three lemmas. Here we say that $/C/$ holds if $\Gamma \Rightarrow \Delta; A$ and $\Gamma'; A \Rightarrow \Delta'$ implies $\Gamma; \Gamma' \Rightarrow \Delta; \Delta'$ for any proper subformula A of C. We also write $\Gamma; \boxed{C} \Rightarrow \Delta$ and $\Gamma \Rightarrow \Delta; \boxed{C}$ to indicate that C is the principal formula of the last inference rule in their proofs. The proof of Lemma 4.3 uses Lemma 4.2, and the proof of Lemma 4.4 uses Lemma 4.3.

Lemma 4.2. *Suppose that $/C/$ holds. Then* $\Gamma \Rightarrow \Delta; \boxed{C}$ *and* $\Gamma'; \boxed{C} \Rightarrow \Delta'$ *imply* $\Gamma; \Gamma' \Rightarrow \Delta; \Delta'$.

Lemma 4.3. *Suppose that $/C/$ holds. Then* $\omega[\Gamma_1 \Rightarrow \Delta_1; C^{n_1}]\cdots[\Gamma_k \Rightarrow \Delta_k; C^{n_k}]$ *and* $\Gamma'; \boxed{C} \Rightarrow \Delta'$ *imply* $\omega[\Gamma_1; \Gamma' \Rightarrow \Delta_1; \Delta']\cdots[\Gamma_k; \Gamma' \Rightarrow \Delta_k; \Delta']$.

Lemma 4.4. *Suppose that $/C/$ holds. Then* $\Gamma \Rightarrow \Delta; C$ *and* $\omega[\Gamma'_1; C^{n_1} \Rightarrow \Delta'_1]\cdots[\Gamma'_k; C^{n_k} \Rightarrow \Delta'_k]$ *imply* $\omega[\Gamma; \Gamma'_1 \Rightarrow \Delta; \Delta'_1]\cdots[\Gamma; \Gamma'_k \Rightarrow \Delta; \Delta'_k]$.

Then we complete the proof of Theorem 4.1 by induction on the structure of the cut formula C.

5. Soundness and completeness of $\mathbf{S_{BBI}}$

This section proves the soundness and completeness of the nested sequent calculus $\mathbf{S_{BBI}}$ with respect to the satisfaction relation in Section 3.2 (Theorems 5.1 and 5.2). It means that the syntactic provability of a sequent coincides with its semantic unsatisfiability, confirming the principle of proof by contradiction embodied in the definition of sequents.

Theorem 5.1 (Soundness). *If* $\Gamma \Rightarrow \Delta$, *then* $\not\models_{\mathcal{W}} \Gamma \Rightarrow \Delta$.

Theorem 5.2 (Completeness). *If* $\not\models_{\mathcal{W}} \Gamma \Rightarrow \Delta$, *then* $\Gamma \Rightarrow \Delta$.

The proof of soundness proceeds by induction on the structure of the proof of $\Gamma \Rightarrow \Delta$. The proof of completeness uses a translation of a sequent W into a formula $[\![W]\!]_{\mathrm{w}}$ in Boolean BI defined as follows:

$$[\![\Gamma \Rightarrow \Delta]\!]_{\mathrm{w}} = [\![\Gamma]\!]_{\mathrm{g}} \wedge \neg[\![\Delta]\!]_{\mathrm{d}}$$

$$\begin{array}{rcl@{\qquad}rcl} [\![\cdot]\!]_{\mathrm{g}} & = & \top & [\![\cdot]\!]_{\mathrm{d}} & = & \bot \\ [\![\Gamma; S]\!]_{\mathrm{g}} & = & [\![\Gamma]\!]_{\mathrm{g}} \wedge [\![S]\!]_{\mathrm{s}} & [\![\Delta; A]\!]_{\mathrm{d}} & = & [\![\Delta]\!]_{\mathrm{d}} \vee A \end{array}$$

$$\begin{array}{rcl} [\![A]\!]_{\mathrm{s}} & = & A \\ [\![\emptyset_{\mathrm{m}}]\!]_{\mathrm{s}} & = & \mathsf{I} \\ [\![W_1, W_2]\!]_{\mathrm{s}} & = & [\![W_1]\!]_{\mathrm{w}} \star [\![W_2]\!]_{\mathrm{w}} \\ [\![W_1\langle\langle W_2 \rangle\rangle]\!]_{\mathrm{s}} & = & \neg([\![W_1]\!]_{\mathrm{w}} \mathrel{-\!\!\star} \neg[\![W_2]\!]_{\mathrm{w}}) \end{array}$$

Recall that a sequent W is a description of a set of nodes with respect to a reference node. $[\![W]\!]_{\mathrm{w}}$ is essentially the same description as W, except that it specifies the relationship between nodes through the use of multiplicative connectives $\star$ and $-\!\!\star$ and negation $\neg$.[2] The translation is characterized by Propositions 5.3 and 5.4.

Proposition 5.3. $\not\models_{\mathcal{W}} W$ *if and only if* $\models \neg[\![W]\!]_{\mathrm{w}}$.

Proposition 5.4. *If* $\cdot \Rightarrow \neg[\![\Gamma \Rightarrow \Delta]\!]_{\mathrm{w}}$, *then* $\Gamma \Rightarrow \Delta$.

Propositions 5.3 and 5.4 allow us to complete the proof of completeness if we additionally show that $\models A$ implies $\cdot \Rightarrow A$ (for $A = \neg[\![\Gamma \Rightarrow \Delta]\!]_{\mathrm{w}}$). Since $\models A$ implies $\vdash A$ by Theorem 2.1, it suffices to prove the following lemma, whose proof exploits the cut elimination property of $\mathbf{S_{BBI}}$ (Theorem 4.1):

Lemma 5.5. *If* $\vdash A$, *then* $\cdot \Rightarrow A$.

The following corollary shows that $\mathbf{S_{BBI}}$ is sound and complete with respect to the Kripke semantics in Section 2:

Corollary 5.6. $\cdot \Rightarrow A$ *if and only if* $\models A$.

6. Display calculus for Boolean BI

This section reviews the display calculus $\mathbf{DL_{BBI}}$ for Boolean BI (without the cut rule) by Brotherston [10]. We establish the equivalence between $\mathbf{S_{BBI}}$ and $\mathbf{DL_{BBI}}$, and show that $\mathbf{S_{BBI}}$ is an optimization of $\mathbf{DL_{BBI}}$.

6.1 Definition and properties of $\mathrm{DL_{BBI}}$

The display calculus $\mathbf{DL_{BBI}}$ uses a judgment $X \vdash_{\mathcal{D}} Y$, called a *consecution*, in its inference rules; X is called an A-structure and Y a C-structure:

$$\begin{array}{rrcl} A\text{-structure} & X & ::= & A \mid \emptyset_{\mathsf{a}} \mid \emptyset_{\mathsf{m}} \mid \sharp Y \mid X; X \mid X, X \\ C\text{-structure} & Y & ::= & A \mid \emptyset_{\mathsf{a}} \mid \sharp X \mid Y; Y \mid X \multimap Y \end{array}$$

A-structures are essentially an extension of bunches in Boolean BI with negative structures $\sharp Y$. C-structures do not use the multiplicative unit $\emptyset_{\mathsf{m}}$ and the multiplicative structural connective ,, but introduce a negative structural connective $\sharp$ and a multiplicative structural connective $\multimap$ which is originally from the display calculus for linear logic [2].

The inference rules of $\mathbf{DL_{BBI}}$ are divided into three groups: structural rules, display rules, and logical rules. Structural rules deal with the structural properties of consecutions. Display rules introduce or eliminate $\sharp Y$, $\sharp X$, and $X \multimap Y$ as necessary in order to "display" a target A-structure or C-structure as the sole element in the left or right side of a consecution. A logical rule focuses on a single formula that has already been "displayed" in the left or right side of a consecution by the display rules. We refer the reader to [10] for the inference rules of $\mathbf{DL_{BBI}}$.

Brotherston [10] presents the following results on $\mathbf{DL_{BBI}}$:[3]

[2] The definition shows that $W_1\langle\langle W_2 \rangle\rangle$ is a meta-level operator corresponding to the logical connective *septraction* in [8, 37].

[3] Similarly to Theorem 4.1, Theorem 6.1 states only the admissibility of the cut rule, but we refer to it as the cut elimination theorem.

Theorem 6.1 (Cut elimination).
If $X \vdash_{\mathcal{D}} A$ *and* $A \vdash_{\mathcal{D}} Y$, *then* $X \vdash_{\mathcal{D}} Y$.

Theorem 6.2 (Soundness and completeness).
$\emptyset_a \vdash_{\mathcal{D}} A$ *if and only if* $\models A$.

6.2 Equivalence between $\mathbf{S_{BBI}}$ and $\mathbf{DL_{BBI}}$

Although the equivalence between $\mathbf{S_{BBI}}$ and $\mathbf{DL_{BBI}}$ is obvious from Corollary 5.6 and Theorem 6.2, it does not illuminate how sequents and consecutions are related. Here we present direct translations between the two calculi and study their similarities and differences.

Given a consecution $X \vdash_{\mathcal{D}} Y$, we translate A-structure X to a sequent $[\![X]\!]_{\mathcal{X}}$ and C-structure Y to another sequent $[\![Y]\!]_{\mathcal{Y}}$. Then we combine $[\![X]\!]_{\mathcal{X}}$ and $[\![Y]\!]_{\mathcal{Y}}$ to build a single sequent $[\![X \vdash_{\mathcal{D}} Y]\!]_{\mathcal{C}}$. Let us write $(\Gamma \Rightarrow \Delta) \uplus (\Gamma' \Rightarrow \Delta')$ for $\Gamma; \Gamma' \Rightarrow \Delta; \Delta'$. We define $[\![X \vdash_{\mathcal{D}} Y]\!]_{\mathcal{C}}$ as follows:

$$\begin{array}{rcl}
[\![X \vdash_{\mathcal{D}} Y]\!]_{\mathcal{C}} & = & [\![X]\!]_{\mathcal{X}} \uplus [\![Y]\!]_{\mathcal{Y}} \\
[\![A]\!]_{\mathcal{X}} & = & A \Rightarrow \cdot \\
[\![\emptyset_a]\!]_{\mathcal{X}} & = & \cdot \Rightarrow \cdot \\
[\![\emptyset_m]\!]_{\mathcal{X}} & = & \emptyset_m \Rightarrow \cdot \\
[\![\sharp Y]\!]_{\mathcal{X}} & = & [\![Y]\!]_{\mathcal{Y}} \\
[\![X_1; X_2]\!]_{\mathcal{X}} & = & [\![X_1]\!]_{\mathcal{X}} \uplus [\![X_2]\!]_{\mathcal{X}} \\
[\![X_1, X_2]\!]_{\mathcal{X}} & = & [\![X_1]\!]_{\mathcal{X}}, [\![X_2]\!]_{\mathcal{X}} \Rightarrow \cdot \\
[\![A]\!]_{\mathcal{Y}} & = & \cdot \Rightarrow A \\
[\![\emptyset_a]\!]_{\mathcal{Y}} & = & \cdot \Rightarrow \cdot \\
[\![\sharp X]\!]_{\mathcal{Y}} & = & [\![X]\!]_{\mathcal{X}} \\
[\![Y_1; Y_2]\!]_{\mathcal{Y}} & = & [\![Y_1]\!]_{\mathcal{Y}} \uplus [\![Y_2]\!]_{\mathcal{Y}} \\
[\![X \multimap Y]\!]_{\mathcal{Y}} & = & [\![X]\!]_{\mathcal{X}} \langle\!\langle [\![Y]\!]_{\mathcal{Y}} \rangle\!\rangle \Rightarrow \cdot
\end{array}$$

Like sequents in $\mathbf{S_{BBI}}$, both A-structure X and C-structure Y are essentially descriptions of a set of nodes, but formulas in X are regarded as true whereas formulas in Y as false in the reference node. We also observe that multiplicative structures X_1, X_2 and $X \multimap Y$ correspond to multiplicative pairs and adjoint pairs in $\mathbf{S_{BBI}}$.

Lemma 6.3 shows that $\mathbf{S_{BBI}}$ is as expressive as $\mathbf{DL_{BBI}}$:

Lemma 6.3.
If $X \vdash_{\mathcal{D}} Y$ *holds in* $\mathbf{DL_{BBI}}$, *then* $[\![X \vdash_{\mathcal{D}} Y]\!]_{\mathcal{C}}$ *holds in* $\mathbf{S_{BBI}}$.

Given a sequent $\Gamma \Rightarrow \Delta$, we translate Γ to an A-structure $[\![\Gamma]\!]_{\mathcal{G}}$ and Δ to a C-structure $[\![\Delta]\!]_{\mathcal{D}}$. Then we combine $[\![\Gamma]\!]_{\mathcal{G}}$ and $[\![\Delta]\!]_{\mathcal{D}}$ to another A-structure $[\![\Gamma \Rightarrow \Delta]\!]_{\mathcal{W}}$ defined as follows:

$$[\![\Gamma \Rightarrow \Delta]\!]_{\mathcal{W}} = [\![\Gamma]\!]_{\mathcal{G}}; \sharp[\![\Delta]\!]_{\mathcal{D}}$$

$$\begin{array}{rclcrcl}
[\![\cdot]\!]_{\mathcal{G}} & = & \emptyset_a & & [\![\cdot]\!]_{\mathcal{D}} & = & \emptyset_a \\
[\![\Gamma; S]\!]_{\mathcal{G}} & = & [\![\Gamma]\!]_{\mathcal{G}}; [\![S]\!]_{\mathcal{S}} & & [\![\Delta; A]\!]_{\mathcal{D}} & = & [\![\Delta]\!]_{\mathcal{D}}; A
\end{array}$$

$$\begin{array}{rcl}
[\![A]\!]_{\mathcal{S}} & = & A \\
[\![\emptyset_m]\!]_{\mathcal{S}} & = & \emptyset_m \\
[\![W_1, W_2]\!]_{\mathcal{S}} & = & [\![W_1]\!]_{\mathcal{W}}, [\![W_2]\!]_{\mathcal{W}} \\
[\![W_1 \langle\!\langle W_2 \rangle\!\rangle]\!]_{\mathcal{S}} & = & \sharp([\![W_1]\!]_{\mathcal{W}} \multimap \sharp[\![W_2]\!]_{\mathcal{W}})
\end{array}$$

$[\![W]\!]_{\mathcal{W}}$ is defined in a similar way to $[\![W]\!]_{\mathrm{w}}$ given in Section 5. For example, $[\![W_1, W_2]\!]_{\mathcal{S}}$ coincides with $[\![W_1, W_2]\!]_{\mathrm{s}}$ if we write , as $\star$, and $[\![W_1 \langle\!\langle W_2 \rangle\!\rangle]\!]_{\mathcal{S}}$ coincides with $[\![W_1 \langle\!\langle W_2 \rangle\!\rangle]\!]_{\mathrm{s}}$ if we write $\sharp$ as $\neg$ and $\multimap$ as $\multimap\!\!\star$. The comparison between $[\![W]\!]_{\mathcal{W}}$ and $[\![W]\!]_{\mathrm{w}}$ reveals a correspondence between structural connectives in $\mathbf{DL_{BBI}}$ and logical connectives in Boolean BI that complies with the translation from $\mathbf{DL_{BBI}}$ to Boolean BI given in [10].

Lemma 6.4 shows that $\mathbf{DL_{BBI}}$ is as expressive as $\mathbf{S_{BBI}}$. In conjunction with Lemma 6.3, it proves the equivalence between $\mathbf{S_{BBI}}$ and $\mathbf{DL_{BBI}}$.

Lemma 6.4. *If* $\Gamma \Rightarrow \Delta$, *then* $[\![\Gamma \Rightarrow \Delta]\!]_{\mathcal{W}} \vdash_{\mathcal{D}} \emptyset_a$.

With Lemmas 6.3 and 6.4, we can now give another indirect proof of Theorem 4.1 by exploiting Theorem 6.1. We need an additional lemma relating the two translations:

Lemma 6.5.
$[\![[\![\Gamma]\!]_{\mathcal{G}}]\!]_{\mathcal{X}} = \Gamma \Rightarrow \cdot$ *and* $[\![[\![\Delta]\!]_{\mathcal{D}}]\!]_{\mathcal{Y}} = \cdot \Rightarrow \Delta$.

Proof of Theorem 4.1. Suppose $\Gamma \Rightarrow \Delta; C$ and $\Gamma'; C \Rightarrow \Delta'$.
$[\![\Gamma \Rightarrow \Delta; C]\!]_{\mathcal{W}} \vdash_{\mathcal{D}} \emptyset_a$ and $[\![\Gamma'; C \Rightarrow \Delta']\!]_{\mathcal{W}} \vdash_{\mathcal{D}} \emptyset_a$ — by Lemma 6.4
$[\![\Gamma]\!]_{\mathcal{G}}; \sharp[\![\Delta]\!]_{\mathcal{D}} \vdash_{\mathcal{D}} C$ and $C \vdash_{\mathcal{D}} \sharp[\![\Gamma']\!]_{\mathcal{G}}; [\![\Delta']\!]_{\mathcal{D}}$ — by the display rules and the rule $\emptyset_a R_{\mathcal{D}}$
$[\![\Gamma]\!]_{\mathcal{G}}; \sharp[\![\Delta]\!]_{\mathcal{D}} \vdash_{\mathcal{D}} \sharp[\![\Gamma']\!]_{\mathcal{G}}; [\![\Delta']\!]_{\mathcal{D}}$ — by Theorem 6.1
$[\![\Gamma; \Gamma']\!]_{\mathcal{G}} \vdash_{\mathcal{D}} [\![\Delta; \Delta']\!]_{\mathcal{D}}$ — by the display rules
$[\![[\![\Gamma; \Gamma']\!]_{\mathcal{G}} \vdash_{\mathcal{D}} [\![\Delta; \Delta']\!]_{\mathcal{D}}]\!]_{\mathcal{C}}$ in $\mathbf{S_{BBI}}$ — by Lemma 6.3
$\Gamma; \Gamma' \Rightarrow \Delta; \Delta'$ — by Lemma 6.5 □

6.3 $\mathbf{S_{BBI}}$ as an optimization of $\mathbf{DL_{BBI}}$

The two translations in Section 6.2 suggest that sequents in $\mathbf{S_{BBI}}$ essentially represent a normal form of consecutions in $\mathbf{DL_{BBI}}$. We say that a consecution is of the normal form if it permits a negative structure $\sharp X$ only in the right side of $\multimap$ according to the revised definition of C-structures:

$$C\text{-structure} \quad Y \quad ::= \quad A \mid \emptyset_a \mid Y; Y \mid X \multimap \sharp X$$

It turns out that every consecution $X \vdash_{\mathcal{D}} Y$ can be converted by the structural rules (for associativity and $\emptyset_a$) and the display rules to its normal form $[\![[\![X \vdash_{\mathcal{D}} Y]\!]_{\mathcal{C}}]\!]_{\mathcal{W}} \vdash_{\mathcal{D}} \emptyset_a$, whose formulas form the same syntactic structure as the sequent $[\![X \vdash_{\mathcal{D}} Y]\!]_{\mathcal{C}}$. Thus we may think of sequents as representing consecutions of the normal form and $\mathbf{S_{BBI}}$ as a sequent calculus that directly manipulates such consecutions.

Note that consecutions of the normal form in $\mathbf{DL_{BBI}}$ still require the negative structural connective $\sharp$ whereas $\mathbf{S_{BBI}}$ requires no such negative structural connective. Hence those display rules dealing with $\sharp$ have no counterparts in $\mathbf{S_{BBI}}$, which implies that proof searches in $\mathbf{S_{BBI}}$ are always simpler than in $\mathbf{DL_{BBI}}$ (except in trivial cases) because of the extra cost of applying such display rules in $\mathbf{DL_{BBI}}$.

Figure 6 shows an example of proving in $\mathbf{DL_{BBI}}$ the same formula as in Figure 5. The proof search proceeds in a similar manner: first creating $\emptyset_m$, next applying a contraction rule to duplicate a C-structure, then consuming the C-structure, and finally applying the rule $Init_{\mathcal{D}}$. We number each proof step to mark the correspondence between proof steps in Figures 5 and 6. Note that the display rule $MD1a_{\mathcal{D}}$ expands to a pair of a traverse rule ($TC_{\mathcal{S}}$ or $TP_{\mathcal{S}}$) and the rule $EC_{\mathcal{S}}$ (at proof steps 3, 5, and 9). We observe that $\mathbf{DL_{BBI}}$ takes extra six proof steps all of which apply display rules (marked in rectangles). This example illustrates that $\mathbf{S_{BBI}}$ is a formal system which can be obtained from an optimization of $\mathbf{DL_{BBI}}$ that dispenses with those display rules dealing with the negative structural connective $\sharp$ and revises all the logical rules accordingly.

7. Nested sequent calculus $\mathbf{CS_{BBI}}$

While the presence of multiplicative connectives from intuitionistic linear logic may suggest the inverse method for implementing a theorem prover for Boolean BI, the contraction property alone makes the inverse method not so ideal as it seems, as already observed in previous work on intuitionistic BI by Donnelly *et al.* [16]. This is especially the case for $\mathbf{S_{BBI}}$, which, unlike sequent calculi for intuitionistic BI, needs to use a graph structure of sequents instead of a tree structure. For example, it is not clear how to generate a minimal graph structure that weakens to a given pair of graph structures (for those inference rules with two sequents in the premise). Thus we choose to use a backward search strategy in our theorem prover.

As the first step, we obtain the nested sequent calculus $\mathbf{CS_{BBI}}$ (Contraction-free $\mathbf{S_{BBI}}$), shown in Figure 7, by embedding the weakening and contraction rules ($WL_{\mathcal{S}}$, $WR_{\mathcal{S}}$, $CL_{\mathcal{S}}$, and $CR_{\mathcal{S}}$) into

Structural rules:

$$\frac{\Gamma; (\Gamma'; W_1, W_2 \Rightarrow \Delta'), W_3; W_1 \oplus S_1, (W_2 \oplus S_2, W_3 \oplus S_3 \Rightarrow \cdot) \Rightarrow \Delta}{\Gamma; (\Gamma'; W_1, W_2 \Rightarrow \Delta'), W_3 \Rightarrow \Delta}\ \mathit{EA}_{\mathcal{C}} \quad \text{where} \left\{ \begin{array}{l} S_1 = W_2\langle\langle \Gamma'; W_3\langle\langle \Gamma \Rightarrow \Delta \rangle\rangle \Rightarrow \Delta' \rangle\rangle \\ S_2 = W_1\langle\langle \Gamma'; W_3\langle\langle \Gamma \Rightarrow \Delta \rangle\rangle \Rightarrow \Delta' \rangle\rangle \\ S_3 = (\Gamma'; W_1, W_2 \Rightarrow \Delta')\langle\langle \Gamma \Rightarrow \Delta \rangle\rangle \end{array} \right.$$

$$\frac{\Gamma; W_2, W_1 \Rightarrow \Delta}{\Gamma; W_1, W_2 \Rightarrow \Delta}\ \mathit{EC}_{\mathcal{C}} \qquad \frac{\Gamma; (\Gamma \Rightarrow \Delta), (\emptyset_{\mathsf{m}} \Rightarrow \cdot) \Rightarrow \Delta}{\Gamma \Rightarrow \Delta}\ \emptyset_{\mathsf{m}}U_{\mathcal{C}}$$

$$\frac{\Gamma; (\Gamma_1 \Rightarrow \Delta_1), (\Gamma_2; \emptyset_{\mathsf{m}} \Rightarrow \Delta_2); \Gamma_1; S \Rightarrow \Delta; \Delta_1}{\Gamma; (\Gamma_1 \Rightarrow \Delta_1), (\Gamma_2; \emptyset_{\mathsf{m}} \Rightarrow \Delta_2) \Rightarrow \Delta}\ \emptyset_{\mathsf{m}}D_{\mathcal{C}} \quad \text{where } S = (\Gamma_2; \emptyset_{\mathsf{m}} \Rightarrow \Delta_2)\langle\langle \Gamma \Rightarrow \Delta \rangle\rangle$$

Traverse rules:

$$\frac{\Gamma_{\mathrm{c}1}; (\Gamma_{\mathrm{c}2} \Rightarrow \Delta_{\mathrm{c}2})\langle\langle \Gamma \Rightarrow \Delta \rangle\rangle \Rightarrow \Delta_{\mathrm{c}1}}{\Gamma; (\Gamma_{\mathrm{c}1} \Rightarrow \Delta_{\mathrm{c}1}), (\Gamma_{\mathrm{c}2} \Rightarrow \Delta_{\mathrm{c}2}) \Rightarrow \Delta}\ \mathit{TC}_{\mathcal{C}} \qquad \frac{\Gamma_{\mathrm{p}}; (\Gamma \Rightarrow \Delta), (\Gamma_{\mathrm{s}} \Rightarrow \Delta_{\mathrm{s}}) \Rightarrow \Delta_{\mathrm{p}}}{\Gamma; (\Gamma_{\mathrm{s}} \Rightarrow \Delta_{\mathrm{s}})\langle\langle \Gamma_{\mathrm{p}} \Rightarrow \Delta_{\mathrm{p}} \rangle\rangle \Rightarrow \Delta}\ \mathit{TP}_{\mathcal{C}} \quad \text{(p for parent, c for child, s for sibling)}$$

Logical rules:

$$\frac{}{\Gamma; A \Rightarrow \Delta; A}\ \mathit{Init}_{\mathcal{C}} \qquad \frac{}{\Gamma; \bot \Rightarrow \Delta}\ \bot L_{\mathcal{C}} \qquad \frac{\Gamma \Rightarrow \Delta; A}{\Gamma; \neg A \Rightarrow \Delta}\ \neg L_{\mathcal{C}} \qquad \frac{\Gamma; A \Rightarrow \Delta}{\Gamma \Rightarrow \Delta; \neg A}\ \neg R_{\mathcal{C}}$$

$$\frac{\Gamma; A \Rightarrow \Delta \quad \Gamma; B \Rightarrow \Delta}{\Gamma; A \vee B \Rightarrow \Delta}\ \vee L_{\mathcal{C}} \qquad \frac{\Gamma \Rightarrow \Delta; A; B}{\Gamma \Rightarrow \Delta; A \vee B}\ \vee R_{\mathcal{C}} \qquad \frac{\Gamma; \emptyset_{\mathsf{m}} \Rightarrow \Delta}{\Gamma; \mathsf{I} \Rightarrow \Delta}\ \mathsf{I}L_{\mathcal{C}} \qquad \frac{}{\Gamma; \emptyset_{\mathsf{m}} \Rightarrow \Delta; \mathsf{I}}\ \mathsf{I}R_{\mathcal{C}}$$

$$\frac{\Gamma; (A \Rightarrow \cdot), (B \Rightarrow \cdot) \Rightarrow \Delta}{\Gamma; A \star B \Rightarrow \Delta}\ \star L_{\mathcal{C}} \qquad \frac{\Gamma; (\Gamma_1 \Rightarrow \Delta_1; A), (\Gamma_2 \Rightarrow \Delta_2) \Rightarrow \Delta; A \star B \quad \Gamma; (\Gamma_1 \Rightarrow \Delta_1), (\Gamma_2 \Rightarrow \Delta_2; B) \Rightarrow \Delta; A \star B}{\Gamma; (\Gamma_1 \Rightarrow \Delta_1), (\Gamma_2 \Rightarrow \Delta_2) \Rightarrow \Delta; A \star B}\ \star R_{\mathcal{C}}$$

$$\frac{\Gamma; (\Gamma_1 \Rightarrow \Delta_1; A)\langle\langle \Gamma_2 \Rightarrow \Delta_2 \rangle\rangle; A \mathrel{-\!\!\star} B \Rightarrow \Delta \quad \Gamma; (\Gamma_1 \Rightarrow \Delta_1)\langle\langle \Gamma_2; B \Rightarrow \Delta_2 \rangle\rangle; A \mathrel{-\!\!\star} B \Rightarrow \Delta}{\Gamma; (\Gamma_1 \Rightarrow \Delta_1)\langle\langle \Gamma_2 \Rightarrow \Delta_2 \rangle\rangle; A \mathrel{-\!\!\star} B \Rightarrow \Delta}\ {-\!\!\star} L_{\mathcal{C}} \qquad \frac{\Gamma; (A \Rightarrow \cdot)\langle\langle \cdot \Rightarrow B \rangle\rangle \Rightarrow \Delta}{\Gamma \Rightarrow \Delta; A \mathrel{-\!\!\star} B}\ {-\!\!\star} R_{\mathcal{C}}$$

Figure 7. Nested sequent calculus $\mathbf{CS_{BBI}}$. We define $(\Gamma \Rightarrow \Delta) \oplus S$ as $\Gamma; S \Rightarrow \Delta$ in the rule $\mathit{EA}_{\mathcal{C}}$.

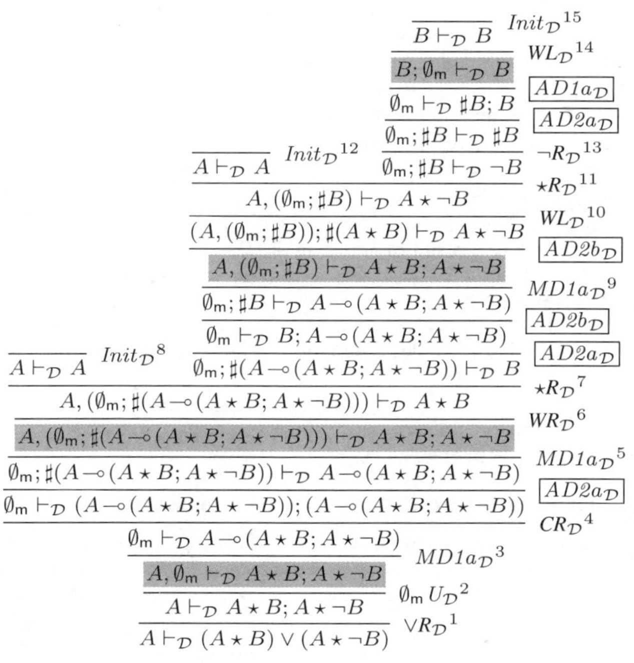

Figure 6. A proof of $A \vdash_{\mathcal{D}} (A \star B) \vee (A \star \neg B)$ in $\mathbf{DL_{BBI}}$ (adapted from Brotherston [9])

all the other rules of $\mathbf{S_{BBI}}$. Similarly to $\mathbf{S_{BBI}}$, the inference rules are divided into structural rules, traverse rules, and logical rules. Since contraction is built into all the inference rules in $\mathbf{CS_{BBI}}$, the premise of every structural rule subsumes the graph structure of nodes represented by the conclusion. Except the rule $\mathit{EC}_{\mathcal{C}}$ which rewrites a node state according to commutativity of sequents, every structural rule has a premise that strictly extends its conclusion with new relations between nodes. Below we further describe the two structural rules $\mathit{EA}_{\mathcal{C}}$ and $\emptyset_{\mathsf{m}}U_{\mathcal{C}}$, in which the premise restructures nodes by changing parent-child and sibling relations but is also able to recover the original structure of nodes expressed in the conclusion.

In the rule $\mathit{EA}_{\mathcal{C}}$, each sequent $W_i \oplus S_i$ ($i = 1, 2, 3$) in the premise represents the same graph structure as the conclusion, except that its reference node is now described by W_i. Extending W_i with S_i in this way is a part of building contraction into the rule $\mathit{EA}_{\mathcal{C}}$ and is thus necessary for the completeness of $\mathbf{CS_{BBI}}$ with respect to Boolean BI. As an example, consider the proof of a sequent

$$(W_1, W_2 \Rightarrow B), W_3 \Rightarrow \cdot$$

where $W_1 = A \Rightarrow \cdot$ and $W_2 = C \mathrel{-\!\!\star} \neg(\neg(A \mathrel{-\!\!\star} B) \star C) \Rightarrow \cdot$ and $W_3 = C \Rightarrow \cdot$. We apply the rule $\mathit{EA}_{\mathcal{C}}$ to generate another sequent

$$(W_1, W_2 \Rightarrow B), W_3; W_1 \oplus S_1, (W_2 \oplus S_2, W_3 \oplus S_3 \Rightarrow \cdot) \Rightarrow \cdot$$

with $S_1 = W_2\langle\langle W_3\langle\langle \cdot \Rightarrow \cdot \rangle\rangle \Rightarrow B \rangle\rangle$ and $S_2 = W_1\langle\langle W_3\langle\langle \cdot \Rightarrow \cdot \rangle\rangle \Rightarrow B \rangle\rangle$ and $S_3 = (W_1, W_2 \Rightarrow B)\langle\langle \cdot \Rightarrow \cdot \rangle\rangle$. Eventually we reach the following sequent which is provable only because of the interaction between S_2 and $A \mathrel{-\!\!\star} B$ via the rule ${-\!\!\star} L_{\mathcal{C}}$:

$$\begin{array}{l} C \mathrel{-\!\!\star} \neg(\neg(A \mathrel{-\!\!\star} B) \star C); \\ \quad (W_3 \oplus S_3)\langle\langle (W_1 \oplus S_1)\langle\langle S_1 \Rightarrow \cdot \rangle\rangle \Rightarrow \neg(A \mathrel{-\!\!\star} B) \star C \rangle\rangle; \\ \quad \boxed{S_2; A \mathrel{-\!\!\star} B} \Rightarrow \cdot \end{array}$$

Hence, if we omit S_i in the premise of the rule $\mathit{EA}_{\mathcal{C}}$, we lose the completeness of $\mathbf{CS_{BBI}}$.

The rule $\emptyset_{\mathsf{m}}U_{\mathcal{C}}$ creates a new child node with a special form of sequent $\emptyset_{\mathsf{m}} \Rightarrow \cdot$, which can be absorbed back into the parent node by the rule $\emptyset_{\mathsf{m}}D_{\mathcal{C}}$. Intuitively $\emptyset_{\mathsf{m}} \Rightarrow \cdot$ describes an empty node whose sibling node can be identified with its parent node. Similarly to the rule $\mathit{EA}_{\mathcal{C}}$, the premise of the rule $\emptyset_{\mathsf{m}}D_{\mathcal{C}}$ combines the conclusion with a new sequent $\Gamma_1; S \Rightarrow \Delta_1$, which represents the same graph structure as the conclusion but has a different reference node. Omitting S in the premise also costs the completeness of $\mathbf{CS_{BBI}}$. For example, if we omit S in the premise of the rule $\emptyset_{\mathsf{m}}D_{\mathcal{C}}$, the sequent in Figure 8 is not provable because its proof depends on the interaction between $A \mathrel{-\!\!\star} B$ and S via the rule ${-\!\!\star} L_{\mathcal{C}}$.

$$
\dfrac{\dfrac{\dfrac{\dfrac{\dfrac{\dfrac{}{\emptyset_{\mathsf{m}}; A; (S' \Rightarrow B)\langle\!\langle A \mathrel{-\!\!\star} B \Rightarrow B \rangle\!\rangle \Rightarrow A}\,\mathit{Init}_C}{A \mathrel{-\!\!\star} B; (\emptyset_{\mathsf{m}}; A \Rightarrow A), (S' \Rightarrow B) \Rightarrow B}\,\mathit{TC}_C}{A \mathrel{-\!\!\star} B; (S' \Rightarrow B), (\emptyset_{\mathsf{m}}; A \Rightarrow A) \Rightarrow B}\,\mathit{EC}_C}{S'; (\emptyset_{\mathsf{m}}; A \Rightarrow A)\langle\!\langle A \mathrel{-\!\!\star} B \Rightarrow B \rangle\!\rangle \Rightarrow B}\,\mathit{TP}_C \qquad \dfrac{\dfrac{}{A \mathrel{-\!\!\star} B; B; (S' \Rightarrow B), (\emptyset_{\mathsf{m}}; A \Rightarrow \cdot) \Rightarrow B}\,\mathit{Init}_C}{S'; (\emptyset_{\mathsf{m}}; A \Rightarrow \cdot)\langle\!\langle A \mathrel{-\!\!\star} B; B \Rightarrow B \rangle\!\rangle \Rightarrow B}\,\mathit{TP}_C}{\boxed{A \mathrel{-\!\!\star} B}; (\top \Rightarrow \cdot), (\emptyset_{\mathsf{m}}; A \Rightarrow \cdot); \top; \boxed{S} \Rightarrow B}\,{\mathrel{-\!\!\star}}L_C}{A \mathrel{-\!\!\star} B; (\top \Rightarrow \cdot), (\emptyset_{\mathsf{m}}; A \Rightarrow \cdot) \Rightarrow B}\,\emptyset_{\mathsf{m}}D_C
$$

$$
\text{where} \left\{ \begin{array}{lcl} S & = & (\emptyset_{\mathsf{m}}; A \Rightarrow \cdot)\langle\!\langle A \mathrel{-\!\!\star} B \Rightarrow B \rangle\!\rangle \\ S' & = & A \mathrel{-\!\!\star} B; (\top \Rightarrow \cdot), (\emptyset_{\mathsf{m}}; A \Rightarrow \cdot); \top \end{array} \right.
$$

Figure 8. A proof of $A \mathrel{-\!\!\star} B; (\top \Rightarrow \cdot), (\emptyset_{\mathsf{m}}; A \Rightarrow \cdot) \Rightarrow B$ in $\mathbf{CS_{BBI}}$

Every inference rule in $\mathbf{CS_{BBI}}$ is invertible, *i.e.*, the premise implies the conclusion and vice versa. We can formally prove that both weakening and contraction are admissible in $\mathbf{CS_{BBI}}$. We can also prove the equivalence between $\mathbf{S_{BBI}}$ and $\mathbf{CS_{BBI}}$.

Theorem 7.1 (Weakening and contraction in $\mathbf{CS_{BBI}}$)**.**
If $\Gamma \Rightarrow \Delta$, *then* $\Gamma; S \Rightarrow \Delta$ *and* $\Gamma \Rightarrow \Delta; A$.
If $\Gamma; S; S \Rightarrow \Delta$, *then* $\Gamma; S \Rightarrow \Delta$.
If $\Gamma \Rightarrow \Delta; A; A$, *then* $\Gamma \Rightarrow \Delta; A$.

Theorem 7.2 (Equivalence between $\mathbf{S_{BBI}}$ and $\mathbf{CS_{BBI}}$)**.**
$\Gamma \Rightarrow \Delta$ *in* $\mathbf{S_{BBI}}$ *if and only if* $\Gamma \Rightarrow \Delta$ *in* $\mathbf{CS_{BBI}}$.

Figure 9 shows an example of proving in $\mathbf{CS_{BBI}}$ the same sequent as in Figure 5. The proof tree is much smaller: the depth decreases from 16 to 8 and the number of applications of rules decreases from 18 to 12. Besides the amount of non-determinism in proof search is now minimal. In Figure 5, after applying the rule $\emptyset_{\mathsf{m}}U_S$ (when read from the conclusion to the premise), we have to decide whether or not to duplicate S by applying the contraction rule CL_S, and if we skip the rule CL_S, proof search fails. In Figure 9, this form of non-determinism does not arise because the contraction rule is embedded into the rule $\emptyset_{\mathsf{m}}U_C$. As a result, except for applying the rule $\emptyset_{\mathsf{m}}U_C$ indefinitely, the only source of non-determinism concerns which of $A \star B$ and $A \star \neg B$ should be considered first by the rule $\star R_C$, which is irrelevant for the purpose of this proof anyway.

Since their role is to change only the reference node without changing the graph structure of nodes, the traverse rule TC_C and the structural rule EC_C in Figure 9 do not increase the complexity of proof search. For example, once we decide to focus on $\neg B$ in $A; (A \Rightarrow \Delta), (\emptyset_{\mathsf{m}} \Rightarrow B; \neg B) \Rightarrow \Delta$, we obtain a unique sequence of rules, namely EC_C followed by TC_C, for exposing $\emptyset_{\mathsf{m}} \Rightarrow B; \neg B$ in the reference node. Thus the cost of proof search is incurred mainly by various decisions on applying the structural and logical rules and not by applications of the traverse rules. Section 8.5 explains how to eliminate the traverse rules altogether in proof search.

8. Backward proof search in $\mathbf{CS_{BBI}}$

This section explains the design of our theorem prover which uses a backward search strategy built on top of $\mathbf{CS_{BBI}}$. Because of the undecidability of Boolean BI [11, 29], our theorem prover implements a semi-decision algorithm. For our purpose, a semi-decision algorithm is still useful because in program verification, we usually attempt to prove formulas that are believed to be true.

Our theorem prover includes a certifier which converts every proof in $\mathbf{CS_{BBI}}$ into an equivalent proof in $\mathbf{S_{BBI}}$ according to our proof of Theorem 7.2. In addition to automated proof search, it also supports an interactive mode, in which the user can issue various tactics to manually change the structure of nodes. Both extensions are a preliminary step toward developing a program verification

```
Algorithm ProveBBI(W, d)
  Input: goal sequent W, search depth d
  Output: true or fail
 1:  for each node w,
 2:    promote w as the reference node
 3:    if Init_C, ⊥L_C, or IR_C is applicable, return true
 4:    if ¬L_C, ¬R_C, ∨R_C, IL_C, ⋆L_C, or −⋆R_C is applicable,
 5:      W' ← result of applying the rule
 6:      return ProveBBI(W', d)
 7:    if ∨L_C is applicable,
 8:      W_1 and W_2 ← result of applying the rule
 9:      return ProveBBI(W_1, d) && ProveBBI(W_2, d)
10:    if ⋆R_C or −⋆L_C is applicable to a fresh node state S,
11:      W_1 and W_2 ← result of applying the rule to S
12:      return ProveBBI(W_1, d) && ProveBBI(W_2, d)
13:  if d = 0, return fail
14:  for each node state S in node w
                    to which EA_C or ∅_mD_C is applicable,
15:    promote w as the reference node
16:    W' ← result of applying the rule to S
17:    if ProveBBI(W', d − 1) = true, return true
18:  for each node w,
19:    promote w as the reference node
20:    W' ← result of applying ∅_mU_C
21:    if ProveBBI(W', d − 1) = true, return true
22:  return fail
```

Figure 10. Pseudocode for the proof search algorithm ProveBBI

system based on full separation logic. For space reasons, we do not describe these extensions.

8.1 Basic structure of the proof search algorithm

Figure 10 shows the pseudocode for the proof search algorithm ProveBBI. Given a goal sequent W and a search depth d as input, it attempts to search for a proof tree for W with at most d applications of the structural rules (except the rule EC_C) along any search path. First it examines every formula in a given sequent and applies the corresponding logical rule if possible (lines 1–12). After checking if $d = 0$ (line 13), it considers the structural rules EA_C, $\emptyset_{\mathsf{m}}D_C$, and $\emptyset_{\mathsf{m}}U_C$ (lines 14–21). It returns either **true** or **fail**, depending on the result of the proof search. For the sake of simplicity, the algorithm ProveBBI assumes that the rule EC_C is embedded into all the other rules. For example, the rule EA_C in Figure 10 indeed refers to one of the four instances obtained by independently applying the rule EC_C to node states W_1, W_2 and $(\Gamma'; W_1, W_2 \Rightarrow \Delta'), W_3$.

The first phase of the algorithm ProveBBI (lines 1–12) exploits the fact that all the logical rules, including $\star R_C$ and ${\mathrel{-\!\!\star}}L_C$, are invertible. Hence it starts by applying the logical rules wherever possible until no more applications are left. For the rules $\star R_C$ and ${\mathrel{-\!\!\star}}L_C$, we make sure that they do not focus more than once on the

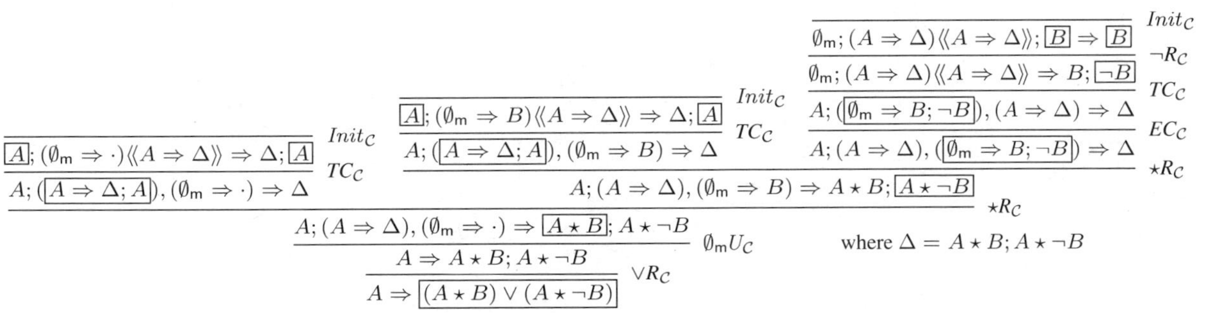

Figure 9. A proof of $A \Rightarrow (A \star B) \vee (A \star \neg B)$ in $\mathbf{CS_{BBI}}$. Each rectangle marks a principal formula or a sequent to be exposed in the reference node.

same pair of a principal formula and a node state (*e.g.*, a pair of $A \mathbin{-\!\!\star} B$ and $(\Gamma_1 \Rightarrow \Delta_1), (\Gamma_2 \Rightarrow \Delta_2)$ in the rule $\star R_C$), since the principal formula survives in the premise.

After the first phase, the algorithm ProveBBI recursively invokes itself to apply the structural rules EA_C, $\emptyset_m D_C$, and $\emptyset_m U_C$ in depth-first order (lines 14–21). For example, with $d = 2$, it considers all sequences of length 2 in the following order: EA_C–EA_C, EA_C–$\emptyset_m D_C$, EA_C–$\emptyset_m U_C$, $\emptyset_m D_C$–EA_C, $\emptyset_m D_C$–$\emptyset_m D_C$, $\emptyset_m D_C$–$\emptyset_m U_C$, $\emptyset_m U_C$–EA_C, $\emptyset_m U_C$–$\emptyset_m D_C$, $\emptyset_m U_C$–$\emptyset_m U_C$. We choose to consider the rules EA_C and $\emptyset_m D_C$ before the rule $\emptyset_m U_C$, which is the least restrictive rule in the sense that it can be applied to any sequent. Note that applying a structural rule does not create new formulas but only gives rise to new pairs of a formula ($A \star B$ or $A \mathbin{-\!\!\star} B$) and a node state to which the rules $\star R_C$ and $\mathbin{-\!\!\star} L_C$ can be applied. A recursive invocation of ProveBBI immediately focuses on these new pairs during its first phase (lines 10–12).

8.2 Explosion in the search space and the number of subgoals

While the algorithm ProveBBI eventually finds a proof tree for every provable sequent if given an unlimited search depth, a naive implementation suffers from two problems that are unique to Boolean BI. The first is an explosion in the search space in terms of the amount of conjunctive non-determinism among the logical rules $\star R_C$ and $\mathbin{-\!\!\star} L_C$ and the structural rules. That is, a typical proof search is quickly overwhelmed with too many choices for applying these rules, which are all invertible and thus can be applied aggressively. This problem is due to the structural rules EA_C, $\emptyset_m D_C$, and $\emptyset_m U_C$, each application of which immediately doubles or quadruples the search space. The second problem is an explosion in the number of subgoals due to the logical rules $\star R_C$ and $\mathbin{-\!\!\star} L_C$, each application of which increments the number of subgoals. These rules can be applied to each formula $A \star B$ or $A \mathbin{-\!\!\star} B$ as many times as there are corresponding node states. For example, if Γ contains n multiplicative pairs, the rule $\star R_C$ creates 2^n subgoals from $\Gamma \Rightarrow A \star B$ during the first phase of the algorithm ProveBBI.

The first problem is closely related to the contraction property built into the structural rules. As an example, consider the structural rule EA_C in Figure 7. The graph structure of the premise has four times more nodes than that of the conclusion because each sequent $W_i \oplus S_i$ $(i = 1, 2, 3)$ represents the same graph structure as the conclusion, as shown in Figure 11. Consequently the premise provides four times more ways to apply the rules of $\mathbf{CS_{BBI}}$, thus quadrupling the search space. In a similar way, each application of the other structural rules $\emptyset_m D_C$ and $\emptyset_m U_C$ doubles the search space. We remark that the first problem is *not* the price to pay for building contraction into the structural rules, since the same problem of search space explosion remains even if we do not build contraction into the structural rules.

The second problem itself is orthogonal to the first problem, but its effect is heavily exacerbated by the first problem. As an example, consider again the structural rule EA_C in Figure 7 where we set $\Delta = A \star (B \star C)$. After an application of the rule EA_C to obtain the graph structure in Figure 11, two applications of the rule $\star R_C$ ensue to copy A to W_1, B to W_2, and C to W_3. If these formulas happen to involve multiplicative connectives, we can again apply the rules $\star R_C$ and $\mathbin{-\!\!\star} L_C$ to propagate their component formulas, which, in turn, may trigger further applications of the rules $\star R_C$ and $\mathbin{-\!\!\star} L_C$, and so on.

To alleviate the first problem, we need to devise a scheme for prioritizing applications of the structural rules (Section 8.3). We can solve the second problem by borrowing an idea from the inverse method (Section 8.4). In addition, we can eliminate the traverse rules altogether (Section 8.5).

8.3 Prioritizing applications of the structural rules

As a solution to the first problem, we assign a priority, either high or low, to every sibling relation between nodes so as to prioritize all applications of the rules EA_C and $\emptyset_m D_C$, and to every node itself so as to prioritize all applications of the rule $\emptyset_m U_C$. When applying a structural rule, the algorithm ProveBBI first considers sibling relations and nodes with a high priority and then those with a low priority. Below we explain how to assign priorities to sibling relations and how to determine priorities for nodes.

For the rule EA_C as shown in Figure 7, we assign priorities to sibling relations in the premise according to Figure 11 with the following interpretation:

- For a sequent inside a rectangle $\boxed{\,W\,}$, every sibling relation in it is assigned the same priority as in the conclusion.
- For a sequent inside a dashed rectangle $[\,W\,]$, every sibling relation in it is assigned a low priority.
- A sibling relation depicted with solid lines $\wedge$ is assigned a high priority.
- A sibling relation depicted with dashed lines $\hat{}$ is assigned a low priority.

The rationale for this assignment is that an application of the rule EA_C is primarily intended to generate sibling relations described by $W_1, (W_2, W_3 \Rightarrow \cdot)$, rather than S_1, S_2, and S_3 in $W_1 \oplus S_1, (W_2 \oplus S_2, W_3 \oplus S_3 \Rightarrow \cdot)$. When applying the rule EA_C, the algorithm ProveBBI focuses first on those node states both of whose sibling relations have a high priority. In a similar way, we assign priorities to sibling relations in the premise of the rules $\emptyset_m D_C$ and $\emptyset_m U_C$ according to Figure 12.

We determine priorities of nodes by analyzing priorities of sibling relations. If a node is involved in a sibling relation with a high

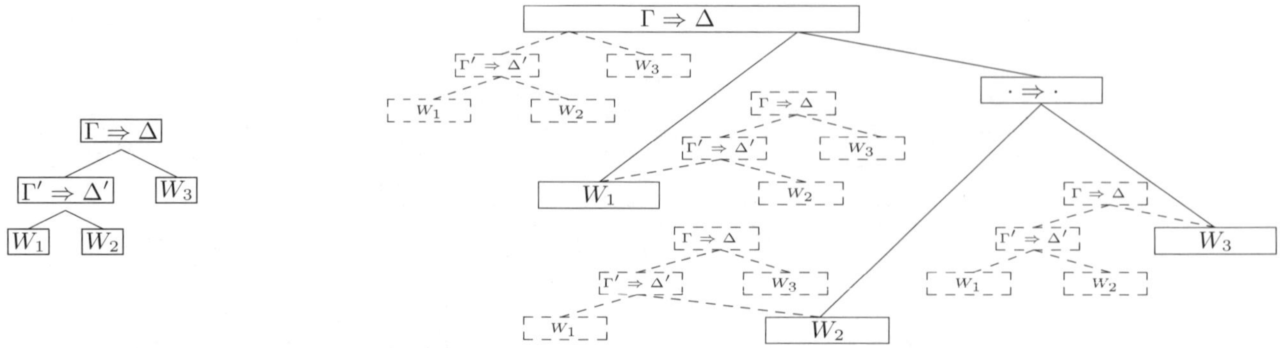

Figure 11. The graph structure of nodes before (conclusion) and after (premise) applying the structural rule EA_C in Figure 7

After applying the rule $\emptyset_m D_C$:

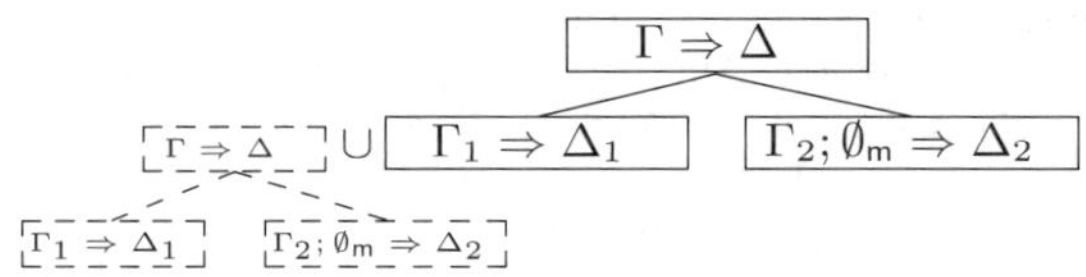

After applying the rule $\emptyset_m U_C$:

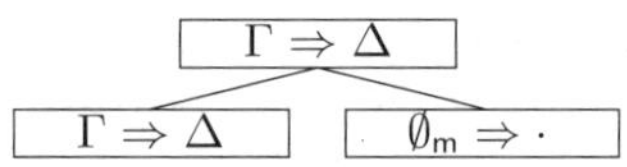

Figure 12. Assigning priorities to sibling relations after applying the rules $\emptyset_m D_C$ and $\emptyset_m U_C$. $(\Gamma \Rightarrow \Delta) \cup (\Gamma' \Rightarrow \Delta')$ is defined as $\Gamma; \Gamma' \Rightarrow \Delta; \Delta'$.

priority, it is more likely to be under active consideration by other structural rules than those nodes with no such involvement. Hence we assign a high priority to every node involved in at least one such sibling relation. For the logical rules $\star L_C$ and $\multimap\!\!\star R_C$, we reuse the priority assigned to the reference node of the conclusion for two new nodes in the premise.

Now we redesign the algorithm ProveBBI as a two-stage algorithm. In the first stage, it applies the structural rules using only sibling relations and nodes with a high priority. Note that it still generates every node with a low priority, which is never used by the structural rules, but may be needed by the logical rules. For example, the two sequents discussed in Section 7 are provable in the first stage precisely because we also generate every node with a low priority. If the proof search fails, it enters the second stage and repeats the proof search without ignoring sibling relations and nodes with a low priority. The second stage is necessary for the completeness of proof search, since some formula requires us to apply the structural rules using those with a low priority as well. In fact, we can find even a formula whose proof tree applies the structural rules using *only* those with a low priority. Section 8.6 presents examples of such formulas.

8.4 Reusing the proof tree from the premise

We solve the problem of an explosion in the number of subgoals with a simple technique of reusing the proof tree from the premise. Suppose that we apply the rule $\star R_C$ or $\multimap\!\!\star L_C$ to produce two subgoals in the premise, without knowing whether this application is necessary or not. If this application is unnecessary, however, every proof tree for the first premise must be a proof tree for the conclusion as well. Hence, upon finding a proof tree for the first subgoal, we "replay" it against the conclusion, and attempt to prove the second subgoal only in the case of a failure. In this way, we can aggressively apply the rules $\star R_C$ and $\multimap\!\!\star L_C$ without worrying about an explosion in the number of subgoals. In essence, we partially simulate the inverse method with a moderate overhead of revisiting proof trees (but without entirely reformulating the nested sequent calculus $\mathbf{CS_{BBI}}$).

8.5 Eliminating the traverse rules

The algorithm ProveBBI invokes the traverse rules to change the reference node (lines 2, 15, 19 in Figure 10), but we can eliminate the traverse rules altogether with a slight change in the representation of sequents. The basic observation is that the traverse rules change only the reference node without altering the graph structure of nodes. Hence, by rewriting every rule in such a way that it directly focuses on any formula or node without requiring a reference node, we can discard the traverse rules.

To this end, we introduce a labelled sequent which assigns a unique label w to every node and annotates all formulas and $\emptyset_m$'s in it with w:

$$
\begin{array}{rccl}
\text{labelled sequent} & L & = & \Xi \vdash \Sigma \Rightarrow \Pi \\
\text{graph structure} & \Xi & ::= & \cdot \mid \Xi, w \sim w_1 \cdot w_2 \\
\text{labelled truth context} & \Sigma & ::= & \cdot \mid \Sigma, A@w \mid \Sigma, \emptyset_m@w \\
\text{labelled falsehood context} & \Pi & ::= & \cdot \mid \Pi, A@w
\end{array}
$$

$w \sim w_1 \cdot w_2$ in the graph structure specifies that w is a parent node of w_1 and w_2. Then we can convert every sequent to a *unique* labelled sequent modulo renaming labels, since a sequent determines a unique graph structure of nodes where each node contains a unique set of true formulas, $\emptyset_m$'s, and false formulas. Let us write $[\![W]\!]$ for the unique labelled sequent converted from sequent W. For a rule deducing W from W' (and W'') in $\mathbf{CS_{BBI}}$, we derive a new rule that deduces $[\![W]\!]$ from $[\![W']\!]$ (and $[\![W'']\!]$) in a single step; for an axiom deducing W in $\mathbf{CS_{BBI}}$, we derive a new axiom deducing $[\![W]\!]$. We refer to the resultant system as the labelled $\mathbf{CS_{BBI}}$:

$$
\frac{W'}{W}\,R \text{ in } \mathbf{CS_{BBI}} \quad \longrightarrow \quad \frac{[\![W']\!]}{[\![W]\!]}\,R_{\mathcal{L}} \text{ in the labelled } \mathbf{CS_{BBI}}
$$

The labelled $\mathbf{CS_{BBI}}$ has no traverse rules because the premise and conclusion of a traverse rule in $\mathbf{CS_{BBI}}$ represent the same graph structure of nodes. Still it is equivalent to $\mathbf{CS_{BBI}}$ because the definition of labelled sequents embeds the traverse rules into all the inference rules:

Proposition 8.1. *W is provable in $\mathbf{CS_{BBI}}$ if and only if $[\![W]\!]$ is provable in the labelled $\mathbf{CS_{BBI}}$.*

Figure 13 shows an example of proving in the labelled $\mathbf{CS_{BBI}}$ the same formula as in Figure 9. The depth decreases from 8 to

$$
\dfrac{
\dfrac{
\dfrac{}{w\sim w_1\cdot w_2 \vdash \Gamma \Rightarrow \Delta;\Delta_1;A@w_1}\,Init_{\mathcal{L}}
\quad
\dfrac{
\dfrac{}{w\sim w_1\cdot w_2 \vdash \Gamma \Rightarrow \Delta;\Delta_1;B@w_2;A@w_1}\,Init_{\mathcal{L}}
\quad
\dfrac{
\dfrac{}{w\sim w_1\cdot w_2 \vdash \Gamma; B@w_2 \Rightarrow \Delta;\Delta_1;B@w_2}\,Init_{\mathcal{L}}
}{w\sim w_1\cdot w_2 \vdash \Gamma \Rightarrow \Delta;\Delta_1;B@w_2;\neg B@w_2;}\,\neg R_{\mathcal{L}}
}{w\sim w_1\cdot w_2 \vdash \Gamma \Rightarrow A\star B@w;\boxed{A\star\neg B@w};\Delta_1;B@w_2}\,\star R_{\mathcal{L}}
}{w\sim w_1\cdot w_2 \vdash \Gamma \Rightarrow \boxed{A\star B@w};A\star\neg B@w;\Delta_1}\,\star R_{\mathcal{L}}
}{
\dfrac{\cdot \vdash A@w \Rightarrow A\star B@w; A\star\neg B@w}{\cdot \vdash A@w \Rightarrow (A\star B)\vee(A\star\neg B)@w}\,\vee R_{\mathcal{L}}
}\,\emptyset_{\mathsf{m}}U_{\mathcal{L}}
\qquad \text{where} \left\{ \begin{array}{lcl} \Gamma & = & A@w; A@w_1; \emptyset_{\mathsf{m}}@w_2 \\ \Delta & = & A\star B@w; A\star\neg B@w \\ \Delta_1 & = & A\star B@w_1; A\star\neg B@w_1 \end{array} \right.
$$

Figure 13. A proof of $\cdot \vdash A@w \Rightarrow (A\star B)\vee(A\star\neg B)@w$ in the labelled $\mathbf{CS_{BBI}}$. The rule $\star R_{\mathcal{L}}$ focuses on the formula inside the rectangle.

6 and the number of applications of rules decreases from 12 to 8. The rule $Init_{\mathcal{L}}$ immediately completes the proof when it detects the same labelled formula in both contexts of a given labelled sequent. The rule $\neg R_{\mathcal{L}}$ also directly focuses on $\neg B@w_2$, regardless of the presence of $w \sim w_1\cdot w_2$ in the graph structure. In this way, the labelled $\mathbf{CS_{BBI}}$ dispenses with the traverse rules, yielding a smaller proof tree than $\mathbf{CS_{BBI}}$.

8.6 Experimental results

We compare a naive implementation of the algorithm ProveBBI with an optimized implementation that incorporates those ideas described in Sections 8.3 and 8.4. Both implementations internally use the labelled $\mathbf{CS_{BBI}}$ to eliminate the traverse rules, as explained in Section 8.5. Our implementations are written in Objective CAML and run on Ubuntu Linux 11.10 with Intel Core i7-960 3.2GHz and 6 gigabytes of main memory.

Figure 14 shows results of running both implementations (*naive* and *optimized*) on 14 representative formulas. For a given formula A, we use sequent $\cdot \Rightarrow A$ and search depth d as input to the algorithm ProveBBI. Except for experiment (c), we set d to the minimum search depth for finding a proof tree. The result is either the return value of ProveBBI (**true** and **fail**) or **error** if the proof search does not terminate within 10 minutes. In measuring the cost in terms of the number of applications of the rules, we exclude the rule $EC_{\mathcal{C}}$ which is already embedded into all the other rules. The elapsed time is in seconds.

Experiment (a) tests nine formulas (all involving multiplicative connectives) of increasing complexity. The two formulas marked $\sharp$ require only those applications of the rule $EA_{\mathcal{C}}$ in which sibling relations with a low priority are visited; hence the proof search finishes in the second stage of the algorithm ProveBBI. Experiment (b) is designed to measure the effectiveness of the two optimizations specifically against the rule $EA_{\mathcal{C}}$. Experiment (c) tests the effect of increasing d for a common formula which can be proven with two applications of the rule $EA_{\mathcal{C}}$ followed by an application of the rule $\emptyset_{\mathsf{m}}D_{\mathcal{C}}$.

We observe that the cost of proof search is mainly driven by search depth d, *i.e.*, the number of applications of the structural rules required to complete proof search. We also observe that the optimized implementation is much less susceptible to the exponential growth of the search space than the naive implementation, thereby demonstrating that the two optimizations in Sections 8.3 and 8.4 are indeed highly effective. In experiment (c), a search depth of 3 eventually produces a proof tree, but only after a number of wrong applications of the rule $EA_{\mathcal{C}}$. An increase of d to 4, however, immediately incurs a wrong application of the rule $EA_{\mathcal{C}}$ which happens to lead to the correct two applications of the rule $EA_{\mathcal{C}}$, which is why it produces a proof tree at a much lower cost (from 5942 to 181). A further increase of d to 5 does not significantly increase the cost, but the elapsed time becomes much longer because of the extra overhead of manipulating much larger sequents.

Overall we find that the optimized implementation is reasonably fast in proving typical formulas of Boolean BI.

9. Related work

9.1 Proof search in the logic of BI and separation logic

Previous work on proof search in the logic of BI mainly focuses on intuitionistic BI, which is another member in the family that inherits its multiplicative connectives from intuitionistic linear logic (like Boolean BI), but additive connectives from intuitionistic propositional logic. Galmiche and Méry [18, 19] present a labelled tableau calculus for a propositional fragment without $\bot$ and develop a theorem prover, called BILL, on top of it. Their later paper [21] extends the calculus for full intuitionistic BI. Donnelly *et al.* [16] investigate the inverse method for a propositional fragment without units ($\top$, $\bot$, and I) and develop a forward theorem prover.

For Boolean BI, no theorem prover has been developed yet because of the lack of a proof theory suitable for proof search. Larchey-Wendling and Gamliche [28] formulate a labelled tableau calculus by extending the labelled tableau calculus for intuitionistic BI in [21], but only in order to investigate the relation between intuitionistic BI and Boolean BI. Brotherston [10] shows that a modular combination of display calculi for classical logic and intuitionistic linear logic gives rise to a display calculus $\mathbf{DL_{BBI}}$ for Boolean BI, the first cut-free syntactic formulation of Boolean BI, and proves the cut elimination property by observing that its rules obey all the syntactic constraints given in [1]. Developing a practical proof search strategy on top of it, however, is far from easy because of the complexity due to its display rules and the difficulty in restricting applications of the contraction rules [9].

Galmiche and Méry [20] present a labelled tableau calculus for separation logic. It lies somewhere between syntactic (tableau) and semantic (labelled) formulations because labels correspond to heaps in separation logic. Their calculus, albeit sound and complete, does not directly translate to a proof search strategy in its current form. It is easy to build a tableau for a given formula according to the calculus, but one needs to check if all branches in the tableau are logically or structurally inconsistent. This requires two semantic functions (a measure and an interpretation) for each branch, and the calculus does not specify how to obtain such semantic functions. For a similar reason, the labelled tableau calculus for Boolean BI in [28] does not directly translate to a proof search strategy. For theorem provers for the decidable fragment of separation logic by Berdine *et al.* [3] (without separating implication), see, for example, [4, 14, 32].

9.2 Nested sequent calculi

A nested sequent calculus is one whose sequent may contain smaller sequents. It has been used as a proof-theoretic formulation of some modal and tense logics [12, 27] for which no sequent calculus of the standard form exists. $\mathbf{S_{BBI}}$ is also a nested sequent calculus because a sequent may contain smaller sequents.

	formula	d	*naive*		*optimized*		
			result	cost	result	cost	time
(a)	$(A \mathrel{-\!\!\star} B) \wedge (\top \star (\mathsf{I} \wedge A)) \rightarrow B$	1	**true**	9	**true**	9	0.001
	$(\mathsf{I} \mathrel{-\!\!\star} \neg(\neg A \star \mathsf{I})) \rightarrow A$	1	**true**	9	**true**	9	0.001
	$\neg((A \mathrel{-\!\!\star} \neg(A \star B)) \wedge ((\neg A \mathrel{-\!\!\star} \neg B) \wedge B))$	1	**true**	26	**true**	19	0.001
	$\mathsf{I} \rightarrow (A \mathrel{-\!\!\star} B \mathrel{-\!\!\star} C) \mathrel{-\!\!\star} A \star B \mathrel{-\!\!\star} C$	2	**true**	700	**true**	76	0.021
	$\mathsf{I} \rightarrow A \star (B \star C) \mathrel{-\!\!\star} A \star B \star C$	2	**true**	2606	**true**	263	0.051
	$\mathsf{I} \rightarrow A \star ((B_1 \mathrel{-\!\!\star} B_2) \star C) \mathrel{-\!\!\star} A \star (B_1 \mathrel{-\!\!\star} B_2) \star C$	2	**true**	12317	**true**	336	0.102
$\sharp$	$\neg((A \mathrel{-\!\!\star} \neg(\neg(D \mathrel{-\!\!\star} \neg(A \star (C \star B))) \star A)) \wedge C \star (D \wedge (A \star B)))$	2	**true**	121000	**true**	380	0.053
	$\neg((C_1 \star (C_2 \star C_3)) \wedge$ $((A \mathrel{-\!\!\star} \neg(\neg(B \mathrel{-\!\!\star} \neg(C_2 \star (C_3 \star C_1))) \star A)) \star (B \wedge (A \star \top))))$	2	**true**	1614053	**true**	43	0.023
$\sharp$	$\neg((A \mathrel{-\!\!\star} \neg(\neg(D \mathrel{-\!\!\star} \neg(C \star B_2 \star (B_1 \star A))) \star A)) \wedge C$ $\star(D \wedge (A \star (B_1 \star B_2))))$	3	**error**	-	**true**	74856	128.4
(b)	$A \star (B \star (C \star D)) \rightarrow D \star (C \star (B \star A))$	2	**true**	2618	**true**	56	0.012
	$A \star (B \star (C \star D)) \rightarrow D \star (B \star (C \star A))$	3	**true**	15686	**true**	34	0.041
	$A \star (B \star (C \star (D \star E))) \rightarrow E \star (D \star (A \star (B \star C)))$	3	**error**	-	**true**	2320	2.2
	$A \star (B \star (C \star (D \star E))) \rightarrow E \star (B \star (A \star (C \star D)))$	4	**error**	-	**true**	2921	28.2
(c)	$\mathsf{I} \rightarrow A \star ((B_1 \mathrel{-\!\!\star} B_2) \star (C \star D)) \mathrel{-\!\!\star} A \star D \star (C \star (B_1 \mathrel{-\!\!\star} B_2))$	2	**fail**	1795	**fail**	1837	0.438
		3	**error**	-	**true**	5942	8.2
		4	**error**	-	**true**	181	7.0
		5	**error**	-	**true**	182	127.0
		6	**error**	-	**error**	-	-

Figure 14. Results of running two implementations (*naive* and *optimized*) of the algorithm ProveBBI. The elapsed time is in seconds.

A nested sequent calculus is often obtained as an optimization of an equivalent display calculus that is not simplified to a sequent calculus of the standard form. Gore *et al.* [22–24] propose such nested sequent calculi for bi-intuitionistic logic and classical tense logic. In particular, their nested sequent calculus $\mathbf{SKt}$ for classical tense logic is similar to $\mathbf{S_{BBI}}$ in that it has two residual rules corresponding to the traverse rules of $\mathbf{S_{BBI}}$. The main difference is that $\mathbf{SKt}$ uses only a tree structure of sequents and has no rule for associativity (which changes parent-child and sibling relations between sequents). Hence it is much easier to embed contraction rules in $\mathbf{SKt}$ than in $\mathbf{S_{BBI}}$ and the problem of search space explosion due to structural rules as in $\mathbf{CS_{BBI}}$ does not exist in $\mathbf{SKt}$.

9.3 Comparison between $\mathbf{S_{BBI}}$ and $\mathbf{DL_{BBI}}$

We have seen in Section 6.3 that for Boolean BI, sequents in $\mathbf{S_{BBI}}$ essentially represent a normal form of consecutions in $\mathbf{DL_{BBI}}$. For intuitionistic BI, Brotherston [10] establishes a stronger result that sequents in its sequent calculus are literally a normal form of consecutions in its display calculus and thus belong to the same syntactic category. He also conjectures that a cut-free sequent calculus for Boolean BI is unlikely to exist if it has no negative structural connective such as $\sharp$ in $\mathbf{DL_{BBI}}$ (see Section 5 in [10]). Our discovery of $\mathbf{S_{BBI}}$ does *not* contradict his conjecture because we can think of sequents in $\mathbf{S_{BBI}}$ as implicitly applying a negative structural connective to falsehood contexts.

What is equally important, however, is that introducing only a negative structural connective is not enough to achieve a cut-free sequent calculus for Boolean BI, which must use a graph structure of sequents in which a sequent may have multiple parent sequents. In the case of $\mathbf{DL_{BBI}}$, the linear structural connective $\multimap$ allows such a graph structure of sequents, but the purpose of introducing $\multimap$ is to obtain the display theorem which is essential to Belnap's proof of the cut elimination theorem for display calculi [1]. Similarly, even though it does not require such a graph structure, the display calculus for intuitionistic BI in [10] also has the same linear structural connective $\multimap$. In contrast, $\mathbf{S_{BBI}}$ introduces an adjoint pair $W\langle\!\langle W' \rangle\!\rangle$ for the sole purpose of allowing such a graph structure of sequents.

10. Conclusion

Despite its close connection with separation logic, Boolean BI has not received much attention from the proof search community. Such a lack of research, which is quite unusual considering the status of separation logic in the field of program verification, is perhaps due to the difficulty of finding a proof theory suitable for theorem proving. Our nested sequent calculus $\mathbf{S_{BBI}}$ as well as a theorem prover based on it may serve as a test bed for developing proof search strategies for Boolean BI. In particular, its use of nested sequents allowing multiple parent sequents may shed new light on how to deal with separating implication in a theorem prover for separation logic.

Acknowledgments

We are grateful to the anonymous reviewers for their helpful comments. This work was supported by the Engineering Research Center of Excellence Program of Korea Ministry of Education, Science and Technology (MEST) / National Research Foundation of Korea (NRF) (Grant 2012-0000472) and Mid-career Researcher Program through NRF funded by the MEST (2010-0022061).

References

[1] N. Belnap. Display logic. *Journal of Philosophical Logic*, 11:375–417, 1982.

[2] N. Belnap. Linear logic displayed. *Notre Dame Journal of Formal Logic*, 31:14–25, 1990.

[3] J. Berdine, C. Calcagno, and P. W. O'Hearn. A decidable fragment of separation logic. In *Proc. FSTTCS*, pages 97–109, 2004.

[4] J. Berdine, C. Calcagno, and P. W. O'Hearn. Smallfoot: Modular automatic assertion checking with separation logic. In *Proc. FMCO*, pages 115–137, 2005.

[5] J. Berdine, C. Calcagno, and P. W. O'Hearn. Symbolic execution with separation logic. In *Proc. APLAS*, pages 52–68, 2005.

[6] J. Berdine, C. Calcagno, B. Cook, D. Distefano, P. W. O'Hearn, T. Wies, and H. Yang. Shape analysis for composite data structures. In *Proc. CAV*, pages 178–192, 2007.

[7] L. Birkedal, N. Torp-Smith, and J. C. Reynolds. Local reasoning about a copying garbage collector. In *Proc. POPL*, pages 220–231, 2004.

[8] R. Brochenin, S. Demri, and É. Lozes. On the almighty wand. In *Proc. CSL*, pages 323–338, 2008.

[9] J. Brotherston. A cut-free proof theory for boolean BI (via display logic). Technical Report DTR09-13, Imperial College London, 2009.

[10] J. Brotherston. A unified display proof theory for bunched logic. In *Proc. MFPS*, pages 197–211, 2010.

[11] J. Brotherston and M. Kanovich. Undecidability of propositional separation logic and its neighbours. In *Proc. LICS*, pages 130–139, 2010.

[12] K. Brünnler. Deep sequent systems for modal logic. In *Proc. Advances in Modal Logic*, pages 107–119, 2006.

[13] B.-Y. E. Chang and X. Rival. Relational inductive shape analysis. In *Proc. POPL*, pages 247–260, 2008.

[14] D. Distefano and M. J. Parkinson. jStar: towards practical verification for Java. In *Proc. OOPSLA*, pages 213–226, 2008.

[15] D. Distefano, P. W. O'Hearn, and H. Yang. A local shape analysis based on separation logic. In *Proc. TACAS*, pages 287–302, 2006.

[16] K. Donnelly, T. Gibson, N. Krishnaswami, S. Magill, and S. Park. The inverse method for the logic of bunched implications. In *Proc. LPAR*, pages 466–480, 2004.

[17] D. Galmiche and D. Larchey-Wendling. Expressivity properties of boolean BI through relational models. In *Proc. FSTTCS*, pages 357–368, 2006.

[18] D. Galmiche and D. Méry. Proof-search and countermodel generation in propositional BI logic. In *Proc. TACS*, pages 263–282, 2001.

[19] D. Galmiche and D. Méry. Semantic labelled tableaux for propositional BI (without bottom). *Journal of Logic and Computation*, 13: 70–753, 2003.

[20] D. Galmiche and D. Méry. Tableaux and resource graphs for separation logic. *Journal of Logic and Computation*, 20:189–231, 2010.

[21] D. Galmiche, D. Méry, and D. J. Pym. The semantics of BI and resource tableaux. *Mathematical Structures in Computer Science*, 15: 1033–1088, 2005.

[22] R. Goré, L. Postniece, and A. Tiu. Cut-elimination and proof-search for bi-intuitionistic logic using nested sequents. In *Proc. Advances in Modal Logic*, pages 43–66, 2008.

[23] R. Goré, L. Postniece, and A. Tiu. Taming displayed tense logics using nested sequents with deep inference. In *Proc. TABLEAUX*, pages 189–204, 2009.

[24] R. Goré, L. Postniece, and A. Tiu. On the correspondence between display postulates and deep inference in nested sequent calculi for tense logics. *Logical Methods in Computer Science*, 7:1–38, 2011.

[25] S. S. Ishtiaq and P. W. O'Hearn. BI as an assertion language for mutable data structures. In *Proc. POPL*, pages 14–26, 2001.

[26] B. Jacobs, J. Smans, and F. Piessens. VeriFast: Imperative programs as proofs. In *Proc. VSTTE*, pages 59–68, 2010.

[27] R. Kashima. Cut-free sequent calculi for some tense logics. *Studia Logica*, 53(1):119–136, 1994.

[28] D. Larchey-Wendling and D. Galmiche. Exploring the relation between intuitionistic BI and boolean BI: an unexpected embedding. *Mathematical Structures in Computer Science*, 19:435–500, 2009.

[29] D. Larchey-Wendling and D. Galmiche. The undecidability of boolean BI through phase semantics. In *Proc. LICS*, pages 140–149, 2010.

[30] S. Magill, J. Berdine, E. M. Clarke, and B. Cook. Arithmetic strengthening for shape analysis. In *Proc. SAS*, pages 419–436, 2007.

[31] N. Marti, R. Affeldt, and A. Yonezawa. Formal verification of the heap manager of an operating system using separation logic. In *Proc. ICFEM*, pages 400–419, 2006.

[32] J. A. Navarro Pérez and A. Rybalchenko. Separation logic + superposition calculus = heap theorem prover. In *Proc. PLDI*, pages 556–566. ACM, 2011.

[33] H. H. Nguyen and W.-N. Chin. Enhancing program verification with lemmas. In *Proc. CAV*, pages 355–369, 2008.

[34] P. W. O'Hearn and D. J. Pym. The logic of bunched implications. *Bulletin of Symbolic Logic*, 5:215–244, 1999.

[35] D. J. Pym. *The Semantics and Proof Theory of the Logic of Bunched Implications*. Kluwer Academic Pub, 2002.

[36] J. C. Reynolds. Separation logic: A logic for shared mutable data structures. In *Proc. LICS*, pages 55–74, 2002.

[37] V. Vafeiadis and M. J. Parkinson. A marriage of rely/guarantee and separation logic. In *Proc. CONCUR*, pages 256–271, 2007.

[38] H. Yang. An example of local reasoning in BI pointer logic: the Schorr-Waite graph marking algorithm. In *Proceedings of the 1st Workshop on Semantics, Program Analysis, and Computing Environments for Memory Management*, pages 41–68, 2001.

From Principles to Programming Languages (and Back)

Shriram Krishnamurthi
Computer Science Department, Brown University
sk@cs.brown.edu

Categories and Subject Descriptors D.3.1 [*Programming Languages*]: Formal Definitions and Theory – semantics; D.2.4 [*Software Engineering*]: Software/Program Verification

Keywords semantics engineering, democracy of languages

The Democracy of Programming Languages

While budding linguists have always had the freedom to tinker, the Web has revolutionized linguistic experiments in two key ways. First, the language-neutrality of network abstractions have made it possible for Web-deployed applications to be written in any language at all, allowing new languages to show off their capabilities. Second, the Web has greatly facilitated the dissemination of these experimental languages. As a result, new languages crop up almost daily, lovingly tended by their designers and user communities and vigorously debated on popular forums. This is a far cry from the programming languages world of just over a decade ago.

Most of these languages are not designed and developed in formal settings. As a result, they lack many of the tools that this conference's audience takes for granted: static analyses, type systems, verification engines, and so on. As we know, these tools not only improve usability, their construction serves as a design check: odd spots in the language design usually manifest themselves as difficulties in building or proving properties about the tool. This leads to a virtuous co-development cycle, or at least forces the language designer to justify the inclusion of such difficult elements.

A cynic might question why every language experiment deserves these tools. Because many of these languages will never see widespread adoption, they may not be worth a significant investment of formal effort. To this, there are three counter-arguments:

1. A language may be intended for in-house use or only to solve a particularly vexing problem in some important system. Thus, the size of its user-base is not a good measure of significance.
2. By the time a language becomes popular, it often already has frameworks, applications, or both, and hence already needs these tools.
3. Because tools are often vital to convincing users to employ the language—all the more given the physical distance between designer and user that the Web enables—the absence of such tools means promising language design experiments may never see the light of day.

It is therefore worth considering a research program that simultaneously serves the democracy of languages while upholding the values we hold dear, such as sound tools that are backed by theorems about their properties.

The Challenges of *Programming* Languages

Languages that developers use to write non-trivial programs rarely resemble the elegant cores we formalize. To have direct impact, three *semantics engineering* questions deserve special attention:

1. Beyond natural language specifications and de-facto normative implementations, language designers increasingly provide conformance test suites. These suites are formal objects (unlike natural language specifications), probably thoughtfully decomposed (unlike many implementations), and kept current (unlike many specifications). How can we ease the transition from conformance suites to formal semantics that match them?
2. Programs are increasingly a rich mix of code in a base language and code written atop frameworks. How can we formulate a semantics for the implicit languages of these APIs? How do we determine the invariants of these languages, to check that base language programs don't violate them?
3. In practice, programs in one language often depend on programs from other languages. While it is tempting to union the semantics of all these languages to reason about such programs, this approach usually leads to an intractable mess of details. Can we define a family of semantics so that we can "zoom" in to the appropriate level of detail? Can such a family accommodate both sound and tractable cross-language reasoning?

Going beyond core languages means also focusing on the needs of the users who employ them. Because programming languages are a developer's primary human-computer interface, the human writing the programs deserves as much attention as the language. In principle, in a complex system with mutual dependence, the two components must be co-designed; but when one of those components is a human, change can usually only be achieved at evolutionary pace. Programming languages, and their environments, therefore need to better account for the established cognitive abilities and disabilities of their users.

The democracy of languages means the future for programming language research is brighter than ever. Furthermore, linguistic thinking applies broadly and is in urgent need. My own group has spent the past decade applying a linguistic mindset—and generating some core results in return—not only to traditional programming and specification languages, but also to industrial access-control languages, Web servers, Web browsers, Excel spreadsheets, Internet routers and firewalls, social networks, and Alice-and-Bob cryptographic diagrams. In all these areas, and more, there is a great need for the clarity and focus on primitives and composition that is characteristic of programming languages thought.

POPL'13, January 23–25, 2013, Rome, Italy.
ACM 978-1-4503-1832-7/13/01.

Library Abstraction for C/C++ Concurrency

Mark Batty
University of Cambridge

Mike Dodds
University of York

Alexey Gotsman
IMDEA Software Institute

Abstract

When constructing complex concurrent systems, abstraction is vital: programmers should be able to reason about concurrent libraries in terms of abstract specifications that hide the implementation details. Relaxed memory models present substantial challenges in this respect, as libraries need not provide sequentially consistent abstractions: to avoid unnecessary synchronisation, they may allow clients to observe relaxed memory effects, and library specifications must capture these.

In this paper, we propose a criterion for sound library abstraction in the new C11 and C++11 memory model, generalising the standard sequentially consistent notion of linearizability. We prove that our criterion soundly captures all client-library interactions, both through call and return values, and through the subtle synchronisation effects arising from the memory model. To illustrate our approach, we verify implementations against specifications for the lock-free Treiber stack and a producer-consumer queue. Ours is the first approach to compositional reasoning for concurrent C11/C++11 programs.

Categories and Subject Descriptors D.2.4 [*Software Engineering*]: Software/Program Verification; F.3.1 [*Logics and Meanings of Programs*]: Specifying and Verifying and Reasoning about Programs

General Terms Languages, Theory, Verification

Keywords Verification, Concurrency, Modularity, C, C++

1. Introduction

Software developers often encapsulate functionality in libraries, and construct complex libraries from simpler ones. The advantage of this is information hiding: the developer need not understand each library's implementation, but only its more abstract *specification*. On a sequential system, a library's internal actions cannot be observed by its client, so its specification can simply be a relation from initial to final states of every library invocation. This does not suffice on a concurrent system, where the invocations can overlap and interact with each other. Hence, a concurrent library's specification is often given as just another library, but with a simpler (e.g., atomic) implementation; the two libraries are called *concrete* and *abstract*, respectively. Validating a specification means showing that the simpler implementation *abstracts* the more complex one, i.e., reproduces all its client-observable behaviours. Library abstraction has to take into account a variety of ways in which a client and library can interact, including values passed at library calls and returns, the contents of shared data structures and, in this paper, the *memory model*.

The memory model of a concurrent system governs what values can be returned when the system reads from shared memory. In a traditional *sequentially consistent (SC)* system, the memory model is straightforward: there is a total order over reads and writes, and each read returns the value of the most recent write to the location being accessed [15]. However, modern processors and programming languages provide *relaxed memory models*, where there is no total order of memory actions, and the order of actions observed by a thread may not agree with program order, or with that observed by other threads.

In this paper, we propose a criterion for library abstraction on the relaxed memory model defined by the new ISO C11 [12] and C++11 [13] standards (henceforth, the 'C11 model'). We handle the core of the C11 memory model, leaving more esoteric features, such release-consume atomics and fences, as future work (see §9). The C11 model is designed to support common compiler optimisations and efficient compilation to architectures such as x86, Power, ARM and Itanium, which themselves do not guarantee SC. It gives the programmer fine-grained control of relaxed behaviour for individual reads and writes, and is defined by a set of axiomatic constraints, rather than operationally. Both of these properties produce subtle interactions between the client and the library that must be accounted for in abstraction.

Our criterion is an evolution of *linearizability* [5, 7, 10, 11], a widely-used abstraction criterion for non-relaxed systems. Like linearizability, our approach satisfies the *Abstraction Theorem*: if one library (a specification) abstracts another (an implementation), then the behaviours of any client using the implementation are contained in the behaviours of the client using the specification. This result allows complex library code to be replaced by simpler specifications, for verification or informal reasoning. Hence, it can be viewed as giving a proof technique for contextual refinement that avoids considering all possible clients. Our criterion is compositional, meaning that a library consisting of several smaller non-interacting libraries can be abstracted by considering each sub-library separately. When restricted to the SC fragment of C11, our criterion implies classical linearizability (but not vice versa).

The proposed criterion for library abstraction gives the first sound technique for specifying C11 and C++11 concurrent libraries. To justify its practicality, we have applied it two typical concurrent algorithms: a non-blocking stack and an array-based queue. To do this, we have adapted the standard linearization point technique to the axiomatic structure of the C11 model. These case studies represent the first step towards verified concurrent libraries for C11 and C++11.

Technical challenges. Apart from managing the mere complexity of the C11 model, defining a criterion for library abstraction

POPL'13, January 23–25, 2012, Rome, Italy.

requires us to deal with several challenges that have not been considered in prior work.

First, the C11 memory model is defined axiomatically, whereas existing techniques for library abstraction, such as linearizability, have focused on operational trace-based models. To deal with this, we propose a novel notion of a *history*, which records all interactions between a client and a library. Histories in our work consist of several partial orders on call and return actions. This is in contrast to variants of linearizability, where histories are linear sequences (for this reason, in the following we avoid the term 'linearizability'). We define an abstraction relation on histories as inclusion over partial orders, and lift this relation to give our abstraction criterion for libraries: one library abstracts another if any history of the former can be reproduced in abstracted form by the latter.

Second, C11 offers the programmer a range of options for concurrently accessing memory, each with different trade-offs between consistency and performance. These choices can subtly affect other memory accesses across the client-library boundary—a particular choice of consistency level inside the library might force or forbid reading certain values in the client, and vice versa. This is an intended feature: it allows C11 libraries to define synchronisation constructs that offer different levels of consistency to clients. We propose a method for constructing histories that captures such client-library interactions uniformly. The Abstraction Theorem certifies that our histories indeed soundly represent *all* possible interactions.

Finally, some aspects of the C11 model conflict with abstraction. Most problematically, the model permits *satisfaction cycles*. In satisfaction cycles, the effect of actions executed down a conditional branch is what causes the branch to be taken in the first place. This breaks the straightforward assumption that faults are confined to either client or library code: a misbehaving client can cause misbehaviour in a library, which can in turn cause the original client misbehaviour! For these reasons, we actually define *two* distinct library abstraction criteria: one for general C11, and one for a language without the feature leading to satisfaction cycles. The former requires an a priori check that the client and the library do not access each others' internal memory locations, which hinders compositionality. The latter lifts this restriction (albeit for a C11 model modified to admit incomplete program runs) and thus provides evidence that satisfaction cycles are to blame for non-compositional behaviour. Our results thus illuminate corner cases in C11 that undermine abstraction, and may inform future revisions of the model.

As we argue in §9, many of the techniques we developed to address the above challenges should be applicable to other models similar to C11.

Structure. In the first part of the paper, we describe informally how algorithms can be expressed and specified in the C11 memory model (§2), and our abstraction criteria (§3). We then present the model formally (§4 and §5), followed by the criteria (§6) and a method for establishing their requirements (§7). Proofs are given in an extended version of the paper [1, §C].

2. C11 Concurrency and Library Specification

In this section we explain the form of our specifications for C11 concurrent libraries, together with a brief introduction to programming in the C11 concurrency model itself. As a running example, we use a version of the non-blocking Treiber stack algorithm [22] implemented using the concurrency primitives in the subset of C11 that we consider. Figure 1a shows its specification, and Figure 1b its implementation, which we have proved to correspond (§7 and [1, §E]). For readability, we present examples in a pseudocode instead of the actual C/C++ syntax. Several important features are highlighted in red—these are explained below.

SPECIFICATION:

```
atomic Seq S;

void init() {
  storeREL(&S,empty);
}

void push(int v) {
  Seq s, s2;
  if (nondet()) while(1);
  atom_sec {
    s = loadRLX(&S);
    s2 = append(s,v);
    CASRLX,REL(&S,s,s2);
  }
}

int pop() {
  Seq s;
  if (nondet()) while(1);
  atom_sec {
    s = loadACQ(&S);
    if (s == empty)
      return EMPTY;
    CASRLX,RLX(&S,s,tail(s));
    return head(s);
  }
}
```

(a)

IMPLEMENTATION:

```
struct Node {
  int data;
  Node *next;
};
atomic Node *T;

void init() {
  storeREL(&T,NULL);
}

void push(int v) {
  Node *x, *t;
  x = new Node();
  x->data = v;
  do {
    t = loadRLX(&T);
    x->next = t;
  } while
    (!CASRLX,REL(&T,t,x));
}

int pop() {
  Node *t, *x;
  do {
    t = loadACQ(&T);
    if (t == NULL)
      return EMPTY;
    x = t->next;
  } while
    (!CASRLX,RLX(&T,t,x));
  return t->data;
}
```

(b)

Figure 1. The Treiber stack. For simplicity, we let pop leak memory. The CASes in the specification always succeed.

Stack specification. As noted in §1, specifications are just alternative library implementations that have the advantage of simplicity, in exchange for inefficiency or nondeterminism. The specification in Figure 1a represents the stack as a sequence abstract data type and provides the three expected methods: `init`, `push` and `pop`. A correct stack implementation should provide the illusion of atomicity of operations to concurrent threads. We specify this by wrapping the bodies of `push` and `pop` in ***atomic sections***, denoted by `atom_sec`. Atomic sections are not part of the standard C11 model—for specification purposes, we have extended the language with a prototype semantics for atomic section (§5). Both `push` and `pop` may non-deterministically diverge, as common stack implementations allow some operations to starve (in concurrency parlance, they are lock-free, but not wait-free). All these are the expected features of a specification on an SC memory model. We now explain the features specific to C11.

The sequence `S` holding the abstract state is declared `atomic`. In C11, programs must not have data races on normal variables; any location where races can occur must be explicitly identified as `atomic` and accessed using the special commands `load`, `store`, and `CAS` (***compare-and-swap***). The latter combines a load and a store into a single operation executed atomically. A CAS takes three arguments: a memory address, an expected value and a new value. The command atomically reads the memory address and, if it contains the expected value, updates it with the new one. Due to our use of atomic sections, the CASes in the specification always succeed. We use CASes here instead of just stores, because, for subtle technical reasons, the latter have a stronger semantics in C11 than our atomic sections (see release sequences in §A).

The `load` and `store` commands are annotated with a ***memory order*** that determines the trade-off between consistency and performance for the memory access; CASes are annotated with two memory orders, as they perform both a load and a store. The choice of memory orders inside a library method can indirectly affect its clients, and thus, a library specification must include them. In the stack specification, several memory operations have the ***release-acquire*** memory orders, denoted by the subscripts REL (for stores) and ACQ (for loads). To explain its effect, consider the following client using the stack according to a typical message-passing idiom:

```
            int a, b, x=0;
                  || do {
x=1;              ||   a = pop();
push(&x);         || } while (a==EMPTY);
                  || b=*a;
```

The first thread writes `1` into `x` and calls `push(&x)`; the second thread pops the address of `x` from the stack and then reads its contents. In general, a relaxed memory model may allow the second thread to read `0` instead of `1`, e.g., because the compiler reorders `x=1` and `push(&x)`. The release-acquire annotations guarantee that this is not the case: when the ACQ load of `S` in `pop` reads the value written by the REL store to `S` in `push`, the two commands ***synchronise***. We define this notion more precisely later, but informally, it means that the ordering between the REL store and ACQ load constrains the values fetched by reads from other locations, such as the read `*a` in the client.

To enable this message-passing idiom, the specification only needs to synchronise from pushes to pops; it need not synchronise from pops to pushes, or from pops to pops. To avoid unnecessary synchronisation, the specification uses the ***relaxed*** memory order (RLX). This order is weaker than release-acquire, meaning that the set of values a relaxed load can read from memory is less constrained; additionally, relaxed loads and stores do not synchronise with each other. However, relaxed operations are very cheap, since they compile to basic loads and stores without any additional hardware barrier instructions. Hence, the specification allows implementations that are efficient, yet support the intended use of the stack for message passing. On the other hand, as we show below, it intentionally allows non-SC stack behaviours.

Stack implementation. Figure 1b gives our implementation of the Treiber stack. The stack is represented by a heap-allocated linked list of nodes, accessed through a top-of-stack pointer `T`. Only the latter needs to be `atomic`, as it is the only point of contention among threads. The `push` function repeatedly reads from the top pointer `T`, initialises a newly created node `x` to point to the value read, and tries to swing `T` to point to `x` using a CAS; `pop` is implemented similarly. For simplicity, we let pop leak memory.

Like the specification, the implementation avoids unnecessary hardware synchronisation by using the relaxed memory order RLX. However, the load of `T` in `pop` is annotated ACQ, since the command `x = t->next` accesses memory based on the value read, and hence, requires it to be up to date.

What does it mean for the implementation in Figure 1b to meet the specification in Figure 1a? As well as returning the right values, it must also faithfully implement the correct synchronisation. To understand how this can be formalised, we must therefore explain how synchronisation works in C11's semantics.

C11 model structure. The C11 memory model is defined axiomatically. An ***execution*** of a program consists of a set of ***actions*** and several partial orders on it. An action describes a memory operation, including the information about the thread that performed it, the address accessed and the values written and/or read. The semantics of a program is given by the set of executions consistent with the program code and satisfying the ***axioms*** of the memory model (see Figure 4 for a flavour of these). Here is a program with one of its executions, whose outcome we explain below:

STORE BUFFERING (SB):

```
storeRLX(&x,0); storeRLX(&y,0)
storeRLX(&x,1) || storeRLX(&y,1)
loadRLX(&y)    || loadRLX(&x)
```

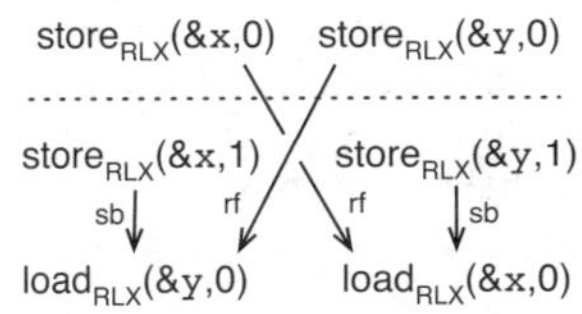

Note that, in diagrams representing executions, we omit thread identifiers from actions. Several of the most important relations in an execution are:

- ***sequenced-before*** (sb), a transitive and irreflexive relation ordering actions by the same thread according to their program order.
- ***initialised-before*** (ib), ordering initial writes to memory locations before all other actions in the execution[1]. Above we have shown ib by a dotted line dividing the two kinds of actions.
- ***reads-from*** (rf), relating reads r to the writes w from which they take their values: $w \xrightarrow{\mathsf{rf}} r$.
- ***happens-before*** (hb), showing the precedence of actions in the execution. In the fragment of C11 that we consider, it is transitive and irreflexive.

Happens-before is the key relation, and is the closest the C11 model has to the notion of a global time in an SC model: a read must not read any write to the same location related to it in hb other than its immediate predecessor. Thus, for writes w_1 and w_2 and a read r accessing the same location, the following shapes are forbidden:

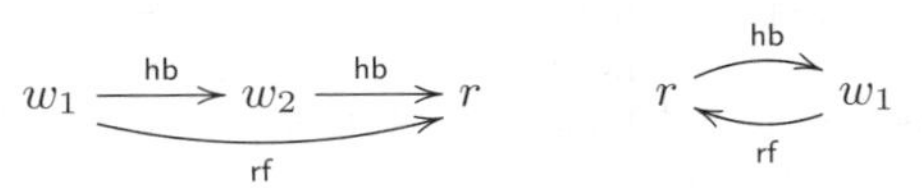

(RD)

However, in contrast to an SC model, hb is partial in C11, and some reads can read from hb-unrelated writes: we might have $w \xrightarrow{\mathsf{rf}} r$, but not $w \xrightarrow{\mathsf{hb}} r$.

Memory orders. By default, memory reads and writes in C11 are ***non-atomic*** (NA). The memory model guarantees that data-race free programs with only non-atomic memory accesses have SC behaviour. A data race occurs when two actions on the same memory location, at least one of which is a write, and at least one of which is a non-atomic access, are unrelated in happens-before, and thus, intuitively, can take place 'at the same time'. Hence, non-expert programmers who write code that is free from both data races and atomic accesses need not understand the details of the relaxed memory model. Data races are considered faults, resulting in undefined behaviour for the whole program.

The three main atomic memory orders, from least to most restrictive, are relaxed, release-acquire and sequentially consistent[2]. We have already seen the first two in the stack example above. The third, ***sequentially consistent*** (SC), does not allow relaxed behaviour: if all actions in a race-free program are either non-atomic or SC, the program exhibits only sequentially-consistent behaviour [2, 4]. However, the SC memory order is more expensive.

The weakest memory order, ***relaxed***, exhibits a number of relaxations, as the C11 model places very few restrictions on which write a relaxed read might read from. For example, consider the (SB)

[1] This is a specialisation of the *additional-synchronises-with* relation from the C11 model [2] to programs without dynamic thread creation, to which we restrict ourselves in this paper (see §4).

[2] Release-consume atomics and fences [2] are left for future work (see §9). We also omit some C11 subtleties that are orthogonal to abstraction (see §4).

example above. The outcome shown there is allowed by C11, but cannot be produced by any interleaving of the threads' actions. C11 disallows it if all memory accesses are annotated as SC.

The ***release-acquire*** memory orders allow more relaxed behaviour than SC, while still providing some guarantees. Consider the following execution of the client of the stack in Figure 1a or 1b we have seen above:

MESSAGE PASSING (MP):

```
int a, b, x=0;

x=1;          || do {a=pop();}
push(&x);     || while
              ||    (a==EMPTY);
              || b=*a;
```

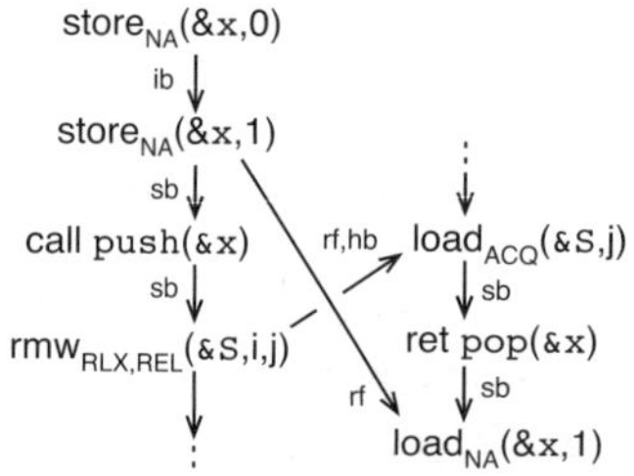

Here rmw (read-modify-write) is a combined load-store action produced by a CAS. In this case, the ACQ load in pop synchronises with the REL store part of the CAS in push that it reads from. This informal notion of synchronisation we mentioned above is formalised in the memory model by including the corresponding rf edge into hb. Then, since $\mathsf{sb} \cup \mathsf{ib} \subseteq \mathsf{hb}$ and hb is transitive, both writes to x happen before the read. Hence, by (RD), the read from x by the second thread is forced to read from the most recent write, i.e., 1.

If all the memory order annotations in the Treiber stack were relaxed, the second thread could read 0 from x instead. Furthermore, without release-acquire synchronisation, there would be a data race between the non-atomic write of x in the first thread and the non-atomic read of x in the second.

The release-acquire memory orders only synchronise between pairs of reads and writes, but do not impose a total order over memory accesses, and therefore allow non-SC behaviour. For example, if we annotate writes in (SB) with REL, and reads with ACQ, then the outcome shown there will still be allowed: each load can read from the initialisation without generating a cycle in hb or violating (RD). We can also get this outcome if we use push and pop operations on two instances of the stack from Figure 1a or 1b instead of load and store. Thus, both the implementation and the specification of the stack allow it to have non-SC behaviour.

To summarise, very roughly, release-acquire allows writes to be delayed but not reordered, while relaxed allows both. Relaxed actions produce even stranger behaviour, including what we call ***satisfaction cycles***:

SATISFACTION CYCLE (SCL):

```
a=loadRLX(&x)      || b=loadRLX(&y)
if (a==8)          || if (b==8)
storeRLX(&y,a)     || storeRLX(&x,8)
```

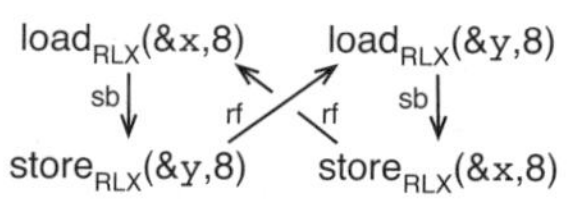

Here, each conditional satisfies its guard from a later write in the other thread. This is possible because relaxed reads and writes do not create any happens-before ordering, and thus neither read is constrained by (RD). Unlike relaxed, release-acquire does not allow satisfaction cycles. If the loads and stores in the example were annotated release-acquire, then both rf edges would also be hb edges. This would produce an hb cycle, which is prohibited by the memory model. Satisfaction cycles are known to be a problematic aspect of the C11 model; as we show in this paper, they also create difficulties for library abstraction.

3. Library Abstraction Informally

Histories. Our approach to abstraction is based on the notion of a ***history***, which concisely records all interactions between the client and the library in a given execution. Clients and libraries can affect one another in several ways in C11. Most straightforwardly, the library can observe the parameters passed by the client at calls, and the client can observe the library's return values. Therefore, a history includes the set of all call and return actions in the execution. However, clients can also observe synchronisation and other memory-model effects inside a method. These more subtle interactions are recorded by two kinds of partial order: *guarantees* and *denies*.

Synchronisation internal to the library can affect the client by forcing reads to read from particular writes. For example, in (MP) from §2, the client is forced to read 1 from x because the push and pop methods synchronise internally in a way that generates an hb ordering between the call to push and the return from pop. If the methods did not hb-synchronise, the client could read from either of the writes to x. The client can thus observe the difference between two library implementations with different internal synchronisation, even if all call and return values are identical. To account for this, the ***guarantee*** relation in a history of an execution records hb edges between library call and return actions.

Even non-synchronising behaviour inside the library can sometimes be observed by the client. For example, the C11 model requires the existence of a total order mo over all atomic writes to a given location. This order cannot go against hb, but is not included into it, as this would make the model much stronger, and would hinder efficient compilation onto very weak architectures, such as Power and ARM [21]. Now, consider the following:

DENY (DN):

```
storeREL(&x,1);

loadACQ(&x); || lib();
lib();       || storeREL(&x,0);
```

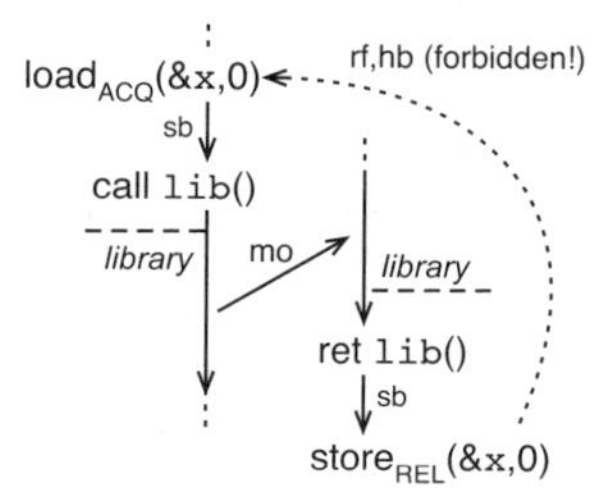

In this execution, a write internal to the invocation of lib in the second thread is mo-ordered after a write internal to the invocation of lib in the first thread. This forbids the client from reading 0 from x. To see this, suppose the contrary holds. Then the ACQ load synchronises with the REL store of 0, yielding an hb edge. By transitivity with the client sb edges, which are included in hb, we get an hb edge from ret lib in the second thread to call lib in the first. Together with the library's sb edges, this yields an hb edge going against the library-internal mo one, which is prohibited by the memory model. To account for such interactions, the ***deny*** relations in a history of an execution record hb or other kinds of edges between return and call actions that the client *cannot* enforce due to the structure of the library, e.g., the hb-edge from ret lib to call lib above.

Abstraction in the presence of relaxed atomics. As we noted in §1, we actually propose two library abstraction criteria: one for the full memory model described in §2, and one for programs without relaxed atomics. We discuss the former first.

Two library executions with the same history are observationally equivalent to clients, even if the executions are produced by different library implementations. By defining a sound abstraction relation over histories, we can therefore establish abstraction between libraries. To this end, we need to compare the histories of libraries under every client context. Fortunately, we need not examine every possible client: it suffices to consider behaviour under a ***most general client***, whose threads repeatedly invoke library methods in any order and with any parameters. Executions under this client generate all possible histories of the library, and thus represent all client-library interactions (with an important caveat, discussed below). We write $[\![\mathcal{L}]\!]I$ for the set of executions of the library $\mathcal{L}$ under the most general client starting from an ***initial state*** I. Initial states are defined formally in §4, but, informally, record initialisation actions such as the ones shown in (SB). The set $[\![\mathcal{L}]\!]I$ gives the denotation of the library considered in isolation from its clients, and in this sense, defines a ***library-local semantics*** of $\mathcal{L}$.

This library-local semantics allows us to define library abstraction. We now quote its definition and formulate the corresponding Abstraction Theorem, introducing some of the concepts used in them only informally. This lets us highlight their most important features that can be discussed independently of the formalities. We fill in the missing details in §6.1, after we have presented the C11 model more fully.

For the memory model with relaxed atomics, a history contains one guarantee and one deny relation.

DEFINITION 1. *A* ***history*** *is a triple* $H = (A, G, D)$, *where* A *is a set of call and return actions, and* $G, D \subseteq A \times A$.

Library abstraction is defined on pairs of libraries $\mathcal{L}$ and sets of their initial states $\mathcal{I}$. It relies on a function $\mathsf{history}(\cdot)$ extracting the history from a given execution of a library, which we lift to sets of executions pointwise. The notation $[\![\mathcal{L}, R]\!]$ and the notion of safety are explained below.

DEFINITION 2. *For histories* (A_1, G_1, D_1) *and* (A_2, G_2, D_2), *we let* $(A_1, G_1, D_1) \sqsubseteq (A_2, G_2, D_2)$ *if* $A_1 = A_2$, $G_1 = G_2$ *and* $D_2 \subseteq D_1$.

For safe $(\mathcal{L}_1, \mathcal{I}_1)$ *and* $(\mathcal{L}_2, \mathcal{I}_2)$, $(\mathcal{L}_1, \mathcal{I}_1)$ ***is abstracted by*** $(\mathcal{L}_2, \mathcal{I}_2)$, *written* $(\mathcal{L}_1, \mathcal{I}_1) \sqsubseteq (\mathcal{L}_2, \mathcal{I}_2)$, *if for any relation* R *containing only edges from return actions to call actions, we have*

$$\forall I_1 \in \mathcal{I}_1, H_1 \in \mathsf{history}([\![\mathcal{L}_1, R]\!]I_1).$$
$$\exists I_2 \in \mathcal{I}_2, H_2 \in \mathsf{history}([\![\mathcal{L}_2, R]\!]I_2).\ H_1 \sqsubseteq H_2.$$

The overall shape of the definition is similar to that of linearizability on SC memory models [11]: any behaviour of the concrete library $\mathcal{L}_1$ relevant to the client has to be reproducible by the abstract library $\mathcal{L}_2$. However, there are several things to note.

First, we allow the execution of the abstract library to deny less than the concrete one, but require it to provide the same guarantee. Intuitively, we can strengthen the deny, because this only allows more client behaviours.

Second, we do not consider raw executions of the most general client of $\mathcal{L}_1$ and $\mathcal{L}_2$, but those whose happens-before relation can be ***extended*** with an arbitrary set R of edges between return and call actions without contradicting the axioms of the memory model; $[\![\mathcal{L}_1, R]\!]I_1$ and $[\![\mathcal{L}_2, R]\!]I_2$ denote the sets of all such extensions. The set R represents the happens-before edges that can be enforced by the client: such happens-before edges are not generated by the most general client and, in the presence of relaxed atomics, have to be considered explicitly (this is the caveat to its generality referred to above). We consider only return-to-call edges, as these are the ones that represent synchronisation inside the client (similarly to how call-to-return edges in the guarantee represent synchronisation inside the library; cf. (MP)). The definition requires that, if an extension of the concrete library is consistent with R, then so must be the matching execution of the abstract one.

Finally, the abstraction relation is defined only between ***safe*** libraries that do not access locations internal to the client and do not have faults, such as data races.

As we show in §7, the specification of the Treiber stack in Figure 1a abstracts its implementation in Figure 1b.

Abstraction theorem. We now formulate a theorem that states the correctness of our library abstraction criterion. We consider programs $\mathcal{C}(\mathcal{L})$ with a single client $\mathcal{C}$ and a library $\mathcal{L}$ (the case of multiple libraries is considered in §6.1). The Abstraction Theorem states that, if we replace the (implementation) library $\mathcal{L}_1$ in a program $\mathcal{C}(\mathcal{L}_1)$ with another (specification) library $\mathcal{L}_2$ abstracting $\mathcal{L}_1$, then the set of client behaviours can only increase. Hence, when reasoning about $\mathcal{C}(\mathcal{L}_1)$, we can soundly replace $\mathcal{L}_1$ with $\mathcal{L}_2$ to simplify reasoning.

In the theorem, $[\![\mathcal{C}(\mathcal{L})]\!]\mathcal{I}$ gives the set of executions of $\mathcal{C}(\mathcal{L})$ from initial states in a set $\mathcal{I}$, $\uplus$ combines the initial states of a client and a library, and $\mathsf{client}(\cdot)$ selects the parts of executions generated by client commands. We call $(\mathcal{C}(\mathcal{L}), \mathcal{I})$ ***non-interfering***, if $\mathcal{C}$ and $\mathcal{L}$ do not access each others' internal memory locations in executions of $\mathcal{C}(\mathcal{L})$ from initial states in $\mathcal{I}$. The notion of safety for $\mathcal{C}(\mathcal{L})$ is analogous to the one for libraries.

THEOREM 3 (Abstraction). *Assume that* $(\mathcal{L}_1, \mathcal{I}_1)$, $(\mathcal{L}_2, \mathcal{I}_2)$, $(\mathcal{C}(\mathcal{L}_2), \mathcal{I} \uplus \mathcal{I}_2)$ *are safe,* $(\mathcal{C}(\mathcal{L}_1), \mathcal{I} \uplus \mathcal{I}_1)$ *is non-interfering and* $(\mathcal{L}_1, \mathcal{I}_1) \sqsubseteq (\mathcal{L}_2, \mathcal{I}_2)$. *Then* $(\mathcal{C}(\mathcal{L}_1), \mathcal{I} \uplus \mathcal{I}_1)$ *is safe and*

$$\mathsf{client}([\![\mathcal{C}(\mathcal{L}_1)]\!](\mathcal{I} \uplus \mathcal{I}_1)) \subseteq \mathsf{client}([\![\mathcal{C}(\mathcal{L}_2)]\!](\mathcal{I} \uplus \mathcal{I}_2)).$$

The requirement of non-interference is crucial, because it ensures that clients can only observe library behaviour through return values and memory-model effects, rather than by 'opening the box' and observing internal states. The drawback of Theorem 3 is that it requires us to establish the non-interference between the client $\mathcal{C}$ and the *concrete* library $\mathcal{L}_1$, e.g., via a type system or a program logic proof. As we show below, we cannot weaken this condition to allow checking non-interference on the client $\mathcal{C}$ using the *abstract* library $\mathcal{L}_2$, as is standard in data refinement on SC memory models [8]. This makes the reasoning principle given by the theorem less compositional, since establishing non-interference requires considering the composed behaviour of the client and the concrete library—precisely what library abstraction is intended to avoid! However, this does not kill compositional reasoning completely, as non-interference is often simple to check even globally. We can also soundly check other aspects of safety, such as data-race freedom, on $\mathcal{C}(\mathcal{L}_2)$. Furthermore, as we show in §6.1, the notion of library abstraction given by Definition 2 is compositional for non-interfering libraries. As we now explain, we can get the desired theorem allowing us to check non-interference on $\mathcal{C}(\mathcal{L}_2)$ for the fragment of the language excluding relaxed atomics.

Abstraction without relaxed atomics. Restricting ourselves to programs without the relaxed memory order (and augmenting the axiomatic memory model to allow incomplete program runs, as described in §4) allows strengthening our result in three ways:

1. We no longer need to quantify over client happens-before edges R, like in Definition 2. Instead, we enrich histories with an additional deny relation, which is easier to deal with in practice than the quantification. Hence, without relaxed atomics, the caveat to the generality of the most general client does not apply.
2. Abstraction on histories can be defined by inclusion on guarantees, rather than by equality.
3. We no longer need to show that the unabstracted program $\mathcal{C}(\mathcal{L}_1)$ is non-interfering. Rather, non-interference is a consequence of the safety of the abstracted program $\mathcal{C}(\mathcal{L}_2)$.

The first two differences make proofs of library abstraction slightly easier, but are largely incidental otherwise. In particular, quantification over client happens-before edges in Definition 2, although unpleasant, does not make library abstraction proofs drastically more complicated. Requiring the guarantees of the concrete and abstract executions to be equal in this definition just results in more verbose specifications in certain cases. In contrast, the last difference is substantial.

The price of satisfaction cycles. For each of the three above differences we have a counterexample showing that Theorem 3 will not hold if we change the corresponding condition to the one required in the case without relaxed atomics. All of these counterexamples involve satisfaction cycles, which can only be produced by relaxed atomics. Our results show that this language feature makes the reasoning principles for C11 programs less compositional. Due to space constraints, here we present only the counterexample for point 3 above; the others are given in [1, §D]. In §6.3, we identify the corresponding place in the proof of the Abstraction Theorem for the language without relaxed atomics where we rely on the absence of satisfaction cycles.

Consider the following pair of libraries $\mathcal{L}_1$ and $\mathcal{L}_2$:

```
L1:  atomic int x;                  L2:  atomic int x;
     int m() {                           int m() {
       storeRLX(&x,42);                    return 42;
       return loadRLX(&x);               }
     }
```

Here x is a library-internal location. We have $\mathcal{L}_1 \sqsubseteq \mathcal{L}_2$, since both method implementations behave exactly the same, assuming that the internal location x is not modified outside the library. Unsafe clients can distinguish between $\mathcal{L}_1$ and $\mathcal{L}_2$. For example, the client

```
print m(); || storeRLX(&x,0);
```

can print 0 when using $\mathcal{L}_1$, but not $\mathcal{L}_2$. However, any non-trivial library behaves erratically when clients corrupt its private data structures, and thus, it is reasonable for abstraction to take into account only well-behaved clients that do not do this. We therefore contend that $\mathcal{L}_1$ *should* be abstracted by $\mathcal{L}_2$ according to any sensible abstraction criterion.

The above misbehaved client violates non-interference when using either $\mathcal{L}_1$ or $\mathcal{L}_2$. However, we can define a more complicated client $\mathcal{C}$ such that $\mathcal{C}(\mathcal{L}_2)$ is non-interfering, but $\mathcal{C}(\mathcal{L}_1)$ is not:

```
a=m()                 || b=loadRLX(&y)
if (a==0)             || if (b==0)
  storeRLX(&y,0)      ||   storeRLX(&x,0)
```

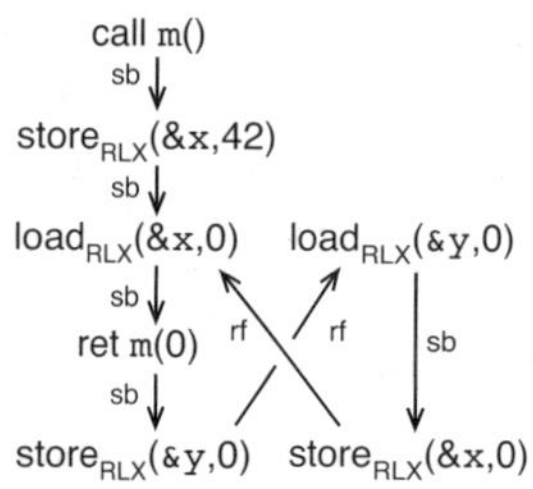

The execution of $\mathcal{C}(\mathcal{L}_1)$ given on the right violates non-interference due to a satisfaction cycle: a fault in the client causes the library to misbehave by returning 0 instead of 42, and the effect of this misbehaviour is what causes the client fault in the first place! Since the abstract library $\mathcal{L}_2$ is completely resilient to client interference, its method will always return 42, and thus, the satisfaction cycle will not appear and the client will not access the variable x. Note that this counterexample is not specific to our notion of library abstraction: *any* such notion for C11 considering $\mathcal{L}_2$ to be a specification for $\mathcal{L}_1$ cannot allow checking non-interference using $\mathcal{L}_2$.

For expository reasons, we have given a very simple counterexample. This program would be easy to detect and eliminate, e.g., using a simple type system: one *syntactic* path in the client is guaranteed to result in the forbidden access to the library's internal state. However, the same kind of behaviour can occur with dynamically-computed addresses: the client stepping out of bounds of an array overwrites the library state, causing it to misbehave, which in turn causes the original client misbehaviour. For this kind of example, proving non-interference becomes non-trivial.

It is unclear to us whether satisfaction cycles are observable in practice. They are disallowed by even the weakest C11 target architectures, such as Power and ARM [21], because these architectures respect read-to-write dependencies created by control-flow. It is also clear that the C11 language designers would like to forbid satisfaction cycles: the C++11 standard [12, Section 29.3, Paragraph 11] states that, although (SCL) from §2 is permitted, "implementations should not allow such behaviour". This apparent contradiction is because certain compiler optimisations, such as common subexpression elimination and hoisting from loops, can potentially create satisfaction cycles (see [16] for discussion). Since avoiding them would require compilers to perform additional analysis and/or limit optimisations, the standard does not disallow satisfaction cycles outright. Our results provide an extra argument that allowing satisfaction cycles is undesirable.

4. C11: Language and Thread-Local Semantics

To define the C11 model, we use a lightly modified version of its formalisation proposed by Batty et al. [2]. In the interests of simplicity, we consider a simple core language, instead of the full C/C++, and omit some of the features of the memory model. We do not handle two categories of features: those that are orthogonal to abstraction, and more esoteric features that would complicate our results. In the first category we have dynamic memory allocation, dynamic thread creation, blocked CASes and non-atomic initialisation of atomic locations (we also do not present the treatment of locks here, although we handle a bounded number of them in our formal development; see §A). In the second category we have memory fences and release-consume atomics, discussed in §9.

The semantics of a C11 program is given by a set of executions, generated in two stages. The first stage, described in this section, generates a set of *action structures* using a sequential thread-local semantics which takes into account only the structure of every thread's statements, not the semantics of memory operations. In particular, the values of reads are chosen arbitrarily, without regard for writes that have taken place. The second stage, described in §5, filters out the action structures that are inconsistent with the C11 memory model. It does this by constructing additional relations and checking the resulting executions against the axioms of the model.

Programming language. We assume that the memory consists of locations from Loc containing values in Val. We assume a function $\mathsf{sort} : \mathsf{Loc} \rightarrow \{\mathsf{ATOM}, \mathsf{NA}\}$, showing whether memory accesses to a given location must be atomic (ATOM) or non-atomic (NA); see §2. The program syntax is as follows:

$$\begin{aligned} C &::= \mathsf{skip} \mid c \mid m \mid C;C \mid \mathsf{if}(x)\ \{C\}\ \mathsf{else}\ \{C\} \mid \\ &\qquad \mathsf{while}(x)\ \{C\} \mid \mathsf{atom\_sec}\ \{c\} \\ \mathcal{L} &::= \{m = C_m \mid m \in M\} \\ \mathcal{C}(\mathcal{L}) &::= \mathsf{let}\ \mathcal{L}\ \mathsf{in}\ C_1 \parallel \ldots \parallel C_n \end{aligned}$$

A program consists of a ***library*** $\mathcal{L}$ implementing methods $m \in \mathsf{Method}$ and its ***client*** $\mathcal{C}$, given by a parallel composition of threads $C_1, \ldots, C_n$. The commands include skip, an arbitrary set of base commands $c \in \mathsf{BComm}$ (e.g., atomic and non-atomic loads and stores, and CASes), method calls $m \in \mathsf{Method}$, sequential composition, branching on the value of a location $x \in \mathsf{Loc}$ and loops. Our language also includes atomic sections, ensuring that a base command executes atomically. Atomic sections are not part of C/C++, but are used here to express library specifications. We assume that every method called by the client is defined in the library, and we disallow nested method calls.

We assume that every method accepts a single parameter and returns a single value. Parameters and return values are passed by every thread via distinguished locations in memory, denoted $\mathsf{param}_t, \mathsf{retval}_t \in \mathsf{Loc}$ for $t = 1..n$, such that $\mathsf{sort}(\mathsf{param}_t) = \mathsf{sort}(\mathsf{retval}_t) = \mathsf{NA}$. The rest of memory locations are partitioned into those owned by the client (CLoc) and the library (LLoc):

$$\mathsf{Loc} = \mathsf{CLoc} \uplus \mathsf{LLoc} \uplus \{\mathsf{param}_t, \mathsf{retval}_t \mid t = 1..n\}.$$

The property of non-interference introduced in §3 then requires that a library or a client access only the memory locations belonging to them (except the ones used for passing parameters and return values). We provide pointers on how we can relax the requirement of static address space partitioning in §9.

Actions. Executions are composed of ***actions***, defined as follows:

$$\begin{aligned} \lambda, \mu \in \mathsf{MemOrd} &::= \mathsf{NA} \mid \mathsf{SC} \mid \mathsf{ACQ} \mid \mathsf{REL} \mid \mathsf{RLX} \\ \varphi \in \mathsf{Effect} &::= \mathsf{store}_\lambda(x, a) \mid \mathsf{load}_\lambda(x, a) \\ &\quad\mid \mathsf{rmw}_{\lambda,\mu}(x, a, b) \mid \mathsf{call}\ m(a) \mid \mathsf{ret}\ m(a) \\ u, v, w, q, r \in \mathsf{Act} &::= (e, g, t, \varphi) \end{aligned}$$

Here $e \in \mathsf{AId}$ is a unique ***action identifier***, and λ, μ are memory orders (§2) of memory accesses. Every instance of an atomic section occurring in an execution has a unique identifier $g \in \mathsf{SectId}$. Atomic sections only have force when multiple actions have the same section identifier, so actions outside any section are simply assigned a unique identifier each. The domains of the rest of the variables are as follows: $t \in \{0, \dots, n\}$, $x \in \mathsf{Loc}$, $a, b \in \mathsf{Val}$. We allow actions by a dummy thread 0 to denote memory initialisation. We only consider actions whose memory orders respect location sorts given by sort, and we do not allow rmw actions of sort NA.

Loading or storing a value a at a location x generates the obvious action. A read-modify-write action $(e, g, t, \mathsf{rmw}_{\lambda,\mu}(x, a, b))$ arises from a successful compare-and-swap command. It corresponds to reading the value a from the location x and atomically overwriting it with the value b; λ and μ give the memory orders of the read and the write, respectively, and have to be different from NA. The value a in $(e, g, t, \mathsf{call}\ m(a))$ or $(e, g, t, \mathsf{ret}\ m(a))$ records the parameter param_t or the return value retval_t passed between the library method and its client. We refer to call and return actions as ***interface actions***.

For an action u we write $\mathsf{sec}(u)$ for its atomic section identifier, and we denote the set of all countable sets of actions by $\mathcal{P}(\mathsf{Act})$. We omit e, g and λ annotations from actions when they are irrelevant. We also write _ for an expression whose value is irrelevant. We use $(t, \mathsf{read}_\lambda(x, a))$ to mean any of the following:

$$\begin{gathered} (t, \mathsf{load}_\lambda(x, a)); \quad (t, \mathsf{rmw}_{\lambda,\_}(x, a, \_)); \\ (t, \mathsf{call}\ \_(a)),\ \text{if } x = \mathsf{param}_t \text{ and } \lambda = \mathsf{NA}; \\ (t, \mathsf{ret}\ \_(a)),\ \text{if } x = \mathsf{retval}_t \text{ and } \lambda = \mathsf{NA}. \end{gathered}$$

We use $(t, \mathsf{write}_\lambda(x, a))$ to mean $(t, \mathsf{store}_\lambda(x, a))$ or $(t, \mathsf{rmw}_{\_,\lambda}(x, \_, a))$. We call the two classes of actions ***read actions*** and ***write actions***, respectively.

Thread-local semantics. The thread-local semantics generates a set of ***action structures***—triples $(A, \mathsf{sb}, \mathsf{ib})$, where $A \in \mathcal{P}(\mathsf{Act})$, and $\mathsf{sb}, \mathsf{ib} \subseteq A \times A$ are the sequenced-before and initialised-before relations introduced in §2. We assume that sb is transitive and irreflexive and relates actions by the same thread; ib relates initialisation actions with thread identifier 0 to the others. We do not require sb to be a total order: in C/C++, the order of executing certain program constructs is unspecified.

For a base command $c \in \mathsf{BComm}$, we assume a set $\langle c \rangle_t \in \mathcal{P}(\mathcal{P}(A) \times \mathcal{P}(A \times A))$ of all pairs of action sets and sb relations that c produces when executed by a thread t (the ib relations are missing, as they are relevant only for a whole program). Note that base commands may include conditionals and loops, and thus can give rise to an arbitrary number of actions; we give a separate explicit semantics to conditionals and loops only because they are used in the most general client in §6.1. Definitions of $\langle c \rangle_t$ for sample base commands c are given in Figure 2. Note that, in the thread-local semantics, a read from memory, such as $\mathsf{load}_\mu(y)$ in the figure, yields an arbitrary value. A CAS command generates an rmw action, if successful, and a load, otherwise.

We define an ***initial state*** of a program $\mathcal{C}(\mathcal{L})$ by a function

$$I \in (\mathsf{LLoc} \uplus \mathsf{CLoc}) \rightharpoonup_{fin} (\mathsf{Val} \times \mathsf{MemOrd}),$$

giving the initial values of memory locations, together with the memory orders of initial writes to them. We define the set of action structures $\langle\!\langle \mathcal{C}(\mathcal{L}) \rangle\!\rangle I$ of a program $\mathcal{C}(\mathcal{L})$ in Figure 3. Note that this set of action structures corresponds to complete runs of $\mathcal{C}(\mathcal{L})$. The clause for atom_sec $\{c\}$ assigns the same atomic section identifier to all actions generated by c. The clause for a call to a method m brackets structures generated by its implementation C_m with call and return actions. We have omitted the clause for loops [1, §B]. For simplicity, we assume that the variable in the condition of a branch is always non-atomic.

Assumptions. We make several straightforward assumptions about the structures in $\langle c \rangle_t$ for $c \in \mathsf{BComm}$:

- Structures in $\langle c \rangle_t$ are finite and contain only load, store and read-modify-write actions by t with unique action identifiers.
- For any $(A, \mathsf{sb}) \in \langle c \rangle_t$, sb is transitive and irreflexive.
- Structures in $\langle c \rangle_t$ are insensitive to the choice of action and atomic section identifiers: applying any bijection to such identifiers from a structure in $\langle c \rangle_t$ produces another structure in $\langle c \rangle_t$.
- Atomic sections in every $(A, \mathsf{sb}) \in \langle c \rangle_t$ are contiguous in sb:

$$\forall u, v, q.\ \mathsf{sec}(u) = \mathsf{sec}(v) \wedge u \xrightarrow{\mathsf{sb}} q \xrightarrow{\mathsf{sb}} v \implies \mathsf{sec}(q) = \mathsf{sec}(u).$$

So as not to obfuscate presentation, we only consider programs $\mathcal{C}(\mathcal{L})$ that use param_t and retval_t correctly. We assume that in any action structure of a program, only library actions by t read param_t and write to retval_t, and only client actions by t read retval_t and write to param_t. We also require that param_t and retval_t be initialised before an access: in any structure $(A, \mathsf{sb}, \mathsf{ib})$ of $\mathcal{C}(\mathcal{L})$,

$$\begin{gathered} (\forall u = (t, \mathsf{call}\ \_) \in A.\ \exists w = (t, \mathsf{write}(\mathsf{param}_t, \_)).\ w \xrightarrow{\mathsf{sb}} u) \wedge \\ (\forall u = (t, \mathsf{ret}\ \_) \in A.\ \exists w = (t, \mathsf{write}(\mathsf{retval}_t, \_)).\ w \xrightarrow{\mathsf{sb}} u). \end{gathered}$$

Additional assumptions without relaxed atomics. For our result without relaxed atomics (§6.2), we currently require the following additional assumptions:

- The structure set $\langle c \rangle_t$ accounts for c fetching any values from the memory locations it reads (see [1, §B] for formalisation).
- Any structure of a base command c inside an atomic section accesses at most one atomic location. This is sufficient for our purposes, since a library specification usually accesses a single such location containing the abstract state of the library.
- We modify the standard C11 model by requiring that a program's semantics include structures corresponding to execution prefixes. In the standard C11 model, all executions are complete (although possibly infinite). We define $\langle C_i \rangle_t^p$ for a thread C_i by

$$\begin{aligned} \langle C_i \rangle_t^p = \{(A_p, \mathsf{sb}_p) \mid \exists (A, \mathsf{sb}) \in \langle C_i \rangle_t. \\ A_p \subseteq A \wedge \forall u \in A, v \in A_p.\ u \xrightarrow{\mathsf{sb}} v \implies u \in A_p\}. \end{aligned}$$

  This is necessary due to the interaction between our prototype atomic section semantics and the C11 model. It weakens the notion of atomicity: atomic sections at the end of a prefix may be partially executed, and therefore more weakly ordered than their completed counterparts. Eliminating it will require a deeper understanding of the relationship between atomicity and the notion of incomplete program runs. See §6.3 for its use in the proof.

5. C11: Axiomatic Memory Model

The axiomatic portion of the C11 model takes a set of action structures of the program, generated by the thread-local semantics in §4, and filters out those which are inconsistent with the memory model. To formulate it, we enrich action structures with extra relations.

Executions. The semantics of a program consists of a set of ***executions***, $X = (A, \mathsf{sb}, \mathsf{ib}, \mathsf{rf}, \mathsf{sc}, \mathsf{mo}, \mathsf{sw}, \mathsf{hb})$, where $A \in \mathcal{P}(\mathsf{Act})$ and the rest are relations on A:

- sb, ib, rf and hb introduced in §4; rf is such that its reverse is a partial function from read to write actions on the same location and with the same value.
- ***sequentially consistent order*** (sc), ordering SC reads from and writes to the same location. The projection of sc to each atomic location is a transitive, irreflexive total order, while writes to distinct locations are unrelated[3].
- ***modification order*** (mo), ordering writes (but not reads!) to the same atomic (i.e., of the sort ATOM) location. The projection of mo to each atomic location is a transitive, irreflexive total order.
- ***synchronises-with*** (sw), defining synchronisation.

We write $\mathsf{r}(X)$ for the component r of the execution X.

We can now define the denotation $[\![\mathcal{C}(\mathcal{L})]\!]$ of a program and the notion of safety and non-interference introduced informally in §3. An execution X is ***valid***, if it satisfies the validity axioms shown in Figure 4; it is ***safe***, if it satisfies the safety axioms in Figure 5, and it is ***non-interfering*** if it satisfies the NONINTERF axiom from Figure 5. We explain the axioms shown in the rest of this section. Intuitively, validity axioms correspond to properties that are enforced by the runtime, while safety axioms correspond to properties that the programmer must ensure to avoid faults. To simplify the following explanations, Figures 4 and 5 do not show axioms dealing with CASes and locks. To keep the presentation tractable, we have also omitted some corner cases from SWDEF and SCREADS in Figure 4. The missing axioms and cases are given in §A, and our results are established for the memory model including these (the correctness of the stack in Figure 1 actually relies on a corner case in SWDEF).

For a program $\mathcal{C}(\mathcal{L})$ and an initial state I, we let $[\![\mathcal{C}(\mathcal{L})]\!]I$ be the set of valid executions X, whether safe or not, such $(A, \mathsf{sb}(X), \mathsf{ib}(X)) \in \langle\mathcal{C}(\mathcal{L})\rangle I$. We write $[\![\mathcal{C}(\mathcal{L})]\!]\mathcal{I}$ to stand for its obvious lifting to sets $\mathcal{I}$ of initial states. A program $\mathcal{C}(\mathcal{L})$ is ***safe*** when run from I if every one of its valid executions is (and similarly for non-interference and sets of initial states). An unsafe program has undefined behaviour.

The validity axioms define sw and hb directly in terms of the other relations (SWDEF and HBDEF). The hb relation is constructed from the sb, ib and sw, and as follows from ACYCLICITY, has to be irreflexive. The $/\!\sim$ operator in the definition of hb is needed to handle atomic sections; for now the reader should ignore it. The sw relation is derived from sc and rf. The rf, sc and mo relations are only constrained by the axioms, not defined directly. We explain the validity axioms by first considering a language fragment with non-atomic memory accesses only and then gradually expanding it to include the other memory orders.

Non-atomic memory accesses. The values read by non-atomic reads are constrained by DETREAD and RFNONATOMIC. DETREAD requires every read to have an associated rf edge when the location read was previously initialised, i.e., when there is a write to it that happened before the read. Executions with reads from uninitialised locations are valid, but, as we explain below, unsafe. RFNONATOMIC requires that a read only reads from the write to the same location immediately preceding it in hb; cf. (RD). In the absence of other synchronisation, this means that a thread can read only from its own previous writes or initial values, since by HBDEF, $\mathsf{sb} \cup \mathsf{ib} \subseteq \mathsf{hb}$. Threads can establish the necessary synchronisation using atomic operations (which we explain now) or locks (which we elide here; see §A).

[3] In the original C11 model [2], sc is a total order on SC operations over all locations. The formulation here is is equivalent to the original one [1, §C], but more convenient for defining library abstraction.

SC atomics. The strong semantics of SC actions is enforced by organising all SC reads and writes over a *single* location into a total order sc, which cannot form a cycle with hb (ACYCLICITY). According to SCREADS, an SC read can only read from the closest sc-preceding write. Thus, if all memory accesses are annotated as SC in (SB) from §2, the result shown there is forbidden. Indeed, by SCREADS and ACYCLICITY, the store of 1 to y has to follow the load of 0 from y in sc, and similarly for x. This yields a cycle in $\mathsf{sb} \cup \mathsf{sc}$, contradicting ACYCLICITY. Note that the model requires the existence of sc, but does not include all of it into hb. As a consequence, one cannot use the ordering of, say, two SC reads in sc to constrain the values that can be read according to RFNONATOMIC.

By SWDEF, an rf edge between an SC write and an SC read generates an sw edge, which is then included into hb by HBDEF. Release-acquire atomics have the same effect, as we now explain.

Release-acquire atomics. By SWDEF, an ACQ read synchronises with the REL write it reads from. For example, if in (SCL) we annotated all writes with REL and all reads with ACQ, then the rf edges would be included into hb and the execution would be prohibited by ACYCLICITY.

For atomics weaker than SC, there is no total order on all operations over a given location analogous to sc; this is why (SB) is allowed. Instead, they satisfy a weaker property of ***coherence***: all writes (but not reads) to a single atomic location are organised into a total modification order mo, which has to be consistent with hb (HBVSMO). SC writes to the location are also included into mo, and in such cases the latter has to be consistent with sc (MOVSSC).

Since reads are not included into mo, we do not have an analogue of SCREADS, and thus, a read has more freedom to choose which write it reads from. The only constraints on atomic accesses weaker than SC are given by coherence axioms—COWR, CORW and CORR. For example, COWR says that a read r that happened after a write w_2 cannot read from a write w_1 earlier in mo.

Relaxed atomics. Like release-acquire atomics, relaxed atomics respect coherence, given by the mo order and the axioms COWR, CORW and CORR. However, rf edges involving them do not generate synchronisation edges sw. The only additional constraint on relaxed reads is given by RFATOMIC, which prohibits reads 'from the future', i.e., from writes later in hb; cf. (RD). This and the fact that coherence axioms enforce no constraints on actions over distinct locations allows (SCL). If all the loads and stores in (SCL) were to the same location, it would be forbidden by CORW.

Safety axioms. The safety axioms in Figure 5 define the conditions under which a program is faulty. DRF constrains pairs of actions over the same location, with at least one write. It requires that such pairs on distinct threads, one of which is a non-atomic access, are related by hb, and on the same thread, by sb (recall that in C/C++, the order of executing certain program constructs is unspecified, and thus, sb is partial). SAFEREAD prohibits reads from uninitialised locations.

The NONINTERF axiom is not part of the C11 memory model, but formalises the property of non-interference required for our results to hold (§3); it is technically convenient for us to consider it together with the other safety axioms. NONINTERF requires that the library and the client only read from and write to the locations they own, except param_t and retval_t used for communication (§4). The axiom classifies an action as performed by the library or the client depending on its position in sb with respect to calls and returns.

Atomic sections. Atomic sections are a widespread idiom for defining library specifications. In an SC memory model, we can

$$\langle \mathsf{store}_\lambda(x, \mathsf{load}_\mu(y))\rangle_t = \{(\{u,v\},\{(u,v)\}) \mid \exists a', e_1, e_2, g_1, g_2.\, e_1 \neq e_2 \wedge g_1 \neq g_2 \wedge u = (e_1, g_1, t, \mathsf{load}_\mu(y, a')) \wedge v = (e_2, g_2, t, \mathsf{store}_\lambda(x, a'))\}$$

$$\langle *y = \mathsf{CAS}_{\lambda,\mu}(x,a,b)\rangle_t = \{(\{u,v\},\{(u,v)\}) \mid \exists e_1, e_2, g_1, g_2, a'.\, e_1 \neq e_2 \wedge g_1 \neq g_2 \wedge a' \neq a \wedge (u = (e_1, g_1, t, \mathsf{rmw}_{\lambda,\mu}(x,a,b)) \wedge v = (e_2, g_2, t, \mathsf{store}_{\mathsf{NA}}(y,1))) \vee (u = (e_1, g_1, t, \mathsf{load}_\lambda(x,a')) \wedge v = (e_2, g_2, t, \mathsf{store}_{\mathsf{NA}}(y,0)))\}$$

Figure 2. Definitions of $\langle c\rangle_t$ for sample base commands. Here $x, y \in \mathsf{Loc}$ and $a, b \in \mathsf{Val}$ are constants.

$$\langle \mathsf{skip}\rangle_t = \{(\emptyset, \emptyset)\}$$

$$\langle C_1; C_2\rangle_t = \{(A_1 \uplus A_2, \mathsf{sb}_1 \cup \mathsf{sb}_2 \cup \{(u,v) \mid u \in A_1 \wedge v \in A_2\}) \mid (A_1, \mathsf{sb}_1) \in \langle C_1\rangle_t \wedge (A_2, \mathsf{sb}_2) \in \langle C_2\rangle_t\}$$

$$\langle \mathsf{if}(x)\ \{C_1\}\ \mathsf{else}\ \{C_2\}\rangle_t = \{(\{u\} \uplus A, \mathsf{sb} \cup \{(u,v) \mid v \in A\}) \mid \exists a.\, (A, \mathsf{sb}) \in \langle C_1\rangle_t \wedge u = (\_, \_, t, \mathsf{load}_{\mathsf{NA}}(x,a)) \wedge a \neq 0\} \cup \{(\{u\} \uplus A, \mathsf{sb} \cup \{(u,v) \mid v \in A\}) \mid (A, \mathsf{sb}) \in \langle C_2\rangle_t \wedge u = (\_, \_, t, \mathsf{load}_{\mathsf{NA}}(x,0))\}$$

$$\langle \mathsf{atom\_sec}\ \{C\}\rangle_t = \{(\{(e,g,t,\varphi) \mid (e,\_,t,\varphi) \in A\}, \{((e_1,g,t,\varphi_1),(e_2,g,t,\varphi_2)) \mid ((e_1,\_,t,\varphi_1),(e_2,\_,t,\varphi_2)) \in \mathsf{sb}\}) \mid (A, \mathsf{sb}) \in \langle C\rangle_t \wedge g \in \mathsf{SectId}\}$$

$$\langle m\rangle_t = \{(A \uplus \{u\} \uplus \{v\}, \mathsf{sb} \cup \{(u,v)\} \cup \{(u,q),(q,v) \mid q \in A\}) \mid (A, \mathsf{sb}) \in \langle C_m\rangle_t \wedge u = (\_,\_,t,\mathsf{call}\ m(\_)) \wedge v = (\_,\_,t,\mathsf{ret}\ m(\_))\}$$

$$\langle \mathsf{let}\ \{m = C_m \mid m \in M\}\ \mathsf{in}\ C_1 \parallel \ldots \parallel C_n\rangle I = \{(A_0 \uplus (\biguplus_{t=1}^n A_t), \bigcup_{t=1}^n \mathsf{sb}_t, (A_0 \times (\biguplus_{t=1}^n A_t))) \mid (\forall t = 1..n.\, (A_t, \mathsf{sb}_t) \in \langle C_t\rangle_t) \wedge (\forall t = 1..n.\, \forall u.\, \exists \text{ finitely many } v.\, (v,u) \in \mathsf{sb}_t) \wedge (A_0 = \biguplus\{(e,g,0,\mathsf{store}_\lambda(x,a)) \mid I(x) = (a,\lambda) \wedge e \in \mathsf{AId} \wedge g \in \mathsf{SectId}\})\}$$

Figure 3. Thread-local semantics. $A \uplus B$ is the union of the sets of actions A and B with disjoint sets of action and atomic section identifiers.

HBDEF. $\mathsf{hb} = ((\mathsf{sb} \cup \mathsf{ib} \cup \mathsf{sw})/{\sim})^+$, where
$R/{\sim} = R \cup \{(u,v) \mid \mathsf{sec}(u) \neq \mathsf{sec}(v) \wedge \exists u', v'.\, \mathsf{sec}(u) = \mathsf{sec}(u') \wedge \mathsf{sec}(v) = \mathsf{sec}(v') \wedge u' \xrightarrow{R} v'\}$

SWDEF$^{\approx}$. $\forall w, r.\, w \xrightarrow{\mathsf{sw}} r \iff \begin{pmatrix} \exists t_1, t_2, \lambda, \mu, x.\, t_1 \neq t_2 \wedge \lambda \in \{\mathsf{SC}, \mathsf{REL}\} \wedge \mu \in \{\mathsf{SC}, \mathsf{ACQ}\} \\ \wedge\, w = (t_1, \mathsf{write}_\lambda(x,\_)) \wedge r = (t_2, \mathsf{read}_\mu(x,\_)) \wedge w \xrightarrow{\mathsf{rf}} r \end{pmatrix}$

ACYCLICITY. $\mathsf{hb} \cup \mathsf{sc}$ is acyclic

DETREAD. $\forall r.\, (\exists x, w'.\, w' \xrightarrow{\mathsf{hb}} r \wedge w' = (\_, \mathsf{write}(x,\_)) \wedge r = (\_, \mathsf{read}(x,\_))) \iff (\exists w.\, w \xrightarrow{\mathsf{rf}} r)$

RFATOMIC.

$\neg\exists r, w.$ 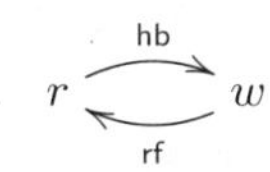

RFNONATOMIC. $\forall w, r, x.\, w \xrightarrow{\mathsf{rf}} r \wedge w = (\_, \mathsf{write}(x,\_)) \wedge r = (\_, \mathsf{read}(x,\_)) \wedge \mathsf{sort}(x) = \mathsf{NA}$
$\implies w \xrightarrow{\mathsf{hb}} r \wedge \neg\exists w'.\, w' = (\_, \mathsf{write}(x,\_)) \wedge w \xrightarrow{\mathsf{hb}} w' \xrightarrow{\mathsf{hb}} r$

SCREADS$^{\approx}$. $\forall w, r.\, w \xrightarrow{\mathsf{rf}} r \wedge r = (\_, \mathsf{read}_{\mathsf{SC}}(x,\_)) \wedge w = (\_, \mathsf{write}_{\mathsf{SC}}(x,\_)) \implies w \xrightarrow{\mathsf{sc}} r \wedge \neg\exists w'.\, w' = (\_, \mathsf{write}(x,\_)) \wedge w \xrightarrow{\mathsf{sc}} w' \xrightarrow{\mathsf{sc}} r$

HBVSMO. $\neg\exists w_1, w_2.$
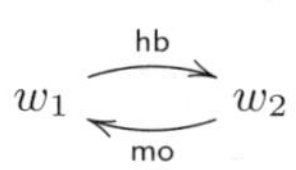

MOVSSC. $\neg\exists w_1, w_2.$
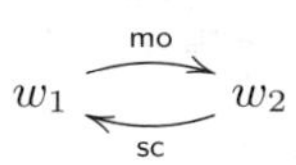

COWR. $\neg\exists w_1, w_2.$
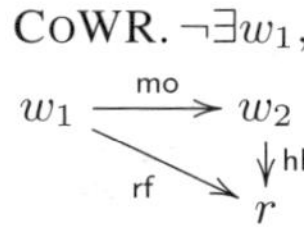

CORW. $\neg\exists r, w_1, w_2.$
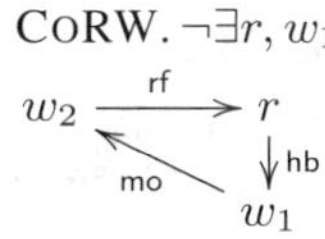

CORR. $\neg\exists r_1, r_2, w_1, w_2.$
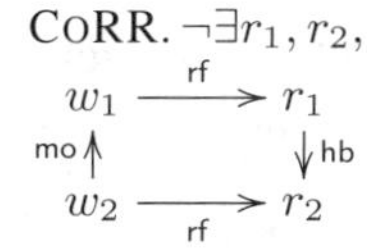

ASMO. $\forall u, v.\, u \xrightarrow{\mathsf{mo}} v \wedge \mathsf{sec}(u) = \mathsf{sec}(v) \implies \neg\exists q.\, u \xrightarrow{\mathsf{mo}} q \xrightarrow{\mathsf{mo}} v \wedge \mathsf{sec}(u) \neq \mathsf{sec}(q)$

ASSC. $\forall u, v.\, u \xrightarrow{\mathsf{sc}} v \wedge \mathsf{sec}(u) = \mathsf{sec}(v) \implies \neg\exists q.\, u \xrightarrow{\mathsf{sc}} q \xrightarrow{\mathsf{sc}} v \wedge \mathsf{sec}(u) \neq \mathsf{sec}(q)$

Figure 4. Selected validity axioms of the C11 memory model. Axioms simplified for the purposes of presentation are marked by $\approx$.

DRF. $\forall u, v, x, t_1, t_2.\, (u, v \in A \wedge u \neq v \wedge u = (t_1, \_(x,\_)) \wedge v = (t_2, \_(x,\_)) \wedge (u = (t_1, \mathsf{write}(x,\_)) \vee v = (t_2, \mathsf{write}(x,\_)))) \implies$
$((t_1 \neq t_2 \implies (u \xrightarrow{\mathsf{hb}} v \vee v \xrightarrow{\mathsf{hb}} u \vee \mathsf{sort}(x) = \mathsf{ATOM})) \wedge (t_1 = t_2 \implies (u \xrightarrow{\mathsf{sb}} v \vee v \xrightarrow{\mathsf{sb}} u)))$

SAFEREAD. $\forall r.\, r \in A \wedge r = (\_, \mathsf{read}(\_,\_)) \implies \exists w.\, w \xrightarrow{\mathsf{rf}} r$

NONINTERF. $\forall u, x, t.\, (u \in A \wedge t \neq 0 \wedge u = (t, \_(x,\_)) \wedge x \notin \{\mathsf{param}_t, \mathsf{retval}_t \mid t = 1..n\}) \implies$
$((\exists v.\, v = (\_, \mathsf{call}\ \_) \wedge v \xrightarrow{\mathsf{sb}} u \wedge \neg\exists q.\, q = (\_, \mathsf{ret}\ \_) \wedge v \xrightarrow{\mathsf{sb}} q \xrightarrow{\mathsf{sb}} u) \iff (x \in \mathsf{LLoc}))$

Figure 5. Selected safety axioms of the C11 memory model

DETREAD$_l$. $\forall r, t.\, ((\exists x.\, r = (\_, \mathsf{read}(x,\_)) \wedge x \neq \mathsf{param}_t \wedge \exists w.\, w \xrightarrow{\mathsf{hb}} r \wedge w = (\_, \mathsf{write}(x,\_))) \iff \exists w'.\, w' \xrightarrow{\mathsf{rf}} r) \wedge$
$(\forall a, b.\, r = (t, \mathsf{read}(\mathsf{param}_t, a)) \in A \wedge u = (\_, \mathsf{call}\ \_(b)) \wedge u \xrightarrow{\mathsf{sb}} r \wedge (\neg\exists v.\, v = (\_, \mathsf{ret}\ \_) \wedge u \xrightarrow{\mathsf{sb}} v \xrightarrow{\mathsf{sb}} r) \implies a = b)$

SAFEREAD$_l$. $\forall r, x, t.\, r \in A \wedge r = (t, \mathsf{read}(x,\_)) \wedge x \neq \mathsf{param}_t \implies \exists w.\, w \xrightarrow{\mathsf{rf}} r$

DETREAD$_c$. $\forall r, t.\, ((\exists x.\, r = (\_, \mathsf{read}(x,\_)) \wedge x \neq \mathsf{retval}_t \wedge \exists w.\, w \xrightarrow{\mathsf{hb}} r \wedge w = (\_, \mathsf{write}(x,\_))) \iff \exists w'.\, w' \xrightarrow{\mathsf{rf}} r) \wedge$
$(\forall a, b.\, r = (t, \mathsf{read}(\mathsf{retval}_t, a)) \wedge u = (\_, \mathsf{ret}\ \_(b)) \wedge u \xrightarrow{\mathsf{sb}} r \wedge (\neg\exists v.\, v = (\_, \mathsf{call}\ \_) \wedge u \xrightarrow{\mathsf{sb}} v \xrightarrow{\mathsf{sb}} r) \implies a = b)$

SAFEREAD$_c$. $\forall r, x, t.\, (r \in A \wedge r = (t, \mathsf{read}(x,\_)) \wedge x \neq \mathsf{retval}_t \implies \exists w.\, w \xrightarrow{\mathsf{rf}} r) \wedge$
$(r \in A \wedge r = (t, \mathsf{read}(\mathsf{retval}_t,\_)) \wedge r \neq (\_, \mathsf{ret}\ \_) \implies \exists u.\, u \xrightarrow{\mathsf{hb}} r \wedge u = (t, \mathsf{ret}\ \_))$

Figure 6. Axioms for library (§6.1) and client (§6.3) executions

define their semantics by simply requiring that no other events are interleaved with actions inside an atomic section. Unfortunately, the relaxed memory model of C11 does not admit such a simple definition. The straightforward solution of imposing a total order on all instances of atomic sections would rule out relaxed specifications that we would like to give, such as the Treiber specification from §2. Hence, we have extended C11 with a prototype notion of atomic sections suitable for its relaxed-memory setting (inspired by the semantics of transactions in [6]). This notion represents only the first step towards a natural specification language for relaxed C11, which is an interesting problem in itself.

The axioms defining the semantics of atomic sections are HBDEF, ASMO and ASSC in Figure 4 and ATOMAS in Figure 7 (deferred to §A for brevity). They capture the expected properties of atomicity. Thus, in HBDEF, we factor $\mathsf{sb} \cup \mathsf{ib} \cup \mathsf{sw}$ over atomic sections using $/\!\sim$: e.g., if an action u happens-before another action v, then u also happens-before any other action from the same atomic section as v. ASMO and ASSC require that actions from the same atomic section be contiguous in mo and sc. ATOMAS constrains relaxed actions, which do not generate hb edges. ASMO, ASSC and ATOMAS are trivially satisfied when every action has a unique atomic section identifier. Additionally, in this case HBDEF simplifies to $\mathsf{hb} = (\mathsf{sb} \cup \mathsf{ib} \cup \mathsf{sw})^+$, which is how it is defined in standard C11 [2]. Thus, if every action executes in a separate atomic section, our augmented model coincides with standard C11.

6. Library Abstraction in Detail

We first define formally the concepts used in the definition of library abstraction (Definition 2) and the Abstraction Theorem (Theorem 3) from §3 for the memory model with relaxed atomics. We then show how the Abstraction Theorem can be strengthened for a fragment of the language excluding them (§6.2) and give the proof outlines for both theorems (§6.3).

6.1 Library Abstraction in the Presence of Relaxed Atomics

History definition. We formally define the history function, which selects a history in the sense of Definition 2 from a library execution. For an execution X, we let

$$\mathsf{history}(X) = (\mathsf{interf}(X), \mathsf{hbL}(X), \mathsf{scL}(X))$$

and lift history to sets of executions pointwise. Here $\mathsf{interf}(X)$ is the projection of $A(X)$ to interface (call and return) actions. The hbL selector computes the guarantee part of the history. We let $\mathsf{hbL}(X)$ be the projection of $\mathsf{hb}(X)$ to pairs of actions of the form $((\_, \mathsf{call}\ \_), (\_, \mathsf{ret}\ \_))$ and pairs of calls and returns (in any order) by the same thread. We record only edges of the above form, since it can be shown that any happens-before edge between interface actions in a library execution under its most general client can be obtained as a transitive closure of such edges. Intuitively, call-to-return edges are the ones that represent the synchronisation between library method invocations, as illustrated by (MP) in §2.

The scL selector computes the deny part of the history. We let $\mathsf{scL}(X)$ be the projection of $((\mathsf{hb}(X) \cup \mathsf{sc}(X))^+)^{-1}$ to pairs of actions of the form $((\_, \mathsf{ret}\ \_), (\_, \mathsf{call}\ \_))$. This component is needed, since the ACYCLICITY axiom (Figure 4) mandates that sc cannot form a cycle with hb, but does not include sc into hb. Thus, when a library relates a call action u to a return action v with hb and sc, the client cannot relate v to u with the same relations, as this would invalidate ACYCLICITY. We add only return-to-call edges into $\mathsf{scL}(X)$, as these are the edges that represent synchronisation inside the client (similarly to how call-to-return edges represent synchronisation inside the library in $\mathsf{hbL}(X)$). One might think that the deny component of the history should have included edges recording potential violations of other similar axioms, e.g., HBVSMO, as suggested by (DN). However, in the case of the model with relaxed atomics, we are forced to quantify over client happens-before edges R in Definition 2. As it happens, this makes it unnecessary to consider axioms other than ACYCLICITY (see the proof of the Theorem 3 in [1, §C]). These axioms, however, have to be taken into account in the case without relaxed atomics (§6.2).

Library-local semantics. We define the most general client as follows. Take $n \geq 1$ and let $\{m_1, \ldots, m_l\}$ be the methods implemented by a library $\mathcal{L}$. We let

$$\mathsf{MGC}_n(\mathcal{L}) = (\mathsf{let}\ \mathcal{L}\ \mathsf{in}\ C_1^{\mathsf{mgc}} \parallel \ldots \parallel C_n^{\mathsf{mgc}}),$$

where C_t^{mgc} is

$$\mathsf{while}(\mathsf{nondet}())\ \{\ \mathsf{if}(\mathsf{nondet}())\ \{m_1\}\ \mathsf{else\ if}(\mathsf{nondet}())\ \{m_2\}\ \ldots\ \mathsf{else}\ \{m_l\}\ \}$$

Here we use the obvious generalisation of loops and conditionals to branch expressions that yield a non-deterministic value. To allow parameters of methods to be chosen arbitrarily, we replace the axioms DETREAD from Figure 4 and SAFEREAD from Figure 5 by DETREAD$_l$ and SAFEREAD$_l$ from Figure 6, which mandate that reads from param_t lack associated rf edges, while nonetheless yielding identical values within a single method call. As part of the proof of the Theorem 3 (§6.3), we show that this client is indeed most general in a certain formal sense (with the caveat concerning the need to extend its executions with client happens-before edges mentioned in §3).

We note that some libraries require their clients to pass only certain combinations of parameters or issue only certain sequences of method calls. Such contracts could be accommodated in our framework by restricting the most general client appropriately; we do not handle them here so as not to complicate the presentation.

For an initial library state $I \in \mathsf{LLoc} \rightharpoonup_{fin} \mathsf{Val} \times \mathsf{MemOrd}$, a ***library execution*** of $\mathcal{L}$ from I is an execution from $[\![\mathsf{MGC}_n(\mathcal{L})]\!]I$ for some $n \geq 1$. A library execution is ***valid*** if it satisfies the validity axioms with DETREAD$_l$ instead of DETREAD; it is ***safe*** if it satisfies the safety axioms with SAFEREAD$_l$ instead of SAFEREAD. We let $[\![\mathcal{L}]\!]I$ be the set of all valid library executions of $\mathcal{L}$ from I and lift $[\![\mathcal{L}]\!]$ to sets of initial states pointwise. We say that a library $\mathcal{L}$ is safe when run from I if so is every execution in $[\![\mathcal{L}]\!]I$; for a set $\mathcal{I}$ of initial states, $(\mathcal{L}, \mathcal{I})$ is safe if $\mathcal{L}$ is safe when run from any $I \in \mathcal{I}$. The notion of a ***non-interfering*** library is defined similarly.

Extended executions. In Definition 2, we use library executions whose happens-before relation is extended with extra edges recording constraints enforced by the client. Consider an execution X and a relation R over interface actions from $A(X)$. The ***extension*** of X with R is an execution that has the same components as X, except the happens-before relation is replaced by $(\mathsf{hb}(X) \cup R)^+$. An extension of a library execution with R is ***admissible*** when it satisfies the corresponding validity axioms, but with HBDEF replaced by

EXTHBDEF. $\mathsf{hb} = ((\mathsf{sb} \cup \mathsf{ib} \cup \mathsf{sw} \cup R)/\!\sim)^+$.

For an initial library state I, we let $[\![\mathcal{L}, R]\!]I$ be the set of admissible executions of $\mathcal{L}$ from I extended with R. This completes the definition of components used in Definition 2.

Execution projections. Finally, we define the client function used in Theorem 3. Consider a valid execution X of $\mathcal{C}(\mathcal{L})$. An action $u \in A$ is a ***library action***, if it is a call or return action, an action of the form $(0, \mathsf{write}(x, \_))$ for $x \in \mathsf{LLoc}$, or if

$$\exists v. v = (\_, \mathsf{call}\ \_) \wedge v \xrightarrow{\mathsf{sb}(X)} u \wedge \neg\exists q. q = (\_, \mathsf{ret}\ \_) \wedge v \xrightarrow{\mathsf{sb}(X)} q \xrightarrow{\mathsf{sb}(X)} u.$$

An action $u \in A$ is a ***client action***, if it is a call or return action, it is an action of the form $(0, \mathsf{write}(x, \_))$ for $x \in \mathsf{CLoc}$, or the negation of the above property holds. We define the execution $\mathsf{lib}(X)$ by restricting the action set to library actions and projecting all the relations in X accordingly. We use a similar projection $\mathsf{client}(X)$ to client actions and lift client and lib to sets of executions pointwise.

Properties of library abstraction. For the fragment of the language with an SC semantics—i.e., allowing only non-atomic memory accesses and SC atomics—Definition 2 implies classical linearizability. This follows from Theorem 3 and the fact that classical linearizability is equivalent to observational abstraction on the SC memory model [7]. However, the converse is not true: since our notion of library abstraction validates Theorem 3 for clients in the full C11, it distinguishes between SC libraries that classical linearizability would consider equivalent (see [1, §D]).

Using Theorem 3, we can obtain the expected property that, like the classical notion of linearizability, our notion of library abstraction is compositional (with a caveat that non-interference among libraries has to be checked globally). Formally, consider libraries $\mathcal{L}_1, \dots, \mathcal{L}_k$ with disjoint sets of declared methods and assume the splitting of the library address space into regions belonging to each library: $\mathsf{LLoc} = \mathsf{LLoc}_1 \uplus \dots \uplus \mathsf{LLoc}_k$. Consider sets of initial states $\mathcal{I}_1, \dots, \mathcal{I}_k$ such that $\forall j = 1..k. \forall I \in \mathcal{I}_j. \mathsf{dom}(I) \subseteq \mathsf{LLoc}_j$. We adjust the notion of library safety so that NONINTERF for $\mathcal{L}_j$ is checked with respect to locations in LLoc_j. Let $(\mathcal{L}'_1, \mathcal{I}'_1), \dots, (\mathcal{L}'_k, \mathcal{I}'_k)$ be corresponding library specifications. We define $\mathcal{L}$, respectively, $\mathcal{L}'$ as the library implementing all methods of $\mathcal{L}_1, \dots, \mathcal{L}_k$, respectively, $\mathcal{L}'_1, \dots, \mathcal{L}'_k$ and having the set of initial states $\mathcal{I}_1 \uplus \dots \uplus \mathcal{I}_k$, respectively, $\mathcal{I}'_1 \uplus \dots \uplus \mathcal{I}'_k$. We assume that any combination of implementations or specifications of different libraries is non-interfering. The following theorem is shown by abstracting $\mathcal{L}_j$ to $\mathcal{L}'_j$ one by one using Theorem 3.

THEOREM 4. *If* $(\mathcal{L}_j, \mathcal{I}_j) \sqsubseteq (\mathcal{L}'_j, \mathcal{I}'_j)$ *for* $j = 1..k$, *then* $\mathcal{L} \sqsubseteq \mathcal{L}'$.

6.2 Library Abstraction without Relaxed Atomics

We call an action with at least one RLX annotation ***relaxed***. In this section, we restrict ourselves to programs whose action structures do not have any relaxed actions, and we augment the C11 thread-local semantics as described in the assumptions of §4. Among other things, these changes allow us to remove the quantification over client happens-before edges R from Definition 2, at the expense of including an additional deny relation into the history.

DEFINITION 5. *An **extended history** is a quadruple* (A, G, D, D'), *where* A *is a set of interface actions, and* $G, D, D' \subseteq A \times A$.

For an execution $X = (A, \mathsf{sb}, \mathsf{ib}, \mathsf{rf}, \mathsf{sc}, \mathsf{mo}, \mathsf{sw}, \mathsf{hb})$, we let

$$\mathsf{Ehistory}(X) = (\mathsf{interf}(X), \mathsf{hbL}(X), \mathsf{scL}(X), \mathsf{denyL}(X)),$$

which we lift to sets of executions pointwise. The selectors interf, hbL and scL are defined as in §6.1.

The relation $\mathsf{denyL}(X)$ is defined similarly to scL, but whereas the latter records client hb and sc edges that can violate ACYCLICITY, the former includes the client hb edges that can violate the axioms HBVSMO, COWR and SCREADS (Figure 4). We do not have to consider other similar axioms, such as RFATOMIC, CORW and CORR since in any valid execution X without relaxed actions, we have $\mathsf{rf}(X) \subseteq \mathsf{hb}(X)$. Due to this, the hb client edges violating, HBVSMO and CORW, COWR and CORR can be covered by the same relations. For the case of HBVSMO and COWR, $\mathsf{denyL}(X)$ includes the dashed edges of all possible instantiations of the following diagrams:

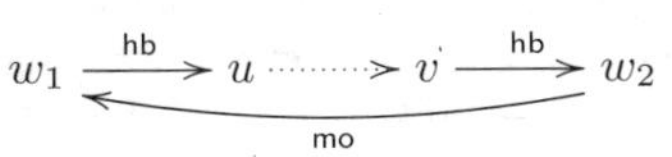

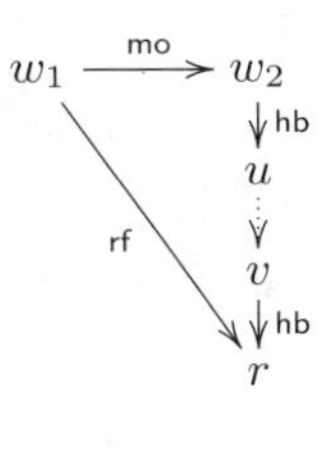

where $u = (\_, \mathsf{ret}\ \_)$ and $v = (\_, \mathsf{call}\ \_)$. This records client hb edges that violate HBVSMO or COWR (cf. (DN) in §3). The diagrams are thus constructed systematically by 'breaking' the hb edge. For the case of SCREADS, $\mathsf{denyL}(X)$ includes edges corresponding to a corner case in this axiom omitted from Figure 4. The full version of the axiom and the corresponding deny diagram are given in §A.

DEFINITION 6. *We let* $(A_1, G_1, D_1, D'_1) \preceq (A_2, G_2, D_2, D'_2)$, *if* $A_1 = A_2$, $G_2 \subseteq G_1$, $D_2 \subseteq D_1$ *and* $D'_2 \subseteq D'_1$.

For safe $(\mathcal{L}_1, \mathcal{I}_1)$ *and* $(\mathcal{L}_2, \mathcal{I}_2)$, $(\mathcal{L}_1, \mathcal{I}_1)$ ***is abstracted by*** $(\mathcal{L}_2, \mathcal{I}_2)$, *written* $(\mathcal{L}_1, \mathcal{I}_1) \preceq (\mathcal{L}_2, \mathcal{I}_2)$, *if*

$$\forall I_1 \in \mathcal{I}_1, H_1 \in \mathsf{Ehistory}([\![\mathcal{L}_1]\!] I_1).\\ \exists I_2 \in \mathcal{I}_2, H_2 \in \mathsf{Ehistory}([\![\mathcal{L}_2]\!] I_2).\ H_1 \preceq H_2.$$

Unlike in Definition 2, here an abstracted history can guarantee *fewer* happens-before edges to the client: without relaxed atomics, removing edges from happens-before can only permit more client behaviours or make the client unsafe. We note that checking the inclusion between the components of the history given by denyL, required by Definition 6, is simpler in practice than quantifying over client happens-before edges R in Definition 2.

For executions X and Y, we write $X \preceq Y$ when all their components except hb are equal, and $\mathsf{hb}(Y) \subseteq \mathsf{hb}(X)$.

THEOREM 7 (Abstraction without relaxed atomics). *Assume that* $(\mathcal{L}_1, \mathcal{I}_1)$, $(\mathcal{L}_2, \mathcal{I}_2)$ *and* $(\mathcal{C}(\mathcal{L}_2), \mathcal{I} \uplus \mathcal{I}_2)$ *are safe and* $(\mathcal{L}_1, \mathcal{I}_1) \preceq (\mathcal{L}_2, \mathcal{I}_2)$. *Then* $(\mathcal{C}(\mathcal{L}_1), \mathcal{I} \uplus \mathcal{I}_1)$ *is safe and*

$$\forall X \in \mathsf{client}([\![\mathcal{C}(\mathcal{L}_1)]\!](\mathcal{I} \uplus \mathcal{I}_1)).\\ \exists Y \in \mathsf{client}([\![\mathcal{C}(\mathcal{L}_2)]\!](\mathcal{I} \uplus \mathcal{I}_2)).\ X \preceq Y.$$

Unlike Theorem 3, this one allows the programmer to check non-interference on $\mathcal{C}(\mathcal{L}_2)$—i.e., with respect to a library specification—and to conclude that $\mathcal{C}(\mathcal{L}_1)$ is non-interfering. Since the abstract library can have a smaller guarantee than the concrete one, the happens-before of the execution $\mathcal{C}(\mathcal{L}_2)$ may also be smaller than that of the execution $\mathcal{C}(\mathcal{L}_1)$.

Like the notion of library abstraction from §6.1, the one proposed here implies classical linearizability for the SC fragment of the language (but not vice versa) and is compositional [1, §C]. However, here the latter property does not require us to check non-interference globally: a composition of several non-interfering libraries is non-interfering.

6.3 Proof Outlines

Client-local semantics. We start by defining the ***client-local semantics*** of a client $\mathcal{C} = C_1 \parallel \dots \parallel C_n$, which is a counterpart of the library-local semantics defined in §6.1. Let M be the set of methods that can be called by $\mathcal{C}$. Consider the program

$$\mathcal{C}(\cdot) = (\mathsf{let}\ \{m = \mathsf{skip} \mid m \in M\}\ \mathsf{in}\ C_1 \parallel \dots \parallel C_n),$$

where every method is implemented by a stub that returns immediately after having been called. Moreover, we allow methods to return arbitrary values by replacing the axioms DETREAD from Figure 4 and SAFEREAD from Figure 5 by DETREAD_c and SAFEREAD_c from Figure 6. We call executions of the above program ***client executions*** of $\mathcal{C}$. A client execution is ***valid***, if it satisfies the validity axioms with DETREAD_c instead of DETREAD; it is ***safe***, if it satisfies the safety axioms with SAFEREAD_c instead of SAFEREAD. For an initial client state $I \in \mathsf{CLoc} \rightharpoonup_{fin} (\mathsf{Val} \times \mathsf{MemOrd})$, let $[\![\mathcal{C}]\!] I$ be the set of all valid client executions of $\mathcal{C}$ from I; for a set $\mathcal{I}$ of initial states we define $[\![\mathcal{C}]\!] \mathcal{I}$ as expected. The notion of an extended client execution is similar to the one of an extended library execution from §6.1. For an extended execution

X we let $\mathsf{core}(X)$ be the execution obtained from X by recomputing $\mathsf{hb}(X)$ from $\mathsf{sb}(X)$, $\mathsf{ib}(X)$ and $\mathsf{sw}(X)$ according to HBDEF.

Client-side history selectors. Consider a client execution X. We define $\mathsf{hbC}(X), \mathsf{scC}(X) \subseteq \mathsf{interf}(X) \times \mathsf{interf}(X)$, which are analogous to hbL and scL from §6.1, but select the information about the client part of the execution that is relevant to the library. We let $\mathsf{hbC}(X)$ be the projection of $\mathsf{hb}(X)$ to pairs of actions of the form $((\_, \mathsf{ret}\ \_), (\_, \mathsf{call}\ \_))$ and pairs of calls and returns (in any order) by the same thread. We select edges of this form as they are the ones that record synchronisation enforced by the client. We let $\mathsf{scC}(X)$ be the projection of $((\mathsf{hb}(X) \cup \mathsf{sc}(X))^+)^{-1}$ to pairs of actions of the form $((\_, \mathsf{call}\ \_), (\_, \mathsf{ret}\ \_))$.

Proof outline for Theorem 3. Consider an execution X of $\mathcal{C}(\mathcal{L}_1)$ from the initial state $I \uplus I_1$, where $I \in \mathcal{I}$ and $I_1 \in \mathcal{I}_1$. We start by decomposing X into a client execution $\mathsf{client}(X)$ and a library execution $\mathsf{lib}(X)$ and showing that

$$\mathsf{client}(X) \in [\![\mathcal{C}, \mathsf{hbL}(\mathsf{core}(\mathsf{lib}(X)))]\!] I;$$
$$\mathsf{lib}(X) \in [\![\mathcal{L}_1, \mathsf{hbC}(\mathsf{core}(\mathsf{client}(X)))]\!] I_1.$$

The second inclusion justifies that the most general client of the library defined in §6.1 is indeed most general, as it can reproduce the behaviour of $\mathcal{L}_1$ under any client $\mathcal{C}$. This comes with the caveat that an execution of the most general client of $\mathcal{L}_1$ has to be extended with $\mathsf{hbL}(\mathsf{core}(\mathsf{lib}(X)))$ to obtain $\mathsf{lib}(X)$, as the library-local semantics does not generate happens-before edges enforced by client synchronisation (and similarly for $\mathsf{client}(X)$ in the first inclusion). The above decomposition step relies on X being non-interfering. Using the fact that $(\mathcal{L}_1, \mathcal{I}_1) \sqsubseteq (\mathcal{L}_2, \mathcal{I}_2)$, we prove that there exist $I_2 \in \mathcal{I}_2$ and $Y \in [\![\mathcal{L}_2, \mathsf{hbC}(\mathsf{core}(\mathsf{client}(X)))]\!] I_2$ such that $\mathsf{history}(\mathsf{lib}(X)) \sqsubseteq \mathsf{history}(Y)$. Here we use the quantification of client happens-before edges R in Definition 2 to handle the extension of the library execution with $\mathsf{hbC}(\mathsf{core}(\mathsf{client}(X)))$. We then compose the executions X and Y into the desired execution of $\mathcal{C}(\mathcal{L}_2)$. This step uses the fact that the deny component of $\mathsf{history}(Y)$ is smaller than that of $\mathsf{history}(\mathsf{lib}(X))$. □

Proof outline for Theorem 7. Unlike in Theorem 3, here we need to consider the case when an execution X of $\mathcal{C}(\mathcal{L}_1)$ has actions violating non-interference. In this case, we identify an "earliest" faulting action u and construct a valid execution that is a prefix of X ending just before u and is thus non-interfering. This is only possible because, without relaxed atomics, we do not have satisfaction cycles, and because the theorem is stated over an augmented thread-local semantics (§4), with prefix executions added to the semantics. We convert the resulting execution into one of $\mathcal{C}(\mathcal{L}_2)$ as in the proof of Theorem 3 and conjoin the action the action u to it. This yields an execution of $\mathcal{C}(\mathcal{L}_2)$ violating non-interference and contradicting the assumption about its safety.

In the case when X is non-interfering, the proof is similar to that of Theorem 3. Some additional work is needed to deal with the fact that Definition 6 does not have a quantification over client happens-before edges and allows the abstract guarantee to be smaller than the concrete one. □

7. Establishing Library Abstraction

In this section, we discuss the proof process for establishing abstraction between libraries in the sense of Definitions 2 and 6. To reason about programs on the C11 memory model, we use axiomatisations of the action structures generated by them, which give a simple mathematical interface to the program semantics. To prove library safety, required by Definitions 2 and 6, we consider all the execution shapes of the most general client, and check these against the C11 safety axioms. We now explain how we prove the correspondence between the executions of concrete and abstract libraries, using Definition 2 for illustration.

Effect points. Consider an execution $X_1 \in [\![\mathcal{L}_1, R]\!] I_1$. We construct an execution $X_2 \in [\![\mathcal{L}_2, R]\!] I_2$ whose history witnesses the existential in Definition 2 using an adapted version of the *linearization point* method for proving linearizability. The method constructs the abstract execution by calling a method specification at a fixed linearization point in every method invocation of the concrete execution; intuitively, it is at this point that the concrete method 'takes effect'. In our adaptation, we construct X_2 by substituting calls to library method implementations in X_1 for the corresponding calls to specifications, and choosing appropriate values for reads and different orders between actions. These values and orders are chosen based on the orders over actions we call ***effect points***, picked for each concrete method invocation in X_1. Thus, the various partial orders over the effect points in the concrete execution dictate the order of precedence for the effects of method invocations in the abstract execution. In contrast with the original linearization point method, the latter order does not have to be linear. We now explain this technique in more detail on an example.

Example: Treiber stack. We have proved the correctness of the stack in Figure 1b with respect to its specification in Figure 1a according to Definition 2 (full details are given in [1, §E]). As effect points in X_1, we pick the rmw actions modifying the stack's top pointer T, which correspond to successful CASes (this is the same choice as the that of linearization points when proving the linearizability of Treiber's stack on an SC memory model). The order $\mathsf{mo}(X_1)$ over these actions defines a total order over successful `push` and `pop` invocations. When substituting invocations of method implementations for invocations of specifications, we use $\mathsf{mo}(X_1)$ to decide $\mathsf{rf}(X_2)$ and $\mathsf{mo}(X_2)$ for the abstract location S. Namely, suppose we have two method invocations U and V in X_1, such that the rmw of U is the immediate predecessor to the rmw of V in $\mathsf{mo}(X_1)$. When substituting corresponding invocations of specification methods U' and V', we set up $\mathsf{rf}(X_2)$ and $\mathsf{mo}(X_2)$ so that the load from S in V' reads from the rmw in U', and $\mathsf{mo}(X_2)$ orders the rmw on S in U' right before rmw on it in V'. Fixing $\mathsf{rf}(X_2)$ and $\mathsf{mo}(X_2)$ in the abstract execution immediately fixes the values of reads, which finishes the construction of X_2.

Example: producer-consumer queue. We have similarly verified a non-blocking producer-consumer queue according to Definition 6 (see [1, §E]). The queue is intended for communication between a single producer thread and a single consumer thread and provides three methods: `init`, `enq` and `deq`. The implementation stores values in a finite cyclic array, while the specification stores them using the abstract data type of a sequence. To ensure that the consumer calling `deq` observes up-to-date values, it must synchronise with the producer calling `enq` using release-acquire atomics.

8. Related Work

Relaxed-memory behaviour has become widespread in real concurrent systems. As a result, some algorithm designers have begun to publish algorithms with memory-model annotations such as fences [3, 17, 18]. However, the corresponding formulations of correctness properties and their proofs are generally informal. While there has been some work on formally verifying programs on weak memory models [14, 20, 23], none has proposed a compositional reasoning method, like we do. Ours is the first approach that formulates the notion of a correct library specification and provides a method for establishing it on C11, or any similarly relaxed model.

Our work is an evolution of *linearizability* [11], a correctness criterion that has been widely adopted in the concurrent algorithms community. In the SC fragment of C11, our definition of library abstraction implies classical linearizability. History abstraction in classical linearizability is defined by linearization of the partial order over non-overlapping methods invocations, and the guarantee portion in our histories can be seen as lifting this to the C11 setting. Classical linearizability has no equivalent to our deny relation; the conflicts between relations that are captured by deny do not occur in an SC setting where all events are totally ordered.

Recent work has formalised the intuition that linearizability corresponds to observational abstraction [7] and has extended it to handle liveness [9], resource-transferring programs [10] and the x86 memory model [5]. The latter work is the closest to this paper; in particular, we borrow the decompose-compose approach in the proof of the Abstraction Theorem (§6.3) from it. However, while its objective is the same as ours—abstraction for relaxed-memory concurrent libraries—the technical challenges and the machinery developed to address them are very different. The x86 memory model can be defined by a small-step operational semantics, which has an underlying total order on abstract machine memory events [19]. Linearizability for x86 is therefore a relatively mild extension to classical linearizability, which simply represents some of these events in (linear) histories. In contrast, C11 constrains relaxed behaviour through partial ordering, controlled by an axiomatic semantics. There are no abstract machine events to linearize, which motivates our novel definition of a history as a set of partial orders and history abstraction as inclusion over them. Furthermore, x86 is a substantially stronger model than C11, with (SB) from §2 being the only significant relaxation [19]. Our approach is the first technique for specifying client-visible effects of relaxations inside libraries on weaker memory models.

9. Conclusion and Future Work

We have proposed the first sound criterion for library abstraction suitable for the C11 memory model and demonstrated its practicality on two small, but typical, relaxed libraries. Our criterion is certainly complex, but much of this complexity arises from the real-world intricacies of the C11 memory model. In turn, the complexity of the model arises from a multitude of target platforms of C and C++—two of the world's most widely-used programming languages. Despite this complexity, the criterion allows developers to establish that C11 libraries satisfy simple, reusable specifications that precisely describe the level of consistency guaranteed. This is an essential ingredient for supporting modular development of complex software on relaxed memory models.

In addition, our approach is the first compositional reasoning technique for an axiomatically defined relaxed memory model, and highlights general principles for abstraction on such models. We have good reason to believe that our techniques can be reused for other memory models, as the conditions for library abstraction fall out naturally from obligations arising when trying to prove the Abstraction Theorem according to the approach in §6.3. In particular, the histories in our approach are constructed uniformly, with deny relations obtained straightforwardly from axioms by 'breaking' hb edges (§6.2). In particular, our preliminary investigations show that these techniques can be used to define a notion of library abstraction for an axiomatic formulation of the x86 memory model [19].

Our specifications describe precisely the level of synchronisation provided by the library, although in some cases this makes them more verbose. This is motivated by the fact that libraries on C11 can offer relaxed interfaces to clients, without either giving up all synchronisation guarantees or enforcing sequential consistency. If information about the internal synchronisation used to ensure library correctness were not described in these interfaces, clients would have to duplicate it, thereby decreasing performance. On the other hand, requiring library interfaces to be SC would rule out libraries that use weaker memory orders to achieve efficiency while preserving basic correctness properties, again decreasing performance. Our prototype atomic section semantics represents a first attempt at a syntactic specification idiom for relaxed algorithms, albeit with limitations as described in §4. We leave a more comprehensive treatment of relaxed atomic sections to future work.

Our two formulations of library abstraction (Definitions 2 and 6) and the Abstraction Theorem (Theorems 3 and 7) identify the feature of the current C/C++ memory model that does not allow fully compositional reasoning about libraries. As we argued in §3, this deficiency is not specific to our definition of library abstraction, but would be inherent to *any* sensible one. We hope that these insights will inform future revisions of the C/C++ memory model.

Our development omits memory fences and release-consume atomics, which are the more advanced features of the C11 memory model. A memory fence is a synchronisation construct that affects many memory actions, rather than just one. Release-consume is a special-purpose memory order which compiles more efficiently to Power and ARM processors. We conjecture that our methods can be used to handle these features. As both of them generate more possible client-library interactions, this will require adding additional relations to histories.

To concentrate on the core challenges of library abstraction in C11, we assumed that the data structures of the client and its libraries are completely disjoint (§4). We hope to lift this restriction by combining our results with a recent generalisation of classical linearizability allowing transfers of memory ownership [10]. Similarly, a previous generalisation of linearizability to handle liveness properties [9] could be used to strengthen specifications of the kind shown in Figure 1a to guarantee properties such as lock-freedom.

Acknowledgements. We would like to thank Hans Boehm, Richard Bornat, Paul McKenney, Robin Morisset, Madan Musuvathi, Peter Sewell, Jaroslav Ševčík, Hongseok Yang and John Wickerson for helpful comments. We acknowledge funding from EPSRC grants EP/F036345 and EP/H005633.

References

[1] M. Batty, M. Dodds, and A. Gotsman. Library abstraction for C/C++ concurrency (extended version). University of York Technical Report YCS-2012-479, 2012.

[2] M. Batty, S. Owens, S. Sarkar, P. Sewell, and T. Weber. Mathematizing C++ concurrency. In *POPL*, 2011.

[3] H.-J. Boehm. Can seqlocks get along with programming language memory models? In *MSPC*, 2012.

[4] H.-J. Boehm and S. V. Adve. Foundations of the C++ concurrency memory model. In *PLDI*, 2008.

[5] S. Burckhardt, A. Gotsman, M. Musuvathi, and H. Yang. Concurrent library correctness on the TSO memory model. In *ESOP*, 2012.

[6] S. Burckhardt, D. Leijen, M. Fähndrich, and M. Sagiv. Eventually consistent transactions. In *ESOP*, 2012.

[7] I. Filipović, P. O'Hearn, N. Rinetzky, and H. Yang. Abstraction for concurrent objects. In *ESOP*, 2009.

[8] I. Filipović, P. O'Hearn, N. Torp-Smith, and H. Yang. Blaiming the client: On data refinement in the presence of pointers. *FAC*, 22, 2010.

[9] A. Gotsman and H. Yang. Liveness-preserving atomicity abstraction. In *ICALP*, 2011.

[10] A. Gotsman and H. Yang. Linearizability with ownership transfer. In *CONCUR*, 2012.

[11] M. P. Herlihy and J. M. Wing. Linearizability: a correctness condition for concurrent objects. *TOPLAS*, 12, 1990.

[12] ISO/IEC. *Programming Languages – C++, 14882:2011*.

[13] ISO/IEC. *Programming Languages – C, 9899:2011*.

[14] M. Kuperstein, M. T. Vechev, and E. Yahav. Partial-coherence abstractions for relaxed memory models. In *PLDI*, 2011.

[15] L. Lamport. How to make a multiprocessor computer that correctly executes multiprocess programs. *IEEE Trans. Comp.*, 28, 1979.

[16] J. Manson. The Java memory model. PhD Thesis. Department of Computer Science, University of Maryland, 2004.

Action structures for locks

$$\langle \mathsf{lock}(\ell)\rangle_t \;= \{(\{(e,g,t,\mathsf{lock}(\ell))\},\emptyset),(\{(e,g,t,\mathsf{block}(\ell))\},\emptyset) \mid e \in \mathsf{AId} \wedge g \in \mathsf{SectId}\}$$

$$\langle \mathsf{unlock}(\ell)\rangle_t = \{(\{(e,g,t,\mathsf{unlock}(\ell))\},\emptyset) \mid e \in \mathsf{AId} \wedge g \in \mathsf{SectId}\}$$

$$\langle \mathsf{let}\ \{m = C_m \mid m \in M\}\ \mathsf{in}\ C_1 \parallel \ldots \parallel C_n\rangle I = \{(A_0 \uplus (\biguplus_{t=1}^{n} A_t), \bigcup_{t=1}^{n} \mathsf{sb}_t, (A_0 \times (\biguplus_{t=1}^{n} A_t))) \mid$$
$$(\forall t = 1..n.\,(A_t,\mathsf{sb}_t) \in \langle C_t\rangle_t) \wedge (\forall t = 1..n.\,\forall u.\,\exists \text{ finitely many } v.\,(v,u) \in \mathsf{sb}_t) \wedge$$
$$(\neg\exists u,v,t.\,(u,v) \in \mathsf{sb}_t \wedge u = (\_,\_,\_,\mathsf{block}(\_))) \wedge (A_0 = \biguplus\{(e,g,0,\mathsf{store}_\lambda(x,a)) \mid I(x) = (a,\lambda) \wedge e \in \mathsf{AId} \wedge g \in \mathsf{SectId}\})\}$$

Additional validity axioms

ATOMRMW. $\forall w,u.\, w \xrightarrow{\mathsf{rf}} u \wedge u = (\_,\mathsf{rmw}(\_)) \implies w \xrightarrow{\mathsf{mo}} u \wedge \neg\exists w'.\, w \xrightarrow{\mathsf{mo}} w' \xrightarrow{\mathsf{mo}} u$

ATOMAS. $\forall w,w',r,u,v,x.\, w \xrightarrow{\mathsf{rf}} r \wedge \mathsf{sec}(u) = \mathsf{sec}(r) \neq \mathsf{sec}(w) = \mathsf{sec}(v) \wedge r = (\_,\mathsf{read}(x,\_)) \wedge \mathsf{sort}(x) = \mathsf{ATOM} \implies \neg(w \xrightarrow{\mathsf{mo}} v)$
$\wedge\ (u = (\_,\mathsf{write}(x,\_)) \implies w \xrightarrow{\mathsf{mo}} u \wedge \neg\exists w''.\, \mathsf{sec}(w'') \neq \mathsf{sec}(u) \wedge w \xrightarrow{\mathsf{mo}} w'' \xrightarrow{\mathsf{mo}} u)$
$\wedge\ (u = (\_,\mathsf{read}(x,\_)) \wedge w' \xrightarrow{\mathsf{rf}} r \wedge \mathsf{sec}(w') \neq \mathsf{sec}(r) \implies w'' = w)$

LOCKS. $\forall u,v.\, u = (\_,\mathsf{lock}(\ell)) \wedge v = (\_,\mathsf{lock}(\ell)) \wedge u \xrightarrow{\mathsf{sc}} v \implies \exists q.\, q = (\_,\mathsf{unlock}(\ell)) \wedge u \xrightarrow{\mathsf{sc}} q \xrightarrow{\mathsf{sc}} v$

SWDEF. $\forall w,r.\, w \xrightarrow{\mathsf{sw}} r \iff (\exists \ell.\, w \xrightarrow{\mathsf{sc}} r \wedge w = (\_,\mathsf{unlock}(\ell)) \wedge r = (\_,\mathsf{lock}(\ell))) \vee$
$(\exists t_1,t_2,\lambda,\mu,x,w'.\, t_1 \neq t_2 \wedge \lambda \in \{\mathsf{SC},\mathsf{REL}\} \wedge \mu \in \{\mathsf{SC},\mathsf{ACQ}\} \wedge w = (t_1,\mathsf{write}_\lambda(x,\_)) \wedge r = (t_2,\mathsf{read}_\mu(x,\_)) \wedge w \xrightarrow{\mathsf{rs}}_{t_1} w' \xrightarrow{\mathsf{rf}} r)$,
where $w \xrightarrow{\mathsf{rs}}_t w' \overset{\mathrm{def}}{\iff} \exists w_1.\, w \xrightarrow{\mathsf{mo}}{}^{*} w_1 \wedge (\forall w_2.\, w \xrightarrow{\mathsf{mo}}{}^{*} w_2 \xrightarrow{\mathsf{mo}}{}^{*} w' \implies (w_2 = (t,\_) \vee w_2 = (\_,\mathsf{rmw}(\_))))$

SCREADS.
$\forall w,r,x.\, w \xrightarrow{\mathsf{rf}} r \wedge r = (\_,\mathsf{read}_{\mathsf{SC}}(x,\_)) \implies$
$((w = (\_,\mathsf{write}_{\mathsf{SC}}(x,\_)) \wedge w \xrightarrow{\mathsf{sc}} r \wedge \neg\exists w'.\, w' = (\_,\mathsf{write}(x,\_)) \wedge w \xrightarrow{\mathsf{sc}} w' \xrightarrow{\mathsf{sc}} r) \vee$
$(\exists \lambda.\, w = (\_,\mathsf{write}_\lambda(x,\_)) \wedge \lambda \neq \mathsf{SC} \wedge \forall w_1.\,(w_1 = (\_,\mathsf{write}(x,\_)) \wedge w_1 \xrightarrow{\mathsf{sc}} r \wedge \neg\exists w_2.\, w_2 = (\_,\mathsf{write}(x,\_)) \wedge w_1 \xrightarrow{\mathsf{sc}} w_2 \xrightarrow{\mathsf{sc}} r) \implies$
$\neg(w \xrightarrow{\mathsf{hb}} w_1)))$

Additional safety axiom

SAFELOCK. $(\forall v,t,\ell.\, v \in A \wedge v = (t,\mathsf{unlock}(\ell)) \implies \exists u.\, u = (t,\mathsf{lock}(\ell)) \wedge u \xrightarrow{\mathsf{sb}} v \wedge \neg\exists q.\, q = (\_,\_(\ell)) \wedge u \xrightarrow{\mathsf{sc}} q \xrightarrow{\mathsf{sc}} v) \wedge$
$(\neg\exists u,v,t,\ell.\, u = (t,\mathsf{lock}(\ell)) \wedge v = (t,\mathsf{block}(\ell)) \wedge u \xrightarrow{\mathsf{sb}} v \wedge \neg\exists q.\, q = (\_,\_(\ell)) \wedge u \xrightarrow{\mathsf{sc}} q \xrightarrow{\mathsf{sc}} v)$

Figure 7. Action structures for locks and additional C11 memory model axioms

[17] M. M. Michael. Scalable lock-free dynamic memory allocation. In *PLDI*, 2004.

[18] M. M. Michael, M. T. Vechev, and V. A. Saraswat. Idempotent work stealing. In *PPOPP*, 2009.

[19] S. Owens, S. Sarkar, and P. Sewell. A better x86 memory model: x86-TSO. In *TPHOLs*, 2009.

[20] T. Ridge. A rely-guarantee proof system for x86-TSO. In *VSTTE*, 2010.

[21] S. Sarkar, P. Sewell, J. Alglave, L. Maranget, and D. Williams. Understanding POWER multiprocessors. In *PLDI*, 2011.

[22] R. K. Treiber. Systems programming: Coping with parallelism. Technical Report RJ 5118, IBM Almaden Research Center, 1986.

[23] I. Wehrman and J. Berdine. A proposal for weak-memory local reasoning. In *LOLA*, 2011.

A. Additional Definitions for the C11 Model

In §4–5, we omitted the treatment of locks and CASes from the description of the memory model and simplified some of the axioms, even though the proofs of our theorems do not make such simplifications. Here we provide the missing definitions.

We handle programs with bounded numbers of locks $\ell \in \mathsf{Lock}$, acquired and released using commands $\mathsf{lock}(\ell)$ and $\mathsf{unlock}(\ell)$, respectively. We thus extend the set of actions as follows: $\varphi\ ::= \ldots \mid \mathsf{lock}(\ell) \mid \mathsf{unlock}(\ell) \mid \mathsf{block}(\ell)$, where $\ell \in \mathsf{Lock}$. An action $(e,g,t,\mathsf{block}(\ell))$ represents a deadlocked attempt to acquire a lock ℓ. We split the set of locks into client and library ones ($\mathsf{Lock} = \mathsf{CLock} \uplus \mathsf{LLock}$) and consider only programs where the client and the library use locks from CLock and LLock, respectively.

In Figure 7, we give the actions structures for lock operations, omitted from Figure 3, and the C11 axioms omitted from Figures 4 and 5. Note that the action structures of a whole program do not include those where a thread executes actions after blocking. To adjust the axioms to the model with locks, we require that the sc relation totally orders actions of the form $(\_,\mathsf{lock}(\_))$, $(\_,\mathsf{block}(\_))$ or $(\_,\mathsf{unlock}(\_))$ for each lock, in addition to SC actions. The axioms ATOMRMW and LOCKS define the behaviour of CAS commands and locks. ATOMAS is an additional axiom for atomic sections, in the spirit of ATOMRMW. SWDEF and SCREADS are full versions of the axioms presented in a simplified form in Figure 4. The former adds synchronisation via ***release sequences*** [2] (defined by the rs relation), and the latter allows SC reads from non-SC writes. SAFELOCK is an additional safety axiom, flagging a double unlock or a double lock in the same thread as a fault.

All the theorems stated in the paper stay valid for this extension of the model. To account for the full version of the SCREADS axiom, we add additional edges to $\mathsf{denyL}(X)$. For $X = (A,\mathsf{sb},\mathsf{ib},\mathsf{rf},\mathsf{sc},\mathsf{mo},\mathsf{sw},\mathsf{hb})$, $\mathsf{denyL}(X)$ includes the dashed edges of all possible instantiations of the following diagram:

$$\begin{pmatrix} w = (\_,\mathsf{write}_\lambda(x,\_)) \wedge \lambda \neq \mathsf{SC} \wedge \\ r = (\_,\mathsf{read}_{\mathsf{SC}}(x,\_)) \wedge \\ w_1 = (\_,\mathsf{write}(x,\_)) \wedge \\ (\neg\exists w_2.\, w_2 = (\_,\mathsf{write}(x,\_)) \wedge \\ w_1 \xrightarrow{\mathsf{sc}} w_2 \xrightarrow{\mathsf{sc}} r) \end{pmatrix} \wedge$$

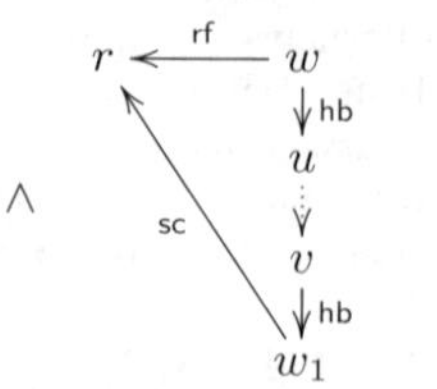

where u is a return, and v is a call. Its counterpart $\mathsf{denyC}(X)$ contains the dashed edges assuming u is a call, and v is a return.

Fault Tolerance via Idempotence

G. Ramalingam and Kapil Vaswani
Microsoft Research, India
grama,kapilv@microsoft.com

Abstract

Building distributed services and applications is challenging due to the pitfalls of distribution such as process and communication failures. A natural solution to these problems is to detect potential failures, and retry the failed computation and/or resend messages. Ensuring correctness in such an environment requires distributed services and applications to be *idempotent*.

In this paper, we study the inter-related aspects of process failures, duplicate messages, and idempotence. We first introduce a simple core language (based on λ-calculus) inspired by modern distributed computing platforms. This language formalizes the notions of a service, duplicate requests, process failures, data partitioning, and *local* atomic transactions that are restricted to a single store.

We then formalize a desired (generic) correctness criterion for applications written in this language, consisting of *idempotence* (which captures the desired safety properties) and *failure-freedom* (which captures the desired progress properties).

We then propose language support in the form of a monad that automatically ensures failfree idempotence. A key characteristic of our implementation is that it is decentralized and does not require distributed coordination. We show that the language support can be enriched with other useful constructs, such as compensations, while retaining the coordination-free decentralized nature of the implementation.

We have implemented the idempotence monad (and its variants) in F# and C# and used our implementation to build realistic applications on Windows Azure. We find that the monad has low runtime overheads and leads to more declarative applications.

Categories and Subject Descriptions D.4.5 [Operating Systems]: Reliability—Fault-tolerance; C.2.4 [Computer-Communication Networks]: Distributed Systems—Client/server, Distributed applications

General Terms Reliability, Languages, Design

Keywords fault tolerance, idempotence, workflow, transaction, monad

1. Introduction

Distributed computing is becoming mainstream. Several modern platforms offer virtualized distributed systems at low entry cost with the promise of scaling out on demand. But distributed computing comes with its own pitfalls, such as process failures, imperfect messaging, asynchrony and concurrency.

Consider the prototypical bank account transfer service in Fig. 1. The goal of the service is to transfer money between bank accounts, potentially in different banks. If the accounts belong to different banks, ensuring that the transfer executes as an *atomic (distributed) transaction* is usually not feasible, and the natural way of expressing this computation is as a *workflow* [10, 20] consisting of two steps, a debit followed by a credit.

What if the process executing the workflow fails in between the debit and credit steps? A natural solution is to detect this failure and ensure that a different process completes the remaining steps of the workflow. A challenging[1] aspect of realizing this solution is figuring out whether the original process failed before or after completing a particular step (either debit or credit). If not done carefully, the debit or credit step may be executed multiple times, leading to further correctness concerns. Services often rely on a central workflow manager to manage process failures during the workflow (using distributed transactions).

Now consider a (seemingly) different problem. Messages sent between the client initiating the transfer and the service may be lost. The only option for a client, when it does not receive a response within some reasonable time, is to resend its request. Yet the client does not want the transfer to occur twice!

In this paper, we study process and communication failures in the context of workflows. The seemingly different problems caused by process and communication failures are, in fact, inter-related. *Idempotence*, a correctness criterion that requires the system to tolerate duplicate requests, is the key to handling both communication and process failures efficiently. Idempotence, when combined with retry, gives us the essence of a workflow, a fault tolerant composition of atomic actions, for free *without the need for distributed coordination*. In the transfer example, a fault tolerant account transfer can be implemented without a central workflow manager if the debit and credit steps can be designed to be idempotent,

Formalizing Failfree Idempotence. In this paper, we introduce a simple core language λ_{FAIL}, inspired by contemporary cloud platforms. This language formalizes process failure, duplicate requests, partitioned data, and *local* transactions. A local transaction provides ACID guarantees but is restricted to access data within a single partition (typically a single server). Computations in λ_{FAIL} are like workflows, but without any fault-tolerance guarantees for the composition (i.e., the computation may fail between transactions).

We then formalize a generic correctness criterion for applications written in λ_{FAIL}. A simple, powerful and tempting criterion is that an application's behavior in the presence of duplicate requests and process failures should be indistinguishable from its behavior in the absence of duplicate requests and failures. We formal-

[1] In general, detecting failures perfectly in an asynchronous, message passing system is impossible [8]. Conservative failure detection can also lead to the same problem of duplicated computation.

POPL'13, January 23–25, 2013, Rome, Italy.

```
let process (request) =
  match request with
  | ("getBalance", (branch, account)) →
      atomic branch {lookup account}
  | ("transfer", (fromBranch, fromAccount, toBranch, toAccount, amt) →
      atomic fromBranch {
        update fromAccount ((lookup fromAccount) − amt)
      };
      atomic toBranch {
        update toAccount ((lookup toAccount) + amt)
      };
      "Transfer complete."
```

Figure 1: A banking service example, in syntactically sugared λ_{FAIL}, that is neither idempotent nor fault-tolerant.

ize a slightly weaker, but more appropriate, correctness criterion, namely *failure-freedom modulo message duplication*. Informally, this criterion permits the system to send duplicate responses. This weakening is appropriate from the perspective of *composition*: if the recipient of the responses can also tolerate duplicate messages, then the sender is freed of the obligation to send the response exactly once.

Automating Idempotence. Next, we address the problem of automatically ensuring idempotence for a service. We present our solution as a monad, the *idempotence* monad. We then show that idempotence, when coupled with a simple retry mechanism, provides a "free" solution to the problem of tolerating process failures, guaranteeing failure-freedom modulo message duplication. We then propose dedicated language support for idempotent computations.

Decentralized Idempotence and Workflow. The idea underlying the idempotence monad is conceptually simple, but tedious to implement manually (i.e., without the monad). Given a unique identifier associated with a computation, the monad essentially adds logging and checking to each effectful step in the workflow to ensure idempotance. An important characteristic of our implementation (of the monad) is that it is designed to work with contemporary distributed storage systems such as key-value tables. Specifically, it does not assume the presence of dedicated storage for logs that can be accessed atomically with each transaction. The monad reuses the underlying store (in this case a key-value table) to simulate a distinct address space for logging.

This leads to a decentralized implementation of idempotence that does not require any centralized storage or any (distributed) coordination between different stores. Thus, the implementation of idempotance preserves the decentralized nature of the underlying computation. This, in turn, leads to a completely decentralized implementation of a (fault-tolerant) workflow, unlike traditional workflow implementations, which use a centralized workflow coordinator and/or a centralized repository for runtime status information.

Extensions. We then extend the idempotence monad with other useful constructs, while preserving the decentralized nature of the construct. One extension allows the application to associate each transaction in a workflow with a compensating action. Another extension allows the application to generate intermediate responses to client requests and then asynchronously retry the requests on client's behalf. This idiom, especially useful in long running computations, frees the client from having to track status of requests, and leads to more responsive clients.

Implementation. We have implemented the idempotence workflow monad in F# targeting the Windows Azure platform. We have implemented several realistic applications using the idempotence workflow monad [2, 4]. We find that the core business logic in these applications can be declaratively expressed using the monad. Our evaluation shows that performance overheads of using the monad over hand-coded implementations are statistically insignificant.

The rest of the paper is organized as follows. In Section 2, we introduce a language λ_{FAIL} and formalize duplicate requests and process failures. We formalize what it means for a λ_{FAIL} application to correctly tolerate duplicate requests and failures. In Section 3, we present the idempotence monad and show how it can be used to tolerate duplicate requests as well as process failures. In Section 4, we describe extensions of the idempotence construct. In Section 5, we evaluate the idempotence monad and our implementation from the perspective of expressiveness, benefits and overheads. Section 6 discusses related work.

2. Failfree Idempotence

In this section we present a language λ_{FAIL} that distils essential elements of distributed computing platforms such as Windows Azure and formalize the concept of failfree idempotence.

2.1 The Language λ_{FAIL}

Informal Overview. A λ_{FAIL} program e represents a service that receives input requests and produces output responses. An input request v is processed by *creating* an agent to evaluate $e\ v$. When the evaluation of $e\ v$ terminates, producing a value v', v' is sent back as the response. Multiple input requests can be processed concurrently, and their evaluation can be interleaved. Shared, mutable, persistent data is stored in *tables*.

Agents. An agent has its own internal state (captured by local variables of the code). An agent may *fail* at any point in time. A failure models problems such as hardware failure, software crashes and reboots . Data stored in tables is *persistent* and is unaffected by agent failures.

Tables. Tables are persistent maps. They provide primitives to *update* the value bound to a key and *lookup* up the value associated with a key. The language provides a *limited* form of an *atomic transaction*, which enables a set of operations on the *same* table to be performed transactionally. Specifically, the construct "`atomic` $t\ e$" evaluates e in the context of table t (lookups and updates are permitted only on table t within e), guaranteeing isolation (no other agent can access t in the middle of e's evaluation) and the all-or-nothing property (no process failure can happen in the middle of e's evaluation).

Example. Fig. 1 presents a simple bank-account-transfer example in syntactically sugared λ_{FAIL}. This example is neither idempotent (e.g., executing the same *transfer* request twice is not equivalent to executing it once) nor fault-tolerant (e.g., if the agent processing a transfer request fails in between the debit and credit steps).

Syntax. Fig. 2 presents the syntax of λ_{FAIL}, which extends λ-calculus with the primitive operations on tables explained above. In the rest of the paper, we will use extensions such as natural numbers, arithmetic operators, and ordered pairs for brevity. These can be encoded in the core language or added to it in the usual fashion. We also use syntactic sugar, such as `lookup` e, where $e \notin \langle \mathsf{Val} \rangle$, as shorthand, e.g., for $(\lambda x.\texttt{lookup}\ x)e$.

Semantic Domains Fig. 2 defines the semantic domains used in the semantics of λ_{FAIL}. Let $\langle \mathsf{Val} \rangle$ denote the set of all basic values: these basically consist of function abstractions. (As usual, natural numbers, string constants, ordered pairs of values, etc. can all be encoded within $\langle \mathsf{Val} \rangle$ or added to it.)

Let $\langle \mathsf{Val} \rangle_{\mathsf{opt}}$ represent the set of *optional* values (of the form `NONE` or `SOME` v). An element of Σ_{ST} (a map from $\langle \mathsf{Val} \rangle$ to

(a) Evaluation Contexts

$$E ::= [\cdot] \mid E\ e \mid v\ E$$

(b) The Set of Evaluation Rules A used to define the standard semantics of λ_{FAIL}.

[INPUT]
$$\frac{v \in \langle \mathsf{Val} \rangle}{\langle e, \mu, \alpha, I, O\rangle \overset{in(v)}{\Rightarrow} \langle e, \mu, \alpha \uplus \{v \rhd (e\ v)\}, I \cup \{v\}, O\rangle}$$

[OUTPUT]
$$\frac{v_o \in \langle \mathsf{Val} \rangle}{\langle e, \mu, \alpha \uplus \{v_i \rhd v_o\}, I, O\rangle \overset{out(v_i, v_o)}{\Rightarrow} \langle e, \mu, \alpha, I, O \cup \{(v_i, v_o)\}\rangle}$$

[NORMAL]
$$\frac{\langle \mu, e\rangle \overset{\omega}{\rightsquigarrow} \langle \mu', e'\rangle}{\langle p, \mu, \alpha \uplus \{v \rhd e\}, I, O\rangle \overset{\epsilon}{\Rightarrow} \langle p, \mu', \alpha \uplus \{v \rhd e'\}, I, O\rangle}$$

[FAIL]
$$\frac{}{\langle p, \mu, \alpha \uplus \{v \rhd e\}, I, O\rangle \overset{\epsilon}{\Rightarrow} \langle p, \mu, \alpha, I, O\rangle}$$

[ATOMIC]
$$\frac{\langle \mu[tn], e()\rangle \overset{\omega\ *}{\twoheadrightarrow} \langle t, v\rangle, v \in \langle \mathsf{Val}\rangle}{\langle \mu, \texttt{atomic}\ tn\ e\rangle \overset{\omega}{\rightsquigarrow} \langle \mu[tn \mapsto t], v\rangle}$$

[UPDATE]
$$\frac{}{\langle t, \texttt{update}\ k\ v\rangle \overset{(t,k,v)}{\twoheadrightarrow} \langle t[k \mapsto (\texttt{SOME}\ v)], 0\rangle}$$

[LOOKUP]
$$\frac{}{\langle t, \texttt{lookup}\ k\rangle \overset{\epsilon}{\twoheadrightarrow} \langle t, t[k]\rangle}$$

[CONTEXT]
$$\frac{\langle t, e\rangle \overset{u}{\twoheadrightarrow} \langle t', e'\rangle}{\langle t, E[e]\rangle \overset{u}{\twoheadrightarrow} \langle t', E[e']\rangle}$$

[CONTEXT]
$$\frac{\langle \mu, e\rangle \overset{\omega}{\rightsquigarrow} \langle \mu', e'\rangle}{\langle \mu, E[e]\rangle \overset{\omega}{\rightsquigarrow} \langle \mu', E[e']\rangle}$$

[LIFT]
$$\frac{e \to e'}{\langle t, e\rangle \overset{\epsilon}{\twoheadrightarrow} \langle t, e'\rangle}$$

[LIFT]
$$\frac{e \to e'}{\langle \mu, e\rangle \overset{\epsilon}{\rightsquigarrow} \langle \mu, e'\rangle}$$

[BETA]
$$\frac{}{(\lambda x.e)\ v \to e[v/x]}$$

[RETRY]
$$\frac{v \in I}{\langle e, \mu, \alpha, I, O\rangle \overset{\epsilon}{\Rightarrow} \langle e, \mu, \alpha \uplus \{v \rhd (e\ v)\}, I, O\rangle}$$

(c) Additional Rules Used To Define the Ideal Semantics of λ_{FAIL}.

[UNIQUE-INPUT]
$$\frac{v \in \langle \mathsf{Val}\rangle, v \notin I}{\langle e, \mu, \alpha, I, O\rangle \overset{in(v)}{\Rightarrow} \langle e, \mu, \alpha \uplus \{v \rhd (e\ v)\}, I \cup \{v\}, O\rangle}$$

[DUPLINPUT]
$$\frac{v \in \langle \mathsf{Val}\rangle, v \in I}{\langle e, \mu, \alpha, I, O\rangle \overset{in(v)}{\Rightarrow} \langle e, \mu, \alpha, I, O\rangle}$$

[DUPLSEND]
$$\frac{v \in O}{\langle e, \mu, \alpha, I, O\rangle \overset{out(v)}{\Rightarrow} \langle e, \mu, \alpha, I, O\rangle}$$

Figure 3: Operational semantics of λ_{FAIL}.

$$\begin{array}{rcl}
 & & x \in \langle \mathsf{Identifier}\rangle \\
v \in \langle \mathsf{Val}\rangle & ::= & x \mid \lambda x.e \\
e \in \langle \mathsf{Exp}\rangle & ::= & v \mid e\ e \mid \texttt{atomic}\ v_1\ v_2 \mid \\
 & & \texttt{update}\ v_1\ v_2 \mid \texttt{lookup}\ v \\
 & & \\
tn \in \langle \mathsf{TableName}\rangle & = & \langle \mathsf{Val}\rangle \\
t \in \Sigma_{ST} & = & \langle \mathsf{Val}\rangle \mapsto \langle \mathsf{Val}\rangle_{\mathsf{opt}} \\
\mu \in \Sigma_T & = & \langle \mathsf{TableName}\rangle \mapsto \Sigma_{ST} \\
\langle \mathsf{Req}\rangle & = & \langle \mathsf{Val}\rangle \\
\langle \mathsf{Resp}\rangle & = & \langle \mathsf{Req}\rangle \times \langle \mathsf{Val}\rangle \\
(v \rhd e) \in \Sigma_A & = & \langle \mathsf{Req}\rangle \times \langle \mathsf{Exp}\rangle \\
\Sigma & = & \langle \mathsf{Exp}\rangle \times \Sigma_T \times \Sigma_A^+ \times 2^{\langle \mathsf{Req}\rangle} \times 2^{\langle \mathsf{Resp}\rangle}
\end{array}$$

Figure 2: The Syntax of λ_{FAIL} and its Semantic Domains.

$\langle \mathsf{Val}\rangle_{\mathsf{opt}}$) represents the value of a single table. An element $\mu \in \Sigma_T$ represents the values of all tables.

As explained earlier, an agent represents a thread of computation spawned to process a given input request. The state of an agent is represented by a pair of the form $v \rhd e$, where v represents the input request being processed and e represents a partially evaluated expression (and represents the local state of the agent). Let Σ_A represent the set of all agent-states.

The state of an executing program is represented by a *system configuration* $\langle e, \mu, \alpha, I, O\rangle \in \Sigma$, where e is the program itself, μ represents the values of all tables, α is the multi-set of currently executing agents, I represents the set of all input requests received so far, and O represents the set of all responses produced so far. (A response to a request v_i is a pair of the form (v_i, v_o) where v_o is the result.) Let Σ represent the set of all configurations.

Let $\uplus$ denote the union operator for multi-sets.

Semantics. Fig. 3 presents an operational semantics for λ_{FAIL} as a labelled transition relation $\overset{\tau}{\Rightarrow}$ on the set of configurations Σ. The evaluation of a program p starts in the initial configuration $\langle\!\langle p\rangle\!\rangle \triangleq \langle p, \mu^I, \emptyset, \emptyset, \emptyset\rangle$, where $\mu^I = \lambda t.\lambda k.\texttt{NONE}$. (Initially, all tables map every key to a default value of $\texttt{NONE}$. We utilize a standard encoding of optional values consisting of either $\texttt{NONE}$ or $\texttt{SOME}\ v$.)

System Transitions. ($\overset{\tau}{\Rightarrow}$) As rule INPUT indicates, the arrival of an input request v spawns a new agent to evaluate $e\ v$. As rule OUTPUT indicates, when an agent's evaluation completes, the resulting value is sent back as a response. The labels on system transitions represent requests and responses. Rule NORMAL describes a normal system transition caused by a potentially effectful execution step performed by a single agent, described below. As the rule indicates, the execution steps of different agents can be interleaved in a non-deterministic order. Rule FAIL indicates that an agent can fail at any point in time.

Agent Transitions. ($\overset{\omega}{\rightsquigarrow}$) Execution steps in the evaluation of a single agent are described by the transition relation $\overset{\omega}{\rightsquigarrow}$ on $\Sigma_T \times \langle \mathsf{Exp} \rangle$. A transition $\langle \mu, e \rangle \overset{\omega}{\rightsquigarrow} \langle \mu', e' \rangle$ indicates that an agent expression e is transformed to an agent expression e', with the side-effect of transforming the table-state from μ to μ'. The label ω represents a sequence of updates to a single table performed atomically in this step. (This label, however, identifies an internal transition not visible externally, which is why the label is omitted in the corresponding system transition in rule NORMAL.) These transitions are of two types: pure (standard λ-calculus evaluation, BETA), and effectful, which take the form of atomic table operations.

Atomic Table Operations. The expression "`atomic t e`" identifies a set of operations to be performed on a *single* table t in an atomic and failfree fashion. Its semantics is defined by rule ATOMIC, which utilizes a transition relation $\overset{u}{\twoheadrightarrow}$ on atomic evaluation configurations of the form $\langle t, e \rangle$, which indicates the atomic evaluation of an expression e at a table t. The labels on such transitions are either ϵ or represent a single update to a table. Rules UPDATE/LOOKUP define the semantics of an update/lookup operation on a table. The rule ATOMIC indicates that no other execution step interleaves with the evaluation of an atomic expression. Note that the evaluation of an atomic expression cannot fail in the middle. In other words, either all effects of the atomic expression evaluation happen or none does.

Retry. The rule RETRY models one of the key ingredients used to tolerate process failures, namely a retry mechanism. The rule indicates that a request must be *retried* periodically. Typically, retrying logic is built into clients. A client will resend a request if it does not receive a response within a pre-defined amount of time. This basic scheme can be optimized, as discussed in Section 4: the system (application) can send an acknowledgement back to the client, after which the client can stop resending a request and the application takes on the responsibility of retrying the request (to ensure progress in the presence of failures). The system can exploit various optimizations in implementing the retry logic, but rule RETRY suffices for our purpose here. As we will soon see, the key reason for adding the RETRY rule to the semantics is to formalize a weakened progress guarantee ("progress modulo retries") that is appropriate in the presence of failures.

2.2 Formalizing Failfree Idempotence

We now formalize a natural correctness goal of any λ_{FAIL} program: namely, that it correctly handles process failures and duplicate messages. We will later see how we can automatically ensure this property for any program. We formalize this correctness criterion as follows. We define an alternative semantics for λ_{FAIL}, which we refer to as the *ideal semantics*, representing an idealized execution platform. We then define a program to be "correct" iff its behavior under the standard semantics is equivalent to its behavior under the ideal semantics.

Ideal Semantics. Let A denote the set of all rules defined in Fig. 3(b). We will define the ideal semantics as a different labelled transition relation on program configurations, by adding and removing some rules to set A. Let $\Rightarrow_S$ denote the labelled transition relation on Σ induced by a given set of rules S. Thus, $\Rightarrow_{\mathsf{A}}$ is the transition relation capturing the standard semantics of λ_{FAIL}.

We first omit rule FAIL eliminating process failures from the ideal semantics. In the ideal semantics, we assume that all input requests are distinct, by replacing the INPUT rule by the UNIQUE-INPUT and DUPLINPUT rules. We also drop rule RETRY. Finally, process failures make it hard to ensure that an application sends an output message exactly once. A common approach to this problem is to weaken the specification and permit the application to send the same output message more than once. We do this by adding rule DUPLSEND. We define IDEAL to be A $\setminus$ { FAIL, RETRY, INPUT} $\cup$ { UNIQUE-INPUT, DUPLINPUT, DUPLSEND}. We refer to $\Rightarrow_{\mathsf{IDEAL}}$ as the ideal semantics for λ_{FAIL}.

Observational Idempotence (Safety). We now consider two (well-studied) notions of behavioral equivalence in formalizing our correctness criterion. Recall that $\langle\!\langle p \rangle\!\rangle$ denotes the initial configuration in an execution of program p (which is the same under both semantics). Given a labelled transition relation $\Rightarrow$ on configurations, an *execution* of a program p (with respect to $\Rightarrow$) is an alternating sequence of states and labels, denoted $\sigma_0 \overset{r_1}{\Rightarrow} \sigma_1 \cdots \sigma_n$, representing a sequence of transitions starting from the initial program state $\sigma_0 = \langle\!\langle p \rangle\!\rangle$. We say that the *observed behavior* $obs(\xi)$ of an execution ξ is the sequence of non-ϵ labels in ξ. Note that $obs(\xi)$ is a sequence of (input) requests and (output) responses. Specifically, it does not include updates to tables, which are internal transitions but not visible externally.

DEFINITION 2.1. *We say that a λ_{FAIL} program p is* observationally idempotent *if for every execution ξ_1 of p under the standard semantics there exists an execution ξ_2 of p under the ideal semantics such that $obs(\xi_1) = obs(\xi_2)$.*

We present a simpler, more abstract, formalization of idempotence in the appendix. However, the preceding definition in terms of the ideal semantics will be useful in formalizing progress properties, as below, and in proving correctness of our implementation.

Failfree Idempotence (Progress). An observationally idempotent program, by definition, gives no progress guarantees. Consider a modified version of the account-transfer example that checks the input request to determine if it is a duplicate request and processes it only if it is not a duplicate. This ensures that the program is idempotent. However, if the agent fails in between the debit and credit steps, we would still have a problem. This motivates the following stronger correctness condition, based on the notion of weak bisimulation. A labelled transition system $(S, \Rightarrow)$ consists of a relation $\overset{\ell}{\Rightarrow} \subseteq S \times S$ for every $\ell \in \langle \mathsf{Label} \rangle$.

DEFINITION 2.2. *A weak bisimulation between two labelled transition systems $(\Sigma_1, \Rightarrow_1)$ and $(\Sigma_2, \Rightarrow_2)$ is a relation $\sim \subseteq \Sigma_1 \times \Sigma_2$ such that for any $\sigma_1 \sim \sigma_2$ we have:*

1. $\sigma_1 \overset{\ell}{\Rightarrow}_1 \sigma_1' \wedge \ell \neq \epsilon \;\Rightarrow\; \exists \sigma_2', \sigma_2''.\sigma_2 \overset{\epsilon}{\Rightarrow}_2^* \sigma_2'' \overset{\ell}{\Rightarrow}_2 \sigma_2' \wedge \sigma_1' \sim \sigma_2'$
2. $\sigma_2 \overset{\ell}{\Rightarrow}_2 \sigma_2' \wedge \ell \neq \epsilon \;\Rightarrow\; \exists \sigma_1', \sigma_1''.\sigma_1 \overset{\epsilon}{\Rightarrow}_1^* \sigma_1'' \overset{\ell}{\Rightarrow}_1 \sigma_1' \wedge \sigma_1' \sim \sigma_2'$
3. $\sigma_1 \overset{\epsilon}{\Rightarrow}_1 \sigma_1' \;\Rightarrow\; \exists \sigma_2'.\sigma_2 \overset{\epsilon}{\Rightarrow}_2^* \sigma_2' \wedge \sigma_1' \sim \sigma_2'$
4. $\sigma_2 \overset{\epsilon}{\Rightarrow}_2 \sigma_2' \;\Rightarrow\; \exists \sigma_1', \sigma_1'.\sigma_1 \overset{\epsilon}{\Rightarrow}_1^* \sigma_1' \wedge \sigma_1' \sim \sigma_2'$

We will write $(\sigma_1, \Sigma_1, \Rightarrow_1) \simeq (\sigma_2, \Sigma_2, \Rightarrow_2)$ to indicate that there exists a weak bisimulation $\sim$ between $(\Sigma_1^r, \Rightarrow_1)$ and $(\Sigma_2^r, \Rightarrow_2)$ under which $\sigma_1 \sim \sigma_2$, where Σ_i^r represents the set of states in Σ_i that are reachable from σ_i via a sequence of $\Rightarrow_i$ transitions. We will omit Σ_1 and Σ_2 in this notation if no confusion is likely.

DEFINITION 2.3. *A λ_{FAIL} program p is said to be* failfree idempotent *iff $(\langle\!\langle p \rangle\!\rangle, \Rightarrow_{\mathsf{A}}) \simeq (\langle\!\langle p \rangle\!\rangle, \Rightarrow_{\mathsf{IDEAL}})$.*

This definition requires a failfree idempotent program to provide progress guarantees: at any point in time, if the system can produce a response r under the ideal semantics, then the system should be capable of producing the same response r under the standard semantics also. However, the inclusion of rule RETRY in the standard semantics means that this progress guarantee holds *provided requests are retried.* Absolute progress guarantees are not possible since an agent may fail before it executes even its first step.

THEOREM 2.4. *A failfree idempotent program is also observationally idempotent.*

```
let imreturn v = fun (guid, tc) → (tc, v)

let imatomic T f =
  fun (guid, tc) →
    atomic T {
      let key = (0, (guid, tc)) in
      match lookup key with
      | Some(v) → (v,tc+1)
      | None →
        let v = f () in (update key v); (v,tc+1)
    }

let imbind (idf, f) =
  fun (guid, tc) →
    let (ntc, v) = idf (guid, tc) in
    f v (guid, ntc)

let imrun idf x =
  let (j,v) = idf x (x, 0) in v

let imupdate key val = update (1,key) val
let imlookup key = lookup (1,key)
```

Figure 4: The Idempotence Monad.

Failfree Idempotent Realization. Failfree idempotence is a generic correctness property we expect of a λ_{FAIL} program. More generally, the following definition combines this property with a "specification" (provided as another λ_{FAIL} program q).

DEFINITION 2.5. *A λ_{FAIL} program p is said to be a* failfree idempotent *realization of q iff* $(\langle\langle p\rangle\rangle, \Rightarrow_{\text{A}}) \simeq (\langle\langle q\rangle\rangle, \Rightarrow_{\text{IDEAL}})$.

3. Realizing Failfree Idempotence

We now present a generic, application-independent, strategy that can be used to ensure failfree idempotence. Informally, a function is idempotent if multiple evaluations of the function on the same argument, potentially concurrently, behave the same as a single evaluation of that function with the same argument. Consider the example in Fig. 1. In this example, the parameter *requestId* serves to distinguish between different transfer requests (and identify duplicate requests). This service can be made idempotent and failfree by (a) using this identifier to *log* debit and credit operations, whenever the operations are performed, and (b) modifying the debit and credit steps to check, using the log, if the steps have already been performed. This strategy can ensure that multiple (potentially partial and concurrent) invocations of *transfer* with the same identifier have the same effect as a single invocation.

Manually ensuring idempotence is tedious and it introduces the possibility of various subtle bugs and in general makes implementation less comprehensible. We now describe a monad-based library that realizes idempotence and failure-freedom in a generic way.

3.1 The Idempotence Monad

The Intuition. A computation performed by a single agent consists of a sequence of steps, "pure" as well as "effectful" ones (namely, atomic local transactions which can read/update a single table.) We use the following strategy to make a computation idempotent:

1. Associate every computation instance (that we wish to make idempotent) with a unique identifier.
2. Associate every step in an idempotent computation with a unique number.
3. Whenever an effectful step is executed, we simultaneously persistently record the fact that this step has executed and save the value produced by this step.
4. Every effectful step is modified to first check if this step has already been executed. If it has, then the previously saved value (for this step) is used instead of executing the step again.

Note that λ_{FAIL} does not have any non-deterministic construct (in a single agent's evaluation). Non-deterministic constructs can be supported by treating them as an effectful step so that once a non-deterministic choice is made, any re-execution of the same step makes the same choice.

Details. We now describe in detail how individual computation steps can be made idempotent and how these idempotent steps can be composed together into idempotent computation. Our solution is essentially a monad (Fig. 4).

We represent an idempotent computation as a function that takes a tuple $(guid, tc)$ as a parameter (where $guid$ and tc represent an identifier and a step number used to uniquely identify steps in a computation) and returns a value along with a new step number. We can "execute" an idempotent computation *idf* as shown by the function `imrun`, using the function's argument itself as the $guid$ value and an initial step number of 0.

The function `imreturn` (the monadic "return") lifts primitive values to idempotent computations. This transformation can be used for any pure (side-effect-free) expressions.

Side-effects (table operations) are permitted only inside the `atomic` construct. The function `imatomic` is used to make a local transaction idempotent. Specifically, "`imatomic` $T\ f_m$" is an idempotent representation for "`atomic` $T\ f$", where f_m is the monadic form of f constructed as described later. As explained above, this is represented as a function that takes a pair $(guid, tc)$ as a parameter and realizes the memoization strategy described above. The pair $(guid, tc)$ is used as a unique identifier for this step. We check whether this step has already executed. If so, we return the previously computed value. If not, we execute this computation step and memoize the computed value. In either case, the step number is incremented in this process and returned.

It is, however, critical to do all of the above steps *atomically* to ensure that even if two agents concurrently attempt to execute the same computation, only one of them will actually execute it. However, note that an atomic expression is allowed to access only a single table. Hence, the "memoized" information for this computation step must be stored in the same table that is accessed by the computation step. However, we must keep our memoization and book-keeping information logically distinct from the program's own data stored in the same table. We achieve this by creating two distinct "address spaces" (of key values) for the table. We convert a key value k used by our idempotence implementation to $(0, k)$ and convert a key value k used by the program itself to $(1, k)$. The functions `imupdate` and `imlookup` do this wrapping for the user's code. Thus, the expression f to be evaluated in the atomic transaction is transformed to its monadic representation f_m by replacing `lookup` and `update` in f by `imlookup` and `imupdate` respectively.

We now consider how to compose individual computation steps in an idempotent computation (the monadic "*bind*" function). Consider a computation of the form "$let\ x\ =\ step1\ in\ step2$" which is equivalent to "$(\lambda x.step2)step1$". We transform $step1$ to its monadic form, say *idf*. We transform $step2$ to its idempotent form, say g. The function *bind*, applied to *idf* and $\lambda x.g$, produces the idempotent form of the whole computation. (A formal and more complete description of the transformation is presented later.)

The result of "`imbind` *idf f*" is defined as follows: it is an idempotent function that takes a parameter $(guid, tc)$, and invokes *idf* (the first step). It uses the value and the step number returned by the idempotent function and invoke the second idempotent function f. Thus the monad effectively threads the step number through the computation, incrementing it in every atomic transaction.

Note that a key characteristic of this implementation is that it is completely decentralized. When a transaction completes, the current agent simply attempts to execute the next (idempotent) transaction in the workflow; no coordination with a centralized transaction manager is required. In general, distributed coordination requires the use of expensive blocking protocols such as 2 phase commit. In contrast, a workflow implementation based on this idea of idempotence coupled with (client-side) retry logic are non-blocking. The implementation does not have a single point-of-failure or single performance bottleneck, which can lead to increased scalability.

Also note that this implementation creates one log entry per transaction. Once logging for idempotence is separated from the core business logic, it can be optimized in several ways. We can avoid redundant logging if the underlying storage engine maintains its own log. Logging can be avoided if the transaction is (declared to be) semantically idempotent.

Example. The monadic library lets us construct the monadic version e_m of any λ_{FAIL} expression e, by using the monadic version of any primitive and the monadic bind in place of function application. E.g., the monadic version of the following code fragment (from the money transfer example)

$$\textit{atomic fb}\ \{\textit{update fa}\ ((\textit{lookup fa}) - \textit{amt})\};$$
$$\textit{atomic tb}\ \{\textit{update ta}\ ((\textit{lookup ta}) + \textit{amt})\};$$

is the following:

$$\texttt{imbind}$$
$$(\texttt{imatomic}\,\textit{fb}\ \{\texttt{imupdate}\,\textit{fa}\ ((\texttt{imlookup}\,\textit{fa}) - \textit{amt})\})$$
$$\{\texttt{imatomic}\ \textit{tb}\ \{\texttt{imupdate}\ \textit{ta}\ ((\texttt{imlookup}\ \textit{ta}) + \textit{amt})\}\}$$

where $\{e\}$ is shorthand for $\lambda x.e$, where x is not free in e.

3.2 Idempotence Monad Programs Are Failfree

In this section, we show that programs written using the idempotence monad are failfree.

Idempotent Executions. Consider any execution of a λ_{FAIL} program. We refer to any transition generated by rule NORMAL as an *execution-step* and identify it by the triple $(v \triangleright e) \overset{\omega}{\dashrightarrow} (v \triangleright e')$. Thus, an *execution-step* $a \overset{\omega}{\dashrightarrow} b$ represents a transition caused by an agent a that transforms to an agent b, with a side-effect ω on the tables. An execution-step $a \overset{\omega}{\dashrightarrow} b$, after an execution ξ, is said to be a *repeated* execution-step if the execution ξ contains some execution-step of the form $a \overset{\omega'}{\dashrightarrow} b'$. (Note that this does not signify a cycle in the execution since the states of the tables could be different in the two corresponding configurations.)

DEFINITION 3.1. *An execution is said to be* operationally idempotent *iff for any two execution-steps $a \overset{\omega}{\dashrightarrow} b$ and $a' \overset{\omega'}{\dashrightarrow} b'$ in the execution (in that order), $a = a'$ implies that $b = b'$ and ω' is empty.*

Note that operational idempotence is a property that involves the side-effects on the tables, unlike observational idempotence. As we show below, it is a stronger property that can be used to establish observational idempotence.

LEMMA 3.2. *Any operationally idempotent execution ξ of a program p (in the standard semantics) is observationally equivalent to some ideal execution ξ' of p (in the ideal semantics): i.e., $obs(\xi) = obs(\xi')$.*

PROOF SKETCH. Let ξ be an operationally idempotent execution of a program p under the standard semantics $\Rightarrow_{\text{A}}$. We show how to construct an execution ξ' of p under the $\Rightarrow_{\text{IDEAL}}$ semantics such that $obs(\xi) = obs(\xi')$.

We first omit any transitions in ξ due to the FAIL rule since their labels are empty.

We next omit the transitions corresponding to repeated execution-steps:

The key point to note here is that an execution-step $a \overset{\omega}{\dashrightarrow} b$ affects the (legality of) subsequent transitions in two ways: indirectly through the side-effects ω on the tables and directly through b (which may take part in subsequent transitions). A repeated execution-step is redundant in any idempotent execution that has no failures (transitions due to the FAIL rule): it has no side-effects on the tables, and if the value b is subsequently used in a non-repeated execution-step, then we can show that another agent identical to b already exists in the configuration.

We then omit any transition due to the RETRY rule. We finally replace INPUT transitions corresponding to a duplicate and replace INPUT transitions corresponding to a non-duplicate input request by a UNIQUE-INPUT transition.

This leaves us with duplicate responses that may be produced by the OUTPUT rule for the same input (due to multiple agents that process it). We replace these transitions by corresponding DUPLSEND transition.

This transformation produces an execution ξ' of p under the $\Rightarrow_{\text{IDEAL}}$ semantics such that $obs(\xi) = obs(\xi')$. ■

Our next goal is to show that all executions of programs written using the idempotence monad are operationally idempotent. However, this claim requires the programs to be *well-typed*, as defined below.

Well-Typed IM Programs. The idempotence monad can be used to write monadic programs in the usual way. The monad may be thought of as defining a new language λ_{IM}, obtained from λ_{FAIL} by replacing the keywords `atomic`, `lookup`, and `update` by the keywords `imatomic`, `imlookup`, `imupdate`, `imbind`, and `imrun`. A λ_{IM} program can also be thought as a λ_{FAIL} program, using the definition of the monad in Fig. 4.

We first mention a few type restrictions used to simplify presentation. We refer to λ-calculus terms as *pure* and their types as pure types. We assume that the types of keys and values of all tables are pure types. We assume that the types of the input request and the output response are also pure types.

We use $\langle \tau_k, \tau_v \rangle$ to denote the type of a table with keys of type τ_k and values of type τ_v. We assume that table names come from some fixed set of identifiers and that the typing environment maps these table names to their types.

The non-pure terms can be classified into two kinds. The first kind are expressions (such as `imupdate` $k\ v$), which are meant to be evaluated in the context of a single table (as part of a local transaction). Fig. 5 presents typing rules for intra-transaction expressions. The type $\tau!\langle \tau_k, \tau_v \rangle$ signifies a term that can be evaluated in the context of a table of type $\langle \tau_k, \tau_v \rangle$, producing a value of type τ. The second kind of expressions are the ones that use the idempotence monad, used to represent workflow computations which execute one or more local transactions. Fig. 6 presents typing rules for such expressions (which are the standard monad typing rules).

In the sequel, we will use the term well-typed IM program to refer to any expression e such that $\Gamma_{tn} \models e : \tau_i \rightarrow_{\text{ID}} \tau_o$, where τ_i and τ_o are, respectively, the types of input and output messages, and Γ_{tn} provides the typings of tables. This is essentialy a program of the form `imrun` e', where e' is constructed from the other monadic constructs.

$$\frac{\Gamma \models e : \tau_k!\langle\tau_k,\tau_v\rangle}{\Gamma \models \texttt{imlookup}\ e : \tau_v!\langle\tau_k,\tau_v\rangle}\ \text{[IMLOOKUP]}$$

$$\frac{\Gamma \models e_1 : \tau_k!\langle\tau_k,\tau_v\rangle \qquad \Gamma \models e_2 : \tau_v!\langle\tau_k,\tau_v\rangle}{\Gamma \models \texttt{imupdate}\ e_1\ e_2 : \text{unit}!\langle\tau_k,\tau_v\rangle}\ \text{[IMUPDATE]}$$

$$\frac{}{x : \tau \models x : \tau!\langle\tau_k,\tau_v\rangle}\ \text{[AT-VAR]}$$

$$\frac{\Gamma, x : \tau_1 \models e : \tau_2!\langle\tau_k,\tau_v\rangle}{\Gamma \models \lambda x.e : (\tau_1 \overset{\langle\tau_k,\tau_v\rangle}{\rightarrow} \tau_2!\langle\tau_k,\tau_v\rangle)}\ \text{[AT-LAMBDA]}$$

$$\frac{\Gamma \models e_1 : (\tau_1 \overset{\langle\tau_k,\tau_v\rangle}{\rightarrow} \tau_2)!\langle\tau_k,\tau_v\rangle \qquad \Gamma \models e_2 : \tau_1!\langle\tau_k,\tau_v\rangle}{\Gamma \models e_1 e_2 : \tau_2!\langle\tau_k,\tau_v\rangle}\ \text{[AT-APPLY]}$$

Figure 5: A type system for intra-transaction expressions.

$$\frac{\Gamma \models e : \tau}{\Gamma \models \texttt{imreturn}\ e : \mathsf{IM}\ \tau}\ \text{[IMRETURN]}$$

$$\frac{\Gamma \models t : \langle\tau_k,\tau_v\rangle \qquad \Gamma \models e : (\text{unit} \overset{\langle\tau_k,\tau_v\rangle}{\rightarrow} \tau)!\langle\tau_k,\tau_v\rangle}{\Gamma \models \texttt{imatomic}\ t\ e : \mathsf{IM}\ \tau}\ \text{[IMATOMIC]}$$

$$\frac{\Gamma \models e_2 : \tau_1 \rightarrow \mathsf{IM}\ \tau_2 \qquad \Gamma \models e_1 : \mathsf{IM}\ \tau_1}{\Gamma \models \texttt{imbind}\ e_1\ e_2 : \mathsf{IM}\ \tau_2}\ \text{[IMBIND]}$$

$$\frac{\Gamma \models e : \tau_1 \rightarrow \mathsf{IM}\ \tau_2}{\Gamma \models \texttt{imrun}\ e : \tau_1 \rightarrow_{\text{ID}} \tau_2}\ \text{[IMRUN]}$$

$$\frac{}{x : \tau \models x : \tau}\ \text{[VAR]}$$

$$\frac{\Gamma, x : \tau_1 \models e : \tau_2}{\Gamma \models \lambda x.e : \tau_1 \rightarrow \tau_2}\ \text{[LAMBDA]}$$

$$\frac{\Gamma, x : \tau_1 \models e : \tau_2}{\Gamma \models \lambda x.e : \tau_1 \rightarrow \tau_2}\ \text{[APPLY]}$$

Figure 6: A type system for idempotence monad.

LEMMA 3.3. *All executions of a well-typed IM program are operationally idempotent.*

PROOF SKETCH. Let us refer to a value of the form $(0, k)$ (used as a key for a table lookup/update operation) as a *system key*. Consider any execution of a well-typed IM program. It is easy to verify that once the value associated with a system key $(0, k)$ in any table is set to be v, it is never subsequently modified.

Consider any two execution-steps $a \overset{\omega}{\dashrightarrow} b$ and $a' \overset{\omega'}{\dashrightarrow} b'$ in the execution (in that order) where $a = a'$. The idempotence property follows trivially whenever these steps are effect-free steps. The only effectful steps are produced by the evaluation of an `imatomic` construct. Since $a = a'$, the *key* value used in the evaluation of `imatomic` in both steps must be identical. The implementation of `imatomic` guarantees that whatever value is produced by the evaluation of `imatomic` in the first step will be memoized with the given value. This guarantees that the second step will find this same value in the table (thanks to the property described earlier). Hence, it will evaluate to the same value and will have no side-effects on the table. It follows that the execution is idempotent. ■

THEOREM 3.4. *Any well-typed IM program is observationally idempotent.*

PROOF SKETCH. Follows immediately from the previous two lemmas. ■

As stated earlier, observational idempotence does not give us any progress guarantees in the presence of failures. We now establish progress guarantees in the form of a weak bisimulation.

DEFINITION 3.5. *Let p be any λ_{FAIL} program. Let Σ^p_{A} denote the set of configurations $\{ \sigma \in \Sigma \mid \langle\langle p \rangle\rangle \Rightarrow^*_{\text{A}} \sigma \}$ that can be produced by the execution of p under the standard semantics. Let Σ^p_{I} denote the set of configurations $\{ \sigma \in \Sigma \mid \langle\langle p \rangle\rangle \Rightarrow^*_{\text{IDEAL}} \sigma \}$ that can be produced by the execution of p under the ideal semantics. We define the relation $\simeq$ between Σ^p_{A} and Σ^p_{I} by $\langle p, \mu_1, \alpha_1, I_1, O_1 \rangle \simeq \langle p, \mu_2, \alpha_2, I_2, O_2 \rangle$ iff $I_1 = I_2$ and $\mu_1 = \mu_2$.*

Note that in the above definition, the condition $I_1 = I_2$ implies that both configurations have received the same set of input requests. The condition $\mu_1 = \mu_2$ implies that the processing of each input request v in both configurations have gone through identical sequences of effectful steps so far. (This follows since every effectful step is memoized and is part of the table state μ_1 and μ_2.)

THEOREM 3.6. *If p is a well-typed IM program, then $\simeq$ is a weak bisimulation between $(\Sigma^p_{\text{A}}, \Rightarrow_{\text{A}})$ and $(\Sigma^p_{\text{I}}, \Rightarrow_{\text{IDEAL}})$.*

PROOF SKETCH. Consider any $\sigma_1 \simeq \sigma_2$. The interesting transitions are those that are effectful (involving an atomic operation) or produce an output. If either σ_1 or σ_2 can perform an interesting transition, we must show that the other can perform an equivalent transition (possibly after a sequence of silent transitions).

Consider the case when an agent $v \triangleright e$ in σ_1 can perform an effectful transition in the standard semantics. Let $v \triangleright e_0$ be the state of the same agent after its most recent `imatomic` evaluation. Then, we must have some side-effect-free evaluation $e_0 \rightarrow e_1 \cdots e_k = e$. Consider configuration σ_2. By definition, we restrict our attention to reachable states. Hence, there exists some execution in the ideal semantics that produces σ_2. This execution must have received input request v and produced an agent $v \triangleright (p\ v)$. Consider the evaluation of this agent. The effectful steps in this agent's evaluation in the ideal semantics must have produced the same sequence of values as in the evaluation in the standard semantics (since the memoized values for these steps are the same in both σ_1 and σ_2). Thus, σ_2 must have some agent of the form $v \triangleright e_i$ for some $0 \leq i \leq k$. This will produce, after zero or more silent transitions, the agent $v \triangleright e$ that can then perform the same effectful transition in the ideal semantics as in the standard semantics.

Consider the case when an agent $v \triangleright e$ in σ_2 can perform an effectful transition in the ideal semantics. We can create a new agent $v \triangleright (p\ v)$ using rule RETRY in the standard semantics. We can then

$$
\begin{array}{rcll}
[x]^{\mathsf{V}} & = & x & \\
[\lambda x.e]^{\mathsf{V}} & = & \lambda x.[e]^{\mathsf{I}} & \\
\\
[x]^{\mathsf{I}} & = & \texttt{imreturn}\, x & \\
[\lambda x.e]^{\mathsf{I}} & = & \texttt{imreturn}\, (\lambda x.[e]^{\mathsf{I}}) & \\
[n\ e]^{\mathsf{I}} & = & \texttt{imbind}\, [n]^{\mathsf{I}}\, (\lambda x.[x\ e]^{\mathsf{I}}) & , n \notin \langle \mathsf{Val} \rangle \\
[v\ n]^{\mathsf{I}} & = & \texttt{imbind}\, [n]^{\mathsf{I}}\, (\lambda x.[v\ x]^{\mathsf{I}}) & , v \in \langle \mathsf{Val} \rangle, n \notin \langle \mathsf{Val} \rangle \\
[v\ v']^{\mathsf{I}} & = & [v]^{\mathsf{V}}\, [v']^{\mathsf{V}} & , v, v' \in \langle \mathsf{Val} \rangle \\
[\texttt{atomic}\, x\ e]^{\mathsf{I}} & = & \langle \texttt{imatomic}\, x\, [e]^{\mathsf{A}}, \mathit{fv} \rangle & \\
& & \text{where } \mathit{fv} = \{x\} \cup \mathit{freevars}(e) & \\
\\
[x]^{\mathsf{A}} & = & x & \\
[\lambda x.e]^{\mathsf{A}} & = & \lambda x.[e]^{\mathsf{A}} & \\
[e_1 e_2]^{\mathsf{A}} & = & [e_1]^{\mathsf{A}} [e_2]^{\mathsf{A}} & \\
[\texttt{update}\, e_1\ e_2]^{\mathsf{A}} & = & \texttt{imupdate}\, [e_1]^{\mathsf{A}}\, [e_2]^{\mathsf{A}} & \\
[\texttt{lookup}\, e]^{\mathsf{A}} & = & \texttt{imlookup}\, [e]^{\mathsf{A}} & \\
\\
\langle e, \{\} \rangle & = & e & \\
\langle e, \{x\} \uplus Y \rangle & = & \langle \texttt{imbind}\, x\ (\lambda x.e), Y \rangle &
\end{array}
$$

Figure 7: Transforming λ_{FAIL} expressions into idempotent expressions.

duplicate the entire execution history of $v \triangleright e$ (which is guaranteed to be the same in both semantics by the definition of $\simeq$). Thanks to the idempotence property, this duplicate execution will have no extra side-effects and will eventually produce the same effectful transition as in the ideal semantics. ∎

THEOREM 3.7. *A well-typed IM program is failfree.*

3.3 Transforming λ_{FAIL} Programs To Idempotent Programs

We have seen that the idempotence monad lets us construct failfree programs. Given any λ_{FAIL}-program e, we can construct its "equivalent" monadic representation using standard techniques (which are conceptually straightforward, though the details are intricate). The transformation is presented in Fig. 7 (based on the transformation in [17]).

We make a few simplifying assumptions (type restrictions) about the source λ_{FAIL} program e in this transformation algorithm (similar to those mentioned in Section 3.2). We assume that the types of keys and values of all tables are pure types. We assume that intra-transaction expressions do not manipulate values of workflow type: e.g., `atomic` t $\{\lambda x.(\texttt{atomic}\ s\ e)\}$ is not allowed.

The translation is defined using multiple translation functions. $[v]^{\mathsf{V}}$ is a translation function that applies only to values (which must be of the form x or $\lambda x.e$). The translation function $[e]^{\mathsf{I}}$ is the heart of the monadic transformation and can be applied to multi-transaction expressions. It uses the idempotence monad to sequence local transactions. The translation function $[e]^{\mathsf{A}}$ is applied to intra-transaction expressions and it is used primarily to replace occurrences of `update` and `lookup` by `imupdate` and `imlookup` respectively. Note that a single local transaction (i.e.intra-transaction expression) evaluation is done using standard evaluation (without using any monad). The auxiliary function $\langle e, X \rangle$ is used to transform the monadic values used in the evaluation of multi-transactions to standard values required in the evaluation of a single local transaction.

Finally, given a top-level λ_{FAIL} program e (which is assumed to be a functional value of the form $\lambda x.e'$), it's monadic form e_m is defined to be `imrun` $[e]^{\mathsf{V}}$. As usual, it can be shown that the translation preserves types: translation of a well-typed λ_{FAIL} program (satisfying the restrictions mentioned above) will produced a well-typed monadic program.

3.4 Failfree Realization Via Idempotence

Given any λ_{FAIL} expression e, we can construct its monadic version e_m as explained above. The preceding results imply that e_m must be failfree. We now establish a stronger result, namely that e_m is a failfree realization of e. (Failure-freedom is a weak correctness criterion. It indicates that a program's behavior under the standard semantics is equivalent to *it's* behavior under the ideal semantics.) The notion of failure-freedom does let us simplify verifying correctness of a program by considering only its behavior under the ideal semantics. In particular, we have:

THEOREM 3.8. *If p and q are weakly bisimilar under the ideal semantics (i.e., if $(\langle\langle p \rangle\rangle, \Rightarrow_{\text{IDEAL}}) \simeq (\langle\langle q \rangle\rangle, \Rightarrow_{\text{IDEAL}})$, and p is failfree, then p is a failfree realization of q.*

PROOF SKETCH. Follows as we can compose the two weak bisimulations together. ∎

This theorem simplifies proving that a program is a failfree realization of another. In particular, we have already seen that a monadic program is failfree (Theorem 3.7). Hence, to prove that e_m is a failfree realization of e, it suffices to show a weak bisimilarity between the *ideal* executions of a λ_{FAIL} program e and the *ideal* executions of its monadic representation e_m.

THEOREM 3.9. *Let e_m be the monadic representation of e. Then, e_m is a failfree realization of e.*

PROOF SKETCH. As explained above, it is sufficient to relate evaluations of e and e_m under the ideal semantics. In this setting, it is intuitively simple to see why the monadic program "e_m" simulates the given program e. The key distinction is that the monadic implementation uses `imatomic` to perform any effectful step. This step will first check the memoized data to see if this step has already executed. In an ideal execution, *this check will always fail*, and the monadic implementation then performs the same effectful step as the original program (and memoizes it). The check is guaranteed to always fail because the keys (g, i) used in distinct executions of `imatomic` are distinct. The value of g will be different for executions corresponding to different inputs x and y. The value i will be different for different steps corresponding to the same input x. ∎

3.5 Idempotent Failfree Computations as a Language Feature

We have now seen how idempotent failfree computations can be automatically realized using the idempotence monad. We now propose a new language construct for idempotent failfree computations.

The construct "`idff` v e" indicates that the computation of e should be failfree and should be idempotent with respect to v: i.e., multiple (potentially concurrent) invocations of this construct with the same value v behaves as though only one of the invocations executed. The above construct permits users to specify the code fragment for which they desire *automatic* idempotence and failure-freedom (provided by the compiler). This enables users to rely on other methods, perhaps application-specific, to ensure these properties elsewhere. (For instance, some computation may be semantically idempotent already.) It also lets the users specify what should be used as *computation identifier* to detect duplicates, as illustrated below.

We refer to this enhanced language as λ_{IDFF}. A formal semantics of λ_{IDFF} appears in the appendix. We illustrate the meaning of the first parameter of `idff` using the incorrect λ_{FAIL} example of Fig. 1. We can wrap the `idff` construct around this example in the following two ways, with different semantics. Note that the input in this example is a pair *(reqId, req)* consisting of a request-id as well as the actual request. Consider:

$$f_1 = \lambda(reqId, req).\ \texttt{idff}\ reqId\ (process\ (reqId, req))$$
$$f_2 = \lambda(reqId, req).\ \texttt{idff}\ (reqId, req)\ (process\ (reqId, req))$$

The behavior of these two functions differ in the cases where multiple inputs arrive with the same request-id but differing in the second parameter *req*. f_1 treats such requests as the same and will process only one of them, while f_2 will treat them as different requests and process them all.

One of the subtle issues with the semantics and implementation of the `idff` construct is the treatment of invocations that have the same id (first parameter) but have different expressions as the second parameter. We take a simple approach with our semantics (that the effect is as if only the first invocation occurred). This has some implications for the underlying implementation (in the presence of failures). One solution is to use a continuation-passing style computation, and memoize the entire continuation in the memoization step (rather than just the value computed for the step).

4. Extensions

We have seen how idempotence can serve as the basis for *fail-free composition* of computations: essentially, a simple form of *fault-tolerant* workflow. In this section, we describe two extensions that enrich this construct, namely compensating actions and asynchronous evaluation, which simplify writing applications. These concepts are not new, but what is interesting is that they can be integrated without affecting the light-weight, decentralized, nature of our idempotence implementation.

4.1 Compensating Actions

The `idff` construct allows us to compose several transactions into an idempotent workflow that appears to execute *exactly once* without process failures. However, the lack of isolation means that when a transaction in the workflow is executed, its precondition may not be satisfied and we may need to abort the workflow. For example, in the transfer example (Fig. 1), the debit step may succeed, but we may be unable to complete the subsequent credit step because the account does not exist. One way of recovering from this failure is to *compensate for* the debit by crediting the amount back to the source account. If compensating actions are correct, the workflow can guarantee all-or-nothing semantics i.e. either all or none of the transactions in the workflow appear to execute.

We first formalize the desired semantics of workflows with compensating actions. We present a language λ_{IDWF} which provides language constructs to associate transactions with compensating actions, and to declare logical failures. Finally, λ_{IDWF} supports a construct `idworkflow` $id\ e$, which composes transactions with compensating actions into a workflow. We present semantics of this construct, and then show how this construct is realized using a *compensation monad*.

Syntax. λ_{IDWF} modifies and extends λ_{FAIL} in the following ways (see Fig. 8). `atomic` $t\ e_a\ e_c$ extends the `atomic` construct of λ_{FAIL} by specifying e_c as the compensation for the atomic transaction e_a. `abort` indicates that a logical failure has occured and the workflow must be aborted. `idworkflow` $id\ e$ represents an idempotent workflow with identifier id, where e is the workflow consisting of a composition of atomic transactions with compensations. Expression of the form $e \oslash e_c$ arise only during evaluation and are not source language constructs.

Semantic Domains. The semantic domains for λ_{IDWF} are the same as for λ_{FAIL} with minor extensions. The runtime expression $e \oslash e_c$ is used to represent a workflow during its execution. Here, e represents the partially evaluated form of a workflow and e_c represents the compensating action to be performed in case the workflow needs to be aborted. Agents can also be of the form $id \blacktriangleright e_w \oslash e_c$, indicating an agent evaluating a workflow.

Semantics. The semantics of λ_{IDWF} is defined using a set of rules consisting of all the rules in A used to define the semantics of λ_{FAIL} except for FAIL and ATOMIC, plus the new rules presented in Fig. 8.

The initiation of a workflow (rule IDWF-BEGIN) creates a new agent of the form $id \blacktriangleright e_w \oslash e_c$, provided no agent has already been created for id. This agent evaluates the workflow e_w and tracks the compensating action e_c to be performed in case of an `abort`. Rule IDWF-END indicates how the computation proceeds once the workflow evaluation is complete (or if a previous workflow with the same id has already been initiated).

The rules ATOMIC and ATOMIC-ABORT define the semantics of transactions in a workflow. Informally, the expression `atomic` $t\ e_a\ e_c$ is evaluated as follows. First, e_a is evaluated atomically to produce a value v. Then, as a side-effect, the compensating action is updated to indicate that $e_c\ v$ should be evaluated as the first step of the compensation before executing the original compensation. Finally, the whole expression evaluates to v. Thus, note that the value produced by the "atomic" action e_a is available to the subsequent computation as well as the compensating action e_c. When a workflow is aborted (rules ATOMIC-ABORT and IDWF-ABORT), the compensation expression is evaluated.

Rule ATOMIC of λ_{FAIL} is replaced by the pair of rules PURE-ATOMIC and PURE-ATOMIC-ABORT, which describe the behavior of a transaction that is not contained within a workflow. PURE-ATOMIC describes the successful completion of a transaction, while PURE-ATOMIC-ABORT describes the case where the transaction is aborted. (The auxiliary relation $\twoheadrightarrow$ used here is defined by the rules for λ_{FAIL}.)

Compensation monad We now describe the *compensation monad* that can be used to realize workflows with compensating actions. For simplicity, we describe an implementation of the compensating monad that focuses only on logical failures and compensations. We assume there are no duplicate requests or process failures. We can realize idempotent workflows with compensating actions by *composing* this monad and the idempotence monad [13].

The compensation monad, shown in Fig. 9, is a combination of the exception monad and the continuation passing style monad. Transactions return a value of the form *Value*(v) (on successful completion) or a special value *Abort* to indicate that the transaction was aborted. Workflows are represented as a function in continuation passing style. The helper function *compensateWith* associates a transaction a with a compensating action to construct a primitive workflow. *compensateWith* constructs a function in continuation passing style. This function first evaluates a(). If a aborts, the whole transaction aborts and returns *Abort*. Otherwise, the continuation is evaluated using the value returned by the transaction. If the continuation itself aborts (because one of the following transactions aborts), we evaluate the compensating action and return the value *Abort*. The monad's *return* simply lifts a value (with no compensation) into a workflow. The monadic *bind* is standard for continuation passing style computations. The function *run* shows how to execute a workflow by passing it an empty continuation.

4.2 Asynchronous evaluation

Workflows are commonly used to perform computations involving several transactions. Consequently, workflows are often long running with highly variable latencies. Large latencies accentuate the

(a) Syntax and Evaluation Context

$$x \in \langle \mathsf{Identifier} \rangle; \qquad v \in \langle \mathsf{Val} \rangle ::= x \mid \lambda x.e$$
$$e \in \langle \mathsf{Exp} \rangle ::= x \mid \lambda x.e \mid e\ e \mid \mathtt{atomic}\ v_t\ v_a\ v_c \mid \mathtt{idworkflow}\ v_i\ v_w \mid \mathtt{abort} \mid \mathtt{update}\ v\ v \mid \mathtt{lookup}\ v \mid e \oslash e_c$$
$$\Sigma_A = \langle \mathsf{Exp} \rangle \times \langle \mathsf{Exp} \rangle + \langle \mathsf{Exp} \rangle \times \langle \mathsf{Exp} \rangle$$
$$E ::= [\cdot] \mid E\ e \mid v\ E \mid E \oslash e$$

(b) Evaluation Rules (in addition to A \ { ATOMIC })

[IDWF-BEGIN]
$$\frac{v \triangleright E[\mathtt{idworkflow}\ id\ w] \in \alpha \qquad \nexists e'.id \blacktriangleright e' \in \alpha}{\langle p, \mu, \alpha, I, O \rangle \stackrel{\epsilon}{\Rightarrow} \langle p, \mu, \alpha \uplus \{id \blacktriangleright (w() \oslash 0)\}, I, O \rangle}$$

[IDWF-END]
$$\frac{id \blacktriangleright u \in \alpha \qquad u \in \langle \mathsf{Val} \rangle}{\langle p, \mu, \alpha \uplus \{v \triangleright E[\mathtt{idworkflow}\ id\ w]\}, I, O \rangle \stackrel{\epsilon}{\Rightarrow} \langle p, \mu, \alpha \uplus \{v \triangleright E[u]\}, I, O \rangle}$$

[NORMAL]
$$\frac{\langle \mu, e \rangle \stackrel{\omega}{\rightsquigarrow} \langle \mu', e' \rangle}{\langle p, \mu, \alpha \uplus \{v \blacktriangleright e\}, I, O \rangle \Rightarrow \langle p, \mu', \alpha \uplus \{v \blacktriangleright e'\}, I, O \rangle}$$

[ATOMIC]
$$\frac{\langle \mu[tn], e_a() \rangle \stackrel{\omega}{\twoheadrightarrow}^{*} \langle t, v \rangle, v \in \langle \mathsf{Val} \rangle}{\langle \mu, E[\mathtt{atomic}\ tn\ e_a\ e_c] \oslash e \rangle \stackrel{\omega}{\rightsquigarrow} \langle \mu[tn \mapsto t], E[v] \oslash ((e_c\ v); e) \rangle}$$

[ATOMIC-ABORT]
$$\frac{\langle \mu[tn], e_a() \rangle \stackrel{\omega}{\twoheadrightarrow}^{*} \langle t, E[\mathsf{abort}] \rangle}{\langle \mu, E[\mathtt{atomic}\ tn\ e_a\ e_c] \oslash e \rangle \stackrel{\epsilon}{\rightsquigarrow} \langle \mu, E[\mathsf{abort}] \oslash e \rangle}$$

[IDWF-ABORT]
$$\frac{}{\langle \mu, (E[\mathtt{abort}]) \oslash e_c \rangle \rightsquigarrow \langle \mu, e_c \rangle}$$

[CONTEXT]
$$\frac{e \rightarrow e'}{\langle \mu, E[e] \oslash e_c \rangle \rightarrow \langle \mu, E[e'] \oslash e_c \rangle}$$

[PURE-ATOMIC]
$$\frac{\langle \mu[tn], e_a() \rangle \stackrel{\omega}{\twoheadrightarrow}^{*} \langle t, v \rangle, v \in \langle \mathsf{Val} \rangle}{\langle \mu, \mathtt{atomic}\ tn\ e_a\ e_c \rangle \stackrel{\omega}{\rightsquigarrow} \langle \mu[tn \mapsto t], v \rangle}$$

[PURE-ATOMIC-ABORT]
$$\frac{\langle \mu[tn], e_a() \rangle \stackrel{\omega}{\twoheadrightarrow}^{*} \langle t, E[\mathtt{abort}] \rangle}{\langle \mu, \mathtt{atomic}\ tn\ e_a\ e_c \rangle \stackrel{\epsilon}{\rightsquigarrow} \langle \mu, 0 \rangle}$$

Figure 8: Syntax and Semantics of λ_{IDWF}.

```
let compensateWith a comp =
  fun f → match a() with
    | Abort → Abort
    | Value(b) → match (f b) with
        | Abort → let _ = comp b in Abort
        | Value(c) → Value(c)

let bind (v, f) = fun g → v (fun a → f a g)
let return a = compensateWith (fun () → a) (fun v → ())
let run a = a (fun x → Value(x))
```

Figure 9: The compensation monad

problem of duplicate requests because clients cannot easily distinguish between a long running workflow and one that has failed to generate a response. While the idempotence monad guarantees correctness in such cases, idempotence does come at a performance cost (due to log lookups). A design pattern commonly used to reduce the number of duplicate requests is for the system to take over the task of retrying (a part of) the request on behalf of the client *asynchronously*, and sending an intermediate response to the client, typically with the transaction identifier. The client can use transaction identifier to periodically poll for the status of the request.

The idempotence monad can be extended to support asynchronous evaluation as follows. At a programmer defined point in the evaluation of the workflow, we create a *checkpoint*. A checkpoint is essentially a closure representing the rest of the workflow, along with relevant state variables. The checkpoint is then persisted, typically in a distributed queue (essentially a worklist). Once the checkpoint has been created, an intermediate response is sent to the client. A set of special agents periodically query the queue, retrieve checkpoints, and continue evaluation, deleting the checkpoint only when the workflow has been fully evaluated.

Supporting asynchronous evaluation requires some additional support from the platform and a minor change to the monad's *bind* function. We assume that the platform provides a *channel* that can only be accessed by the idempotence monad (hence not exposed in λ_{FAIL}). Messages can be sent to this channel using the function *send* and received using the function *recv*. We assume the channel supports the following handshake protocol for messages in order to guarantee at-least-once processing of messages. In this protocol, *recv* does not delete messages from the channel. Instead, an agent that receives a message must acknowledge the message (using *ack*) before the message is permanently deleted. If an agent crashes after receiving a message and before acknowledging it, the message reappears in the channel and may be processed by other agents. (Windows Azure provides such a channel implementation, which our implementation uses.)

The changes to the idempotence monad are illustrated in Figure 10. Instead of invoking the remainder of the workflow, the modified *bind* (Fig. 10) creates a closure for the rest of the workflow and persists the closure in a special queue (*"worklist"*) (using the function *send*). Special agent processes (*agent*) retrieve the checkpoints (using *recv*) and continue evaluating the rest of workflow. If an agent manages to evaluate the workflow without failing, it deletes the workflow from the queue (using *ack*). In our implementation, the choice of using asynchronous evaluation (and the particular step at which to create a checkpoint) is left to the programmer. We evaluate the benefits of these optimizations in Section 5.

```
let agent () =
  while (true)
    let (msgid, msg) = recv "worklist"in
    let (f, params) = msg in
    let result = f params in
    let _ = ack "worklist" (msgid,msg) in result

let bind (idf, f) =
  fun (guid, tc) →
    let (ntc, v) = idf (guid, tc)
    send "worklist" (f a (guid, ntc + 1))
```

Figure 10: The idempotence monad with asynchronous evaluation

```
let saveSurvey response = idworkflow {
  do! addAtomic "responses" response.Id response
  return! atomic{
    let! summary = readAtomic "summaries" response.SurveyName
    do summary.Merge(response)
    return! writeAtomic "summaries" response.SurveyName summary }}
```

Figure 11: The save survey operation expressed as in idempotent workflow.

5. Evaluation

We have implemented the idempotence workflow monad and its variants in C# and F#, targeting Windows Azure, a platform for hosting distributed applications. Azure provides a key-value store with explicit support for data partitioning, where partitions are units of serializability. In this section, we focus on evaluating the expressiveness and performance overheads of the idempotence monad.

Sample applications We found several real world applications whose core logic can be declaratively expressed as workflows. We briefly describe an expense management application [4] and a survey application [3]. Other applications we have implemented include applications for online auctions [2], blogging and banking.

Survey application. The Surveys application enables users to design a survey, publish the survey, and collect the results of surveys. The most performance critical scenario in this application is when a user submits a survey. This operation involves two steps, recording the response and updating the survey summary with the response. For scalability, survey responses and summaries are stored in different data partitions. Figure 11 shows an implementation of this operation using workflows. The syntax here is from the actual F# implementation and differs from λ_{FAIL} in non-essential ways. The workflow is composed of two transactions, a transaction that saves the response and a transaction that updates the summary. In this implementation, survey responses do not reflect in the summary immediately. In general, *deferred writes* are often acceptable as long as the writes will eventually appear to occur exactly once, a guarantee workflows provide. The use of the idempotence monad guarantees that even if multiple requests are received with the same survey, the workflows appears to execute just once.

Auction application. The auction application allows users to bid for items on auction and track the status of their bids. Sellers can register items for auction with a time limit and a minimum bid price. Auction sites are often high volume sites, and both latency and scalability is important. The most critical operation in this application is the operation that processes new bids. This operation can be expressed as a workflow composed of several transaction.

	Hand-coded	**Molecules**
Banking	94	7296
Blogging	243	6484
Auction	107	7256
Surveys	530	9004
Expense	378	6504

Figure 12: Average message size (in bytes) of the hand-coded and workflow implementations.

The first transaction checks if the bid is valid and then checks if the bid beats the current maximum bid, in which case the bid is recorded in a bids table. The second transaction marks the current winner and loosing bidders in a separate table. The web front-end is programmed to poll this table periodically for the latest bid status. Subsequent transactions update other tables such as an aggregate table that maintains the most frequently bid items, more frequent bidders etc. With the idempotent workflow monad, it is easy to guarantee that each bid is processed exactly once even if clients retry with little change in complexity.

Overheads. There are two sources of overheads associated with idempotent workflows compared to hand-coded implementations. First, asynchronous evaluation requires serialization and deserialization closures, which can be expensive. Compiler generated closures tend to capture a lot more state than hand-coded implementations. Idempotent workflows also add unnecessary logging to transactions that are already idempotent.

Fig. 12 shows the average size of messages sent in hand-coded and workflow monad based implementations. As expected, the workflow based implementation generates significantly larger messages. However, experiments on Windows Azure show that the size of the message does not significantly influence the read/write latency or throughput of channels [1], as confirmed by our experiments below.

Next, we evaluate the overall performance overheads of using the idempotence monad relative to hand-coded implementations. For each benchmark application, we evaluate three versions - the original hand-coded version, and two monad based versions. The first version (*synchronous*) evaluates the workflow synchronously in the context of the current agent and delegates the responsibility of retrying operations to the client. The second version uses asynchronous evaluation.

We hosted each of the applications on Windows Azure and ensured that each variant was assigned the same hardware resources i.e. 5 virtual machines, each with a 4-core processor and 7 GB RAM. We assigned two virtual machines each for the front end agents that service browser requests and agents that interact with the storage system and one virtual machine for a background agent uses for asynchronous/check-pointed evaluation. In the synchronous evaluation variant, we assigned an additional virtual machine to the storage interaction agent. For each benchmark, we created a workload that simulates users exercising performance critical scenarios in the application. For example, in the surveys application, the workload consists of a mix of surveys response requests and survey analysis requests. In each case, the workload is biased towards write requests (e.g. 75% responses and 25% analysis requests in the survey application) to ensure that molecular transactions are on the critical path. We ran the workload for 3 minutes (with a 30 seconds warm-up period) and measured throughput (number of requests serviced per second) and latency (average response time) for varying number of simultaneous users.

Fig. 13 shows the measured throughput and latency for the surveys application. In the baseline version, both throughput and

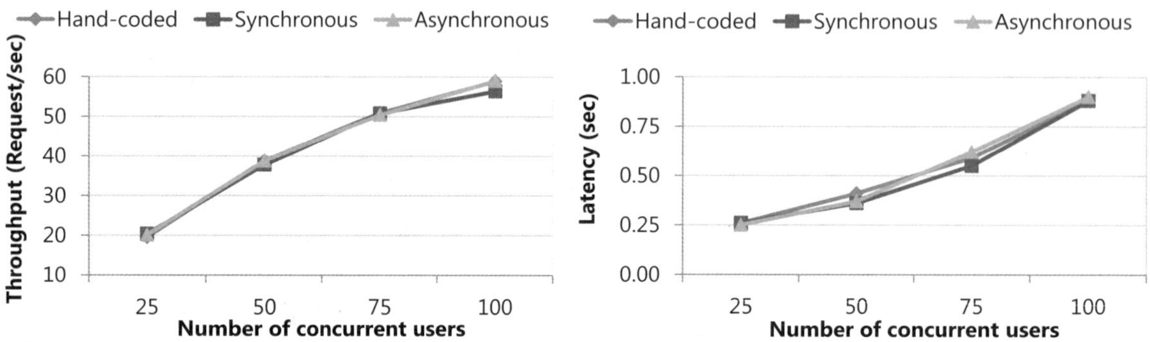

Figure 13: Average throughput and latency for various versions of the survey application.

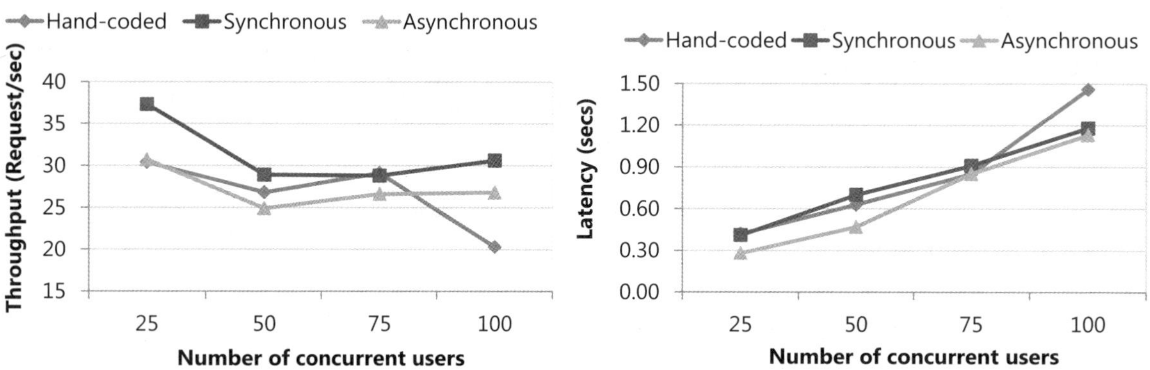

Figure 14: Average throughput and latency for various versions of the auction application.

latency increase almost linearly with the number of users. All monad based implementations closely follow this trend, suggesting very little additional overhead due to our implementation. The throughput (60 operations/second) and latencies are along expected lines. The expected throughput of Azure tables is 500 reads/writes per second, whereas our "operation" is a workflow consisting of two transactions.

The auction application (Fig. 14) has slightly different performance characteristics. The throughput of this application is lower than the surveys application and it decreases with load. This is expected since the workflow is significantly longer. Synchronous evaluation achieves better throughput than the hand-coded implemented (which is asynchronous) at almost the same latency. As expected, asynchronous evaluation improves latency, especially at low loads, but at the cost of reduced throughput (up to 25% lower). At high loads, all monad based implementations perform better than the hand-coded implementation. This is due to a few low level optimizations (such as batching of requests) performed by our implementation. We leave a more detailed performance analysis and optimization of the idempotence monad for future work.

6. Related Work

Our work builds on previous literature in the topics of building reliable distributed systems and transactional workflow. Idempotence has been widely and informally recognized as an important property of distributed systems. Our key contributions include: (a) A formal specification of the desired correctness properties, both safety (idempotence) as well as progress (failure freedom). (b) An automatic technique for guaranteeing failfree idempotence, presented as a monad. This implementation technique is decentralized and does not require distributed coordination. (c) Language constructs for idempotent workflow.

The need to move beyond atomic transactions to sequential compositions of atomic transactions (i.e., workflows) motivated the early work on Sagas and long running transactions [10, 20]. These constructs are weaker than distributed transactions and are generally used to orchestrate processes that run for extended periods. Kamath et al [12] discusses several issues relating to the implementation of transaction managers in Sagas and workflows. A distinguishing aspect of our work is that it exploits the fact that a service is required to be observationally idempotent (from its clients' perspective) to simplify the internal implementation of the workflow. In particular, this lets us avoid the need for distributed coordination with workflow managers.

Modern web applications often exploit horizontal partitioning for scalability, which involves storing data in a number of different databases or non-relational data-stores. This leads to a need for workflow-style computations even within a single intra-enterprise application. Since scalability is key (and the motivation for data partitioning), conventional workflow engines are rarely considered for use in this context. Instead, the programmer usually realizes the workflow manually, exposing themselves to all the subtleties of realizing such workflow correctly. Pritchett [16] describes programming methodologies for use in these scenarios. Our goal is to provide lightweight language mechanisms that can be used to realize idempotent workflows correctly in such scenarios.

Helland [11] explains in detail why idempotence is an essential property for reliable systems.

Frolund *et al.* [9] define a correctness criteria known as *X-Ability* for replicated services. A history is said to be *x-able* if it is equivalent to some history where every request is processed exactly once. Much like failfree idempotence, X-Ability is both a safety and liveness criteria. Our notion of failfree idempotence is generalizes X-Ability beyond replication requests to workflows. There are also significant differences in our implementation techniques.

Our work is also related to open nested multi-level transactions [15, 19]. These two constructs share the use of compensating actions, but are semantically different. Open nested transactions provide a way for dealing with conflicts at a higher level of abstraction, which often leads to increased concurrency.

Our basic setting is similar to Argus [14]. However, the construct that Argus provides programmers to deal with process failures is a conventional transaction. As with sagas, we show that many applications can be expressed using workflows (as we cover in Section 2) with compensating actions to compensate for the lack of isolation. The transactor programming model [7] also provide primitives for dealing with process failures in a distributed system. However, there is no shared state in the transactor model. The primitives provided by the transactor model (stabilize, checkpoint, and rollback) are different from the primitives we study.

Bruni et al [5] formalize compensating actions in an abstract language. Their formalism, however, does not explicitly model state. Their paper, in fact, suggests study of compensation in the context of imperative features (state, variables, control-flow constructs) as future work. Our work provides a compensation-based transactional construct as a library in a real language (F#) for a real system (Azure), in addition to the theoretical treatment in the setting of lambda-calculus with mutable shared state.

Luis et. al [6] propose an abstract model of compensating actions (based on process calculus) for reasoning about correctness for workflows that use compensating actions.

Faulty lambda calculus [18] is a programming language and a type system for fault tolerance. However, λ_{FAIL} is addresses process failures, while faulty lambda calculus addresses transient data corruption errors.

Acknowledgments

We would like to acknowledge Siddharth Agarwal, Nirmesh Malviya, Khilan Gudka, and Dheeraj Singh for their contributions.

References

[1] Azurescope: Benchmarking and Guidance for Windows Azure. `http://azurescope.cloudapp.net/BenchmarkTestCases/#4f2bdbcc-7c23-4c06-9c00-f2cc12d2d2a7`, June 2011.

[2] Bid Now Sample. `http://bidnow.codeplex.com`, June 2011.

[3] The Tailspin Scenario. `http://msdn.microsoft.com/en-us/library/ff966486.aspx`, June 2011.

[4] Windows Azure Patterns and Practices. `http://wag.codeplex.com/`, 2011.

[5] Roberto Bruni, Hernán Melgratti, and Ugo Montanari. Theoretical Foundations for Compensations in Flow Composition Languages. In *Proceedings of POPL*, pages 209–220, 2005.

[6] Luis Caires, Carla Ferreira, and Hugo Vieira. A Process Calculus Analysis of Compensations. In *Trustworthy Global Computing*, volume 5474 of *Lecture Notes in Computer Science*, pages 87–103. 2009.

[7] John Field and Carlos A. Varela. Transactors: A Programming Model for Maintaining Globally Consistent Distributed State in Unreliable Environments. In *Proceedings of POPL*, pages 195–208, 2005.

[8] M.J. Fischer, N.A. Lynch, and M.S. Paterson. Impossibility of Distributed Consensus with one Faulty Process. *Journal of the ACM (JACM)*, 32(2):374–382, 1985.

[9] Svend Frolund and Rachid Guerraoui. X-Ability: A Theory of Replication. *Distributed Computing*, 14, 2000.

[10] Hector Garcia-Molina and Kenneth Salem. Sagas. In *Proc. of ICMD*, pages 249–259, 1987.

[11] Pat Helland. Idempotence is not a medical condition. *ACM Queue*, 10(4):30–46, 2012.

[12] Mohan Kamath and Krithi Ramamritham. Correctness Issues in Workflow Management. *Distributed Systems Engineering*, 3(4):213, 1996.

[13] Sheng Liang, Paul Hudak, and Mark Jones. Monad Transformers and Modular Interpreters. In *In Proc. of POPL*, pages 333–343, 1995.

[14] Barbara Liskov. Distributed programming in argus. *Communications of ACM*, 31:300–312, March 1988.

[15] J. Eliot B. Moss. Nested Transactions: An Approach to Reliable Distributed Computing, 1981.

[16] Dan Pritchett. Base: An acid alternative. *Queue*, 6(3):48–55, May 2008.

[17] Philip Wadler and Peter Thiemann. The Marriage of Effects and Monads. *ACM Trans. Comput. Log.*, 4(1):1–32, 2003.

[18] David Walker, Lester Mackey, Jay Ligatti, George A. Reis, and David I. August. Static Typing for a Faulty Lambda Calculus. In *In ACM International Conference on Functional Programming*, 2006.

[19] Gerhard Weikum and Hans-J. Schek. Concepts and Applications of Multilevel Transactions and Open Nested Transactions. In *Database Transaction Models for Advanced Applications*, pages 515–553, 1992.

[20] Gerhard Weikum and Gottfried Vossen. *Transactional Information Systems: Theory, Algorithms, and the Practice of Concurrency Control*. 2001.

A. An Abstract Definition of Idempotence

We now present a more abstract definition of idempotence in terms of histories.

Basics. The users of the system issue requests to the system. Let I denote a set of input messages (or *requests*). The system responds to requests with a *response*. Let O denote a set of output values. An output message or response is a pair $(i, o) \in I \times O$ indicating that the output value o is produced in response to input request i.

A *history* π is a sequence $e_1 e_2 \cdots e_k$ of requests and responses (i.e., each e_i can be either a request or a response). We will restrict our attention to histories that satisfy the simple property that every response corresponds to an earlier request in the history. We define a *specification* Φ to be a set of histories. In the sequel, we use a set of histories to specify desired safety properties of the system.

In the sequel, let $q \in I$ range over requests and let $r \in I \times O$ range over responses. Let α, β, and γ range over sequences of requests and responses.

DEFINITION A.1. *A specification Φ is said to be* asynchronous *if it satisfies the following properties.*

1. $\alpha\beta q\gamma \in \Phi \Rightarrow \alpha q\beta\gamma \in \Phi$.
2. $\alpha r\beta\gamma \in \Phi \Rightarrow \alpha\beta r\gamma \in \Phi$.

The above conditions are a natural restriction on specifications because of messaging delays that cannot be controlled. The above property is also related to the notion of linearizability. Given any sequential specification Φ_s, "linearizable Φ_s" can be defined as the smallest asynchronous specification that contains Φ_s. Every linearizable specification satifies the asynchronous property defined above, but not all asynchronous specifications are linearizable.

Idempotence. Two requests q_1 and q_2 (in the same history) are said to be *duplicates* if $q_1 = q_2$. Two responses (q_1, r_1) and (q_2, r_2) (in the same history) are said to be *duplicates* if $q_1 = q_2$.

DEFINITION A.2. *A specification Φ is said to* idempotent *iff:*

1. *Duplicate requests have no effect: $\alpha q \beta q \gamma \in \Phi$ iff $\alpha q \beta \gamma \in \Phi$.*
2. *Duplicates responses have the same value:*

$$\alpha(q, o_1)\beta(q, o_2)\gamma \in \Phi \Rightarrow o_1 = o_2.$$

3. *Duplicate responses are allowed: $\alpha r \beta r \gamma \in \Phi$ iff $\alpha r \beta \gamma \in \Phi$.*

(The above definition is intended for asynchronous specifications. Hence, the asynchrony conditions have been used to simplify the definition.)

Idempotence Closure. We define a history to be *repetitionless* if it contains no duplicate requests or duplicate responses. We define a specification Φ to be *repetitionless* if all histories in Φ are repetitionless.

Given a repetitionless specification Φ, we define its idempotence closure $idem(\Phi)$ to be the smallest specification that contains Φ and is idempotent.

We now summarize our goal: given a program p that satisfies a repetitionless specification Φ in the absence of process failures and duplicate requests, construct a program p' that satisfies $idem(\Phi)$ even in the presence of process failures and duplicate requests.

Extension The above definitions can be generalized to permit requests to be of the form (k, v), where k is a unique-identifier (key) for an input request, and allowing responses to be of the form (k, o), where k is the unique-identifier of the input request for which the response is produced. Note that the above definition does not capture the progress conditions of *failure-freedom*.

B. The Semantics of λ_{IDFF}

We adapt the earlier operational semantics of λ_{FAIL} as shown in Fig. 15 to define the semantics of λ_{IDFF}. We extend the definition Σ_A, the set of agents: previously, an agent was of the form $v \triangleright e$. Now, an agent may now also be of the form $v \blacktriangleright e$, indicating a `idff` evaluation of expression e with identifier v.

$$\text{Syntax Extension: } e \in \langle\mathsf{Exp}\rangle ::= \cdots \mid \texttt{idff}\ v_1\ v_2$$

$$\text{Semantic Domain Changes: } \Sigma_A = \langle\mathsf{Exp}\rangle \times \langle\mathsf{Exp}\rangle + \langle\mathsf{Exp}\rangle \times \langle\mathsf{Exp}\rangle$$

Additional Evaluation Rules:

[IDFF-NEW]

$$\frac{v \triangleright E[\texttt{idff}\ id\ e] \in \alpha \qquad \nexists e'.id \blacktriangleright e' \in \alpha}{\langle p, \mu, \alpha, I, O\rangle \stackrel{\epsilon}{\Rightarrow} \langle p, \mu, \alpha \uplus \{id \blacktriangleright e()\}, I, O\rangle}$$

[IDFF-USE]

$$\frac{id \blacktriangleright w \in \alpha \qquad w \in \langle\mathsf{Val}\rangle}{\langle p, \mu, \alpha \uplus \{v \triangleright E[\texttt{idff}\ id\ e]\}, I, O\rangle \stackrel{\epsilon}{\Rightarrow} \langle p, \mu, \alpha \uplus \{v \triangleright E[w]\}, I, O\rangle}$$

[NORMAL]

$$\frac{\langle \mu, e\rangle \stackrel{\ell}{\rightsquigarrow} \langle \mu', e'\rangle}{\langle p, \mu, \alpha \uplus \{v \blacktriangleright e\}, I, O\rangle \Rightarrow \langle p, \mu', \alpha \uplus \{v \blacktriangleright e'\}, I, O\rangle}$$

Figure 15: The language λ_{IDFF}, defined via extensions to language λ_{FAIL}. Rules IDFF-NEW and IDFF-USE must be duplicated for $v \blacktriangleright E[\texttt{idff}\ id\ e]$ as well.

Rule IDFF-NEW handles the evaluation of the construct `idff` v e, when no preceding `idff` computation with the same identifier v has been initiated. This has the effect of creating a new agent $v \blacktriangleright e$. Rule IDFF-USE allows the computation `idff` v e to proceed once the created agent completes evaluation (as indicated by the presence of an agent of the form $v \blacktriangleright w$, where w is a value). The same rule also applies to "duplicate" evaluations with the same id.

Deadlock-freedom-by-design: Multiparty Asynchronous Global Programming

Marco Carbone Fabrizio Montesi

IT University of Copenhagen

{carbonem,fmontesi}@itu.dk

Abstract

Over the last decade, *global descriptions* have been successfully employed for the verification and implementation of communicating systems, respectively as *protocol specifications* and *choreographies*. In this work, we bring these two practices together by proposing a purely-global programming model. We show a novel interpretation of *asynchrony* and *parallelism* in a global setting and develop a typing discipline that verifies choreographies against protocol specifications, based on multiparty sessions. Exploiting the nature of global descriptions, our type system defines a new class of deadlock-free concurrent systems (*deadlock-freedom-by-design*), provides type inference, and supports session mobility. We give a notion of Endpoint Projection (EPP) which generates correct entity code (as π-calculus terms) from a choreography. Finally, we evaluate our approach by providing a prototype implementation for a concrete programming language and by applying it to some examples from multicore and service-oriented programming.

Categories and Subject Descriptors D.3.1 [*Programming Languages*]: Formal Definitions and Theory; F.3.2 [*Semantics of Programming Languages*]: Process Models

General Terms Design, Languages, Theory

Keywords Concurrency, Choreography, Types, Sessions.

1. Introduction

Global descriptions represent a powerful paradigm for designing communicating systems where the programmer gives a global view of how messages are exchanged during execution, instead of separately defining the behaviour of each *endpoint* (entity). Then, the local behaviour of each endpoint can be automatically generated by means of *EndPoint Projection* (EPP). The paradigm has been studied in formal models [10, 15, 22, 26], standards [1, 37], and language implementations [23, 33, 36]. Global descriptions have a great impact on the quality of software, as they represent "formal blueprints" of how communicating systems should behave and offer a concise view of the message flows enacted by a system. In particular, they (i) lower the possibility of introducing programming errors and (ii) ease the task (both manual and automatic) of detecting them. Global descriptions can be used at different levels of abstraction, ranging from abstract descriptions of *protocols* to descriptions of concrete system implementations, dubbed *choreographies*. These different incarnations respectively underpin two recent and successful development methodologies.

In the first methodology, programmers design abstract protocols using global descriptions [22, 23]. These are automatically projected onto *abstract endpoint* specifications which are finally used for the static verification of manually written endpoint code:

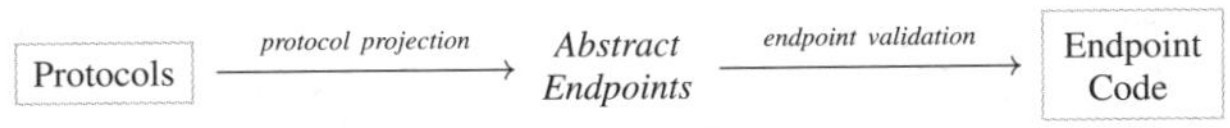

The approach above has the benefit of producing very clear protocol specifications. However, it deprives the programmer from a global view of the system when dealing with its implementation. A major consequence is that programming becomes error-prone when dealing with the actual interleaving of different protocol instances. For example, it can easily lead to deadlocked systems [7].

The second methodology deals with system implementations using choreographies [36, 37]. Programmers can write a choreography and then automatically project an executable system from it:

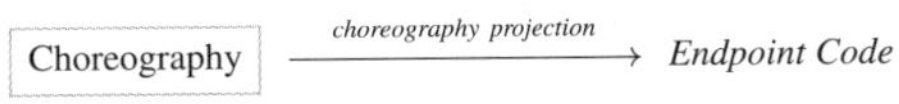

Here, the main advantage is the precise view given by choreographies on the possible system executions. However, choreographies lack in abstraction wrt global protocol descriptions and their programming needs to be disciplined with additional tools. Current disciplines for choreography-driven programming are based on writing abstract endpoint descriptions and then using them to check the behaviour of each endpoint, directly on the choreography or its EPP [15, 36]. Hence, in these models, we lose a global view of the system when describing its protocol specifications.

Inspired by these observations and by private conversations with our industry collaborators [2, 20, 31, 35, 37], we ask:

Can we design a unified framework that combines global descriptions of protocols and implementations?

Clearly, a positive answer would retain the advantages of global descriptions for *both* the writing of protocols and that of implementations. Moreover, a natural following question is whether such a unified framework could offer more than just the sum of the parts: are there other advantages that can arise from the combination of global protocol descriptions with choreographies?

In order to answer the questions above, we build and analyse a model for a fully global framework. In our model, developers design both protocols and implementations from a global viewpoint. Endpoint implementations can then be automatically generated:

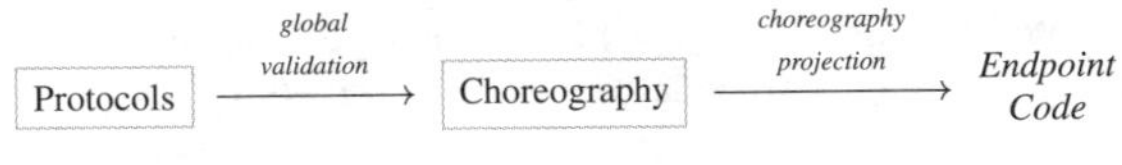

POPL'13, January 23–25, 2013, Rome, Italy.

The challenge of reaching our objective is twofold. First, since we aim at designing a model where choreographies can instantiate different protocols multiple times and interleave their execution, the model should ensure that these interleavings will not lead to bad behaviour. Second, it is not clear how common aspects of concurrent systems such as *asynchrony* (communications are asynchronous) and *parallelism* (parallel executions) should influence the interpretation of a choreography: choreographies describe communications as atomic actions, making concurrency less explicit.

Main contributions. We provide the following contributions:

Multiparty Choreographies. We introduce a choreography model with *multiparty* protocol instances (*sessions*) as first-class elements (§ 3) and provide an EPP that, under simple restrictions, correctly generates endpoint code from a choreography (§ 5).

Asynchrony and Parallelism. Our framework gives a novel and concise interpretation of asynchrony and parallelism, by inferring the implicit concurrent behaviour specified in a choreography (§ 3).

Typing and Type inference. We provide a type system (§ 4) for checking choreographies against protocol specifications given as multiparty session types [22]. Our type analysis plays a major role in ensuring the correctness of EPP code. Interestingly, due to the global nature of choreographies, our framework can generate correct endpoint code that is not allowed by current multiparty session typings (§ 5, Typing expressiveness). We also give a type inference technique supporting the opposite methodology, i.e., extracting the protocols implemented in a choreography (§ 4, Type inference).

Delegation. This is the first work to provide a choreography model supporting *session delegation*, a mobility mechanism for delegating the continuation of a protocol (§ 3). Due to asynchrony and parallelism, typing delegation (§ 4) is nontrivial since messages prior to and after delegation may be interleaved, making it difficult to check that channel ownerships are consistently respected.

Deadlock-freedom-by-design. Our framework seamlessly guarantees deadlock freedom (§ 5, Corollary 1), a notoriously hard problem in multiparty sessions types [7]. This feature follows from using a choreography as initial design tool.

Implementation and Evaluation. We provide a prototype implementation of our framework (§ 6), featuring a programming language (Chor), an IDE, and an EPP that support the development of concurrent systems using our global methodology. We use Chor to evaluate our programming model against examples of different nature, from multicore to distributed programming (§ 7).

Proofs and full definitions can be found in [14].

2. Model Preview

In this section we give an informal description of our model, whose key elements are *protocols* and *choreographies*. A protocol is an abstract specification of the structure of some communications in a system, whereas a choreography describes a concrete system implementing one or more protocols. We represent protocols with *global types* [22], global descriptions where entities are abstracted as *roles* that communicate following a given conversation structure.

Example 1 (Two-buyer protocol). In this protocol, two buyers B1 and B2 wish to share the purchase of a product from a seller S:

1. $\texttt{B1 -> S} : \langle \textbf{string} \rangle;\ \texttt{S -> B1} : \langle \textbf{int} \rangle;\ \texttt{S -> B2} : \langle \textbf{int} \rangle;\ \texttt{B1 -> B2} : \langle \textbf{int} \rangle;$
2. $\texttt{B2 -> S} : \{\ ok : \texttt{B2 -> S} : \langle \textbf{string} \rangle;\ \texttt{S -> B2} : \langle \textbf{date} \rangle,\quad quit : \mathsf{end}\ \}$

Above, B1, B2 and S are called *roles*. Buyer B1 sends to a seller S a purchase request of type **string**. Then, S sends a quote to B1 and another potential buyer B2. Thereafter, B1 tells B2 the amount she wishes to contribute with. Afterwards, B2 notifies S of whether she has accepted (*ok* or *quit*). If so, B2 sends to S a string (address) and, finally, S replies with a delivery date of type **date**. □

In this paper, we introduce a choreography model for globally implementing protocols such as the one above. Its core elements are *threads* and *sessions*. A thread represents a (logical) processing unit that executes a sequence of instructions. Each thread has its own local variables, and can exchange messages with other threads by performing I/O communications. Threads can be programmed to be already active or dynamically created at runtime. A session is an instance of a protocol and implements communications between some threads. Sessions can be dynamically created by threads.

Example 2 (Two-buyer choreography). We give a choreography implementing the two-buyer protocol in Example 1.

1. $\mathsf{b_1[B1], b_2[B2]}\ \textbf{start}\ \mathsf{s[S]} : a(k);$
2. $\mathsf{b_1[B1]}.book\ \texttt{->}\ \mathsf{s[S]}.x_1 : k;$
3. $\mathsf{s[S].quote}(x_1)\ \texttt{->}\ \mathsf{b_1[B1]}.y_1 : k;$
4. $\mathsf{s[S].quote}(x_1)\ \texttt{->}\ \mathsf{b_2[B2]}.z_1 : k;$
5. $\mathsf{b_1[B1].contrib}(y_1)\ \texttt{->}\ \mathsf{b_2[B2]}.z_2 : k;$
6. $\mathsf{if}\ (z_1 - z_2 \leq 100)@\mathsf{b_2}$
7. $\mathsf{then}\ \mathsf{b_2[B2]}\ \texttt{->}\ \mathsf{s[S]} : k[ok];$
8. $\quad \mathsf{b_2[B2]}.addr\ \texttt{->}\ \mathsf{s[S]}.x_2 : k;$
9. $\quad \mathsf{s[S]}.ddate\ \texttt{->}\ \mathsf{b_2[B2]}.z_3 : k$
10. $\mathsf{else}\ \mathsf{b_2[B2]}\ \texttt{->}\ \mathsf{s[S]} : k[quit]$

In Line 1, threads $\mathsf{b_1}$, $\mathsf{b_2}$ and freshly spawned thread s start a session k through public channel a playing roles B1, B2 and S respectively. In Lines 2-5, $\mathsf{b_1}$ asks s for book "*book*" and gets back the quote "quote(*book*)" which is also sent to $\mathsf{b_2}$. Note that, e.g., $\mathsf{b_1}$ uses its local variable y_1 to receive the evaluation of "quote(*book*)". Then, $\mathsf{b_1}$ tells $\mathsf{b_2}$ the amount she wishes to contribute for the purchase, namely "contrib(quote(*book*))". In Line 6, $\mathsf{b_2}$ evaluates the offer received by $\mathsf{b_1}$ in the guard $(z_1 - z_2 \leq 100)@\mathsf{b_2}$. If positive, $\mathsf{b_2}$ communicates her decision with the selection $\mathsf{b_2[B2]}\ \texttt{->}\ \mathsf{s[S]} : k[ok]$, sends her address *addr* and receives the delivery date *ddate* (Lines 7-9). Otherwise, $\mathsf{b_2}$ aborts by selecting *quit* in Line 10. □

Observe that the structure of session k in Example 2 is that of the protocol given in Example 1. The only differences are that data has become explicit and that we introduced the **start** primitive. The latter allows threads to synchronise on a public name, e.g., a, and create new threads and sessions. In Line 1 of Example 2, $\mathsf{b_1}$ and $\mathsf{b_2}$ are already active threads while s is a service thread, i.e., a dynamically spawned thread. Active threads appear on the left-hand side of the **start** keyword, whereas (fresh) service threads appear on its right-hand side. Role annotations, e.g., $\mathsf{b_1[B1]}$, relate each thread to the role it plays in a session.

Example 3 (Two-buyer-helper choreography). Choreographies can also describe multiple, interleaved instances of multiple protocols. Hereafter, we extend the two-buyer choreography from Example 2 with two other sessions, k' and k'', that $\mathsf{b_1}$ and $\mathsf{b_2}$ will respectively use for getting help in the transaction.

...as Lines 1-5 in Example 2...

C_1:
6. $\mathsf{b_1[B]}\ \textbf{start}\ \mathsf{h_1[H]} : b(k');$
7. $\mathsf{b_1[B].(contrib}(y_1)/2)\ \texttt{->}\ \mathsf{h_1[H]}.y : k';$
8. $\mathsf{b_1[B]}\ \texttt{->}\ \mathsf{h_1[H]} : k'[done];$

C_2:
9. $\mathsf{b_2[B]}\ \textbf{start}\ \mathsf{h_2[H]} : b(k'');$
10. $\mathsf{b_2[B]}.((z_1 - z_2)/2)\ \texttt{->}\ \mathsf{h_2[H]}.z : k'';$
11. $\mathsf{b_2[B]}\ \texttt{->}\ \mathsf{h_2[H]} : k''[del];$
12. $\mathsf{b_2[B]}.z_1\ \texttt{->}\ \mathsf{h_2[H]}.z' : k'';$
13. $\mathsf{b_2[B]}\ \texttt{->}\ \mathsf{h_2[H]} : k''\langle\!\langle k[\mathsf{B2}] \rangle\!\rangle;$

C_3:
14. $\mathsf{if}\ ((z/z') \leq 30\%)@\mathsf{h_2}$
15. $\mathsf{then}\ \mathsf{h_2[B2]}\ \texttt{->}\ \mathsf{s[S]} : k[ok];$
16. $\quad \mathsf{h_2[B2]}.addr\ \texttt{->}\ \mathsf{s[S]}.x_2 : k;$
17. $\quad \mathsf{s[S]}.ddate\ \texttt{->}\ \mathsf{h_2[B2]}.z'' : k$
18. $\mathsf{else}\ \mathsf{h_2[B2]}\ \texttt{->}\ \mathsf{s[S]} : k[quit]$

The choreography starts with the first 5 lines of that in Example 2. In block C_1, $\mathsf{b_1}$ starts a new session with a helper $\mathsf{h_1}$, asks it to contribute for half of its part (Line 7), and informs it that it does not need to do more (Line 8). On the other hand, in block C_2, b_2 does the same with another thread h_2 until Line 11. Differently now, b_2 asks h_2 to continue session k *by taking on its role* (Line 11). Then, it sends the total price received from s to h_2 (Line 12) and *delegates* the session reference (Line 13). Finally, in block C_3, h_2 completes the two-buyer protocol instead of b_2, checking that its own contribution is less than 30% of the total price. Note that h_1 and h_2 are started through the same public channel b, which acts as a reusable shared channel in multiparty session types [22]. □

Our model has two features that interestingly influence choreography interpretation in subtly different ways. Firstly, *parallelism*: thread executions may concurrently proceed without any predetermined ordering unless causal constraints are introduced. Secondly, *asynchrony*: communications are asynchronous, so a thread may send a message to another thread and then immediately proceed before the message has actually been delivered by the network.

For instance, in Example 3, the threads whose behaviour is described in blocks C_1 and C_2 are different (b_1 and h_1 for C_1, b_2 and h_2 for C_2). Therefore, their executions may interleave due to parallelism. E.g., b_2 and h_2 may start session k'' *before* b_1 and h_1 start session k'. Even more, k'' may be completely executed before k' is started. Hence, the interpretation of $C_1; C_2$ should be equivalent to that of $C_2; C_1$, and, in general, to that of any interleaving of C_1 and C_2. Furthermore, in Lines 3 and 4 of Example 2, where s sends the quote to b_1 and then b_2, it may happen that b_2 (Line 4) receives the quote before b_1 due to asynchronous messaging. Parallelism and asynchrony are respectively handled by our *swapping* relation and our asynchronous semantics, both formalised in the next section.

In general, we say that our relaxed sequential operator lifts the programmer from expressing the degree of concurrency (asynchrony and parallelism) of a system. Indeed, our framework will automatically infer the latter by looking at the thread identifiers. We made this choice in favour of design minimality and simplicity. In real tools, combining the sequential operator with explicit primitives for, e.g., parallelism, may be preferrable for clarity purposes. We discuss this in § 9, Sequential and Parallel Operators.

3. Choreographies with Multiparty Sessions

We introduce the *Global Calculus (GC)*, a choreography model with multiparty asynchronous sessions.

Syntax. The syntax of our calculus is reported in Figure 1.

$$
\begin{array}{rcll}
C & ::= & \eta; C & \textit{(sequence)} \\
& \mid & \mathsf{if}\, e@\tau\, \mathsf{then}\, C_1\, \mathsf{else}\, C_2 & \textit{(conditional)} \\
& \mid & \mathbf{0} & \textit{(inaction)} \\
& \mid & \mathsf{rec}\, X(\widetilde{x@\tau}, \tilde{k}, \tilde{\tau}) = C'\, \mathsf{in}\, C & \textit{(recursion)} \\
& \mid & X(\widetilde{e@\tau}, \tilde{k}, \tilde{\tau}) & \textit{(call)} \\
& \mid & (\boldsymbol{\nu} r)\, C & \textit{(restriction)} \\
\eta & ::= & \tau_1[\mathsf{p}].e\ \texttt{->}\ \tau_2[\mathsf{q}].x : k & \textit{(communication)} \\
& \mid & \tau_1[\mathsf{p}]\ \texttt{->}\ \tau_2[\mathsf{q}] : k[l] & \textit{(selection)} \\
& \mid & \tau_1[\mathsf{p}]\ \texttt{->}\ \tau_2[\mathsf{q}] : k\langle\!\langle k'[\mathsf{p}'] \rangle\!\rangle & \textit{(delegation)} \\
& \mid & \tau_1[\mathsf{p}_1], \ldots, \tau_n[\mathsf{p}_n]\ \mathbf{start}\ \tau_{n+1}[\mathsf{p}_{n+1}], \ldots, \tau_m[\mathsf{p}_m] : a(k) & \textit{(start)}
\end{array}
$$

Figure 1. Global Calculus with Multiparty Sessions, syntax.

C is a choreography, τ is a thread, and k is a session (identifier). Interactions between threads are specified by the term $\eta; C$ which reads: *the system may execute the interaction η and continue as C*. We distinguish four different kinds of interaction: *(start)*, *(communication)*, *(selection)*, and *(delegation)*. *(start)* denotes session initiation: threads τ_i (for $1 \leq i \leq m$) start a new multiparty session through public channel a and tag it with a fresh identifier k, called session channel. The first n threads, dubbed the *active threads*, are already running, while $\tau_{n+1}, \ldots, \tau_m$, dubbed the *service threads*, are dynamically created and started. We assume that $m \geq 2$ (a session has at least two participants) and $n \geq 1$ (a session is started by at least one running thread). The p_i's denote the roles played by the threads in the session. *(communication)* denotes a communication where thread τ_1 sends, over session k, the evaluation of a first-order expression e to thread τ_2, which binds it to variable x[1]. In *(selection)*, τ_1 communicates to τ_2 her selection of branch l. Through *(delegation)*, τ_1 delegates to τ_2 over k her role p' in session k'.

GC also offers other standard programming language constructs. In *(conditional)*, expression e is labelled with a thread name, indicating where it is evaluated. *(recursion)* and *(call)* model standard recursive procedures, where each variable in $\tilde{x}$ or expression in $\tilde{e}$, respectively, is located at a thread in $\tilde{\tau}$. In *(call)*, we assume that each expression can only be either a variable or a value. *(restriction)*, which is only used at runtime and cannot be used in programs, models name restriction. r (for restricted name) can be a thread or a session channel. The term $\mathbf{0}$ denotes termination.

In a term $\eta; C$, η can bind session channels, threads and variables. When η is a *(start)*, $\tau_1, \ldots, \tau_n$ are free while k and $\tau_{n+1}, \ldots, \tau_m$ are bound (since they are freshly created). If η is a *(communication)*, variable x is bound. As usual, r is bound in $(\boldsymbol{\nu} r)\ C$. We often omit $\mathbf{0}$, empty vectors, and irrelevant variables. In the remainder, $(\boldsymbol{\nu} r_1, \ldots, r_n)$ is a shortcut for $(\boldsymbol{\nu} r_1) \ldots (\boldsymbol{\nu} r_n)$.

Semantics. Above, we stated that the term $\eta; C$ specifies a system that *may* execute the interaction η and then continue as C. Threads, however, are assumed to run in parallel. As a consequence, some actions in C may be performed before η. For example, blocks C_1 and C_2 from Example 3 describe the behaviour of different threads. Therefore, as discussed in § 2, in an actual system run of these threads, their executions may interleave due to parallelism. To deal with such cases, we define the *swapping* congruence relation $\simeq_C$, which allows permutations of this kind of interaction sequences[2]. $\simeq_C$ is defined as the smallest congruence satisfying the rules in Figure 2. $\simeq_C$ exchanges terms with different threads. The top rule swaps two conditionals: C_1' and C_2 are swapped to preserve the semantics of the term wrt the evaluations of the conditions. The bottom-left rule swaps two interactions η and η' that do not share any thread names (calculated by $\mathsf{thr}(\eta)$). The bottom-right rule swaps an interaction η out of a conditional if it prefixes both branches and does not involve the thread that checks the condition.

Asynchronous messaging can cause situations as the one discussed for Lines 3 and 4 of Example 2 in § 2, where s sends the quote to b_1, then to b_2, and b_2 may receive the quote before b_1. Unlike for parallelism, we address this issue directly in the operational semantics. This is because asynchrony is somehow asymmetric: even though the receiving actions may interleave in a different order wrt that in the choreography, the sending actions instead will surely happen in the specified order, since the thread performing the outputs is the same. This is different from parallelism, where the ordering of *both* receiving and sending actions may change. It is unsafe to manipulate the syntax of the choreography for simulating asynchrony, since when we will generate the code for the sender thread (cf. § 5) remembering the order of outputs will be important.

Figure 3 contains the rules defining the labelled reduction semantics for GC, whose labels λ are defined as:

$$\lambda \ ::= \ \eta \ \mid \ \mathsf{if}@\tau \ \mid \ (\boldsymbol{\nu} r)\, \lambda$$

[1] For clarity, we annotate threads with roles. This is necessary only for *(start)* since roles can be inferred from session identifiers in all other terms.

[2] Handling parallelism with a congruence simplifies our development, since swaps in a choreography do not influence the behaviour of its EPP [14].

$$\frac{\tau \neq \tau'}{\text{if } e@\tau \text{ then } (\text{if } e'@\tau' \text{ then } C_1 \text{ else } C_2) \text{ else } (\text{if } e'@\tau' \text{ then } C_1' \text{ else } C_2') \simeq_C \text{if } e'@\tau' \text{ then } (\text{if } e@\tau \text{ then } C_1 \text{ else } C_1') \text{ else } (\text{if } e@\tau \text{ then } C_2 \text{ else } C_2')}$$

$$\frac{\mathsf{thr}(\eta) \cap \mathsf{thr}(\eta') = \emptyset}{\eta; \eta' \simeq_C \eta'; \eta} \qquad \frac{\tau \notin \mathsf{thr}(\eta)}{\text{if } e@\tau \text{ then } (\eta; C_1) \text{ else } (\eta; C_2) \simeq_C \eta; \text{if } e@\tau \text{ then } C_1 \text{ else } C_2}$$

Figure 2. Global Calculus with Multiparty Sessions, swap relation $\simeq_C$.

$\lfloor^{\mathrm{C}}|_{\mathrm{ACT}}\rceil$ $\quad \eta \in \{\textit{(selection)}, \textit{(delegation)}, \textit{(start)}\} \Rightarrow \eta; C \xrightarrow{\eta} (\boldsymbol{\nu}\tilde{r})\, C \quad (\tilde{r} = \mathsf{bn}(\eta))$

$\lfloor^{\mathrm{C}}|_{\mathrm{COM}}\rceil$ $\quad \eta = \tau_1[\mathsf{p}].e \texttt{ -> } \tau_2[\mathsf{q}].x : k \Rightarrow \eta; C \xrightarrow{\eta[v/e]} C[v/x@\tau_2] \quad (e \downarrow v)$

$\lfloor^{\mathrm{C}}|_{\mathrm{ASYNC}}\rceil$ $\quad C \xrightarrow{\lambda} (\boldsymbol{\nu}\tilde{r})\, C' \Rightarrow \eta; C \xrightarrow{\lambda} (\boldsymbol{\nu}\tilde{r})\, \eta; C' \quad \begin{pmatrix} \mathsf{snd}(\eta) \in \mathsf{fn}(\lambda) & \tilde{r} = \mathsf{bn}(\lambda) & \eta \neq \textit{(start)} \\ \mathsf{rcv}(\eta) \notin \mathsf{fn}(\lambda) & \tilde{r} \notin \mathsf{fn}(\eta) & \end{pmatrix}$

$\lfloor^{\mathrm{C}}|_{\mathrm{IF}}\rceil$ $\quad \text{if } e@\tau \text{ then } C_1 \text{ else } C_2 \xrightarrow{\text{if}@\tau} C_i \quad (i = 1 \text{ if } e \downarrow \text{true}, \ i = 2 \text{ otherwise})$

$\lfloor^{\mathrm{C}}|_{\mathrm{CTX}}\rceil$ $\quad C_1 \xrightarrow{\lambda} C_1' \Rightarrow \text{rec } X(\widetilde{x@\tau}, \tilde{k}, \tilde{\tau}) = C_2 \text{ in } C_1 \xrightarrow{\lambda} \text{rec } X(\widetilde{x@\tau}, \tilde{k}, \tilde{\tau}) = C_2 \text{ in } C_1'$

$\lfloor^{\mathrm{C}}|_{\mathrm{RES}}\rceil$ $\quad C \xrightarrow{\lambda} C' \Rightarrow (\boldsymbol{\nu}r)\, C \xrightarrow{(\nu r)\,\lambda} (\boldsymbol{\nu}r)\, C'$

$\lfloor^{\mathrm{C}}|_{\mathrm{EQ}}\rceil$ $\quad C_1 \mathcal{R} C_1' \quad C_1' \xrightarrow{\lambda} C_2' \quad C_2' \mathcal{R} C_2 \Rightarrow C_1 \xrightarrow{\lambda} C_2 \qquad \mathcal{R} \in \{\simeq_C, \equiv\}$

Figure 3. Global Calculus with Multiparty Sessions, semantics.

A label is either an interaction η, an internal action if$@\tau$ by thread τ (conditional), or another label with restricted name r (when new threads or session channels are created). Rule $\lfloor^{\mathrm{C}}|_{\mathrm{ASYNC}}\rceil$ captures the asynchronous behaviour of endpoint systems, allowing a thread to send a message and then proceed freely before the intended receiver actually receives it. In the rule, the sender of η performs the action λ in the continuation C without waiting for the message in η to be delivered. We check that the receiver of η is not involved in λ since otherwise causality between η and λ would be violated. Finally, η is kept for the later observation of the message delivery. Rule $\lfloor^{\mathrm{C}}|_{\mathrm{ACT}}\rceil$ models interactions that are not *(communication)*. In the reductum, if η is a *(start)* then $\tilde{r}$ contains the freshly created service threads and the session channel. For all other cases, $\tilde{r}$ is empty. In $\lfloor^{\mathrm{C}}|_{\mathrm{COM}}\rceil$, we substitute variable x with value v (the evaluation of the expression e in a system that we leave unspecified) with the *smart substitution* $C[v/x@\tau]$, which substitutes x with v only under the free name τ in C, modelling local variables. In rule $\lfloor^{\mathrm{C}}|_{\mathrm{EQ}}\rceil$, the relation $\mathcal{R}$ can be either the swapping relation $\simeq_C$ or *structural congruence* $\equiv$. Structural congruence handles name restriction and recursion unfolding. We just mention the rule for unfolding: $\text{rec } X(\widetilde{x@\tau}, \tilde{k}, \tilde{\tau}) = C' \text{ in } X(\widetilde{v@\tau}, \tilde{k}, \tilde{\tau}) \equiv \text{rec } X(\widetilde{x@\tau}, \tilde{k}, \tilde{\tau}) = C' \text{ in } C'[\tilde{v}/\tilde{x}@\tilde{\tau}]$. All other rules are standard and can be found in [14].

Choreographies enjoy deadlock-freedom since every term but $\mathbf{0}$ has a corresponding semantic rule that can reduce it. Formally,

Theorem 1 (Deadlock-Freedom). *Let $C \not\equiv \mathbf{0}$ and contain no free variable names. Then, there exist C', λ such that $C \xrightarrow{\lambda} C'$.*

4. Typing Choreographies

We now present our typing system which allows to specify protocols in terms of global types [7, 22] and then check whether session behaviours in a choreography respect them.

Syntax. Figure 4 contains the syntax of global types. $\mathsf{p} \texttt{ -> } \mathsf{q} : \langle U \rangle; G$ abstracts an interaction from role p to role q with continuation G, where U, referred to as the *carrying type*, is the type of the exchanged message. U can either be a basic type S or $G@\mathsf{p}$. Communicating $G@\mathsf{p}$ means that a sender role *delegates* to another role her role p in protocol G. In $\mathsf{p} \texttt{ -> } \mathsf{q} : \{l_i : G_i\}_{i \in I}$, role p can select one label l_i and continue as G_i. All other terms are standard.

G	::=	$\mathsf{p} \texttt{ -> } \mathsf{q} : \langle U \rangle; G$	*(communication)*
	|	$\mathsf{p} \texttt{ -> } \mathsf{q} : \{l_i : G_i\}_{i \in I}$	*(choice)*
	|	end	*(inaction)*
	|	rec $\mathbf{t}$; G	*(recursion)*
	|	$\mathbf{t}$	*(call)*
U	::=	$S \mid G@\mathsf{p}$	*(values)*
S	::=	**bool** | **int** | **string** | ...	*(sort)*

Figure 4. Global Types, syntax.

Semantics. We give a semantics for global types, which expresses the (abstract) execution of protocols. $G \xrightarrow{\alpha} G'$ is the smallest relation on the recursion-unfolding of global types satisfying the rules given in Figure 5. A label α shows which interaction is consumed. Since our discussion on asynchrony and parallelism applies also to protocols, we need to capture these aspects also in their semantics. Similarly to $\lfloor^{\mathrm{C}}|_{\mathrm{ASYNC}}\rceil$, $\lfloor^{\mathrm{G}}|_{\mathrm{ASYNC\text{-}COM}}\rceil$ models asynchrony in global types by allowing a sender role to proceed before the corresponding receiver has actually received the message. $\lfloor^{\mathrm{G}}|_{\mathrm{ASYNC\text{-}BRANCH}}\rceil$ does the same for branching. Observe that since we are allowing an asynchronous action from inside branch G_j to take place, we restrict the branching to the choice $l_j : G_j$ in order to disable the other branches. In $\lfloor^{\mathrm{G}}|_{\mathrm{SWAP}}\rceil$, the relation $\simeq_G$ for global types models parallelism and is defined similarly to $\simeq_C$; formally, it is the smallest congruence satisfying the rules in Figure 6. The rules are similar to the ones for $\simeq_C$ where conditional is now replaced by branching.

Type checking. We now introduce our multiparty session typing, which checks that sessions in a program (choreography without restrictions) follow the protocol specifications given as global types. We use three kinds of typing environments:

(Service Env) $\quad \Gamma ::= \Gamma,\ a\langle \tilde{\mathsf{p}} \mid\mid \tilde{\mathsf{q}} \rangle : G \ \mid\ \Gamma,\ x@\tau : S \ \mid\ \emptyset \ \mid\ \Gamma,\ X : (\Gamma, \Theta, \Delta)$

(Thread Env) $\quad \Theta ::= \Theta,\ \tau : k[\mathsf{p}] \mid \emptyset$

(Session Env) $\quad \Delta ::= \Delta,\ k : G \mid \emptyset$

A *service environment* Γ carries the global type of each public channel, specifying how a session has to be executed after initialisation. In $a\langle \tilde{\mathsf{p}} \mid\mid \tilde{\mathsf{q}} \rangle$, $\tilde{\mathsf{p}}$ and $\tilde{\mathsf{q}}$ are the roles of the active and service

$$\lfloor^{G}|_{\text{COM}}\rceil \quad \mathtt{p} \texttt{ -> } \mathtt{q} : \langle U \rangle; G \xrightarrow{\mathtt{p} \texttt{ -> } \mathtt{q}:\langle U \rangle} G \qquad \lfloor^{G}|_{\text{BRANCH}}\rceil \quad \mathtt{p} \texttt{ -> } \mathtt{q} : \{l_i : G_i\}_{i \in I \cup \{j\}} \xrightarrow{\mathtt{p} \texttt{ -> } \mathtt{q}:l_j} G_j$$

$$\lfloor^{G}|_{\text{REC}}\rceil \quad \frac{G[\mathsf{rec}\ \mathbf{t}; G/\mathbf{t}] \xrightarrow{\alpha} G'}{\mathsf{rec}\ \mathbf{t}; G \xrightarrow{\alpha} G'} \qquad \lfloor^{G}|_{\text{SWAP}}\rceil \quad \frac{G_1 \simeq_{\mathcal{G}} G_1' \xrightarrow{\alpha} G_2' \simeq_{\mathcal{G}} G_2}{G_1 \xrightarrow{\alpha} G_2}$$

$$\lfloor^{G}|_{\text{ASYNC-COM}}\rceil \quad \frac{G \xrightarrow{\alpha} G' \quad \mathtt{p} \in \mathsf{roles}(\alpha), \mathtt{q} \notin \mathsf{roles}(\alpha)}{\mathtt{p} \texttt{ -> } \mathtt{q} : \langle U \rangle; G \xrightarrow{\alpha} \mathtt{p} \texttt{ -> } \mathtt{q} : \langle U \rangle; G'} \qquad \lfloor^{G}|_{\text{ASYNC-BRANCH}}\rceil \quad \frac{G_j \xrightarrow{\alpha} G_j' \quad \mathtt{p} \in \mathsf{roles}(\alpha), \mathtt{q} \notin \mathsf{roles}(\alpha)}{\mathtt{p} \texttt{ -> } \mathtt{q} : \{l_i : G_i\}_{i \in I \cup \{j\}} \xrightarrow{\alpha} \mathtt{p} \texttt{ -> } \mathtt{q} : \{l_j : G_j'\}}$$

Figure 5. Global Types, semantics.

$$\lfloor^{GS}|_{\text{COM-COM}}\rceil \quad \frac{\{\mathtt{p},\mathtt{q}\} \cap \{\mathtt{p}',\mathtt{q}'\} = \emptyset}{\mathtt{p} \texttt{ -> } \mathtt{q} : \langle U \rangle;\ \mathtt{p}' \texttt{ -> } \mathtt{q}' : \langle U' \rangle \quad \simeq_{\mathcal{G}} \quad \mathtt{p}' \texttt{ -> } \mathtt{q}' : \langle U' \rangle;\ \mathtt{p} \texttt{ -> } \mathtt{q} : \langle U \rangle}$$

$$\lfloor^{GS}|_{\text{COM-CHOICE}}\rceil \quad \frac{\{\mathtt{p},\mathtt{q}\} \cap \{\mathtt{p}',\mathtt{q}'\} = \emptyset}{\mathtt{p} \texttt{ -> } \mathtt{q} : \{l_i : \mathtt{p}' \texttt{ -> } \mathtt{q}' : \langle U \rangle;\ G_i\}_{i \in I} \quad \simeq_{\mathcal{G}} \quad \mathtt{p}' \texttt{ -> } \mathtt{q}' : \langle U \rangle;\ \mathtt{p} \texttt{ -> } \mathtt{q} : \{l_i : G_i\}_{i \in I}}$$

$$\lfloor^{GS}|_{\text{CHOICE-CHOICE}}\rceil \quad \frac{\{\mathtt{p},\mathtt{q}\} \cap \{\mathtt{p}',\mathtt{q}'\} = \emptyset}{\mathtt{p} \texttt{ -> } \mathtt{q} : \{l_i : \mathtt{p}' \texttt{ -> } \mathtt{q}' : \{l_j' : G_{ij}\}_{j \in J}\}_{i \in I} \quad \simeq_{\mathcal{G}} \quad \mathtt{p}' \texttt{ -> } \mathtt{q}' : \{l_j' : \mathtt{p} \texttt{ -> } \mathtt{q} : \{l_i : G_{ij}\}_{i \in I}\}_{j \in J}}$$

Figure 6. Global Types, swap relation $\simeq_{\mathcal{G}}$.

threads respectively. Γ also keeps the *sort* types of variables and all environments necessary for typing recursive procedures. A *thread environment* Θ keeps track of which role each thread is playing in a session. Finally, a *session environment* Δ records the type of each running session k. We assume that we can write $\Gamma, a : G$ only if a does not occur in Γ; the same holds for Δ wrt sessions k. Furthermore, we can write $\Theta, \tau : k[\mathtt{p}]$ only if τ is not associated to any other role in the same session k in Θ. Consequently, a thread can participate in multiple sessions playing different roles, but it cannot participate in the same session with more than one role.

Typing judgements have the shape $\Gamma;\ \Theta \vdash C \triangleright \Delta$. Intuitively, C is well-typed provided that public channels are used according to Γ, threads play roles according to Θ, and session channels are used according to Δ. Figure 7 contains the typing rules. Rule $\lfloor^{GT}|_{\text{START}}\rceil$ types a *(start)* term by checking that, in the subterm C, session k is used according to the type G of public channel a. Also, each thread τ_i is checked to play role $\mathtt{p}_i$ in C when using session k. We require all roles $\mathtt{p}_i$ to occur in G ($\mathsf{roles}(G)$), enforcing that each thread communicates at least once in the session. We abuse notation $\tau_{n+1}, \ldots, \tau_m \notin \Theta$ for checking that threads $\tau_{n+1}, \ldots, \tau_m$ are not (associated to any session) in Θ, ensuring their freshness. In $\lfloor^{GT}|_{\text{COM}}\rceil$ we check that, given an interaction between τ_1 and τ_2 over session channel k, (i) the global type for k in the session environment requires a communication of type S between role $\mathtt{p}$ and role $\mathtt{q}$, (ii) τ_1 plays role $\mathtt{p}$ and τ_2 plays role $\mathtt{q}$ according to Θ, and (iii) expression e and variable x have type S according to Γ. Rule $\lfloor^{GT}|_{\text{SEL}}\rceil$ deals with selection and is similar to $\lfloor^{GT}|_{\text{COM}}\rceil$, although we now check that the chosen label is among the ones allowed by the type. $\lfloor^{GT}|_{\text{DEL}}\rceil$ addresses session delegation: it transfers the ownership of role $\mathtt{p}'$ in session k' and checks that the carrying type in the session type of k is the type of the continuation of k'. $\lfloor^{GT}|_{\text{REC}}\rceil$ types a recursive procedure and the choreography in which it is used. The recursion body is checked using only the types of its parameters (stored in Γ), public channels (Γ_{srv}), and giving the possibility to invoke other procedures (Γ_{rec}). All other rules are standard.

For instance, the protocol in Example 1 types channel a in Example 2.

Runtime typing. For showing that *well-typed programs never go wrong*, we need to extend our typing to runtime choreographies. In particular, we need to deal with two issues: asynchronous delegations and parallelism. Hereby, we give an intuition of these issues and how we deal with them (see [14] for details).

Asynchronous Delegation. We check runtime choreographies with new judgements of the form $\Gamma; \Theta \vdash_{\Sigma} C \triangleright \Delta$. The extra environment Σ, the *delegation environment*, contains information about channels that may have been already delegated by rule $\lfloor^{C}|_{\text{ASYNC}}\rceil$. E.g., consider the following choreography:

$$C = \underbrace{\tau_1[\mathtt{p}].e \texttt{ -> } \tau_2[\mathtt{q}].x : k;}_{\eta_1} \ \underbrace{\tau_1[\mathtt{p}'] \texttt{ -> } \tau_3[\mathtt{q}'] : k'\langle\langle k[\mathtt{p}]\rangle\rangle;}_{\eta_2} \ \underbrace{\tau_3[\mathtt{p}].e' \texttt{ -> } \tau_4[\mathtt{r}].y : k}_{\eta_3}$$

By $\lfloor^{C}|_{\text{ASYNC}}\rceil$, C may execute η_2 before η_1 and reduce to $\eta_1; \eta_3$. When typing $\eta_1; \eta_3$, we need to remember the delegation η_2 in Σ, since we cannot construct a thread environment Θ for typing both η_1 and η_3. Therefore, the choreography $\eta_1; \eta_3$ would be well-typed with $\Sigma = \eta_2$ but not with $\Sigma = \emptyset$. Parallelism can actually make things worse, e.g., $\eta_3; \eta_1$, a swap of $\eta_1; \eta_3$, is clearly still safe at endpoint, since the output in η_1 has already been executed and thus τ_1 will no longer use k. Our type system uses Σ also to gracefully handle these cases. To exemplify how we formalise this mechanism, we show the runtime typing version of rule $\lfloor^{GT}|_{\text{COM}}\rceil$:

$$\frac{\begin{array}{c}(\Theta \vdash \tau_1 : k[\mathtt{p}] \ \vee\ \mathsf{delegates}(\Sigma, \tau_1, k[\mathtt{p}])) \\ \Theta \vdash \tau_2 : k[\mathtt{q}] \qquad \neg\mathsf{delegated}(\Sigma, k[\mathtt{q}]) \\ \Gamma, x@\tau_2 : S;\ \Theta \vdash_{\Sigma} C \triangleright k : G, \Delta \qquad \Gamma \vdash e@\tau_1 : S\end{array}}{\Gamma;\ \Theta \vdash_{\Sigma} \tau_1[\mathtt{p}].e \texttt{ -> } \tau_2[\mathtt{q}].x : k; C \triangleright k : \mathtt{p} \texttt{ -> } \mathtt{q} : \langle S \rangle; G, \Delta}$$

The rule above differs from $\lfloor^{GT}|_{\text{COM}}\rceil$ in Figure 7 only in the role checks for the two interacting threads, given in the first two lines. In the first line, we check that thread τ_1 plays role $\mathtt{p}$ in session k, using Θ, *or* that τ_1 has asynchronously delegated $\mathtt{p}$ to another thread, using Σ through the auxiliary predicate $\mathsf{delegates}$. This covers our example above, where C reduces to $\eta_1; \eta_3$. In the second line, we check that τ_2 plays role $\mathtt{q}$, as before in rule $\lfloor^{GT}|_{\text{COM}}\rceil$ for programs. However, now we also need to check that τ_2 has not asynchronously delegated its role to another thread, using another auxiliary predicate $\mathsf{delegated}$ on Σ. This condition is necessary for guaranteeing that $\mathtt{q}$ is played only by one thread, in order to avoid races on the receiving of messages for $\mathtt{q}$ in session k.

Parallelism. Consider the following protocol:

$$G = \mathtt{p}_1 \texttt{ -> } \mathtt{p}_2 : \langle \mathbf{int} \rangle;\quad \mathtt{p}_3 \texttt{ -> } \mathtt{p}_4 : \langle \mathbf{string} \rangle$$

$$\lfloor^{\mathrm{GT}}|\textsc{Start}\rceil\ \frac{\begin{array}{c}\Gamma \vdash a\langle \mathtt{p}_1,\dots,\mathtt{p}_n \mid\mid \mathtt{p}_{n+1},\dots,\mathtt{p}_m\rangle : G \qquad \{\mathtt{p}_1,\dots,\mathtt{p}_m\} = \mathsf{roles}(G)\\ \Gamma;\ \Theta, \tau_1 : k[\mathtt{p}_1],\dots,\tau_m : k[\mathtt{p}_m] \vdash C \rhd \Delta, k : G \qquad \tau_{n+1},\dots,\tau_m \notin \Theta\end{array}}{\Gamma;\ \Theta \vdash \tau_1[\mathtt{p}_1],\dots,\tau_n[\mathtt{p}_n]\ \mathbf{start}\ \tau_{n+1}[\mathtt{p}_{n+1}],\dots,\tau_m[\mathtt{p}_m] : a(k); C \rhd \Delta} \qquad \lfloor^{\mathrm{GT}}|\textsc{Var}\rceil\ \frac{\Gamma = \Gamma_{\mathsf{srv}}, \Gamma' \qquad \Delta'\ \mathsf{end\ only}}{\Gamma, X : (\Gamma', \Theta, \Delta);\ \Theta \vdash X(\widetilde{x@\tau}, \tilde{k}, \tilde{\tau}) \rhd \Delta, \Delta'}$$

$$\lfloor^{\mathrm{GT}}|\textsc{Com}\rceil\ \frac{\Gamma \vdash e@\tau_1 : S \qquad \Theta \vdash \tau_1 : k[\mathtt{p}],\ \tau_2 : k[\mathtt{q}] \qquad \Gamma,\ x@\tau_2 : S;\ \Theta \vdash C \rhd k : G, \Delta}{\Gamma;\ \Theta \vdash \tau_1[\mathtt{p}].e\ \texttt{->}\ \tau_2[\mathtt{q}].x : k; C \rhd k : \mathtt{p}\ \texttt{->}\ \mathtt{q} : \langle S\rangle; G,\ \Delta} \qquad \lfloor^{\mathrm{GT}}|\textsc{Zero}\rceil\ \frac{\Delta\ \mathsf{end\ only}}{\Gamma;\ \Theta \vdash \mathbf{0} \rhd \Delta}$$

$$\lfloor^{\mathrm{GT}}|\textsc{Sel}\rceil\ \frac{\Theta \vdash \tau_1 : k[\mathtt{p}],\ \tau_2 : k[\mathtt{q}] \qquad \Gamma;\ \Theta \vdash C \rhd k : G_j,\ \Delta \qquad j \in I}{\Gamma;\ \Theta \vdash \tau_1[\mathtt{p}]\ \texttt{->}\ \tau_2[\mathtt{q}] : k[l_j]; C \rhd k : \mathtt{p}\ \texttt{->}\ \mathtt{q} : \{l_i : G_i\}_{i \in I}} \qquad \lfloor^{\mathrm{GT}}|\textsc{If}\rceil\ \frac{\Gamma \vdash e@\tau : \mathbf{bool} \qquad \Gamma;\ \Theta \vdash C_1 \rhd \Delta \qquad \Gamma;\ \Theta \vdash C_2 \rhd \Delta}{\Gamma;\ \Theta \vdash \mathsf{if}\ e@\tau\ \mathsf{then}\ C_1\ \mathsf{else}\ C_2 \rhd \Delta}$$

$$\lfloor^{\mathrm{GT}}|\textsc{Del}\rceil\ \frac{\Theta \vdash \tau_1 : k[\mathtt{p}],\ \tau_2 : k[\mathtt{q}] \qquad \Gamma;\ \Theta, \tau_2 : k'[\mathtt{p}'] \vdash C \rhd k : G,\ k' : G',\ \Delta}{\Gamma;\ \Theta, \tau_1 : k'[\mathtt{p}'] \vdash \tau_1[\mathtt{p}]\ \texttt{->}\ \tau_2[\mathtt{q}] : k\langle\langle k'[\mathtt{p}']\rangle\rangle; C \rhd k : \mathtt{p}\ \texttt{->}\ \mathtt{q} : \langle G'@\mathtt{p}'\rangle; G,\ k' : G',\ \Delta}$$

$$\lfloor^{\mathrm{GT}}|\textsc{Rec}\rceil\ \frac{\Gamma, X : (\Gamma|_{\widetilde{x@\tau}}, \Theta|_{\tilde{\tau}}, \Delta|_{\tilde{k}});\ \Theta \vdash C \rhd \Delta \qquad \Gamma_{\mathsf{rec}}, \Gamma_{\mathsf{srv}}, \Gamma|_{\widetilde{x@\tau}}; \Theta|_{\tilde{\tau}} \vdash C' \rhd \Delta|_{\tilde{k}}}{\Gamma;\ \Theta \vdash \mathsf{rec}\ X(\widetilde{x@\tau}, \tilde{k}, \tilde{\tau}) = C'\ \mathsf{in}\ C \rhd \Delta}$$

Figure 7. Global Calculus with Multiparty Sessions, typing rules.

which can correctly type public channel a in the choreography:

$$C \quad = \quad \begin{array}{l}\tau_1[\mathtt{p}_1], \tau_2[\mathtt{p}_2]\ \mathbf{start}\ \tau_3[\mathtt{p}_3], \tau_4[\mathtt{p}_4] : a(k);\\ \tau_1[\mathtt{p}_1].e\ \texttt{->}\ \tau_2[\mathtt{p}_2].x : k; \quad \tau_3[\mathtt{p}_3].e'\ \texttt{->}\ \tau_4[\mathtt{p}_4].y : k\end{array}$$

Since $\{\tau_1, \tau_2\} \cap \{\tau_3, \tau_4\} = \emptyset$, we can swap C with C' such that:

$$C' \quad = \quad \begin{array}{l}\tau_1[\mathtt{p}_1], \tau_2[\mathtt{p}_2]\ \mathbf{start}\ \tau_3[\mathtt{p}_3], \tau_4[\mathtt{p}_4] : a(k);\\ \tau_3[\mathtt{p}_3].e'\ \texttt{->}\ \tau_4[\mathtt{p}_4].y : k; \quad \tau_1[\mathtt{p}_1].e\ \texttt{->}\ \tau_2[\mathtt{p}_2].x : k\end{array}$$

Public channel a in C' does not have type G anymore, but C' is clearly still correct since we can easily follow its swap from C in type G using swapping for global types:

$$G \quad \simeq_{\mathcal{G}} \quad \mathtt{p}_3\ \texttt{->}\ \mathtt{q}_4 : \langle \mathbf{string}\rangle;\ \mathtt{p}_1\ \texttt{->}\ \mathtt{p}_2 : \langle \mathbf{int}\rangle$$

Our type system, however, does not deal with swappings in global types, and would reject C'. We made this choice so that programmers do not need to think about the swap relations when writing programs, which could make error messages confusing in some cases. However, at runtime, we must consider swaps in order to preserve well-typedness wrt reductions (Subject Reduction). Therefore, our runtime type system augments rules $\lfloor^{\mathrm{GT}}|\textsc{Start}\rceil$ and $\lfloor^{\mathrm{GT}}|\textsc{Del}\rceil$ for typing up to $\simeq_{\mathcal{G}}$.

Properties. We can now present the expected main properties of our type system. In the sequel, we say that $\Delta \xrightarrow{k:\alpha} \Delta'$ whenever $k : G$ is in Δ such that $G \xrightarrow{\alpha} G'$ and Δ' is the result of substituting $k : G$ in Δ with $k : G'$. Also, we write $\Delta \simeq_{\mathcal{G}} \Delta'$ iff $\mathsf{dom}(\Delta) = \mathsf{dom}(\Delta')$ and $\Delta(k) \simeq_{\mathcal{G}} \Delta'(k)$ for all $k \in \mathsf{dom}(\Delta)$.

Theorem 2. *Assume* $\Gamma;\ \Theta \vdash_{\Sigma} C \rhd \Delta$. *Then,*

- *(Subject Swap)* $C \simeq_{\mathcal{C}} C'$ *implies* $\Gamma;\ \Theta \vdash_{\Sigma} C' \rhd \Delta'$ *where* $\Delta \simeq_{\mathcal{G}} \Delta'$.
- $C \xrightarrow{\lambda} C'$ *implies that there exists* Δ' *such that*
  - *(Subject Reduction)* $\Gamma;\ \Theta' \vdash_{\Sigma'} C' \rhd \Delta'$ *for some* Θ', Σ'.
  - *(Session Fidelity) if* λ *is a communication on session* k *then* $\Delta \xrightarrow{k:\alpha} \Delta'$ *with* α *and* λ *on the same roles; else,* $\Delta = \Delta'$.

Type inference. We exploit the close correspondence between protocols and choreographies to perform *type inference* of public channels. Thus, we can automatically extract protocols from choreographies. First, we define *subtyping* as set inclusion on branching labels, similarly to the covariant typing of rule $\lfloor^{\mathrm{GT}}|\textsc{Sel}\rceil$ in Figure 7. Then, we modify our rules to determine the *principal type* of a choreography. Hereby, we discuss this aspect informally (cf. [14] for the formalisation). We change rule $\lfloor^{\mathrm{GT}}|\textsc{Sel}\rceil$ to require a singleton branching type for the label of interest. Then, $\lfloor^{\mathrm{GT}}|\textsc{If}\rceil$ will have to compute the least upper bound (lub) of the session environments Δ_1 and Δ_2 (for C_1 and C_2 in the branches), by *merging* their branching types. Similarly, rule $\lfloor^{\mathrm{GT}}|\textsc{Start}\rceil$ will need to update service types in Γ with the lub of all the global types of each session started through the same public channel a. Recursion is handled in a standard manner [34].

For example, from b in Example 3, we can infer the type: $\mathtt{B}\ \texttt{->}\ \mathtt{H} : \langle\mathbf{int}\rangle;\ \mathtt{B}\ \texttt{->}\ \mathtt{H} : \{\mathit{done} : \mathtt{end},\ \mathit{del} : \mathtt{B}\ \texttt{->}\ \mathtt{H} : \langle\mathbf{int}\rangle; \mathtt{B}\ \texttt{->}\ \mathtt{H} : \langle(\ldots\text{as Line 2 in Example 1}\ldots)@\mathtt{B2}\rangle\}$.

5. Endpoint Projection and its Properties

We now address endpoint code generation. First, we recall an endpoint model that we shall use as a target language. Then, we show how to generate endpoint code for each thread in a choreography and, finally, how to obtain the code for the entire system. Our code generation, the *EndPoint Projection (EPP)*, will satisfy the *EPP Theorem*, which gives a correspondence between the asynchronous semantics of choreographies and the one of endpoint terms.

Endpoint model. We model endpoint code with the calculus for multiparty sessions [7], whose syntax includes conditional, parallel, the inactive process and recursion plus the following terms, where unboxed terms denote programs:

$$\begin{array}{llll} P, Q ::= & \ldots & & \\ \mid & \overline{a}[\mathtt{p}_1,\dots,\mathtt{p}_m](k); P & \mid a[\mathtt{p}](k); P & \mid\ !a[\mathtt{p}](k); P \\ \mid & c?\mathtt{p}(x); P & \mid c?\mathtt{p}(\!(k')\!); P & \mid c?\mathtt{p}\ \&\ \{l_i : P_i\}_{i \in I} \\ \mid & c!\mathtt{p}\langle e\rangle; P & \mid c!\mathtt{p}\langle\!\langle c'\rangle\!\rangle; P & \mid c!\mathtt{p} \oplus l; P \\ \mid & \boxed{k : h} & \mid \boxed{(\boldsymbol{\nu} k)\ P} & \end{array}$$

$$c ::= k \mid \boxed{k[\mathtt{q}]} \qquad \boxed{h} ::= \boxed{(\mathtt{p}, \mathtt{q}, \boldsymbol{w}) \cdot h} \mid \boxed{\varnothing}$$

$$\boxed{\boldsymbol{w}} ::= \boxed{v} \mid \boxed{l} \mid \boxed{k[\mathtt{p}]}$$

The first row contains the terms for implementing a session **start**: request, accept and replicated accept respectively. Request and accept are used by active threads, while the latter models a process for spawning service threads. The second row concerns in-session inputs of a value, channel (delegation), or label (branching). For $c = k$, $k?\mathtt{p}$ is an input from role $\mathtt{p}$ over session k. Dually, the third row has outputs, where $\mathtt{p}$ in $k!\mathtt{p}$ is the role the message is sent to.

Example 4. $P_{\mathsf{s}} \mid P_{\mathsf{b}_1} \mid P_{\mathsf{b}_2}$ *is an endpoint implementation of Example 2 where:*

$$
\begin{aligned}
P_{\mathsf{s}} = \;& !a[\mathtt{S}](k);\; k?\mathtt{B1}(x_1);\; k!\mathtt{B1}\langle \mathsf{quote}(x_1)\rangle;\; k!\mathtt{B2}\langle \mathsf{quote}(x_1)\rangle;\\
& k?\mathtt{B2}\,\&\left\{\begin{array}{ll} ok: & k?\mathtt{B2}(x_2);\\ & k!\mathtt{B2}\langle ddate\rangle,\\ quit: \mathbf{0} & \end{array}\right\}
\end{aligned}
$$

$$
\begin{aligned}
P_{\mathsf{b}_1} =\;& \overline{a}[\mathtt{B1},\mathtt{B2},\mathtt{S}](k);\; k!\mathtt{S}\langle book\rangle;\; k?\mathtt{S}(y_1);\; k!\mathtt{B2}\langle \mathsf{contrib}(y_1)\rangle\\
P_{\mathsf{b}_2} =\;& a[\mathtt{B2}](k);\; k?\mathtt{S}(z_1);\; k?\mathtt{B1}(z_2);\; \mathsf{if}\ (z_1 - z_2 \leq 100)\\
& \quad \mathsf{then}\ k!\mathtt{S} \oplus ok;\; k!\mathtt{S}\langle addr\rangle;\; k?\mathtt{S}(z_3)\\
& \quad \mathsf{else}\ k!\mathtt{S} \oplus quit
\end{aligned}
$$

□

Boxed terms are used only at runtime. A session queue $k : h$ is a FIFO queue h for session channel k. A message in h contains the sender and receiver roles, and the carried message $\boldsymbol{w}$ (a value v, a label l or a delegated channel $k[\mathsf{p}]$). Messages with different pairs of roles can be permuted by structural congruence (omitted), simulating a queue per each pair of roles [7]. Since messages in a queue have both a receiver and a sender role, in-session inputs and outputs are annotated with the executing role at runtime. E.g., the term $k[\mathsf{q}]!\mathsf{p} \oplus l; P$ is an executing process which will put the message $(\mathsf{q}, \mathsf{p}, l)$ in the queue k with sender q and receiver p. Figure 8 contains a selection of the rules defining the semantics of terms, where $R = \prod_{j \in J} !a[\mathsf{p}_j](k_j); Q_j$, $I = \{1, \ldots, n\}$ and $J = \{n+1, \ldots, m\}$. The first rule initiates a session, creating an empty session queue $k : \varnothing$ and substituting every occurrence of session channel k (which will be restricted) with $k[\mathsf{p}_j]$ where p_j is the role that must be played by process P_j. Replicated services in R model spawning of new processes. The second rule puts value v, the evaluation of e, in the queue for k. The last rule is about branching: it fetches a label l_j from the queue and then continues as process P_j. Labels, denoted by μ, annotate reductions to make their actions observable. E.g., label $!\mathsf{p} \texttt{ -> } \mathsf{q} : k\langle v\rangle$ denotes a communication from role p to role q on session channel k carrying v. Similarly, the label for branching starts with a ?, denoting input.

Thread projection. We denote with $C \downharpoonright_\tau$ the projection of the behaviour of a thread in a choreography onto an endpoint term. A selection of the rules defining $C \downharpoonright_\tau$ is reported in Figure 9. Thread projection adds no further ad-hoc communications wrt the originating choreography. In a start, we project the first thread to an endpoint request, threads $\tau_2, \ldots, \tau_n$ to accepts and threads $\tau_{n+1}, \ldots, \tau_m$ to replicated accepts. For selection, the sender is projected to an output and the receiver to a branching. Projections of communication and delegation (omitted) follow the same principle. In a choreography conditional, τ is projected to a local conditional, whereas for all other threads we require their projected behaviours to be merged by the *merging* partial operator $\sqcup$ [15]. $P \sqcup Q$ is isomorphic to P and Q up to branching, where all branches of P or Q with distinct labels are also included. As a full example, the thread projections of the choreography in Example 2 (Two-buyer choreography) are the processes reported in Example 4.

Linearity. The expressivity of the *(start)* primitive may introduce races on public channels. For example, the choreography

$$\tau_1[\mathsf{p}], \tau_2[\mathsf{q}]\ \mathbf{start}\ : a(k); \quad \tau_3[\mathsf{p}], \tau_4[\mathsf{q}]\ \mathbf{start}\ : a(k') \qquad (1)$$

features four threads starting two different sessions on the same public channel. If we run their projections in parallel, we have a race between τ_1 and τ_3 and another between τ_2 and τ_4 for synchronising on a. This may result in τ_1 starting a session with τ_4 and τ_2 starting a session with τ_3, violating the choreography.

In the sequel an *interaction node*, denoted by n, is an abstraction of a node in a choreography syntax tree. n can either be $\tau_1, \ldots, \tau_n\ \mathbf{start}\ \tau_{n+1}, \ldots, \tau_m : a$ (abstracting a *(start)* node) or $\tau_1 \texttt{ -> } \tau_2$ (abstracting a session interaction). We write $\mathsf{n}_1 \prec \mathsf{n}_2 \in C$ whenever n_1 precedes n_2 in the choreography C.

Definition 1 (Dependency). *We write* $\mathsf{n}_1 \prec_\tau \mathsf{n}_2 \in C$ *if* $\mathsf{n}_1 \prec \mathsf{n}_2 \in C$ *and either*

1. $\mathsf{n}_1 = \tau_1, \ldots, \tau_n\ \mathbf{start}\ \tau_{n+1}, \ldots, \tau_m : a$ *and* $\mathsf{n}_2 = \tau \texttt{ -> } \tau'$ *if* $\tau = \tau_i$, $1 \leq i \leq m$*; or,*
2. $\mathsf{n}_1 = \tau_1, \ldots, \tau_n\ \mathbf{start}\ \tau_{n+1}, \ldots, \tau_m : a$ *and* $\mathsf{n}_2 = \tau'_1, \ldots, \tau'_n\ \mathbf{start}\ \tau'_{n+1}, \ldots, \tau'_m\ : a$ *where* $\tau = \tau_i$ *for* $1 \leq i \leq m$ *and* $\tau \in \mathsf{fn}(\mathsf{n}_2)$*; or,*
3. $\mathsf{n}_1 = \tau' \texttt{ -> } \tau$ *and* $\tau \in \mathsf{fn}(\mathsf{n}_2)$.

$\mathsf{n}_1 \prec_\tau \mathsf{n}_2 \in C$ implies that the projection of τ for the originating node of n_2 will not be enabled before that for n_1. We use dependencies to define *linearity*:

Definition 2 (Linearity). *If* $\mathsf{n}_i = \tau^i_1, \ldots, \tau^i_n\ \mathbf{start}\ \tau^i_{n+1}, \ldots, \tau^i_m :$ a $(i = 1, 2,\ n \geq 2)$ *are in* C *and are not in different branches of a (cond), we say* C *is* linear *if either* $\forall j \in \{1, \ldots, n\}.\exists j' \in \{1, \ldots, m\}.\ \mathsf{n}_1 \prec_{\tau^1_{j'}} \ldots \prec_{\tau^2_j} \mathsf{n}_2$ *or* $\forall j \in \{1, \ldots, n\}.\exists j' \in \{1, \ldots, m\}.\ \mathsf{n}_2 \prec_{\tau^2_{j'}} \ldots \prec_{\tau^1_j} \mathsf{n}_1$.

Linearity checks that, for all start nodes $\mathsf{n}_1 \prec \mathsf{n}_2 \in C$ on the same a, each active thread in n_2 depends on some thread in n_1, avoiding races between active threads. This is not necessary for service threads, since they will be merged by our EPP. Linearity is preserved by our semantics and is decidable, since a choreography is linear whenever its one-time unfolding of recursions is linear.

Example 5. *In (1), we cannot build any dependency unless, e.g.,* $\tau_1 = \tau_3$ *and* $\tau_2 = \tau_4$*. Instead, the following choreography is linear with dependencies between* τ_1 *and* τ_3 *and between* τ_2 *and* τ_4*.*

$$\tau_1[\mathsf{p}], \tau_2[\mathsf{q}]\ \mathbf{start}\ : a(k);\ \tau_1[\mathsf{p}_1] \texttt{ -> } \tau_3[\mathsf{p}_3] : k';\ \tau_2[\mathsf{p}_2] \texttt{ -> } \tau'_2[\mathsf{p}_4] : k';\ \tau'_2[\mathsf{p}_5] \texttt{ -> } \tau_4[\mathsf{p}_6] : k';\ \tau_3[\mathsf{p}], \tau_4[\mathsf{q}]\ \mathbf{start}\ : a(k)$$

□

EPP. Since different service threads may be started on the same public channel and play the same role, we use $\sqcup$ for merging their behaviours into a single replicated process. We identify such threads with $\lfloor C \rfloor^a_\mathsf{p}$, the *service grouping operator* [14]. We can finally give the complete definition of EPP:

Definition 3 (Endpoint Projection). *Let* $C \equiv (\boldsymbol{\nu} \tilde{\tau}\tilde{k})\ C_f$ *where* C_f *is restriction-free, i.e., there are no subterms* $(\boldsymbol{\nu} r)\ C'$ *in* C_f*. Then, the EPP of* C *is:*

$$C \downharpoonright = (\boldsymbol{\nu}\tilde{k}) \Bigg(\underbrace{\prod_{\tau \in \mathsf{fn}(C_f)} C_f \downharpoonright_\tau}_{\text{(i)}} \;\Big|\; \underbrace{\prod_{k \in \mathsf{fn}(C_f)} k : \varnothing}_{\text{(ii)}} \Bigg) \;\Big|\; \underbrace{\prod_{a,\mathsf{p}} \Big(\bigsqcup_{\tau \in \lfloor C_f \rfloor^a_\mathsf{p}} C_f \downharpoonright_\tau \Big)}_{\text{(iii)}}$$

The EPP of C is the parallel composition of (i) the projections of all active threads; (ii) the queues for all active sessions; and (iii) the replicated processes obtained by merging the projections of all service threads with same public channel and role. Note how swapping has no influence on EPP, since we now have parallel composition at the endpoint level, i.e., if $C \simeq_C C'$ then $C \downharpoonright \equiv C' \downharpoonright$.

Example 6. *Let* C *be the two-buyer-helper choreography from Example 3. Since* h_1 *and* h_2 *are grouped under* $\lfloor C \rfloor^b_{\mathtt{H}}$*, the EPP of* C *will merge their behaviour into a single process (say,* P_h*). I.e.,* $C \downharpoonright = C \downharpoonright_{\mathsf{b}_1} \mid C \downharpoonright_{\mathsf{b}_2} \mid C \downharpoonright_{\mathsf{s}} \mid P_\mathsf{h}$ *where* P_h *is:*

$$
\begin{aligned}
& !b[\mathtt{H}](k');\\
& \quad k'?\mathtt{B}(z);\; k'?\mathtt{B}\,\&\left\{\begin{array}{ll} done: & \mathbf{0},\\ del: & k'?\mathtt{B}(z');\; k'?\mathtt{B}((k));\\ & \mathsf{if}\ (z - z' \leq 100)\\ & \mathsf{then}\ k!\mathtt{S} \oplus ok;\, k!\mathtt{S}\langle addr\rangle;\, k?\mathtt{S}(z'')\\ & \mathsf{else}\ k!\mathtt{S} \oplus quit \end{array}\right\}
\end{aligned}
$$

□

$$\lfloor^{\text{P}}|\text{START}\rceil \quad \overline{a}[\mathtt{p}_1,\ldots,\mathtt{p}_m](k);P \mid \textstyle\prod_{i\in I} a[\mathtt{p}_i](k_i);P_i \mid R \xrightarrow{\mathtt{p}_1,\ldots,\mathtt{p}_n\ \mathbf{start}\ \mathtt{p}_{n+1},\ldots,\mathtt{p}_m:a(k)} (\boldsymbol{\nu} k)\left(P[k[\mathtt{p}_1]/k] \mid \textstyle\prod_{i\in I} P_i[k[\mathtt{p}_i]/k_i] \mid \textstyle\prod_{j\in J} Q_j[k[\mathtt{p}_j]/k_j] \mid k:\varnothing\right) \mid R$$

$$\lfloor^{\text{EP}}|\text{SEND}\rceil \quad k[\mathtt{p}]!\mathtt{q}\langle e\rangle;P \mid k:h \xrightarrow{!\mathtt{p}\ \texttt{->}\ \mathtt{q}:k\langle v\rangle} P \mid k:h\cdot(\mathtt{p},\mathtt{q},v) \quad (e\downarrow v)$$

$$\lfloor^{\text{EP}}|\text{BRANCH}\rceil \quad k[\mathtt{q}]?\mathtt{p}\,\&\,\{l_i:P_i\}_{i\in I} \mid k:(\mathtt{q},\mathtt{p},l_j)\cdot h \xrightarrow{?\mathtt{p}\ \texttt{->}\ \mathtt{q}:k[l_j]} P_j \mid k:h \quad (j\in I)$$

Figure 8. Endpoint calculus, selected reduction rules.

$$\left(\begin{array}{l}\tau_1[\mathtt{p}_1],\ldots,\tau_n[\mathtt{p}_n]\ \mathbf{start}\\ \quad\tau_{n+1}[\mathtt{p}_{n+1}],\ldots,\tau_m[\mathtt{p}_m]:a(k);C\end{array}\right)\lfloor_{\tau_i} = \begin{cases}\overline{a}[\mathtt{p}_1,\ldots,\mathtt{p}_m](k);(C\lfloor_{\tau_i}) & \text{if } i=1\\ a[\mathtt{p}_i](k);(C\lfloor_{\tau_i}) & \text{if } 2\le i\le n\\ !a[\mathtt{p}_i](k);(C\lfloor_{\tau_i}) & \text{if } n+1\le i\le m\\ C\lfloor_{\tau_i} & \text{otherwise}\end{cases}$$

$$(\,\tau_1[\mathtt{p}]\ \texttt{->}\ \tau_2[\mathtt{q}]:k[l];C\,)\lfloor_\tau = \begin{cases}k!\mathtt{q}\oplus l;(C\lfloor_\tau) & \text{if } \tau=\tau_1\\ k?\mathtt{p}\,\&\,\{l:(C\lfloor_\tau)\} & \text{if } \tau=\tau_2\\ C\lfloor_\tau & \text{otherwise}\end{cases}$$

$$(\,\mathsf{if}\ e@\tau\ \mathsf{then}\ C_1\ \mathsf{else}\ C_2\,)\lfloor_{\tau'} = \begin{cases}\mathsf{if}\ e\ \mathsf{then}\ (C_1\lfloor_{\tau'})\ \mathsf{else}\ (C_2\lfloor_{\tau'}) & \text{if } \tau=\tau'\\ (C_1\lfloor_{\tau'})\sqcup(C_2\lfloor_{\tau'}) & \text{otherwise}\end{cases}$$

Figure 9. Thread projection, selected rules.

EPP Theorem. We now present our *EPP Theorem*, which formalises the relationship between the semantics of a well-typed, linear choreography and the semantics of its EPP. Without loss of generality, we consider only *strict reductions*, denoted by $\rightsquigarrow$, i.e. reductions where restricted names not under a prefix are never renamed. $\rightsquigarrow^*$ denotes the closure of $\rightsquigarrow$. The entailment $\tilde{\lambda} \vdash \tilde{\mu}$ checks that the endpoint actions $\tilde{\mu}$ *implement* the global actions $\tilde{\lambda}$ (cf. [14]).

Theorem 3 (EPP). *Let $C \equiv (\boldsymbol{\nu}\tilde{\tau}\tilde{k})\ C_f$ be linear and well-typed, with C_f restriction-free. Then,*

1. *(Completeness) $C \overset{\lambda}{\rightsquigarrow} C'$ implies there exists P such that (i) $C'\lfloor \prec P$ and either (ii) $C\lfloor \overset{\mu}{\rightsquigarrow} P$ where $\lambda \vdash \mu$ or (iii) $C\lfloor \overset{\mu_1}{\rightsquigarrow}\overset{\mu_2}{\rightsquigarrow} P$ where $\lambda \vdash \mu_1,\mu_2$.*
2. *(Soundness) $C\lfloor \overset{\tilde{\mu}}{\rightsquigarrow}{}^* P$ implies there exist P' and C' such that (i) $P \overset{\tilde{\mu}'}{\rightsquigarrow}{}^* P'$; (ii) $C \overset{\tilde{\lambda}}{\rightsquigarrow}{}^* C'$ and $\tilde{\lambda} \vdash \tilde{\mu},\tilde{\mu}'$; and (iii) $C'\lfloor \prec P'$.*

Above, the *pruning relation* $P \prec Q$ is such that $P \sim Q$ ($\sim$ is bisimilarity) and that P has some unused branches and replicated accepts. Point 1. states that an EPP can mimic (up to pruning) all the reductions of its originating choreography; on the other hand, point 2. says that an EPP always eventually reduces (up to pruning) to the projection of a (possibly reached after multiple reductions) reductum of its originating choreography. Both points ensure that the observables of a choreography and its EPP are correctly related.

By Theorems 1 and 3, we can formalise our *deadlock-freedom-by-design* property. Below, $\xrightarrow{\tilde{\mu}}{}^*$ is the closure of $\xrightarrow{\mu}$.

Corollary 1 (Deadlock-freedom-by-design)**.** *Let C be linear and well-typed. Then, for any P such that $C\lfloor \xrightarrow{\tilde{\mu}}{}^* P$, we have that either $P \xrightarrow{\mu'} P'$ for some P', μ' or $\mathbf{0} \prec P$.*

Moreover, our EPP code enjoys standard communication safety:

Corollary 2 (Safety)**.** *Let C be linear, well-typed and $C\lfloor \xrightarrow{\tilde{\mu}}{}^* P$. Then,*

1. *(Linearity) P has no races on any a or k with same role $\mathtt{p}$;*
2. *(Error-freedom) if P has an enabled input $k[\mathtt{p}]?\mathtt{q}$ that can consume a message $(\mathtt{p},\mathtt{q},\boldsymbol{w})$ from a session queue $k:h$ in P, then $\boldsymbol{w}$ is of the same type of the input (value, label, or delegated channel).*

Typing expressiveness. Previously proposed typing disciplines for session types ensure properties similar to ours, but performing type analysis directly on endpoint programs [7, 15, 22]. Our typing discipline subsumes a larger class of safe deadlock-free systems, by exploiting the extra information that we gain from defining implementations with choreographies. In particular, our typing system allows for two novel features wrt standard multiparty session typing: inter-protocol coherence and partial protocol implementation.

Let us discuss inter-protocol coherence. Consider the protocol:

$$G = \mathtt{p}\ \texttt{->}\ \mathtt{q}:\{l_1:\mathtt{r}\ \texttt{->}\ \mathtt{p}:\langle\mathbf{int}\rangle,\ l_2:\mathtt{r}\ \texttt{->}\ \mathtt{q}:\langle\mathbf{int}\rangle\}$$

Above, $\mathtt{p}$ communicates to $\mathtt{q}$ a choice between labels l_1 and l_2. In the first case another role, $\mathtt{r}$, is expected to communicate an integer to $\mathtt{p}$. Otherwise, $\mathtt{r}$ will communicate an integer to $\mathtt{q}$. A potential use case for G could be that $\mathtt{r}$ possesses some good, and $\mathtt{p}$ decides where the good should be sent to ($\mathtt{p}$ itself or $\mathtt{q}$). Previous work on global types cannot type any system implementing G, since G cannot be projected onto a correct set of endpoint types [38]. Indeed, in the protocol, $\mathtt{r}$ is not informed of the choice made by $\mathtt{p}$ and thus cannot know whether it should communicate with $\mathtt{p}$ or $\mathtt{q}$ afterwards. We refer to this problem by saying that G is not *coherent* for previous type systems based on global types. In our framework, we do not consider protocol coherence because protocols such as G above can easily be implemented by interleaving them with other ones. For example, consider the following choreography:

1. $\tau_1[\mathtt{p}]\ \mathbf{start}\ \tau_2[\mathtt{q}],\tau_3[\mathtt{r}]:a(k);\quad \tau_2[\mathtt{p}'],\tau_3[\mathtt{q}']\ \mathbf{start}\ :b(k');$
2. $\mathsf{if}\ e@\tau_1\ \mathsf{then}\quad \tau_1[\mathtt{p}]\ \texttt{->}\ \tau_2[\mathtt{q}]:k[l_1];\ \tau_2[\mathtt{p}']\ \texttt{->}\ \tau_3[\mathtt{q}']:k'[l_1];$
3. $\qquad\qquad\qquad \tau_3[\mathtt{r}].\mathit{some\_int}\ \texttt{->}\ \tau_1[\mathtt{p}].x:k$
4. $\qquad\quad \mathsf{else}\quad \tau_1[\mathtt{p}]\ \texttt{->}\ \tau_2[\mathtt{q}]:k[l_2];\ \tau_2[\mathtt{p}']\ \texttt{->}\ \tau_3[\mathtt{q}']:k'[l_2];$
5. $\qquad\qquad\qquad \tau_3[\mathtt{r}].\mathit{some\_int}\ \texttt{->}\ \tau_2[\mathtt{q}].y:k$

The choreography above can be typed correctly using G as type for a (we omit the typing for b). In order to notify τ_3, playing role $\mathtt{r}$, of the choice performed by τ_1, playing role $\mathtt{p}$, we make use of an additional session between τ_2 and τ_3. We use this session, k', after τ_2 receives the choice from τ_1. Observe that the choreography is typable and can be correctly projected by our EPP. The key aspect of this example is that our framework leaves the task of defining a coherent system to the implementation (the choreography). Hence, protocols can be designed at a higher level of abstraction. E.g., in G we do not specify how $\mathtt{r}$ is notified of the choice. We call this aspect *inter-protocol coherence*, since it is the composition of protocols in a choreography that is checked for coherence (by checking whether its EPP is defined), and not each protocol by itself.

We now discuss partial protocol implementation with the following choreography:

$$\begin{array}{ll} \tau[\mathsf{p}], \tau'[\mathsf{q}]\ \mathbf{start}\ : a(k); & \tau[\mathsf{p}] \texttt{ -> } \tau'[\mathsf{q}] : k[l_1]; \\ \tau[\mathsf{p}], \tau'[\mathsf{q}]\ \mathbf{start}\ : a(k'); & \mathsf{if}\ e@\tau\ \mathsf{then}\ \tau[\mathsf{p}] \texttt{ -> } \tau'[\mathsf{q}] : k'[l_2] \\ & \qquad\quad \mathsf{else}\ \ \tau[\mathsf{p}] \texttt{ -> } \tau'[\mathsf{q}] : k'[l_3] \end{array}$$

The choreography above is typable in our system (a's type is $\mathsf{p} \texttt{ -> } \mathsf{q} : \{l_1 : \mathsf{end},\ l_2 : \mathsf{end},\ l_3 : \mathsf{end}\}$). However, the endpoint projection for τ' would not be typable with standard contra-variant input typing, which requires that *at least* all the branches in the type are implemented. Again, this is a consequence of using choreographies: since in the choreography we know exactly which outputs will correspond to which inputs, we can ensure that the protocol branches that τ' does not implement will never be used.

6. Implementation

Following our model, we have implemented the Chor programming language [16]. Our implementation is open source and comes with a complete IDE, developed as an Eclipse [19] plugin.

Chor features all GC primitives (Figure 1), an implementation of our typing discipline (Figure 7), and an EPP implementation for projecting choreographies onto executable endpoints (from § 5). Chor also provides some syntax extensions for enhanced usability, e.g., protocols may refer to other protocols and choreographies allow local code for local state manipulation and user interactions.

We give an overview of the development methodology offered by our framework, and detail some aspects of our implementation.

Development methodology. In the development methodology suggested by Chor (see Figure 10), developers can first use our IDE to write protocol specifications and choreographies. The programmer is supported by on-the-fly verification which takes care of checking (i) the syntactic correctness of program terms and (ii) the type compliance of the choreography wrt the protocol specifications, using our typing discipline. Program errors are reported using syntax highlighting, allowing for an interactive programming experience.

Once the global program is completed, developers can automatically project to an endpoint implementation, given in the Jolie programming language (cf. Executable artifacts). Nevertheless, Chor is designed to be extended to multiple endpoint languages: potentially, each thread in a choreography could be implemented with a different endpoint technology. We plan future extensions to support projecting endpoints to e.g., Java, C#, or WS-BPEL [30].

Each Jolie endpoint program comes with its own deployment information, given as a term separated from the code implementing the behaviour of the projected thread. This part can be optionally customised by the programmer, which can be useful for running the programs on some specific network or communication technology.

Finally, the Jolie endpoint programs can be executed. As expected, they will implement the originating choreography.

Executable artifacts. Our EPP implementation targets Jolie, an open-source service-oriented language [3, 29]. Choosing Jolie has several reasons: (i) Jolie offers constructs similar to those of our endpoint calculus, e.g., communications and input choices, making part of our EPP straightforward; (ii) Jolie has a formal semantics and a reference implementation, which we used for implementing some abstract aspects of our model such as message queues and session channels; and (iii) Jolie supports a wide range of compatibility with other technologies as detailed below.

Deployment. By default, our endpoint programs will operate on top of TCP/IP sockets. However, since Jolie also supports other communication technologies – e.g. local memory IPC and Bluetooth – and data formats – e.g. HTTP and SOAP [4] – programmers may customise deployment information of each endpoint. Hence, some endpoints may communicate over, e.g., HTTP, while others, e.g., using fast binary data formats. Additionally, different endpoints may be deployed in different machines and/or networks.

Notably, customising the deployment of an endpoint program does not necessarily require updating the code of the others. Supporting this flexibility has required a careful implementation of session starts (rule $\lfloor^{\text{EP}}|_{\text{START}}\rceil$), which are coordinated by special "start services". The (endpoint projections of the) active threads willing to start a session contact the appropriate start service. Then, the start service spawns the (projections of the) service threads by calling the external services that implement them. In every message exchange, each endpoint informs the start service of the *binding information* (e.g., IP address and data format) on which the endpoint can be reached. Finally, the start service informs all participants about all necessary bindings, so that each party can dynamically update its references to the others (e.g., socket connections).

Another key feature concerning different communication technologies is that our queue implementation is based on the latest *correlation sets* implementation in Jolie [28]. Correlation sets allow to program incoming message queueing by correlating some data values inside messages with those inside of a thread local state. Our EPP handles this programming to implement a separate queue for each role in a session as required by our model. Afterwards, the programmer can customise correlation for each deployment artifact. For instance, some threads may identify sessions using HTTP cookies (as in common web applications), while others may use SOAP headers (as in the WS-Addressing specifications [5]).

Delegation. Session delegation is a nontrivial mechanism at the level of endpoint implementation. The main concern lies in updating channel references (bindings). For instance, assume that a session k has some thread participants, say τ and $\tilde{\tau}$. Suppose now that τ delegates its role on k to another thread τ' through a different session. In such a situation, all the threads in $\tilde{\tau}$ need their external references to be updated for reaching τ' instead of τ when communicating with the session/role pair delegated by τ. In our endpoint model this necessity is completely abstracted away by the synchronisations on the centralised message queues (one per session). However, in our implementation, message queues are completely distributed: each thread owns a message queue which must be reached explicitly by other threads. [24] presents a survey of possible solutions to this problem in asynchronous scenarios. The main challenge is that $\tilde{\tau}$ may send messages to τ before getting notified of the delegation, and τ must thus resend these messages to τ', adding extra communications. In our EPP implementation, each thread in $\tilde{\tau}$ knows when the delegation will happen using the information from the choreography. Hence, we are always in the optimal case where no messages are lost.

7. Examples

Choreography-based programming can have several applications, ranging from multicore programming to distributed Web Services. Below, we present and discuss two possible example applications.

Streaming-AVP. In this example, we show how to combine two different protocols for implementing a streaming service for movie files. We start by giving the protocol for streaming:

$$\mathsf{rec}\ \mathbf{t};\ \mathtt{S} \texttt{ -> } \mathtt{C} : \langle \mathbf{bytes} \rangle;\ \mathtt{S} \texttt{ -> } \mathtt{C} : \{\ again : \mathbf{t},\ \ end : \mathsf{end}\ \}$$

In the protocol above, S is a streaming server sending byte packets to a client C. After each packet, S communicates to C whether there are more bits to be sent or the stream is over (choices $again$ and end). The other protocol (AVP, for Audio-Video Processing) is

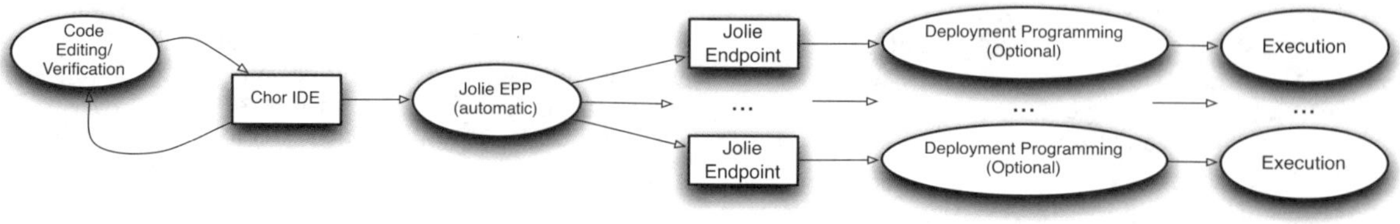

Figure 10. Development methodology with the Chor language.

defined by the following global type:

$$\text{rec } \mathbf{t}; \mathtt{F} \text{ -> } \mathtt{A}: \langle\mathbf{bytes}\rangle; \mathtt{F} \text{ -> } \mathtt{V}: \langle\mathbf{bytes}\rangle; \mathtt{A} \text{ -> } \mathtt{S}: \langle\mathbf{bytes}\rangle; \mathtt{V} \text{ -> } \mathtt{S}: \langle\mathbf{bytes}\rangle; \mathtt{F} \text{ -> } \mathtt{A}: \{\ \mathit{again}: \mathtt{A} \text{ -> } \mathtt{V}: \langle\mathbf{bytes}\rangle;\ \mathtt{V} \text{ -> } \mathtt{S}: \langle\mathbf{bytes}\rangle; \mathbf{t},\ \mathit{end}: \mathsf{end}\ \}$$

Four roles participate in this protocol: a filesystem F, an audio decoder A, a video decoder V, and a sink S. The flow of information in this protocol consists of F sending the raw audio information to A and the raw video information to V, read from the movie file. Then both A and V send the processed decoded information to the sink S.

The goal of this example is to show how to interleave the two protocols so that the information produced by an implementation of AVP is forwarded to a client (e.g., a display) as pictured below:

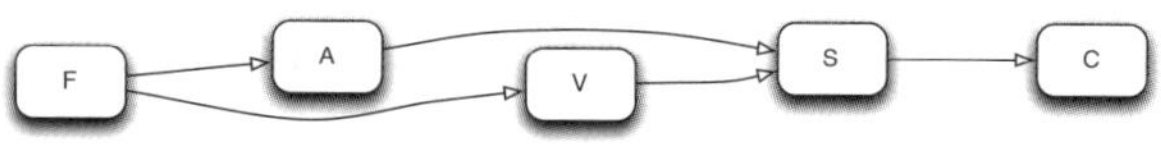

We implement such a system as follows:

$$\begin{array}{l} \mathsf{c}[\mathtt{C}]\ \mathbf{start}\ \mathsf{s}[\mathtt{S}] : a(\mathit{stream});\ \mathsf{s}[\mathtt{S}]\ \mathbf{start}\ \mathsf{f}[\mathtt{F}], \mathsf{a}[\mathtt{A}], \mathsf{v}[\mathtt{V}] : b(\mathit{avp}); \\ \text{rec } \mathsf{AVPStreaming}(\epsilon, (\mathit{avp}, \mathit{stream}), (f, a, v, s, c)) = C \text{ in} \\ \quad \mathsf{AVPStreaming}(\epsilon, (\mathit{avp}, \mathit{stream}), (f, a, v, s, c)) \end{array}$$

The choreography above starts two sessions (on a and b) corresponding to the two protocols specified above. Note that the streamer in the first protocol and the file system, the audio decoder and the video decoder in the second where chosen to be service threads. The core of the choreography is the term C defined as:

```
1.  f[F].audioByteChunk -> a[A].audioByteChunk : avp;
2.  f[F].videoByteChunk -> v[V].videoByteChunk : avp;
3.  a[A].decodeA(audioByteChunk) -> s[S].audioPkt : avp;
4.  v[V].decodeV(videoByteChunk) -> s[S].videoPkt : avp;
5.  s[S].(audioPkt + videoPkt) -> c[C].pkt : stream;
6.  if (more())@f
7.     f[F] -> a[A] : avp[again]; a[A] -> v[V] : avp[again];
8.     v[V] -> s[S] : avp[again]; s[S] -> c[C] : stream[again];
9.     AVPStreaming(ε, (avp, stream), (f, a, v, s, c))
10. else
11.    f[F] -> a[A] : avp[end]; a[A] -> v[V] : avp[end];
12.    v[V] -> s[S] : avp[end]; s[S] -> c[C] : stream[end]
```

Choreography C can be repeated several times. Lines 1-5 describe how the filesystem sends audio and video information to the threads implementing the audio and video decoders respectively. Then, the audio and video decoder resend the processed information to the thread implementing the sink. The same thread implements the streamer in the other protocol and therefore sends to the client data obtained by composing the audio and video (this is like multiplexing). Lines 7-9 correspond to the if-branch where the file server will communicate to the other threads that there is more data to process. Similarly, termination is communicated to the other threads in the else-branch (Lines 11-12). Clearly, the choreography above is well-typed wrt the two given global types.

As an example, the following process is the EPP for s:

$$\begin{array}{l} !a[\mathtt{S}](\mathit{stream});\ \bar{b}[\mathtt{S}, \mathtt{F}, \mathtt{A}, \mathtt{V}](\mathit{avp}); \\ \text{rec } \mathsf{AVPStreaming}(\epsilon, (\mathit{avp}, \mathit{stream})) = \\ \left(\begin{array}{l} \mathit{avp}?\mathtt{A}(\mathit{audiopacket});\ \mathit{avp}?\mathtt{V}(\mathit{videopacket}); \\ \mathit{stream}!\mathtt{C}\langle \mathit{audiopacket} + \mathit{videopacket}\rangle; \\ \mathit{avp}?\mathtt{V}\ \& \left\{ \begin{array}{l} \mathit{again}: \mathit{stream}!\mathtt{C} \oplus \mathit{again}; \\ \qquad \mathsf{AVPStreaming}(\epsilon, (\mathit{avp}, \mathit{stream})) \\ \mathit{end}: \mathit{stream}!\mathtt{C} \oplus \mathit{end} \end{array} \right\} \end{array} \right) \\ \text{in } \mathsf{AVPStreaming}(\epsilon, (\mathit{avp}, \mathit{stream})) \end{array}$$

OpenID and Logging. We give an example using a variant of OpenID [32], a protocol where a client (called user) authenticates to a server (called relying party) through a third-party identity provider. We define the protocol with the following global type:

$$\mathtt{U} \text{ -> } \mathtt{RP} : \langle\mathbf{string}\rangle;\ \mathtt{RP} \text{ -> } \mathtt{IP} : \langle\mathbf{string}\rangle;\ \mathtt{U} \text{ -> } \mathtt{IP} : \langle\mathbf{string}\rangle;$$

$$\mathtt{IP} \text{ -> } \mathtt{RP} : \left\{ \begin{array}{ll} \mathit{ok}: & \mathtt{RP} \text{ -> } \mathtt{U} : \{\mathit{ok} : \mathtt{RP} \text{ -> } \mathtt{U} : \langle G@\mathtt{C}\rangle; \mathsf{end}\}, \\ \mathit{fail}: & \mathtt{RP} \text{ -> } \mathtt{U} : \{\mathit{fail} : \mathsf{end}\} \end{array} \right\}$$

Above, RP abstracts the relying party, IP the identity provider and U the user. First, U sends her username to RP, which forwards it to IP. Then, U sends her password to IP, which will notify RP of whether the username/password credentials are valid (*ok* or *fail*). Finally, RP forwards the notification to U. If successful, RP also delegates to U role C in a session of type G, where $G = \mathtt{S} \text{ -> } \mathtt{C} : \langle\mathbf{string}\rangle$.

This example interleaves OpenID with another protocol where a client C asks a log server S for either a secret or a public log. Finally, S replies with the corresponding log content. Formally,

$$\mathtt{C} \text{ -> } \mathtt{S} : \{\mathit{secret} : \mathtt{S} \text{ -> } \mathtt{C} : \langle\mathbf{string}\rangle,\ \mathit{public} : \mathtt{S} \text{ -> } \mathtt{C} : \langle\mathbf{string}\rangle\}$$

Now, we can program our system as follows:

```
1.  rp[RP], u[U] start ip[IP] : publicOpenID(k);
2.  u[U].user -> rp.user : k;
3.  rp[RP].user -> ip[IP].username : k;
4.  u[U].pwd -> ip[IP].password : k;
5.  if (check(username, password))@ip
6.    ip[IP] -> rp[RP] : k[ok];
7.    rp[RP] -> u[U] : k[ok];
8.    if (high(username))@rp
9.      rp[C] start s[S] : log(k');
10.     rp[C] -> s[S] : k'[secret];
11.     rp[RP] -> u[U] : k⟨⟨k'[C]⟩⟩;
12.     s[S].secret_msg -> u[C].logContent : k'
13.   else
14.     rp[C] start s[S] : log(k');
15.     rp[C] -> s[S] : k'[public];
16.     rp[RP] -> u[U] : k⟨⟨k'[C]⟩⟩;
17.     s[S].public_msg -> u[C].logContent : k'
18. else
19.   ip[IP] -> rp[RP] : k[fail];
20.   ip[IP] -> u[U] : k[fail]
```

where rp, u, ip, and s are the endpoints of the system. Line 1 describes the initiation of a protocol instance between rp, u and ip, by means of the public name a. In Lines 2-4, u sends its credentials to rp and ip (only username to rp). Then, ip checks the data received

(Line 5) and communicates the outcome to rp (Lines 6 and 19). In both cases, the selection is forwarded to u (Lines 7 and 20). In the if-branch, rp checks the user access level. If high, it starts a new session (log) spawning s (Line 9) and asks for a secret log (Line 10). Consequently, rp will delegate its role in session k' to the user u through session k. Finally, u will get the requested log. The system works similarly in the public log case (Lines 14-17).

We conclude by showing the EPP for service thread s:

$$!log[\mathtt{S}](k');\ k'?\mathtt{C}\,\&\left\{\begin{array}{l} secret : k'!\mathtt{C}\langle private\_msg\rangle, \\ public : k'!\mathtt{C}\langle public\_msg\rangle \end{array}\right\}$$

Note how the thread projections of s for the different branches of the choreography (Lines 9-12 and 14-17) would yield different code which is then merged into the one above.

Other examples. In the Chor website [16] we provide other examples, which can also be directly tested in the Chor IDE. The examples include other applications of OpenID, usage of the choreography language for programming a use case of the Ocean Observatories Initiative [31], and other web services applications.

8. Related Work

Global methods for communicating systems occur in different forms, including MSC [25], security protocols [8, 9, 12] and automata theory [21]. However, these works are not intended as fully-fledged programming languages since they do not deal with, e.g., different layers of abstraction or value passing.

This is the first work proposing an asynchronous semantics for a choreography language based on sessions. To the best of our knowledge, the notion of *delayed input* [27] is the most similar result to the asynchrony modelled by our semantics.

The closest work to ours is [15], which proposes a *synchronous* choreography model without delegation based on *binary* (endpoint) session types. Our framework shows that switching to multiparty asynchronous sessions with delegation introduces more complexity, but also that such complexity can be elegantly hidden from the programmer. Moreover, [15] has implicit threads and deals with a stronger sequential operator, requiring two syntactic restrictions on choreographies, i.e., well-threadedness and connectedness. In contrast, our approach needs no such restrictions because of explicit threads and a more relaxed sequential operator. Finally, [15] ensures EPP correctness based on a type preservation result, while we guarantee the same without the need for an endpoint typing.

Multiparty session types have been previously used for checking endpoint systems [7, 17, 22]. We have shown that they can be adopted for typing choreographies, defining a new class of correct well-typed endpoint systems (through EPP). Our global types as well as our endpoint model are taken by [7]. Other works have given an asynchronous semantics to global types: [22] defines a semantics in terms of that of the projection of global types while [18] interprets global types as asynchronous communication automata. Our linearity notion is inspired by [22].

[7] guarantees *progress* for multiparty sessions by building additional restrictions on top of (endpoint) session typing. Processes satisfying progress do not get stuck provided that they can be run in parallel with other processes that would unlock stuck states. In our work progress, implied by deadlock-freedom, is an immediate consequence of our EPP Theorem, yielding a simpler analysis.

9. Discussion and Future Extensions

We discuss some aspects of choreography-driven programming and future extensions in relation to the work presented in this article.

Approach. It may be unclear how the choreography-driven approach may deal with standard aspects of programming such as *choreography composition* and *endpoint code reuse*.

Choreography composition is fundamental for supporting distributed (team) development. Our framework supports it with (i) service merging and (ii) procedures. (i) Our EPP merges service threads started on the same public channel and role into a single process. This allows two choreographies to be composed into a bigger system, whenever their respective service threads are mergeable. Mergeability can be assured by using a design pattern, i.e. enforcing service threads that need to be merged to start with distinct branches. (ii) Procedures can be written and typed separately, so to create libraries that can be used by other choreographies (code reuse). As future work, we plan to extend Chor with a namespacing system to fully support this methodology.

Endpoint code reuse may be necessary when parts of the system being designed are already implemented. For instance, we may want to reuse an existing identity provider service in § 7, OpenID and Logging. Our model does not currently offer a way of integrating existing endpoint code with the EPP of a choreography. We discuss some potential solutions, which we leave as future work.

Using *bisimulation* techniques, we can verify some existing service code to be bisimilar to the code that would be generated by the EPP [10]. Alternatively, we could use a type system, such as multiparty session typing [7, 22], for guaranteeing that the existing code has a behaviour "compatible" with the choreography.

Both the techniques mentioned above can be adjusted to allow for refinement, i.e. the legacy code may do extra actions as long as they do not interfere with the good behaviour of the choreography. The resulting system would still guarantee communication safety and session fidelity (protocol compliance). Deadlock-freedom would also still be guaranteed, provided that the legacy code has been verified to be deadlock-free. Note that our implementation of delegation (§ 6, Delegation) would need to fall back to the protocol presented in [24] for those sessions whose behaviour is partly implemented by legacy code, since the latter cannot refer to the necessary information provided by the choreography.

GC features. Based on our conversations with our industry collaborators, we discuss some relevant aspects and extensions of GC.

Sequential and Parallel operators. The relaxed semantics of our sequential operator ";" allows our framework to express parallelism with a minimal syntax. However, an explicit parallel operator may make choreographies more readable. We discuss here two possible extensions in this sense, based upon a hypothetical operator $C_1 \mid C_2$ equipped with the classical interleaving semantics of parallel composition. We use the following choreography as reference example:

$$C_{\mathsf{par}} \ = \ \tau_1[\mathtt{p}_1].e \texttt{ -> } \tau_2[\mathtt{p}_2].x : k \ \mid \ \tau_3[\mathtt{p}_3].e' \texttt{ -> } \tau_2[\mathtt{p}_4].y : k'$$

Whenever $\tau_1, \tau_2, \tau_3, \tau_4$ are all different, C_{par} can be encoded using our sequential operator:

$$C_{\mathsf{seq}} \ = \ \tau_1[\mathtt{p}_1].e \texttt{ -> } \tau_2[\mathtt{p}_2].x : k;\ \tau_3[\mathtt{p}_3].e' \texttt{ -> } \tau_2[\mathtt{p}_4].y : k'$$

In fact, thanks to our swap relation $\simeq_C$, C_{par} would behave exactly as C_{seq} . If the two interactions in C_{par} share a thread name, e.g., $\tau_2 = \tau_4$, the parallel operator $\mid$ would not be syntax sugar anymore, since the projection of τ_2 would be a parallel composition of two input actions. This also means that τ_2 would no longer be a simple sequential thread, raising the complexity of our framework and going out of the scope of the present work.

Public channel passing. We leave the treatment of public channel name passing as future work. The main challenge is to statically establish where such channels can be located in the endpoints.

Interactional exceptions. Our language does not offer specific features for error/exception recovery. A possible extension is to include exceptions in our choreography language in the spirit of what is informally suggested by [13] for binary sessions.

Dynamic join. We plan to extend our model to allow threads to dynamically join and leave an existing session, similarly to [11, 17].

We conjecture that asynchrony and parallelism will influence these extensions in a nontrivial way.
Multiple roles. In our model, a thread can play only one role per session. However, there are cases in which multiple roles in a protocol may be implemented by a single thread, which would be useful both for system simplification and resource saving. We plan to extend our typing system to allow for this occurrences. [6, 11] follow a similar direction, but using endpoint implementations.
Global deployment. Chor projects Jolie programs with a default deployment configuration that can be edited afterwards for each endpoint. This may be inconvenient for the programmer, since a choreography may describe many participants. Therefore, we plan to introduce a global deployment language for choreographies, from which the deployment configuration of each endpoint could be automatically generated. We envision that this extension could be relevant for facilitating checks on the correctness of a deployment configuration of a system, e.g., consistent I/O connections.
Security. Global descriptions are particularly suitable for the study of security-related aspects in distributed systems [8, 9, 12]. Our choreographies give a global view of how sessions are interleaved and how their references are transmitted. It would be interesting to see how this aspect may influence the security analysis of a system.
Scaffolding. Since in our model a protocol and a session behaviour in a choreography have similar structures, we could implement a scaffolding tool in our IDE that, given a protocol, would generate a prototype choreography with "dummy" data that implements it. Then, programmers would refine and interleave different prototypes to obtain the desired behaviour.

10. Conclusions

We presented a fully-fledged model for defining asynchronous system implementations as global programs. We developed a type system for checking choreographies against multiparty protocol specifications. Moreover, through type inference, developers can also use choreographies as implementation prototypes to infer new protocol standards. Our EPP generates correct endpoint code, ensuring nontrivial properties such as deadlock freedom and communication safety. Finally, we provided a prototype implementation of our framework and applied it to some realistic examples.

Acknowledgements. We are grateful to N. Yoshida, J. Bengtson, T. Hildebrandt, K.Honda, C. Schürmannn, V. Vasconcelos, and the anonymous reviewers for their comments. The Danish Agency for Science, Technology and Innovation supported Carbone.

References

[1] BPMN. `http://www.omg.org/spec/BPMN/2.0/`.

[2] italianaSoftware. `http://www.italianasoftware.com/`.

[3] Jolie language. `http://www.jolie-lang.org/`.

[4] SOAP Specifications. `http://www.w3.org/TR/soap/`.

[5] WS-Addressing. `http://www.w3.org/TR/ws-addr-core/`.

[6] P. Baltazar, L. Caires, V. T. Vasconcelos, and H. T. Vieira. A Type System for Flexible Role Assignment in Multiparty Communicating Systems. In *Proc. of TGC*, 2012. To appear.

[7] L. Bettini, M. Coppo, L. D'Antoni, M. D. Luca, M. Dezani-Ciancaglini, and N. Yoshida. Global progress in dynamically interleaved multiparty sessions. In *CONCUR*, volume 5201 of *LNCS*, pages 418–433. Springer, 2008.

[8] K. Bhargavan, R. Corin, P.-M. Deniélou, C. Fournet, and J. J. Leifer. Cryptographic protocol synthesis and verification for multiparty sessions. In *Proc. of CSF*, pages 124–140, 2009.

[9] S. Briais and U. Nestmann. A formal semantics for protocol narrations. *Theoretical Computer Science*, 389(3):484–511, 2007.

[10] N. Busi, R. Gorrieri, C. Guidi, R. Lucchi, and G. Zavattaro. Choreography and orchestration conformance for system design. In *Proc. of Coordination*, volume 4038 of *LNCS*, pages 63–81. Springer-Verlag, 2006.

[11] L. Caires and H. T. Vieira. Conversation types. *Theoretical Computer Science*, 411(51-52):4399–4440, 2010.

[12] C. Caleiro, L. Viganò, and D. A. Basin. On the semantics of Alice&Bob specifications of security protocols. *Theor. Comput. Sci.*, 367(1-2):88–122, 2006.

[13] M. Carbone. Session-based choreography with exceptions. In *Proc. of PLACES*, volume 241, pages 35–55. ENTCS, 2008.

[14] M. Carbone and F. Montesi. Typed multiparty global programming. Technical Report 149, IT University of Copenhagen, 2011. `http://www.itu.dk/people/fabr/papers/multichor`.

[15] M. Carbone, K. Honda, and N. Yoshida. Structured communication-centred programming for web services. In *Proc. of ESOP*, volume 4421 of *LNCS*, pages 2–17. Springer-Verlag, 2007.

[16] Chor. Programming Language. `http://www.chor-lang.org/`.

[17] P.-M. Deniélou and N. Yoshida. Dynamic multirole session types. In *Proc. of POPL*, pages 435–446. ACM, 2011.

[18] P.-M. Deniélou and N. Yoshida. Multiparty session types meet communicating automata. In *Proc. of ESOP*, LNCS, pages 194–213. Springer-Verlag, 2012.

[19] Eclipse. The Eclipse IDE. `http://www.eclipse.org/`.

[20] Enea. ENEA: Italian National agency for new technologies, Energy and sustainable economic development. `http://www.enea.it/`.

[21] X. Fu, T. Bultan, and J. Su. Realizability of conversation protocols with message contents. *International Journal on Web Service Res.*, 2 (4):68–93, 2005.

[22] K. Honda, N. Yoshida, and M. Carbone. Multiparty asynchronous session types. In *Proc. of POPL*, volume 43(1), pages 273–284. ACM, 2008.

[23] K. Honda, A. Mukhamedov, G. Brown, T.-C. Chen, and N. Yoshida. Scribbling interactions with a formal foundation. In *Proc. of ICDCIT*, volume 6536 of *LNCS*, pages 55–75. Springer, 2011.

[24] R. Hu, N. Yoshida, and K. Honda. Session-based distributed programming in java. In *ECOOP*, pages 516–541, 2008.

[25] International Telecommunication Union. Recommendation Z.120: Message Sequence Chart, 1996.

[26] I. Lanese, C. Guidi, F. Montesi, and G. Zavattaro. Bridging the gap between interaction- and process-oriented choreographies. In *Proc. of SEFM*, pages 323–332. IEEE, 2008.

[27] M. Merro and D. Sangiorgi. On asynchrony in name-passing calculi. *Mathematical Structures in Computer Science*, 14(5):715–767, 2004.

[28] F. Montesi and M. Carbone. Programming services with correlation sets. In *ICSOC*, pages 125–141, 2011.

[29] F. Montesi, C. Guidi, and G. Zavattaro. Composing Services with JOLIE. In *Proc. of ECOWS*, pages 13–22, 2007.

[30] OASIS. Web Services Business Process Execution Language. `http://docs.oasis-open.org/wsbpel/2.0/wsbpel-v2.0.html`.

[31] OOI. Ocean Observatories. `http://www.oceanobservatories.org`.

[32] OpenID. Specifications. `http://openid.net/developers/specs/`.

[33] PI4SOA. http://www.pi4soa.org, 2008.

[34] B. C. Pierce. *Types and Programming Languages*. MIT Press, MA, USA, 2002.

[35] Qualit-E. Funded by Cognizant. `http://www.cognizant.com/`.

[36] Savara. JBoss Community. `http://www.jboss.org/savara/`.

[37] W3C WS-CDL Working Group. Web services choreography description language version 1.0. http://www.w3.org/TR/ws-cdl-10/, 2004.

[38] N. Yoshida, P.-M. Deniélou, A. Bejleri, and R. Hu. Parameterised multiparty session types. In *FOSSACS'10*, volume 6014 of *LNCS*, pages 128–145, 2010.

The Type Discipline of Behavioral Separation

Luís Caires   João C. Seco

CITI and Departamento de Informática
Faculdade de Ciências e Tecnologia, Universidade Nova de Lisboa

Abstract

We introduce the concept of behavioral separation as a general principle for disciplining interference in higher-order imperative concurrent programs, and present a type-based approach that systematically develops the concept in the context of an ML-like language extended with concurrency and synchronization primitives. Behavioral separation builds on notions originally introduced for behavioral type systems and separation logics, but shifts the focus from the separation of static program state properties towards the separation of dynamic usage behaviors of runtime values. Behavioral separation types specify how values may be safely used by client code, and can enforce fine-grained interference control disciplines while preserving compositionality, information hiding, and flexibility. We illustrate how our type system, even if based on a small set of general primitives, is already able to tackle fairly challenging program idioms, involving aliasing at various types, concurrency with first-class threads, manipulation of linked data structures, behavioral borrowing, and invariant-based separation.

Categories and Subject Descriptors D.3.3 [*Programming Languages*]: Language Constructs and Features; F.3.3 [*Logics and Meanings of Programs*]: Verifying and Reasoning about Programs; F.3.3 [*Logics and Meanings of Programs*]: Type structure

Keywords Behavioral Types, Separation, Interference, Concurrency, Higher Order Programming

1. Introduction

The purpose of this work is to introduce and develop the concept of *behavioral separation* as a general principle for disciplining interference in higher-order imperative concurrent programs.

Statically verifying that higher-order imperative programs do not go wrong in the presence of possible interference has proven to be a challenging task, and a fertile ground for research since the seminal work of Reynolds [36]. In general, two program fragments interfere when the effects generated by one fragment may change the state visible to the other, typically due to aliasing or to concurrency. Some forms of interference are "bad", and may cause catastrophic failure, such as read/write races when accessing the same memory cell. Other forms of interference are "good" and even required, such as the interference between a producer and a consumer running concurrently, and sharing a thread-safe state-full queue, or the interference between the head and tail references of a linked list structure. "Interference is the essence of concurrency", as Cliff Jones frequently recalled [26]. An ongoing issue to overcome is then to find techniques for disciplining interference between different usages of the same objects and ensure safety, while being able to address increasingly sophisticated programming idioms.

Significant advances have been achieved recently towards these general goals, in particular by the separation logics of O'Hearn and Reynolds [33, 39] and by several substructural type and effect systems, e.g., [1, 3, 8]. Namely, separation logic supports expressive forms of local reasoning, based on the use of the separating conjunction in combination with fractional permissions [5, 9] to characterize the fine structure of program states. Extending such state-based techniques to tackle the sophisticated program idioms arising in modern higher-order imperative concurrent programming is thus both promising and challenging [40].

In this work, we radically depart from a state-based view towards a behavioral view of program assertions, and introduce the notion of behavioral separation. Behavioral separation builds on concepts originating in behavioral type systems and separation logics, but shifts the focus from the separation of static program state properties towards the separation of dynamic usage behaviors of runtime values. More concretely, we develop a type structure that systematically explores the concept of behavioral separation to enforce safety of programs, ruling out "bad" interferences in the presence of aliasing and concurrency. Our presentation is grounded on a core ML-like programming language with concurrency primitives, designed as a convenient abstraction for a large family of languages supporting higher-order imperative concurrent programming.

Behavioral types [16, 21, 24], based on process algebras, characterize the interface of a system not just as a specification of the static type of exchanged messages, but more importantly as a specification of its dynamic behavior. Likewise, our behavioral separation types specify how program values may be safely used by client code, but, unlike pure behavioral types, are able to capture fine-grained interference control disciplines. A key novelty of our approach consists in uniformly combining in the same type structure "temporal" operations, such as sequential separation, important to capture constraints on traces, with "spatial" operations, such as parallel separation and isolation, important to discipline aliasing and concurrency. Remarkably, we carry out our development in the context of a clean substructural type theory, in which all type operators satisfy natural algebraic properties, based on a λ-calculus extended with imperative references and concurrency constructs.

Behavioral separation types promote information hiding, compositionality, and flexibility, since type assertions talk about separation constraints on usage behaviors as externally perceived by the programs which use them, rather than about the internal structure of program state or code. As will be clear from our examples, behavioral separation types are also expressive and flexible enough for proving safety of programs combining features still challenging for

POPL'13, January 23–25, 2013, Rome, Italy.

(and even out of reach of) existing proof methods, including general higher-order store, aliasing / sharing at all types, linked data structures, borrowing of local behavior, first-class threads, and invariant-based separation, based on typed synchronization constructs.

2. Overview

In this section, we motivate the general concept of behavioral separation, informally introducing our core programming language and the various behavioral separation type operators by going through a sequence of examples. Consider first the following implementation of a collection ADT, where we assume list elements to be natural numbers and the representation data structure to be a linked list.

$$\begin{array}{l}
\textbf{let } \mathit{newNode} = \lambda[].\textbf{var } \mathit{next}, \mathit{elt} \textbf{ in} \\
\qquad\qquad\qquad [\ \mathit{setElt} = \lambda e.(\mathit{elt} := e), \\
\qquad\qquad\qquad\ \ \mathit{getElt} = \mathit{elt}, \\
\qquad\qquad\qquad\ \ \mathit{setNext} = \lambda p.(\mathit{next} := p), \\
\qquad\qquad\qquad\ \ \mathit{getNext} = \mathit{next}\ ] \textbf{ in} \\
\textbf{let } \mathit{newColl} = \\
\quad \lambda[].\textbf{var } \mathit{hd}, \mathit{id} \textbf{ in} \\
\quad\ [\ \mathit{init} = \lambda i.(\mathit{hd} := \mathtt{NULL}; \mathit{id} := i), \\
\quad\ \ \ \mathit{getId} = \mathit{id}, \\
\quad\ \ \ \mathit{add} = \lambda e.\textbf{let } n = (\mathit{newNode}\ \textbf{nil}) \textbf{ in} \\
\qquad\qquad\quad ((n.\mathit{setElt}\ e); (n.\mathit{setNext}\ \mathit{hd}); \mathit{hd}{:=}\mathtt{NODE}(n)), \\
\quad\ \ \ \mathit{scan} = \textbf{var } s \textbf{ in } (\\
\qquad\qquad\quad s := \mathit{hd}; \\
\qquad\qquad\quad \textbf{rec } L.\textbf{case } s \textbf{ of} \\
\qquad\qquad\qquad\quad \mathtt{NULL} \rightarrow \textbf{nil} \\
\qquad\qquad\qquad\quad \mathtt{NODE}(n) \rightarrow (s := n.\mathit{getNext}; L))]
\end{array}$$

We define four operations on collections: the initializer *init*, which sets the collection identifier (a string); the *getId* operation, which returns the collection identifier; the *add* operation, which adds a new element to the collection; and the *scan* operation, which traverses the linked list, visiting each node in sequence. We model ADT "objects" by tuples of closures sharing memory locations, and "classes" by object generating functions, along standard lines. In our language, tuple fields are bound to expressions (quoted code), to be evaluated only after field selection (as e.g. in [38]). The **var** x **in** e block creates a ML-style heap allocated variable, where the created cell can survive the lifetime of the body e, embedded in the value returned (cf. **let** x = **ref**(**nil**) **in** e in ML).

In the code shown above, the private hd variable refers to the head of the linked list, and is shared by the *add* and *scan* operations. We represent references to list elements by variant values, with options NULL(**nil**) abbreviated NULL and representing the null reference, and NODE(n), representing a list node. In NODE(n), n is a tuple with fields *setElt*, *getElt*, *setNext*, and *getNext*. Notice that the latter two fields access the heap variable *next*, which references the next node, if any, and is local to the given node.

Using standard functional and product types we could assign to *newColl* a type as $\mathtt{0}{\rightarrow}SC$, where 0 is a "unit" type, and SC a record type representing the collection "objects". Such a record type would essentially specify a flat interface, listing the signature of the operations available, each one modeled as a typed field. Quite differently, in our system types specify value *usage behaviors*, rather than value structure. As a first example consider

$$SC \triangleq \mathit{init}{:}\mathtt{str}{\mapsto}\mathtt{0}\,;(\mathit{getId}{:}\mathtt{str}\ \&\ \mathit{add}{:}\mathtt{nat}{\mapsto}\mathtt{0}\ \&\ \mathit{scan}{:}\mathtt{0})^*$$

The type SC specifies a (possible) usage behavior offered by a collection. Intuitively, the type SC says that collections may be used by first calling the *init* "method", and then the *getId*, *add*, and *scan* "methods", in iterated choice. First, it offers a label selection usage, denoted by the label selection type $\mathit{init}{:}\mathtt{str}{\mapsto}\mathtt{0}$. The usage consists in selecting the *init* label to get a value of type $\mathtt{str}\mapsto\mathtt{0}$. The stop type 0 specifies that no usage is available.

The operator $(-){\mapsto}(-)$ is our primitive functional type. $U \mapsto V$ is a type for functions which do not interfere unsafely with their argument, and specifies a *single usage* of a value as a function, at the appropriate argument U and return type V. The $U{\mapsto}V$ does not correspond to a standard function type $U{\rightarrow}V$, which can nevertheless be encoded in our system as will become clear later. It does neither correspond to the linear arrow, nor to the arrows of separation [33, 39] or bunched logic [32], even if it is closely connected to all of these. In a state-full, concurrent programming world, there are just too many ways of using a function object. In conjugation with other type operators, the functional type $U{\mapsto}V$ allows much of such variety to be modularly approached.

Sequencing of behaviors is expressed by the sequential separation type operator $(-)\,;(-)$. A value typed by $U\,;V$ first offers to clients the usage behavior U and only after V. In our example, after the $\mathit{init}{:}\mathtt{str}{\mapsto}\mathtt{0}$ usage behavior, the collection value offers a usage $(\mathit{getId}{:}\mathtt{str}\ \&\ \mathit{add}{:}\mathtt{nat}{\mapsto}\mathtt{0}\ \&\ \mathit{scan}{:}\mathtt{0})^*$. This last type specifies the iterated choice between the selection of fields *getId*, *add*, and *scan*, each one yielding a value of respectively type str, $\mathtt{nat}\mapsto\mathtt{0}$, and 0. Choice between alternative behaviors is expressed using intersection types. A value typed by $U\ \&\ V$ offers to clients the choice between behaviors U and V, since it can provide both U and V, alternatively. The star type U^* denotes the iteration of U.

Clearly, the type operators just described may express rich sequential protocols. Still, they are not expressive enough to express aliased or concurrent usages, due to the strict linearity they enforce. A more flexible and still safe usage type for our collection would allow, after initialization, the *getId* operation to be always available, concurrently with a *add* or a *scan* operation. To express this possibility we use the parallel separation type operator $(-)\,|(-)$.

In general, a $U \mid V$ type asserts that behaviors U and V may be safely used by causally independent clients, either due to aliasing or to concurrency, without incurring in unsafe interference. Such a parallel usage only completes when both behaviors U and V complete. Exploring parallel separation, we may assign to function *newColl* the more flexible type $\mathtt{0}{\mapsto}CC$ where

$$CC \triangleq (\mathit{init}{:}\mathtt{str}{\mapsto}\mathtt{0})\,;(!\mathit{getId}{:}\mathtt{str}\,|(!\mathit{scan}{:}\mathtt{0}\,;\mathit{add}{:}\mathtt{nat}{\mapsto}\mathtt{0})^*)$$

The type CC asserts that, after initialization, a collection provides two independently usable behaviors, one of type $!\mathit{getId}{:}\mathtt{str}$ and other of type $(!\mathit{scan}{:}\mathtt{0}\,;\mathit{add}{:}\mathtt{nat}{\mapsto}\mathtt{0})^*$, composed using the parallel separation type operator $(-)\,|(-)$.

The type operator $!(-)$, used in $!\mathit{getId}{:}\mathtt{str}$ and $!\mathit{scan}{:}\mathtt{0}$, specifies an unbounded number, possibly zero, of separated parallel usages (parallel in the sense of $(-)\,|(-)$). In particular, the type $!\mathit{getId}{:}\mathtt{str}$ allows an unbounded number of (possibly concurrent) aliases to access the field $\mathit{getId}{:}\mathtt{str}$. Then, the type $(!\mathit{scan}{:}\mathtt{0}\,;\mathit{add}{:}\mathtt{nat}{\mapsto}\mathtt{0})^*$ specifies a usage consisting of the interleaved repetition of some parallel usages of the $\mathit{scan}{:}\mathtt{0}$ behavior followed by the $\mathit{add}{:}\mathtt{nat}{\mapsto}\mathtt{0}$ behavior. Only after all the *scan* operations selected in the $!\mathit{scan}{:}\mathtt{0}$ phase conclude, will $\mathit{add}{:}\mathtt{nat}{\mapsto}\mathtt{0}$ become again available. Since there is no obligation to pick any $\mathit{scan}{:}\mathtt{0}$ operation in the $!\mathit{scan}{:}\mathtt{0}$ phase, the type CC also allows any number of $\mathit{add}{:}\mathtt{nat}{\mapsto}\mathtt{0}$ operations to be sequentially performed.

Notice that the behavior of a newly created collection c is completely separated, or isolated, from context: no behavioral dependencies exist between $c{:}CC$ and the behavior of other values in a program using the collection. We express isolation, which plays an important role in our framework, by a specific type operator $\circ(-)$. We thus assign to the function *newColl* the type $\mathtt{0}\mapsto\circ CC$.

Let us now consider some code snippets using the collection type just defined, and discuss valid (and invalid) typings.

$$\textbf{let } c = \mathit{newColl}\ [] \textbf{ in } (c.\mathit{init}\ \text{“}\mathit{my}\text{”}); c.\mathit{scan}; (c.\mathit{add}\ 1)$$

$$\textbf{let } c = \mathit{newColl}\ [] \textbf{ in } (c.\mathit{init}\ \text{“}\mathit{my}\text{”}); (c.\mathit{add}\ 1); c.\mathit{getId}; c.\mathit{scan}$$

Both code fragments are validated by our type system. In the first one, it is clear that the usage of c follows the intended type. In the second one, the intended usage type of c is also not violated, even if behaviors that appear parallel separated in the type (e.g., $c{:}getId{:}\mathtt{str}$ and $c{:}scan{:}0$) are sequentially used in the code. Clearly, if a value may be safely used according to $U \mid V$, it may also be safely used according to $U \,;\, V$. Subsumption principles as this one are captured by subtyping, a pre-order on types written $U <: V$. In particular, subtyping satisfies the exchange law [19]

$$(A\,;C) \mid (B\,;D) <: (A \mid B) \;\; ; (C \mid D)$$

of which $U \mid V <: U\,;V$ is a special case.

The next examples illustrate behavioral "borrowing", where fragments of the behavior of c are temporarily used by some function, before being given back to the caller context.

$$\begin{array}{l}\textbf{let}\ c = newColl\ []\ \textbf{in}\\ \quad \textbf{let}\ f = \lambda x.(x.init\ \text{"your"})\ \textbf{in}\ (f\ c); (c.add\ 2)\end{array}$$

$$\begin{array}{l}\textbf{let}\ c = newColl\ []\ \textbf{in}\\ \quad \textbf{let}\ g = \lambda x.(x.scan)\ \textbf{in}\\ \qquad (c.init\ \text{"my"}); (g\ c); c.scan; (c.add\ 2); (g\ c)\end{array}$$

In the second case the borrowing function is used twice, at different places of the global behavior. The borrowed type is declared in the function domain, e.g., $f{:}(init{:}\mathtt{str} \mapsto 0) \mapsto 0$. On the other hand

$$\begin{array}{l}\textbf{let}\ c = newColl\ []\ \textbf{in}\\ \quad \textbf{let}\ h = \lambda x.(x.init\ \text{"your"})\ \textbf{in}\ (c.add\ 2); (h\ c)\end{array}$$

attempts to use add before $init$, and is rejected by our type system.

More interesting examples illustrate borrowing of behavior through the store, which our type system is able to handle in a natural way, even in a higher-order setting. Consider the following code snippet. It respects the expected behavioral constraints on the value c and the heap allocated variable a, even if the behavior of c is temporarily accessible at a, and is in fact typeable in our system.

$$\begin{array}{l}\textbf{let}\ c = newColl\ []\ \textbf{in var}\ a\ \textbf{in}\\ \quad (a := c; (a.init\ \text{"my"}); (a.add\ 1); (a.add\ 1); c.scan))\end{array}$$

Heap variables are assigned behavioral separation types expressed in terms of use $\mathtt{use}$, read $\mathtt{rd}(U)$ and write $\mathtt{wr}(U)$ capabilities, and related by subtyping axioms. We show some of them here

$$\mathtt{var} <: \mathtt{use}\,;\mathtt{var} \quad \mathtt{use} <: \mathtt{wr}(U)\,;\mathtt{rd}(U) \quad \mathtt{rd}(!U) <: !\mathtt{rd}(U)$$

$$\mathtt{rd}(U\,;V) <: \mathtt{rd}(U)\,;\mathtt{rd}(V) \quad \mathtt{rd}(U \mid V) <: \mathtt{rd}(U) \mid \mathtt{rd}(V)$$

The first two axioms say that a single use of a variable consists in writing on it a value of type U, followed by a matching read phase. The following axioms specify how the reading phase may be behaviorally separated, depending on the type of the stored value.

The next example illustrates higher-order borrowing through the store, the function attached to the add field is itself stored in memory, before being called.

$$\begin{array}{l}\textbf{let}\ c = newColl\ []\ \textbf{in}\ ((c.init\ \text{"my"});\\ \quad \textbf{var}\ a\ \textbf{in}\ (a := c.add; (a\ 1); c.scan))\end{array}$$

This code does not violate any constraints imposed by the type of c, even if a collection "method" (a functional value) is extracted by selecting $c.add$ and stored in the temporary heap variable a.

These last two examples get past our typing discipline, because the type system keeps track of global separation constraints between all the values in the scope, and relies on sequential and parallel frame reasoning to *locally* replace behaviors in behavioral separation type assertions. In the last example, the function of type $\mathtt{nat} \mapsto 0$ is required to be used (exactly once) before $scan$ is selected in c, even if its behavior is temporarily stored in the variable a, respecting the initial footprint of $c.add$ of in the global behavioral separation type. The type pre-condition of $a := c.add$ is $a{:}\mathtt{use} \mid (c{:}add{:}\mathtt{nat} \mapsto 0\,; c{:}scan{:}0\,; \cdots)$, and the post-condition is $a{:}\mathtt{rd}(add{:}\mathtt{nat} \mapsto 0)\,; c{:}scan{:}0\,; \cdots$. Notice that this last type sequentially constrains the behaviors of a and c, forcing a to be read before using c. The ability to specify global separation constraints, involving several values, seems essential for the expressiveness of our system. As a further illustration of this point, consider

$$\textbf{let}\ c = newColl\ []\ \textbf{in let}\ m = c.init\ \textbf{in}\ c.scan$$

Here, the $init$ qualifier is selected, but since the associated functional behavior (bound to m) is not actually exercised, the initialization of the local hd variable is not performed, causing the $scan$ operation to "crash" in the **case** expression. Of course, this code does not type check under our current assumptions, since it does not preserve the frame conditions imposed by the intended behavioral separation protocols. Indeed, $c.scan$ would need to be typed under the pre-condition $(m{:}\mathtt{str} \mapsto 0)\,; c{:}scan{:}0\,; \cdots$, which states that m must be used (as a function) before progressing with the continuation behavior of collection c, which is not possible.

The type system systematically uses local reasoning and frame principles on behavioral separation assertions to modularly compute effects of program fragments. As another example, consider

$$\begin{array}{l}\textbf{var}\ s\ \textbf{in}\ (s := \text{"hi"};\\ \quad \textbf{let}\ F = \lambda x.(\textbf{let}\ c = newColl\ []\ \textbf{in}\ (c.init\ x; c))\ \textbf{in}\\ \quad (\textbf{let}\ u = (F\ s)\ \textbf{in}\ (s := \text{"ok"}; u.add\ 1)))\end{array}$$

So F returns an initialized collection. The pre-condition type assertion to typing $(F\ s)$ is $s{:}\mathtt{rd}(\mathtt{str})\,;\mathtt{var} \mid F{:}(\mathtt{str} \mapsto \circ CC)$. We assume that the type of strings $\mathtt{str}$ is shareable ($\mathtt{str} <: !\mathtt{str}$), so that reading from s does not "empty" the variable. To type function application, we collect the footprints of argument and function as $(s{:}\mathtt{rd}(\mathtt{str}) \mid F{:}(\mathtt{str} \mapsto \circ CC))\,; s{:}\mathtt{rd}(\mathtt{str})\,;\mathtt{var}$. After typing **let** $u = (F\ s)$, the type assertion is $u{:}\circ CC\,; s{:}\mathtt{rd}(\mathtt{str}); \mathtt{var}$. Apparently, this says that u must be fully used as $\circ CC$ before the variable s can used again, which is not sensible. However, the behavior $\circ CC$ is isolated, as expressed by $\circ(-)$, so the use of s does not causally depend on it: by the subtyping law $(\circ U)\,;V <: (\circ U) \mid V$, we actually reach $u{:}\circ CC \mid s{:}\mathtt{rd}(\mathtt{str}); \mathtt{var}$, and then $u{:}\circ CC \mid s{:}\mathtt{var}$ (by $\mathtt{rd}(\mathtt{str}) <: \mathtt{rd}(0) <: 0$). Isolated types offer a safe escape from the strict locality discipline, allowing isolated behaviors to be fully (and soundly) separated from a global type in which they might appear embedded. As a further illustration, the following code is typeable by assigning $\circ CC \mapsto 0$ to f so that it captures the argument full behavior (storing it in heap variable a) rather than borrowing it.

$$\begin{array}{l}\textbf{let}\ c = newColl\ []\ \textbf{in}\\ \quad \textbf{var}\ a\ \textbf{in let}\ f = \lambda x.a := x\ \textbf{in}\ ((f\ c); (a.init\ \text{"my"}))\end{array}$$

We now consider some examples with concurrency. The parallel expression $(e_1 \| e_2)$ clearly brings up the possibility of interference. The next couple of examples are safe, and type-check in our system

$$\begin{array}{l}\textbf{let}\ c = newColl\ []\ \textbf{in}\\ \quad ((c.init\ \text{"my"}); (c.add\ 1); (c.scan \| c.scan))\end{array}$$

$$\begin{array}{l}\textbf{let}\ c = newColl\ []\ \textbf{in let}\ f = \lambda x.(x.scan)\ \textbf{in}\\ \quad ((c.init\ \text{"my"}); ((f\ c) \| c.scan); (c.getId \| (c.add\ 2)); (f\ c))\end{array}$$

On the other hand, the code snippets

$$\textbf{let}\ c = newColl\ []\ \textbf{in}\ ((c.init\ \text{"my"}); ((c.add\ 1) \| (c.scan)))$$

$$\begin{array}{l}\textbf{let}\ c = newColl\ []\ \textbf{in}\\ \quad \textbf{let}\ f = \lambda x.((x.add\ 0) \| (c.add\ 1))\ \textbf{in}\ ((c.init\ \text{"my"}); (f\ c))\end{array}$$

violate the intended behavioral separation constraints, and are rejected by the type system. In the last case, although the function f may be given type $(add{:}\mathtt{nat} \mapsto 0) \mapsto 0$, the application $(f\ c)$ is not typeable, since the type CC cannot provide footprints for separately typing function and argument (no parallel separated add

capabilities are available on c). On the other hand, the following similar looking code is safe and well-typed.

$$\textbf{let } c = newColl\ [] \textbf{ in}$$
$$\textbf{let } f = \lambda x.(x.scan \| c.scan) \textbf{ in } ((c.init\ \text{“}my\text{”}); (f\ c))$$

The form $(e_1 \| e_2)$ is actually derived from primitive **fork** and **wait** thread-based concurrency constructs. Thread references are first-class values in our language, created by the **fork**(e) expression. The interesting operation on threads is to wait for their return value. Let

$$\textbf{let } c = newColl\ [] \textbf{ in } ((c.init\ \text{“}my\text{”});$$
$$\textbf{var } a \textbf{ in } (a := \textbf{fork}(c.scan); c.scan; \textbf{wait}(a); (c.add\ 1)))$$

This code is well-typed under the current typing assumptions for c, as enforced by the parallel and sequential frame conditions, since the footprints of the **fork** and **wait** expressions match the expectations of the global behavioral type. On the other hand,

$$\textbf{let } c = newColl\ [] \textbf{ in } ((c.init\ \text{“}my\text{”});$$
$$\textbf{var } a \textbf{ in } (a := \textbf{fork}(c.scan); (c.add\ 1); \textbf{wait}(a)))$$

is not well-typed under the same assumptions: it breaks the separation constraints required by the type of c. Such type requires $c.scan$ and $(c.add\ 1)$ to be sequentially separated, but overlapping may occur at runtime, causing unsafe interference.

As noticed before, it is not sound to assign to our collection a type allowing the add operation to be used concurrently with $scan$ operations. That would violate the intended usage protocol of the internal state, causing a write/read race on heap variable hd. However, our language allows “critical regions” in the code to be sequentialized, and eventually typed by invariant-based separation. Invariant-based separation allows isolated behaviors to be repeatedly interleaved in the global behavior, as far as the associated invariant conditions, expressed by a conveniently chosen type assertion, are preserved. In our example, this could be achieved, e.g., by adding a new local heap variable inv to the collection, and wrapping the uses of hd in add and $scan$ as follows

$$add = \lambda e.\textbf{sync}(inv)(\ldots)$$
$$scan = \textbf{var } s \textbf{ in sync}(inv)(s := hd); \textbf{rec } L.\textbf{case } s \textbf{ of} \cdots)$$

To type this code, we associate an assertion $hd{:}\mathtt{rd}(!\circ PNode)\,;\mathtt{var}$ to the heap variable inv, which expresses an invariant condition protecting its footprint. Our type system is then able to assign to the concurrent collection the following type, which allows, after initialization, operations $getId$, add and $scan$ to be unboundedly aliased, or shared by several active threads.

$$C \triangleq (init{:}\mathtt{str}{\mapsto}\mathtt{0})\,;(!getId{:}\mathtt{str} \mid !scan{:}\mathtt{0} \mid !add{:}\mathtt{nat}{\mapsto}\mathtt{0})$$

Of course, the main novelty to highlight here is not the familiar reasoning technique for lock invariants, but the way our type discipline elegantly captures it. Even if based on a few fairly general principles, it can be effectively used to reason about safety properties of higher-order concurrent programs involving difficult to handle scenarios of aliasing and concurrency. We are not aware of related proposals, able to address the same set of (realistic) programming idioms, and based on a a similarly general foundation, as we have achieved here. This paper makes the following contributions:

- We motivate and introduce the concept of behavioral separation as a general principle for disciplining interference in higher-order imperative concurrent programs.
- We present a behavioral separation type system for a λ-calculus with imperative and concurrency constructs. We show soundness of the system, proving type preservation under reduction (Theorems 4.3 and 4.5) and progress (Theorem 4.4).
- We illustrate, by means of many examples, how our type system, even if based on a small set of very general primitives, is already able to tackle fairly challenging program idioms.

$a, b, c, m, n, t \ldots \in$	Λ	*(Names)*
$x, y, z \ldots \in$	$\mathcal{V}$	*(Variables)*
$l, s \ldots \in$	$\mathcal{L}$	*(Labels)*
$X, Y \ldots \in$	χ	*(Expression Vars)*

e, f	$::=$	x	*(Variable)*
	$\mid$	$\lambda x.e$	*(Abstraction)*
	$\mid$	$e_1 e_2$	*(Application)*
	$\mid$	**let** $x = e_1$ **in** e_2	*(Definition)*
	$\mid$	**var** a **in** e	*(Heap variable decl)*
	$\mid$	$a := e$	*(Assignment)*
	$\mid$	a	*(Dereference)*
	$\mid$	$[l_1 = e_1, \ldots]$	*(Tupling)*
	$\mid$	$e.l$	*(Selection)*
	$\mid$	$l(e)$	*(Variant)*
	$\mid$	**case** e **of** $l_i(x_i) \to e_i$	*(Conditional)*
	$\mid$	**rec**$(X)e$	*(Recursion)*
	$\mid$	X	*(Recursion variable)*
	$\mid$	**fork** e	*(New thread)*
	$\mid$	**wait** e	*(Wait)*
	$\mid$	**sync**$(a)e$	*(Synchronized block)*
	$\mid$	$sy(a)e$	*(inSynchronized block)*
	$\mid$	n	*(Thread identifier)*

Figure 1. Programming Language.

3. Programming Language

Our programming language, presented in Figure 1, is a λ-calculus with mutable heap allocated variables, tuples, variants, and concurrency primitives. To keep it close to familiar high-level languages such as Java, we consider unstructured (fork/join) thread-oriented concurrency primitives, and a synchronization construct. Our language is fairly simple yet expressive enough to support challenging imperative higher-order concurrent programming idioms.

To formally define it, we assume given an infinite set of names Λ, an infinite set of variables $\mathcal{V}$, and an infinite set of method labels $\mathcal{L}$. Names in Λ are used to identify threads and heap locations. For simplicity sake, we omit basic values, and literals for booleans or integers; their addition as primitives is straightforward.

The functional core includes abstraction $\lambda x.e$ and application $e_1 e_2$, following call-by-value evaluation. The tuple expression $[l_1 = e_1, \ldots]$ denotes a record collecting expressions e_i, each one qualified by the label l_i. As in [37], and without any loss of generality, we consider lazy tuples, where the expression e_i is only evaluated after selection of the label l_i. Lazy tuples allow different qualifications of the same entity to be subject to different interference constraints, both along the time and space dimensions, and are convenient for encoding objects as tuples of “methods”. The empty tuple [] is also written **nil**.

The **let** expression represents local definition and sequential composition: in **let** $x = e_1$ **in** e_2, the subexpression e_1 is evaluated first, its result bound to x, and then e_2 is executed using the value x. We abbreviate **let** $x = e_1$ **in** e_2 by $(e_1; e_2)$ if x is not free in e_2.

The construct $l(e)$ injects the value of expression e into the variant label l. The **case** construct corresponds to a standard destructor for labeled sum types. The expression **case** e **of** $l_i(x_i) \to e_i$ first evaluates e to a variant value $l_i(v)$ (if this is not the case, execution will get stuck). Then, v is bound to x_i, e_i evaluated and its value returned as the result of the whole **case** expression.

Variable declaration **var** a **in** e, variable access a, and assignment $a := e$ are interpreted as usual.

The expression **fork** e spawns a new thread dedicated to the evaluation of expression e, and immediately returns the new thread identifier (a name) to the caller (thread identifiers are values, and do not appear in source programs). Both the calling thread and the newly created one proceed execution concurrently. The expression **wait** e suspends the caller until the thread resulting from evaluating e terminates with some result (if ever). Such result will then be returned as the result of the **wait** expression.

Our language includes a simple synchronization primitive. The primitive relies on endowing each heap variable with a lock. Such locks are available for flexible use in programs, pretty much as object locks are used, e.g., in Java programs (either to lock the variable itself, or to protect any other relevant region of the state). At each moment, a lock may be either taken or free. The expression $\mathbf{sync}(n)e$ evaluates the expression e in exclusion, using the lock associated to heap variable n (cf. the Java synchronized block); only one thread may acquire the lock of n in linear ("write") mode.

To track entry and exit of synchronization blocks in the operational semantics, we use the auxiliary construct $sy(n)e$. No occurrences of this construct, or of location or thread names are expected to appear in source programs, these elements belong to the runtime syntax of the full language, as shown in Figure 1.

The operational semantics of our programming language is defined by a reduction system using evaluation contexts. A state consists of a pair $h;\ T$, where h is a heap and T is a set of threads. A reduction step has the form

$$\boxed{h;\ T \rightarrow h';\ T'} \qquad (h;\ T \text{ reduces to } h';\ T')$$

expressing a computation step from state $h;\ T$ to state $h';\ T'$. In any such step, new heap cells may be allocated, threads may be created, evolve, or terminate. Each thread in T is represented by an element of the form $t\langle e\rangle$, where t is the thread name (from Λ), and e is the runtime expression under execution by the thread. We write $t\langle e\rangle \cdot T$ for the disjoint union of T and $\{t\langle e\rangle\}$. A heap h is a mapping from heap locations (names) to values. Each heap binding $n_k \mapsto v$ also has an integer-valued counter k associated, to be used as a semaphore, important to support the synchronization primitives. We write $h(n_k \mapsto v)$ to denote a heap such that $n_k \mapsto v \in h$, and $h[n_k \mapsto v]$ to denote the heap obtained from h after storing v at location n, with lock value k. We now introduce values $\mathcal{V}$ and evaluation contexts $\mathcal{E}$, given by

$$\begin{array}{lcl} v, u \in \mathcal{V} & ::= & \lambda x.e \mid [\, l_1 = e_1, \dots \,] \mid l(v) \mid t \mid x \\ \mathcal{E} & ::= & \square \mid \mathbf{let}\ x = \mathcal{E}\ \mathbf{in}\ e \mid \mathcal{E}.l \mid \mathcal{E}e \mid v\mathcal{E} \mid l(\mathcal{E}) \\ & \mid & \mathbf{wait}(\mathcal{E}) \mid sy(n)\mathcal{E} \mid \mathbf{case}\ \mathcal{E}\ \mathbf{of}\ \overline{l_i(x_i) \rightarrow e_i} \end{array}$$

A value in our language is either an abstraction, a tuple (including the empty tuple **nil**), a variant value, a thread name, or a variable. Without loss of generality, we restrict assignments in our source language to the simple form $a := v$ where v is a value, and use $a := e$ as an abbreviation for **let** $x = e$ **in** $a := x$. The rules defining the reduction relation are presented in Figure 2.

We write $\{v/x\}$ for the capture avoiding substitution of v for x, defined as expected. Notice that there is no order assumed between elements in a thread set T, so any thread $t\langle e\rangle \in T$ may be (non-deterministically) scheduled in a reduction step. Most reduction rules are easy to interpret, and do not deserve much explanation. In rules (Red var) and (Red fork) the side condition $(\boldsymbol{\nu} n)$ state that name n must be fresh in the respective left hand side.

Rules (Red sync*) rely on the integer-valued lock associated to the each heap location n. When the lock is zero, the lock is free. Rule (Red syncin) checks that the lock k associated to v is free, before decrementing it to -1, and allowing execution to enter the critical region e: the expression $sy(n)e$ signals that the execution of e is taking place inside a critical region protected by the lock of n. The lock is released after the body of the $sy(n)e$ block reduces to a value u, in rule (Red syncout).

(Red rec)
$$h;\ t\langle \mathcal{E}[\, \mathbf{rec}(X)e \,]\rangle \cdot T \rightarrow h;\ t\langle \mathcal{E}[\, e\{\mathbf{rec}(X)e/X\} \,]\rangle \cdot T$$
(Red let)
$$h;\ t\langle \mathcal{E}[\, \mathbf{let}\ x = v\ \mathbf{in}\ e \,]\rangle \cdot T \rightarrow h;\ t\langle \mathcal{E}[\, e\{v/x\} \,]\rangle \cdot T$$
(Red beta)
$$h;\ t\langle \mathcal{E}[\, (\lambda x.e)v \,]\rangle \cdot T \rightarrow h;\ t\langle \mathcal{E}[\, e\{v/x\} \,]\rangle \cdot T$$
(Red sel)
$$h;\ t\langle \mathcal{E}[\, [\, \overline{l = e} \,].l_i \,]\rangle \cdot T \rightarrow h;\ t\langle \mathcal{E}[\, e_i \,]\rangle \cdot T$$
(Red case)
$$h;\ t\langle \mathcal{E}[\, \mathbf{case}\ l_i(v)\ \mathbf{of}\ \overline{l(x) \rightarrow e} \,]\rangle \cdot T \rightarrow h;\ t\langle \mathcal{E}[\, e_i\{v/x_i\} \,]\rangle \cdot T$$
(Red var)
$$h;\ t\langle \mathcal{E}[\, \mathbf{var}\ a\ \mathbf{in}\ e \,]\rangle \cdot T \rightarrow h[n \mapsto \mathbf{nil}];\ t\langle \mathcal{E}[\, e\{n/a\} \,]\rangle \cdot T \qquad (\boldsymbol{\nu} n)$$
(Red assign)
$$h(n_k \mapsto v);\ t\langle \mathcal{E}[\, n := u \,]\rangle \cdot T \rightarrow h[n_k \mapsto u];\ t\langle \mathcal{E}[\, \mathbf{nil} \,]\rangle \cdot T$$
(Red deref)
$$h(n_k \mapsto v);\ t\langle \mathcal{E}[\, n \,]\rangle \cdot T \rightarrow h(n_k \mapsto v);\ t\langle \mathcal{E}[\, v \,]\rangle \cdot T$$
(Red fork)
$$h;\ t\langle \mathcal{E}[\, \mathbf{fork}\ e \,]\rangle \cdot T \rightarrow h;\ t\langle \mathcal{E}[\, n \,]\rangle \cdot n\langle e\rangle \cdot T \qquad (\boldsymbol{\nu} n)$$
(Red wait)
$$h;\ t\langle \mathcal{E}[\, \mathbf{wait}\ n \,]\rangle \cdot n\langle v\rangle \cdot T \rightarrow h;\ t\langle \mathcal{E}[\, v \,]\rangle \cdot T$$
(Red syncin)
$$h(n_0 \mapsto v);\ t\langle \mathcal{E}[\, \mathbf{sync}(n)e \,]\rangle \cdot T \rightarrow h[n_{-1} \mapsto v];\ t\langle \mathcal{E}[sy(n)e]\rangle \cdot T$$
(Red syncout)
$$h(n_{-1} \mapsto u);\ t\langle \mathcal{E}[\, sy(n)v \,]\rangle \cdot T \rightarrow h[n_0 \mapsto u];\ t\langle \mathcal{E}[v]\rangle \cdot T$$

Figure 2. Reduction.

4. Type System

In this section, we technically present our type system. As already discussed, types describe behavioral usages of values. We start by systematically introducing each type operator, discussing on the way their basic algebraic properties and related subsumption laws.

DEFINITION 4.1 (Types). *Type operators are given by*

$$\begin{array}{lcllcl} T, U & ::= & 0 & \textit{(stop)} & \mid\ T \mapsto V & \textit{(function)} \\ & \mid & T \,;U & \textit{(sequential)} & \mid\ T \mid U & \textit{(parallel)} \\ & \mid & T \,\&\, U & \textit{(intersection)} & \mid\ l{:}T & \textit{(qualification)} \\ & \mid & \oplus_{l \in I} l{:}T_l & \textit{(sum)} & \mid\ !T & \textit{(shared)} \\ & \mid & \circ T & \textit{(isolated)} & \mid\ \tau(T) & \textit{(thread)} \\ & \mid & \mathtt{rec}(X)T & \textit{(recursion)} & \mid\ X & \textit{(recursion var)} \end{array}$$

We assume some primitive type constructors $\mathtt{c}$, $\mathtt{c}(U)$, such as `str`, `nat`, to represent basic data types, and `var`, $\mathtt{rd}(U)$, etc, to represent behavioral separation types for heap allocated variables. The *stop type* 0 types any value exposing no behavioral capability, in particular it types **nil**. The *sequential type* $T\,;U$ asserts of a value that it can be safely used first according to type T, and only afterwards according to type U. The sequential type expresses behavioral separation along the temporal dimension. Sequential types induce a monoid with identity 0 in the type structure, expressed by

$$U\,;(V\,;T) \mathrel{<:>} (U\,;V)\,;T \qquad U\,;0 \mathrel{<:>} U \qquad 0\,;U \mathrel{<:>} U$$

The *parallel type* $T \mid U$ asserts of a value that it can be subject to two safe independent parallel usages, specified by type T and type U respectively. By "independent parallel usage" of a value we mean any form of sharing, arising not just in concurrent programs, but also in sequential programs, due to aliasing. The parallel type thus expresses behavioral separation along the spatial dimension. It builds on the fundamental idea of separation (cf. separation logic [39]), but focusing on the independence of usage behaviors, as perceived from a "client" viewpoint , rather than on the disjointness of underlying resources (to highlight this understanding of $T \mid U$, we refrain from using the notation $T * U$). A key insight on $(- \mid -)$ is that behaviors typed by parallel separation do not interfere in unsafe ways, even if they rely (and write) on shared resources (e.g., as a result of invariant based separation, developed in Section 4.5).

An usage of type $U \mid V$ only concludes when both U and V conclude: in a type such as $(U \mid V) \,;T$, the usage T is only available when $(U \mid V)$ conclude. So our type language provides an abstract way of splitting "permissions", without using explicit fractions (cf. [9]). Parallel types induce a commutative monoid with identity $\mathtt{0}$

$$U \,|(V \mid T) \mathrel{<:>} (U \mid V) \mid T \quad U \mid V \mathrel{<:>} V \mid U \quad U \mid \mathtt{0} \mathrel{<:>} U$$

Sequential and parallel composition are related by the exchange law [4, 19], the following causality preserving distribution principle

$$(A\,;C) \mid (B\,;D) \mathrel{<:} (A \mid B) \;;(C \mid D)$$

A special case is the familiar interleaving law $U \mid V \mathrel{<:} V\,;U$.

The (linear) *intersection* type $U \,\&\, V$ asserts of a value that it may be safely used according to type U and according to type V. The client code using such a value can therefore freely decide to pick either the U or the V behavior (but not both, since we exploit a linear interpretation of $\&$). The following basic laws hold.

$$U \,\&\, V \mathrel{<:} U \quad U \,\&\, V \mathrel{<:} V \quad U \mathrel{<:} U \,\&\, U$$

Notice that $(- \mid -)$, $(-\,;-)$ and $(- \,\&\, -)$ induce a CKA [19].

The *recursive* type $rec(X).A$, with X guarded in A, is interpreted co-inductively. We define $U^* \triangleq \mathtt{rec}(X)(\mathtt{0} \,\&(U\,;X))$.

The *shared* type $!T$ asserts of a value that it can be safely subject to an unbounded number of parallel separated usages (cf. $(- \mid -)$), each one specified by type T. In particular, it may be unboundedly aliased at type T. The following laws hold for the type $!T$

$$!U \mathrel{<:} U \quad !U \mathrel{<:} !!U \quad \mathtt{0} \mathrel{<:} !\mathtt{0} \quad !U \mid !V \mathrel{<:} !(U \mid V)$$
$$!U \mathrel{<:} \mathtt{0} \quad !U \mathrel{<:} !U \mid !U$$

Notice that $!(-)$ satisfies the fundamental co-monadic laws for the linear logic exponential; so our notation highlights the connection.

The *function* type $T \mapsto V$ asserts of a value that it can be safely used (once) as a function that when given as argument a value of type T, exercises on it a usage of type T, and returns a result of type V. Type $U \mapsto V$ is adjoint to $U|V$, so that the behavioral separation interpretation ensures the intended safety property: no unsafe interference can arise even if function and argument share state-full resources, since they are behaviorally separated. So $U \mapsto V$ is a type for functions that do not unsafely interfere with their arguments, as in the sharing interpretation of the arrow $\twoheadrightarrow$ in [32], but does not completely forbid interference to ensure safety. Moreover, unlike in the standard linear logic interpretation of the arrow $(U \multimap V)$, a function of type $U \mapsto V$ can use its parameter more than once, as long as it globally respects the behavioral type U (as in [12]).

The *isolated* type $\circ T$ asserts of a value that it may be used as specified by the type T, but, more crucially, that such usage is fully isolated, not subject to any external (global) constraints. A value of type $\circ T$ is completely separated (in terms of behavior) from the rest of the "world". In particular, $\circ T$ says that the usage T is not borrowed from some larger computation. We may see a value of type $\circ T$ as offering a self-contained suspended behavior of type T, that may be used at any future step in the computation. No liveness commitments are imposed on client code to use a value of type $\circ T$, unless it actually starts to use it at type T. In particular, a value of type $\circ T$ may be safely dropped, since nothing causally depends on it: a safe use for a value of type $\circ T$ is not to use it at all. Moreover, since nothing can causally depend on a value of type $\circ T$, we expect the law $(\circ U)\,;V \mathrel{<:} (\circ U) \mid V$ to hold. We also have

$$\mathtt{0} \mathrel{<:} \circ\mathtt{0} \quad \circ A \mid \circ B \mathrel{<:} \circ(A \mid B) \quad \circ A \mathrel{<:} A \quad \circ A \mathrel{<:} \circ\circ A$$
$$\circ A \mathrel{<:} \mathtt{0} \quad !\circ A \mathrel{<:} \circ !A \quad (\circ A \mid B)\,;C \mathrel{<:} \circ A \,|(B\,;C)$$

The first five laws express familiar algebraic principles (cf. the basic laws for $!(-)$). The last two laws are proper to $\circ(-)$. In particular, the last one expresses the key property of $\circ(-)$, global behavioral isolation: a behavior of type $\circ T$ is isolated, and can be freely used anytime, concurrently with anything. No other behavior can causally depend from a behavior of type $\circ T$. By exchange, we may derive the "postponing" law $(\circ A)\,;B \mathrel{<:} B\,;(\circ A)$.

The *qualified* type $l{:}T$ asserts of a value that it offers a usage of type T under the label l. It describes a label selection capability of a tuple, classifying the usage type of the value in field l. As in [38], general tuple types may be defined by combining qualified types with other type constructors, e.g. $(l_1{:}T_1 \,\&\ldots\&\, l_n{:}T_n)^*$.

The *sum* type $\oplus_{l \in i} l_i{:}T_i$ asserts of a value that it is a labeled value that can be used according to type T_i if it is labeled with l_i. Client code using such a value must branch on the possible labels, before actually using the selected behavior. The sum type thus corresponds to a standard labeled disjoint union, useful to describe variants or options. We abbreviate $(\mathtt{NULL}{:}\mathtt{0} \oplus \mathtt{NODE}{:}U)$ by $\mathtt{Opt}(U)$.

The *thread* type $\tau(T)$ asserts of a value that it references a running thread that upon termination returns a value of type T.

Types for heap allocated variables are conveniently described in our system by specific primitives, expressing usage, write and read capabilities. The type of a freshly allocated heap variable is `var`. The type `var` denotes the generic heap variable usage protocol, and is axiomatized by several subtyping laws, presented in Section 4.1.

As previously discussed, a type classifies a single value. In order to type program expressions, which may use in general several different values, we introduce a notion of *type assertion*. A type assertion corresponds to the usual notion of type environment, assigning types to the various free identifiers in a program. However, our type assertions finely describe behavioral dependencies between the several identifiers in its domain, by placing basic type assignments of the form $x{:}T$ embedded in a larger global type.

DEFINITION 4.2 (Type Assertion). *Type assertions are given by*

$$A, B ::= x{:}T \mid A\,;B \mid A|B \mid A \,\&\, B \mid !A \mid \circ A \mid X \mid \mathtt{rec}(X)A$$

For an example, under the assumptions expressed by the type assertion $(f{:}U \mapsto V\,;y{:}U) \mid z{:}U$, the function f can be applied to z but not to y, so $(f\ z)$ is well typed but $(f\ y)$ is not, since the behavior $y{:}U$ is only available after $f{:}U \mapsto V$ is used.

We denote by $Dom(A)$ the (finite) set of variables appearing in a type assertion A. If A has a singleton domain $\{x\}$ (that is, refers to a single variable x), we implicitly identify it with the singular assertion $x{:}(A)_x$ where the type $(A)_x$ is given by

$$\begin{array}{ll} (x{:}T)_x = T & (A\,;B)_x = (A)_x\,;(B)_x \\ (A \mid B)_x = (A)_x \,|(B)_x & (A \,\&\, B)_x = (A)_x \,\&(B)_x \\ (!A)_x = !(A)_x & (\circ A)_x = \circ(A)_x \\ (X)_x = X & (\mathtt{rec}(X)A)_x = \mathtt{rec}(X)(A)_x \end{array}$$

Therefore, we identify, e.g., $x{:}(up\,;dn)$ with $(x{:}up)\,;(x{:}dn)$, and $\mathtt{rec}(X)((x{:}up \mid x{:}dn)\,;X)$ with $x{:}\mathtt{rec}(X)((up \mid dn)\,;X)$.

We define *type assertion contexts* $\mathcal{A}[-]$ as the one hole syntactic contexts associated to type assertions. We also consider *active assertion contexts* $\mathcal{E}[-]$, where the hole occurs unguarded, defined

$$\mathcal{E}[-] ::= \Box \mid \mathcal{E}[-]\,;A \mid \mathcal{E}[-] \,|\, A \mid A \,|\, \mathcal{E}[-]$$

4.1 Subtyping

Type assertions are related by a subtyping relation. We write $A \mathrel{<:} B$ to state that A is a subtype of B, meaning that the usage behavior

A <:> $A \mid 0$ $\quad A \mid B$ <: $B \mid A$ $\quad A \mid (B \mid C)$ <:> $(A \mid B) \mid C$

A <:> $A ; 0$ $\quad A$ <:> $0 ; A$ $\quad A ; (B ; C)$ <:> $(A ; B) ; C$

$(A ; C) \mid (B ; D)$ <: $(A \mid B) ; (C \mid D)$

$A \,\&\, B$ <: A $\quad A \,\&\, B$ <: B $\quad A$ <: $A \,\&\, A$

0 <: $\circ 0$ $\quad \circ A$ <: 0 $\quad \circ A$ <: A $\quad \circ A$ <: $\circ\circ A$ $\quad \circ A \mid \circ B$ <: $\circ(A \mid B)$

$!\circ A$ <: $\circ !A$ $\quad (\circ A \mid B) ; C$ <: $\circ A \mid (B ; C)$ $\quad !A \mid !B$ <: $!(A \mid B)$

0 <: $!0$ $\quad !A$ <: 0 $\quad !A$ <: A $\quad !A$ <: $!!A$ $\quad !A$ <: $!A \mid !A$

$\texttt{rec}(X)A$ <:> $A\{\texttt{rec}(X)A/X\}$ $\quad$ `var` <: `use ; var`

`use` <: `use ; use` $\quad$ `use` <: $\texttt{wr}(U) ; \texttt{rd}(U)$ $\quad \texttt{wr}(0)$ <: 0 $\quad \texttt{rd}(0)$ <: 0

$\texttt{rd}(U; V)$ <: $\texttt{rd}(U); \texttt{rd}(V)$ $\quad \texttt{rd}(U \mid V)$ <: $\texttt{rd}(U) \mid \texttt{rd}(V)$

$\texttt{rd}(!U)$ <: $!\texttt{rd}(!U)$ $\quad \texttt{rd}(\circ U) ; \texttt{var}$ <: $\circ(\texttt{rd}(\circ U) ; \texttt{var})$

Figure 3. Subtyping.

B is subsumed by usage behavior A. Intuitively, A <: B means that if some value may be safely used according to A then it may also be safely used according to B.

$\boxed{A <: B}$ $\quad$ (A is a subtype of B)

Notice that subtyping also apply to types by letting U <: V if and only if $x{:}U$ <: $x{:}V$. Subtyping axioms, defined in Figure 3, express the basic algebraic laws of the type operators discussed above. We abbreviate by A <:> B the fact that A <: B and B <: A. To save space, we abbreviate rules of the form $x{:}U$ <: $x{:}V$ by U <: V, and omit subtyping congruence rules. All type operators satisfy the expected (covariant) subtyping congruence principles, with some exceptions, e.g., the arrow $U \mapsto V$, which is contravariant in the domain U, and $\texttt{wr}(V)$, which is contravariant on V (see [13]).

Particularly interesting are the axioms defining the `var` behavior. We may derive `var` <: $\circ$`var`: clearly a fresh heap variable offers an isolated behavior. The first axioms state that a variable can be subject to an unbounded number of uses, each use composed by a write and a read phase. Other axioms specify how the reading phase may be behaviorally separated, depending on the type of the stored value. For example, the axiom for $\texttt{rd}(U \mid V)$ says that if a value of type $U \mid V$ can be read from the variable, then the variable can also be subject to independent reading at types U and V. This point is crucial: e.g., a heap variable may be shared or aliased, only if the stored value also may be. Notice that the axiom for `use`, allowing a different type U to be picked at different unfoldings of `var`, naturally support strong updates [2] (updating a heap variable to hold values of unrelated types at different points in time).

4.2 Typing

Type judgments of our system have the form

$\boxed{A \vdash_z e :: B}$ $\quad$ (e types from A to z in B)

where A and B are type assertions, e is an expression, and the index z is a variable. We refer to A as the pre-condition, and to B as the post-condition of the typing judgment. The behavioral type of (the value of) e, as determined by the type system, appears embedded in assertion B. The variable z stands for such a value, and can only occur free in B (not in A or e). This idea of scoping the return value z over the post-condition appears in the Hoare triple types of [31], although here the type of z cannot be given apart from B. For an example, consider $a{:}\texttt{use} \vdash_z (\lambda x.a := x) :: z{:}\circ U \mapsto 0 ; a{:}\texttt{rd}(\circ U)$. This judgment asserts that evaluating the expression $(\lambda x.a := x)$ in a state providing $a{:}\texttt{use}$ returns a functional value (identified by z in the post-condition) that must be used exactly once before the heap variable a can be read. We now progressively present the several rules of our type system, discussing each one on the way.

4.2.1 Structural Rules

The identity axiom

$$x{:}U \vdash_z x :: z{:}U \ (\mathit{Id})$$

asserts that access to the identifier x simply returns the associated value, usable according to the type in the pre-condition (N.B: (Id) has the proviso that U is free from heap variable types: typing rules for heap variable dereference are given below). The type system includes four other structural rules. A crucial one is subtyping (Sub), which embeds into typing the basic subsumption principles. It allows assertions in type rules to be considered up to <:> , and plays a role similar to the consequence rule in Hoare logics.

$$\frac{A <: A' \quad A' \vdash_x e :: B' \quad B' <: B}{A \vdash_x e :: B} \ (\mathit{Sub})$$

The rule for **let** corresponds to cut (x not free in the conclusion)

$$\frac{A \vdash_x e_1 :: B \quad B \vdash_y e_2 :: C}{A \vdash_y \textbf{let}\ x\ =\ e_1\ \textbf{in}\ e_2 :: C} \ (\mathit{Let})$$

The following parallel and sequential structural rules express basic "frame" principles. Rule (Par) allows the footprint of an expression to be enlarged along the spatial dimension, while rule (Seq) allows the footprint to be enlarged along the temporal dimension.

$$\frac{A \vdash_x e :: B}{A \mid C \vdash_x e :: B \mid C} \ (\mathit{Par}) \qquad \frac{A \vdash_x e :: B}{A ; C \vdash_x e :: B ; C} \ (\mathit{Seq})$$

Given these two rules, the following "deep" frame rule is admissible for any active type assertion context $\mathcal{E}[-]$.

$$\frac{A \vdash_x e :: B}{\mathcal{E}[A] \vdash_x e :: \mathcal{E}[B]} \ (\mathit{Frame})$$

4.2.2 Functional Type

We have the following typing rules for the λ-calculus core.

$$\frac{A | x{:}U \vdash_y e :: y{:}T}{A\ \vdash_z \lambda x.e :: z{:}U {\mapsto} T} \ (\mathit{VAbs})$$

$$\frac{A \vdash_z e_1 :: z{:}U{\mapsto}T \quad B \vdash_x e_2 :: x{:}U}{A \mid B\ \vdash_y e_1 e_2 :: y{:}T} \ (\mathit{App})$$

These rules are similar to the arrow rules in linear or bunched [32] type systems, even if our semantics for $\mapsto$ is different. Given the interpretation of $A \mid B$, (App) ensures that functions do not interfere with their arguments unsafely upon application. Notice that the type of the argument x is left 0 in the post-condition of the premise of (VAbs), forcing the function body to fully exercise the behavior U of its parameter, consistently with the "argument-borrowing" semantics of our functional type. The type of an "argument-capturing" function may be rendered $(\circ U) \mapsto V$, and the type of a function that can safely share the behavior of its argument with its own behavior may specified $(!U) \mapsto V$. Behavioral separation types allow many fine-grained variations of functional behavior to be specified (e.g., $!(U \mapsto V)$ - a shareable function; $(U \mapsto V)^*$ - a non shareable but repeatedly usable function, etc). Notice that in our typed language (as, e.g., in the monadic λ-calculus) one cannot encode **let** by application and abstraction.

4.2.3 Tuple Type

The rules for tuples and field selection have the expected form.

$$\frac{A \vdash_x e :: x{:}U}{A \vdash_z [\ldots l = e \ldots] :: z{:}l{:}U} (\mathit{Tuple}) \qquad \frac{A \vdash_z e :: z{:}l{:}T}{A \vdash_x e.l :: x{:}T} (\mathit{Sel})$$

Recall that field contents of tuples are evaluated lazily, as in [37], so $(Tuple)$ allows a single field to be type checked.

4.2.4 Intersection Type

We include as primitive the introduction rule And.

$$\frac{A \vdash_y e :: B \quad A \vdash_y e :: C}{A \vdash_y e :: B \ \& \ C}(And) \qquad \frac{A \vdash_y e :: B_1 \ \& \ B_2}{A \vdash_y e :: B_i}(AndE)$$

Technically, we choose to absorb the elimination principles for intersection in the subtyping relation (e.g., $A \,\&\, B <: A$). However, familiar elimination rules $AndE$ are admissible (using (Sub)).

4.2.5 Behavioral-Separation Types

Structured behavioral-separation usages are assigned to basic values (abstractions, tuples) by the following type rules:

$$0 \vdash_y v :: 0 \ (VStop) \qquad \frac{A \vdash_y v :: C \quad B \vdash_y v :: D}{A\,;B \vdash_y v :: C\,;D}(VSeq)$$

$$\frac{!A_1 \mid \ldots \mid !A_n \vdash_x v{::}B}{!A_1 \mid \ldots \mid !A_n \vdash_x v{::}!B}\ (VShr) \qquad \frac{A \vdash_y v{::}C \quad B \vdash_y v{::}D}{A \mid B \vdash_y v :: C \mid D}(VPar)$$

Rule $(VShr)$ expresses that a value can be subject to any number of shared usages, if it only relies on resources which may also be safely used by any number of shared usages. Interestingly, these rules allow values to satisfy crisper frame principles than the structural rules in Section 4.2.1, which apply to general expressions. For example, the following "fat" identity axiom and left-sequential frame rule turn out to be admissible for values, even if the corresponding principles are not sound for arbitrary expressions.

$$A \vdash_y v :: A \ (VId) \qquad \frac{B \vdash_y v :: C}{A\,;B \vdash_y v :: A\,;C}\ (VLSeq)$$

4.2.6 Isolated Type

The rule (Iso) assigns to the post-condition of an expression an isolated type if it only depends on values of isolated type.

$$\frac{\circ A_1 \mid \ldots \mid \circ A_n \vdash_x e :: B}{\circ A_1 \mid \ldots \mid \circ A_n \vdash_x e :: \circ B}\ (Iso)$$

The type rules for $!A$ and $\circ A$ are therefore similar, and express the basic comonadic principle associated to these type constructors (cf. the introduction rule for ! in intuitionistic linear logic), even if their meaning is quite different (sharing versus isolation).

A remarkable property of any type T of the form $!\circ U$ is that $T <:> T \mid T$ and $T <:> \circ T$, so that T is both shared and isolated.

4.2.7 Sum Type

Sum types are also handled by familiar looking typing rules.

$$\frac{A \vdash_y e_c :: y : \oplus_{i \in I} l_i{:}T_i \quad x_i{:}T_i \mid B \vdash_z e_i :: C}{A \mid B \vdash_z \textbf{case}\ e_c\ \textbf{of}\ \overline{l(x) \rightarrow e} :: C}\ (Case)$$

$$\frac{A \vdash_z e :: z{:}T_j}{A \vdash_z l_j(e) :: z{:} \oplus_{i \in I} l_i{:}T_i}\ (Option)$$

As for function application, the type rule for case ensures that the matched value is separated from the corresponding case branch, so to avoid unsafe interference.

4.2.8 Heap Variable Types

We have already explained how heap allocated variables are modeled in our system as special values, subject to a specific usage protocol defined by certain subtyping axioms. The type rule for a variable declaration types the body under the assumption of a separated complete protocol for the new variable, specified by `var`.

$$\frac{a{:}\texttt{var} \mid A \vdash_x e :: C}{A \vdash_x \textbf{var}\ a\ \textbf{in}\ e :: C}\ (Var)$$

Rules for dereference and assignment are more interesting. We consider two typing rules for dereference, and two typing rules for assignment. The alternative typings express boundary cases on usage of the variable protocol, which are not naturally captured by a single typing rule. We distinguish between reading just a "piece" of the behavior stored in the variable $(RdVB)$, from reading the whole remaining stored behavior $(RdVF)$.

$$a{:}\texttt{rd}(U) \vdash_x a :: x{:}U \ (RdVB)$$

$$a{:}\texttt{rd}(U); \texttt{use} \vdash_x a :: x{:}U \mid a{:}\texttt{use} \ (RdVF)$$

Rule $(RdVF)$ states that even if the precondition states that the next `use` of variable a is guarded by a read usage $\texttt{rd}(U)$, the variable content $x{:}U$ is separated of the residual variable behavior $a{:}\texttt{use}$, specifying an "empty" variable. Rule $(RdVF)$ expresses an important invariant ensured by the type system: the behavior stored in any heap variable is always separated from the continuation behavior of the variable object itself (after all of its content gets read off). So the post-condition in the conclusion of $(RdVF)$ always holds, even if the type of the heap variable content is not explicitly declared as isolated (not of the form $\circ U$).

We also have two rules for assignment, depending on wether the behavior stored in the heap variable is isolated or borrowed.

$$\frac{A \vdash_z v :: z{:}\circ U \mid a{:}\texttt{wr}(\circ U)}{A \vdash_z a := v :: 0}\ (WrVF)$$

$$\frac{A \vdash_z v :: z{:}U \mid a{:}\texttt{use}}{A \vdash_z a := v :: a{:}\texttt{rd}(U)}\ (WrVB)$$

In both rules, the stored value is required to be parallel separated from the heap variable, which must be in a ready-for-write state. Rule $(WrVF)$ handles the case in which the value behavior to be stored is isolated. Here, we only require the write capability, as the stored value may be used anytime later. Rule $(WrVB)$ handles the case in which the value behavior to be stored may be not isolated. In this case, one must ensure that all associated reads will happen before any sequential continuation of $z{:}U$, so a whole `use` is required in the premise, leaving the associated read usage active in the post-condition. It is interesting to see why a rule as $(WrVF)$, but considering a non-isolated type for the stored value, would not be sound. Let us consider a simple counterexample.

$$\begin{array}{l}
r{:}U \mid a{:}\texttt{wr}(U) \vdash_x r :: x{:}U \mid a{:}\texttt{wr}(U) \\
r{:}U \mid a{:}\texttt{wr}(U) \vdash_x a := r :: 0 \\
r{:}U\,;V \mid a{:}\texttt{wr}(U) \vdash_x a := r :: r{:}V \\
r{:}U\,;V \mid a{:}\texttt{wr}(U); \texttt{rd}(U) \vdash_x a := r :: r{:}V\,; a{:}\texttt{rd}(U) \\
r{:}U\,;V \mid a{:}\texttt{use} \vdash_x a := r :: r{:}V\,; a{:}\texttt{rd}(U)
\end{array}$$

This candidate derivation states that after executing $a := r$ the behavior $r{:}V$ is available before reading the variable a, thus violating the requirement that r must be used as $U\,;V$. A correct typing is:

$$\begin{array}{l}
r{:}U \mid a{:}\texttt{use} \vdash_x r :: x{:}U \mid a{:}\texttt{use} \\
r{:}U \mid a{:}\texttt{use} \vdash_x a := r :: a{:}\texttt{rd}(U) \\
r{:}U\,;V \mid a{:}\texttt{use} \vdash_x a := r :: a{:}\texttt{rd}(U)\,; r{:}V
\end{array}$$

Typing rules for assignment require separation between heap variable and stored value. This may suggest that typing of circular chains of references through the heap may be difficult, if not impossible. Although it is clear that linear behaviors cannot refer circularly to themselves, that is not the case for general behavioral separation types: some safe circular chains may still support separated behaviors, due to the presence of qualified tuples, or just because of sharing (including invariant based separation). We illustrate the point in Section 4.5, by typing a version of Landin's knot.

In the discussion above, we omitted recursion and recursive types. To accommodate recursion typing judgements are equipped with a recursion variable environment η, which maps expression variables Z to type judgments and type variables X to type assertions (we have elided the recursion environment in rules where it does not play any relevant role). This technique is inspired in familiar approaches to co-inductive types [34]), see [13] for details.

We collect the rules of the basic system in Figure 4. For clarity's sake, we present the type system in two steps, first without synchronization constructs, extended in Section 4.5 to the full language.

4.3 Typing the Collection Implementation

We get back to the running example in the Introduction. We claimed that a collection value may be assigned the type $\circ CC$, and the function $newColl$ the type $\mathtt{0} \mapsto \circ CC$. We now discuss how such type is actually assigned by our type system. We first type the list nodes. Consider the following abbreviations

$$InitNode \triangleq setElt{:}(\mathtt{nat} \mapsto 0)\,;\, setNext{:}(!\circ PNode \mapsto 0)$$
$$INode \triangleq !getNext{:}PNode \mid !getElt{:}\mathtt{nat}$$
$$Node \triangleq InitNode\,;\,!\circ INode \qquad PNode \triangleq !\mathtt{Opt}(INode)$$

The type $PNode$ defines the behavior of a pointer to a list of (initialized) nodes, as created by the function $newNode$. We use option types to type list pointers: either the "null" pointer, tagged $\mathtt{NULL}(-)$ or a value of type $INode$, tagged by $\mathtt{NODE}(-)$.

Directed by rules $VSeq$, $VShr$ and $Tuple$, the system assigns type $Node$ to the tuple $[setElt = \cdots]$ by checking that it can be subject to the given behavioral separation usage, while safely using its local resources (the variables $next$ and elt). The variable elt gets assigned type $\mathtt{wr(nat)}\,;!\mathtt{rd(nat)}$: it is written just once (in the operation $setElt$), and available for shared reading from then on. Notice that $\mathtt{var} <: \mathtt{wr(nat)}\,;!\mathtt{rd(nat)}$, since $\mathtt{nat}$ is assumed shared ($\mathtt{nat} <: !\mathtt{nat}$). Variable $next$ is typed $\mathtt{wr}(\circ PNode)\,;!\mathtt{rd}(PNode)\,;\mathtt{var}$. After initialization (execution of the behavior $InitNode$), the node type evolves to $!\circ INode$; only operations $getNext$ and $getElt$ are available, usable by an unbounded number of aliases or concurrent clients. The shared behavior $INode$ of the list nodes supports sharing of the linked list and allows the type $!scan{:}\mathtt{0}$ to be assigned within CC. Recall

$$CC \triangleq (init{:}\mathtt{str}{\mapsto}\mathtt{0})\,;(!getId{:}\mathtt{str} \mid (!scan{:}\mathtt{0}\,;add{:}\mathtt{nat}{\mapsto}\mathtt{0})^*)$$

Checking $newCollection$ against type $0 \mapsto \circ CC$, involves verifying that the "object" tuple $[init = \cdots]$ representing a collection can be safely subject to the behavioral separation usage specified by CC. After $init$, the variable hd is assigned type $\mathtt{rd}(!\circ PNode)\,;\mathtt{var}$. This type is kept invariant between iterated executions of the add and $scan$ operations.

It is particularly interesting to see how the $scan$ operation is typed. The footprint precondition is $hd{:}\mathtt{rd}(!\circ PNode)$ (note that $!\circ PNode <: !\circ PNode\,;!\circ PNode$). After the assignment $s := hd$, the type assertion is $s{:}\mathtt{rd}(PNode)\,;\mathtt{var}$. We detail the derivation of the scan loop, showing the key judgments.

1 $s{:}\mathtt{use} \vdash^{\eta}_{x} \textbf{nil} :: s{:}\mathtt{use}$
2 $n{:}INode \mid s{:}\mathtt{use} \vdash^{\eta}_{x} s := n.getNext :: s{:}\mathtt{rd}(PNode)\,;\mathtt{use}$
3 $s{:}\mathtt{rd}(PNode)\,;\mathtt{use} \vdash^{\eta}_{x} L :: s{:}\mathtt{use}$
4 $n{:}INode \mid s{:}\mathtt{use} \vdash^{\eta}_{x} s := n.getNext; L :: s{:}\mathtt{use}$
5 $s{:}\mathtt{rd}(PNode)\,;\mathtt{use} \vdash^{\eta}_{x} \textbf{case}\ s\ \textbf{of}\ \ldots :: s{:}\mathtt{use}$
6 $s{:}\mathtt{rd}(PNode)\,;\mathtt{use} \vdash^{\emptyset}_{x} \textbf{rec}\ L.\textbf{case}\ \ldots :: s{:}\mathtt{use}$
7 $s{:}\mathtt{rd}(PNode)\,;\mathtt{var} \vdash^{\emptyset}_{x} \textbf{rec}\ L.\textbf{case}\ \ldots :: s{:}\mathtt{var}$

Derivation of 2 uses (WrVB). 5 is derived from 1 and 4 by (Case). 7 is derived from 6 by (Seq) and (Sub). Let $\eta(L) = s{:}\mathtt{rd}(PNode)\,;\mathtt{use} \vdash_x s{:}\mathtt{use}$ be the recursion environment introduced by (Rec) deriving 6 from 5, and used by (RecVar) in 3. Fully detailed typing derivations for the collection and other examples in this paper are given in [13].

4.4 Type Preservation and Progress

We now state the main correctness results for the basic type system, namely the subject reduction property and progress for well-typed programs. Type preservation and progress ensure that in a well typed program all values are properly used according to their assigned behavioral-separation types. In particular, given the structure of types assigned to variables, no write/write or read/write races while writing to heap variables are possible (it is not the case that $\mathtt{use} <: (\mathtt{wr}(U) \mid \mathtt{wr}(V))\,;T$ or $\mathtt{use} <: (\mathtt{rd}(U) \mid \mathtt{wr}(V))\,;T$).

We thus introduce rules typing for runtime configurations $h\ ;\ S$

$$\emptyset\ ;\ \emptyset \rhd \mathtt{0}\ (E) \qquad \frac{h\ ;\ S \rhd \mathcal{E}[C] \quad C \vdash_x e :: x{:}T}{h\ ;\ S \cdot t\langle e\rangle \rhd \mathcal{E}[t{:}\tau(T)]}\ (T)$$

$$\frac{h\ ;\ S \rhd A \quad A <: B}{h\ ;\ S \rhd B}\ (S) \qquad \frac{h\ ;\ S \rhd A \quad A \vdash_x v :: B}{h, n \mapsto v\ ;\ S \rhd B\{n{:}\mathtt{var}/x\}}\ (H)$$

In rule (T), $\mathcal{E}$ is an active type assertion context. The notation $B\{n{:}\mathtt{var}/x\}$ (with n fresh in B) represents the update of assertion B where the behavior pieces assigned to $x \in Dom(B)$ are substituted in place by reads to a new heap variable n: essentially, all occurrences of the form $x{:}U$ in type B are replaced by $n{:}\mathtt{rd}(U)$ and a $n{:}\mathtt{var}$ is inserted in sequential and linear position relative to all $n{:}\mathtt{rd}(U)$'s. We can now state our first type preservation result.

THEOREM 4.3. *If* $h\ ;\ S \rhd A$ *and* $h\ ;\ S \to h'; S'$ *then* $h'; S' \rhd A$.

An expression e is live, noted $live(e)$, if it is not a value. A set S of threads is live, noted $live(S)$ if there is some thread $t\langle e\rangle$ in S such that $live(e)$. We can then prove

THEOREM 4.4. *If* $h\ ;\ S \rhd A$ *and* $live(S)$ *then* $h\ ;\ S \to h'; S'$.

Detailed proofs and definitions are given in [13].

4.5 Invariant-based Separation

We now extend the basic type system to cover the full core language with $\textbf{sync}(a)e$ blocks, and invariant-based reasoning. As explained in Section 3, each heap variable is equipped with an associated lock (pretty much like a Java object is). To each lock, a resource invariant, expressed by an isolated typing assertion, is associated for verification purposes. We only accept for lock invariant a heap assertion R such that $R <: \circ R$ (let us call "heap assertion" any type assertion that just refers to heap variable types - $\mathtt{var}$, $\mathtt{use}$, etc). Handling lock invariants requires some additional structure in our type system: we add to typing judgments an invariant mapping ι, that associates to heap location locks their invariants:

$$\boxed{A \vdash^{\iota}_{z} e :: B} \quad (e \text{ types from } A \text{ to } z \text{ in } B \text{ under } \iota)$$

The invariant mapping is propagated untouched by all typing rules, except in the new rule for variable declaration, which may introduce a lock invariant, and in the rules for $\textbf{sync}(n)e$ and $sy(n)e$, which make use the lock invariant associated to heap location n:

$$\frac{\iota(a) \mid A \vdash^{\iota\backslash a}_{x} e :: \iota(a) \mid B}{A \vdash^{\iota}_{x} \textbf{sync}(a)e :: B}\ (Sync) \qquad \frac{A \vdash^{\iota\backslash a}_{x} e :: \iota(a) \mid B}{A \vdash^{\iota}_{x} sy(a)e :: B}\ (Sy)$$

$$\frac{A <: B \mid R \quad a{:}\mathtt{var} \mid B \vdash^{\iota\{R/a\}}_{x} e :: C}{A \vdash^{\iota}_{x} \textbf{var}\ a\ \textbf{in}\ e :: C}\ (Var)$$

Without loss of generality, we assume that the invariant associated to some heap variable's lock does not talk about the variable itself, but only about other heap variables in scope. Interestingly, notice that the rule for **sync** directly expresses an anti-frame principle [35]. Consider the code snippet describing an "atomic" variable.

$$\begin{array}{l} \textbf{let}\ atomic = \lambda v. \\ \quad \textbf{var}\ s\ \textbf{in}\ s := v; \\ \quad\quad \textbf{var}\ lock\ \textbf{in}\ [\ set = \lambda x.\textbf{sync}(lock)s := x, \\ \quad\quad\quad\quad get = \textbf{sync}(lock)s\ ]\ \textbf{in}\ \ldots \end{array}$$

$$\mathsf{0} \vdash_y v :: \mathsf{0}\ (\mathit{VStop}) \quad x{:}U \vdash_y x :: y{:}U\ (\mathit{Id}) \quad \frac{\circ A_1 \mid \ldots \mid \circ A_n \vdash_x e :: B}{\circ A_1 \mid \ldots \mid \circ A_n \vdash_x e :: \circ B}\ (\mathit{Iso}) \quad \frac{!A_1 \mid \ldots \mid !A_n \vdash_x v :: B}{!A_1 \mid \ldots \mid !A_n \vdash_x v :: !B}\ (\mathit{VShr})$$

$$\frac{A <: A' \quad A' \vdash_x e :: B' \quad B' <: B}{A \vdash_x e :: B}\ (\mathit{Sub}) \quad \frac{A \vdash_y e :: B \quad A \vdash_y e :: C}{A \vdash_y e :: B \ \&\ C}\ (\mathit{And}) \quad \frac{A \vdash_x e_1 :: B \quad B \vdash_y e_2 :: C}{A \vdash_y \textbf{let } x = e_1 \textbf{ in } e_2 :: C}\ (\mathit{Let})$$

$$\frac{A \vdash_x e :: B}{A\,;\,C \vdash_x e :: B\,;\,C}\ (\mathit{Seq}) \quad \frac{A \vdash_x e :: B}{A \mid C \vdash_x e :: B \mid C}\ (\mathit{Par}) \quad \frac{A \vdash_x e_1 :: x{:}U \mapsto T \quad B \vdash_y e_2 :: y{:}U}{A \mid B \vdash_z e_1 e_2 :: z{:}T}\ (\mathit{App})$$

$$\frac{A \vdash_x e :: x{:}U}{A \vdash_x [\ldots l = e \ldots] :: x{:}l{:}U}\ (\mathit{Tuple}) \quad \frac{A \vdash_x e :: x{:}l{:}T}{A \vdash_x e.l :: x{:}T}\ (\mathit{Sel}) \quad \frac{A \mid x{:}U \vdash_z e :: z{:}T}{A \vdash_z \lambda x.e :: z{:}U \mapsto T}\ (\mathit{VAbs}) \quad \frac{\eta(Z) = (A \vdash_x B)}{A \vdash^{\eta}_x Z :: B}\ (\mathit{RecVar})$$

$$\frac{A \vdash_y e_c :: y : \oplus_{i \in I} l_i{:}T_i \quad x_i{:}T_i \mid B \vdash_z e_i :: C}{A \mid B \vdash_z \textbf{case } e_c \textbf{ of } \overline{l(x) \rightarrow e} :: C}\ (\mathit{Case}) \quad \frac{A \vdash_z e :: z{:}T_j}{A \vdash_z l_j(e) :: z{:} \oplus_{i \in I} l_i{:}T_i}\ (\mathit{Option}) \quad \frac{A \vdash^{\eta\{Z/(A \vdash_x B)\}}_x e :: B}{A \vdash^{\eta}_x \textbf{rec}(Z)e :: B}\ (\mathit{Rec})$$

$$\frac{A \vdash_y v :: C \quad B \vdash_y v :: D}{A\,;\,B \vdash_y v :: C\,;\,D}\ (\mathit{VSeq}) \quad \frac{A \vdash_y v :: C \quad B \vdash_y v :: D}{A \mid B \vdash_y v :: C \mid D}\ (\mathit{VPar}) \quad \frac{\eta(X) = A}{A \vdash^{\eta}_x v :: X}\ (\mathit{VRecVar}) \quad \frac{A \vdash^{\eta\{X/A\}}_x v :: B}{A \vdash^{\eta}_x v :: \mathtt{rec}(X)B}\ (\mathit{VRec})$$

$$\frac{a{:}\mathtt{var} \mid A \vdash_x e :: C}{A \vdash_x \textbf{var } a \textbf{ in } e :: C}\ (\mathit{Var}) \quad \frac{A \vdash_z v :: z{:}U \mid a{:}\mathtt{use}}{A \vdash_z a := v :: a{:}\mathtt{rd}(U)}\ (\mathit{WrVB}) \quad a{:}\mathtt{rd}(U); \mathtt{use} \vdash_x a :: x{:}U \mid a{:}\mathtt{use}\ (\mathit{RdVF})$$

$$\frac{A \vdash_z v :: z{:}\circ U \mid a{:}\mathtt{wr}(\circ U)}{A \vdash_z a := v :: \mathsf{0}}\ (\mathit{WrVF}) \quad a{:}\mathtt{rd}(U) \vdash_x a :: x{:}U\ (\mathit{RdVB}) \quad \frac{A \vdash_x e :: x{:}T}{A \vdash_x \textbf{fork } e :: x{:}\tau(T)}\ (\mathit{Fork}) \quad \frac{A \vdash_x e :: x{:}\tau(T)}{A \vdash_x \textbf{wait } e :: x{:}T}\ (\mathit{Wait})$$

Figure 4. Typing Rules.

Let U be a shared isolated type (a type such that $U <: !\circ U$, see Section 4.2.6). We can then derive the typing

$$\mathit{atomic}{:}U \mapsto (!\mathit{set}{:}(U \mapsto 0) \mid !\mathit{get}{:}U)$$

by associating to *lock* the invariant $s{:}\mathtt{rd}(U)\,;\mathtt{var}$. This type states that *atomic* is a function that returns a state-full variable "object" that can be safely used concurrently by an arbitrary number of setters and getters. Notice that if any of the two sync blocks is removed, *atomic* would only be typed by a behavioral-separation type that sequentializes the *get* and *set* operations somehow. For example, if both sync blocks are removed, a possible typing is

$$\mathit{atomic}{:}U \mapsto (!\mathit{get}{:}U\,;\,\mathit{set}{:}(U \mapsto 0))^*$$

which would still allow sharing (aliasing, or concurrent usage) of the *get* "method" but not of the *set* "method".

This example illustrates how the (concurrency control) monitor construction can be explained as a type coercion operator in our type structure, e.g., coercing $(A\,;B) \,\&\, (B\,;A)$ to $A \mid B$. Recall that by the exchange law we can derive $A \mid B <: (A\,;B) \,\&\, (B\,;A)$, expressing the basic interleaving principle that a value of type $A \mid B$ can be used according to $(A;B) \,\&\, (B\,;A)$. Conversely, given a value providing the behavior $(A\,;B) \,\&\, (B\,;A)$, we may in general coerce it to the behavior $A \mid B$, by wrapping it inside a monitor enforcing the appropriate usage protocol by means of locking. The monitored object then exports two behaviorally parallel separated interfaces A and B, even if there is potentially sharing / interference between the implementations of A and B. Our type system naturally assigns $A \mid B$ to the monitored object, relying on the modular type rules for locking and on standard invariant-based reasoning.

Invariant based reasoning is also useful in a non-concurrent setting, in which case we may consider the **sync** operator essentially as a typing device for potentially shared (aliased) usages. We elaborate on this point using a simple, yet non-trivial example: a FIFO queue implemented with a linked list data structure with head and tail pointers (code listed in Figure 5). We describe the type *Node* assigned to node value in the list:

$$\mathit{Node} \triangleq \mathit{HeadT} \mid \mathit{TailT} \qquad \mathit{SHeadT} \triangleq \mathtt{Opt}(\mathit{HeadT})$$
$$\mathit{HeadT} \triangleq \circ \mathit{unlink}{:}\circ \mathit{SHeadT} \qquad \mathit{TailT} \triangleq \circ \mathit{link}{:}\circ \mathit{SHeadT} \mapsto \mathsf{0}$$

```
SQueue ≜
let new =
  λ[].var next in
      next := NULL;
      var lock in
        [ unLink = sync(lock)let x = next
                                in (next := NULL; x)
          link = λx.sync(lock)next := x ]
in var head, tail in (
      head := NULL; tail := NULL;
      [ enq = let n = (new nil) in
                case tail of
                NULL → (head := NODE(n);
                          tail := NODE(n))
                NODE(y) → (y.link NODE(n));
                          tail := NODE(n)),
        deq = case head of
              NULL → head := NULL
              NODE(y) → (head := y.unLink;
                   case head of
                   NULL → tail := NULL; head := NULL
                   NODE(y) → head := NODE(y)) ]
```

Figure 5. A FIFO Queue Implemented with a Linked List

Our type system assigns to function *new* the type $!(\mathsf{0} \mapsto \mathit{Node})$. *Node* is a parallel separation type, exposing, on the one hand, the behavior to be assigned to the head pointer or to the previous node in the list, and, on the other hand, the behavior to be assigned to the tail pointer. The safe separation of behaviors is enforced by the use of invariant based separation, associating to *lock* the invariant $\mathit{next}{:}\mathtt{rd}(\circ \mathit{SHeadT})\,;\mathtt{var}$. So, for example, aliasing of n in $(\mathit{head} := \mathtt{NODE}(n); \mathit{tail} := \mathtt{NODE}(n))$ type checks since given $n{:}\mathit{Node}$ we may separate and assign type *SHeadT* to the first occurrence of $\mathtt{NODE}(n)$ and $\mathtt{Opt}(\mathit{TailT})$ to the second.

We then derive $\vdash_q \mathit{SQueue} :: \mathit{SQueueI}$ where

$$\mathit{SQueueI} \triangleq (q{:}\mathit{enq}{:}\mathsf{0} \,\&\, q{:}\mathit{deq}{:}\mathsf{0})^*$$

This type says that the declared behavioral separation protocols are enforced, even in the presence of possible interference between the state accessible from $head$ and $tail$. Additionally, type $Node$ clearly says that both $link$ and $unlink$ operation are used at most once in each list node, the first through the $tail$ alias, the other by the $head$ alias, and that this describes the full behavior of a node. Type $SQueueI$ above declares a sequential behavior for the queue, where enq and deq operations cannot be selected concurrently. A (typeable) concurrent queue can be defined by guarding the sequential implementation described with appropriate **sync** blocks:

$$
\begin{array}{l}
\textbf{let}\, CQueue = \textbf{var}\ head, tail\ \textbf{in}\ (\\
\quad head := \texttt{NULL};\ tail := \texttt{NULL}; \\
\quad \textbf{var}\ qinv\ \textbf{in} \\
\quad [\ \ enq = \textbf{sync}(qinv)(\ldots) \\
\quad\ \ \ deq = \textbf{sync}(qinv)(\ldots)\ \ ]
\end{array}
$$

For type checking this code we associate to $qinv$ the invariant $head{:}\texttt{rd}(\circ SHeadT)\,\texttt{;}\,\texttt{var}\mid tail{:}\texttt{rd}(\circ STailT)\,\texttt{;}\,\texttt{var}$. We then derive $\vdash_q CQueue :: QueueCI$ for $QueueCI \triangleq\ !enq{:}0 \mid !q{:}deq{:}0$. The $QueueCI$ interface type explicitly says that the queue can be safely used by many concurrent clients, as in. e.g.,

$$\textbf{let}\ q = CQueue\ \textbf{in}\ (q.enq;\ q.enq \| q.deq;\ q.deq)$$

Notice that in the assertion typing $SQueue$ only sequential types appear, that is, no $(- \mid -)$ or $!(-)$. So only a single thread may be visiting the code of $SQueue$. This means (informal claim) that the lock $lock$ associated to each list node will always be free. So, the **sync** blocks in $Node$ are operationally irrelevant, and may be seen as an auxiliary device for bracketing code regions subject to invariant-based type checking of separation. On the other hand, **sync** blocks are of course essential to $CQueue$, if it is to be actually used according to the more permissive type $QueueCI$.

As a further example, we present a code fragment tying a Landin's knot, thus creating a circular chain of references in the higher-order store. We may verify that it can be typed by assigning to the (operationally useless) lock $linv$ the invariant $a{:}\texttt{rd}(!\circ(0 \mapsto 0))\,\texttt{;}\,\texttt{var}$, and to the function f the type $!\circ(0 \mapsto 0)$.

$$
\begin{array}{l}
\textbf{var}\ a\ \textbf{in}\ (\ a := \lambda x.x; \\
\quad \textbf{var}\ linv\ \textbf{in let}\ f = \lambda y.(\textbf{sync}(linv)(a)\ y) \\
\quad\quad \textbf{in}\ (\textbf{sync}(linv)(a := f);\ (f\ \textbf{nil}))\ )
\end{array}
$$

In principle, our type system could be refined to distinguish between two different scenarios for invariant based reasoning, one already useful to handle interference in sequential code, another one to handle interference in truly concurrent code, only the latter would require real locks to be introduced in the code. We leave this discussion for future consideration, for the issue seems orthogonal to the main purpose of this paper. The key point to highlight here is that our typing principles for the **sync** construct seem to capture a useful and general form of invariant reasoning about safe interference in the context of a behavioral separation type system.

We can now state the type preservation result for the full core language. To that end, typing for runtime configurations is generalized to consider the declaration of invariants. This is achieved by a global invariant mapping ι, which assigns lock invariants to locations: essentially, the rule (H) of Section 4.4 is replaced by the following rules, covering the two possible lock states (see [13]).

$$\frac{h\ ;\ S \rhd_\iota A \mid R \quad A \vdash^\iota_x v :: B}{h, n_0 \mapsto v\ ;\ S \rhd_{\iota\{R/n\}} B\{n{:}\texttt{var}/x\}}\ \text{(HU)}$$

$$\frac{h\ ;\ S \rhd_\iota A \quad A \vdash^\iota_x v :: B}{h, n_{-1} \mapsto v\ ;\ S \rhd_{\iota\{R/n\}} B\{n{:}\texttt{var}/x\}}\ \text{(HL)}$$

THEOREM 4.5. *If* $h\ ;\ S \rhd_\iota A$ *and* $h\ ;\ S \rightarrow h'; S'$ *then* $h'; S' \rhd_\iota A$.

A progress property also holds for the full core language with concurrency and synchronization primitives, but in a slightly weaker sense, due to the possibility of deadlock on **sync** blocks (see [13]).

5. Related Work

The concept of separation results from a research stream whose origins can be traced back to the seminal works of Reynolds on syntactic control of interference [36, 37]. Separation logics extend classical Hoare logic with new connectives, in particular the separation conjunction, which allows to specify the fine-grained structure of states in programs manipulating references, and enables local reasoning to successfully tackle programs with references [39] and concurrency [33]. More recently, separation logic has motivated the introduction of Hoare Type Theory [31], and has been extended to languages with higher-order store [40]. These works focus on the identification of higher-order frame principles for state-based local reasoning. The idea of assigning a parallel separation type to some value, even when there is (safe) interference between the implementations of the separated behaviors, is reminiscent of concepts explored in fictional separation [25], concurrent abstract predicates [17], and superficially substructural types [28]. Again, these works are carried out within state-based separation logics. We have shown how a type based approach to behavioral separation, in principle less precise for specification purposes than a full logic, can already be used to enforce interference safety on programming languages idioms and features not yet in the scope of such approaches, such as higher-order store and first class concurrency. Work on spatial logics for concurrent systems [11, 15] offered remote inspiration for our approach, but explored different notions of "separation", useful to reasoning about distribution and mobility, rather than about interference. Although the fundamental notion of separation applies to many kinds of computational structures [14, 20], the idea of combining separation with behavioral types to discipline interference in a realistic programming language, as we do here, does not seem to have been considered before.

Various forms of behavioral types have been independently introduced by several authors with the intent of classifying usage patterns of computational objects [16, 21, 24]. Some of these works have motivated more refined verification techniques, for example, to check resource usage disciplines [23] in functional programs. A particular case of behavioral types are the so-called session types, intended to discipline message exchanges between partners in distributed systems. Although initially proposed for systems with interaction between exactly two partners [21], session types have been extended to systems with an arbitrary number of participants [22]. Our notion of type assertion is loosely related with the notion of global type introduced in [22], in the sense that it needs to talk about the joint behavior of several entities. A version of session types to discipline interactions between concurrent objects was developed in [18], but does not attempt to deal with interference or aliasing. More recently, the first author and Pfenning developed an interpretation of session types in linear logic [12], which also inspired some aspects of the theory presented here. Connections between session types and separation logic have also been investigated in [41], but focusing on disciplining the transference of resources in process communications. In prior work, we attempted a very preliminary approach to the concept of behavioral separation [10]. However, the developments in this paper clarify the notion of behavioral separation type in the context of a clean substructural type theory, based on a λ-calculus with imperative and concurrency constructs, and are much more general and expressive.

Several works have proposed type-based approaches to discipline aliasing and concurrency control in various programming languages, usually exploiting type and effect systems [1, 8]. Ownership types have also been studied to discipline aliasing and concurrency [6, 7]. Some of these works have led to the development of powerful programming tools [27]. Typically, these works do not focus on capturing the dynamic behavior of resources at a deeper level, as we do here, but on tracking occurrences of identifiers, locks, permissions, regions, and data dependencies, essentially resorting to linearity. An important exception is typestate, which uses a state-based approach to specify resource usage protocols in object oriented languages [3]. A key ingredient of the typestate approach is the use of primitive permissions to capture usage idioms, rather than resource behavior. In parallel research we are investigating combinations of separation with typestate [29]. Techniques to support expressive borrowing idioms in the context of typestate have been recently proposed in [30].

6. Concluding Remarks

We have introduced behavioral separation as a general principle for disciplining interference, due either to aliasing or concurrency, by combining concepts from separation logic and behavioral type systems. We have designed a behavioral separation type system that illustrates the concept using a higher-order imperative functional language extended with concurrency and synchronization primitives. Our type system is proven sound using proof theoretic techniques.

We have also shown that the expressiveness of our approach goes beyond the state of the art for type-based verification of aliasing and concurrency, and provided several challenging examples involving fine-grained state manipulation, thread based concurrency, and synchronization constructs. Further examples, including the implementation of a concurrent queue based on a double linked list can be found in [13]. In ongoing work, we have already designed an algorithm that can effectively type check programs in our core language with a reasonable annotation burden – these results will be reported elsewhere. We are also investigating generalizations to invariant-based separation, along the lines suggested in Section 4.5, and the extension of our basic framework with dependent types, which would support more precise specifications.

Acknowledgments. Thanks to Peter O'Hearn for insightful remarks on safe interference, to Jorge A. Perez, Rodrigo Rodrigues, and to the anonymous reviewers for useful comments. Work co-supported by FCT Pest UI527 2011; PDTC/104583; CMU-PT NGN-44.

References

[1] M. Abadi, C. Flanagan, and S. N. Freund. Types for safe locking: Static race detection for Java. *ACM TOPLAS*, 28(2):207–255, 2006.

[2] A. Ahmed, M. Fluet, and G. Morrisett. L^3: A Linear Language with Locations. *Fundam. Inform.*, 77(4):397–449, 2007.

[3] K. Bierhoff and J. Aldrich. Modular Typestate Checking of Aliased Objects. In *OOPSLA 2007*, pages 301–320, 2007.

[4] S. L. Bloom and Z. Ésik. Free Shuffle Algebras in Language Varieties. *Theoretical Computer Science*, 163(1&2):55–98, 1996.

[5] R. Bornat, C. Calcagno, P. W. O'Hearn, and M. Parkinson. Permission accounting in separation logic. In *POPL 2005*, pages 259–270, 2005.

[6] C. Boyapati, R. Lee, and M. C. Rinard. Ownership types for safe programming: preventing data races and deadlocks. In *OOPSLA 2002*, pages 211–230. ACM, 2002.

[7] C. Boyapati, B. Liskov, and L. Shrira. Ownership types for object encapsulation. In *POPL 2003*, 2003.

[8] C. Boyapati and M. C. Rinard. A Parameterized Type System for Race-Free Java Programs. In *OOPSLA 2001*, pages 56–69, 2001.

[9] J. Boyland. Checking Interference with Fractional Permissions. In *SAS 2003*, volume 2694 of *LNCS*, pages 55–72. Springer-Verlag, 2003.

[10] L. Caires. Spatial-Behavioral Types for Concurrency and Resource Control in Distributed Systems. *Theoretical Computer Science*, 402(2-3):120–141, 2008.

[11] L. Caires and L. Cardelli. A Spatial Logic for Concurrency (Part I). *Information and Computation*, 186(2):194–235, 2003.

[12] L. Caires and F. Pfenning. Session Types as Intuitionistic Linear Propositions. In *CONCUR'10*, volume 6269 of *LNCS*, pages 222–236. Springer-Verlag, 2010.

[13] L. Caires and J. C. Seco. The Type Discipline of Behavioral Separation. Technical report, TR-DI-FCT-UNL, 2012.

[14] C. Calcagno, P. W. O'Hearn, and H. Yang. Local Action and Abstract Separation Logic. In *LICS 2007*, pages 366–378, 2007.

[15] L. Cardelli and A. D. Gordon. Anytime, Anywhere. Modal Logics for Mobile Ambients. In *POPL 2000*, pages 365–377. ACM, 2000.

[16] S. Chaki, S. Rajamani, and J. Rehof. Types as models: Model Checking Message-Passing Programs. In *POPL 2002*, pages 45–57, 2002.

[17] T. Dinsdale-Young, M. Dodds, P. Gardner, M. J. Parkinson, and V. Vafeiadis. Concurrent Abstract Predicates. In *ECOOP 2010*, volume 6183 of *LNCS*, pages 504–528. Springer-Verlag, 2010.

[18] S. J. Gay, V. Thudichum Vasconcelos, A. Ravara, N. Gesbert, and A. Z. Caldeira. Modular Session Types for Distributed Object-oriented Programming. In *POPL 2010*, pages 299–312, 2010.

[19] C. A. R. Hoare, B. Möller, G. Struth, and I. Wehrman. Concurrent Kleene Algebra. In *CONCUR'09*, volume 5710 of *LNCS*, pages 399–414. Springer-Verlag, 2009.

[20] T. Hoare and P. W. O'Hearn. Separation Logic Semantics for Communicating Processes. *EN Theo. Computer Science*, 212:3–25, 2008.

[21] K. Honda, V. T. Vasconcelos, and M. Kubo. Language Primitives and Type Discipline for Structured Communication-Based Programming. In *ESOP 1998*, volume 1381 of *LNCS*, pages 122–138. Springer, 1998.

[22] K. Honda, N. Yoshida, and M. Carbone. Multiparty Asynchronous Session Types. In *POPL 2008*, pages 273–284. ACM, 2008.

[23] A. Igarashi and N. Kobayashi. Resource Usage Analysis. In *POPL 2002*, pages 331–342, 2002.

[24] A. Igarashi and N. Kobayashi. A Generic Type System for the Pi-Calculus. *Theoretical Computer Science*, 311(1-3):121–163, 2004.

[25] J. B. Jensen and L. Birkedal. Fictional Separation Logic. In *ESOP 2012*, LNCS, pages 377–396. Springer-Verlag, 2012.

[26] Cliff B. Jones. Splitting Atoms Safely. *Theoretical Computer Science*, 375(1-3):109–119, 2007.

[27] R. Bocchino Jr., S. Heumann, N. Honarmand, S. Adve, V. Adve, A. Welc, and T. Shpeisman. Safe Nondeterminism in a Deterministic-by-default Parallel Language. In *POPL 2011*, pages 535–548, 2011.

[28] N. R. Krishnaswami, A. Turon, D. Dreyer, and D. Garg. Superficially Substructural Types. In *ICFP'12*, pages 41–54. ACM, 2012.

[29] Militão, F. and Aldrich, J. and Caires, L. Aliasing control with view-based typestate. In *FTFJP '10*, pages 7:1–7:7. ACM, 2010.

[30] K. Naden, R. Bocchino, J. Aldrich, and K. Bierhoff. A Type System for Borrowing Permissions. In *POPL 2012*, pages 557–570, 2012.

[31] A. Nanevski, J. G. Morrisett, and L. Birkedal. Hoare Type Theory, Polymorphism and Separation. *J. Fun. P.*, 18(5-6):865–911, 2008.

[32] P. W. O'Hearn. On Bunched Typing. *J. Fun. P.*, 13(4):747–796, 2003.

[33] P. W. O'Hearn. Resources, Concurrency, and Local Reasoning. *Theor. Comput. Sci.*, 375(1-3):271–307, 2007.

[34] B. Pierce. *Types and Programming Languages*. MIT Press, 2002.

[35] François Pottier. Hiding local state in direct style: A higher-order anti-frame rule. In *LICS'08*, pages 331–340, 2008.

[36] J. C. Reynolds. Syntactic Control of Interference. In *POPL 78*, pages 39–46, 1978.

[37] J. C. Reynolds. Syntactic Control of Interference, Part 2. In *ICALP 89*, volume 372 of *LNCS*, pages 704–722. Springer, 1989.

[38] J. C. Reynolds. *Design of the programming language FORSYTHE*, pages 173–233. Birkhauser Boston Inc., Cambridge, MA, USA, 1997.

[39] J. C. Reynolds. Separation Logic: A Logic for Shared Mutable Data Structures. In *LICS 2012*, 2002.

[40] J. Schwinghammer, L. Birkedal, B. Reus, and H. Yang. Nested Hoare Triples and Frame Rules for Higher-order Store. *Logical Methods in Computer Science*, 7(3), 2011.

[41] J. Villard, E. Lozes, and C. Calcagno. Proving copyless message passing. In *APLAS 2009*, volume 5904 of *LNCS*, pages 194–209. Springer-Verlag, 2009.

Views: Compositional Reasoning for Concurrent Programs

Thomas Dinsdale-Young
Imperial College
td202@doc.ic.ac.uk

Lars Birkedal
IT University of Copenhagen
birkedal@itu.dk

Philippa Gardner
Imperial College
pg@doc.ic.ac.uk

Matthew Parkinson
Microsoft Research
mattpark@microsoft.com

Hongseok Yang
University of Oxford
hongseok00@gmail.com

Abstract

Compositional abstractions underly many reasoning principles for concurrent programs: the concurrent environment is abstracted in order to reason about a thread in isolation; and these abstractions are composed to reason about a program consisting of many threads. For instance, separation logic uses formulae that describe part of the state, abstracting the rest; when two threads use disjoint state, their specifications can be composed with the separating conjunction. Type systems abstract the state to the types of variables; threads may be composed when they agree on the types of shared variables.

In this paper, we present the "Concurrent Views Framework", a metatheory of concurrent reasoning principles. The theory is parameterised by an abstraction of state with a notion of composition, which we call *views*. The metatheory is remarkably simple, but highly applicable: the rely-guarantee method, concurrent separation logic, concurrent abstract predicates, type systems for recursive references and for unique pointers, and even an adaptation of the Owicki-Gries method can all be seen as instances of the Concurrent Views Framework. Moreover, our metatheory proves each of these systems is sound without requiring induction on the operational semantics.

Categories and Subject Descriptors F.3.1 [*Specifying and Verifying and Reasoning about Programs*]: Logics of programs

General Terms Theory, Verification

Keywords concurrency; axiomatic semantics; compositional reasoning

1. Introduction

This paper aims to find the core principles underlying compositional reasoning systems for (first-order) concurrent programs. Compositional reasoning means that we consider each component in isolation without having to know the precise concurrent, or sequential, context in which it will be placed. This is essential for reasoning about incomplete code or libraries: the context is not known. In a concurrent setting, compositional reasoning allows a thread to be considered in isolation, rather than considering all possible interleavings of a program.

Type systems and program logics are two common forms of compositional reasoning. They strike a balance between invariant properties that must be preserved during the execution of a concurrent program, and operations that may be performed. Standard type systems and rely-guarantee methods [20] focus on preserving global properties: for example, the typing of the memory. Such approaches are good at handling sharing and interference, but work less well with stateful behaviour. Contrastingly, separation logic [18, 27] focuses on local portions of the state, which can be manipulated independently. This approach is good at handling stateful behaviour, but works less well with sharing and interference. There have been forays into the middle ground such as linear types [1, 23, 29] and related capability systems [7], which allow strong (type-changing) updates to memory, and SAGL [15], RGSep [31], LRG [14] and deny-guarantee [9, 13], which combine ideas from rely-guarantee and separation logic to enable reasoning about fine-grained concurrency in the heap. These developments have led to increasingly elaborate reasoning systems, each introducing new features to tackle specific applications of compositional reasoning and ad-hoc metatheory to justify these features.

Given the diversity of these approaches, it is not clear that they have significant common ground. Can the ad-hoc metatheory of each be generalised to give a paradigm in which all can be understood?

We argue that in fact the above reasoning systems employ a common approach to compositionality. They provide thread-specific abstractions of the state, which embody enough information to prove properties about the behaviour of a thread whilst allowing for the possible behaviours of other threads.

We introduce the "Concurrent Views Framework" ("Views Framework" or "Views" for short), which captures this compositional reasoning by introducing the notion of *views*. Intuitively, a thread's view consists of abstract *knowledge* about the current state of the machine and the thread's *rights* to change the state of the machine. The knowledge of a thread must be *stable* under the operations of concurrent threads: no other thread may have rights to invalidate the thread's knowledge. Conversely, no thread can have knowledge that another thread has the right to invalidate. Views are *compositional*: knowledge and rights may be distributed between threads and recombined.

To illustrate the Views Framework, first consider type systems for an imperative concurrent language. In a simple type system, the types of variables are invariant. Each thread's view is provided by

POPL'13, January 23–25, 2013, Rome, Italy.

a typing context, which embodies the knowledge that the values of variables agree with their types, and the rights to change the state such that this typing is preserved. When views are composed, they must agree on the types of all variables they share. In a type system that permits strong (*i.e.* type-changing) updates, threads again have knowledge that variables agree with their types, but may make updates that change the types of variables. Threads' views may be consistently composed only if they describe disjoint sets of variables, which each thread can be seen to *own*. Note that, since heap locations may be aliased by multiple variables, it is not in general permissible to update their types. However, a type system may include unique reference types, that confer ownership of heap locations, and hence allow type-changing updates. In this paper, we show how a simple type system (§2.2), a type system with strong updates, recursive types and subtyping (§7.1), and a type system with unique references (§7.2) can all be formalised in Views.

Now consider program logics for the same concurrent language. With concurrent separation logic, the views are assertions that describe the part of the state *owned* by a thread. These views embody knowledge about the owned part of the state, and confer the exclusive right to modify it. Views are composed with the separating conjunction, which enforces disjoint ownership of the state, so that no thread may alter state owned by another thread. More elaborate logics, such as deny-guarantee [13] and concurrent abstract predicates (CAP) [9], allow assertions to describe shared state and ownership of specific capabilities to update the shared state. Here, the *stability* of assertions is important: an assertion about the shared state must be invariant under operations for which other threads may have capabilities. In this paper, we represent a wide range of example program logics in our Views Framework, including several separation logics (§§3.1, 3.2, 7.4), the Owicki-Gries [24] (§7.3) and rely-guarantee methods [20] (§4) and CAP (§7.5). A fuller description of all our examples can be found in the technical report [11], along with Coq formalisations of many of them.

The Views Framework embodies the essential ingredients for sound compositional reasoning. Given a set of views with a composition operator (denoted $*$), together with an axiomatisation for the atomic commands, Views provides a generic program logic. For soundness, we require a *reification function* from views to sets of machine states and an *axiom soundness* property. The reification function relates partial, abstract views to complete, concrete machine states. Axiom soundness ensures that the axioms for the atomic commands are sound with respect to the reification, in the context of an arbitrary environment view. This embeds compositionality in the *meaning* of 'program C updates the view from p to q': for all environment views r, it must update $p * r$ to $q * r$. This approach has previously been used for extending sequential separation logic for higher-order languages, where it is otherwise difficult to characterise locality properties of commands, which are sufficient for ensuring compositionality [2, 3]. We show that the interpretation also provides a simpler and more general metatheory for logics of *concurrent* programs, identifying simple properties needed to prove soundness in contrast with the complex soundness results in the literature.

The Views Framework provides a generalised frame rule. This rule is essential for directly encoding the weakening rule from rely-guarantee and rules for manipulating resource invariants in concurrent separation logic. The new rule allows a function to be applied uniformly to the pre- and postcondition of a command. Without this rule the encoding of concurrent separation logic, rely-guarantee and Owicki-Gries method would require a far more complex representation of the high-level reasoning with permissions, such as deny-guarantee.

Given the wide range of examples that are instances of our framework, we believe "Views" embodies the core principles underlying compositional reasoning about concurrent programs.

Overview. In §2 we present our core contribution — the Concurrent Views Framework — defining the parameters and properties necessary to instantiate our general program logic. As a pedagogical example, we show how a simple type system may be encoded in Views. In §3, we show how separation algebras and interference can be used to construct instances of the Views Framework, illustrating these constructions with separation logic. In §4, we present a novel generalisation of the frame rule for the Views Framework. This rule makes it possible to encode contextual rules, which we illustrate by the weakening rule of the rely-guarantee method. We present a general combination rule in §5, which generalises the rules of disjunction and conjunction. We give a sufficient condition for its soundness and consider the special cases of disjunction and conjunction. We outline the general soundness proof for the framework in §6. In §7, we show the versatility of Views through five further example instances: recursive types, unique types, the Owicki-Gries method, atomic concurrent separation logic, and concurrent abstract predicates. Finally, we discuss related work in §8 and conclude in §9.

We have formalised all of the metatheory of the paper, as well as many of the examples, in Coq (see [11]).

2. Concurrent Views Framework

In this section, we present the Concurrent Views Framework. In §2.1, we present the programming language and its operational semantics, which is parameterised by a notion of state and a set of primitive atomic commands and their semantics as state transformers. In §2.2, we provide a set of rules for compositional reasoning, which is parameterised by an abstraction of the state equipped with a composition operation — a *views semigroup* — and an axiomatisation of the atomic commands. In §2.3, we give a general soundness result for the framework with respect to the operational semantics, which is parameterised by a relationship between the abstract views and the concrete states, and requires each axiom to satisfy a soundness property with respect to the semantics of the corresponding atomic command. To illustrate the Views Framework, we interleave its definition with an example of how to instantiate it for a simple type system for a heap update language.

2.1 Programming Language and Operational Semantics

We define the Views Framework on a simple programming language that is built from standard composite commands, and parameterised by a set of atomic commands. This enables us to consider many examples without having to change the metatheory.

Parameter A (Atomic Commands). *Assume a set of (syntactic)* atomic commands Atom, *ranged over by* a.

Definition 1 (Language Syntax). *The set of (syntactic)* commands, Comm, *ranged over by* C, *is defined by the following grammar:*

$$C ::= a \mid \mathtt{skip} \mid C;C \mid C+C \mid C \parallel C \mid C^*.$$

The operational semantics is parameterised by a model of machine states and an interpretation of the atomic commands as state transformers.

Parameter B (Machine States). *Assume a set of* machine states $\mathcal{S}$, *ranged over by* s.

Parameter C (Interpretation of Atomic Commands). *Assume a function* $[\![-]\!] : \mathsf{Atom} \to \mathcal{S} \to \mathcal{P}(\mathcal{S})$ *that associates each atomic command with a non-deterministic state transformer. (Where necessary, we lift non-deterministic state transformers to sets of states: for* $S \in \mathcal{P}(\mathcal{S})$, $[\![a]\!](S) = \bigcup\{[\![a]\!](s) \mid s \in S\}$.*)*

For machine state s, the set of states $[\![a]\!](s)$ is the set of possible outcomes of running the atomic command a. If the set is empty, then the command blocks. Here, we consider partial correctness, and so ignore executions that deadlock — that is, reach a state (other than `skip`) in which every thread is blocked. If we wish to guarantee against some exceptional behaviour, it should be modelled with an exception state, rather than by blocking.

We define the operational semantics of the language using a labelled transition system. Transitions are between commands, and are labelled by atomic commands or id. id labels computation steps in which the state is not changed.

Definition 2 (Transition Labels). *The set of* transition labels, $\mathsf{Label} \stackrel{\text{def}}{=} \mathsf{Atom} \uplus \{\mathsf{id}\}$, *extends the set of atomic commands with a designated identity label,* id. *Labels are ranged over by* α. $[\![-]\!]$ *is extended to* Label *by defining* $[\![\mathsf{id}]\!] \stackrel{\text{def}}{=} \lambda s.\, \{s\}$.

The labelled transition system splits the control-flow aspect of execution, represented by the transitions between commands, and the state-transforming aspect of execution, represented by the labelling of the transitions. This makes it easy to reinterpret programs over a more abstract state-space, while preserving the control-flow structure, which simplifies the soundness proof of our logic.

Definition 3 (Labelled Transition System and Operational Semantics). *The labelled transition relation* $- \xrightarrow{-} - : \mathsf{Comm} \times \mathsf{Label} \times \mathsf{Comm}$ *is defined by the following rules:*

$$\frac{C_1 \xrightarrow{\alpha} C_1'}{C_1; C_2 \xrightarrow{\alpha} C_1'; C_2} \quad \frac{}{\mathtt{skip}; C_2 \xrightarrow{\mathsf{id}} C_2} \quad \frac{}{C_1 + C_2 \xrightarrow{\mathsf{id}} C_i}\, i \in \{1,2\}$$

$$\frac{}{C^* \xrightarrow{\mathsf{id}} C; C^*} \quad \frac{}{C^* \xrightarrow{\mathsf{id}} \mathtt{skip}} \quad \frac{}{\mathtt{skip} \parallel C_2 \xrightarrow{\mathsf{id}} C_2} \quad \frac{}{C_1 \parallel \mathtt{skip} \xrightarrow{\mathsf{id}} C_1}$$

$$\frac{}{a \xrightarrow{a} \mathtt{skip}} \quad \frac{C_1 \xrightarrow{\alpha} C_1'}{C_1 \parallel C_2 \xrightarrow{\alpha} C_1' \parallel C_2} \quad \frac{C_2 \xrightarrow{\alpha} C_2'}{C_1 \parallel C_2 \xrightarrow{\alpha} C_1 \parallel C_2'}$$

The multi-step operational transition relation $-,- \rightarrow^* -,- : (\mathsf{Comm} \times \mathcal{S}) \times (\mathsf{Comm} \times \mathcal{S})$ *is defined by the following rules:*

$$\frac{}{C, s \rightarrow^* C, s} \quad \frac{C_1 \xrightarrow{\alpha} C_2 \quad s_2 \in [\![\alpha]\!](s_1) \quad C_2, s_2 \rightarrow^* C_3, s_3}{C_1, s_1 \rightarrow^* C_3, s_3}$$

Heap Update Language

For our examples, we use a language with simple atomic primitives for manipulating a heap. We therefore define instances of Parameters A, B and C accordingly.

Definition 4 (Atomic Heap Commands) **: Parameter A.** *Assume a set of variable names* Var, *ranged over by* x *and* y, *and a set of values* Val, *ranged over by* v, *of which a subset* $\mathsf{Loc} \subseteq \mathsf{Val}$ *represents heap addresses, ranged over by* l. *The syntax of atomic heap commands,* $\mathsf{Atom_H}$, *is defined by the grammar:*

$$a ::= x := y \;\big|\; [x] := v \;\big|\; [x] := y \;\big|\; x := [y] \;\big|\; x := \mathsf{ref}\ y.$$

Definition 5 (Heap States) **: Parameter B.** *Machine states are partial functions from variables and locations to values. There is also an exceptional faulting state, denoted* $\lightning$, *which represents the result of an invalid memory access. Formally,*

$$\mathcal{S}_\mathsf{H} \stackrel{\text{def}}{=} ((\mathsf{Var} \uplus \mathsf{Loc}) \rightharpoonup_{\text{fin}} \mathsf{Val}) \uplus \{\lightning\}.$$

Definition 6 (Heap Command Interpretation) **: Parameter C.** *The interpretation of the atomic heap-update commands is given by:*

$$\begin{aligned}
[\![x := y]\!](s) &\stackrel{\text{def}}{=} y \in \mathrm{dom}(s) \rhd \{s[x \mapsto s(y)]\} \\
[\![[x] := v]\!](s) &\stackrel{\text{def}}{=} x, s(x) \in \mathrm{dom}(s) \rhd \{s[s(x) \mapsto v]\} \\
[\![[x] := y]\!](s) &\stackrel{\text{def}}{=} x, y, s(x) \in \mathrm{dom}(s) \rhd \{s[s(x) \mapsto s(y)]\} \\
[\![x := [y]]\!](s) &\stackrel{\text{def}}{=} y, s(y) \in \mathrm{dom}(s) \rhd \{s[x \mapsto s(s(y))]\} \\
[\![x := \mathsf{ref}\ y]\!](s) &\stackrel{\text{def}}{=} y \in \mathrm{dom}(s) \rhd \\
&\qquad \{s[x \mapsto l, l \mapsto s(y)] \mid l \in \mathsf{Loc} \setminus \mathrm{dom}(s)\}
\end{aligned}$$

where $b \rhd s = $ *if* b *then* s *else* $\lightning$. *Here we extend* dom *to* $\mathcal{S}_\mathsf{H}$ *by taking* $\mathrm{dom}(\lightning) = \emptyset$.

2.2 Views and Program Logic

Reasoning systems typically do not require the user to reason directly about the state; they provide an abstract representation of the state that supports a particular form of reasoning. For example, in a simple type system the state is abstracted by a type context, Γ, which maps variables, x, to types, τ. A type represents a property about the variable, *e.g.* that it is a pointer to a cell in the heap. In a program logic like separation logic, the state is abstracted by assertions, P, Q, that describe parts of the memory. Complex assertions may be used to represent interesting structures, such as a lock x with an invariant P: $\mathsf{Lock}(x, P)$. Such assertions may not merely describe the state, but also enforce a protocol that threads must obey — for instance, only releasing a lock after establishing its invariant. These abstract representations do not precisely describe the memory, just certain properties it satisfies. They also can contain additional information — about typing, ownership and protocols, for instance — that is not present in the underlying state.

These abstractions form the key parameter of the framework: the *views*. We have one basic requirement for views, which is that they form a commutative semigroup.

Parameter D (View Commutative Semigroup). *Assume a commutative semigroup* $(\mathsf{View}, *)$. *The variables* p, q, r *are used to denote elements of* View.

If the semigroup has a unit, u, then we call it a *view monoid*, written $(\mathsf{View}, *, u)$. The unit is not required for the theory, but simplifies its use.

Intuitively, views are resources that embody *knowledge* about the state and the protocol threads must obey, and *rights* to modify the state in accordance with the implied protocol. The semigroup operation $*$ (*view composition*) combines the knowledge and rights of two views.

Since composition is used to combine the views of different threads, it must ensure consistency between these views. For example, to combine two typing contexts, they must agree on the type of any variables they have in common. Since threads only maintain the types in their view, if agreement was not enforced then one thread might violate another's expectations.

In separation logic, composition (separating conjunction) enforces that ownership is exclusive: no two views can simultaneously have ownership of a heap cell. In variants that allow assertions about shared state, such as deny-guarantee, composition also forces consistency between such assertions.

This consistency is typically implemented by a special inconsistent view that is the result of composing two views that are not consistent. The inconsistent view is usually a (unique) zero element of the semigroup: when composed with any other view, the result is the inconsistent view.

We define a *program logic* for our programming language, in which views provide the pre- and postconditions of the commands.

The program logic is parameterised by the set of axioms for atomic commands.

Parameter E (Axiomatisation). *Assume a set of axioms* $\mathsf{Axiom} \subseteq \mathsf{View} \times \mathsf{Label} \times \mathsf{View}$.

Definition 7 (Entailment). *The* entailment relation $\models\, \subseteq \mathsf{View} \times \mathsf{View}$ *is defined by:*

$$p \models q \overset{\text{def}}{\iff} (p, \mathsf{id}, q) \in \mathsf{Axiom}.$$

Definition 8 (Program Logic). *The program logic's judgements are of the form* $\vdash \{p\}\, C\, \{q\}$*, where* $p, q \in \mathsf{View}$ *provide the precondition and postcondition of command* $C \in \mathsf{Comm}$*. The proof rules for these judgements are as follows:*

$$\frac{(p, a, q) \in \mathsf{Axiom}}{\vdash \{p\}\, a\, \{q\}} \qquad \frac{\vdash \{p\}\, C\, \{q\}}{\vdash \{p * r\}\, C\, \{q * r\}} \qquad \frac{}{\vdash \{p\}\, \mathtt{skip}\, \{p\}}$$

$$\frac{\vdash \{p\}\, C_1\, \{q\} \quad \vdash \{p\}\, C_2\, \{q\}}{\vdash \{p\}\, C_1 + C_2\, \{q\}} \qquad \frac{\vdash \{p\}\, C\, \{p\}}{\vdash \{p\}\, C^*\, \{p\}}$$

$$\frac{\vdash \{p\}\, C_1\, \{r\} \quad \vdash \{r\}\, C_2\, \{q\}}{\vdash \{p\}\, C_1; C_2\, \{q\}} \qquad \frac{\vdash \{p_1\}\, C_1\, \{q_1\} \quad \vdash \{p_2\}\, C_2\, \{q_2\}}{\vdash \{p_1 * p_2\}\, C_1 \parallel C_2\, \{q_1 * q_2\}}$$

$$\frac{p \models p' \quad \vdash \{p'\}\, C\, \{q\}}{\vdash \{p\}\, C\, \{q\}} \qquad \frac{\vdash \{p\}\, C\, \{q'\} \quad q' \models q}{\vdash \{p\}\, C\, \{q\}}$$

The intended semantics of $\vdash \{p\}\, C\, \{q\}$ is that if the program C is run to termination from an initial state that is described by the view p, then the resulting state will be described by the view q. This is a partial correctness interpretation: the judgements say nothing about non-terminating executions.

The proof rules are standard rules from disjoint concurrent separation logic. They include the frame rule, which captures the intuition that a program's view can be extended with a composable view, and the disjoint concurrency rule, which allows the views of two threads to be composed. Note that, although in separation logic the concurrency rule imposes disjointness, in Views it does not; it just imposes composability. The last two rules are rules of consequence: they allow the precondition to be strengthened or the postcondition weakened with respect to the axiomatically-specified relation $\models$. If $\models$ is reflexive, these rules may be combined into a single rule.

Simple Type System

Consider a simple type system for our heap update language, where variables and heap cells are typed from the set Type, ranged over by τ, and defined by:

$$\tau ::= \mathsf{val} \mid \mathsf{ref}\ \tau.$$

The type val indicates that a variable or heap cell contains some unspecified value, while the type $\mathsf{ref}\ \tau$ indicates that it contains the address of a heap cell whose contents is typed as τ. A typing context $\Gamma : \mathsf{Var} \rightharpoonup \mathsf{Type}$ is a partial function which assigns types to variables.

Within the Views Framework, typing contexts are views. Composition, $\cup_\bot$, is the union of contexts (as relations), with a special *inconsistent typing context*, $\bot$, used to denote the composition of typing contexts that disagree on the type of some variable.

Definition 9 (Simple Type Views) **: Parameter D.** *The view monoid for the simple type system is defined as:*

$$((\mathsf{Var} \rightharpoonup \mathsf{Type}) \uplus \{\bot\}, \cup_\bot, \emptyset)$$

Judgements of the type system have the form $\Gamma \vdash C$. We treat this as syntax for $\vdash \{\Gamma\}\, C\, \{\Gamma\}$ in the Views Framework. It remains to give axioms for the type system.

Definition 10 (Simple Type Axioms) **: Parameter E.** *The axioms for the simple type system are defined schematically as:*

$$\mathbf{x} : \tau, \mathbf{y} : \tau \vdash \mathbf{x} := \mathbf{y} \qquad \mathbf{x} : \mathsf{ref}\ \mathsf{val} \vdash [\mathbf{x}] := v$$

$$\mathbf{x} : \tau, \mathbf{y} : \mathsf{ref}\ \tau \vdash \mathbf{x} := [\mathbf{y}] \qquad \mathbf{x} : \mathsf{ref}\ \tau, \mathbf{y} : \tau \vdash \mathbf{x} := \mathsf{ref}\ \mathbf{y}$$

$$\mathbf{x} : \mathsf{ref}\ \tau, \mathbf{y} : \tau \vdash [\mathbf{x}] := \mathbf{y}$$

The inference rules of the type system are as follows:

$$\frac{}{\Gamma \vdash \mathtt{skip}} \qquad \frac{\Gamma \vdash C_1 \quad \Gamma \vdash C_2 \quad \mathsf{op} \in \{;, +\}}{\Gamma \vdash C_1\, \mathsf{op}\, C_2}$$

$$\frac{\Gamma_1 \vdash C_1 \quad \Gamma_2 \vdash C_2}{\Gamma_1, \Gamma_2 \vdash C_1 \| C_2} \qquad \frac{\Gamma \vdash C}{\Gamma \vdash C^*} \qquad \frac{\Gamma \vdash C}{\Gamma, \Gamma' \vdash C}$$

Each of these rules is justified by the rules of the Views program logic, where we interpret Γ_1, Γ_2 as $\Gamma_1 \cup_\bot \Gamma_2$. The most interesting of these is the last, the weakening rule, which is an instance of the frame rule, with the frame Γ'.

2.3 Reification and Soundness

In order to relate the program logic to the operational semantics, it is necessary to define a relationship between the abstract views and the concrete machine states. In a type system, this would be given by a judgement $\Gamma \vdash s$ asserting that state s is well-typed with respect to the context Γ. In separation logic, it would be given by a Kripke model, where the judgement $s \models P$ asserts that formula P holds in state s. In the Views Framework, we model this relationship with a *reification function*.

Parameter F (Reification). *Assume a* reification function $\lfloor - \rfloor : \mathsf{View} \to \mathcal{P}(\mathcal{S})$ *which maps views to sets of machine states.*

Note that the reification function has very few restrictions. The semigroup structure of views is not reflected at the level of machine states: the notion of composition is purely an abstraction. The space of machine states need not be covered completely by the reification; this is useful for giving fault-avoiding interpretations to our proof judgements. Furthermore, inconsistent views may be mapped to the empty set of machine states.

Choosing an appropriate reification function is important. We could, for instance, map all views to the empty set and claim soundness of an arbitrary logic. However, judgements in the logic would convey no information about the operational semantics, as they would not describe the execution of a program from any initial state at all. Consequently, soundness is always with respect to the choice of reification function.

Soundness requires that the axioms concerning atomic commands are satisfied by the operational interpretation of the commands. We define an abstract notion of executing a small step of the program. To be able to make the step from p to q with the action α, we must ensure that the operational interpretation of the action satisfies the specification, and moreover it also preserves any possible environment view.

Definition 11 (Action Judgement). *The* action judgement *is defined as:*

$$\alpha \Vdash \{p\}\{q\} \overset{\text{def}}{\iff}$$
$$[\![\alpha]\!](\lfloor p \rfloor) \subseteq \lfloor q \rfloor \ \wedge\ \forall r \in \mathsf{View}.\, [\![\alpha]\!](\lfloor p * r \rfloor) \subseteq \lfloor q * r \rfloor.$$

For a view monoid, this definition simplifies to:

$$\alpha \Vdash \{p\}\{q\} \iff \forall r \in \mathsf{View}.\, [\![\alpha]\!](\lfloor p * r \rfloor) \subseteq \lfloor q * r \rfloor. \quad (1)$$

Semantic entailment is a special case of the action judgement, for the label id.

Definition 12 (Semantic Entailment). $p \preceq q \overset{\text{def}}{\iff} \mathsf{id} \Vdash \{p\}\{q\}$.

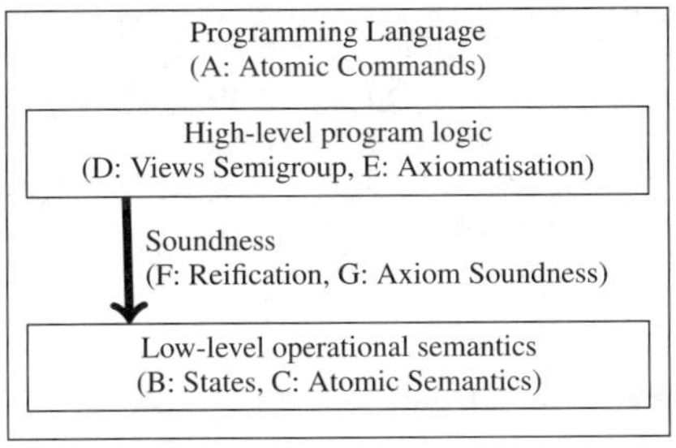

Figure 1. Overview of the Views Framework

For each axiom (p, α, q), the interpretation of α must update view p to q while preserving any environment view. This is captured by the following property:

Property G (Axiom Soundness). *For every* $(p, \alpha, q) \in \mathsf{Axiom}$,

$$\alpha \Vdash \{p\}\{q\}.$$

This property is both necessary and sufficient for the soundness of the program logic. We state the soundness result here, and provide more details in §6.

Theorem (Soundness). *Assume that* $\vdash \{p\}\, C\, \{q\}$ *is derivable in the program logic. Then, for all* $s \in \lfloor p \rfloor$ *and* $s' \in \mathcal{S}$, *if* $(C, s) \to^* (\mathtt{skip}, s')$ *then* $s' \in \lfloor q \rfloor$.

Simple Type System: Soundness

We reify typing contexts as the set of states which are well-typed with respect to the context. Consequently, we must define a notion of typing for states.

Definition 13 (State Typing). *The state typing judgement* $\Gamma; \Theta \vdash s$, *where* $\Gamma : \mathsf{Var} \rightharpoonup \mathsf{Type}$, $s \in \mathcal{S}_\mathsf{H}$ *and* $\Theta : \mathsf{Loc} \rightharpoonup \mathsf{Type}$ *ranges over heap typing contexts, is defined as follows:*

$$\Gamma; \Theta \vdash s \overset{\text{def}}{\iff} \forall x \in \mathrm{dom}\,(\Gamma)\,.\,\Theta \vdash s(x) : \Gamma(x) \\ \land \forall l \in \mathrm{dom}\,(\Theta)\,.\,\Theta \vdash s(l) : \Theta(l)$$

where $\Theta \vdash v : \tau \overset{\text{def}}{\iff} \tau = \mathsf{val} \lor \tau = \mathsf{ref}\ (\Theta(v))$.

The state typing essentially ensures that every typed variable and location has a value consistent with its type. Specifically, this means that references must refer to addresses that have the appropriate type. Note that it would not be possible to have x and y referencing the same location in the typing context $x : \mathsf{ref\ val}, y : \mathsf{ref\ ref\ val}$. This is necessary, since otherwise an update to the location via x could invalidate the type of y.

Definition 14 (Simple Type Reification) **: Parameter F.** *The simple type reification,* $\lfloor - \rfloor_{\mathsf{TS}} : \mathsf{View}_{\mathcal{M}_\mathsf{TS}} \to \mathcal{P}(\mathcal{S}_\mathsf{H})$, *is defined as follows:*

$$\lfloor \Gamma \rfloor_{\mathsf{TS}} \overset{\text{def}}{=} \{s \in \mathcal{S}_\mathsf{H} \mid \exists \Theta.\, \Gamma; \Theta \vdash s\}.$$

To establish soundness, we need only show Property G (Axiom Soundness). This is straightforward; for further details, consult [11]. Importantly, this works because we do not require locality at the low level of the semantics, only at the high level. Thus, standard separation algebra approaches [6, 12] would not work for this example.

2.4 Summary

The parameters of the Views Framework are summarised in Figure 1. The language (§2.1) is parameterised by a set of atomic commands, and its semantics is determined by a notion of state and the semantics of the atomic commands as state transformers. The Views program logic (§2.2) is parameterised by a semigroup of views and an axiomatisation of the atomic commands. The soundness of the logic (§2.3) is with respect to a reification of views into concrete states, and is established by proving the axiom soundness property.

In the following sections, we consider numerous instances of the Views Framework. In doing so, we elaborate the metatheory with common constructions and additional proof rules.

Remark. The Views Framework is more general than existing axiomatisations of separation logic [6], in that it does not restrict views to be sets of (machine) states but allows them to be elements in any semigroup. In fact, choosing this views semigroup and an accompanying reification function well is the most important step of using our framework. A good choice of the views semigroup leads to a program logic where a verifier works on the right level of abstraction of machine states. Also, it picks an appropriate scope for the universal quantification in the axiom soundness property, and gives an effective set of axioms for atomic commands. This influence of the views semigroup on axiom soundness corresponds to selecting a notion of locality properties for commands, which was usually done in a fixed manner in the work on separation logic.

3. Constructing Views

We can instantiate of the framework directly, but instantiations often have common structure which can be used to simplify the process. We present two general approaches to constructing views as sets, whose elements themselves belong to a (partial) monoid.

3.1 Separation Algebras

Calcagno *et al.* [6] introduced the concept of *separation algebras* to generalise separation logic. For many examples, we use a generalisation of separation algebras with multiple units [5, 12] (and without the cancellativity requirement) to construct a view monoid.

Parameter H (Separation Algebra). *A separation algebra* $(\mathcal{M}, \bullet, I)$ *is a partial, commutative monoid with multiple units. Namely, it is a set* $\mathcal{M}$ *equipped with a partial operator* $\bullet : \mathcal{M} \times \mathcal{M} \rightharpoonup \mathcal{M}$ *and a unit set* $I \subseteq \mathcal{M}$ *satisfying:*

- Commutativity: $m_1 \bullet m_2 = m_2 \bullet m_1$ *when either is defined;*
- Associativity: $m_1 \bullet (m_2 \bullet m_3) = (m_1 \bullet m_2) \bullet m_3$ *when either is defined;*
- Existence of Unit: *for all* $m \in \mathcal{M}$ *there exists* $i \in I$ *such that* $i \bullet m = m$; *and*
- Minimality of Unit: *for all* $m \in \mathcal{M}$ *and* $i \in I$, *if* $i \bullet m$ *is defined then* $i \bullet m = m$.

Definition 15 (Separation View Monoid) **: Parameter D.** *Each separation algebra* $(\mathcal{M}, \bullet, I)$ *induces a* separation view monoid $(\mathcal{P}(\mathcal{M}), *, I)$, *where* $p_1 * p_2 \overset{\text{def}}{=} \{m_1 \bullet m_2 \mid m_1 \in p_1, m_2 \in p_2\}$.

Separation algebras are typically constructed by adding instrumentation to machine states; this instrumentation determines how states may be composed, typically by recording ownership or invariant properties. While previous work has required cancellativity, we do not.

Remark. For Separation View Monoids, it is common to choose entailment ($\models$) to be subset inclusion ($\subseteq$).

Disjoint Concurrent Separation Logic

To illustrate the separation algebra, we present a simple separation logic for disjoint concurrency.

Definition 16 (DCSL Separation Algebra) **: Parameter H.** *The separation algebra for disjoint concurrent separation logic is* $(\mathcal{M}_{\mathsf{DCSL}}, \uplus, \{\emptyset\})$*, where* $\mathcal{M}_{\mathsf{DCSL}} \stackrel{\text{def}}{=} (\mathsf{Var} \uplus \mathsf{Loc}) \rightharpoonup_{\text{fin}} \mathsf{Val}$*,* $\uplus$ *is the union of partial functions with disjoint domains, and the unit,* $\emptyset$*, is the partial function with the empty domain.*

Elements of $\mathcal{M}_{\mathsf{DCSL}}$ declare ownership of the variables and heap addresses that belong to their domains, as well as defining their values. Significantly, they do not declare information about parts of the state which are not owned. Views $p, q \in \mathcal{P}(\mathcal{M}_{\mathsf{DCSL}})$ are sets of these abstract states. Thus, p and q describe resources, which hold information about part of the state.

Judgements of disjoint concurrent separation logic are, as in the Views Framework, triples of the form $\vdash \{p\}\, C\, \{q\}$. The view $\mathbf{x} \Rightarrow v$ denotes the singleton set of the partial function mapping variable $\mathbf{x}$ to value v, and $\mathbf{x} \Rightarrow \_$ denotes the set of all partial functions that map only variable $\mathbf{x}$ to a value. Similarly, the views $l \mapsto v$ and $l \mapsto \_$ map heap address l to v or any value respectively. The view $\exists v.\, p(v)$ is the (infinite) join of $p(v)$ for all values of v.

Definition 17 (DCSL Axiomatisation) **: Parameter E.** *The axiomatisation for separation logic is given by the schemas:*

$$\{\mathbf{x} \Rightarrow \_ * \mathbf{y} \Rightarrow v\}\ \mathbf{x} := \mathbf{y}\ \{\mathbf{x} \Rightarrow v * \mathbf{y} \Rightarrow v\}$$

$$\{\mathbf{x} \Rightarrow l * l \mapsto \_\}\ [\mathbf{x}] := v\ \{\mathbf{x} \Rightarrow l * l \mapsto v\}$$

$$\{\mathbf{x} \Rightarrow l * l \mapsto \_ * \mathbf{y} \Rightarrow v\}\ [\mathbf{x}] := \mathbf{y}\ \{\mathbf{x} \Rightarrow l * l \mapsto v * \mathbf{y} \Rightarrow v\}$$

$$\{\mathbf{y} \Rightarrow l * l \mapsto v * \mathbf{x} \Rightarrow \_\}\ \mathbf{x} := [\mathbf{y}]\ \{\mathbf{y} \Rightarrow l * l \mapsto v * \mathbf{x} \Rightarrow v\}$$

$$\{\mathbf{x} \Rightarrow \_ * \mathbf{y} \Rightarrow v\}\ \mathbf{x} := \mathsf{ref}\ \mathbf{y}\ \{\exists l.\, \mathbf{x} \Rightarrow l * l \mapsto v * \mathbf{y} \Rightarrow v\}$$

For the soundness of a view model based on separation algebra, we typically provide a reification function for elements of the separation algebra. This is then lifted to give a reification for views.

Parameter I (Separation Algebra Reification). $\lfloor - \rfloor : \mathcal{M} \to \mathcal{P}(\mathcal{S})$.

Definition 18 : Parameter F. $\lfloor p \rfloor = \bigcup_{m \in p} \lfloor m \rfloor$.

Given this construction of a view monoid and reification function, Property G has an equivalent formulation that is typically simpler to check.

Property J (Axiom Soundness II). *For every* $(p, \alpha, q) \in \mathsf{Axiom}$*, and every* $m \in \mathcal{M}$*,* $[\![\alpha]\!]\lfloor p * \{m\} \rfloor \subseteq \lfloor q * \{m\} \rfloor$.

Remark. The case where $\alpha = \mathsf{id}$ will always hold if $p \vDash q$ implies that $p \subseteq q$, justifying subset inclusion as a natural choice for the entailment relation.

Disjoint Concurrent Separation Logic: Soundness

Since separation-logic views are sets of partial functions from variables and locations to values, they can be seen as sets of heap states. Thus, we can define a simple notion of reification.

Definition 19 (DCSL Reification) **: Parameter I.** *The DCSL reification,* $\lfloor - \rfloor_{\mathsf{DCSL}} : \mathcal{M}_{\mathsf{DCSL}} \to \mathcal{P}(\mathcal{S})$*, is defined as follows:*

$$\lfloor s \rfloor_{\mathsf{DCSL}} \stackrel{\text{def}}{=} \{s\}.$$

Our axioms for atomic commands are sound in the sense of Property J. Taking entailment to be $\subseteq$ gives the standard rule of consequence.

Note that the reification function does not cover the machine state space: there is no view p with $\lightning \in \lfloor p \rfloor$. This means that our separation-logic triples do not permit memory faults to occur, in accordance with the standard interpretation.

3.2 Separation Algebras with Interference

Views model partial, abstracted information about machine states that is stable — immune to interference from other threads. In logics with fine-grained permissions such as those used in deny-guarantee (DG) [13] and concurrent abstract predicates (CAP) [9], the elements of the separation algebra are not stable by construction, but an additional obligation is added to only mention stable sets of elements. This can simply be seen as another way of constructing a view monoid from a separation algebra and an *interference relation*.

Parameter K (Interference Relation). *An* interference relation $\mathcal{R} \subseteq \mathcal{M} \times \mathcal{M}$ *on a separation algebra* $(\mathcal{M}, \bullet, I)$ *is a preorder satisfying the properties:*

- *for all* $m_1, m_2, m, m' \in \mathcal{M}$ *with* $m = m_1 \bullet m_2$ *and* $m\, \mathcal{R}\, m'$*, there exist* $m_1', m_2' \in \mathcal{M}$ *with* $m_1\, \mathcal{R}\, m_1'$*,* $m_2\, \mathcal{R}\, m_2'$ *and* $m' = m_1' \bullet m_2'$*; and*
- *for all* $i \in I$ *and* $m \in \mathcal{M}$ *with* $i\, \mathcal{R}\, m$*,* $m \in I$*.*

Definition 20 (Stabilised View Monoid) **: Parameter D.** *An interference relation* $\mathcal{R}$ *on a separation algebra* $(\mathcal{M}, \bullet, I)$ *generates a* stabilised view monoid $(\mathcal{R}(\mathsf{View}_{\mathcal{M}}), *, I)$*, where*

$$\mathcal{R}(\mathsf{View}_{\mathcal{M}}) = \{p \in \mathcal{P}(\mathcal{M}) \mid \mathcal{R}(p) \subseteq p\}$$

The notation $\mathcal{R}(p)$ *means* $\{m \in \mathcal{M} \mid \exists m_p \in p.\, m_p\, \mathcal{R}\, m\}$*. The composition* $*$ *is as in Definition 15. That* $\mathcal{R}(\mathsf{View}_{\mathcal{M}})$ *is closed under* $*$ *and includes* I *follows from the conditions in Parameter K.*

Remark. Unlike in CAP [9] and DG [13], we do not need to provide a guarantee relation to say what a thread can do. That is dealt with by axiom soundness.

In this setting, Property G has an equivalent formulation that is typically simpler to check.

Property L (Axiom Soundness III). *For every* $(p, \alpha, q) \in \mathsf{Axiom}$*, and every* $m \in \mathcal{M}$ *then* $[\![\alpha]\!](\lfloor p * \{m\} \rfloor) \subseteq \lfloor q * \mathcal{R}(\{m\}) \rfloor$.

Separation Logic with Ownership

We illustrate how interference can be used to construct views, by showing how separation logic can be constructed this way. Rather than using the separation algebra introduced in Section 3.1, we construct a view monoid for disjoint concurrent separation logic by instrumenting machine states (excluding $\lightning$) with an ownership mask, which provides explicit permissions for stating which variables and addresses are "owned".

Definition 21 (MSL Separation Algebra) **: Parameter H.** *The masked-separation-logic separation algebra is* $(\mathcal{M}_{\mathsf{MSL}}, \bullet_{\mathsf{MSL}}, I_{\mathsf{MSL}})$*, where*

$$\mathcal{M}_{\mathsf{MSL}} \stackrel{\text{def}}{=} (\mathsf{Var} \uplus \mathsf{Loc}) \rightharpoonup_{\text{fin}} (\mathsf{Val} \times \{0, 1\}),$$

$$\begin{aligned} m_1 \bullet m_2 = m \stackrel{\text{def}}{\iff}\ & \\ & \mathrm{dom}\,(m_1) = \mathrm{dom}\,(m_2) = \mathrm{dom}\,(m) \\ & \wedge \forall k \in \mathrm{dom}\,(m) \,.\, m_1(k){\downarrow_1} = m_2(k){\downarrow_1} = m(k){\downarrow_1} \\ & \qquad \wedge m_1(k){\downarrow_2} + m_2(k){\downarrow_2} = m(k){\downarrow_2} \end{aligned}$$

$$\text{and } I \stackrel{\text{def}}{=} \{m \in \mathcal{M}_{\mathsf{MSL}} \mid \forall k \in \mathrm{dom}\,(m) \,.\, m(k){\downarrow_2} = 0\}.$$

where $\downarrow_i$ *accesses the i-th component of a tuple.*

For each variable (or address), the first component of the partial function represents its value, and the second component indicates whether or not the variable (or location) is owned. If a variable, or location, is undefined then it is not allocated. Composition requires that the state components are the same as that of the composite, and that their ownership masks sum to give the mask of the composite. This ensures that each variable and location is uniquely owned. This composition is well-defined, associative and commutative.

If we constructed a view model based on this separation algebra, the commands we could reason about would be very limited: they could not alter the (machine) state. This is because programs are required to preserve all frames, and therefore all values. However, the intention is that only variables and locations that are owned are preserved by other threads. Thus, instead of preserving all frames, we wish only to preserve all *stable* frames for a suitable notion of stability. This can be obtained by defining an interference relation:

Definition 22 (MSL Interference Relation) **: Parameter K.**

$$m \, \mathcal{R} \, m' \overset{\text{def}}{\iff} \forall k \in \mathrm{dom}\,(m) \,.\, m(k){\downarrow_2} > 0 \implies m'(k) = m(k)$$

This relation expresses that the environment can do anything that does not alter the variables and locations owned by the thread. It is not difficult to see that the interference relation satisfies the decomposition property: any change that does not alter the variables or locations owned by either thread does not alter the variables or locations owned by each thread individually.

If we consider the view monoid induced by the separation algebra under this interference relation, $\mathcal{R}(\mathsf{View}_{\mathsf{MSL}})$, we obtain a notion of view that is specific about variables and locations that are owned, but can say nothing at all about variables and locations that are not owned. Thus, threads are at liberty to mutate variables and heap locations they own, and allocate locations that are not owned by other threads, since these operations preserve stable frames. (Note that composition plays an important role here: it enforces that the environment cannot also own variables and locations that belong to the thread.)

We define an operation $\iota : R(\mathsf{View}_{\mathsf{MSL}}) \to \mathsf{View}_{\mathsf{DCSL}}$ by:

$$\iota(p) \overset{\text{def}}{=} \left\{ m \in \mathcal{M}_{\mathsf{DCSL}} \;\middle|\; \begin{array}{l} \exists m' \in p.\, \forall k, v. \\ \quad m(k) = v \iff m'(k) = (v, 1) \end{array} \right\}$$

This operation in fact defines an isomorphism between the two view monoids, so we can really think of the separation logic model as being constructed in this way.

This construction of separation logic parallels the approach of implicit dynamic frames [28]. There, assertions about the state and about ownership are decoupled. Assertions are required to be *self framing*, a property which corresponds directly to stability.

Separation logic with fractional permissions [4] can be defined by using fractions from the interval $[0, 1]$ instead of a bit mask. In §7.5, we discuss how the more complex permissions model of CAP can also be expressed using separation algebras with interference.

4. Generalised Frame Rule

When reasoning uses a context, it is common to have weakening rules on that context, such as the weakening rule of the type system in §2.2. In the views representation, weakening rules become rules that perform the same manipulation on the pre- and postcondition of the specification. In the simple type system, the weakening rule corresponded to the frame rule. However, for certain examples the frame rule is not powerful enough to represent the required context manipulation directly. We therefore introduce a generalised version of the frame rule.

Rely-Guarantee

We motivate the need for generalized frame rules by considering the rely-guarantee method [20]. Rely-guarantee judgements take the form $R, G \vdash \{P\}\; C\; \{Q\}$. Here, P and Q are assertions (interpreted as sets of states). R and G are relations on states — *rely* and *guarantee* relations — that describe how the environment and the program C respectively are allowed to update the state. The assertions P and Q are required to be stable under R.

The atomic step rule takes the following form:

$$\frac{[\![a]\!]{\restriction_P} \subseteq G \quad [\![a]\!](P) \subseteq Q}{R, G \vdash \{P\}\; a\; \{Q\}} \tag{2}$$

where $A{\restriction_P} \overset{\text{def}}{=} \{(s, s') \in A \mid s \in P\}$. The first condition ensures that G describes the possible behaviours of the program.

The rely-guarantee method is epitomised by the following rule for parallel composition:

$$\frac{\begin{array}{ll} G_1 \subseteq R_2 & R_1, G_1 \vdash \{P_1\}\; C_1\; \{Q_1\} \\ G_2 \subseteq R_1 & R_2, G_2 \vdash \{P_2\}\; C_2\; \{Q_2\} \end{array}}{R_1 \cap R_2, G_1 \cup G_2 \vdash \{P_1 \cap P_2\}\; C_1 \| C_2\; \{Q_1 \cap Q_2\}}$$

This rule requires that the behaviours of each thread, abstracted by G_1 and G_2, are contained in the interference expected by the other thread, represented by R_2 and R_1. The context of the composition relies on the environment doing no more than both threads expect, while the guarantee must account for the behaviours of each thread.

The above rules suggest encoding rely-guarantee into the Views Framework with views consisting of triples (P, R, G) of assertions and rely and guarantee relations, where P is stable under R. Composition would then follow the parallel rule, resulting in the special inconsistent view $\bot$ when the relies and guarantees do not meet the side-conditions.

Definition 23 (RG View Monoid) **: Parameter D.** *The set* View_{RG} *of rely-guarantee views is defined as:*

$$\{(P, R, G) \in \mathcal{P}(\mathcal{S}) \times \mathcal{P}(\mathcal{S}^2) \times \mathcal{P}(\mathcal{S}^2) \mid R(P) \subseteq P\} \uplus \{\bot\}.$$

Composition is defined as:

$$(P_1, R_1, G_1) * (P_2, R_2, G_2) = (P_1 \cap P_2, R_1 \cap R_2, G_1 \cup G_2) \quad \text{provided } G_1 \subseteq R_2 \text{ and } G_2 \subseteq R_1;$$

with all other cases resulting in $\bot$. *The unit is* $(\mathcal{S}, \mathcal{S}^2, \emptyset)$.

We encode the rules by placing the rely and guarantee both into the pre- and postcondition.

$$R, G \vdash \{P\}\; C\; \{Q\} \overset{\text{def}}{\iff} \vdash \{(P, R, G)\}\; C\; \{(Q, R, G)\}.$$

For all rely-guarantee judgements we assume the pre- and postcondition are stable with respect to the rely, and thus (P, R, G) and (Q, R, G) are both valid views. Using this encoding, the structural rules (including parallel) follow trivially from the rules of the Views program logic, and the atomic rule (2) can be considered to define a set of atomic axioms (Parameter E).

Views are reified to the set of states satisfying their assertions.

Definition 24 (RG Reification) **: Parameter F.**

$$\lfloor (P, R, G) \rfloor = P \qquad \lfloor \bot \rfloor = \emptyset.$$

Lemma 1 (RG Axiom Soundness) **: Property G.** *If* $[\![a]\!]{\restriction_P} \subseteq G$ *and* $[\![a]\!](P) \subseteq Q$ *then* $a \Vdash \{(P, R, G)\}\{(Q, R, G)\}$.

Proof. We must show that, for every $(P_1, R_1, G_1) \in \mathsf{View}_{RG}$,

$$[\![a]\!]\lfloor (P, R, G) * (P_1, R_1, G_1) \rfloor \subseteq \lfloor (Q, R, G) * (P_1, R_1, G_1) \rfloor.$$

We can assume composition is defined as the undefined case is trivial, and as reification ignores the rely-guarantee components, we can simplify this to:

$$(G \subseteq R_1 \;\wedge\; G_1 \subseteq R \;\wedge\; R(P) \subseteq P \;\wedge\; R_1(P_1) \subseteq P_1) \implies [\![a]\!](P \cap P_1) \subseteq Q \cap P_1.$$

Showing that the result is in Q follows directly from the second premise, and that it is in P_1 from the first premise using routine relational reasoning. □

While we have established the soundness of most of the rules, we have not yet considered rely-guarantee's weakening rule:

$$\frac{R_1 \subseteq R_2 \quad G_2 \subseteq G_1 \quad R_2, G_2 \vdash \{P\}\, C\, \{Q\}}{R_1, G_1 \vdash \{P\}\, C\, \{Q\}}$$

This rule simply increases the restrictions on the environment: it may do less ($R_1 \subseteq R_2$) but must tolerate more ($G_2 \subseteq G_1$).

If we try to encode the context weakening rule using the frame rule induced by the composition above, we require:

$$R_1 \subseteq R_2 \wedge G_2 \subseteq G_1 \overset{?}{\Longrightarrow} \exists R_3, G_3.\ (P, R_1, G_1) = (P, R_2, G_2) * (P, R_3, G_3).$$

However, this does not hold when $R_2 \not\subseteq G_1$. We could use a more elaborate structure to represent the pair of relations such as the deny-guarantee structure [13], which can then be encoded into our framework. However, this loses the original elegance of rely-guarantee, and does not capture the intuition behind it. Instead, we provide a new generalisation of the frame rule that can capture this reasoning directly.

We introduce a generalised frame rule, which applies a function to the pre- and postconditions of a specification. The rule is parameterised by a function $f : \mathsf{View} \to \mathsf{View}$:

$$\frac{\vdash \{p\}\, C\, \{q\}}{\vdash \{f(p)\}\, C\, \{f(q)\}}$$

By choosing particular functions, f, we can encode a range of reasoning rules, in particular the standard frame rule: for the frame r, pick the function

$$f_{*r} \overset{\text{def}}{=} \lambda p.\, p * r.$$

Now, for the rule to be sound we must prove the following property for the f function and the action judgement used in axiom soundness.

Property M (f-step Preservation).

$$\forall \alpha, p, q.\quad \alpha \Vdash \{p\}\{q\} \implies \alpha \Vdash \{f(p)\}\{f(q)\}.$$

This property is sufficient for the soundness of the generalised frame rule. The proof of soundness is essentially the same as for the frame rule, and has been checked in Coq [11].

Remark. The generalised frame rule is analogous to the frame rule of context logic [5], where contexts are applied by a non-commutative operation to the pre- and postconditions. One could construct a context algebra by taking views as the data and the functions satisfying Property M as the contexts, and thus see the generalised frame rule as an instance of the context logic rule. Conversely, one could view the application of a context as a function satisfying Property M, and hence see the context logic frame rule as an instance of the generalised frame rule.

Rely-Guarantee: Weakening

Returning to our motivating example, we can now show how to encode rely-guarantee weakening rule using the generalised frame rule. The weakening rule can be restated in an equivalent form as:

$$\frac{R, G \vdash \{P\}\, C\, \{Q\}}{R \cap R', G \cup G' \vdash \{P\}\, C\, \{Q\}}$$

Thus we justify this instance of the rule using the generalised frame rule choosing f to be the function that restricts the rely by R', and extends the guarantee by G':

$$f_{(R',G')} \overset{\text{def}}{=} \lambda_\perp(P, R, G).\, (P, R \cap R', G \cup G')$$

where $(\lambda_\perp x.\, f(x))\, v$ is $f(v)$ if v is not $\perp$, and is $\perp$ otherwise. Thus we are required to show the following.

Lemma 2 ($f_{(R',G')}$-step Preservation) **: Property M.**

$$\alpha \Vdash \{(P_1, R_1, G_1)\}\{(P_2, R_2, G_2)\} \implies$$
$$\alpha \Vdash \{(P_1, R_1 \cap R', G_1 \cup G')\}\{(P_2, R_2 \cap R', G_2 \cup G')\}.$$

This holds because the changes to the rely and guarantee only serve to further restrict the set of environment views that we must consider in the action judgement, and the assumption ensures $R_1 \subseteq R_2$ and $G_1 \supseteq G_2$.

5. Combination Rule

The views proof system we have presented so far has omitted two common rules: disjunction and conjunction. One key reason for this is that such rules are not applicable to every instantiation of the framework. For example, the simple type system of §2.2 does not naturally support a disjunction or conjunction rule.

Both of these rules may be expressed as special cases of a general rule for combining multiple specifications of a single program. This general rule is parameterised by a notion of view combination (such as disjunction or conjunction), which maps indexed families of views into single views. By choosing the index set, I, we can define combination operations at different cardinalities.

Parameter N (View I-Combination). *Assume a function* $\bigoplus_I : (I \to \mathsf{View}) \to \mathsf{View}$.

The combination rule is as follows:

$$\frac{\forall i \in I. \vdash \{p_i\}\, C\, \{q_i\}}{\vdash \{\bigoplus_{i \in I} p_i\}\, C\, \{\bigoplus_{i \in I} q_i\}}$$

This rule is justified sound by the following property:

Property O (Primitive Combination). *For all* $\alpha \in \mathsf{Label}$,

$$(\forall i \in I.\, \alpha \Vdash \{p_i\}\{q_i\}) \implies \alpha \Vdash \{\textstyle\bigoplus_{i \in I} p_i\}\{\textstyle\bigoplus_{i \in I} q_i\}.$$

Remark. This combination rule generalises the *generalised frame rule* from the previous section, which is simply a unary instance of the combination rule.

Disjunction. In the case of disjunction, there is often a natural operator $\bigvee$ that has the following properties:

Property P (Join Distributivity). $p * \bigvee_{i \in I} q_i = \bigvee_{i \in I} (p * q_i)$.

Property Q (Join Morphism). $\lfloor \bigvee_{i \in I} p_i \rfloor = \bigcup_{i \in I} \lfloor p_i \rfloor$.

Together, these two properties imply Property O.

Separation Algebras

When views are constructed from a separation algebra, as in §3.1, the views themselves are sets, and so it is natural to consider set union ($\bigcup$) as a notion of disjunction. By the definition of a separation view monoid (Definition 15), it follows that $\bigcup$ satisfies the join distributivity property (Property P). The join morphism property (Property Q) likewise follows directly from the element-wise definition of reification (Definition 18). Consequently, the obvious rule of disjunction is sound for logics built from separation algebras in this way, such as separation logic.

For a stabilised view monoid (Definition 20), note that the interference relation preserves unions (since it is applied element-wise). From this, it follows that $\bigcup$ again satisfies the required properties to provide a rule of disjunction.

Conjunction. It is possible to give properties analogous to Properties P and Q, relating a conjunction $\bigwedge$ with $\bigcap$. Such properties are sufficient to establish Property O, however, it is not often that an instantiation of Views is equipped with a $\bigwedge$ operator with these properties. For instance, in separation logic, $*$ does not distribute over conjunction. In cases, such as separation logic, where a conjunction rule is sound, Property O can typically used to directly justify it.

It is less common for instantiations to have a conjunction rule than a disjunction rule. One explanation for this is that views typically add instrumentation that is not present in the concrete state (such as type information). This information can evolve independently of the concrete state, leading to different specifications for the same program that make incompatible changes to the instrumentation, which cannot be combined with a conjunction rule.

Disjoint Concurrent Separation Logic

For disjoint concurrent separation logic, consider the binary conjunction operation given by set intersection, $\cap$. We can prove that this gives a sound rule of conjunction by establishing Property O, using two useful facts. Firstly, for views constructed from separation algebras, the action judgement need only account for singleton environment views:

$$\alpha \Vdash \{p\}\{q\} \iff \forall m.\, [\![\alpha]\!] (\lfloor p * \{m\} \rfloor) \subseteq \lfloor q * \{m\} \rfloor.$$

(This fact justifies the sufficiency of axiom soundness II (Property J).) Secondly, singleton views are precise:

$$(p_1 \cap p_2) * \{m\} = (p_1 * \{m\}) \cap (p_2 * \{m\}).$$

(Note that this is not a general property of separation algebras, but can be established for separation logic.)

Suppose that $\alpha \Vdash \{p_1\}\{q_1\}$ and $\alpha \Vdash \{p_2\}\{q_2\}$. Using the above facts, and Definition I, we can establish that

$$\begin{aligned} &[\![\alpha]\!] (\lfloor (p_1 \cap p_2) * \{m\} \rfloor) \\ &\quad \subseteq [\![\alpha]\!] (\lfloor p_1 * \{m\} \rfloor) \cap [\![\alpha]\!] (\lfloor p_2 * \{m\} \rfloor) \\ &\quad \subseteq \lfloor (q_1 * \{m\}) \rfloor \cap \lfloor (q_2 * \{m\}) \rfloor \\ &\quad = \lfloor (q_1 \cap q_2) * \{m\} \rfloor. \end{aligned}$$

This is sufficient for Property O to hold for binary intersection.

This argument extends to infinitary intersection. Notably, however, it does not apply to the nullary case, which would give $\vdash \{\top\}\, C\, \{\top\}$ for every program C (where $\top = \mathcal{M}_{\text{DCSL}}$). This would be unsound, since $\lightning \notin \lfloor \top \rfloor$, yet there are programs which may fault when run from an arbitrary initial state.

6. Soundness

In this section, we sketch the soundness of the framework. The following results have been machine checked with Coq, and the proof scripts are available [11].

There are two key properties of the action judgement. The first is that it is closed under the composition of a view, and the second that it is closed under the semantic entailment order (Definition 12).

Lemma 3 (Basic Locality)**.** *For all $p, q, r \in \mathsf{View}$, $\alpha \in \mathsf{Label}$, if $\alpha \Vdash \{p\}\{q\}$ then $\alpha \Vdash \{p * r\}\{q * r\}$.*

Lemma 4 (Basic $\preceq$-closure)**.** *For all $p, p', q, q' \in \mathsf{View}$, $\alpha \in \mathsf{Label}$, if $p \preceq p'$, $\alpha \Vdash \{p'\}\{q'\}$ and $q' \preceq q$ then $\alpha \Vdash \{p\}\{q\}$.*

To prove the soundness, we use a semantic judgment that ensures every step of the machine correctly preserves the context using the action judgment. The semantic judgement is defined coinductively: it is a greatest fixed point.

Definition 25 (Semantic Judgement)**.** *For command $C \in \mathsf{Comm}$ and views $p, q \in \mathsf{View}$, the semantic judgement $\Vdash \{p\}\, C\, \{q\}$ is defined to be the maximal relation such that $\Vdash \{p\}\, C\, \{q\}$ holds if and only if the following two conditions are satisfied:*

1. *for all $\alpha \in \mathsf{Label}$, $C' \in \mathsf{Comm}$, if $C \xrightarrow{\alpha} C'$, then there exists $p' \in \mathsf{View}$ such that $\alpha \Vdash \{p\}\{p'\}$ and $\Vdash \{p'\}\, C'\, \{q\}$;*
2. *if $C = \mathtt{skip}$ then $p \preceq q$.*

We can understand the semantic judgment, $\Vdash \{p\}\, C\, \{q\}$, as creating a trace of views for each possible interleaving of the commands in C, where each trace starts in p, and if it is a finite trace, then it ends in q. That is, if $\alpha_1\alpha_2 \dots \alpha_n$ is a finite trace of C, then there exists a sequence $p_1 \dots p_{n+1}$, such that $p = p_1$, $p_{n+1} \preceq q$ and $\alpha_i \Vdash \{p_i\}\{p_{i+1}\}$. If $\alpha_1\alpha_2 \dots$ is an infinite trace of C, then there exists a sequence $p_1 p_2 \dots$, such that $p = p_1$ and $\alpha_i \Vdash \{p_i\}\{p_{i+1}\}$.

For each of the proof rules there is a corresponding lemma establishing that it holds for the semantic judgement. We present two particularly interesting ones here.

Lemma 5 (Soundness of Frame)**.** *If $\Vdash \{p\}\, C\, \{q\}$ then*

$$\Vdash \{p * r\}\, C\, \{q * r\}.$$

Proof. By coinduction. The case $C = \mathtt{skip}$ is trivial. Assume that $\Vdash \{p\}\, C\, \{q\}$ and $C \xrightarrow{\alpha} C'$. By these assumptions, there exists p' such that $\alpha \Vdash \{p\}\{p'\}$ and $\Vdash \{p'\}\, C'\, \{q\}$. It suffices to show that $\alpha \Vdash \{p * r\}\{p' * r\}$ and $\Vdash \{p' * r\}\, C'\, \{q * r\}$. The first follows from Lemma 3 and the second from the coinductive hypothesis. □

Remark. The soundness of the generalised frame rule and the combination rule are proved by a similar argument to the frame rule. For the combination rule, we require the axiom of choice for the indexing set; this allows us to select a "next" view (p' in the above proof) for each index.

Lemma 6 (Soundness of Parallel)**.** *If $\Vdash \{p_1\}\, C_1\, \{q_1\}$ and $\Vdash \{p_2\}\, C_2\, \{q_2\}$ then $\Vdash \{p_1 * p_2\}\, C_1 \parallel C_2\, \{q_1 * q_2\}$.*

Proof. By coinduction. Assume that $C_1 \parallel C_2 \xrightarrow{\alpha} C'$. Either one thread takes a step or one thread has finished executing.

If the latter, $C' = C_i$, $C_j = \mathtt{skip}$ and $\alpha = \mathsf{id}$, where $\{i, j\} = \{1, 2\}$. It must be that $p_j \preceq q_j$, so $\mathsf{id} \Vdash \{p_i * p_j\}\{p_i * q_j\}$ by definition of $\preceq$. Furthermore, $\Vdash \{p_i * q_j\}\, C_i\, \{q_i * q_j\}$ follows from Lemmas 5.

If the former, assume that $C' = C_1' \parallel C_2$ and $C_1 \xrightarrow{\alpha} C_1'$. (The case where C_2 reduces is similar.) By assumption, there exists p_1' such that $\alpha \Vdash \{p_1\}\{p_1'\}$ and $\Vdash \{p_1'\}\, C_1\, \{q_1\}$. It suffices to show that $\alpha \Vdash \{p_1 * p_2\}\{p_1' * p_2\}$ and $\Vdash \{p_1' * p_2\}\, C_1' \parallel C_2\, \{q_1 * q_2\}$. The first follows from Lemma 3 and the second from the coinductive hypothesis. □

By similar lemmas for the other proof rules, we establish that the proof judgement of the logic implies the semantic judgement.

Lemma 7. *If $\vdash \{p\}\, C\, \{q\}$ is derivable in the program logic, then $\Vdash \{p\}\, C\, \{q\}$.*

To establish soundness, we link the semantic judgement to the multi-step operational semantics.

Lemma 8. *If $\Vdash \{p\}\, C\, \{q\}$, then for all $s \in \lfloor p \rfloor$ and $s' \in \mathcal{S}$, if $(C, s) \to^* (\mathtt{skip}, s')$ then $s' \in \lfloor q \rfloor$.*

This lemma follows from the definitions. Soundness now follows immediately from the preceding two lemmas.

Theorem (Soundness)**.** *Assume that $\vdash \{p\}\, C\, \{q\}$ is derivable in the program logic. Then, for all $s \in \lfloor p \rfloor$ and $s' \in \mathcal{S}$, if $(C, s) \to^* (\mathtt{skip}, s')$ then $s' \in \lfloor q \rfloor$.*

7. Further Examples

We provide five additional instantiations to illustrate the flexibility of our metatheory: recursive types, unique types, Owicki-Gries method, separation logic with resource invariants, and Concurrent Abstract Predicates. The recursive types example demonstrates that Views captures more realistic types. It also illustrates how the rule of consequence can be used for subtyping. The connection between strong update type systems and separation logic has been an open problem for around ten years; the unique types example makes tentative steps towards connecting them using the Views Framework. The Owicki-Gries example illustrates that even underlying traditionally non-compositional reasoning is a compositional core. The penultimate example shows how resource invariants can be added to the views formulation of separation logic by using the generalised frame rule. The final example, CAP, illustrates that the metatheory scales to recent complex logics.

7.1 Recursive Types

In this example, we give a type system for references to pairs and recursive types, which allows us to represent simple lists and trees. The syntax of types is

$$\tau \ ::= \ \mathsf{val} \ \big| \ \mathsf{null} \ \big| \ \mathsf{ref}\ \tau\ \tau \ \big| \ \tau? \ \big| \ \mu X.\tau \ \big| \ X$$

The type null represents the type inhabited just by the value 0. The reference type, ref τ_1 τ_2, is a pointer to a pair of locations with types τ_1 and τ_2 respectively. The nullable type $\tau?$ allows null, as well as values of type τ. Note that ref cannot be a null pointer Finally, the fixed-point operator and type variables make it possible to represent recursive data types. For example, we can define lists as:

$$\mathsf{list}\ \tau \overset{\text{def}}{=} \mu X.\,(\mathsf{ref}\ \tau\ \mathsf{X})?$$

As with the simple type system, views consist of type contexts and the inconsistent context. Unlike in that example, however, we compose typing contexts with disjoint union. This allows us to consider variables as uniquely owned by threads, rather than shared, and consequently reason about strong (type-changing) updates of variables.

Definition 26 (Recursive Type View Monoid) **: Parameter D.** *The view monoid for recursive types is* $((\mathsf{Var} \rightharpoonup \mathsf{Type})_\bot, \uplus_\bot, \emptyset)$.

We extend the heap-update language introduced in §2.1 to work with pairs instead of single heap cells. We assume that values are integers, and locations are positive integers. $x := \mathsf{ref}\ y\ z$ allocates a pair of consecutive locations in the heap, initialising them with values y and z. The first and second components of a pair x may be accessed independently by $x.\mathsf{fst}$ and $x.\mathsf{snd}$. To encode case splitting on a pointer being null we use two commands: $?x{=}0$, which blocks if x is not null, and performs the identity action otherwise; and $?x{\neq}0$ which blocks if x is null, and performs the identity action otherwise. These allow us to encode choice as

$$\mathsf{ifNull}\ x\ \mathsf{then}\ C_1\ \mathsf{else}\ C_2 \overset{\text{def}}{=} (?x{=}0; C_1) + (?x{\neq}0; C_2)$$

Since we wish to allow type-changing updates, commands are specified with both a pre- and a post-type context: $\Gamma_1 \vdash C \dashv \Gamma_2$. In the Views Framework, we naturally interpret this as syntax for $\vdash \{\Gamma_1\}\ C\ \{\Gamma_2\}$.

In order to introduce nullable types, and to fold and unfold recursive types, we introduce a notion of subtyping. The subtyping relation, $\prec$, is defined as the least pre-order satisfying:

$$\begin{array}{cc} \tau \prec \tau? & \mathsf{null} \prec \tau? \\ \mu X.\tau \prec \tau[\mu X.\tau/X] & \tau[\mu X.\tau/X] \prec \mu X.\tau \end{array}$$

Definition 27 (Context Subtyping)**.** *Subtyping is lifted to contexts in the obvious way:*

$$\Gamma_1 \prec \Gamma_2 \overset{\text{def}}{\iff} \forall x : \tau_2 \in \Gamma_2 . \exists x : \tau_1 \in \Gamma_1 . \tau_1 \prec \tau_2.$$

Definition 28 (Recursive Type Axiomatisation) **: Parameter E.** *The typing rules for atomic commands include the following:*

$$\frac{}{x : \tau? \vdash ?x{=}0 \dashv x : \mathsf{null}} \qquad \frac{}{x : \tau? \vdash ?x{\neq}0 \dashv x : \tau}$$

$$\frac{}{x : \mathsf{ref}\ \tau_1\ \tau_2, y : \tau_1 \vdash x.\mathsf{fst} := y \dashv x : \mathsf{ref}\ \tau_1\ \tau_2, y : \tau_1}$$

$$\frac{}{x : \mathsf{ref}\ \tau_1\ \tau_2, y : \_ \vdash y := x.\mathsf{fst} \dashv x : \mathsf{ref}\ \tau_1\ \tau_2, y : \tau_1}$$

$$\frac{}{x : \_, y : \tau_1, z : \tau_2 \vdash x := \mathsf{ref}\ y\ z \dashv x : \mathsf{ref}\ \tau_1\ \tau_2, y : \tau_1, z : \tau_2}$$

Typing rules for the snd *component are analogous to those for* fst. *We give the axioms for entailment as*

$$\Gamma_1 \vDash \Gamma_2 \overset{\text{def}}{\iff} \Gamma_1 \prec \Gamma_2$$

The challenging aspect of this instantiation is giving the reification, which requires us to define a notion of being well-typed. We define a relation $\Theta \vdash v : \tau$ that expresses that a value v has type τ in a heap typing Θ, that maps locations to types. Note that values range over integers.

$$\frac{}{\Theta \vdash v : \mathsf{val}} \qquad \frac{}{\Theta \vdash 0 : \tau?} \qquad \frac{}{\Theta \vdash 0 : \mathsf{null}}$$

$$\frac{\Theta \vdash v : \tau[\mu X.\tau/X]}{\Theta \vdash v : \mu X.\tau} \qquad \frac{\Theta \vdash v : \tau}{\Theta \vdash v : \tau?} \qquad \frac{}{\Theta \vdash v : \mathsf{ref}\ \Theta(v)\ \Theta(v+1)}$$

We can then define reification as the set of states that are well typed with respect to a view. That is, those states for which there is a heap typing such that the value of each variable and heap location is correctly typed by the view and the heap typing.

Definition 29 (Recursive Type Reification) **: Parameter F.**

$$s \in \lfloor \Gamma \rfloor_\mu \overset{\text{def}}{\iff} \exists \Theta . \forall x \in \mathrm{dom}(\Gamma \cup \Theta). \Theta \vdash s(x) : (\Gamma \cup \Theta)(x)$$

To show the type system is sound we simply show axiom soundness (Property G) for the axioms and subtyping relation.

7.2 Unique Types

The previous example used an atomic allocate and instantiate instruction, $x := \mathsf{ref}\, y\, z$. But this is not realistic as this would be done in many operations. In this example we extend the types from the previous section to allow us to separate allocation from instantiation. We give a new high-level syntax to types, that allows us to represent a unique reference at the top-level:

$$t \ ::= \ \tau \mid \mathsf{uref}\ \tau\ \tau$$

We change Γ to map to these extended types.

We can then give rules for the atomic commands to allocate and update a unique reference

$$\frac{}{x : \_ \vdash x := \mathsf{ref} \dashv x : \mathsf{uref\ val\ val}}$$

$$\frac{}{x : \mathsf{uref}\ \_\ \tau_2, y : \tau_1 \vdash x.\mathsf{fst} := y \dashv x : \mathsf{uref}\ \tau_1\ \tau_2, y : \tau_1}$$

These rules allow us to alter the type of something in the heap. This is sound as we are currently the only thread to have access to the location.

We use the subtyping relation to cast away the uniqueness by adding the following to the subtype relation:

$$\mathsf{uref}\ \tau_1\ \tau_2 \prec \mathsf{ref}\ \tau_1\ \tau_2$$

We define a function that forgets the uniqueness information, so that we can reuse the previous definitions:

$$\llbracket\Gamma\rrbracket \stackrel{\text{def}}{=} \lambda x.\,\text{if } \Gamma\,x = \mathsf{uref}\,\tau_1\,\tau_2 \text{ then } \mathsf{ref}\,\tau_1\,\tau_2 \text{ else } \Gamma\,x$$

Our notion of a memory satisfying a type context is the same as before with an additional constraint that each unique reference can be removed from the memory and the memory is well-typed without it in the smaller context.

$$s \in \lfloor\Gamma\rfloor_{u\mu} \stackrel{\text{def}}{=} s \in \lfloor\llbracket\Gamma\rrbracket\rfloor_{\mu} \wedge \\ \forall x : \mathsf{uref}\,\_\,\_ \in \Gamma.\, s\lfloor_{s(x),s(x+1)} \in \lfloor\llbracket\Gamma\lfloor_x\rrbracket\rfloor_{\mu}$$

where $f\lfloor_x \stackrel{\text{def}}{=} \lambda y.\,\text{if } x{\neq}y \text{ then } f\,y \text{ else } \bot$. Note this does not mean that the location of a unique reference cannot occur in another stack or heap location, but it cannot occur as something potentially considered as a reference. Technically,

$$x : \mathsf{uref}\,\tau_1\,\tau_2, y : \_ \vdash y := x \dashv x : \mathsf{uref}\,\tau_1\,\tau_2, y : \mathsf{val}$$

is a sound axiom in this model. We require this kind of property of our model as we only distinguish between integers and references at the type level. The concrete model does not separate them. Thus, it is possible for the allocator to use a location for which the integer is currently in use, but this does not matter. If it is being treated as a location, then it would already be allocated and thus the allocator would not double allocate it.

The axioms and subtyping satisfy the required properties (Property G).

7.3 Owicki-Gries Method

We present a version of the Owicki-Gries method [24] that can be encoded trivially into the Views Framework. However, we omit the auxiliary variable rule, and leave this to future work.

Normally, the Owicki-Gries method has a non-compositional check on parallel composition: each command used by one thread, when restricted to its precondition, preserves all the assertions used in the proof of other thread. We explicitly account for the assertions used in a proof, and the commands and preconditions as contexts to our judgements. Specifically,

$$\mathbb{P}, \mathbb{A} \vdash \{P\}\, C\, \{Q\}$$

means that executing C in a state satisfying P, if it terminates, then the state will satisfy Q, and the proof only uses assertions in $\mathbb{P}$,[1] and its atomic commands are described by $\mathbb{A}$. Thus the rule for an atomic command is

$$\frac{P \in \mathbb{P} \quad Q \in \mathbb{P} \quad (P, a) \in \mathbb{A} \quad \llbracket a\rrbracket(P) \subseteq Q}{\mathbb{P}, \mathbb{A} \vdash \{P\}\, a\, \{Q\}} \tag{3}$$

The parallel rule is

$$\frac{\begin{array}{ll}\mathbb{P}_1, \mathbb{A}_1 \vdash \{P_1\}\, C_1\, \{Q_1\} & \forall P \in \mathbb{P}_2, (P', a) \in \mathbb{A}_1.\, \llbracket a\rrbracket(P{\wedge}P') \subseteq P \\ \mathbb{P}_2, \mathbb{A}_2 \vdash \{P_2\}\, C_2\, \{Q_2\} & \forall P \in \mathbb{P}_1, (P', a) \in \mathbb{A}_2.\, \llbracket a\rrbracket(P{\wedge}P') \subseteq P\end{array}}{\mathbb{P}_1 \cup \mathbb{P}_2, \mathbb{A}_1 \cup \mathbb{A}_2 \vdash \{P_1{\wedge}P_2\}\, C_1 \| C_2\, \{Q_1{\wedge}Q_2\}}$$

The two side-conditions (right premises) are the standard "non-compositional" interference freedom checks. Again, as with rely-guarantee, this parallel rule induces a composition operation that we can use to build a view model.

[1] The precise definition actually requires that the proof only uses assertions that are intersections of some elements of $\mathbb{P}$. Otherwise, we would require the parallel rule to additionally require its pre- and postconditions to be in $\mathbb{P}$. This requirement is only evident in the soundness proof, and does not alter the reasoning provided by the Owicki Gries method that we present.

Definition 30 (Owicki-Gries View Monoid) **: Parameter D.** *The Owicki-Gries view monoid* $(\mathsf{View}_{OG}, *, (\emptyset, \emptyset, \mathcal{S}))$ *is defined by*

$$\mathsf{View}_{OG} \stackrel{\text{def}}{=} \left\{(\mathbb{P}, \mathbb{A}, P) \,\middle|\, \exists \mathbb{P}' \subseteq \mathbb{P}.\, P = \bigcap \mathbb{P}'\right\} \uplus \{\bot\}$$

with composition given by

$$(\mathbb{P}_1, \mathbb{A}_1, P_1) * (\mathbb{P}_2, \mathbb{A}_2, P_2) \stackrel{\text{def}}{=} (\mathbb{P}_1 \cup \mathbb{P}_2, \mathbb{A}_1 \cup \mathbb{A}_2, P_1 \cap P_2) \\ \textit{provided } \forall P \in \mathbb{P}_1, (P', a) \in \mathbb{A}_2.\, \llbracket a\rrbracket(P \wedge P') \subseteq P \\ \forall P \in \mathbb{P}_2, (P', a) \in \mathbb{A}_1.\, \llbracket a\rrbracket(P \wedge P') \subseteq P$$

and otherwise defined to be $\bot$.

The proof rules follow from the Views Framework using the obvious encoding. The atomic rule (3) determines the atomic axioms (Parameter E). We can provide a weakening rule, that allows the context to be enlarged, as a simple application of the generalised frame rule.

For soundness, we define reification (Parameter F) as simply taking the assertion component of a view (and $\emptyset$ in the case of $\bot$). Axiom soundness (Property G) follows from the premises of (3) by the consistency requirement of composition. Step preservation (Property M) for weakening follows trivially from axiom soundness, given that the atomic rule (3) is closed under enlarging the context.

7.4 Atomic CSL

We consider a concurrent separation logic with a single resource invariant that must be preserved by each atomic command [25]. This logic has a simple rule for atomic commands:

$$\frac{\vdash_{\mathsf{DCSL}} \{I * P\}\, a\, \{I * Q\}}{I \vdash \{P\}\, a\, \{Q\}}$$

If the atomic command meets the specification in standard separation logic (§3.1) with the invariant, I, added to both the pre- and postcondition, then it meets the specification in this logic. We interpret this in the Views Framework by defining views to be pairs of shared invariants and local assertions. Composition on these views requires invariants to agree.

Definition 31 (Atomic CSL View Semigroup) **: Parameter D.** *The atomic CSL view semigroup is*

$$((\mathsf{View}_{\mathsf{DCSL}} \times \mathsf{View}_{\mathsf{DCSL}}) \uplus \{\bot\}, *_{\mathsf{ACSL}})$$

where $(I_1, P_1) *_{\mathsf{ACSL}} (I_2, P_2)$ *is defined to be* $(I_1, P_1 *_{\mathsf{DCSL}} P_2)$ *if* $I_1 = I_2$*, and* $\bot$ *otherwise.*

We encode the judgement $I \vdash \{P\}\, C\, \{Q\}$ as

$$\vdash \{(I, P)\}\, C\, \{(I, Q)\}\,.$$

There are two rules for manipulating the context (the resource invariant). The first is a frame rule for the resource invariant, and the second allows local state to be added to the resource invariant:

$$\frac{I \vdash \{P\}\, C\, \{Q\}}{I * I' \vdash \{P\}\, C\, \{Q\}} \qquad \frac{I * I' \vdash \{P\}\, C\, \{Q\}}{I \vdash \{P * I'\}\, C\, \{Q * I'\}}$$

These rules can be interpreted as instances of the generalised frame rule. For the invariant frame rule, the following function is suitable:

$$f_h(I') \stackrel{\text{def}}{=} \lambda_\bot(I, P).\, (I * I', P).$$

For the local invariant rule, a more complicated function is necessary:

$$f_s(I, I') \stackrel{\text{def}}{=} \lambda_\bot(I_1, P).\, \text{if } I_1 = I * I' \text{ then } (I, P * I') \text{ else } \bot.$$

The function ensures that the resource invariant in the premise is $I * I'$, if not then the function maps to the inconsistent view, thus making the rule and the property vacuous.

For soundness, we define the reification to take the composition of the invariant and local-state assertion in the sense of DCSL.

Definition 32 (Atomic CSL Reification) **: Parameter F.**

$$\lfloor (I, P) \rfloor \stackrel{\text{def}}{=} I *_{\mathsf{DCSL}} P \qquad\qquad \lfloor \bot \rfloor \stackrel{\text{def}}{=} \emptyset$$

This is the only example we present in the paper that does not have a unit. However, the model does have a zero, $\bot$, and satisfies

$$\forall x.\, \exists u.\, x * u = x \wedge \forall y.\, y * u = y \vee y * u = \bot.$$

This property is sufficient to show the simplification of $\alpha \Vdash \{p\}\{q\}$ given in (1), provided $\lfloor \bot \rfloor = \emptyset$.

Axiom soundness (Property G) can easily be established given the soundness of DCSL. The context rules require us to prove Property M. For the first, we can appeal to the frame rule of DCSL, with the frame I'. For the second, the function $f_s(I, I')$ either renders the judgement trivial or preserves the reification, so Property M holds.

Remark. If we wish to establish the conjunction rule for this logic, we can do so if the resource invariant is precise[2], given that assume DCSL has a conjunction rule. We must show (for the binary case)

$$\alpha \Vdash \{(I, P_1)\}\{(I, Q_1)\} \wedge \alpha \Vdash \{(I, P_2)\}\{(I, Q_2)\} \implies \alpha \Vdash \{(I, P_1 \wedge P_2)\}\{(I, Q_1 \wedge Q_2)\}.$$

Using the DCSL rule of conjunction, we know

$$\alpha \Vdash_{\mathsf{DCSL}} \{(I * P_1) \wedge (I * P_2)\}\{(I * Q_1) \wedge (I * Q_2)\}.$$

Using the DCSL rule of consequence, we know

$$\alpha \Vdash_{\mathsf{DCSL}} \{I * (P_1 \wedge P_2)\}\{(I * Q_1) \wedge (I * Q_2)\}.$$

And, moreover, if I is precise, then this implies

$$\alpha \Vdash_{\mathsf{DCSL}} \{I * (P_1 \wedge P_2)\}\{I * (Q_1 \wedge Q_2)\}.$$

This establishes primitive combination (Property O), which is sufficient for the conjunction rule to be sound.

7.5 Concurrent Abstract Predicates

Concurrent Abstract Predicates (CAP) [9] extends separation logic with shared regions that can be mutated by multiple threads through atomic operations. Each shared region is associated with some interference environment which stipulates how it may be mutated, by defining a collection of actions. Threads can mutate the shared state only by performing actions for which they have a capability resource, which may be exclusive or non-exclusive. An example of a CAP assertion is the following:

$$\exists r.\, [\textsc{Lock}]^r_\pi * \boxed{(x \mapsto 0 * [\textsc{Unlock}]^r_1) \vee x \mapsto 1}^{\,r}_{I(r)} \qquad (4)$$

This assertion represents a shared mutex in the heap at address x. The boxed part of the assertion describes the shared region: either the mutex is available (x has value 0) or it is locked (x has value 1). If it is available, the exclusive capability $[\textsc{Unlock}]^r_1$ belongs to the region. The thread itself has a non-exclusive capability $[\textsc{Lock}]^r_\pi$, which will permit it to lock the mutex. The actions corresponding to the capabilities are defined by the interference environment $I(r)$:

$$I(r) \stackrel{\text{def}}{=} \left(\begin{array}{ll} \textsc{Lock} & : x \mapsto 0 * [\textsc{Unlock}]^r_1 \rightsquigarrow x \mapsto 1, \\ \textsc{Unlock} : & x \mapsto 1 \rightsquigarrow x \mapsto 0 * [\textsc{Unlock}]^r_1 \end{array} \right)$$

The interference environment stipulates that a thread holding a $\textsc{Lock}$ capability may (atomically) update x from 0 to 1 in the shared region, simultaneously removing the capability $[\textsc{Unlock}]^r_1$; a thread holding an $\textsc{Unlock}$ capability may update x from 1 to 0 while returning $[\textsc{Unlock}]^r_1$ to the shared region. By locking the mutex, a thread acquires the exclusive capability to unlock it. This guarantees that only one thread can have locked the mutex at a time, and only that thread can unlock it. Having locked the mutex (through an atomic compare-and-swap operation), a thread's view may be described by the following assertion:

$$\exists r.\, [\textsc{Unlock}]^r_1 * [\textsc{Lock}]^r_\pi * \boxed{x \mapsto 1}^{\,r}_{I(r)} \qquad (5)$$

Whereas in (4) the thread does not know whether the mutex is locked or not, in (5) it knows that it is locked. It can only make such an assertion because it holds the exclusive capability $[\textsc{Unlock}]^r_1$; without that, the assertion would not be stable. (In separation logic, capabilities are always directly associated with the information they pertain to, as in $l \mapsto 7$, whereas in CAP they can be separated.)

In the rest of this section, we informally describe the parameters for the Views Framework. We do not give their formal details, and direct the reader to Dinsdale-Young's thesis [8] and our technical report [11] for the full definition and explanation.

CAP assertions are modelled by sets of states instrumented with ownership, capabilities and region information. Each instrumented state consists of three components. The first is the thread-local state, which consists of capability resources as well as separation-logic-style heap resources. The second is a mapping that associates region identifiers with their states. The third is an interference environment that associates the action identifiers used in capabilities with their interpretations as actions. Instrumented states form a separation algebra (Parameter H): composition of instrumented states is defined as requiring equality between the second and third components, while combining the resources in the first component. For the formal definition, see [8, §8.3.1].

To use CAP, we must work with stable assertions — views — in order to account for possible interactions between threads. These stable assertions are defined by closure under an interference relation (Parameter K), which allows the environment to update regions in any way for which it can have a suitable capability. The interference relation is constructed as the transitive closure of three relations, which model region update (in accordance with actions the environment may have capability to perform), region construction and region destruction. See [8, p319, Definition 8.14] for the formal definition and [8, p337, Lemma 112] for the proof of the decomposition property.

Reification (Parameter I) for CAP is given by combining the heap components of the local and shared states, dropping the capabilities and interference environment. The atomic rule of CAP effectively establishes axiom soundness (Property L) by means of a guarantee relation that obliges atomic operations to preserve stable frames [8, p345, Lemma 125; p338, Lemma 114].

Remark. In our MSL example, interference was not essential. Since the interference relations were equivalences, views were sets of equivalence classes, and it was easy to define canonical representations of these classes. CAP, on the other hand, is difficult to model without considering interference explicitly. One reason for this might be that interference is directional, and not simply an equivalence. Consequently, expressing entailments as inclusions between closed sets is likely to be the simplest way of constructing a suitable view model. Another reason is that it is convenient to construct views from assertions that are not themselves stable, hence it is convenient to have a model in which we can represent both stable and unstable assertions.

8. Related Work

Our composition operator provides a logical notion of separation, which, as we have demonstrated by examples, need not be realized by physical separation in the concrete machine. This idea of fictional separation has been used in recent work on separation logics

[2] I is precise, iff $\forall p, q.\, (I * p) \wedge (I * q) \implies I * (p \wedge q)$.

for concurrent languages [9, 13, 15, 31]. Similar ideas are also useful in a purely sequential setting to enable modular reasoning about abstract data structures implemented using physical sharing, but for which a logical notion of separation can be defined [10, 19, 21, 22].

The soundness of Pottier's capability system [26] is based on an axiom that is similar to our definition of interference relation, and the soundness proof of concurrent abstract predicates [9] also uses an equivalent lemma. Our framework does not have an explicit notion of guarantee, so many of the other properties required in both Pottier's work and concurrent abstract predicates are not required. Feng's LRG [14] also provides conditions such that the stable predicates can be composed. The condition requires fences to delimit the scope of interference, which we do not require.

9. Conclusions

We have introduced "Views" as a general framework in which a wide variety of compositional reasoning approaches can be constructed, understood and proved sound. We find it surprising and revealing that diverse approaches such as separation logic, rely-guarantee, the Owicki-Gries method and type systems can be understood in an elegant, unifying setting. While the power of the Views Framework is in the variety of systems that it encapsulates, its virtue is in providing a common semantic footing for them: each of the approaches we have studied can be proved sound by appeal to the general soundness result of Views, without recourse to induction over the operational semantics.

We have shown how Views captures a broad selection of existing reasoning systems. Of course, the true test is whether Views can be used to develop new and interesting systems. We are already finding this to be the case. Concurrent abstract predicates has been extended with higher-order features, using Views extended with step-indexing to prove soundness [30]. The Views Framework has been extended to reason about $C^\sharp$ with interesting permission annotations to ensure isolation between threads [17]. Views are also helping in the development of sound logics for local reasoning about intrinsically structured data, such as file systems [16]; in this setting, decomposing data into fragments that record how they are connected is central, and is elegantly justified by the semantic entailment of Views.

In 2002, Reynolds noted the close relationship between separation logic and type systems and wondered "whether the dividing line between types and assertions can be erased" [27]. We have shown that, at least in the first-order case, types and assertions are simply different kinds of *view*. Ultimately, we have identified core principles underlying compositional reasoning about concurrent programs, and formalised them in a unifying framework: Views.

Acknowledgments We thank Tony Hoare, Peter O'Hearn, Azalea Raad, John Wickerson, Adam Wright and the anonymous referees of POPL'12, LICS'12, CONCUR'12 and POPL'13 for helpful feedback and comments on the paper. Dinsdale-Young, Gardner and Yang acknowledge support from EPSRC.

References

[1] A. Ahmed, M. Fluet, and G. Morrisett. L^3: A linear language with locations. *Fundam. Inform.*, 77(4):397–449, 2007.

[2] L. Birkedal, N. Torp-Smith, and H. Yang. Semantics of separation-logic typing and higher-order frame rules for Algol-like languages. *LMCS*, 2(5:1), 2006.

[3] L. Birkedal, B. Reus, J. Schwinghammer, and H. Yang. A simple model of separation logic for higher-order store. In *ICALP*, 2008.

[4] R. Bornat, C. Calcagno, P. O'Hearn, and M. Parkinson. Permission accounting in separation logic. In *POPL'05*, 2005.

[5] C. Calcagno, P. Gardner, and U. Zarfaty. Local reasoning about data update. *ENTCS*, 172:133–175, 2007.

[6] C. Calcagno, P. W. O'Hearn, and H. Yang. Local action and abstract separation logic. In *LICS*, 2007.

[7] A. Charguéraud and F. Pottier. Functional translation of a calculus of capabilities. In *ICFP*, pages 213–224, 2008.

[8] T. Dinsdale-Young. *Abstract Data and Local Reasoning*. PhD thesis, Imperial College, Department of Computing, 2010.

[9] T. Dinsdale-Young, M. Dodds, P. Gardner, M. J. Parkinson, and V. Vafeiadis. Concurrent abstract predicates. In *ECOOP*, 2010.

[10] T. Dinsdale-Young, P. Gardner, and M. Wheelhouse. Abstraction and refinement for local reasoning. In *VSTTE*, 2010.

[11] T. Dinsdale-Young, L. Birkedal, P. Gardner, M. Parkinson, and H. Yang. Views: Compositional reasoning for concurrent programs (technical report and addditional material). `http://sites.google.com/site/viewsmodel/`, 2012.

[12] R. Dockins, A. Hobor, and A. W. Appel. A fresh look at separation algebras and share accounting. In *APLAS*, 2009.

[13] M. Dodds, X. Feng, M. J. Parkinson, and V. Vafeiadis. Deny-guarantee reasoning. In *ESOP*, pages 363–377, 2009.

[14] X. Feng. Local rely-guarantee reasoning. In *POPL*, 2009.

[15] X. Feng, R. Ferreira, and Z. Shao. On the relationship between concurrent separation logic and assume-guarantee reasoning. In *ESOP*, pages 173–188, 2007.

[16] P. Gardner, G. Nzik, and A. Wright. Reasoning about POSIX file systems using structural separation logic. Draft, 2012.

[17] C. Gordon, M. Parkinson, J. Parsons, A. Bromfield, and J. Duffy. Uniqueness and reference immutability for safe parallelism. In *OOPSLA*, 2012.

[18] S. S. Ishtiaq and P. W. O'Hearn. BI as an assertion language for mutable data structures. In *POPL*, pages 14–26, 2001.

[19] J. B. Jensen and L. Birkedal. Fictional separation logic. In *ESOP*, 2012.

[20] C. B. Jones. Tentative steps toward a development method for interfering programs. *ACM TOPLAS*, 5(4):596–619, 1983.

[21] N. Krishnaswami, L. Birkedal, and J. Aldrich. Verifying event-driven programs using ramified frame properties. In *TLDI*, 2010.

[22] N. Krishnaswami, A. Turon, D. Dreyer, and D. Garg. Superficially substructural types. In *ICFP*, 2012.

[23] G. Morrisett, D. Walker, K. Crary, and N. Glew. From system F to typed assembly language. *TOPLAS*, 21(3):527–568, 1999.

[24] S. Owicki and D. Gries. An axiomatic proof technique for parallel programs I. *Acta Informatica*, 6(4):319–340, 1976.

[25] M. J. Parkinson, R. Bornat, and P. O'Hearn. Modular verification of a non-blocking stack. In *POPL*, 2007.

[26] F. Pottier. Syntactic soundness proof of a type-and-capability system with hidden state. Technical report, INRIA, 2011.

[27] J. C. Reynolds. Separation logic: A logic for shared mutable data structures. In *LICS*, 2002.

[28] J. Smans, B. Jacobs, and F. Piessens. Implicit dynamic frames: Combining dynamic frames and separation logic. In *ECOOP*, 2009.

[29] F. Smith, D. Walker, and J. G. Morrisett. Alias types. In *ESOP*, 2000.

[30] K. Svendsen, L. Birkedal, and M. Parkinson. A specification of the joins library in higher-order separation logic. Technical report, IT University of Copenhagen, 2012.

[31] V. Vafeiadis and M. J. Parkinson. A marriage of rely/guarantee and separation logic. In *CONCUR*, pages 256–271, 2007.

High-Level Separation Logic for Low-Level Code

Jonas B. Jensen
IT University of Copenhagen
jobr@itu.dk

Nick Benton Andrew Kennedy
Microsoft Research Cambridge
{nick,akenn}@microsoft.com

Abstract

Separation logic is a powerful tool for reasoning about structured, imperative programs that manipulate pointers. However, its application to unstructured, lower-level languages such as assembly language or machine code remains challenging. In this paper we describe a separation logic tailored for this purpose that we have applied to x86 machine-code programs.

The logic is built from an assertion logic on machine states over which we construct a specification logic that encapsulates uses of frames and step indexing. The traditional notion of Hoare triple is not applicable directly to unstructured machine code, where code and data are mixed together and programs do not in general run to completion, so instead we adopt a continuation-passing style of specification with preconditions alone. Nevertheless, the range of primitives provided by the specification logic, which include a higher-order frame connective, a novel read-only frame connective, and a 'later' modality, support the definition of derived forms to support structured-programming-style reasoning for common cases, in which standard rules for Hoare triples are derived as lemmas. Furthermore, our encoding of scoped assembly-language labels lets us give definitions and proof rules for powerful assembly-language 'macros' such as while loops, conditionals and procedures.

We have applied the framework to a model of sequential x86 machine code built entirely within the Coq proof assistant, including tactic support based on computational reflection.

Categories and Subject Descriptors F.3.1 [*Logics and meanings of programs*]: Specifying and Verifying and Reasoning about Programs—Assertions, Invariants, Logics of programs, Mechanical verification, Pre- and post-conditions, Specification techniques; D.3.2 [*Programming Languages*]: Language Classifications—Macro and assembly languages; D.2.4 [*Software Engineering*]: Software / Program Verification—Correctness proofs, formal methods

General Terms Languages, theory, verification

Keywords Separation logic, machine code, proof assistants

1. Introduction

Formal verification is one of the most important techniques for building reliable computer systems. Research in software verification typically, and quite reasonably, concerns reasoning about the high-level programming languages with which most programmers work. But to build genuinely trustworthy systems, one really needs to verify the machine code that actually runs, whether it be hand-crafted or the output of a compiler. This is particularly important for establishing security properties, since failures of abstraction between the high and low-level models often lead to vulnerabilities (and because hand-crafted machine code is often found in security-critical places, such as kernels). A further motivation for verifying low-level code is that real systems are composed of components written in many different languages; machine code is the only truly universal lingua franca by which we can reason about properties of such compositions. Finally, experience shows that hand-written low-level programs are simply much harder to get right than higher-level ones, increasing the credibility gap between formal and informal verifications.

Verifying low-level, unstructured programs [18, 39], and compilers that produce them [24], both have a long history. And since such verifications are, like low-level programs themselves, extremely lengthy and error-prone, some form of mechanical assistance is absolutely crucial. This assistance often takes the form of automated decision procedures for first-order logic and various more specialized theories, combined by an SMT solver [21]. Here, however, our focus is on deductive Hoare-style verification of machine-code programs using an interactive proof assistant, in our case Coq. This requires more manual effort on the part of the user, but allows one to work with much richer mathematical models and specifications, which are particularly important for modularity. Both approaches to mechanization also have considerable history, with much pioneering work applying interactive provers to low-level code having been done with the Boyer-Moore prover in the 1980s [25, 41]. Recently, however, an exciting confluence of advances in foundational theory, program logics (most notably separation logic [35]) and the technology of proof assistants, together with increased interest in formal certification, have led to an explosion of work on mechanized verification of real (or at least, realistic) software, including compilers and operating systems. Although many of these formalizations do involve reasoning about machine code or assembly language programs, program logics for low-level code are generally much less satisfactory, and more ad hoc, than those for high-level languages.

The design of a high-level program logic tends to follow closely the structure and abstractions provided by the language. Commands in a while-language, for example, may be modelled as partial functions from stores to stores, which are only combined in certain very restricted ways. The classical Hoare triple, relating a predicate on inputs to a predicate on outputs, is a natural (indeed, inevitable) and generally satisfactory form of specification for such functions. Furthermore, the structured form of programs leads to particularly elegant, syntax-directed program logic rules for composing verifications. Machine code, by contrast, has almost nothing in the way of inherent structure or abstractions to guide one, supports chal-

POPL'13, January 23–25, 2013, Rome, Italy.

lenging patterns of programming and also involves a host of messy complexities.

The messy complexities include large instruction sets with variable-length encodings, the need to work with bit-level operations and arithmetic mod 2^{32}, alignment, a plethora of flags, registers, addressing modes, and so on. These inevitably cause some pain, but are just the sort of thing proof assistants are good at checking precisely and, with a well-engineered formalization, removing some of the drudgery from.[1] There is, of course, complexity of a quite different order associated (at both high- and low-level) with concurrency – especially relaxed memory models on multiprocessors – which we do not address at all in this paper. Even in the sequential case, however, the lack of inherent structure in low-level code is a fundamental problem.

Machine code features unstructured control flow. A contiguous block of instructions potentially has many entry points and many exits, with the added complication that the same bytes may decode differently according to the entry point. Machine code is almost entirely untyped and higher-order, with no runtime tagging: any word in memory or a register may be treated as a scalar value, a pointer or a code pointer, and common coding patterns do make use of this flexibility: stealing bits in pointers, storing metadata at offsets from code pointers, computing branches, and so on. Finally, code and data live in the same heap, allowing code generation, self-modifying code and code examination, for example for interpreting instructions. The most basic abstractions, such as memory allocation or function calling, are not built in, but are conventions that must be specified, followed and verified at appropriate points. Furthermore, code that implements even the simplest of these abstractions, such as first-order function calls, uses features of machine code whose high-level analogues (higher-order, dynamically allocated local state) are challenging to reason about – and a subject of active research – even in very high-level languages such as ML.

Some logics, type systems and analyses for machine code deal with these complexities by imposing structure and restrictions on the code they deal with. For example, one can enforce a traditional basic block structure, hard-code memory allocation as a special pseudo-instruction or treat calling and a call-stack specially [5, 27, 31, 40]. Such techniques can work well for verifying code that looks like it came from a C compiler, but we would like something more generally applicable, able to verify smoothly higher-order code, systems code such as schedulers and allocators, and code that uses clever bit-level representation tricks. In previous work, for example on compiling a functional language to a rather idealized assembly language [7], one of us has proved useful results in Coq using a shallow embedding of step-indexed, separated predicates and relations, a notion of biorthogonality ('perping') for code pointers, explicit second-order quantification for framing, and a more-or-less ad hoc collection of lemmas for instructions, quantifier manipulation and entailment. Given sufficient effort, such an approach can undeniably be pushed through, but the proofs and specifications are very clumsy; although some of the connectives have respectable properties, there is certainly no sense that one is working in a well-structured program logic, with a well-behaved proof theory. Applying such a naive approach in the context of real machine code, with the above-mentioned messy complexities and in which we would clearly need to build numerous higher-level proof abstractions, seemed unlikely to work well.

Separation logics for higher-level languages, by contrast, do have a good proof theory. In particular, work on *higher-order* frame rules allows local reasoning about higher-order programs, allowing invariants to be framed onto commands in context by distributing them through the specifications of parameters [9]. A major goal of the work described here is to bring the power and concision of higher-order frame rules to reasoning about machine-code programs. At first sight, it may seem unclear how to incorporate even the first-order frame rule

$$\frac{\{P\}\,C\,\{Q\}}{\{P * R\}\,C\,\{Q * R\}}$$

into a system for reasoning about machine code. Firstly, the frame rule is typically justified using a global property of commands with respect to a semantics defined over partial heaps: if a command executes without faulting in some heap, then it does so in any extension of that heap and moreover, if it terminates it preserves the extension. Partial heaps in the semantics model a built-in allocator, but, as in our previous work in low-level code [6, 7], we do not wish to define the ground semantics (with respect to which we interpret specifications) using partial heaps: whatever memory is in the machine is there all the time, and the allocator is just another piece of code to be specified and verified in our framework.

Secondly, the postcondition of a triple corresponds to the single exit point of a first-order command. Machine code fragments do not have single exits, or even a natural, local notion of terminating execution. We are ultimately concerned with the observable behaviour of whole programs, and do not wish to restrict ourselves to a form of specification that relies on the non-observable, intensional property of reaching a particular intermediate program counter value. We thus take our basic form of safety specifications to be one that only involves a precondition: execution from a given address in a state satisfying the precondition is safe. As Chlipala [16] observes, it is not obvious how to attach a frame soundly to such a specification. We address these problems by going beyond a shallow embedding of specifications of individual program points, to an embedding of a fully-fledged specification logic [23, 34], making the context within which code fragments are proved explicit, and with a semantics that captures (but a surface notation which hides) the way in which frames are preserved.

The specification logic allows one to work with subtle patterns of invariant preservation, but does not impose particular forms of specification. Rather, it provides building blocks from which more complex patterns, including Hoare triples, may be built. The rich, well-behaved theory of the core logic allows derived rules for new forms of specification to be expressed and proved concisely.

We have formalized our specification logic in the Coq proof assistant, and instantiated it for the particular case of a model for sequential x86 machine code. Our formalization also includes a range of reflective tactics for solving separation entailments and performing specification logic proofs at a high level of abstraction. This paper mainly discusses the logic in a machine-independent way, but we use the x86 instantiation for examples and motivation.

In summary, the contributions of this work include:

1. A separation logic for unstructured machine code that supports both first- and higher-order frame rules.
2. Accounts of specification-level connectives including framing, a 'read-only' frame, a 'later' modality and a full range of intuitionistic connectives, all with good logical properties.
3. Examples of higher-level patterns, such as Hoare triples, and associated proof rules being defined smoothly within the logic.
4. An certified assembler, supporting convenient macro definitions with internal label generation and natural derived proof rules, with examples including while-program constructs and procedure calling.

[1] Logics for high-level languages often ignore fixed-length arithmetic, even when that is what is provided by real implementations.

5. A semantics involving no instrumention or other modifications to the underlying machine model. Memory can be total, and step-counting and auxiliary variables happen only in the logic.
6. All this is formalized in Coq, with an instantiation for x86 machine code and tactic support for high-level proving. The formalization is available via the authors' web pages.

2. Machine model

Our separation logic is not tied to any particular machine architecture, but in order to illustrate its application we will be presenting examples from 32-bit x86, the architecture for which we have built a model in Coq.[2] In this section we present enough concrete detail of this model to support subsequent sections.

We have modelled a subset of the 32-bit x86 instruction set, considering sequential execution only, but treating memory, registers and flags in sufficient detail to obtain accurate specification of its behaviour.

Machine words and arithmetic We model n-bit machine words simply as n-nary tuples of boolean values, deploying an indexed type in Coq for the purpose. The x86 architecture makes various use of 8-bit (BYTE), 16-bit (WORD), 32-bit (DWORD) and 64-bit (QWORD) values, and so nat-dependent types in Coq are a boon to specification. Logical and arithmetic operations are defined directly in terms of bits, although to prove useful properties of arithmetic it proved handy to map words into arithmetic modulo 2^n, making use of the `ssreflect` library for algebraic identities [20].

Machine state The state of the machine is described by a triple of registers, flags and memory state:

$$\begin{aligned}\mathbb{S} = {} & (\mathsf{reg} \to \mathsf{DWORD}) \times \\ & (\mathsf{flag} \to \{\mathsf{true}, \mathsf{false}, \mathsf{undef}\}) \times \\ & (\mathsf{DWORD} \to (\mathsf{BYTE} \uplus \{\mathsf{unmapped}\}))\end{aligned}$$

Register state is a straightforward mapping from the x86's nine core registers (EAX, EBX, ECX, EDX, ESI, EDI, EBP, ESP and EIP) to 32-bit values. The EIP instruction pointer register is the x86's program counter and points to the next instruction to be decoded by the processor. Rather than model the special EFLAGS as a monolithic register, we split it up into boolean-valued flags. The undef value represents the undefined state in which many instructions leave flags. Any dependence of execution on an undefined state, such as in a conditional branch instruction, is then treated as unspecified behaviour. Memory is modelled straightforwardly as 32-bit-addressable bytes, with the possibility that any byte might be missing or inaccessible. For now, we are not interested in finer distinctions such as read-only or no-execute, though it would be a simple matter to incorporate these notions. It is however important to note that the 'partiality' of memory has nothing to do with the partial states of separation logic; indeed we could choose to model and fully specify the x86 support for fault handling, using the very same logic.

Instructions Any machine model must of course include a datatype of instructions. The x86 instruction set is notoriously large and baroque but by careful subsetting and factoring our datatype is made reasonably concise. Figure 1 presents the instruction datatype, with only some names changed for the purposes of this paper.

Instruction decoding The x86 instruction format is also complex, being variable in length and not canonical: a single instruction can sometimes be encoded in many ways. We have implemented an instruction decoder as a partial function

$$\mathsf{decode} : \mathsf{DWORD} \times (\mathsf{DWORD} \to (\mathsf{BYTE} \uplus \{\mathsf{unmapped}\})) \rightharpoonup \mathsf{DWORD} \times \mathsf{Instr}$$

such that if $\mathsf{decode}(i, m) = (j, \iota)$ then memory m from address i up to but not including address j is defined and decodes to instruction ι. The decoder reads memory incrementally, returning an undefined value if memory is inaccessible or out of range, or if the contents do not describe an instruction in our chosen subset. (There is no need to specify explicitly a maximum instruction length.) Lifting decode to machine states, and threading the updating of the EIP register through, yields a partial function in $\mathbb{S} \rightharpoonup \mathbb{S} \times \mathsf{Instr}$.

Instruction execution Instruction execution is given by a partial function on states $\mathbb{S} \times \mathsf{Instr} \rightharpoonup \mathbb{S}$, which when composed with instruction decoding gives rise to a small-step transition function on machine states $\mathsf{step} : \mathbb{S} \rightharpoonup \mathbb{S}$. When this function is undefined, it means that either a fault occurred (such as the decoding of an illegal instruction or an access to unmapped memory), or behaviour is simply unspecified (such as branching on an undefined flag).

Typeof d = if d then DWORD else BYTE
Scale = S_1 | S_2 | S_4 | S_8
MemSpec = Reg × option (NonSPReg × Scale) × DWORD
RegMem = RegMemR (r:Reg) | RegMemM(ms:MemSpec)
RegImm d = RegImmI (c:Typeof d) | RegImmR (r:Reg)
Src = SrcI (c:DWORD) | SrcM (ms:MemSpec) | SrcR(r:Reg)
DstSrc d =
| RR (dst:Reg) (src:Reg)
| RM (dst:Reg) (src:MemSpec)
| MR (dst:MemSpec) (src:Reg)
| RI (dst:Reg) (src:Typeof d)
| MI (dst:MemSpec) (src:Typeof d)
BinOp = ADC | ADD | AND | CMP | OR | SBB | SUB | XOR
UnaryOp = INC | DEC | NOT | NEG | POP
BitOp = BT | BTC | BTR | BTS
ShiftOp = ROL | ROR | RCL | RCR | SHL | SHR | SAL | SAR
Count = ShiftCL | ShiftImm (b:BYTE)
Condition = O | B | Z | BE | S | P | L | LE
Instr =
| UOP (d:bool) (op:UnaryOp) (dst:RegMem)
| BOP d (op:BinOp) (ds:DstSrc d)
| BITOP (op:BitOp) (dst:RegMem false)
| TEST d (dst:RegMem) (src:RegImm d)
| MOV d (ds:DstSrc d)
| SHIFTOP (d:bool) (op:ShiftOp) (dst:RegMem) (c:Count)
| MUL (src:RegMem)
| LEA (reg:Reg) (src:RegMem)
| JCC (cc:Condition) (dir:bool) (tgt:DWORD)
| PUSH (src:Src)
| POP (dst:RegMem)
| CALL (src:Src) | JMP (src:Src)
| RET ($size$:WORD)
| CLC | STC | CMC | HLT

Figure 1. Instruction datatype

[2] There is no particular reason for choosing x86 over x64 or ARM.

3. Assertion logic

3.1 Partial states

Assertions in separation logic describe a subset, or 'footprint', of the machine state. For high-level imperative programs with dynamic allocation this footprint consists of a subset of the heap. Indeed a common idiom is to prove that some code starts or finishes with an 'empty' heap.

Here, there is no such thing: we have the whole machine at our disposal, and we must carve out our own abstractions such as heaps or stacks, so the footprint is simply that part of the state that we care about right now. We also find it useful to use separation in describing the manipulation of registers and flags, and so define *partial* states as follows, noting the resemblance to the definition of total states in Section 2.

$$\begin{aligned}\Sigma = {} & (\mathsf{reg} \rightharpoonup \mathsf{DWORD}) \times \\ & (\mathsf{flag} \rightharpoonup \{\mathsf{true}, \mathsf{false}, \mathsf{undef}\}) \times \\ & (\mathsf{DWORD} \rightharpoonup (\mathsf{BYTE} \uplus \{\mathsf{unmapped}\}))\end{aligned}$$

There is a partial binary operation $\uplus$ on elements of Σ, defined when its operands have disjoint domains on all three tuple components and yielding a tuple with the union of each of the maps. This makes $(\Sigma, \uplus)$ a *separation algebra* [15]; i.e., a partial commutative monoid.

3.2 Assertion logic

An assertion is a predicate on partial states:

$$\mathsf{asn} \triangleq \mathcal{P}(\Sigma)$$

Since $(\Sigma, \uplus)$ is a separation algebra, its powerset asn forms a complete boolean BI algebra, i.e., a model of the assertion language of classical separation logic, where the connectives are defined in the standard way [15]:

$$\forall x{:}T.\ P(x) \triangleq \bigcap_{x:T} P(x) \qquad \exists x{:}T.\ P(x) \triangleq \bigcup_{x:T} P(x)$$
$$P \Rightarrow Q \triangleq \{\sigma \mid \sigma \in P \Rightarrow \sigma \in Q\} \qquad \mathsf{emp} \triangleq \{([], [], [])\}$$
$$P * Q \triangleq \{\sigma \mid \exists \sigma_1, \sigma_2.\ \sigma = \sigma_1 \uplus \sigma_2 \wedge \sigma_1 \in P \wedge \sigma_2 \in Q\}$$
$$P \mathrel{-\!\!*} Q \triangleq \{\sigma_2 \mid \forall \sigma_1.\ \forall \sigma = \sigma_1 \uplus \sigma_2.\ \sigma_1 \in P \Rightarrow \sigma \in Q\}$$

The propositional connectives $(\wedge, \top)$ and $(\vee, \bot)$ are just binary and nullary special cases of $\forall$ and $\exists$ respectively. As usual, entailment is defined as $P \vdash Q \triangleq P \subseteq Q$, and we write $\vdash P$ for $\top \vdash P$ and $P \equiv Q$ whenever $P \vdash Q$ and $Q \vdash P$.

There is a notion of points-to [35] for registers and for flags:

$$r \mapsto v \triangleq \{([r \mapsto v], [], [])\} \qquad f \mapsto b \triangleq \{([], [f \mapsto b], [])\}$$

The meaning of the points-to assertion for memory, $i..j \mapsto v$, depends on the type of v; this is done using a *type class* [37] in our Coq implementation. For BYTE and DWORD types, points-to means that memory from address i to j contains that value. In these cases, j is uniquely determined to be $i+1$ or $i+4$ respectively. For syntactic assembly instructions ι, it means that the memory at $i..j$ decodes to ι. In other words, $\mathsf{decode}(i, m) = (j, \iota)$ where m is the memory component of the state. Instruction encoding is not unique, so more than one byte sequence in memory may decode to the same ι. We write $i \mapsto v$ to mean $\exists j.\ i..j \mapsto v$.

Discussion. Another option would have been to let the registers and flags behave like the 'stack' in traditional separation logic [35] and not split them over $*$. This is the approach taken by Shao et al. [14, 31] and Chlipala [16], but it leads to the side condition on the frame rules that the program may not modify any registers mentioned by the frame. In a setting where programs have multiple entry and exit points and may be self-modifying, it is not even clear what that side condition means or how to check it, so we instead make registers and flags split across $*$, following Myreen et al. [29].

4. Specification logic

4.1 Safety

We extend the single-step partial function step : $\mathbb{S} \rightharpoonup \mathbb{S}$ to a function run : $\mathbb{N} \times \mathbb{S} \rightharpoonup \mathbb{S}$, where $\mathsf{run}(k, s)$ is the state that results from successful execution of k instructions starting from state s.

Unlike the high-level languages typically modelled with Hoare logics, a CPU has no natural notion of finishing a computation. It will run forever until it either faults or loses power[3]. This means that we cannot apply the standard Hoare-logic approach of describing a computation by a precondition and a postcondition since there is no meaningful time to check the postcondition.

Instead, specifications revolve around *safety*. We characterise the safe machine configurations as the set of pairs $(k, P) : \mathbb{N} \times \mathsf{asn}$ such that the machine will run for at least k steps without faulting if started from a state in P:

$$\mathsf{safe} \triangleq \{(k, P) \mid \forall \sigma \in P.\ \forall s \sqsupseteq \sigma.\ \exists s' : \mathbb{S}.\ \mathsf{run}(k, s) = s'\}$$

The relation $s \sqsupseteq \sigma$ states that all the mappings in σ are also found in s. This is how we connect the partial states found in assertions to the total states executed by the machine.

Example 1. It is safe to sit in a tight loop forever. That is,

$$\forall k, i.\ (k, (\mathsf{EIP} \mapsto i * i \mapsto \mathsf{jmp}\ i)) \in \mathsf{safe}$$

The EIP register is the instruction pointer, and jmp i is an unconditional jump to address i. The proof goes by induction on k. ◇

The number k plays the role of a *step index* [2]. We are ultimately always interested in proving computations safe for an arbitrary number of steps, but exposing an intermediate step index gives us a value on which we can do induction.

As a running example, we will attempt to specify the unconditional jump instruction. We can show that for all i, a, k, R,

$$\begin{aligned}&(k, Q * R) \in \mathsf{safe} \Rightarrow (k+1, P * R) \in \mathsf{safe} && \text{where}\\ &P = (\mathsf{EIP} \mapsto i * i \mapsto \mathsf{jmp}\ a) && \text{and}\\ &Q = (\mathsf{EIP} \mapsto a * i \mapsto \mathsf{jmp}\ a)\end{aligned}$$

In words, if you need to show that $P * R$ is a safe configuration for $k+1$ steps, it suffices to show that $Q * R$ is safe for k steps. When a specification follows this pattern, we can think of P as a precondition, Q as a postcondition, and R as a frame.

The specification does not say that $Q * R$ will ever hold. Rather, it requires that if $Q * R$ does hold, then we are in a safe configuration. This can be seen as a CPS version of Hoare logic, which is appropriate for machine code since nothing ever returns or finishes at this level [5, 31, 38].

We will refine this specification in later examples as we develop constructions at higher levels of abstraction.

4.2 Specification logic

Reasoning directly about membership of safe is awkward since the step index and frame are explicit and visible even though their use always follows the same pattern. The solution is to instead consider safe as a formula in a *specification logic*. We define a specification to be a set of of (k, P)-pairs that is closed under decreasing k and under starring arbitrary assertions onto P:

$$\mathsf{spec} \triangleq \{S \subseteq \mathbb{N} \times \mathsf{asn} \mid \forall (k, P) \in S, k' \leq k, R.\ (k', P * R) \in S\}$$

[3] Even when it faults, it will typically reboot and so keep running, but this behaviour is outside of our model.

Intuitively, a specification S : spec describes how many steps the machine has to execute before it no longer holds and what frames the execution will preserve. This idea comes from the work of Birkedal, Torp-Smith and Yang on higher-order frame rules [8, 10], and spec is essentially a step-indexed version of Krishnaswami's specification logic model [23].

The definition of spec is such that safe $\in$ spec. Furthermore, spec is a *complete Heyting algebra* and thus a model of intuitionistic logic. This gives us a notion of entailment ($\vdash \triangleq \subseteq$) and the logical connectives ($\forall, \exists, \wedge, \vee, \top, \bot, \Rightarrow$) with the expected rules. The definitions of the connectives follow a standard Kripke model:

$$\forall x\colon T.\ S(x) \triangleq \bigcap_{x:T} S(x) \qquad \exists x\colon T.\ S(x) \triangleq \bigcup_{x:T} S(x)$$

$$S \Rightarrow S' \triangleq \{(k, P) \mid \forall k' \leq k.\ \forall R.\ (k', P * R) \in S \Rightarrow (k', P * R) \in S'\}$$

Again, the propositional connectives $(\wedge, \top)$ and $(\vee, \bot)$ are just binary and nullary special cases of $\forall$ and $\exists$ respectively.

Notice how the semantics of $\Rightarrow$ requires arbitrary frames to be preserved across the implication. This was not a choice we made – it is the only definition that makes $\Rightarrow$ be the right adjoint of $\wedge$, and it falls out of giving standard Kripke semantics.

We also get two new connectives: the *later* connective $\triangleright$ and the *frame* connective $\otimes$. We will define and discuss these in the next two subsections. They will enable us to state the specification of the jmp instruction from Section 4.1 more succinctly:

$$\triangleright\, \mathsf{safe}\otimes(\mathsf{EIP}\mapsto a * i\mapsto \mathsf{jmp}\ a) \vdash \mathsf{safe}\otimes(\mathsf{EIP}\mapsto i * i\mapsto \mathsf{jmp}\ a) \quad (1)$$

We can even factor out the duplicated part of the assertion and just write

$$\vdash (\triangleright\, \mathsf{safe} \otimes (\mathsf{EIP} \mapsto a) \Rightarrow \mathsf{safe} \otimes (\mathsf{EIP} \mapsto i)) \otimes i \mapsto \mathsf{jmp}\ a$$

or, informally, reading from right to left: 'given that i points to instruction jmp a, it is safe to execute with the instruction pointer set to i if it is later safe to execute with the instruction pointer set to a'.

4.3 Frame connective

Following the literature on higher-order frame rules [8, 10, 23], we define the *frame connective* $\otimes$: spec $\times$ asn $\rightarrow$ spec as

$$S \otimes R \triangleq \{(k, P) \mid (k, P * R) \in S\}$$

This is also known as the invariant extension connective [8] because an intuitive reading of $S \otimes R$ is that the computation described by S is allowed to additionally depend on and maintain the invariant R. Note that, by unpacking the definitions,

$$\vdash \mathsf{safe} \otimes P \quad \text{iff} \quad \forall k, R.\ (k, P * R) \in \mathsf{safe}$$

relating judgements in the specification logic with the safety of executions. Since we defined spec such that any S can be extended by any invariant, we can immediately prove the higher-order frame rule:

$$\frac{}{S \vdash S \otimes R}\ \text{FRAME}$$

The frame connective distributes over all other connectives, including $\triangleright$ and itself. That means, for example, that

$$\frac{}{(S \Rightarrow S') \otimes R \ \equiv\ S \otimes R \Rightarrow S' \otimes R}\ \otimes\text{-}\Rightarrow$$

It also interacts with emp and $*$ as follows.

$$\frac{}{S \otimes \mathsf{emp} \ \equiv\ S}\ \otimes\text{-EMP}$$

$$\frac{}{S \otimes R_1 \otimes R_2 \ \equiv\ S \otimes (R_1 * R_2)}\ \otimes\text{-}*$$

Example 2. We can now start to see why FRAME should be thought of as a frame rule. Assume we have proved for some P and Q that

$$\vdash \mathsf{safe} \otimes Q \Rightarrow \mathsf{safe} \otimes P.$$

Then by FRAME, $\otimes$-$\Rightarrow$ and $\otimes$-$*$, we can derive

$$\vdash \mathsf{safe} \otimes (Q * R) \Rightarrow \mathsf{safe} \otimes (P * R).$$

Visually this looks like the standard frame rule, and it performs the same function: to extend both pre- and post-condition by an invariant. $\diamond$

The formula $S \otimes R$ is covariant in S with respect to entailment, meaning that

$$\frac{S \vdash S'}{S \otimes R \vdash S' \otimes R}\ \otimes\text{-}\vdash$$

The variance in R is more complicated and will be discussed in Section 7.1.

Example 3. To illustrate informally how FRAME generalises the standard first-order frame rule, consider a program in a high-level functional programming language f_1 : (unit $\rightarrow$ unit) $\rightarrow$ unit, whose specification is, for some particular P, Q and R,

$$\forall g.\ \{P * R\}\ g\ ()\ \{Q * R\} \Rightarrow \{P * R\}\ f_1(g)\ \{Q * R\}$$

That is, f_1 forwards the specification of g. Most likely, f_1 simply applies its argument to the unit value, but assume that it has been verified separately and we should not see its implementation.

If we have g_1 with specification $\{P\}\ g_1\ ()\ \{Q\}$, we cannot immediately apply $f_1(g_1)$ since the specification does not match what f_1 requires. However, we can apply the ordinary frame rule to deduce that g_1 also has the specification $\{P * R\}\ g_1\ ()\ \{Q * R\}$, and then we can call $f_1(g_1)$ if we are in a state satisfying $P * R$.

Now instead consider an f_2 with the specification

$$\forall g.\ \{P\}\ g\ ()\ \{Q\} \Rightarrow \{P\}\ f_2(g)\ \{Q\}$$

and a g_2 with specification $\{P * R\}\ g_2\ ()\ \{Q * R\}$. It is impossible with just the standard frame rule to call $f_2(g_2)$ since the specification of g_2 cannot be refined to match what is assumed by f_2. But with the higher-order frame rule, we can instead refine the specification of f_2 to be

$$\forall g.\ (\{P\}\ g\ ()\ \{Q\} \Rightarrow \{P\}\ f_2(g)\ \{Q\}) \otimes R \equiv$$
$$\forall g.\ \{P\}\ g\ ()\ \{Q\} \otimes R \Rightarrow \{P\}\ f_2(g)\ \{Q\} \otimes R \equiv$$
$$\forall g.\ \{P * R\}\ g\ ()\ \{Q * R\} \Rightarrow \{P * R\}\ f_2(g)\ \{Q * R\}$$

It is now compatible with our g_2.

Without the higher-order frame rule, we would have had to either re-verify the implementation of f_2 or generalise the original specification of f_2 to explicitly quantify over all possible frames that may be threaded through. The latter option is essentially what the definition of spec does, but this is invisible and implicit. $\diamond$

Using $\otimes$ to give concise and modular specifications to higher-order functions is as important here as in any other separation logic, but that is not our main reason for including $\otimes$. We do it because it allows our logic to have a frame rule despite the program being unstructured and low-level. Chlipala [16] uses explicit second-order quantification in place of a frame rule, whilst Shao et al. [14, 31] have a frame rule that only applies to judgements in a very restrictive specification logic; in particular, it does not apply directly to specifications of function pointers.

4.4 Later connective

Just as we hide the explicit frames using $\otimes$, we hide the step indexes using the *later* connective, $\triangleright$. This is a trick pioneered by Nakano [30] that exploits the fact that we are never interested in the absolute number of steps but only that they are the same or differ by exactly one between two specification formulas. We define

$$\triangleright S \triangleq \{(k, P) \mid \forall k' < k.\ (k', P) \in S\}$$

Because any S : spec is closed under decreasing steps, an equivalent definition is that $(0, P) \in \triangleright S$ for all P, and $(k{+}1, P) \in \triangleright S$ iff $(k, P) \in S$. The closure under decreasing steps is expressed logically as the rule

$$\frac{}{S \vdash \triangleright S}\ \triangleright\text{-WEAKEN}$$

As mentioned in Section 4.1, the purpose of step indexes is to serve as a handle for induction. We can phrase the induction principle on natural numbers using the following rule [3, 30], which is named for its similarity to a corresponding rule in Gödel-Löb logic [3].

$$\frac{\triangleright S \vdash S}{\vdash S}\ \text{LÖB}$$

The Löb rule is a reformulation of the strong induction principle for natural numbers: if $(\forall k' < k.\ P(k')) \Rightarrow P(k)$ for all k, then $P(n)$ holds for any n. It is a powerful rule in that it almost allows assuming the formula one wants to prove, except that the assumption may only be used after taking one step of computation.

Example 4. Recall the specification of a tight loop from Example 1. We can now express and prove that inside the specification logic in just two steps:

$$\frac{\dfrac{}{\triangleright \mathsf{safe} \otimes (\mathsf{EIP} \mapsto i * i \mapsto \mathsf{jmp}\ i) \vdash \mathsf{safe} \otimes (\mathsf{EIP} \mapsto i * i \mapsto \mathsf{jmp}\ i)}\ (1)}{\vdash \mathsf{safe} \otimes (\mathsf{EIP} \mapsto i * i \mapsto \mathsf{jmp}\ i)}\ \text{LÖB} \qquad \diamond$$

The $\triangleright$ connective distributes over every other connective we have mentioned except for $\bot$ and existential quantification over empty types.

Discussion. Like we saw in the rule for jmp (Equation (1)), every step of computation allows us to relax our remaining proof obligation by adding a $\triangleright$. For example, we could prove that

$$\vdash (\triangleright\triangleright \mathsf{safe} \otimes (\mathsf{EIP} \mapsto j) \Rightarrow \mathsf{safe} \otimes (\mathsf{EIP} \mapsto i)) \otimes i..j \mapsto (\mathsf{nop}; \mathsf{nop}) \quad (2)$$

where nop is the no-operation instruction. There are *two* $\triangleright$'s on the 'postcondition' of (2) because it takes two steps of computation to get there. It turns out, however, that it is never useful to have more than one $\triangleright$ applied to a specification since the purpose of step indexes is to do induction, and induction will always give us the necessary assumptions on the immediate predecessor of the number of interest.

Furthermore, we have found that $\triangleright$ is not necessary in code that only moves forward. Löb induction only makes sense when verifying loops, and a loop requires some form of backward jump unless we consider highly-contrived self-modifying code. Therefore, in practice, we would state (2) without any $\triangleright$-connective at all.

4.5 Read-only frame

The instruction rules we have discussed so far are too weak for some purposes. Recall the rule for jmp:

$$\vdash (\triangleright \mathsf{safe} \otimes (\mathsf{EIP} \mapsto a) \Rightarrow \mathsf{safe} \otimes (\mathsf{EIP} \mapsto i)) \otimes i \mapsto \mathsf{jmp}\ a$$

Because the meaning of $i \mapsto \mathsf{jmp}\ a$ is only that the memory starting at i decodes to jmp a, the rule would be satisfied in a semantics where the jmp instruction not only performed the jump but also replaced its own machine code in memory with a different byte sequence that also decoded to jmp a. This would be a problem for programs whose code needs to stay unmodified; e.g., to verify that the checksum of the code remains the same.

Our solution is to make this specification more precise by employing the *read-only frame* connective, defined as

$$S \oslash R \triangleq \forall \sigma \in R.\ S \otimes \{\sigma\}.$$

A more precise specification for jmp is then

$$\vdash (\triangleright \mathsf{safe} \otimes (\mathsf{EIP} \mapsto a) \Rightarrow \mathsf{safe} \otimes (\mathsf{EIP} \mapsto i)) \oslash i \mapsto \mathsf{jmp}\ a$$

Intuitively, $S \oslash R$ requires S not only to preserve the truth of R but to leave unmodified the underlying state fragment that made R true. The state may be changed temporarily, just as R might be broken, as long as it is restored at the end of the computation described by S.

Like for $\otimes$, there is a frame rule:

$$\frac{}{S \vdash S \oslash R}\ \text{FRAME-RO}$$

The $\oslash$ connective does not distribute over every other connective like $\otimes$ does, but it does distribute over $\forall, \wedge, \top, \otimes, \oslash, \triangleright$. It only distributes in one direction over $\exists$ and $\Rightarrow$:

$$\frac{}{(\exists a.\ S(a) \oslash R) \vdash (\exists a.\ S(a)) \oslash R}$$

$$\frac{}{(S \Rightarrow S') \oslash R \vdash S \oslash R \Rightarrow S' \oslash R}$$

The formula $S \oslash R$ is covariant in S and contravariant in R with respect to entailment, meaning that

$$\frac{S \vdash S' \qquad R' \vdash R}{S \oslash R \vdash S' \oslash R'}\ \oslash\text{-}\vdash$$

Another convenient property is that existential quantifiers can be moved in and out of the frame:

$$\frac{}{S \oslash (\exists x.\ R(x)) \equiv \forall x.\ S \oslash R(x)}$$

These last two properties of $\oslash$ about variance and commuting with existentials do not generally hold for $\otimes$. The cases where they hold are discussed in Sections 7.1 and 7.2. We explore further properties of $\oslash$ in Section 7.3.

Discussion. This connective is reminiscent of fractional permissions [12] but more coarse-grained and light-weight. We mention connections to other notions of weak ownership [22] in Section 9.

Our definition of $\oslash$ may not be the only good one, but we have examined three other candidate definitions and found that the one given above had the most convenient properties for our purposes. The candidates relate to each other as follows.

$$\begin{array}{rl} \forall R' \vdash R * \top.\ S \otimes R' & \vdash \\ \forall R' \vdash R.\ S \otimes R' & \vdash \\ \forall \sigma \in (R * \top).\ S \otimes \{\sigma\} & \equiv \\ \forall \sigma \in R.\ S \otimes \{\sigma\} & \end{array}$$

5. High-level assembly code

5.1 Basic blocks

Using safe and the connectives discussed so far, we can specify code with multiple entry points and exit points, jumps to code pointers, self-modification, and so on. In practice, though, most code is much simpler. For code that behaves like a *basic block*, with control flow always coming in at the top and going out at the bottom, we can describe its behaviour with a Hoare triple, defined in the specification logic as:

$$\{P\}\ c\ \{Q\} \triangleq \forall i, j.\ (\mathsf{safe} \otimes (\mathsf{EIP} \mapsto j * Q) \Rightarrow \mathsf{safe} \otimes (\mathsf{EIP} \mapsto i * P)) \oslash i..j \mapsto c$$

Example 5. The instruction mov r, v (move literal v to register r) can be specified as $\vdash \{r?\}$ mov r, v $\{r \mapsto v\}$, where $r?$ is shorthand for $\exists v.\ r \mapsto v$. This is much more compact and readable than writing the specification in terms of safe. ◇

This triple satisfies the structural rules we expect from a Hoare triple in separation logic:

$$\frac{P \vdash P' \quad S \vdash \{P'\}\, c\, \{Q'\} \quad Q' \vdash Q}{S \vdash \{P\}\, c\, \{Q\}}$$

$$\frac{S \vdash \forall x.\ \{P(x)\}\, c\, \{Q\}}{S \vdash \{\exists x.\ P(x)\}\, c\, \{Q\}} \qquad \frac{S \vdash \{P\}\, c\, \{Q\}}{S \vdash \{P * R\}\, c\, \{Q * R\}}$$

The frame rule for the triple follows from FRAME and the fact that $\otimes$ distributes into the triple:

$$\frac{}{\{P\}\, c\, \{Q\} \otimes R \equiv \{P * R\}\, c\, \{Q * R\}}\ \otimes\text{-TRIPLE}$$

There is no rule of conjunction for the triple since this would be unsound in the presence of FRAME [8].

Discussion. This kind of triple is certainly not the only useful one. One could also adapt the position-indexed triples of Myreen and Gordon [29] to this setting, allowing use of the triple metaphor in specifying code with multiple entry and exit points. It would be a matter of taste whether this seemed more convenient to work with than reasoning directly in terms of safe.

The triple defined here can be thought of as encoding a very simple calling convention: inlining; i.e., concatenation of code. We envision defining triples for other conventions as needed and proving similar properties about them. See Section 5.5 for another example.

It is a valid question to ask why there is no $\triangleright$ on the postcondition part of the triple so it would read $\triangleright$ safe $\otimes$ (EIP $\mapsto j * Q$). It would give stronger specifications for single instructions like in Example 5, but as discussed in Section 4.4, it would also be unnecessary since control flow always moves forward in a triple. We will also see in Section 5.3 that there are useful values of c that take no computation steps.

5.2 Rules for x86 instructions

With a variety of logical building blocks in place, we can give appealingly simple rules for x86 instructions. These split into instructions that do not touch the instruction pointer, for which we can use the Hoare-triple form, and control flow instructions, for which we describe their effect on the instruction pointer explicitly.

Example 6. The following rule for 'add register indirect with offset' is a typical instance. Here d is a literal DWORD offset, and addition of two 32-bit values produces a pair (c, v) where v is the 32-bit (truncated) result, and c is the carry into bit 32.

$$\begin{array}{ll} \vdash & \{r_1 \mapsto v_1 * \mathsf{OF?} * \mathsf{SF?} * \mathsf{ZF?} * \mathsf{CF?} * \mathsf{PF?}\} \\ & \mathsf{add}\ r_1, [r_2 + d] \\ & \{r_1 \mapsto v * \mathsf{OF} \mapsto \neg(\mathsf{msb}\ v_1 \oplus \mathsf{msb}\ v_2) \oplus \mathsf{msb}\ v \\ & \quad * \mathsf{SF} \mapsto \mathsf{msb}\ v * \mathsf{ZF} \mapsto (v = 0) * \mathsf{CF} \mapsto c * \mathsf{PF} \mapsto \mathsf{lsb}\ v\} \\ & \otimes (r_2 \mapsto w * w + d \mapsto v_2) \\ & \text{where } v_1 + v_2 = (c, v) \end{array}$$

The $\neg$ and $\oplus$ operators are boolean negation and xor respectively. The instruction affects flags OF, SF, ZF, CF and PF whose values initially are arbitrary ($F?$ is shorthand for $\exists f.\ F \mapsto f$, where f may be undef). Notice the framing of invariant registers and memory. ◇

Example 7. For the jump-if-zero instruction, we specify two 'postconditions', the first for when the branch is taken, and the second for when it isn't.

$$\begin{array}{l} \vdash (\triangleright\, \mathsf{safe} \otimes (b \wedge \mathsf{EIP} \mapsto a * \mathsf{ZF} \mapsto b) \wedge \\ \quad \mathsf{safe} \otimes (\neg b \wedge \mathsf{EIP} \mapsto j * \mathsf{ZF} \mapsto b) \\ \quad \Rightarrow \mathsf{safe} \otimes (\mathsf{EIP} \mapsto i * \mathsf{ZF} \mapsto b)) \\ \oslash\ i..j \mapsto \mathsf{jz}\ a \end{array}$$

Note the use of the *later* connective when the (possibly backwards) branch is taken. ◇

Our approach is to give a very general specification to each instruction and then on top of that provide convenience definitions for common cases. In a sense, our rules are therefore just a logical reformulation of the operational semantics, which may seem a bit unimpressive but turns out to be a strong platform on which to build higher-level layers of abstraction.

5.3 Instruction encoding and assembly language

We have implemented an encoder for syntactic instructions, and it has the property that

$$i..j \mapsto \mathsf{encode}(i, \iota) \vdash i..j \mapsto \iota$$

That is, if the memory at $i..j$ contains the sequence of bytes $\mathsf{encode}(i, \iota)$, then that memory will decode to the instruction ι. The instruction decoder referred to here is the same one that is part of the operational semantics for the machine. The encode function takes i as parameter because the encoding of x86 instructions is not generally position-independent.

This encoder is the main ingredient in our *assembler*: a certified and executable Coq function that takes a *program* as input and produces a list of bytes as output. A program is a value in the following inductive definition.

$$p ::= (\iota) \mid \mathsf{skip} \mid p; p \mid l\!: \mid \mathsf{LOCAL}\ l;\ p$$

That is, a program is essentially a list of instructions with label markers 'l:' interspersed. A label l may be declared local to program p with the LOCAL l; p construction. A label is simply a memory address; i.e., a 32-bit word, and it can therefore be used as an argument to jump instructions. The following is a closed program that loops forever.

$$\mathsf{LOCAL}\ l;\ l\!:\ \mathsf{jmp}\ l$$

The LOCAL constructor in our Coq implementation has type (DWORD $\to$ program) $\to$ program, so writing LOCAL l; p is just syntactic sugar for LOCAL$(\lambda l.\ p(l))$. The benefit of modelling label scopes with function spaces is that Coq handles all aspects of label naming transparently, including the necessary capture-avoidance and α-conversion. The downside is that it is not viable to statically rule out ill-formed programs, such as programs that place the same label more than once.

The assembler function, assemble, is partial and maps an address and a program to a sequence of bytes. It is undefined if the program is ill-formed. Where defined, it has the correctness property that

$$i..j \mapsto \mathsf{assemble}(i, p) \vdash i..j \mapsto p$$

Here, $i..j \mapsto p$ is defined recursively as follows.

$$\begin{array}{ll} i..j \mapsto (\iota) & \triangleq i..j \mapsto \iota \\ i..j \mapsto \mathsf{skip} & \triangleq i = j \wedge \mathsf{emp} \\ i..j \mapsto p_1; p_2 & \triangleq \exists i'.\ i..i' \mapsto p_1 * i'..j \mapsto p_2 \\ i..j \mapsto \mathsf{LOCAL}\ l;\ p & \triangleq \exists l.\ i..j \mapsto p(l) \\ i..j \mapsto l\!: & \triangleq i = j = l \wedge \mathsf{emp} \end{array}$$

Recall that the definition of triples $\{P\}\ c\ \{Q\}$ in Section 5.1 did not require c to have a particular type; the definition and its rules are valid for any c that can occur on the right of a points-to. Thus, we can put a program p in a triple, and it turns out that the following rules hold.

$$\frac{}{\vdash \{P\}\ \mathsf{skip}\ \{P\}} \qquad \frac{S \vdash \{P\}\ p_1\ \{Q\} \quad S \vdash \{Q\}\ p_2\ \{R\}}{S \vdash \{P\}\ p_1; p_2\ \{R\}}$$

$$\frac{S \vdash \{P\}\ \iota\ \{Q\}}{S \vdash \{P\}\ (\iota)\ \{Q\}} \qquad \frac{S \vdash \forall l.\ \{P\}\ p(l)\ \{Q\}}{S \vdash \{P\}\ \mathsf{LOCAL}\ l;\ p\ \{Q\}}$$

There is no useful rule for the case of l: in a triple.

Example 8. We cannot specify jmp with a triple in any useful way, but we can specify the special case of a tight loop shown above:

$$\vdash \{\mathsf{emp}\}\ \mathsf{LOCAL}\ l;\ l\colon \mathsf{jmp}\ l\ \{\bot\}$$

The proof is by first applying the triple rule for LOCAL, then unfolding the definition of the triple and applying the result of Example 4. ◇

5.4 Assembly macros

A useful assembly language has not only labels but also macros; i.e., parameterised definitions that expand to instruction sequences when invoked. We get macros almost for free since assembly programs are written and parsed inside Coq and can be intermixed with all the features of its term language. This includes let-bindings, fixpoint computations, custom syntax, coercions, overloading and other features of a modern dependently-typed programming language.

An example of a very useful macro is the following definition of while(p_1, t, b, p_2), where p_1 is a loop test, p_2 is a loop body, t encodes the combination of processor flags to be branched on, and b is a boolean that indicates whether the test should be inverted.

$$\begin{aligned}\mathsf{while}(p_1,t,b,p_2) \triangleq\ & \mathsf{LOCAL}\ l_1, l_2;\\ & \mathsf{jmp}\ l_1;\\ l_2\colon\ & p_2;\\ l_1\colon\ & p_1;\\ & \mathsf{jcc}\ t, b, l_2\end{aligned}$$

The jcc instruction is the general *conditional jump* on x86. We see here how LOCAL lets us declare labels that will be fresh for every invocation of the while macro. Real-world macro assemblers also have that functionality, although the scope is usually tied to the nearest named macro or global label. Our Coq notations for assembly syntax, including LOCAL, are chosen to be compatible with *MASM*, the Microsoft assembler.

Macros such as while give us the usual convenience of not having to write similar code many times. But even better, it lets us avoid writing similar proofs many times. If the body and test can be specified in terms of a triple, then the loop as a whole also has a triple specification:

$$\frac{S \vdash \{P\}\ p_1\ \{\exists b'.\ I(b') * \mathsf{cond}(t,b')\} \qquad S \vdash \{I(b) * \mathsf{cond}(t,b)\}\ p_2\ \{P\}}{S \vdash \{P\}\ \mathsf{while}(p_1,t,b,p_2)\ \{I(\neg b) * \mathsf{cond}(t,\neg b)\}}\ \textsc{While}$$

Here, cond(t, b) translates t, of type Condition from Figure 1, to an assertion that tests the relevant flags. For example, $\mathsf{cond}(\mathsf{Z}, b) = \mathsf{ZF} \mapsto b$, where ZF is the *zero flag*. There are two loop invariants, P and I, representing the state before and after executing the test p_1 since this may have side effects.

The proof of the WHILE rule involves $\triangleright$-operators and the LÖB rule, but these technicalities do not leak out into the rule statement.

With if and while macros and the sequence operator on programs, we have the building blocks to easily write and verify programs with structured control flow. These constructs also facilitate using our assembly language as the target of a verified compiler from a structured language, which is something we hope to investigate more in future work.

5.5 Procedure calls

The triple $\{P\}\ c\ \{Q\}$ encodes and abstracts the often-occurring programming pattern of structured control flow. Another crucial pattern to capture is procedure calls. We will here show the theory of a very simple calling convention [29]: store the return address in register EDX and jump to the procedure entry point. The following macro calls the procedure whose code is at address f.

$$\begin{aligned}\mathsf{call}\ f \triangleq\ & \mathsf{LOCAL}\ i_{\mathrm{ret}};\\ & \mathsf{mov\ EDX}, i_{\mathrm{ret}};\\ & \mathsf{jmp}\ f;\\ i_{\mathrm{ret}}\colon\ & \end{aligned}$$

The calling convention does not specify how to pass arguments or return values; this is instead part of individual procedure specifications. A more realistic calling convention would maintain a stack of arguments and return addresses to allow deep call hierarchies and reentrancy, but this would clutter our examples with arithmetic side conditions because the stack has to be finite [29].

The following definition describes the behaviour of a procedure starting at f with precondition P and postcondition Q.

$$\begin{aligned}f{\mapsto}\{P\}\{Q\} \triangleq \forall i_{\mathrm{ret}}.\ & \mathsf{safe} \otimes (\mathsf{EIP} \mapsto i_{\mathrm{ret}} * \mathsf{EDX?} * Q) \Rightarrow\\ & \mathsf{safe} \otimes (\mathsf{EIP} \mapsto f * \mathsf{EDX} \mapsto i_{\mathrm{ret}} * P)\end{aligned}$$

Recall that EDX? is shorthand for $\exists v.\ \mathsf{EDX} \mapsto v$. This definition satisfies the usual rules for a triple-like formula, including

$$\frac{}{f{\mapsto}\{P\}\{Q\} \otimes R \equiv f{\mapsto}\{P * R\}\{Q * R\}}\ \otimes\text{-}\textsc{Proc}$$

In contrast with the triple defined in Section 5.1, this definition of a procedure specification does not mention the code stored at f. The code should be mentioned separately from its behaviour such that the footprint of the code covers both the caller and the callee.

The rule for calling a procedure looks fairly standard:

$$\frac{}{\triangleright f{\mapsto}\{P\}\{Q\} \vdash \{P\}\ \mathsf{call}\ f\ \{Q\} \otimes \mathsf{EDX?}}\ \textsc{Call}$$

It reveals that EDX is overwritten as part of the calling convention. The $\triangleright$ modality on the premise, together with LÖB, permits recursion [3].

Example 9. This is the first of three examples to illustrate independent verification of caller and callee. Consider the following definition of a program that calls some procedure at f twice:

$$p_{\mathrm{caller}}(f) \triangleq \mathsf{call}\ f;\ \mathsf{call}\ f$$

If the intention with this program is to compose it with a procedure that satisfies

$$S_{\mathrm{callee}}(f) \triangleq \forall a.\ f{\mapsto}\{\mathsf{EAX} \mapsto a\}\{\mathsf{EAX} \mapsto a+2\},$$

then we can specify the caller as

$$S_{\mathrm{callee}}(f) \vdash \{\mathsf{EAX} \mapsto a\}\ p_{\mathrm{caller}}(f)\ \{\mathsf{EAX} \mapsto a+4\} \otimes \mathsf{EDX?}$$

We can prove this specification directly from the program sequencing rule and CALL. No $\triangleright$ connective is put on the assumption since no recursion is intended. ◇

If a procedure body p is structured and returns at its very end, we can prove its specification through the following rule.

$$\frac{S \vdash \{P\}\ p\ \{Q\} \oslash \mathsf{EDX?}}{S \vdash f{\mapsto}\{P\}\{Q\} \oslash f \mapsto (p;\ \mathsf{jmp\ EDX})}\ \textsc{Body}$$

In words, this means that calling f behaves as (P, Q) when in memory where the program (p; jmp EDX) is at address f, assuming we can prove the given triple, which is allowed to access EDX as long as it restores its value in the end.

Example 10. The following program almost satisfies S_{callee} as defined in Example 9.

$$p_{\mathrm{callee}} \triangleq \mathsf{inc\ EAX};\ \mathsf{inc\ EAX};\ \mathsf{jmp\ EDX}$$

We say *almost* because the inc instruction affects the status flags of the CPU as a side effect. The caller is not interested in the flags, but they have to be in the specification of p_{callee} since they do get affected. Let flags be the assertion that all flags are of some (existential) value. Then we can prove

$$\vdash S_{\text{callee}}(f) \otimes \mathsf{flags} \oslash f \mapsto p_{\text{callee}}.$$

The proof is by applying BODY, whose conclusion matches the above specification after rewriting by $\otimes$-PROC. ◇

The next example demonstrates how to compose a caller and a callee, even if the callee has a larger footprint than what the caller assumes. This shows how to execute the informal reasoning from Example 3 in our logic.

Example 11. We can now compose the implementations of the caller from Example 9 and the callee from Example 10 to obtain the following closed program. We arbitrarily choose to place the callee in memory before the caller.

$$p_{\text{main}}(entry) \triangleq \mathsf{LOCAL}\ f;\ f\colon p_{\text{callee}};\ entry\colon p_{\text{caller}}(f)$$

We can give the following specification to this program, which says that the code between $entry$ and j will increment EAX by 4 and step on EDX and the flags.

$$\begin{aligned}\vdash (&\mathsf{safe} \otimes (\mathsf{EIP} \mapsto j * \mathsf{EAX} \mapsto a+4) \Rightarrow\\ &\mathsf{safe} \otimes (\mathsf{EIP} \mapsto entry * \mathsf{EAX} \mapsto a)\\ )&\otimes (\mathsf{EDX}? * \mathsf{flags}) \oslash (i..j \mapsto p_{\text{main}}(entry))\end{aligned}$$

The crucial step in proving this specification is to satisfy the caller's assumption, S_{callee}, with the callee specification, which is essentially $S_{\text{callee}} \otimes \mathsf{flags}$. The former entails the latter, but here we would need the entailment to go the other way. Instead, we exploit that FRAME is a higher-order frame rule [9] and lets us frame an assertion on to the left and right side of an entailment simultaneously. This is allowed by the rules $\otimes$-$\vdash$ and $\oslash$-$\vdash$ from Sections 4.3 and 4.5. Abbreviating

$$S_{\text{caller}}(f) \triangleq \forall a.\ \{\mathsf{EAX} \mapsto a\}\ p_{\text{caller}}(f)\ \{\mathsf{EAX} \mapsto a+4\} \otimes \mathsf{EDX}?,$$

we can derive

$$\dfrac{\dfrac{\dfrac{}{S_{\text{callee}}(f) \vdash S_{\text{caller}}(f)}\ \text{Ex. 9}}{\begin{array}{l}S_{\text{callee}}(f) \otimes \mathsf{flags} \vdash\\ S_{\text{caller}}(f) \otimes \mathsf{flags}\end{array}}\ \otimes\text{-}\vdash}{\begin{array}{l}S_{\text{callee}}(f) \otimes \mathsf{flags} \oslash f \mapsto p_{\text{callee}} \vdash\\ S_{\text{caller}}(f) \otimes \mathsf{flags} \oslash f \mapsto p_{\text{callee}}\end{array}}\ \oslash\text{-}\vdash$$

We know from Example 10 that $\vdash S_{\text{callee}}(f) \otimes \mathsf{flags} \oslash f \mapsto p_{\text{callee}}$, so by transitivity of $\vdash$ we conclude $\vdash S_{\text{caller}}(f) \otimes \mathsf{flags} \oslash f \mapsto p_{\text{callee}}$. From this, it is straightforward to derive our desired specification for p_{main}. ◇

The preceding example showed how to use FRAME as a *second-order* [9], or, *hypothetical* [32] frame rule. The procedure involved was first-order at run-time, though. The following example involves a proper higher-order procedure; i.e., a procedure that takes a pointer to another procedure as argument.

Example 12. The simplest example of a higher-order procedure is 'apply', which in a functional programming language would be defined as

$$\mathsf{apply}(g, x) = g(x).$$

In our set-up, an apply procedure that takes its g argument in register EBX is implemented simply as

$$p_{\text{apply}} \triangleq \mathsf{jmp\ EBX}.$$

Its specification reflects how it forwards the behaviour (P, Q) of g:

$$\begin{aligned}\vdash (&g \mapsto \{P * \mathsf{EBX}?\}\{Q\} \Rightarrow\\ &f \mapsto \{P * \mathsf{EBX} \mapsto g\}\{Q\}) \oslash f \mapsto p_{\text{apply}}.\end{aligned}$$ ◇

6. Practical verification

We have used our Coq development not only to build a machine model and to validate the logic developed in this paper; it is also an environment for building and verifying actual machine-code programs.

In this section we describe the Coq tactic support that we have developed for making machine code verification manageable, and present a slightly larger example of assembly language (seven instructions!) in order to give a flavour of the Coq proof of its correctness.

6.1 Example: memory allocation

We illustrate the use of the logic, rules, and Coq tactics with a slightly more challenging example: the specification of a memory allocator and its simplest possible realisation, the bumping of a pointer and checking it against a limit.

Its specification is as follows, parameterized by the number of bytes n to be allocated and an address $fail$ to jump to on failure.

$$\begin{aligned}&\mathsf{allocSpec}(n, fail, inv, code) \triangleq \forall i, j.\\ &\quad(\mathsf{safe} \otimes (\mathsf{EIP} \mapsto fail * \mathsf{EDI}?) \land\\ &\quad\ \mathsf{safe} \otimes (\mathsf{EIP} \mapsto j * \exists a.\ (\mathsf{EDI} \mapsto a{+}n) * (a\,..\,a{+}n \mapsto \_)) \Rightarrow\\ &\quad\ \mathsf{safe} \otimes (\mathsf{EIP} \mapsto i * \mathsf{EDI}?))\\ &\quad\otimes (\mathsf{ESI}? * \mathsf{flags} * inv) \oslash (i..j \mapsto code)\end{aligned}$$

The specification is framed by an assertion that register ESI is used as scratch storage, flags are updated arbitrarily, and an internal invariant inv is maintained. The latter might be the well-formedness of some representation of free lists, or in our trivial allocator, simply a pair of pointers.

The calling convention is 'inline', in other words, the allocator is just a macro consisting of assembly in $code$. In Section 6.5, we will wrap a slightly less trivial calling convention around it.

Control either drops through, if successful, or branches to address $fail$, if memory cannot be allocated. On success, the allocator leaves an address a in EDI that is just beyond the n bytes of memory that were allocated; on failure, EDI is trashed.

Perhaps surprisingly, even a bump-and-check implementation consists of seven instructions:

$$\begin{aligned}\mathsf{allocImp}(info, n, fail) \triangleq\ &\mathsf{mov\ ESI}, info;\\ &\mathsf{mov\ EDI}, [\mathsf{ESI}];\\ &\mathsf{add\ EDI}, n;\\ &\mathsf{jc}\ fail;\\ &\mathsf{cmp}\ [\mathsf{ESI}+4],\ \mathsf{EDI};\\ &\mathsf{jc}\ fail;\\ &\mathsf{mov}\ [\mathsf{ESI}],\ \mathsf{EDI}.\end{aligned}$$

The implementation invariant inv is the following:

$$\begin{aligned}&\mathsf{inv}(info) \triangleq \exists base, limit.\\ &\quad info \mapsto base * (info+4 \mapsto limit) * (base\,..\,limit \mapsto \_).\end{aligned}$$

In other words, at address $info$ there is a pair of pointers $base$ and $limit$ that bound a piece of mapped memory.

6.2 Applying instruction rules

During a proof, we typically keep the goal in the form

$$S_{\text{ctx}} \vdash (S \Rightarrow \mathsf{safe} \otimes P) \oslash R.$$

The specifications discussed in this paper are easy to put into that form by applying distributivity rules for $\otimes$ and decurrying nested implications, and we have implemented a tactic to do this automatically. Typically, R describes the code to be executed, and P describes the instruction pointer and the remaining state that will go into proving the precondition of the next instruction.

We may use the full range of specification-logic rules on this goal, but eventually we will want to apply the lemma appropriate for the code that EIP is pointing to in P. We assume that the lemma has the same form as the goal and apply a lemma through the following rule.

$$\frac{\begin{array}{l} S'_{\text{ctx}} \vdash (S' \Rightarrow \mathsf{safe} \otimes P') \oslash R' \\ S_{\text{ctx}} \vdash S'_{\text{ctx}} \\ P \quad \vdash P' * R_{\text{P}} \\ R \quad \vdash R' * \top \\ S_{\text{ctx}} \vdash (S \Rightarrow S' \otimes R_{\text{P}}) \oslash R \end{array}}{S_{\text{ctx}} \vdash (S \Rightarrow \mathsf{safe} \otimes P) \oslash R} \text{ SPECAPPLY}$$

The top premise is the lemma to be applied, and the bottom premise is the remaining proof obligation that describes the symbolic state after having applied the lemma. If the lemma is an instruction rule, the three middle premises correspond to satisfying its preconditions at the level of specifications, data memory and code memory respectively. The latter two can be dealt with by our entailment checker, described in the next subsection.

6.3 Assertion entailment solving

Much of the activity in a formal separation logic proof is proving entailment between assertions. This happens every time a precondition needs to be discharged, and if it is not automated, the proofs will drown in the details of fragile manual context manipulation and rewriting modulo associativity and commutativity.

Typically, we are given a description of the current state P and a precondition P', and we must show $P \vdash P' * R$ for our own choice of frame R, which represents all the left-over state that was not consumed by the precondition and can therefore be framed out. Our approach to this automation is similar to other separation-logic tools [4, 16]: if P and P' consist only of $*$, emp and atomic assertions, we iterate through the conjuncts of P', attempting to unify each with a conjunct found in P and let the two cancel out.

Typically, P' is full of holes corresponding to universally-quantified variables that have yet to be instantiated. The holes are represented in Coq as *unification variables*, which are identifiers that will receive a value upon being unified with a subformula from P. Several subformulas of P may unify, but typically only one choice will permit the entailment as a whole to be solved. For example, we may be proving

$$\mathsf{EAX} \mapsto i * j \mapsto 2 * i \mapsto 1 \vdash \mathsf{EAX} \mapsto U_1 * U_1 \mapsto U_2 * \top,$$

where U_1 and U_2 are unification variables of type DWORD. If our algorithm should attempt to unify the atom $U_1 \mapsto U_2$ with the atom $j \mapsto 2$, it will succeed, but the remaining proof obligation will be

$$\mathsf{EAX} \mapsto i * i \mapsto 1 \vdash \mathsf{EAX} \mapsto j * \top$$

The algorithm succeeds even if it did not solve the goal entirely, leaving the rest to be proved interactively, but in this case there is no solution for the remaining part of the goal.

Rather than try to support backtracking, which does not combine well with interactive proof, we make the algorithm greedy but predictable: subformulas of P' are unified from left to right. In our current example, this would first fix the choice of U_1 to be i, and the second conjunct of P' would therefore become $i \mapsto U_2$, which rules out the bad unification choice from before.

There is of course no guarantee that this always works, but we have found that it virtually always works in practice as long as preconditions are written with this left-to-right order in mind. This happens naturally since it is also more readable for humans who read from left to right. If the algorithm should still fail, it remains possible to manually instantiate the unification variables.

The entailment solving algorithm is implemented with a hybrid approach, where the unification is done by Coq's built-in higher-order unification engine, while the cancellation of identical terms is done with *proof by reflection* [17], which has good performance.

If an entailment has existential quantifiers on the left-hand side, we can apply the rule

$$\frac{\forall x.\ (\mathcal{C}[P(x)] \vdash Q)}{\mathcal{C}[\exists x.\ P(x)] \vdash Q}$$

where $\mathcal{C}$ is formula with a hole that contains only $*$-connectives in the path from the root to the hole. This lets us effectively move the quantified variable into the Coq variable context.

If an entailment has existential quantifiers on the right-hand side, we will eventually need to instantiate them with witnesses. This can be done with the rule

$$\frac{\exists x.\ (P \vdash \mathcal{C}[Q(x)])}{P \vdash \mathcal{C}[\exists x.\ Q(x)]}$$

We immediately apply the rule, but we instantiate x with a *unification variable*, which in practice defers instantiation until a unification forces it to happen as described above.

We have extended the tactic for moving quantifiers into the context so it also works on specification-logic entailments. For example, given the goal

$$S' \vdash \forall x_1.\ S \Rightarrow \mathsf{safe} \otimes (\exists x_3.\ P(x_1, x_3)) \oslash (\exists x_2.\ R(x_2)),$$

the extended tactic will introduce x_1, x_2 and x_3 into the Coq variable context and leave the new goal

$$S' \vdash S \Rightarrow \mathsf{safe} \otimes P(x_1, x_3) \oslash R(x_2).$$

The rules allowing x_2 and x_3 to be pulled out are given in Sections 4.5 and 7.2 respectively.

6.4 Proving the allocator

Correctness consists of proving the following, for any *info*, n, *fail*.

$$\vdash \mathsf{allocSpec}(n, \mathit{fail}, \mathsf{inv}(\mathit{info}), \mathsf{allocImp}(\mathit{info}, n, \mathit{fail})).$$

Here is a fragment of the Coq proof script that deals with the second instruction in the implementation. (We make use of `ssreflect` extensions to standard Coq tactic notation [20].)

```
(* mov EDI, [ESI] *)
rewrite {2}/inv. specintros => base limit.
specapply MOV_RMO_rule.
- by ssimpl.
```

For this instruction, almost everything is handled automatically. The initial `rewrite` simply unfolds the invariant inv to expose the existential quantifiers. The custom tactic `specintros` pulls the existentially-quantified variables from deep within the goal to introduce them into the Coq context. The tactic '`specapply` l' will first normalise both the goal and lemma l to have the form required by the SPECAPPLY rule from Section 6.2. It will then invoke SPECAPPLY with l as the first premise. In this case, l is `MOV_RMO_rule`, the rule for instructions of the form mov $r_1, [r_2]$. The second and fourth premises are trivial, leaving only the precondition of the mov rule as a subgoal. This can be discharged by our `ssimpl` tactic, which implements entailment checking as described in Section 6.3.

In fact none of the instructions needs more than four lines of proof, and we hope to reduce this further through the use of additional lemma and tactic support once we have more experience with proving.

6.5 Wrapping the allocator

Having verified a component, such as the allocator, it is reasonably straightforward to use to the logic to verify higher-level abstractions in a modular way. As an example, we show the wrapping of the allocator in a procedure for consing onto a list.

We start with the inductive 'list segment' assertion of separation logic (originally due to Burstall [13]):

$$\mathsf{listSeg}(p, e, vs) \triangleq \begin{cases} \exists q.\ (p \mapsto v) * (p{+}4 \mapsto q) * \mathsf{listSeg}(q, e, vs') & \text{if } vs = v :: vs' \\ p = e \wedge \mathsf{emp} & \text{otherwise} \end{cases}$$

Here, vs is a list of DWORDs and the assertion says that memory contains a linked list starting at p and ending at e with elements given by vs. A possible specification for our cons function is

$$\begin{array}{l} \mathsf{consSpec}(r_1, r_2, \mathit{info}, i, j, \mathit{code}) \triangleq \forall h, t, e, vs. \\ \quad (i \mapsto \{r_1 \mapsto h * r_2 \mapsto t * \mathsf{listSeg}(t, e, vs) * \mathsf{EDI}?\} \\ \qquad\quad \{r_1? * r_2? * ((\mathsf{EDI} \mapsto 0 * \mathsf{listSeg}(t, e, vs)) \vee \\ \qquad\qquad\qquad (\exists q.\ \mathsf{EDI} \mapsto q * \mathsf{listSeg}(q, e, h :: vs))\} \\ \quad) \otimes (\mathsf{ESI}? * \mathsf{flags} * \mathsf{inv}(\mathit{info})) \oslash (i..j \mapsto \mathit{code}) \end{array}$$

specifying a procedure that is passed a value h in r_1 and a pointer to a list starting at t in r_2. On return, EDI is either zero, and the original linked list is preserved, or EDI points to a linked list segment ending at e with h added as the new head element. An implementation is given by

```
cons(r1, r2, info) ≜ LOCAL fail; LOCAL succeed;
                      allocImp(info, 8, fail);
                      sub EDI, 8;
                      mov [EDI], r1;
                      mov [EDI + 4], r2;
                      jmp succeed;
                     fail:
                      mov EDI, 0;
                     succeed:
                      jmp EDX
```

The proof that for any $r_1, r_2, \mathit{info}, i$ and j,

$$\vdash \mathsf{consSpec}(r_1, r_2, \mathit{info}, i, j, \mathsf{cons}(r_1, r_2, \mathit{info}))$$

is entirely modular, relying on the BODY rule and the previous result that allocImp meets allocSpec.

7. Properties of the frame connectives

We now return to the frame connective, $\otimes$, defined in Section 4.3. In previous literature on higher-order frame rules [8–10, 33], the R in $S \otimes R$ tends to be inert and does not interact with its environment until it has distributed inwards across all connectives and has been merged into the pre- and post-conditions of a triple. Only at that point will the rule of consequence and the existential rule for triples be used to interact with R.

Since we only see triples in certain special cases, as described in Section 5.1, we are interested in specification-level generalisations of the consequence and existential rules, just as FRAME is a specification-level generalisation of the frame rule for triples. The use of these generalised rules in practice is similar to their counterparts in ordinary Hoare logic.

7.1 Specification-level rule of consequence

The standard Hoare rule of consequence states that $\{P\}\ c\ \{Q\}$ is contravariant in P and covariant in Q with respect to entailment. Analogously, the generalisation we present here describes the variance of $S \otimes R$ in R. It turns out that $S \otimes R$ is not always covariant nor always contravariant in R; it can be either, depending on S. We encode this as two predicates on S:

$$\mathsf{frame}_+(S) \triangleq \forall P, Q.\ (P \vdash Q) \Rightarrow (S \otimes P \vdash S \otimes Q)$$
$$\mathsf{frame}_-(S) \triangleq \forall P, Q.\ (P \vdash Q) \Rightarrow (S \otimes Q \vdash S \otimes P)$$

These definitions directly give rise to our two specification-level rules of consequence:

$$\frac{\mathsf{frame}_+(S) \quad P \vdash Q}{S \otimes P \vdash S \otimes Q} \qquad \frac{\mathsf{frame}_-(S) \quad P \vdash Q}{S \otimes Q \vdash S \otimes P}$$

All we did so far was to switch the problem to proving $\mathsf{frame}_+(S)$ or $\mathsf{frame}_-(S)$ for particular S, but it turns out that there is a very schematic set of rules for this. Writing $f : (V_1, \ldots, V_n) \longrightarrow V$ to mean

$$\begin{array}{l} \forall S_1, \ldots, S_n.\ \mathsf{frame}_{V_1}(S_1) \wedge \ldots \wedge \mathsf{frame}_{V_n}(S_n) \\ \qquad \Rightarrow \mathsf{frame}_V(f(S_1, \ldots, S_n)), \end{array}$$

we can tabulate the rules for various connectives concisely:

$$\begin{array}{r} \mathsf{safe} : - \\ \top, \bot : + \text{ and } - \\ \triangleright, \otimes, \oslash, \forall, \exists : + \longrightarrow + \text{ and } - \longrightarrow - \\ \wedge, \vee : (+,+) \longrightarrow + \text{ and } (-,-) \longrightarrow - \\ \Rightarrow : (-,+) \longrightarrow + \text{ and } (+,-) \longrightarrow - \end{array}$$

Notice that all the logical connectives preserve either covariance or contravariance of their operands (modulo the flip that happens for implication), but there is no way to combine the variances.

Example 13. For all P_1 and P_2, $\mathsf{frame}_-(\triangleright \mathsf{safe} \otimes P_1 \wedge \mathsf{safe} \otimes P_2)$. $\diamond$

Example 14. For all P, $\mathsf{frame}_+(\mathsf{safe} \otimes P \Rightarrow \bot)$. $\diamond$

There are no definitions analogous to $\mathsf{frame}_+(S)$ and $\mathsf{frame}_-(S)$ for the read-only frame connective since $S \oslash R$ is always contravariant in R. But as we will see in Section 7.3, the frame family of predicates plays an important role for $\oslash$ too.

It is no coincidence that these rules for variance have not been studied in the previous literature. There is no rule for frame_+ or frame_- on Hoare triples, and in a logic where the only atomic specifications are the triple and $\top, \bot$, then any S that satisfies $\mathsf{frame}_+(S)$ or $\mathsf{frame}_-(S)$ is equivalent to either $\top$ or $\bot$.

7.2 Specification-level existential rule

The *existential rule* in Hoare logic allows moving an existential quantifier from the precondition of a Hoare triple out into the logical variable context. Just as we have generalised the frame and consequence rules, we can generalise the existential rule to work with other specifications than triples. Using the same approach as in Section 7.1, we define

$$\mathsf{frame}_\exists(S) \triangleq \forall P.\ \big((\forall x.\ S \otimes P(x)) \vdash S \otimes (\exists x.\ P(x))\big)$$

We can then state the specification-level existential rule as

$$\frac{\mathsf{frame}_\exists(S) \quad S' \vdash \forall x.\ S \otimes P(x)}{S' \vdash S \otimes (\exists x.\ P(x))}$$

The following rules, using the notation introduced in Section 7.1, let us schematically prove $\mathsf{frame}_\exists$.

$$\begin{array}{r} \mathsf{safe} : \exists \\ \triangleright, \otimes, \oslash, \forall : \exists \longrightarrow \exists \\ \wedge : (\exists, \exists) \longrightarrow \exists \\ \Rightarrow : (-, \exists) \longrightarrow \exists \end{array}$$

The natural converse of $\mathsf{frame}_\exists(S)$, with the entailment in the other direction, is equivalent to $\mathsf{frame}_-(S)$. This gives an intuitive justification of the rule for implication above.

Example 15. For all P, c, Q, we have $\mathsf{frame}_\exists(\{P\}\ c\ \{Q\})$. This is seen by unfolding the definition of the triple and applying the above rules. $\diamond$

7.3 Further properties of read-only frame connective

The read-only frame and the frame connectives are interchangeable in certain cases:

1. For singleton frames: $S \oslash \{\sigma\} \equiv S \otimes \{\sigma\}$.
2. If $\mathsf{frame}_{\exists}(S)$ then $S \oslash R \vdash S \otimes R$.
3. If $\mathsf{frame}_{-}(S)$ then $S \otimes R \vdash S \oslash R$.

Whereas two adjacent frame connectives can always be merged and split by the $\otimes$-$*$ rule, this is not always possible for the read-only frame connective:

1. If $\mathsf{frame}_{\exists}(S)$ then $S \oslash (R * R') \vdash S \oslash R \oslash R'$.
2. Unconditionally, $S \oslash R \oslash R' \vdash S \oslash (R * R')$.

8. Related work

This paper builds on previous work on higher-order frame rules, assembly-language verification and guarded recursion.

Separation logic for assembly code. Our work shares many goals with the work of Myreen et al. [28, 29]. They have built a separation logic for subsets of ARM and x86 in the HOL4 proof assistant. Their logic emphasises total correctness, but since assembly-language programs do not terminate, total correctness does not mean guaranteed termination as it usually would. Instead, a postcondition Q means that execution will eventually reach a machine state in Q. This makes specifications much more intensional than in our case, preventing, for example, relocating and patching (or interpreting) code in memory in an externally-unobservable way unless this has been somehow explicitly allowed by the specification.

The logic of Myreen et al. lacks labels in assembly programs, relying instead on explicit instruction address arithmetic. Their entire specification logic takes place in a generalised Hoare triple with multiple pre- and postconditions and offset transformer functions. This is general enough to support jumps, function calls and self-modifying code, but it remains a triple and is thus restricted to what can be expressed with preconditions, postconditions and code blocks.

The CAP family of logics from Shao et al. are also Hoare logics for low-level code, all verified in Coq. The family includes XCAP [31], GCAP [14], SCAP and ISCAP [40]. Unfortunately, neither of them is a generalisation of any of the others, so each has its strengths and weaknesses. All except GCAP and SCAP have high-level heap manipulation commands such as allocation or function calls built into the machine semantics.

All except GCAP have the program residing in a map from labels to instruction sequences, which is a high level of abstraction and cannot support treating code as data. As Myreen [28] and hopefully this paper have shown, it is not difficult to treat code as data and support function pointers if the logic is fundamentally set up for it. In contrast, GCAP supports it with some awkwardness by attempting to impose the map-from-labels abstraction on top of what is actually happening in the machine.

Affeldt et al [1] have formalized in Coq a separation logic for first-order MIPS assembly code, extending a simpler logic due to Saabas and Uustalu [36], and applied it to verifying provable security of implementations of cryptographic primitives.

Chlipala's Bedrock project [16] is also a Coq framework for verifying low-level code with separation logic. Like our framework, Bedrock has 'while' and 'if' macros and associated proof principles for common patterns of structured code. Chlipala emphasises automated verification, and the program logic is therefore not very expressive. There is no frame rule, so frames are instead passed around explicitly in procedure specifications. Chlipala explains the problem with defining a frame rule for programs with unstructured jumps; here we have demonstrated how this may be solved.

None of the logics discussed above feature a higher-order frame rule.

Higher-order frame rules. The frame rule was extended by O'Hearn et al. [32] to the *hypothetical frame rule*, which allowed framing invariants onto a context of procedure specifications in addition to the triple under consideration. This allowed greater modularity in separate verification of caller and callee, but it still required programs to have structured control flow.

The higher-order frame rule was proposed by Birkedal et al. and used in a separation-logic type system for a programming language with higher-order functions and ground store [8–10]. It has later been extended to languages with higher-order store and used by Krishnaswami [23] and by Pottier [33]. In all cases, it has been for high-level functional programming languages, whereas we have applied it to machine code. We believe we are the first to complement the higher-order frame rule with a higher-order rule of consequence and a higher-order existential rule (Sections 7.1 and 7.2).

Typed assembly language. The work of Appel et al. on typed assembly language and foundational proof-carrying code has demonstrated that step indexing [2] is a viable technique for describing the behaviour of low-level programs. The 'Very Modal Model' paper [3] popularised Nakano's *later* operator, which we also use here, and demonstrated its applicability to assembly code.

The work on typed assembly language focuses on safety of reference types coming from high-level languages and does not attempt to verify code for full functional correctness as we do.

9. Future work

The logic described in this paper will form the foundation for broader research on language-based security in verified systems software.

Although the focus of this paper is on the general design of a separation logic for machine code, and is thus largely parametric in the underlying machine model, one's confidence in the real world validity of verifications in the logic is undeniably limited by one's confidence in the accuracy of that model. Our x86 model was hand-constructed from reading the Intel manuals and, although small programs extracted from Coq seem to run as expected on real hardware, has not been subject to any systematic testing or verification. Indeed, there is one aspect of the Intel specification that we knowingly do not currently model, namely the presence of a code cache: instructions written to memory are, on post-Pentium processors, not guaranteed to be picked up by subsequent execution until a jump or other synchronizing instruction has occurred. We plan to treat the code cache following the approach of Myreen [28], which we expect to be unproblematic. More generally, however, we would like to work with a more trustworthy machine model; these have previously been obtained by extensive testing [19, 26] and semi-automated extraction from the text of reference manuals [11].

An important feature currently missing from our machine model is I/O. By adding this we would incorporate *observations* beyond the simple notion of 'safe' execution, but we believe that our framework is generic enough that the safe specification can be generalized to safety properties involving observable input and output transitions. We have not so far given any serious thought to how one might also prove liveness properties in a comparably extensional way, though that is clearly an interesting subject for future work. It would also be useful to extend our logic to deal with binary relations, rather than unary predicates, on machine states. Such an extension would allow us to verify information flow and abstraction properties [7].

We have already begun to experiment with verified compilation, building a tiny imperative language, its compiler, program logic and proof of correctness, all within Coq. It is straightforward to mix machine code with higher-level languages, as our logic provides a common framework for specifying their interaction at a suitably high level. We plan to develop a number of domain-specific 'little languages' within the same framework.

Low-level code often makes sophisticated use of low-level data structures whose 'ownership' properties cannot easily be captured by the default model of separation described here. We might instead employ 'fictional separation logic' [22]; it is interesting to note that even our use of partial states Σ to describe the machine state $\mathbb{S}$ in a more fine-grained way is reminiscent of fictional separation.

Acknowledgements. We would like to thank Lars Birkedal and Kasper Svendsen for many discussions on higher-order frame rules and their applications.

References

[1] R. Affeldt, D. Nowak, and K. Yamada. Certifying assembly with formal security proofs: the case of BBS. *Sci. Comput. Prog.*, 77(10-11), 2012.

[2] A. W. Appel and D. McAllester. An indexed model of recursive types for foundational proof-carrying code. *ACM Trans. Program. Lang. Syst.*, 2001.

[3] A. W. Appel, P.-A. Melliès, C. D. Richards, and J. Vouillon. A very modal model of a modern, major, general type system. In *Proceedings of POPL*, 2007.

[4] J. Bengtson, J. B. Jensen, and L. Birkedal. Charge! – a framework for higher-order separation logic in Coq. In *Proc. of ITP*, 2012.

[5] N. Benton. A typed, compositional logic for a stack-based abstract machine. In *APLAS*, volume 3780 of *LNCS*, 2005.

[6] N. Benton. Abstracting allocation: The new new thing. In *Computer Science Logic (CSL 2006)*, volume 4207 of *LNCS*, 2006.

[7] N. Benton and N. Tabareau. Compiling functional types to relational specifications for low level imperative code. In *TLDI*, 2009.

[8] L. Birkedal, N. Torp-Smith, and H. Yang. Semantics of separation-logic typing and higher-order frame rules. In *Proc. of LICS*, 2005.

[9] L. Birkedal, N. Torp-Smith, and H. Yang. Semantics of separation-logic typing and higher-order frame rules for Algol-like languages. *Logical Methods in Computer Science*, 2006.

[10] L. Birkedal and H. Yang. Relational parametricity and separation logic. *Logical Methods in Computer Science*, 2008.

[11] F. Blanqui, C. Helmstetter, V. Joloboff, J.-F. Monin, and X. Shi. Designing a CPU model: from a pseudo-formal document to fast code. In *3rd Workshop on Rapid Simulation and Performance Evaluation: Methods and Tools (RAPIDO 2011)*, 2011.

[12] R. Bornat, C. Calcagno, P. W. O'Hearn, and M. J. Parkinson. Permission accounting in separation logic. In *Proceedings of POPL*, 2005.

[13] R. M. Burstall. Some techniques for proving correctness of programs which alter data structures. *Machine Intelligence*, 7, 1972.

[14] H. Cai, Z. Shao, and A. Vaynberg. Certified self-modifying code. In *Proc. of PLDI*, 2007.

[15] C. Calcagno, P. W. O'Hearn, and H. Yang. Local action and abstract separation logic. In *Proc. of LICS*, 2007.

[16] A. Chlipala. Mostly-automated verification of low-level programs in computational separation logic. In *Proc. of PLDI*, 2011.

[17] A. Chlipala. *Certified Programming with Dependent Types*. MIT Press, to appear.

[18] R. W. Floyd. Assigning meanings to programs. In J. T. Schwartz, editor, *Mathematical Aspects of Computer Science*, volume 19 of *Proc. of Symposia in Applied Mathematics*, Providence, Rhode Island, 1967. AMS.

[19] A. C. J. Fox and M. O. Myreen. A trustworthy monadic formalization of the ARMv7 instruction set architecture. In *1st International Conference on Interactive Theorem Proving (ITP 2010)*, volume 6172 of *LNCS*, 2010.

[20] G. Gonthier, A. Mahboubi, and E. Tassi. A small scale reflection extension for the Coq system. Technical Report 6455, INRIA, 2011.

[21] C. Hawblitzel and E. Petrank. Automated verification of practical garbage collectors. In *POPL*, 2009.

[22] J. B. Jensen and L. Birkedal. Fictional separation logic. In *Proc. of ESOP*, volume 7211 of *LNCS*. Springer, 2012.

[23] N. R. Krishnaswami. *Verifying Higher-Order Imperative Programs with Higher-Order Separation Logic*. PhD thesis, Carnegie Mellon University, 2012.

[24] J. McCarthy and J. Painter. Correctness of a compiler for arithmetic expressions. In *Mathematical Aspects of Computer Science*, volume 19 of *Proc. of Symposia in Applied Mathematics*. AMS, 1967.

[25] J. Strother Moore. A mechanically verified language implementation. *Journal of Automated Reasoning*, 5, 1989.

[26] G. Morrisett, G. Tan, J. Tassarotti, J.B. Tristan, and E. Gan. Rocksalt: Better, faster, stronger SFI for the x86. In *33rd ACM SIGPLAN Conference on Programming Language Design and Implementation (PLDI 2012)*. ACM, 2012.

[27] G. Morrisett, D. Walker, K. Crary, and N. Glew. From System F to typed assembly language. *ACM Transactions on Programming Languages and Systems*, 21(3), 1999.

[28] M. O. Myreen. Verified just-in-time compiler on x86. In *Proc. of POPL*, 2010.

[29] M. O. Myreen and M. J. C. Gordon. Hoare logic for realistically modelled machine code. In *Proc. of TACAS*, 2007.

[30] H. Nakano. A modality for recursion. In *Proc. of LICS*, 2000.

[31] Z. Ni and Z. Shao. Certified assembly programming with embedded code pointers. In *Proc. of POPL*, 2006.

[32] P. W. O'Hearn, H. Yang, and J. C. Reynolds. Separation and information hiding. In *Proc. of POPL*, 2004.

[33] F. Pottier. Hiding local state in direct style: a higher-order anti-frame rule. In *Proc. of LICS*, 2008.

[34] J. C. Reynolds. An introduction to specification logic. In *Logics of Programs*, 1983.

[35] J. C. Reynolds. Separation logic: A logic for shared mutable data structures. In *Proc. of LICS*, 2002.

[36] A. Saabas and T. Uustalu. A compositional natural semantics and Hoare logic for low-level languages. *Theor. Comput. Sci.*, 373(3), 2007.

[37] M. Sozeau and N. Oury. First-class type classes. In *Proc. of TPHOLs*, 2008.

[38] G. Tan and A. W. Appel. A compositional logic for control flow. In *7th International Conference on Verification, Model Checking, and Abstract Interpretation (VMCAI 2006)*, 2006.

[39] A. M. Turing. Checking a large routine. In *Report of a Conference on High Speed Automatic Calculating Machines*, 1949.

[40] X. Jiang W. Wang, Z. Shao and Y. Guo. A simple model for certifying assembly programs with first-class function pointers. In *Proc. of TASE*, 2011.

[41] W. D. Young. A mechanically verified code generator. *Journal of Automated Reasoning*, 5, 1989.

How Languages Can Save Distributed Computing

Andrew C. Myers

Department of Computer Science
Cornell University
Ithaca, New York, United States
andru@cs.cornell.edu

1. Current abstractions are failing us

Current networked computing platforms make available to users an immense and growing amount of computing power and storage. This should be an exciting time for computing, and it is. To users, it might seem an infinitely powerful Internet Computer exists with a manifestation on each of their several computing devices.

However, distributed applications are still relatively primitive and unreliable; they are too centralized on clusters provisioned by individual organizations; users find it hard to share code or even data without opening themselves up to attacks.

The grit in the gears of progress is the difficulty of building applications for the Internet Computer. Our programming models are simply too difficult and low-level for programmers to use effectively. We need higher-level programming models and programming languages that get us closer to programming the Internet Computer directly.

The software stack Industry-standard programming models involve developing the application logic in a programming language such as Java. (The situation is not very different in most other programming languages, except that library and tool support are typically weaker.) This application logic sits atop a large stack of abstractions, whose abbreviations seem to proliferate: SQL, HTTP, EJB, RMI, XML, AJAX, SOAP, JSON, etc. Because these abstractions don't hide the software layers below, applications must be written in a way that is aware of too much of the stack. This structure makes the application complex and unreliable, and more likely to have security vulnerabilities. Further, as it filters through these layers, information within the program is transformed through multiple representations as it migrates from persistent storage to remote clients and back, creating fragility and inefficiency.

Of course, there are reasons why the software stack has evolved to this complex state. Distributed programs must handle distributed code and data securely and efficiently. They usually span multiple domains of trust: a user client and a server, at least, though applications that bring together information and code from multiple domains are becoming more common.

If past history is any guide, industry will keep incrementally adding new layers to the software stack. On the current trajectory, our computers will become increasingly difficult and unpleasant to program, and less secure. Something better is needed, and languages can help.

2. A higher-level abstraction: Fabric

In Fabric [1, 6], we have been exploring a very different approach to building distributed applications, centered around a high-level programming language in which code and data can be used in a uniform and transparent way, regardless of where that code and data is located on the network. Objects at the language level may be persisted at remote nodes in the network. Analogously to the current use of JavaScript, the code for those objects may be located at remote, untrusted nodes and dynamically loaded by the using node. Dynamic loading is important because we want to (securely) support the kinds of activities already common in the web ecosystem, in which programmers share and swap code and data freely.

There are two challenges in realizing this vision: first, to develop a programming model that in an abstract way exposes to the programmer the underlying systems issues: persistence, distribution, failure, and security. Second, to realize this model in an implementation that, even in a completely decentralized system, respects the properties that the language-level abstraction purports to offer. These properties can easily be in tension with each other. For example, the distributed protocols needed to ensure consistency can easily enable distrusted participants to infer confidential information.

The language abstraction The Fabric programming language closely resembles Java, but differs in some important respects.

- Similarly to the Jif programming language [7], it adds information security annotations that specify the confidentiality and integrity of information manipulated by the program. The security of the system is enforced both statically and dynamically by using these policies to control information flow. Fabric goes beyond Jif by adding annotations that control new attacks on confidentiality and integrity that arise in a distributed setting: covert channels created by requests for remote objects, and attacks on integrity that might be launched by downloaded mobile code.
- All information, including distributed and persistent data and code, is presented to the programmer as language-level objects. The system automatically takes care of caching, migrating, and persisting these objects to support efficient, secure, consistent execution. There is no need to have a relational database as part of the software stack.

Categories and Subject Descriptors D.3.2 [*Programming Languages*]: Language Classifications—Concurrent, distributed, and parallel languages; D.4.6 [*Operating Systems*]: Security and Protection—information flow controls

Keywords security, information flow, abstractions

POPL'13, January 23–25, 2013, Rome, Italy.
ACM 978-1-4503-1832-7/13/01.

- Distribution is exposed explicitly to the programmer through annotations on constructors and method calls that indicate where allocation or computation, respectively, should occur. For example, a method call `o.m@n()` transfers control to network node `n` to run the code.
- The consistency and durability of computations of these distributed, persistent objects is supported by a language-level transaction mechanism. The statement `atomic` $\{S\}$ executes statement S as though in isolation from everything else happening on the network, even when S contains distributed computation.

Implementing the abstraction Fabric aims to provide this high-level programming abstraction, yet with an implementation that runs code securely and efficiently on a completely decentralized collection of nodes. The threat model is similar to that of the web, so malicious nodes are assumed to be part of Fabric and to be able to join and then provide code and data to other nodes. The Fabric compiler and run-time system together ensure that information does flow to any node that is not trusted to enforce its confidentiality policy, and that information does not flow from any node that is not trusted to enforce its integrity policy. The inherent compositionality of information flow control then ensures that all information flows across the distributed system respect the information security policies, even though these policies are interpreted and enforced in a decentralized way.

Cooperation between nodes requires explicit trust, so information security policies are expressed in terms of principals. Nodes are principals in Fabric, and like all other principals, are represented by objects that can describe their trust in other principals. Complex trust relationships can thus be expressed, enabling enforcement of complex information security controls.

Nodes serve three roles in Fabric: as *workers*, which do computation over cached copies of objects persistently stored elsewhere; as *stores*, which record the authoritative versions of persistent objects and ensure durability; and as *dissemination nodes*, which make object data highly available. These different kinds of nodes support a variety of different distributed architectures, including web-like client–server structures, but also more general structures, such as clients that directly interact or clients that use information and code from multiple servers.

Fabric works differently from middleware systems such as RMI or CORBA because worker nodes cache copies of remote objects rather than representing remote objects as proxies. This implementation choice is important for security and for performance. Execution stays on the current node unless there is an explicit transfer of control through a remote method call. Computing on object copies means that remote nodes do not learn when objects they store are used. A hierarchical two-phase commit protocol ensures consistency while protecting the confidentiality and integrity of information from untrusted participants.

The prototype implementation of Fabric is publicly available [5].

3. Conclusions

The Fabric project is developing a new language and system to support the kinds of activities now happening on the web: the free exchange of code and data across a decentralized, distributed system. Fabric eliminates much of the complexity of the current web-based distributed programming model, by raising the level of abstraction at which applications are developed. This makes the resulting system simpler overall, by eliminating software layers and data conversions that are not essential to application functionality. By exposing security considerations in information flow policies, it supports secure composition of code and data from different trust domains.

Fabric is one approach to raising the level of abstraction, and clearly could be extended usefully in various ways. There have been several other recent language-based attempts to raise the level of abstraction for programming distributed systems, particularly for web applications [2–4, 8]. Some of these show that the Fabric abstraction is not the only candidate for an effective high-level programming abstraction. For example, abstractions centered around streams are likely to be useful for some applications.

If we are to obtain a clean, high-level language-level abstraction for programming future distributed computing systems, it is to be hoped that the programming language community will be involved. However, this will require that language researchers confront some traditionally "systems" issues such as persistence, distribution, and security, and to develop effective abstractions for handling these issues. To program the Internet Computer, programming-language research will need to break out of its abstraction layer.

References

[1] Owen Arden, Michael D. George, Jed Liu, K. Vikram, Aslan Askarov, and Andrew C. Myers. Sharing mobile code securely with information flow control. In *Proc. IEEE Symposium on Security and Privacy*, pages 191–205, May 2012.

[2] Adam Chlipala. Static checking of dynamically-varying security policies in database-backed applications. In *Proc. 9th USENIX Symp. on Operating Systems Design and Implementation (OSDI)*, October 2010.

[3] Stephen Chong, Jed Liu, Andrew C. Myers, Xin Qi, K. Vikram, Lantian Zheng, and Xin Zheng. Secure web applications via automatic partitioning. In *Proc. 21st ACM Symp. on Operating System Principles (SOSP)*, October 2007.

[4] Ezra Cooper, Sam Lindley, Philip Wadler, and Jeremy Yallop. Links: Web programming without tiers. In *Proc. 5th International Symposium on Formal Methods for Components and Objects*, November 2006.

[5] Jed Liu, Owen Arden, Michael D. George, K. Vikram, and Andrew C. Myers. Fabric 0.2. Software release, `http://www.cs.cornell.edu/projects/fabric`, October 2012.

[6] Jed Liu, Michael D. George, K. Vikram, Xin Qi, Lucas Waye, and Andrew C. Myers. Fabric: A platform for secure distributed computation and storage. In *Proc. 22nd ACM Symp. on Operating System Principles (SOSP)*, pages 321–334, 2009.

[7] Andrew C. Myers, Lantian Zheng, Steve Zdancewic, Stephen Chong, and Nathaniel Nystrom. Jif 3.0: Java information flow. Software release, `http://www.cs.cornell.edu/jif`, July 2006.

[8] M. Serrano, E. Gallesio, and F. Loitsch. HOP, a language for programming the Web 2.0. In *Proc. 1st Dynamic Languages Symposium*, pages 975–985, October 2006.

Quantitative Relaxation of Concurrent Data Structures

Thomas A. Henzinger* Christoph M. Kirsch+ Hannes Payer+ Ali Sezgin* Ana Sokolova+

*IST Austria
{tah,asezgin}@ist.ac.at

+University of Salzburg
firstname.lastname@cs.uni-salzburg.at

Abstract

There is a trade-off between performance and correctness in implementing concurrent data structures. Better performance may be achieved at the expense of relaxing correctness, by redefining the semantics of data structures. We address such a redefinition of data structure semantics and present a systematic and formal framework for obtaining new data structures by quantitatively relaxing existing ones. We view a data structure as a sequential specification containing all "legal" sequences over an alphabet of method calls. Relaxing the data structure corresponds to defining a distance from *any* sequence over the alphabet to the sequential specification: the k-relaxed sequential specification contains all sequences over the alphabet within distance k from the original specification. In contrast to other existing work, our relaxations are semantic (distance in terms of data structure states). As an instantiation of our framework, we present two simple yet generic relaxation schemes, called out-of-order and stuttering relaxation, along with several ways of computing distances. We show that the out-of-order relaxation, when further instantiated to stacks, queues, and priority queues, amounts to tolerating bounded out-of-order behavior, which cannot be captured by a purely syntactic relaxation (distance in terms of sequence manipulation, e.g. edit distance). We give concurrent implementations of relaxed data structures and demonstrate that bounded relaxations provide the means for trading correctness for performance in a controlled way. The relaxations are monotonic, which further highlights the trade-off: increasing k increases the number of permitted sequences, which as we demonstrate can lead to better performance. Finally, since a relaxed stack or queue also implements a pool, we obtain new concurrent pool implementations that outperform the state-of-the-art ones.

Categories and Subject Descriptors D.3.1 [*Programming languages*]: Formal definitions and theory—semantics; E.1 [*Data Structures*]: Lists, stacks, and queues; D.1.3 [*Programming languages*]: Programming techniques—concurrent programing

General Terms Theory, Algorithms, Design, Performance

Keywords (concurrent) data structures, relaxed semantics, quantitative models, costs

POPL'13, January 23–25, 2013, Rome, Italy.

1. Introduction

Concurrent data structures may be a performance and scalability bottleneck and thus prevent effective use of increasingly parallel hardware [18]. There is a trade-off between scalability (performance) and correctness in implementing concurrent data structures. A remedy to the scalability problem is to relax the semantics of concurrent data structures. The semantics is given by some notion of equivalence with sequential behavior. The equivalence is determined by a consistency condition, most commonly linearizability [7], and the sequential behavior is inherited from the sequential version of the data structure (e.g., the sequential behavior of a concurrent stack is a regular stack). Therefore, relaxing the semantics of a concurrent data structure amounts to either weakening the consistency condition (linearizability being replaced with sequential consistency or quiescent consistency) or redefining (relaxing) its sequential specification. In this paper, we present a framework for relaxing sequential specifications in a quantitative manner.

For an example of a relaxation, imagine a *k*-stack in which each `pop` removes one of the most recent *k* elements and an operation `size` which returns a value that is at most *k* away from the correct size. It is intuitively clear that such a *k*-stack relaxes a regular stack, but current theory does not provide means to quantify the relaxation. Our framework does, it provides a way to formally describe and quantitatively assess such relaxations.

We view a data structure as a sequential specification *S* consisting of all semantically correct sequences of method calls. We identify the sequential specification with a particular labeled transition system (LTS) whose states are sets of sequences in *S* with indistinguishable future behavior and transitions are labeled by method calls. A sequence is in the sequential specification if and only if it is a finite trace of this LTS.

Our framework for quantitative relaxation of concurrent data structures amounts to specifying costs of transitions and paths. In the LTS, only *correct* transitions are allowed, e.g., a transition labeled by `pop(a)` is only possible in a state of a stack with `a` as top element. In a relaxation, we are exactly interested in allowing the *wrong* transitions, but they will have to incur cost. Our framework makes this possible in a controlled quantitative way.

The framework is instantiated through specifying two cost functions: A local function, *transition cost*, that assigns a penalty to each wrong transition, and a global function, *path cost*, that accumulates the local costs (using, e.g., maximum, sum, or average) to obtain the overall distance of a sequence. Via this local-global dichotomy, we are able to achieve a separation of concerns, modularity and flexibility: Different transition costs can be used with the same path cost, or vice versa, leading to different relaxations. Once the distance of a sequence from the original sequential specification *S* is defined in this way, a *k*-relaxation of the data structure becomes the set of all sequences within distance *k* from *S*.

Returning to the stack example above, we can set the transition cost of a `pop` transition at a state to be the number of elements that are between the popped element and the top of the stack. We can define the path cost to be the maximum transition cost that occurs along a sequence. Then, the corresponding k-relaxation precisely captures what we intuitively described.

We instantiate the framework on two levels. On the abstract level, we present two generic relaxations called out-of-order and stuttering relaxation, which provide a way to assign transition costs, together with several different path cost functions for *any* data structure. On the concrete level, we instantiate the out-of-order relaxation to stacks, queues, and priority queues. We spell out the effects of the relaxation in these concrete cases and prove that they indeed correspond to the intuitive idea of bounded relaxed out-of-order behavior. We also instantiate the stuttering relaxation to a Compare-And-Swap (CAS) object and a shared counter and prove correspondence results as well.

We show that the relaxation framework is indeed of practical value: we give an efficient new implementation of an out-of-order stack and fit an existing efficient implementation of an out-of-order queue [11] in our framework as well. The experimental results demonstrate ideal behavior: linear scalability and performance. In particular, the relaxed stack implementation we present outperforms and outscales state-of-the-art stack, queue, and pool algorithms on various workloads. We also present implementations for a stuttering CAS, a stuttering shared counter using this stuttering CAS and a different stuttering shared counter, all of which further demonstrate increased scalability and performance.

The main contributions of this paper are: (1) the framework for quantitative relaxation of data structures, and (2) efficient concurrent implementations. The way to the framework is paved by formally capturing the semantics of a data structure. Other contributions made possible by the framework are: the generic out-of-order and stuttering relaxations of data structures; characterizations of the out-of-order relaxation in concrete terms for stacks, queues, and priority queues; characterization of the stuttering relaxation in concrete terms for CAS and shared counters.

The structure of the paper is as follows. In the remainder of this section, we provide motivation for the main features of our work. We present the formal view on data structures in Section 2, followed by the framework for quantitative relaxation in Section 3. Throughout the formal part we use a stack as running example. We present the two generic instances, out-of-order and stuttering relaxations, in Section 4 and instantiate them further to concrete data structures in Section 5 and Section 6, respectively. We discuss related work in Section 7. In Section 8 we present implementation details and in Section 9 experimental results confirming our original scalability and performance goal. We wrap up with concluding remarks in Section 10.

In the related work survey, we put special emphasis on quasi-linearizability [2], the only other work we are aware of that also tackled the problem of quantitatively relaxing sequential data structures for better performance in the concurrent setting. As opposed to our semantic (state-based) approach in assigning distances to sequences, the relaxation of [2] is syntactic (permutation-based). We argue that (1) the semantic approach is more expressive than the syntactic one, and (2) it allows the designer of a data structure to formally capture the intent of a specific relaxation more easily and naturally.

Highlights

Relaxation improves performance. A relaxation of the sequential specification of a data structure can lead to a distribution of contention points, diminishing the need for, and thus, the cost of synchronization. For instance, instead of requiring that each pop operation updates the top pointer of a concurrent stack, allowing a relaxation which sets the size of the window from which a removal is deemed acceptable to some $k > 1$ (most recent elements) effectively reduces contention for the top pointer. In Section 9, we show that even such a simple relaxation for stacks with $k = 80$ on a 40-core (2 hyperthreads per core) server machine can lead to an eight-fold increase in performance compared to the existing state-of-the-art implementations of strict stacks.

Note that a larger sequential specification increases the potential for better performance. Since our relaxations are monotonic, increasing k increases the performance potential. However, the extent to which this potential can be utilized in practice depends on many factors among which is the choice of hardware.

Generality. Consider three different sequences belonging to three different data structures, stack, queue, and priority queue, respectively:

```
push(a)push(b)push(c)push(d)
enq(a)enq(c)enq(b)enq(d)
ins(a)ins(b)ins(d)ins(c)
```

where for the priority queue `b` has top priority, followed by `a` and `c` that have the same medium priotity, and `d` has low priority.

If these sequences are extended with a removal operation (`pop`, `deq`, `rem`, respectively), the expected return values are `d` (element at the top of the stack), `a` (element at the head of the queue), and `b` (element with the highest priority).

Imagine instead, that the removal operation returns `c` for all of these three sequences. At first sight, that `c` is returned seems to be arbitrary. However, a careful examination reveals a common pattern: In each sequence, `c` is not the current, but *next* (possible) value to be removed. That is, in the stack it is the element immediately below the top element; in the queue it is the element immediately after the head element; in the priority queue it is an element with the second highest priority. It then seems natural to view all these relaxations as an instantiation of a common relaxation scheme.

Our framework allows one to precisely express this and other common types of relaxations. For instance, our generic out-of-order relaxation provides exactly this for data structures in which information is retrieved according to some order, temporal in the case of queue and stack, logical in the case of a priority queue. The generic relaxation removes the need of relaxing each data structure separately.

Modularity. Let us now consider the situation immediately following the removal of `c` from the stack as was depicted above. We have the following sequence:

```
push(a)push(b)push(c)push(d)pop(c)
```

The stack now contains the elements `a`, `b`, and `d`, the last of which is on top. One might desire a particular relaxation where two consecutive out-of-order removals are not allowed, and hence, the next removal has to return `d`. Yet another might find it acceptable that at all times one of the top two elements are removed; it does not matter how long the top element remains on the stack. Our framework allows one to express both. Each transition incurs a transition cost. Observe that in both relaxations the same cost (out-of-order removal cost) is assigned to each transition. Each sequence of transition costs incurs a path cost, and this is what distinguishes the two relaxations. The first will require that there are no two consecutive transitions with non-zero cost; the second will require that the maximum of any transition cost is at most 1. We thus obtain a modular framework in which existing relaxations can be tailored by modifying transition costs, path costs, or both.

Measurability. The code given in Figure 1(a) represents a CAS-based strict shared counter. The shared variable `c` is a counter, and each thread tries to increment the value of the counter. Representative of many concurrent implementations, this code leads to poor scalability as all threads trying to increment the counter will compete for access to `c`.

```
while(true):
  x = c;
  if (CAS(&c,x,x+1)):
    return x+1;
```
(a) Single counter.

```
while(true):
  x,v = getMaxAndValueAt(c, f(t));
  if (CAS(&c[f(t)],v,x+1)):
    return x+1;
```
(b) Distributed counter.

Figure 1. Shared counters

Next, consider a modified version of this shared counter, given in Figure 1(b). Unlike the strict implementation, here we use an array `c` of k counters and the logical value of the shared counter is taken to be the maximum value among all the counters in `c`. Each thread `t` can write only to the slot with index `f(t)`. Each attempt of `t` incrementing the counter starts by reading the value contained in `f(t)` (stored in `v`) and the maximum value of all the counters in `c` (stored in `x`). Then, it tries to update its counter to $\mathtt{x}+1$ provided that `f(t)` is not updated by a concurrent thread.

The behavior of this code depends crucially on the value chosen for the size k of the array. For instance, if $k = 1$, then this implementation will be behaviorally equivalent to the single counter code. For other values of k, it is evident that there will be a discrepancy between the behaviors of the two codes.

We go beyond this qualitative notion (existence vs. absence of relaxation) and provide a measure for any relaxation defined in our framework. The distributed counter given in Figure 1(b) is in fact a k-stuttering relaxation of the shared counter of Figure 1(a). This way an application developer using a quantitatively relaxed data structure can evaluate the gain in performance for k-relaxation vs. the effort of modifying an application that uses it, and try to optimize k. For instance, if the relaxed shared counter is used as a performance counter counting the occurrence of a given event, e.g. context switches in a multi-processor scheduler, not all occurrences of events will be registered. Knowing that the number of unregistered event occurrences within one counter increment can not exceed k (the size of `c`) is a crucial information for the application designer.

Transparency. Now consider the code given in Figure 2. This code is very similar to the strict shared counter code of Figure 1(a) except for the call to the method `kCAS` instead of `CAS`. The `kCAS` is a relaxed version of `CAS` such that up to at most k many concurrent threads trying to update the value of the `CAS` object can complete with false positive (see Section 6 and Section 8 for details).

Although the `kCAS` and the distributed counter of Figure 1(b) take fundamentally different approaches in relaxing the strict semantics of a counter, they both implement a k-stuttering relaxation. This illustrates another use of our framework: It can be used as a simpler way to establish abstract equivalence, thus providing transparency for a higher-level application. If one shows that two implementations implement the same relaxation, then a client application using either implementation will observe the same behavior, regardless of the differences in actual implementation details.

```
while(true):
  x = c;
  if (kCAS(&c,x,x+1)):
    return x+1;
```
Figure 2. `kCAS` counter.

2. Data structures, specifications, states

Let Σ be a set of methods including input and output values. We will refer to Σ as the sequential alphabet. A *sequential history* $\mathbf{s}$ is an element of Σ^*, i.e., a sequence over Σ. As usual, by ε we denote the empty sequence in Σ^*. A *data structure* is a *sequential specification* S which is a prefix-closed set of sequential histories, $S \subseteq \Sigma^*$.

EXAMPLE 2.1. The set of methods of a stack, with data in a set D, is

$$\Sigma_{\mathbb{S}} = \{\mathtt{push(d)} \mid \mathtt{d} \in D\} \cup \{\mathtt{pop(d)} \mid \mathtt{d} \in D \cup \{\mathtt{null}\}\}.$$

The sequential specification $S_{\mathbb{S}}$ consists of all stack-valid sequences, i.e., sequences in which each pop pops the top of the stack and each push pushes an element at the top. For instance, the sequence $\mathbf{s}_{\mathbb{S}} = \mathtt{push(a)pop(a)push(b)}$ is in the sequential specification $S_{\mathbb{S}}$, whereas the sequence $\mathbf{t}_{\mathbb{S}} = \mathtt{push(a)push(b)pop(a)}$ is not.

The following definition is the core of our way of capturing semantics. Let S be a sequential specification.

DEFINITION 2.2. *Two sequential histories* $\mathbf{s}, \mathbf{t} \in S$ *are* S-equivalent, *written* $\mathbf{s} \equiv_S \mathbf{t}$, *if for any sequence* $\mathbf{u} \in \Sigma^*$, $\mathbf{su} \in S$ *if and only if* $\mathbf{tu} \in S$.

It is clear that $\equiv_S$ is an equivalence relation. By $[\mathbf{s}]_S$ we denote the S-equivalence class of $\mathbf{s}$. Intuitively, two sequences in the sequential specification are S-equivalent if they lead to the same "state". The following simple property follows directly from the definition of S-equivalence.

LEMMA 2.3. *If* $\mathbf{s} \equiv_S \mathbf{t}$ *and* $\mathbf{su} \in S$, *then* $\mathbf{su} \equiv_S \mathbf{tu}$.

The intuition about states is made explicit in the next definition. In addition, we point out particular "minimal" representatives of a state.

DEFINITION 2.4. *A state of a data structure with sequential specification S is an equivalence class $[\mathbf{s}]_S$ with respect to $\equiv_S$. For a state $q = [\mathbf{s}]_S$, the kernel of q is the set*

$$\ker(q) = \{\mathbf{t} \in [\mathbf{s}]_S \mid \mathbf{t} \textit{ has minimal length }\}.$$

A sequence $\mathbf{s} \in S$ is a kernel sequence if $\mathbf{s} \in \ker([\mathbf{s}]_S)$.

EXAMPLE 2.5. One can easily show that kernel sequences of a stack are all sequences in $\{\mathtt{push(d)} \mid d \in D\}^*$. Moreover, for any state $q = [\mathbf{s}]_{S_{\mathbb{S}}}$ of a stack, there is a unique sequence in $\ker(q)$, i.e., $|\ker(q)| = 1$. This implies that different sequences in $\mathbf{s} \in \{\mathtt{push(d)} \mid \mathtt{d} \in D\}^*$ represent different states.

Having identified states, a data structure corresponds to a labeled transition system (LTS) that we define next.

DEFINITION 2.6. *Let S be a (sequential specification of a) data structure. Its corresponding LTS is* $\mathrm{LTS}(S) = (Q, \Sigma, \rightarrow, q_0)$ *with*

- *set of states* $Q = S/\equiv_S = \{[\mathbf{s}]_S \mid \mathbf{s} \in S\}$,
- *set of labels* Σ,
- *transition relation* $\rightarrow \subseteq Q \times \Sigma \times Q$ *given by*

$$[\mathbf{s}]_S \xrightarrow{m} [\mathbf{s}m]_S \textit{ if and only if } \mathbf{s}m \in S, \textit{ and}$$

- *initial state* $q_0 = [\varepsilon]_S$.

Note that the transition relation is well defined (independent of the choice of a representative) due to Lemma 2.3. Also q_0 is well defined since S is prefix closed. We write $q \xrightarrow{m}$ if there is an m-labeled transition from q to some state; $q \overset{m}{\not\rightarrow}$ if there is no m-labeled transition from q. We also write $q \xrightarrow{\mathbf{u}}$ if there is a $\mathbf{u}$-labeled path of transitions starting from q, and $q \overset{\mathbf{u}}{\not\rightarrow}$ if it is not the case that $q \xrightarrow{\mathbf{u}}$. The following immediate observation provides the exact correspondence between the sequential specification of a data structure and its LTS: S is the set of finite traces of the initial state of $LTS(S)$.

LEMMA 2.7. *Let S be a sequential specification with* $\mathrm{LTS}(S) = (Q, \Sigma, \rightarrow, q_0)$. *Then for any* $\mathbf{u} \in \Sigma^*$ *we have* $\mathbf{u} \in S$ *if and only if* $q_0 \xrightarrow{\mathbf{u}}$.

EXAMPLE 2.8. Since different stack-kernel sequences represent different states, cf. Example 2.5, the transitions of $LTS(S_S)$ are fully described by

$$[\mathbf{s}]_{S_S} \overset{\texttt{push(a)}}{\rightarrow} [\mathbf{s}\cdot\texttt{push(a)}]_{S_S}$$
$$[\mathbf{s}]_{S_S} \overset{\texttt{pop(a)}}{\rightarrow} [\mathbf{s}']_{S_S} \quad \text{if } \mathbf{s} = \mathbf{s}'\cdot\texttt{push(a)}, \text{ and}$$
$$[\mathbf{s}]_{S_S} \overset{\texttt{pop(null)}}{\rightarrow} [\varepsilon]_{S_S} \text{ if } \mathbf{s} = \varepsilon$$

where $\mathbf{s}$ is a kernel sequence in $\{\texttt{push(d)} \mid d \in D\}^*$. Note that if $\mathbf{s} = \mathbf{s}'\cdot\texttt{push(a)}$, then $[\mathbf{s}\cdot\texttt{pop(a)}]_{S_S} = [\mathbf{s}']_{S_S}$.

3. Framework for quantitative relaxations

We are now ready to present the framework for quantitatively relaxing data structures. Let $S \subseteq \Sigma^*$ be a data structure with $\mathrm{LTS}(S) = (Q, \Sigma, \rightarrow, q_0)$. Our goal is to relax S to a so-called k-relaxed specification $S_k \subseteq \Sigma^*$ in a bounded way, with k providing the bound.

Giving a relaxation for a data structure S amounts to the following three steps:

1. **Completion.** From $\mathrm{LTS}(S) = (Q, \Sigma, \rightarrow, q_0)$ we construct the completed labeled transition system
$$\mathrm{LTS}_c(S) = (Q, \Sigma, Q \times \Sigma \times Q, q_0)$$
with transitions from any state to any other state by any method.
2. **Transition costs.** From $\mathrm{LTS}_c(S)$ a quantitative labeled transition system $\mathrm{QLTS}(S) = (Q, \Sigma, Q \times \Sigma \times Q, q_0, C, \mathrm{cost})$ is constructed. Here C is a well-ordered cost domain, hence it has a minimum that we denote by 0, and $\mathrm{cost}\colon Q \times \Sigma \times Q \rightarrow C$ is the transition cost function satisfying
$$\mathrm{cost}(q, m, q') = 0 \quad \text{if and only if} \quad q \overset{m}{\rightarrow} q' \text{ in } \mathrm{LTS}(S).$$
We write $q \overset{m,k}{\rightarrow} q'$ for the quantitative transition with $\mathrm{cost}(q, m, q') = k$. A quantitative path of $\mathrm{QLTS}(S)$ is a sequence
$$\kappa = q_1 \overset{m_1,k_1}{\rightarrow} q_2 \overset{m_2,k_2}{\rightarrow} q_3 \ldots q_n \overset{m_n,k_n}{\rightarrow} q_{n+1}.$$
The sequence $\tau = (m_1, k_1)(m_2, k_2)\ldots(m_n, k_n) \in (\Sigma \times C)^*$ is the quantitative trace of κ, notation $\mathrm{qtr}(\kappa)$, and the sequence $\mathbf{u} = m_1 \ldots m_n$ is the trace of the quantitative path κ and of the quantitative trace $\mathrm{qtr}(\kappa)$, notation $\mathrm{tr}(\kappa) = \mathrm{tr}(\mathrm{qtr}(\kappa)) = \mathbf{u}$. By $\mathrm{qtr}(\mathbf{u})$ we denote the set of all quantitative traces of quantitative paths starting in the initial state with trace $\mathbf{u}$ and by $\mathrm{qtr}(S)$ the set of all quantitative traces of quantitative paths starting in the initial state.
3. **Path cost function.** We choose a monotone path cost function $\mathrm{pcost}\colon \mathrm{qtr}(S) \rightarrow C$. Monotonicity here is with respect to prefix order: if a quantitative trace τ is a prefix of a quantitative trace τ', then $\mathrm{pcost}(\tau) \leqslant \mathrm{pcost}(\tau')$.

Having performed these three steps, we can define the k-relaxed specification.

DEFINITION 3.1. *The k-relaxed specification S_k for $k \in C$ contains all sequences that have a distance at most k from S,*

$$S_k = \{\mathbf{u} \in \Sigma^* \mid d_S(\mathbf{u}) \leqslant k\}$$

where $d_S(\mathbf{u})$ is the distance of $\mathbf{u}$ to the sequential specification S given by

$$d_S(\mathbf{u}) = \min\{\mathrm{pcost}(\tau) | \tau \in \mathrm{qtr}(\mathbf{u})\}.$$

REMARK 3.2. Both the distance d_S and the relaxed specification S_k are actually parametric in the transition cost function as well as in the path cost function. For simplicity, we prefer a light, overloaded notation that does not explicitly mention these parameters. Also, for some applications one may wish for two different cost domains, one for the transition, one for the path cost, of which only the second one needs to be well ordered. Again for simplicity, we restrict the presentation to a single cost domain.

Some obvious properties of the quantified relaxations resulting from our framework are:

- $S_0 = S$, ensured by the condition on the transition cost function.
- Every relaxation S_k is prefix closed, ensured by the monotonicity of the path cost function.
- The relaxations are monotone, i.e., if $k \leqslant m$, then $S_k \subseteq S_m$.

To conclude, in order to relax a data structure all that one needs is a cost domain C, a transition cost for each transition in the completed LTS (item 2. above), and a path cost function (item 3. above).

REMARK 3.3. The current framework does not allow for relaxations that leave the original state space of $LTS(S)$. An example of such is a prophetic relaxation of e.g. stack, where sequences with $\texttt{pop(a)}$ preceding $\texttt{push(a)}$ need to be assigned finite distance. This can be done by slightly changing the definition of $LTS_c(S)$: Instead of keeping the original states $S/\equiv_S$, one can take as set of states the quotient $\Sigma^*/\sim$ where $\sim$ is an equivalence that coincides with $\equiv_S$ when restricted to S. For simplicity and since we do not use such relaxations in this paper, our current definition of $LTS_c(S)$ keeps the states unchanged.

4. Generic relaxations

In this section we illustrate the relaxation framework on two generic examples. The value and generality of these particular examples become evident in Section 5 and Section 6 when we instantiate them to concrete data structures. Let $S \subseteq \Sigma^*$ be a data structure with $\mathrm{LTS}(S) = (Q, \Sigma, \rightarrow, q_0)$. We first fix the cost domain to $C = \mathbb{N} \cup \{\infty\}$.

4.1 Out-of-order relaxation

For the out-of-order generic relaxation we define a transition cost function $scost\colon Q \times \Sigma \times Q \rightarrow C$, called *segment cost*, and mention two other related transition cost functions.

DEFINITION 4.1. *Let $t = (q, m, q')$ be a transition in $\mathrm{LTS}_c(S)$. Let $\mathbf{v}$ be a sequence with minimal length satisfying one of the following two conditions:*

(1) There exist sequences $\mathbf{u}$, $\mathbf{w}$ such that $\mathbf{uvw} \in \ker(q)$ and $\mathbf{uw}$ is a kernel sequence and either
  (i) $[\mathbf{uw}]_S \overset{m}{\rightarrow} [\mathbf{u'w}]_S$ and $q' = [\mathbf{u'vw}]_S$, or
  (ii) $[\mathbf{uw}]_S \overset{m}{\rightarrow} [\mathbf{uw'}]_S$ and $q' = [\mathbf{uvw'}]_S$.

(2) There exist sequences $\mathbf{u}$, $\mathbf{w}$ such that $\mathbf{uw} \in \ker(q)$ and $\mathbf{uvw}$ is a kernel sequence and either
  (i) $[\mathbf{uvw}]_S \overset{m}{\rightarrow} [\mathbf{u'vw}]_S$ and $q' = [\mathbf{u'w}]_S$, or
  (ii) $[\mathbf{uvw}]_S \overset{m}{\rightarrow} [\mathbf{uvw'}]_S$ and $q' = [\mathbf{uw'}]_S$.

Then the segment cost is given by the length of $\mathbf{v}$, $scost(t) = |\mathbf{v}|$. If such a sequence $\mathbf{v}$ does not exist for t, then $scost(t) = \infty$.

Intuitively, segment cost of a relaxed transition is the length of the shortest subword ($\mathbf{v}$) whose removal (1) or insertion (2) into the kernel sequence enables a transition. Observe that the transition can be taken in $\mathrm{LTS}(S)$ if and only if its segment cost is 0, obtained by setting $\mathbf{v} = \varepsilon$. We will see in the next section that this cost quantifies *out-of-order* updates or observations, such as returning an element other than the top element in a stack or removing an element other than the head of a queue. We note that segment cost just as any transition cost can also be used per method, i.e., some methods may be relaxed, some not.

4.2 Stuttering relaxation

For the stuttering generic relaxation, we define the so-called *stuttering cost.*

DEFINITION 4.2. *Let $t = (q, m, q')$ be a transition in $\mathrm{LTS}_c(S)$. Then, the* stuttering cost, *stcost is defined as*

$$stcost(q,m,q') = \begin{cases} 0 & \text{if } q \xrightarrow{m} q' \\ 1 & \text{if } q = q' \wedge q \stackrel{m}{\nrightarrow} q' \wedge q \xrightarrow{m} \\ \infty & \text{otherwise} \end{cases}$$

where $\rightarrow$ is the transition relation of $LTS(S)$.

Intuitively, the stuttering relaxation allows for (already enabled) transitions to have no effect on the state. If, in the specification S, q goes to $\hat{q}$ with method m and $q \neq \hat{q}$, then the stuttering cost of applying m at q *and* staying at q after the transition is 1. All other transitions which are not part of the original specification are set to have infinite cost.

An example of an unbounded (except in the maximal size of the queue) stuttering relaxation is presented in [15], where workers are allowed to work on the same task by a relaxed queue semantics and an element in the queue can be dequeued a number of times (up to the maximal size of the queue). In favor of bounded stuttering we note that, typically, implementations can benefit from retiring (completing rather than retrying) mutator method calls when there is too much contention and have the client handle false positives.

4.3 Path cost functions

Let $S \subseteq \Sigma^*$ be a data structure and $\tau = (m_1, k_1)(m_2, k_2)\dots(m_n, k_n)$ a quantitative trace in $\mathrm{qtr}(S)$. We define the following generic path cost functions (to be used with any transition cost):

- The *maximal cost*, $\mathrm{pcost}_{max}\colon \mathrm{qtr}(S) \to \mathbb{N} \cup \{\infty\}$, maps τ to the maximal transition cost along it. Formally,

$$\mathrm{pcost}_{max}(\tau) = \max\{k_i \mid 1 \leqslant i \leqslant n\}.$$

- The φ-*interval cost*, $\mathrm{pcost}_{[\varphi]}\colon \mathrm{qtr}(S) \to \mathbb{N} \cup \{\infty\}$, for φ a binary predicate (first order formula with two free variables making statements about positions in the quantitative trace), maps τ to the length of a maximal consecutive quantitative subtrace that satisfies φ. Hence, we have

$$\mathrm{pcost}_{[\varphi]}(\tau) = \max\{j - i + 1 \mid \varphi(i,j) \text{ and } 1 \leqslant i \leqslant j \leqslant n\}.$$

- The φ-*interval restricted maximal cost*, $\mathrm{pcost}_{max|[\varphi]}\colon \mathrm{qtr}(S) \to \mathbb{N} \cup \{\infty\}$, for φ as in the φ-interval cost, is given by

$$\mathrm{pcost}_{max|[\varphi]}(\tau) = \max\{l_{i,j} \mid \varphi(i,j) \text{ and } 1 \leqslant i \leqslant j \leqslant n\},$$

  where

$$l_{i,j} = \max\{k_r + (r - i + 1) \mid i \leqslant r \leqslant j\}.$$

We instantiate the out-of-order relaxation along with the maximal, φ-interval, and φ-interval restricted maximal cost on stacks, queues, and priority queues in Section 5. The φ-interval restricted maximal cost is more complex and less intuitive than the other path cost functions, but when instantiated it provides valuable relaxation examples that are efficiently implementable. In Section 6 we apply the stuttering relaxation along with the φ-interval cost on a CAS object and on a shared counter. Note that the other two cost functions do not make much sense together with the stuttering cost (the maximal cost is two-valued and the φ-interval restricted maximal cost amounts to the φ-interval cost plus one).

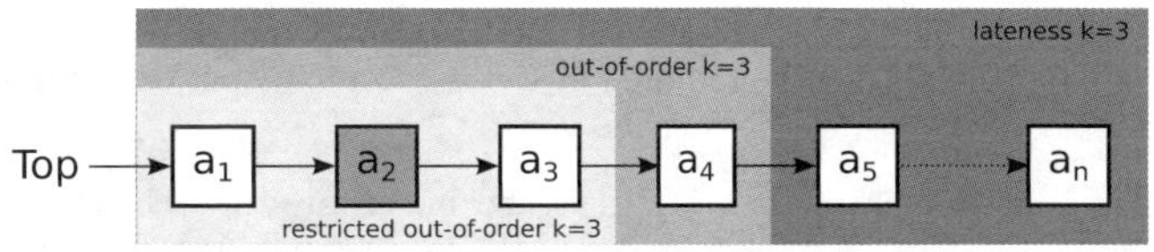

Figure 3. The ranges of elements which may be returned by a pop operation of a k-stack with restricted out-of-order, out-of-order, and lateness relaxation with $k = 3$. The element a_2 is already removed.

5. Out-of-order stacks, queues, and priority queues

In this section we apply the relaxation of Section 4.1 to stacks, FIFO queues, and priority queues. Due to lack of space, here we leave out some common methods, e.g., `top` (for stack), `head` (for queue), `size` (for all). Inclusion of these methods does not change the results, in particular Propositions 5.1-5.3, presented in this section.

Stack. We have already given the set of methods of a stack, its states, and its LTS in Example 2.1, Example 2.5, and Example 2.8. Let us recall that the sequential specification S_S consists of all stack-valid sequences, i.e., sequences in which each `pop` pops the top of the stack, and each `push` pushes an element at the top.
Let $\mathbf{s}$ be a kernel sequence. A kernel sequence $\mathbf{s}'$ is

- `push(a)`-out-of-order-k from $\mathbf{s}$ if $\mathbf{s}' = \mathbf{u} \cdot \mathtt{push(a)} \cdot \mathbf{v}$ where $\mathbf{s} = \mathbf{uv}$, $\mathbf{v}$ is minimal, and $|\mathbf{v}| = k$;
- `pop(a)`-out-of-order-k from $\mathbf{s}$ if $\mathbf{s}' = \mathbf{uv}$ where $\mathbf{s} = \mathbf{u} \cdot \mathtt{push(a)} \cdot \mathbf{v}$, $\mathbf{v}$ is minimal, and $|\mathbf{v}| = k$;
- `pop(null)`-out-of-order-k from $\mathbf{s}$ if $\mathbf{s} = \mathbf{s}'$ and $|\mathbf{s}| = k$;

By inspecting all cases, we can show the following proposition.

PROPOSITION 5.1. *Let $\mathbf{s}$ and $\mathbf{s}'$ be two kernel sequences of a stack. Then $[\mathbf{s}]_{S_S} \xrightarrow{m,k} [\mathbf{s}']_{S_S}$ in the out-of-order relaxation with segment cost if and only if $\mathbf{s}'$ is m-out-of-order-k from $\mathbf{s}$.*

As mentioned in Section 4.1, the relaxations can be applied method-wise. We implemented k-relaxed stacks with only `push` and `pop` methods, of which only `pop` is relaxed according to the segment cost.The interpretation of the path cost functions from Section 4.3 and the corresponding relaxations are as follows:

- The maximal cost represents the maximal distance from the top of a popped element, leading to an *out-of-order k-stack.* Hence, in an out-of-order k-stack, each `pop` pops an element that is at most k away from the top.

Let $\varphi(i, j)$ be the following first order formula with free variables i and j:

$$\forall r \in [i, j].\, k_r \neq 0$$

- The φ-interval cost represents lateness, i.e., the maximal number of consecutive pops needed to pop the top, leading to a *lateness k-stack.* Hence, in a lateness k-stack at most the k-th consecutive pop pops the top.
- The φ-interval restricted maximal cost represents the maximal size of a "shrinking window" starting from the top from which elements can be popped, leading to a *restricted out-of-order k-stack.* In a restricted out-of-order k-stack, each pop removes an element at most $k - l$ away from the top, where l is the current lateness of the top.

Figure 3 presents a snapshot of a relaxed stack in each of the three out-of-order relaxations. It shows a state of a stack in which the element a_2, marked in grey, has been removed after the last removal of the top or the last push had happened. The ranges show which elements may be returned by a pop operation applied to this state in each out-of-order relaxed version for $k = 3$.

FIFO queue. We now briefly describe the out-of-order relaxation of a queue.The set of methods for a FIFO queue, with data set D, is

$$\Sigma_Q = \{\texttt{enq(d)} \mid \texttt{d} \in D\} \cup \{\texttt{deq(d)} \mid \texttt{d} \in D \cup \{\texttt{null}\}\}.$$

The sequential specification S_Q consists of all queue-valid sequences, i.e., sequences in which each deq deques the head of the queue and each enq enqueues at the tail of the queue. For instance, the following sequence $\mathbf{s}_Q = \texttt{enq(a)enq(b)deq(a)}$ is in the sequential specification S_Q, whereas the sequence $\mathbf{t}_Q = \texttt{enq(a)enq(b)deq(b)}$ is not.

One can easily show that kernel sequences of a FIFO queue are all sequences in $\{\texttt{enq(d)} \mid \texttt{d} \in D\}^*$. Moreover, also here, for any state $q = [\mathbf{s}]_{S_Q}$ of the FIFO queue, there is a unique sequence in $\ker(q)$, i.e., $|\ker(q)| = 1$. Hence different sequences in $\mathbf{s} \in \{\texttt{enq(d)} \mid \texttt{d} \in D\}^*$ represent different states. As a consequence, the transition relation of $LTS(S_Q)$ can be described in a concise way. Let $\mathbf{s}$ be a kernel sequence of a queue. We have,

$$[\mathbf{s}]_{S_Q} \overset{\texttt{enq(a)}}{\rightarrow} [\mathbf{s}\cdot\texttt{enq(a)}]_{S_Q},$$
$$[\mathbf{s}]_{S_Q} \overset{\texttt{deq(a)}}{\rightarrow} [\mathbf{s}']_{S_Q} \quad \text{if } \mathbf{s} = \texttt{enq(a)}\cdot\mathbf{s}', \text{ and}$$
$$[\mathbf{s}]_{S_Q} \overset{\texttt{deq(null)}}{\rightarrow} [\varepsilon]_{S_Q} \text{ if } \mathbf{s} = \varepsilon.$$

In a similar way as for stack, we can define when a queue kernel sequence is m-out-of-order-k from another kernel sequence, for m being a queue method. Furthermore, the analogue of Proposition 5.1 (obtained by replacing "stack" by "FIFO queue") holds for queues as well which we state below.

PROPOSITION 5.2. *Let* $\mathbf{s}$ *and* $\mathbf{s}'$ *be two kernel sequences of a queue. Then* $[\mathbf{s}]_{S_Q} \overset{m,k}{\rightarrow} [\mathbf{s}']_{S_Q}$ *in the out-of-order relaxation with segment cost if and only if* $\mathbf{s}'$ *is* m*-out-of-order-*k *from* $\mathbf{s}$.

The maximal path cost function leads to analogous out-of-order k-queue. For lateness and restricted out-of-order k-queues we need to employ slightly different path cost functions.

Priority queue. The data set of a priority queue needs to be well-ordered, since data items carry priority as well. We take the data set to be $\mathbb{N}$. The smaller the number, the higher the priority. The set of methods is

$$\Sigma_{\mathcal{P}} = \{\texttt{ins(n)} \mid \texttt{n} \in \mathbb{N}\} \cup \{\texttt{rem(n)} \mid \texttt{n} \in \mathbb{N} \cup \{\texttt{null}\}\}.$$

The sequential specification $S_{\mathcal{P}}$ consists of all priority-queue-valid sequences, i.e., sequences in which each rem removes an element with highest available priority.

Kernel sequences of a priority queue are all sequences in $\{\texttt{ins(n)} \mid \texttt{n} \in \mathbb{N}\}^*$. Unlike for stack and queue, there may be more than one sequence representing a state of a priority queue. For a state q, if $\mathbf{s} \in \ker(q)$, then also any permutation of $\mathbf{s}$ is in $\ker(q)$. Nevertheless, the order provides a canonical representative of a state: the unique kernel sequence ordered in non-increasing priority[1]. Let $\mathbf{s}$ be a canonical kernel sequence. The transitions of $LTS(S_{\mathcal{P}})$ are fully described by

$$[\mathbf{s}]_{S_{\mathcal{P}}} \overset{\texttt{ins(n)}}{\rightarrow} [\mathbf{s}\cdot\texttt{ins(n)}]_{S_{\mathcal{P}}},$$
$$[\mathbf{s}]_{S_{\mathcal{P}}} \overset{\texttt{rem(n)}}{\rightarrow} [\mathbf{s}']_{S_{\mathcal{P}}} \quad \text{if } \mathbf{s} = \texttt{ins(n)}\cdot\mathbf{s}', \text{ and}$$
$$[\mathbf{s}]_{S_{\mathcal{P}}} \overset{\texttt{rem(null)}}{\rightarrow} [\varepsilon]_{S_{\mathcal{P}}} \text{ if } \mathbf{s} = \varepsilon.$$

Again, we define when a canonical kernel sequence is m-out-of-order-k from another canonical kernel sequence, where m is a priority queue method. We have the following result.

PROPOSITION 5.3. *Let* $\mathbf{s}$ *and* $\mathbf{s}'$ *be two kernel sequences of a priority queue. Then* $[\mathbf{s}]_{S_{\mathcal{P}}} \overset{m,k}{\rightarrow} [\mathbf{s}']_{S_{\mathcal{P}}}$ *in the out-of-order relaxation with segment cost if and only if* $\mathbf{s}'$ *is* m*-out-of-order-*k *from* $\mathbf{s}$.

Analogous relaxations are again possible, only the path cost functions are more complex since they need to capture when an element with higher priority than all existing elements in the priority queue is inserted.

[1] The canonical representative is a matter of choice. Equally justified is using the unique kernel sequence ordered in non-decreasing priority, in which case the transitions of a priority queue resemble more the transitions of a stack, highlighting the duality between FIFO queues and stacks.

6. Stuttering relaxed CAS and shared counter

In this section, we instantiate the relaxation from Section 4.2 to two concrete examples.

CAS. The set of methods for a Compare-And-Swap (CAS) object with a data set D and an initial data value $\texttt{init} \in D$ can, for our purposes, be modeled as

$$\Sigma_{CAS} = \{\texttt{cas(d,d',b)} \mid \texttt{d},\texttt{d}' \in D, \texttt{b} \in \{\texttt{T},\texttt{F}\}\}.$$

The sequential specification S_{CAS} is defined inductively as follows: The empty sequence ε is in S_{CAS} and any sequence of length one and shape $\texttt{cas(init,d,T)}$ is in S_{CAS} for $\texttt{d} \in D$. If $\mathbf{s} \in S_{CAS}$, let $\mathbf{t}$ be the maximal prefix of $\mathbf{s}$ such that $\mathbf{s} = \mathbf{t}\cdot m \cdot \mathbf{u}$ for $m = \texttt{cas(d,d',T)}$. Then $\mathbf{s}\cdot m' \in S_{CAS}$ if either

(1) $m' = \texttt{cas(d',d'',T)}$, or

(2) $m' = \texttt{cas(d'',d''',F)}$ and $\texttt{d}'' \neq \texttt{d}'$.

Let $\mathbf{s} \in S_{CAS}$ and let as before $\mathbf{t}$ be the maximal prefix of $\mathbf{s}$ such that $\mathbf{s} = \mathbf{t}\cdot m\cdot\mathbf{u}$ for $m = \texttt{cas(d,d',T)}$. Then, it is not difficult to show that, $s \equiv \texttt{cas(init,d',T)}$. Hence, there is a unique kernel sequence in each equivalence class and it has length one. The transitions of $LTS(S_{CAS})$ are given by

$$[\varepsilon]_{S_{CAS}} \overset{\texttt{cas(init,d,T)}}{\rightarrow} [\texttt{cas(init,d,T)}]_{S_{CAS}},$$

$$[\texttt{cas(init,d,T)}]_{S_{CAS}} \overset{\texttt{cas(d,d',T)}}{\rightarrow} [\texttt{cas(init,d',T)}]_{S_{CAS}}, \text{ and}$$

$$[\texttt{cas(init,d,T)}]_{S_{CAS}} \overset{\texttt{cas(d',d'',F)}}{\rightarrow} [\texttt{cas(init,d,T)}]_{S_{CAS}} \text{ if } \texttt{d} \neq \texttt{d}'.$$

Intuitively, the state of the CAS object is given by one data value d, initially set to init. In such a state, a transition by method $\texttt{cas(d,d',T)}$ is enabled since the comparison of the first argument and the current value succeeds (returns T, true) leading to the new state value $\texttt{d}'$, that is, a successful comparison results in a swapped value. A transition by method $\texttt{cas(d',d'',F)}$ in which the comparison fails (returns F, false) is enabled if indeed $\texttt{d} \neq \texttt{d}'$ after which no swap happens and the state value remains d. The state with data value d is formally represented by the equivalence class of a sequence with a single method $\texttt{cas(init,d,T)}$.

Now let us formalize the notion of allowing invisible failures for CAS object updates. For this purpose we define another object called failCAS over the same set of methods, with a somewhat different set of legal sequences. We call a sequence

$$\texttt{cas(d,d',T)}\cdot\mathbf{y}\cdot\texttt{cas(d,d'',T)}$$

over Σ_{CAS} a *false positive sequence* if $\texttt{cas(d,d',T)}\cdot\mathbf{y} \in S_{CAS}$, $\mathbf{y}$ is a sequence of symbols of the form $\texttt{cas(d''',-,F)}$ with $\texttt{d}''' \neq \texttt{d}$, and $\texttt{d} \neq \texttt{d}'$. Then, $\mathbf{s} = s_0 \dots s_n \in S_{failCAS}$ if there exists a set of positions $0 = i_0 < i_1 < \ldots < i_r = n$ for $\mathbf{s}$ such that each sequence $s_{i_{j-1}} \cdots s_{i_j}$, for $1 \leqslant j \leqslant r$, is either a false positive sequence or is in S_{CAS}. Let the *failure count* of $\mathbf{x} \in S_{failCAS}$ be the maximum number of consecutive false positive sequences $\mathbf{x}$ contains.

The corresponding relaxation in our framework is obtained by using stuttering cost on the CAS object and φ-interval cost for the predicate $\varphi(i,j)$ given by

$$\forall r \in [i,j].(k_r \neq 0 \vee \exists \mathtt{d}, \mathtt{d}' \in D.(m_r = \mathtt{cas}(\mathtt{d},\mathtt{d}',\mathtt{F}))),$$

leads to a k-CAS in which up to k methods may stutter at the same state (fail to perform a swap even though the data values match). It is then easy to show the following correspondence result.

PROPOSITION 6.1. *A sequence* $\mathbf{x} \in S_{failCAS}$ *has failure count* k *if and only if* $\mathbf{x}$ *is in the specification of* k*-CAS.*

Shared counter. The set of methods of a shared counter is

$$\Sigma_{SC} = \{\mathtt{get\&Inc(n)} \mid \mathtt{n} \in \mathbb{N}\}.$$

The sequential specification S_{SC} of a shared counter contains the empty sequence ε and a sequence $\mathbf{s}$ of length $n > 0$ is in S_{SC} if and only if $\mathbf{s}(\mathtt{i}) = \mathtt{get\&Inc(i)}$, for all $1 \leqslant \mathtt{i} \leqslant n$.

One can easily show that each state of a shared counter is a singleton, i.e., for $\mathbf{s}, \mathbf{t} \in S_{SC}$ we have $\mathbf{s} \equiv \mathbf{t}$ if and only if $\mathbf{s} = \mathbf{t}$. The unique sequence representing a state is automatically a kernel sequence. The transitions of $LTS(S_{SC})$ are obviously given by

$$[\varepsilon]_{S_{SC}} \xrightarrow{\mathtt{get\&Inc(1)}} [\mathtt{get\&Inc(1)}]_{S_{SC}}, \text{ and}$$

$$[\mathbf{s}]_{S_{SC}} \xrightarrow{\mathtt{get\&Inc(n+1)}} [\mathbf{s} \cdot \mathtt{get\&Inc(n+1)}]_{S_{SC}},$$

if $\mathbf{s}(\mathtt{i}) = \mathtt{get\&Inc(i)}$, for all $1 \leqslant \mathtt{i} \leqslant n$.

We define a failing shared counter analogously to a failing CAS object. A sequence $\mathbf{s}$ is a behavior of failSC if either $\mathbf{s} \in \{\varepsilon, \mathtt{get\&Inc(1)}\}$, or $\mathbf{t} = \mathbf{u} \cdot \mathtt{get\&Inc(n)}$ is a behavior of failSC and $\mathbf{s} = \mathbf{t} \cdot \mathtt{get\&Inc(n}+a\mathtt{)}$, for $a \in \{0,1\}$. The *failure count* of $\mathbf{s} \in S_{failSC}$ is one less than the length of a maximal subsequence of identical symbols in $\mathbf{s}$.

The corresponding relaxation of the shared counter is obtained by the stuttering cost and the φ-interval cost, for $\varphi(i,j) = \forall r \in [i,j].k_r \neq 0$. Thus, we get the k-stuttering shared counter, k-SC, in which a method can stutter (fail to produce a new, incremented by one, value) at most k times. For instance, the sequence

$$\mathtt{get\&Inc(1)get\&Inc(2)get\&Inc(2)get\&Inc(2)get\&Inc(3)}$$

is in the sequential specification of the 2-stuttering shared counter, 2-SC. We again have the following correspondence result.

PROPOSITION 6.2. *A sequence* $\mathbf{x} \in S_{failSC}$ *has failure count* k *if and only if* $\mathbf{x}$ *is in the specification of* k*-SC.*

7. Related work

The general topic of this paper is part of a recent trend towards scalable but semantically weaker concurrent data structures [18]. We first discuss work related to our framework and then focus on work related to our implementations.

Framework. The relaxation framework generalizes previous work on so-called semantical deviation and k-FIFO queues [10, 12] which correspond to restricted out-of-order k-FIFO queues here.

Our work is closely related to relaxing the semantics of concurrent data structures through quasi-linearizability [2]. Just like quasi-linearizability, we provide quantitative relaxations of concurrent data structures. Unlike quasi-linearizability which uses syntactic distances, our relaxations are based on semantical distances from a sequence to the sequential specification. We briefly present the quasi-linearizability approach, identify two main issues, and how our method overcomes these.

We call two sequences $\mathbf{x}$, $\mathbf{x}'$, both of length n, permutation equivalent, written $\mathbf{x} \sim \mathbf{x}'$, if there exists a permutation p on $\{1,\ldots,n\}$ such that for all $1 \leqslant i \leqslant n$, $\mathbf{x}(i) = \mathbf{x}'(p(i))$. We write $\mathbf{x} \sim_p \mathbf{x}'$ to emphasize the permutation witnessing $\mathbf{x} \sim \mathbf{x}'$. In such a case, the permutation distance between $\mathbf{x}$ and $\mathbf{x}'$ is given as $\max\{|i - p(i)| \mid 1 \leqslant i \leqslant n\}$.

Let S be a sequential specification over Σ. In [2], the distance of a sequence $\mathbf{x} \in \Sigma^*$ to S is defined via a collection D of subsets of Σ. Let $\mathbf{y} \in \Sigma^*$ be a sequence such that $\mathbf{z} = \mathbf{xy}$ has a permutation equivalent $\mathbf{z}' \in S$. Then, for $A \in D$, the A-cost of obtaining $\mathbf{z}'$ from $\mathbf{z}$ is the permutation distance between $\mathbf{z}|A$ and $\mathbf{z}'|A$, where $|$ denotes restriction. Let k_A denote the minimal A-cost over all $\mathbf{y}$. Then, $\mathbf{x}$ is quasi-linearizable with quasi-linearization factor $Q\colon D \to \mathbb{N}$, if for all $A \in D$, $k_A \leqslant Q(A)$. Observe that the distance for $\mathbf{x}$ is obtained by quantifying over all possible extensions of $\mathbf{x}$ whose permutations are in S. We now show that this definition fails to capture desired relaxation distances.

1. *Not precise.* Consider the following sequence:

$$\mathtt{enq(1)enq(2)enq(3)deq(1)deq(2)enq(4)deq(4)}$$

In order to assign a relaxation cost of 1 to this sequence belonging to an out-of-order queue, quasi-linearizability employs a scheme where only enqueue operations are allowed to commute. Formally, quasi-linearizability uses $D = \{Enq, Deq\}$ with $Q(Enq) = k$ and $Q(Deq) = 0$, where Enq (resp., Deq) contains all enq (resp., deq) symbols. However, with this scheme the sequence $\mathtt{deq(i)}^n$ which removes elements from an empty queue will always be in any k-relaxation of the queue because setting

$$\mathbf{z} = \mathtt{deq(i)}^n\mathtt{enq(i)}^n, \quad \mathbf{z}' = \mathtt{enq(i)}^n\mathtt{deq(i)}^n$$

will give $k_{Enq} = k_{Deq} = 0$, independent of the value n. This means that the following implementation is a 0-relaxation of queue.

```
enq(x): { while(true);}  deq(): { return random();}
```

This implementation is clearly not implementing a queue, nor any intended bounded relaxation of a queue, but all the sequences it generates will have zero distance relative to D as given above. Thus, quasi-linearizability cannot exactly capture intended relaxations and might allow wrong behaviors. Observe that we have already shown in Proposition 5.2 that out-of-order k-queues can never generate such erroneous behavior.

2. *Not general.* For a stack, consider the sequence

$$\begin{aligned}\mathbf{x} \quad = \quad & \mathtt{push(a)[push(i)pop(i)]}^n \\ & \mathtt{push(b)[push(j)pop(j)]}^m \\ & \mathtt{pop(a)[push(1)pop(1)]}^r\end{aligned}$$

where all symbols, a, b, ... have distinct values. Prior to the removal of a, the stack contains a and b, with the latter at the top position. The distance in the out-of-order relaxation induced by maximal path cost and segment cost in this case is 1 since the element popped is immediately after the top entry. However, with quasi-linearization factor Q, it is impossible to precisely capture out-of-order penalty for data structures like stacks. First, consider the case where we pick $\mathbf{z} = \mathbf{x}$, which we can do since $\mathbf{x}$ has a permutation equivalent valid stack sequence. In order to get a permutation $\mathbf{x}'$ of $\mathbf{x}$ such that $\mathbf{x}'$ is a valid sequence of a stack, either one of pop(a) or push(b) has to move over m copies of push and pop operations, or one of push(a) or push(b) has to move over n copies of push and pop operations. So either D is empty which allows for any sequence to be in the relaxation or it is always possible to pick the values for n and m such that the penalty is arbitrarily large. Second, consider the case where we extend **x** with **y** such that **xy** has a permutation equivalent valid stack behavior. But because of the $2r$-long suffix of **x**, a similar reasoning as in the previous case applies to this case as well.

Similarly, a stuttering relaxation will not have a finite quasi-linearizability distance, since no permutation of (an extension of) a stuttering sequence is in the original sequential specification.

Consistency conditions. As opposed to relaxing the sequential specification of a concurrent data structure, one may also relax the consistency condition, e.g., quiescent consistency [4] instead of linearizability. We note that linearizable out-of-order relaxation of a stack is incomparable to a quiescently consistent stack. To see this, first, consider a concurrent history **c** with two threads t_1 and t_2. The history **c** starts with the invocation of `push(a)` by t_1, followed by a sequence `pop(i)`^{n}`push(i)`^{n} all executed by t_2. This history is quiescently consistent for stack because the reordering of methods (even those that do not overlap in time) is allowed as long as they are not separated by a quiescent state. On the other hand, any linearization of **c** will have to observe out-of-order pop operations since the operations of t_2 do not overlap. So, for each k, there exists a history which is quiescently consistent for stack but is not in the specification of an out-of-order k-stack. Second, consider the sequential history `push(a)push(b)pop(a)` which has an out-of-order relaxation distance of 1. Since the history is sequential, quiescent consistency will not allow any reordering. Thus, for any k, there exists a history which is in the specification of an out-of-order k-stack but not quiescently consistent. A comprehensive overview of variants of weaker and stronger consistency conditions than linearizability can be found in [6].

Implementations. Work related to our implementations and experiments is discussed in more detail in Section 8 and Section 9. Here we briefly refer to all the work considered. Our relaxed stack implementation is closely related to the very recent efficient lock-free implementation of a relaxed k-FIFO queue [11] (by some of us and a third coauthor), but the change from queue to stack semantics imposes a significant difference as well. The k-FIFO queue [11] is in turn related to implementations of relaxed FIFO queues such as the Random Dequeue and Segment Queue [2] as well as Scal queues [10, 12]. Both the Random Dequeue Queue and the Segment Queue implement the restricted out-of-order relaxation. The Segment Queue [2] and the k-FIFO queue [11] implement a queue of segments. However, the implementations are quite different with significant impact on performance, see Section 9. Our relaxed stack implementation implements a stack of segments. Scal queues are relaxed queues with, in general, unbounded relaxation. Since any relaxed stack or queue implementation also implements a pool, we compare our work also to state-of-the-art pool implementations [1, 3, 19].

In [5], the authors show that implementing deterministic data structure semantics requires expensive synchronization mechanisms which may prohibit scalability in high contention scenarios. We agree with that and show in our implementations and experiments that the non-determinism introduced in the sequential specification provides scalability and performance benefits. In [15], the authors present a work-stealing queue with relaxed semantics where queue elements may be returned any number of times instead of just once. In comparison to other state-of-the-art work-stealing queues with non-relaxed semantics this may provide better performance and scalability. Again the introduced non-determinism pays off. Overview of different relaxations on hardware and software level is presented in [9, 18].

8. Implementations of relaxed data structures

In this section we present the new implementation of a restricted out-of-order stack (k-stack, for short) and present the two new implementations of a stuttering shared counter. It is interesting to note that the "restricted" relaxation seems to be crucial for obtaining performance[2], which is why we focus on it.

8.1 k-Stack

The top pointer of a concurrent stack may become a scalability bottleneck under high contention [20]. The main idea behind our k-stack implementation is to reduce contention on the top pointer by maintaining a stack of so-called k-segments[3]. We implemented the stack that holds the k-segments similarly to the lock-free stack of [20] with the difference that there is always at least one k-segment, even if it is empty, on the stack. This avoids unnecessary removal and adding of a k-segment, e.g. in the empty state. A k-segment (or just segment, when no confusion arises) contains k "atomic values" (see next paragraph) which may either point to `null` indicating an empty slot or may hold a so-called item. Both push and pop operations are served by the top segment. Hence, up to k stack operations may be performed in parallel. A push operation tries to insert an element in the top segment. It adds a new segment to the stack if the top segment is full. A pop operation tries to remove an element from the top segment. It removes the top segment from the stack if it is empty and is not the only segment on the stack. Additionally, each segment contains an atomic counter `remove` that counts how many threads are trying to remove it from the stack. The counter is initially set to zero.

The pseudo code of the lock-free k-stack algorithm with $k > 0$ is depicted in Figure 4. The occurrence of the ABA problem is made unlikely through version numbers. We refer to values enhanced with version numbers as atomic values. Hence an atomic value has two fields, the actual value `val` and its version number `ver`.

The methods `init`, `try_add_new_ksegment`, and `try_remove_ksegment` implement the stack of segments. In the latter, the atomic counter `remove` is updated and the method `empty` that performs an empty check is called. We discuss the method `empty` within the pop method, as it is also called there.

Let `item` represent an element to be pushed on the k-stack. The `push` method first tries to find an empty slot for the `item` using the `find_empty_slot` method (line 45). The `find_empty_slot` method randomly selects an index in the top k-segment and then linearly searches for an empty slot starting with the selected index and wrapping around at index k. Then the `push` method checks if the k-stack state has been consistently observed by testing whether `top` changed in the meantime (line 46) which would trigger a retry. If an empty slot is found (line 47) the method tries to insert the `item` at the location of the empty slot using a compare-and-swap (`CAS`) operation (line 49). If the insertion is successful the method verifies whether the insertion is also valid by calling the `committed` method (line 50), as discussed below. If any of these steps fails, a retry is performed. If no empty slot is found in the current top segment, the `push` method tries to add a new segment to the stack of segments (line 53) and then retries.

The `committed` method (line 24) validates an insertion, it ensures that the inserted element is really inserted *on the stack.* This method is the core and the main novelty of the algorithm. It returns `true` when the insertion is valid and `false` when it is not valid. An insertion is invalidated if a concurrent thread removes the segment to which the element was inserted before the effect of the

[2] For an efficient implementation one needs a sequential specification that fits the properties of the hardware that it will run on.

[3] The same high-level idea is used in the Segment Queue [2] and the k-FIFO queue [11] discussed in the next subsection.

```
1 global top;
2
3 void init():
4   new_ksegment = calloc(sizeof(ksegment));
5   top = atomic_value(new_ksegment, 0);
6
7 void try_add_new_ksegment(top_old):
8   if top_old == top:
9     new_ksegment = calloc(sizeof(ksegment));
10    new_ksegment->next = top_old;
11    top_new = atomic_value(new_ksegment, top_old.ver+1);
12    CAS(&top, top_old, top_new);
13
14 void try_remove_ksegment(top_old):
15  if top_old == top:
16    if top_old->next != null:
17      atomic_increment(&top_old->remove);
18      if empty(top_old):
19        top_new = atomic_value(top_old->next,
             top_old.ver+1);
20        if CAS(&top, top_old, top_new):
21          return;
22      atomic_decrement(&top_old->remove);
23
24 bool committed(top_old, item_new, index):
25  if top_old->s[index] != item_new:
26    return true;
27  else if top_old->remove == 0:
28    return true;
29  else:  //top_old->remove >= 1
30    item_empty = atomic_value(EMPTY, item_new.ver+1);
31    if top_old != top:
32      if !CAS(&top_old->s[index], item_new, item_empty):
33        return true;
34    else:
35      top_new = atomic_value(top_old.val, top_old.ver+1);
36      if CAS(&top, top_old, top_new):
37        return true;
38      if !CAS(&top_old->s[index], item_new, item_empty):
39        return true;
40  return false;
41
42 void push(item):
43  while true:
44    top_old = top;
45    item_old, index = find_empty_slot(top_old);
46    if top_old == top:
47      if item_old.val == EMPTY:
48        item_new = atomic_value(item, item_old.ver+1);
49        if CAS(&top_old->s[index], item_old, item_new):
50          if committed(top_old, item_new, index):
51            return true;
52      else:
53        try_add_new_ksegment(top_old);
54
55 item pop():
56  while true:
57    top_old = top;
58    item_old, index = find_item(top_old);
59    if top_old == top:
60      if item_old.val != EMPTY:
61        item_empty = atomic_value(EMPTY, item_old.ver+1);
62        if CAS(&top_old->s[index], item_old, item_empty):
63          return item_old.val;
64      else:
65        if only_ksegment(top_old):
66          if empty(top_old):
67            if top_old == top:
68              return null;
69        else:
70          try_remove_ksegment(top_old);
```

Figure 4. Lock-free k-stack algorithm

insertion took place. Therefore, an insertion is valid if the inserted item already got popped at validation time by a concurrent thread (line 25, 32, 38) or the segment where the item was inserted was not removed by a concurrent thread (line 27). A `remove` counter larger than zero indicates that the segment has been removed or concurrent threads are trying to remove the segment from the stack (line 29). If the current top segment is not equal to the segment where the item was inserted we have to conservatively assume that the segment was removed from the stack (line 31) and undo the insertion (line 32). If the current top segment is equal to the segment where the item was inserted, a race with concurrent popping threads may occur which may not have observed the insertion of the item and may try to remove the k-segment from the stack in the meantime. This would result in loss of the inserted item. To prevent that, the method tries to increment the version number in the `top` atomic value using `CAS` (line 36) forcing threads that concurrently try to remove that k-segment to retry. If this fails, a concurrent pop operation may have changed `top` (line 20) which would make the insertion potentially invalid. Hence, in case of losing the race, the method tries to undo the insertion using `CAS` (line 38).

The `pop` method returns an item if the k-stack is not empty. Otherwise it returns `null`. Similar to the `push` method, the `pop` method first tries to find an item in the top segment using the `find_item` method (line 58). The `find_item` method randomly selects an index in the top k-segment and then linearly searches for an item starting with the selected index and wrapping around at index k. Then, the `pop` method checks if the k-stack state has been consistently observed by checking whether `top` changed in the meantime (line 59) which would trigger a retry. If an item was found (line 60) the method tries to remove it using `CAS` (line 62) and returns it if the removal was successful (line 63). Otherwise a retry is performed. If no item is found and the current segment is the only segment on the stack (line 65) an empty check is performed using the method `empty` (line 66). This method stores the values of the k slots of the segment in a local array (if they are empty) and subsequently checks in another pass over the segment slots whether the values in the slots changed in the meantime. If a non-empty slot was found, the empty method immediately returns `false`. If the empty check succeeded and the top did not change in the meantime (line 67), `null` is returned (line 68). Otherwise, if no item is found in the current segment and there is more than one segment in the stack, the method tries to remove the segment (line 70) and performs a retry.

Correctness: k-Stack

We now prove that the k-stack implementation is correct for the relaxed stack semantics.

PROPOSITION 8.1. *The k-stack algorithm is linearizable with respect to restricted out-of-order k-stack.*

Proof. Without loss of generality, we assume that each item pushed on the stack is unique. A segment `s'` is *reachable* from a segment `s` if either `s'=s` or `s'` is reachable from `s->next`. An item `i` is *on the stack*, if `push(i)` has already committed and there exists a segment reachable from the top segment containing a slot whose value is `i`. Note that reachability is important, i.e., only having a slot containing the item is not enough to guarantee that the item is logically on the stack, because the slot could be in a segment (to be) removed by a concurrent pop operation.

We begin by identifying a linearization point of each method call. The goal is to show that the sequential history obtained from a concurrent history by ordering methods according to their linearization points is in the specification of a restricted out-of-order k-stack. The linearization point of `push` is the reading of the empty slot (line 45) in the last iteration (successful insertion) of the main loop. The linearization point of `pop` that does not return `null` is the reading of a non-empty slot (line 58) in the last iteration (successful removal) of the main loop. The linearization point of a `null`-returning `pop` is the point after the first pass of the segment in the call to `empty` method (line 66) which returns `true`.

The correctness argument is based on the following facts.

1. An item is pushed on the stack exactly once. This is a consequence of our unique-items assumption and the control flow of `push(i)`, the only method that can modify a slot to contain `i`.

2. An item is popped at most once. If an item `i` is on the stack, then it can only be removed once, because of 1. and the existence of a unique statement which replaces `i` with empty. If `i` is in some slot but not on the stack, then `push(i)` will erase `i` and retry insertion before committing. We have to show that while `i` is in some slot but not on the stack, no pop operation can return `i`. Clearly, the call to method `committed` by `push(i)` must return `false`. This implies that until `committed` completes, the slot where `i` resides is not modified by any other thread. Otherwise, either after the first `if` statement (line 25) or following failed `CAS` attempts (lines 32 and 38) of replacing `i` with empty will lead to returning true. Furthermore, when control reaches the only exit point for returning `false`, it is guaranteed that there is no slot containing `i`. Thus, if `i` is not on the stack, no pop operation could have replaced it with empty.

3. If a pop operation returns `null`, then during its execution, there must be a state at which there are no items on the stack. Since returning `null` is without any side-effect, it suffices to prove the existence of a state which corresponds to a logically empty stack. The call to `empty` is only done when the top segment is the only segment in the stack. In the `empty` method, the value of `top` is checked at the beginning and after the first pass to ensure that the pointer is not updated by concurrent operations. Hence, the stack is indeed logically empty at the linearization point since the second pass succeeds.

4. An item `j` cannot be popped before an item `i`, if they are both on the stack, and `i`, `j` are in segments `s`, `s'`, respectively, with `s'` reachable from `s` and `s'` $\neq$ `s`. The segment `s'` can become a top segment only after the segment `s` has been removed by some pop operation. Moreover, if a segment becomes unreachable from the top segment, it remains unreachable. These two observations imply that the linearization point of `pop(i)` must precede the linearization point of `pop(j)` which can only happen when `s'` is a top segment.

5. An item `i` on the stack is popped only if it is one of the $k-l$ youngest items on the stack, where l is the current lateness of the youngest item. By youngest we mean most recently pushed. Recall that lateness is the number of pops that were performed after the pop of the previous youngest item or the push of the current youngest one. Assume `i` is popped from the stack at the current moment in time and at that point the youngest item is `t` with current lateness l. This means that ever since `t` is the youngest item on the stack, no push operation was performed and there have been l pop operations performed none of which removed `t`. Let `j` be any of these l popped items. Since `t` is the last item pushed and it is still on the stack, `t` is in the top segment. Since `j` is removed before `t`, by 4. it must have also resided in the top segment. For the same reason, also `i` is in the top segment prior to its removal. Hence, at the moment in which `pop(i)` happens, there are at most $k-l$ items in the top segment.

Now, 5. shows that the sequential behavior obtained by ordering methods according to their linearization points satisfies the restricted-out-of-order k-stack. Moreover, 3. shows an even stricter behavior, a linearizable empty check.[4] Thus, any concurrent execution generated by the given algorithm is linearizable for restricted out-of-order k-stack. Observe that already 1. and 2. show that the k-stack has pool semantics. □

[4] We could easily relax the linearizable empty check to fit the restricted out-of-order specification, by removing line 66 in the code. However, a linearizable empty check is a valuable feature of a concurrent implementation.

```
struct blk_original {
  pidtype X;
  bool Y;
  val_t V;
  bool C;
  val_t D;
};
```

(a) CAS.

```
struct blk_modified {
  pidtype X[k];
  bool Y[k];
  val_t V;
  bool C[k];
  val_t D;
};
```

(b) k-CAS.

Figure 5. Wait-free CAS and k-CAS state structures.

Without any particular difficulty, but with a somewhat lengthy argument, one can show that the k-stack algorithm is lock-free by showing that whenever a thread retries an operation, another thread completes its operation ensuring progress of at least one thread.

8.2 k-Stuttering shared counters

We implemented the two versions of a stuttering k-shared counter, as discussed in the introduction. The first version is based on a k-relaxed stuttering version of a wait-free software CAS operation [13] (k-CAS for short). It uses a structure `blk_original`, shown in Figure 5(a), to keep track of the state of concurrent CAS operations. The atomic value is located in field `V` and the CAS operation uses the decision fields `X`, `Y`, and `C` to determine which thread gets permission to change `V`. We modified the `blk_original` structure so that the fields `X`, `Y`, and `C` are arrays of size k depicted in structure `blk_modified` in Figure 5(b). We keep the main CAS operation unmodified but use a balancing function that maps threads to array indices i smaller than k (the thread ID modulo k). A thread determines the state of its CAS operation by just accessing position i in the arrays `X`, `Y`, and `C`. On success, a thread writes the new value into `V`. Hence, up to k concurrent threads may perform the k-CAS operation in parallel and change `V` resulting in a loss of at most $k-1$ state changes, which further results in at most $k-1$ lost shared counter updates.

The second version of the k-shared counter is the k-distributed counter depicted in Figure 1(b).

It is not difficult to show that both implementations are linearizable with respect to the k-stuttering shared counter and they are lock-free.

9. Experiments

We evaluate the performance and scalability of the k-stack, several existing quantitatively relaxed FIFO queues, and the k-stuttering shared counter implementations. All experiments ran on an Intel-based server machine with four 10-core 2.0GHz Intel Xeon processors (40 cores, 2 hyperthreads per core), 24MB shared L3-cache, and 128GB of memory running Linux 2.6.39. We implemented a benchmarking framework to analyze our k-stack and k-shared counter implementations, as well as the implementations of relaxed queues. The benchmarking framework can be configured for a different number of threads (n), number of operations each thread performs (o), and the computational load performed between each operation (c). The computational load between two consecutive operations is created by iteratively calculating π and c is the number of iterations performed. We use $c = 2000$ which takes a total of $4600ns$ on average in our experiments. The framework uses static preallocation for memory used at runtime with touching each page before running the benchmark to avoid paging issues.

9.1 k-Stack

We compare our k-stack implementation with a standard lock-based stack (LS), which acquires a global lock for each stack operation, and a non-blocking stack (NS) [20], which uses a CAS operation to manipulate the top pointer of the stack. Moreover, we compare our k-stack with different pools. The lock-free (BAG) [19]

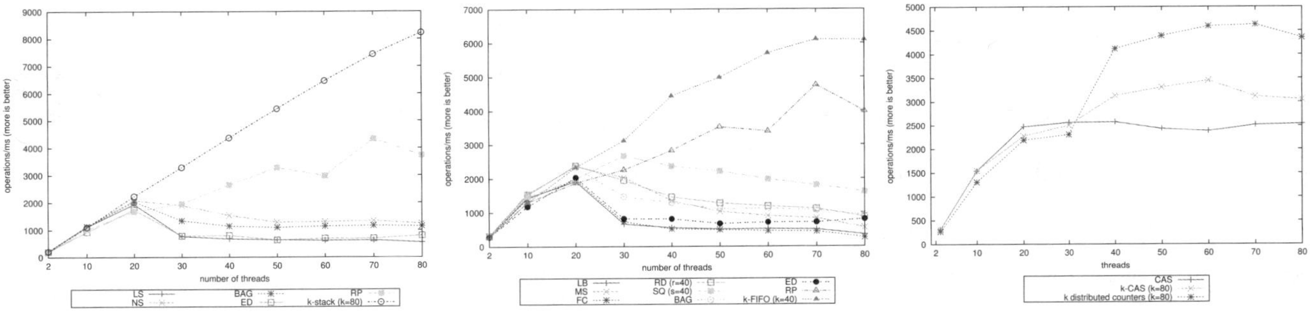

(a) Stack (b) FIFO queue (c) Shared counter

Figure 6. Benchmarks on a 40-core (2 hyperthreads per core) server with an increasing number of threads

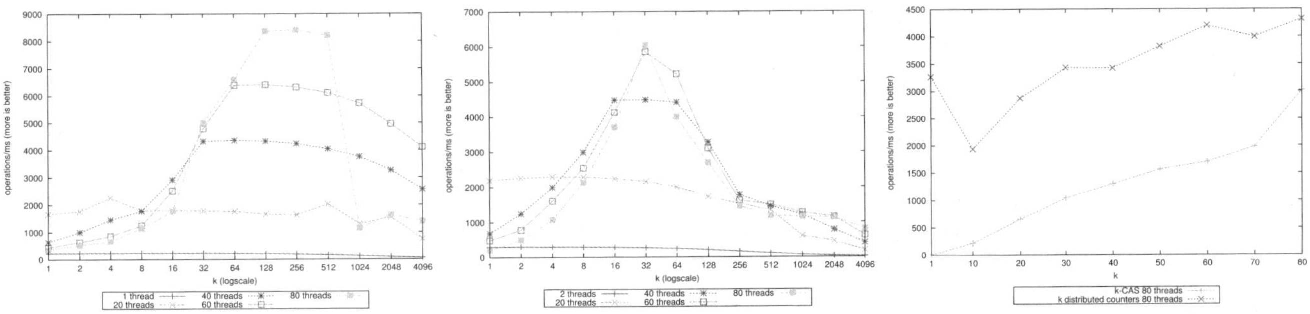

(a) Stack (b) FIFO queue (c) Shared counter

Figure 7. Benchmarks on a 40-core (2 hyperthreads per core) server with increasing k

pool is based on thread-local lists of elements. Threads put elements on their local list and take elements from their local list if it is not empty. If it is empty they take elements from the lists of other threads. The lock-free elimination-diffraction pool (ED) [1] uses a set of FIFO queues to store elements. Access to these queues is balanced using elimination arrays and a diffraction tree. The synchronous rendezvousing pool (RP) [3] implements a single elimination array using a ring buffer. A get operation marks a slot identified by its thread id and waits for a take operation to insert an element. Take operations scan the array for pending get operations.

Figure 6(a) depicts the performance analysis of our k-stack. We configure $k = 80$, which is a good k (on average) for a broad range of thread combinations and workloads on our server machine. This is no surprise since the server machine has (logically) 80 cores. The analysis is done on a producer-consumer workload where half of the threads are producers and half are consumers. The k-stack outscales and outperforms all considered stack and pool implementations. Figure 7(a) shows the effect of k on performance and scalability. There exists an optimal k with respect to performance, which is also robust in the sense that there exists only a single range of close-to-optimal k. For large k performance decreases due to higher sequential overhead, e.g. scanning for elements in almost empty k-segments. Note that an increase in performance above $k = 80$ is not to be expected on the given architecture.

9.2 Quantitatively relaxed FIFO queues

We also evaluate the existing implementations of a k-FIFO queue [11] and different FIFO queues, quasi-linearizable FIFO queues, and the pools introduced in the previous section. The k-FIFO queue [11] implements a restricted out-of-order k-queue as a lock-free linked list of k-segments. An enqueue operation is served by the tail k-segment and a dequeue operation is served by the head k-segment. Hence, up to k enqueue and k dequeue operations may be performed in parallel. The k-FIFO queue is empty if head and tail point to the same k-segment which does not contain any elements. The lock-based (strict) FIFO queue (LB) locks a global lock for each queue operation. The lock-free Michael-Scott (strict) FIFO queue (MS) [14] uses `CAS` operations to change head, tail, and next pointer in a linked list of elements. The flat-combining (strict) FIFO queue (FC) [8] is based on the approach that a single thread performs the queue operations of multiple threads by locking the whole queue, collecting pending queue operations, and applying them to the queue. The Random Dequeue Queue (RD) [2] implements a quasi-linearizable FIFO with quasi-factor r where r defines the range $[0, r-1]$ of a random number. It actually implements a restricted out-of-order r-FIFO queue. RD is based on MS where the dequeue operation was modified in a way that the random number determines which element is returned starting from the oldest element. The Segment Queue (SQ) [2] is a quasi-linearizable FIFO queue with quasi-factor s. It is logically similar (both implement a queue of segments and hence a restricted out-of-order queue) to the k-FIFO queue but does not provide a linearizable empty check, i.e., it may return `null` in the not-empty state. Also, SQ comes with a different segment management strategy than the k-FIFO queue, which results on average in significantly more CAS operations.

Figure 6(b) depicts the performance analysis of the queues. We configure $k = r = s = 40$, which turns out be a good k (on average) for a broad range of thread combinations and workloads on our server machine. This is no surprise since then the level of possible parallelism is $2k = 80$, the number of (logical) cores. We use a producer-consumer workload where half of the threads are producers and half consumers. The k-FIFO queue outscales and outperforms all considered FIFO queue, quasi-linearizable FIFO queue, and pool implementations. Figure 7(b) shows the effect of k on performance and scalability. Again, there exists a robust and optimal k with respect to performance. Also here, for large k performance decreases due to larger sequential overhead.

9.3 k-Shared counter

We compare our k-CAS-based shared counter and distributed shared counter implementations with a shared counter implementation based on a regular CAS operation depicted in Figure 6(c). The threads perform in total one million counter increment operations in each benchmark run. The CAS version performs best until 30 threads. After that the k-CAS-based shared counter and the distributed shared counter version outperform it. Figure 7(c) shows the effect of k on performance and scalability. In the k-CAS version performance monotonically increases with larger k, whereas in the distributed shared counter version performances decreases until $k = 10$, but monotonically increases after that. Our educated guess is that this is caused by the trade-off between two possible sources of contention: (1) CAS on the same memory location, and (2) bad caching, i.e., accessing many different locations in memory. The distributed shared counter decreases (1) but increases (2). However, except for small values of k, we observe that the gain is larger than the loss.

10. Final remarks

We have presented a framework for quantitative relaxation of concurrent data structures together with generic as well as further concrete instances of it. Our main motivation is the belief that relaxed data structures may decrease contention and thus provide the potential for scalable and well-performing implementations. Indeed, the potential advantage which we demonstrate utilizable is striking. The lessons learned can be summarized as follows: The way from a sequential implementation to efficient concurrent implementation is always hard. Just because a sequential specification is relaxed, it does not necessarily mean that an efficient implementation immediately follows. However, efficient implementations that benefit from quantitative relaxations are possible, as we demonstrate in this paper. In our opinion, the framework provides a firm formal ground for quantitative relaxation of concurrent data structures and paves the road to designing efficient concurrent implementations.

Our current results open up several directions for future work. One important issue is the applicability of relaxed data structures. Demonstrating applicability can either be achieved by exploring applications that tolerate a relaxation, e.g. provide less accurate but nevertheless acceptable results, or showing that end-to-end quality may remain the same despite the actual relaxation of semantics. In the latter case, relaxations do not influence correctness in the sense of [16, 17]. Another evident but difficult goal would be to synthesize well-performing implementations from relaxations. As a first step we believe it is important to study the main principles that lead to good performance. This is another line of future work that we plan to undertake in small steps.

Acknowledgements

This work has been supported by the European Research Council advanced grant QUAREM, the National Research Network RiSE on Rigorous Systems Engineering (Austrian Science Fund S11404-N23), and an Elise Richter Fellowship (Austrian Science Fund V00125). We thank the anonymous referees for their constructive and inspiring comments and suggestions. Ana Sokolova wishes to thank Dexter Kozen and in particular Joel Ouaknine: had they not saved her life, she would have missed a lot of the fun involved in working on this paper and seeing it finished.

References

[1] Y. Afek, G. Korland, M. Natanzon, and N. Shavit. Scalable producer-consumer pools based on elimination-diffraction trees. In *Proc. European Conference on Parallel Processing (Euro-Par)*, pages 151–162. Springer, 2010.

[2] Y. Afek, G. Korland, and E. Yanovsky. Quasi-linearizability: Relaxed consistency for improved concurrency. In *Proc. Conference on Principles of Distributed Systems (OPODIS)*, pages 395–410. Springer, 2010.

[3] Y. Afek, M. Hakimi, and A. Morrison. Fast and scalable rendezvousing. In *Proc. International Conference on Distributed Computing (DISC)*, pages 16–31, Berlin, Heidelberg, 2011. Springer-Verlag.

[4] J. Aspnes, M. Herlihy, and N. Shavit. Counting networks. *Journal of the ACM*, 41:1020–1048, 1994.

[5] H. Attiya, R. Guerraoui, D. Hendler, P. Kuznetsov, M. Michael, and M. Vechev. Laws of order: expensive synchronization in concurrent algorithms cannot be eliminated. In *Proc. of Principles of Programming Languages (POPL)*, pages 487–498. ACM, 2011.

[6] M. Herlihy and N. Shavit. *The Art of Multiprocessor Programming*. Morgan Kaufmann Publishers Inc., 2008.

[7] M. Herlihy and J. Wing. Linearizability: a correctness condition for concurrent objects. *ACM Transactions on Programming Languages and Systems (TOPLAS)*, 12(3):463–492, 1990.

[8] D. H. I. Incze, N. Shavit, and M. Tzafrir. Flat combining and the synchronization-parallelism tradeoff. In *Proc. Symposium on Parallelism in Algorithms and Architectures (SPAA)*, pages 355–364. ACM, 2010.

[9] C. Kirsch and H. Payer. Incorrect systems: It's not the problem, it's the solution. In *Proc. Design Automation Conference (DAC)*. ACM, 2012.

[10] C. Kirsch, H. Payer, H. Röck, and A. Sokolova. Brief announcement: Scalability versus semantics of concurrent FIFO queues. In *Proc. Symposium on Principles of Distributed Computing (PODC)*. ACM, 2011.

[11] C. Kirsch, M. Lippautz, and H. Payer. Fast and scalable k-fifo queues. Technical Report 2012-04, Department of Computer Sciences, University of Salzburg, June 2012.

[12] C. Kirsch, H. Payer, H. Röck, and A. Sokolova. Performance, scalability, and semantics of concurrent FIFO queues. In *Proc. International Conference on Algorithms and Architectures for Parallel Processing (ICA3PP)*, pages 273–287. LNCS 7439, 2012.

[13] V. Luchangco, M. M., and N. Shavit. On the uncontended complexity of consensus. In *Proc. International Symposium on Distributed Computing (DISC)*, pages 45–59. Springer-Verlag, 2003.

[14] M. Michael and M. Scott. Simple, fast, and practical non-blocking and blocking concurrent queue algorithms. In *Proc. Symposium on Principles of Distributed Computing (PODC)*, pages 267–275. ACM, 1996.

[15] M. Michael, M. Vechev, and V. Saraswat. Idempotent work stealing. In *Proc. Principles and Practice of Parallel Programming (PPoPP)*, pages 45–54. ACM, 2009.

[16] S. Misailovic, S. Sidiroglou, H. Hoffmann, and M. C. Rinard. Quality of service profiling. In *Proc. 32nd ACM/IEEE International Conference on Software Engineering (ICSE) - Volume 1*, pages 25–34. ACM, 2010.

[17] A. Sampson, W. Dietl, E. Fortuna, D. Gnanapragasam, L. Ceze, and D. Grossman. Enerj: approximate data types for safe and general low-power computation. In *Proc. 32nd ACM SIGPLAN Conference on Programming Language Design and Implementation (PLDI)*, pages 164–174. ACM, 2011.

[18] N. Shavit. Data structures in the multicore age. *Communications ACM*, 54:76–84, March 2011.

[19] H. Sundell, A. Gidenstam, M. Papatriantafilou, and P. Tsigas. A lock-free algorithm for concurrent bags. In *Proc. Symposium on Parallelism in Algorithms and Architectures (SPAA)*, pages 335–344, New York, NY, USA, 2011. ACM.

[20] R. Treiber. Systems programming: Coping with parallelism. Technical Report RJ5118, IBM Almaden Research Center, April 1986.

Plan B: A Buffered Memory Model for Java

Delphine Demange[2] Vincent Laporte[2,1] Lei Zhao[1] Suresh Jagannathan[1] David Pichardie[3,1] Jan Vitek[1]

[1]Purdue University [2]ENS Cachan Bretagne - IRISA [3]INRIA Rennes

Abstract

Recent advances in verification have made it possible to envision trusted implementations of real-world languages. Java with its type-safety and fully specified semantics would appear to be an ideal candidate; yet, the complexity of the translation steps used in production virtual machines have made it a challenging target for verifying compiler technology. One of Java's key innovations, its memory model, poses significant obstacles to such an endeavor. The Java Memory Model is an ambitious attempt at specifying the behavior of multithreaded programs in a portable, hardware agnostic, way. While experts have an intuitive grasp of the properties that the model should enjoy, the specification is complex and not well-suited for integration within a verifying compiler infrastructure. Moreover, the specification is given in an axiomatic style that is distant from the intuitive reordering-based reasonings traditionally used to justify or rule out behaviors, and ill suited to the kind of operational reasoning one would expect to employ in a compiler. This paper takes a step back, and introduces a *Buffered Memory Model* (BMM) for Java. We choose a pragmatic point in the design space sacrificing generality in favor of a model that is fully characterized in terms of the reorderings it allows, amenable to formal reasoning, and which can be efficiently applied to a specific hardware family, namely x86 multiprocessors. Although the BMM restricts the reorderings compilers are allowed to perform, it serves as the key enabling device to achieving a verification pathway from bytecode to machine instructions. Despite its restrictions, we show that it is backwards compatible with the Java Memory Model and that it does not cripple performance on TSO architectures.

Categories and Subject Descriptors D.3.1 [*Programming Languages*]: Formal Definitions and Theory; F.3.1 [*Specifying and Verifying and Reasoning about Programs*]

Keywords Concurrency; Java; Memory Model; Verified Compilation

1. Introduction

Formally verified systems are becoming a reality [18, 20]. Recent successes have shown that it is possible to construct reasonably efficient compilers along with a machine-checked proof of correctness. Building on our experience with the Fiji real-time virtual machine [26] and verified compilation for relaxed memory architectures (CompcertTSO) [35], we have embarked on a project to produce a verified platform for a variant of the Java language that abides by the Safety Critical Specification for Java [12]. To build a verifying compiler requires starting from a formal semantics of the source language and, simultaneously, developing and proving the

POPL'13, January 23–25, 2013, Rome, Italy.

$x \leftarrow 0 \quad y \leftarrow 0 \quad z \leftarrow 0$

$r_1 \leftarrow z$	$r_2 \leftarrow x$
`if` $(r_1 = 1)$ $\{x \leftarrow 1;\ \ y \leftarrow 1\}$	$r_3 \leftarrow y$
`else` $\{y \leftarrow 1;\ \ x \leftarrow 1\}$	`if` $(r_2 = 1\ \&\ r_3 = 1)$ $z \leftarrow 1$

Figure 1. JMM. x, y and z are shared memory variables, r_i are local. In the JMM, no execution yields $r_1 = r_2 = r_3 = 1$. However, manually reordering the writes to x and y so that they are performed in the same order in both branches allows the compiler to eliminate the conditional and hoist the assignments above the store to r_1, thus making such an execution permissible. Alternative definitions of the JMM [5] allow this execution, but the justification is complex, involving subtle notions of speculations and non-local reasoning over execution traces.

correctness of optimizations and transformations, with an associated formal operational semantics developed for each of the compiler's intermediate representations all the way through to the backend target. Although we expected Java to be a challenge because of the complexity of the transformations used in high-performance virtual machines like Fiji, the Java memory model [22] also complicates the task of devising a tractable formal semantics for the source and intermediate representations.

The Java Memory Model (JMM) was designed to specify the behavior of concurrent programs across all modern architectures and compiler optimizations currently in use in production virtual machines. The complexity underlying the JMM stems from the need to give a semantics to *all* programs, even racy ones, and the desire to be maximally portable. This degree of generality comes at the price of complexity. When explaining the semantics of racy programs, textbooks [11] elide key JMM notions such as the definition of a legal execution. This issue remains the subject of much active research [4, 5, 10, 15, 21]. Consider Fig. 1 which shows a program where, according to [22], no execution can yield $r_1 = r_2 = r_3 = 1$. But, if the programmer were to manually reorder the instructions in the else-branch, a seemingly insignificant refactoring, this result would be allowed. Such unintuitive behavior is unfortunate. From the verifying compiler writer's point of view, the situation is not much better – it is an open problem to write correctness proofs for a compiler with respect to the JMM's current definition, especially if the target platform enforces its own relaxed (or weak) memory semantics. Indeed, even in the absence of formal proofs, existing Java compilers are not JMM compliant [34]. (And in the process of writing this paper we discovered that our own virtual machine was not JMM compliant.)

Often the JMM is informally discussed in terms of allowed instruction reorderings combined with *sequentially consistent* (SC) interleavings. To illustrate, assume for a moment that reordering of independent, non-volatile, statements was allowed, then we could admit $r_1 = r_2 = 1$ as the value of the program on the left.

$x \leftarrow 0$	$y \leftarrow 0$	reordering with speculative loads $\longrightarrow$	$x \leftarrow 0$	$y \leftarrow 0$
$r_1 \leftarrow x$	$r_2 \leftarrow y$		$y \leftarrow 1$	$x \leftarrow 1$
$y \leftarrow 1$	$x \leftarrow 1$		$r_1 \leftarrow x$	$r_2 \leftarrow y$

This would be true because after reordering, the result is an SC execution. With this approach, reasoning would be easy – determining the validity of an execution would boil down to considering combinations of permitted reorderings. Unfortunately, the JMM reorderings are complex, and reasoning about transformations is rarely intuitive. To rule an execution illegal requires showing that it is not an SC execution if the program is data-race free, or that it includes an *out-of-thin-air* read. Formalizing these notions leads to a complex definition involving race-committing sequences. This is a level of complexity that is challenging for most programmers to tackle. In [5], four test cases from Pugh et al. [28] were found to be flawed, but a later paper [37], using an automatic verification tool, contradicted this interpretation on two of the examples. Such a lack of clarity for programs less than 10 instructions long does not bode well for the viability of the model.

The complexity of the JMM arises in large part by its desire to be portable across all platforms and thus hardware agnostic. But, this is a challenging goal given the vastly different relaxed memory subsystems found on modern architectures, and the range of optimizations modern compilers perform, many of which are often ill-understood. For example, operational definitions of the Power architecture [31] are substantially different from those defined for x86 [36]; the former supports out-of-order unbounded speculative executions and subtle notions of partial coherence, while the latter is expressed in terms of more intuitive store buffers and limited memory reorderings. It is unclear how one might define a tractable formal language memory model that can be effectively tailored to both. Neither is there a clear specification of the optimizations that ought to be supported.

Of course, we could greatly simplify the problem by drastically limiting the behaviors admitted by Java with an easily understood albeit more restrictive model such as sequential consistency. Valid program executions would be limited to those that can be expressed purely in terms of a sequential interleaving of thread actions; but under SC, reordering of shared-memory reads and writes is prohibited. While simple to state and easy to understand, we choose to not follow this approach because SC would likely cripple performance of Java programs on all modern microprocessors due to the large number of fences needed to enforce SC on relaxed hardware; this would be especially true for racy programs implementing sophisticated lock-free algorithms of the kind found, for example, in optimized libraries such as `java.util.concurrent`.

Instead, we propose an alternative memory model that has a tractable semantics and designed to be mapped to x86 multiprocessors that support a Total Store Ordering relaxed memory semantics [30, 36]. We introduce the *Buffered Memory Model* (BMM), a memory model for Java that can be fully characterized in terms of the memory reorderings it allows on top of sequentially consistent executions. The BMM comes in two forms. The first is an axiomatic specification that can be used to relate it to the JMM, and which provides an intuitive method to describe valid and invalid program executions. The second form is a fully operational abstract machine with write buffers attached to each thread. This semantics can be readily used by a verifying compiler infrastructure like CompcertTSO. BMM is backwards compatible: existing software that has been written against the JMM can be run directly since the JMM is a superset of the BMM (i.e., every legal BMM execution is legal under the JMM). This ensures that legacy software that has been validated and tested with the JMM in mind will remain correct. The contributions of this paper are thus as follows:

- An axiomatic definition of the BMM, an alternative memory model for Java programs, fully characterized in term of memory event reorderings, and a compliance proof with the JMM.
- A formalization of BMM_o, an operational definition of the semantics of Java programs, equipped with a simple mapping to the Total Store Order (TSO) memory model enabling it easily be used with the x86 family of multiprocessor architectures and with verified compilers like CompcertTSO targeting such platforms.
- A proof that BMM and BMM_o are equivalent. We prove the data race freedom (DRF) theorem for BMM and the legality of reordering optimizations under the BMM.
- An upper bound on the cost of preserving BMM semantics on a production virtual machine running on a TSO hardware, benchmark results measuring the cost and overhead of BMM enforcement, compared to JMM-compliant implementations, and an illustration of the subtle performance implications of the memory model with a case study on the implementation of biased locking.

We note that the design rationale for the BMM is very much dictated by our overarching goal of constructing a verifying compiler for Java. As a result, BMM is not intended to be general-purpose, and does not apply directly to all architectures and compiler optimizations. Instead, we view it as a starting point for further research on verified compilation and memory models.

The BMM, the statements of results and key lemmas are expressed in Coq; our proofs are rigorous but non-mechanised. The details are available online, along with the version of Fiji and LLVM used in our benchmarks: `http://r.cs.purdue.edu/bmm`

2. Related Work

Language Memory Models. Languages like Java and C++ have sophisticated memory models to answer questions related to data visibility and updates for concurrent programs. The JMM does this using committing-sequences, that make it subtle, complex, and unsound [10, 34]. Huisman and Petri [15] proved its DRF guarantee. They tackled the inconsistencies of [22], related to memory initialization by adding hypotheses. Aspinall and Ševčík [5] proposed an alternative definition of the JMM that does not suffer from these issues. They restrict their definition to the finite case, as we do here. Recently, Lochbihler [21] extended the formalization by including infinite executions and dynamic allocations. This work proves type-safety for correctly synchronized programs. Such a mechanized proof is a *tour de force* since it covers a large fragment of Java. However, the proof structure is quite different from the simulation proof we need to perform within the scope of a verified optimizing compiler. There has also been recent work on memory models for C++. Boehm and Adve [6] provide a semantics for data-race free C++ programs, including a semantics for *low-level atomics*. In Java, it is mandatory to also give well-defined semantics to racy programs to avoid security breaches.

Weak Memory Model Formalizations. Work in this area has focussed primarily on characterizing hardware memory models. Early studies [1, 2, 13] outlined a range of hardware memory models, and attempted to rigorously formalize the vendor's documentations. Alglave et al. [3] defined a general framework for formalizing hardware models using partial orders. Operational characterizations have been examined in [25, 30, 31]. Burckhardt *et al.* [9] define an expressive denotational framework where a memory model is a set of dynamic reorderings, aggregation or splitting rewriting rules. TSO boils down to a store-load reordering and a store-load aggregation rule. The BMM follows this line of work by providing provably equivalent axiomatic and operational models that make it intuitive and suitable to verification.

Proofs, Verified Compilation, and Weak Memory Models. Defining multithreaded semantics in terms of reordering is also the approach taken by Miné [24]: the semantics of multithreaded C programs is defined as the interleavings of the programs possibly obtained by the syntactic transformations defining the memory model.

From a certified compiler perspective, an operational definition of the JMM is desirable. There are several attempts to provide such a semantics [7, 8, 10, 16] but none of them has been used in a proof assistant. Our operational semantics is inspired by the TSO memory model proposed in [35] which has been formalized in Coq. Ševčík [32] identifies some trace transformations that are valid under the JMM. Transformations are however defined semantically. This gap is filled in [33] where the program transformations are proved to be correct, but this is done under a DRF assumption. [33] also identifies the need for characterizing memory models in terms of the transformations they permit, and this is the goal of the axiomatic formalization of BMM.

3. BMM: Two Models for the Price of One

While the BMM covers the whole of Java, the most challenging parts of reasoning about concurrent programs are those that manipulate shared memory in a potentially racy way. Following the JMM's design, we separate operations that are purely thread-local from those that deal with shared memory. The BMM is parametrized by an abstract notion of intra-thread semantics to deal with the former. We mention a few of the high-level concepts and our design choices before focusing on the memory model proper. (More details about this part of our model is in the online Coq development.)

Java Values. The JVM operates on two kinds of values: primitives and references. Primitives include `long` and `double` values that are 64-bits wide. Updates to these variables is not guaranteed to be atomic on a 32-bit machine. Our intra-thread semantics captures this. The treatment of references is delicate. Several instruction like `instanceof`, `checkcast`, `invokevirtual` require reading the class of an object pointed to by a reference. These operations are not relevant to the memory model because they refer to immutable meta-data. We explicitly avoid reading from shared memory in those cases since that would directly entail reasoning about the memory model. Instead, our semantics attaches type information to references in the spirit of formalizations of the bytecode verifier. As a consequence, the type of an object can be conceptually read without going to shared memory. We also give to each thread its own allocation pool. This matches the notion of field initialization that is advocated in the JMM. We do not need to initialize objects with a default value when we allocate them because each memory address has a well-typed initial value from the very beginning of the program execution.

Final Fields. The JMM provides complex rules for fields annotated `final`. Compilers are allowed to perform aggressive optimizations on reads. The surprising thing is that `final` fields may change between reads. This occurs if the programmer leaks an object during its construction. The result is a very non-intuitive semantics which stands more as a warning for the programmer who does not follow a safe publication pattern than a real semantics. Our position is to forbid unsafe publications [14] (which happens to be a restriction imposed by Safety Critical Java as well). This allows us to keep an intuitive semantics for `final` fields and let compilers aggressively optimize them.

Class Initialization. Lazy class loading is an important mechanism for concurrent programming; see for example the *initialization on demand holder idiom* [27]. Our semantic supports this by tracking the current initialization status of each class.

Synchronization Actions. Their treatment in the paper is slightly simplified. Our formal semantics needs to handle more synchronization actions than those explained here. For example, when spawning a thread, an exception `IllegalThreadStateException` can occur if the thread has already been started. It means that, for a given execution and a given thread, there can be only one successful spawn event but several other failed spawn events. A so-called JMM *synchronizes-with* edge must exist between the successful spawn and all failed spawn events.

3.1 A Reordering-based Memory Model

We propose a memory model that can be *fully* characterized by reorderings over SC executions and that has a simple specification. In the BMM, (1) all SC executions are allowed and, (2) any execution from which an SC execution can be derived by reordering a non-volatile read action with a preceeding non-volatile write action is allowed; both actions must operate over disjoint memory locations and the actions can be separated by a sequence of reads that see the write action. Thus, for instance in the following program

$$\begin{array}{c} x{\leftarrow}0 \quad y{\leftarrow}0 \\ \hline \begin{array}{c||c} x{\leftarrow}1 & y{\leftarrow}1 \\ r_1{\leftarrow}y & r_2{\leftarrow}x \end{array} \\ r_1 = r_2 = 0 \text{ is } \textbf{allowed} \end{array}$$

it suffices to reorder one of the threads for the result to be permissible under an SC execution. Fig. 2 gives some prohibited executions. Thanks to this reordering-based definition, all three examples are easily seen to be illegal since no reordering is applicable and no SC execution can exhibit such behaviors.

$$\begin{array}{c} x{\leftarrow}0 \quad y{\leftarrow}0 \\ \hline \begin{array}{c||c} x{\leftarrow}1 & r_1{\leftarrow}y \\ y{\leftarrow}1 & r_2{\leftarrow}x \end{array} \\ r_1 = 1, r_2 = 0 \text{ is } \textbf{illegal} \end{array} \qquad \begin{array}{c} x{\leftarrow}0 \quad y{\leftarrow}0 \\ \hline \begin{array}{c||c||c} x{\leftarrow}1 & r_1{\leftarrow}x & r_2{\leftarrow}y \\ & y{\leftarrow}1 & r_3{\leftarrow}x \end{array} \\ r_1 = r_2 = 1, r_3 = 0 \text{ is } \textbf{illegal} \end{array}$$

$$\begin{array}{c} x{\leftarrow}0 \quad y{\leftarrow}0 \\ \hline \begin{array}{c||c||c||c} x{\leftarrow}1 & r_1{\leftarrow}x & y{\leftarrow}1 & r_3{\leftarrow}y \\ & r_2{\leftarrow}y & & r_4{\leftarrow}x \end{array} \\ r_2 = r_4 = 0, r_1 = r_3 = 1 \text{ is } \textbf{illegal} \end{array}$$

Figure 2. BMM executions.

3.2 A Buffered Operational Memory Model

While more intuitive for the programmer, the reordering-based definition of BMM lacks an operational form. What we seek with an operational model is a companion proof technique to provide a formal correspondence proof between the different layers of a verified compiler. Operational semantics have been long advocated as a vehicle within which to conduct such proofs by facilitating the use of simulation diagrams. Thanks to their inductive form, they can be used to reason about global program behavior in terms of elementary single steps. Axiomatic models generally do not enjoy the same kind of proof technique. In [34], to prove validity of some program transformations, the authors had to reason on whole prefixes of traces. This uncomfortable situation comes from the fact that in the JMM, a trace of $n+1$ execution steps is not easily defined in term of its n first steps. At the hardware level, operational semantics have been provided in [31, 36]. It is not surprising to see that no proof connects the JMM with any of these operational models. Thus, our second memory model, called BMM_o, introduces a *store buffer*: each hardware thread effectively has a FIFO buffer of pending memory writes, so that reads performed on different processors can occur before writes have propagated to main memory.

3.3 Reconciling the Two Models

While the axiomatic form of BMM has an intuitive definition and supports a subset of the executions permitted by the JMM, its operational variant has been specified to fit cleanly within the store

	SC	C++	JMM	BMM
DRF theorem	✓	✓	✓	✓
Reordering memory accesses	×	✓	✓	⊗
Redundant memory accesses elimination/introduction	✓	✓	⊗	⊗
Operational semantics	✓	✓	×	✓
Semantics for all programs	✓	×	✓	✓
Programmer can understand the semantics of racy programs	✓	×	×	✓
Sound with respect to JMM (does not break legacy Java)	✓	×	✓	✓
Lock optimizations	✓	✓	⊗	⊗

Table 1. Expressivity and properties of memory models. ✓ if a property holds, × if it does not, and ⊗ if there are restrictions. The models differ in the reordering they permit, how they are formalized, the programs they consider, and their support for legacy code. BMM is weaker than the JMM in terms of allowed reorderings, but its operational semantics is useful for verifying compiler optimizations, and its simpler axiomatic version is easier for programmers to understand. Reordering memory accesses is illegal under original JMM [10, 22] but legal under the alternative version of [34].

buffering operations provided by x86-based relaxed memory hardware. The two models are reconciled with an equivalence proof. For this purpose, the BMM reorderings have been carefully chosen to align with the behaviors permitted under $\mathsf{BMM_o}$. These two semantics have different uses. In Sec. 5.1, we use the reordering view to prove the JMM compatibility. In Sec. 8 we use the operational semantics to study the validity of compiler-driven program transformations. Tab. 1 gives an overview of the properties of the BMM.

4. Background on the Java Memory Model

We introduce key notions from the JMM. A language memory model formally specifies what values can be read by each thread depending upon the writes performed by this thread or others. These interactions are categorized using inter-thread actions.

Inter-thread Actions. The shared memory of a program is split into a set of disjoint *addresses* which are instance fields, static fields or array positions but not local variables. For each address $x \in \mathbb{X}$, we can determine if it is volatile or not with the function $\mathsf{volatile} : \mathbb{X} \to \mathrm{bool}$. In the literature, external actions are distinguished from other memory actions. In this work, we model external actions using volatile writes [1], that can be identified with the function $\mathsf{external} : \mathbb{X} \to \mathrm{bool}$.[2] We assume a set $\mathbb{T}$ of threads, a set $\mathbb{L}$ of locks, and a set $\mathbb{V}$ of values. The set of inter-thread actions is given below, where superscript i denotes the unique identifier of memory actions.

$$
\begin{array}{lll}
\mathbb{A} ::= & \mathsf{w}_t^i x, v & \text{(thread } t \text{ writes value } v \text{ to address } x) \\
\mid & \mathsf{r}_t^i x & \text{(thread } t \text{ reads from address } x) \\
\mid & \mathsf{l}_t^i l & \text{(thread } t \text{ acquires a lock on monitor } l) \\
\mid & \mathsf{u}_t^i l & \text{(thread } t \text{ releases a lock on monitor } l) \\
\mid & \mathsf{s}_t t' & \text{(thread } t \text{ creates a new thread } t') \\
\mid & \mathsf{b}_t & \text{(thread } t \text{ starts)} \\
\mid & \mathsf{j}_t^i t' & \text{(thread } t \text{ detects } t' \text{ has terminated)} \\
\mid & \mathsf{e}_t & \text{(thread } t \text{ ends)} \\
\mid & \mathsf{w}_0 x & \text{(default write action to address } x)
\end{array}
$$

$$x \in \mathbb{X} \qquad v \in \mathbb{V} \qquad l \in \mathbb{L} \qquad t, t' \in \mathbb{T} \qquad i \in \mathbb{N}$$

[1] E.g., a call by a thread t to a function f with arguments args that returns value v is modeled as a volatile write to the abstract location $\mathsf{f(args)}$.

[2] We require that, $\forall x, \mathsf{external}(x) \Rightarrow \mathsf{volatile}(x)$

Action $\mathsf{w}_0 x$ initializes address x; it has no emitting thread.[3] Thread start (b_t) and end (e_t) can happen only once and thus do not require identifiers. For any action a that is not a default write action, we write $T(a)$ the emitting thread of this action. For any write action w, we write $V(w)$ the value written by that action; initialization actions write a default value according to the type of the related address. We use some notations for sets of actions:

$$
\begin{array}{ll}
\mathbb{A}_\mathrm{r} = \{\mathsf{r}_t^i x \mid t \in \mathbb{T},\ x \in \mathbb{X}\} & \text{(reads)} \\
\mathbb{A}_\mathrm{w} = \{\mathsf{w}_t^i x, v; \mathsf{w}_0 x \mid t \in \mathbb{T},\ x \in \mathbb{X},\ v \in \mathbb{V}\} & \text{(writes)} \\
\mathbb{A}_\mathrm{d} = \{\mathsf{w}_0 x \mid x \in \mathbb{X}\} & \text{(initializations)} \\
\mathbb{A}_\mathrm{b} = \{\mathsf{b}_t \mid t \in \mathbb{T}\} & \text{(begins)} \\
\mathbb{A}_\mathrm{s} = \{\mathsf{w}_t^i x, v; \mathsf{r}_t^i x \mid t \in \mathbb{T},\ x \in \mathbb{X},\ \mathsf{volatile}(x)\} & \\
\quad \cup \{\mathsf{l}_t^i l; \mathsf{u}_t^i l \mid t \in \mathbb{T},\ l \in \mathbb{L}\} & \text{(synchronizations)} \\
\quad \cup \{\mathsf{s}_t t'; \mathsf{b}_t; \mathsf{j}_t^i t'; \mathsf{e}_t \mid t, t' \in \mathbb{T}\} & \\
\mathbb{A}_\mathrm{x} = \{\mathsf{w}_t^i x, v \mid t \in \mathbb{T},\ \mathsf{external}(x)\} & \text{(external actions)}
\end{array}
$$

The JMM is based on a *happens-before* model [19]. An execution is described in terms of partial orders between memory actions. The same external behavior may be associated with many different interleavings of thread actions. An interleaving can be seen as a total order on actions: "this action occurs before that one according to global time". Such an interleaving is in fact a consistent extension of a partial order called "happens before" that precisely relates causal dependencies between actions. For example, the program Fig. 3a may exhibit an interleaving of thread-actions

$$\mathsf{b}_{t_1} :: \mathsf{b}_{t_2} :: \mathsf{w}_{t_1} x, 1 :: \mathsf{r}_{t_1} y :: \mathsf{w}_{t_2} y, 1 :: \mathsf{r}_{t_2} x$$

but there is no causal dependency between the read performed in t_1 and the one performed in t_2. Fig. 3b presents the causality relation behind such a linear presentation. Each gray region is dedicated to the actions owned by a same thread.

$x \leftarrow 0 \quad y \leftarrow 0$

$x \leftarrow 1$	$y \leftarrow 1$
$r_1 \leftarrow y$	$r_2 \leftarrow x$

(a) Code of threads t_1, t_2.

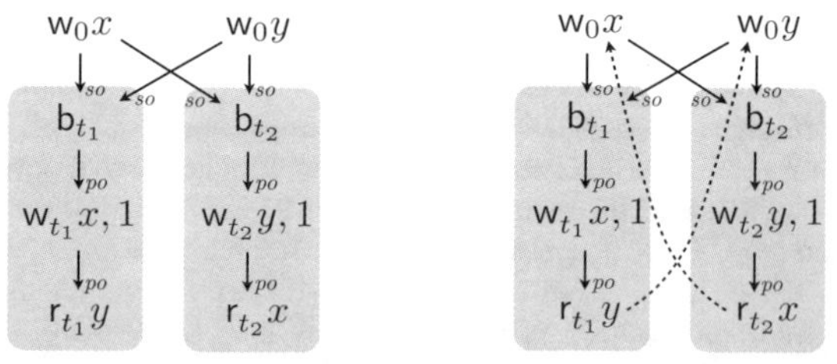

(b) Causality relation (c) Axiomatic execution

Figure 3. Happens-before execution with and without write-seen arrows.

The unique identifier is omited here. Any sequence of solid arrows between actions a and b means a *should happen before* b. Apart from address initialization and thread starts, few actions are actually constrained in this example. We distinguish two kinds of arrows: $\xrightarrow{po}$ reflects program order between actions of a same thread; $\xrightarrow{so}$ reflects the synchronization relation between events. In more complex

[3] Unlike [5, 22], we stick to the JMM: every address is virtually given a default value at the start of the program, even if the corresponding location is not allocated yet.

examples, it may relate an unlock of a monitor with its subsequent lock or the write of a volatile address with a subsequent read. Dotted arrows indicate which write was seen by each read action. These arrows form what we call an axiomatic execution. The write seen must satisfy some minimal constraints that we will make clear with the notion of well-formed execution.

Notations. When a partial order is total we write it directly as a sequence of elements that uniquely characterizes it. When a partial order $\xrightarrow{o}$ is a disjoint union (indexed by $\mathbb{T}$) of orders, we write its restriction on thread t as $[\xrightarrow{o}]_t$. A list of elements can be thought of as a total order. We write $a \xrightarrow{tr} b$ when elements a, b are ordered with regards to a list tr. We call any irreflexive transitive relation an *order*. Two such relations R and R' are said to be *consistent* when they satisfy: $\forall x,\ y,\ \neg(xRy \wedge yR'x)$. We write $tr\downarrow_A$ for the sequence tr filtered to the elements of the set A.

DEFINITION 4.1 (Axiomatic execution). *An execution E is described by a tuple $E = \langle P, A, \xrightarrow{po}, \xrightarrow{so}, W\rangle$ where:*

- *P is a program and $A \subseteq \mathbb{A} \setminus \mathbb{A}_{\mathrm{d}}$ is a set of actions,*
- *$\xrightarrow{po} \subseteq A \times A$ is the* program order*, a disjoint union of total orders on actions of each thread,*
- *$\xrightarrow{so} \subseteq (A \cup \mathbb{A}_{\mathrm{d}}) \times (A \cup \mathbb{A}_{\mathrm{d}})$ is the* synchronization order*: the union of a total order on $A \cap \mathbb{A}_{\mathrm{s}}$ of all synchronization actions in A, and the cartesian product $\mathbb{A}_{\mathrm{d}} \times (A \cap \mathbb{A}_{\mathrm{s}})$,*
- *$W \in \mathbb{A}_{\mathrm{r}} \rightharpoonup \mathbb{A}_{\mathrm{w}}$ is a* write-seen *function that maps each read action r from A to a write action w of $A \cup \mathbb{A}_{\mathrm{d}}$ (r and w must operate on the same address).*

We now explain how to extract the happens-before relation from the program order and the synchronization order of an execution.

DEFINITION 4.2 (Synchronizes-with relation). *An action a* synchronizes-with *an action b (written $a \xrightarrow{sw} b$) in an execution $E = \langle P, A, \xrightarrow{po}, \xrightarrow{so}, W\rangle$ if $a \xrightarrow{so} b$ and a, b satisfy one of the following conditions:*

- *$a \in \mathbb{A}_{\mathrm{d}}$ and $b \in A \cap \mathbb{A}_{\mathrm{b}}$ (default writes synchronizes-with starts),*
- *a is a spawn of a thread t and b is the start of the thread t,*
- *a is a write to a volatile address x and b is a read from x,*
- *a is an unlock on monitor l and b is a lock on monitor l,*
- *a is the end of the thread t and b is a join action on t.*

DEFINITION 4.3 (Happens-before order). *The* happens-before *order of an execution is the transitive closure of the union of its synchronizes-with relation and its program order.*

$$\xrightarrow{hb} = (\xrightarrow{sw} \cup \xrightarrow{po})^{+}$$

Intra-thread Semantics. Our formalization requires an abstract notion of intra-thread semantic state $\mathrm{State}_{\mathrm{intra}}$ and an intra-thread labeled transition relation

$$\overset{\cdot}{\twoheadrightarrow} \subseteq \mathrm{State}_{\mathrm{intra}} \times \mathrm{Label}_{\mathrm{intra}} \times \mathrm{State}_{\mathrm{intra}}$$

given to each thread $t \in \mathbb{T}$. Transition labels are in the set $\mathrm{Label}_{\mathrm{intra}} = (\mathbb{A} \setminus \mathbb{A}_{\mathrm{r}}) \cup (\mathbb{A}_{\mathrm{r}} \times \mathbb{V}) \cup \{\tau\}$: a thread can either take an action step, or a silent step (with label τ) that is memory irrelevant. For a read action step, the value read is paired with the action in the label. The requirements on the intra-thread semantics are:

- $\overset{\cdot}{\twoheadrightarrow}$ only relates states of the same thread,
- there is an *initial* state Ready: no transition leads to it and a thread t steps from it if and only if it emits the b_t action,
- non-silent labels are tagged with the emitting thread,
- there is a *final* state Done: a step of a thread t leads to it if and only if its last transition is labeled by e_t.

DEFINITION 4.4 (Intra-traces). *Let $tr = a_1 :: \cdots :: a_n$ be a sequence of actions in set A and let W be a write-seen function on A. Given a thread $t \in \mathbb{T}$ in program P, tr is an* intra-trace *of t if there exist $s_0, s_1, \ldots, s_m \in \mathrm{State}_{\mathrm{intra}}$ ($m \geq n$) and $l = l_1 :: \cdots :: l_m \in \mathrm{list}(\mathrm{Label}_{\mathrm{intra}})$ such that:*

- *for all $a \in \{a_1, \ldots, a_n\}$, $T(a) = t$,*
- *s_0 is the initial intra-thread state* Ready*,*
- *for all $i \in \{1, \ldots, m\}$, $s_{i-1} \xrightarrow{l_i}\!\!\!\!\rightarrow s_i$,*
- *the projection $b_1 :: \cdots :: b_n$ of l to non-silent labels is such that $b_i = (a_i, V(W(a_i)))$ if a_i is a read action or $b_i = a_i$ otherwise.*

We write $P[t]$ for the set of such pairs (tr, W) for P.

DEFINITION 4.5 (Well-formed execution). *An execution $\langle P, A, \xrightarrow{po}, \xrightarrow{so}, W\rangle$, is* well-formed *if*

- *A is finite,*
- *$\xrightarrow{so}$ is consistent with $\xrightarrow{po}$,*
- *Locking is proper: for all lock actions $\mathsf{l}^i_t l \in A$ and all threads t' different from the thread t, the number of lock actions on l emitted by t' before $\mathsf{l}^i_t l$ in $\xrightarrow{so}$ is the same as the number of unlock actions on l emitted by t' before $\mathsf{l}^i_t l$ in $\xrightarrow{so}$, and each unlock action $\mathsf{u}^i_t l \in A$ occurs after a matching lock action:*

$$\forall \mathsf{l}^i_t l, \forall t' \neq t, |\{\mathsf{l}^j_{t'} l \mid \mathsf{l}^j_{t'} l \xrightarrow{so} \mathsf{l}^i_t l\}| = |\{\mathsf{u}^j_{t'} l \mid \mathsf{u}^j_{t'} l \xrightarrow{so} \mathsf{l}^i_t l\}|$$
$$\forall \mathsf{u}^i_t l, |\{\mathsf{l}^j_t l \mid \mathsf{l}^j_t l \xrightarrow{po} \mathsf{u}^i_t l\}| > |\{\mathsf{u}^j_t l \mid \mathsf{u}^j_t l \xrightarrow{po} \mathsf{u}^i_t l\}|$$

- *$\xrightarrow{po}$ is intra-thread consistent: for all thread $t \in \mathbb{T}$, $([\xrightarrow{po}]_t, W) \in P[t]$,*
- *$\xrightarrow{so}$ is consistent with W: for every read r of a volatile address x we have $W(r) \xrightarrow{so} r$ and for any write w to x different from $W(r)$, either $w \xrightarrow{so} W(r) \xrightarrow{so} r$ or $W(r) \xrightarrow{so} r \xrightarrow{so} w$,*
- *$\xrightarrow{hb}$ is consistent with W: for all reads r of x, $r \xrightarrow{hb} W(r)$ does not hold and there is no intervening write w to x, i.e. such that $W(r) \xrightarrow{hb} w \xrightarrow{hb} r$.*

A distinguished subfamily of well-formed executions is the set of Sequentially Consistent axiomatic executions.

DEFINITION 4.6 (Sequentially Consistent (SC) execution). *A well-formed execution $E = \langle P, A, \xrightarrow{po}, \xrightarrow{so}, W\rangle$ is SC if there exists a total order $\xrightarrow{to}$ on A such that*

- *$\xrightarrow{to}$ is consistent with $\xrightarrow{po}$ and $\xrightarrow{so}$,*
- *for each read action $r \in A$ accessing address x, $W(r)$ is the last write on x before r in $\xrightarrow{to}$.*

The set of well-formed executions of a program forms the *Happens-Before* memory model. It is relatively easy to manipulate but it is not a satisfactory memory model because it allows *out-of-thin-air* values [22] and does not fulfill the DRF theorem. The JMM considers a subset of this model; these are known as *legal* executions. The exact definition of legal executions is subtle. In a nutshell, a well-formed execution E is legal if there exists a sequence $E_0, E_1, \ldots, E_n = E$ of well-formed executions such that in E_0, each read sees a write that it does not race with. Then progressively, each execution E_i allows some reads through data races but in a well-founded order until the execution E itself is reached. Thanks to this definition, one obtains almost directly that: in a DRF program all reads see writes that happen-before them and each execution is sequentially consistent; and no out-of-thin-air value can be read, by the causality order on races.

Whereas the DRF guarantee of the JMM is easily achieved, the complex definition of the race-committing sequence makes it hard to justify whether a given reordering is allowed or not. Our approach is to define the BMM with explicit reorderings, introduced in the next section.

5. BMM: An Axiomatic Memory Model

We now formally define the axiomatic view of our memory model. The semantics is built on top of two simple notions: sequential consistency and reordering of actions. The transformations of executions are expressed with the notion of local reordering.

DEFINITION 5.1 (Local reordering). *Given an execution* $E = \langle P, A, \xrightarrow{po}, \xrightarrow{so}, W\rangle$, $E' = \langle P', A, \xrightarrow{po'}, \xrightarrow{so}, W\rangle$ *is a local reordering of* E *from an action list* l *to a list* l' *in thread* t *if*

- $[\xrightarrow{po}]_t = \alpha \cdot l \cdot \beta$ *and* $[\xrightarrow{po'}]_t = \alpha \cdot l' \cdot \beta$,
- $[\xrightarrow{po}]_{t'} = [\xrightarrow{po'}]_{t'}$ *for all threads* $t' \neq t$,
- *for all* $(tr, W) \in P'[t]$ *where* tr *is of the form* $\alpha \cdot l' \cdot \beta$, *there exists* $(\alpha \cdot l \cdot \beta, W) \in P[t]$,
- $P[t'] = P'[t']$ *for all thread* $t' \neq t$,
- l *and* l' *contain the same set of actions,*
- *no element of* l *or* l' *is a synchronization action.*

Such a reordering is written $E \xrightarrow{t:[l \longrightarrow l']} E'$.

Intuitively, we reorder the intra-thread trace $[\xrightarrow{po}]_t$ by transforming l into l'. BMM exposes two reorderings to the programmer. The first one is a *Write-Read* reordering which reorders a read before a previous adjacent write to a different address. Here is a simple example:

$$x \leftarrow 1;\ r \leftarrow y \quad \xrightarrow{\text{WR}} \quad r \leftarrow y;\ x \leftarrow 1$$

DEFINITION 5.2 (Write-Read reordering). *A* Write-Read *reordering,* $E \xrightarrow{\text{WR}} E'$, *of an execution* $E = \langle P, A, \xrightarrow{po}, \xrightarrow{so}, W\rangle$ *with respect to actions* w *and* r *in* t, *is a local reordering* E' *such that*

$$E \xrightarrow{t:[w::r \longrightarrow r::w]} E'$$

where w *and* r *operate on different addresses.*

Fig. 4 illustrates the use of the Write-Read reordering on a classical litmus test program. To understand the BMM semantics, a key observation must be made: the execution on the left is not sequentially consistent but after two WR reorderings we obtain a sequentially consistent execution. It is then tempting to ask if a BMM execution is any execution that can be transformed into an SC execution after

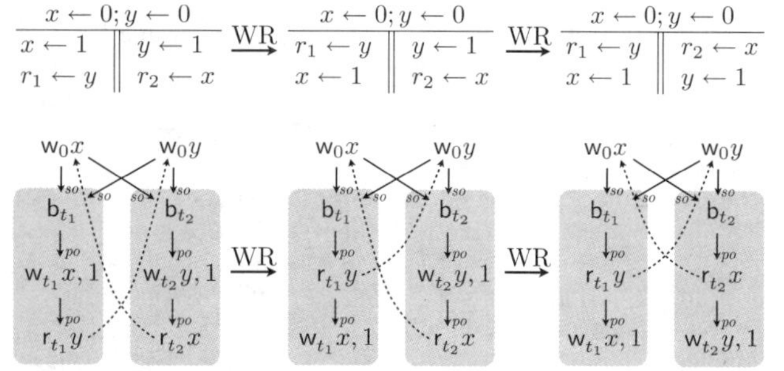

Figure 4. Write-Read reordering example.

some WR reorderings. Unfortunately, such a definition would not allow us to capture executions exhibited by TSO-hardware, so we need to work a bit harder.

The program on the top-left part of Fig. 5 illustrates this issue. In this program, the configuration $r_1 = 1, r_2 = 0, r_3 = 1; r_4 = 1, r_5 = 0$ is reachable under a TSO architecture, but it is not a SC execution and no WR reordering can be applied to this program. We introduce a second category of reorderings that is allowed in BMM that permits such executions.

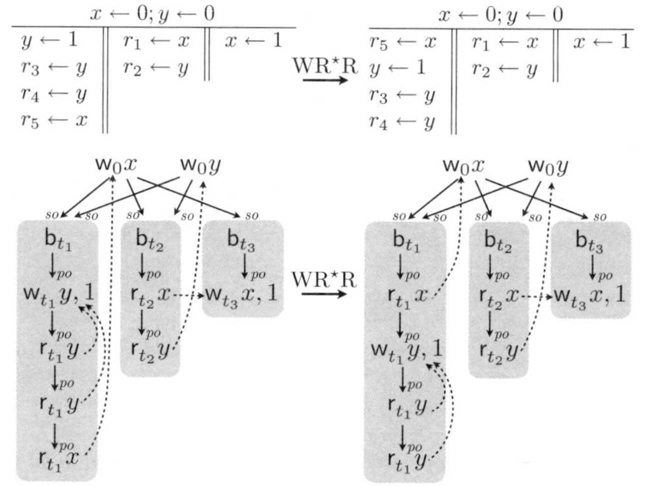

Figure 5. Write-Read-Read reordering example.

DEFINITION 5.3 (Write-Read-Read reordering). *A* Write-Read-Read *reordering of* $E = \langle P, A, \xrightarrow{po}, \xrightarrow{so}, W\rangle$ *w.r.t. a tuple of action* $(w, \vec{r}, r')$ *of* A, *is a local reordering* E' *such that*

$$E \xrightarrow{t:[w::\vec{r}::r' \longrightarrow r'::w::\vec{r}]} E'$$

Reads in $\vec{r} = r_1, \ldots, r_n$ *have* w *as write-seen, and* r' *and* w *target different addresses. Such a reordering is written* $E \xrightarrow{\text{WR}^\star\text{R}} E'$.

In Fig. 5, we apply this transformations to the previous program. This time, a reordering is possible and leads to an SC execution. Note that $\text{WR}^\star\text{R}$ is a generalization of the previous WR reordering. We prove in Sec. 7 that this new reordering exactly captures a TSO operational semantics. Formally, a BMM execution is any execution that can be transformed using $\text{WR}^\star\text{R}$ reorderings until reaching an SC execution.

DEFINITION 5.4 (BMM executions). BMM *executions are:*

$$\text{BMM} = \left\{ E \mid \exists E', E \xrightarrow{RO} E' \text{ and } E' \text{is SC} \right\}$$

with $\xrightarrow{RO} = (\xrightarrow{\text{WR}^\star\text{R}})^*$.

We write BMM(P) for the set of executions of a program P. The BMM observable behaviors of a program P is then defined as the set of sequences of external actions:

$$Obs(P) = \left\{ \xrightarrow{so} \downarrow_{\mathbb{A}_x} \mid \langle P, A, \xrightarrow{po}, \xrightarrow{so}, W\rangle \in \text{BMM}(P) \right\}$$

The definition of BMM is a least post-fixpoint. Every time we must prove that BMM is included in some set of well-formed executions, we can rely on the following characterization.

LEMMA 5.1 (BMM least post-fixpoint characterisation). BMM *is the least set* S *of well-formed executions such that*

- *all* SC *executions are in* S,
- S *is backward-closed by* BMM *reorderings: for any well-formed executions* E, E' *such that* $E \xrightarrow{RO} E'$, *if* $E' \in S$ *then* $E \in S$.

Proof. First, BMM satisfies the two above properties. Now, let S be a set of well-formed executions satisfying both properties. We show that BMM $\subseteq S$. Let $E \in$ BMM. If E is SC, then $E \in S$. Otherwise, there exists an SC execution E' such that $E \xrightarrow{RO} E'$. But E' is in S, so E is in S too. □

We use this lemma to show that BMM is a subset of the JMM executions and to show the equivalence between BMM and $\text{BMM}_\circ$.

5.1 BMM is a Subset of JMM

The current Java Memory Model defines the set of legal executions as a subset of all well-formed executions that are justifiable using a sequence of intermediate justifications. In order to connect our model with the JMM, rather than unfolding the details of this formal definition, we rely on the following JMM properties:

- JMM accepts all sequentially consistent executions,
- JMM allows reordering of non-volatile memory accesses hitting different locations [34].

THEOREM 5.2. *Let* JMM *be the set of all legal executions permitted by the* JMM. *Then,* BMM $\subseteq$ JMM.

Proof. We use here Lemma 5.1. We first know that JMM contains all SC executions. Then, suppose that $E \xrightarrow{RO} E'$ with $E' \in$ JMM. In the JMM, reordering non volatile memory accesses hitting different addresses is allowed [34]. We use this property to un-transform E' into E. Hence, E is also in JMM, meaning that JMM is backward-closed by $\text{WR}^\star\text{R}$. □

5.2 DRF Guarantee

We establish that BMM enjoys the important property that any reasonable memory model should have, namely a *data-race-free guarantee* - data-race free programs have SC executions only. We first define the standard notions of concurrent conflicting memory action, data-race, and data-race-free programs:

DEFINITION 5.5 (Conflicting actions). *Two non-volatile actions* $a, b \in \mathbb{A}_r \cup \mathbb{A}_w$ *are* conflicting *if they target the same address and* $T(a) \neq T(b)$ *and at least one of them is a write.*

DEFINITION 5.6 (Data-races). *Let* $\langle P, A, \xrightarrow{po}, \xrightarrow{so}, W\rangle$ *be a* BMM SC *execution. Two conflicting actions* a, b *form a* data-race *if they are not ordered by* $\xrightarrow{hb}$.

DEFINITION 5.7 (DRF). *A program* P *is* data-race free, *written* $DRF(P)$, *if all of its* SC *executions are free of data-race.*

THEOREM 5.3 (DRF guarantee). *For all* P, *if* $DRF(P)$, *then for all execution* $E \in$ BMM(P), E *is* SC.

Proof. Let P be such that $DRF(P)$, and $E \in$ BMM(P). By Theorem 5.2, $E \in$ JMM(P). But JMM satisfies the DRF guarantee [32], so E is sequentially consistent. □

6. $\text{BMM}_\circ$: An Operational Memory Model

In this section, we provide an operational view of the BMM. The reorderings allowed in its axiomatic version can be implemented by a $\text{BMM}_\circ$ machine that attaches a write-buffer to each running thread. The $\text{BMM}_\circ$ semantics is also parametrized by an intra-thread semantics. Hence, we need to consider an extra set of actions: the silent actions in $\mathbb{A}_{\text{sil}}$ that are either the unbuffering $\overline{\text{B}}(a)$ of a write action $a \in \mathbb{A}_w \setminus \mathbb{A}_d$ by thread $T(a)$ or a silent step τ_t by thread t.

$$\mathbb{A}_{\text{sil}} ::= \overline{\text{B}}(a) \mid \tau_t$$

$$\frac{ts(t) \xrightarrow{\tau}\!\!\!\!\rightarrow s}{ts, b, m \xrightarrow{\tau_t} ts[t \mapsto s], b, m}\,[\text{TAU}]$$

$$\frac{ts(t) \xrightarrow{\mathsf{r}_t^i x \mid V(w)}\!\!\!\!\rightarrow s \quad w = \text{rd}_t(b, m, x) \quad \neg\mathsf{volatile}(x)}{ts, b, m \xrightarrow{\mathsf{r}_t^i x \mid w} ts[t \mapsto s], b, m}\,[\text{READ}]$$

$$\frac{ts(t) \xrightarrow{\mathsf{w}_t^i x, v}\!\!\!\!\rightarrow s \quad \neg\mathsf{volatile}(x)}{ts, b, m \xrightarrow{\mathsf{w}_t^i x, v} ts[t \mapsto s], b[t \mapsto (\mathsf{w}_t^i x, v) :: b(t)], m}\,[\text{WRITE}]$$

$$\frac{b(t) = l \cdot [\mathsf{w}_t^i x, v]}{ts, b, m \xrightarrow{\overline{\text{B}}(\mathsf{w}_t^i x, v)} ts, b[t \mapsto l], m[x \mapsto (\mathsf{w}_t^i x, v)]}\,[\text{UNBUFF}]$$

$$\frac{ts, m \xrightarrow{\lambda}_{\mathsf{synch}} ts', m' \quad b(t) = []}{ts, b, m \xrightarrow{\lambda} ts', b, m'}\,[\text{SYNCH}]$$

Figure 6. $\text{BMM}_\circ$ machine (labelled transition system).

The idea behind $\text{BMM}_\circ$ is to provide a generative, operational machine that executes an input operational execution, modifying a memory state, made of thread buffers and a shared memory. The input of the $\text{BMM}_\circ$ machine is an operational execution, made of a program and a trace of *operational actions*. An operational action $a \in \mathbb{A}_{\text{op}}$ is either an action in $\mathbb{A} \setminus (\mathbb{A}_d \cup \mathbb{A}_r)$, or a pair in $\mathbb{A}_r \times \mathbb{A}_w$ (for each read action we record the write action that it sees, and refer to it as its *write-seen*), or a silent action in $\mathbb{A}_{\text{sil}}$.

DEFINITION 6.1 (Operational execution). *An operational execution is a pair* (P, tr) *where* P *is a program and* $tr \in \text{list}(\mathbb{A}_{\text{op}})$ *is finite and such that no action appear more than once in* tr.

The $\text{BMM}_\circ$ machine is then defined by a transition system, parametrized by an intra-thread semantics. We now describe its states and transitions. A $\text{BMM}_\circ$ state $\in$ State is a record

$$\begin{array}{lcll} ts & \in & \mathbb{T} \rightharpoonup \text{State}_{\text{intra}}; & \text{(intra-thread state of threads)} \\ b & \in & \mathbb{T} \rightharpoonup \text{list}(\mathbb{A}_w \setminus \mathbb{A}_d); & \text{(one buffer per thread)} \\ m & \in & \mathbb{X} \rightarrow \mathbb{A}_w & \text{(one write action per address)} \end{array}$$

The state first keeps track of each intra-thread state in $\text{State}_{\text{intra}}$. Each thread is given a write buffer; all non-volatile write actions are first written to this buffer. When unbuffered, these writes are committed to the shared memory m, that maps addresses to write actions. Given a memory state (buffers b and memory m), the $\text{BMM}_\circ$ machine specifies the write action a thread t can read when accessing the address x:

$$\text{rd}_t(b, m, x) = \begin{cases} w & \text{if } w \text{ is the first write to } x \text{ in } b(t) \\ m(x) & \text{if there is no write to } x \text{ in } b(t) \end{cases}$$

If a pending write to this address appears in the buffer of t, we take the most recent in the execution (*i.e.* the first in the buffer). Otherwise we consult the memory. If no write has been performed yet at this address we will retrieve the default value for this address.

The $\text{BMM}_\circ$ machine is defined as a labeled transition system where steps are labeled by operational actions. The salient semantic rules are given Fig. 6. In all rules (except BUFF) the $\text{BMM}_\circ$ machine makes a step that the intra-thread semantics can match. Rule TAU corresponds to a intra-thread silent step (when e.g. the thread operates on registers). The $\text{BMM}_\circ$ memory state does not change in this case. On a non-volatile read (READ) the value is obtained from

$$\frac{ts(t) \overset{\mathsf{r}^i_t x|V(w)}{\twoheadrightarrow} s \quad w = m(x) \quad \mathsf{volatile}(x)}{ts, m \xrightarrow{\mathsf{r}^i_t x|w}_{\mathsf{synch}} ts[t \mapsto s], m}\text{[READV]} \qquad \frac{ts(t) \overset{\mathsf{w}^i_t x,v}{\twoheadrightarrow} s \quad \mathsf{volatile}(x)}{ts, m \xrightarrow{\mathsf{w}^i_t x,v}_{\mathsf{synch}} ts[t \mapsto s], m[x \mapsto (\mathsf{w}^i_t x, v)]}\text{[WRITEV]}$$

$$\frac{ts(t) \overset{\mathsf{b}_t}{\twoheadrightarrow} s}{ts, m \xrightarrow{\mathsf{b}_t}_{\mathsf{synch}} ts[t \mapsto s], m}\text{[BEGIN]} \qquad \frac{ts(t) \overset{\mathsf{s}_t t'}{\twoheadrightarrow} s \quad t' \notin \mathrm{dom}(ts)}{ts, m \xrightarrow{\mathsf{s}_t t'}_{\mathsf{synch}} ts[t \mapsto s][t' \mapsto \mathrm{Ready}], m}\text{[SPAWN]} \qquad \frac{ts(t) \overset{\mathsf{l}^i_t l}{\twoheadrightarrow} s}{ts, m \xrightarrow{\mathsf{l}^i_t l}_{\mathsf{synch}} ts[t \mapsto s], m}\text{[LOCK]}$$

$$\frac{ts(t) \overset{\mathsf{e}_t}{\twoheadrightarrow} s}{ts, m \xrightarrow{\mathsf{e}_t}_{\mathsf{synch}} ts[t \mapsto s], m}\text{[END]} \qquad \frac{ts(t') = \mathrm{Done} \quad ts(t) \overset{\mathsf{j}^i_t t'}{\twoheadrightarrow} s}{ts, m \xrightarrow{\mathsf{j}^i_t t'}_{\mathsf{synch}} ts[t \mapsto s], m}\text{[JOIN]} \qquad \frac{ts(t) \overset{\mathsf{u}^i_t l}{\twoheadrightarrow} s}{ts, m \xrightarrow{\mathsf{u}^i_t l}_{\mathsf{synch}} ts[t \mapsto s], m}\text{[UNLOCK]}$$

Figure 7. $\mathsf{BMM}_\circ$ machine (synchronization actions).

the memory state using the rd function. For this action, the intra-thread event is a pair $\mathsf{r}^i_t x \mid v$ composed of a read and a value. The intra-thread semantics accepts any value here but the purpose of the rule is to constrain it using thread-local buffers and shared memory. On a non-volatile write (WRITE), the write action is put onto the thread's buffer. A write action can be unbuffered at any time, in which case the write is committed into shared memory (UNBUFF). All synchronizing actions are emitted by threads whose buffers are empty. They are gathered under the SYNCH rule whose definition (relying on a relation $\rightarrow_{\mathsf{synch}}$) is in Fig. 7. Reads from and writes to volatile locations directly access the memory so that all threads have a consistent view (READV and WRITEV). When a thread ends (END), its state is kept in the $\mathsf{BMM}_\circ$ state, enabling other threads to join it (JOIN), and preventing it to from being restarted (SPAWN).

We then define a $\mathsf{BMM}_\circ$ execution as a constrained operational execution that is accepted by the $\mathsf{BMM}_\circ$ machine: the input trace is properly locked and can be executed by the machine, with the intended meaning that the input execution is intra-thread consistent.

DEFINITION 6.2 ($\mathsf{BMM}_\circ$ execution). *An operational execution (P, tr) is in $\mathsf{BMM}_\circ(P)$ if there exists states $s_0, s_1, \ldots, s_n$ in* State *satisfying the following:*

- *tr is properly locked (see Definition 4.5, using $\xrightarrow{tr}$ instead of $\xrightarrow{po}$ and $\xrightarrow{so}$),*
- *s_0 is an initial state: the memory maps every address to the corresponding default write ($\forall x, m(x) = \mathsf{w}_0 x$), buffers are empty and $s_0.ts$ is defined for exactly one thread, mapping it to the* Ready *state,*
- *$tr = a_1 :: \cdots :: a_n \in \mathrm{list}(\mathbb{A}_{\mathrm{op}})$,*
- *for all $i \in \{1, \ldots, n\}, s_{i-1} \xrightarrow{a_i} s_i$.*

The $\mathsf{BMM}_\circ$ behaviors of program P are external action traces obtained by projecting all executions of P accepted by the $\mathsf{BMM}_\circ$ machine on $\mathbb{A}_{\mathrm{x}}$:

$$Obs_\circ(P) = \{tr \downarrow_{\mathbb{A}_{\mathrm{x}}} \mid (P, tr) \in \mathsf{BMM}_\circ(P)\}$$

7. Equivalence of BMM and $\mathsf{BMM}_\circ$

We show that BMM and $\mathsf{BMM}_\circ$ are equivalent relaxed memory models: they allow the exact same set of behaviors for any program.

THEOREM 7.1. *For all program P, $\quad Obs_\circ(P) = Obs(P)$.*

The proof relies on an operator ρ that bridges the gap between BMM and $\mathsf{BMM}_\circ$ by building axiomatic executions from operational ones.

DEFINITION 7.1 (ρ operator). *Let $E_\circ = (P, tr)$ be an execution, ρ is defined as $\rho(E_\circ) = \langle P, A, \xrightarrow{po}, \xrightarrow{so}, W\rangle$ where*

- *A is the set of non-silent actions in tr,*
- *for all $a, b \in A$, $a \xrightarrow{po} b$ iff $T(a) = T(b)$ and $a \xrightarrow{tr} b$,*
- *for all $a, b \in A$, $a \xrightarrow{so} b$ iff $a, b \in \mathbb{A}_{\mathrm{s}}$ and $a \xrightarrow{tr} b$,*
- *for all pairs $\mathsf{r}^i_t x \mid w$ in tr, $W(\mathsf{r}^i_t x) = w$.*

We show that $\rho(\mathsf{BMM}_\circ) = \mathsf{BMM}$. Each inclusion is proved and Theorem 7.1 follows from the following lemma.

LEMMA 7.2. *Let $E_\circ = (P, tr)$ be an operational execution and $\langle P, A, \xrightarrow{po}, \xrightarrow{so}, W\rangle = \rho(E_\circ)$, then $tr \downarrow_{\mathbb{A}_{\mathrm{x}}} = (\xrightarrow{so} \downarrow_{\mathbb{A}_{\mathrm{x}}})$.*

Proof. By definition of ρ, we know that for all $a, b \in A$, $a \xrightarrow{so} b$ iff $a, b \in \mathbb{A}_{\mathrm{s}}$ and $a \xrightarrow{tr} b$. □

We define auxiliary notions needed for the proof. An operational execution $E_\circ$ is well-formed if $\rho(E_\circ)$ is well-formed, and it is SC_ρ if $\rho(E_\circ)$ is SC. Similarly, we define operational reorderings relying on ρ: an execution $E'_\circ$ is an operational reordering of $E_\circ$ if $\rho(E_\circ) \xrightarrow{\mathrm{WR}^\star\mathrm{R}} \rho(E'_\circ)$. We abuse notations and write it $E_\circ \xrightarrow{\mathrm{WR}^\star\mathrm{R}} E'_\circ$, and lift this notion to trace reorderings $\xrightarrow{RO}$. To lighten the notations in this section, we keep implicit the unique identifier of actions and write w^t_x for $\mathsf{w}^i_t x, v$ (the value written is omitted). When considering operational actions in a trace we generally omit the write action w attached to a read action.

7.1 $\rho(\mathsf{BMM}_\circ) \subseteq \mathsf{BMM}$

We prove that every $\mathsf{BMM}_\circ$ execution trace can be reordered into a SC trace. The proof relies on a reordering scheme explained in the following lemma.

LEMMA 7.3. *Let $E_\circ = (P, tr) \in \mathsf{BMM}_\circ(P)$, with $tr = \alpha \cdot [\mathsf{w}^t_x] \cdot \beta$ an execution such that $\overline{\mathrm{B}}(\mathsf{w}^t_x) \notin \beta$. We write*

- *$\mathcal{W}^t = \{\mathsf{w}^t_y \in \beta \mid y \in \mathbb{X}\}$, write actions belonging to thread t,*
- *$\mathcal{R}^t = \{\mathsf{r}^t_y \in \beta \mid \mathsf{w}^t_x \cdot \beta = \gamma_1 \cdot \mathsf{w}^t_y \cdot \gamma_2 \cdot \mathsf{r}^t_y \cdot \gamma_3,\ y \in \mathbb{X},\ \gamma_1, \gamma_2, \gamma_3 \in \mathrm{list}(\mathbb{A}_{\mathrm{op}})\}$, read actions seeing a write performed by t in $[\mathsf{w}^t_x] \cdot \beta$,*
- *$\beta \setminus (\mathcal{W}^t \cup \mathcal{R}^t)$ the remaining actions in β.*

Then, there exist P', β_1, β_2 such that $E'_\circ = (P', tr') \in \mathsf{BMM}_\circ(P')$, $E_\circ \xrightarrow{RO} E'_\circ$ and $tr' = \alpha \cdot \beta_1 \cdot [\mathsf{w}^t_x] \cdot \beta_2$ where,

- *$\beta_1 = \beta \downarrow_{\beta \setminus (\mathcal{W}^t \cup \mathcal{R}^t)}$,*
- *β_2 contains the elements of $\mathcal{W}^t \cup \mathcal{R}^t$,*
- *$[\mathsf{w}^t_x] \cdot \beta_2$ matches the pattern $(\mathsf{w}^t_{x_1}; (\mathsf{r}^t_{x_1})^*) \cdot \ldots \cdot (\mathsf{w}^t_{x_n}; (\mathsf{r}^t_{x_n})^*)$,*
- *for all δ, $(P, tr \cdot \delta) \in \mathsf{BMM}_\circ(P)$ then $(P', tr' \cdot \delta) \in \mathsf{BMM}_\circ(P')$.*

Before going into the detail of the proof, we give an intuition on how we use it. This lemma is applied to a part of an execution in which a write action, performed by t, stays in its buffer. This is illustrated in the following figure, where the grey regions denote subsequences of actions whose owning thread is not t. The bold stroke action w^t_x is the write action that remains in t's buffer until the end of tr. We will use this action as a pivot on all the actions performed in the rest of tr, so that the resulting trace tr' is as illustrated: (a) all grey actions are shifted before the pivot, remaining in the same relative order, by changing the interleaving; (b) actions of thread t are handled with the $\mathrm{WR}^\star\mathrm{R}$ reordering rule. Because write actions of t cannot be moved, they are kept to the right of the pivot.

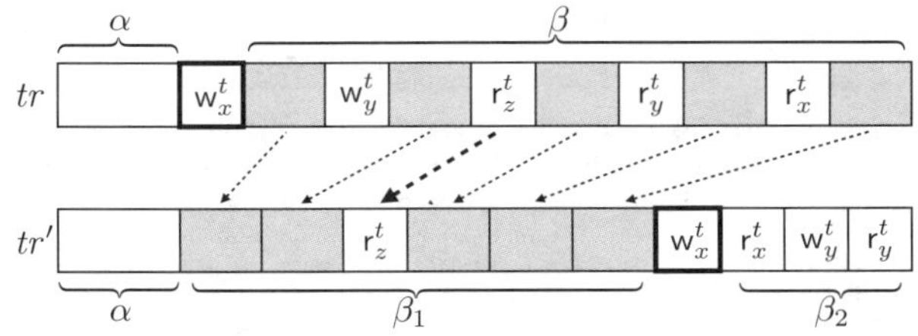

Handling read actions of t is more involved: either they see a write that occurred (necessarily in thread t) after the pivot in tr, and they are accumulated in a pattern $(\mathsf{w}^t_{x_1}; (\mathsf{r}^t_{x_1})^*) \cdot \ldots \cdot (\mathsf{w}^t_{x_n}; (\mathsf{r}^t_{x_n})^*)$, or they see a write that occurs before the pivot, and $\mathrm{WR}^\star\mathrm{R}$ is applied repeatedly on this pattern, until they are swapped before w^t_x.

Proof. Let $E_\circ = (P, tr) \in \mathsf{BMM}_\circ(P)$, with $tr = (\alpha \cdot [\mathsf{w}^t_x] \cdot \beta)$ and $\overline{\mathsf{B}}(\mathsf{w}^t_x) \notin \beta$. The sub-trace $[\mathsf{w}^t_x] \cdot \beta$ can be decomposed as $[\mathsf{w}^t_x] \cdot \beta = \beta_p \cdot \beta_t$ with $\beta_p = [\mathsf{w}^t_y; (\mathsf{r}^t_y)^*]^+$ (we take the shortest β_t). We now proceed by induction on the length of β_t.

- Base case: β_t is empty. We don't need any reordering transformation to reach the expected pattern.
- Inductive case. We proceed by case analysis on the first element of $\beta_t = a :: \beta'_t$ and show that a can be either (i) integrated inside the pattern β_p or (ii) be moved before this pattern:
  - If $a = \mathsf{r}^t_k$, when k is one of the addresses of β_p. Here, we integrate in β_p by applying an $\mathrm{WR}^\star\mathrm{R}$ as many times as needed to make it part of the right $\mathsf{w}^t_k(\mathsf{r}^t_k)^*$ pattern such that $\beta_p = \beta_{p1} \cdot (\mathsf{w}^t_k(\mathsf{r}^t_k)^*) \cdot \beta_{p2}$. Note $\mathrm{WR}^\star\mathrm{R}$ can be applied because the pattern only concerns thread t, and the visibility conditions required by $\mathrm{WR}^\star\mathrm{R}$ are fulfilled. The right-most such pattern before a, i.e. such that there is no w^t_k in β_{p2}, is the only one that can ensure the write-seen of a to be preserved, according to $\mathsf{BMM}_\circ$. Thus the resulting trace $\left(P', \alpha \cdot \beta_{p1} \cdot (\mathsf{w}^t_k(\mathsf{r}^t_k)^* a) \cdot \beta_{p2} \cdot \beta'_t\right)$ is $\mathsf{BMM}_\circ$.
  - If $a = \mathsf{r}^t_k$, when k is not any of the addresses of β_p. We apply the same reasoning as in the previous case, rewriting the trace with $\mathrm{WR}^\star\mathrm{R}$, but in this case, this simply amounts to put a before w^t_x, because $\mathrm{WR}^\star\mathrm{R}$ will be applied on the whole β_p (and the write-seen is trivially kept valid).
  - If $a = \overline{\mathsf{B}}(a')$, then $a' \in \alpha$ because there is no unbuffering action in β_p. This unbuffering could have been done just before w^t_x. This unbuffering does not modify the visibility constraints of the new trace, as it cannot overwrite any of the write actions in β_p. For any trace δ, if $(P, \alpha \cdot \beta_p \cdot [a] \cdot \beta'_t \cdot \delta) \in \mathsf{BMM}_\circ(P)$ then the trace $(P, \alpha \cdot [a] \cdot \beta_p \cdot \beta'_t \cdot \delta)$ is also in $\mathsf{BMM}_\circ$ (P): any read in δ that sees a' in the first trace can still see it in the second trace because no write action in β_p is unbuffered before δ.
  - For all other cases ($a = \mathsf{r}^{t''}_k$, where $t'' \neq t$, $a = \mathsf{w}^{t''}_k$, with $t'' \neq t$, and $a \in \mathbb{A}_s$), we can just change the interleaving to move a before β_p and conclude easily.

For each resulting trace, we show that we are under the induction hypothesis premises. Hence, we conclude by induction.

□

This reordering scheme is extensively used for proving Lemma 7.4, stating that the reordering interpretation of BMM can be simulated in the operational world.

LEMMA 7.4. *Let $E_\circ = (P, tr) \in \mathsf{BMM}_\circ(P)$. Then there exist P', tr' such that $E_\circ \xrightarrow{RO} (P', tr')$, with $(P', tr') \in \mathsf{BMM}_\circ(P')$ is SC_ρ.*

In order to prove the lemma by induction, we need to prove a stronger result, that includes an additional property on the shape of the two operational traces tr and tr'. This so-called *write-swapping* property is formally defined as follows.

DEFINITION 7.2 (Write-swapping). *Let tr and tr' two sequences of actions. The* write-swapping *property holds on (tr, tr') if for any write actions w_1, w_2 to the same address,*

- *if $w_1 \xrightarrow{tr} w_2$ and $w_2 \xrightarrow{tr'} w_1$ (write actions have been swapped) then the trace tr is of the form $tr = \alpha \cdot [w_1] \cdot \beta \cdot [w_2] \cdot \gamma$ and $\overline{\mathsf{B}}(w_1) \notin \beta$.*
- *if $w_1 \xrightarrow{tr} w_2$ and $w_1 \xrightarrow{tr'} w_2$ (write actions have not been swapped) then if $\overline{\mathsf{B}}(w_1)$ occurs before w_2 in tr, it is also the case in tr'.*

Proof. We prove Lemma 7.4 by strong induction on the size of the execution $|tr| = n$. Assume the property holds for any integer $k < n$. Let $E_\circ = (P, tr) \in \mathsf{BMM}_\circ(P)$ an execution of size n.

We assume $n > 0$ (the case $n = 0$ holds trivially). So tr is of the form $tr = tr_1 \cdot [a]$. By induction on tr_1, we get P_2 and tr_2 such that $(P, tr_1) \xrightarrow{RO} (P_2, tr_2)$, with $E^2_\circ = (P_2, tr_2) \in \mathsf{BMM}_\circ(P_2) \cap \mathrm{SC}_\rho$, plus a write-swapping on (tr_1, tr_2).

We extend $E^2_\circ$ to $(P_2, tr_2 \cdot [a])$. If action a is not a read action, we can conclude directly. Otherwise, $a = \mathsf{r}^{t_3}_x$, the extended trace is in $\mathsf{BMM}_\circ(P_2)$, and the write-swapping property holds. It remains to show that it is SC_ρ. If it is not, we proceed by case analysis:

Case 1: There is a thread $t \neq t_3$ whose buffer is not empty at the end of tr_2. Formally, there is a write action w^t_y in tr_2 such that $\overline{\mathsf{B}}(\mathsf{w}^t_y) \notin tr_2$. $tr_2.[a]$ is of the form $\alpha \cdot [\mathsf{w}^t_y] \cdot \beta \cdot [\mathsf{r}^{t_3}_x]$. Applying Lemma 7.3 on w^t_y, we get P_3 and tr_3 such that $(P_2, tr_2.[a]) \xrightarrow{RO} (P_3, tr_3)$ with $E^3_\circ = (P_3, tr_3) \in \mathsf{BMM}_\circ(P_3)$ and $tr_3 = \alpha \cdot \beta_1 \cdot [\mathsf{r}^{t_3}_x] \cdot [\mathsf{w}^t_y] \cdot \beta_2$ with $[\mathsf{w}^t_y] \cdot \beta_2$ matching the pattern $[\mathsf{w}^t_\cdot; (\mathsf{r}^t_\cdot)^*]^+$. By induction on $\alpha \cdot \beta_1 \cdot [\mathsf{r}^{t_3}_x]$, we get P_4 and tr_4 such that $\left(P_3, \alpha \cdot \beta_1 \cdot [\mathsf{r}^{t_3}_x]\right) \xrightarrow{RO} (P_4, tr_4)$, with $E^4_\circ = (P_4, tr_4) \in \mathsf{BMM}_\circ(P_4) \cap \mathrm{SC}_\rho$, plus a write-swapping property on the traces. We concatenate the suffix $[\mathsf{w}^t_y] \cdot \beta_2$ to extend tr_4 to an execution in $\mathsf{BMM}_\circ(P_4) \cap \mathrm{SC}_\rho$. The sequential consistency holds thanks to the pattern of $[\mathsf{w}^t_y] \cdot \beta_2$. The write-swapping is preserved by the concatenation.

Case 2: All threads distinct from t_3 have their buffer empty at the end of tr_2. Formally, for every write action $\mathsf{w}^t_y \in tr_2$ such that $t \neq t_3$, $\overline{\mathsf{B}}(\mathsf{w}^t_y) \in tr_2$. Let $\mathsf{w}^{t_1}_x$ be the write seen by $\mathsf{r}^{t_3}_x$.

- If $\overline{\mathsf{B}}(\mathsf{w}^{t_1}_x) \notin tr_2$, it means that $t_1 = t_3$. The trace $tr_2.[a]$ is of the form: $\alpha \cdot [\mathsf{w}^{t_1}_x] \cdot \beta \cdot [\mathsf{r}^{t_3}_x]$. We apply Lemma 7.3 on $\mathsf{w}^{t_1}_x$. The trace $\alpha \cdot \beta_1 \cdot [\mathsf{w}^{t_1}_x] \cdot \beta_2$ we obtain is in $\mathsf{BMM}_\circ$ and by the shape of β_1 and β_2 it is SC_ρ. We must show $\mathsf{w}^{t_1}_x$ is now the most recent write to x in β_2. But any other write there would be from thread t_1 and $\mathsf{r}^{t_3}_x$ could thus not see $\mathsf{w}^{t_1}_x$.
- If $\overline{\mathsf{B}}(\mathsf{w}^{t_1}_x) \in tr_2$, then the trace $tr_2.[a]$ is of the form $\alpha \cdot [\mathsf{w}^{t_1}_x] \cdot \beta \cdot [\overline{\mathsf{B}}(\mathsf{w}^{t_1}_x)] \cdot \gamma \cdot [\mathsf{r}^{t_3}_x]$. No $\mathsf{w}^{t_2}_x$ more recent than $\mathsf{w}^{t_1}_x$ can appear in γ: either it is unbuffered in γ and it would overwrite $\mathsf{w}^{t_1}_x$ or it is not unbuffered but then $t_2 = t_3$ and $\mathsf{w}^{t_1}_x$ could not be seen by $\mathsf{r}^{t_3}_x$. No unbuffering $\overline{\mathsf{B}}(\mathsf{w}^{t_2}_x)$ can either appear in γ since it would overwrite $\mathsf{w}^{t_1}_x$.

By Lemma 7.3 on $\mathsf{w}_x^{t_1}$ and β, we get a trace tr_3 such that $tr_3 \cdot [\overline{\mathrm{B}}(\mathsf{w}_x^{t_1})] \cdot \gamma \cdot [\mathsf{r}_x^{t_3}] = \alpha \cdot \beta_1 \cdot [\mathsf{w}_x^{t_1}] \cdot \beta_2 \cdot [\overline{\mathrm{B}}(\mathsf{w}_x^{t_1})] \cdot \gamma \cdot [\mathsf{r}_x^{t_3}]$. In this trace, the most recent write to x is now $\mathsf{w}_x^{t_1}$. The subtrace $\alpha \cdot \beta_1 \cdot [\mathsf{w}_x^{t_1}] \cdot \beta_2 \cdot [\overline{\mathrm{B}}(\mathsf{w}_x^{t_1})]$ is SC because $\alpha \cdot [\mathsf{w}_x^{t_1}] \cdot \beta \cdot [\overline{\mathrm{B}}(\mathsf{w}_x^{t_1})]$ was. It remains to show that all reads in γ still see the most recent writes. By induction on $tr_3 \cdot [\overline{\mathrm{B}}(\mathsf{w}_x^{t_1})] \cdot \gamma$, an SC execution is rebuilt, that keeps the same write-seen.

□

Finally, we obtain the first inclusion as a corollary of Lemma 7.4.

COROLLARY 7.5. $\rho(\mathsf{BMM}_\circ) \subseteq \mathsf{BMM}$.

Proof. Let $E_\circ = (P, tr) \in \mathsf{BMM}_\circ(P)$. By Lemma 7.4, we have $E_\circ \xrightarrow{RO} E'_\circ$, with $E'_\circ = (P', tr') \in \mathsf{BMM}_\circ(P')$ is SC_ρ. By definition, $\rho(E_\circ) \xrightarrow{RO} \rho(E'_\circ)$ and $\rho(E'_\circ)$ is SC. Hence, $\rho(E_\circ) \in \mathsf{BMM}(P)$. □

7.2 $\mathsf{BMM} \subseteq \rho(\mathsf{BMM}_\circ)$

We use here the post-fixpoint characterization of BMM (Lemma 5.1). We first show that $\rho(\mathsf{BMM}_\circ)$ contains all SC axiomatic executions. Let $E = \langle P, A, \xrightarrow{po}, \xrightarrow{so}, W\rangle \in \mathsf{BMM}$ be an SC execution. Then there exists a total order $\xrightarrow{to}$ on A, compatible with $\xrightarrow{po}$ and $\xrightarrow{so}$ such that all read actions in A see the last write to their address w.r.t. $\xrightarrow{to}$. We claim that $E_\circ = (P, tr)$ can be build, with $tr\downarrow_{\mathbb{A}} = \xrightarrow{to}$, and that $E_\circ \in \mathsf{BMM}_\circ(P)$. Silent actions are inserted in $\xrightarrow{to}$ so that each write action is immediately unbuffered, and that tr is intra-thread consistent – an equivalent condition was required for $E \in \mathsf{BMM}(P)$. Finally $\rho(E_\circ) = E$. We also show that $\rho(\mathsf{BMM}_\circ)$ is backward-closed by $\mathrm{WR^{\star}R}$. Let E and E' two well-formed axiomatic executions such that $E' \in \rho(\mathsf{BMM}_\circ)$ and $E \xrightarrow{\mathrm{WR^{\star}R}} E'$. $E' \in \rho(\mathsf{BMM}_\circ)$ so there exists $E'_\circ \in \mathsf{BMM}_\circ$ such that $E' = \rho(E'_\circ)$. $\mathrm{WR^{\star}R}$ is a valid transformation under $\mathsf{BMM}_\circ$ (see Sec. 8.1), meaning that there exists $E_\circ \in \mathsf{BMM}_\circ$ such that $\rho(E_\circ) = E$. Hence, $E \in \rho(\mathsf{BMM}_\circ)$.

8. Validity of Transformations

One of the objectives of any memory model is to take into account the reorderings performed by the hardware and to allow compilers to perform some program transformations that deal directly with memory accesses or locks. Tab. 2 gives standard transformations and their validity under various memory models [32, 34].

For a proof of validity we rely on the operational model: we consider a $\mathsf{BMM}_\circ$ trace of a transformed program and show there exists a valid $\mathsf{BMM}_\circ$ trace of the original program with the same behavior. For a proof of invalidity, we provide a counter-example and use the intuitive reordering memory model of BMM: given a program P and a transformed program P', we show that there exists an execution that is valid for P' but invalid for P (both under BMM). This table demonstrate that, despite its restricted set of reorderings, BMM allows useful transformations.

8.1 Validity of WR and $\mathrm{WR^{\star}R}$

Among the set of transformations, the validity of the local reordering $\mathrm{WR^{\star}R}$ is crucial for the memory model inclusion.

DEFINITION 8.1 (Valid reordering). *A local reordering $\xrightarrow{\Phi}$ between axiomatic executions is said to be valid with respect to $\mathsf{BMM}_\circ$ if for all axiomatic execution E and all operational execution $E_\circ$, $E \xrightarrow{\Phi} \rho(E_\circ)$ and $E_\circ \in \mathsf{BMM}_\circ$ implies that there exists $E'_\circ \in \mathsf{BMM}_\circ$ such that $E = \rho(E'_\circ)$.*

We can show that both WR and $\mathrm{WR^{\star}R}$ are valid.

Transformation	SC	JMM	BMM
Trace preserving transformation	✓	✓	✓
Reordering normal memory accesses	×	✓	⊗
Redundant read after read elimination	✓	×	✓
Redundant read after write elimination	✓	✓	✓
Irrelevant read elimination	✓	✓	✓
Irrelevant read introduction	✓	×	✓
Redundant write before write elimination	✓	✓	✓
Redundant write after read elimination	✓	×	×
Roach motel reordering	✓	×	⊗

We write ✓ for a valid transformation and × when it is generally wrong, ⊗ for limited applicability: only $\mathrm{WR^{\star}R}$ applies to normal memory accesses; a read can be delayed past a lock and a write can take over an unlock.

Table 2. Validity of transformations in memory models.

LEMMA 8.1. $\xrightarrow{\mathrm{WR}}$ *is valid.*

Proof. Let $E = \langle P, A, \xrightarrow{po}, \xrightarrow{so}, W\rangle$ be an axiomatic execution and $E_\circ = (P', tr')$ an operational execution with $E \xrightarrow{\mathrm{WR}} \rho(E_\circ)$ and $E_\circ \in \mathsf{BMM}_\circ$. By hypothesis, we know that $tr' = \beta \cdot [\mathsf{r}_t^j x] \cdot \gamma \cdot [\mathsf{w}_t^i y, v] \cdot \delta$ and γ does not contain any action owned by t except some unbuffering actions. The write action $\mathsf{w}_t^i y, v$ can be performed just after $\mathsf{r}_t^j x$ since the unbuffering in γ are independent of it and no read action in γ can see $\mathsf{w}_t^i y, v$ (it is still in its buffer). Hence the trace $\beta \cdot [\mathsf{r}_t^j x] \cdot [\mathsf{w}_t^i y, v] \cdot \gamma \cdot \delta$ is still in $\mathsf{BMM}_\circ$ for the same value-seen and write-seen information. After a swap we obtain a trace $tr'' = \beta \cdot [\mathsf{w}_t^i y, v] \cdot [\mathsf{r}_t^j x] \cdot \gamma \cdot \delta$ that belongs to $\mathsf{BMM}_\circ(P)$ (by definition of $\xrightarrow{\mathrm{WR}}$) and $\rho(P, tr'') = E$. □

LEMMA 8.2. $\xrightarrow{\mathrm{WR^{\star}R}}$ *is valid.*

Proof. Let $E = \langle P, A, \xrightarrow{po}, \xrightarrow{so}, W\rangle$ be an axiomatic execution and let $E_\circ = (P', tr')$ be an operational execution such that $E \xrightarrow{\mathrm{WR^{\star}R}} \rho(E_\circ)$ and $E_\circ \in \mathsf{BMM}_\circ$. By hypothesis, the traces tr' is of the form $tr' = \beta \cdot [\mathsf{r}_t^j x] \cdot \gamma \cdot [\mathsf{w}_t^i y, v] \cdot \gamma_1 \cdot [\mathsf{r}_t^{i_1} y] \cdots \gamma_n \cdot [\mathsf{r}_t^{i_n} y] \cdot \delta$. Each $\gamma, \gamma_1, \ldots, \gamma_n$ does not contain any action owned by t except some unbuffering actions. As in the previous proof, the action $\mathsf{w}_t^i y, v$ can be performed just after $\mathsf{r}_t^j x$. All read actions $\mathsf{r}_t^{i_1} y, \ldots, \mathsf{r}_t^{i_n} y$ see the write $\mathsf{w}_t^i y, v$ in tr' and can thus also be performed earlier. The trace $\beta \cdot [\mathsf{r}_t^j x] \cdot [\mathsf{w}_t^i y, v] \cdot [\mathsf{r}_t^{i_1} y] \cdots [\mathsf{r}_t^{i_n} y] \cdot \gamma \cdot \gamma_1 \cdots \gamma_n \cdot \delta$ is still in $\mathsf{BMM}_\circ(P')$ for the same value-seen and write-seen (the moved reads see $\mathsf{w}_t^i y, v$ directly from t's buffer). We then conclude with a swap: the trace $tr'' = \beta \cdot [\mathsf{w}_t^i y, v] \cdot [\mathsf{r}_t^{i_1} y] \cdots [\mathsf{r}_t^{i_n} y] \cdot [\mathsf{r}_t^j x] \cdot \gamma \cdot \gamma_1 \cdots \gamma_n \cdot \delta$ belongs to $\mathsf{BMM}_\circ(P)$ and $\rho(P, tr'') = E$. □

8.2 Other Valid Transformations

Given $E' = (P', tr')$, for each transformation we observe the shape of tr' and provide a corresponding $\mathsf{BMM}_\circ$ trace of an untransformed program. We assume that the intra-thread semantics accepts the transformation. All read and write actions are non-volatile.

Redundant Read after Read Elimination.

$$tr' = \beta \cdot [\mathsf{r}_t^i x] \cdot \gamma$$

Trace $\beta \cdot [\mathsf{r}_t^i x] \cdot [\mathsf{r}_t^j x] \cdot \gamma$ is in $\mathsf{BMM}_\circ$. $\mathsf{r}_t^j x$ and $\mathsf{r}_t^i x$ see the same write.

Redundant Read after Write Elimination.

$$tr' = \beta \cdot [\mathsf{w}_t^i x, v] \cdot \gamma$$

Trace $\beta \cdot [\mathsf{w}_t^i x, v] \cdot [\mathsf{r}_t^j x] \cdot \gamma$ is in $\mathsf{BMM}_\circ$. $\mathsf{r}_t^j x$ sees $\mathsf{w}_t^i x, v$ in its buffer.

Irrelevant Read Elimination.

$$tr' = \beta \cdot \delta$$

Trace $\beta \cdot [\mathsf{r}^i_t x] \cdot \gamma$ is in $\mathsf{BMM_o}$. $\mathsf{r}^i_t x$ sees the first write to x in the buffer or pick the current write attached to x in memory.

Irrelevant Read Introduction.

$$tr' = \beta \cdot [\mathsf{r}^i_t x] \cdot \delta$$

Trace $\beta \cdot \gamma$ is in $\mathsf{BMM_o}$. The visibility of the other actions is preserved.

Redundant Write before Write Elimination.

$$tr' = \beta \cdot [\mathsf{w}^j_t y, v] \cdot \gamma$$

We distinguish two cases. If $\gamma = \gamma_1 \cdot \overline{\mathsf{B}}(\mathsf{w}^j_t y, v) \cdot \gamma_2$. The trace $\beta \cdot [\mathsf{w}^i_t y, v'] \cdot [\mathsf{w}^j_t y, v] \cdot \gamma_1 \cdot \overline{\mathsf{B}}(\mathsf{w}^i_t y, v') \cdot \overline{\mathsf{B}}(\mathsf{w}^j_t y, v) \cdot \gamma_2$ is in $\mathsf{BMM_o}$. Adding the unbuffering preserves the visibility of $\mathsf{w}^j_t y, v$ since $\mathsf{w}^i_t y, v'$ is never seen. Otherwise, $\overline{\mathsf{B}}(\mathsf{w}^j_t y, v) \notin \gamma$. The trace $tr' = \beta \cdot [\mathsf{w}^i_t y, v'] \cdot [\mathsf{w}^j_t y, v] \cdot \gamma$ is in $\mathsf{BMM_o}$. $\mathsf{w}^i_t y, v'$ is never seen.

Roach-motel: Read-lock Reordering. A read before a lock can be reordered (no action emitted by the thread t in γ).

$$tr' = \beta \cdot [\mathsf{l}^i_t l] \cdot \gamma \cdot [\mathsf{r}^j_t x] \cdot \delta$$

We assume tr' is properly locked so no synchronization action on l is in γ. Hence the following interleaving is a valid trace of the transformed program: $\beta \cdot \gamma \cdot [\mathsf{l}^i_t l] \cdot [\mathsf{r}^j_t x] \cdot \delta$. Then the trace $\beta \cdot \gamma \cdot [\mathsf{r}^j_t x] \cdot [\mathsf{l}^i_t l] \cdot \delta$ is in $\mathsf{BMM_o}$.

Roach-motel: Unlock-write Reordering. A write after an unlock can be reordered. Since the buffer must be empty, the transformed trace has the following shape, where $\mathsf{w}^i_t x, v$ is the last non silent action of thread t.

$$tr' = \beta \cdot [\mathsf{w}^i_t x, v] \cdot \gamma \cdot [\overline{\mathsf{B}}(\mathsf{w}^i_t x, v)] \cdot \delta \cdot [\mathsf{u}^j_t l] \cdot \eta$$

There is no action emitted by thread t in γ except some unbufferings. No action in γ emitted by the other threads can see the write $\mathsf{w}^i_t x, v$. Then, changing the scheduling, we can obtain the following $\mathsf{BMM_o}$ traces: $\beta \cdot \gamma \cdot [\mathsf{w}^i_t x, v] \cdot [\overline{\mathsf{B}}(\mathsf{w}^i_t x, v)] \cdot \delta \cdot [\mathsf{u}^j_t l] \cdot \eta$. By hypothesis, there is no action emitted by the thread t in δ; besides there is no lock/unlock action on l in δ. Therefore changing the scheduling again can lead to the following $\mathsf{BMM_o}$ (properly locked) trace: $\beta \cdot \gamma \cdot [\mathsf{w}^i_t x, v] \cdot [\overline{\mathsf{B}}(\mathsf{w}^i_t x, v)] \cdot [\mathsf{u}^j_t l] \cdot \delta \cdot \eta$. Finally, the following trace is a $\mathsf{BMM_o}$ execution of the untransformed program: $\beta \cdot \gamma \cdot [\mathsf{u}^j_t l] \cdot [\mathsf{w}^i_t x, v] \cdot [\overline{\mathsf{B}}(\mathsf{w}^i_t x, v)] \cdot \delta \cdot \eta$.

8.3 Invalid Transformations

The BMM helps understand why some transformations are invalid.

Redundant Write after Read Elimination. Here v is volatile.

$x{\leftarrow}0$	$y{\leftarrow}0$
$r_1{\leftarrow}x$	$x{\leftarrow}1$
$y{\leftarrow}1$	$v{\leftarrow}0$
$x{\leftarrow}r_1$	$r_2{\leftarrow}y$
$r_3{\leftarrow}x$	

$r_1{=}r_2{=}0, r_3{=}1$ invalid

redund. write → after read elim.

$x{\leftarrow}0$	$y{\leftarrow}0$
$r_1{\leftarrow}x$	$x{\leftarrow}1$
$y{\leftarrow}1$	$v{\leftarrow}0$
	$r_2{\leftarrow}y$
$r_3{\leftarrow}x$	

$r_1{=}r_2{=}0, r_3{=}1$ valid

On the left, we see why the execution is not valid: it isn't SC and no reordering is possible. After the redundant write elimination, the execution becomes valid because the read $r_3{\leftarrow}x$ can be reordered with the write $y{\leftarrow}1$ to give a SC execution. This transformation thus introduced new behaviors.

Roach-motel: Unlock-read Reordering. Reordering reads and unlocks is not allowed. Here, the reads cannot both see the default writes, whereas they could if one of them was hoisted into the critical section and reordered with the preceeding write.

$x \leftarrow 0$	$y \leftarrow 0$
lock l	lock l'
$x \leftarrow 1$	$y \leftarrow 1$
unlock l	unlock l'
$r_1{\leftarrow}y$	$r_2{\leftarrow}x$

Roach-motel: Write-lock Reordering. Reordering writes and locks is not allowed. The reads cannot both see the default writes, whereas they could if one of the writes was hoisted into the critical section and reordered with the next read.

$x \leftarrow 0$	$y \leftarrow 0$
$x \leftarrow 1$	$y \leftarrow 1$
lock l	lock l'
$r_1{\leftarrow}y$	$r_2{\leftarrow}x$
unlock l	unlock l'

9. Empirical Evaluation of the BMM

We have shown that BMM is more restrictive than the JMM. It is, therefore, natural to ask how severe these restrictions are in practice, i.e. what is the performance impact imposed by BMM when incorporated within a production virtual machine running on a TSO architecture. In this section, we present results from a preliminary study that provides a coarse upper-bound approximation of the overheads incurred by BMM conformance. Our experiment is as follows. Starting with a production virtual machine, we switch the backend from a non-verifying optimizing compiler to one that preserves TSO semantics. Then, we modify any Java-level optimizations performed by the VM to be BMM compliant. We expect that the performance results are going to be an upper bound on the costs of BMM, since we limited the optimizations performed by the VM and ensured that they precisely respect the reorderings allowed by BMM. This enforcement is realized through the injection of *memory fences*, operations that effectively flush the contents of store buffers; we make no attempt to optimize or verify the placement of such fences [38].

Specifically, we start with the Fiji open-source real-time VM [26]. We selected Fiji because it has competitive performance, we understand the optimizations it performs well, and it is representative of a real-world system. The Fiji compiler takes bytecode as input and, in the configuration we use here, transforms it into ANSI C code, which is fed to `gcc`. The Fiji compiler includes a variety of classic optimizations as well as Java-specific techniques. To achieve BMM compliance in the back-end, we replace `gcc` with LLVM_{TSO}, an LLVM branch with optimizations either modified or disabled to preserve compliance with the TSO memory model [23]. This is a close approximation of what we would write to support BMM in the backend. Within Fiji, we carefully examined all optimization passes to ensure compliance with BMM; redundant code elimination (RCE) is the only optimization for which compliance could not be guaranteed; RCE is performed over local operations as well as heap loads; as a result, the optimization permits write-read or read-read operations to be reordered, violating BMM semantics. We modified the optimization to disallow processing any heap loads.

We evaluated the modified system on a variety of benchmarks, including SPECjvm98, SPECjbb2000, and a subset of DaCapo2006 (2006-10-MR2 Release) and DaCapo2009 (9.12 Bach Release). The whole benchmark suite is a mix of concurrent and sequential programs, which we think are well suited to exhibit the throughput overheads of missed optimization opportunities and superfluous fences. (The concurrent programs we consider are `mtrt`, `avora9`, `jbb2000`, `lusearch6`, and `lusearch9`). The experiments were run on an 8-Core Xeon 3.16 GHz processors and 8 GB memory machine installed with Fedora 13 Linux (kernel 2.6.34). SPECjvm98 was executed for 15 iterations with the first 5 iterations being warm-up. We report the mean of the last 10 iterations. The standard deviation was negligible. The SPECjbb2000 and DaCapo benchmarks were all executed with their default configurations, except that the workload

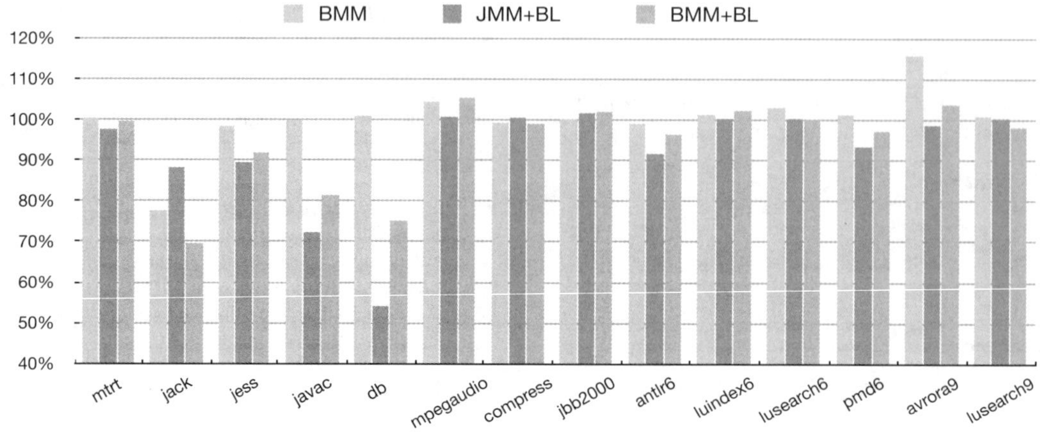

Figure 8. Fiji VM. Execution time normalized to JMM configuration. See Tab. 3 for configurations.

Name	LLVM	RCE	Biased-locking
JMM (baseline)	regular	regular	off
BMM	tso	modified	off
JMM +BL	regular	regular	on with no fence
BMM +BL	tso	modified	on with 2 fences

Table 3. Evaluation configurations.

was set to the maximum wherever possible and that the number of warehouses (for SPECjbb2000) and the number of threads (for DaCapo2009) were set to 8 to exercise the maximum concurrency.

We evaluate how BMM impacts performance by examining performance relative to a system that uses an unmodified version of Fiji and LLVM; in this baseline configuration, there are no optimizations that are either modified or disabled within either Fiji or LLVM; specifically, the baseline implementation allows Fiji to perform RCE transformations, and LLVM to perform non-TSO compliant reorderings. The results are shown in Fig. 8 with column BMM. The numbers are normalized with respect to this baseline. First, observe that adding TSO support to LLVM and crippling RCE has almost no impact on performance on most of benchmarks with the exception of `jack` and `avrora9`; for the former, BMM is 22% faster while 16% slower for the latter. The average slowdown is 1%. In general, these results provide anecdotal evidence that BMM is essentially performance neutral. On more relaxed architectures the story is, of course, likely to be different.

Biased Locking. While inspecting the code of the Fiji VM, we stumbled upon an interesting optimization. Fiji has several implementations of the Java concurrency control primitives. One optimization that is supported is called biased locking [17]. Biased locking is an implementation of locking operations that is efficient when one thread repeatedly acquires and releases the same monitor [29], a pattern that is frequent in Java. Roughly, a monitor can be *biased* to one thread that can then acquire and release it without any synchronization. However, when a thread needs a lock that is biased to another thread, that bias needs to be *revoked* using synchronizing instructions. As shown in Fig. 8 under column JMM+BL, turning on biased locking in Fiji results in a maximum speed up of roughly 45% (and an average of 8%). This optimization thus appears to be important to performance.

Fiji's biased locking is implemented without any CAS or fences. Although we believe this is what most of modern Java VM do, its correctness is unclear given the current formal definition of JMM. Biased locking implies a roach motel reordering and this kind of reordering has been shown to be invalid by Sevčik [34]. According to the "JSR–133 cookbook" and other folklore,[4] *biased locking is permitted under JMM*, but to the best of our knowledge, there is no formal proof on the number of fences required to ensure correctness.

The BMM requires two fences, as we will prove next, one at the lock and one at the unlock. With two fences, the benefits of biased locking is 30% at best (and on average 6%).

Validity of Biased Locking. We explain how to reason about biased locking under BMM. Since the implementation of the locking mechanism cannot be described with Java constructs only, we introduce two actions available only at a lower-level language in the compilation chain: a *memory fence* f_t and a *fake unlock* $\tilde{\mathsf{u}}^i_t l$. The memory fence can be emitted by a thread if and only if its buffer is empty. The effect of the action is to ensure the buffer is empty prior to any subsequent action being performed.

$$\frac{ts(t) \xrightarrow{\mathsf{f}_t} s}{ts, m \xrightarrow{\mathsf{f}_t}_{\mathsf{synch}} ts[t \mapsto s], m}\,[\textsc{Fence}]$$

The fake unlock models the bias revocation; this action is taken into account as a regular unlock in what makes a trace properly locked. However, it imposes no restrictions on the state of buffers.

$$\frac{ts(t) \xrightarrow{\tilde{\mathsf{u}}^i_t l} s}{ts, b, m \xrightarrow{\tilde{\mathsf{u}}^i_t l} ts[t \mapsto s], b, m}\,[\textsc{FakeUnlock}]$$

At this level of abstraction we do not describe *how* the biased locking is to be implemented, but the intuition is that the conjunction of a fence and a fake unlock corresponds to an unlock. The general case of a thread silently reacquiring the same lock can be seen as a trace transformation (there is no $\mathsf{l}_t l$ in β and no $\mathsf{l}_t l$ nor $\mathsf{u}_t l$ in γ):

$$\alpha \cdot [\mathsf{l}^i_t l] \cdot \beta \cdot [\mathsf{u}^j_t l] \cdot \gamma \cdot [\mathsf{l}^k_t l] \cdot \delta \xrightarrow{\mathrm{BL}} \alpha \cdot [\mathsf{l}^i_t l] \cdot \beta \cdot [\mathsf{f}_t] \cdot \gamma \cdot [\mathsf{f}_t] \cdot \delta$$

This transformation is indeed valid: consider a BMM_o execution (P', tr') with $tr' = \alpha \cdot [\mathsf{l}^i_t l] \cdot \beta \cdot [\mathsf{f}_t] \cdot \gamma \cdot [\mathsf{f}_t] \cdot \delta$. If the intra-thread semantics allows to replace the first fence by an action $\mathsf{u}^j_t l$ and the second one by an action $\mathsf{l}^k_t l$, then the untransformed trace $tr = \alpha \cdot [\mathsf{l}^i_t l] \cdot \beta \cdot [\mathsf{u}^j_t l] \cdot \gamma \cdot [\mathsf{l}^k_t l] \cdot \delta$ is also BMM_o: the Fence rule ensures that when the f_t action is emitted the buffer of thread t is empty so the Unlock/Lock rules can be applied. Moreover the trace tr is properly locked. The revocation of a biased lock corresponds to the following trace transformation.

$$\alpha \cdot [\mathsf{l}^i_t l] \cdot \beta \cdot [\mathsf{u}^j_t l] \cdot \gamma \cdot \delta \xrightarrow{\mathrm{BL}'} \alpha \cdot [\mathsf{l}^i_t l] \cdot \beta \cdot [\mathsf{f}_t] \cdot \gamma \cdot [\tilde{\mathsf{u}}^{j'}_t l] \cdot \delta$$

[4] `https://blogs.oracle.com/dave/entry/biased_locking_in_hotspot`

Since there is no lock on monitor l in γ, if the transformed trace is properly locked, then so is the initial one. The action f_t ensures t's buffer is empty after β. The UNLOCK rule can thus be applied.

10. Conclusions

This work presents BMM, a memory model that has been designed as part of a broader undertaking to build a verifying compiler for multithreaded safety-critical Java. The key characteristics required for such a memory model are ease-of-understanding both for programmers and compiler writers, and a practical realization within a compiler framework that does not impose onerous restrictions on important program optimizations. We believe BMM is a promising step in this direction. Its axiomatic definition is expressed using intuitive and simple memory reordering notions, making it suitable for reasoning about program transformations, while its operational view can conveniently serve as a basis for a verifying compiler infrastructure. Its backward compatibility with JMM entails that we can use BMM on legacy code. It thus provides a key missing piece for a verified infrastructure for Java on the x86 processor family.

The question of how to obtain a more relaxed model, one that would allow efficient implementations on architectures such as Power and ARM, while at the same time remaining amenable to incorporation within verified compilers, remains a subject for future research. Although these more relaxed platforms still guarantee coherence (all threads must respect a single linear order of writes), they allow other non-intuitive behaviors such as out-of-order writes, speculative execution, etc., as well as having a substantially more complex notion of dependence; these complexities make formalization and axiomatic reasoning challenging [31]. We believe that more experience with BMM, with respect to both applications and optimizations, is necessary before we can transplant the intuitions underlying our development here to these other environments.

Acknowledgments

We would like to thank Hans Boehm, Cliff Click, Doug Lea, Gustavo Petri, Filip Pizlo, Jaroslav Ševčík and Peter Sewell for their useful feedback on this work. We thank Dan Marino for his help with LLVM_{TSO}.

References

[1] S. V. Adve and K. Gharachorloo. Shared memory consistency models: A tutorial. *Computer*, 29(12), 1996.

[2] S. V. Adve and M. Hill. A Unified Formalization of Four Shared-Memory Models. *Par. and Distr. Systems, IEEE Transactions on*, 1993.

[3] J. Alglave, L. Maranget, S. Sarkar, and P. Sewell. Fences in Weak Memory Models. In *Proc. of CAV*, 2010.

[4] D. Aspinall and J. Ševčík. Java Memory Model Examples: Good, Bad and Ugly. In *Proc. of VAMP*, 2007.

[5] D. Aspinall and J. Ševčík. Formalising Java's Data Race Free Guarantee. In *Proc. of TPHOLs*, 2007.

[6] H.-J. Boehm and S. V. Adve. Foundations of the C++ concurrency memory model. *SIGPLAN Not.*, 43, 2008.

[7] G. Boudol and G. Petri. Relaxed Memory Models: an Operational Approach. In *Proc. of POPL*, 2009.

[8] G. Boudol and G. Petri. A Theory of Speculative Computation. In *Proc. of ESOP*, 2010.

[9] S. Burckhardt, M. Musuvathi, and V. Singh. Verifying Local Transformations on Relaxed Memory Models. In *Proc. of CC*, 2010.

[10] P. Cenciarelli, A. Knapp, and E. Sibilio. The Java Memory Model: Operationally, denotationally, axiomatically. In *Proc. of ESOP*, 2007.

[11] B. Goetz, T. Peierls, J. Bloch, J. Bowbeer, D. Holmes, and D. Lea. *Java Concurrency in Practice*. Addison-Wesley Longman, 2006.

[12] T. Henties, J. Hunt, D. Locke, K. Nilsen, M. Schoeberl, and J. Vitek. Java for safety-critical applications. In *SafeCert*, 2009.

[13] L. Higham, J. Kawash, and N. Verwaaland. Defining and Comparing Memory Consistency Models. In *Proc. of PDCS*, 1997.

[14] L. Hubert, T. Jensen, V. Monfort, and D. Pichardie. Enforcing Secure Object Initialization in Java. In *Proc. of ESORICS*, 2010.

[15] M. Huisman and G. Petri. The Java Memory Model: a Formal Explanation. In *Proc. of VAMP*, 2007.

[16] R. Jagadeesan, C. Pitcher, and J. Riely. Generative Operational Semantics for Relaxed Memory Models. In *Proc. of ESOP*, 2010.

[17] K. Kawachiya, A. Koseki, and T. Onodera. Lock Reservation: Java Locks can Mostly do Without Atomic Operations. In *Proc. of OOPSLA*, 2002.

[18] G. Klein and T. Nipkow. A Machine-Checked Model for a Java-like Language, Virtual Machine, and Compiler. *ACM Trans. Program. Lang. Syst.*, 28(4), 2006.

[19] L. Lamport. Time, Clocks, and the Ordering of Events in a Distributed System. *Commun. ACM*, 21(7), 1978.

[20] X. Leroy. A Formally Verified Compiler Back-end. *J. Autom. Reasoning*, 43(4), 2009.

[21] A. Lochbihler. Java and the Java memory Model – a Unified, Machine-Checked Formalisation. In *Proc. of ESOP*, 2012.

[22] J. Manson, W. Pugh, and S. V. Adve. The Java Memory Model. In *Proc. of POPL*, 2005.

[23] D. Marino, A. Singh, T. D. Millstein, M. Musuvathi, and S. Narayanasamy. A Case for an SC-Preserving Compiler. In *Proc. of PLDI*, 2011.

[24] A. Miné. Static Analysis of Run-Time Errors in Embedded Critical Parallel C Programs. In *Proc. of ESOP*, 2011.

[25] S. Owens, S. Sarkar, and P. Sewell. A Better x86 Memory Model: x86-TSO. In *Proc. of TPHOLs*, 2009.

[26] F. Pizlo, L. Ziarek, E. Blanton, P. Maj, and J. Vitek. High-level Programming of Embedded Hard Real-Time Devices. In *Proc. of EuroSys*, 2010.

[27] W. Pugh. The Initialization On Demand Holder idiom, 2004. `http://www.cs.umd.edu/~pugh/java/memoryModel/jsr-133-faq.html#dcl`.

[28] W. Pugh. Causality test cases for the Java Memory Model, 2004. `http://www.cs.umd.edu/~pugh/java/memoryModel/CausalityTestCases.html`.

[29] K. Russell and D. Detlefs. Eliminating Synchronization-Related Atomic Operations with Biased Locking and Bulk Rebiasing. In *Proc. of OOPSLA*, 2006.

[30] S. Sarkar, P. Sewell, F. Z. Nardelli, S. Owens, T. Ridge, T. Braibant, M. O. Myreen, and J. Alglave. The Semantics of x86-CC Multiprocessor Machine Code. In *Proc. of POPL*, 2009.

[31] S. Sarkar, P. Sewell, J. Alglave, L. Maranget, and D. Williams. Understanding Power Multiprocessors. In *Proc. of PLDI*, 2011.

[32] J. Ševčík. *Program Transformations in Weak Memory Models*. PhD thesis, The University of Edinburgh, 2009.

[33] J. Ševčík. Safe optimisations for shared-memory concurrent programs. In *Proc. of PLDI*, 2011.

[34] J. Ševčík and D. Aspinall. On Validity of Program Transformations in the Java Memory Model. In *Proc. of ECOOP*, 2008.

[35] J. Ševčík, V. Vafeiadis, F. Z. Nardelli, S. Jagannathan, and P. Sewell. Relaxed-memory Concurrency and Verified Compilation. In *Proc. of POPL*, 2011.

[36] P. Sewell, S. Sarkar, S. Owens, F. Z. Nardelli, and M. O. Myreen. x86-TSO: A rigorous and usable programmer's model for x86 multiprocessors. *Commun. ACM*, 53(7), 2010.

[37] E. Torlak, M. Vaziri, and J. Dolby. MemSAT: Checking Axiomatic Specifications of Memory Models. In *Proc. of PLDI*, 2010.

[38] V. Vafeiadis and F. Z. Nardelli. Verifying fence elimination optimisations. In *Proc. of SAS*, 2011.

Logical Relations for Fine-Grained Concurrency

Aaron Turon
Northeastern University
turon@ccs.neu.edu

Jacob Thamsborg
IT University of Copenhagen
thamsborg@itu.dk

Amal Ahmed
Northeastern University
amal@ccs.neu.edu

Lars Birkedal
IT University of Copenhagen
birkedal@itu.dk

Derek Dreyer
MPI-SWS, Germany
dreyer@mpi-sws.org

Abstract

Fine-grained concurrent data structures (or FCDs) reduce the granularity of critical sections in both time and space, thus making it possible for clients to access different parts of a mutable data structure in parallel. However, the tradeoff is that the implementations of FCDs are very subtle and tricky to reason about directly. Consequently, they are carefully designed to be *contextual refinements* of their coarse-grained counterparts, meaning that their clients can reason about them as if all access to them were sequentialized.

In this paper, we propose a new semantic model, based on Kripke logical relations, that supports direct proofs of contextual refinement in the setting of a type-safe high-level language. The key idea behind our model is to provide a simple way of expressing the "local life stories" of individual pieces of an FCD's hidden state by means of *protocols* that the threads concurrently accessing that state must follow. By endowing these protocols with a simple yet powerful transition structure, as well as the ability to assert invariants on both heap states and specification *code*, we are able to support clean and intuitive refinement proofs for the most sophisticated types of FCDs, such as conditional compare-and-set (CCAS).

Categories and Subject Descriptors D.3.1 [*Programming Languages*]: Formal Definitions and Theory; F.3.1 [*Logics and Meanings of Programs*]: Specifying and Verifying and Reasoning about Programs

Keywords Refinement, fine-grained concurrency, linearizability, separation logic, logical relations, data abstraction, local state

1. Introduction

Suppose you want to take a sequential mutable data structure and adapt it to a concurrent setting, so that multiple threads can safely access it in parallel. The simplest way to do it is to treat all of the operations on the data structure as critical sections governed by a common lock. This *coarse-grained* approach to concurrency is easy for clients to reason about, since it essentially sequentializes all access to the data structure, but by the same token it also thwarts any speedup one might hope to gain from parallelism. In contrast, *fine-grained* concurrent data structures (or FCDs) reduce the granularity of critical sections in both time and space, often down to a single primitive atomic instruction like "compare-and-set" (CAS), so that clients can exploit parallelism by having different threads manipulate different parts of the data structure simultaneously.

POPL'13, January 23–25, 2013, Rome, Italy.

As FCDs are very tricky to reason about directly, they are carefully designed to be *contextual refinements* of their course-grained counterparts. This means essentially that, performance gains aside, no client can tell they are working with the fine-grained version of a data structure instead of the coarse-grained version. Put another way, the FCD is a faithful *implementation* of its coarse-grained *specification*. Thus, clients can safely reason about the FCD as if all access to it were sequentialized, while at the same time reaping the efficiency benefits of parallelism.

Contextual refinement is clearly an essential property that clients of an FCD expect to hold [20]. The question is how to prove it. In this paper, we propose a new semantic model that supports **direct** proofs of contextual refinement in the setting of a type-safe **high-level language**. The key idea behind our model is to provide a simple way of expressing the **protocols** that govern the hidden state of an FCD and that the threads concurrently accessing it must follow. By endowing these protocols with a simple yet powerful transition structure, as well as the ability to assert invariants on both heap states and specification *code*, we are able to support intuitive refinement proofs for **the most sophisticated types of FCDs**. We now examine these selling points in more detail.

Direct: Rather than prove contextual refinement directly, most prior approaches have focused on proving a related property on traces called *linearizability* [21]. Linearizability is often viewed as being synonymous with contextual refinement, but in fact this has only recently been shown by Filipovic *et al.* [14] to be the case (and only for a particular class of languages). As Filipovic *et al.* argue, refinement is the property that clients of an FCD actually want, and linearizability is one technique for proving it. We instead provide a direct proof technique for contextual refinement, which sidesteps any discussion of linearizability.

High-level language: Most prior work has only considered FCDs coded in first-order C-like languages. However, one of the most widely-used FCD libraries, `java.util.concurrent`, is written in a type-safe high-level language (Java) and indeed *depends* on the abstraction facilities of Java to ensure that the private state of its FCDs is hidden from clients. Our approach is the first to prove contextual refinement for `java.util.concurrent`-style FCDs in the setting of a higher-order language with abstract types, recursive types, and general mutable references, thus establishing the correctness of these FCDs when linked with unknown well-typed client code.

How? To achieve these first two aims, we employ a *step-indexed Kripke logical relations (SKLR)* model [2, 3, 9, 4]. SKLRs have been actively developed in recent years as an effective tool for reasoning about representation independence for higher-order stateful ADTs, and thus provide a solid foundation for reasoning about contextual refinement of concurrent objects in a realistic, high-level setting. To adapt SKLRs to reasoning about FCDs, we follow the approach of recent work by Birkedal *et al.* [5] and employ a "small-step-style" model, which accounts properly for the possibility that threads are preempted after every step of computation. Birkedal *et al.*'s model, however, is limited in its ability to reason about interference between threads, which is ubiquitous in FCDs. We therefore generalize their model with support for *protocols*.

Protocols: To understand how an FCD works, it helps to think of each *piece* of the data structure (*e.g.,* each node of a linked list) as being subject to a *protocol* that tells its "life story": how it came to be allocated, how its contents evolve over time, and how it eventually "dies" by being disconnected (or deleted) from the data structure. This protocol describes the rules by which all threads must play as they access the shared state of the FCD.

A number of FCDs additionally require their protocols to support *role-playing*—that is, a mechanism by which different threads participating in the protocol can dynamically acquire certain "roles". These roles may enable them to make certain transitions that other threads cannot. A simple example of this is a locking protocol, under which the thread that acquires the lock adopts the unique role of "lock-holder" and thus knows that no other thread has the ability to release the lock.

How? Following recent work by Dreyer *et al.* in the setting of SKLRs [9], our model supports a direct encoding of protocols as *state transition systems (STSs)* of a certain kind. In comparison to Dreyer *et al.*'s work, we deploy STSs at a much finer granularity and use them to tell *local life stories* about individual nodes of a data structure. Of course, there are also "global" constraints connecting up the life stories of the individual nodes, but to a large extent we are able to reason about FCDs at the level of these local life stories and their local interactions with one another.

In order to account for role-playing, we enrich our STSs with a notion of *tokens*. Intuitively, the idea is that, while the STS defines the basic roadmap for the possible changes to the state of the FCD, some of the roads on that map are toll roads that may only be traversed by threads owning certain tokens. This idea is highly reminiscent of recent work on "concurrent abstract predicates" [7], but we believe our approach is simpler and more direct.

The most sophisticated types of FCDs: In proving refinement for each operation of an FCD, a key step is identifying its *linearization point*, the point during its execution at which the operation can be considered to have "committed", *i.e.,* the point at which its coarse-grained spec can be viewed as having executed atomically. What sets the most sophisticated FCDs apart from the pack, and makes them so challenging to verify, is that their linearization points are hard to identify in a thread-local and temporally-local way.

For example, the "elimination stack" FCD [19] provides side channels by which a "push" and "pop" operation can mutually decide to cancel each other out without touching the stack itself. This works by having one operation (say, push) use the side channel to offer its argument to be pushed; if a thread running the pop operation sees this offer, it can commit both the push and pop at once. Although it is very kind of the pop thread to *cooperate* with the push thread by helping it complete its operation in this way, it also means that the linearization point for push occurs during the execution of pop, thus making thread-local verification difficult.

In other algorithms like CCAS [18, 15], the *nondeterminism* induced by shared-state concurrency has the effect that it is impossible to determine where the linearization point has occurred until after the fine-grained operation has completed its execution. This in turn makes it challenging to reason about refinement in a temporally-local way, *i.e.,* showing that each step of the algorithm, considered in isolation, obeys the FCD's shared-state protocol.

How? The whole point of SKLRs is to provide a way of describing local knowledge about the hidden resources of an abstract data type, but in prior work those "hidden resources" have been synonymous with "local variables" or "a private piece of the heap". To support reasoning about thread cooperation and nondeterminism, we make two orthogonal generalizations to the notion of resources.

First, to model cooperation, we extend resources to also include *specification code*. This extension makes it possible for "the right to commit an operation" (*e.g.,* push, in the example above) to be treated as a shareable resource, which one thread may pass to other "helper" threads to run on its behalf. Second, to model nondeterminism, we extend resources to include *sets of specification states*. This extension makes it possible to *speculate* about all the possible specification states that our FCD implementation could be viewed as refining, so that we can wait until the implementation has finished executing to decide which one we want to choose.

Both of these extensions are formally and conceptually simple—especially in comparison to prior approaches relying on ghost and prophecy variables [1]—and we will demonstrate their utility on both illustrative toy examples (Sections 2.5 and 2.6) and a more realistic FCD example toward the end of the paper (Section 4).

2. The main ideas

2.1 The language

We study FCDs within a variant of the polymorphic lambda calculus, extended with tagged sums, general mutable references (higher-order state), equi-recursive types, CAS, and **fork**. These features suffice for modeling the kinds of FCDs used within java.util.concurrent, which (a) are polymorphic, (b) use recursive, linked data structures, and (c) rely on the abstraction facilities of the language for data hiding.[1] Figure 1 presents the syntax of the language together with excerpts of the static and dynamic semantics. In examples, we will employ a few other features that trivially extend the language defined here, *e.g.,* immutable pairs and records.

While the language is essentially standard, there are a few unusual aspects that help keep our treatment of FCDs concise. Terms are not annotated with types, but polymorphism is nevertheless introduced and eliminated by explicit type abstraction ($\Lambda.e$) and application ($e\ \_$). Reference and tuple types are combined into the type $\mathbf{ref}(\overline{\tau})$, useful for constructing objects with many mutable fields. The term $e[i]$ reads and projects the i-th component from a tuple reference e, while $e[i] := e'$ assigns a new value to that component. When e is a single-cell reference, we will usually write $e := e'$ instead of $e[1] := e'$. Finally, the type $\mathbf{ref}_?(\overline{\tau})$ of "option references" provides an *untagged union* of the unit and reference types, with explicit coercions **null** and **some**(e). Because reading and writing operations work on references, and not option references (which must be separately eliminated by cases), there are no null-pointer errors. The net effect of flattening these types is fewer layers of indirection, which simplifies verification.

The type system imposes two important restrictions. First, recursive types $\mu\alpha.\tau$ are required to be *productive*, meaning that all free occurrences of α in τ must appear under a non-μ type constructor. More subtle is the restriction on CAS, which can only be used on components of *comparable type* σ. This constraint is needed because CAS performs an equality comparison of word-sized values at the hardware level; it is only reasonable to apply it at types whose representation allows such a comparison, *i.e.,* base types and locations. Tagged sums are allocated on the heap and hence represented using locations, making them comparable as well. Figure 1 presents the nonstandard typing rules; the remaining rules are standard (see appendix [35]). Note that we use u to denote values that can be stored in the heap.

A threadpool T is a finite map from thread identifiers to expressions. A program configuration $h; T$ pairs a heap with a thread pool. We define a small-step, call-by-value operational semantics as a re-

[1] We will use closures as our primary means of hiding local state.

$$
\begin{array}{rcl}
\tau & ::= & \mathbf{1} \mid \mathbf{B} \mid \mathbf{N} \mid \tau + \tau \mid \mathbf{ref}(\overline{\tau}) \mid \mathbf{ref_?}(\overline{\tau}) \mid \mu\alpha.\tau \mid \forall\alpha.\tau \mid \alpha \mid \tau \to \tau \\
\sigma & ::= & \mathbf{1} \mid \mathbf{B} \mid \mathbf{N} \mid \tau + \tau \mid \mathbf{ref}(\overline{\tau}) \mid \mathbf{ref_?}(\overline{\tau}) \mid \mu\alpha.\sigma \\
e & ::= & () \mid \mathbf{true} \mid \mathbf{false} \mid \mathbf{if}\ e\ \mathbf{then}\ e\ \mathbf{else}\ e \mid n \mid e + e \mid x \mid \Lambda.e \mid e\ \_ \mid e\ e \\
 & \mid & \mathbf{rec}\ f(x).e \mid \mathbf{new}\ \overline{e} \mid e[i] \mid e[i] := e \mid \mathsf{CAS}(e[i], e, e) \mid \ell \mid \mathbf{fork}\ e \\
 & \mid & \mathbf{null} \mid \mathbf{some}(e) \mid \mathbf{case}(e, \mathbf{null} \Rightarrow e, \mathbf{some}(x) \Rightarrow e) \\
 & \mid & \mathbf{inj}_i\ e \mid \mathbf{case}(e, \mathbf{inj}_1\ x \Rightarrow e, \mathbf{inj}_2\ y \Rightarrow e) \\
v & ::= & \mathbf{rec}\ f(x).e \mid \Lambda.e \mid () \mid n \mid \mathbf{true} \mid \mathbf{false} \mid \ell \mid x \qquad u ::= (\overline{v}) \mid \mathbf{inj}_i\ v \\
\Gamma & ::= & \cdot \mid \Gamma, x : \tau \qquad \Delta ::= \cdot \mid \Delta, \alpha \qquad \Omega ::= \Delta; \Gamma \\
K & ::= & [\,] \mid \mathbf{some}(K) \mid \mathbf{case}(K, \mathbf{null} \Rightarrow e, \mathbf{some}(x) \Rightarrow e) \mid K\ \_ \mid \cdots \\
T & \in & \text{ThreadPool} \triangleq \mathbb{N} \xrightarrow{\text{fin}} \text{Exp} \qquad h \in \text{Heap} \triangleq \text{Loc} \xrightarrow{\text{fin}} \text{HeapVal}
\end{array}
$$

Type rules $\boxed{\Omega \vdash e : \tau}$

$$
\frac{\Omega \vdash e : \mathbf{ref}(\overline{\tau}) \quad \tau_i = \sigma \quad \Omega \vdash e_o : \sigma \quad \Omega \vdash e_n : \sigma}{\Omega \vdash \mathsf{CAS}(e[i], e_o, e_n) : \mathbf{B}}
\qquad
\frac{\Omega \vdash e : \mathbf{1}}{\Omega \vdash \mathbf{fork}\ e : \mathbf{1}}
$$

$$
\frac{\Omega \vdash e : \mathbf{ref}(\overline{\tau})}{\Omega \vdash \mathbf{some}(e) : \mathbf{ref_?}(\overline{\tau})}
\qquad
\frac{\Omega, \alpha \vdash e : \tau}{\Omega \vdash \Lambda.e : \forall\alpha.\tau}
\qquad
\frac{\Omega \vdash e : \forall\alpha.\tau}{\Omega \vdash e\ \_ : \tau[\tau'/\alpha]}
$$

Primitive reductions $\boxed{h; e \hookrightarrow h'; e'}$

$$
\begin{array}{rcll}
h; \ell[i] & \hookrightarrow & h; v_i & \text{when } h(\ell) = (\overline{v}) \\
h; \mathsf{CAS}(\ell[i], v_o, v_n) & \hookrightarrow & h[\ell[i] = v_n]; \mathbf{true} & \text{when } h(\ell)[i] = v_o \\
h; \mathsf{CAS}(\ell[i], v_o, v_n) & \hookrightarrow & h; \mathbf{false} & \text{when } h(\ell)[i] \neq v_o
\end{array}
$$

$$
\begin{array}{ll}
h; \mathbf{case}((), \mathbf{null} \Rightarrow e_1, \mathbf{some}(x) \Rightarrow e_2) \hookrightarrow h; e_1 & \\
h; \mathbf{case}(\ell, \mathbf{null} \Rightarrow e_1, \mathbf{some}(x) \Rightarrow e_2) \hookrightarrow h; e_2[\ell/x] & \\
h; \mathbf{new}\ (\overline{v}) \hookrightarrow h \uplus [\ell \mapsto (\overline{v})]; \ell & h; \mathbf{null} \hookrightarrow h; () \\
h; \mathbf{inj}_i\ v \hookrightarrow h \uplus [\ell \mapsto \mathbf{inj}_i\ v]; \ell & h; \mathbf{some}(\ell) \hookrightarrow h; \ell \\
h; \Lambda.e\ \_ \hookrightarrow h; e &
\end{array}
$$

Program reduction $\boxed{h; T \to h'; T'}$

$$
\frac{h; e \hookrightarrow h'; e'}{h; T \uplus [i \mapsto K[e]] \to h'; T \uplus [i \mapsto K[e']]}
$$

$$
h; T \uplus [i \mapsto K[\mathbf{fork}\ e]] \to h; T \uplus [i \mapsto K[()]] \uplus [j \mapsto e]
$$

Figure 1. Our language: $F^{\mu!}$ with **fork** and CAS

lation $\to$ between program configurations, allowing the creation of new threads and the nondeterministic interleaving of existing ones. We use evaluation contexts K to specify a left-to-right evaluation order within each thread.

2.2 A finer look at FCDs

The granularity of a concurrent data structure is a measure of the locality of synchronization between threads accessing it. Coarse-grained data structures provide exclusive, global access for the duration of a critical section: a thread holding the lock can access as much of the data structure as needed, secure in the knowledge that it will encounter a consistent, frozen representation. By contrast, fine-grained data structures localize or eliminate synchronization, forcing threads to do their work on the basis of limited knowledge about its state—sometimes as little as what the contents of a single word are at a single moment.

The local, highly-concurrent nature of FCDs is best understood by example. In Figure 2, we give a variant of Michael and Scott's lock-free queue [29].[2] The queue maintains a reference, head, to a *nonempty* linked list; the first node of the list is considered a "sentinel" whose data does not contribute to the queue.

Nodes are dequeued from the front of the list, so we examine the deq code first. If the queue is *logically* nonempty, it contains at least two nodes: the sentinel (physical head), and its successor (logical head). Intuitively, the deq operation should atomically update the head reference from the sentinel to its successor; after doing so, the old logical head becomes the new sentinel, and the next node, if any, becomes the new logical head. Because there is no lock protecting head, however, a concurrent operation could update it at any time. Thus, deq employs *optimistic concurrency*: after gaining access to the sentinel by dereferencing head, it does some additional work—finding the logical head—while optimistically assuming that head has not changed behind its back. In the end, optimism meets reality through CAS, which performs an atomic update only when head is unchanged. If its optimism was misplaced, deq must start from scratch. After all, the queue's state may have entirely changed in the interim.

The key thing to notice is just how little knowledge deq has as it executes. Immediately after reading head, the most that can be said is that the resulting node *was once* the physical head of the queue. The power of CAS is that it mixes instantaneous knowledge—the head *is now* n—with instantaneous action—the head *becomes* n'. The weakness of CAS is that this potent mixture applies only to a single word of memory. For deq, this weakness is manifested in the lack of knowledge CAS has about the new value n', which *should* still be the successor to the physical head n at the instant of the CAS. Because CAS cannot check this fact, it must be established *pessimistically*, *i.e.*, guaranteed to be true on the basis of the queue's internal protocol. We will see in a moment how to formulate such a protocol, but first, we examine the more subtle enq.

In a singly-linked queue implementation, one would expect to have both head and tail pointers, and indeed the full Michael-Scott queue includes a "tail" pointer. However, because CAS operates on only one word at a time, it is impossible to use a single CAS operation to both link in a new node and update a tail pointer. The classic algorithm allows the tail pointer to lag behind the true tail by at most one node, while the implementation in `java.util.concurrent` allows multi-node lagging. These choices affect performance, of course, but from a correctness standpoint one needs to make essentially the same argument whether one has a lagging tail, or simply traverses from head as we do.

In all of these cases, it is necessary to *find* the actual tail of the list (whose successor is **null**) by doing some amount of traversal. Clearly, this requires at least that the actual tail be reachable from the starting point of the traversal; the loop invariant of the traversal is then that the tail is reachable from the current node. But in our highly-concurrent environment, we must account for the fact that the data structure is changing under foot, even as we traverse it. The node that was the tail of the list when we *began* the traversal might not even be *in* the data structure by the time we finish.

2.3 The story of a node

We want, ultimately, to prove that MSQ refines its coarse-grained specification CGQ. The latter uses a lock to protect its internal state; sync(e) { e' } is a simple derived form that wraps acquisition/release of the non-reentrant spinlock e around the code e'.[3] Ideally, the proof would proceed in the same way one's intuitive reasoning does, *i.e.*, by considering the execution of a single function by a single thread one line at a time, reasoning about what is known at each program point. To achieve this goal, we must solve two closely-related problems: we must characterize the possible interference from concurrent threads, and we must characterize the knowledge that our thread can gain.

We solve both of these problems by introducing a notion of *protocol*, based on the abstract state transition systems of Dreyer *et al.* [9], but with an important twist: we apply these transition systems at the level of *individual nodes*, rather than as a description

[2] We use the shorthand $\mathsf{cons}(e, e') \triangleq \mathbf{some}(\mathbf{new}\ (e, e'))$.

[3] The definition of sync is given in the appendix [35].

```
MSQ: ∀α.1 → { enq : α → 1, deq : 1 → ref?(α) }
MSQ ≜ Λ. λ(). let head = new (new (null, null)) in {
  deq = rec try(). let n = head[1] in case n[2]
                of some(n′) ⇒ if CAS(head[1], n, n′)
                                then n′[1] else try()
                 | null      ⇒ null,       (∗ queue is empty ∗)
  enq = λx. let n = cons(some(new x), null) in
              let rec try(c) = case c[2]
                of some(c′) ⇒ try(c′)
                 | null      ⇒ if CAS(c[2], null, n)
                                then () else try(c)
              in try(head[1])
}
CGQ ≜ Λ. λ(). let head = new null, lock = new false in {
  deq = λ(). sync(lock) {
    case head[1] of some(n) ⇒ head[1] := n[2]; some(new n[1])
                   | null    ⇒ null
  },
  enq = λx. sync(lock) { ... }   (∗ elided ∗)
}
```

Per-node protocol:

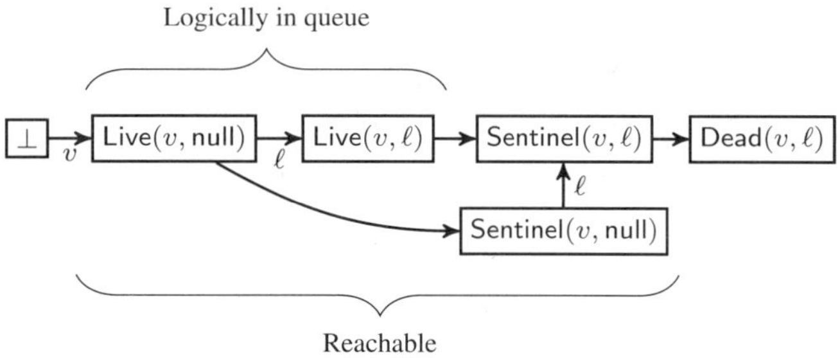

Global interpretation:

$$I(s) \triangleq \mathsf{head}_\mathrm{I} \mapsto_\mathrm{I} \ell_0 * \ell_0 \mapsto_\mathrm{I} (v_0, v_\mathrm{I}) * \exists v_\mathrm{S}.\ \mathsf{head}_\mathrm{S} \mapsto_\mathrm{S} v_\mathrm{S}$$
$$* \ \mathsf{lock} \mapsto_\mathrm{S} \mathbf{false} * \mathsf{link}(v_\mathrm{I}, v_\mathrm{S}, s_L) * \overline{(s(\ell_i') \neq \bot \wedge \ell_i \mapsto_\mathrm{I} (v_i, \ell_i'))}$$
$$\text{when } s = [\ell_0 \mapsto \mathsf{Sentinel}(v_0, v_\mathrm{I})] \uplus s_L \uplus \overline{[\ell_i \mapsto \mathsf{Dead}(v_i, \ell_i')]}$$

$$\mathsf{link}(\mathbf{null}, \mathbf{null}, \emptyset) \triangleq \mathsf{emp}$$
$$\mathsf{link}(\ell_\mathrm{I}, \ell_\mathrm{S}, [\ell_\mathrm{I} \mapsto \mathsf{Live}(v_\mathrm{I}, v_\mathrm{I}')] \uplus s) \triangleq \exists v, v_\mathrm{S}, v_\mathrm{S}'.\ v \preceq^{\mathcal{V}} v_\mathrm{S} : \alpha *$$
$$v_\mathrm{I} \mapsto_\mathrm{I} v * \ell_\mathrm{I} \mapsto_\mathrm{I} (v_\mathrm{I}, v_\mathrm{I}') * \ell_\mathrm{S} \mapsto_\mathrm{I} (v_\mathrm{S}, v_\mathrm{S}') * \mathsf{link}(v_\mathrm{I}', v_\mathrm{S}', s)$$

Figure 2. A variant of Michael and Scott's queue

of the entire data structure. These transition systems describe what we call the *local life stories* of each piece of an FCD. The diagram in Figure 2 is just such a story. Every heap location can be seen as a *potential* node in the queue, but all but finitely many are "unborn" (state $\bot$). After birth, nodes go through a progression of life changes. Some changes are manifested physically. The transition from Live(v, **null**) to Live(v, ℓ), for example, occurs when the successor field of the node is updated to link in a new node. Other changes reflect evolving relationships. The transition from Live to Sentinel, for example, does not represent an internal change to the node, but rather a change in the node's position in the data structure. Finally, a node "dies" when it becomes unreachable.

The benefit of these life stories is that they account for knowledge and interference together, in a local and abstract way. Knowledge is expressed by asserting that a given node is *at least* at a certain point in its life story. This kind of knowledge is inherently stable under interference, because *all* code must conform to the protocol, and is therefore constrained to a forward march through the STS. The life story gathers together in one place all the knowledge and interference that is relevant to a given node, even knowledge like "reachability" which is ostensibly a global property. This allows us to draw global conclusions from local information, which is precisely what is needed when reasoning about FCDs. For example, notice that no node can die with a **null** successor field. A successful CAS on the successor field from **null** to some location—like the one performed in enq—entails that the successor field was instantaneously **null** (local information), which by the protocol means the node was instantaneously reachable (global information), which entails that the CAS makes a new node reachable. Similarly, the protocol makes it immediately clear that the queue is free from any ABA problems [34], because nodes cannot be reincarnated and their fields, once non-**null**, never change.

To formalize this reasoning, we must connect the abstract account of knowledge and interference provided by the protocol to concrete constraints on the queue's representation. We do this by giving a *state-dependent invariant* I for the data structure, where "state" refers to abstract STS states. For the queue, we have the following set of states for each node's local STS:

$$S_0 \triangleq \{\bot\} \cup \{\mathsf{Live}(v, v') \mid v, v' \in \mathrm{Val}\}$$
$$\cup \ \{\mathsf{Sentinel}(v, v') \mid v, v' \in \mathrm{Val}\} \cup \{\mathsf{Dead}(v, \ell) \mid v \in \mathrm{Val}, \ell \in \mathrm{Loc}\}$$

along with the transition relation $\rightsquigarrow_0$ given in the diagram, where the annotated edges denote branches for choosing particular concrete v and ℓ values. The data structure as a whole is governed by a *product* STS with states $S \triangleq \mathrm{Loc} \xrightarrow{\text{fin}} S_0$, where $\xrightarrow{\text{fin}}$ indicates that all but finitely many locations are in the $\bot$ (unborn) state in their local STS. The transition relation $\rightsquigarrow$ for the product STS is just the pointwise lifting of the one for each node's STS: $s \rightsquigarrow s'$ iff $\forall \ell.\ s(\ell) \rightsquigarrow_0 s'(\ell)$. Thus, at the abstract level, the product STS is simply a collection of independent, local STSs.

At the concrete level of the invariant I, however, we record the constraints that tie one node's life story to another's; see Figure 2. The invariant is essentially a *relational* version of the recursive "list" predicate from separation logic [33]. The relational nature is apparent in the fact that the invariant makes assertions about *both* the implementation ($\mapsto_\mathrm{I}$) *and* specification ($\mapsto_\mathrm{S}$) heap, carving out the portion of each corresponding to an instance of MSQ and CGQ, respectively. It is thus a kind of linking invariant (or "refinement map") [22, 1], as one would expect to find in any refinement proof.

At a high level, the invariant says: the state of the product STS must decompose into exactly one sentinel node (at location ℓ_0), a collection of Live nodes s_L, and a collection of Dead nodes at locations $\overline{\ell_i}$ (the overbar notation represents a list). The link assertion recursively asserts that each Live node in the implementation corresponds to some node in the specification, and that a node is Live iff it is reachable from the sentinel. Since the queue is parametric over the type α of its data, the data stored in each live implementation node must *refine* the data stored in the specification node at type α (written $v_1 \preceq^{\mathcal{V}} v_2 : \alpha$; see Section 3). The invariant also accounts for two representation differences between MSQ and CGQ. First, the node data in the implementation is stored in a **ref**?(α), while the specification stores the data directly. Second, the specification has a lock. The invariant requires that the lock is always free (**false**) because, as we show that MSQ refines CGQ, we always run entire critical sections of CGQ at once, going from unlocked state to unlocked state. These "big steps" of the CGQ correspond to the linearization points of the MSQ.

Finally—and crucially—Dead nodes must have non-**null** successor pointers whose locations are in a non-$\bot$ state. This property is the key for giving a simple, *local* loop invariant for enq, namely, that the current node c is *at least* in a Live state. It follows that if the successor pointer of c is not **null**, it must be another node at least in the Live state. If, on the other hand, the successor node of c *is* **null**, we know that c is both not Dead, and at least Live, which means that c must be (at that instant) reachable from the implementation's head pointer.

The proof outlines for MSQ and the other examples in this section are given in the appendix [35].

2.4 Role-playing and tokens

Although Michael and Scott's queue is already tricky to verify, there is a specific sense in which its protocol in Figure 2 is simple: it treats all threads equally. All threads see a level playing field with a single notion of "legal" transition, and any thread is free to make any legal transition according to the protocol. Many FCDs, however, require more refined protocols in which different threads can play different *roles*—granting them the rights to make different sets of transitions—and in which threads can acquire and release these roles dynamically as they execute.

In fact, one need not look to complex FCDs for instances of this dynamic role-playing—the simple lock used in the coarse-grained "spec" of the Michael-Scott queue is a perfect and canonical example. In a protocol governing a single lock (*e.g.*, lock, in CGQ), there are two states: Unlocked and Locked. Starting from the Unlocked state, all threads should be able to acquire the lock and transition to the Locked state. But not vice versa: once a thread has acquired the lock and moved to the Locked state, it has adopted the role of "lock-holder" and should know that *it* is the only thread with the right to release the lock and return to Unlocked.

To support this kind of role-playing, we enrich STSs with a notion of *tokens*, which are used to grant authority over certain types of actions in a protocol. Each STS may employ its own appropriately chosen set of tokens, and each thread may *privately own* some subset of these tokens. The idea, then, is that certain transitions are only legal for the thread that privately owns certain tokens. Formally speaking, this is achieved by associating with each state in the STS a set of tokens that are currently *free*, *i.e.*, not owned by any thread.[4] We then stipulate *the law of conservation of tokens*: for a thread to legally transition from state s to state s', the (disjoint) union of its private tokens and the free tokens must be the same in s and in s'.

For instance, in the locking protocol, there is just a single token—call it TheLock. In the Unlocked state, the STS asserts that TheLock must belong to the free tokens and thus that *no* thread owns it privately, whereas in the Locked state, the STS asserts that TheLock does *not* belong to the free tokens and thus that *some* thread owns it privately. Pictorially, • denotes that TheLock is in the free tokens, and ○ denotes that it is not:

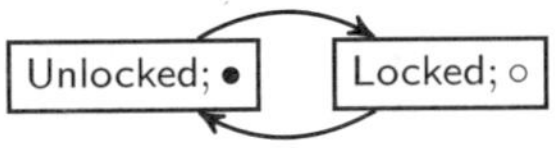

When a thread acquires the physical lock and transitions to the Locked state, it must add TheLock to its private tokens in order to satisfy conservation of tokens. Thereafter, no other thread may transition back to Unlocked because doing so requires putting TheLock back into the free tokens of the STS, which is something only the private owner of TheLock can do. Usually the invariant for the Unlocked state owns all of the hidden state for the data structure, while the Locked invariant owns nothing. Thus, a thread taking the lock also acquires the resources it protects, but must return these resources on lock release (in the style of CSL [31]).

As this simple example suggests, tokens induce very natural *thread-relative* notions of *rely* and *guarantee* relations on states of an STS. For any thread i, the total tokens A of an STS must equal the disjoint union of i's private tokens A_i, the free tokens A_{free} in the current state s, and the "frame" tokens A_{frame} (*i.e.*, the combined private tokens of all other threads but i). The *guarantee* relation says which future states thread i may transition to, namely those that are accessible by a series of transitions that i can "pay for" using its private tokens A_i. Dually, the *rely* relation says which future states other threads may transition to, namely those that are accessible by a series of transitions that can be paid for *without* using i's private tokens A_i (*i.e.*, only using the tokens in A_{frame}). These two relations play a central role in our model (Section 3).

[4] Another perspective is that the free tokens are owned by the STS itself, as opposed to the threads participating in the protocol; *cf.* CSL [31].

```
redFlag ≜ λ(). let flag = new true, chan = new 0 in {
  flip = rec try().
    if CAS(chan, 1, 2) then () else
    if CAS(flag, true, false) then () else
    if CAS(flag, false, true) then () else
    if CAS(chan, 0, 1) then
      if CAS(chan, 1, 0) then try() else chan := 0
    else try(),
  read = λ(). flag[1]
}
blueFlag ≜ λ(). let flag = new true, lock = new false in {
  flip = λ(). sync(lock) { flag := not flag[1] },
  read = λ(). sync(lock) { flag[1] }
}
```

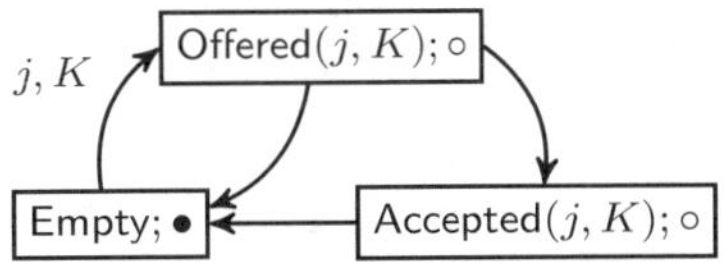

$$
\begin{aligned}
Q &\triangleq \exists x : \mathbf{B}.\ flag_{\mathrm{I}} \mapsto_{\mathrm{I}} x * flag_{\mathrm{S}} \mapsto_{\mathrm{S}} x * \mathsf{lock} \mapsto_{\mathrm{S}} \mathbf{false} \\
I(\mathsf{Empty}) &\triangleq Q * chan \mapsto_{\mathrm{I}} 0 \\
I(\mathsf{Offered}(j, K)) &\triangleq Q * chan \mapsto_{\mathrm{I}} 1 * j \rightarrowtail_{\mathrm{S}} K[\mathsf{flip}_{\mathrm{S}}()] \\
I(\mathsf{Accepted}(j, K)) &\triangleq Q * chan \mapsto_{\mathrm{I}} 2 * j \rightarrowtail_{\mathrm{S}} K[()]
\end{aligned}
$$

Figure 3. Red flags versus blue flags

2.5 Cooperation and specifications-as-resources

As explained in the introduction, some FCDs use side channels, separate from the main data structure, to enable threads executing different operations to *cooperate*. To illustrate this, we use a toy example—inspired specifically by "elimination stacks" [19]—that isolates the essential challenge of reasoning about cooperation, minus the full-blown messiness of a real data structure.

Figure 3 shows the example, in which redFlag is a lock-free implementation of blueFlag. The latter is a very simple data structure, which maintains a hidden boolean *flag*, and provides operations to flip it and read it. One obvious lock-free implementation of flip would be to keep running CAS(*flag*, **true**, **false**) and CAS(*flag*, **false**, **true**) repeatedly until one of them succeeds. However, to demonstrate cooperation, redFlag does something more "clever": in addition to maintaining *flag*, it also maintains a side channel *chan*, which it uses to enable two flip operations to cancel each other out without ever modifying *flag* at all!

More specifically, *chan* adheres to the following protocol, which is visualized in Figure 3 (ignore the K's for now). If $chan \mapsto_{\mathrm{I}} 0$, it means the side channel is not currently being used (it is in the Empty state). If $chan \mapsto_{\mathrm{I}} 1$, it means that some thread j has offered to perform a flip using the side channel and moved it into the Offered$(j, -)$ state. If $chan \mapsto_{\mathrm{I}} 2$, it means that another thread has accepted thread j's offer and transitioned to Accepted$(j, -)$—thus silently performing both flip's at once (since they cancel out)—but that thread j has not yet acknowledged that its offer was accepted.

Like the locking example, this protocol uses a single token—call it Offer—which is free in state Empty but which thread j moves into its private tokens when it transitions to the Offered$(j, -)$ state. After that transition, due to its ownership of Offer, thread j is the only thread that has the right to revoke that offer by setting *chan* back to 0 and returning to Empty. On the other hand, *any* thread may transition from Offered$(j, -)$ to Accepted$(j, -)$, since the two states have identical free tokens, namely, none. Once in the

$\mathsf{Accepted}(j, -)$ state, though, thread j is again the only thread able to Empty the channel.

The implementation of flip in redFlag then works as follows. First, we use CAS to check if another thread has offered to flip (*i.e.,* if $chan \mapsto_{\mathrm{I}} 1$), and if so, we accept the offer by setting *chan* to 2. We then immediately return, having implicitly committed both flips right then and there, without ever accessing *flag*. If that fails, we give up temporarily on the side-channel shenanigans and instead try to perform a bona fide flip by doing $\mathsf{CAS}(flag, \mathbf{true}, \mathbf{false})$ and $\mathsf{CAS}(flag, \mathbf{false}, \mathbf{true})$ as suggested above. If *that* fails as well, then we attempt to make an offer on the side channel by changing *chan* from 0 to 1. If our attempt succeeds, then we (rather stupidly[5]) try to immediately revoke the offer and loop back to the beginning. If perchance another thread has preempted us at this point and accepted our offer (*i.e.,* if $\mathsf{CAS}(chan, 1, 0)$ fails, implying that another thread has updated *chan* to 2), then that other thread must have already committed our flip on our behalf, so we simply set *chan* back to 0, thus making the side channel free for other threads to use, and return. Finally, if all else fails, we loop again.

As far as the refinement proof is concerned, there are essentially two interesting points here. The first concerns the $\mathsf{CAS}(chan, 1, 0)$ step. As we observed already, the failure of this CAS implies that *chan* must be 2. Why? Because of the way our protocol uses tokens. After the previous $\mathsf{CAS}(chan, 0, 1)$ succeeded, we knew that we had successfully transitioned to the $\mathsf{Offered}(j, -)$ state, and thus that our thread j now controls the Offer token. Our ownership of Offer tells us that other threads can only transition to a limited set of states via the rely ordering (*i.e.,* without owning Offer): they can either leave the state where it is, or they can transition to $\mathsf{Accepted}(j, -)$. Thus, when we observe that *chan* is not 1, we know it *must* be 2.

The second, more interesting point concerns the *semantics* of cooperation. If we make an offer on *chan*, which is accepted by another thread, it should imply that the other thread performed our flip for us, so we don't have to. At least that's the intuition, but how is that intuition enforced by the protocol? That is, when we observe that our offer has been accepted, we do so merely by inspecting the current value of *chan*. But how do we know that the other thread that updated *chan* from 1 to 2 actually "performed our flip" for us? For example, as perverse as this sounds, what is to prevent redFlag from performing $chan := 2$ as part of its implementation of read?

Our key to enforcing that the semantics of cooperation is respected is to treat *specification code* as a kind of resource. We introduce a new assertion, $j \rightarrowtail_{\mathrm{S}} e$, which describes the knowledge that thread j (on the spec side) is poised to run the term e. Ordinarily, this knowledge is kept private to thread j itself, but in a cooperative protocol, the whole idea is that j should be able to pass control over its spec code e to other threads, so that they may execute some steps of e on its behalf.

Specifically, this assertion is used to give semantic meaning to the $\mathsf{Offered}(j, K)$ and $\mathsf{Accepted}(j, K)$ states in our protocol (see the interpretation of F in Figure 3). In the former state, we know that $j \rightarrowtail_{\mathrm{S}} K[\mathsf{flip}_{\mathrm{S}}()]$, which tells us that thread j has offered its spec code $K[\mathsf{flip}_{\mathrm{S}}()]$ to be run by another thread, whereas in the latter state, we know that $j \rightarrowtail_{\mathrm{S}} K[()]$, which tells us that j's flip has been executed. (The K is present here only because we do not want to place any restrictions on the evaluation context of the flip operation.) These interpretations demand that whatever thread accepts the offer by transitioning from $\mathsf{Offered}(j, K)$ to $\mathsf{Accepted}(j, K)$ must take the responsibility not only of updating *chan* to 2 but also of executing $\mathsf{flip}_{\mathrm{S}}()$—and *only* $\mathsf{flip}_{\mathrm{S}}()$—on j's behalf. When j subsequently moves back to the Empty state, it regains private control over its specification code, so that other threads may no longer execute it.

[5] At this point in a real implementation, it would make sense to wait a while for other threads to accept our offer, but we elide that detail since it is irrelevant for reasoning about correctness.

$$
\begin{array}{rcl}
\mathsf{rand} & \triangleq & \lambda().\ \mathbf{let}\ y = \mathbf{new\ false\ in}\ (\mathbf{fork}\ y := \mathbf{true}); y[1] \\
\mathsf{lateChoice} & \triangleq & \lambda x.\ x := 0; \mathsf{rand}() \\
\mathsf{earlyChoice} & \triangleq & \lambda x.\ \mathbf{let}\ r = \mathsf{rand}()\ \mathbf{in}\ x := 0; r
\end{array}
$$

$$
\begin{array}{l}
\langle x_{\mathrm{I}} \preceq^{\mathcal{V}} x_{\mathrm{S}} : \mathbf{ref}(\mathsf{N}) \wedge j \rightarrowtail_{\mathrm{S}} K[\mathsf{earlyChoice}(x_{\mathrm{S}})] \rangle \\
\quad x_{\mathrm{I}} := 0 \\
\langle x_{\mathrm{I}} \preceq^{\mathcal{V}} x_{\mathrm{S}} : \mathbf{ref}(\mathsf{N}) \wedge (j \rightarrowtail_{\mathrm{S}} K[\mathbf{true}] \oplus j \rightarrowtail_{\mathrm{S}} K[\mathbf{false}]) \rangle \\
\quad \mathsf{rand}() \\
\langle \mathsf{ret}.\ (\mathsf{ret} = \mathbf{true} \vee \mathsf{ret} = \mathbf{false}) \wedge (j \rightarrowtail_{\mathrm{S}} K[\mathbf{true}] \oplus j \rightarrowtail_{\mathrm{S}} K[\mathbf{false}]) \rangle \\
\langle \mathsf{ret}.\ j \rightarrowtail_{\mathrm{S}} K[\mathsf{ret}]) \rangle
\end{array}
$$

Figure 4. Late choice versus early choice

2.6 Nondeterminism and speculation

Another tricky aspect of reasoning about FCDs (like the "conditional CAS" example we consider in Section 4) is dealing with nondeterminism. The problem is that when proving that an FCD refines some coarse-grained spec, we want to reason in a temporally-local fashion—*i.e.,* using something akin to a *simulation* argument, by which the behavior of each step of FCD code is matched against zero or more steps of spec code—but nondeterminism, it would seem, foils this plan.

To see why, consider the "late choice/early choice" example in Figure 4. This example is really simple: it does not maintain any hidden state (hence no protocol), and is not in fact an FCD at all, but it nevertheless illustrates the core difficulty with nondeterminism. We want to show that lateChoice refines earlyChoice. Both functions flip a coin (*i.e.,* use rand() to nondeterministically choose a boolean value) and set a given variable x to 0, but they do so in opposite orders. Intuitively, though, the order shouldn't matter: there is no way to observe the coin flip until the functions return. However, if we try to reason about the refinement using a simulation argument, we run into a problem. The first step of lateChoice is the setting of x to 0. To simulate this step in earlyChoice, we need to match the assignment of x to 0 as well, since the update is an externally observable effect. But to do that we must first flip earlyChoice's coin. While we have the freedom to choose the outcome of the flip,[6] the trouble is that we don't know what the outcome should be: lateChoice's coin flip has yet to be executed.

The solution is simple: speculate! That is, if you don't know which spec states to step to in order to match an implementation step, then keep your options open and maintain a *speculative set of specification states* that are reachable from the initial spec state and consistent with any observable effects of the implementation step. In the case of lateChoice/earlyChoice, this means that we can simulate the first step of lateChoice (the setting of x to 0) by executing the *entire* earlyChoice function *twice*. In both speculative states x is set to 0, but in one the coin flip returns **true**, and in the other it returns **false**.

This reasoning is captured in the Hoare-style proof outline given in Figure 4. The precondition $j \rightarrowtail_{\mathrm{S}} K[\mathsf{earlyChoice}(x_{\mathrm{S}})]$—an instance of the assertions on specification code introduced in the previous section—denotes that initially the spec side is poised to execute earlyChoice. After we execute $x := 0$ in lateChoice, we speculate that the coin flip on the spec side could result in earlyChoice either returning **true** or returning **false**. This is represented by the speculative assertion $(j \rightarrowtail_{\mathrm{S}} K[\mathbf{true}] \oplus j \rightarrowtail_{\mathrm{S}} K[\mathbf{false}])$ appearing in the postcondition of this first step, in which the $\oplus$ operator provides a *speculative choice* between two subassertions characterizing possible spec states. In the subsequent step, lateChoice flips its coin,

[6] For *every* implementation execution, we must construct *some* specification execution.

yielding a return value ret of either **true** or **false**. We can then refine the speculative set of specification states to whichever one (either $j \rightarrowtail_S K[\textbf{true}]$ or $j \rightarrowtail_S K[\textbf{false}]$) matches ret, and simply drop the other state from consideration. In the end, what matters is that we are left with at least one spec state that has been produced by a sequence of steps matching the observable behavior of the implementation's steps.

The idea of speculation is not new: it is implicit in Lynch and Vaandrager's notion of *forward-backward simulation* [28]. What is new here is that we capture speculation assertionally without using prophecy variables, which allows us to *compose* speculations without fuss. For example, we can use speculative reasoning in a private, thread-local way (as in the choice example) while separately using it within the protocol governing some shared state (as in the CCAS example, Section 4). We give a more detailed comparison to related work in Section 5.

3. The formal model

In this section, we develop the syntax and semantics of a logic for concurrent programs in our higher-order, polymorphic language. We leave a proof theory for future work, and instead work "in the model" (semantically) when verifying examples.

3.1 Overview: proving refinement via hiding and protocols

Our logic is ultimately used to prove contextual refinements, so it is important to first make clear what that entails, both formally and practically. To define contextual refinement, we first introduce a standard typing judgment for contexts,

$$C : (\Omega, \tau) \rightsquigarrow (\Omega', \tau')$$

so that whenever $\Omega \vdash e : \tau$, we have $\Omega' \vdash C[e] : \tau'$. Then if $\Omega \vdash e_I : \tau$ and $\Omega \vdash e_S : \tau$, we say e_I *contextually refines* e_S, written $\Omega \models e_I \preceq e_S : \tau$, if:

$$\begin{array}{l} \text{for every } i, j \text{ and } C : (\Omega, \tau) \rightsquigarrow (\emptyset, \mathbf{N}) \text{ we have} \\ \quad \forall n.\forall T_I. \quad \emptyset; [i \mapsto C[e_I]] \rightarrow^* h_1; [i \mapsto n] \uplus T_I \\ \implies \exists T_S. \quad \emptyset; [j \mapsto C[e_S]] \rightarrow^* h_2; [j \mapsto n] \uplus T_S \end{array}$$

Refinement formalizes "observable behavior" as anything a client of an expression could "test." A context C captures the notion of an unknown (but well-typed!) client, which can interact arbitrarily with the two expressions. If e_I behaves in a way that its spec, e_S, does not, it should be possible to find a context C whose main thread returns a number with e_I that, with e_S, it does not.

The only practical way to *prove* refinement is to find some other, more structured way of characterizing observable behavior—one that does not require detailed reasoning about particular contexts. In a high-level language, FCDs hide their internal state within the functions they export (their "methods"), thereby greatly limiting the scope of interaction they have with their clients. In particular, a client context can neither observe nor alter the internal state directly; all interactions are mediated by the methods. From the perspective of an FCD, then, the behavior of a client can be reduced to a collection of possibly-concurrent method invocations. And from the perspective of a client, the behavior of an FCD can be reduced to the answers it returns from those invocations.

How can we prove that an arbitrary collection of concurrent method calls to an FCD will yield the same answers as its spec? Protocols are the key: they capture the effect methods can have on the internal state—and thereby the effect they have on each other—*abstractly, i.e.,* without reference to FCD code. Protocols enable us to reason locally, about one method invocation at a time. Instead of considering an arbitrary sequence of prior method invocations, we simply start from an arbitrary protocol state. And instead of considering arbitrary concurrent invocations, we simply force our local reasoning to withstand arbitrary "rely" moves in a protocol.

$$\begin{array}{rcl} P & ::= & v = v \mid \mathsf{emp} \mid v \mapsto_I u \mid v \mapsto_S u \mid i \rightarrowtail_S e \mid P * P \\ & \mid & P \Rightarrow P \mid P \wedge P \mid P \vee P \mid \exists x.P \mid \forall x.P \\ & \mid & P \oplus P \mid \varphi \mid \iota \mid \triangleright P \mid T@m\ \langle x.\ P\rangle \\ \varphi & ::= & \langle P\rangle\ e\ \langle x.\ Q\rangle \mid v \preceq^{\mathcal{V}} v : \tau \mid \Omega \vdash e \preceq^{\mathcal{E}} e : \tau \\ \iota & ::= & (\theta, I, s, A) \quad \text{where} \begin{cases} I \in \theta.S \rightarrow \text{Assert}, & s \in \theta.S, \\ A \subseteq \theta.A, & A \# \theta.F(s) \end{cases} \\ \theta & ::= & (S, A, \rightsquigarrow, F) \text{ where } S, A \text{ sets}, \rightsquigarrow \subseteq S \times S,\ F \in S \rightarrow \wp(A) \\ m & ::= & i \mid \mathsf{none} \end{array}$$

Figure 5. Syntax of assertions

3.2 Assertions

In program logics for first-order languages, there is a strict separation between assertions about *data* (*e.g.,* heap assertions) and assertions about *code* (*e.g.,* Hoare triples). But the distinction makes less sense for higher-order languages, where code *is* data and hence claims about data must include claims about code. Our logic is therefore built around a single notion of assertion, P, shown in Figure 5, that plays several disparate roles.

Assertions are best understood one role at a time. The first role they play is similar to that of heap assertions in separation logic: they capture knowledge about a part of the (implementation's) heap, *e.g.,* $x \mapsto_I 0$, and support the composition of such knowledge, *e.g.,* $x \mapsto_I 0 * y \mapsto_I 1$. In this capacity, assertions make claims contingent on the current state, which may be invalidated in a later state.

On the other hand, some assertions are *pure*, meaning that if they hold in a given state, they will hold in any possible future state. The syntactic subclass of *code assertions* φ all have this property, and they include *Hoare triples* $\langle P\rangle\ e\ \langle x.\ Q\rangle$. The Hoare triple says: for any future state satisfying P, if the (implementation) expression e is executed until it terminates with a result, the final state will satisfy Q (where x is the value e returned). So, for example, $\langle \mathsf{emp}\rangle$ **new** $0\ \langle x.\ x \mapsto_I 0\rangle$ is a *valid* assertion, *i.e.,* it holds in any state. More generally, the usual rules of separation logic apply, including the frame rule, the rule of consequence—and sequencing. The sequencing rule works, even in our concurrent setting, because heap assertions describe a portion of heap that is *privately owned* by the expression in the Hoare triple. In particular, that portion of the heap is guaranteed to be neither observed nor altered by threads concurrent with the expression.

The next role assertions play is expressing knowledge about *shared* resources. All shared resources are governed by a protocol. For hidden state, the protocol can be chosen freely, modulo proving that exported methods actually follow it. For visible state, however, *e.g.,* a reference that is returned directly to the context, the protocol is forced to be a trivial one—roughly, one that allows the state to take on any well-typed value at any time, accounting for the arbitrary interference an unknown context could cause (see Section 3.4).

Claims about shared resources are made through *island assertions* ι (inspired by LADR [10]), which first of all assert the *existence* of said resources. We call each shared collection of resources an *island*, because each collection is disjoint from the others and is governed by an independent protocol. An island assertion gives the protocol governing its resources:

- The component $\theta = (S, A, \rightsquigarrow, F)$ formalizes the STS for the protocol, where S is its set of states, A is its set of possible tokens, $\rightsquigarrow$ is its transition relation, and F is a function telling which tokens are free at each state. (We will use dot notation like $\theta.S$ to project named components from compound objects.)
- The component I tells how each state of the STS is *interpreted* as an assertion characterizing the concrete, hidden resources that are actually owned by the island in that state.

Domains

$$\begin{aligned}
\text{StateSet} &\triangleq \{ \Sigma \subseteq \text{Heap} \times \text{ThreadPool} \mid \Sigma \text{ finite, nonempty} \} \\
\text{Resource} &\triangleq \{ \eta \in \text{Heap} \times \text{StateSet} \} \\
\text{Island}_n &\triangleq \left\{ (\theta, J, s, A) \;\middle|\; \begin{array}{l} \theta \in \text{STS},\ s \in \theta.S,\ A \subseteq \theta.A,\ A \# \theta.F(s), \\ J \in \theta.S \to \text{UWorld}_n \overset{\text{mon}}{\to} \wp(\text{Resource}) \end{array} \right\} \\
\text{World}_n &\triangleq \left\{ W = (k, \omega) \;\middle|\; k < n,\ \omega \in \mathbb{N} \overset{\text{fin}}{\rightharpoonup} \text{Island}_k \right\} \\
\text{UWorld}_n &\triangleq \{ U \in \text{World}_n \mid U = |U| \} \\
\text{VRel}_n &\triangleq \left\{ V \in \text{UWorld}_n \overset{\text{mon}}{\to} \wp(\text{Val} \times \text{Val}) \right\}
\end{aligned}$$

Island and world operations

$$\begin{aligned}
|(\theta, J, s, A)| &\triangleq (\theta, J, s, \emptyset) \qquad |(k, \omega)| \triangleq (k, \lambda i.|\omega(i)|) \\
\text{frame}(\theta, J, s, A) &\triangleq (\theta,\ J,\ s,\ \theta.A - \theta.F(s) - A) \\
\text{frame}(k, \omega) &\triangleq (k,\ \lambda i.\text{frame}(\omega(i))) \\
\lfloor(\theta, J, s_0, A)\rfloor_k &\triangleq (\theta, \lambda s.I(s) \restriction \text{UWorld}_k, s_0, A) \\
\triangleright(k+1, \omega) &\triangleq (k, \lambda i.\lfloor\omega(i)\rfloor_k) \\
\text{interp}(\theta, J, s, A) &\triangleq J(s)
\end{aligned}$$

Composition

$$\begin{aligned}
&\text{State sets} & \Sigma_1 \otimes \Sigma_2 &\triangleq \{ h_1 \uplus h_2; T_1 \uplus T_2 \mid h_i; T_i \in \Sigma_i \} \text{ when } \textit{all} \text{ compositions are defined} \\
&\text{Resources} & (h_1, \Sigma_1) \otimes (h_2, \Sigma_2) &\triangleq (h_1 \uplus h_2, \Sigma_1 \otimes \Sigma_2) \\
&\text{Islands} & (\theta, J, s, A) \otimes (\theta', J', s', A') &\triangleq (\theta, J, s, A \uplus A') \quad \text{when } \theta = \theta',\ s = s',\ J = J' \\
&\text{Worlds} & (k, \omega) \otimes (k', \omega') &\triangleq (k, \lambda i.\omega(i) \otimes \omega'(i)) \quad \text{when } k = k',\ \text{dom}(\omega) = \text{dom}(\omega')
\end{aligned}$$

Protocol conformance

$$\begin{aligned}
\theta \vdash (s, A) \rightsquigarrow (s', A') &\triangleq s \rightsquigarrow_\theta s',\ \theta.F(s) \uplus A = \theta.F(s') \uplus A' \\
(\theta, J, s, A) \overset{\text{guar}}{\sqsubseteq} (\theta', J', s', A') &\triangleq \theta = \theta',\ J = J',\ \theta \vdash (s, A) \rightsquigarrow^* (s', A') \\
(k, \omega) \overset{\text{guar}}{\sqsubseteq} (k', \omega') &\triangleq k \geq k',\ \forall i \in \text{dom}(\omega).\ \lfloor\omega(i)\rfloor_{k'} \overset{\text{guar}}{\sqsubseteq} \omega'(i) \\
W \overset{\text{rely}}{\sqsubseteq} W' &\triangleq \text{frame}(W) \overset{\text{guar}}{\sqsubseteq} \text{frame}(W')
\end{aligned}$$

World satisfaction:

$$\eta : W, \eta' \triangleq W.k > 0 \implies \eta = \eta' \otimes \overline{\eta_i},\ \forall i \in \text{dom}(W.\omega).\ \eta_i \in \text{interp}(W.\omega(i))(\triangleright|W|)$$

Figure 6. Semantic structures and operations on them

In addition, island assertions express knowledge about the state of the protocol (the component s) and any privately-owned tokens (the component A). This last bit of knowledge gives a *lower bound* on the actual state of the protocol, which may in fact by in any "rely-future" state of s, *i.e.*, any state that can be reached from s by the environment without using the privately-owned tokens A.

Finally, assertions play two refinement-related roles. The first is to express refinement itself, either between two closed values ($v_I \preceq^{\mathcal{V}} v_S : \tau$) or between open expressions ($\Omega \vdash e_I \preceq^{\mathcal{E}} e_S : \tau$)—the syntactic counterpart to semantic refinement (Section 3.1). Until this point, we have avoided saying anything about spec terms, but in order to prove refinement we need to show that the observable behavior of an implementation can be mimicked by its spec. This brings us to an essential idea:

$$\begin{aligned} e_I \preceq^{\mathcal{E}} e_S : \tau \quad &\approx \quad \text{(roughly!)} \\ &\forall j.\ \langle j \rightarrowtail_S e_S \rangle\ e_I\ \langle x_I.\ \exists x_S.\ x_I \preceq^{\mathcal{V}} x_S : \tau \wedge j \rightarrowtail_S x_S \rangle \end{aligned}$$

By treating spec code as a resource, we can reduce refinement reasoning to Hoare-style reasoning. Thus, the final role assertions play is to express knowledge about—and ownership of—spec resources, which include portions both of the heap (*e.g.*, $x \mapsto_S 0$) and of the threadpool (*e.g.*, $j \rightarrowtail_S e_S$). These resources can be shared and hence governed by protocols, just as implementation-side resources can.

When proving refinement for an FCD, we will prove something like the above Hoare triple for an arbitrary application of each of its methods—usually in the scope of an island assertion giving the protocol for its shared, hidden state. For each method invocation, we start from an arbitrary state of that protocol, and are *given ownership of* the spec code corresponding to the invocation, which we may choose to transfer to the protocol to support cooperation (as explained in Section 2.5). But in the end, when the implementation's invocation has finished and returned a value x_I, we must have regained exclusive control over its spec, which must have mimicked it by producing a value x_S that x_I refines.

The remaining forms of assertions include standard logical connectives, and two more technical forms of assertions—$\triangleright P$ and $T@m\ \langle x.\ P\rangle$—which we explain in the Section 3.4.

3.3 Semantic structures

The semantics of assertions is given using two judgments, one for general assertions ($W, \eta \models^\rho P$) and the other for code assertions ($U \models^\rho \varphi$), where P and φ contain no free term variables but may contain free type variables bound by ρ. To explain these judgments, we begin with the semantic structures of *worlds* W, *resources* η and *environments* ρ, together with operations on them needed to interpret assertions—all defined in Figure 6.

Resources The *resources* $\eta = (h, \Sigma)$ that assertions claim knowledge about and ownership of include both implementation heaps h, and speculative sets Σ of spec configurations. (Recall that a *configuration* $\varsigma = h; T$ consists of a heap and a threadpool.) Resources can be combined at every level, which is necessary for interpreting the $*$ operator on assertions. For heaps and threadpools, composition is done via $\uplus$, the usual disjoint union. The composition of state sets is just the set of state compositions—but it is only defined when *all* such state compositions are defined, so that speculative sets Σ have a single "footprint" consisting of all the locations/threads existing in *any* speculative state. To ensure that this footprint is finite, we require that speculation is itself finite. Finally, composition of resources is the composition of their parts.

Islands and possible worlds All assertions are interpreted in the context of some *possible world* W, which contains a collection ω of islands—this is the "Kripke" in Kripke logical relations. Semantic islands look very much like syntactic island assertions: the only difference is that STS states are interpreted semantically via J, rather than syntactically via I. Unfortunately, this creates a circularity: J is meant to interpret its syntactic counterpart I, and since assertions are interpreted in the contexts of worlds, the interpretation must be relative to the current world—but we are in the middle of *defining* worlds! The step index k in worlds is used to stratify away circularities in the definition of worlds and the logical relation; it and its attendant operators $\triangleright$ and $\lfloor - \rfloor_k$ are completely standard, and so for space reasons we direct the interested reader to earlier work for a detailed explanation [9, 10]. The less interested reader should simply ignore step indices from here on.

There is one additional subtlety, however: it is crucial that all participants in a protocol agree on the protocol's interpretation of a state, which must therefore be insensitive to which tokens a particular participant owns. We guarantee this by giving the interpretation J access to only the *unprivileged* part of a participant's world, $|W|$, which has been stripped of any tokens; see the constraint on the type of J.

To determine the meaning of assertions like $\iota * \iota'$, we must allow islands to be composed. Semantic island composition $\otimes$ is defined only when the islands agree on all aspects of the protocol, including its state; their owned tokens are then (disjointly) combined. Note, however, that because island *assertions* are rely-closed, an assertion like $\iota * \iota'$ does *not* require ι and ι' to assert the same state. It merely requires that there is some state that is in both of their rely-futures. Worlds are composable only when they define the same islands and those islands are composable.

Environments Type variables are interpreted by an *environment* ρ that maps them to relations $V \in$ VRel. This interpretation of types captures the usual relational parametricity [32], in which the interpretation of an abstract type may relate values of potentially different types on the the implementation and specification sides.

Protocol conformance The judgment $\theta \vdash (s, A) \rightsquigarrow (s', A')$ codifies the law of conservation of tokens (Section 2.4) for a single step.[7] We use this judgment in defining a *guarantee* relation governing the changes an expression can make to an island's state, given the tokens it owns. An expression can likewise *rely* on its environment to only change the island ι according to the tokens that the environment owns, *i.e.,* the tokens owned by frame(ι).

The rely and guarantee views of a protocol give rise to *two* notions of future worlds. In both cases, the world may grow to include new islands, but any existing islands are constrained by their rely and guarantee relations, respectively. The guarantee relation on islands may include changes to both the state of the STS and the privately-owned tokens. The rely relation only allows the state to change, since only the (implicit) environmental participant making the move may gain or lose tokens. Island interpretations J are required to be monotone with respect to the rely relation on worlds (written $\overset{\text{mon}}{\rightarrow}$), which ensures that making a rely move in one island cannot possibly invalidate the interpretation of another.

World satisfaction Worlds describe shared state abstractly, in terms of protocol states. Expressions, on the other hand, are executed against some *concrete* resources. The *world satisfaction relation* $\eta : W, \eta'$ defines when a given collection of concrete resources η "satisfies" a world, meaning that it breaks into a disjoint portion for each island, with each portion satisfying its island's current interpretation. The parameter η' represents additional resources that are *private*, and therefore disjoint from those governed by the world, which is convenient for defining the semantics of assertions below.

3.4 Semantics

The semantics of assertions given in Figure 7 satisfies a fundamental property: if $W, \eta \models^\rho P$ and $W \overset{\text{rely}}{\sqsubseteq} W'$ then $W', \eta \models^\rho P$. All assertions are therefore "stable" under arbitrary interference from other threads. This should not be a surprise: assertions are either statements about private resources (for which interference is impossible) or about shared islands (for which interference is assumed, *e.g.,* we are careful to only assert *lower bounds* on the state of an island). The only subtlety is in the semantics of implication, which must be explicitly rely-closed to ensure stability. The semantics of the basic assertions about private resources and islands are entirely straightforward, as are those for the basic logical connectives (we omit $=$, $\vee$ and $\exists$).

The value refinement assertion $v_1 \preceq^{\mathcal{V}} v_2 : \tau$ requires that any observations a context can make of v_1 at type τ can also be made of v_2. Those readers familiar with Kripke logical relations will recognize it as essentially the standard definition of logical approximation between values. Base type values must be identical. For function types, we check that the bodies of the functions are related when given related arguments, which, due to the semantics of implication, might happen in a rely-future world. For recursive types, we check that the values are related at the unfolded type, which is well-founded due to the productivity requirement on recursive types (and our strategic uses of $\triangleright$ in type constructors). Values that are exposed to the context at heap-allocated type—**ref** and sum types—are forced to be governed by a trivial island allowing *all* type-safe updates (in the case of **ref**'s) and *no* updates (in the case of sums). Hidden state, on the other hand, is by definition state that does not escape directly to the context, and so we need say nothing about it for value refinement.

The fact that refinement is a pure assertion (insensitive to the state of private resources or the ownership of private tokens) is essential for soundness, for a simple reason: once a value has reached the context, it can be copied and used concurrently. We therefore cannot claim that any *one* copy of the value privately owns some resources. Note that, if P is impure, we use $U \models^\rho P$ as shorthand for $\forall \eta.\ U, \eta \models^\rho P$.

For expression refinement $\Omega \vdash e_1 \preceq^{\mathcal{E}} e_2 : \tau$, we first close off any term or type variables bound by Ω with the appropriate universal quantification. Closed expression refinement is defined in terms of a Hoare triple, almost in the way we suggested in Section 3.2. The main difference in the actual definition is that we additionally quantify over the unknown evaluation context K in which a specification is running; this annoyance appears to be necessary for proving that refinement is a precongruence.

Hoare triples are defined via the *threadpool simulation* assertion $T@m\ \langle x.\ P\rangle$, which is the engine that powers our model. Threadpool simulation accounts for the fact that an expression can fork threads as it executes, but that we care about the return value only from the initial thread, m. To satisfy $T@m\ \langle x.\ P\rangle$ at some W and η, the threads in T must first of all continuously obey the protocols of W, given private ownership of η. That is, every atomic step taken by a thread must transform its shared resources in a way that corresponds to a guarantee move in the protocol, and it must preserve as a frame any private resources of its environment, but it may change private resources η in any way it likes. In between each such atomic step, the context might get a chance to run, which we model by quantifying over an arbitrary rely-future world. If at any point the main thread m terminates, it must do so in a state satisfying P, where x is bound to the value the main thread returned. Afterward, any lingering threads are still required to obey the protocol.

That threadpool simulation is, in fact, a simulation is due to its use of the *speculative stepping relation* $\Sigma \rightrightarrows \Sigma'$, which requires any changes to the spec state to represent feasible execution steps: every new state must be reachable from some old state, but we are free to introduce multiple new states originating in the same old state, and we are free to drop irrelevant old states on the floor. As a result of how simulation is defined, such changes to the spec state can only be made to those pieces that are under the threadpool's control, either as part of its private resources (allowing arbitrary feasible updates) or its shared ones (allowing only protocol-permitted updates).

3.5 Soundness for refinement

Our key theorem is:

Theorem 1 (Soundness). If $U \models^\emptyset \Omega \vdash e_1 \preceq^{\mathcal{E}} e_2 : \tau$ for all U then $\Omega \models e_1 \preceq e_2 : \tau$.

[7] We use the more readable notation $s \rightsquigarrow_\theta s'$ in place of $\theta.\rightsquigarrow (s, s')$.

Private and shared-state assertions: $W, \eta \models^{\rho} R$ iff

R	Requirements
φ	$\lvert W \rvert \models^{\rho} \varphi$
emp	$W = \lvert W \rvert, \eta = (\emptyset, \{\emptyset; \emptyset\})$
$v \mapsto_{\mathrm{I}} u$	$\eta = ([v \mapsto u], \{\emptyset; \emptyset\})$
$v \mapsto_{\mathrm{S}} u$	$\eta = (\emptyset, \{[v \mapsto u]; \emptyset\})$
$i \rightarrowtail_{\mathrm{S}} e$	$\eta = (\emptyset, \{\emptyset; [i \mapsto e]\})$
$P \wedge Q$	$W, \eta \models^{\rho} P$ and $W, \eta \models^{\rho} Q$
$P \Rightarrow Q$	$\forall W' \overset{\text{rely}}{\sqsupseteq} W.\ W', \eta \models^{\rho} P \implies W', \eta \models^{\rho} Q$
$\forall x.P$	$\forall v.\ W, \eta \models^{\rho} P[v/x]$
$\triangleright P$	$W.k > 0 \implies \triangleright W, \eta \models^{\rho} P$
$P_1 * P_2$	$W = W_1 \otimes W_2,\ \eta = \eta_1 \otimes \eta_2,\ W_i, \eta_i \models^{\rho} P_i$
$P_1 \oplus P_2$	$\eta.\Sigma = \Sigma_1 \cup \Sigma_2,\ W, (\eta.h, \Sigma_i) \models^{\rho} P_i$
(θ, I, s, A)	$\exists i.\ W \overset{\text{rely}}{\sqsupseteq} (W.k, [i \mapsto (\theta, [\![I]\!], s, A)])$
	where $[\![I]\!] \triangleq \lambda s.\lambda U.\{\eta \mid U, \eta \models^{\rho} I(s)\}$

Hoare triples:

$U \models^{\rho} \langle P \rangle\, e\, \langle x.\ Q \rangle \ \triangleq\ \forall i.\ U \models^{\rho} P \Rightarrow [i \mapsto e]@i\, \langle x.\ Q \rangle$

Value refinement: $U \models^{\rho} v_1 \preceq^{\mathcal{V}} v_2 : \tau_0$ iff

τ_0	Requirements
τ_b	$v_1 = v_2,\ \vdash v_i : \tau_b$ for $\tau_b \in \{\mathbf{1}, \mathsf{B}, \mathsf{N}\}$
α	$(v_1, v_2) \in \rho(\alpha)(U)$
$\tau \to \tau'$	$v_i = \mathbf{rec}\ f(x).e_i, U \models^{\rho} \triangleright(x : \tau \vdash e_1[v_1/f] \preceq^{\mathcal{E}} e_2[v_2/f] : \tau')$
$\forall \alpha.\tau$	$v_i = \Lambda.e_i, \quad U \models^{\rho} \triangleright(\alpha \vdash e_1 \preceq^{\mathcal{E}} e_2 : \tau)$
$\mu\alpha.\tau$	$U \models^{\rho} v_1 \preceq^{\mathcal{V}} v_2 : \tau[\mu\alpha.\tau/\alpha]$
$\mathbf{ref}_{?}(\overline{\tau})$	$U \models^{\rho} v_1 \preceq^{\mathcal{V}} v_2 : \mathbf{1} \vee v_1 \preceq^{\mathcal{V}} v_2 : \mathbf{ref}(\overline{\tau})$
$\mathbf{ref}(\overline{\tau})$	$U \models^{\rho} \mathrm{inv}(\exists \overline{x}, \overline{y}.\ \bigwedge \overline{x \preceq^{\mathcal{V}} y : \tau} \wedge v_1 \mapsto_{\mathrm{I}} (\overline{x}) * v_2 \mapsto_{\mathrm{S}} (\overline{y}))$
$\tau_1 + \tau_2$	$\exists i.\ U \models^{\rho} \exists x, y.\ x \preceq^{\mathcal{V}} y : \tau_i \wedge \mathrm{inv}(v_1 \mapsto_{\mathrm{I}} \mathbf{inj}_i\ x * v_2 \mapsto_{\mathrm{S}} \mathbf{inj}_i\ y)$

Expression refinement: $U \models^{\rho} \Omega \vdash e_1 \preceq^{\mathcal{E}} e_2 : \tau$ iff

Ω	Requirements
$\cdot$	$\forall K, j.\ U \models^{\rho} \langle j \rightarrowtail_{\mathrm{S}} K[e_2] \rangle\, e_1\, \langle x.\ \exists y.\ x \preceq^{\mathcal{V}} y : \tau \wedge j \rightarrowtail_{\mathrm{S}} K[y] \rangle$
$x{:}\tau', \Omega'$	$\forall v_1, v_2.\ U \models^{\rho} v_1 \preceq^{\mathcal{V}} v_2 : \tau' \ \Rightarrow\ \Omega' \vdash e_1[v_1/x] \preceq^{\mathcal{E}} e_2[v_2/x] : \tau$
α, Ω'	$\forall V.\ U \models^{\rho[\alpha \mapsto V]} \Omega' \vdash e_1 \preceq^{\mathcal{E}} e_2 : \tau$

Invariant protocols: $\mathrm{inv}(P) \ \triangleq\ ((\{1\}, \emptyset, \emptyset, \lambda\_.\emptyset), \lambda\_.P, 1, \emptyset)$

Spec stepping: $\Sigma \rightrightarrows \Sigma' \ \triangleq\ \forall \varsigma' \in \Sigma'.\ \exists \varsigma \in \Sigma.\ \varsigma \to^{*} \varsigma'$

Threadpool simulation:

$W_0, \eta \models^{\rho} T@m\, \langle x.\ Q \rangle \ \triangleq\ \forall W \overset{\text{rely}}{\sqsupseteq} W_0,\ \eta_F \# \eta.$ if $W.k > 0$ and $h, \Sigma : W, \eta \otimes \eta_F$ then:

if $h; T \to h'; T'$ then $\exists \Sigma', \eta', W' \overset{\text{guar}}{\sqsupseteq} W.\ \ \Sigma \rightrightarrows \Sigma',\ \ h', \Sigma' : W', \eta' \otimes \eta_F,\ \ W'.k = W.k - 1,\ \ W', \eta' \models^{\rho} T'@m\, \langle x.\ Q \rangle$

if $T = T_0 \uplus [m \mapsto v]$ then $\exists \Sigma', \eta', W' \overset{\text{guar}}{\sqsupseteq} W.\ \ \Sigma \rightrightarrows \Sigma',\ \ h, \Sigma' : W', \eta' \otimes \eta_F,\ \ W'.k = W.k,\ \ W', \eta' \models^{\rho} Q[v/x] * T_0@\mathsf{none}\, \langle x.\ \mathsf{tt} \rangle$

Figure 7. The semantics of assertions

The proof of this theorem, given in the appendix [35], is built on novel lemmas expressing key framing properties for the threadpool simulation assertion, the most important being:

Lemma 1 (Framing). If $W_1, \eta_1 \models^{\rho} T_1@m_1\ \langle x.\ Q_1 \rangle$ and $W_2, \eta_2 \models^{\rho} T_2@m_2\, \langle x.\ Q_2 \rangle$ with $m_1 = \mathsf{none}$ or $m_1 \in \mathrm{dom}(T_1)$, then $W_1 \otimes W_2, \eta_1 \otimes \eta_2 \models^{\rho} T_1 \uplus T_2@m_1\, \langle x.\ Q_1 \rangle$.

These lemmas allow us to prove that refinement assertions are *congruent* (*i.e.,* they compose), which is the difficult part of soundness. We can also derive the following inference rules for *valid*, pure assertions (true at every world):

$$\frac{\langle P \rangle\, e\, \langle x.\ P' \rangle \quad \forall x.\langle P' \rangle\, e'\, \langle y.\ P'' \rangle}{\langle P \rangle\ \mathbf{let}\ x = e\ \mathbf{in}\ e'\, \langle y.\ P'' \rangle} \qquad \frac{\langle P \rangle\, e\, \langle x.\ Q \rangle}{\langle P * R \rangle\, e\, \langle x.\ Q * R \rangle}$$

$$\frac{P \Rightarrow P' \quad \langle P' \rangle\, e\, \langle x.\ Q' \rangle \quad Q' \Rightarrow Q}{\langle P \rangle\, e\, \langle x.\ Q \rangle} \qquad \frac{\triangleright P \Rightarrow P}{P}$$

The first three of these inference rules are the expected ones for a separation logic (our assertions also model intuitionistic BI). The last rule is the Löb rule, which allows us to reason about recursive functions by assuming their specification holds one step later [10]. In giving proof outlines in the next section, we make implicit use of these rules, and also drop the variable binding in the postcondition when it is irrelevant.

4. Case study: conditional CAS

With the details of our model in hand, we are now in a position to tackle, in detail, a rather complex FCD: Harris *et al.*'s *conditional CAS* [18, 15], which performs a compare-and-set on one word of memory, but only succeeds when some other word (the *control flag*) is non-zero at the same instant. This data structure is the workhorse that enables Harris *et al.* to build their remarkable lock-free multi-word CAS from single-word CAS.

As with the Michael-Scott queue, we have boiled down conditional CAS to its essence, retaining its key verification challenges while removing extraneous detail. Thus, we study lock-free conditional *increment* on a counter, with a fixed control flag per instance of the counter; see the specification $\mathsf{counter}_{\mathrm{S}}$ in Figure 8. These simplifications eliminate the need to track administrative information about the operation we are trying to perform but do not change the algorithm itself, so adapting our proof of conditional increment to full CCAS is a straightforward exercise.

4.1 The protocol

To explain our implementation, $\mathsf{counter}_{\mathrm{I}}$, we begin with its representation and the protocol that governs it. The control flag f is represented using a simple boolean reference; all of the action is in the counter c, which has type $\mathbf{ref}(\mathsf{N} + \mathsf{N})$. A value $\mathbf{inj}_1\ n$ represents an "inactive" counter with logical value n. A value $\mathbf{inj}_2\ n$, in contrast, means that the counter is undergoing a conditional increment, and had the logical value n when the increment began. Because $\mathbf{inj}_2\ n$ records the original value, a concurrent thread attempting another operation on the data structure can help finish the in-progress increment. This helping is actually not so selfless: really, one thread is just "helping" another thread get out of its way.

The question is how to perform a conditional increment without using any locks. Remarkably, the algorithm simply reads the flag f, and then—in a separate step—updates the counter c with a CAS; see the $\mathsf{complete}$ function. It is possible, therefore, for one thread performing a conditional increment to read f as true, at which point another thread sets f to false; the original thread then proceeds with incrementing the counter, even though the control flag is false! Proving that $\mathsf{counter}_{\mathrm{I}}$ refines $\mathsf{counter}_{\mathrm{S}}$ despite this blatant race

```
counters_S ≜
  let c = new 0, f = new false, lock = new false
  let setFlag(b) = sync(lock) { f := b }
  let get()      = sync(lock) { c[1] }
  let cinc()     = sync(lock) { c[1] := c[1] + if f[1] then 1 else 0 }
  in (get, setFlag, cinc)

counter_I ≜
  let c = new inj_1 0, f = new false
  let setFlag(b) = f := b
  let complete(x, n) = if f[1] then CAS(c, x, inj_1 (n + 1))
                                else CAS(c, x, inj_1 n)
  let rec get() = let x = c[1] in case x of
      inj_1 n ⇒ n
    | inj_2 n ⇒ complete(o, n); get()
  let rec cinc() = let x = c[1] in case x of
      inj_1 n ⇒ let y = inj_2 n in
        if CAS(c, x, y) then complete(y, n); () else cinc()
    | inj_2 n ⇒ complete(x, n); cinc()
  in (get, setFlag, cinc)
```

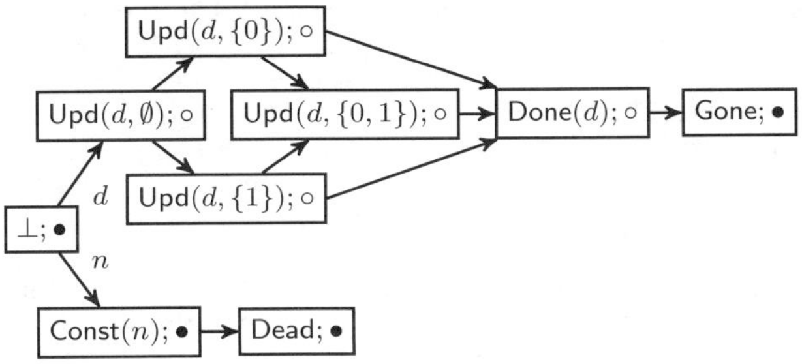

$$d ::= n, j, K \qquad B \subseteq \{0,1\} \qquad A \triangleq \mathrm{Loc} \qquad S \triangleq \mathrm{Loc} \xrightarrow{\mathrm{fin}} S_0$$

$$S_0 \triangleq \{\bot, \mathsf{Upd}(d,B), \mathsf{Done}(d), \mathsf{Gone}, \mathsf{Const}(n), \mathsf{Dead}\}$$

$$\begin{aligned} I(s) \triangleq\ & \exists b : \mathbf{B}.\ f_I \mapsto_I b * f_S \mapsto_S b * \mathsf{lock} \mapsto_S \mathbf{false} \\ * \ & \exists! \ell_c.\ s(\ell) \in \{\mathsf{Const}(-), \mathsf{Upd}(-,-)\} \\ * \ & \begin{cases} \mathsf{linkUpd}(\ell_c, n, j, K, B) & s(\ell_c) = \mathsf{Upd}(n, j, K, B) \\ \mathsf{linkConst}(\ell_c, n) & s(\ell_c) = \mathsf{Const}(n) \end{cases} \\ * \ & \bigstar_{s(\ell)=\mathsf{Done}(n,j,K)} \ell \mapsto_I \mathbf{inj}_2\ n * j \rightarrowtail_S K[()] \\ * \ & \bigstar_{s(\ell)=\mathsf{Gone}} \ell \mapsto_I \mathbf{inj}_2\ - \quad * \quad \bigstar_{s(\ell)=\mathsf{Dead}} \ell \mapsto_I \mathbf{inj}_1\ - \end{aligned}$$

$$\mathsf{linkConst}(\ell_c, n) \triangleq c_I \mapsto_I \ell_c * \ell_c \mapsto_I \mathbf{inj}_1\ n * c_S \mapsto_S n$$

$$\begin{aligned} \mathsf{linkUpd}(\ell_c, n, j, K, B) \triangleq\ & c_I \mapsto_I \ell_c * \ell_c \mapsto_I \mathbf{inj}_2\ n \\ * & \begin{pmatrix} c_S \mapsto_S n * j \rightarrowtail_S K[\mathsf{cinc}()] & \\ \oplus\ c_S \mapsto_S n * j \rightarrowtail_S K[()] & \text{if } 0 \in B \\ \oplus\ c_S \mapsto_S (n+1) * j \rightarrowtail_S K[()] & \text{if } 1 \in B \end{pmatrix} \end{aligned}$$

Figure 8. Conditional increment, a simplification of CCAS

```
let complete(x, n) =                ⟨x ∝ Upd(n, j, K, ∅)⟩
  if f[1] then                      ⟨x ∝ Upd(n, j, K, {1})⟩
    CAS(c, x, inj_1 (n + 1))        ⟨x ∝ Done(n, j, K)⟩
  else                              ⟨x ∝ Upd(n, j, K, {0})⟩
    CAS(c, x, inj_1 n)              ⟨x ∝ Done(n, j, K)⟩

let rec cinc() =                    ⟨j ↣_S K[cinc_S()] * (θ, I, ∅, ∅)⟩
  let x = c[1] in                   ⟨j ↣_S K[cinc_S()] *
                                      (x ∝ Const(−) ∨ x ∝ Upd(−, −))⟩
  case x of
   inj_1 n ⇒                        ⟨j ↣_S K[cinc_S()] * x ∝ Const(n)⟩
    let y = inj_2 n in              ⟨j ↣_S K[cinc_S()] * x ∝ Const(n) *
                                      y ↦ inj_2 n⟩
    if CAS(c, x, y) then            ⟨x ∝ Dead(n) ∧ y ∝• Upd(n, j, K, ∅)⟩
                                 ∴  ⟨y ∝• Upd(n, j, K, ∅)⟩
      complete(y, n);               ⟨y ∝• Done(n, j, K)⟩
      ()                            ⟨ret. ret = () ∧ j ↣_S K[()] ∧ y ∝ Gone⟩
                                 ∴  ⟨ret. ret = () ∧ j ↣_S K[()]⟩
    else                            ⟨j ↣_S K[cinc_S()] * (θ, I, ∅, ∅)⟩
      cinc()                        ⟨ret. ret = () ∧ j ↣_S K[()]⟩

  | inj_2 n ⇒                       ⟨j ↣_S K[cinc_S()] * x ∝ Upd(n, −, −, −)⟩
    complete(x, n);                 ⟨j ↣_S K[cinc_S()] * x ∝ Done(n, −, −)⟩
                                 ∴  ⟨j ↣_S K[cinc_S()] * (θ, I, ∅, ∅)⟩
    cinc()                          ⟨ret. ret = () ∧ j ↣_S K[()]⟩
```

Figure 9. Proof outline for conditional increment

condition will require all the features of our model, working in concert.

An initial idea is that when the *physical* value of the counter is $\mathbf{inj}_2\ n$, its *logical* value is ambiguous: it is either n or $n+1$. This idea will only work if we can associate such logical values with feasible executions of the spec's cinc code, since "logical" value really means the spec's value. The difficulty is in choosing *when* to take spec steps. If we wait to execute the spec code until a successful CAS in complete, we may be too late: as the interleaving above shows, the flag may have changed by then. But we cannot execute the spec when we read the flag, either: the CAS that follows it may fail, in which case some *other* thread must have executed the spec.

The way out of this conundrum is for threads to interact via a speculative protocol, shown in Figure 8. Recall that injections into sum types are heap-allocated, so every value c takes on has an identity: its location. The protocol gives the life story for every possible location in the heap as a potential value of c, with the usual constraint that all but finitely many locations are in the unborn ($\bot$) state. The first step of the protocol reflects the choice latent in the sum type: either this location is a quiescent $\mathbf{inj}_1\ n$ (represented initially by $\mathsf{Const}(n)$) or an active increment operation $\mathbf{inj}_2\ n$ (represented initially by $\mathsf{Upd}(d, \emptyset)$). The *logical descriptor* d gives the old value n of the counter, together with the thread id j and specification evaluation context of the thread attempting the increment. The latter information is necessary because thread j temporarily donates its spec to the protocol, permitting helping threads to execute the spec on its behalf. Following the pattern laid out in Section 2.5, in return for donating its spec, thread j receives a token—call it Attempt—which will later permit it, and only it, to recover its spec. As usual, we depict the token with a bullet.

The life story for a quiescent $\mathbf{inj}_1\ n$ is quite mundane: either it is the current value pointed to by c, or it is Dead. An active cell $\mathbf{inj}_2\ n$ leads a much more exciting life. In the first phase of life, $\mathsf{Upd}(d, B)$, the cell records which *branches* $B \subseteq \{0, 1\}$ of the complete code have been entered by a thread. Initially, no thread has executed complete, so the set is empty. If a thread subsequently reads that $f = \mathbf{true}$ in the first step of executing complete, it moves to the set $\{1\}$, since it is now committed to the branch that adds 1 to the initial value n. Crucially, this step coincides with a *speculative* run of the specification; the un-run spec is also retained, in case some other thread commits to the 0 branch. The branch-accumulation process continues until some thread (perhaps not the original instigator of the increment) actually succeeds in performing its CAS in complete. At that point, the increment is Done, and its $\mathbf{inj}_2\ n$ cell is effectively dead, but not yet Gone: in the end, the thread that instigated the original increment reclaims its spec, whose execution is guaranteed to be finished.

4.2 The proof

We now formally justify that $\mathsf{counter_I}$ refines $\mathsf{counter_S}$ by giving a concrete interpretation to the protocol and providing a Hoare-style proof outline for complete and cinc. The outline for get is then a straightforward exercise.

To formalize the protocol, we first give the set of states S_0 for an *individual* life story; see Figure 8. The states S for the data structure are then a product of individual STS states indexed by location, with all but finitely many locations required to be in state $\bot$. The set of tokens A for the product STS is just the set of locations, *i.e.,* there is one token per location (and hence per individual life story). The transition relation $\rightsquigarrow$ on the product STS lifts the one for individual life stories: $s \rightsquigarrow s' \triangleq \forall \ell.\ s(\ell) = s'(\ell) \lor s(\ell) \rightsquigarrow s'(\ell)$. If F_0 is the free-token function for an individual STS, we can then define the product STS as follows:

$$\theta \;\triangleq\; (S, A, \rightsquigarrow, \lambda s.\{\ell \mid F_0(s(\ell)) = \{\mathsf{Attempt}\}\})$$

The interpretation I for states of the product STS given in Figure 8 is fairly straightforward. The implementation and specification flag values must always match. There must exist a unique location ℓ_c ("$\exists! \ell_c$") in a "live" state of Const or Upd. This unique live location will be the one currently pointed to by c. In the Upd state, it also owns speculative spec resources according to the branch set B. Finally, Done nodes retain a finished spec, while Dead and Gone nodes are simply garbage $\mathbf{inj}_1\,(-)$ and $\mathbf{inj}_2\,(-)$ nodes, respectively.

To show the refinement $\mathsf{counter_I} \preceq^{\mathcal{E}} \mathsf{counter_S} : \tau$, where $\tau = (\mathbf{1} \to \mathbf{N} \times \mathbf{B} \to \mathbf{1} \times \mathbf{1} \to \mathbf{1})$, it suffices to show the following Hoare triple for every j, K:

$$\langle j \mapsto_{\mathrm{S}} K[\mathsf{counter_S}]\rangle\ \mathsf{counter_I}\ \left\langle z_{\mathrm{I}}.\ \exists z_{\mathrm{S}}.\ z_{\mathrm{I}} \preceq^{\mathcal{V}} z_{\mathrm{S}} : \tau \land j \mapsto_{\mathrm{S}} K[z_{\mathrm{S}}]\right\rangle$$

The execution of $\mathsf{counter_I}$ is short and simple: it allocates the hidden state of the data structure, and then immediately returns three procedures for manipulating that state. In the proof of the triple, after the hidden state is allocated, we construct an island to govern it and add the island to the world (a guarantee extension). The new island is described by the assertion $\exists \ell.\ (\theta, I, [\ell \mapsto \mathsf{Const}(0)], \emptyset)$, which says that it follows the conditional increment protocol (θ and I), is in some rely-future state of $[\ell \mapsto \mathsf{Const}(0)]$ (in which every location other than ℓ is unborn), and currently owns no tokens. Adding this island requires us to show that the initial values of the hidden state in the implementation and specification satisfy the invariant at this state, which they clearly do.

We must then show, in the context of this extended world, that each of the implementation procedures refines the corresponding specification procedure; we give the detailed proof for cinc, *i.e.,*

$$\langle j \mapsto_{\mathrm{S}} K[\mathsf{cinc_S}()] * (\theta, I, \emptyset, \emptyset)\rangle\ \mathsf{cinc_I}()\ \langle \mathsf{ret}.\ \mathsf{ret} = () \land j \mapsto_{\mathrm{S}} K[()]\rangle$$

In the precondition, we weaken our knowledge about the island to simply saying that it is in a rely-future state of $\emptyset$ (where *every* location maps to $\bot$), since this is all we need to know.

The locality of the local life stories is manifested in our ability to make isolated, abstract assertions about a particular location governed by the data structure. Because every location is in some rely-future state of $\bot$, we can focus on a location x of interest by asserting that the product STS is in a rely-future state of $[x \mapsto s_0]$, where $s_0 \in S_0$. For readability, we employ the following shorthand for making such local assertions about the island:

$$x \propto s_0 \;\triangleq\; (\theta, I, [x \mapsto s_0], \emptyset) \qquad x \propto_{\bullet} s_0 \;\triangleq\; (\theta, I, [x \mapsto s_0], \{x\})$$

Thus empowered, we can glean some additional insight about the algorithm: that the complete function satisfies the triple

$$\langle x \propto \mathsf{Upd}(n, j, K, \emptyset)\rangle\ \mathsf{complete}(x, n)\ \langle \mathsf{ret}.\ x \propto \mathsf{Done}(n, j, K)\rangle$$

In reading this triple, it is crucial to remember that assertions are closed under rely moves—so $x \propto \mathsf{Upd}(n, j, K, \emptyset)$ means that the location x *was once* a live, in-progress update. The interesting thing about the triple is that, regardless of the exact initial state of x, on exit we *know* that x is at least Done—and there's no going back.

The proof outline for complete at the top of Figure 9 states that, after reading the value of the flag, the location x is in an appropriately speculative state. To *prove* that fact, we must consider the rely-future states of $\mathsf{Upd}(n, j, K, \emptyset)$, and show that for each such state we can reach (via a guarantee move) a rely-future state of $\mathsf{Upd}(n, j, K, \{1\})$ or $\mathsf{Upd}(n, j, K, \{0\})$, depending on the value read. For example, if the initial state is s_0 and we read that the flag is true, we take a guarantee move to s_0' as follows:

If s_0 is	then s_0' is	If s_0 is	then s_0' is
$\mathsf{Upd}(d, \emptyset)$	$\mathsf{Upd}(d, \{1\})$	$\mathsf{Upd}(d, \{1\})$	$\mathsf{Upd}(d, \{1\})$
$\mathsf{Upd}(d, \{0\})$	$\mathsf{Upd}(d, \{0, 1\})$	$\mathsf{Upd}(d, \{0, 1\})$	$\mathsf{Upd}(d, \{0, 1\})$
$\mathsf{Done}(d)$	$\mathsf{Done}(d)$	Gone	Gone

If the initial state already included the needed speculation (or was Done or Gone), there is nothing to show; otherwise, changing the state requires speculative execution of the spec. We perform a similar case analysis at the CAS step, but there we start with the knowledge that the appropriate speculation has already been performed—which is exactly what we need if the CAS succeeds. If, on the other hand, the CAS fails, it *must* be the case that x is at least Done: if it were still in an Upd state, the CAS would have succeeded.

With complete out of the way, the proof of cinc is relatively easy; see the bottom of Figure 9.[8] When entering the procedure, all that is known is that the island exists, and that the specification is owned. The thread first examines c to see if the counter is quiescent, which is the interesting case. If the subsequent CAS succeeds in installing an active descriptor $\mathbf{inj}_2\ n$, that descriptor is the new live node (in state $\mathsf{Upd}(n, j, K, \emptyset)$)—and the thread, being responsible for this transition, gains ownership of the descriptor's token. The resulting assertion $y \propto_{\bullet} \mathsf{Upd}(n, j, K, \emptyset)$ is equivalent to

$$y \propto \mathsf{Upd}(n, j, K, \emptyset) * y \propto_{\bullet} \mathsf{Upd}(n, j, K, \emptyset)$$

which means that we can use $y \propto_{\bullet} \mathsf{Upd}(n, j, K, \emptyset)$ as a *frame* in an application of the frame rule to the triple for $\mathsf{complete}(y, n)$. This gives us the framed postcondition

$$y \propto \mathsf{Done}(n, j, K) * y \propto_{\bullet} \mathsf{Upd}(n, j, K, \emptyset)$$

which is equivalent to $y \propto_{\bullet} \mathsf{Done}(n, j, K)$. Since our thread still owns the token, we know the state is *exactly* $\mathsf{Done}(n, j, K)$, and in the next step (where we return the requisite unit value) we trade the token in return for our spec—which *some* thread has executed.

5. Discussion and related work

We have presented a model for a **high-level language** with concurrency that enables **direct refinement proofs** for sophisticated FCDs, via a notion of **local protocol** that encompasses the fundamental phenomena of **role-playing**, **cooperation**, and **nondeterminism**. In this section, we survey the most closely related work along each of these axes.

High-level language Birkedal *et al.* [5] recently developed the first logical-relations model for a *higher-order* concurrent language similar to the one we consider here. Their aim was to show the soundness of a sophisticated Lucassen-and-Gifford-style [27] type-and-effect system, and in particular to prove the soundness of a Parallelization Theorem for disjoint concurrency expressed by the effect system (when the Bernstein conditions are satisfied). The worlds used in the logical relation capture the all-or-nothing approach to interference implied by the type-and-effect system. As a result, the model has rather limited support for reasoning about FCDs: it can only prove correctness of algorithms that can withstand arbitrary interference.

We are unaware of any other proof methods that handle higher-order languages, shared-state concurrency, *and* local state.

Direct refinement proofs Herlihy and Wing's seminal notion of *linearizability* [21] has long been the gold standard of correctness for FCDs, but as Filipović *et al.* argue [14], what clients of an FCD *really* want is a contextual refinement property. Filipović *et al.* go on

[8] The steps labeled with $\therefore$ indicate uses of the rule of consequence.

to show that, under certain (strong) assumptions about a programming language, linearizability implies contextual refinement for that language. More recently, Gotsman and Yang generalized both linearizability and this result (the so-called *abstraction theorem*) to include potential ownership transfer of memory between FCDs and their clients [16]. While it is possible to compose this abstraction theorem with a proof of linearizability to prove refinement, there are several advantages to our approach of proving refinement directly. First of all, it allows us to treat refinement as an assertion in our logic, which means that we can *compose* proofs of refinement when reasoning about compound FCDs, and do so while working within a single logic. Second, it allows us to leverage recent work for reasoning about refinement and hidden state, *e.g.,* Dreyer *et al.*'s STS-based logical relations [9]. Third, it allows us to reason about FCDs that use higher-order features, *e.g.,* the universal FCD construction given in [20], which would otherwise require extending the definition of linearizability to the higher-order case. Finally, it allows us to seamlessly combine reasoning about fine-grained concurrency with other kinds of reasoning, *e.g.,* relational parametricity [32].

Turon and Wand developed the first logic for reasoning directly about contextual refinement for FCDs [36]. Their model is based on ideas from rely-guarantee and separation logic and was developed for a simple first-order language, using an extension of Brookes's trace-based denotational semantics [6]. While it is capable of proving refinement for simple FCDs, such as Treiber's stack, it does not easily scale to more sophisticated algorithms.

More recently, Liang *et al.* proposed RGSim [25], a compositional inter-language simulation relation based on rely-guarantee for verifying program transformations in a concurrent setting. Liang *et al.* also use their method to prove that some simple, but realistic, FCDs are simulated by their spec. While the original paper on RGSim did not relate simulation to refinement or linearizability, new (currently unpublished) work has done so [24].

Local protocols O'Hearn *et al.*'s work on *Linearizability with hindsight* [30] clearly articulates the need for local protocols in reasoning about FCDs, and demonstrates how a certain mixture of local and global constraints leads to insightful proofs about lock-free traversals. At the heart of the work is the remarkable *Hindsight Lemma*, which justifies conclusions about reachability in the past based on information in the present. Since O'Hearn *et al.* are focused on providing proofs for a particular class of algorithms, they do not formalize a general notion of protocol, but instead focus on a collection of invariants specific to the traversals they study. We have focused, in contrast, on giving a simple but general account of local protocols that suffices for *temporally-local* reasoning about a range of FCDs. It remains to be seen, however, whether our techniques yield a satisfying temporally-local correctness proof for the kinds of traversals O'Hearn *et al.* study, or whether (as O'Hearn *et al.* argue) these traversals are best understood non-locally.

The notion of protocol most closely related to ours is Dinsdale-Young *et al.*'s *Concurrent abstract predicates* (CAP) [7]. CAP extends separation logic with shared, hidden regions similar to our islands. These regions are governed by a set of *abstract predicates*, which can be used to make localized assertions about the state of the region. In addition, CAP provides a notion of named *actions* which characterize the possible changes to the region. Crucially, actions are treated as a kind of *resource* which can be gained, lost, or split up (in a fractional permissions style), and executing an action can result in a change to the available actions. It is incumbent upon users of the logic to show that their abstract predicates and actions cohere, by showing that every abstract predicate is "self-stable" (remains true after any available action is executed).

While CAP's notion of protocol is very expressive, it is also somewhat "low-level" compared to our STS-based protocols, which would require a somewhat unwieldy encoding to express in CAP. In addition, our protocols make a clear separation between *knowledge* bounding the state of the protocol (treated as a copyable assertion) and *rights* to change the state (treated as a linear resource: tokens), which are mixed in CAP. Another major difference is that CAP exposes the internal protocol of a data structure as part of the specification seen by a client—which means that the spec for a given FCD often depends on how the client is envisioned to use it. Additional specs (and additional correctness proofs) may be necessary for other clients. By contrast, we take a coarse-grained data structure as an all-purpose spec; if clients then want to use that data structure according to some sophisticated internal protocol, they are free to do so. Finally, our protocols support speculation and spec code as a resource, neither of which are supported in CAP.

Role-playing The classic treatment of role-playing in shared-state concurrency is Jones's *rely-guarantee* reasoning [23], in which threads *guarantee* to make only certain updates, so long as they can *rely* on their environment to make only certain (possibly different) updates. More recent work has combined rely-guarantee and separation logic (SAGL [13] and RGSep [38]), in some cases even supporting a frame rule over the rely and guarantee constraints themsevles (LRG [12]). This line of work culminated in Dodds *et al.*'s *deny-guarantee* reasoning [8]—the precursor to CAP—which was designed to facilitate a more dynamic form of rely-guarantee to account for non-well-bracketed thread lifetimes. In the deny-guarantee framework, actions are classified into those that both a thread and its environment can perform, those that neither can perform, and those that only one or the other can perform. The classification of an action is manifested in terms of two-dimensional fractional permissions (the dimensions being "deny" and "guarantee"), which can be split and combined dynamically. Our STSs express dynamic evolution of roles in an arguably more direct and visual way, through tokens.

Cooperation Vafeiadis's thesis [37] set a high-water mark in verification of the most sophisticated FCDs (such as CCAS [18, 15]). Building on his RGSep logic, Vafeiadis established an informal methodology for proving linearizability by employing several kinds of ghost state (including prophecy variables and "one-shot" resources, the latter representing linearization points). By cleverly storing and communicating this ghost state to another thread, one can perform thread-local verification and yet account for cooperation: the other thread "fires" the single shot of the one-shot ghost resource. While this account of cooperation seems intuitively reasonable, it lacks any formal metatheory justifying its use in linearizability or refinement proofs. Our computational resources generalize Vafeiadis's "one-shot" ghost state, since they can (and do) run computations for an arbitrary number of steps, and we have justified their use in refinement proofs—showing, in fact, that the technique of logical relations can be expressed in a "unary" (Hoare logic) style by using these computational resources.

Concurrently with our work, Liang and Feng have extended their RGSim framework to account for cooperation [24]. The new simulation method is parameterized by a "pending thread inference map" Θ, which plays a role somewhat akin to our worlds. For us, worlds impose a relation between the current protocol state, the current implementation heap, and the current, speculative spec resources. By contrast, Θ imposes a relation between the current implementation heap and the current spec thread pool. To recover something like our protocols, one instead introduces *ghost state* into the implementation heap, much as Vafeiadis does; as a result, Θ can be used to do thread-local reasoning about cooperative FCDs. However, there are several important differences from our approach. First, there is no notion of *composition* on thread inference maps, which take the perspective of the global implementation heap and global pool of spec threads. Thus thread inference maps do not work as resources that can be owned, split up, transferred and recombined. Second, the assertions that are used in pre- and post-conditions cannot talk directly about the thread inference map; they must control it indirectly, via ghost state. Third, the simulation approach does not support speculation or high-level language features like higher-order functions or polymorphism. Finally, it requires encoding protocols via traditional ghost state and rely/guarantee, rather than through standalone, visual protocols.

Groves and Colvin propose [17] a radically different approach for dealing with cooperation, based on Lipton's method of *reduction* [26]. Reduction, in a sense, "undoes" the effects of concurrency by showing that interleaved actions commute with one another—much like linearizability. Groves and Colvin are able to *derive* an elimination stack from its spec by a series of transformations, justifying each by considering possible interleavings and proving, very roughly, that the relevant actions commute. Elmas *et al.* also developed a method for proving linearizability using reduction and abstraction [11], and while they do not study cooperation explicitly, it is likely that their method can cope with it too.

Nondeterminism Forward simulation is well-known to be sensitive to differences in the timing of nondeterminism (also known as the "branching" structure of a transition system) [39]. On the other hand, forward simulation is appealingly *local*, since it considers only one step of a program at a time (as opposed to *e.g.*, trace semantics). To retain temporally-local reasoning but permit differences in nondeterminism (as in the late/early choice example), it suffices to use a combination of forward and *backward* simulation or, equivalently, history and *prophecy* variables [28, 1]. Lynch and Vaandrager showed that there are also *hybrids* of forward and backward simulations, which relate a *single* state in one system to a *set* of states in the other—much like our speculation. Our technique goes further, though, in combining this *temporally*-local form of reasoning with *thread*-local reasoning: hybrid simulations work at the level of complete systems, whereas our threadpool simulations can be composed into larger threadpool simulations. Composability allows us to combine thread-private uses of speculation with shared uses of speculation in protocols; moreover, it is crucial in showing soundness for contextual refinement.

References

[1] M. Abadi and L. Lamport. The existence of refinement mappings. *Theoretical Computer Science*, 82(2):253–284, 1991.

[2] A. Ahmed. Step-indexed syntactic logical relations for recursive and quantified types. In *ESOP*, 2006.

[3] A. Ahmed, D. Dreyer, and A. Rossberg. State-dependent representation independence. In *POPL*, 2009.

[4] L. Birkedal, B. Reus, J. Schwinghammer, K. Støvring, J. Thamsborg, and H. Yang. Step-indexed Kripke models over recursive worlds. In *POPL*, 2011.

[5] L. Birkedal, F. Sieczkowski, and J. Thamsborg. A concurrent logical relation. In *CSL*, Sept. 2012.

[6] S. Brookes. Full abstraction for a shared variable parallel language. *Information and Computation*, 127(2):145–163, 1996.

[7] T. Dinsdale-Young, M. Dodds, P. Gardner, M. Parkinson, and V. Vafeiadis. Concurrent abstract predicates. In *ECOOP*, June 2010.

[8] M. Dodds, X. Feng, M. Parkinson, and V. Vafeiadis. Deny-guarantee reasoning. In *ESOP*, 2009.

[9] D. Dreyer, G. Neis, and L. Birkedal. The impact of higher-order state and control effects on local relational reasoning. In *ICFP*, 2010.

[10] D. Dreyer, G. Neis, A. Rossberg, and L. Birkedal. A relational modal logic for higher-order stateful ADTs. In *POPL*, 2010.

[11] T. Elmas, S. Qadeer, A. Sezgin, O. Subasi, and S. Tasiran. Simplifying linearizability proofs with reduction and abstraction. In *TACAS*, 2010.

[12] X. Feng. Local rely-guarantee reasoning. In *POPL*, pages 315–327. ACM, 2009.

[13] X. Feng, R. Ferreira, and Z. Shao. On the relationship between concurrent separation logic and assume-guarantee reasoning. In *ESOP*, 2007.

[14] I. Filipović, P. O'Hearn, N. Rinetzky, and H. Yang. Abstraction for concurrent objects. *Theoretical Computer Science*, 411, 2010.

[15] K. Fraser and T. Harris. Concurrent programming without locks. *ACM Trans. Comput. Syst.*, 25(2), 2007.

[16] A. Gotsman and H. Yang. Linearizability with ownership transfer. In *CONCUR*, 2012.

[17] L. Groves and R. Colvin. Trace-based derivation of a scalable lock-free stack algorithm. *Form. Asp. Comput.*, 21(1-2):187–223, 2009.

[18] T. Harris, K. Fraser, and I. Pratt. A practical multi-word compare-and-swap operation. In *DISC*, 2002.

[19] D. Hendler, N. Shavit, and L. Yerushalmi. A scalable lock-free stack algorithm. In *SPAA*, 2004.

[20] M. Herlihy and N. Shavit. *The Art of Multiprocessor Programming*. Morgan Kaufmann, 2008.

[21] M. P. Herlihy and J. M. Wing. Linearizability: a correctness condition for concurrent objects. *TOPLAS*, 12(3):463–492, 1990.

[22] C. A. R. Hoare. Proof of correctness of data representations. *Acta Informatica*, 1(4):271–281, 1972.

[23] C. B. Jones. Tentative steps toward a development method for interfering programs. *TOPLAS*, 5(4):596–619, 1983.

[24] H. Liang and X. Feng. Modular verification of linearizability with non-fixed linearization points. Manuscript, July 2012.

[25] H. Liang, X. Feng, and M. Fu. A rely-guarantee-based simulation for verifying concurrent program transformations. In *POPL*, 2012.

[26] R. J. Lipton. Reduction: a method of proving properties of parallel programs. *Commun. ACM*, 18(12):717–721, 1975.

[27] J. Lucassen and D. Gifford. Polymorphic effect systems. In *POPL*, 1988.

[28] N. Lynch and F. Vaandrager. Forward and backward simulations I: untimed systems. *Inf. Comput.*, 121(2):214–233, 1995.

[29] M. M. Michael and M. L. Scott. Nonblocking algorithms and preemption-safe locking on multiprogrammed shared memory multiprocessors. *J. Parallel Distrib. Comput.*, 51(1):1–26, 1998.

[30] P. O'Hearn, N. Rinetzky, M. Vechev, E. Yahav, and G. Yorsh. Verifying linearizability with hindsight. In *PODC*, 2010.

[31] P. W. O'Hearn. Resources, concurrency, and local reasoning. *Theor. Comput. Sci.*, 375(1-3):271–307, 2007.

[32] J. C. Reynolds. Types, Abstraction and Parametric Polymorphism. In *Information Processing*, 1983.

[33] J. C. Reynolds. Separation logic: A logic for shared mutable data structures. In *LICS*, 2002.

[34] R. Treiber. Systems programming: coping with parallelism. Technical report, Almaden Research Center, 1986.

[35] A. Turon, J. Thamsborg, A. Ahmed, L. Birkedal, and D. Dreyer. Logical relations for fine-grained concurrency (Technical appendix), 2012. URL: `http://www.ccs.neu.edu/home/turon/relcon`.

[36] A. Turon and M. Wand. A separation logic for refining concurrent objects. In *POPL*, 2011.

[37] V. Vafeiadis. *Modular fine-grained concurrency verification*. PhD thesis, University of Cambridge, 2008.

[38] V. Vafeiadis and M. Parkinson. A marriage of rely/guarantee and separation logic. In *CONCUR*, 2007.

[39] R. J. van Glabbeek. The linear time - branching time spectrum. In *CONCUR*, 1990.

Linear Dependent Types for Differential Privacy

Marco Gaboardi[⋆‡] Andreas Haeberlen[⋆] Justin Hsu[⋆] Arjun Narayan[⋆] Benjamin C. Pierce[⋆]

[⋆]University of Pennsylvania [‡]Università di Bologna–INRIA EPI Focus

Abstract

Differential privacy offers a way to answer queries about sensitive information while providing strong, provable privacy guarantees, ensuring that the presence or absence of a single individual in the database has a negligible statistical effect on the query's result. Proving that a given query has this property involves establishing a bound on the query's *sensitivity*—how much its result can change when a single record is added or removed.

A variety of tools have been developed for certifying that a given query is differentially private. In one approach, Reed and Pierce [34] proposed a functional programming language, *Fuzz*, for writing differentially private queries. *Fuzz* uses linear types to track sensitivity and a probability monad to express randomized computation; it guarantees that any program with a certain type is differentially private. *Fuzz* can successfully verify many useful queries. However, it fails when the sensitivity analysis depends on values that are not known statically.

We present *DFuzz*, an extension of *Fuzz* with a combination of linear indexed types and lightweight dependent types. This combination allows a richer sensitivity analysis that is able to certify a larger class of queries as differentially private, including ones whose sensitivity depends on runtime information. As in *Fuzz*, the differential privacy guarantee follows directly from the soundness theorem of the type system. We demonstrate the enhanced expressivity of *DFuzz* by certifying differential privacy for a broad class of iterative algorithms that could not be typed previously.

Categories and Subject Descriptors D.3.2 [*Programming Languages*]: Language Classifications—Specialized application languages; F.3.3 [*Theory of computation*]: Studies of Program Constructs—Type structure

General Terms Design, Languages, Theory

Keywords differential privacy, type systems, linear logic, dependent types

1. Introduction

An enormous amount of data accumulates in databases every day—travel reservations, hospital records, location data, etc. This information could potentially be very valuable, e.g., for scientific and medical research, but much of it cannot be safely released due to privacy concerns. Moreover, aggregation and anonymization are not sufficient to safeguard privacy: recent experience with the Netflix prize [30], for example, has shown how easy it is to leak sensitive information accidentally, even when the data is carefully sanitized before it is released.

Differential privacy [4, 12, 13] is a promising approach to this problem: it offers strong statistical privacy guarantees for certain types of queries, even in worst-case scenarios. Intuitively, this is accomplished by a) admitting only queries whose result does not depend too much on the data of any single individual, and b) adding some random noise to the result of each query. Thus, if we pick any individual I and remove all of I's data from the database before answering a query, the probability that the result is any given value v remains almost the same. This limits the amount of information that can be learned about a single individual by observing the result of the query.

Many specific queries have been shown to be differentially private, including machine learning algorithms such as empirical risk minimization [5] and k-means, combinatorial optimization algorithms such as vertex cover and k-medians [18], and many others. But checking that a given query is differentially private can be both tedious and rather subtle. The key challenge is to prove an upper bound on the query's *sensitivity*, i.e., the maximum change in the query's output that can result from changing the data of a single individual. (Briefly, higher-sensitivity queries require more noise to maintain privacy.) Since most data analysts are not experts in differential privacy, they cannot benefit from its strong guarantees unless they have access to suitable tools.

The approach we focus on is to provide analysts with a *programming language for differentially private queries*: the analyst can formulate queries in this language and then submit them to a special compiler, which determines their "privacy cost" and rejects them if this cost exceeds a budget that has been specified by the analyst. This approach is attractive because differential privacy is compositional; for instance, the privacy cost of a sequence of differentially private computations is simply the sum of the individual costs. Thus, we can reason about large, complex queries by manually inspecting a few simple primitives and then suitably composing the analysis results of larger and larger subqueries. This is the basis of previous systems like *PINQ* [26], which provides a SQL-like language, *Airavat* [36], which implements a MapReduce framework, and *Fuzz* [20, 33, 34], a higher-order functional language.

The analysis in Fuzz is based on a type system [33, 34] that certifies queries as differentially private via two components: numeric annotations at the type level to describe the sensitivity of functions and a probability monad to represent probabilistic computations. *Fuzz* can certify many useful queries, but it fails for other important kinds of queries, including some fairly simple ones. For instance, iterative algorithms such as k-means can only be analyzed

POPL'13, January 23–25, 2013, Rome, Italy.

when the number of iterations is a constant, and there are other instances (such as a program that computes a cumulative distribution function for an arbitrary list of cutoffs) where even the *type* of the program cannot be expressed in *Fuzz*! *Fuzz* fails for these programs because their overall sensitivities are not simply a static composition of the sensitivities of subprograms; rather, they depend on some input data, such as the number of iterations or the list of numeric cutoffs. Numeric sensitivity annotations are not sufficient to express such *dependencies* between input data and sensitivity; however, as we show in this paper, these dependencies can be expressed with dependent types.

Dependent types enable static reasoning about information that will be available to a program only at runtime. But we must make a choice at the outset regarding the complexity of the dependencies we wish to support: richer dependencies would expand the range of queries that can be certified as differentially private, but systems with rich dependent types tend to require extensive program annotations, which would make *DFuzz* more difficult to use by non-experts. At the extreme end of this spectrum would be a system like CertiPriv [3], which can certify a broad range of differentially private queries but requires the programmer to supply most of the proof. To preserve our goal of usability by non-experts, we instead work near the other end, choosing a *lightweight* form of dependent types that requires few annotations but still yields a powerful analysis.

We introduce a language called *DFuzz*—Dependent *Fuzz*—that combines a rich form of type-level sensitivity annotations with lightweight dependent types. The sensitivity annotations we consider are arithmetic expressions over real numbers. Our dependent types are a simple form of *indexed types*, where indices describe the size of data types and provide the programmer with dependent pattern matching in the style of Dependent ML [38]. Sensitivity annotations and dependent types combine well, and the resulting language possesses strong metatheoretic properties. Most importantly, our type system (like that of *Fuzz*) natively captures the concept of differential privacy, since *DFuzz* enjoys an extension of the metric preservation property of [33, 34]. To demonstrate the capabilities of *DFuzz*, we show that it can certify several examples from the differential privacy literature quite naturally, including Iterative Database Construction [19], k-means [4], k-medians [18], and the Cumulative Distribution Function [27].

In summary, we offer the following contributions:

- *DFuzz*, a core calculus for differential privacy that combines the earlier sensitivity analysis of Reed and Pierce [34] with lightweight dependent types inspired by Dependent ML [38] (Section 3);
- the fundamental metatheory for *DFuzz*, including an adaptation of the usual basic metatheory—substitution, preservation and progress—as well as a generalization of the metric preservation theorem from [33, 34] (Sections 4 and 5); and
- four example programs that express algorithms from the differential privacy literature and can be successfully certified by *DFuzz* (Section 6).

We discuss related work in Section 7 and future research directions in Section 8.

2. Background and Overview

Differential privacy We begin by reviewing some basic definitions. Suppose the private data is collected in a database that contains rows of the same type, and each individual's data is in a single row. Let $\mathbf{db}$ be the type of such databases, and assume for the moment that we are interested in real-valued queries. Then the key definition of differential privacy (based on [13]) is:

2.1 Definition: A randomized function $f : \mathbf{db} \to \mathbb{R}$ is ϵ-*differentially private* if, for all possible sets of outputs $S \subseteq \mathbb{R}$ and for any two databases b, b' that differ in only one row,

$$\mathtt{Pr}[f(b) \in S] \leq e^{\epsilon} \cdot \mathtt{Pr}[f(b') \in S].$$

Intuitively, this means that the presence or absence of one individual's data has only a small effect on the distribution of f's (randomized) outputs. Here ϵ is a privacy parameter; the larger ϵ is, the more information about individuals is potentially revealed by the result. For small ϵ, the factor e^{ϵ} can be thought of as $1 + \epsilon$. We will often refer to ϵ as the *privacy cost* of running f.

We can extend the definition to data types other than $\mathbf{db}$ and $\mathbb{R}$ if we assign to each data type a *metric* that measures the distance between values. We write $\vdash v \sim_r v' : \tau$ to indicate that two values v and v' of type τ are at most r apart. Thus we obtain:

2.2 Definition: A randomized function $q : \tau \to \sigma$ is ϵ-differentially private if, for all sets S of closed values of type σ and for all $v, v' : \tau$ such that $\vdash v \sim_r v' : \tau$, we have:

$$Pr[q(v) \in S] \leq e^{\epsilon r} Pr[q(v') \in S]$$

To determine whether a given query has this property, the following definition is useful:

2.3 Definition: A function $f : \tau \to \sigma$ is *c-sensitive* for $c \in \mathbb{R}^{\geq 0}$ if, for all $v, v' : \tau$ with $\vdash v \sim_r v' : \tau$, we have $\vdash f(v) \sim_{c \cdot r} f(v') : \sigma$.

In other words, a c-sensitive function magnifies changes in its inputs by at most a factor of c. When a function q is not c-sensitive for any $c \in \mathbb{R}^{\geq 0}$ in the sense of the above definition, we will refer to it as ∞-sensitive. Real-valued functions with limited sensitivity can be converted into ϵ-differentially private queries using the *Laplace mechanism* (introduced in [13]). Here, we write $\mathcal{L}_{\beta}$ to denote the Laplace distribution with scaling parameter β.

2.4 Proposition: Let $f : \mathbf{db} \to \mathbb{R}$ be a c-sensitive function, and let $q : \mathbf{db} \to \mathbb{R}$ be the randomized function $q = \lambda b.\ f(b) + N$, where N is a random variable distributed according to $\mathcal{L}_{c/\epsilon}$. Then q is ϵ-differentially private.

In other words, the Laplace mechanism converts f into a randomized function q by adding noise from the Laplace distribution. Note that the parameter of the distribution—the 'magnitude' of the noise—depends on both c and ϵ: the stronger the privacy requirement (smaller ϵ) and the higher the sensitivity of f (larger c), the more noise must be added to f's result to preserve privacy.

Linear types for differential privacy The key idea behind static type systems for differential privacy is to provide a compositional analysis that tracks both the privacy cost ϵ and the sensitivity c of a function. For context, we sketch the analysis in *Fuzz* [33, 34], on which our work is based.

Fuzz has a *linear type system*: functions can have types of the form $!_r\sigma \multimap \tau$, where the *modality* $!_r$ is annotated with a numeric upper bound r on the function's sensitivity. For instance, the term $\lambda x.(2 \cdot x)$ can be given the type $!_2\mathbb{R} \multimap \mathbb{R}$ to express the fact that $f(x) = 2 \cdot x$ is 2-sensitive in its argument x.[1] *Fuzz* checks these types with standard typing judgments of the form $\Gamma \vdash e : \sigma$, where the type environment Γ additionally contains hypotheses about sensitivity. For instance, a typing judgment $x :\, !_c\sigma \vdash e : \tau$ means that e can be given type τ if e is at most c-sensitive in the free variable x.

[1] In [33, 34] the symbol ! appears both in types (as here) and in terms (to help guide typechecking algorithms). Here, for simplicity, we elide uses in terms.

As an illustration, consider the slightly more complex program $(\lambda z.3 \cdot z + 8)(5 \cdot x)$ It is easy to see that $x : !_5\mathbb{R} \vdash 5 \cdot x : \mathbb{R}$ and $\vdash \lambda z.3 \cdot z + 8 : !_3\mathbb{R} \multimap \mathbb{R}$, and *Fuzz* thus uses the typing rule

$$\frac{\Gamma \vdash e : !_r\tau \multimap \sigma \quad \Delta \vdash g : \tau}{\Gamma + r\Delta \vdash e\, g : \sigma}$$

to infer $x : !_{15}\mathbb{R} \vdash (\lambda z.3 \cdot z + 8)(5 \cdot x) : \mathbb{R}$. This reflects the fact that $3 \cdot (5 \cdot x) + 8 = 15 \cdot x + 8$ is 15-sensitive in x. To turn this (deterministic) program into a (randomized) differentially private one, *Fuzz* introduces a *probability monad* $\bigcirc$ and assigns monadic types to randomized computations. Accordingly, the concept of sensitivity is generalized so that the privacy cost of a differentially private function is interpreted as its sensitivity. Specifically, the type system guarantees that any program that can be given a type $!_\epsilon\mathbf{db} \multimap \bigcirc\mathbb{R}$ is differentially private, with privacy cost ϵ. [2]

The full *Fuzz* type system is described in [33, 34], which also show how several practical programs can be successfully type-checked; one of these is k-means clustering, a machine learning algorithm that takes a list of points and computes centers around which the points cluster. However, as mentioned above, a key limitation of *Fuzz* is that its sensitivity annotations are purely numeric. In the case of k-means clustering, this is a major inconvenience: the sensitivity depends on the number of iterations of the algorithm, but *Fuzz* types cannot express the fact that a function's sensitivity in one parameter may depend on the value of another—the only way out is to hard-code the number of iterations. For instance, in *Fuzz* a k-means program performing two iterations can be typed as:

$$\mathit{2iter\text{-}k\text{-}means} : !_\infty\mathbf{L}(\mathbb{R}\otimes\mathbb{R}) \multimap !_{6\epsilon}\mathbf{Bag}(\mathbb{R}\otimes\mathbb{R}) \multimap \bigcirc(\mathbf{L}(\mathbb{R}\otimes\mathbb{R}))$$

This type says that *2iter-k-means* is a program that, when provided with an initial list of centers (of type $\mathbf{L}(\mathbb{R} \otimes \mathbb{R})$), produces a 6ϵ-differentially private algorithm that maps a dataset to a new list of centers. A k-means program that performs a different number of iterations would have a different type. Worse, in Section 6, we will see several examples of practical algorithms whose *types* cannot be expressed in *Fuzz*, e.g., the IDC algorithm [19], in which the desired sensitivity is itself a parameter. This means that we cannot even add such operations to *Fuzz* as primitives.

In *DFuzz*, we overcome this limitation by adding dependent types. In particular, we add a lightweight form of dependent types that allow us to give the following type to a general algorithm for k-means:

$$\begin{aligned} \mathit{k\text{-}means} : \forall i, k.(&!_\infty\mathbf{N}[i] \multimap !_\infty\mathbf{L}(\mathbb{R}\otimes\mathbb{R})[k] \\ &\multimap !_{3i\epsilon}\mathbf{Bag}(\mathbb{R}\otimes\mathbb{R}) \multimap \bigcirc(\mathbf{L}(\mathbb{R}\otimes\mathbb{R})[k]))\end{aligned}$$

This type gives more precise information about the behavior of *k-means*: it says that *k-means* is a program that, when provided with a natural number i specifying the number of iterations (the sensitivity annotation is ∞ since this parameter does not need to be kept private) and a list of k centers, produces a $3i\epsilon$-differentially private algorithm that maps the dataset to a list of k centers. In the next section, we describe *DFuzz*'s dependent types in more detail.

3. DFuzz

The main novelty of *DFuzz* is the way it combines a lightweight form of dependent types, *à la* Dependent ML [38], with a sensitivity analysis inspired by the one in [33, 34]. This combination requires several ingredients, which are formally defined in Figure 1 (type grammar), Figure 2 (program syntax), Figure 3 (kinding rules), Figure 4 (subtyping rules), Figures 5, 6, 7 (typing rules), and Figure 8 (selected operational semantics rules). We describe each of these components below, omitting some secondary details for brevity. (In particular, we elide some linear data types like $\otimes$, $\&$, and $\oplus$. A full description is available in [14].)

[2] In [34], a *fixed* value of ϵ was baked into the metric on distributions. In contrast, we use the convention from [33], where the privacy parameter ϵ is not fixed, and is made explicit in the type annotation.

κ	::=	$\iota \mid \upsilon$	(kinds)
Z	::=	$\mathbf{N}[S] \mid \mathbf{L}(\tau)[S] \mid \mathbb{R}[R] \mid \mathcal{P}[S]$	(precise types)
α	::=	$\mathbb{R} \mid \mathtt{db}$	(basic types)
a	::=	$\forall i : \kappa.\tau \mid \exists i : \kappa.\tau$	(quantified types)
τ	::=	$a \mid Z \mid \alpha \mid A \multimap \tau \mid \bigcirc\tau$	(types)
A	::=	$!_R\tau$	(modal types)
S	::=	$i \mid 0 \mid S+1$	(size terms)
R	::=	$k \mid r \mid S \mid R+R \mid R\cdot R \mid \infty$	(sensitivity terms)
Φ	::=	$\emptyset \mid S=0 \mid S=i+1 \mid \Phi\wedge\Phi$	(assumptions)
$\mathcal{C}$	::=	$S=S \mid R\leq R$	(constraints)
ϕ	::=	$\emptyset \mid \phi, i:\kappa$	(kind environments)
Γ	::=	$\emptyset \mid \Gamma, x:A$	(type environments)

Figure 1. *DFuzz* Types

$$\begin{array}{rcll}
p & ::= & (r_1, \ldots, r_n) & \text{(probabilities)} \\
e, g & ::= & x \mid \lambda x.e \mid e\,e \mid \mathtt{f} \mid \mathbf{fix}\, x.e & \text{(expressions)} \\
& & \mid 0 \mid \mathbf{s}\, e \mid \mathtt{nil} \mid \mathtt{cons}[S](e, e) & \\
& & \mid \mathbf{case_N}\, e\, \mathbf{of}\, 0 \to e \mid x[i] + 1 \to e & \\
& & \mid \mathbf{case_L}\, e\, \mathbf{of}\, \mathtt{nil} \to e \mid \mathtt{cons}[i](y, x) \to e & \\
& & \mid \Lambda i.e \mid e[I] \mid \mathbf{pack}(e, I)\, \mathbf{as}\, \exists i : \kappa.\sigma & \\
& & \mid \mathbf{unpack}\, e\, \mathbf{as}\, (x, i)\, \mathbf{in}\, e & \\
& & \mid p \mid \mathbf{return}\, e \mid \{e, (e_1, \ldots, e_n)\} & \\
& & \mid \mathbf{let}\, \bigcirc x = e\, \mathbf{in}\, e & \\
v & ::= & \lambda x.e \mid \mathtt{f} \mid \mathbf{fix}\, x.e \mid () & \text{(values)} \\
& & \mid 0 \mid \mathbf{s}\, v \mid \mathtt{nil} \mid \mathtt{cons}[S](v, v) & \\
& & \mid \Lambda i.e \mid \mathbf{pack}(v, I)\, \mathbf{as}\, \exists i : \kappa.\sigma & \\
& & \mid p \mid \mathbf{return}\, v \mid \{v, (e_1, \ldots, e_n)\} & \\
s & ::= & \mathbf{do}\, e \mid \{p, (s_1, \ldots, s_n)\} & \text{(states)} \\
f & ::= & \mathbf{do}\,\mathbf{return}\, v \mid \{p, (f_1, \ldots, f_n)\} & \text{(final states)}
\end{array}$$

Figure 2. *DFuzz* Syntax

Sizes and sensitivities The special feature of *DFuzz* types (Figure 1) is that they can contain *size* or *sensitivity* information. This information is described by means of terms in a small language at the type level. A *size term*, written S, is a term that conforms to the grammar

$$S ::= i \mid 0 \mid S+1$$

where i is a size variable. Size terms are simple expressions over natural numbers; they are used to describe the size of data types. A *sensitivity term*, denoted R, is a term that conforms to the grammar

$$R ::= k \mid r \mid S \mid R+R \mid R\cdot R \mid \infty$$

where k is a sensitivity variable and r is a non-negative real constant, i.e., $r \in \mathbb{R}^{\geq 0}$. Sensitivity terms are simple expressions that consist of positive real numbers and the symbol ∞; they are used to describe program sensitivity. An annotation of ∞ means that

$$\frac{}{\phi \vdash 0 : \iota}\ (k.0) \qquad \frac{}{\phi \vdash \infty : \upsilon}\ (k.\infty) \qquad \frac{\phi(i) = \kappa}{\phi \vdash i : \kappa}\ (k.Ax) \qquad \frac{r \in \mathbb{R}^{\geq 0}}{\phi \vdash r : \upsilon}\ (k.\mathbb{R}) \qquad \frac{\phi \vdash S : \iota}{\phi \vdash S + 1 : \iota}\ (k.+1)$$

$$\frac{\phi \vdash R_1 : \upsilon \quad \phi \vdash R_2 : \upsilon}{\phi \vdash R_1 + R_2 : \upsilon}\ (k.+) \qquad \frac{\phi \vdash R_1 : \upsilon \quad \phi \vdash R_2 : \upsilon}{\phi \vdash R_1 \cdot R_2 : \upsilon}\ (k.\cdot) \qquad \frac{\phi \vdash S : \iota}{\phi \vdash S : \upsilon}\ (k.<:)$$

Figure 3. Kinding rules

$$\frac{}{\phi; \Phi \models \sigma \sqsubseteq \sigma}\ (st.R) \qquad \frac{\phi; \Phi \models \sigma_1 \sqsubseteq \sigma_2 \quad \phi; \Phi \models \sigma_2 \sqsubseteq \sigma_3}{\phi; \Phi \models \sigma_1 \sqsubseteq \sigma_3}\ (st.T) \qquad \frac{\phi; \Phi \models \sigma_3 \sqsubseteq \sigma_1 \quad \phi; \Phi \models \sigma_2 \sqsubseteq \sigma_4}{\phi; \Phi \models \sigma_1 \multimap \sigma_2 \sqsubseteq \sigma_3 \multimap \sigma_4}\ (st.\multimap)$$

$$\frac{\phi, i : \kappa; \Phi \models \sigma_1 \sqsubseteq \sigma_2 \quad i \notin \mathrm{FSV}(\Phi)}{\phi; \Phi \models \forall i : \kappa.\sigma_1 \sqsubseteq \forall i : \kappa.\sigma_2}\ (st.\forall) \qquad \frac{\phi; \Phi \models R_2 \leq R_1 \quad \phi; \Phi \models \sigma_1 \sqsubseteq \sigma_2}{\phi; \Phi \models !_{R_1}\sigma_1 \sqsubseteq !_{R_2}\sigma_2}\ (st.!)$$

$$\frac{\phi, i : \kappa; \Phi \models \sigma_1 \sqsubseteq \sigma_2 \quad i \notin \mathrm{FSV}(\Phi)}{\phi; \Phi \models \exists i : \kappa.\sigma_1 \sqsubseteq \exists i : \kappa.\sigma_2}\ (st.\exists) \qquad \frac{\phi; \Phi \models S = S'}{\phi; \Phi \models \mathbf{N}[S] \sqsubseteq \mathbf{N}[S']}\ (st.\mathbf{N}) \qquad \frac{\phi; \Phi \models S = S' \quad \phi; \Phi \models \sigma \sqsubseteq \tau}{\phi; \Phi \models \mathbf{L}(\sigma)[S] \sqsubseteq \mathbf{L}(\tau)[S']}\ (st.\mathbf{L}(\sigma))$$

Figure 4. Subtyping rules

$$\frac{}{\phi; \Phi; \Gamma, x : !_1\sigma \vdash x : \sigma}\ (Ax) \qquad \frac{\phi; \Phi; \Gamma \vdash e : \sigma \quad \phi; \Phi \models \sigma \sqsubseteq \tau}{\phi; \Phi; \Gamma \vdash e : \tau}\ (\sqsubseteq.R) \qquad \frac{\phi; \Phi; \Gamma \vdash e : \sigma \quad \phi; \Phi \models \Delta \sqsubseteq \Gamma}{\phi; \Phi; \Delta \vdash e : \sigma}\ (\sqsubseteq.L)$$

$$\frac{\phi; \Phi; \Gamma, x : !_\infty\sigma \vdash e : \sigma}{\phi; \Phi; \infty \cdot \Gamma \vdash \mathbf{fix}\ x.e : \sigma}\ (\mathit{fix}) \qquad \frac{\phi; \Phi; \Gamma, x : !_R\sigma \vdash e : \tau}{\phi; \Phi; \Gamma \vdash \lambda x.e : !_R\sigma \multimap \tau}\ (\multimap I) \qquad \frac{\phi; \Phi; \Gamma \vdash e : !_R\sigma \multimap \tau \quad \phi; \Phi; \Delta \vdash g : \sigma}{\phi; \Phi; \Gamma + R \cdot \Delta \vdash e\ g : \tau}\ (\multimap E)$$

Figure 5. Core Typing Rules

$$\frac{\phi; \Phi; \Gamma \vdash e : \mathbf{N}[S]}{\phi; \Phi; \Gamma \vdash \mathbf{s}\, e : \mathbf{N}[S+1]}\ (\mathbf{s}) \qquad \frac{}{\phi; \Phi; \Gamma \vdash \mathtt{nil} : \mathbf{L}(\sigma)[0]}\ (n) \qquad \frac{\phi; \Phi; \Gamma \vdash e : \sigma \quad \phi; \Phi; \Delta \vdash g : \mathbf{L}(\sigma)[S]}{\phi; \Phi; \Gamma + \Delta \vdash \mathtt{cons}[S](e, g) : \mathbf{L}(\sigma)[S+1]}\ (c)$$

$$\frac{}{\phi; \Phi; \Gamma \vdash 0 : \mathbf{N}[0]}\ (0) \qquad \frac{\phi; \Phi; \Gamma \vdash e : \mathbf{N}[S] \quad \phi; \Phi \wedge S = 0; \Delta \vdash g_1 : \sigma \quad \phi, i : \iota; \Phi \wedge S = i + 1; \Delta, x : !_R\mathbf{N}[i] \vdash g_2 : \sigma}{\phi; \Phi; \Delta + R \cdot \Gamma \vdash \mathbf{case}_{\mathbf{N}}\ e\ \mathbf{of}\ 0 \to g_1 \mid x[i] + 1 \to g_2 : \sigma}\ (\mathbf{case})_{\mathbf{N}}$$

$$\frac{\phi; \Phi; \Gamma \vdash e : \mathbf{L}(\tau)[S] \quad \phi; \Phi \wedge S = 0; \Delta \vdash g_1 : \sigma \quad \phi, i : \iota; \Phi \wedge S = i + 1; \Delta, x : !_R\mathbf{L}(\tau)[i], y : !_R\tau \vdash g_2 : \sigma}{\phi; \Phi; \Delta + R \cdot \Gamma \vdash \mathbf{case}_{\mathbf{L}}\ e\ \mathbf{of}\ \mathtt{nil} \to g_1 \mid \mathtt{cons}(y, x[i]) \to g_2 : \sigma}\ (\mathbf{case})_{\mathbf{L}(\tau)}$$

$$\frac{\phi, i : \kappa; \Phi; \Gamma \vdash e : \tau \quad i \notin \mathrm{FSV}(\Phi; \Gamma)}{\phi; \Phi; \Gamma \vdash \Lambda i.e : \forall i : \kappa.\tau}\ (\forall I) \qquad \frac{\phi; \Phi; \Gamma \vdash e : \tau\{I/i\} \quad \phi \vdash I : \kappa}{\phi; \Phi; \Gamma \vdash \mathbf{pack}(e, I)\ \mathbf{as}\ \exists i : \kappa.\tau : \exists i : \kappa.\tau}\ (\exists I)$$

$$\frac{\phi; \Phi; \Gamma \vdash e : \forall i : \kappa.\tau \quad \phi \vdash I : \kappa}{\phi; \Phi; \Gamma \vdash e[I] : \tau\{I/i\}}\ (\forall E) \qquad \frac{\phi; \Phi; \Gamma \vdash e : \exists i : \kappa.\tau \quad \phi, i : \kappa; \Phi; \Delta, x : !_R\tau \vdash g : \sigma \quad i \notin \mathrm{FSV}(\Phi; \Delta; \sigma; R)}{\phi; \Phi; \Delta + R \cdot \Gamma \vdash \mathbf{unpack}\ e\ \mathbf{as}\ (x, i)\ \mathbf{in}\ g : \sigma}\ (\exists E)$$

$$\frac{\phi; \Phi\ \text{imply}\ f\ R\text{-sensitive}\ \sigma \to \tau}{\phi; \Phi; \Gamma \vdash \mathtt{f} : !_R\sigma \multimap \tau}\ (\mathit{Ext})$$

Figure 6. Data Types and Polymorphism Typing Rules

$$\frac{\phi; \Phi; \Gamma \vdash e : \sigma}{\phi; \Phi; \infty\Gamma \vdash \mathbf{return}\ e : \bigcirc\sigma}\ (\bigcirc I) \qquad \frac{\phi; \Phi; \Gamma \vdash e : \bigcirc\sigma \quad \phi; \Phi; \Delta, x : !_\infty\sigma \vdash g : \bigcirc\tau}{\phi; \Phi; \Gamma + \Delta \vdash \mathbf{let}\ \bigcirc x = e\ \mathbf{in}\ g : \bigcirc\tau}\ (\bigcirc E) \qquad \frac{}{\phi; \Phi; \Gamma \vdash (r_1, \ldots, r_n) : \mathcal{P}[n]}\ (\mathcal{P})$$

$$\frac{\phi; \Phi; \Gamma \vdash e : \mathcal{P}[n] \quad \phi; \Phi; \Delta \vdash e_i : \bigcirc\sigma \quad (\forall i)}{\phi; \Phi; \Gamma + \Delta \vdash \{e, (e_1, \ldots, e_n)\} : \bigcirc\sigma}\ (\{e\}) \qquad \frac{\phi; \Phi; \Gamma \vdash p : \mathcal{P}[n] \quad \phi; \Phi; \Delta \vdash s_i : \sigma \quad (\forall i)}{\phi; \Phi; \Gamma + \Delta \vdash \{p, (s_1, \ldots, s_n)\} : \sigma}\ (\{s\}) \qquad \frac{\phi; \Phi; \Gamma \vdash e : \bigcirc\sigma}{\phi; \Phi; \Gamma \vdash \mathbf{do}\ e : \sigma}\ (\mathbf{do})$$

Figure 7. Probability Layer Typing Rules

there is no guaranteed bound on the sensitivity. The binary operators $+$ and $\cdot$ are the symbolic counterparts on sensitivities of sum and product on values. Their precise meaning is described below. We will use the metavariable I to range over sizes and sensitivities.

Any size term is also a sensitivity term. This is important for expressing *dependencies* between sizes (for example, number of iterations) and sensitivities (for example, privacy cost). To ensure the correct behavior of size and sensitivity terms, and to prevent undesired substitutions, we consider size and sensitivity terms to be typed as well; to avoid confusion, we refer to the types for size and sensitivity terms as *kinds*. *DFuzz* uses two kinds: ι for size annotations and υ for sensitivity annotations. Kinds are assigned to terms via *kind judgments* of the form

$$\phi \vdash I : \kappa$$

where ϕ is a *kind environment*, i.e., a set of kind assignments to size and sensitivity variables. The rules for deriving the judgment $\phi \vdash I : \kappa$ are presented in Figure 3. Notice that we have a *subkind* relation on terms that is induced by the rule $(k.{<:})$. This relation allows us to consider size terms as sensitivity terms. For notational convenience, we will sometime write sizes and sensitivities terms without making explicit their kind.

We can interpret size terms over the domain $\mathbb{N}$ of natural numbers and sensitivity terms over the domain $\mathbb{R}^{\geq 0} \cup \{\infty\}$ of non-negative extended real numbers. To interpret expressions with free variables we need, as usual, a notion of *assignment*—that is, a mapping ρ from size variables to elements of $\mathbb{N}$ and from sensitivity variables to elements of $\mathbb{R}^{\geq 0} \cup \{\infty\}$. We write $\mathrm{dom}(\rho)$ for the domain of ρ; this is a set of variable-kind mappings of the shape $i : \kappa$ where each variable i appears at most once.

Given a term $\phi \vdash I : \kappa$ and an assignment ρ such that $\phi \subseteq \mathrm{dom}(\rho)$, we inductively define the interpretation $[\![I]\!]_\rho$:

- $[\![0]\!]_\rho = 0$
- $[\![i]\!]_\rho = \rho(i)$
- $[\![S+1]\!]_\rho = [\![S]\!]_\rho + 1$
- $[\![r]\!]_\rho = r$
- $[\![R_1 + R_2]\!]_\rho = [\![R_1]\!]_\rho \mathbin{\hat{+}} [\![R_2]\!]_\rho$
- $[\![R_1 \cdot R_2]\!]_\rho = [\![R_1]\!]_\rho \mathbin{\hat{\cdot}} [\![R_2]\!]_\rho$
- $[\![\infty]\!]_\rho = \infty$

where $\hat{+}$ and $\hat{\cdot}$ are the usual sum and product extended to ∞:

$$\begin{aligned} &\infty \mathbin{\hat{+}} r = r \mathbin{\hat{+}} \infty = \infty && \text{for every } r \in \mathbb{R}^{\geq 0} \cup \{\infty\}, \\ &\infty \mathbin{\hat{\cdot}} r = r \mathbin{\hat{\cdot}} \infty = \infty && \text{for every } r \neq 0, \text{ and} \\ &\infty \mathbin{\hat{\cdot}} 0 = 0 \mathbin{\hat{\cdot}} \infty = 0 \end{aligned}$$

(Note that this definition implicitly coerces size terms—natural numbers—into real numbers as needed.) The well-definedness of the interpretation is ensured by the following lemma:

3.1 Lemma: Let $\phi \vdash I : \kappa$ and $\phi \subseteq \mathrm{dom}(\rho)$. Then:

- If $\kappa = \iota$, then $[\![I]\!]_\rho \in \mathbb{N}$.
- If $\kappa = \upsilon$, then $[\![I]\!]_\rho \in \mathbb{R}^{\geq 0} \cup \{\infty\}$.

Proof: By induction on the derivation proving $\phi \vdash S : \kappa$. □

Data types and dependent pattern matching Our syntax of types offers just two representative algebraic data types: natural numbers $\mathbf{N}[S]$ and lists $\mathbf{L}(\sigma)[S]$ with elements of type σ (see Figure 1). We could have gone further and included general algebraic datatype declarations and pattern matching, but this would add to the complexity of the notation without (we believe) raising new conceptual issues; we leave this generalization to future work.

Intuitively, the size of a natural number corresponds to its value (we consider a unary encoding of the natural numbers, and we assume the natural number 0 to be of size 0), and the size of a list corresponds to the number of elements in it (we assume `nil` to be of size 0). Types like $\mathbf{N}[S]$ and $\mathbf{L}(\sigma)[S]$ are inhabited only by terms whose evaluation produces a value of size S (if it terminates). The approach is reminiscent of Hayashi's singleton types [21].

To illustrate why size terms are helpful for expressiveness, let us consider the list data type in more detail. Values of the list type are built through the constructors `nil` and $\mathtt{cons}[S](e, g)$ (see Figure 2), where `cons` carries the size S of the expression g as additional information. This information is used to support a simple form of *dependent pattern matching*: the $\mathbf{case_L}$ destructor can, in addition to the usual term-level pattern matching, also perform type-level pattern matching. This is described by the following reduction rule (see Figure 8)

$$\mathbf{case_L}\ \mathtt{cons}[S](e_1, e_2)\ \mathbf{of}\ \mathtt{nil} \to g_1 \mid \mathtt{cons}[i](y, x) \to g_2 \\ \mapsto g_2\{e_1/y\}\{e_2/x\}\{S/i\}$$

in which the size S is propagated to the term g_2. In a similar way, in the reduction rule (Op-Case$_\mathbf{s}$) in Figure 8 for dependent pattern matching on $\mathbf{N}[S]$, the information n is propagated to the term g_2.

The data type elimination rules in Figure 6 are crucial to making this technique work. For instance, the elimination rule for the list data type

$$\frac{\phi; \Phi; \Gamma \vdash e : \mathbf{L}(\tau)[S] \qquad \phi; \Phi \wedge S = 0; \Delta \vdash g_1 : \sigma \\ \phi, i : \iota; \Phi \wedge S = i+1; \Delta, x : !_R \mathbf{L}(\tau)[i], y : !_R \tau \vdash g_2 : \sigma}{\phi; \Phi; \Delta + R \cdot \Gamma \vdash \mathbf{case_L}\ e\ \mathbf{of}\ \mathtt{nil} \to g_1 \mid \mathtt{cons}[i](y, x) \to g_2 : \sigma}$$

adds assumptions (explained in detail below) to the contexts used to typecheck the two branches of the **case** construct, reflecting information gleaned by the **case** about the size S of the test value e. In the first branch, it is assumed that $S = 0$; this extra piece of information enables us to remember, at the typing judgment level, that e has been matched to `nil`. Conversely, in the second branch, it is assumed that $S = i + 1$, giving us a name i for the size of the tail of the list e, which appears in the type assumed for the pattern variable x. A similar mechanism is used in the elimination rule for the $\mathbf{N}[S]$ data type.

Assumptions and constraints More formally, a judgment

$$\phi; \Phi; \Gamma \vdash e : \sigma$$

contains, besides the usual environment Γ for term variables and the kind environment ϕ, an extra parameter Φ that records the assumptions under which the typing is obtained. Intuitively, the expression e can be assigned the type σ for any value of its free size variables satisfying Φ. Since assumptions Φ record the size constraints generated by the pattern matching rules, we consider assumptions that conform to the following grammar:

$$\Phi ::= \emptyset \mid S = 0 \mid S = i + 1 \mid \Phi \wedge \Phi$$

An assumption Φ is well defined when it is associated with a kind environment ϕ that determines the kinds of the free size variables in Φ. We write $\phi \vdash \Phi$ in this case. Given an assumption $\phi \vdash \Phi$ and an assignment ρ such that $\phi \subseteq \mathrm{dom}(\rho)$, the interpretation $[\![\Phi]\!]_\rho$ is defined inductively as follows:

- $[\![\emptyset]\!]_\rho = \mathbf{true}$
- $[\![S = 0]\!]_\rho = ([\![S]\!]_\rho \mathrel{\hat{=}} 0)$
- $[\![S = i + 1]\!]_\rho = ([\![S]\!]_\rho \mathrel{\hat{=}} [\![i]\!]_\rho \mathbin{\hat{+}} 1)$
- $[\![\Phi_1 \wedge \Phi_2]\!]_\rho = [\![\Phi_1]\!]_\rho \wedge [\![\Phi_2]\!]_\rho$

where $\hat{=}$ is equality on natural numbers. The use of assumptions is crucial for the subtyping relation (Figure 4). Indeed, subtyping judgments involve judgments of the shape

$$\phi; \Phi \models \mathcal{C}$$

where $\mathcal{C}$ is a *constraint* of the form $R \leq R'$ or $S = S'$. The meaning of a constraint $\mathcal{C}$ also follows directly from the interpretation of the size and sensitivity terms it contains. Given an assignment ρ for the size and sensitivity variables appearing in $\mathcal{C}$, the interpretation $[\![\mathcal{C}]\!]_\rho$ is defined inductively as

- $[\![R \leq R']\!]_\rho = ([\![R]\!]_\rho \hat{\leq} [\![R']\!]_\rho)$
- $[\![S = S']\!]_\rho = ([\![S]\!]_\rho \hat{=} [\![S']\!]_\rho)$

where $\hat{\leq}$ is the expected extension of $\leq$ to cover ∞. The judgment $\phi; \Phi \models \mathcal{C}$ asserts that the constraint $\mathcal{C}$ is a logical consequences of the assumption Φ, i.e. for every ρ such that $[\![\Phi]\!]_\rho = \mathbf{true}$ we have $[\![\mathcal{C}]\!]_\rho = \mathbf{true}$. Analogously, we will also use the notation $\phi; \Phi \models \Psi$ to denote the fact that the assumption Ψ is a logical consequence of the assumption Φ. We will see how these judgments are used later when we present the subtyping rules in detail.

Generalized sensitivities and the scaling modality Sensitivity terms are the key ingredients in the sensitivity analysis. They appear as decorations of the *scaling modality* $!_R$. The scaling modality is used to define types with the shape $!_R\sigma$, which are used in turn in function types and in term environments. Suppose that a given expression e can be assigned the function type $!_R\sigma \multimap \tau$:

$$\phi; \Phi; \Gamma \vdash e \;:\; !_R\sigma \multimap \tau$$

Then we know that e is a function that maps elements of type σ to elements of type τ as long as Φ is satisfied, and that in this case R is an upper bound on the function's sensitivity.

Two points merit further explanation. First, a static analysis cannot always describe the exact sensitivity of a program; we are always dealing with conservative upper bounds. Second, we say that R "describes" this upper bound because it is not necessarily a number: it can depend on size or sensitivity variables from ϕ, which can themselves be involved in assumptions from Φ. This dependency is central to the expressivity of *DFuzz*.

Modal types also appear in type environments. A typing judgment of the form

$$\phi; \Phi; x_1 : !_{R_1}\sigma_1, \ldots, x_n : !_{R_n}\sigma_n \vdash e : \sigma$$

says that the expression e is a function whose sensitivity in the ith argument is described by the sensitivity term R_i. Notice that this means that every function type comes with a sensitivity term associated to its input type. Indeed, here—unlike [33, 34]—we are implicitly using the standard linear logic decomposition of the intuitionistic implication $\sigma \rightarrow \tau = !\sigma \multimap \tau$ and the observation that it suffices to have modal types appearing in negative position. For convenience, we will similarly use the notation $\sigma \rightarrow \tau$ as a shorthand for non-sensitive functions, i.e., functions of a type $!_R\sigma \multimap \tau$ where $[\![R]\!] = \infty$.

Modal types can be combined by arithmetic operations

$$!_R\sigma + !_T\sigma = !_{R+T}\sigma \text{ and } T \cdot !_R\sigma = !_{T \cdot R}\sigma$$

and these operations are lifted to type environments. The sum of two contexts is defined inductively as:

- $\emptyset + \emptyset = \emptyset$
- $(\Gamma, x : A) + (\Delta, x : B) = (\Gamma + \Delta), x : A + B$
- $(\Gamma, x : A) + \Delta = \Gamma + (\Delta, x : A) = (\Gamma + \Delta), x : A$, if $x \notin \mathrm{dom}(\Gamma, \Delta)$

The product of a type environment with a sensitivity term T is:

- $T \cdot \emptyset = \emptyset$
- $T \cdot (\Gamma, x : A) = T \cdot \Gamma, x : T \cdot A$

It is worth emphasizing that the sum $\Gamma + \Delta$ of two type environments Γ and Δ is defined only in the case that for each $x \in \mathrm{dom}(\Gamma) \cap \mathrm{dom}(\Delta)$ the type $A+B$ is defined, where $x : A \in \Gamma$ and $x : B \in \Delta$. This in turn requires that there is a type σ such that $A = !_{R_1}\sigma$ and $B = !_{R_2}\sigma$. In all the binary rules in Figure 5 we implicitly assume this condition.

A sensitivity term can also appear as the annotation of a precise type $\mathbb{R}[R]$. This class of types is close in spirit to the data types $\mathbf{N}[S]$ and $\mathbf{L}(\sigma)[S]$, since it classifies terms whose value is described by R. However, we have no destructor operation for this kind of type. We will see in Section 5.4 that these types can be used to dynamically specify the sensitivity of certain operations.

Subtyping and quantifiers The assumptions introduced by pattern matching play a crucial role in the subtyping relation $\sqsubseteq$, which is defined by the rules in Figure 4. A subtyping judgment has the shape

$$\phi; \Phi \vdash \sigma \sqsubseteq \tau$$

where ϕ is a kind environment and Φ is an assumption. Intuitively, the subtyping relation $\phi; \Phi \vdash \sigma \sqsubseteq \tau$ says that (1) σ and τ are equal up to their decorations with size and sensitivity terms, and (2) the decoration of τ is more permissive than the decoration of σ under the assumption Φ. One main purpose of the subtyping relation is to capture the fact that an R-sensitive function is also R'-sensitive for $R \leq R'$. This is ensured by the rule for the scaling modality:

$$\frac{\phi; \Phi \models R_2 \leq R_1 \quad \phi; \Phi \models \sigma_1 \sqsubseteq \sigma_2}{\phi; \Phi \models !_{R_1}\sigma_1 \sqsubseteq !_{R_2}\sigma_2} \; (st.!)$$

Indeed, the combination of this rule and the rule for function types

$$\frac{\phi; \Phi \models \sigma_3 \sqsubseteq \sigma_1 \quad \phi; \Phi \models \sigma_2 \sqsubseteq \sigma_4}{\phi; \Phi \models \sigma_1 \multimap \sigma_2 \sqsubseteq \sigma_3 \multimap \sigma_4} \; (st.\multimap)$$

(which, as usual, is contravariant in its first argument) ensures that $\phi; \Phi \vdash !_R\sigma \multimap \tau \sqsubseteq !_{R'}\sigma \multimap \tau$ iff $\phi; \Phi \models R \leq R'$. In other words, if we can prove that $R \leq R'$ under assumption Φ, then every expression that can be given the type $!_R\sigma \multimap \tau$ can *also* be given the type $!_{R'}\sigma \multimap \tau$.

Subtyping is also needed for putting the dependent pattern matching mechanism to work, to unify the contexts and the types in the two branches of a **case** rule. This is obtained by using subtyping judgments on data types. For instance, for natural numbers we have a rule

$$\frac{\phi; \Phi \models S = S'}{\phi; \Phi \models \mathbf{N}[S] \sqsubseteq \mathbf{N}[S']} \; (st.\mathbf{N})$$

that allows us to obtain the type $\mathbf{N}[S']$ from the type $\mathbf{N}[S]$ if we have $\phi; \Phi \models S = S'$.

Subtyping can be applied by using the rule $(\sqsubseteq.R)$ in Figure 5. Moreover, it can be extended to type environments: the judgment $\phi; \Phi \models \Gamma \sqsubseteq \Delta$ holds if for every $x : A \in \Delta$ we have $x : B \in \Gamma$ and $\phi; \Phi \models B \sqsubseteq A$. Note that the type environment Γ can contain variable assignments for variables that do not appear in Δ. Thus the rule $(\sqsubseteq.L)$ in Figure 5 can also be seen as a kind of weakening.

In order to be able to express the size and sensitivity dependencies in a uniform way, , we additionally enrich the type language with a universal quantifier $\forall$ and an existential quantifier $\exists$ over size and sensitivity variables (Figure 6). For instance, the type

$$\forall i : \iota.(\mathbf{N}[i] \multimap !_i\mathbb{R} \multimap \mathbb{R})$$

can be assigned to a program that, given a value of type $\mathbf{N}[S]$, returns an S-sensitive function of type $!_S\mathbb{R} \multimap \mathbb{R}$, for any size term $\vdash S : \iota$. Similarly, the type

$$\forall i : \iota.(\mathbf{N}[i] \multimap \exists k : \upsilon.(!_j\mathbb{R} \multimap \mathbb{R}))$$

abstracts the sensitivity of the function that is returned when a term of this type is provided with a value of type $\mathbf{N}[S]$. Finally, the type

$$\exists i : \iota.\mathbf{N}[i]$$

is the type of the ordinary natural numbers.

The probability layer To ensure differential privacy, we need to be able to write probabilistic computations. This is achieved in *DFuzz* by considering a grammar of programs with two layers (Figure 2) . We have an *expression layer* that contains the constructors and destructors for each data type, and an additional *probability state layer* that contains the program constructions for describing probabilities over expressions and values. To mediate between the two layers, we use a monadic type $\bigcirc\tau$, similar to the one found in Ramsey and Pfeffer's stochastic lambda calculus [32].

In order to describe probabilistic states, we need to have probability vectors p, i.e., lists of real numbers from the interval $[0, 1]$ that sum up to 1. Probability vectors can be typed by means of a precise type of the shape $\mathcal{P}[S]$, where the size term S describes the length of the vector. Though S can range over variables, the typing rules for vectors only use types $\mathcal{P}[n]$ indexed by a constant natural number n. A *probabilistic state* s then is either an object of the shape $\{p, (s_1, \ldots, s_n)\}$ where p is a probabilistic vector, or an object of the shape $\mathbf{do}\, e$. Intuitively, the former associates a discrete probability distribution, described by p, to a list of probabilistic states $(s_1, \ldots, s_n)$, whereas the latter turns an expression into a probabilistic state. Probabilistic states represent probabilistic computations in the sense that their evaluation results in *final states* that assign probabilities to values. For an example, the state

$$\{(0.2, 0.8), (\mathbf{do\,return}\,1, \\ \{(0.5, 0.5), (\mathbf{do\,return}\,2, \mathbf{do\,return}\,3)\})\}$$

is a final state in which the value 1 is returned with probability 0.2 and the values 2 and 3 are each returned with probability $0.8 \cdot 0.5 = 0.4$.

We use three monadic expression forms to ensure that only expressions representing probabilistic computations can be turned into probabilistic states. The expression $\mathbf{return}\, e$ can be seen as representing the distribution that deterministically yields e; the monadic sequencing $\mathbf{let}\bigcirc x = e\,\mathbf{in}\, e'$ can be seen as a program that draws a sample x from the probabilistic computation e and then continues with the computation e'; and the explicit probability construction $\{e, (e_1, \ldots, e_n)\}$ associates an expression e representing a probability vector with a list of random computations $(e_1, \ldots, e_n)$. The typing rules (Figure 7) ensure that we consider only well-formed expressions. In particular, the rule

$$\frac{\phi; \Phi; \Gamma \vdash e : \mathcal{P}[n] \quad \phi; \Phi; \Delta \vdash e_i : \bigcirc\sigma \quad (\forall i)}{\phi; \Phi; \Gamma + \Delta \vdash \{e, (e_1, \ldots, e_n)\} : \bigcirc\sigma} \;(\{e\})$$

ensures that (1) e represents a probability vector, and (2) every e_i is a probabilistic computation. Notice also that this rule is responsible for the well-formedness of the probabilistic states. It ensures that we associate lists of expressions of length n only with probability vectors of the same length. This is the reason for introducing the precise type $\mathcal{P}[n]$.

As a last remark, notice that the different components of a state represent independent computations, so, even though evaluation of expressions is defined sequentially, we define evaluation on states in parallel.

Sensitivity and primitive operations One last component that is necessary to make the framework practical is a way to add *trusted* primitive operations, i.e., operations that are known to preserve the properties of the type system. This is intuitively the meaning of the following typing rule from Figure 6:

$$\frac{\phi; \Phi \text{ imply } f\ R\text{-sensitive } \sigma \to \tau}{\phi; \Phi; \Gamma \vdash \mathtt{f} : !_R\sigma \multimap \tau} \;(\mathit{Ext})$$

which says that we can add to *DFuzz* any primitive operation $\mathtt{f}$ of type $!_R\sigma \multimap \tau$ as long as we know that this operation represents a mathematical function f that maps values in the type σ to values in the type τ and that is R-sensitive under the assumption Φ.

At the operational level, the evaluation rules for the primitive operation $\mathtt{f}$ must respect the behavior of the function f. This is obtained by means of the two following rules (Figure 8):

$$\frac{e \mapsto e'}{\mathtt{f}\, e \mapsto \mathtt{f}\, e'} \;(\text{Op-Ext-Tr}) \qquad \frac{}{\mathtt{f}\, v \mapsto f(v)} \;(\text{Op-Ext})$$

We can also extend *DFuzz* with additional primitive types, as long as they are equipped with a metric that respects the properties we describe in Section 5.

4. Basic Metatheory

In this section, we develop fundamental properties of *DFuzz*. In order to show the usual properties one would expect from our programming language—type preservation and progress—we additionally need to prove some properties that are particular to our use of size and sensitivity annotations. These will also be useful to prove the Metric Preservation Theorem in the next section. We give just proof sketches; full proofs are in [14].

4.1 Properties of Sizes and Sensitivities

As we saw earlier, typing judgments in *DFuzz* have the form

$$\phi; \Phi; \Gamma \vdash e : \sigma$$

i.e., they are indexed by a set of kind assignments to index variables ϕ and an assumption Φ. Intuitively, the fact that the subtyping can prove statements using the assumptions in Φ is what makes the dependent pattern matching work: it enables us to recover the same type from the different branches.

Here, we prove some properties of the typing with respect to the assumption Φ. The first says that strengthening the assumption preserves the typing.

4.1.1 Lemma [Assumption Strengthening]: Suppose that $\phi; \Psi \models \Phi$. Then, we have:

1. If $\phi; \Phi \models \mathcal{C}$, then $\phi; \Psi \models \mathcal{C}$.
2. If $\phi; \Phi \models \sigma \sqsubseteq \tau$, then $\phi; \Psi \models \sigma \sqsubseteq \tau$.
3. If $\phi; \Phi; \Gamma \vdash e : \sigma$, then $\phi; \Psi; \Gamma \vdash e : \sigma$.
4. If $\phi; \Phi; \Gamma \vdash s : \sigma$, then $\phi; \Psi; \Gamma \vdash s : \sigma$.

Proof: (1) follows directly from the transitivity of the logical implication; (2) follows by induction on the derivation proving $\phi; \Phi \models \sigma \sqsubseteq \tau$, using Point 1 when needed. (3) follows by induction on the derivation proving $\phi; \Phi; \Gamma \vdash e : \sigma$, using Point 2 when needed. (4) follows by induction on the derivation proving $\phi; \Phi; \Gamma \vdash s : \sigma$, using Point 3 when needed. □

The environment ϕ can contain free size and sensitivity variables; these can be thought of as placeholders for any size or sensitivity index term, and they can be instantiated with a concrete index term when necessary. This is captured by the next lemma:

4.1.2 Lemma [Instantiation]:

1. If $\phi, i : \kappa; \Phi \models \mathcal{C}$, then, for every $\phi \vdash I : \kappa$, we have $\phi; \Phi\{I/i\} \models \mathcal{C}\{I/i\}$.
2. If $\phi, i : \kappa; \Phi \models \sigma \sqsubseteq \tau$, then, for every $\phi \vdash I : \kappa$, we have $\phi; \Phi\{I/i\} \models \sigma\{I/i\} \sqsubseteq \tau\{I/i\}$.

$$\frac{}{(\mathbf{case_N}\ 0\ \mathbf{of}\ 0 \rightarrow e_1 \mid x[i]+1 \rightarrow e_2) \mapsto e_1}\ (\text{Op-Case}_0) \qquad \frac{}{(\mathbf{case_N}\ \mathbf{s}\ n\ \mathbf{of}\ 0 \rightarrow e_1 \mid x[i] \rightarrow e_2) \mapsto e_2\{n/x\}\{n/i\}}\ (\text{Op-Case}_\mathbf{s})$$

$$\frac{e \mapsto e'}{(\mathbf{case_L}\ e\ \mathbf{of}\ \mathtt{nil} \rightarrow e_1 \mid \mathtt{cons}[i](x,y) \rightarrow e_2) \mapsto (\mathbf{case_L}\ e'\ \mathbf{of}\ \mathtt{nil} \rightarrow e_1 \mid \mathtt{cons}[i](x,y) \rightarrow e_2)}\ (\text{Op-Case-List-Tr})$$

$$\frac{e \mapsto e'}{\mathtt{f}\ e \mapsto \mathtt{f}\ e'}\ (\text{Op-Ext-Tr}) \qquad \frac{}{(\mathbf{case_L}\ \mathtt{nil}\ \mathbf{of}\ \mathtt{nil} \rightarrow e_1 \mid \mathtt{cons}(x, y[i]) \rightarrow e_2) \mapsto e_1}\ (\text{Op-Case}_{\mathtt{nil}}) \qquad \frac{}{\mathtt{f}\ v \mapsto f(v)}\ (\text{Op-Ext})$$

$$\frac{}{(\mathbf{case_L}\ \mathtt{cons}[S](v,w)\ \mathbf{of}\ e_1 \mid \mathtt{cons}(x, y[i]).e_2) \mapsto e_2\{v/x\}\{w/y\}\{S/i\}}\ (\text{Op-Case}_\mathbf{c}) \qquad \frac{}{(\mathbf{fix}\ x.e)v \mapsto e\{\mathbf{fix}\ x.e/x\}v}\ (\text{Op-fix}_{\multimap})$$

$$\frac{}{(\mathbf{fix}\ x.e)[I] \mapsto e\{\mathbf{fix}\ x.e/x\}[I]}\ (\text{Op-fix}_\forall) \qquad \frac{e \mapsto e'}{\mathbf{unpack}\ e\ \mathbf{as}\ (x,i)\ \mathbf{in}\ g \mapsto \mathbf{unpack}\ e'\ \mathbf{as}\ (x,i)\ \mathbf{in}\ g}\ (\text{Op-}\exists\text{-Tr-1})$$

$$\frac{e \mapsto e'}{\mathbf{pack}(e, I)\ \mathbf{as}\ \exists i : \kappa.\sigma \mapsto \mathbf{pack}(e', I)\ \mathbf{as}\ \exists i : \kappa.\sigma}\ (\text{Op-}\exists\text{-Tr-2})$$

$$\frac{}{\mathbf{unpack}\ (\mathbf{pack}(v, I)\ \mathbf{as}\ \exists i : \kappa.\sigma)\ \mathbf{as}\ (x,i)\ \mathbf{in}\ e \mapsto e\{I/i\}\{v/x\}}\ (\text{Op-}\exists)$$

$$\frac{e \mapsto e'}{\mathbf{return}\ e \mapsto \mathbf{return}\ e'}\ (\text{Op-Return-Tr}) \qquad \frac{e \mapsto e'}{\{e, (e_1, \ldots, e_n)\} \mapsto \{e', (e_1, \ldots, e_n)\}}\ (\text{Op-P-Exp-Tr})$$

$$\frac{e \mapsto e'}{\mathbf{let}\ \bigcirc x = e\ \mathbf{in}\ e_0 \mapsto \mathbf{let}\ \bigcirc x = e'\ \mathbf{in}\ e_0}\ (\text{Op-}\bigcirc\text{-Tr}) \qquad \frac{}{\mathbf{let}\ \bigcirc x = \mathbf{return}\ v\ \mathbf{in}\ e' \mapsto e'\{v/x\}}\ (\text{Op-}\bigcirc\text{-Return-Tr})$$

$$\frac{}{\mathbf{let}\ \bigcirc x = \{p, (e_i)_{i \in 1 \ldots n}\}\ \mathbf{in}\ e' \mapsto \{p, (\mathbf{let}\ \bigcirc x = e_i\ \mathbf{in}\ e')_{i \in 1 \ldots n}\}}\ (\text{Op-}\bigcirc) \qquad \frac{}{\mathbf{do}\ \{p, (e_i)_{i \in 1 \ldots n}\} \mapsto \{p, (\mathbf{do}\ e_i)_{i \in 1 \ldots n}\}}\ (\text{Op-Do})$$

$$\frac{e \mapsto e'}{\mathbf{do}\ e \mapsto \mathbf{do}\ e'}\ (\text{Op-Do-Tr}) \qquad \frac{\emptyset \neq I \subseteq 1 \ldots n \qquad s_i \mapsto s'_i \qquad s_j = s'_j = f_j \qquad (\forall i \in I, j \notin I)}{\{p, (s_i)_{i \in 1 \ldots n}\} \mapsto \{p, (s'_i)_{i \in 1 \ldots n}\}}\ (\text{Op-P-State-Tr})$$

Figure 8. Selected Evaluation Rules

3. If $\phi, i : \kappa; \Phi; \Gamma \vdash e : \sigma$, then, for every $\phi \vdash I : \kappa$, we have $\phi; \Phi\{I/i\}; \Gamma\{I/i\} \vdash e\{I/i\} : \sigma\{I/i\}$.
4. If $\phi, i : \kappa; \Phi; \Gamma \vdash s : \sigma$, then, for every $\phi \vdash I : \kappa$, we have $\phi; \Phi\{I/i\}; \Gamma\{I/i\} \vdash s\{I/i\} : \sigma\{I/i\}$.

Proof: (1) follows directly from the definition of constraint satisfiability; (2) follows by induction on the derivation proving $\phi, i : \kappa; \Phi \models \sigma \sqsubseteq \tau$, using Point 1 when needed. (3) follows by induction on the derivation proving $\phi, i : \kappa; \Phi; \Gamma \vdash e : \sigma$, using Point 2 when needed. (4) follows by induction on the derivation proving $\phi, i : \kappa; \Phi; \Gamma \vdash s : \sigma$, using Point 3 when needed. □

4.2 Type Soundness and Type Preservation

Using the properties on size and sensitivities annotations detailed in the previous section, we are now ready to prove the usual properties we want a programming language to enjoy: substitution, type preservation, and progress.

4.2.1 Theorem [Substitution]: If $\phi; \Phi; \Gamma, x : !_R\tau \vdash e : \sigma$ and $\phi; \Phi; \Delta \vdash g : \tau$, then $\phi; \Phi; \Gamma + R \cdot \Delta \vdash e\{g/x\} : \sigma$.

Proof: By induction on the derivation proving $\phi; \Phi; \Gamma, x : !_R\tau \vdash e : \sigma$. □

The proof of the Substitution Lemma is straightforward, except for the management of the term variable environments. The proof of Type Preservation, however, is not as straightforward because it requires managing the constraints and the size and sensitivity annotations in various places.

4.2.2 Theorem [Type Preservation]:

1. If $\vdash e : \sigma$ and $e \mapsto e'$, then $\vdash e' : \sigma$.
2. If $\vdash s : \sigma$ and $s \mapsto s'$, then $\vdash s' : \sigma$.

Proof: Part (1) proceeds by induction on the derivation proving $\vdash e : \sigma$ and case analysis on the possible derivations for $e \mapsto e'$, using the Substitution Lemma (4.2.1). Lemmas (4.1.1) and (4.1.2) are needed when the step taken comes from a dependent pattern matching rule. Part (2) now follows by induction on the derivation proving $\vdash s : \sigma$ and case analysis on the possible derivations for $s \mapsto s'$, using Point 1 when needed. □

We can also prove Progress as usual:

4.2.3 Theorem [Progress]:

1. If $\vdash e : \sigma$, then either $e \mapsto e'$, or e is a value.
2. If $\vdash s : \sigma$, then either $s \mapsto s'$, or s is final.

Proof: Both parts proceed by induction on the given derivation, using part (1) as needed in part (2). □

5. Metric Preservation and ϵ-Differential Privacy

The design of the *DFuzz* type system is intimately related to the metric relation we present in this section. This connection is captured by the Metric Preservation Theorem (5.2.7), which states that the evaluations of two well typed expressions at a given distance result in two values at the same distance or less.

5.1 Metric Relations

To formalize the notion of sensitivity, we need a metric relation on programs and states that captures an appropriate notion of "information distance" for each type. For this purpose, we first introduce a metric relation $\sim_r$ on values and final states, and then extend it to a metric relation $\approx_r$ on expressions and states through substitutions of related values. Concretely, we begin with metric judgments on values and final states

$$\vdash v \sim_r v' : \sigma \qquad \vdash f \sim_r f' : \sigma$$

asserting, respectively, that values v, v' and final states f, f' are related at type σ and that they are no more than r apart, where $r \in \mathbb{R}^{\geq 0}$.

Using these metric judgments, we can also relate substitutions of values for variables in an environment Γ. First, we need some notation. Let Γ° be the environment obtained from Γ as follows:

$$\Gamma^\circ = \{x_i : \sigma_i \mid x_i : !_{R_i}\sigma_i \in \Gamma\}$$

Suppose that γ is a vector of positive reals indexed by variables in $\mathrm{dom}(\Gamma)$, i.e. $\gamma = (x_1 := r_1, \ldots, x_n := r_n)$. Then, we also define a metric judgment with shape:

$$\vdash \delta \sim_\gamma \delta' : \Gamma^\circ$$

This asserts that the substitutions δ and δ' of values for the variables in $\mathrm{dom}(\Gamma)$ are related at the types described by Γ°, and that they are no more than γ apart. That is, for every value $v_i = \delta(x_i)$ and $v'_i = \delta'(x_i)$ we have $\vdash v_i \sim_{\gamma(x_i)} v'_i$.

Finally, we have judgments for expressions and states:

$$\Gamma \vdash e \approx_r e' : \sigma \qquad \Gamma \vdash s \approx_r s' : \sigma$$

These assert that the expressions e, e' and states s, s' are related at the type σ, and that they are no more then r apart, in the type environment Γ.

Given an environment $\Gamma = (x_1 : !_{R_1}\sigma_1, \ldots, x_n : !_{R_n}\sigma_n)$ and a variable-indexed vector of positive reals $\gamma = (x_1 := r_1, \ldots, x_n := r_n)$, we define $\gamma[\![\Gamma]\!]$ as $\sum_{i=1}^{n} r_i \cdot [\![R_i]\!]$. By definition, $\gamma[\![\Gamma]\!]$ can assume values in $\mathbb{R}^{\geq 0} \cup \{\infty\}$. In what follows, we will be particularly interested in the cases where $\gamma[\![\Gamma]\!]$ is finite.

All these metric judgments are defined inductively by the rules in Figure 9 where $|b_1 \triangle b_2|$ is the size of the symmetric difference between the two databases b_1 and b_2. It is worth noting that the metric on expressions considers only expressions that are typable with no constraints and no free size variables. This ensures that the index r in the relations $\sim_r$ and $\approx_r$ is actually a value $r \in \mathbb{R}^{\geq 0}$.

The metric presented here, like the one used in [33], differs significantly from the one presented in [34] in its treatment of non-value expressions and states. In particular, we do not require the relation on expressions to be closed under reduction. This makes the proof of metric preservation easier, and, as we will see, it is sufficient to ensure differential privacy.

5.2 Metric Preservation

The Metric Preservation Theorem (5.2.7), which we present at the end of this section, can be seen as an extension of the Type Preservation Theorem (4.2.2). We can read it as asserting that the evaluation of expressions and states preserves not only their types but also the distances between related input values, up to a constant factor given by the metric relation.

The proof of the metric preservation theorem involves five major steps. The goal of these steps is to ensure that the different metric relations respect the properties of the type system. The first step is to show that the metric on expressions and states internalizes a sort of weakening:

5.2.1 Lemma:

1. If $\Delta \vdash e \approx_r e' : \sigma$ and $r \leq p$, then $\Delta \vdash e \approx_p e' : \sigma$.
2. If $\Delta \vdash s \approx_r s' : \sigma$ and $r \leq p$, then $\Delta \vdash s \approx_p s' : \sigma$.

Proof: The proof of (1) is by inversion on the rule proving $\Delta \vdash e \approx_r e' : \sigma$, using the fact that, if $\vdash v \sim_{r'} v' : \tau$ and $r' \leq p'$, then $\vdash v \sim_{p'} v' : \tau$. The base case of (2) follows from (1); the inductive case follows directly by induction hypothesis. □

The second step is to show that the metric relation is well behaved with respect to the subtyping relation. This is formalized by the following lemma.

5.2.2 Lemma [Subtyping on metrics]:

1. If $\vdash e \approx_r e' : \sigma$, and $\emptyset; \emptyset \vdash \sigma \sqsubseteq \tau$, then $\vdash e \approx_r e' : \tau$.
2. If $\vdash s \approx_r s' : \sigma$, and $\emptyset; \emptyset \vdash \sigma \sqsubseteq \tau$, then $\vdash s \approx_r s' : \tau$.

Proof: (1) by induction on the derivation proving $\vdash e \approx_r e' : \sigma$; (2) by induction on the derivation proving $\vdash s \approx_r s' : \sigma$. □

The third technical lemma is an intermediate step to show that the two metric relations $\sim_r$ and $\approx_r$ coincide on expressions and states that happen to be values and final states, respectively.

5.2.3 Lemma:

1. Suppose $\emptyset; \emptyset; \Gamma \vdash e : \tau$. If $\vdash \delta_1 \sim_\gamma \delta_2 : \Gamma^\circ$ and $\delta_1 e$ is a value, then $\delta_2 e$ must also be a value, and $\vdash \delta_1 e \sim_{\gamma[\![\Gamma]\!]} \delta_2 e : \tau$.
2. Suppose $\emptyset; \emptyset; \Gamma \vdash s : \tau$. If $\vdash \delta_1 \sim_\gamma \delta_2 : \Gamma^\circ$ and $\delta_1 s$ is final, then $\delta_2 s$ must also be final, and $\vdash \delta_1 s \sim_{\gamma[\![\Gamma]\!]} \delta_2 s : \tau$.

5.2.4 Corollary:

1. $\vdash v \approx_r v' : \tau$ iff $\vdash v \sim_r v' : \tau$.
2. $\vdash f \approx_r f' : \tau$ iff $\vdash f \sim_r f' : \tau$.

The last important property that the metric inherits from the *DFuzz* type system is a substitution property on the judgments involving the relation $\approx_r$.

5.2.5 Lemma [Substitution into $\approx$]: The following rule is admissible:

$$\frac{\Delta_1 \vdash e_1 \approx_{r_1} e'_1 : \tau_1 \qquad \Delta_2, x' : !_R\tau_1 \vdash e_2 \approx_{r_2} e'_2 : \tau_2}{R \cdot \Delta_1 + \Delta_2 \vdash e_2\{e_1/x\} \approx_{r_1[\![R]\!]+r_2} e'_2\{e'_1/x\} : \tau_2}$$

Combining these four results, we can prove the main lemma:

5.2.6 Lemma [Metric Compatibility]: Suppose $\vdash \delta \sim_\gamma \delta' : \Gamma^\circ$ such that $\gamma[\![\Gamma]\!] \in \mathbb{R}^{\geq 0}$. Then:

1. If $\emptyset; \emptyset; \Gamma \vdash e : \sigma$ and $\delta e \mapsto g$, then $\exists g'.\ \delta' e \mapsto g'$ and $\vdash g \approx_{\gamma[\![\Gamma]\!]} g' : \sigma$.
2. If $\emptyset; \emptyset; \Gamma \vdash s : \sigma$ and $\delta s \mapsto s_f$, then $\exists s'_f.\ \delta' s \mapsto s'_f$ and $\vdash s_f \approx_{\gamma[\![\Gamma]\!]} s'_f : \sigma$.

Proof: By induction on the typing derivation proving $\emptyset; \emptyset; \Gamma \vdash e : \sigma$ and $\emptyset; \emptyset; \Gamma \vdash f : \sigma$, respectively, with further case analysis on the evaluation step taken and using Corollary (5.2.4) and the Substitution Lemma (5.2.5). □

The Metric Compatibility lemma is the main ingredient we need to prove that well-typed programs map related input values to related output values:

5.2.7 Theorem [Metric Preservation]:

1. If $\vdash e \approx_r e' : \sigma$ and $e \mapsto e_f$, then $\exists e'_f.\ e' \mapsto e'_f$ and $\vdash e_f \approx_r e'_f : \sigma$.
2. If $\vdash s \approx_r s' : \sigma$ and $s \mapsto s_f$, then $\exists s'_f.\ s' \mapsto s'_f$ and $\vdash s_f \approx_r s'_f : \sigma$.

Proof: (1) By inversion on the rule proving the judgment $\vdash e \approx_r e' : \sigma$, using the Metric Compatibility Lemma (5.2.6); (2) by induction on the derivation proving the judgment $\vdash s \approx_r s' : \sigma$, again using Lemma (5.2.6). □

We can then make a corresponding statement about the complete evaluation $\hookrightarrow$ of two expressions or two states, where $\hookrightarrow$ is the reflexive, transitive closure of the step relation $\mapsto$:

5.2.8 Theorem [Big-Step Metric Preservation]:

1. If $\vdash e \approx_r e' : \sigma$ and $e \hookrightarrow v$, then there exists v' such that $e' \hookrightarrow v'$ and $\vdash v \sim_r v' : \sigma$.
2. If $\vdash s \approx_r s' : \sigma$ and $s \hookrightarrow f$, then there exists f' such that $e' \hookrightarrow f'$ and $\vdash f \sim_r f' : \sigma$.

$$\frac{\emptyset;\emptyset;\emptyset \vdash v : \sigma}{\vdash v \sim_0 v : \sigma} \qquad \frac{\emptyset;\emptyset;\emptyset \vdash f : \sigma}{\vdash f \sim_0 f : \sigma} \qquad \frac{\emptyset;\emptyset;\emptyset \vdash n : \mathbf{N}[S]}{\vdash n \sim_0 n : \mathbf{N}[S]} \qquad \frac{\emptyset;\emptyset;\emptyset \vdash r : \mathbb{R}[R]}{\vdash r \sim_0 r : \mathbb{R}[R]} \qquad \frac{\emptyset;\emptyset;\emptyset \vdash \mathtt{nil} : \mathbf{L}(\sigma)[0]}{\vdash \mathtt{nil} \sim_0 \mathtt{nil} : \mathbf{L}(\sigma)[0]}$$

$$\frac{\vdash v_1 \sim_{r_1} v_1' : \sigma \quad \vdash v_2 \sim_{r_2} v_2' : \mathbf{L}(\sigma)[S]}{\vdash \mathtt{cons}[S](v_1, v_2) \sim_{r_1+r_2} \mathtt{cons}[S](v_1', v_2') : \mathbf{L}(\sigma)[S+1]} \qquad \frac{\vdash v \sim_r v' : \sigma \qquad r \leq r'}{\vdash v \sim_{r'} v' : \sigma} \qquad \frac{|r_1 - r_2| = r}{\vdash r_1 \sim_r r_2 : \mathbb{R}} \qquad \frac{|b_1 \triangle b_2| = r}{\vdash b_1 \sim_r b_2 : \mathbf{db}}$$

$$\frac{x : !_R\sigma \vdash e \approx_r e' : \tau}{\vdash \lambda x.e \sim_r \lambda x.e' : !_R\sigma \multimap \tau} \qquad \frac{x : !_\infty\sigma \vdash e \approx_r e' : \sigma}{\vdash \mathbf{fix}\, x.e \sim_r \mathbf{fix}\, x.e' : \sigma} \qquad \frac{\vdash v \sim_r v' : \sigma\{I/i\}}{\vdash \mathbf{pack}(v, I)\ \mathbf{as}\ \exists i : \kappa.\sigma \sim_r \mathbf{pack}(v', I)\ \mathbf{as}\ \exists i : \kappa.\sigma : \exists i : \kappa.\sigma}$$

$$\frac{\forall \vdash R : \kappa \quad \vdash v\{R/i\} \sim_r v'\{R/i\} : \sigma\{R/i\}}{\vdash \Lambda i.v \sim_r \Lambda i.v' : \forall i : \kappa.\sigma} \qquad \frac{|\ln(r_i/r_i')| \leq s \qquad (\forall i)}{\vdash (r_1, \ldots, r_n) \sim_s (r_1', \ldots, r_n') : \mathcal{P}[n]}$$

$$\frac{\vdash p \sim_r p' : \mathcal{P}[n] \qquad \vdash f_i \sim_s f_i' : \tau \quad (\forall i)}{\vdash \{p, (f_1, \ldots, f_n)\} \sim_{r+s} \{p', (f_1', \ldots, f_n')\} : \tau} \qquad \frac{\vdash p \sim_r p' : \mathcal{P}[n] \qquad \vdash e_i \approx_s e_i' : \bigcirc\tau \quad (\forall i)}{\vdash \{p, (e_1, \ldots, e_n)\} \sim_{r+s} \{p', (e_1', \ldots, e_n')\} : \bigcirc\tau}$$

$$\frac{\vdash p \sim_r p' : \mathcal{P}[n] \qquad \Gamma \vdash s_i \approx_s s_i' : \tau \quad (\forall i)}{\Gamma \vdash \{p, (s_1, \ldots, s_n)\} \approx_{r+s} \{p', (s_1', \ldots, s_n')\} : \tau} \qquad \frac{\Gamma \vdash e \approx_r e' : \bigcirc\tau}{\Gamma \vdash \mathbf{do}\, e \approx_r \mathbf{do}\, e' : \tau} \qquad \frac{\vdash \delta_1 \sim_\gamma \delta_2 : \Gamma^\circ \quad \emptyset;\emptyset;\Gamma,\Delta \vdash e : \sigma}{\Delta \vdash \delta_1 e \approx_{\gamma[\![\Gamma]\!]} \delta_2 e : \sigma}$$

$$\frac{\vdash v_i \sim_{r_i} v_i' : \sigma_i \quad (\forall i)}{\{v_1/x_1, \cdots, v_n/x_n\} \sim_{(x_1:=r_1,\cdots,x_n:=r_n)} \{v_1'/x_1, \cdots, v_n'/x_n\} : (x_1 : \sigma_1, \ldots, x_n : \sigma_n)}$$

Figure 9. Metric Rules

5.3 Well-Typed Programs are ϵ-Differentially Private

The Big-Step Metric Preservation Theorem (5.2.8) ensures that programs map related inputs to related outputs. Combined with the properties of the probability layer, this allow us to show that well-typed programs are differentially private.

To formalize this, we need to define the probability $\mathtt{Pr}_f[v]$ that a final state f yields a value v. We recursively define:

$$\mathtt{Pr}_{\mathbf{do\ return}\ v'}[v] = \begin{cases} 1 & \text{if } v = v' \\ 0 & \text{otherwise} \end{cases}$$

$$\mathtt{Pr}_{\{(p_1,\ldots,p_n),(f_1,\ldots,f_n)\}}[v] = \sum_{i=1}^{n} p_i\, \mathtt{Pr}_{f_i}[v]$$

Note that, by the typing rule for probabilistic states ($\{s\}$), the tuples $(p_1, \ldots, p_n), (f_1, \ldots, f_n)$ must have the same length. The metric on probability distributions is carefully chosen so that the metric on final states corresponds to the relation on probability distributions needed in the definition of differential privacy.

5.3.1 Lemma: Let $\vdash f : \sigma$ and $\vdash f' : \sigma$ be two closed final states such that $f \sim_r f' : \sigma$ for some $r \in \mathbb{R}^{\geq 0}$. Then, for every value $\vdash v : \sigma$,

$$\mathtt{Pr}_f[v] \leq e^r \mathtt{Pr}_{f'}[v].$$

Thus, we can show that the type system can verify that a program is ϵ-differentially private.

5.3.2 Theorem [ϵ-Differential Privacy]: The execution of any closed program e such that

$$\vdash e : !_\epsilon\sigma \multimap \bigcirc\tau$$

is an ϵ-differentially private function from σ to τ. That is, for all closed values $v, v' : \sigma$ such that $\vdash v \sim_r v' : \sigma$, and all closed values $w : \tau$, if $\mathbf{do}(e\ v) \hookrightarrow f$ and $\mathbf{do}(e\ v') \hookrightarrow f'$, then

$$\mathtt{Pr}_f[w] \leq e^{r\epsilon} \mathtt{Pr}_{f'}[w].$$

Proof: By using the fact that $\vdash \{v/x\} \sim_{(x:=r)} \{v'/x\} : (x : \sigma)$, we have that $\vdash \mathbf{do}(e\ x)\{v/x\} \approx_{r\epsilon} \mathbf{do}(e\ x)\{v'/x\} : \tau$. So, by the Big-step Metric Preservation Theorem (5.2.8), we obtain $f \approx_{r\epsilon} f' : \tau$. We conclude by Corollary (5.2.4) and Lemma (5.3.1). □

The above theorem shows that in order to ensure that the execution of a program e corresponds to an ϵ-differentially private randomized function from values in σ to values in τ, it is sufficient to check that the program e has a type of this form:

$$\vdash e : !_\epsilon\sigma \multimap \bigcirc\tau$$

5.4 Primitive Operations for Privacy

As outlined in Section 3, one important property of *DFuzz* is that it can be extended by means of primitive operations. In particular, we are interested in adding two basic building blocks, allowing us to build more involved differentially private examples. The first operation we add is the *Laplace mechanism* (Proposition (2.4)), with the following signature:

$$\mathit{add\_noise} : \forall \epsilon : \upsilon.\mathbb{R}[\epsilon] \to !_\epsilon\mathbb{R} \multimap \bigcirc\mathbb{R}$$

Note that, unlike the version presented in *Fuzz*, this primitive allows the level of noise (and thus, the level of privacy) to be specified by the user.

Another primitive operation that fits well in our framework is the *exponential mechanism* [28]

$$\begin{aligned} \mathit{exp\_noise} : &\forall s : \upsilon, \epsilon : \upsilon.\mathbb{R}[s] \to \mathbf{Bag}(\sigma) \to (\sigma \to !_s\mathbf{db} \multimap \mathbb{R}) \\ &\to \mathbb{R}[\epsilon] \to !_\epsilon\mathbf{db} \multimap \bigcirc\sigma \end{aligned} \tag{1}$$

where $\mathbf{Bag}(\sigma)$ is a primitive type representing a multiset of objects of type σ. The exponential mechanism takes a set of possible outputs, a *quality score* that assigns to each element in the range a number (depending on the database), and the database itself. The quality score is at most s-sensitive in the database, and here we allow this sensitivity to be passed in as a parameter. The algorithm privately outputs an element of the range that approximately maximizes the quality score.

6. Case Studies

To illustrate how *DFuzz*'s dependent types expand the range of programs that can be certified as differentially private, we now present four examples of practical algorithms that can be implemented in *DFuzz*, but not in *Fuzz*. Each algorithm is taken from a different paper from the differential privacy literature (specifically, [4, 18, 19, 27]). The first three algorithms rely on the following new feature that is enabled by *DFuzz*'s dependent types:

Iterative privacy: The ability to express a dependency between the total privacy cost of a function and a parameter that is chosen at runtime, such as a number of iterations.

The last example illustrates how allowing slightly more complex sensitivity annotations can increase the expressivity, and it also shows another important use for dependent types:

Privacy-utility tradeoff: The ability of a function to control its own privacy cost, e.g., by scaling the precision of an iterated operation to make the total cost independent of the number of iterations.

We are experimenting with a prototype implementation of *DFuzz*, and we present the examples in the actual syntax used by the prototype, an extension of *Fuzz* that closely follows the concrete syntax from Figure 2 (for instance, we write `sample x=e; e'` to denote **let** $\bigcirc x = e$ **in** e'); we only omit instantiations of size/sensitivity terms for brevity. The examples also use some additional constructs, such as `(a,b)` for tensor products of types `a` and `b`, with associated primitive operations. Details of these extensions are available in [14].

6.1 Iterative Privacy

***k-means* [4]** Our first example (Figure 10) is k-means clustering, an algorithm from data mining that groups a set of data points into k clusters. Given a set of points and an initial guess for the k cluster centers, the algorithm iteratively refines the clusters by first associating each point with the closest center, and then moving each center to the middle of its associated points; the differentially private version ensures privacy by adding some noise to the refined centers. The k-means algorithm can be implemented in *DFuzz* as follows: Here, `iterate` is a caller-supplied procedure performing

```
function kmeans
  (iters : Nat[i]) (eps : num[e])
  (db :[3 * i * e] (num,num) bag)
  (centers : list(num,num)[j])
  (iterate : num[e] -> (num,num) bag -o[3*e]
    list(num,num)[j] -> Circle list(num,num)[j])
  : Circle list(num,num)[j]
  {
    case iters of
      0      => return centers
    | n + 1 => sample next_centers =
                    kmeans n eps db centers iterate;
                 iterate eps db next_centers
  }
```

Figure 10. k-means in *DFuzz*

an update of the centers (details omitted for brevity).

Note that the sensitivity of `kmeans` in the database `db` depends on two other parameters: the number of iterations `[i]` and the privacy cost per iteration `[e]` that the analyst is willing to tolerate. This is enabled by the dependent types in *DFuzz*; in contrast, *Fuzz* is only able to typecheck a simplified version of k-means in which both parameters are hard-coded.

***Iterative Database Construction* [19]** Our second example (Figure 11) is an algorithm that can efficiently answer *exponentially* many queries with good accuracy. This is done by first constructing a public approximation of the private database, which can then be used to answer queries without further privacy cost. IDC builds the approximation iteratively: given an initial guess, it uses a *private distinguisher (PA)* to find a query that would be inaccurate on the current approximation and then applies a *database update algorithm (DUA)* to refine the approximation. PA and DUA are parameters of the algorithm, and the sensitivity of an IDC instance depends on the sensitivities of its PA. This can be expressed in *DFuzz* as follows: Several choices for PA and DUA have been proposed in the

```
function IDC
  (iter : Nat[i]) (eps : num[e])
  (db :[2 * i * e] db_type) (qs : query bag)
  (PA : (query bag) -> approx_db
      -> db_type -o[e] Circle query)
  (DUA : approx_db -> query -> num -> approx_db)
  (eval_q : query -> db_type -o[1] num)
  : Circle approx_db {
  case iter of
    0      => return init_approx
  | n + 1 =>
      sample approx = (IDC n eps db qs PA DUA);
      sample q = PA qs approx db;
      sample actual = add_noise eps (eval_q q db);
      return (DUA approx q actual)
  }
```

Figure 11. Iterative Database Function in *DFuzz*

literature; some can be written directly in *DFuzz* (e.g., the exponential distinguisher from [22]), and others can be added as trusted primitives (e.g., the sparse distinguisher from [35]). By contrast, a parametric IDC cannot be written in plain *Fuzz* because there is no way to express the dependency between the sensitivity of the PA/DUA and the sensitivity of the overall algorithm.

***Cumulative Distribution Function* [27]** Our third example (Figure 12) is an algorithm that computes the CDF function. Given a database of numeric records and a list of buckets defined by cutoff values, it computes the number of records in each bucket. [27] presents three variants of this algorithm with different privacy/utility tradeoffs, only one of which was previously supported in *Fuzz*. To understand why, consider the following version, implemented in *DFuzz*: Note that the sensitivity in this version depends

```
function cdf
  (eps : num[e]) (buckets : list(num)[i])
  (db :[i * e] num bag) : Circle list(num)[i]
  {
    case buckets of
      []        => return []
    | (x :: y) =>
        let (lt,gt) = bag_split (fun n => n<x) db;
        sample count = add_noise eps (bag_size lt);
        sample bigger = cdf eps y gt;
        return (count :: bigger)
  }
```

Figure 12. Cumulative Distribution Function in *DFuzz*

on the number of cutoff values or "buckets." Since *Fuzz* cannot capture such a dependency, this CDF variant is not just impossible to write in *Fuzz*—it cannot even be added as a trusted primitive, since there is no way to express its type signature. In contrast, *DFuzz* can directly support this program, and it could also support the last version in [27] with a small extension that we discuss in Section 8.

6.2 Privacy-Utility Tradeoff

Our fourth and most complex example shows how *DFuzz* enables programmers to write functions that control their own privacy cost, and it also illustrates how small extensions to the language for sensitivity annotations can further increase expressivity. The extension we use here introduces a new operation $R_1 \tilde{\oslash} R_2$ on sensitivity terms R_1 and R_2 that provides a limited form of division. The interpretation is extended accordingly as follows:

$$\llbracket R_1 \tilde{\oslash} R_2 \rrbracket_\rho = \frac{r}{s} \quad \text{if } \llbracket R_1 \rrbracket_\rho = r \wedge \llbracket R_2 \rrbracket_\rho = s \wedge r, s \notin \{0, \infty\}$$
$$\llbracket R_1 \tilde{\oslash} R_2 \rrbracket_\rho = 0 \quad \text{if } \llbracket R_1 \rrbracket_\rho = 0 \vee \llbracket R_2 \rrbracket_\rho = \infty$$
$$\llbracket R_1 \tilde{\oslash} R_2 \rrbracket_\rho = \infty \quad \text{otherwise}$$

The behavior of the $\tilde{\oslash}$ operator is different from that of the ordinary division operator: $\tilde{\oslash}$ does not enjoy the usual properties of division with respect to multiplication and addition, i.e., it is *not* the inverse of multiplication, and it does *not* enjoy the usual distributivity laws. However, it does have two key properties. First, Lemma (3.1) still holds for the system that includes $\tilde{\oslash}$. If the usual division $\div$ were added instead, the interpretation would no longer be total because $r \div 0$ and $\infty \div \infty$ are in general undefined when $\div$ is the inverse of $\cdot$ and enjoys the usual distributivity laws. The choice of $\tilde{\oslash}$ ensures the preservation of the metatheoretic results of Sections 4 and 5. Second, the interpretation of $\tilde{\oslash}$ satisfies the following inequality (the need for which will become apparent shortly) for every ρ:

$$\llbracket (R_1 \tilde{\oslash} (R_2 + 1)) \cdot R_2 \rrbracket_\rho \leq \llbracket R_1 \rrbracket_\rho \qquad (2)$$

In terms of $\tilde{\oslash}$, we can add a *safe division* primitive to the language for terms:

$$div : \forall i : \upsilon . \forall j : \upsilon . \mathbb{R}[i] \to \mathbb{R}[j+1] \to \mathbb{R}[i \tilde{\oslash} (j+1)]$$

Note that the div operation is simply a restriction of the usual division to positive real numbers that we make total by restricting the domain of the denominator to reals greater than or equal to 1.

***k*-medians [18]** With this extension, we can implement our fourth example (Figure 13): an algorithm for *k-medians*, a classic problem in combinatorial optimization. Given a database V of locations, with distances between locations, a desired number k of (say) factories to build, and a private demand set $D \subseteq V$, the goal is to select a set $F \subseteq V$ of k locations to minimize the cost, defined to be the sum of the distances from each demand point to the closest factory. In the program, the distances are given implicitly via the *cost function*, which maps sets of factory locations to costs. The algorithm starts with an initial random choice F_0 of k locations and runs several iterations, each time using the exponential mechanism (Equation (1) in Section 5.4) to find the best location to swap for a location in the candidate set of factories. After building up a collection of candidate factory sets, the mechanism uses the exponential mechanism once more to choose the best configuration.

The helper function `kmedians_aux` runs the main loop, which repeatedly tries to improve the cost of a set of locations by replacing a location from the set with one that is not in the set. The outer `kmedians` function simply chooses an initial (random) set of factory locations and sets up the privacy and iteration constants.

The program uses several primitive functions for manipulating bags: `bagcontains` checks the membership in bags, `bagproduct` builds the Cartesian product of two bags, `bagadd` adds an element to a bag, `bagswap` swaps two element in a bag, and `bagselect` chooses subset of a given size from a bag uniformly at random. The helper function `score` measures how much a swap can improve the cost of a set of locations. It can also be written in *DFuzz* (see [14]).

The key challenge in implementing k-medians is that it scales the privacy level of the exponential mechanism to achieve a *constant* overall privacy cost, independent of the number of iterations. To derive the correct type for `kmedians`, *DFuzz* must prove that, in the call to the auxiliary function `kmedians_aux`, the sensitivity of `D` is at most `eps`. This involves checking a subtyping application that requires the following inequality between sensitivity terms:

$$((e \tilde{\oslash} (i+1)) \tilde{\oslash} (2 \cdot s + 1)) \cdot (2 \cdot s) \cdot i \leq e$$

This inequality follows from two applications of Equation (2). Thus, with the additional $\tilde{\oslash}$ operator, algorithms that scale their privacy cost depending on the number of iterations can be expressed and verified in *DFuzz*, using dependent types.

```
function kmedians_aux
  (iter : Nat[i]) (F0 : (loc bag)) (delta : num[s])
  (cost : (loc bag) -> (loc bag) -o[s] num)
  (eps : num[e]) (V : loc bag)
  (D :[e * (2 * s) * i] loc bag)
  : Circle (loc bag, (loc bag) bag)
  {
    case iter of
    | 0 => return (F0, (bag F0))
    | x + 1 =>
       sample pair = kmedians_aux x F0 delta cost
                                          eps V D;
       let (Fi, Fs) = pair;
       let (_, F_comp) =
          bagsplit (fun l => bagcontains V l) Fi;
       swaps = bagproduct Fi F_comp;
       sample best = exp_noise delta swaps
                         (score cost Fi)
                         (eps * (2 * delta)) D;
       let (a, b) = best;
       Fnew = bagswap a b Fi;
       return (Fnew, bagadd Fs Fnew)
  }

function kmedians
  (T : Nat[i]) (delta : num[s]) (V : loc bag)
  (cost : (loc bag) -> (loc bag) -o[s] num)
  (D :[2 * e] loc bag) (eps : num[e])
  (k : Nat[n]) : Circle (loc bag)
  {
    sample F1 = bagselect k V;
    eps' = div(div(eps,(T + 1)),(2 * delta)+1);
    sample result = kmedians_aux T F1
                      delta cost eps' V D;
    let (_, Fs) = result;
    exp_noise delta Fs cost eps D
  }
```

Figure 13. k-medians in *DFuzz*

7. Related Work

Differential privacy Our system provides differential privacy [12], one of the strongest privacy guarantees that has been proposed to date. Alternatives include randomization, l-diversity, and k-anonymity, which are generally less restrictive but can be vulnerable to certain attacks on privacy [24]. Differential privacy offers a provable bound on the amount of information an attacker can learn about any individual, even with access to auxiliary information.

PINQ [26] is an SQL-like differentially private query language embedded in C#; Airavat [36] is a MapReduce-based solution using a modified Java VM. Both PINQ and Airavat check privacy at runtime, while *DFuzz* uses a static check. The other previous work in this area is *Fuzz* [20, 33, 34], on which *DFuzz* is based. *DFuzz* has a richer type system: while *Fuzz* uses linear types to track sensitivity, *DFuzz* uses a combination of linear indexed types and lightweight dependent types, which substantially expands the set of differentially private queries that can be certified successfully.

Another recent language-based solution is CertiPriv [3]. This is a machine-assisted framework—built on top of the Coq proof assistant—for reasoning about differential privacy from first principles. CertiPriv can certify even more queries than *DFuzz*, including queries that do not rely on standard building blocks such as the Laplace mechanism—indeed, it can be used to prove the correctness of the Laplace mechanism itself. However, this comes at the cost of much higher complexity and less automation, making CertiPriv more suitable for experts who are expanding the boundaries of differential privacy. In contrast, *DFuzz*'s certification is automatic, allowing it to target a broader class of potential users.

Other work in this area include Xu [39], who considered differential privacy in a distributed setting, using a probabilisitc process calculus, and Mohan et al. [29], who introduce a platform for private data analysis that optimizes error for certain queries.

Linear dependent types Linear types, inspired by Girard's linear logic [15], have emerged as key tools to support fine grained reasoning about resource management [37]. In this context, the idea of using indexed modalities $!_p$ for counting multiple uses of the same resource, as we do, emerged early on. Bounded Linear Logic [16] introduced modalities indexed by polynomial expressions. Those are similar to our sensitivity annotations with the essential difference that they are polynomials over natural numbers, while we consider polynomials over the reals augmented with ∞. This approach has been extended in [9] by constrained universal and existential quantifiers, providing mechanisms for polymorphism and abstraction over polynomial expressions similar to the ones made available by our quantifiers over size and sensitivity variables.

Different forms of lightweight dependent types form the basis for programming languages such as Dependent ML, ATS, and Epigram. Moreover, they have also started to be incorporated in more standard programming languages, such as Haskell [40]. In all these approaches the types can express richer properties of the program that can then be ensured automatically by type checking.

ATS [7] is a language that combines linear and dependent types. Its type system is enriched with a notion of resources that is a type-level representation of memory locations. The management of location resources uses a linear discipline. This aspect makes ATS useful for reasoning about properties of memory and pointers. However, linear types as used in ATS are not enough to reason about the sensitivity of programs.

Linear indexed types and lightweight dependent types have also been combined in [8] with the aim of providing a general framework for implicit complexity. The approach in [8] is similar in spirit to the one developed in the current paper; however, it considers only type-level terms that represent natural numbers, and its typing judgments are parametric in an equational program providing for the semantics of the type-level language. Moreover, [8] allows a further dependency between different modal operators that is not needed for our analysis. More recently, Krishnaswami et al. [23] proposed a language that combines linear (non-indexed) types with dependent types in order to provide program modules with a refined control of their state.

Related notions of privacy and sensitivity The study of database privacy and statistical databases has a long history. Recent work includes Dalvi, Ré, and Suciu's study of probabilistic database management systems [10], and Machanavajjhala et al.'s comparison of different notions of privacy with respect to real-world census data [25].

Quantitative Information Flow is concerned with how much one piece of a program can affect another, but measures this in terms of how many bits of entropy leak during one execution. While Differential Privacy and Quantitative Information Flow are clearly related concepts, the question of establishing formal relations between them has been approached only recently [1, 2].

Provenance analysis in databases tracks the input data actually used to compute a query's output, and is also capable of detecting that the same piece of data was used multiple times to produce a given answer [17].

Palamidessi and Stronati [31] recently proposed a constraint-based approach to compute the sensitivity of relational algebra queries. Their analysis is able in particular to compute the exact sensitivity for a wide range of queries. In contrast, the goal of our approach is to provide an upper bound on the sensitivity not only of relational queries but also for higher order functional programs.

Chaudhuri et al. in [6] study automatic program analyses that establish sensitivity (which they call robustness) of numerical programs. Their approach can also used to ensure differential privacy, although they do not study this application in depth. Our approach differs in that we ensure differential privacy through a logically motivated type system, rather than a program analysis.

8. Conclusions and Future Work

We have presented a new core language, *DFuzz*, for differentially private queries. Like its predecessor, *Fuzz*, *DFuzz* has a type system with strong metatheoretic properties, which guarantee that all queries of a certain type are differentially private. The key novelty in *DFuzz* is a lightweight form of linear dependent types that track size and sensitivity information; this considerably expands the range of programs that can be certified as differentially private. We have demonstrated the expressivity of *DFuzz* using four example algorithms from the differential privacy literature that can be implemented in *Fuzz* only in greatly simplified form, or not at all.

Prototype We are currently working on an algorithmic version of *DFuzz* and a prototype implementation. The key implementation challenge is related to checking the subtype relation. A natural approach to this problem is to generate numeric and logical constraints that would have to be satisfied in order to type the program, and to then pass these constraints to an external solver. In the case of *DFuzz*, some of the constraints are over real numbers, but they are of a form that is supported by the Z3 solver [11]. Since *DFuzz*'s additional constructs and annotations are erasable at runtime, a prototype can share a backend with *Fuzz*, and is thus able to take advantage of *Fuzz*'s defenses against side channels [20].

Possible extensions The languages for size and sensitivity annotations we have used in this paper are fairly restrictive, but this is merely a design choice, and not an inherent limitation of the approach. As we have shown in the k-medians example, allowing more complex size and sensitivity annotations can increase the expressivity, though it may also make the generated constraints harder to solve.

There are other simple increments to the annotation languages that would increase *DFuzz*'s expressivity. For example, [27] provides a higher-utility algorithm for the cumulative distribution function that uses a divide-and-conquer approach. The resulting sensitivity is proportional to the *logarithm* of the number of buckets. If logarithms of sizes were added to the annotation language, it would become possible to implement this algorithm. (Of course, this addition would again come at the cost of increasing the difficulty of constraint solving.) Another possible direction would be to include more general data types, as in [38], in addition to the precise types $\mathbf{L}(\sigma)[S]$ and $\mathbf{N}[S]$ we have focused on. For instance, the private Facility Location algorithm, as presented in [18], is similar to k-medians, but, instead of a fixed number of factories to build, we are given a fixed cost per factory, and the goal is to minimize the total cost. This algorithm requires recursion over generalized trees, which we speculate could be implemented in *DFuzz* if support for sized versions of these data types were added.

Limitations and future work We designed *DFuzz* to certify algorithms for which the differential privacy property can essentially be proven with a rich compositional sensitivity analysis to show that the noise is drawn from an appropriate distribution. However, in the differential privacy literature there are algorithms whose analysis requires more involved reasoning. One example is the private version of the Unweighted Vertex Cover algorithm that was presented in [18]. One way to handle the analysis for this algorithm would be to use the probabilistic *relational* reasoning that is the basis of the CertiPriv framework [3]. The ability to reason about relations between different programs and data, i.e., about closely neighboring databases, seems crucial to this approach. However, by using the CertiPriv framework, one loses the ability to reason about differential privacy in an automated way. One natural way to preserve the automatic approach and to nevertheless expand the scope of the analysis would be to combine the approach of *DFuzz* with a limited form of relational reasoning.

Acknowledgments We thank Emilio Jesús Gallego Arias for many valuable comments on the final version of this work. We thank Mário S. Alvim, Loris D'Antoni, Sanjeev Khanna, Aaron Roth, and the anonymous reviewers for their helpful comments. This research was supported by ONR grants N00014-09-1-0770 and N00014-12-1-0757, and NSF grant #1065060. Marco Gaboardi was supported by the European Community's Seventh Framework Programme (FP7/2007-2013) under grant agreement n° 272487.

References

[1] M. S. Alvim, M. E. Andres, K. Chatzikokolakis, and C. Palamidessi. On the relation between Differential Privacy and Quantitative Information Flow. In *Proc. ICALP*, 2011.

[2] G. Barthe and B. Köpf. Information-theoretic Bounds for Differentially Private Mechanisms. In *Proc. CSF*, 2011.

[3] G. Barthe, B. Köpf, F. Olmedo, and S. Zanella Béguelin. Probabilistic relational reasoning for differential privacy. In *Proc. POPL*, 2012.

[4] A. Blum, C. Dwork, F. McSherry, and K. Nissim. Practical privacy: the SuLQ framework. In *Proc. PODS*, 2005.

[5] K. Chaudhuri, C. Monteleoni, and A. D. Sarwate. Differentially private empirical risk minimization. *J. Mach. Learn. Res.*, 12:1069–1109, July 2011.

[6] S. Chaudhuri, S. Gulwani, R. Lublinerman, and S. NavidPour. Proving programs robust. In *Proc. FSE*, 2011.

[7] C. Chen and H. Xi. Combining programming with theorem proving. In *Proc. ICFP*, pages 66–77, 2005.

[8] U. Dal Lago and M. Gaboardi. Linear dependent types and relative completeness. In IEEE LICS '11, pages 133–142, 2011.

[9] U. Dal Lago and M. Hofmann. Bounded linear logic, revisited. In *TLCA*, volume 5608 of *LNCS*, pages 80–94. Springer, 2009.

[10] N. Dalvi, C. Ré, and D. Suciu. Probabilistic databases: diamonds in the dirt. *Commun. ACM*, 52(7):86–94, 2009.

[11] L. de Moura and N. Bjørner. Z3: An efficient SMT solver. In *Proc. TACAS*, 2008.

[12] C. Dwork. Differential privacy. In *Proc. ICALP*, 2006.

[13] C. Dwork, F. McSherry, K. Nissim, and A. Smith. Calibrating noise to sensitivity in private data analysis. In *Proc. TCC*, 2006.

[14] M. Gaboardi, A. Haeberlen, J. Hsu, A. Narayan, and B. C. Pierce. Linear dependent types for differential privacy (extended version). `http://privacy.cis.upenn.edu/papers/dfuzz-long.pdf`.

[15] J. Girard. Linear logic. *Theor. Comp. Sci.*, 50(1):1–102, 1987.

[16] J. Girard, A. Scedrov, and P. Scott. Bounded linear logic. *Theoretical Computer Science*, 97(1):1–66, 1992.

[17] T. J. Green, G. Karvounarakis, and V. Tannen. Provenance semirings. In *Proc. PODS*, 2007.

[18] A. Gupta, K. Ligett, F. McSherry, A. Roth, and K. Talwar. Differentially private combinatorial optimization. In *Proc. SODA*, 2010.

[19] A. Gupta, A. Roth, and J. Ullman. Iterative constructions and private data release. In *Proc. TCC*, 2012.

[20] A. Haeberlen, B. C. Pierce, and A. Narayan. Differential privacy under fire. In *Proc. USENIX Security*, 2011.

[21] S. Hayashi. Singleton, union and intersection types for program extraction. In *Proc. TACS*, volume 526 of *LNCS*, pages 701–730. Springer Berlin / Heidelberg, 1991.

[22] S. P. Kasiviswanathan, H. K. Lee, K. Nissim, S. Raskhodnikova, and A. Smith. What can we learn privately? In *Proc. FOCS*, Oct. 2008.

[23] N. R. Krishnaswami, A. Turon, D. Dreyer, and D. Garg. Superficially substructural types. In *Proc. ICFP*, 2012.

[24] N. Li, T. Li, and S. Venkatasubramanian. t-closeness: Privacy beyond k-anonymity and l-diversity. In *Proc. ICDE*, 2007.

[25] A. Machanavajjhala, D. Kifer, J. Abowd, J. Gehrke, and L. Vilhuber. Privacy: Theory meets practice on the map. In *Proc. ICDE*, 2008.

[26] F. McSherry. Privacy integrated queries: an extensible platform for privacy-preserving data analysis. In *Proc. SIGMOD*, 2009.

[27] F. McSherry and R. Mahajan. Differentially-private network trace analysis. In *Proc. SIGCOMM*, 2010.

[28] F. McSherry and K. Talwar. Mechanism design via differential privacy. In *Proc. FOCS*, 2007.

[29] P. Mohan, A. Thakurta, E. Shi, D. Song, and D. Culler. GUPT: privacy preserving data analysis made easy. In *Proc. SIGMOD*, 2012.

[30] A. Narayanan and V. Shmatikov. Robust de-anonymization of large sparse datasets. In *Proc. IEEE S&P*, 2008.

[31] C. Palamidessi and M. Stronati. Differential privacy for relational algebra: Improving the sensitivity bounds via constraint systems. In *Proc. QAPLS*, volume 85 of *EPTCS*, pages 92–105, 2012.

[32] N. Ramsey and A. Pfeffer. Stochastic lambda calculus and monads of probability distributions. In *Proc. POPL*, 2002.

[33] J. Reed, M. Gaboardi, and B. C. Pierce. Distance makes the types grow stronger: A calculus for differential privacy (extended version). `http://privacy.cis.upenn.edu/papers/fuzz-long.pdf`.

[34] J. Reed and B. C. Pierce. Distance makes the types grow stronger: A calculus for differential privacy. In *Proc. ICFP*, Sept. 2010.

[35] A. Roth and T. Roughgarden. The median mechanism: Interactive and efficient privacy with multiple queries. In *Proc. STOC*, 2010.

[36] I. Roy, S. T. V. Setty, A. Kilzer, V. Shmatikov, and E. Witchel. Airavat: security and privacy for MapReduce. In *Proc. NSDI*, 2010.

[37] D. Walker. *Advanced Topics in Types and Programming Languages*, chapter Substructural Type Systems. The MIT Press, 2005.

[38] H. Xi and F. Pfenning. Dependent types in practical programming. In *Proc. POPL*, 1999.

[39] L. Xu. Modular reasoning about differential privacy in a probabilistic process calculus. Manuscript, 2012.

[40] B. A. Yorgey, S. Weirich, J. Cretin, S. Peyton Jones, D. Vytiniotis, and J. P. M. es. Giving Haskell a promotion. In *Proc. TLDI*, 2012.

Fully Abstract Compilation to JavaScript

Cédric Fournet Nikhil Swamy Juan Chen Pierre-Evariste Dagand Pierre-Yves Strub[1] Benjamin Livshits

Microsoft Research and MSR-INRIA[1]

{fournet, nswamy, juanchen, livshits}@microsoft.com dagand@cis.strath.ac.uk pierre-yves@strub.nu

Abstract

Many tools allow programmers to develop applications in high-level languages and deploy them in web browsers via compilation to JavaScript. While practical and widely used, these compilers are ad hoc: no guarantee is provided on their correctness for whole programs, nor their security for programs executed within arbitrary JavaScript contexts. This paper presents a compiler with such guarantees. We compile an ML-like language with higher-order functions and references to JavaScript, while preserving all source program properties. Relying on type-based invariants and applicative bisimilarity, we show full abstraction: two programs are equivalent in all source contexts if and only if their wrapped translations are equivalent in all JavaScript contexts. We evaluate our compiler on sample programs, including a series of secure libraries.

Categories and Subject Descriptors D.2.4 [*Software/ Program Verification*]: Validation; D.3.4 [*Processors*]: Compilers; D.4.6 [*Operating Systems*]: Security and Protection—Verification.

Keywords Program equivalence; full abstraction; refinement types.

1. Introduction

Many tools allow programmers to develop applications in high-level languages and deploy them in web browsers via compilation to JavaScript. These include industrial compilers like GWT for Java, WebSharper and Pit for F#, and Dart, as well as several academic efforts like Links (Cooper et al. 2006) and Hop (Serrano et al. 2006). While practical and, in some cases, widely used, these compilers are *ad hoc*: no guarantee is provided on their correctness for whole programs, nor their security for programs executed within arbitrary JavaScript contexts.

The lack of security against JavaScript contexts is of particular concern, since compiled code is routinely linked with libraries authored directly in JavaScript. Libraries like jQuery and Prototype are widely used, provide improved support for several core web-programming tasks, but do so by making use of highly dynamic features of JavaScript, e.g., by redefining properties of predefined objects. Less well-known libraries are also routinely included in pages, often by simply including a pointer to the code served from a potentially untrustworthy URL. It is also common practice to include rich third-party content (e.g., advertisement scripts) in the same context as trusted JavaScript code. In all those cases, linking with a malicious or buggy script can easily break invariants of compiled code, compromise its security, and, in general, render any reasoning principles of the source programming language inapplicable to the JavaScript code that is actually executed.

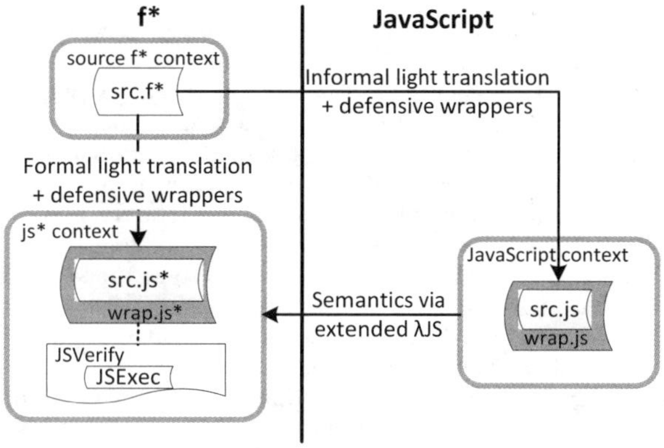

Figure 1. Architecture

This paper presents a correct and secure compiler from a variant of ML with higher-order functions and references to JavaScript. Our main result is *full abstraction*: two programs are equivalent in all source contexts if and only if their translations are equivalent in all JavaScript contexts. Full abstraction is an ideal compiler property, inasmuch as it enables local reasoning on source code, without the need to understand the details of the compiler or the target platform. In our case, programmers can rely on their experience with ML, with static scopes and types, or trust source-level verification tools—and largely ignore the rather tricky semantics of JavaScript.

Which semantics for JavaScript? Compared to ML, the semantics of JavaScript is daunting. There are several different ECMA standards and various implementations (mainly by web browsers) that deviate from the standard in idiosyncratic ways. Maffeis et al. (2008) give an operational semantics for the ECMAScript 3 standard, which while extremely detailed, is also unwieldy in that it is not easily amenable to formal proof or to testing. An alternative approach is to give a semantics via translation to a simpler language, and then to test this translation semantics for compliance with browser implementations. This is the approach of Guha et al. (2010), who give a translation of JavaScript into a mostly standard, dynamically typed lambda calculus called λJS. The translation semantics is convenient for our purposes (e.g., it is executable) and not necessarily less precise or more complex. So, following λJS, we give a semantics to JavaScript by elaboration to F* (Swamy et al. 2011), a variant of ML with richer types. We intend this semantics to capture the main features of the ECMAScript 5 standard, including features like getters and setters that were missing in λJS. Our semantics also includes a number of experimental findings pertaining to implementation-specific features of JavaScript such as the `arguments`, `caller`, and `callee` properties.

A high-level view of the paper Figure 1 outlines our technical development. On the left, we have f*, a subset of F* that includes higher-order functions, mutable references, exceptions, and fatal errors, but excludes polymorphism for simplicity. Its semantics is parameterized by a type signature that defines the basic constants available to a program. On the right, we have concrete JavaScript.

Our compiler takes an f* program (src.f*) with an arbitrary signature and emits JavaScript syntax in two phases. The first phase (the 'light translation') is compositional and translates f* constructs to the corresponding ones in JavaScript, e.g., function closures to function closures, yielding src.js. For code meant to be executed in untrusted JavaScript contexts, we supplement the light translation with carefully crafted defensive wrappers (wrap.js) to securely import and export values at every source type while preserving the translation invariant.

To reason formally about our compiler, we reflect its output within an arbitrary JavaScript context back into f*. Specifically, we employ a variant of the λJS semantics to translate JavaScript to js*, an instance of f* with a signature JSExec that provides runtime support for js* programs. Our proof of full abstraction relies on refinement typing to establish several key invariants of the translation. For this typing, we introduce JSVerify, a precise typed model of JSExec expressed using monadic refinement types in f*. Then, we develop a new eager-normal-form variant of applicative bisimilarity for contextual equivalence in f* and use it to show the main result of the paper, i.e., that two f* programs are equivalent with respect to an arbitrary f* context if, and only if, their defensively wrapped light translations are equivalent with respect to an arbitrary js* context. We summarize our main contributions below.

- We describe a compiler from f* (§3) to JavaScript, including defensive wrappers to safely mediate interactions between translated programs and their context. (§4)
- We introduce js*, a model of JavaScript within f* that includes security-relevant features of ECMAScript 5 and popular JavaScript implementations. (§5)
- We formalize our compiler as a translation from f* to js*. We show that it is a forward simulation that preserves a typing and heap invariant. This yields safety and correctness for translations of closed programs executed in isolation. Additionally, by typing, we show that the defensive wrappers support safely exchanging values of various types with an untrusted context. (§6)
- We develop a new co-inductive proof technique for f*, with labeled bisimulations to capture the interactions of configurations of related terms with their abstract context, such that bisimilarity coincides with contextual equivalence. (§7)
- We prove our compiler from f* to js* fully abstract. (§8)
- We close with a brief discussion and experimental evaluation of our compiler implementation. (§9)

Disclaimer As usual, full abstraction holds only within our formal semantics of JavaScript, and various side channels may still exist in JavaScript implementations, based, for instance, on stack or heap exhaustion, or timing analysis.

This presentation necessarily omits many details. Additional materials, including a technical report with the full formal development, an F* implementation with a JavaScript back-end, sample source and compiled programs, and an updated F* theory in Coq are available at `http://research.microsoft.com/fstar`.

Related work Programming language abstractions have long been recognized as an essential means for protection (Morris 1973); their secure implementations are often specified as full abstraction (Abadi 1998; Abadi et al. 2002; Abadi and Plotkin 2010; Agten et al. 2012). Conversely, many attacks can be interpreted as failures of abstraction, and several counterexamples to full abstraction exist. For example, Mitchell (1993) notes that Lisp with FEXPR has no abstraction contexts, and Kennedy (2006) points out the lack of full abstraction in translations from C# to .NET.

Many powerful co-inductive techniques exist for program equivalence, with various combinations of types, higher-order functions, private mutable state, and exceptions (Sumii and Pierce 2005; Lassen 2005). As discussed in §7, ours combines their features so that bisimulations precisely capture the invariants of wrapped translation within untrusted JavaScript contexts. Although employing logical relations instead of bisimulations, Ahmed and Blume (2008) also use type-directed wrappers to prove that typed closure conversion in the polymorphic λ-calculus is fully abstract. However, unlike us, they do not use the wrappers in the translation itself.

There has been recent work on protecting JavaScript programs from malicious contexts. For example, Taly et al. (2011) apply a dataflow analysis to check that programs in a subset of ECMAScript 5's strict mode (lacking getters and setters) do not leak private data to an adversary. Using this analysis, the authors were able to prove the safety of object-capability idioms used by the Caja (2012) framework that rewrites JavaScript applications to confine security-critical objects, such as the DOM, behind object capabilities. This confinement property is related to the invariant enforced by our wrappers, which we check by typing. Taly et al., however, do not deal with full abstraction.

2. Challenges in secure JavaScript programming

To illustrate the difficulty of writing secure JavaScript code, we naively implement a protection mechanism around a trusted, external function `rawSend` for posting messages to some target domain (Figure 2). By calling `mkSend(rawSend)`, we should obtain a function that enforce the following policy:

- Send messages only to whitelisted URLs (to avoid privacy leaks); of at most 5 characters (to bound resource usage); that includes a secret credential (to identify the service users).
- Do not leak the `rawSend` function or the secret credential, to prevent bypassing our protection mechanism.

Our implementation calls a `sanitize` function, hypothetically provided by some other trusted library. As typical in JavaScript, linking is performed dynamically through the global name-space.

For simplicity, we use our mechanism to protect an anonymous function that prints the message and its target on the console. The resulting protected `send` function is exported to the global name-space and therefore made available to untrusted scripts:

```
send = mkSend(function (target, msg) {
  console.info("Sent " + msg + " to " + target);});
```

In isolation, our code seems to enforce our policy. However, we are going to demonstrate how, by carefully manipulating the context, a malicious script can bypass our protection mechanism. We do not claim any novelty in describing these attacks (Caja 2012; Taly et al. 2011; Meyerovich and Livshits 2010): with these examples, we aim at giving our reader a glimpse at the challenges met by security-conscious JavaScript programmers as well as prepare the ground for our defensive wrappers in §6.

Attack 1: Overwriting global objects Importing objects from the global name-space is risky: by definition, every script has access to this name-space. For instance, a script can maliciously overwrite the `sanitize` function right before calling the `send` operation:

```
sanitize = function (s,msg) { return msg; };
send("http://www.microsoft.com/owa", "too long!");
```

To prevent this attack, we must run `mkSend` before any hostile script (first-starter privilege) and store a private copy of `sanitize` as well as any other trusted library function it may call.

```
function mkSend(rawSend){
  var whiteList = {"http://www.microsoft.com/mail":true,
                   "http://www.microsoft.com/owa":true};
  function newSend(target, msg){
    msg = "[" + secret_credential + "]" + msg;
    if (whiteList[target]){
      rawSend(target,window.sanitize(5,msg));}
    else { console.error("Rejected.");}};
  return newSend ;}
function sanitize(size,msg) {
  return msg.substring(0,size);}
```

Figure 2. Naive implementation of a secure `send`

Attack 2: Dynamic source code inspection Unsurprisingly, hiding secrets in source code is to be avoided. Supposing that we wanted to keep the `whiteList` secret, a malicious script can use the `toString` method on the `mkSend` function to retrieve its content:

```
var targets = mkSend.toString().match(/\'.*?\':true/g)
targets = targets.map(function (s) {
        return s.replace(/\'(.*?)\':true/,"$1") });
```

A mere regular expression matching on the resulting string lets us extract the list of valid targets. This is not, as such, a violation of the specification, yet it is a rather unusual feature.

Attack 3: Redefining `Object` Since JavaScript is a prototype-oriented programming language, one can dynamically modify properties of any object in the system. In particular, one can add a field to the prototype of the canonical object, `Object`, hence extending the white list without even referring to `whiteList` itself:

```
Object.prototype["http://www.evil.com"] = true;
send("http://www.evil.com","msg");
```

To preclude this attack, we must ensure that any given field is indeed part of the `whiteList` object, and not inherited from its prototype chain. To this end, we could use a safe private copy (obtained by starting first) of the `hasOwnProperty` method.

Attack 4: Side-effectful implicit coercions Part of the complexity of JavaScript comes from its treatment of coercions: should the need arise, objects are automatically coerced at run-time. Instead of a string, one can, for instance, pass an object with a `toString` method that returns a string in the `whiteList` on the first use and another string as the actual send operation is performed:

```
var count = 0;
var target = { toString: function() {
    return count++ == 0 ? "http://www.microsoft.com/owa"
                        : "http://www.evil.com" }};
send(target, "msg");
```

To tame these implicit coercions, we may explicitly check that the input arguments are of the correct type, using the `typeof` operator. Alternatively, we may force a coercion upon receiving the arguments and store the result—this is the case for `msg` in Figure 2.

Attack 5: Walking the call stack Finally, stepping outside ECMA standards, most implementations of the `Function` object provide a `caller` property that points to the current caller of the function being executed. Abusing this mechanism, any callback (such as an implicit coercion or a getter) grants access to the arguments of its caller `newSend`, including `msg` after concatenation with `secret_credential`:

```
var c;
var target = { toString: function toStr () {
  c = toStr.caller.arguments[1].match(/\[(.*?)\]/)[1];
  return "http://www.microsoft.com/mail" }}
send(target, "msg");
```

This code enables one to retrieve the credential by matching the `msg` argument. Similarly, one could retrieve any secret on the call stack. To guard against this attack, we must explicitly clear the `caller` field of our functions before any potential callback.

Our proposal The examples above show that local reasoning about code in JavaScript can be compromised through a variety of attacks. Hence, writing secure code in JavaScript is a hardship: one must take a great deal of attack vectors into account, and one ends up maintaining extremely cumbersome programs, which makes them more error-prone. We propose that programmers instead use a source language with static types and scopes to write security-sensitive code. A compiler should then securely translate the source language to JavaScript, freeing the programmer from thinking about the subtle semantics of JavaScript. In this context, ML appears to be a particularly effective source language: it has static types and scopes; it is functional, so we can rely on closures and higher-order functions also available in JavaScript; and, being impure, we can adopt a programming style that approaches idiomatic JavaScript. In ML, the example of Figure 2 can be written as shown below, which clearly meets the stated security goals.

```
let mkSend rawSend =
  let whiteList = ["http://www.microsoft.com/mail";
                   "http://www.microsoft.com/owa"] in
  fun target msg →
    let msg = "[" ^ secret_credential ^ "]" ^ msg in
    if mem target whiteList then rawSend target (sanitize 5 msg)
    else consoleError "Rejected."
```

3. Syntax and semantics of f*

In this paper, we use f*, a fragment of F* (Swamy et al. 2011) similar to ML, with the syntax shown below and a standard, small-step, call-by value semantics (see the full paper). We have extended the original presentation and formal development of F* with exceptions, fatal errors, and primitive support for a mutable store.

Values range over variables, memory locations, abstraction over terms, and n-ary, fully applied data constructors. We add a form of results r, which, in addition to values, includes exceptions **raise** v and fatal **error**. Expressions are in a partial administrative normal form, with, for instance, function application $e\ v$ requiring the argument to be a value. We also have pattern matching, reference allocation, assignment and dereference, and exception handlers.

Syntax of f*

v	$::=$	$x \mid \ell \mid \lambda x{:}t.e \mid D\,\bar{t}\,\bar{v}$	values
r	$::=$	$v \mid \textbf{raise}\ v \mid \textbf{error}$	results
e	$::=$	$r \mid e\ v \mid \textbf{let}\ x = e\ \textbf{in}\ e' \mid v_1 := v_2 \mid \mathsf{ref}\ v \mid !v \mid$ $\textbf{try}\ e\ \textbf{with}\ x.e \mid \textbf{match}\ v\ \textbf{with}\ D\ \bar{\alpha}\ \bar{x} \to e\ \textbf{else}\ e'$	terms
t	$::=$	$T \mid \mathsf{ref}\ t \mid t \to t'$	types
H	$::=$	$\cdot \mid (\ell \mapsto_t v) \mid H, H'$	store
$F[\_]$	$::=$	$\_ \mid F\ v \mid F\ t \mid \textbf{let}\ x = F\ \textbf{in}\ e$	exn. ctx
$E[\_]$	$::=$	$\_ \mid E\ v \mid E\ t \mid \textbf{let}\ x = E\ \textbf{in}\ e \mid \textbf{try}\ E\ \textbf{with}\ x.e$	eval. ctx
S	$::=$	$\cdot \mid D{:}t \mid T{::}\kappa \mid S, S'$	signature
Γ	$::=$	$\cdot \mid \Gamma, x{:}t \mid \Gamma, \alpha \mid \Gamma, \ell{:}t \mid \ldots$	type env.

An f* runtime state, written $H \mid e$, is a pair of a store mapping locations to values and a program expression. The reduction relation has the form $H \mid e \to_S H' \mid e'$ where the index S is a fixed inductive signature that defines all constructors. This signature includes at least a type exn for exceptions, types ref t for references, and unit. We also freely use common primitive types like int and bool, and expect these to be in the signature as well. Our syntax does not include a fixpoint form because recursion can be encoded with recursive datatypes in the signature. We consider several instantiations of the signature S in this paper, to define our source language (§4) and to embed dynamically typed JavaScript within f* (§5).

Syntactic sugar We write applications $e\ e'$ as abbreviations of **let** $x = e'$ **in** $e\ x$, for some fresh x. A similar transformation applies to pattern matching, reference operations, exception raising, etc. We write **if** e **then** e_1 **else** e_2 for **match** e **with** true $\to e_1$ **else** e_2, and $e_1; e_2$ for **let** $\_ = e_1$ **in** e_2. Additionally, in code listings, we rely on the concrete syntax of F*, which closely resembles OCaml and F#.

Plain types F* includes various dependent typing features, but we ignore this in f*, and restrict the types to a monomorphic subset of ML including function types $t \to t'$, references, and recursive datatypes. Nevertheless, we have extended our Coq-based metatheory of the full F* language to include exceptions, state and errors, and proved subject reduction for the reduction of open terms, i.e., terms that may contain free variables, which is used in §7 and §8. We present a specialized version of this theorem below, where we use the type judgment for F* runtime states. This is written here as $S;\Gamma \vdash H \,|\, e : t$, denoting that in an environment including the signature S, free variables Γ, and the typed domain of H (written $\sigma(H)$, including $\ell : t$ for each $\ell \mapsto_t v$ in H), the store H is well-typed and the expression e has type t. When the signature S is evident from the context, we simply write $\Gamma \vdash H \,|\, e : t$.

Theorem 1 (Type soundness for open-term reduction)**.** *Given S, Γ, H, e, and t such that $S;\Gamma \vdash H \,|\, e : t$, either (1) e is a result; or (2) e is an open redex, i.e., $e \in \{E[x\ v], E[\textbf{match}\ x\ \textbf{with} \ldots], E[x := v], E[!x]\}$; or (3) there exist H', e' such that $H \,|\, e \to_S H' \,|\, e'$ and $S;\Gamma \vdash H' \,|\, e' : t$.*

Contextual equivalence We only observe well-typed terms and compare them at the same plain types. Following Theorem 1, we define basic observations on runtime states s: (1) s returns, that is, $s \to_S^* H \,|\, r$, with three kinds of results: any value (written $s \Downarrow$); any exception (written $s \Downarrow \textbf{raise}$); or an error (written $s \Downarrow \textbf{error}$); or (2) s diverges (written $s \Uparrow$) when it has an infinite sequence of reductions; or (3) (only in case s is open), s reduces to a redex with a free variable in evaluation context.

We define contextual equivalence for closed values and expressions, considering all typed evaluation contexts. (Equivalence between open terms can be re-stated using closed function values.)

Definition 1 (Contextual Equivalence)**.** *Two (closed, typed) runtime states s and s' have the same behavior, written $s \approx_{\mathsf{e}}^{\bullet} s'$, when they either both return the same kind of result, or both diverge.*

Two (closed, typed) terms are equivalent, written $e \approx_{\mathsf{e}} e'$, when they have the same behavior in all evaluation contexts.

4. A compiler from f* to JavaScript

We present our compiler from f* to JavaScript, using the f* program below as a running example.

```
let mkLog _ = let log = ref (Nil : list string) in
              let add x = log := Cons x !log in
              let iter f = List.iter f !log in
              (add, iter)
```

Calls to mkLog return an abstract interface to a log, with functions add and iter to extend the log with a string and to operate on its contents, respectively. Reasoning in f*, it is clear for instance that the log only contains strings and that it grows monotonically.

In this section, we illustrate informally how our compiler ensures that all source invariants are preserved in the translation to JavaScript. In subsequent sections, we justify it by formalizing our compiler as a translation from f* to js* and proving it fully abstract.

The light translation Our compiler proceeds in two phases. The first phase is compositional and purely syntax-directed: the translation function $\llbracket e \rrbracket$, shown in Figure 3, translates f* constructs to their JavaScript counterparts. Following standard practice, we assume uniqueness of variable names. We also use an auxiliary function, *locals*(e), that collects the let- and pattern-bound names not enclosed within additional λs of expression e.

We translate functions in f* to functions in JavaScript as follows: Local variable declarations in JavaScript always occur at the top of a function body, so we collect the source locals and declare them upfront. When reading a variable x (the second rule), we simply lookup the JavaScript variable with the same name x. In the third rule, we translate let-bindings to JavaScript *sequence expressions* (x=e0,e1)—in JavaScript, this expression evaluates e0, assigns the result to x, and then evaluates e1.

$$
\begin{array}{ll}
\multicolumn{2}{l}{\llbracket \lambda x{:}t.e \rrbracket \mapsto \texttt{function(x)}\{\overline{\texttt{var y;}}\texttt{return}\llbracket e \rrbracket\texttt{;}\} \quad \text{where } \bar{y} = \text{locals}(e)} \\
\llbracket x \rrbracket \mapsto \texttt{x} & \llbracket \textbf{let}\ x = e_1\ \textbf{in}\ e_2 \rrbracket \mapsto \texttt{(x=}\llbracket e_1 \rrbracket, \llbracket e_2 \rrbracket\texttt{)} \\
\llbracket e_1\ v_2 \rrbracket \mapsto \llbracket e_1 \rrbracket(\llbracket v_2 \rrbracket) & \llbracket D\ \bar{v} \rrbracket \mapsto \{\texttt{"tag"}{:}\mathit{str}\ D, \overline{\mathit{str}\ i{:}\llbracket v_i \rrbracket}\} \\
\llbracket \mathsf{ref}\ v \rrbracket \mapsto \{\texttt{"ref"}{:}\llbracket v \rrbracket\} & \llbracket v_1 := v_2 \rrbracket \mapsto (\llbracket v_1 \rrbracket\texttt{.ref=}\llbracket v_2 \rrbracket, \texttt{undefined}) \\
\llbracket !v \rrbracket \mapsto \llbracket v \rrbracket\texttt{.ref} & \llbracket \textbf{error} \rrbracket \mapsto \texttt{alert("error")} \\
\multicolumn{2}{l}{\llbracket \textbf{match}\ v\ \textbf{with}\ D\ \bar{x} \to e_1\ \textbf{else}\ e_2 \rrbracket \mapsto} \\
\multicolumn{2}{l}{\qquad (\llbracket v \rrbracket\texttt{.tag === }\mathit{str}\ D)\texttt{?}(\overline{\texttt{x}_i\texttt{=}\llbracket v \rrbracket\texttt{[}\mathit{str}\ i\texttt{]}}, \llbracket e_1 \rrbracket)\texttt{:}\llbracket e_2 \rrbracket}
\end{array}
$$

Figure 3. Light translation from f* to JavaScript

Function application is straightforward. We translate data values $D\ v_0 \ldots v_{n-1}$ to objects with a tag field recording the name of the constructor as a string, and with fields "0", ..., *str* $(n-1)$ containing the translations of the arguments—the meta-function *str* encodes its argument as a JavaScript string. References have a single field "ref". When assigning a reference, we update the ref field and then evaluate to undefined, our representation of the ():unit value in JavaScript. We model fatal error in JavaScript by calling the alert function, which pops up a dialog in most browser environments—several other possibilities exist for modeling fatal errors. Finally, we translate matching to JavaScript *conditional expressions*, e?e0:e1. Observe that the only statement forms we use are within functions, where we use var declarations and return. By relying only on the expression forms of JavaScript, we obtain a simple compositional translation.

For simplicity, the input of the translation does not contain exceptions and their handlers, but we still study their properties for all f* evaluation contexts (including exceptions). Technically, we also require that f* does not have ref unit and similar types whose values are all contextually equivalent in f* but whose translations may be distinguished in JavaScript using untyped equality. Finally, we do not formalize the translation of polymorphic data constructors, although they are supported by our compiler implementation.

At top level, our formalization applies to the translation of programs enclosed within a function. Our implementation augments this with simple handling for top-level let-bindings. Running this on the declaration of mkLog, we obtain the following JavaScript, where List.iter refers to the translation of the f* function List.iter.

```
function mkLog (u) {
 var log; var add; var iter;
 return
   (log={"ref":{"tag":"Nil"}},
   (add=(function(x){
     return (log.ref={"tag":"Cons", "0":x, "1":log.ref},
            undefined); }),
   (iter=(function(f){
     return (List.iter(f)(log.ref));}),
   {"tag":"Pair", "0":add, "1":iter})));}
```

Type-directed defensive wrappers Providing a JavaScript context with direct access to mkLog is not fully abstract: an adversary could, for example, call mkLog, obtain iter, and then call it with a function f that (as in attack 5 of §2) walks the stack, accesses log directly from the arguments of List.iter, and breaks its invariants. To protect our code, we apply type-directed wrappers that build a firewall between the lightly translated f* code and its context.

Our wrappers are JavaScript functions indexed by source types t. They come in pairs: a 'down' wrapper, written $\downarrow t$, takes a light translation of a source value $v{:}t$ and exports it safely to the context; an 'up' wrapper, written $\uparrow t$, takes any JavaScript value supplied by the context and attempts to extract from it a value that is a light translation of some source $v{:}t$; this may fail.

In addition to ensuring that the translated f* code and its context interact at the expected types, the wrappers seek to enforce a strict heap separation between the code and the context. Specifically, we

```
function downunit(x) { return x;}
function upunit(x) { return undefined;}
function downbool(x) { return x;}
function upbool(z) { return (z ? true : false);}
function downstring(x) { return x;}
function upstring(x) { return (x + "");}

function downpair(dn_a, dn_b) {
  return function (p) {
    return {"tag":"Pair",
            "0":dn_a(p["0"]),"1":dn_b(p["1"])};}}
function uppair(up_a, up_b) {
  return function(z) {
    return {"tag":"Pair",
            "0":up_a(z["0"]),"1":up_b(z["1"])};}}

function downfun (up_a,down_b) {
  return function (f) {
    return function (z) {
      return (down_b (f (up_a(z)))); }}}
function upfun (down_a,up_b) {
  return function (f) {
    return function (x) {
      var z = down_a x;
      var y = undefined;
      function stub() {
        arguments.callee.caller = undefined;
        arguments.callee.arguments = undefined;
        y = up_b(f(z)); }
      stub(); return y; };};}
```

Figure 4. Selected wrappers in JavaScript

ensure that the context never obtains a direct reference to an object that is used by the light translation; references from f* objects to objects owned by the context (we call such objects untrusted, or un, objects) are also problematic, since the contents of un objects are unreliable, e.g., they may change unexpectedly. So, access to f* objects by the attacker, and vice versa, are mediated by wrappers.

Figure 4 lists some wrappers used by our compiler. For immutable base types shared between f* and JavaScript, such as strings, the 'down' wrapper does nothing, whereas the 'up' wrapper forces a coercion. There are various JavaScript idioms that serve to induce coercions at particular types, e.g., for Booleans, we use an explicit conditional expression; for numbers, we use unary addition; for strings, we concatenate with the empty string, etc. This ensures, for instance, that `true` and `false` are indeed the only imported Boolean values, foiling problems like attack 4 from §2.

For datatypes such as pairs and lists (and any allocated data), we must ensure that wrapping preserves heap separation. Thus, we allocate a fresh representation and recursively wrap their contents. The 'up' wrapper is safe even as its code accesses fields (which may trigger callbacks to the context via implicit coercions or getters) because the imported content is kept as a local value on the 'up' wrapper stack. Our code includes wrapper generators; for instance, `downpair` takes as parameter two 'down' wrappers for types a and b and returns a 'down' wrapper for pairs containing an a and a b.

For functions, the situation is more complex, since the 'up' wrapper has no way to check that its argument is the valid representation of a source f* function. Instead, the wrapping is deferred: the function `downfun`, corresponding to $\downarrow(a \to b)$, exports a function `f` by wrapping it with another function that first imports the argument `x`, then applies `f`, and finally exports the result. In the other direction, one might have expected `upfun` (for $\uparrow(a \to b)$) to be strictly dual to $\downarrow(a \to b)$, i.e., export the argument, apply the function, and import the result. However, this is insufficient. As attack 5 of §2 illustrates, the JavaScript calling convention provides a function with access to the function object and arguments of its caller. If a trusted function were to call an untrusted one directly, the latter obtains a reference to the arguments of the former, breaking our heap separation discipline.

To this end, following the code of `upfun` in Figure 4, the wrapper for importing an untrusted function `f` (purportedly the translation of an $a \to b$ value) is itself a function, callable from any trusted context, that first exports its argument into a local variable `z`, then calls a fresh, single-use `stub`. The `stub` makes the call to `f` on behalf of the trusted code, but before doing so, it clears its own `caller` and `arguments` object. When the call to `f` proceeds, the context obtains a reference to the `stub`, but cannot walk the stack beyond the stub and compromise trusted code. After the untrusted call completes, `up_b` wraps up the result and stores it in `y`. (Returning the value directly is dangerous, since the attacker has a pointer to the `stub` closure, so, it may be able to call this closure later and receive the protected value.) After the `stub` completes, the wrapper returns the contents of the local variable `y`. Thus, to an attacker that attempts to traverse the call stack via the `caller`/`callee` properties, the stack (growing downward) appears as depicted alongside. Walking upward, untraversable `stub` objects delimit regions of the stack that transition from untrusted to trusted code. Additionally, the up and down wrappers mediate all calls across trust boundaries.

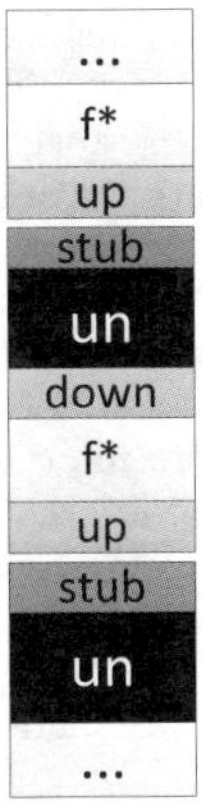

Top-level translation Continuing with our example, we list below the script that makes `mkLog` available to an arbitrary JavaScript context after suitable wrapping. Rather than placing `mkLog` directly into the global name-space (i.e., the `window` object in a web browser), our compiler generates a function `init` that takes the `window` object as a parameter, defines the lightly translated code of `mkLog` in a local variable, and exports it to `window.mkLog` after unfolding and applying the down-wrapper $\downarrow(\text{unit} \to (\text{string} \to \text{unit} * (\text{string} \to \text{unit}) \to \text{unit}))$. After running `init(window)`, our script overwrites `init` to prevent any later use (such as `init.toString()`).

```
function init(w) {
  function mkLog(u){...} // light translation shown above
  w.mkLog=
   downfun(upunit,
           downpair(downfun(upstring, downunit),
                    downfun(upfun(downstring, upunit),
                            downunit)))(mkLog); }
init(window); init=undefined;
```

Threats and countermeasures We briefly review potential threats to full abstraction, and informally discuss how we handle them.

- Modifying `Object.prototype` can override the default behavior of objects, e.g. when accessing their properties. As an invariant, translated f* code never triggers a prototype chain traversal, so our translation does not depend on `Object.prototype`.
- By changing `Function.prototype.apply`, an adversary can interpose code at function calls. However, ECMAScript 5 states that this interception does not affect primitive function calls.
- `Function.toString` returns the static source of a function closure as a string. Our wrappers ensure that, for any function `g` handed to the adversary, `g.toString()` always returns the text of its down wrapper, that is, the constant string `"function (z) { return (down_b (f (up_a(z)))); }"`
- Implicit coercions are pre-empted by systematically forcing coercions in 'up' wrappers.
- Stack walks via `callee` and `caller` properties are countered by the stub mechanism described above.
- Some browsers provide `(new Error()).stack`, which dumps the current stack as a string. Assuming that our code runs first, we disable it in the `init` function, using the code below.

```
var oldErr=Error; window.Error=function(){
  var x=oldErr(); x.stack=""; return x;};
```

Are these countermeasures sufficient? The rest of the paper, culminating with the main results of §8, provide a positive answer, at least within our semantics of JavaScript.

5. A semantics of JavaScript in f*

We begin our formal development with a semantics of JavaScript by translation to js*, the instance of f* with inductive signature JSExec described below; this allows us to carry out our full-abstraction argument entirely within a single language. We base our semantics on λJS, a dynamically typed language to which Guha et al. (2010) translate JavaScript. We extend λJS to include some features of ECMAScript 5 that were missing in the original formulation (which targeted ECMAScript 3), as well as browser-specific features that are relevant for full abstraction. Concurrently, Politz et al. (2012) have extended λJS to cover the strict mode of ECMAScript 5.

We focus on a few main features of js*: dynamic typing, object properties, function creation, the calling convention, control operators, and `eval`. We refer to our technical report for a complete presentation, including a formal translation from λJS to js*.

Dynamic typing. In order to type any JavaScript values, JSExec defines dyn, a standard 'type dynamic', as follows.

```
type dyn = Null : dyn | Undef : dyn | Bool: bool → dyn
  | Str: string → dyn | Num: float → dyn
  | Obj: loc → dyn | Fun: dyn → (dyn → dyn → dyn) → dyn
and obj = list (string * property)
and loc = ref obj
and property = Data: attrs → dyn → property
  | Accessor: attrs → (dyn * dyn) → property
type exn = Break: int→ dyn→ exn | Exn: dyn→ exn | Return: dyn→ exn
```

The type dyn has a constructor for each JavaScript primitive type. For instance, the JavaScript string literal `"Rome"` is represented as Str `"Rome"`: dyn. Objects are references to maps from string (property names) to property, the type of values or accessors (getters and setters). Their property attributes attrs specify, for instance, whether they are writable or enumerable. (Our translation does not rely on attributes for security.) Getters and setters are treated as functions, called to perform property lookups or assignments. Functions in JavaScript are also objects—one may set properties on them, writing, for instance, `function foo(){}; foo.x = 17.` To handle this, we represent JavaScript functions as js* values Fun o f, constructed from a function object o:dyn and a closure f. All functions in JavaScript receive an implicit `this` parameter and, following λJS, a single argument object with a field for each of their explicit arguments. Thus, the closure f within Fun o f has type dyn → dyn → dyn. We discuss the three kinds of exceptions shortly.

Function creation and application While outside the ECMAScript specification, most browsers implement a quirk in their calling convention. Functions `f` receive their (variable number of) arguments in single `arguments` objects. These objects include a `callee` field that points to the function object of `f`. Conversely, function objects include an arguments field that points back to the argument object of their last activation, if any, and a caller field that points back to the function object of their last caller. (This field may point to `f` itself, if it makes recursive calls, or be `null`, for top-level calls.) These fields are implicitly updated at every call. In particular, all JavaScript functions are recursive through the store, since they are given access to their own object.

To model this calling convention, JSExec defines several operations. First, a lookup function looks up the property name f in the map of an object (accounting for function values as well).

```
let lookup (d:dyn) (f:string) = match d with
  Obj loc | Fun (Obj loc) _ → assoc f !loc | _ → None
```

Similarly, a modify function updates properties within object maps. In this section, we use shorthands for these functions:

$$e\langle f\rangle \triangleq \textbf{match}\ \mathsf{lookup}\ e\ f\ \textbf{with}\ \mathsf{Some(Data\ \_\ x)}\rightarrow \mathsf{x}\ |\ \_\rightarrow \mathsf{Undef}$$
$$e_1\langle f\rangle = e_2 \triangleq \mathsf{modify}\ e_1\ f\ e_2$$

To allocate functions, JSExec defines mkFun as follows:

```
let mkFun (s:string) (code: dyn → dyn → dyn → dyn) =
  let o = alloc () in let f = Fun o (code o) in
  o⟨"@code"⟩ = f; o⟨"@toString"⟩ = Str s; o⟨"prototype"⟩ = ...; ...; f
```

For instance, we formally translate `function (x){ return x;}` to mkFun `"function(x)..."` (**fun** o this args → select o args `"0"`) where the first argument is a string literal that represents the source text of the function and the second argument is a js* closure that receives three objects: the (soon-to-be-created) function object o, the 'this' parameter, and the actual arguments. The call to mkFun allocates o, partially applies the closure to o, and sets various properties on o before returning f.

To call functions, JSExec provides apply, which receives four arguments: caller, the object of the calling function; callee, the function to be called; a this pointer; and an args object.

```
let apply (caller:dyn) (callee:dyn) (this:dyn) (args:dyn) : dyn =
  match callee with | (Fun o f) →
    let caller0 = o⟨"caller"⟩ in let args0 = o⟨"arguments"⟩ in
    try o⟨"caller"⟩ = caller⟨"@code"⟩; o⟨"arguments"⟩ = args;
      args⟨"callee"⟩ = callee; f this args
    with Break _ → error | e → raise e
    finally (o⟨"caller"⟩ = caller0; o⟨"arguments"⟩ = args0) | ...
```

Following the code, apply calls f with argument this and args. First, however, it saves the callee's caller and arguments fields, sets these fields for the current call, and sets a pointer from args to callee. Conversely, once the call returns, apply restores the callee's fields to their old value. (The derived f* form **try** ... **with** ... **finally**, detailed below, ensures that the fields are restored even if the call raises an exception.) Experimentally, this reflects major browser implementations of JavaScript.

Property access In JavaScript, properties of objects are looked up first in the object's own property map, then in the object's prototype (stored in a special property "@proto"), walking the prototype chain as needed. Once found, if the property happens to be a getter, then the getter function is called, otherwise its value is returned. This is implemented by the select function, shown below. Since calling the getter requires passing a caller object, we write select caller l f to select field f from object l in the context of the function object caller. (Recall that the translation of our example function included a call to select passing its object o as a parameter.)

```
let rec getProperty (l:dyn) (f:string) = match lookup l f with
  | Some p → Some p
  | None → match lookup l "@proto" with
    | Some (Data _ l') → getProperty l' f | None → None
let select (caller:dyn) (l:dyn) (f:string): dyn =
  match getProperty l f with
    | Some(Accessor _ (g, _)) → apply caller g l (mkEmptyArgs())
    | Some(Data _ d) → d | _ → Undef
```

A similar function, update caller l f v, sets property f on object l to value v. This function traverses the prototype chain looking for a setter for property f. If a setter is found, update calls it with caller and v; otherwise it calls modify l f v.

Exceptions and control operators We model exceptions and the other imperative control operators of JavaScript using f* exceptions. JavaScript has a `return` statement to end the current call, and a `break l` statement to return control to the code location labeled `l`, which must be defined within the same function body. λJS desugars both to a single form, which we represent as the exception Break l v. Additionally, we use exceptions Exn v for JavaScript exceptions, and Return v to encode finally clauses, as follows.

try e_1 **with** e_2 **finally** $e_3 \triangleq$ **try** (**try** e_1 **with** e_2) **finally** e_3
try e_1 **finally** $e_2 \triangleq$ **try raise** (Return e_1)
with y. **match** y **with** | Return r $\rightarrow e_2$; r | _ $\rightarrow e_2$; **raise** y

Dynamic evaluation JSExec does not support `eval`, as this would involve parsing, translating, and loading js⋆ code at run time. On the other hand, js⋆ contexts can implement any 'primitive' function `eval` using the datatypes of JSExec, together with any values they obtain by interacting with our wrapped translation. As such, our full-abstraction result applies also to contexts that use `eval`.

Typability We conclude this section with a simple result: every λJS program translated to js⋆ is well-typed against JSExec. In the statement below, $[\![e]\!]$ is the translation of a λJS expression to js⋆.

Theorem 2 (Typability of λJS translation)**.** *For all λJS programs* e *with free variables* $\overline{x}$, *we have* $JSExec; \overline{x{:}\mathsf{dyn}} \vdash [\![e]\!] : \mathsf{dyn}$.

Contextual equivalence in JavaScript (discussion) After translation to js⋆, we formally compare JavaScript programs using the contextual equivalence of §3 (Definition 1). This equivalence relies on the observation of fatal errors, which are not primitive in JavaScript, but informally account for any code with an immediate observable effect, such as `alert("error")` or `window.location = "http://error.com"`. This equivalence in js⋆ is also *a priori* finer than JavaScript equivalence, inasmuch as it quantifies over all well-typed js⋆ contexts, not just those obtained by translating JavaScript contexts. Thus, we err on the safe side: most of our results would apply unchanged for variants and extensions of JSExec (as long as its signature is unchanged), for instance, to model additional features of JavaScript implementations. Conversely, §8 shows that translations of JavaScript contexts are complete at least for interacting with wrapped translated f⋆ programs.

6. A type-preserving simulation from f⋆ to js⋆

Formally, our compiler can be viewed as the translation from f⋆ to JavaScript (§4) composed with the embedding of JavaScript into js⋆ (§5). In this light, its correctness is far from obvious. For example, even though superficially we translate f⋆ functions to JavaScript functions, several corner cases of their semantics lurk beneath the surface syntax. As we have seen, functional values translate to expressions that allocate several objects, and are subject to a calling convention with side-effects.

This section proves several safety properties for the f⋆-to-js⋆ compiler. In order to carry out these proofs, we use an alternative, monadic type system for f⋆ due to Schlesinger and Swamy (2012), as well as an application of this type system to JavaScript provided by Swamy et al. (2012). Specifically, we use JSVerify, a variant of JSExec with monadically refined types that allows us to state and prove precise typing and heap invariants of js⋆ programs. Using this machinery, we prove that the light translation preserves types and is a (weak) forward simulation. Additionally, we prove that the defensive wrappers successfully maintain several key invariants, including separating un objects from the others. While useful in their own right for whole programs (e.g., we can prove that when a source f⋆ program has no assertion failures, then neither does its translation), these properties serve primarily as lemmas that facilitate the main results of §8.

Monadic f⋆ The type system of monadic f⋆ is based on a monad of predicate transformers called the *Dijkstra state monad*. The type of this monad is written DST t wp, and stands for stateful computations yielding a t result and with specification described by the weakest pre-condition predicate transformer wp. The transformer wp takes a post-condition formula post, relating a result of type t and a final heap, and returns a pre-condition formula pre, a predicate on an initial heap. Given a program e : DST t wp and a particular post-condition post to be proven, the f⋆ type checker

Syntax of types in monadic f⋆

t	$::=$	$T \mid a \mid t\ t \mid x{:}t\{\phi\} \mid \forall a{::}\kappa.t \mid x{:}t \rightarrow t \mid \overline{x{:}t} \rightarrow \mathsf{DST}\ t\ \phi$	types
ϕ	$::=$	$\top \mid \bot \mid \phi \wedge \phi \mid \phi \vee \phi \mid \neg\ \phi \mid \phi \Longrightarrow \phi' \mid \forall x{:}t.\phi \mid \exists x{:}t.\phi$	formulas
	$\mid$	$P \mid \lambda x{:}t.\phi \mid \Lambda a{::}\kappa.\phi \mid \phi\ u \mid \phi\ \phi$	
κ	$::=$	$\star \mid E \mid x{:}t \Rightarrow \kappa \mid \alpha{::}\kappa \Rightarrow \kappa$	kinds
u	$::=$	$v \mid t \mid \mathsf{V}\ v \mid \mathsf{E}\ v \mid \mathsf{err} \mid \mathsf{Sel}\ u\ u \mid \mathsf{Upd}\ u\ u\ u \mid u_1 + u_2 \ldots$	logic term

builds a verification condition wp post and uses Z3, an SMT solver (de Moura and Bjørner 2008), to try to discharge the proof.

We give the syntax of monadic f⋆ types above. As in §3, the type language is parameterized by a signature S that also defines a set of type constructors T. Types include variables a, type applications $t\ t'$, refinement types $x{:}t\{\phi\}$, and polymorphic types $\forall a{::}\kappa.t$. Data constructors are n-ary and are given pure dependent function types $\forall \overline{a{::}\kappa}.\overline{x{:}t} \rightarrow t'$. General function types have the form $\overline{x{:}t} \rightarrow \mathsf{DST}\ t'\ \phi$, with a monadic co-domain dependent on the curried arguments $\overline{x{:}t}$.

Formulas ϕ include the usual connectives (implication is written $\Longrightarrow$, distinguishing it from the kind constructor $\Rightarrow$ discussed below). Predicates P may be interpreted (e.g. equality), although uninterpreted predicates can be introduced by the signature S. Formulas also include a strongly normalizing applicative language of functions over logical terms and other predicates. We write $\lambda x{:}t.\phi$ and $\Lambda a{::}\kappa.\phi$ for predicate literals or, in the latter case, for transformers from a predicate (or type) a of kind κ to ϕ. Formulas can be applied to other formulas or to logical terms u.

The type system is parametric in the logic used to interpret formulas. By default, we use a first-order logic with uninterpreted functions and theories of functional arrays, arithmetic, datatypes, and equality. For example, we use type heap and interpreted functions Sel: heap $\rightarrow$ ref $\alpha \rightarrow \alpha$ and Upd: heap $\rightarrow$ ref $\alpha \rightarrow \alpha \rightarrow$ heap from the select/update theory of functional arrays (McCarthy 1962) to model the store. Logic terms also include three kinds of result constructors: V v is a result value; E v is an exceptional result; and err is the error value. We define *asResult* $v \triangleq$ V v, *asResult* (**raise** v) $\triangleq$ E v, and *asResult* **error** $\triangleq$ E. Additionally, we write Result r ϕ as an abbreviation asserting that ϕ x is valid when r = V x.

We have two base kinds: $\star$ is the kind given to value types, while E is the kind of types that stand for erasable specifications, with the sub-kinding relation $\star \leq E$. We include dependent function kinds, both from types to kinds, and from kinds to kinds. In most cases, unless we feel it adds clarity, we omit writing kinds.

The main judgments in the monadic type system are $S;\Gamma \vdash^D v : t$ for values and $S;\Gamma \vdash^D e : \mathsf{DST}\ t\ \phi$ for expressions. They rely on an auxiliary judgment, $S;\Gamma \models \phi$, stating that formula ϕ is derivable from the logical refinements of context Γ. For example, we can type the program $\lambda x{:}\mathsf{ref\ int}.x := !x + 1$ as x:ref int $\rightarrow$ DST unit Λpost.λh:heap.post (V ()) (Upd h x ((Sel h x) + 1)). This is the type of a function from integer references x to unit, where the weakest pre-condition for any predicate post relating a unit result to the output heap is the formula post (V ()) (Upd h ((Sel h x) + 1)), indicating that the function always returns normally with () and updates the input heap h with the contents of location x incremented.

The judgments for typing terms extend naturally to a judgment on runtime states, written $S;\Gamma \vdash^D H \mid e : \mathsf{DST}\ t\ \phi$. The soundness theorem for monadic f⋆ is a refinement of Theorem 1; it also applies to open reductions. In its statement below, we rely on a function *asHeap* that interprets a store H as a Sel/Upd value of type heap.

Theorem 3 (Monadic soundness)**.** *Given S, Γ, H, e, t, ϕ such that $S;\Gamma \vdash^D H \mid e : DST\ t\ \phi$, and a post-condition ψ such that $S;\Gamma \models \phi\ \psi\ (asHeap\ H)$ is derivable; either: (1) e is a result and $S;\Gamma \models \psi\ (asResult\ e)\ (asHeap\ H)$; (2) e is an open redex; or (3) there exist H', e', ϕ', such that $H \mid e \rightarrow_S H' \mid e'$, $S;\Gamma \vdash^D H' \mid e' : DST\ t\ \phi'$ and $S;\Gamma \models \phi'\ \psi\ (asHeap\ H')$.*

We sometimes use a monad iDST, an abbreviation for the DST monad augmented with a heap invariant: iDST t wp is the type of a computation that, when run with an input heap h satisfying HeapInv h ∧ wp post h, diverges or produces an output heap h' and result r:t satisfying HeapInv h' ∧ DeltaHeap h h' ∧ post r h'. We describe the heap invariants enforced by iDST below, referring to our online material for the full definitions.

JSVerify: a precise typed model of JSExec We now present a few key elements in JSVerify, an interface for JSExec written using the precise types of monadic f*. We start by showing how we recover the precision of the source type system by refining the type dyn introduced in §5. A central feature of this refinement is JSVerify's model of a partitioned js* heap. We conclude this subsection with a lemma relating JSExec to JSVerify.

Dynamic typing We structure our formal development by translating the types of f* into logical formulas. Specifically, we use a refinement of type dynamic developed by Swamy et al. (2012) to embed the simple type language of f* within the refinement logic of monadic f*. For example, rather than typing Str "Rome" simply as dyn, we type it as x:dyn{TypeOf x = string}, where TypeOf is an uninterpreted function from values to E-kinded types.

We show a few cases in the definition of type dyn used in JSVerify below. The full listing of JSVerify is available online.

```
type dyn = ...
| Str: string → d:dyn{TypeOf d=string}
| Obj: l:loc → d:dyn{TypeOf d=TypeOf l}
| Fun: ∀wp. o:dyn{∃ l. o=Obj l ∧ ...}
   → (this:dyn → args:dyn → iDST dyn (wp o args this))
   → d:dyn{TypeOf d=WP wp}
```

As in JSExec, an object is a value Obj l, for some heap reference l:loc. In addition, the refinement on the Obj constructor recalls the refinement on the underlying loc. The Fun constructor takes two value arguments, an object o and a function closure, as before. In addition, it now takes a specificational argument: a predicate transformer wp for the function closure. The refinement on the argument o requires it to be an object (in addition to some other properties, which we elide from this presentation). The function closure is itself typed within the iDST monad with weakest precondition wp. The type of Fun recalls the predicate transformer of the closure in its result type, i.e., TypeOf d=WP wp where WP is a type-level coercion from the kind of wp to E.

Invariants of a partitioned heap Our proof strategy involves enriching the type of heap references to keep track of a logical partition of the js* heap into five compartments. This partition allows us to prove several invariants, e.g., that there are no references from objects in the attacker-controlled part of the heap to elsewhere. These five heap compartments are as follows:

Inv: *the invariant heap* Let-bound variables, arguments and data are immutable in f* but are held in heap locations in js*. To keep track of these locations, we place them in a logical compartment called the Inv heap. A complication that we handle is that these locations are not strictly immutable—JavaScript forces us to preallocate locals, requiring a mutation after allocation, and the calling convention also involves implicit effects. Still, we prove that, once set, all the relevant fields of objects in the Inv heap never change.

Ref: *the heap of source references* Locations used to represent the translation of f* values of type ref t are placed in the Ref heap, where an invariant ensures that the content of a Ref heap cell, once initialized, always holds a translation of a t-typed source value.

Abs: *the abstract heap of function objects* Recall that every function in js* is associated with a heap-allocated object whose contents is updated at every function call. We place these unstable locations in the Abs heap, and ensure that translated source programs never read or write from these locations, i.e., function objects are abstract.

Un: *the untrusted heap* This heap compartment is used to model locations under control of the attacker. Our full-abstraction result relies crucially on a strict heap separation to ensure that locations from the other compartments never leak into the Un heap (with one exception, discussed next).

Stub: *the heap of declassified function objects* Function objects corresponding to stubs in the `upfun` wrapper are allocated in a compartment of their own. These objects initially belong to the f* translation, but, once used, they become accessible from the Un heap. To this end, we implement (and type) a logical declassification protocol, allowing us to prove that, as their ownership is transferred to the attacker, stub objects do not leak any information.

To keep track of these heap compartments, JSVerify enriches the representation of heap allocated objects with (ghost) metadata, outlined below. We have a tag for each compartment. The type tobj, which is a wrapper around the type obj, associates it with its tag and a predicate p, an invariant on the contents of the object.

```
type tag = Inv: tag | Ref: tag | Abs: tag | Un: tag | Stub: tag
type tobj = TO: ∀p::obj ⇒ E . t:tag
                  → o:obj{(t=Ref ⟹ "ref" ∈ dom o ∧ p o)
                          ∧ t =Inv ⟹ ...}
                  → v:tobj{TypeOf v=PT p t}
type loc = TL: ∀p::obj ⇒ E . t:tag → ref (v:tobj{TypeOf v=PT p t})
             → v:loc{TypeOf v=PT p t}
```

Values of type tobj are triples TO p t o. Its third component o is typed as an obj (that is, a map from strings to properties) refined with a formula stating, for example, that if the object is in the Ref heap, then it contains the `"ref"` field, and that it satisfies the invariant p. A similar, but more complex invariant applies to objects in the Inv compartment (due to object initialization and implicit effects). The result type of TO records both the invariant p and the tag of the object in the refinement. The type loc is also a triple, TL p t r, where r is a reference to a tagged object. We memoize the tag and invariant of the content of r with the reference itself, and the type of TL ensures that the tags of the content and the loc agree.

Translation of types A source type t in f* is translated to the refined js* type $[\![t]\!] \triangleq$ d:dyn{ϕ_t d} where ϕ_t is a predicate on dyn-typed js* values. We show a few cases below, where SelObj selects an object from the heap, and SelProp selects a property.

$$\begin{aligned}
\phi_{\mathsf{string}} &= \lambda \mathsf{d}.\mathsf{TypeOf\ d{=}string} \\
\phi_{\mathsf{ref}\ t} &= \lambda \mathsf{d}.\mathsf{TypeOf\ d{=}PT}\ (\lambda \mathsf{o}.\ \phi_t\ (\mathsf{SelProp\ o}\ \texttt{"ref"}))\ \mathsf{Ref} \\
\phi_{t \to t'} &= \lambda \mathsf{d}.\mathsf{TypeOf\ d{=}WP}\ \lambda_\ \mathsf{a}\ _.\Lambda \mathsf{p}.\lambda \mathsf{h}.\phi_t\ (\mathsf{SelProp(SelObj\ h\ a)}\ \texttt{"0"}) \\
&\qquad \wedge \ldots \wedge \forall \mathsf{r\ h'}.\ \mathsf{Result\ r}\ \phi_{t'} \Longrightarrow \mathsf{p\ r\ h'}
\end{aligned}$$

The translation for primitive types like string is simple: the refinement formula ϕ_{string} requires the translated value to be a Str _ : dyn. The translation of ref t requires an object in the Ref heap, whose `"ref"` field satisfies predicate ϕ_t. The translation of function types $\phi_{t \to t'}$ requires the compiled value to be a Fun wp _ _ term, where (among other requirements) the predicate transformer wp requires its zeroth argument to satisfy ϕ_t, and requires proving the post-condition on a result r that satisfies $\phi_{t'}$ (if it is a value).

Interface of JSVerify To enforce our invariants, JSVerify exposes a monadic version of the JSExec interface. To operate on un values, for instance, it provides aliases to the functions select, update, and apply of §5. An un value is either a primitive value, or an object (or function) allocated in the Un heap, or a declassified Stub object. The function selectUn allows a (non-internal) field to be selected from an un object. Its pre-condition requires both the caller and the object o to be un-values, and requires the post-condition p to be proven for any IsUn result and heap (since, via getters, selecting a field can trigger arbitrary code). The specification for updating an un object is similar. Calling an un function requires that the caller be an un value, both this and args be un, and ensures that the result is also un. In all cases, the use of the iDST monad requires and ensures the heap invariant as well.

```
type IsUn x = TypeOf x=string ∨ ... ∨ GetTag x = Un
              ∨ (GetTag x = Stub ∧ Declassified x)
type un = x:dyn{IsUn x}
val selectUn:caller:dyn{GetTag caller = Un}
          →o:un →f:string{¬ IsInternalField f}
          →iDST dyn (Λp.λh. ∀r h'. Result r IsUn ⟹ p r h')
val updateUn: caller:dyn{GetTag caller = Un}
          →o:un →f:string{¬ IsInternalField f} →v:un
          →iDST dyn (Λp.λh. ∀r h'. Result r IsUn ⟹ p r h')
val applyUnUn: caller:un →callee:dyn{GetTag callee = Un}
          →this:un →args:un{GetTag args = Un}
          →iDST dyn (Λp.λh. ∀r h'. Result r IsUn ⟹ p r h')
```

Accessing the other heaps imposes stricter requirements but also provides more guarantees.

Relating JSExec and JSVerify To relate our two interfaces, we prove a lemma that shows that any js⋆ program well-typed against JSExec is also well-typed against JSVerify, as long as it interacts only with the Un-fragment of JSVerify. To state this lemma, and in the rest of the paper, we use the following syntactic shorthands:

- We write $S;\Gamma \vdash^D e : t$ for a computation with a trivial pre-condition returning a t-result, i.e., $S;\Gamma \vdash^D e : \mathsf{iDST}\ t\ \mathsf{wp}_\top$, where $S;\Gamma \models \forall \mathsf{h.HeapInv\ h} \Longrightarrow \mathsf{wp}_\top(\lambda\_\mathsf{h'.HeapInv\ h'} \land \mathsf{DeltaHeap\ h\ h'})\mathsf{h}$.
- $S;\Gamma \vdash^D H\,|\,e : t$ stands for $S;\Gamma \vdash^D H\,|\,e : \mathsf{iDST}\ t\ \mathsf{wp}$, where $S;\Gamma \models \mathsf{wp}\ (\lambda\_\mathsf{h'.HeapInv\ h'} \land \mathsf{DeltaHeap\ h\ h'})\ \mathsf{h}$ and $\mathsf{h} = asHeap\ H$.
- Γ^D is the lifting of function types in the context Γ, where a type $\mathsf{t} \to \mathsf{t'}$ is lifted to $\mathsf{x{:}t} \to \mathsf{iDST\ t'\ wp}_\top$. When it is clear from the context, we write types like $\mathsf{t} \to \mathsf{t'}$, leaving the lifting implicit.
- $tagUn(H\,|\,e)$ is the runtime state obtained by adding Un-tags to each object and loc-typed constant in $H\,|\,e$.

Lemma 2 (Universal monadic typability of js⋆)**.** *If JSExec;*$\Gamma \vdash H\,|\,e : t$*, then JSVerify;*$\Gamma^D \vdash^D tagUn(H\,|\,e) : t$

Henceforth, we write $\Gamma \vdash^D H\,|\,e : t$ for monadic typing, leaving the signature of JSVerify in the context implicit.

Formal light translation of f⋆ runtime states We now formalize the light translation as a relation $\Gamma \vdash_f H\,|\,e : t \leadsto_I H'\,|\,e'$ for the translation of the f⋆ runtime configuration $H\,|\,e$ of type t into a js⋆ configuration $I, H'\,|\,e'$, where H' is the Ref compartment and I consists of both the Inv and Abs compartments. The subscript f is a js⋆ value, representing the object of the function that encloses e; it is Null at the top-level. Figure 5 gives five representative translation rules, simplifying them by eliding type arguments. The rules are to be interpreted as inlining the definitions from JSVerify into the translated term, rather than leaving them as free variables.

The first rule translates a data constructor to an object literal, which in JSVerify is represented as an Inv location that is allocated and immediately initialized with the contents of the constructor. This is particularly important—the alternative of allocating an object first, and then setting its fields is not secure, since, in general, this could cause a traversal of the prototype chain, triggering attacker code in case the attacker has installed a setter on the publicly available `Object.prototype`. In contrast, the allocation of an object literal never causes a prototype traversal.

The second rule translates a let- or λ-bound source variable x to a js⋆ expression that selects from the "0" field of an object stored in the Inv heap, whose location is bound to a js⋆ variable of the same name. The invariant guarantees that the "0" field is set in the immediate object, again preventing any prototype traversal.

$$\frac{\forall i. \Gamma \vdash_f v_i : t_i \leadsto_I e_i}{\Gamma \vdash_f D_{\bar{t} \to T}\ \bar{v} : T \leadsto_I \mathsf{mkInv}\ [(\texttt{"tag"}, \mathsf{Str}\ (str\ D)); \overline{(str\ i, e_i)}]}$$

$$\frac{\Gamma(x) = t}{\Gamma \vdash_f x : t \leadsto_I \mathsf{selectInv}\ f\ x\ \texttt{"0"}}$$

$$\frac{\Gamma, x{:}t_x \vdash_o e : t \leadsto_I e' \quad \overline{x_i : t_i} = \mathrm{locals}(e) \quad src \text{ any string constant}}{\Gamma \vdash_f \lambda x{:}t_x.e{:}t_x \to t \leadsto_I \mathsf{mkFunAbs}\ src\ \lambda o\,\_x.\mathbf{let}\ \overline{x_i = \mathsf{mkLocInv}()}\ \mathbf{in}\ e'}$$

$$\frac{\Gamma \vdash_f e : t' \to t \leadsto_I e' \qquad \Gamma \vdash_f v : t' \leadsto_I v'}{\Gamma \vdash_f e\ v : t \leadsto_I \mathsf{applyAnyAbs}\ f\ e'\ \ell_{global}\ (\mathsf{mkInv}\ (\mathsf{TO\ Inv}\ [(\texttt{"0"}, v')]))}$$

$$\frac{v_\ell = \mathsf{Obj}\ (\mathsf{TL\ Inv}\ \ell) \quad \Gamma \vdash_f v : t \leadsto_I v' \quad I(l) = \mathsf{TO\ Inv}\ [(\texttt{"0"}, v')]}{\Gamma \vdash_f v : t \leadsto_I \mathsf{selectInv}\ \varphi_t\ f\ v_\ell\ \texttt{"0"}}$$

Figure 5. Light translation from f⋆ to js⋆ (selected rules)

The third rule translates a closure. Function objects in the light translation are always allocated in the Abs heap. So, we use an alias of JSExec.mkFun from JSVerify called mkFunAbs, which builds the function object. We translate the body of the function using the variable o as the caller object, passed as an argument to applyAbs (an alias of JSExec.apply for calling an Abs function) at every call-site in the body of e, as shown in the next rule. Again, the arguments are passed as an object literal.

The last rule is useful primarily for translating runtime expressions, rather than source values. f⋆ has an applicative semantics with a standard β-reduction rule. However, in js⋆, values are passed as pointers to the Inv (or sometimes Abs) heap. Without this last rule, this mismatch would cause considerable technical difficulties in our forward simulation proof. For example, in f⋆ we may have $(\lambda x.(x,x))\ D \to_S (D,D)$ for some constructor D. When translating the left-hand side, we may allocate only one D in js⋆, whereas, the translation of the right-hand side would allocate two objects. To reflect both possibilities, the light translation is a non-deterministic relation on runtime states, indexed by the js⋆ heap I, representing pre-allocated data. So, in the last rule, if we find a location ℓ in the I heap which already contains a value that is a valid translation of the source value v, then, rather than allocate a fresh location, we may simply translate v to the expression that selects from ℓ. As such, our translation relation conveniently hides the details of data allocation and aliasing—our typed invariant and §8 show that those details are not observable anyway.

Correctness of the light translation We present our main results for the light translation, first stating that it preserves the typing and heap invariants, then that it is a forward simulation: every f⋆ reduction is matched by one or more js⋆ reductions.

Type preservation states that if an f⋆ state $H\,|\,e$ well-typed at t is translated to a js⋆ state $H'\,|\,e'$ (with Inv and Abs heaps I), then the js⋆ state is well-typed in the iDST monad against JSVerify. The lemma ensures that when h0 (the logical value corresponding to I and H') satisfies the heap invariant, the js⋆ state diverges, or produces a result r and post-heap h1, where h1 satisfies the heap invariant and DeltaHeap h0 h1; and that Result r ϕ_t is valid. As a base case, the heap invariant on the empty heap (produced when translating a source program, rather than an intermediate runtime configuration) is trivially satisfied. A technical requirement, due to JavaScript's hoisting of local variables, is that all the let-bound variables of the translated term already exist in the heap I.

Lemma 3 (Type preservation)**.** *If* $\Gamma \vdash_f H\,|\,e : t \leadsto_I H'\,|\,e'$ *then, for* $\Gamma' = [\![\Gamma]\!], \Gamma_{locals(e)}$*, there exists* ψ *such that* $\Gamma' \vdash^D H', I\,|\,e' :$ *iDST dyn* ψ *and, for* $h0 = asHeap\ (I, H')$*, if HeapInv h0 and LocalsOK* $locals(e)$ *h0, then*

$$\Gamma' \models \psi\ (\lambda x\ h1.\ \mathit{HeapInv\ h1} \land \mathit{DeltaHeap\ h0\ h1} \land \mathit{Result}\ x\ \phi_t)\ h0$$

Our next lemma ensures that the formal light translation is a forward simulation. That is, every reduction step of an f* program $H \mid e$ is matched by one or more reductions of its js* translation. We use an auxiliary function *Abs I*, standing for the set of objects that may be used as the caller object in js*:

$$Abs\ I = \{\mathsf{Null}\} \cup \{\mathsf{Obj}\ \ell \mid \ell \in \mathrm{dom}(I) \wedge \mathsf{GetTag}\ \ell = \mathsf{Abs}\}$$

Lemma 4 (Forward simulation). *For any source reduction step* $H \mid e \rightarrow_S H_1 \mid e_1$ *and any translation* $\Gamma \vdash_f H \mid e \rightsquigarrow_I H' \mid e'$, *where* $f \in Abs\ I$, *there exist reduction steps* $I, H' \mid e' \rightarrow_S^{+} I, I', H_1' \mid e_1'$, *and a translation* $\Gamma \vdash_g H_1 \mid e_1 \rightsquigarrow_{I,I'} H_1' \mid e_1'$, *where* $g \in Abs\ (I, I')$.

Defensive wrappers We now consider the properties of the second phase of our compiler, i.e., the defensive wrappers. Figure 6 lists the js* code of `downfun` and `upfun`—it is instructive to compare with the JavaScript wrappers shown in Figure 4. This code is typed against JSVerify, making use of the heap-partition-aware variants of functions in JSExec. This allows us to record the code positions that may trigger callbacks to untrusted code (which leaks the caller's object to the context). Specifically, we use the following variants of mkFun, apply, select, and update.

- abs-functions reside in the Abs heap and are created by mkFunAbs. They may be called with any caller using applyAnyAbs.
- un-functions are created by mkFunUn with an object o:un. They are called using applyUnUn, that is, only by callers with an un object (since this object is possibly leaked to the callee) and un arguments. Similarly, Un objects are selected using selectUn, possibly triggering a callback to the context (due to a getter).
- stub-functions specifically support our 'upfun' wrapper. They are created by mkFunStub with an object in the Stub compartment. They can be called *at most once* by any caller using applyAnyStub, after which they are declassified and released to the context. Prior to the declassification, stub objects are safe—they can be updated without triggering callbacks.
- Local variables and data constructors are allocated in the Inv heap using mkLocalInv and mkInv, respectively. These local variables may be set at most once, using setInv, then selected many times using selectInv. These calls never trigger callbacks.
- Mutable references are allocated using mkRef, and accessed using selectRef and updateRef. Locations in the Ref compartment are always well-typed, and the accesses never trigger callbacks.

For a given source type t, $\downarrow t$ is an abs-function that takes values of type $[\![t]\!]$ and returns values of type un. Conversely, $\uparrow t$ is an un-function that takes values of type un and (attempts to) return a value of type $[\![t]\!]$. To facilitate proofs of these typing properties, we instrument the js* wrappers with calls to JSVerify, rather than JSExec, as already noted. Additionally, we require two verification hints in the code of upfun. First, we add a call to a ghost function declassify, which is used to record in the refinement logic that the stub object has been released to the attacker and should henceforth be typed as un. A pre-condition of declassify u callee is that the all the fields of callee must already by typeable as un. Hence, we clear the contents of its `"caller"` and `"arguments"` fields. However, the callee object also has an internal field called `"@code"` containing a reference to the function closure itself, which the adversary can use to call the stub directly, once it has access to the stub function object (e.g., by using `Function.prototype.apply`). JavaScript provides no way to clear the `"@code"` field directly. To handle this case, we carefully ensure that, after declassification, the function closure can be typed as a function from un to un. Thus, the stub returns its result via a side-effect to the reference by. Typing this idiom requires one level of indirection: we initialize the reference by to None and, each time the stub is called and successfully imports the translation of

```
let downfun =
  mkFunAbs "downfun" (fun _ _ (apair:inv) →
    mkFunAbs "downfun_a2b" (fun _ _ (af:inv) →
      mkFunUn "downfun_f" (fun (u:un) (_:un) (az:un) →
        let up_a = selectInv u apair "0" in
        let z = selectUn u az "0" in
        let x = applyUnUn u up_a global (mkArgUn z) in
        let f = selectInv u af "0" in
        let y = applyAnyAbs u f global (mkArgInv x) in
        let down_b = selectInv u apair "1" in
        applyAnyAbs u down_b global (mkArgInv y))))
let upfun =
  mkFunAbs "upfun" (fun _ _ (apair:inv) →
    mkFunUn "upfun_a2b" (fun _ _ (af:un) →
      mkFunAbs "upfun_f" (fun (o:abs) _ (ax:inv) →
        let az = mkLocalInv() in
        let by = mkRef (mkInv [("tag", Str "None")]) in
        let down_a = selectInv apair "0" in
        let x = selectInv o ax "0" in
        setInv o az "0" (applyAnyAbs o down_a global (mkArgInv x));
        let stub = mkFunStub "stub" (fun (u:stub) (_:un) (a0:stub) →
          let callee = selectStub u a0 "callee" in
          updateStub u callee "caller" Undef;
          updateStub u callee "arguments" Undef;
          declassify u callee; (* ghost *)
          let f = selectUn u af "0" in
          let z = selectInv u az "0" in
          let y = applyUnUn u f global (mkArgUn(z)) in
          let up_b = selectInv u apair "1" in
          let b = applyUnUn u up_b global (mkArgUn y) in
          let someb = mkInv [("tag", Str "Some"); ("0", b)] in
          updateRef u by "ref" someb)
        applyAnyStub o stub global (allocStub());
        selectInv o (selectRef o by "ref") "0")))
```

Figure 6. Function wrappers in js* (omitting most types)

a source value v:b, it updates by with the translation of Some v. (In Figure 4, we collapse the option reference into a single mutable location, which is a simple semantics preserving transformation.)

Equipped with these types, we show that a down-wrapped light translation has type un. Likewise, we show that, if an up-wrapped un value returns normally, then it returns a value typed as the translation of its source type. In the lemma statement, we write $\downarrow t\ e$ for the application of a down wrapper to e, i.e., applyAnyAbs $(\_ : abs)\ \downarrow t\ (\_ : un)\ e$; and $\uparrow t\ e$ is applyUnUn $(\_ : un)\ \uparrow t\ (\_ : un)\ e$. In conjunction with Lemma 2, this shows that a wrapped term can be safely embedded in any JavaScript context.

Lemma 5 (Typing of wrapped terms).
If $\Gamma \vdash^D v : [\![t]\!]$ *then* $\Gamma \vdash^D \downarrow t\ v : un$; *if* $\Gamma \vdash^D v : un$ *then* $\Gamma \vdash^D \uparrow t\ v : [\![t]\!]$.

7. Contextual equivalence by bisimulation in f*

Contextual equivalence is a precise and intuitive notion of equivalence, both in JavaScript and in f*, but it leads to complicated direct proofs, as one needs to reason about any reduction in any context. To structure our full-abstraction proof, and to analyze interactions between translations of equivalent f* expressions and their js* contexts, we develop a custom labeled bisimulation proof technique. Although formally independent of JavaScript, the design of our bisimulation is guided by its application to source f* and js* in §8:

- Our bisimulation must support f* types, higher order functions, mutable state, exceptions, divergence, and errors.
- Functions exported using 'down' wrappers may share private state, so we need to jointly relate *configurations* of functions, rather than single functions. (See also Sumii and Pierce 2005.)
- Our wrappers stop at imported and exported functions; thus, to extend wrapping from terms to configurations and maintain wrapping as a transition invariant, we use a variant of normal

form bisimulation (Lassen 2005): our configurations have free variables standing for the functions imported from the context; thus, any callback yields a transition output with a continuation.

Next, we define these bisimulation configurations and we study their behavior, first using concrete context closures, then more abstract labeled transitions. The main result of the section is that labeled bisimilarity coincides with contextual equivalence.

We use interfaces to specify how configurations may interact with their context. An interface declares some exported functions (previously sent to the context), some imported functions (previously received from the context), some continuations (for ongoing calls to the context), and some memory (shared with the context).

Definition 6 (Interface). *An interface $\mathcal{I} = \sigma;\Gamma$ consists of heap types σ (for the heap shared with the context) and a type environment Γ that binds variables to function types t, each annotated with one of three sorts:*

- *$z :_{\mathsf{z}} t$ for functions imported from the context;*
- *$x :_{\mathsf{x}} t$ for functions exported to the context; and*
- *$k :_{\mathsf{k}} t$ for continuations of calls to the context.*

We let Γ_{z} be the projection of Γ on imported functions, and similarly for Γ_{x} and Γ_{k}. We often elide these annotations, writing for instance $y : t \in \Gamma$ for any binding of Γ. When $y \in \mathrm{dom}(\Gamma)$, we write $\Gamma|y$ for the prefix of Γ such that Γ is of the form $\Gamma|y, y{:}t, \Gamma'$.

Our configurations represent *pairs* of related f* runtime states, both waiting for their next interaction with the context. We introduce notations for pairs of related terms in configurations: for any phrase of syntax M, we write $\overline{M}$ for pairs of Ms, and write $M_{\urcorner}$ and $M_{\ulcorner}$ for their left and right projections, respectively. Further, we treat propositions φ with pairs $\overline{M}^{n}_{i=1}$ as $\varphi\{M^i_{\urcorner}/\overline{M}^i\} \wedge \varphi\{M^i_{\ulcorner}/\overline{M}^i\}$.

In this section and §8, we omit the inductive signature S in typing judgments, and write ';' instead of ',' to separate references from functions in typing environments.

Definition 7 (Configuration). *Given an interface $\mathcal{I} = \sigma;\Gamma$, a well-formed configuration $\mathcal{C} = \overline{I}\,|\,\overline{\rho}$ (written $\mathcal{I} \vdash \mathcal{C}$) consists of two heaps $\overline{I}$ such that $\sigma;\Gamma_{\mathsf{z}} \vdash \overline{I}$ and two substitutions $\overline{\rho}$ from every $y{:}t \in \Gamma_{\mathsf{x}} \uplus \Gamma_{\mathsf{k}}$ to values $\overline{v}$ such that $\sigma, \sigma(\overline{I}); (\Gamma|y)_{\mathsf{z}} \vdash \overline{v} : t$.*

In the definition, $\overline{I}$ is a pair of private heaps, with $I_{\urcorner}$ and $I_{\ulcorner}$ having possibly different domains, both disjoint from σ. (The typing judgments imply $\mathrm{dom}(\sigma) \cap \mathrm{dom}(\sigma(I)) = \emptyset$.) The substitutions $\overline{\rho}$ map every variable in $\Gamma_{\mathsf{x}} \uplus \Gamma_{\mathsf{k}}$ to functions; in particular, continuations are just functions. The environment $(\Gamma|y)_{\mathsf{z}}$ let us type them with free variables standing for previously-imported functions.

Next, we lift the contextual equivalence of §3 from terms to configurations, relying on generalized contexts and context closure:

Definition 8 (Configuration Context). *Given an interface $\sigma;\Gamma$, a well-formed evaluation context $\mathcal{E} = O\,|\,Z, e : t$ consists of*

- *a heap O such that $\sigma \subseteq \sigma(O)$ and $\sigma(O);\Gamma_{\mathsf{x}} \vdash O$;*
- *a substitution Z from every $z{:}t \in \Gamma_{\mathsf{z}}$ to a value v such that $\sigma(O);(\Gamma|z)_{\mathsf{x}} \vdash v : t$*
- *a call-stack: a typed expression $e : t$ defined by induction on Γ_{k}:*
  - *when $\Gamma_{\mathsf{k}} = \emptyset$, the stack is any e such that $\sigma(O);\Gamma_{\mathsf{x}} \vdash e : t$;*
  - *when $\Gamma_{\mathsf{k}} = k : t_1 \to t_2, \Gamma'_{\mathsf{k}}$, the stack is any $E[k\; e_1]$ such that $\sigma(O);(\Gamma|k)_{\mathsf{x}}, y : t_2 \vdash E[y] : t$ and $e_1 : t_1$ is a stack for Γ'_{k}.*

Definition 9 (Context Closure). *Given a context $O\,|\,Z, e : t$ and a configuration $\overline{I}\,|\,\overline{\rho}$ with the same interface and disjoint heaps ($\mathrm{dom}(O) \cap \mathrm{dom}(\overline{I}) = \emptyset$), we let $\mathcal{E}[\mathcal{C}] \triangleq (O, \overline{I}\,|\,e)\{\overline{\rho}, Z\}$ be the two runtime states obtained by composing the context with both sides of the configuration and jointly applying the substitutions $\overline{\rho}$ and Z in the order recorded in Γ (substituting first the latest variables).*

These runtime states are closed and well-typed: $\vdash \mathcal{E}[\mathcal{C}] : t$

Definition 10 (Contextual equivalence for Configurations).

$$\approx_E \triangleq \{\mathcal{I} \vdash \mathcal{C} \text{ such that } \forall \mathcal{E}, \mathcal{E}[\mathcal{C}]_{\urcorner} \approx^{\bullet}_{\mathsf{e}} \mathcal{E}[\mathcal{C}]_{\ulcorner}\}$$

Our definition generalizes plain contextual equivalences: for instance, contextual equivalence $\approx_{\mathsf{e}}$ on functions of type t coincides with $\approx_E$ on configurations with signature $\emptyset; x :_{\mathsf{x}} t$. More generally, we can reduce contextual equivalence of two open expressions $x_i : t_i \vdash \overline{e} : t$ to the function-value equivalence of $\vdash \lambda x_i.\overline{e} : t_i \to t$.

Labeled bisimulations To keep the context implicit, we define interactions between the configuration and its context as labeled transitions of the form $\mathcal{I} \vdash \mathcal{C} \xrightarrow{\alpha\,;\,\beta} \mathcal{I}' \vdash \mathcal{C}'$ where α and β range over input and output labels, respectively. The input label (e.g., a function call with parameters, or returning a result to a previous call) is provided by the context to the configuration, and the output label is its response (e.g., a returned value or a callback). The transition occurs only if both terms in the configuration $\mathcal{C}$ have matching behaviors (e.g., both return the same result, call the same callback, etc). Thus, the transition relation characterizes pairs of f* runtime states that have similar interactions with their context.

Definition 11 (Input Label). *Given an interface $\sigma;\Gamma$, an input label $\alpha = \Gamma'_{\mathsf{z}}\; O\,|\,y\,r$ consists of*

- *a signature Γ'_{z} disjoint from Γ;*
- *a heap O such that $\sigma \subseteq \sigma(O)$ and $\sigma(O);\Gamma_{\mathsf{x}}, \Gamma'_{\mathsf{z}} \vdash O$;*
- *a value parameter v such that $\sigma(O);\Gamma'_{\mathsf{z}} \vdash v : t$;*
- *a query $q = y\,r$, of one of the three forms below:*
  - *$x\,r$, a call to any $x : t \to t' \in \Gamma_{\mathsf{x}}$; or*
  - *$k\,v$, a return with $\Gamma_{\mathsf{k}} = \Gamma'_{\mathsf{k}}, k : t \to t'$; or*
  - *$k\,(\textbf{raise}\,v)$, an exception with $\Gamma_{\mathsf{k}} = \Gamma'_{\mathsf{k}}, k : t'$ and $t = t_e$.*

such that, moreover, the values within O and v with a function type are pairwise distinct variables in Γ'_{z}.

Intuitively, an input label represents a minimal, open context that calls a function previously exported by the configuration, or returns from a previous call from the configuration to the context; O represents some shared heap, and Γ'_{z} some fresh variables standing for any function imported by this input from the context. In combination, we obtain a pair of well-typed (open) runtime states $\Gamma_{\mathsf{z}}, \Gamma'_{\mathsf{z}} \vdash O, \overline{I}\,|\,y\overline{\rho}\,v$ applying the function associated with y in $\overline{\rho}$ to v. In the last two forms of query, the condition on Γ_{k} ensures that the context returns only at the top of the stack (with a value or an exception). The final condition ensures that no function values are passed directly to the configuration. In particular, the context cannot directly pass a function x previously received from the configuration. Instead, the context can pass a fresh variable z, and can later call x whenever z is called back.

Definition 12 (Output Label). *Given an interface $\sigma;\Gamma$ and an input label $\Gamma'_{\mathsf{z}}\; O\,|\,y\,r : t$, an output label is one of the following:*

- ***error** for failure;*
- *$\Uparrow$ for divergence;*
- *$\Gamma''_{\mathsf{x}}\; O'\,|\,v'$ for normal returns, such that $\Gamma''_{\mathsf{x}} \vdash O'\,|\,v' : t$;*
- *$\Gamma''_{\mathsf{x}}\; O'\,|\,\textbf{raise}\,v'$ for exceptions, such that $\Gamma''_{\mathsf{x}} \vdash O'\,|\,v' : t_e$; or*
- *$\Gamma''_{\mathsf{x}}\; O'\,|\,z\,v' : t''$ for callbacks, such that $\Gamma''_{\mathsf{x}} \vdash O'\,|\,v' : t'$ and $z : t' \to t'' \in \Gamma'_{\mathsf{z}}$.*

In the last three cases, we require that Γ''_{x} and Γ' be disjoint; that O' extend O with the locations reachable from v' and O; and that all values within O' and v' with function types be distinct variables defining the domain of Γ''_{x}.

For convenience, to deal with both kinds of inputs, we write $\Gamma \setminus_{\mathsf{k}} y$ for Γ when $y{:}_{\mathsf{x}}\,\_ \in \Gamma$ and for $\Gamma \setminus y$ when $\Gamma_{\mathsf{k}} = \Gamma'_{\mathsf{k}}, y : \_$. We also let Γ^{+} abbreviate $\Gamma \setminus_{\mathsf{z}} y, \Gamma'_{\mathsf{z}}, \Gamma''_{\mathsf{x}}$ in the interface after the output.

As with input labels, we require that v' in output results do not contain names from $\Gamma_{\mathsf{x}}, \Gamma_{\mathsf{z}}$.

In combination, compatible inputs and outputs define transitions between interfaces. Transitions between configurations (defined shortly) can be seen as their refinement, of the form

$$\sigma;\Gamma \vdash \mathscr{C} \xrightarrow{\Gamma'_{\mathsf{z}}\ O\,|\,q\,v{:}t\ ;\ \Gamma''_{\mathsf{x}}\ O'|z\,v'{:}t''} \sigma(O');\Gamma^{+} \vdash \mathscr{C}'$$

A plain labeled simulation on pair of terms would require that, for every transition on one side, there exists a matching transition on the other side. In our case, since configurations already account for both sides, we define transitions as a *partial* relation between configurations: we have a transition only when both sides perform matching outputs. For uniformity, we use two additional terminal configurations, **error** and $\Uparrow$, with no input, to represent the outcome of transitions that lead to failure and divergence, respectively.

For a given configuration $\mathscr{I} \vdash \mathscr{C}$, the additional locations in O in the input label may clash with the private locations of $\bar{I}$; our transitions implicitly assume that this is not the case, as we can always pick another input label with fresh names, and that the output label is well-formed.

Definition 13 (Transition). *Given interface $\sigma;\Gamma$ and input label $\alpha = \Gamma'_{\mathsf{z}}\ O\,|\,y\,r : t$, configuration transitions are (partially) defined below, with one rule for each form of output:*

$$\frac{O\rho_b, I_b\,|\,y\rho_b\,v \Downarrow \textbf{error} \text{ for } b = \Lsh,\Rsh}{\sigma;\Gamma \vdash \bar{I}\,|\,\bar{\rho} \xrightarrow{\alpha\,;\,\textbf{error}} \textbf{error}} \qquad \frac{O\rho_b, I_b\,|\,y\rho_b\,v \Uparrow \text{ for } b = \Lsh,\Rsh}{\sigma;\Gamma \vdash \bar{I}\,|\,\bar{\rho} \xrightarrow{\alpha\,;\,\Uparrow} \Uparrow}$$

$$\frac{O\rho_b, I_b\,|\,y\rho_b\,v \to_S{}^{*}\ O'\rho'_b, I^{\circ}{}_b\,|\,r'\rho'_b \text{ for } b = \Lsh,\Rsh}{\sigma;\Gamma \vdash \bar{I}\,|\,\bar{\rho} \xrightarrow{\alpha\,;\,\Gamma''_{\mathsf{x}}\ O'|r'} \sigma,\sigma';\Gamma^{+} \vdash \overline{I'}\,|\,\bar{\rho},\bar{\rho}'}$$

$$\frac{O\rho_b, I_b\,|\,y\rho_b\,v \to_S{}^{*}\ O'\rho'_b, I^{\circ}{}_b\,|\,E_b[z\,v'\rho'_b] \text{ for } b = \Lsh,\Rsh}{\sigma;\Gamma \vdash \bar{I}\,|\,\bar{\rho} \xrightarrow{\alpha\,;\,\Gamma''_{\mathsf{x}}\ O'|z\,v'} \sigma,\sigma';\Gamma^{+}, k :_{\mathsf{k}} t \vdash \overline{I'}\,|\,\bar{\rho}, k \mapsto \lambda r.\overline{E}[r], \bar{\rho}'}$$

Definition 14 (Bisimilarity). *A bisimulation φ is a set of configurations closed by transitions: for every $\mathscr{I} \vdash \mathscr{C} \in \varphi$ with input label α, there exists an output label β and $\mathscr{I}' \vdash \mathscr{C}' \in \varphi$ such that*

$$\mathscr{I} \vdash \mathscr{C} \xrightarrow{\alpha\,;\,\beta} \mathscr{I}' \vdash \mathscr{C}'$$

Applicative bisimilarity, written $\approx_A$, is the largest bisimulation.

As usual, to prove $\mathscr{C} \subseteq \approx_A$ for a given configuration $\mathscr{C}$, it suffices to build some φ that includes $\mathscr{C}$ and show that it is a bisimulation. (See the full paper for additional discussion and examples.)

We now relate labeled transitions on configurations to the reductions of runtime states obtained by context closure.

Lemma 15. *Let $\mathscr{C} \in \approx_A$. The two sides of any context closure $\mathscr{E}[\mathscr{C}]$ either return some identical result; or diverge; or reduce to some $\mathscr{E}'[\mathscr{C}']$ with $\mathscr{C} \xrightarrow{\alpha\,;\,\beta} \mathscr{C}'$ and $\mathscr{C}' \in \approx_A$.*

Lemma 16. *For every transition $\mathscr{I} \xrightarrow{\alpha\,;\,\beta} \mathscr{I}'$, there is a context $\mathscr{E}_T$ for $\mathscr{I}$ such that, for any $\mathscr{C} : \mathscr{I}$ with input α, we have $\mathscr{E}_T[\mathscr{C}] \in \approx^{\bullet}_{\mathsf{e}}$ if and only if $\mathscr{C}$ performs this transition.*

Lemma 17. *For every transition $\mathscr{I} \vdash \mathscr{C} \xrightarrow{\alpha\,;\,\beta} \mathscr{I}' \vdash \mathscr{C}'$ and context-closure $\mathscr{E}'[\mathscr{C}']$, there is a context closure $\mathscr{E}[\mathscr{C}]$ such that $\mathscr{E}[\mathscr{C}] \to_S{}^{*} \approx^{\bullet}_{\mathsf{e}} \mathscr{E}'[\mathscr{C}']$.*

Theorem 4. $\approx_E = \approx_A$.

8. Full abstraction for wrapped translations

We are finally ready to prove full abstraction, relating contextual equivalences in f* and js*. Relying on Theorem 4, we use labeled bisimulations rather than contextual equivalences: the main idea is to extend the wrapped translation from source expressions to source configurations, and to systematically relate their source and target transitions. We begin by establishing a corollary of type soundness for reasoning about untrusted callbacks. Then, we establish operational properties for wrappers, setting up notations for configuration translations (Definition 21).

Untrusted callbacks As we import untrusted values, callbacks triggered by getters are innocuous, since the context can provide arbitrary values anyway. To deal with them in the bisimulation, we use a corollary of open subject reduction, where we use I to refer to the union of the translation of the source Ref heap H, together with the Inv, Abs, and the private locations in the Stub heap.

Lemma 18 (Untrusted Callbacks). *For every typed open runtime state $s \triangleq O_{un}, I\,|\,e$, where $\Gamma'_{\mathsf{z}} \vdash^{D} s : t'$ and Γ'_{z} defines only functions $z : un \to un$, one of the following holds: $s \Uparrow$; or $s \to_S{}^{*}\ O'_{un}, I^{+}\,|\,r$; or $s \to_S{}^{*}\ O'_{un}, I^{+}\,|\,E[z\,(\_ : un) : un]$.*

Properties of wrappers For functional types, the full paper defines $\downarrow t\{x'\}$, the js* open function value obtained by reducing $\downarrow t\ x'$. Similarly, $\uparrow t\{z\}$ is the function obtained by reducing $\uparrow t\ z$—this latter operation just distributes up and down wrappers around the argument and return of z, so the value always exists. In both cases, we remove the Fun constructor, and retain the function closure within. The main operational property for down wrappers is that, as we export a translation of a source value, we obtain a freshly-allocated un value that depends only on the source value—not on the choice of its translation. Its proof is by induction on v relying on monadic typing (§6) and is mutually inductive with the proof of Lemma 20, which reasons about importing values from the context. For clarity, we present the two lemmas separately.

Lemma 19 (Running down). *Let $\Gamma_x \vdash v : t$ such that $\downarrow t$ is defined and Γ_{x} binds the functions of v. Let Γ'_x declare $x : un \to un \to un$ and ρ substitute $\downarrow t'\{x\}$ for every $x :_{\mathsf{x}} t' \in \Gamma_{\mathsf{x}}$. There exist O_{un} and v' such that, for any light translation $\Gamma_{\mathsf{x}} \vdash_f v : t \leadsto_I e'$, we have $I\,|\downarrow t\ e' \to_S{}^{*}\ O_{un}, I^{+}\,|\,v'\rho$ and $\Gamma'_x \vdash^{D} O_{un}, I^{+}\,|\,v'\rho : \mathsf{un}$.*

Intuitively, O_{un} is the new un memory allocated to copy the exported value, while Γ'_{x} declares the exported wrapped-down translations of the function variables in v.

The next lemma shows that 'up' wrappers return (at most) light translations of a source value that depend only on the untrusted context. Besides, those wrappers may trigger untrusted callbacks in the process, diverge, fail, or raise an exception. (In addition to divergence in any callbacks that may be triggered, we may get divergence, for instance, as we try to import a circular list.)

Lemma 20 (Running up). *For all values $u : un$ and states $s \triangleq O_{un}, H, I\,|\uparrow t\ u$, such that $\Gamma'_{\mathsf{z}} \vdash^{D} s : [\![t]\!]$, if s returns with final state $O'_{un}, H', I^{+}\,|\,v' : [\![t]\!]$ (after any number of untrusted callbacks) then $\Gamma_{\mathsf{z}} \vdash_f H''\,|\,v : t \leadsto_{I^{+}} H'\,|\,v'$ for some source runtime state $H''\,|\,v$.*

Candidate bisimulation We define the full translation of source configurations. (The full translation of programs is a special case.) As in §4, this translation is non-deterministic; it includes consistent translations of every piece of the source configuration. It is designed to be closed by js* transitions. To keeps track of all allocated stubs, it also includes the translation of H_{stub}, an auxiliary store (not present in the source configuration) with one option reference for every stub. As can be expected of a defensive translation, its interface consists entirely of untrusted locations and functions.

We refer to the full paper for auxiliary definitions of the evaluation contexts $E_{\Downarrow t}[\_]$ for frames that transition from untrusted callers to translated callees, $F[F'[\_]]$ for frames that transition from translated callbacks to untrusted callees, $stub_{s,r}$ for f* stub closures with object s and reference r (variable by in Figure 4), and $U[\_]$ that ranges over their continuations after declassification. This definition also omits partially-applied functions, e.g. $\downarrow t\{x\}$ applied to a this object and waiting for its arguments object.

Definition 21 (Configuration Translation). *A translation of the source configuration* $\emptyset;\Gamma \vdash \mathscr{C} = \overline{H} \,|\, \overline{\rho}$ *is any configuration of the form* $\sigma';\Gamma' \vdash \overline{I}', \overline{H}' \,|\, \overline{\rho}'$ *such that, for* $b = \Lsh, \Rsh$ *we have*

(1) $\Gamma \vdash H_b \uplus H_{\mathsf{stub}} \rightsquigarrow_{I_b} H_b^\circ$.

(2) *For every* $x :_{\mathsf{x}} t \in \Gamma$, *we have* $\Gamma \vdash x\,\rho_b \rightsquigarrow_{I_b} v_b^\circ$ *and* $x\,\rho_b^\circ = \downarrow t\{v_b^\circ\}$.

(3) *For every* $k :_{\mathsf{k}} t \to t' \in \Gamma$, *we have* $\Gamma \vdash k\,\rho_b \rightsquigarrow_{I_b} E_b^\circ[\_]$, *using the light translation of expressions with an additional rule translating* $[\_]$ *to* $[\_]$, *and* $k\,\rho_b^\circ$ *is* $E_{\Downarrow t'}[E_b^\circ[F[F'[U[\_]]]]]$ *for some typed continuation* $U[\_]$ *reachable from* $stub_{s,r}$.

(4) *For every* $r \mapsto \mathsf{v} : \mathsf{option}\, t' \in H_{\mathsf{stub}}$, ρ_b° *also defines* $stub_{s,r}$ *and any typed continuations* $U[\_]$ *reachable from* $stub_{s,r}$.

(5) $\overline{I}'$, $\overline{H}'$, *and* $\overline{\rho}'$ *are obtained from* $\overline{I}^\circ$, $\overline{H}^\circ$, *and* $\overline{\rho}^\circ$ *by replacing every instance of* z *with* $\uparrow t\{z\}$ *for every* $z :_{\mathsf{z}} t \in \Gamma$.

(6) σ' *declares* un *objects (including function objects for the exported functions* x*) and the function objects* s *of the stubs of* (4).

(7) Γ' *declares* $[\![z :_{\mathsf{z}} t]\!] = z :_{\mathsf{z}} \mathsf{un} \to \mathsf{un} \to \mathsf{un}$, $[\![x :_{\mathsf{x}} t]\!] = x :_{\mathsf{x}} \mathsf{un} \to \mathsf{un} \to \mathsf{un}$, *or* $[\![k :_{\mathsf{k}} t]\!] = k :_{\mathsf{k}} \mathsf{un} \to \mathsf{un}$ *for every declaration in* Γ *and every definition of* (4),

The lemma statements below account for the non-determinism of our translation: for soundness, $[\![\_]\!]$ collects all configuration translations defined above; for completeness, $[\![\_]\!]'$ collects all configuration translations without stub callbacks. We obtain our main theorem for programs seen as singleton configurations.

Lemma 22 (Soundness). *If* $\mathscr{I} \vdash \mathscr{C} \in \approx_E$ *then* $[\![\mathscr{I} \vdash \mathscr{C}]\!] \subseteq \approx_E$.

Lemma 23 (Completeness). *If* $[\![\mathscr{I} \vdash \mathscr{C}]\!]' \cap \approx_E \neq \emptyset$ *then* $\mathscr{I} \vdash \mathscr{C} \in \approx_E$.

Theorem 5 (Full abstraction). *For all translations* $\vdash \overline{v} : t \rightsquigarrow_\emptyset \overline{e}$ *such that* $\downarrow t$ *is defined,* $v_0 \approx_{\mathsf{e}} v_1$ *in* $\mathsf{f}^\star$ *if and only if* $\downarrow t\; e_0 \approx_{\mathsf{e}} \downarrow t\; e_1$ *in* $\mathsf{js}^\star$.

9. Preliminary case studies and discussion

Although we leave an extensive evaluation of our compiler as future work, we have already used it to program several small case studies (available on the web)—we briefly describe two of these here.

Secure subsystems A traditional challenge in JavaScript programming involves combining code from multiple, mutually distrusting sources, while maintaining a degree of control over the resulting mash-up. One design towards this objective could be to implement a subsystem in f* that mediates mash-up interactions, prove it correct using monadic f*, and then deploy it using our compiler.

To illustrate our point, we have implemented an interference-free local store on top of the `localStorage` object in HTML 5, which offers a key-value store per web page. The challenge is that this resource is shared between all scripts running in a web page: they can all read, write, and even clear the whole storage without any access control. To enable mash-ups to use local storage, we implement a secure API `setItem`, `getItem`, and `removeItem` that multiplexes access to `localStorage` while ensuring isolation.

Advising JavaScript Meyerovich and Livshits (2010) propose ConScript, a browser-based implementation of *aspect-oriented advice* for JavaScript, itself expressed as JavaScript code. In preliminary experiments, we have been able to implement 6 ConScript policies in f*. Being written in f* makes the advice simpler: we can prove correctness of the advice by contextual equivalence at the source level, and, unlike ConScript, we do not require any browser modifications.

Performance The benefits of running secure JavaScript come at a price, as any interactions with untrusted code are mediated by wrappers. The cost of wrapping, however, is proportionate only to the number of "boundary crossings" between trusted and untrusted code. When executing within f*, there is little overhead due to security protections. Nevertheless, we expect to improve our translation, with an eye towards performance, along several axes. For example, our current representation of datatypes is naïve. We might instead use JavaScript's `ArrayBuffer`, which offers a packed data representation. For the wrappers, rather than exporting data by copying, we plan to investigate using `Object.freeze`, a new feature that dynamically renders the fields of an object immutable. We are also considering using a lazy semantics for the wrappers that import data (possibly using proxies of the forthcoming ES6 standard). This would necessitate reflecting the callbacks in the source semantics, as lazy importing may trigger callbacks to the context as imported data is read, but the performance gains may make this a good tradeoff.

Conclusions It is increasingly common for compilers to target JavaScript, contributing to a growing view of JavaScript as the "assembly language of the Web". Our work provides a foundation for such compilers, particularly when compiled code must interact with code from other, less trustworthy sources. Relying on full abstraction, developers who program in higher level languages such as ML can reliably and securely deploy their code, without having to worry about the intricacies of JavaScript.

References

M. Abadi. Protection in programming-language translations. In *ICALP*, volume 1443, pages 868–883, 1998.

M. Abadi and G. D. Plotkin. On protection by layout randomization. In *IEEE CSF*, pages 337–351, 2010.

M. Abadi, C. Fournet, and G. Gonthier. Secure implementation of channel abstractions. *Information and Computation*, 174(1):37–83, Apr. 2002.

P. Agten, R. Strackx, B. Jacobs, and F. Piessens. Secure compilation to modern processors. In *IEEE CSF*, pages 171–185, 2012.

A. Ahmed and M. Blume. Typed closure conversion preserves observational equivalence. In *ICFP*, 2008.

Caja. Attack vectors for privilege escalation, 2012. URL `http://code.google.com/p/google-caja/wiki/AttackVectors`.

E. Cooper, S. Lindley, P. Wadler, and J. Yallop. Links: Web programming without tiers. In *FMCO*, 2006.

L. de Moura and N. Bjørner. Z3: An efficient SMT solver. In *TACAS*, 2008.

A. Guha, C. Saftoiu, and S. Krishnamurthi. The essence of JavaScript. In *ECOOP*, 2010.

A. Kennedy. Securing the .NET programming model. *TCS*, 364(3), 2006.

S. Lassen. Eager normal form bisimulation. *LICS*, 2005.

S. Maffeis, J. C. Mitchell, and A. Taly. An operational semantics for JavaScript. In *APLAS*, 2008.

J. McCarthy. Towards a mathematical science of computation. In *IFIP Congress*, pages 21–28, 1962.

L. A. Meyerovich and V. B. Livshits. Conscript: Specifying and enforcing fine-grained security policies for JavaScript in the browser. In *IEEE S&P*, 2010.

J. C. Mitchell. On abstraction and the expressive power of programming languages. *Science of Computer Programming*, 21(2):141 – 163, 1993.

J. H. Morris. Protection in programming languages. In *CACM (16)*, 1973.

J. Politz, M. Carroll, B. Lerner, J. Pombrio, and S. Krishnamurthi. A tested semantics for getters, setters, and eval in JavaScript. In *DLS*, 2012.

C. Schlesinger and N. Swamy. Verification condition generation with the Dijkstra state monad. Technical Report MSR-TR-2012-45, Mar. 2012.

M. Serrano, E. Gallesio, and F. Loitsch. Hop: a language for programming the web 2.0. In *OOPSLA Companion*, pages 975–985, 2006.

E. Sumii and B. C. Pierce. A bisimulation for type abstraction and recursion. In *POPL*, 2005.

N. Swamy, J. Chen, C. Fournet, P.-Y. Strub, K. Bhargavan, and J. Yang. Secure distributed programming with value-dependent types. In *ICFP*, 2011.

N. Swamy, J. Weinberger, C. Schlesinger, J. Chen, and B. Livshits. Towards JavaScript verification with the Dijkstra state monad. Technical Report MSR-TR-2012-37, Mar 2012.

A. Taly, U. Erlingsson, J. C. Mitchell, M. S. Miller, and J. Nagra. Automated analysis of security-critical JavaScript APIs. In *IEEE S&P*, 2011.

Towards Fully Automatic Placement of Security Sanitizers and Declassifiers

Benjamin Livshits
Microsoft Research
livshits@microsoft.com

Stephen Chong
Harvard University
chong@seas.harvard.edu

Abstract

A great deal of research on sanitizer placement, sanitizer correctness, checking path validity, and policy inference, has been done in the last five to ten years, involving type systems, static analysis and run-time monitoring and enforcement. However, in pretty much all work thus far, the burden of sanitizer placement has fallen on the developer. However, sanitizer placement in large-scale applications is difficult, and developers are likely to make errors, and thus create security vulnerabilities.

This paper advocates a radically different approach: we aim to fully automate the placement of sanitizers by analyzing the flow of tainted data in the program. We argue that developers are better off leaving out sanitizers *entirely* instead of trying to place them.

This paper proposes a fully automatic technique for sanitizer placement. Placement is *static* whenever possible, switching to *run time* when necessary. Run-time taint tracking techniques can be used to track the source of a value, and thus apply appropriate sanitization. However, due to the run-time overhead of run-time taint tracking, our technique avoids it wherever possible.

Categories and Subject Descriptors D.2.4 [*Software/Program Verification*]: Validation; D.3.4 [*Processors*]: Compilers; D.4.6 [*Operating Systems*]: Security and Protection—Information flow controls

General Terms Languages, Security, Verification

Keywords Security analysis, vulnerability prevention

1. Introduction

Tracking of explicit information flow has received a great deal of attention in recent years. Two primary applications for explicit information flow tracking stand out prominently:

- preventing injection attacks within web applications such as cross-site scripting (XSS) and SQL injection; and
- preventing private data leaks, such as those recently observed in a variety of popular mobile applications [10].

POPL'13, January 23–25, 2013, Rome, Italy.

These attacks have motivated a great deal of research in the last five to ten years on sanitizer placement, sanitizer correctness [15, 45], checking path validity, and policy inference [23, 41], involving type systems [8, 32], static analysis [17, 18, 22, 42, 43, 47], and run-time monitoring and enforcement [6, 7, 11, 25].[1]

Much academic work in this space focuses on finding missing sanitizers and is applied to relatively small applications. Several projects have explored the use of run-time techniques, motivated in part by the scalability and precision challenges that static analysis typically encounters. Additional motivation for exploring run-time techniques comes from the complexity of large-scale web applications with multiple, potentially nested sanitizers, which recent assessments [38, 39] suggest is well beyond the ability of developers to address using static reasoning and code reviews.

We also feel that the run-time approach is most practical in the long run. However, the overhead of run-time approaches can be considerable. Prior work on sanitizer placement advocates dynamic sanitizer placement through a combination of *inline* instrumentation [25] and *library-based* instrumentation [6, 7]. The main advantage of library-based instrumentation is reduced overhead: only library code (as opposed to application code) needs to be instrumented. However, library-based approaches do not deal well with information propagated through non-library code and data structures such as `char[]`, `byte[]`, and custom character-level sanitizers. Custom character-level sanitizers are quite common, and sanitizers typically deal with string data at the level of characters [15]. The overhead of these approaches varies, but is generally between 1–20%, depending on the application. In the case of library-based instrumentation, the "depth" of the data propagation path largely determines the overhead. In large enterprise applications, we know that data can undergo a high number of transformations during its lifetime [28], resulting in higher overhead than experiments with smaller applications would lead us to believe. Prior research has proposed the use of pointer analysis as a way to reduce the number of instrumentation points [2, 24]. However, the number of program points that are deemed to be reachable from sources and may flow to sinks is still quite large in practice, leading to a high number of instrumentation points. We feel that it is crucial to develop novel ways to decrease the performance penalty for inline instrumentation to make it practical.

[1] For simplicity, in the rest of this paper, we shall talk primarily about sanitizer placement (for integrity preservation). Our techniques apply equally well to the placement of declassifiers (for confidentiality preservation).

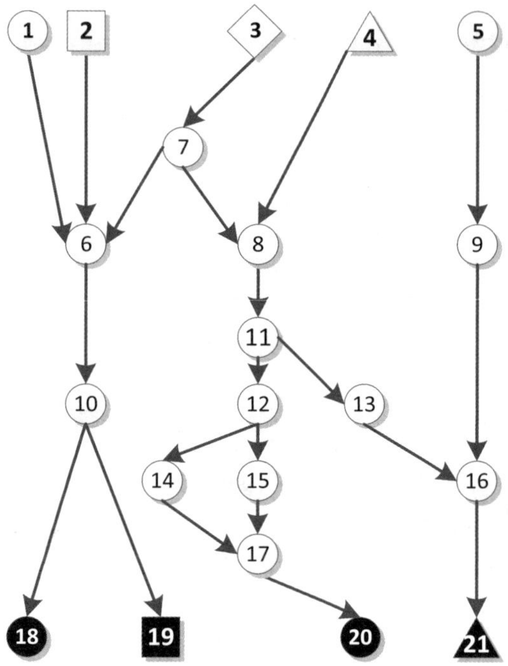

Figure 1. Motivating example of a small, but illustrative flow graph. Sources are at the top; sinks are at the bottom.

We aim to *fully automate* the placement of sanitizers by analyzing the flow of tainted data. A key observation is that, given a policy, sources and sinks within the application *induce* restrictions on the placement of sanitizers. It is difficult for developers to place sanitizers so as to satisfy all of these restrictions, especially in large-scale applications [39]. In fact, we argue that developers are better off leaving out sanitizers *entirely*, allowing them to be placed automatically.

In this paper we propose a fully automatic technique for sanitizer placement. The goal is to minimize both run-time overhead and code bloat due to instrumentation. Sanitizer placement is *static* whenever possible, switching to *run-time techniques* when necessary. We perform analyses on the inter-procedural dataflow graph of the program to identify where sanitizers can be placed, and where values must be tracked at run-time in order to determine which sanitizer to apply. In order to reduce run-time overhead, we resort to run-time tracking only when necessary.

1.1 Sanitization Policies

Large applications come with libraries of sanitizers. Developers are heavily discouraged from writing their own sanitizers. This is in part because most of the time, they get them wrong [4, 15]. Since sanitizers are implemented as library functions, they are typically pure functions, with type `String` → `String`.

Policies can be given in the form of a table that for every type of data source and data sink indicates the appropriate sanitizer for values that flow from that source to that sink. Policies are declarative specifications, and can both provide developer guidance and simplify the code review process. Section 2 gives examples of policies.

1.2 Dataflow Graphs and Policies

Figure 1 shows a simple dataflow graph that will be used as an example throughout this paper. The policy for this example graph is shown in Figure 2. Source types (○, □, ◇, △) are shown in rows and sink types (●, ■, ▲) are shown in columns. We use ⊘ as a special kind of source type and sink type, for data production or consumption that is not relevant to security (such as constant strings or other trusted sources of data). Thus, we assume that every source and sink of data has a type that appears in the table.

Entries in the table indicate which sanitizer should be applied to data. We use metavariable $\mathcal{P}$ to range over policies, I to range over source types, O to range over sink types, and S to range over sanitizers. We write $\mathcal{P}(I, O)$ for the entry in policy $\mathcal{P}$ for source I and sink O. We assume that a node cannot be both a source and a sink, and write $\tau(n)$ for the source type or sink type of node n. For example, in Figure 1, where n_i is the node labeled with integer i we have $\tau(n_3) = \diamond$ and $\tau(n_{19}) = $ ■. Since n_{11} is neither a source nor a sink, $\tau(n_{11})$ is undefined.

	●	■	▲	⊘
○	S_1	S_1	S_4	⊥
□	S_1	S_2	⊥	⊥
◇	S_2	S_1	S_3	⊥
△	⊥	⊥	S_3	⊥
⊘	⊥	⊥	⊥	⊥

Figure 2. Example policy. Sources shown vertically; sinks shown horizontally. ⊥ means no sanitization required.

For example, let $\mathcal{P}$ be the policy in Figure 2. Data originating from a source of type □ and going to a sink of type ● should have sanitizer S_1 applied to it. If $\mathcal{P}(I, O) = \bot$ then no sanitization should be applied data flowing from source type I to sink type O. This may indicate, for example, that constant string data should not be sanitized before being displayed to the user.

1.3 Contributions

This paper makes the following contributions:

- **Fully automatic sanitizer placement.** We argue that sanitizer placement should be automatic, given a policy and an application, instead of the current approach of the developer being responsible for getting it right.
- **Node-based placement.** We propose a simple node-based strategy for static sanitizer placement. While it is simple to implement and incurs no run-time overhead, it is incorrect for many dataflow graphs.
- **Edge-based placement.** We propose an edge-based strategy for sanitizer placement, which attempts to place sanitizers statically and "spills over" into run time whenever necessary. This strategy is appropriate to use when the simple node-based strategy fails.
- **Correctness.** We define the correctness of sanitization of values in a dataflow graph, and prove that our edge-based strategy for placement is correct.
- **Experiments.** We extensively evaluate how our placement strategies affect the number of instrumentation points on both large applications (up to 1.8 million lines of code) and synthetically generated dataflow graphs. While the node-based approach only instruments a fraction of all nodes, in most cases it fails to provide sanitization on all paths. The edge-based approach, while it requires more sophisticated analysis, provides full sanitization, while reducing the number of instrumentation points by 6.19× on average. Our edge-based technique works even better in the case of a precise underlying dataflow graph: for sparser synthetically generated

graphs, we see a reduction in the number of instrumentation points as high as 27×, compared to the naïve version.

1.4 Paper Organization

Section 2 presents examples that highlight the need for automated sanitizer placement. Section 3 gives an overview to our approach for automatic sanitizer placement. Section 4 presents dataflow analyses and algorithms to implement our approach. Section 5 describes our experimental evaluation. Related work is discussed in Section 6. Finally, Sections 7 and 8 describe future work and conclude.

2. Motivating Examples

Our examination of large-scale applications has shown that data processing is typically performed via a fixed set of sanitizers whose proper selection depends on the kind of source and sink and can be expressed as a table, as in Figure 2 [39]. Sanitization policies in this section illustrate the complexity of real-world data manipulation scenarios.

2.1 Web Applications

	URL	CSS
input	encodeForURL	encodeForCSS

The OWASP Enterprise Security API (ESAPI) is an open-source web-application security library. Usage guidelines of ESAPI reveal that the correct sanitization to apply to data depends on how the data will be used, that is, on the sink context. To sanitize a user-provided URL, function `ESAPI.encoder().encodeForURL(`*input*`)` should be used. But to sanitize user input that will be used to construct a CSS attribute, function `ESAPI.encoder().encodeForCSS(`*input*`)` should be used.

2.2 Web Application Roles

In large-scale web applications, sanitization requirements often vary based on who is interacting with the application. This is referred to as *role-based* sanitization. For example, Wordpress allows authors to insert certain HTML tags in their blog posts that commenters may not [46]. Similar approaches are taken by phpBB and Drupal. This complexity is reflected in sanitization libraries such as AntiXSS [27], OWASP HTML Sanitizer Library [30], and HTML Purifier [48], where the developer can select different policies for sanitization of HTML.

This source sensitivity arises because not all users are created equal, and that authentication provides a degree of trust (and increase of capabilities) that is not warranted for non-authenticated users.

2.3 Encrypted Cloud

	output	cloud
input	$\perp$	encrypt
cloud	decrypt	$\perp$

Consider a web application using a public cloud provider for storage. The web application wants to use the cloud for scalability and to reduce storage hardware costs, but does not fully trust the cloud to protect the confidentiality of its data. The application therefore will use encryption when serializing data to the database, and decryption when deserializing.

In this scenario, the sources are of types *input* and *cloud* and sinks are of types *output* and *cloud*. The policy would encrypt data before it goes into the cloud and decrypt it on the way out of the cloud. The correct sanitization to apply (if any) depends on both the source and sink of data.

2.4 Mobile App Privacy and Security

Previous studies have shown that applications on Android and other mobile platforms leak user data to untrusted parties. One solution is that the developer needs to filter out private data before it is allowed to go outside [9, 10]. However, the app often has legitimate reasons to send user input and data outside. Consider a gmail app that needs to communicate with its "parent" site, or its *host*, in this case, `mail.google.com`. It is necessary to send information to that hosting URL, including keystrokes, files on the local system if those are to be attached to email, etc. There is perhaps no compelling need to send user data to `AdMob.com`, a third-party mobile advertisement provider whose library is embedded in the app [10], and so data sent to a third-party should be cleansed, i.e., should have sensitive information removed, a form of declassification. This highlights the need to treat the hosting site differently from third-party sites.

Source types for this scenario are *user input*, *data from host*, and *data from 3rd-party site*. Sink types are *screen output*, *isolated app storage*, *send to host*, and *send to 3rd-party site*. Data sent to a third party site that does not originate from the third party site should be cleansed. Also, third-party data being shown to the screen might need to be pretty-printed or checked for integrity in some way, which we we refer to in the table below as `ascii-sanitizer`. No other sanitization or declassification is required.

	screen output	isolated app storage	to host	to 3rd-party site
user input	$\perp$	$\perp$	$\perp$	cleanse
host	$\perp$	$\perp$	$\perp$	cleanse
3rd-party site	ascii-sanitizer	$\perp$	$\perp$	$\perp$

2.5 Properties of the Placement Problem

Sink sensitivity: Sanitization is *sink sensitive*: sanitization to apply to data depends on how the data will be used.

Source sensitivity: Sanitization is *source sensitive*: the correct sanitizer to use on data depends on where the data comes from. Source sensitivity also makes full automatic sanitization (as advocated by Samuel et al. [38]) difficult.

Context-sensitivity: As elaborated in ScriptGard [39] and by Weinberger et al. [46], sanitization is context-sensitive: to choose the proper sanitizer, the nested context needs to be determined. Consider the following snippet of HTML code, which displays a comment (the value *untrusted*) when the element is clicked.

```
<div class='comment-box'
  onclick='displayComment(untrusted, this)'>
    ... hidden comment ...
</div>
```

The untrusted comment is in two nested contexts: it is in the `onclick` attribute of an HTML tag, and it is in a single-quoted JavaScript string context. To properly sanitize the untrusted comment, we must ensure that the untrusted comment does not contain either JavaScript or HTML meta-characters. In general, more than one sanitizer may be needed on a path between a given source and a sink. We model this using a single function to represent the *composition* of sanitizers, as required.

Not idempotent or reversible: Note that sanitizers are *not* guaranteed to be either idempotent or reversible, meaning that we cannot apply them more than once. A recent study [15] shows that out of 24 sanitizers considered, 19 are idempotent, and that only 2 are reversible. Moreover, order is important, as less than 30% of pairs of sanitizers commute. Finally, over-sanitization is also a significant issue, which often leads to malformed double-encoded data.

3. Overview

In this section we define the problem and present an overview of two solutions: a completely static node-based solution, and an edge-based solution that uses static analysis and run-time taint tracking. The static node-based solution incurs no run-time overhead, but doesn't always result in correct sanitization. The edge-based solution is always correct, but may incur run-time overhead due to taint tracking.

3.1 Valid Sanitizer Placement Problem

A *dataflow graph* $G = \langle N, E\rangle$ is a directed graph over a set of nodes N with edges E that describes how data flows through a system. Nodes represent computation and/or storage locations, and edges represent the flow of data in the system. As the program performs computation, values traverse the dataflow graph, following edges in the graph, with nodes representing both computation performed on values, and where values are stored during execution. A dataflow graph may have cycles in it. This work is not directly concerned with the precision or soundness of the analysis used to produce the dataflow graph: improvements to the precision and soundness of analyses for dataflow graph construction will seamlessly improve the quality and soundness of our results. Our focus is to ensure correct sanitization of data in a program, and as such we require an interprocedural dataflow graph.

Suppose policy $\mathcal{P}$ describes which sanitizer should be applied to data traversing a dataflow graph. We aim to provide sanitization for values traversing the dataflow graph, according to the following correctness definition.

Definition 1. *Given a dataflow graph* $G = \langle N, E\rangle$, *sanitization for the graph is* valid for policy $\mathcal{P}$ *if for all source nodes s, and all sink nodes t:*

- *if* $\mathcal{P}(\tau(s), \tau(t)) = S$ *then every value that flows from s to t has sanitizer S applied exactly once, and no other sanitizer is applied.*
- *if* $\mathcal{P}(\tau(s), \tau(t)) = \bot$ *then every value that flows from s to t has no sanitizer applied.*

We require that a sanitizer be applied at most once on any given path because sanitizers are not necessarily idempotent [15]: applying it multiple times might result in incorrect sanitization. We require that sanitizers are not applied needlessly. We model multiple (potentially nested) sanitizers as a single (composite) sanitizer.

We consider two strategies for sanitizer placement: a node-based formulation (Section 3.2) that is efficient, but may fail to produce valid sanitization; and an edge-based formulation (Section 3.3) that always provides correct sanitization, but may require run-time taint tracking in order to determine the correct sanitizer to apply.

We assume that the dataflow graph $G = \langle N, E\rangle$ does not contain any node that has both multiple in-coming edges and multiple out-going edges. This assumption is without loss of generality, since if a graph does not satisfy this requirement, it can easily be transformed to one that does by the insertion of synthetic nodes. This assumption is required for the correctness of the edge-based formulation, and is analogous to assumptions in control-flow graph analysis of the absence of *critical edges*: edges that go from nodes with multiple successors to nodes with multiple predecessors.

	Possible	Exclusive
S_1	1, 2, 3, 6, 7, 10, 18, 19	1
S_2	2, 3, 6, 7, 8, 10, 11, 12, 14, 15, 17, 19, 20	
S_3	3, 4, 7, 8, 11, 13, 16, 21	13
S_4	5, 9, 16, 21	5, 9
$\bot$	4, 8, 11, 12, 14, 15, 17, 20	

Figure 3. S_i-possible and S_i-exclusive nodes for Figure 1.

3.2 Node-based Formulation

We say that a node n is S_i*-possible* if it is on a path from a source node s to a sink node t that requires sanitizer S_i, that is, $\mathcal{P}(\tau(s), \tau(t)) = S_i$. Thus, if n is S_i-possible, then at least some of the data passing through node n requires application of S_i. We say a node n is S_i*-exclusive* if it is S_i-possible, and it is not S_j-posible for any $j \neq i$. In other words, node n is S_i-exclusive if it is S_i-possible, and for any source s and sink t, if n is on a path from s to t, then that path requires sanitizer S_i (i.e., $\mathcal{P}(\tau(s), \tau(t)) = S_i$).

Definition 2. *Node* $n \in N$ *is* S_i-possible *if there is a source node s and sink node t such that n is on a path from s to t and* $\mathcal{P}(\tau(s), \tau(t)) = S_i$.

Definition 3. *Node* $n \in N$ *is* S_i-exclusive *if it is* S_i*-possible and for all source nodes s and sink nodes t, if n is on a path from s to t then* $\mathcal{P}(\tau(s), \tau(t)) = S_i$.

Figure 3 shows possible and exclusive nodes for sanitizers S_1, S_2, S_3, and $\bot$ for the dataflow graph of Figure 1. Note that while possible nodes are plentiful, exclusive nodes are rarer. In fact, S_2 and $\bot$ have no exclusive nodes at all. Note that node n_{13} is on a path both from n_3 to n_{21}, and from n_4 to n_{21}. However, it is S_3-exclusive because both $\tau(n_3) = \Diamond$ and $\tau(n_4) = \triangle$ require the same sanitizer when going to sink $\blacktriangle$: $\mathcal{P}(\Diamond, \blacktriangle) = \mathcal{P}(\triangle, \blacktriangle) = S_3$.

For sparser dataflow graphs, exclusive nodes will be more plentiful. Exclusive nodes are good candidates at which to apply a sanitizer to all data passing through the node. However, exclusive nodes are not necessarily unique: there may be multiple S_i-exclusive nodes on a single path from a source to a sink. If there are multiple S_i-exclusive nodes on a path, we need to choose just one of them at which to apply sanitizer S_i. Since in many common applications of data sanitization, a sanitized value is larger than the unsanitized value (e.g., escaping special characters in a string will increase the length of the string), we prefer to perform sanitization as late as possible. We say that node n is S_i*-latest-exclusive* if it is S_i-exclusive, and for every path going through n, it is the last S_i-exclusive node on that path.

Definition 4. *Node* $n \in N$ *is* S_i-latest-exclusive *if n is* S_i*-exclusive and for every source node s and sink node t, and for every path from s to t, if n is on that path, then n is the last* S_i*-exclusive node on the path.*

By this definition, we see that in Figure 1 nodes n_1, n_9, and n_{13} are latest exclusive nodes (for sanitizers S_1, S_4 and S_3 respectively). Node n_5 is not an S_4-latest exclusive node, since there is another S_4-exclusive node later on a path from n_5. It is easy to see from the definition that for any path from source node s to sink node t with $\mathcal{P}(\tau(s), \tau(t)) = S_i$, there is at most one S_i-latest-exclusive node on that path.

There may, however, be no S_i-latest-exclusive node on a path: if there is a path from source node s to sink node t with

$\mathcal{P}(\tau(s), \tau(t)) = S_i$, but there is no S_i-latest-exclusive node on that path, then node-based placement will not sanitize values traveling from s to t on that path. Thus, placing sanitizers only at latest-exclusive nodes may fail to produce a valid placement (Definition 1).

As will be seen in Section 5, the static node-based approach does not produce a valid placement for all but simple and sparse dataflow graphs.

3.3 Edge-based Formulation

We consider instead an edge-based formulation that is able to always find a correct placement of sanitizers in a dataflow graph, although it may be necessary to record and track at run time some information about the path that a value has taken in the graph in order to determine the correct sanitizer (if any) to apply to the value.

Figure 4 summarizes the key concepts used in our edge-based solution. We provide full definitions and intuition for each of these terms below.

We say that an edge e is *source dependent* if the sanitization to apply to values traversing e depends on which source produced the value.

Definition 5. *An edge e is* source dependent *if there exist sources s_0 and s_1 and sinks t such that e is on a path from s_0 to t and on a path from s_1 to t and $\mathcal{P}(\tau(s_0), \tau(t)) \neq \mathcal{P}(\tau(s_1), \tau(t))$ (i.e, the sanitizer to use depends on the source).*

Similarly, we say an edge is *sink dependent* if the sanitization to apply to values traversing it depends on which sink the value will go to.

Definition 6. *An edge e is* sink dependent *if there exist source s and sinks t_0 and t_1 such that e is on a path from s to t_0 and on a path from s to t_1 and $\mathcal{P}(\tau(s), \tau(t_0)) \neq \mathcal{P}(\tau(s), \tau(t_1))$ (i.e., the sanitizer to use depends on the sink).*

Intuitively, if an edge is sink dependent, then when a value traverses the edge, we do not yet know which sanitizer to apply. By contrast, if an edge is source dependent, we do not know which sanitizer to apply to values traversing the edge unless we know from which source the value originated. If an edge is neither source dependent nor sink dependent, then all values traversing the edge are meant to have the same sanitizer applied.

We say that edge e is *source (sink) independent* if it is not source (sink) dependent.

In Figure 1, the edge from node n_6 to node n_{10} is both source dependent and sink dependent. It is sink dependent because it is on paths from n_2 to both n_{18} and n_{19}, but $\mathcal{P}(\tau(n_2), \tau(n_{18})) = S_1 \neq S_2 = \mathcal{P}(\tau(n_2), \tau(n_{19}))$. It is source dependent since it is on paths from both n_1 and n_2 to n_{19} and $\mathcal{P}(\tau(n_1), \tau(n_{19})) = S_1 \neq S_2 = \mathcal{P}(\tau(n_2), \tau(n_{19}))$.

The edge from node n_7 to node n_8 is source independent (since only one source node can reach it), but is sink dependent.

3.3.1 Trigger Edges

To apply a sanitizer at a source-dependent edge, we must know from which source a value originated. We can use run-time tracking to "taint" a value so that we can determine its source. However, run-time taint tracking can be expensive, and we do not need to track all values manipulated by the system, just those for which we need to know the source in order to determine which sanitizer to apply.

We identify edges where it is necessary to start run-time tracking of values, and edges where, if we were tracking, it suffices to stop tracking. Edge e is an *in-trigger edge* if it is a source-independent edge but has an edge after it that is source dependent. In-trigger edges are the edges where we have sufficient information to know where a value came from, and need to start run-time tracking because the origin of a value affects which sanitizer to apply. If e is an in-trigger edge from node n_1 to n_2, then there must be at least one other edge going to node n_2, since n_2 is a node where paths from different sources merge.

Definition 7. *Edge e is an* in-trigger edge *if it is a source-independent edge from node n_1 to node n_2 such that there exists a source-dependent edge $n_2 \to n_3$.*

Edge e is an *out-trigger edge* if it is a source-independent edge that is preceded by a source-dependent edge e'. If we were tracking run-time values as they traverse edge e', then we no longer need to track them when they traverse edge e. If e is an out-trigger edge from node n_1 to n_2, then there must be at least one other edge leaving n_1, since n_1 is a node where paths from different sources to different sinks split.

Definition 8. *Edge e is an* out-trigger edge *if it is a source-independent edge from node n_1 to node n_2 such that there exists a source-dependent edge $n_0 \to n_1$.*

Once we have sanitized a value, we will not need to perform run-time tracking for the value. (This is an invariant that our run-time discipline will enforce: only values that require sanitization and have not yet been sanitized will be tagged at run time.) Because run-time tracking of values can be expensive, we typically want to perform sanitization as early as possible. We can only perform sanitization at sink-independent edges (because at sink-dependent edges, the sanitization to apply depends on the future use of the value). *Sanitization edges* are the earliest possible edges at which we can perform sanitization: they are sink-independent edges that are the earliest sink-independent edge for some path from a source to a sink. That is, if e is a sanitization edge, then for at least one path from a source to a sink, it is the earliest sink-independent edge.

Definition 9. *Edge e is a* sanitization edge *if it is a sink-independent edge and there is a source node s and sink node t such that e is the earliest sink-independent edge on a path from s to t.*

Figure 5 shows the source-dependent edge, sink-dependent edges, in-trigger edges, out-trigger edges, and sanitization edges for our running example from Figure 1. For example, edge $n_4 \to n_8$ is an in-trigger edge, since it is source independent, but has a successor edge $n_8 \to n_{11}$ that is source dependent. Edge $n_{10} \to n_{19}$ is a sanitization edge as it is the earliest sink-independent edge on the path from node n_2 to n_{19}. Note that edge $n_{13} \to n_{16}$ is not a sanitization edge, even though it is sink independent. This is because any path that goes through $n_{13} \to n_{16}$ must first go through the sink independent edge $n_{11} \to n_{13}$.

In addition, Figure 5 shows for each edge e the *policy table at e*. This is simply the policy table $\mathcal{P}$ restricted to the source types I and sink types O such that e is on a path from a source node of type I to a sink node of type O. Policy tables at edges are a useful concept for computing an appropriate placement, and will be used in Section 4.

Definition 10. *The* edge policy *at edge e is the restriction of the (global) policy $\mathcal{P}$ to include only source types I and*

Term	Brief description
Source-dependent edge	Sanitizer to apply to values traversing the edge depends on which source type the value came from.
Sink-dependent edge	Sanitizer to apply to values traversing the edge depends on which sink type the value will go to.
In-trigger edge	Source-independent edge with a source-dependent successor.
Out-trigger edge	Source-independent edge with a source-dependent predecessor.
Sanitization edge	Earliest sink-independent edge on *some* path from a source to a sink.
Tag edge	In-trigger edge that isn't dominated by sanitization edges. Start run-time tagging of values.
Untag edge	Either a sanitization edge, or an out-trigger edge that is not dominated by sanitization edges. Stop run-time tagging of values.
Carry edge	Edge that (a) is reachable from a tag edge without an intervening untag edge, and (b) can reach an untag edge, and (c) is neither a tag nor an untag edge. Instrument to propagate run-time taint values.

Figure 4. Summary of terms for edge-based placement.

sink types O such that e is on a path from a source node of type I to a sink node of type O. We write $\mathcal{P}_e$ for the edge policy at edge e.

3.3.2 Tag, Untag, and Carry edges

In-trigger edges and out-trigger edges help us identify where we may need to start, and can stop, run-time tracking of values. However, we can refine these notions to reduce the amount of run-time tracking we must perform.

Intuitively, run-time tracking is necessary only when a sanitization edge needs to distinguish values coming from different sources. These are exactly the sanitization edges that are source dependent. We need to propagate taint information only along source-dependent edges, and only until we sanitize the value.

This also means that we only need to *start* taint tracking (which we refer to as "tagging" data) when data values move from a source-independent edge to a source-dependent edge and the data is not yet sanitized (and will need sanitization in the future). Similarly, we can *stop* taint tracking (which we refer to as "untagging" data) when tagged data is sanitized, or when it moves from a source-dependent edge to a source-independent edge.

Specifically, a *tag edge* (where we tag values at run time, and start the run-time taint tracking) are in-trigger edges such that a value traversing the edge might be unsanitized and require sanitization in the future. A value is unsanitized if it has not gone through a sanitization edge, and thus the tag edges are in-trigger edges that are not dominated[2] by a sanitization edge. Note that an edge dominates itself, and thus a tag edge cannot also be a sanitization edge.

Definition 11. *Edge e is a* tag edge *if e is an in-trigger edge that is not dominated by sanitization edges.*

An *untag edge* is an edge such that a tagged value can reach it (i.e., it is not dominated by sanitization edges), and we no longer need to track the tagged values. It is either a sanitization edge (since after sanitization we no longer need to track taint), or an out-trigger edge.

Definition 12. *An* untag edge *is either (a) an out-trigger edge that is not dominated by a sanitization edge; or (b) a sanitization edge.*

At tag edges we tag values and start taint tracking, and continue taint tracking the tagged value until it reaches an untag edge: if the untag edge is a sanitization edge, we apply the appropriate sanitizer; otherwise, the untag

[2]We define domination in dataflow graphs as follows. Edge e is *dominated* by edge e' if any path from any source that ends with edge e must contain e'.

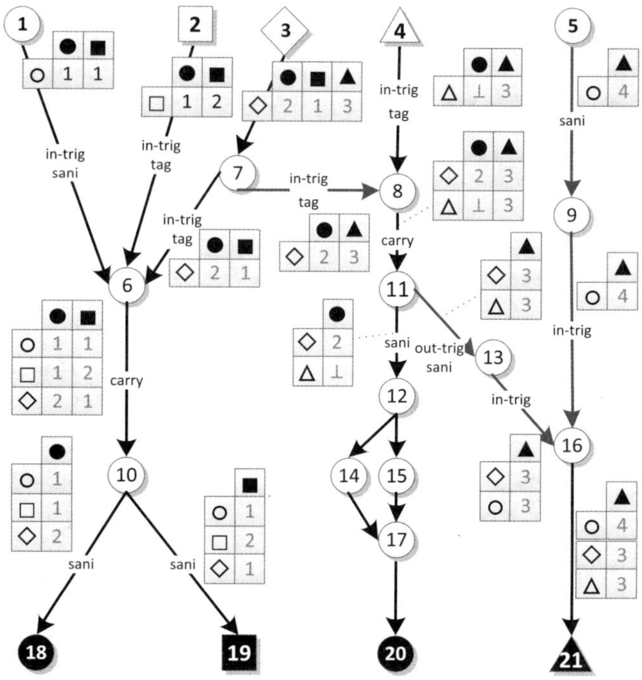

Figure 5. Policy tables are shown at every node and trigger edges are marked.

edge is an out-trigger edge and we can stop taint tracking. (Note that if we stop taint-tracking a value at an untag edge, we may potentially resume taint tracking if the value later encounters another in-trigger edge not dominated by sanitization edges.) Edges between tag edges and untag edges will need to propagate tag values. We refer to these edges as *carry edges.*

Definition 13. *Edge e is a* carry edge *if e is on a path from a tag edge to an untag edge such that the path does not contain an untag edge. That is, if edges $e_0, \ldots, e_n$ are a path where e_0 is a tag edge, e_n is an untag edge, and $e_1, \ldots, e_{n-1}$ are not tag edges, then edges $e_1, \ldots, e_{n-1}$ are carry edges.*

In Figure 5, edge $n_7 \rightarrow n_6$ is a tag edge: it is an in-trigger edge (since it is source independent and successor edge $n_6 \rightarrow n_{10}$ is source dependent) that is not dominated by sanitizer edges. By contrast, edge $n_{13} \rightarrow n_{16}$ is an in-trigger edge, but it is not a tag edge, since it is dominated by sanitizer edge $n_{11} \rightarrow n_{13}$. This means that any values traversing $n_{13} \rightarrow n_{16}$ will already be sanitized, and so there is no need to track their source type in order to determine which sanitizer to apply. In Figure 5, all untag edges are sanitization edges.

Edge $n_6 \rightarrow n_{10}$ is a carry edge, as it is on a path from tag edge $n_1 \rightarrow n_6$ to untag edge $n_{10} \rightarrow n_{18}$ without an intervening untag edge. Edge $n_6 \rightarrow n_{10}$ will propagate the tags that tag edges $n_1 \rightarrow n_6$, $n_2 \rightarrow n_6$, and $n_7 \rightarrow n_6$ create, and enable sanitization edges $n_{10} \rightarrow n_{18}$ and $n_{10} \rightarrow n_{18}$ to apply the appropriate sanitization.

3.3.3 Run-Time Taint Tracking for Sanitization

We have defined several different kinds of edges that are relevant to the run-time discipline for applying correct sanitization to values: sanitization edges, tag edges, untag edges, and carry edges. We summarize what the instrumentation for these edges is required to do at run time:

- **tag edge:** when a value traverses a tag edge, if the value is not tagged then tag the value with *one of the source types* reaching it. A reaching source node, and its type, can be statically determined by examining the edge policy. Multiple source types may reach the tag edge, and any can be used, since tag edges are source independent.
- **untag edge:** when a tagged value traverses an untag edge, untag it.
- **sanitization edge:** If the sanitization edge is not preceded by a carry edge, then no tagged values can reach this edge, and all values traversing this edge should have the same sanitizer applied. Otherwise, apply sanitization only if the value is tagged by looking up the tag (which is a source type) in the edge's policy table to find the appropriate sanitizer to apply (which might be $\perp$, in which case no sanitization is applied).
- **carry edge:** when a value traverses a carry edge, any taint on the value must be propagated.

For example, in Figure 5, consider a value flowing from source node n_3 to sink node n_{20}. At tag edge $n_7 \rightarrow n_8$, the value will be tagged with its originating source type $\tau(n_3) = \diamondsuit$. The value with its tag will be propagated over carry edge $n_8 \rightarrow n_{11}$. Upon reaching sanitization edge $n_{11} \rightarrow n_{12}$, its tag will be examined, and the appropriate sanitizer (S_3) applied. Note that the tag was needed for $n_{11} \rightarrow n_{12}$ to determine which sanitizer to apply, since a value from source node n_4 could also traverse that edge, requiring no sanitization ($\perp$).

Note that if an edge e is not a tag edge, untag edge, sanitization edge, or carry edge, then e requires no instrumentation, as no tagged value will traverse e, and e does not need to perform any tagging, untagging, or sanitization. For example, in Figure 5, edges between nodes n_{12} and n_{20} require no instrumentation.

3.3.4 Correctness of Edge-based Placement

The edge-based placement produces a valid placement (Definition 1). We present here the key lemma that proves this.

Lemma 1. *For every path from a source node s to a sink node t, the following conditions hold for values flowing along that path.*

1. *There is at least one sanitization edge on the path.*
2. *If $\mathcal{P}(\tau(s), \tau(t)) = \perp$ then no sanitization will be applied.*
3. *If $\mathcal{P}(\tau(s), \tau(t)) \neq \perp$ then sanitizer $\mathcal{P}(\tau(s), \tau(t))$ will be applied at the first sanitization edge.*
4. *No sanitization will be applied at the second or subsequent sanitization edges.*

Proof: Condition (1) holds from the definition of sanitization edges, and because an edge whose target is a sink node must be sink independent.

Let $e_0, \ldots, e_n$ be a path from a source node to a sink node, and let e_i be the first sanitization edge. Conditions (2) and (3) hold by the following argument. If e_i is source independent then all values traversing e_i will have the same sanitization applied (either sanitizer S if $\mathcal{P}(\tau(s), \tau(t)) = S$, or no sanitization if $\mathcal{P}(\tau(s), \tau(t)) = \perp$). Suppose that e_i is source dependent. Then there must be some other source s' such that there is a path from s' to e_i and some output t' reachable from e_i such that $\mathcal{P}(\tau(s), \tau(t')) \neq \mathcal{P}(\tau(s'), \tau(t'))$. Since e_0 is source independent and e_i is source dependent and the first sanitizer edge, there must be some edge e_j on the path $e_0, \ldots e_{i-1}$ such that e_j is a tag edge, and all edges $e_{j+1}, \ldots, e_{i-1}$ are carry edges. Thus, at e_j, the value will be tagged with source type $\tau(s)$ (or some other source type I such that $\mathcal{P}(\tau(s), \tau(t)) = \mathcal{P}(I, \tau(t))$), the carry edges will propagate this tag, and so at sanitization edge e_i, the correct sanitization will be applied.

Suppose that condition (4) does not hold. Then there is some edge e_k in path $e_{i+1}, \ldots, e_n$ such that e_k is a sanitization edge, and e_k applies sanitization to values traversing path $e_o, \ldots, e_n$. Since e_k is a sanitization edge, it is the earliest sink-independent edge on some path from source to a sink, and so there must be some other source node s' that can reach e_k. Since e_k is the first sink-independent edge on a path from s', there must be another edge leaving *source*(e_k) (where *source*(e) denotes the source node of edge e) such that on that edge, some sink node t' is reachable that is not reachable from e_k, and $\mathcal{P}(\tau(s'), \tau(t)) \neq \mathcal{P}(\tau(s'), \tau(t'))$. More over, since *source*(e_k) has multiple edges coming from it, by assumption that the dataflow graph has no nodes with both multiple successors and multiple predecessors, node *source*(e_k) has a single predecessor, edge e_{k-1}, and so e_{k-1} is also on the path from s' to e_k. Therefore, edge e_{k-1} must be source dependent: since e_i can reach t', and e_i is sink independent, it means that either $\mathcal{P}(\tau(s), \tau(t')) \neq \mathcal{P}(\tau(s'), \tau(t'))$ or $\mathcal{P}(\tau(s), \tau(t)) \neq \mathcal{P}(\tau(s'), \tau(t))$.

Now consider whether e_{k-1} is a carry edge. **Suppose e_{k-1} is a carry edge.** We will show that none of the edges on $e_i, ..., e_{k-1}$ can be a tag edge, and thus, a value coming from e_i cannot be tagged, and so at sanitizer e_k, no sanitization will be applied. This contradicts the assumption that condition (4) doesn't hold.

Note that e_i is not a tag edge, as it is a sanitization edge. Then there must be some tag edge e_m between e_i and e_{k-1}. Since it is not dominated by sanitizer edges, there must be a path from a source node s_0 (such that $\tau(s_0) \neq \tau(s)$) to *source*(e_m) without a sanitization edge. Since e_m is an in-trigger edge, it is source independent. That means that for all sink types O reachable from e_m, and all source types I that can reach e_m, we have $\mathcal{P}_{e_m}(\tau(s), O) = \mathcal{P}_{e_m}(I, O)$. But any sink type O reachable from e_m is also reachable from e_i, and e_i is sink independent. That means that for any sink types O_1 and O_2 we have $\mathcal{P}_{e_m}(\tau(s), O_1) = \mathcal{P}_{e_m}(\tau(s), O_2)$. Together these imply that e_m is sink independent, since for any source I that can reach e_m and sinks O_1 and O_2 that can be reached from e_m we have:

$$\begin{aligned}
\mathcal{P}_{e_m}(I, O_1) &= \mathcal{P}_{e_m}(\tau(s), O_1) && e_m \text{ is source independent} \\
&= \mathcal{P}_{e_i}(\tau(s), O_1) && O_1 \text{ is reachable from } e_i \\
&= \mathcal{P}_{e_i}(\tau(s), O_2) && e_i \text{ is sink independent,} \\
& && \text{and } O_2 \text{ is reachable from } e_i
\end{aligned}$$

$$= \mathcal{P}_{e_m}(\tau(s), O_2)$$
$$= \mathcal{P}_{e_m}(I, O_2) \qquad e_m \text{ is source independent}$$

But then e_m is the first sink-independent edge on the path from I_0 to e_m, and so it is a sanitization edge. This is a contradiction, as e_m is a tag edge.

Suppose e_{k-1} is not a carry edge. Edge e_k is an untag edge (since it is a sanitization edge). Note that e_{k-1} is not a tag edge, since it is source dependent. But since e_{k-1} is source dependent, and e_k is the first sanitization edge on the path from s' to e_k, then there must be a tag edge on the path from s' to e_k without any intervening untag edges between it and e_k. Therefore e_{k-1} is a carry edge, which is a contradiction. ∎

The correctness of the edge-based placement follows trivially from Lemma 1 and the fact that no edge other than a sanitizer edge applies sanitization.

3.3.5 Optimizations

There are several opportunities for optimization in the edge-based placement approach.

Remove un-needed sanitization edges: For simplicity of the presentation and the proof, we have defined the behavior of tag edges and sanitization edges treating "no sanitization" $\perp$ as if it were a sanitizer. If a sanitizer is not preceded by a carry edge, and the policy dictates that no sanitization should be applied, then the sanitization edge does not perform any computation, and should not be instrumented. Similarly, if a tag edge is tagging a value with a source type that will never require sanitization, then the tag edge can be removed, and the value never tagged. This optimization is valid because a sanitization edge that may receive tagged values will never sanitize an untagged value.

Sanitization edges preceded by carry edges: For simplicity we required that any sanitization edge preceded by a carry edge needed to check the run-time tag before applying sanitization. There are some situations (statically determinable) where a sanitization edge will be preceded by a carry edge, yet all values going through it should have the same sanitization applied. In Figure 5 edge $n_{11} \to n_{13}$ is an example of this: the preceding edge $n_8 \to n_{11}$ is a carry edge, but $n_{11} \to n_{13}$ is source independent and the first sanitization edge on any path that goes through it. Thus, all values traversing $n_{11} \to n_{13}$ will have sanitizer S_3 applied, so there is no need to examine the tag.

Attaching tags to run-time values: We envision the run-time taint tracking being implemented simply by attaching tags to run-time values. This is a strategy that works well for dynamic languages such as Java, PHP, or JavaScript. The tags can be quite compact: we have described it above as tagging a value with the source type that it originated from (or a source type with equivalent sanitization requirements), but it would suffice to use bit strings that uniquely identify a source type. The number of sources depends on the policy, but will typically be small, meaning that a tag of 3–4 bits would suffice. There are opportunities for efficient implementation of taint-tracking when the tags are this small, such as placing the tag within the value header at run time. With this tagging approach, instrumentation for carry edges becomes trivial, since tags will be copied if they exist. Thus, the only instrumentation required will be to tag values as they traverse tag edges, untag them as they traverse untag edges, and apply sanitization at sanitization edges.

Semi-lattice	L	set of source types	
Top	$\top$	$\emptyset$	
Initial value	*init*(n)	$\emptyset$	
Transfer function	$TF(n)$	add $\tau(n)$ to set	if n is a source
		identity	otherwise
Meet operator	$\sqcap(x, y)$	union $x \cup y$	
Direction		*forward*	

(a) Available source types.

Semi-lattice	L	set of sink types	
Top	$\top$	$\emptyset$	
Initial value	*init*(n)	$\emptyset$	
Transfer function	$TF(n)$	add $\tau(n)$ to set	if n is a sink
		identity	otherwise
Meet operator	$\sqcap(x, y)$	union $x \cup y$	
Direction		*backward*	

(b) Anticipated sink types.

Figure 6. Available source types and anticipated sink types.

Efficient lookup for sanitization: Since the number of possible tags that can reach a given sanitization edge is small and known statically, we can pre-compute a lookup table for each sanitization edge that maps the tag number to the required sanitizer, thus minimizing run-time calculations.

Early vs. late sanitizer placement: The static node-based placement strategy performs sanitization as late as possible, at latest-exclusive nodes. The edge-based placement performs sanitization as early as possible, at the earliest sink-independent edges. The reason for this difference is that for the purely static node-based placement, it is slightly better to perform sanitization late, as many common sanitizers increase the size of data, and thus place additional pressure on memory. By contrast, for edge-based placement, early sanitization will reduce the amount of run-time taint tracking required, and we believe the cost of any run-time taint tracking outweighs the cost of increased size of data from sanitization.

4. Placement Algorithms

In this section, we propose concrete algorithms for computing the sets and relations described in Section 3. At the core of these computations, we have dataflow analysis, as described in Aho et al. [1]. As we will see, we can often stage our computation and break it down into a series of two or three analyses, one after another. As Knoop et al. [20] observe, this is often advantageous compared to a more complex equation-based approach, because each analysis stage completes quickly.

4.1 Node-based Placement

To implement the node-based placement strategy we compute the set of nodes that are S_i-possible and S_i-exclusive for each sanitizer S_i for i ranging from 1 to k. To combine the computation of these properties for different sanitizers S_i, we use *bit vectors* as our representation. Generally, a 1 at position i for a value at node $n \in N$ means that the property (either possibility or exclusiveness) holds for S_i.

First, we compute *available* source types and *anticipated* sink types at every node using a dataflow analysis, as shown in Figure 6. We specify dataflow analyses by giving the semi-

Semi-lattice	L	bit vector of length k	
Top	$\top$	$\bar{0}$	
Initial value	$init(n)$	$\bar{0}$	
Transfer function	$TF(n)$	bit $i = 1$	if n is S_i-exclusive
		identity	otherwise
Meet operator	$\sqcap(x, y)$	bitwise or $x \mid y$	
Direction		*backward*	

Figure 7. Computes exclusive_anticipated(i).

lattice of dataflow facts, the initial values of start nodes (source nodes for forward analyses, sink nodes for backwards analyses), the transfer function for nodes, and the direction of the dataflow analysis. This is a complete specification of the dataflow analyses.

We then combine the *available* sources and *anticipated* sinks information as described in Algorithm 1, to determine for each node which sanitizers are possible at every node. This is done by *projecting* the policy table to only the available source types and anticipated sink types. We write $Project(\mathcal{P}, S, T)$ for the policy table that contains only the rows of policy table $\mathcal{P}$ for sink types S, and only the columns of $\mathcal{P}$ for sink types T. If at node n, sanitizer S_i appears in policy table $Project(\mathcal{P}, available(n), anticipated(n))$, then n is S_i-possible.

Algorithm 1. Possible nodes.

```
for all n ∈ N do
   for all S_i ∈ Project(P, available(n), anticipated(n)) do
      possible(S_i) = possible(S_i) ∪ {n}
```

The nodes that are S_i-exclusive are a subset of nodes that are S_i-possible. Computing S_i-exclusive nodes is a simple matter of removing from the set of S_i-possible nodes any node that is S_j-possible, for any $i \neq j$, as shown in Algorithm 2.

Algorithm 2. Exclusive nodes.

```
for all i ∈ [1..k] do
   exclusive(S_i) = possible(S_i)
   for all j ∈ [1..k] do
      if i ≠ j then
         for all n ∈ possible(S_i) do
            if n ∈ possible(S_j) then
               exclusive(S_i) = exclusive(S_i) \ {n}
```

The last step is to compute latest-exclusive nodes: S_i-exclusive nodes that for some path from a source to a sink are the last S_i-exclusive node on that path. Figure 7 describes a backward dataflow analysis that identifies, for each S_i, which nodes can reach an S_i-exclusive node. We write exclusive_anticipated(S_i) for the set of nodes that can reach a S_i-exclusive node. Latest-exclusive nodes are simply the set of exclusive nodes, minus the set of anticipated-exclusive nodes (Algorithm 3).

Algorithm 3. Latest-exclusive nodes

```
for all i ∈ [1..k] do
   latest_exclusive(S_i) = exclusive(S_i)
   for all n ∈ exclusive_anticipated(S_i) do
      latest_exclusive(S_i) = latest_exclusive(S_i) \ {n}
```

We place sanitizer S_i at all nodes that are S_i-latest-exclusive. Latest-exclusive nodes may be rare, especially in dense graphs. For the graph in Figure 1, this algorithm will place sanitizers only at nodes n_1, n_{13}, and n_9. However, this is clearly insufficient, because not all values traversing the graph will be sanitized, such as values flowing from source node n_3 to sink node n_{20}.

Semi-lattice	L	*Bool*	
Top	$\top$	*true*	
Initial value	$init(n)$	*true*	
Transfer function	$TF(n)$	*true*	if $\exists S_i.\ n \in$ latest_exclusive(S_i)
		identity	otherwise
Meet operator	$\sqcap(x, y)$	conjunction $x \wedge y$	
Direction		*forward*	

Figure 8. Detect whether static placement is valid.

Figure 8 describes a dataflow analysis to detect whether all paths from sources to sinks go through a latest-exclusive node. Dataflow facts are booleans, indicating whether all paths to the node have gone through a latest-exclusive node. (By construction, a path can have at most one latest-exclusive node, so there is no need to count the number of latest-exclusive nodes on a path.) The static placement is valid if and only if the dataflow analysis produces a value of *true* at all sink nodes. If the static placement is valid, then it can be used to correctly sanitize all values, with no run-time overhead. If the placement is not valid, then the edge-based placement can be used to ensure correct sanitization, albeit with some run-time overhead.

4.2 Edge-based Placement

To implement the edge-based solution, we must identify several different sets of edges, summarized in Figure 4. We present algorithms to compute each of these sets of edges.

Source-dependent edges and sink-dependent edges: First, we compute the available source types and anticipated sink types for every edge, similar to the dataflow analyses in Figure 6. However, whereas Figure 6 computes dataflow facts for nodes, we need to compute dataflow facts for edges.

Next, for each edge e we compute edge policy $\mathcal{P}_e$: policy table $\mathcal{P}$ restricted to the available source types and anticipated sink types of edge e. We use edge policies to identify source-dependent edges and sink-dependent edges. Edge e is source dependent if and only if $\mathcal{P}_e$ has more than one unique sanitizer in any column. Edge e is sink dependent if and only if $\mathcal{P}_e$ has more than one unique sanitizer in any row.

In-trigger and out-trigger edges: Recall that in-trigger edges are source-independent edges with a source-dependent successor edge, and out-trigger edges are source-independent edges with a source-dependent predecessor edge. We can compute these edges efficiently simply by inspection of the dataflow graph. Let in_trigger denote the set of in-trigger edges, and out_trigger denote the set of out-trigger edges.

Sanitization edges: Sanitization edges are sink-independent edges that are the earliest sink-independent edge on *some* path from a source to a sink. They are the edges at which sanitization will be performed: at sink-independent edges the sanitization to apply to a value does not depend on which sink the value will go to.

Figure 9 presents a dataflow algorithm for computing sanitization edges. Note that the analysis computes dataflow facts for edges. Dataflow facts are pairs of boolean values. The first value is true for an edge if and only if all paths to the edge go through a sink-independent edge. The second boolean value is true for sanitization edges: edges that are the first sink-independent edge on some path, which is exactly the edges that are sink independent and have at least

Semi-lattice	L	*Bool* $\times$ *Bool*
Top	$\top$	*(true, true)*
Initial value	$init(e)$	*(false, false)*
Transfer function	$TF(e)$	$(f_1(e), f_2(e))$
	$f_1(e)(a,b)$	$= \begin{cases} true & \text{if } e \text{ is sink independent} \\ a & \text{otherwise} \end{cases}$
	$f_2(e)(a,b)$	$= \begin{cases} true & \text{if } f_1(e) = true \text{ and } a = false \\ false & \text{otherwise} \end{cases}$
Meet operator	$\sqcap(x,y)$	pointwise $\wedge$
Direction		*forward*

Figure 9. Computes $\mathsf{sanitization}(e)$.

Semi-lattice	L	*Bool*
Top	$\top$	*true*
Initial value	$init(e)$	*false*
Transfer function	$TF(e)$	$\begin{cases} true & \text{if } e \text{ is a sanitization edge} \\ identity & \text{otherwise} \end{cases}$
Meet operator	$\sqcap(x,y)$	$x \wedge y$
Direction		*forward*

Figure 10. Computes $\mathsf{dom\_sani}(e)$: whether edge e is dominated by sanitization edges.

one path to it that does not go through a sink-independent edge. Note that the transfer function for edge e is given as a pair of functions, $f_1(e)$ and $f_2(e)$, each of which is a function from the input dataflow fact (a pair of boolean values, (a, b)) to a boolean value.

Tag and untag edges: Tag and untag edges are where we, respectively, start and stop run-time tracking of values. The definition of both tag and untag edges relies on identifying edges that are dominated by a sanitization edge, for which we use the dataflow analysis in Figure 10. We write $\mathsf{dom\_sani}(e)$ if edge e is dominated by sanitization edges. If e is a sanitization edge, then $\mathsf{dom\_sani}(e)$ is true.

The following algorithm computes the set of tag and untag edges. Tag edges are in-trigger edges that are not dominated by sanitization edges. Untag edges are either sanitization edges, or out-trigger edges that are not dominated by sanitization edges.

Algorithm 4. Tag and untag edges.

for all $e \in E$ do
  if $e \in \mathsf{in\_trigger} \wedge \neg\mathsf{dom\_sani}(e)$ then
    $\mathsf{tag} = \mathsf{tag} \cup \{e\}$
  if $(e \in \mathsf{out\_trigger} \wedge \neg\mathsf{dom\_sani}(e)) \vee e \in \mathsf{sanitization}$ then
    $\mathsf{untag} = \mathsf{untag} \cup \{e\}$

Carry edges: Finally, carry edges are those on a path from a tag to an untag edge that does not pass through an untag edge. The set of carry edges can be computed by first performing a forward dataflow analysis to compute $\mathsf{tag\_available}$—the set of edges that are reachable from a tag edge without an intervening untag edge—and then performing a backward dataflow analysis to compute $\mathsf{untag\_anticipated}$, the set of edges that can reach an untag edge. These dataflow analyses are shown in Figure 11. Carry edges are the non-tag, non-untag edges that are in both the

Semi-lattice	L	*Bool*	
Top	$\top$	*false*	
Initial value	$init(e)$	*false*	
Transfer function	$TF(e)$	$\begin{cases} true & \text{if } e \in \mathsf{tag} \\ false & \text{if } e \in \mathsf{untag} \\ identity & \text{otherwise} \end{cases}$	
Meet operator	$\sqcap(x,y)$	$x \vee y$	
Direction		*forward*	

(a) Computes $\mathsf{tag\_available}$: reachable from tag edge without intervening untag edge.

Semi-lattice	L	*Bool*
Top	$\top$	*false*
Initial value	$init(e)$	*false*
Transfer function	$TF(e)$	$\begin{cases} true & \text{if } e \in \mathsf{untag} \\ identity & \text{otherwise} \end{cases}$
Meet operator	$\sqcap(x,y)$	$x \vee y$
Direction		*backward*

(b) Computes $\mathsf{untag\_anticipated}$: can reach untag edge.

Figure 11. Dataflow analyses for carry edge computation.

Benchmark	DLLs	DLL (KB)	LOC
Alias Management	3	65	10,812
Chat Application	3	543	6,783
Bicycle Club App	3	62	14,529
Software	15	118	11,941
Sporting Field Management	3	290	15,803
Commitment Management	7	369	25,602
New Hire	11	565	5,595
Expense Report Approval	4	421	78,914
Customer Support Portal	14	2,447	66,385
Relationship Management	5	3,345	1,810,585

Figure 12. Benchmark applications, sorted by code size.

$\mathsf{tag\_available}$ and $\mathsf{untag\_anticipated}$ sets, as defined in the following algorithm.

Algorithm 5. Carry edges.

for all $e \in E$ do
  if $e \in \mathsf{tag\_available} \wedge e \in \mathsf{untag\_anticipated}$ then
    if $e \notin \mathsf{tag} \wedge e \notin \mathsf{untag}$ then
      $\mathsf{carry} = \mathsf{carry} \cup \{e\}$

5. Experimental Evaluation

Our evaluation focuses on comparing the number of instrumentation points using our sanitizer placement algorithms compared to a baseline implementation that performs dynamic taint tracking between all sources and sinks. Our target applications are long-running server applications. Runtime overhead of taint tracking is typically workload specific (e.g., [10]), so we choose not to evaluate run-time overhead directly. Reducing the number of instrumentation points is a valuable goal, since long-running applications with diverse workloads have high code coverage over time, hitting increasingly many instrumentation points. Section 5.1 presents the results of applying our techniques to large C# web applications written in ASP.NET. Section 5.2 evaluates our approach against large, synthetically constructed graphs.

5.1 Large Applications

Figure 12 contains a summary of information about our macro-benchmarks. These are relatively large business web

Application	Graph nodes	Taint sources	Taint sinks	Tainted nodes forward	Tainted nodes backward	Tainted nodes both	Tainted nodes ratio	Exclusive nodes all	Exclusive nodes l.e.	Exclusive nodes ratio	Sanitization coverage
Terralever	156	64	69	140	140	76	48%	122	50	32%	82%
Alias Management	59	11	12	22	21	11	18%	19	9	15%	86%
Contoso Bicycle Club	161	50	54	145	133	87	54%	94	40	24%	50%
Windows Experience Catalog	204	47	83	186	160	101	49%	120	49	24%	93%
Commitment Management	356	135	132	299	296	183	51%	221	86	24%	79%
New Hire	502	142	183	401	409	229	45%	275	110	21%	70%
Expense Report Approval	805	214	322	722	637	408	50%	389	170	21%	82%
Customer Support Portal	3,881	967	1,219	3,488	3,263	2,266	58%	1,721	770	19%	—
Relationship Management	3,639	1,054	982	3,321	3,104	2,241	61%	1,565	637	17%	—

Figure 13. Node-based analysis and its effectiveness.

Application	Total edges	Taint sources	Taint sinks	Tainted forward	Tainted backward	Tainted both	Tainted ratio	Dependent source	Dependent sink	Triggers in	Triggers out	Triggers sanitizer	Edge count tag	Edge count untag	Edge count carry	Instr. total	Instr. ratio
Terralever	142	96	89	140	137	136	95%	3	1	8	0	97	1	5	0	6	**22.66**
Alias Management	962	11	10	13	14	13	1%	0	0	0	0	11	0	2	0	2	**6.5**
Contoso Bicycle Club	182	80	70	170	174	164	90%	32	27	29	9	84	2	6	7	15	**10.93**
Windows Experience	430	68	162	386	364	358	83%	133	125	14	117	193	2	31	123	156	2.29
Commitment Management	461	177	188	420	409	386	83%	110	114	45	41	215	6	30	108	144	2.68
New Hire	873	258	347	680	771	652	74%	181	192	108	75	342	27	67	126	220	2.96
Expense Report Approval	1,389	367	503	1,286	1,296	1,208	86%	189	197	131	143	577	23	99	144	266	**4.54**
Customer Support Portal	8,985	1,505	2,167	8,534	8,469	8,069	89%	4,315	4,364	901	1,331	2,875	232	541	3,917	4,690	1.72
Relationship Management	17,732	2,376	2,594	17,227	17,358	16,888	95%	11,227	11,585	2,057	2,020	4,407	428	533	10,725	11,686	1.44

Figure 14. Edge-based analysis and its effectiveness. Reduction in number of instrumented edges is shown in last column.

applications written on top of the ASP.NET framework, consisting of several separate DLLs, as shown in column 2. Not all code contained within the application source tree is actually deployed to the Web server. Most of the time, the number and size of deployed DLLs primarily consisting of .NET bytecode is a good measure of the application size, as shown in column 3. Note that in several cases, libraries supplied in the form of DLLs without the source code constitute the biggest part of an application. Finally, to provide another measure of the application size, column 4 shows the traditional line-of-code metric for *all* the code within the application. Note that correct manual sanitization for these applications is a challenge, as explored in the Merlin project [23]; we therefore believe that fully automatic placement is a better alternative.

Policy: There are applications ranging from tens of thousands of lines of code to over a million in the case of the Relationship Management application.

We classified sources and sinks into three categories: normal, file, resource, based on their functionality (i.e., `TextWriter.Write` is a file-related sink).

	normal	file	∅
normal	S_1	S_2	⊥
resource	S_3	S_4	⊥
∅	⊥	⊥	⊥

We used the policy shown in the table in this paragraph for these applications. Finally, we completely disregarded existing sanitizers, fully automating sanitizer placement.

5.1.1 Node-based Placement

Figure 13 contains the results of applying the node-based placement strategy. Applications are represented as graphs, some nodes of which are marked as sources or sinks. Dataflow graphs are computed by the CAT.NET tool [26], and are fairly sparse. Nodes of the graph are parameters and return results of individual methods in the application or its libraries. Edges represent data flow as inferred by CAT.NET. A different static analysis tool could also be used to construct these graphs; the precision and soundness of CAT.NET results is orthogonal to our approach. The number of nodes (column 2) as well as sources and sinks (3–4) ranges from dozens to lower thousands.

Columns 5–8 summarize information about tainted nodes in the graph. Column 5 is forward-tainted nodes (i.e., nodes that can be reached from a source node). Column 6 is backward-tainted nodes (i.e., nodes that can reach a target node). Column 7 is both forward- and backward-tainted nodes (i.e., nodes that are on a path from a source node to a sink node) and column 8 is the fraction of these nodes compared to all nodes in the graph. We can see that for a well-connected graph, the percentage of such nodes can be quite high, going higher than 60%. The implication is that a *very high* fraction of nodes needs to be instrumented to propagate the taint forward at run time.

Columns 9–11 capture our exclusive node computation. Column 9 is the number of exclusive nodes and column 10 is the number of latest exclusive nodes. Column 11 is the fraction of latest exclusive nodes within the nodes of the graph. Finally, column 12 shows the *coverage*, which is the fraction of all source-sink paths that are properly sanitized with latest exclusive nodes.[3] Two key take-aways from this table are as follows:

- the naïve approach of taint-tracking on all nodes on a path from a source to a sink is *very expensive*, with as many as 60+% of nodes needing to be instrumented; and
- while instrumenting just the latest exclusive nodes requires less instrumentation, the obtained coverage is sig-

[3]Coverage numbers are not available for the largest two application; the large number of paths in the dataflow graph cannot be enumerated in reasonable time.

nificantly less than 100%, so the static node-based approach is generally *unacceptable* for sanitizer placement.

5.1.2 Edge-based Placement

Figure 14 shows the results of applying the edge-based placement strategy. Column 2 shows the number of edges in the graph. Columns 3–4 show the number of sources and sinks, respectively; note that we use a slightly different policy for which nodes as marked as sources and sinks compared to Figure 13. Columns 5–7 show the number of forward and backward-tainted edges and edges tainted in both directions. Column 8 shows the percentage of edges tainted in both directions as a fraction of the number of edges in the graph.

Columns 9–10 show the number of source-dependent edges and sink-dependent edges. Columns 11–13 show the number of in-trigger edges, out-trigger edges, and sanitizer edges. Columns 14–16 show the counts for the other kinds of edges computed by the edge-based formulation. Finally, columns 17 and 18 show the number of edges needing instrumentation and the savings compared to the naïve approach of instrumenting edges that are both forward- and backward-tainted. We highlight particularly noticeable savings in bold. (As described in Section 3.3.5, we do not count unneeded sanitization edges when counting edges that require instrumentation.) Three key take-aways from this table are:

- We see that for most applications, the percentage of edges that are forward- and backward-tainted is quite high, indicating that the underlying dataflow analysis of CAT.NET is quite imprecise, leading to a great deal of connectivity within the dataflow graph.
- Savings in terms of the number of instrumentation points in the last column of Figure 14 are 6.19× on average.
- In general, our analysis is not as effective at reducing the number of instrumentation points for densely-connected graphs (the last several rows) as it is for the sparser graphs (the first several rows).

5.2 Synthetic Graphs

Finally, we evaluate our (edge-based) algorithm on some synthetically constructed graphs. To build such graphs, we start with 100 sources, 100 sinks, and 1,000 regular nodes. We randomize the type of the sources with equal probability between ⊘, □, ○, ◇, and △, and the type of sinks between ⊘, ●, ■, and ▲, using the policy in Figure 2 for proper sanitizer placement. We connect sources to sinks by performing a random walk of length 10 starting at a random source and ending at a random sink through the graph, creating edges as we pass from node to node. We use a density parameter d to vary how many such walks we perform, affecting the number of edges.

Figure 15 shows the improvements with edge-based instrumentation compared to naïve, taint-based instrumentation as the number of edges grows. We can see that for sparse graphs, the improvements are most noticeable, peaking at over 27×, gradually becoming less pronounced (only 48% improvement for 550 edges).

The improvements obtained with our strategy depends on the quality of the underlying dataflow graph. Results in Figure 15 suggest that our strategy performs better with *sparser* dataflow graphs, and performs worse when the dataflow graph is more highly connected. Since more precise analyses produce sparser dataflow graphs (since there are fewer conservative over-approximations of dataflow), investment

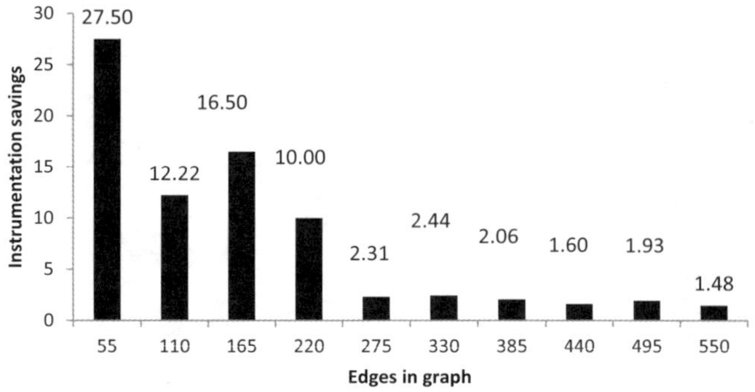

Figure 15. Synthetic graph results.

in precise static dataflow graph construction may improve the results of sanitization placement. This conclusion resonates with the experience of a number of projects that use static analysis to reduce the number of run-time instrumentation points: if static analysis is imprecise, the effect of this reduction is not very significant.

6. Related Work

The most closely-related work is that of King et al. [19], which considers the problem of resolving type errors in security-typed programs [36] by automatically placing mediation statements in a program (which explicitly declassify information or authorize the possibly dangerous information flow). They construct a graph representation of information flow in a program, such that source nodes are high-security inputs, and sink nodes are low-security outputs. A min-cut in this graph corresponds to a minimal set of program points such that insertion of mediation statements at these program points would allow the program to type check.

Their problem is similar to ours, in that every path from a source to a sink must have a mediation statement. However, their problem is simpler than ours, because all paths require the same kind of mediation statement. By contrast, our policies allow different source-sink pairs to require different sanitization. As such, we are unable to use a min-cut approach to identify sanitization program points. Also, in our setting, it is important to prevent over-sanitization: values should have the appropriate sanitization applied exactly once. By contrast, it is permissible (though perhaps undesirable) for a path from a source to a sink to have multiple mediation statements.

Samuel et al. [38] share our goal of automatic sanitization, but the details are very different. Our approach is designed to work on large legacy applications written in languages such as Java or C#, whereas they focus on much smaller programs in Google Closure. Their technique is based on constraint satisfaction using a custom solver, and has potential for scalability issues, whereas our approach uses dataflow analysis with well-understood scalability properties.

Graph-based analysis for information security: Several researchers have used program dependence graphs for analyzing information security of programs [12, 14, 40]. Program dependence graphs include both data dependencies and control dependencies, unlike the dataflow graphs we use in this work, which typically contain just data dependencies. Hammer et al. [13] consider enforcement of declassification [37] using program dependence graphs. However, Hammer et al. require certain nodes in a program dependence to be annotated as declassifiers, whereas we seek to *infer* where to insert declassifiers and sanitizers.

Software security analysis of web applications: Program analysis has a long history of being used for finding security bugs in web applications. Static analysis has been advocated for PHP, Java, and other languages [17, 18, 22, 47]. Multiple run-time analysis systems for information flow tracking have also been proposed [11, 25, 29, 31].

Automating placement: Most recently, we have seen increased interest in automating security-critical decisions for the developer [38, 46]. The use of a security type system for enforcing correctness is another case of cooperating with the developer to achieve better code quality and correctness guarantees [33].

Sanitizer correctness: Balzarotti et al. [3] show that custom sanitizer routines are often incorrectly implemented. Our concerns in this paper are complimentary to sanitizer correctness. The Cross-Site Scripting Cheat Sheet shows over two hundred examples of strings that exercise common corner cases of web sanitizers [34]. The BEK project proposes a systematic domain-specific languages for writing and checking sanitizers [15, 45].

Specification inference: Livshits et al. [23] propose an approach to inferring information flow specifications (sources, sanitizers, and sinks) using factor graphs. Kremenek et al. [21] propose belief inference as a way to infer specifications for static analysis checkers. Vaughan and Chong [44] propose policy inference to discover correct declassification policies.

Graph algorithms: LCM and PRE: A range of graph-theoretical algorithms from compiler literature is relevant for our work. In particular, Knoop et al. [20] describe lazy code motion. Rüthing et al. describe a variant of it called sparse code motion [35]. Partial redundancy elimination of PRE is described by Hosking et al. [16] and Briggs and Cooper [5].

7. Future Work

The design of our placement strategies is motivated by real-world concerns (for example, in the edge-based strategy, we perform sanitization as early as possible to reduce the amount of run-time taint-tracking). However, we do not offer a formal notion of optimality of our algorithms. This is in part because it is unclear what we should aim to optimize. Possible candidates include reducing the number of instrumentation points or run-time overhead for the worst-case or average-case workloads. Exploring these different notions of optimality in order to decide which is best requires building a more complete prototype.

Our matrix-based policy specification allows different sanitizers to be specified for all source-sink pairs. However, this may not be sufficiently expressive in all cases. For example, how do we properly sanitize the result of concatenating string data from two different kinds of sources? We see at least two possible solutions to this lack of expressiveness. One is to treat as sinks computations that combine two or more source types, effectively forcing proper sanitization to take place on values before computation occurs. An alternative that works for some compositional operations (e.g., string concatenation) is to perform finer-grained byte-level tagging, so that the appropriate sanitizer can be applied to the appropriate bytes of the value.

Another shortcoming of our matrix-based policy specification is that we collapse a sequence of sanitizers into a single one. This might prove to be a disadvantage in some settings, where keeping them separate would create interesting optimization opportunities.

We have described our approach as working on dataflow graphs that describe data dependencies. We believe our approach could be extended to work on graphs that also record control dependencies. However, it may be difficult to ensure that sanitizer and declassifiers correctly account for potentially dangerous control dependencies.

We also believe that the approach outlined here can apply to settings other than security. Consider the challenge of manually placing `catch` blocks in a program written in Java or C#. This problem has a similar structure to the sanitizer placement problem: instead of the dataflow graph we have the call graph of the program; for source nodes, we have statements that can throw exceptions; instead of sanitizers we have `catch` blocks. Finally, there is only one sink, the top-most `main` function, by the exit of which we generally need to catch all run-time-catchable exceptions.

8. Conclusions

Traditionally, developers have been responsible for properly dealing with the possibility of injection attacks and information leaks in their code, leading to numerous bugs, especially in large, complex code bases. The algorithms presented in this paper pave the way for completely automatic placement of sanitizers and declassifiers.

We proposed two strategies for automatic sanitizer placement. The first is a node-based entirely static approach that has no run-time overhead, but in many settings will not correctly sanitize all values. The second strategy is an edge-based approach that attempts to place sanitizers statically, but uses run-time taint-tracking when necessary to determine the appropriate sanitization to apply to values. The edge-based placement strategy will always sanitize values correctly, and reduces the number of nodes that require instrumentation, sometimes by as much as 27×, compared to naïve taint-tracking of values between sources and sinks.

Acknowledgments

We thank the anonymous reviewers for their helpful comments. We appreciate the helpful comments of Trent Jaeger and Somesh Jha. This research is supported in part by the National Science Foundation under Grant No. 1054172.

References

[1] A. V. Aho, M. Lam, R. Sethi, and J. D. Ullman. *Compilers: Principles, Techniques, and Tools.* Addison-Wesley, 2007.

[2] D. Avots, M. Dalton, B. Livshits, and M. S. Lam. Improving software security with a C pointer analysis. In *Proceedings of the International Conference on Software Engineering*, May 2005.

[3] D. Balzarotti, M. Cova, V. Felmetsger, N. Jovanovic, E. Kirda, C. Kruegel, and G. Vigna. Saner: Composing Static and Dynamic Analysis to Validate Sanitization in Web Applications. In *Proceedings of the IEEE Symposium on Security and Privacy*, May 2008.

[4] D. Bates, A. Barth, and C. Jackson. Regular expressions considered harmful in client-side XSS filters. In *Proceedings of the International World Wide Web Conference*, 2010.

[5] P. Briggs and K. D. Cooper. Effective partial redundancy elimination. In *Proceedings of the Conference on Programming Language Design and Implementation*, 1994.

[6] B. Chess and J. West. Dynamic taint propagation: Finding vulnerabilities without attacking. *Information Security Technical Reports*, 13, January 2008.

[7] E. Chin and D. Wagner. Efficient character-level taint tracking for Java. In *Proceedings of the Workshop on Secure Web Services*, 2009.

[8] S. Chong, K. Vikram, and A. C. Myers. Sif: enforcing confidentiality and integrity in Web applications. In *Proceedings of Usenix Security Symposium*, 2007.

[9] M. Egele, C. Kruegel, E. Kirda, and G. Vigna. PiOS: Detecting privacy leaks in iOS applications. In *Proceedings of the Annual Network and Distributed System Security Symposium*, Feb. 2011.

[10] W. Enck, P. Gilbert, B.-G. Chun, L. P. Cox, J. Jung, P. McDaniel, and A. N. Sheth. TaintDroid: an information-flow tracking system for realtime privacy monitoring on smartphones. In *Proceedings of the Usenix Conference on Operating Systems Design and Implementation*, 2010.

[11] V. Haldar, D. Chandra, and M. Franz. Dynamic taint propagation for Java. In *Proceedings of the Annual Computer Security Applications Conference*, Dec. 2005.

[12] C. Hammer and G. Snelting. Flow-sensitive, context-sensitive, and object-sensitive information flow control based on program dependence graphs. *International Journal of Information Security*, 8(6):399–422, Dec. 2009.

[13] C. Hammer, J. Krinke, and F. Nodes. Intransitive noninterference in dependence graphs. In *2nd International Symposium on Leveraging Application of Formal Methods, Verification and Validation*, Nov. 2006.

[14] C. Hammer, J. Krinke, and G. Snelting. Information flow control for java based on path conditions in dependence graphs. In *IEEE International Symposium on Secure Software Engineering*, Mar. 2006.

[15] P. Hooimeijer, B. Livshits, D. Molnar, P. Saxena, and M. Veanes. Fast and precise sanitizer analysis with BEK. In *Proceedings of the Usenix Security Symposium*, Aug. 2011.

[16] A. L. Hosking, N. Nystrom, D. Whitlock, Q. Cutts, and A. Diwan. Partial redundancy elimination for access path expressions. *Software Practice and Experience*, 31, May 2001.

[17] Y.-W. Huang, F. Yu, C. Hang, C.-H. Tsai, D.-T. Lee, and S.-Y. Kuo. Securing Web application code by static analysis and runtime protection. In *Proceedings of the International Conference on World Wide Web*, 2004.

[18] N. Jovanovic, C. Kruegel, and E. Kirda. Pixy: A static analysis tool for detecting Web application vulnerabilities (short paper). In *Proceedings of the IEEE Symposium on Security and Privacy*, 2006.

[19] D. King, S. Jha, D. Muthukumaran, T. Jaeger, S. Jha, and S. A. Seshia. Automating security mediation placement. In *Proceedings of the European Symposium on Programming*, 2010.

[20] J. Knoop, O. Rüthing, and B. Steffen. Lazy code motion. *SIGPLAN Notes*, 39:460–472, April 2004.

[21] T. Kremenek, P. Twohey, G. Back, A. Y. Ng, and D. R. Engler. From uncertainty to belief: Inferring the specification within. In *Symposium on Operating Systems Design and Implementation*, Nov. 2006.

[22] B. Livshits and M. S. Lam. Finding security errors in Java programs with static analysis. In *Proceedings of the Usenix Security Symposium*, 2005.

[23] B. Livshits, A. V. Nori, S. K. Rajamani, and A. Banerjee. Merlin: Specification inference for explicit information flow problems. In *Proceedings of the Conference on Programming Language Design and Implementation*, June 2009.

[24] M. Martin, B. Livshits, and M. S. Lam. Finding application errors and security flaws using PQL: a program query language. In *Proceedings of the Conference on Object Oriented Programming Systems Languages and Applications*, pages 365–383, 2005.

[25] M. Martin, B. Livshits, and M. S. Lam. SecuriFly: runtime vulnerability protection for Web applications. Technical report, Stanford University, 2006.

[26] Microsoft Corporation. Microsoft Code Analysis Tool .NET (CAT.NET). `http://www.microsoft.com/en-us/download/details.aspx?id=19968`, 3 2009.

[27] Microsoft Corporation. Microsoft web protection library. `http://wpl.codeplex.com/`, 2012.

[28] N. Mitchell, G. Sevitsky, and H. Srinivasan. The diary of a datum: an approach to modeling runtime complexity in framework-based applications. In *Proceedings of the European Conference on Object-Oriented Programming, Systems, Languages, and Applications*, 2005.

[29] A. Nguyen-Tuong, S. Guarnieri, D. Greene, J. Shirley, and D. Evans. Automatically hardening Web applications using precise tainting. In *Proceedings of the IFIP International Information Security Conference*, 2005.

[30] OWASP. OWASP-Java-HTML-sanitizer. `http://code.google.com/p/owasp-java-html-sanitizer/`, 2011.

[31] T. Pietraszek and C. V. Berghe. Defending against injection attacks through context-sensitive string evaluation. In *Proceedings of the Recent Advances in Intrusion Detection*, Sept. 2005.

[32] W. Robertson and G. Vigna. Static enforcement of web application integrity through strong typing. In *Proceedings of the Usenix Security Symposium*, 2009.

[33] W. Robertson and G. Vigna. Static enforcement of web application integrity through strong typing. In *Proceedings of the Usenix Security Symposium*, Aug. 2009.

[34] RSnake. XSS cheat sheet for filter evasion. `http://ha.ckers.org/xss.html`.

[35] O. Rüthing, J. Knoop, and B. Steffen. Sparse code motion. In *Proceedings of the Symposium on Principles of Programming Languages*, 2000.

[36] A. Sabelfeld and A. C. Myers. Language-based information-flow security. *IEEE Journal on Selected Areas in Communications*, 21(1):5–19, Jan. 2003.

[37] A. Sabelfeld and D. Sands. Dimensions and principles of declassification. In *Proceedings of the 18th IEEE Computer Security Foundations Workshop*, pages 255–269. IEEE Computer Society, June 2005.

[38] M. Samuel, P. Saxena, and D. Song. Context-sensitive auto-sanitization in web templating languages using type qualifiers. In *Proceedings of the Conference on Computer and Communications Security*, Oct. 2011.

[39] P. Saxena, D. Molnar, and B. Livshits. ScriptGard: Automatic context-sensitive sanitization for large-scale legacy web applications. In *Proceedings of the Conference on Computer and Communications Security*, Oct. 2011.

[40] B. Scholz, C. Zhang, and C. Cifuentes. User-input dependence analysis via graph reachability. Technical Report 2008-171, Sun Microsystems Labs, 2008.

[41] V. Srivastava, M. D. Bond, K. S. McKinley, and V. Shmatikov. A security policy oracle: detecting security holes using multiple API implementations. In *Proceedings of the Conference on Programming Language Design and Implementation*, 2011.

[42] Z. Su and G. Wassermann. The essence of command injection attacks in Web applications. In *Proceedings of the Symposium on Principles of Programming Languages*, 2006.

[43] O. Tripp, M. Pistoia, S. J. Fink, M. Sridharan, and O. Weisman. TAJ: effective taint analysis of web applications. In *Proceedings of the Conference on Programming Language Design and Implementation*, 2009.

[44] J. Vaughan and S. Chong. Inference of expressive declassification policies. In *Proceedings of IEEE Symposium on Security and Privacy*, May 2011.

[45] M. Veanes, P. Hooimeijer, B. Livshits, D. Molnar, and N. Bjorner. Symbolic finite state transducers: Algorithms and applications. In *Proceedings of the Sympolisium on Principles of Programming Languages*, Jan. 2012.

[46] J. Weinberger, P. Saxena, D. Akhawe, M. Finifter, R. Shin, and D. Song. A systematic analysis of XSS sanitization in web application frameworks. In *Proceedings of the European Symposium on Research in Computer Security*, Sept. 2011.

[47] Y. Xie and A. Aiken. Static detection of security vulnerabilities in scripting languages. In *Proceedings of the Usenix Security Symposium*, 2006.

[48] E. Z. Yang. HTML purifier. `http://code.google.com/p/owasp-java-html-sanitizer/`, 2011.

The Principles and Practice of Probabilistic Programming

Noah D. Goodman
Stanford University
ngoodman@stanford.edu

Categories and Subject Descriptors D [*3*]: m

Keywords probabilistic models, probabilistic programs

Probabilities describe degrees of belief, and probabilistic inference describes rational reasoning under uncertainty. It is no wonder, then, that probabilistic models have exploded onto the scene of modern artificial intelligence, cognitive science, and applied statistics: these are all sciences of inference under uncertainty. But as probabilistic models have become more sophisticated, the tools to formally describe them and to perform probabilistic inference have wrestled with new complexity. Just as programming beyond the simplest algorithms requires tools for abstraction and composition, complex probabilistic modeling requires new progress in model representation—*probabilistic* programming languages. These languages provide compositional means for describing complex probability distributions; implementations of these languages provide *generic* inference engines: tools for performing efficient probabilistic inference over an arbitrary program.

In their simplest form, probabilistic programming languages extend a well-specified deterministic programming language with primitive constructs for random choice. This is a relatively old idea, with foundational work by Giry, Kozen, Jones, Moggi, Saheb-Djahromi, Plotkin, and others [see e.g. 7]. Yet it has seen a resurgence thanks to new tools for probabilistic inference and new complexity of probabilistic modeling applications. There are a number of recent probabilistic programming languages [e.g. 8, 9, 11–17], embodying different tradeoffs in expressivity, efficiency, and perspicuity. We will focus on the probabilistic programming language Church [6] for simplicity, but the design of probabilistic languages to best support complex model representation and efficient inference is an active and important topic.

Church extends (the purely functional subset of) Scheme with elementary random primitives, such as flip (a bernoulli), multinomial, and gaussian. In addition, Church includes language constructs that simplify modeling. For instance, mem, a higher-order procedure that memoizes its input function, is useful for describing persistent random properties and lazy model construction. (Interestingly, memoization has a semantic effect in probabilistic languages.) If we view the semantics of the underlying deterministic language as a map from programs to executions of the program, the semantics of the probabilistic language will be a map from programs to distributions over executions. When the program halts with probability one, this induces a proper distribution over return values. Indeed, *any* computable distribution can be represented as the distribution induced by a Church program in this way (see [3, §6], [1, §11], and citations therein).

```
(define (rejection-query thunk condition)
  (let ((val (thunk)))
    (if (condition val)
        val
        (rejection-query thunk condition))))
```

```
(query
  ...defines...
  query-expression
  condition-expression)
```

```
(define (thunk)
  ...defines...
  (pair query-expression
        condition-expression))
(define condition rest)
```

Figure 1. (Top) Defining conditional inference in Church as a stochastic recursion: rejection sampling represents the conditional probability of the thunk conditioned on the condition predicate being true. We typically use special query syntax (Bottom, left), which can be desugared into a query thunk (Bottom, right).

Probabilistic graphical models [10], aka Bayes nets, are one of the most important ideas of modern AI. Probabilistic programs extend probabilistic graphical models, leveraging concepts from programming language research. Indeed, graphical models can be seen as flow diagrams for probabilistic programs—and just as flow diagrams for deterministic programs are useful but not powerful enough to represent general computation, graphical models are a useful but incomplete approach to probabilistic modeling. For an example of this, we need look no further than the fundamental operation for inference, probabilistic conditioning, which forms a posterior distribution over executions from the prior distribution specified by the program. Conditioning is typically viewed as a special operation that happens *to* a probabilistic model (capturing observations or assumptions), not one that can be expressed *as* a model. However, because probabilistic programs allow *stochastic recursion*, conditioning can be defined as an ordinary probabilistic function (Fig. 1, Top). (However see [1] for complications in the case of continuous values.)

A wide variety of probabilistic models are useful for diverse tasks, including unsupervised learning, vision, planning, and statistical model selection. Due to space limitations, we only mention two characteristic examples here. The first, Fig. 2, captures key concepts for commonsense reasoning about the game tug-of-war. This "conceptual library" of probabilistic functions can be used to reason about many patterns of evidence, via different queries, without needing to specify ahead of time the set of people, the teams, or the matches. The program thus enables a very large numbers of different inferences to be modeled, and the model predictions match human intuitions quite well (a correlation of 0.98 between

POPL'13, January 23–25, 2013, Rome, Italy.
ACM 978-1-4503-1832-7/13/01.

```
;;Strength is a persistent property of each person,
    hence memoized:
(define strength
  (mem (lambda (person) (gaussian 1.0 1.0))))

;;Laziness varies from match to match:
(define (lazy person) (flip 0.3))

;;When a person is lazy they pull less:
(define (pulling person) (if (lazy person)
                             (/ (strength person) 2)
                             (strength person)))

;;Total pulling of the team is the sum:
(define (total-pulling team) (sum (map pulling team)))

;;The winning team pulls hardest:
(define (winner team1 team2)
  (if (< (total-pulling team1) (total-pulling team2))
      team2
      team1))
```

Figure 2. Modeling intuitive concepts in the tug-of-war domain. While this model is simple, probabilistic queries can explain human reasoning from diverse evidence with high quantitative accuracy [4].

```
;;The basic listener: how is the world, given that the
    utterance is true?
(define (literal-listener utterance)
  (query
    (define world (world-prior))
    world
    ((meaning utterance) world)))

;;The speaker: what should I say, so that the listener
    infer the right world?
(define (speaker world)
  (query
    (define utterance (language-prior))
    utterance
    (equal? world (literal-listener utterance))))

;;The smart listener: how is the world, given that a
    speaker chose this utterance to express it?
(define (listener utterance)
  (query
    (define world (world-prior))
    world
    (equal? utterance (speaker world))))
```

Figure 3. A probabilistic model of natural language pragmatics using nested-query to model reasoning-about-reasoning.

model and human judgements in the experiments of [4]). The ability to model many inferences is inherited from the productivity of the underlying programming language, while the ability to capture complex, graded commonsense reasoning is inherited from probabilistic inference.

A more subtle model is shown in Fig. 3. Here we model pragmatic inference in natural language following [2, 5, 18]. Critically, because query is an ordinary function that may be nested in itself, we are able to model a listener reasoning about a speaker, who reasons about a naive listener. This model formalizes the idea that a listener is trying to infer what the speaker intended, while a speaker is trying to make the listener form a particular belief. Versions of this model again predict human judgements with high quantitative accuracy [2, 5].

The critical obstacle to probabilistic programming as a practical tool is efficient implementation of the inference operator. It is clear that the expected runtime for the rejection-query operator in Fig. 1 increases as the probability of satisfying the condition decreases. Hence, while rejection is useful as a definition, it is impractical for real modeling tasks, where the condition is typically very unlikely. An obvious alternative that does not take longer when the condition is less likely is to enumerate all execution paths of the program, for instance by using co-routines. Unfortunately, naive enumeration takes time proportional to the number of executions, which grows exponentially in the number of random choices. This can be ameliorated in some cases by using dynamic programming. Indeed it is possible to do inference for the simple pragmatics model in Fig. 3 by using a sophisticated dynamic programming approach [18].

For other classes of program, such as the tug-of-war model, Fig. 2, it can be better to switch to an approximate inference technique based on Markov chain Monte Carlo. One such algorithm [6] can be derived from the Metropolis Hastings recipe: a random change to a single random choice is made on each step, leading to a random walk in the space of program executions. This walk is guaranteed to visit executions in proportion to their probability. We individuate random choices using their position in the execution—this can be achieved by a code transformation, resulting in a very lightweight inference process [20].

Each step of this MCMC process requires re-executing the program, in order to compute updated probabilities. Several orders of magnitude in speed increases are seen by just-in-time compiling this probability update [21]. To do so, we separate structural random choices (those that can influence control flow) from non-structural. When we encounter a new setting of the structural choices we partially-evaluate the program to straight-line code, which is aggressively optimized. Structural choices can sometimes be found automatically by flow analysis, but in other instances must be annotated by hand.

The distinction between structural and non-structural choices can also be used to construct an algorithm that more effectively explores the space of executions for "open universe" models—those that define distributions over a variable number of entities [22]. This class of programs is especially well-suited to complex procedural modeling in computer graphics. For instance, Yeh et al. [22] describe models for layout of virtual worlds. These procedural models typically have many real-valued random choices. In this setting Hamiltonian Monte Carlo, which exploits the gradient of the score to make more well-directed steps in execution space, can be a useful additional tool. The needed gradient can be derived automatically by a non-standard interpretation of the program [19].

The sampling of inference algorithms described above suggests an important generalization: advanced statistical inference techniques can be implemented for arbitrary programs by leveraging methods developed in programming language research (program analysis, non-standard interpretation, partial evaluation, etc.). Existing research only scratches the surface of potential interactions between statistics, AI, and PL. Though technically demanding, this interaction may be the critical ingredient in bringing complex probabilistic modeling to the wider world.

Acknowledgments

Thanks to Dan Roy, Cameron Freer, and Andreas Stuhlmüller for helpful comments. This work was supported by ONR grant N00014-09-0124.

References

[1] N. Ackerman, C. Freer, and D. Roy. Noncomputable conditional distributions. In *Logic in Computer Science (LICS), 2011 26th Annual IEEE Symposium on*, pages 107–116. IEEE, 2011.

[2] M. Frank and N. Goodman. Predicting pragmatic reasoning in language games. *Science*, 336(6084):998–998, 2012.

[3] C. E. Freer and D. M. Roy. Computable de Finetti measures. *Annals of Pure and Applied Logic*, 163(5):530–546, 2012. doi: 10.1016/j.apal.2011.06.011.

[4] T. Gerstenberg and N. D. Goodman. Ping pong in Church: Productive use of concepts in human probabilistic inference. In *Proceedings of the 34th annual conference of the cognitive science society*, 2012.

[5] N. Goodman and A. Stuhlmüller. Knowledge and implicature: Modeling language understanding as social cognition. *Topics in Cognitive Science*, 2013.

[6] N. Goodman, V. Mansinghka, D. Roy, K. Bonawitz, and J. Tenenbaum. Church: A language for generative models. In *In UAI*, 2008.

[7] C. Jones and G. Plotkin. A probabilistic powerdomain of evaluations. In *Logic in Computer Science (LICS), 1989 4th Annual IEEE Symposium on*, pages 186–195, Jun 1989. doi: 10.1109/LICS.1989.39173.

[8] A. Kimmig, B. Demoen, L. De Raedt, V. S. Costa, and R. Rocha. On the implementation of the probabilistic logic programming language ProbLog. *Theory and Practice of Logic Programming*, 11(2-3):235–262, 2011.

[9] O. Kiselyov and C. Shan. Embedded probabilistic programming. In *Domain-Specific Languages*, pages 360–384, 2009.

[10] D. Koller and N. Friedman. *Probabilistic graphical models: principles and techniques*. MIT press, 2009.

[11] A. McCallum, K. Schultz, and S. Singh. Factorie: Probabilistic programming via imperatively defined factor graphs. In *Neural Information Processing Systems Conference (NIPS)*, 2009.

[12] B. Milch, B. Marthi, S. Russell, D. Sontag, D. L. Ong, and A. Kolobov. BLOG: Probabilistic models with unknown objects. In *International Joint Conference on Artificial Intelligence (IJCAI)*, pages 1352–1359, 2005.

[13] A. Pfeffer. IBAL: A probabilistic rational programming language. In *International Joint Conference on Artificial Intelligence (IJCAI)*, pages 733–740. Morgan Kaufmann Publ., 2001.

[14] A. Pfeffer. Figaro: An object-oriented probabilistic programming language. *Charles River Analytics Technical Report*, 2009.

[15] D. Poole. The independent choice logic and beyond. *Probabilistic inductive logic programming*, pages 222–243, 2008.

[16] M. Richardson and P. Domingos. Markov logic networks. *Machine Learning*, 62:107–136, 2006.

[17] T. Sato and Y. Kameya. PRISM: A symbolic-statistical modeling language. In *International Joint Conference on Artificial Intelligence (IJCAI)*, 1997.

[18] A. Stuhlmüller and N. Goodman. A dynamic programming algorithm for inference in recursive probabilistic programs. *arXiv preprint arXiv:1206.3555*, 2012.

[19] D. Wingate, N. Goodman, A. Stuhlmueller, and J. Siskind. Nonstandard interpretations of probabilistic programs for efficient inference. In *Advances in Neural Information Processing Systems 23*, 2011.

[20] D. Wingate, A. Stuhlmueller, and N. Goodman. Lightweight implementations of probabilistic programming languages via transformational compilation. In *Proceedings of the 14th international conference on Artificial Intelligence and Statistics*, page 131, 2011.

[21] L. Yang, P. Hanrahan, and N. Goodman. Incrementalizing mcmc on probabilistic programs through tracing and slicing. Under review.

[22] Y. Yeh, L. Yang, M. Watson, N. Goodman, and P. Hanrahan. Synthesizing open worlds with constraints using locally annealed reversible jump mcmc. *ACM Transactions on Graphics (TOG)*, 31 (4):56, 2012.

A Model-Learner Pattern for Bayesian Reasoning

Andrew D. Gordon (Microsoft Research and University of Edinburgh) Mihhail Aizatulin (Open University)
Johannes Borgström (Uppsala University) Guillaume Claret (Microsoft Research)
Thore Graepel (Microsoft Research) Aditya V. Nori (Microsoft Research)
Sriram K. Rajamani (Microsoft Research) Claudio Russo (Microsoft Research)

Abstract

A Bayesian model is based on a pair of probability distributions, known as the *prior* and *sampling* distributions. A wide range of fundamental machine learning tasks, including regression, classification, clustering, and many others, can all be seen as Bayesian models. We propose a new probabilistic programming abstraction, a *typed Bayesian model*, based on a pair of probabilistic expressions for the prior and sampling distributions. A *sampler* for a model is an algorithm to compute synthetic data from its sampling distribution, while a *learner* for a model is an algorithm for probabilistic inference on the model. Models, samplers, and learners form a generic programming pattern for model-based inference. They support the uniform expression of common tasks including model testing, and generic compositions such as mixture models, evidence-based model averaging, and mixtures of experts. A formal semantics supports reasoning about model equivalence and implementation correctness. By developing a series of examples and three learner implementations based on exact inference, factor graphs, and Markov chain Monte Carlo, we demonstrate the broad applicability of this new programming pattern.

Categories and Subject Descriptors D.3.3 [*Programming Languages*]: Language Constructs and Features—Patterns

Keywords Bayesian reasoning, machine learning, model-learner pattern, probabilistic programming

1. Introduction

Background: Bayesian Models and Inference We give the simple, general structure of a Bayesian model (see MacKay (2003) for instance); many examples follow later in the paper. Let y be the output of the model, such as the object to be predicted or observed, and let x be any input information on which to condition, such as the feature vector in classification or regression. Let w be the parameters of the model and let h be the hyperparameters. The key ingredients of a Bayesian model are the two conditional probability distributions:

- the *prior distribution* $p(w|h)$ over the parameters;
- the *sampling distribution* $p(y|x,w)$ over the output.

POPL'13, January 23–25, 2013, Rome, Italy.

The parameters w parameterize the sampling distribution over the output, while the hyperparameters h parameterize the prior distribution over the parameters.

Given training data $d = (x,y)$, we obtain by Bayes' rule expressions for computing the following distributions:

- the *posterior distribution* $p(w|d,h)$;
- the *posterior predictive distribution* $p(y'|x',d,h)$, assuming that (x',y') are independent from and identically distributed as (x,y).

This fundamental Bayesian model represents a wide variety of machine learning tasks. There are also a great many machine learning algorithms for *probabilistic inference*, that is, for computing exactly or approximately the posterior $p(w|d,h)$, and for using $p(y'|x',d,h)$ to make predictions.

Background: Probabilistic Programming for Inference Probabilistic programming language systems allow automatic generation of bespoke machine-learning algorithms. Such systems include AutoBayes (Schumann et al. 2008), Alchemy (Domingos et al. 2008), BUGS (Gilks et al. 1994), Church (Goodman et al. 2008), Csoft (Winn and Minka 2009), FACTORIE (McCallum et al. 2009), Figaro (Pfeffer 2010), Fun (Borgström et al. 2011), HANSEI (Kiselyov and Shan 2009), HBC (Daumé III 2008), IBAL (Pfeffer 2001), Probabilistic cc (Gupta et al. 1999), PFP (Erwig and Kollmansberger 2006), and Probabilistic Scheme (Radul 2007), amongst others.

The user writes a short probabilistic program, often embedded within a larger conventional program, and the system produces an algorithm for learning distributions given by the probabilistic program. Hence, probabilistic programming saves development costs compared to the alternative of writing the inference algorithm from scratch. Probabilistic programming is more flexible than the alternative of relying on a fixed algorithm for a particular task, as one can easily compose, refactor, and write variations of models. On the other hand, for some tasks a fixed algorithm may be more efficient, but much progress is being made on inference engines for probabilistic programs.

Still, the current practice of probabilistic programming is low-level, irregular, and unstructured. Probabilistic programs represent Bayesian models, but simply intermingle the code for defining parameters, predicting outputs, observing data, and so on. The absence of such structure is a missed opportunity. For example, in our own experience with Fun, we have over a dozen samples, but very little code re-use even though each sample performs similar tasks such as training, parameter learning, and prediction. We also duplicate code for the task of testing a model by sampling parameters, generating synthetic data from the predictive distribution, and then comparing with the outcome of learning the parameters from the synthetic data. Moreover, there is repetition of common probabilistic patterns such as constructing mixture models. Other probabilistic programming systems share these problems.

Our Proposal: The Model-Learner Pattern The central idea of the paper is to add structure and code re-use to probabilistic programming by representing a Bayesian model by a generic type Model<TH,TW,TX,TY>. A value of this type is a record containing a hyperparameter together with probabilistic expressions for the prior and sampling distributions. The type parameters correspond to the constituents of a Bayesian model: hyperparameters h : TH, parameters w : TW, inputs x : TX, and outputs y : TY. The aim of the model-learner pattern is to make construction, use, and re-use of models easier (rather than to make inference more efficient). We are aware of no probabilistic system that encourages writing Bayesian models in a generic format.

Common patterns of constructing Bayesian models can be written as functions on these typed models. Given any model, we can derive a *sampler* object, which has general methods to draw samples from the prior and sampling distributions, for test purposes. Given any model and a suitable algorithm, we can derive a *learner* object, which has general methods to train on data, and to compute the posterior distribution and posterior predictive distributions.

Fun We evaluate the model-learner pattern by developing the idea in detail using Fun (Borgström et al. 2011), a probabilistic language embedded within F#, a dialect of ML for .NET. (The model-learner pattern can be developed in other probabilistic languages too, with or without types, but Fun has both a precise formal semantics and an efficient implementation.) As background, Section 2 recalls the syntax, type system, and informal semantics of Fun.

Model-Learner Pattern, and a Reference Learner Section 3 describes our notions of models, samplers, and learners using Fun, independently of any particular implementation of probabilistic inference. Theorem 1 asserts that the reference learner does indeed compute the posterior and posterior predictive distributions.

Learners based on Exact Inference and Factor Graphs We present in Section 4 a learner for discrete models that uses Algebraic Decision Diagrams (ADDs) as a compact representation of joint distributions. Theorem 2 shows correctness of the ADD backend. We show by example that Bayesian networks can be presented as models, and solved using ADDs, with performance comparable to other systems. Section 5 describes inference using probabilistic graphical models in Infer.NET (Minka et al. 2009). We describe our typed API for inferring distributions using Infer.NET.

Theory We enhance the previous semantics of Fun. The original version of Fun and its semantics (Borgström et al. 2011) did not include sums or observations on composite types, did not describe a semantics of Fun in the probability monad, and did not consider how to compute a density function for a probabilistic expression. In Section 6, we recall the measure-transformer semantics of Fun from previous work (Borgström et al. 2011). We extend Fun and the measure-transformer semantics with sum types, and give an inductive definition for observations on composite types. We identify a normal form with a single outermost observation, Theorem 3, enabling a semantics for many Fun expressions using the standard probability monad. These results provide a firm foundation for our semantics of the model-learner pattern.

Generic Mixtures Section 7 shows how generic compositions such as mixture models, evidence-based model averaging, and mixtures of experts can be seen as *model combinators*, that is, F# functions for producing models from models. Fun itself is first-order in the sense that functions are not values, but our combinators are higher-order functions in the host language F#. Theorem 4 shows that we can compute the evidence for a model (a measure of how well the model fits the observed data) using a simple if-expression, enabling a simple definition of these combinators and setting us apart from many other probabilistic languages.

Third Learner: via Markov chain Monte Carlo In Section 8, we develop the theory and implementation of a learner based on Markov chain Monte Carlo (MCMC) techniques. This learner is built on Filzbach (Purves and Lyutsarev 2012), a generic MCMC system. Given training data $d = (x, y)$, Bayesian MCMC computations explore different values for parameter w, and for each w require us to compute the density of the posterior function, that is, $p(w|d,h)$. Hence, to implement a learner, we need to compute the density of a probabilistic expression. We present a algorithm based on the direct symbolic evaluation of a probabilistic expression with only deterministic let bindings, verify its correctness as Theorem 5, and report our implementation. With our method, the user provides only a model, and our system automatically computes the density of the posterior; hence, we save the user effort compared to existing practice with Filzbach (and other MCMC systems) where the user provides code for both the sampling distribution and the density calculation.

Table of Model Types Table 1 at the end of the paper summarizes our collection of typed models. Our examples demonstrate that a wide range of tasks, including regression, classification, topic modelling, all fit the model-learner pattern. All our example models have been tested via at least one of our three learner backends. Our Infer.NET learner generates code of the same form as one would execute directly, so there is no performance penality. Our initial Filzbach learner used an interpretive log-posterior function, which was much less efficient than typical log-posterior functions written in C. Our current implementation now uses run-time code generation to compile the log-posterior function, yielding performance competitive with the C-code; further gains may be achieved by runtime specialization of this function to the data at hand. Our practical examples are evidence that a wide range of machine learning tasks are executable using the model-learning pattern, with no loss in performance in principle. but with the advantage of automatic synthesis of test data from the model, and in the case of MCMC-based systems such as Filzbach, the automatic construction of the density function.

Section 9 discusses related work and Section 10 concludes.

Contributions of the Paper The new conceptual insight is that code-based machine learning can be structured around *typed Bayesian models*, which are records containing a hyperparameter together with probabilistic expressions for prior and sampling distributions. Our specific technical contributions:

- Definition of a type of Bayesian models, with combinators for compositionally constructing models, and operations to derive samplers and learners from an arbitrary model.
- Many Bayesian examples expressed as such executable models.
- A formal semantics for models, learning, and prediction in terms of Fun, and its semantics using measure transformers and the probability monad.
- Learners based on Algebraic Decision Diagrams, message-passing on factor graphs, and MCMC.

Our generic format for models, and generic learner and sampler interfaces have several advantages over conventional probabilistic programming. An end-user may assemble new models from pre-existing models and combinators, without writing models from scratch. Our API is accessible from other languages such as C#. It is easy to add a new inference algorithm as a new learner. Finally, we enable generic programming for code re-use.

Most of the listings in the paper are directly imported from our F# code, and are a mixture of quoted probabilistic Fun code and deterministic functions in full F#.

A full version with additional details and proofs is available (Gordon et al. 2013).

2. Fun: Probabilistic Expressions (Review)

We recall the core calculus Fun (Borgström et al. 2011), enriched here with sum types to support the normal form of Section 6. Fun is a first-order functional language, without recursion. Our implementation efficiently supports a richer language with arrays and array comprehensions, and Vector and Matrix types, whose semantics can be seen as shorthands for constructs in this core.

We let c range over constant data of base and unit type, n over integers and r over real numbers. We write $\mathrm{ty}(c) = t$ to mean that constant c has type t.

Values and Types of Fun:

$U,V ::= x \mid c \mid (V,V) \mid \textbf{inl}\ V \mid \textbf{inr}\ V$	value
$a,b ::= \textbf{int} \mid \textbf{real}$	base type
$t,u ::= \textbf{unit} \mid (t_1 * t_2) \mid (t_1 + t_2)$	compound type

Let **bool** $\triangleq$ **unit** + **unit**. We let $\mathbf{V}_t$ be the set of closed values of type t (real numbers, integers, and so on). Semantically we consider **real** to be the reals, but our implementation uses double-precision floats. We assume a collection of deterministic functions on these types, including arithmetic and logical operators, and **fst** and **snd** projections on pairs. Each function f of arity n has a signature of the form **val** $f\colon t_1 * \cdots * t_n \to t_{n+1}$. We assume standard families of primitive probability distributions of type $\mathsf{PDist}\langle t\rangle$, such as the following.

Distributions: $\mathrm{Dist} : (x_1 : t_1 * \cdots * x_n : t_n) \to \mathsf{PDist}\langle t\rangle$

$\mathsf{Bernoulli} : (\mathsf{bias} : \textbf{real}) \to \mathsf{PDist}\langle \textbf{bool}\rangle$
$\mathsf{Beta} : (\mathsf{a} : \textbf{real} * \mathsf{b} : \textbf{real}) \to \mathsf{PDist}\langle \textbf{real}\rangle$
$\mathsf{Gaussian} : (\mathsf{mean} : \textbf{real} * \mathsf{prec} : \textbf{real}) \to \mathsf{PDist}\langle \textbf{real}\rangle$
$\mathsf{Gamma} : (\mathsf{shape} : \textbf{real} * \mathsf{scale} : \textbf{real}) \to \mathsf{PDist}\langle \textbf{real}\rangle$

A Bernoulli distribution is a biased coin flip; the bias lies in the unit interval $[0,1]$ and is the probability of **true**. A Beta distribution, often used as a prior distribution on the bias of a Bernoulli distribution, is a distribution on the unit interval; when $\mathsf{a} = 1$ and $\mathsf{b} = 1$, it is the uniform distribution on the unit interval. A Gaussian distribution is parameterized by its mean and precision; the *standard deviation* σ follows from the identity $\sigma^2 = 1/\mathsf{prec}$. A Gamma distribution, often used as a prior distribution on the precision of a Gaussian distribution, is a distribution on the positive reals.

The expressions of Fun are in a syntax akin to administrative normal form, with **let**-expressions for sequential composition.

Expressions of Fun:

$M,N ::=$	expression
V	value
$f(V_1,\ldots,V_n)$	deterministic application
$\textbf{let}\ x = M\ \textbf{in}\ N$	let (scope of x is N)
$\textbf{match}\ V\ \textbf{with inl}\ x : M \mid \textbf{inr}\ y : N$	matching (scope of x is M, scope of y is N)
$\textbf{random}(\mathrm{Dist}(V))$	primitive distribution
$\textbf{observe}\ f(V_1,\ldots,V_n)$	observation
fail	failure

We rely on several standard syntactic conventions. We write **if** V **then** M **else** N for **match** V **with inl** $\_ : M \mid$ **inr** $\_ : N$. We write $M;N$ for **let** $x = M$ **in** N when x is not free in N. Although formally Fun uses administrative normal form, we often allow arbitrary expressions M in places where values V are expected, assuming the insertion of suitable **let**-expressions. We allow arbitrary length tuples, formed by multiple pairings. We make use of records, and arrays and array comprehensions, where the size of each array is known statically; we consider operations on records and on statically-sized arrays to be reducible to operations on tuples.

Observation and failure expressions represent conditioning. We usually write observations in the form **observe** $f(\overline{V})$, where $\overline{V}$ is short for $V_1,\ldots,V_n$. Such an observation expresses (unnormalized) conditioning on the event that the indicator function $f(\overline{V})$ yields a zero, defined as a closed value where every instance of c is 0. The primitive **fail** represents an impossible event. It has the same meaning as an observation such as **observe**$(1+1)$ whose indicator function cannot yield zero. Note that **observe** is a no-op on **bool**, since any Boolean is a zero according to the above definition. We write **observe** $(x = V)$ for **observe** $(x - V)$ when $V = (c_1,\ldots,c_n)$ and $x - V$ is the component-wise difference.

We write $\Gamma \vdash M : t$ to mean that in type environment $\Gamma = x_1 : t_1,\ldots,x_n : t_n$ (x_i distinct) the expression M has type t. We write $\diamond$ for the empty type environment. Apart from the following, the typing rules are standard.

Selected Typing Rules: $\Gamma \vdash M : t$

(FUN OBSERVE)
$$\frac{\Gamma \vdash f(\overline{V}) : t}{\Gamma \vdash \textbf{observe}\ f(\overline{V}) : \textbf{unit}}$$

(FUN RANDOM)
$$\frac{\mathrm{Dist} : (x_1 : t_1 * \cdots * x_n : t_n) \to \mathsf{PDist}\langle t\rangle \qquad \Gamma \vdash V : (t_1 * \cdots * t_n)}{\Gamma \vdash \textbf{random}(\mathrm{Dist}(V)) : t}$$

Fun is designed as a subset of F#, so we represent Fun expressions using F#'s features for reflection (Syme 2006): quotation, evaluation, and antiquotation. We represent a closed term M of type t by the F# quotation <@ M @> of F# type Expr<t>. More generally, if $\diamond, x_1 : t_1,\ldots,x_n : t_n \vdash M : t$ we represent M by the F# quotation <@ **fun** $(x_1,\ldots,x_n) \to M$ @>. Suppose E is a quotation: E.Eval evaluates E to its value, and inside a quotation, the % symbol denotes antiquotation—the expression $(\%E)$ embeds the expression E within the quotation.

The semantics of Fun is detailed in Section 6; as usual, for precision concerning mixes of discrete and continuous probabilities, we turn to measure theory. Formally, the semantics of a closed Fun expression M is a finite measure $\mathscr{M}[\![M]\!]$ over its return type. A subtlety is that the semantics may or may not be a *probability distribution*, that is, one whose total measure is 1. Still, until Section 6, we think simply of all Fun expressions as defining probability distributions (implicitly normalising the measure), and use conventional mathematical notations for probability (as in the start of Section 1). We assume some familiarity with basic concepts such as joint distributions and marginalization.

Let an *inference engine* be an algorithm that given a quotation of a closed Fun expression M of type t returns a possibly approximate representation of the distribution $\mathscr{M}[\![M]\!]$. We can represent an inference engine as a function Expr<t> $\to$ DistT where DistT is the type of the representation.

3. Models, Samplers, and Learners

This section explains the central idea of the paper: that the prior and sampling distributions constituting a Bayesian model may be represented by a pair of typed Fun expressions. We introduce the distributions using conventional mathematical notations, alongside our formal notation using Fun expressions. We begin by explaining the idea for a specific example, and then generalize.

3.1 A Specific Bayesian Model: Linear Regression in Fun

As outlined in the introduction, a Bayesian model consists of a *prior distribution* $p(w|h)$ over parameter w, given hyperparameter h, together with a *sampling distribution* $p(y|x,w)$ over output y, given input information x and parameter w. Viewed as a function of the parameters w, with y fixed, the sampling distribution is also known as the *likelihood function*.

The prior distribution represents our uncertain beliefs about the parameters, given hyperparameter h. The sampling distribution represents our view of how output y is produced from input x given parameter w.

We consider the problem of linear regression, that is, of finding the best fitting line given a set of points. Our input data are $d = (x,y)$ where $x = [|x_1;\ldots;x_n|]$ and $y = [|y_1;\ldots;y_n|]$ are arrays of coordinates. Intuitively, we fit a noisy line $y_i = Ax_i + B + \varepsilon$ to the data, where the noise ε is drawn from a Gaussian distribution with *mean* 0 and *precision Prec*.

The expression prior h below expresses our initial uncertainty about the parameters A, B, and *Prec* of the noisy line, where hyperparameter h provides parameters for these distributions. (A standard alternative to a constant hyperparameter is to consider a prior over the hyperparameter, known as the *hyperprior*; we discuss hyperpriors in the full version.) The probabilistic expression gen(w,x) defines how to generate each y_i from x_i and parameters w. (In the Fun code below, we use record and array notations which are eventually treated as operations on tuples.)

The Prior and Sampling Distributions:

```
let prior h = { A = random (Gaussian(h.MeanA, h.PrecA))
                B = random (Gaussian(h.MeanB, h.PrecB))
                Prec = random (Gamma(h.Shape, h.Scale)) }
let gen (w,x) = [| for xi in x →
        (w.A * xi) + w.B + random(Gaussian(0.0, w.Prec)) |]
```

These expressions formalize the prior and sampling distributions. The prior distribution $p(w|h)$ is the density of $\mathcal{M}[\![\text{prior } h]\!]$ at w, while the sampling distribution $p(y|x,w)$ is the density of $\mathcal{M}[\![\text{gen}(w,x)]\!]$ at y. We assemble the two components of our model in the function predictive below, to obtain the *prior predictive distribution* $p(y|x,h)$, the density of $\mathcal{M}[\![\text{predictive}(h,x)]\!]$ at y.

The Prior Predictive Distribution:

```
let predictive (h,x) = let w = prior h in gen(w,x)
```

The semantics of the **let**-expression is obtained by forming the joint distribution of $\mathcal{M}[\![\text{prior } h]\!]$ and $\mathcal{M}[\![\text{gen}(w,x)]\!]$, and marginalizing with respect to $\mathcal{M}[\![\text{gen}(w,x)]\!]$. Formally, the semantics is obtained as the following integral.

$$p(y|x,h) = \int p(y|x,w)p(w|h)dw \tag{1}$$

We may sample from the prior predictive distribution by choosing h and input x as shown by the following F# output.

```
val h = {MeanA=0.0; PrecA=1.0; MeanB=5.0; PrecB=0.3;
    Shape=1.0; Scale=1.0}
val x = [|0.0; 1.0; 2.0; 3.0; 4.0; 5.0|]
```

We first sample w from the prior distribution $w =$ prior h, and then the output $y =$ gen(w,x).

```
val w = {A = 0.70; B = 4.33; Prec = 0.58;} // sampled prior(h)
val y = [|4.85; 5.19; 7.36; 4.49; 8.10; 8.06|] // sampled gen(w,x)
```

We express the posterior and posterior predictive distributions as Fun expressions, using **observe** to condition on the data (x,y).

The Posterior and Posterior Predictive Distributions:

```
let posterior (h,x,y) = let w = prior h in observe (y=gen(w,x)); w
let posterior_predictive(h,x,y,x') =
  let w = posterior (h,x,y) in gen(w,x')
```

Given observed data $d = (x,y)$, via Bayes' Rule we obtain a *posterior distribution*, that is, the prior in light of the data.

$$p(w|d,h) = \frac{p(y|x,w)p(w|h)}{p(d|h)} \tag{2}$$

The normalization constant $p(d|h) = \int p(y|x,w)p(w|h)dw$ is known as the *evidence* or *marginal likelihood*. We also obtain the *(posterior) predictive* distribution:

$$p(y'|x',d,h) = \int p(y'|x',w)p(w|d,h)dw \tag{3}$$

Using a particular inference engine for Fun we may obtain concrete representations of the normalized distributions. In the case of our running example, we try to infer the parameters used to generate our sample data y. By running our Infer.NET implementation of Fun to compute the distribution posterior(h,x,y) we obtain the following approximations.

```
{ A = Gaussian(0.5576, 0.05089); // actual A=0.70
  B = Gaussian(4.936, 0.404); // actual B=4.33
  Prec = Gamma(1.695, 0.46)[mean=0.78];} // actual Prec=0.58
```

Moreover, suppose we have new input $x' = [|6.0;7.0;8.0;9.0|]$. By running our Infer.NET implementation of Fun to compute the distribution posterior_predictive(h,x,y,x') we obtain the following.

```
[| Gaussian(8.282, 0.1858); Gaussian(8.839, 0.1654);
   Gaussian(9.397, 0.1469); Gaussian(9.954, 0.1303); |]
```

To summarize, we modelled a noisy line by distributions written as the Fun expressions prior h and gen(w,x). We ran these expressions to draw samples from the predictive distribution, so as to create a *synthetic dataset* $d = (x,y)$. We wrote Fun expressions for the posterior and posterior predictive distributions, and ran an inference engine to learn the posterior and to make predictions given fresh data. These tasks are the essence of Bayesian reasoning. The remainder of this section proposes generic types and interfaces for these tasks.

3.2 Typed Bayesian Models in General

In general, let a *typed Bayesian model* be a value of the record type Model<TH,TW,TX,TY>, where the type parameters correspond to the different data of a Bayesian model: hyperparameters h : TH, parameters w : TW, inputs x : TX, and outputs y : TY.

Typed Bayesian Model:

```
type Model<'TH,'TW,'TX,'TY> =
  { HyperParameter: 'TH
    Prior: Expr<'TH →'TW>
    Gen: Expr<'TW * 'TX →'TY> }
```

Given a model m, the Fun expression $h =$ m.HyperParameter is the hyperparameter, the Fun expression (%m.Prior) h is the prior distribution $p(w|h)$, and the Fun expression (%m.Gen)(w,x) is the sampling distribution $p(y|x,w)$. (We treat F# expressions such as (%m.Prior) h as being closed Fun expressions, although strictly speaking they are F# expressions that evaluate via antiquotation and function application to closed Fun expressions.)

The following module packages our linear regression code as a typed model M1. We use F# quotations <@...@> to treat the bodies of prior and gen above as Fun expressions.

Linear Regression Model:

```
module LinearRegression =
  type TH = {MeanA: real; PrecA: real; ... }
  type TW<'TA,'TB,'TN> = {A:'TA; B:'TB; Prec:'TN}
  type TX = real[]
  type TY = real[]
  let M1 = { HyperParameter = h
             Prior = <@ fun h → prior h @>
             Gen = <@ fun (w,x) → gen(w,x) @> }
         : Model<TH,TW<real,real,real>,TX,TY>
```

3.3 Sampling Parameters and Data

Given any model m, with h = m.HyperParameter, we construct a new *sampler* S by sampling w from $p(w|h)$, and providing the methods:

- S.Parameters : TW is w sampled from the prior $p(w|h)$;
- S.Sample(x) : TY samples the sampling distribution $p(y|x,w)$.

The Sampler Interface:

```
type ISampler<'TW,'TX,'TY> = interface
    abstract Parameters: 'TW
    abstract Sample: x:'TX → 'TY
  end
```

Hence, a sampler draws from the prior predictive distribution. We omit our sampler code, which uses Eval to evaluate quotations.

3.4 Learning Parameters and Making Predictions

Given any model m, with h = m.HyperParameter, and an inference engine, we may construct a new *learner* L with the following interface.

The Learner Interface:

```
type ILearner<'TDistW,'TX,'TY,'TDistY> = interface
    abstract Train: x:'TX * y:'TY → unit
    abstract Posterior: unit → 'TDistW
    abstract Predict: x:'TX → 'TDistY
  end
```

The type 'TDistW represents distributions over parameter 'TW, while the type 'TDistY represents distributions over output 'TY. Different learners may use different representations. Our ADD learner exactly represents distributions over Booleans using an ADD data structure, while our Infer.NET learner yields approximate parameters of the marginal distributions of each dimension of the distribution and our MCMC learner represents a distribution as an ensemble of samples.

We can think of a Fun quotation as an exact representation of a conditional distribution on its return type, independent of any inference engine. Using this idea, we present below our *reference learner*, which captures the intended exact semantics of our API, by assembling suitable quotations. The mutable variable d takes as values Fun expressions that represent the current parameter distribution, initially the posterior. Each call to Train updates d by conditioning with the training data. Calls to Posterior and Predict return suitable quotations for the posterior and posterior predictive distributions. (Compare with the posterior and posterior_predictive functions in Section 3.1.)

Reference Learner L for Model m:

```
let h = m.HyperParameter
let d = ref <@ (%m.Prior) h @>
{ new ILearner<Expr<'TW>,'TX,'TY,Expr<'TY>> with
   member l.Train(x:'TX,y:'TY) =
         d := <@ let w = (% !d) in
                  observe(y = ((%m.Gen) (w,x)))
                  w @>
   member l.Posterior():Expr<'TW> = (!d)
   member l.Predict(x:'TX):Expr<'TY> =
         <@ let w = (% !d) in (%m.Gen) (w,x) @> }
```

Theorem 1. *After n calls to* Train *with arguments* $d = \{(x_i,y_i)\}_{i=1}^n$,

- L.Posterior *represents the posterior distribution* $p(w|d,h)$*;*
- L.Predict(x') *represents the predictive distribution* $p(y'|x',d,h)$.

Our reference learner code is in fact the basis of our exact learner based on ADDs. Our other learners use numeric representations of intermediate distributions, rather than a quotation.

For example, a generic usage of our samplers and learners is to test whether an inference algorithm can recover known parameters from synthetic data. Consider a learner L constructed from a model m, hyperparameter h, and some inference engine. Given some input x, we may test the effectiveness of L by constructing a new sampler S for m and h, and running the following.

```
let w: TW = S.Parameters // fixed parameters
L.Train(x,S.Sample(x)) // train on synthetic data
let wD: TDistW = L.Posterior() // inferred distribution on w
... // test how probable w is according to wD
```

We abstract this pattern (as a function) in Section 3.6.

3.5 Generic Combinator for IID Models

If we assume that the data is a collection $d = \{(x_i,y_i)\}_{i=1}^n$ of identically and independently distributed (IID) observations, then the sampling distribution factorizes according to:

$$p(\{y_i\}_{i=1}^n|\{x_i\}_{i=1}^n,w) = \prod_{i=1}^n p(y_i|x_i,w) \tag{4}$$

Hence, we arrive at our first model combinator, IIDArray. Given a model that sends TX to TY, IIDArray builds a new model with the same prior, but which sends TX[] to TY[]. Learning with any model built from this combinator is an instance of *batch learning*, where multiple data items are processed simultaneously. (In the code below, we use an F# quotation of a **fun**-abstraction to represent a Fun expression with two free variables w and xs, as described in Section 2.)

Combinator to Lift Model to Act on Arrays:

```
module IIDArray =
 let M(m:Model<'TH,'TW,'TX,'TY>) =
   {HyperParameter = m.HyperParameter
    Prior = m.Prior
    Gen = <@ fun (w,xs) → [|for x in xs → (%m.Gen)(w,x)|] @> }
   : Model<'TH,'TW,'TX[],'TY[]>
```

For example, M2 below is linear regression on a single (x,y) point, and M3, obtained by our combinator, is equivalent to our original model M1. Models in the style of M2 are useful because we may assemble them with other combinators before applying IIDArray, as shown in Section 7.

Linear Regression, Again and Again:

```
let M2 =
  { HyperParameter = h
    Prior = <@ fun h → prior h @> // as before
    Gen = <@ fun(w,x) →
      (w.A * x) + w.B + random(Gaussian(0.0,w.Prec)) @>
  }: Model<TH,TW<real,real,real>,real,real>
let M3 = IIDArray.M(M2)
```

3.6 Generic Loopback Testing

A common method to test the effectiveness of a learner on a particular model is to generate IID sample data for different x_i for a fixed w, and then evaluate the posterior distribution for w obtained by training on that data. We here give a generic procedure for such a loopback test.

Functions for loopback testing:

```
let test (toLearner: Model<'TH,'TW,'TX,'TY> →
                      ILearner<'DistW,'TX,'TY,'DistY>)
         (m:Model<'TH,'TW,'TX,'TY>)
         (x:'TX) : 'TW * 'DistW =
  let L = toLearner(m)
  let S = Sampler.FromModel(m)
  let y = S.Sample(x)
  do L.Train(x,y)
  (S.Parameters,L.Posterior())
let testMany l m xs = test l (IIDArray.M(m)) xs
```

Since the details of evaluating the inferred posterior depend on its learner-specific representation, test simply returns the parameters and posterior distribution to the caller. Notice how testMany is constructed by a simple application of the model combinator IIDArray.M.

Here is an application of testMany to our running example, linear regression, using the Infer.NET learner we describe below:

Loopback testing of linear regression:

```
let toL m = InferNetLearner.LearnerFromModel(m,Marginalize)
let (w,dW) = testMany toL M2 [| −100.0 .. 1.0 .. 100.0 |]
```

On one test run, we obtained:

```
w= { A = 0.3477837603;
     B = −27.13593566;
     Prec = 2.103660906;}
dW={ A = Gaussian(0.3479, 1.467e06);
     B = Gaussian(−27.09, 435.0);
     Prec = Gamma(99.74, 0.02203)[mean=2.197];}
```

Here the learner has inferred close approximations to A, B and Prec, with very high precision especially for A.

4. A Learner using Exact Inference

The exact learner uses symbolic evaluation of Boolean functions representing discrete distributions in order to give an answer that is either an *exact* marginal of each variable or the *exact* joint distribution. Let Bernoulli Fun be the finite fragment of Fun where the only sum type is **bool** = **unit** + **unit**, the only matches are conditionals, there are no instances of **observe**, and every **random** expression takes the form **random** (Bernoulli(c)) for some real $c \in (0,1)$. The semantics of a closed Bernoulli Fun program is a sub-probability distribution over its discrete return type, that is, a measure that may sum to less than 1.

4.1 Inference by Symbolic Evaluation of Programs

The procedure POST symbolically evaluates a Bernoulli Fun expression M, and computes the posterior sub-distribution over the result of M given a valuation of its free variables. The algorithm relies on the following notations. We write **let** $x:t = N$ **in** M for the corresponding untyped **let**-expression when $\Gamma \vdash N : t$. We write $\mathtt{ite}(v = U, V_T, V_F)$ for the conditional statement that returns V_T when $v = U$ and V_F otherwise. A valuation σ is a finite map from variables to closed values; A Γ-valuation σ is a finite map $x_1 \mapsto V_1, \dots, x_n \mapsto V_n$ where each $V_i \in \mathbf{V}_{t_i}$. We let $\diamond$ denote the empty valuation, and write $S(\Gamma)$ for the set of Γ-valuations. If $\Gamma \vdash V : t$ and σ is a Γ-valuation, $V\sigma$ is the closed value resulting from substituting $\sigma(x)$ for x in V for all $x \in \mathrm{dom}(\Gamma)$. Given an open expression M, where $\Gamma \vdash M : t$, POST is a function from valuations $\sigma \in S(\Gamma)$ to discrete sub-probability distributions over $\mathbf{V}_t$. By uncurrying, the semantics of M can also be expressed as a function from $S(\Gamma) \times \mathbf{V}_t$ to sub-probabilities $[0,1]$. The algorithm POST (M) computes this function by structural recursion on M. The POST function is a forward analysis that computes the posterior distribution, and is named by analogy with the standard post-condition computation in program analysis.

Post Calculation $\mathrm{POST}(M) : S(\Gamma) \times \mathbf{V}_t \to$ **real when** $\Gamma \vdash M : t$

$$\mathrm{POST}(V) = \lambda\sigma, v.\mathtt{ite}(v = V\sigma, 1, 0)$$

$$\mathrm{POST}(f(V_1,\dots,V_n)) = \lambda\sigma, v.\mathtt{ite}(v = f(V_1\sigma,\dots,V_n\sigma), 1, 0)$$

$$\mathrm{POST}(\mathsf{Bernoulli}(r)) = \lambda\sigma, v.\mathtt{ite}(v = \mathbf{true}, r, 1-r)$$

$$\mathrm{POST}(\mathbf{if}\ V\ \mathbf{then}\ N_1\ \mathbf{else}\ N_2) = \lambda\sigma, v.\mathrm{POST}(V)[\sigma, \mathbf{true}] \cdot \mathrm{POST}(N_1)[\sigma, v] + \mathrm{POST}(V)[\sigma, \mathbf{false}] \cdot \mathrm{POST}(N_2)[\sigma, v]$$

$$\mathrm{POST}(\mathbf{let}\ x:t = N_1\ \mathbf{in}\ N_2) = \lambda\sigma, v.\textstyle\sum_{u \in \mathbf{V}_t} \mathrm{POST}(N_1)[\sigma, u] \cdot \mathrm{POST}(N_2)[(\sigma, x \mapsto u), v]$$

$$\mathrm{POST}(\mathbf{fail}) = \lambda(\sigma, ()).0$$

The POST computation uses four different types of operations on functions: (1) pointwise product, (2) pointwise sum, (3) if-then-else, (4) summation over a variable, or existential quantification. The operations (1) and (2) are used, for example, in the case for **if**, operation (3) is used in the cases for values, deterministic functions, and Bernoulli, and operation (4) is used in the **let** case. Each of these operations is directly supported by ADD packages such as CUDD (Somenzi 2012) and takes time proportional to the product of the sizes of the arguments in the worst case.

Theorem 2. *Let M be a Bernoulli Fun program with $\diamond \vdash M : t$. For all values $V \in \mathbf{V}_t$, $\mathrm{POST}(M)[\diamond, V] = \mathscr{M}[\![M]\!]\ \{V\}$.*

The ADD learner builds on the reference learner, calling the POST algorithm on the Fun expression returned from its Posterior and Predict methods. An ADD learner has the following type, where ADD<'T> is the type of a decision diagram that maps values of type 'T to probabilities.

```
: ILearner<ADD<'TW>, 'TX, 'TY, ADD<'TY>>
```

In our experiments, the performance of the ADD learner is competitive with algorithms implemented in SamIam (Darwiche 2009). Claret et al. (2012) report performance in detail for symbolic evaluation of a related imperative probabilistic language.

4.2 Example: Bayes Net for Sprinkler

The sprinkler model is a classical example of a Bayes net (Pearl and Shafer 1995). In our variant, the model describes the conditional probabilities of rain having fallen and the sprinkler having been on, given that the grass is observed to be wet. In detail, given prior distributions for rain and sprinkling, and the view that rain has a

90% chance of wetting the grass, sprinkling an 80% chance, and some other cause a 10% chance, what is the posterior distribution for rain and sprinkling, given that the grass is wet. We perform inference using the ADD learner described above, yielding an exact posterior.

Sprinkler model

```
module Sprinkler =
  type TH = {RainH: real; SprinklerH: real}
  type TW<'b> = {Rain: 'b; Sprinkler: 'b}
  type TX = IsGrassWet // a unit type
  type TY = bool
  let M:Model<TH,TW<bool>,TX,TY> =
   {HyperParameter = {RainH=0.3; SprinklerH=0.5}
    Prior = <@ fun h →
     {Rain = random(Bernoulli(h.RainH))
      Sprinkler = random(Bernoulli(h.SprinklerH))} @>
    Gen = <@ fun (w,x) →
      (random (Bernoulli(0.9)) && w.Rain) ||
      (random (Bernoulli(0.8)) && w.Sprinkler) ||
      random (Bernoulli(0.1)) @>}
```

Given an ADD learner L for this model, here is the outcome of L.Train(IsGrassWet, **true**); L.Posterior.

```
[({Rain = false; Sprinkler = false;}, 0.05777484318);
 ({Rain = true; Sprinkler = false;}, 0.2253218884);
 ({Rain = false; Sprinkler = true;}, 0.4737537141);
 ({Rain = true; Sprinkler = true;}, 0.2431495543)];
```

5. A Learner based on Factor Graph Inference

Infer.NET is a probabilistic programming system which generates efficient, scalable inference algorithms based on message-passing on factor graphs. We compile a Fun expression to the input format of Infer.NET, Csoft, and perform inference (Borgström et al. 2011).

Since the original description of Fun, we have made a series of enhancements which make the present paper possible. These include the API described next, support for arrays, and a compiler based on multiple transformations of the Fun expression.

5.1 Learner for Message-Passing Algorithms in Infer.NET

We describe our interface for creating learners based on Infer.NET, but omit the details of the implementation, which rely on the existing translation from Fun to Infer.NET.

Infer.NET computes marginal posterior distributions from joint distributions involving observed and unobserved variables. For example, given a probabilistic program defining a joint distribution on pairs of type **bool** × **real**, Infer.NET computes the marginal of the first projection as a value d_1 say of the distribution type Bernoulli, and computes the approximate marginal of the second projection as a value d_2 say of type Gaussian. (Bernoulli and Gaussian are Infer.NET types representing the distribution as a record of its parameters.) Infer.NET uses the distribution families of the priors on these projections as (approximate) distribution types for the marginals. Let a *marginal type* G be a nesting of tuples, records and arrays, over distribution types such as Bernoulli and Gaussian. Let joint(G) be G with each occurrence of an Infer.NET type replaced with its range; for instance, joint(Bernoulli) = **bool** and joint(Gaussian) = **real**.

We perform inference using Infer.NET using the following function, where CompoundDistribution is a dynamically typed value representing the composite of the marginal distributions.

Core Inference for Infer.NET Fun:

```
val inferDynamic: Expr<'TA →'TB> →
                         'TA →CompoundDistribution
```

Next, we describe use of automatic coercions to achieve better static typing than with inferDynamic. A *compound distribution for G* is a value of CompoundDistribution representing a value of type G. A *G-coercion* is a function CompoundDistribution → G that coerces a compound distribution for G to the corresponding value.

To create a learner for m : Model<TH,TW,TX,TY> we ask the user to supply F# marginal types GW and GY such that joint(GW) = TW and joint(GY) = TY, plus a MarginalizeModel<GW,GY>, which is a pair of a GW-coercion and a GY-coercion. (We have helper functions to construct these coercions, but we omit the details.) The resulting learner does approximate inference on the model m. After each call to Train, we run inference and record the result at marginal type GW. Calling Posterior returns the current distribution. Calling Predict runs inference, and we return the result at marginal type GY.

Constructing an Infer.NET Learner:

```
type MarginalizeModel<'GW,'GY> =
  { MarginalizePrior: CompoundDistribution →'GW
    MarginalizeGen: CompoundDistribution →'GY }

val Learner: (Model<'TH,'TW,'TX,'TY> * 'TH
            * MarginalizeModel<'GW,'GY>
          →ILearner<'GW,'TX,'TY,'GY>
```

5.2 Example: Gaussian

Here is the model for the ubiquitous Gaussian. The parameters are its Mean and Precision. Their priors are a Gaussian and a Gamma. In turn, the hyperparameter consists of the parameters for the priors. The sampling distribution simply draws from the Gaussian, ignoring the input of type TX = **unit**. (A model that ignores its input is said to be *unsupervised*.)

Gaussian Model:

```
module GaussianModel =
 type GammaW<'TA,'TB> = {Shape: 'TA; Scale: 'TB}
 type TW<'TA,'TB> = {Mean:'TA; Precision:'TB}
 type TH = { Gaussian: TW<real,real>
             Gamma: GammaW<real,real> }
 let M: Model<TH,TW<real,real>,unit,real> =
  {HyperParameter = {Gaussian={Mean=0.0;Precision=1.0}
                     Gamma={Shape=1.1;Scale=2.0}}
   Prior= <@ fun h →{Mean= let m = h.Gaussian.Mean
                           let p = h.Gaussian.Precision
                           random(Gaussian(m,p))
                     Precision=let sh = h.Gamma.Shape
                               let sc = h.Gamma.Scale
                               random(Gamma(sh,sc))}@>
   Gen= <@ fun (w,x) →let m,p = w.Mean,w.Precision
                      random(Gaussian(m,p)) @> }
```

We obtain a learner of the following type. The subject of the marginal type for y, Gaussian, is **real**, while the subject of the marginal type for w, TW<Gaussian,Gamma>, is TW<**real**,**real**>. (We make TW generic so it can express both these types).

```
: ILearner<TW<Gaussian,Gamma>,unit,real,Gaussian>
```

After inference, we can inspect the parameters of the inferred Gaussian and Gamma distributions to learn the inferred mean and variance of the data, and the remaining uncertainty thereof.

Probit is a standard binary classifier built from a Gaussian. Its model shares the same prior, and its output is a probabilistic Boolean dependent on its input. We use this model in Section 7.

Probit Model:

```
let Probit : Model<TH,TW<real,real>,real,bool> =
  {HyperParameter = M.HyperParameter
   Prior = M.Prior
   Gen = <@ fun (w,x) →
             x < random(Gaussian(w.Mean,w.Precision)) @> }
```

We have a range of other models including multivariate linear regression, the Bayes Point Machine classifier (Minka 2001), the LDA (Latent Dirichlet Allocation) topic modelling (Blei et al. 2003), and TrueSkill (Herbrich et al. 2006), but we omit the details.

6. Semantics of Models: Measures and Monads

In this section, we review the measure-transformer semantics of Fun (Borgström et al. 2011), and extend it with sum types and observations on composite types. Based on our experience with Fun models, their structure often includes a single outermost **observe** statement. Here, we show that given a certain *compatibility* constraint on its semantics, any Fun expression can be transformed to one with a single outermost **observe**, preserving the semantics. As part of the proof, we show that the measure-transformer semantics of **observe**-free Fun models is closely related to their semantics when considered as programs of the stochastic lambda-calculus of Ramsey and Pfeffer (2002). This clarifies the relationship between our measure-transformer semantics and the probability monad, in particular for programs with none or only a single outermost observation.

6.1 Measure Transformer Semantics for Fun Expressions

In this section, we recall the measure-transformers used in Borgström et al. (2011), and augment these with operations on sum types and failure. We also give an inductive definition of the semantics of observations on composite types, and recall the compositional denotational semantics of a Fun expression as a measure transformer, augmented with sum types. For more explanations and intuitions, see (Borgström et al. 2011). We conclude by introducing the notion of *compatible* measure, and show that it is sufficient (but not necessary) for all observations to be well-defined.

We define the measurable sets of type t, written $\mathcal{M}_t$, as the Lebesgue-measurable subsets of $\mathbf{V}_t$, which in particular contains all closed sets. We write $f : t \to u$ to mean that f is a measurable function from type t to type u, that is, that $f^{-1}(A) \in \mathcal{M}_t$ for all $A \in \mathcal{M}_u$. Let $\mathtt{M}\,t$ be the set of finite measures on t, that is, additive functions from $\mathcal{M}_t$ to the non-negative real numbers. Let the sub-probability distributions $\mathtt{S}\,t$ be the finite measures whose range is contained in $[0,1]$. Let $t \rightsquigarrow u$ be the set of measure transformers from t to u, defined as the partial functions $\mathtt{M}\,t \rightharpoonup \mathtt{M}\,u$. If $\Gamma = x_1 : t_1,\ldots,x_n : t_n$ we let $\mathrm{range}(\Gamma) \triangleq t_1 * \cdots * t_n$. We make use of the following constructions on measures.

- The Dirac δ measure is $\delta_V(A) \triangleq 1$ if $V \in A$, 0 otherwise.
- Given a function $f : t \to u$ and a measure $\mu \in \mathtt{M}\,t$, there is a measure $\mu f^{-1} \in \mathtt{M}\,u$ given by $(\mu f^{-1})(B) \triangleq \mu(f^{-1}(B))$. We can add two measures on the same set as $(\mu_1 + \mu_2)(A) \triangleq \mu_1(A) + \mu_2(A)$. The disjoint sum $(\mu_1 \uplus \mu_2)$ of two measures is defined as $(\mu_1 \uplus \mu_2)(A \uplus B) = \mu_1(A) + \mu_2(B)$.
- Given a measure μ on t, a measurable set $A \in \mathcal{M}_t$ and a function $f : t \to \mathbf{real}$, we write $\int_A f\,d\mu$ or equivalently $\int_A f(x)\,d\mu(x)$ for standard (Lebesgue) integration. This integration is always well-defined if μ is finite and f is bounded.
- Given a measure μ on t, a function $D\mu : t \to \mathbf{real}$ is a *density* for μ iff $\mu(A) = \int_A (D\mu)\,d\lambda$ for all A, where λ is the completion of the standard measure on t (which is built by taking products and disjoint sums of the counting measure on **int** and the interval (Borel) measure on **real**).

The semantics of a Fun program is given in terms of the following measure transformers, which encapsulate standard theorems in finite measure theory.

Measure Transformer Combinators:

$\mathtt{pure} \in (t \to u) \to (t \rightsquigarrow u)$
$\ggg \in (t_1 \rightsquigarrow t_2) \to (t_2 \rightsquigarrow t_3) \to (t_1 \rightsquigarrow t_3)$
$\mathtt{extend} \in (t \to \mathtt{S}\,u) \to (t \rightsquigarrow (t * u))$
$\mathtt{observe} \in (t \to \mathbf{real}) \to (t \rightsquigarrow t)$
$\Vert \in (t_1 \rightsquigarrow u) \to (t_2 \rightsquigarrow u) \to ((t_1 + t_2) \rightsquigarrow u)$
$\mathtt{fail} \in (t \rightsquigarrow t)$

To lift a pure measurable function to a measure transformer, we use the combinator pure. Given $f : t \to u$, we let $\mathtt{pure}\,f\;\mu\;A \triangleq \mu f^{-1}(A)$, where $\mu \in \mathtt{M}\,t$ and A is a measurable set from u.

To sequentially compose two measure transformers we use standard function composition, defining $T \ggg U \triangleq U \circ T$.

The combinator extend extends the domain of a measure using a function yielding sub-probability distributions. We let $\mathtt{extend}\,m\;\mu\;AB \triangleq \int_{\mathbf{V}_t} m(x)(\{y \mid (x,y) \in AB\})\,d\mu(x)$.

The combinator observe computes the conditional density of a measure μ over t on the event that an indicator function p of type $t \to \mathbf{real}$ is zero. Note that this conditioning is *unnormalized*. We consider the family of events $p(x) = r$ where r ranges over $\mathbb{R}$. We let $\mathbf{B}^r_\varepsilon$ be the closed ball of radius ε around r (that is, $[x-\varepsilon, r+\varepsilon]$), and define $\dot{\mu}[A||p=r] \in \mathbb{R}$ (the μ-density at $p = r$ of A) by:

Conditional Density: $\dot{\mu}[A||p=r]$

$\dot{\mu}[A||p=r] \triangleq \lim_{\varepsilon\to 0} \mu(A \cap p^{-1}(\mathbf{B}^r_\varepsilon)) / \int_{\mathbf{B}^r_\varepsilon} 1\,d\lambda$ if the limit exists

We define $\mathtt{observe}\,p\;\mu\;A \triangleq \dot{\mu}[A||p=0]$. As an example, if $t = u * \mathbf{real}$, $p = \lambda(x,y).(y-c)$ and μ has continuous density $D\mu$ then

$$\mathtt{observe}\,p\;\mu\;A = \int_{\{x|(x,c)\in A\}} D\mu(x,c)\,d\lambda(x) \quad (5)$$

and $\int_{\mathbb{R}} \dot{\mu}[A||p=x]\,d\lambda(x) = \mu(A)$. Notice that $\mathtt{observe}\,p\;\mu\;A$ is greater than $\mu(A)$ if the density at $p = 0$ is greater than 1, so we cannot consider only transforming (sub-)probability distributions.

Support for sum types (new) To add support for sum types, we introduce a new measure transformer. We let $(T_1 \Vert T_2)\;\mu\;A \triangleq T_1(X \mapsto \mu(X \uplus \varnothing))(A) + T_2(X \mapsto \mu(\varnothing \uplus X))(A)$. We also let $\mathtt{fail}\;\mu\;A \triangleq 0$.

Observations on composite types (new) The Fun language of Borgström et al. (2011) permits observations only on atomic types. To achieve a normal form (Theorem 3) we here extend observations to composite types. We write $\mathtt{obs}\;f@u$ if $f : t \to u$; then the measure transformer $\mathtt{obs}\;f$ has type $t \rightsquigarrow t$. Below we let $1_b \triangleq 1$, $1_{\mathbf{unit}} \triangleq ()$, $1_{t*u} \triangleq (1_t, 1_u)$ and $1_{t+u} \triangleq 1_t$. We write $\mathtt{split}\;p = \mathtt{pure}\;\lambda s.\mathtt{if}\;p(s)\;\mathtt{then}\;\mathbf{inl}\;s\;\mathtt{else}\;\mathbf{inr}\;s$.

Observations on Composite Types: $\mathtt{obs}\;f@u$

$\mathtt{obs}\;f@\mathbf{real} \triangleq \mathtt{observe}\;f$
$\mathtt{obs}\;f@\mathbf{int} \triangleq \mathtt{split}\;(\lambda s.f(s) = 0) \ggg (\mathtt{pure\;id} \Vert \mathtt{fail})$
$\mathtt{obs}\;f@\mathbf{unit} \triangleq \mathtt{pure\;id}$
$\mathtt{obs}\;f@(u_1 * u_2) \triangleq \mathtt{obs}\;(\mathtt{snd} \circ f)@u_2 \ggg \mathtt{obs}\;(\mathtt{fst} \circ f)@u_1$
$\mathtt{obs}\;f@(u_1 + u_2) \triangleq \mathtt{split}\;f \ggg$
$\quad (\mathtt{obs}\;(\mathtt{either\;id}\;\lambda\_.1_{u_1}) \circ f@u_1$
$\quad \Vert\;\mathtt{obs}\;(\mathtt{either}\;\lambda\_.1_{u_2}\;\mathtt{id}) \circ f@u_2)$

Observation at **real** type is primitive; it is trivial at **unit** type. At **int** we `fail` unless f returns 0. For products, we observe each component in turn. For sum types, we split the set of states depending on the branch of the sum picked by f, and run the observation in each branch. Note that observations on discrete types yield a series of `splits` where some branches `fail`, and that `obs` $\lambda\_.1$@**int** $=$ `fail`.

Measure transformer semantics We can then give a compositional semantics of a Fun program as a measure transformer, taking a measure over assignments to its free variables and returning a joint measure over variable assignments and return value. To bind the values of a valuation to the corresponding variables we use $\text{pat}(\diamond) = ()$ and $\text{pat}(xs,x) := (\text{pat}(xs),x)$ as patterns and in return values. Below we define the measure transformer semantics of a program as $\mathscr{A}\llbracket M \rrbracket_{xs}$ where xs are the free variables in the program. We use an auxiliary definition $\mathscr{A}\llbracket M \rrbracket^{y}_{xs}$ for the semantics of the program M in the scope of y. For closed terms M we obtain $\mathscr{M}\llbracket M \rrbracket$ by transforming the trivial probability measure.

Each signature **val** $f\colon t_1 * \cdots * t_n \to t_{n+1}$ means that f is a total function with $f : \mathbf{V}_{t_1*\cdots*t_n} \to \mathbf{V}_{t_{n+1}}$. If $\text{Dist} : t \to \text{PDist}\langle u \rangle$ and $V \in \mathbf{V}_t$, there is a corresponding measure $\mu_{\text{Dist}(V)}$ on $\mathbf{V}_u$. This measure is a probability measure for legal values of V, and otherwise, such as in Bernoulli(3.0), it is the zero measure.

To apply $|||$ below we need to lift a sum to the top level of a type. We do this with `lift1` $: t*(u_1+u_2) \to (t*u_1)+(t*u_2)$ defined as $\lambda x,y.$`match` y `with inl` z : `inl`(x,z) | `inr` z : `inr`(x,z).

Measure Transformer Semantics of Fun: $\mathscr{M}\llbracket M \rrbracket$, $\mathscr{A}\llbracket M \rrbracket_{xs}\ \mu$

$\mathscr{M}\llbracket M \rrbracket\ A \triangleq \mathscr{A}\llbracket M \rrbracket_{\diamond}\ \delta_{()}\ \{()\} \times A$

$\mathscr{A}\llbracket M \rrbracket^{y}_{xs} \triangleq \mathscr{A}\llbracket M \rrbracket_{xs,y} \ggg \texttt{pure}\ \lambda(\text{pat}(xs,y),z).(\text{pat}(xs),z)$

$\mathscr{A}\llbracket V \rrbracket_{xs} \triangleq \texttt{pure}\ \lambda\,\text{pat}(xs).(\text{pat}(xs),V)$
$\mathscr{A}\llbracket f(V_1,\dots,V_n) \rrbracket_{xs} \triangleq \texttt{pure}\ \lambda\,\text{pat}(xs).(\text{pat}(xs),f(\overline{V}))$

$\mathscr{A}\llbracket \textbf{match}\ V\ \textbf{with inl}\ x:\ M\ \mid \textbf{inr}\ y:\ N \rrbracket_{xs} \triangleq$
$\qquad \mathscr{A}\llbracket V \rrbracket_{xs} \ggg \texttt{pure lift1} \ggg (\mathscr{A}\llbracket M \rrbracket^{x}_{xs} \mathbin{|||} \mathscr{A}\llbracket N \rrbracket^{y}_{xs})$

$\mathscr{A}\llbracket \textbf{let}\ x = M\ \textbf{in}\ N \rrbracket_{xs} \triangleq \mathscr{A}\llbracket M \rrbracket_{xs} \ggg \mathscr{A}\llbracket N \rrbracket^{x}_{xs}$
$\mathscr{A}\llbracket \textbf{random}(\text{Dist}(V)) \rrbracket_{xs} \triangleq \texttt{extend}\ \lambda\,\text{pat}(xs).\mu_{\text{Dist}(V)}$
$\mathscr{A}\llbracket \textbf{observe}\ f(\overline{V}) \rrbracket_{xs} \triangleq \texttt{obs}\ \lambda\,\text{pat}(xs).f(\overline{V}) \ggg \mathscr{A}\llbracket () \rrbracket_{xs}$
$\mathscr{A}\llbracket \textbf{fail} \rrbracket_{xs} \triangleq \texttt{fail} \ggg \mathscr{A}\llbracket () \rrbracket_{xs}$

Note that $\mathscr{A}\llbracket \textbf{observe}\ 1+1 \rrbracket_{xs} = \mathscr{A}\llbracket \textbf{fail} \rrbracket_{xs}$. Indeed, **fail** suffices to implement all observations on discrete types (by inlining `obs`, implementing `split` using **if**).

Proposition 1 (Static Adequacy)**.** *If* $\Gamma \vdash M : t$ *then* $\mathscr{A}\llbracket M \rrbracket_{\text{dom}(\Gamma)} \in \text{range}(\Gamma) \rightsquigarrow (\text{range}(\Gamma) \times \text{t})$.

As seen above, (`observe` p) μ might be undefined, if its defining limit does not exist. We here give a sufficient condition for the limit to exist. We inductively define compatibility of a measure with respect to all the observations in a composition of measure transformer combinators as follows. We write $\mu \models T$ for "μ is compatible with respect to T".

Compatibility: $\mu \models T$ $\qquad$ ($T \in t \rightsquigarrow u$ **and** $\mu \in \mathtt{M}\ t$)

$\mu \models \texttt{pure}\ f \qquad \mu \models \texttt{extend}\ m \qquad \mu \models \texttt{fail}$

$\mu_1 \uplus \mu_2 \models T_1 \mathbin{|||} T_2$ iff $\mu_1 \models T_1$ and $\mu_2 \models T_2$
$\mu \models T \ggg U$ iff $\mu \models T$ and $(T\ \mu) \models U$

$\mu \models \texttt{observe}\ p$ iff p is an affine function,
and there is ε such that $D\mu$ is continuous on $p^{-1}(\mathbf{B}^0_\varepsilon)$
and p is not constant on any open subset of $p^{-1}(\mathbf{B}^0_\varepsilon)$.

Proposition 2. *If* $\mu \models T$*, then* $T\mu$ *is defined.*

Compatibility is not necessary for $T\mu$ to be defined:

Hybrid Measure:

let hybrid1 = **if random**(Bernoulli(0.5)) **then** 1.0
$\qquad$ **else random**(Gaussian(0.0,1.0))
let hybrid2 = (**random**(Gaussian(0.0,r)),hybrid1)

The measure $\mu = \mathscr{M}\llbracket\text{hybrid2}\rrbracket$ is the average of a two-dimensional Gaussian distribution and a line mass at $y = 1.0$. Here $\mu \models$ `observe` $\lambda(x,y).y$, but we do not have $\mu \models$ `observe` $\lambda(x,y).x$ because the line $x = 0.0$ crosses the line mass at $y = 1.0$, where the density fails to exist. However, by the definition of `observe` we get (`observe` $\lambda(x,y).x$) $\mathscr{M}\llbracket\text{hybrid2}\rrbracket = \sqrt{r}\cdot\phi(0.0)\cdot\mathscr{M}\llbracket(0.0,\text{hybrid1})\rrbracket$ where $\phi(0.0) \approx 0.3989$ is the probability density of the standard normal distribution at 0.0. Note that as the precision r above grows, the weight of the resulting distribution grows, with no upper bound.

6.2 Monadic Semantics for Fun with fail

If M does not contain any occurrence of **observe** or **fail** then M is a term in the language of (Ramsey and Pfeffer 2002) which has a semantics using the probability monad (Giry 1982). To treat **fail** we work in the sub-probability monad (Panangaden 1999), where the set of admissible distributions μ also admits $|\mu| < 1$ (cf. the semantics of Barthe et al. (2012)).

The valuation σ maps the free variables of M to closed values.

Monadic Semantics of Fun with fail: $\mathscr{P}\llbracket M \rrbracket\ \sigma$

$(\mu \gg= f)\ A \triangleq \int f(x)(A)\,d\mu(x)$	Monadic bind
$(\texttt{return}\ v)\ A \triangleq 1$ if $v \in A$, else 0	Monadic return
$\texttt{zero}\ A \triangleq 0$	Monadic zero

$\mathscr{P}\llbracket V \rrbracket\ \sigma \triangleq \texttt{return}\ (V\sigma)$
$\mathscr{P}\llbracket f(V_1,\dots,V_n) \rrbracket\ \sigma \triangleq \texttt{return}\ f(V_1\sigma,\dots,V_n\sigma)$

$\mathscr{P}\llbracket \textbf{match}\ V\ \textbf{with inl}\ x:\ M\ \mid \textbf{inr}\ y:\ N \rrbracket\ \sigma \triangleq \mathscr{P}\llbracket V \rrbracket\ \sigma \gg=$
$\qquad \texttt{either}\ (\lambda v.\mathscr{P}\llbracket M \rrbracket\ (\sigma, x \mapsto v))\ (\lambda v.\mathscr{P}\llbracket N \rrbracket\ (\sigma, y \mapsto v))$

$\mathscr{P}\llbracket \textbf{let}\ x = M\ \textbf{in}\ N \rrbracket\ \sigma \triangleq \mathscr{P}\llbracket M \rrbracket\ \sigma \gg= \lambda v.\mathscr{P}\llbracket N \rrbracket\ (\sigma, x \mapsto v)$
$\mathscr{P}\llbracket \textbf{random}(\text{Dist}(V)) \rrbracket\ \sigma \triangleq \mu_{\text{Dist}(V\sigma)}$
$\mathscr{P}\llbracket \textbf{fail} \rrbracket\ \sigma \triangleq \texttt{zero}$

Proposition 3. *If* $x_1 : t_1,\dots,x_n : t_n \vdash M : t$ *and* $xs = x_1,\dots,x_n$ *and all observations in* M *are* **fail**, *then*
$\mathscr{A}\llbracket M \rrbracket_{xs} = \texttt{extend}\ \lambda(v_1,\dots,v_n).\mathscr{P}\llbracket M \rrbracket\ (x_1 \mapsto v_1,\dots,x_n \mapsto v_n)$.

In particular, if $\diamond \vdash M : t$ we have $\mathscr{M}\llbracket M \rrbracket = \mathscr{P}\llbracket M \rrbracket\ \diamond$.

6.3 A Normal Form for Fun Expressions

Observation Translation: O$\llbracket M \rrbracket$ $\qquad$ (*o* **does not appear in** *N*)

$\text{O}\llbracket \textbf{observe}\ f(\overline{V}) \rrbracket \triangleq (), f(\overline{V})$

$\text{O}\llbracket \textbf{let}\ x = M\ \textbf{in}\ N \rrbracket \triangleq$
$\qquad \textbf{let}\ x,o = \text{O}\llbracket M \rrbracket\ \textbf{in let}\ y,o' = \text{O}\llbracket N \rrbracket\ \textbf{in}\ y,(o',o)$

$\text{O}\llbracket \textbf{match}\ V\ \textbf{with inl}\ x:\ M_1\ \mid \textbf{inr}\ y:\ M_2 \rrbracket \triangleq \textbf{match}\ V\ \textbf{with}$
$\qquad \mid \textbf{inl}\ x \to \textbf{let}\ r,o = \text{O}\llbracket M_1 \rrbracket\ \textbf{in}\ r, \textbf{inl}\ o$
$\qquad \mid \textbf{inr}\ y \to \textbf{let}\ r,o = \text{O}\llbracket M_2 \rrbracket\ \textbf{in}\ r, \textbf{inr}\ o$

$\text{O}\llbracket M \rrbracket \triangleq M, ()$ $\qquad$ otherwise

Proposition 4. *If* $\Gamma \vdash M : t$ *then there is* u *such that* $\Gamma \vdash \text{O}\llbracket M \rrbracket : t * u$.

Theorem 3. *If* $\Gamma \vdash M : t$ *and* $N =$ **let** r,o = O$\llbracket M \rrbracket$ **in observe** o;r *and* $\mu \models \mathscr{A}\llbracket N \rrbracket_{\text{dom}(\Gamma)}$ *then* $\mathscr{A}\llbracket M \rrbracket_{\text{dom}(\Gamma)}\ \mu = \mathscr{A}\llbracket N \rrbracket_{\text{dom}(\Gamma)}\ \mu$.

Corollary (Normal form for closed terms)**.** *If* $\diamond \vdash M : t$ *and* N *is as above and* $\delta_{()} \models \mathscr{A}\llbracket N \rrbracket_{\diamond}$ *then* $\mathscr{M}\llbracket M \rrbracket = \mathscr{M}\llbracket N \rrbracket$.

The program M = **observe** (**fst** (hybrid2)) does not satisfy the compatibility precondition of the normal form theorem. This can be checked using static analyses (Bhat et al. 2012a) that can determine if $\mathscr{M}[\![O[\![M]\!]]\!]$ is absolutely continuous and thus admits a density. A more sensitive analysis could additionally determine the discontinuities of the density function in many cases, allowing to check compatibility statically.

The results of this section imply that **observe**-free models (that is, generative ones), and models with discrete observations only, have measure-transformer semantics that correspond to their monadic semantics, so we can use the latter for its simplicity.

7. Generic Probabilistic Conditionals

Perhaps surprisingly, the lowly **if** expression gives rise to three useful and interesting ways of composing Bayesian models: mixture models, model averaging and a mixture of experts. We also show how to use the **if** expression as a general means for computing model evidence and evidence ratios.

7.1 Bayesian Mixture Models

Given a number of models m_k with $k = 1 \dots K$ with the same types of inputs x_i and IID data y_i, we can create a mixture of these models by introducing an indicator variable z_i (conditionally independent given w) for each sample y_i that indicates which mixture component m_k it was generated by. This composition is helpful when the data can be generated by one of several known models. Below, we write w_k and h_k for the parameters and the hyperparameter associated with model k, and $\overline{w}$ for $w_1, \dots, w_K$. The sampling distribution is then given by:

$$p(\{y_i\}_{i=1}^n | \{x_i\}_{i=1}^n, w, \overline{w}) = \prod_{i=1}^{n} \sum_{k=1}^{K} p(z_i = k|w) p(y_i|x_i, m_k, w_k) \quad (6)$$

We here give a generic combinator for creating a mixture of two models, given a prior over the probability of choosing the first distribution.

Mixture Model Combinator

```
let M (m1:Model<'TH1,'TW1,'TX,'TY>,
       m2:Model<'TH2,'TW2,'TX,'TY>)
     : Model<(BetaW *'TH1*'TH2),
             (real * 'TW1*'TW2),'TX,'TY> =
  {HyperParameter = (uniformBeta,
                     m1.HyperParameter,m2.HyperParameter)
   Prior = <@ fun (bw,h1,h2) →
            (random(Beta(bw.trueCount,bw.falseCount)),
             (%m1.Prior) h1, (%m2.Prior) h2) @>
   Gen= <@ fun ((bias,w1,w2),x) →
          if breakSymmetry(random(Bernoulli(bias)))
          then (%m1.Gen) (w1,x)
          else (%m2.Gen) (w2,x) @>}
```

(The call to breakSymmetry is a pragma for the Infer.NET backend—it avoids the pitfall of learning symmetric solutions.)

We can create a mixture of two Gaussian models, where we have no prior knowledge of the probability of each model being used.

Mixture of two Gaussian models

```
let m = M(GaussianModel.M,GaussianModel.M)
```

Such a model is useful for fitting a scalar property of two populations of unknown sizes.

7.2 Model Evidence by a Conditional

An important concept in Bayesian machine learning is the notion of *model evidence*, which intuitively is the likelihood of the model given a particular set of observations. It is for instance used to choose between different models of the same data (*model selection* (MacKay 2003, ch.22)), and as an objective function to maximize in certain inference techniques.

If M is a closed term we define $\mathscr{E}(M) \triangleq |\mathscr{M}[\![M]\!]|$, that is, the total measure of the semantics $\mathscr{M}[\![M]\!]$. Note that $\mathscr{E}(M)$ may be different from 1 if M contains instances of **observe** or **fail**, as discussed in Section 6. More generally, if $\Gamma \vdash M : t$ we let $\mathscr{E}(M,\mu) \triangleq |\mathscr{A}[\![M]\!]_{\mathrm{dom}(\Gamma)}\ \mu|$. When choosing between two (or more) different models M and N (for the same data), we typically want to choose the model that has the highest likelihood given the observations (of the data).

The presence of arbitrary **if**-expressions in the language allows to compute the evidence of a model in a uniform way. More generally, the ratio of the evidence of two models (also known as the Bayes factor) can be computed as the ratio between the probabilities of the two possible outcomes of a Boolean variable (compare Minka and Winn (2008)), by inferring the posterior probability of an a priori unbiased selector variable being true.

Evidence ratio by if-expression: $\mathscr{E}[\![M,N]\!]$

$\mathscr{E}[\![M,N]\!] \triangleq$ **let** x = **random**(Bernoulli(0.5)) **in**
if x **then** M; () **else** N; ()
x

Lemma 5. *If* $\Gamma \vdash M : t$ *and* $\Gamma \vdash N : u$ *and* $\mu \in \mathtt{M}\,(\mathrm{range}(\Gamma))$ *then*

$$\frac{\mathscr{E}(M,\mu)}{\mathscr{E}(N,\mu)} = \frac{\mathscr{A}[\![\mathscr{E}[\![M,N]\!]]\!]_{\mathrm{dom}(\Gamma)}\ \mu\ \{(s,\mathbf{true}) \mid s \in \mathbf{V}\mathrm{range}(\Gamma)\}}{\mathscr{A}[\![\mathscr{E}[\![M,N]\!]]\!]_{\mathrm{dom}(\Gamma)}\ \mu\ \{(s,\mathbf{false}) \mid s \in \mathbf{V}\mathrm{range}(\Gamma)\}}.$$

Proof: By expanding $\mathscr{A}[\![\mathscr{E}[\![M,N]\!]]\!]_{\mathrm{dom}(\Gamma)}$. ■

Given Lemma 5, we can compute the evidence of a model M from its evidence ratio to the trivial model (), which has evidence 1.

Theorem 4. *If* $\diamond \vdash M : t$ *we have* $\mathscr{E}(M) = 2 \cdot \mathscr{M}[\![\mathscr{E}[\![M,()]\!]]\!]\ \{\mathbf{true}\}$. *For open terms, if* $\Gamma \vdash M : t$ *and* $\mu \in \mathtt{M}\,(\mathrm{range}(\Gamma))$ *then* $\mathscr{E}(M,\mu) = 2 \cdot (\mathscr{A}[\![\mathscr{E}[\![M,()]\!]]\!]_{\mathrm{dom}(\Gamma)}\ \mu\ \{(s,\mathbf{true}) \mid s \in \mathbf{V}\mathrm{range}(\Gamma)\})$.

For this way of computing model evidence to work, it is critical that **observe** denotes *unnormalized* conditioning. It does not generalize to languages such as Church (Goodman et al. 2008), where observations (queries) correspond to a renormalized distribution: in such a language $\mathscr{M}[\![\mathscr{E}[\![M,N]\!]]\!]\ \{\mathbf{true}\} = 0.5$ for all admissible M,N. The technique also does not work in languages where the probability distribution of a program is the limit of its successive approximations, such as Probabilistic cc (Gupta et al. 1999). In such a language $\mathscr{M}[\![\mathscr{E}[\![M,()]\!]]\!]\{\mathbf{true}\} \leq 0.5$ for all M. Frameworks based on Gibbs sampling such as BUGS also fail, since **if**-expressions "containing [random] variables require a facility for computing the evidence of a submodel, which Gibbs sampling does not provide" (Minka and Winn 2008).

7.3 Model averaging

In Section 7.1 we were combining models m_k by choosing a model for each data point. Another standard notion of composition is *model averaging* (Hoeting et al. 1999), where we have some prior belief $p(m_k|h)$ about how likely each model m_k is to have generated all of the data, that is then updated based on the evidence of each model given the data, that we here assume to be IID.

$$p(\{y_i\}_{i=1}^n | \{x_i\}_{i=1}^n, w, \overline{w}) = \sum_{k=1}^{K} p(z = k|w) \prod_{i=1}^{n} p(y_i|x_i, m_k, w_k) \quad (7)$$

We show below a combinator for the case $K = 2$. The parameter of the combined model includes a random **bool** switch, which is inspected to generate each output y_i from the model m_{switch}.

Combinator for Model Averaging:

```
let M (m1:Model<'TH1,'TW1,'TX,'TY>,
       m2:Model<'TH2,'TW2,'TX,'TY>)
     : Model<(real*'TH1*'TH2),
             (bool*'TW1*'TW2),'TX,'TY> =
 {HyperParameter = (0.5,
                    m1.HyperParameter,m2.HyperParameter)
  Prior = <@ fun (bias,h1,h2) →
             (random(Bernoulli(bias)),
              (%m1.Prior) h1, (%m2.Prior) h2) @>
  Gen = <@ fun ((switch,w1,w2),x) →
             if switch then (%m1.Gen) (w1,x)
             else (%m2.Gen) (w2,x) @>}
```

The posterior distribution over the bias gives us the evidence ratio between the two models m1 and m2 (cf. Lemma 5), multiplied with the prior odds.

$$\frac{p(z=1|d,h)}{p(z=2|d,h)} = \frac{p(d|m_1,h_1)}{p(d|m_2,h_2)}\frac{p(z=1|h)}{p(z=2|h)} \tag{8}$$

7.4 Mixture of Experts

A powerful supervised counterpart to the unsupervised mixture models discussed in 7.1 is the Mixture of Experts model (Jacobs et al. 1991), and its hierarchical variants (Bishop and Svensén 2003; Jordan and Jacobs 1994). The idea is to use a so-called gating model $p(z_i|x_i,w)$ to decide for each input x_i which model to use for generating the corresponding output y_i. We consider a mixture of K models with conditional sampling distributions $p(y_i|x_i,m_k,w_k)$, priors $p(w_k|h_k)$ and a gating model $p(z_i|x_i,w)$ with prior $p(w|h)$ resulting in the combined sampling distribution

$$p(\{y_i\}_{i=1}^n|\{x_i\}_{i=1}^n,w,\overline{w}) = \prod_{i=1}^{n}\sum_{k=1}^{K} p(z=k|x_i,w)p(y_i|x_i,m_k,w_k) \tag{9}$$

As before, we here implement the binary case with two data models m_k with $k \in \{T,F\}$, with independent priors given their parameters: $p(w,w_F,w_T|h,h_T,h_F) = p(w|h)p(w_T|h_T)p(w_F|h_F)$.

Combinator for Mixture of Experts:

```
let M(mc:Model<'TH,'TW,'TX,bool>,
      m1:Model<'TH1,'TW1,'TX,'TY>,
      m2:Model<'TH2,'TW2,'TX,'TY>)
    : Model<'TH*'TH1*'TH2,'TW*'TW1*'TW2,'TX,'TY> =
 {HyperParameter = (mc.HyperParameter,
                    m1.HyperParameter,m2.HyperParameter)
  Prior = <@ fun (hc,h1,h2) →
       (%mc.Prior) hc, (%m1.Prior) h1, (%m2.Prior) h2 @>
  Gen = <@ fun ((wc,w1,w2),x) →
           if (%mc.Gen) (wc,x) then (%m1.Gen) (w1,x)
           else (%m2.Gen) (w2,x) @>}
```

The hierarchical Mixture of Experts model (Bishop and Svensén 2003; Jordan and Jacobs 1994) can easily be obtained by a tree of calls to the above combinator. It is also straightforward to build an n-ary version of this combinator from the above construction, or a variation that operates on arrays of models with identical type parameters.

Some Examples of Hierarchical Mixtures of Experts

```
let m = ExpertMixture.M(Probit,M2,M2)
let n = IIDArray.M(ExpertMixture.M(Probit,m,m))
```

The model M2 fits a line to the data. The model m above attempts to fit two different lines l_1 and l_2, and to find a point x_0 where the data gradually shifts from being fitted to l_1 (for $x \ll x_0$) and being fitted to l_2 (for $x \gg x_0$). The model n attempts to fit four lines with three separating points, and operates on arrays of IID data.

8. A Learner based on Monte Carlo Inference

Markov chain Monte Carlo (MCMC) methods are an important class of inference algorithms for Bayesian models because they make it possible to obtain samples from the posterior for a wide variety of models, even if that posterior is not in a simple family of parametric probability distributions or densities. The idea of MCMC is to construct a Markov chain in the parameter space of the model whose equilibrium distribution is the posterior distribution over model parameters. Neal (1993) provides an excellent review of MCMC methods. As an example implementation, we consider Filzbach (Purves and Lyutsarev 2012), an implementation of an adaptive MCMC sampler based on the Metropolis-Hastings algorithm (Hastings 1970; Metropolis et al. 1953). All that is required to apply an MCMC algorithm to a particular model is the ability to calculate posterior probabilities for a given set of parameters. The algorithm then generates an ensemble of samples from the posterior. This ensemble serves as a representation of the posterior, or to calculate desired marginal distributions of individual parameters or other integrals under the posterior distribution.

8.1 Direct Calculation of Log-Posterior

Bhat et al. (2012a) report an algorithm (but not an implementation), for computing the densities of the distribution computed by a probabilistic program, and a type system that guarantees their existence. Their algorithm uses integration at every **let**-expression; we here implement a simplified version without integrals but instead limited to deterministic **let**-bound variables only. This pattern is common in the real-world models we have studied, for greater efficiency and simplicity. (In unpublished work, Bhat et al. (2012b) implement a more general algorithm for calculating densities of Fun programs.)

We describe a recursive function PRE, which is an effective partial algorithm for calculating the log-density for the parameters of a generative model written in Fun. (It is standard to compute logs to avoid underflow when dealing with very small probabilities.) The PRE function is a backward analysis that computes the density function, and is named by analogy with the standard pre-condition computation in program analysis.

Log-density calculation $\text{PRE}(V,\sigma,M) \in \mathbb{R} \cup \{-\infty,\bot\}$

$\text{PRE}(V,\sigma,U) = \log(1.0)$ **if** $U\sigma = V$ **else** $\log(0.0)$

$\text{PRE}(V,\sigma,f(V_1,\dots,V_n)) = \log(1.0)$ **if** $f(V_1\sigma,\dots,V_n\sigma) = V$
$\log(0.0)$ **otherwise**

$\text{PRE}(V,\sigma,\textbf{random}(\text{Dist}(U))) = \log(D(\mu_{\text{Dist}(U\sigma)}(V)))$

$\text{PRE}(V,\sigma,\textbf{match } U \textbf{ with inl } x:\ M \mid \textbf{inr } y:\ N) =$
$\text{PRE}(V,(\sigma,x \mapsto U'),M)$ **if** $U\sigma = \textbf{inl } U'$
$\text{PRE}(V,(\sigma,y \mapsto U'),N)$ **if** $U\sigma = \textbf{inr } U'$

$\text{PRE}(V,\sigma,\textbf{let } x = M \textbf{ in } N) = \text{PRE}(V,(\sigma,x \mapsto U),N)$
if M is deterministic and $M\sigma$ evaluates to U
$\bot$ **otherwise**

$\text{PRE}(V,\sigma,\textbf{fail}) = \log(0.0)$

$\text{PRE}(V,\sigma,\textbf{observe } f(\overline{V})) = \bot$

When defined (that is, not $\perp$), the $\text{PRE}(V,\sigma,M)$ function computes the log-posterior density of the parameters (in σ) given the data V.

Theorem 5. *If* $\Gamma \vdash M : t$ *and* σ *is a* Γ*-valuation and* $V \in \mathbf{V}_t$ *and* $\text{PRE}(V,\sigma,M) \neq \perp$ *then* $\text{PRE}(V,\sigma,M) = \log((D(\mathscr{P}[\![M]\!]\ \sigma))(V))$.

The log-posterior of the parameters V_w is then obtained by adding the log-density of the prior at V_w, which is obtained by calling $\text{PRE}(V_w, h \mapsto V_h, \text{Prior})$, where V_h is the hyperparameter, to the log-posterior density $\text{PRE}(V_y, w \mapsto V_w, M)$.

Here is the actual log-posterior function we pass to Filzbach from our MCMC learner (space precludes more detail):

```
let (Lambda(vh,p)) = m.Prior
let (Lambda(vw,e)) =
    <@ fun w → [|for x in xs → (%m.Gen) (w,x)|] @>
let likelihood : 'TW → real =
    (* fun w → PRE(ys,[vw,w],e) + PRE(w,[vh,h],p) *)
    Compile(fun w → <@ (%PRE(<@ ys @>,[vw,w],e)) +
                         (%PRE(w,[vh,<@ h @>],p)) @>)
```

Here, (xs,ys) is the observed data (from training) and m is the original model. Though not shown here, the MCMC learner represents distributions simply as an ensemble (an array) of samples.

8.2 Example: Purves' PlantGrowth

As a typical example, we present a simplified model of *plant growth*, adapted from a Filzbach example. Given an array of (deterministic) temperature data, temps, the model generates the mass of a plant on harvest day x, assuming that $0 \leq x < |\text{temps}|$.

The parameter of the model is a record of numbers: the plant's initial mass (imass), daily growth rate (alpha), optimum temperature for growth (topt), temperature sensitivity (trho) and the deviation of some noise (sigma). Each field is given a Gaussian prior.

The harvest mass is calculated by iterating a daily growth function (the argument of Array.Fold below) on the initial mass. This deterministic computation is finally perturbed by some noise, drawn from a Gaussian of unknown precision (prec obtained from sigma).

PlantGrowth Model (Prior omitted due to lack of space) :

```
<@ fun (w,x) → // first grow plant deterministically...
    let prec = 1.0/(w.sigma * w.sigma)
    let mass = // compute the mass after x days
        Array.fold // compute next mass in a time series
          (fun mass_i airtemp_i →
            let r = (airtemp_i−w.topt)/w.trho
            mass_i + (w.alpha * mass_i) * exp (−1.0*(r*r)))
          w.imass (Array.sub temps 0 x)
    random(Gaussian(mass,prec)) @> // ... finally add noise
```

To perform inference on this model, a Filzbach user must also provide a function computing the log-posterior of the model's parameters given some observed data (here, pairs of harvest days and masses). It is this function that Filzbach's MCMC algorithm attempts to maximize over the parameter space. Moreover, the user typically also needs to write an explicit generative model for producing predictions, based either on the mean of the obtained posterior parameter distribution or, better yet, by *error propagation* using an ensemble of parameters drawn from this posterior. Instead, we use the PRE algorithm described above to automatically compute the log-posterior function from the generative model.

(Adaptation of our learner to related methods (such as the computation of either the *maximum likelihood* (MLE) or the *maximum a posteriori probability* (MAP) estimate) appears straightforward but is beyond the scope of the paper.)

9. Related Work

Formal Semantics of Probabilistic Languages There is a long history of formal semantics for probabilistic languages with sampling primitives, often with recursive computation. One of the first semantics is for Probabilistic LCF (Saheb-Djahromi 1978), which augments the core functional language LCF with weighted binary choice, for discrete distributions. Kozen (1981) develops a probabilistic semantics for while-programs with random assignment. He develops two equivalent semantics; one more operational, and the other denotational. McIver and Morgan (2005) develop a theory of abstraction and refinement for probabilistic while programs with real-valued variables, based on weakest preconditions.

Jones and Plotkin (1989) investigate the probability monad, and apply it to languages with discrete probabilistic choice. Ramsey and Pfeffer (2002) give a stochastic λ-calculus with a measure-theoretic semantics in the probability monad, and provide an embedding within Haskell; they also do not consider observations.

Several languages (such as PFP (Erwig and Kollmansberger 2006)), IBAL (Pfeffer 2007), HANSEI (Kiselyov and Shan 2009), CertiPriv (Barthe et al. 2012) and the informal sampling semantics of Csoft (Minka et al. 2009)) have Boolean assertions or **fail** statements that give rise to sub-probabilities. Such languages support the mixture operations and evidence calculations of Section 7, for discrete observations only.

The concurrent constraint programming language PCC of Gupta et al. (1999) allows describing continuous probability distributions using independent sampling and constraints. However, their semantics of constraints is different than that of Fun observations. This makes PCC less suitable for compositional Bayesian modelling, since computation of model evidence using an if statement (Theorem 4) does not work: the program `choose` X `from` $\{0,1\}$ `in if` $X = 1$ `then` $[b,P]$ yields probability at most 0.5 of b being true.

In contrast, the measure-transformer semantics of Fun allows computing $\mathscr{E}(M) > 1$ for well-fitted models with continuous observations using the one-sided if statement of Theorem 4, as do the direct factor graph semantics of Csoft (Minka et al. 2009) using gates (Minka and Winn 2008).

Probabilistic Languages for Machine Learning Previous programming models for machine learning mainly represent particular implementation strategies, rather than general Bayesian models.

An exception is Church (Goodman et al. 2008), which represents probability distributions over Lisp terms as Lisp programs, and uses various inference techniques. However, since every admissible term denotes a probability distribution, $\mathscr{E}[\![M,()]\!]$ always yields true with probability 0.5.

Early work includes that of Koller et al. (1997) where a probabilistic model is represented as a functional program with probabilistic choice. FACTORIE (McCallum et al. 2009) is a library for imperatively constructing factor graphs. BUGS (Gilks et al. 1994) uses Gibbs sampling for Bayesian inference on Bayesian networks, represented as imperative probabilistic programs. IBAL (Pfeffer 2007) integrates Bayesian parameter estimation and decision-theoretic utility maximisation, but only works with discrete datatypes. Alchemy (Domingos et al. 2008) represents Markov logic networks, which are inherently discrete. Park et al. (2005) also define a probabilistic functional language, where as in Church terms always denote probability distributions.

PMML (Guazzelli et al. 2009) is an XML format for representing trained instances of a range of models, including association rules, neural networks, decision trees, support vector machines, etc. PMML does not represent arbitrary graphical or generative models. In our terms, a PMML model corresponds roughly to a trained learner. We have not developed any format for persisting trained learners; a format based on PMML may be suitable.

Example / Learner	TH	TW	TDistW	TX	TY	TDistY
Sprinkler / A	SP.TH	SP.TW<**bool**>	ADD<SP.TW<**bool**>>	SP.TX	**bool**	ADD<**bool**>
TwoCoins / A	TC.TH	TC.TW<**bool**>	ADD<TC.TW<**bool**>>	TC.TX	**bool**	ADD<**bool**>
Two Coins / IN	TC.TH	TC.TW<**bool**>	TC.TW<Bernoulli>	TC.TX	**bool**	Bernoulli
Friends / A	**bool**[][]	**bool** list list	ADD<**bool** list list>	**int** $*$ **int** $*$ **int**	**bool**	ADD<**bool**>
Students / A	**int** $*$ **int**	**bool** list list	ADD<**bool** list list>	**int** $*$ **int** $*$ **int**	**bool**	ADD<**bool**>
Gaussian / IN	GM.TH	GM.TW<$\mathscr{R}$,$\mathscr{R}$>	GM.TW<$\mathscr{N}$,Γ>	**unit**	**real**	$\mathscr{N}$
Gaussian Mix/ IN	MX1.TH	$\mathscr{R}*$ GaussW$*$GaussW	$\beta*$ GM.TW<$\mathscr{N}$,Γ>$*$GM.TW<$\mathscr{N}$,Γ>	**unit**	**real**	$\mathscr{N}$
Gaussian Mix / F	MX2.TH	(GaussW$*$GaussW)	(GaussW$*$GaussW)[]	**unit**	**real**	$\mathscr{R}$[]
PlantGrowth / F	**unit**	PG.TW	PG.TW[]	**int**	**real**	$\mathscr{R}$[]
TrueSkill / IN	TS.TH	TS.TW<$\mathscr{R}$>	TS.TW<$\mathscr{N}$>	TrueSkill.TX	**bool**	Bernoulli
Lin. Reg. / IN	LR.TH	LR.TW<$\mathscr{R}$,$\mathscr{R}$,$\mathscr{R}$>	LR.TW<$\mathscr{N}$,$\mathscr{N}$,Γ>	**real**	**real**	$\mathscr{N}$
MV Gaussian / IN	MVG.TH	MVG.TW<$\vec{\mathscr{R}}$,$\mathscr{M}$>	MVG.TW<$\vec{\mathscr{N}}$,$\mathscr{W}$>	**unit**	$\vec{\mathscr{R}}$	$\vec{\mathscr{N}}$

$\mathscr{R}$= **real** $\mathscr{N}$= Gaussian β= Beta Γ= Gamma
$\vec{\mathscr{R}}$= Vector $\mathscr{M}$= PositiveDefiniteMatrix
$\mathscr{W}$ = Wishart // *generalizes* Γ *to multiple dimensions*
$\vec{\mathscr{N}}$= VectorGaussian // *multivariate Gaussian distribution*
GaussW= {Mean:$\mathscr{R}$; Precision:$\mathscr{R}$}
BetaW = {trueCount: $\mathscr{R}$; falseCount: $\mathscr{R}$}
SP.TH = {RainH: $\mathscr{R}$; SprinklerH: $\mathscr{R}$}
SP.TW<'TB> = {Rain: 'TB; Sprinkler: 'TB}
SP.TX = IsGrassWet // *a unit type*
TC.TH = {Bias1: $\mathscr{R}$; Bias2: $\mathscr{R}$}
TC.TW<'TB> = {Heads1: 'TB; Heads2: 'TB}
TC.TX = AreEitherHeads // *a unit type*
GM.TW<'TM,'TP> = {Mean:'TM; Precision:'TP}
GM.TH ={ Gaussian: GaussW, Gamma: GammaW }

MX1.TH = BetaW $*$ GM.TH $*$ GM.TH
MX2.TH = GM.TH $*$ GM.TH
PG.TW = {alpha:$\mathscr{R}$;topt:$\mathscr{R}$;trho:$\mathscr{R}$;imass:$\mathscr{R}$;sigma:$\mathscr{R}$}
TS.TH = { Players: **int**; G: GaussW; P: GammaW }
TS.TW<'TA> = { Skills: 'TA[]}
TS.TX = { P1:**int**; P2: **int** }
LR.TH = {MeanA: $\mathscr{R}$; PrecA: $\mathscr{R}$; MeanB: $\mathscr{R}$; PrecB: $\mathscr{R}$; Shape: $\mathscr{R}$; Scale: $\mathscr{R}$}
LR.TW<'TA,'TB,'TN> = {A:'TA; B:'TB; Prec:'TN}
MVG.TH = {NCols:**int**; MeanVectorPrecisionCount:$\mathscr{R}$; WishartShapeConstant:$\mathscr{R}$; WishartScaleConstant:$\mathscr{R}$}
MVG.TW<'TM,'TC> = {Mean:'TM; Covariance:'TC}

Table 1. Rows show types for L : ILearner(TDistW,TX,TY,TDistY) for m : Model<TH,TW,TX,TY> (A=ADD, IN=Infer.NET, F=Filzbach)

Inference using ADDs The idea of using ADDs for probabilistic inference has been explored before. Sanner and McAllester (2005) define Affine Algebraic Decision Diagrams to perform inference over Bayesian networks and Markov Decision Processes. Kwiatkowska et al. (2006) have used a variants of ADDs to perform probabilistic model checking in the PRISM project. Bozga and Maler (1999) have used ADDs to symbolically simulate Markov chains. Chavira and Darwiche (2007) use ADDs to compactly represent factors in a Bayesian network and thereby perform efficient inference via variable elimination. In contrast, the ADD backend described in this paper avoids factor graphs altogether and uses ADDs to represent symbolic program states (which are distributions) at every program point, much like a data-flow analysis or an abstract interpreter (Cousot and Cousot 1977).

Mardziel et al. (2011) develop an approximate representation for discrete distributions based on abstract interpretations, with application to knowledge-based security policies.

10. Conclusions

We proposed typed programming abstractions, models and learners, for packaging, composing, and training and predicting with Bayesian models. We are aware of no prior generic abstractions for Bayesian models.

Future work includes adding functions over recursive types, and general recursion to the Fun language. We will also investigate the possibility of relaxing the condition of compatibility of a measure with respect to a model.

Acknowledgements Conversations about this work with Chris Bishop, John Bronskill, Tom Minka, Drew Purves, Robert Simmons, Matthew Smith, and John Winn were invaluable. Sooraj Bhat, Jael Kriener, and Sameer Singh commented on a draft.

References

G. Barthe, B. Köpf, F. Olmedo, and S. Zanella Béguelin. Probabilistic relational reasoning for differential privacy. In J. Field and M. Hicks, editors, *POPL*, pages 97–110. ACM, 2012.

S. Bhat, A. Agarwal, R. W. Vuduc, and A. G. Gray. A type theory for probability density functions. In J. Field and M. Hicks, editors, *POPL*, pages 545–556. ACM, 2012a.

S. Bhat, J. Borgström, A. D. Gordon, and C. Russo. Deriving probability density functions from probabilistic functional programs. Draft paper, 2012b.

C. M. Bishop and M. Svensén. Bayesian hierarchical mixtures of experts. In C. Meek and U. Kjärulff, editors, *Uncertainty in Artificial Intelligence (UAI'03)*, pages 57–64. Morgan Kaufmann, 2003.

D. M. Blei, A. Y. Ng, and M. I. Jordan. Latent Dirichlet allocation. *Journal of Machine Learning Research*, 3:993–1022, 2003.

J. Borgström, A. D. Gordon, M. Greenberg, J. Margetson, and J. Van Gael. Measure transformer semantics for Bayesian machine learning. In *European Symposium on Programming (ESOP'11)*, volume 6602 of *LNCS*, pages 77–96. Springer, 2011. Download available at `http://research.microsoft.com/fun`.

M. Bozga and O. Maler. On the representation of probabilities over structured domains. In *Computer Aided Verification (CAV '99)*, pages 261–273, 1999.

M. Chavira and A. Darwiche. Compiling Bayesian networks using variable elimination. In *International Joint Conference on on Artificial Intelligence (IJCAI '07)*, pages 2443–2449, 2007.

G. Claret, S. K. Rajamani, A. V. Nori, A. D. Gordon, and J. Borgström. Bayesian inference for probabilistic programs via symbolic execution. Technical Report MSR–TR–2012–86, Microsoft Research, 2012.

P. Cousot and R. Cousot. Abstract interpretation: a unified lattice model for the static analysis of programs by construction or approximation of fixpoints. In *POPL*, pages 238–252, 1977.

A. Darwiche. *Modeling and Reasoning with Bayesian Networks*. CUP, 2009.

H. Daumé III. *HBC: Hierarchical Bayes Compiler*, 2008. Available at `http://www.cs.utah.edu/~hal/HBC/`.

P. Domingos, S. Kok, D. Lowd, H. Poon, M. Richardson, and P. Singla. Markov logic. In L. De Raedt, P. Frasconi, K. Kersting, and S. Muggleton, editors, *Probabilistic inductive logic programming*, pages 92–117. Springer-Verlag, Berlin, Heidelberg, 2008.

M. Erwig and S. Kollmansberger. Functional pearls: Probabilistic functional programming in Haskell. *J. Funct. Program.*, 16(1):21–34, 2006.

W. R. Gilks, A. Thomas, and D. J. Spiegelhalter. A language and program for complex Bayesian modelling. *The Statistician*, 43:169–178, 1994.

M. Giry. A categorical approach to probability theory. In B. Banaschewski, editor, *Categorical Aspects of Topology and Analysis*, volume 915 of *Lecture Notes in Mathematics*, pages 68–85. Springer Berlin / Heidelberg, 1982.

N. Goodman, V. K. Mansinghka, D. M. Roy, K. Bonawitz, and J. B. Tenenbaum. Church: a language for generative models. In *Uncertainty in Artificial Intelligence (UAI'08)*, pages 220–229. AUAI Press, 2008.

A. D. Gordon, M. Aizatulin, J. Borgström, G. Claret, T. Graepel, A. Nori, S. Rajamani, and C. Russo. A model-learner pattern for Bayesian reasoning. Technical Report MSR-TR-2013-1, Microsoft Research, 2013.

A. Guazzelli, M. Zeller, W. Chen, and G. Williams. PMML: An open standard for sharing models. *The R Journal*, 1(1), May 2009.

V. Gupta, R. Jagadeesan, and P. Panangaden. Stochastic processes as concurrent constraint programs. In *POPL*, pages 189–202, 1999.

W. K. Hastings. Monte Carlo sampling methods using Markov chains and their applications. *Biometrika*, 57(1):97–109, 1970.

R. Herbrich, T. Minka, and T. Graepel. Trueskill^{tm}: A Bayesian skill rating system. In *Advances in Neural Information Processing Systems (NIPS'06)*, pages 569–576, 2006.

J. A. Hoeting, D. Madigan, A. E. Raftery, and C. T. Volinsky. Bayesian model averaging: A tutorial. *Statistical Science*, 14(4):382–401, 1999.

R. A. Jacobs, M. I. Jordan, S. J. Nowlan, and G. E. Hinton. Adaptive mixtures of local experts. *Neural Computation*, 3:79–87, 1991.

C. Jones and G. D. Plotkin. A probabilistic powerdomain of evaluations. In *Logic in Computer Science (LICS'89)*, pages 186–195. IEEE Computer Society, 1989.

M. I. Jordan and R. A. Jacobs. Hierarchical mixtures of experts and the EM algorithm. *Neural Computation*, 6(2):181–214, 1994.

O. Kiselyov and C. Shan. Monolingual probabilistic programming using generalized coroutines. In *Uncertainty in Artificial Intelligence (UAI'09)*, 2009.

D. Koller, D. A. McAllester, and A. Pfeffer. Effective Bayesian inference for stochastic programs. In *AAAI/IAAI*, pages 740–747, 1997.

D. Kozen. Semantics of probabilistic programs. *Journal of Computer and System Sciences*, 22(3):328–350, 1981.

M. Z. Kwiatkowska, G. Norman, and D. Parker. Quantitative analysis with the probabilistic model checker PRISM. In *Quantitative Aspects of Programming Languages (QAPL 2005)*, volume 153(2) of *ENTCS*, pages 5–31, 2006.

D. J. C. MacKay. *Information Theory, Inference, and Learning Algorithms*. CUP, 2003.

P. Mardziel, S. Magill, M. Hicks, and M. Srivatsa. Dynamic enforcement of knowledge-based security policies. In *Computer Security Foundations Symposium (CSF'11)*, pages 114–128, 2011.

A. McCallum, K. Schultz, and S. Singh. Factorie: Probabilistic programming via imperatively defined factor graphs. In *Advances in Neural Information Processing Systems (NIPS'09)*, pages 1249–1257, 2009.

A. McIver and C. Morgan. *Abstraction, refinement and proof for probabilistic systems*. Monographs in computer science. Springer, 2005.

N. Metropolis, A. W. Rosenbluth, M. N. Rosenbluth, A. H. Teller, and E. Teller. Equation of state calculations by fast computing machines. *Journal of Chemical Physics*, 21:1087–1092, 1953.

T. Minka. *A family of algorithms for approximate Bayesian inference*. PhD thesis, MIT, 2001.

T. Minka and J. M. Winn. Gates. In *Advances in Neural Information Processing Systems (NIPS'08)*, pages 1073–1080. MIT Press, 2008.

T. Minka, J. Winn, J. Guiver, and A. Kannan. Infer.NET 2.3, Nov. 2009. Software available from `http://research.microsoft.com/infernet`.

R. M. Neal. Probabilistic inference using Markov chain Monte Carlo methods. Technical Report CRG-TR-93-1, Dept. of Computer Science, University of Toronto, September 1993.

S. Park, F. Pfenning, and S. Thrun. A probabilistic language based upon sampling functions. In *POPL*, pages 171–182. ACM, 2005.

J. Pearl and G. Shafer. Probabilistic reasoning in intelligent systems: Networks of plausible inference. *Synthese-Dordrecht*, 104(1):161, 1995.

P. Panangaden. The category of Markov kernels. *Electronic Notes in Theoretical Computer Science*, 22:171–187, 1999.

A. Pfeffer. IBAL: A probabilistic rational programming language. In B. Nebel, editor, *International Joint Conference on Artificial Intelligence (IJCAI'01)*, pages 733–740. Morgan Kaufmann, 2001.

A. Pfeffer. The design and implementation of IBAL: A general-purpose probabilistic language. In L. Getoor and B. Taskar, editors, *Introduction to Statistical Relational Learning*. MIT Press, 2007.

A. Pfeffer. Practical probabilistic programming. In P. Frasconi and F. A. Lisi, editors, *Inductive Logic Programming (ILP 2010)*, volume 6489 of *Lecture Notes in Computer Science*, pages 2–3. Springer, 2010.

D. Purves and V. Lyutsarev. *Filzbach User Guide*, 2012. Available at `http://research.microsoft.com/en-us/um/cambridge/groups/science/tools/filzbach/filzbach.htm`.

A. Radul. Report on the probabilistic language scheme. In *Proceedings of the 2007 symposium on Dynamic languages (DLS'07)*, pages 2–10. ACM, 2007.

N. Ramsey and A. Pfeffer. Stochastic lambda calculus and monads of probability distributions. In *POPL*, pages 154–165, 2002.

N. Saheb-Djahromi. Probabilistic LCF. In *Mathematical Foundations of Computer Science (MFCS)*, volume 64 of *LNCS*, pages 442–451. Springer, 1978.

S. Sanner and D. A. McAllester. Affine Algebraic Decision Diagrams (AADDs) and their application to structured probabilistic inference. In *International Joint Conference on on Artificial Intelligence (IJCAI '05)*, pages 1384–1390, 2005.

J. Schumann, T. Pressburger, E. Denney, W. Buntine, and B. Fischer. AutoBayes program synthesis system users manual. Technical Report NASA/TM–2008–215366, NASA Ames Research Center, 2008.

F. Somenzi. CUDD: CU decision diagram package, release 2.5.0, 2012. Software available from `http://vlsi.colorado.edu`.

D. Syme. Leveraging .NET meta-programming components from F#: integrated queries and interoperable heterogeneous execution. In A. Kennedy and F. Pottier, editors, *ML Workshop*, pages 43–54. ACM, 2006.

J. Winn and T. Minka. Probabilistic programming with Infer.NET. Machine Learning Summer School lecture notes, available at `http://research.microsoft.com/~minka/papers/mlss2009/`, 2009.

Hyperstream Processing Systems

Nonstandard Modeling of Continuous-Time Signals

Kohei Suenaga
Kyoto University
ksuenaga@kuis.kyoto-u.ac.jp

Hiroyoshi Sekine Ichiro Hasuo
University of Tokyo
{nue_of_k,ichiro}@is.s.u-tokyo.ac.jp

Abstract

We exploit the apparent similarity between (discrete-time) *stream processing* and (continuous-time) *signal processing* and transfer a deductive verification framework from the former to the latter. Our development is based on rigorous semantics that relies on *nonstandard analysis (NSA)*.

Specifically, we start with a discrete framework consisting of a Lustre-like stream processing language, its Kahn-style fixed point semantics, and a program logic (in the form of a type system) for partial correctness guarantees. This stream framework is transferred *as it is* to one for *hyperstreams*—streams of streams, that typically arise from sampling (continuous-time) signals with progressively smaller intervals—via the logical infrastructure of NSA. Under a certain continuity assumption we identify hyperstreams with signals; our final outcome thus obtained is a deductive verification framework of signals. In it one verifies properties of signals using the (conventionally discrete) proof principles, like fixed point induction.

Categories and Subject Descriptors F.3.1 [*Logics and Meanings of Programs*]: Specifying and Verifying and Reasoning about Programs—Logics of programs; F.3.2 [*Logics and Meanings of Programs*]: Semantics of Programming Languages—Denotational semantics

Keywords hybrid system; stream processing; signal processing; type system; nonstandard analysis

1. Introduction

Signal By *signals* we mean values that depend on continuous time, that is, functions $s : \mathbb{R}_{\geq 0} \to \mathbb{C}$.[1] Signals are everywhere in the real world: they are the most straightforward model of physical quantities like position, velocity, voltage, etc. Signals have been studied extensively in the theory of *dynamical systems*, or more recently from the engineering viewpoint of *control theory*.

[1] The use of complex numbers $\mathbb{C}$—instead of $\mathbb{R}$—as the range is due to our use of i (the imaginary unit) in our leading example in §6. This choice is not important: our theory behaves the same for both $\mathbb{C} \cong \mathbb{R}^2$ and $\mathbb{R}$.

POPL'13, January 23–25, 2013, Rome, Italy.

Hybrid system In the modern world where more and more physical systems are under the control of computers (cars, plants, pacemakers, etc.), signals that are not entirely smooth—with discrete *jumps* caused by digital control—have gained their significance. They play an important role in the study of *hybrid systems*, an aspect of the more general topic of *cyber-physical systems*. Simulink, an industry-standard tool for modeling and simulation of hybrid systems, supports the design of a hybrid system as a *signal processing system* composed of interconnected blocks (above right). A signal processing system is one that receives, processes and outputs signals.

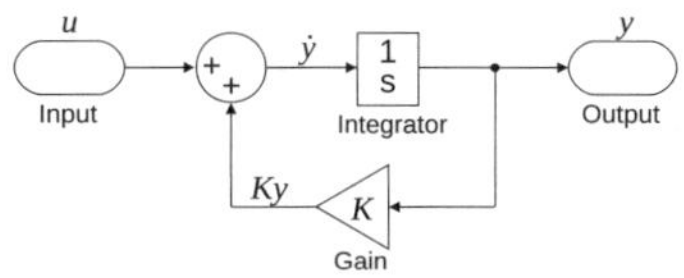

Stream processing Study of formal verification—or computer science in general—has traditionally been focused on discrete data (this is changing rapidly, though). There *stream processing system* is a heavily studied notion, together with related notions like *dataflow network* and *reactive programming* [29]. A *stream* is an infinite sequence $(a_0, a_1, \dots)$ of data; thus it is a time-varying value $s : \mathbb{N} \to \mathbb{C}$ with a discrete notion of time. It bears an obvious similarity to the notion of signal. Moreover, common graphical presentations of stream processing systems look very much like Simulink block diagrams.

This similarity is the starting point of the current work. The difference between signals and streams is whether the time domain is continuous ($\mathbb{R}_{\geq 0}$) or discrete ($\mathbb{N}$). If one can unify this difference, the discrete techniques for streams that have been accumulated in computer science can be readily applied to signals. This is what we do, by the mathematical vehicle of *nonstandard analysis (NSA)*. NSA allows us to think of continuous-time *flow* dynamics as if it is a succession of discrete-time *jumps* each of which is infinitely small.

Nonstandard Analysis NSA is an alternative formalization of analysis—convergence, continuity, differentiation, etc.—that uses the explicit notion of *infinitesimal* (i.e. infinitely small) number. Leibniz's original formulation of analysis was based on infinitesimals; but a naive use of such immediately leads to a contradiction. It was Robinson [24] who gave a logically rigorous foundation for infinitesimals using the notion of *ultrafilter*.

In our previous work [13, 30] we used NSA to represent flow dynamics by means of `while` loops—each iteration of a loop changes values infinitesimally. What is remarkable about NSA is its logical infrastructure: its famous result called the *transfer principle* states that a formula is valid for real numbers if and only if it is valid for hyperreals (i.e. reals extended with infinitesimals). Therefore, reals vs. hyperreals (i.e. discrete vs. continuous, in the setting of [13, 30]) are *the same* from a logical point of view. This allowed us in [13, 30] to transfer a logical (i.e. deductive) verification technique for discrete programs *as it is* to hybrid systems.

In the current work we use the same idea to fill in the gap between signal processing and stream processing. We similarly transfer a deductive verification method, too. In it we employ the formalism of a (first-order functional) stream processing language SPROC—it is modeled after the widely-accepted language Lustre [9]—to represent stream processing systems.

NSA is in fact not only about "analysis": its use is found in many branches of mathematics, such as general topology [14, Chap. III] and posets [35]. In this paper we present another instance of such, namely *domain theory* upgraded with NSA (Appendix B, part of which already appeared in [3]). We use it in the definition of denotational semantics of SPROC^{dt}.

Overview of the technical development On the right, in (1), is the overview of our development. It is centered around two key ideas: *hyperstream sampling* and *sectionwise execution*.

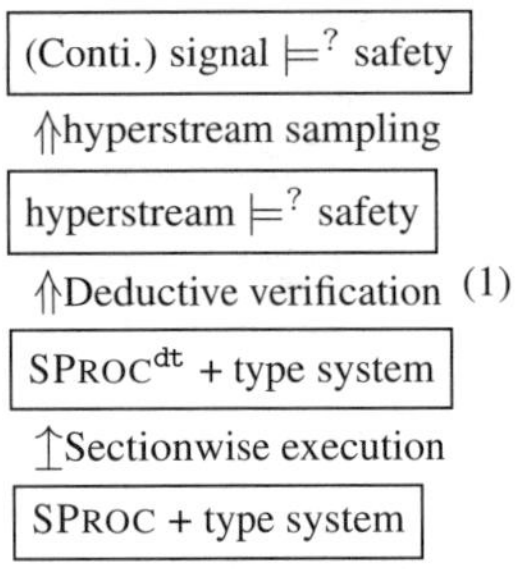

(1)

Hyperstream sampling Typically, a computer science approach to the study of continuous-time signals starts off with *sampling* a signal f. A sampling interval $\delta > 0$ results in a stream $(f(i\delta))_{i\in\mathbb{N}} = \bigl(f(0), f(\delta), f(2\delta), \dots\bigr)$. Obviously such sampling cannot be *exact*—we cannot know what happens to f during δ seconds of the sampling interval.

Then a natural idea is to consider infinitely many sampling intervals that are progressively small, as shown on the right. This results in a stream of streams $\Bigl(\bigl(f(\frac{i}{j+1})\bigr)_{i\in\mathbb{N}}\Bigr)_{j\in\mathbb{N}}$, that is

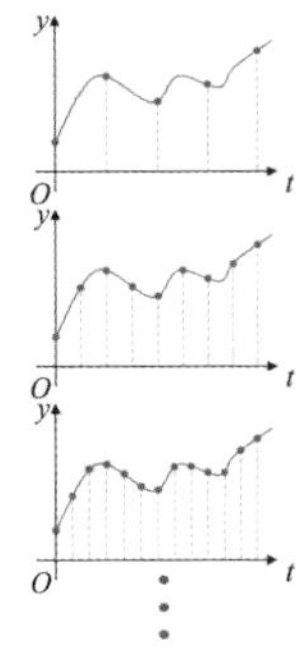

$$\begin{pmatrix} (f(0), f(1), f(2), \dots), \\ (f(0), f(\frac{1}{2}), f(1), \dots), \\ (f(0), f(\frac{1}{3}), f(\frac{2}{3}), \dots), \\ \dots \end{pmatrix} . \qquad (2)$$

Roughly a *hyperstream* is such a stream of streams.

This *hyperstream sampling* still cannot be exact for all signals f: after all, there are only countably many sampling points, while $\mathbb{R}_{\geq 0}$ is uncountable. However, if f satisfies some continuity assumption, we could reconstruct the value $f(t)$ for $t \in \mathbb{R}_{\geq 0}$ as a certain limit of sampled values. Specifically, based on the figure below on the right, we "vertically" collect the following values from the sampling result (2).

$$f(\lceil t \rceil),\ f(\tfrac{\lceil 2t \rceil}{2}),\ f(\tfrac{\lceil 3t \rceil}{3}),\ \dots \quad \longrightarrow \quad f(t) \qquad (3)$$

This construction is called *smoothing*; here $\lceil\_\rceil$ is "rounding up."

We will formalize these sampling and smoothing operations (Smth and Smp) in §5. There we propose a class of functions (i.e. a continuity requirement) that makes hyperstream sampling indeed exact, that is, $\mathsf{Smth} \circ \mathsf{Smp} = \mathrm{id}$.

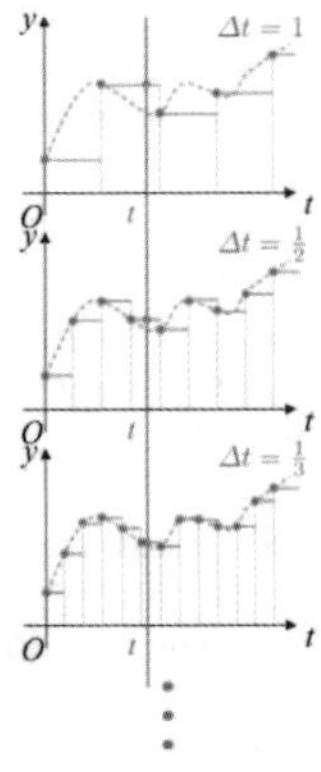

In this paper in fact we use a refined notion of hyperstream: it is not simply a stream of streams (described above) but is the **-transform* of the notion of stream. The intuition behind this refined notion is: a hyperstream is a stream $(f(0), f(\mathtt{dt}), f(2\mathtt{dt}), \dots)$ with an infinitesimal sampling interval $\mathtt{dt}$. The j-th stream $(f(0), f(\frac{1}{j+1}), f(\frac{2}{j+1}), \dots)$ in (2) then occurs as its j-th approximation. *-transform is an NSA construction; its benefit is that we can transfer a logical theory of streams *as it is* to that of hyperstreams, via the celebrated *transfer principle* in NSA.

This idea of using an infinitesimal sampling interval is already presented in [3, §2.3], where they establish $\mathsf{Smth} \circ \mathsf{Smp} = \mathrm{id}$ for functions $f : \mathbb{R}_{\geq 0} \to \mathbb{R}$ that are everywhere *continuous* (they also hint an extension to piecewise continuity). Since we aim at hybrid applications, our class of functions (Def. 5.1) is broader and contains some Zeno examples such as a bouncing ball.

Sectionwise execution The second key idea is about integrating NSA into program semantics and transferring the latter from discrete to continuous/hybrid. For this purpose we use the idea called *sectionwise execution*; it was first used in our previous work [13, 30] for a language with `while` loops. Here we briefly review the idea as presented in [13, 30], adapting it later to the current setting of stream processing.

Its very first example is the program c_{elapse} on the right. Here $\mathtt{dt}$ is a constant that denotes an infinitesimal value; if that is the case the `while` loop will not terminate within finitely many steps. Nevertheless it is somehow intuitive to imagine the "execution" of the program to increase t from 0 to 1, in a smooth and continuous manner.

$t := 0$;
`while` $t \leq 1$ `do`
$t := t + \mathtt{dt}$

To put this intuition into rigorous program semantics, we think of the following *sectionwise execution*. For each natural number i we consider the *i-th section* of the program c_{elapse}, that is denoted by $c_{\mathsf{elapse}}|_i$ and shown on the right. Concretely, $c_{\mathsf{elapse}}|_i$ is obtained by replacing the infinitesimal $\mathtt{dt}$ in c_{elapse} with $\frac{1}{i+1}$. Informally $c_{\mathsf{elapse}}|_i$ is the "i-th approximation" of the original c_{elapse}.

$t := 0$;
`while` $t \leq 1$ `do`
$t := t + \frac{1}{i+1}$

A section $c_{\mathsf{elapse}}|_i$ does terminate within finite steps and yields $1 + \frac{1}{i+1}$ as the value of t. Now we collect the outcome of sectionwise execution and obtain a sequence

$$(1+1,\ 1+\tfrac{1}{2},\ 1+\tfrac{1}{3},\ \dots,\ 1+\tfrac{1}{i},\ \dots) \qquad (4)$$

which is intuitively thought of as a progressive approximation of the actual outcome of the original program c_{elapse}. Indeed, in the language of NSA, the sequence (4) represents a hyperreal number r that is infinitesimally close to 1.

In [30], based on this idea, we presented a framework for modeling and verification of hybrid systems. It consists of an imperative language WHILE and a Hoare-style program logic HOARE, augmented with a constant $\mathtt{dt}$ and called WHILE^{dt} and HOARE^{dt}. Exploiting the transfer principle in NSA—which roughly states that reals and hyperreals are "logically the same"—we showed that the rules of HOARE^{dt} (precisely the same as those of HOARE) are sound and relatively complete. Underlying is the denotational semantics of programs defined in the above sectionwise way. In [13] we applied several static analysis techniques (mainly for invariant discovery) to this setting. We also implemented an automated verification tool.[2]

It was speculated in [13, 30] that the use of $\mathtt{dt}$ is not only for `while` programs but is probably a general methodology for transferring a discrete verification framework to continuous/hybrid. Our current work is one such example: the framework of a stream processing language and a program logic (in the form of a type system) is transferred to the one for *hyperstream processing*. Here "sectionwise execution" takes the following concrete form. As a hyperstream processing language we introduce SPROC^{dt}; it is a stream processing language SPROC, augmented with a constant $\mathtt{dt}$ for an infinitesimal interval. The denotation $[\![p]\!]$ of an SPROC^{dt}

[2] We note that "programs" in WHILE^{dt} are not executable in general; this is already clear in the example of c_{elapse}. We rather think of WHILE^{dt} as a *modeling* language, on which we can carry out static, deductive verification. The same is true of the language SPROC^{dt} introduced in the current paper.

program p—say p takes a hyperstream and returns a hyperstream—is defined by

$$[\![p]\!]\Big(\big((a_{i,j})_i\big)_j\Big) \;:=\; \Big([\![p|_j]\!]\big((a_{i,j})_i\big)\Big)_j \; ; \qquad (5)$$

that is, the section $p|_j$ (an SPROC program) is applied to the j-th stream of the input hyperstream, and their outcome is bundled up.

Example 1.1 (The sine curve). Here is a program $\mathsf{pg}_{\mathsf{Sine}}$ in SPROC^{dt}.

$$\begin{array}{l}\texttt{node Sine() returns } (s) \\ \texttt{where } s = 0\ \texttt{fby}^1\ (s + c \times \texttt{dt});\quad c = 1\ \texttt{fby}^1\ (c - s \times \texttt{dt}) \qquad (6) \\ \texttt{node Main() returns } (\texttt{proj}_1\ \texttt{Sine}())\end{array}$$

The third line (declaring Main) is bureaucracy and can be ignored for the moment. The core part is the mutual recursive definition of the hyperstreams s and c, whose intuition we now explain. The operator $\texttt{fby}^1$ means delay by one step (i.e. dt seconds):

$$(a_0, a_1, \ldots)\ \texttt{fby}^1\ (b_0, b_1, \ldots) \;=\; (a_0, b_0, b_1, \ldots)\ .$$

Therefore the (recursive) equation $s = 0\ \texttt{fby}^1\ (s + c \times \texttt{dt})$ means, for each n (that in fact ranges over *hypernatural numbers*),

$$s(n) = \begin{cases} 0 & \text{if } n = 0, \\ s(n-1) + c(n-1) \times \texttt{dt} & \text{otherwise.}\end{cases}$$

This yields the following equations.

$$s(0) = 0 \qquad \frac{s(n) - s(n-1)}{\texttt{dt}} = c(n-1) \qquad (7)$$

The value $s(n-1)$ is that of one step before $s(n)$, i.e. dt seconds before $s(n)$. Thus the equations (7) are identified with the differential equation $\sin'(t) = \cos(t)$ with the initial value $\sin(0) = 0$.

Intuitively, the section-wise execution of $\mathsf{pg}_{\mathsf{Sine}}$ realizes the sine curve as the limit of the approximations with $\texttt{dt} = 1, \frac{1}{2}, \frac{1}{3}, \ldots$. This is like the graphs on the right.

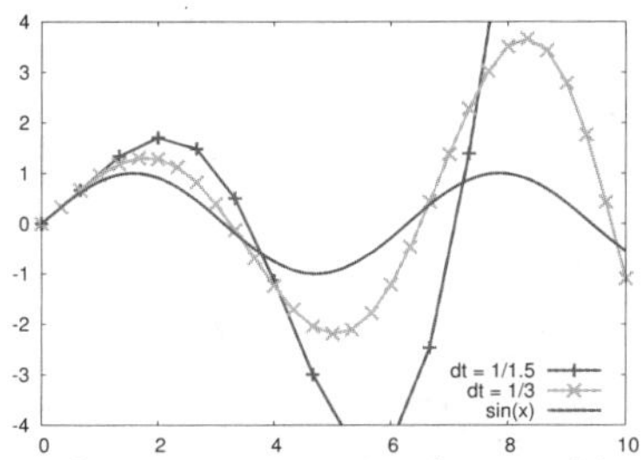

In the current work we employ a more advanced part of NSA than used in [13, 30]. It allows us to transfer statements not only on arithmetic facts but also on set-theoretical ones. More precisely, we can now transfer formulas of the first-order language $\mathscr{L}_X$ (Def. 2.5) that has $\in$ as a binary predicate. The details of this part of NSA is rather complicated but most of them are not needed; in §2.2 we list the minimal set of necessarily definitions and results.

A usage scenario Our technical framework summarized in (1) is supposed to be used in the following way.

We are given two data: a continuous-time signal f and a safety property P. The goal is to verify that f satisfies P. Towards that goal, one first *models* f by an SPROC^{dt} program pg_f. Typically we are not given f as a mathematical entity (i.e. a function $f : \mathbb{R}_{\geq 0} \to \mathbb{C}$), but we get its formal specification written in some formalism like ODEs and Simulink diagrams. In this case, modeling of f amounts to *translation* of a specification (say in ODEs) into an SPROC^{dt} program. This modeling part is briefly discussed in §5.3 but a more extensive treatment is left as future work.

The question then becomes whether the SPROC^{dt} program pg_f satisfies the safety property P. For that we can use a type system for SPROC^{dt}: P is translated into a suitable type ν_{P}; and we try to derive a judgment $\mathsf{pg}_f \vdash \nu_{\mathsf{P}}$ using the typing rules. The typing rules include the well-established proof principle of *fixed point induction*.

Once the derivation is done, by type soundness (Thm. 4.20) it guarantees that the hyperstream $[\![\mathsf{pg}_f]\!]$ denoted by pg_f satisfies ν_{P}. Finally by Thm. 5.12 it implies that the signal $\mathsf{Smth}([\![\mathsf{pg}_f]\!])$ satisfies P. Thus we are done, under the condition that the SPROC^{dt} modeling of f is correct (i.e. $\mathsf{Smth}([\![\mathsf{pg}_f]\!]) = f$).

Note that the last paragraph is all about the metatheory. The actual verification task is derivation of a type judgment, and this is done in the same deductive style as the verification of (discrete-time) stream processing. In its course the NSA metatheory is completely concealed.

Organization of the paper In §2 we list the definitions and results of NSA that are used later. A prototype stream language SPROC is introduced in §3, together with its Kahn-style denotational semantics and a type system for safety guarantee. It is modeled after Lustre and is nothing novel; but the SPROC framework is carefully designed so that it allows the transfer to SPROC^{dt} in §4. Finally in §5 we translate signals into hyperstreams, and also the safety guarantee for hyperstreams (obtained by the SPROC^{dt} type system) to that for signals. §6 is devoted to a verification example. Our intention is to use the current framework for hybrid systems (as mentioned above)—definitions like Def. 5.1 are worked out so that it accommodates many common hybrid dynamics. Our leading example (Example 1.1, which is used in §6) is however a totally continuous one; this is due to the limited space. In §7 we conclude.

We defer most of the proofs to the extended version [31]. In this paper we sometimes refer to "Appendix"; it is found in [31].

Related work The current work shares with [4] the observation of the similarity between signal processing and stream processing. In [4] they extend Lustre by ODEs. They go on to a compilation framework that separates discrete and continuous parts of a program, passing the latter to an external solver to approximate continuous dynamics. For the correctness of the compilation they introduce NSA-based formal semantics [5], which like ours takes continuous dynamics as a succession of infinitesimal jumps. They also employ a type system for the separation of discrete and continuous parts of a program. Despite these similarities, the current work's objective is quite different from theirs—we aim to exploit NSA's logical infrastructure to transfer deductive (i.e. logical) verification from discrete stream processing to continuous-time signal processing. The extension of Lustre by ODEs in [5] is not designed towards this objective.

Formal verification of Simulink diagrams has been studied e.g. in [10, 28, 33]. In [28] Simulink diagrams are translated into hybrid automata, which are amenable to model checking. In [33] translation of a discrete fragment of Simulink into Lustre is presented. [10] combines symbolic analysis and numerical simulation, towards the goal of enhanced simulation coverage. All these papers agree on one point: Simulink lacks formal semantics. In [7, 10] Simulink semantics is defined "operationally" by formalizing the simulation algorithms used in the implementation of Simulink. We hope our hyperstream modeling will serve as a basis of denotational semantics of Simulink.

Turning to the purely discrete world, formal verification of stream processing systems is studied often in the abstract interpretation community [11]. Application of these results to our current deductive approach is an interesting direction of future work.

For hybrid systems in general, there have been extensive research efforts from the formal verification community. Unlike the current work where we turn flow into jump via dt, most of them feature acute distinction between flow- and jump-dynamics. These include: model-checking approaches based on hybrid automata [2]; deductive approaches, one of the most notable of which is a recent series of work by Platzer and his colleagues (including [21, 23]). Interestingly in [23] it is argued that being hybrid imposes no additional burden to deductive verification. This concurs with our NSA view that being discrete and being continuous/hybrid are "logically the same."

Some verification techniques from the static analysis community have been successfully used in hybrid applications (modeled with explicit differential equations) [17, 25–27]. The basic idea of the current work—also of our previous [13, 30]—is to transfer discrete verification techniques *as they are* to continuous/hybrid settings.

It is never our intention to champion the superiority of discrete techniques to continuous ones. The formal verification community has worked out a stock of discrete techniques; our case is that their application domain can be pushed further to continuous/hybrid. Indeed we see ODEs as an extremely efficient formalism for continuous dynamics. We plan to incorporate them into our NSA framework.

The use of NSA as a foundation of hybrid system modeling is not proposed for the first time; see e.g. [3, 5, 6]. Compared to this existing body of work, we claim our novelty is the use of NSA's logical infrastructure (especially the transfer principle) for deductive verification, based on a concrete modeling language.

In particular, the basic idea of the current paper (namely, stream processing + NSA = signal processing) as well as two important technical ideas (namely: infinitesimal sampling intervals and domain theory in NSA) are already in [3]. Unlike the current paper where we introduce a concrete programming (or modeling) language SPROC^{dt}, in [3] they work with an abstract (graphical) language of string diagrams for monoidal categories.

Notations and terminology The syntactic equality is denoted by $\equiv$.

An infinite stream $s = (a_0, a_1, \dots)$ over S is identified with a function $s : \mathbb{N} \to S$. We write $s(i)$ for its i-th element, i.e. $s(i) = a_i$.

For a nonnegative real $r \in \mathbb{R}_{\geq 0}$, $\lceil r \rceil \in \mathbb{N}$ denotes the least natural number that is not smaller than r, that is, $r \leq \lceil r \rceil < r + 1$.

In this paper we use some domain theory, for which our principal reference is [1]. We will be using ω-cpo's—calling them simply "cpo's"—while in [1] most results are formulated in terms of directed cpo's. The equivalence between these two "cpo's" is found in [1, Prop. 2.1.15]. We also assume the least element $\perp$ in cpo's.

2. A Nonstandard Analysis Primer

Here we list the minimal set of necessary definitions and results in nonstandard analysis (NSA). More details are found e.g. in [12, 14].

2.1 Infinitesimals in NSA

First we present an elementary part of NSA. We fix an *index set* $I = \mathbb{N}$, and an *ultrafilter* $\mathcal{F} \subseteq \mathcal{P}(I)$ that extends the cofinite filter $\mathcal{F}_c := \{S \subseteq I \mid I \setminus S \text{ is finite}\}$. Its properties to be noted: 1) for any $S \subseteq I$, exactly one of S and $I \setminus S$ belongs to $\mathcal{F}$; 2) if S is *cofinite* (i.e. $I \setminus S$ is finite), then S belongs to $\mathcal{F}$.

Definition 2.1 (Hypernumber $d \in {}^*X$)**.** For a *base set* X (typically it is $\mathbb{N}$, $\mathbb{R}$ or $\mathbb{C}$), we define the set ${}^*X$ of *hypernumbers* by ${}^*X := X^I/{\sim_\mathcal{F}}$. It is the set of infinite sequences on X modulo the following equivalence $\sim_\mathcal{F}$: we define $(a_0, a_1, \dots) \sim_\mathcal{F} (a'_0, a'_1, \dots)$ by

$$\{i \in I \mid a_i = a'_i\} \in \mathcal{F} \ , \tag{8}$$

for which we say "$a_i = a'_i$ for almost every i."

Therefore, given that two sequences $(a_i)_i$ and $(a'_i)_i$ coincide except for finitely many indices i, they represent the same hypernumber. The predicates other than $=$ (such as $<$) are defined in the same way. A notable consequence is the existence of an infinitesimal number: a hyperreal $\omega^{-1} := [\,(1, \frac{1}{2}, \frac{1}{3}, \dots)\,]$ is positive ($0 < \omega^{-1}$) but is smaller than any (standard) positive real $r = [(r, r, \dots)]$.

Definition 2.2 (Shadow)**.** A hyperreal r is *limited* if it is not infinite, i.e. if there is a standard positive real $K \in \mathbb{R}$ such that $-K < r < K$. It is well-known (see [12, 14]) that a limited hyperreal r has a unique standard real that is infinitely close to r. This standard real is called the *shadow* of r and denoted by $\mathrm{sh}(r)$.

The notion of shadow is a generalization of that of limit: if $(a_i)_i$ converges then $\mathrm{sh}\big([(a_0, a_1, \dots)]\big) = \lim_{i \to \infty} a_i$. See e.g. [12, 14].

Remark 2.3. It is common in NSA to take an index set I that is bigger than $\mathbb{N}$, and an ultrafilter $\mathcal{F} \subseteq \mathcal{P}(I)$ over I. The merit of doing so is that the resulting monomorphism ${}^*(\_)$ (§2.2) can be chosen to be an *enlargement*; see [14, Chap. II]. In this paper, however, we favor concreteness and choose $I = \mathbb{N}$ as the index set.

2.2 NSA in Superstructure

What we need from the logical machinery of NSA goes beyond the elementary fragment presented above. It employs a set theory-like formal language $\mathscr{L}_X$ and a so-called *superstructure* as a model. The definitions and results listed below are all well-established and commonly used in NSA. We follow [14, Chap. II], in which more details can be found.

Superstructure A superstructure is a "universe," constructed step by step from a certain base set X. We assume $\mathbb{N} \subseteq X$.

Definition 2.4 (Superstructure)**.** A *superstructure* $V(X)$ over X is:

$$V(X) := \textstyle\bigcup_{n \in \mathbb{N}} V_n(X) \ , \quad \text{where}$$
$$V_0(X) := X \quad \text{and } V_{n+1}(X) := V_n(X) \cup \mathcal{P}(V_n(X)) \ .$$

(Ordered) pairs (a, b) and tuples $(a_1, \dots, a_m)$ are defined in $V(X)$ as is usually done in set theory, e.g. $(a, b) := \{\{a\}, \{a, b\}\}$. The set $V(X)$ is closed under many set formation operations. For example the function space $a \to b$ is thought of as a collection of special binary relations ($a \to b \subseteq \mathcal{P}(a \times b)$), hence is in $V(X)$.

****-Transform*** We use the following predicate logic $\mathscr{L}_X$.

Definition 2.5 (The language $\mathscr{L}_X$)**.** *Terms* in $\mathscr{L}_X$ consist of: variables $x, y, x_1, x_2, \dots$; and a constant a for each entity $a \in V(X)$.

Formulas in $\mathscr{L}_X$ are constructed as follows.

- The predicate symbols are $=$ and $\in$; both are binary. The *atomic formulas* are of the form $s = t$ or $s \in t$ (where s and t are terms).
- Any Boolean combination of formulas is a formula. We use the symbols $\wedge, \vee, \neg$ and $\Rightarrow$.
- Given a formula A, a variable x and a term s, the expressions $\forall x \in s.\, A$ and $\exists x \in s.\, A$ are formulas.

Note that quantifiers always come with a bound s. The language $\mathscr{L}_X$ depends on the choice of X (it determines the set of constants). We shall also use the following syntax sugars in $\mathscr{L}_X$, as is common in NSA. Their translation into proper $\mathscr{L}_X$ formulas is straightforward.

(s, t)	pair	$(s_1, \dots, s_m)$	tuple
$s \times t$	direct product		
$s \subseteq t$	inclusion, short for $\forall x \in s.\, x \in t$		
$s(t)$	function application; short for x s.t. $(t, x) \in s$		
$s \circ t$	function composition, $(s \circ t)(x) = s(t(x))$		
$s \leq t$	inequality in $\mathbb{N}$; short for $(s, t) \in\, \leq$ where $\leq\, \subseteq \mathbb{N}^2$		

Remark 2.6. We note that $\mathscr{L}_X$ resides on a different level from the languages that we introduce later, such as SPROC, SPROC^{dt} and their assertion languages. $\mathscr{L}_X$ is used to define the semantics of those object-level languages, and is a *meta language* in this sense.

Definition 2.7 (Semantics of $\mathscr{L}_X$)**.** We interpret $\mathscr{L}_X$ in the superstructure $V(X)$ in the obvious way. Let A be a closed formula; we say A is *valid* if A is true in $V(X)$.

Validity is defined only for closed formulas.

The so-called *ultrapower construction* yields a canonical map

$$^*(\_) \;:\; V(X) \longrightarrow V(^*X) \;, \qquad a \longmapsto {}^*a \tag{9}$$

that is called the *$*$-transform*. It is a map from the universe $V(X)$ of standard entities to $V(^*X)$ of nonstandard entities. We skip the details of its construction; later in this section we take a closer look.

The map $^*(\_)$ becomes a *monomorphism*, a notion in NSA. Most notably it satisfies the *transfer principle* (Lem. 2.9).

Definition 2.8 ($*$-transform of formulas)**.** Let A be a formula in $\mathscr{L}_X$. The *$*$-transform* of A, denoted by $^*A$, is a formula in $\mathscr{L}_{^*X}$ obtained by replacing each constant a occurring in A with the constant $^*a$ that designates the element $^*a \in V(^*X)$.

Lemma 2.9 (The transfer principle)**.** *For any closed formula A in $\mathscr{L}_X$, A is valid (in $V(X)$) if and only if $^*A$ is valid (in $V(^*X)$).* □

The transfer principle is a powerful result and we will totally rely on it in the semantics of SPROC^{dt}. Here are the first examples of its use.

Lemma 2.10. *1. For $a \in V(X) \setminus X$ we obtain an injective map*

$$^*(\_) \;:\; a \longrightarrow {}^*a \;, \qquad (b \in a) \longmapsto ({}^*b \in {}^*a) \tag{10}$$

as a restriction of $^*(\_)$ in (9).

2. *If a is a finite set, the map (10) is an isomorphism $a \xrightarrow{\cong} {}^*a$.*
3. *Let $a \to b$ be the set of functions from a to b. We have $^*(a \to b) \subseteq {}^*a \to {}^*b$.*
4. *$^*(a_1 \times \cdots \times a_m) = {}^*a_1 \times \cdots \times {}^*a_m$; and $^*(a_1 \cup \cdots \cup a_m) = {}^*a_1 \cup \cdots \cup {}^*a_m$.*
5. *For a binary relation $r \subseteq a \times a$, we have $^*r \subseteq {}^*a \times {}^*a$. Moreover, r is an order if and only if $^*r$ is an order.* □

Internal Sets The distinction between *internal* and *external* entities is central in NSA. In this paper however it is much of formality, since all the entities we use are internal. Here we present only the relevant definitions, leaving their intuitions to [14, §II.6]. In Appendix B, especially Rem. B.8, we will see that being internal is crucial for transfer.

Definition 2.11 (Internal entity)**.** An element $b \in V(^*X)$ is *internal* with respect to $^*(\_) : V(X) \to V(^*X)$ if there is $a \in V(X)$ such that $b \in {}^*a$. It is *external* if it is not internal.

Lemma 2.12. *$f : {}^*a \to {}^*b$ is internal if and only if $f \in {}^*(a \to b)$.* □

The ultrapower construction We collect some necessary facts about the ultrapower construction of the monomorphism $^*(\_)$ in (9). Its details are beyond our scope; they are found in [14, §II.4].

The map $^*(\_)$ in fact factorizes into the following three steps.

$$\begin{array}{ccc} V(X) & \xrightarrow{\quad ^*(\_) \quad} & V(^*X) \\ {\scriptstyle \overline{(\_)}}\downarrow & & \uparrow{\scriptstyle M} \\ \bigcup_{n\in\mathbb{N}} \big(V_n(X) \setminus V_{n-1}(X)\big)^I & \xrightarrow[\;[\_]\;]{} & \prod^0_{\mathcal{F}} V(X) \end{array} \tag{11}$$

The first factor $\overline{(\_)}$ maps $a \in V(X)$ to the constant function $\overline{a}$ such that $\overline{a}(i) = a$ for each $i \in I$; recall that we have chosen $I = \mathbb{N}$ (Rem. 2.3). The second $[\_]$ takes a quotient modulo the ultrafilter $\mathcal{F}$; finally the third factor M is the so-called *Mostowski collapse*.

For an intuition let us exhibit these maps in the simple setting of §2.1. The first factor $\overline{(\_)}$ corresponds to forming constant streams: $a \mapsto \overline{a} = (a, a, \dots)$. The second $[\_]$ is quotienting modulo $\sim_{\mathcal{F}}$ of (8). The third map M does nothing—it is a book-keeping function that is only needed in the extended setting of superstructures.

The next result [14, Thm. 4.5] is about "starting from the lower-left corner" in (11). It follows from the definition of M and is a crucial step in the proof of the transfer principle (Lem. 2.9). It serves as an important lemma, too, later for the semantics of SPROC^{dt}.

Lemma 2.13 (Łoś' theorem)**.** *Let A be a formula in $\mathscr{L}_X$ with its free variables contained in $\{x_1, \dots, x_m\}$; and $a_1, \dots, a_m \in \bigcup_{n\in\mathbb{N}} \big(V_n(X) \setminus V_{n-1}(X)\big)^I$. Then*

$$\begin{array}{l} ^*A\big[\, M[a_1]/x_1, \dots, M[a_m]/x_m \,\big] \text{ is valid} \\ \iff \quad \{ i \in I \mid A[a_1(i)/x_1, \dots, a_m(i)/x_m] \text{ is valid} \} \in \mathcal{F} \;. \end{array}$$

As a special case, let $S \in V(X)$, then

$$M[a] \in {}^*S \quad \iff \quad a(i) \in S \text{ for almost every } i. \qquad \square$$

Corollary 2.14. *Let $a, b \in V(X)$; and for each $i \in I$, $f_i \in (a \to b)$ and $x_i \in a$. Then $M[(f_i)_{i\in I}]$ is an internal function $^*a \to {}^*b$; and $M[(x_i)_{i\in I}] \in {}^*a$. Moreover,*

$$M[(f_i(x_i))_{i\in I}] = \Big(M[(f_i)_{i\in I}]\Big)\Big(M[(x_i)_{i\in I}]\Big) \;. \qquad \square$$

3. The Stream Processing Language SPROC

In this section we introduce the language SPROC for stream processing, together with its denotational semantics and a type system. The last is much like a Hoare-style program logic for partial correctness. The whole framework is nothing surprising: SPROC is modeled after Lustre [9]; its semantics is defined as usual, following Kahn [15]; and the type system is rudimentary with a limited expressive power. The point is their clean logical foundations, which allow us to transfer the whole framework—via NSA—to SPROC^{dt} (§4).

3.1 SPROC: Syntax

For an example of an SPROC program, see Example 1.1. It is an SPROC^{dt} program, but the two languages are very close.

Definition 3.1 (SPROC)**.** We fix a set $\mathbf{SVar}$ of *stream variables* and, for each $m, n \in \mathbb{N}$, a set $\mathbf{NdName}_{m,n}$ of *node names* of arity (m, n). These sets are assumed to be disjoint. The syntax of SPROC is defined in Table 1. Some of its details are in order.

The set $\mathbf{SExp}_{\mathbb{C}}$ consists of the *$\mathbb{C}$-stream expressions*. A constant $c \in \mathbb{C}$ stands for the $\mathbb{C}$-stream $(c, c, \dots)$. The operator $^\wedge$ is for the power: $(a_0, a_1, \dots) \wedge (b_0, b_1, \dots) = (a_0^{b_0}, a_1^{b_1}, \dots)$. For each $j \in \mathbb{N}$ we have an operator $\mathtt{fby}^j$ ("followed by"). It means

$$(a_0, a_1, \dots) \;\mathtt{fby}^j\; (b_0, b_1, \dots) \;=\; (a_0, \dots, a_{j-1}, b_0, b_1, \dots) \;. \tag{12}$$

The expression $\mathtt{proj}_k\, f(e_1, \dots, e_m)$ invokes the node whose name is f (declared elsewhere in the same program), feeds it with the input $(e_1, \dots, e_m)$, and returns the k-th component of its output.

The set $\mathbf{SExp}_{\mathbb{B}}$ consists of the expressions for streams in the Boolean values $\mathbb{B} = \{\mathrm{tt}, \mathrm{ff}\}$. The operators $=$, $\mathtt{isReal}$ and $<$ are the obvious extensions of $= \,:\, \mathbb{C}^2 \to \mathbb{B}$, $\mathtt{isReal} : \mathbb{C} \to \mathbb{B}$ and $< : \mathbb{C}^2 \to \mathbb{B}$. The last is defined by

$$c_1 < c_2 \;:=\; \begin{cases} \mathrm{tt} & \text{if } c_1, c_2 \in \mathbb{R} \text{ and } c_1 < c_2, \\ \mathrm{ff} & \text{otherwise.} \end{cases} \tag{13}$$

Each *node* $\mathsf{nd} \in \mathbf{Nodes}$ comes with a certain arity (m, n) and its name f is chosen from $\mathbf{NdName}_{m,n}$. It takes m-many $\mathbb{C}$-streams as input and returns n-many $\mathbb{C}$-streams as output. In the node nd in Table 1, the variable x_i is for an input stream; and the local variable y_i is used in the (mutually) recursive computation inside the node (specified by $y_1 = e'_1; \ldots; y_l = e'_l$). These x_i's and y_i's together constitute the set of *bound variables* in nd. The restriction in Table 1 dictates that only these variables are allowed to occur in nd.

Finally, a *program* of SPROC is a finite sequence of nodes, with the last one designated as the *main* node. The restriction in Table 1 means that we can invoke a node only if it is declared in the program.

3.2 SPROC: Denotational Semantics

We define the semantics of SPROC in the denotational style, exploiting the cpo structure of streams. This approach to the denotational semantics of stream processing systems dates back to Kahn [15]. Specifically, our semantic domains are as follows.

Definition 3.2 ($\mathbb{C}^\infty, \mathbb{B}^\infty$). By $\mathbb{C}^\infty$ we denote the set of finite and infinite streams over $\mathbb{C}$. That is, $\mathbb{C}^\infty := \mathbb{C}^* \cup \mathbb{C}^{\mathbb{N}}$. We also define $\mathbb{B}^\infty$ for $\mathbb{B} = \{\mathrm{tt}, \mathrm{ff}\}$ by $\mathbb{B}^\infty := \mathbb{B}^* \cup \mathbb{B}^{\mathbb{N}}$.

Notation 3.3. In what follows it is convenient to regard a finite stream as if it is an infinite stream. Using $\perp$ ("undefined"), we identify $(a_0, a_1, \ldots, a_m)$ with an infinite stream

$$(a_0, a_1, \ldots, a_m, \perp, \perp, \ldots) \ .$$

The intuition is: "production of the element a_{m+1} never terminated; thus the elements henceforth never got produced." Hence in $(a_n)_{n\in\mathbb{N}} \in \mathbb{C}^\infty$, if $a_m = \perp$ then $a_{m'} = \perp$ for any $m' \geq m$.

The following result underpins Kahn's approach [15].

Lemma 3.4. *The prefix order $\sqsubseteq$ on $\mathbb{C}^\infty$ makes it a cpo, that is, any ascending chain $s_0 \sqsubseteq s_1 \sqsubseteq \cdots$ has a supremum $\bigsqcup_i s_i$. Its least element is the empty stream ε. The same holds for $\mathbb{B}^\infty$ too.* □

Based on this observation, we introduce the semantics as follows.

Definition 3.5 (Variable/node environment). A *(stream) variable environment* is a function $J : \mathbf{SVar} \to \mathbb{C}^\infty$ that assigns $J(x) \in \mathbb{C}^\infty$ to each stream variable x. A *node environment* K assigns, to each node name $f \in \mathbf{NdName}$, a continuous function

$$K(f) \in \big((\mathbb{C}^\infty)^{m_f} \to_{\mathrm{ct}} (\mathbb{C}^\infty)^{n_f} \big) \ . \qquad (14)$$

Here (m_f, n_f) is the arity of f; and the set $(\mathbb{C}^\infty)^{m_f} \to_{\mathrm{ct}} (\mathbb{C}^\infty)^{n_f}$ is that of *continuous* (i.e. $\bigsqcup$-preserving, but not necessarily $\perp$-preserving) functions from $(\mathbb{C}^\infty)^{m_f}$ to $(\mathbb{C}^\infty)^{n_f}$, with respect to the order $\sqsubseteq$ in Lem. 3.4. Therefore K is an element of the following set.

$$K \in \textstyle\prod_{f\in\mathbf{NdName}} \big((\mathbb{C}^\infty)^{m_f} \to_{\mathrm{ct}} (\mathbb{C}^\infty)^{n_f} \big) \ . \qquad (15)$$

We denote the sets of (stream) variable environments and node environments by $\mathbf{SVarEnv}$ and $\mathbf{NdEnv}$, respectively.

Lemma 3.6. *The sets $\mathbf{SVarEnv}$ and $\mathbf{NdEnv}$ are cpo's, with the pointwise extension of the order structure of $\mathbb{C}^\infty$. Specifically, between $K, K' \in \mathbf{NdEnv}$, we have $K \sqsubseteq K'$ if and only if*

$$\begin{aligned} &\forall m, n \in \mathbb{N}. \forall f \in \mathbf{NdName}_{m,n}. \forall \vec{s} \in (\mathbb{C}^\infty)^m. \\ &\qquad \forall k \in [1, n]. \quad \pi_k\big(K(f)(\vec{s})\big) \sqsubseteq \pi_k\big(K'(f)(\vec{s})\big) \ . \end{aligned}$$

Here π_k is the k-th projection $\pi_k : (\mathbb{C}^\infty)^n \to \mathbb{C}^\infty$. The order on $\mathbf{SVarEnv}$ is similar. □

Using these environments we define the semantics of SPROC expressions as follows. We go step by step.

Definition 3.7 ($[\![e]\!]_{J,K}$ and $[\![b]\!]_{J,K}$). In Table 2 we define the denotation $[\![e]\!]_{J,K} \in \mathbb{C}^\infty$ of a $\mathbb{C}$-stream expression $e \in \mathbf{SExp}_{\mathbb{C}}$, under variable and node environments J and K.

Here the definition of $[\![e_1 \ \mathtt{aop} \ e_2]\!]_{J,K}$ simply says that aop is applied elementwise. Recall that a finite stream $(a_0 \ldots a_m)$ is identified with $(a_0, \ldots, a_m, \perp, \perp, \ldots)$; the operator $\mathtt{aop}_\perp$ returns $\perp$ if any of its arguments is $\perp$. This is the same for $\mathtt{if}_\perp \ldots \mathtt{then} \ldots \mathtt{else} \ldots$, $\wedge_\perp$, $\neg_\perp$, etc. that appear later in Table 2. The definition of $[\![e_1 \ \mathtt{fby}^j \ e_2]\!]_{J,K}$ is the equation (12) put in formal terms. Recall that $\perp$ means "nontermination" (Notation 3.3). In the definition of $[\![\mathtt{proj}_k \ f(e_1, \ldots, e_m)]\!]_{J,K}$, recall that π_k is the k-th projection (see Lem. 3.6); also note the type of K (see (14)).

We simultaneously interpret $\mathbb{B}$-stream expressions, as in Table 2. Recall our definition of $<$ between complex numbers (see (13)).

The semantics of intra/inter-node recursion is by least fixed points.

Definition 3.8 ($[\![\mathrm{nd}]\!]_K$). Let nd be a node

$$\mathrm{nd} :\equiv \left[\begin{array}{l} \mathtt{node} \ f(x_1, \ldots, x_m) \ \mathtt{returns} \ (e_1, \ldots, e_n) \\ \mathtt{where} \ y_1 = e'_1; \ldots; y_l = e'_l \end{array} \right] \qquad (16)$$

of arity (m, n). We define its denotation

$$[\![\mathrm{nd}]\!]_K : (\mathbb{C}^\infty)^m \longrightarrow (\mathbb{C}^\infty)^n \qquad (17)$$

as follows. Given $\vec{s} = (s_1, \ldots, s_m) \in (\mathbb{C}^\infty)^m$ as input, first we solve the following recursive equation, and obtain a variable environment J_0 as its least solution.

$$J_0 = J_0 \left[\begin{array}{l} x_1 \mapsto s_1, \ \ldots, \ x_m \mapsto s_m, \\ y_1 \mapsto [\![e'_1]\!]_{J_0,K}, \ \ldots, \ y_l \mapsto [\![e'_l]\!]_{J_0,K} \end{array} \right] \qquad (18)$$

On the right-hand side, $[x_1 \mapsto s_1, \ldots]$ means a function update. The variable environment J_0 thus obtained is used in:

$$[\![\mathrm{nd}]\!]_K(s_1, \ldots, s_m) := \big([\![e_1]\!]_{J_0,K}, \ldots, [\![e_n]\!]_{J_0,K} \big) \in (\mathbb{C}^\infty)^n \ .$$

Definition 3.9 ($[\![\mathrm{pg}]\!]$). Let pg be a program $[\mathrm{nd}_1, \ldots, \mathrm{nd}_N; \mathrm{nd}_{\mathrm{Main}}]$; $f_1, \ldots, f_N$ and f_{Main} be the names of $\mathrm{nd}_1, \ldots, \mathrm{nd}_N$ and $\mathrm{nd}_{\mathrm{Main}}$; and $(m_{\mathrm{Main}}, n_{\mathrm{Main}})$ be the arity of $\mathrm{nd}_{\mathrm{Main}}$. We define the denotation $[\![\mathrm{pg}]\!] : (\mathbb{C}^\infty)^{m_{\mathrm{Main}}} \to (\mathbb{C}^\infty)^{n_{\mathrm{Main}}}$ as follows. We define a node environment K_0 to be the least solution of the following recursive equation.

$$K_0 = K_0 \left[\begin{array}{l} f_1 \mapsto [\![\mathrm{nd}_1]\!]_{K_0}, \ \ldots, \ f_N \mapsto [\![\mathrm{nd}_N]\!]_{K_0}, \\ f_{\mathrm{Main}} \mapsto [\![\mathrm{nd}_{\mathrm{Main}}]\!]_{K_0} \end{array} \right] \qquad (19)$$

The node environment K_0 thus obtained is used in the following. (Note the type; see (17))

$$[\![\mathrm{pg}]\!] := [\![\mathrm{nd}_{\mathrm{Main}}]\!]_{K_0} \quad : (\mathbb{C}^\infty)^{m_{\mathrm{Main}}} \to (\mathbb{C}^\infty)^{n_{\mathrm{Main}}}$$

We need the following lemmas for Def. 3.8–3.9 to make sense. These follow from the fact that all the constructs in the denotational semantics are continuous, which is proved in Appendix A.

Lemma 3.10. *For any node* nd *and any $K \in \mathbf{NdEnv}$, the function $[\![\mathrm{nd}]\!]_K : (\mathbb{C}^\infty)^m \to (\mathbb{C}^\infty)^n$ is continuous. Therefore the function on the right-hand side of (19) is indeed a node environment.* □

Lemma 3.11. *The recursive equations (18–19) have least solutions.*

Proof. By the continuity of the relevant operations, including

$$\begin{aligned} \Phi : \ & \mathbf{SVarEnv} \longrightarrow \mathbf{SVarEnv} \ , \\ & J \longmapsto J \left[\begin{array}{l} x_1 \mapsto s_1, \ \ldots, \ x_m \mapsto s_m, \\ y_1 \mapsto [\![e'_1]\!]_{J,K}, \ \ldots, \ y_l \mapsto [\![e'_l]\!]_{J,K} \end{array} \right] , \end{aligned} \qquad (20)$$

and Lem. 3.6. □

3.3 SPROC: Type System for Safety Guarantee

We now present a "program logic" for SPROC. SPROC is a first-order functional language; therefore, as usual, our logic takes the form of a *type system*. There we identify types with predicates.

Our type system is rather restricted and is aimed (solely) at the *partial* guarantee of safety, that is, it gives no guarantee in the

$$
\begin{array}{rcll}
\mathbf{SExp}_{\mathbb{C}} \ni e & ::= & x \mid c \mid e_1 + e_2 \mid e_1 \times e_2 \mid e_1 \mathbin{\char`^} e_2 \mid e_1\ \mathtt{fby}^j\ e_2 \mid \mathtt{if}\ b\ \mathtt{then}\ e_1\ \mathtt{else}\ e_2 \mid \mathtt{proj}_k\ f(e_1, \dots, e_m) & \\
& & \quad \text{where } x \in \mathbf{SVar};\ c \in \mathbb{C};\ j \in \mathbb{N};\ b \in \mathbf{SExp}_{\mathbb{B}};\ f \in \mathbf{NdName}_{m,n};\ \text{and } k \in [1, n] & \\
\mathbf{SExp}_{\mathbb{B}} \ni b & ::= & \mathtt{true} \mid \mathtt{false} \mid b_1 \wedge b_2 \mid \neg b \mid e_1 = e_2 \mid \mathtt{isReal}(e) \mid e_1 < e_2 & \text{where } e, e_i \in \mathbf{SExp}_{\mathbb{C}} \\
\mathbf{Nodes} \ni \mathsf{nd} & ::= & \left[\begin{array}{l} \mathtt{node}\ f(x_1, \dots, x_m)\ \mathtt{returns}\ (e_1, \dots, e_n) \\ \mathtt{where}\ y_1 = e'_1; y_2 = e'_2; \dots ; y_l = e'_l \end{array}\right] & \begin{array}{l} \text{where } f \in \mathbf{NdName}_{m,n};\ x_i, y_i \in \mathbf{SVar};\ e_i, e'_i \in \mathbf{SExp}_{\mathbb{C}}; \\ x_1, \dots, x_m, y_1, \dots, y_n \text{ are all distinct; and the variables occurring} \\ \text{in } e_i, e'_i \text{ are restricted to } x_i \text{ and } y_i \end{array} \\
\mathbf{Programs} \ni \mathsf{pg} & ::= & [\mathsf{nd}_1, \mathsf{nd}_2, \dots, \mathsf{nd}_m; \mathsf{nd}_{\mathsf{Main}}] & \begin{array}{l} \text{where } \mathsf{nd}_i, \mathsf{nd}_{\mathsf{Main}} \in \mathbf{Nodes}; \text{ and the node names occurring in } \mathsf{nd}_i \text{ or } \mathsf{nd}_{\mathsf{Main}} \\ \text{are restricted to } f_1, \dots, f_m \text{ and } f_{\mathsf{Main}}, \text{ the (distinct) names of } \mathsf{nd}_1, \dots, \mathsf{nd}_m \text{ and } \mathsf{nd}_{\mathsf{Main}} \end{array}
\end{array}
$$

Table 1. Syntax of SPROC

$$
\begin{array}{l}
[\![x]\!]_{J,K} := J(x) \qquad [\![c]\!]_{J,K} := (c, c, \dots) \qquad [\![e_1\ \mathtt{aop}\ e_2]\!]_{J,K} := \big([\![e_1]\!]_{J,K}(n)\ \mathtt{aop}_{\bot}\ [\![e_2]\!]_{J,K}(n) \big)_{n \in \mathbb{N}} \quad \text{where } \mathtt{aop} \in \{+, \times, \char`^\} \\
[\![e_1\ \mathtt{fby}^j\ e_2]\!]_{J,K} := \begin{cases} \big([\![e_1]\!]_{J,K}(0), [\![e_1]\!]_{J,K}(1), \dots, [\![e_1]\!]_{J,K}(j-1), [\![e_2]\!]_{J,K}(0), [\![e_2]\!]_{J,K}(1), \dots \big) & \text{if the length of } [\![e_1]\!]_{J,K} \text{ is at least } j \\ \big([\![e_1]\!]_{J,K}(0), [\![e_1]\!]_{J,K}(1), \dots, [\![e_1]\!]_{J,K}(k-1), \bot, \bot \dots \big) & \text{if the length of } [\![e_1]\!]_{J,K} \text{ is } k \text{ and } k < j \end{cases} \\
[\![\mathtt{if}\ b\ \mathtt{then}\ e_1\ \mathtt{else}\ e_2]\!]_{J,K} := \big(\mathtt{if}_{\bot}\ [\![b]\!]_{J,K}(n)\ \mathtt{then}\ [\![e_1]\!]_{J,K}(n)\ \mathtt{else}\ [\![e_2]\!]_{J,K}(n) \big)_{n \in \mathbb{N}} \\
[\![\mathtt{proj}_k\ f(e_1, \dots, e_m)]\!]_{J,K} := \pi_k\Big(K(f)\big([\![e_1]\!]_{J,K}, \dots, [\![e_m]\!]_{J,K} \big) \Big) \\
[\![\mathtt{true}]\!]_{J,K} := (\mathrm{tt}, \mathrm{tt}, \dots) \quad [\![\mathtt{false}]\!]_{J,K} := (\mathrm{ff}, \mathrm{ff}, \dots) \quad [\![b_1 \wedge b_2]\!]_{J,K} := \big([\![b_1]\!]_{J,K}(n) \wedge_{\bot} [\![b_2]\!]_{J,K}(n) \big)_{n \in \mathbb{N}} \quad [\![\neg b]\!]_{J,K} := \big(\neg_{\bot} [\![b]\!]_{J,K}(n) \big)_{n \in \mathbb{N}} \\
[\![e_1 = e_2]\!]_{J,K} := \big([\![e_1]\!]_{J,K}(n) =_{\bot} [\![e_2]\!]_{J,K}(n) \big)_{n \in \mathbb{N}} \qquad [\![\mathtt{isReal}(e)]\!]_{J,K} := \Big(\mathtt{isReal}_{\bot}\big([\![e]\!]_{J,K}(n) \big) \Big)_{n \in \mathbb{N}} \\
[\![e_1 < e_2]\!]_{J,K}(n) := \begin{cases} [\![e_1]\!]_{J,K}(n) <_{\bot} [\![e_2]\!]_{J,K}(n) & \text{if } n = 0 \text{ or } [\![e_1 < e_2]\!]_{J,K}(n-1) \neq \bot \\ \bot & \text{if } [\![e_1 < e_2]\!]_{J,K}(n-1) = \bot \end{cases}
\end{array}
$$

Table 2. Denotation $[\![e]\!]_{J,K}$, $[\![b]\!]_{J,K}$

case of nontermination. Our focus on partial safety is influenced by [18]; and is much like common Hoare-style program logics. We leave as future work verification of liveness properties; the latter necessarily involves the analysis of termination (i.e. *productivity* in stream processing).

Remark 3.12. For functional stream processing languages, Nakano's type system [20] with the $\bullet$ modality is well-known. Its concern is for the productivity (i.e. totality, termination) of stream computation; this is orthogonal to ours (partial safety). In [16] semantics of stream processing subject to Nakano's types is proposed using ultrametric spaces—as an alternative to the Kahn-style cpo semantics which we have used—with its merit being that one can form a semantic domain consisting solely of *total* streams (i.e. $\mathbb{C}^{\mathbb{N}}$ instead of $\mathbb{C}^{\infty}$). Application of these results to SPROC, and further to SPROC^{dt}, is left as future work.

3.3.1 SPROC: Type Syntax

Our type syntax is borrowed from that of *dependent type systems*. The latter are known for their expressiveness and have been used for verification of higher-order programs (e.g. in [32]). Our type system, as a feasibility study of the methodology, is much more restricted. See Example 3.14.

$$
\begin{array}{rcl}
\mathbf{AExp} \ni a & ::= & v \mid c \mid a_1 + a_2 \mid a_1 \times a_2 \mid a_1 \mathbin{\char`^} a_2 \mid \lceil a_1 \rceil \\
& & \quad \text{where } v \in \mathbf{Var} \text{ and } c \in \mathbb{C} \\
\mathbf{Fml} \ni P & ::= & \mathtt{true} \mid \mathtt{false} \mid P_1 \wedge P_2 \mid P_1 \vee P_2 \mid \neg P \mid \\
& & a_1 = a_2 \mid \mathtt{isReal}(a) \mid a_1 < a_2 \mid a_1 \leq a_2 \mid \\
& & \forall v \in \mathbb{N}.\, P \mid \forall v \in \mathbb{C}.\, P \\
& & \quad \text{where } v \in \mathbf{Var} \text{ and } a, a_i \in \mathbf{SExp}_{\mathbb{C}} \\
\mathbf{SType}_{\mathbb{C}} \ni \tau & ::= & \prod_{v \in \mathbb{N}} \{u \in \mathbb{C} \mid P\} \quad \text{where } u, v \in \mathbf{Var}, \\
& & \quad P \in \mathbf{Fml} \text{ and } \mathrm{FV}(P) \subseteq \{u, v\} \\
\mathbf{SType}_{\mathbb{B}} \ni \beta & ::= & \prod_{v \in \mathbb{N}} P \quad \text{where } v \in \mathbf{Var}, \\
& & \quad P \in \mathbf{Fml} \text{ and } \mathrm{FV}(P) \subseteq \{v\} \\
\mathbf{NdType}_{m,n} \ni \nu & ::= & (\tau_1, \dots, \tau_m) \to (\tau'_1, \dots, \tau'_n) \\
& & \quad \text{where } \tau_i, \tau'_i \in \mathbf{SType}_{\mathbb{C}}
\end{array}
$$

Table 3. Type Syntax for SPROC

Definition 3.13 (Types for SPROC)**.** The syntax of our type system for SPROC is shown in Table 3.

The set $\mathbf{AExp}$ is that of *arithmetic expressions*, each of which denotes a number in $\mathbb{C}$. We assume a countable set $\mathbf{Var}$ of variables; note that this is different from the set $\mathbf{SVar}$ of *stream* variables. The *rounding up* operation $\lceil \_ \rceil$ (see §1) is included for a later use. The set $\mathbf{Fml}$ is that of *assertion formulas*; it follows the usual syntax of first-order predicate logic.

A *type* $\tau \in \mathbf{SType}_{\mathbb{C}}$ *for* $\mathbb{C}$*-streams* is an expression $\prod_{v \in \mathbb{N}} \{u \in \mathbb{C} \mid P\}$. It consists of variables u, v, a formula P, and the delimiter $\prod_{\_ \in \mathbb{N}} \{\_ \in \mathbb{C} \mid \_\}$. Its informal meaning is

$$\{u \in \mathbb{C} \mid P[0/v]\} \times \{u \in \mathbb{C} \mid P[1/v]\} \times \{u \in \mathbb{C} \mid P[2/v]\} \times \cdots \ ;$$

that is, the set of streams s such that its n-th element $u = s(n)$ and $v = n$ satisfy P, for each $n \in \mathbb{N}$. A *type* $\beta \in \mathbf{SType}_{\mathbb{B}}$ *for* $\mathbb{B}$*-streams* is similar: $t \models \prod_{v \in \mathbb{N}} P$ if $t(n)$ is equivalent to P, with $v = n$, for each $n \in \mathbb{N}$.

A *node type* $\nu \equiv (\tau_1, \dots, \tau_m) \to (\tau'_1, \dots, \tau'_n) \in \mathbf{NdType}_{m,n}$ represents the set of nodes of arity (m, n) that, when fed with streams satisfying $\tau_1, \dots, \tau_m$, output streams satisfying $\tau'_1, \dots, \tau'_n$.

In the expression $\prod_{v \in \mathbb{N}} \{u \in \mathbb{C} \mid P\} \in \mathbf{SType}_{\mathbb{C}}$, the variables u and v are *bound*. We identify types modulo renaming of these bound variables. The same is true of v in $\prod_{v \in \mathbb{N}} P \in \mathbf{SType}_{\mathbb{C}}$.

Example 3.14. The $\mathbb{C}$-stream type $\prod_{v \in \mathbb{N}} \{u \mid v \geq 3 \Rightarrow u \leq 1\}$ specifies that the elements $s(3), s(4), \dots$ of a stream s are real and ≤ 1. Our types can thus express rudimentary safety properties.

Regarding the limitation of the expressive power, it is straightforward to extend the type system with stream types of arity $k > 1$: $\prod_{v \in \mathbb{N}} \{ (u_1, \dots, u_k) \mid P \}$, where $\mathrm{FV}(P) \subseteq \{u_1, \dots, u_k, v\}$. This extension allows us to speak about correlations among distinct streams. So can we about correlations between input and output: we can prepare auxiliary output streams that copy input streams, and compare them with the output. Furthermore we can express temporal properties: to see if a stream s is increasing, we can check if the pair $(0\ \mathtt{fby}^1\ s, s)$ satisfies the binary type $\prod_{v \in \mathbb{N}} \{(u_1, u_2) \mid u_1 < u_2\}$. In this paper we restrict the presentation to unary stream types for the sake of simplicity.

This is not to say that the type system is amply expressive. For example, the type judgment $\Delta; x : \tau, y : \sigma \vdash \mathtt{if}\ x = y\ \mathtt{then}\ y\ \mathtt{else}\ x : \tau$ (whose validity is not hard to see) cannot be derived by the typing rules. In its derivation one would need a $\mathbb{B}$-stream type $\prod_{v\in\mathbb{N}}\{x(v) = y(v)\}$, which is prohibited due to the free variables x, y in it.

Anyway, the syntactic restrictions in Table 3—compared to a fully-fledged dependent type system—simplify the type system drastically. For example, we do not need the well-formedness condition of type environments, which is usually needed in dependent type systems (see e.g. [32]). Relaxing these restrictions is future work.

3.3.2 SPROC: Type Semantics

Definition 3.15 (Valuation). A *valuation* is either $\bot$ ("undefined") or a function $L : \mathbf{Var} \to \mathbb{C}$. The set of valuations is denoted by $\mathbf{Val}$, that is, $\mathbf{Val} = (\mathbf{Var} \to \mathbb{C}) \cup \{\bot\}$.

The function update $L[u_1 \mapsto c_1, \ldots, u_m \mapsto c_m]$, with $L \in \mathbf{Val}$, $u_i \in \mathbf{Var}$ and $c_i \in \mathbb{C} \cup \{\bot\}$, is defined by:

$$L[\vec{u} \mapsto \vec{c}] \; := \; \begin{cases} \bot & \text{if any of } c_i \text{ is } \bot \\ \text{(the usual function update)} & \text{otherwise.} \end{cases} \tag{21}$$

Therefore: if the length of $s \in \mathbb{C}^\infty$ is not more than n, valuation $L[u \mapsto s(n)]$ is defined to be $\bot$.

Definition 3.16 (Semantics of $\mathbf{AExp}$, $\mathbf{Fml}$). The *denotation* $[\![a]\!]_L \in \mathbb{C} \cup \{\bot\}$, of an arithmetic expression $a \in \mathbf{AExp}$ under a valuation $L \in \mathbf{Val}$, is defined in the usual manner. We define $\models$ between valuations and formulas in the usual manner, too. For example,

$$\begin{aligned} L \models \mathtt{isReal}(a) &\overset{\text{def.}}{\iff} L = \bot \text{ or } [\![a]\!]_L \in \mathbb{R} \;, \\ L \models \forall v \in \mathbb{N}.P &\overset{\text{def.}}{\iff} L = \bot \text{ or } L[v \mapsto n] \models P \text{ for any } n \in \mathbb{N} \;, \end{aligned}$$

and so on. In particular, the valuation $\bot \in \mathbf{Val}$ satisfies any formula.

A formula P is *valid* ($\models P$) if $L \models P$ for any $L \in \mathbf{Val}$.

Definition 3.17 (Semantics of types). Between a $\mathbb{C}$-stream $s \in \mathbb{C}^\infty$ and a $\mathbb{C}$-stream type $\tau \in \mathbf{SType}_\mathbb{C}$, $s \models \tau$ is defined by

$$\begin{aligned} & s \models \textstyle\prod_{v\in\mathbb{N}}\{u \in \mathbb{C} \mid P\} \overset{\text{def.}}{\iff} \\ & \quad L[v \mapsto n, u \mapsto s(n)] \models P \text{ for each } n \in \mathbb{N} \text{ and } L \in \mathbf{Val}. \end{aligned}$$

Note that the valuation L in the definition is vacuous, because of the restriction that $\mathrm{FV}(P) \subseteq \{u, v\}$. Note also that when $s(n) = \bot$, then $L[v \mapsto n, u \mapsto s(n)]$ is $\bot$ (Def. 3.15), which satisfies P. This reflects our focus on *partial correctness*: when the computation does not terminate—i.e. when the length of $s \in \mathbb{C}^\infty$ is l, and its $(l+1)$-th element never gets produced—it does not matter what the type τ specifies about the $(l+1)$-th and later elements of s.

Similarly, between a $\mathbb{B}$-stream $t \in \mathbb{B}^\infty$ and a $\mathbb{B}$-stream type $\beta \in \mathbf{SType}_\mathbb{B}$, the *satisfaction relation* $t \models \beta$ is defined as follows.

$$\begin{aligned} t \models \textstyle\prod_{v\in\mathbb{N}} P \overset{\text{def.}}{\iff} & \text{ for each } n \in \mathbb{N},\, t(n) = \bot \text{ or} \\ & \big(t(n) = \mathtt{tt} \Leftrightarrow L[v \mapsto n] \models P \text{ for each } L \in \mathbf{Val}\big) \end{aligned}$$

That is, "$t(n)$ if and only if $P[n/v]$."

Finally, between a continuous function $g : (\mathbb{C}^\infty)^m \to_{\mathrm{ct}} (\mathbb{C}^\infty)^n$ and a node type $\nu \in \mathbf{NdType}_{m,n}$, the *satisfaction relation* $\models$ is:

$$\begin{aligned} & g \models (\tau_1, \ldots, \tau_m) \to (\tau'_1, \ldots, \tau'_n) \overset{\text{def.}}{\iff} \\ & \forall s_1, \ldots, s_m, s'_1, \ldots, s'_n \in \mathbb{C}^\infty. \\ & \left[\begin{array}{l} s_1 \models \tau_1 \wedge \cdots \wedge s_m \models \tau_m \wedge (s'_1, \ldots, s'_n) = g(s_1, \ldots, s_m) \\ \quad \Longrightarrow \quad s'_1 \models \tau'_1 \wedge \cdots \wedge s'_n \models \tau'_n \end{array}\right] \end{aligned}$$

3.3.3 SPROC: Type Derivation

In type judgments we have two kinds of environments.

Definition 3.18 (Type environment). A *stream type environment* $\Gamma = \{x_1 : \tau_1, \ldots, x_m : \tau_m\}$ is a finite set of pairs of a stream variable $x_i \in \mathbf{SVar}$ and a $\mathbb{C}$-stream type $\tau_i \in \mathbf{SType}_\mathbb{C}$. We require $x_1, \ldots, x_m$ to be distinct.

Similarly, a *node type environment* $\Delta = \{f_1 : \nu_1, \ldots, f_m : \nu_m\}$ is a finite set, where $f_i \in \mathbf{NdName}$ is a node name and $\nu \in \mathbf{NdType}$ is a node type with the same arity.

We denote the sets of stream and node type environments by $\mathbf{STEnv}$ and $\mathbf{NdTEnv}$, respectively.

Notation 3.19. We sometimes write $\Gamma(x)$. In this case it is assumed that $x : \tau$ is in Γ with some τ; and $\Gamma(x)$ denotes this (unique) τ.

Definition 3.20 (Type judgment). In our type system for SPROC we have four classes of type judgments. Here $\vdash$ is a (mere) delimiter.

- $\Delta; \Gamma \vdash e : \tau$, meaning: the $\mathbb{C}$-stream expression e is of the type τ if the variables denote the streams conforming to Γ and the node names denote the nodes conforming to Δ.
- $\Delta; \Gamma \vdash b : \tau_b$, meaning the same, between $\mathbb{B}$-stream expressions and $\mathbb{B}$-stream types.
- $\Delta \vdash \mathsf{nd} : \nu$, meaning: the node nd is of the node type ν if the node names denote the nodes that conform to Δ.
- $\vdash \mathsf{pg} : \nu$, meaning: pg's main node $\mathsf{nd}_{\mathsf{Main}}$ is of the node type ν.

Definition 3.21 (Type derivation). The typing rules for SPROC are as shown in Table 4. We write $\Vdash \mathcal{J}$ if the type judgment $\mathcal{J}$ is derivable.

3.3.4 SPROC: Type Soundness

Definition 3.22. Between a stream variable environment $J \in \mathbf{SVarEnv} = (\mathbf{SVar} \to \mathbb{C}^\infty)$ and a stream type environment $\Gamma = \{x_1 : \tau_1, \ldots, x_m : \tau_m\} \in \mathbf{STEnv}$, we define $J \models \Gamma$ by

$$J \models \Gamma \overset{\text{def.}}{\iff} J(x_i) \models \tau_i \text{ for each } i \in [1, m].$$

Here the latter $\models$ is as defined in Def. 3.17.

Similarly, between a node environment $K \in \mathbf{NdEnv}$ and a node type environment $\Delta = \{f_1 : \nu_1, \ldots, f_m : \nu_m\} \in \mathbf{NdTEnv}$, we define $K \models \Delta$ if and only if $K(f_i) \models \nu_i$ for each $i \in [1, m]$.

Lemma 3.23. *The $\mathbb{C}$-stream $\bot \in \mathbb{C}^\infty$ (i.e. the empty stream) satisfies any type τ, that is, $\bot \models \tau$. The same for $\bot \in \mathbb{B}^\infty$. Similarly we have $\bot \models \Gamma$ for $\bot \in \mathbf{SVarEnv}$; and $\bot \models \Delta$ for $\bot \in \mathbf{NdEnv}$.* □

Definition 3.24 (Validity of type judgments). We say a type judgment $\Delta; \Gamma \vdash e : \tau$ is *valid*, and write $\models \;\; \Delta; \Gamma \vdash e : \tau$, if for any $J \in \mathbf{SVarEnv}$ and $K \in \mathbf{NdEnv}$, $J \models \Gamma$ and $K \models \Delta$ imply $[\![e]\!]_{J,K} \models \tau$. The *validity* of the other three classes of type judgments is defined in the same manner.

Theorem 3.25 (Type soundness). *A derivable type judgment is valid, that is, $\Vdash \mathcal{J}$ implies $\models \mathcal{J}$.*

Proof. The proof is mostly straightforward by induction. In Appendix D we show some exemplary cases. The cases (NODE) and (PROG) involve the principle of fixed point induction. □

4. The Hyperstream Processing Language SPROC^{dt}

4.1 SPROC^{dt}: Syntax

Definition 4.1 (SPROC^{dt}). The syntax of SPROC^{dt} is the same as that of SPROC (Table 1), except that we have two additional constructs—$\mathtt{dt}$ and $\mathtt{fby}^{\frac{r}{\mathtt{dt}}}$—in the set $\mathbf{SExp}_\mathbb{C}$.

$$\begin{aligned} \mathbf{SExp}_\mathbb{C} \ni e \;::=\;& x \mid c \mid e_1 + e_2 \mid \cdots \text{ (The same as in Table 1)} \\ & \mid \mathtt{dt} \mid e_1 \;\mathtt{fby}^{\frac{r}{\mathtt{dt}}}\; e_2 \qquad \text{where } r \in \mathbb{R}_{\geq 0} \end{aligned}$$

In SPROC^{dt} we call the elements of $\mathbf{SExp}_\mathbb{C}$ *$\mathbb{C}$-hyperstream expressions*. The same for $\mathbf{SExp}_\mathbb{B}$, too. Intuitively, the stream expression

$$\dfrac{}{\Delta;\Gamma\vdash x:\Gamma(x)}\ (\textsc{SVar}) \qquad \dfrac{}{\Delta;\Gamma\vdash c:\prod_{v\in\mathbb{N}}\{u\in\mathbb{C}\mid u=c\}}\ (\textsc{Const})$$

$$\dfrac{\Delta;\Gamma\vdash e_i:\prod_{v\in\mathbb{N}}\{u_i\in\mathbb{C}\mid P_i\}\text{ for }i=1,2 \quad \models\forall v\in\mathbb{N}.\forall u_1,u_2,u\in\mathbb{C}.(P_1\wedge P_2\wedge u=(u_1\,\mathtt{aop}\,u_2)\Rightarrow P)}{\Delta;\Gamma\vdash e_1\,\mathtt{aop}\,e_2:\prod_{v\in\mathbb{N}}\{u\in\mathbb{C}\mid P\}}\ (\textsc{Aop})\quad (\mathtt{aop}\in\{+,\times,\hat{}\,\})$$

$$\dfrac{\Delta;\Gamma\vdash e_i:\prod_{v\in\mathbb{N}}\{u\in\mathbb{C}\mid P_i\}\text{ for }i=1,2 \quad \models\forall v\in\mathbb{N}.\forall u\in\mathbb{C}.\big((v<j\wedge P_1\Rightarrow P)\wedge(v\geq j\wedge P_2[v-j/v]\Rightarrow P)\big)}{\Delta;\Gamma\vdash e_1\,\mathtt{fby}^j\,e_2:\prod_{v\in\mathbb{N}}\{u\in\mathbb{C}\mid P\}}\ (\textsc{Fby}^j)$$

$$\dfrac{\Delta;\Gamma\vdash b:\prod_{v\in\mathbb{N}}P_b \quad \Delta;\Gamma\vdash e_i:\prod_{v\in\mathbb{N}}\{u\in\mathbb{C}\mid P_i\}\text{ for }i=1,2 \quad \models\forall v\in\mathbb{N}.\forall u\in\mathbb{C}.(P_b\wedge P_1\Rightarrow P)\wedge(P_b\wedge P_2\Rightarrow P)}{\Delta;\Gamma\vdash \mathtt{if}\ b\ \mathtt{then}\ e_1\ \mathtt{else}\ e_2:\prod_{v\in\mathbb{N}}\{u\in\mathbb{C}\mid P\}}\ (\textsc{If})$$

$$\dfrac{\Delta;\Gamma\vdash e_i:\tau_i\text{ for }i\in[1,m] \quad \Delta(f)=(\tau_1,\dots,\tau_m)\to(\tau'_1,\dots,\tau'_n)}{\Delta;\Gamma\vdash \mathtt{proj}_k\,f(e_1,\dots,e_m):\tau'_k}\ (\textsc{NdCall})$$

$$\dfrac{\Delta;\Gamma\vdash e:\prod_{v\in\mathbb{N}}\{u\in\mathbb{C}\mid P'\} \quad \models\forall v\in\mathbb{N}.\forall u\in\mathbb{C}.\,P'\Rightarrow P}{\Delta;\Gamma\vdash e:\prod_{v\in\mathbb{N}}\{u\in\mathbb{C}\mid P\}}\ (\textsc{CStConseq})$$

$$\dfrac{\Delta;\Gamma\vdash b_i:\prod_{v\in\mathbb{N}}P_i\text{ for }i=1,2}{\Delta;\Gamma\vdash b_1\wedge b_2:\prod_{v\in\mathbb{N}}(P_1\wedge P_2)\text{ for }i=1,2}\ (\textsc{And}) \qquad (\textsc{True}),\ (\textsc{False}),\ (\textsc{Neg})\text{ are similar}$$

$$\dfrac{\Delta;\Gamma\vdash e_i:\prod_{v\in\mathbb{N}}\{u_i\in\mathbb{C}\mid P_i\}\text{ for }i=1,2 \quad \models\forall v\in\mathbb{N}.\forall u_1,u_2\in\mathbb{C}.\big(P_1\wedge P_2\Rightarrow(P\Leftrightarrow u_1=u_2)\big)}{\Delta;\Gamma\vdash e_1=e_2:\prod_{v\in\mathbb{N}}P}\ (\textsc{Equal})$$

$$\dfrac{\Delta;\Gamma\vdash e:\prod_{v\in\mathbb{N}}\{u\in\mathbb{C}\mid P'\} \quad \models\forall v\in\mathbb{N}.\forall u\in\mathbb{C}.\big(P'\Rightarrow(P\Leftrightarrow\mathtt{isReal}(u))\big)}{\Delta;\Gamma\vdash \mathtt{isReal}(e):\prod_{v\in\mathbb{N}}P}\ (\textsc{IsReal})$$

$$\dfrac{\Delta;\Gamma\vdash e_i:\prod_{v\in\mathbb{N}}\{u_i\in\mathbb{C}\mid P_i\}\text{ for }i=1,2 \quad \models\forall v\in\mathbb{N}.\forall u_1,u_2\in\mathbb{C}.\big(P_1\wedge P_2\Rightarrow(P\Leftrightarrow(\mathtt{isReal}(u_1)\wedge\mathtt{isReal}(u_2)\wedge u_1<u_2))\big)}{\Delta;\Gamma\vdash e_1<e_2:\prod_{v\in\mathbb{N}}P}\ (\textsc{Less})$$

$$\dfrac{\Delta;\Gamma\vdash b:\prod_{v\in\mathbb{N}}P' \quad \models\forall v\in\mathbb{N}.\,P'\Leftrightarrow P}{\Delta;\Gamma\vdash b:\prod_{v\in\mathbb{N}}P}\ (\textsc{BStConseq})$$

$$\dfrac{\Gamma(x_i)\equiv\tau_i\text{ for }i\in[1,m] \quad \Delta;\Gamma\vdash e'_j:\Gamma(y_j)\text{ for }j\in[1,l] \quad \Delta;\Gamma\vdash e_k:\tau''_k\text{ for }k\in[1,n]}{\Delta\vdash\left[\begin{array}{l}\mathtt{node}\ f(x_1,\dots,x_m)\ \mathtt{returns}\ (e_1,\dots,e_n)\\ \mathtt{where}\ y_1=e'_1;\dots;y_l=e'_l\end{array}\right]:(\tau_1,\dots,\tau_m)\to(\tau''_1,\dots,\tau''_n)}\ (\textsc{Node})$$

$$\dfrac{\begin{array}{l}\Delta\vdash\mathsf{nd}:(\tau'_1,\dots,\tau'_m)\to(\sigma'_1,\dots,\sigma'_n)\\ \models\forall v\in\mathbb{N}.\,\forall u\in\mathbb{C}.\,P_i\Rightarrow P'_i\text{ for }i\in[1,m] \qquad \models\forall v\in\mathbb{N}.\,\forall u\in\mathbb{C}.\,Q'_j\Rightarrow Q_j\text{ for }j\in[1,n]\\ \big(\text{where }\tau_i\equiv\prod_{v\in\mathbb{N}}\{u\in\mathbb{C}\mid P_i\},\ \tau'_i\equiv\prod_{v\in\mathbb{N}}\{u\in\mathbb{C}\mid P'_i\},\ \sigma_j\equiv\prod_{v\in\mathbb{N}}\{u\in\mathbb{C}\mid Q_j\},\ \sigma'_j\equiv\prod_{v\in\mathbb{N}}\{u\in\mathbb{C}\mid Q'_j\}\big)\end{array}}{\Delta\vdash\mathsf{nd}:(\tau_1,\dots,\tau_m)\to(\sigma_1,\dots,\sigma_n)}\ (\textsc{NdConseq})$$

$$\dfrac{\Delta\vdash\mathsf{nd}_i:\Delta(f_i)\text{ for }i\in[1,m] \quad \Delta\vdash\mathsf{nd}_{\mathsf{Main}}:\nu}{\vdash[\mathsf{nd}_1,\dots,\mathsf{nd}_m;\mathsf{nd}_{\mathsf{Main}}]:\nu}\ (\textsc{Prog}) \quad (f_i\text{ is the name of the nodes }\mathsf{nd}_i)$$

Table 4. Typing rules for SPROC

dt represents the constant stream $(\mathtt{dt},\mathtt{dt},\dots)$; each dt therein is thought of as a positive infinitesimal *sampling interval*. In addition to $\mathtt{fby}^j$ for the delay by j steps, we now have $\mathtt{fby}^{\frac{r}{\mathtt{dt}}}$ for delay by infinite steps. With dt being the sampling interval, $1/\mathtt{dt}$ is the *sampling frequency*. Therefore delay by $\frac{r}{\mathtt{dt}}$ steps means delay "by r seconds."

For the semantics of $\text{SPROC}^{\mathrm{dt}}$ we use the second key idea of *sectionwise execution* (see §1). In it an $\text{SPROC}^{\mathrm{dt}}$ program is first split up into its *sections*; each section is an SPROC program and hence is interpreted in a usual manner (§3.2). The outcome of each section is bundled up and constitutes the outcome of the original $\text{SPROC}^{\mathrm{dt}}$ program. In §4.2 we formalize this idea in the NSA terms of §2.2.

Definition 4.2 (Section $e|_i$ of $\text{SPROC}^{\mathrm{dt}}$ expressions)**.** Let p be an $\text{SPROC}^{\mathrm{dt}}$ expression. For each $i\in\mathbb{N}$, its *i-th section* $p|_i$ is the SPROC expression obtained from p, by replacing 1) the stream expression dt with $\frac{1}{i+1}$; 2) the operator $\mathtt{fby}^{\frac{r}{\mathtt{dt}}}$ with $\mathtt{fby}^{\lceil r(i+1)\rceil}$.

4.2 $\text{SPROC}^{\mathrm{dt}}$: Semantics

We repeat the development of the semantics of SPROC—replacing streams with hyperstreams, via *-transform—and interpret $\text{SPROC}^{\mathrm{dt}}$. Here we rely on domain theory formulated in an NSA setting. Its details are found in Appendix B (part of which already appeared in [3]).

Definition 4.3 (Variable/node environment for $\text{SPROC}^{\mathrm{dt}}$)**.** The set of *(stream) variable environments* for $\text{SPROC}^{\mathrm{dt}}$ is the *-transform $^*\mathbf{SVarEnv}$ of $\mathbf{SVarEnv}$ for SPROC. Recall that $\mathbf{SVarEnv}=(\mathbf{SVar}\to\mathbb{C}^\infty)$; by Lem. 2.12, a variable environment for $\text{SPROC}^{\mathrm{dt}}$ is precisely an internal function $J:{}^*\mathbf{SVar}\to{}^*(\mathbb{C}^\infty)$.

Similarly, the set of *node environments* for $\text{SPROC}^{\mathrm{dt}}$ is the *-transform $^*\mathbf{NdEnv}$ of that for SPROC.

We shall first define the denotation $[\![e]\!]_{J,K}\in{}^*(\mathbb{C}^\infty)$ of a hyperstream expression $e\in\mathbf{SExp}_{\mathbb{C}}$ in $\text{SPROC}^{\mathrm{dt}}$, under $J\in{}^*\mathbf{SVarEnv}$ and $K\in{}^*\mathbf{NdEnv}$. This is done sectionwise; we proceed exploiting the NSA machinery in §2.2, finally leading to Def. 4.4.

Given $e\in\mathbf{SExp}_{\mathbb{C}}$ in $\text{SPROC}^{\mathrm{dt}}$, each section $e|_i$ (Def. 4.2) is an SPROC expression. Its denotation (Def. 3.7) yields a function

$$[\![e|_i]\!]\ :\ \mathbf{SVarEnv}\times\mathbf{NdEnv}\longrightarrow_{\mathrm{ct}}\mathbb{C}^\infty\ ;$$

its continuity is proved in Lem. A.3. We collect $[\![e|_i]\!]$ for each i; this results, using Lem. 2.13, in the following function.

$$\begin{aligned} M\big[([\![e|_i]\!])_{i\in\mathbb{N}}\big] &\in {}^*(\mathbf{SVarEnv}\times\mathbf{NdEnv}\to_{\mathrm{ct}}\mathbb{C}^\infty)\\ &\overset{\text{Lem. B.6 \& 2.10}}{=} ({}^*\mathbf{SVarEnv}\times{}^*\mathbf{NdEnv}\to_{^*\mathrm{ct}}{}^*(\mathbb{C}^\infty)) \end{aligned} \tag{22}$$

The last denotes the space of **-continuous functions* (Def. B.5), whose details can safely be skipped for the moment.

Definition 4.4 ($[\![e]\!]$, $[\![b]\!]$)**.** The *denotation* $[\![e]\!]$, of a $\mathbb{C}$-hyperstream expression $e\in\mathbf{SExp}_{\mathbb{C}}$ in $\text{SPROC}^{\mathrm{dt}}$, is defined as follows using (22).

$$\llbracket e \rrbracket := M\big[\,(\llbracket e|_i \rrbracket)_{i\in\mathbb{N}}\big] \ :\ {}^*\mathbf{SVarEnv} \times {}^*\mathbf{NdEnv} \to_{^*\mathrm{ct}} {}^*(\mathbb{C}^\infty)$$

The denotation $\llbracket b \rrbracket : {}^*\mathbf{SVarEnv} \times {}^*\mathbf{NdEnv} \to_{^*\mathrm{ct}} {}^*(\mathbb{B}^\infty)$ of $b \in \mathbf{SExp}_\mathbb{B}$ in SPROC$^\mathrm{dt}$ is defined in the same manner.

We now interpret nodes and programs in SPROC$^\mathrm{dt}$. There are two equivalent ways to do so; here we present the "sectionwise" definition that is similar to Def. 4.4. This is more convenient for the later use in §4.3; see Rem. 4.6 for the other definition.

Definition 4.5 ($\llbracket \mathsf{nd} \rrbracket$, $\llbracket \mathsf{pg} \rrbracket$)**.** Given a node nd in SPROC$^\mathrm{dt}$ of arity (m, n), its denotation $\llbracket \mathsf{nd} \rrbracket$ is defined by

$$\llbracket \mathsf{nd} \rrbracket := M\big[\,\big(\llbracket \mathsf{nd}|_i \rrbracket\big)_{i\in\mathbb{N}}\big] \ :\ {}^*\mathbf{NdEnv} \to_{^*\mathrm{ct}} \big({}^*(\mathbb{C}^\infty)^m \to_{^*\mathrm{ct}} {}^*(\mathbb{C}^\infty)^n\big)\ ,$$

where $\llbracket \mathsf{nd}|_i \rrbracket : \mathbf{NdEnv} \to_{\mathrm{ct}} ((\mathbb{C}^\infty)^m \to_{\mathrm{ct}} (\mathbb{C}^\infty)^n)$ is as defined in Def. 3.8 (its continuity is proved in Lem. A.6).

For a program pg in SPROC$^\mathrm{dt}$ of arity (m, n), its denotation $\llbracket \mathsf{pg} \rrbracket$ is defined similarly by

$$\llbracket \mathsf{pg} \rrbracket := M\big[\,\big(\llbracket \mathsf{pg}|_i \rrbracket\big)_{i\in\mathbb{N}}\big] \ :\ {}^*(\mathbb{C}^\infty)^{m_\mathsf{Main}} \to_{^*\mathrm{ct}} {}^*(\mathbb{C}^\infty)^{n_\mathsf{Main}}\ .$$

Remark 4.6. A drawback of the sectionwise definition of $\llbracket \mathsf{nd} \rrbracket$ (Def. 4.5) is that the relationship between $\llbracket \mathsf{nd} \rrbracket$ and $\llbracket e \rrbracket$ (for e occurring in nd) is not visible at all. Conceptually this is unnatural.

In fact, we can define $\llbracket \mathsf{nd} \rrbracket$ directly from $\llbracket e \rrbracket$—like we did in §3.2—by solving a "hyperdomain equation" in the hyperdomain ${}^*\mathbf{SVarEnv}$. For the latter we use the technique presented in [3]; see Appendix B, especially Lem. B.7. The two definitions indeed coincide; see Appendix C for details.

4.3 SPROC$^\mathrm{dt}$: Type System for Safety Guarantee

We introduce a type system for SPROC$^\mathrm{dt}$ as a "*-transform" of that for SPROC. It might be hard at this stage to make sense of a hyperstream s satisfying a type τ; it will be used in our main theorem (Thm. 5.12).

4.3.1 SPROC$^\mathrm{dt}$: Type Syntax

$$\begin{array}{rcl}
\mathbf{AExp} \ni a & ::= & v \mid c \mid a_1 + a_2 \mid a_1 \times a_2 \mid a_1 \wedge a_2 \mid \lceil a_1 \rceil \mid \\
& & \mathtt{dt} \mid \frac{1}{\mathtt{dt}} \quad \text{where } v \in \mathbf{Var} \text{ and } c \in \mathbb{C} \\
\mathbf{Fml} \ni P & ::= & \mathtt{true} \mid \mathtt{false} \mid P_1 \wedge P_2 \mid P_1 \vee P_2 \mid \neg P \mid \\
& & a_1 = a_2 \mid \mathtt{isReal}(a) \mid a_1 < a_2 \mid a_1 \le a_2 \mid \\
& & \forall v \in {}^*\mathbb{N}.\, P \mid \forall v \in {}^*\mathbb{C}.\, P \\
& & \quad \text{where } v \in \mathbf{Var} \text{ and } a, a_i \in \mathbf{AExp} \\
\mathbf{SType}_\mathbb{C} \ni \tau & ::= & \prod_{v \in {}^*\mathbb{N}} \{u \in {}^*\mathbb{C} \mid P\} \quad \text{where } u, v \in \mathbf{Var}, \\
& & \quad P \in \mathbf{Fml} \text{ and } \mathrm{FV}(P) \subseteq \{u, v\} \\
\mathbf{SType}_\mathbb{B} \ni \beta & ::= & \prod_{v \in {}^*\mathbb{N}} P \quad \text{where } v \in \mathbf{Var}, \\
& & \quad P \in \mathbf{Fml} \text{ and } \mathrm{FV}(P) \subseteq \{v\} \\
\mathbf{NdType}_{m,n} \ni \nu & ::= & (\tau_1, \dots, \tau_m) \to (\tau'_1, \dots, \tau'_n) \\
& & \quad \text{where } \tau_i, \tau'_i \in \mathbf{SType}_\mathbb{C}
\end{array}$$

Table 5. Type Syntax for SPROC$^\mathrm{dt}$

Definition 4.7 (Types for SPROC$^\mathrm{dt}$)**.** The syntax of the SPROC$^\mathrm{dt}$ type system is in Table 5. It is almost the same as that for SPROC (Table 3). The differences are: 1) we have $\mathtt{dt} \in \mathbf{AExp}$ that represents an infinitesimal sampling interval; 2) quantifiers in $\mathbf{Fml}$ and stream types are taken over hypernumbers ${}^*\mathbb{N}$, ${}^*\mathbb{C}$, instead of standard numbers.

We define sections of type expressions. This is like Def. 4.2.

Definition 4.8 (Section of type expressions)**.** The *i-th section* $p|_i$ of an SPROC$^\mathrm{dt}$ type expression p is obtained from p by: 1) replacing dt with $\frac{1}{i+1}$; 2) replacing $\frac{1}{\mathtt{dt}}$ with $i + 1$; 3) replacing hyperquantifiers $\forall v \in {}^*\mathbb{D}$ (where $\mathbb{D} \in \{\mathbb{N}, \mathbb{C}\}$) with standard quantifiers $\forall v \in \mathbb{D}$; and 4) replacing hyperquantifiers $v \in {}^*\mathbb{N}$ and $u \in {}^*\mathbb{C}$ in the stream types $\prod_{v\in{}^*\mathbb{N}}\{u \in {}^*\mathbb{C} \mid P\}$ and $\prod_{v\in{}^*\mathbb{N}} P$ by the corresponding standard quantifiers. A section $p|_i$ is obviously an SPROC type expression.

4.3.2 SPROC$^\mathrm{dt}$: Type Semantics

Definition 4.9 (Valuation for SPROC$^\mathrm{dt}$)**.** The set of *valuations* for SPROC$^\mathrm{dt}$ is ${}^*\mathbf{Val}$, the *-transform of the set $\mathbf{Val} = (\mathbf{Var} \to \mathbb{C}) \cup \{\bot\}$ in Def. 3.15. By 2.10, a valuation for SPROC$^\mathrm{dt}$ is either an internal function $L : {}^*\mathbf{Var} \to {}^*\mathbb{C}$, or $L = \bot$.

The function update $L[\overrightarrow{u_i} \mapsto \overrightarrow{c_i}]$, with $L \in {}^*\mathbf{Val}$, $u_i \in \mathbf{Var}$ and $c_i \in {}^*\mathbb{C} \cup \{\bot\}$, is the *-transform of the corresponding operation in SPROC (Def. 3.15). Namely, the latter induces a function (by (21))

$$\begin{aligned}
\Theta : \mathbf{Val} \times \big(\mathbf{Var} \times (\mathbb{C} \cup \{\bot\})\big)^m &\to \mathbf{Val}, \\
(L', \overrightarrow{(u', c')}) &\mapsto L'[\vec{u'} \mapsto \vec{c'}].
\end{aligned} \tag{23}$$

Its *-transform under ${}^*(\_)$ in (9) is an internal function ${}^*\Theta : {}^*\mathbf{Val} \times \big({}^*\mathbf{Var} \times ({}^*\mathbb{C} \cup \{\bot\})\big)^m \to {}^*\mathbf{Val}$. We precompose the injection $\mathbf{Var} \hookrightarrow {}^*\mathbf{Var}$ from Lem. 2.10.1, and obtain

$$\Theta' \ :\ {}^*\mathbf{Val} \times \big(\mathbf{Var} \times ({}^*\mathbb{C} \cup \{\bot\})\big)^m \longrightarrow {}^*\mathbf{Val}\ .$$

We define the function update by $L[\vec{u} \mapsto \vec{c}] := \Theta'(L, \overrightarrow{(u, c)})$.

Definition 4.10 (Semantics of $\mathbf{AExp}$, $\mathbf{Fml}$)**.** The denotation $\llbracket a \rrbracket_L \in {}^*\mathbb{C} \cup \{\bot\}$ of $a \in \mathbf{AExp}$ under a valuation $L \in {}^*\mathbf{Val}$ is defined as follows. It is $\bot$ when $L = \bot$; otherwise

$$\begin{array}{rll}
\llbracket v \rrbracket_L := & L({}^*v)\ , & \llbracket c \rrbracket_L := {}^*c\ , \\
\llbracket \mathtt{dt} \rrbracket_L := & M\big[(\tfrac{1}{i+1})_{i\in I}\big] = [(1, \tfrac{1}{2}, \tfrac{1}{3}, \dots)]\ , & \\
\llbracket a_1\ \mathtt{aop}\ a_2 \rrbracket_L := & \llbracket a_1 \rrbracket_L\ {}^*\mathtt{aop}\ \llbracket a_2 \rrbracket_L & \text{where } \mathtt{aop} \in \{+, \times, \wedge\}.
\end{array}$$

In the first line, ${}^*(\_) : \mathbf{Var} \to {}^*\mathbf{Var}$ and ${}^*(\_) : \mathbb{C} \to {}^*\mathbb{C}$ are from Lem. 2.10.1. In the second line recall that $I = \mathbb{N}$ (Rem. 2.3); thus $\llbracket \mathtt{dt} \rrbracket_L$ is in fact the infinitesimal number ω^{-1} exhibited in §2.1. In the last line, ${}^*\mathtt{aop} : ({}^*\mathbb{C})^2 \to {}^*\mathbb{C}$ is the *-transform of aop.

The *satisfaction relation* $L \models P$ between $L \in {}^*\mathbf{Val}$ and $P \in \mathbf{Fml}$ is defined in the usual manner. For example,

$$\begin{aligned}
L \models a_1 < a_2 \ &\stackrel{\text{def.}}{\iff} \\
&L = \bot \text{ or } \big(\llbracket a_1 \rrbracket_L, \llbracket a_2 \rrbracket_L \in {}^*\mathbb{R}\ \wedge\ \llbracket a_1 \rrbracket_L {}^*\!\!<_\bot \llbracket a_2 \rrbracket_L\big)\ .
\end{aligned}$$

A formula P is *valid* (written $\models P$) if $L \models P$ for any $L \in {}^*\mathbf{Val}$.

We shall characterize this semantics in a sectionwise manner, so that we can later apply Łoś' theorem (Lem. 2.13). For each $a \in \mathbf{AExp}$ in SPROC$^\mathrm{dt}$, its section $a|_i$ determines by Def. 3.16 a function $\llbracket a|_i \rrbracket : \mathbf{Val} \to \mathbb{C} \cup \{\bot\}$. Thus by Lem. 2.13 we have

$$M\big[(\llbracket a|_i \rrbracket)_{i\in I}\big] \ \in {}^*(\mathbf{Val} \to \mathbb{C} \cup \{\bot\}) \stackrel{\text{Lem. 2.10}}{\subseteq} ({}^*\mathbf{Val} \to {}^*\mathbb{C} \cup \{\bot\})\ . \tag{24}$$

Similarly, a formula $P \in \mathbf{Fml}$ for SPROC$^\mathrm{dt}$ determine

$$\begin{aligned}
M\big[(_ \models P|_i\,)_{i\in I}\big] \quad &\in {}^*(\mathbf{Val} \to \mathbb{B}) \subseteq ({}^*\mathbf{Val} \to \mathbb{B})\ , \\
M\big[(\models P|_i\,)_{i\in I}\big] \quad &\in {}^*\mathbb{B} \stackrel{\cong}{\Rightarrow} \mathbb{B}.
\end{aligned} \tag{25}$$

Lemma 4.11. *Between Def. 4.10 and (24–25), the following hold.*

$$\begin{array}{lcl}
\llbracket a \rrbracket_L & = & \big(M[(\llbracket a|_i \rrbracket)_{i\in I}]\big)(L) \\
L \models P & \iff & \big(M\big[(_ \models P|_i\,)_{i\in I}\big]\big)(L) = \mathrm{tt} \\
\models P & \iff & M\big[(\models P|_i\,)_{i\in I}\big] = \mathrm{tt}
\end{array}$$

□

The next definition is parallel to Def. 3.17.

Definition 4.12. The *satisfaction relation* $\models$ between a hyperstream

$$s \in {}^*(\mathbb{C}^\infty) \subseteq ({}^*\mathbb{N} \to {}^*\mathbb{C} \cup \{\bot\}) \quad (\text{where } \subseteq \text{ is due to Lem. B.3})$$

and a $\mathbb{C}$-hyperstream type $\tau \equiv \prod_{v\in{}^*\mathbb{N}}\{u \in {}^*\mathbb{C} \mid P\}$ is defined by:

$$\begin{aligned}
s \models \textstyle\prod_{v\in{}^*\mathbb{N}}\{u \in {}^*\mathbb{C} \mid P\} \ &\stackrel{\text{def.}}{\iff} \\
L[v \mapsto n, u \mapsto s(n)] &\models P \text{ for each } n \in {}^*\mathbb{N} \text{ and } L \in {}^*\mathbf{Val}.
\end{aligned}$$

In the setting of the previous definition, each section $\tau|_i \equiv \prod_{v\in\mathbb{N}}\{u \in \mathbb{C} \mid P|_i\}$ determines a function (by Def. 3.17)

$$(\_ \models \textstyle\prod_{v\in\mathbb{N}}\{u\in\mathbb{C}\mid P|_i\}) \;:\; \mathbb{C}^\infty \longrightarrow \mathbb{B} \;;$$

therefore by Lem. 2.13 we obtain

$$M\big[(\_ \models \textstyle\prod_{v\in\mathbb{N}}\{u\in\mathbb{C}\mid P|_i\})_{i\in I}\big] \;:\; {}^*(\mathbb{C}^\infty) \longrightarrow \mathbb{B} \;. \tag{26}$$

Lemma 4.13. *Between Def. 4.12 and (26), the following holds.*

$$s \models \tau \iff \Big(M\big[(\_ \models \textstyle\prod_{v\in\mathbb{N}}\{u\in\mathbb{C}\mid P|_i\})_{i\in I}\big]\Big)(s) = \mathtt{tt}$$

□

Similarly, for $\mathbb{B}$-hyperstream types and node types, the satisfaction relations $\models$ are defined much like in Def. 3.17. See Appendix D.6. They have the following sectionwise characterizations, too.

Lemma 4.14.

$$t \models \textstyle\prod_{v\in{}^*\mathbb{N}} P \iff \Big(M\big[(\_ \models \prod_{v\in\mathbb{N}} P|_i)_{i\in I}\big]\Big)(t) = \mathtt{tt} \;;$$
$$g \models (\vec{\tau}) \to (\vec{\tau'}) \iff \Big(M\big[(\_ \models (\overrightarrow{\tau|_i}) \to (\overrightarrow{\tau'|_i}))_{i\in I}\big]\Big)(g) = \mathtt{tt}$$ □

4.3.3 SPROC^{dt}: Type Derivation

Typing rules in SPROC^{dt} are almost the same as in SPROC. In particular the use of hypernumbers is transparent; this reflects the NSA idea that standard numbers and hypernumbers are logically the same.

Definition 4.15 (Type environment)**.** A *stream type environment* and a *node type environment* for SPROC^{dt} are defined in the same way as in SPROC (Def. 3.18): the former is a finite subset $\Gamma = \{x_i : \tau_i\} \subseteq \mathbf{Var} \times \mathbf{SType}_{\mathbb{C}}$. We denote the sets of stream and node type environments by **STEnv** and **NdTEnv**, respectively.

Definition 4.16 (Type derivation)**.** The type judgments and the typing rules for SPROC^{dt} are the same as for SPROC (Table 4), except for:

- they are $*$-transformed, that is, the quantifiers ($\prod_{v\in\mathbb{N}}\{u \in \mathbb{C} \mid \_\}$, $\forall x \in \mathbb{C}$, etc.) are replaced by the corresponding hyperquantifiers ($\prod_{v\in{}^*\mathbb{N}}\{u \in {}^*\mathbb{C} \mid \_\}$, $\forall x \in {}^*\mathbb{C}$, etc.);
- we have the following two additional rules. (FBY$^{\frac{r}{\mathrm{dt}}}$) is similar to (FBY^j); there $\lceil\frac{r}{\mathrm{dt}}\rceil$ is short for $\lceil r \times \frac{1}{\mathrm{dt}}\rceil$.

$$\frac{}{\Delta;\Gamma \vdash \mathtt{dt} : \prod_{v\in\mathbb{N}}\{u\in\mathbb{C} \mid u = \mathtt{dt}\}}\;(\mathrm{dt})$$

$$\frac{\begin{array}{c}\Delta;\Gamma\vdash e_1 : \prod_v\{u \mid P_1\} \qquad \Delta;\Gamma\vdash e_2 : \prod_v\{u \mid P_2\}\\ \models \forall v \in {}^*\mathbb{N}.\forall u \in {}^*\mathbb{C}.\big((v < \frac{r}{\mathrm{dt}} \wedge P_1 \Rightarrow P)\wedge \\ (v \geq \frac{r}{\mathrm{dt}} \wedge P_2[(v - \lceil\frac{r}{\mathrm{dt}}\rceil)/v] \Rightarrow P)\big)\end{array}}{\Delta;\Gamma\vdash e_1\; \mathtt{fby}^{\frac{r}{\mathrm{dt}}}\; e_2 : \prod_{v\in{}^*\mathbb{N}}\{u \in {}^*\mathbb{C} \mid P\}}\;(\mathrm{FBY}^{\frac{r}{\mathrm{dt}}})$$

4.3.4 SPROC^{dt}: Type Soundness

Definition 4.17. The *satisfaction relation* $J \models \Gamma$ between $J \in {}^*\mathbf{SVarEnv}$ (Def. 4.3) and $\Gamma \in \mathbf{STEnv}$ (Def. 4.15) is

$$J \models \Gamma \quad\stackrel{\text{def.}}{\iff}\quad J({}^*x_i) \models \Gamma(x_i) \text{ for each } i \in [1, m],$$

where ${}^*x_i$ is the image under ${}^*(\_) : \mathbf{Var} \to {}^*\mathbf{Var}$ (Lem. 2.10.1). The *satisfaction relation* $K \models \Delta$ between $K \in {}^*\mathbf{NdEnv}$ and $\Delta \in \mathbf{NdTEnv}$ is defined in the same way.

Definition 4.18 (Validity of type judgments)**.** We say a type judgment $\Delta;\Gamma \vdash e : \tau$ is *valid*, and write $\models \Delta;\Gamma \vdash e : \tau$, if for any $J \in {}^*\mathbf{SVarEnv}$ and $K \in {}^*\mathbf{NdEnv}$, $J \models \Gamma$ and $K \models \Delta$ imply $[\![e]\!]_{J,K} \models \tau$. The *validity* of the other three classes of type judgments is defined in the same manner.

Lemma 4.19. *Validity of a judgment is determined sectionwise:*

$$\models \Delta;\Gamma\vdash e : \tau \iff M\big[(\models \Delta|_i;\Gamma|_i \vdash e|_i : \tau|_i)_{i\in I}\big] = \mathtt{tt} \;.$$

□

Finally we come to soundness. Its proof is totally modular, exploiting the sectionwise characterizations of $\models$'s. It is notable that the content of rules does not matter, as long as they are sound for SPROC.

Theorem 4.20 (Type soundness of SPROC^{dt})**.** *A derivable type judgment is valid in* SPROC^{dt}*, that is,* $\Vdash \mathcal{J}$ *implies* $\models \mathcal{J}$. □

5. Signals as Hyperstreams

We introduce a translation between (continuous-time) signals and hyperstreams. This enables SPROC^{dt} to model signals, and its type system to provide signals' safety guarantees. Such signals cannot just be *any* function $f : \mathbb{R}_{\geq 0} \to \mathbb{C}$; we introduce a certain class of functions that makes the translation work (Def. 5.1). The class is closed under common operations like integration and differentiation, too.

The basic idea of a translation between signals and hyperstreams (§5.2) is already in [3], where they establish the correctness of their translation for functions $f : \mathbb{R}_{\geq 0} \to \mathbb{R}$ that are everywhere continuous (they also hint an extension to piecewise continuity). Since we aim at hybrid applications, our class of functions (Def. 5.1) is broader and contains some Zeno examples such as a bouncing ball.

In §5.1–5.2, for simplicity, we prove results for the $\mathbb{R}$-valued signals and streams. Extension to $\mathbb{C}$-valued ones is straightforward—we can separate real and imaginary parts and identify $\mathbb{C}$ with $\mathbb{R}^2$.

5.1 Signals

Functions that are right continuous with left limits everywhere play an important role in the theory of stochastic processes. They are called *càdlàg*; our class of (continuous enough) *signal* is based on this.

Definition 5.1 (Signal)**.** A function $f : \mathbb{R}_{\geq 0} \to \mathbb{R}$ is *of class Càdlàg*^{n} if: 1) it is right differentiable; 2) it has left limits $\lim_{t\to t_0-0} f(t)$ for each $t_0 \in \mathbb{R}_{>0}$; and 3) its right derivative f^r is of class *Càdlàg*$^{n-1}$. A function $f : \mathbb{R}_{\geq 0} \to \mathbb{R}$ is *of class Càdlàg*^{0} if it is right continuous and has left limits everywhere. A function f is *of class Càdlàg*$^\infty$ if it is of class *Càdlàg*^{n} for all $n \in \mathbb{N}$.

A function $f : \mathbb{R}_{\geq 0} \to \mathbb{R}$ is said to be a *signal* if it is of class *Càdlàg*$^\infty$ and, for any $t \in \mathbb{R}_{\geq 0}$, there is $\varepsilon > 0$ such that f is of class C^∞ in the interval $(t, t+\varepsilon)$. **Signals** denotes the set of signals.

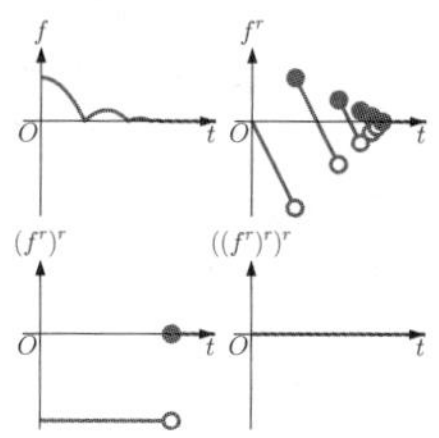

Many common hybrid dynamics are indeed signals in our sense; but not all of them. A bouncing ball—a first example of the *Zeno behavior*—is modeled as a signal (on the right). However, if we reverse time and flip horizontally, the resulting is not a signal: the halting point t_0 has no interval $(t_0, t_0+\varepsilon)$ in which the function is of class C^∞.

Another nonexample arises from the *compare-to-constant* operation in Simulink. The function

$$f(t) = \quad e^{-\frac{1}{t}} \sin\tfrac{1}{t} \quad (\text{if } t > 0)\;; \qquad 0 \quad (\text{if } t \leq 0)$$

oscillates around $t = 0$ very fast but very small (due to the factor $e^{-\frac{1}{t}}$); it is a signal. However, comparison with 0 results in a nonsignal—it is clearly not right continuous at $t = 0$.

Our notion of signal still has reasonable closure properties.

Lemma 5.2. *A signal $f \in$ **Signals** is right differentiable and Riemann integrable, resulting again in signals.* □

Remark 5.3. The notion of càdlàg function is used mostly in the context of stochastic systems. This is also the case in the hybrid system literature [8, 22]. Our use of the notion suggests it might also be related to the question of *samplability* (see e.g. [34]), though the details are yet to be worked out.

5.2 Signals as Hyperstreams

We define the *(hyperstream) sampling map* Smp and the *smoothing map* Smth, and show that they form faithful translation of signals into hyperstreams, that is roughly, $\mathsf{Smth}(\mathsf{Smp}(f)) = f$. Recall that in §5.1–5.2 we are restricting to $\mathbb{R}$-valued hyperstreams.

$$\mathbf{Signals} \xrightarrow{\mathsf{Smp}} {}^*(\mathbb{R}^\infty), \qquad \mathbf{Signals} \hookleftarrow (\mathbb{R}_{\geq 0} \to {}^*\mathbb{R} \cup \{\bot\}) \xleftarrow{\mathsf{Smth}} {}^*(\mathbb{R}^\infty)$$

Definition 5.4 (Smp). $\mathsf{Smp} : \mathbf{Signals} \to {}^*(\mathbb{R}^\infty)$ is defined by

$$\mathsf{Smp}(f) := M\Big[\Big((f(\tfrac{j}{i+1}))_{j\in\mathbb{N}}\Big)_{i\in I}\Big] .$$

This is exactly the hyperstream sampling (2) put in the NSA terms. Here $(f(\frac{j}{i+1}))_{j\in\mathbb{N}}$ is in $\mathbb{R}^\infty$, for each $i \in I = \mathbb{N}$; hence by Lem. 2.13 we have $M\big[((f(\frac{j}{i+1}))_{j\in\mathbb{N}})_{i\in I}\big]$ belong to ${}^*(\mathbb{R}^\infty)$.

The converse *smoothing* operation (3) need not yield a signal, or even a function $\mathbb{R}_{\geq 0} \to \mathbb{R}$. The stream in (3) need not converge; that is, in the NSA terms, the hyperreal $\big[\big(f(\lceil t\rceil), f(\frac{\lceil 2t\rceil}{2}), \dots\big)\big]$ can be an infinite number. This results in the extended output type $\mathbb{R}_{\geq 0} \to {}^*\mathbb{R} \cup \{\bot\}$ in the following definition of Smth.

Definition 5.5 (Smth). The mapping $\mathsf{Smth} : {}^*(\mathbb{R}^\infty) \to (\mathbb{R}_{\geq 0} \to {}^*\mathbb{R} \cup \{\bot\})$ is defined as follows. Let $h \in {}^*(\mathbb{R}^\infty)$ and $t \in \mathbb{R}_{\geq 0}$; the latter induces a function $(\lceil (i+1)t\rceil)_{i\in I}$ from $I = \mathbb{N}$ to $\mathbb{N}$. Lem. 2.13 yields $M\big[(\lceil (i+1)t\rceil)_{i\in I}\big]$ as an element of ${}^*\mathbb{N}$; this is fed to $h \in {}^*(\mathbb{R}^\infty) \subseteq ({}^*\mathbb{N} \to {}^*\mathbb{R} \cup \{\bot\})$ (Lem. B.3) and we define

$$\mathsf{Smth}(h)(t) := h\Big(M\big[(\lceil (i+1)t\rceil)_{i\in I}\big]\Big) .$$

"$\mathsf{Smth} \circ \mathsf{Smp} = \mathrm{id}$" is put precise using shadow (Def. 2.2).

Theorem 5.6. *For each $f \in \mathbf{Signals}$ and $t \in \mathbb{R}_{\geq 0}$, the hyperreal $\mathsf{Smth}(\mathsf{Smp}(f))(t)$ is limited and $\mathrm{sh}\big(\mathsf{Smth}(\mathsf{Smp}(f))(t)\big) = f(t)$.* □

5.3 Modeling Signals in SPROC^{dt}

From this point on we are back in the $\mathbb{C}$-valued setting. We rely on the definitions and results in §5.1–5.2 extended from $\mathbb{R}$ to $\mathbb{C}$.

Soundness of signal verification via SPROC^{dt} relies on the correct modeling of a signal f as an SPROC^{dt} program pg_f (cf. the usage scenario in §1). Its extensive treatment—especially the translation of ODEs and Simulink diagrams into SPROC^{dt} programs—will be presented in another venue. Here we present some basic results.

Definition 5.7 (SPROC^{dt} model). Let $f \in \mathbf{Signals}$. A hyperstream expression $e \in \mathbf{SExp}_{\mathbb{C}}$ in SPROC^{dt} is said to be a *model* of f under J, K, if $\mathrm{sh}\big(\mathsf{Smth}(\llbracket e\rrbracket_{J,K})(t)\big) = f(t)$ for all $t \in \mathbb{R}_{\geq 0}$. It is similarly defined for an SPROC^{dt} program pg to be a *model* of f.

Proposition 5.8. *Let e_1, e_2 be models of signals f_1, f_2 under J, K.*

1. *For each $c \in \mathbb{C}$, the constant symbol $c \in \mathbf{SExp}_{\mathbb{C}}$ is a model of the constant signal $\overline{c}(t) = c$.*
2. *$(e_1 \;\mathtt{aop}\; e_2)$ is a model of the signal $(f_1 \;\mathtt{aop}\; f_2)$ (computed pointwise) under J, K, for $\mathtt{aop} \in \{+, \times, \hat{}\}$.*
3. *$(e_1 \;\mathtt{fby}^{\frac{r}{\mathtt{dt}}}\; e_2)$ is a model, under J, K, of the signal $(f_1 \;\mathtt{fby}^{r\,\mathrm{sec.}}\; f_2)$. The latter is defined below; it is easily seen to be a signal.*

$$(f_1 \;\mathtt{fby}^{r\,\mathrm{sec.}}\; f_2)(t) := \begin{cases} f_1(t) & \text{if } t < r, \\ f_2(t-r) & \text{if } t \geq r. \end{cases} \qquad \square$$

As to Lem. 5.2, we also have SPROC^{dt} programs for right differentiation and Riemann integration. We leave them to another venue.

In Example 1.1 we have used an SPROC^{dt} model (6) of the sine curve, where the latter is defined using an ODE. Its (intuitively obvious) correctness can be proved by showing that $\mathsf{Smth}(\llbracket \mathsf{pg}_{\mathsf{Sine}}\rrbracket)$ is a solution of the ODE defining the sine curve.

5.4 Safety Guarantee for Signals

In translating safety guarantees from SPROC^{dt} to signals, the property $\tau \equiv \prod_v \{u \mid P\}$ cannot be just anything—after all, Smp samples only countably many $t \in \mathbb{R}$. A sufficient condition is given by τ's being *(topologically) closed*. It means that the set $\{(u, v) \mid \models P\}$ is closed in $\mathbb{C}^2$. The type syntax for signals is restricted accordingly; in particular, adding $<$, $\neg$ or $\exists$ makes topological closedness fail.

Definition 5.9 (Type Syntax for Signals).

$$\begin{array}{rcl}
\mathbf{AExp} \ni a & ::= & v \mid c \mid a_1 \;\mathtt{aop}\; a_2 \\
& & \quad\text{where } v \in \mathbf{Var}, c \in \mathbb{C}, \mathtt{aop} \in \{+, \times, \hat{}\} \\
\mathbf{Fml} \ni P & ::= & \mathtt{true} \mid \mathtt{false} \mid P_1 \vee P_2 \mid P_1 \wedge P_2 \mid a_1 = a_2 \mid \\
& & \mathtt{isReal}(a) \mid a_1 \leq a_2 \mid \forall v \in \mathbb{C}.\, P \\
& & \quad\text{where } v \in \mathbf{Var}, a, a_i \in \mathbf{AExp} \\
\mathbf{SgType} \ni \tau & ::= & \prod_{w\in\mathbb{R}_{\geq 0}} \{u \in \mathbb{C} \mid P\} \quad \text{where } u, w \in \mathbf{Var}, \\
& & \quad P \in \mathbf{Fml} \text{ and } \mathrm{FV}(P) \subseteq \{u, w\} \\
\mathbf{SgPrType}_{m,n} \ni \nu & ::= & (\tau_1, \dots, \tau_m) \to (\tau'_1, \dots, \tau'_n) \\
& & \quad\text{where } \tau_i, \tau'_i \in \mathbf{SgType}
\end{array}$$

The set $\mathbf{SgType}$ is that of *signal types*.

Definition 5.10 (Semantics of Signal Types). A *valuation* L is the same as in Def. 3.15; $L \models P$ with $P \in \mathbf{Fml}$ is defined as usual, too.

Between $f \in \mathbf{Signals}$ and $\tau \in \mathbf{SgType}$, $f \models \tau$ is defined by:

$$\begin{array}{l} f \models \prod_{w\in\mathbb{R}_{\geq 0}} \{u \in \mathbb{C} \mid P\} \overset{\text{def.}}{\iff} \\ \qquad \forall t \in \mathbb{R}_{\geq 0}.\, \forall L \in \mathbf{Val}.\; L[w \mapsto t, u \mapsto f(t)] \models P . \end{array}$$

As in Def. 3.17, L in the above is vacuous since $\mathrm{FV}(P) \subseteq \{u, w\}$.

Definition 5.11 (Translation p^{HS} of types). To each type expression p for signals (Def. 5.9), we assign an SPROC^{dt} type expression p^{HS}. It is defined by replacing: 1) the signal type $\prod_{w\in\mathbb{R}_{\geq 0}} \{u \in \mathbb{C} \mid P\}$ with the hyperstream type $\prod_{v\in{}^*\mathbb{N}} \{u \in \mathbb{C} \mid P^{\mathrm{HS}}[(v \times \mathtt{dt})/w]\}$; 2) quantifiers $\forall v \in \mathbb{C}$ with hyperquantifiers $\forall v \in {}^*\mathbb{C}$.

The idea of p^{HS} is to represent time w in P by the step number v multiplied by the sampling interval $\mathtt{dt}$.

Theorem 5.12 (Soundness). *Let $f \in \mathbf{Signals}$ be a signal, and $\tau \equiv \prod_{w\in\mathbb{R}_{\geq 0}} \{u \in \mathbb{C} \mid P\} \in \mathbf{SgType}$ be a signal type. Assume further that an SPROC^{dt} program pg is a model of f (Def. 5.7). Then:*

$$\Vdash \vdash \mathsf{pg} : () \to (\tau^{\mathrm{HS}}) \quad \Longrightarrow \quad f \models \tau . \qquad \square$$

We expect the opposite direction $\Leftarrow$ of the theorem to fail in general—the left-hand side guarantees safety also for a time t that is infinitely large. We also note that, while the signal type syntax (Def. 5.9) is more restricted than that of SPROC^{dt} (§4.3), in deriving the left-hand side of the theorem one can safely use the full SPROC^{dt} type system.

6. An Example: The Sine Curve

We verify the range of the sine curve. Specifically, we show that $\mathsf{pg}_{\mathsf{Sine}}$ in Example 1.1 satisfies, for any real constants $t_0 > 0$ and $\varepsilon > 0$,

$$\llbracket \mathsf{pg}_{\mathsf{Sine}}\rrbracket \models \prod_{w\in\mathbb{R}_{\geq 0}} \{u \in \mathbb{C} \mid t_0 \leq w \vee u \leq 1 + \varepsilon\} . \tag{27}$$

Our intuition of the formula in (27) is $w < t_0 \Rightarrow u \leq 1 + \varepsilon$; due to the restricted syntax of signal types (Def. 5.9) it is written as in (27). By Thm. 5.12, it suffices to derive the following type judgment using the typing rules of SPROC^{dt}.

$$\vdash \mathsf{pg}_{\mathsf{Sine}} : () \to (\tau_{\mathsf{goal}}) \;, \text{ where} \quad \tau_{\mathsf{goal}} :\equiv \prod_{v\in{}^*\mathbb{N}}\{u \in {}^*\mathbb{C} \mid t_0 \le v \times \mathtt{dt} \vee u \le 1+\varepsilon\} \;. \tag{28}$$

In its derivation, the most significant step (below) uses the principle of fixed point induction to deal with the intra-node recursion (s and c) in $\mathsf{pg}_{\mathsf{Sine}}$. This step is an instance of the (NODE) rule (Table 4):

$$\frac{\begin{array}{ll}(a) & \Delta_0; \{s : \tau_{s\text{-inv}}, c : \tau_{c\text{-inv}}\} \vdash 0\;\mathtt{fby}^1\;(s + c \times \mathtt{dt}) : \tau_{s\text{-inv}}\\ (b) & \Delta_0; \{s : \tau_{s\text{-inv}}, c : \tau_{c\text{-inv}}\} \vdash 1\;\mathtt{fby}^1\;(c - s \times \mathtt{dt}) : \tau_{c\text{-inv}}\\ (c) & \Delta_0; \{s : \tau_{s\text{-inv}}, c : \tau_{c\text{-inv}}\} \vdash s : \tau_{s\text{-inv}}\end{array}}{\Delta_0; \left\{\begin{array}{l}s : \tau_{s\text{-inv}}\\ c : \tau_{c\text{-inv}}\end{array}\right\} \vdash \left[\begin{array}{l}\mathtt{node\ Sine()\ returns}\ (s)\\ \mathtt{where}\ s = 0\;\mathtt{fby}^1\;(s + c \times \mathtt{dt});\\ \qquad c = 1\;\mathtt{fby}^1\;(c - s \times \mathtt{dt})\end{array}\right] : \begin{array}{l}() \to\\ (\tau_{s\text{-inv}})\end{array}} \tag{29}$$

Here the type environment $\Gamma_{\mathsf{inv}} := \{s : \tau_{s\text{-inv}}, c : \tau_{c\text{-inv}}\}$ plays the role of an invariant. The types are concretely as follows.

$$\begin{aligned}\tau_{s\text{-inv}} &\equiv \textstyle\prod_{v\in{}^*\mathbb{N}}\{u \in {}^*\mathbb{C} \mid u = \frac{1}{2}\mathrm{i}(1 - \mathrm{i}\cdot\mathtt{dt})^v - \frac{1}{2}\mathrm{i}(1 + \mathrm{i}\cdot\mathtt{dt})^v\}\\ \tau_{c\text{-inv}} &\equiv \textstyle\prod_{v\in{}^*\mathbb{N}}\{u \in {}^*\mathbb{C} \mid u = \frac{1}{2}(1 - \mathrm{i}\cdot\mathtt{dt})^v + \frac{1}{2}(1 + \mathrm{i}\cdot\mathtt{dt})^v\}\end{aligned}$$

Here i is the imaginary unit. Δ_0 in (29) is $\{\mathtt{Sine} : () \to \tau_{\mathsf{goal}}\}$.

It is straightforward to derive the assumptions (a–c) of (29). The derivation of (a) is in Appendix D.12. (b) is similar; (c) is by (SVAR).

Therefore we have derived the conclusion of (29). To it we apply the (NDCONSEQ) and (PROG) rules and derive our final goal $\vdash \mathsf{pg}_{\mathsf{Sine}} : () \to (\tau_{\mathsf{goal}})$. The former requires the side condition

$$\begin{aligned}&\models \forall v \in {}^*\mathbb{N}.\, \forall u \in {}^*\mathbb{C}.\, \big(\, u = \tfrac{1}{2}\mathrm{i}(1 - \mathrm{i}\cdot\mathtt{dt})^v - \tfrac{1}{2}\mathrm{i}(1 + \mathrm{i}\cdot\mathtt{dt})^v\\ &\qquad \Rightarrow\; (t_0 \le v \times \mathtt{dt} \vee u \le 1 + \varepsilon)\,\big) \;.\end{aligned} \tag{30}$$

Its is proved in a discrete manner, using Lem. 2.13. See Appendix D.

As is always with the Hoare-style logics, invariant discovery is the hardest part in SPROC^{dt} type derivation. In this example we discovered the invariants $\tau_{s\text{-inv}}$, $\tau_{c\text{-inv}}$ by solving the recurrence relations derived from the program. This is a totally discrete business.

7. Conclusions and Future Work

Starting from a familiar framework of a stream processing language SPROC, its Kahn-style denotational semantics and a type system as a program logic, we extended it with a constant dt and obtained a framework for hyperstreams. Translation of signals into hyperstreams enables us to use deductive verification in SPROC^{dt} for certain safety guarantees of signals. The logical infrastructure of NSA provides the framework with a rigorous mathematical basis.

Some directions of future work are mentioned in the *related work* part of §1; here we add a couple. In this paper we have made one discretization technique (namely *discrete sampling*) "hyper" and thus exact. We are interested in use of NSA in other discretization techniques such as the Fourier transform.

Type inference for SPROC^{dt} is future work. Due to its character as a program logic, the situation would be much like with Hoare-style logics: even type checking (i.e. proof search) would be undecidable; and the biggest challenge would be in invariant discovery.

Acknowledgments

Thanks are due to the participants of NII Shonan Meeting *Hybrid Systems: Theory and Practice, Seriously* for useful discussions; in particular to Manuela Luminita Bujorianu for drawing our attention to càdlàg functions. We are also grateful to the anonymous referees for their useful suggestions and critical questions; and to Samuel Mimram for letting know of their work [3] (which, to our shame, we were not aware of until the last stage of the paper's preparation).

K.S. is supported by Grant-in-Aid for Research Activity Start-up No. 24800035, JSPS, and by Hakubi Project, Kyoto Univesity; H.S. & I.H. are supported by Grants-in-Aid for Young Scientists (A) No. 24680001, JSPS, and by Aihara Innovative Mathematical Modelling Project, FIRST Program, JSPS/CSTP.

References

[1] S. Abramsky and A. Jung. Domain theory. In S. Abramsky, D. M. Gabbai, and T. S. E. Maibaum, editors, *Handbook of Logic in Computer Science*, volume 3, pages 1–168. Oxford Univ. Press, 1994.

[2] R. Alur, C. Courcoubetis, N. Halbwachs, T. A. Henzinger, P.-H. Ho, X. Nicollin, A. Olivero, J. Sifakis, and S. Yovine. The algorithmic analysis of hybrid systems. *Theor. Comp. Sci.*, 138(1):3–34, 1995.

[3] R. Beauxis and S. Mimram. A non-standard semantics for Kahn networks in continuous time. In M. Bezem, editor, *CSL*, volume 12 of *LIPIcs*, pages 35–50. Schloss Dagstuhl - Leibniz-Zentrum fuer Informatik, 2011. ISBN 978-3-939897-32-3.

[4] A. Benveniste, T. Bourke, B. Caillaud, and M. Pouzet. Divide and recycle: types and compilation for a hybrid synchronous language. In J. Vitek and B. D. Sutter, editors, *LCTES*, pages 61–70. ACM, 2011.

[5] A. Benveniste, T. Bourke, B. Caillaud, and M. Pouzet. Non-standard semantics of hybrid systems modelers. *J. Comput. Syst. Sci.*, 78(3): 877–910, 2012.

[6] S. Bliudze and D. Krob. Modelling of complex systems: Systems as dataflow machines. *Fundam. Inform.*, 91(2):251–274, 2009.

[7] O. Bouissou and A. Chapoutot. An operational semantics for Simulink's simulation engine. In R. Wilhelm, H. Falk, and W. Yi, editors, *LCTES*, pages 129–138. ACM, 2012. ISBN 978-1-4503-1212-7.

[8] M. L. Bujorianu and J. Lygeros. Theoretical foundations of stochastic hybrid systems. In *International Symposium on Mathematical Theory of Networks and Systems (MTNS 2004)*, 2004.

[9] P. Caspi, D. Pilaud, N. Halbwachs, and J. Plaice. Lustre: A declarative language for programming synchronous systems. In *POPL*, pages 214–227. ACM Press, 1987. ISBN 0-89791-215-2.

[10] A. Chapoutot and M. Martel. Abstract simulation: A static analysis of simulink models. In T. Chen, D. N. Serpanos, and W. Taha, editors, *ICESS*, pages 83–92. IEEE, 2009.

[11] A. Gamatié and L. Gonnord. Static analysis of synchronous programs in signal for efficient design of multi-clocked embedded systems. In J. Vitek and B. D. Sutter, editors, *LCTES*, pages 71–80. ACM, 2011.

[12] R. Goldblatt. *Lectures on the Hyperreals: An Introduction to Nonstandard Analysis*. Springer-Verlag, 1998.

[13] I. Hasuo and K. Suenaga. Exercises in *Nonstandard Static Analysis* of hybrid systems. In P. Madhusudan and S. A. Seshia, editors, *CAV*, volume 7358 of *Lect. Notes Comp. Sci.*, pages 462–478. Springer, 2012.

[14] A. E. Hurd and P. A. Loeb. *An Introduction to Nonstandard Real Analysis*. Academic Press, 1985.

[15] G. Kahn. The semantics of simple language for parallel programming. In *IFIP Congress*, pages 471–475, 1974.

[16] N. R. Krishnaswami and N. Benton. Ultrametric semantics of reactive programs. In *LICS*, pages 257–266. IEEE Computer Society, 2011. ISBN 978-0-7695-4412-0.

[17] E. A. Lee and H. Zheng. Operational semantics of hybrid systems. In Morari and Thiele [19], pages 25–53. ISBN 3-540-25108-1.

[18] Z. Manna and A. Pnueli. *Temporal Verification of Reactive Systems: Safety*. Springer, 1995. ISBN 978-0-387-94459-3.

[19] M. Morari and L. Thiele, editors. *Hybrid Systems: Computation and Control, 8th International Workshop, HSCC 2005, Zurich, Switzerland, March 9-11, 2005, Proceedings*, volume 3414 of *Lecture Notes in Computer Science*, 2005. Springer. ISBN 3-540-25108-1.

[20] H. Nakano. A modality for recursion. In *LICS*, pages 255–266. IEEE Computer Society, 2000. ISBN 0-7695-0725-5.

[21] A. Platzer. *Logical Analysis of Hybrid Systems—Proving Theorems for Complex Dynamics*. Springer, 2010. ISBN 978-3-642-14508-7.

[22] A. Platzer. Stochastic differential dynamic logic for stochastic hybrid programs. In N. Bjørner and V. Sofronie-Stokkermans, editors, *CADE*, volume 6803 of *Lecture Notes in Computer Science*, pages 446–460. Springer, 2011. ISBN 978-3-642-22437-9.

[23] A. Platzer. The complete proof theory of hybrid systems. In *LICS*, 2012.

[24] A. Robinson. *Non-standard analysis*. Princeton Univ. Press, 1996.

[25] E. Rodríguez-Carbonell and A. Tiwari. Generating polynomial invariants for hybrid systems. In Morari and Thiele [19], pages 590–605. ISBN 3-540-25108-1.

[26] S. Sankaranarayanan. Automatic invariant generation for hybrid systems using ideal fixed points. In K. H. Johansson and W. Yi, editors, *HSCC*, pages 221–230. ACM, 2010. ISBN 978-1-60558-955-8.

[27] S. Sankaranarayanan, H. B. Sipma, and Z. Manna. Constructing invariants for hybrid systems. *Formal Meth. in Sys. Design*, 32(1): 25–55, 2008.

[28] P. Schrammel and B. Jeannet. From hybrid data-flow languages to hybrid automata: a complete translation. In T. Dang and I. M. Mitchell, editors, *HSCC*, pages 167–176. ACM, 2012. ISBN 978-1-4503-1220-2.

[29] R. Stephens. A survey of stream processing. *Acta Inf.*, 34(7):491–541, 1997.

[30] K. Suenaga and I. Hasuo. Programming with infinitesimals: A while-language for hybrid system modeling. In L. Aceto, M. Henzinger, and J. Sgall, editors, *ICALP (2)*, volume 6756 of *Lect. Notes Comp. Sci.*, pages 392–403. Springer, 2011. ISBN 978-3-642-22011-1.

[31] K. Suenaga, H. Sekine, and I. Hasuo. Hyperstream processing systems: Nonstandard modeling of continuous signal processing. Extended version with proofs, 2013. `www-mmm.is.s.u-tokyo.ac.jp/~ichiro/papers.html`.

[32] T. Terauchi. Dependent types from counterexamples. In M. V. Hermenegildo and J. Palsberg, editors, *POPL*, pages 119–130. ACM, 2010. ISBN 978-1-60558-479-9.

[33] S. Tripakis, C. Sofronis, P. Caspi, and A. Curic. Translating discrete-time simulink to Lustre. *ACM Trans. Embedded Comput. Syst.*, 4(4): 779–818, 2005.

[34] Z. Wan and P. Hudak. Functional reactive programming from first principles. In M. S. Lam, editor, *PLDI*, pages 242–252. ACM, 2000. ISBN 1-58113-199-2.

[35] K. R. Wicks. Nonstandard analysis of ordered sets. *Order*, 12:265–293, 1995.

HALO: Haskell to Logic through Denotational Semantics

Dimitrios Vytiniotis
Simon Peyton Jones
Microsoft Research

Dan Rosén
Koen Claessen
Chalmers University

Abstract

Even well-typed programs can go wrong in modern functional languages, by encountering a pattern-match failure, or simply returning the wrong answer. An increasingly-popular response is to allow programmers to write *contracts* that express semantic properties, such as crash-freedom or some useful post-condition. We study the *static verification* of such contracts. Our main contribution is a novel translation to first-order logic of both Haskell programs, and contracts written in Haskell, all justified by denotational semantics. This translation enables us to prove that functions satisfy their contracts using an off-the-shelf first-order logic theorem prover.

Categories and Subject Descriptors D.3 [*Software*]: Applicative (functional) languages

General Terms verification, languages

Keywords static contract checking, first-order logic

1. Introduction

Haskell programmers enjoy the benefits of strong static types and purity: static types eliminate many bugs early on in the development cycle, and purity simplifies equational reasoning about programs. Despite these benefits, however, bugs may still remain in purely functional code and programs often crash if applied to the wrong arguments. For example, consider these Haskell definitions:

```
f xs = head (reverse (True : xs))
g xs = head (reverse xs)
```

Both `f` and `g` are well typed (and hence do not "go wrong" in Milner's sense), but `g` will crash when applied to the empty list, whereas `f` cannot crash regardless of its arguments. To distinguish the two we need reasoning that goes well beyond that typically embodied in a standard type system.

Many variants of *dependent type systems* (Norell 2007; Swamy et al. 2011; Xi 2007) or *refinement type systems* (Knowles and Flanagan 2010; Rondon et al. 2008) have been proposed to address this problem, each offering different degrees of expressiveness or automation. Another line of work aiming to address this challenge, studied by many researchers as well (Blume and McAllester 2006; Findler and Felleisen 2002; Knowles and Flanagan 2010; Siek and Taha 2006; Wadler and Findler 2009), allows programmers to annotate functions with *contracts*, which are forms of behavioural specifications. For instance, we might write the following contract for `reverse`:

$$\texttt{reverse} \in (xs : \texttt{CF}) \rightarrow \{ys \mid \texttt{null}\ xs\ \texttt{<=>}\ \texttt{null}\ ys\}$$

This contract annotation asserts that if `reverse` is applied to a crash-free (`CF`) argument list `xs` then the result `ys` will be empty (`null`) if and only if `xs` is empty. What is a crash-free argument? Since we are using lazy semantics, a list could contain cons-cells that yield errors when evaluated, and the `CF` precondition asserts that the input list is not one of those. Notice also that `null` and `<=>` are just ordinary Haskell functions, perhaps written by the programmer, even though they appear inside contracts.

With this property of `reverse` in hand, we might hope to prove that `f` satisfies the contract

$$\texttt{f} \in \texttt{CF} \rightarrow \texttt{CF}$$

But how do we verify that `reverse` and `f` satisfy the claimed contracts? Contracts are often tested dynamically, but our plan here is different: we want to verify contracts *statically* and *automatically*.

It should be clear that there is a good deal of logical reasoning to do, and a now-popular approach is to delegate the task to an off-the-shelf theorem prover such as Z3 (De Moura and Bjørner 2008) or Vampire (Hoder et al. 2010), or search for counterexamples with a finite model finder (Claessen and Sörensson 2003). With that in mind, we make the following new contributions:

- We give a translation of Haskell programs to first-order logic (FOL) theories. It turns out that lazy programs have a very natural translation into first-order logic (Section 3).
- We give a translation of contracts to FOL formulae, and an axiomatisation of the language semantics in FOL (Section 3.5).
- Our main contribution is to show that if we can prove the formula that arises from a contract translation for a given program, then the program does indeed satisfy this contract. Our proof uses the novel idea of employing the denotational semantics as a first-order model (Section 4).
- We show how to use this translation in practice for static contract checking with a FOL theorem prover (Section 4.5), and how to prove goals by induction (Section 5).

This work is a first step towards practical contract checking for Haskell programs, laying out the theoretical foundations for further engineering and experimentation. Nevertheless, we have already implemented a prototype for Haskell programs that uses GHC as a front-end. We have evaluated the practicality of our approach on many examples, including lazy and higher-order programs, and goals that require induction. We report this initial encouraging evaluation in Section 6.

POPL'13, January 23–25, 2013, Rome, Italy.

Programs, definitions, and expressions

$$\begin{array}{lcll}
P & ::= & d_1 \ldots d_n & \\
d & ::= & f\ \overline{a}\ \overline{(x{:}\tau)} = u & \\
u & ::= & e \mid \texttt{case}\ e\ \texttt{of}\ \overline{K\ \overline{y} \to e} & \\
e & ::= & x & \text{Variables} \\
 & \mid & f[\overline{\tau}] & \text{Function variables} \\
 & \mid & K[\overline{\tau}](\overline{e}) & \text{Data constructors} \\
 & \mid & e\ e & \text{Applications} \\
 & \mid & \texttt{BAD} & \text{Runtime error}
\end{array}$$

Syntax of closed values

$$v, w \ ::= \ K^n[\overline{\tau}](\overline{e}^n) \mid f^n[\overline{\tau}]\ \overline{e}^{m<n} \mid \texttt{BAD}$$

Contracts

$$\begin{array}{lcll}
\texttt{C} & ::= & \{x \mid e\} & \text{Base contracts} \\
 & \mid & (x : \texttt{C}_1) \to \texttt{C}_2 & \text{Arrow contracts} \\
 & \mid & \texttt{C}_1 \& \texttt{C}_2 & \text{Conjunctions} \\
 & \mid & \texttt{CF} & \text{Crash-freedom}
\end{array}$$

Types

$$\begin{array}{lcll}
\tau, \sigma & ::= & T\ \overline{\tau} & \text{Datatypes} \\
 & \mid & a \mid \tau \to \tau &
\end{array}$$

Type environments and signatures

$$\begin{array}{lcl}
\Gamma & ::= & \cdot \mid \Gamma, x \\
\Delta & ::= & \cdot \mid \Delta, a \mid \Delta, x{:}\tau \\
\Sigma & ::= & \cdot \mid \Sigma, T{:}n \mid \Sigma, f{:}\forall \overline{a}.\tau \mid \Sigma, K^n{:}\forall \overline{a}.\overline{\tau}^n \to T\ \overline{a}
\end{array}$$

Auxiliary functions

$$\begin{array}{lcl}
(\cdot)^- & = & \cdot \\
(\Delta, a)^- & = & \Delta^- \\
(\Delta, (x{:}\tau))^- & = & \Delta^-, x
\end{array}$$

Figure 1: Syntax of λ_{HALO} and its contracts

To our knowledge no one has previously presented a translation of lazy higher-order programs to first-order logic, in a provably sound way with respect to a denotational semantics. Furthermore, our approach to static contract checking is distinctly different to previous work: instead of wrapping and symbolic execution (Xu 2012; Xu et al. 2009), we harness purity and laziness to directly use the denotational semantics of programs and contracts and discharge the obligations with a FOL theorem prover, side-stepping the wrapping process. Instead of generating verification conditions by pushing pre- and post- conditions through a program, we directly ask a theorem prover to prove a contract for the FOL encoding of a program. We discuss related work in Section 8.

2. A higher-order lazy language and its contracts

To formalise the ideas behind our implementation, we define a tiny source language λ_{HALO}: a polymorphic, higher-order, call-by-name λ-calculus with algebraic datatypes, pattern matching, and recursion. Our actual implementation treats all of Haskell, by using GHC as a front end to translate Haskell into language λ_{HALO}.

2.1 Syntax of λ_{HALO}

Figure 1 presents the syntax of λ_{HALO}. A program P consists of a set of recursive function definitions $d_1 \ldots d_n$. Each definition has a left hand side that binds its type-variable and term-variable parameters; if f has n term-variable parameters we say that it has arity n, and sometimes write it f^n. The right hand side u of a definition is either a `case` expression or a `case`-free expression e. A `case`-free expression consists of variables x, function variables $f[\overline{\tau}]$ fully applied to their type arguments, applications $e_1\ e_2$, and data constructor applications $K[\overline{\tau}](\overline{e})$. The latter return values of datatypes $T\ \overline{\tau}$. As a notation, we use $\overline{x}^n$ for sequences of elements of size n. When n is omitted $\overline{x}$ has a size which is implied by the context or is not interesting.

A program *crashes* if it evaluates the special value BAD. For example, we assume that the standard Haskell function `error` simply invokes BAD, thus:

```
error :: String -> a
error s = BAD
```

Moreover, we assume that all incomplete pattern-matches are completed, with the missing case yielding BAD. For example:

```
head :: [a] -> [a]
head (x:xs) = x
head []     = BAD
```

In our context, BAD is our way to saying what it means for a program to "go wrong", and verification amounts to proving that a program cannot invoke BAD.

Our language embodies several convenient syntactic constraints: (i) λ-abstractions occur only at the top-level, (ii) `case`-expressions can only immediately follow a function definition, and (iii) constructors are fully applied. Any Haskell program can be transformed into this restricted form by lambda-lifting, `case`-lifting, and eta-expansion respectively, and our working prototype does just this. However this simpler language is notationally convenient for the translation of programs to first-order logic.

λ_{HALO} is an explicitly-typed language, and we assume the existence of a typing relation $\Sigma \vdash P$, which checks that a program conforms to the definitions in the signature Σ. A signature Σ (Figure 1) records the declared data types, data constructors and types of functions in the program P. The well-formedness of expressions is checked with a typing relation $\Sigma\,;\Delta \vdash u : \tau$, where Δ is a typing environment, also in Figure 1. We do not give the details of the typing relation since it is standard. Our technical development and analysis in the following sections assume that the program has been checked for type errors. The typing judgement should check that all pattern matches are exhaustive; as mentioned above, missing cases should return BAD.

The syntax of closed values is also given in Figure 1. Since we do not have arbitrary λ-abstractions, values can only be partial function applications $f^n[\overline{\tau}]\ \ \overline{e}^{m<n}$, data constructor applications $K[\tau](\overline{e})$, and the error term BAD.

The operational semantics of λ_{HALO} is entirely standard, and we do not give it here. We write $P \vdash u \Downarrow v$ to mean "in program P, right-hand side u evaluates to value v",

2.2 Contracts

We now turn our attention to contracts. The syntax of contracts is given in Figure 1 and includes base contracts $\{x \mid e\}$, arrow contracts $(x : \texttt{C}_1) \to \texttt{C}_2$, conjunctions $\texttt{C}_1\&\texttt{C}_2$ and crash-freedom CF. Previous work (Xu et al. 2009) includes other constructs as well, but the constructs we give here are enough to verify many programs and exhibit the interesting theoretical and practical problems.

We write $e \in C$ to mean "the expression e satisfies the contract C", and similarly for functions f. We will say what contracts mean formally in Section 4.3. However, here is their informal meaning:

$$
\begin{array}{llll}
\text{Terms} & & & \\
s, t & ::= & x & \text{Variables} \\
 & | & f(\overline{t}) & \text{Function applications} \\
 & | & K(\overline{t}) & \text{Constructor applications} \\
 & | & sel\_K_i(t) & \text{Constructor selectors} \\
 & | & f_{ptr} \mid app(t, s) & \text{Pointers and application} \\
 & | & unr \mid bad & \text{Unreachable, bad} \\
\text{Formulae} & & & \\
\varphi & ::= & \mathsf{cf}(t) & \text{Crash-freedom} \\
 & | & t_1 = t_2 & \text{Equality} \\
 & | & \varphi \wedge \varphi \mid \varphi \vee \varphi \mid \neg\varphi & \\
 & | & \forall x . \varphi \mid \exists x . \varphi & \\
\text{Abbreviations} & & & \\
app(t, \overline{s}^n) & = & (\ldots(app(t, s_1), \ldots s_n)\ldots) & \\
\varphi_1 \Rightarrow \varphi_2 & = & \neg\varphi_1 \vee \varphi_2 &
\end{array}
$$

Figure 2: Syntax of FOL

- $e \in \{x \mid e'\}$ means that e does not evaluate to a value or $e'[e/x]$ evaluates to `True` or does not evaluate to a value. Notice that e' is an arbitrary expression (in our implementation, arbitrary Haskell expressions), rather than being restricted to some well behaved meta-language. This is great for the programmer because the language and its library functions are familiar, but poses a challenge for verification because these expressions in contracts may themselves diverge or crash.
- $e \in (x : \mathtt{C}_1) \rightarrow \mathtt{C}_2$ means that whenever e' satisfies $\mathtt{C}_1$, it is the case that $(e\, e')$ satisfies $\mathtt{C}_2[e'/x]$.
- $e \in \mathtt{C}_1 \& \mathtt{C}_2$ means that e satisfies both $\mathtt{C}_1$ and $\mathtt{C}_2$.
- $e \in \mathtt{CF}$ means that e is *crash free*; that is e does not crash regardless of what context it is plugged into (see Section 3.6).

3. Translating λ_{HALO} to first-order logic

Our goal is to answer the question "does expression e satisfy contract C?". Our plan is to translate the expression and the contract into a first-order logic (FOL) term and formula respectively, and get an FOL prover to do the heavy lifting. In this section we formalise our translation, and describe how we use it to verify contracts.

3.1 The FOL language

We begin with the syntax of the FOL language, which is given in Figure 2. There are two syntactic forms, *terms* and *formulae*. Terms include saturated function applications $f(\overline{t})$, that is, fully applied to all the arguments that were declared at their definition. They also include saturated constructor applications $K(\overline{t})$, variables, and, for each data constructor K^n in the signature Σ with arity n, a set of *selector functions* $sel\_K_i(t)$ for $i \in 1 \ldots n$. The terms $app(t, s)$ and f_{ptr} concern the higher-order aspects of λ_{HALO} (namely unsaturated applications), which we discuss in Section 3.3. Finally we introduce two new syntactic constructs unr and bad. As an abbreviation we often use $app(t, \overline{s})$ for the sequence of applications to each s_i, as Figure 2 shows.

A formula φ in Figure 2 is just a FOL formula, augmented with a predicate $\mathsf{cf}(t)$ for crash-freedom, which we discuss in Section 3.6.

3.2 Translation of expressions to FOL

What exactly does it mean to translate an expression to first-order logic? We are primarily interested in reasoning about equality, so we might hope for this informal guiding principle:

$$\boxed{\mathcal{P}\llbracket P \rrbracket = \varphi} \quad \mathcal{P}\llbracket \overline{d} \rrbracket = \bigwedge \overline{\mathcal{D}\llbracket d \rrbracket}$$

$$\boxed{\mathcal{D}\llbracket d \rrbracket = \varphi}$$

$$
\begin{array}{rcl}
\mathcal{D}\llbracket f\ \overline{a}\ \overline{(x{:}\tau)} = u \rrbracket & = & \forall \overline{x} . \mathcal{U}(f(\overline{x}))\llbracket u \rrbracket \\
 & & \wedge\ \forall \overline{x} .\ f(\overline{x}) = app(f_{ptr}, \overline{x})
\end{array}
$$

$$\boxed{\mathcal{U}(s)\llbracket u \rrbracket = \varphi}$$

$$
\begin{array}{l}
\mathcal{U}(s)\llbracket e \rrbracket \ = \ (s = \mathcal{E}\llbracket e \rrbracket) \\
\mathcal{U}(s)\llbracket \mathtt{case}\ e\ \mathtt{of}\ \overline{K\ \overline{y} \rightarrow e'} \rrbracket \\
\qquad = \ (t = bad \Rightarrow s = bad) \\
\qquad \wedge\ (\forall \overline{y} . t = K_1(\overline{y}) \Rightarrow s = \mathcal{E}\llbracket e'_1 \rrbracket)\ \wedge \ldots \\
\qquad \wedge\ (t \neq bad\ \wedge t \neq K_1(\overline{sel\_K_{1i}(t)})\ \wedge\ \ldots \Rightarrow s = unr) \\
\quad \text{where}\ \ t = \mathcal{E}\llbracket e \rrbracket
\end{array}
$$

$$\boxed{\mathcal{E}\llbracket e \rrbracket = t}$$

$$
\begin{array}{rcl}
\mathcal{E}\llbracket x \rrbracket & = & x \\
\mathcal{E}\llbracket f[\overline{\tau}] \rrbracket & = & f_{ptr} \\
\mathcal{E}\llbracket K[\overline{\tau}](\overline{e}) \rrbracket & = & K(\overline{\mathcal{E}\llbracket e \rrbracket}) \\
\mathcal{E}\llbracket e_1\ e_2 \rrbracket & = & app(\mathcal{E}\llbracket e_1 \rrbracket, \mathcal{E}\llbracket e_2 \rrbracket) \\
\mathcal{E}\llbracket \mathtt{BAD} \rrbracket & = & bad
\end{array}
$$

$$\boxed{\mathcal{C}\llbracket e \in \mathtt{C} \rrbracket = \varphi}$$

$$
\begin{array}{rcl}
\mathcal{C}\llbracket e \in \{x \mid e'\} \rrbracket & = & t = unr \\
 & \vee & t'[t/x] = unr \\
 & \vee & t'[t/x] = \mathit{True} \\
 & \text{where} & t = \mathcal{E}\llbracket e \rrbracket \text{ and } t' = \mathcal{E}\llbracket e' \rrbracket \\
\mathcal{C}\llbracket e \in (x{:}\mathtt{C}_1) \rightarrow \mathtt{C}_2 \rrbracket & = & \forall x . \mathcal{C}\llbracket x \in \mathtt{C}_1 \rrbracket \Rightarrow \mathcal{C}\llbracket e\ x \in \mathtt{C}_2 \rrbracket \\
\mathcal{C}\llbracket e \in \mathtt{C}_1 \& \mathtt{C}_2 \rrbracket & = & \mathcal{C}\llbracket e \in \mathtt{C}_1 \rrbracket \wedge \mathcal{C}\llbracket e \in \mathtt{C}_2 \rrbracket \\
\mathcal{C}\llbracket e \in \mathtt{CF} \rrbracket & = & \mathsf{cf}(\mathcal{E}\llbracket e \rrbracket)
\end{array}
$$

Figure 3: Translation of programs and contracts to logic

$$\boxed{\text{Theory } \mathcal{T}}$$

Axioms for bad and unr

$$
\begin{array}{ll}
\text{AxAppBad} & \forall x . app(bad, x) = bad \\
\text{AxAppUnr} & \forall x . app(unr, x) = unr \\
\text{AxDisjBU} & bad \neq unr
\end{array}
$$

Axioms for data constructors

$$
\begin{array}{ll}
\text{AxDisjC} & \forall \overline{x}^n \overline{y}^m . K(\overline{x}) \neq J(\overline{y}) \\
 & \text{for every } (K{:}\forall \overline{a} . \overline{\tau}^n \rightarrow T\ \overline{a}) \in \Sigma \\
 & \text{and } (J{:}\forall \overline{a} . \overline{\tau}^m \rightarrow S\ \overline{a}) \in \Sigma \\
 & \text{and } K \neq J \\
\text{AxDisjCBU} & (\forall \overline{x}^n . K(\overline{x}) \neq unr\ \wedge K(\overline{x}) \neq bad) \\
 & \text{for every } (K{:}\forall \overline{a} . \overline{\tau}^n \rightarrow T\ \overline{a}) \in \Sigma \\
\text{AxInj} & \forall \overline{y}^n .\ sel\_K_i(K(\overline{y})) = y_i \\
 & \text{for every } K^n \in \Sigma \text{ and } i \in 1..n
\end{array}
$$

Axioms for crash-freedom

$$
\begin{array}{ll}
\text{AxCfC} & \forall \overline{x}^n . \mathsf{cf}(K(\overline{x})) \Leftrightarrow \bigwedge \mathsf{cf}(\overline{x}) \\
 & \text{for every } (K{:}\forall \overline{a} . \overline{\tau}^n \rightarrow T\ \overline{a}) \in \Sigma \\
\text{AxCfBU} & \mathsf{cf}(unr) \wedge \neg\mathsf{cf}(bad)
\end{array}
$$

Figure 4: Theory $\mathcal{T}$: axioms of the FOL constants

If we can prove[1] in FOL that $\mathcal{E}\{\!\{e_1\}\!\} = \mathcal{E}\{\!\{e_2\}\!\}$ then e_1 and e_2 are semantically equivalent.

where $\mathcal{E}\{\!\{e\}\!\}$ is the translation of e to a FOL term. That is, we can reason about the equality of Haskell terms by translating them into FOL, and then using a FOL theorem prover. The formal statement of this property is Corollary 4.5.

The translation of programs, definitions, and expressions to FOL is given in Figure 3. The function $\mathcal{P}\{\!\{P\}\!\}$ translates a program to a conjunction of formulae, one for each definition d, using $\mathcal{D}\{\!\{d\}\!\}$ to translate each definition. The first clause in $\mathcal{D}$s right-hand side uses $\mathcal{U}$ to translate the right hand side u, and quantifies over the $\overline{x}$. We will deal with the second clause of $\mathcal{D}$ in Section 3.3.

Ignoring `case` for now (which we discuss in Section 3.4), the formula $\mathcal{U}(f(\overline{x}))\{\!\{e\}\!\}$ simply asserts the equality $f(\overline{x}) = \mathcal{E}\{\!\{e\}\!\}$. That is, we use a new function f in the logic for each function definition in the program, and assert that any application of f is equal to (the logical translation of) f's right hand side. Notice that we erase type arguments in the translation since they do not affect the semantics. You might think that the translation $f(\overline{x}) = \mathcal{E}\{\!\{e\}\!\}$ is entirely obvious but, surprisingly, it is only correct because we are in a call-by-name setting. The same equation is problematic in a call-by-value setting – an issue we return to towards the end of Section 4.4.

Lastly $\mathcal{E}\{\!\{e\}\!\}$ deals with expressions. We will deal with functions and application shortly (Section 3.3), but the other equations for $\mathcal{E}\{\!\{e\}\!\}$ are straightforward. Notice that $\mathcal{E}\{\!\{\texttt{BAD}\}\!\} = \mathit{bad}$, and recall that `BAD` is the λ_{HALO}-term used for an inexhaustive `case` or a call to `error`. It follows from our guiding principle that for any e, if we manage to prove in FOL that $\mathcal{E}\{\!\{e\}\!\} = \mathit{bad}$, then the source program e must be semantically equivalent to `BAD`, meaning that it definitely crashes.

3.3 Translating higher-order functions

If λ_{HALO} was a first-order language, the translation of function calls would be easy:

$$\mathcal{E}\{\!\{f[\overline{\tau}]\ \overline{e}\}\!\} = f(\overline{\mathcal{E}\{\!\{e\}\!\}})$$

At first it might be surprising that we can also translate a *higher-order* language λ_{HALO} into first order logic, but in fact it is easy to do so, as Figure 3 shows. We introduce into the logic (a) a single new function *app*, and (b) a nullary constant f_{ptr} for each function f (see Figure 2). Then, the equations for $\mathcal{E}\{\!\{e\}\!\}$ translate application in λ_{HALO} to a use of *app* in FOL, and any mention of function f in λ_{HALO} to a use of f_{ptr} in the logic. For example:

$$\mathcal{E}\{\!\{\texttt{map f xs}\}\!\} = \mathit{app}(\mathit{app}(\texttt{map}_{ptr}, \texttt{f}_{ptr}), \texttt{xs})$$

assuming that `map` and `f` are top-level functions in the λ_{HALO}-program, and `xs` is a local variable. Once enough *app* applications stack up, so that $\texttt{map}_{ptr}$ is applied to two arguments, we can invoke the `map` function directly in the logic, an idea we express with the following axiom:

$$\forall xy\ .\ \mathit{app}(\mathit{app}(\texttt{map}_{ptr}, x), y) = \texttt{map}(x, y)$$

These axioms, one for each function f, are generated by the second clause of the rules for $\mathcal{D}\{\!\{d\}\!\}$ in Figure 3. (The notation $\mathit{app}(f, \overline{x})$ is defined in Figure 2.) You can think of $\texttt{map}_{ptr}$ as a "pointer to", or "name of" of, `map`. The *app* axiom for `map` translates a saturated use of `map`'s pointer into a call of `map` itself.

[1] From an appropriate axiomatisation of the semantics of programs.

3.4 Data types and `case` expressions

The second equation for $\mathcal{U}(s)\{\!\{u\}\!\}$ in Figure 3 deals with `case` expressions, by generating a conjunction of formulae, as follows:

- If the scrutinee t is *bad* (meaning that evaluating it invokes `BAD`) then the result s of the `case` expression is also *bad*. That is, `case` is strict in its scrutinee.
- If the scrutinee is an application of one of the constructors K_i mentioned in one of the `case` alternatives, then the result s is equal to the corresponding right-hand side, e_i', after quantifying the variables $\overline{y}$ bound by the `case` alternative.
- Otherwise the result is *unr*. The bit before the implication $\Rightarrow$ is just the negation of the previous preconditions; the formula $t{\neq}K_1(\mathit{sel\_K}_1(t))$ is the clumsy FOL way to say "t is not built with constructor K_1".

Why do we need the last clause? Consider the function `not`:

```
not :: Bool -> Bool
not True = False
not False = True
```

Suppose we claim that $\texttt{not} \in \texttt{CF} \rightarrow \texttt{CF}$, which is patently true. But if we lack the last clause above, the claim is *not* true in every model; for example `not` might crash when given the (ill-typed but crash-free) argument 3. The third clause above excludes this possibility by asserting that the result of `not` is the special crash-free constant *unr* if the scrutinee is ill-typed (i.e. not *bad* and not built with the constructors of the type). This is the whole reason we need *unr* in the first place. In general, if $\mathcal{E}\{\!\{e\}\!\} = \mathit{unr}$ is provable in the logic, then e is ill-typed, or divergent.

Of course, we also need to axiomatise the behaviour of data constructors and selectors, which is done in Figure 4:

- AxDisjCBU explains that a term headed by a data constructor cannot also be *bad* or *unr*.
- AxInj explains how the selectors $\mathit{sel\_K}_i$ work.
- AxDisjC tells the prover that all data constructors are pairwise disjoint. There are a quadratic number of such axioms, which presents a scaling problem. For this reason FOL provers sometimes offer a built-in notion of data constructors, so this is not a problem in practice, but we ignore this pragmatic issue here.

A small point is that AxCfBU actually implies AxDisjBU but for presentational reasons we keep both axioms.

3.5 Translation of contracts to FOL

Now that we know how to translate *programs* to first order logic, we turn our attention to translating *contracts*. We do not translate a contract *per se*; rather we translate the claim $e \in \texttt{C}$. Once we have translated $e \in \texttt{C}$ to a first-order logic formula, we can ask a prover to prove it using axioms from the translation of the program, or axioms from Figure 4. If successful, we can claim that indeed e does satisfy C. Of course that needs proof, which we address in Section 4.4.

Figure 3 presents the translation $\mathcal{C}\{\!\{e \in \texttt{C}\}\!\}$; there are four equations corresponding to the syntax of contracts in Figure 1. The last three cases are delightfully simple and direct. Conjunction of contracts turns into conjunction in the logic; a dependent function contract turns into universal quantification and implication; and the claim that e is crash-free turns into a use of the special term $\mathsf{cf}(t)$ in the logic. We discuss crash-freedom in Section 3.6.

The first equation, for predicate contracts $e \in \{x \mid e'\}$, is sightly more complicated. The first clause $t = \mathit{unr}$, together with the axioms for *unr* in Figure 4, ensures that *unr* satisfies every contract. The second and third say that the contract holds if e' diverges or is semantically equal to `True`. The choices embodied in this rule were discussed at length in earlier work (Xu et al. 2009) and we do not repeat it here.

3.6 Crash-freedom

The claim $e \in$ `CF`, pronounced "e is crash-free", means that e cannot crash *regardless of context*. So, for example `(BAD, True)` is not crash-free because it can crash if evaluated in the context `fst (BAD, True)`. Of course, the context itself should not be the source of the crash; for example `(True,False)` is crash-free even though `BAD (True,False)` will crash.

We use the FOL term $\mathsf{cf}(t)$ to assert that t is crash-free. The axioms for cf are given in Figure 4. AXCFC says that a data constructor application is crash-free if and only iff its arguments are crash-free. AXCFBU says that unr is crash-free, and that bad is not. That turns out to be all that we need.

3.7 Summary

That completes our formally-described — but so far only informally-justified — translation from a λ_{HALO} program and a set of contract claims, into first-order logic. To a first approximation, we can now hand the generated axioms from the program and our axiomatisation to an FOL theorem prover and ask it to use them to prove the translation of the contract claims.

4. Soundness through denotational semantics

Our account so far has been largely informal. How can we be sure that if the FOL prover says "Yes! This FOL formula is provable", then the corresponding λ_{HALO} program indeed satisfies the claimed contract?

To prove this claim we take a denotational approach. Most of what follows is an adaptation of well-known techniques to our setting and there are no surprises — we refer the reader to (Winskel 1993) or (Benton et al. 2009) for a short and modern exposition of the standard methodology.

4.1 Technical preliminaries

We will assume a program P, well-formed in a signature Σ, so that $\Sigma \vdash P$. Given a signature Σ we define a strict bi-functor F on complete partial orders (cpos), below:

$$
\begin{array}{rcll}
F(D^-, D^+) & = & (\ \prod_{n_1} D^+ & K_1^{n_1} \in \Sigma \\
& + & \ldots & \ldots \\
& + & \prod_{n_k} D^+ & K_k^{n_k} \in \Sigma \\
& + & (D^- \Rightarrow_c D^+) & \\
& + & \mathbf{1}_{bad} \ \ )_\bot &
\end{array}
$$

The bi-functor F is the lifting of a big sum: that sum consists of (i) products, one for each possible constructor (even across different data types), (ii) the continuous function space from D^- to D^+, and (iii) a unit cpo to denote `BAD` values. The notation $\prod_n D$ abbreviates n-ary products of cpos (the unit cpo $\mathbf{1}$ if $n = 0$). The product and sum constructions are standard, but note that we use their non-strict versions. The notation $C \Rightarrow_c D$ denotes the cpo induced by the space of continuous functions from the cpo C to the cpo D. We use the notation $\mathbf{1}_{bad}$ to denote a single-element cpo – the bad subscript is just there for readability. The notation $D_\bot$ is *lifting*.

Observe that we have dropped all type information from the source language. The elements of the products corresponding to data constructors are simply D^+ (instead of more a precise description from

$$
\begin{array}{rcl}
\multicolumn{3}{l}{[\![e]\!]_{\langle \cdot,\cdot \rangle} : (\mathit{FunVar} \Rightarrow_c D_\infty) \times (\mathit{Var} \Rightarrow_c D_\infty) \Rightarrow_c D_\infty} \\
[\![x]\!]_{\langle \sigma,\rho \rangle} & = & \rho(x) \\
[\![f\ [\overline{\tau}]]\!]_{\langle \sigma,\rho \rangle} & = & \sigma(f) \\
[\![K\ [\overline{\tau}]\ (\overline{e})]\!]_{\langle \sigma,\rho \rangle} & = & \mathsf{K}(\overline{[\![e]\!]_{\langle \sigma,\rho \rangle}}) \\
[\![e_1\ e_2]\!]_{\langle \sigma,\rho \rangle} & = & \mathsf{app}([\![e_1]\!]_{\langle \sigma,\rho \rangle}, [\![e_2]\!]_{\langle \sigma,\rho \rangle}) \\
[\![\mathtt{BAD}]\!]_{\langle \sigma,\rho \rangle} & = & \mathsf{Bad}
\end{array}
$$

$$
\begin{array}{rcl}
\multicolumn{3}{l}{[\![u]\!]_{\langle \cdot,\cdot \rangle} : (\mathit{FunVar} \Rightarrow_c D_\infty) \times (\mathit{Var} \Rightarrow_c D_\infty) \Rightarrow_c D_\infty} \\
[\![e]\!]_{\langle \sigma,\rho \rangle} & = & [\![e]\!]_{\langle \sigma,\rho \rangle} \\
[\![\mathtt{case}\ e\ \mathtt{of} \overline{K\ \overline{y} \to e_K}]\!]_{\langle \sigma,\rho \rangle} & = & [\![e_K]\!]_{\langle \sigma,\rho,\overline{y \mapsto d} \rangle} \\
& & \quad \text{if } [\![e]\!]_{\langle \sigma,\rho \rangle} = \mathsf{K}(\overline{d}) \\
& & \quad \text{and } K \text{ is a } \mathtt{case} \text{ branch} \\
& = & \mathsf{Bad} \quad \text{if } [\![e]\!]_{\langle \sigma,\rho \rangle} = \mathsf{Bad} \\
& = & \bot \quad \text{otherwise}
\end{array}
$$

$$
\begin{array}{l}
[\![P]\!] : (\mathit{FunVar} \Rightarrow_c D_\infty) \Rightarrow_c (\mathit{FunVar} \Rightarrow_c D_\infty) \\
[\![P]\!]_\sigma f \ = \ \mathsf{Fun}(\lambda d_1 . \ldots \mathsf{Fun}(\lambda d_n . [\![u]\!]_{\langle \sigma,\overline{x \mapsto d} \rangle}) \ldots) \\
\qquad\qquad \text{if } (f\ \overline{a}\ \overline{x} = u) \in P \\
\qquad = \bot \quad \text{otherwise}
\end{array}
$$

Figure 5: Denotational semantics of λ_{HALO}

type information) and the return types of data constructors are similarly ignored. This is not to say that a more type-rich denotational semantics is not possible (or desirable even) but this simple denotational semantics turns out to be sufficient for formalisation and verification.

Now we can define D_∞ as the solution to this recursive domain equation

$$D_\infty \approx F(D_\infty, D_\infty)$$

We can show that D_∞ exists using the standard *embedding-projection* pairs methodology. Moreover, we define the value domain V_∞ thus:

$$
\begin{array}{rlr}
V_\infty = & \prod_{n_1} D_\infty & K_1^{n_1} \in \Sigma \\
& + \ldots & \ldots \\
& + \prod_{n_k} D_\infty & K_k^{n_k} \in \Sigma \\
& + (D_\infty \Rightarrow_c D_\infty) & \\
& + \mathbf{1}_{bad} &
\end{array}
$$

The following continuous functions also exist:

$$
\begin{array}{rcl}
\mathsf{roll} & : & (V_\infty)_\bot \Rightarrow_c D_\infty \\
\mathsf{unroll} & : & D_\infty \Rightarrow_c (V_\infty)_\bot
\end{array}
$$

However in what follows we will always elide these functions to reduce clutter.

To denote elements of V_∞ we use the following notation.

- $\mathsf{K}(d_1, \ldots, d_n)$ denotes the injection of the n-ary product of D_∞ into the component of the sum V_∞ corresponding to the n-ary constructor K.
- $\mathsf{Fun}(d)$ is the injection of an element of $D_\infty \Rightarrow_c D_\infty$ into the function component of V_∞
- Bad is the unit injection into V_∞.

4.2 Denotational semantics of expressions and programs

Figure 5 gives the denotational interpretations of expressions e, right hand sides u, and programs P, in terms of the domain-theoretic language and combinators we have defined.

First, the denumerable set of term variable names $x_1, \ldots$ induces a discrete cpo *Var* and the denumerable set of function variable names $f_1, \ldots$ induces a discrete cpo *FunVar*. We define, *semantic term environments* to be the cpo $(Var \Rightarrow_c D_\infty)$, and *semantic function environments* to be the cpo $(FunVar \Rightarrow_c D_\infty)$.

Figure 5 defines the denotational semantics of expressions $[\![e]\!]$ as a continuous map from these two environments to D_∞. It is entirely straightforward except for application, which depends on the continuous function $\mathsf{app} : D_\infty \times D_\infty \Rightarrow_c D_\infty$, defined thus[2]:

$$\begin{array}{rcll} \mathsf{app}(d,a) & = & d_f(a) & \text{if } d = \mathsf{Fun}(d_f) \\ & = & \mathsf{Bad} & \text{if } d = \mathsf{Bad} \\ & = & \bot & \text{otherwise} \end{array}$$

That is, application applies the payload d_f if the function d comes from the appropriate component of V_∞, propagates Bad, and otherwise returns $\bot$.

The semantics of right-hand sides $[\![u]\!]$ is defined similarly. The semantics of a `case` expression is the semantics of the matching branch, if one exists. Otherwise, like application, it propagates Bad. In all other cases we return $\bot$, not Bad; all the missing cases can only be constructors of different datatypes than the datatype that K belongs to, because all `case` expressions are complete (Section 2.1). This treatment corresponds directly to our treatment of unr in Section 3.4.

Finally, Figure 5 gives the semantics of a program P, which should be read recalling its syntax in Figure 1. Since $[\![P]\!]$ is continuous, its limit exists and is an element of the cpo $FunVar \Rightarrow_c D_\infty$.

Definition 4.1. *We will refer to the limit of the $[\![P]\!]$ as $[\![P]\!]^\infty$ in what follows. Moreover, to reduce notational overhead below, for a program with no free variables we will use notation $[\![e]\!]$ to mean $[\![e]\!]_{\langle [\![P]\!]^\infty, \cdot \rangle}$, and $[\![e]\!]_\rho$ to mean $[\![e]\!]_{\langle [\![P]\!]^\infty, \rho \rangle}$*

Although we have not presented a formal operational semantics, we state the usual soundness and adequacy results:

Theorem 4.1 (Soundness and adequacy)**.** *Assume $\Sigma \vdash P$ and u with no free term variables. Then (i) if $P \vdash u \Downarrow v$ then $[\![u]\!] = [\![v]\!]$; and (ii) if $[\![e]\!] \neq \bot$, then $\exists v$ such that $P \vdash e \Downarrow v$.*

The proof of adequacy is routine domain theory so we only sketch the high-level road-map: The proof proceeds by defining a *logical relation* between semantics and syntax, via the use of a bi-functor on admissible relations between elements of D_∞ and closed expressions (Pitts 1996). Adequacy then follows from the *fundamental theorem* of this logical relation, which asserts that every expression is related to its denotation.

4.3 Denotational semantics of contracts

Now we are ready to say formally what it means for a function to satisfy a contract. We define the semantics of a contract as the set of denotations that satisfy it:

$$[\![\mathtt{C}]\!]_\rho \subseteq D_\infty$$

where `C` is a contract with free term variables in the semantic environment ρ. Figure 6 gives the definition of this function. A base contract $\{x \mid e\}$ is satisfied by $\bot$ or or by a computation that causes the predicate e to become $\bot$ or return *True*[3]. The denotation of an arrow contract, and of conjunction, are both straightforward.

The `CF` contract is a little harder. Intuitively an expression is crash-free iff it cannot crash if plugged into an arbitrary crash-free context. Of course this is a self-referential definition so how do we know it makes sense? The original paper (Xu et al. 2009) specified that an expression is crash free iff it cannot crash when plugged into a context that *syntactically* does not contain the `BAD` value. This is a reasonable definition in the operational semantics world, but here we can do better because we are working with elements of D_∞. Using techniques developed by Pitts (Pitts 1996) we can define crash-freedom denotationally as the greatest solution to the recursive equation for F^∞_{cf} in Figure 6. Technically, since the equation involves mixed-variance recursion, to show that such a fixpoint exists we have to use minimal invariance. Minimal invariance can be used with strict bi-functors to show that every element in the "negative" fixpoint of a bi-functor is contained in the "positive" fixpoint, by constructing a sequence of approximations whose limit is the identity (this *is* the minimal invariance property), and showing that every approximation of that element is contained in the positive fixpoint. Admissibility does the rest.

$$\boxed{[\![\mathtt{C}]\!]_\rho \subseteq D_\infty}$$

$$[\![x \mid e]\!]_\rho = \{d \mid d = \bot \vee [\![e]\!]_{\rho, x \mapsto d} \in \{\mathsf{True}, \bot\}\}$$

$$[\![(x{:}\mathtt{C}_1) \to \mathtt{C}_2]\!]_\rho = \{d \mid \forall d' \in [\![\mathtt{C}_1]\!]_\rho \,.\, \mathsf{app}(d,d') \in [\![\mathtt{C}_2]\!]_{\rho, x \mapsto d'}\}$$

$$[\![\mathtt{C}_1 \& \mathtt{C}_2]\!]_\rho = \{d \mid d \in [\![\mathtt{C}_1]\!]_\rho \wedge d \in [\![\mathtt{C}_2]\!]_\rho\}$$

$$[\![\mathtt{CF}]\!]_\rho = F^\infty_{\mathsf{cf}}$$

where

$$\begin{array}{rl} F^\infty_{\mathsf{cf}} = & \{\bot\} \\ & \cup \{\, \mathsf{K}(\overline{d}) \mid K^n \in \Sigma,\ d_i \in F^\infty_{\mathsf{cf}} \} \\ & \cup \{\, \mathsf{Fun}(d) \mid \forall d' \in F^\infty_{\mathsf{cf}} \,.\, d(d') \in F^\infty_{\mathsf{cf}} \} \end{array}$$

Figure 6: Denotations of contracts

Hence the definition F^∞_{cf} is well-formed; in addition the following is true and will be useful later on for induction:

Lemma 4.2. *$\bot \in F^\infty_{\mathsf{cf}}$ and F^∞_{cf} is admissible, that is, if all elements of a chain are in F^∞_{cf} then so is its limit.*

4.4 Soundness of the logic translation

We have developed a formal semantics for expressions as well as contracts, so it is time we see how we can use this semantics to show that our translation to first-order logic is sound with respect to this semantics.

Our plan is to give an interpretation (in the FOL sense of the term) to our translated FOL terms, using the carrier set D_∞ as our model. Happily this is straightforward to do:

$$\begin{array}{rcl} \mathcal{I}(f(\overline{t})) & = & \mathsf{app}([\![f]\!], \overline{\mathcal{I}(t)}) \\ \mathcal{I}(app(t_1,t_2)) & = & \mathsf{app}(\mathcal{I}(t_1), \mathcal{I}(t_2)) \\ \mathcal{I}(f_{ptr}) & = & [\![f]\!] \\ \mathcal{I}(K(\overline{t})) & = & \mathsf{K}(\overline{\mathcal{I}(t)}) \\ \mathcal{I}(sel\_K_i(t)) & = & d_i \quad \text{if } \mathcal{I}(t) = \mathsf{K}(\overline{d}) \\ & = & \bot \quad \text{otherwise} \\ \mathcal{I}(unr) & = & \bot \\ \mathcal{I}(bad) & = & \mathsf{Bad} \end{array}$$

The essential soundness theorem that states that our interpretation makes sense is the following.

Theorem 4.3 (Interpretation respects denotations)**.** *Assume that $\Sigma \vdash P$ and expression e does not contain any free variables. Then, if $\mathcal{E}\{\!\{e\}\!\} = t$ then $\mathcal{I}(t) = [\![e]\!]$. (Recall that notation $[\![e]\!]$ abbreviates the semantics of e in the program P, see Definition 4.1)*

[2] A small technical remark: we write the definition with pattern matching notation $\mathsf{app}(d,a)$ (instead of using π_1 for projecting out d and π_2 for projecting out a) but that is fine, since $\times$ is not a lifted construction.

[3] In previous work (Xu et al. 2009) the base contract also required *crash-freedom*. We changed this choice only for reasons of taste; both choices are equally straightforward technically.

The proof is an easy induction on the size of the term e.

Our soundness results are expressed with the following theorem:
Theorem 4.4. *If* $\Sigma \vdash P$ *then* $\langle D_\infty, \mathcal{I}\rangle \models \mathcal{T} \wedge \mathcal{P}\{\!\{P\}\!\}$.

As a corollary we get our "guiding principle" from the introduction.
Corollary 4.5. *Assume that* $\Sigma \vdash P$ *and* e_1 *and* e_2 *contain no free term variables. The following are true:*

- $[\![e_1]\!] = [\![e_2]\!]$ *iff* $\mathcal{I}(\mathcal{E}\{\!\{e_1\}\!\}) = \mathcal{I}(\mathcal{E}\{\!\{e_2\}\!\})$.
- *If* $\mathcal{T} \wedge \mathcal{P}\{\!\{P\}\!\} \vdash \mathcal{E}\{\!\{e_1\}\!\} = \mathcal{E}\{\!\{e_2\}\!\}$ *then* $[\![e_1]\!] = [\![e_2]\!]$.

Proof. The first part follows directly from Theorem 4.3. For the second part the left-hand side implies that $\mathcal{E}\{\!\{e_1\}\!\}$ and $\mathcal{E}\{\!\{e_2\}\!\}$ are equal in all models of $\mathcal{T} \wedge \mathcal{P}\{\!\{P\}\!\}$, in particular (using Theorem 4.4) by $\langle D_\infty, \mathcal{I}\rangle$ and by the first part the case is finished. □

Theorem 4.6. *Assume that* e *and* C *contain no free term variables. Then the FOL translation of the claim* $e \in$ C *holds in the model if and only if the denotation of* e *is in the semantics of* C. *Formally:*

$$\langle D_\infty, \mathcal{I}\rangle \models \mathcal{C}\{\!\{e \in \mathtt{C}\}\!\} \quad \Leftrightarrow \quad [\![e]\!] \in [\![\mathtt{C}]\!]$$

Completeness of axiomatisation The D_∞ domain has a complex structure and there are many more facts that hold about elements of D_∞ that are not reflected in any of our axioms in $\mathcal{T}$. For instance, here are some admissible axioms that are valid:

$$\begin{array}{l} \forall \overline{x}^n \,.\, app(f_{ptr}, \overline{x}) \neq unr \wedge app(f_{ptr}, \overline{x}) \neq bad \\ \quad \wedge\ \forall \overline{y}^k \,.\, app(f_{ptr}, \overline{x}) \neq K(\overline{y}) \\ \text{for every } (f\ \overline{a}\ \overline{x}^m = u) \in P \text{ and } K \in \Sigma \text{ with } m > n \end{array}$$

These axioms assert that partial applications cannot be equated to any constructor, ⊥ nor Bad. If the reader is worried that without a complete formalisation of all equalities of D_∞ it is impossible to prove any programs correct, we would like to reassure them that that is not the case, as we shall see in the next section.

The translation and lazy vs strict semantics We have mentioned previously (Section 3.2) that the translation that we have presented is only valid in a call-by-name setting, and here we explain why.

Whenever we use universal quantification in the logic, we really quantify over *any* denotation, including ⊥ and Bad. In a call-by-name language, given a function `f x = True`, the axiom $\forall x \,.\, f(x) = \mathsf{True}$ is true in the intended denotational model. However, in a call-by-value setting, x is allowed to be interpreted as ⊥. That means that the unguarded axiom is actually not true, because $f\ \bot \neq \mathsf{True}$. Instead we need the following variation:

$$\forall x \,.\, x \neq bad \wedge x \neq unr \Rightarrow f(x) = t$$

Moreover, the axioms for the $app(\cdot, \cdot)$ combinator have to be modified to perform checks that the argument is not ⊥ or Bad before actually calling a function. In a call-by-name language these guards are needed only for `case` and the function part of app.

4.5 Contract checking as satisfiability

Having established the soundness of our translation, it is time we see in this section how we can use this sound translation to verify a program. The following theorem is then true:
Theorem 4.7 (Soundness). *Assume that* e *and* C *contain only function symbols from* P *and no free term variables. Let* $\mathcal{T}_{all} = \mathcal{T} \wedge \mathcal{P}\{\!\{P\}\!\}$. *If* $\mathcal{T}_{all} \wedge \neg\mathcal{C}\{\!\{e \in \mathtt{C}\}\!\}$ *is unsatisfiable then* $\langle D_\infty, \mathcal{I}\rangle \models \mathcal{C}\{\!\{e \in \mathtt{C}\}\!\}$ *and consequently* $[\![e]\!] \in [\![\mathtt{C}]\!]$.

Proof. If there is no model for this formula then its negation must be valid (true in all models), that is $\neg\mathcal{T}_{all} \vee \mathcal{C}\{\!\{e \in \mathtt{C}\}\!\}$ is valid. By completeness of first-order logic $\mathcal{T}_{all} \vdash \mathcal{C}\{\!\{e \in \mathtt{C}\}\!\}$. This means that all models of $\mathcal{T}_{all}$ validate $\mathcal{C}\{\!\{f \in \mathtt{C}\}\!\}$. In particular, for the denotational model we have that $\langle D_\infty, \mathcal{I}\rangle \models \mathcal{T}_{all}$ and hence $\langle D_\infty, \mathcal{I}\rangle \models \mathcal{C}\{\!\{e \in \mathtt{C}\}\!\}$. Theorem 4.6 finishes the proof. □

Hence, to verify a program e satisfies a contract C we need to do the following:

- Generate formulae for the theory $\mathcal{T} \wedge \mathcal{P}\{\!\{P\}\!\}$
- Generate the negation of a contract translation: $\neg\mathcal{C}\{\!\{e \in \mathtt{C}\}\!\}$
- Ask a FOL theorem prover for a model for the conjunction of the above formulae

Incremental verification Theorem 4.7 gives us a way to check that an expression satisfies a contract. Assume that we are given a program P with a function $f \in dom(P)$, for which we have already shown that $\langle D_\infty, \mathcal{I}\rangle \models \mathcal{C}\{\!\{f \in \mathtt{C}_f\}\!\}$. Suppose next that we are presented with a "next" goal, to prove that $\langle D_\infty, \mathcal{I}\rangle \models \mathcal{C}\{\!\{h \in \mathtt{C}_h\}\!\}$. We may consider the following variations of how to do this:

- Ask for the unsatisfiability of:
  $$\mathcal{T} \wedge \mathcal{P}\{\!\{P\}\!\} \wedge \neg\mathcal{C}\{\!\{h \in \mathtt{C}_h\}\!\}$$
  The soundness of this query follows from Theorem 4.7 above.
- Ask for the unsatisfiability of:
  $$\mathcal{T} \wedge \mathcal{P}\{\!\{P\}\!\} \wedge \mathcal{C}\{\!\{f \in \mathtt{C}_f\}\!\} \wedge \neg\mathcal{C}\{\!\{h \in \mathtt{C}_h\}\!\}$$
  This query adds the *already proven* contract for f to the theory. If this formula is unsatisfiable, then its negation is valid, and we know that the denotational model is a model of the theory *and* of $\mathcal{C}\{\!\{f \in \mathtt{C}_f\}\!\}$ and hence it must also be a model of $\mathcal{C}\{\!\{h \in \mathtt{C}_h\}\!\}$.
- Ask for the unsatisfiability of:
  $$\mathcal{T} \wedge \mathcal{P}\{\!\{P \setminus f\}\!\} \wedge \mathcal{C}\{\!\{f \in \mathtt{C}_f\}\!\} \wedge \neg\mathcal{C}\{\!\{h \in \mathtt{C}_h\}\!\}$$
  This query removes the axioms associated with the *definition* of f, leaving only its *contract* available. This makes the proof of h's contract insensitive to changes in f's implementation. Via a similar reasoning as before, such an invocation is sound as well.

Incremental verification essentially implies that our approach does not require a whole-program analysis: once a contract is proved about a function, it can be assumed, even if the definition of the function is not exported, and subsequently used to prove contracts of other functions that may call it. Exporting only the contract but not a definition of a function can be beneficial for efficiency reasons when verifying further goals; the drawback is that the exported contracts might not be precise enough for proving these further goals. Our framework supports any of those strategies.

5. Induction

An important practical extension is the ability to prove contracts about recursive functions using induction. For instance, we might want to prove that `length` satisfies `CF` → `CF`.

```
length []     = Z
length (x:xs) = S (length xs)
```

In the second case we need to show that the result of `length xs` is crash-free but we do not have this information so the proof gets stuck, often resulting in the FOL-solver looping.

A naive approach would be to perform induction over the list argument of `length` – however in Haskell datatypes may be lazy infinite streams and ordinary induction is not a valid proof principle. Fortunately, we can still appeal to *fixpoint induction*. The fixpoint induction scheme that we use for `length` above would be to *assume* that the contract holds for the occurence of some function `length_rec` inside the body of its definition, and then try to prove it for the function:

```
length []     = Z
length (x:xs) = S (length_rec xs)
```

Formally, our induction scheme is:

Definition 5.1 (Induction scheme)**.** *To prove that* $[\![g]\!] \in [\![\mathtt{C}]\!]$ *for a function* $g\ \overline{a}\ \overline{x{:}\tau} = e[g]$ *(meaning* e *contains some occurrences of* g*), we perform the following steps:*

- *Generate function symbols* g°, $g^{\bullet}$
- *Generate the theory formula*

$$\varphi = \mathcal{T} \wedge \mathcal{P}\{\!\{P \cup g^{\bullet}\ \overline{a}\ \overline{x{:}\tau} = e[g^{\circ}]\}\!\}$$

- *Prove that the query* $\varphi \wedge \mathcal{C}\{\!\{g^{\circ} \in \mathtt{C}\}\!\} \wedge \neg\mathcal{C}\{\!\{g^{\bullet} \in \mathtt{C}\}\!\}$ *is unsatisfiable.*

Why is this approach sound? The crucial step here is the fact that contracts are admissible predicates.

Theorem 5.1 (Contract admissibility)**.** *If* $d_i \in [\![\mathtt{C}]\!]$ *for all elements of a chain* $d_1 \sqsubseteq d_2 \sqsubseteq \ldots$ *then the limit of the chain* $\sqcup d_i \in [\![\mathtt{C}]\!]$*. Moreover,* $\bot \in [\![\mathtt{C}]\!]$*.*

Proof. By induction on the contract C; for the CF case we get the result from Lemma 4.2. For the predicate case we get the result from the fact that the denotations of programs are continuous in D_∞. The arrow case follows by induction. □

We can then prove the soundness of our induction scheme.

Theorem 5.2. *The induction scheme in Definition 5.1 is correct.*

Proof. We need to show that: $[\![P]\!]^{\infty}(g) \in [\![\mathtt{C}]\!]$ and hence, by admissibility it is enough to find a chain whose limit is $[\![P]\!]^{\infty}(g)$ and such that every element is in $[\![\mathtt{C}]\!]$. Let us consider the chain $[\![P]\!]^{k}(g)$ so that $[\![P]\!]^{0}(g) = \bot$ and $[\![P]\!]^{k+1}(g) = [\![P]\!]_{([\![P]\!]^{k})}(g)$ whose limit is $[\![P]\!]^{\infty}(g)$. We know that $\bot \in [\![\mathtt{C}]\!]$ so, by using contract admissiblity, all we need to show is that if $[\![P]\!]^{k}(g) \in [\![\mathtt{C}]\!]$ then $[\![P]\!]^{k+1}(g) \in [\![\mathtt{C}]\!]$.

To show this, we can assume a model where the denotational interpretation $\mathcal{I}$ has been extended so that $\mathcal{I}(g^{\circ}) = [\![P]\!]^{k}(g)$ and $\mathcal{I}(g^{\bullet}) = [\![P]\!]^{k+1}(g)$. By proving that the formula

$$\varphi \wedge \mathcal{C}\{\!\{g^{\circ} \in \mathtt{C}\}\!\} \wedge \neg\mathcal{C}\{\!\{g^{\bullet} \in \mathtt{C}\}\!\}$$

is unsatisfiable, since $\langle D_\infty, \mathcal{I}\rangle \models \varphi$ and $\langle D_\infty, \mathcal{I}\rangle \models \mathcal{C}\{\!\{g^{\circ} \in \mathtt{C}\}\!\}$, we get $\langle D_\infty, \mathcal{I}\rangle \models \mathcal{C}\{\!\{g^{\bullet} \in \mathtt{C}\}\!\}$, and hence $[\![P]\!]^{k+1}(g) \in [\![\mathtt{C}]\!]$. □

Note that contract admissibility is *absolutely essential* for the soundness of our induction scheme, and is not a property that holds of every predicate on denotations. For example, consider the following Haskell definition:

```
ones = 1 : ones
f (S x) = 1 : f x
f Z     = [0]
```

Let us try to check if the $\forall x.\mathtt{f}(x) \neq \mathtt{ones}$ is true in the denotational model, using fixpoint induction. Importanttly, by $\neq$ here we really mean the negation of logical equality – *not* a Haskell function that computes a Bool. The case for $\bot$ holds, and so does the case for the Z constructor. For the S x case, we can assume that $\mathtt{f}(x) \neq \mathtt{ones}$ and we can easily prove that this implies that $\mathtt{f}(\mathtt{S}\ x) \neq \mathtt{ones}$. Nevertheless, the property is *not true* – just pick a counterexample $[\![\mathtt{s}]\!]$ where s = S s. What happened here is that the property is denotationally true of all the elements of the following chain

$$\bot \sqsubseteq \mathsf{S}(\bot) \sqsubseteq \mathsf{S}(\mathsf{S}(\bot)) \sqsubseteq \ldots$$

but is false in the limit of this chain. In other words $\neq$ is not admissible and our induction scheme is plain nonsense for non-admissible predicates.

Finally, we have observed that for many practical cases, a straightforward generalization of our lemma above for mutually recursive definitions is required. Indeed, our tool performs mutual fixpoint induction when a recursive group of functions is encountered. We leave it as future work to develop more advanced techniques such as strengthening of induction hypotheses or identifying more sophisticated induction schemes.

6. Implementation and practical experience

Our prototype contract checker is called halo. It uses GHC to parse, typecheck, and desugar a Haskell program, translates it into first order logic (exactly as in Section 3), and invokes a FOL theorem prover (Equinox, Z3, Vampire, etc) on the FOL formula. The desugared Haskell program is expressed in GHC's intermediate language called Core (Sulzmann et al. 2007), an explicitly-typed variant of System F. It is straightforward to translate Core into our language λ_{HALO}.

6.1 Expressing contracts in Haskell

How does the user express contracts? We write contracts in Haskell itself, using higher-order abstract syntax and a GADT, in a manner reminiscent of the work on *typed contracts* for functional programming (Hinze et al. 2006):

```
data Contract t where
  (:->) :: Contract a
        -> (a -> Contract b)
        -> Contract (a -> b)
  Pred  :: (a -> Bool) -> Contract a
  CF    :: Contract a
  (:&:) :: Contract a -> Contract a -> Contract a
```

A value of type Contract t is a a contract for a function of type t. The connectives are :-> for dependent contract function space, CF for crash-freedom, Pred for predication, and :&: for conjunction. One advantage of writing contracts as Haskell terms is that we can use Haskell itself to build new contract combinators. For example, a useful derived connective is non-dependent function space:

```
(-->) :: Contract a -> Contract b -> Contract (a -> b)
c1 --> c2 = c1 :-> (\_ -> c2)
```

A contract is always associated with a function, so we pair the two in a Statement:

```
data Statement where
    (:::) :: a -> Contract a -> Statement
```

In our previous mathematical notation we might write the following contract for head:

$$\mathtt{head} \in \mathtt{CF}\ \&\ \{\mathtt{xs} \mid \mathtt{not}\ (\mathtt{null}\ \mathtt{xs})\} \to \mathtt{CF}$$

Here is how we express the contract as a Haskell definition:

```
c_head :: Statement
c_head = head ::: CF :&: Pred (not . null) --> CF
```

If we put this definition in a file Head.hs, together with the supporting definitions of head, not, and null, then we can run halo Head.hs. The halo program translates the contract and the supporting function definitions into FOL, generates a TPTP [4] file, and invokes a theorem prover. And indeed c_head is verified by all theorem provers we tried.

For recursive functions halo uses fixpoint induction, as described in Section 5.

[4] A widely supported format for FOL (Sutcliffe 2009).

6.2 Practical considerations

To make the theorem prover work as fast as possible we trim the theories to include only what is needed to prove a property. Unnecessary function pointers, data types and definitions for the current goal are not generated.

When proving a series of contracts, it is natural to do so in dependency order. For example:

```
reverse :: [a] -> [a]
reverse [] = []
reverse (x:xs) = reverse xs ++ [x]

reverse_cf :: Statement
reverse_cf = reverse ::: CF --> CF
```

To prove this contract we must first prove that (++) $\in$ CF $\to$ CF $\to$ CF; then we can prove `reverse`'s contract assuming the one for `(++)`. At the moment, `halo` asks the programmer to specify which auxiliary contracts are useful, via a second constructor in the `Statement` type:

```
reverse_cf = reverse ::: CF --> CF
                  'Using' append_cf
```

6.3 Dependent contracts

`halo` can prove dependent contracts. For example:

$$\texttt{filter} \in (\texttt{p} : \texttt{CF} \to \texttt{CF}) \to \texttt{CF} \to \texttt{CF} \ \& \ \{\texttt{ys} \mid \texttt{all p ys}\}$$

This contract says that under suitable assumptions of crash-freedom, the result of `filter` is both crash-free and satisfies `all p`. Here `all` is a standard Haskell function, and `p` is the functional argument itself.

In our source-file syntax we use `(:->)` to bind `p`.

```
filter_all :: Statement
filter_all =
  filter ::: (CF --> CF) :-> \p ->
             CF --> (CF :&: Pred (all p))
```

The contract looks slightly confusing since it uses two "arrows", one from `:->`, and one from the `->` in the lambda. This contract is proved by applying fixed point induction.

6.4 Higher order functions

Our tool also deals with (very) higher order functions. Consider this function `withMany`, from library `Foreign.Util.Marshal`:

```
withMany :: (a -> (b -> res) -> res)
         -> [a] -> ([b] -> res) -> res
withMany _       []     f = f []
withMany withFoo (x:xs) f = withFoo x (\x' ->
      withMany withFoo xs (\xs' -> f (x':xs')))
```

For `withMany`, our tool proves

$$\texttt{withMany} \in \ (\texttt{CF} \to (\texttt{CF} \to \texttt{CF}) \to \texttt{CF}) \to (\texttt{CF} \to (\texttt{CF} \to \texttt{CF}) \to \texttt{CF})$$

6.5 Experimental Results

We have run `halo` on a collection of mostly-small tests, some of which can be viewed in Figure 7. Our full testsuite and tables can be downloaded from `http://www.cse.chalmers.se/~koen/halo`. The test cases include:

Description	*equinox*	*Z3*	*Vampire*	*E*	*Axioms*
`ack` CF	-	0.04	0.03	-	40
`all` CF	-	0.00	3.36	0.04	39
`(++)` CF	-	0.03	3.30	0.38	31
`concatMap` CF	-	0.03	6.60	-	40
`length` CF	0.87	0.00	0.80	0.01	30
`(+)` CF	44.33	0.00	3.32	0.10	30
`(*)` CF	6.44	0.03	3.36	-	36
`factorial` CF	6.69	0.02	4.18	31.04	40
`exp` CF	-	0.03	3.36	-	41
`(*)` accumulator CF	-	0.03	3.32	-	37
`exp` accumulator CF	-	0.04	4.20	0.12	42
`factorial` accum. CF	-	0.03	3.32	-	41
`reverse` CF	13.40	0.03	28.77	-	36
`(++)`/any morphism	-	0.03	-	-	58
`filter` satisfies `all`	-	0.03	-	-	47
`iterate` CF	5.54	0.00	0.00	0.00	30
`repeat` CF	0.06	0.00	0.00	0.01	26
`foldr1`	-	0.01	1.04	24.78	50
`head`	18.62	0.00	0.00	0.01	42
`fromJust`	0.05	0.00	0.00	0.00	36
`risersBy`	-	-	1.53	-	58
`shrink`	-	0.04	-	-	79
`withMany` CF	-	0.00	-	-	39

Figure 7: Theorem prover running time in seconds on some of the problems in the test suite on contracts that hold, together with the number of axioms the generated TPTP files comprises.

- Crash-freedom of standard library functions, such as `(++)`, `iterate`, and `concatMap`.
- Crash-freedom of functions with more complex recursive patterns (Ackermann's function, functions with accumulators).
- Partial functions given appropriate preconditions (`foldr1`, `head`, `fromJust`).
- The `risers` example from Catch (Mitchell and Runciman 2008).
- Some non-trivial post-conditions, such as the example above with `filter` and `all`, and also `any p xs || any p ys` = `any p (xs ++ ys)`.

We tried four theorem provers, Equinox, Z3, Vampire and E, and gave them 60 seconds for each problem. For our problems, Z3 seems to be the most successful. To give an idea of the sizes of the FOL problems, we additionally include the number of FOL axioms that are associated with each verification task in Figure 7. This number ranges between 26-79 but does not appear to be directly associated to the running time.

7. Discussion

Contracts that do not hold In practice, programmers will often propose contracts that do not hold. For example, consider the following definitions:

```
length []     = Z
length (x:xs) = S (length xs)

isZero Z = True
isZero _ = False
```

Suppose that we would like to check the (false) contract:

$$\texttt{length} \in \texttt{CF} \to \{x \mid \texttt{isZero}\ x\}$$

A satisfiability-based checker will diverge trying to construct a counter model for the negation of the above query; we have confirmed that this is indeed the behaviour of several tools (Z3, Equinox, E). Why? When a counter-model exists, it will include tables for the function symbols in the formula. Recall that functions in FOL are total over the domain of the terms in the model. This means that function tables may be *infinite* if the terms in the model are infinite. Several (very useful!) axioms, such as discrimination (AXDISJC), may in fact force the models to be infinite.

In our example, the table for `length` is indeed infinite since `[]` is always disjoint from `Cons x xs` for any `x` and `xs`. Even if there is a finitely-representable infinite model, the theorem prover may search forever in the "wrong corner" of the model.

From a practical point of view this is unfortunate; it is not acceptable for the checker to loop when the programmer writes an erroneous contract. Tantalisingly, there exists a very simple counterexample, e.g. `[Z]`, and that single small example is all the programmer needs to see the falsity of the contract.

Addressing this problem is a challenging (but essential) direction for future work, and we are currently working on a modification of our theory that admits the denotational model, but also permits *finite models* corresponding to counterexample traces. If the theory can guarantee the existence of a finite model in case of a counterexample, a finite model finder such as Paradox (Claessen and Sörensson 2003) will find it.

A tighter correspondence to operational semantics? Earlier work gave a declarative specfication of contracts using *operational semantics* (Xu et al. 2009). In this paper we have instead used a *denotational semantics* for contracts (Figure 6). It is natural to ask whether or not the two semantics are identical.

From computational adequacy, Theorem 4.1 we can easily state the following theorem:

Corollary 7.1. *Assume that* e *and* $\texttt{C}$ *contain no term variables and assume that* $\mathcal{C}\{\!\{e \in \{x \mid e_p\}\}\!\} = \varphi$. *It is the case that* $\langle D_\infty, \mathcal{I}\rangle \models \varphi$ *if and only iff either* $P \not\vdash e \Downarrow$ *or* $P \not\vdash e_p[e/x] \Downarrow$ *or* $P \vdash e_p[e/x] \Downarrow True$.

Hence, the operational and denotational semantics of *predicate contracts* coincide. However, the correspondence is not precise for *dependent function contracts*. Recall the operational definition of contract satisfaction for a function contract:

$$e \in (x{:}\texttt{C}_1) \to \texttt{C}_2 \text{ iff}$$
$$\text{for all } e' \text{ such that } (e' \in \texttt{C}_1) \text{ it is } e\ e' \in \texttt{C}_2[e'/x]$$

The denotational specification (Figure 6) says that for all denotations d' such that $d' \in [\![\texttt{C}_1]\!]$, it is the case that $\mathsf{app}([\![e]\!], d') \in [\![\texttt{C}_2]\!]_{x \mapsto d'}$.

Alas there are *more* denotations than images of terms in D_∞, and we can easily show that the correspondence breaks, exploiting the infamous *parallel-or* function as a test. We omit the details due to lack of space.

This is not a serious problem in practice. After all the two definitions mostly coincide, and they precisely coincide in the base case. At the end of the day, we are interested in whether `main` $\in$ `CF`, and we have proven that if is crash-free denotationally, it is definitely crash-free in any operationally-reasonable term.

Finally, is it possible to define an operational model for our FOL theory that interpreted equality as contextual equivalence? Probably this could be made to work, although we believe that the formal clutter from syntactic manipulation of terms could be worse than the current denotational approach.

Polymorphic crash-freedom Observe that our axiomatisation of crash-freedom in Figure 4 includes only axioms for data constructors. In fact, our denotational interpretation F^∞_{cf} allows more axioms, such as:

$$\forall xy\,.\,\mathsf{cf}(x) \land \mathsf{cf}(y) \Rightarrow \mathsf{cf}(app(x,y))$$

This axiom is useful if we wish to give directly a `CF` contract to a value of arrow type. For instance, instead of specifying that `map` satisfies the contract (`CF` $\to$ `CF`) $\to$ `CF` $\to$ `CF` one may want to say that it satisfies the contract `CF` $\to$ `CF` $\to$ `CF`. With the latter contract we need the previous axiom to be able to apply the function argument of `map` to a crash-free value and get a crash-free result.

In some situations, the following axiom might be beneficial as well:

$$(\forall \overline{x}\,.\,\mathsf{cf}(f(\overline{x}))) \Rightarrow \mathsf{cf}(f_{ptr})$$

If the result of applying a function to any possible argument is crash-free then so is the function pointer. This allows us to go in the inverse direction as before, and pass a function pointer to a function that expects a `CF` argument. However notice that this last axiom introduces a quantified assumption, which might lead to significant efficiency problems.

Ideally we would like to say that $[\![\texttt{CF}]\!] = [\![\texttt{CF} \to \texttt{CF}]\!]$, but that is not quite true. In particular,

$$(\forall x\,.\,\mathsf{cf}(app(y,x))) \Rightarrow \mathsf{cf}(y)$$

is *not* valid in the denotational model. For instance consider the value $\mathsf{K}(\mathsf{Bad})$ for y. The left-hand side is going to always be true, because the application is ill-typed and will yield $\bot$, but y is not itself crash-free.

8. Related work

There are very few practical tools for the automatic verification of arbitrary *lazy and higher-order* functional programs, though the automated verification of higher-order programs, at least for restricted strongly-normalizing languages, has been studied before, for instance by the ACL2 community. Furthermore, our approach of directly translating the denotational semantics of programs does not appear to be well-explored in the literature.

Catch (Mitchell and Runciman 2008) is one of the very few tools that address the verification of lazy Haskell, and have been evaluated on real programs. Using static analysis, Catch can detect pattern match failures, and hence prove that a program cannot crash. Some annotations may be necessary for the analysis to succeed. Our aim in this paper is to achieve similar goals, and moreover to be in a position to assert functional correctness.

Liquid Types (Rondon et al. 2008) is an influential approach to call-by-value functional program verification. Contracts are written as refinements in a fixed language of predicates (which may include recursive predicates) and the extracted conditions are discharged using an SMT-solver. Because the language of predicates is fixed, predicate abstraction can very effectively *infer* precise refinements, even for recursive functions, and hence the annotation burden is very low. In our case, since the language of predicates is, *by design*, the very same programming language with the same semantics, inference of function specifications is harder. The other important difference is that liquid types requires all *uses* of a function to satisfy its precondition, whereas in the semantics that we have chosen, bad uses are allowed but the programmer gets no guarantees back.

Rather different to Liquid Types, Dminor (Bierman et al. 2010) allows refinements to be written in the very same programming language. Contrary to our case however, in Dminor the expressions that refine types must be pure — that is, terminating — and have a unique denotation (e.g. not depending on the store). Driven from a typing relation that includes logic entailment judgements, verification conditions are extracted and discharged automatically using Z3. Similar in spirit, the Fstar (Swamy et al. 2011) compiler also extracts verification conditions that are discharged using Z3 or interactive theorem provers. Hybrid type systems such as Sage (Knowles and Flanagan 2010) attempt to prove as many of the goals statically, and defer the rest as runtime tests.

Boogie (Barnett et al. 2005) is a verification back end that supports procedures as well as pure functions. By using Z3, Boogie verifies programs written in the BoogiePL intermediate language, which could potentially be used as the back end of our translation as well. Recent work on performing induction on top of an induction-free SMT solver proposes a "tactic" for encoding induction schemes as first-order queries, which is reminiscent of the way that we perform induction (Leino 2012).

The recent work on the Leon system (Suter et al. 2011) presents an approach to the verification of *first-order* and *call-by-value* recursive functional programs, which appears to be very efficient in practice. It works by extending SMT with recursive programs and "control literals" that guide the pattern matching search for a counter-model, and is guaranteed to find a model if one exists (whereas that is not yet the case in our system, as we discussed earlier). It does not include a special treatment of the $\bot$ value nor pattern match failures seem to be in the scope of that project, but rather partial functional correctness.

The tool Zeno (Sonnex et al. 2012) verifies equational properties of functional programs. Its proof search is based on induction, equality reasoning and operational semantics. While guaranteeing termination, it can also start new induction proofs driven by syntactic heuristics. However, it only considers finite and total subsets of values, and we want to reason about Haskell programs as they appear in the wild: possibly non-terminating, with lazy infinite values, and run time crashes.

First-order logic has been used as a target for higher-order languages in other verification contexts as well. Users of the interactive theorem prover Isabelle have for many years had the opportunity to use automated first-order provers to discharge proof obligations. This work has recently culminated in the tool Sledgehammer (Blanchette et al. 2011), which not only uses first-order provers, but also SMT solvers as back ends. There has also been a version of the dependently typed programming language Agda in which proof obligations could be sent to an automatic first-order prover (Abel et al. 2005). Both of these use a translation from a typed higher-order language of well-founded definitions to first-order logic. A work that comes very close to ours, in that they deal with a lazy, general recursive language with partial functions, is by Bove et al. (2012), who use Agda as a logical framework to reason about general recursive functional programs, and combine interaction in Agda with automated proofs in FOL.

There exists more work on translating the semantics of programs or their properties in higher-order logics (e.g. CIC), for instance the work on Characteristic Formulae (Charguéraud 2011) and the work on Hoare-logic VCC-based verification (Rgis-Gianas and Pottier 2008). The former is interpreting a program as a higher-order predicate transformer whereas the latter introduces a higher-order typed Hoare-logic and extracts verification conditions which are proved interactively in Coq or with an automated theorem prover. We aim to stay within the realm of first-order logic to exploit automation offered by the advances in FOL theorem provers and model finders. At the same time we do lose expressivity, as our predicate language are only plain-old Haskell functions. On the other hand this gives us admissibility practically for free even in the absense of inductive types. But even in the case of the previous work of Régis-Gianas and Pottier, positivity conditions have to be imposed on datatypes to make sure that the logical specification can be embedded in a logic built in CIC. Like Liquid types, that work enforces contract preconditions in all call sites. Finally, in the higher-order logic world, the recent work of Huffman (Huffman 2012) can be used to translate Haskell programs and reason about their semantics in HOLCF; the main application being the verification of monad transformers.

The previous work on static contract checking for Haskell (Xu et al. 2009) was based on *wrapping*. A term was effectively wrapped with an appropriately nested contract test, and symbolic execution or aggressive inlining was used to show that `BAD` values could never be reached in this wrapped term. In follow-up work, Xu (Xu 2012) proposes a variation, this time for a *call-by-value* language, which performs symbolic execution along with a "logicization" of the program that can be used (via a theorem prover) to eliminate paths that can provably not generate `BAD` value,. The "logicization" of a program has a similar spirit to our translation to logic. Furthermore, the logicization of programs is dependent on whether the resulting formula is going to be used as a goal or assumption in a proof. Improving Xu's work, Tobin-Hochstadt and Van Horn (Tobin-Hochstadt and Horn 2012) propose a system in the same space of symbolic execution but they enrich the language of contracts to handle arbitrary, potentially divergent or crashing functions. We believe that our approach, which is to directly encode the semantics of programs, might be simpler to specify and reason about. That said, symbolic execution has the advantage of querying a theorem prover on many small goals, instead of a single big goal. We have some ideas about how to break large satisfiability queries to smaller ones, guided by the symbolic evaluation of functions, and we consider integrating this methodology.

Finally, higher-order model checking (Kobayashi 2009a,b) aims at verifying properties about the execution of functional programs (for instance it can also verify temporal properties of programs) based on a translation of programs to higher-order recursion schemes. Higher-order model checking is an area of active research, aiming to improve the efficiency and applicability of the original approach.

9. Conclusions and future work

Static verification for functional programming languages seems an under-studied (compared to the imperative world) and very promising area of research. In practical terms, our most immediate goal is to ensure that we can find finite counter-examples quickly, and present them comprehensibly to the user, rather allowing the theorem prover to diverge. As mentioned in Section 7 we have well-developed ideas for how to do this. It would also be interesting to see if *triggers* in SMT 2.0 could also be used to support that goal.

We would like to add support for primitive data types, such as `Integer`, using theorem provers such as `T-SPASS` to deal with the `tff` (typed first-order arithmetic) part of TPTP. Another approach might be to generate theories in the SMT 2.0 format, understood by Z3, which has support for integer arithmetic and more. Another important direction is finding ways to split our big verification goals into smaller ones that can be proven significantly faster. Finally, we would like to investigate whether we can automatically strengthen contracts to be used as induction hypotheses in inductive proofs, deriving information from failed attempts.

Acknowledgements Thanks to the POPL 2013 reviewers and Richard Eisenberg for their feedback, and to Nathan Collins for early work on a prototype of our translation.

References

Andreas Abel, Thierry Coquand, and Ulf Norell. Connecting a logical framework to a first-order logic prover. In *5th International Workshop on Frontiers of Combining Systems (FroCoS)*, LNCS. Springer Verlag, 2005.

Michael Barnett, Bor-Yuh Evan Chang, Robert DeLine, Bart Jacobs, and K. Rustan M. Leino. Boogie: A modular reusable verifier for object-oriented programs. In *Formal methods for Components and Objects*, pages 364–387, 2005.

Nick Benton, Andrew Kennedy, and Carsten Varming. Some domain theory and denotational semantics in coq. In *Proceedings of the 22nd International Conference on Theorem Proving in Higher Order Logics*, TPHOLs '09, pages 115–130, Berlin, Heidelberg, 2009. Springer-Verlag.

Gavin M. Bierman, Andrew D. Gordon, Cătălin Hriţcu, and David Langworthy. Semantic subtyping with an SMT solver. In *Proceedings of the 15th ACM SIGPLAN International Conference on Functional programming*, ICFP '10, pages 105–116, New York, NY, USA, 2010. ACM.

Jasmin Blanchette, Sascha Böhme, and Lawrence Paulson. Extending Sledgehammer with SMT solvers. In *Conference on Automated Deduction (CADE)*, LNCS. Springer Verlag, 2011.

Matthias Blume and David McAllester. Sound and complete models of contracts. *J. Funct. Program.*, 16(4-5):375–414, July 2006. ISSN 0956-7968.

Ana Bove, Peter Dybjer, and Andrés Sicard-Ramírez. Combining interactive and automatic reasoning in first order theories of functional programs. In Lars Birkedal, editor, *15th International Conference on Foundations of Software Science and Computational Structures, FoSSaCS 2012*, volume 7213 of *LNCS*, pages 104–118, March 2012.

Arthur Charguéraud. Characteristic formulae for the verification of imperative programs. In *Proceedings of the 16th ACM SIGPLAN International Conference on Functional Programming*, ICFP '11, pages 418–430, New York, NY, USA, 2011. ACM.

Koen Claessen and Niklas Sörensson. New techniques that improve MACE-style model finding. In *Proc. of Workshop on Model Computation (MODEL)*, 2003.

Leonardo De Moura and Nikolaj Bjørner. Z3: an efficient SMT solver. In *Proceedings of the Theory and Practice of Software, 14th International Conference on Tools and Algorithms for the Construction and Analysis of Systems*, TACAS'08/ETAPS'08, pages 337–340, Berlin, Heidelberg, 2008. Springer-Verlag.

Robert Bruce Findler and Matthias Felleisen. Contracts for higher-order functions. In *Proceedings of the seventh ACM SIGPLAN International Conference on Functional programming*, ICFP '02, pages 48–59, New York, NY, USA, 2002. ACM.

Ralf Hinze, Johan Jeuring, and Andres Löh. Typed contracts for functional programming. In *Proceedings of the 8th International Conference on Functional and Logic Programming*, FLOPS'06, pages 208–225, Berlin, Heidelberg, 2006. Springer-Verlag.

Kryštof Hoder, Laura Kovács, and Andrei Voronkov. Interpolation and symbol elimination in Vampire. In *Proceedings of the 5th International Conference on Automated Reasoning*, IJCAR'10, pages 188–195, Berlin, Heidelberg, 2010. Springer-Verlag.

Brian Huffman. Formal verification of monad transformers. In *Proceedings of the 17th ACM SIGPLAN International Conference on Functional Programming*, ICFP '12, pages 15–16, New York, NY, USA, 2012. ACM.

Kenneth Knowles and Cormac Flanagan. Hybrid type checking. *ACM Trans. Program. Lang. Syst.*, 32(2):6:1–6:34, February 2010. ISSN 0164-0925.

Naoki Kobayashi. Types and higher-order recursion schemes for verification of higher-order programs. In *Proceedings of the 36th ACM SIGPLAN-SIGACT Symposium on Principles of Programming Languages*, POPL '09, pages 416–428, New York, NY, USA, 2009a. ACM.

Naoki Kobayashi. Model-checking higher-order functions. In *Proceedings of the 11th ACM SIGPLAN Conference on Principles and Practice of Declarative Programming*, PPDP '09, pages 25–36, New York, NY, USA, 2009b. ACM.

K. Rustan M. Leino. Automating induction with an SMT solver. In *Proceedings of the 13th International Conference on Verification, Model Checking, and Abstract Interpretation*, VMCAI'12, pages 315–331, Berlin, Heidelberg, 2012. Springer-Verlag.

Neil Mitchell and Colin Runciman. Not all patterns, but enough: an automatic verifier for partial but sufficient pattern matching. In *Proceedings of the 1st ACM SIGPLAN Symposium on Haskell*, Haskell '08, pages 49–60, New York, NY, USA, 2008. ACM.

Ulf Norell. *Towards a practical programming language based on dependent type theory*. PhD thesis, Chalmers University of Technology, 2007.

Andrew M. Pitts. Relational properties of domains. *Inf. Comput.*, 127(2): 66–90, 1996.

Patrick M. Rondon, Ming Kawaguci, and Ranjit Jhala. Liquid types. In *Proceedings of the 2008 ACM SIGPLAN Conference on Programming Language Design and Implementation*, PLDI '08, pages 159–169, New York, NY, USA, 2008. ACM.

Yann Rgis-Gianas and Franois Pottier. A Hoare logic for call-by-value functional programs. In *Proceedings of the Ninth International Conference on Mathematics of Program Construction (MPC'08)*, pages 305–335, July 2008.

Jeremy G. Siek and Walid Taha. Gradual typing for functional languages. In *IN SCHEME AND FUNCTIONAL PROGRAMMING WORKSHOP*, pages 81–92, 2006.

William Sonnex, Sophia Drossopoulou, and Susan Eisenbach. Zeno: an automated prover for properties of recursive data structures. In *Proceedings of the 18th International Conference on Tools and Algorithms for the Construction and Analysis of Systems*, TACAS'12, pages 407–421, Berlin, Heidelberg, 2012. Springer-Verlag.

Martin Sulzmann, Manuel M. T. Chakravarty, Simon Peyton Jones, and Kevin Donnelly. System F with type equality coercions. In *Proceedings of the 2007 ACM SIGPLAN International Workshop on Types in Languages Design and Implementation*, TLDI '07, pages 53–66, New York, NY, USA, 2007. ACM.

G. Sutcliffe. The TPTP Problem Library and Associated Infrastructure: The FOF and CNF Parts, v3.5.0. *Journal of Automated Reasoning*, 43 (4):337–362, 2009.

Philippe Suter, Ali Sinan Köksal, and Viktor Kuncak. Satisfiability modulo recursive programs. In *Proceedings of the 18th International Conference on Static analysis*, SAS'11, pages 298–315, Berlin, Heidelberg, 2011. Springer-Verlag.

Nikhil Swamy, Juan Chen, Cédric Fournet, Pierre-Yves Strub, Karthikeyan Bhargavan, and Jean Yang. Secure distributed programming with value-dependent types. In *International Conference on Functional Programming*, pages 266–278, 2011.

Sam Tobin-Hochstadt and David Van Horn. Higher-order symbolic execution via contracts. In *Proceedings of the ACM SIGPLAN Conference on Object-Oriented Programming, Systems, Languages, and Applications*, OOPSLA '12, 2012.

Philip Wadler and Robert Bruce Findler. Well-typed programs can't be blamed. In *Proceedings of the 18th European Symposium on Programming Languages and Systems*, ESOP '09, pages 1–16, Berlin, Heidelberg, 2009. Springer-Verlag.

Glynn Winskel. *The formal semantics of programming languages - an introduction*. Foundation of computing series. MIT Press, 1993.

Hongwei Xi. Dependent ML: an approach to practical programming with dependent types. *J. Funct. Program.*, 17(2):215–286, March 2007. ISSN 0956-7968.

Dana N. Xu. Hybrid contract checking via symbolic simplification. In *Proceedings of the ACM SIGPLAN 2012 Workshop on Partial Evaluation and Program Manipulation*, PEPM '12, pages 107–116, New York, NY, USA, 2012. ACM.

Dana N. Xu, Simon Peyton Jones, and Koen Claessen. Static contract checking for Haskell. In *Proceedings of the 36th annual ACM SIGPLAN-SIGACT Symposium on Principles of Programming Languages*, POPL '09, pages 41–52, New York, NY, USA, 2009. ACM.

Sigma*: Symbolic Learning of Input-Output Specifications

Matko Botinčan
University of Cambridge
matko.botincan@cl.cam.ac.uk

Domagoj Babić *
Facebook, Inc.
babic@eecs.berkeley.edu

Abstract

We present Sigma*, a novel technique for learning symbolic models of software behavior. Sigma* addresses the challenge of synthesizing models of software by using symbolic conjectures and abstraction. By combining dynamic symbolic execution to discover symbolic input-output steps of the programs and counterexample guided abstraction refinement to over-approximate program behavior, Sigma* transforms arbitrary source representation of programs into faithful input-output models. We define a class of stream filters—programs that process streams of data items—for which Sigma* converges to a complete model if abstraction refinement eventually builds up a sufficiently strong abstraction. In other words, Sigma* is complete relative to abstraction. To represent inferred symbolic models, we use a variant of symbolic transducers that can be effectively composed and equivalence checked. Thus, Sigma* enables fully automatic analysis of behavioral properties such as commutativity, reversibility and idempotence, which is useful for web sanitizer verification and stream programs compiler optimizations, as we show experimentally. We also show how models inferred by Sigma* can boost performance of stream programs by parallelized code generation.

Categories and Subject Descriptors D.2.4 [*Software Engineering*]: Software Verification—Formal methods; D.3.4 [*Programming Languages*]: Processors—Optimization

General Terms Languages, Theory, Verification

Keywords Inductive learning, Specification synthesis, Behavioral properties, Equivalence checking, Stream programs, Compiler optimization, Parallelization

1. Introduction

Modern software systems often process large amounts of data in a stream-like fashion. By streams, we mean sequences of data items, processed in some order. Such stream processing is inherent to many domains such as digital signal processing, embedded applications, network event processing, financial applications, web applications, and even to common desktop software. Likewise, big-data services running on a cloud often continuously process streams of moving data and batches of past data.

* This work was done while the second author was with UC Berkeley.

POPL'13, January 23–25, 2013, Rome, Italy.

We focus on a simple notion of programs that applies to many of these systems, called a *filter*. Filters are typically small fragments of code, but they facilitate large scale stream-processing [15, 18, 23, 26, 29, 32, 54]. A filter iteratively reads a bounded number of items from an input stream at once, performs some computation on those items, and writes the results to an output stream. Filters exchange data via stream(s) with other parts of the program, and can also be glued together into more complex structures. Unfortunately, reasoning about even these relatively simplistic programs is difficult as their low-level implementation details often obscure the high-level input-output behavior that we want to reason about.

Our aim is to provide ways for automated analysis of the input-output behavior of programs such as stream filters. Although the internal implementation of such programs may be rather delicate, many of their properties rely solely on their input-output behavior. To exemplify a couple of such properties, let us consider intentionally simple filters P and P' (coming from, say, two revisions of the code or from two different vendors), that implement a difference encoder (used in, e.g., JPEG compression [53]):[1]

P
```
out(peek(0));
while (true) {
  out(peek(1)-peek(0));
  in ();
}
```

P'
```
state = 0;
while (true) {
  out(peek(0)-state);
  state = in();
}
```

P and P' are syntactically different and have different operational semantics but they exhibit the same input-output behavior. Behavioral equivalence of P and P' ensures that the two implementations can be used interchangeably—for instance, a behaviorally equivalent stateless (or with few states) implementation might be preferable over a stateful (or with many states) one, as the former can be made amenable to data-parallel execution by a simple replication. For another property, consider a filter Q that looks like P but instead of the difference calculates the sum of the two consecutive values. If we connect P's output stream to Q's input stream in a pipeline then the resulting composition will have the same behavior as if we were to connect Q's output to P's input. Knowing that P and Q are commutative with respect to each other we can reorder them (e.g., for performance reasons) without affecting the behavior of the pipeline.

In this paper, we present a technique called Σ^* that enables automated analyses of input-output properties of programs by *learning*. Σ^* uses dynamic symbolic execution [16, 28, 49] to discover symbolic input-output steps of a program, and counterexample guided abstraction refinement [7, 20] to over-approximate program behavior, and combines the two techniques into a sound and complete (relative to abstraction) symbolic learning algorithm. Σ^* works on the control-flow graph without assuming any specific

[1] In these code snippets, function **out**() writes a data item to the output stream, **peek**() returns the item at the given offset in the input stream without consuming it, and **in**() consumes and returns the current item from the input stream.

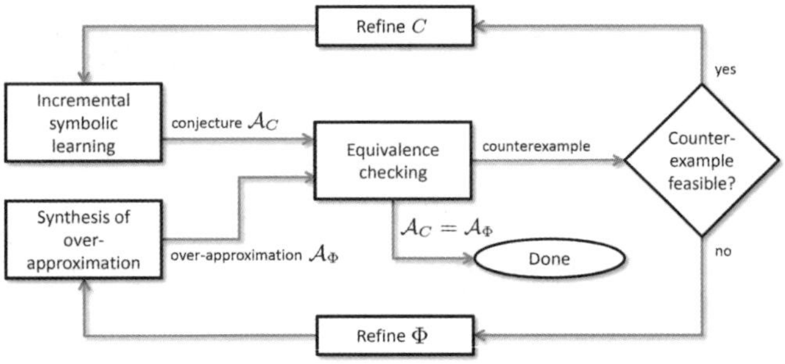

Figure 1: The Design of Σ^*. Arrows indicate the data flow.

syntactic structure of the program and, by learning, synthesizes a faithful *symbolic model* of program behavior. It represents the models using a variant of symbolic transducers (STs) [14], which generalize classical finite-state machines by allowing transitions labeled with arbitrary predicates as input guards and terms as output. Assuming formulae from a decidable theory, STs can be effectively composed and equivalence-checked, enabling analysis of various behavioral properties such as commutativity, reversibility, and idempotence.

Σ^* targets applications beyond just verification. As we show, Σ^* enables domain-specific compiler optimizations (e.g., filter fusion and reordering [2, 45]) for a wider class of stream programs than currently possible. Also, STs inferred by Σ^* lend themselves to vectorized implementation (e.g., by utilising SIMD instructions [57], GPU architecture [15, 56] or field-programmable gate arrays [35, 39]) and data-parallel execution (e.g., by replication or using speculative techniques such as [48]).

Overview of Σ^***.** In a nutshell, Σ^* can be seen as an extension of Angluin's L^* automata-learning algorithm [5] to learning models of programs. L^*, designed to learn regular languages in a black-box manner, is not applicable to the general software setting for two reasons. Firstly, L^* requires a priori knowledge of the concrete alphabet of the language. While that fits certain scenarios (such as inference of component interfaces [4, 27, 51], where the alphabet corresponds to the set of component's methods), the exact alphabet of software internals (including, for instance, all values that arise during the execution) is hard to specify in advance. Even if known, such alphabets are typically large (or practically infinite), so treating them concretely as in L^* hinders scalability. Secondly, L^* merely conjectures the inferred model and to check the conjecture relies upon an oracle (a teacher) that can answer equivalence queries. An omniscient oracle for equivalence checking against software artifacts is, however, computationally intractable.

Therefore, Σ^* is built around two key ideas:

1. Σ^* uses dynamic symbolic execution to discover constraints on input values (path predicates) and terms generating output values, and builds symbolic alphabet out of these. By using symbolic alphabets to represent equivalence classes of input-output steps, Σ^* enables discovery of complete input-output behavior independently of the concrete alphabet size.
2. Instead of equivalence checking against the program, Σ^* builds an abstraction that is a finite-state symbolic over-approximation of program behavior that we wish to learn. Checking equivalence of (deterministic) symbolic conjectures and such (possibly non-deterministic) over-approximations can be done algorithmically. Σ^* implements an algorithm that either generates a *separating sequence* (counterexample) showing how the conjecture and abstraction differ, or proves they are equivalent.

Starting with the trivial symbolic conjecture and the coarsest abstraction, Σ^* iteratively refines the conjecture or the abstraction until the two become equivalent (see Figure 1). If the counterexample returned by the equivalence checking algorithm is spurious (i.e., the program does not produce the same sequence of outputs as the abstraction), we refine the abstraction. Otherwise, the counterexample represents a behavior that the conjecture failed to capture, and we refine the conjecture. Upon termination, the final conjecture is in a certain sense minimal behaviorally equivalent model of the program.

The symbolic conjecture maintained by Σ^* is a variant of symbolic finite-state transducers [14] that we call symbolic *lookback* transducers (SLTs). To generate outputs, SLTs use a sliding window over a bounded number of past inputs (SLTs can also be augmented with *lookahead* to allow peeking of incoming inputs). Along with conjectures, we also synthesize over-approximations of program behavior in the form of SLTs. We use predicate abstraction [7, 30] to abstract away the internal control flow of a program, however, in doing so we keep the input-output data flow intact. We then transform the obtained abstraction into an equivalent non-deterministic SLT. To check equivalence of the conjecture and the over-approximation, we use our algorithm for equivalence checking of a deterministic and non-deterministic SLT.

The main technical result of the paper is that Σ^* is relatively complete with respect to the abstraction. Assuming that the program behavior can be represented with an SLT, Σ^* terminates with an SLT behaviorally equivalent to the program if the overapproximation scheme eventually produces an inductive invariant implying the program's input-output relation. Since synthesis of the overapproximating SLT is guided by abstraction refinement, relative completeness of Σ^* is conditioned by completeness of the predicate selection method in refinement of the predicate abstraction [9, 42].

Other classes of program behavior could be learned by varying the type of symbolic conjectures. For programs whose behavior cannot be represented within the given class of symbolic models, Σ^* will end up conjecturing more refined models ad infinitum. However, if Σ^* is interrupted before convergence, the conjecture is guaranteed to be correct up to the explored depth.

Applications. To demonstrate practical utility of Σ^*, we report three experimental studies conducted with our implementation:

- *Web Sanitizers Verification.* We analyzed sanitizers from Google AutoEscape web sanitization framework and found out that 86% of them (12 out of 14) can be represented as SLTs. Σ^* successfully inferred all 12 sanitizers fully automatically, enabling their further analysis with systems such as Bek [37].
- *Stream Filter Optimization.* We applied Σ^* to infer filters from various stream processing applications [18, 23, 33, 45, 54]. We show how Σ^* enables optimizations such as reordering and fusion that are not possible with the current state-of-the-art.
- *Parallelization.* We show how SLT models of filters enable automated parallelization. From a variety of SLTs, we generated SIMD implementations using Intel SSE intrinsics and GPU implementations using NVIDIA CUDA, and obtained speedups of up to 3.89 against the most optimized `gcc` code.

Contributions. We claim the following contributions.

- *Symbolic Learning Framework* Σ^*. We present an automated learning framework Σ^* for learning symbolic models of programs's input-output behavior. The key insight behind Σ^*, besides use of symbolic alphabets to represent program steps, is use of over-approximation to detect convergence.
- *Symbolic Lookback Transducers.* We introduce a carefully limited variant of symbolic transducers that is amenable to learning

```
prev = 0; cur = 0; i = 0;
while (true) {
    cur = peek(0);
    if (i < 2)              out(cur);
    else
        if (cur < prev) out(cur + prev);
        else            out(cur - prev);
    prev = in();
    i++;
}
```

Figure 2: Code Snippet for the Running Example in §2.

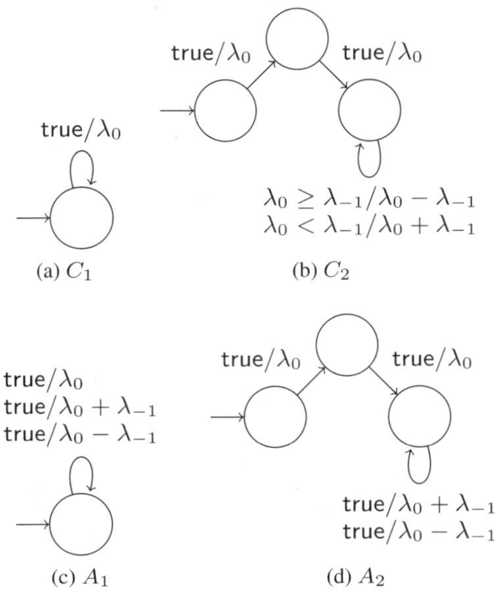

Figure 3: Conjectures and Abstractions for the Example in Figure 2.

and develop an equivalence checking algorithm. We experimentally show that SLTs are useful in practice through three case studies, two of which demonstrate novel use of transducers.

- *Synthesis of Over-approximations.* We show how to transform predicate abstraction of a program into an SLT over-approximating the program behavior, and how to refine it. The key step of the synthesis is finitization of the unabstracted components of states that correspond to the input-output flow.
- *Relative Completeness.* Our main technical result is that Σ^* converges to a sound and complete model of SLT programs, as long as the abstraction refinement eventually builds a strong enough set of predicates. Effectively, this result reduces the completeness of learning to the completeness of abstraction.

2. Σ^* Illustrated by Example

We begin by showing how Σ^* works on the example given in Figure 2. The program reads input in an infinite loop using commands **peek**() and **in**(); **peek**(0) reads the current input symbol and leaves it in the input stream, while **in**() reads the current input symbol and moves onto the next one. Both commands halt if there is no more input to read. In the first two iterations, the program prints the last read symbol (using command **out**), and in every subsequent iteration it outputs the sum or difference of the last two symbols, depending on their relative ordering.

We represent learned conjectures and synthesized abstractions in the example as SLTs with lookback 1. Each transition is labeled by a symbolic predicate-term pair of the form p/t. The transition is taken when the predicate p evaluates to true for a given sequence of concrete input symbols. The term t describes the computed output. Predicates and terms are expressions over input symbols and constants. We use λ_0 to denote the current symbol and λ_{-i} to denote symbols read i transitions before. SLTs with lookback k are allowed to read only the current and the last k symbols.

We use (dynamic) symbolic execution [16, 28, 49] to gather sequences of predicates and output terms occurring along the paths in the program execution. For instance, given an input of length four, a possible execution might take twice the then branch of the first if, then the else branch of the second if, and finally the then branch of the second if. For that execution we would obtain a predicate sequence (the path condition) $\vec{p} = \mathsf{true} \cdot \mathsf{true} \cdot (\mathsf{cur}_3 \geq \mathsf{prev}_2) \cdot (\mathsf{cur}_4 < \mathsf{prev}_3)$, and an output sequence $\vec{t} = \mathsf{cur}_1 \cdot \mathsf{cur}_2 \cdot (\mathsf{cur}_3 - \mathsf{prev}_2) \cdot (\mathsf{cur}_4 + \mathsf{prev}_3)$. In sequences such as $\vec{p}$ and $\vec{t}$, we use "$\cdot$" to denote the concatenation operator.

To obtain predicates and output terms formulated with regard to the input, we relativize all references of variables in $\vec{p}$ and $\vec{t}$ so that they become expressed with respect to the current position in the input stream. For instance, the relativized version of $\vec{p}$ would be the sequence $\mathsf{true} \cdot \mathsf{true} \cdot (\lambda_0 \geq \lambda_{-1}) \cdot (\lambda_0 < \lambda_{-1})$, and of $\vec{t}$, the sequence $\lambda_0 \cdot \lambda_0 \cdot (\lambda_0 - \lambda_{-1}) \cdot (\lambda_0 + \lambda_1)$. As for SLTs, the variable λ_{-j} in each element $\vec{p}|_i$ of the sequences above corresponds to the input symbol j positions before the current position (i) in the input stream. Thus, e.g., λ_0 in the third and fourth element of the sequences correspond to the last two symbols read by the program. To generate a concrete input from relativized path conditions, we need to derelativize them and pass the derelativized formula to an SMT solver. In the case above, the solver might return a concrete sequence $0 \cdot 1 \cdot 3 \cdot 2$ satisfying the relativized path condition.

Σ^* begins processing the example by learning the first conjecture C_1 (Figure 3a), and compares it against predicate abstraction A_1 of the program with respect to an empty set of predicates (Figure 3c). Note that, unlike in the classic predicate abstraction, we keep the input-output data flow intact. Equivalence checking of C_1 and A_1 produces the first symbolic counterexample, say a predicate $\vec{p_1} = \mathsf{true}$ and output $\vec{t_1} = (\lambda_0 + \lambda_{-1})$, which is a behavior captured by the abstraction, but not the conjecture. Any concrete sequence satisfying those two formulae is a concrete counterexample. For example, take input $\lambda_{-1} = 1, \lambda_0 = 1$. The program will produce output λ_0 for that input without reading λ_{-1}, showing that $\vec{p_1}/\vec{t_1}$ is spurious because symbolic outputs do not match. We refine the abstraction with respect to a new set of predicates, obtained by some predicate selection method (e.g., by taking atomic predicates in the weakest precondition computed along the path [6]). Suppose such method returns $\{i = 0, i \geq 2\}$ at this instance. The refined abstraction A_2 is shown in Figure 3d. Equivalence checking of A_2 and C_1 produces the second symbolic counterexample, say $\vec{p_2} = \mathsf{true} \cdot \mathsf{true} \cdot \mathsf{true}$ and $\vec{t_2} = \lambda_0 \cdot \lambda_0 \cdot (\lambda_0 - \lambda_{-1})$. Any sequence of three symbols will satisfy $\vec{p_2}$ and it turns out that counterexample is not spurious. Thus, we have to refine the conjecture.

After processing the counterexample, Σ^* learns conjecture C_2 shown in Figure 3b. C_2 is correct, but Σ^* does not know that yet, because equivalence checking of C_2 and A_2 returns the third counterexample, say $\vec{p_3} = \mathsf{true} \cdot \mathsf{true} \cdot (\lambda_0 < \lambda_{-1})$ and $\vec{t_3} = \lambda_0 \cdot \lambda_0 \cdot (\lambda_0 + \lambda_1)$. The third counterexample is not spurious either. Thus, once again, we need to refine the abstraction. Using the same method for refinement as above, we extend the set of predicates with $\lambda_0 < \lambda_{-1}$. Predicate abstraction computes A_3, which is equivalent to C_2, and the process terminates, faithfully inferring the program's input-output relation, i.e., the specification of program's input-output behavior.

For the following example with nested loops, Σ^* terminates inferring a SLT with lookback 0, shown on the right.

```
while (true) {
    x = in();
    while (x != 'a') {
        x = in();
        out(x);
    }
}
```

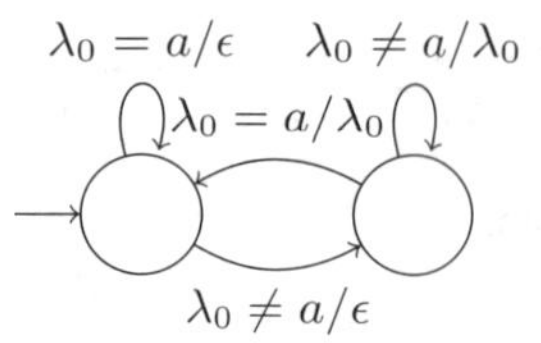

3. Transductive Programs

We now turn to the formal development of Σ^*. In this section, we formalize the syntax and semantics of programs that transform an input stream into an output stream of symbols. Behavior of certain such programs can be represented by SLTs (§4). We also formally define concepts associated with the dynamic symbolic execution, which we use in development of over-approximations (§5) and learning (§6). To simplify exposition, henceforth we assume programs working with streams of integers.

3.1 Preliminaries

Let $\mathbb{Z}$ be the set of integers, $\mathbb{N} = \{i \in \mathbb{Z} \mid i > 0\}$ the set of naturals, and $\mathbb{B} = \{\mathsf{false}, \mathsf{true}\}$ the set of booleans. For a set D, we denote by D^* the free monoid generated by D with concatenation as the operation and the empty word ϵ as identity. We refer to words in D^* as sequences. Sequences of predicates (resp. terms) we denote by $\vec{p} = p_1 \cdots p_m$ (resp. $\mathbf{t} = t_1 \cdots t_n$). For sequences of sequences of terms, we write $\vec{t}$. We denote the length of $\vec{p}$ by $|\vec{p}|$, the i-th element of $\vec{p}$ by $\vec{p}|_i$ and the subsequence $p_i \cdots p_{i+k}$ by $\vec{p}|_{[i,i+k]}$. For $f\colon D \to C$ and $D' \subseteq D$, we write $f|_{D'}$ to denote the restriction of f on D'. For $\vec{a}$ and $\vec{b}$ such that $n \triangleq |\vec{a}| = |\vec{b}|$, we write $f[\vec{a} \leftarrow \vec{b}]$ to denote the function f' such that for all $i \in \{1, \ldots, n\}$, $f'(\vec{a}|_i) = \vec{b}|_i$ and for all $x \notin \{\vec{a}|_1, \ldots, \vec{a}|_n\}$, $f'(x) = f(x)$. We use $\mathbf{t}[x \mapsto y]$ to denote the term obtained from $\mathbf{t}$ by simultaneously replacing all free occurrences of x with y. $\mathsf{Vars}(t)$ denotes the set of all free variables in t.

3.2 Syntactic Representation

We first define syntactic representation of programs. Let V be the set of program variables. Expressions (terms) $\mathit{Exp}[\mathsf{V}]$, predicates $\mathit{BExp}[\mathsf{V}]$, and atomic commands $\mathit{Cmd}[\mathsf{V}]$ over V are given by:

$$\begin{array}{rcll} e & ::= & \mathsf{k} \mid x \mid \mathsf{f}(\mathbf{e}) \mid \ldots & \in \mathit{Exp}[\mathsf{V}] \\ b & ::= & \mathsf{false} \mid \mathsf{true} \mid \neg b \mid b \wedge b \mid b \vee b \mid & \\ & & e = e \mid e \neq e \mid \mathsf{R}(\mathbf{e}) \mid \ldots & \in \mathit{BExp}[\mathsf{V}] \\ c & ::= & \mathsf{assume}(b) \mid x := e \mid x := \mathsf{peek}(\mathsf{k}) \mid & \\ & & x := \mathsf{in}() \mid \mathsf{out}(e) & \in \mathit{Cmd}[\mathsf{V}] \end{array}$$

where $\mathsf{k} \in \mathbb{Z}$, $x \in \mathsf{V}$, while f and R are constructors for terms and predicates. As long as the quantifier-free theory of $\mathit{Exp}[\mathsf{V}]$ with equality and satisfiability of $\mathit{BExp}[\mathsf{V}]$ are decidable, particular details of the grammar are not important. The command $x := \mathsf{peek}(\mathsf{k})$ reads a data item at offset k from the current symbol in the input stream and stores the item to x if the input is available, otherwise it causes the program to halt. The $\mathsf{in}()$ command works like $\mathsf{peek}(0)$ but in addition consumes the item from the input stream and moves onto the next input symbol. The command $\mathsf{out}(e)$ writes the value of e to the output stream.

We represent programs using control-flow automata [36] over the language of atomic commands. The control-flow automaton is determined by a set of control nodes N containing a distinguished node $\mathsf{s_N} \in \mathsf{N}$ representing the starting point of the program and a function $\mathsf{succ}\colon \mathsf{N} \times \mathit{Cmd}[\mathsf{V}] \rightharpoonup \mathsf{N}$ representing labeled edges. All nodes either have a single successor or have all outgoing edges labeled with a label of the form $\mathsf{assume}(b)$. In the latter case, we assume that all corresponding predicates b are mutually exclusive and that their disjunction is a tautology.

$$\begin{array}{rcl} [\![\mathsf{k}]\!]_\sigma & = & \mathsf{k} \\ [\![x]\!]_\sigma & \doteq & \begin{cases} \sigma(x) & \text{if } x \in \mathsf{V}, \\ x & \text{if } x \in \mathsf{V_I}, \\ \text{undefined} & \text{otherwise} \end{cases} \\ [\![\mathsf{f}(\mathbf{e})]\!]_\sigma & \doteq & \mathsf{f}([\![e_1]\!]_\sigma, \ldots, [\![e_n]\!]_\sigma) \end{array}$$

Figure 4: Symbolic Evaluation of Expressions.

$$\begin{array}{lcl} (\mathsf{n}, \sigma, \rho, \imath, \jmath) & \overset{\mathsf{assume}(b)}{\rightsquigarrow} & (\mathsf{n}', \sigma, \rho, \imath, \jmath) \\ (\mathsf{n}, \sigma, \rho, \imath, \jmath) & \overset{x:=e}{\rightsquigarrow} & (\mathsf{n}', \sigma[x \leftarrow [\![e]\!]_\sigma], \rho, \imath, \jmath) \\ (\mathsf{n}, \sigma, \rho, \imath, \jmath) & \overset{x:=\mathsf{peek}(\mathsf{k})}{\rightsquigarrow} & (\mathsf{n}', \sigma[x \leftarrow [\![in_{\imath+\mathsf{k}}]\!]_\sigma], \rho, \imath, \jmath) \\ (\mathsf{n}, \sigma, \rho, \imath, \jmath) & \overset{x:=\mathsf{in}()}{\rightsquigarrow} & (\mathsf{n}', \sigma[x \leftarrow [\![in_\imath]\!]_\sigma], \rho, \imath+1, \jmath) \\ (\mathsf{n}, \sigma, \rho, \imath, \jmath) & \overset{\mathsf{out}(e)}{\rightsquigarrow} & (\mathsf{n}', \sigma, \rho[out_\jmath \leftarrow [\![e]\!]_\sigma], \imath, \jmath+1) \end{array}$$

Figure 5: Symbolic Semantics of Commands.

3.3 Symbolic Semantics

Given a program $\mathcal{P}$ we now define its symbolic semantics. We formalize the contents of the input and the output stream with sets of variables $\mathsf{V_I} \triangleq \{in_1, in_2, \ldots\}$ (in-variables) and $\mathsf{V_O} \triangleq \{out_1, out_2, \ldots\}$ (out-variables), respectively. On a particular run of $\mathcal{P}$, all except finitely many of these variables are undefined, and for those which are defined, $in_\imath$ corresponds to the $\imath$-th element of the input stream, and $out_\jmath$ to the $\jmath$-th element of the output stream. By $\vec{in}$ we refer to the sequence of in-variables $in_1 in_2 \ldots$ and we use ℓ_{in} to denote the length of the data sequence in the input stream.

We evaluate expressions on a memory $\sigma \in \mathsf{Mem} \triangleq \mathsf{V} \rightharpoonup \mathit{Exp}[\mathsf{V_I}]$ as indicated in Figure 4. We execute commands on states of the form $\mathsf{State} \triangleq \mathsf{N} \times \mathsf{Mem} \times \mathsf{OutStr} \times \mathbb{N} \times \mathbb{N}$. The third component, $\mathsf{OutStr} \triangleq \mathsf{V_O} \rightharpoonup \mathit{Exp}[\mathsf{V_I}]$, represents the symbols in the output stream. The last two components of the state, the in-index and the out-index, store indices of the current element in the input stream and the output stream, respectively. We denote the components of a state $s \in \mathsf{State}$ by $s.\mathsf{n}$, $s.\sigma$, $s.\rho$, $s.\imath$, and $s.\jmath$, respectively. The initial state is $s_0 = (\mathsf{s_N}, \emptyset, \emptyset, 1, 1)$.

We represent the symbolic semantics of $\mathcal{P}$ by a labeled transition system (LTS) $\mathcal{T} = (\mathsf{State}, C, \rightsquigarrow)$ with State as the set of states, $C \subseteq \mathit{Cmd}[\mathsf{V}]$ as the finite set of labels, and $\rightsquigarrow$ as the labeled transition relation. The relation $\rightsquigarrow\ \subseteq \mathsf{State} \times C \times \mathsf{State}$ is defined by the rules given in Figure 5, showing the effect of each command on a state. In each rule we have $n' = \mathsf{succ}(n, c)$. We write $s \overset{c}{\rightsquigarrow} s'$ to denote the transition $(s, c, s') \in \rightsquigarrow$.

3.4 Dynamic Symbolic Traces, Path Predicates and Outputs

The LTS $\mathcal{T}$ encodes the symbolic semantics of $\mathcal{P}$ with respect to any input. Given a concrete input $\vec{a} \in \mathbb{Z}^*$, we can construct a sequence of states in $\mathcal{T}$ representing the (dynamic) symbolic trace of $\mathcal{P}$ driven by $\vec{a}$, as in [16, 28, 49]. We start with the initial state s_0 and at each step we follow the transition $s_i \overset{c}{\rightsquigarrow} s_{i+1}$, such that if c is of the form $\mathsf{assume}(b)$ then b is true in $s_i.\sigma[\vec{in} \leftarrow \vec{a}]$. We stop if we ever reach a state s_f, which we call ending, such that the in-index $s_f.\imath$ equals $\ell_{\mathsf{in}} + 1$ or s_f has an outgoing $\overset{\_:=\mathsf{peek}(\mathsf{k})}{\rightsquigarrow}$-transition with k such that $s_f.\imath + \mathsf{k} > \ell_{\mathsf{in}}$. We define the symbolic trace of

$\mathcal{P}$ on input $\vec{a}$, denoted $\tau_{\mathcal{P}}(\vec{a})$, as the finite sequence $s_0 s_1 \ldots s_f$ if an ending state is reached, or as the infinite sequence $s_0 s_1 \ldots$ otherwise.

We refer to a state s_i as *in-state* if $s_i = s_0$, $s_i = s_f$ or the incoming transition reads an input symbol, i.e., $s_{i-1} \overset{\_:=\mathsf{in}()}{\rightsquigarrow} s_i$. Let $\tau^{\mathsf{in}}_{\mathcal{P}}(\vec{a}) \triangleq \tilde{s}_0 \tilde{s}_1 \ldots \tilde{s}_n$ be the sequence of in-states from $\tau_{\mathcal{P}}(\vec{a})$. We define *big-step transition* as a transition between two successive states in $\tau^{\mathsf{in}}_{\mathcal{P}}(\vec{a})$. For $1 \leq i \leq n$, let p_i be the conjunction of predicates b of the form $\mathsf{assume}(b)$ encountered on all transitions between $\tilde{s}_{i-1}$ and $\tilde{s}_i$. In case no $\overset{\mathsf{assume}(\_)}{\rightsquigarrow}$-transitions exist between $\tilde{s}_{i-1}$ and $\tilde{s}_i$ we set p_i to true. Furthermore, for $1 \leq i \leq n$, let $\mathbf{t}_i$ be the sequence of symbolic outputs (as written to out-variables by $\overset{\mathsf{out}(\_)}{\rightsquigarrow}$-transitions) between $\tilde{s}_{i-1}$ and $\tilde{s}_i$. If no output is generated we set $\mathbf{t}_i$ to ϵ.

We define *path predicates* of $\mathcal{P}$ on input $\vec{a}$ as the sequence $\pi_{\mathcal{P}}(\vec{a}) \triangleq p_1 \cdots p_n$. Analogously, we define the *symbolic output* of $\mathcal{P}$ on $\vec{a}$ by $\theta_{\mathcal{P}}(\vec{a}) \triangleq \mathbf{t}_1 \cdots \mathbf{t}_n$. The *concrete output* of $\mathcal{P}$ on $\vec{a}$ is defined by $\gamma_{\mathcal{P}}(\vec{a}) \triangleq \theta_{\mathcal{P}}(\vec{a})[\vec{in} \mapsto \vec{a}]$.

3.5 Transductive and k-lookback Programs

In order to be able to learn program behavior, we have to make some assumptions about programs. Firstly, when considering the input-output behavior of a program, no path in a program should end up in a loop without reading an input, i.e., we will not allow infinite periods of silence during which the program would not read any input. This first assumption will allow us to extend incomplete conjectures of program behavior with new big-step transitions. Secondly, we will assume that programs produce uniformly bounded number of output symbols per each big-step transition. This second assumption is inherent to symbolic transducers [14], on which we base SLTs (§4), the model of program behaviour used in Σ^*.

More formally, let $\mathcal{T}$ be the LTS of $\mathcal{P}$ and ξ any symbolic trace in $\mathcal{T}$ starting with s_0 and ending with an in-state. Let us denote by $\#in(\xi)$ the number of $\overset{\_:=\mathsf{in}()}{\rightsquigarrow}$-transitions in ξ and by $\#out(\xi)$ the number of $\overset{\mathsf{out}(\_)}{\rightsquigarrow}$-transitions in ξ. We say that $\mathcal{P}$ is *transductive* if there are no infinite symbolic traces in $\mathcal{T}$ with only finitely many in-states, and there exists $M \in \mathbb{N}$ such that for every ξ as above we have $\#out(\xi) < M \cdot \#in(\xi)$. As a consequence, if $\mathcal{P}$ is transductive then for every input $\vec{a}$, $\tau_{\mathcal{P}}(\vec{a})$ is finite and $|\theta_{\mathcal{P}}(\vec{a})| = |\gamma_{\mathcal{P}}(\vec{a})| < M \cdot |\vec{a}|$.

Besides transductiveness, we impose an additional requirement that is specific to the type of transducers that we use to represent program behavior in Σ^*, but that could be relaxed if we would use more expressive models (such as, e.g., transducers with registers [3, 14]). This additional requirement asks that transductive programs produce outputs from a bounded number of inputs in the past. More formally, we say that $\mathcal{P}$ is *k-lookback* if $\mathcal{P}$ is transductive and for every ξ as above, each $\overset{\mathsf{out}(e)}{\rightsquigarrow}$-transition in ξ depends only on previous k inputs, i.e., if $s \overset{\mathsf{out}(e)}{\rightsquigarrow} s'$ then $\mathsf{Vars}([\![e]\!]_{s.\sigma}) \subseteq \{in_{s.\imath-k}, \ldots, in_{s.\imath}\}$. In §5 and §6 we focus on a class of k-lookback programs whose behavior can be represented with SLTs.

3.6 Input Relativization

In development of over-approximations (§5) and the learning algorithm (§6), we will need to rephrase symbolic expressions pertaining to program states so that they use the offset from the current position in the input stream rather than from the beginning. We show how to relativize these expressions so that the offset becomes relative to the current in-index.

Let $\mathsf{V}_\lambda \triangleq \{\ldots, \lambda_{-1}, \lambda_0, \lambda_1, \ldots\}$ be an infinite set of λ-variables, indexed by a relative offset. We use λ-variables so that λ_0 stands for the current symbol in the input stream, λ_{-i} for the symbol i positions back and λ_i for the symbol i positions ahead. Let $\vec{in} \overset{\imath}{\mapsto} \vec{\lambda}$ denote a variable substitution that maps each in-variable $in_\jmath$ to λ-variable $\lambda_{\jmath-\imath}$. We define *relativization* of a state $s = (\mathsf{n}, \sigma, \rho, \imath, \jmath)$ by $\Lambda(s) \triangleq (\mathsf{n}, \sigma[\vec{in} \overset{\imath}{\mapsto} \vec{\lambda}], \rho[\vec{in} \overset{\imath}{\mapsto} \vec{\lambda}], \jmath)$. Intuitively, $\Lambda(s)$ relativizes symbolic expressions in s with respect to the current in-index. For general transductive programs, expressions in σ- and ρ-components of $\Lambda(s)$ may use unboundedly many λ-variables as the expressions can refer to inputs from arbitrary far in the past. However, k-lookback programs use only up to k λ-variables with negative index, namely, $\lambda_{-k}, \ldots, \lambda_{-1}$.

4. Symbolic Transducers with Lookback

In the last section, we formalized the syntax and semantics of programs. In this section, we introduce symbolic lookback transducers (SLTs) with a constructive equivalence checking algorithm. We use SLTs to represent synthesized over-approximations (§5) and symbolic conjectures in the learning algorithm (§6).

4.1 Background

Finite-state transducers are an extension of classic finite-state automata obtained by allowing output on transitions (see [46]). Symbolic finite-state transducers [14] extend finite-state transducers by symbolic transitions, which are defined using predicates for input guards and symbolic terms for output. Our notion of SLTs extends symbolic finite-state transducers with a sliding window over input, which allows a transducer to generate outputs based on a bounded number of inputs from the past.

4.2 Definitions

We now formally define symbolic finite-state transducers with k-lookback — k-SLTs. We specialize our exposition for the case when the alphabet of input and output symbols is $\mathbb{Z}$, but generalization is easy. We omit k, when it is not important.

Instead of reading a single symbol from the input tape at a time, the tape head of a k-SLT is effectively a window of size $k+1$, reading the current and the last k symbols. Equivalently, such a transducer can be seen as a transducer with k registers updated in a FIFO manner on each transition—the newly read symbol is inserted, while the oldest is removed from the queue. Rather than using registers, we use the set of λ-variables $\mathsf{V}^k_\lambda := \{\lambda_{-k}, \ldots, \lambda_{-1}, \lambda_0\}$ so that λ_0 is the current symbol and λ_{-i} is the symbol i positions back.

Definition 1. *A symbolic finite transducer with lookback k (k-SLT) is a tuple $\mathcal{A} = (Q, q_0, \Delta)$ where Q is a finite set of states, $q_0 \in Q$ is the initial state and $\Delta \subseteq Q \times BExp[\mathsf{V}^k_\lambda] \times Q \times Exp[\mathsf{V}^k_\lambda]^*$ is a finite transition relation.*

In other words, SLT is a variant of a symbolic sequential ϵ-input-free (i.e., real-time) transducer having only final states,[2] and in general can be non-deterministic and does not have to be bounded-valued.

We say that SLT $\mathcal{A}$ is *deterministic* if for every two transitions $q \xrightarrow{\varphi/\mathbf{t}} r$ and $q \xrightarrow{\varphi'/\mathbf{t}'} r'$ if $\varphi \wedge \varphi'$ is satisfiable then $r = r'$ and $(\varphi \wedge \varphi') \Rightarrow \mathbf{t} = \mathbf{t}'$ is valid. SLTs that are inferred by the Σ^*'s learning algorithm will always be deterministic and even more, transitions from every state will have mutually disjoint guards.

We next formally define how SLTs produce output. Before defining a run of an SLT, we introduce some convenient notation.

[2] It is unclear how to learn transducers with non-final states, as such transducers allow inherent ambiguity in where the output is produced. Indeed, existing algorithms for learning concrete transducers (e.g., [50, 58]) require all states to be final.

For brevity, we refer to the sequence $\lambda_{-k} \dots \lambda_0$ as $\overleftarrow{\lambda}$. To process the input, k-SLT prepends it with k dummy symbols $\bot \notin \mathbb{Z}$. Any operation with $\bot$ yields $\bot$ and every comparison with $\bot$ (except $\bot = \bot$) is false. For a sequence $\vec{a}$, let us denote $\vec{a}^{\bot} \triangleq \bot^k \cdot \vec{a}$.

A *run of* k-SLT $\mathcal{A} = (Q, q_0, \Delta)$ on $\vec{a} \in \mathbb{Z}^n$ is a finite sequence of states $q_0 \dots q_n$ such that there exists a sequence of transitions

$$q_0 \xrightarrow{\varphi_1/\mathbf{t}_1} q_1 \xrightarrow{\varphi_2/\mathbf{t}_2} q_2 \cdots q_{n-1} \xrightarrow{\varphi_n/\mathbf{t}_n} q_n,$$

where $\varphi_1, \dots, \varphi_n \in BExp[\mathsf{V}^k_\lambda]$ and $\mathbf{t}_1, \dots, \mathbf{t}_n \in Exp[\mathsf{V}^k_\lambda]^*$ such that for all $1 \le i \le n$, $\vec{a}^{\bot}|_{[i,i+k]}$ satisfies φ_i. We say that $\mathcal{A}$ on the input $\vec{a}$ *produces the output* $\vec{o} \in \mathbb{Z}^*$ and write $\vec{a} \twoheadrightarrow_{\mathcal{A}} \vec{o}$ if for all $1 \le i \le n$, $\mathbf{o}_i = \mathbf{t}_i \left[\overleftarrow{\lambda} \mapsto \vec{a}^{\bot}|_{[i,i+k]}\right]$, where $\vec{o}|_i = \mathbf{o}_i$.

If $\mathcal{A}$ is deterministic, the run is uniquely determined by the input sequence. For a deterministic $\mathcal{A}$ and $\vec{a} \in \mathbb{Z}^*$, let us denote by $\pi_{\mathcal{A}}(\vec{a})$, $\theta_{\mathcal{A}}(\vec{a})$ and $\gamma_{\mathcal{A}}(\vec{a})$ the corresponding sequences $\varphi_1 \cdots \varphi_n$, $\mathbf{t}_1 \cdots \mathbf{t}_n$, and $\mathbf{o}_1 \cdots \mathbf{o}_n$, respectively.

We define the *transduction* of (a possibly nondeterministic) $\mathcal{A}$ as a function $\mathcal{T}_{\mathcal{A}} : \mathbb{Z}^* \to 2^{\mathbb{Z}^*}$ defined by $\mathcal{T}_{\mathcal{A}}(\vec{a}) \triangleq \{\vec{o} \mid \vec{a} \twoheadrightarrow_{\mathcal{A}} \vec{o}\}$. We say that $\mathcal{A}$ is *single-valued* if for all $\vec{a}$, $|\mathcal{T}_{\mathcal{A}}(\vec{a})| \le 1$.

4.3 Composition of SLTs

SLTs are closed under composition. Given a k-SLT $\mathcal{A}$ and a l-SLT $\mathcal{B}$, their composition is a $(k+l)$-SLT $\mathcal{A} \circ \mathcal{B}$ such that $\mathcal{T}_{\mathcal{A}\circ\mathcal{B}}(\vec{a}) = \{\mathcal{T}_{\mathcal{B}}(\vec{o}) \mid \vec{o} \in \mathcal{T}_{\mathcal{A}}(\vec{a})\}$. The composition of SLTs can be constructed similarly as the composition of symbolic finite-state transducers [14].

4.4 Equivalence Checking

Unfortunately, general equivalence checking of SLTs is undecidable as it is already undecidable to check equivalence of concrete non-deterministic ϵ-free finite-state transducers [41]. While the technique of Bjørner et al. [14] could be adapted to SLTs to decide the single-valued case, that would not suffice in our case as over-approximations of programs (§5) need not to be bounded-valued. Fortunately, our learning conjectures are always deterministic, so in fact we only need to check equivalence between a deterministic and a (possibly) non-deterministic SLT.

We present an efficient algorithm for equivalence checking between deterministic and non-deterministic SLTs, which is a symbolic adaptation of the algorithm from Demers et al. [22] for deciding single-valuedness of finite-state transducers. To check whether a deterministic and non-deterministic SLT are equivalent, it suffices to check whether their union (which is a non-deterministic SLT) is single-valued. Checking whether a non-deterministic SLT $\mathcal{A} = (Q, q_0, \Delta)$ is single-valued is efficiently decidable in $\mathcal{O}(|Q|^2)$ time [22] by checking whether a linear grammar generated from $\mathcal{A}$ generates a language of palindromes [38].

Let (N, T, P, S) be a linear context-free grammar, with a finite set of non-terminals (resp. terminals) N (resp. T), a finite set of productions P of the form $N ::= TNT \mid \epsilon$, and the start symbol $S \in N$. From a k-SLT $\mathcal{A}$, generate a grammar $\mathcal{G} = (Q \times Q, BExp[\mathsf{V}^k_\lambda] \times Exp[\mathsf{V}^k_\lambda]^*, P, [q_0, q_0])$, where P is defined as $[s_1, s_2] ::= (\varphi_1, \mathbf{t}_1)[s_1', s_2'](\varphi_2, \mathbf{t}_2)$, such that $(s_i, \varphi_i, \mathbf{t}_i, s_i') \in \Delta$, $\bigwedge_i \varphi_i$ is satisfiable, and $\mathbf{t}_i \neq \bot$. By $\bot$, our learning algorithm denotes outputs on transitions that are either infeasible because of the constraints on the path condition, or subsumed by other predicates. $\mathcal{A}$ is single-valued iff $\mathcal{G}$ generates a set of palindromes. Checking whether the outputs match under the guards reduces to checking the validity of formula $(\bigwedge_i \varphi_i) \Rightarrow \mathbf{t}_1 = \mathbf{t}_2$, which can be done with $\mathcal{O}(|Q|^2)$ calls to the prover. If $\mathcal{A}$ is not single valued then we construct a witness for disequality between the deterministic and the non-deterministic SLT called *separating sequence* by finding the shortest path from the start symbol to the first reachable rule that does not generate a palindrome.

4.5 Extension with Lookahead

SLTs can be straightforwardly extended to incorporate lookahead. In our model of SLTs, the sliding window begins at the current input tape head position and covers k last symbols. Such window can also be made to cover symbols ahead of the current head position by using additional λ-variables $\lambda_1, \dots, \lambda_l$ such that λ_i stands for the symbol i positions ahead. A k-SLT with a lookahead l can be reduced to a $(k+l)$-SLT, so equivalence checking of SLTs with lookahead can be reduced to equivalence checking of SLTs.

5. Synthesis of Over-Approximations

We now show how to synthesize sound program over-approximations for a class of programs with finite lookback. Overapproximations are computed in two steps. In the first step, we construct an over-approximation of the program that is based on predicate abstraction [8, 30]. In the second step, we transform the obtained abstraction to an equivalent non-deterministic SLT. We refine such an SLT by augmenting the set of predicates in predicate abstraction.

5.1 Abstraction of Transductive Programs

The goal of the abstraction is to abstract away the internal computation of the program but in doing so to keep all of its original input-output behavior. Let us consider the LTS $\mathcal{T} = (\mathsf{State}, C, \rightsquigarrow)$ of a transductive program $\mathcal{P}$ as defined in §3.3. We parameterize our abstraction by a set of predicates Φ over program variables, interpreted over $\mathsf{V} \rightharpoonup \mathbb{Z}$. Let us denote by $\mathsf{Pred}(\Phi)$ the set of boolean combinations over predicates from Φ (i.e., all minterms). We define the abstraction of $\mathcal{T}$ as the LTS $\mathcal{T}^\sharp = (\mathsf{State}^\sharp, C, \rightsquigarrow^\sharp)$ constructed as follows. The set of abstract states $\mathsf{State}^\sharp$ is given by

$$\mathsf{State}^\sharp \triangleq \mathsf{N} \times \mathsf{Pred}(\Phi) \times (\mathsf{V_D} \rightharpoonup Exp[\mathsf{V_I}]) \times \mathsf{OutStr} \times \mathbb{N} \times \mathbb{N}$$

where the valuations of program variables are mapped to predicates in $\mathsf{Pred}(\Phi)$ satisfied by the valuation, while the data variables $\mathsf{V_D} \subseteq \mathsf{V}$ that are live (i.e., for which there exists data flow to output terms), are kept intact along with other components of the state. Using the approximate post operator on $\mathsf{Pred}(\Phi)$ computed with predicate abstraction we obtain the transition relation $\rightsquigarrow^\sharp$ on abstract states. We rely on the soundness of the predicate abstraction to obtain the following.

Proposition 2. *For every input $\vec{a}$, if $\tau_{\mathcal{P}}(\vec{a}) = s_0 \dots s_n$ is a trace in $\mathcal{T}$, then there exists a trace $\tau^\sharp_{\mathcal{P}}(\vec{a}) = s_0' \dots s_n'$ in $\mathcal{T}^\sharp$ such that for every $0 \le i \le n$, $s_i.\mathsf{n} = s_i'.\mathsf{n}$, $s_i.\rho = s_i'.\rho$ $s_i.\imath = s_i'.\imath$, $s_i.\jmath = s_i'.\jmath$, $s_i.\sigma|_{\mathsf{V_D}} = s_i'.\sigma$ and $s_i.\sigma$ satisfies $s_i'.\varphi$. Consequently, the output $\gamma^\sharp_{\mathcal{P}}(\vec{a})$ corresponding to the trace $\tau^\sharp_{\mathcal{P}}(\vec{a})$ is equal to $\gamma_{\mathcal{P}}(\vec{a})$.*

5.2 Translation to SLTs

We now translate the abstract LTS $\mathcal{T}^\sharp = (\mathsf{State}^\sharp, C, \rightsquigarrow^\sharp)$ into an equivalent (possibly non-deterministic) SLT. We define an equivalence relation $\sim$ on $\mathsf{State}^\sharp$ as follows. For $s, s' \in \mathsf{State}^\sharp$, we let $s \sim s'$ iff[3] for $\Lambda(s) = (n, \varphi_\lambda, \sigma_\lambda, \rho_\lambda, \jmath)$ and $\Lambda(s') = (n', \varphi_\lambda', \sigma_\lambda', \rho_\lambda', \jmath')$ we have $n = n'$, $\varphi_\lambda \Leftrightarrow \varphi_\lambda'$ and $\sigma_\lambda = \sigma_\lambda'$.

Relation $\sim$ can have infinitely many equivalence classes in general, however, we focus on programs having finite-index $\sim$, as we can represent such programs with SLTs and learn with Σ^*.

Definition 3. *We say that $\mathcal{P}$ is* SLT-representable *if for any choice of Φ, the corresponding relation $\sim$ is of finite index.*

SLT-representable programs necessary have a bounded lookback.

Let us define $\mathsf{paths}^\sharp_{\mathsf{in}}(s, t)$ as the set of all $\rightsquigarrow^\sharp$-sequences of states between s and t such that there is a single input transition

[3] We extend the definition of input-relativization to $s = (\mathsf{n}, \varphi, \sigma, \rho, \imath, \jmath) \in \mathsf{State}^\sharp$ by $\Lambda(s) \triangleq (\mathsf{n}, \varphi[\vec{in} \xmapsto{\imath} \overleftarrow{\lambda}], \sigma[\vec{in} \xmapsto{\imath} \overleftarrow{\lambda}], \rho[\vec{in} \xmapsto{\imath} \overleftarrow{\lambda}], \jmath)$.

between states on the path from s to t. For $\xi \in \mathsf{paths}^\sharp_{\mathsf{in}}(s,t)$, let us denote by $\pi^\sharp(\xi)$ the conjunction of assumed predicates on transitions in ξ and let $\theta^\sharp(\xi)$ be the produced symbolic output. We need the following lemma for our translation to an SLT to be well-defined.

Lemma 4. *If $s \sim s'$ and $t \sim t'$ then for every path $\xi \in \mathsf{paths}^\sharp_{\mathsf{in}}(s,t)$, there exists an equivalent path $\xi' \in \mathsf{paths}^\sharp_{\mathsf{in}}(s',t')$ such that $\pi^\sharp(\xi) = \pi^\sharp(\xi')$ and $\theta^\sharp(\xi) = \theta^\sharp(\xi')$.*

We define $\mathcal{A}_\Phi$ to be the SLT (Q, q_0, Δ) with $Q \triangleq \{[s]_\sim \mid s \text{ is } in\text{-state}\}$ as the set of states, $q_0 \triangleq [s_0]_\sim$ as the initial state and Δ as the transition relation such that $[s] \xrightarrow{\varphi/\mathbf{t}} [s'] \in \Delta$ iff there exist $\xi \in \mathsf{paths}^\sharp_{\mathsf{in}}(s,s')$, such that $\pi^\sharp(\xi) = \varphi$ and $\theta^\sharp(\xi) = \mathbf{t}$. Intuitively, $\mathcal{A}_\Phi$ represents all isomorphism classes of big-step transitions between the abstracted in-states.

Lemma 5. *If $\mathcal{P}$ is SLT-representable then $\mathcal{A}_\Phi$ is an SLT.*

We can now show that $\mathcal{A}_\Phi$ captures exactly the behavior of $\mathcal{T}^\sharp$ thus $\mathcal{A}_\Phi$ soundly over-approximates the behavior of $\mathcal{P}$.

Proposition 6. *For all $\vec{a}$, $\gamma^\sharp_{\mathcal{P}}(\vec{a}) = \vec{o}$ iff $\vec{a}^\perp \twoheadrightarrow_{\mathcal{A}_\Phi} \vec{o}$.*

Corollary 7. *For all $\vec{a}$, if $\gamma_{\mathcal{P}}(\vec{a}) = \vec{o}$ then $\vec{a}^\perp \twoheadrightarrow_{\mathcal{A}_\Phi} \vec{o}$.*

5.3 Refinement

Suppose that $\mathcal{A}_\Phi$ strictly over-approximates the behavior of an SLT-representable $\mathcal{P}$ on some input $\vec{a}$, i.e., there exist $\vec{o}$ and $\vec{o}'$, $\vec{o} \neq \vec{o}'$, such that $\gamma_{\mathcal{P}}(\vec{a}) = \vec{o}$ and $\vec{a} \twoheadrightarrow_{\mathcal{A}_\Phi} \vec{o}'$. Then we need to refine the abstraction $\mathcal{A}_\Phi$. We do so by adding enough predicates to Φ to evidence infeasibility of the spurious run in $\mathcal{A}_\Phi$ that generates $\vec{o}'$.

Our approach to finding a new set of predicates for refining $\mathcal{A}_\Phi$ is based on standard counterexample feasibility analysis with weakest preconditions [6]. The basic idea is to build a predicate α from the spurious trace in $\mathcal{A}_\Phi$ generating $\vec{o}'$ so that α is unsatisfiable if and only if the given trace is infeasible in $\mathcal{P}$. Starting with false, α is obtained by applying the weakest precondition of commands in $\mathcal{P}$ along the trace, until the beginning of the trace. To maintain the syntactic form of assume-predicates collected along the trace, we keep all substitutions in α explicitly. The set of all atomic predicates in α is then used to augment Φ.[4] Although more involved methods (e.g., based on Craig interpolation) are possible, our empirical evaluation shows that this heuristic works well in practice for our target classes of programs.

Completeness of the predicate selection method. Since our abstraction is based on predicate abstraction and fully precise isomorphic representation of other components of the state, $\mathcal{A}_\Phi$ in fact defines the strongest inductive invariant containing the reachable set of states of $\mathcal{P}$ that is expressible as a Boolean combination of the given set of predicates, while faithfully preserving the input-output relation in the relativized form. If there exists a quantifier-free inductive invariant ψ which can be built using some set of predicates Φ such that ψ uniquely identifies the reachable states of $\mathcal{P}$, then the construction of abstraction would converge. Assuming a complete decision procedure for the underlying theory and a predicate selection method that would eventually build such Φ, by the relative completeness of predicate abstraction [9, 42], we could generate an invariant as strong as ψ.

Although it is not clear how to construct such ψ directly from $\mathcal{P}$, we can construct it if the number of states n of an SLT $\mathcal{A}_{\mathcal{P}}$ that is behaviorally equivalent to $\mathcal{P}$ is known a priori—by explicitly encoding a checking sequence [46] that distinguishes $\mathcal{A}_{\mathcal{P}}$ from all other transducers up to n states. To abstract away the complexity of such construction, we assume existence of a predicate selection method that eventually yields a set Φ resulting in an abstraction $\mathcal{A}_\Phi$ equivalent to $\mathcal{P}$. We will say that a predicate selection method is *complete* if it is guaranteed to eventually generate a sufficient set of predicates to construct $\mathcal{A}_\Phi$ equivalent to $\mathcal{P}$. Our main result expresses completeness of our learning algorithm relative to existence of such a complete predicate selection method. However, we emphasize that the predicate selection mechanism does not affect the soundness of Σ^*, nor the quality of inferred models, only the eventual convergence.

[4] In some examples we employ additional heuristic that uses templates built from syntactic predicates in the code.

6. Learning

In this section, we describe Σ^*'s learning algorithm and prove its main properties. Our algorithm iteratively builds conjectures similarly as L^*. To make the presentation reasonably self-contained, we first give a brief overview of L^* (§6.1). We then define the representation of conjectures (§6.2), followed by the detailed presentation of the learning algorithm (§6.3) and its properties (§6.4).

6.1 Background: Overview of L^*

Here we give an informal overview of the classic L^*. See the paper of Angluin [5] for a more detailed description (or Shahbaz and Groz [50] for the Mealy machines version of L^*).

The goal of L^* is to learn an unknown regular language D by generating a deterministic finite automaton (DFA) that accepts D. L^* starts by asking a teacher, who knows D, membership queries over a known concrete alphabet to check whether certain words are in D. The results of these queries are recorded in a so-called observation table. Membership queries are iteratively asked until certain technical conditions are met, upon which L^* conjectures an automaton. L^* asks the teacher an equivalence query to check if the conjectured language is equivalent to D. The teacher either confirms the equivalence or returns a counterexample, which is a word that distinguishes D from the conjecture. L^* uses the counterexample to devise new membership queries, refining the conjecture. This procedure is repeated until the conjecture becomes equivalent to D. If D is indeed a regular language then L^* is guaranteed to find a (minimal) DFA for D after at most a polynomial number of membership and equivalence queries.

In Σ^*, we answer the membership queries by using a combination of concrete and symbolic execution [16, 28, 49], and the equivalence queries by equivalence checking learned conjectures and increasingly refined abstractions, using the equivalence checking algorithm for SLTs (§4.4).

6.2 Definitions

We proceed by giving notational conveniences used in the section and defining Σ^*'s representation of the observation table.

We first define a relativization function for path predicates and symbolic outputs by $\Lambda(s_1 \ldots s_n) \triangleq s_1[\vec{in} \overset{1}{\mapsto} \overleftarrow{\lambda}] \ldots s_n[\vec{in} \overset{n}{\mapsto} \overleftarrow{\lambda}]$, where $\vec{in} \overset{i}{\mapsto} \overleftarrow{\lambda}$ is the variable substitution defined in §3.6 and $\vec{s}$ is either a path predicate or symbolic output. If $\vec{s}$ is a symbolic output $\vec{t}$, the same relativization function is applied to each individual term in the subsequence, i.e., if $\mathbf{t} = t_1 \ldots t_m$ then $\mathbf{t}[\vec{in} \overset{i}{\mapsto} \overleftarrow{\lambda}] = t_1[\vec{in} \overset{i}{\mapsto} \overleftarrow{\lambda}] \ldots t_m[\vec{in} \overset{i}{\mapsto} \overleftarrow{\lambda}]$. We next define $\mathsf{witness}$ as a function that takes a sequence of relativized predicates, derelativizes them by applying the inverse of the Λ substitution, computes a conjunction of derelativized predicates $\bigwedge_{1 \leq i \leq |\vec{p}|} (\Lambda^{-1}(\vec{p}))\,|_i$, passes the conjunction to an SMT solver, and returns a concrete sequence of input symbols of length $|\vec{p}|$ satisfying the conjunction, or $\perp$ if the conjunction is infeasible. Finally, we point out that all equality (resp. inequality) checks $=$ (resp. $\neq$) over predicates and terms in this section are syntactic equality (resp. inequality) checks.[5]

Σ^* constructs symbolic observation table similarly as L^*, but table entries are path predicates and symbolic outputs (§3.4), rather than concrete words. The finished table can be easily translated into an SLT, representing a conjecture. As in L^*, such conjecture will always be deterministic.

Definition 8. Symbolic observation table *is a quadruple* $(R, S, E, T) \subseteq (BExp[\mathsf{V}_\lambda]^*, BExp[\mathsf{V}_\lambda]^*, BExp[\mathsf{V}_\lambda]^*, BExp[\mathsf{V}_\lambda]^* \times BExp[\mathsf{V}_\lambda]^* \rightarrow (Exp[\mathsf{V}_\lambda] \cup \{\bot, \epsilon\})^*)$, *where*

- *$R \subseteq S$ represents a set of identified states,*
- *S (resp. E) is a prefix- (resp. suffix-) closed set of relativized path predicates, and*
- *T is a map indexed by $\vec{p}_\mathsf{p} \in S, \vec{p}_\mathsf{s} \in E$, containing the suffix of the relativized symbolic output generated when processing $\vec{p}_\mathsf{s}$ immediately after $\vec{p}_\mathsf{p}$, i.e., if $\vec{a} = \mathsf{witness}(\vec{p}_\mathsf{p} \cdot \vec{p}_\mathsf{s})$ and $\vec{t} = \Lambda(\theta_\mathcal{P}(\vec{a}))$ then $T[\vec{p}_\mathsf{p}, \vec{p}_\mathsf{s}] = \vec{t}_\mathsf{s}$, where $\vec{t}_\mathsf{s}$ is a suffix of $\vec{t}$ such that $|\vec{t}_\mathsf{s}| = |\vec{p}_\mathsf{s}|$.*

For $\vec{p} \in S$, we define a $\vec{p}$-row in the observation table as an E-indexed set, denoted $\vec{p}$-row. We denote outputs generated by infeasible transitions in the table by $\bot$.

Intuitively, R represents a set of shortest paths leading to discovered states, $S \supseteq R$ contains exactly path predicates from R and additionally all the sequences that extend sequences from R by exactly one big-step transition. The role of S is to exercise all the transitions in the inferred SLT. Finally, E is the set of distinguishing tests that distinguish different states.

The classic L^* makes a conjecture when the table is *closed*, which means that every sequence in S has a representative in R, i.e., $\forall \vec{p} \in S \,.\, \exists \vec{r} \in R \,.\, \vec{p}\text{-}row = \vec{r}\text{-}row$. We define closedness in the same way as L^*. From a closed table, we can easily construct a complete (for all states and input symbols, all transitions are defined) SLT using standard techniques (e.g., see [5, 50]).[6]

6.3 The Learning Algorithm

We begin by describing the FILLROWS algorithm that computes the missing entries of the observation table, continue with the EXTENDTABLE algorithm that explores the successor states of all states discovered at certain step, and end with the Σ^*'s learning algorithm.

Algorithm 1 computes the missing entries in the observation table. If the entry is missing for some prefix $\vec{p}_\mathsf{p} \in S$ and suffix $\vec{p}_\mathsf{s} \in E$, we first try to compute a concrete witness $\vec{a}$ by splicing together the prefix and the suffix (Line 2). While the sets S (and R) contain path predicates that are collected along prefixes of some feasible paths in $\mathcal{P}$ starting from the initial state, the set E contains suffixes of feasible paths. Naturally, when we arbitrarily splice prefixes and suffixes of different paths, the resulting formula might be infeasible. If feasible, we execute $\vec{a}$ on $\mathcal{P}$ using concolic execution (Line 4) and collect the predicates ($\vec{r}$) and output terms ($\vec{t}$) from big-step transitions. Note that the collected predicates might differ from $\vec{p}_\mathsf{p} \cdot \vec{p}_\mathsf{s}$, but at least the prefix (corresponding to $\vec{p}_\mathsf{p}$) will always match. The outputs corresponding to mismatched

input and output : Observation table OT
1 **forall the** $\vec{p}_\mathsf{p} \in S, \vec{p}_\mathsf{s} \in E$ *such that* $T[\vec{p}_\mathsf{p}, \vec{p}_\mathsf{s}]$ *is undefined* **do**
2 $\quad \vec{a} := \mathsf{witness}(\vec{p}_\mathsf{p} \cdot \vec{p}_\mathsf{s})$
3 $\quad$ **if** $\vec{a} \neq \bot$ **then**
4 $\quad\quad (\vec{r}, \vec{t}) := (\Lambda(\pi_\mathcal{P}(\vec{a})), \Lambda(\theta_\mathcal{P}(\vec{a})))$ `// assert(`$|\vec{r}| = |\vec{t}|$`)`
5 $\quad\quad \vec{t}_\mathsf{s} := \epsilon$
6 $\quad\quad$ **forall the** $1 \leq i \leq |\vec{t}|$ **do**
7 $\quad\quad\quad$ **if** $i > |\vec{p}_\mathsf{p}|$ **then**
8 $\quad\quad\quad\quad$ **if** $(\vec{p}_\mathsf{p} \cdot \vec{p}_\mathsf{s})|_i = \vec{r}|_i$ **then** $\vec{t}_\mathsf{s} := \vec{t}_\mathsf{s} \cdot \vec{t}|_i$
9 $\quad\quad\quad\quad$ **else** $\vec{t}_\mathsf{s} := \vec{t}_\mathsf{s} \cdot \bot$
10 $\quad\quad\quad$ **else**
$\quad\quad\quad\quad$ `// assert(`$\vec{p}_\mathsf{p}|_i = \vec{r}|_i$`)`
11 $\quad\quad T[\vec{p}_\mathsf{p}, \vec{p}_\mathsf{s}] := \vec{t}_\mathsf{s}$
12 $\quad$ **else**
13 $\quad\quad T[\vec{p}_\mathsf{p}, \vec{p}_\mathsf{s}] := \bot$
`// Close the table`
14 **forall the** $\vec{p} \in S$ *s.t.* $\neg\exists \vec{r} \in R \,.\, \vec{p}\text{-}row = \vec{r}\text{-}row$ **do**
15 $\quad R := R \cup \vec{p}$ `// New state`
16 Return OT

Algorithm 1: The FILLROWS Algorithm.

predicates and infeasible path conditions are marked $\bot$. Lines 6–9 replace the output terms at positions where the $\vec{p}_\mathsf{p} \cdot \vec{p}_\mathsf{s}$ and $\vec{r}$ sequences differ syntactically. Finally, lines 14–15 close the table.

Algorithm 2 takes a state representative $\vec{r}$, i.e., a path predicate that holds on the shortest path to the identified state, and finds all the outgoing big-step transitions from that state, adding the predicates from those transitions to E and the entire sequence ($\vec{r}$ extended by one transition) to S. The only interesting part of the algorithm is the discovery of new transitions and the corresponding predicates. In the first iteration, Line 6 extends the representative sequence $\vec{r}$ with predicate true, effectively allowing the solver to produce an arbitrary value for the last element of the concrete input sequence. Executing the obtained concrete sequence and collecting predicates along the path, we identify the first big-step transition guard predicate (r_s). In every following iteration, we negate a disjunction of the predicates discovered so far, until the disjunction becomes valid (test at Line 4). All infeasible traces lead to a ghost state that has one self-loop transition labeled $\mathsf{true}/\bot$. The algorithm creates such a state automatically, if needed, by filling the corresponding row with $\bot$, as even the prefix to the ghost state is infeasible.

Finally, Algorithm 3 infers a symbolic transducer. Lines 1–9 discover all the big-step transitions from the initial state and the corresponding predicates. All the discovered predicates are added to the set E. In the next three lines, we extend and close the table, producing the first $\mathcal{A}_C$ conjecture and the first abstraction $\mathcal{A}_\Phi$ of $\mathcal{P}$. The loop beginning on Line 15 checks the equivalence between the conjecture and abstraction. If they are equivalent, the algorithm terminates returning the exact transducer implemented by $\mathcal{P}$. Otherwise, the counterexample is checked against $\mathcal{P}$. If it is spurious, we refine the abstraction, otherwise, we refine the conjecture. We use Shahbaz and Groz's [50] technique for processing the counterexamples adapted for our symbolic setting. First, we collect the predicates from $\mathcal{P}$ along the path determined by the counterexample and discard the longest prefix that is already in S. We denote the remaining suffix by $\vec{p}_\mathsf{s}$. We add all suffixes of $\vec{p}_\mathsf{s}$ to E (Line 24), to assure that E remains suffix closed.

6.4 Properties

First, we state the main properties of Σ^*, and then proceed with the proof of relative completeness and a discussion of computational complexity.

[5] At the cost of more complex exposition, we could use semantic equality and check that output terms are equal under the guard restrictions. Such an approach might allow us to learn more compact SLTs.

[6] In L^*, one also defines the *consistency* property, which would in our setting say that if two sequences $\vec{p}_1, \vec{p}_2$ from R are equivalent, then both states reached by $\gamma_\mathcal{P}(\mathsf{witness}(\vec{p}_1))$ and $\gamma_\mathcal{P}(\mathsf{witness}(\vec{p}_2))$ must produce the same output in the next big-step transition given the same input symbol. We maintain the consistency of our symbolic observation table by always assuring that each state has only one representative in the R set.

input and output : Observation table OT

forall the $\vec{r} \in R$ **do** `// Extend all sequences from` R
  if $\neg\exists \vec{p_s} \in E \,.\, |\vec{p_s}| = 1 \wedge \vec{r} \cdot \vec{p_s} \in S$ **then**
    $s := \mathsf{false}$
    while $s \not\Leftrightarrow \mathsf{true}$ **do**
      $r_s := \epsilon$
      $\vec{a} := \mathsf{witness}(\vec{r} \cdot \neg s)$
      if $a = \bot$ **then**
        $r_s := \neg s$
        $s := \mathsf{true}$
      else
        $\vec{p} := \Lambda(\pi_{\mathcal{P}}(\vec{a}))$
        `// assert(`$|\vec{p}| = |\vec{r}| + 1$`)` $r_s := \vec{p}|_{|\vec{r}|+1}$
        $s := s \vee r_s$
      $E := E \cup \{r_s\}$
      $S := S \cup \{\vec{r} \cdot r_s\}$
      $OT :=$ FILLROWS(OT)
Return OT

Algorithm 2: The EXTENDTABLE Algorithm.

init : $R = \{\epsilon\}, S = \{\epsilon\}, E = \emptyset, T = \emptyset, i = 0, s = \mathsf{false}$
result : k-SLT $\mathcal{A}_C$

repeat `// Fill 1st row`
  if $s \Leftrightarrow \mathsf{false}$ **then**
    $a :=$ randomly generated array of type $\mathbb{Z}[1]$
  else
    $a := \mathsf{witness}(\neg s)$
  $p := \Lambda\left(\pi_{\mathcal{P}}(a)|_1\right)$ `// 1st pred. from path predicate`
  $E := E \cup p$
  $T[\epsilon, p] := \Lambda\left(\theta_{\mathcal{P}}(a)|_1\right)$
  $s := s \vee p$
until $s \Leftrightarrow \mathsf{true}$
$(R, S, E, T) :=$ EXTENDTABLE(FILLROWS(R, S, E, T))
Compute $\mathcal{A}_C$ from (R, S, E, T)
Compute initial $\mathcal{A}_\Phi$ of $\mathcal{P}$
while true **do**
  Let $(\vec{a}, \vec{o})$ be a separating sequence between $\mathcal{A}_C$ and $\mathcal{A}_\Phi$
  if $\vec{a} = \epsilon$ **then**
    Return $\mathcal{A}_C$
  if $\gamma_{\mathcal{P}}(\vec{a}) \neq \vec{o}$ **then** `// Spurious counterexample?`
    Refine $\mathcal{A}_\Phi$ of $\mathcal{P}$ on $(\vec{a}, \vec{o})$
  else
    $\vec{p} := \Lambda(\pi_{\mathcal{P}}(\vec{a}))$
    Let $\vec{p_p}$ be the longest prefix of $\vec{p}$ s.t. $\vec{p_p} \in S$
    Let $\vec{p_s}$ be s.t. $\vec{p} = \vec{p_p} \cdot \vec{p_s}$
    $E := E \cup \mathit{Suffix}\,(\vec{p_s})$
    $(R, S, E, T) :=$ EXTENDTABLE(FILLROWS(R, S, E, T))
    Compute $\mathcal{A}_C$ from (R, S, E, T)

Algorithm 3: The Σ^*'s Learning Algorithm.

Lemma 9. *Let $T = (R, S, E, T)$ be a symbolic observation table. Then Σ^* preserves the following invariants:*

1. *R and S (resp. E) are always prefix- (resp. suffix-) closed.*
2. *For every $\vec{p} \in S$ there is a unique $\vec{r} \in R$ such that $\vec{p}$-row $=$ $\vec{r}$-row.*
3. *For every $\vec{r} \in R$, there are $r_s^1, \ldots, r_s^n$ such that $\bigvee_{i=1}^{n} r_s^i \Leftrightarrow$ true and for all i, it holds that $\vec{r} \cdot r_s^i \in S$.*
4. *The conjecture $\mathcal{A}_C$ is closed at the end of each step.*

Correctness. R represents the part of the symbolic execution tree of $\mathcal{P}$ on which the conjecture faithfully represents the behavior of $\mathcal{P}$, which is stated with the following proposition.

Proposition 10 (Bounded correctness)**.** *After each step, for all $\vec{r} \in R$ and $\vec{a}$ such that $\vec{a} = \mathsf{witness}(\vec{r})$, $\gamma_{\mathcal{P}}(\vec{a}) = \gamma_{\mathcal{A}_C}(\vec{a})$ holds.*

One can rephrase bounded correctness as a guarantee given by Σ^* in case Σ^* is interrupted before reaching a convergence. In other words, we can consider Σ^* as performing bounded model checking of the program with a state-space exploration strategy guided by the learned model.

Completeness. The following lemma ensures that a progress is made after each conjecture refinement.

Lemma 11. *If at some step of Σ^*, $(\vec{a}, \vec{o})$ is a separating sequence such that $\gamma_{\mathcal{P}}(\vec{a}) = \vec{o}$, then at the end of the step, for all $\vec{a}'$ such that $\vec{a}' = \mathsf{witness}(\pi_{\mathcal{P}}(\vec{a}))$, $\gamma_{\mathcal{A}_C}(\vec{a}') = \gamma_{\mathcal{P}}(\vec{a}')$ holds.*

We state the completeness of Σ^* relative to the completeness of the predicate selection method.

Theorem 12 (Relative completeness)**.** *If $\mathcal{P}$ is SLT-representable and the predicate selection method for refinement is complete, then Σ^* terminates with $\mathcal{A}_C$ being behaviorally equivalent to $\mathcal{P}$.*

Proof. First note that when $\mathcal{A}_\Phi$ is single-valued, then by the soundness of abstraction, $\mathcal{A}_\Phi$ is in fact behaviorally equivalent to $\mathcal{P}$. As the predicate selection method is assumed to be complete, we will eventually obtain a single-valued $\mathcal{A}_\Phi$.

The equivalence check of $\mathcal{A}_\Phi$ and $\mathcal{A}_C$ always returns the shortest separating sequence (if one exists). There can be only finitely many shortest separating sequences of a given length, and at each step such a sequence is used either to refine the conjecture or to refine the abstraction. Therefore, the number of conjecture refinements must also be finite. □

Computational complexity. Next, we analyze the complexity of Σ^*. Let n be the number of states of the inferred SLT, k the maximal number of outgoing big-step transitions from any state, m the maximal length of any counterexample, and c the number of counterexamples. There can be at most $n - 1$ counterexamples, as each counterexample distinguishes at least one state. Since we initialize E with k predicates, $|E|$ can grow to at most $k+m(n-1)$. The size of S is at most $n \cdot k$. Thus, the table can contain at most $n \cdot k \cdot (k + m \cdot n - m) = \mathcal{O}(n \cdot k^2 + m \cdot n^2 \cdot k)$ entries. The k factor is likely to be small in practice, and our equivalence checking algorithm finds the minimal counterexample. The SMT solver is called once per each state (i.e., representative in R) and for each outgoing transition. For each equivalence check, we might need to call the solver n^2 times. Thus, the total worst-case number of calls to the solver is $\mathcal{O}(n \cdot k + n^2)$, not including the number of calls required for abstraction refinement, which depends on the abstraction technique used.

7. Applications

In this section, we demonstrate practical utility of Σ^* by applying it in three different application domains and reporting experimental results obtained with our prototype implementation.

We built our implementation on top of KLEE [17] with STP [25] and CPAchecker [13]. We patched KLEE to generate relativized symbolic traces and answer membership queries for the learning algorithm (§6), and used STP in the equivalence checking algorithm (§4.4). We used CPAchecker for counterexample-guided predicate abstraction refinement (§5).

All experiments were run on a machine with Intel Core2 Quad 2.8 GHz CPU and NVIDIA GeForce GTX 460 GPU (with 7

Benchmark	Learned	Int. bits	#States	#Transitions	Lookback	$\#\mathcal{A}_C$ refinements	$\#\mathcal{A}_\Phi$ refinements	$\|\Phi\|$
`EncodeHtml` [37]	✓	8	1	2	0	0	1	10
`GetTags` [14]	✓	48	3	7	1	4	5	6
`CleanseAttribute`	✓	40	2	4	1	0	3	14
`CleanseCss`	✓	40	1	2	0	0	2	16
`CssUrlEscape`	✓	40	1	11	0	0	1	12
`HtmlEscape`	✓	8	$L+1$	$7 \cdot L$	L	L	$L+3$	$L+11$
`JavascriptEscape`	✓	16	3	16	2	2	6	20
`JavascriptNumber`	✓	41	17	19	16	17	23	41
`JsonEscape`	✓	8	$L+1$	$11 \cdot L$	L	L	$L+3$	$L+12$
`PreEscape`	✓	8	$L+1$	$5 \cdot L$	L	L	$L+3$	$L+6$
`UrlQueryEscape`	✓	8	2	11	0	2	5	19
`XMLEscape`	✓	8	$L+1$	$7 \cdot L$	L	$L-1$	$L+2$	$L+11$
`PrefixLine`	–	8						
`SnippetEscape`	–	8						

Table 1: Experimental Results. The benchmarks that Σ^* successfully learned are denoted by ✓. The last benchmark could be learned if Σ^* were extended to handle subsequential transducers. *Int. bits* is the size of the internal control and data state in bits, *#States* the number of states in the final SLT, *#Transitions* the number of transitions in the final SLT, *$\#\mathcal{A}_C$ refinements* the number of refinements of the conjecture, *$\#\mathcal{A}_\Phi$ refinements* the number of refinements of the abstraction, and $|\Phi|$ the size of the set of predicates in the final abstraction. In each of the four benchmarks whose rows contain symbolic expressions dependent on L, the particular L denotes the bound on the size of the buffer internally used by the benchmark. The value of L depends on the characteristics of the input language of the benchmark and is a priori fixed in our four benchmarks (e.g., for `HtmlEscape`, it is bounded by the maximal length of tag names, attribute names and special symbols).

1.42 GHz multiprocessors, 48 cores each). The learning algorithm inferred all learnable benchmarks described below in less than three seconds.

7.1 Web Sanitizers Verification

To make web applications more secure, sanitization is used to remove possibly malicious elements from user's input. Although small in numbers of lines of code, sanitizers in real-world applications are surprisingly difficult to implement correctly [10, 37], often because low-level implementation tricks are obscuring the intended input-output behavior. By automatically inferring input-output models of sanitizers, we can automatically check their properties such as commutativity, reversibility, and idempotence using tool such as Bek [37].

We evaluated Σ^* on the sanitizers from Google AutoEscape (GA) web sanitization framework, the same benchmarks used by Hooimeijer et al. [37]. We dropped the `ValidateUrl` sanitizer, as it is effectively just a wrapper for calling other sanitizers. In addition to GA sanitizers, we added to our benchmark suite the sanitizers `EncodeHtml` [37] and `GetTags` [14].

We found out that 86% of GA sanitizers (12 out of 14) along with `EncodeHtml` and `GetTags` are SLT-representable and were successfully learned by Σ^* (Table 1). In comparison, the authors of [37] had to invest several hours of a human expert's time into manual synthesis of each transducer from the source code. Only two sanitizers could not be inferred by Σ^*. `PrefixLine` is effectively a 0-SLT, but it is implemented by calling the `memchr` function in guards, which could only be represented by nondeterminism, as `memchr`'s return value could be arbitrarily far ahead from the start of the input string. `SnippetEscape` generates output from a predefined set of symbols only at the end of the input, but it could be learned if Σ^* were extended to subsequential transducers by generalizing Vilar's algorithm [58] to the symbolic setting.

7.2 Stream Filter Optimization

Stream programs often consist of many interacting filters that have to be optimized against various goals (e.g., speed, latency, throughput, ...). Two vital filter optimizations are reordering and fusion. For instance, reordering might be profitable when it would place a filter that is selective (i.e., drops some data) before a costly filter that does some processing. However, we must ensure that the

Benchmark	Linear	Stateless
Saxpy kernel [56]	+	+
Radix-2 complex FFT filter [43]	+	+
FIR filter [45]	+	+
Zig-zag descrambling filter in MPEG-2 [23]	+	+
Clsfr in L3-Switch bridge [18]	–	+
FM demodulator in StreamIt [54]	–	+
MPEG-2 internal parser in StreamIt [54]	–	–
GSM encoder/decoder in MiBench [33]	–	–

Table 2: Properties of Eight Filters Inferred by Σ^*. First four filters are linear and can be optimized with existing techniques. Σ^* enables fusion and reordering optimizations for all eight filters. By stateless, we mean single-state transducers.

two filters are commutative in order for reordering to be safe. Filter fusion is used when it would be profitable to trade pipeline parallelism for lower communication cost.

We conducted a set of experiments to explore ability of Σ^* to enable stream filter optimizations such as reordering and fusion. Table 2 shows eight filters inferred by Σ^* indicating their two key properties: whether they encode a linear or non-linear output function, and whether they are stateless (i.e., have a single state) or stateful (i.e., have more then one state). First four filters can be optimized with existing techniques for optimizing linear filters [2, 45]. To our knowledge, no optimization techniques used in existing stream program compilers can optimize the remaining filters in Table 2. On the other hand, Σ^* enables fusion and reordering optimizations for all eight filters.

7.3 Parallelization

Finally, we show how SLT models of filters enable automated parallelization. We consider two approaches to improving utilization of hardware concurrency by mapping filters to (1) multiple cores and (2) SIMD instructions. Stateless filters are inherently data-parallel and lend themselves naturally to both multi-core and vectorized implementations by simple replication. Stateful filters normally cannot be parallelized this way as their next invocation depends on the previous invocation. However, SLT filters have usually small, a priori known, number of states, so we can run each replica of an SLT filter from each state in parallel and merge suitable outputs.

To provide some insight into possible practical speedups, we generated SIMD implementations using Intel SSE4 intrinsics and GPU implementations using NVIDIA CUDA 4.2 of 11 single-state SLTs (3 from Table 1, 6 from Table 2, and 2 hand-crafted) and one three-state SLT inferred by Σ^*. Original source code representations of all SLTs are stateful and some of them are with non-affine loop nests. For the stateless SLTs, we obtained speedups in the range of 1.72 to 3.89 for the SSE versions, and 1.5 to 2.7 for the CUDA versions. For the 3-state SLT, the speedup of the CUDA version was 2.3. CUDA versions were run using 1024 threads (resp. 1024 threads in 3 blocks) for the single-state (resp. three-state) SLTs. We established the baseline by running the sequential version of SLTs compiled with `gcc` with all optimizations (`-O3`) and SSE flags turned on.

8. Discussion

Predicate abstraction. To obtain complete models, Σ^* relies on convergence of the abstraction. One could rightfully ask why we need the whole learning machinery of Σ^* as we presume the abstraction eventually becoming equivalent (although, in a possibly non-deterministic form) to the behavioral model. Our program is deterministic, so as long as the abstraction is not single-valued it must contain infeasible behavior. Therefore, we could consider a procedure that just iteratively refines the abstraction until the abstraction becomes single-valued.

Setting aside how to efficiently refine abstractions alone, an abstraction-only approach suffers from a fundamental limitation: models generated by the abstraction can be unboundedly larger than the ones learned by Σ^*. For instance, consider the program from Figure 1 in [31], which is considered as an example on which predicate abstraction does not work well. Let us adapt the example by adding reading an input and writing some output in the loop, and enclosing it with an outer **while**(`true`)-loop to become a transductive program. Then Σ^* infers a single-state SLT, while by using predicate abstraction alone we would obtain an SLT with 1000 states.

SLT limitations. Along with the dependency on the abstraction, ability of Σ^* to infer complete models of program behavior is limited by the expressive power of symbolic conjectures. We have judiciously restricted SLTs so as to be able to represent interesting real-world examples while still being able to learn and equivalence check them efficiently. However, there are still other interesting classes of programs that are not SLT-representable. At the cost of additional complexity, we believe it would be possible to extend Σ^* to work with symbolic versions of more expressive transducers such as subsequential [58] and streaming transducers [3] and in this way enable learning of larger classes of programs.

Incomplete models. While the main concern of this paper is learning of exact behavioral models, incomplete models inferred by Σ^* could also be useful, e.g., for automated testing based on dynamic symbolic execution [16, 28, 49]. The learning component of Σ^* can be seen as systematically exploring all paths in the execution tree of a program, but in addition conjecturing the behavior of not yet explored branches. Conjectures could be used to guide the exploration strategy, similarly as in MACE [19], which showed how concrete transducer conjectures enable more effective testing of protocol implementations.

9. Other Related Work

Learning of symbolic transducers. Previous work on learning some notion of symbolic transducers [1, 12, 40] focuses on limited variations that a priori fix the shape of predicates and generate concrete values. Learning algorithms for these transducers postulate existence of an equivalence checking oracle and work over concrete alphabets, relying on the shape restrictions to translate the L^*-inferred concrete transducer to a symbolic one. As software artefacts feature predicates that are unknown prior to the analysis, if techniques [1, 12, 40] were to be applied in the software setting, they would need to exhaustively enumerate predicates, whose set is unbounded.

Learning in verification. Techniques for learning various types of automata have been applied in a wide variety of verification settings: inference of interface invariants [4, 27, 51], learning-guided concolic execution [19], compositional verification [21], and regular model checking [34]. In those settings, except for [27], learning is performed using concrete alphabets in a black-box manner, even though source code is usually available. Independently to us, Giannakopoulou et al. [27] have recently developed a technique for learning component interfaces that combines L^* with symbolic execution to discover method input guards. However, their approach treats method invocations as a single input step with no output, and, unlike Σ^*, assumes that each method has a finite number of paths. Under this later constraint, equivalence checking can be done by merely executing a sufficiently large number of membership queries. Alur and Černý's approach to synthesis of interface specifications with JIST [4] also uses predicate abstraction as Σ^*. However, predicate abstraction in JIST is used to check whether the synthesized interfaces are safe for a given safety property. In general, such interfaces are approximate and may incorporate infeasible behavior. In addition, the paper [4] does not demonstrate that the technique can be fully automated. In contrast, Σ^* is fully automated and infers faithful models upon termination.

Property checking. Although the goal of Σ^* is different, it resembles some ideas used in property checking. Most closely related, collecting predicates on conditional statements as in automated testing [16, 28, 49] has been previously combined with predicate abstraction in the SYNERGY algorithm [31]. While SYNERGY uses a combination of *must* and *may* analyses to check safety properties faster, Σ^* uses *must* (learning) and *may* (abstraction) to infer a more compact input-output relation.

Optimizations of filters. The closest work to our application of Σ^* for stream compiler optimizations is on optimizations of linear filters [45] and (slightly more general) linear state space systems [2] in StreamIt. In another line of work [47], fusion of filters for Brook has been developed using an affine model. Soulé et al. [52] developed a proof calculus that allows analysis of non-linear filters, but they can perform reordering optimizations only if filters are stateless. In contrast, Σ^* allows fusion and reordering of stateful filters with non-linear input-output relations. Approaches for numerical static analysis of linear filters (e.g., [24]) do not relate directly to ours as their goal is to obtain deep numerical properties of filters (such as numerical bounds) for safety-critical applications.

Automated parallelization. Thies et al. [55] extract pipeline partitions from legacy streaming applications written in C by relying on programmer-provided annotations indicating pipeline boundaries. In contrast, our approach does not require any annotations. For synchronous dataflow streaming applications, parallelism has been exploited either by replicating stateless filters [15, 29, 44], or by using affine partitioning of loop nests [47]. In contrast, Σ^* enables parallelization of non-linear stateful filters with non-affine loop bounds. There is a massive amount of work on general cross-loop iteration dependence scheduling (e.g., see [11]). Σ^* is aimed at complementing such advanced techniques by enabling naïve parallelization of behaviorally simple loop nests that are not necessary polyhedral, disjoint or with a clear pipeline structure.

Acknowledgments

This work was supported by the Gates trust, the Lawrence Livermore National Lab grant B597718, and by the NSERC PDF fellowship. Thanks to Mike Dodds, Eric Koskinen, Matthew Parkinson, Dawn Song, John Wickerson and the anonymous reviewers for comments and suggestions.

References

[1] F. Aarts, B. Jonsson, and J. Uijen. Generating models of infinite-state communication protocols using regular inference with abstraction. In *Proc. of the 22nd IFIP WG 6.1 Int. Conf. on Testing Software and Systems*, pages 188–204, 2010.

[2] S. Agrawal, W. Thies, and S. P. Amarasinghe. Optimizing stream programs using linear state space analysis. In *Proc. of the 2005 Int. Conf. on Compilers, Architecture, and Synthesis for Embedded Systems*, pages 126–136, 2005.

[3] R. Alur and P. Černý. Streaming transducers for algorithmic verification of single-pass list-processing programs. In *Proc. of the 38th ACM SIGPLAN-SIGACT Symp. on Principles of Programming Languages*, pages 599–610, 2011.

[4] R. Alur, P. Černý, P. Madhusudan, and W. Nam. Synthesis of interface specifications for Java classes. In *Proc. of the 32nd ACM SIGPLAN-SIGACT Symp. on Principles of Programming Languages*, pages 98–109, 2005.

[5] D. Angluin. Learning regular sets from queries and counterexamples. *Information and Computation*, 75(2):87–106, 1987.

[6] T. Ball. Formalizing counterexample-driven refinement with weakest preconditions. In *Engineering Theories of Software Intensive Systems*, volume 195 of *NATO Science Series*, pages 121–139. 2005.

[7] T. Ball, R. Majumdar, T. Millstein, and S. Rajamani. Automatic predicate abstraction of C programs. In *Proc. of the 2001 ACM SIGPLAN Conference on Programming Language Design and Implementation*, pages 203–213, 2001.

[8] T. Ball, A. Podelski, and S. K. Rajamani. Boolean and cartesian abstraction for model checking C programs. In *Proc. of the 7th Int. Conf. on Tools and Algorithms for the Construction and Analysis of Systems*, pages 268–283, 2001.

[9] T. Ball, A. Podelski, and S. K. Rajamani. Relative completeness of abstraction refinement for software model checking. In *Proc. of the 8th Int. Conf. on Tools and Algorithms for the Construction and Analysis of Systems*, pages 158–172, 2002.

[10] D. Balzarotti, M. Cova, V. Felmetsger, N. Jovanovic, E. Kirda, C. Kruegel, and G. Vigna. Saner: Composing static and dynamic analysis to validate sanitization in web applications. In *IEEE Symposium on Security and Privacy*, pages 387–401, 2008.

[11] M. M. Baskaran, N. Vydyanathan, U. Bondhugula, J. Ramanujam, A. Rountev, and P. Sadayappan. Compiler-assisted dynamic scheduling for effective parallelization of loop nests on multicore processors. In *Proc. of the 14th ACM SIGPLAN Symp. on Principles and Practice of Parallel Programming*, pages 219–228, 2009.

[12] T. Berg, B. Jonsson, and H. Raffelt. Regular inference for state machines using domains with equality tests. In *Proc. of the Theory and practice of software, 11th Int. Conf. on Fundamental approaches to software engineering*, pages 317–331, 2008.

[13] D. Beyer and M. E. Keremoglu. Cpachecker: A tool for configurable software verification. In *Proc. of the 23rd Int. Conf. on Computer Aided Verification*, pages 184–190, 2011.

[14] N. Bjørner, P. Hooimeijer, B. Livshits, D. Molnar, and M. Veanes. Symbolic finite state transducers: Algorithms and applications. In *Proc.of the 39th ACM SIGPLAN-SIGACT Symp. on Principles of Programming Languages*, 2012.

[15] I. Buck, T. Foley, D. R. Horn, J. Sugerman, K. Fatahalian, M. Houston, and P. Hanrahan. Brook for GPUs: stream computing on graphics hardware. *ACM Trans. Graph.*, 23(3):777–786, 2004.

[16] C. Cadar and D. R. Engler. Execution generated test cases: How to make systems code crash itself. In *Proc. of the 12th Int. SPIN Workshop on Model Checking Software*, pages 2–23, 2005.

[17] C. Cadar, D. Dunbar, and D. Engler. KLEE: Unassisted and automatic generation of high-coverage tests for complex systems programs. In *Proc. of the 8th USENIX Symp. on Operating Systems Design and Implementation*, pages 209–224, 2008.

[18] M. K. Chen, X.-F. Li, R. Lian, J. H. Lin, L. Liu, T. Liu, and R. Ju. Shangri-La: achieving high performance from compiled network applications while enabling ease of programming. In *Proc. of the ACM SIGPLAN 2005 Conference on Programming Language Design and Implementation*, pages 224–236, 2005.

[19] C. Y. Cho, D. Babić, P. Poosankam, K. Z. Chen, E. X. Wu, and D. Song. MACE: Model-inference-assisted concolic exploration for protocol and vulnerability discovery. In *USENIX Security Symposium*, 2011.

[20] E. M. Clarke, O. Grumberg, S. Jha, Y. Lu, and H. Veith. Counterexample-guided abstraction refinement. In *Proc. of the 12th Int. Conf. on Computer Aided Verification*, pages 154–169, 2000.

[21] J. M. Cobleigh, D. Giannakopoulou, and C. S. Păsăreanu. Learning assumptions for compositional verification. In *Proc. of the 9th Int. Conf. on Tools and Algorithms for the Construction and Analysis of Systems*, volume 2619, pages 331–346, 2003.

[22] A. J. Demers, C. Keleman, and B. Reusch. On some decidable properties of finite state translations. *Acta Informatica*, 17:349–364, 1982.

[23] M. Drake, H. Hoffmann, R. M. Rabbah, and S. P. Amarasinghe. MPEG-2 decoding in a stream programming language. In *Proc. of the 20th International Parallel and Distributed Processing Symposium*, 2006.

[24] J. Feret. Static analysis of digital filters. In *Programming Languages and Systems, 13th European Symposium on Programming*, pages 33–48, 2004.

[25] V. Ganesh and D. L. Dill. A decision procedure for bit-vectors and arrays. In *Proc. of the 19th Int. Conf. on Computer Aided Verification*, pages 519–531, 2007.

[26] B. Gedik, H. Andrade, K.-L. Wu, P. S. Yu, and M. Doo. Spade: the System S declarative stream processing engine. In *SIGMOD Conference*, pages 1123–1134, 2008.

[27] D. Giannakopoulou, Z. Rakamaric, and V. Raman. Symbolic learning of component interfaces. In *19th Int. Symp. on Static Analysis*, pages 248–264, 2012.

[28] P. Godefroid, N. Klarlund, and K. Sen. DART: directed automated random testing. In *Proc. of the ACM SIGPLAN 2005 Conf. on Programming Language Design and Implementation*, pages 213–223, 2005.

[29] M. I. Gordon, W. Thies, and S. P. Amarasinghe. Exploiting coarse-grained task, data, and pipeline parallelism in stream programs. In *Proc. of the 12th Int. Conf. on Architectural Support for Programming Languages and Operating Systems*, pages 151–162, 2006.

[30] S. Graf and H. Saidi. Construction of abstract state graphs with PVS. In *Proc. of the 9th Int. Conf. on Computer Aided Verification*, pages 72–83, 1997.

[31] B. S. Gulavani, T. A. Henzinger, Y. Kannan, A. V. Nori, and S. K. Rajamani. SYNERGY: a new algorithm for property checking. In *Proc. of the 14th ACM SIGSOFT Int. Symp. on Foundations of Software Engineering*, pages 117–127, 2006.

[32] J. Gummaraju, J. Coburn, Y. Turner, and M. Rosenblum. Streamware: programming general-purpose multicore processors using streams. In *Proc. of the 13th Int. Conf. on Architectural Support for Programming Languages and Operating Systems*, pages 297–307, 2008.

[33] M. R. Guthaus, J. S. Ringenberg, D. Ernst, T. M. Austin, T. Mudge, and R. B. Brown. MiBench: A free, commercially representative embedded benchmark suite. In *Proc. of the Workload Characterization. WWC-4 IEEE Int. Workshop*, pages 3–14, 2001.

[34] P. Habermehl and T. Vojnar. Regular model checking using inference of regular languages. *Electr. Notes Theor. Comput. Sci.*, 138:21–36, 2005.

[35] A. Hagiescu, W.-F. Wong, D. F. Bacon, and R. M. Rabbah. A computing origami: folding streams in FPGAs. In *Proc. of the 46th Design Automation Conference*, pages 282–287, 2009.

[36] T. A. Henzinger, R. Jhala, R. Majumdar, and G. Sutre. Lazy abstraction. In *Proc. of the 29th ACM SIGPLAN-SIGACT Symp. on Principles of Programming Languages*, pages 58–70, 2002.

[37] P. Hooimeijer, B. Livshits, D. Molnar, P. Saxena, and M. Veanes. Fast and precise sanitizer analysis with BEK. In *USENIX Security Symposium*, 2011.

[38] J. E. Hopcroft. On the equivalence and containment problems for context-free languages. *Theory of Computing Systems*, 3:119–124, 1969.

[39] A. Hormati, M. Kudlur, S. A. Mahlke, D. F. Bacon, and R. M. Rabbah. Optimus: efficient realization of streaming applications on FPGAs. In *Proc. of the 2008 Int. Conf. on Compilers, Architecture, and Synthesis for Embedded Systems*, pages 41–50, 2008.

[40] F. Howar, B. Steffen, B. Jonsson, and S. Cassel. Inferring canonical register automata. In *Proc. of the 13th Int. Conf. on Verification, Model Checking, and Abstract Interpretation*, pages 251–266, 2012.

[41] O. H. Ibarra. The unsolvability of the equivalence problem for ϵ-free NGSM's with unary input (output) alphabet and applications. In *Proc. of the 18th Annual Symp. on Foundations of Computer Science*, pages 74–81, 1977.

[42] R. Jhala and K. L. McMillan. A practical and complete approach to predicate refinement. In *Proc. of the 12th Int. Conf. on Tools and Algorithms for the Construction and Analysis of Systems*, pages 459–473, 2006.

[43] U. J. Kapasi, W. J. Dally, S. Rixner, J. D. Owens, and B. Khailany. The imagine stream processor. In *Proc. of the 20th Int. Conf. on Computer Design, VLSI in Computers and Processors*, pages 282–288, 2002.

[44] M. Kudlur and S. A. Mahlke. Orchestrating the execution of stream programs on multicore platforms. In *Proc. of the ACM SIGPLAN 2008 Conference on Programming Language Design and Implementation*, pages 114–124, 2008.

[45] A. A. Lamb, W. Thies, and S. P. Amarasinghe. Linear analysis and optimization of stream programs. In *Proc. of the ACM SIGPLAN 2003 Conference on Programming Language Design and Implementation*, pages 12–25, 2003.

[46] D. Lee and M. Yannakakis. Principles and methods of testing finite state machines-a survey. In *Proc. of the IEEE*, volume 84, pages 1090–1123, 1996.

[47] S.-W. Liao, Z. Du, G. Wu, and G.-Y. Lueh. Data and computation transformations for Brook streaming applications on multiprocessors. In *Proc. of the 4th IEEE/ACM Int. Symp. on Code Generation and Optimization*, pages 196–207, 2006.

[48] P. Prabhu, G. Ramalingam, and K. Vaswani. Safe programmable speculative parallelism. In *Proc. of the 2010 ACM SIGPLAN Conf. on Programming Language Design and Implementation*, pages 50–61, 2010.

[49] K. Sen, D. Marinov, and G. Agha. CUTE: a concolic unit testing engine for C. In *Proc. of the 10th European Software Engineering Conf. held jointly with 13th ACM SIGSOFT Int. Symp. on Foundations of Software Engineering*, pages 263–272, 2005.

[50] M. Shahbaz and R. Groz. Inferring Mealy machines. In *Proc. of the 2nd World Congress on Formal Methods*, pages 207–222, 2009.

[51] R. Singh, D. Giannakopoulou, and C. S. Pasareanu. Learning component interfaces with may and must abstractions. In *Proc. of the 22nd Int. Conf. on Computer Aided Verification*, pages 527–542, 2010.

[52] R. Soulé, M. Hirzel, R. Grimm, B. Gedik, H. Andrade, V. Kumar, and K.-L. Wu. A universal calculus for stream processing languages. In *Programming Languages and Systems, 19th European Symposium on Programming*, pages 507–528, 2010.

[53] W. Thies and S. P. Amarasinghe. An empirical characterization of stream programs and its implications for language and compiler design. In *Proc. of the 19th International Conference on Parallel Architecture and Compilation Techniques*, pages 365–376, 2010.

[54] W. Thies, M. Karczmarek, and S. P. Amarasinghe. StreamIt: A language for streaming applications. In *Proc. of the 11th International Conference on Compiler Construction*, pages 179–196, 2002.

[55] W. Thies, V. Chandrasekhar, and S. P. Amarasinghe. A practical approach to exploiting coarse-grained pipeline parallelism in C programs. In *40th Annual IEEE/ACM Int. Symp. on Microarchitecture*, pages 356–369, 2007.

[56] A. Udupa, R. Govindarajan, and M. J. Thazhuthaveetil. Software pipelined execution of stream programs on GPUs. In *Proc. of the 7th Int. Symp. on Code Generation and Optimization*, pages 200–209, 2009.

[57] M. Veanes, D. Molnar, B. Livshits, and L. Litchev. Generating fast string manipulating code through transducer exploration and SIMD integration. Technical Report MSR-TR-2011–124, Microsoft Research, 2011.

[58] J. M. Vilar. Query learning of subsequential transducers. In *Proc. of the 3rd Int. Colloquium on Grammatical Inference: Learning Syntax from Sentences*, pages 72–83, 1996.

Checking NFA Equivalence with Bisimulations up to Congruence

Filippo Bonchi Damien Pous *

CNRS, ENS Lyon, Université de Lyon, LIP (UMR 5668)

{filippo.bonchi,damien.pous}@ens-lyon.fr

Abstract

We introduce *bisimulation up to congruence* as a technique for proving language equivalence of non-deterministic finite automata. Exploiting this technique, we devise an optimisation of the classical algorithm by Hopcroft and Karp [18]. We compare our approach to the recently introduced antichain algorithms, by analysing and relating the two underlying coinductive proof methods. We give concrete examples where we exponentially improve over antichains; experimental results moreover show non negligible improvements.

Categories and Subject Descriptors F.4.3 [*Mathematical Logic*]: Decision Problems; F.1.1 [*Models of computation*]: Automata; D.2.4 [*Program Verification*]: Model Checking

Keywords Language Equivalence, Automata, Bisimulation, Coinduction, Up-to techniques, Congruence, Antichains.

1. Introduction

Checking language equivalence of finite automata is a classical problem in computer science, which finds applications in many fields ranging from compiler construction to model checking.

Equivalence of deterministic finite automata (DFA) can be checked either via minimisation [17] or through Hopcroft and Karp's algorithm [2, 18], which exploits an instance of what is nowadays called a *coinduction proof principle* [25, 27, 29]: two states recognise the same language if and only if there exists a *bisimulation* relating them. In order to check the equivalence of two given states, Hopcroft and Karp's algorithm creates a relation containing them and tries to build a bisimulation by adding pairs of states to this relation: if it succeeds then the two states are equivalent, otherwise they are different.

On the one hand, minimisation algorithms have the advantage of checking the equivalence of all the states at once (while Hopcroft and Karp's algorithm only check a given pair of states). On the other hand, they have the disadvantage of needing the whole automata from the beginning, while Hopcroft and Karp's algorithm can be executed "on-the-fly" [13], on a lazy DFA whose transitions are computed on demand.

* Work partially funded by the PiCoq project, ANR-10-BLAN-0305 and by the COGIP (PEPS-CNRS) project.

POPL'13, January 23–25, 2013, Rome, Italy.

This difference is fundamental for our work and for other recently introduced algorithms based on *antichains* [1, 31]. Indeed, when starting from non-deterministic finite automata (NFA), the powerset construction used to get deterministic automata induces an exponential factor. In contrast, the algorithm we introduce in this work for checking equivalence of NFA (as well as those in [1, 31]) usually does not build the whole deterministic automaton, but just a small part of it. We write "usually" because in few bad cases, the algorithm still needs exponentially many states of the DFA.

Our algorithm is grounded on a simple observation on determinised NFA: for all sets X and Y of states of the original NFA, the union (written $+$) of the language recognised by X (written $[\![X]\!]$) and the language recognised by Y ($[\![Y]\!]$) is equal to the language recognised by the union of X and Y ($[\![X+Y]\!]$). In symbols:

$$[\![X+Y]\!] = [\![X]\!] + [\![Y]\!] \tag{1}$$

This fact leads us to introduce a sound and complete proof technique for language equivalence, namely *bisimulation up to context*, that exploits both *induction* (on the operator $+$) and *coinduction*: if a bisimulation R equates both the (sets of) states X_1, Y_1 and X_2, Y_2, then $[\![X_1]\!] = [\![Y_1]\!]$ and $[\![X_2]\!] = [\![Y_2]\!]$ and, by (1), we can immediately conclude that also $X_1 + X_2$ and $Y_1 + Y_2$ are language equivalent. Intuitively, bisimulations up to context are bisimulations which *do not need to relate* $X_1 + X_2$ and $Y_1 + Y_2$ when X_1 (resp. X_2) and Y_1 (resp. Y_2) are already related.

To illustrate this idea, let us check the equivalence of states x and u in the following NFA. (Final states are overlined, labelled edges represent transitions.)

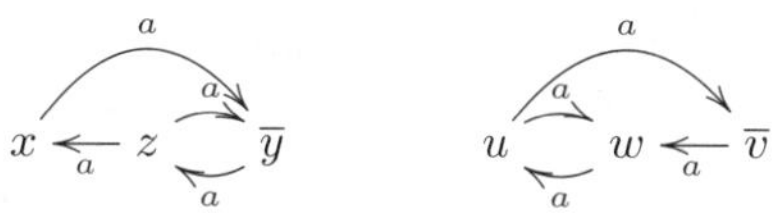

The determinised automaton is depicted below.

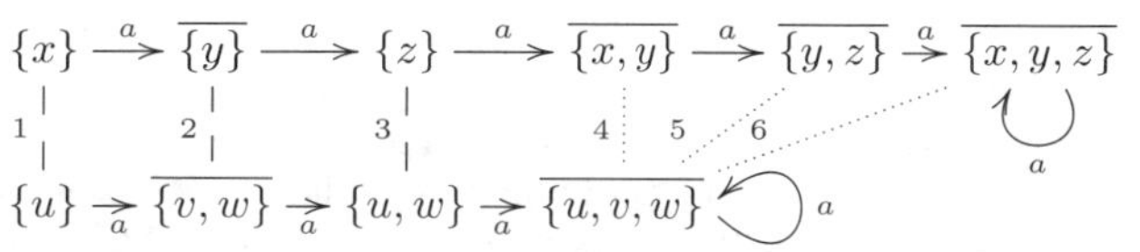

Each state is a set of states of the NFA, final states are overlined: they contain at least one final state of the NFA. The numbered lines show a relation which is a bisimulation containing x and u. Actually, this is the relation that is built by Hopcroft and Karp's algorithm (the numbers express the order in which pairs are added).

The dashed lines (numbered by 1, 2, 3) form a smaller relation which is not a bisimulation, but a bisimulation up to context: the equivalence of states $\{x,y\}$ and $\{u,v,w\}$ could be immediately deduced from the fact that $\{x\}$ is related to $\{u\}$ and $\{y\}$ to $\{v,w\}$, without the need of further exploring the determinised automaton.

Bisimulations up-to, and in particular bisimulations up to context, have been introduced in the setting of concurrency theory [25, 28] as a proof technique for bisimilarity of CCS or π-calculus processes. As far as we know, they have never been used for proving language equivalence of NFA.

Among these techniques one should also mention *bisimulation up to equivalence*, which, as we show in this paper, is implicitly used in the original Hopcroft and Karp's algorithm. This technique can be briefly explained by noting that not all bisimulations are equivalence relations: it might be the case that a bisimulation relates (for instance) X and Y, Y and Z but not X and Z. However, since $[\![X]\!] = [\![Y]\!]$ and $[\![Y]\!] = [\![Z]\!]$, we can immediately conclude that X and Z recognise the same language. Analogously to bisimulations up to context, a bisimulation up to equivalence *does not need to relate* X and Z when they are both related to some Y.

The techniques of up-to equivalence and up-to context can be combined resulting in a powerful proof technique which we call *bisimulation up to congruence*. Our algorithm is in fact just an extension of Hopcroft and Karp's algorithm that attempts to build a bisimulation up to congruence instead of a bisimulation up to equivalence. An important consequence when using up to congruence is that we do not need to build the whole deterministic automata, but just those states that are needed for the bisimulation up-to. For instance, in the above NFA, the algorithm stops after equating z and $u + v$ and does not build the remaining four states. Despite their use of the up to equivalence technique, this is not the case with Hopcroft and Karp's algorithm, where all accessible subsets of the deterministic automata have to be visited at least once.

The ability of visiting only a small portion of the determinised automaton is also the key feature of the antichain algorithm [31] and its optimisation exploiting similarity [1]. The two algorithms are designed to check *language inclusion* rather than equivalence, but we can relate these approaches by observing that the two problems are equivalent ($[\![X]\!] = [\![Y]\!]$ iff $[\![X]\!] \subseteq [\![Y]\!]$ and $[\![Y]\!] \subseteq [\![X]\!]$; and $[\![X]\!] \subseteq [\![Y]\!]$ iff $[\![X]\!] + [\![Y]\!] = [\![Y]\!]$ iff $[\![X + Y]\!] = [\![Y]\!]$).

In order to compare with these algorithms, we make explicit the coinductive up-to technique underlying the antichain algorithm [31]. We prove that this technique can be seen as a restriction of up to congruence, for which *symmetry* and *transitivity* are not allowed. As a consequence, the antichain algorithm usually needs to explore more states than our algorithm. Moreover, we show how to integrate the optimisation proposed in [1] in our setting, resulting in an even more efficient algorithm.

In summary, the contributions of this work are: (1) the observation that Hopcroft and Karp implicitly use bisimulations up to equivalence, (2) an efficient algorithm for checking language equivalence (and inclusion), based on a powerful up to technique, and (3) a comparison with antichain algorithms, by recasting them into our coinductive framework.

Outline

Section 2 recalls Hopcroft and Karp's algorithm for DFA, showing that it implicitly exploits bisimulation up to equivalence. Section 3 describes the novel algorithm, based on bisimulations up to congruence. We compare this algorithm with the antichain one in Section 4, and we show how to exploit similarity in Section 5. Section 6 is devoted to benchmarks. Sections 7 and 8 discuss related and future works. Omitted proofs can be found in [6].

Notation

We denote sets by capital letters $X, Y, S, T \ldots$ and functions by lower case letters $f, g, \ldots$ Given sets X and Y, $X \times Y$ is their Cartesian product, $X \uplus Y$ is the disjoint union and X^Y is the set of functions $f : Y \to X$. Finite iterations of a function $f : X \to X$ are denoted by f^n (formally, $f^0(x) = x$, $f^{n+1}(x) = f(f^n(x))$). The collection of subsets of X is denoted by $\mathcal{P}(X)$. The (omega) iteration of a function $f : \mathcal{P}(X) \to \mathcal{P}(X)$ is denoted by f^ω (formally, $f^\omega(Y) = \bigcup_{n\geq 0} f^n(Y)$). For a set of letters A, $A^\star$ denotes the set of all finite words over A; ϵ the empty word; and $w_1 w_2$ the concatenation of words $w_1, w_2 \in A^\star$. We use 2 for the set $\{0, 1\}$ and $2^{A^\star}$ for the set of all languages over A.

2. Hopcroft and Karp's algorithm for DFA

A deterministic finite automaton (DFA) over the alphabet A is a triple (S, o, t), where S is a finite set of states, $o : S \to 2$ is the output function, which determines if a state $x \in S$ is final ($o(x) = 1$) or not ($o(x) = 0$), and $t : S \to S^A$ is the transition function which returns, for each state x and for each letter $a \in A$, the next state $t_a(x)$. For $a \in A$, we write $x \xrightarrow{a} x'$ to mean that $t_a(x) = x'$. For $w \in A^\star$, we write $x \xrightarrow{w} x'$ for the least relation such that (1) $x \xrightarrow{\epsilon} x$ and (2) $x \xrightarrow{aw'} x'$ iff $x \xrightarrow{a} x''$ and $x'' \xrightarrow{w'} x'$.

For any DFA, there exists a function $[\![-]\!] : S \to 2^{A^\star}$ mapping states to languages, defined for all $x \in S$ as follows:

$$[\![x]\!](\epsilon) = o(x) \ , \qquad [\![x]\!](aw) = [\![t_a(x)]\!](w) \ .$$

The language $[\![x]\!]$ is called the language accepted by x. Given two automata (S_1, o_1, t_1) and (S_2, o_2, t_2), the states $x_1 \in S_1$ and $x_2 \in S_2$ are said to be *language equivalent* (written $x_1 \sim x_2$) iff they accept the same language.

Remark 1. *In the following, we will always consider the problem of checking the equivalence of states of one single and fixed automaton (S, o, t). We do not loose generality since for any two automata (S_1, o_1, t_1) and (S_2, o_2, t_2) it is always possible to build an automaton $(S_1 \uplus S_2, o_1 \uplus o_2, t_1 \uplus t_2)$ such that the language accepted by every state $x \in S_1 \uplus S_2$ is the same as the language accepted by x in the original automaton (S_i, o_i, t_i). For this reason, we also work with automata without explicit initial states: we focus on the equivalence of two arbitrary states of a fixed DFA.*

2.1 Proving language equivalence via coinduction

We first define bisimulation. We make explicit the underlying notion of progression which we need in the sequel.

Definition 1 (Progression, Bisimulation). *Given two relations $R, R' \subseteq S \times S$ on states, R progresses to R', denoted $R \rightarrowtail R'$, if whenever $x \; R \; y$ then*

1. *$o(x) = o(y)$ and*
2. *for all $a \in A$, $t_a(x) \; R' \; t_a(y)$.*

A bisimulation *is a relation R such that $R \rightarrowtail R$.*

As expected, bisimulation is a sound and complete proof technique for checking language equivalence of DFA:

Proposition 1 (Coinduction). *Two states are language equivalent iff there exists a bisimulation that relates them.*

2.2 Naive algorithm

Figure 1 shows a naive version of Hopcroft and Karp's algorithm for checking language equivalence of the states x and y of a deterministic finite automaton (S, o, t). Starting from x and y, the algorithm builds a relation R that, in case of success, is a bisimulation. In order to do that, it employs the set (of pairs of states) *todo* which, intuitively, at any step of the execution, contains the pairs (x', y') that must be checked: if (x', y') already belongs to R, then it has already been checked and nothing else should be done. Otherwise, the algorithm checks if x' and y' have the same outputs (i.e., if both are final or not). If $o(x') \neq o(y')$, then x and y are different. If $o(x') = o(y')$, then the algorithm inserts (x', y') in R and, for all $a \in A$, the pairs $(t_a(x'), t_a(y'))$ in *todo*.

```
                    Naive(x, y)

(1) R is empty; todo is empty;
(2) insert (x, y) in todo;
(3) while todo is not empty, do
 (3.1)   extract (x', y') from todo;
 (3.2)   if (x', y') ∈ R then continue;
 (3.3)   if o(x') ≠ o(y') then return false;
 (3.4)   for all a ∈ A,
           insert (t_a(x'), t_a(y')) in todo;
 (3.5)   insert (x', y') in R;
(4) return true;
```

Figure 1. Naive algorithm for checking the equivalence of states x and y of a DFA (S, o, t); R and *todo* are sets of pairs of states. The code of $\texttt{HK}(x, y)$ is obtained by replacing step 3.2 with `if` $(x', y') \in e(R)$ `then continue`.

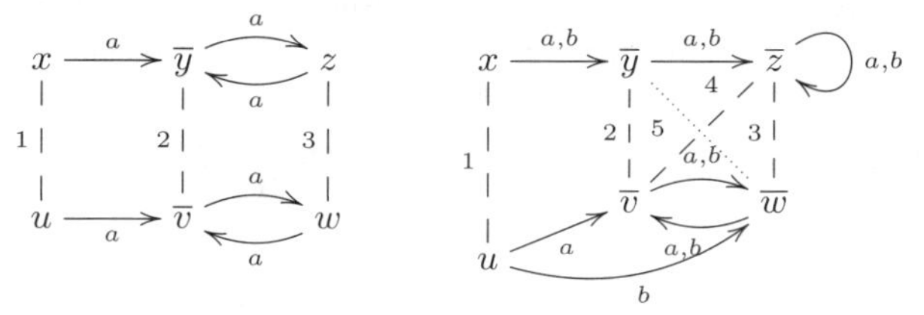

Figure 2. Checking for DFA equivalence.

Proposition 2. *For all $x, y \in S$, $x \sim y$ iff* $\texttt{Naive}(x, y)$.

Proof. We first observe that if $\texttt{Naive}(x, y)$ returns true then the relation R that is built before arriving to step 4 is a bisimulation. Indeed, the following proposition is an invariant for the loop corresponding to step 3:

$$R \rightarrowtail R \cup todo$$

This invariant is preserved since at any iteration of the algorithm, a pair (x', y') is removed from *todo* and inserted in R after checking that $o(x') = o(y')$ and adding $(t_a(x'), t_a(y'))$ for all $a \in A$ in *todo*. Since *todo* is empty at the end of the loop, we eventually have $R \rightarrowtail R$, i.e., R is a bisimulation. By Proposition 1, $x \sim y$.

We now prove that if $\texttt{Naive}(x, y)$ returns false, then $x \not\sim y$. Note that for all (x', y') inserted in *todo*, there exists a word $w \in A^\star$ such that $x \overset{w}{\to} x'$ and $y \overset{w}{\to} y'$. Since $o(x') \neq o(y')$, then $[\![x']\!](\epsilon) \neq [\![y']\!](\epsilon)$ and thus $[\![x]\!](w) = [\![x']\!](\epsilon) \neq [\![y']\!](\epsilon) = [\![y]\!](w)$, that is $x \not\sim y$. □

Since both Hopcroft and Karp's algorithm and the one we introduce in Section 3 are simple variations of this naive one, it is important to illustrate its execution with an example. Consider the DFA with input alphabet $A = \{a\}$ in the left-hand side of Figure 2, and suppose we want to check that x and u are language equivalent.

During the initialisation, (x, u) is inserted in *todo*. At the first iteration, since $o(x) = 0 = o(u)$, (x, u) is inserted in R and (y, v) in *todo*. At the second iteration, since $o(y) = 1 = o(v)$, (y, v) is inserted in R and (z, w) in *todo*. At the third iteration, since $o(z) = 0 = o(w)$, (z, w) is inserted in R and (y, v) in *todo*. At the fourth iteration, since (y, v) is already in R, the algorithm does nothing. Since there are no more pairs to check in *todo*, the relation R is a bisimulation and the algorithm terminates returning true.

These iterations are concisely described by the numbered dashed lines in Figure 2. The line i means that the connected pair is inserted in R at iteration i. (In the sequel, when enumerating iterations, we ignore those where a pair from *todo* is already in R so that there is nothing to do.)

Remark 2. *Unless it finds a counter-example,* $\texttt{Naive}$ *constructs the* smallest *bisimulation that relates the two starting states (see Proposition 8 in [6]). On the contrary, minimisation algorithms [17] are designed to compute the* largest *bisimulation relation for a given automaton. For instance, taking automaton on the left of Figure 2, they would equate the states x and w which are language equivalent, while* $\texttt{Naive}(x, u)$ *does not relate them.*

2.3 Hopcroft and Karp's algorithm

The naive algorithm is quadratic: a new pair is added to R at each non-trivial iteration, and there are only n^2 such pairs, where $n = |S|$ is the number of states of the DFA. To make this algorithm (almost) linear, Hopcroft and Karp actually record a set of *equivalence classes* rather than a set of visited pairs. As a consequence, their algorithm may stop earlier when an encountered pair of states is not already in R but in its reflexive, symmetric, and transitive closure. For instance, in the right-hand side example from Figure 2, we can stop when we encounter the dotted pair (y, w) since these two states already belong to the same equivalence class according to the four previous pairs.

With this optimisation, the produced relation R contains at most n pairs (two equivalence classes are merged each time a pair is added). Formally, and ignoring the concrete data structure to store equivalence classes, Hopcroft and Karp's algorithm consists in simply replacing step 3.2 in Figure 1 with

```
(3.2)   if (x', y') ∈ e(R) then continue;
```

where $e\colon \mathcal{P}(S \times S) \to \mathcal{P}(S \times S)$ is the function mapping each relation $R \subseteq S \times S$ into its symmetric, reflexive, and transitive closure. We hereafter refer to this algorithm as $\texttt{HK}$.

2.4 Bisimulations up-to

We now show that the optimisation used by Hopcroft and Karp corresponds to exploiting an "up-to technique".

Definition 2 (Bisimulation up-to)**.** *Let $f\colon \mathcal{P}(S \times S) \to \mathcal{P}(S \times S)$ be a function on relations on S. A relation R is a* bisimulation up to f *if $R \rightarrowtail f(R)$, i.e., whenever $x \; R \; y$ then*

1. *$o(x) = o(y)$ and*
2. *for all $a \in A$, $t_a(x) \; f(R) \; t_a(y)$.*

With this definition, Hopcroft and Karp's algorithm just consists in trying to build a bisimulation up to e. To prove the correctness of the algorithm, it suffices to show that any bisimulation up to e is contained in a bisimulation. We use for that the notion of compatible function [26, 28]:

Definition 3 (Compatible function)**.** *A function $f\colon \mathcal{P}(S \times S) \to \mathcal{P}(S \times S)$ is* compatible *if it is monotone and it preserves progressions: for all $R, R' \subseteq S \times S$,*

$$R \rightarrowtail R' \text{ entails } f(R) \rightarrowtail f(R') .$$

Proposition 3. *Let f be a compatible function. Any bisimulation up to f is contained in a bisimulation.*

Proof. Suppose that R is a bisimulation up to f, i.e., that $R \rightarrowtail f(R)$. Using compatibility of f and by a simple induction on n, we get $\forall n, f^n(R) \rightarrowtail f^{n+1}(R)$. Therefore, we have

$$\bigcup_n f^n(R) \rightarrowtail \bigcup_n f^n(R) ,$$

in other words, $f^\omega(R) = \bigcup_n f^n(R)$ is a bisimulation. This latter relation trivially contains R, by taking $n = 0$. □

We could prove directly that e is a compatible function; we however take a detour to ease our correctness proof for the algorithm we propose in Section 3.

Lemma 1. *The following functions are compatible:*

- id: *the identity function;*
- $f \circ g$: *the composition of compatible functions f and g;*
- $\bigcup F$: *the pointwise union of an arbitrary family F of compatible functions: $\bigcup F(R) = \bigcup_{f \in F} f(R)$;*
- f^ω: *the (omega) iteration of a compatible function f.*

Lemma 2. *The following functions are compatible:*

- *the constant reflexive function: $r(R) = \{(x, x) \mid x \in S\}$;*
- *the converse function: $s(R) = \{(y, x) \mid x\ R\ y\}$;*
- *the squaring function: $t(R) = \{(x, z) \mid \exists y, x\ R\ y\ R\ z\}$.*

Intuitively, given a relation R, $(s \cup \mathrm{id})(R)$ is the symmetric closure of R, $(r \cup s \cup \mathrm{id})(R)$ is its reflexive and symmetric closure, and $(r \cup s \cup t \cup \mathrm{id})^\omega(R)$ is its symmetric, reflexive and transitive closure: $e = (r \cup s \cup t \cup \mathrm{id})^\omega$. Another way to understand this decomposition of e is to recall that for a given R, $e(R)$ can be defined inductively by the following rules:

$$\frac{}{x\ e(R)\ x}\,r \qquad \frac{x\ e(R)\ y}{y\ e(R)\ x}\,s \qquad \frac{x\ e(R)\ y\ \ y\ e(R)\ z}{x\ e(R)\ z}\,t \qquad \frac{x\ R\ y}{x\ e(R)\ y}\,\mathrm{id}$$

Theorem 1. *Any bisimulation up to e is contained in a bisimulation.*

Proof. By Proposition 3, it suffices to show that e is compatible, which follows from Lemma 1 and Lemma 2. □

Corollary 1. *For all $x, y \in S$, $x \sim y$ iff $\mathtt{HK}(x, y)$.*

Proof. Same proof as for Proposition 2, by using the invariant $R \rightarrowtail e(R) \cup todo$. We deduce that R is a bisimulation up to e after the loop. We conclude with Theorem 1 and Proposition 1. □

Returning to the right-hand side example from Figure 2, Hopcroft and Karp's algorithm constructs the relation

$$R_{\mathtt{HK}} = \{(x, u), (y, v), (z, w), (z, v)\}$$

which is not a bisimulation, but a bisimulation up to e: it contains the pair (x, u), whose b-transitions lead to (y, w), which is not in $R_{\mathtt{HK}}$ but in its equivalence closure, $e(R_{\mathtt{HK}})$.

3. Optimised algorithm for NFA

We now move from DFA to non-deterministic automata (NFA). We start with standard definitions about semi-lattices, determinisation, and language equivalence for NFA.

A *semi-lattice* $(X, +, 0)$ consists of a set X and a binary operation $+\colon X \times X \to X$ which is associative, commutative, idempotent (ACI), and has $0 \in X$ as identity. Given two semi-lattices $(X_1, +_1, 0_1)$ and $(X_2, +_2, 0_2)$, an *homomorphism* of semi-lattices is a function $f\colon X_1 \to X_2$ such that for all $x, y \in X_1$, $f(x +_1 y) = f(x) +_2 f(y)$ and $f(0_1) = 0_2$. The set $2 = \{0, 1\}$ is a semi-lattice when taking $+$ to be the ordinary Boolean or. Also the set of all languages $2^{A^\star}$ carries a semi-lattice where $+$ is the union of languages and 0 is the empty language. More generally, for any set X, $\mathcal{P}(X)$ is a semi-lattice where $+$ is the union of sets and 0 is the empty set. In the sequel, we indiscriminately use 0 to denote the element $0 \in 2$, the empty language in $2^{A^\star}$, and the empty set in $\mathcal{P}(X)$. Similarly, we use $+$ to denote the Boolean or in 2, the union of languages in $2^{A^\star}$, and the union of sets in $\mathcal{P}(X)$.

A non-deterministic finite automaton (NFA) over the input alphabet A is a triple (S, o, t), where S is a finite set of states, $o\colon S \to 2$ is the output function (as for DFA), and $t\colon S \to \mathcal{P}(S)^A$ is the transition relation, which assigns to each state $x \in S$ and input letter $a \in A$ a set of possible successor states.

The *powerset construction* transforms any NFA (S, o, t) in the DFA $(\mathcal{P}(S), o^\sharp, t^\sharp)$ where $o^\sharp\colon \mathcal{P}(S) \to 2$ and $t^\sharp\colon \mathcal{P}(S) \to \mathcal{P}(S)^A$ are defined for all $X \in \mathcal{P}(S)$ and $a \in A$ as follows:

$$o^\sharp(X) = \begin{cases} o(x) & \text{if } X = \{x\} \text{ with } x \in S \\ 0 & \text{if } X = 0 \\ o^\sharp(X_1) + o^\sharp(X_2) & \text{if } X = X_1 + X_2 \end{cases}$$

$$t_a^\sharp(X) = \begin{cases} t_a(x) & \text{if } X = \{x\} \text{ with } x \in S \\ 0 & \text{if } X = 0 \\ t_a^\sharp(X_1) + t_a^\sharp(X_2) & \text{if } X = X_1 + X_2 \end{cases}$$

Observe that in $(\mathcal{P}(S), o^\sharp, t^\sharp)$, the states form a semi-lattice $(\mathcal{P}(S), +, 0)$, and $o^\sharp$ and $t^\sharp$ are, by definition, semi-lattices homomorphisms. These properties are fundamental for the up-to technique we are going to introduce; in order to highlight the difference with generic DFA (which usually do not carry this structure), we introduce the following definition.

Definition 4. *A* determinised NFA *is a DFA $(\mathcal{P}(S), o^\sharp, t^\sharp)$ obtained via the powerset construction of some NFA (S, o, t).*

Hereafter, we use a new notation for representing states of determinised NFA: in place of the singleton $\{x\}$, we just write x and, in place of $\{x_1, \ldots, x_n\}$, we write $x_1 + \cdots + x_n$.

For an example, consider the NFA (S, o, t) depicted below (left) and part of the determinised NFA $(\mathcal{P}(S), o^\sharp, t^\sharp)$ (right).

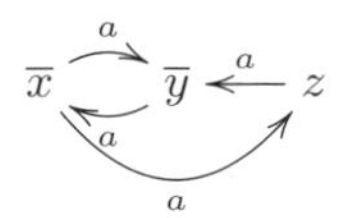

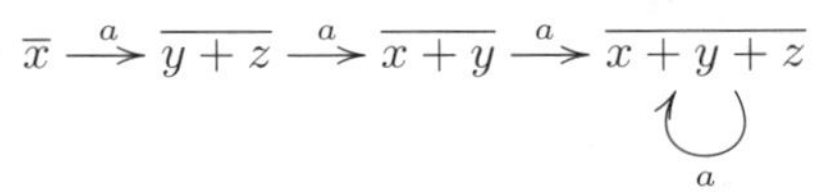

In the determinised NFA, x makes one single a-transition going into $y + z$. This state is final: $o^\sharp(y + z) = o^\sharp(y) + o^\sharp(z) = o(y) + o(z) = 1 + 0 = 1$; it makes an a-transition into $t_a^\sharp(y + z) = t_a^\sharp(y) + t_a^\sharp(z) = t_a(y) + t_a(z) = x + y$.

The language accepted by the states of an NFA (S, o, t) can be conveniently defined via the powerset construction: the language accepted by $x \in S$ is the language accepted by the singleton $\{x\}$ in the DFA $(\mathcal{P}(S), o^\sharp, t^\sharp)$, in symbols $[\![\{x\}]\!]$. Therefore, in the following, instead of considering the problem of language equivalence of states of the NFA, we focus on language equivalence of *sets* of states of the NFA: given two sets of states X and Y in $\mathcal{P}(S)$, we say that X and Y are language equivalent ($X \sim Y$) iff $[\![X]\!] = [\![Y]\!]$. This is exactly what happens in standard automata theory, where NFA are equipped with sets of initial states.

3.1 Extending coinduction to NFA

In order to check whether two sets of states X and Y of an NFA (S, o, t) are language equivalent, we can simply employ the bisimulation proof method on $(\mathcal{P}(S), o^\sharp, t^\sharp)$. More explicitly, a bisimulation for an NFA (S, o, t) is a relation $R \subseteq \mathcal{P}(S) \times \mathcal{P}(S)$ on sets of states, such that whenever $X\ R\ Y$ then (1) $o^\sharp(X) = o^\sharp(Y)$, and (2) for all $a \in A$, $t_a^\sharp(X)\ R\ t_a^\sharp(Y)$. Since this is just the old definition of bisimulation (Definition 1) applied to $(\mathcal{P}(S), o^\sharp, t^\sharp)$, we get that $X \sim Y$ iff there exists a bisimulation relating them.

Remark 3 (Linear time v.s. branching time)**.** *It is important not to confuse these bisimulation relations with the standard Milner-and-Park bisimulations [25] (which* strictly *imply language equivalence): in a standard bisimulation R, if the following states x and*

y of an NFA are in R,

then each x_i should be in R with some y_j (and vice-versa). Here, instead, we first transform the transition relation into

$$x \xrightarrow{a} x_1 + \cdots + x_n \qquad\qquad y \xrightarrow{a} y_1 + \cdots + y_m \ ,$$

using the powerset construction, and then we require that the sets $x_1 + \cdots + x_n$ and $y_1 + \cdots + y_m$ are related by R.

3.2 Bisimulation up to congruence

The semi-lattice structure $(\mathcal{P}(S), +, 0)$ carried by determinised NFA makes it possible to introduce a new up-to technique, which is not available with plain DFA: *up to congruence*. This technique relies on the following function.

Definition 5 (Congruence closure). *Let $u\colon \mathcal{P}(\mathcal{P}(S) \times \mathcal{P}(S)) \to \mathcal{P}(\mathcal{P}(S) \times \mathcal{P}(S))$ be the function on relations on sets of states defined for all $R \subseteq \mathcal{P}(S) \times \mathcal{P}(S)$ as:*

$$u(R) = \{(X_1 + X_2,\ Y_1 + Y_2) \mid X_1\ R\ Y_1 \text{ and } X_2\ R\ Y_2\}\,.$$

The function $c = (r \cup s \cup t \cup u \cup \mathrm{id})^\omega$ is called the congruence closure *function.*

Intuitively, $c(R)$ is the smallest equivalence relation which is closed with respect to $+$ and which includes R. It could alternatively be defined inductively using the rules r, s, t, and id from the previous section, and the following one:

$$\frac{X_1\ c(R)\ Y_1 \qquad X_2\ c(R)\ Y_2}{X_1 + X_2\ c(R)\ Y_1 + Y_2}\ u$$

We call bisimulations up to congruence the bisimulations up to c. We report the explicit definition for the sake of clarity:

Definition 6 (Bisimulation up to congruence). *A bisimulation up to congruence for an NFA (S, o, t) is a relation $R \subseteq \mathcal{P}(S) \times \mathcal{P}(S)$ on sets of states, such that whenever $X\ R\ Y$ then*

1. $o^\sharp(X) = o^\sharp(Y)$ and
2. for all $a \in A$, $t^\sharp_a(X)\ c(R)\ t^\sharp_a(Y)$.

We then show that bisimulations up to congruence are sound, using the notion of compatibility:

Lemma 3. *The function u is compatible.*

Proof. We assume that $R \rightarrowtail R'$, and we prove that $u(R) \rightarrowtail u(R')$. If $X\ u(R)\ Y$, then $X = X_1 + X_2$ and $Y = Y_1 + Y_2$ for some X_1, X_2, Y_1, Y_2 such that $X_1\ R\ Y_1$ and $X_2\ R\ Y_2$. By assumption, we have $o^\sharp(X_1) = o^\sharp(Y_1)$, $o^\sharp(X_2) = o^\sharp(Y_2)$, and for all $a \in A$, $t^\sharp_a(X_1)\ R'\ t^\sharp_a(Y_1)$ and $t^\sharp_a(X_2)\ R'\ t^\sharp_a(Y_2)$. Since $o^\sharp$ and $t^\sharp$ are homomorphisms, we deduce $o^\sharp(X_1 + X_2) = o^\sharp(Y_1 + Y_2)$, and for all $a \in A$, $t^\sharp_a(X_1 + X_2)\ u(R')\ t^\sharp_a(Y_1 + Y_2)$. ☐

Theorem 2. *Any bisimulation up to congruence is contained in a bisimulation.*

Proof. By Proposition 3, it suffices to show that c is compatible, which follows from Lemmas 1, 2 and 3. ☐

In the Introduction, we already gave an example of bisimulation up to context, which is a particular case of bisimulation up to congruence (up to context corresponds using just the function $(r \cup u \cup \mathrm{id})^\omega$, without closing under s and t).

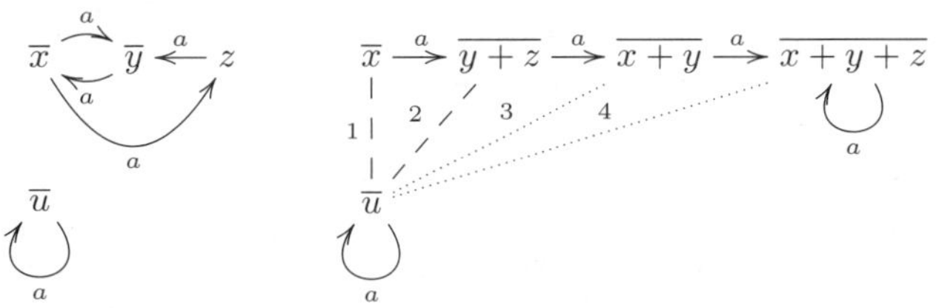

Figure 3. Bisimulations up to congruence, on a single letter NFA.

```
                    Naive(X,Y)

(1) R is empty; todo is empty;
(2) insert (X,Y) in todo;
(3) while todo is not empty, do
  (3.1)  extract (X',Y') from todo;
  (3.2)  if (X',Y') ∈ R then continue;
  (3.3)  if o#(X') ≠ o#(Y') then return false;
  (3.4)  for all a ∈ A,
           insert (t#_a(X'), t#_a(Y')) in todo;
  (3.5)  insert (X',Y') in R;
(4) return true;
```

Figure 4. On-the-fly naive algorithm, for checking the equivalence of sets of states X and Y of an NFA (S, o, t). The code for on-the-fly $\mathtt{HK}(X, Y)$ is obtained by replacing the test in step 3.2 with $(X', Y') \in e(R)$; the code for $\mathtt{HKC}(X, Y)$ is obtained by replacing this test with $(X', Y') \in c(R \cup todo)$.

A more involved example illustrating the use of all ingredients of the congruence closure function (c) is given in Figure 3. The relation R expressed by the dashed numbered lines (formally $R = \{(x,\ u), (y + z,\ u)\}$) is neither a bisimulation nor a bisimulation up to equivalence since $y{+}z \xrightarrow{a} x{+}y$ and $u \xrightarrow{a} u$, but $(x{+}y,\ u) \notin e(R)$. However, R is a bisimulation up to congruence. Indeed, we have $(x + y,\ u) \in c(R)$:

$$\begin{aligned} x + y\ c(R)\ & u + y && ((x, u) \in R)\\ c(R)\ & y + z + y && ((y + z, u) \in R)\\ =\ & y + z &&\\ c(R)\ & u && ((y + z, u) \in R)\end{aligned}$$

In contrast, we need four pairs to get a bisimulation up to e containing (x, u): this is the relation depicted with both dashed and dotted lines in Figure 3.

Note that we can deduce many other equations from R; in fact, $c(R)$ defines the following partition of sets of states:

$$\{0\}, \{y\}, \{z\}, \{x, u, x{+}y, x{+}z, \text{ and the 9 remaining subsets}\}.$$

3.3 Optimised algorithm for NFA

Algorithms for NFA can be obtained by computing the determinised NFA on-the-fly [13]: starting from the algorithms for DFA (Figure 1), it suffices to work with sets of states, and to inline the powerset construction. The corresponding code is given in Figure 4. The naive algorithm (`Naive`) does not use any up to technique, Hopcroft and Karp's algorithm (`HK`) reasons up to equivalence in step 3.2, and the optimised algorithm, referred as `HKC` in the sequel, relies on up to congruence: step 3.2 becomes

```
(3.2)  if (X',Y') ∈ c(R ∪ todo) then continue;
```

Observe that we use $c(R \cup todo)$ rather than $c(R)$: this allows us to skip more pairs, and this is safe since all pairs in $todo$ will eventually be processed.

Corollary 2. *For all $X, Y \in \mathcal{P}(S)$, $X \sim Y$ iff* $\texttt{HKC}(X, Y)$.

Proof. Same proof as for Proposition 2, by using the invariant $R \rightarrowtail c(R \cup todo)$ for the loop. We deduce that R is a bisimulation up to congruence after the loop. We conclude with Theorem 2 and Proposition 1. □

The most important point about these three algorithms is that they compute the states of the determinised NFA lazily. This means that only *accessible* states need to be computed, which is of practical importance since the determinised NFA can be exponentially large. In case of a negative answer, the three algorithms stop even before all accessible states have been explored; otherwise, if a bisimulation (possibly up-to) is found, it depends on the algorithm:

- With `Naive`, all accessible states need to be visited, by definition of bisimulation.
- With `HK`, the only case where some accessible states can be avoided is when a pair (X, X) is encountered: the algorithm skips this pair so that the successors of X are not necessarily computed (this situation rarely happens in practice—it actually never happens when starting with disjoint automata). In the other cases where a pair (X, Y) is skipped, then X and Y are necessarily already related to some other states in R, so that their successors will eventually be explored.
- With `HKC`, only a small portion of the accessible states is built (check the experiments in Section 6). To see a concrete example, let us execute `HKC` on the NFA from Figure 3. After two iterations, $R = \{(x, u), (y + z, u)\}$. Since $x + y \; c(R) \; u$, the algorithm stops without building the states $x + y$ and $x + y + z$. Similarly, in the example from the Introduction, `HKC` does not construct the four states corresponding to pairs 4, 5, and 6.

This ability of `HKC` to ignore parts of the determinised NFA comes from the up to congruence technique, which allows one to infer properties about states that were not necessarily encountered before. As we shall see in Section 4, the efficiency of antichain-based algorithms [1, 31] also comes from their ability to skip large parts of the determinised NFA.

3.4 Computing the congruence closure

For the optimised algorithm to be effective, we need a way to check whether some pairs belong to the congruence closure of some relation (step `3.2`). We present here a simple solution based on set rewriting; the key idea is to look at each pair (X, Y) in a relation R as a pair of rewriting rules:

$$X \to X + Y \qquad\qquad Y \to X + Y \;,$$

which can be used to compute normal forms for sets of states. Indeed, by idempotence, $X \; R \; Y$ entails $X \; c(R) \; X + Y$.

Definition 7. *Let $R \subseteq \mathcal{P}(S) \times \mathcal{P}(S)$ be a relation on sets of states. We define $\rightsquigarrow_R \subseteq \mathcal{P}(S) \times \mathcal{P}(S)$ as the smallest irreflexive relation that satisfies the following rules:*

$$\frac{X \; R \; Y}{X \rightsquigarrow_R X + Y} \qquad \frac{X \; R \; Y}{Y \rightsquigarrow_R X + Y} \qquad \frac{Z \rightsquigarrow_R Z'}{U + Z \rightsquigarrow_R U + Z'}$$

Lemma 4. *For all relations R, the relation $\rightsquigarrow_R$ is convergent.*

In the sequel, we denote by $X{\downarrow_R}$ the normal form of a set X w.r.t. $\rightsquigarrow_R$. Intuitively, the normal form of a set is the largest set of its equivalence class. Recalling the example from Figure 3, the common normal form of $x + y$ and u can be computed as follows (R is the relation $\{(x, u), (y + z, u)\}$):

$$x + y \rightsquigarrow x + y + u \rightsquigarrow x + y + z + u \leftsquigarrow x + u \leftsquigarrow u$$

Theorem 3. *For all relations R, and for all $X, Y \in \mathcal{P}(S)$, we have $X{\downarrow_R} = Y{\downarrow_R}$ iff $(X, Y) \in c(R)$.*

Thus, for checking $(X, Y) \in c(R \cup todo)$ we only have to compute the normal form of X and Y with respect to $\rightsquigarrow_{R \cup todo}$. Note that each pair of $R \cup todo$ may be used only once as a rewriting rule, but we do not know in advance in which order to apply these rules. Therefore, the time required to find one rule that applies is in the worst case rn where $r = |R \cup todo|$ is the size of the relation $R \cup todo$, and $n = |S|$ is the number of states of the NFA (assuming linear time complexity for set-theoretic union and containment of sets of states). Since we cannot apply more than r rules, the time for checking whether $(X, Y) \in c(R \cup todo)$ is bounded by $r^2 n$.

We tried other solutions, notably by using binary decision diagrams [9]. We have chosen to keep the presented rewriting algorithm for its simplicity and because it behaves well in practice.

3.5 Complexity hints

The complexity of `Naive`, `HK` and `HKC` is closely related to the size of the relation that they build. Hereafter, we use $v = |A|$ to denote the number of letters in A.

Lemma 5. *The three algorithms require at most $1 + v \cdot |R|$ iterations, where $|R|$ is the size of the produced relation; moreover, this bound is reached whenever they return true.*

Therefore, we can conveniently reason about $|R|$.

Lemma 6. *Let $R_{\texttt{Naive}}$, $R_{\texttt{HK}}$, and $R_{\texttt{HKC}}$ denote the relations produced by the three algorithms. We have*

$$|R_{\texttt{HKC}}|, |R_{\texttt{HK}}| \leq m \qquad\qquad |R_{\texttt{Naive}}| \leq m^2 \;, \tag{2}$$

where $m \leq 2^n$ is the number of accessible states in the determinised NFA and n is the number of states of the NFA. If the algorithms return true, we moreover have

$$|R_{\texttt{HKC}}| \leq |R_{\texttt{HK}}| \leq |R_{\texttt{Naive}}| \;. \tag{3}$$

As shown below in Section 4.2.4, $R_{\texttt{HKC}}$ can be exponentially smaller than $R_{\texttt{HK}}$. Notice however that the problem of deciding NFA language equivalence is PSPACE-complete [24], and that none of the algorithms presented here is in PSPACE: all of them store a set of visited pairs, and in the worst case, this set can become exponentially large with all of them. (This also holds for the antichain algorithms [1, 31] which we describe in Section 4.) Instead, the standard PSPACE algorithm does not store any set of visited pairs: it checks all words of length smaller than 2^n. While this can be done in polynomial space, this systematically requires exponential time.

3.6 Using `HKC` for checking language inclusion

For NFA, language inclusion can be reduced to language equivalence in a rather simple way. Since the function $[\![-]\!] \colon \mathcal{P}(S) \to 2^{A^\star}$ is a semi-lattice homomorphism (see Theorem 7 in [6]), for any given sets of states X and Y, $[\![X+Y]\!] = [\![Y]\!]$ iff $[\![X]\!] + [\![Y]\!] = [\![Y]\!]$ iff $[\![X]\!] \subseteq [\![Y]\!]$. Therefore, it suffices to run $\texttt{HKC}(X+Y, Y)$ to check the inclusion $[\![X]\!] \subseteq [\![Y]\!]$.

In such a situation, all pairs that are eventually manipulated by `HKC` have the shape $(X'+Y', Y')$ for some sets X', Y'. Step `3.2` of `HKC`, where it checks whether the current pair belongs to the congruence closure of the relation, can thus be simplified. First, the pairs in the current relation can only be used to rewrite from right to left. Second, the following lemma allows one to avoid unnecessary normal form computations:

Lemma 7. *For all sets X, Y and for all relations R, we have $X+Y\ c(R)\ Y$ iff $X \subseteq Y{\downarrow_R}$.*

Proof. We first prove that for all X, Y, $X{\downarrow_R} = Y{\downarrow_R}$ iff $X \subseteq Y{\downarrow_R}$ and $Y \subseteq X{\downarrow_R}$, using the fact that the normalisation function ${\downarrow_R}\colon X \mapsto X{\downarrow_R}$ is monotone and idempotent. The announced result follows by Theorem 3 since $Y \subseteq (X+Y){\downarrow_R}$ is always true and $X+Y \subseteq Y{\downarrow_R}$ iff $X \subseteq Y{\downarrow_R}$. □

At this point, the reader might wonder whether checking the two inclusions separetly is more convenient than checking the equivalence directly. Hereafter, we show that this is not the case.

Lemma 8. *Let X, Y be two sets of states; let $R_\subseteq$ and $R_\supseteq$ be the relations computed by HKC$(X+Y, Y)$ and HKC$(X+Y, X)$, respectively. If $R_\subseteq$ and $R_\supseteq$ are bisimulations up to congruence, then the following relation is a bisimulation up to congruence:*

$$R_= = \{(X', Y') \mid (X'+Y', Y') \in R_\subseteq \text{ or } (X'+Y', X') \in R_\supseteq\}.$$

On the contrary, checking the equivalence directly actually allows one to skip some pairs that cannot be skipped when reasoning by double inclusion. As an example, consider the DFA on the right of Figure 2. The relation computed by $\mathtt{HKC}(x, u)$ contains only four pairs (because the fifth one follows from transitivity). Instead, the relations built by $\mathtt{HKC}(x, x+u)$ and $\mathtt{HKC}(u+x, u)$ would both contain five pairs: transitivity cannot be used since our relations are now oriented (from $y \leq v$, $z \leq v$ and $z \leq w$, we cannot deduce $y \leq w$). Another example, where we get an exponential factor by checking the equivalence directly rather than through the two inclusions, can be found in Section 4.2.4.

In a sense, the behaviour of the coinduction proof method here is similar to that of standard proofs by induction, where one often has to strengthen the induction predicate to get a (nicer) proof.

4. Antichain algorithm

In [31], De Wulf et al. have proposed the *antichain* approach for checking language inclusion of NFA. We show that this approach can be explained in terms of *simulations up to upward-closure* that, in turn, can be seen as a special case of bisimulations up to congruence. Before doing so, we recall the standard notion of antichain and we describe the antichain algorithm (AC).

Given a partial order $(X, \sqsubseteq)$, an *antichain* is a subset $Y \subseteq X$ containing only incomparable elements (that is, for all $y_1, y_2 \in Y$, $y_1 \not\sqsubseteq y_2$ and $y_2 \not\sqsubseteq y_1$). AC exploits antichains over the set $S \times \mathcal{P}(S)$, where the ordering is given by $(x_1, Y_1) \sqsubseteq (x_2, Y_2)$ iff $x_1 = x_2$ and $Y_1 \subseteq Y_2$.

In order to check $[\![X]\!] \subseteq [\![Y]\!]$ for two sets of states X, Y of an NFA (S, o, t), AC maintains an antichain of pairs (x', Y'), where x' is a state of the NFA and Y' is a state of the determinised automaton. More precisely, the automaton is explored non-deterministically (via t) for obtaining the first component of the pair and deterministically (via $t^\sharp$) for the second one. If a pair such that x' is accepting ($o(x') = 1$) and Y' is not ($o^\sharp(Y') = 0$) is encountered, then a counter-example has been found. Otherwise all derivatives of the pair along the automata transitions have to be inserted into the antichain, so that they will be explored. If one of these pairs p is larger than a previously encountered pair p' ($p' \sqsubseteq p$) then the language inclusion corresponding to p is subsumed by p' so that p can be skipped; otherwise, if $p \sqsubseteq p_1, \dots, p_n$ for some pairs $p_1, \dots, p_n$ that are already in the antichain, then one can safely remove these pairs: they are subsumed by p and, by doing so, the set of visited pairs remains an antichain.

Remark 4. *An important difference between HKC and AC consists in the fact that the former inserts pairs in todo without checking whether they are redundant (this check is performed when the pair is processed), while the latter removes all redundant pairs whenever a new one is inserted. Therefore, the cost of an iteration with HKC is merely the cost of the corresponding congruence check, while the cost of an iteration with AC is merely that of inserting all successors of the corresponding pair and simplifying the antichain.*

Note that the above description corresponds to the "forward" antichain algorithm, as described in [1]. Instead, the original antichain algorithm, as first described in [31], is "backward" in the sense that the automata are traversed in the reversed way, from accepting states to initial states. The two versions are dual [31] and we could similarly define the backward counterpart of HKC and HK. We however stick to the forward versions for the sake of clarity.

4.1 Coinductive presentation

Leaving apart the concrete data structures used to manipulate antichains, we can rephrase this algorithm using a coinductive framework, like we did for Hopcroft and Karp's algorithm.

First define a notion of *simulation*, where the left-hand side automaton is executed non-deterministically:

Definition 8 (Simulation). *Given two relations $T, T' \subseteq S \times \mathcal{P}(S)$, T* s-progresses to *T', denoted $T \rightarrowtail_s T'$, if whenever $x\ T\ Y$ then*

1. *$o(x) \leq o^\sharp(Y)$ and*
2. *for all $a \in A$, $x' \in t_a(x)$, $x'\ T'\ t_a^\sharp(Y)$.*

A simulation *is a relation T such that $T \rightarrowtail_s T$.*

As expected, we obtain the following coinductive proof principle:

Proposition 4 (Coinduction). *For all sets X, Y, we have $[\![X]\!] \subseteq [\![Y]\!]$ iff there exists a simulation T such that for all $x \in X$, $x\ T\ Y$.*

(Note that like for our notion of bisimulation, the above notion of simulation is weaker than the standard one from concurrency theory [25], which *strictly* entails language inclusion—Remark 3.)

To account for the antichain algorithm, where we can discard pairs using the preorder $\sqsubseteq$, it suffices to define the *upward closure* function $\uparrow\colon \mathcal{P}(S \times \mathcal{P}(S)) \to \mathcal{P}(S \times \mathcal{P}(S))$ as

$$\uparrow T = \{(x, Y) \mid \exists (x', Y') \in T \text{ s.t. } (x', Y') \sqsubseteq (x, Y)\}\ .$$

A pair belongs to the upward closure $\uparrow T$ of a relation $T \subseteq S \times \mathcal{P}(S)$, if and only if this pair is subsumed by some pair in T. In fact, rather than trying to construct a simulation, AC attempts to construct a simulation up to upward closure.

Like for HK and HKC, this method can be justified by defining the appropriate notion of s-compatible function, showing that any simulation up to an s-compatible function is contained in a simulation, and showing that the upward closure function ($\uparrow$) is s-compatible.

Theorem 4. *Any simulation up to $\uparrow$ is contained in a simulation.*

Corollary 3. *For all $X, Y \in \mathcal{P}(S)$, $[\![X]\!] \subseteq [\![Y]\!]$ iff AC(X, Y).*

4.2 Comparing HKC and AC

The efficiency of the two algorithms strongly depends on the number of pairs that they need to explore. In the following (Sections 4.2.3 and 4.2.4), we show that HKC can explore far fewer pairs than AC: when checking language inclusion of automata that share some states, or when checking language equivalence. We would also like to formally prove that (a) HKC never explores more than AC, and (b) when checking inclusion of disjoint automata, AC never explores more than HKC. Unfortunately, the validity of these statements highly depends on numerous assumptions about the two algorithms (e.g., on the exploration strategy) and their potential proofs seem complicated and not really informative. For these reasons, we preferred to investigate the formal correspondence at the level of the coinductive proof techniques, where it is much cleaner.

4.2.1 Language inclusion: HKC can mimic AC

As explained in Section 3.6, we can check the language inclusion of two sets X, Y by executing $\mathtt{HKC}(X{+}Y, Y)$. We now show that for any simulation up to upward closure that proves the inclusion $[\![X]\!] \subseteq [\![Y]\!]$, there exists a bisimulation up to congruence of the same size which proves the same inclusion. For $T \subseteq S \times \mathcal{P}(S)$, let $\widehat{T} \subseteq \mathcal{P}(S) \times \mathcal{P}(S)$ denote the relation $\{(x+Y, Y) \mid x\ T\ Y\}$.

Lemma 9. *We have* $\widehat{\uparrow T} \subseteq c(\widehat{T})$.

Proof. If $(x+Y, Y) \in \widehat{\uparrow T}$, then there exists $Y' \subseteq Y$ such that $(x, Y') \in T$. By definition, $(x+Y', Y') \in \widehat{T}$ and $(Y, Y) \in c(\widehat{T})$. By the rule (u), $(x+Y'+Y, Y'+Y) \in c(\widehat{T})$ and since $Y' \subseteq Y$, $(x+Y, Y) \in c(\widehat{T})$. □

Proposition 5. *If T is a simulation up to $\uparrow$, then $\widehat{T}$ is a bisimulation up to c.*

Proof. First observe that if $T \rightarrowtail_s T'$, then $\widehat{T} \rightarrowtail u^\omega(\widehat{T'})$. Therefore, if $T \rightarrowtail_s \uparrow T$, then $\widehat{T} \rightarrowtail u^\omega(\widehat{\uparrow T})$. By Lemma 9, $\widehat{T} \rightarrowtail u^\omega(c(\widehat{T})) = c(\widehat{T})$. □

(Note that transitivity and symmetry are not used in the above proofs: the constructed bisimulation up to congruence is actually a bisimulation up to context $(r \cup u \cup id)^\omega$.)

The relation $\widehat{T}$ is not the one computed by HKCsince the former contains pairs of the shape $(x+Y, Y)$, while the latter has pairs of the shape $(X+Y, Y)$ with X possibly not a singleton. However, note that manipulating pairs of the two kinds does not change anything since by Lemma 7, $(X+Y, Y) \in c(R)$ iff for all $x \in X$, $(x+Y, Y) \in c(R)$.

4.2.2 Inclusion: AC can mimic HKC on disjoint automata

As shown in Section 4.2.3 below, HKC can be faster than AC, thanks to the up to transitivity technique. However, in the special case where the two automata are disjoint, transitivity cannot help, and the two algorithms actually match each other.

Suppose that the automaton (S, o, t) is built from two disjoint automata (S_1, o_1, t_1) and (S_2, o_2, t_2) as described in Remark 1. Let R be the relation obtained by running $\mathtt{HKC}(X_0{+}Y_0, Y_0)$ with $X_0 \subseteq S_1$ and $Y_0 \subseteq S_2$. All pairs in R are necessarily of the shape $(X{+}Y,\ Y)$ with $X \subseteq S_1$ and $Y \subseteq S_2$. Let $\overline{R} \subseteq S \times \mathcal{P}(S)$ denote the relation $\{(x, Y) \mid \exists X,\ x \in X \text{ and } X{+}Y\ R\ Y\}$.

Lemma 10. *If S_1 and S_2 are disjoint, then* $\overline{c(R)} \subseteq \uparrow(\overline{R})$.

Proof. Suppose that $x\ \overline{c(R)}\ Y$, i.e., $x \in X$ with $X+Y\ c(R)\ Y$. By Lemma 7, we have $X \subseteq Y{\downarrow_R}$, and hence, $x \in Y{\downarrow_R}$. By definition of R the pairs it contains can only be used to rewrite from right to left; moreover, since S_1 and S_2 are disjoint, such rewriting steps cannot enable new rewriting rules, so that all steps can be performed in parallel: we have $Y{\downarrow_R} = \sum_{X'+Y' R Y' \subseteq Y} X'$. Therefore, there exist some X', Y' with $x \in X'$, $X'{+}Y'\ \ R\ Y'$, and $Y' \subseteq Y$. It follows that $(x, Y') \in \overline{R}$, hence $(x, Y) \in \uparrow(\overline{R})$. □

Proposition 6. *If S_1 and S_2 are disjoint, and if R is a bisimulation up to congruence, then $\overline{R}$ is a simulation up to upward closure.*

Proof. First observe that for all relations R, R', if $R \rightarrowtail R'$, then $\overline{R} \rightarrowtail_s \overline{R'}$. Therefore, if $R \rightarrowtail c(R)$, then $\overline{R} \rightarrowtail_s \overline{c(R)}$. We deduce $\overline{R} \rightarrowtail_s \uparrow(\overline{R})$ by Lemma 10. □

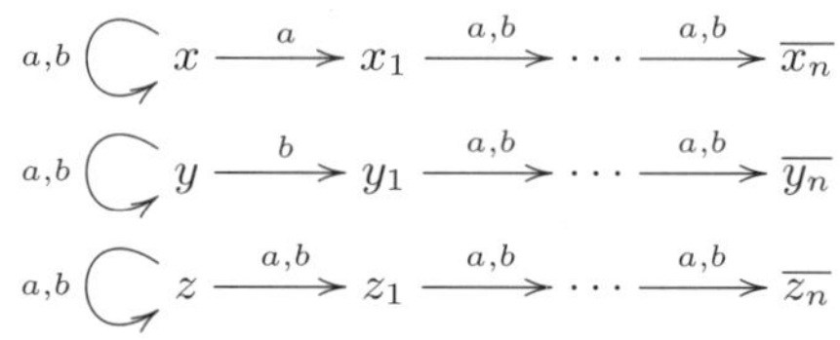

Figure 5. Family of examples where HKC exponentially improves over AC and HK; we have $x + y \sim z$.

4.2.3 Inclusion: AC cannot mimic HKC on merged automata

The containment of Lemma 10 does not hold when S_1 and S_2 are not disjoint since c can exploit transitivity while $\uparrow$ cannot. For a concrete grasp, take $R = \{(x+y, y), (y+z, z)\}$ and observe that $(x, z) \in \overline{c(R)}$ but $(x, z) \notin \uparrow(\overline{R})$. This difference makes it possible to find bisimulations up to c that are much smaller than the corresponding simulations up to $\uparrow$, and for HKC to be more efficient than AC. An example, where HKC is exponentially better than AC for checking language inclusion of automata sharing some states, is given in [7].

4.2.4 Language equivalence: AC cannot mimic HKC

AC can be used to check language equivalence, by checking the two underlying inclusions. However, checking equivalence directly can be better, even in the disjoint case. To see this on a simple example, consider the DFA on the right-hand side of Figure 2. If we use AC twice to prove $x \sim u$, we get the following antichains

$$T_1 = \{(x,u), (y,v), (y,w), (z,v), (z,w)\}$$
$$T_2 = \{(u,x), (v,y), (w,y), (v,z), (w,z)\}$$

containing five pairs each. Instead, four pairs are sufficient with HK or HKC, thanks to up to symmetry and up to transitivity.

For a more interesting example, consider the family of NFA given in Figure 5, where n is an arbitrary natural number. Taken together, the states x and y are equivalent to the state z: they recognise the language $(a{+}b)^\star(a{+}b)^{n+1}$. Alone, the state x (resp. y) recognises the language $(a{+}b)^\star a(a{+}b)^n$ (resp. $(a{+}b)^\star b(a{+}b)^n$).

For $i \leq n$, let $X_i = x{+}x_1{+}\ldots{+}x_i$, $Y_i = y{+}y_1{+}\ldots{+}y_i$, and $Z_i = z{+}z_1{+}\ldots{+}z_i$; for $N \subseteq [1..i]$, furthermore set

$$X_i^N = x + \sum_{j \in N} x_j \ , \qquad \overline{Y}_i^N = y + \sum_{j \in [1..n] \setminus N} y_j \ .$$

In the determinised NFA, $x+y$ can reach all the states of the shape $X_i^N{+}\overline{Y}_i^N$, for $i \leq n$ and $N \subseteq [1..i]$. For instance, for $n{=}i{=}2$, we have $x{+}y \overset{aa}{\to} x{+}y{+}x_1{+}x_2$, $x{+}y \overset{ab}{\to} x{+}y{+}y_1{+}x_2$, $x{+}y \overset{ba}{\to} x{+}y{+}x_1{+}y_2$, and $x{+}y \overset{bb}{\to} x{+}y{+}y_1{+}y_2$. Instead, z reaches only $n{+}1$ distinct states, those of the form Z_i.

The smallest bisimulation relating $x+y$ and z is

$$R = \{(X_i^N + \overline{Y}_i^N,\ Z_i) \mid i \leq n, N \subseteq [1..i]\},$$

which contains $2^{n+1}{-}1$ pairs. This is the relation computed by $\mathtt{Naive}(x, y)$ and $\mathtt{HK}(x, y)$—the up to equivalence technique (alone) does not help in HK. With AC, we obtain the antichains $T_x + T_y$ (for $[\![x+y]\!] \subseteq [\![z]\!]$) and T_z (for $[\![x+y]\!] \supseteq [\![z]\!]$), where:

$$T_x = \{(x_i,\ Z_i) \mid i \leq n\},$$
$$T_y = \{(y_i,\ Z_i) \mid i \leq n\},$$
$$T_z = \{(z_i,\ X_i^N + \overline{Y}_i^N) \mid i \leq n, N \subseteq [1..i]\}.$$

Note that T_x and T_y have size $n+1$, and T_z has size $2^{n+1}{-}1$.

The language recognised by x or y are known for having a minimal DFA with 2^n states [19]. So, checking $x + y \sim z$ via minimisation (e.g., [17]) would also require exponential time.

This is not the case with HKC, which requires only polynomial time in this case. Indeed, $\texttt{HKC}(x{+}y, z)$ builds the relation

$$\begin{aligned} R' = \{&(x+y,\ z)\} \\ \cup \{&(x + Y_i + y_{i+1},\ Z_{i+1}) \mid i < n\} \\ \cup \{&(x + Y_i + x_{i+1},\ Z_{i+1}) \mid i < n\} \end{aligned}$$

which is a bisimulation up to congruence and which only contains $2n + 1$ pairs. To see that this is a bisimulation up to congruence, consider the pair $(x{+}y{+}x_1{+}y_2,\ Z_2)$ obtained from $(x{+}y,\ z)$ after reading the word ba. This pair does not belong to R' but to its congruence closure. Indeed, we have

$$\begin{aligned} x{+}y{+}x_1{+}y_2 \; c(R') \; & Z_1{+}y_2 && (x{+}y{+}x_1 \; R' \; Z_1) \\ c(R') \; & x{+}y{+}y_1{+}y_2 && (x{+}y{+}y_1 \; R' \; Z_1) \\ c(R') \; & Z_2 && (x{+}y{+}y_1{+}y_2 \; R' \; Z_2) \end{aligned}$$

(Check Lemma 18 in [6] for a complete proof.)

5. Exploiting Similarity

Looking at the example in Figure 5, a natural idea would be to first quotient the automaton by graph isomorphism. By doing so, we would merge the states x_i, y_i, z_i, and we would obtain the following automaton, for which checking $x{+}y \sim z$ is much easier.

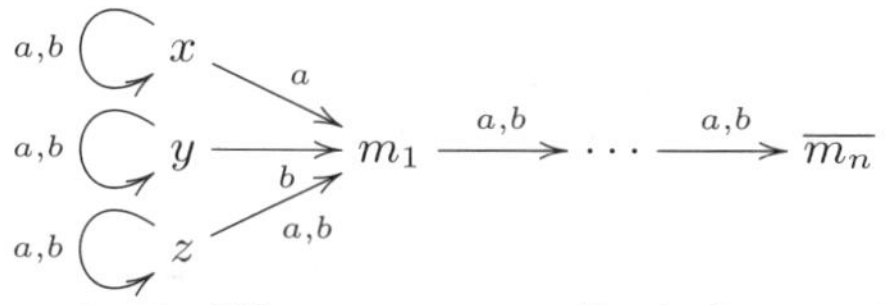

As shown in [1, 12], one can actually do better with the antichain algorithm, by exploiting any preorder contained in language inclusion (e.g., similarity [25]). In this section, we rephrase this technique for antichains in our coinductive framework, and we show how this idea can be embedded in HKC, resulting in an even stronger algorithm.

5.1 AC with similarity: AC'

For the sake of clarity, we fix the preorder to be *similarity*, which can be computed in quadratic time [14] (or even less [16]):

Definition 9 (Similarity). Similarity *is the largest relation on states* $\preceq \subseteq S \times S$ *such that* $x \preceq y$ *entails:*

1. $o(x) \leq o(y)$ *and*
2. *for all* $a \in A, x' \in S$ *such that* $x \xrightarrow{a} x'$, *there exists some* y' *such that* $y \xrightarrow{a} y'$ *and* $x' \preceq y'$.

One extends similarity to a preorder $\preceq^{\forall\exists} \subseteq \mathcal{P}(S) \times \mathcal{P}(S)$ on sets of states, and to a preorder $\sqsubseteq^{\preceq} \subseteq (S \times \mathcal{P}(S)) \times (S \times \mathcal{P}(S))$ on antichain pairs, as:

$$\begin{aligned} X \preceq^{\forall\exists} Y \quad & \text{if} \quad \forall x \in X, \exists y \in Y, x \preceq y \ , \\ (x', Y') \sqsubseteq^{\preceq} (x, Y) \quad & \text{if} \quad x \preceq x' \text{ and } Y' \preceq^{\forall\exists} Y \ . \end{aligned}$$

The new antichain algorithm [1], which we call AC', is similar to AC, but the antichain is now taken w.r.t. the new preorder $\sqsubseteq^{\preceq}$. Formally, let $\curlywedge\colon \mathcal{P}(S \times \mathcal{P}(S)) \to \mathcal{P}(S \times \mathcal{P}(S))$ be the function defined for all relations $T \subseteq S \times \mathcal{P}(S)$ by $x \curlywedge T \; Y$ if

$$x \preceq^{\forall\exists} Y \text{ or } (x', Y') \sqsubseteq^{\preceq} (x, Y) \text{ for some } (x', Y') \in T \ .$$

While AC consists in trying to build a simulation up to $\uparrow$, AC' tries to build a simulation up to $\curlywedge$, i.e., it skips a pair (x, Y) if either (a) it is subsumed by another pair of the antichain or (b) $x \preceq^{\forall\exists} Y$.

Theorem 5. *Any simulation up to* $\curlywedge$ *is contained in a simulation.*

Corollary 4. *The antichain algorithm proposed in [1] is sound and complete: for all sets* X, Y, $[\![X]\!] \subseteq [\![Y]\!]$ *iff* $\texttt{AC'}(X, Y)$.

Optimisation 1(a) and optimisation 1(b) in [1] are simply (a) and (b), as discussed above. Another optimisation, called Optimisation 2, is presented in [1]: if $y_1 \preceq y_2$ and $y_1, y_2 \in Y$ for some pair (x, Y), then y_1 can be safely removed from Y. Note that while this is useful to store smaller sets, it does not allow one to explore less since the pairs encountered with or without Optimisation 2 are always equivalent w.r.t. the ordering $\sqsubseteq^{\preceq}$: $Y \preceq^{\forall\exists} Y \setminus y_1$ and, for all $a \in A$, $t_a^\sharp(Y) \preceq^{\forall\exists} t_a^\sharp(Y \setminus y_1)$.

5.2 HKC with similarity: HKC'

Although HKC is primarily designed to check language equivalence, we can also extend it to exploit the similarity preorder. It suffices to notice that for any similarity pair $x \preceq y$, we have $x{+}y \sim y$.

Let $\overline{\preceq}$ denote the relation $\{(x{+}y,\ y) \mid x \preceq y\}$, let r' denote the constant function to $\overline{\preceq}$, and let $c' = (r' \cup s \cup t \cup u \cup id)^\omega$. Accordingly, we call HKC' the algorithm obtained from HKC (Figure 4) by replacing $(X, Y) \in c(R \cup todo)$ with $(X, Y) \in c'(R \cup todo)$ in step 3.2. Notice that the latter test can be reduced to rewriting thanks to Theorem 3 and the following lemma.

Lemma 11. *For all relations* R, $c'(R) = c(R \cup \overline{\preceq})$.

In other words to check whether $(X, Y) \in c'(R \cup todo)$, it suffices to compute the normal forms of X and Y w.r.t. the rules from $R \cup todo$ plus the rules $x + y \leftarrow y$ for all $x \preceq y$.

Theorem 6. *Any bisimulation up to* c' *is contained in a bisimulation.*

Proof. Consider the constant function $r''\colon \mathcal{P}(\mathcal{P}(S) \times \mathcal{P}(S)) \to \mathcal{P}(\mathcal{P}(S) \times \mathcal{P}(S))$ mapping all relations to $\sim$. Since language equivalence ($\sim$) is a bisimulation, we immediately obtain that this function is compatible. Thus so is the function $c'' = (r'' \cup s \cup t \cup u \cup id)^\omega$. We have that $\overline{\preceq}$ is contained in $\sim$, so that any bisimulation up to c' is a bisimulation up to c''. Since c'' is compatible, such a relation is contained in a bisimulation, by Proposition 3. ☐

Note that in the above proof, we can replace $\overline{\preceq}$ by any other relation contained in $\sim$. Intuitively, bisimulations up to c'' correspond to classical *bisimulations up to bisimilarity* [25] from concurrency.

Corollary 5. *For all sets* X, Y, *we have* $X \sim Y$ *iff* $\texttt{HKC'}(X, Y)$.

5.3 Relationship between HKC' and AC'

Like in Section 4.2.1, we can show that for any simulation up to $\curlywedge$ there exists a corresponding bisimulation up to c', of the same size.

Lemma 12. *For all relations* $T \subseteq S \times \mathcal{P}(S)$, $\widehat{\curlywedge T} \subseteq c'(\widehat{T})$.

Proposition 7. *If* T *is a simulation up to* $\curlywedge$, *then* $\widehat{T}$ *is a bisimulation up to* c'.

However, even for checking inclusion of disjoint automata, AC' cannot mimic HKC', because now the similarity relation allows one to exploit transitivity. To see this, consider the example given in Figure 6, where we want to check that $[\![z]\!] \subseteq [\![x + y]\!]$, and for which the similarity relation is shown on the right-hand side.

Since this is an inclusion of disjoint automata, HKC and AC, which do not exploit similarity, behave the same (cf. Sections 4.2.1 and 4.2.2). Actually, they also behave like HK and they require $2^{n+1}{-}1$ pairs. On the contrary, the use of similarity allows HKC' to prove the inclusion with only $2n + 1$ pairs, by computing the

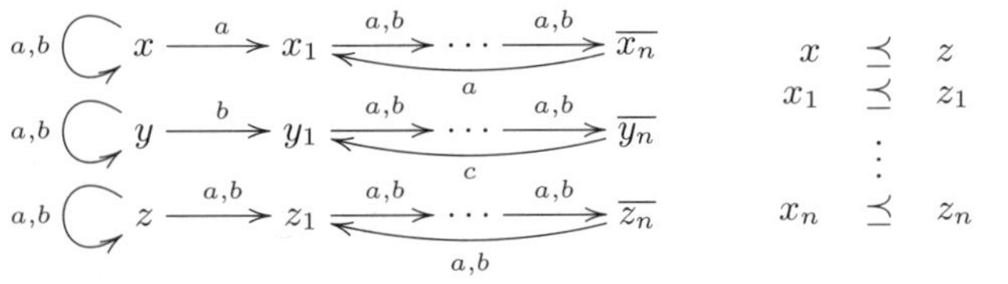

Figure 6. Family of examples where HKC' exponentially improves over AC', for inclusion of disjoint automata: we have $[\![z]\!] \subseteq [\![x{+}y]\!]$.

following bisimulation up to c' (Lemma 19 in [6]):

$$\begin{aligned} R'' = \; & \{(z{+}x{+}y,\ x{+}y)\} \\ & \cup \{(Z_{i+1}{+}X_i{+}y{+}y_{i+1},\ X_i{+}y{+}y_{i+1}) \mid i < n\} \\ & \cup \{(Z_{i+1}{+}X_{i+1}{+}y,\ X_{i+1}{+}y) \mid i < n\}\ , \end{aligned}$$

where $X_i = x{+}x_1{+}\ldots{+}x_i$ and $Z_i = z{+}z_1{+}\ldots{+}z_i$.

Like in Section 4.2.4, to see that this is a bisimulation up to c' (where we do exploit similarity), consider the pair obtained after reading the word ab: $(Z_2{+}x{+}y{+}x_2{+}y_1,\ x{+}y{+}x_2{+}y_1)$. This pair does not belong to R'' or $c(R'')$, but it does belong to $c'(R'')$. Indeed, by Lemmas 7 and 11, this pair belong to $c'(R'')$ iff $Z_2 \subseteq (x{+}y{+}x_2{+}y_1)\downarrow_{R''\cup\preceq}$, and we have

$$\begin{aligned} & x{+}y{+}x_2{+}y_1 \\ \rightsquigarrow_{R''\cup\preceq}\ & Z_1{+}x{+}y{+}y_1{+}x_2 && (Z_1{+}x{+}y{+}y_1\ R''\ x{+}y{+}y_1) \\ \rightsquigarrow_{R''\cup\preceq}\ & Z_1{+}X_1{+}y{+}y_1{+}x_2 = Z_1{+}X_2{+}y{+}y_1 && (x_1 \preceq z_1) \\ \rightsquigarrow_{R''\cup\preceq}\ & Z_2{+}X_2{+}y{+}y_1{+}x_2 && (Z_2{+}X_2{+}y\ R''\ X_2{+}y) \end{aligned}$$

On the contrary, AC' is not able to exploit similarity in this case, and it behaves like AC: both of them compute the same antichain T_z as in the example from Section 4.2.4, which has $2^{n+1}{-}1$ elements.

In fact, even when considering inclusion of disjoint automata, the use of similarity tends to virtually merge states, so that HKC' can use the up to transitivity technique which AC and AC' lack.

5.4 A short recap

Figure 7 summarises the relationship amongst the presented algorithms, in the general case and in the special case of language inclusion of disjoint automata. In this diagram, an arrow X$\rightarrow$Y (from an algorithm X to Y) means that (a) Y can explore less states than X, and (b) Y can mimic X, i.e., the proof technique of Y is at least as powerful as the one of X. (The labels on the arrows point to the sections showing these relations; unlabelled arrows are not illustrated in this paper, they are easily inferred from what we have shown.)

6. Experimental assessment

To get an intuition of the average behaviour of HKC on various NFA, and to compare it with HK and AC, we provide some benchmarks on random automata and on automata obtained from model-checking problems. In both cases, we conduct the experiments on a MacBook pro 2.4GHz Intel Core i7, with 4GB of memory, running OS X Lion (10.7.4). We use our OCaml implementation [7] for HK, HKC, and HKC', while we use the `libvata` C++ library [21] for AC and AC'.[1] (To our knowledge, `libvata` is the most efficient implementation currently available for these algorithms, even though this library was designed for tree automata rather than plain NFA.)

6.1 Random automata

For a given size n, we generate a thousand random NFA with n states and two letters. According to [30], we use a linear transition density of 1.25 (which means that the expected out-degree of each state and with respect to each letter is 1.25): Tabakov and Vardi empirically showed that one statistically gets more challenging NFA with this particular value. We generate NFA without accepting states: by doing so, we make sure that the algorithms never encounter a counter-example, so that they always continue until they find a (bi)simulation up to: these runs correspond to their worst cases for all possible choices of accepting states for the given NFA.[2]

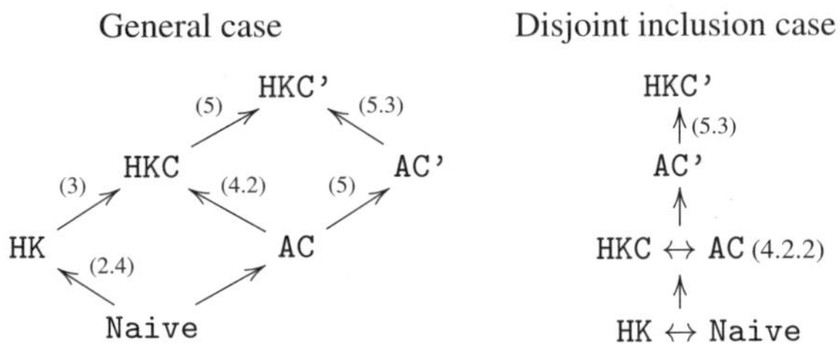

Figure 7. Relationship between the various algorithms.

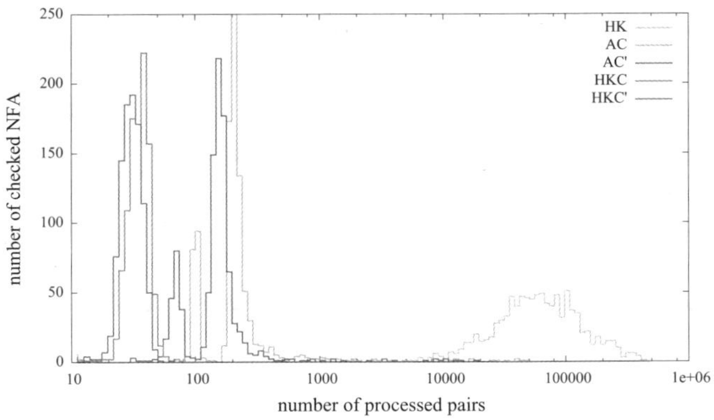

Figure 8. Distributions of the number of processed pairs, for the 1000 NFA with 100 states and 2 letters from Table 1.

We run all algorithms on these NFA, starting from two distinct singleton sets, to measure the required time and the number of processed pairs: for HK, HKC, and HKC', this is the number of pairs put into the bisimulation up to (R); for AC and AC', this is the number of pairs inserted into the antichain. The timings for HKC' and AC' do not include the time required to compute similarity.

We report the median values (50%), the last deciles (90%), the last percentiles (99%), and the maximum values (100%) in Table 1. For instance, for $n = 70$, 90% of the examples require less than 155ms with HK; equivalently, 10% of the examples require more than 155ms. (For a few tests, `libvata` ran out of memory, whence the ∞ symbols in the table.) We also plotted on Figure 8 the distribution of the number of processed pairs when $n = 100$.

HKC and AC are several orders of magnitude better than HK, and HKC is usually two to ten times faster than AC. Moreover, for the first four lines, HKC is much more predictable than AC, i.e., the last percentiles and maximal values are of the same order as the median value. (AC seems to become more predictable for larger values of n.) The same relative behaviour can be observed between HKC' and AC'; moreover, HKC alone is apparently faster than AC'.

Also recall that the size of the relations generated by HK is a lower bound for the number of accessible states of the determinised

[1] More precisely, the upward algorithms provided by default in `libvata`.

[2] To get this behaviour for AC and AC', we actually had to trick `libvata`, which otherwise starts by removing non-coaccessible states, and thus reduces any of these NFA to the empty one.

$n = \|S\|$	algo.	required time (seconds)				number of processed pairs				mDFA size
		50%	90%	99%	100%	50%	90%	99%	100%	50%
50	HK	0.007	0.022	0.050	0.119	2511	6299	12506	25272	∼1000
	AC	0.002	0.003	0.142	1.083	112	245	2130	5208	
	HKC	0.000	0.000	0.000	0.000	21	26	32	63	
	AC'	0.002	0.002	0.038	0.211	79	131	1098	1926	
	HKC'	0.000	0.000	0.000	0.000	18	23	28	58	
70	HK	0.047	0.155	0.413	0.740	10479	28186	58782	87055	∼6000
	AC	0.002	0.003	1.492	4.163	150	285	8383	15575	
	HKC	0.000	0.000	0.000	0.000	27	34	40	49	
	AC'	0.002	0.003	0.320	0.884	110	172	3017	6096	
	HKC'	0.000	0.000	0.000	0.000	23	29	36	44	
100	HK	0.373	1.207	3.435	5.660	58454	164857	361227	471727	∼30000
	AC	0.003	0.004	3.214	36.990	204	298	13801	48059	
	HKC	0.000	0.000	0.000	0.001	36	44	54	70	
	AC'	0.003	0.004	0.738	6.966	152	211	4087	18455	
	HKC'	0.000	0.000	0.000	0.001	31	39	46	64	
300	AC	0.009	0.010	0.028	0.750	562	622	2232	14655	–
	HKC	0.001	0.002	0.003	0.009	86	104	118	132	
	AC'	0.012	0.013	0.022	0.970	433	484	920	14160	
	HKC'	0.001	0.001	0.002	0.006	76	91	104	116	
500	AC	0.014	0.015	0.039	∞	918	986	2571	∞	–
	HKC	0.002	0.005	0.008	0.018	130	154	176	193	
	AC'	0.025	0.028	0.042	∞	710	772	1182	∞	
	HKC'	0.002	0.004	0.007	0.013	115	136	154	169	
1000	AC	0.029	0.031	0.038	∞	1808	1878	2282	∞	–
	HKC	0.007	0.022	0.055	0.093	228	271	304	337	
	AC'	0.074	0.080	0.092	∞	1409	1488	1647	∞	
	HKC'	0.008	0.019	0.041	0.077	202	238	265	299	

Table 1. Running the five presented algorithms to check language equivalence on random NFA with two letters.

NFA (Lemma 6 (2)); one can thus see in Table 1 that `HKC` usually explores an extremely small portion of these DFA (e.g., less than one per thousand for $n = 100$). The last column reports the median size of the minimal DFA for the corresponding parameters, as given in [30]. `HK` usually explores much more states than what would be necessary with a minimal DFA, while `HKC` and `AC` need much less.

6.2 Automata from regular model-checking

Checking language inclusion of NFA can be useful for model-checking, where one sometimes has to compute a sequence of NFA by iteratively applying a transducer, until a fixpoint is reached [8]. To know that the fixpoint is reached, one typically has to check whether an NFA is contained in another one.

Abdulla et al. [1] use such benchmarks to test their algorithm (`AC'`) against the plain antichain algorithm (`AC` [31]). We reuse them to test `HKC'` against `AC'` in a concrete scenario. We take the sequences of automata kindly provided by L. Holik, which come from those used in [1] and arise from the model checking of various programs (the bakery algorithm, bubble sort, and a producer-consumer system). For all these sequences, we check the inclusions of consecutive pairs, in both directions. We separate the results into those for which a counter-example is found, and those for which the inclusion holds.

The results are given in Table 2. As expected, `HKC` and `AC` roughly behave the same: we have inclusions of disjoint automata. `HKC'` is however quite faster than `AC'`: up to transitivity can be exploited thanks to similarity pairs. Like in Table 1, the timings do not include the time required to compute similarity, which is given separately (computed using `libvata`). Also note that over the 546 positive answers, 368 are obtained immediately by similarity.

7. Related work

A similar notion of bisimulation up to congruence has already been used to obtain decidability and complexity results about context-free processes, under the name of *self-bisimulations*. Caucal [10] introduced this concept to give a shorter and nicer proof of the result by Baeten et al. [4]: bisimilarity is decidable for normed context-free processes. Christensen et al [11] then generalised the result to all context-free processes, also by using self-bisimulations. Hirshfeld et al. [15] used a refinement of this notion to get a polynomial algorithm for bisimilarity in the normed case.

There are two main differences with the ideas we presented here. First, the above papers focus on bisimilarity rather than language equivalence (recall that although we use bisimulation relations, we check language equivalence since we work on the determinised NFA—Remark 3). Second, we consider a notion of bisimulation up to congruence where the congruence is taken with respect to non-determinism (union of sets of states). Self-bisimulations are also bisimulations up to congruence, but the congruence is taken with respect to word concatenation. We cannot consider this operation in our setting since we do not have the corresponding monoid structure in plain NFA.

Other approaches, that are independent from the algebraic structure (e.g., monoids or semi-lattices) and the behavioural equivalence (e.g., bisimilarity or language equivalence) are shown in [5, 22, 23, 26]. These propose very general frameworks into which our up to congruence technique fits as a very special case. To our knowledge, bisimulation up to congruence has never been proposed as a technique for proving language equivalence of NFA.

8. Conclusions and future work

We showed that the standard algorithm by Hopcroft and Karp for checking language equivalence of DFA relies on a bisimulation up to equivalence proof technique; this allowed us to design a new algorithm (`HKC`) for the non-deterministic case, where we exploit a novel technique called up to congruence.

We then compared `HKC` to the recently introduced antichain algorithms [31] (`AC`): when checking the inclusion of disjoint automata, the two algorithms are equivalent, in all the other cases

algorithm	inclusions (546 pairs)				counter-examples (518 pairs)			
	50%	90%	99%	100%	50%	90%	99%	100%
AC	0.036	0.860	4.981	5.084	0.009	0.094	1.412	2.887
HKC	0.049	0.798	6.494	6.762	0.000	0.014	0.916	2.685
AC'	0.013	0.167	1.326	1.480	0.012	0.107	1.047	1.134
HKC'	0.000	0.034	0.224	0.345	0.001	0.005	0.025	0.383
sim_time	0.039	0.185	0.574	0.618	0.038	0.193	0.577	0.593

Table 2. Timings, in seconds, for language inclusion of disjoint NFA generated from model-checking.

HKC is more efficient since it can use transitivity to prune a larger portion of the state-space.

The difference between these two approaches becomes even more striking when considering some optimisation exploiting similarity. Indeed, as nicely shown with AC' [1], the antichains approach can widely benefit from the knowledge one gets by first computing similarity. Inspired by this work, we showed that both our proof technique (bisimulation up to congruence) and our algorithm (HKC) can be easily modified to exploit similarity. The resulting algorithm (HKC') is now more efficient than AC' even for checking language inclusion of disjoint automata.

We provided concrete examples where HKC and HKC' are exponentially faster than AC and AC' (Sections 4.2.4 and 5.3) and we proved that the coinductive techniques underlying the formers are at least as powerful as those exploited by the latters (Propositions 5 and 7). We finally compared the algorithms experimentally, by running them on both randomly generated automata, and automata resulting from model checking problems. It appears that for these examples, HKC and HKC' perform better than AC and AC'.

Our implementation of the presented algorithms is available online [7], together with Coq proof scripts, and with an applet making it possible to run the algorithms on user-provided examples.

As future work, we plan to extend our approach to tree automata. In particular, it seems promising to investigate if further up-to techniques can be defined for regular tree expressions. For instance, the algorithms proposed in [3, 20] exploit some optimisation which suggest us coinductive up-to techniques.

Acknowledgments

We are grateful to M. Bonsangue, J. Rutten, and A. Silva for the stimulating discussions that eventually led to this work; and to L. Doyen, P. Habermehl, L. Holík and B. Koenig for their help with antichain algorithms.

References

[1] P. A. Abdulla, Y.-F. Chen, L. Holík, R. Mayr, and T. Vojnar. When simulation meets antichains. In *Proc. TACAS*, vol. 6015 of *LNCS*, pages 158–174. Springer, 2010.

[2] A. V. Aho, J. E. Hopcroft, and J. D. Ullman. *The Design and Analysis of Computer Algorithms*. Addison-Wesley, 1974.

[3] A. Aiken and B. R. Murphy. Implementing regular tree expressions. In *FPCA*, vol. 523 of *LNCS*, pages 427–447. Springer, 1991.

[4] J. C. M. Baeten, J. A. Bergstra, and J. W. Klop. Decidability of bisimulation equivalence for processes generating context-free languages. In *Proc. PARLE (II)*, vol. 259 of *LNCS*, pages 94–111. Springer, 1987.

[5] F. Bartels. *On generalized coinduction and probabilistic specification formats*. PhD thesis, Vrije Universiteit Amsterdam, 2004.

[6] F. Bonchi and D. Pous. Extended version of this abstract, with omitted proofs. `http://hal.inria.fr/hal-00639716/`, 2012.

[7] F. Bonchi and D. Pous. Web appendix for this paper. `http://perso.ens-lyon.fr/damien.pous/hknt`, 2012.

[8] A. Bouajjani, P. Habermehl, and T. Vojnar. Abstract regular model checking. In *Proc. CAV*, vol. 3114 of *LNCS*. Springer, 2004.

[9] R. E. Bryant. Graph-based algorithms for boolean function manipulation. *IEEE Trans. Computers*, 35(8):677–691, 1986.

[10] D. Caucal. Graphes canoniques de graphes algébriques. *ITA*, 24:339–352, 1990.

[11] S. Christensen, H. Hüttel, and C. Stirling. Bisimulation equivalence is decidable for all context-free processes. *Information and Computation*, 121(2):143–148, 1995.

[12] L. Doyen and J.-F. Raskin. Antichain Algorithms for Finite Automata. In *Proc. TACAS*, vol. 6015 of *LNCS*. Springer, 2010.

[13] J.-C. Fernandez, L. Mounier, C. Jard, and T. Jron. On-the-fly verification of finite transition systems. *Formal Methods in System Design*, 1 (2/3):251–273, 1992.

[14] M. R. Henzinger, T. A. Henzinger, and P. W. Kopke. Computing simulations on finite and infinite graphs. In *Proc. FOCS*, pages 453–462. IEEE Computer Society, 1995.

[15] Y. Hirshfeld, M. Jerrum, and F. Moller. A polynomial algorithm for deciding bisimilarity of normed context-free processes. *Theoretical Computer Science*, 158(1&2):143–159, 1996.

[16] L. Holík and J. Šimáček. Optimizing an LTS-Simulation Algorithm. *Computing and Informatics*, 2010(7):1337–1348, 2010.

[17] J. E. Hopcroft. An n log n algorithm for minimizing in a finite automaton. In *Proc. International Symposium of Theory of Machines and Computations*, pages 189–196. Academic Press, 1971.

[18] J. E. Hopcroft and R. M. Karp. A linear algorithm for testing equivalence of finite automata. TR 114, Cornell Univ., December 1971.

[19] J. E. Hopcroft and J. D. Ullman. *Introduction to Automata Theory, Languages and Computation*. Addison-Wesley, 1979.

[20] H. Hosoya, J. Vouillon, and B. C. Pierce. Regular expression types for XML. *ACM Trans. Program. Lang. Syst.*, 27(1):46–90, 2005.

[21] O. Lengál, J. Simácek, and T. Vojnar. Vata: A library for efficient manipulation of non-deterministic tree automata. In *TACAS*, vol. 7214 of *LNCS*, pages 79–94. Springer, 2012.

[22] M. Lenisa. From set-theoretic coinduction to coalgebraic coinduction: some results, some problems. *ENTCS*, 19:2–22, 1999.

[23] D. Lucanu and G. Rosu. Circular coinduction with special contexts. In *Proc. ICFEM*, vol. 5885 of *LNCS*, pages 639–659. Springer, 2009.

[24] A. Meyer and L. J. Stockmeyer. Word problems requiring exponential time. In *Proc. STOC*, pages 1–9. ACM, 1973.

[25] R. Milner. *Communication and Concurrency*. Prentice Hall, 1989.

[26] D. Pous. Complete lattices and up-to techniques. In *Proc. APLAS*, vol. 4807 of *LNCS*, pages 351–366. Springer, 2007.

[27] J. Rutten. Automata and coinduction (an exercise in coalgebra). In *Proc. CONCUR*, vol. 1466 of *LNCS*, pages 194–218. Springer, 1998.

[28] D. Sangiorgi. On the bisimulation proof method. *Mathematical Structures in Computer Science*, 8:447–479, 1998.

[29] D. Sangiorgi. *Introduction to Bisimulation and Coinduction*. Cambridge University Press, 2011.

[30] D. Tabakov and M. Vardi. Experimental evaluation of classical automata constructions. In *Proc. LPAR*, vol. 3835 of *LNCS*, pages 396–411. Springer, 2005.

[31] M. D. Wulf, L. Doyen, T. A. Henzinger, and J.-F. Raskin. Antichains: A new algorithm for checking universality of finite automata. In *Proc. CAV*, vol. 4144 of *LNCS*, pages 17–30. Springer, 2006.

Synthesis of Biological Models from Mutation Experiments

Ali Sinan Köksal[1] Yewen Pu[1] Saurabh Srivastava[1]
Rastislav Bodík[1] Jasmin Fisher[2] Nir Piterman[3]

[1]University of California, Berkeley [2]Microsoft Research, Cambridge [3]University of Leicester

koksal@cs.berkeley.edu, yewenpu@mit.edu, saurabhs@cs.berkeley.edu,
bodik@cs.berkeley.edu, jasmin.fisher@microsoft.com, nir.piterman@le.ac.uk

Abstract

Executable biology presents new challenges to formal methods. This paper addresses two problems that cell biologists face when developing formally analyzable models.

First, we show how to automatically synthesize a concurrent in-silico model for cell development given in-vivo experiments of how particular mutations influence the experiment outcome. The problem of synthesis under mutations is unique because mutations may produce non-deterministic outcomes (presumably by introducing races between competing signaling pathways in the cells) and the synthesized model must be able to replay all these outcomes in order to faithfully describe the modeled cellular processes. In contrast, a "regular" concurrent program is correct if it picks any outcome allowed by the non-deterministic specification. We developed synthesis algorithms and synthesized a model of cell fate determination of the earthworm *C. elegans*. A version of this model previously took systems biologists months to develop.

Second, we address the problem of under-constrained specifications that arise due to incomplete sets of mutation experiments. Under-constrained specifications give rise to distinct models, each explaining the same phenomenon differently. Addressing the ambiguity of specifications corresponds to analyzing the space of plausible models. We develop algorithms for detecting ambiguity in specifications, i.e., whether there exist alternative models that would produce different fates on some unperformed experiment, and for removing redundancy from specifications, i.e., computing minimal non-ambiguous specifications.

Additionally, we develop a modeling language and embed it into Scala. We describe how this language design and embedding allows us to build an efficient synthesizer. For our *C. elegans* case study, we infer two observationally equivalent models expressing different biological hypotheses through different protein interactions. One of these hypotheses was previously unknown to biologists.

This work was supported in part by NSF grant 1019343 to the Computing Research Association for the CIFellows Project, and by NSF grant CCF-1139011.

POPL'13, January 23–25, 2013, Rome, Italy.

Categories and Subject Descriptors F.3.1 [*Logics and Meaning of Programs*]: Specifying and Verifying and Reasoning about Programs

Keywords Program Synthesis, Specification Ambiguity Analysis, Executable Biology

1. Introduction

Diseases can be caused by perturbed gene and protein regulatory networks. For example, disease X may be related to the levels of proteins P and R, and P may negatively regulate R. Once the level of P is decreased, high levels of R may cause disease X. To avoid the disease, we may want to increase the level of P. One way to infer protein regulatory networks is to carry out *mutation experiments*, in which cells are genetically modified to suppress or enhance the activity of a certain protein, leading the cell to exhibit abnormal behavior such as uncontrolled cell divisions. If, by suppressing the activity of protein P, the resulting phenotype can be attributed to, say, an increased activity of a known protein R, we can infer from this mutation experiment that P negatively regulates R. From many such inferences, experimental biologists deduce regulatory networks that describe the causal events leading to specific cell fates and other behaviors.

Experimental biologists are concerned about the correctness of their models that give a dynamic explanation of how the observed outcomes are produced. Executable biology [14] addresses this concern by building executable models that can be verified against performed experiments. Treating cells as concurrent agents models the fact that cells do not evolve at synchronous rates [19, 20]. Verification ensures that a concurrent model is correct for all variations of cell growth rates, by exploring all possible executions of the model [15].

Unfortunately, turning informal maps of regulatory networks common in biological literature into executable models is laborious because it involves explicitly defining timing delay and strength of how multiple proteins regulate each other. In our previous work, some of us developed a model of vulval cell fate specification (*i.e.*, how vulval cells make the decision to develop into a particular cell type) in the *C. elegans* worm [12]. This model correctly predicted an unknown protein-protein interaction, however it took several months to tweak the details of the model before it was verified against the experimental data. Whenever new experiments are added, or when the model is extended with new components, similar tweaks are required.

This paper develops techniques for synthesizing executable models from experimental observations and prior biological knowledge. Two challenges make this synthesis problem interesting. First, the outcomes of some cellular systems, such as fates of stem cells, are non-deterministic. For example, in the *C. elegans* system that we study, some mutations cause the six observed vulval precursor cells (VPCs) to acquire one of two alternative fates, presumably due to races in the communication among cells. The desired executable model must be able to reproduce all the observed behavior in order to be correct. We synthesize concurrent cell models such that, for each observable outcome, there exists a schedule that leads the model to produce the outcome. This requirement makes our synthesis task a new problem, which is more complex than what has been previously addressed.

Second, the incomplete set of mutation experiments forms only a partial specification. Because only certain genes are mutated from the total combinatorial set of possible mutations, we cannot be certain that an executable model that verifies against these mutations, whether it is synthesized or manually constructed, is the sole explanation of the cellular regulatory process. This is because there could exist an alternative model that is observationally identical on the current specification but observationally distinct on an additional mutation. Finding such an additional mutation would uncover *ambiguity* in the current specification.

To confirm that we have synthesized a unique model, we go beyond synthesis and develop methods for the analysis of the space of plausible models, i.e., models that agree with the specification. If observationally distinct models exist, we suggest a new mutation that differentiates them. If no alternative models exist, we determine the smallest set of experiments that is sufficient to arrive at the unique model. Finding such a minimal set is interesting because, should biologists decide to redo the experiments for validation, they only need to perform the experiments that suffice to synthesize a unique model. Finally, it is interesting to ask whether there are observationally identical but internally different models. Such models present regulatory networks where the network function is "implemented" via different protein interactions. These models cannot be distinguished by observing phenotypes; we must, say, instrument proteins with fluorescent markers (similar to tracing the program) and observe the cell during its development. This is a harder experiment, but the cost of instrumentation is reduced with the help of formal methods, as we can identify which genes to mark given the internal differences between the observationally identical models.

We have built an efficient verifier, synthesizer and specification ambiguity analyzer that implements algorithms for the analyses described above. Our synthesizer takes as input the mutations, the results observed under mutations and a template structure of the cells, and from them it generates a verified model. The template of the cell defines the cell components, and a superset of their interconnections (inhibition, activation), allowing biologists to formally state existing knowledge on the system being modeled. Additionally, the granularity of the discretized concentration levels for each component is set a priori. What we synthesize is the internal logic and timing of the components, i.e., how their concentration changes in terms of their incoming signals, and we therefore off-load the most difficult task of systems biology modeling to a computation search engine.

This paper makes the following contributions:

1. We designed SBL, a domain-specific language for expressing our models using an execution model with restricted asynchrony called bounded asynchrony [15]. We embed SBL into the Scala programming language [25] and build a lightweight synthesizer, which is publicly available [21]. We describe how to translate SBL programs into formulas in order to solve synthesis and specification analysis problems (Sections 3 and 4).
2. We formulate the verification problem (Section 5.1) and the program synthesis problem (Section 5.2). We observe that unlike previous synthesis tasks, e.g., concurrent synthesis [28] or synthesis from examples [17] or invariants [30], which are expressed as formulas with two levels of quantification (2QBF), this problem is expressed as a formula with three levels of quantification (3QBF), which makes it a new kind of problem. We develop efficient algorithms for solving this problem that reduce to three communicating SAT solvers.
3. We develop methods for analyzing the specifications and the space of plausible models (Section 5.3): We describe algorithms for determining whether internally or externally distinguishable models exist, and for finding minimal non-ambiguous specifications. These algorithms build on our 3QBF synthesis procedure, and can potentially guide new wet-lab experiments by computing mutation experiments that disambiguate alternative models.
4. We evaluate our framework by describing that it efficiently (1) generates valid models for the *C. elegans* VPCs. The model fixes a bug in previous modeling, an incorrect modeling of a component's behavior when it is mutated; (2) shows that no behaviorally distinct models exist (even after extending the experiment space to consider mutations for each component in the VPCs), but two internally different models were synthesized, one of which expresses a previously unknown biological hypothesis; and (3) prunes the specification from forty-eight mutation experiments to a minimal set of four experiments (Section 6).

2. Technical Overview

This section presents an overview of the program synthesis and specification analysis methods we have developed for modeling biological systems. We describe how scientists typically conduct mutation experiments to infer informal genetic regulatory networks, discuss how these models can be formalized, present our programming language for expressing, verifying and synthesizing formal biological models, and outline our synthesis and specification analysis algorithms for programs in this language.

2.1 Background on Mutation Experiments.

Here we give a brief background on mutation experiments, in the context of developmental systems biology. The role of these experiments is to understand cellular genetic regulatory networks, in particular those that control stem cell differentiation. These regulatory networks are of interest in part because their failure may trigger disease:

> Cancer is fundamentally a disease of failure of regulation of tissue growth. In order for a normal cell to transform into a cancer cell, the genes which regulate cell growth and differentiation must be altered. (Wikipedia)

Hence, to understand cancer, one needs to understand cell differentiation. There are two common mechanisms for cell differentiation: (1) a single cell divides into cells of different types based on the asymmetric accumulation of substances inside the cell; and (2) multiple identical cells differentiate by mutually communicating with the goal of arriving at coordinated fates [13]. We focus on the second mechanism, and aim to mechanistically explain cell differentiation by modeling intercellular communication.

The specific goal of developmental biologists is to infer the program that stem cells "execute" to agree on their fates. This program executes within one cell division cycle during which a pluripotent cell decides its fate, potentially by communicating with other cells.

One method for inferring this program is to mutate a set of genes in the cell and observe the resulting changes in the cell development. These experiments are particularly attractive because phenotype changes resulting from the cell taking a different fate are visually observable, avoiding the need for the more expensive tracing of temporal protein levels by the means of tagging cell proteins with fluorescent genes.

From gene mutation experiments, biologists infer protein interactions, namely which proteins are activated or inhibited by the mutated protein. For example, Yoo *et al.* [32] infers:

> In this assay, depletion of [genes] lst-2, lst-3, lst-4, or dpy-23, as well as ark-1, caused [a phenotype change, namely] ectopic vulval induction, suggesting that they function as negative regulators of the EGFR-MAPK [protein] pathway [due to the phenotype change being linked to inhibition of the pathway].

Biologists unify such piecemeal information to create informal models of cellular programs, such as the one in Figure 1 from [12]. This model shows how five cells—an anchor cell (AC), three vulval precursor cells (VPC), as well as the hyp7 cell—communicate to determine the fate of the VPCs. Each VPC contains the same set of components, which is composed of receptors (let-23 and lin12) and proteins (lst, sem-5, let-60 and mpk-1). The edges between these components show the activation (→) vs. inhibition (⊣) relationships between them.

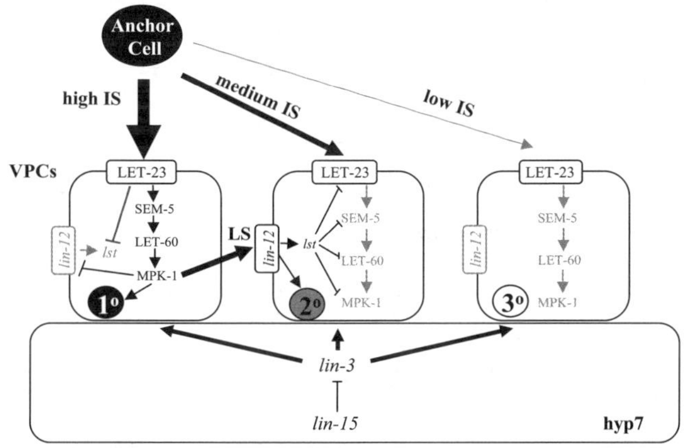

Figure 1. An informal diagram of cell fate specification in a system of three VPC cells [12]. These cells react to the inductive signal (IS) from the anchor cell and communicate among themselves using the lateral signal (LS) to decide one of three fates.

While these informal models may capture all known interactions among cell components, they do not describe the dynamics of the cell, such as what race conditions permit the cells to take non-deterministic fates that have been observed under some mutations. Due to this lack of dynamic information, one cannot be certain that these diagrams accurately describe the cell fate specification mechanism.

2.2 Executable Biology

The goal of *executable biology* [14] is to create executable models that allow the observation of the dynamic behavior of biological systems. Furthermore, these models are verified against experimental observations. For concurrent discrete models, verification, say, with model checking, ensures that all executions of the model agree with the observed outcomes. By verifying the program under the non-deterministic interleaving of cell steps, we ensure that a program is a faithful model of a cell system where cells may progress at varying rates[1] [15, 20].

It is challenging to create verifiable, concurrent models of communication between cells. To transform the informal model in Figure 1 into an executable model, the designer must model (1) protein levels; (2) timing delay or rates at which proteins react with other components; and (3) how a protein behaves when both an activator and an inhibitor of the protein are active. We have previously developed a verified model of *C. elegans* VPC cells; that model took several months to develop [12]. This paper develops methods for automatically synthesizing executable models of concurrent cellular systems.

Non-deterministic experiment outcomes. A mutation experiment may produce different outcomes when run repeatedly. A correct model must reproduce *all* non-deterministic outcomes of a given mutation experiment. We synthesize concurrent cell models that satisfy this requirement by ensuring that each outcome that must be observed is reproduced by the model under some interleaving of cell steps.

For biological reasons, we use a restricted model of concurrency, *bounded asynchrony* [15]. Because neighboring cells always advance at relatively similar rates, rather than at arbitrary speeds, fully asynchronous models are too unconstrainted to reproduce the observation in certain mutation experiments. One-bounded asynchrony is one way to achieve restricted asynchrony, ensuring that between two execution steps of a cell, no other cell can take more than two steps.

Because of the requirement to reproduce all possible outcomes, model synthesis in this setting is a more complex synthesis task than what has been previously addressed. In this paper, we advance the state-of-the-art in solving this new synthesis problem.

2.3 Modeling Language

We have developed a high-level programming model, SBL, inspired by biological diagrams such as the one in Figure 1. SBL introduces programming abstractions for cells, cell components, and interaction between components.

Programs in SBL (Figure 2) are composed of cells, which execute according to a schedule s that adheres to the *1-bounded-asynchrony* constraint. The schedule is of bounded length; the number of steps in the schedule corresponds to the desired discretization of the cell division cycle. Multiple cells can take simultaneous steps. Cells are composed of components, which model proteins or cell receptors. Components communicate with other components in the same cell or in other cells; communicating components are connected with directed edges, which correspond either to activation or inhibition relationships. Components of a cell execute synchronously; all take one step when the cell is scheduled. Components have state—a discretized concentration—usually modeled at 2-5 levels. When the component executes, it updates its next state based on its current state and the states of its activators or inhibitors. Each component is modeled with an update function $(L, L^k) \rightarrow L$, where L are levels and k is the number of components activators and inhibitors, combined.

Thanks to these abstractions, SBL programs are syntactically smaller compared to models expressed in the Reactive Modules language [1], which was the modeling language used in earlier work [12]. As a result, we are able to develop efficient synthesis algorithms for programs in SBL.

EXAMPLE 1. *To illustrate, we consider the problem of designing a simple distributed protocol. Mutations in this setting correspond to*

[1] Another way to model varying cell rates is to use stochasticity. In stochastic models [2, 24], this non-determinism takes the form of protein models making probabilistic transitions, accounting for variability of protein level change rates in nature. However, moving non-determinism from protein modeling into the scheduler allows protein models to be deterministic, which in turn enables discrete verification techniques.

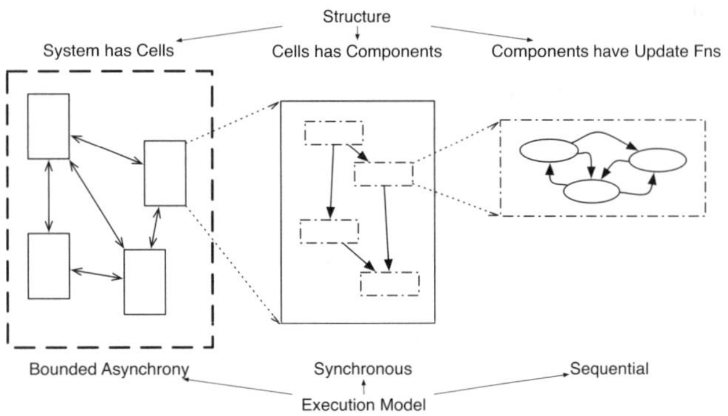

Figure 2. Hierarchical organization of programs in SBL. The system is composed of cells, which in turn are composed of components. At each time step, components update their discrete state using an update function, in terms of their previous state and incoming signals from other components. Edges between components denote which components can communicate between them. Cells group together components that always move synchronously, and they adhere to a restricted form of concurrency.

environment effects on the system being designed, and the specification consists of input-output pairs defining the desired behavior for given environments.

The goal is to design a weak consensus protocol for a three-node system. (In a biological system, these nodes would be cells, and node components would be proteins in the cells.) Two nodes (called sensors N1 and N2) are listening to a signal from a master node (a base station BS). When the base station sends a signal, at least one of the sensors must make a decision to take a measurement. When a sensor takes a measurement, it sends a release message to the other sensor permitting the other sensor not to take a measurement in order to save its power. The decision to make a measurement is made on the basis of (1) the strength from the base station; in normal conditions, the sensor that received the stronger signal should take measurement as it is closer to the base station; and (2) receiving the release message from the other signal. The environment may cause the communication between the two sensors to be down, sensors must take a measurement if no signal was received from their peer. Similar to a system of cells progressing at similar rates, we assume that sensors have bounded skew, i.e., *they run under bounded asynchronous schedules.*

An implementation of this protocol is presented in Figure 3. Figure 3(a) presents a hierarchical view of how cell communication is organized, and which components each cell contains. On the left is the top-most level with three nodes; the base station node (BS) contains one component, the base node, which emits a constant high (H) or low (L) signal to nodes N1 and N2. These nodes decide to commit or to delegate by communicating with each other. Figure 3(b), (c) and (d) show a graphical representation of update functions for three components in nodes N1 and N2 (the remaining simpler update functions have been omitted from the figure).

2.4 Language Extensions for Verification

To make programs in our language amenable to verification, we now introduce component mutations, formalize specifications, and define a correctness condition for programs.

We model cell mutation with an adversary who perturbs the cell program such that a set of adversary-selected cell components receive adversary-supplied semantics. Typically, a cell component is mutated either to be suppressed or to stay at a high concentration level throughout the execution of the program, although we also support other mutation types.

The set of mutation experiments performed in the lab serve as our correctness specification. Let F be the set of possible outcomes of a mutation experiment. For example, if a cell can take one of three fates, the outcomes of an experiment with six cells is a six-tuple from $F = \{1, 2, 3\}^6$. Let M be the set of possible mutations that one can apply on a cell; typically, all cells involved in an experiment are mutated identically. The set of experiments *Exp* is a subset of $M \times F$, where $(m, f) \in$ *Exp* if the fate f has been observed on the mutation m. With n cell components and three possible mutations per component (e.g., no mutation; suppressed; high level), M is exponential in the number of components of the cell. As a result, biologists do not carry out all mutations.

Having an incomplete set of experiments implies that we have to accommodate partial specifications. While the set of experiments *Exp* is a subset of $M \times F$, we assume that once a mutation has been carried out, the lab has observed all possible outcomes for this mutation by repeating the experiment a sufficient number of times. This is a reasonable assumption for systems that have been reliably studied by many independent labs, such as our case study, vulval fate specification in *C. elegans* (Section 6). Without this assumption, we would have no upper bound on the specification, as any (m, f) pair could potentially be observed in experiments that have not been performed so far. The assumption allows us to synthesize with both positive examples (outcomes that must be produced by the model for an experiment) and negative ones (outcomes that must never be observed for an experiment). To model such full knowledge for a single mutation, our specification is a (partial) map $E : M \rightarrow 2^F$. The domain of E is the set of performed mutations. If $m \in dom(E) \wedge f \notin E(m)$, we assume that mutation m cannot result in fate f; the pair (m, f) is a negative example. We say that a program $P : M \rightarrow F$ is a *correct model* of E if, for each $m \in dom(E)$, the execution $P(m)$ may produce each element of $E(m)$ by controlling some aspect of the execution of P, namely the schedule that controls the concurrent execution of cells in the program.

Correctness Condition. To define a correctness condition, we view an SBL program as a function $P : (M, S) \rightarrow F$, where M and F are domains of mutations (input configurations) and fates, while S is the set of schedules adhering to bounded asynchrony. The explicit schedule allows us to formulate a correctness condition $correct(P, E)$ of a program P on a specification $E : M \rightarrow 2^F$, which has two parts:

1. *demonic scheduling:* A demonic scheduler cannot make the model produce a fate that is outside the specification, *i.e.*, $demonic(P) = \forall m \in dom(E).\forall s \in S : P(m, s) \in E(m)$.
2. *angelic scheduling:* An angelic scheduler must be able to produce each fate in the specification, *i.e.*, $angelic(P) = \forall m \in dom(E).\forall f \in E(m).\exists s \in S : P(m, s) = f$.

The demonic requirement asks that the model is an underapproximation of the specification, while the angelic requirement asks that it is an overapproximation. Angelic scheduling adds a layer of difficulty that is handled through the construction of a novel verifier (Section 5.1).

EXAMPLE 2. *The specification for Example 1, expressed as a set of experiments, is shown in Figure 4. The left column shows the mutations (environment effects) M, while the right column shows the desired outcomes F. It is interesting to note that we are using the mutations as the environment adversary; the mutations describe situations under which the nodes N1 and N2 must operate according to the expected outcomes. For example, the last row describes the situation in which the signal arriving at N1 is high, while the*

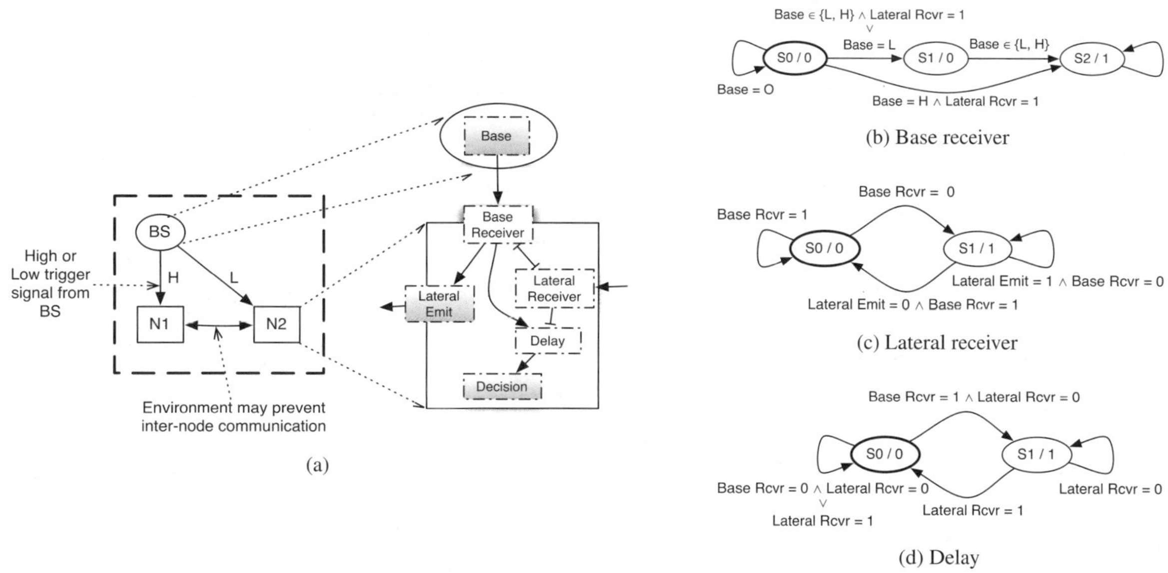

Figure 3. (a) Hierarchical view of node connections, and of their components. The top node is the base station, and the bottom nodes are distributed sensors which may not communicate with each other due to environment effects. (b), (c), (d) Graphical representation of update functions for base receiver, lateral receiver and delay components in the distributed sensors. Each state is labeled with its name and the output value that the state maps to.

Base station trigger	Inter-node comm.	N1	N2
N1=H, N2=H	Y	C	D
		D	C
		C	C
N1=L, N2=L	Y	C	D
		D	C
		C	C
N1=H, N2=L	Y	C	D
N1=L, N2=H	Y	D	C
N1=H, N2=H	N	C	C
N1=L, N2=L	N	C	C
N1=H, N2=L	N	C	C
N1=L, N2=H	N	C	C

Figure 4. The specification for the distributed protocol example, giving required outcomes for nodes N1 and N2 under a range of scenarios of base station trigger signals and cases of whether the two nodes can communicate between themselves (Y) or not (N). C = Commit, D = Delegate.

signal arriving at N2 is low, and the communication between nodes is down. We can think of this mutation as the adversary lowering the signal to N2 and preventing the communication between the two sensor nodes. The outcome C means that a node has committed to taking a measurement while D means that the measurement was delegated to the peer node.

2.5 Language Extensions for Synthesis

In order to allow synthesis of update functions in our programs, we extend our language such that these can be left unspecified. We describe partial programs in SBL and we define the synthesis problem.

The input to the synthesizer is the specification E and a *partial program* $P^?$ to be completed by the synthesizer, if feasible, into a program P^h such that the predicate $correct(P^h, E)$ holds. A partial program is a program template in which certain fragments are parameterized and need to be supplied by the synthesizer. Our language allows parameterization of (1) cell component behavior; and (2) how components communicate. Because update functions model timing delay and change rates of proteins, we found them to be the hardest part of the model to produce manually. By parameterizing update functions, we can indirectly leave unspecified also the connections between components: for example, if a biologist is unsure whether a protein P is inhibited by a protein Q or a protein R, both Q and R can be connected to P; if Q turns out not to influence P, the synthesizer is able to produce an update function for P that disregards the state of Q. The parameterized update functions are constrained to agree with the activation and inhibition semantics specified in the partial program by restricting their structure. This is achieved by stating monotonicity invariants on how a protein's input concentrations can influence its concentration; these invariants are described in Section 4.2.

From the user standpoint, the partial program $P^?$ encodes biological assumptions; it defines the components in the cells as well as a superset of connections between them. It thus (1) conveys the desire to model particular proteins and (2) states the knowledge of which (superset of) pairs of proteins communicate. Partial programs encoding biological assumptions form the basis for the ambiguity analysis described in Section 2.6.

Our synthesis problem is to find update functions h that yield a correct model:

DEFINITION 2.1 (Synthesis problem). *For a partial program $P^?$ to be completed with hole values h into P^h, the synthesis problem is to find the update functions h that yield a correct model:*

$$S(h) := \exists h : demonic(P^h) \wedge angelic(P^h)$$

A correct model must reproduce all observed experiments, and this is captured in the $angelic(P)$ correctness condition, which is a formula with two levels of quantification (2QBF). This makes the synthesis problem a 3QBF problem, while typical synthesis problems are 2QBF (of the form $\exists$ *hole* $\forall$ *input* : ϕ).

Formulas with more than one level of quantification cannot be handed off directly to an SMT solver, because the performance of SMT solvers is only reliable for existential (one quantifier) formulas. One way to tackle 2QBF problems is to develop a counterexample-guided inductive synthesis (CEGIS) algorithm. In the classical CEGIS algorithm, an inductive synthesizer produces a program that is correct on a small sample of inputs; a verifier then checks this candidate program on remaining inputs [29]. To handle the 3QBF synthesis problem $S(h)$, we develop a novel two-part CEGIS algorithm, where an inductive synthesizer communicates with two verifiers, one for each of the two correctness conditions, and collects two kinds of counterexamples, one from each verifier (Section 5.2).

EXAMPLE 3. *The update functions for Example 1, presented in Figures 3(b), (c) and (d) are produced by our synthesizer. These update functions control how these components react to signals from the base station and the peer sensor. The synthesizer takes four seconds to generate these update functions. Intuitively, a sensor's protocol is simple: if you receive a weak signal, wait a little while and wait for the release signal from the other sensor. If it does not arrive, take a measurement. Still, even for this simple protocol, designing the update functions manually is not trivial.*

2.6 Ambiguity Analysis

Assume that a biologist produces an executable model that verifies against all performed experiments. Now imagine that after he publishes his conclusions from this model, another biologist performs a new mutation experiment whose outcome invalidates the model as well as the conclusions drawn from it. (Given a new mutation experiment m_{n+1}, a model P becomes invalid if it cannot reproduce an outcome observed for m_{n+1}, or if it produces an outcome that has never been observed after performing m_{n+1} sufficiently many times.)

Naturally, we are interested in the question of whether one can ascertain the validity of a model in the absence of complete experiments. In particular, under what assumptions can a model be considered the sole explanation of biological phenomena?

We view this question as analysis of ambiguity in the specification E, and define an *alternative model query* that answers the question. We first introduce aggregate outcomes and specification ambiguity.

DEFINITION 2.2 (Aggregate outcome). *Let P be a model and m a mutation. The* aggregate outcome *of P on m, denoted $P[m]$, is the set of outcomes produced by P mutated with m over the set S of all schedules: $P[m] := \{P(m,s) \mid \forall s \in S\}$*

A specification E is ambiguous for a partial program $P^?$ (that expresses a set of biological assumptions) if we can find two completions P^{h_1} and P^{h_2} that disagree on some new experiment. Of course, one of these models would become invalid given the new experiment.

DEFINITION 2.3 (Specification ambiguity). *Given a partial program $P^?$, a specification E is ambiguous, denoted $Amb(E, P^?)$, if $\exists m \in M \ \exists h_1, h_2.\ correct(P^{h_1}, E) \wedge correct(P^{h_2}, E) \wedge P^{h_1}[m] \neq P^{h_2}[m]$.*

Note that m must be a new experiment, *i.e.*, $m \in M \setminus dom(E)$, because the two models must agree with the specification E on all mutations in $dom(E)$.

In Section 6, we show that the specification for our case study is unambiguous given provided biological assumptions (*i.e.*, , there is no need for more experiments at the desired level of modeling). We also show that removing some historically important experiments indeed makes the specification ambiguous, permitting alternative explanations for coordination between cells.

DEFINITION 2.4 (Alternative model query). *Given a partial program $P^?$ stating biological assumptions and an existing (perhaps previously synthesized) model P (that need not be an instantiation of $P^?$), the* alternative model query *finds a mutation m and a new model P^h such that $P[m] \neq P^h[m]$, or shows that no such h and m exist.*

We develop an algorithm to solve this query in Section 5.3.1.

EXAMPLE 4. *We now ask whether we can find alternative models for Example 1 using the alternative model query. Suppose we relaxed the specification and do not care about the outcome on the case $N1 = L$, $N2 = L$. We ask our synthesizer to generate models under this relaxed specification such that they differ from the model in Example 1. Our synthesizer generates an alternative model that has much simpler behavior (as it need not be non-deterministic under the row that we ignored). The update functions are shown in Figure 5. When we ask for a mutation that distinguishes among the models, the synthesizer produces the omitted row. (Note that this last query is a special case of the alternative model query, such that both input programs are fully specified.)*

Now consider an experimental scenario where one wants to validate a set of experiments performed in the literature by performing them again. Is it possible to identify the smallest set of experiments whose replication is sufficient to yield a non-ambiguous specification?

To answer this question, we define a *minimization query* that computes such a minimal set.

DEFINITION 2.5 (Minimization query). *Given a non-ambiguous specification E, the* minimization query *computes a minimal non-ambiguous specification E_m from E,* i.e., $\neg Amb(E_m, P^?) \wedge \neg\exists E', E' \subset E_m \wedge \neg Amb(E', P^?)$.

An algorithm that solves the minimization query is presented in Section 5.3.2.

In our case study, we show that, under our assumptions $P^?$, one needs to replicate about 10% of experiments. This result suggests that computing which experiments to perform might reduce unnecessary laboratory work.

EXAMPLE 5. *We explored the minimization query for Example 1. Our synthesizer prunes E down to the first three rows of Figure 4 as a minimally unambiguous specification. This is somewhat surprising but it gives substantial insight into the problem, as the user can now understand that the specification of the four cases with lost communication was redundant, while the user may have presumed that it was necessary.*

3. Language

In this section, we present the formal semantics of our language, by first defining the language constructs, and then giving operational semantics rules for execution.

The basic construct in SBL is a *component*. We denote the set of all components in a program by *Comp*. Components are connected via a set of directed edges, defined by the relation $Edges \subseteq Comp \times Comp$. Edges model channels of communication between cell components. For each component c, we say a component c' is an *input component* of c if there is an edge $(c', c) \in Edges$. For each c, we define the set of input components $Input_c$ as $\{c' : (c', c) \in Edges\}$. A component c has a state σ_c that takes values from a finite domain L_c. Each component c is also associated with an update function, denoted f_c, that updates its state σ_c, given the current value of its input components. The function f_c has domain $L_c \times \Pi_{c' \in Input_c} L_{c'}$ and range L_c. The update

$$\textsc{Run-Program}\ \frac{S = s :: ss \qquad \bar{\bar{\sigma}}_{init} \xrightarrow{s,Cells,Edges} \bar{\bar{\sigma}}' \qquad \langle \bar{\bar{\sigma}}', ss \rangle \xrightarrow{Cells,Edges} \langle \bar{\bar{\sigma}}_{final}, [\,] \rangle}{\langle \bar{\bar{\sigma}}_{init}, S \rangle \xrightarrow{Cells,Edges} \langle \bar{\bar{\sigma}}_{final}, [\,] \rangle}$$

$$\textsc{Run-Program-Base}\ \frac{}{\langle \bar{\bar{\sigma}}, [\,] \rangle \xrightarrow{Cells,Edges} \langle \bar{\bar{\sigma}}, [\,] \rangle}$$

$$\textsc{Advance-Cells}\ \frac{\forall cell \in Cells\ \bar{\sigma}_{cell} \xrightarrow{\bar{\bar{\sigma}},cell,Edges,s(cell)} \bar{\sigma}'_{cell} \qquad \bar{\bar{\sigma}}' = \cup_{cell \in Cells}\{\bar{\sigma}'_{cell}\}}{\bar{\bar{\sigma}} \xrightarrow{s,Cells,Edges} \bar{\bar{\sigma}}''}$$

$$\textsc{Cell-Enabled}\ \frac{\forall \sigma_c \in \bar{\sigma}\ \sigma_c \xrightarrow{c,\bar{\bar{\sigma}},Edges} \sigma'_c \qquad \bar{\sigma}' = \cup_{c \in cell}\{\sigma'_c\}}{\bar{\sigma} \xrightarrow{\bar{\bar{\sigma}},cell,Edges,1} \bar{\sigma}'} \qquad \textsc{Cell-Disabled}\ \frac{}{\bar{\sigma} \xrightarrow{\bar{\bar{\sigma}},cell,Edges,0} \bar{\sigma}}$$

$$\textsc{Advance-Component}\ \frac{\Sigma = \{\sigma_{c'} : (c', c) \in Edges\} \qquad f_c(\Sigma, \sigma) = \sigma'}{\sigma \xrightarrow{c,\bar{\bar{\sigma}},Edges} \sigma'}$$

Figure 6. Small-step semantics for program execution. RUN-PROGRAM runs a schedule by advancing the cells according to each micro-step in the schedule, with RUN-PROGRAM-BASE as the base case. ADVANCE-CELLS rule updates the states of cells, depending on the current micro-step s. If a cell is enabled, it is advanced by applying the CELL-ENABLED rule. Conversely, if a cell is disabled, the CELL-DISABLED rule keeps its state unchanged. ADVANCE-NODE rule updates the state of a component by invoking the update function on the states of all input component states and its own state

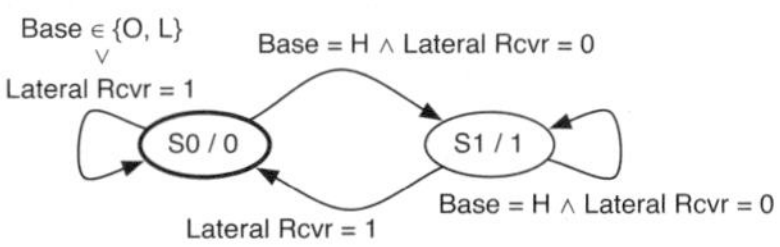

(a) Base receiver

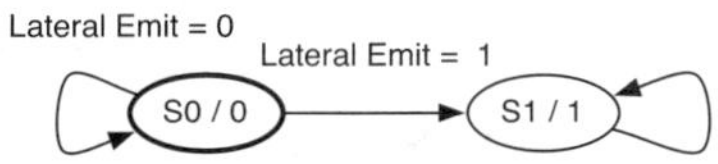

(b) Lateral receiver

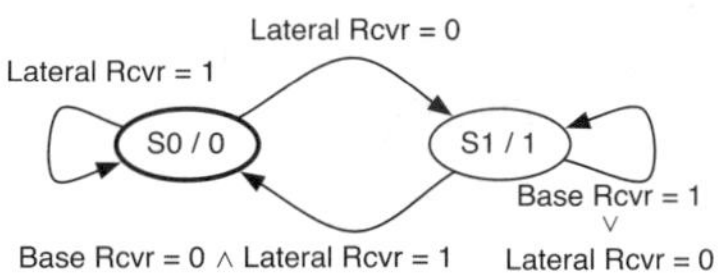

(c) Delay

Figure 5. Update functions generated using the alternative query model to differentiate from the model in Example 1 under ambiguous specification, obtained by removing row 2 of Figure 4.

function for a component is chosen from a sequence of functions $F_c := [f_{c,1}, \ldots, f_{c,k}]$ that describe possible alternative behaviors of that component under different mutations, i.e., the natural and altered behaviors of the component.

A *cell* is a set of components. Within a cell, we have a synchronous execution model, i.e. all components of a cell update their state simultaneously. The state of a cell $\bar{\sigma}$ is defined as the set of states of the components that the cell contains. We denote the set of all cells in a program by $Cells$. $Cells$ forms a partition on all the components in the program. A pair of cells $(cell_1, cell_2)$ are said to be *communicating* if there exists a pair of components $(comp_1, comp_2)$ connected by an edge in the respective cells.

The pair $(Cells, Edges)$ constitutes a *program*. The program state $\bar{\bar{\sigma}}$ is the set of all cell states in the program. The input to a program is a *configuration* (*i.e.*, a mutation). A configuration is a function from components to integers, that expresses for each component c the index of the function in F_c that should be used as the update function f_c. The output of a program is defined as the state of user-designated components in the final state reached in an execution.

Partial Programs. The sequence F_c of functions associated with component c need not be specified concretely. When at least one component function is not concretely specified, we say the program is *partial*. Typically, users will only concretely specify the behaviors under well-understood mutations that would not make sense to redefine. For example, a typical example in the biological case is the knock-out mutation which subdues the function of the component and fixes it to the OFF state.

Operational semantics Figure 6 shows the small-step semantic rules for program execution. Here, we assume that the program starts in the initial state $\bar{\bar{\sigma}}_{init}$, and that it has already been preprocessed by fixing a particular update function for each component according to the input configuration. The semantics are defined recursing down the program structure. The RUN-PROGRAM rule executes the program by moving all cells in accordance with a schedule S. The ADVANCE-CELLS rule captures the intuition that each schedule step s partitions the cells into the sets *enabled* (for which $s(cell) = 1$) and *disabled* (for which $s(cell) = 0$). Rules CELL-ENABLED and CELL-DISABLED describe how cell states are updated for enabled and disabled cells, respectively. For the disabled cells, the state remains unchanged. Enabled cells are advanced by applying the ADVANCE-COMPONENT rule for each component, which corresponds to updating the component state by reading the state of connected neighbors and using the component's update function.

Bounded Asynchrony. The concurrency notion that our execution model admits is bounded asynchrony. This model faithfully represents biological systems where complete synchrony is too strict, and complete asynchrony does not accurately model cells that progress at similar but not identical rates.

Fisher et al. [15] define bounded asynchrony with schedules consisting of micro- and macro-steps. Each micro-step consists of a subset of the components stepping synchronously. This is what we have been calling a schedule up to this point. Next we block micro-steps together into a macro-step. Each k-bounded macro-step consists of all components taking k steps split across multiple micro-steps. For example, let us consider three nodes and the schedule 110 (micro-step) indicates the first two take a step while the third waits. Suppose the second schedule is the micro-step 001. Then the two micro-steps together make a macro-step in which all nodes take one step and which is therefore 1-bounded.

Schedules over micro-steps are much more expensive to enumerate than schedules over macro-steps, especially 1-bounded macro-steps. Schedules over 1-bounded macro-steps (where each node necessarily moves once), can be succinctly encoded without loss of information as pairwise happens-before between connected nodes. That is, a 1-bounded macro-schedule is an assignment of $<$, $>$, or $=$ to each edge in the node topology[2]. The following lemma holds:

LEMMA 1 (Fisher et al. [15]). *A micro-schedule exists if and only if a realizable macro-schedule exists over the node topology.*

Here a realizable macro-schedule is one that does not cause an inconsistent ordering of nodes in a cycle. We use this result critically to efficiently encode partial programs as formulas (Section 4), and restrict schedules to be 1-bounded.

Using macro-steps allows us to define a compact symbolic encoding of our programs into formulas, which would have not been possible with micro-steps.

4. Translating Programs into Formulas

We now describe how to translate execution of SBL programs to SMT formulas, enabling verification and synthesis. We first give rewrite rules that construct a formula corresponding to the symbolic execution of a program. We then describe additional constraints that encode biological domain knowledge to be used in synthesis of programs.

4.1 Translation of Program Execution

The translation of program execution is parameterized by the following symbolic variables:

- For each time step t and each pair of connected cells (c_1, c_2), we define a channel configuration variable $channel_{t,c_1,c_2}$ that must hold exactly one of the three values "$<$", "$>$" and "$=$". These variables encode the symbolic schedule for program execution. Variables $channel_{t,c_1,c_2}$ and $channel_{t,c2,c1}$ are asserted to be consistent in the following way:

$$\begin{gathered} channel_{t,c1,c2} = \text{``}>\text{''} \Leftrightarrow channel_{t,c2,c1} = \text{``}<\text{''} \\ \wedge \\ channel_{t,c1,c2} = \text{``}<\text{''} \Leftrightarrow channel_{t,c2,c1} = \text{``}>\text{''} \\ \wedge \\ channel_{t,c1,c2} = \text{``}=\text{''} \Leftrightarrow channel_{t,c2,c1} = \text{``}=\text{''} \end{gathered}$$

- For each component c, we represent each function $f_i \in F_c$ as a lookup table with symbolic values for each value in its domain $L_c \times \Pi_{c' \in Input_c} L_{c'}$. Entries of the lookup table are represented by the variables $table_{v_c, v_{c_1}, \ldots, v_{c_n}}$ that take values in L_c.
- For each component c, we represent its mutation symbolically as a variable m_c, that encodes the index of the function to use among F_c. If m_c has value i, then the function $f_{c,i}$ will be used as the update function of component c.
- For each component c at each execution step, we create a variable $\sigma_{t,c}$ that takes values in the domain of L_c. These variables represent the component state symbolically over the execution of the program.

Translation rules for compiling program execution to an SMT formula are shown in Figure 7.

T_{RUN} is the top-level rule for translating the execution of a program, unrolling the execution for k steps. T_{READ} uses the symbolic macro-schedule values to assert the input states that should be read by each component at a given macro-step. If a cell $cell$ runs before or at the same time as another cell $cell'$ (i.e. the macro-step variable between the two cells at a time step has value "$<$", or "$=$"), the components in $cell$ reads their input states from $cell'$ at the previous time step. On the other hand, if $cell$ runs after $cell'$, it reads its input states from the current time step. Finally, T_{UPDATE} asserts that the state of a component is updated in terms of its symbolic mutation, input state, own state, and update function. The outermost conjunction enumerates over possible update functions. For each mutation, the inner conjunction enumerates possible input value tuples of the update function. The symbolic state is updated given symbolic lookup variables for the chosen mutation.

This translation does not impose any constraints on the parameterized update functions, and therefore encodes a very large space of possible update functions. To help with the program synthesis task, we need to restrict this space. This is achieved in Section 4.2 by asserting biologically motivated constraints on the structure of the parameterized update functions.

4.2 Domain-Specific Constraints on Update Functions

The translation in Section 4.1 does not impose restrictions on the structure of the update functions that are left unspecified by the user. When modeling biological systems, formulating a hypothesis typically involves stating high-level invariants about whether a component *activates or* inhibits another one. In this section, we describe how the space of update functions is restricted using this high-level knowledge.

We first formalize how the high-level biological invariants are stated by defining a partial labeling of edges with activation and inhibition semantics.

DEFINITION 4.1 (Edge labeling). *Given a partial program $P^?$, the partial function label : Edges $\rightarrow$ {activating, inhibiting} annotates edges in $P^?$ as either activating or inhibiting.*

As a component's state expresses its activation level, we assume the existence of a total order on its possible states. This will allow us to state the properties that restrict the space of update functions.

DEFINITION 4.2 (State ordering). *Let c be a component, and L_c the set of possible state values for c. The state ordering $\leq_c$ is a total order on L_c.*

Using the edge labeling and the state ordering for each component, we now define a partial order on the combined input values for a component.

DEFINITION 4.3 (Input ordering). *Given a component c with update function $f_c : L_c \times L_{c_1} \times \ldots \times L_{c_n} \rightarrow L_c$, the partial order $\preceq_c$ on elements of $L_{c_1} \times \ldots \times L_{c_n}$ is defined as:*

$$\begin{aligned} &(v_1, \ldots, v_n) \preceq_c (u_1, \ldots, u_n) \\ &\quad := \forall i \in \{1, \ldots, n\}. \\ &\qquad (label((c_i, c)) = activating \wedge v_i \leq_{c_i} u_i) \vee \\ &\qquad (label((c_i, c)) = inhibiting \wedge v_i \geq_{c_i} u_i) \end{aligned}$$

[2] Technically, for micro-steps it is the sequence of ordered bell numbers or Fubini numbers [16], while for 1-bounded macro-steps it is $3^{\text{num edges}}$.

$$\text{T}_{\text{RUN}}[\![Cells, Edges]\!] \quad := \quad \bigwedge_{t\in\{1,\dots,k\}} \bigwedge_{cell\in Cells} \bigwedge_{c\in cell} \text{T}_{\text{READ}}[\![t, c, Edges]\!] \wedge \text{T}_{\text{UPDATE}}[\![t, c, Edges]\!]$$

$$\text{T}_{\text{READ}}[\![t, c, Edges]\!] \quad := \quad \bigwedge_{\substack{(c',c)\in Edges \\ c'\in cell' \\ c\in cell}} \begin{pmatrix} ((channel_{t,cell',cell}=\text{“<”})\Rightarrow(\sigma_{read,t,c,c'}=\sigma_{t-1,c'})) \\ \wedge \\ ((channel_{t,cell',cell}=\text{“=”})\Rightarrow(\sigma_{read,t,c,c'}=\sigma_{t-1,c'})) \\ \wedge \\ ((channel_{t,cell',cell}=\text{“>”})\Rightarrow(\sigma_{read,t,c,c'}=\sigma_{t,c'})) \end{pmatrix}$$

$$\text{T}_{\text{UPDATE}}[\![t, c, Edges]\!] \quad := \quad \bigwedge_{f_i\in F_c} m_c = i \Rightarrow \left(\bigwedge_{(v_c,v_{c_1},\dots,v_{c_n})\in dom(f_i)} \begin{matrix} (\sigma_{t-1,c},\sigma_{read,t,c_1,c},\dots,\sigma_{read,t,c_n,c})=(v_c,v_{c_1},\dots,v_{c_n}) \\ \Rightarrow \\ \sigma_{t,c}=table_{v_c,v_{c_1},\dots,v_{c_n}} \end{matrix} \right)$$

Figure 7. Translation rules for symbolic execution of programs.

Intuitively, $\preceq$ is a partial order on the strength of the input values to a component, based on the activation and inhibition annotations. We now describe two kinds of invariants that restrict the space of possible update functions.

Input monotonicity Our first property is motivated by the following observation: If there is an activating edge from component c_1 to component c_2, then an increase in σ_{c_1} should not have by itself the effect of decreasing σ_{c_2}. Conversely, if c_1 and c_2 are connected through an inhibiting edge, then a decrease in the value of σ_{c_1} should not result by itself in the decrease of σ_{c_2}:

$$\forall i_1, i_2 \in L_{c_1} \times \ldots \times L_{c_n}. \forall v \in L_c.$$
$$i_1 \preceq_c i_2 \Rightarrow f_c(v, i_1) \leq_c f_c(v, i_2)$$

State monotonicity The second property that we assert imposes a monotonicity constraint on f_c in terms of the value of σ_c. This property expresses that, for the same input value, a greater the activation level of the component cannot be updated to a smaller value:

$$\forall i \in L_{c_1} \times \ldots \times L_{c_n}. \forall v_1, v_2 \in L_c.$$
$$v_1 \leq_c v_2 \Rightarrow f_c(v_1, i) \leq_c f_c(v_2, i)$$

We found that asserting constraints that encode these two invariants based on user annotations on component connections is crucial for ensuring that the structure of update functions agree with existing biological knowledge.

5. Synthesis and Querying Spaces of Models

In section 4, we described how we translate program execution to formulas. In this section, we present algorithms that leverage this translation for verification and synthesis, as well as specification ambiguity analysis.

The formula that encodes program execution parameterizes (1) update functions (which are the holes in partial programs); (2) schedules; and (3) input configurations (*i.e.*, mutations). The space for update functions and the space for schedules are typically very large. However, specifications are typically wet-lab experiments which are sparse and inherently small (of order 10^2 experiments). Based on this observation, we develop algorithms that unroll quantifications for input configurations only.

In the following, we refer to the symbolic output parameter of translating the execution of P with input m and schedule s as $P(m, s)$, and we denote by E the specification (given as a partial function from M to 2^F).

5.1 Verifying Programs

The correctness condition presented in Section 2.4 is defined as:

$$correct(P) := demonic(P) \wedge angelic(P)$$

The properties $demonic(P)$ and $angelic(P)$ are in 1QBF and 2QBF respectively. As a result, the correctness condition $correct(P)$ is in 2QBF.

We verify correctness conditions $demonic(P)$ and $angelic(P)$ separately, using a verifier V_d that searches for demonic schedules that lead to the violation of the specification, and a verifier V_a that checks whether all non-deterministic outcomes for a given mutation can be reached for some angelic schedule.

Verifying for demonic schedules. The formula $demonic(P)$ states that the set $E(m)$ is an upper bound for all observed outcomes of P with input m:

$$demonic(P) := \forall m \in dom(E). \forall s \in S.\ P(m, s) \in E(m)$$

To check this property, we attempt to disprove it by searching for a demonic schedule that produces an unobserved outcome for an input in $dom(E)$, the domain of E. Given the observation that there is a small set of input values in $dom(E)$, we solve this formula by unrolling the existential quantification over this set, and by querying symbolically for a demonic schedule. The condition $P(m, s) \notin E(m)$ is expressed by unrolling over values in $E(m)$, which is also a small set. We thus solve the 1QBF formula:

$$\bigvee_{m\in dom(E)} \exists s. \bigwedge_{f\in E(m)} P(m, s) \neq f$$

If this formula is satisfiable, P does not satisfy *demonic*, and we obtain a concrete counterexample (m, s) such that running P on input m and schedule s leads to an unobserved fate. If it is unsatisfiable, then P is correct with respect to *demonic*.

Verifying for angelic schedules. The *angelic* condition states that all outcomes in the set that m maps to must be observable, i.e. appear in some execution of P on m:

$$angelic(P) := \forall m \in dom(E),\ f \in E(m). \exists s.\ P(m, s) = f$$

This amounts to searching for an angelic schedule for each $f \in E(m)$. We reduce the 2QBF correctness property to an efficiently solvable 1QBF problem by unrolling values of the domain $dom(E)$, again based on the assumption that this is a small domain. To unroll $angelic(P)$, we construct the following query for each $m \in dom(E)$ and for each $f \in E(m)$:

$$\exists s.\ P(m, s) = f$$

If the above formula is unsatisfiable for some m and f, then no angelic schedule can be found for reaching that outcome when running P, and (m, f) is a counterexample input/output pair witnessing that $angelic(P)$ does not hold. If the formula is satisfiable for each $m \in dom(E)$ and for each $f \in E(m)$, then verification for angelic schedules succeeds.

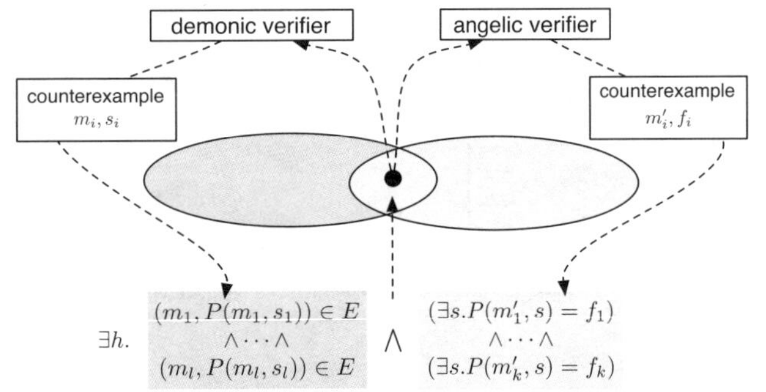

Figure 8. The synthesizer consists of three communicating solvers. The two verifiers generate two kinds of counterexamples, and the synthesizer generates models that satisfy the constraints for all counterexamples.

A program verifies against the specification E if it verifies against both V_d and V_a.

5.2 Synthesizing Programs

In our language, it is possible to define a partial program $P^?$ that admits freedom in the update functions of its components. We now present a synthesis algorithm for finding update functions in $P^?$ such that the completed program P^h is correct with respect to the correctness condition *correct*(P). Our procedure leverages the two verifiers V_d and V_a to check correctness properties $demonic$ and $angelic$ respectively, in order to solve the following synthesis problem:

$$S(h) := \exists h.\ demonic(P^h) \wedge angelic(P^h)$$

This formula is in 3QBF, due to the quantifier alternation $\exists\forall\exists$ resulting from $angelic(P^h)$ being nested within the quantification over h.

We solve $S(h)$ by developing a counterexample-guided inductive synthesis (CEGIS) algorithm, which decomposes the 3QBF problem into two 1QBF solvers (an inductive synthesizer and the demonic verifier V_d) and one 2QBF solver (the angelic verifier V_a). The inductive synthesizer produces a candidate model that is correct on all counterexamples and sends this model to both verifiers. If both approve the model, the synthesis successfully terminates. If either fails, counterexamples are produced, refining the correctness constraints placed on the inductive synthesizer, making it eventually produce a correct model (or conclude that no model exists in the model space described by $P^?$). The solver architecture is shown in Figure 8.

Precisely, the synthesizer maintains two sets of counterexamples, $CE_1 \subseteq dom(E) \times S$ and $CE_2 \subseteq dom(E) \times F$. The first set contains pairs of inputs and schedules, and is computed with counterexamples given by the verifier for demonic schedules. The second one is a subset of the input/output specifications, and is in turn computed with counterexamples found by the verifier for angelic schedules. Starting with initial sets CE_1 and CE_2, the synthesizer solves at each step the following formula to find a candidate model:

$$\exists h. \quad \left(\bigwedge_{(m,s)\in CE_1} P^h(m,s) \in E(m) \right) \wedge \left(\bigwedge_{(m,f)\in CE_2} \exists s.\ P^h(m,s) = f \right)$$

If the above formula is unsatisfiable, the partial program cannot be completed, i.e. synthesis fails. Otherwise, the valuation of h defines a candidate model that we attempt to verify using verifiers V_d and V_a. If at least one of the verifiers returns with a counterexample, the synthesizer attempts to find a new candidate after updating the sets CE_1 and CE_2 with the counterexamples returned by either verifier. If a candidate model is validated by both verifiers, we obtain the completed program P^h that is correct with respect to the specification E.

5.3 Querying for Ambiguity Analysis

Given the above procedure for synthesizing programs, we are now interested in querying spaces of possible models. In particular, we analyze ambiguity of specifications. If a specification is underspecified, we aim to reduce ambiguity by expanding it. If, on the other hand, it is overspecified, our goal is to reduce the specification size without introducing ambiguity.

Computing Aggregate Outcome We first give an iterative algorithm to find aggregate outcome set for a given program p and a given input m. The aggregate outcome set $P[m]$ is the set of outcomes of P on m over all schedules. We approach the task by first computing the outcome of P on m under an initial schedule s. We then enlarge the set of observed outcomes Obs by searching for a schedule leading the program to produce a previously unseen outcome. To find such an outcome, we build a formula that states that the new outcome must differ from each value in the Obs set inferred so far. Each step of the algorithm thus attempts to extend Obs by solving the following formula:

$$\exists s. \bigwedge_{f\in Obs} P(m,s) \neq f$$

If this formula is satisfiable, we obtain an outcome that we add to the set Obs, and then attempt to solve the formula with the updated set. If it is unsatisfiable, we have obtained all outcomes that can be produced by P on input m.

5.3.1 Alternative Models

To ascertain that a given hypothesis is the sole explanation to a biological phenomenon, a biologist would like to learn whether there exists another hypothesis that differs from the first on its observable outcome on an unperformed experiment, but is correct on the known experiments. Given a program P_1 that expresses the first hypothesis, and a partial program $P_2^?$ that expresses a space of alternatives for the second, we can state this query formally as:

$$\exists m.\exists h.correct(P_2^h) \wedge P_2^h[m] \neq P_1[m]$$

If this query is satisfiable, then there is an alternative program P_2^h and a new experiment m such that performing the experiment m will invalidate at least one of P_1 and P_2^h. We now describe an algorithm to solve this query.

Given the hypothesis that the space of mutation experiments M is small, we approach this task by unrolling the existential quantification over m. The problem then reduces to synthesizing P_2^h for a given mutation m, such that $P_2^h[m] \neq P_1[m]$.

$P_2^h[m]$ can differ from $P_1[m]$ in two distinct ways: (1) It can either contain an output value not in $P_1[m]$; or (2) it can be a strict subset of $P_1[m]$. We give one algorithm for each case.

Case 1. A program P_2^h that produces an outcome not seen in $P_1[m]$ can be found by augmenting the synthesis query described in Section 5.2 with a constraint asserting that there exists a schedule that leads P_2^h to produce an outcome not in $P_1[m]$, *i.e.*, $P_2^h[m] \setminus P_1[m] \neq \emptyset$. We solve the following formula to answer this query:

$$\exists h.\ correct(P_2^h) \wedge \exists s.P_2^h(m,s) \notin P[m]$$

This formula is satisfiable if and only if there exists a completion of program P_2^h that produces an outcome not in $P[m]$. It is 3QBF, and is handled using the mechanism of a synthesizer communicating with two verifiers to perform inductive synthesis described in Section 5.2.

Case 2. Alternatively, P_2^h may be found by attempting to synthesize a model that always produces outcomes in a strict subset of $P_1[m]$. This is achieved by discarding elements of $P_1[m]$ one at a time, to see if such a model can be found. We do not need consider all subsets of $P_1[m]$, as we only state that $P_1[m] \setminus \{f\}$ is only an upper bound of the possible outcomes for input m.

$$\exists h. \qquad correct(P_2^h) \wedge \left(\bigvee_{f \in P_1[m]} \forall s.\ P_2^h(i,s) \in P_1[m] \setminus \{f\}\right)$$

This formula is satisfiable if and only if there exists a completion of program P_2^h such that its observable outcome set is a strict subset of observable outcomes of P_1 on input m. Similarly to Case 1, we use the scheme of cooperating solvers described in Section 5.2 to solve this formula.

5.3.2 Minimization

In a context where performing experiments is an expensive process, a researcher may want to obtain a minimal non-ambiguous specification that sufficiently constrains the space of models to validate a hypothesis. Given a partial program $P^?$ that expresses a hypothesis, and a specification E that is non-ambiguous with respect to $P^?$, the task of finding a minimal non-ambiguous specification E_m is stated as:

$$\neg Amb(E_m, P^?) \wedge \neg\exists E', E' \subset E_m \wedge \neg Amb(E', P^?)$$

We compute a minimal specification E_m by iteratively restricting the domain of E for the partial program $P^?$. This can be done by invoking the *alternative model* query once for each mutation in $dom(E)$.

At each step, we check whether program $P^?$ can be completed to a program P^h that decides a set of outputs $P^h[m]$ distinct from $E(m)$, considering as specification the set of currently non-redundant input values. This check is performed using the *alternative model query* described in Section 5.3.1. If synthesis fails, m is marked as redundant. Otherwise, removing m from the specification leads to ambiguity, and as a result m should be kept in the final set of pruned inputs. Upon considering all inputs in the domain of E, a minimal specification is obtained by removing from the domain of E those inputs that are marked as redundant.

6. Case Study: *C. elegans* vulval development

We attempt to synthesize a model for the vulval precursor cells (VPCs) that start off identical but through coordination among themselves and with the Anchor Cell (AC) agree on specific fates. From informal descriptions of protein interactions found in biological literature, we develop our template $VPC^?$. The template is shown in Figure 9(a) (derived from Figure 1.)

From the template, we observed that there are nodes with extremely simplistic on-off behavior. These are LS, the downstream nodes of the cascade (sem5, let60, and mpk1) and the fate nodes. While we can introduce holes in them (with expected performance degradation, yet not being intractable), biologists have a very clear understanding of these nodes, and so expect to see a simple and known behavior in them. Additionally, introducing holes in these nodes leaves too much freedom to the synthesizer, such that generated models do not have a biological interpretation.

Therefore we run our tool with unknown update functions for lin12, let23, and lst. The generated update functions satisfy the specification and template structure of the program. On the other hand, lin12, which has a very well understood behavior, colludes with the other components to give models that are hard to explain to the biologists. Therefore, we additionally allow the user to specify the behavior of lin12 concretely and synthesize let23 and lst. Let23 and lst are indeed the most complex functions in their timing delays (and have the most complex interconnection dependences). Indeed, in our attempts prior to synthesis (when designing the verifier) to write the model by hand, we actually failed. Additionally, the models previously written did not maintain the requisite lin12 behavior. Therefore, our synthesizer was solving a problem that had been impossible to solve manually, even after considerable effort.

The specification consists of forty-eight experimental observations of the fate outcomes of six VPC cells in sequence. Some of these observation have non-deterministic outcome fates. A fragment of the specification is shown in Figure 9(b).

From the template and these experiments, our synthesizer generated update function solutions to let23 and lst that were confirmed by the biologists to be plausible behaviors. The output from the synthesizer is shown in Figure 10(a).

It is important to note that this is a very significant achievement. Previously, when we had written down a model for VPCs in RM [12] it had the following flaws: (1) The previous model did not satisfy a biological invariant required on the lin12 component, and all efforts to fix the model failed, (2) RM is too expressive and therefore there were cases where the model "read the future" which was hard to interpret biologically, (3) the model lacked readability prohibiting debugging, extension, and biological interpretation. Our synthesized alternative model solves all these. Our first biologically relevant result is therefore that through synthesis we have revalidated the (experimentally-confirmed) prediction from previous work, *without the vagaries of human modeling*.

6.0.3 Specification ambiguity for *C. elegans* VPC models

Next, we analyzed the ambiguity in the specification. The important biological unknown is the specific node within the cascade let23-sem5-let60-mpk1 that sends out the inhibitory signal to lin12 and lst. We attempted experimenting with all four options under our definition of understanding the specification ambiguity:

Alternative models for particular input configuration 44 of the 48 experimental observations are deterministic. We wanted to know how many models exist if only the deterministic outcomes are asserted. We found that under this relaxed specification, *all* four options of inhibition coming from any node of the cascade work.

Then using the alternative model query from Section 5.3, we asked for a model including any one of the four remaining outcomes. The synthesizer eliminates two that have inhibition emanating from let60 and mpk1. This was significant since it formally confirmed the biologist's intuition that the inhibition comes from higher up in the cascade. Additionally, it showed that sem5 (in addition to let23, which was conjectured earlier) was a valid possibility for the inhibitor.

Input configuration for disambiguating models Next, we attempted to observationally distinguish these two remaining valid models. Our 48 observations mutate the entire cascade (all nodes let23 to mpk1) together. We wanted to infer if a finer-grained mutation exists that distinguishes these two remaining mechanistic hypotheses. We expanded the experimental set by enumerating all possibilities of the cascade nodes (2^4 possibilities of expansion for each of the 48 rows) leading to 384 experiments. Our synthesizer shows that *no other mutations exist* that would observationally distinguish these two hypotheses. This saves the biologist significant effort (336 experiments, each of which are expensive and time-consuming) as they now know that mutation experiments will not

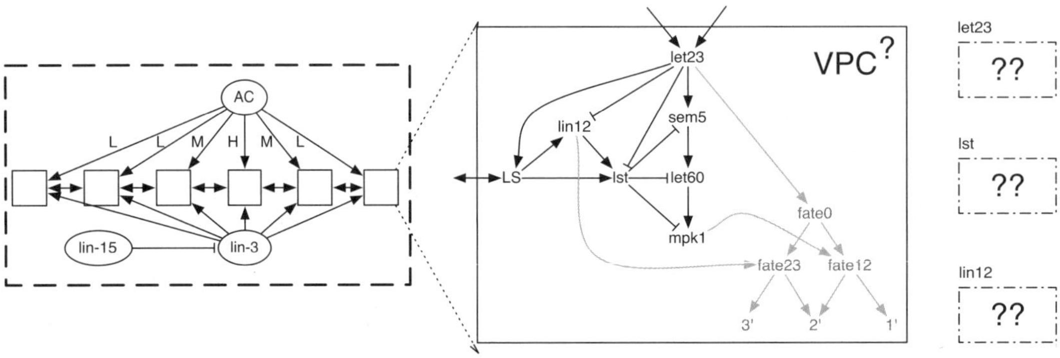

Exp#	Mutations					Fate pattern					
	AC	lin12	lin15	Vul	lst	P3.p	P4.p	P5.p	P6.p	P7.p	P8.p
1	Formed	wt	wt	wt	wt	3	3	2	1	2	3
5	Formed	wt	ko	wt	wt	1/2	1/2	2	1	2	1/2
7	Formed	wt	ko	ko	wt	3	3	3	3	3	3
13	Formed	ko	ko	wt	wt	1	1	1	1	1	1

Figure 9. (a) The template $VPC^?$ we use for our experiments, which is derived as simply the union of connections known to biologists [12] as informally shown by Figure 1. The "fate" nodes are instrumentation nodes to help read out the outcome. (b) A small fraction of the specification E (4 rows out of 48), obtained from literature in biology [12]. A fate pattern of $1/2$ indicates that both 1 and 2 are outcomes observed in experiments.

suffice to distinguish these explanations and out-of-band experiments need to be performed.

Inferring the minimal specification We run our minimization query from Section 5.3 for each of the VPC queries, with significant results. We infer that, for the space we are searching over, only four experimental observations suffice to yield a unique model. This set contains all non-deterministic outcomes, and additionally others that together constrain the system enough to yield the unique model that is explained by the 48 experiments.

Wet-lab predictions Our exploration demonstrated that (1) let23 is not the only possibility for inhibition, but sem5 is as well; (2) let60 and mpk1 cannot play that role; and (3) the models using let23 and sem5 cannot be distinguished observationally. These suggest a possible inhibition from sem5, that cannot be distinguished through mutation experiments on the components included in our model, therefore other types of experiments would need to be done.

7. Performance evaluation

We implemented our language as an embedded DSL in Scala. Our synthesis and analysis framework, also implemented in Scala, uses the Z3 theorem prover [10] as its underlying constraint solver. We interface with Z3 through the Scala^{Z3} library [22]. Our framework consists of 5K lines of code.

We show performance results for the evaluation of our synthesis procedure in Figure 11(a). For each example, we present total execution time, maximum memory usage, number of calls to the underlying SMT solver Z3, average call time, the structure of holes in the partial programs, as well as the search space for synthesizing update functions. VPC1, VPC2, VPC3 and VPC4 are models of the fate decision in *C. elegans* vulval precursor cell development that express each different biological hypotheses about the cells through their topology. VPC1 and VPC2 are synthesized using a specification E with domain size 48, while VPC3 and VPC4 are synthesized using a specification E' whose domain is restricted to 44 elements. Sensors is the example introduced in Section 2. For each example, we report the total running time for synthesis, the maximum memory usage, number of calls to the underlying SMT solver Z3, the average time Z3 takes to solve these queries, a description of holes in the partial program as a sequence of number of states for each unspecified update function, and the size of the search space for synthesizing these functions.

In all cases, we find that even for a complicated synthesis problem such as the VPCs, our synthesizer is efficient.

In Figure 11(b), we present performance results for the pruning procedure described in Section 5.3.2. We report the domain size for the result of the procedure and the initial domain size in the *pruned/total* column.

As expected, the time for pruning is significantly higher than for only synthesis. This is because multiple synthesis and verification queries are solved in the process of minimization. However, compared to the amount of time this could potentially save the biologists, *i.e.*, months or even years of work in doing redundant experiments, our inference times are insignificant.

8. Related Work

Inference of biological models While model checking of (manually written) logical biological models has been an active area of research, we are not aware of work that synthesizes these models. In contrast, a growing body of literature exists on inference of non-logical models. The first class of such models uses ordinary differential equations (ODEs). An example of ODE model inference from temporal and spatial data is the work by Aswani *et al.*, who reduce the amount of prior knowledge needed to infer an accurate model [3]. Rizk *et al.* find parameters for ODE models by optimizing a notion of continuous degree of satisfaction of temporal logic formulas [27]. Because ODE models are continuous, these techniques do not appear directly applicable for inference of logical models based on concurrent systems.

Machine learning has also been used to infer biological models. Barker *et al.* use time series data of protein levels to infer whether a protein is an activator or a suppressor of another protein [4]. Time series data of concentrations is not available in our setting, so these approaches do not apply to the inference of our models.

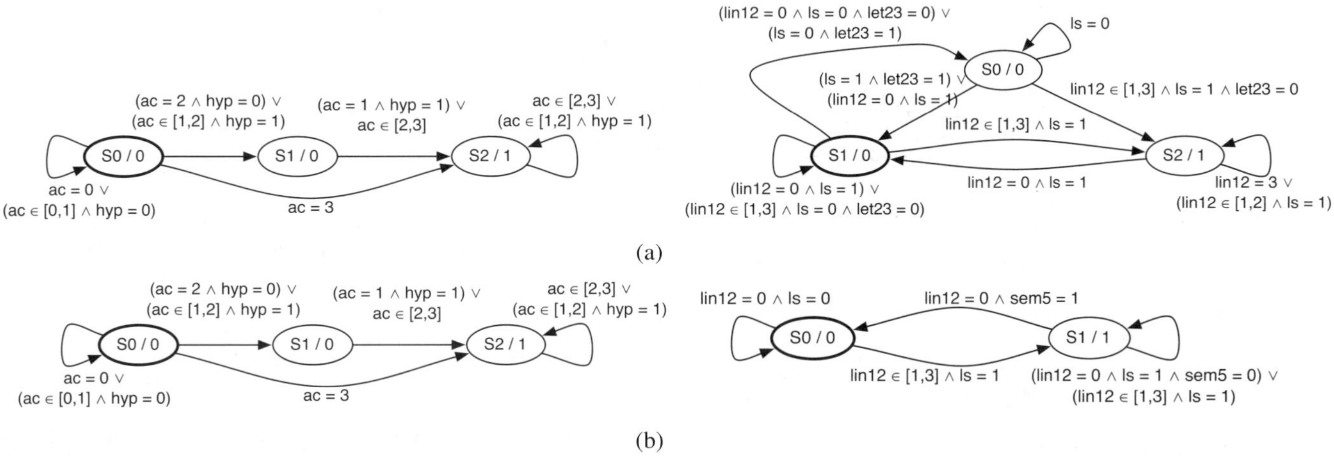

Figure 10. Synthesized update functions given two different connection topologies, for let23, and lst. (a) The topology with lst and lin12 inhibited by let23. The template allows for three let23 states and three lst states. (b) The topology with lst and lin12 inhibited by sem5. The template allows for three let23 states and two lst states.

example	time	mem.	# calls	$\frac{time}{\# calls}$	holes	search space
VPC1	96.64	2.34	282	0.09	(3, 3)	$2.25 \cdot 10^{34}$
VPC2	87.77	2.33	285	0.08	(3, 2)	$1.21 \cdot 10^{21}$
VPC3	48.29	0.77	139	0.10	(4, 3)	$1.47 \cdot 10^{42}$
VPC4	49.18	1.26	133	0.09	(5, 3)	$7.25 \cdot 10^{50}$
Sensors	4.30	2.40	51	0.01	(3, 2, 2)	$2.53 \cdot 10^{13}$

(a)

example	time	mem.	# calls	$\frac{time}{\# calls}$	$\frac{pruned}{total}$
VPC1	2964.82	2.20	3805	0.54	4/48
VPC2	1845.94	1.69	3544	0.31	3/48
VPC3	273.77	1.31	491	0.29	4/44
VPC4	316.32	1.35	482	0.37	4/44
Sensors	14.46	0.71	167	0.04	3/8

(b)

Figure 11. All times are in seconds, and memory usage is in gigabytes. (a) Evaluation results for synthesis. The number of levels (*i.e.*, states) for each synthesized update function is shown in the *holes* column. (b) Evaluation results for specification pruning. We report for each example the size of the pruned specification domain and the size of the original specification domain.

Stochastic modeling An alternative to modeling biological systems using non-deterministic concurrency is to use stochasticity [2, 18, 24]. If we were interested in making predictions on the system's output behavior, *i.e.*, the *most likely* the behavior of the cell for a given mutation, we might select a model that predicts concentrations of proteins under varying initial parameters, including those not yet measured in the lab. Such predictive models are often stochastic.

In contrast, we care to only discover a mechanistic explanation for the cellular system (*i.e.*, how proteins communicate to agree on a particular cell fate). It is appropriate here to rely on a discrete model because the modeling problem is to find a program that reproduces each observed outcome on at least one execution — as opposed to some ratio of all executions. The existence of such a schedule is sufficient to determine the need to have the crucial protein-protein interaction.

Synthesis algorithms for concurrent systems. Our synthesis algorithm extends the synthesis algorithm for concurrent data structures [28]. That work showed how to extend the CEGIS algorithm [29] from the sequential setting into the semantics of concurrent programs. The resulting algorithm however did not handle the richer specification used in this paper (*i.e.*, the angelic correctness). Indeed, new algorithms had to be developed for the specifications of this paper. The Paraglider project developed synthesizers for concurrent data structures by deriving them from high-level specifications [31]. It is not clear how these derivation algorithms can be adapted to synthesis of concurrent systems under input-output examples such as ours.

Model checking [5–7, 11, 18] and abstract interpretation [9] have been applied to analyze various biological systems. All such efforts to manually construct and validate models have severely demonstrated the need for a synthesis system.

Various other paradigms have been used to model biological systems, including Petri nets [8], boolean networks [23], and process algebras [26]. While our techniques are not directly applicable, our success in synthesis for a model previously expressed in the expressive RM formalism demonstrates potential for synthesis in these other formalisms as well.

9. Conclusion

We present a language and develop algorithms for synthesizing concurrent models from experiments that perform mutations on biological cells and observe the results of the mutation on developed cells. We synthesize models that reproduce all non-deterministic outcomes of experiments. This variant of synthesis requires a 3QBF algorithm, which we design by allowing three solvers to communicate counterexamples. We also develop algorithms for analyzing specification ambiguity, ascertaining that a model is the sole biological explanation whenever possible under given biological assumptions, and computing minimal non-ambiguous specifications. We carried out a significant case study, synthesizing a model of vulval cell fate specification in the *C. elegans* earthworm that expresses a previously unknown biological hypothesis.

References

[1] Rajeev Alur and Thomas A. Henzinger. Reactive modules. *Formal Methods in System Design*, 15(1):7–48, 1999.

[2] A. Arkin, J. Ross, and H. H. McAdams. Stochastic kinetic analysis of developmental pathway bifurcation in phage lambda-infected Escherichia coli cells. *Genetics*, 149(4):1633–1648, Aug 1998.

[3] Anil Aswani, Soile V. E. Keränen, James Brown, Charless C. Fowlkes, David W. Knowles, Mark D. Biggin, Peter Bickel, and Claire J. Tomlin. Nonparametric identification of regulatory interactions from spatial and temporal gene expression data. *BMC Bioinformatics*, 11:413, 2010.

[4] Nathan A. Barker, Chris J. Myers, and Hiroyuki Kuwahara. Learning genetic regulatory network connectivity from time series data. *IEEE/ACM Trans. Comput. Biology Bioinform.*, 8(1):152–165, 2011.

[5] Grégory Batt, Calin Belta, and Ron Weiss. Temporal logic analysis of gene networks under parameter uncertainty. *IEEE Transactions of Automatic Control*, page 2008.

[6] Grégory Batt, Delphine Ropers, Hidde de Jong, Johannes Geiselmann, Radu Mateescu, Michel Page, and Dominique Schneider. Analysis and verification of qualitative models of genetic regulatory networks: A model-checking approach. In *IJCAI*, 2005.

[7] Nathalie Chabrier and François Fages. Symbolic model checking of biochemical networks. CMSB '03, 2003.

[8] C. Chaouiya. Petri net modelling of biological networks. *Brief. Bioinformatics*, 8(4):210–219, Jul 2007.

[9] Vincent Danos, Jérôme Feret, Walter Fontana, and Jean Krivine. Abstract interpretation of cellular signalling networks. VMCAI'08, pages 83–97.

[10] Leonardo de Moura and Nikolaj Bjørner. Z3: Efficient SMT solver. In *TACAS'08: Tools and Algorithms for the Construction and Analysis of Systems*, volume 4963/2008 of *Lecture Notes in Computer Science*, pages 337–340, 2008.

[11] David L. Dill. Model checking cell biology. In *CAV*, page 2, 2012.

[12] J. Fisher, N. Piterman, A. Hajnal, and T. A. Henzinger. Predictive modeling of signaling crosstalk during C. elegans vulval development. *PLoS Comput. Biol.*, 3(5):e92, May 2007.

[13] Jasmin Fisher, David Harel, and Thomas A. Henzinger. Biology as reactivity. *Commun. ACM*, 54(10):72–82, 2011.

[14] Jasmin Fisher and Thomas A. Henzinger. Executable cell biology. *Nature Biotechnology*, 25(11):1239–1249, November 2007.

[15] Jasmin Fisher, Thomas A. Henzinger, Maria Mateescu, and Nir Piterman. Bounded asynchrony: Concurrency for modeling cell-cell interactions. In *FMSB*, pages 17–32, 2008.

[16] `https://oeis.org/A000670`.

[17] Sumit Gulwani. Automating string processing in spreadsheets using input-output examples. In *Proceedings of the 38th annual ACM SIGPLAN-SIGACT symposium on Principles of programming languages*, POPL '11, pages 317–330. ACM.

[18] J. Heath, M. Kwiatkowska, G. Norman, D. Parker, and O. Tymchyshyn. Probabilistic model checking of complex biological pathways. *Theoretical Computer Science*, 319(3):239–257, 2008.

[19] Na'aman Kam, Irun R. Cohen, and David Harel. The immune system as a reactive system: Modeling t cell activation with statecharts. In *HCC*, pages 15–22, 2001.

[20] Na'aman Kam, David Harel, Hillel Kugler, Rami Marelly, Amir Pnueli, E. Jane Albert Hubbard, and Michael J. Stern. Formal modeling of c. elegans development: A scenario-based approach. In *CMSB*, pages 4–20, 2003.

[21] `http://www.cs.berkeley.edu/~koksal/`.

[22] Ali Sinan Köksal, Viktor Kuncak, and Philippe Suter. Scala to the Power of Z3: Integrating SMT and Programming. In *CADE*, pages 400–406, 2011.

[23] S. Li, S. M. Assmann, and R. Albert. Predicting essential components of signal transduction networks: a dynamic model of guard cell abscisic acid signaling. *PLoS Biol.*, 4(10):e312, Oct 2006.

[24] H. H. McAdams and A. Arkin. Stochastic mechanisms in gene expression. *Proc. Natl. Acad. Sci. U.S.A.*, 94(3):814–819, Feb 1997.

[25] Martin Odersky, Lex Spoon, and Bill Venners. *Programming in Scala: a comprehensive step-by-step guide*. Artima Press, 2008.

[26] Aviv Regev and Ehud Shapiro. The pi-calculus as an abstraction for biomolecular systems. 2004.

[27] Aurélien Rizk, Grégory Batt, François Fages, and Sylvain Soliman. Continuous valuations of temporal logic specifications with applications to parameter optimization and robustness measures. *Theor. Comput. Sci.*, 412(26):2827–2839, 2011.

[28] Armando Solar-Lezama, Christopher Grant Jones, and Rastislav Bodik. Sketching concurrent data structures. In *Proceedings of the 2008 ACM SIGPLAN conference on Programming language design and implementation*, PLDI '08, pages 136–148. ACM.

[29] Armando Solar-Lezama, Liviu Tancau, Rastislav Bodik, Sanjit Seshia, and Vijay Saraswat. Combinatorial sketching for finite programs. In *ASPLOS-XII*, pages 404–415, New York, NY, USA, 2006. ACM.

[30] Saurabh Srivastava, Sumit Gulwani, and Jeffrey S. Foster. From program verification to program synthesis. In *POPL*, 2010.

[31] Martin Vechev and Eran Yahav. Deriving linearizable fine-grained concurrent objects. *SIGPLAN Not.*, 43(6):125–135, June 2008.

[32] A. S. Yoo, C. Bais, and I. Greenwald. Crosstalk between the EGFR and LIN-12/Notch pathways in C. elegans vulval development. *Science*, 303(5658):663–666, Jan 2004.

Sub-Polyhedral Scheduling Using (Unit-)Two-Variable-Per-Inequality Polyhedra

Ramakrishna Upadrasta
INRIA and LRI, Université Paris-Sud (11)
Ramakrishna.Upadrasta@inria.fr

Albert Cohen
INRIA and École Normale Supérieure
Albert.Cohen@inria.fr

Abstract

Polyhedral compilation has been successful in the design and implementation of complex loop nest optimizers and parallelizing compilers. The algorithmic complexity and scalability limitations remain one important weakness. We address it using sub-polyhedral under-aproximations of the systems of constraints resulting from affine scheduling problems. We propose a sub-polyhedral scheduling technique using (Unit-)Two-Variable-Per-Inequality or (U)TVPI Polyhedra. This technique relies on simple polynomial time algorithms to under-approximate a general polyhedron into (U)TVPI polyhedra. We modify the state-of-the-art PLuTo compiler using our scheduling technique, and show that for a majority of the Polybench (2.0) kernels, the above under-approximations yield polyhedra that are non-empty. Solving the under-approximated system leads to asymptotic gains in complexity, and shows practically significant improvements when compared to a traditional LP solver. We also verify that code generated by our sub-polyhedral parallelization prototype matches the performance of PLuTo-optimized code when the under-approximation preserves feasibility.

Categories and Subject Descriptors D.3.4 [*Programming Languages*]: Processors—Compilers, Optimization

General Terms Approximations, Complexity, Scheduling, Optimization, Performance

Keywords Approximation Algorithms, Complexity Theory, Compiler Optimizations, Parallelism, Loop Transformations, Affine Scheduling, Optimization, Geometric Algorithms

1. Motivation

Polyhedral compilation is well established as the most effective framework to reason with loop programs. At its heart lie the representation of loop nests as polyhedra, and the search for their semantics-preserving loop transformations. In general, semantics preservation amounts to the *feasibility of rational polyhedra*, while performance and profitability are related to *optimization on rational polyhedra*. This simplicity is both the strength as well as the weakness of polyhedral compilation. Strength because polyhedral abstractions are extremely powerful to analyze loops, encoding multitudes of useful transformations, with the ability to automatically parallelize and tile them on newer architectures being one of the main practical applications. And weakness because the richness of polyhedra itself becomes an obstacle due to the complexity of its core algorithms. This latter issue creates a practical challenge when programs of non-trivial size are being compiled. Our view is that using approximations of polyhedra alleviates and provides a solution for this scalability challenge.

In a previous paper [53], we proposed different directions for sub-polyhedral compilation, where approximations of general convex polyhedra could be used so that the problems that are being solved by polyhedral compilers can be made scalable with worst-case polynomial time guarantee. This was followed by the introduction of sub-polyhedral scheduling in [54], where we proposed using (U)TVPI sub-polyhedral under-approximations to reduce the complexity of affine scheduling.

In the current paper, we build from the above works and make solid progress towards polyhedral schedulers that are intrinsically scalable in the program size. Our techniques rely on strongly polynomial algorithms, i.e., whose time complexity is polynomial only in the number of integers in the input and not on the bit-size of the input encoding. For example, we are able to substitute linear programming with min-cost flow and shortest paths problems, which are solvable using graph theoretic methods like the well known Bellman-Ford algorithm.

Our method applies to latency and depth minimization approaches like Feautrier's algorithm [25], as well as methods centered on loop tiling like Bondhugula et al.'s PLuTo [13, 29].

1.1 Polyhedral compilation

Affine scheduling [21] now is a part and parcel of many compilers which aspire to compile for parallel architectures (GCC, LLVM, IBM XL, Reservoir Labs R-Stream). The seminal work of Feautrier [25] opened the avenue of constraint-based affine transformation methods, building on the affine form of the Farkas lemma. This approach has been refined, extended and applied in many directions. To cite only two recent achievements at the two extremes of the complexity spectrum: the tiling-centric PLuTo algorithm of Bondhugula et al. [13] extending the Forward Communication Only (FCO) principle of Griebl et al. [29] for coarse-grain parallelization, and the complete, convex characterization of Vasilache [55] and decoupled exploration heuristic of Pouchet et al. [39]. Much progress has been made in the understanding of the theoretical and practical complexity of polyhedral compilation problems. Nevertheless, when considering multidimensional affine transformations, none of these are strongly polynomial in the size of the program. The lowest complexity heuristics such as PLuTo are reducible to linear programming, which is only weakly polynomial, its traditional Simplex implementation being associated with

POPL'13, January 23–25, 2013, Rome, Italy.

large memory requirements and having a worst-case exponential complexity.

1.2 Unscalability of a current scheduler

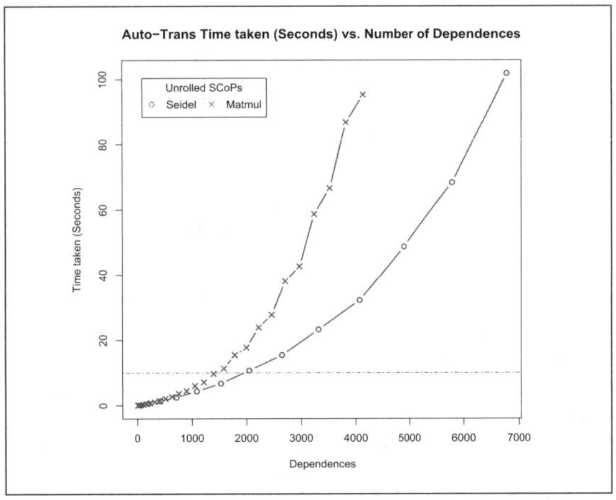

Figure 1. Unscalability for Large Loop Programs

In this section, we show an example of unscalability of current methods in PLuTo. We have artificially unrolled two typical kernels from PolyBench [40], `matmul` and `seidel`, by a variable number of times so as to increase the number of dependences in the loop nests. We have also enclosed the unrolled loops in two "time loops", mimicking the behavior of a scientific computing kernel. The above transformations induce thousands of dependences in the input program. The compilation times are shown in Figure 1. with `matmul` in blue (crosses) and `seidel` in red (circles).

We checked that the compilation time (`auto_trans` time of PLuTo) increases in a roughly n^5 complexity in the number of statements in the system. The rest of the modules of PLuTo—in particular, dependence analysis and code generation (CLooG)—took significantly less than the above.

It may seem that the above unrolling based method is an artificial way to induce unscalability, with inlining being a better candidate for the same in real world benchmarks. While unrolling is much simpler to simulate, limitations of current infrastructures do not provide a platform to study the asymptotic time complexity associated with code size increases associated with inlining. Hence, the above examples could only be taken as representatives of the unscalability problem. But it should also be remembered that when discussing the solution time with respect to the input code size increase, the number of constraints in the overall LP problem is linear in the number of dependences in the input code. So, a method like the above which gives a representative sample to increase the size of the LP program is not a limitation.

Further, in current benchmarks for loop nest optimization—like the PolyBench—the range of dependences is in tens, and it can arguably be said that presently there exists no scalability problem like in the above artificial examples. But, polyhedral compilers will soon face such large problems, arising from aggressive interprocedural optimization, domain-specific program generation, or simply as the applicability restrictions continue to be lifted [10, 51]. In addition, there could be a restriction of the time limit in just-in-time compilers that would further exacerbate the scalability problem, such as just-in-time applications of LLVM/Polly [30]. Note that IBM XL, LLVM, and R-Stream have schedulers similar to PLuTo.

In the following, we aim for lower complexity feasibility and optimization algorithms, with worst-case strongly polynomial bounds, and closer to n^2 time complexity for large-scale and/or just-in-time compilation applications.

1.3 Contributions

In this paper, we make the following contributions:

- We show that state-of-the-art parallelization and affine scheduling heuristics such as PLuTo can be adapted to (U)TVPI subpolyhedra, thereby reducing their algorithmic complexity.
- Using elementary polyhedral concepts, we present a simple and powerful framework (an approximation scheme) which can be used for designing Under-Approximation (UA) algorithms of general convex polyhedra, linearizing the UA problem.
- We evaluate these methods by integrating them into PLuTo. We show that for a significant percentage of Farkas-polyhedra arising from a wide range of test cases from affine scheduling, the (U)TVPI-UAs proposed above are precise enough to preserve feasibility. We show that our approximations when solved with a Bellman-Ford algorithm show considerable improvement in running time over a well established Simplex implementation. Further, we show that preliminary integration of the above UA polyhedra into PLuTo yields code in most cases that does not suffer significant increase in execution time.
- We show how our framework is general enough to extend to various other problems in compiler scheduling, either within the affine transformations or beyond.

The paper is structured as follows. Section 2 introduces TVPI and UTVPI sub-polyhedra. Section 3 introduces polyhedral scheduling, our method to tackle with the scalability problem, and the mathematical framework for the linearization of the under-approximati problem and for establishing its correctness. Section 4 proposes simple algorithms that under-approximate a general convex polyhedron into a (U)TVPI polyhedron. Section 5 discusses the theoretical and practical implications of the above algorithms. In Section 6, we discuss the various methods for having better control of feasibility in the presence of multiple polyhedra. In Section 7 we discuss the results of implementing these algorithms in PLuTo. In Section 8 we discuss extensions and related work, and we conclude in Section 9.

2. Sub-Polyhedra: TVPI and UTVPI

In this section, we briefly cover some basics of TVPI and UTVPI approximations of polyhedra. A more extensive discussion on these, including other flavors of sub-polyhedra as used by the static analysis community can be found in our earlier work [53]. For a polyhedron described in constraint form, let m be the number of inequalities, n be the number of variables and B the upper bound on the absolute value of the coefficients describing the system.

2.1 TVPI sub-polyhedra

In TVPI polyhedra, each constraint is of the form: $ax_i + bx_j \leq c$ $a, b, c \in \mathbb{Q}$. TVPI are obviously closed under projection, and hence many algorithms on geometric operations that are developed for planar polyhedra (polygons) are directly applicable to general TVPI, giving rise to simple algorithms with low complexity. Furthermore, the dual of a TVPI program is a generalized min-cost flow problem, which can be solved using graph algorithms. So, the linear programming community has been interested in TVPI polyhedra because it can be dealt with strongly polynomial time algorithms.

Application of graph theory to linear programming using TVPI systems was pioneered by Shostak [46]. Aspvall and Shiloach [4] showed the polynomiality of the feasibility problem of TVPI-LP formulations by introducing a unique strongly polynomial time procedure that can be used to decide the range of a particular variable with respect to a given constant. This latter procedure is a Bellman-Ford style propagation of values assigned to variables through inequalities in the system, and is the heart of all subsequent algorithms in the TVPI literature. The following result by Wayne [58] is the best to date for the TVPI optimization problem:

Lemma 2.1.1 [LP optimization on TVPI] Linear programming optimization on TVPI systems can be solved in $\mathcal{O}(m^3n^2 \log m \log B)$ worst case time.

It is well known that for general polyhedra, the optimization and the feasibility problems have the same weakly-polynomial time hardness. But it is interesting to note that till date, they have different complexities on TVPI systems. The feasibility problem on TVPI systems has lower complexity than the above weakly polynomial time result by Wayne on the optimization problem. Network flow based ("combinatorial") strongly polynomial time algorithms for the feasibility problem were given by Cohen and Megiddo [16]. Hochbaum and Naor [32] showed that feasibility of TVPI polyhedra can be determined in strongly polynomial time:

Lemma 2.1.2 [Feasibility on TVPI] Feasibility of TVPI systems can be solved in $\mathcal{O}(mn^2 \log m)$ worst case time.

The above nearly cubic time algorithm by Hochbaum-Naor is surprisingly simple. It embeds the mentioned decision procedure of Aspvall-Shiloach into a binary search, along with a selected application of Chernikova on a planar polyhedron. It can be seen that the above result can as well be used to derive strongly polynomial time cubic bounds for Fourier-Motzkin elimination, and for projection of variables from TVPI systems.

TVPI systems have been used for various problems in abstract interpretation and verification [47].

2.2 UTVPI sub-polyhedra (octagons)

Octagons have constraints of the form $ax_i + bx_j \leq c; a, b \in \{0, \pm 1\}, c \in \mathbb{Q}$, and are called so because in 2-dimensions, their geometric shape is octagonal. They are also referred to as Unit Two Variables Per Inequality (UTVPI) because of the nature of their constraints. Since UTVPI $\subset$ TVPI, the complexity bounds of TVPI polyhedra apply to UTVPI polyhedra as well. But, as the dual of the LP formulation of shortest-paths problem has just difference constraints [1] with the form $x_i - x_j \leq c$, general UTVPI systems can be solved with same quadratic complexity as Bellman-Ford, giving the following lemma:

Lemma 2.2 [Feasibility on UTVPI] Feasibility of UTVPI systems can be solved in $\mathcal{O}(mn)$ worst case time and in $\mathcal{O}(m+n)$ space.

The above decision algorithm can also return a feasibility certificate of the UTVPI polyhedron.

UTVPI polyhedra have successfully been used for various problems in abstract interpretation and program verification [38]. Also, they have well supported implementations, in Apron [34], the Astrée analyzer [12, 17], and in the Parma Polyhedra Library (PPL) [5].

2.3 Sub-polyhedra vs. general (convex) polyhedra

The use of sub-polyhedra by the static analysis community has different requirements than our proposed application to affine scheduling. In the former, they serve as abstract domains and provide operations like union, intersection, projection etc., which are efficiently solved by (U)TVPI polyhedra providing better worst-case complexity. The objective functions in polyhedral scheduling are very simple functionals with unit coefficients, and lexicographic minima. Our (U)TVPI sub-polyhedral approximate solutions are based on the assumption that the objective function itself could be approximated and any valid feasibility certificate is usually enough. In this aspect, sub-polyhedra fare better than general convex polyhedra for which efficient algorithms are usually based on the widely used Simplex [18] algorithm.

The worst-case complexity of LP is known to be (weakly) polynomial in time [44], and the Simplex algorithm, while taking exponential time on worst-case scenario squashed cube inputs (as shown by Klee-Minty), is known to run well in practice [11].

In practice, we are more interested in the average-case complexity of LP, to evaluate the merit of our approximation methods. Let $Z(m, n)$ be the complexity of LP using the Simplex algorithm with m constraints and n variables. Determining typical value of Z is not an easy task, as it is well known to depend on many details of the algorithm, like relative ratio of m and n, pivoting rule, method of exploiting sparsity, and even many implementation details. In this paper however, we will be using the following folklore result which does not count the bit-size complexity: on a *typical* input, $Z = \mathcal{O}((m+n)mn)$ on *average*.

In the above empirical estimate, we assume that the Gaussian elimination steps of the Simplex are very fast, exploiting sparsity, and assuming a linear number $\mathcal{O}(m+n)$ of pivoting steps. Also, the above estimate is practically very accurate for the LP programs we observe, despite the recent invalidation of Hirsch conjecture [43, 61]. Note that advanced algorithmic analyses using novel perturbation-based probabilistic techniques have even been proposed by Spielman and Teng [48] to establish the average-case polynomial running time; but these results go way beyond the empirical estimate we need to evaluate our algorithms.

3. Polyhedral Scheduling and Approximations

In this section, we show how the above classes of sub-polyhedra could be used to help in overcoming the scalability challenge in affine scheduling.

3.1 Polyhedral scheduling and Farkas lemma

Let us first recall some essential notations and results about polyhedral compilation.

The input to any polyhedral scheduling algorithm is a polyhedral dependence graph G, which is a result of a dependence analysis, and is defined to be a multi-graph $G = (V, E)$, where V is the set of statements, and each particular dependence edge $e \in E$ is annotated with a parametrized polyhedron $\mathcal{D}_e$. Each of the constraints of $\mathcal{D}_e$ is affine and involves (I, N) where vectors I and N are the iteration and parameter vectors, respectively.

In Feautrier's algorithm [25], these are converted into a per-dependence edge polyhedron $P_e(\mu, \lambda)$, with μ-variables being the Farkas multipliers that come from domain constraints and λ-variables being the Farkas multipliers that come from dependence constraints. This conversion is done by application of the affine form of the Farkas lemma [44, Corollary 7.1h] given as:

Lemma 3.1 [Affine Form of Farkas's Lemma] Let $\mathcal{D}$ be a nonempty polyhedron defined by p inequalities $\mathbf{a}_k\mathbf{x} + b_k \geq 0$, for any $k \in \{1, \ldots, p\}$. An affine form Φ is non-negative over $\mathcal{D}$ if and only if it is a non-negative affine combination of the affine forms used to define $\mathcal{D}$, meaning:

$$\Phi(\mathbf{x}) \equiv \lambda_0 + \sum_{k=1}^{p} \lambda_k(\mathbf{a}_k\mathbf{x} + b_k);\ \forall k \in [0, p]\ \lambda_k \geq 0$$

The nonnegative values λ_k are called Farkas' multipliers.

In the per-edge Farkas polyhedron $P_e(\mu, \lambda)$, both of the newly created λ and μ variables are called the Farkas multipliers. By putting together all the per-edge Farkas polyhedra, one obtains an overall Farkas polyhedron $P = \cap_{e \in E} P_e$, which is amenable to Linear Programming. Any rational point that satisfies P is considered a valid schedule.

The above application of the Farkas lemma results in all the constraints in the Feautrier's scheduler, with some additional variables to model the strong/strict satisfaction of dependences at a given dimension of the affine schedule. In PLuTo, a different but conceptually similar method results in a majority of dependence constraints of the same form as Feautrier's.

It has been shown elsewhere [27, 53] that these methods result in an LP problem of size $m \times n \approx (d \cdot |E|) \times (d \cdot |V|)$, where d is the mean depth of the loop nests. Assuming a usual simplex method—whose complexity has been alluded in the previous section—for solving systems with bounded d leads to a close to $\mathcal{O}(|E|^2|V|) = \mathcal{O}(|V|^5)$ asymptotic complexity (not counting the bit-size complexity, and assuming $|E| = \mathcal{O}(|V|^2)$), closely matching the curves in Figure 1 and leading to unscalability problems.

3.2 Schedule space under-approximation

In this paper, we propose that P be Under-Approximated (UA) to improve the scalability of the scheduling algorithm. This means that instead of searching for an optimal feasible point in P, we search in $P_a = \mathrm{UA}(P)$. The above approximation is legal and only leads to a conservative approximation of losing schedules, though it is well proven [39] that P is highly redundant with respect to schedule points. The overall process has to ensure that the approximation algorithm, as well as the solution finding time be scalable algorithms. We can restrict these requirements further and say that both of these algorithms should have *worst-case strongly polynomial time* running times matching the complexities of (U)TVPI polyhedra introduced in Section 2.

The above approximation can also be done on a per-dependence-edge basis. In this method, the per-dependence-edge Farkas polyhedra P_e are under-approximated, and the solution is found from the overall polyhedron obtained by putting together all the per-dependence UAs. Namely, by doing $P_a = \mathrm{UA}(P) = \cap_{e \in E} \mathrm{UA}(P_e)$. If the above approximation leads to a non-empty polyhedron, then we can find schedule using $\mathrm{UA}(P)$ instead of P.

In the above, we are exploiting the property that each of the individual P_e's of polyhedral compilation are guaranteed to be non-empty [25] directly as a result of dependence analysis. It also helps that each of the per-dependence-edge Farkas polyhedra P_e are comparably much smaller than the overall polyhedron.

In the rest of this section, we define a simple and sound mathematical background to build (U)TVPI approximations of polyhedra, to linearize the problem of finding approximations, and to prove that the algorithms we construct in later sections return valid approximations. For giving these sufficiency conditions, we take two approaches: an intuitive and geometric explanation using duality/polarity in next section, followed by a more direct way using the equivalent Farkas solution.

3.3 Convexity and approximations

Starting with a polyhedron given in constraint form as $P = \{\mathbf{x} | A\mathbf{x} + \mathbf{b} \geq \mathbf{0}\}$, we show that simple approximations of P can be obtained by reasoning about over-approximations of the dual (polar), associated with the transpose matrix $[A \,|\, \mathbf{b}]^T$. To accomplish the above, we introduce some basic lemmas about convexity and then show how these geometric concepts help reasoning about under-approximations and over-approximations in a unified manner. The reader may refer to standard books for a complete coverage [44, 61]. A more detailed presentation of this material can be found in [52, 54].

3.3.1 Homogenization and conical polarity

In projective geometry, homogenization can be done on polyhedra in $\mathcal{H}$-form—constraint form—or in $\mathcal{V}$-form—vertex form or generator form. The following definition is when P is in $\mathcal{H}$-form.

Definition 3.3.1a [Homogenization] Let $P = P(A, \mathbf{b})$ ($P = \{\mathbf{x} | A\mathbf{x} + \mathbf{b} \geq \mathbf{0}\}$) be a $\mathcal{H}$-polyhedron, then its homogenization is a cone and is also a $\mathcal{H}$-polyhedron:

$$\mathrm{homog}(P) = \left(\begin{pmatrix} A & \mathbf{b} \\ \mathbf{0}^T & 1 \end{pmatrix}, \begin{pmatrix} \mathbf{0} \\ 0 \end{pmatrix} \right) = C(P) \quad (1)$$

It can be noted that if A is a $m \times n$-matrix (m constraints and n variables), and $\mathbf{b}$ is a $m \times 1$-vector, then the homogenized constraint system C (or $\mathrm{homog}(P)$) is of size $(m+1) \times (n+1)$. Note that the constants dimension has become an additional dimension in the $(n+1)$-dimensional space. We would be referring to this dimension as *homogenizing* dimension and the other dimensions as *non-homogenizing* dimensions. Though the homogenization is a rather trivial process, involving special marking of the dimensions, it however needs to be mentioned because this paper deals with (U)TVPI constraints having at most two non-zero coefficients in the non-homogenizing dimensions.

The following is the definition of polar of a polyhedron:

Definition 3.3.1b [Conical Polarity] For $C \subseteq \mathbb{R}^n$, the polar set is defined by

$$C^* = \{\mathbf{c} \in (\mathbb{R}^n)^* : \mathbf{cx} \leq 0 \text{ for all } \mathbf{x} \in C\} \subseteq (\mathbb{R}^n)^*$$

From the above definition, K, the polar cone corresponding to P can directly be constructed from $\mathrm{homog}(P)$ in (1), and whose generator vectors are columns of the following matrix:

$$K = \mathrm{cone} \begin{pmatrix} A^T & \mathbf{0} \\ \mathbf{b}^T & 1 \end{pmatrix} \quad (2)$$

In matricial form, K is of size $(n+1) \times (m+1)$, the transpose of constraint matrix of (1), and can also be written as the following:

$$K = \mathrm{cone}\left\{ \begin{pmatrix} \mathbf{a}_1^T \\ b_1 \end{pmatrix}, \ldots, \begin{pmatrix} \mathbf{a}_j^T \\ b_j \end{pmatrix}, \ldots, \begin{pmatrix} \mathbf{a}_m^T \\ b_m \end{pmatrix}, \begin{pmatrix} \mathbf{0} \\ 1 \end{pmatrix} \right\} \quad (3)$$

3.3.2 Polarity, (U)TVPI and (U)TCPV

Though a polyhedron can be represented in either of $\mathcal{H}/\mathcal{V}$-forms there is certain naturality in describing the primal in $\mathcal{H}$-form for problems that occur in polyhedral compilation. The polar can be built in linear time in $\mathcal{V}$-form as in (3). But converting the primal to $\mathcal{V}$-form or the polar to $\mathcal{H}$-form is very costly; it involves the Chernikova algorithm which takes exponential time. In the following lemma, we will implicitly be using the above *dual* interpretation, *without* making an actual call to Chernikova.

Lemma 3.3.2 [(U)TVPI and (U)TCPV] For a TVPI-polyhedron, the polar has vertices and rays (generators) which have not more than two non-zero components in the non-homogenizing dimensions. For a UTVPI-polyhedron, the polar has generators which have not more than two non-zero components each in the non-homogenizing dimensions, with them being from $\{-1, +1\}$. We define the polar of a (U)TVPI constraint as *(Unit-)Two-Components-Per-Vector* or *(U)TCPV* vector. Further, we define the polar of a (U)TVPI polyhedron as a *(U)TCPV polyhedron*.

3.3.3 Under-approximation and over-approximation

The following lemma and its corollary are standard results:

Lemma 3.3.3a [Polarity and Inclusivity] For any two cones K_1 and K_2, $K_1 \subseteq K_2 \Leftrightarrow K_1^* \supseteq K_2^*$.

Corollary 3.3.3b [Toggling between OA/UA] $(\mathrm{OA}(K^*))^* \subseteq K$

The above corollary means that by taking the polar of a cone and taking the resultant's Over-Approximation (OA) one obtains a cone whose polar is an UA of the original cone. By using it, the problem of finding a UA of a polyhedron in $\mathcal{H}$-form is reduced to the problem of finding a OA of its polar cone in $\mathcal{V}$-form. More specifically, if we let P_a (respectively K_a) be the approximation of P (respectively K), we have the following:

$$K_a \supseteq K \Leftrightarrow P_a \subseteq P \quad (4)$$

So, the objective in the polar space of finding the TCPV-OA of cone K given in $\mathcal{V}$-form as in (3), is equivalent to finding a cone K_a such that:

$$K \in \mathrm{cone}\,(K_a) \quad (5)$$

By this equation, if each column of K as in (3) can be written as a conical sum of the vectors in K_a, then the approximation remains a valid approximation. If each vector in K_a is a (U)TCPV vector, then the corresponding P_a would be a (U)TVPI approximation of P.

3.4 Approximation scheme for TVPI-UA

In this section, we formulate the sufficient conditions to prove that the UAs we will construct in Section 4 are valid approximations. In fact, with the Farkas lemma in Section 3.1 and the equivalent homogenization-polarity intuition in Section 3.3, we do have all the necessary ammunition to construct an approximation scheme which allows us to built TVPI-UAs of general polyhedra. (UTVPI-UAs are simple extensions of the material in this section.)

In the rest of this section, for ease of exposition, we assume that the polyhedron P is 3-dimensional; these are also called 3VPI polyhedra. Generalization to $n > 3$ is straightforward.[1]

Let the j-th column of K, with $1 \le j \le m$, be $K^j = (\mathbf{a}_j, b_j)^T = \begin{pmatrix} a_{j,1} & a_{j,2} & a_{j,3} & b_j \end{pmatrix}^T$. Then we have

$$K^j = \begin{pmatrix} a_{j,1} \\ a_{j,2} \\ a_{j,3} \\ b_j \end{pmatrix} \in \mathrm{cone} \begin{pmatrix} t_1^{j,1} & t_2^{j,1} & 0 \\ t_1^{j,2} & 0 & t_3^{j,2} \\ 0 & t_2^{j,3} & t_3^{j,3} \\ p_1^j & p_2^j & p_3^j \end{pmatrix} = \mathrm{cone}(T^j) \quad (6)$$

where the (t,p)-variables constitute the elements of the unknown T-matrix and are to be found out.

It can be noticed that each column of the matrix T^j is a TCPV vector and hence is a TVPI constraint in the primal space. The above is what we call an *approximation scheme*. In this scheme:

Definition 3.4 [Approximation scheme] A non-TVPI constraint $a_{j,1}x_1 + a_{j,2}x_2 + a_{j,3}x_3 + b_j \ge 0$ in the original system is replaced by the set of constraints $\mathrm{UA}(x_1, x_2, x_3) = \{t_1^{j,1}x_1 + t_1^{j,2}x_2 + p_1^j \ge 0; t_2^{j,1}x_1 + t_2^{j,3}x_3 + p_2^j \ge 0; t_3^{j,2}x_2 + t_3^{j,3}x_3 + p_3^j \ge 0\}$.

In the above scheme, every column vector of K which has more than two non-zero components is replaced by a set of TCPV vectors such that the original vector remains in the conical sum of the replacements. The conical combination of the replacement vectors would hence be an OA of the original vector K^j satisfying (5). The above scheme remains valid as long as the (t,p) variables and the (a,b) constants satisfy the convexity requirement. One way for ensuring the same is by making the (t,p)-variables satisfy the following additional constraints, which we would be referring to as *context constraints* for reasons that will be exposed later:

$$\{t_1^{j,1} + t_2^{j,1} = a_{j,1}; t_1^{j,2} + t_3^{j,2} = a_{j,2}; t_2^{j,3} + t_3^{j,3} = a_{j,3}; \\ p_1^j + p_2^j + p_3^j = b_j\} \quad (7)$$

If such a set of T matrices can be found for each non-TCPV vector of K, then we have $K_a = \{T^1, T^2, \ldots, T^m\}$ and the resultant TCPV approximation would be $K \in \mathrm{cone}\,\{T^1, T^2, \ldots, T^m\}$. We have the following theorem:

Theorem 3.4 [TVPI and UA] P_a is a valid TVPI-UA of the original Polyhedron P.

Proof We employ the affine form of Farkas lemma, with the premise of non-emptiness of P guaranteed because of the per-constraint method. For the UA to be proper, the affine form corresponding to the original constraint $\mathbf{a}_j\mathbf{x} + b_j$ should be expressible as a positive sum of the replacement TVPI vectors: $a_{j,1}x_1 + a_{j,2}x_2 + a_{j,3}x_3 + b_j \equiv \lambda_0^j + \lambda_1^j(t_1^{j,1}x_1 + t_1^{j,2}x_2 + p_1^j) + \lambda_2^j(t_2^{j,1}x_1 + t_2^{j,3}x_3 + p_2^j) + \lambda_3^j(t_3^{j,2}x_2 + t_3^{j,3}x_3 + p_3^j)$, where the λ-multipliers satisfy $\lambda_0^j, \lambda_1^j, \lambda_2^j, \lambda_3^j \ge 0$. Pairwise matching for each of the x-variables yields:

$$\{a_{j,1} = \lambda_1^j t_1^{j,1} + \lambda_2^j t_2^{j,1}; a_{j,2} = \lambda_1^j t_1^{j,2} + \lambda_3^j t_3^{j,2}; \\ a_{j,3} = \lambda_2^j t_2^{j,3} + \lambda_3^j t_3^{j,3}; b_j = \lambda_0^j + \lambda_1 p_1^j + \lambda_2^j p_2^j + \lambda_3^j p_3^j\} \quad (8)$$

Setting $\lambda_1^j = \lambda_2^j = \lambda_3^j = 1$ yields the context constraints defined in (7) proving the validity of the approximation, except for the additional λ_0^j in the homogenizing-dimension-matching. Setting $\lambda_0^j = 0$ is safe, and we will see later that it actually contributes to the quality of the approximation. ∎

The problem remains to find such a set of (t,p) variables satisfying the above context constraints (7), so that the approximation remains valid. It can be seen that searching for the (t,p) variables directly could lead to a non-linear (quadratic) formulation. Even searching for t-variables that satisfy the above constraints turns out to be non-linear. But, as they are existentially quantified, the equations can be solved using advanced quantifier elimination techniques like [49], which are well known to be unscalable beyond small inputs and certainly not polynomial.

The next section proposes some linearizations of the above mentioned approximation scheme, so that the approximation algorithms remain scalable. This is done first as a heuristic where both (t,p)-variables are arbitrarily fixed, then as a more careful method where only the t-variables are fixed, while the p-variables are found by an LP formulation.

4. TVPI and UTVPI UA Algorithms

In this section, we use the framework developed in earlier section and develop worst-case polynomial time algorithms for obtaining (U)TVPI under-approximations of Polyhedra.

4.1 The median method for TVPI-UA

In this section, we introduce a simple, per-constraint, strongly polynomial heuristic, using the framework developed in Section 3.4. The main idea of this approximation is (5), saying that the original vector can be approximated by any set of the replacement TCPV vectors, as long as the former remains in the cone of the latter.

Definition 4.1 [Median method: 3-d case] The inequality $ax + by + cz + 1 \ge 0$ can be approximated by the set of inequalities $\{ax + by + \frac{2}{3} \ge 0; ax + cz + \frac{2}{3} \ge 0; by + cz + \frac{2}{3} \ge 0;\}$.

[1] It is also possible to reduce a general polyhedron into an equivalent 3VPI one. According to Shostak [46], the transformation has been suggested by R. Tarjan. It is similar to the reduction of an arbitrary boolean satisfiability ("SAT") problem to a 3SAT problem. This transformation is not an approximation, which is the subject of this paper.

Geometric intuition for the above derives from the observation of the polar space, where the above approximation is the following:

$$\begin{bmatrix} a \\ b \\ c \\ 1 \end{bmatrix} \in \text{cone} \begin{pmatrix} \frac{1}{2}a & \frac{1}{2}a & 0 \\ \frac{1}{2}b & 0 & \frac{1}{2}b \\ 0 & \frac{1}{2}c & \frac{1}{2}c \\ \frac{1}{3} & \frac{1}{3} & \frac{1}{3} \end{pmatrix}$$

The intuition for the above approximation comes from (6). The values of the t-variables and p-variables need to satisfy (7). As explained earlier, the t-variables have to be instantiated a priori to avoid solving a non-linear problem. The method in this section fixes the p variables also in a heuristic manner by dividing the available "budget" in the homogenizing dimensions equally between the values in the homogenizing dimensions of the replacement TCPV vectors. We call it the median method because the original vector is the median of the replacement vectors in the polar space.

General n-d case The above can be easily generalized to n-d polyhedra. Let s be the sparsity of a polyhedron, i.e., the number of non-zero variables (outside the homogenizing dimension) for a specific constraint, with $1 \leq s \leq n$. Let $q = \binom{s}{2} = s(s-1)/2$ and let $r = s - 1$. The resultant set of TCPV vectors corresponding to the particular constraint are $n+1$ dimensional, with cardinality q. The coefficients of the non-homogenizing dimensions are divided by r, while the homogenizing dimension is uniformly divided by q.

In each of the cases, it can be seen that the approximation being proposed is a TCPV approximation, making its polar a TVPI approximation. It can also be verified using the construction given in the earlier sections and equations (5) and (6) that the UA proposed in each case is a valid approximation.

Example 1 Let the input system be the triangular pyramid (3d-simplex) $\{x, y, z \geq 0; x + y + z \leq 1\}$. Only the inequality $x + y + z \leq 1$ is not TVPI and is approximated by the set of inequalities $\{x+y \leq \frac{2}{3}; x+z \leq \frac{2}{3}; y+z \leq \frac{2}{3}\}$. It can be seen that the approximation is a non-empty TVPI system (it is a UTVPI system), with vertices $\{(0,0,0), (\frac{2}{3},0,0), (0,\frac{2}{3},0), (0,0,\frac{2}{3}), (\frac{1}{3},\frac{1}{3},\frac{1}{3})\}$, each of which are inside the vertices of the original system $\{(0,0,0), (1,0,0), (0,1,0), (0,0,1)\}$. (The above example is similar [21, 25] to the Farkas system induced in the compilation of the matrix-vector-product: $\texttt{s[i]}+= \texttt{A} * \texttt{x[i]}$.) □

With reference to the choice of Farkas multiplier λ_0 in Theorem 3.4, it can be seen that setting $\lambda_0 = 0$ in the above example has the advantage that the three replacement TVPI hyperplanes intersect exactly on the original non-TVPI hyperplane. Any other strictly positive choice for λ_0 would mean that the point of intersection would lie strictly inside the positive half-space of the original and thus giving rise to an UA which is in a way less effective.

Example 2 Let the input system be the skewed triangular pyramid $\{x, y, z \geq 0; 1000x + 100y + 10z \leq 1\}$. Only the inequality $1000x + 100y + 10z \leq 1$ is not TVPI and is approximated by the set of inequalities $\{1000x + 100y \leq \frac{2}{3}; 1000x + 10z \leq \frac{2}{3}; 100y + 10z \leq \frac{2}{3}\}$. It can be seen that the resultant approximation is a non-empty TVPI system with vertices: $\{(0,0,0), (\frac{1}{1500},0,0), (0,\frac{1}{150},0), (0,0,\frac{1}{15}), (\frac{1}{3000},\frac{10}{3000},\frac{100}{3000})\}$, each of which are inside the vertices of the original system, which are $\{(0,0,0), (\frac{1}{1000},0,0), (0,0,\frac{1}{10}), (0,\frac{1}{100},0)\}$. □

It can be seen that the median method is simple and easy to implement, but does not have any guarantee of ensuring that the resultant approximation is non-empty. In the next section, we will generalize this method to formulate a parametrized approximation and formulate an LP problem to find the approximation.

4.2 LP-based parametrized TVPI approximation

To ease the exposition, we will primarily deal with 3-dimensional polyhedra again; higher dimensional extensions are straightforward.

The median method can easily be extended by defining the approximation as a *parametrization* on the values in the homogenizing dimension entries: as $\text{UA}_2(\mathbf{a}_j\mathbf{x} \geq b_j) = \{(\mathbf{x}, \mathbf{p}^j) | a_{j,1}x_1 + a_{j,2}x_2 \geq 2p_1^j; a_{j,1}x_1 + a_{j,3}x_3 \geq 2p_2^j; a_{j,2}x_2 + a_{j,3}x_3 \geq 2p_3^j; \sum \mathbf{p}^j = b_j; \}$ where the values of the 3-dimensional $\mathbf{p}^j$-vector are unknown and have to be found out.

In the above approximation, it can be observed that the coefficients in the non-homogenizing dimensions (t-variable values) have been fixed, much similar to their choice in the median method. But, the coefficients in the homogenized dimension (p-variable values) are unknown and have to be found out. The context constraint $\sum \mathbf{p}^j = p_1^j + p_2^j + p_3^j = b_j$ is not arbitrary. It is determined by the choice of the multipliers for the t-variables so that the K^j vector is in the convex-sum of T^j, as given in (6).

The resultant system is $\mathcal{S}_{HD}(\mathbf{x}, \mathbf{p}^j) = \{(\mathbf{x}, \mathbf{p}^j) | \mathbf{a}_1\mathbf{x} \geq b_1; \ldots; \mathbf{a}_{j-1}\mathbf{x} \geq b_{j-1}; \text{UA}_2(\mathbf{a}_j\mathbf{x} \geq b_j); \mathbf{a}_{j+1}\mathbf{x} \geq b_{j+1}; \ldots; \mathbf{a}_m\mathbf{x} \geq b_m; \}$. In the following discussion, we show that the higher dimensional system $\mathcal{S}_{HD}(\mathbf{x}, \mathbf{p}^j)$ can be interpreted in two ways, a geometric and an algorithmic ways, each having its own merits.

4.2.1 A parametrized approximation

$\mathcal{S}_{HD}$ can geometrically be considered as a parametrized approximation, with $\mathbf{p}^j$ being the parametric vector and the context constraint $\sum \mathbf{p}^j = b_j$ considered as the parametric context. When the values of the vector $\mathbf{p}^j$ are known, then the system:

$$\mathcal{S}_2(\mathbf{x}) = \mathcal{S}_{HD}(\mathbf{x}, \mathbf{p}^j)|\mathbf{p}^j \qquad (9)$$

is a non-parametrized LP problem, which can be tested for feasibility in the usual $\mathbf{x}$-variables. Since the context constraint $\sum \mathbf{p}^j = b_j$ is respected, it follows from the proofs of earlier sections that $\mathcal{S}_2(\mathbf{x})$ is a proper approximation of $\mathcal{S}(\mathbf{x})$. If the value of the vector $\mathbf{p}^j$ is not known, $\mathcal{S}_2(\mathbf{x})$ can be considered as a parametrized approximation of $\mathcal{S}(\mathbf{x})$. Note that the context constraint is only on the p-variables, while the t-variables have been assigned a fixed value.

4.2.2 An LP formulation

Algorithmically we can consider $\mathcal{S}_{HD}(\mathbf{x}, \mathbf{p}^j)$ to be a non-parametric LP system with unknown variables $(\mathbf{x}, \mathbf{p}^j)$. Such an interpretation is possible because there exist no non-linear terms in the definition of $\mathcal{S}_2(\mathbf{x}, \mathbf{p}^j)$ and it is only the feasibility of the approximation that is interesting. Supposing the system $\mathcal{S}_{HD}(\mathbf{x}, \mathbf{p}^j)$ is solved for feasibility, with the unknown variables vector as $(\mathbf{x}, \mathbf{p}^j)$, and a valid assignment for the values of both $\mathbf{x}$-variables as well as the $\mathbf{p}^j$-variables is found, then the system $\mathcal{S}_2(\mathbf{x})$ as given by (9) can be considered an approximation of the system $\mathcal{S}(\mathbf{x})$, as long as the $\mathbf{p}^j$-variables satisfy the constraint $\sum \mathbf{p}^j = b_j$. On the other hand, $\mathcal{S}_{HD}(\mathbf{x}, \mathbf{p}^j)$ is a higher dimensional system than $\mathcal{S}(\mathbf{x})$ and hence cannot be considered as an approximation of the latter. It is an intermediate form useful for algorithmic purposes.

Example 3 Here is a reduced example from Banerjee's book [8]. $\mathcal{S}(x, y, z) = \{(x, y, z) \mid -z + 3 \geq 0; x - z \geq 0; -y + z - 1 \geq 0; -x + y + z + 1 \geq 0\}$. It is clearly not a TVPI system as the fourth constraint is non-TVPI. The median method applied to this constraint yields the system $\mathcal{S}_1(x, y, z) = \{(x, y, z) | -z + 3 \geq 0; x - z \geq 0; -y + z - 1 \geq 0; -x + y + \frac{2}{3} \geq 0; -x + z + \frac{2}{3} \geq 0; y + z + \frac{2}{3} \geq 0\}$, which turns out to be an empty system. On the other hand, the method in this section would lead to the following higher dimensional system: $\mathcal{S}_{HD}(x, y, z, p_1, p_2, p_3) = \{(x, y, z, p_1, p_2, p_3) | -z+3 \geq 0; x-z \geq 0; -y+z-1 \geq 0; -x+$

$y+2p_1 \geq 0; -x+z+2p_2 \geq 0; y+z+2p_3 \geq 0; p_1+p_2+p_3 = 1\}$, where the variables p_1, p_2, p_3 are additional context variables and the last constraint $p_1 + p_2 + p_3 = 1$ is a context constraint. When system $\mathcal{S}_{HD}$ is solved for a feasible point, and the set of p-variables that are obtained as solution $(\frac{1}{2}, 0, \frac{1}{2})$ are substituted, we obtain $\mathcal{S}_2(x, y, z) = \{(x, y, z) | -z+3 \geq 0; x - z \geq 0; -y + z - 1 \geq 0; -x + y + 1 \geq 0; -x + z \geq 0; y + z + 1 \geq 0\}$. The reader can verify the satisfiability of the two approximations $\mathcal{S}_1$ and $\mathcal{S}_2$. □

The above method involves only one call to a standard LP solver. The disadvantage is that the system $\mathcal{S}_{HD}(\mathbf{x}, \mathbf{p})$ has $n + \binom{\|\mathbf{a}_j\|}{2} = n + \|\mathbf{a}_j\|(\|\mathbf{a}_j\| - 1)/2 \approx \mathcal{O}(n + \|\mathbf{a}_j\|^2)$ dimensions, where $\|\mathbf{a}_j\|$ is the number of non-zero elements in the vector $\mathbf{a}_j$. As the method involves a call to an LP solver, its theoretical cost is not strongly polynomial time.

4.3 Multiple constraint LP formulations

When there exist multiple non-TVPI constraints in $\mathcal{S}(\mathbf{x})$, each one of them has to approximated to find a TVPI approximation of the polyhedron. Let m_k be the number of non-TVPI constraints in $\mathcal{S}(\mathbf{x})$, with $m_k \leq m$. Without loss of generality, we can assume that the constraints have been ordered such that the non-TVPI constraints come first, followed by the TVPI constraints. This means that the constraints of $\mathcal{S}(\mathbf{x})$ are $\{1, \ldots, m_k, \ldots, m\}$, with the constraints $\{1, \ldots, m_k\}$ being non-TVPI constraints and the constraints $\{m_k + 1, \ldots, m\}$ being TVPI constraints.

4.3.1 One-shot method

A straightforward way in which one can find a TVPI approximation of the above non-TVPI system $\mathcal{S}(\mathbf{x})$ is to construct a system $\mathcal{S}_{HD}(\mathbf{x}, \mathbf{p}^1, \ldots, \mathbf{p}^{m_k})$ in which all the non-TVPI constraints in $\mathcal{S}(\mathbf{x})$ are approximated using the scheme described in Section 4.2.2. This system can be solved using an LP formulation in variables as $\{\mathbf{x}, \mathbf{p}^1, \ldots, \mathbf{p}^{m_k}\}$. An approximation of $\mathcal{S}(\mathbf{x})$ could be found as $\mathcal{S}_{HD}(\mathbf{x}, \mathbf{p}^1, \ldots, \mathbf{p}^{m_k}) | \mathbf{p}^1, \ldots, \mathbf{p}^{m_k}$. It can easily be shown that the latter system is a proper approximation as long as the context constraints $\sum \mathbf{p}^1 = b_1, \ldots, \sum \mathbf{p}^{m_k} = b_{m_k}$ are respected.

But, finding the approximations of all the non-TVPI constraints simultaneously in the above fashion would lead to a large LP system. $\mathcal{S}_{HD}(\mathbf{x}, \mathbf{p}^1, \ldots, \mathbf{p}^{m_k})$ could have up to $n + \sum_{l=1}^{m_k} \binom{\|\mathbf{a}_l\|}{2} = n + \sum_{l=1}^{m_k} \|\mathbf{a}_l\|(\|\mathbf{a}_l\| - 1)/2$-dimensions which could be as large as $\mathcal{O}(n + \|\widehat{\mathcal{S}_{m_k}}\|^3)$, with $\|\widehat{\mathcal{S}_{m_k}}\|$ being the average number of non-zero coefficients in the non-TVPI constraints in $\mathcal{S}(\mathbf{x})$.

4.3.2 Iterative methods

We can also iterate the above process described in Section 4.2.2 for each of the m_k non-TVPI constraints in $\mathcal{S}(\mathbf{x})$ on an iterative basis. Clearly, there could be choice in the methods in whether the original system is being updated with the approximation constraints of each non-TVPI constraint or not. We refer to the case when the original system is immediately updated as the *incremental* method. We refer to the case when the approximations of all non-TVPI constraints are found by constructing LP formulations on the same LP system as the *independent* method.

It could be noticed that each of the above methods involves multiple LP calls: one for each non-TVPI constraint $\mathcal{S}(\mathbf{x})$. This means making upto $\mathcal{O}(m)$ LP calls in total for building the approximation system. But, the dimension of each of the LP systems is in the order of $\mathcal{O}(n + \|\widehat{\mathcal{S}_{m_k}}\|^2)$, which is much more reasonable than the previous one-shot formulation.

4.4 Per constraint UTVPI-UA of TVPI

Let us sketch a simple per-constraint algorithm that takes a TVPI constraint and returns its UTVPI under-approximation.

From Lemma 3.3.2, a vector in the polar space needs to be TCPV, and should have equal magnitude components in the non-homogenizing dimensions for the original to be UTVPI. So, the intuition for this algorithm is similar to the TCPV-OA, namely that reasoning about the original TCPV vectors in the polar space and computing a set of UTCPV vectors which OA the original TCPV vector resulting in an OA.

Suppose the TCPV vector has components as (a, b, p) in the (x_i, x_j, x_0) dimension (with x_0 being the homogenizing dimension), then we can replace it with two UTCPV vectors. The replacement has to just take care of the fact that the new UTCPV vectors are such that the original vector is in the conical sum of the replacements. As the case when $a = b$ means that the vector is already a UTCPV vector, the other cases can be handled in the following way: $\begin{cases} a > b: & \text{cone}\{(b, b, \frac{p}{2})^T, (a-b, 0, \frac{p}{2})^T\} \\ a < b: & \text{cone}\{(a, a, \frac{p}{2})^T, (0, b-a, \frac{p}{2})^T\} \end{cases}$.
In either of the above cases, it can be noticed that the first vector is a UTCPV vector and the second is an interval vector. The first case is illustrated in Figure 2.

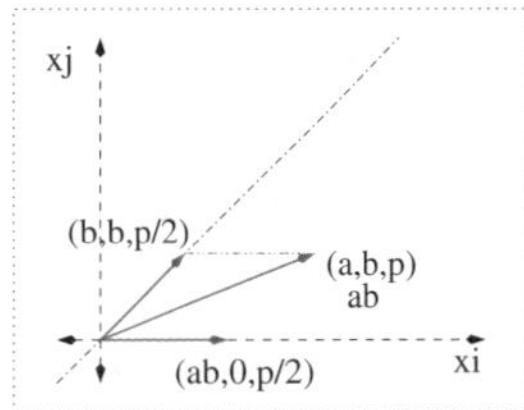

Figure 2. TCPV to UTCPV approximation

Lemma 4.4 [Validity of the above UTVPI approximation] Given a TVPI constraint, the above method returns a valid UTVPI-UA of the constraint.

Proof The geometric proof derives from the observation that the sum of the corresponding UTCPV replacement vectors is the original vector. Hence every vector in the polar space that is reachable by the original vector is reachable by these replacement vectors, meaning that they give an OA in the polar space. In the primal space, the replacements necessarily give an UA (Cor. 3.3.3b). ■

Example 4 Let $P^{\mathcal{V}} = \text{conv}\{(1,1), (4,1), (1,2)\}$, with the $\mathcal{H}$-form of P being $P^{\mathcal{H}} = \{1 \leq x \leq 4; 1 \leq y \leq 2; x + 3y \leq 7\}$. It can be seen that P is a TVPI system, but not a UTVPI system, as the third constraint is a non-UTVPI constraint. The UTVPI approximation by the above method is $\{1 \leq x \leq 4; 1 \leq y \leq 2; x + y \leq \frac{7}{2}; 2y \leq \frac{7}{2}\}$ which can be seen to be non-empty. □

The cost of finding the UA is linear and the method is simple to implement, just like the median method mentioned in Section 4.1. Just like that method, this method does not have any guarantee that the approximated system is non-empty.

4.5 LP based parametrized UTVPI approximation

This approximation is similar to the parametrized TVPI approximation of Section 4.2, in the sense of searching for p variables instead of t's. We are not covering it for lack of space.

5. Metrics and Discussion

Let us now study the size of the new system, the complexity of the conversion, the overall complexity of finding a solution, and discuss some fundamental and methodological limitations of our approach.

5.1 Sizes

Let the original matrix be of size $m \times n$: m constraints and n variables with m_k and m_t being the number of non-TVPI and

TVPI constraints respectively. Also let the overall sparsity factor of the system be $\hat{s}$, which means that for a constraint in the input system, on average $\hat{s}$ variable elements are non-zero. It will be seen in Sections 7.1 that for practical purposes, $\hat{s}$ is a small constant (little more than 4) and relatively independent of n.

TVPI-UA For a system described as above, each of the TVPI-UA methods (given in Sections 4.1 and 4.2) replace a non-TVPI constraint $\mathbf{a}_j$ with the same number of $\binom{\|\mathbf{a}_j\|}{2} = \|\mathbf{a}_j\|(\|\mathbf{a}_j\|-1)/2$ TVPI constraints. Doing the above process for each of the m_k non-TVPI constraints creates an approximated TVPI system of size $m_a \times n$, where $m_a = m_t + \widehat{\|\mathcal{S}_{m_k}\|}(\widehat{\|\mathcal{S}_{m_k}\|} - 1)m_k/2$. It can be assumed that the new system is approximately of the size $\hat{s}^2 m \times n$. In the rare case that $\hat{s} = n$ (which means that the constraint matrix does not have any zero entries) then the size of the resultant TVPI constraint system is $\frac{n(n-1)m}{2} \times n$ which is of the order of $n^2 m \times n$.

UTVPI-UA For UTVPI approximation given in Section 4.4, we have the same order of complexity of additional constraints as in the TVPI-UA case, though double in number.

Constraint graph The Bellman-Ford algorithm constructs a constraint graph, or incidence matrix, of nearly twice the size of the input UTVPI system before solving it: a $m \times n$ input system results in $(2n + 1)$ nodes and $(2m + 2n)$ edges, due to simple transformations of addition of positive and negative forms of each variable [38, Section 2.2], and addition of a pseudo-source-vertex for the shortest-paths problem [1]. The former is a relaxation of UTVPI into difference constraints and is exact for rational points [38], though some (odd) integer points in the original are lost.

5.2 Complexity of conversion

Both the median method of TVPI approximation covered in Section 4.1 and the UTVPI approximation covered in Section 4.4 are strongly polynomial time algorithms as they do not use any LP call when constructing the approximation. The parametric approximation covered in Section 4.2.2 is a weakly polynomial time algorithm for it needs to solve an LP problem for finding the homogenizing dimension values.

For the case of multiple constraints, complexity of conversion is one LP call for the one-shot algorithm of Section 4.3.1, and one LP call per non-TVPI constraint for both incremental and independent algorithms. Each of the above numbers are weakly polynomial time, but are worst-case times nonetheless.

5.3 Complexity of finding a solution

For the TVPI approximation, as the worst-case complexity of Hochbaum-Naor is $\mathcal{O}(mn^2 \log m)$ [32], applying it to the resultant approximated system would lead to $\mathcal{O}(\hat{s}^2 mn^2 \log \hat{s}m)$ time with constraint sparsity $\hat{s}$, and $\mathcal{O}(n^4 m \log nm)$ in the unlikely case when $\hat{s} = O(n)$.

For the UTVPI approximation, as the theoretical worst-case complexity of solving UTVPI systems is $\mathcal{O}(mn)$ (if we use the traditional Bellman-Ford algorithm on the difference constraints), the corresponding complexities would be $\mathcal{O}(\hat{s}^2 mn)$, and $\mathcal{O}(n^3 m)$ respectively. We will see in Section 7.1 empirical evidence suggesting that TVPI constraints are *always* UTVPI in practice, making this method very attractive.

5.4 Pre/post-processing

It can be noticed that our algorithms do not ask for removal of redundant inequalities, which is as hard as determining if the input system is feasible.

Polyhedra in compilation have lot of duplicate constraints, which gets reflected in the approximations as well. Compilers like PLuTo remove these by methods like textual matching which leads to a large decrease in the number of constraints. A more advanced scheme, finely-tuned to UTVPI constraints, would use a hashing or radix-sort technique (like in [3]) packing the UTVPI constraint in a few integers: exploiting the fact that the non-homogenizing dimension values are from $\{0, \pm 1\}$, while the homogenizing dimension values are *always* from a very small set $[-5, 5]$. It would bring the simplification complexity to linear time. We thus believe that the problem of duplicate elimination is asymptotically insignificant.

The following example shows an inherent limitation of the process of TVPI-UA itself.

Example 5 The polyhedron described using the constraints $\{x + y + z \geq -1; x + y + z \leq 1\}$ is not TVPI. Though it is unbounded in both directions, the only TVPI approximations that are possible of the above polyhedron are bounded TVPI polyhedra, which can be considered a failure of the UA approach. □

The above kinds of polyhedra can be considered as degenerate cases and identified by a pre-processing step that removes the lineality space from the input polyhedron. Further, the Farkas polyhedra that arise in polyhedral scheduling are always pointed polyhedra and can never have non-trivial lineality space.

5.5 Integer scaling and TU polyhedra

The parametric approximations of Sections 4.2 and 4.5 can ensure that the resulting difference constraints are integer constraints of the type $x_i - x_j \leq c$, where $c \in \mathbb{Z}$. This would involve scaling up the pseudo-parametric variables, changing the context constraints accordingly, and *solving an ILP problem*—instead of the usual LP problem—though on a per-P_e basis. Such a local transformation will not only induce integer schedules because incidence matrices are a sub-class of network matrices, but also has the additional property that all vertices of the resultant overall polyhedron are integral (because such matrices are Totally Unimodular [44, Chapter 19]). We will show in Section 8 that this method would help in polynomial time approximations of NP-Complete problems and code-generation.

6. Feasibility Control With Many Polyhedra

The previous sections discuss algorithms for the under approximation of one single polyhedron, so that the UA polyhedron can be solved as a means of trading expressiveness (e.g., the ability to find "good" affine transformations) for scalability. In affine scheduling however, the overall system P is an intersection of many polyhedra, each of them arising from a dependence-edge as in the case of Feautrier's scheduler [25, 26], or the above along with some additional constraints as in the case of Bondhugula's scheduler [13, 29]. More specifically:

- Feautrier's scheduler to minimize latency: $P_L = \cap_{e \in E} P_e$, where P_e is the per-dependence-edge Farkas polyhedron. A given dependence edge induces a (weak satisfaction) constraint in the system until it is strongly satisfied by outer dimensions of the multidimensional affine schedule (i.e., the sink of a dependence is scheduled at a strictly higher time step than the source).
- Bondhugula's FCO scheduler to expose loop tiling opportunties: $P_{FCO} = \cap_{e \in E} P_e \cap_{v \in V} H_v \cap_{v \in V} N_v$, where P_e is similar to Feautrier's scheduler's per-dependence polyhedron, enforcing weak dependence satisfaction only, but *at all dimensions* of the multidimensional affine schedule; while H_v collects the per-statement linear independence constraints, and N_v collects the per-statement non-negativity or trivial solution avoidance constraints.

These two cases are different because, thanks to the conditions in [26], the polyhedron built by Feautrier's multi-dimensional scheduler is known to be *always* feasible. This condition however is not necessarily true for FCO-based systems: though the number of problematic, additional constraints $|H_V| + |N_V|$ is small (around $2|V|$ or less than 10%) when compared to Farkas multiplier constraints $|P_E|$, the overall polyhedron could be empty, complicating the UA procedure.

The feasibility preservation problem is to find a non-empty $\mathrm{UA}(P)$ in each of the above cases, *without* making any queries—like an LP call—on the overall system P.[2]

In this section we discuss practical methods to increase the control on feasibility for the overall approximated system.

6.1 Feautrier's scheduler

Let us first discuss a technique for Feautrier's scheduler. Let us start by approximating each of the P_e by calling the one-shot algorithm discussed in Section 4.3.1, and construct the overall approximation by putting all the individual approximations together: $\mathrm{UA}(P) = \cap_{e \in E} \mathrm{UA}(P_e)$. The overall approximation is the result of $|E|$ calls to the one-shot procedure. This will be affordable because each of the P_e-s are quite small.

Feautrier's algorithm always finds a (rational) multi-dimensional affine schedule, which guarantees that P is a feasible polyhedron. The main question is whether feasibility will be preserved when intersecting the per-dependence approximations. It may sound as a surprise that the answer is yes. Notice that he original schedule of the source program is always feasible. The key idea is to *seed* the approximation of the per-dependence P_e polyhedra, forcing this original schedule into the UA. It simply amounts to substituting the values of the coefficients of the original schedule in the Farkas constraints, and adding the resulting (in)equalities to the systems before applying the one-shot UA method.

This result is important because of the large number of affine scheduling heuristics deriving from Feautrier's algorithm. Feautrier's fine-grain parallelization method is already useful for loop vectorization [26]. Our seeding approach is directly applicable to coarse-grain parallelization heuristics as well [36].

We could stop there and declare success. But more advanced methods combining tiling for locality enhancement and parallelism extraction require additional effort to preserve feasibility. The next section studies the most successful of these heuristics, pushing us to enhance the under-approximation method to tackle feasibility preservation in presence of more complex affine constraints.

6.2 FCO scheduling in PLuTo

In this section, we discuss the approximation of P in the context of Bondhugula's FCO scheduler, as implemented in PLuTo. Here, seeding with the original schedule is not possible since the loops of the source program may not be directly permutable/tilable. We study a variety of Per-Dependence constraint clustering techniques.

PD1: Fully-separate Each P_e is approximated alone, and all the additional constraints are approximated together as in: $\mathrm{UA}(P) = \cap_{e \in E} \mathrm{UA}(P_e) \cap \mathrm{UA}(\cap_{v \in V} H_v \cap_{v \in V} N_v)$. The overall approximation is the result of $|E| + 1$ applications of the one-shot method.

PD2: Total augmentation Each P_e is augmented with *all* the additional constraints, and this augmented polyhedron is approximated, as in: $\mathrm{UA}(P) = \cap_{e \in E} \mathrm{UA}(P_e \cap_{v \in V} H_v \cap_{v \in V} N_v)$. The overall approximation is the intersection of $|E|$ one-shot approxiations, and each element in H_V and N_V could be approximated multiple-times.

PD3: Selected augmentation Each P_e is augmented with *its section* of the additional constraints H_u and N_u (for statements u on either side of dependence edge) and the augmented per-dependence polyhedron is approximated. If $e : v_1 \to v_2$, $\mathrm{UA}(P) = \cap_e \mathrm{UA}(P_e \cap H_{v_1} \cap H_{v_2} \cap N_{v_1} \cap N_{v_2})$. The overall approximation is the intersection of $|E|$ one-shot approximations.

PD4: Just Farkas Each P_e is approximated independently, just like in Feautrier's scheduler, while the additional constraints are thrown away. The overall approximation is the intersection of $|E|$ one-shot approximations.

This method clearly does not give an UA. It is meant to better characterize the source of the infeasibility in the previous three methods. Indeed, considering the intersection of UAs of per-dependence, weak-satisfaction constraints we know that the P_e's are homogeneous cones. This tells us that the origin can be used as a seed to build a non-empty approximation.

7. Experimental Results

We conduct systematic experiments, tiling and parallelizing the PolyBench (2.0) [40] with the source-to-source polyhedral optimizer PLuTo (PLuTo-0.6). Subsequent to our experiments, later versions of PolyBench(3.x) have been released, and which have similar numbers. Farkas systems are extracted from PLuTo. We compare the default linear programming calls to PIP [24] with the TVPI-UA and then the UTVPI-UA algorithms. The UTVPI-UA is further relaxed into a constraint graph (or incidence matrix) which is fed to a custom implementation of the Bellman-Ford algorithm.

Note that we still use PIP for the much smaller linear programming problems arising from the feasibility enhancing heuristics. Also, Pluto makes use of PIP in parts unrelated with the scalability of affine scheduling problems: the PIP calls from PLuTo originate from the functions `dep_satisfaction_test` (DS), `get_dep_direction` (DIR) and `find_permutable_hyperplanes` (FPH).

We focus on FPH calls which correspond to affine scheduling problems. There are a lot more calls of the DS and DIR variety when compared to the FPH calls, optimization of the former pair of LP calls is entirely a different problem from the FPH variety in many ways. Primarily, the former need to be *over-approximated* [21, 53] as otherwise, it results in incorrect transformations. The latter of course are the main topic of this paper and need to be *under-approximated* leading to a conservative approximation and perhaps loss of useful schedules.

7.1 Features of the polyhedra

Here we are referring to Table 1.a. The initial three columns refer to the size of the loop nest: L is the number of loops, S the number of statements, and D the number of dependences. The next sets of columns indicate the polyhedral characteristics of the different varieties of calls from PLuTo. As the DS and DIR variety are similar types of calls, they have been summarized together. The remaining 8 columns (Table 1.b) will be discussed in the next section.

The number of polyhedra of different types are indicated in the P columns ($\mathrm{P_{DS}}$, $\mathrm{P_{DIR}}$ and $\mathrm{P_{FPH}}$). As written earlier, there are lot more polyhedral calls of DS/DIR than when compared to FPH. But the former are smaller calls and are linearly dependent on the size of the loop nest. For a particular benchmark and variety of polyhedra (DS/DIR or FPH), n and $\hat{m}$ columns indicate the number of variables (unknowns), and average number of constraints in the particular LP formulation respectively. $\hat{m}_t$ column indicates the average number of TVPI constraints for that benchmark and variety of polyhedra.

DS/DIR As it can be expected, most of the constraints in the DS/DIR polyhedra are TVPI constraints. In these polyhedra, there

[2] If such a query could be made, then it could as well be used to solve for the objective function resulting in the schedule...

	Loop nest			$P_{DS}(1)/P_{DIR}(2)$					P_{FPH}							Median		LP (indep)		PD2		PD4	
Bench	#L	#S	#D	$\#P_1$	$\#P_2$	n	$\hat{m}$	$\hat{m}_t$	#P	n	$\hat{m}$	$\hat{m}_t$	$\widehat{\lVert\mathcal{S}_{m_k}\rVert}$	$\hat{m}_a$	$\hat{m}_u$	YY	YN	YY	YN	YY	YN	YY	YN
adi	12	4	54	90	564	9	20	19	3	20	200	65	5	1844	614	0	3	0	3	0	3	3	0
corcol	12	6	14	38	194	9	17	16	3	22	22	13	5	130	77	1	2	0	3	3	0	3	0
covcol	13	7	26	41	228	15	25	24	3	24	18	14	4	29	55	3	0	3	0	3	0	3	0
dsyr2k	3	1	3	9	18	8	18	17	3	7	8	6	3	11	18	3	0	3	0	3	0	3	0
dsyrk	3	1	3	9	18	8	18	17	3	7	8	7	3	11	18	3	0	3	0	3	0	3	0
fdtd-2d	11	4	48	39	168	10	22	21	3	20	96	35	6	1010	367	0	3	1	2	0	3	3	0
gemver	7	4	13	29	161	6	13	12	2	14	21	15	4	48	47	0	2	2	0	1	1	2	0
jacobi-1d	4	2	10	16	88	7	14	13	2	10	32	14	5	232	104	0	2	0	2	0	2	2	0
jacobi-2d	6	2	14	21	84	9	19	18	3	12	65	15	7	1135	212	0	3	0	3	0	3	3	0
lu	5	2	10	12	60	11	23	22	3	10	35	17	5	232	106	0	3	0	3	0	3	3	0
matmul	3	1	3	9	18	10	21	21	3	9	9	7	4	20	24	3	0	3	0	3	0	3	0
mvt	4	2	11	31	68	6	13	12	2	9	20	12	3	46	52	0	2	2	0	2	0	3	0
seidel	3	1	27	37	162	12	24	23	3	8	33	15	5	168	179	0	3	3	0	0	3	3	0
ssymm	8	3	15	33	126	8	19	19	3	14	15	10	3	22	36	3	0	3	0	3	0	3	0
strmm	3	1	4	8	24	8	17	16	3	7	12	8	3	20	30	0	3	3	0	0	3	3	0
tmm	3	1	3	9	18	10	21	21	3	9	11	8	4	23	30	3	0	3	0	3	0	3	0
																19	26	29	16	24	21	45	0

Table 1. (a) Problem size, Polyhedral and TVPI-ness characteristics, (b) UA effectiveness

is *never* more than 1 constraint per polyhedron which is non-TVPI. In all the cases, whenever a constraint is TVPI, it is *always* a UTVPI constraint, having the same absolute magnitude for the two coefficients, when it has two entries.

FPH In the FPH variety, it can be noticed that the sizes of some of the FPH polyhedra are small and comparable to the DS/DIR polyhedra. This is either the result of a small problem size or because PLuTo uses Fourier-Motzkin elimination, along with a syntactic heuristic to reduce the duplicate constraints. As it can be expected, $\hat{m}_t$, number of TVPI constraints in the original system, is highly benchmark dependent. But, just like in DS/DIR polyhedra, a TVPI constraint is always a UTVPI constraint.

$\widehat{\lVert\mathcal{S}_{m_k}\rVert}$ is the average number of non-zero coefficients in the non-TVPI constraints for that benchmark. It can be seen that this number, though again being benchmark dependent, is a small constant when compared to the dimension size n. $\hat{m}_a$ is the number of constraints in the new (approximated TVPI) system. As seen earlier, $\hat{m}_a = \widehat{\lVert\mathcal{S}_{m_k}\rVert}(\widehat{\lVert\mathcal{S}_{m_k}\rVert} - 1)(m - m_t)/2 + m_t$.

The relative growth of the approximated system with respect to the original one is defined as the ratio between the sum of entries in the $\hat{m}_a$ and $\hat{m}$ columns. We found the average value of this to be 8, meaning that the overall sparsity factor $\hat{s}$ is a little more than 4. Sometimes the growth of the approximated system is significant, but it has to be remembered that $\hat{m}_a$ is the number of constraints without any simplification, while m is obtained after systematic simplification and elimination of duplicates in PLuTo.

For comparison purposes with $\hat{m}_a$, we have added the $\hat{m}_u$ column, which is the average unsimplified system size when the simplification techniques used in PLuTo are turned off. It can be observed that $\hat{m}_u$ and $\hat{m}_a$ are of comparable sizes. Our experience is that when the approximated system undergoes simplification and duplication removal techniques, it leads to a much smaller system, comparable to the one in m columns. Also, asymptotically, the size increase that only depends on sparsity does not matter much.

7.2 UA feasibility

Here we are referring to Table 1.b. These numbers are for TVPI-UA. (The results for UTVPI-UA are similar and are not being given because of space constraint.) These columns refer to the median method discussed in Section 4.1, to the LP based independent method discussed in Section 4.3.2 and the per-dependence methods discussed in Section 6 respectively. All the columns except for the LP-indep method refer to the per-dependence methods. Only the LP-indep method was implemented on the overall Farkas system, one that is obtained after putting together all the individual systems and after simplification by PLuTo.

The PLuTo calls of the FPH variety are for LexMin. In the current table, we discuss the feasibility results only. The columns YY (Yes-Yes), YN (Yes-No), denote the feasibility (Y) or infeasibility (N) of the original and approximated systems respectively. They have been highlighted accordingly. Since the FPH system is used to find an optimization point in the overall system, a YN entry would mean loss of parallelization.

It can be seen that the LP-indep method (29 YY and 16 YN cases or 10 out of 16 PolyBench problems) performs much better than the median method (19 YY and 26 YN cases or 6 out of 16 PolyBench problems). The latter performs not as poorly as the simplicity of the approach would hint to. We expect the incremental method to have much better performance than the current independent method. The results of PD1 (not shown) fare marginally better than the median method. The results of PD2 are close to LP-indep (24 YY and 21 YN cases or 8 out of 16 PolyBench loop nests). Advanced clustering strategy PD3 has not been implemented. PD4 (Just Farkas) gives 100% feasibility preservation results (45 YY and 0 YN), making it quite attractive. The next sections study the impact on compilation time and on the performance of the generated code.

7.3 Scalability comparison: Simplex vs. Bellman-Ford

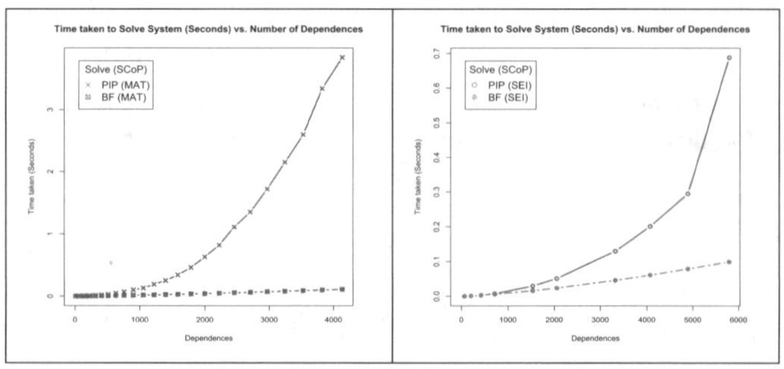

Figure 3. Simplex (PIP) vs. Bellman-Ford (BF)

Figure 3 shows the running times of the Simplex on the original system vs. Bellman-Ford (BF) on a UTVPI approximated system (PD4). The former uses the quite well used dual-simplex implementation of PIP [24] (similar [50] to many LP solvers like CPLEX [11]) called on a *rational polyhedron for feasibility*, while the latter is our own implementation of a standard Bellman-Ford algorithm called for testing for presence of *negative weight cycles*.

The input programs `matmul` and `seidel` are the same as in Figure 1, and each call of `auto_trans` of PLuTo to find schedule hyperplanes has tens of calls of the above variety, which explains the difference in scales. Prior to solving either of these, the duplicates were eliminated using a syntactic matching like currently in PLuTo. Even on the systems with duplicates, the improvements were similar, though being more prominent.

It can be seen from the graphs that for their respective inputs, BF (worst-case $\mathcal{O}(\hat{s}^2mn) \approx \mathcal{O}(|E||V|) \approx \mathcal{O}(|V|^3)$) is asymptotically as well as empirically faster than PIP's Simplex (observed $\mathcal{O}((m+n)mn) \approx \mathcal{O}(|V|^5)$), answering positively the scalability challenge. The regression coefficients (linear R^2) for the above formulae are around 99.9%. The curves for BF appear linear because the x-axis counts the number of dependences, which is practically $\mathcal{O}(|V|^2)$. Though the memory improvements are not shown in the above graphs, the linear memory of BF is considerably lighter than the quadratic memory of Simplex.

The relatively lesser magnitudes and hence lesser improvements of `seidel` when compared to `matmul` could be attributed to the fact that while the former has just uniform dependences which are easily amenable to the Gaussian eliminations of PIP, the latter has more complex affine dependences and also induces many more Farkas multiplier variables.

7.4 UA generated code performance

		Perf. Comparison (Seconds)			
Benchmark	Orig	Par cur	Par new	Til cur	Til new
gemver	0.31	0.15 (2x)	0.15 (2x)	0.15 (2x)	0.15 (2x)
mvt	1.40	0.27 (5x)	0.28 (5x)	0.42 (5x)	0.43 (5x)
seidel	11.8	3.6 (3x)	3.6 (3x)	11.5 (1x)	11.5 (1x)

Table 2. UA Code Performance

We are referring here to Table 2, limiting ourselves to a subset of the YY cases in the previous table that our current implementation could handle; we will later consider all YY and YN cases with a more robust implementation. In each case, we replaced the original system(s) by the approximated TVPI ones obtained by the independent LP method. The cost function was unchanged and the solution was found using PIP. It can be seen that performance gains closely match the default polyhedral method in PLuTo, despite the approximation taking place. The impact of YN approximations on PLuTo's effectiveness is yet to be studied, but we express some hope on PLuTo's loop distribution heuristic to break infeasible systems.

8. Extensions and Related Work

In this section we will first see how our framework can be applied to other (scalability) problems, either in affine scheduling framework or beyond, and then cover some related work.

8.1 Applications to other loop transformation problems

One important strength of our under-approximation framework is its ability to trade precision for scalability using (U)TVPI approximations of polyhedra. Scalability arises from the excellent worst-case complexities of sub-polyhedral operations, and the ability to largely implement the approximation as an independent optimization problem for each dependence-edge. The latter property is another strength of our approach, which happens to be general enough to be applied to other compilation problems, related and unrelated to scheduling.

Darte-Vivien's scheduling As the framework of Feautrier which we build from is the most powerful among the class of algorithms that find affine schedules [56], the LP formulation in Darte-Vivien's scheduling [22] can directly be approximated by our method.

Shifting 1-d loops for pipelining and compaction To solve the cyclic scheduling (decomposed software pipelining) problem, Calland et al. [14] give an LP formulation whose constraint matrix is built from incidence matrices of the original and a retimed dependence graph, and prove it to be a Totally Unimodular (TU) matrix. As given, the formulation is not a (U)TVPI polyhedron having at most 3 non-zero elements per row. But, it can benefit from our framework as the constraints are constructed on a per-dependence-edge basis, and the constraint matrix elements belong to the set $\{0, \pm 1\}$. Darte-Huard's loop shifting for compaction [19] uses a very similar framework to the above paper, where an LP formulation which is a variation of a min-cost flow problem is used, and hence could as well benefit from a (U)TVPI approximation resulting in a strongly polynomial time algorithm.

n-d loop alignment for fusion Darte-Huard show that external shifting in the multi-dimensional loop alignment problem is NP-Complete [20]. They provide an ILP formulation constructed on a per-dependence-edge basis, with 4 variables per constraint and general coefficients (not just $\{0, \pm 1\}$). A possible heuristic for their formulation that builds on our techniques would be to under-approximate each per-edge constraint and to solve the overall system using the Bellman-Ford algorithm. This is correct because rational relaxation and subsequent UA may result in less integer points, but no new ones. The overall UA, if non-empty, can be solved in polynomial time. Further, it can be made to directly result in an integer multi-dimensional shift using the integer scaling discussed earlier in Section 5.5. In this method, an *ILP problem* is solved on a per-P_e-basis, while solving a *normal Bellman-Ford problem* on the overall UA polyhedron resulting in an integer multi-dimensional shift. In this aspect, UTVPI polyhedra are very special, and such a polynomial time shifting algorithm will not be possible even with a TVPI-UA, as solving integer-TVPI polyhedra is known to be NP-Complete [35].

Simpler code generated As seen earlier, by the TU property, a restriction of the homogenizing dimensions to integers can ensure that *all the vertices* of the resultant UTVPI-UA are integers. Using these UAs in scheduling has the additional advantage of simpler code being generated, even with affine schedules generated through (rational) linear programming (PLuTo uses integer linear programming by default). Rational schedule coefficients may indeed induce modulos in loop bounds and conditional expressions of the generated code, a risk completely eliminated with our approach.

8.2 Related work

Feautrier's scalable modular scheduling Feautrier's approach [27] starts with Gaussian elimination, and suggests a Minkowski decomposition (generator representation) of P_e for projection. We consider this approach as complementary to ours in the sense of per-dependence methods, but the use of generator representation makes it less likely to be scalable than ours.

Approximations in loop optimization Previous approaches to approximations in loop optimization concerned themselves with restricting the kinds of input programs or the kinds of transformations being searched for [21, 60]. The most notable examples of the above are the Dependence Levels of Allen and Kennedy [2] and Direction Vectors of Wolf and Lam [59]. Each of the above are less powerful than the affine scheduling model of Feautrier [25]. Our approach tackles the scalability problem from within the affine scheduling model and is more powerful.

(U)TVPI in loop optimization UTVPI polyhedra have previously been used by Balasundaram and Kennedy [7] in task level loop parallelization and pipelining applications, by data dependence analysis, domain simplification and (limited form of) code generation. Their use is similar to the framework of classical dependence over-approximations [21, 53, 60]. Our use of (U)TVPI is more powerful than theirs because of our affine scheduling framework and UA algorithms. Further, Pugh [42] and Maydan et al. [37] also hint that (U)TVPI polyhedra could be solved with better complexity and hence used in dependence analysis citing some statistics from parallelization benchmarks. Our statistics in Table 1.a could be seen as extensions of the above.

(U)TVPI in static analysis General polyhedra are known [31, 33, 38] to be considerably more expensive than (U)TVPI polyhedra for abstract domain operations. Hence, sub-polyhedra have been widely employed in abstract interpretation problems by the static analysis community as a means of trading precision for scalability. A comparison of the use of sub-polyhedra, along with their applicability to polyhedral compilation can be found in [53]. Of the many classes of sub-polyhedra, (U)TVPI polyhedra have extensively been used [6, 38, 47], with impressive results such as in Astrée [12, 17].

Approximations to sub-polyhedra We are not aware of any previous algorithm for finding approximations of general polyhedra into sub-polyhedra other than finding the interval ("box") polyhedral OAs. The literature is scarce about polyhedral approximations and more so for UAs. (The naïve method of projecting out the extra variables on a per-constraint basis using Fourier-Motzkin method leads to an over-approximation with no bound on the complexity.) Vivien-Wicker [57] propose an algorithm to find the parallelepiped-OA of a 3d-polyhedron in vertex representation. Miné [38, Section 4.3] adapts the vertex method for finding the UTVPI-OA of a general polyhedron. Simon et al. [47, Section 3.2.6] propose an iterative algorithm for the TVPI-OA of a general polyhedron using LP. Our algorithm for TVPI-UA in Section 4.3 can be seen as complementary to the latter, though our algorithm formulates the LP problem by searching only for the replacements in the homogenizing dimension.

Feasibility and optimization algorithms The state of the art in feasibility testing for TVPI systems is by Hochbaum-Naor [32], and for optimization of TVPI systems by Wayne [58]. We are not aware of existing implementations of the above algorithms. The state of the art for feasibility and optimization of UTVPI systems is by the well understood Bellman-Ford algorithm [41], which involves constructing a nearly $2m \times 2n$ size constraint graph encoding the difference constraints [23] and testing it for presence of negative weight cycles using the shortest-path problem. The latter has been extensively studied, beginning from [9, 28] to most recently in [15]. Efficient, though closure based methods for the same [6, 38] are available in Apron [34] and PPL [5]. More general forms than ours, like boolean formulae involving UTVPI constraints have been considered in constraint programming, like by Seshia et al. [45].

9. Conclusions and Future Work

We have presented sub-polyhedral scheduling using (U)TVPI polyhedra. We have proposed worst-case polynomial time algorithms to compute (U)TVPI under-approximations from a general convex polyhedron. We have shown initial results of the above approximations as well as their integration in PLuTo. Our experiments clearly indicate an asymptotic improvement in scalability, answering positively the scalability challenge.

To stay within polynomial time, care was taken to linearize the under-approximation model, avoiding the exponential vertex and ray construction associated with the Chernikova algorithm. The most difficult problem is the lack of a scalable way to reliably preserve the non-emptiness of the underapproximation when the original polyhedron is non-empty. The one-shot linear programming method offers this guarantee, but not in strongly polynomial time. We explore different heuristics relying on bounded-size linear programs to trade complexity for feasibility. We know this problem is difficult because a strongly polynomial method with this guarantee could directly lead to a solution of finding strongly polynomial feasibility test for general polyhedra.

The scalability experiments indicate an asymptotic improvement of Bellman-Ford over linear programming. Future experiments should include a fast duplicate elimination, a complete evaluation of the performance impact of the approximation on all PolyBench using an approximated objective function compatible with the Bellman-Ford algorithm, and a complementary study of the memory complexity (known to be overwhelmingly in our favor).

An illustration of the power of our approximation scheme has been shown on important affine scheduling problems. Future work would involve applying the scheme to a wider range of compilation problems, including ILP or mixed-ILP formulations, so that either heuristics with better complexity measures are obtained, or the resulting approximations provide practical improvements on complex systems.

Acknowledgments We are grateful to Paul Feautrier for the tremendously helpful suggestions and insights. We are also thankful to Cédric Bastoul and Armin Größlinger for their feedback at different stages. Our work also benefited from Uday Bondhugula's PLuTo framework, and from the detailed comments from anonymous reviewers. This work was partly supported by the French Nano2012 project Mediacom, in collaboration with STMicroelectronics, and by the European FP7 project CARP id. 287767.

References

[1] R. K. Ahuja, T. L. Magnanti, and J. B. Orlin. *Network flows: theory, algorithms, and applications*. Prentice-Hall, Inc., NJ, USA, 1993.

[2] R. Allen and K. Kennedy. Automatic translation of fortran programs to vector form. *ACM Trans. Program. Lang. Syst.*, 9(4):491–542, Oct. 1987.

[3] A. Andersson and S. Nilsson. Implementing radixsort. *J. Exp. Algorithmics*, 3, Sept. 1998.

[4] B. Aspvall and Y. Shiloach. A polynomial time algorithm for solving systems of linear inequalities with two variables per inequality. *SIAM J. Comput.*, 9(4):827–845, 1980.

[5] R. Bagnara, P. M. Hill, and E. Zaffanella. The Parma Polyhedra Library: Toward a complete set of numerical abstractions for the analysis and verification of hardware and software systems. *Science of Computer Programming*, 72(1–2):3–21, 2008.

[6] R. Bagnara, P. M. Hill, and E. Zaffanella. Weakly-relational shapes for numeric abstractions: improved algorithms and proofs of correctness. *Formal Methods in System Design*, 35(3):279–323, 2009.

[7] V. Balasundaram and K. Kennedy. A technique for summarizing data access and its use in parallelism enhancing transformations. In *PLDI*, pages 41–53, 1989.

[8] U. Banerjee. *Loop Transformations for Restructuring Compilers: The Foundations*. Kluwer Academic Publishers, Boston, 1992.

[9] R. Bellman. On a routing problem. *Quarterly of Applied Mathematics*, 16:87–90, 1958.

[10] M.-W. Benabderrahmane, L.-N. Pouchet, A. Cohen, and C. Bastoul. The polyhedral model is more widely applicable than you think. In *Proceedings of the International Conference on Compiler Construction (ETAPS CC'10)*, number 6011 in LNCS, Paphos, Cyprus, Mar. 2010. Springer-Verlag.

[11] R. E. Bixby. Solving real-world linear programs: A decade and more of progress. *Oper. Res.*, 50(1):3–15, Jan. 2002.

[12] B. Blanchet, P. Cousot, R. Cousot, J. Feret, L. Mauborgne, A. Miné, D. Monniaux, and X. Rival. A static analyzer for large safety-critical software. In *PLDI*, pages 196–207. ACM, 2003.

[13] U. Bondhugula, A. Hartono, J. Ramanujam, and P. Sadayappan. A practical automatic polyhedral parallelizer and locality optimizer. In *PLDI*, pages 101–113, 2008.

[14] P.-Y. Calland, A. Darte, and Y. Robert. Circuit retiming applied to decomposed software pipelining. *IEEE Trans. Parallel Distrib. Syst.*, 9(1):24–35, Jan. 1998.

[15] B. V. Cherkassky, L. Georgiadis, A. V. Goldberg, R. E. Tarjan, and R. F. Werneck. Shortest-path feasibility algorithms: An experimental evaluation. *J. Exp. Algorithmics*, 14:7:2.7–7:2.37, Jan. 2010.

[16] E. Cohen and N. Megiddo. Improved algorithms for linear inequalities with two variables per inequality. *SIAM J. Comput.*, 23:1313–1350, December 1994.

[17] P. Cousot, R. Cousot, J. Feret, L. Mauborgne, A. Miné, and X. Rival. Why does Astrée scale up? *Formal Methods in System Design*, 35(3):229–264, Dec 2009.

[18] G. B. Dantzig. *Linear Programming and Extensions*. Princeton University Press, Princeton, NJ, 1963.

[19] A. Darte and G. Huard. Loop shifting for loop compaction. *Int. J. Parallel Program.*, 28(5):499–534, Oct. 2000.

[20] A. Darte and G. Huard. Complexity of multi-dimensional loop alignment. In *Proceedings of the 19th Annual Symposium on Theoretical Aspects of Computer Science*, STACS '02, pages 179–191, London, UK, UK, 2002. Springer-Verlag.

[21] A. Darte, Y. Robert, and F. Vivien. *Scheduling and Automatic Parallelization*. Birkhaüser, 2000.

[22] A. Darte and F. Vivien. Optimal fine and medium grain parallelism detection in polyhedral reduced dependence graphs. *Int. J. Parallel Program.*, 25:447–496, December 1997.

[23] H. Edelsbrunner, G. Rote, and E. Welzl. Testing the necklace condition for shortest tours and optimal factors in the plane. *Theor. Comput. Sci.*, 66(2):157–180, 1989.

[24] P. Feautrier. Parametric integer programming. *RAIRO Recherche Opérationnelle*, 22(3):243–268, 1988. http://www.piplib.org/.

[25] P. Feautrier. Some efficient solutions to the affine scheduling problem: I. one-dimensional time. *IJPP*, 21:313–348, October 1992.

[26] P. Feautrier. Some efficient solutions to the affine scheduling problem: Part ii: Multidimensional time. *Int. J. Parallel Program.*, 21:389–420, December 1992.

[27] P. Feautrier. Scalable and structured scheduling. *International Journal of Parallel Programming*, 34(5):459–487, 2006.

[28] L. R. Ford, Jr. and D. R. Fulkerson. *Flows in Networks*. Princeton University Press, 1962.

[29] M. Griebl, P. Feautrier, and A. Größlinger. Forward communication only placements and their use for parallel program construction. In W. Pugh and C.-W. Tseng, editors, *LCPC*, volume 2481 of *Lecture Notes in Computer Science*, pages 16–30. Springer, 2002.

[30] T. Grosser, H. Zheng, A. Raghesh, A. Simbürger, A. Größlinger, and L.-N. Pouchet. Polly - Polyhedral Optimization in LLVM. In *IMPACT 2011, in conjunction with CGO 2011*, Chamonix, France, Apr 2011.

[31] N. Halbwachs, D. Merchat, and L. Gonnord. Some ways to reduce the space dimension in polyhedra computations. *Form. Methods Syst. Des.*, 29:79–95, July 2006.

[32] D. S. Hochbaum and J. Naor. Simple and fast algorithms for linear and integer programs with two variables per inequality. *SIAM J. Comput.*, 23(6):1179–1192, 1994.

[33] J. Jaffar, M. J. Maher, P. J. Stuckey, and R. H. C. Yap. Beyond finite domains. In A. Borning, editor, *PPCP*, volume 874 of *Lecture Notes in Computer Science*, pages 86–94. Springer, 1994.

[34] B. Jeannet and A. Miné. Apron: A library of numerical abstract domains for static analysis. In *CAV*, pages 661–667, 2009.

[35] J. C. Lagarias. The computational complexity of simultaneous diophantine approximation problems. *SIAM J. Comput.*, 14(1):196–209, 1985.

[36] A. W. Lim and M. S. Lam. Communication-free parallelization via affine transformations. In *POPL*, pages 201–214, Paris, France, jan 1997.

[37] D. E. Maydan, J. L. Hennessy, and M. S. Lam. Efficient and exact data dependence analysis. In *Proceedings of the ACM SIGPLAN 1991 conference on Programming language design and implementation*, PLDI '91, pages 1–14, New York, NY, USA, 1991. ACM.

[38] A. Miné. The octagon abstract domain. *Higher-Order and Symbolic Computation*, 19(1):31–100, 2006.

[39] L.-N. Pouchet, U. Bondhugula, C. Bastoul, A. Cohen, J. Ramanujam, P. Sadayappan, and N. Vasilache. Loop transformations: convexity, pruning and optimization. In *POPL*, pages 549–562, 2011.

[40] L.-N. Pouchet, U. Bondhugula, et al. The polybench benchmarks. http://www.cse.ohio-state.edu/~pouchet/software/polybench.

[41] V. R. Pratt. Two easy theories whose combination is hard. Technical report, Massachusetts Institute of Technology, Cambridge, Mass, 1977. http://boole.stanford.edu/pub/sefnp.pdf.

[42] W. Pugh. A practical algorithm for exact array dependence analysis. *Commun. ACM*, 35(8):102–114, Aug. 1992.

[43] F. Santos. A counterexample to the hirsch conjecture. *Annals of Mathematics*, 176:383–412, 2012.

[44] A. Schrijver. *Theory of linear and integer programming*. John Wiley & Sons, Inc., New York, NY, USA, 1986.

[45] S. A. Seshia, K. Subramani, and R. E. Bryant. On solving boolean combinations of UTVPI constraints. *Journal on Satisfiability, Boolean Modeling and Computation (JSAT)*, 3(1-2):67–90, 2007.

[46] R. Shostak. Deciding linear inequalities by computing loop residues. *J. ACM*, 28:769–779, October 1981.

[47] A. Simon and A. King. The two variable per inequality abstract domain. *Higher Order Symbol. Comput.*, 23(1):87–143, Mar. 2010.

[48] D. A. Spielman and S.-H. Teng. Smoothed analysis of algorithms: Why the simplex algorithm usually takes polynomial time. *J. ACM*, 51:385–463, May 2004.

[49] A. Tarski. *A decision method for elementary algebra and geometry*. Univ. of California Press, Berkeley, 2nd edition, 1951.

[50] M. J. Todd. The many facets of linear programming. *Mathematical Programming*, 91:417–436, 2002.

[51] K. Trifunovic, A. Cohen, D. Edelsohn, F. Li, T. Grosser, H. Jagasia, R. Ladelsky, S. Pop, J. Sjödin, and R. Upadrasta. Graphite two years after: First lessons learned from real-world polyhedral compilation. In *GCC Research Opportunities Workshop (GROW'10)*, Pisa, Italy, Jan. 2010.

[52] R. Upadrasta. *Scalability Challenges in the Polyhedral Model: An Algorithmic Approach using (Unit-)Two-variable Per Inequality Sub-Polyhedra*. PhD thesis, Université Paris-Sud (11), Orsay, France, January 2013.

[53] R. Upadrasta and A. Cohen. Potential and Challenges of Two-Variable-Per-Inequality Sub-Polyhedral Compilation. In *First International Workshop on Polyhedral Compilation Techniques (IMPACT'11), in conjunction with CGO'11*, Chamonix, France, Apr. 2011.

[54] R. Upadrasta and A. Cohen. A Case for Strongly Polynomial Time Sub-Polyhedral Scheduling Using Two-Variable-Per-Inequality Polyhedra. In *Second International Workshop on Polyhedral Compilation Techniques (IMPACT'12), in conjunction with HiPEAC'12*, Paris, France, Jan. 2012.

[55] N. Vasilache. *Scalable Program Optimization Techniques In The Polyhedral Model*. PhD thesis, Paris-Sud 11 University, Sept. 2007.

[56] F. Vivien. On the optimality of feautrier's scheduling algorithm. *Concurrency and Computation: Practice and Experience*, 15(11-12):1047–1068, 2003.

[57] F. Vivien and N. Wicker. Minimal enclosing parallelepiped in 3d. *Comput. Geom. Theory Appl.*, 29:177–190, November 2004.

[58] K. D. Wayne. A polynomial combinatorial algorithm for generalized minimum cost flow. In *Proceedings of the thirty-first annual ACM symposium on Theory of computing*, STOC '99, pages 11–18, New York, NY, USA, 1999. ACM.

[59] M. E. Wolf and M. S. Lam. A loop transformation theory and an algorithm to maximize parallelism. *IEEE Trans. Parallel Distrib. Syst.*, 2(4):452–471, Oct. 1991.

[60] Y.-Q. Yang, C. Ancourt, and F. Irigoin. Minimal data dependence abstractions for loop transformations. In K. Pingali, U. Banerjee, D. Gelernter, A. Nicolau, and D. A. Padua, editors, *LCPC*, volume 892 of *Lecture Notes in Computer Science*, pages 201–216. Springer, 1994.

[61] G. Ziegler. *Lectures on polytopes*. Graduate texts in mathematics. Springer Science, 2006.

Optimizing Data Structures in High-Level Programs

New Directions for Extensible Compilers based on Staging

Tiark Rompf [*‡] Arvind K. Sujeeth [†] Nada Amin [*] Kevin J. Brown [†] Vojin Jovanovic [*]
HyoukJoong Lee [†] Manohar Jonnalagedda [*] Kunle Olukotun [†] Martin Odersky [*]

[*] EPFL: {first.last}@epfl.ch [‡] Oracle Labs [†] Stanford University: {asujeeth, kjbrown, hyouklee, kunle}@stanford.edu

Abstract

High level data structures are a cornerstone of modern programming and at the same time stand in the way of compiler optimizations. In order to reason about user or library-defined data structures, compilers need to be extensible. Common mechanisms to extend compilers fall into two categories. Frontend macros, staging or partial evaluation systems can be used to programmatically remove abstraction and specialize programs before they enter the compiler. Alternatively, some compilers allow extending the internal workings by adding new transformation passes at different points in the compile chain or adding new intermediate representation (IR) types. None of these mechanisms alone is sufficient to handle the challenges posed by high level data structures. This paper shows a novel way to combine them to yield benefits that are greater than the sum of the parts.

Instead of using staging merely as a front end, we implement internal compiler passes using staging as well. These internal passes delegate back to program execution to construct the transformed IR. Staging is known to simplify program generation, and in the same way it can simplify program transformation. Defining a transformation as a staged IR interpreter is simpler than implementing a low-level IR to IR transformer. With custom IR nodes, many optimizations that are expressed as rewritings from IR nodes to staged program fragments can be combined into a single pass, mitigating phase ordering problems. Speculative rewriting can preserve optimistic assumptions around loops.

We demonstrate several powerful program optimizations using this architecture that are particularly geared towards data structures: a novel loop fusion and deforestation algorithm, array of struct to struct of array conversion, object flattening and code generation for heterogeneous parallel devices. We validate our approach using several non trivial case studies that exhibit order of magnitude speedups in experiments.

Categories and Subject Descriptors D.3.4 [*Programming Languages*]: Processors – Code generation, Optimization, Run-time environments; D.1.3 [*Programming Techniques*]: Concurrent Programming – Parallel programming

General Terms Design, Languages, Performance

Keywords Staging, Code Generation, Data Structures, Extensible Compilers

POPL'13, January 23–25, 2013, Rome, Italy.


```
// Vectors
object Vector {
  def fromArray[T:Numeric](a: Array[T]) =
    new Vector { val data = a }
  def zeros[T:Numeric](n: Int) =
    Vector.fromArray(Array.fill(n)(i => zero[T]))
}
abstract class Vector[T:Numeric] {
  val data: Array[T]
  def +(that: Vector[T]) =
    Vector.fromArray(data.zipWith(that.data)(_ + _))      ...
}
// Matrices
abstract class Matrix[T:Numeric] { ... }
// Complex Numbers
case class Complex(re: Double, im: Double) {
  def +(that: Complex) = Complex(re + that.re, im + that.im)
  def *(that: Complex) = ...
}
// (elided Numeric[Complex] type class implementation)
```

Figure 1. Skeleton of a high-level Scala linear algebra package

1. Introduction

Compiling high-level programs to efficient low-level code is hard, particularly because such programs use and define high-level abstractions. The compiler cannot see through abstractions ("abstraction penalty"), and it cannot reason about domain-specific properties ("general purpose bottleneck"). Among the most important abstractions are data structure and collection operations, and those also commonly present the most difficulties to an optimizing compiler.

Let us consider an example of high level programming in Scala. We would like to implement a dense linear algebra package. Figure 1 shows a skeleton implementation of Vectors and Matrices as a thin layer over Arrays, using high-level collection operations (fill, zipWith) internally. Vectors and Matrices contain numeric values (type class Numeric). We also define Complex numbers as a new numeric type.

With these definitions at hand, we can write programs like the following:

```
def diag(k:Int) = k * Matrix.identity(n)
val m1 = (v1+v2).transpose * (v1+v2)
val m2 = diag(l)
if (scale) println(m1*m2) // == m1*(k*id) == k*m1*id == k*m1
else println(m1)          // no need to compute m2
```

This code is elegant and high level, demonstrating how Scala's focus on abstraction and generalization increases development productivity. But unfortunately the code will run very slowly, one or two orders of magnitude slower than a tuned low-level implementation using just arrays and while loops (see Section 5).

What exactly is going wrong? Some of the reasons are:

1. Neither the Scala compiler nor the just-in-time compiler inside the JVM can apply generic optimizations, like common subexpression or dead code elimination (CSE, DCE), to non-trivial matrix or vector computations.
2. The involved compilers have no notion of domain-specific laws like m*id=m (where m is a matrix and id the identity matrix), which could be used for optimization.
3. Programming in a functional programming style creates lots of intermediate objects.
4. The uniform heap-allocated object representation on the JVM is inefficient for complex numbers.

In order to enable a compiler to reason about programs with high-level abstractions, we need mechanisms to extend the compiler so that it is able to resolve those abstractions. There are two common approaches. The first is to translate the abstractions away before the program reaches the compiler proper, so that the compiler does not need to be aware of them. This is the idea behind macro systems and staging. Partial evaluation (PE) can also be used to specialize programs before they reach the actual compiler. The second option is to teach the compiler new domain-specific rules. Usually, compiler extensibility is understood as a means to add new phases. Some extensible compilers also allow adding new IR types but often it is not clear how new nodes interact with existing generic optimizations.

However, neither of these approaches alone is sufficient to handle the challenges posed by high-level data structures and abstractions. Going back to our example, if all we have is staging or macros, then the expression `m*id`, which is equivalent to `m`, will be expanded into while loops before it even reaches the compiler, so no simplification to `m` can take place. In general, limited forms of simplification can be added (see C++ expression templates [51]) but to be fully effective, the full range of generic compiler optimizations (CSE, constant propagation, etc) would need to be duplicated, too. If on the other hand all we have is a facility to add new compiler passes, then we can add an optimization pass that simplifies `m*id` to `m`, but we need another pass that expands matrix multiplications into loops. These passes need to be implemented as low-level IR to IR transformations, which is much more difficult than the macro or staging approach that can use regular (multi-stage) computation to express the desired target code. Implementing optimizations as separate passes also leads to phase ordering problems if multiple optimizations are added independently.

We argue that what we really want is the best of both worlds: On the one hand, we want to treat operations symbolically so that they can be matched by transformation rules. But on the other hand we also want the power of staging to programmatically define the result of a transformation. In addition to that, we need a way to define transformations independently but avoid phase ordering problems when optimizations are applied.

Contributions In this paper, we present an extensible compiler architecture that solves this challenge, while still keeping the programming effort required to express optimizations and transformations low. Our approach achieves large speedups on high-level programs by fusing collection operations, changing data layout and applying further optimizations on high-level objects, enabled by intermediate languages with staging and a facility to combine independently specified optimizations without phase ordering issues.

To illustrate at a high level how our system works, consider again the linear algebra case. We use staging to obtain an intermediate representation from the initial program. In order to avoid the problems of the pure staging or macro approach, we apply optimizations at different levels, and we combine as many optimizations as possible together in a single pass to avoid many of the traditional phase-ordering problems. Linear algebra optimizations are implemented by the library author as rewrite rules that rewrite symbolic expressions into staged program fragments. The system applies rewriting speculatively using optimistic assumptions and rolls back intermediate transformations when they later turn out to be unsound. This strategy eliminates phase ordering problems that are due to one optimization module having to make pessimistic assumptions about the outcome of another one. Once no further simplification is possible on the linear algebra level, we want to switch to a lower level representation which consists of arrays and loops. We implement this kind of 'lowering' transform as a staged interpreter over the intermediate program. Since the interpreter again uses staging, it constructs a new program and thus acts as a program transformer. By default, this interpreter maps each expression to a structurally equivalent one. The library author extends it to map linear algebra operations to their lower level representation. On this lower level, the system applies another set of optimizations (e.g. loop fusion) in a combined pass, re-applying global optimizations to take advantage of new opportunities exposed by changing the representation. This process can be repeated for any desired number of lowering steps.

In particular, we make the following contributions:

- We use staging to build extensible multi-pass compilers that can also profitably combine modular optimizations into single passes: Staged IR interpreters act as IR transformers and speculative rewriting allows combining independently specified optimization while keeping optimistic assumptions.
- We use a graph-based intermediate representation that may contain structured, compound expressions. Splitting and merging compound expressions allows reusing existing optimization on their pieces (e.g. DCE to remove unused parts of a data structure). This approach extends to powerful data format conversions (e.g. array-of-struct to struct-of-array).
- We present a novel data parallel loop fusion algorithm that uniformly handles horizontal and vertical fusion and also includes asymmetric traversals (`flatMap`, `groupBy`).
- We demonstrate how this compiler architecture can solve tough optimization problems related to data structures in a number of nontrivial case studies.

We build on our previous work on Lightweight Modular Staging (LMS) [39] and highlight similarities and differences to previous work as we go along. The speculative rewriting approach is based on earlier work by Lerner, Grove and Chambers [29].

Organization We start out by reviewing partial evaluation and staging (§2). Insights from this section will help understand how we use staging for program transformation (§3), where we first present symbolic optimizations using speculative rewriting (§3.2) before delving into lowering passes as staged IR interpreters (§3.3). A third transformation we explore is the splitting and merging of compound expressions to reuse existing optimizations (§3.4). We then present how these techniques can be used to perform data structure optimizations (§4): our generic staged struct abstraction (§4.1), which extends to unions and inheritance (§4.2), an array of struct to struct of array transform (§4.3), and loop fusion (§4.4). We then present a set of case studies where our transformations are particularly appealing (§5): linear algebra (§5.1), regular expression matching (§5.2), collection and query operations (§5.3), and string templating (§5.4). Finally we discuss our results (§6), review related work (§6.1) and conclude (§6.2).

2. Background

Many computations can naturally be separated into stages distinguished by frequency of execution or availability of information. Multi-stage programming (MSP, *staging* for short) as established by Taha and Sheard [46] make the stages explicit and allows programmers to delay evaluation of a program expression to a later stage (thus, *staging* an expression). The present stage effectively acts as a code generator that, when run, produces the program of the next stage.

Staging is closely related to partial evaluation [20], which specializes programs to statically known parts of their input. For the purpose of this paper, we can treat partial evaluation (and in particular binding-time analysis (BTA)) as automatic staging and staging as programmer-controlled partial evaluation.

A key difference is that partial evaluation strictly specializes programs and usually comes with soundness guarantees whereas adding staging annotations to a program in an MSP language such as MetaOCaml [7] provides more freedom for composing staged fragments but requires some care so as not to change the computed result.

Much of the research on staging and partial evaluation was driven by the desire to simplify compiler development. For example, specializing an interpreter to a particular program yields a compiled program with the interpreter overhead removed (the first Futamura projection [15]). Self applicable partial evaluators can generate compilers from interpreters and compiler generators.

The exposition in this paper uses Scala and Lightweight Modular Staging (LMS) [39], a library-only staging approach. Contrary to dedicated MSP languages based on quasi quotation, LMS uses only types to distinguish the computational stages. Expressions belonging to the second stage have type Rep[T] in the first stage when yielding a computation of type T in the second stage. Expressions of a plain type T will be evaluated in the first stage and become constants in stage two. The plain Scala type system propagates information about which expressions are staged and thus performs a semi-automatic local BTA. Thus, LMS shares some of the benefits of automatic PE and manual staging.

Example: Zero-Overhead Traversal Abstractions Arrays in Scala are bare JVM arrays which need to be traversed using while loops and indices. The Scala standard library provides an enrichment that adds a foreach method:

```
array foreach { i => println(i) }
```

Adding foreach is achieved using an implicit conversion:

```
implicit def enrichArray[T](a: Array[T]) = new {
  def foreach(f: T => Unit): Unit =
    { var i = 0; while (i < a.length) { f(a(i)); i += 1 } }
}
```

This implementation has non-negligible abstraction overhead (closure allocation, interference with JVM inlining, etc). We would like to tell the compiler, whenever it sees a foreach invocation, to just put the while loop there instead. This is a simple case where macros or staging can help.

Using LMS, we just change the method argument types. Figure 2 shows a set of staged array and vector operations. The LMS framework provides overloaded variants of many operations that lift those operations to work on Rep types, i.e. staged expressions rather than actual data.

It is important to note the difference between types `Rep[A=>B]` (a staged function object) and `Rep[A]=>Rep[B]` (a function on staged values). By using the latter, foreach ensures that the function parameter is always evaluated and unfolded at staging time. Macro systems that only allow lifting expression trees support only types `Rep[A=>B]`. This limits expressiveness and there are no guarantees that higher order functions are evaluated at staging time.

In addition to the LMS framework, we use the Scala-Virtualized compiler [32] which redefines several core language features as method calls and thus makes them overloadable as well. For example, the code

```
// Array
implicit def enrichArray[T](a: Rep[Array[T]]) = new {
  def foreach(f: Rep[T] => Rep[Unit]): Rep[Unit] =
    { var i = 0; while (i < a.length) { f(a(i)); i += 1 } }
  def zipWith(b: Rep[Array[T]])(f: (Rep[T],Rep[T]) => Rep[T]) =
    Array.fill(a.length min b.length) { i => f(a(i), b(i)) }
}
// Vector
trait Vector[T] extends Struct { val data: Array[T] }
implicit def enrichVector[T:Numeric](a: Rep[Vector[T]]) = new {
  def +(b: Rep[Vector[T]]) =
    Vector.fromArray(a.data.zipWith(b.data)(_ + _))       ...
}
// (companion objects define Array.fill and Vector.fromArray)
```

Figure 2. Staged Array and Vector Ops.

```
var i = 0; while (i < n) { i = i + 1 }
```

will be desugared as follows:

```
val i = __newVar(0); __while(i < n, { __assign(i, i + 1) })
```

Methods `__newVar`, `__assign`, `__while` are overloaded to work on Rep types. These methods need to be suitably defined and made available in scope. Scala-Virtualized also provides overloaded field access and object construction methods. In the declaration of vectors or complex numbers, extending `Struct` serves as a marker to automatically lift object construction and field accesses to the domain of Rep types. This means that staged field accesses such as `v.data` are transparently available on `Rep[Vector[T]]` values and (in this case) would return `Rep[Array[T]]` values. Similarly,

```
new Vector { val data = /* type Rep[Array[T]] */ }
```

will return a `Rep[Vector[T]]` object.

Generic Programming with Type Classes Figure 2 uses the type class `Numeric` to abstract over particular numeric types. The type class pattern [55], which decouples data objects from generic dispatch fits naturally with a staged programming model. We can define a staged variant of the standard `Numeric` type class and, with addition on numeric vectors defined in Figure 2, make vectors themselves instance of Numeric:

```
class Numeric[T] { def num_plus[T](a:Rep[T],b:Rep[T]): Rep[T] }
implicit def vecIsNumeric[T:Numeric] = new Numeric[Vector[T]] {
  def num_plus(a: Rep[Vector[T], b: Rep[Vector[T]]) = a + b
}
```

This allows us to pass, say, a staged `Vector[Int]` to any function that works over generic types `T:Numeric`, such as vector addition itself. The same holds for `Vector[Vector[Int]]`. Without staging, type classes are implemented by passing an implicit dictionary, the type class instance, to generic functions. Here, type classes are a purely stage-time concept. All generic code is specialized to the concrete types and no type class instances exist (and hence no virtual dispatch occurs) when the staged program is run.

Maintaining Evaluation Order Compared to staging or macro systems based on quasi quotation, LMS preserves program semantics in more cases. In particular, adding Rep types does not change the relative evaluation order of statements within a stage. In

```
compute() foreach { i => println(i) }
```

the staged foreach implementation from Figure 2 will evaluate compute() only once, whereas purely syntactic expansion would produce this target code:

```
while (i < compute().length) { println(compute()(i)); i += 1 }
```

LMS performs on-the fly ANF conversion, similar to earlier work on PE with effects [49]. Systems based on quasi quotation could profitably use the same method to maintain evaluation order but we are unaware of any sustem that does. Instead, most other systems leave it up to the programmer to insert let-bindings in the right places, which can easily lead to subtle errors.

Limitations of Front-End Staging and Macros Despite the given benefits, for top performance it is often not sufficient to use staging (or macros, or partial evaluation) as a front end. Let us consider a simple yet non-trivial example:

```
val v1 = ...
v1 + Vector.zeros(n)
```

Staging will replace the zero vector creation and the subsequent addition with arrays and loops. What we would like instead, however, is to apply a symbolic simplification rule v+zero->v to remove the zero addition before expansion takes place.

Let us imagine that our system would allow us to implement the vector plus operation in such a way that it can inspect its arguments to look for invocations of `Vector.zeros`. This would cover the simple case above but we would still run into problems if we complicate the use case slightly:

```
val v1 = ...
val v2 = Vector.zeros(n)
v1 + v2
```

To handle programs like this, it is not sufficient to just inspect the (syntactic) arguments. We need to integrate the staging expansion with some form of forward data flow propagation, otherwise the argument to plus is just an identifier.

The deeper problem is that we are forced to commit to a single data representation. Even if we combine staging with an extensible compiler we need to make a decision: Should we treat vectors as symbolic entities with algebraic laws, implemented as IR nodes amenable to optimization? Or should we stage them so that the compiler sees just loops and arrays without abstraction overhead?

The following sections will discuss mechanisms to integrate these approaches and for treating data structures in a more abstract way.

3. Program Transformation via Staging

Staging usually is a method for generating programs: A multi-stage program builds an object program which is then compiled normally again. We show that staging is also useful as a tool for transforming programs. Any transformation can be broken down into a traversal and a generation part. Not surprisingly, staging helps with the generation part. In our case, internal compiler passes are IR interpreters that happen to be staged so that they return a new program as the result. This way they can delegate back to program execution to build the result of a program transformation.

Staging for program transformation has a number of benefits. First, building a (staged) IR interpreter is far simpler than building a non-trivial IR to IR transformer. Second, optimizations can be added gradually to a staged program, starting, e.g., with the code from Figure 2. Third, the program (or library) itself is in control of the translation and can influence what kind of code is generated.

One of the key aspects of our approach is to distinguish two kinds of transforms: Optimizations and Lowerings. Lowerings translate programs into a lower-level representation (e.g. linear algebra operations into arrays and loops). Lowerings have a natural ordering so they can be profitably arranged in separate passes. Optimizations, by contrast, have no clear ordering and are prone to phase ordering problems. Thus, they need to be combined for maximum effectiveness. Also, most lowerings are mandatory whereas optimizations are usually optional. Of course the distinction is not always clear cut but many transforms fall into only one of the categories. In any case, it is important that all applicable optimizations are applied exhaustively before lowering takes place. Otherwise, high-level optimization opportunities may be missed. After a lowering step, there may be new opportunities for optimization. Thus, our system performs a sequence of optimization, lowering, optimization steps, until the lowest-level representation is reached. The final representation is unparsed to target code.

We recap the LMS extensible IR (§3.1) and first consider optimizations (§3.2), then lowerings (§3.3). Afterwards we descibe the treatment of compound expressions (§3.4).

3.1 The LMS Extensible Graph IR

We now turn to the level of 'primitive' staged operations. Using LMS we do not directly produce the second stage program in source form but instead as an extensible intermediate representation (IR). We refer the reader to our previous work for details on the IR [37–39, 41] but give a short recap here. The overall structure is that of a "sea of nodes" dependency graph [9].

In Figure 3, which will be the running example for this section, we recast the vector implementation from Figure 2 in terms of custom IR nodes. The user-facing interface is defined in trait `Vectors`, with abstract methods (vec_zeros, vec_plus) that are implemented in trait `VectorsExp` to create IR nodes of type `VectorZeros` and `VectorPlus`, respectively.

The framework provides IR base classes via trait `BaseExp`, mixed into `VectorsExp` (but not `Vectors`, to keep the IR hidden from user code). Expressions are atomic:

```
abstract class Exp[T]
case class Const[T](x: T) extends Exp[T]
case class Sym[T](n: Int) extends Exp[T]
```

Trait `BaseExp` defines `Rep[T]=Exp[T]`, whereas `Rep[T]` is left as an abstract type in trait `Base`.

Custom (composite) IR nodes extend `Def[T]`. They refer to other IR nodes only via symbols. There is also a type `Block[T]` to define nested blocks (not used in Figure 3). Taking a closer look at vec_zero reveals that its expected return type is `Exp[T]` but the result value is of type `Def[T]`. This conversion is achieved implicitly by `toAtom`:

```
implicit def toAtom[T](d: Def[T]): Exp[T] = reflectPure(d)
```

Method `reflectPure` maintains the correct evaluation order by binding the argument d to a fresh symbol (on the fly ANF conversion).

```
def reflectPure[T](d: Def[T]): Sym[T]
def reifyBlock[T](b: =>Exp[T]): Block[T]
```

The counterpart `reifyBlock` (note the by-name argument) captures performed statements into a block object. Additional reflect methods exist to mark IR nodes with various kinds of side effects (see [41] for details).

3.2 Combining Optimizations: Speculative Rewriting

Many optimizations that are traditionally implemented using an iterative dataflow analysis followed by a transformation pass can also be expressed using various flavors of (possibly context dependent) rewriting. Whenever possible we tend to prefer a rewriting variant because rewrite rules are easy to specify separately and do not require programmers to define abstract interpretation lattices.

Rewrites and Smart Constructors LMS performs forward optimizations eagerly while constructing the IR. Hash-consing implements CSE and smart constructors apply pattern rewriting, including various kinds of constant propagation. This can be seen as adding "online" PE to the existing "offline" stage distinction defined by Rep types [42, 45]. In Figure 3, trait `VectorsExpOpt` can be mixed in with `VectorsExp` and overrides vec_plus to simplify zero additions. Rewriting is integrated with other forward optimizations: Pattern matches of the form `case Def(VectorZeros(n)) => ...` will look up the available definition of a symbol. Here is a simple example program, before (left) and after constant folding (middle):

```
val x = 3 * y        val x = 3 * y        println(6 * y)
println(2 * x)       println(6 * y)
```

DCE will later remove the multiplication and the binding for x (right).

```scala
// Vector interface
trait Vectors extends Base {
  // elided implicit enrichment boilerplate:
  //   Vector.zeros(n) = vec_zeros(n), v1 + v2 = vec_plus(a,b)
  def vec_zeros[T:Numeric](n: Rep[Int]): Rep[Vector[T]]
  def vec_plus[T:Numeric](a: Rep[Vector[T]], b: Rep[Vector[T]]): Rep[Vector[T]]
}
// low level translation target
trait VectorsLowLevel extends Vectors {
  def vec_zeros_ll[T:Numeric](n: Rep[Int]): Rep[Vector[T]] =
    Vector.fromArray(Array.fill(n) { i => zero[T] })
  def vec_plus_ll[T:Numeric](a: Rep[Vector[T]], b: Rep[Vector[T]]) =
    Vector.fromArray(a.data.zipWith(b.data)(_ + _))
}
// IR level implementation
trait VectorsExp extends BaseExp with Vectors {
  // IR node definitions and constructors
  case class VectorZeros(n: Exp[Int]) extends Def[Vector[T]]
  case class VectorPlus(a: Exp[Vector[T]],b: Exp[Vector[T]]) extends Def[Vector[T]]
  def vec_zeros[T:Numeric](n: Rep[Int]): Rep[Vector[T]] = VectorZeros(n)
  def vec_plus[T:Numeric](a: Rep[Vector[T]], b: Rep[Vector[T]]) = VectorPlus(a,b)
  // mirror: transformation default case
  def mirror[T](d: Def[T])(t: Transformer) = d match {
    case VectorZeros(n) => Vector.zeros(t.transformExp(n))
    case VectorPlus(a,b) => t.transformExp(a) + t.transformExp(b)
    case _ => super.mirror(d)
  }
}
// optimizing rewrites (can be specified separately)
trait VectorsExpOpt extends VectorsExp {
  override def vec_plus[T:Numeric](a:Rep[Vector[T]],b:Rep[Vector[T]])=(a,b)match{
    case (a, Def(VectorZeros(n))) => a
    case (Def(VectorZeros(n)), b) => b
    case _ => super.vec_plus(a,b)
  }
}
// transformer: IR -> low level impl
trait LowerVectors extends ForwardTransformer {
  val IR: VectorsExp with VectorsLowLevel; import IR._
  def transformDef[T](d: Def[T]): Exp[T] = d match {
    case VectorZeros(n) => vec_zeros_ll(transformExp(n))
    case VectorPlus(a,b) => vec_plus_ll(transformExp(a), transformExp(b))
    case _ => super.transformDef(d)
  }
}
```

Figure 3. Vector Implementation with IR and Lowering.

Applying Rewrites Speculatively Many optimizations are mutually beneficial. In the presence of loops, optimizations need to make optimistic assumptions for the supporting analysis to obtain best results. If multiple analyses are run separately, each of them effectively makes pessimistic assumptions about the outcome of all others. Combined analyses avoid the phase ordering problem by solving everything at the same time. The challenge, of course, is to automatically combine analyses and transformations that are implemented independently of one another.

Since the forward optimizations described above are applied at IR construction time where loop information is incomplete, LMS previously allowed rewrites and CSE only for purely functional operations and not in the presence of imperative loops. These pessimistic assumptions, together with monolithic compound expressions (see Section 3.4) prevented effective combinations of separate rewrites.

Lerner, Grove, and Chambers showed a method of composing separately specified optimizations by interleaving analyses and transformations [29]. We use a modified version of their algorithm that works on structured loops instead of CFGs and using dependency information and rewriting instead of explicit data flow lattices. To the best of our knowledge, we are the first to extend this approach to extensible compilers and a purely rewriting based environment. Usually, rewriting is semantics preserving, i.e. pessimistic. The idea is to drop that assumption. As a corollary, we need to rewrite speculatively and be able to rollback to a previous state to get optimistic optimization. The algorithm proceeds as follows: for each encountered loop, apply all possible transforms to the loop body, given empty initial assumptions. Analyze the result of the transformation: if any new information is discovered throw away the transformed loop body and retransform the original with updated assumptions. Repeat until the analysis result has reached a fixpoint and keep the last transformation as result. This process can be costly for deeply nested loops, but compares favorably to the alternative of running independent transformations one after another until a global fixpoint is reached [29].

Here is an example of speculative rewriting, showing the untransformed program (left), the initial optimistic iteration (middle), and the fixpoint (right) reached after the second iteration:

```scala
var x = 7                    var x = 7          var x = 7 //dead
var c = 0                    var c = 0          var c = 0
while (c < 10) {             while (true) {     while (c < 10) {
  if (x < 10) print("!")       print("!")         print("!")
  else x = c                   print(7)           print(7)
  print(x)                     print(0)           print(c)
  print(c)                     c = 1              c += 1
  c += 1                     }                  }
}
```

This algorithm allows us to do all forward data flow analyses and transforms in one uniform, combined pass driven by rewriting. In the example above, during the initial iteration (middle), separately specified rewrites for variables and conditionals work together to determine that x=c is never executed. At the end of the loop body we discover the write to c, which invalidates our initial optimistic assumption c=0. We rewrite the original body again with the new information (right). This time there is no additional knowledge discovered so the last speculative rewrite becomes the final one.

Speculative rewriting as used here is still a fully static transform– not to be confused with speculative dynamic optimizations performed inside virtual machines that may incur multiple profiling, compilation and deoptimization cycles.

3.3 Separate Lowering Passes: Transformers

Previously LMS had a single code generation pass that scheduled the IR graph, performing DCE and code motion. We generalize this facility to allow arbitrary traversals of the program tree which results from scheduling the IR graph. Similar to other optimizations, DCE and code motion work on high-level (possibly composite) IR nodes.

Generic IR Traversal and Transformation Once we have a traversal abstraction, transformation falls out naturally by building a traversal that constructs a new staged program. The implementation is shown in Figure 4. Transformation needs a default case, which we call *mirroring* (see trait `VectorsExp` in Figure 3). Mirroring an IR node will call back to the corresponding smart constructor, after applying a transformer to its arguments. Mirroring loops is slightly more complicated than what is shown in Figure 3 because of the bound variable:

```scala
case ArrayFill(n,i,y) =>
  Array.fill(transformExp(n), { j =>
    t.withSubst(i -> j) { transformBlock(y) } }
```

Implementing Custom Transformers In our running example, we would like to treat linear algebra operations symbolically first, with individual IR nodes like `VectorZeros` and `VectorPlus`. In Figure 3, the smart constructor `vec_plus` implements a rewrite that simplifies V+Z to V. CSE, DCE, etc. will all be performed on these high level nodes.

After all those optimizations are applied, we want to transform our operations to the low-level array implementation from Figure 2 in a separate lowering pass. Trait `LowerVectors` in Figure 3 implements this transformation by delegating back to user-space code,

```
// traversal
trait ForwardTraversal {
  val IR: Expressions; import IR._
  def traverseBlock[T](b: Block[T]): Unit =
    focusExactScope(block) { stms =>
      stms foreach traverseStm }
  def traverseStm[T](s: Stm[T]): Unit =
    blocks(stm.rhs) foreach traverseBlock
}
// transform
trait ForwardTransformer extends ForwardTraversal {
  val IR: Expressions; import IR._
  var subst: Map[Exp[_],Exp[_]]
  def transformExp[T](s: Exp[T]): Exp[T] = // lookup s in subst
  def transformBlock[T](b: Block[T]): Exp[T] = scopeSubst {
    traverseBlock(b); transformExp(b.res) }
  def transformDef[T](d: Def[T]): Exp[T] = mirror(d, this)
  override def traverseStm(s: Stm[T]) = {
    val e = transformDef(s.rhs); subst += (s.sym -> e); e }
}
```

Figure 4. Traversal and Transformer Interface.

namely method `vec_plus_ll` in trait `VectorsLowLevel`. The result of the transform is a staged program fragment just like in Figure 2.

This setup greatly simplifies the definition of the lowering transform, which would otherwise need to assemble the `fill` or `zipWith` code using low level IR manipulations. Instead we benefit directly from the staged `zipWith` definition from Figure 2. Also, further rewrites will take place automatically. Essentially all simplifications are performed eagerly, after each transform phase. Thus we guarantee that CSE, DCE, etc. have been applied on high-level operations before they are translated into lower-level equivalents, on which optimizations would be much harder to apply. To give a quick example, the initial program

```
val v1 = ...
val v2 = Vector.zeros(n)
val v3 = v1 + v2
v1 + v3
```

will become

```
val v1 = ...
Vector.fromArray(v1.data.zipWith(v1.data)(_ + _))
```

after lowering (modulo unfolding of staged zipWith).

Worklist Transformers and Delayed Rewriting Transformers can be extended with a worklist, which is useful if the result may contain terms that need further transformation. With a worklist transformer, we can register individual rewrites for particular nodes. Running the transformer applies the rewrites, which may register new replacements for the next iteration. The process stops if no further work is required (empty work list).

Delayed rewriting is a simplified interface that allows specifying lowerings together with the operations and the regular immediate rewrites. This helps to reduce the boilerplate needed to define transformations. For example, here is the `VectorZeros` lowering from Figure 3 recast as delayed rewrite:

```
def vec_zeros[T:Numeric](n: Rep[Int]) =
  VectorZeros(n) atPhase(lowering) {
    Vector.fromArray(Array.fill(n) { i => zero[T] })
  }
```

The `atPhase` block is registered with worklist transformer `lowering`. Before lowering, the IR node remains a `VectorZeros` node, which allows other smart constructor rewrites to kick in that expect this pattern.

3.4 Compound Expressions: Split and Merge

Since our IR contains structured expressions like loops and conditionals, optimizations need to reason about compound statements. This is not easy: for example, a simple DCE algorithm will not be able to remove only pieces of a compound expression. Our solution is simple yet effective: We eagerly split many kinds of compound statements, assuming optimistically that only parts will be needed. Splitting is implemented just like any other rewrite, and thus integrates well with other unrelated optimizations (see Section 3.2). We find out which parts are needed through the regular DCE algorithm and afterwards, we reassemble the remaining pieces.

Effectful Statements A good example of statement splitting is effectful conditionals:

```
var a, b, c = ...      var a, b, c = ...      var a, c = ...
if (c) {               if (c)  a = 9          if (c) a = 9
  a = 9; b = 1         if (c)  b = 1          else   c = 3
} else                 if (!c) c = 3          println(a+c)
  c = 3                println(a+c)
println(a+c)
```

From the conditional in the initial program (left), splitting creates three separate expressions, one for each referenced variable (middle). DCE removes the middle one because variable b is not used, and the remaining conditionals are merged back together (right). Of course successful merging requires to keep track of how expressions have been split. An extension of this simple merge facility which attempts to merge expressions that may not have been split before is loop fusion (Section 4.4).

Data Structures Splitting is also very effective for data structures, as often only parts of a data structure are used or modified. This will be discussed in more detail in Section 4 below but here is already a quick example. Assume c1 and c2 are complex numbers:

```
val c3 = if (test) c1 else c2
println(c3.re)
```

The conditional will be split for each field of a struct. Internally the above will be represented as:

```
val c3re = if (test) c1re else c2re
val c3im = if (test) c1im else c2im    // dead
val c3 = Complex(c3re, c3im)           // dead
println(c3re)
```

The computation of the imaginary component as well as the struct creation for the result of the conditional are never used and thus they will be removed by DCE.

4. Data Structure Optimizations

High level data structures are a cornerstone of modern programming and at the same time stand in the way of compiler optimizations. We illuminate the main issues compilers have with data structures as used by the two dominant programming paradigms.

OOP Object oriented programming treats every data value as an object. This is a powerful pattern that makes it easy to extend languages with new functionality. In Scala, e.g., it is easy to add a complex number class. But there is a price to be paid: allocating each complex number as a separate object will not perform well. Furthermore, if we are working with arrays of complex numbers we get much better performance if we use a struct of array representation. Staging and embedded compilers allow us to abstract away the object abstraction and reason about individual pieces of data that objects are composed of and possibly rearrange that data in more efficient ways.

FP Functional programs create lots of intermediate results. This is particularly bad for collection operations. Theoretically, compilers can leverage referential transparency. But impure functional languages need sophisticated effects analysis, which is hard if there is a lot of abstraction. Our staged programs are much simpler because abstraction is stripped away. We can do better and simpler effects analysis. A simple liveness analysis can turn copying into in-place modification. A novel loop fusion algorithm (data parallel and asymmetric, includes `flatMap` and `groupBy`) removes many intermediate results (Section 4.4).

```
// generic struct interface
trait StructExp extends BaseExp {
  abstract class StructTag
  case class Struct[T](tag: StructTag, elems: Map[String,Rep[Any]]) extends Def[T]
  case class Field[T](struct: Rep[Any], key: String) extends Def[T]
  def struct[T](tag: StructTag, elems: Map[String,Rep[Any]]) = Struct(tag, elems)
  def field[T](struct: Rep[Any], key: String): Rep[T] = struct match {
    case Def(Struct(tag, elems)) => elems(key).asInstanceOf[Rep[T]]
    case _ => Field[T](struct, key)
  }
}
// splitting array construction
case class ArraySoaTag(base: StructTag, len: Exp[Int]) extends StructTag
override def arrayFill[T](size: Exp[Int], v: Sym[Int], body: Def[T]) = body match {
  case Block(Def(Struct(tag, elems))) =>
    struct[T](ArraySoaTag(tag,size),
      elems.map(p => (p._1, arrayFill(size, v, Block(p._2)))))
  case _ => super.arrayFill(size, v, body)
}
// splitting array access
override def infix_apply[T](a: Rep[Array[T]], i: Rep[Int]) = a match {
  case Def(Struct(ArraySoaTag(tag,len),elems)) =>
    struct[T](tag, elems.map(p => (p._1, infix_apply(p._2, i))))
  case _ => super.infix_apply(a,i)
}
override def infix_length[T](a: Rep[Array[T]]): Rep[Int] = a match {
  case Def(Struct(ArraySoaTag(tag, len), elems)) => len
  case _ => super.infix_length(a)
}
```

Figure 5. Generic Struct interface and SoA Transform.

4.1 A Generic Struct Interface

Product types, i.e. records or structs are one of the core data structure building blocks. It pays off to have a generic implementation that comes with common optimizations (Figure 5). Trait `StructExp` defines two IR node types for struct creation and field access. The struct creation node takes a hash map that relates (static) field identifiers with (dynamic) values and a `tag` that can hold further information about the data representation. The method `field` tries to look up the desired value directly if the argument is a Struct node. With this struct abstraction we can implement the data structure splitting and merging example from Section 3.4 by overriding the if-then-else smart constructor to create a conditional for each field in a struct.

4.2 Unions and Inheritance

The struct abstraction can be extended to sum types and inheritance using a tagged union approach [21, 34]. We add a `clzz` field to each struct that refers to an expression that defines the object's class. Being a regular struct field, it is subject to all common optimizations. We extend the complex number example with two subtraits:

```
trait Complex
trait Cartesian extends Complex with Struct {
  val re: Double; val im: Double }
trait Polar extends Complex with Struct {
  val r: Double; val phi: Double }
```

Splitting transforms work as before: e.g. conditional expressions are forwarded to the fields of the struct. But now the result struct will contain the union of the fields found in the two branches, inserting null values as appropriate. A conditional is created for the `clzz` field only if the exact class is not known at staging time. Given straightforward factory methods `Cartesian` and `Polar`, the expression

```
val a = Cartesian(1.0, 2.0); val b = Polar(3.0, 4.0)
if (x > 0) a else b
```

produces this generated code:

```
val (re, im, r, phi, clzz) =
  if (x > 0) (1.0, 2.0, null, null, classOf[Cartesian])
  else (null, null, 3.0, 4.0, classOf[Polar])
struct("re"->re, "im"->im, "r"->r, "phi"->phi, "clzz"->clzz)
```

The `clzz` fields allows virtual dispatch via type tests and type casting, e.g. to convert any complex number to its cartesian representation:

```
def infix_toCartesian(c: Rep[Complex]) : Rep[Cartesian] =
  if (c.isInstanceOf[Cartesian]) c.asInstanceOf[Cartesian]
  else { val p = c.asInstanceOf[Polar]
    Cartesian(p.r * cos(p.phi), p.r * sin(p.phi)) }
```

Appropriate rewrites ensure that if the argument is known to be a Cartesian, the conversion is a no-op. The type test that inspects the clzz field is only generated if the type cannot be determined statically. If the clzz field is never used it will be removed by DCE.

4.3 Struct of Array and Other Data Format Conversions

A natural extension of the splitting mechanism is a generic array-of-struct to struct-of-array transform (AoS to SoA). The mechanism is analogous to that for conditionals. We override the array constructor `arrayFill` that represents expressions of the form `Array.fill(n) { i => body }` to create a struct with an array for each component of the body if the body itself is a Struct (Figure 5). Note that we tag the result struct with an `ArraySoaTag` to keep track of the transformation. We also override the methods that are used to access array elements and return the length of an array to do the right thing for transformed arrays.

The SoA data layout is beneficial in many cases. Consider for example calculating complex conjugates (i.e. swapping the sign of the imaginary components) over a vector of complex numbers.

```
def conj(c: Rep[Complex]) = if (c.isCartesian) {
    val c2 = c.toCartesian; Cartesian(c.re,-c.im)
  } else { val c2 = c.toPolar; Polar(c.r, -c.phi) }
```

To make the test case more interesting we perform the calculation only in one branch of a conditional:

```
val vector1 = Array.fill(100) { i => Cartesian(...) }
if (test) vector1.map(conj) else vector1
```

All the real parts remain unchanged so the array holding them need not be touched at all. Only the imaginary parts have to be transformed, cutting the total required memory bandwidth in half. Uniform array operations like this are also a much better fit for SIMD execution. The generated intermediate code is:

```
val vector1re,vector1im = ...
val vector1clzz = // array holding classOf[Cartesian] values
val vector2im = if (test) Array.fill(vector1size) {
  i => -vector1im(i) } else vector1im
struct(ArraySoaTag(Complex, vector1size),
  Map("re"->vector1re,"im"->vector2im,"clzz"->vector1clzz))
```

Note how the conditionals for the "re" and "clzz" fields have been eliminated since the fields do not change (the initial array contains cartesian numbers only). If the `struct` expression will not be referenced in the final code DCE removes the "clzz" array.

In the presence of conditionals that produce array elements of different types, a possible optimization would be to use a sparse representation for the arrays that make up the result SoA (similar to DPH [21]). However, all the usual sparse vs dense tradeoffs apply.

One concern with data representation conversions is what happens if an array is returned from a staged code fragment to the enclosing program. In this case, the compiler will generate conversion code to return a plain array-of-struct copy of the data.

4.4 Loop Fusion and Deforestation

The use of independent and freely composable traversal operations such as `v.map(..).sum` is preferable to explicitly coded loops. However, naive implementations of these operations would be expensive and entail lots of intermediate data structures. We present a novel loop fusion algorithm for data parallel loops and traversals. The core loop abstraction is

$$\texttt{loop(s)}\ \overline{\texttt{x} = \mathcal{G}}\ \{\ \texttt{i} \Rightarrow \overline{E[\texttt{x} \leftarrow \texttt{f(i)}]}\ \}$$

Generator kinds: $\mathcal{G}$ ::= Collect | Reduce($\oplus$) | Bucket($\mathcal{G}$)
Yield statement: xs ← x
Contexts: $E[.]$ ::= loops and conditionals

Horizontal case (for all types of generators):

```
loop(s) x1=G1 { i1 => E1[ x1 ← f1(i1) ] }
loop(s) y1=G2 { i2 => E2[ x2 ← f2(i2) ] }
──────────────────────────────────────────
loop(s) x1=G1, x2=G2 { i =>
    E1[ x1 ← f1(i) ]; E2[ x2 ← f2(i) ] }
```

Vertical case (consume collect):

```
loop(s) x1=Collect { i1 => E1[ x1 ← f1(i1) ] }
loop(x1.size) x2=G { i2 => E2[ x2 ← f2(x1(i2)) ] }
──────────────────────────────────────────
loop(s) x1=Collect, x2=G { i =>
    E1[ x1 ← f1(i); E2[ x2 ← f2(f1(i)) ]] }
```

Vertical case (consume bucket collect):

```
loop(s) x1=Bucket(Collect) { i1 =>
    E1[ x1 ← (k1(i1), f1(i1)) ] }
loop(x1.size) x2=Collect { i2 =>
  loop(x1(i2).size) y=G { j =>
    E2[ y ← f2(x1(i2)(j)) ] }; x2 ← y }
──────────────────────────────────────────
loop(s) x1=Bucket(Collect), x2=Bucket(G) { i =>
  E1[ x1 ← (k1(i), f1(i));
    E2[ x2 ← (k1(i), f2(f1(i))) ]] }
```

Figure 6. Loop fusion.

where s is the size of the loop and i the loop variable ranging over $[0, s)$. A loop can compute multiple results $\overline{x}$, each of which is associated with a generator $\mathcal{G}$. There are three kinds of generators: Collect, which creates a flat array-like data structure, Reduce($\oplus$), which reduces values with the associative operation $\oplus$, or Bucket($\mathcal{G}$), which creates a nested data structure, grouping generated values by key and applying $\mathcal{G}$ to those with matching key. Loop bodies consist of *yield* statements x←f(i) that pass values to generators (of this loop or an outer loop), embedded in some outer context $E[.]$ that might consist of other loops or conditionals. Note that a yield statement x←.. does not introduce a binding for x, but passes a value to the generator identified by x. For Bucket generators, yield takes (key,value) pairs.

This model is expressive enough to represent many common collection operations:

```
x=v.map(f)      loop(v.size) x=Collect   { i => x ← f(v(i)) }
x=v.sum         loop(v.size) x=Reduce(+) { i => x ← v(i) }
x=v.filter(p)   loop(v.size) x=Collect   { i => if (p(v(i)))
                                                   x ← v(i) }
x=v.flatMap(f)  loop(v.size) x=Collect   { i => val w = f(v(i))
                                     loop(w.size) { j => x ← w(j) }}
x=v.distinct    loop(v.size) x=Bucket(Reduce(rhs)) { i =>
                                                x ← (v(i), v(i)) }
```

Operation distinct uses a bucket reduction with function rhs, which returns the right-hand side of a tuple element, to return a flat sequence that contains only the rightmost occurence of a duplicate element.

Other operations are accommodated by generalizing slightly. Instead of implementing a groupBy operation that returns a sequence of (Key, Seq[Value]) pairs we can return the keys and values in separate data structures. For a given selector function f that computes a key from a value, the equivalent of (ks,vs)=v.groupBy(f).unzip is:

```
loop(v.size) ks=Bucket(Reduce(rhs)),vs=Bucket(Collect) { i =>
  ks ← (f(v(i)), v(i)); vs ← (f(v(i)), v(i)) }
```

This loop ranges over the size of v and produces two result collections ks, a flat sequence of keys, and vs, a nested collections of values that belong to the key in ks at the same index.

The fusion rules are summarized in Figure 6. Fusion of two loops is only permitted if there are no other dependencies between the loops, for example caused by side effects. Since we are working with a graph-based IR, dependency information is readily available. Vertical fusion, which absorbs a consumer loop into the producer loop, is only permitted if the consumer loop does not have any dependencies on its loop variable other than acessing the consumed collection at this index. In a data parallel setting, where loops are chunked, the producer may not be able to compute the exact index of an element in the collection it is building. Multiple instances of f1(i) are subject to CSE and not evaluated twice. Substituting x1(i2) with f1(i) will remove a reference to x1. If x1 is not used anywhere else, it will also be subject to DCE. Within fused loop bodies, unifying index variable i and substituting references will trigger the usual forward rewriting and simplification. Thus, fusion not only removes intermediate data structures but also provides additional optimization opportunities inside fused loop bodies (including fusion of nested loops).

```
def preferences(ratings: Rep[Matrix[Int]],
                sims: Rep[Matrix[Double]]) = {
  sims.mapRowsToVector { testProfile =>
    val num = sum(0, ratings.numRows) {
      i => testProfile(ratings(i,1))*ratings(i,2) }
    val den = sum(0, ratings.numRows) {
      i => abs(testProfile(ratings(i,1))) }
    num/(den+1)
}}
```

Figure 7. Snippet from collaborative filtering to be optimized

Fixed size array construction Array(a,b,c) can be expressed as

```
loop(3) x=Collect { case 0 => x ← a
                    case 1 => x ← b case 2 => x ← c }
```

and concatenation xs ++ ys as Array(xs,ys).flatMap(i=>i):

```
loop(2) x=Collect { case 0 => loop(xs.size) { i => x ← xs(i) }
                    case 1 => loop(ys.size) { i => x ← ys(i) }}
```

Fusing these patterns with a consumer will duplicate the consumer code into each match case. Therefore, implementations should impose cutoff mechanisms to prevent code explosion. Code generation does not need to emit actual loops for fixed array constructions but can just produce the right sequencing of yield operations.

5. Case Studies

We present several case studies to illuminate how our compiler architecture and in particular the staging aspect enable advanced optimizations related to data structures.

All experiments were performed on a Dell Precision T7500n with two quad-core Xeon 2.67GHz processors and 96GB of RAM. Scala code was run on the Oracle Java SE Runtime Environment 1.7.0 and the Hotspot 64-bit server VM with default options. We ran each application ten times (to warm up the JIT) and report the average of the last 5 runs. For each run we timed the computational portion of the application.

5.1 Linear Algebra

We first consider two examples using an extended version of the staged linear algebra library presented in Section 1. In the first example, we use staged transformation, partial evaluation, rewrite rules, and fusion together to transparently optimize a logical operation on a sparse matrix into a much more efficient version that only operates on its non-zero values. In the second example, we show how staged transformations can elegantly specialize loops to different computing devices by selecting a dimension to unroll and expressing the unrolled loop as a simple while loop in the source language.

Sparse User-Defined Operators Figure 7 shows an excerpt from a collaborative filtering application. This snippet computes a user's

```
trait SparseMatrix[A] extends Matrix[A] with Struct {
  val numRows: Rep[Double],     val numCols:    Rep[Double],
  val _data:   Rep[Array[A]],  val _nnz:       Rep[Int],
  val _rowPtr: Rep[Array[Int]],val _colIndices:Rep[Array[Int]]
}
trait SparseVector[A] extends Vector[A] with Struct {
  val length:  Rep[Int],       val _data: Rep[Array[A]],
  val _indices: Rep[Array[Int]],val _nnz:  Rep[Int]
}
```

Figure 8. Data structure definition for sparse matrix and vector

preference for other users given the user's previous ratings and a pre-computed NxN similarity matrix. The code is written in a representation-agnostic way – it works whether sims is dense or sparse using generic operations. Our goal is to transform the function mapRowsToVector into an efficient sparse operation if sims is sparse and the user-provided function argument to mapRowsToVector returns 0 when the input is a vector (row) containing only 0s. By expressing this as a transformation (rather than during construction), the IR node for mapRowsToVector can take part in other analyses and rewritings prior to being lowered to operate on the underlying arrays.

Figure 8 defines new data structures for sparse matrices and vectors in the manner described in Section 4. Using these definitions, we define the transformed version of mapRowsToVector as follows:

```
def infix_mapRowsToVector[A,B](x: Rep[Matrix[A]],
                               f: Rep[Vector[A]] => Rep[B]) = {
  def isZeroFunc(f: Rep[Vector[A]] => Rep[B], len: Rep[Int]) =
    // use symbolic evaluation to test the user-defined
    // function f against a zero-valued argument
    f(Vector.zeros[A](len)) match {
      case Const(x) if (x == defaultValue[B]) => true
      case _ => false
    }
  if (x.isInstanceOf[SparseMatrix] && isZeroFunc(f,x.numRows))
    MatrixMapRowsToVec(x,f) atPhase(lowering) {
      // transform to operate only on non-zero values
      new SparseVector[B] {
        val length = x.numRows
        val _indices = asSparseMat(x).nzRowIndices // elided
        val _data = _indices.map(i=>f(x(i)))
        val _nnz = _indices.length
      }
    }
  else MatrixMapRowsToVec(x,f) // default
}
```

Staging is the critical ingredient that allows this transformation to be written expressively and correctly. We first use the programmatic struct support with inheritance from Section 4.1 to operate uniformly on dense and sparse matrices and to obtain access to the underlying representation in order to perform the transformation. If the argument is a sparse matrix, mapRowsToVector calls isZeroFunc, which symbolically evaluates the user-defined function f at staging time to discover if it actually has no effect on empty rows in the argument matrix. This discovery is in turn enabled by further rewrite rules that implement symbolic execution by optimizing operations for constant values. For example, we define sum as:

```
override def sum[A:Numeric](start: Exp[Int], end: Exp[Int],
                            block: Exp[Int] => Exp[A]) =
  block(fresh[Int]) match {
    case Const(x) if x == 0 => unit(0.asInstanceOf[A])
    case _ => super.sum(start,end,block)
  }
```

We are able to successfully perform this transformation of mapRowsToVector because LMS re-applies all rewrite rules as the transformed IR is constructed. After the transformation, the code is further optimized by fusing together the two sum statements in Figure 7 (but the fused summation is still only run on non-zero rows). Figure 9 shows the results of running the collaborative filtering snippet with input data of varying sparsity. As expected, the transformation provides greater benefit with increasing sparsity because we switched from a representation-agnostic implementation to a representation-sensitive one. We also implicitly parallelize the transformed map function, resulting in good speedup over the sequential baseline automatically.

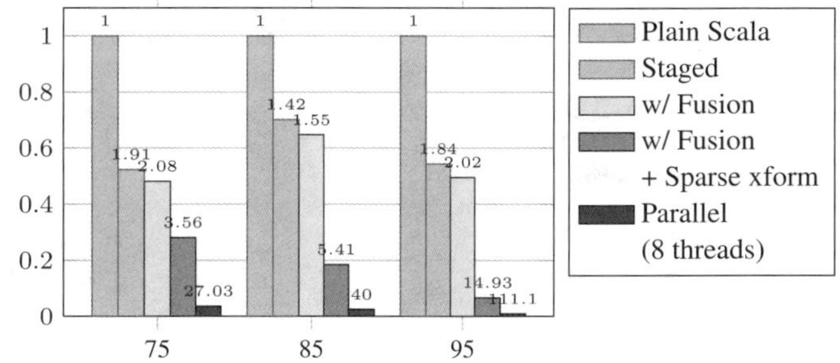

Figure 9. LinAlg Benchmark. The y-axis shows the normalized execution time of the collaborative filtering snippet on a 10kx10k matrix with various optimizations. The x-axis represents the percentage of sparse rows in the test data. Speedup numbers are reported at the top of each bar.

```
// x = input matrix, k = num clusters
// c = distance from each sample to nearest centroid
val newLocations = Matrix.fromArray {
  // returns an Array[Vector[Double]]
  Array.range(0,k) { j =>
    val (points,weightedpoints) = sum(0, x.numRows) {
      i => if (c(i) == j) (1,x(i))
    }
    val d = if (points == 0) 1 else points
    weightedpoints / d
}}
```

Figure 10. Snippet from k-means clustering to be optimized

Loop Parallelization for Heterogeneous Processors The final linear algebra example we will consider is the parallelization of a loop in the well-known k-means clustering algorithm. Figure 10 shows the snippet, which updates the cluster locations in the current iteration to the mean of all the samples currently assigned to that cluster.

K-means clustering is a statistical algorithm that is amenable to both multicore parallelization and GPU execution [28]. However, the Array.range statement in Figure 10 poses a challenge: each of the k cluster locations can be computed in parallel, or we can compute the inner sum statement in parallel. Since $k \ll$ x.numRows usually, on multicore machines with a smaller number of hardware threads (< 16) it is better to parallelize the outer (fromArray) dimension, but on massively parallel machines such as GPUs it is much better to parallelize the inner (sum) dimension.

If we internally represent parallel operators such as Array.range and sum as loops, a parallelization framework (such as Delite [5]) can automatically generate parallel and/or GPU code for them. Using the notation from Section 3.3, we can then define a device-specific transformation as follows:

```
trait LoopTransformerExp extends LinAlgExp { self =>
  val t = new LoopTransformer { val IR: self.type = self }
  def hasNestedLoop(l: Loop[_]): Boolean // elided
  def transformCollectToWhile(l: Collect[_]) = {
```

```
    // construct transformed representation
    var i = 0
    val size = t.transformExp(l.size)
    val res = alloc(size)
    while (i < size) {
      t.transformBlock(l.update)
        (res,i,t.transformBlock(l.func)(i))
      i += 1
    }
    res
}}
trait LoopTransformer extends ForwardTransformer {
  val IR: LoopTransformerExp
  import IR._
  override def transformStm(stm: Stm): Exp[Any] = stm match {
    case TP(s,l:Loop[_]) if (generateGPU && hasNestedLoop(l)) =>
      l.body match {
        case c:Collect[_] => transformCollectToWhile(c)
        case _ => super.transformStm(stm)
      }
    case _ => super.transformStm(stm)
}}
```

This transformation unwraps the `Array.range` function, which is internally represented by a loop, into an explicit **while** loop to expose any nested parallel operators. Although we elide it here, it is easy to add a heuristic to decide (statically if known or dynamically if not) whether or not to unwrap a loop based on its size. Note that due to staging, the transformed representation can be written as simple source code, which is easier to understand than direct IR manipulations. The transformation is only triggered if we are attempting to generate GPU code; if we are generating CPU code, we parallelize the outer loop to maximize our hardware utilization.

5.2 Regular Expression Matchers

Specializing string matchers and parsers is a popular benchmark in the partial evaluation literature [2, 10, 42]. Usually, specialization produces a set of mutually recursive functions, which is also our starting point. However this code does not achieve top performance compared to fast automata libraries. We show that treating generated functions as data objects and transforming them into a more efficient form yields performance that exceeds that of an optimized library.

We consider "multi-threaded" regular expression matchers, that spawn a new conceptual thread to process alternatives in parallel. Of course, these matchers do not actually spawn OS-level threads, but rather need to be advanced manually by client code. Thus, they are similar to coroutines. Here is an example for the fixed regular expression .*AAB:

```
def findAAB(): NIO = {
  guard(C('A')) {
    guard(C('A')) {
      guard(C('B'), true) {
        stop()
  }}} ++
  guard(W) { findAAB() } // in parallel ...
}
```

The first argument to guard is a character classs, `C(.)` defines a singleton character class and `W` denotes the wildcard. We added combinators on top of the core abstractions that can produce matchers from more conventional regular expressions: `many(seq)(star(W), C('A'), C('A'), C('B'))` for the example above. We can easily add a parser for textual regular expressions on top of these combinators.

NFA to DFA Conversion Internally, the given matcher uses an API that models nondeterministic finite automata (NFA):

```
def exploreNFA[A:Manifest](xs: NIO, cin: Rep[Char])(
    k: (Boolean, NIO) => Rep[A]): Rep[A] = xs match {
  case Nil => k(false, Nil)
  case NTrans(W, e, s)::rest =>
    val (xs1, xs2) = xs.partition(_.c != W)
    exploreNFA(xs1,cin)(continueWith(k, x2))
  case NTrans(cset, e, s)::rest =>
    if (cset contains cin) {
      val xs1 = // restrict rest: knowing cset
      exploreNFA(xs1,cin)((flag,acc) => k(
        flag || e(), acc ++ s()))
    } else {
      val xs1 = // restrict rest: knowing_not cset
      exploreNFA(xs1, cin)(k)
    }
}
```

Figure 11. NFA Exploration

```
type NIO = List[NTrans]
case class NTrans(c: CharSet, x: () => Boolean, s: () => NIO)
def guard(c: CharSet, x: => Boolean = false)(s: => NIO): NIO = {
  List(NTrans(c, () => x, () => s))
}
def stop(): NIO = Nil
```

An NFA state consists of a list of possible transitions. Each transition may be guarded by a set and it may have a flag to be signaled if the transition is taken. It also knows how to compute the following state. For simplicity, we use set of characters for the guard and a boolean for the flag, but of course, we could use generic types as well. Note that the API does not mention where input is obtained from (files, streams, etc.).

We will translate NFAs to DFAs using staging. The `Automaton` class is part of the unstaged DFA API. The staged API is just a thin wrapper.

```
case class Automaton[I, O](out: O, next: I => Automaton[I,O])
type DfaState = Automaton[Char,Boolean]
type DIO = Rep[DfaState]
def dfa_trans(e: Boolean)(f: Rep[Char] => DIO): DIO
```

Translating an NFA to a DFA is accomplished by creating a DFA state for each encountered NFA configuration:

```
def convertNFAtoDFA(flag: Boolean, state: NIO): DIO = {
  val cstate = canonicalize(state)
  dfa_trans(flag) { c: Rep[Char] => exploreNFA(cstate, c) {
    convertNFAtoDFA
  }
}}
convertNFAtoDFA(false, findAAB())
```

The LMS framework memoizes functions which, with the state canonicalization (e.g. we need to remove duplicates), ensures termination if the NFA is in fact finite. Indeed, our approach is conceptually similar to generating a DFA using derivatives of regular expressions [6, 35]: both approaches rely on identifying (approximately) equivalent automaton states; furthermore, computing a symbolic derivative is similar to advancing the NFA by a symbolic character, as explained next.

We use a separate function to explore the NFA space (see Figure 11), advancing the automaton by a symbolic character `cin` to invoke its continuation `k` with a new automaton, i.e. the possible set of states after consuming `cin`. The given implementation needs only to treat the wildcard character set (denoted by `W`) specially. The other character sets (single character or range) are treated generically, and it would be straightforward to add more cases without changing this function. The algorithm tries to remove as many redundant checks and impossible branches as possible (it relies on

```
def naiveFindAAB():
Automaton[Char, Boolean] = {
  val x1 = {x2: (Char) =>
    /*matched nothing*/
    val x3 = x2 == 'A'
    val x18 = if (x3) {
      x17
    } else {
      x13
    }

    x18
  }

  val x12 = Automaton(true,x1)
  val x7 = {x8: (Char) =>
    /*matched AA*/
    /* ... */
  }
  val x10 = Automaton(false,x7)
  val x4 = {x5: (Char) =>
    /*matched A*/
    /* ... */
  }
  val x17 = Automaton(false,x4)
  val x13 = Automaton(false,x1)
  x13
}
```

```
def optFindAAB(input: String):
Boolean = {
  val n = input.length
  if (n==0) return false
  var id = 0
  var i = 0
  val n_dec = n-1
  while (i < n_dec) {
    val x18 = input.charAt(i)
    // first case analysis
    // for next state id
    id = id match {
     case 0 =>
      /*matched nothing*/
       val x26 = x18 == 'A'
       val x27 = if (x26) 2
       else 0
       x27
     case 1 =>
       /*matched AA ... */
     case 2 =>
       /*matched A ...*/
    }
    i += 1
  }
  val x18 = input.charAt(i)
  // second case analysis
  // for final boolean flag
  id == 1 && x18 == 'B'
}
```

Figure 12. Generated matcher code for regular expression .*AAB. Optimized code on the right.

the knowing and knowing_not binary functions on character sets). This only works because the guards are staging-time values.

The generated code is shown in Figure 12 on the left. Each function corresponds to one DFA state.

One straightforward optimization is to signal early stopping if the boolean flag remains the same in all possible next states. To do so, we change the `DfaState` so that the output can encode two boolean values: the original flag and whether we can stop early. This does not help for matching .*AAB, but it does for .*AAB.*, as we can stop as soon as we find an occurrence of AAB.

Transforming Closures Our final implementation generates a complete matcher from a `String` input to a `Boolean` output. The generated code does not have functions nor `Automaton` states. Instead, we generate a case statement for each function. We do this twice: in the middle of matching the input, the value of the case analysis is the next functional state, while for the last character matching, its value is the boolean flag output. Because all the cases are inlined, we achieve early stopping by simply returning from the function with the boolean flag output in the midst of the first case analysis. The optimized code is shown in Figure 12 on the right.

Figure 13 shows benchmarking results. We compare our "naive" implementation (Staged 1), which includes the early stopping optimization, to the JDK and dk.brics.automaton [31] libraries. On average, our "naive" implementation is more than 2.5x faster than JDK's and about 3x slower than dk.brics.automaton. In order to speed up our implementation, we experimented with various staged transformations. Our final implementation (Staged 2) beats dk.brics.automaton by nearly a factor of 2 and JDK by a factor of 15. For comparison, we also tried a completely unstaged plain Scala version, where we directly evaluate the code instead of staging it, and it is 140x slower than JDK.

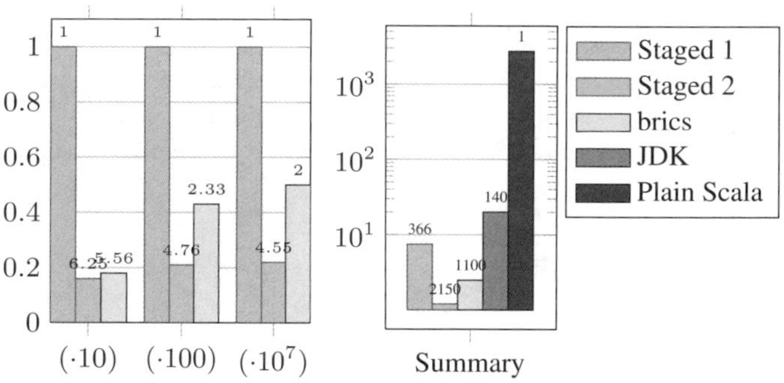

Figure 13. Regexp Benchmark. The first graph shows the relative execution time of matching an 10, 100, or 10^7 long input string of the form A+B on the regular expression .*AAB. The second graph summarizes the relative performance over many different inputs and regular expressions. Speedups are reported on top of each bar.

```
// lineItems: Array[LineItem]
val q = lineItems filter (_.l_shipdate <= Date(''1998-12-01'')).
groupBy (_.l_linestatus) map { case (key,g) => new {
  val lineStatus = key
  val sumQty = g.map(_.l_quantity).sum
  val sumDiscountedPrice =
    g.map(l => l.l_extendedprice*(1.0-l.l_discount)).sum
  val avgPrice = g.map(_.l_extendedprice).sum / g.size
  val countOrder = g.size
}} sortBy(_.lineStatus)
```

Figure 14. Sample query (similar to Q1 of the TPC-H benchmark)

5.3 Collection and Query Operations

Next we consider the case of executing queries on in-memory collections. Figure 14 shows a simplified version (for illustration purposes) of TPC-H Query 1 written using the standard Scala collections API. A straightforward execution of this query as written will be substantially slower than what could be achieved with an optimized low-level imperative implementation. In particular executing this code in Scala will perform a new array allocation for the output of each collection operation. Furthermore, every element of the arrays will be a heap allocated object since both `LineItem` and the anonymous class for the result are implemented as JVM classes. These classes however contain only fields, no methods, and as such we can apply struct optimizations to them during staging. Since the fields of these structs can all be represented as JVM primitive types, we can eliminate all of the heap allocated objects at runtime by performing array-of-struct (AoS) to struct-of-array (SoA) transformations for each array. Furthermore since `LineItem` as defined by TPC-H contains 16 fields, while Query 1 only accesses 7 of those fields, the DCE engine eliminates the arrays of the other 9 fields all together once the SoA form is created.

Fusion Optimization In addition, we eliminate the intermediate array and map data structures produced by each of the collection operations by fusing operations (Section 4.4) at two levels. At the inner level, creating the output struct requires multiple reduction operations. Horizontal fusion combines the reductions for each field into a single loop. On the outer level, the query groups the collection according to a key function and then maps each group (sub-collection) down to a single element. We fuse the `groupBy` and `map` together by using the rule for consuming a bucket-collect operation. Essentially the fusing algorithm observes that the output element of each group can be computed directly by reducing the entire input collection into the buckets defined by the key function of the `groupBy`. Furthermore, the vertical consume-collect rule fuses the `filter` with the `groupBy` by predicating the addition of each element

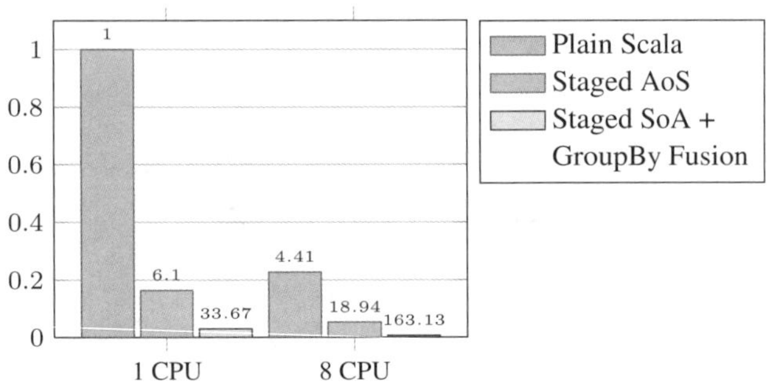

Figure 15. Performance of TPC-H Query 1 with staging optimizations. The y-axis shows the normalized execution time for 30 million records with speedups reported at the top of each bar.

to the appropriate group (and after `groupBy-map` fusion, predicating the reduction of each element into the appropriate group). Finally, horizontal fusion combines the operations for each field (array in the SoA form) into a single loop. Therefore, the program produces the output collection directly from the input with a single loop and no intermediate arrays. Sorting the output yields the final result.

We perform one final optimization during code generation of the fused loop. In order to implement `Bucket(Reduce)` operations we internally allocate a generic HashMap instance to manage the buckets. However, when n `Bucket(Reduce)` operations with the same key function appear in the same loop, we do not allocate a HashMap for each operation. Instead we use a single HashMap to determine an array index for each key, and then use that index to access the n arrays allocated to hold the result of each operation, eliminating the overhead of computing the same bucket location multiple times.

Performance Results We evaluate these optimizations in Figure 15. The execution times are normalized to the plain Scala library implementation of the query (leftmost bar). The middle bar shows the benefits of staging but without applying SoA transformations or groupBy fusion. Here staging is only applying basic optimizations such as common subexpression elimination and code motion. In particular the staged version contains the following key improvements. Higher-order abstractions such as anonymous functions have been eliminated, construction of the `Date` object within the filter has been lifted out of the loop and converted into an `Int`, pairs of primitive types have been packed into a single primitive type with twice the bits (e.g., a `Pair[Char,Char]` is encoded as an `Int`), and the map-reduce chains in the inner loop have been fused. Since we do not perform SoA transformations in this version, the `LineItem` struct is generated as a custom JVM class and the unused fields remain in the generated code. These optimizations provide approximately 6x speedup over the library implementation.

The rightmost bar shows the results of adding AoS to SoA transformations and all of the fusion optimizations described above, namely fusing the filter, groupBy, and map operations into a single loop. These optimizations provide approximately 5.5x speedup over the basic staging optimizations and 34x speedup over the library implementation. In addition, this version scales better when parallelized across multiple cores as it parallelizes over the size of the input collection rather than over the number of groups. Ultimately, with staging optimizations and parallel code generation, we were able to attain 163x speedup with 8 cores over a single-threaded library implementation.

Heterogeneous Targets AoS to SoA conversion greatly improves the ability to generate code for GPUs. In this example, however, the data transfer cost overwhelms any speedup for end-to-end runs. Another interesting target besides multi-core and GPU devices are "Big Data" cluster frameworks such as Hadoop or Spark. We can use the same collections API to target several different frameworks by adding appropriate framework-specific lowerings. A recent paper [1] contains more details and demonstrates good speedups.

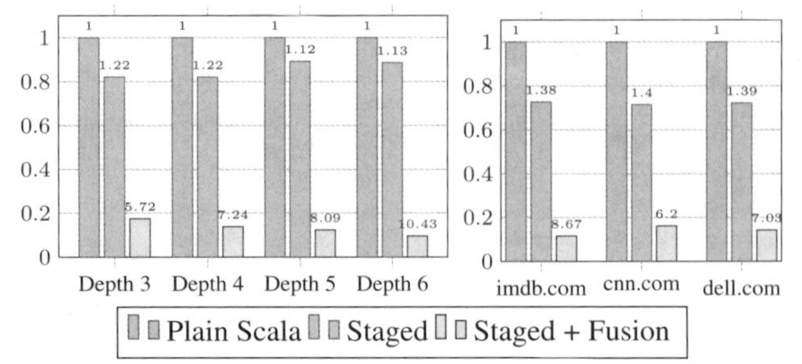

Figure 16. Synthetic file system to HTML (left, x-axis represents the template nesting depth. Depths 1 and 2 are omitted due to very short running times). Commercial websites (right). The y-axis shows normalized running time compared to plain Scala, speedup numbers are shown at the top of each bar.

5.4 String Templates

String template libraries are in wide use today to transform structured data into a flat string representation (e.g. XML, HTML, or JSON). While the semantics are simple and easy to express in a functional way, template engine implementations are often intricate because data copying and intermediate data structures need to be avoided to obtain good performance. We present the core of a template engine based on purely functional collection operations (list construction, concatenation and comprehensions), with loop fusion (Section 4.4) taking care of removing intermediate data structures.

A simple HTML menu can be rendered like this:

```
def link(uri: Rep[String], name: Rep[String]) =
  List("<a href='", uri, "'>", name, "</a>")
def renderItem(i: Rep[Item]) =   List("<li><ul>") ++
  i.subitems.flatMap(link(i.name, i.link)) ++ List("</ul></li>")
def usersTable(items: Rep[List[Item]]) = List("<ul>") ++
  items.flatMap(x => renderItem(x)) ++ List("</ul>")
```

When executing this code without fusion optimization, each `flatMap` operation traverses the lists produced by the nested template one more time. Each concat (++) operation incurs an additional traversal. This results in performance that, for fixed output size, decreases linearly with the level of template nesting. The asymptotic worst case complexity is thus quadratic in the output size, whereas an imperative implementation would be linear.

Since all function calls are unfolded at staging time, our fusion transformation (Section 4.4) is able to remove the unnecessary traversals and data structures, provided that only core collection operations are used to express templates. The generated code traverses the input data structure just once, emitting strings directly into a single output buffer.

Benchmark results are reported in Figure 16. We demonstrate the ability of obtaining asymptotic speedups on a synthetic benchmark that generates HTML representations of a file system structure with growing levels of nesting: with fusion enabled, speedups grow with the depth of nesting. Furthermore, we implemented mock templates to resemble the structure of three public web sites, yielding speedups of up to 8.6x over the plain, unstaged Scala implementation.

6. Discussion

As shown in Section 5, our system is able to achieve order of magnitude (and in one case even asymptotic) speedups on a varied range of non-trivial high level programs. While we are not aware of any other system that demonstrably achieves comparable results on a similar range of programs, these results bear the question whether they could be achieved with similar effort using other means.

As suggested by one of the reviewers, a simpler design would be to perform optimizations dynamically. For example, one could implement vectors and matrices as a hierarchy of classes, with a special class for zero vectors, instead of distinguishing zero vectors statically in the IR. This is certainly a valid design, but it comes with a number of drawbacks. First, runtime distinctions introduce interpretive overhead, indirection and virtual calls, which also make it harder for the compiler to generate efficient code. Second, while dynamic information may be more precise than static information at some times, the possibilities for dynamic optimizations are very limited in other key aspects: For example, it is not clear how to integrate DCE or any other optimization that requires non-local knowledge (liveness, horizontal fusion).

Another question posed by a reviewer was whether staging really simplifies transformation compared to state-of-the art rewriting systems such as those included in language workbenches like Spoofax [24] or JetBrains MPS [19]. While these systems are impressive, we believe they serve a different purpose and that the capability to programmatically remove abstraction at all intermediate levels, with strong guarantees about the residual code, is hard to overstate in the context of program optimization. For example, the code in Figure 3 transforms symbolic linear algebra operations to the same zero-overhead traversals shown in Figure 2, with higher order functions and type class instances removed by staging, without dedicated compiler analysis. Staging enables us to express a program (or model) transformer as an interpreter; this is an advantage because writing an interpreter in an expressive language is arguably simpler than implementing a transformer, even with good toolkit support. A key aspect is linguistic reuse of abstractions of the meta language. For example, our recent work on JavaScript generation using LMS [27] re-uses Scala's CPS transform [40] at staging-time to generate asynchronous code that is in continuation passing style (CPS). By contrast, WebDSL [17], which is implemented in Spoofax, has to implement the CPS transform afresh, for each language construct of the object language.

Working with a graph-based IR also makes a qualitative difference compared to expression trees. Most importantly, it becomes much easier to implement transforms that require dependency information. Our fusion algorithm (Section 4.4), for example, does not require loops to be syntactically close or adjacent to be fused:

```
def calcSum() = array.sum
def calcCount() = array.filter(_ > 0).count
println("sum: " + calcSum())
println("avg: " + (calcSum() / calcCount()))
```

Staging will inline the `calcSum` and `calcCount` calls and the fusion algorithm will combine all traversals into a single loop. Any algorithm that only considers dependent traversal expressions will miss the horizontal fusion opportunities across the two `println` statements. This is commonly the case for pure front-end approaches based e.g. on C++ expression templates.

Another key aspect of our design is the different treatment of lowering transforms (handled in separate passes one after the other) and optimizations (combined into joint simplification passes using speculative rewriting). We believe this distinction is essential to make optimizations reliable by avoiding phase ordering problems and making sure that high-level optimizations are applied exhaustively before lowerings take place.

Finally, there is the question of programmer effort required to achieve similar results. From our perspective, the most important aspects are that the optimizations we present can be applied gradually, and that they are reusable for all clients of an optimized library. We expect that end user programmers will not usually write any transformations on their own, but they can add rewrites if they need. Library developers who wish to add optimizations need to implement functionality corresponding to the code we show (e.g. in Figure 3) but they can do so in a gradual way: Start with code similar to Figure 1, add staging (Figure 2), and, if that is not sufficient, add further optimizations (Figure 3). Delayed rewriting (Section 3.3) can further reduce boilerplate. The guarantees provided by the type system (non-`Rep[T]` expressions evaluated at staging time) and smart constructors (no IR node constructed if rewrites match) help ensure that optimizations take place in the intended way. As a debugging aid, transformed code can be emitted at any time.

6.1 Related Work

Extensible compilers have been studied for a long time, recent examples in the Java world are Polyglot [33] and JastAdd [13]. The Glasgow Haskell Compiler also allows custom rewrite rules [22]. There are also elaborate approaches to library specific optimizations inspired by formal methods. ROSE [36] is a framework for building source-to-source translators that derives automated optimizations from semantics annotations on library abstractions. COBALT [30] is a domain-specific language for implementing optimizations that are amenable to automated correctness reasoning. Tate et al. [48] present a method of generating compiler optimizations automatically from program examples before and after a transformation.

Delite [5, 28, 41] is a parallelization framework for DSLs developed on top of LMS. Previously, Delite had a notion of a multi-level IR: some IR nodes could be viewed from several different angles at the same time (say, as a parallel loop and as a matrix operation). This caused problems because "earlier", more high-level views had to be carried along and obsolete or fully exploited information was never discarded, limiting the choices of the compiler. We have used the techniques presented in this work to extend Delite and to implement domain-specific optimizations (similar to those presented in the case studies) for existing Delite DSLs such as OptiML [44]. Delite was also used as the parallel execution engine for the case studies in this paper. Compared to Delite, this paper presents a general extensible compiler architecture, not limited to domain specific languages. Previous publications on LMS [38, 39] presented only the pure front-end, single pass instantiation. The use of `Rep[T]` types to define binding times in LMS is inspired by earlier work on finally tagless or polymorphic language embedding [8, 18].

Tobin-Hochstadt et al. [50] propose languages as libraries in Racket and make pervasive use of macros for translation. Our approach of using staging is similar in spirit. Earlier work on realistic compilation by program transformation in the context of Scheme was presented by Kelsey and Hudak [25].

The ability to compile high-level languages to lower-level programming models has been investigated in several contexts. Elliot et al. [14] pioneered embedded compilation and used a simple image synthesis DSL as an example. Telescoping languages [26] is a strategy to automatically generate optimized domain-specific libraries. In C++, expression templates [51] are popular to implement limited forms of domain specific optimizations [23, 52]. The granularity is restricted to parts of a larger template expression.

Nystrom et al. [34] shows a library based approach to translating Scala programs to OpenCL code. This is largely achieved through Java bytecode translation. A similar approach is used by Lime [3] to compile high-level Java code to a hardware description language such as Verilog.

Our compiler infrastructure implements a set of advanced optimizations in a reusable fashion. Related work includes program transformations using advanced rewrite rules [4], combining analyses and optimizations [9, 29, 53] as well as techniques for eliminating intermediate results [12, 54] and loop fusion [16]. An interesting alternative to speculative rewriting is equality saturation [47], which encodes many ways to express an operation in the IR.

As an example of using partial evaluation in program transformation, Sperber and Thiemann [43] perform closure conversion and tail call introduction by applying offline partial evaluating to a suitable interpreter. More recently, Cook et al. [11] perform model transformation by partial evaluation of model interpreters. Partial evaluation corresponds to constant folding and specialization whereas our approach allows arbitrary compiler optimizations, arbitrary computation at staging/specialization time to remove abstraction overhead and provides strong guarantees about what becomes part of the residual code (type `Rep[T]` residual, vs `T` static).

6.2 Conclusion

We have demonstrated a compiler architecture that achieves order of magnitude speedups on high-level programs by fusing collection operations, changing data layout and applying further optimizations on high-level objects, enabled by intermediate languages with staging and a facility to combine optimizations without phase ordering problems. Our system combines several novel pieces with existing techniques, which together provide optimization power that is greater than the sum of the parts.

Acknowledgments

We thank the POPL reviewers for their valuable feedback and suggestions. This research was sponsored by the European Reserach Council (ERC) under grant 587327 "DOPPLER", DARPA through Oracle order US103282, DARPA contract HR0011-11-C-0007 "SEEC", NSF grant SHF CCF-1111943, the Stanford Pervasive Parallelism Lab affiliates program (supported by Oracle, AMD, Intel, NVIDIA) and additional support from Oracle.

References

[1] S. Ackermann, V. Jovanovic, T. Rompf, and M. Odersky. Jet: An embedded dsl for high performance big data processing. BigData, 2012. http://infoscience.epfl.ch/record/181673/files/paper.pdf.

[2] M. S. Ager, O. Danvy, and H. K. Rohde. Fast partial evaluation of pattern matching in strings. *ACM Trans. Program. Lang. Syst.*, 28(4): 696–714, 2006.

[3] J. Auerbach, D. F. Bacon, P. Cheng, and R. Rabbah. Lime: a java-compatible and synthesizable language for heterogeneous architectures. OOPSLA, 2010.

[4] M. Bravenboer, A. van Dam, K. Olmos, and E. Visser. Program transformation with scoped dynamic rewrite rules. *Fundam. Inf.*, 69: 123–178, July 2005.

[5] K. J. Brown, A. K. Sujeeth, H. Lee, T. Rompf, H. Chafi, M. Odersky, and K. Olukotun. A heterogeneous parallel framework for domain-specific languages. PACT, 2011.

[6] J. A. Brzozowski. Derivatives of regular expressions. *J. ACM*, 11(4): 481–494, 1964.

[7] C. Calcagno, W. Taha, L. Huang, and X. Leroy. Implementing multi-stage languages using asts, gensym, and reflection. In *GPCE*, 2003.

[8] J. Carette, O. Kiselyov, and C. chieh Shan. Finally tagless, partially evaluated: Tagless staged interpreters for simpler typed languages. *J. Funct. Program.*, 19(5):509–543, 2009.

[9] C. Click and K. D. Cooper. Combining analyses, combining optimizations. *ACM Trans. Program. Lang. Syst.*, 17:181–196, March 1995.

[10] C. Consel and O. Danvy. Partial evaluation of pattern matching in strings. *Inf. Process. Lett.*, 30(2):79–86, 1989.

[11] W. R. Cook, B. Delaware, T. Finsterbusch, A. Ibrahim, and B. Wiedermann. Model transformation by partial evaluation of model interpreters. Technical Report TR-09-09, UT Austin Department of Computer Science, 2008.

[12] D. Coutts, R. Leshchinskiy, and D. Stewart. Stream fusion: from lists to streams to nothing at all. In *ICFP*, 2007.

[13] T. Ekman and G. Hedin. The jastadd system - modular extensible compiler construction. *Sci. Comput. Program.*, 69(1-3):14–26, 2007.

[14] C. Elliott, S. Finne, and O. de Moor. Compiling embedded languages. In W. Taha, editor, *Semantics, Applications, and Implementation of Program Generation*, volume 1924 of *Lecture Notes in Computer Science*, pages 9–26. Springer Berlin / Heidelberg, 2000.

[15] Y. Futamura. Partial evaluation of computation process - an approach to a compiler-compiler. *Higher-Order and Symbolic Computation*, 12 (4):381–391, 1999.

[16] C. Grelck, K. Hinckfuß, and S.-B. Scholz. With-loop fusion for data locality and parallelism. IFL, 2006.

[17] D. M. Groenewegen, Z. Hemel, L. C. L. Kats, and E. Visser. WebDSL: a domain-specific language for dynamic web applications. In *OOPSLA Companion*, 2008.

[18] C. Hofer, K. Ostermann, T. Rendel, and A. Moors. Polymorphic embedding of DSLs. GPCE, 2008.

[19] JetBrains. Meta Programming System, 2009. URL http://www.jetbrains.com/mps/.

[20] N. D. Jones, C. K. Gomard, and P. Sestoft. *Partial evaluation and automatic program generation*. Prentice-Hall, Inc., Upper Saddle River, NJ, USA, 1993.

[21] S. L. P. Jones, R. Leshchinskiy, G. Keller, and M. M. T. Chakravarty. Harnessing the Multicores: Nested Data Parallelism in Haskell. In *FSTTCS*, 2008.

[22] S. P. Jones, A. Tolmach, and T. Hoare. Playing by the rules: rewriting as a practical optimisation technique in ghc. Haskell, 2001.

[23] S. Karmesin, J. Crotinger, J. Cummings, S. Haney, W. Humphrey, J. Reynders, S. Smith, and T. J. Williams. Array design and expression evaluation in pooma ii. In *ISCOPE*, 1998.

[24] L. C. L. Kats and E. Visser. The Spoofax language workbench. rules for declarative specification of languages and IDEs. In *SPLASH/OOPSLA Companion*, 2010.

[25] R. Kelsey and P. Hudak. Realistic compilation by program transformation. In *POPL*, 1989.

[26] K. Kennedy, B. Broom, A. Chauhan, R. Fowler, J. Garvin, C. Koelbel, C. McCosh, and J. Mellor-Crummey. Telescoping languages: A system for automatic generation of domain languages. *Proceedings of the IEEE*, 93(3):387–408, 2005.

[27] G. Kossakowski, N. Amin, T. Rompf, and M. Odersky. Javascript as an embedded dsl. In *ECOOP*, 2012.

[28] H. Lee, K. J. Brown, A. K. Sujeeth, H. Chafi, T. Rompf, M. Odersky, and K. Olukotun. Implementing domain-specific languages for heterogeneous parallel computing. *IEEE Micro*, 31(5):42–53, 2011.

[29] S. Lerner, D. Grove, and C. Chambers. Composing dataflow analyses and transformations. *SIGPLAN Not.*, 37:270–282, January 2002.

[30] S. Lerner, T. D. Millstein, and C. Chambers. Automatically proving the correctness of compiler optimizations. In *PLDI*, 2003.

[31] A. Møller. dk.brics.automaton – finite-state automata and regular expressions for Java, 2010. http://www.brics.dk/automaton/.

[32] A. Moors, T. Rompf, P. Haller, and M. Odersky. Scala-virtualized. PEPM, 2012.

[33] N. Nystrom, M. R. Clarkson, and A. C. Myers. Polyglot: An extensible compiler framework for java. In *CC*, 2003.

[34] N. Nystrom, D. White, and K. Das. Firepile: run-time compilation for gpus in scala. GPCE, 2011.

[35] S. Owens, J. Reppy, and A. Turon. Regular-expression derivatives reexamined. *J. Funct. Program.*, 19(2):173–190, Mar. 2009.

[36] D. J. Quinlan, M. Schordan, Q. Yi, and A. Sæbjørnsen. Classification and utilization of abstractions for optimization. In *ISoLA (Preliminary proceedings)*, 2004.

[37] T. Rompf. *Lightweight Modular Staging and Embedded Compilers: Abstraction Without Regret for High-Level High-Performance Programming*. PhD thesis, EPFL, 2012.

[38] T. Rompf and M. Odersky. Lightweight modular staging: a pragmatic approach to runtime code generation and compiled dsls. GPCE, 2010.

[39] T. Rompf and M. Odersky. Lightweight modular staging: a pragmatic approach to runtime code generation and compiled dsls. *Commun. ACM*, 55(6):121–130, 2012.

[40] T. Rompf, I. Maier, and M. Odersky. Implementing first-class polymorphic delimited continuations by a type-directed selective cps-transform. In *ICFP*, 2009.

[41] T. Rompf, A. K. Sujeeth, H. Lee, K. J. Brown, H. Chafi, M. Odersky, and K. Olukotun. Building-blocks for performance oriented dsls. DSL, 2011.

[42] A. Shali and W. R. Cook. Hybrid partial evaluation. OOPSLA, 2011.

[43] M. Sperber and P. Thiemann. Realistic compilation by partial evaluation. In *PLDI*, 1996.

[44] A. K. Sujeeth, H. Lee, K. J. Brown, T. Rompf, M. Wu, A. R. Atreya, M. Odersky, and K. Olukotun. OptiML: an implicitly parallel domain-specific language for machine learning. ICML, 2011.

[45] E. Sumii and N. Kobayashi. A hybrid approach to online and offline partial evaluation. *Higher-Order and Symbolic Computation*, 14(2-3): 101–142, 2001.

[46] W. Taha and T. Sheard. Metaml and multi-stage programming with explicit annotations. *Theor. Comput. Sci.*, 248(1-2):211–242, 2000.

[47] R. Tate, M. Stepp, Z. Tatlock, and S. Lerner. Equality saturation: a new approach to optimization. In *POPL*, 2009.

[48] R. Tate, M. Stepp, and S. Lerner. Generating compiler optimizations from proofs. In *POPL*, 2010.

[49] P. Thiemann and D. Dussart. Partial evaluation for higher-order languages with state. Technical report, 1999. URL http://www.informatik.uni-freiburg.de/~thiemann/papers/mlpe.ps.gz.

[50] S. Tobin-Hochstadt, V. St-Amour, R. Culpepper, M. Flatt, and M. Felleisen. Languages as libraries. PLDI '11, 2011.

[51] T. L. Veldhuizen. Expression templates, C++ gems. SIGS Publications, Inc., New York, NY, 1996.

[52] T. L. Veldhuizen. Arrays in blitz++. In *ISCOPE*, 1998.

[53] T. L. Veldhuizen and J. G. Siek. Combining optimizations, combining theories. Technical report, Indiana University, 2008.

[54] P. Wadler. Deforestation: Transforming programs to eliminate trees. *Theor. Comput. Sci.*, 73(2):231–248, 1990.

[55] P. Wadler and S. Blott. How to make ad-hoc polymorphism less adhoc. In *POPL*, 1989.

Principled Parsing for Indentation-Sensitive Languages

Revisiting Landin's Offside Rule

Michael D. Adams

Portland State University

http://michaeldadams.org/

Abstract

Several popular languages, such as Haskell, Python, and F#, use the indentation and layout of code as part of their syntax. Because context-free grammars cannot express the rules of indentation, parsers for these languages currently use *ad hoc* techniques to handle layout. These techniques tend to be low-level and operational in nature and forgo the advantages of more declarative specifications like context-free grammars. For example, they are often coded by hand instead of being generated by a parser generator.

This paper presents a simple extension to context-free grammars that can express these layout rules, and derives GLR and LR(k) algorithms for parsing these grammars. These grammars are easy to write and can be parsed efficiently. Examples for several languages are presented, as are benchmarks showing the practical efficiency of these algorithms.

Categories and Subject Descriptors D.3.1 [*Programming Languages*]: Formal Definitions and Theory—Syntax; D.3.4 [*Programming Languages*]: Processors—Parsing; F.4.2 [*Mathematical Logic and Formal Languages*]: Grammars and Other Rewriting Systems—Parsing

General Terms Algorithms, Languages

Keywords Parsing, Indentation, Offside rule

1. Introduction

Languages such as Haskell [Marlow (ed.) 2010] and Python [Python] use the indentation of code to delimit various grammatical forms. In Haskell, the contents of a `let`, `where`, `do`, or `case` expression can be indented relative to the surrounding code instead of being explicitly delimited by curly braces. In Python, the body of a multi-line function or compound statement must be indented relative to the surrounding code; there is no alternative, explicitly-delimited syntax. For example, in Haskell one may write:

```
mapAccumR f = loop
  where loop acc (x:xs) = (acc'', x' : xs')
          where (acc'', x') = f acc' x
                (acc', xs') = loop acc xs
        loop acc [] = (acc, [])
```


POPL '13, January 23–25, 2013, Rome, Italy.

The indentation of the bindings after each `where` keyword determines the parse structure of this code. For example, the indentation of the last line determines that it is part of the bindings introduced by the first `where` instead of the second `where`.

Likewise, in Python one may write:

```
def factorial(x):
  result = 1
  for i in range(1, x + 1):
    result = result * i
  return result
print factorial(5)
```

Here the indentation determines that the `for` loop ends before the `return` and the `factorial` function ends after the `return`.

While Haskell and Python are well known for being indentation-sensitive languages, quite a few other languages also use indentation. Landin's ISWIM [Landin 1966] introduced the concept of the offside rule for indentation, which requires that all tokens in an expression be indented at least as far as the first token of the expression. Variations on this rule are used by Haskell, Miranda [Turner 1989], occam [INMOS Limited 1984], Orwell [Wadler 1985], Curry [Hanus (ed.) 2006], and Habit [HASP Project 2010]. F# is indentation sensitive when its lightweight syntax is enabled [Syme et al. 2010, §15.1]. The block styles in the YAML [Ben-Kiki et al. 2009] data serialization language are indentation sensitive, as are many forms in the Markdown [Gruber] and reStructuredText [Goodger 2012] markup languages. Even Scheme has an indentation-sensitive syntax in the form of SRFI-49 [Möller 2005], though it is not often used.

Whitespace sensitivity may be controversial, but regardless of whether it is a good idea from a language design perspective, it is important that the grammars of layout-sensitive languages be precisely specified. Unfortunately, many language specifications are informal in their description of layout or use formalisms that are not amenable to practical implementation. The task of parsing layout is thus often left to *ad hoc*, handwritten code.

The lack of a standard formalism for expressing these layout rules and of parser generators for such a formalism increases the complexity of writing parsers for these languages. Often, practical parsers for these languages have significant structural differences from the language specification. For example, the layout rule for Haskell is specified in terms of an extra pass between the lexer and the parser that inserts explicit delimiters. This extra pass uses information about whether the parsing that occurs later in the pipeline will succeed or fail on particular inputs. Due to the resulting cyclic dependency, Haskell implementations do not actually structure their parsers this way. As a result, the structural differences between the implementation and the specification make it difficult to determine if one accurately reflects the other.

This paper aims to resolve this situation by proposing a grammar formalism for expressing layout rules. This formalism is both theoretically sound and practical to implement. Indentation-sensitive grammars are easy and convenient to write, and fast and efficient parsers can be implemented for them. The primary contributions of this paper are:

- a grammar formalism for expressing indentation-sensitive languages, which is informally described in Section 2 and formally defined later in Section 4;
- a demonstration in Section 3 of the expressivity of these grammars by showing how to express the layout rules of ISWIM, Miranda, Haskell, and Python in terms of these grammars;
- a development in Section 5 of GLR and LR(k) parsing algorithms for these grammars, which is possible by a careful factoring of item sets into state and indentation sets; and
- a demonstration in Section 6 of the practical performance of these parsing techniques relative to existing *ad hoc* techniques.

Section 7 of this paper reviews related work. Section 8 concludes.

Note that Section 5 of this paper assumes a fair amount of familiarity with standard parsing techniques and in particular the work by Knuth [1965] on LR(k) parsing. Other than Section 5, however, this paper assumes only a basic knowledge of context-free grammars.

2. The Basic Idea

In order to support indentation-sensitive parsing, we use a modification of traditional, context-free grammars. We parse over a sequence of terminals where every terminal is annotated with the column at which it occurs in the source code. We call this its indentation. During parsing, we also annotate each non-terminal with an indentation. The grammar specifies a numerical relation that the indentation of each non-terminal must have with the indentation of its immediate children. These relations are usually chosen so the indentation of a non-terminal is the minimum column at which any token in the non-terminal is allowed to occur. Thus, the indentation of a non-terminal usually coincides with the intuitive notion of how far a block of code is indented. Formally, however, the indentation of a non-terminal has no meaning other than that it must appropriately relate to the indentation of the non-terminal's children.

We call these grammars indentation-sensitive context-free grammars (IS-CFG) to contrast them with traditional indentation-insensitive context-free grammars (II-CFG). Section 3 gives examples of IS-CFGs for real world languages, and Section 4 formally defines this class of grammars.

As a simple example, we may write $A \to \texttt{'('}^{=} A^{>} \texttt{')'}^{=}$ to mean that (and) must be at the same indentation as the A on the left of the production arrow but the A on the right must be at a greater indentation. We may also write $A \to \texttt{'['}^{\geq} A^{>} \texttt{']'}^{\geq}$ to mean the same except that [and] must be at a greater or equal indentation than the A on the left of the production arrow. In addition, we may write $A \to A^{=} A^{=}$ to mean that the indentation of both occurrences of A on the right of the production must be at indentations equal to that of the A on the left of the production. Combined with the production $A \to \varepsilon$, these form a grammar of nested parentheses and square brackets. In that grammar, matching parentheses must align vertically, and things enclosed in parentheses must be indented more than the parentheses are indented. Things enclosed in square brackets merely must be indented more than the surrounding code. Figure 1 shows examples of parse trees for this grammar on the words $(^1 [^4 (^5)^5]^7)^1$ and $(^1 [^8 (^6)^6 [^8]^9]^4 (^3)^3)^1$ where we write X^i to mean that i is the indentation of X. In these parse trees, take particular note of how the indentations of the non-terminals and terminals relate according to the indentation relations specified in the grammar.

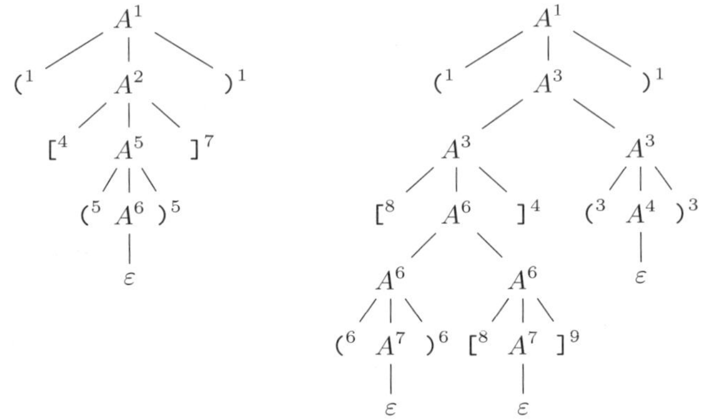

Figure 1. Example IS-CFG parse trees for $(^1 [^4 (^5)^5]^7)^1$ and $(^1 [^8 (^6)^6 [^8]^9]^4 (^3)^3)^1$ respectively.

In general, we write a production as $A \to X_1^{\rhd_1} X_2^{\rhd_2} \cdots X_n^{\rhd_n}$, where $\rhd_1, \rhd_2, \cdots, \rhd_n$ are relations between indentations, to mean that the indentation of A relates to the indentations of each $X_1, X_2, \cdots, X_n$ according to $\rhd_1, \rhd_2, \cdots, \rhd_n$. That is to say, this production requires $j_1 \rhd_1 i, j_2 \rhd_2 i, \cdots, j_n \rhd_n i$ if i is the indentation of A and $j_1, j_2, \cdots, j_n$ are the respective indentations of $X_1, X_2, \cdots, X_n$.

While in principle any set of indentation relations can be used, we restrict ourselves to the relations $=$, $>$, $\geq$, and $\circledast$. The $=$, $>$, and $\geq$ relations have their usual meanings. The $\circledast$ relation is $\{(i, j) \mid i, j \in \mathbb{N}\}$ and effectively disassociates the indentation of a child from that of its parent.

Indentation-sensitive languages typically have forms that require the first token of a subexpression to be at the same indentation as the subexpression itself even though the non-terminal for that subexpression does not normally require this. Thus for every non-terminal or terminal, X, we introduce the non-terminal $|X|$ that is identical to X except that its indentation is always equal to the indentation of its first token. This is merely syntactic sugar, as we can introduce the production $|a| \to a^{=}$ for each terminal a and the production $|A| \to |X_m|^{=} X_{m+1}^{\rhd_{m+1}} \cdots X_n^{\rhd_n}$ for each production $A \to X_1^{\rhd_1} X_2^{\rhd_2} \cdots X_n^{\rhd_n}$ where $n \geq 1$ and each $m \leq n$ such that $X_1, X_2, \cdots, X_{m-1}$ are all nullable. For example, with the above grammar, $|A|$ would have the productions $|A| \to |\texttt{'('}|^{=} A^{>} \texttt{')'}^{=}$ and $|A| \to |\texttt{'['}|^{\geq} A^{>} \texttt{']'}^{\geq}$ from the first two productions for A. It would also have $|A| \to |A^{=}| A^{=}$ and $|A| \to |A^{=}|$ from the third production for A. By replacing $\rhd_m$ with $=$, the first symbol of each production is forced to have the same indentation as the non-terminal on the left of the production. By transitivity, this is the indentation of the first token in the non-terminal. This is a straightforward, mechanical transformation requiring no input from the user.

3. Indentation-Sensitive Languages

Despite this system's simplicity, it can express a wide array of layout rules. This section demonstrates this by presenting the layout rules of several languages in terms of IS-CFGs. Where possible, we use the non-terminal names from the original grammar of each language. Though not shown here, sketches for other indentation-sensitive languages have been constructed for occam,[1] Orwell, Curry, Habit, and SRFI-49.

[1] The additional indentation relation $\{(i + 2, i) \mid i \in \mathbb{N}\}$ is required by occam as it has forms that require increasing indentation by exactly 2.

3.1 ISWIM and Miranda

With ISWIM, Landin [1966] introduced several innovations still used in programming languages today. Among these is the use of indentation to indicate program structure. Landin defines an "offside rule"[2] that specifies that:

> The southeast quadrant that just contains the phrase's first symbol must contain the entire phrase, except possibly for [parenthesized] subsegments. [Landin 1966]

This rule requires that all the tokens in a particular non-terminal be at a column that is at least as far right (i.e., in the southeast quadrant) as the column of the first token.

The IS-CFG for ISWIM is similar to the II-CFG for ISWIM that ignores the offside rule except that we annotate each production of the IS-CFG with appropriate indentation relations. As an example, consider the productions in Figure 2 where we have applied the offside rule to only the right-hand side of `where` clauses.[3] Note that the productions for $|\texttt{expr}|$ are created automatically from the productions for `expr` as specified in Section 2. We do likewise for the terminals.[4] Using this grammar to parse the expression

```
x + v where
 x = -(
y + z) + w
```

results in the parse tree in Figure 3.

For productions that do not involve the offside rule, such as the productions for addition and negation, we annotate the non-terminals with $=$ and the terminals with $\geq$. This means that these productions do not change the current indentation and terminals are allowed at any column greater than or equal to the current indentation. For example, the expressions for `x + v`, `(y + z)`, and all the variable references are all at the same indentation as their respective parents. For those expressions, no special indentation rule is in effect and we simply use $=$ to propagate the indentation from parent to child. The terminals use $\geq$ so they can be at that or any greater indentation. If a non-terminal is too far left (e.g., if `w` was at column 5), then the $\geq$ constraint is violated and the code would be rejected. This is a common pattern that we will see in other grammars as well.

Next, consider forms that involve the offside rule. Wherever a non-terminal A should trigger the offside rule, we simply use $|A|^{\geq}$ instead of $A^{=}$. An example is the right-hand side of a `where` clause where we use $|\texttt{expr}|^{\geq}$ instead of $\texttt{expr}^{=}$. Because we use $\geq$ instead of $=$, the right-hand side is allowed to be at a greater indentation than its parent. We see this in the example parse tree where the right-hand side of the `where` clause has an indentation of 6 while its parent has an indentation of 1. If the top-level `expr` were at indentation 7, however, such a parse with a right-hand side at indentation 6 would be rejected. We also use $|\texttt{expr}|$ instead of `expr` so that the first token of the right-hand side of the `where` clause has the same indentation as the entire right-hand side. As a consequence, in the example parse tree, the indentations on the path from the right-hand side of the `where` to the `'-'` are all exactly 6.

Finally, since parenthesized expressions are exempt from the indentation constraints of the surrounding code, the production for parenthesized expressions uses $\texttt{expr}^{\circledast}$ instead of $\texttt{expr}^{=}$. This frees the indentation of the expression inside the parentheses from any indentation constraints coming from the context of the expression. This is used in the example parse tree where the `y + z` expression has an indentation of 0 even though the `(y + z)` expression has an indentation of 6. Uses of the offside rule inside the parentheses still have effect, of course.

Productions written by the user:

$$
\begin{aligned}
\texttt{expr} &\to \texttt{expr}^{=}\ \texttt{'where'}^{\geq}\ \texttt{ID}^{\geq}\ \texttt{'='}^{\geq}\ |\texttt{expr}|^{\geq}\\
\texttt{expr} &\to \texttt{expr}^{=}\ \texttt{'+'}^{\geq}\ \texttt{expr}^{=}\\
\texttt{expr} &\to \texttt{'-'}^{\geq}\ \texttt{expr}^{=}\\
\texttt{expr} &\to \texttt{'('}^{\geq}\ \texttt{expr}^{\circledast}\ \texttt{')'}^{\geq}\\
\texttt{expr} &\to \texttt{ID}^{\geq}
\end{aligned}
$$

Productions added by desugaring:

$$
\begin{aligned}
|\texttt{expr}| &\to |\texttt{expr}|^{=}\ \texttt{'where'}^{\geq}\ \texttt{ID}^{\geq}\ \texttt{'='}^{\geq}\ |\texttt{expr}|^{\geq}\\
|\texttt{expr}| &\to |\texttt{expr}|^{=}\ \texttt{'+'}^{\geq}\ \texttt{expr}^{=}\\
|\texttt{expr}| &\to |\texttt{'-'}|^{=}\ \texttt{expr}^{=}\\
|\texttt{expr}| &\to |\texttt{'('}|^{=}\ \texttt{expr}^{\circledast}\ \texttt{')'}^{\geq}\\
|\texttt{expr}| &\to |\texttt{ID}|^{=}
\end{aligned}
$$

$$
\begin{array}{lll}
|\texttt{'='}| \to \texttt{'='}^{=} & |\texttt{'+'}| \to \texttt{'+'}^{=} & |\texttt{'-'}| \to \texttt{'-'}^{=}\\
|\texttt{'('}| \to \texttt{'('}^{=} & |\texttt{')'}| \to \texttt{')'}^{=} & |\texttt{ID}| \to \texttt{ID}^{=}\\
|\texttt{'where'}| \to \texttt{'where'}^{=} & &
\end{array}
$$

Figure 2. IS-CFG productions for ISWIM.

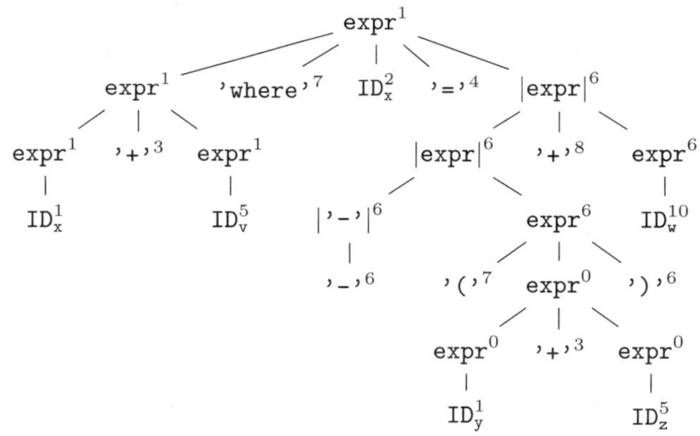

Figure 3. IS-CFG parse tree for ISWIM.

The Miranda language uses the same offside rule as ISWIM except for two differences. The first is that expressions inside parentheses *are* subject to indentation constraints imposed by the context outside the parentheses. The production for parenthesized expressions thus uses $=$ instead of $\circledast$ and is simply:

$$\texttt{expr} \to \texttt{'('}^{\geq}\ \texttt{expr}^{=}\ \texttt{')'}^{\geq}$$

The second difference is that the language specification adopts the notational convention that for any non-terminal `x`,

> `x(;)` means that `x` is followed by an optional semicolon and is subject to the offside rule..., so that every token of `x` must lie below or to the right of the first. Provided the layout makes it clear where `x` terminates, the trailing semicolon may be omitted. [Turner 1989, §25]

This notation is easily handled by introducing, for each non-terminal A, the non-terminal $A\texttt{(;)}$ and the two productions $A\texttt{(;)} \to |A|^{\geq}$ and $A\texttt{(;)} \to |A|^{\geq}\ \texttt{';'}$.

[2] Landin spells it as both "offside" and "off-side". We adopt the spelling consistent with the rule from sports.

[3] Landin is not clear about whether his offside rule applies to all syntactic forms. His examples imply that it does not. For the sake of example, we also simplify `where` and omit the multiple bindings case. That case uses the same techniques as Haskell's statement blocks.

[4] Of course, the productions generated for the terminals `'='`, `'+'`, `')'` and `'where'` are unreachable from the rest of the grammar and can be omitted.

```
L (<n>:ts) (m:ms) = ';' : (L ts (m:ms))     if m = n
                  = '}' : (L (<n>:ts) ms)  if n < m
L (<n>:ts)     ms = L ts ms
L ({n}:ts) (m:ms) = '{' : (L ts (n:m:ms)) if n > m
L ({n}:ts)     [] = '{' : (L ts [n])       if n > 0
L ({n}:ts)     ms = '{' : '}' : (L (<n>:ts) ms)
L ('}':ts) (0:ms) = '}' : (L ts ms)
L ('}':ts)     ms = parse-error
L ('{':ts)     ms = '{' : (L ts (0:ms))
L ( t :ts) (m:ms) = '}' : (L (t:ts) ms)
                     if m ≠ 0 and parse-error(t)
L ( t :ts)     ms =  t  : (L ts ms)
L        []    [] =  []
L        [] (m:ms) = '}' : L [] ms          if m ≠ 0
```

Figure 4. Haskell's L function [Marlow (ed.) 2010, §10.3].

```
case      → 'case'^> exp^= 'of'^> altBlock^=

-- Explicitly delimited blocks
altBlock  → '{'^> alts^⊛ '}'^⊛

-- Layout-delimited blocks
altBlock  → altLayout^>
altLayout → altLayout^= |alts|^=
altLayout →             |alts|^=

-- Clause sequences
alts  →                 alt^=
alts  → alts^= ';'^>    alt^=
```

Figure 5. Grammatical productions for case.

3.2 Haskell

3.2.1 Language

Haskell uses a more sophisticated offside rule than does ISWIM. Indentation-sensitive blocks (e.g. the bodies of do, case, or where expressions) are made up of one or more statements or clauses that not only are indented relative to the surrounding code but also are indented to the same column as each other. Thus, lines that are more indented than the block continue the current clause, lines that are at the same indentation as the block start a new clause, and lines that are less indented than the block are not part of the block. In addition, semicolons (;) and curly braces ({ and }) can explicitly separate clauses and delimit blocks, respectively. Explicitly delimited blocks are exempt from indentation restrictions arising from the surrounding code.

While the indentation rules of Haskell are intuitive to use in practice, the way that they are formally expressed in the Haskell language specification [Marlow (ed.) 2010, §10.3] is not nearly so intuitive. The indentation rules are specified in terms of both the lexer and an extra pass between the lexer and the parser. Roughly speaking, the lexer inserts special $\{n\}$ tokens where a new block might start and special $<n>$ tokens where a new clause within a block might start. The extra pass then translates these tokens into explicit semicolons and curly braces.

The special tokens are inserted according to the following rules:

- If a let, where, do, or of keyword is not followed by the lexeme {, the token $\{n\}$ is inserted after the keyword, where n is the indentation of the next lexeme if there is one, or 0 if the end of file has been reached.
- If the first lexeme of a module is not { or module, then it is preceded by $\{n\}$ where n is the indentation of the lexeme.
- Where the start of a lexeme is preceded only by white space on the same line, this lexeme is preceded by $<n>$, where n is the indentation of the lexeme, provided that it is not, as a consequence of the first two rules, preceded by $\{n\}$. [Marlow (ed.) 2010, §10.3]

Between the lexer and the parser, an indentation resolution pass converts the lexeme stream into a stream that uses explicit semicolons and curly braces to delimit clauses and blocks. The stream of tokens from this pass is defined to be L tokens [] where tokens is the stream of tokens from the lexer and L is the function in Figure 4. Thus the context-free grammar has to deal with only semicolons and curly braces. It does not deal with layout.

This L function is fairly intricate, but the key clauses are the ones dealing with $<n>$ and $\{n\}$. After a let, where, do, or of keyword, the lexer inserts a $\{n\}$ token. If n is a greater indentation than the current indentation, then the first clause for $\{n\}$ executes, an open brace ({) is inserted, and the indentation n is pushed on the second argument to L (i.e., the stack of indentations). If a line starts at the same indentation as the top of the stack, then the first clause for $<n>$ executes and a semicolon (;) is inserted to start a new clause. If it starts at a smaller indentation, then the second clause for $<n>$ executes and a close brace (}) is inserted to close the block started by the inserted open brace. Finally, if the line is at a greater indentation, then the third clause executes, no extra token is inserted, and the line is a continuation of the current clause. The effect of all this is that {, ;, and } tokens are inserted wherever layout indicates that blocks start, new clauses begin, or blocks end, respectively. The other clauses in L handle a variety of other edge cases and scenarios.

Note that L uses parse-error to signal a parse error, but uses parse-error(t) as an oracle that predicts the future behavior of the parser that runs after L. Specifically,

> if the tokens generated so far by L together with the next token t represent an invalid prefix of the Haskell grammar, and the tokens generated so far by L followed by the token "}" represent a valid prefix of the Haskell grammar, then parse-error(t) is true. [Marlow (ed.) 2010, §10.3]

This handles code such as

```
let x = do f; g in x
```

where the block starting after the do needs to be terminated before the in. This requires knowledge about the parse structure in order to be handled properly, and thus parse-error(t) is used to query the parser for this information.

In addition to the operational nature of this definition, the use of the parse-error(t) predicate means that L cannot run as an independent pass; its execution must interact with the parser. In fact, the Haskell implementations GHC [GHC 2011] and Hugs [Jones 1994] do not use a separate pass for L. Instead, the lexer and parser share state consisting of a stack of indentations. The parser accounts for the behavior of parse-error(t) by making close braces optional in the grammar and appropriately adjusting the indentation stack when braces are omitted. The protocol relies on "some mildly complicated interactions between the lexer and parser" [Jones 1994] and is tricky to use. While preparing the parser in Section 6, we found that even minor changes to the error propagation of the parser affected whether syntactically correct programs were accepted by this style of parser.

While we may believe the correctness of these parsers based on their many years of use and testing, the significant and fundamental structural differences between their implementation and the language specification are troubling.

3.2.2 Grammar

Haskell's layout rule is more complicated than those of ISWIM and Miranda, but is also easily specified as an IS-CFG. By using an IS-CFG there is no need for an intermediate `L` function, and the lexer and parser can be cleanly separated into self-contained passes. The functionality of `parse-error(t)` is simply implicit in the structure of the grammar.

Figure 5 shows example productions for `case` expressions. For productions that do not change the indentation, we annotate non-terminals with a default indentation relation of $=$ and terminals with a default indentation relation of $>$. We use $>$ instead of $\geq$ because Haskell distinguishes tokens that are at an indentation equal to the current indentation from tokens that are at a strictly greater indentation. The former start a new clause while the latter continue the current clause.

In Haskell, a block can be delimited by either explicit curly braces or use of the layout rule. In Figure 5, this is reflected by the two different productions for `altBlock`. If `altBlock` expands to `'{'`$^>$ `alts`$^\circledast$ `}`$^\circledast$, then the $\circledast$ relation allows `alts` to not respect the indentation constraints from the surrounding code.[5] Since Haskell's layout rule allows closing braces to occur at any column, we use $\circledast$ instead of the usual $>$ on `'}'`. On the other hand, if `altBlock` expands to `altLayout`$^>$, then the $>$ relation increases the indentation. In the productions for `altLayout`, the use of $|$`alts`$|$ instead of `alts` ensures that the first tokens of the `alts` all align to the same column. Note that within an `alts`, each `alt` must be separated by a semicolon (`;`). Thus, because `altLayout` refers to `alts` instead of `alt`, each instance of `alt` can be separated using either layout or a semicolon. When using curly braces to explicitly delimit a block, semicolons must always be used.

Other grammatical forms that use the layout rule follow the same general pattern as `case` with only minor variation to account for differing base cases (e.g., `let` uses `decl` in place of `alt`) and structures (e.g., a `do` block is a sequence of `stmt` ending in an `exp`).

A subtlety of Haskell's layout rule is that tokens on the same line as, but after, a closing brace may not have to respect the current indentation. This is because the `L` function considers the indentation of only the first token of a line (i.e., where `<`n`>` is inserted) and tokens after a `let`, `where`, `do` or `of` keyword (i.e., where `{`n`}` is inserted). One might view this as an artifact of how the language specification uses `L` to define layout, but this aspect of Haskell's layout rule is still expressible by having the lexer annotate tokens whose indentation is to be ignored with an indentation of infinity.[6] Since terminals have an indentation relation of $>$, the infinite indentation of these tokens will always match. We have the lexer handle this instead of the parser because it is the linear order of tokens instead of the grammatical structure of the syntax that controls what tokens are indentation sensitive. For example, the token after the `do` keyword is indentation sensitive regardless of the structure of the expression following the `do`. This requires the lexer to maintain a bit of extra state indicating whether we are at the start of a line or after a `let`, `where`, `do` or `of` keyword, but this is a fairly light requirement as the lexer is presumably already tracking state to determine the column of each token.

Finally, GHC also supports an alternative indentation rule that is enabled by the `RelaxedLayout` extension. It allows opening braces to be at any column regardless of the current indentation [GHC 2011, §1.5.2]. This is easily implemented by changing the first production for `altBlock` to be:

$$\texttt{altBlock} \;\rightarrow\; \texttt{'\{'}^{\circledast}\ \texttt{alts}^{\circledast}\ \texttt{'\}'}^{\circledast}$$

[5] This assumes no tokens are at column 0, which we reserve for this purpose.

[6] Of course, column information for error reporting should still use the actual position of the token.

3.3 Python

3.3.1 Language

Python represents a different approach to specifying indentation sensitivity. It is explicitly line oriented and features `NEWLINE` in its grammar as a terminal that separates statements. The grammar uses `INDENT` and `DEDENT` tokens to delimit indentation-sensitive forms. An `INDENT` token is emitted by the lexer whenever the start of a line is at a strictly greater indentation than the previous line. Matching `DEDENT` tokens are emitted when a line starts at a lesser indentation.

In Python, indentation is used only to delimit statements, and there are no indentation-sensitive forms for expressions. This, combined with the simple layout rules, would seem to make parsing Python much simpler than for Haskell, but Python has line joining rules that complicate matters.

Normally, each new line of Python code starts a new statement. If, however, the preceding line ends in a backslash (\), then the current line is "joined" with the preceding line and is a continuation of the preceding line. In addition, tokens on this line are treated as if they had the same indentation as the backslash itself.

Python's *explicit* line joining rule is simple enough to implement directly in the lexer, but Python also has an *implicit* line joining rule. Specifically, expressions

> in parentheses, square brackets or curly braces can be split over more than one physical line without using backslashes. ... The indentation of the continuation lines is not important. [Python, §2.1.6]

This means that `INDENT` and `DEDENT` tokens must not be emitted by the lexer between paired delimiters. For example, the second line of the following code should not emit an `INDENT` and the indentation of the third line should be compared to the indentation of the first line instead of the second line.

```
x = [
  y ]
  z = 3
```

Thus, while the simplicity of Python's indentation rules is attractive, they contain hidden complexity that requires interleaving the execution of the lexer and parser.

3.3.2 Grammar

Though Python's specification presents its indentation rules quite differently from Haskell's specification, once we translate it to an IS-CFG, it shares many similarities with that of Haskell. The lexer still needs to produce `NEWLINE` tokens, but it does not produce `INDENT` or `DEDENT` tokens. As with Haskell, we start with a grammar where the non-terminals and terminals are annotated with indentation relations of $=$ and $>$, respectively.

In Python, the only form that changes indentation is the `suite` non-terminal, which represents a block of statements contained inside a compound statement. For example, one of the productions for `while` is:

$$\texttt{while\_stmt} \;\rightarrow\; \texttt{'while'}^{>}\ \texttt{test}^{=}\ \texttt{':'}^{>}\ \texttt{suite}^{=}$$

A `suite` has two forms. The first is for a single-line statement and is the same as with the standard Python grammar. The second is for multi-line statements. The following productions handle both of these two cases.

$$\begin{aligned}
\texttt{suite} &\rightarrow \texttt{stmt_list}^{=}\ \texttt{NEWLINE}^{>}\\
\texttt{suite} &\rightarrow \texttt{NEWLINE}^{>}\ \texttt{block}^{>}\\
\texttt{block} &\rightarrow \texttt{block}^{=}\ |\texttt{statement}|^{=}\\
\texttt{block} &\rightarrow |\texttt{statement}|^{=}
\end{aligned}$$

When a suite is of the multi-line form (i.e., using the second production), the initial NEWLINE token ensures that the suite is on a separate line from the preceding header. The block inside a suite must then be at some indentation greater than the current indentation. Such a block is a sequence of statement forms that all start with their first token at the same column. In Python's grammar, the productions for statement already include a terminating NEWLINE, so NEWLINE is not needed in the productions for block.

For implicit line joining, we employ the same trick as for parenthesized expressions in ISWIM and braces in Haskell. For any production that contains parentheses, square brackets or curly braces, we annotate the part contained in the delimiters with the $\circledast$ indentation relation. Since the final delimiter is also allowed to appear at any column, we annotate it with $\circledast$. For example, one of the productions for list construction becomes:

$$\texttt{atom} \rightarrow \texttt{'['}^{>}\ \texttt{listmaker}^{\circledast}\ \texttt{]}^{\circledast}$$

There remain a few subtleties with Python's line joining rules that we must address. First, as with Haskell, tokens after a closing delimiter can appear at any column. For example, the following code is validly indented according to Python's rules:

```
while True:
        x = 1 + (
2) + 3
```

To handle this we use the same trick as for Haskell and annotate tokens that are not at the start of a line with an infinite indentation.

Second, while a lexer based on regular expressions can detect the start of a line and thus produce finite indentations for the first token of a line but infinite indentations for other tokens, it cannot detect matching parentheses to determine that NEWLINE tokens should be omitted inside delimited forms. Thus non-terminals that occur inside delimited forms need to allow the insertion of NEWLINE tokens at arbitrary locations. This may mean there have to be two forms of a non-terminal (i.e., for expressions inside versus outside a delimited form), but this is a fairly mechanical transformation that can be automated by the use of syntactic sugar similar to the syntactic sugar for $|A|$. Alternatively, it may be possible to use a grammar that does not use NEWLINE tokens at all and instead, like for Haskell, uses vertical alignment to delimit statements.

Finally, as with the standard Python parser, the lexer still handles the explicit line joining that is triggered by a line ending in a backslash (\). It gives the tokens of an explicitly joined line the same indentation as the backslash itself, and the backslash is not emitted as a token.

3.4 Conventions and syntactic sugar

In an IS-CFG, every symbol in every production must be annotated with an indentation relation. In many indentation-sensitive languages, however, productions often allow terminals to appear at any indentation greater than the current indentation but do not themselves change the current indentation. Thus we can simplify the job of writing an IS-CFG by adopting the convention that if a symbol on the right-hand side of a production is not explicitly annotated with an indentation relation, then it implicitly defaults to $=$ if it is a non-terminal and $>$ if it is a terminal. For example, with this convention, the only productions in Figure 5 that need explicit annotations are those for altBlock. All other productions simply use the defaults. Using this convention most productions in a grammar do not have to be annotated with indentation relations. They thus look like ordinary II-CFG productions, and only the forms that explicitly deal with indentation must be explicitly annotated.

In addition, just as II-CFGs often allow the use of alternation bars (|) or Kleene stars (*) to simplify writing grammars, it is often convenient to allow symbols on the right-hand side of a production to be annotated with a composition of indentation relations. Thus we might write $\texttt{A} \rightarrow \texttt{C}^{>\circledast}$ instead of the more verbose

$$\texttt{A} \rightarrow \texttt{B}^{\circledast}$$
$$\texttt{B} \rightarrow \texttt{C}^{>}$$

These conventions are merely notational conveniences and do not affect the fundamental theory.

4. Indentation-Sensitive Grammars

The formalism for IS-CFGs that this paper proposes is an extension of II-CFGs. Thus to review the standard definition of II-CFGs, recall that a grammar is a four-tuple $G = (N, \Sigma, \delta, S)$ where N is a finite set of non-terminal symbols, Σ is a finite set of terminal symbols, δ is a finite production relation, and $S \in N$ is the start symbol. The relation δ is a subset of $N \times (N \cup \Sigma)^*$, and we write $A \rightarrow X_1 X_2 \cdots X_n$ for a tuple $(A, X_1 X_2 \cdots X_n)$ that is an element of δ.

As a notational convention let A, B, C be elements of N, let a, b, c be elements of Σ, and let X, Y, Z be elements of $N \cup \Sigma$. Let U, V, W be elements of $(N \cup \Sigma)^*$, and u, v, w be elements of Σ^*.

We define a rewrite relation $(\Rightarrow) \subseteq (N \cup \Sigma)^* \times (N \cup \Sigma)^*$ such that $UAV \Rightarrow UX_1X_2 \cdots X_nV$ iff $A \rightarrow X_1 X_2 \cdots X_n$. We define $(\Rightarrow^*)$ as the reflexive, transitive closure of $(\Rightarrow)$.

The language recognized by a grammar is then defined as $\mathcal{L}(G) = \{w \in \Sigma^* \mid S \Rightarrow^* w\}$ and is the set of words reachable by the rewrite relation from the start symbol.

An IS-CFG is also a four-tuple, $G = (N, \Sigma, \delta, S)$, except that δ and S account for indentations. S is an element of $N \times \mathbb{N}$ and records the indentation of the initial non-terminal. The production relation, δ, is an element of $N \times ((N \cup \Sigma) \times \mathbb{I})^*$ where $\mathbb{I}$ is the domain of indentation relations and each indentation relation is a subset of $\mathbb{N} \times \mathbb{N}$. In principle, these indentation relations can be any subset of $\mathbb{N} \times \mathbb{N}$, but for our purposes we restrict $\mathbb{I}$ to the relations $=, >, \geq$ and $\circledast$.

Here and in the remainder of this paper, we restrict ourselves to finite indentations, but everything generalizes straightforwardly to languages with infinite indentations.

As a notational convention, let i, j and l be indentations and $\rhd$ be an indentation relation. For the sake of compactness, we adopt the notations X^i and $X^{\rhd}$, respectively, for a pair of X and either an indentation i or an indentation relation $\rhd$. Thus we write $A \rightarrow X_1^{\rhd_1} X_2^{\rhd_2} \cdots X_n^{\rhd_n}$ for a tuple $(A, (X_1, \rhd_1)(X_2, \rhd_2) \cdots (X_n, \rhd_n))$ that is an element of δ.

As with II-CFGs, we define a rewrite relation

$$(\Rightarrow) \subseteq ((N \cup \Sigma) \times \mathbb{N})^* \times ((N \cup \Sigma) \times \mathbb{N})^*$$

where $UA^iV \Rightarrow UX_1^{j_1} X_2^{j_2} \cdots X_n^{j_n} V$ iff $A \rightarrow X_1^{\rhd_1} X_2^{\rhd_2} \cdots X_n^{\rhd_n}$ and $j_1 \rhd_1 i, j_2 \rhd_2 i, \cdots, j_n \rhd_n i$. The $(\Rightarrow^*)$ relation, the language $\mathcal{L}(G)$, derivations, and parse trees are all defined as with II-CFGs except that they are in terms of this new rewrite relation.

Note that every II-CFG is encodable as an IS-CFG by translating every production $A \rightarrow X_1 X_2 \cdots X_n$ to $A \rightarrow X_1^{\circledast} X_2^{\circledast} \cdots X_n^{\circledast}$ and every word $a_1 a_2 \cdots a_m$ to $a_1^{i_1} a_2^{i_2} \cdots a_m^{i_m}$ with arbitrary $i_1, i_2, \cdots, i_m \in \mathbb{N}$. Conversely, erasing the indentations and indentation relations in an IS-CFG results in an II-CFG. Note that translating from an II-CFG to an IS-CFG will not introduce ambiguities, but translating from an IS-CFG to an II-CFG might.

5. Parsing

Of course, a grammar is not practically useful if we cannot effectively parse with it. In this section, we show how to modify traditional parsing techniques for II-CFGs to handle IS-CFGs. We show this for both GLR and LR(k) parsing. This can also be done for

CYK, SLR, LALR, GLL, and LL(k), but we do not present those here as they are straightforward once the techniques for LR(k) parsing are understood.

In order to derive GLR and LR(k) parsing algorithms, we first prove a number of basic properties about indentation relations and IS-CFGs (Section 5.1). Then, we model IS-CFGs by using infinite II-CFGs (Section 5.2). Next, we consider traditional rewrite systems (Section 5.3) and parsing algorithms (Section 5.4) applied to this infinite II-CFG. Finally, we factor out the parts of these constructions representing indentations so that these algorithms can be expressed finitely (Sections 5.5, 5.6 and 5.7) and discuss some practical efficiency considerations (Section 5.8). The key insights here are, first, expressing the semantics of an IS-CFG in terms of an infinite II-CFG and, second, factoring the representation of item sets into a finite representation.

5.1 Basic properties

There are a few technical definitions and properties that we will use in our parsing algorithms. We present these without discussion.

Definition 1. A non-terminal A is *nullable* if $A^i \Rightarrow^* \varepsilon$ for all i.

Lemma 2 (Composition of indentation relations). *Every finite sequence of compositions of elements from $\mathbb{I}$ is one of $=$, $\geq$, $\circledast$, $\geq\circledast$, $>^n$, or $>^n\circledast$ for some $n \geq 1$.*

Proof. $=$ is a left and right identity under composition. $\circledast$ is a left annihilator under composition. The compositions of $>$ with $\geq$ and $\geq$ with $>$ are both $>$. □

Lemma 3 (Closure of indentation relations). *The closure of $\mathbb{I}$ under finite sequences of composition and either finite or infinite sets of unions is the set of unions of one or more of $=$, $\geq$, $\circledast$, $\geq\circledast$, $>^n$, and $>^m\circledast$ for some $n, m \geq 1$ where each of these is in the union only once. We call this closure $\bar{\mathbb{I}}$ and as a notational convention let $\bar{\triangleright}$ be an element of $\bar{\mathbb{I}}$.*

Proof. By Lemma 2, every finite composition is of the form $=$, $\geq$, $\circledast$, $\geq\circledast$, $>^n$, or $>^m\circledast$. Since $>^n \supseteq >^{n'}$ if $n' \geq n$ and $>^m\circledast \supseteq >^{m'}\circledast$ if $m' \geq m$, at most one occurrence of $>^n$ and one occurrence of $>^m\circledast$ needs to be in the union. □

Lemma 4 (Indentations of unique parses). *If $A^i \Rightarrow^* W$, then the set of all indentations i' such that $A^{i'} \Rightarrow^* W$ using the same sequence of productions is either the set $\mathbb{N}$, a singleton or the upper bounded set $\{i \mid i \leq n\}$ for some $n \in \mathbb{N}$. Furthermore, if it is a singleton or upper bounded set, then the maximum indentation is limited to be at most the maximum indentation in W.*

Proof. Consider the derivation as a parse tree. Each edge can be annotated with the indentation relation between parent and child nodes. The relation between the indentation of the root A^i and each leaf a^j is then a composition of the edges in the path from A^i to a^j. The possible values of i are the values compatible with every leaf indentation and the root's relation to them. By Lemma 2 every such relation is one of $=$, $\geq$, $\circledast$, $\geq\circledast$, $>^p$ or $>^q\circledast$ and for a particular leaf the compatible root indentations are thus are either $\mathbb{N}$, a singleton, or $\{i \mid i \leq m\}$ for some $m \in \mathbb{N}$. The intersection of these over all the leaves in the parse tree is thus either the set $\mathbb{N}$, a singleton, or $\{i \mid i \leq n\}$ for some $n \in \mathbb{N}$. □

Lemma 5 (Indentations of ambiguous parses). *If $A^i \Rightarrow^* W$, then the set of all indentations i' such that $A^{i'} \Rightarrow^* W$ using any sequence of productions is either the set $\mathbb{N}$ or a finite subset of $\mathbb{N}$. Moreover, the finite subsets of $\mathbb{N}$ are bounded by the maximum indentation in W.*

Proof. By Lemma 4 and the union over all parses. □

5.2 Translating IS-CFGs to infinite II-CFGs

The first step of our approach is to model the IS-CFG by an infinite II-CFG. Of course we do not actually compute with this infinite grammar, but it provides a mathematical model from which we derive a computable parsing algorithm. Given an IS-CFG $G = (N, \Sigma, \delta, S)$, this II-CFG is $G' = (N', \Sigma', \delta', S')$ where:

$$\begin{aligned} N' &= N \times \mathbb{N} \\ \Sigma' &= \Sigma \times \mathbb{N} \\ \delta' &= \Big\{ A^i \to X_1^{j_1} X_2^{j_2} \cdots X_n^{j_n} \\ &\qquad | A \to X_1^{\triangleright_1} X_2^{\triangleright_2} \cdots X_n^{\triangleright_n} \in \delta, \\ &\qquad i, j_1, j_2, \cdots, j_n \in \mathbb{N}, \\ &\qquad j_1 \triangleright_1 i, j_2 \triangleright_2 i, \cdots, j_n \triangleright_n i \} \\ S' &= S \end{aligned}$$

This grammar has an infinite number of non-terminals, terminals and productions per non-terminal, but we still limit derivations to finite lengths.

Note that traditional parsing algorithms on this grammar may not terminate due to the infinite size of G', so we formally model G' as the limit of successive approximations where each approximation bounds the maximum indentation in any non-terminal, terminal or production to successively greater values. We gloss over this detail in the remainder of this paper.

Lemma 6 (Equivalence). *$S \Rightarrow^* W$ for G iff $S' \Rightarrow^* W$ for G'.*

Proof. By induction on the number of reductions and the fact that for all W and W', $W \Rightarrow W'$ in G iff $W \Rightarrow W'$ in G'. □

5.3 Rewrite system

In this subsection, we consider LR(k) parsing in terms of a rewrite system that concisely specifies what it means for a parser to be LR(k). In later subsections, we derive more conventional stack-based parsing algorithms. In this development, we closely follow the original presentation of LR(k) parsing by Knuth [1965] with only minor changes to use current notational conventions.

Recall that an LR(k) parser is one that always produces a rightmost derivation, and a rightmost derivation is one in which the rightmost non-terminal is always expanded before any other non-terminals. The symbols resulting from such an expansion step are called the handle. For example, if

$$S \Rightarrow^* UX^jV \Rightarrow UY_1^{l_1} \cdots Y_p^{l_p} V \Rightarrow^* W$$

is a rightmost derivation, then a handle of $UY_1^{l_1} \cdots Y_p^{l_p} V$ is $Y_1^{l_1} \cdots Y_p^{l_p}$. Note that in order for this to be a rightmost derivation, V necessarily contains only elements of Σ, though U and $Y_1^{l_1} \cdots Y_p^{l_p}$ may contain elements of both Σ and N.

Since an LR(k) parser works from the result of a rightmost derivation back to the start symbol, LR(k) parsing can be accomplished by iteratively searching for the handle of a string and performing the appropriate reduction. Again following Knuth [1965], given the infinite II-CFG $G' = (N', \Sigma', \delta', S')$ we construct the right-linear (and thus regular) grammar $G'' = (N'', N' \cup \Sigma', \delta'', S'')$ for recognizing prefixes that end in a handle. Here the non-terminals are

$$N'' = \Big\{ \Big[A^i, a_1^{j_1} a_2^{j_2} \cdots a_k^{j_k} \Big] \Big| A^i \in N', a_1^{j_1}, a_2^{j_2}, \cdots, a_k^{j_k} \in \Sigma' \Big\}$$

and represent the part of the string that contains the handle. The $a_1^{j_1} a_2^{j_2} \cdots a_k^{j_k}$ track the k terminals expected after the handle and are the lookahead. For each $A^i \to X_1^{j_1} \cdots X_m^{j_m} X_{m+1}^{j_{m+1}} \cdots X_n^{j_n}$ in δ' and each $u = a_1^{l_1} a_2^{l_2} \cdots a_k^{l_k}$, we include the following in δ'':

$$\left[A^i, u\right] \to X_1^{j_1} \cdots X_n^{j_n} u$$
$$\left[A^i, u\right] \to X_1^{j_1} \cdots X_m^{j_m} \left[X_{m+1}^{j_{m+1}}, v\right]$$
$$\text{for each } v \in H_k\left(X_m^{j_m} \cdots X_n^{j_n} u\right)$$

Here, u and v are the lookaheads expected by the parser. $H_k(W)$ computes such lookaheads by computing the k-length prefixes of $\mathcal{L}(W)$ and is defined as

$$H_k(W) = \left\{a_1^{l_1} a_2^{l_2} \cdots a_k^{l_k} \middle| W \Rightarrow^* a_1^{l_1} a_2^{l_2} \cdots a_k^{l_k} U\right\}$$

where the reduction relation $\Rightarrow^*$ is for G'.

The intuition here is that the first production expands to the handle along with a lookahead string and the second production expands to an intermediate non-terminal that in turn eventually expands to the handle.

Since this grammar is regular, it can be implemented by a state machine [Brzozowski 1964], which leads to the following rewrite based algorithm for parsing.

Algorithm 7. *Given input string W, if $S = W$ then stop and accept the string. Otherwise, find all prefixes of W that match the regular language $\mathcal{L}(G'')$. If there are no such matches, then reject the string. Otherwise, non-deterministically choose one of the matches, and let the last production of the match be*

$$\left[A^i, u\right] \to X_1^{j_1} X_2^{j_2} \cdots X_n^{j_n} u$$

Replace this occurrence of $X_1^{j_1} X_2^{j_2} \cdots X_n^{j_n}$ in W with A^i as it is a handle of W, and repeat this algorithm with the new value of W.

Note that this algorithm is non-deterministic and accepts the word if any path through the algorithm accepts the word. We allow this because productions in G (e.g., $A \to B^{\circledast}$ and $A \to C^{>}$) may produce multiple productions when translated to G' (e.g., all $A^i \to B^j$ and $A^i \to C^k$ such that $k > i$). These may introduce ambiguities in G' even when there are no ambiguities in G. Once we convert to a finite version of the parsing algorithm, we will eliminate this non-determinism.

5.4 Parsing with stacks

Of course, rewriting the entire string and restarting the automaton from the start as done in Algorithm 7 is inefficient. Instead, we can save a trace of the states visited. When a handle is reduced, we rewind to the state just before the first symbol of the handle and proceed from there. This is the essential idea behind the traditional LR(k) parser development by Knuth [1965]. We apply this idea to our infinite II-CFG to obtain the following construction.

We begin with the notion of an item. We denote an item by

$$\left[A^i \to X_1^{j_1} \cdots X_m^{j_m} \bullet X_{m+1}^{j_{m+1}} \cdots X_n^{j_n}; u\right]$$

where $A^i \to X_1^{j_1} \cdots X_n^{j_n}$ is a production in G' and $u \in (\Sigma')^k$ is the lookahead. The algorithm maintains a stack of sets of items $\mathcal{S}_0\mathcal{S}_1 \cdots \mathcal{S}_n$ where $\mathcal{S}_n$ is the top element of the stack. We use the notation $\mathcal{S}_0\mathcal{S}_1 \cdots \mathcal{S}_n \mid a_1 a_2 \cdots a_k w$ to denote that $\mathcal{S}_0\mathcal{S}_1 \cdots \mathcal{S}_n$ is the current stack and $a_1 a_2 \cdots a_k w$ is the input remaining to be consumed by the parser.

To parse a word w, we start with the configuration

$$\mathcal{S}_0 \mid w \dashv_1^{i_0} \dashv_2^{i_0} \cdots \dashv_k^{i_0}$$

where $\mathcal{S}_0 = \left\{\left[\hat{S} \to \bullet S'; \dashv_1^0 \dashv_2^0 \cdots \dashv_k^0\right]\right\}$. We let $\hat{S}$ be a fresh non-terminal and $\dashv_1, \dashv_2, \cdots, \dashv_k$ be fresh terminals that pad the string to have at least k tokens of lookahead. We then run the following parsing algorithm.

Algorithm 8. *Given configuration $\mathcal{S}_0\mathcal{S}_1 \cdots \mathcal{S}_n \mid a_1^{i_1}, a_2^{i_2} \cdots a_k^{i_k} w$, if $\left[\hat{S} \to S\bullet; u\right] \in \mathcal{S}_n$ and $a_1^{i_1}, a_2^{i_2} \cdots a_k^{i_k} w = \dashv_1^{i_0} \dashv_2^{i_0} \cdots \dashv_k^{i_0}$, then accept. Otherwise:*

1. *Compute the closure, $\mathcal{S}'$, of $\mathcal{S}_n$ where $\mathcal{S}'$ is the least set of items satisfying the recurrence*

$$\begin{aligned}\mathcal{S}' = \mathcal{S}_n \cup \Big\{ & \left[X_{m+1}^{j_{m+1}} \to \bullet Y_1^{l_1} \cdots Y_p^{l_p}; v\right] \\ & \Big| \left[A^i \to X_1^{j_1} \cdots X_m^{j_m} \bullet X_{m+1}^{j_{m+1}} \cdots X_n^{j_n}; u\right] \in \mathcal{S}_n, \\ & X_{m+1}^{j_{m+1}} \to Y_1^{l_1} \cdots Y_p^{l_p} \in \delta' \\ & v \in H_k\left(X_{m+1}^{j_{m+1}} \cdots X_n^{j_n} u\right)\Big\}\end{aligned}$$

2. *Compute the acceptable lookahead set $\mathcal{K}$ where*

$$\begin{aligned}\mathcal{K} = \Big\{v \Big| & \left[A^i \to X_1^{j_1} \cdots X_m^{j_m} \bullet X_{m+1}^{j_{m+1}} \cdots X_n^{j_n}; u\right] \in \mathcal{S}', \\ & v \in H_k\left(X_{m+1}^{j_{m+1}} \cdots X_n^{j_n} u\right)\Big\}\end{aligned}$$

3. *For each production $A^i \to X_1^{j_1} \cdots X_n^{j_n}$ in δ', compute the acceptable lookahead set $\mathcal{K}\left(A^i \to X_1^{j_1} \cdots X_n^{j_n}\right)$ where*

$$\mathcal{K}\left(A^i \to X_1^{j_1} \cdots X_n^{j_n}\right) = \left\{u \middle| \left[A^i \to X_1^{j_1} \cdots X_n^{j_n} \bullet; u\right] \in \mathcal{S}'\right\}$$

4. *Let $GOTO\left(\mathcal{S}, Z^l\right) =$*

$$\begin{aligned}\Big\{ & \left[A^i \to X_1^{j_1} \cdots X_m^{j_m} X_{m+1}^{j_{m+1}} \bullet X_{m+2}^{j_{m+2}} \cdots X_n^{j_n}; v\right] \\ & \Big| \left[A^i \to X_1^{j_1} \cdots X_m^{j_m} \bullet X_{m+1}^{j_{m+1}} X_{m+2}^{j_{m+2}} \cdots X_n^{j_n}; u\right] \in \mathcal{S}, \\ & X_{m+1}^{j_{m+1}} = Z^l\Big\}\end{aligned}$$

   and non-deterministically choose one of the following.

   (a) *If $a_1^{i_1} a_2^{i_2} \cdots a_k^{i_k} \in \mathcal{K}$, then do a shift action by looping back to the start of the algorithm with the new configuration*

$$\mathcal{S}_0\mathcal{S}_1 \cdots \mathcal{S}_n GOTO\left(\mathcal{S}_n, a_1^{i_1}\right) \mid a_2^{i_2} \cdots a_k^{i_k} w$$

   (b) *If $a_1^{i_1} a_2^{i_2} \cdots a_k^{i_k} \in \mathcal{K}\left(A^i \to X_1^{j_1} \cdots X_n^{j_n}\right)$ for some production $A^i \to X_1^{j_1} \cdots X_n^{j_n}$, then do a reduce action by looping back to the start of the algorithm with the new configuration*

$$\mathcal{S}_0\mathcal{S}_1 \cdots \mathcal{S}_{n-m} GOTO\left(\mathcal{S}_{n-m}, A^i\right) \mid a_1^{i_1} a_2^{i_2} \cdots a_k^{i_k} w$$

5.5 Finite representations of stacks

Algorithm 8 contains both non-determinism and infinite sets. Here we depart from Knuth [1965] in order to eliminate these. Up to this point, our parser is simply a standard LR(k) parser, albeit on an infinite II-CFG, and we rely on the correctness of the standard LR(k) parsing algorithm for our correctness. From here forward, we ensure correctness by ensuring that our modified version of the algorithm models the same item sets as Algorithm 8, albeit using a more efficient representation.

As a first step, consider the sets of items that form the stack. Each item is of the form

$$\left[A^i \to X_1^{j_1} \cdots X_m^{j_m} \bullet X_{m+1}^{j_{m+1}} \cdots X_n^{j_n}; u\right]$$

where $A^i \in N \times \mathbb{N}$, $X_1^{j_1}, \cdots, X_n^{j_n} \in (N \cup \Sigma) \times \mathbb{N}$, and $u \in (\Sigma \times \mathbb{N})^k$. Observe that the indentations to the left of the bullet,

$j_1, \cdots, j_m$, do not effect the parsing process, and multiple items that differ only in the values of $j_1, \cdots, j_m$ can therefore be represented by a single item. This reduces the state space slightly, but we can go further and also factor out $j_{m+1}, \cdots, j_n$ by observing that the algorithm preserves the following completeness property for item sets.

Definition 9 (Item-set completeness)**.** We say that an item set, $\mathcal{S}$, is complete if for every $A \to X_1^{\rhd_1} \cdots X_n^{\rhd_n} \in \delta$,

$$\left[A^i \to X_1^{j_1} \cdots X_m^{j_m} \bullet X_{m+1}^{j_{m+1}} \cdots X_n^{j_n}; u\right] \in \mathcal{S}$$

implies that

$$\mathcal{S} \supseteq \Big\{ \left[A^i \to X_1^{j_1} \cdots X_m^{j_m} \bullet X_{m+1}^{j'_{m+1}} \cdots X_n^{j'_n}; u\right] \\ \big| j'_{m+1}, \cdots, j'_n \in \mathbb{N}, j'_{m+1} \rhd_{m+1} i, \cdots, j'_n \rhd_n i \Big\}$$

This property is preserved by each loop through Algorithm 8, as stated in the following lemma.

Lemma 10. *If every item set on the stack is complete at the start of a loop through Algorithm 8, then every item set on the new stack at the start of the next loop is also complete.*

Proof. For every production $X_{m+1} \to Y_1^{\rhd_1} \cdots Y_p^{\rhd_p}$, if the closure step adds the item $\left[X_{m+1}^{j_{m+1}} \to \bullet Y_1^{l_1} \cdots Y_p^{l_p}; v\right]$, then by construction it adds all items of the form $\left[X_{m+1}^{j_{m+1}} \to \bullet Y_1^{l'_1} \cdots Y_p^{l'_p}; v\right]$ where $l'_1 \rhd_1 j_{m+1}, \cdots, l'_p \rhd_1 j_{m+1}$. Thus this step of the algorithm preserves completeness.

The *GOTO* operation filters the set of items by requiring that $X_{m+1}^{j_{m+1}} = Z^l$, but afterwards $X_{m+1}^{j_{m+1}}$ is moved to the left of the bullet and is therefore no longer relevant to the completeness of the item set. Since j_{m+1} is related to $j_{m+2}, \cdots, j_n$ only indirectly through i, the remaining $j_{m+2}, \cdots, j_n$ are complete given the i that remain in the item set. □

Since the item sets in the stack are all complete, we no longer need to represent the individual $j_1, \cdots, j_n$. The only indentations we need to record are i, the indentation of the non-terminal on the left-hand side of the production, and the indentations in u, the expected lookahead. Thus, we can represent items that differ only in the values of $j_1, \cdots, j_n$ with

$$\left[A \to X_1^{\rhd_1} \cdots X_m^{\rhd_m} \bullet X_{m+1}^{\rhd_{m+1}} \cdots X_n^{\rhd_n}; L\right]$$

where $A \to X_1^{\rhd_1}, \cdots, X_n^{\rhd_n} \in \delta$ and $L \subseteq \mathbb{N} \times (\Sigma \times \mathbb{N})^k$. We call L the indentation-and-lookahead set. Each element of L is a pair of i, the indentation for A, and u, the lookahead word.

With this factoring we can implement a GLR parser [Tomita 1985] by letting $k = 0$ and translating Algorithm 8 to use this representation of item sets. Since $k = 0$, the lookahead is always the empty string and L is simply a set of indentations. By examining the algorithm we can further determine that this set will always be either the set $\mathbb{N}$, a finite subset of $\mathbb{N}$, or the union of a finite subset of $\mathbb{N}$ with the set of all elements of $\mathbb{N}$ greater than j for some $j \in \mathbb{N}$. These sets are all finitely representable and thus computable. Finally, the standard technique of elaborating the possible item sets and the transitions between them can be used to construct a state machine for a push-down automaton that recognizes G. During this elaboration, we keep the set of indentations, L, abstract. This ensures that there are only finitely many item sets to be elaborated. At runtime, both the current state and the stack elements then simply store a reference to one of these pre-elaborated item sets along with a concrete indentation set. Any non-determinism remaining in the algorithm is handled using the standard stack representation used by GLR parsers.

5.6 Parsing LR(k) grammars

After having factored the representation of the item sets this far, we eliminate the non-determinism in the algorithm by restricting the algorithm to only LR(k) grammars. Recall that an LR(k) grammar is defined to have a unique rightmost derivation for any given word. Thus there is always a unique handle at each parsing step, and thus in the non-deterministic choice at the end of Algorithm 8 there is never more than one allowed choice. Otherwise, we have a shift/reduce or a reduce/reduce conflict, and the grammar is not an LR(k) grammar.

With the original representation of item sets, we did not apply this criterion because there might be multiple reductions that differ only in their indentations. For example, if we have $A \to B^{\circledast}$ in G, then both $A^1 \to B^1$ and $A^2 \to B^1$ are in G'. These could lead to spurious reduce/reduce conflicts. However, now that items are identified in terms of productions from δ (e.g., $A \to B^{\circledast}$) instead of productions from δ' (e.g., $A^1 \to B^1$), these conflicts no longer occur. Any remaining shift/reduce or reduce/reduce conflicts reflect a conflict in the original grammar, G, and are not artifacts of the translation to G'.

The last remaining source of ambiguity is the indentation-and-lookahead set, L, which can grow infinitely. To resolve this we change the representation of L from being a subset of $\mathbb{N} \times (\Sigma \times \mathbb{N})^k$ to being a subset of $\mathbb{N}$ along with an element of $\left(\bar{\mathbb{I}} \times \bar{\mathbb{I}} \times \Sigma\right)^k \times \bar{\mathbb{I}}$.

We write such an item as

$$\left[A \to X_1^{\rhd_1} \cdots X_m^{\rhd_m} \bullet X_{m+1}^{\rhd_{m+1}} \cdots X_n^{\rhd_n}; \right. \\ \left. I; (\bar{\rhd}_{1,1}, \bar{\rhd}_{1,2}, a_1) \cdots (\bar{\rhd}_{k,1}, \bar{\rhd}_{k,2}, a_k)\, \bar{\rhd}_{k+1}\right]$$

This represents the item

$$\left[A \to X_1^{\rhd_1} \cdots X_m^{\rhd_m} \bullet X_{m+1}^{\rhd_{m+1}} \cdots X_n^{\rhd_n}; L\right]$$

where $S = B^{i_0}$ and

$$\begin{aligned} L = \Big\{ & \left(i, a_1^{j_1} \cdots a_k^{j_k}\right) \\ & | \, i \in I, \\ & i \; \bar{\rhd}_{1,1} \, l_1, \;\; l_1 \, \bar{\rhd}_{2,1} \; l_2, \;\; \cdots, \;\; l_{k-1} \, \bar{\rhd}_{k,1} \, l_k, \\ & j_1 \, \bar{\rhd}_{1,2} \, l_1, \;\; j_2 \, \bar{\rhd}_{2,2} \, l_2, \;\; \cdots, \;\; j_k \quad \bar{\rhd}_{k,2} \, l_k, \\ & l_k \, \bar{\rhd}_{k+1} \, i_0 \Big\} \end{aligned}$$

The intuition behind this representation is best understood in terms of the sort of parse tree that could lead to the item that is trying to parse an A with lookaheads of $a_1 \cdots a_k$. This situation is depicted in Figure 6. Note that there are no terminals between any of A, or $a_1, a_2, \cdots, a_k$, and in the general case, we consider a node to be an ancestor of itself so some of $C_1^{l_1}, C_2^{l_2}, \cdots, C_k^{l_k}$ or B^{i_0} may actually be the same node.

The lookahead token $a_1^{j_1}$ is in the lookahead only because A shares with it the ancestor C_1 at indentation l_1. The $\bar{\rhd}_{1,1}$ and $\bar{\rhd}_{1,2}$ relations record the possible indentation relations between C_1 and, respectively, A and $a_1^{j_1}$. The second lookahead token $a_2^{j_2}$ is in the lookahead only because C_1, the common ancestor of the item and the first lookahead token, also shares with a_2 the common ancestor C_2 at indentation l_2. The $\bar{\rhd}_{2,1}$ and $\bar{\rhd}_{2,2}$ relations record the possible indentation relations between C_2 and, respectively, C_1 and a_2. And so on, until we reach the final ancestor, C_k, at indentation l_k. This ancestor has a minimum indentation at which it can occur so we use $\bar{\rhd}_{k+1}$ to record the indentation relation between C_k and B, the start terminal.

The lookahead computation, H_k, that is defined in Section 5.3 must of course be modified to account for this representation. We omit this because, while conceptually simple, its formal definition is fairly intricate.

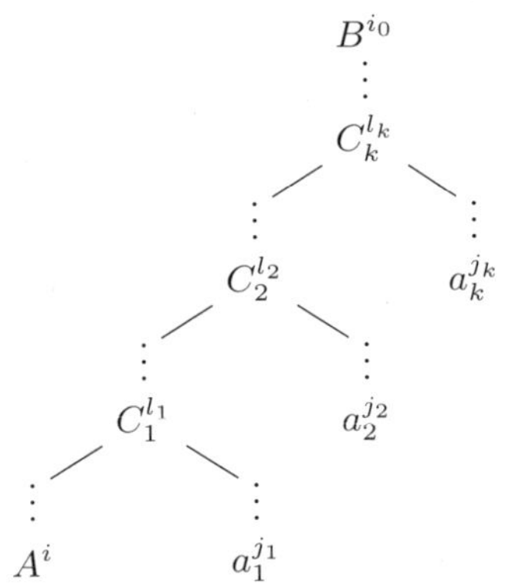

Figure 6. The structure of lookahead tokens in a parse tree.

With this representation, the lookahead set is finitely represented so the only potentially infinite part remaining is the indentation set. However, as before, we can show that these sets are always either the set $\mathbb{N}$, a finite subset of $\mathbb{N}$, or the union of a finite subset of $\mathbb{N}$ with the set of all elements of $\mathbb{N}$ greater than j for some $j \in \mathbb{N}$. Indentation sets are thus finitely representable, and we have completely reduced the parsing algorithm to a finite representation.

We can now construct an LR(k) parser just as we constructed the GLR parser at the end of Section 5.5. As before, to do this we translate Algorithm 8 to use the new item set representation, keep the indentation sets abstract while we elaborate the possible item sets to form the states of the push-down automaton, and at runtime augment the automaton states and stack entries with concrete indentation sets.

5.7 Correctness of item set representation

We must consider carefully the correctness of the parsing algorithm based on the item-set representation given in Section 5.6. At first glance, the representation looks like it could lead to lookaheads matching when they should not. Indeed, the following grammar of variable references (i.e., ID) and do blocks with vertically aligned statements shows how this can arise:

$$\begin{array}{lll}
\texttt{expr} & \to & \texttt{ID}^{>} \\
\texttt{expr} & \to & \texttt{'do'}^{>}\ |\texttt{stmts}|^{>} \\
\texttt{stmts} & \to & |\texttt{expr}|^{=} \\
\texttt{stmts} & \to & \texttt{stmts}^{=}\ |\texttt{expr}|^{=}
\end{array}$$

For example, consider the parse of the word $\texttt{'do'}^{1}\ \texttt{'do'}^{4}\ \texttt{ID}^{7}\ \texttt{ID}^{2}$ which may come from the code:

```
do do x
 y
```

Note that y does not align with either the second do or the x, and thus this code should be rejected. Put another way, the valid lookaheads when looking ahead at the ID for y but before reducing x to expr are $\texttt{ID}^4$, $\texttt{ID}^7$, $\texttt{'do'}^4$, and $\texttt{'do'}^7$. The string should thus be rejected since $\texttt{ID}^2$, the token for y, is not in that set. But the LR(1) lookahead set using the new representation is $\{((\geq, =, \texttt{ID})>), ((\geq, =, \texttt{'do'})>)\}$. Since the current indentation is 7 and there exist l such that $7 \geq l$, $2 = l$, and $l > 0$, the string will not be immediately rejected.

This representation thus appears to over approximate the set of indentations for a particular lookahead. This means that in the non-deterministic choice at the end of Algorithm 8 there could be more reductions possible than there should be. However, as we restrict ourselves to LR(k) grammars, this turns out to not be a problem. This is because there are only four cases where these spurious reductions occur:

Case 1. There should be *no* reductions or shifts possible, but the approximation makes *one* extra reduction possible.

In this case, the parser should reject the program, but will instead reduce and continue parsing. However, this case happens only when some other item set further up the stack also checks the lookahead tokens. Though the string is not rejected immediately, it will be rejected once we reach that point in the stack. In our example, once x reduces to expr and then do x reduces to an expr that finally reduces to stmts, the lookahead set will be $\{((=, =, \texttt{ID})>), ((=, =, \texttt{'do'})>)\}$. Since the indentation at that point is 4 but the next token is ID^2, the parser will reject the program. The program might not be rejected as soon as we expect, but it is eventually rejected. This case may arise even when the grammar is LR(k).

Case 2. There should be *no* shifts or reductions possible, but the approximation makes *two or more* extra reductions possible.

The representation for lookaheads in Section 5.6 is designed so that every lookahead word that it represents comes from a valid parse. Thus if this representation generates multiple possible reductions, then there is some string that would also generate those multiple possible reductions with the original representation in Algorithm 8. In that case, the grammar is not LR(k), and the grammar should be rejected by the parser generator.

Case 3. There should be *one* reduction or shift possible, but the approximation makes *one or more* extra reductions possible.

The same reasoning applies as in the preceding case.

Case 4. There should be *two or more* reductions or shifts possible.

Then the original grammar is not LR(k), and the grammar should be rejected by the parser generator.

This means that the representation in Section 5.6 is valid for any grammar that is LR(k), and furthermore we can detect when a grammar is not LR(k) by using this representation.

5.8 An efficiency consideration

Note that each item in an item set may have a different set of indentations. For example, we may have an item set containing both of the following two items:

$$[A \to \bullet a^{>} b^{=}; I; u]$$
$$[A \to \bullet a^{=} b^{=}; I; u]$$

Even if they start with the same indentation set, I, after reading an a, the indentation sets for these items will be different from each other. For the first item, the indentation set will be restricted to indentations strictly greater than the indentation for a. For the second item, the indentations will be restricted to indentations equal to that of a. Thus, different items can have different indentation sets, and a naive factoring (e.g., sharing I between items in an item set) is insufficient. This does not preclude the possibility of a clever refactoring like the one done with the lookahead sets, but we have been unable to find such a factoring that works in all cases. Nevertheless, as a practical matter the following techniques seem to work well.

Observe that we need to keep only the indentation sets for items before the closure is taken. Items generated by the closure operation can be annotated with the $\trianglerighteq$ that can lead to them and this value can be incorporated into the lookahead check. In addition, when we can determine that some set of items will always have the same indentation set, we can represent them using a common

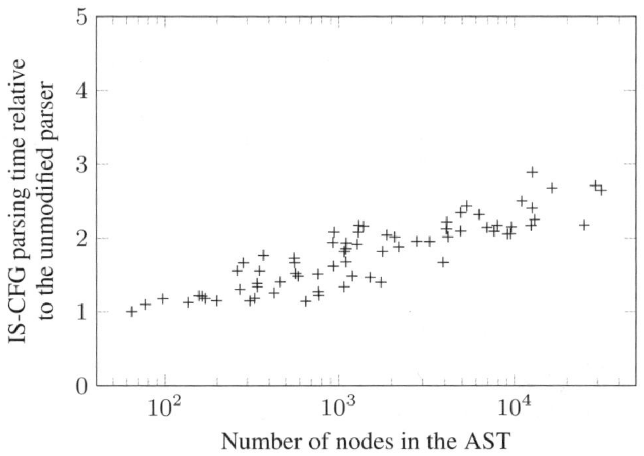

Figure 7. Benchmark results.

indentation set. These techniques reduce the number of indentation sets that must be passed from one state to another, and based on the experience implementing the Haskell parser in Section 6, the resulting number of such sets is usually one.

6. Implementation

In order to verify the real-world practicality of this parsing technique, we modified the Happy parser generator [Marlow and Gill 2009] to support the parsing techniques presented in this paper. The parser is LALR instead of LR(k), but the techniques shown in Section 5 generalize straightforwardly to LALR. Note that this implementation is only a prototype and is only intended for testing the practical feasibility of parsing with IS-CFGs. In particular, no significant effort was put into optimizing the performance of the generated parser.

The Haskell parser from the `haskell-src` package [Marlow et al. 2011] uses techniques for implementing layout similar to those used by GHC. However, it is packaged as a standalone parser, and this makes it easy to isolate for benchmarking purposes. This parser was modified to use an IS-CFG instead of using shared state between the lexer and parser. Both the modified and unmodified versions were then run on the preprocessed source files from the `base` package [bas 2012]. Two modules (`GHC.Float` and `GHC.Constants`) could not be preprocessed due to missing header files. Of the 178 remaining Haskell modules, 85 cannot be parsed by the unmodified `haskell-src` parser due to syntactic extensions, such as rank-2 types, that are not supported by `haskell-src`. This left 93 source files that are parsable by the unmodified parser. All of these files parsed and produced the same parse tree when parsed using the IS-CFG based parser.

Figure 7 shows the parsing times of the modified parser relative to the unmodified parser when run on these files. These benchmarks were compiled using GHC version 7.0.3 with the `-O2`, `-optl-static` and `-optl-pthread` flags and were run on a 64-bit, 3.2GHz Xeon running Ubuntu 12.04 with 4GB of RAM. Timing measurements were collected using Criterion version 0.6.0.1 with 1000 samples per benchmark.

Note that the `haskell-src` parser is designed to run both the lexer and the parser simultaneously so they can share information about indentations. It is difficult to separate the execution of the parser from the execution of the lexer, so the lexing time is included in the times for both that parser and the IS-CFG based one.

As expected, the IS-CFG based parser runs in approximately linear time. It is geometrically on average 1.73 times slower than the unmodified `haskell-src` parser. There is a slight upward trend in the factor by which the IS-CFG based parser is slower than the unmodified parser. This is primarily due to the fact that we are graphing the ratio between the performance of the modified and unmodified parsers and the unmodified parser has low-order performance overheads that are more significant on small inputs. Given that this is a prototype implementation with little optimization, the fact that the IS-CFG version is only one to three times slower than the standard `haskell-src` parser is promising. This overhead is likely due to the manipulation of the indentation sets as the representation of indentation sets is naive. Since in practice only certain sorts of sets are common (e.g., singletons and the set $\mathbb{N}$), an improved version could optimize for these sorts of sets. In addition, we could take advantage of the tokens with an indentation of infinity by adding a fast path through the parser that short circuits the indentation computations.

7. Related Work

The `uulib` parser library [Swierstra 2011] and the `indents` [Anklesaria 2012] and `indentparser` [Kurur 2012] extensions to the Parsec [Leijen and Martini 2012] parser library provide support for indentation-sensitive parsing. To the best of our knowledge there is no published, formal theory for the sort of indentation that these parsers implement. They are all combinator-based, top-down parsers and use some variation of threading state through a parser monad to track the current indentation.

Hutton [1992] describes an approach to parsing indentation-sensitive languages that is based on filtering the token stream. This idea is further developed by Hutton and Meijer [1996]. In both cases, the layout combinator searches the token stream for appropriately indented tokens and passes only those tokens to the combinator for the expression to which the layout rule applies. As each use of layout scans the remaining tokens in the input, this can lead to quadratic running time. Given that the layout combinator filters tokens before parsing occurs, this technique also cannot support subexpressions, such as parenthesized expressions in Python, that are exempt from layout constraints. Thus, this approach is incapable of expressing many real-world languages including ISWIM, Habit, Haskell, and Python.

Erdweg et al. [2012] propose a method of parsing indentation-sensitive languages by effectively filtering the parse trees generated by a GLR parser. The GLR parser generates all possible parse trees irrespective of layout. Indentation constraints on each parse node then remove the trees that violate the layout rules. For performance reasons, this filtering is interleaved with the execution of the GLR parser when possible. Aside from the fact that they require a GLR parser and thus generate parse trees that might not be used, a critical difference between their system and the one presented in this paper is that their indentation constraints are in terms of the set of tokens under a non-terminal whereas the system in this paper uses constraints between non-terminals and their immediate children. Thus, the two approaches look at the problem from different perspectives. Erdweg et al. [2012] do not consider the question of an LR(k) parser.

Brunauer and Mühlbacher [2006] take a unique approach to specifying the indentation-sensitive aspects of a language. They use a scannerless grammar that uses individual characters as tokens and has non-terminals that take an integer counter as parameter. This integer is threaded through the grammar and eventually specifies the number of spaces that must occur within certain productions. The grammar encodes the indentation rules of the language by carefully arranging how this parameter is threaded through the grammar and thus how many whitespace characters should occur at each point in the grammar.

While encoding indentation sensitivity this way is formally precise, it comes at a cost. The YAML specification [Ben-Kiki et al. 2009] uses the approach proposed by Brunauer and Mühlbacher [2006] and as a result has about a dozen and a half different non-terminals for various sorts of whitespace and comments. With this encoding, the grammar cannot use a separate tokenizer and must be scannerless, each possible occurrence of whitespace must be explicit in the grammar, and the grammar must carefully track which non-terminals produce or expect what sorts of whitespace. The authors of the YAML grammar establish naming conventions for non-terminals that help manage this, but the result is still a grammar that is difficult to comprehend and even more difficult to modify.

While this approach bears some similarity to the technique proposed in this paper, a key difference is that their method uses the parameters of non-terminals to generate explicit whitespace characters and thus incurs a significant accounting overhead in the design of the grammar. On the other hand, the system presented in this paper operates at a higher level, using the parameter to indicate the column or indentation at which non-terminals and terminals should occur. This is a subtle distinction, but it has a profound impact. As shown in Section 3, layout rules are comparatively simple to encode this way, and as shown in Section 5, this formalism is amenable to traditional parsing techniques such as LR(k) parsing.

Note that none of the systems reviewed above present an LR(k) parsing algorithm. They use either top-down parsers or, in the case of Erdweg et al. [2012], a GLR parser.

8. Conclusion

This paper presents a grammatical formalism for indentation-sensitive languages. It is both expressive and easy to use. We derive provably correct GLR and LR(k) parsers for this formalism. Though not shown here, CYK, SLR, LALR, GLL and LL(k) parsers can also be constructed by appropriately using the key technique of factoring item sets. Experiments on a Haskell parser using this formalism show that the parser runs between one and three times slower than a parser using traditional *ad hoc* techniques for handling indentation sensitivity. Improvements in the handling of indentation sets may reduce this overhead. Using these techniques, the layout rules of a wide variety of languages can be expressed easily and parsed effectively.

Acknowledgments

Feedback from Andrew Tolmach, R. Kent Dybvig, Tim Sheard, Mark P. Jones, Nathan Collins, Steffen Lösch and the anonymous referees helped improve the presentation of this paper.

References

base version 4.5.1.0, June 2012. URL `http://hackage.haskell.org/package/base/`.

Sam Anklesaria. indents version 0.3.3, May 2012. URL `http://hackage.haskell.org/package/indents/`.

Oren Ben-Kiki, Clark Evans, and Ingy döt Net. *YAML Ain't Markup Language (YAML) Version 1.2*, 3rd edition, October 2009. URL `http://www.yaml.org/spec/1.2/spec.html`.

Leonhard Brunauer and Bernhard Mühlbacher. Indentation sensitive languages. Unpublished manuscript, July 2006. URL `http://www.cs.uni-salzburg.at/~ck/wiki/uploads/TCS-Summer-2006.IndentationSensitiveLanguages/`.

Janusz A. Brzozowski. Derivatives of regular expressions. *Journal of the ACM (JACM)*, 11(4):481–494, October 1964. ISSN 0004-5411. doi: 10.1145/321239.321249.

Sebastian Erdweg, Tillmann Rendel, Christian Kästner, and Klaus Ostermann. Layout-sensitive generalized parsing. In *Software Language Engineering*, Lecture Notes in Computer Science. Springer Berlin / Heidelberg, 2012. URL `http://sugarj.org/layout-parsing.pdf`. To appear.

The Glorious Glasgow Haskell Compilation System User's Guide, Version 7.2.1. The GHC Team, August 2011. URL `http://www.haskell.org/ghc/docs/7.2.1/html/users_guide/`.

David Goodger. *reStructuredText Markup Specification*, January 2012. URL `http://docutils.sourceforge.net/docs/ref/rst/restructuredtext.html`. Revision 7302.

John Gruber. *Markdown: Syntax*. URL `http://daringfireball.net/projects/markdown/syntax`. Retrieved on June 24, 2012.

Michael Hanus (ed.). Curry: An integrated functional logic language (version 0.8.2). Technical report, March 2006. URL `http://www.informatik.uni-kiel.de/~curry/report.html`.

HASP Project. The Habit programming language: The revised preliminary report, November 2010. URL `http://hasp.cs.pdx.edu/habit-report-Nov2010.pdf`.

Graham Hutton. Higher-order functions for parsing. *Journal of Functional Programming*, 2(03):323–343, July 1992. doi: 10.1017/S0956796800000411.

Graham Hutton and Erik Meijer. Monadic parser combinators. Technical Report NOTTCS-TR-96-4, Department of Computer Science, University of Nottingham, 1996.

INMOS Limited. *occam programming manual*. Prentice-Hall international series in computer science. Prentice-Hall International, 1984. ISBN 978-0-13-629296-8.

Mark P. Jones. The implementation of the Gofer functional programming system. Research Report YALEU/DCS/RR-1030, Yale University, New Haven, Connecticut, USA, May 1994.

Donald E. Knuth. On the translation of languages from left to right. *Information and Control*, 8(6):607–639, December 1965. ISSN 0019-9958. doi: 10.1016/S0019-9958(65)90426-2.

Piyush P. Kurur. indentparser version 0.1, January 2012. URL `http://hackage.haskell.org/package/indentparser/`.

P. J. Landin. The next 700 programming languages. *Communications of the ACM*, 9(3):157–166, March 1966. ISSN 0001-0782. doi: 10.1145/365230.365257.

Daan Leijen and Paolo Martini. parsec version 3.1.3, June 2012. URL `http://hackage.haskell.org/package/parsec/`.

Simon Marlow and Andy Gill. *Happy User Guide*, 2009. URL `http://www.haskell.org/happy/doc/html/`. For Happy version 1.18.

Simon Marlow, Sven Panne, and Noel Winstanley. haskell-src version 1.0.1.5, November 2011. URL `http://hackage.haskell.org/package/haskell-src`.

Simon Marlow (ed.). *Haskell 2010 Language Report*, April 2010. URL `http://www.haskell.org/onlinereport/haskell2010/`.

Egil Möller. *SRFI-49: Indentation-sensitive syntax*, May 2005. URL `http://srfi.schemers.org/srfi-49/srfi-49.html`.

Python. *The Python Language Reference*. URL `http://docs.python.org/reference/`. Retrieved on June 26, 2012.

S. Doaitse Swierstra. uulib version 0.9.14, August 2011. URL `http://hackage.haskell.org/package/uulib/`.

Don Syme et al. *The F# 2.0 Language Specification*. Microsoft Corporation, April 2010. URL `https://research.microsoft.com/en-us/um/cambridge/projects/fsharp/manual/spec.html`. Updated April 2012.

Masaru Tomita. *Efficient Parsing for Natural Language: A Fast Algorithm for Practical Systems*. Kluwer International Series in Engineering and Computer Science. Kluwer Academic Publishers, 1985. ISBN 978-0-89838-202-0.

D. A. Turner. *Miranda System Manual*. Research Software Limited, 1989. URL `http://www.cs.kent.ac.uk/people/staff/dat/miranda/manual/`.

Philip Wadler. An introduction to Orwell. Technical report, Programming Research Group at Oxford University, 1985.

The Ramifications of Sharing in Data Structures

Aquinas Hobor
National University of Singapore
hobor@comp.nus.edu.sg

Jules Villard
University College London
j.villard@cs.ucl.ac.uk

Abstract

Programs manipulating mutable data structures with intrinsic sharing present a challenge for modular verification. Deep aliasing inside data structures dramatically complicates reasoning in isolation over parts of these objects because changes to one part of the structure (say, the left child of a dag node) can affect other parts (the right child or some of its descendants) that may point into it. The result is that finding intuitive and compositional proofs of correctness is usually a struggle. We propose a compositional proof system that enables local reasoning in the presence of sharing.

While the AI "frame problem" elegantly captures the reasoning required to verify programs without sharing, we contend that natural reasoning about programs with sharing instead requires an answer to a different and more challenging AI problem, the "ramification problem": reasoning about the indirect consequences of actions. Accordingly, we present a RAMIFY proof rule that attacks the ramification problem head-on and show how to reason with it. Our framework is valid in any separation logic and permits sound compositional and local reasoning in the context of both specified and unspecified sharing. We verify the correctness of a number of examples, including programs that manipulate dags, graphs, and overlaid data structures in nontrivial ways.

Categories and Subject Descriptors F.3.1 [*Specifying and Verifying and Reasoning about Programs*]: Logics of programs; D.2.4 [*Software/Program Verification*]: Correctness proofs, Formal methods

General Terms Languages, Theory, Verification.

Keywords Aliasing, Heap/Shape, Modularity, Separation logic.

1. Introduction

Data structures with intrinsic sharing, such as acyclic and unrestricted graphs as well as various kinds of overlaid data structures, are pervasive in computing. An example of an overlaid data structure can be found in the Linux deadline I/O scheduler, in which the set of events forms both a singly linked list and a binary sorted tree, depending on which links one follows. Programs manipulating data structures with sharing are often short, but the reason that they are correct can be subtle, and previous work has not come up with general, intuitive and compositional principles for reasoning about such programs. The key difficulty is that deep aliasing dramatically complicates reasoning in isolation over parts of these objects: changes to one part of the structure (say, the left child of a dag) can affect other parts (the right child or its descendants) that may point into it.

We propose a compositional proof system for programs manipulating shared data structures. Our framework directly addresses the intrinsic sharing present in the data structures and achieves compositionality via applications of the following *ramify rule*:

$$\textsc{Ramify}\quad \frac{\{P\}\ c\ \{Q\} \qquad \mathit{ramify}(R, P, Q, R')}{\{R\}\ c\ \{R'\}}$$

At first glance there seems to be no connection between the known spec $\{P\}\ c\ \{Q\}$ and the desired spec $\{R\}\ c\ \{R'\}$. The connection is given by the *ramification*, indicated by the $\mathit{ramify}(R, P, Q, R')$ premise, which asserts (semantically, although this paper also provides ways to reason syntactically about it) that the "global" assertion R becomes R' after a "local" transformation from P to Q.

The term "ramification" comes from artificial intelligence [Fin87, Thi01] and refers to the problem of understanding the indirect (global) consequences of (local) actions (*e.g.* relocating a bookcase might reduce the ambient light by blocking the window). Ramification is contrasted with the simpler "frame" problem, which centers on maintaining knowledge after unrelated actions (*e.g.*, relocating the bookcase does not change the number of moons of Jupiter).

Program verification has had significant success handling the frame problem, especially with the frame rule of separation logic [Rey02]:

$$\textsc{Frame}\quad \frac{\{P\}\ c\ \{Q\}}{\{P * F\}\ c\ \{Q * F\}}$$

Here the *separating conjunction* $*$ ensures that P and F cover *disjoint* pieces of heap, allowing the frame rule to guarantee that F is unchanged under the action of c. The frame rule buys us compositionality in the presence of the heap: we can reason about the effect a program has on the portions of heap it accesses, and reuse that spec in any bigger heap. This has given rise to concise, compositional proofs of programs, even in the presence of *some* forms of sharing where one knows *what* is shared *by whom*.

Unfortunately, we usually cannot use the frame rule directly when verifying programs that manipulate data structures with *unrestricted* sharing because such structures cannot easily be massaged into the form $P * F$: for example, the left and right descendants of a dag node are not usually disjoint. The reason to focus on ramification rather than frame is that the former allows us to reuse specs for c in far more diverse settings than the latter permits. Of course, with great power comes great responsibility: having isolated the parts of the proof that require careful examination of indirect effects on the global structure, we are left with ramification obligations to prove.

As it turns out, ramifications are expressible as separation logic entailments: $\mathit{ramify}(R, P, Q, R') \stackrel{\text{def}}{=} R \vdash P * (Q \mathrel{-\!\!*} R')$. These entailments feature the "magic wand" connective of separation logic ("for all states σ_1 satisfying Q and disjoint from the current state σ_2, the combination of both states $\sigma_1 \oplus \sigma_2$ satisfies R'"), which is notor-

POPL'13 January 23–25, 2013, Rome, Italy.

iously hard to reason about in general given the universal quantification over states. However, appearances of $-\!\!*$ in ramifications are restricted to a particular idiom that, together with $*$, denotes an *update* to the state. Guided by this intuition, we are able to reduce these spatial entailments to more abstract reasoning about the nature of the update on the structure's mathematical representation (*e.g.*, graphs as sets of nodes and edges and transformations on said graphs). The verification process thus divides into two parts: first, showing that a concrete program correctly implements some transformation on an abstract mathematical structure; and second, showing that those mathematical transformations produce the desired specification.

This division gives us the freedom to describe data structures with intrinsic sharing in the most natural way. We will present examples that use the separating conjunction $*$ of separation logic to reason about genuine disjointness (*e.g.*, between the parent of a dag node and its children), the overlapping conjunction $\uplus$ to reason about unspecified sharing (*e.g.*, between the left and right children of a dag node), and the classical conjunction to reason about complete sharing (*e.g.*, an overlaid data structure).

In contrast to previous work, we achieve *compositional* reasoning and *embrace* the sharing. Approaches based on separation logic favored convoluted invariants that hacked the state into the disjoint pieces required by the frame rule. Often the predicate definitions depended heavily on the program at hand (*e.g.* the dag definition used could depend on the order of traversal in the algorithm [BCO04]). In other words, previous attempts to reason about shared data structures with separation logic have stood on their head to avoid the sharing. Other approaches suffered from these problems at least as much and often gave up compositionality altogether [Bor00].

Our key contributions are as follows:

- We present the RAMIFY rule which enables local reasoning while accounting for global effects precisely when they are required. Ramification can reason about programs that manipulate data structures with unrestricted sharing while enabling the small specifications, compositionality, and expressiveness that have led to separation logic's success.
- Although the ramify rule leads to more natural Hoare proofs, the entailment checks can be nontrivial. We have developed a "ramification library" of lemmas that help simplify the ramification conditions. Crucially, we also show how to *prove* ramifications concerned with certain general graph and dag updates in a way that enables a separation of concern between heap manipulations and mathematical reasoning about graphs.
- We have applied the ramify rule to a variety of algorithms that manipulate data structures with nontrivial sharing. Although some of the examples are not long, all involve intricate reasoning due to the heavy use of sharing. We think that a strength of our approach is that the Hoare invariants at each program point are natural and seem to follow our "programmer's intuition" much more closely than traditional proofs.
- We give a semantic account of ramification, and show that RAMIFY and FRAME are each derivable from the other, meaning that our framework is applicable in any separation logic. Moreover, we identify the precise constraints on the underlying model that enable the overlapping conjunction $\uplus$, and show that most separation logics in the literature can therefore follow our recipe and use it to reason about unspecified sharing.

The rest of the paper is organized as follows: we first recall some important concepts from separation logic (§2). We then motivate and present the ramify rule (§3), and show how to reason about it (§4). Based on this, we provide proof sketches for three examples that showcase different aspects of ramification: marking a dag (§5), removing from an overlaid data structure (§6), and Cheney's garbage collector (§7). Finally, we show how ramification is applicable in virtually any separation logic (§8), compare to related works, and conclude.

2. Separation Logic and Trees

Recall the framework of separation logic [IO01, Rey02] while considering the following `mark` procedure, written in C, that recursively marks binary trees, dags, or graphs:

```
1 struct node {int m; struct node *l,*r;};
2 void mark(struct node *x) {
3   if (!x || x->m) return;
4   struct node *l = x->l, *r = x->r;
5   x->m = 1; mark(l); mark(r); }
```

Separation logic allows straightforward inductive definitions of predicates to describe tree-like data structures in the heap. The following definition disregards the actual contents and location of each node, but does make sure that the structure is acyclic (thanks to the $*$ between the root and the subtrees) and that no sharing occurs between subtrees (thanks to the $*$ between the children):

$$\mathsf{tree}(x) \stackrel{\text{def}}{=} (x = 0 \wedge \mathsf{emp}) \vee \exists d, l, r.\, x \mapsto d, l, r * \mathsf{tree}(l) * \mathsf{tree}(r)$$

The definition of tree uses the standard *classical* separation logic operators. A heaplet h satisfies the points-to predicate $x \mapsto y$ when h contains *only* the location x, whose value is y, and the separating conjunction $P * Q$ asserts that P and Q hold on disjoint subheaps. We use $x \mapsto d, l, r$ as a shorthand for $(x+0) \mapsto d * (x+1) \mapsto l * (x+2) \mapsto r$ (simplifying the memory model so that *e.g.*, each datum occupies one unit of space).

It is well-known how to use separation logic to prove the `mark` procedure memory safe for trees. Moreover, the separation logic proof mirrors the programmer's intuitions beautifully. The crux of the verification is to handle the recursive calls via the frame rule, *e.g.*, at line 5, taking the spec of `mark` as a premise:

$$\dfrac{\{\mathsf{tree}(\mathtt{l})\}\ \mathtt{mark(l)}\ \{\mathsf{tree}(\mathtt{l})\}}{\begin{array}{l}\{\mathtt{t} \mapsto 1, \mathtt{l}, \mathtt{r} * \mathsf{tree}(\mathtt{l}) * \mathsf{tree}(\mathtt{r})\}\\ \mathtt{mark(l)}\\ \{\mathtt{t} \mapsto 1, \mathtt{l}, \mathtt{r} * \mathsf{tree}(\mathtt{l}) * \mathsf{tree}(\mathtt{r})\}\end{array}}\ \textsc{Frame} \quad (1)$$

This is a canonical example of how inductive predicates, the separating conjunction, and the frame rule fit together to produce concise proofs. Unrolling the tree predicate yields $*$-conjoined formulas, so the proof system, via its frame rule, is able to perform surgery on the symbolic state and work on each sub-state independently.

3. Ramifications for Sharing

We now turn to the case of data structures with sharing, and introduce our RAMIFY rule. We begin by defining inductive predicates for dags and graphs before presenting the proof sketch that we aspire to for the `mark` procedure when applied to dags.

3.1 Dag and Graph Predicates

Our first task is to define a dag predicate. Since the separating conjunction $*$ prevents sharing, our first attempt updates tree to utilize regular conjunction $\wedge$ between the children instead:

$$\mathsf{dag}_0(x) \stackrel{\text{def}}{=} (x = 0 \wedge \mathsf{emp}) \vee \exists l, r.\, x \mapsto l, r * (\mathsf{dag}_0(l) \wedge \mathsf{dag}_0(r))$$

Unfortunately, in *classical* separation logic, $\mathsf{dag}_0(x)$ actually describes a linked list because the conjunction forces the two sub-dags to occupy *exactly* the same space in memory ($h \models P \wedge Q$ if $h \models P$ and $h \models Q$). However, Reynolds points out that dag_0 is correct in *intuitionistic* separation logic, in which $x \mapsto y$ holds on any heap that contains *at least* x, rather than *only* x [Rey02, §6]. Translated into our classical setting this is equivalent to defining dags as follows:

$$\mathsf{dag}_1(x) \stackrel{\text{def}}{=} (x = 0 \wedge \mathsf{emp}) \vee \exists l, r.\, x \mapsto l, r * ((\mathsf{dag}_1(l) * \mathsf{true}) \wedge (\mathsf{dag}_1(r) * \mathsf{true}))$$

If our first attempt was in some sense "too small", then our second is "too big": $\mathsf{dag}_1(x)$ holds on any heap that contains *at least* a dag rooted at x. As usual in intuitionistic separation logic, it is impossible to fully verify certain algorithms (*e.g.* showing that dag disposal completely frees the structure) using dag_1.

What we want is a way to get the overlapping features of the intuitionistic conjunction without actually becoming intuitionistic. We turn to another connective, scarcely studied in the published literature, which we dub the *overlapping conjunction* and write $\circledast$, and which precisely characterizes the desired sharing:

$$h \models P \circledast Q \stackrel{\text{def}}{=} \exists h_1, h_2, h_3.\ (h_1 \oplus h_2 \oplus h_3 = h) \wedge (h_1 \oplus h_2 \models P) \wedge (h_2 \oplus h_3 \models Q)$$

The $\oplus$ is the combination operator on the underlying separation algebra [COY07] (often some kind of disjoint union). Contrast the definition of $\circledast$ with the standard definition of $*$:

$$h \models P * Q \stackrel{\text{def}}{=} \exists h_1, h_2.\ (h_1 \oplus h_2 = h) \wedge (h_1 \models P) \wedge (h_2 \models Q)$$

Here are some properties of $\circledast$ for reference and to aid intuition.

Lemma 3.1

$$P \circledast \mathsf{emp} \dashv\vdash P \quad (2)$$
$$P \wedge Q \vdash P \circledast Q \quad (3)$$
$$P * Q \vdash P \circledast Q \quad (4)$$
$$P \circledast Q \vdash P * \mathsf{true} \quad (5)$$
$$P \circledast Q \dashv\vdash \exists R.\ (R \mathrel{-\!\!*} P) * (R \mathrel{-\!\!*} Q) * R \quad (6)$$
$$P \circledast Q \dashv\vdash Q \circledast P \quad (7)$$
$$P \circledast (Q \circledast R) \dashv\vdash (P \circledast Q) \circledast R \quad (8)$$
$$covar(F_1) \Rightarrow covar(F_2) \Rightarrow covar(\lambda P.\ F_1(P) \circledast F_2(P)) \quad (9)$$

Equations (2), (3), (4) and (5) are immediate from the definition of $\circledast$. We use quantification over predicates in (6). Commutativity (7) is direct from (6) and the commutativity of $*$. In contrast, associativity (8) is trickier and requires cross split (see §8.3). Finally, Lem. (9) enables $\circledast$ to be used in covariant[1] recursive predicates, just like $*$ and $\wedge$. Whenever we write recursive definitions using $\circledast$, including dag and graph below, we are implicitly using (9).

The key point to $\circledast$ is that we can use it in exactly the same places that feature the kinds of sharing that the intuitionistic $\wedge$ captures, but it does not "over-approximate" the resulting structure. That is, it allows us to define a classical dag (with a data field) as:

$$\mathsf{dag}(x) \stackrel{\text{def}}{=} (x = 0 \wedge \mathsf{emp}) \vee \exists d, l, r.\ x \mapsto d, l, r * (\mathsf{dag}(l) \circledast \mathsf{dag}(r)) \quad (10)$$

The separating conjunction $*$ between the root x and its children prevents cycles in the data structure. Pleasingly, the definition for graphs simply replaces this remaining $*$ with another $\circledast$:

$$\mathsf{graph}(x) \stackrel{\text{def}}{=} (x = 0 \wedge \mathsf{emp}) \vee \exists d, l, r.\ x \mapsto d, l, r \circledast \mathsf{graph}(l) \circledast \mathsf{graph}(r) \quad (11)$$

We will equip dag and graph with mathematical dags δ and graphs γ to enable proofs of functional correctness, writing $\mathsf{dag}(x, \delta)$ and $\mathsf{graph}(x, \gamma)$ respectively; δ and γ need not be "tight" and so can include vertices that are unreachable from x. Mathematical trees lack sharing and are hence directly definable as terms; mathematical dags δ and graphs γ are more complicated and so we defer the associated formal definitions until §4.2; one key notation is $\delta(x) = (d, l, r)$, which indicates that the mathematical node x is associated with data d and successors l and r.

Unspecified Sharing Observe that $\circledast$ models *unspecified sharing*: *i.e.*, the dag predicate does not say which parts of a dag are shared. In contrast, *specified sharing* requires the precise identification of the shared part, *e.g.* on a dag identifying which nodes are shared between the left and right children; often this is very difficult.

[1] $covar(F) \stackrel{\text{def}}{=} (P \vdash Q) \Rightarrow F(P) \vdash F(Q)$

```
1  void mark(struct node *x) { // {dag(x,δ)}
2    struct node *l,*r;
3    if (x == 0 || x->m == 1) return;
4    l = x->l; r = x->r;
5  // {x ↦ 0,l,r * (dag(l,δ) ⊛ dag(r,δ)) ∧ δ(x) = (0,l,r)}
6    x->m = 1;
7  // {x ↦ 1,l,r * (dag(l,δ) ⊛ dag(r,δ)) ∧ δ(x) = (0,l,r)}
8    mark(l);
9  //↯(23) { x ↦ 1,l,r * (dag(l,m(δ,l)) ⊛ dag(r,m(δ,l))) ∧
           δ(x) = (0,l,r) }
10   mark(r);
11 //↯(24) { x ↦ 1,l,r * (dag(l,δ') ⊛ dag(r,δ')) ∧
           δ(x) = (0,l,r) ∧ δ' = m(m(δ,l),r) }
12 } // {dag(x,m(δ,x))}
```

Figure 1: Proof sketch for marking a binary dag. The steps that induce ramifications are indicated with $\lightning_i$, where the associated ramification entailment is equation number i.

On the other hand, sometimes specified sharing is exactly what the doctor ordered. Although the overlapping conjunction is extremely useful, our framework is not based around it, and one of our key contributions is that RAMIFY can handle both specified and unspecified sharing. For an example of specified sharing, see §6, which uses $\wedge$ instead of $\circledast$; moreover, see §8.3 for how we can use the explicit overlapping conjunction of Cherini and Blanco [CB09].

3.2 Ramifications of Manipulating Dags

Fig. 1 presents the annotated[2] proof sketch of the functional correctness of `mark` when applied to dags using the small spec $\{\mathsf{dag}(\mathtt{l}, \delta)\}$ `mark(l)` $\{\mathsf{dag}(\mathtt{l}, m(\delta, \mathtt{l}))\}$. The function $m(\delta, x)$, whose formal definition is deferred until §5, indicates the mathematical dag derived from δ via marking starting from node x. Notice that this specification immediately implies that if the initial dag is unmarked then the final dag is completely marked.

As is the case for many recursive programs on graph-like data structures, part of the state tracking the recursive exploration of the graph resides in the call stack, which remembers which states have been only partially processed. Our spec accounts for this complexity while remaining local (*i.e.*, it only describes the portion of memory accessed by `mark`), enabling compositional reasoning. Moreover, we enjoy straightforward invariants at each program point.

Although the invariants are natural, the proof in separation logic is far from obvious. Things are straightforward enough until we reach the first recursive call at line 8. For tree we applied the frame rule in equation 1, which worked very well. While we can easily frame away the $\mathtt{x} \mapsto 1, \mathtt{l}, \mathtt{r}$ from the precondition (line 7), disentangling the two dag predicates into $\mathsf{dag}(\mathtt{l}, \delta)$ on the one hand and a $*$-disjoint frame on the other would necessitate describing the shape of the right child once everything that is shared with the left child has been removed, which is exactly what we wish to avoid. The second recursive call, in line 10, presents exactly the same problem: we wish to frame but cannot. These two recursive calls require a new proof pattern that we call *ramification*.

3.3 The RAMIFY Rule

While the proof outline of Fig. 1 provides all the invariants needed to prove `mark` on dags, FRAME cannot be applied directly to reason about the effect of applying the `mark` spec on the left child because the left and right child are not disjoint. To solve this issue, we introduce the *ramification rule*, which allows the reasoning to

[2] We often write *e.g.* $\delta(\mathtt{x}) = \ldots$ when what we really mean is $\mathtt{x} \Downarrow v \wedge \delta(v) = \ldots$, where $\mathtt{x} \Downarrow v$ means that the variable x evaluates to the value v in the current state, because mathematical graphs take values rather than variables. We elide these kinds of details for the presentation.

progress through commands that have indirect global effects:

$$\textsc{Ramify}\quad \frac{\{P\}\,c\,\{Q\} \qquad R \vdash P * (Q \mathrel{-\!\!*} R') \qquad \mathit{fv}(Q \mathrel{-\!\!*} R') \cap \mathit{modif}(c) = \varnothing}{\{R\}\,c\,\{R'\}}$$

RAMIFY isolates the complicated leap in reasoning at each recursive call site so that the assertions at each program point remain natural, such as in Fig. 1 (*e.g.*, the assertions are free from $\mathrel{-\!\!*}$). No free variables of $Q \mathrel{-\!\!*} R'$ may be modified by c. As usual, magic wand (separating implication) is the adjunct[3] of $*$:

$$h \vDash P \mathrel{-\!\!*} Q \stackrel{\text{def}}{=} \forall h'.\, h \bot h' \Rightarrow h' \vDash P \Rightarrow h \oplus h' \vDash Q$$

Here $h \bot h'$ asserts the *compatibility* of h and h' ($\exists h''.\, h \oplus h' = h''$). Informally, ramify can be read as "the result of applying c in a state R is R' if replacing P inside R with Q yields R'". Magic wand binds *more loosely* than any other operator.

Ramify is sufficiently abstract that it can be hard to appreciate. As an initial demonstration of its power, observe that the frame rule (modulo some restrictions on free variables as discussed below) is a direct consequence because $P * F \vdash P * (Q \mathrel{-\!\!*} Q * F)$.

Next, let us apply ramification to verify the following spec, in which $\mathtt{x} \mapsto -$ is the standard notation for $\exists x'.\, \mathtt{x} \mapsto x'$.

$$\{\mathtt{x} \mapsto - \circledast \mathtt{y} \mapsto -\}\ \mathtt{*x = a}\ \{\mathtt{x} \mapsto \mathtt{a} \circledast \mathtt{y} \mapsto -\}$$

RAMIFY emits two subgoals. The first precisely matches the standard small axiom for store update in separation logic:

$$\{\mathtt{x} \mapsto -\}\ \mathtt{*x = a}\ \{\mathtt{x} \mapsto \mathtt{a}\}$$

The second is the following ramification entailment, whose proof is direct from the associated definitions:

$$x \mapsto - \circledast y \mapsto - \vdash x \mapsto - * (x \mapsto a \mathrel{-\!\!*} x \mapsto a \circledast y \mapsto -) \quad (12)$$

Free variables Notice that RAMIFY has a side condition to pacify the usual free variable bugaboo. Usually this is no big deal, but it causes trouble when we want to use ramification to verify commands of the form `x =`$f(\ldots)$, since `x` *is* modified and we may want to refer to it in the postcondition. One sufficient solution, which pleasingly removes all free variable side conditions, is to use variables as resource [BCY06], but this introduces other complications. Another solution is to use the following variant of the ramify rule:

$$\textsc{RamifyAssign}\quad \frac{\{P\}\, x' = f(\ldots)\, \{Q\} \qquad R \vdash P * (Q \mathrel{-\!\!*} [x \mapsto x']R')}{\{R\}\, x = f(\ldots)\, \{R'\}}\ \dagger$$

$^\dagger x' \notin \mathit{fv}(R, R', P) \cup \mathit{vars}(f) \ \wedge\ \mathit{fv}(Q \mathrel{-\!\!*} R') \cap \mathit{modif}(f) = \varnothing$

RAMIFYASSIGN is a consequence of RAMIFY and the usual rules for assignment and sequence if we are allowed to make the local program transformation from `x =`$f(\ldots)$ to x'`=`$f(\ldots)$`; x =` x' in which x' is always chosen fresh. From now on we will sweep free variable issues under the rug, silently using RAMIFYASSIGN when needed.

Lookup Because points-to facts may be buried inside shared parts of the state, we find it convenient to use the *global* rule for lookup [Rey02] instead of the standard *local* one of separation logic:

$$\textsc{Lookup}\quad \frac{}{\{\exists x'.\, (y \mapsto x' * \mathsf{true}) \wedge [x \mapsto x']P\}\ \mathtt{x = *y}\ \{P\}}\ x' \notin \mathit{fv}(P, y)$$

In fact, RAMIFYASSIGN is able to derive LOOKUP from the standard local separation logic axiom.

4. Reasoning about Ramifications

To set the stage for the verification of our examples, we now present techniques for general reasoning about ramifications and link abstract mathematical reasoning about graphs to spatial ramifications.

4.1 Ramification Library

Our *ramification library* is a collection of lemmas that help reduce complicated ramifications and related entailments. Some of the more general-purpose lemmas, which can handle simplifications such as removing frames that occur within ramifications, are grouped in Fig. 2. Other lemmas in our library are specific to certain data structures such as graphs; we will meet some of these in §4.3.

Some of the lemmas in Fig. 2 require that various predicates be *precise*, which means that whenever P is satisfied on a sub-state ($h_1 \leqslant h_3 \stackrel{\text{def}}{=} \exists h_2.\, h_1 \oplus h_2 = h_3$), that sub-state must be unique:

$$\mathit{precise}(P) \stackrel{\text{def}}{=} \forall h_1, h_2, h_3.\, h_1 \leqslant h_3 \Rightarrow h_2 \leqslant h_3 \Rightarrow h_1 \vDash P \Rightarrow h_2 \vDash P \Rightarrow h_1 = h_2$$

All the predicates we consider here are indeed precise, so this is never a concern in this paper.

Lemmas 4.3 and 4.4 use $-\!\!\circledast$, the existential magic wand:

$$h \vDash P \mathrel{-\!\!\circledast} Q \stackrel{\text{def}}{=} \exists h'.\, h \bot h' \wedge h' \vDash P \wedge h \oplus h' \vDash Q$$

This operator can be tricky because one does not know *which* copy of P has been pulled out of Q, but is handy sometimes.

Lem. 4.1 allows one to frame away F *within* an overlapping conjunction in order to focus on an easier entailment. Perhaps surprisingly, both P and Q need to be precise for it to hold.

Lem. 4.2 and 4.3 are analogues of Lem. 4.1 for classical conjunctions. Although Lem. 4.2 is more immediate, the premise $R \vdash P * (Q \mathrel{-\!\!*} R')$ may sometimes be difficult to establish. In particular, one would need to show that P can always be found in a state satisfying R, which is not necessarily the case; it is true in the original ramification because the state satisfies $(P * F) \wedge R$. Lem. 4.3 remedies this by requiring the subtler condition that *if* P may be found in R, then *any* way of adding Q instead of P yields R'. We use this lemma to prove the `pop` program in §6.

Lem. 4.4 allows one to ignore parts of the state that remain invariant during an update. For instance, a procedure may require some piece of state in its precondition that is not modified and thus percolates unchanged to its postcondition. For the lemma to apply, that piece has to be described precisely enough by F that R' is invariant under swapping it for any other satisfying F (third premise). Precision of P is required to force the same sub-state of R to satisfy both $F * \mathsf{true}$ and $Q \mathrel{-\!\!*} R'$ (second and last premises), and $R \vdash P * F * \mathsf{true}$ makes sure that R always contains $P * F$.

Finally, Lem. 4.5 and 4.6 allow one to split a ramification over either disjoint or overlapping pieces of states into independant ramifications over each of these states. This is crucial to make the proof of some ramification entailments modular, for instance when reasoning about the effects of an update on both a global graph and a set of overlapping pointers as in our proof of Cheney's algorithm (see §7), or when proving the dag copying program of §A.

This ramification library is by no means exhaustive, nor do we use all of it in the examples presented here. Rather, we think that these lemmas demonstrate that ramification entailments can be reasoned about using the intuition that they represent *updates* to the state. The lemmas we will present in §4.3 for ramifications on graphs and dags further reinforce that claim.

4.2 Exact Graph and Dag Predicates

In this section, we define mathematical graphs γ and dags δ; we will provide ways to reason about ramifications which involve them in the next section. Before we do so, however, let us consider whether our job would be any easier if we were only worried about shape instead of functional correctness, *e.g.* if we tried to verify `mark` with the spec $\{\mathtt{dag(x)}\}\ \mathtt{mark(x)}\ \{\mathtt{dag(x)}\}$.

As in Fig. 1, the proof is straightforward until the first recursive call on line 8. After framing away the root pointer $\mathtt{x} \mapsto 1, l, r$, we apply RAMIFY, which emits the following entailment, in which P

[3] That is, $*$ and $\mathrel{-\!\!*}$ are related by $P * Q \vdash R \Leftrightarrow P \vdash Q \mathrel{-\!\!*} R$.

4.1: Frame within $\circledast$ Ramification

$$\frac{\mathit{precise}(P,Q) \qquad P \circledast R \vdash P * (Q \mathrel{-\!\!*} Q \circledast R')}{(P * F) \circledast R \vdash P * (Q \mathrel{-\!\!*} (Q * F) \circledast R')}$$

4.2: Frame within $\wedge$ Ramification 1

$$\frac{\mathit{precise}(P) \qquad R \vdash P * (Q \mathrel{-\!\!*} R')}{(P * F) \wedge R \vdash P * (Q \mathrel{-\!\!*} (Q * F) \wedge R')}$$

4.3: Frame within $\wedge$ Ramification 2

$$\frac{P \mathrel{-\!\circledast} R \vdash Q \mathrel{-\!\!*} R'}{(P * F) \wedge R \vdash P * (Q \mathrel{-\!\!*} (Q * F) \wedge R')}$$

4.4: Exact Frame within Ramification

$$\frac{\mathit{precise}(P) \qquad R \vdash P * F * \mathsf{true} \qquad F \mathrel{-\!\circledast} R' \vdash F \mathrel{-\!\!*} R' \qquad R \vdash P * (Q \mathrel{-\!\!*} R')}{R \vdash P * F * (Q * F \mathrel{-\!\!*} R')}$$

4.5: Disjoint Ramification

$$\frac{R \vdash P * (P' \mathrel{-\!\!*} R') \qquad S \vdash Q * (Q' \mathrel{-\!\!*} S')}{R * S \vdash P * Q * (P' * Q' \mathrel{-\!\!*} R' * S')}$$

4.6: $\circledast$-piecewise Ramification

$$\frac{\mathit{precise}(P,P') \qquad \forall i.\, P \circledast Q_i \vdash P * (P' \mathrel{-\!\!*} P' \circledast Q_i')}{P \circledast Q_1 \circledast Q_2 \vdash P * (P' \mathrel{-\!\!*} P' \circledast Q_1' \circledast Q_2')}$$

Figure 2: Some general-purpose lemmas from our ramification library.

and Q are the pre- and postconditions from the recursive call:

$$\overbrace{\mathsf{dag}(\mathtt{l}) \circledast \mathsf{dag}(\mathtt{r})}^{R} \vdash \overbrace{\mathsf{dag}(\mathtt{l})}^{P} * (\overbrace{\mathsf{dag}(\mathtt{l})}^{Q} \mathrel{-\!\!*} \overbrace{\mathsf{dag}(\mathtt{l}) \circledast \mathsf{dag}(\mathtt{r})}^{R'})$$

Unfortunately, this entailment turns out to be invalid. Recall that our ramification $P * (Q \mathrel{-\!\!*} R')$ idiom represents a state update, in which P is substituted for Q in R to yield R'. Here this means substituting one $\mathsf{dag}(\mathtt{l})$ for another $\mathsf{dag}(\mathtt{l})$, which on its surface seems reasonable. The problem is that the "ramified away" state $(Q \mathrel{-\!\!*} R')$ can have dangling pointers into the "local" state P; if P is mangled too badly as it is transformed into Q then those pointers break in the recombined state R' (here $\mathsf{dag}(\mathtt{l}) \circledast \mathsf{dag}(\mathtt{r})$):

In this example, the update on dag l has freed node s and allocated a fresh node l'' instead. Although l is still a dag afterwards, r is not, so we will not be able to prove $\mathsf{dag}(\mathtt{l}) \circledast \mathsf{dag}(\mathtt{r})$.

This is not an artificial problem stemming from our approach. In fact, the failure of the ramification entailment indicates that $\{\mathsf{dag}(\mathtt{l})\}$ `mark(l)` $\{\mathsf{dag}(\mathtt{l})\}$ is too weak of an inductive specification: overly aggressive changes to the pointer structure of the left sub-dag could make the recursive call to the right sub-dag crash, and we must reflect that reality in the specification for `mark`.

There are several solutions to this problem, but for this paper choose the most powerful: proving functional correctness. In §8.3 we will discuss some other possibilities that can yield more lightweight shape proofs at the cost of some additional formalism.

Mathematical graphs We define the mathematical representation of a directed binary graph as a quadruple (V, D, L, E), where V is a finite set of vertices, D is some set of data, $L : V \to D$ is a labeling function associating each vertex v with some data d, and $E : V \to (V \uplus \{0\}) \times (V \uplus \{0\})$ associates each vertex with up to two successors. To ease the matching between a mathematical graph and its heap representation we usually take $V \subset \mathsf{Loc}$ and $D \subseteq \mathsf{Val}$.

Given a mathematical graph $\gamma = (V, D, L, E)$, we often write $x \in \gamma$ for $x \in V \uplus \{0\}$, $S \subseteq \gamma$ for $S \subseteq V \uplus \{0\}$, and $\gamma(x)$ for $(L(x), E(x).1, E(x).2)$. We define the update of γ at node v, written $[v \mapsto (d,l,r)]\gamma$, where $l, r \in V \cup \{v\} \uplus \{0\}$ and $d \in D$, as:

$$[v \mapsto (d,l,r)](V,D,L,E) \stackrel{\text{def}}{=} (V \cup \{v\}, D, [v \mapsto d]L, [v \mapsto (l,r)]V)$$

A node y is the *successor* of a node $x \in \gamma$, written $x \overset{\gamma}{\leadsto} y$, or simply $x \leadsto y$ when γ is clear from context, if either $E(x) = (y, z)$ or $E(x) = (z, y)$ for some z. A node y is *reachable* from x, written $x \overset{\gamma}{\leadsto}^* y$ or $x \leadsto^* y$, if (x, y) is in the reflexive transitive closure $\leadsto$. The reachability set of $x \in \gamma$, written $\mathit{reach}(\gamma, x)$, is defined as:

$$\mathit{reach}(\gamma, x) \stackrel{\text{def}}{=} \{y \mid x \overset{\gamma}{\leadsto}^* y\}$$

We also lift reachability to sets of vertices $S = \{v_1, \ldots, v_n\} \subseteq V$:

$$\mathit{reach}(\gamma, S) \stackrel{\text{def}}{=} \mathit{reach}(\gamma, v_1) \cup \cdots \cup \mathit{reach}(\gamma, v_n)$$

Given a graph $\gamma = (V, D, L, E)$ and a set of vertices $S \subseteq V$, it is often useful to restrict γ to those vertices *reachable from* (respectively *not* reachable from) the vertices in S, written $\gamma \downarrow S$ (and respectively $\gamma \uparrow S$). Accordingly, we define (where $f \downharpoonright S$ is the function obtained from f by restricting the domain to the set S):

$$\gamma \downarrow S \stackrel{\text{def}}{=} (V' = \mathit{reach}(\gamma, S) \quad , D, L \downharpoonright V', E \downharpoonright V')$$
$$\gamma \uparrow S \stackrel{\text{def}}{=} (V' = V \backslash (\mathit{reach}(\gamma, S)), D, L \downharpoonright V', E \downharpoonright V')$$

The quadruple $(V', D', L', E') = \gamma \uparrow S$ is not necessarily a graph, since the edge function E' may point outside of the new set of edges V'. However, $\gamma \downarrow S$ is always a graph: the subgraph of γ reachable from S. We sometimes write $\gamma \downarrow x$ and $\gamma \uparrow x$ for $\gamma \downarrow \{x\}$ and $\gamma \uparrow \{x\}$. By convention, if $S \nsubseteq V$ then $(V, D, L, E) \downarrow S$ is the empty graph.

Spatial graphs We tie a mathematical graph γ to a spatial (in-heap) graph by adding γ as a parameter to graph:

$$\mathsf{graph}(x, \gamma) \stackrel{\text{def}}{=} \begin{array}{l} (x = 0 \wedge \mathsf{emp}) \vee \exists d, l, r.\, \gamma(x) = (d, l, r) \wedge \\ x \mapsto d, l, r \circledast \mathsf{graph}(l, \gamma) \circledast \mathsf{graph}(r, \gamma) \end{array}$$

Note that $\mathsf{graph}(x, \gamma)$ "owns" only the spatial representation of the portion of γ that is reachable from x; γ may contain other nodes. This is expressed by the following lemma, that "explodes" a graph into its individual nodes. We use the *iterative star* notation, defined as emp if the set that is being iterated over is empty and as follows otherwise, given a predicate $P(x)$ on x:

$$\bigstar_{x \in \{x_1, \ldots, x_n\}} P(x) \stackrel{\text{def}}{=} P(x_1) * \cdots * P(x_n)$$

Lemma 4.7 *For every graph $\gamma = (V, E)$ and node $x \in \gamma$,*

$$\mathsf{graph}(x, \gamma) \dashv\vdash \bigstar_{v \in \mathit{reach}(\gamma, x)} v \mapsto \gamma(v)$$

Generally speaking, reasoning at this level is undesirable in program proofs, and ramification crucially allows us to remain at the level of graph instead. However, this lemma is useful both as a sanity check and to prove the general lemmas about ramifying graphs given in the next section.

We likewise enrich dag with a mathematical graph δ:

$$\mathsf{dag}(x, \delta) \stackrel{\text{def}}{=} \begin{array}{l} (x = 0 \wedge \mathsf{emp}) \vee \exists d, l, r.\, \delta(x) = (d, l, r) \wedge \\ x \mapsto d, l, r * (\mathsf{dag}(l, \delta) \circledast \mathsf{dag}(r, \delta)) \end{array}$$

Moreover, the predicate $\mathsf{dag}(x, \delta)$ is satisfiable *if and only if* $\delta \downarrow x$ is indeed a dag, as enforced by the $*$ in the spatial predicate:

Lemma 4.8 *For every graph δ and variable x,*

$$\mathsf{dag}(x, \delta) \dashv\vdash \mathsf{graph}(x, \delta) \wedge (\delta \downarrow x \textit{ is acyclic})$$

Finally, we define the following shorthand for describing multiple sub-graphs of the same graph from a root set $S = \{v_1, \ldots, v_n\}$:

$$\mathsf{graphs}(S, \gamma) \stackrel{\text{def}}{=} \mathsf{graph}(v_1, \gamma) \circledast \cdots \circledast \mathsf{graph}(v_n, \gamma)$$
$$\mathsf{dags}(S, \delta) \stackrel{\text{def}}{=} \mathsf{dag}(v_1, \delta) \circledast \cdots \circledast \mathsf{dag}(v_n, \delta)$$

If $S = \varnothing$ then both predicates denote emp.

4.3 Reasoning about Graph and Dag Ramifications

One advantage of proving functional correctness is that we can tightly connect our mathematical reasoning with our spatial reasoning. Here we state lemmas that do just that.

First, the spatial graph (and thus dag) predicates are precise.

Lemma 4.9 *For all S and γ, $precise(\mathsf{graphs}(S,\gamma))$.*

Our next lemma lets us *reroot* collections of sub-graphs provided that we preserve the set of reachable nodes:

Lemma 4.10 *If $reach(\gamma, S) = reach(\gamma, S')$, then*

$$\mathsf{graphs}(S,\gamma) \dashv\vdash \mathsf{graphs}(S',\gamma)$$

Our third lemma helps us extend a graph with fresh nodes.

Lemma 4.11 (Graph Growth)

$$x \mapsto d,x,x \vdash \mathsf{graph}(x,[x \mapsto (d,x,x)]) \quad (13)$$

$$x \mapsto d,x,r * \mathsf{graph}(r,\gamma) \vdash \mathsf{graph}(x,[x \mapsto (d,x,r)]\gamma) \quad (14)$$

$$x \mapsto d,l,r * \mathsf{graphs}(\{l,r\},\gamma) \vdash \mathsf{graph}(x,[x \mapsto (d,l,r)]\gamma) \quad (15)$$

$$x \mapsto d,l,r * \mathsf{dags}(\{l,r\},\delta) \vdash \mathsf{dag}(x,[x \mapsto (d,l,r)]\delta) \quad (16)$$

First, (13) a graph cell x whose successors are both itself corresponds to a singleton graph $[x \mapsto (d,x,x)]$.[4] Second, (14) if a node x has a loop to itself on the left and a pointer to an existing graph on the right,[5] then we can add x to the graph; not shown is the mirrored case when the loop is on the right. Third, (15) if x links to two (possibly equal) graph nodes then we can again add x to the graph. The first two cases need to be stated separately because $x \notin \gamma$ means that $\mathsf{graph}(x,\gamma)$ is $\perp$. Finally, (16) is the analogue of (15) for dags; we do not need analogues for (13) and (14) because dags must be acyclic.

The frame rule, combined with the $*$ between a parent and its descendants and equation (16), is enough to mutate the root of a dag. However, an unrestricted graph has $\uplus$ between the parent and its successors, so we need to use RAMIFY to update the root. The following lemma helps discharge the associated ramifications:

Lemma 4.12 (Single Graph Node Update)

$$\frac{\gamma(x) = (d,l,r) \qquad \gamma' = [x \mapsto (d',l',r')]\gamma}{\begin{array}{c}\mathsf{graphs}(\{x,l',r'\} \cup S,\gamma) \vdash x \mapsto d,l,r * \\ (x \mapsto d',l',r' \mathrel{-\!\!*} \mathsf{graphs}(\{x,l,r\} \cup S,\gamma'))\end{array}} \quad (17)$$

$$\frac{\gamma(x) = (d,l,r) \qquad \gamma' = [x \mapsto (d',l,r)]\gamma}{\mathsf{graph}(x,\gamma) \vdash x \mapsto d,l,r * (x \mapsto d',l,r \mathrel{-\!\!*} \mathsf{graph}(x,\gamma'))} \quad (18)$$

Lem. 4.11 handles the cases in which we are adding a fresh node, so in (17)-(18) we need only consider the case in which $\{x,l,r,l',r'\} \subseteq \gamma$. The case of interest is (17), a full update to node x, where we are updating not only the data d to d' but also the pointers l and r to l' and r' respectively. The precondition is a $\uplus$-joined set of subgraphs of γ, including x, l', and r', as well as arbitrary others S. After the update, the state contains subgraphs at x (which now contains l' and r') and S, as well as the old l and r (previously contained in the old x), which may now be disconnected from $\{x\} \cup S$. In practice we often care about far simpler updates; (18) is a direct consequence of (17), and handles the case in which we only wish to update the data field.

Next, we observe that an update that preserves the set of reachable nodes cannot remove any overlapping points-to fact. The same remark is true of dags as well, replacing graphs with dags everywhere in the lemma below.

[4] $[x \mapsto (d,x,x)] \stackrel{\text{def}}{=} (\{x\}, D, [x \mapsto d], [x \mapsto (x,x)])$

[5] Observe that r can be equal to 0, in which case $\mathsf{graph}(r,\gamma)$ is just emp.

Lemma 4.13 (Points-to preservation)

$$\frac{reach(\gamma',S') \supseteq reach(\gamma,S)}{\begin{array}{c}\mathsf{graphs}(S,\gamma) \uplus x \mapsto - \vdash \mathsf{graphs}(S,\gamma) * \\ (\mathsf{graphs}(S',\gamma') \mathrel{-\!\!*} \mathsf{graphs}(S',\gamma') \uplus x \mapsto -)\end{array}}$$

Our final lemma applies when we wish to update an entire subgraph (typically with a function call) rather than a single node.

Lemma 4.14 (Subgraph Update)

$$\frac{reach(\gamma',S_1') \supseteq reach(\gamma,S_1) \qquad \gamma' \uparrow S_1' = \gamma \uparrow S_1}{\begin{array}{c}\mathsf{graphs}(S_1,\gamma) \uplus \mathsf{graphs}(S_2,\gamma) \vdash \mathsf{graphs}(S_1,\gamma) * \\ (\mathsf{graphs}(S_1',\gamma') \mathrel{-\!\!*} \mathsf{graphs}(S_1',\gamma') \uplus \mathsf{graphs}(S_2,\gamma'))\end{array}} \quad (19)$$

$$\frac{reach(\delta',S_1') \supseteq reach(\delta,S_1) \qquad \delta' \uparrow S_1' = \delta \uparrow S_1}{\begin{array}{c}\mathsf{dags}(S_1,\delta) \uplus \mathsf{dags}(S_2,\delta) \vdash \mathsf{dags}(S_1,\delta) * \\ (\mathsf{dags}(S_1',\delta') \mathrel{-\!\!*} \mathsf{dags}(S_1',\delta') \uplus \mathsf{dags}(S_2,\delta'))\end{array}} \quad (20)$$

First, (19) lets us ramify an update to a subgraph (or set of subgraphs) as long as all previously reachable nodes are still reachable (to prevent *e.g.* the dangling pointer problem outlined in §3.3) and the mathematical update is local. Second, (20) gives us the same property for dags (if our newly substituted sub-dag does not contain a cycle then our whole dag will not suddenly become cyclic).

5. Proving `mark` on Dags

We are ready at last to polish off the proof of `mark` from Fig. 1.

Mathematical marking One of our goals is to translate mathematical reasoning into spatial reasoning. Define the mathematical marking $m(\gamma,r)$ of a graph $\gamma = (V,D,L,E)$ starting from the vertex $r \in V$ as marking all nodes reachable via *unmarked nodes* from r. Formally, define a new relation $\overset{\gamma}{\leadsto}_0$ as follows:

$$x \overset{\gamma}{\leadsto}_0 y \text{ iff } \exists z.\, \gamma(x) = (0,y,z) \vee \gamma(x) = (0,z,y)$$

As before, we omit the subscript γ when it is clear from context and write $\overset{\gamma}{\leadsto}{}_0^*$ for the reflexive transitive closure. The marking $m(\gamma,r)$ of γ from r is then (V,D,L',E) where, for all $x \in V$,

$$L'(x) \;=\; \begin{cases} 1 & \text{if } r \leadsto_0^* x \\ L(x) & \text{otherwise} \end{cases}$$

We also need to describe the effect of marking a single node in γ, accomplished with $m_1(\gamma,x)$, that sets the marked bit of node x in γ to 1. The following lemma about mathematical markings now becomes crucial to prove the functional correctness of `mark`.

Lemma 5.1 *For all graphs γ and nodes $x,y \in \gamma$,*

$$m(m(\gamma,x),y) \;=\; m(m(\gamma,y),x) \quad (21)$$

Moreover, if $\gamma(x) = (d,l,r)$, then

$$m(m(m_1(\gamma,x),l),r) = m(m_1(m(\gamma,l),x),r) =$$
$$m_1(m(m(\gamma,l),r),x) = m(m_1(m(\gamma,r),x),l) = m(\gamma,x) \quad (22)$$

That is, (21) we can swap the order of two mathematical markings, and (22) regardless of which order we mark the root and children (either child first by equation 21), at the end we are fully marked.

Spatial marking Our first remaining tasks are the ramifications on lines 9 and 11. In both cases we frame away the root node and then apply RAMIFY, yielding the following entailments:

$$\begin{array}{r}\mathsf{dag}(\mathtt{l},\delta) \uplus \mathsf{dag}(\mathtt{r},\delta) \vdash \mathsf{dag}(\mathtt{l},\delta) * (\mathsf{dag}(\mathtt{l},m(\delta,\mathtt{l})) \mathrel{-\!\!*} \\ \mathsf{dag}(\mathtt{l},m(\delta,\mathtt{l})) \uplus \mathsf{dag}(\mathtt{r},m(\delta,\mathtt{l})))\end{array} \quad (23)$$

$$\begin{array}{l}\mathsf{dag}(\mathtt{l},m(\delta,\mathtt{l})) \uplus \mathsf{dag}(\mathtt{r},m(\delta,\mathtt{l})) \\ \vdash \mathsf{dag}(\mathtt{r},m(\delta,\mathtt{l})) * (\mathsf{dag}(\mathtt{r},m(m(\delta,\mathtt{l}),\mathtt{r})) \mathrel{-\!\!*} \\ \quad \mathsf{dag}(\mathtt{l},m(m(\delta,\mathtt{l}),\mathtt{r})) \uplus \mathsf{dag}(\mathtt{r},m(m(\delta,\mathtt{l}),\mathtt{r})))\end{array} \quad (24)$$

Observe that the first ramification directly implies the second by instantiating δ with $m(\delta,\mathtt{l})$ in the first entailment and using the commutativity of $\circledast$ to swap the roles of $\mathtt{l}$ and $\mathtt{r}$. To prove (23), we apply Lem. 4.14 to reduce the spatial ramification entailment to a pair of mathematical subgoals. The first mathematical subgoal,

$$reach(m(\delta, \mathtt{l}), \mathtt{l}) \supseteq reach(\delta, \mathtt{l}),$$

i.e., that every vertex reachable from $\mathtt{l}$ in the old dag δ is still reachable from $\mathtt{l}$ in the new dag $m(\delta, \mathtt{l})$, is immediate because the mathematical marking function m changes neither the vertices nor the edges of the dag δ. The second mathematical subgoal,

$$m(\delta, \mathtt{l}) \uparrow \mathtt{l} = \delta \uparrow \mathtt{l},$$

i.e., that the part of δ that is *not* reachable from $\mathtt{l}$ is identical to the part of $m(\delta, \mathtt{l})$ that is *not* reachable $\mathtt{l}$, is almost as simple. By the definition of m, we know that the only difference between δ and $m(\delta, \mathtt{l})$ is that the new labeling function has marked vertices reachable via unmarked paths in δ from $\mathtt{l}$; all other labels are maintained. Since the second mathematical subgoal only cares about changes to the portion of the mathematical graph that is not reachable from $\mathtt{l}$, and those labels are unchanged, we are done.

Finally, to establish the postcondition in line 12 from line 11, apply Lem. 4.11 to derive $\mathsf{dag}(\mathtt{x}, m_1(m(m(\delta, \mathtt{l}), \mathtt{r}), \mathtt{x}))$, which by Lem. 5.1 is equivalent to our postcondition.

5.1 Observations

Our proof of `mark` (*i.e.*, Fig. 1 and §5) is short and our invariants at each program point are straightforward. We were able to reuse our initial ramification (23) to prove our second (24). Essentially all of the spatial difficulties were handled by our ramification library. Moreover, by Lem. 5.1 our proof is easy to modify to accommodate trivial changes in the program like moving the update in line 6 to after one or both of the recursive calls in lines 8 and 10, swapping the order of the recursive calls, etc. Our ability to accommodate these kinds of changes is an indication of the power of using ramification to separate mathematical and spatial reasoning from each other.

In contrast, previous work on verifying these kinds of algorithms used complex and brittle invariants so that they could always apply the frame rule. For example, consider Bornat *et al.* [BCO04], which is the progenitor of most previous work in applying separation logic to reason about data structures with intrinsic sharing.

Bornat *et al.* define mathematical dags as tree-shaped terms whose nodes are either labeled proper nodes (written $x : \mathsf{Node}\ \delta_l\ \delta_r$) or references to a label elsewhere in the dag (written $\mathsf{Ptr}\ x$) to express sharing. Their spatial pdag predicate grants ownership of a node at the point that corresponds to where it is declared in the mathematical definition (roughly speaking, $\mathsf{pdag}\ x\ (x : \mathsf{Node}\ \delta_l\ \delta_r) \stackrel{\text{def}}{=} x \mapsto v, l, r * \mathsf{pdag}\ l\ \delta_l * \mathsf{pdag}\ r\ \delta_r$), but not when it is referenced again (similarly, $\mathsf{pdag}\ x\ (\mathsf{Ptr}\ x) \stackrel{\text{def}}{=} \mathsf{emp}$). Each node can only be declared once (although it may be referenced many times), and the order in which they are declared must match the order in which the program traverses the dag, as the authors note [BCO04, §8, p. 7]:

> This predicate is specifically designed to support a left to right scan, as are the formulae on which it is based. It seems difficult to avoid this complication.

Unfortunately, the consequences of this style of definition ricochet to many other parts of the associated verification, including the statement of the specification of `mark` and its exact implementation. Changes in one part of the system (*e.g.*, swapping the order of traversal) required changes to other parts of the system (*i.e.*, the definition of pdag, the specification of `mark`, and the invariants at each program point). Altogether, the style of hacking the state into many disjoint pieces to reason about data structures with intrinsic sharing pays a heavy price to enable the frame rule, resulting in "dauntingly subtle" [BCO04, §8.4, p. 9] definitions and verifications.

In contrast, our definition of mathematical graphs is traditional, our dag predicate is natural, and our specification for `mark` is straightforward. None of these depend on internal implementation specifics of the algorithm such as traversal orders. Moreover, our program invariants are easy to understand, easy to update to accommodate minor changes in the algorithm, and easy to verify using ramification and our ramification library. Verifications utilizing ramifications are both more natural and more robust than those in previous work.

Marking possibly cyclic graphs The `mark` function can also mark unrestricted graphs. Because Lemmas 4.14 and 5.1 both apply to graphs as well as dags, the only substantial change to the the proof in Fig. 1 is for line 6. Here dags only require the frame rule due to the $*$ between a parent and its children but unrestricted graphs require an additional ramification due to the additional $\circledast$:

$$\begin{array}{l} \mathtt{x} \mapsto 0, \mathtt{l}, \mathtt{r} \circledast \mathsf{graphs}(\{\mathtt{l}, \mathtt{r}\}, \gamma) \vdash \mathtt{x} \mapsto 0, \mathtt{l}, \mathtt{r} * \\ \qquad (\mathtt{x} \mapsto 1, \mathtt{l}, \mathtt{r} -\!\!\circledast\ \mathtt{x} \mapsto 1, \mathtt{l}, \mathtt{r} \circledast \mathsf{graphs}(\{\mathtt{l}, \mathtt{r}\}, m_1(\gamma, \mathtt{x}))) \end{array}$$

This ramification follows directly from Lem. 4.12.

Termination Our work here is primarily concerned with partial correctness, but suppose we were interested in total correctness as well. The dag argument is simpler: each recursive call is on a strictly smaller subheap thanks to the $*$ between a parent and its children; notice that this argument is valid regardless of whether we mark the root first, at line 6, or after one or both recursive calls. In contrast, the termination argument on unrestricted graphs is more complicated because the $\circledast$ between root and successors means that the subheap may not be any smaller at the recursive calls. Instead, each recursive call must be on a graph with fewer unmarked nodes; if we recurse before coloring the root then we may not terminate.

5.2 Other Graph Algorithms

To prove that ramification can apply equally well to programs that, unlike `mark`, mutate the link structure of the graph, we also verified `copy_dag` and `dispose_graph`. The full details are in Appendices A and B respectively; here we give only the key insights.

Copying dags The goal of the `copy_dag` function is to make a deep (structure-preserving) copy of its argument. It uses a data field in each original node to record the location of its corresponding copy (or 0 if the node has not yet been copied). Just as with `mark`, a straightforward recursive implementation is compact and works as follows. If the root is already copied then return immediately; otherwise, recursively copy the left and right children, allocate a new node to be the root's copy, and set its fields as appropriate.

To make the verification hang together, we need to add a new feature to our separation logic: *regions* [LG88]. Briefly, regions indicate disjoint zones in the heap, and a spatial predicate P can be tagged with a region identifier α to become P_α, indicating that P is entirely contained in region α. Predicates in different regions are always disjoint, even when connected by sharing operators such as $\circledast$.

Regions are useful when we are faced with the following problem, in which $\sharp$ is some sharing operator such as $\wedge$ or $\circledast$:

$$(P * Q) \sharp (R * S) \ \stackrel{?}{\dashv\vdash}\ (P \sharp R) * (Q \sharp S)$$

That is, we have some disjoint formulas P and Q, which overlap with two additional disjoint formulas R and S, and we wish to shuffle resources around until the P and Q are overlapping with each other and are disjoint from the overlapping Q and S.

The $\dashv$ direction is immediate. Unfortunately, verifying `copy_dag` requires the $\vdash$ direction after making both recursive calls and reaching the following invariant, in which $\mathtt{l}$ and $\mathtt{r}$ are the left and right children of the root and $\mathtt{ll}$ and $\mathtt{rr}$ are their respective copies:

$$(\mathsf{dag}(\mathtt{l}, \delta) * \mathsf{dag}(\mathtt{ll}, \delta')) \circledast (\mathsf{dag}(\mathtt{r}, \delta) * \mathsf{dag}(\mathtt{rr}, \delta'))$$

Now we need to apply the rule of consequence to disentangle the original children from their overlapping copies:

$$(\mathsf{dag}(\mathtt{l}, \delta) \circledast \mathsf{dag}(\mathtt{r}, \delta)) * (\mathsf{dag}(\mathtt{ll}, \delta') \circledast \mathsf{dag}(\mathtt{rr}, \delta'))$$

```
1  struct node { struct node *next,*l,*r; };
2  void pop(void) { //{list(s) ∧ tree(t)}
3    if (!s) return;
4    struct node *c = s;
5  // {(s ↦ n,l,r ∗ list(n)) ∧ tree(t) ∧ c = s}
6    s = c->next;
7  // {(c ↦ s,l,r ∗ list(s)) ∧ tree(t)}
8  // {(c ↦ s,l,r ∗ list(s)) ∧ (sktree(t,π ⊎ {c}) ∗ ptrs(π ⊎ {c}))}
9    t = tree_del(t,c);
10 //↯{(c ↦ s,−,− ∗ list(s)) ∧ (sktree(t,π) ∗ c ↦ −,−,− ∗ ptrs(π))}
11 // {(list(s) ∧ tree(t)) ∗ c ↦ −,−,−}
12   free(c);
13 } // {list(s)) ∧ tree(t)}
```

Figure 3: Removal from a threaded tree.

The problem is that the implication is just not true without carrying around some additional information via regions: specifically, that the original dag is in region α while the copy is being created in region β. In general regions help because they ensure that P does not have any overlap with S despite the intermediate sharing operator $\sharp$:

$$(P_\alpha * Q_\beta)\sharp(R_\alpha * S_\beta) \dashv\vdash (P\sharp R)_\alpha * (Q\sharp S)_\beta \qquad (25)$$

Others have run across the same problem in diverse contexts including RGSep [Vaf07] and shape analysis for overlaid lists and trees [LYP11] and have turned to regions for similar reasons.

Interestingly, our verification also uses regions in an novel way to split one large ramification entailment (equation 35) into two smaller entailments via Lem. 4.5 from our ramification library. This second use of regions is not vital to verify `copy_dag`, but it does simplify things nicely. Other than the use of regions, the verification proceeds straightforwardly.

Disposing graphs Disposing a graph is usually done in two steps: first, suppress all sharing between nodes of the graph, so that each node has at most one predecessor, thus computing a spanning tree of the graph; and then dispose the tree. Apx. B contains the novel verification for the first step; verifying the second is standard. The real proof effort is on the mathematical side; the spatial aspects of the verification are no more complicated than `mark` and `copy_dag`, and do not require regions. Because our definition for graph uses $\circledast$, we are able to establish emp at the end, indicating that we have completely freed the structure.

6. Overlaid Data Structures

Reasoning about threaded trees Our examples so far have focused on graph manipulations. Ramification is also applicable in other interesting contexts, including overlaid data structures. Here we focus on one kind of overlaid structure: *threaded trees*, which overlay lists and trees. Each node has *three* links to other nodes of the data structure: a "next" pointer of a singly-linked list, and the "left" and "right" fields of a binary tree. This is a popular type of overlaid data structure: the linked list may record the set of elements some order of particular interest (*e.g.*, first-inserted to most recent), while the tree provides efficient out-of-order lookup.

Our case study is a procedure that removes the first element of the linked list from the data structure, inspired by what can be found in the Linux deadline I/O scheduler [LYP11]. The code and annotations are shown in Fig. 3. It assumes two global variables s and t that point respectively to the head of the linked list and the root of the tree. The precondition states that the two shapes span *exactly* the same memory cells, enforced by the conjunction $\wedge$. Removing from the list (line 6) merely advances the head pointer, but we cannot stop there because it leaves the overlaid structure in an inconsistent state (the items in the list and the tree must be identical).

Removing from the tree is likely to be operationally complex, potentially involving operations to rebalance, reroot, or otherwise rotate parts of the tree. Thus, we abstract this operation and assume that it is performed by a function `tree_del(t,c)`. Its spec has to express two particular facts to ensure that it is well-behaved w.r.t. the overlaid list structure: it must not tamper with the list fields, and the resulting new tree should cover the same nodes as before except for c. We enforce the first constraint by not giving any access rights on the list fields to the procedure, *i.e.* by restricting its precondition to the "skeleton" of the tree, and the second constraint by recording the set of nodes encompassed in the tree shape. We therefore define the following predicate that skips the list fields of each node:

$$\begin{aligned}\mathsf{sktree}(x,\pi) \stackrel{\text{def}}{=} {}& (x = 0 \wedge \mathsf{emp} \wedge \pi = \varnothing) \vee \exists l, r, \pi_l, \pi_r.\\ & x+1 \mapsto l, r * \mathsf{sktree}(l,\pi_l) * \mathsf{sktree}(r,\pi_r) \wedge\\ & \pi = \{x\} \uplus \pi_l \uplus \pi_r\end{aligned}$$

The tree predicate can be split into a skeleton and a bag of points-to predicates, using the *pointers* predicate ptrs:

$$\mathsf{ptrs}(\{x_1,\ldots,x_n\}) \stackrel{\text{def}}{=} x_1 \mapsto - * \cdots * x_n \mapsto -$$

$$\mathsf{tree}(t) \Leftrightarrow \exists\pi.\, \mathsf{sktree}(t,\pi) * \mathsf{ptrs}(\pi) \qquad (26)$$

The list predicate is defined in the standard way for nil-terminated acyclic lists with two data fields:

$$\mathsf{list}(l) \stackrel{\text{def}}{=} (l = 0 \wedge \mathsf{emp}) \vee \exists l', x, y.\, l \mapsto l', x, y * \mathsf{list}(l')$$

We moreover assume that each address is aligned as a multiple of 3, to prevent *skewing*, in which a node in the tree might overlap two nodes in the list in a state satisfying $\mathsf{list}(s) \wedge \mathsf{tree}(t)$.

A general observation about how overlaid data structures are manipulated is that changes to fields of only one structure do not affect the other, *e.g.*, list induction easily proves that

$$x \mapsto n, l, r \mathrel{-\!\!\circledast} \mathsf{list}(s) \vdash x \mapsto n, l', r' \mathrel{-\!\!*} \mathsf{list}(s)$$

This reads as: if a state may be completed by a node to form a linked list, then completing it by any other node at the same location and with the same next field also yields a list. The same property for *skeleton* trees follows by induction on the size of the tree:

$$\mathsf{sktree}(t,\pi) \mathrel{-\!\!\circledast} \mathsf{list}(s) \vdash \mathsf{sktree}(t',\pi) \mathrel{-\!\!*} \mathsf{list}(s) \qquad (27)$$

Verification The spec of `tree_del` follows the discussion above: $\{\mathsf{sktree}(t,\pi \uplus \{c\})\}$`u=tree_del(t,c)`$\{\mathsf{sktree}(u,\pi) * c{+}1 \mapsto -,-\}$

The proof sketched in Fig. 3 is mostly straightforward: if s is nil then the list is empty, hence so is the tree and the postcondition is trivially satisfied; otherwise, we unfold the list predicate, which enables the lookup at line 6. After that, we split the tree according to (26) and apply the following ramification:

$$\begin{aligned}&(\mathtt{c} \mapsto \mathtt{s}, l, r * \mathsf{list}(\mathtt{s})) \wedge (\mathsf{sktree}(\mathtt{t}, \pi \uplus \{\mathtt{c}\}) * \mathsf{ptrs}(\pi \uplus \{\mathtt{c}\}))\\ \vdash{}& \mathsf{sktree}(\mathtt{t}, \pi \uplus \{\mathtt{c}\}) * (\mathtt{c}+1 \mapsto -,- * \mathsf{sktree}(t',\pi) \mathrel{-\!\!*}\\ &\quad (\mathtt{c} \mapsto \mathtt{s},-,- * \mathsf{list}(\mathtt{s})) \wedge\\ &\quad (\mathtt{c}+1 \mapsto -,- * \mathsf{sktree}(t',\pi) * \mathsf{ptrs}(\pi \uplus \{\mathtt{c}\})))\end{aligned}$$

This ramification follows a general pattern, and we can reduce it to a much simpler one by noticing that the right-hand side conjunct is automatically handled by Lem. 4.3 from our ramification library, which can remove frames that occur within $\wedge$ ramifications. This yields the following simpler proof obligation:

$$\begin{aligned}&\mathsf{sktree}(t,\pi \uplus \{c\}) \mathrel{-\!\!\circledast} c \mapsto x, y, z * \mathsf{list}(s)\\ \vdash{}& c+1 \mapsto -,- * \mathsf{sktree}(t',\pi) \mathrel{-\!\!*} c \mapsto x,-,- * \mathsf{list}(s)\end{aligned}$$

This entailment is similar to (27). The rest of the proof is immediate.

7. Cheney's Garbage Collector

It is time for the acid test: verifying the functional correctness of Cheney's garbage collector [Che70]. The general setting is as follows. There are two disjoint, equally large regions of memory, the *from-space* and the *to-space*, starting respectively at the address pointed to by `from` and `to`. Programs manipulate *objects* in the from-space. When the program wishes to allocate but the from-space has run out of room, we garbage collect by copying the entire graph of reachable objects into the to-space before swapping `from` and `to` and resuming normal execution. If the former from-space had any unreachable objects then the new from-space has some free space.

In the tradition of previous work, we make a number of simplifications. We assume that there is a single root from which all *active* objects are reachable, *i.e.* any object *not* reachable from that root can be safely reclaimed. We also restrict our study to even-aligned two-field objects that contain only pointers (including the null pointer) rather than arbitrary integers. Our proof can be modified to verify the unsimplified algorithm; *e.g.*, we can allow data by the usual systems hack of requiring that data be odd and pointers be even.

Remarkably, Cheney's algorithm migrates the graph from one space to the other using only a *constant* amount of extra memory, which is in short supply during garbage collection. Contrast this with our dag-copying example of §A that required *linear* additional space (in both the data fields and the function stack). The cost is that we mangle the original graph, which we can live with because afterwards it will be garbage. The trick is that Cheney rewires the first field in each already-copied object in the from-space to point to its copy in the to-space. The collector can determine whether an object has already been copied, and moreover discover the copy's address, by checking if its first field points into the to-space.

Following [Gas11], we implement the algorithm as two functions: `collect` and `copy_ref`, shown in Fig. 4. In addition to the `to` and `from` pointers (fixed for the duration of the collection), they maintain two additional pointers into the to-space. First, the `scan` pointer separates the fully-processed "scanned" objects, whose pointers point into the to-space, from the partially-processed "queued" objects, whose pointers point into the from-space. Second, the `free` pointer distinguishes the first unused address in the to-space.

Initially (line 3), `scan` = `free` = `to`, meaning that no objects have been copied and the entire to-space is free. The process is initiated by copying the object pointed to by the root `r` (line 4), which allocates two cells of memory at the beginning of the to-space by increasing `free` and fills them with the values in the original object, now enqueued. After that the program loops (lines 5–12) until no queued objects remain, calling `copy_ref` on both object fields (lines 8 and 11) before incrementing `scan` to indicate that the object has been scanned. Each call to `copy_ref` swings the from-space pointers into the to-space, queuing newly encountered nodes as necessary. Fig. 5 presents an intermediate state in the execution, with one node copied and scanned and one node queued for scanning.

Formal specification To represent states of the execution we use the following definitions. Mathematical graphs are pairs (V, E), *i.e.* we remove D and L, and the spatial predicate is accordingly

$$\mathsf{graph}(x,\gamma) \stackrel{\text{def}}{=} \begin{array}{l}(x = 0 \wedge \mathsf{emp}) \vee \exists l, r.\, \gamma(x) = (l, r) \wedge \\ x \mapsto l, r \circledast \mathsf{graph}(l,\gamma) \circledast \mathsf{graph}(r,\gamma)\end{array}$$

We define shorthand to express whether a node is in the from- or to-space and whether it has been copied (recall that `to`, `from` and `size` are constant throughout the execution):

$$\begin{aligned} \mathit{from}(x) &\stackrel{\text{def}}{=} x = 0 \vee \mathtt{from} \leqslant x < \mathtt{from} + \mathtt{size} \\ \mathit{to}(x) &\stackrel{\text{def}}{=} x = 0 \vee \mathtt{to} \leqslant x < \mathtt{to} + \mathtt{size} \\ \mathit{copied}(\gamma, x) &\stackrel{\text{def}}{=} x \neq 0 \wedge \mathit{from}(x) \wedge \mathit{to}(\gamma(x).1) \end{aligned}$$

We write $\mathit{from}(\gamma)$ for $\forall v \in \gamma.\, \mathit{from}(v)$ and similarly for $\mathit{to}(\gamma)$. The memory also contains a *pool* of free addresses, starting at some x, and the whole from-space, which we use to collect nodes that the algorithm disconnects (*i.e.*, from-space objects that are no longer reachable from the to-space and are therefore fresh garbage):

$$\begin{aligned} \mathsf{pool}(x) &\stackrel{\text{def}}{=} \mathsf{ptrs}(\{x, \ldots, \mathtt{to} + \mathtt{size} - 1\}) \\ \mathsf{fromsp} &\stackrel{\text{def}}{=} \mathsf{ptrs}(\{\mathtt{from}, \ldots, \mathtt{from} + \mathtt{size} - 1\}) \end{aligned}$$

The main end-to-end property of a garbage collector is that the final graph is *isomorphic* to the original one. In the middle of a

```
1  void collect(void **r) {
2  // {(r ↦ r_0 ∗ graph(r_0, γ_0) ⊛ fromsp) ∗ pool(to) ∧ from(γ_0)}
3    scan = free = to;
4    copy_ref(r);
5    while (scan != free)
6  // { r ↦ to ∗ (graph(to, γ) ⊛ fromsp) ∗ pool(free) ∧
//     γ@to ≈ γ_0@r_0 ∧ cheney(γ, scan, free) }
7  { // { r ↦ to ∗ (graph(to, γ) ⊛ scan ↦ q_0, q_1 ⊛ graph(q_0, γ) ⊛
  //     graph(q_1, γ) ⊛ fromsp) ∗ pool(free) ∧ γ@to ≈ γ_0@r_0 ∧
  //     cheney(γ, scan, free) ∧ scan ⩽ free − 2 }
8      copy_ref(scan);
9  //↯ { r ↦ to ∗ (graph(to, γ') ⊛ scan ↦ q'_0, q_1 ⊛ graph(q'_0, γ') ⊛
//     graph(q_0, γ') ⊛ graph(q_1, γ') ⊛ fromsp) ∗ pool(free) ∧
//     γ@to ≈ γ_0@r_0 ∧ scan ⩽ free − 2 ∧
//     cheney(γ', scan + 1, free) ∧ γ'@to ≈ γ@to }
10 // { r ↦ to ∗ (graph(to, γ') ⊛ fromsp) ∗ pool(free) ∧
//     γ'@to ≈ γ_0@r_0 ∧ cheney(γ', scan + 1, free) ∧
//     scan ⩽ free − 2 }
11     copy_ref(scan + 1);
12     scan = scan + 2; }
13 } // { r ↦ to ∗ graph(to, γ) ∗ fromsp ∗ pool(free) ∧
  //     to(γ) ∧ γ@to ≈ γ_0@r_0 }
14
15 void copy_ref(void **p) {
16 // {(p ↦ q ⊛ graph(q, γ)) ∗ pool(f) ∧ cheney(γ, p, f) ∧ free = f}
17   if (*p) {
18 // { (p ↦ q ⊛ q ↦ a, b ⊛ graph(a, γ) ⊛ graph(b, γ)) ∗
//     pool(f) ∧ cheney(γ, p, f) ∧ free = f }
19   void *obj = *p;
20   void *fwd = *obj;
21 // { (p ↦ obj ⊛ obj ↦ fwd, b ⊛ graph(fwd, γ) ⊛ graph(b, γ)) ∗
//     pool(f) ∧ cheney(γ, p, f) ∧ free = f }
22   if (to <= fwd && fwd < to + size){
23 // { (p ↦ obj ⊛ obj ↦ fwd, b ⊛ graph(fwd, γ) ⊛ graph(b, γ)) ∗
//     pool(f) ∧ cheney(γ, p, f) ∧ free = f ∧ to(fwd) }
24     *p = fwd;
25 //↯ { (p ↦ fwd ⊛ obj ↦ fwd, b ⊛ graph(fwd, γ') ⊛ graph(b, γ')) ∗
//     pool(f) ∧ cheney(γ, p, f) ∧ free = f ∧ to(fwd) ∧
//     cheney(γ', p + 1, f) ∧ γ' = [p ↦ fwd]γ }
26   } else {
27 // { (p ↦ obj ⊛ obj ↦ fwd, b ⊛ graph(fwd, γ) ⊛ graph(b, γ)) ∗
//     pool(f) ∧ cheney(γ, p, f) ∧ free = f ∧ from(fwd) }
28     void *new = free;
29     free = free + 2;
30     *new = *obj;
31     *(new + 1) = *(obj + 1);
32 // { (p ↦ obj ⊛ obj ↦ fwd, b ⊛ graph(fwd, γ) ⊛ graph(b, γ)) ∗
//     new ↦ fwd, b ∗ pool(free) ∧ free = f + 2 ∧
//     cheney(γ, p, f) ∧ from(fwd) ∧ new = f }
33 // { (p ↦ obj ⊛ obj ↦ fwd, b ⊛ new ↦ fwd, b ⊛
//     graph(fwd, γ_1) ⊛ graph(b, γ_1)) ∗ pool(free) ∧
//     free = f + 2 ∧ cheney(γ, p, f) ∧ from(fwd) ∧
//     new = f ∧ γ_1 = [new ↦ fwd, b]γ }
34     *obj = new;
35 //↯ { (p ↦ obj ⊛ obj ↦ new, b ⊛ new ↦ fwd, b ⊛
//     graph(fwd, γ_2) ⊛ graph(b, γ_2)) ∗ pool(free) ∧
//     cheney(γ, p, f) ∧ free = f + 2 ∧ from(fwd) ∧
//     new = f ∧ γ_2 = [obj ↦ new][new ↦ fwd, b]γ }
36     *p = new;
37 //↯ { (p ↦ new ⊛ obj ↦ new, b ⊛ new ↦ fwd, b ⊛
//     graph(fwd, γ') ⊛ graph(b, γ')) ∗ pool(free) ∧
//     cheney(γ, p, f) ∧ free = f + 2 ∧ from(fwd) ∧
//     new = f ∧ γ' = [p ↦ new][obj ↦ new][new ↦ fwd, b]γ }
38 }}} // { (p ↦ q' ⊛ graph(q', γ') ⊛ graph(q, γ')) ∗ pool(free) ∧
    //     cheney(γ', p + 1, free) ∧ γ@to ≈ γ'@to ∧
    //     γ' ↑ {p, q, q'} = γ ↑ {p, q} ∧ free ⩾ f }
```

Figure 4: Proof sketch of Cheney's garbage collector.

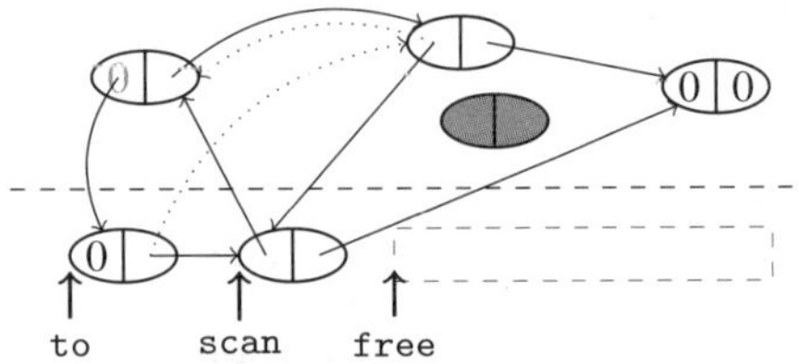

Figure 5: Transient state of the memory during garbage collection. Previous field values are indicated by 0 or dotted pointer arrows.

$$\begin{aligned}
&\mathit{cheney}(\gamma, s, f) \stackrel{\text{def}}{=} \mathit{to}(s) \wedge \mathit{to}(f) \wedge \\
&|\{v \mid \mathit{copied}(\gamma, v)\}| = (f - \texttt{to})/2 \wedge && (28)\\
&\{\texttt{to}, \ldots, f-2\} \subseteq \gamma \downarrow \texttt{to} \wedge && (29)\\
&\forall v \in \gamma.\, \forall a, b.\, \gamma(v) = (a, b) \Rightarrow \\
&\quad \begin{pmatrix} \mathit{to}(v) \wedge ((v < s \wedge \mathit{to}(a)) \vee (v \geqslant s \wedge \mathit{from}(a))) \wedge \\ ((v{+}1 < s \wedge \mathit{to}(b)) \vee (v{+}1 \geqslant s \wedge \mathit{from}(b))) \end{pmatrix} \vee && (30)\\
&\quad (\mathit{from}(v) \wedge \mathit{from}(b) \wedge (\mathit{to}(a) \Rightarrow \gamma@b \approx \gamma@(\gamma(a).2))) && (31)
\end{aligned}$$

Figure 6: Cheney graphs. Parameter s is the first unscanned address and f is the beginning of the free space. There are as many nodes in the to-space as there are copied nodes (28), which ensures that we never exhaust our free space at line 29. Every cell in the to-space is reachable (29). For each object, either (30) it is in the to-space and either scanned with fields pointing to the to-space, or queued with fields pointing to the from-space; or (31) it is in the from-space, with fields either entirely pointing to the from-space or with first field pointing to its copy in the to-space, in which case the second fields of the object and its copy point to isomorphic sub-graphs.

collection, the loop invariant is more complex; for Cheney it is that the graph rooted at `to` is isomorphic to the original one *up-to* a canonicalization function, $\mathit{canon}(\gamma)$. The canonicalization of a graph $\gamma = (V, E)$ "skips" already copied nodes by following their first field (which points to their copies). Formally, $\mathit{canon}(\gamma)$ is the graph (V', E') where $V' = \{v \in V \mid \neg\mathit{copied}(\gamma, v)\}$ and, if $E(x) = (v_1, v_2)$, then $E'(x) = (v'_1, v'_2)$ with

$$v'_i = \begin{cases} E(v_i).1 & \text{if } \mathit{copied}(\gamma, v_i) \\ v_i & \text{otherwise} \end{cases}$$

We write $\gamma@x \approx \gamma'@x'$ to denote *graph isomorphism* between $\mathit{canon}(\gamma) \downarrow x$ and $\mathit{canon}(\gamma') \downarrow x'$. Both $\mathit{from}(\gamma)$ and $\mathit{to}(\gamma)$ imply $\mathit{canon}(\gamma) = \gamma$, so at the end of garbage collection, when the entire graph has been moved into the to-space, we will have standard isomorphism between the old graph and the new.

The main constraints satisfied by the graph are enforced in the mathematical world by the *cheney* predicate shown in Fig. 6. Additionally, the following invariant is implicit throughout the proof:

$$\texttt{to} \leqslant \texttt{scan} \leqslant \texttt{free} < \texttt{to}{+}\texttt{size} \wedge \mathit{even}(\texttt{from}, \texttt{to}, \texttt{scan}, \texttt{free}, \gamma)$$

Here *even* forces all objects and global pointers to be aligned on even boundaries. Notice that a graph entirely in the from-space is automatically a Cheney graph: $\mathit{from}(\gamma) \Rightarrow \mathit{cheney}(\gamma, \texttt{to}, \texttt{to})$. Similarly, if $\texttt{to} \in \gamma$ and $s = f$ then $\mathit{cheney}(\gamma, s, f) \Rightarrow \mathit{to}(\gamma)$. These observations are enough to go from the precondition to the loop invariant, and from the loop invariant to the postcondition.

Verification of `copy_ref` We omit the (simpler) spec of `copy_ref` that applies the first time it is called in `collect` (line 4) and focus instead on the calls made from the main loop (lines 8 and 11). `copy_ref` swings one field of a queued object from its original target in the from-space to its target's copy in the to-space. If the target is 0 then no action is required and the post is direct from the pre. Otherwise, we can unfold the graph (line 16) to expose the target object in the from-space. We then examine its first field, `fwd`.

If `fwd` is in the to-space, then the target object has a copy located there and we swing the pointer to it. The ramification immediately follows from Lem. 4.12, slightly modified to handle single-field updates, and updates the graph to $\gamma' = [\texttt{p} \mapsto \texttt{fwd}]\gamma$ (where a single field update $[x \mapsto y]\gamma$ corresponds to $[x \mapsto y, \gamma(x).2]\gamma$ if x is even and to $[x-1 \mapsto \gamma(x).1, y]\gamma$ if x is odd). The actual proof effort at that point is to mathematically establish $\mathit{cheney}(\gamma', \texttt{p}{+}1, \texttt{free})$ and $\gamma@\texttt{to} \approx \gamma'@\texttt{to}$. The former holds because the only update is that `p` changed from queued in γ to scanned in γ' ($\texttt{p} < \texttt{p}+1$) and from pointing to the from-space to the to-space. For the latter, notice that $\mathit{canon}(\gamma)(\texttt{p}) = \texttt{fwd}$, so swinging `p` to point to `fwd` gives the same canonical graph: $\mathit{canon}(\gamma) = \mathit{canon}(\gamma')$, hence $\gamma@\texttt{to} \approx \gamma'@\texttt{to}$.

If the object has not been copied yet, we reserve two units of space at the position of the `free` pointer (by advancing it, line 27), and fill them with the object's fields. Since the pool of free space is kept $*$-separated from the current graph of objects, FRAME is able to deal nicely with the heap mutations up to the assignment at line 35. Now we rewrite the state to integrate the new object into the main graph (Lem. 4.11), then swing both the current field `p` and the first field of the target object `obj` to point to the copy `new`, yielding two successive ramifications that update the global graph accordingly, which we can discharge with Lem. 4.12. Once again, RAMIFY and our library allow us to progress past updates to the shared state; the actual complexity resides in establishing mathematical facts about graphs in the postcondition. Their proof is similar to the case in which `fwd` was in the to-space to begin with. We have to prove that `new` is reachable from `to`, as required by 29, which holds because `p` is reachable from `to` and points to it. The isomorphism holds because `new` and `obj` have identical contents.

Verification of `collect` The main function first copies the root node in the graph using an alternative (simpler) spec for `copy_ref` to establish the loop invariant (line 6, in which we leave out the case $r_0 = 0$ of an empty graph). It then enters a loop that updates both fields of the first unscanned object in succession (which may queue up new objects), repeating until all objects have been scanned. The looping condition allow us to go from the invariant at line 6 to the assertion at line 7 (in particular, $\texttt{to} \leadsto^* \texttt{scan}$ by (29) so Lem. 4.10 applies). The ramification at line 9 makes interesting use of our ramification library. Lem. 4.13 tells us that each individual pointer in fromsp (as well as the other field of `scan`) is preserved. Combining this with Lem. 4.6 yields that the whole of fromsp is preserved. The graphs are updated thanks to Lem. 4.14. We finally combine both our conclusions with another application of Lem. 4.6. To deduce line 10, we fold back the sub-graph rooted at `scan` into the main one rooted at `to`, which leaves the following spatial deduction, which holds because, together, $\mathsf{graph}(\texttt{to}, \gamma')$ and fromsp contain the whole allocated heap:

$$\mathsf{graph}(\texttt{to}, \gamma') \circledast \mathsf{graph}(q_0, \gamma') \circledast \mathsf{fromsp} \vdash \mathsf{graph}(\texttt{to}, \gamma') \circledast \mathsf{fromsp}$$

The second call to `copy_ref` is analogous to the first, and after we advance `scan` we reach the loop invariant.[6]

Related work Cheney's garbage collector has been a benchmark of sorts for heap-aware verification, especially in separation logic [MAY06, TSBR08, Gas11]. Previous verifications worked by exploding the spatial graph into its individual nodes, and grouping those into several *disjoint* groups corresponding to the intersections of various heap regions (from and to-space, scanned and unscanned,

[6] In the above proof, the global variable `free` is modified by `copy_ref`, but appears in our ramified assertions. We circumvent this issue by treating `free` as a resource: we remove our knowledge about `free` when `copy_ref` is called, and only get to assume what is in `copy_ref`'s post-condition in the post-ramified state (*e.g.* line 9).

$$\dfrac{\dfrac{}{R \vdash P * (Q \mathrel{-\!\!*} R')}\text{Hyp.} \qquad \dfrac{\dfrac{}{\{P\}\ c\ \{Q\}}\text{Hyp.} \quad \dfrac{}{\mathit{modif}(c) \cap \mathit{fv}(Q \mathrel{-\!\!*} R') = \varnothing}\text{Hyp.}}{\{P * (Q \mathrel{-\!\!*} R')\}\ c\ \{Q * (Q \mathrel{-\!\!*} R')\}}\text{Frame} \qquad \dfrac{}{Q * (Q \mathrel{-\!\!*} R') \vdash R'}\text{Modus Ponens}}{\{R\}\ c\ \{R'\}}\text{Consequence}$$

Figure 7: Proof of RAMIFY.

etc.). Our approach uses a single, *generic* inductive graph predicate, and the intricacies of reasoning about those regions is handled at the level of mathematical graphs. This division of labor yields, in our opinion, a much more pleasant and concise proof, which enjoys relatively intuitive and natural invariants.

8. Universality, Strongest Posts, and Extensions

Here we discuss the general applicability of the ramify rule as well as an alternative form of the rule. We also discuss a number of extensions to apply ramifications to more examples, including the overlapping conjunction $\uplus$, regions, and higher-order settings.

8.1 Universality of Ramification

In §3.3 we showed that the frame rule was a consequence of the ramify rule. Somewhat surprisingly, the converse is also true.

Theorem 8.1 (RAMIFY)

$$\dfrac{\{P\}\ c\ \{Q\} \qquad R \vdash P * (Q \mathrel{-\!\!*} R')}{\{R\}\ c\ \{R'\}} \quad \begin{array}{l}\mathit{fv}(Q \mathrel{-\!\!*} R') \cap \\ \mathit{modif}(c) = \varnothing\end{array}$$

Proof By the short derivation given in Fig. 7. □

Because theorem 8.1 only requires frame and consequence, ramify is valid in any separation logic. This is very handy, because it means that we do not need to modify the numerous flavors of separation logic in previous work to incorporate ramification: it has been there all along, just waiting for its importance to be recognized.

8.2 Weakest preconditions and strongest postconditions

In fact, our ramify rule appears in the separation logic folklore as a weakest precondition rule, codified as follows:

Lemma 8.1 (Weakest Pre) *Given a postcondition R' and a specification $\{P\}\ c\ \{Q\}$, then $P * (Q \mathrel{-\!\!*} R')$ is the weakest precondition,* i.e., *given any specification $\{R\}\ c\ \{R'\}$, then $R \vdash P * (Q \mathrel{-\!\!*} R')$.*

Our examples demonstrate that we can successfully ramify with weakest precondition. Can we also succeed with strongest postcondition, *i.e.*, with the following "forward ramify" rule:

FWRAMIFY
$$\dfrac{\{P\}\ c\ \{Q\} \qquad R \vdash P * \mathsf{true} \qquad (P \mathrel{-\!\!\circledast} R) * Q \vdash R'}{\{R\}\ c\ \{R'\}}$$

The $(P \mathrel{-\!\!\circledast} R) * Q \vdash R'$ pattern is reminiscent of a pattern used in RGSep [VP07] to characterize *stability* by setting R' to R. In RGSep the focus is on concurrency, and a thread's collaborators may take an unknown number of actions. In our setting we know that a given specification will execute exactly once, which we leverage by allowing the consequent to be the more general R' rather than R. When P is precise, FWRAMIFY gives the strongest postcondition:

Lemma 8.2 (Strongest Post) *Given precondition R and $\{P\}\ c\ \{Q\}$, if P is precise then $(P \mathrel{-\!\!\circledast} R) * Q$ is the strongest postcondition.*

As it happens, whenever P is precise, RAMIFY and FWRAMIFY are each derivable from the other. However, precision is actually only needed when starting from FWRAMIFY, and so we consider RAMIFY to be fundamental. Moreover, although we were able to prove some of the examples using FWRAMIFY, we found its $\mathrel{-\!\!\circledast}$ idiom to be harder to reason about than the $\mathrel{-\!\!*}$ idiom in RAMIFY.

8.3 Extensions supporting ramification

We can ramify in any separation logic, but verifying certain programs can require various extensions, such as regions in §A. Here we detail other extensions, starting with a more careful look at $\uplus$.

The overlapping conjunction $\uplus$ Although the overlapping conjunction $\uplus$ appears occasionally in the literature (under such names as "fusion", "relevance conjunction", and "sepish"), its properties are not well-understood for abstract separation logics.

A separation algebra [COY07] is a partial commutative monoid with cancellation $(S, \oplus)$ that provides an abstract model for separation logic. Although the overlapping conjunction $\uplus$ can be defined in any separation algebra, it is not necessarily easy to use: in fact, several critical properties require stronger separation algebra axioms. We propose using a variant described by Dockins *et al.* [DHA09] that has multiple units, *disjointness* (*i.e.*, $x \oplus x = y \Rightarrow x = y$), and a kind of distributivity property called "cross split":

$$\begin{array}{l} a \oplus b = z \wedge c \oplus d = z \Rightarrow \exists ac, ad, bc, bd. \\ \quad ac \oplus ad = a \wedge bc \oplus bd = b \wedge ac \oplus bc = c \wedge ad \oplus bd = d \end{array}$$

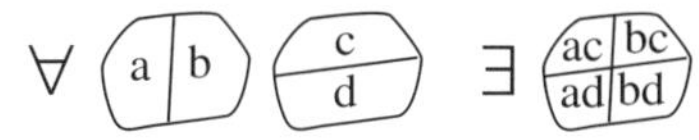

That is, if an element (*e.g.*, a heaplet) can be split in two different ways, then there are *four* subobjects which partition the original and respect the original splittings. Cross split is not discussed much in the literature, but we discovered that it is vital for reasoning about the overlapping conjunction $\uplus$, which is not even associative without it. In fact, virtually all of our proofs that use $\uplus$ assume cross split.

Many—but by no means all—separation algebras used in practice satisfy cross split, including the canonical model of heaplets as partial maps from addresses to values (quarters are found by set intersection on the domain). Users of our theory must therefore verify that the separation algebras they care about satisfy cross split.

Explicit overlapping conjunction Cherini and Blanco proposed a generalization of $P \uplus Q$ that tagged the shared core with an explicit description C [CB09], defined as follows:

$$\begin{array}{l} h \models P\langle \uplus : C \rangle Q \ \stackrel{\text{def}}{=}\ \exists h_1, h_2, h_3.\ (h_1 \oplus h_2 \oplus h_3 = s) \wedge \\ \quad (h_1 \oplus h_2 \models P) \ \wedge\ (h_2 \models C) \ \wedge\ (h_2 \oplus h_3 \models Q) \end{array}$$

This *explicit overlapping conjunction* is more expressive than $\uplus$:

$$P\langle \uplus : \mathsf{true} \rangle Q \ \dashv\vdash\ P \uplus Q$$

Moreover, Cherini and Blanco developed the following proof rule:

EXPRAMIFY
$$\dfrac{\{P\}\ c\ \{Q\} \qquad (C \mathrel{-\!\!\circledast} R) * C' \vdash R' \qquad Q \vdash C' * \mathsf{true}}{\{P\langle \uplus : C \rangle R\}\ c\ \{Q\langle \uplus : C' \rangle R'\}}$$

Unfortunately, EXPRAMIFY is not useful to verify any of our examples because we focus on *unspecified sharing*—that is, we do not know exactly what the overlap is (*e.g.*, the precise nodes shared between the children of a dag node), and hence cannot pick C or C' other than true. In general unspecified sharing is more difficult to verify than specified sharing, which is apparent when one tries to apply EXPRAMIFY:

$$(\mathsf{true} \mathrel{-\!\!\circledast} R) * \mathsf{true} \vdash R'$$

In other words, start from R, remove an unrestricted subheap, replace it with a second unrestricted heap, and now prove R'. Yikes!

Conversely, ExpRamify cannot verify our overlaid example (§6) because instead of C and C' being too weak, they represent the entire structure (*i.e.*, $P = C = R$ and $Q = C' = R'$). Applying ExpRamify then makes no progress because the "simpler" Hoare subproof $\{P\}\ c\ \{Q\}$ is actually identical to the goal.

All of that said, Cherini and Blanco demonstrate how to use ExpRamify to verify programs that operate in the special case of *specified partial sharing—i.e.*, when nontrivial C and C' are known and not the entire P, Q, R, or R'. Happily, ExpRamify is derivable from Ramify, so we can reuse all of their verifications.

Fractional shares, actions, and tight regions In §4.2 we pointed out that naïve attempts to verify `mark` using the shape-only $\mathsf{dag}(x)$ predicate were unsound. In this paper we focused on functional correctness instead, but we also experimented various other methods for guaranteeing that the graph is not overly mangled, including fractional shares [DHA09], actions in the style of RGSep [Vaf07], and a variant of regions that could prevent memory deallocation. Each method had some benefits but also required some additional formalism; the tradeoffs were unclear.

Higher-order settings In recent years there have been several flavors of separation logic to reason about higher-order state such as the resource invariants of concurrent separation logic with first-class locks [HAZ08]. Although we did not do any ramifications for genuine higher-order settings (which are often very complicated in ways unrelated to their higher-orderness), we did check a few of the ramifications from this paper in Coq within the framework of approximating separation algebras [HDA10], and believe that the higher-orderness by itself poses no fundamental difficulties.

9. Related Work

There is a large body of work, orthogonal to ours, tackling the design and proof of *algorithms* for data structures with sharing. Its counterpart in program verification spans a range of domains, and we begin this section with other separation logic based analyses.

Our reasoning about graphs owes a lot to the overlapping conjunction $\circledast$, which has roots in relevant logic [Urq72]. Many people have rediscovered it in the context of separation logic [Rey03, GMS12], who defined inductive graphs and dags as we did, but did not provide a means to reason about them. Cherini and Blanco were able to reason about a *specified* version of $\circledast$ using a more domain-specific framework than ours, as discussed in §8.3.

More recently, Mehnert *et al.* and Krishnaswami *et al.* have used some form of ramification to verify respectively implementations of snapshottable trees [MSBS12] and programs that follow the subject-observer pattern [KBA10], both of which involved unspecified sharing. Their ramifications are restricted to ad-hoc "ramification operators" tailored for each example, and the logic itself is domain-specific and done modulo a predicate on the global heap. It would be interesting to try and recast their proofs in our setting. Lee *et al.* devised an automatic analysis for threaded trees that instruments the results of separate analyses for lists and for trees [LYP11].

Moreover, several works have dealt with *definite* sharing in separation logic, *e.g.* doubly linked lists [Rey00], trees with parent pointers, skip or cyclic lists, etc. In these cases, one always knows *what* is shared and *by whom*. On the other hand, handling *indefinite* sharing, such as in this paper, was achieved only by resorting to tricks that specified or avoided the sharing. Yang's proof of the Schorr-Waite graph marking algorithm [Yan01, §7] (later mechanized in Isabelle/HOL [MN05]) does not define a spatial graph predicate, but rather describes the graph by its spanning tree. Attempts to lift this kind of reasoning to other algorithms on dags and graphs has led to convoluted predicates that explicitly deal with sharing and hack data structures into $*$-conjoined pieces, often in ways tied to the behavior of the program at hand [BCO04].

Several other frameworks have dealt with sharing in programs. In shape analysis, Hob can prove data structure consistency when one can expose a *backbone* into which objects ultimately point [WKL+06], and TVLA has been used to prove partial correctness of a mark-and-sweep garbage collector and the Schorr-Waite algorithm [MSRF04]. Hawblitzel and Petrank have used Boogie to automatically verify garbage collectors [HP09]. However, these works do not provide *compositional* reasoning for sharing.

It would be interesting to see if we can import ramification into other frameworks, such as Dafny [Lei10], whose reasoning about the heap is based on dynamic frames (a cousin of separation logic).

10. Conclusion

We have presented a new paradigm, ramification, valid in any separation logic, for the compositional verification of programs that manipulate data structures with both specified and unspecified sharing. We gave a ramification library that helps simplify ramification entailments in general and reduces local spatial updates to abstract mathematical reasoning. We have demonstrated the applicability of our framework by providing concise, local specifications for a range of examples and data structures, including Cheney's garbage collector. These initial successes lead us to believe that ramification provides a robust basis for elegant, compositional reasoning about sharing in data structures.

Acknowledgments

We deeply thank Peter O'Hearn for his continuous help and encouragement. We also benefited from discussions with Josh Berdine, Richard Bornat, Gareth Smitch, David Walker, Hongseok Yang, and especially with Matthew Parkinson, who first suggested that our initial semantic account of ramification was expressible as a separation logic entailment. Finally, we thank the anonymous reviewers for their suggestions and enthusiasm.

This research was supported by a Lee Kuan Yew Postdoctoral Fellowship and EPSRC Programme Grant "Resource Reasoning".

References

[BCO04] R. Bornat, C. Calcagno, and P. O'Hearn. Local reasoning, separation and aliasing. In *SPACE*, 2004.

[BCY06] R. Bornat, C. Calcagno, and H. Yang. Variables as resource in separation logic. *ENTCS*, 155, 2006.

[Bor00] R. Bornat. Proving pointer programs in Hoare logic. In *MPC*, 2000.

[CB09] R. Cherini and J. O. Blanco. Local reasoning for abstraction and sharing. In *SAC*, 2009.

[Che70] C. J. Cheney. A nonrecursive list compacting algorithm. *C. ACM*, 13(11), 1970.

[COY07] C. Calcagno, P. W. O'Hearn, and H. Yang. Local action and abstract separation logic. In *LICS*, 2007.

[DHA09] R. Dockins, A. Hobor, and A. W. Appel. A fresh look at separation algebras and share accounting. In *APLAS*, 2009.

[Fin87] J. Finger. *Exploiting constraints in design synthesis*. PhD thesis, Stanford University, 1987.

[Gas11] H. Gast. Developer-oriented correctness proofs - a case study of Cheney's algorithm. In *ICFEM*, 2011.

[GMS12] P. Gardner, S. Maffeis, and G. D. Smith. Towards a program logic for JavaScript. In *POPL*, 2012.

[HAZ08] A. Hobor, A. W. Appel, and F. Zappa Nardelli. Oracle semantics for concurrent separation logic. In *ESOP*, 2008.

[HDA10] A. Hobor, R. Dockins, and A. W. Appel. A logical mix of approximation and separation. In *APLAS*, ENTCS, 2010.

[HP09] C. Hawblitzel and E. Petrank. Automated verification of practical garbage collectors. In *POPL*, 2009.

[IO01] S. S. Ishtiaq and P. W. O'Hearn. BI as an assertion language for mutable data structures. In *POPL*, 2001.

[KBA10] N. Krishnaswami, L. Birkedal, and J. Aldrich. Verifying event-driven programs using ramified frame properties. In *TLDI*, 2010.

[Lei10] K. R. M. Leino. Dafny: An automatic program verifier for functional correctness. In *LPAR*, 2010.

[LG88] J. M. Lucassen and D. K. Gifford. Polymorphic effect systems. In *POPL*, 1988.

[LYP11] O. Lee, H. Yang, and R. Petersen. Program analysis for overlaid data structures. In *CAV*, 2011.

[MAY06] N. Marti, R. Affeldt, and A. Yonezawa. Formal verification of the heap manager of an operating system using separation logic. In *ICFEM*, 2006.

[MN05] F. Mehta and T. Nipkow. Proving pointer programs in higher-order logic. *Inf. Comput.*, 199(1-2), 2005.

[MSBS12] H. Mehnert, F. Sieczkowski, L. Birkedal, and P. Sestoft. Formalized verification of snapshotable trees: Separation and sharing. In *VSTTE*, 2012.

[MSRF04] R. Manevich, S. Sagiv, G. Ramalingam, and J. Field. Partially disjunctive heap abstraction. In *SAS*, 2004.

[Rey00] J. C. Reynolds. Intuitionistic reasoning about shared mutable data structure. In *Millennial Perspectives in Computer Science*, Cornerstones of Computing, 2000.

[Rey02] J. C. Reynolds. Separation logic: A logic for shared mutable data structures. In *LICS*, 2002.

[Rey03] J. C. Reynolds. A short course on separation logic. `http://www.cs.cmu.edu/afs/cs.cmu.edu/project/fox-19/member/jcr/wwwaac2003/notes7.ps`, 2003.

[Thi01] M. Thielscher. The qualification problem: A solution to the problem of anomalous models. *Artificial Intelligence*, 131(1), 2001.

[TSBR08] N. Torp-Smith, L. Birkedal, and J. C. Reynolds. Local reasoning about a copying garbage collector. *ACM TOPLAS*, 30(4), 2008.

[Urq72] A. Urquhart. Semantics for relevant logics. *J. Symb. Log.*, 37(1), 1972.

[Vaf07] V. Vafeiadis. *Modular fine-grained concurrency verification*. PhD thesis, University of Cambridge, 2007.

[VP07] V. Vafeiadis and M. J. Parkinson. A marriage of rely/guarantee and separation logic. In *CONCUR*, 2007.

[WKL+06] T. Wies, V. Kuncak, P. Lam, A. Podelski, and M. C. Rinard. Field constraint analysis. In *VMCAI*, 2006.

[Yan01] H. Yang. *Local Reasoning for Stateful Programs*. PhD thesis, University of Illinois, 2001.

```
struct node {struct node *c,*l,*r;};
struct node *
copy_dag(struct node *x) { // {icdag(x, δ)}
  struct node *l,*r,*ll,*rr,*y;
  if (!x) return 0;
  if (x->c) return x->c;
  l = x->l; r = x->r;
  y = malloc(sizeof(struct node));
  x->c = y;
// { x ↦α y, l, r ∗ (icdag(l, δ) ⊛ icdag(r, δ)) ∗ y ↦β −, −, − ∧
//   δ(x) = (0, l, r) }
  ll = copy_dag(l);
// ↯(35) { x ↦α y, l, r ∗ (ddag(l, ll, δ′) ⊛ icdag(r, δ′)) ∗
//         y ↦β −, −, − ∧ δ(x) = (0, l, r) ∧ δ′ ⩾l δ }
  rr = copy_dag(r);
// ↯(36) { x ↦α 0, l, r ∗ (ddag(l, ll, δ″) ⊛ ddag(r, rr, δ″)) ∗
//         y ↦β −, −, − ∧ δ(x) = (0, l, r) ∧ δ′ ⩾l δ ∧ δ″ ⩾r δ′ }
  y->c = 0; y->l = ll; y->r = rr;
// { x ↦α y, l, r ∗ y ↦β 0, ll, rr ∗
//   (ddag(l, ll, δ″) ⊛ ddag(r, rr, δ″)) ∧
//   δ(x) = (0, l, r) ∧ δ′ ⩾l δ ∧ δ″ ⩾r δ′ }
  return y;
} // {ddag(x, y, δ‴) ∧ δ‴ ⩾x δ}
```

Figure 8: Proof sketch of dag copy.

A. Copying Dags

The program in Fig. 8 makes a deep (structure-preserving) copy of a dag, using a data field in each original node to record the location of its copy when it exists (or 0 otherwise). Initially, all the copy fields of dag(`x`) must be set to 0, and at the end all the nodes reachable from `x` will have been copied into a new dag whose root is returned by `copy_dag`. In the intermediate recursive calls, parts of the dag rooted at the argument will have already been copied.

To cut down on the amount of formalism we must present to verify a reasonable-looking specification for `copy_dag`, we will utilize regions in the following ad-hoc way. We assume two regions, α and β, bound at the "top level", in the meta context. The initial dag must come in region α, and `malloc` always allocates in region β; afterwards the new copy will be in β and the original will remain in α. This specification is not as general as one would want, since *e.g.* it prevents us from verifying the copying of a copy; a far better specification would take the regions as parameters, but all of the extra wizardry would be in the (orthogonal) region management system rather than in the ramifications. Ideally, such a system would have features such as general-purpose region creation, destruction, and merging, as well as a good handle on region variable scoping.

Describing completed and in-process dag copies We represent an entirely copied dag $\delta = (V, D, L, E)$ rooted at x and its copy rooted at y by the predicate $\mathsf{ddag}(x, y, \delta)$ (or *double dag*):

$$\mathsf{ddag}(x, y, \delta) \stackrel{\text{def}}{=} \begin{array}{l}(x = y = 0 \wedge \mathsf{emp}) \vee (\mathsf{dag}_\alpha(x, \delta) \ast \\ \quad \mathsf{dag}_\beta(y, copy(\delta)) \wedge L(x) = y \wedge y \neq 0)\end{array}$$

The nodes in the first dag are described by the graph δ. Because we store the addresses of the copy in the data fields, δ is also enough to describe the copy via $copy(\delta) = (V', D, L', E')$, where

$$\begin{aligned} V' &= \{v' \mid \exists v \in V.\, L(v) = v' \wedge v' \neq 0\} \\ L'(v) &= 0 \\ E'(v) &= (l', r') \text{ if } \begin{cases} \exists v' \in V.\, \delta(v') = (v, l, r) \wedge \\ (l = l' = 0 \vee L(l) = l') \wedge \\ (r = r' = 0 \vee L(r) = r') \end{cases} \end{aligned}$$

The predicate ddag describes the postcondition for `copy_dag`; our next task is to define the precondition. Because some parts of the dag may have already been copied, the *in-copy dag* predicate $\mathsf{icdag}(x, \delta)$ describes a single dag in region α and a *set* of dags in region β corresponding to any previously copied sub-dags.

$$\mathsf{icdag}(x, \delta) \stackrel{\text{def}}{=} \mathsf{dag}_\alpha(x, \delta) \ast \mathsf{dags}_\beta(pr(x, \delta), copy(\delta))$$

$pr(x, \delta)$ (processed roots) finds the roots of the copied sub-dags:

$$pr(x, \delta) \stackrel{\text{def}}{=} \begin{cases} \varnothing & \text{if } x = 0 \\ pr(l, \delta) \cup pr(r, \delta) & \text{if } \delta(x) = (0, l, r) \\ \{x\} & \text{otherwise} \end{cases} \qquad (32)$$

Observe that when x is copied, *i.e.* $\delta(x) = (y, l, r)$ and $y \neq 0$, then

$$\mathsf{icdags}(x, \delta) \dashv\vdash \mathsf{ddags}(x, y, \delta) \qquad (33)$$

We will use this equivalence to move between the precondition and the postcondition when we discover that the dag is already copied.

When we wish to reason entirely about the copies we write $\mathsf{cdags}(x, \delta)$ (*i.e., copy dags*) for $\mathsf{dags}(pr(x, \delta), copy(\delta))$. Note that if x is not yet copied, *i.e.* $\delta(x) = (0, l, r)$, then, using the second case in the definition of pr, we deduce that

$$\mathsf{cdags}(x, \delta) \dashv\vdash \mathsf{cdags}(l, \delta) \circledast \mathsf{cdags}(r, \delta), \text{ and thus}$$

$$\mathsf{icdags}(x, \delta) \dashv\vdash x \mapsto_\alpha 0, l, r \ast (\mathsf{icdags}(l, \delta) \circledast \mathsf{icdags}(r, \delta)) \; (34)$$

Finally, to reflect the fact that already copied parts of the dag will not be changed by `copy_dag`, we define the relation $\delta' \geqslant_x \delta$ between two dags $\delta = (V, D, L, E)$ and $\delta' = (V, D, L', E)$, true when $\delta' \uparrow x = \delta \uparrow x$ and $\delta' \downarrow x$ is "more copied" than $\delta \downarrow x$:

$$\forall v \in reach(\delta, x).\; \begin{array}{l}(L(v) \neq 0 \Rightarrow L'(v) = L(v)) \wedge \\ (L'(v) = 0 \Rightarrow L(v) = 0)\end{array}$$

We will write $\delta' \geqslant \delta$ when $\exists x.\, \delta' \geqslant_x \delta$.

Verification of `copy_dag` Now we annotate the program in Fig. 8 with the key assertions to prove the following specification:

$$\{\mathsf{icdag}(x,\delta)\}\ \texttt{y = copy\_dag(x)}\ \{\mathsf{ddag}(x,y,\delta') \wedge \delta' \geqslant_x \delta\}$$

If the dag is empty then the postcondition is trivially satisfied (line 5); if the node has already been copied (line 6) then equation 33 yields the postcondition. The real meat of the algorithm is in the ramifications from the two recursive call sites and the entailment of the postcondition from line 16. The two ramifications are as follows:

$$\begin{aligned}&\mathsf{icdag}(\mathtt{l},\delta) \circledast \mathsf{icdag}(\mathtt{r},\delta)\\ &\vdash \mathsf{icdag}(\mathtt{l},\delta) * (\mathsf{ddag}(\mathtt{l},\mathtt{ll},\delta') \wedge \delta' \geqslant_{\mathtt{l}} \delta \mathrel{-\!\!*} \\ &\qquad \mathsf{ddag}(\mathtt{l},\mathtt{ll},\delta') \circledast \mathsf{icdag}(\mathtt{r},\delta') \wedge \delta' \geqslant_{\mathtt{l}} \delta)\end{aligned} \tag{35}$$

$$\begin{aligned}&\mathsf{ddag}(\mathtt{l},\delta') \circledast \mathsf{icdag}(\mathtt{r},\delta')\\ &\vdash \mathsf{icdag}(\mathtt{r},\delta') * (\mathsf{ddag}(\mathtt{r},\mathtt{rr},\delta'') \wedge \delta'' \geqslant_{\mathtt{r}} \delta' \mathrel{-\!\!*} \\ &\qquad \mathsf{ddag}(\mathtt{l},\mathtt{ll},\delta'') \circledast \mathsf{ddag}(\mathtt{r},\mathtt{rr},\delta'') \wedge \delta'' \geqslant_{\mathtt{r}} \delta')\end{aligned} \tag{36}$$

As with `mark`, the second ramification follows from the first by swapping the roles of $\mathtt{r}$ and $\mathtt{l}$ and observing that when $\delta' \geqslant \delta$

$$\mathsf{ddag}(x,y,\delta) \vdash \mathsf{icdag}(x,\delta') \Leftrightarrow \mathsf{ddag}(x,y,\delta') \Leftrightarrow \mathsf{ddag}(x,y,\delta)$$

Regions let us split the first ramification (35) using the Lem. 4.5 from our ramification library, yielding two simpler ramifications in which $\delta' \geqslant_{\mathtt{l}} \delta$, and, by the definition of ddag, $\mathtt{l}=\mathtt{ll}=0 \vee \delta'(\mathtt{l})=(\mathtt{ll},-,-)$. The first half of (35), in region α,

$$\begin{aligned}\mathsf{dag}(\mathtt{l},\delta) \circledast \mathsf{dag}(\mathtt{r},\delta) \vdash{}& \mathsf{dag}(\mathtt{l},\delta) * (\mathsf{dag}(\mathtt{l},\delta') \mathrel{-\!\!*} \\ & \mathsf{dag}(\mathtt{l},\delta') \circledast \mathsf{dag}(\mathtt{r},\delta')),\end{aligned} \tag{37}$$

is direct from Lem. 4.14. The second half of (35), in region β, is

$$\begin{aligned}\mathsf{cdags}(\mathtt{l},\delta) \circledast \mathsf{cdags}(\mathtt{r},\delta) \vdash{}& \mathsf{cdags}(\mathtt{l},\delta) * (\mathsf{dag}(\mathtt{ll},\delta'_c) \mathrel{-\!\!*} \\ & \mathsf{dag}(\mathtt{ll},\delta'_c) \circledast \mathsf{cdags}(\mathtt{r},\delta'))\end{aligned} \tag{38}$$

where $\delta'_c = copy(\delta')$. This ramification is more involved because the copied roots of δ' starting from $\mathtt{r}$ may differ from the previous ones in δ. Instantiating Lem. 4.14 with $S_1 = pr(\delta,\mathtt{l})$, $S_2 = pr(\delta,\mathtt{r})$ and $S'_1 = \{\mathtt{ll}\}$ yields this entailment, which is only halfway there, because it features the sub-dags rooted at $pr(\delta,\mathtt{r})$, whereas we want those rooted at $pr(\delta',\mathtt{r})$:

$$\begin{aligned}&\mathsf{cdags}(\mathtt{l},\delta) \circledast \mathsf{cdags}(\mathtt{r},\delta) \vdash \mathsf{cdags}(\mathtt{l},\delta) * \\ &\quad (\mathsf{dag}(\mathtt{ll},\delta'_c) \mathrel{-\!\!*} \mathsf{dag}(\mathtt{ll},\delta'_c) \circledast \mathsf{dags}(pr(\delta,\mathtt{r}),\delta'_c))\end{aligned}$$

To complete this proof, we remark that the copied roots of $\mathtt{r}$ in δ' and in δ satisfy the following relations, hence Lem. 4.10 applies:

$$\begin{aligned}pr(\delta,\mathtt{r}) &\subseteq reach(\delta'_c, pr(\delta',\mathtt{r})) && (\delta' \geqslant \delta)\\ pr(\delta',\mathtt{r}) &\subseteq pr(\delta,\mathtt{r}) \cup reach(\delta'_c,\mathtt{ll}) && (\delta' \geqslant_{\mathtt{l}} \delta)\end{aligned}$$

To reach the postcondition from line 16, the sub-copies on each side of the overlapping conjunction need to be disentangled from the original sub-dags using regions and equation 25 in the following derivations, where $\delta(\mathtt{x})=(0,\mathtt{l},\mathtt{r})$, $\delta' \geqslant_{\mathtt{l}} \delta$, and $\delta'' \geqslant_{\mathtt{r}} \delta'$:

$$\begin{aligned}&\mathtt{x} \mapsto_\alpha \mathtt{y},\mathtt{l},\mathtt{r} * \mathtt{y} \mapsto_\beta 0,\mathtt{ll},\mathtt{rr} * \\ &(\mathsf{dag}_\alpha(\mathtt{l},\delta'') * \mathsf{dag}_\beta(\mathtt{ll},copy(\delta''))) \circledast \\ &(\mathsf{dag}_\alpha(\mathtt{r},\delta'') * \mathsf{dag}_\beta(\mathtt{rr},copy(\delta''))) \\ \vdash{}& \mathsf{dag}_\alpha(\mathtt{x},\delta''') * \mathsf{dag}_\beta(\mathtt{y},copy(\delta''')) \wedge \delta''' = [\mathtt{x} \mapsto (\mathtt{y},\mathtt{l},\mathtt{r})]\delta'' \\ \vdash{}& \mathsf{ddag}(\mathtt{x},\mathtt{y},\delta''') \wedge \delta''' \geqslant_{\mathtt{x}} \delta\end{aligned} \tag{39}$$

The last deduction step uses this mathematical fact:

$$\delta(x) = (0,l,r) \wedge \delta'(x) = (y,l,r) \wedge \delta' \geqslant_l \delta \wedge \delta' \geqslant_r \delta \Rightarrow \delta' \geqslant_x \delta$$

B. Disposing a Graph

Let us show how to verify the depth-first search spanning tree procedure for binary graphs, as presented in Fig. 9.

The desired top-level specification for `spanning` is that, starting from an unmarked graph γ, we remove some edges (indicated by the predicate $\sqsubseteq$) and get a tree τ that covers the same set of nodes:

$$\begin{aligned}&\{\mathsf{graph}(x,\gamma) \wedge unmarked(\gamma)\}\\ &\texttt{spanning(x)}\\ &\{\mathsf{tree}(x,\tau) \wedge \tau \sqsubseteq \gamma \wedge reach(\tau,x) = reach(\gamma,x)\}\end{aligned}$$

The predicate $(V,D,L,E) \sqsubseteq (V',D',L',E')$ is true when $(V',D',L') = (V,D,L)$, and E has "fewer edges" than E':

$$\forall v \in V.\, E'(v) = (l',r') \Rightarrow E(v) = (l,r) \wedge l \in \{l',0\} \wedge r \in \{r',0\}$$

```
1  void spanning(struct node *x) {
2  // {graph(x, γ) ∧ γ(x) = (0, −, −)}
3    struct node *l,*r;
4    l = x->l; r = x->r;
5  // {x ↦ 0, l, r ⊛ graph(l, γ) ⊛ graph(r, γ) ∧ γ(x) = (0, l, r)}
6    x->m = 1;
7  //↯ { x ↦ 1, l, r ⊛ graph(l, γ1) ⊛ graph(r, γ1) ∧
       γ(x) = (0, l, r) ∧ γ1 = m1(γ, x) }
8    if (l && !l->m)
9  //  { x ↦ 1, l, r ⊛ graph(l, γ1) ⊛ graph(r, γ1) ∧
       γ(x) = (0, l, r) ∧ γ1 = m1(γ, x) ∧ γ1(l) = (0, −, −) }
10     spanning(l);
11   else x->l = 0;
12 //↯ { (x ↦ 1, l, r ⊛ tree(l, γ2) ⊛ graphs(pr(l, γ1), γ2) ⊛
       graph(r, γ2) ∧ γ(x) = (0, l, r) ∧ γ1 = m1(γ, x) ∧
       γ1(l) = (0, −, −) ∧
       γ2 ⊑ m(γ1, l) ∧ reach(γ2, l) = reach0(γ1, l)) ∨ ··· }
13   if (r && !r->m) spanning(r);
14   else x->r = 0;
15 //↯ { ((x ↦ 1, l, r ⊛ tree(l, γ3) ⊛ graphs(pr(l, γ1), γ3) ⊛
        tree(r, γ3) ⊛ graphs(pr(r, γ2), γ3) ∧ γ(x) = (0, l, r) ∧
        γ1 = m1(γ, x) ∧ γ1(l) = (0, −, −) ∧ γ2(r) = (0, −, −) ∧
        γ2 ⊑ m(γ1, l) ∧ reach(γ2, l) = reach0(γ1, l) ∧
        γ3 ⊑ m(γ2, r) ∧ reach(γ3, r) = reach0(γ2, r))
     ∨ (x ↦ 1, l, 0 ⊛ tree(l, γ3') ⊛ graphs(pr(l, γ1), γ3') ⊛
        graph(r, γ3') ∧ γ(x) = (0, l, r) ∧ γ1 = m1(γ, x) ∧
        γ1(l) = (0, −, −) ∧ (γ2(r) = (1, −, −) ∨ r = 0) ∧
        γ2 ⊑ m(γ1, l) ∧ reach(γ2, l) = reach0(γ1, l) ∧
        γ3' = [x ↦ (1, l, 0)]γ2)
     ∨ ··· }
16 } // { tree(x, γ') ⊛ graphs(pr(x, γ), γ') ∧
         γ' ⊑ m(γ, x) ∧ reach0(γ, x) = reach(γ', x) }
```

Figure 9: Spanning tree of a binary graph.

During the execution, the graph will be partially marked, and the effect of `spanning` on such graphs is thus subtler. Assuming that the root x of the graph γ has not been marked yet, it transforms the *unmarked* part of γ that is reachable from x (it was not apparent in the top-level specification, wherein $reach_0(\gamma,x) = reach(\gamma,x)$) into a tree covering the same nodes, overlapped with some subgraphs. As seen in Fig. 9, these extra subgraphs are precisely those that start at a marked node reachable from x via unmarked nodes in the original graph, using the pr predicate (32) from Apx. A.

The proof of `spanning` has four main branches, corresponding to whether each of the left and right sub-graphs has to be examined or not (notice that `spanning` assumes a non-empty graph as a precondition). In Fig. 9, we only show the proof sketch corresponding to the case where the left sub-graph was non-empty and unmarked. Marking the root $\mathtt{x}$ is done as in `mark` for graphs. To handle the recursive call of line 10, we have to prove the following ramification:

$$\begin{aligned}&\mathsf{graph}(\mathtt{l},\gamma_1) \circledast \mathsf{graph}(\mathtt{x},\gamma_1) \vdash \mathsf{graph}(\mathtt{l},\gamma_1) * \\ &\quad (\mathsf{tree}(\mathtt{l},\gamma_2) \circledast \mathsf{graphs}(pr(\mathtt{l},\gamma_1),\gamma_2) \mathrel{-\!\!*} \\ &\qquad \mathsf{tree}(\mathtt{l},\gamma_2) \circledast \mathsf{graphs}(pr(\mathtt{l},\gamma_1),\gamma_2) \circledast \mathsf{graph}(\mathtt{x},\gamma_2))\end{aligned}$$

Rewriting $\mathsf{tree}(\mathtt{l},\gamma_2)$ as $\mathsf{graph}(\mathtt{l},\gamma_2) \wedge (\gamma_2 \downarrow \mathtt{l}$ is a tree$)$, using an analogue of Lem. 4.8 for trees turns this ramification into an application of Lem. 4.14. The same trick can be used to obtain the first disjunct of line 15 (corresponding to the case where `spanning(r)` was applied), while the second disjunct is an application of Lem. 4.12.

Because the nodes covered by the sub-trees at $\mathtt{l}$ and $\mathtt{r}$ are marked and form the same set as the nodes reachable via unmarked paths in the graphs before each recursive call, we can disentangle both trees and the roots in the first disjunct of line 15 to form the spatial part

$$\begin{aligned}&(\mathtt{x} \mapsto 1,\mathtt{l},\mathtt{r} * \mathsf{tree}(\mathtt{l},\gamma_3) * \mathsf{tree}(\mathtt{r},\gamma_3))\\ &\circledast \mathsf{graphs}(pr(\mathtt{l},\gamma_1),\gamma_3) \circledast \mathsf{graphs}(pr(\mathtt{r},\gamma_2),\gamma_3)\end{aligned}$$

The post follows from the pure facts. The other disjuncts are similar.

Complete Instantiation-Based Interpolation

Nishant Totla
Indian Institute of Technology Bombay
nishant.totla@gmail.com

Thomas Wies
New York University
wies@cs.nyu.edu

Abstract

Craig interpolation has been a valuable tool for formal methods with interesting applications in program analysis and verification. Modern SMT solvers implement interpolation procedures for the theories that are most commonly used in these applications. However, many application-specific theories remain unsupported, which limits the class of problems to which interpolation-based techniques apply. In this paper, we present a generic framework to build new interpolation procedures via reduction to existing interpolation procedures. We consider the case where an application-specific theory can be formalized as an extension of a base theory with additional symbols and axioms. Our technique uses finite instantiation of the extension axioms to reduce an interpolation problem in the theory extension to one in the base theory. We identify a model-theoretic criterion that allows us to detect the cases where our technique is complete. We discuss specific theories that are relevant in program verification and that satisfy this criterion. In particular, we obtain complete interpolation procedures for theories of arrays and linked lists. The latter is the first complete interpolation procedure for a theory that supports reasoning about complex shape properties of heap-allocated data structures. We have implemented this procedure in a prototype on top of existing SMT solvers and used it to automatically infer loop invariants of list-manipulating programs.

Categories and Subject Descriptors D.2.4 [*Software Engineering*]: Software/Program Verification; F.3.1 [*Logics and Meaning of Programs*]: Specifying and Verifying and Reasoning about Programs; I.2.3 [*Artificial Intelligence*]: Deduction and Theorem Proving

General Terms Algorithms, Theory, Reliability, Verification

Keywords Craig Interpolants, Decision Procedures, Satisfiability Module Theories, Program Analysis, Data Structures

1. Introduction

In his pioneering work [37], McMillan recognized the usefulness of Craig interpolants [13] for the automated construction of abstractions of systems. Since then, interpolation-based algorithms have been developed for a number of problems in program analysis and verification [1, 15, 17, 24, 25, 31, 34, 39]. An important requirement for most of these algorithms is that interpolants are *ground* (i.e., quantifier-free). This is because the computed interpolants again serve as input to decision procedures that only support quantifier-free formulas. Modern SMT solvers implement ground interpolation procedures for the theories that are most commonly used in program verification. This includes theories such as linear arithmetic [8, 9, 23, 38], the theory of uninterpreted function symbols with equality [19, 38, 50], and combinations of such theories [11, 21, 38, 50]. However, many application-specific theories remain unsupported. This limits the class of problems and programs to which interpolation-based algorithms can be applied.

In this paper, we present a generic framework that enables the modular construction of ground interpolation procedures for application-specific theories via a reduction to existing interpolation procedures. We focus on cases where an application-specific theory can be formalized as an extension of a *base theory* with additional symbols and universally quantified axioms. As an example of such a *theory extension*, consider the theory of arrays over integers. Here, the base theory is the theory of linear integer arithmetic, the extension symbols are the array selection and update functions, and the extension axioms are McCarthy's read over write axioms [36], which give meaning to the extension symbols. Theory extensions often appear in practice, e.g., as part of the background theories of verification systems such as BOOGIE [3] and WHY [18], and the tools that are built on top of these systems.

Our starting point is the approach to instantiation-based interpolation for local theory extension presented in [47]. Local theory extensions [46] are extensions for which satisfiability of ground formulas can be decided via a reduction to satisfiability in the base theory. The reduction works by instantiating the extension axioms only with terms that already appear in the input formula. In [47], this instantiation-based reduction approach is applied to the problem of computing ground interpolants in local theory extensions. This technique is used, e.g., in the interpolation procedures underlying the software model checker ARMC [44] and the interpolating prover CSIsat [6]. In [47], the instantiation-based interpolation approach was shown to be complete for a syntactically defined class of local theory extensions. Unfortunately, many interesting application-specific theories do not fall into this class.

Instead of imposing syntactic restrictions, we identify a stronger condition on the theory extension than just locality to ensure completeness of instantiation-based interpolation. We then relate this condition to a semantic property of the models of the theory extension. We refer to this property as the *partial amalgamation property*. This property allows us to systematically construct theory extensions for which the instantiation-based approach produces a complete ground interpolation procedure. The resulting framework then applies to a more general class of theory extensions than [47].

We discuss several non-trivial examples of theories that are relevant in program verification and to which our framework applies. In particular, we consider the theory of arrays with difference function [10]. Using our approach we obtain an alternative ground interpolation procedure for this theory. Unlike the procedure presented in [10], our procedure does not require a dedicated decision proce-

POPL'13, January 23–25, 2013, Rome, Italy.

dure for this specific array theory. Instead, it reduces the interpolation problem to existing interpolation procedures for uninterpreted functions and linear arithmetic.

The second example that we discuss in detail is a variation of Nelson's theory of linked lists with reachability predicates [41], which was studied more recently in [35]. We show that this theory does not admit ground interpolation, unless it is extended (among others) with an additional *join* function. Given two heap nodes, the join function returns the *join point* of the two list segments that start in the given nodes (if such a join point exists). Incidentally, the join function is not just of theoretical interest, but is also useful to express properties about the heap that are important for verifying frame conditions. We prove that our extended theory of linked lists with reachability has partial amalgamation. Using our approach we then obtain the first ground interpolation procedure for a theory that supports reasoning about complex shape properties of heap-allocated data structures. This interpolation procedure has promising applications in CEGAR-based shape analysis [5, 42] and may also provide a new perspective on the construction of shape domains in parametric shape analysis [45].

To show the feasibility of our approach, we have implemented a prototype of our interpolation framework and instantiated it for the theory of linked lists presented in this paper. We have successfully applied the resulting interpolation procedure to automatically infer loop invariants for the verification of list-manipulating programs.

Summary. The main contributions of this paper can be summarized as follows:

- We present a new framework to modularly construct interpolation procedures for application-specific theories.
- We present a model-theoretic criterion that allows us to identify the theories for which our interpolation framework is complete.
- We present examples of theories that are important for program verification and to which our framework applies. In particular, we present the first decidable theory for reasoning about complex shape properties of heap-allocated data structures that admits ground interpolation.
- We report on our experience with a prototype implementation of our framework, which we have successfully used to infer loop invariants of simple list-manipulating programs.

An extended version of this paper including proofs of key lemmas and theorems is available as a technical report [48].

2. Motivation and Overview

We motivate our approach using the concrete application of interpolation to the problem of inferring invariants for program verification. Consider the reverse function given in Figure 1. This function takes a pointer x to a singly-linked list as input, reverses the list, and then returns a pointer to the head of the reversed list.

Our goal is to verify that the reverse function preserves acyclicity, i.e., if the input list is acyclic, then so is the output list. We can express acyclicity of list x by saying that null is reachable from x by following the n pointer fields in the heap. Using the notation that we formally introduce in Section 5.2, this is denoted by the *reachability predicate* $\mathsf{x} \xrightarrow{\mathsf{n}} \mathsf{null}$. Hence, the property we want to verify is that if the pre-condition $\mathsf{x} \xrightarrow{\mathsf{n}} \mathsf{null}$ holds at the entry point of function reverse, then the same formula holds again at the return point.

The graph in Figure 1 depicts an intermediate state of the heap that is observed during the execution of reverse when the function is applied to an acyclic list of length six. This state is observed at the entry point of the while loop, after the first three iterations of the loop. An appropriate inductive loop invariant for a Hoare proof of

```
typedef struct Node {
  struct node* n;
  int data;
} *List;
```

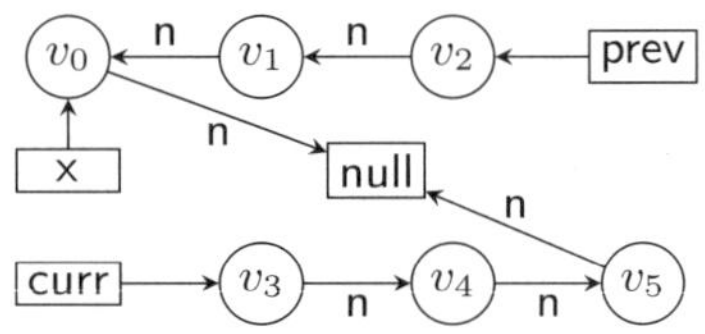


```
List reverse (List x) {
  List prev, curr, succ;
  curr = x;
  prev = null;
  while (curr != null) {
    succ = curr.n;
    curr.n = prev;
    prev = curr;
    curr = succ;
  }
  x = prev;
  return x;
}
```

Figure 1. C code for in-place reversal of a linked list. The graph depicts a reachable program state at the entry point of the while loop in function reverse.

our verification goal must capture the situation depicted in Figure 1, but abstract from the concrete length of the list segments. That is, the loop invariant must express that the list segments pointed to by prev and curr are acyclic (in fact, only the former is strictly necessary for the proof), and that the two list segments are disjoint. An appropriate inductive loop invariant is given by the following formula:

$$\mathsf{prev} \xrightarrow{\mathsf{n}} \mathsf{null} \wedge \mathsf{curr} \xrightarrow{\mathsf{n}} \mathsf{null} \wedge (\mathsf{prev} \overset{\mathsf{n}}{\curlyvee} \mathsf{curr}) = \mathsf{null} \quad (1)$$

The term $(\mathsf{prev} \overset{\mathsf{n}}{\curlyvee} \mathsf{curr})$ denotes the *join point* of the list segments starting from prev and curr, i.e., $(\mathsf{prev} \overset{\mathsf{n}}{\curlyvee} \mathsf{curr})$ is the first node that is reachable from both prev and curr by following n pointer fields in the heap, unless such a node does not exist, in which case its value is prev. The formula $(\mathsf{prev} \overset{\mathsf{n}}{\curlyvee} \mathsf{curr}) = \mathsf{null}$, thus, implies the disjointness of the two list segments. Note that this formula cannot be expressed in terms of the reachability predicate, unless we allow universal quantification over heap nodes.

We next describe how to compute inductive loop invariants such as (1) using our instantiation-based interpolation approach.

2.1 Interpolation-Based Program Verification

Given an unsatisfiable conjunction of formulas $A \wedge B$, an interpolant for $A \wedge B$ is a formula I such that I is implied by A, the conjunction $I \wedge B$ is unsatisfiable, and I only speaks about common symbols of A and B. A popular approach to interpolation-based verification uses bounded model checking to generate infeasible error traces of the analyzed program. These infeasible error traces are then translated into unsatisfiable formulas $A \wedge B$, where A and B encode a partition of the trace into a prefix and suffix trace. An interpolant I for $A \wedge B$ then describes a set of program states that (1) includes all states that are reachable by executing the prefix of the trace and (2) only includes states from which no feasible execution of the suffix is possible. The interpolant I is then used as a candidate invariant to refine the search for additional infeasible error traces. This process is continued until a fixed point is reached, i.e., until an inductive invariant has been computed that proves the program correct. We illustrated this approach through an example.

The left-hand side of Figure 2 shows an error trace of function reverse that is obtained by unrolling the while loop three times. The first and last assume statements correspond to the pre-condition, respectively, the negated post-condition of reverse. This error trace is infeasible, i.e., there is no execution that reaches the end of the trace (note that a failing assume statement blocks an execution). The right-hand side of Figure 2 shows an encoding of this error trace into a first-order formula using static single assignments. Note that the symbols $\bullet \xrightarrow{\bullet} \bullet$, $\bullet.\bullet$, and $\bullet[\bullet := \bullet]$ are interpreted. That

Trace		Trace formula
assume x $\xrightarrow{n}$ null;	A	$x_0 \xrightarrow{n_0} \mathsf{null}\ \wedge$
curr = x;	A	$\mathsf{curr}_0 = x_0\ \wedge$
prev = null;	A	$\mathsf{prev}_0 = \mathsf{null}\ \wedge$
assume curr != null;	A	$\mathsf{curr}_0 \neq \mathsf{null}\ \wedge$
succ = curr.n;	A	$\mathsf{succ}_1 = \mathsf{curr}_0.\mathsf{n}_0\ \wedge$
curr.n = prev;	A	$\mathsf{n}_1 = \mathsf{n}_0[\mathsf{curr}_0 := \mathsf{prev}_0]\ \wedge$
prev = curr;	A	$\mathsf{prev}_1 = \mathsf{curr}_0\ \wedge$
curr = succ;	A	$\mathsf{curr}_1 = \mathsf{succ}_1\ \wedge$
assume curr != null;	B	$\mathsf{curr}_1 \neq \mathsf{null}\ \wedge$
succ = curr.n;	B	$\mathsf{succ}_2 = \mathsf{curr}_1.\mathsf{n}_1\ \wedge$
curr.n = prev;	B	$\mathsf{n}_2 = \mathsf{n}_1[\mathsf{curr}_1 := \mathsf{prev}_1]\ \wedge$
prev = curr;	B	$\mathsf{prev}_2 = \mathsf{curr}_1\ \wedge$
curr = succ;	B	$\mathsf{curr}_2 = \mathsf{succ}_2\ \wedge$
assume curr != null;	B	$\mathsf{curr}_2 \neq \mathsf{null}\ \wedge$
succ = curr.n;	B	$\mathsf{succ}_3 = \mathsf{curr}_2.\mathsf{n}_2\ \wedge$
curr.n = prev;	B	$\mathsf{n}_3 = \mathsf{n}_2[\mathsf{curr}_2 := \mathsf{prev}_2]\ \wedge$
prev = curr;	B	$\mathsf{prev}_3 = \mathsf{curr}_2\ \wedge$
curr = succ;	B	$\mathsf{curr}_3 = \mathsf{succ}_3\ \wedge$
assume curr==null;	B	$\mathsf{curr}_3 = \mathsf{null}\ \wedge$
x = prev;	B	$x_1 = \mathsf{prev}_3\ \wedge$
assume !(x $\xrightarrow{n}$ null);	B	$\neg(x_1 \xrightarrow{n_3} \mathsf{null})$

Figure 2. Spurious error trace of function reverse and its encoding as a trace formula

is, they are given meaning by a specific first-order theory, here the theory of linked lists with reachability that we introduce in Section 5.2. The symbol $\bullet \xrightarrow{\bullet} \bullet$ is interpreted as described above. The symbol $\bullet.\bullet$ denotes field dereference and the symbol $\bullet[\bullet := \bullet]$ field update. The remaining symbols such as curr_0 and n_1 are uninterpreted. We call this formula the *trace formula* of the error trace because the valuations of uninterpreted symbols that make the trace formula true exactly correspond to the feasible executions of the trace. Since the error trace is infeasible, its trace formula is unsatisfiable. We can now split the trace formula into two parts A and B, say, where A corresponds to the prefix of the trace up to the end of the first iteration of the while loop and B to the remainder of the trace. This is depicted in Figure 2. Since $A \wedge B$ is unsatisfiable, we can interpolate the two formulas. A possible ground interpolant for this choice of A and B is:

$$\mathsf{prev}_1 \xrightarrow{\mathsf{n}_1} \mathsf{null} \wedge \mathsf{curr}_1 \xrightarrow{\mathsf{n}_1} \mathsf{null} \wedge \mathsf{prev}_1 \overset{\mathsf{n}_1}{\curlyvee} \mathsf{curr}_1 = \mathsf{null} \qquad (2)$$

Note that this is a valid interpolant for A and B. In particular, it only speaks about uninterpreted symbols that are common to both A and B. Further note that (modulo renaming of variables) formula (2) exactly corresponds to the inductive loop invariant (1) of reverse. Formula (2) is also the exact interpolant that the prototype implementation of our interpolation framework produces for this particular conjunction $A \wedge B$. We next describe through an example how our interpolation framework works in detail.

2.2 Instantiation-Based Interpolation through an Example

Our interpolation framework is parameterized by a theory extension. This theory extension consists of the base theory, for which we assume that a ground interpolation procedure exists, and the symbols and axioms that extend the base theory. In our example, we consider the theory of linked lists with reachability, where the base theory is the *empty theory*. That is, the base theory only supports uninterpreted constants and equality. The extension symbols are the symbols $\bullet \overset{\bullet}{\curlyvee} \bullet$, $\bullet.\bullet$, and $\bullet[\bullet := \bullet]$, which we described earlier, as well as the *constrained* reachability predicate $\bullet \xrightarrow{\bullet/\bullet} \bullet$. Intuitively, $a \xrightarrow{f/c} b$ means that b is reachable via an f-path from a that does not go through c. In particular, $a \xrightarrow{f} b$ is simply a shorthand for $a \xrightarrow{f/b} b$. The meaning of the extension symbols is given by the extension axioms shown in Figure 6 of Section 5.2. All free variables appearing in these axioms are implicitly universally quantified. Note in particular how the constrained reachability predicate is used to define reachability with respect to an updated field $f[u := v]$ in terms of reachability with respect to field f. In the following, we denote this set of extension axioms by $\mathcal{K}$.

Instantiation-based interpolation reduces the computation of interpolants in the theory extension to the problem of computing interpolants in the base theory, thus, effectively building new interpolation procedures by reusing existing ones. The reduction works by *turning* the interpreted extension symbols into uninterpreted ones. This is accomplished by generating finitely many ground instances $\mathcal{K}[T]$ of the extension axioms $\mathcal{K}$ for a finite set of terms T that is computed from the input formula $A \wedge B$. The set of terms T is chosen such that the formula $\mathcal{K}[T] \wedge A \wedge B$ is already unsatisfiable in the base theory. If in addition, the set $\mathcal{K}[T]$ does not contain instances that mix non-shared symbols of A and B, then $\mathcal{K}[T]$ can be divided into $\mathcal{K}[T] = \mathcal{K}[T_A] \cup \mathcal{K}[T_B]$ where $\mathcal{K}[T_A]$ contains only symbols of A and $\mathcal{K}[T_B]$ only symbols of B. That is, we obtain an instance $A_0 \wedge B_0$ of an interpolation problem for the base theory (modulo uninterpreted functions) where $A_0 = \mathcal{K}[T_A] \wedge A$ and $B_0 = \mathcal{K}[T_B] \wedge B$. We then compute a ground interpolant I_0 for $A_0 \wedge B_0$ using the interpolation procedure for the base theory. Finally, from I_0 we reconstruct a ground interpolant I for $A \wedge B$.

We illustrate this approach by computing an interpolant for the following formula $A \wedge B$:

$$\underbrace{c \xrightarrow{f} a \wedge a.f = c}_{A} \wedge \underbrace{c \xrightarrow{f} b \wedge \neg b \xrightarrow{f} c}_{B} \qquad (3)$$

Note that this conjunction is unsatisfiable in the theory of linked lists with reachability because A implies that c lies on an f cycle, while B implies that this is not the case.

From the formula $A \wedge B$ we compute the sets of terms T_A and T_B that we use to instantiate the extension axioms. In our example, we use $T_A = \{a, c, c.f\}$ and $T_B = \{b, c, c.f\}$. Figure 3 then shows the resulting sets of ground clauses $A_0 = A \cup \mathcal{K}[T_A]$ and $B_0 = B \cup \mathcal{K}[T_B]$. Note that we omit all instances of extension axioms that are not needed to prove unsatisfiability of $A_0 \wedge B_0$.

To see why the conjunction $A_0 \wedge B_0$ is unsatisfiable, suppose that $a = c$. Then clause 2 in A_0 implies $c.f = c$. If on the other hand $a \neq c$, then clauses 4 and 2 imply $a \xrightarrow{f} c$. Hence together with 8 and 6 this implies $a \xrightarrow{f/a} c.f \vee c.f \xrightarrow{f} a$. If $c.f \xrightarrow{f} a$, then 3 implies $c.f \xrightarrow{f} c$. If $a \xrightarrow{f/a} c.f$ then from 7 follows again $c.f \xrightarrow{f} c$ because otherwise clause 5 gives $a = c$, which contradicts the assumption. Thus, A_0 implies the formula $I \equiv c = f.c \vee c.f \xrightarrow{f} c$. Using similar reasoning we can show that $I \wedge B_0$ is unsatisfiable. Since I only speaks about common symbols of A_0 and B_0, it is an interpolant for $A_0 \wedge B_0$ and hence also for $A \wedge B$.

Note that in the above derivation of the interpolant I, all function and predicate symbols in A_0 and B_0 where treated as uninterpreted symbols, i.e., we can compute I by applying an interpolation procedure for the theory of uninterpreted functions with equality to the formula $A_0 \wedge B_0$. We thus reduced the problem of computing ground interpolants in the theory of linked lists with reachability to computing ground interpolants in the combination of the base theory (which is empty in our case) with the theory of uninterpreted functions and equality.

The crux of this instantiation-based reduction approach is whether it is indeed always possible to compute sets of terms T_A and T_B from $A \wedge B$ such that the reduced formula $A_0 \wedge B_0$ is an interpolation problem for the base theory. That is, to find T_A and T_B

A_0	B_0
$1: c \xrightarrow{f} a$	$1: c \xrightarrow{f} b$
$2: a.f = c$	$2: \neg b \xrightarrow{f} c$
$3: c.f \xrightarrow{f} a \wedge a \xrightarrow{f} c \Rightarrow c.f \xrightarrow{f} c$	$3: c \xrightarrow{f/b} c.f \wedge c.f \xrightarrow{f/b} c \wedge c.f \xrightarrow{f} b \Rightarrow c \xrightarrow{f/c} c.f$
$4: a \xrightarrow{f/c} a.f \vee a = c$	$4: c.f \xrightarrow{f} c \wedge c \xrightarrow{f} b \Rightarrow c.f \xrightarrow{f} b$
$5: a \xrightarrow{f/a} c \Rightarrow a = c$	$5: c \xrightarrow{f/c} f.c \Rightarrow c = c.f$
$6: c \xrightarrow{f/a} c.f \vee c = a$	$6: c \xrightarrow{f/b} f.c \vee c = b$
$7: a \xrightarrow{f} c \wedge a \xrightarrow{f/a} c.f \Rightarrow a \xrightarrow{f/c} c.f \wedge c.f \xrightarrow{f} c \vee a \xrightarrow{f/a} c \wedge c \xrightarrow{f/a} c.f$	$7: c.f = c \wedge c \xrightarrow{f} b \Rightarrow c = b$
$8: c \xrightarrow{f/a} c.f \wedge c \xrightarrow{f} a \Rightarrow a \xrightarrow{f/a} c.f \vee c.f \xrightarrow{f} a$	$8: c.f \xrightarrow{f} c \wedge c.f \xrightarrow{f} b \Rightarrow c.f \xrightarrow{f/c} b \wedge b \xrightarrow{f} c \vee c.f \xrightarrow{f/b} c \wedge c \xrightarrow{f} b$
$9: \ldots$	$9: \ldots$

Figure 3. Interpolation problem $A_0 \wedge B_0$ that is obtained from (3) after instantiation of the extension axioms. All function and predicate symbols are uninterpreted.

such that (1) $A_0 \wedge B_0$ is unsatisfiable and (2) A_0, B_0 do not share terms that are not already shared by A, B. It is here where our semantic completeness criterion of partial amalgamation comes into play. It allows us to systematically construct these sets of terms.

3. Preliminaries

In the following, we define the syntax and semantics of formulas. We further recall the notions of partial structures and (Ψ-)local theory extensions as defined in [28, 46]. Finally, we define the problem that interpolation problems we are considering.

Sorted first-order logic. We present our problem in sorted first-order logic with equality. A *signature* Σ is a tuple (S, Ω), where S is a countable set of sorts and Ω is a countable set of function symbols f with associated arity $n \geq 0$ and associated sort $s_1 \times \cdots \times s_n \to s_0$ with $s_i \in S$ for all $i \leq n$. Function symbols of arity 0 are called *constant symbols*. We assume that all signatures contain a dedicated sort $\mathsf{bool} \in S$ and dedicated equality symbols $=_s \in \Omega$ of sort $s \times s \to \mathsf{bool}$ for all sorts $s \in S \setminus \{\mathsf{bool}\}$. Note that we generally treat predicate symbols of sort $s_1, \ldots, s_n$ as function symbols of sort $s_1 \times \ldots \times s_n \to \mathsf{bool}$ and we typically drop sort annotations from equality symbols. Terms are built as usual from the function symbols in Ω and (sorted) variables taken from a countably infinite set X that is disjoint from Ω. A term t is said to be *ground*, if no variable appears in t.

A Σ-*atom* A is a Σ-term of sort bool. We use infix notation for atoms built from the equality symbol. A Σ-*formula* F is defined via structural recursion as either one of A, $\neg F_1$, $F_1 \wedge F_2$, or $\forall x : s.F_1$, where A is a Σ-atom, F_1 and F_2 are Σ-formulas, and $x \in X$ is a variable of sort $s \in S$. We typically omit sort annotations from quantifiers if this causes no confusion. We use syntactic sugar for Boolean constants ($\top$, $\bot$), disjunctions ($F_1 \vee F_2$), implications ($F_1 \Rightarrow F_2$), and existential quantification ($\exists x.F_1$).

Total and partial structures. Given a signature $\Sigma = (S, \Omega)$, a *partial* Σ-*structure* M is a function that maps each sort $s \in S$ to a non-empty set $M(s)$ and each function symbol $f \in \Omega$ of sort $s_1 \times \cdots \times s_n \to s_0$ to a partial function $M(f) : M(s_1) \times \cdots \times M(s_n) \rightharpoonup M(s_0)$. We denote by $[M]$ the *support* of M which is the non-disjoint union of the interpretation of all sorts in M. We assume that all partial structures interpret the sort bool by the two-element set of Booleans $\{0, 1\}$. We further assume that all structures M interpret each symbol $=_s$ by the equality relation on $M(s)$. A partial structure M is called *total structure* or simply *structure* if it interprets all function symbols by total functions. For a Σ-structure M where Σ extends a signature Σ_0 with additional sorts and function symbols, we write $M|_{\Sigma_0}$ for the Σ_0-structure obtained by restricting M to Σ_0. Given partial Σ-structures M and N, a *weak embedding* of M into N is a total injective function $h : [M] \to [N]$ such that for all $f \in \Sigma$, and $a_1, \ldots, a_n \in M$, if $M(f)$ is defined on $(a_1, \ldots, a_n)$ then $N(f)$ is defined on $(h(a_1), \ldots, h(a_n))$ and $h(M(f)(a_1, \ldots, a_n)) = N(f)(h(a_1), \ldots, h(a_n))$. If h is a weak embedding between M and N, then we denote this by $h : M \to N$. We say that M *weakly embeds* into N if a weak embedding of M into N exists. A weak embedding between total structures is simply called *embedding*. If M weakly embeds into N and $[M] \subseteq [N]$, we call M a (partial) *substructure* of N, which (abusing notation) is denoted by $M \subseteq N$.

Given a total structure M and a *variable assignment* $\beta : X \to M$, the evaluation $t_{M,\beta}$ of a term t in M, β is defined as usual. For the evaluation of a ground term t in M we write just $M(t)$. A quantified variable of sort s ranges over all elements of $M(s)$. From the interpretation of terms the notions of satisfiability, validity, and entailment of atoms, formulas, clauses, and sets of clauses in total structures are derived as usual. In particular, we use the standard interpretation of propositional connectives in classical logic. We write $M, \beta \models F$ if M satisfies F under β where F is a formula, a clause, or a set of clauses. We write $M \models F$ if F is valid in M. In this case we also call M a *model* of F. The interpretation $t_{M,\beta}$ of a term t in a partial structure M is as for total structures, except that if $t = f(t_1, \ldots, t_n)$ for $f \in \Omega$ then $t_{M,\beta}$ is undefined if either $t_{i\,M,\beta}$ is undefined for some i, or $(t_{1\,M,\beta}, \ldots, t_{n\,M,\beta})$ is not in the domain of $M(f)$. We say that a partial structure M *weakly satisfies* a literal L under β, written $M, \beta \models_w L$, if (i) L is an atom A and either $A_{M,\beta} = 1$ or $A_{M,\beta}$ is undefined, or (ii) L is a negated atom $\neg A$ and either $A_{M,\beta} = 0$ or $A_{M,\beta}$ is undefined. The notion of weak satisfiability is extended to (sets of) clauses as for total structures. A clause C (respectively, a set of clauses) is *weakly valid* in a partial structure M if M weakly satisfies C for all assignments β. We then call M a *weak partial model* of C.

Theories and theory extensions. A *theory* $\mathcal{T}$ over signature Σ is simply a set of Σ-formulas. We consider theories $\mathcal{T}$ defined as a set of Σ-formulas that are consequences of a given set of clauses $\mathcal{K}$. We call $\mathcal{K}$ the *axioms* of the theory $\mathcal{T}$ and we often identify $\mathcal{K}$ and $\mathcal{T}$. For a theory $\mathcal{T}$ and formulas (clauses, sets of clauses) F and G, we use $F \models_{\mathcal{T}} G$ as a short-hand for $\mathcal{T} \cup F \models G$.

Let $\Sigma_0 = (S_0, \Omega_0)$ be a signature and assume that signature $\Sigma_1 = (S_0 \cup S_e, \Omega_0 \cup \Omega_e)$ extends Σ_0 by new sorts S_e and function symbols Ω_e. We call the elements of Ω_e *extension symbols* and terms starting with extension symbols *extension terms*. A theory $\mathcal{T}_1$ over Σ_1 is an *extension* of a theory $\mathcal{T}_0$ over Σ_0, if $\mathcal{T}_1$ is obtained from $\mathcal{T}_0$ by adding a set of (universally quantified) Σ_1-clauses $\mathcal{K}$.

Ψ-local theory extensions. The following definition captures one specific variant of (Ψ-)local theory extensions that is discussed together with other variants of this notion in [46] and [28].

Let $\mathcal{T}$ be a theory over signature $\Sigma_0 = (S_0, \Omega_0)$ and $\mathcal{T}_1 = \mathcal{T}_0 \cup \mathcal{K}$ a theory extension of $\mathcal{T}_0$ with finite $\mathcal{K}$ and signature $\Sigma_1 = (S_0 \cup S_e, \Omega_0 \cup \Omega_e)$. In the following, when we refer to a set of ground clauses G, we assume they are over the signature Σ_1^c which extends Σ_1 with a set of new constant symbols Ω^c. For a set of clauses $\mathcal{K}$, we denote by $\mathsf{st}(\mathcal{K})$ the set of all ground subterms that appear in $\mathcal{K}$. An *embedding closure* for $\mathcal{T}_1$ is a function Ψ associating with a set of (universally quantified) clauses $\mathcal{K}$ and a finite set of ground terms T a finite set $\Psi(T)$ of ground terms such that (i) all ground subterms in $\mathcal{K}$ and T are in $\Psi(T)$; (ii) Ψ is monotone, i.e., for all sets of ground terms T, T' if $T \subseteq T'$ then $\Psi(T) \subseteq \Psi(T')$; (iii) Ψ is idempotent, i.e., for all sets of ground terms T, $\Psi(\Psi(T)) \subseteq \Psi(T)$. (iv) Ψ is compatible with any map h between constants, i.e., $\Psi(h(T)) = h(\Psi(T))$ where h is homomorphically extended to terms. For a set of ground clauses G, we denote by $\Psi(G)$ the set $\Psi(\mathsf{st}(G))$. Let $\mathcal{K}[\Psi(G)]$ be the set of instances of $\mathcal{K}$ in which all extension terms are in $\Psi(G)$. We say that $\mathcal{T}_1 = \mathcal{T}_0 \cup \mathcal{K}$ is a *Ψ-local theory extension* if there exists an embedding closure Ψ such that for every finite set of ground clauses G, $\mathcal{T}_1 \cup G \models \bot$ iff $\mathcal{T}_0 \cup \mathcal{K}[\Psi(G)] \cup G \models \bot$. Theory extension $\mathcal{T}_1 = \mathcal{T}_0 \cup \mathcal{K}$ is a *local theory extension*, if it is a Ψ-local extension, where Ψ is defined as $\Psi(T) = \mathsf{st}(\mathcal{K}) \cup \mathsf{st}(T)$.

Craig interpolation modulo theories. We use a notion of Craig interpolation modulo theories where interpreted symbols are considered to be shared between formulas. Let Σ be a signature and $\mathcal{T}$ a Σ-theory. Let further Σ^c be the signature Σ extended with fresh constant symbols Ω^c. We say that a Σ^c-term t is *shared* between two sets of Σ^c-terms T_A and T_B, if all constants from Ω^c in t appear in both T_A and T_B, i.e., $\mathsf{st}(t) \cap \Omega^c \subseteq \mathsf{st}(T_A) \cap \mathsf{st}(T_B)$. We say that t is *T_A-pure* if $\mathsf{st}(t) \cap \Omega^c \subseteq \mathsf{st}(T_A)$, respectively, t is *T_B-pure* if $\mathsf{st}(t) \cap \Omega^c \subseteq \mathsf{st}(T_B)$. We extend these notions from sets of terms T_A and T_B to clauses and sets of clauses, as expected.

Given a conjunction $A \wedge B$ of Σ^c-formulas A, B that is unsatisfiable in $\mathcal{T}$, a *Craig interpolant* for $A \wedge B$ is a Σ^c-formula I such that: (a) I is a consequence of A in $\mathcal{T}$: $A \models_{\mathcal{T}} I$, (b) the conjunction of I and B is unsatisfiable in $\mathcal{T}$: $I \wedge B \models_{\mathcal{T}} \bot$, and (c) all terms in $\mathsf{st}(I)$ are shared between A and B. We say that $\mathcal{T}$ *admits ground interpolation* if for all finite sets of Σ^c-ground clauses A and B with $A \cup B \models_{\mathcal{T}} \bot$, there exists a finite set of Σ^c-ground clauses I that is a Craig interpolant for $A \wedge B$.

4. Instantiation-Based Interpolation

We now present our framework for instantiation-based interpolation. In the following, when we refer to a theory extension $\mathcal{T}_1 = \mathcal{T}_0 \cup \mathcal{K}$, we denote by Σ_0 the signature of $\mathcal{T}_0$ and by $\Sigma_1 = \Sigma_0 \cup \Sigma_e$ the signature of $\mathcal{T}_1$, where $\Sigma_e = (S_e, \Omega_e)$ are the extension symbols and sorts.

In the case of local theories, the instantiation-based reduction approach to interpolation works as follows [47]. Suppose we are given sets of ground clauses A and B over Σ_1, whose conjunction is unsatisfiable in $\mathcal{T}_1$. The goal is to compute a ground interpolant I for $A \wedge B$. Locality tells us that we can reduce the problem of checking (un)satisfiability of $A \cup B$ in $\mathcal{T}_1$ to checking (un)satisfiability of $\mathcal{K}[A \cup B] \cup A \cup B$ in $\mathcal{T}_0$. Here, $\mathcal{K}[A \cup B]$ is the (finite) set of instances of clauses in $\mathcal{K}$ that are obtained by replacing the free variables appearing below extension terms in $\mathcal{K}$ with ground subterms appearing in $\mathcal{K} \cup A \cup B$, such that all resulting ground extension terms in $\mathcal{K}[A \cup B]$ already appear in $A \cup B$. The instances $\mathcal{K}[A \cup B]$ can be partitioned into A-pure instances $\mathcal{K}_A$ (obtained by instantiating clauses in $\mathcal{K}$ with terms from A only), B-pure instances $\mathcal{K}_B$ (obtained by instantiating clauses in $\mathcal{K}$ with terms from B only), and mixed instances $\mathcal{K}_C$ (obtained by instantiating clauses in $\mathcal{K}$ with terms from both A and B). If it is possible to find a finite set of non-mixed terms that separates the mixed instances $\mathcal{K}_C$ into sets of A-pure instances $\mathcal{K}_{C,A}$ and B-pure instances $\mathcal{K}_{C,B}$, then we obtain an interpolation problem for the base theory $A_0 \cup B_0 \models_{\mathcal{T}_0} \bot$. Here, A_0 and B_0 are the results of applying Ackermann's expansion to eliminate the extension symbols from the sets of clauses $\mathcal{K}_A \cup \mathcal{K}_{C,A} \cup A$, respectively, $\mathcal{K}_B \cup \mathcal{K}_{C,B} \cup B$. From a ground interpolant I_0 for $A_0 \wedge B_0$ one can then easily reconstruct a ground interpolant I for $A \wedge B$.

The question is whether it is indeed possible to separate the instances $\mathcal{K}_C$ into A-pure and B-pure parts. The result in [47] identifies sufficient conditions on the theory extension to ensure this. Unfortunately, these restrictions are quite severe. In particular, the axioms in $\mathcal{K}$ are required to be Horn clauses of a specific form, which rules out many interesting applications. Instead of imposing such syntactic restrictions on the theory, we first identify a stronger completeness condition on the theory extension than just (Ψ-)locality and then relate this condition to a semantic condition on the models of the theory. By combining these two results, we obtain a framework of complete instantiation-based ground interpolation procedures for a more general class of theory extensions.

proc Interpolate
  input
    $\mathcal{T}_1 = \mathcal{T}_0 \cup \mathcal{K}$: theory extension
    $\mathsf{Interpolate}_0$: ground interpolation procedure for $\mathcal{T}_0 \cup \mathcal{T}_{\mathsf{EUF}}$
    W : amalgamation closure for $\mathcal{T}_1$
    A, B : sets of ground Σ_1^c-clauses with $A \cup B \models_{\mathcal{T}_1} \bot$
  begin
    $A_0 := A \cup \mathcal{K}[W(A, B)]$
    $B_0 := B \cup \mathcal{K}[W(B, A)]$
    $I := \mathsf{Interpolate}_0(A_0, B_0)$
    return I
  end

Figure 4. Generic instantiation-based interpolation procedure.

4.1 W-Separable Theories

To formalize the set of terms that is required to separate the mixed instances of A and B, we introduce the notion of an *amalgamation closure*. An *amalgamation closure* for a theory extension $\mathcal{T}_1 = \mathcal{T}_0 \cup \mathcal{K}$ is a function W associating with finite sets of ground terms T_A and T_B, a finite set $W(T_A, T_B)$ of ground terms such that (i) all ground subterms in $\mathcal{K}$ and T_A are in $W(T_A, T_B)$; (ii) W is monotone, i.e., for all $T_A \subseteq T_A'$, $T_B \subseteq T_B'$, $W(T_A, T_B) \subseteq W(T_A', T_B')$; (iii) W is a closure, i.e., $W(W(T_A, T_B), W(T_B, T_A)) \subseteq W(T_A, T_B)$; (iv) W is compatible with any map h between constants satisfying $h(c_1) \neq h(c_2)$, for all constants $c_1 \in \mathsf{st}(T_A)$, $c_2 \in \mathsf{st}(T_B)$ that are not shared between T_A and T_B, i.e., for any such h we require $W(h(T_A), h(T_B)) = h(W(T_A, T_B))$; and (v) $W(T_A, T_B)$ only contains T_A-pure terms. For sets of ground clauses A, B we write $W(A, B)$ as a shorthand for $W(\mathsf{st}(A), \mathsf{st}(B))$. For the remainder of this section W always refers to an amalgamation closure.

We next identify the cases where the instances of extension axioms can be separated.

Definition 1. *We say that a theory extension $\mathcal{T}_1 = \mathcal{T}_0 \cup \mathcal{K}$ is W-*separable *if for all sets of ground clauses A and B, $\mathcal{T}_1 \cup A \cup B \models \bot$ iff $\mathcal{T}_0 \cup \mathcal{K}[W(A, B)] \cup A \cup \mathcal{K}[W(B, A)] \cup B \models \bot$.*

From this definition we directly obtain the following theorem.

Theorem 2. *If $\mathcal{T}_1 = \mathcal{T}_0 \cup \mathcal{K}$ is W-separable, then it is Ψ-local where Ψ is defined by $\Psi(T) = W(T, T)$, for all sets of ground terms T.*

Our generic instantiation-based interpolation procedure is described in Figure 4. Procedure Interpolate reduces the given interpolation problem $A \wedge B$ for the theory extension $\mathcal{T}_1 = \mathcal{T}_0 \cup \mathcal{K}$, to an interpolation problem $A_0 \wedge B_0$ in $\mathcal{T}_0 \cup \mathcal{T}_{\mathsf{EUF}}$, where $\mathcal{T}_{\mathsf{EUF}}$ is the theory of uninterpreted function symbols with equality. For W-separable theory extensions, procedure Interpolate is sound and complete, provided that a complete ground interpolation procedure $\mathsf{Interpolate}_0$ for $\mathcal{T}_0 \cup \mathcal{T}_{\mathsf{EUF}}$ exists:

Theorem 3. *Let $\mathcal{T}_1 = \mathcal{T}_0 \cup \mathcal{K}$ be a theory extension such that:*

1. $\mathcal{T}_0 \cup \mathcal{T}_{\mathsf{EUF}}$ *has a ground interpolation procedure* $\mathsf{Interpolate}_0$,
2. *all free variables in* $\mathcal{K}$ *appear below extension symbols, and*
3. $\mathcal{T}_1 \supseteq \mathcal{T}_0$ *is* W*-separable.*

Then Interpolate *is a ground interpolation procedure for* $\mathcal{T}_1$.

4.2 Identifying W-Separable Theories

We now present our semantic criterion to identify W-separable theories. Let us begin by recalling the model theoretic notion of amalgamation [32]. An *amalgam* for a theory $\mathcal{T}$ is a tuple (M_A, M_B, M_C) where M_A, M_B, M_C are models of $\mathcal{T}$ with $M_A \supseteq M_C \subseteq M_B$ and $[M_C] = [M_A] \cap [M_B]$. Theory $\mathcal{T}$ has the *amalgamation property* if for every amalgam (M_A, M_B, M_C) of $\mathcal{T}$, there exists a model M_D of $\mathcal{T}$, and embeddings $h_A : M_A \to M_D$ and $h_B : M_B \to M_D$ such that $h_A|_{[M_C]} = h_B|_{[M_C]}$. If in addition $h_A[M_A] \cap h_B[M_B] = h_A[M_C] = h_B[M_C]$ where for any sets $X \subseteq Y$ and function f with domain Y, $f X = \{ f(x) \mid x \in X \}$, then $\mathcal{T}$ is said to have the *strong amalgamation property*. Note that $\mathcal{T}$ has the strong amalgamation property iff for all models M_A, M_B, M_C of $\mathcal{T}$ with $M_A \supseteq M_C \subseteq M_B$ and $[M_C] = [M_A] \cap [M_B]$ there exists a model M_D of $\mathcal{T}$ with $M_A \subseteq M_D \supseteq M_B$.

It is well-known that amalgamation and ground interpolation are strongly related:

Theorem 4 ([2]). *A theory* $\mathcal{T}$ *has ground interpolation iff* $\mathcal{T}$ *has the amalgamation property.*

Theorem 4 provides an effective tool to check whether a given theory admits ground interpolation. Unfortunately, the amalgamation property only tells us that ground interpolants exist, not how to compute them (other than by brute-force enumeration). To remedy this fact, we define a related notion of *partial* amalgamation that refers to partial instead of total models and weak embeddings instead of embeddings. This notion allows us to characterize W-separable theories. Together with Theorem 3, we then obtain a powerful model theoretic criterion that does not just allow us to prove the existence of ground interpolants, but also tells us how to generically construct the accompanying interpolation procedure by applying Theorem 3.

For a weak partial model M of a theory extension $\mathcal{T}_1 = \mathcal{T}_0 \cup \mathcal{K}$, we denote by $T(\Omega_e, M)$ the set of terms $T(M) = \{ f(a_1, \dots, a_n) \mid a_i \in [M], f \in \Omega_e, M(f)(a_1, \dots, a_n) \text{ defined} \}$ where we treat the elements of the support $[M]$ as constant symbols that are interpreted by themselves. Further, we denote by $\mathsf{PMod}(\mathcal{T}_1)$ the set of all weak partial Σ_1-models M of $\mathcal{T}_1$ in which all symbols in Σ_0 are totally defined and $T(M)$ is finite. Let W be an amalgamation closure for theory extension $\mathcal{T}_1 = \mathcal{T}_0 \cup \mathcal{K}$. A *partial* W*-amalgam* for $\mathcal{T}_1 = \mathcal{T}_0 \cup \mathcal{K}$ is a tuple (M_A, M_B, M_C) where (i) $M_A, M_B, M_C \in \mathsf{PMod}(\mathcal{T}_1)$; (ii) M_C is a substructure of both M_A and M_B; (iii) $[M_C] = [M_A] \cap [M_B]$; (vi) both $T(M_A)$ and $T(M_B)$ are closed under W, i.e., $W(T(M_A), T(M_B)) \subseteq T(M_A)$ and $W(T(M_B), T(M_A)) \subseteq T(M_B)$; and (v) $T(M_A) \cap T(M_B) \subseteq T(M_C)$.

Definition 5. *A theory extension* $\mathcal{T}_1 = \mathcal{T}_0 \cup \mathcal{K}$ *is said to have the* partial amalgamation property *with respect to* W *if for all partial* W*-amalgams* (M_A, M_B, M_C) *there exists a model* M_D *of* $\mathcal{T}_1$*, and weak embeddings* $h_A : M_A \to M_D$ *and* $h_B : M_B \to M_D$ *such that* $h_A|_{[M_C]} = h_B|_{[M_C]}$.

To simplify matters, we assume that the extension axioms $\mathcal{K}$ are in a specific normal form: a clause C is called Σ_1*-flat* if no term that occurs in C below a predicate symbol or the symbol $=$ contains nested function symbols. A clause C is called Σ_1*-linear* if (i) whenever a variable occurs in two non-variable terms in C that do not start with a predicate or the equality symbol, the two terms are identical, and if (ii) no such term contains two occurrences of the same variable. Note that every set of extension axioms can be syntactically transformed into one that is Σ_1-flat and Σ_1-linear.

Intuitively, a weak partial model M of $A_0 \wedge B_0$ corresponds to a partial W-amalgam (M_A, M_B, M_C) where M_A is obtained from M by restricting M to the terms in A_0, M_B is obtained by restricting M to the terms in B_0, and M_C is obtained by restricting M to the common terms of A_0 and B_0. Partial amalgamation then tells us that we can always obtain a total model of $A_0 \wedge B_0$ from M. This is what the following theorem says:

Theorem 6. *Let* $\mathcal{T}_1 = \mathcal{T}_0 \cup \mathcal{K}$ *be a theory extension with* $\mathcal{K}$ Σ_1*-linear and* Σ_1*-flat. If* $\mathcal{T}_1$ *has the partial amalgamation property with respect to* W*, then* $\mathcal{T}_1$ *is* W*-separable.*

Finally, in order to apply Theorem 3, we need to be able to identify the cases where a ground interpolation procedure $\mathsf{Interpolate}_0$ for the theory $\mathcal{T}_0 \cup \mathcal{T}_{\mathsf{EUF}}$ exists. One possibility is that we view $\mathcal{T}_0 \cup \mathcal{T}_{\mathsf{EUF}}$ as the disjoint combination of the theories $\mathcal{T}_0$ and $\mathcal{T}_{\mathsf{EUF}}$. In this case, we require that $\mathcal{T}_0$ is decidable, has the strong amalgamation property, and is stably infinite. Since $\mathcal{T}_{\mathsf{EUF}}$ satisfies the same properties, a ground interpolation procedure for the disjoint combination of the theories $\mathcal{T}_0$ and $\mathcal{T}_{\mathsf{EUF}}$ exists, as follows from [11, Corollary 1].

Corollary 7. *Let* $\mathcal{T}_1 = \mathcal{T}_0 \cup \mathcal{K}$ *be a theory extension such that:*

1. *satisfiability of sets of ground clauses is decidable for* $\mathcal{T}_0$,
2. $\mathcal{T}_0$ *is stably infinite*
3. $\mathcal{T}_0$ *has the strong amalgamation property,*
4. *all free variables in* $\mathcal{K}$ *appear below extension symbols, and*
5. $\mathcal{T}_1 \supseteq \mathcal{T}_0$ *is* W*-separable.*

Then Interpolate *is a ground interpolation procedure for* $\mathcal{T}_1$ *where* $\mathsf{Interpolate}_0$ *is the ground interpolation procedure for the disjoint theory combination* $\mathcal{T}_0 \cup \mathcal{T}_{\mathsf{EUF}}$.

Alternatively, we can view $\mathcal{T}_0 \cup \mathcal{T}_{\mathsf{EUF}}$ as a local extension of $\mathcal{T}_0$ and use results from [47] to obtain the procedure $\mathsf{Interpolate}_0$. This yields different requirements on the base theory than the ones stated in Corollary 7. See the technical report [48] for further details.

5. Examples

Our framework of complete instantiation-based interpolation applies to many known local theory extensions, including those described in [47]. In the following, we discuss two non-trivial examples that go beyond the theories considered in [47].

5.1 Theory of Arrays with Difference Function

Our first example is the theory of arrays with difference function that has been recently investigated in [10]. We define this theory of arrays as a theory extension $\mathcal{T}_{\mathsf{arr}} = \mathcal{T}_0 \cup \mathcal{K}_{\mathsf{arr}}$ that is parametric in its base theory $\mathcal{T}_0$. For this purpose, we assume that the base theory $\mathcal{T}_0$ is over signature $\Sigma_0 = (S_0, \Omega_0)$ with sorts index and elem in S_0, and that $\mathcal{T}_0$ satisfies the assumptions of Corollary 7. Examples of appropriate base theories are the empty theory (in which case Ω_0 contains only equality predicates), the theory of uninterpreted function symbols with equality, and the theory of linear arithmetic, interpreting the sort index as integers.

The theory $\mathcal{T}_{\mathsf{arr}}$ extends $\mathcal{T}_0$ with a fresh sort array and extension symbols rd : array $\times$ index $\to$ elem, wr : array $\times$ index $\times$ elem $\to$ array, and $diff$: array $\times$ array $\to$ index. The function symbols rd and wr stand for the usual array selection and update function whose meaning is given by McCarthy's read over write axioms [36]:

$$rd(wr(a,i,e),i) = e, \tag{4}$$

$$i \neq j \Rightarrow rd(wr(a,i,e),j) = rd(a,j) \tag{5}$$

The function *diff* is defined as follows: for any two distinct arrays a and b, the term $diff(a,b)$ denotes an index at which a and b differ. This is formalized by the following axiom:

$$a \neq b \Rightarrow rd(a, diff(a,b)) \neq rd(b, diff(a,b)) \quad (6)$$

Note that this axiom is obtained by skolemizing the extensionality axiom for arrays

$$\forall ab.\, a \neq b \Rightarrow \exists i.\, rd(a,i) \neq rd(b,i)$$

where *diff* is the introduced Skolem function for the existentially quantified variable i. The set of extension axioms $\mathcal{K}_{\text{arr}}$ of our theory of arrays consists of the flattened and linearized versions of the axioms (4), (5), and (6) where a, b, i, j and e are implicitly universally quantified variables. For instance, the linearized and flattened version of axiom (4) is

$$b = wr(a,i,e) \wedge i = j \Rightarrow rd(b,j) = e$$

It is well-known that the standard theory of arrays (i.e., the one given by axioms (4) and (5)) does not admit ground interpolation. We illustrate this through an example due to Ranjit Jhala: consider the ground formulas $A \equiv b = wr(a,i,e)$ and $B \equiv j \neq k \wedge rd(a,j) \neq rd(b,j) \wedge rd(a,k) \neq rd(b,k)$ whose conjunction is unsatisfiable. There exists no ground interpolant for (A,B) that only contains the shared constants a, b and the theory symbols wr and rd. However, as has been observed in [10], such a ground interpolant can be constructed if one includes the difference function *diff* in the theory. An appropriate ground interpolant for (A,B) in the extended theory is given by $b = wr(a, diff(a,b), rd(b, diff(a,b)))$. In fact, the authors of [10] have shown that including the *diff* function is sufficient for ground interpolation. We now give an alternative proof of this result by showing that $\mathcal{T}_{\text{arr}}$ has the partial amalgamation property. This leads to an alternative interpolation procedure for theory $\mathcal{T}_{\text{arr}}$ that can be easily implemented on top of an existing interpolation procedure for the base theory.

In order to define an appropriate amalgamation closure W_{arr}, we need to generalize the example above. That is, we have to define W_{arr} in such a way that there exists no partial W_{arr}-amalgams (M_A, M_B, M_C) with arrays a and b that are shared between M_A and M_B, and M_A, M_B disagree on the number of indices at which a and b differ. To this end, inductively define for any terms a and b of sort array and $k \geq 0$ the term $a \overset{k}{\rightsquigarrow} b$ as follows:

$a \overset{k}{\rightsquigarrow} b = a$ if $k = 0$ and
$a \overset{k}{\rightsquigarrow} b = wr(a \overset{k-1}{\rightsquigarrow} b, diff(a \overset{k-1}{\rightsquigarrow} b, b), rd(b, diff(a \overset{k-1}{\rightsquigarrow} b, b)))$

for all $k > 0$. Note that if in some $\mathcal{T}_{\text{arr}}$-model two arrays a and b differ in exactly k positions, then $b = a \overset{k}{\rightsquigarrow} b$. Now define W_{arr} as follows:

$W_{\text{arr}}(T_A, T_B) =$
  let $T_0 = \mathsf{st}(T_A \cup \{ a \overset{k}{\rightsquigarrow} b \mid a, b \in \mathsf{st}(T_A \cap T_B) \})$ in
  let $T_1 = \mathsf{st}(T_0 \cup \{ rd(a, diff(a,b)) \mid a, b \in \mathsf{st}(T_A) \})$ in
  $T_1 \cup \{ rd(a,i) \mid a, i \in \mathsf{st}(T_1), rd(b,i) \in T_1 \cup \mathsf{st}(T_B) \}$

where k is the number of non-shared terms of the form $wr(a,i,e)$ in $T_A \cup T_B$. Note that $W_{\text{arr}}(T_A, T_B)$ can be represented in space that is polynomial in the size of $T_A \cup T_B$. Hence, also $\mathcal{K}_{\text{arr}}[W(A,B)] \cup \mathcal{K}_{\text{arr}}[W(B,A)]$ is polynomial in A, B for finite sets of ground clauses A, B.

Clearly W_{arr} satisfies properties (i), (ii), (iv), and (v) of amalgamation closures. To see that it also satisfies (iii), note that W_{arr} does not increase the number of non-shared terms of the form $wr(a,i,e)$.

Lemma 8. *W_{arr} is an amalgamation closure.*

Theorem 9. *The theory $\mathcal{T}_{\text{arr}} = \mathcal{T}_0 \cup \mathcal{K}_{\text{arr}}$ has the partial amalgamation property with respect to W_{arr}.*

5.2 Theory of Linked Lists with Reachability

Our second example is an extension of Nelson's theory of linked lists with reachability [41], which is also at the core of the LISBQ logic studied in [35]. This theory is useful for reasoning about the correctness of programs that manipulate list-like heap-allocated data structures. We show that neither Nelson's original theory, nor its variation in [35] admit ground interpolation. Using counterexamples to the partial amalgamation property for Nelson's theory, we then systematically develop an extension of the theory, which admits ground interpolation. As a result, we obtain the first complete ground interpolation procedure for a non-trivial theory of linked data structures.

As in the previous example, we define our theory of lists with reachability as a theory extension $\mathcal{T}_{\text{llr}} = \mathcal{T}_0 \cup \mathcal{K}_{\text{llr}}$ that is parametric in its base theory $\mathcal{T}_0$. We require that the base theory is over the signature $\Sigma_0 = (S_0, \Omega_0)$ with a dedicated sort addr in S_0 and that $\mathcal{T}_0$ satisfies the assumptions of Corollary 7. Theory $\mathcal{T}_{\text{llr}}$ extends the base theory with an additional sort field and extension symbols rd, wr, df, jp, lb, and R. The associated sorts are as follows:

$$\begin{aligned}
rd &: \mathsf{field} \times \mathsf{addr} \to \mathsf{addr} \\
wr &: \mathsf{field} \times \mathsf{addr} \times \mathsf{addr} \to \mathsf{field} \\
df &: \mathsf{field} \times \mathsf{field} \to \mathsf{addr} \\
jp, lb &: \mathsf{field} \times \mathsf{addr} \times \mathsf{addr} \to \mathsf{addr} \\
R &: \mathsf{field} \times \mathsf{addr} \times \mathsf{addr} \times \mathsf{addr} \to \mathsf{bool}
\end{aligned}$$

Before we present the axioms of the theory extension, we define the meaning of the extension symbols in terms of a set of structures $\mathcal{M}_{\text{llr}}$ in which the interpretation of extension symbols is determined by the interpretation of the sorts addr and field. We call the structures in $\mathcal{M}_{\text{llr}}$ *heap models*. In a heap model $M \in \mathcal{M}_{\text{llr}}$, the sort addr represents a set of memory addresses and the sort field a set of address-valued pointer fields. We use a Bornat/Burstall-style memory model [7], i.e., each field is represented as a function from addresses to addresses. The base theory may, e.g., interpret the sort addr as integers to model pointer arithmetic, or it may leave this sort uninterpreted to obtain a more abstract memory model.

In a heap model, the extension symbols rd and wr are interpreted as function application and function update, respectively. For notational convenience, we write $x.f$ and $f[x := y]$ in formulas for terms of the form $rd(f,x)$, respectively, $wr(f,x,y)$. An atom $R(f,a,b,c)$ holds in a heap model M, if there exists a path in the function graph spanned by field f that connects addresses a and b, and the shortest such path does not visit address c. In formulas, we write $x \xrightarrow{f/u} y$ instead of $R(f,x,y,u)$ and we write $x \xrightarrow{f} y$ as a short-hand for $x \xrightarrow{f/y} y$. Note that $a \xrightarrow{f} b$ holds in a heap model M iff a and b are related by the reflexive transitive closure of f. The function symbol jp is interpreted such that $jp(f,a,b)$ denotes the *join point* of addresses a and b, i.e., $jp(f,a,b)$ is the first address on the f-path starting in a that is also on the f-path starting in b, unless these paths are disjoint. In the latter case, we define $jp(f,a,b) = a$. Note that even if the f-paths starting in a and b are not disjoint, we might still have $jp(f,a,b) \neq jp(f,b,a)$ if the two paths form a cycle. In formulas, we write $x \overset{f}{\curlyvee} y$ as a shorthand for $jp(f,x,y)$. The function symbol lb is interpreted such that if b is reachable from a via f, then $lb(f,a,b)$ is the last address before b on the shortest f-path from a to b. The function symbol df is interpreted as in the theory of arrays, i.e., $df(f,g)$ denotes an address for which f and g take different values in case f and g are not the same functions.

$$M(rd)(f,a) = f(a)$$
$$M(wr)(f,a,b) = f[a \mapsto b]$$
$$M(R)(f,a,b,c) = 1 \text{ iff}$$
$$(a,b) \in \{\, (d, f(d)) \mid d \in M(\mathsf{addr}) \wedge d \neq c \,\}^*$$
$$M(df)(f,g) \in \{\, a \in M(\mathsf{addr}) \mid f(a) \neq g(a) \,\} \text{ if } f \neq g$$
$$M(jp)(f,a,b) = c \text{ iff}$$
$$(a,c) \in \{\, (d, f(d)) \mid (b,d) \notin f^* \,\}^* \wedge ((b,c) \in f^* \vee a = c)$$
$$M(lb)(f,a,f(b)) = b \text{ if } M(R)(f,a,b,f(b)) = 1$$

Figure 5. Restrictions on the interpretation of extension symbols in a heap model M

Formally, for a binary relation P over a set X (respectively, a unary function $P : X \to X$), we denote by P^* the reflexive transitive closure of P. The set of heap models $\mathcal{M}_{\mathsf{llr}}$ is then defined as the set of all structures M such that (i) $M|_{\Sigma_0}$ is a model of $\mathcal{T}_0$, (ii) $M(\mathsf{field})$ is the set of all functions $M(\mathsf{addr}) \to M(\mathsf{addr})$, (iii) the interpretation of the extension symbols in M satisfies the restrictions specified in Figure 5, and (iv) for every $a \in M(\mathsf{addr})$, $f \in M(\mathsf{field})$, the set $\{\, b \in M(\mathsf{addr}) \mid a \xrightarrow{f} b \vee b \xrightarrow{f} a \,\}$ is finite. Condition (iv) is not strictly necessary, but it provides a more precise characterization of the models that we obtain from partial amalgams of $\mathcal{T}_{\mathsf{llr}}$.

We make the following simplifying assumption, which restricts the set of input formulas that we consider.

Assumption 10. *The set of uninterpreted constants Ω^c contains at most one constant of sort* field.

Assumption 10 means that we will only consider input formulas $A \wedge B$ in which all terms of sort field are related by a finite sequence of field writes. That is, there will be no models of such formulas in which the interpretation of two terms of sort field appearing in $A \wedge B$ differ at more than n addresses, where n is the number of field writes in $A \wedge B$.

The extension axioms $\mathcal{K}_{\mathsf{llr}}$ are the set of clauses that is obtained by computing the conjunctive normal form of the axioms given in Figure 6, and linearizing and flattening the resulting set of clauses. The following lemma states that the resulting theory extension $\mathcal{T}_{\mathsf{llr}}$ is a sound axiomatization of heap models.

Lemma 11. *All heap models are models of $\mathcal{T}_{\mathsf{llr}}$.*

As we shall see later, the extension axioms are also sufficient to fully characterize heap models, i.e., every ground formula that is satisfiable modulo $\mathcal{T}_{\mathsf{llr}}$ is also satisfiable in some heap model. However, let us first explain why the theory without the function jp does not have ground interpolation. To this end, consider the situation illustrated in Figure 7. The graphs M_A, M_B, and M_C depict (partial) heap models where the dashed edges denote binary reachability $x \xrightarrow{f} y$. Transitive and reflexive edges are omitted for readability. The structures M_A and M_B are almost identical. They only differ in the order in which the list segments starting in c_1 and c_2 join the list segment starting in c_0. In M_A the segment of c_1 joins before the one of c_2 and in M_B it is the other way around. We express M_A and M_B in terms of formulas A and B as follows:

$$A \equiv \quad c_0 \xrightarrow{f/c_1} a_0 \wedge c_1 \xrightarrow{f/c_0} a_0 \wedge a_0 \xrightarrow{f} a_1 \wedge c_2 \xrightarrow{f/a_0} a_1 \wedge a_1 \xrightarrow{f} c_3 \wedge a_0 \neq a_1$$
$$B \equiv \quad c_0 \xrightarrow{f/c_2} b_0 \wedge c_2 \xrightarrow{f/c_0} b_0 \wedge b_0 \xrightarrow{f} b_1 \wedge c_1 \xrightarrow{f/b_0} b_1 \wedge b_1 \xrightarrow{f} c_3 \wedge b_0 \neq b_1$$

$$\begin{aligned}
&\mathsf{Reflexive}\ x \xrightarrow{f/u} x\\
&\mathsf{Step}\ x \xrightarrow{f/u} x.f \vee x = u\\
&\mathsf{SelfLoop}\ x.f = x \wedge x \xrightarrow{f} y \Rightarrow x = y\\
&\mathsf{Sandwich}\ x \xrightarrow{f/x} y \Rightarrow x = y\\
&\mathsf{Reach}\ x \xrightarrow{f/u} y \Rightarrow x \xrightarrow{f} y\\
&\mathsf{Linear1}\ x \xrightarrow{f} y \Rightarrow x \xrightarrow{f/y} u \vee x \xrightarrow{f/u} y\\
&\mathsf{Linear2}\ x \xrightarrow{f/u} y \wedge x \xrightarrow{f/v} z \Rightarrow\\
&\qquad x \xrightarrow{f/u} z \wedge z \xrightarrow{f/u} y \vee x \xrightarrow{f/v} y \wedge y \xrightarrow{f/v} z\\
&\mathsf{Transitive1}\ x \xrightarrow{f/u} y \wedge y \xrightarrow{f/u} z \Rightarrow x \xrightarrow{f/u} z\\
&\mathsf{Transitive2}\ x \xrightarrow{f/z} y \wedge y \xrightarrow{f/z} u \wedge y \xrightarrow{f} z \Rightarrow x \xrightarrow{f/u} y\\
&\mathsf{Join1}\ x \xrightarrow{f} (x \overset{f}{\curlyvee} y)\\
&\mathsf{Join2}\ x \xrightarrow{f} z \wedge y \xrightarrow{f} z \Rightarrow y \xrightarrow{f} (x \overset{f}{\curlyvee} y)\\
&\mathsf{Join3}\ x \xrightarrow{f} z \wedge y \xrightarrow{f} z \Rightarrow x \xrightarrow{f/z} (x \overset{f}{\curlyvee} y)\\
&\mathsf{Join4}\ y \xrightarrow{f} (x \overset{f}{\curlyvee} y) \vee (x \overset{f}{\curlyvee} y) = x\\
&\mathsf{LastBefore}\ x \xrightarrow{f/y.f} y \Rightarrow lb(f, x, y.f) = y\\
&\mathsf{ReachWrite}\ x \xrightarrow{f[u:=v]/w} y \Leftrightarrow\\
&\qquad x \xrightarrow{f/w} y \wedge x \xrightarrow{f/u} y \vee\\
&\qquad x \xrightarrow{f/w} u \wedge v \xrightarrow{f/w} y \wedge v \xrightarrow{f/u} y \wedge u \neq w\\
&\mathsf{ReadWrite1}\ x.(f[x := y]) = y\\
&\mathsf{ReadWrite2}\ x \neq y \Rightarrow y.(f[x := z]) = y.f\\
&\mathsf{Diff}\ f \neq g \Rightarrow df(f,g).f \neq df(f,g).g
\end{aligned}$$

Figure 6. Axioms of theory extension $\mathcal{T}_{\mathsf{llr}}$

The conjunction $A \wedge B$ is unsatisfiable because A and B do not agree on the order of the join points of the list segments. An appropriate ground interpolant for $A \wedge B$ is given by

$$\neg(c_0 \overset{f}{\curlyvee} c_2) \xrightarrow{f} (c_0 \overset{f}{\curlyvee} c_1)$$

All other ground interpolants for $A \wedge B$ also rely on the join function. Hence, if we drop the join function from the theory $\mathcal{T}_{\mathsf{llr}}$, we lose ground interpolation. This is also reflected in a violation of the amalgamation property. If we drop joins, the models M_A and M_B have a common substructure M_C, which we also depict in Figure 7. There is no model M_D in which both M_A and M_B can be embedded while preserving the common substructure M_C.

The function lb plays a similar role than jp in that it is also needed for the completeness of ground interpolation. A corresponding counterexample to partial amalgamation can be found in the extended version of this paper [48]. We omit further details here because the function lb appears to be of less practical importance than the join function.

Although the full theory $\mathcal{T}_{\mathsf{llr}}$ admits ground interpolation, it is still difficult to devise an amalgamation closure W_{llr} that allows us to prove partial amalgamation for this theory. We illustrate this using the unsatisfiable formula (3) in Section 2.2. One ground interpolant for $A \wedge B$ is $c.f \xrightarrow{f} c$, which expresses that c lies on

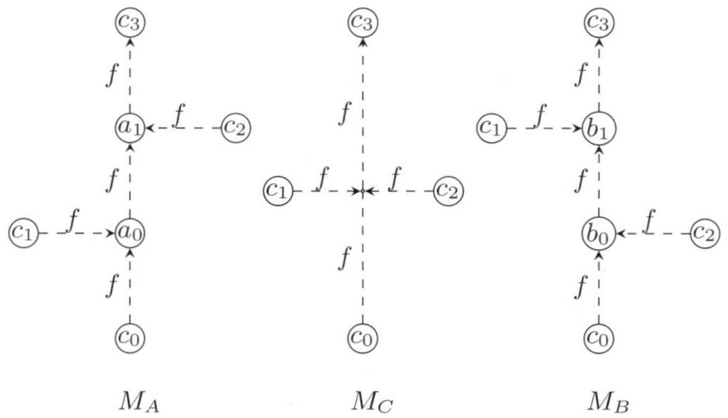

Figure 7. An amalgam (M_A, M_C, M_B) of the theory of linked lists without join that witnesses a violation of amalgamation

a cycle. In order to prove the partial amalgamation property for theory $\mathcal{T}_{\mathsf{llr}}$, we have to ensure that the shared substructure of every partial amalgam already contains all information about which of the shared terms c lie on a cycle. Since we can express this using the formula $c.f \xrightarrow{f} c$ we may attempt to define the amalgamation closure W_{llr} such that for every shared field f and every shared address c defined in the common substructure, also $c.f$ is defined. However, since $c.f$ is again shared, such an operator W_{llr} would inevitably fail to satisfy condition (iii) of amalgamation closures.

We can avoid this problem by further extending $\mathcal{T}_{\mathsf{llr}}$ with an additional predicate symbol Cy : field $\times$ addr $\rightarrow$ bool such that $Cy(f, c)$ holds iff $c.f \xrightarrow{f} c$. The corresponding extension axioms defining Cy are as follows

$$\text{Cycle1 } x \xrightarrow{f} y \wedge y \xrightarrow{f} x \Rightarrow Cy(f, x) \vee x = y$$

$$\text{Cycle2 } Cy(f, x) \wedge x \xrightarrow{f} y \Rightarrow y \xrightarrow{f} x$$

Note that in these axioms we do not use $c.f$ to define $Cy(f, c)$, which avoids the problem with the definition of the amalgamation closure mentioned above. We denote by $\mathcal{K}_{\mathsf{llrc}}$ the set of extension axioms obtained by adding these axioms to $\mathcal{K}_{\mathsf{llr}}$ and we denote by $\mathcal{T}_{\mathsf{llrc}}$ the resulting theory extension $\mathcal{T}_{\mathsf{llrc}} = \mathcal{T}_0 \cup \mathcal{K}_{\mathsf{llrc}}$.

To define the amalgamation closure for $\mathcal{T}_{\mathsf{llrc}}$, we first define the terms $f \overset{k}{\rightsquigarrow} g$ for all terms f, g of sort field and $k \geq 0$, as in the case of the array theory, except that we replace array reads by field reads and array writes by field writes. The amalgamation closure for $\mathcal{T}_{\mathsf{llrc}}$ is then defined as follows:

$$\begin{aligned}
& W_{\mathsf{llrc}}(T_A, T_B) = \\
& \quad \text{let } T_0 = \mathsf{st}(T_A \cup \{\, f \overset{k}{\rightsquigarrow} g \mid f, g \in \mathsf{st}(T_A \cap T_B) \,\}) \text{ in} \\
& \quad \text{let } T_1 = \mathsf{st}(T_0 \cup \{\, df(f, g).f \mid f, g \in \mathsf{st}(T_A) \,\}) \text{ in} \\
& \quad \text{let } T_2 = T_1 \cup \{\, a.f \mid f, a \in \mathsf{st}(T_1), a.g \in T_1 \cup \mathsf{st}(T_B) \,\} \text{ in} \\
& \quad \text{let } T_3 = T_2 \cup \{\, lb^1(f, a, b.f) \mid a, b.f \in T_2 \,\} \text{ in} \\
& \quad \text{let } T_4 = T_3 \cup \{\, (a \overset{f}{\curlyvee} b)^1 \mid a, b, f \in T_3 \text{ shared with } T_B \,\} \text{ in} \\
& \quad \text{let } T_5 = T_4 \cup \{\, a \xrightarrow{f/c} b \mid a, b, c, f \in T_4 \,\} \text{ in} \\
& \quad \text{let } T_6 = T_5 \cup \{\, Cy(f, a) \mid f, a \in T_5 \text{ shared with } T_B \,\} \text{ in} \\
& \quad T_6
\end{aligned}$$

where k is the number of non-shared terms of the form $f[a := b]$ in $T_A \cup T_B$, $lb^1(f, a, b.f)$ denotes $lb(f, a, b.f)$ if lb does not appear in a or else it denotes a, and similarly $(a \overset{f}{\curlyvee} b)^1$ denotes $a \overset{f}{\curlyvee} b$ if no join appears in a and b, or else a. The intermediate set of terms T_2 in the definition of $W_{\mathsf{llrc}}(T_A, T_B)$ is similar to the set of terms computed by W_{arr} for the theory of arrays. The set of terms T_4 ensures that the joins of all shared terms are defined. Note that in models of $\mathcal{T}_{\mathsf{llrc}}$ we have for all a, b, c and f, $(a \overset{f}{\curlyvee} b) \overset{f}{\curlyvee} c = a \overset{f}{\curlyvee} c$ or $(a \overset{f}{\curlyvee} b) \overset{f}{\curlyvee} c = b \overset{f}{\curlyvee} c$, and similarly $a \overset{f}{\curlyvee} (b \overset{f}{\curlyvee} c) = a \overset{f}{\curlyvee} b$ or $a \overset{f}{\curlyvee} (b \overset{f}{\curlyvee} c) = a \overset{f}{\curlyvee} c$. Because of this property and Assumption 10, we can avoid the construction of terms with nested occurrences of joins. The set T_5 ensures that the reachability predicate is fully defined in all partial models. Finally, T_6 ensures that the predicate Cy is defined for all shared terms.

Lemma 12. *W_{llrc} is an amalgamation closure.*

We can now prove that theory $\mathcal{T}_{\mathsf{llrc}}$ has the partial amalgamation property. In fact, we can prove a slightly stronger statement:

Lemma 13. *For every partial W_{llrc}-amalgam (M_A, M_B, M_C) of $\mathcal{T}_{\mathsf{llrc}}$ there exists a total model M_D of $\mathcal{T}_{\mathsf{llrc}}$, and weak embeddings $h_A : M_A \rightarrow M_D$ and $h_B : M_B \rightarrow M_D$ such that $h_A|_{[M_C]} = h_B|_{[M_C]}$. Moreover, $M_D|_{\Sigma_{\mathsf{llr}}}$ is isomorphic to a heap model.*

Theorem 14. *The theory $\mathcal{T}_{\mathsf{llrc}} = \mathcal{T}_0 \cup \mathcal{K}_{\mathsf{llrc}}$ has the partial amalgamation property with respect to W_{llrc}.*

Theorem 14 does not just give us a complete ground interpolation procedure for $\mathcal{T}_{\mathsf{llrc}}$, but also for $\mathcal{T}_{\mathsf{llr}}$. This is because we can always rewrite atoms of the form $Cy(f, c)$ in interpolants for theory $\mathcal{T}_{\mathsf{llrc}}$ into atoms $c.f \xrightarrow{f} c$, obtaining an interpolant for $\mathcal{T}_{\mathsf{llr}}$.

Corollary 15. *Theory $\mathcal{T}_{\mathsf{llr}}$ admits ground interpolation.*

Finally, we can show that satisfiability of ground formulas modulo $\mathcal{T}_{\mathsf{llr}}$ is equivalent to satisfiability of ground formulas modulo heap models. This is a consequence of Lemma 13 and Lemma 11.

Theorem 16. *Let G be a finite set of ground $\Sigma^{\mathsf{c}}_{\mathsf{llr}}$-clauses. Then $\mathcal{T}_{\mathsf{llr}} \cup G \models \bot$ iff $M \not\models G$ for all $M \in \mathcal{M}_{\mathsf{llr}}$.*

Note that the number of terms in $W_{\mathsf{llrc}}(T_A, T_B)$ is polynomial in the size of $T_A \cup T_B$ and, hence, so is the number of generated instances of extension axioms. Together with Theorem 14 this implies that satisfiability of ground formulas modulo $\mathcal{T}_{\mathsf{llr}}$ is decidable in NP, provided $\mathcal{T}_0 \cup \mathcal{T}_{\mathsf{EUF}}$ is also decidable in NP.

6. Combining Interpolation and Abstraction

We now turn towards more practical concerns. A common problem in interpolation-based algorithms is that interpolants are not unique. Often the interpolation procedure produces interpolants that are not useful for a specific application. This may cause, e.g., that the refinement loop of a software model checker diverges because the generated interpolants do not sufficiently abstract from the infeasible error traces.

To illustrate this problem, consider the program shown in Figure 8. The function concat takes two lists x and y as input and concatenates them by first traversing x and then swinging the pointer of the last node of x to y. A second while loop then traverses x again to check whether y is reachable after the concatenation. Suppose we want to use interpolation-based verification to check that the assert statement in concat never fails. The right-hand side of Figure 8 shows the trace formula for a spurious error trace of concat, which is obtained by unrolling both loops twice. The trace formula is unsatisfiable, hence we can compute an interpolant for the indicated choice of $A \wedge B$. One valid interpolant is as follows:

$$\mathsf{x.n_1.n_1} \neq \mathsf{null} \vee \mathsf{y} = \mathsf{null}$$

This interpolant is rather useless for obtaining an inductive invariant that allows us to prove our verification goal. The interpolant only rules out the one given error trace and fails to abstract from its specifics, i.e., the length of the traversed list. We would rather like to obtain the alternative interpolant $\mathsf{x} \xrightarrow{\mathsf{n_1}} \mathsf{y}$, which is the inductive loop invariant we are seeking. But how can we ensure that the

```
void concat (List x, List y) {
  List curr, prev;
  prev = null;
  curr = x;
  while (curr != null) {
    prev = curr;
    curr = curr.n;
  }
  if (prev == null) x = y;
  else prev.n = y;

  curr = x;
  while (curr != null &&
         curr != y) {
    curr = curr.n
  }
  assert (curr == y);
}
```

$$A \left\{ \begin{array}{ll} \mathsf{prev}_0 = \mathsf{null} & \wedge \\ \mathsf{curr}_0 = \mathsf{x} & \wedge \\ \mathsf{curr}_0 \neq \mathsf{null} & \wedge \\ \mathsf{prev}_1 = curr_0 & \wedge \\ \mathsf{curr}_1 = \mathsf{curr}_0.\mathsf{n}_0 & \wedge \\ \mathsf{curr}_1 = \mathsf{null} & \wedge \\ \mathsf{prev}_2 = \mathsf{curr}_1 & \wedge \\ \mathsf{curr}_2 = \mathsf{curr}_1.\mathsf{n}_0 & \wedge \\ \mathsf{curr}_2 = \mathsf{null} & \wedge \\ \mathsf{prev}_2 \neq \mathsf{null} & \wedge \\ \mathsf{n}_1 = \mathsf{n}_0[\mathsf{prev}_2 := y] & \wedge \end{array} \right.$$

$$B \left\{ \begin{array}{ll} \mathsf{curr}_3 = \mathsf{x} & \wedge \\ \mathsf{curr}_3 \neq \mathsf{null} & \wedge \\ \mathsf{curr}_3 \neq \mathsf{y} & \wedge \\ \mathsf{curr}_4 = \mathsf{curr}_3.\mathsf{n}_1 & \wedge \\ \mathsf{curr}_4 \neq \mathsf{null} & \wedge \\ \mathsf{curr}_4 \neq \mathsf{y} & \wedge \\ \mathsf{curr}_5 = \mathsf{curr}_4.\mathsf{n}_1 & \wedge \\ (\mathsf{curr}_5 = \mathsf{null} \vee & \\ \;\mathsf{curr}_5 = \mathsf{y}) & \wedge \\ \mathsf{curr}_5 \neq \mathsf{y} & \end{array} \right.$$

Figure 8. C code for concatenation of two lists. The second while loop checks whether y is reachable from x after the concatenation. The right-hand side shows the trace formula for an infeasible error trace that is obtained by unfolding both while loops twice.

proc InterpolateWithAbstraction
- **input**
  - $\mathcal{T}_1 = \mathcal{T}_0 \cup \mathcal{K}$: theory extension
  - $\mathsf{Interpolate}_0$: ground interpolation procedure for $\mathcal{T}_0 \cup \mathcal{T}_{\mathsf{EUF}}$
  - $\mathsf{GetModel}_0$: model generation procedure for $\mathcal{T}_0 \cup \mathcal{T}_{\mathsf{EUF}}$
  - W : amalgamation closure for $\mathcal{T}_1$
  - α : abstraction function for weak partial models $\mathsf{PMod}(\mathcal{T}_1)$
  - A, B : sets of ground Σ_1^c-clauses with $A \cup B \models_{\mathcal{T}_1} \bot$
- **begin**
  - $I := \bot$
  - **while** $\neg I \wedge A \wedge \mathcal{K}[W(A,B)] \not\models_{\mathcal{T}_0 \cup \mathcal{T}_{\mathsf{EUF}}} \bot$ **do**
    - $M_A := \mathsf{GetModel}_0(\neg I \wedge A \wedge \mathcal{K}[W(A,B)])$
    - $A_0 := \alpha(M_A) \cup \mathcal{K}[W(\alpha(M_A), B)]$
    - $B_0 := B \cup \mathcal{K}[W(B, \alpha(M_A))]$
    - **if** $A_0 \cup B_0 \not\models_{\mathcal{T}_0 \cup \mathcal{T}_{\mathsf{EUF}}} \bot$ **then**
      - $A_0 := M_A \cup \mathcal{K}[W(M_A, B)]$
      - $B_0 := B \cup \mathcal{K}[W(B, M_A)]$
    - $I := I \vee \mathsf{Interpolate}_0(A_0, B_0)$
  - **return** I
- **end**

Figure 9. Instantiation-based interpolation procedure with user-defined abstraction of partial models.

interpolation procedure finds the right interpolant? What accounts for a "good" interpolant often depends on the concrete application. It is therefore difficult to devise generic strategies that can be hard-wired into the interpolation procedure.

Our approach enables the user of the interpolation procedure to inject domain-specific knowledge that helps to guide the proof search and improves the quality of the produced interpolants. This can be done as follows. Note that a partial model M can be thought of as a symbolic representation of a set of total models, namely the set of all models into which M weakly embeds. In fact, for many local theory extensions we can represent a ground formula A as a finite set of partial models each of which is represented as a finite set of ground unit clauses. We can then guide the interpolation procedure as follows: instead of interpolating $A \wedge B$ directly, we enumerate partial models M_A of A, which we interpolate one by one with B. However, before we compute the interpolant of $M_A \wedge B$ for a given partial model M_A, we first apply a user-defined abstraction function α that *widens* M_A by dropping certain clauses. For instance, in the case of the theory of linked-lists we may want to drop all clauses containing the function symbol for field dereference from partial models and only keep information about reachability and joins.

This idea of combining interpolation and abstraction is realized in procedure InterpolateWithAbstraction given in Figure 9, which refines our earlier procedure in Figure 4. Procedure InterpolateWithAbstraction takes as additional arguments the user-defined abstraction function α and a procedure $\mathsf{GetModel}_0$ that is able to generate partial models for satisfiable formulas in the theory $\mathcal{T}_0 \cup \mathcal{T}_{\mathsf{EUF}}$. The while loop enumerates the partial models of A. In each iteration, we only consider partial models that are not yet subsumed by the already computed interpolants I. This ensures that only few partial models have to be considered in practice. The conditional statement in the body of the while loop guarantees that the interpolation procedure falls back to the full partial model M_A in the cases where the abstraction function is too coarse and does not preserve unsatisfiability of $M_A \wedge B$.

Procedure InterpolateWithAbstraction enables us to easily incorporate domain-specific abstraction and widening techniques into the interpolation procedure while still treating the underlying interpolation procedure for the base theory as a black box. The ability of modern SMT solvers to generate models for satisfiable formulas makes it easy to implement this approach.

7. Implementation and Evaluation

We have implemented our framework in a prototype tool and instantiated it for the theory of linked lists with reachability that we presented in Section 5.2. The prototype is written in OCaml. It implements a variation of the algorithm presented in Figure 9. We use the SMT solver Z3 v.4.0 [14] for the generation of partial models and MathSAT 5 [22] for interpolation of formulas in the base theory. Communication with both provers is done via their SMT-LIB 2 [4] interfaces. The difference between the implementation and the vanilla algorithm in Figure 9 is that we use the incremental solving capability of the SMT solver to get a more fine-grained abstraction of partial models. Instead of falling immediately back to the full partial model M_A whenever the abstract partial model is too weak to prove unsatisfiability, we sort the clauses of M_A in a particular order and then push them one by one on the assertion stack of the solver. Each time we push a new clause onto the stack, we check whether the conjunction of the stack with B is still satisfiable. Once it becomes unsatisfiable, we compute the interpolant. The order in which the clauses of the partial model are pushed is determined by a weight associated with each clause, where lighter clauses are considered first. The weight function encodes the domain-specific knowledge that guides the proof search of the solver. In our implementation we have chosen the weight function such that highest weight is given to clauses that contain dereferences of pointer fields. This makes it more likely that the computed interpolants abstract from the length of the lists.

The number of generated instances of extension axioms is polynomial in the size of the input formulas, which means that the underlying decision problem remains in NP. However, in practice the eager instantiation approach can still be a performance bottle neck with thousands of clauses generated even for small examples. We therefore implemented several optimizations to reduce the number

benchmark	#unroll.	$\#M_A$	#inst.	time (s)
reverse	3	1	5,003	0.4
concat	2-2	1	9,953	0.6
delete	2	2	27,934	2.3
insertBefore	2	2	28,176	2.3
splice	2	4	135,446	12.1

Table 1. Summary of experiments. The columns list the benchmark name, the number of loop unrollings in the error trace, the number of generated partial models for A, the number of generated instances of extension axioms, and the total computation time.

of instances of axioms that we generate. First, we compute the congruence closure for the terms appearing in the original input formula and then only instantiate axioms by selecting one representative term per congruence class. We have found this to work particularly well for trace formulas, which typically contain many equalities. Second, we use a more lazy instantiation approach where we first compute a subset of the terms in the amalgamation closure that is likely to be sufficient for proving unsatisfiability. For example, in our experiments we never needed to generate instances with terms that contain the df function. Apart from these obvious optimizations, our instance generation procedure is still rather naive.

To evaluate the feasibility of our approach, we have used our implementation to automatically infer loop invariants for verifying properties of simple list-manipulating programs. In particular, we checked functional correctness properties and whether certain shape invariants are preserved. For this purpose, we manually generated spurious error traces from the considered programs by unrolling their loops a few times. Our prototype accepts such error traces as input and converts them into trace formulas which are then interpolated. Our experiments where conducted on a Linux laptop with a dual-core processor and 4GB RAM. Table 1 shows the summary of our experiments. In all cases, the obtained interpolant was an inductive loop invariant of the program and strong enough to prove the program correct. Roughly 40% of the running time is spent on I/O with the provers. However, the main bottle neck of the implementation is the eager instantiation of extension axioms. We believe that the running times can be significantly improved by using more sophisticated model-driven instantiation approaches such as [20, 29], which instantiate axioms incrementally.

8. Related Work

Our notion of partial amalgamation is closely related to the (strong) amalgamation property [32], whose role in ground interpolation for disjoint theory combinations has been recently studied [11]. Our use of amalgamation properties is orthogonal to [11], as we consider (non-disjoint) theory extensions rather than disjoint theory combinations. In a sense, partial amalgamation is the adaptation of the weak embedability condition in [46] to the case of interpolation. Our approach can thus be thought of as the symbioses of the two orthogonal approaches described in [46, 47] and [11]. Note that neither of the interpolation techniques presented in [47] and [11] can be applied directly to the theory of lists considered in this paper. The approach in [47] is restricted to extension axioms of a very specific syntactic form: Horn clauses in which all predicate symbols are binary and where additional guard constraints on the quantified variables apply. All three restrictions are violated by the axioms of the list theory. The approach in [11] could be used, in principle, to obtain an interpolation procedure for the combination of a theory of lists with uninterpreted heap nodes and, e.g., the theory of linear integer arithmetic (for interpreting heap nodes as addresses). However, the technique in [11] assumes that interpolation procedures for the component theories already exist. There is no interpolation procedure for the list theory component to start with. Hence, the combination technique of [11] cannot be applied. Other reduction-based approaches to interpolation that are less closely related include [33], which is based on quantifier elimination.

Ground interpolation procedures for specific theories have been developed, e.g., for linear arithmetic over reals [23, 38] and integers [8, 9], uninterpreted functions with equality [19, 38, 50], functional lists [50], as well as, combinations of these theories [11, 21, 38, 50]. These are the procedures that our approach builds on. We discussed two specific theories for which ground interpolation reduces to these existing procedures: the theory of arrays with difference functions [10], and the theory of linked-lists with reachability [35, 41] extended with join. We believe that our approach applies to many other theory extensions that are of importance in program verification, such as our theory of imperative trees [49].

Interpolation approaches that use resolution-based automated theorem provers have been studied, e.g., in [26, 40]. Unlike our approach, these methods target undecidable fragments of first-order logic and infer quantified interpolants. Sometimes, such quantified interpolants are needed to obtain inductive invariants. We can use our approach to infer quantified interpolants by applying techniques explored in [1]. One interesting observation is that these quantified interpolants themselves often constitute local theory extensions and can therefore be treated systematically by our framework, if they become part of subsequent interpolation problems. To out knowledge, McMillan's [40] interpolating version of the theorem prover SPASS, is the only other interpolation-based system that has been used to infer shape invariants of heap-allocated data structures. Unlike our theory of linked-lists, McMillan's axiomatization of reachability predicates is incomplete.

Recent works have explored techniques to influence the quality of computed interpolants, e.g., by reducing the size of unsatisfiability proofs from which interpolants are generated [27], restricting the language in which interpolants can be expressed [1, 30], or by controlling the interpolant strength [16]. Our technique of guiding the proof search of the interpolation procedure through user-defined abstraction functions is orthogonal to these approaches. In spirit, it is most closely related to [30]. The key difference is that we do not need to modify the underlying interpolation procedure, which would contradict our modular approach to interpolation. The idea of using the ability of SMT solvers to generate models for abstraction has been previously explored, e.g., in [43]. Whether the approach of combining interpolation and abstraction can be explained more concisely in terms of abstract interpretation, e.g., in the spirit of [12], remains a question for future research.

9. Conclusion

We have presented a new instantiation-based interpolation framework that enables the modular construction of ground interpolation procedures for application-specific theories. We introduced the semantic notion of partial amalgamation to systematically identify and construct theories for which our framework yields complete interpolation procedures. We gave examples of both new and existing theories to which our framework applies. Using a prototype implementation we demonstrated that our framework enables new applications of interpolation-based algorithms in program verification. Therefore, we see this work as a starting point for a new line of research that studies efficient instantiation-based interpolation procedures for applications in program verification.

Acknowledgments

This work was supported in part by the European Research Council (ERC) Advanced Investigator Grant QUAREM and by the Austrian Science Fund (FWF) project S11402-N23.

References

[1] F. Alberti, R. Bruttomesso, S. Ghilardi, S. Ranise, and N. Sharygina. Lazy abstraction with interpolants for arrays. In *LPAR*, volume 7180 of *LNCS*, pages 46–61. Springer, 2012.

[2] P. Bacsich. Amalgamation properties and interpolation theorems for equational theories. *Algebra Universalis*, 5:45–55, 1975.

[3] M. Barnett and K. R. M. Leino. To goto where no statement has gone before. In *VSTTE*, volume 6217 of *LNCS*, pages 157–168, 2010.

[4] C. Barrett, A. Stump, and C. Tinelli. The SMT-LIB Standard: Version 2.0, 2010.

[5] D. Beyer, T. A. Henzinger, and G. Théoduloz. Lazy shape analysis. In *CAV*, volume 4144 of *LNCS*, pages 532–546. Springer, 2006.

[6] D. Beyer, D. Zufferey, and R. Majumdar. CSIsat: Interpolation for LA+EUF. In *CAV*, volume 5123 of *LNCS*, pages 304–308, 2008.

[7] R. Bornat. Proving Pointer Programs in Hoare Logic. In *MPC*, volume 1837 of *LNCS*, pages 102–126. Springer, 2000.

[8] A. Brillout, D. Kroening, P. Rümmer, and T. Wahl. An Interpolating Sequent Calculus for Quantifier-Free Presburger Arithmetic. *J. Autom. Reasoning*, 47(4):341–367, 2011.

[9] A. Brillout, D. Kroening, P. Rümmer, and T. Wahl. Beyond Quantifier-Free Interpolation in Extensions of Presburger Arithmetic. In *VMCAI*, volume 6538 of *LNCS*, pages 88–102. Springer, 2011.

[10] R. Bruttomesso, S. Ghilardi, and S. Ranise. Rewriting-based quantifier-free interpolation for a theory of arrays. In *RTA*, volume 10 of *LIPIcs*, pages 171–186, 2011.

[11] R. Bruttomesso, S. Ghilardi, and S. Ranise. From strong amalgamability to modularity of quantifier-free interpolation. In *IJCAR*, volume 7364 of *LNCS*, pages 118–133. Springer, 2012.

[12] P. Cousot, R. Cousot, and L. Mauborgne. The reduced product of abstract domains and the combination of decision procedures. In *FOSSACS*, volume 6604 of *LNCS*, pages 456–472. Springer, 2011.

[13] W. Craig. Three uses of the Herbrand-Gentzen theorem in relating model theory and proof theory. *The Journal of Symbolic Logic*, 22(3):269–285, 1957.

[14] L. de Moura and N. Bjørner. Z3: An efficient SMT solver. In *TACAS*, pages 337–340, 2008.

[15] K. Dräger, A. Kupriyanov, B. Finkbeiner, and H. Wehrheim. SLAB: A Certifying Model Checker for Infinite-State Concurrent Systems. In *TACAS*, volume 6015 of *LNCS*, pages 271–274. Springer, 2010.

[16] V. D'Silva, D. Kroening, M. Purandare, and G. Weissenbacher. Interpolant strength. In *VMCAI*, volume 5944 of *LNCS*, pages 129–145. Springer, 2010.

[17] E. Ermis, M. Schäf, and T. Wies. Error invariants. In *FM*, volume 7436 of *LNCS*, pages 187–201. Springer, 2012.

[18] J.-C. Filliâtre and C. Marché. The Why/Krakatoa/Caduceus Platform for Deductive Program Verification. In *CAV*, volume 4590 of *LNCS*, pages 173–177. Springer, 2007.

[19] A. Fuchs, A. Goel, J. Grundy, S. Krstic, and C. Tinelli. Ground interpolation for the theory of equality. In *TACAS*, volume 5505 of *LNCS*, pages 413–427. Springer, 2009.

[20] Y. Ge and L. M. de Moura. Complete instantiation for quantified formulas in satisfiabiliby modulo theories. In *CAV*, volume 5643 of *LNCS*, pages 306–320. Springer, 2009.

[21] A. Goel, S. Krstic, and C. Tinelli. Ground interpolation for combined theories. In *CADE*, volume 5663 of *Lecture Notes in Computer Science*, pages 183–198. Springer, 2009.

[22] A. Griggio. A Practical Approach to Satisfiability Modulo Linear Integer Arithmetic. *JSAT*, 8:1–27, January 2012.

[23] A. Griggio, T. T. H. Le, and R. Sebastiani. Efficient interpolant generation in satisfiability modulo linear integer arithmetic. In *TACAS*, volume 6605 of *LNCS*, pages 143–157. Springer, 2011.

[24] M. Heizmann, J. Hoenicke, and A. Podelski. Nested interpolants. In *POPL*, pages 471–482. ACM, 2010.

[25] T. A. Henzinger, R. Jhala, R. Majumdar, and K. L. McMillan. Abstractions from proofs. In *31st POPL*, 2004.

[26] K. Hoder, L. Kovács, and A. Voronkov. Interpolation and symbol elimination in vampire. In *IJCAR*, volume 6173 of *LNCS*, pages 188–195. Springer, 2010.

[27] K. Hoder, L. Kovács, and A. Voronkov. Playing in the grey area of proofs. In *POPL*, pages 259–272. ACM, 2012.

[28] C. Ihlemann, S. Jacobs, and V. Sofronie-Stokkermans. On local reasoning in verification. In *TACAS*, pages 265–281, 2008.

[29] S. Jacobs. Incremental instance generation in local reasoning. In *CAV*, volume 5643 of *LNCS*, pages 368–382. Springer, 2009.

[30] R. Jhala and K. L. McMillan. A practical and complete approach to predicate refinement. In *TACAS*, volume 3920 of *LNCS*, pages 459–473. Springer, 2006.

[31] R. Jhala and K. L. McMillan. Interpolant-based transition relation approximation. *Logical Methods in Computer Science*, 3(4), 2007.

[32] B. Jónsson. Universal relational systems. *Math. Scand.*, 4:193–208, 1956.

[33] D. Kapur, R. Majumdar, and C. G. Zarba. Interpolation for data structures. In *SIGSOFT FSE*, pages 105–116. ACM, 2006.

[34] D. Kroening and G. Weissenbacher. Interpolation-Based Software Verification with Wolverine. In *CAV*, volume 6806 of *LNCS*, pages 573–578. Springer, 2011.

[35] S. K. Lahiri and S. Qadeer. Back to the future: revisiting precise program verification using SMT solvers. In *POPL*, pages 171–182. ACM, 2008.

[36] J. McCarthy. Towards a mathematical science of computation. In *IFIP Congress*, pages 21–28, 1962.

[37] K. L. McMillan. Interpolation and SAT-Based Model Checking. In *CAV*, volume 2725 of *LNCS*, pages 1–13. Springer, 2003.

[38] K. L. McMillan. An interpolating theorem prover. *Theor. Comput. Sci.*, 345(1):101–121, 2005.

[39] K. L. McMillan. Lazy abstraction with interpolants. In *CAV*, volume 4144 of *LNCS*, pages 123–136. Springer, 2006.

[40] K. L. McMillan. Quantified invariant generation using an interpolating saturation prover. In *TACAS*, volume 4963 of *LNCS*, pages 413–427. Springer, 2008.

[41] G. Nelson. Verifying reachability invariants of linked structures. In *POPL*, pages 38–47. ACM, 1983.

[42] A. Podelski and T. Wies. Counterexample-guided focus. In *POPL*, pages 249–260. ACM, 2010.

[43] T. W. Reps, S. Sagiv, and G. Yorsh. Symbolic implementation of the best transformer. In *VMCAI*, volume 2937 of *LNCS*, pages 252–266. Springer, 2004.

[44] A. Rybalchenko and V. Sofronie-Stokkermans. Constraint solving for interpolation. In *VMCAI*, volume 4349 of *LNCS*, pages 346–362. Springer, 2007.

[45] M. Sagiv, T. Reps, and R. Wilhelm. Parametric shape analysis via 3-valued logic. *ACM TOPLAS*, 24(3):217–298, 2002.

[46] V. Sofronie-Stokkermans. Hierarchic reasoning in local theory extensions. In *CADE*, pages 219–234, 2005.

[47] V. Sofronie-Stokkermans. Interpolation in local theory extensions. *Logical Methods in Computer Science*, 4(4), 2008.

[48] N. Totla and T. Wies. Complete instantiation-based interpolation. Technical Report TR2012-950, New York University, 2012.

[49] T. Wies, M. Muñiz, and V. Kuncak. An efficient decision procedure for imperative tree data structures. In *CADE*, volume 6803 of *LNCS*, pages 476–491. Springer, 2011.

[50] G. Yorsh and M. Musuvathi. A combination method for generating interpolants. In *CADE*, volume 3632 of *LNCS*, pages 353–368, 2005.

Automatic Detection of Floating-Point Exceptions

Earl T. Barr   Thanh Vo   Vu Le   Zhendong Su
Department of Computer Science, University of California at Davis
{etbarr, vo, vmle, su}@ucdavis.edu

Abstract

It is well-known that floating-point exceptions can be disastrous and writing exception-free numerical programs is very difficult. Thus, it is important to automatically detect such errors. In this paper, we present Ariadne, a practical symbolic execution system specifically designed and implemented for detecting floating-point exceptions. Ariadne systematically transforms a numerical program to explicitly check each exception triggering condition. Ariadne symbolically executes the transformed program using real arithmetic to find candidate real-valued inputs that can reach and trigger an exception. Ariadne converts each candidate input into a floating-point number, then tests it against the original program. In general, approximating floating-point arithmetic with real arithmetic can change paths from feasible to infeasible and vice versa. The key insight of this work is that, for the problem of detecting floating-point exceptions, this approximation works well in practice because, if one input reaches an exception, many are likely to, and at least one of them will do so over both floating-point and real arithmetic. To realize Ariadne, we also devised a novel, practical linearization technique to solve nonlinear constraints. We extensively evaluated Ariadne over 467 scalar functions in the widely used GNU Scientific Library (GSL). Our results show that Ariadne is practical and identifies a large number of real runtime exceptions in GSL. The GSL developers confirmed our preliminary findings and look forward to Ariadne's public release, which we plan to do in the near future.

Categories and Subject Descriptors D.2.3 [*Software Engineering*]: Coding Tools and Techniques; D.2.4 [*Software Engineering*]: Software/Program Verification — Reliability, Validation; D.2.5 [*Software Engineering*]: Testing and Debugging — Symbolic execution; F.3.1 [*Logics and Meanings of Programs*]: Specifying and Verifying and Reasoning about Programs

General Terms Algorithms, Languages, Reliability, Verification

Keywords Floating-point exceptions; symbolic execution

1. Introduction

On June 4, 1996, the European Space Agency's Ariane 5 rocket veered off course and self-destructed because the assignment of a floating-point number to an integer caused an overflow [40]. The loss is estimated to have been US$370 million. Scientific results increasingly rest on software that is usually numeric and may invalidate results when buggy [33]. In February 2010, Toyota implicated control software in its spate of brake failures [3]. Haptic controllers are being used for remote surgery [36]. Numerical software, which uses floating-point arithmetic, is prominent in critical control systems in devices in national defense, transportation, and health care. Clearly, we are increasingly reliant on it.

Floating-point numbers are a finite precision encoding of real numbers. Floating-point operations are not closed and may throw exceptions: their result may have an absolute value greater than the largest floating-point number and *overflow*; it may be nonzero and smaller than the smallest nonzero floating-point number and *underflow*; or it may lie between two floating-point numbers, require rounding, and be *inexact*. *Dividing-by-zero* and the *invalid* application of an operation to operands outside its domain, like taking the square root of a negative number, also generate exceptions. The IEEE 754 standard defines these exceptions [24].

Writing numerical software that does not throw floating-point exceptions is difficult [19, 22]. For example, it is easy to imagine writing `if (x != y){ z = 1 / (x-y); }` and then later contending with the program mysteriously failing due to a spurious Divide-by-Zero [19]. As another example, consider a straightforward implementation to compute the 2-norm of a vector [22, 23]:

```
sum = 0;
for (i = 0; i < N; i++)
  sum = sum + x[i] * x[i];
norm = sqrt(sum);
```

For many slightly large or small vector components, this code may overflow or underflow when evaluating `x[i]*x[i]` or adding the result to `sum`. In spite of exceptions during its computation, the norm itself may, nonetheless, be representable as an unexceptional floating-point number. Even when some exceptions are caught and handled, others may not be; these are *uncaught exceptions*. The Divide-by-Zero in the first example is an uncaught exception.

Symbolic analysis has been successfully used to test and validate software [7, 18, 38]. However, little work has considered symbolic analysis of floating-point code, although much work has pursued formalizing IEEE floating-point standards in various proof systems such as Coq, HOL, and PVS. One natural approach is to equip a satisfiability modulo theory (SMT) solver with a theory for floating-point. This has proved to be a challenging problem; ongoing efforts simplify and deviate from the IEEE floating-point standard [37].

For detecting floating-point exceptions, our core insight is that, if an exception can occur at a particular operation, then that exception defines a neighborhood in which exception-triggering inputs are numerous. If one of these inputs triggers the exception over the reals, then another is likely to do so over floating-point arithmetic. Guided by this insight, we propose to symbolically execute a numeric program over the reals to search for an exception-triggering input. To this end, we transform a numeric program to explicitly check the operands of each floating-point operation before executing it. If a check fails, the transformed program signals the floating-

POPL'13, January 23–25, 2013, Rome, Italy.

point exception that would have occurred if the guarded operation had executed, then terminates. In the transformed program, the constraints are over real, not floating-point numbers, so we can directly feed them into an SMT solver equipped with the theory of reals, such as Microsoft's Z3 [9]. If we can reach any of these injected program points, we can query the SMT solver for an input that triggers that exception. This input is unlikely to be a floating-point number, so we search the neighborhood of that input for a candidate floating point number that also triggers the exception over real arithmetic. To undo the inaccuracy of symbolic execution over the reals, we then test that candidate against the original program, concretely executed over floating-point arithmetic.

Our approach, which we have christened Ariadne, automatically detects floating-point exceptions. While not all exceptions are bugs, the utility of Ariadne rests on three observations: 1) over- and underflows can be disastrous, as the loss of the Ariane 5 demonstrates; 2) the GSL developers confirmed as bugs several of the exceptions Ariadne found; and 3) Invalid and Divide-by-Zero exceptions are likely to be bugs. Ariadne reports only *real* exceptions: when it reports inputs that cause a program to throw a particular floating-point exception, that program run on those inputs will certainly throw that exception. When Ariadne finds an exception, developers can use the inputs to fix the bug and to construct a test case to add to their test suite.

To realize Ariadne, we extended the symbolic execution engine KLEE [7] to use Z3 (version 3.1) as its SMT solver instead of STP [16], which does not support the theory of reals. Interesting numeric code often results in multivariate, nonlinear constraints. In particular, the constraints we encountered while analyzing the GNU Scientific Library, were usually multivariate and nonlinear (Section 5). We fed these constraints to iSAT, the state of the art nonlinear SMT solver [13], but it only handled less than 1%, rejecting most of our constraints because they contain large constant values that exceed iSAT's bounds. We also directly gave them to Z3, which had recently added support for multivariate, nonlinear constraints but it could only handle a small percentage. These results motivated us to devise a novel, practical method for handling nonlinear constraints involving rational functions (to support division), which we also incorporated into KLEE; this method works effectively over the constraints arising in our problem setting. A new algorithm for solving nonlinear constraints, realized in a prototype called nlsat, was developed concurrently with our work and added to Z3 [25]. We ran nlsat on 10,000 of our constraints, uniformly selected at random, and compared its performance to that of our solver, Z3-ARIADNE (Section 5). Z3-ARIADNE resolved 9,119 of the constraints (5,510 being satisfiable), while nlsat resolved 5,248 of the constraints, and returned unknown, timed out, or had parse errors on the rest.

Our contributions follow:

- The insight that, for the problem of detecting floating-point exceptions, real arithmetic can effectively model floating-point arithmetic, since when one input triggers a floating-point exception, many are likely to do so and, of those, some will do so over both real and floating-point arithmetic;
- An LLVM and KLEE-based implementation of our technique and its evaluation on the GNU Scientific Library (GSL);
- A tool that automatically converts fixed precision numeric code into arbitrary precision numeric code to detect potentially avoidable overflows and underflows; and
- A practical method for handling nonlinear constraints involving rational functions over the reals.

We evaluated our tool on the GNU Scientific Library (GSL) version 1.14. We analyzed all functions in the GSL that take scalar inputs, which include elementary and many differential equation

```
double av1(double x, double y) {
   return (x+y)/2.0;
}

double av2(double x, double y) {
   return x/2.0 + y/2.0;
}

double av3(double x,double y) {
   return x + (y-x)/2.0;
}

double av4(double x, double y) {
   return y + (x-y)/2.0;
}

double average(double x, double y) {
   int samesign;
   if ( x >= 0 ) {
      if (y >=0)
         samesign = 1;
      else
         samesign = 0;
   } else {
      if (y >= 0)
         samesign = 0;
      else
         samesign = 1;
   }
   if ( samesign ) {
      if ( y >= x)
         return av3(x,y);
      else
         return av4(x,y);
   } else
      return av1(x,y);
}
```

Figure 1: Sterbenz' average function.

functions. Across the 467 functions we analyzed, our tool discovered inputs that generated 2091 floating-point exceptions. 91.9% of these are Underflows and Overflows, while the remainder are Divide-by-Zero and Invalid exceptions. Some of these exceptions are highly nontrivial, as a particular Divide-by-Zero we describe in detail in Section 5.2 illustrates. We reported preliminary results to the GSL community; they confirmed that our warnings were valid and look forward to the public release of our tool. These results show that modeling floating-point numbers as reals to find exceptions is a sweet spot in the trade-off between practicality and precision.

To motivate and clarify our problem, Section 2 presents and explains numerical code that contains floating-point exceptions. We open Section 3 with terminology, then describe the two transformations on which Ariadne rests: the first reifies the exceptions a floating-point operation may throw into program points and the second symbolically handles external functions. We close Section 3 with the algorithms we use to solve multivariate, nonlinear constraints. Section 4 describes the realization of Ariadne. In Section 5, we present the results of analyzing the GSL special functions with Ariadne. We discuss closely related work in Section 6 and conclude in Section 7.

2. Illustrative Example

Floating-point arithmetic is unintuitive. Sterbenz [39] illustrates this fact by computing $\frac{x+y}{2}$, the average of two numbers. Even for a "simple" function like this, it requires considerable knowledge to

```
1  int gsl_sf_bessel_Knu_scaled_asympx_e(
2     const double nu, const double x,
3     gsl_sf_result * result
4  ) { /* x >> nu*nu+1 */
5    double mu   = 4.0*nu*nu;
6    double mum1 = mu-1.0;
7    double mum9 = mu-9.0;
8    double pre  = sqrt(M_PI/(2.0*x));
9    double r    = nu/x;
10   result->val = pre * (1.0 + mum1/(8.0*x)
11               + mum1*mum9/(128.0*x*x));
12   result->err = 2.0 * GSL_DBL_EPSILON
13               * fabs(result->val)
14               + pre * fabs(0.1*r*r*r);
15   return GSL_SUCCESS;
16 }
```

Figure 2: A function from GSL's special function collection.

implement it well. The four functions av1–4 in Figure 1 are a few possible average formulas. They are all equivalent over the reals, but not over floating-point numbers. For instance, av1 overflows when x and y have the same sign and are sufficiently large, and av2 is inaccurate and requires a second expensive division. Sterbenz performs a very interesting analysis of this problem and defines average that uses av1, av3, and av4 according to the signs of the inputs x and y. Sterbenz proved average to be free of overflows. Our tool Ariadne explores all the paths in average and does not find any overflows, as expected. To run Ariadne, we issue "ariadne sterbenz.c" at the command line to compile and apply the operand checking, explicit floating-point exception transformation, then symbolically execute the result to produce sterbenz.out, which contains the analysis results. Ariadne discovers 6 underflows, reporting, for example x = -3.337611e-308 and y = 2.225074e-308, as an input pair that triggers this exception at line 2.

We close with a function that contains each of the four floating-point exceptions Ariadne detects, drawn from our test corpus, the GSL special functions. Figure 2 contains the GSL's implementation of gsl_sf_bessel_Knu_scaled _asympx_e. Run on this function, Ariadne reports that the square-root operation at line 8 throws an Invalid exception when x < 0 and a Divide-by-Zero when x = 0. When nu = -5.789604e+76 and x = 2.467898e+03, the evaluation of mum1*mum9 at lines 10–11 overflows. Finally, when nu = -7.458341e-155 and x = 2.197413e+03, the evaluation of mu = 4.0*nu*nu at line 5 underflows.

3. Approach

Figure 3 depicts the architecture of Ariadne, which has two main phases. Phase one transforms an input numeric program into a form that explicitly checks for floating-point exceptions before each floating-point operation and, if one occurs, throws it and terminates execution. The transformed program contains conditionals, such as x > DBL_MAX, that cannot hold during concrete execution, where DBL_MAX denotes the maximum floating-point value. The transformed program, including its peculiar conditionals, are amenable to symbolic execution and any program point that symbolic execution reaches without throwing an exception has the property that none of its floating-point variables contain a special value, such as NaN (Not a Number) or ∞. Thus, the numeric constraints generated during symbolic execution involve those floating-point values that are a subset of $\mathbb{R}$ and suitable input to an SMT solver supporting the theory of reals. During phase two, Ariadne symbolically executes the transformed program, and for each path that reaches a floating-point exception injected in phase one, it attempts to solve the corresponding path constraint. If a satisfying assignment is found, Ariadne attempts to trigger the exception in the original code. If it succeeds, Ariadne reports the assignment as a concrete input that triggers the exception. Our symbolic execution is standard; the key challenge in its realization is how to effectively solve the collected numerical constraints, many of which are multivariate, nonlinear.

Exception	Example	Default Result
Overflow	$\lvert x+y\rvert > \Omega$	$\pm\infty$
Underflow	$\lvert x/y\rvert < \lambda$	Subnormals
Divide-by-Zero	$x/0$	$\pm\infty$
Invalid	$0/0, 0\times\infty, \sqrt{-1}$	NaN
Inexact	nearest$(x \text{ op } y) \neq x \text{ op } y$	Rounded result

Table 1: Floating-point exceptions; $x, y \in \mathbb{F}$ [23, §2.3].

We first present pertinent background in numerical analysis and introduce notation (Section 3.1), then describe our transformation (Section 3.2) and how we solve numerical constraints (Section 3.3).

3.1 Background and Notation

Four integer parameters define a floating-point number system $\mathbb{F} \subset \mathbb{R}$: the base (radix) β, the precision t, the minimum exponent $e_{\min}$, and the maximum exponent $e_{\max}$. With these parameters and the mantissa $m \in \mathbb{Z}$ and the exponent $e \in \mathbb{Z}$,

$$\mathbb{F} = \{\ \pm m\beta^{e-t} \mid (0 \le m \le \beta^t - 1 \wedge e_{\min} \le e \le e_{\max}) \\ \vee (0 < m < \beta^{t-1} \wedge e = e_{\min})\ \}$$

The floating-point numbers for which $\beta^{t-1} \le m \le \beta^t \wedge e_{\min} \le e \le e_{\max}$ holds are *normal*; the numbers for which $0 \le m < \beta^{t-1} \wedge e = e_{\min}$ holds are *subnormal* [23, §2.1]. $\Omega = \beta^{e_{\max}}(1-\beta^{-t})$ denotes the maximum floating-point number; $-\Omega$, the minimum. $\lambda = \beta^{e_{\min}-1}$ is the smallest normalized floating-point number; $æ = \beta^{e_{\min}-t}$ is the smallest denormalized.

Floating-point operations can generate exceptions shown in Table 1. Some applications of the operations on certain operands are undefined and cause the Divide-by-Zero and Invalid exceptions. Finite precision causes the rest. Inexact occurs frequently [19, 26] and is often an unavoidable consequence of finite precision. For example, when dividing 1.0 by 3.0, an Inexact exception occurs because the ratio $1/3$ cannot be exactly represented as a floating-point number. For this reason, Ariadne focuses on discovering Overflow, Underflow, Invalid, and Divide-by-Zero exceptions.

Throughout this section, we abuse $\mathbb{Q}$ to denote its arbitrary precision subset. Let $fp : \mathbb{Q} \to \mathbb{F}$ convert a rational into the nearest floating-point value, rounding down. For $next : \mathbb{F} \times \mathbb{F} \to \mathbb{F}$, $next(x, y)$ returns the floating-point number next to x in the direction of y.

To model path constraints, we consider formulas ϕ in the theory of reals. For a formula ϕ, $fv(\phi) = \vec{x}$ denotes the free variables in ϕ. We use S to denote satisfiable or SAT; $\bar{S}$ to denote unsatisfiable or UNSAT; and U for UNKNOWN. Below, we define algorithms that return satisfying bindings to variables or UNSAT or UNKNOWN. For this purpose, we define $A^n_{\mathbb{F}} = (V \times \mathbb{F})^n \uplus \{\bar{S}, U\}$ to be a disjoint union that is either an n length vector of simultaneous assignments over $\mathbb{F}$ to the variables V, or is UNSAT or UNKNOWN. For ISSAT: $A^n_{\mathbb{F}} \to \mathbb{B}$, ISSAT$(a)$ returns true if $a \notin \{\bar{S}, U\}$.

3.2 Program Transformation

We first define T, the term rewriting system we use to inject explicit floating-point exception handling into numeric code. For simplicity of presentation, we assume that nested arithmetic expressions have been flattened. We assume that the program terminates after throwing a floating-point exception.

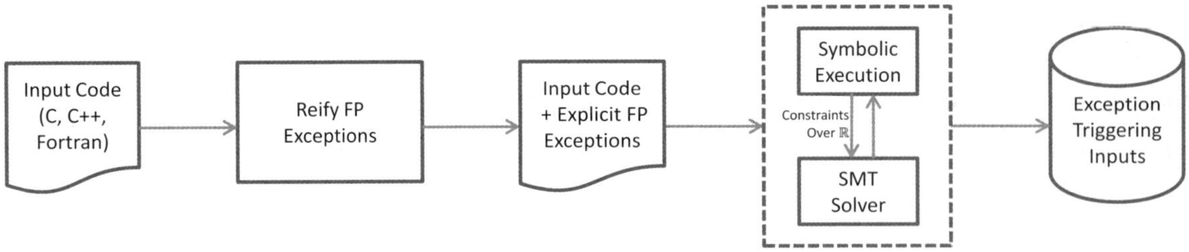

Figure 3: The architecture of Ariadne.

3.2.1 Basic Arithmetic Operations

The operator $\odot \in \{+,-,*\}$, and variables x and y bind to floating-point expressions. We have the following *local rewriting rules*:

$$T(x \odot y) \quad = \quad \begin{cases} \text{Overflow} & \text{if } |x \odot y| > \Omega \\ \text{Underflow} & \text{if } 0 < |x \odot y| < \lambda \\ x \odot y & \text{otherwise} \end{cases}$$

$$T(x\ /\ y) \quad = \quad \begin{cases} \text{Invalid} & \text{if } x = 0 \wedge y = 0 \\ \text{Divide-by-Zero} & \text{if } x \neq 0 \wedge y = 0 \\ \text{Overflow} & \text{if } |x| > |y|\Omega \\ \text{Underflow} & \text{if } 0 < |x| < |y|\lambda \\ x\ /\ y & \text{otherwise} \end{cases}$$

We also have a global contextual rewriting rule $T(C[e]) = C[T(e)]$, where e denotes an expression of the form $x \odot y$ or $x\ /\ y$, and $C[\cdot]$ denotes a program context. Ignoring time-dependent behavior, it is evident that $[\![p]\!] = [\![T(p)]\!]$ when the numeric program p terminates without throwing a floating-point exception, where $[\![\cdot]\!]$ denotes the semantics of its operand.

Figure 4a shows a concrete example of how T, specialized to C, transforms a subtraction expression (line 6 of example in Figure 2). The result of the subtraction is checked and, if an exception could occur, execution terminates. The division transformation, depicted in Figure 4b, is the most involved transformation. The original expression is taken from line 9 of the example in Figure 2. A floating-point division operation can throw four distinct exceptions, each of which the transformed code explicitly checks. For instance, given the inputs `nu = 0.0` and `x = 0.0`, the original expression would have terminated normally and returned NaN, but the transformed code would detect and output an Invalid exception, then terminate.

3.2.2 Elementary Mathematical Functions

Calls into an unanalyzed library usually terminate symbolic execution. Calls to elementary mathematical functions, such as `sqrt`, `log`, `exp`, `cos`, `sin` and `pow`, are frequent in our constraints. These functions are often handled in hardware, like `sqrt`. We next describe simple, yet effective, transformations to deal with these functions. Indeed, during our experiments, these transformations enabled us to find approximately 41% of the floating-point exceptions we report. When all of an elementary function's operands are within its domain, these well-tested, ubiquitous functions do not return specials. To handle an unanalyzed elementary function, therefore, we insert checks that its operands are in its domain and signal the appropriate exception if a check fails, then bind a fresh symbolic variable to the call. These symbolic variables are *dependent*, since they depend on other symbolic variables. Input symbolic variables are *independent*.

We add the obvious constraints on the range of dependent variables. For instance, we add the constraint $d^2 = x$, for `sqrt`, which

```
double z = mu - 1.0;
double abs1 = fabs(z);
if (DBL_MAX < abs1) {
   perror("Overflow!\n");
   exit(1);
}
if (0 < abs1 && abs1 < DBL_MIN) {
   perror("Underflow!\n");
   exit(1);
}
double mum1 = z;
```

(a) Subtraction (line 6 of example in Figure 2).

```
if (x == 0) { // denominator is zero
   if (nu == 0) {
      perror("Invalid!\n");
   } else {
      perror("DivZero!\n");
   }
   exit(1);
}
double abs1 = fabs(nu);
double abs2 = fabs(x);
if (abs1 > abs2 * DBL_MAX) {
   perror("Overflow!\n");
   exit(1);
}
if (0 < abs1 && abs1 < abs2 * DBL_MIN) {
   perror("Underflow!\n");
   exit(1);
}
double r = nu/x;
```

(b) Division (line 9 of example in Figure 2).

Figure 4: Ariadne transformations realized in C: Ariadne symbolically executes this code over arbitrary precision rationals, where the conditionals can be tested; `fabs` returns the absolute value of a double.

has a polynomial representation, as shown in Figure 5. On line 8 of the example in Figure 2, we replace the call to `sqrt` with the fresh symbolic variable d and add the constraint $d^2 = \text{M\_PI}/(2.0 * x)$. A dependent symbolic variable can depend on another dependent variable, as when `log(log(x))` is encountered. Dependent variables allow us to defer a call's evaluation until that variable appears in a path constraint that we feed to the solver. The binding of a dependent variable to a function call is recorded in a table, for use during its evaluation, when we concretize a dependent variable and the variables on which it depends (Section 3.3.1). Table 2 shows the contents of the dependent symbolic variable table when the

$$T(\texttt{sqrt}(x)) = \begin{cases} \text{Invalid} & \text{if } x < 0 \\ d, \text{ where } d \cdot d = x & \text{otherwise} \end{cases}$$

$$T(\texttt{exp}(x)) = \begin{cases} \text{Overflow} & \text{if } x > \texttt{log}(\Omega) \\ \text{Underflow} & \text{if } x < \texttt{log}(\lambda) \\ d & \text{otherwise} \end{cases}$$

$$T(\texttt{log}(x)) = \begin{cases} \text{Invalid} & \text{if } x \leq 0 \\ d & \text{otherwise} \end{cases}$$

$$T(\texttt{cos}(x)) = d \quad \text{where } -1 \leq d \leq 1$$

$$T(\texttt{sin}(x)) = d \quad \text{where } -1 \leq d \leq 1$$

$$T(\texttt{pow}(x,y)) = \begin{cases} \text{Invalid} & \text{if } x = 0 \wedge y \leq 0 \\ d & \text{otherwise} \end{cases}$$

Figure 5: Rewriting rules for elementary mathematical functions.

Dependent variable	Expression
d_0	$\texttt{sin}(\frac{x}{y})$
d_1	$\texttt{log}(x^2 + \frac{1}{x})$

Table 2: A dependent symbolic variable table.

transformation encounters $\texttt{sin}(\frac{x}{y})$ and $\texttt{log}(x^2 + \frac{1}{x})$, which use the independent variables x, y. In Figure 5, we rewrite calls to pow to throw Invalid if its operands are outside its domain. Our rewriting of pow could make additional checks for exceptions, such as $y > 0 \wedge y\texttt{log}(x) > \texttt{log}(\Omega)$, but we found the described handling of pow and the other elementary functions to be very effective over the functions we analyzed.

3.3 Solving Numeric Constraints

Designing SMT solvers that can effectively support multivariate, nonlinear constraints over the reals is an active area of research. Off-the-shelf SMT solvers focus on linear constraints and do not support general nonlinear constraints over the real domain because linear constraints are prevalent in integer programs and solving nonlinear constraints is very expensive (although decidable over the reals). However, real-world numeric applications contain many nonlinear constraints. In our experiment over the GSL special functions, 81% of queries are nonlinear, 73% are multivariate and 62% are both nonlinear and multivariate.

Algorithm 1 is the Ariadne solver for floating-point exceptions. During symbolic execution, it is called to solve the numeric path constraints to the program points that represent exceptions, injected during the program transformation (Section 3.2). In addition to the path constraint ϕ, the Ariadne exception solver takes T, the dependent symbolic variable table built during the transformation phase (Section 3.2.2), p, the original, untransformed numeric program itself, the possible exception e, and l, the location (program point) in p of the operation that may throw e.

To solve ϕ, Algorithm 1 first checks whether ϕ contains any multivariate numerical constraints. It it does, Algorithm 1 concretizes ϕ using T to convert ϕ into a univariate formula. On line 5, it calls the CONCRETIZE method, which interacts with the underlying SMT solver to bind variables that appear in multivariate numeric constraints to values in $\mathbb{F}$ (Section 3.3.1); it returns ϕ_c with the selected variables replaced with concrete values and $\vec{a}_c$, which records those variable to value bindings. Algorithm 1 calls SOLVEUNIVARIATE (Algorithm 2) to solve a univariate formula. When SOLVEUNIVARIATE finds a satisfying assignment, Algorithm 1 returns the bindings from the calls to both CONCRETIZE

Algorithm 1 ARIADNESOLVE: $\Phi \times \mathbb{T} \times P \times \mathbb{E} \times \mathbb{N} \to A^n_{\mathbb{F}}$ solves a numeric path constraint over the reals. This topmost algorithm handles formulae that contain multivariate numerical constraints. When ϕ contains such a constraint, the solver tries various concretizations up to its MAX_CONCRETIZATIONS bound. Note that $n = |fv(\phi)|$, for $\phi \in \Phi$.

inputs $\phi \in \Phi$, a numeric constraint from p.
$T \in \mathbb{T}$, a table of dependent symbolic variables.
$p \in P$, the numeric program under analysis.
$e \in \mathbb{E}$, the potential exception.
$l \in \mathbb{N}$, the location of e.
ISMULTIVARIATE : $\Phi \to \mathbb{B}$ returns true when passed a formula that contains a multivariate numerical constraint.

1: **if** $\neg$ISMULTVARIATE$(\phi) \wedge |T| = 0$ **then**
2:   **return** SOLVEUNIVARIATE$(\phi, \langle\rangle, p, e, l)$ *// Algorithm 2*
3: **else**
4:   **for** 1..MAX_CONCRETIZATIONS **do**
5:     $\phi_c, \vec{a}_c :=$ CONCRETIZE(ϕ, T) *// Algorithm 3*
6:     $\vec{a} :=$ SOLVEUNIVARIATE$(\phi_c, \vec{a}_c, p, e, l)$ *// Algorithm 2*
7:     **if** ISSAT$(\vec{a})$ **then**
8:       **return** $\vec{a}$
9:     **end if**
10:   **end for**
11:   **return** U *// Return UNKNOWN.*
12: **end if**

Algorithm 2 SOLVEUNIVARIATE: $\Phi \times A^n_{\mathbb{F}} \times P \times \mathbb{E} \times \mathbb{N} \to A^n_{\mathbb{F}}$ linearizes nonlinear univariate constraints in ϕ, finds a floating-point solution to the resulting constraints, then checks whether a satisfying solution triggers the given exception at the specified location.

inputs $\phi \in \Phi$, a formula whose numeric constraints are univariate.
$\vec{a}_c \in A^n_{\mathbb{F}}$, the concretized bindings.
$p \in P$, the numeric program under analysis.
$e \in \mathbb{E}$, the potential exception.
$l \in \mathbb{N}$, the location of e.

1: $\phi' :=$ LINEARIZE(ϕ) *// Algorithm 4*
2: $\vec{a} := \vec{a}_c +$ SOLVEOVER$\mathbb{F}(\phi')$ *// Algorithm 5*
3: **if** ISSAT$(\vec{a}) \wedge p(\vec{a})$ does *not* throw e at l **then**
4:   **return** U *// Return UNKNOWN.*
5: **end if**
6: **return** $\vec{a}$

and SOLVEUNIVARIATE. Algorithm 1 tries different concretizations up to MAX_CONCRETIZATIONS times. Our experiments validate our core insight that, if an exception is reachable, many inputs reach it: varying MAX_CONCRETIZATIONS did not greatly change Ariadne's detection rate (See Section 5.1).

To convert a nonlinear univariate formula into a linear formula, Algorithm 2 applies a linearization technique that finds the roots of each nonlinear polynomial constraint, then rewrites the constraints into an equivalent disjunction of interval checks (Section 3.3.2). When ϕ is linear, $\phi' = \phi$. While ϕ' is univariate and linear upon input to SOLVEOVER$\mathbb{F}$ on line 2, it remains a formula in the theory of reals, so the underlying SMT solver, used in CONCRETIZE in Algorithm 1 and here in the SOLVEOVER$\mathbb{F}$ function, may return a solution in $\mathbb{Q} \setminus \mathbb{F}$. The SOLVEOVER$\mathbb{F}$ algorithm (Section 3.3.3) finds a floating-point solution in $\mathbb{F}^n$ for its input, if one exists.

The SOLVEOVER$\mathbb{F}$ function's solution reaches and triggers an exception when symbolically executed using real arithmetic, but may not when concretely executed using floating-point arithmetic. For instance, consider "if$(x+1 > \Omega)$ Overflow". The binding $x = \Omega$ is valid solution in the theory of reals and SOLVEOVER$\mathbb{F}$ can return it, since $x \in \mathbb{F}$. Under concrete execution with standard floating-point semantics, however, the difference in magnitude of the operands means that the result of the addition operation must be truncated to fit into the finite precision of floating-point which "absorbs" the 1 into x's value of Ω. Under floating-point arithmetic, this Overflow is unreachable and the binding produced during symbolic execution is a false positive. Approximating floating-point arithmetic with real arithmetic can also produce false negatives, again due to rounding.

Thus, each satisfying solution SOLVEOVER$\mathbb{F}$ produces is a candidate solution that Ariadne must concretely check. In Algorithm 2, line 3 performs the requisite concrete check over floating-point. Here, the Ariadne exception solver executes p on the candidate satisfying assignments — both those found by SOLVEOVER$\mathbb{F}$ and $\vec{a}_c$ from concretization — to determine whether p actually throws the e at l, the location of the floating-point operation under scrutiny.

Ariadne is certainly correct when it reports that executing a program on an input vector throws a particular floating-point exception at a particular operation. However, Ariadne cannot guarantee that a program is exception-free, for three reasons: it 1) approximates floating-point semantics with constraints over the reals, which notably ignore rounding (*i.e.* Inexact); 2) concretizes multivariate into univariate constraints; and 3) rewrites loop conditions to bound the number of iterations. The decision to approximate floating-point arithmetic with real arithmetic is the core design decision of this work. This decision favors practicality in the trade-off between practicality and precision; it allows us to use off-the-shelf SMT solvers, such as Z3. It is also what necessitates the concrete execution check to confirm that a path to an exception is indeed satisfiable; it also means that we may fail to detect exceptions. That said, deployed numerical software is usually robust, *i.e.* small changes in its input cause small changes in its output, so error accumulation due to rounding is typically small. Thus, an "ideal" execution over the reals should closely approximate the actual execution over floating-point, especially for invalid, overflow and underflow exceptions. Concretization means that Ariadne might abandon a path as unsatisfiable, when that path is, in fact, satisfiable and contains exceptions; analyzing programs with externally imposed loop bounds also means that Ariadne may fail to explore paths that contain exceptions. All of these cases mean that Ariadne may miss exceptions. In spite of these limitations, Ariadne is an effective testing technique that detects many floating-point exceptions, as our results in Section 5 demonstrate. In particular, we empirically show that concretization is quite effective in our setting (Section 5.1).

3.3.1 Concretization

Before querying its SMT solver in Algorithm 1, Ariadne must convert multivariate to univariate polynomial constraints and can no longer defer the concrete evaluation of elementary functions, in the form of dependent symbolic variables. Algorithm 3 takes the input formula ϕ and the analyzed program's dependent symbolic variable table T and handles these two problems. The algorithm first identifies V_T, the dependent variables that appear in both T and ϕ, then the independent variables on which they depend. We define V_T to avoid needlessly concretizing independent variables whose dependent variables do not appear in ϕ. Algorithm 3 then identifies all the independent variables that appear in a multivariate, numeric constraint in ϕ and not in V_T. Then it builds and topologically sorts the DAG G to concretize the variables in G so that it has all the information it needs to evaluate the expressions in T.

On line 8, the choose function nondeterministically selects an element from a set, but could be defined to implement an arbitrary selection policy, such as selecting the free variable with the highest degree or that appears most often[1]. Since I_u is a greedy over-approximation of the hitting set of variables in the multivariate numeric constraints in ϕ, Algorithm 3 may over-concretize, as when ϕ contains three multivariate constraints and Algorithm 3 picks variables to concretize in the first two that completely concretize the third constraint. When this happens, we simply hope to do better in a subsequent call to CONCRETIZE in Algorithm 1.

Algorithm 3 CONCRETIZE : $\Phi \times \mathbb{T} \rightarrow \Phi \times A_{\mathbb{F}}^{n-1}$ builds a DAG that contains the symbolic variables that appear in multivariate numeric constraints and all variables in T, then concretizes them in topological sort order. The CONCRETIZE function must process T, because Ariadne can no longer defer handling elementary functions, since it is about to query the underlying SMT solver.

inputs ϕ, a numeric constraint.
T, a dependent symbolic variable table.

1: $\vec{a} := \langle\rangle$ contains concretized variable bindings.
2: $D_\phi = fv(\phi) \cap \{d \mid (d,e) \in T\}$ is the set of dependent symbolic variables in T that appear in ϕ.
3: $V_T = D_\phi \cup \{v \mid d \in D_\phi \wedge (d,e) \in T \wedge v \in fv(e)\}$ is the set of dependent symbolic variables in T and the variables on which they depend that appear in ϕ.
4: $M_\phi = \{m \mid m$ is a multivariate, numeric constraint in $\phi \wedge |fv(m) \setminus V_T| > 1\}$ is the set of multivariate, numeric constraints in ϕ that will remain multivariate after T has been concretized.
5: $I_m = \bigcup_{m \in M_\phi} fv(m) \setminus V_T$ is the set of independent variables in M_ϕ that will remain after T has been concretized.
6: $I_u := \emptyset$ is the set of variables that will remain symbolic after the constraints in M_ϕ have either been converted to univariate or entirely concretized.
7: **while** $M_\phi \neq \emptyset$ **do** // *Greedily approximate the hitting set of* M_ϕ.
8: $\quad I_u := I_u \cup \text{choose}(fv(m) \setminus V_T)$, for some $m \in M_\phi$
9: $\quad M_\phi := \{c \mid c \in M_\phi \wedge fv(c) \cap I_u = \emptyset\}$ // *Remove those constraints covered by the choice made in the previous line.*
10: **end while**
11: $G = (V,E)$, where $V = V_T \cup I_m \setminus I_u$ and $(u,v) \in E$ when v depends on u, *i.e.* $u \in fv(T(v))$.
12: $\forall x \in$ TOPOSORT(G) **do**
13: $\quad$ **if** INDEGREE$(x) = 0$ **then** // *Independent symbolic variables.*
14: $\quad\quad c :=$ BINDVARIABLE(ϕ, x)
15: $\quad\quad$ **return** ϕ, U **if** $c = U$
16: $\quad$ **else** // *Dependent symbolic variables.*
17: $\quad\quad c :=$ EVAL$(T(x), \vec{a})$
18: $\quad$ **end if**
19: $\quad \vec{a} := \vec{a} + (x,c)$
20: $\quad \phi := \phi[c/x]$
21: **end for**
22: **return** $\phi, \vec{a}$

The fact that concretization is quite effective in our setting supports our core insight: in practice, our constraints either have no solution or many. Our symbolic variables are defined over intervals; if an input triggers an exception, there will almost always be many such inputs. An experiment in Section 5.1 demonstrates the robustness of our concretization results.

To clarify the presentation, we introduce the helper function CHECKBINDING: $\Phi \times V \times \mathbb{F} \rightarrow \mathbb{B}$ to check that a candidate binding does not trivially falsify a formula. For the call CHECKBINDING(ϕ, x, c), we have

$\forall \phi_i \in \phi$ **do**
$\quad$ **return false if** EVALEXPR$(\phi_i[c/x]) =$ **false**

[1] Preliminary experiments using degree or count of occurrences did not outperform uniform selection.

Algorithm 4 LINEARIZE: $\Phi \to \Phi$ rewrites a nonlinear polynomial constraint into an equivalent disjunction of linear interval predicates. Here, polysolver is a placeholder for any polynomial solver; our implementation uses the one in the GSL-1.14 (Section 4).

input $\phi = \bigwedge c_i$, a univariate numeric path constraint.
  $\forall c_i \in \phi$ **do** // *All constraints in* ϕ.
    if $c_i = R(x) \prec 0 \wedge \text{degree}(R(x)) > 1$ **then**
      $\{x_1, x_2, \cdots, x_n\} = \text{polysolver}(R(x))$
      $I = (\infty, x_1), \cdots, (x_n, \infty)$, where $x_i < x_j$ when $i < j$.
      I^- is those intervals in which $R(x) < 0$.
      I^+ is those intervals in which $R(x) > 0$.
      $\text{eq} := \bigvee_{i=1}^{n} x = x_i$
      $\text{lt} := \bigvee_{i \in I^-} x \in i$
      $\text{gt} := \bigvee_{i \in I^+} x \in i$
      $\psi :=$ **match** $\prec$ **with**
        $= \to \text{eq}$
        $| < \to \text{lt}$
        $| > \to \text{gt}$
        $| \leq \to \text{eq} \vee \text{lt}$
        $| \geq \to \text{eq} \vee \text{gt}$
      $\phi := \phi[\psi / c_i]$
    end if
  end for
  return ϕ

  end for
  return true

The $\phi_i[c/x]$ notation means to rewrite every appearance of x in ϕ_i with c. The function EVALEXPR walks the expression tree that results from the substitution and evaluates constant expressions. It returns false if the recursive evaluation of constant expressions reduces the expression tree to false. For example, consider the simple numeric constraint $5x > 0$: EVALEXPR would return false for any assignment to x less than or equal to zero and true otherwise. Its complexity is $O(n)$, where n is the number of nodes in the expression tree. The function CHECKBINDING checks a single binding; to test a bounded number of bindings, we define BINDVARIABLE: $\Phi \times V \to \mathbb{F} \cup \{U\}$:

  for 1..MAX_BINDINGS **do**
    $c :=$ RANDOM($\mathbf{dom}(x)$)
    return c **if** CHECKBINDING(ϕ, x, c)
  end for
  return U // *Return UNKNOWN.*

In our setting, topological sort means that the condition at line 13 will be true until all the independent symbolic variables that appear in an expression in T are exhausted, at which point the condition will always be false and dependent variables will be processed. At line 17, we evaluate the expression $T(x)$ in the context of $\vec{a}$ to find a concrete binding for x. For example, consider $T(x) = log(y^2 + \frac{1}{y})$ in Table 2. When y is concretized to 1, $x = log(2) = 1$.

Algorithm 3 may convert ϕ into a ground formula, *i.e.*, a formula with no free variables. When this happens, LINEARIZE echoes the ground formula and SOLVEOVER$\mathbb{F}$ returns true or false via $\bar{S}$. Otherwise, Algorithm 3 returns a rewritten ϕ that contains no multivariate numeric constraints. During the topological sort, Algorithm 3 calls EVALEXPR for each independent symbolic variable over expression trees whose maximum number of nodes is bounded by ϕ. For each dependent variable, we must evaluate its corresponding expression, at cost α. Thus, the complexity of Algorithm 3 is $O(|I||\phi| + |D|\alpha + |E|)$, where $V = I \cup D$.

3.3.2 Linearizing Univariate Nonlinear Constraints

Given a univariate, nonlinear constraint, we transform it into a disjunction of linear constraints, suitable for an off-the-shelf SMT

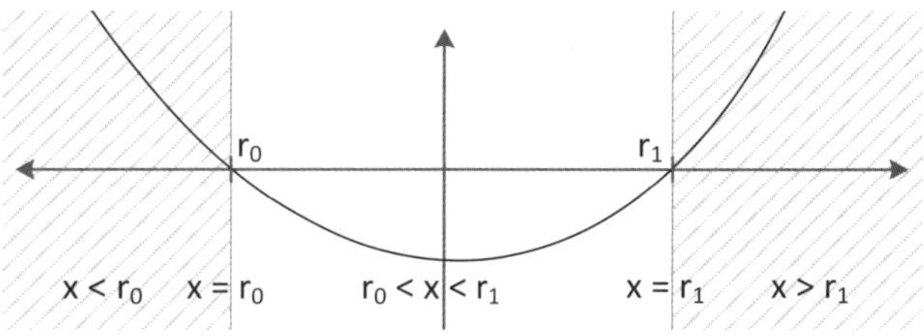

Figure 6: The roots of the univariate polynomial constraint $R(x) = (x - r_0)(x - r_1)$ define intervals that determine its sign.

solver. Algorithm 4 linearizes a formula in the theory of reals into an equivalent formula by replacing each comparison involving a nonlinear polynomial with an equivalent linear disjunction.

Figure 6 gives the high-level intuition that underlies this linearization. The roots of $R(x) = (x - r_0)(x - r_1)$ define intervals that determine its sign, as shown in the figure. We simply need to encode the intervals that the roots define and the sign of $R(x)$ when x falls into each interval into disjunctive linear constraints. To form these intervals, we must find the roots of a univariate polynomial constraint. Thus, the complexity of Algorithm 4 is quadratic. The correctness of the technical details of this rewriting rests on Lemma 3.1, which we present next.

Lemma 3.1. *For a rational function $f(x) = \frac{P(x)}{Q(x)}$ where $x \in \mathbb{R}$, there exists a polynomial $R(x)$ of degree m whose $n \leq m$ distinct real roots $x_1, \cdots, x_n$ define $n+1$ intervals that can be partitioned into I^-, those intervals in which $R(x)$ is negative, and I^+, where $R(x)$ is positive. Using the roots and these intervals, we have*

$$f(x) = 0 \equiv \bigvee_{i=1}^{n} x = x_i$$

$$f(x) < 0 \equiv \bigvee_{i \in I^-} x \in i$$

$$f(x) > 0 \equiv \bigvee_{i \in I^+} x \in i$$

Proof. The rational function $f(x) = \frac{P(x)}{Q(x)}$, by definition. For $\prec \in \{<, >, =\}$, $\frac{P(x)}{Q(x)} \prec 0 \equiv P(x)Q(x) \prec 0 \wedge Q(x) \neq 0$ (multiply by $Q(x)^2$), so our problem reduces to that of solving the predicate $R(x) \prec 0$ which either has the form $P(x)Q(x)$ or $Q(x)$. We normalize $R(x)$ so that its leading coefficient is positive. From the Fundamental Theorem of Algebra, we have $R(x) = (x - x_1)(x - x_2) \cdots (x - x_m)$, where m is the degree of $R(x)$. Complex roots with a non-zero imaginary part cannot equal zero and when $a + bi, b \neq 0$ is a root, its conjugate is also a root, so the product of the non-real complex factors of $R(x)$ is positive, and do not determine its sign, $R(x) = 0$ holds whenever x equals any of the real roots of $R(x)$, *i.e.* $(x = x_1) \vee \cdots \vee (x = x_n)$. Otherwise, x falls into one of the $n+1$ intervals defined by the roots of $R(x)$. Evaluating $R(x)$ in each of these intervals partitions them into I^+, those intervals in which $R(x)$ is positive, and I^-, those intervals in which $R(x)$ is negative. Thus, when $R(x) \neq 0$, it is negative whenever x falls into any of the intervals in I^- and positive whenever x is in some interval in I^+. □

3.3.3 Finding a Floating-point Solution

Given a univariate, linear constraint ϕ, we need to find a solution over $\mathbb{F}$. Algorithm 5 loops over the intervals that ϕ defines. It tries to solve ϕ at line 2, then substitutes the nearest float less than or equal to the solution into ϕ and tries to solve the resulting formula at line 5. If that fails, it then substitutes the nearest float greater than or

Algorithm 5 SOLVEOVER$\mathbb{F}$: $\Phi \to A^n_{\mathbb{F}}$ takes a path constraint and returns a satisfying assignment over $\mathbb{F}$ if one exists.

input $\phi \in \Phi$, a path constraint.
1: **while true do**
2: $\quad \vec{a} :=$ SMT.SOLVE(ϕ)
3: $\quad$ **return** $\vec{a}$ **if not** ISSAT($\vec{a}$)
4: $\quad (x, v) = \vec{a}$
5: $\quad \vec{a} :=$ SMT.SOLVE($\phi[fp(v)/x]$)
6: $\quad$ **return** $\vec{a}$ **if** ISSAT($\vec{a}$)
7: $\quad \vec{a} :=$ SMT.SOLVE($\phi[\text{next}(fp(v), \Omega)/x]$)
8: $\quad$ **return** $\vec{a}$ **if** ISSAT($\vec{a}$)
9: $\quad \phi := \phi \wedge (x < fp(v) \vee x > \text{next}(fp(v), \Omega))$
10: **end while**

equal to the solution into ϕ and tries to solve the resulting formula at line 7. If this fails, it rules out the interval under consideration at line 9 and considers the next interval. The complexity of this step is linear in the number of intervals; we prove its correctness next.

Lemma 3.2. *Algorithm 5 finds a floating-point solution to a univariate linear constraint, if one exists.*

Proof. The solution for a univariate system of linear inequalities is a set of intervals. A linear inequality has the form $ax + b > 0$. Either $a = 0$ and b determines the truth value of the inequality, or the solution of the clause falls into one of two intervals defined by the root of the clause. Thus, the path constraint ϕ defines a set of intervals $\bigcup[a_i, b_i]$[2]. For $x \in [a_i, b_i]$, let x_f be the largest floating-point number less than or equal to x. If either $x_f \in [a_i, b_i]$ or $\text{next}(x_f, \Omega) \in [a_i, b_i]$ then a floating-point value exists that satisfies the path constraints. Otherwise, we have $x_f \notin [a_i, b_i] \wedge \text{next}(x_f, \Omega) \notin [a_i, b_i] \wedge [a_i, b_i] \cap [x_f, next(x_f, \Omega)] \neq \emptyset$ which implies $x_f < a_i < b_i < \text{next}(x_f, \Omega)$. In this case, there is no floating-point number in the interval $[a_i, b_i)]$. So we add the constraint $x < x_f \vee x > \text{next}(x_f, \Omega)$ to rule out $[a_i, b_i]$ and consider a different interval. If the algorithm exhausts all the intervals without finding a satisfying floating-point value, no floating-point value for x satisfies the path constraint. □

4. Implementation

In this section, we present the implementation of our floating-point exception detection tool, Ariadne. Ariadne's implementation mirrors its operation: it consists of transformation or analysis components. The transformation rests on LLVM 2.7 [29]. Its arbitrary precision transformation uses GMP [14]. Its analysis phases extends version 2.7 of the KLEE symbolic execution engine [7] and uses the polynomial solver from GSL 1.14 to rewrite constraints [15]. We are indebted to the community for having made these tools available. To give back, we will also publicly release our tool.

4.1 Transformations

Our transformations are implemented as an LLVM analysis and transform pass and operate on LLVM IR. For this reason, our transformations are language agnostic and, in particular, can handle C, C++ and Fortran, the three languages in which most numerical software is written. The principle transformations are reify exception, loop bound, and arbitrary precision.

Reify Exception This transformation makes potential floating-point exceptions explicit. Before each floating-point operation, it injects operand guards to check for exceptions. The bodies of these checks signal the relevant exception and contain a program point that can only be reached if the guarded operation can throw that exception, as described in Section 3.2. It also handles elementary functions and constructs the dependent symbolic variable table (Section 3.2.2). Given an input module, it iterates over every instruction, in every basic block, in every function. It rewrites at the instruction-level, matching the `Call` instruction, arithmetic (`FAdd`, `FSub`, `FMul`, `FDiv`) and conversion (`FPToSI`, `FPToUI`) floating-point operations. When handling the `Call` instruction, the transformation detects and handles elementary functions (Section 3).

Loop Bound Symbolic execution maintains state for each path; path explosion can exhaust resources and prevent symbolic execution from reaching interesting program points. Loops exacerbate this problem. The loop bound transformation takes a bound parameter that it rewrites every loop in its input to obey. Our loop transformation operates on LLVM bytecode, after loop normalization. Here, we show how it works conceptually:

```
                         int i = 0; // a fresh variable
while( expr ) {    ⇒    while( i++ < BOUND && expr ) {
    body                     body
}                        }
```

Arbitrary Precision In Section 5.3, we propose a classifier that separates likely to be avoidable over- and under-flows from those that are likely to be unavoidable. The idea is to transform a program that throws a floating-point exception into an equivalent program that uses arbitrary precision rationals instead of floats, then run the transformed program to check whether 1) it terminates and 2) the result can be converted into floating-point without over- or under-flowing. The arbitrary precision transformation (AP), converts each float type annotation into `mpq_t`, the GMP library's arbitrary precision rational type. AP converts each arithmetic operation to the corresponding GMP function. AP recursively traverses structures. AP rewrites internal function prototypes and definition and marshals and unmarshals the parameters to external functions.

4.2 Analysis

Concurrently and separately from KLEE-FP [4], we added support for floating point types and operations to KLEE. Our goal is not to support symbolic reasoning on the equivalence between floating-point values like KLEE-FP, but to replace KLEE's underlying SMT solver, STP, which does not support satisfiability reasoning over the reals. We modified KLEE 1) to use version 3.1 of the Z3 SMT solver from Microsoft, which supports the theory of real numbers, and 2) to support floating-point symbolic variables, update its internal expressions when encountering floating-point operations, and output those expressions, labeling the symbolic variables with type `real`, as input to Z3. To implement linearization (Section 3.3.2) and find the roots of polynomials, we extended KLEE to use the GSL polynomial solver package and to internally represent every expression as a rational function, *i.e.* a fraction of two polynomials.

Limitations KLEE requires heap-allocated memory to have concrete size. Memory contents can be symbolic and KLEE handles symbolic pointers by cloning. Ariadne inherits this memory handling strategy from KLEE. We also restrict symbolic variables to floating-point parameters and assign random values to integer parameters. We do not handle parameters whose type is pointer or **`struct`**. We intend to support these features in the future.

5. Evaluation

We first motivate our creation of a new multivariate, nonlinear solver, then present exceptions it found and discuss its performance as an automatic floating-point exception detector. Ariadne finds many overflows and underflows (Xflows), many of which may be an unavoidable consequence of finite precision. We close with the presentation of an Xflow classifier that seeks to separate avoidable from unavoidable Xflows and the $\mathbb{F} \to \mathbb{Q}$ type transformation on which it rests.

[2] We consider the closed intervals; open intervals can be handled similarly.

We ran our experiments on a machine running Ubuntu 10.04.2 LTS (kernel 2.6.32-30-server) with 128GB RAM and 3 Intel Xeon X7542 6-Core 2.66GHz 18MB Cache, for a total of 18 cores. The Ariadne engine is described in Section 4. We choose to analyze the special functions of the GNU scientific library (GSL) version gsl-1.14, because the first phase of Ariadne focuses on scalar functions and most of GSL's special functions take and return scalars. We examined all the special functions in the GSL, even though some are static and others share their core implementation. The GSL is a mature, well-maintained, well-tested, widely deployed scientific library [15]. It is for these reasons that we selected it for analysis: finding nontrivial exceptions in it is both challenging and important. In spite of these challenges, Ariadne found nontrivial exceptions.

Since Ariadne analyzes programs not functions, we applied a transformation to each special function in the GSL library that synthesizes a `main` that creates symbolic variables and calls the analyzed function, in addition to applying the transformations described in Section 3.2 and Section 4.1.

5.1 Experimental Setup

External functions and loops cause difficulties for static analyzes, like the symbolic analysis underlying Z3-ARIADNE. We handle a subset of external functions as described in Section 3.2.2. For loops, a classic workaround tactic is to impose a timeout. Another is to bound the loops. We did both. We imposed two timeouts — per-query and per-run. To bound loops, we implemented a transformation that injects a bound into each loop, as described in Section 4.1. Although we could have restricted the use of this loop bound transformation to functions whose analysis failed, we re-ran the analysis on all functions at each loop bound, seeking the Pareto optimal balance of loop bound and time-to-completion. The infinity loop bound means that we did not apply our loop bound transformation.

Concretization We performed the analysis described here with maximum concretizations set to 1 (so we only tried a single concretization per query), as we found that this setting effectively balances performance and precision: higher numbers of concretizations had minimal impact on our results. When we uniformly sampled 1% of queries for intensive concretization, our results were stable. At 1,000 concretizations, 6% of the UNSAT results at 1 concretization became SAT; at 1,000,000, 8% of the UNSAT results became SAT. These results validate our trade-off of performance against precision.

Z3-ARIADNE Our goal is to build a precise and practical tool to detect floating-point exceptions. To this end, we hybridized the Ariadne solver with Z3: we handed each query, even multivariate, nonlinear ones, to Z3 first, and only queried the Ariadne solver on those queries to which Z3 reported UNKNOWN. We name this hybrid solver Z3-ARIADNE.

Result Reporting Multiple paths or multiple inputs along a single path might reach an exception-triggering program point. If that exception is a bug, its fix might require a single condition, implying that all the bug-triggering inputs are in an equivalence class, or logic bounded by the number of distinct inputs that trigger it. Thus, we report exceptions as $[X,Y]$ where X counts unique exception locations found and Y counts the unique input to location pairs.

Preconditions The public API of the GSL documents some preconditions, so do some of the comments internal to its source code. To get a handle on Z3-ARIADNE's false positive rate, we selected, uniformly at random, 20 of the 315 functions in which Z3-ARIADNE reported exceptions. We manually examined the public API and the source of these 20 functions to 1) identify their preconditions and 2) check whether the exception-triggering inputs Z3-ARIADNE reported against these functions violated those preconditions. Two of the 20 functions were static; against these two functions, Z3-ARIADNE reports 7 input to exception pairs. Even though they had no explicit preconditions in their comments, their call sites may implicitly encode preconditions, so we conservatively deemed these 7 pairs to be false positives. Six functions had publicly documented preconditions. Against these 6 functions, Z3-ARIADNE reported 16 exception pairs, 2 of which violated the function's precondition and are false positives. Against the remaining 12, Z3-ARIADNE reported 64 input to exception pairs. In this experiment, therefore, Z3-ARIADNE's false positive rate was $\frac{9}{77}$ or 12%.

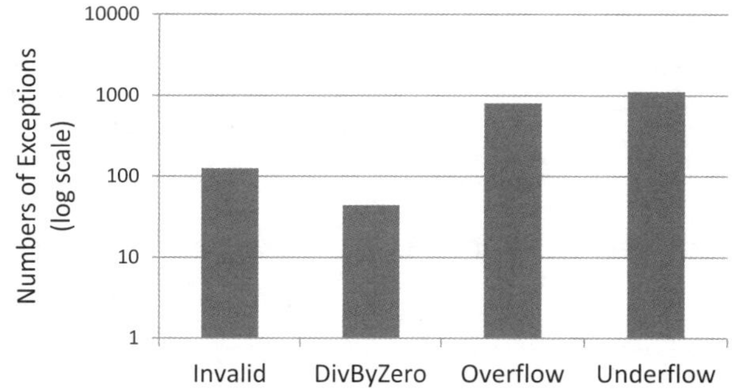

Figure 7: Ariadne found 2091 input-to-location pairs that trigger floating-point exceptions in the GNU Scientific library, distributed as shown.

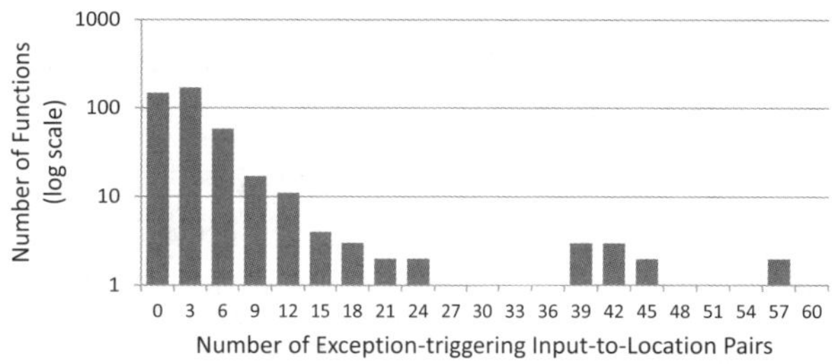

Figure 8: Bar plot of the number of functions (y-axis) with the specified number of input-to-location pairs that trigger floating-point exceptions (x-axis).

Path Injection For each operation, the Ariadne transformation doubles (quadruples in the case of division) the paths to the operation. The reason is that `fabs` uses a conditional to compute the absolute value of its operand. Consider "`double pre = 1.0/sqrt(2.0*M_PI*x);`". Here, the expression passed to `sqrt` actually contains only one multiplication because the compiler replaces the constant multiplication `2.0*M_PI` with a single constant. Considering only the multiplication in the operand of the `sqrt`, Ariadne injects the following pseudocode:

```
1 if ( x > 0  ) y = (2.0*M_PI*x)
2 else y = -(2.0*M_PI*x)
3 if (y > DBL_MAX) Overflow
4 if (y < DBL_MIN) Underflow
5 double pre  = 1.0/sqrt(y);
```

In this example, Ariadne finds `x = 2.861117e+307` that traverses 1, 3 and `x = -2.861117e+307` that traverses 1, 2, 3; both inputs satisfy the conditional and trigger Overflow.

5.2 Analysis Performance and Results

Z3-ARIADNE found a total of 2091 input-to-location pairs that triggered exceptions, distributed as shown in Figure 7. Z3-ARIADNE

Function (prefix gsl_sf_)	Line	Inputs
conicalP_1_e	989	2.0e+01, 1.0e+00
bessel_Jnu_asympx_e	234	0.0, 0.0
exprel_n_CF_e	89	-1.0e+00, 1.340781e+154
bessel_Knu_scaled_asympx_e	317	0.0, 0.0

Table 3: 4 of the 44 Divide-by-Zero exceptions Ariadne found.

Function (prefix gsl_sf_bessel_)	Line	Inputs
Inu_scaled_asymp_unif_e	361	-2.225074e-308, 0.0
Knu_scaled_asympx_e	317	-7.458341e-155, -8.654053e+01
Jnu_asympx_e	234	-5.0e-01, 0.0
Inu_scaled_asympx_e	302	-1.5e+00, -3.921032e+03

Table 4: 4 of the 125 Invalid exceptions Ariadne found.

finds many more Xflows than Invalid or Divide-by-Zero exceptions because programmers strive to avoid the latter and because Xflows can mask these exceptions, as when an underflow occurs in the evaluation of a denominator and terminates exploration of that path before the division is evaluated. Figure 8 shows the distribution of functions in terms of the potential exceptions they contain. As expected, this distribution is skewed: Given the maturity and popularity of the GSL, it is not surprising that most of its functions contain no latent floating-point exceptions. Ariadne reports the most exceptions, 152, in `gsl_sf_bessel_Inu_scaled_asympx_e` defined in `gsl/specfunc/bessel.c`:

Perhaps the most serious exceptions are Divide-by-Zero and Invalid exceptions. For a selection of these exceptions, Table 3 and Table 4 show the function in which we found this type of exceptions, the line number, and exception triggering inputs. For example, Ariadne found a Divide-by-Zero exception in `gsl_sf_conicalP_1_e` in `gsl/specfunc/legendre_con.c`. Line 989 of this file is "`const int stat_V = conicalP_1_V( th, x/sh, lambda, 1.0, &V0, &V1);`". When `lambda = 20` and `x = 1, sh = sqrt(x - 1.0) * sqrt(x + 1.0) = 0`, so `x/sh` throws Divide-by-Zero, 122 lines and 8 control points from function entry.

Table 5 shows the results from our analysis of the scalar GSL special functions. The data shows that, over the GSL special functions, the loop bound (the first column) has little impact on the results. We believe that the reason for this is that the analyzed functions do not make heavy use of looping constructs.

Z3-ARIADNE attempts to explore all paths within the per-run time bound it is given. When Z3-ARIADNE does not exhaust its per-run timeout when analyzing a function, we increment the "No Timeout" column. Z3-ARIADNE successfully explores a path when it determines that the path is satisfiable; when it finds an exception, that exception is *real*, *i.e.* it certainly occurs with the reported inputs, even though Z3-ARIADNE does not model rounding, because Z3-ARIADNE confirms candidate input-to-exception pairs via its concrete execution check (Section 3.3).

Z3-ARIADNE's abandonment of a path as unsatisfiable is provisional for the three reasons discussed in Section 3.3: it approximates floating-point semantics with reals, which notably ignores rounding; it concretizes multivariate into univariate constraints; and it bounds loops. Of these three, we can have some confidence when Z3-ARIADNE reports UNSAT due to concretization, because, as we describe above, concretization is effective due to the fact that the variables in our numerical constraints in practice either have few or many solutions. The former case causes Z3-ARIADNE to report unsatisfiable constraints. When reporting UNSAT, Z3-ARIADNE's precision is good, so the third column reports the count of functions Z3-ARIADNE fully explored without encountering a per-query time-out, *i.e.* U. In some of the functions it fully explored, Z3-ARIADNE discovered no exceptions; the count of these functions is in column four. The set of functions whose cardinality appears in the "No Timeout" column contains the "All Paths Explored" functions which contain the "No Exception Discovered" functions. We note that, while most of the functions in which Z3-ARIADNE discovered no exceptions at the infinity bound are loop-free, four are not.

During Z3-ARIADNE's analysis of the GSL, Z3 handled 48% of the total queries, while Ariadne handled the rest. Of the total queries made, we can guarantee the results for 76% at the infinity bound. The remaining 24% represent UNSAT results of which we cannot be certain, since they involve concretization. That said, our intensive concretization experiment shows that 92% of them are likely to be UNSAT, with 1M concretizations, we found 8% additional SAT. $24\% \cdot 8\% = 1.9\%$, so Z3-ARIADNE is likely to incorrectly resolve around 2% of its constraints.

The loop bound transformation monotonically reduces the number of paths in a program, so each of the function columns should be monotonically increasing. This pattern does not hold over "No Timeout" column. There are two reasons for this variation. First, Z3 randomly hangs on some of the nonlinear, multivariate constraints Z3-ARIADNE feeds it, in spite of its per-query timeout. Second, KLEE flips coins during path scheduling to ensure better coverage. In short, some of the analysis runs at certain loop bounds were simply unlucky.

The three columns that contain the ratios of SAT $\frac{|S|}{|Q|}$, UNSAT $\frac{|\bar{S}|}{|Q|}$, and UNKNOWN $\frac{|U|}{|Q|}$ queries report on Z3-ARIADNE's overall effectiveness. Recall that in Z3-ARIADNE, Ariadne only handles Z3's unknown queries. The Ariadne ratio column reports Ariadne effectiveness at solving Z3's unknowns in our context. Let $S_A, \bar{S}_A$ and U_A be the SAT, UNSAT and UNKNOWN queries that Ariadne handles. The Ariadne ratio then is $\frac{|S_A \cup \bar{S}_A|}{|S_A \cup \bar{S}_A \cup U_A|}$. In short, Ariadne found a substantial fraction of the exceptions and resolved 76–82% of the queries that Z3 was unable to handle.

The "Unique" exception field shows $[X,Y]$, where X is the number of exception locations and Y is the number of unique input to exception location pairs found by Z3-ARIADNE only at the specified loop bound. In the case of the number of input to location pairs, only the pair is unique, not the path it take nor the exception it reaches. At loop bound 64, the unique exception field in Table 5 contains $[3,145]$. This means that the analysis discovered 3 exceptions that it did not also find at another bound and 145 input to exception pairs, found only at this bound. The "Shared" also reports exceptions and paths to exceptions, but without the constraint that those exceptions and input to exception pairs were only discovered at the specified loop bound.

Our analysis is embarrassingly parallelizable, so the test harness partitions the functions onto available cores (in our case 18), then analyzes each function, one by one, against each loop bound. It records the analysis time per function per loop bound. The sum of all the analysis times for all the functions at each loop bound is reported in the total time column. Again, we see that, with our corpus, the loop bound does not have much impact on analysis time.

5.3 Classifying Overflows and Underflows

Some overflows and underflows (Xflows) are an unavoidable consequence of finite precision. The addition $\Omega + \Omega$ is a case in point. Some Xflows, however, may be avoided by changing the order of evaluation in or outright replacing the algorithm used to compute a solution. Because a developer's time is precious, we introduce the *avoidable Xflow classifier* to distinguish potentially avoidable Xflows from those that are not.

Let $A : \mathbb{F}^n \to \mathbb{F}$ be an algorithm implemented using floating-point and $\mathscr{A}$ be that same algorithm implemented using arbitrary

Loop Bound	No Timeout	All Paths Explored	No Exception Discovered	$\frac{\|S\|}{\|Q\|}$	$\frac{\|\bar{S}\|}{\|Q\|}$	$\frac{\|U\|}{\|Q\|}$	Ariadne Ratio	Exceptions Unique	Exceptions Shared	Total Time (hours)
infinity	363	136	45	0.57	0.30	0.13	0.76	[20,174]	[636,847]	89
64	370	149	54	0.57	0.32	0.11	0.80	[3,145]	[658,874]	85
32	368	149	54	0.57	0.32	0.11	0.81	[1,162]	[651,859]	87
16	367	149	54	0.57	0.32	0.11	0.81	[0,142]	[652,858]	87
8	368	149	54	0.57	0.32	0.11	0.81	[3,144]	[652,862]	86
4	366	149	54	0.58	0.32	0.10	0.82	[0,138]	[644,853]	89
2	367	149	54	0.56	0.33	0.11	0.81	[4,134]	[644,863]	86
1	372	149	54	0.56	0.33	0.11	0.81	[4,144]	[655,872]	84

Table 5: The results of Z3-ARIADNE's analysis of the 467 GSL special functions at the specified loop bounds. Here, Q is the set of all queries issued during analysis and S, $\bar{S}$ and U partition Q into its SAT, UNSAT and UNKNOWN queries.

	Overflows	Underflows
Avoidable?	98	180
Total	155	217
Ratio	0.63	0.83

Table 6: Potentially avoidable overflows and underflows.

precision arithmetic over $\mathbb{Q}$. When $A(\vec{i})$ overflows or underflows, we deem that exception *potentially avoidable* if $\mathscr{A}(\vec{i})$ falls within the range of normal floating-point numbers, *i.e.* $|\mathscr{A}(\vec{i})| \in [\lambda, \Omega]$.

This classifier rests on the intuition that, if the evaluation of a floating-point expression over arbitrary precision arithmetic falls within the range of normal floating-point numbers, then it may be possible to find an alternate expression that evaluates to that same result over floating-point without generating intermediate values that trigger floating-point exceptions. For example, consider Sterbenz' `av3`, where $x + \frac{y-x}{2}$. When $x = -\Omega, y = \Omega$, the subtraction overflows under floating-point, but the final result is 0, a normal floating-point number. Further, we know that `av1` is the algebraically equivalent (over the reals) expression $\frac{x+y}{2}$ that, in this case, generates the correct answer without intermediate overflow.

To realize our Xflow classifier, we wrote a transformer that takes a numeric program and replaces its **`float`** and **`double`** types with an arbitrary precision rational type, for whose implementation we use `mpq_t` from GMP [14]. In addition to rewriting types, our arbitrary precision transformer also rewrites floating-point operations into rational operations. For instance, `z = x + y` becomes `mpq_add(z,x,y)`.

Xflows dominated the exceptions we found, comprising 91.9% of all exceptions. We defined and realized our classifier with the aim of filtering these Xflows. Nonetheless, the number of potentially avoidable Xflows remains high in Table 6. Note that GSL is a worst case for us. In a numerical library such as the GSL, these ratios are high because the range of many mathematical functions is small but their implementation relies on floating-point operations whose operands have extremal magnitude.

6. Related Work

Ariadne is related to the large body of work on symbolic execution [27], such as recent representative work on KLEE [7] and DART [18]. Our work directly builds on KLEE and uses its standard symbolic exploration strategy. To the best of our knowledge, it is the first symbolic execution technique applied to the detection of floating-point runtime exceptions. We have proposed a novel programming transformation concept to reduce floating-point analysis to reasoning on real arithmetic and developed practical techniques to solve nonlinear constraints.

Our work is also closely related to the static analysis of numerical programs. The main difference of our work from these is our focus on bug detection rather than proving the absence of error — every exception we detect is a real exception, but we may miss some. We next briefly discuss representative efforts in this area.

Majumdar *et al.* extended the Splat concolic testing engine to support floating-point and nonlinear constraints, then tackled the problems of path coverage, range and robustness analysis [30]. Lakhotia *et al.* empirically evaluated two search-based techniques for solving numerical constraints — alternating variable method and evolution strategies [28]. Their goal was to improve the solution of numerical constraints in general, not in our specific context of detecting floating-point exceptions. They found that these techniques do not decisively outperform Pex' custom solvers. Godefroid and Kinder observed that numerical operations rarely appear in conditionals and therefore not in the path constraint [17]. They leverage this observation to build an analysis that aims to prove the memory safety of floating-point operations and the non-interference of the numeric and non-numeric parts of the subject program. This is in marked contrast with our work, where our transformation explicitly adds numeric conditions and solves the resulting constraints in order to detect floating-point exceptions.

Goubault [20] developed an abstract interpretation-based static analysis [5] to analyze errors introduced by the approximation of floating-point arithmetic. Goubault and Putot later refined this work with a more precise abstract domain [21]. Brillout *et al.* encode floating-point operations as functions on bit vectors, then successively both over- and under-approximate the resulting formulae [2]. Martel [31] presents a general concrete semantics for floating-point operations to explain the propagation of roundoff errors in a computation. In later work [32], Martel applies this concrete semantics and designed a static analysis for checking the stability of loops [23]. Miné [34] proposes an abstract interpretation-based approach to detect floating point errors. Underflows and round-off errors are considered tolerable and thus not considered real run-time errors. Monniaux [35] summarizes the typical errors when using program analysis techniques to detect bugs in or verify correctness of numerical programs. Astree [6] statically analyzes C programs and attempts to prove the absence of overflows and other runtime errors, both over integers and floating-point numbers.

Also related are different approaches to model the floating point computation for numerical programs. Fang *et al.* [11, 12] propose the use of affine arithmetic to model floating-point errors. Darulova *et al.* augment Scala with two new data types: AffineFloat, which computes error bounds while remaining compatible with the Double type and SmartFloat, which generalizes AffineFloat to sets of inputs [8]. Two projects that address floating-point accuracy problems are Fluctuat [10] and a recent paper that dynamically shadows floating-point values and operations with higher precision operands and operators in order to detect accuracy loss, catastrophic cancellation in particular [1]. Ariadne complements these papers, since its focus is the detection of floating-point exceptions, not floating-point accuracy.

7. Conclusion and Future Work

We have presented our design and implementation of Ariadne, a symbolic execution engine for detecting floating-point runtime exceptions. We have also reported our extensive evaluation of Ariadne over a few hundred GSL scalar functions. Our results show that Ariadne is practical, primarily enabled by our novel combination of program rewriting to expose floating-point exceptional conditions and techniques for nonlinear constraint solving. Our immediate future work is to publicly release the tool to benefit numerical software developers. We would also like to investigate approaches to support non-scalar functions, such as those functions that accept or return vectors or matrices.

8. Acknowledgments

We thank Jian Zhang, Mark Gabel, David Hamilton, and the anonymous reviewers for constructive feedback on earlier drafts of this paper. We also thank Zhaojun Bai, William M. Kahan, and Ren-Cang Li for helpful discussions on this work. This research was supported in part by NSF (grants 0702622, 0917392, and 1117603) and the US Air Force (grant FA9550-07-1-0532). The information presented here does not necessarily reflect the position or the policy of the government and no official endorsement should be inferred.

References

[1] F. Benz, A. Hildebrandt, and S. Hack. A dynamic program analysis to find floating-point accuracy problems. In *PLDI*, 2012.

[2] A. Brillout, D. Kroening, and T. Wahl. Mixed abstractions for floating-point arithmetic. In *FMCAD*, 2009.

[3] CNN. Toyota: Software to blame for Prius brake problems. `http://www.cnn.com/2010/WORLD/asiapcf/02/04/japan.prius.complaints/index.html`.

[4] P. Collingbourne, C. Cadar, and P. H. Kelly. Symbolic crosschecking of floating-point and SIMD code. In *EuroSys*, 2011.

[5] P. Cousot and R. Cousot. Abstract interpretation: A unified lattice model for static analysis of programs by construction or approximation of fixpoints. In *POPL*, 1977.

[6] P. Cousot, R. Cousot, J. Feret, L. Mauborgne, A. Miné, D. Monniaux, and X. Rival. The ASTRÉE analyzer. In *ESOP*, 2005.

[7] D. E. Daniel Dunbar, Cristian Cadar. KLEE: Unassisted and automatic generation of high-coverage tests for complex systems programs. In *OSDI*, 2008.

[8] E. Darulova and V. Kuncak. Trustworthy numerical computation in Scala. In *OOPSLA*, 2011.

[9] L. De Moura and N. Bjørner. Z3: An efficient SMT solver. In *TACAS*, 2008.

[10] D. Delmas, E. Goubault, S. Putot, J. Souyris, K. Tekkal, and F. Védrine. Towards an industrial use of FLUCTUAT on safety-critical avionics software. In *FMICS*, 2009.

[11] C. F. Fang, T. Chen, and R. A. Rutenbar. Floating-point error analysis based on affine arithmetic. In *ICASSP*, 2003.

[12] C. F. Fang, R. A. Rutenbar, M. Püschel, and T. Chen. Toward efficient static analysis of finite-precision effects in DSP applications via affine arithmetic modeling. In *DAC*, 2003.

[13] M. Fränzle, C. Herde, T. Teige, S. Ratschan, and T. Schubert. Efficient solving of large non-linear arithmetic constraint systems with complex Boolean structure. *JSAT*, 1(3-4):209–236, 2007.

[14] FSF. GMP: The GNU multiple precision arithmetic library. `/http://gmplib.org/`.

[15] FSF. GSL: GNU scientific library. `http://www.gnu.org/s/gsl/`.

[16] V. Ganesh and D. L. Dill. A decision procedure for bit-vectors and arrays. In *CAV*, 2007.

[17] P. Godefroid and J. Kinder. Proving memory safety of floating-point computations by combining static and dynamic program analysis. In *ISSTA*, 2010.

[18] P. Godefroid, N. Klarlund, and K. Sen. DART: Directed automated random testing. In *PLDI*, 2005.

[19] D. Goldberg. What every computer scientist should know about floating-point arithmetic. *ACM Computing Surveys*, 23(1), 1991.

[20] E. Goubault. Static analyses of the precision of floating-point operations. In *SAS*, 2001.

[21] E. Goubault and S. Putot. Static analysis of numerical algorithms. In *SAS*, 2006.

[22] J. Hauser. Handling floating-point exceptions in numeric programs. *TOPLAS*, 18(2), 1996.

[23] N. J. Higham. *Accuracy and stability of numerical algorithms*. Society for Industrial and Applied Mathematics, 2nd edition, 2002.

[24] IEEE Computer Society. IEEE standard for floating-point arithmetic, 2008.

[25] D. Jovanović and L. de Moura. Solving non-linear arithmetic. In *IJCAR*, 2012.

[26] W. Kahan. A demonstration of presubstitution for ∞/∞ (Grail), 2005.

[27] J. C. King. Symbolic execution and program testing. *Communications of the ACM*, 19, 1976.

[28] K. Lakhotia, N. Tillmann, M. Harman, and J. De Halleux. FloPSy: search-based floating point constraint solving for symbolic execution. In *ICTSS*, 2010.

[29] C. Lattner and V. Adve. LLVM: A compilation framework for lifelong program analysis & transformation. In *CGO*, 2004.

[30] R. Majumdar, I. Saha, and Z. Wang. Systematic testing for control applications. In *MEMOCODE*, 2010.

[31] M. Martel. Propagation of roundoff errors in finite precision computations: a semantics approach. In *ESOP*, 2002.

[32] M. Martel. Static analysis of the numerical stability of loops. In *SAS*, 2002.

[33] Z. Merali. Computational science: ...error ...why scientific programming does not compute. *Nature*, 467:775–777, 2010.

[34] A. Miné. Relational abstract domains for the detection of floating-point run-time errors. In *ESOP*, 2004.

[35] D. Monniaux. The pitfalls of verifying floating-point computations. *TOPLAS*, 30(3):12:1–12:41, 2008.

[36] K. L. Palmerius. Fast and high precision volume haptics. In *Proceedings of the IEEE World Haptics Conference*. IEEE, 2007.

[37] P. Rümmer and T. Wahl. An SMT-LIB theory of binary floating-point arithmetic. In *SMT at FLoC*, 2010.

[38] K. Sen. CUTE: a concolic unit testing engine for C. In *FSE*, 2005.

[39] P. H. Sterbenz. *Floating-Point Computation*. Prentice-Hall, 1974.

[40] Wikipedia. Ariane 5 flight 501. `http://en.wikipedia.org/wiki/Ariane_5_Flight_501`.

Subjective Auxiliary State for Coarse-Grained Concurrency

Ruy Ley-Wild   Aleksandar Nanevski

IMDEA Software Institute

{ruy.leywild, aleks.nanevski}@imdea.org

Abstract

From Owicki-Gries' Resource Invariants and Jones' Rely/Guarantee to modern variants based on Separation Logic, axiomatic logics for concurrency require auxiliary state to explicitly relate the effect of all threads to the global invariant on the shared resource. Unfortunately, auxiliary state gives the proof of an individual thread access to the auxiliaries of all other threads. This makes proofs sensitive to the global context, which prevents local reasoning and compositionality.

To tame this historical difficulty of auxiliary state, we propose *subjective auxiliary state*, whereby each thread is verified using a *self* view (i.e., the thread's effect on the shared resource) and an *other* view (i.e., the collective effect of all the other threads). Subjectivity generalizes auxiliary state from stacks and heaps to user-chosen partial commutative monoids, which can eliminate the dependence on the global thread structure.

We employ subjectivity to formulate Subjective Concurrent Separation Logic as a combination of subjective auxiliary state and Concurrent Separation Logic. The logic yields simple, compositional proofs of coarse-grained concurrent programs that use auxiliary state, and scales to support higher-order recursive procedures that can themselves fork new threads. We prove the soundness of the logic with a novel denotational semantics of action trees and a definition of safety using rely/guarantee transitions over a large subjective footprint. We have mechanized the denotational semantics, logic, metatheory, and a number of examples by a shallow embedding in Coq.

Categories and Subject Descriptors D.2.4 [*Software Engineering*]: Program Verification—Correctness proofs; D.3.3 [*Programming Languages*]: Language Constructs and Features—Concurrent programming structures

Keywords concurrency, verification, local reasoning, rely-guarantee thinking, dependent type theory

1. Introduction

Auxiliary state (*a.k.a.* ghost state) is a necessary evil that compensates for the "expressive weakness" [13] of axiomatic program logics for concurrency. It is necessary in proofs to partially expose the internal behavior of threads in order to relate local program assertions to global invariants, and in the metatheory to establish completeness [20]. But it is evil because the proof of an individual thread becomes sensitive to the global thread structure of the context in which it is used. This prevents local reasoning and limits the compositionality of all logics that use auxiliary state.

$$
\begin{array}{c}
\{y \mathrel{\mapstochar\rightharpoonup} \alpha * z \mathrel{\mapstochar\rightharpoonup} \beta\} \\
\begin{array}{c|c}
\begin{array}{c} \{y \mathrel{\mapstochar\rightharpoonup} \alpha\} \\ \left\langle \begin{array}{c} \{y \mathrel{\mapstochar\rightharpoonup} \alpha * \exists \beta. I_2(\alpha,\beta)\} \\ x := [x]+1; y := [y]+1; \\ \{y \mathrel{\mapstochar\rightharpoonup} \alpha{+}1 * \exists \beta. I_2(\alpha{+}1,\beta)\} \end{array} \right\rangle \\ \{y \mathrel{\mapstochar\rightharpoonup} \alpha{+}1\} \end{array}
&
\begin{array}{c} \{z \mathrel{\mapstochar\rightharpoonup} \beta\} \\ \left\langle \begin{array}{c} \{z \mathrel{\mapstochar\rightharpoonup} \beta * \exists \alpha. I_2(\alpha,\beta)\} \\ x := [x]+1; z := [z]+1; \\ \{z \mathrel{\mapstochar\rightharpoonup} \beta{+}1 * \exists \alpha. I_2(\alpha,\beta{+}1)\} \end{array} \right\rangle \\ \{z \mathrel{\mapstochar\rightharpoonup} \beta{+}1\} \end{array}
\end{array} \\
\{y \mathrel{\mapstochar\rightharpoonup} \alpha{+}1 * z \mathrel{\mapstochar\rightharpoonup} \beta{+}1\}
\end{array}
$$

Figure 1. Two incr threads in Concurrent Separation Logic with fractional permissions.

We illustrate the problem of auxiliary state through the classical concurrent incrementor example of Owicki and Gries. The program $\mathsf{incr}(n) \mathrel{\widehat{=}} \langle x := [x] + n \rangle$ enters a *critical section* $\langle - \rangle$ to gain access to the shared state x and increment it by n. We want to verify incr with a *compositional* specification that can be used to deduce the overall effect on x by several incr's in parallel. For example, if k threads concurrently call $\mathsf{incr}(1)$, we should be able to deduce that the overall effect is for x to increment by k.

In Owicki and Gries' **Resource Invariants** (RI) [21], the shared state is specified by a *resource invariant* I that holds whenever all threads are outside the critical section. By *mutual exclusion*, when a thread enters a critical section it acquires exclusive access to the shared state satisfying the invariant. It may mutate the shared state and violate the invariant, but it must restore the invariant before releasing the resource and leaving the critical section. RI is notably useful for *coarse-grained* concurrency, where interference is confined to critical sections. Because the invariant abstracts away from having to reason explicitly about concurrent interference, RI enables sequential reasoning about individual threads.

An invariant that *only* refers to x, however, has no way to identify each thread's effect on the total value, thus, at best it can show that x increments by an unspecified amount. This suffices to prove memory safety, but not to deduce a noninvariant property such as x increments by k. Owicki and Gries' solution (and most axiomatic logics follow suit) is for each thread to have *auxiliary state* that exposes its effect on the shared state to the invariant; auxiliaries are updated for the sake of verification, but aren't needed for execution.

For two parallel incr threads, in **Concurrent Separation Logic** (CSL) [19] with fractional permissions [1] (Figure 1), the *binary* invariant $I_2(\alpha, \beta) \mathrel{\widehat{=}} x \mapsto \alpha{+}\beta * y \mathrel{\mapstochar\rightharpoonup} \alpha * z \mathrel{\mapstochar\rightharpoonup} \beta$ says that the shared state x contains the sum $\alpha{+}\beta$, auxiliary state y captures the first thread's cumulative effect on (i.e., contribution to) x, and likewise z for the second thread.[1] Ownership of an auxiliary is split in half

POPL'13, January 23–25, 2013, Rome, Italy.

[1] We take Separation Logic heaps as our model of state. The separating conjunction $p{*}q$ means that the heap splits into disjoint subheaps that satisfy

between the invariant and the owning thread, to ensure that only the owner can update the auxiliary. The program is instrumented with *shaded* code to update auxiliaries, and with {braced} assertions that say what holds at specific program points. The final assertion and the invariant imply that x increments by 2.

However, if instead we wanted to prove the effect of three parallel increments, we would have to use a different *ternary* invariant $I_3(\alpha, \beta, \gamma) \mathrel{\widehat{=}} x \mapsto \alpha{+}\beta{+}\gamma * y \mapsto \alpha * z \mapsto \beta * w \mapsto \gamma$. Even though the two-thread program is a subprogram of the three-thread one, the former's proof is specific to the binary invariant I_2 and cannot be reused in the latter's proof. Thus, in RI and its logical descendants such as CSL, even a simple program as incrementation lacks a single proof that can be reused in different contexts.

In this sense, axiomatic proofs with auxiliary state have limited compositionality: it is not always possible to prove a subprogram and reuse its proof directly in a larger context. The problem is that when an invariant mentions auxiliary state, the auxiliaries reveal thread identities (e.g., w in I_3 identifies the new thread). Therefore, when the verification of a thread sees the invariant in the critical section, it becomes dependent on the global thread structure, which breaks local reasoning. Even worse, when threads are forked dynamically (e.g., an iterator forks a separate thread to process each element in a list), the invariant must be defined in terms of dynamically-allocated auxiliary state that mirrors the forking pattern, which makes the invariant even more context specific.

For *fine-grained* concurrency, where interference may occur between any two memory operations, Jones' **Rely/Guarantee** (RG) [12] explicitly specifies thread and environment interference on the shared state. This can reduce and sometimes even eliminate the auxiliary state required in RI proofs. However, RG and most of its logical descendants (e.g., RGSep [26], SAGL [9], Deny-Guarantee [7]) still require noncompositional auxiliary state for the incrementor. To our knowledge, the only exceptions are Concurrent Abstract Predicates (CAP) [6] and HLRG [10], which *can* verify the incrementor without auxiliary state. However, both logics use RG-style specifications that impose complex reasoning about interference explicitly in the proof. We consider this should be avoided for reasoning about any coarse-grained algorithm, because critical sections are used exactly to abstract away from interference.

We present **Subjective Concurrent Separation Logic** (SCSL), a prototype logic for a stateful language with higher-order recursive procedures, fork-join concurrency, and a lock-protected critical section (Section 4). SCSL combines the classical techniques of Resource Invariants and Separation Logic, and tames the difficulties of auxiliary state with a novel *subjective* perspective.

Subjective auxiliary state gives two complementary thread-oriented views on auxiliary state: a *self* view $\mathsf{a_S}$ of the thread's own auxiliary contribution, and an *other* view $\mathsf{a_O}$ that agglomerates all other threads' contributions. To eliminate the dependency on the number of threads in the environment, subjective auxiliary state generalizes from stack variables and heap locations to a user-chosen *partial commutative monoid* (PCM). For various examples, choosing an optimized PCM can blur the global thread structure, in contrast to auxiliary stacks or heaps. Since stacks and heaps are PCMs [4], subjective auxiliary state subsumes classical auxiliary state. Thus, when a suitable auxiliary PCM cannot be found, a proof can always fall back on using an auxiliary stack or heap.

p and q that are passed to each subthread of a parallel composition; $\ell \mathrel{\stackrel{\frac{1}{2}}{\mapsto}} v$ is a *half fractional permission* that allows dereferencing ℓ with contents v; $\ell \mathrel{\stackrel{\frac{1}{2}}{\mapsto}} v * \ell \mathrel{\stackrel{\frac{1}{2}}{\mapsto}} v$ is equivalent to $\ell \mapsto v$, which also allows updating ℓ. Strictly speaking, the invariant is the unparameterized assertion $\exists\alpha.\exists\beta.I_2(\alpha, \beta)$ where the auxiliary contributions α and β are existentially quantified; we concentrate on the parameterized I_2 to simplify the presentation and omit the details of how fractional permissions relate the free and bound variables.

Intuitively, subjectivity synthesizes the thread/environment dichotomy espoused by Rely/Guarantee and the PCM structure of state elucidated by Separation Logic. In contrast to the *temporal* emphasis of Rely/Guarantee transitions, subjective auxiliary state creates a *spatial* dichotomy between thread and environment auxiliaries. In contrast to the exclusively *local*, small footprint, view of state in Separation Logic, the $\mathsf{a_O}$ view of the environment embodies *non-local* information about the run-time context, but the PCM-agglomeration makes it abstract enough to retain the CSL-style local reasoning.

The critical point concerns how to combine proofs of two threads into a proof of their **parallel composition**. When one thread updates its $\mathsf{a_S}$, then it implicitly also updates another thread's $\mathsf{a_O}$. How do we ensure that the proof of the other thread remains a valid subproof in the combination, when it sees its $\mathsf{a_O}$ view change?

We resolve this question by proving a CSL-style rule of parallel composition with a novel *subjective separating conjunction* connective $\circledast$ for splitting auxiliary views. The rule ensures that if the initial views of two threads are coherent at the fork point, then there exists a coherent combination of the views at the join point. This suffices to use the proofs of threads as black boxes and establish the combined verification of their parallel composition. We also prove a frame rule with $\circledast$ that surprisingly does not require cancellativity of the auxiliary PCM.

We show that SCSL yields simple, compositional proofs for a few coarse-grained concurrent programs from the literature (Sections 2 and 3). Although the programs are relatively simple, their proofs in existing logics either require auxiliaries which leads to noncompositionality, or can avoid auxiliaries but are technically complex. Moreover, we show that SCSL scales to higher-order recursive procedures which can themselves fork new thread, depending on run time values; to our knowledge, this combination is not supported by any existing logic[2]. Although we focus on RI proofs for coarse-grained concurrency, we believe subjectivity will also synergize well with RG for fine-grained concurrency.

We give SCSL a novel denotational **model** that represents computations as *action trees* and establish **soundness** of the logic by a definition of safety that crucially relies on subjectivity, not only of the user-chosen auxiliary PCM, but also of heap and lock ownership (Section 5). We embed SCSL into the higher-order logic Calculus of Inductive Constructions [18], and thus inherit a number of features from dependent type theory: abstraction over programs (i.e., higher-order procedures), types (i.e., polymorphism), and predicates (i.e., datatypes, objects, modules). These features are essential for modular programming and verification, but, aside from abstract predicates [22, 6], have not been considered in the axiomatic concurrency logic literature. The embedding allowed us to mechanize the semantics, logic, soundness proof, and a number of examples in Coq; the Coq sources are available online [16].

2. SCSL and Proving the Incrementor

2.1 Subjective Auxiliary State

Subjective Concurrent Separation Logic (SCSL) has a single lock with global scope which is associated with a user-chosen partial commutative monoid (PCM) $(\mathbb{U}, \oplus, \mathbb{0})$ for auxiliary state and an invariant I_* indexed by $\mathbb{U}$. A PCM is a set $\mathbb{U}$ with an associative and commutative join operation $\oplus$ and unit element $\mathbb{0}$. Intuitively, the unit $\mathbb{0}$ describes a null effect; the join $\oplus$ combines the effects of two parallel threads, which mirrors the associativity and commutativity of parallel composition; and partiality indicates inconsistent views (e.g., two threads owning a lock simultaneously).

[2] We don't, however, support higher-order heaps that can store procedures.

By working with an auxiliary PCM, we can take the $\oplus$-total $\tau \in \mathbb{U}$ of *all* threads' combined contributions: if each thread i contributes σ_i, then $\tau = \bigoplus_i \sigma_i$. The single total auxiliary value τ serves to define a *unary* invariant $I_*(\tau)$ that doesn't depend on the number of threads, in contrast to CSL proofs where auxiliaries expose all threads in the invariant (e.g., $y \mapsto \alpha$ identifies the left thread and $z \mapsto \beta$ the right thread in the CSL proof from Section 1).

To preserve locality, however, assertions can't directly refer to the total τ, because all threads can interfere on its value. Instead, each thread i has two complementary subjective *views* of τ: a *self* view $\mathsf{a_S} \rightarrowtail \sigma_i$ of the thread's own auxiliary contribution, and an *other* view $\mathsf{a_O} \hookrightarrow \omega_i$ where $\omega_i = \bigoplus_{j \neq i} \sigma_j$ is the $\oplus$-subtotal of all other threads' contributions.[3] Although different threads i and j may have different views $(\mathsf{a_S}, \mathsf{a_O})$, all views are mutually *coherent* in that they yield the same $\oplus$-total: $\sigma_i \oplus \omega_i = \tau = \sigma_j \oplus \omega_j$. We use $\mathsf{a_S} \rightarrowtail \sigma_i$ throughout the program to track the thread's contribution as it changes, but only use $\mathsf{a_O} \hookrightarrow \omega_i$ in the critical section to track that the environment's contribution remains fixed when it can't access the shared resource (Section 2.4).

2.2 Parallel Composition and Subjective Separation

For the incrementor, we choose the PCM $(\mathbb{N}, +, 0)$ of natural numbers under addition and the unary invariant $I_*(\tau) \mathrel{\widehat{=}} x \mapsto \tau$, which hides the identity of threads and thus permits a compositional proof of incr. The SCSL specification of $\mathsf{incr}(n)$ is:

$$\forall n{:}\mathsf{nat}.\{\mathsf{a_S} \rightarrowtail \sigma\}\mathsf{incr}(n) : \mathsf{unit}\{\mathsf{a_S} \rightarrowtail \sigma + n\}$$

incr takes an argument n and increments the thread's contribution $\mathsf{a_S}$ from σ to $\sigma + n$,[4] and returns unit.[5] Since the value of $\mathsf{a_S}$ is thread-specific, the SCSL specification does not expose thread identities (*cf.* how y identified the left thread in the CSL proof).

The environment's contribution $\mathsf{a_O}$ does not appear in the specification and is thus unconstrained, but it will show up in the proof of incr. Since incr only mutates shared state, the local heap is implicitly empty in the pre and post. By framing, incr is safe to run in any larger private heap, which remains unchanged upon termination.

To prove two parallel increments, we use the SCSL PAR rule:

$$\frac{\{p_1\}C_1\{q_1\} \qquad \{p_2\}C_2\{q_2\}}{\{p_1 \circledast p_2\}C_1 \parallel C_2\{q_1 \circledast q_2\}}\ \textsc{Par}$$

The ***subjective separating conjunction*** $\circledast$ connective splits the heap into two disjoint subheaps; the novelty is that $\circledast$ also splits the *contents* of $\mathsf{a_S}$: $\mathsf{a_S} \rightarrowtail \alpha \circledast \mathsf{a_S} \rightarrowtail \beta$ is equivalent to $\mathsf{a_S} \rightarrowtail \alpha \oplus \beta$. For comparison, the CSL PAR rule uses the separating conjunction $*$ to split the heap and *ownership* of auxiliaries among parallel threads.

The SCSL proof of incr is compositional: we can instantiate σ and n in the proof of incr, which is otherwise used as a black box, to show that $\mathsf{incr}(i) \parallel \mathsf{incr}(j)$ increments x by $i{+}j$.

$$\begin{array}{c}
\{\mathsf{a_S} \rightarrowtail \alpha{+}\beta\}\\
\{\mathsf{a_S} \rightarrowtail \alpha \circledast \mathsf{a_S} \rightarrowtail \beta\}\\
\begin{array}{c||c}
\{\mathsf{a_S} \rightarrowtail \alpha\} & \{\mathsf{a_S} \rightarrowtail \beta\}\\
\mathsf{incr}(i) & \mathsf{incr}(j)\\
\{\mathsf{a_S} \rightarrowtail \alpha{+}i\} & \{\mathsf{a_S} \rightarrowtail \beta{+}j\}
\end{array}\\
\{\mathsf{a_S} \rightarrowtail \alpha{+}i \circledast \mathsf{a_S} \rightarrowtail \beta{+}j\}\\
\{\mathsf{a_S} \rightarrowtail (\alpha{+}i){+}(\beta{+}j)\}
\end{array}$$

The parallel composition starts with a contribution $\mathsf{a_S} \rightarrowtail \alpha{+}\beta$. When the parent thread forks two child threads, the parent's view $\mathsf{a_S}$ splits between its children, while the children's $\mathsf{a_O}$'s are implicitly induced to preserve coherence (i.e., the left child's environment includes the right child, and vice versa). By coherence, the combination of views is the same irrespective of the viewer.[6]

viewer:		parent $\Leftrightarrow$	$\text{child}_1 \circledast$	child_2
views:	self $\mathsf{a_S}$ (explicit)	$\alpha{+}\beta$	α	β
	other $\mathsf{a_O}$ (implicit)	ω	$\beta{+}\omega$	$\alpha{+}\omega$
combined views:	$\mathsf{a_S}{+}\mathsf{a_O}$		$\alpha{+}\beta{+}\omega$	

The left thread instantiates the incr proof with α and i to show that the overall contribution increments from α to $\alpha{+}i$; and analogously for the right thread. The soundness of parallel composition ensures that, dually, at the join point the children's $\mathsf{a_S}$'s can be combined back into the parent's $\mathsf{a_S}$: the subthreads' $\mathsf{a_S}$'s are added and the parallel composition ends with $\mathsf{a_S}$ incremented by $i{+}j$ over the initial value. $\mathsf{a_O}$ is implicitly unconstrained and unknown in the parent, and thus remains so in both child threads.

We can directly reuse the two-thread SCSL proof compositionally in a three-thread program *without having to change the invariant or subproof for the particular context*. The three-thread program increments the initial contribution $\alpha{+}\beta{+}\gamma$ by $i{+}j{+}k$ with a structurally similar proof as the two-thread program.

$$\begin{array}{c}
\{\mathsf{a_S} \rightarrowtail \alpha{+}\beta{+}\gamma\}\\
\{\mathsf{a_S} \rightarrowtail \alpha{+}\beta \circledast \mathsf{a_S} \rightarrowtail \gamma\}\\
\begin{array}{c||c}
\{\mathsf{a_S} \rightarrowtail \alpha{+}\beta\} & \{\mathsf{a_S} \rightarrowtail \gamma\}\\
\mathsf{incr}(i) \parallel \mathsf{incr}(j) & \mathsf{incr}(k)\\
\{\mathsf{a_S} \rightarrowtail (\alpha{+}i){+}(\beta{+}j)\} & \{\mathsf{a_S} \rightarrowtail \gamma{+}k\}
\end{array}\\
\{\mathsf{a_S} \rightarrowtail (\alpha{+}i){+}(\beta{+}j) \circledast \mathsf{a_S} \rightarrowtail \gamma{+}k\}\\
\{\mathsf{a_S} \rightarrowtail (\alpha{+}i){+}(\beta{+}j){+}(\gamma{+}k)\}
\end{array}$$

Here, the initial $(\mathsf{a_S}, \mathsf{a_O})$ views are $(\alpha{+}\beta{+}\gamma, \omega)$ for some ω, which induce views for the three threads: $(\alpha, \beta{+}\gamma{+}\omega)$, $(\beta, \alpha{+}\gamma{+}\omega)$, and $(\gamma, \alpha{+}\beta{+}\omega)$; all have the coherent total $\alpha{+}\beta{+}\gamma{+}\omega$.

Furthermore, we can substitute programs with the same specification. For example, the parallel $\mathsf{incr}(i) \parallel \mathsf{incr}(j)$ and the sequential $\mathsf{incr}(i); \mathsf{incr}(j)$ with a different number of threads can be given the same specification $\{\mathsf{a_S} \rightarrowtail \alpha{+}\beta\} - \{\mathsf{a_S} \rightarrowtail \alpha{+}\beta{+}i{+}j\}$. Therefore we can use them interchangeably in the three-increment program and the overall proof remains the same. In Section 3.2, we show that this approach scales to prove a concurrent iterator, where the number of threads depends on a run-time value.

2.3 Assertions

In SCSL, an assertion is a predicate over a *world* w of the form $h; \mu; \sigma; \omega$. h is the thread's private heap (a finite map from pointers to values), which is a PCM with the empty heap as unit and disjoint

$h; \mu; \sigma; \omega \models \mathsf{a_S} \rightarrowtail \sigma'$	iff $(h, \mu, \sigma) = (\mathsf{empty}, \cancel{\mathsf{Own}}, \sigma')$
$h; \mu; \sigma; \omega \models \mathsf{m_S} \rightarrowtail \mu'$	iff $(h, \mu, \sigma) = (\mathsf{empty}, \mu', \mathbb{0})$
$h; \mu; \sigma; \omega \models \ell \mapsto v$	iff $(h, \mu, \sigma) = ([\ell \Rightarrow v], \cancel{\mathsf{Own}}, \mathbb{0})$
$h; \mu; \sigma; \omega \models \mathsf{a_O} \hookrightarrow \omega'$	iff $\omega = \omega'$
$h; \mu; \sigma; \omega \models \mathsf{emp}$	iff $(h, \mu, \sigma) = (\mathsf{empty}, \cancel{\mathsf{Own}}, \mathbb{0})$
$h; \mu; \sigma; \omega \models p_1 * p_2$	iff $h_1; \mu_1; \sigma_1; \omega \models p_1$ and $h_2; \mu_2; \sigma_2; \omega \models p_2$ where $(h, \mu, \sigma) = (h_1 \oplus h_2, \mu_1 \oplus \mu_2, \sigma_1 \oplus \sigma_2)$ for some h_i, μ_i, σ_i
$h; \mu; \sigma; \omega \models p_1 \circledast p_2$	iff $h_1; \mu_1; \sigma_1; \sigma_2 \oplus \omega \models p_1$ and $h_2; \mu_2; \sigma_2; \sigma_1 \oplus \omega \models p_2$ where $(h, \mu, \sigma) = (h_1 \oplus h_2, \mu_1 \oplus \mu_2, \sigma_1 \oplus \sigma_2)$ for some h_i, μ_i, σ_i
$w \models p_1 \wedge p_2$	iff $w \models p_1$ and $w \models p_2$
$[\mu, \sigma, \omega]\, p$ abbreviates	$(\mathsf{m_S} \rightarrowtail \mu * \mathsf{a_S} \rightarrowtail \sigma * p) \wedge \mathsf{a_O} \hookrightarrow \omega$

Figure 2. Semantics of assertions $h; \mu; \sigma; \omega \models p$ (fragment).

[3] For the moment, $\mathsf{a_S} \rightarrowtail \sigma$ and $\mathsf{a_O} \hookrightarrow \omega$ should be read as asserting the contents of each auxiliary view, but don't directly permit mutation; their formal meaning is explained in Section 2.3.

[4] We use Greek letters, such as σ, for *logical variables* that scope over the pre- and postcondition to relate initial and final states.

[5] The SCSL judgments include an explicit return type (Section 4). Hereafter we omit the return type unless it requires commentary.

[6] This pattern recurs in the semantics, not only for auxiliaries but also for heaps and lock ownership (Section 5.5).

union $\uplus$ as join (undefined if the heaps overlap). μ is an element of the lock ownership PCM mtx, with elements Own (to indicate the viewer owns the lock and is thus in a critical section) and $\cancel{\mathsf{Own}}$; the join $\oplus$ is defined with unit $\cancel{\mathsf{Own}}$, but $\mathsf{Own} \oplus \mathsf{Own}$ is undefined because two threads cannot enter a critical section simultaneously. σ and ω are the thread and environment's respective auxiliary contributions from $\mathbb{U}$.

In our subjective terminology, the components h, μ and σ are the *self* views on the thread's world, as they describe the state of the thread itself. On the other hand, ω is the *other* view, as it describes the abstract effect of the thread's environment on the shared state.

Figure 2 gives the interpretation of assertions.[7] The thread's auxiliary pointer assertion $\mathsf{a_S} \rightarrowtail \sigma'$ constrains the σ component of the world to be σ', and the h and μ components to be the respective PCM units, but the ω component is unconstrained because the environment may enter the critical section and change its contribution in tandem with the shared state. Thus, the $\mathsf{a_S} \rightarrowtail -$ assertions in the specification of incr implicitly mean the private heap is empty and the lock isn't owned. The pointer assertion $\ell \mapsto v$ and lock (*a.k.a.* mutex) pointer assertion $\mathsf{m_S} \rightarrowtail \mu'$ are defined analogously. The environment's auxiliary pointer assertion $\mathsf{a_O} \hookrightarrow \omega'$ constrains the ω component of the world to be ω', but is *intuitionistic* in that it doesn't constrain the h, μ, or σ components. The auxiliary pointer assertions use a half arrow tip to suggest that they can't be mutated directly (though we don't use permissions).

The $p_1 \circledast p_2$ assertion splits the self components h, μ, and σ between p_1 and p_2, and induces the other component to maintain coherence (i.e., $\sigma_2 \oplus \omega$ for p_1, and dually for p_2). The $p_1 * p_2$ assertion also splits the self components h, μ, and σ, but doesn't change the other component ω.

The SCSL rules for memory and locking commands typically use the assertion $[\mu', \sigma', \omega']\, p$, which abbreviates $(\mathsf{m_S} \rightarrowtail \mu' * \mathsf{a_S} \rightarrowtail \sigma' * p) \wedge \mathsf{a_O} \hookrightarrow \omega'$ and holds in a world $h; \mu; \sigma; \omega$ if $(\mu, \sigma, \omega) = (\mu', \sigma', \omega')$ and h satisfies the heap predicate p. The asymmetry between the $\mathsf{a_S} \rightarrowtail -$ and $\mathsf{a_O} \hookrightarrow -$ assertions stems from the fact that $\mathsf{a_S}$ must be tracked throughout the program, in particular when it is split at forking points, but $\mathsf{a_O}$ is implicitly induced to preserve coherence at forking points and is only tracked in the critical section.

2.4 Critical Sections and Local Auxiliary Functions

The following proof outline of incr is parametric in σ_i and n. In SCSL, we enter and exit *critical sections* using explicit lock and unlock commands, which illustrates how lock ownership works in tandem with auxiliaries.

	$\{\mathsf{a_S} \rightarrowtail \sigma_i\}$	precondition
	$\{[\cancel{\mathsf{Own}}, \sigma_i, -]\, \mathsf{emp}\}$	by CONSEQ
1	$\mathsf{lock};$	
	$\{\exists \omega_i . [\mathsf{Own}, \sigma_i, \omega_i]\, I_*(\sigma_i + \omega_i)\}$	by lock
2	$tmp \leftarrow \mathsf{read}\ x;$	
	$\{\exists \omega_i . [\mathsf{Own}, \sigma_i, \omega_i]\, x \mapsto (\sigma_i + \omega_i) \wedge tmp = \sigma_i + \omega_i\}$	by read
3	$\mathsf{write}\ x\ (tmp + n);$	
	$\{\exists \omega_i . [\mathsf{Own}, \sigma_i, \omega_i]\, x \mapsto ((\sigma_i + \omega_i) + n)\}$	by write
	$\{\exists \omega_i . [\mathsf{Own}, \sigma_i, \omega_i]\, I_*((\sigma_i + n) + \omega_i)\}$	by CONSEQ
4	unlock_{Φ_n}	
	$\{\exists \omega_i . [\cancel{\mathsf{Own}}, \Phi_n(\sigma_i), -]\, \mathsf{emp}\}$	by unlock
	$\{\mathsf{a_S} \rightarrowtail \sigma_i + n\}$	by CONSEQ

First, the precondition $\mathsf{a_S} \rightarrowtail \sigma_i$ is turned into the equivalent explicit assertion $[\cancel{\mathsf{Own}}, \sigma_i, -]\, \mathsf{emp}$, where "$-$" indicates that the environment's contribution is existentially quantified and thus unknown.

The lock operation (line 1) uses the SCSL rule:

$$\{[\cancel{\mathsf{Own}}, \sigma_i, -]\, \mathsf{emp}\}\mathsf{lock}\{\exists \omega_i . [\mathsf{Own}, \sigma_i, \omega_i]\, I_*\, (\sigma_i \oplus \omega_i)\}$$

where the PCM operation $\oplus$ is instantiated with $+$. Locking changes the ownership status from $\cancel{\mathsf{Own}}$ to Own and preserves the thread's contribution σ_i. Prior to locking, the environment may enter the critical section and change its contribution in tandem with the shared state, thus $\mathsf{a_O}$ is unconstrained in the precondition and existentially named ω_i in the postcondition. The thread also acquires the shared state satisfying $I_*(\tau)$, which is equivalent to $I_*(\sigma_i \oplus \omega_i)$ by the coherence of views.

By mutual exclusion, other threads j can't access or change the shared resource, so their contributions σ_j and consequently $\mathsf{a_O} \hookrightarrow \omega_i (= \bigoplus_{j \neq i} \sigma_j)$ remain fixed throughout the critical section. This invariance is explicitly specified by the commands in the critical section. For example, the SCSL read rule:

$$\{[\mu_i, \sigma_i, \omega_i]\, x \mapsto \nu\}\mathsf{read}\ x \left\{ \begin{array}{c} [\mu_i, \sigma_i, \text{if } \mu = \mathsf{Own} \text{ then } \omega_i \text{ else } -] \\ x \mapsto \nu \wedge \mathsf{res} = \nu \end{array} \right\}$$

includes the standard Separation Logic specification that initial heap contains a pointer x with value ν; in the postcondition, the heap is preserved and ν is bound to the dedicated result variable. Moreover, the lock status μ_i and thread contribution σ_i may be arbitrary and are preserved across the read. However, the environment's contribution is subject to a conditional on the lock ownership: if the thread Owns the lock because it's in a critical section, then $\mathsf{a_O}$ remains fixed at ω_i, otherwise $\mathsf{a_O}$ is undetermined in the postcondition. The other memory commands determine the heap as in Separation Logic and preserve the auxiliaries just like read.

By sequential composition, the read (line 2) binds the contents of x (i.e., $\sigma_i + \omega_i$ by the invariant) to the local variable tmp, and extends the assertion with an equation that describes tmp. The write (line 3) increments x by n, which is reflected in the assertion about the contents of x. Since the thread Owns the lock, the read and write preserve the auxiliaries as σ_i and ω_i.

That the environment's auxiliary $\mathsf{a_O} \hookrightarrow \omega_i$ is fixed throughout the critical section becomes crucial at the unlock command when the invariant $I_*(\sigma_i' \oplus \omega_i)$ must be restored for some *new* thread contribution σ_i' and the *same* environment contribution ω_i from the moment of locking. This emulates the Owicki-Gries discipline that an auxiliary is only updated by its owner in the critical section.

Since we generalize auxiliary state from heap to PCM $\mathbb{U}$, we must also generalize from stack- and heap-mutating auxiliary code to *auxiliary functions* Φ on $\mathbb{U}$. The unlock rule:

$$\{[\mathsf{Own}, \sigma_i, \omega_i]\, I_*\, (\Phi(\sigma_i) \oplus \omega_i)\}\mathsf{unlock}_\Phi\{[\cancel{\mathsf{Own}}, \Phi(\sigma_i), -]\, \mathsf{emp}\}$$

requires the unlock command to be decorated by a mathematical function Φ such that the heap initially satisfies the invariant $I_*(\Phi(\sigma_i) \oplus \omega_i)$ relative to a *new* thread contribution $\Phi(\sigma_i)$, rather than the former thread contribution σ_i. In the postcondition, lock ownership and the invariant heap are released, the thread's auxiliary is updated from σ_i to $\sigma_i' \mathrel{\widehat{=}} \Phi(\sigma_i)$ (which implicitly changes other threads' ω_j). The environment's auxiliary again becomes undetermined, because the thread is no longer in the critical section and the environment can change its contribution at will.

In the incrementor proof, the auxiliary function on unlock (line 4) is $\Phi_n(\sigma) \mathrel{\widehat{=}} \sigma{+}n$, which corresponds to the auxiliary update code used in Section 1 to increment the auxiliaries y and z. By unlocking, the thread's auxiliary $\mathsf{a_S}$ is updated from σ_i to $\Phi_n(\sigma_i) = \sigma_i{+}n$ and the invariant subheap is released. Finally, the existential ω_i can be eliminated because it doesn't appear in the assertion, and we return to the more succinct $\mathsf{a_S} \rightarrowtail \sigma_i + n$.

The structured form of auxiliary update via unlock_Φ has several advantages when compared to the classical auxiliary code from Section 1. First, since Φ is a pure function, it can't perform side

[7] We write $[\ell \Mapsto v]$ for the singleton heap that maps ℓ to v, $[h|\ell \Mapsto v]$ for the heap that maps ℓ to v and behaves like h on other locations, and $h \setminus \ell$ for the heap h without ℓ. By taking the lock and auxiliary units $h; \cancel{\mathsf{Own}}; \mathbb{0}; \mathbb{0} \models p$ we recover the standard Separation Logic relation $h \models_{\mathsf{SL}} p$.

effects to leak the contents of auxiliary state into the heap and thus change the program's semantics.

Second, Φ doesn't directly name $\mathsf{a_S}$. Instead, the proof implicitly applies Φ to the $\mathsf{a_S}$ value of the viewing thread. Thus, Φ can't possibly mutate other threads' auxiliary contributions. In this sense, SCSL differs from a number of related systems [2, 23, 24] which require ownership-tracking permissions to control which auxiliaries can be changed by what auxiliary code (e.g., how the left thread updates y and the right thread updates z in Section 1).

Most importantly, Φ can update the appropriate $\mathsf{a_S}$ without knowing the viewing thread's identity, whereas the CSL proof updates specific auxiliaries in each thread (e.g., y in the left thread, and z in the right thread in Section 1). The independence from the thread's identity facilitates reusability: the *same invariant, auxiliary code, and proof of* incr *can be used without any change*, in contexts with two or three concurrent threads (Section 2.2), or with any number of threads as we illustrate with the iterator (Section 3.2).

To ensure the soundness of parallel composition and framing, however, the auxiliary function Φ must be *local* in the following formal sense, where $\mathsf{valid}(\alpha)$ means α is a defined PCM element. Obviously, the incrementor's Φ_n is local.

Definition 1. *A partial function Φ on a PCM $\mathbb{U}$ is* local, *written $\Phi : \mathbb{U} \rightharpoonup_{\mathsf{L}} \mathbb{U}$, if for all $\alpha, \beta \in \mathbb{U}$,* $\mathsf{valid}\,(\alpha \oplus \beta)$ *and* $\mathsf{valid}\,(\Phi(\alpha))$ *imply $\Phi\,(\alpha \oplus \beta) = \Phi(\alpha) \oplus \beta$.*

Intuitively, Φ can be applied to $\mathsf{a_S}$ with $\mathsf{a_O}$ "framed" on by $\oplus$-combination: it will act on $\mathsf{a_S}$ but simply propagate $\mathsf{a_O}$ without change. This property makes Φ appropriate for modeling auxiliary code for a thread to modify its auxiliary $\mathsf{a_S}$, but is unaffected by and doesn't affect the auxiliary $\mathsf{a_O}$ of other threads running in parallel.

3. More Examples

3.1 Coarse-Grained Set with Disjoint Interference

We adapt a coarse-grained set example from Concurrent Abstract Predicates [6] (in Section 6 we compare with this approach). If threads perform *logically* disjoint operations (i.e., add or remove distinct elements), then we can prove their parallel composition with local reasoning. This is possible even if the operations interfere *physically* on the data structure; for example, if the set is implemented with a splay tree, the memory shape will depend on the order of operations. Fortunately, at the level of abstraction of set membership, the proof isn't sensitive to the noncommutativity of physical operations. Alternatively, we could specify the logical disjointness using classical auxiliary state, but it leads to the same problems as in the incrementor.

We assume a set library, whose procedures sadd and sremove are sequential and can be run in a critical section preserving the auxiliaries:

$$\begin{array}{cc} \{v \notin \Sigma \wedge [\mathsf{Own}, \sigma, \omega]\,\mathsf{set}(x, \Sigma)\} & \{[\mathsf{Own}, \sigma, \omega]\,\mathsf{set}(x, \Sigma \uplus \{v\})\} \\ \mathsf{sadd}(x, v) & \mathsf{sremove}(x, v) \\ \{[\mathsf{Own}, \sigma, \omega]\,\mathsf{set}(x, \Sigma \uplus \{v\})\} & \{[\mathsf{Own}, \sigma, \omega]\,\mathsf{set}(x, \Sigma)\} \end{array}$$

Here v is drawn from some universe V of values, and $\mathsf{set}(x, \Sigma)$ is a spatial predicate that means the finite subset $\Sigma \subseteq V$ is represented at pointer x. We can obtain a coarse-grained concurrent library by wrapping each procedure in a critical section:

$$\begin{array}{l} \mathsf{cadd}(v) \mathrel{\widehat{=}} \mathsf{lock};\ \mathsf{sadd}(x, v) \quad\quad ;\ \mathsf{unlock} \\ \mathsf{cremove}(v) \mathrel{\widehat{=}} \mathsf{lock};\ \mathsf{sremove}(x, v);\ \mathsf{unlock} \end{array}$$

Although the coarse-grained implementation is inefficient because threads must contend for the entire data structure, we can choose suitable auxiliaries $\mathsf{in}(v)$ and $\mathsf{out}(v)$ to specify the procedures in a *local* manner that only depends on the element being manipulated:

$$\begin{array}{c} \{\mathsf{a_S} \rightarrowtail \mathsf{out}(v)\}\quad \mathsf{cadd}(x, v) \quad \{\mathsf{a_S} \rightarrowtail \mathsf{in}(v)\} \\ \{\mathsf{a_S} \rightarrowtail \mathsf{in}(v)\}\ \mathsf{cremove}(x, v)\ \{\mathsf{a_S} \rightarrowtail \mathsf{out}(v)\} \end{array}$$

We can thus reason locally in each thread to prove the effect of concurrently adding or removing three distinct elements:

$$\begin{array}{c} \{\mathsf{a_S} \rightarrowtail (\mathsf{in}(a) \oplus \mathsf{out}(b) \oplus \mathsf{in}(c))\} \\ \begin{array}{c} \{\mathsf{a_S} \rightarrowtail \mathsf{in}(a)\} \\ \mathsf{cremove}(a) \\ \{\mathsf{a_S} \rightarrowtail \mathsf{out}(a)\} \end{array} \;\Bigg\|\; \begin{array}{c} \{\mathsf{a_S} \rightarrowtail \mathsf{out}(b)\} \\ \mathsf{cadd}(b) \\ \{\mathsf{a_S} \rightarrowtail \mathsf{in}(b)\} \end{array} \;\Bigg\|\; \begin{array}{c} \{\mathsf{a_S} \rightarrowtail \mathsf{in}(c)\} \\ \mathsf{cremove}(c) \\ \{\mathsf{a_S} \rightarrowtail \mathsf{out}(c)\} \end{array} \\ \{\mathsf{a_S} \rightarrowtail (\mathsf{out}(a) \oplus \mathsf{in}(b) \oplus \mathsf{out}(c))\} \end{array}$$

To verify the concurrent library in SCSL, the auxiliaries should maintain the distributed, partitioned knowledge of which elements are in or out of the data structure. We pick the auxiliary PCM $(V \rightharpoonup_{\mathsf{fin}} \mathsf{bool}, \uplus, \emptyset)$ of finite partial maps from V to bool, with the join $\uplus$ taking the union of maps with disjoint domain, and the empty map $\emptyset$ as unit. Given such a finite map φ, the invariant $I_*\ (\varphi) \mathrel{\widehat{=}} \mathsf{set}(x, \varphi^{-1}[\mathsf{true}])$ states that the set contains exactly the elements that φ maps to true. We define $\mathsf{in}(v), \mathsf{out}(v) : V \rightharpoonup_{\mathsf{fin}} \mathsf{bool}$ to map v to true and false, respectively, and be undefined elsewhere.

Then we can prove cadd (and cremove similarly) as follows:

$$\begin{array}{ll} \{\mathsf{a_S} \rightarrowtail \mathsf{out}(v)\} & \text{precondition} \\ \{[\cancel{\mathsf{Own}}, \mathsf{out}(v), -]\ \mathsf{emp}\} & \text{by C}\textsc{onseq} \\ \mathsf{lock}; & \\ \{\exists \varphi_{\mathsf{O}}.[\cancel{\mathsf{Own}}, \mathsf{out}(v), \varphi_{\mathsf{O}}]\ I_*(\mathsf{out}(v) \uplus \varphi_{\mathsf{O}})\} & \text{by L}\textsc{ock} \\ \mathsf{sadd}(x, v); & \\ \{\exists \varphi_{\mathsf{O}}.[\cancel{\mathsf{Own}}, \mathsf{out}(v), \varphi_{\mathsf{O}}]\ I_*(\mathsf{in}(v) \uplus \varphi_{\mathsf{O}})\} & \text{by sadd} \\ \mathsf{unlock}_{\Phi_v}; & \\ \{[\cancel{\mathsf{Own}}, \mathsf{in}(v), -]\ \mathsf{emp}\} & \text{by U}\textsc{nlock} \\ \{\mathsf{a_S} \rightarrowtail \mathsf{in}(v)\} & \text{by C}\textsc{onseq} \end{array}$$

When the program locks, the environment's auxiliary φ_{O} comes into scope. The initial invariant $I_*(\mathsf{out}(v) \uplus \varphi_{\mathsf{O}})$ is equivalent to sadd's precondition with $\Sigma{=}(\mathsf{out}(v) \uplus \varphi_{\mathsf{O}})^{-1}[\mathsf{true}]{=}\varphi_{\mathsf{O}}^{-1}[\mathsf{true}]$; sadd's postcondition $\mathsf{set}(x, \varphi_{\mathsf{O}}^{-1}[\mathsf{true}] \uplus \{v\})$ restores the invariant $I_*(\mathsf{in}(v) \uplus \varphi_{\mathsf{O}})$. Unlocking turns $\mathsf{a_S}$ into $\Phi_v(\mathsf{out}(v)){=}\mathsf{in}(v)$, where

$$\Phi_v(\varphi) \mathrel{\widehat{=}} \lambda u. \begin{cases} \text{true} & u = v \text{ and } v \in \mathsf{dom}\ \varphi \\ \varphi(u) & u \neq v \text{ and } u, v \in \mathsf{dom}\ \varphi \\ \text{undefined} & \text{otherwise} \end{cases}$$

Φ_v turns a finite map φ with $v \in \mathsf{dom}\ \varphi$ into a φ' that behaves like φ on all elements, except that it maps v to true; if $v \notin \mathsf{dom}\ \varphi$, then $\Phi_v(\varphi)$ is undefined. It is straightforward to check that Φ_v is local.

3.2 Higher-order Iterator

We can prove a *higher-order* iterator that *dynamically forks* a procedure f (itself possibly concurrent) to process each element in a list.[8] In SCSL, we can prove the iterator with a *hypothetical* f:

$$\begin{array}{l} \forall n{:}A.\ \{\mathsf{a_S} \rightarrowtail \psi(n)\} f(n){:}\mathsf{unit}\{\mathsf{a_S} \rightarrowtail \phi(n)\} \\ \quad \vdash \forall ns{:}\mathsf{list}\ A.\ \{\mathsf{a_S} \rightarrowtail \overline{\psi}(ns)\}\mathsf{iter}(ns){:}\mathsf{unit}\{\mathsf{a_S} \rightarrowtail \overline{\phi}(ns)\} \end{array}$$

which assumes $f(n)$ changes the local auxiliary contribution from $\psi(n)$ to $\phi(n)$, relative to some ambient type A, PCM $(\mathbb{U}, \oplus, \mathbb{0})$, invariant I_*, and functions $\psi, \phi : A \to \mathbb{U}$. The overall effect of $\mathsf{iter}\ f\ ns$ is to change the local auxiliary contribution from $\overline{\psi}(ns)$ to $\overline{\phi}(ns)$, where $\overline{\psi}(ns)$ is $\bigoplus_{n \in ns} \psi(n)$ and similarly for $\overline{\phi}$.

By embedding SCSL into the type theory of the Calculus of Inductive Constructions (CiC) (Section 5), however, we can explicitly λ-abstract over f and give iter the specification (i.e., CiC type):

$$\begin{array}{l} \mathsf{iter} : \forall f{:}(\forall n{:}A.\ \{\!|\mathsf{a_S} \rightarrowtail \psi(n)|\!\}\mathsf{unit}\{\!|\mathsf{a_S} \rightarrowtail \phi(n)|\!\}). \\ \quad\quad \forall ns{:}\mathsf{list}\ A.\ \{\!|\mathsf{a_S} \rightarrowtail \overline{\psi}(ns)|\!\}\mathsf{unit}\{\!|\mathsf{a_S} \rightarrowtail \overline{\phi}(ns)|\!\} \end{array}$$

[8] We use pure lists and pattern-matching for clarity, although we can also prove the iterator for heap-allocated lists.

The proof outline for iter is:

$$
\begin{array}{l}
\mathsf{iter} \mathrel{\widehat{=}} \lambda f.\,\mathsf{fix\ loop}.\,ns. \\
\left(\begin{array}{l}
\mathsf{match}\ ns\ \mathsf{with} \\
\mid \mathsf{nil} \Rightarrow \{\mathsf{as} \rightarrowtail \overline{\psi}(\mathsf{nil})\}\ \mathsf{ret}\ ()\ \{\mathsf{as} \rightarrowtail \overline{\phi}(\mathsf{nil})\} \\
\mid n'{::}ns' \Rightarrow \\
\left(\begin{array}{c}
\{\mathsf{as} \rightarrowtail \overline{\psi}(n'{::}ns')\} \\
\{\mathsf{as} \rightarrowtail (\psi(n') \oplus \overline{\psi}(ns'))\} \\
\{\mathsf{as} \rightarrowtail \psi(n') \circledast \mathsf{as} \rightarrowtail \overline{\psi}(ns')\} \\
\begin{array}{c|c}
\{\mathsf{as} \rightarrowtail \psi(n')\} & \{\mathsf{as} \rightarrowtail \overline{\psi}(ns')\} \\
f\ n' & \mathsf{loop}\ ns' \\
\{\mathsf{as} \rightarrowtail \phi(n')\} & \{\mathsf{as} \rightarrowtail \overline{\phi}(ns')\}
\end{array} \\
\{\mathsf{as} \rightarrowtail \phi(n') \circledast \mathsf{as} \rightarrowtail \overline{\phi}(ns')\} \\
\{\mathsf{as} \rightarrowtail (\phi(n') \oplus \overline{\phi}(ns'))\} \\
\{\mathsf{as} \rightarrowtail \overline{\phi}(n'{::}ns')\} \\
\mathsf{ret}\ () \\
\{\mathsf{as} \rightarrowtail \overline{\phi}(n'{::}ns')\}
\end{array}\right)
\end{array}\right)
\end{array}
$$

iter is defined *recursively* by fix with two arguments: loop for recursive calls and the list ns. The body pattern-matches the list: for nil, it returns unit and the overall effect preserves the local contribution $\overline{\psi}(\mathsf{nil}) = \mathbb{0} = \overline{\phi}(\mathsf{nil})$; otherwise for $n'{::}ns'$, it concurrently applies f to the head element n' and recurses on the tail ns', then returns unit, so the contribution changes from $\overline{\psi}(n'{::}ns')$ to $\overline{\phi}(n'{::}ns')$.

Defining xincr2 to be either the sincr2 $\mathrel{\widehat{=}} \lambda n.(\mathsf{incr}(n); \mathsf{incr}(n))$ or cincr2 $\mathrel{\widehat{=}} \lambda n.(\mathsf{incr}(n) \parallel \mathsf{incr}(n))$ has the same effect of incrementing by twice the argument (Section 2.2), independently of whether the program is sequential or concurrent:

$$\forall n{:}\mathbb{N}.\{\mathsf{as} \rightarrowtail 0\}\ \mathsf{xincr2}(n)\ \{\mathsf{as} \rightarrowtail 2 \times n\}$$

Then, we can show that iterating xincr2 increments by twice the sum of the list, using $\psi(\_) = 0$ and $\phi(n) = 2 \times n$:

$$\forall ns{:}\mathsf{list}\ \mathbb{N}.\{\mathsf{as} \rightarrowtail 0\}\ \mathsf{iter\ xincr2}\ ns\ \{\mathsf{as} \rightarrowtail 2 \times \textstyle\sum_{n \in ns} n\}$$

Finally, we can iterate again to add up a list of lists of numbers, using $\psi(\_) = 0$ and $\phi(ns) = \sum_{n \in ns} n$ for the outer iter:

$$\forall nss{:}\mathsf{list}\ (\mathsf{list}\ \mathbb{N}).\{\mathsf{as} \rightarrowtail 0\}\ \mathsf{iter}\ (\mathsf{iter\ xincr2})\ nss\ \{\mathsf{as} \rightarrowtail 2 \times \sum_{n \in ns \in nss} n\}$$

We can also iterate the concurrent set cadd procedure to show that if initially none of the elements of the list are in the set, then afterwards all of the elements are in the list, using $\psi(v) = \mathsf{out}(v)$ and $\phi(v) = \mathsf{in}(v)$:

$$\forall vs{:}\mathsf{list}\ V.\{\mathsf{as} \rightarrowtail \overline{\mathsf{out}}(vs)\}\ \mathsf{iter\ cadd}\ vs\ \{\mathsf{as} \rightarrowtail \overline{\mathsf{in}}(vs)\}$$

Although iter has a dynamic forking pattern that depends on the list argument and although f may spawn multiple threads, subjective auxiliary state gives the iterator a *robust* specification. We can use the *same* proof of iter for different types of list elements (e.g., $\mathbb{N}$, list $\mathbb{N}$, and V), different lists (e.g., any number of elements), and procedures with different internal concurrency (e.g., one thread in sincr2, two threads in cincr2, and argument-dependent in (iter xincr2)).

4. Language and Logic

Language In the tradition of axiomatic program logics, the language of SCSL splits into purely-functional *expressions* e (v when the expression is a value), and *commands* C with effects of divergence, state, and concurrency, and *procedures* F for commands with arguments. Expressions are classified by types A, which, for the purposes of this section, range over base types unit, nat, bool, and pointers ptr (isomorphic to nat), all with the usual values.

The syntax of commands and procedures is:

$$
\begin{array}{rl}
C ::= & \mathsf{lock} \mid \mathsf{unlock}_{\Phi} \mid x \leftarrow C_1; C_2 \mid C_1 \parallel C_2 \\
& \mid \mathsf{if}\ e\ \mathsf{then}\ C_1\ \mathsf{else}\ C_2 \mid F(e) \\
F ::= & f \mid \mathsf{alloc} \mid \mathsf{dealloc} \mid \mathsf{read} \mid \mathsf{write} \mid \mathsf{ret} \mid \mathsf{fix}\, f.x.C
\end{array}
$$

Commands and procedures include memory and locking operations, a monadic unit ret v that returns v and terminates, a monadic bind (i.e., sequential composition) $x \leftarrow C_1;\ C_2$ runs C_1 then substitutes its result v_1 for x to run C_2 (we write $C_1; C_2$ when $x \notin \mathsf{FV}(C_2)$), fork-join parallel composition $C_1 \parallel C_2$, a conditional, a procedure application $F(e)$, a procedure variable f, or a fixed-point $\mathsf{fix}\, f.x.C$ for recursive procedures. Note that memory operations and ret are technically procedures because they take arguments.

Like in a monadic functional language, such as Haskell, commands return values. This enables avoiding mutable variables (i.e., a stack) in favor of immutable variables, which can be substituted with expressions. A stack imposes a number of technical difficulties in a Hoare-style logic [2, 23, 24], especially for supporting procedures [14], so we prefer to avoid it.

In Section 5, we embed SCSL into the Calculus of Inductive Constructions (CiC), which immediately provides us with a pure language of expressions and specifications-level objects such as assertions and auxiliary functions. The embedding also gives us access to arbitrary CiC inductive types (e.g., list) and constructs for pattern-matching against them. We can also write procedures that abstract over *commands* and *procedures* (*cf.* the iterator in Section 3.2). Presenting the full syntax of CiC is beyond the scope of this paper, so we only present the fragment relevant to effectful programs and Hoare-style reasoning about them.

Specifications SCSL is parametrized in the auxiliary PCM $\mathbb{U}$ and a resource invariant I_* index by $\mathbb{U}$ that describes the single, global resource protected by the lock and unlock commands.

A command C satisfies the Hoare triple $\{p\}C : A\{q\}$ if it respects mutual exclusion and is memory-safe when executed from a world satisfying p, and concurrently with *any* environment that respects mutual exclusion. Furthermore, if C terminates, it returns a value of type A in a world satisfying q. q may use a dedicated variable res of type A to name the return result.

We use a *procedure triple*, $\forall x{:}B.\ \{p\}F\ (x) : A\{q\}$, to specify a potentially recursive procedure F taking an argument x of type B to a result of type A. The assertions p and q may depend on x. We use Cartesian products $A_1 \times A_2$ for functions with more than one argument, but curry the function for readability.

The SCSL judgments are *hypothetical* under a context Γ that maps *program variables* x to their type and *procedure variables* f to their specification. Each specification is allowed to depend on the variables declared to the left.

$$\Gamma ::= \cdot \mid \Gamma, x{:}A \mid \Gamma, \forall x{:}B.\{p\}f(x) : A\{q\}$$

Γ does not bind logical variables. In first-order Hoare logics, logical variables are implicitly universally quantified with global scope. In SCSL, we limit their scope to the Hoare triple in which they appear. This is required for specifying recursive procedures, where a logical variable may be instantiated differently in each recursive call [14]. We also assume a formation requirement on Hoare triples $\mathsf{FLV}(p) \supseteq \mathsf{FLV}(q)$, i.e., that all free logical variables of the postcondition also appear in the precondition.

Figure 3 presents the inference rules for the SCSL judgments for Hoare triples $\Gamma \vdash \{p\}\ C : A\ \{q\}$ and $\Gamma \vdash \forall x : B.\{p\}\ F\ (x) : A\{q\}$. We have discussed the memory and locking commands in Section 2, so we proceed to describe the remaining inference rules.

Parallel composition The parallel composition $C_1 \parallel C_2$ forks into two children threads for C_1 and C_2, and when they terminate with return values v_i of type A_i, the threads are joined into a single return of the pair (v_1, v_2) of type $A_1 \times A_2$. The rule reads as follows: (1) the parallel composition precondition $p_1 \circledast p_2$ can be split into p_1 and p_2, (2) each thread C_i must be verified separately with precondition p_i and postcondition q_i, and (3) the postconditions q_1 and q_2 can be recombined into the parallel composition postcondi-

$$
\begin{array}{llll}
\Gamma \vdash \forall x{:}A. & \{[\mu,\sigma,\omega]\,\mathsf{emp}\} & \mathsf{alloc}\ x : \mathsf{ptr} & \{[\mu,\sigma,\mathsf{if}\ \mu = \mathsf{Own}\ \mathsf{then}\ \omega\ \mathsf{else}\ -]\ \mathsf{res} \mapsto x\} \\
\Gamma \vdash \forall x{:}\mathsf{ptr}. & \{[\mu,\sigma,\omega]\,x \mapsto -\} & \mathsf{dealloc}\ x : \mathsf{unit} & \{[\mu,\sigma,\mathsf{if}\ \mu = \mathsf{Own}\ \mathsf{then}\ \omega\ \mathsf{else}\ -]\ \mathsf{emp}\} \\
\Gamma \vdash \forall x{:}\mathsf{ptr}. & \{[\mu,\sigma,\omega]\,x \mapsto \nu\} & \mathsf{read}\ x : A & \{[\mu,\sigma,\mathsf{if}\ \mu = \mathsf{Own}\ \mathsf{then}\ \omega\ \mathsf{else}\ -]\ x \mapsto \nu \wedge \mathsf{res} = \nu\} \\
\Gamma \vdash \forall x{:}\mathsf{ptr}.\forall y{:}A. & \{[\mu,\sigma,\omega]\,x \mapsto -\} & \mathsf{write}\ x\ y : \mathsf{unit} & \{[\mu,\sigma,\mathsf{if}\ \mu = \mathsf{Own}\ \mathsf{then}\ \omega\ \mathsf{else}\ -]\ x \mapsto y\} \\
\Gamma \vdash & \{[\cancel{\mathsf{Own}},\sigma,-]\,\mathsf{emp}\} & \mathsf{lock} : \mathsf{unit} & \{\exists \omega.[\mathsf{Own},\sigma,\omega]\ I_*\ (\sigma \oplus \omega)\} \\
\Gamma \vdash & \{[\mathsf{Own},\sigma,\omega]\ I_*\ (\Phi(\sigma) \oplus \omega)\} & \mathsf{unlock}_\Phi : \mathsf{unit} & \{[\cancel{\mathsf{Own}},\Phi(\sigma),-]\,\mathsf{emp}\} \\
\Gamma \vdash \forall x{:}A. & \{[\mu,\sigma,\omega]\,\mathsf{emp}\} & \mathsf{ret}\ x : A & \{[\mu,\sigma,\mathsf{if}\ \mu = \mathsf{Own}\ \mathsf{then}\ \omega\ \mathsf{else}\ -]\ \mathsf{emp} \wedge \mathsf{res} = x\}
\end{array}
$$

$$
\frac{\begin{array}{c}\Gamma \vdash \{e = \mathsf{true} \wedge p\} C_1 : A\{q\} \\ \Gamma \vdash \{e = \mathsf{false} \wedge p\} C_2 : A\{q\}\end{array}}{\Gamma \vdash \{p\}\mathsf{if}\ e\ \mathsf{then}\ C_1\ \mathsf{else}\ C_2 : A\{q\}}\ \textsc{If}
\qquad
\frac{\Gamma \vdash \{p_1\} C : A\{q_1\} \quad \Gamma \vdash \{p_2\} C : A\{q_2\}}{\Gamma \vdash \{p_1 \wedge p_2\} C : A\{q_1 \wedge q_2\}}\ \textsc{Conj}
\qquad
\frac{\Gamma \vdash \{p\} C : A\{q\} \quad \alpha \notin \mathsf{dom}\ \Gamma}{\Gamma \vdash \{\exists \alpha{:}A.p\} C : A\{\exists \alpha{:}A.q\}}\ \textsc{Exist}
$$

$$
\frac{\Gamma \vdash \{p_1\} C : A\{q_1\} \quad \Gamma \vdash (p_1, q_1) \sqsubseteq (p_2, q_2)}{\Gamma \vdash \{p_2\} C : A\{q_2\}}\ \textsc{Conseq}
\qquad
\frac{\Gamma \vdash \{p\} C : A\{q\}}{\Gamma \vdash \{p \circledast r\} C : A\{q \circledast r\}}\ \textsc{Frame}
$$

$$
\frac{\Gamma \vdash \{p\} C_1 : B\{q\} \quad \Gamma, x{:}B \vdash \{[x/\mathsf{res}]q\} C_2 : A\{r\} \quad x \notin \mathsf{FV}(r)}{\Gamma \vdash \{p\} x \leftarrow C_1; C_2 : A\{r\}}\ \textsc{Seq}
\qquad
\frac{\Gamma \vdash \{p_1\} C_1 : A_1\{q_1\} \quad \Gamma \vdash \{p_2\} C_2 : A_2\{q_2\}}{\Gamma \vdash \{p_1 \circledast p_2\} C_1 \parallel C_2 : A_1 \times A_2\{[\mathsf{res}.1/\mathsf{res}]q_1 \circledast [\mathsf{res}.2/\mathsf{res}]q_2\}}\ \textsc{Par}
$$

$$
\frac{\forall x{:}B.\{p\} f(x) : A\{q\} \in \Gamma}{\Gamma \vdash \forall x{:}B.\{p\} f(x) : A\{q\}}\ \textsc{Hyp}
\qquad
\frac{\Gamma, \forall x{:}B.\{p\} f(x) : A\{q\}, x{:}B \vdash \{p\} C : A\{q\}}{\Gamma \vdash \forall x{:}B.\{p\}(\mathsf{fix}\,f.x.C)(x) : A\{q\}}\ \textsc{Fix}
\qquad
\frac{\Gamma \vdash \forall x{:}B.\{p\} F(x) : A\{q\} \quad \Gamma \vdash e : B}{\Gamma \vdash \{[e/x]p\} F(e) : A\{[e/x]q\}}\ \textsc{App}
$$

Figure 3. Subjective CSL rules $\Gamma \vdash \{p\} C : A\{q\}$ and $\Gamma \vdash \forall x{:}B.\{p\} F(x) : A\{q\}$.

tion $q_1 \circledast q_2$, with the projections from the resulting pair substituted for the dedicated variable res.

The precondition $p_1 \circledast p_2$ expresses that the initial world for the parent thread has the form $h_1 \oplus h_2; \mu_1 \oplus \mu_2; \sigma_1 \oplus \sigma_2; \omega$. The left child receives the world $h_1; \mu_1; \sigma_1; \sigma_2 \oplus \omega$ in its precondition p_1, and dually for the right child and p_2. The splitting of h, μ and σ components reflects that the children divide the local heap and contribution of the parent thread. The left child's environment contribution $\sigma_2 \oplus \omega$ reflects that upon forking C_2 becomes part of C_1's environment, and a dual remark applies to the right child.

The parallel composition rule thus states that if a partition satisfying the preconditions can be found of the initial world, then a partition satisfying both postconditions can be found of the ending world. Intuitively, the rule is sound because the required partition of the ending state can be obtained by executing C_1, C_2, and their common environment in an interleaved manner, while updating their respective values of $\mathsf{a_S}$ and $\mathsf{a_O}$. Whenever one thread's $\mathsf{a_S} \rightarrowtail \sigma_i$ is updated, the $\mathsf{a_O} \hookrightarrow \omega_j$'s of the other two threads must be updated correspondingly in order to preserve the coherence between views, that is, that every thread i sees the same total $\tau = \sigma_i \oplus \omega_i$.

Fixed points We support a combinator fix for general recursion, rather than just while-loops. The iterator (Section 3.2) requires fix because of its dynamic forking structure; it isn't tail recursive and thus difficult to write using a while-loop. The inference rule requires proving a Hoare triple for the procedure body, under a hypothesis that the recursive calls satisfy the same triple. In practice, when writing recursive programs, the assertions p and q have to be supplied by hand (they cannot be inferred automatically), and they essentially correspond to a loop invariant.

Framing The FRAME rule allows splitting the world into $p \circledast r$, verifying the command with precondition p and postcondition q, then recombining the postcondition with the framed world into $q \circledast r$. Note that the rule uses $\circledast$ which allows auxiliaries to also be framed. Somewhat surprisingly, the auxiliary PCM $\mathbb{U}$ need not be *cancellative*.[9] This allows us to prove a concurrent maximum program (not shown) that uses the PCM $(\mathbb{N}, \max, 0)$ which is *not* cancellative, yet we can frame the thread's auxiliary contribution.

[9] Cancellativity means that if $\alpha \oplus \beta = \beta \oplus \gamma$, then $\beta = \gamma$; a property that the heap PCM satisfies and is often associated with the FRAME rule.

Cancellativity for *heaps* is required in the soundness proofs for CSL (and SCSL) in order to uniquely determine the heap transfered between the thread and the shared resource upon locking and unlocking [19, 3]. In SCSL, the auxiliary PCM need not be cancellative, because there is no analogous transfer of auxiliaries.

Other Rules The procedure APPlication rule uses the typing judgment for expressions $\Gamma \vdash e : A$, which is the customary one from a typed λ-calculus, so we omit its rules; in Section 5, this judgment will correspond to CiC's typing judgment.

The CONSEQ rule uses the judgment $\Gamma \vdash (p_1, q_1) \sqsubseteq (p_2, q_2)$, which generalizes the customary side conditions $p_2 \Rightarrow p_1$ for strengthening the precondition and $q_1 \Rightarrow q_2$ for weakening the postcondition, to deal with the local scope of logical variables (*cf.* Section 5.4). The other rules are standard from Hoare logic.

5. Semantics

We define semantic objects of *actions* for heap mutation and *action trees* for control flow, which yield finite, partial *approximations* of the behavior of SCSL commands; their *operational semantics* gives the low-level execution relative to the full heap (Section 5.1). We define the high-level notions of *coherent configuration* to maintain an explicit partition between the shared state heaplet and the thread's and environment's private heaplets and auxiliaries, and *subjective rely/guarantee* transitions between configurations for environment and thread interference that respect *mutual exclusion* (Section 5.2). Both the operational semantics and subjective rely/guarantee transitions use a large footprint, although SCSL enjoys small footprint specifications.

We relate the low-level operational semantics to the high-level subjective rely/guarantee transitions by a *modal* always predicate (Section 5.3) that ensures a tree is resilient to any amount of subjective rely interference, and that all operational steps by a tree are memory-safe and correspond to subjective guarantee interference.

The denotational semantics (Section 5.4) interprets judgments by the *monadic Hoare type* $\{\!|p|\!\}A\{\!|q|\!\}$, which is a *complete lattice* of trees that are always-safe to run from any initial configuration that satisfies precondition p and if they terminate produce a final configuration that satisfies postcondition q. The complete lattice structure makes the semantic domain suitable for modeling recursion. A command is denoted by the set of its tree approximations, and a procedure is denoted by a function into a set of trees.

$$\frac{\ell \notin \mathsf{dom}\,h}{h;\mathsf{Alloc}\;v \rightsquigarrow_{\mathsf{a}} [h|\ell \Rightarrow v];\ell} \qquad \frac{\ell \in \mathsf{dom}\,h}{h;\mathsf{Dealloc}\;\ell \rightsquigarrow_{\mathsf{a}} h \setminus \ell;()}$$

$$\frac{h(\ell) = v : A}{h;\mathsf{Read}_A\;\ell \rightsquigarrow_{\mathsf{a}} h;v} \qquad \frac{\ell \in \mathsf{dom}\,h}{h;\mathsf{Write}\;\ell\;v \rightsquigarrow_{\mathsf{a}} [h|\ell \Rightarrow v];()} \qquad \frac{}{h;\mathsf{Idle} \rightsquigarrow_{\mathsf{a}} h;()}$$

$$\frac{h(\ell) = v_1}{h;\mathsf{CAS}\;\ell\;v_1\;v_2 \rightsquigarrow_{\mathsf{a}} [h|\ell \Rightarrow v_2];\mathsf{true}} \qquad \frac{h(\ell) = v \qquad v \neq v_1}{h;\mathsf{CAS}\;x\;v_1\;v_2 \rightsquigarrow_{\mathsf{a}} h;\mathsf{false}}$$

$$\frac{h;a \rightsquigarrow_{\mathsf{a}} h';v}{h;\mathsf{Cons}\;a\;\Phi\;k \overset{\mathsf{nil}}{\rightsquigarrow}_{\mathsf{t}} h';(k\;v)} \qquad \frac{}{h;\mathsf{Par}\;(\mathsf{Ret}\;v_1)\;(\mathsf{Ret}\;v_2)\;k \overset{\mathsf{nil}}{\rightsquigarrow}_{\mathsf{t}} h;k\;(v_1,v_2)}$$

$$\frac{h;t_1 \overset{\pi}{\rightsquigarrow}_{\mathsf{t}} h';t_1'}{h;\mathsf{Par}\;t_1\;t_2\;k \overset{\mathsf{L}::\pi}{\rightsquigarrow}_{\mathsf{t}} h';\mathsf{Par}\;t_1'\;t_2\;k} \qquad \frac{h;t_2 \overset{\pi}{\rightsquigarrow}_{\mathsf{t}} h';t_2'}{h;\mathsf{Par}\;t_1\;t_2\;k \overset{\mathsf{R}::\pi}{\rightsquigarrow}_{\mathsf{t}} h';\mathsf{Par}\;t_1\;t_2'\;k}$$

Figure 4. Action stepping $h;a \rightsquigarrow_{\mathsf{a}} h';v$ (top) and tree stepping $h;t \overset{\pi}{\rightsquigarrow}_{\mathsf{t}} h';t'$ (bottom).

The *soundness* of SCSL (Section 5.5) follows from showing that the denotation of memory operations satisfy the appropriate always predicate, and that always satisfies certain closure conditions. In Section 6, we discuss the relationship of our denotational semantics to existing semantics for CSL.

We choose the Calculus of Inductive Constructions (CiC) [18] as our meta logic. This has several important benefits. First, we can define a *shallow embedding* of SCSL into CiC that allows us to program and prove directly *with the semantic objects*, thus immediately lifting SCSL to a full-blown programming language and verification system with higher-order functions, abstract types, abstract predicates, and a module system. We also gain a powerful dependently-typed λ-calculus, which we use to formalize all semantic definitions and metatheory, including the definition of action trees by *iterated inductive definitions* [17, 18], specification-level functions (e.g., auxiliary functions Φ), and programming-level higher-order procedures (e.g., the iterator). Finally, we were able to mechanize the entire semantics and metatheory [16] in the Coq proof assistant implementation of CiC.

We use set-theoretic and type-theoretic notation as appropriate. The reader unconcerned with the fine points of the type theory, may read a typing judgment $x{:}A$ as a set membership predicate $x \in A$.

5.1 Actions, Trees, and Operational Semantics

The type family action A of A-returning **actions** includes constructors for the SCSL memory commands, an idle action returning unit, and a compare-and-swap CAS used to implement locking:

$$\begin{array}{llll} \mathsf{Alloc}\;(v{:}B) & : \mathsf{action\ ptr} & \mathsf{Read}_A\;(x{:}\mathsf{ptr}) & : \mathsf{action}\;A \\ \mathsf{Dealloc}\;(x{:}\mathsf{ptr}) & : \mathsf{action\ unit} & \mathsf{Write}\;(x{:}\mathsf{ptr})\;(v{:}B) & : \mathsf{action\ unit} \\ \mathsf{Idle} & & : \mathsf{action\ unit} & \\ \multicolumn{4}{l}{\mathsf{CAS}\;(x{:}\mathsf{ptr})\;(v_1{:}B)\;(v_2{:}B) : \mathsf{action\ bool}} \end{array}$$

The operational semantics of actions $h;a \rightsquigarrow_{\mathsf{a}} h';v$ (Figure 4, top) steps an A-returning action a relative to an initial heap h, and produces an ending heap h' and result v of type A. The operational semantics of the basic memory operations is standard. The CAS action takes a pointer ℓ and two values v_1 and v_2, it atomically checks whether ℓ contains v_1 and, if so, replaces it with v_2 and returns true; otherwise, it preserves the heap and returns false.

The type family tree A of A-returning **trees** is defined by an *iterated inductive definition*:

$$\begin{array}{ll} \mathsf{Bottom} & : \mathsf{tree}\;A \\ \mathsf{Ret}\;(v{:}A) & : \mathsf{tree}\;A \\ \mathsf{Cons}\;(a{:}\mathsf{action}\;B)\;(\Phi{:}\mathbb{U} \rightharpoonup_{\mathsf{L}} \mathbb{U})(k{:}B \to \mathsf{tree}\;A) & : \mathsf{tree}\;A \\ \mathsf{Par}\;(t_1{:}\mathsf{tree}\;B_1)\;(t_2{:}\mathsf{tree}\;B_2)\;(k{:}B_1 \times B_2 \to \mathsf{tree}\;A) & : \mathsf{tree}\;A \end{array}$$

Since trees have finite depth, they can only *approximate* divergent computations, thus the Bottom tree indicates an incomplete approximation. Ret v is a terminal computation that returns value $v : A$. Cons $a\;\Phi\;k$ sequentially composes a B-returning action a with a continuation k that takes a's return value and generates the rest of the approximation; the tree also carries a local auxiliary function $\Phi{:}\mathbb{U} \rightharpoonup_{\mathsf{L}} \mathbb{U}$ for mutating auxiliary state (Section 5.2). Par $t_1\;t_2\;k$ is the parallel composition of trees t_1 and t_2, and a continuation k that takes the pair of their results when they join. CiC's iterated inductive definition permits the recursive occurrences of tree to be *nonuniform* (e.g., tree B_i in Par) and *nested* (e.g., the *positive* occurrence of tree A in the continuation). Since the CiC function space $\to$ includes case-analysis, the continuation may branch upon the argument, which captures the pure computation of conditionals. This closely corresponds to the operational intuition and leads to a straightforward denotational semantics.

To explicitly quantify over the nondeterminism of concurrent interleaving, we define a schedule ζ to be a list of paths, where a path π is a list of L or R symbols that traverse the Left or Right branches of Par trees and select a β-redex (i.e., an action or the parallel composition of two Ret trees).

The small-step operational semantics of trees $h;t \overset{\pi}{\rightsquigarrow}_{\mathsf{t}} h',t'$ (Figure 4, bottom) is defined inductively on π to step tree t from initial heap h to a reduced tree t' in ending heap h'. Stepping is undefined for the Bottom and Ret trees. For the Cons and Par trees, the path π selects a β-redex and performs the appropriate reduction. Note that only the heap and action in the tree are needed to define stepping, which captures the intuition that auxiliary state $\mathbb{U}$ and auxiliary functions Φ have no bearing on the operational semantics.

The denotation of SCSL Hoare triples will establish that "well-specified programs don't go wrong". We follow a Milner-style approach where only well-typed (i.e., well-specified) programs are given meaning and ensure that every action and tree encountered in the operational semantics is memory-safe relative to the given heap; thus we can avoid explicit fault states in the operational semantics and defining the semantics of unsafe programs.

Definition 2 (Action and auxiliary function at a path)**.** *Given a tree t and path π, the action a and local auxiliary function Φ appear in t at path π, written $(a, \Phi) = t \mathbin{@} \pi$, iff*

$$\begin{array}{llll} & \pi = \mathsf{nil} & \textit{and}\; t = \mathsf{Cons}\;a\;\Phi\;k & \\ \textit{or} & \pi = \mathsf{nil} & \textit{and}\; t = \mathsf{Par}\;(\mathsf{Ret}\;\_)\;(\mathsf{Ret}\;\_)\;k & \textit{and}\;(a,\Phi) = (\mathsf{Idle}, \mathsf{id}) \\ \textit{or} & \pi = \mathsf{L}::\pi' & \textit{and}\; t = \mathsf{Par}\;t_1\;\_\;\_ & \textit{and}\;(a,\Phi) = t_1 \mathbin{@} \pi' \\ \textit{or} & \pi = \mathsf{R}::\pi' & \textit{and}\; t = \mathsf{Par}\;\_\;t_2\;\_ & \textit{and}\;(a,\Phi) = t_2 \mathbin{@} \pi' \end{array}$$

We write $a = t \mathbin{@} \pi$ instead of $(a, -) = t \mathbin{@} \pi$ when we are interested only in the action a, and likewise for Φ.

Definition 3 (Safety)**.** *1. Action a is safe for the heap h, if there exist h' and v such that $h; a \rightsquigarrow_{\mathsf{a}} h', v$.*

2. Tree t is safe for a heap h and path π, if $a = t@\pi$ implies that a is safe for h.

3. Tree t is safe for a heap h and a schedule ζ if either (1) $\zeta = \mathsf{nil}$, or (2) if $\zeta = \pi{::}\zeta'$ then t is safe for h and π, and t' is safe for h' and ζ' for all h' and t' such that $h;t \overset{\pi}{\rightsquigarrow}_{\mathsf{t}} h';t'$.

4. Tree t is safe for a heap h, written memsafe $h\;t$*, if it is safe for h, for any schedule ζ.*

Intuitively, t is memory-safe for heap h if no matter which steps one takes through t starting from h, the actions in the tree will not attempt to dereference a non-existent or ill-typed memory cell, or deallocate an unallocated cell. Bottom and Ret trees are trivially safe because they don't step. A Cons tree is safe if it's head action is safe and the continuation is safe. A Par tree is safe if both of it's subtrees are safe, and when they return the continuation is safe.

5.2 Coherent Configurations and Subjective Rely/Guarantee

The operational semantics yields execution over the full heap, but doesn't contain enough information for enforcing SCSL specifications regarding mutual exclusion for critical sections over the resource invariant and auxiliaries. We need to extend heaps with additional information which is the *logical state* of SCSL.

We define *coherent configurations* $(h_\mathsf{S}; \mu_\mathsf{S}; \sigma_\mathsf{S} \mid h_\mathsf{R} \mid h_\mathsf{O}; \mu_\mathsf{O}; \sigma_\mathsf{O})$ consisting of the thread's private heap h_S, lock ownership status μ_S, and auxiliary σ_S; the shared heap h_R containing the dedicated lock location lk and the shared resource satisfying the resource invariant I_*; and the environment's private state h_O, μ_O, and σ_O. Subjectivity thus appears in the semantics as the logical partition of heaps, lock ownership status, and auxiliaries from the point of view of the thread being specified. Although environment threads have their own private states, the configuration conflates them into a single private state for the environment as a whole.

Coherent configurations are defined relative to the user-chosen auxiliary PCM $\mathbb{U}$ and resource invariant I_* over $\mathbb{U}$ and heap such that $I_*\ (\alpha)$ is *precise*[10] for all $\alpha \in \mathbb{U}$. As in CSL, precision is required to uniquely determine the invariant heaplet to be transferred between the shared and private heaplets. Moreover, we assume a reserved location lk for implementing the lock.

Definition 4 (Coherent Configuration). *A* coherent configuration *is a 7-tuple* $c = (h_\mathsf{S}; \mu_\mathsf{O}; \sigma_\mathsf{O} \mid h_\mathsf{R} \mid h_\mathsf{O}; \mu_\mathsf{O}; \sigma_\mathsf{O})$ *such that:*

1. $\mathsf{valid}\ (h_\mathsf{S} \oplus h_\mathsf{R} \oplus h_\mathsf{O})$, $\mathsf{valid}\ (\mu_\mathsf{S} \oplus \mu_\mathsf{O})$, $\mathsf{valid}\ (\sigma_\mathsf{S} \oplus \sigma_\mathsf{O})$
2. $\mu_\mathsf{S} \oplus \mu_\mathsf{O} = \overline{\mathsf{Own}} \Rightarrow h_\mathsf{R} \models_\mathsf{SL} \mathsf{lk} \mapsto \mathsf{false} * I_*\ (\sigma_\mathsf{S} \oplus \sigma_\mathsf{O})$
3. $\mu_\mathsf{S} \oplus \mu_\mathsf{O} = \mathsf{Own} \Rightarrow h_\mathsf{R} \models_\mathsf{SL} \mathsf{lk} \mapsto \mathsf{true}$

Intuitively, all components of a configuration join in a valid way (1). Mutual exclusion means that (2) when nobody owns lk ($\mu_\mathsf{S} \oplus \mu_\mathsf{O} = \overline{\mathsf{Own}}$), then the shared heap contains the lock lk set to false and a heaplet satisfying $I_*(\sigma_\mathsf{S} \oplus \sigma_\mathsf{O})$ relative to the total auxiliary; and (3) if either the thread or its environment owns lk ($\mu_\mathsf{S} \oplus \mu_\mathsf{O} = \mathsf{Own}$), then the shared heap only contains the lock lk set to true because the owner has acquired the invariant heaplet.

The large footprint configuration is needed to define the transitions and establish the soundness of the logic. However, the operational semantics only uses the full heap $h_\mathsf{S} \oplus h_\mathsf{R} \oplus h_\mathsf{O}$, and the assertions only require the small footprint of the world $h_\mathsf{S}; \mu_\mathsf{S}; \sigma_\mathsf{S}; \sigma_\mathsf{O}$. Recall that the environment's auxiliary σ_O is needed in the critical section to establish its invariance and prove that I_* is preserved (*cf.* the proof of incr in Section 2.4); but the environment's components h_O and μ_O are omitted from assertions because they are not needed for local verification of a thread.

Definition 5. *A configuration* $c = (h_\mathsf{S}; \mu_\mathsf{S}; \sigma_\mathsf{S} \mid h_\mathsf{R} \mid h_\mathsf{O}; \mu_\mathsf{O}; \sigma_\mathsf{O})$ *has heap* $\mathsf{hp}(c) \mathrel{\widehat{=}} h_\mathsf{S} \oplus h_\mathsf{R} \oplus h_\mathsf{O}$ *and world* $\mathsf{wd}(c) \mathrel{\widehat{=}} h_\mathsf{S}; \mu_\mathsf{S}; \sigma_\mathsf{S}; \sigma_\mathsf{O}$.

Given the spatial description of configurations, we can define the temporal notions of *subjective rely/guarantee* transitions $\leadsto^*_\mathsf{R}$ and $\overset{\Phi}{\leadsto}_\mathsf{G}$ for environment and thread interference on a configuration that respect mutual exclusion and auxiliary updates.

Definition 6 (Subjective guarantee). *The* subjective guarantee *transition* $c \overset{\Phi}{\leadsto}_\mathsf{G} c'$ *holds relative to* $\Phi : \mathbb{U} \rightharpoonup_\mathsf{L} \mathbb{U}$ *if the configurations* c *and* c' *have one of the forms (where* $d_\mathsf{O} = h_\mathsf{O}; \mu_\mathsf{O}; \sigma_\mathsf{O}$*):*

Priv	$c = (h_\mathsf{S}$	$; \mu_\mathsf{S}\ ; \sigma_\mathsf{S}$	$\mid h_\mathsf{R}$	$\mid d_\mathsf{O})$
	$c' = (h'_\mathsf{S}$	$; \mu_\mathsf{S}\ ; \sigma_\mathsf{S}$	$\mid h_\mathsf{R}$	$\mid d_\mathsf{O})$
Acq	$c = (h_\mathsf{S}$	$; \overline{\mathsf{Own}}; \sigma_\mathsf{S}$	$\mid [\mathsf{lk} \Mapsto \mathsf{false}] \oplus h_\mathsf{inv}$	$\mid d_\mathsf{O})$
	$c' = (h_\mathsf{S} \oplus h_\mathsf{inv}$	$; \mathsf{Own}; \sigma_\mathsf{S}$	$\mid [\mathsf{lk} \Mapsto \mathsf{true}]$	$\mid d_\mathsf{O})$
Rel	$c = (h_\mathsf{S} \oplus h_\mathsf{inv}$	$; \mathsf{Own}; \sigma_\mathsf{S}$	$\mid [\mathsf{lk} \Mapsto \mathsf{true}]$	$\mid d_\mathsf{O})$
	$c' = (h_\mathsf{S}$	$; \overline{\mathsf{Own}}; \Phi(\sigma_\mathsf{S})$	$\mid [\mathsf{lk} \Mapsto \mathsf{false}] \oplus h_\mathsf{inv}$	$\mid d_\mathsf{O})$

Subjective guarantee transitions correspond to the changes that a thread can perform: mutation on the thread's Private heap, Acquiring the resource by locking and transferring the invariant heaplet from the shared state to the thread's private heap, and dually Releasing the resource. In the last case, the auxiliary function Φ uniquely determines how to change the thread's view σ_S. Note that in any case, the environment's private state is preserved.

The environment threads make complementary transitions on the shared state and the environment's private state. However, as we will define Hoare triples to abstract over arbitrary environment interference, a coarser view suffices to describe mutual exclusion.

Definition 7 (Subjective rely). *The* subjective rely *transition* $c \leadsto^*_\mathsf{R} c'$ *holds if the configurations have the form* $c = (h_\mathsf{S}; \mu_\mathsf{S}; \sigma_\mathsf{S} \mid h_\mathsf{R} \mid h_\mathsf{O}; \mu_\mathsf{O}; \sigma_\mathsf{O})$ *and* $c' = (h_\mathsf{S}; \mu_\mathsf{S}; \sigma_\mathsf{S} \mid h'_\mathsf{R} \mid h'_\mathsf{O}; \mu'_\mathsf{O}; \sigma'_\mathsf{O})$*, and if* $\mu_\mathsf{S} = \mathsf{Own}$ *then* $\sigma'_\mathsf{O} = \sigma_\mathsf{O}$.

A subjective rely transition represents arbitrary environment interference that respects mutual exclusion. The environment can mutate its private state and the shared state arbitrarily as long as coherence is preserved. If the thread Owns the lock, then the environment's auxiliary must remain fixed. Intuitively, $\leadsto^*_\mathsf{R}$ is the *reflexive-transitive* closure of the *transpose* of $\leadsto_\mathsf{G}$, i.e., where mutation is done on the environment's private state instead of the thread's private state, and with any possible auxiliary function Φ. Note that in any case, the thread's private state is preserved.

5.3 Modal Predicates

We next define a number of *modal* predicates over *all* possible steps of execution to relate the operational semantics over heaps and the subjective rely/guarantee transitions over coherent configurations.

Definition 8 (Modal predicates). *The predicates* $\mathsf{always}^\zeta\ c\ t\ p$, $\mathsf{always}\ c\ t\ P$*, and* $\mathsf{after}\ c\ t\ Q$ *are defined relative to a schedule* ζ*, configuration* c*, A-returning tree* t*, and predicates* $P : \mathsf{config} \to \mathsf{tree}\ A \to \mathsf{prop}$ *and* $Q : \mathsf{config} \to A \to \mathsf{prop}$*:*

$$\begin{array}{l}\mathsf{always}^\zeta\ c\ t\ P \mathrel{\widehat{=}} \\ \quad \forall c_\mathsf{R}.\ c \leadsto^*_\mathsf{R} c_\mathsf{R} \Rightarrow \\ \qquad \left(\begin{array}{l}\mathsf{memsafe}\ (\mathsf{hp}(c_\mathsf{R}))\ t \wedge P\ c_\mathsf{R}\ t \wedge \\ \forall \pi\ \zeta'\ h_\mathsf{G}\ t'.\ \zeta = \pi{::}\zeta' \ \wedge\ \mathsf{hp}(c_\mathsf{R}); t \overset{\pi}{\leadsto}_\mathsf{t} h_\mathsf{G}; t' \Rightarrow \\ \qquad \left(\begin{array}{r}\exists c_\mathsf{G}\ \Phi.\ \mathsf{hp}(c_\mathsf{G}) = h_\mathsf{G} \wedge \Phi = t \mathbin{@} \pi \wedge \\ c_\mathsf{R} \overset{\Phi}{\leadsto}_\mathsf{G} c_\mathsf{G} \wedge \mathsf{always}^{\zeta'}\ c_\mathsf{G}\ t'\ P\end{array}\right)\end{array}\right) \\ \ \ \mathsf{always}\ c\ t\ P \mathrel{\widehat{=}} \forall \zeta.\ \mathsf{always}^\zeta\ c\ t\ P \\ \quad \mathsf{after}\ c\ t\ Q \mathrel{\widehat{=}} \mathsf{always}\ c\ t\ (\lambda c'\ t'.\ \forall v'.\ t' = \mathsf{Ret}\ v' \Rightarrow Q\ c'\ v')\end{array}$$

$\mathsf{always}\ c\ t\ P$ expresses the fact that starting from configuration c, the tree t remains memory-safe and the user-chosen predicate P holds of all intermediate configurations and trees, for any schedule ζ and under any environment interference. The helper predicate $\mathsf{always}^\zeta\ c\ t\ P$ is defined by induction on ζ: the environment is allowed to make arbitrary subjective rely interference from c to c_R, the resulting configuration must have a heap that's memory safe for t and the predicate $P\ c_\mathsf{R}\ t$ holds; moreover, if the schedule is $\pi{::}\zeta'$ and t steps to h_G and t', then there must be a subjective guarantee transition from c_R to c_G whose heap is h_G, and the predicate recurses on ζ', c_G, and t'. Mutual exclusion is thus ensured because all transitions conform to subjective rely/guarantee transitions.

$\mathsf{after}\ c\ t\ Q$ encodes that t is memory safe and respects mutual exclusion; however, $Q\ c'\ v'$ only holds if t steps completely to $\mathsf{Ret}\ v'$ in configuration c'.

---

[10] A heap predicate p is *precise* if it determines a unique subheap: for every heap h with subheaps h_1, h_2, if $h_1 \models_\mathsf{SL} p$ and $h_2 \models_\mathsf{SL} p$ then $h_1 = h_2$.

5.4 SCSL Denotational Semantics

The denotational semantics of SCSL commands and judgments are defined simultaneously. The mutual recursion is neccessary because the denotation of judgments depends on the denotation of commands and procedures, while the denotation of a fixed point procedure depends on the denotation of its procedure triple to determine the lattice in which to take the fixed point.

We denote SCSL programs as *sets* T of trees of increasing precision including the Bottom tree, which is the coarsest possible approximation of any program:

$$\mathsf{prog}\ A \ \widehat{=}\ \{T \subseteq \mathcal{P}(\mathsf{tree}\ A) \mid \mathsf{Bottom} \in T\}.$$

To model recursion, we construct a complete lattice of Hoare types to get fixed points. We use the after predicate to ensure the tree approximations are memory safe, respect mutual exclusion, and satisfy their SCSL specifications.

Definition 9 (Hoare types). *Fix precondition* $p : \mathsf{world} \to \mathsf{prop}$ *postcondition* $q : A \to \mathsf{world} \to \mathsf{prop}$, *with free logical variables* $\mathsf{FLV}(p, q)$. *The Hoare type* $\{\!|p|\!\}A\{\!|q|\!\}$ *is defined as follows.*

$$\{\!|p|\!\}A\{\!|q|\!\} \ \widehat{=}\ \{T \in \mathsf{prog}\ A \mid \forall \mathsf{FLV}(p,q)\ (c{:}\mathsf{config})\ (t \in T).\ (\mathsf{wd}(c) \models p) \Rightarrow \mathsf{after}\ c\ t\ (\lambda c'\ v'.\, \mathsf{wd}(c') \models q\ v')\}$$

Intuitively, the denotation of a SCSL judgment $\{p\}C{:}A\{q\}$ is the set of trees T denoting the command C, together with a proof that for any initial configuration c whose world $\mathsf{wd}(c)$ satisfies the precondition p, then after executing any tree $t \in T$ from c produces some result value v' and final configuration c' whose world $\mathsf{wd}(c')$ satisfies postcondition q. The definition quantifies over the free logical variables of p and q in order to give these variables local scope, as stipulated in Section 4.

SCSL assertions (Section 2.3) are arbitrary CiC predicates of type $\mathsf{world} \to \mathsf{prop}$ over worlds, where $\mathsf{world} \ \widehat{=}\ \mathsf{heap} \times \mathsf{mtx} \times \mathbb{U} \times \mathbb{U}$. For example, the predicate $\mathsf{a}_S \rightarrowtail \sigma'$ is defined as $\lambda w{:}\mathsf{world}.\ (\exists h\ \mu\ \omega.\, w = h; \mu; \sigma'; \omega)$. We retain the $w \models p$ notation for the application $p\ w$.

Lemma 1. *The type* $\{\!|p|\!\}A\{\!|q|\!\}$ *is a complete lattice, with set union as the join operator, and* $\{\mathsf{Bottom}\}$ *as the unit element.*

The type $\forall x{:}B.\ \{\!|p|\!\}A\{\!|q|\!\}$ *of functions mapping* $x : B$ *into* $\{\!|p|\!\}A\{\!|q|\!\}$, *where* A, p, q *may depend on* x, *is also a complete lattice, with the join operator on functions defined pointwise, and the constant* $\{\mathsf{Bottom}\}$ *function as the unit element.*

The **denotation of judgments** $[\![\Gamma \vdash J]\!]$ (Figure 5, top) turns SCSL judgments into CiC typing judgments ($\vdash_{\mathsf{CiC}}$). A command specification $\{p\} - {:}A\{q\}$ is denoted by the CiC type $\{\!|p|\!\}A\{\!|q|\!\}$, and a procedure specification $\forall x{:}B.\ \{p\} - {:}A\{q\}$ is denoted by the CiC monadic function type $\forall x{:}B.\ \{\!|p|\!\}A\{\!|q|\!\}$.

The $(p_1, q_1) \sqsubseteq (p_2, q_2)$ judgment generalizes the usual side conditions on the rule of CONSEQuence: (1) $p_2 \Rightarrow p_1$ for strengthening the precondition and (2) $q_1 \Rightarrow q_2$ for weakening the postcondition, and adapts them to the local interpretation of logical variables. The first conjunct in the denotation existentially quantifies the respective logic variables of p_2 and of p_1 to generalize (1); the quantification is existential to match the definition of Hoare types, which quantify universally over $\mathsf{FLV}(p, q)$ and have a negative occurrence of the precondition. The second conjunct generalizes (2) by universally quantifying the respective logic variables, taking into account that the logic variables of q_i are constrained by the precondition p_i.

The **denotation of commands and procedures** (Figure 5, bottom) is subsidiary to that of judgments because the fixed-point construction is indexed by the argument and return types, and the pre- and postconditions. An A-returning command C is denoted by a set of approximating trees in $\mathsf{prog}\ A$, and an A-returning procedure F with argument B is denoted by a set of trees in $B \to \mathsf{prog}\ A$.

$$
\begin{array}{ll}
[\![\cdot]\!] & \widehat{=}\ \cdot \\
[\![\Gamma, x{:}A]\!] & \widehat{=}\ [\![\Gamma]\!], x : A \\
[\![\Gamma, \forall x{:}B.\ \{p\}\, f(x){:}A\, \{q\}]\!] & \widehat{=}\ [\![\Gamma]\!], f : \forall x{:}B.\ \{\!|p|\!\}A\{\!|q|\!\} \\
\\
[\![\Gamma \vdash \{p\}\ C : A\, \{q\}]\!] & \widehat{=}\ [\![\Gamma]\!] \vdash_{\mathsf{CiC}} [\![C]\!] : \{\!|p|\!\}A\{\!|q|\!\} \\
[\![\Gamma \vdash \forall x{:}B.\{p\}F(x) : A\{q\}]\!] & \widehat{=}\ [\![\Gamma]\!] \vdash_{\mathsf{CiC}} [\![F]\!] : \forall x{:}B.\ \{\!|p|\!\}A\{\!|q|\!\} \\
[\![\Gamma \vdash e : A]\!] & \widehat{=}\ [\![\Gamma]\!] \vdash_{\mathsf{CiC}} e : A \\
[\![\Gamma \vdash (p_1, q_1) \sqsubseteq (p_2, q_2)]\!] & \widehat{=} \\
\quad [\![\Gamma]\!] \vdash_{\mathsf{CiC}} \forall w\ w'{:}\mathsf{world}.\ (w \models (\exists \bar{v}_2.\, p_2) \Rightarrow (\exists \bar{v}_1.\, p_1)) \wedge & \\
\quad ((\forall \bar{v}_1.\, w \models p_1 \Rightarrow w' \models q_1) \Rightarrow (\forall \bar{v}_2.\, w \models p_2 \Rightarrow w' \models q_2)) & \\
\quad \text{where } \bar{v}_i \ \widehat{=}\ \mathsf{FLV}(p_i, q_i) &
\end{array}
$$

$$
\begin{array}{rcl}
[\![\mathsf{alloc}_A]\!]\ (x{:}A) & \widehat{=} & \{\mathsf{Bottom}, \mathsf{Cons}\ (\mathsf{Alloc}\ x)\ \mathsf{id}\ \mathsf{Ret}\} \\
[\![\mathsf{dealloc}]\!]\ (x{:}\mathsf{ptr}) & \widehat{=} & \{\mathsf{Bottom}, \mathsf{Cons}\ (\mathsf{Dealloc}\ x)\ \mathsf{id}\ \mathsf{Ret}\} \\
[\![\mathsf{read}_A]\!]\ (x{:}\mathsf{ptr}) & \widehat{=} & \{\mathsf{Bottom}, \mathsf{Cons}\ (\mathsf{Read}_A\ x)\ \mathsf{id}\ \mathsf{Ret}\} \\
[\![\mathsf{write}_A]\!]\ (x{:}\mathsf{ptr})\ (y{:}A) & \widehat{=} & \{\mathsf{Bottom}, \mathsf{Cons}\ (\mathsf{Write}\ x\ y)\ \mathsf{id}\ \mathsf{Ret}\} \\
[\![\mathsf{lock}]\!] & \widehat{=} & \{t_k \mid k \in \mathbb{N}\} \\
\text{where}\quad t_0 & \widehat{=} & \mathsf{Bottom}, \\
t_{k+1} & \widehat{=} & \mathsf{Cons}\ (\mathsf{CAS}\ \mathsf{lk}\ \mathsf{false}\ \mathsf{true})\ \mathsf{id} \\
& & \quad (\lambda x.\, \mathsf{if}\ x\ \mathsf{then}\ \mathsf{Ret}\ ()\ \mathsf{else}\ t_k) \\
[\![\mathsf{unlock}_\Phi]\!] & \widehat{=} & \{\mathsf{Bottom}, \mathsf{Cons}\ (\mathsf{Write}\ \mathsf{lk}\ \mathsf{false})\ \Phi\ \mathsf{Ret}\} \\
[\![\mathsf{ret}_A]\!]\ (x{:}A) & \widehat{=} & \{\mathsf{Bottom}, \mathsf{Ret}\ x\} \\
[\![x \leftarrow C_1; C_2]\!] & \widehat{=} & [\![C_1]\!]; (\lambda x.\ [\![C_2]\!]) \\
[\![C_1 \parallel C_2]\!] & \widehat{=} & [\![C_1]\!] \parallel [\![C_2]\!] \\
[\![\mathsf{if}\ e\ \mathsf{then}\ C_1\ \mathsf{else}\ C_2]\!] & \widehat{=} & \mathsf{if}\ e\ \mathsf{then}\ [\![C_1]\!]\ \mathsf{else}\ [\![C_2]\!] \\
[\![F\ (e)]\!] & \widehat{=} & [\![F]\!]\ (e) \\
[\![\mathsf{fix}\ f^{B,A,p,q}.\ x.\ C]\!] & \widehat{=} & \mathsf{lfp}_{\forall x:B.\ \{\!|p|\!\}A\{\!|q|\!\}}\ (\lambda f.\lambda x.\ [\![C]\!])
\end{array}
$$

Figure 5. Denotational semantics of SCSL judgments (top), and commands and procedures (bottom).

Each SCSL memory command is denoted by a pair of approximations: Bottom, and a Cons tree with the appropriate action and a Ret continuation. We use the identity function on $\mathbb{U}$ as our auxiliary function (which is obviously local) because memory commands don't change auxiliary state.

The lock command is denoted by the set of approximations of a loop around a CAS to atomically change the contents of the dedicated lock lk from false to true, until it succeeds. Intuitively, this is an explicit least fixed point construction. The unlock_Φ command writes false into the dedicated pointer lk and updates the auxiliary state according to the user-provided local auxiliary function Φ.

The sequential composition of commands uses the sequential composition $(T_1; K_2) \in \mathsf{prog}\ B$ of a set of trees $T_1 \in \mathsf{prog}\ A$ and a function into a set of trees $K_2 \in A \to \mathsf{prog}\ B$, which concatenates $t_1 \bowtie K_2$ each tree $t_1 \in T_1$ with a continuation in K_2.

$$
\begin{array}{rcl}
T_1; K_2 & \widehat{=} & \bigcup\{t_1 \bowtie K_2 \mid t_1 \in T_1\} \\
\text{where}\quad \mathsf{Ret}\ v \bowtie K & \widehat{=} & K\ v \\
\mathsf{Par}\ t_1\ t_2\ k \bowtie K & \widehat{=} & \{\mathsf{Par}\ t_1\ t_2\ k' \mid \forall x.\, k'\ x \in (k\ x \bowtie K)\} \\
\mathsf{Cons}\ a\ \Phi\ k \bowtie K & \widehat{=} & \{\mathsf{Cons}\ a\ \Phi\ k' \mid \forall x.\, k'\ x \in (k\ x \bowtie K)\} \\
\mathsf{Bottom} \bowtie K & \widehat{=} & \{\mathsf{Bottom}\}
\end{array}
$$

The definition is well-founded because the continuation k' approximates trees in $k\ x \bowtie K$ for every x, as permitted by the iterated inductive definition.

The parallel composition of commands uses the parallel composition $T_1 \parallel T_2 \in \mathsf{prog}\ (A_1 \times A_2)$ of sets of trees $T_1 \in \mathsf{prog}\ A_1$ and $T_2 \in \mathsf{prog}\ A_2$, which includes Bottom and all the pairwise parallel compositions of trees in T_1 and T_2.

$$T_1 \parallel T_2 \ \widehat{=}\ \{\mathsf{Bottom}\} \cup \{\mathsf{Par}\ t_1\ t_2\ \mathsf{Ret} \mid t_1 \in T_1 \wedge t_2 \in T_2\}$$

Since all SCSL program constructors preserve *monotonicity*, the $\mathsf{fix}\, f.x.C$ procedure can take the least fixed point lfp of the function $\lambda f.\, \lambda x.\ [\![C]\!]$ by the Knaster-Tarski theorem.

5.5 Modal Lemmas and Soundness Theorem

We culminate with the proof of soundness of the interpretation. We have carried all of these proofs in Coq [16], they usually proceed by an induction on the schedule ζ.

The Determinacy lemma means subjective guarantee transitions from a configuration that result in equal heaps, also result in equal configurations (i.e., with equal auxiliaries and heap partitions). Thus, stepping a tree in always uniquely determines the auxiliary state, which is crucial for the soundness of the CONJunction rule.

Lemma 2 (Determinacy of Subjective Guarantee transitions). *If* $c \overset{\Phi}{\rightsquigarrow}_{\mathsf{G}} c_1$, $c \overset{\Phi}{\rightsquigarrow}_{\mathsf{G}} c_2$, *and* $\mathsf{hp}(c_1) = \mathsf{hp}(c_2)$, *then* $c_1 = c_2$.

The Universal lemma states that the modal always commutes with universal quantification, which yields to the soundness of an infinitary CONJunction rule. The assumption $\mathsf{always}\ c\ t\ (\lambda c'\ t'.\, \mathsf{True})$ makes the lemma hold when the quantification over x is vacuous.

Lemma 3 (Universal). *If* $\mathsf{always}\ c\ t\ (\lambda c'\ t'.\, \mathsf{True})$, *then* always *commutes with universal quantification:*

$\mathsf{always}\ c\ t\ (\lambda c'\ t'.\, \forall x.\, P\ x\ c'\ t')$ *iff* $\forall x.\, \mathsf{always}\ c\ t\ (\lambda c'\ t'.\, P\ x\ c'\ t')$.

The Normality lemma corresponds to weakening the postcondition, which is needed for the proof of the CONSEQ rule.

Lemma 4 (Normality for after). *If* $\mathsf{after}\ c\ t\ Q_1$ *and* $Q_1\ c'\ v' \Rightarrow Q_2\ c'\ v'$ *for all* c' *and* v', *then* $\mathsf{after}\ c\ t\ Q_2$.

Closure under sequential composition justifies the SEQ rule: q holds at the end of a concatenated tree if the final configuration of the prefix can be used as an initial configuration for the suffix to show q holds after.

Lemma 5 (Closure under sequential composition). *If* $t_{12} \in t_1 \bowtie T_2$ *and* $\mathsf{after}\ c\ t_1\ (\lambda c'\ v'.\forall t'.\, t' \in T_2\ v' \Rightarrow \mathsf{after}\ c'\ t'\ Q)$, *then* $\mathsf{after}\ c\ t_{12}\ Q$.

Closure under parallel composition justifies the PAR rule. Intuitively, it holds because when (an approximation t_2 of) C_2 takes a step over its private and shared state, it amounts to $\rightsquigarrow_{\mathsf{R}}^{*}$ environment interference on (an approximation t_1 of) C_1, and vice versa. Note that the pattern of rearranging subjective thread/environment components recurs at the level of triples $d = h; \mu; \sigma$: the parallel composition uses $(d_1 \oplus d_2, d_{\mathsf{O}})$ and the left and right child threads use $(d_1, d_2 \oplus d_{\mathsf{O}})$ and $(d_2, d_1 \oplus d_{\mathsf{O}})$, respectively.

Lemma 6 (Closure under parallel composition). *If* $\mathsf{after}\ (d_1 \mid h_{\mathsf{R}} \mid d_2 \oplus d_{\mathsf{O}})\ t_1\ Q_1$ *and* $\mathsf{after}\ (d_2 \mid h_{\mathsf{R}} \mid d_1 \oplus d_{\mathsf{O}})\ t_2\ Q_2$, *then* $\mathsf{after}\ (d_1 \oplus d_2 \mid h_{\mathsf{R}} \mid d_{\mathsf{O}})\ (\mathsf{Par}\ t_1\ t_2\ \mathsf{Ret})\ (Q_1 \circledast Q_2)$, *where*

$$\begin{aligned} Q_1 \circledast Q_2 \mathrel{\widehat{=}} \lambda c'\ v'.\, \exists d_1'\ d_2'\ h_{\mathsf{R}}'\ d_{\mathsf{O}}'.\ & c' = (d_1' \oplus d_2' \mid h_{\mathsf{R}}' \mid d_{\mathsf{O}}') \wedge \\ & Q_1\ (d_1' \mid h_{\mathsf{R}}' \mid d_2' \oplus d_{\mathsf{O}}')\ (v'.1) \wedge \\ & Q_2\ (d_2' \mid h_{\mathsf{R}}' \mid d_1' \oplus d_{\mathsf{O}}')\ (v'.2) \end{aligned}$$

Finally, the Frame lemma can be viewed as an instance of the Parallel lemma, by taking C_2 to be the idle thread that does not change the heap or auxiliaries.

Lemma 7 (Frame). *If* $\mathsf{after}\ (d_1 \mid h_{\mathsf{R}} \mid d_2 \oplus d_{\mathsf{O}})\ t\ Q$, *then* $\mathsf{after}\ (d_1 \oplus d_2 \mid h_{\mathsf{R}} \mid d_{\mathsf{O}})\ t\ Q'$, *where*

$$\begin{aligned} Q' \mathrel{\widehat{=}} \lambda c'\ v'.\, \exists d_1'\ h_{\mathsf{R}}'\ d_{\mathsf{O}}'.\ & c' = (d_1' \oplus d_2, h_{\mathsf{R}}', d_{\mathsf{O}}') \wedge \\ & Q\ (d_1' \mid h_{\mathsf{R}}' \mid d_2 \oplus d_{\mathsf{O}}')\ v \end{aligned}$$

Theorem 1 (Soundness). *If* $\Gamma \vdash J$, *then* $[\![\Gamma \vdash J]\!]$.

Proof. By induction on the derivation of J. Each basic command is sound because the pre- and postconditions are stable under environment interference, the precondition implies the command is memsafe, and the resulting configuration satisfies the postcondition. The SEQ, PAR and FRAME rules are sound by Lemmas 5, 6, and 7. The fix rule is sound by the Knaster-Tarski theorem. The CONJ rule is sound by Lemma 3, and the CONSEQ rule by Lemma 4. The EXISTential rule and IF rules are derivable. Since SCSL procedures are interpreted as (monadic) CiC functions. the procedure APPlication and HYPothesis rules are sound by the function application and hypothesis rules of CiC. □

6. Related Work

Owicki and Gries' Resource Invariants (RI) [21] emphasizes a spatial specification of shared state that usually suffices for coarse-grained concurrency. Jones' Rely/Guarantee (RG) [12] emphasizes a temporal specification of thread and environment interference on shared state that is appropriate for fine-grained concurrency and can avoid some of the auxiliary state that appears in RI proofs.

The combination of RI or RG with Separation Logic in Concurrent Separation Logic (CSL) [19], RGSep [26], SAGL [9, 8], and Deny-Guarantee [7] has proved fruitful for the compositional verification of stateful, concurrent programs. However, to prove noninvariant properties as in the incrementor example, those logics still require auxiliary state to relate local program assertions to global (spatial or temporal) invariants. Auxiliary state makes the proof of a single thread sensitive to the global thread structure, which prevents local reasoning and leads to noncompositionality. In SCSL, subjective auxiliary state suffices to overcome this noncompositionality and recovers local reasoning in a CSL-style logic. On the other hand, RG specifications give fine-grained descriptions of possible interference, which to our knowledge isn't possible with subjective auxiliary state and RI alone.

Whereas CSL and existing variants use *local* specifications that only refer to the program's private state, SCSL gains expressivity through the $\mathsf{a_O}$ view to provide *non-local* information about the environment's auxiliary contribution, but retains CSL-style *local reasoning* by leveraging the PCM structure of auxiliaries to avoid sensitivity to the environment's thread structure.

Concurrent Abstract Predicates (CAP) [6] by Dinsdale-Young et al.'s is an axiomatic logic that *can* prove the incrementor and coarse-grained set *without* auxiliary state. A CAP proof involves defining a set of actions, which are RG-style transitions on private and shared state, which includes concrete heap and abstract capabilities that identify enabled actions (thus there is a subtle mutual recursion between an action and the capability to perform the action). Deductions in a proof use the actions to move heap and capabilities between the private and shared states. Intermediate assertions must be checked to be stable under the environment's action interference, which is standard in RG-style proofs. Whereas our prototype SCSL only provides one lock with global scope, CAP provides multiple shared regions each with an associated set of protocols (i.e., RG interference specifications).

Although CAP overcomes the need for auxiliary state, in our opinion the corresponding proofs of the incrementor and coarse-grained set are more indirect than the noncompositional RI proofs based on auxiliary state. Moreover, we consider the complexity of fine-grained interference reasoning should be unnecessary for coarse-grained concurrency, where critical sections are meant to abstract away from interference. To achieve compositional proofs of the same programs in SCSL, it suffices to pick a PCM and resource invariant, and to conduct RI-style sequential reasoning in the critical section. Although SCSL assertions go beyond private state in mentioning the environment's contribution $\mathsf{a_O}$, it is only tracked in the critical section where it is known to remain fixed, so we can avoid reasoning about stability under interference.

Since SCSL follows the RI tradition, it is best suited for coarse-grained concurrency; by contrast, CAP is more general because the interference specifications yield compositional proofs for both coarse- and fine-grained concurrency. Moreover, abstract predicates enable **modularity** by giving different library implementations the same specification, thus hiding their internal concurrency. Since the SCSL embedding into CiC gives us access to abstraction over predicates (as well as over types and higher-order modules), SCSL already supports this kind of modularity. However, to reach the expressive power of CAP, we have to investigate how to combine subjectivity with RG for fine-grained concurrency.

Jacobs and Piessens' **fine-grained concurrency specifications** [11] provide an alternative means for modularity: a procedure can be verified parametrically in the caller's invariant, auxiliary state and code, which are then instantiated by each call site. This allows verifying the increment procedure once, but the two- and three-thread programs must use different invariants and each procedure call must use different auxiliary state and update code. In SCSL, we can also parametrize a procedure in the caller's invariant and auxiliaries as illustrated by the iterator. Moreover, subjectivity overcomes the need for different invariants and auxiliary state, and local auxiliary functions can update the auxiliary without sensitivity to the thread's identity.

To our knowledge, SCSL is the first axiomatic concurrency logic to support **higher-order procedures**, which is necessary to prove the iterator where the argument procedure exposes its effects and is general enough to support polymorphic instantiation (e.g., iter (iter xincr2) in Section 3.2). A first-order iterator has been proved in CAP [5], where the procedure applied to each element is hard-coded and doesn't expose any state or concurrency effects.

Fu et al.'s **HLRG** logic [10] combines rely/guarantee and temporal reasoning over explicit history traces. This eliminates the need for auxiliary state, but, as in CAP, at the expense of more involved reasoning than necessary in the case of coarse-grained algorithms. HLRG only handles a single top-level parallel composition of a fixed number of threads; by contrast, SCSL allows parallel composition in any command and the number of forked threads can vary dynamically, which is necessary to prove the iterator.

The denotational **semantics** of SCSL is inspired by Brookes' domain-theoretic model for CSL [3], but differs in several crucial respects. Brookes uses store (*a.k.a.* stack), heap, and resource (*a.k.a.* lock) actions to represent the operation and its result. We use actions to represent heap operations, and only by stepping an action do we obtain its result. We can avoid a stack altogether because our commands return values which are bound to immutable variables (*a.k.a.* identifiers). Since we implement the lock with a dedicated heap location, we avoid a separate notion of resource actions.

Brookes denotes a command as a set of *action traces*, which are *finite or infinite* sequences of actions including all possible results. For example, reading ℓ has the denotation $\{(\mathsf{Read}\ \ell, m)\}_{m\in\mathbb{Z}}$. We avoid enumerating all possible results by shifting to *action trees*: the Cons tree pairs an action (in our sense) with a continuation that takes the result of the operation and generates a tree for the rest of the computation. Since we are concerned with safety properties, it suffices to consider *finite* tree approximations.

Brookes' parallel composition is given by a *fairmerge* interleaving of traces. For example, reading ℓ in parallel has the denotation $\{(\mathsf{Read}\ \ell, m)\ (\mathsf{Read}\ \ell, n)\}_{m,n\in\mathbb{Z}}$, the case $m \neq n$ is a *non-sequential* trace that accounts for the environment mutating ℓ between the two reads and is needed for compositionality. We avoid dealing with non-sequential traces by including a Parallel tree constructor and unfolding the execution in the always predicate.

Brookes includes a fault state to account for races (i.e., one thread writes to a location while another thread also reads or writes), accessing a nonexistent location, and unlocking without restoring the resource invariant. We avoid an explicit fault state by ensuring that "well-specified programs don't go wrong": every heap operation encountered during an execution is safe to execute. We do not identify races because threads must interfere on the implicit lock location, but it is immediate from the interpretation of Hoare triples that parallel threads can otherwise only mutate their private heaps, which are disjoint.

Besides Brookes' denotational model, Vafeiadis [25] and Feng et al. [9] give operational proofs of CSL's soundness. We are similar to those approaches in two ways: (1) the explicit use of RG-style specifications in the semantics to describe interference over the shared resource, and (2) the use of step-indexing in the definition of safety, although we use tree paths whereas they use natural numbers. Since we interpret SCSL Hoare triples as monadic functions in CiC, however, operational methods do not suffice and we must resort to a semantic proof of soundness.

Existing approaches to the soundness of CSL use a *small* footprint in the sense that their semantic definitions of safety only refer to the thread's private state and (in some cases) the shared state. Similarly, the combination of RG and Separation Logic in RGSep [26] and SAGL [9, 8] only describe interference over the shared state. By contrast, our subjective rely/guarantee transitions use a *large* footprint, which encompasses the shared state as well as the thread and environment's private state of heap, lock ownership, and user-chosen auxiliary state. While our subjective rely/guarantee transitions are hard-coded for RI, we expect that the logic can be generalized to user-chosen RG interference and thus we will be able to verify fine-grained concurrency.

The concept of **local action** appears in Abstract Separation Logic [4] to model stateful, non-deterministic programs. A local action is a function $f : \Sigma \to \mathcal{P}(\Sigma)^\top$ where Σ is a *separation algebra* (i.e., a *cancellative* PCM) of states σ. The codomain is a set of possible next-states to express nondeterminism or an error marker $\top$ to indicate that the action faults. The function must satisfy the *locality condition*: if valid $(\sigma_1 \oplus \sigma_2)$, then $f(\sigma_1 \oplus \sigma_2) \sqsubseteq \{\sigma_1' \oplus \sigma_2 \mid \sigma_1' \in f(\sigma_1)\}$. By contrast, our local auxiliary functions Φ are deterministic because there is at most one possible next-state and we implicitly avoid the error marker by using the validity conditions. Since auxiliary *functions* can be noncomputable, we conjecture they will enable more expressive specifications than the traditional use of (computable) auxiliary *code*.

Krishnaswami et al. [15] use a PCM to abstractly represent the states of various program modules in a setting of a sequential higher-order language. Similar to our resource invariant, their module invariants are also predicates over the combined abstract states of all the modules.

7. Conclusion and Future Work

We propose Subjective Concurrent Separation Logic (SCSL) as a combination of Resource Invariants and Separation Logic with *subjective auxiliary state*, which tames the objective thread structure exposed by classical auxiliary state. The approach is enabled by generalizing auxiliaries from stack and heap to user-chosen partial commutative monoids (PCM), and from auxiliary code to local auxiliary functions. Each thread has a subjective perspective that splits auxiliary state into contributions by the *self* (the thread itself) and the *other* (its environment). The auxiliary PCM crucially permits agglomerating all environment thread's contributions, which makes proofs insensitive to the internal concurrency of the environment. SCSL provides parallel composition and frame rules that use the *subjective separating conjunction* to split auxiliary contributions in a coherent manner; surprisingly, the rules are sound even if the auxiliary PCM is not cancellative.

For an incrementor and a coarse-grained set with logically disjoint interference, we show that suitable choice of auxiliary PCM yields simple, compositional proofs independent of the number of parallel threads; by contrast, existing logics either use auxiliary state which makes proofs sensitive to the global thread structure, or achieve compositionality at the expense of complex Rely/Guarantee reasoning. We also prove a higher-order iterator with dynamic thread creation, whose verification is independent of the internal concurrency of the function applied to each element. In future work, we will study how subjective auxiliary state scales to more complex, real-world programs.

We prove the soundness of SCSL by a shallow embedding into the Calculus of Inductive Constructions using a novel denotational semantics of action trees and a definition of safety that uses rely/guarantee transitions over a large subjective footprint encompassing heaps, lock ownership, and user-chosen auxiliaries.

Since SCSL provides a single lock with global scope, a proof is committed to a single auxiliary PCM and resource invariant. In future work, we will scale the logic to multiple locks with delimited scope and refinement across auxiliary PCMs and resource invariants. We will also study the combination of subjective auxiliary state Rely/Guarantee reasoning for fine-grained programs in the presence of richer language constructs such as separate fork and join commands.

Acknowledgments

This research has been partially supported by Spanish MICINN Project TIN2010-20639 Paran10; AMAROUT grant PCOFUND-GA-2008-229599; and Ramon y Cajal grant RYC-2010-0743.

References

[1] Richard Bornat, Cristiano Calcagno, Peter W. O'Hearn, and Matthew J. Parkinson. Permission accounting in separation logic. In *POPL*, 2005.

[2] Richard Bornat, Cristiano Calcagno, and Hongseok Yang. Variables as resource in separation logic. *ENTCS*, 155, 2006.

[3] Stephen Brookes. A semantics for concurrent separation logic. *Theor. Comput. Sci.*, 375(1-3), 2007.

[4] Cristiano Calcagno, Peter W. O'Hearn, and Hongseok Yang. Local action and abstract separation logic. In *LICS*, 2007.

[5] Pedro da Rocha Pinto, Thomas Dinsdale-Young, Mike Dodds, Philippa Gardner, and Mark J. Wheelhouse. A simple abstraction for complex concurrent indexes. In *OOPSLA*, 2011.

[6] Thomas Dinsdale-Young, Mike Dodds, Philippa Gardner, Matthew J. Parkinson, and Viktor Vafeiadis. Concurrent abstract predicates. In *ECOOP*, 2010.

[7] Mike Dodds, Xinyu Feng, Matthew J. Parkinson, and Viktor Vafeiadis. Deny-guarantee reasoning. In *ESOP*, 2009.

[8] Xinyu Feng. Local rely-guarantee reasoning. In *POPL*, 2009.

[9] Xinyu Feng, Rodrigo Ferreira, and Zhong Shao. On the relationship between concurrent separation logic and assume-guarantee reasoning. In *ESOP*, 2007.

[10] Ming Fu, Yong Li, Xinyu Feng, Zhong Shao, and Yu Zhang. Reasoning about optimistic concurrency using a program logic for history. In *CONCUR*, 2010.

[11] Bart Jacobs and Frank Piessens. Expressive modular fine-grained concurrency specification. In *POPL*, 2011.

[12] Cliff B. Jones. Specification and design of (parallel) programs. In *IFIP Congress*, 1983.

[13] Cliff B. Jones. The role of auxiliary variables in the formal development of concurrent programs. Technical Report CS-TR-1179, University of Newcastle upon Tyne, Computing Science, 2009.

[14] Thomas Kleymann. Hoare logic and auxiliary variables. *Formal Aspects of Computing*, 11, 1999.

[15] Neelakantan R. Krishnaswami, Aaron Turon, Derek Dreyer, and Deepak Garg. Superficially substructural types. In *ICFP*, 2012.

[16] Ruy Ley-Wild and Aleksandar Nanevski. Supporting Material. https://software.imdea.org/~aleks/scsl/, July 2012.

[17] Per Martin-Löf. Haupstatz for the intuitionistic theory of iterated inductive definitions. In *Scandinavian Logic Symposium*, 1971.

[18] The Coq development team. *The Coq proof assistant reference manual*. LogiCal Project, 2004. Version 8.0.

[19] Peter W. O'Hearn. Resources, concurrency, and local reasoning. *Theor. Comput. Sci.*, 375(1-3), 2007.

[20] Susan S. Owicki. *Axiomatic Proof Techniques for Parallel Programs*. PhD thesis, Cornell University, 1975.

[21] Susan S. Owicki and David Gries. Verifying properties of parallel programs: An axiomatic approach. *Commun. ACM*, 19(5), 1976.

[22] Matthew J. Parkinson and Gavin M. Bierman. Separation logic and abstraction. In *POPL*, 2005.

[23] Matthew J. Parkinson, Richard Bornat, and Cristiano Calcagno. Variables as resource in Hoare logics. In *LICS*, 2006.

[24] Uday S. Reddy and John C. Reynolds. Syntactic control of interference for separation logic. In *POPL*, 2012.

[25] Viktor Vafeiadis. Concurrent separation logic and operational semantics. *ENTCS*, 276, 2011.

[26] Viktor Vafeiadis and Matthew J. Parkinson. A marriage of rely/guarantee and separation logic. In *CONCUR*, 2007.

Author Index

NOTES

NOTES